For Reference

Not to be taken from this room

D1256456

THE MOTION PICTURE GUIDE

THIS VOLUME IS DEDICATED TO
BETTE DAVIS
JOAN CRAWFORD
INGRID BERGMAN
SALLY FIELD
CLAUDETTE COLBERT
GRETA GARBO
MARLENE DIETRICH
CAROLE LOMBARD
BARBARA STANWYCK
SHIRLEY MAC LAINE
JEAN ARTHUR
OLIVIA DE HAVILLAND
GLORIA SWANSON
IRENE DUNNE
and all the leading ladies

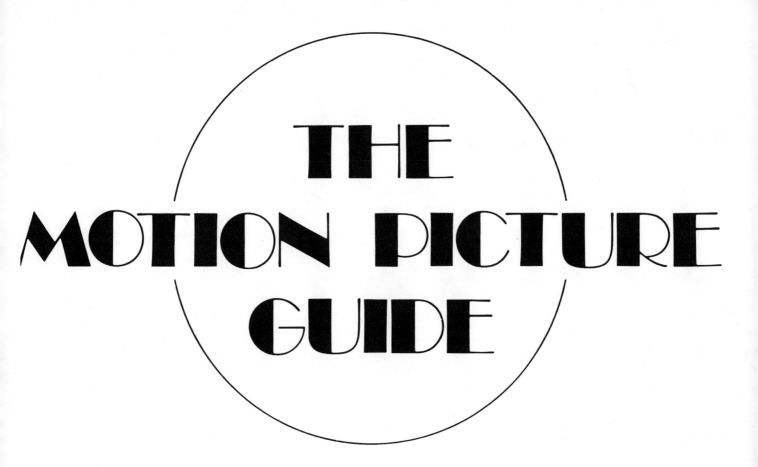

THE MOTION PICTURE GUIDE

T-V

1927-1983

Jay Robert Nash
Stanley Ralph Ross

CINEBOOKS, INC.

Chicago, 1987

Publishers of THE COMPLETE FILM RESOURCE CENTER

Publishers: Jay Robert Nash, Stanley Ralph Ross; **Associate Publisher:** Kenneth H. Petchenik; **Executive Editor:** Jim McCormick; **Senior Editor:** David Tardy; **Associate Editors:** Oksana Lydia Creighton, Jeffrey H. Wallenfeldt; **Senior Staff Writer:** James J. Mulay; **Staff Writers:** Arnie Bernstein, Daniel Curran, Phil Pantone, Michael Theobald, Brian Brock; **Director of Production:** William Leahy; **Production Editor:** Shelby Payne; **Production Assistants:** Jeanette Hori, Michaela Tuohy; **Chief Researcher:** William C. Clogston.

Editorial and Sales Offices: CINEBOOKS, 990 Grove, Evanston, Illinois 60201.

Library of Congress Catalog Card Number: 85-071145
ISBN: 0-933997-00-0 THE MOTION PICTURE GUIDE (10 Vols.)
0-933997-08-6 THE MOTION PICTURE GUIDE, Vol. VIII (T–V)

Printed in the United States
First Edition
This volume contains 3,256 entries.

1 2 3 4 5 6 7 8 9 10

HOW TO USE INFORMATION IN THIS GUIDE

ALPHABETICAL ORDER

All entries have been arranged alphabetically throughout this and all subsequent volumes. In establishing alphabetical order, all articles (A, An, The) appear after the main title (AFFAIR TO REMEMBER, AN). In the case of foreign films the article precedes the main title (LES MISERABLES appears in the letter L) which makes, we feel, for easier access and uniformity. Contractions are grouped together and these will be followed by non-apostrophized words of the same letters. B.F.'s DAUGHTER is at the beginning of the letter B, not under BF.

TITLES

It is important to know what title you are seeking; use the *complete* title of the film. The film ADVENTURES OF ROBIN HOOD, THE, cannot be found under merely ROBIN HOOD. Many films are known under different titles and we have taken great pains to cross-reference these titles. (AKA, also known as) as well as alternate titles used in Great Britain (GB). In addition to the cross-reference title only entries, AKAs and alternate titles in Great Britain can be found in the title line for each entry. An alphabetically arranged comprehensive list of title changes appears in the Index volume (Vol. X).

RATINGS

We have rated each and every film at critical levels that include acting, directing, script, and technical achievement (or the sad lack of it). We have a *five-star* rating, unlike all other rating systems, to signify a film superbly made on every level, in short, a masterpiece. At the lowest end of the scale is *zero* and we mean it. The ratings are as follows: *zero* (not worth a glance), °(poor), °°(fair), °°°(good), °°°°(excellent), °°°°°(masterpiece, and these are few and far between). Half-marks mean almost there but not quite.

YEAR OF RELEASE

We have used in all applicable instances the year of United States release. This sometimes means that a film released abroad may have a different date elsewhere than in these volumes but this is generally the date released in foreign countries, not in the U.S.

FOREIGN COUNTRY PRODUCTION

When possible, we have listed abbreviated names of the foreign countries originating the production of a film. This information will be found within the parenthesis containing the year of release. If no country is listed in this space, it is a U.S. production.

RUNNING TIME

A hotly debated category, we have opted to list the running time a film ran at the time of its initial U.S. release but we will usually mention in the text if the film was drastically cut and give the reasons why. We have attempted to be as accurate as possible by consulting the most reliable sources.

PRODUCING AND DISTRIBUTING COMPANIES

The producing and/or distributing company of every film is listed in abbreviated entries next to the running time in the title line (see abbreviations; for all those firms not abbreviated, the entire firm's name will be present).

COLOR OR BLACK-AND-WHITE

The use of color or black-and-white availability appears as c or bw following the producing/releasing company entry.

CASTS

Whenever possible, we give *the complete cast and the roles played* for each film and this is the case in 95% of all entries, the only encyclopedia to ever offer such comprehensive information in covering the entire field. The names of actors and actresses are in Roman lettering, the names of the roles each played in Italic inside parentheses.

SYNOPSIS

The in-depth synopsis for each entry (when such applies) offers the plot of each film, critical evaluation, anecdotal information on the production and its personnel, awards won when applicable and additional information dealing with the production's impact upon the public, its success or failure at the box office, its social significance, if any. Acting methods, technical innovations, script originality are detailed. We also cite other productions involving an entry's personnel for critical comparisons and to establish the style or genre of expertise of directors, writers, actors and technical people.

REMAKES AND SEQUELS

Information regarding films that have sequels, sequels themselves or direct remakes of films can be found at the very end of each synopsis.

DUBBING AND SUBTITLES

We will generally point out in the synopsis when a foreign film is dubbed in English, mostly when the dubbing is poor. When voices are dubbed, particularly when singers render vocals on songs mimed by stars, we generally point out these facts either in the cast/role listing or inside the synopsis. If a film is in a foreign language and subtitled, we signify the fact in a parenthetical statement at the end of each entry (In Italian, English subtitles).

CREDITS

The credits for the creative and technical personnel of a film are extensive and they include: p (producer, often executive producer); d (director); w (screenwriter, followed by adaptation, if any, and creator of original story, if any, and other sources such as authors for plays, articles, short stories, novels and non-fiction books); ph (cinematographer, followed by camera system and color process when applicable, i.e., Panavision, Technicolor); m (composer of musical score); ed (film editor); md (music director); art d (art director); set d (set decoration); cos (costumes); spec eff (special effects); ch (choreography); m/l (music and lyrics); stunts, makeup, and other credits when merited. When someone receives two or more credits in a single film the credits may be combined (p&d, John Ford) or the last name repeated in subsequent credits shared with another (d, John Ford; w, Ford, Dudley Nichols).

GENRES/SUBJECT

Each film is categorized for easy identification as to genre and/or subject and themes at the left-hand bottom of each entry. (Western, Prison Drama, Spy Drama, Romance, Musical, Comedy, War, Horror, Science-Fiction, Adventure, Biography, Historical Drama, Children's Film, Animated Feature, etc.) More specific subject and theme breakdowns will be found in the Index (Vol. X).

PR AND MPAA RATINGS

The Parental Recommendation provides parents having no knowledge of the style and content of each film with a guide; if a film has excessive violence, sex, strong language, it is so indicated. Otherwise, films specifically designed for young children are also indicated. The Parental Recommendation (**PR**) is to be found at the right-hand bottom of each entry, followed, when applicable, by the **MPAA** rating. The PR ratings are as follows: **AAA** (must for children); **AA** (good for children); **A** (acceptable for children); **C** (cautionary, some objectionable scenes); **O** (completely objectionable for children).

KEY TO ABBREVIATIONS

Foreign Countries:

Arg.	Argentina
Aus.	Australia
Aust.	Austria
Bel.	Belgium
Braz.	Brazil
Brit.	Great Britain (GB when used for alternate title)
Can.	Canada
Chi.	China
Czech.	Czechoslovakia
Den.	Denmark
E. Ger.	East Germany
Fin.	Finland
Fr.	France
Ger.	Germany (includes W. Germany)
Gr.	Greece
Hung.	Hungary
Ital.	Italy
Jap.	Japan
Mex.	Mexico
Neth.	Netherlands
Phil.	Philippines
Pol.	Poland
Rum.	Rumania
S.K.	South Korea
Span.	Spain
Swed.	Sweden

Key to Abbreviations (continued)

Switz.	Switzerland
Thai.	Thailand
USSR	Union of Soviet Socialist Republics
Yugo.	Yugoslavia

Production Companies, Studios and Distributors (U.S. and British)

AA	ALLIED ARTISTS
ABF	Associated British Films
AE	Avco Embassy
AEX	Associated Exhibitors
AH	Anglo-Hollandia
AIP	American International Pictures
AM	American
ANCH	Anchor Film Distributors
ANE	American National Enterprises
AP	Associated Producers
AP&D	Associated Producers & Distributors
ARC	Associated Releasing Corp.
Argosy	Argosy Productions
Arrow	Arrow Films
ART	Artcraft
Astra	Astra Films
AY	Aywon
BA	British Actors
B&C	British and Colonial Kinematograph Co.
BAN	Banner Films
BI	British Instructional
BIFD	B.I.F.D. Films
BIP	British International Pictures
BJP	Buck Jones Productions
BL	British Lion
Blackpool	Blackpool Productions
BLUE	Bluebird
BN	British National
BNF	British and Foreign Film
Boulting	Boulting Brothers (Brit.)
BP	British Photoplay Production
BPP	B.P. Productions
BRIT	Britannia Films
BRO	Broadwest
Bryanston	Bryantston Films (Brit.)
BS	Blue Streak
BUS	Bushey (Brit.)
BUT	Butchers Film Service
BV	Buena Vista (Walt Disney)
CAP	Capital Films
CC	Christie Comedy
CD	Continental Distributing
CHAD	Chadwick Pictures Corporation
CHES	Chesterfield
Cineguild	Cineguild
CL	Clarendon
CLIN	Clinton
COL	COLUMBIA
Colony	Colony Pictures
COM	Commonwealth
COMM	Commodore Pictures
COS	Cosmopolitan (Hearst)
DE	Dependable Exchange
DGP	Dorothy Gish Productions
Disney	Walt Disney Productions
DIST	Distinctive
DM	DeMille Productions
DOUB	Doubleday
EAL	Ealing Studios (Brit.)
ECF	East Coast Films
ECL	Eclectic
ED	Eldorado
EF	Eagle Films
EFF & EFF	E.F.F. & E.F.F. Comedy
EFI	English Films Inc.
EIFC	Export and Import Film Corp.
EL	Eagle-Lion
EM	Embassy Pictures Corp.

EMI	EMI Productions
EP	Enterprise Pictures
EPC	Equity Pictures Corp.
EQ	Equitable
EXCEL	Excellent
FA	Fine Arts
FC	Film Classics
FD	First Division
FN	First National
FOX	20TH CENTURY FOX (and Fox Productions)
FP	Famous Players (and Famous Players Lasky)
FRP	Frontroom Productions
Gainsborough	Gainsborough Productions
GAU	Gaumont (Brit.)
GEN	General
GFD	General Films Distributors
Goldwyn	Samuel Goldwyn Productions
GN	Grand National
GOTH	Gotham
Grafton	Grafton Films (Brit.)
H	Harma
HAE	Harma Associated Distributors
Hammer	Hammer Films (Brit.)
HD	Hagen and Double
HM	Hi Mark
HR	Hal Roach
IA	International Artists
ID	Ideal
IF	Independent Film Distributors (Brit.)
Imperator	Imperator Films (Brit.)
IP	Independent Pictures Corp.
IN	Invincible Films
INSP	Inspirational Pictures (Richard Barthelmess)
IV	Ivan Film
Javelin	Javelin Film Productions (Brit.)
JUR	Jury
KC	Kinema Club
KCB	Kay C. Booking
Knightsbridge	Knightsbridge Productions (Brit.)
Korda	Alexander Korda Productions (Brit.)
Ladd	Ladd Company Productions
LAS	Lasky Productions (Jesse L. Lasky)
LFP	London Films
LIP	London Independent Producers
Lorimar	Lorimar Productions
LUM	Lumis
Majestic	Majestic Films
Mascot	Mascot Films
Mayflowers	Mayflowers Productions (Brit.)
Metro	Metro
MFC	Mission Film Corporation
MG	Metro-Goldwyn
MGM	METRO-GOLDWYN-MAYER
MON	Monogram
MOR	Morante
MS	Mack Sennett
MUT	Mutual
N	National
NG	National General
NGP	National General Pictures (Alexander Korda, Brit.)
NW	New World
Orion	Orion Productions
Ortus	Ortus Productions (Brit.)
PAR	PARAMOUNT
Pascal	Gabriel Pascal Productions (Brit.)
PDC	Producers Distributors Corp.

ix

Key to Abbreviations (continued)

PEER	Peerless
PWN	Peninsula Studios
PFC	Pacific Film Company
PG	Playgoers
PI	Pacific International
PIO	Pioneer Film Corp.
PM	Pall Mall
PP	Pro Patria
PRC	Producers Releasing Corporation
PRE	Preferred
QDC	Quality Distributing Corp.
RAY	Rayart
RAD	Radio Pictures
RANK	J. Arthur Rank (Brit.)
RBP	Rex Beach Pictures
REA	Real Art
REG	Regional Films
REN	Renown
REP	Republic
RF	Regal Films
RFD	R.F.D. Productions (Brit.)
RKO	RKO RADIO PICTURES
Rogell	Rogell
Romulus	Romulus Films (Brit.)
Royal	Royal
SB	Samuel Bronston
SCHUL	B.P. Schulberg Productions
SEL	Select
SELZ	Selznick International (David O. Selznick)
SF	Selznick Films
SL	Sol Lesser
SONO	Sonofilms
SP	Seven Pines Productions (Brit.)
SRP	St. Regis Pictures
STER	Sterling
STOLL	Stoll
SUN	Sunset
SYN	Syndicate Releasing Co.
SZ	Sam Zimbalist
TC	Two Cities (Brit.)
T/C	Trem-Carr
THI	Thomas H. Ince
TIF	Tiffany
TRA	Transatlantic Pictures
TRU	Truart
TS	Tiffany/Stahl
UA	UNITED ARTISTS
UNIV	UNIVERSAL (AND UNIVERSAL INTERNATIONAL)
Venture	Venture Distributors
VIT	Vitagraph
WAL	Waldorf
WB	WARNER BROTHERS (AND WARNER BROTHERS-SEVEN ARTS)
WEST	Westminster
WF	Woodfall Productions (Brit.)
WI	Wisteria
WORLD	World
WSHP	William S. Hart Productions
ZUKOR	Adolph Zukor Productions

Foreign

ABSF	AB Svensk Film Industries (Swed.)
Action	Action Films (Fr.)
ADP	Agnes Delahaie Productions (Fr.)
Agata	Agata Films (Span.)
Alter	Alter Films (Fr.)
Arch	Archway Film Distributors
Argos	Argos Films (Fr.)
Argui	Argui Films (Fr.)
Ariane	Les Films Ariane (Fr.)
Athos	Athos Films (Fr.)
Belga	Belga Films (Bel.)
Beta	Beta Films (Ger.)
CA	Cine-Alliance (Fr.)
Caddy	Caddy Films (Fr.)
CCFC	Compagnie Commerciale Francais Einematographique (Fr.)
CDD	Cino Del Duca (Ital.)
CEN	Les Films de Centaur (Fr.)
CFD	Czecheslovak Film Productions
CHAM	Champion (Ital.)
Cinegay	Cinegay Films (Ital.)
Cines	Cines Films (Ital.)
Cineriz	Cinerez Films (Ital.)
Citel	Citel Films (Switz.)
Como	Como Films (Fr.)
CON	Concordia (Fr.)
Corona	Corona Films (Fr.)
D	Documento Films (Ital.)
DD	Dino De Laurentiis (Ital.)
Dear	Dear Films (Ital.)
DIF	Discina International Films (Fr.)
DPR	Films du Palais-Royal (Fr.)
EX	Excelsa Films (Ital.)
FDP	Films du Pantheon (Fr.)
Fono	Fono Roma (Ital.)
FS	Filmsonor Productions (Fr.)
Gala	Fala Films (Ital.)
Galatea	Galatea Productions (Ital.)
Gamma	Gamma Films (Fr.)
Gemma	Gemma Cinematografica (Ital.)
GFD	General Film Distributors, Ltd. (Can.)
GP	General Productions (Fr.)
Gray	(Gray Films (Fr.)
IFD	Intercontinental Film Distributors
Janus	Janus Films (Ger.)
JMR	Macques Mage Releasing (Fr.)
LF	Les Louvre Films (Fr.)
LFM	Les Films Moliere (Fr.)
Lux	Lux Productions (Ital.)
Melville	Melville Productions (Fr.)
Midega	Midega Films (Span.)
NEF	N.E.F. La Nouvelle Edition Francaise (Fr.)
NFD	N.F.D. Productions (Ger.)
ONCIC	Office National pour le Commerce et L'Industrie Cinematographique (Fr.)
Ortus	Ortus Films (Can.)
PAC	Production Artistique Cinematographique (Fr.)
Pagnol	Marcel Pagnol Productions (Fr.)
Parc	Parc Films (Fr.)
Paris	Paris Films (Fr.)
Pathe	Pathe Films (Fr.)
PECF	Productions et Editions Cinematographique Francais (Fr.)
PF	Parafrench Releasing Co. (Fr.)
PIC	Produzione International Cinematografica (Ital.)
Ponti	Carlo Ponti Productions (Ital.)
RAC	Realisation d'Art Cinematographique (Fr.)
Regina	Regina Films (Fr.)
Renn	Renn Productions (Fr.)
SDFS	Societe des Films Sonores Tobis (Fr.)
SEDIF	Societe d'Exploitation ed de Distribution de Films (Fr.)
SFP	Societe Francais de Production (Fr.)
Sigma	Sigma Productions (Fr.)
SNE	Societe Nouvelle des Establishments (Fr.)
Titanus	Titanus Productions (Ital.)
TRC	Transcontinental Films (Fr.)
UDIF	U.D.I.F. Productions (Fr.)
UFA	Deutsche Universum-Film AG (Ger.)
UGC	Union Generale Cinematographique (Fr.)
Union	Union Films (Ger.)
Vera	Vera Productions (Fr.)

T

(NOTE: 1984 releases appear in Volume IX)

T-BIRD GANG*½   (1959) 75m Filmgroup bw (AKA:THE PAY-OFF)

Ed Nelson (*Alex*), John Brinkley (*Frank*), Pat George (*Marla*), Beach Dickerson (*Barney*), Tony Miller (*Raymond*).

Out to avenge the murder of his father, Brinkley goes undercover and joins a gang led by Nelson. Brinkley's life is saved by Nelson's right-hand man, and that precipitates the collapse of the gang. Sleazy exploitation picture good for some laughs.

p, Roger Corman; d, Richard Harbinger; w, John Brinkley, Tony Miller; m, Shelley Manne.

Crime   (PR:C MPAA:NR)

T-MEN****   (1947) 91m EL bw

Dennis O'Keefe (*Dennis O'Brien*), Alfred Ryder (*Tony Genaro*), Mary Meade (*Evangeline*), Wallace Ford (*Schemer*), June Lockhart (*Tony's Wife*), Charles McGraw (*Moxie*), Jane Randolph (*Diana*), Art Smith (*Gregg*), Herbert Heyes (*Chief Carson*), Jack Overman (*Brownie*), John Wengraf (*Shiv*), Jim Bannon (*Lindsay*), William Malten (*Paul Miller*), Reed Hadley (*Narrator*), Vivian Austin (*Genevieve*), James Seay (*Hardy*), Lyle Latell (*Isgreg*), John Newland (*Jackson Lee*), Victor Cutler (*Snapbrim*), Tito Vuolo (*Pasquale*), John Parrish (*Harry*), Curt Conway (*Shorty*), Ricki Van Dusen (*Girl on Plane*), Irmgard Dawson (*Hostess on Plane*), Robert Williams (*Detective Captain*), Anton Kosta (*Vantucci*), Paul Fierro (*Chops*), Louis Bacigalupi (*Boxcar*), Trevor Bardette (*Rudy*), William Yip (*Chinese Merchant*), Al Bridge (*Agent in Phone Booth*), Keefe Brasselle (*Cigar Attendant*), Les Sketchley (*Big Guy*), George M. Manning, Paul Hogan (*Men*), Jerry Jerome, Bernie Sell, Ralph Brooks, John Ardell (*Dice Players*), Sandra Gould (*Girl at Phone*), Cuca Martinez (*Dancer in Club*), Salvadore Barroga (*Housekeeper*), Tom McGuire, Mira McKinney (*Couple at Car*), Frank Ferguson (*Secret Service Man*), Cecil Weston (*Woman Proprietor*), Frank Hyer (*Ollie*), George Carleton (*Morgue Attendant*).

One of director Anthony Mann's finest forays into *film noir*, T-MEN was Mann's first wholly successful financial and artistic triumph. O'Keefe and Ryder are two treasury agents determined to crack a successful counterfeiting ring after a fellow agent is killed during the investigation. In order to obtain first-class information, the agents pose as underworld hoods and infiltrate a powerful Detroit mob family headed by Kosta. They discover that Ford, a sleazy little hood with a penchant for steam baths who operates out in Los Angeles, may hold the key to the counterfeiting ring and O'Keefe travels west, combing every steam bath in Los Angeles to find him. O'Keefe manages to worm his way into the counterfeiting ring by passing off a phony bill which he claims to have the plates for (provided by the Treasury Department from their stock of confiscated counterfeit plates). He sends for Ryder to come from Detroit and the men bide their time by bargaining for the supposed plates while using the situation to investigate further. The agents ingratiate themselves with Ford, though they cannot uncover the secret to the operation that will enable them to crack the case. Ford fears he'll soon be knocked off by the boys in Detroit, and he is right for they have sent McGraw to kill him. Ford begins to suspect that Ryder is a T-Man (they run into Ryder's wife on the street) and he informs McGraw of his suspicions in the hope that he'll be allowed to live. McGraw accepts the news and then locks Ford in a steam bath and turns the steam on full blast. The sadistic killer stands and watches as the hysterical Ford tries to smash the glass in the tiny window to no avail. The lethal steam bath seems to take forever, but Ford finally dies. Meanwhile, Ryder finally cracks the secret of the counterfeiting operation, just as McGraw and the gang, O'Keefe among them, arrive to kill him. Ryder knows full well what is about to happen and he manages to slip O'Keefe the essential information before he is murdered by McGraw. O'Keefe relays the information to the Treasury Department and then must work to save his own life because a member of the mob, Malten, has recognized the plates to be the work of a counterfeiter he knew in prison. The climax takes place aboard a ship where McGraw closes in on O'Keefe; as the men play cat and mouse along the twisted mass of metal pipes and ladders, a small army of T-Men descend on the ship. O'Keefe traps McGraw behind a steel door (now it is he who bangs for his life) as the law catches up with him. McGraw goes down in a hail of bullets and the counterfeiting ring is smashed. When PRC studios and Britain's J. Arthur Rank organization merged to form Eagle-Lion, the new owners encouraged better scripts and more artistic creativity while providing bigger budgets to achieve their goals. Director Mann rose to the occasion and began a series of facsinating *film noir* crime dramas (T- MEN, RAW DEAL, and THE BLACK BOOK) with superb cinematographer John Alton. Presented in a documentary-like style with narration by Reed Hadley, T-MEN shifts from the bureaucratic staunchness of the voice-over to the shadowy, out-of-control world of *film noir*. In what would become a major theme in Mann's later work (especially in the westerns with Jimmy Stewart), the film examines the thin line between the law and the lawless, the hunters and the hunted. Though lawmen O'Keefe and Ryder plunge themselves into the criminal element with fervor, they are party to acts only sanctioned by society if one wears a badge. These themes are illustrated beautifully by Alton's visuals, which see the agents in the same dark, shadowy light as the criminals. The film is at its most shocking during the steam bath murder and the scene is intense and horrifying enough to disturb most sensitive viewers. Mann and Alton's work for Eagle-Lion was so distinguished that MGM took note and signed them both on.

p, Aubrey Schenck; d, Anthony Mann; w, John C. Higgings (based on a story by Virginia Kellogg); ph, John Alton; m, Paul Sawtell; ed, Fred Allen; md, Irving Friedman; art d, Edward C. Jewell; set d, Armor Marlowe; cos, Frances Ehren; spec eff, George J. Teague; makeup, Ern Westmore, Joe Stinton.

Crime   Cas.   (PR:C MPAA:NR)

T.A.G.: THE ASSASSINATION GAME*½   (1982) 92m New World c

Robert Carradine (*Alex*), Linda Hamilton (*Susan*), Bruce Abbott (*Gersh*), Kristine DeBell (*Nancy*), Frazer Smith (*Carpenter*), Perry Lang (*Frank*), John Mengatti (*Randy*), Michael Winslow (*Gowdy*), Ivan Bonar.

A silly college game, in which the kids go about hunting each other with rubber-tipped dart guns, acts as the spark for one of the contestants, Abbott, to actually murder his rivals when he starts to take the game too seriously. He knows he's licked, and in the frustration uses a real gun to do in the contenders. Carradine plays the school reporter who follows Hamilton around as she goes about stalking her prey, and in the process falls in love with her. Although the film has the possibilities of being a dark psychological look into an innocent obsession becoming a social menace, director Castle didn't concentrate on this facet alone but went off into various other tangents which hurt the film's overall impact.

p, Peter Rosten, Dan Rosenthal; d&w, Nick Castle; ph, Willy Kurant (DeLuxe Color); m, Craig Safan; ed, Tom Walls; prod d, Peter Politanoff; art d, Randy Moore, Craig Stearns; makeup, Bob Germaine.

Drama/Thriller   Cas.   (PR:C MPAA:PG)

THX 1138***   (1971) 88m American Zoetrope/WB c

Robert Duvall (*THX 1138*), Donald Pleasence (*SEN 5241*), Don Pedro Colley (*SRT*), Maggie McOmie (*LUH 3417*), Ian Wolfe (*PTO*), Sid Haig (*NCH*), Marshall Efron (*TWA*), John Pearce (*DWY*), Johnny Weissmuller, Jr, Robert Feero (*Chrome Robots*), Irene Forrest (*IMM*), Claudette Bessing (*ELC*), Gary Alan Marsh (*CAM*), John Seaton (*OUE*), Eugene I. Sullivan (*JOT*), Raymond J. Walsh (*TRG*), Mark Lawhead (*Shell Dweller*), Susan Baldwin (*Control Officer*), James Wheaton (*Voice of OMM*), Henry Jacobs (*Mark 8 Student*), Bill Love (*Mark 8 Instructor*), Doc Stortt (*Monk*), Gary Austin (*Man in Yellow*), Scott L. Menges (*Child No. 1*), Toby L. Stearns (*Child No. 2*), Paul K. Haje (*Prosecutor*), Ralph Chesse (*Proctor*), Dion M. Chesse (*Defense*), Bruce Chesse (*Pontifay*), Mello Alexander, Barbara J. Artis (*The Holograms Dancers*), Morris D. Erby (*Newscaster*), Willie C. Barnes, Richard Quinnell (*Comics*), Jean M. Durand (*Listener*), Scott Beach, Neva Beach, Tarrance McGovern, Julie Payne, James Cranna, Ruth Silveira, Bruce Mackey, David Ogden Stiers (*The Announcers*).

This was Lucas' film debut, made after Francis Ford Coppola saw the short version that won Lucas the 1967 National Student Film Festival award while he was still a student at the University of Southern California. This picture stars a young Duvall playing a man who, along with McOmie and Pleasence, attempts to escape from a futuristic society located beneath the Earth's surface. Reminiscent of the repressive societies described in Ergenev Zamatin's We, George Orwell's 1984, and Aldous Huxley's Brave New World, Duvall's society has outlawed love and sex, with drugs as mandatory additions to diet. McOmie plays Duvall's love interest. She awakens him to the pleasures of love after she and Duvall stop taking the repressive drugs. They are arrested and in prison he discovers she is pregnant. While in jail, they hook up with Pleasence, who persuades the two to escape with him. In the escape attempt, McOmie and Duvall are separated and she is killed. He discovers the test tube that contains his fetus, and he and Pleasence continue their escape. After a suspenseful chase scene in which Pleasence is killed, Duvall makes it to the outer world of Earth.

p, Lawrence Sturhahn; d, George Lucas; w, Lucas, Walter Murch (based on a story by Lucas); ph, Dave Meyers, Albert Kihn (Techniscope, Technicolor); m, Lalo Schifrin; ed, Lucas; art d, Michael Haller; cos, Donald Longhurst; stunts, Jon Ward, Duffy Hamilton.

Fantasy   Cas.   (PR:C MPAA:PG)

TNT JACKSON zero   (1975) 70m Premier/New World c

Jeanne Bell (*TNT Jackson*), Stan Shaw (*Charlie*), Pat Anderson (*Elaine*), Ken Metcalf (*Sid*), Chiquito, Leo Martin, Chris Cruz, Percy Gordon, June Gamble.

Black exploitation film stars former Playmate Bell as a tough-talking black woman who's an expert in martial arts. She travels to Hong Kong in search of her missing brother, and unwittingly links up with his murderer, Shaw. Unknown to her, he's in charge of a heroin ring she's also come to investigate. His boss, Metcalf, mistakenly believes that Bell is responsible for supplying information to the police, when in fact the real leak is his lover, Anderson. Plenty of high-kicking kung-fu action, with Bell getting her shirt ripped off in practically every fight scene. Bloody ending has Anderson and Metcalf dying together, and Bell chopping the life out of Shaw.

p&d, Cirio Santiago; w, Dick Miller, Ken Metcalf; ph, Felipe J. Sacdalan (Metrocolor); m, Tito Sotto; ed, Gervasio Santos, Barbara Pokras; art d, Ben Otico.

Martial Arts (PR:O MPAA:R)

T.P.A. (SEE: PRESIDENT'S ANALYST, THE, 1967)

T.R. BASKIN*½ (1971) 89m PAR c (GB: DATE WITH A LONELY GIRL)

Candice Bergen (*T.R. Baskin*), Peter Boyle (*Jack Mitchell*), James Caan (*Larry Moore*), Marcia Rodd (*Dayle Wigoda*), Erin O'Reilly (*Kathy*), Howard Platt (*Arthur*), William Wise (*Gary*), Jane Alderman (*Marsha*), Joy Mandel (*Linda*), Fawne Harriman (*Alice*), Hope Hommersand (*Eilene*), Mariann Walters (*Interviewer*), Dick Sasso (*Cab Driver*), Mike Nussbaum (*Office Manager*), Thomas Erhart (*Landlord*), Jim Kodl (*Doorman*), Eleanor Merriam (*YWCA Woman*), Sandy Lipton (*Saleslady*), Linda Crittenden, Pam Hoffman (*Receptionists*).

Bergen stars as a naive country girl who comes to the big city of Chicago in search of love, adventure, and an interesting career. She finds none of these, but instead lives in a drab apartment, has a boring, meaningless job, and two unsuccessful affairs with Boyle and Caan. Although she raises some interesting questions, Bergen's character does not evoke the sympathy nor the interest intended. In the end, we are still left with questions but no answers.

p, Peter Hyams; d, Herbert Ross; w, Hyams; ph, Gerald Hirschfeld (Technicolor); m, Jack Elliott; ed, Maury Winetrobe; prod d&art d, Albert Brenner; set d, William B. Fosser; makeup, Lilliam Toth.

Drama/Comedy (PR:C MPAA:GP)

TA CHI (SEE: LAST WOMEN OF SHANG, 1964, Jap.)

TABLE BAY (SEE: CODE 7, VICTIM 5!, 1964, Brit.)

TABLE FOR FIVE** (1983) 122m WB c

Jon Voight (*J. P. Tannen*), Richard Crenna (*Mitchell*), Marie Christine Barrault (*Marie*), Millie Perkins (*Kathleen*), Roxana Zal (*Tilde*), Robby Kiger (*Truman-Paul*), Son Hoang Bui (*Trung*), Maria O'Brien (*Mandy*), Nelson Welch (*Old Man*), Bernie Hern (*Bickering Husband*), Moria Turner (*Bickering Wife*), Cynthia Kania, Kevin Costner (*Newlyweds*), Marion Russell (*Rodessa*), Gustaf Unger, Bertil Unger (*Twins*), Erik Holland (*Captain*), Helle Franz (*Ventriloquist*), Peggy Kubena (*Blonde*), James Lawrence (*Communications Officer*), Ora Rubinstein (*Girl on Airplane*), Robert Schaffel (*Frank*), Rupert Sykes (*Ship's Officer*), Hugo Valentino (*Ugo*), Ronald Hoiseck (*Maitre d'*), Enrico Pini (*Taxi Driver*), Said (*Jeep Driver*).

Sentimental soaper with good performances but an overlong script and some false notes. Shot mostly on the S. S. Vistafjord, which was actually making a cruise, it's the story of a man who comes to grips with a family he'd allowed to slip away. Voight and Perkins are divorced and she's remarried to attorney Crenna, a sharp, thoughtful man who takes his stepfather role seriously. After vaguely ignoring his three children for years, irresponsible Voight decides to squire them on a luxury cruise through the Mediterranean. His children are Zal, Kiger, and Bui, an adopted Asian child. Once aboard the ship, Voight learns that he has little in common with his progeny. They are close to each other but estranged from him and annoyed that he is spending more time coveting the glamorous female passengers than in spending any time with them. Voight senses their feelings and says that if he can't suddenly be their father again, is it possible that they can consider him an older pal? Voight meets Barrault and enjoys her company and manages to get to know her, despite Zal's attempts to break up this shipboard romance. The ship stops at Rome, Athens, and Cairo, and many of the scenes are set against the natural wonders of those locations with travelog footage to the Sphinx, the Colosseum, and various Greek monuments that dot Athens. Barrault becomes part of the entourage and the other two children more or less accept her. On the briney, Voight gets a call from the U.S. which tells him that Perkins has been killed in an automobile accident. Crenna is the man who gives Voight the news and says that he will fly to Europe to get the children. When he arrives, he learns that Voight has not yet told the children about their mother and is asking for a bit more time to break the tragedy to them. Crenna knows that he can probably take the children legally because Voight has already proven himself an unfit father. In the end, with Barrault's prodding, Voight decides that these children are worth fighting for and he will go to any lengths to keep them. The moral issue of natural parents versus adoptive parents is examined but no real solution is offered. Zal is excellent as the daughter and later appeared on several TV shows where she demonstrated her abilities and indicated that she has a bright acting future. Screenwriter Seltzer came up

with the idea after having experienced a real-life adoption drama of his own. He was in Vietnam doing research on a project, met a young orphan girl, and decided to adopt her. But it took too long for the beaurocracy to fall into place and he hired an older Vietnamese boy to look after the youngster. Later, both kids barely managed to make it out of the ravaged country on one of the last planes. Perkins, after being off the screen for some years, doesn't seem to have aged and still shows that the promise she had in THE DIARY OF ANNE FRANK has come to fruition. More should be seen of her. In two small roles, identical twins Gustaf and Bertil Unger, who are well-known in the Hollywood community as foreign press representatives. They are "mirror" twins in that one wears a monocle in his left eye, the other in his right. TABLE FOR FIVE was a nice attempt at a family film that eventually failed at the box office because there wasn't enough of an edge to it. Lieberman, a TV commercials director with lots of experience working with children, makes his debut. With other, more powerful material, he will be a force to reckon with. Producer Schaffel inserts himself in the small role of "Frank" and shows why he became a producer.

p, Robert Schaffel; d, Robert Lieberman; w, David Seltzer; ph, Vilmos Zsigmond (DeLuxe Color); m, Miles Goodman, John Morris; ed, Michael Kahn; prod d, Robert R. Boyle; art d, Norman Newberry; set d, Arthur Jeph Parker; cos, Vicki Sanchez, Sandy Berke, Silvio Scarano.

Drama **Cas.** (PR:C MPAA:PG)

TABU (FUGITIVOS DE LAS ISLAS DEL SUR)
(SEE: DRUMS OF TABU, 1967, Ital/Span.)

TAFFY AND THE JUNGLE HUNTER** (1965) 87m Zimbalist/AA c

Jacques Bergerac (*David Claveau*), Manuel Padilla (*Beau*), Shary Marshall (*Rosa Wynn, Governess*), Hari [Harry] Rhodes (*Kahli, Native Chief*), Taffy (*Elephant*), Margo (*Chimpanzee*), Robert DoQui.

Jungle adventure in which a young boy, Padilla, runs away to the jungle with his beloved elephant and pet chimp. A widespread search has his governess, Marshall, finding the boy and coming to terms with her fear of lions, when a beast is about to make a hearty meal out of the boy.

p, William Faris; d, Terry O. Morse; w, Arthur Hoerl, Alfred Zimbalist (based on a story by Donald Zimbalist); ph, Brydon Baker (Technicolor); m, Shorty Rogers; ed, Faris; m/l, "Taffy," A. Zimbalist, Rogers; makeup, Louis Haszillo.

Adventure (PR:AA MPAA:NR)

TAGGART** (1964) 85M UNIV c

Tony Young (*Kent Taggart*), Dan Duryea (*Jason*), Dick Foran (*Stark*), Elsa Cardenas (*Consuela Stark*), Jean Hale (*Miriam Stark*), Emile Meyer (*Ben Blazer*), David Carradine (*Cal Dodge*), Peter Duryea (*Rusty Bob Blazer*), Tom Reese (*Vince August*), Ray Teal (*Ralph Taggart*), Claudia Barrett (*Lola*), Stuart Randall (*Sheriff*), Harry Carey, Jr (*Lt. Hudson*), Bill Henry (*Army Sergeant*), Sarah Selby (*Maude Taggart*), George Murdock (*Army Scout*), Arthur Space (*Colonel*), Bob Steele (*Cook*).

Sex is what separates this western from the typical oater, making for a neat movie with plenty of action thrown in as well. Young plays the son of landowners who are killed by Peter Duryea and his parents who intend to increase their already expansive property lines. In revenge, Young kills Peter Duryea and his folks, but before dying, Duryea's father hires three gunmen to track down Young. Young manages to kill two of them before running away to Indian country, where he meets with Foran, an aging miner, his Mexican wife, Cardenas, and their daughter, Hale. He is tracked there by the lone surviving gunman, Dan Duryea, who is immediately taken prisoner by Foran. When Cardenas makes a play for Young and is rejected, she frees Duryea and makes off with him and her husband's gold. On the way she is killed by Indians. Foran, Young, and Hale join a nearby fort in helping stave off an Indian attack, and there they stumble upon Duryea. The gunman manages to kill Foran before being killed himself by Young, who shoots him after Duryea's horse collapses under him from the weight of the gold. Young and Hale are left to begin a new life together.

p, Gordon Kay; d, R.G. Springsteen; w, Robert Creighton Williams (based on a novel by Louis L'Amour); ph, William Margulies (Technicolor); m, Herman Stein; ed, Tony Martinelli; md, Joseph Gershenson; art d, Alexander Golitzen, Raymond Beal; set d, John McCarthy, James M. Walters, Sr.; makeup, Bud Westmore.

Western (PR:C MPAA:NR)

TAHITI HONEY** (1943) 69m REP bw

Simone Simon, Dennis O'Keefe, Michael Whalen, Lionel Stander, Wally Vernon, Tommey Adams, Tom Seidal, Dan Seymour.

A romance film, with touches of comedy, about O'Keefe as a pianist abandoned in Tahiti. To beef up his band, he takes on singer Simon, much to the dislike of the other band members. They head to San Francisco, only to bomb out in their few engagements. She wants to change the type of music they play and when the band finally relents everything starts going well for the boys. While this is going on, O'Keefe and Simon strike up a romance despite her engagement to a sailor. After a little competition from a different sailor, everything ends on a happy note, with the boys in the Navy and the band a success. Songs include "Tahiti Honey" (Jule Styne, George H. Brown, Sol Meyer); "You Could Hear a Pin Drop", "Any Old Port in a Storm", "This Gets Better Every Minute, "Koni Plenty Hu-Hu", "Of Course I'm a Cossack" (Charles Newman, Lew Pollack).

p&d, John H. Auer; w, Lawrence Kimble, Fredrick Kohner, H. W. Hanemann based on a story by Kohner); ph, Jack Marta; ed, Richard Van Enger; md, Morton Scott; art d, Russell Kimball.

Musical   **(PR:A   MPAA:NR)**

TAHITI NIGHTS**   (1945) 63m COL bw

Jinx Falkenburg (*Luana*), Dave O'Brien (*Jack*), Mary Treen (*Mata*), Florence Bates (*Queen Liliha*), Cy Kendall (*Chief Enoka*), Eddie Bruce (*Chopstick*), Pedro de Cordoba (*Tonga*), Hilo Hattie (*Temata*), Carole Mathews (*Betty Lou*), The Vagabonds, Isabel Withers, Peter Cusanelli, Charles Opunui, Chris Willbowbird.

O'Brien is a happy-go-lucky band leader ready to do a gig on a Tahitian island. When he arrives, he finds out there have already been plans made for him to wed the local princess. Not a bad story, but slow pace grinds everything almost to a halt. Best song of the whole affair is "Let Me Love You Tonight" (Mitchell Parrish, Rene Touzet). Another well done tune is "Cockeyed Mayor of Jaunakakai" (R. Alex Anderson, Al Stillman).

p, Sam White; d, Will Jason; w, Lillie Hayward; ph, Benjamin Kline; ed, Jerome Thoms; art d, George Brooks; set d, George Montgomery; m/l, Harry Owens.

Musical   **(PR:A   MPAA:NR)**

TAHITIAN, THE*   (1956) 79m Crane-Knott-Long c

Ana (*Herself*), Vahio (*Himself*), Taia Tepava (*Medicine Man*), Tehapaitua Salmon (*Chief Morro*), Dr. George Thooris (*Dr. De Motte*), Dr. Henry K. Beye (*Dr. Stuart*), Ben Bambridge (*Ben*), William A. Robinson (*Robinson*), Tetoa Mauu (*Tetoa*), Denise Pottier (*Singer*), Miri Rei (*Narrator*).

When a group of scientists try to stop a filaria epidemic spreading through some natives from mosquitoes, the local medicine man refuses to let a modern remedy be used on his tribe. The chief also is against the plan until his son is infested with the threadlike parasitic worms that cause the horrible disease. He quickly changes his mind and modern technologies triumph. The cast is comprised of unprofessional actors and the results show. Though some of the native dances and music give the film a realistic edge, most high school thespian productions have better performances. In addition the filmmakers are woefully inept, showing no talent at all for story construction. A narration attempts to tie it all together but it just doesn't work.

p, Cornelius Crane, James Knott, Lotus Long; d, Knott; w, Knott, Long, Annabel Ross; ph, Knott (Eastmancolor); m, Eddie Lund; ed, Otto Meyer.

Drama   **(PR:A   MPAA:NR)**

TAIHEIYO HITORIBOTCHI (SEE: ALONE ON THE PACIFIC, 1964, Jap.)

TAIHEIYO NO ARASHI (SEE: I BOMBED PEARL HARBOR, 1961, Jap.)

TAIL SPIN**   (1939) 84m FOX bw

Alice Faye (*Trixie Lee*), Constance Bennett (*Gerry Lester*), Nancy Kelly (*Lois Allen*), Joan Davis (*Babe Dugan*), Charles Farrell (*Bud*), Jane Wyman (*Alabama*), Kane Richmond (*Dick "Tex" Price*), Wally Vernon (*Chick*), Joan Valerie (*Sunny*), Edward Norris (*Speed Allen*), J. Anthony Hughes (*Al Moore*), Harry Davenport (*T. P. Lester*), Mary Gordon (*Mrs. Lee*), Harry Rosenthal (*Cafe Manager*), Irving Bacon (*Storekeeper*), Sam Hayes (*Announcer*).

This picture's story centers around the women fliers of the time and their trials and tribulations, the results of how they will do almost anything to win the cross country races. Faye is a young woman determined to win, but she runs into trouble when her plane takes a dive. She gets some other people to back her, but then runs into trouble with the wealthy and aristocratic Bennett. The two end up competing not only in racing airplanes, but also for the same man. Faye is liked by everyone else in the race, so her fellow competitors give her a helping hand along the way. Film is marred by many death scenes, including a suicide of one of the men fliers.

p, Darryl F. Zanuck; d, Roy Del Ruth; w, Frank Wead; ph, Karl Freund; ed, Allen McNeil; md, Louis Silvers; art d, Bernard Herzbrun, Rudolph Sternad; set d, Thomas Little; cos, Gwen Wakeling; m/l, "Are You in the Mood For Mischief," Mack Gordon, Harry Revel.

Drama   **(PR:A   MPAA:NR)**

TAILOR MADE MAN, A*½   (1931) 77m MGM bw

William Haines (*John Paul Bart*), Dorothy Jordan (*Tanya*), Joseph Cawthorn (*Huber*), Marjorie Rambeau (*Kitty DuPuy*), William Austin (*Jellicot*), Ian Keith (*Dr. Von Sonntag*), Hedda Hopper (*Mrs. Stanlaw*), Hale Hamilton (*Mr. Stanlaw*), Joan Marsh (*Beanie*), Martha Sleeper (*Corrine*), Henry Armetta (*Peter, Tailor*), Walter Walker (*Abraham Nathan*), Forrester Harvey (*Pomeroy*).

Remake of the 1922 silent version stars Haines as a small-time tailor pants-presser who finagles his way into the world of big business by "borrowing" Austin's dress suit. He crashes Hopper's party that Austin is also attending, and holds his breath hoping Austin won't recognize his suit. He achieves success in the end, however, when he saves the company from going under. Unfortunately, the weak storyline and Haines' poor acting ability leave a lot of loose threads to this picture.

d, Sam Wood; w, Edgar Allen Woolf (based on the play "The Importer" by Harry James Smith); ph, Alfred Gilks; ed, George Hively; art d, Cedric Gibbons.

Drama   **(PR:A   MPAA:NR)**

TAINTED MONEY   (SEE: SHOW THEM NO MERCY, 1935)

TAKE, THE**   (1974) 91m World Film Services/COL c

Billy Dee Williams (*Sneed*), Eddie Albert (*Chief Berrigan*), Frankie Avalon (*Danny James*), Sorrell Booke (*Oscar*), Tracy Reed (*Nancy*), Albert Salmi (*Dolek*), Vic Morrow (*Manso*), A. Martinez (*Tallbear*), James Luisi (*Benedetto*).

In television police show style, Williams, in one of his first starring roles, plays a police lieutenant who is taking money under the table, while at the same time attempting to break up the mob in an effort to impress his superiors. He is spurred on by Booke in this film that uses plenty of old standards, such as fistfights and car chases, in order to keep the weak storyline interesting. To justify Williams' behavior, the film shows flashbacks of his traumatic childhood, along with the sufferings he endured as a young adult that helped to shape his life. Watch for Avalon in a small part as the shifty-eyed crook.

p, Howard Brandy; d, Robert Hartford-Davis; w, Del Reisman, Franklin Coen (based on the novel Sir, You Bastard by G. F. Newman); ph, Duke Callaghan (Metrocolor); m, Fred Karlin; ed, Aaron Stell; art d, Kirk Axtel.

Action Drama   **(PR:C   MPAA:PG)**

TAKE A CHANCE*½   (1933) 80m Rowland-Brice/PAR bw

James Dunn (*Duke Stanley*), Cliff Edwards (*Louie Webb*), June Knight (*Toni Ray*), Lillian Roth (*Wanda Hill*), Charles "Buddy" Rogers (*Kenneth Raleigh*), Lillian Bond (*Thelma Green*), Charles Richmond (*Andrew Raleigh*), Dorothy Lee (*Consuelo Raleigh*), Robert Gleckler (*Mike Caruso*), Lona Andre (*Miss Miami Beach*), Harry Shannon (*Bartender*), George McKay (*Steve*), Mildred Webb (*Chorus Girl*), Marjorie Main (*Woman*).

This was taken from a successful Broadway production that starred Ethel Merman. Unfortunately, Merman wasn't in the film version in this scattered reproduction that had almost no direction. Dunn and Edwards are a couple of lame-brains, trying to rise above their carnival level to the big time. But enthusiastic performances can't save this one from being forgotten. Songs include: "Turn Out the Light" (Buddy De Sylva, Richard A. Whiting, Nacio Herb Brown), "It's only a Paper Moon" (Billy Rose, E. Y. Harburg, Harold Arlen), "Come Up and See Me Sometime" (Arthur Swanstron, Louis Alter), "Night Owl" (Herman Hupfeld), "New Deal Rhythm" (Roger Edens, Harburg), "Should I Be Sweet," "Rise 'n' Shine" (De Sylva, Vincent Youmans), "Eadie was a Lady" (DeSylva, Brown, Whiting).

d, Lawrence Schwab, Monte Brice; w, Schwab, Buddy DeSylva, Brice (based on a play by DeSylva, Sid Silvers, Nacio Brown, Schwab, Richard Whiting, Vincent Youmans); ph, William Steiner; m, Jay Gorney, Lou Alter, Herman Hupfeld; ch, Bob Connally.

Musical   **(PR:A   MPAA:NR)**

TAKE A CHANCE**   (1937, Brit.) 73m Grosvenor/ABF bw

Claude Hulbert (*Alastair Pallivant*), Binnie Hale (*Wilhelmina Ryde*), Henry Kendall (*Archie Burton*), Enid Stamp-Taylor (*Cicely Burton*), Gwen Farrar (*Lady Meriton*), Jack Barty (*Joe Cooper*), Harry Tate (*Sgt. Tugday*), Guy Middleton (*Richard Carfax*), Kynaston Reeves (*Blinkers Grayson*), Percy Walsh, Townsend Whitling, Billy Bray, Bob Emery.

Lackluster comedy has Kendall ready to wager on his longshot horse, then finding the odds against it shortening. His buddy Hulbert discovers that Kendall's cheating wife, Taylor, is giving information to her lover. Hulbert's true love, Hale, ends up winning a pile of money on the horse. Amazingly trivial, the film evaporates from the memory before the seat can fold up.

p, Harcourt Templeman; d, Sinclair Hill; w, D. B. Wyndham-Lewis, G. H. Moresby-White (based on a play by Walter Hackett); ph, John W. Boyle.

Comedy   **(PR:A   MPAA:NR)**

TAKE A GIANT STEP**   (1959) 100m Sheila/UA bw

Johnny Nash (*Spencer Scott*), Estelle Hemsley (*Grandma*), Ruby Dee (*Christine the Maid*), Frederick O'Neal (*Lem Scott*), Ellen Holly (*Carol*), Pauline Meyers (*Violet*), Beah Richards (*May Scott*), Royce Wallace (*Rose*), Frances Foster (*Poppy*), Dell Erickson (*Bobby*), Dee Pollack (*Tony*), Frank Killmond (*Gussie*), Joseph Sonessa (*Johnny*), Sherman Raskin (*Alan*).

While the filmmakers' intentions were well placed, the handling of the story didn't hold up. The film, with a screenplay by Louis S. Peterson and Julius J. Epstein, studies the difficulties a black teenager faces growing up in a white world. Nash, as the boy, is ostracized by his white friends' parents. His own parents are unresponsive to his needs, so he turns to the maid, Dee. In the stage version the relationship between the boy and the maid had heavy sexual overtones, but the film downplays that aspect of the story. Scenes depicting Nash's relationship with his white friends seem staged and awkward. However, strong performances by Nash and supporting players make the film worth viewing.

p, Julius J. Epstein; d, Philip Leacock; w, Louis S. Peterson, Epstein (based on a play by Peterson); ph, Arthur Arling; m, Jack Marshall; ed, Frank Gross; art d, Edward Carrere; cos, Bill Thomas; m/l, title song, Jay Livingston, Ray Evans (sung by Johnny Nash).

Drama   **(PR:A   MPAA:NR)**

TAKE A GIRL LIKE YOU**   (1970, Brit.) 101m Albion/COL c

Hayley Mills (*Jenny Bunn*), Oliver Reed (*Patrick Standish*), Noel Harrison (*Julian Ormerod*), John Bird (*Dick Thompson*), Sheila Hancock (*Martha Thompson*), Aimi MacDonald (*Wendy*), Geraldine Sherman (*Anna*), Ronald Lacey (*Graham*), John Fortune (*Sir Gerald*), Imogen Hassall (*Samantha*), Pippa Steel (*Ted*), Penelope Keith (*Tory Lady*), Nicholas Courtney (*Panel Chairman*), George Woodbridge (*Publican*), Jimmy Gardner (*Voter*), Nerys Hughes (*Teacher*), Jean Marlow (*Mother*), Howard Goorney (*Labor Agent*).

Story focuses on carouser Reed's obsession with deflowering the innocent Mills. She is a naive teacher who moves into a London suburb and becomes friends with Sherman, who is dating Reed. Reed is attracted to Mills, but he gets nowhere with her. At Harrison's party, Mills becomes convinced that Reed is sincere, and they agree to rendezvous the following Saturday. But before the day arrives, Mills bumps into Harrison, who tells Mills Reed has told him of the couple's plan. She decides to sleep with Harrison instead of Reed, who catches them in bed together. Mills tells Reed she wanted him to pursue her with more effort.

p, Hal E. Chester; d, Jonathan Miller; w, George Melly (based on the novel by Kingsley Amis); ph, Dick Bush (Technicolor); m, Stanley Myers; ed, Jack Harris, Rex Pyke; art d, Jack Shampan; set d, Tim Abadie; m/l, title song, Bill Martin, Phil Coulter (sung by Foundations), "It Takes a Lot of Loving," Myers, Hal Shaper (sung by Harmony Grass); makeup, George Partleton.

Comedy   **(PR:O   MPAA:R)**

TAKE A HARD RIDE**   (1975, U.S./Ital.) 103m Fanfare Music-Euro-General-Cine Y Television/FOX c

Jim Brown (*Pike*), Lee Van Cleef (*Kiefer*), Fred Williamson (*Tyree*), Catherine Spaak (*Catherine*), Jim Kelly (*Kashtok*), Barry Sullivan (*Sheriff Kane*), Dana Andrews (*Morgan*), Harry Carey, Jr (*Dumper*), Robert Donner (*Skave*), Charles McGregor (*Cloyd*), Leonard Smith (*Cangey*), Ronald Howard (*Halsey*), Ricardo Palacios (*Calvera*), Robin Levitt (*Chico*), Buddy Joe Hooken (*Angel*).

The Canary Islands provide the vivid scenery for this film, which stars ex-football player Jim Brown. Brown is a cowboy intent on delivering $86,000 to his dying boss' wife. As Brown begins his trek, he is joined by smooth-talking gambler Williamson, who has other plans for the cash. Williamson helps Brown fight off others who are pursuing him. Van Cleef is the ruthless bounty hunter who stays on the pair's trail throughout the entire film. The stunt work and second-unit direction was done by Hal Needham, who would go on to direct SMOKEY AND THE BANDIT and other stunt-oriented films.

p, Harry Bernsen, Leon Chooluck; d, Anthony M. Dawson [Antonio Margheriti]; w, Eric Bercovici, Jerry Ludwig; ph, Riccardo Pallotini (DeLuxe Color); m, Jerry Goldsmith; ed, Stanford C. Allen; art d, Julio Molina.; spec eff, Luciano D'Achille, Antonio Molina; makeup, Carmen Martin; stunts, Hal Needham, Juan Majon.

Western   **(PR:C   MPAA:PG)**

TAKE A LETTER, DARLING**½   (1942) 93m PAR bw (GB: GREEN-EYED WOMAN)

Rosalind Russell (*A. M. MacGregor*), Fred MacMurray (*Tom Verney*), Macdonald Carey (*Jonathan Caldwell*), Constance Moore (*Ethel Caldwell*), Robert Benchley (*G. B. Atwater*), Charles Arnt (*Bud Newton*), Cecil Kellaway (*Uncle George*), Kathleen Howard (*Aunt Minnie*), Margaret Seddon (*Aunt Judy*), Dooley Wilson (*Moses*), George H. Reed (*Sam*), Margaret Hayes (*Sally*), Sonny Boy Williams (*Mickey Dowling*), John Holland (*Secretary*), Florine McKinney (*Young Mother*), Dorothy Granger (*Switchboard Operator*), Amo Ingraham (*Tall Willowy Brunette*), Katharine

"Karin" Booth (*Blonde Stenographer*), Lynda Grey (*Model*), Keith Richards, Jack Rice (*Salesmen*), Lorin Raker (*Mr. Horner*), Jean Del Val (*Headwaiter*), Francis Sales (*Waiter*), Arthur Loft (*Mr. French*), Janet Graves, Douglas Dean (*Dancers*), James Millican (*Chauffeur*), George Dolenz (*Assistant Headwaiter*), Isabel Randolph (*Mrs. French*), Stanley Mack (*Boarder*), Reginald Sheffield, Reginald Simpson (*Husbands*), Virginia Brissac (*Mrs. Dowling the Landlady*), Eddie Acuff (*Man Who Picks Teeth*), Nell Craig (*Assistant Saleslady*), Betty Farrington (*Francesco's Fitter*), Sid D'Albrook (*Overalled Man*), David James (*Baby*).

Russell is an advertising executive who becomes concerned about the way the wives of some of her clients are becoming jealous of her. To put up an appearance of being spoken for, she hires MacMurray, a struggling artist looking for a way to keep food on his table while working on his canvases. His job is to be Russell's assistant and pretend to be her fiance. Enter Moore as one of Russell's clients who wants MacMurray to handle her account personally, and then some. Russell's strictly business attitude melts in the face of this unexpected competition and she finds herself thoroughly jealous about her hired beau. While a slick studio product, technically adept and well-acted, the film is utterly predictable. From the time MacMurray makes his entrance, it's only a matter of time before he and Russell end up in each other's arms. Russell's first film as a free-lance actress after the expiration of her MGM contract. Her role was originally intended for Claudette Colbert, but Colbert was suddenly reassigned to THE PALM BEACH STORY (1942) after Carole Lombard, planned for that role, was killed in a plane crash while on a war bond-selling tour. MacMurray is his usual bland, likable self, not terribly convincing as an artist. Macdonald Carey makes one of his first screen appearances, but the best reason to view this film now is to see the delightful Robert Benchley, as Russell's partner, at work in a number of funny routines.

p, Fred Kohlmar; d, Mitchell Leisen; w, Claude Binyon (based on a story by George Beck); ph, John Mescall; m, Victor Young; ed, Doane Harrison, Thomas Scott; art d, Hans Dreier, Roland Anderson; cos, Leisen, Irene.

Comedy   **(PR:A   MPAA:NR)**

TAKE A POWDER*   (1953, Brit.) 58m RLT/Apex bw

Julien Vedey (*Prof. Schultz*), Max Bacon (*Maxie*), Isabel George (*Betty*), Maudie Edwards (*Matron*), Neville Gates (*Bill*), Fred Kitchen, Jr (*Dr. Fowler*), Alexis Chesnakov (*Dr. Stroganoff*), Larry Taylor (*Spike*), Bobby Beaumont, Joe Cunningham, Mark Singleton, Gordon Craig, Muriel White, Diana Wynne.

Bacon is a nostrum-peddling quack who is mistaken for a missing atomic scientist and given a hospital to run. Stupefyingly unfunny from beginning to end.

p, Lionel Tomlinson; d, Tomlinson, Julien Vedey; w, Rex Diamond, Vedey (based on a story by Vedey), ph, Ernest Palmer.

Comedy   **(PR:A   MPAA:NR)**

TAKE ALL OF ME*½   (1978, Ital.) 90m Group I International c

Richard Johnson (*Richard Lasky*), Pamela Vincent (*Stella Glisset*), Maria Antonietta Beluzzi (*Simone*).

This melodrama features Johnson as a hard-bitten pianist who, never having made the big time, is bitter toward society. He meets Vincent, who is dying of leukemia. She builds his confidence, and he manages to get booked to do a concert in Paris. While his career is on the rebound, she is slowly dying, ending up on her deathbed the night before the performance. He will not leave her side, but she insists he play. He finally relents, and she finds the strength to make it backstage to hear his moment of triumph. Also interspersed are flashbacks of their short romance. As he plays, she dies, knowing he is happy.

p, Mario Cotone; d, Luigi Cozzi; w, Cozzi, Michele Delle Aie, Daniele Del Guidice, Sonia Molteni; ph, Roberto Piazzoli (Technicolor); m, Stelvio Cipriani.

Drama   **(PR:O   MPAA:R)**

TAKE CARE OF MY LITTLE GIRL**   (1951) 93m FOX c

Jeanne Crain (*Liz Erickson*), Dale Robertson (*Joe Blake*), Mitzi Gaynor (*Adelaide*), Jean Peters (*Dallas*), Jeffrey Hunter (*Chad Carnes*), Betty Lynn (*Marge*), Helen Westcott (*Merry Coombs*), Lenka Peterson (*Ruth*), Carol Brannon (*Casey*), Natalie Schafer (*Mother Clark*), Beverly Dennis (*Janet*), Kathleen Hughes (*Jenny*), Peggy O'Connor (*June*), Charlene Hardey (*Ellie*), Janet Stewart (*Polly*), Gail Davis (*Thelma*), Judy Walsh (*Justine*), John Litel (*Mr. Erickson*), Irene Martin (*Marcia*), Penny McGuiggan (*Helen*), Pattee Chapman (*Paula*), Mary Thomas (*Vivian*), Palma Shard (*Georgette*), Jean Romaine (*Rosalyn*), Margia Dean (*Claire*), William A. Mahan (*Pete Grayson*), Marjorie Crossland (*Olive Erickson*), June Alden (*Girl in Gym*), Billy Lechner (*Bellboy*), Jill Kraft (*Sid Goldman*), George Nader (*Jack Gruber*), Grandon Rhodes (*Prof. Benson*), Dusty Anderson (*Cashier*), Harry Harvey (*Clerk*), Garnet Marks (*Doctor*), Virginia Hunt (*Lyn Hippenstahl*), Eleanor Lawson, Shirley Tegge (*Freshmen*), King Donovan (*Cab Driver*).

This film, which takes a critical look at the sorority system, stars Crain as a spoiled but intelligent coed whose goal is to be accepted into her mother's prestigious sorority. She watches as the sorority she joins spurns her best friend, and abandons her values to help a classmate, a member of the top fraternity, cheat on an exam. After undergoing several hardships, Crain realizes the sorority system isn't all it is cracked up to be. Robertson plays the boy friend who convinces her she doesn't need to join a sorority to succeed in school.

p, Julian Blaustein; d, Jean Negulesco; w, Julius J. and Philip G. Epstein (based on the novel by Peggy Goodin); ph, Harry Jackson (Technicolor); m, Alfred Newman; ed, William Reynolds; art d, Lyle Wheeler, Joseph C. Wright; cos, William Travilla.

Drama   **(PR:A   MPAA:NR)**

TAKE DOWN**½   (1979) 107m American Film Consortium/BV c

Edward Herrmann (*Ed Branish*), Kathleen Lloyd (*Jill Branish*), Lorenzo Lamas (*Nick Kilvitus*), Maureen McCormick (*Brooke Cooper*), Nick Beauvy (*Jimmy Kier*), Stephen Furst (*Randy Jensen*), Kevin Hooks (*Jasper Mac-gruder*), Vincent Roberts (*Bobby Cooper*), Darryl Peterson (*Ted Yacabobich*), "T" Oney Smith (*Chauncey Washington*), Salvador Feliciano (*Tom Palum-bo*), Boyd Silversmith (*Jack Gross*), Scott Burgi (*Robert Stankovich*), Lynn Baird (*Doc Talada*), Ron Bartholomew (*Warren Overpeck*), Kip Otanez (*Zeno Chicarelli*), Larry Miller (*LeRoy Barron*), Gary Petersen (*Thad Lardner*), Oscar Roland (*Mr. Kilvitus*), Hyde Clayton (*Principal*), Prentiss Rowe (*Referee*), Elizabeth Grand (*Mrs. Kilvitus*), Christy Neal (*Suzette Smith*), Bob Kawa (*Rockville Coach*), Fred Carl Rowland (*Orem Coach*).

Herrmann, while waiting to hear from Harvard about a teaching post, is given the chore of coaching a high school wrestling team. The team has been pathetic through the years and Herrmann comes to realize his job involves more baby sitting than coaching. The team needs a 185-pounder, and the only student who fits the bill is an indifferent Lamas. Herrmann coaxes him out and the kid responds to all the attention. The team has all the predictable characters--the funny man, the little guy everyone protects, and the student who can only wrestle well to music. This was the first independent production distributed by Buena Vista following Walt Disney's death.

p&d, Keith Merrill; w, Merrill, Eric Hendershot (based on an idea by Hendershot); ph, Reed Smoot (Deluxe Color); m, Merrill B. Jenson; ed, Richard Fetterman; art d, Douglas G. Johnson.

Drama   **Cas.**   **(PR:C   MPAA:PG)**

TAKE HER BY SURPRISE**½   (1967, Can.) 80m Somerset/Cannon
bw (AKA: TAKEN BY SURPRISE; VIOLENT LOVE)

Paul Negri (*Walter Dorland*), Nuel Beckett (*Miklos*), Joan Armstrong (*Margaret Dorland*), Peter F. Adamson (*Korba*), Solveigh Schattmann (*Social Worker*), Michelle Albert (*Korba's Assistant*), Dara Wells (*Carla*), Marjorie Spencer (*Audience Volunteer*), Edward McCormack (*Mr. Kimble*), Marjorie McCormack (*Mrs. Kimble*).

When mobster Negri wants his wife (Armstrong) killed, he hires pyschopath Beckett, a known sex offender, to do the job. Negri gets Adamson to hypnotize Beckett, who is sent to the cabin in Canada where Armstrong is vacationing. Beckett tries to rape her before killing her, but she is able to knock him out. She hides in a barn, but Beckett finds her. A struggle ensues, and he falls from the hayloft and is killed. Negri, who thinks he now is a widower, arrives at the cabin and finds his wife with the gun he had given to Beckett. She shoots him and wanders away.

p, John Somerset [John S. Gaisford]; d, Rudi Dorn; ph, Gerhard Alsen; m, John Bath; ed, Glenn Ludlow; cos, Christine; makeup, Peggy Stevens, Marjorie Spencer.

Drama   **(PR:A   MPAA:NR)**

TAKE HER, SHE'S MINE**½   (1963) 98m FOX c

James Stewart (*Frank Michaelson*), Sandra Dee (*Mollie Michaelson*), Audrey Meadows (*Anne Michaelson*), Robert Morley (*Pope-Jones*), Philippe Forquet (*Henri Bonnet*), John McGiver (*Hector G. Ivor*), Robert Denver (*Alex*), Monica Moran (*Linda*), Jenny Maxwell (*Sarah*), Cynthia Pepper (*Adele*), Maurice Marsac (*Mons. Bonnet*), Irene Tsu (*Miss Wu*), Charla Doherty (*Liz Michaelson*), Marcel Hillaire (*Policeman*), Charles Robinson (*Stanley Bowdry*), Janine Grandel (*Mme. Bonnet*), Marie Baker.

A lighthearted family comedy about a teenage girl, Dee, whose first steps into womanhood send her father, Stewart, into a frenzy. Dee's involvement with radical anti-nuclear causes and long-haired hippies shakes up the ultraconservative and overprotective Stewart. When Dee gets sent to Paris on an art scholarship, Stewart becomes even more frantic. His worst fears are confirmed when he picks up a Life magazine and finds his daughter posing for the paintings of Forquet, a Picasso-influenced artist. Stewart runs off to Paris to keep an eye on Dee, but in the process gets himself in big trouble with the gendarmes. He is mistakenly arrested when a seedy cafe is raided, and struggles to prove his innocence. Later, at a costume ball in which Stewart dresses as Daniel Boone, Dee introduces Forquet to her father. The young couple profess their love for each other, easing Stewart's nerves and enabling him to return to the States. Although he is reassured

of Dee's safety, he is soon worrying about his younger daughter, Doherty. Although TAKE HER, SHE'S MINE is a pretty simple-minded, wholesome story, it still serves as a fine piece of family-oriented comedy. Stewart, as always, is a pleasure to watch, praise which also holds true for Meadows ("Alice Norton" in TV's "The Honeymooners") as his wife. Scripted by Johnson from a Phoebe and Henry Ephron stage play, TAKE HER, SHE'S MINE was one of three screenplays which hit the desk of Darryl F. Zanuck when he took over the presidency of 20th Century-Fox in 1962. Johnson's script was agreed to, paid for, and cast with Stewart by former head of production Peter Lavathes. When Zanuck took over he tossed out the other two scripts, keeping only Johnson's. Zanuck, however, wanted a number of changes before he would agree to a final okay. Johnson refused to write another word without additional payment and the situation almost ended in a lawsuit. Zanuck finally agreed to pay Johnson to rewrite the final third of the script, moving the locale to Paris in an effort to make the film more internationally acceptable. As Dorris Johnson and Ellen Leventhal cite in their book The Letters Of Nunnally Johnson, Johnson consented to the rewrite and "went back and finished up a very lousy third act, all taken on the back lot, and the French didn't understand that any more than the Americans."

p&d, Henry Koster; w, Nunnally Johnson (based on the play by Phoebe Ephron, Henry Ephron); ph, Lucien Ballard (CinemaScope, DeLuxe Color); m, Jerry Goldsmith; ed, Marjorie Fowler; md, Goldsmith; art d, Jack Martin Smith, Malcolm Brown; set d, Walter M. Scott, Stuart A. Reiss; cos, Travilla; spec eff, L. B. Abbott, Emil Kosa, Jr.; makeup, Ben Nye.

Comedy   **(PR:A   MPAA:NR)**

TAKE IT ALL***   (1966, Can.) 99m Films Cassiopee-Orion/Lopert bw
(A TOUT PRENDRE)

Johanne (*Johanne [Harelle]*), Claude Jutra (*Claude*), Victor Desy (*Victor*), Tania Fedor (*The Mother*), Guy Hoffmann (*The Priest*), Monique Joly (*Monique*), Monique Mercure (*Barbara*), Patrick Straram (*Nicolas*), Francois Tasse (*An Actor*).

Most of the dialog was supposedly ad-libbed during the actual shooting of this Canadian drama. Jutra is an intellectual who comes across the alluring Johanne, a black model, at a party in Montreal. The pair engage in an affair, and she becomes pregnant. Jutra considers but rejects the idea of marriage, as it would cost him his freedom. Johanne ends up losing the child and he ends the affair, returning to what he loves best, making laughter for the world through his writing. This unconventional film originally was shot by Jutra in 16mm in 1962, and makes a statement about his egotistical concerns during a real or imaginary affair. There is some confusion over who was responsible for the English narration added to the film. Some sources credit poet-musician Leonard Cohen, while others seem to credit Jutra. (In French; English subtitles.)

p, Claude Jutra, Robert Hershorn; d, Jutra; w, Jutra, Johanne, Victor Desy (based on an original idea by Jutra); ph, Michel Brault, Jean-Claude Labrecque, Bernard Gosselin; m, Jean Cousineau, Maurice Blackburn, Serge Garant; ed, Jutra, Camile Adam, Eric de Bayser, Pierre Bernard, Brault, Gilles Groulx, Werner Nold.

Drama   **(PR:A   MPAA:NR)**

TAKE IT BIG**   (1944) 75m PAR bw

Jack Haley (*Jack North*), Harriet Hilliard (*Jerry Clinton*), Mary Beth Hughes (*Gaye Livingstone*), Richard Lane (*Eddie Hampton*), Arline Judge (*Pert Martin*), Fritz Feld (*Dr. Dittenhoffer*), Lucile Gleason (*Sophie*), Fuzzy Knight (*Cowboy Joe*), Frank Forest (*Harvey Phillips*), George Meeker (*John Hankinson*), Nils T. Granlund, Ozzie Nelson and His Orchestra (*Themselves*), Ralph Peters (*House Detective*), Pansy the Horse, Rochelle and Beebe.

Haley is part of an act in which he plays the back end of a horse. He finds out he has inherited a dude ranch, and shows up at the fancy place he now thinks is his. He discovers, however, that he actually owns the run-down A-Bar-B. He pulls the place out of bankruptcy by putting on a show with help from Hilliard, Forest, and Nelson. Neither Haley's comedic touch, nor Hilliard's and Forest's voices can help the weak plot. Forest, who previously worked in radio, performs a scene from Gioacchino Antonio Rossini's opera "Barber of Seville." Jerry Seelen and Lester Lee contributed several songs to the film. "Sunday, Monday and Always" (Johnny Burke, Jimmy Van Heusen), became a hit when performed in DIXIE (1943) by Bing Crosby. Other songs are "Love and Learn," "Life Can Be Beautiful," "Take It Big," and "I'm a Big Success with You."

p, William H. Pine, William C. Thomas; d, Frank McDonald; w, Howard J. Green, Joe Bigelow; ph, Fred Jackman, Jr.; m, Rudy Schrager; ed, Victor Lewis, Howard Smith; art d, F. Paul Sylos.

Musical   **Cas.**   **(PR:A   MPAA:NR)**

TAKE IT FROM ME*½   (1937, Brit.) 78m WB-FN bw (GB: TRANSATLANTIC TROUBLE)

Max Miller (Albert Hall), Betty Lynne (Lilli Maguet), Buddy Baer (Kid Brody), Clem Lawrence (Timber Wood), Zillah Bateman (Lady Foxham), James Stephenson (Lewis), Charlotte Parry (Mrs. Murphy), Joan Miller (Secretary).

Lightweight comedy features Baer as a boxer who becomes flirtatious Bateman's "protege" after he knocks out her previous favorite in a fight. They sail to England on an ocean liner, and en route Baer's manager (Miller) is mistaken by gold digger Lynne for a millionaire. Lynne learns the truth, dumps Miller, and pursues Baer instead.

p, Irving Asher; d, William Beaudine; w, John Meehan, Jr., J.O.C. Orton; ph, Basil Emmott.

Comedy   **(PR:A   MPAA:NR)**

TAKE IT OR LEAVE IT**   (1944) 70m FOX bw

Phil Baker, Phil Silvers (Themselves), Edward Ryan (Eddie), Marjorie Massow (Kate Collins), Stanley Prager (Herb Gordon), Roy Gordon (Dr. Edward Preston), Nana Bryant (Miss Burke), Carleton Young (Program Director), Ann Corcoran (Secretary), Nella Walker (Mrs. Preston), Renie Riano (Mrs. Bramble), Frank Jenks (Taxi Driver), B.S. Pully (Truck Driver).

Baker hosted a popular radio program, and this film tries to cash in on his popularity. Ryan is a young husband who needs $1,000 to pay his pregnant wife's doctor. He takes his wife and buddy to a popular game show broadcast and becomes a participant. Goodhearted Baker realizes that Ryan needs more than just the $64 in prize money, so he adds some zeroes. Ryan makes his bucks in the "scenes from famous movies" category, which let the makers of the film slip in 20th Century-Fox movie clips featuring Shirley Temple, Al Jolson, and Sonja Henie.

ph, Joseph LaShelle; ed, Harry Reynolds; md, Emil Newman; art d, Lyle Wheeler, Leland Fuller; spec eff, Fred Sersen, cos, Kay Nelson.

Musical   **(PR:A   MPAA:NR)**

TAKE ME AWAY, MY LOVE*   (1962, Gr.) 90m Bezant/Greek Motion Pictures bw

Christina Sylba (Lilia), George Foundas (Memas), Andrew Barkoulis (Alkis), Betty Sabba (Sophia).

Sordid melodrama which sees a sleazy nightclub owner, Foundas, force his young hostess, Sylba, into the unsavory world of prostitution. Barkoulis, a reporter in love with Sylba, uncovers Foundas' crime syndicate and rescues the girl.

p, K. Drista, G. Dambakare; d, E. Giannopoulou; w, Dritsa.

Crime   **(PR:O   MPAA:NR)**

TAKE ME HIGH**   (1973, Brit.) 90m EMI c

Cliff Richard, Debbie Watling, Hugh Griffith, George Cole, Anthony Andrews, Richard Wattis.

When a struggling eatery has some trouble promoting a new hamburger, the manager of a local bank steps in to help. An unbelievable musical, sans dancing, definitely aimed at youngsters. Richard, an occasional film performer, was better known as a minor British pop star. Look for a young Andrews, who would become an accomplished actor in just a few years with the television mini-series "Brideshead Revisited."

p, Kenneth Harper; d, David Askey; w, Christopher Penfold; ph, Norman Warwick (Technicolor); m, Tony Cole; m/l, Cole.

Musical   **(PR:A   MPAA:NR)**

TAKE ME OUT TO THE BALL GAME****   (1949) 93m MGM c (GB: EVERYBODY'S CHEERING)

Frank Sinatra (Dennis Ryan), Esther Williams (K.C. Higgins), Gene Kelly (Eddie O'Brien), Betty Garrett (Shirley Delwyn), Edward Arnold (Joe Lorgan), Jules Munshin (Nat Goldberg), Richard Lane (Michael Gilhuly), Tom Dugan (Slappy Burke), Murray Alper (Zalinka), Wilton Graff (Nick Donford), Mack Gray, Charles Regan (Henchmen), Saul Gorss (Steve), Douglas Fowley (Karl), Eddie Parkes (Dr. Winston), James Burke (Cop in Park), The Blackburn Twins (Specialty), Gordon Jones (Sen. Catcher), Jack Bruce, John "Red" Burger, Aaron Phillips, Edward Cutler, Ellsworth Blake, Harry Allen, Joseph Roach, Hubert Kerns, Pete Kooy, Robert Simpson, Richard Landry, Jack Boyle, Richard Beavers (Wolves' Team), Virginia Bates, Joi Landing (Girls on Train), Mitchell Lewis (Fisherman), Esther Michaelson (Fisherman's Wife), Almira Sessions, Isabel O'Madigan, Gil Perkins, Robert Stephenson, Charles Sullivan, Edna Harris (Fans), Frank Scannell (Reporter), Henry Kulky (Burly Acrobat), Dorothy Abbott (Girl Dancer), Jackie Jackson (Kid), Si Jenks (Sam), Jack Rice (Room Clerk), Ed Cassidy (Teddy Roosevelt), Dick Wessel (Umpire), Sally Forrest (Dancer).

Sinatra and Kelly are a popular song-and-dance team on the vaudeville circuit who spend their summers playing baseball in a semi-professional

league. Ready to begin a new season, the pair are surprised and delighted to find Williams is the new team owner as well as their manager. Both find her attractive, but Williams is only interested in fielding a good team. Kelly takes a job moonlighting as a dance director for a nightclub chorus line, and Williams angrily benches him for violating training rules. Kelly then falls under the spell of Arnold, a seemingly benevolent man who in reality is a big-time gambler. He has interests in an opposing team, and wants Kelly to help throw some games so as to ensure his investment. Eventually Kelly catches on, and Arnold tries to keep him from playing in an important game. Kelly manages to get to the ball park in time, helping Williams and his teammates to win the pennant. Williams at last falls for Kelly, while her friend Garrett ends up winning Sinatra's heart. This is an amiable film, marked by the enjoyable cast and some lively, if not memorable, music. TAKE ME OUT TO THE BALL GAME was Sinatra and Kelly's follow-up to ANCHORS AWEIGH (1945), and the two are again well-matched partners. Williams essays her role with grit, toeing the line as the no-nonsense manager, yet always keeping a certain femininity. This is one of her few roles where she barely gets near a pool (only once in fact), but even sans water Williams musters a good performance. The film was based on an original idea of Kelly and Stanley Donen's, which closely resembled a minor 1930 film, THEY LEARNED ABOUT WOMEN. After concocting the story (for which they received $25,000), Kelly and Donen asked for the chance to direct. However, this was resolved amicably when it was decided to bring Berkeley on as director. This would be his last directoral effort, a favor granted to the once mighty talent by producer Freed. Berkeley had suffered from many personal problems, which had led to a nervous breakdown, and now he wanted to make a fresh start. He had asked Freed to help him out, and the producer–who had received generous help in his early career from Berkeley– responded by giving Berkeley another chance behind the camera. Kelly and Donen were allowed to direct TAKE ME OUT TO THE BALL GAME's musical sequences. Freed was impressed by their talents, and allowed the pair to direct the next Kelly-Sinatra film, ON THE TOWN, later that year. Production went smoothly on TAKE ME OUT TO THE BALL GAME. "We had weeks of grinding rehearsals," Garrett recalled, "...and we became very close....we were doing a two shot of a little scene together and they shot the master shot, then they shot over my shoulder to get a closeup of Frank and started to move the camera away. He yelled, 'Hey, wait a minute. How about a closeup of my girl here?' They gave me that closeup because of Frank." Sinatra was never known as much of a dancer, but Kelly made the most he could of Sinatra's talents, working dance routines around his abilities without ever compromising the work. The songs include: "Take Me Out to the Ball Game" (Albert von Tilzer, Jack Norworth), "The Hat My Father Wore on St. Patrick's Day" (William Jerome, Jean Schwartz, sung by Kelly), "O'Brien to Ryan to Goldberg" (Roger Edens, Betty Comden, Adolph Green, sung by Kelly, Sinatra, Jules Munshin), "The Right Girl for Me" (Edens, Comden, Green, sung by Sinatra), "It's Fate, Baby, It's Fate" (Edens, Comden, Green, sung by Sinatra, Garrett), "Yes Indeedy" (Edens, Comden, Green, sung by Kelly, Sinatra), "Strictly U.S.A." (Edens, Comden, Green).

p, Arthur Freed; d, Busby Berkeley; w, Harry Tugend, George Wells (uncredited) Harry Crane (based on a story by Gene Kelly and Stanley Donen); ph, George Folsey (Technicolor); m, Robert Edens; ed, Blanche Sewell; md, Adolph Deutsch; art d, Cedric Gibbons, Daniel B. Cathcart; set d, Edwin B. Willis, Henry W. Grace; cos, Helen Rose, Valles; spec eff, Warren Newcombe, Peter Ballbusch; ch, Kelly, Donen; makeup, Jack Dawn.

Musical   **(PR:AA   MPAA:NR)**

TAKE ME OVER**   (1963, Brit.) 60m COL bw

Temperance Seven (The Twenties Group), John Paul (Campbell Carter), John Rutland (Sid Light), Diane Aubrey (Carole Carter), Mark Burns (Bill Light), Mildred Mayne (Typist), Totti Truman-Taylor (Woman).

Undistinguished musical which sees a hotel builder try all sorts of outrageous schemes in order to buy an antique store and coffee shop that are vital to the success of his new venture. A change of genre for lower-case thriller director Lynn.

p, William McLeod; d, Robert Lynn; w, Dail Ambler.

Musical   **(PR:A   MPAA:NR)**

TAKE ME TO PARIS**   (1951, Brit.) 72m Byron/ABF-Pathe bw

Albert Modley (Albert), Roberta Huby (Linda Vane), Bruce Seton (Gerald Vane), Claire Guilbert (Annette), Richard Molinas (Pojo), George Bishop (Mr. Armstrong), Leonard Sharp (Walter), Jim Gerald (Butcher), Argus (Jules), Lottie Beck, Marc Valbel, Gerald Rex, Paul Bonifas.

A goofy little comedy which sees some shady stable boys from Britain and France team up in a scheme to smuggle counterfeit cash across the English Channel under a horse blanket. Their plan goes awry when the horse they had picked out is injured and withdrawn from the race. Seeking a replacement, the crooks are forced to rely on the laughingstock of the stables, Dunderhead. Dunderhead's much-maligned jockey, Modley, overhears the criminals, plan and succeeds in ruining their scheme while winning the big race astride Dunderhead.

p, Henry Halstead; d, Jack Raymond; w, Max Catto; ph, James Wilson.

Comedy (PR:A MPAA:NR)

TAKE ME TO TOWN** (1953) 81m UNIV c

Ann Sheridan (*Vermilion O'Toole*), Sterling Hayden (*Will Hall*), Philip Reed (*Newton Cole*), Lee Patrick (*Rose*), Phyllis Stanley (*Mrs. Stoffer*), Lee Aaker (*Corney*), Harvey Grant (*Petey*), Dusty Henley (*Bucket*), Larry Gates (*Ed Daggett*), Forrest Lewis (*Ed Higgins*), Dorothy Neumann (*Felice Pickett*), Ann Tyrell (*Louise Pickett*), Robert Anderson (*Chuck*), Frank Sully (*Sammy*), Lane Chandler (*Mike*), Guy Williams (*Hero*), Alice Kelley (*Heroine*), Ruth Hampton, Jackie Loughery, Valerie Jackson, Anita Ekberg (*Dancehall Girls*), Fess Parker (*Long John*), Dusty Walker (*Singer*), Mickey Little, Jimmy Karath, Jerry Wayne (*Boys*), The Pickett Sisters.

A pleasant outdoor adventure-comedy with a few songs sprinkled through to lift the proceedings out of the very ordinary. Sheridan is a saloon singer on the run from Gates, a federal agent. There are some charges against her which have been trumped up but she has no faith in the judicial system so she's taken refuge in a Northwest lumber area and hopes to submerge herself in the tall timber. Hayden is a logger and a part-time preacher. He is widowed and is raising three children, Aaker, Grant, and Henley, but they need more than a dad who spends half his time chopping trees and the other half denouncing the Devil. When the kids meet Sheridan, they think she'd make a swell mother for them and they do their best to arrange that situation with Hayden. In the meantime local man-hungry widow Stanley is resentful of Sheridan's appearance as she was hoping to nab Hayden herself. Hayden comes to love Sheridan but she is shunned by the rest of the conservative community until she shows her mettle by killing a bear, getting rid of Reed, a former boy friend from her sordid past, making friends with Patrick, the woman who runs the town's dancehall, and, finally, when the place needs some money to erect a new house of worship, Sheridan calls upon her show business expertise and pulls a Mickey Rooney-Judy Garland as she stages a program that gets everyone hootin' and hollerin' and donating money for the church as Gates arrives to announce that the charges have been dropped. Songs include: "The Tale of Vermilion O'Toole" (Frederick Herbert, sung over titles by Dusty Walker), "Holy, Holy, Holy" (traditional, sung by choir), "Oh, You Red-Head" (Herbert, Milton Rosen, sung by Sheridan, Patrick, chorus), "Take Me to Town" (Lester Lee, Dan Shapiro, sung by the Pickett Sisters.) In a small role, that's Fess Parker as "Long John" and if you really have a sharp eye you'll notice comely Swedish actress Anita Ekberg in either her first or second film. In 1953, she also made THE GOLDEN BLADE at the same studio. Another very attractive dance hall girl was Jackie Loughery, former "Miss USA" (1952) who later married "Dragnet's" Jack Webb.

p, Ross Hunter, Leonard Goldstein; d, Douglas Sirk; w, Richard Morris (based on his story "Flame of the Timberline"); ph, Russell Metty (Technicolor); m, Joseph Gershenson; ed, Milton Carruth; art d, Bernard Herzbrun, Hilyard Brown, Alexander Golitzen; set d, Russell A. Gausman, Julia Heron; cos, Bill Thomas; ch, Hal Belfer.

Adventure/Comedy/Musical (PR:A MPAA:NR)

TAKE ME TO THE FAIR (SEE: IT HAPPENED AT THE WORLD'S FAIR, 1963)

TAKE MY LIFE*½ (1942) 70m Toddy-Consolidated bw

Harlem Tuff Kids: Freddie Jackson (*Harlem Tuff Kid Johnny*), Eugene Jackson (*Tuff Kid Bill*), Paul White (*Tuff Kid Icky*), Eddie Lynn (*Tuff Kid Stinky*), DeForrest Covan (*Tuff Kid Shadow*), Monte Hawley (*Dr. Thurman*), Jeni Le Gon (*Helen Stanley*), Lovey Lane (*Renie DeVere*), Robert Webb (*Ace Baldwin*), Jack Carr (*Sgt. Holmes*), Harry Leverette (*Cpl. Mack*), Guernsey Morrow (*Dr. Moore*), Herbert Skinner (*Dr. Johnson*), Arthur Ray (*Rev. Wyman*).

An all-black cast is featured in this melodrama about a group of teenage boys who are led down the road to tragedy by their evil companions. Featuring little action and an abundance of dialog, the film attempts to be a morality play, murder story, comedy, and government propaganda short, all rolled into one. The moral issues, including prison reform, are treated in an overly dramatic and preachy way, and the message is lost.

p&d, Harry M. Popkin; w, Billie Myers, Edward Dewey (based on a story by Myers); ph, Clark Ramsey; ed, Martin J. Cohn.

Drama (PR:A MPAA:NR)

TAKE MY LIFE*½ (1948, Brit.) 79m Cineguild/EL-Rank bw

Hugh Williams (*Nicholas Talbot*), Greta Gynt (*Philippa Bentley*), Marius Goring (*Sidney Flemming*), Francis L. Sullivan (*Prosecuting Counsel*), Henry Edwards (*Inspector Archer*), Rosalie Crutchley (*Elizabeth Rusman*), Marjorie Mars (*Mrs. Newcombe*), Maurice Denham (*Defending Counsel*), Leo Britt (*John Newcombe*), David Wallbridge (*Leslie Newcombe*), Ronald Adam (*Deaf Man*), Herbert Walton (*Mike Grieve*), Henry Morrell (*Judge*), Leo Bieber (*Conductor*).

Cinematographer Ronald Neame takes his first crack at directing in this film about an opera star's husband who is framed on a murder charge. All the evidence points to him since he was the dead woman's ex-fiance; only his wife believes he is innocent. The only evidence is some written music on a piece of torn paper. With this clue, Gynt embarks on a plan to clear her husband's name and she succeeds.

p, Anthony Havelock-Allan; d, Ronald Neame; w, Winston Graham, Valerie Taylor, Margaret Kennedy; (based on a story by Graham and Taylor); ph, Guy Green; m, William Alwyn; ed, Jack Harris, Geoffrey Foot; prod d, John Bryan; md, Muir Mathieson; art d, Wilfred Shingleton; cos, Joy Ricardo.

Murder Mystery (PR:A MPAA:NR)

TAKE MY TIP** (1937, Brit.) 74m GAU/GFD bw

Jack Hulbert (*Lord George Pilkington*), Cicely Courtneidge (*Lady Hattie Pilkington*), Harold Huth (*Buchan*), Frank Cellier (*Paradine*), Frank Pettingell (*Willis*), Robb Wilton (*Foreman*), Philip Buchel (*Dancing Guest*), H.F. Maltby (*Patchett*), Eliot Makeham (*Digworthy*), Paul Sheridan (*Clerk in Hotel*).

A lighthearted, silly musical comedy about a pair of wealthy folks who have been swindled out of their money, and set out to catch the crook. They dress up as servants in a hotel that their butler owns and, through assuming several identities, get their fortune back. Hulbert and Courtneidge were musical comedy stars for several years in England before entering films. Songs include "I Was Anything But Sentimental" and "I'm Like a Little Birdie Out of My Cage."

p, Michael Balcon; d, Herbert Mason; w, Sidney Gilliat, Michael Hogan, Jack Hulbert; ph, Bernard Knowles; ch, Philip Buchel, Scott Courtney.

Comedy (PR:A MPAA:NR)

TAKE OFF THAT HAT** (1938, Brit.) 86m Viking bw

Scott and Whaley (*Cuthbert and Pussyfoot*), C. Denier Warren (*Ginsberg*), Fred Duprez (*Burroughs*), Inga Andersen, Billy Russell, Gipsy Nina, Olly Alston and His Band, The Sherman Fisher Girls.

A chaotic comedy-variety show loosely tied together by the black comedian team of Scott and Whaley. The duo fake a winning ticket on the soccer pool and end up with thousands of dollars which they spend on a lavish, ultra-modern apartment. They turn every knob and push every button in sight which causes the water, heat, and appliances to go wild. After getting things relatively under control, the men are visited by a variety of strange people, including a clown who tunes their piano with construction tools. It's all very bizarre and a number of musical interludes are worked into the story as well. The film was reissued a year later with 27 minutes removed.

p&d, Eric Humphris; w, Edmund Dalby, C. Denier Warren; ph, Desmond Dickinson.

Comedy/Musical (PR:A MPAA:NR)

TAKE ONE FALSE STEP*** (1949) 94m UNIV bw

William Powell (*Prof. Andrew Gentling*), Shelley Winters (*Catherine Sykes*), Marsha Hunt (*Martha Wier*), Dorothy Hart (*Helen Gentling*), James Gleason (*Gledhill*), Felix Bressart (*Prof. Morris Avrum*), Art Baker (*Henry Pritchard*), Sheldon Leonard (*Pacciano*), Howard Freeman (*Dr. Markheim*), Houseley Stevenson (*Thatcher*), Paul Harvey (*Mr. Arnspiger*), Francis Pierlot (*Dr. Watson*), Jess Barker (*Arnold Sykes*), Mikel Conrad (*Freddie*), Enid Markey (*Clara*), Tony Curtis (*Hot Rod Driver*), Sandra Gould (*Newspaper Girl*), Dorothy Vaughan (*Leona*), Minerva Urecal (*Woman Gas Station Attendant*), Maurice Marsac (*Louis the Maitre d'*), Tommy Ivo (*Boy*), Ralph Peters (*Portly Man*), Harland Tucker (*Clerk*), Lyle Latell (*Reporter*), George Lynn, Charles J. Flynn, Edmund Cobb, Charles McAvoy (*Policemen*), Lennie Bremen (*Truck Driver*), Herbert Heywood (*Attendant*), Jack Rice (*Good Humor Man*), Marjorie Bennett (*Waitress*), Frank Cady, Paul Brinegar (*Players*), Helen Crozier (*Maid*), Jim Toney (*Bartender*), Ethyl May Halls (*Woman at Window*).

This is an unusual blend of comedy and violence that well combines the different genres' elements. Powell, ever the debonair gentleman, plays a college professor whose sedate life with spouse Hart is given a sudden jolt when his old girl friend Winters re-enters his life. He agrees to meet her for dinner to talk over old times. After their date Winters mysteriously disappears and all evidence points towards murder. Powell has been trying to get a prim and proper philanthropist to donate a sizable amount of cash to his school and knows any link with a murder case will dash whatever hopes he has for this. Before the police learn that Powell had been with Winters, the teacher decides to begin an investigation of his own, following the trail from Los Angeles to San Francisco. Here the story takes some violent turns as Powell encounters a vicious police dog, as well as witnessing a man crushed by the wheels of an unrelenting train. Powell's encounters with some rather shady characters, as well as his growing fear of rabies as a result of his dog bite, only add to the terrifying aspects of the story. Starting off as a light comedy, the plot takes several surprising twists, changing the very nature of the story with sudden and shocking impact. Though not as engaging a mystery as any of Powell's THIN MAN films, the picture holds its own with the odd combination of laughs and thrills. At the time of this film's production Winters was studying Shakespeare under the tutelage of Charles Laughton. One day she was awakened from her usual lunch-hour nap and summoned to the offices of William Goetz, a studio exeutive. In her book *Shelley Also Known As Shirley* Winters recalled that "Mr. Goetz informed me that the cameraman was complaining that I had rings under my eyes that even makeup and special lighting could not completely wipe out. ...'you've just got to get some sleep. We've got lots of money invested in you, and we're building your career' [Goetz was quoted as saying.] I explained that I was studying Shakespeare... every night in order to train myself to become a better actress. There was a long pause while he stared at me in disbelief. Finally, he said, 'We don't do much Shakespeare out here at the Valley lot, so you sleep at night, you hear me?'"

p&d, Chester Erskine; w, Erskine, Irwin Shaw (based on the novel *Night Call* by Irwin and David Shaw); ph, Franz Planer; m, Walter Scharf; ed, Russell Schoengarth; art d, Bernard Herzbrun, Emrich Nicholson; set d, Ruby Levitt; cos, Orry-Kelly; makeup, Bud Westmore, Emile LaVigne.

Crime   **(PR:C MPAA:NR)**

TAKE THE HEIR**   (1930) 63m Screen Story Syndicate/Big 4 bw

Edward Everett Horton (*Smithers*), Dorothy Devore (*Susan*), Frank Elliott (*Lord Tweedham*), Edythe Chapman (*Lady Tweedham*), Otis Harlan (*John Walker*), Kay Deslys (*Muriel Walker*), Margaret Campbell (*Mrs. Smythe-Bellingham*).

Elliott, an oft-inebriated Englishman, inherits the estate of a wealthy uncle in America. Because of his condition his valet, Horton, must take up his employer's guise. He goes to the home of the executor of the will (Harlan) and is immediately smitten with maid Devore. Unfortunately, Deslys, Harlan's plump daughter, sets her eyes on Horton and attempts to woo him with not-too-subtle affections. Several plot twists later Horton's identity is revealed and he wins Devore's heart while Elliott ends up with Deslys. A mildly amusing comedy.

p, John R. Freuler, C.A. Stimson; d, Lloyd Ingraham; w, Beatrice Van; ph, Allen Siegler; m, J.M. Coopersmith.

Comedy   **(PR:AA MPAA:NR)**

TAKE THE HIGH GROUND***   (1953) 101m MGM c

Richard Widmark (*Sgt. Thorne Ryan*), Karl Malden (*Sgt. Laverne Holt*), Elaine Stewart (*Julie Mollison*), Russ Tamblyn (*Paul Jamison*), Carleton Carpenter (*Merton Tolliver*), Steve Forrest (*Lobo Naglaski*), Jerome Courtland (*Elvin Carey*), William Hairston (*Daniel Hazard*), Robert Arthur (*Donald Q. Dover IV*), Maurice Jara (*Franklin D. No Bear*), Chris Warfield (*Soldier*), Bert Freed (*Sgt. Vince Opperman*), Regis Toomey (*Chaplain*), Fort Bliss Personnel.

Dore Schary produced a number of rough Army films and TAKE THE HIGH GROUND fits right into the mold. This time it's about how a diverse group of raw civilians become fighting machines. Widmark has a lock on this role and plays it well as the top sergeant in charge of getting this group of basic wimps ready for battle in a short period of time so they can save their own lives. While Widmark is the tough guy, Malden plays the good-hearted leader, with a soft spot in his heart for the men, and a sympathetic ear. It also shows the inner conflicts the men face, the conflicts among themselves, and the troubles their women must endure when the men are shipped out.

p, Dore Schary; d, Richard Brooks; w, Millard Kaufman; ph, John Alton (Ansco Color); m, Dimitri Tiomkin; ed, John Dunning; art d, Cedric Gibbons; m/l, Tiomkin, Ned Washington.

War   **(PR:A MPAA:NR)**

TAKE THE MONEY AND RUN***½   (1969) 85m
                                   Heywood-Hillary-Palomar/CINERAMA c

Woody Allen (*Virgil Starkwell*), Janet Margolin (*Louise*), Marcel Hillaire (*Fritz*), Jacquelyn Hyde (*Miss Blaire*), Lonny Chapman (*Jake*), Jan Merlin (*Al*), James Anderson (*Chain Gang Warden*), Howard Storm (*Fred*), Mark Gordon (*Vince*), Micil Murphy (*Frank*), Minnow Moskowitz (*Joe Agneta*), Nate Jacobson (*Judge*), Grace Bauer (*Farmhouse Lady*), Ethel Sokolow (*Mother Starkwell*), Henry Leff (*Father Starkwell*), Don Frazier (*Psychiatrist*), Mike O'Dowd (*Michael Sullivan*), Jackson Beck (*Narrator*).

Woody Allen's first directorial achievement is a frequently hilarious, sometimes misfiring satire of crime movies. Allen plays the typical shlemiel, a put-upon wimp who becomes a compulsive criminal. Told in a semi-documentary fashion with a rumbling narration by Beck (who was heard as the narrator on radio's "Superman" for years), it portends what Allen was to do years later in ZELIG. Allen begins his criminal career by robbing vending machines. His parents, Leff and Sokolow, are seen talking about their misguided son while wearing eyeglass-nose-mustache disguises so they won't be recognized by the neighbors when this "documentary" is released. After an attempt at heisting money from an armored car, Allen is caught and sent to a prison where the inmates are a compendium of every inmate ever seen in a prison film (thus making it very funny for anyone who has ever seen that kind of movie). Allen tries to escape by carving a gun out of a bar of soap (a takeoff on what John Dillinger did). It's a bust and two more years are added to his sentence. To get out, Allen volunteers to be a guinea pig in a dangerous medical experiment and he is rewarded by a parole. On the streets again, he tries to become legitimate but the call to criminality overtakes him. He plans to snatch the purse of Margolin, a lovely laundress, but changes his mind when he falls in love, saying: "After the first 15 minutes, I knew I wanted to marry her. And after the first half hour, I totally gave up the idea of snatching her purse." (A comment which shows the order in which the compulsive criminal places priorities.) Now in love and needing money, Allen tries to rob a bank and hands his scrawled note to the tellers. An argument erupts when the bank's employees can't read his handwriting. He is again thrown into jail, where Margolin makes regular visits to keep his spirits buoyed. Through a mistake, Allen gets out of jail. He marries Margolin and moves to another state where he takes an office job in a sincere attempt to go straight. Hyde, one of his fellow employees at the office, discovers his true identity and tries to blackmail him. She wants his body and will stop at nothing to get it. Allen retaliates at a turkey dinner she's prepared by attempting to stab her to death with an overcooked drumstick. Margolin becomes pregnant and Allen thinks he has to try one more robbery to make enough money to care for his burgeoning family. He attempts to crack another bank and winds up incarcerated once more. Attached to five other convicts in a chain gang, Allen leads them out of jail and to a farm house where Bauer is frightened of the sextet. (Some very funny moments here when one of the men wants to go to the bathroom and they all have to watch in close-order steps because they are attached by chains.) The escapees break the chains, after an anxious moment with some dumb cops, and go their separate ways. Allen returns to Margolin and now tops the "Most Wanted" list. He is soon apprehended and taken to jail where he reflects on his life, patiently carving up another bar of soap as the picture ends. One-liners galore, lots of episodic scenes and some good satire, with the intercutting of actual news footage to establish the era (President Richard Nixon and Dwight Eisenhower are prominent). A bit of an homage to Claude Lelouch in the love scenes between Allen and Margolin, then into the jail sequences that can only be appreciated if one has seen I AM A FUGITIVE FROM A CHAIN GANG, THE LAST MILE, or any of many jail movies. A spotty picture with many delicious moments, including a sequence where Allen hires an over-the-hill movie director (Hillaire) to pretend he is shooting a film about a bank robbery. Allen and his men will use that as a cover to actually rob the institution and everything is going well until a rival gang arrives with the same intention in mind. Several inside jokes make it hard for many people in the hinterlands to fathom. Allen had written WHAT'S NEW PUSSYCAT?, coscripted WHAT'S UP TIGER LILY? and had his play used as the basis for DON'T DRINK THE WATER. From this picture on, he was to become an eminent comedy writer-director-actor of the 1970s, and continued into the next decade. Cinematographer Said was replaced on the movie and received no credit, despite having worked on it for a few weeks. Allen's co-author on this and BANANAS was Rose, who decided to leave New York and try his hand at solo screenwriting in California.

p, Charles H. Joffe; d, Woody Allen; w, Allen, Mickey Rose; ph, Lester Shorr, (uncredited) Fouad Said (Eastmancolor); m, Marvin Hamlisch; ed, Ralph Rosenblum, James T. Heckert, Ron Kalish, Paul Jordan; md, Kermit Levinsky; art d, Fred Harpman; set d, Marvin March; spec eff, A. D. Flowers; makeup, Stanley R. Dufford.

Comedy   **Cas.**   **(PR:C MPAA:M)**

TAKE THE STAGE   (SEE: CURTAIN CALL AT CACTUS CREEK,
                                                                  1950)

TAKE THE STAND*½   (1934) 78m Liberty bw (GB: THE GREAT
                                                       RADIO MYSTERY)

Jack LaRue, Thelma Todd, Gail Patrick, Russell Hopton, Berton Churchill, Vince Barnett, Leslie Fenton, Sheila Terry, Paul Hurst, DeWitt Jennings, Bradley Page, Oscar Apfel, Jason Robards, Sr, Richard Tucker, Arnold Gray, Edward Kane, Lew Kelly, Al Hill.

This story about newspaper columnists, based loosely on Earl Derr Biggers' novel, Take the Stand, is a simple, if not boring, story about a group of people all having good reason to rub out an abrasive columnist. All gather in his office and just when he is starting his radio broadcast, the words, "don't shoot" are heard over the air. Detective Hopton gets on the case and finds LaRue has been done in by an icicle. Not much of a buildup leaves little emotion for the climax.

p, M.H. Hoffman; d, Phil Rosen; w, Albert Demond (based on the novel *The Deuce of Hearts* by Earl Derr Biggers); ph, Harry Neumann, Tom Galligan; ed, Mildred Johnston.

Drama   **(PR:A MPAA:NR)**

TAKE THIS JOB AND SHOVE IT**
                                   (1981) 100m Cinema Group/AE c

Robert Hays (*Frank Maclin*), Art Carney (*Charlie Pickett*), Barbara Hershey (*J.M. Halstead*), David Keith (*Harry Meade*), Tim Thomerson (*Ray Binkowski*), Martin Mull (*Dick Ebersol*), Eddie Albert (*Samuel Ellison*), Penelope Milford (*Lenore Meade*), David Allan Coe (*Mooney*), Lacy J. Dalton (*Mrs. Mooney*), Charlie Rich (*Hooker*), George Lindsay (*Semitruck Driver*), Johnny Paycheck (*Man with Hamburgers*), Len Lesser (*Roach*), Royal Dano (*Beeber*), Virgil Frye (*Cleach*), Bruce Fischer (*Jimmy*), Mike Genovese

(Marvin), Suzanne Kent (Charmaine), Robert Swan (Virgil), James Karen (Loomis), Wally Engelhardt (Doomar), Sharon Ernster (Doreen), Joan Prather (Madelene), Fran Ryan (Mrs. Hinkle), Carole Mallory (B-Jo), Brenda King (Secretary), David Selburg (Harvard Type), Stephan B. Meyers (Harry, Jr.), Mary Pat Hennagir (Patricia Ann), Mare O'Brien (Mary), Brad Alan Waller (Dugan), James Whittle (Installer).

Not a big hit at the box office, but picked up a big following when it hit cable television. This film was the first put out by the Cinema group. Hays is the young executive assigned to reshape the direction of a small-town brewery his large corporation has just taken over. He has all the executive trappings, sports car, condo, etc., and is not ready to go back to his small home town. He arrives, meets his old buddies, whom he now has to get to shape up or ship out. As he turns into the whip cracker corporate execs praise him while his old friends turn against him. Finally, he realizes what counts in life and wins back his buddies. The problems of the blue-collar worker are focused on here and the film offers more than just laughter. The film was based on the song sung by Johnny Paycheck and penned by country singer-writer, David Allen Coe.

p, Greg Blackwell; d, Gus Trikonis; w, Barry Schneider (based on a story by Jeffrey Bernini, Schneider from a song by David Allen Coe); ph, James Devis (CFI); m, Billy Sherrill; ed, Richard Belding; art d, Jim Dultz.

Comedy/Drama　　　　　　Cas.　　　　　(PR:C-O　MPAA:PG)

TAKEN BY SURPRISE　　　(SEE: TAKE HER BY SURPRISE, 1967, Can.)

TAKERS, THE　　　　　　　(SEE: MALAGA, 1962, Brit.)

TAKING OF PELHAM ONE, TWO, THREE, THE* ½**　　(1974) 104m Palomar-Palladium/UA c

Walter Matthau (Lt. Garber), Robert Shaw (Blue), Martin Balsam (Green), Hector Elizondo (Grey), Earl Hindman (Brown), James Broderick (Denny Doyle, Motorman), Dick O'Neill (Correll, Dispatcher), Lee Wallace (The Mayor), Tom Pedi (Caz Dolowicz, Supervisor), Beatrice Winde (Mrs. Jenkins), Jerry Stiller (Lt. Rico Patrone), Nathan George (Patrolman James), Rudy Bond (Police Commissioner), Kenneth McMillan (Borough Commander), Doris Roberts (Mayor's Wife), Julius Harris (Inspector Daniels), Cynthia Belgrave (The Maid), Anna Berger (Mother), Gary Bolling (Homosexual), Carol Cole (Secretary), Alex Colon (Delivery Boy), Joe Fields (Salesman), Mari Gorman (Hooker), Michael Gorrin (Old Man), Thomas LaFleur (Older Son), Maria Landa (Spanish Woman), Louise Larabee (Alcoholic), George Lee Miles (Pimp), William Snickowski (Hippie/Plainclothes Policeman), Jerry Holland (Budy Carmondy), Ruth Attaway (Mayor's Nurse), Tony Roberts (Warren LaSalle, Mayor's Aide).

This exciting and suspenseful drama of a subway car held for ransom begins with Matthau, a New York transit cop, giving some visiting Japanese a guided tour of the subway control center. Matthau mocks and insults the party, not realizing that his guests speak English. Meanwhile, in the subway tunnels of New York, a train pulls out of the Pelham station at 1:23 p.m. Aboard are four men wearing identical hats, glasses, mustaches, and raincoats. The group, led by Shaw, separates one car from the train, taking the conductor (Broderick) and the passengers on board hostage. Their demands are chillingly simple: the city must pay one million dollars ransom in exactly one hour or else they will begin killing hostages. A dialog begins over the radio between Matthau and Shaw as the detective tries to negotiate a safe release for the hostages. One of the kidnapers (Balsam) is suffering from a bad cold and Matthau blesses him with each sneeze. Eventually Shaw has Broderick killed when the demands have not been met. The ransom money is finally delivered and the gang makes their plan to escape. Knowing that the train will only run when a man's hand grips the throttle, the kidnapers rig a device that will send the car off with no one but the passengers aboard. The car begins rolling, picking up speed as it moves. Snickowski, a plainclothes cop who had been aboard all along, leaps off in an attempt to follow the gang. As the train moves faster and faster towards certain disaster, Matthau becomes convinced the kidnapers are no longer aboard. The passengers panic except for Gorrin, an old man who knows the Transit Authority can stop the train. A brake is electronically turned on and the passengers are safe. Meanwhile, the gang begins removing their hats, raincoats, glasses, and phony mustaches. Balsam gets away with his share of the loot and goes home. Matthau confronts Shaw in the subway tunnel and tells him that he's under arrest. Shaw asks if his crimes will merit the death penalty. When Matthau replies yes, Shaw saves the legal system the trouble by electrocuting himself on the third rail. Matthau approaches the badly injured Snickowski and tells him that help is on the way. Now the hunt is on for the remaining gang members. A list of disgruntled ex-transit workers is drawn up as suspects, seeing as only they would have the technical know-how to pull off such a crime. Matthau and his partner go to Balsam's apartment, where the frightened man hurriedly hides the loot before letting the cops in. A bundle of money remains on the floor but Balsam manages to kick it under his bed during the course of the interview. Matthau and his partner leave and Balsam sneezes as they close the door. Matthau blesses him and with a sour look on his face, realizes that Balsam is his man. Though Matthau and Shaw spend most of the film communicating through a microphone, the tension between the two is well developed.

The editing back and forth is sharp, accentuating the two strong performances and adding to the suspense. Shaw is excellent as the cold-blooded killer, with a steely performance that fascinates as well as frightens. The one low point is the slice-of-life group of passengers aboard the subway. Each hostage is a stereotype, ranging from a mother and two bratty children, to a streetwise pimp, to Gorrin's know-it-all old man. The direction is sharp, using the small, darkened world of the subway to its fullest, and backed by Shire's exciting jazz score which compliments the suspense. The film was advertised in many large cities with posters displayed in subway stations, but this ad campaign emphasizing every commuter's nightmare was dumped when subway riders across the country complained.

p, Gabriel Katzka, Edgar J. Scherick; d, Joseph Sargent; w, Peter Stone (based on the novel by John Godey); ph, Owen Roizman (Panavision, Technicolor); m, David Shire; ed, Gerald Greenberg, Robert Q. Lovett; art d, Gene Rudolf; cos, Anna Hill Johnstone.

Crime　　　　　　　　　　Cas.　　　　　(PR:O　MPAA:R)

TAKING OFF**　　　　(1971) 92m Forman-Crown-Hausman UNIV c

Lynn Carlin (Lynn Tyne), Buck Henry (Larry Tyne), Linnea Heacock (Jeannie Tyne), Georgia Engel (Margot), Tony Harvey (Tony), Audra Lindley (Ann Lockston), Paul Benedict (Ben Lockston), Vincent Schiavelli (Schiavelli), David Gittler (Jamie), Ike and Tina Turner (Themselves), Rae Allen (Mrs. Divito), Corinna Cristobal (Corinna Divito), Allen Garfield (Norman), Barry Del Rae (Schuyler), Frank Berle (Committee Man), Phillip Bruns (Policeman), Gail Busman (Nancy Lockston), Robert Dryden (Dr. Bronson), Madeline Geffen (Committee Woman), Anna Gyory (Ellen Lubar), Jack Hausman (Dr. Besch), Carrie Kotkin (Laurie), Herman Meeker (SPFC President), Ultra Violet, Lillian Halpert (SPFC Members), Sari Freeman, Jamie Freeman, Nina Hart, Michelle Scheideler, Debbie Robbins, Nancy Bell, Nancy Ferland, Jane Bedrick, Susan Chafitz, Meryl Schneiderman, Janie Rosenberg, Kay Beckett, Bobo Bates, Carly Simon, Mary Mitchell, Catherine Heriza, Shellen Lubin, Jinx Rubin, Caren Klugman (Audition Singers).

Czech-born Forman's first U.S. movie is a crackerjack look at the sociology of the country he had just adopted. Had it been made by an American, chances are lots of what Forman's "new eyes" had perceived would have been lost. Heacock is a runaway teenager who has settled in New York's East Village after coming from a typical suburban home in Forest Hills, Queens, where her parents are Carlin and Henry. She's auditioning as a singer but suddenly freezes and can't perform. In her parents' home, Henry and Carlin are at a loss to find Heacock and are baring their woes to best pals Engel and Harvey. The two men leave their wives to talk and go off to report Heacock's disappearance at the police station. Before they can get to the authorities, they stop for a quick, consoling drink at a tavern, and one leads to another. Soon they are sloshed. Back at the house, Engel is telling Carlin about her bedroom antics with her husband when Heacock walks in. Carlin is happy to see her but angry that she'd left and in a fit of pique accuses her of being a junkie. Harvey and Henry enter and Henry hits Heacock with a drunken slap. There's a huge row between Henry and Carlin, who is angered at his staggering behavior and the fact that he's hit their daughter. Heacock uses the squabble to again leave. On the following day, a sober Henry travels to the seamy East Village in an attempt to find Heacock and he meets Lindley, a woman in the same boat. Lindley's daughter has also run away and she thinks that the East Village is the place where most of these teens go. Lindley and her husband, Benedict, belong to an organization known as The Society for Parents of Fugitive Children (SPFC). Henry and Carlin go to a meeting of this support group where Schiavelli (using his own name for the part) turns the whole middle-aged group on with grass. He says that they must smoke this dope in order to better understand what their children are attracted to. At first, the older folks show no effects, and many claim that they don't feel any response to the marijuana. Then a woman begins singing at the top of her lungs, and soon the others join in, like a bunch of drunks standing on the street corner singing "Heart Of My Heart." Engel and Benedict are invited by Henry and Carlin back to their home for a nightcap. It turns out that Engel and Benedict are "swingers" and they suggest a friendly game of strip poker. Oiled by several drinks, the evening gets raunchy. Heacock has come home once more and looks down from the second story to see Henry nude on the card table singing snatches of opera while Carlin sits topless, on a laughing jag. After Engel and Benedict depart, Henry and Carlin put their clothes on and get into a discussion with Heacock. She informs them that she is now seeing a young man. They decide that they can become closer to Heacock if they see the kind of boy she likes, so they tell her to invite the youth to their home for a family dinner. When he shows up, they are shocked to see that he's a long-haired, hirsute lad. Upon seeing him, Carlin bursts into tears. Henry attempts to be pleasant to the boy, Gittler, and wonders whether his kind of music can actually make him a living. When Gittler shyly admits that he made nearly $300,000 that year, Henry and Carlin look at the bearded boy in a new light. The dinner ends and the family gathers round the piano. Carlin plays while Henry sings "Stranger in Paradise" from "Kismet" (music by Borodin, lyrics by Wright and Forrest). Other songs include "Air" (written by Mike Heron, played by The Incredible String Band), "Goodbye, So Long" (Ike Turner, performed by Ike and Tina Turner), "Love" (written and performed by Nina Hart), "Long Time Physical Effects" (written and performed by Carly Simon), "And Even the Horses Had Wings" (written and performed by Bobo Bates), "Let's Get a Little Sentimental" (Mike Leander), "Lessons in Love" (written and performed by Catherine Heriza), "Ode to a Screw" (Tom Eyen, Peter Cornell), "Feeling Sort of Nice" (written and performed by Shellen Lubin), and opera music from "Stabat Mater" by Anton Dvorak. The movie is more satire than farce and satire "is what closes on Saturday nights," said George S. Kaufman. Kaufman was right and this movie did nowhere near the business it deserved, although it did serve to introduce Forman to the U.S. audience after his European successes with LOVES OF A BLONDE and THE FIREMAN'S BALL. Henry had done cameo appearances in THE GRADUATE and CATCH-22 and here has a full-fledged leading role. His work is exemplary and he more than holds his own with the other, more experienced actors. Carlin first came to prominence in FACES although her career never went as far as her talent could take her. Heacock was an amateur whom Forman spotted in Central Park. Forman enjoys using nonprofessionals and always seems to evoke excellent results from them. The promise of this first U.S. movie paid off when Forman distinguished himself with ONE FLEW OVER THE CUCKOO'S NEST, AMADEUS, and the overlooked classic, RAGTIME. It's a well-made comedy that avoids the obvious at every turn. The script was written by a formidable quartet composed of Forman, playwright Guare (whose "The House of Blue Leaves" won several Tony Awards in June, 1986), French author Carriere (who co-wrote BELLE DU JOUR and THE MILKY WAY), and Klein. Lots of laughs and lots of wincing in this movie which lays bare the generation gap in a unique fashion and makes movies such as SUMMERTREE (a film on the same subject directed by Anthony Newley) look like a high school film student's failing term project.

p, Alfred W. Crown; d, Milos Forman; w, Forman, John Guare, Jean-Claude Carriere, John Klein; ph, Miroslav Ondricek (Movielab Color); ed, John Carter; art d, Robert Wightman; cos, Peggy Farrell; makeup, Irving Buckman.

Comedy/Drama　　　　　　　　　　**(PR:O　MPAA:R)**

TAKING SIDES　　　　　　(SEE: LIGHTNING GUNS, 1950)

TAKING TIGER MOUNTAIN** (1983, U.S./Welsh) 81m The Players Chess Club bw/c (TRECHI MYNYDD Y TEIGR)

Barry Wooller, Judy Church, Lou Montgomery, Bill Paxton, the Voices of June Allen, Scott Pitcock.

In a world devastated by nuclear war, a group of militant women brainwash and gender-shift a young man and send him-her off to Wales to assassinate the operator of a white slavery gang. Loosely based on a short piece by underground author William S. Burroughs, "Bladerunner," the title of which was appropriated by Ridley Scott for his 1982 film, which was in turn based on a novel titled Do Androids Dream of Electric Sheep? by Philip K. Dick. A low-budget production from beginning to end, the film still has some interesting themes rambling through it, though they are mostly neglected by the direction.

d, Tom Huckabee, Kent Smith; w, Huckabee, Smith, Paul Cullum (partly based on the story "Bladerunner" by William S. Burroughs); ph, Smith; m, Radio Free Europe, Randy Kelleher, David Boone; prod d, Bill Paxton.

Science Fiction　　　　　　　　　　**(PR:O　MPAA:NR)**

TALE OF FIVE CITIES, A (SEE: TALE OF FIVE WOMEN, A, 1951, Brit.)

TALE OF FIVE WOMEN, A** (1951, Brit.) 86m UA bw (GB: A TALE OF FIVE CITIES)

Bonar Colleano (Bob Mitchell), Lana Morris (Delia), Barbara Kelly (Lesley), Anne Vernon (Jeannine), Eva Bartok (Katalin), Gina Lollobrigida (Maria), Karin Himbold (Charlotte), Geoffrey Sumner ("Wingco"), Lily Kahn (Charlady), Philip Leaver (Italian Official), Annette Poivre (Annette), Danny Green (Levinsky), Carl Jaffe (Charlotte's Brother), Charles Irwin, MacDonald Parke, Arthur Gomez, Aletha Orr, Andrew Irvine, Terence Alexander, Dany Dauberson.

A good idea that gets too stretched out despite some lovely background scenery of the European capitals. Colleano is a British soldier who doesn't have an accent because he had worked in the U.S. for a while. He suffers amnesia during WW II and is sent back to the U.S. where officials think he belongs. He is taken in by a New York family and they take him all over Europe. He searches for women he knew in the past, but can't even remember if he is married. Too slow moving as Colleano tries to regain his memory.

p, Maurice J. Wilson, Alexander Paal, Boris Morros; d, Montgomery Tully, Romollo Macellini, Geza von Cziffra, Wolfgang Stuadte, E.E. Reinert; w, Richard Llewellyn, Pietro Tellini, Gunther Weisenborn, Jacques Companeez, Patrick Kirwin, Wilson; ph, La Torre, Ludwig Berger, Friedel Behn-Grund, Roger Dormoy, Gordon Lang; m, Hans May, Joseph Hajos; ed, Maurice Rootes; art d, Robert Renzo, Fritz Jonstorff, Walter Kurtz, Jean D'Eaubonne, Don Russell.

Drama　　　　　　　　　　　　**(PR:A　MPAA:NR)**

TALE OF THE COCK　　　　(SEE: CHILDISH THINGS, 1969)

TALE OF THREE WOMEN, A* (1954, Brit.) 85m Danzigers/PAR bw

Derek Bond, Hazel Court, David Horne, Jack Watling, Gene Anderson, Karel Stepanek, Catherine Finn, Oliver Johnston, Peter Gawthorne, Helene Cordet, Michael Ripper, Philip Leaver, Patricia Owens, Gordon McLeod, Robert Perceval, Digby Wolfe, Gilbert Harding (Narrator).

Tedious collection of three crime dramas with women at their centers. In the first, Court turns in her murderous lover in a fit of remorse. The second has kleptomaniac Watling saved from jail by fiancee Anderson. In the third, Stepanek murders his accountant, but when wife Finn learns that he is having an affair with another woman, she turns him in. Nothing here of note.

p, Edward J. and Harry Lee Danziger; d, Paul Dickson, Thelma Connell; w, Paul Tabori, James Eastwood, George Mikes; ph, Jack Cox, James Wilson.

Crime　　　　　　　　　　　　**(PR:A　MPAA:NR)**

TALE OF TWO CITIES, A**** 　　　　　(1935) 120m MGM bw

Ronald Colman (Sydney Carton), Elizabeth Allan (Lucie Manette), Edna May Oliver (Miss Pross), Blanche Yurka (Mme. DeFarge), Reginald Owen (Stryver), Basil Rathbone (Marquis St. Evremonde), Henry B. Walthall (Dr. Manette), Donald Woods (Charles Darnay), Walter Catlett (Barsad), Fritz Leiber, Sr. (Gaspard), H.B. Warner (Gabelle), Mitchell Lewis (Ernest DeFarge), Claude Gillingwater (Jarvis Lorry), Billy Bevan (Jerry Cruncher), Isabel Jewell (Seamstress), Lucille La Verne (La Vengeance), Tully Marshall (Woodcutter), Fay Chaldecott (Lucie the Daughter), Eily Malyon (Mrs. Cruncher), E.E. Clive (Judge in Old Bailey), Lawrence Grant (Prosecuting Attorney in Old Bailey), John Davidson (Morveau), Tom Ricketts (Tellson, Jr.), Donald Haines (Jerry Cruncher, Jr.), Ralf Harolde (Prosecutor), Nigel de Brulier, Boyd Irwin, Sr., Sam Flint, Winter Hall, (Aristocrats), Ed Piel, Sr. (Cartwright), Edward Hearn (Leader), Richard Alexander (Executioner), Cyril McLaglen (Headsman), Frank Mayo (Jailer), Walter Kingsford (Victor the Jailer), Barlowe Borland (Jacques No. 116), Rolfe Sedan (Condemned Dandy), Robert Warwick (Tribunal Judge), Dale Fuller, Tempe Piggott (Old Hags), Montague Shaw (Chief Registrar), Chappell Dossett (English Priest), Forrester Harvey (Joe, Coach Guard), Jimmy Aubrey (Innkeeper), Billy House (Border Guard).

Probably the best film production of Charles Dickens' classic novel (and there have been many, at least six besides this), A TALE OF TWO CITIES follows the turmoil of the French Revolution and its innocent and not-so-innocent victims. Colman is a London barrister, disillusioned with the world and deeply in love with Allan. She, however, considers him only a friend, and marries Woods, the scion of French nobility and a doppelganger for Colman. Woods' uncle is the hated Rathbone, who turns the peasants against him when he tramples a young boy under the hooves of his horses, then seems more concerned about the condition of the animals than that of the boy, who dies. The father of the boy breaks into Rathbone's manor and kills him, and soon the revolution is in full swing, the people storming the Bastille and executing aristocrats right and left. Anyone connected with the hated Rathbone is a target, and Woods is lured back to Paris and arrested, awaiting the guillotine. Back in London, Colman is still devoted to Allan, and now her little daughter as well. She is frantic as she awaits news of her husband. Colman, tired of this world and seeing no hope of happiness for himself, goes to Paris where he manages to free Woods and take his place awaiting death. In the cell that night he meets seamstress Jewell, who recognizes him. He asks her to keep quiet for his sake then they talk all through the night; he even holds her hand as they ascend the scaffold. His last words are so inextricably linked with Colman's performance that they are almost impossible to say without slipping into Colman's distinctive accent: "It is a far, far better thing that I do than I have ever done; it is a far, far better rest that I go to than I have ever known." A superb, lavish production that holds up well today, thanks to the skillful efforts of the MGM stock company playing every small role to perfection. Colman gives one of the best performances of his life, a role he had long wanted to play. In an interview in 1928, seven years before this film, he said: "He 'Carton' has lived for me since the first instant I discovered him in the pages of the novel." Without his mustache for the first time, Colman's performance as the world-weary martyr is a stunner. Equally memorable is Yurka as the sinister Mme. DeFarge, endlessly cackling as she sews a long scarf and decides who the next victim of the Terror is to be. She was the 67th actress to test for the part and she later called it "the plum role of the season." The little seamstress with whom Colman goes to the guillotine was also memorably played by Jewell, known around Hollywood till that time then as a wisecracking comedienne. Director Conway refused to even test her for the part, but Selznick countermanded him and gave her the role. Enormous sets of the Bastille and other Paris landmarks were built, and the scene where the Bastille is stormed was staged with over 17,000 howling extras under the directorial hand of Jacques Tourneur. Tourneur was also sent with the second unit crew to Bakersfield to film a scene of Woods riding between a row of poplar trees. As soon as they arrived, a rainstorm rolled in and persisted for five days. Each day Selznick sent increasingly more threatening memos, each signed at the bottom with the familiar DOS. Finally Tourneur sent back a memo explaining that he understood how the scene was to be shot and that he would be more than happy to do it, but, he added, "Unfortunately it has been raining for five long days and I cannot control this for it is an act of GOD," the final word in the same spot and style as Selznick's usual initials. Tourneur was fired, but quickly rehired. The film became a huge success and gave Selznick the freedom to walk away from MGM (and his father-in-law, Louis B. Mayer) and set up Selznick International Pictures.

p, David O. Selznick; d, Jack Conway; w, W.P. Lipscomb, S.N. Behrman (based on the novel by Charles Dickens); ph, Oliver T. Marsh; m, Herbert Stothart; ed, Conrad A. Nervig; art d, Cedric Gibbons, Fredric Hope; set d, Edwin B. Willis; cos, Dolly Tree; revolutionary sequences staged by Val Lewton, Jacques Tourneur.

Historical Drama   **Cas.**   **(PR:A MPAA:NR)**

TALE OF TWO CITIES, A*   (1958, Brit.) 117m RFD/RANK bw

Dirk Bogarde (Sydney Carton), Dorothy Tutin (Lucie Manette), Cecil Parker (Jarvis Lorry), Stephen Murray (Dr. Manette), Athene Seyler (Miss Pross), Paul Guers (Charles Darnay), Marie Versini (Marie Gabelle), Ian Bannen (Gabelle), Alfie Bass (Jerry Cruncher), Ernest Clark (Stryver), Rosalie Crutchley (Mme. Defarge), Freda Jackson (Vengeance), Duncan Lamont (Ernest Defarge), Christopher Lee (Marquis St. Evremonde), Leo McKern (Attorney General), Donald Pleasence (Barsad), Eric Pohlmann (Sawyer), Dominique Boschero.

This is the sixth attempt to bring the Charles Dickens novel to the screen (previously filmed in 1911, 1917, 1922, 1925, 1935). It's the long-told story of a frivolous young lawyer who spends most of his time drinking. But he meets the woman of his dreams, and eventually, awakened to responsibility in aiding victims of the French Revolution, gives his life for her in the ultimate sacrifice. Christopher Lee, who would go on to countless other roles as a heartless villain, is excellent as the amoral Marquis St. Evremonde. Of interest to those who yearn for historical–and literary–accuracy in films is the fact that this version of the classic was the first to be produced in Britain, with location scenes for the French Revolution sequences shot in Bourges and Valencay. This TALE strives for the careful attention to detail that mark the best BBC-produced literary translations today. In addition, the subtle quality of Bogarde's performance lends an entirely different quality to the pivotal role of Sydney Carton. Unlike Ronald Colman's misty-eyed nobility as he approaches the guillotine in the 1935 version, Bogarde faces his death as the inevitable result of his devotion to a cause that is larger than life itself. Perhaps not as melodramatic as the Hollywood version, but, to some, infinitely more satisfying.

p, Betty E. Box; d, Ralph Thomas; w, T.E.B. Clarke (based on the novel by Charles Dickens); ph, Ernest Steward; m, Richard Addinsell; ed, Alfred Roome; md, Muir Mathieson; art d, Carmen Dillon; cos, Beatrice Dawson.

Drama   **Cas.**   **(PR:A MPAA:NR)**

TALENT SCOUT   (1937) 62m WB-FN bw (GB: STUDIO ROMANCE)

Donald Woods (Steve Stewart), Jeanne Madden (Doris Pierce/Mary Brannigan), Fred Lawrence (Raymond Crane), Rosalind Marquis (Bernice Fox), Joseph Crehan (A.J. Lambert), Charles Halton (M.B. Carter), David Carlyle [Robert Paige] (Bert Smith), Teddy Hart (Moe Jerome), Mary Treen (Janet Morris), Al Herman (Jack Scholl), Helen Valkis (Ruth), John Pearson (Jed Hudkins), Frank Faylen (Master of Ceremonies), John Harron (Charlie), Mary Doyle (Miss Grant), Harry Fox (Robert Donnolly).

This film gave the studio execs a chance to look at some rising young stars by collecting them in a single film. It's supposed to be a look behind the scenes of how Hollywood works. All the typical characters are there: the funny young comedian, the uppity prima donna, and the sweet-natured girl singer. Plot has Woods searching for Madden after he has been fired as a talent scout for a local studio. He finds Madden and sees her as his ticket back to the big time. He cons his old employers into giving her a test which she fails miserably, but he gets her on the payroll anyway. Naturally, she goes on to fame and fortune and falls for her leading man. Troubles ensue, however, so Woods must come to the rescue in order to save his true love–and provide the obligatory happy ending. Songs include: "In the Silent Picture Days," "I Am the Singer, You Are My Song," "Born to Love," and "I Was Wrong" (M.K. Jerome, Jack Scholl).

d, William Clemens; w, George Bilson, William Jacobs (based on a story by Bilson); ph, Rex Wimpy; ed, Terry Morse.

Musical   **(PR:A MPAA:NR)**

TALES AFTER THE RAIN   (SEE: UGETSU MONOGATARI, 1953, Jap.)

TALES FROM THE CRYPT*   (1972, Brit.) 92m Amicus-Metromedia Producers/Cinerama c

Ralph Richardson (Crypt Keeper), Geoffrey Bayldon (Guide), "All Through the House": Joan Collins (Joanne Clayton), Marty Goddey (Richard Clayton), Oliver MacGreevy (Maniac), Chloe Franks (Carol Clayton), "Reflection of Death": Ian Hendry (Carl Maitland), Paul Clere (Maitland's Son), Sharon Clere (Maitland's Daughter), Angie Grant (Susan), Susan Denny (Mrs. Maitland), Frank Forsyth (Tramp), "Blind Alleys": Nigel Patrick (William Rogers), Patrick Magee (George Carter), Tony Wall (Attendant), Harry Locke (Cook), George Herbert (Old Blind Man), John Barrard, Carl Bernard, Ernest C. Jennings, Chris Cannon, Hugo De Vernier, Louis Mansi (Other Blind Men), "Poetic Justice": Peter Cushing (Grimsdyke), Robin Phillips (James Elliot), David Markham (Edward Elliot), Edward Evans (Mr. Ramsay), Ann Sears (Mrs. Carter), Irene Gawne (Mrs. Phelps), Kay Adrian (Mrs. Davies), Clifford Earl (Police Sergeant), Manning Wilson (Vicar), Dan Caulfield (Postman), Robert Hutton (Mr. Baker), Melinda Clancy (Miss Carter), Stafford Medhurst (Mrs. Phelps' Son), Carlos Baker (Mrs. Davies' Son), "Wish You Were Here": Richard Greene (Ralph Jason), Roy Dotrice (Charles Gregory), Barbara Murray (Enid Jason), Peter Thomas (Pallbearer), Hedger Wallace (Detective).

Max Rosenberg and Milton Subotsky collaborated on many horror films such as THE HOUSE THAT DRIPPED BLOOD and THE SKULL. This time they piece five short stories together through five main characters who start on the same tour of a cemetery. Ralph Richardson as the crypt keeper gives the stories continuity. All the tales are interpreted extremely well, and spawned the film VAULT OF HORROR the following year.

p, Milton Subotsky, Max J. Rosenberg; d, Freddie Francis; w, Subotsky (based on the stories "Tales from the Crypt" and "The Vault of Horror" by Al Feldstein, Johnny Craig, William Gaines, appearing in "Cartoon" Magazines); ph, Norman Warwick, John Harris (Eastmancolor); m, Douglas Gamley; ed, Teddy Darvas; md, Gamley; art d, Tony Curtis; set d, Helen Thomas; m/l, "Toccata," "Fugue in D Minor," Johann Sebastian Bach (played by Nicolas Kynaston); makeup, Roy Ashton.

Horror   **Cas.**   **(PR:C MPAA:PG)**

TALES FROM THE CRYPT PART II
          (SEE: VAULT OF HORROR, 1973, Brit.)

TALES OF A SALESMAN*½   (1965) 53m Lawtone/Rossmore c (AKA: TALES OF A TRAVELING SALESMAN)

David Reed (Herman), Pope Hook (Sales Manager), Terri Collins, Terri Dean, Karen Wyatt, Carol Dark, Vicki Reim.

A poorly conceived comedy about traveling salesmen and what they do to increase sales. Here's the gimmick: As his wife tries to rouse Reed from his sleep, he has a dream about his boss (Hook). The man is telling Reed to increase his production. Then a ghost shows up and offers to help him out. As the ghost checks out the prospective customers, he spies five women scarcely clad. From there, TALES OF A SALESMAN becomes a voyeur's paradise as the women run around nearly naked and play silly games to arouse Reed. One "classic" scene has a woman seductively fondling the cherry in her drink. Finally the ghost comes back to Reed to show him that all is not lost and good prospects abound if he will only open his eyes and look for them. Don't expect IT'S A WONDERFUL LIFE from this minor travesty.

p, John Lawrence; d, Don Russell; w, Lawrence; ph, William Zsigmond (DeLuxe Color).

Comedy   **(PR:C MPAA:NR)**

TALES OF A TRAVELING SALESMAN
          (SEE: TALES OF A SALESMAN, 1965)

TALES OF BEATRIX POTTER   (SEE: PETER RABBIT AND TALES OF BEATRIX POTTER, 1971, Brit.)

TALES OF HOFFMANN, THE½   (1951, Brit.) 138m The Archers-LFP/Lopert c

"Prolog and Epilog": Moira Shearer (Stella), Robert Rounseville (Hoffmann), Robert Helpmann (Lindorff), Pamela Brown (Nicklaus, sung by Monica Sinclair), Frederick Ashton (Kleinzack), Meinhart Maur (Luther, sung by Fisher-Morgan), John Ford (Nathaniel, sung by Rene Soames), Richard Golding (Hermann, sung by Owen Brannigan), Philip Leaver (Andreas), Edmund Audran (Cancer), "The Tale of Olympia": Shearer (Olympia, sung by Dorothy Bond), Leonide Massine (Spalanzani, sung by Graham Clifford), Robert Helpmann (Coppelius, sung by Bruce Dargavet), Ashton (Cochenille, sung by Murray Dickie), Tale of Giulietta": Ludmilla Tcherina (Giulietta, sung by Margherita Grandi), Helpmann (Dapertutto, sung by Dargavet), Massine (Schlemil, sung by Richard Standon), Lionel Harris (Pitichinaccio, sung by Dickie), "The Tale of Antonia": Ann Ayars (Antonia), Mogens Wieth (Crespel, sung by Brannigan), Massine (Franz, sung by Clifford), Helpmann (Dr. Miracle, sung by Dargavel), Jean Alexander (Mother's Voice), The Sadlers Wells Chorus.

This overly long opera follows the life and loves of a young university student (Rounseville in the title role). The poor fellow never succeeds in love–one time falling for a doll created by a magician, and another time falling in love with a girl who will die if she sings, and, of course, she does just that. All of the "tales" are done in exquisite detail and contain lavish dance numbers, including a stunning ballet sequence choreographed by dancer Ashton and performed by him and Shearer of THE RED SHOES. But while the dizzying array of design elements and magnificent vocal performances are impressive, 138 minutes is just too long to keep any but the pure opera devotee's interest. THE TALES OF HOFFMANN was a front-runner at the Cannes Film Festival, but producers refused to cut the last scene and so lost in the long run. The film, for all its spectacular sets and cast and crew members involved only took nine weeks to make. The final act was cut for the British version to make it more appealing to the masses.

p,d&w, Michael Powell, Emeric Pressburger (based on the opera by Jacques Offenbach); ph, Christopher Challis (Technicolor); m, Offenbach; ed, Reginald Mills; prod d, Arthur Lawson; md, Sir Thomas Beecham conducting The Royal Philharmonic Orchestra; art d, set d&cos, Hein Heckroth; English libretto, Dennis Arundell (based on the original by Jules Barbier).

Opera   **(PR:A   MPAA:NR)**

TALES OF MANHATTAN****   (1942) 118m FOX bw

Sequence A: Charles Boyer (*Paul Orman*), Rita Hayworth (*Ethel Halloway*), Thomas Mitchell (*John Halloway*), Eugene Pallette (*Luther*), Helene Reynolds (*Actress*), Robert Grieg (*Lazar*), Jack Chefe (*Tailor*), William Halligan (*Oliver Webb*), Charles Williams (*Paul's Agent*), Eric Wilton (*Halloway's Butler*), Sequence B: Ginger Rogers (*Diane*), Henry Fonda (*George*), Cesar Romero (*Harry Wilson*), Gail Patrick (*Ellen*), Roland Young (*Edgar the Butler*), Marion Martin (*Squirrel*), Frank Orth (*Secondhand Dealer*), Connie Leon (*Mary*), Sequence C: Charles Laughton (*Charles Smith*), Elsa Lanchester (*Elsa Smith*), Victor Francen (*Auturo Bellini*), Christian Rub (*Wilson*), Adeline DeWalt Reynolds (*Grandmother*), Sig Arno (*Piccolo Player*), Forbes Murray (*Dignified Man*), Buster Brodie (*Call Boy*), Frank Jaquet (*Musician*), Will Wright (*Skeptic*), Frank Dae (*Elderly Man*), Rene Austin (*Susan*), Frank Darien (*Latecomer*), Dewey Robinson (*Bar Proprietor*), Tom O'Grady (*Latecomer*), Curly Twyfford (*Bird Man*), Gino Corrado (*Spectator*), Sequence D: Edward G. Robinson (*Larry Browne*), George Sanders (*Williams*), James Gleason (*Father Joe*), Harry Davenport (*Professor Lyons*), James Rennie (*Hank Bronson*), Harry Hayden (*Soupy Davis*), Morris Ankrum (*Judge Barnes*), Don Douglas (*Henderson*), Mae Marsh (*Molly*), Barbara Lynn (*Mary*), Paul Renay (*Spud Johnson*), Ted Stanhope (*Chauffeur*), Esther Howard (*Woman*), Joseph Bernard (*Postman*), Alex Pollard (*Waiter*), Don Brady (*Whistler*), Sequence E: Paul Robeson (*Luke*), Ethel Waters (*Esther*), Eddie "Rochester" Anderson (*Rev. Lazarus*), J. Carrol Naish (*Costello*), Clarence Muse (*Grandpa*), George Reed (*Christopher*), Cordell Hickman (*Nicodemus*), John Kelly (*Monk*), Lonnie Nichols (*Brad*), Charles Gray (*Rod*), Phillip Hurlie (*Jeff*), Archie Savage (*Man*), Rita Christiani, Laura Vaughn, Ella Mae Lashley, Olive Ball, Maggie Dorsey (*Women*), Charles Tannen (*Pilot*), Hall Johnson Choir (*Themselves*), Johnny Lee (*Carpenter*), Blue Washington (*Black Man*).

TALES OF MANHATTAN is an episodic film, following the travels of a fancy tail coat which goes from riches to rags over the course of the story. Boyer is a famous actor who buys the evening coat, only to be told the garment carries a curse. Later, while in a dalliance with his mistress, Hayworth, he is shot by Hayworth's jealous husband, Mitchell. Fortunately Boyer survives the shooting (having never even been hit by the bullet), and quickly has his valet sell the jacket. It ends up in Romero's hands, but his fiancee, Rogers, finds a steamy love letter in one of the pockets. To escape her fury, Romero insists the coat belongs to his pal, Fonda. Rogers, thinking Fonda is a fiery lover because of the note, runs off with him, leaving Romero with nothing but the coat. The cursed garment ends up in a pawnshop, where it's picked up by Lanchester. She gives it to her husband, Laughton, who is readying himself to conduct a symphony he has written. Because the coat is too small for Laughton's frame, it splits. Francen, Laughton's benefactor, takes over conducting chores and the coat makes another trip. This time it ends up on the bowery. Gleason, a mission priest, gives the jacket to Robinson, a lawyer who is down on his luck. The padre insists Robinson should wear the coat to a college reunion. Robinson does, and while there he is accused by Sanders of picking someone's pocket. Robinson admits to being broke, and with that, three of his former classmates decide to help him get back on his feet. The coat next ends up with Naish, a crook who wears it while he pulls off a job. He puts his loot in the pockets, then boards a plane. During the flight the jacket begins to burn, and, forgetting he's stuffed it with $40,000, Naish throws the jacket out the window. The money flutters to the ground where it is picked up by Robeson and Waters, two poor sharecroppers. They take the money to Anderson, the local preacher, while the coat ends up hanging on a scarecrow. TALES OF MANHATTAN is held together by a thin string, unfolding with a good deal of charm. The episodes flow smoothly from one to another, belying the fact that different writers worked on the different episodes. Duvivier's direction is the key, keeping the episodes from becoming a disjointed effort. Eagle (later to change his name to Sam Spiegel) and Morros found the idea, based on Ferenc Molnar story, to be an intriguing one. A slew of writers, including such varied talents as Hecht, Stewart, and Keaton, were hired to work on the different episodes, while Duvivier, who had directed the similarly episodic UN CARNET DU BAL in France was hired to helm the project. Audiences took to the film, and it enjoyed a thriving box office. There were, however, some accusations of racism regarding the simplistic presentation of blacks in the final episode, and Robeson himself later denounced the film. Originally there was to be a sixth episode, featuring W.C. Fields and Margaret Dumont. This episode was to have followed Robinson's, and featured the bulbous nosed comedian as a lecturer who buys the jacket at

a second hand shop run by Phil Silvers. He then wears it to a swanky affair at Dumont's home, where he delivers a lecture on-- what else?--the evils of alcohol. While Fields goes on about the damage demon rum does to one's liver, his audience quickly gets snockered on some cocanut milk Fields' has spiked. Fields only worked for five days on the sequence, getting $50,000 for the part, double that of anyone else in the star-studded cast. Fields ad-libbed much of his dialog, and was praised for the sequence by preview audiences. However, it was decided that this episode interrupted the natural flow of the story and the 20-minute piece was excised. The songs here include: "Glory Day" (Leo Robin, Ralph Rainger), "Fare Thee Well to El Dorado," "A Journey to Your Lips," "A Tale of Manhattan" (Paul Francis Webster, Saul Chaplin), "All God's Children Got Shoes," "Great Getting Up in the Morning."

p, Boris Morros, S.P. Eagle 'Sam Speigel'); d, Julien Duvivier; w, Ben Hecht, Ferenc Molnar, Donald Ogden Stewart, Samuel Hoffenstein, Alan Campbell, Ladislas Fodor, Laszlo Vadnai, Laslo Gorog, Lamar Trotti, Henry Blankford, (uncredited) Buster Keaton, Ed Beloin, Bill Morrow; ph, Joseph Walker; m, Sol Kaplan; ed, Robert Bischoff; md, Edward Paul; art d, Richard Day, Boris Leven; set d, Thomas Little; cos, Irene, Dolly Tree, Bernard Newman, Gwen Wakeling, Oleg Cassini; makeup, Guy Pearce.

Comedy   **(PR:AA   MPAA:NR)**

TALES OF ORDINARY MADNESS**   (1983, Ital.) 101m 23
                                                Giugno-Ginis- Miracle/Fred Baker c

Ben Gazzara (*Charles Serking*), Ornella Muti (*Cass*), Susan Tyrrell (*Vera*), Tanya Lopert (*Vicky*), Roy Brocksmith (*Bartender*), Katia Berger (*Girl on Beach*), Hope Cameron (*Landlady*), Judith Drake (*Fat Woman*), Patrick Hughes (*Pimp*), Wendy Welles (*Teenage Runaway*), Jay Julien (*Publisher*), Leopold Stratton, Anthony Pitillo, Peter Jarvis.

A journey through the weird eyes of Italian director Marco Ferreri. An aging beat poet (Gazzara) shuffles his way through life and the seamier sides of the U.S. Almost laughable, but supposedly a serious look at life as Gazzara meets all types of low-life women in an attempt to find himself. Filled with symbolism. (Muti represents mutilation.) Gazzara should never have wandered into this one.

p, Jacqueline Ferreri; d, Marco Ferreri; w, Marco Ferreri, Sergio Amidei, Anthony Foutz (based on short stories by Charles Bukowski); ph, Tonino delli Colli (Eastmancolor); m, Philippe Sarde; ed, Ruggero Mastroianni; prod d&art d, Dante Ferretti; cos, Nicoletta Ercole, Rita Corradini.

Drama   **Cas.**   **(PR:O   MPAA:NR)**

TALES OF PARIS**½   (1962, Fr./Ital.) 100m Francos Incei Times
                         Film Corp. bw (LES PARISIENNES; LE PARIGINE; AKA: OF BEDS
                                                                    AND BROADS)

"The Tale of Ella": Dany Saval (*Ella*), Darry Cowl (*Hubert*), Henri Tisot (*Eric*), Jacques Ary (*Pidoux*), Francoise Giret (*Juliette*), Serge Marquand (*Taxi Driver*), Les Chaussettes Noires (*Singers*), "The Tale of Antonia": Dany Robin (*Antonia*), Jean Poiret (*Jean-Pierre*), Christian Marquand (*Christian*), Bernard Lavalette (*Richard*), "The Tale of Francoise": Francoise Arnoul (*Francoise*), Francoise Brion (*Jacqueline*), Paul Guers (*Michel*), "The Tale of Sophie": Catherine Deneuve (*Sophie*), Johnny Hallyday (*Jean*), Gillian Hills (*Theodora*), Elina Labourdette (*The Mother*), Jose-Luis de Vilallonga (*Her Suitor*), Berthe Grandval (*Suzanne*), Gisele Sandre (*Andree*).

Four short romantic stories that focus on the trials and tribulations of young people in love who pursue their dreams in the City of Love. In "Tale of Ella," Saval is late for a nightclub rehearsal and hails a taxi. After bullying her way into the car, she meets a meek man who is almost afraid of her, but not quite. He is actually a famous producer Saval would kill to meet. Not only does he win her hand in marriage, but he also gives her a new part in an upcoming film. "The Tale of Antonia" is one of a housewife's revenge. Robin is living the good life of a doctor's wife when she hears through the grapevine that a past boy friend (Marquand) is bad-mouthing her lovemaking. To get even, she seduces him, then calmly announces that he's a bore and she's happier with her husband. Arnoul has been listening long enough about how her friend has complete control over her lover in "The Tale of Francoise" so she sets out to see if the claims are true. Seems that Brion thinks--no actually knows--that her lover will always be true to her. Arnoul checks him out for herself and to her delight, finds that her friend is sadly mistaken. Deneuve is tired of playing the goody-goody and so to show her classmates how much she knows of the world, she conjures up a make-believe lover. To prove it, she has her friends gather where her supposed boy friend lives (actually her best friend's place) and goes through the window to meet him. There Deneuve meets a young singer and actually falls in love. Finally she wants to tell the truth, but her friends prefer the old story better.

p, Francis Cosne; m, Georges Garvarentz; ed, Leonide Azar; art d, Jean Andre; m/l, Charles Aznavour; "The Tale of Ella": d, Jacques Poitrenaud; w, Isabelle Phat, Marc Aurian, Jean-Loup Dabadie, Poitrenaud, Cosne; ph, Henri Alekan; "The Tale of Antonia": d, Michel Boisrond; w, Annette Wademant, Boisrond, Cosne; ph, Alekan; "The Tale of Francoise": d, Claude Barma; w, Jacques Armand, Claude Brule, Barma, Cosne; ph, Armand Thirard; "The Tale of Sophie": d, Marc Allegret; w, Roger Vadim, Allegret,

Cosne; ph, Thirard.

Comedy   (PR:A MPAA:NR)

TALES OF ROBIN HOOD½**   (1951) 61m Lippert bw

Robert Clarke (*Robin Hood*), Mary Hatcher (*Maid Marian*), Paul Cavanagh (*Sir Guy*), Wade Crosby (*Little John*), Whit Bissell (*Will Stutely*), Ben Welden (*Friar Tuck*), Robert Bice (*Will Scarlett*), Keith Richards (*Sir Alan*), Bruce Lester (*Alan A-Dale*), Tiny Stowe (*Sheriff of Nottingham*), Lester Matthews (*Sir Fitzwalter*), John Vosper (*Earl of Chester*), Norman Bishop (*Much*), Margia Dean (*Betty*), Lorin Raker (*Landlord*), George Slocum (*Captain of the Guards*), John Doucette (*Wilfred*), John Harmon, Matt McHugh, David Stollery.

Lack of well-known names doesn't help this story about Robin and his Band of Merry Men. Actually this minor retelling of the legend is well assembled. It's aided by a fresh plot twist that has Clarke and the boys fighting the oppressive Normans who have conquered the noble Saxons. He finally runs them out of the forest (for a while) and wins the heart of Hatcher to boot. Filled with plenty of sword fights and robbings of the rich. A nicely done film that was overlooked by many.

p, Hal Roach, Jr.; d, James Tinling; w, Leroy H. Zehren; ph, George Robinson; m, Leon Klatzkin; ed, Richard Currier; art d, McClure Capps.

Adventure   (PR:A MPAA:NR)

TALES OF TERROR*½**   (1962) 90m Alta Vista/AIP c (AKA: POE'S TALES OF TERROR)

"Morella": Vincent Price (*Locke*), Maggie Pierce (*Lenora*), Leona Gage (*Morella*), Ed Cobb (*Driver*), "The Black Cat": Price (*Fortunato*), Peter Lorre (*Montresor*), Joyce Jameson (*Annabel*), Lenny Weinrib, John Hacketl (*Policemen*), Wally Campo (*Bartender*), Alan Dewit (*Chairman*), "The Case of Mr. Valdemar": Price (*Valdemar*), Basil Rathbone (*Carmichael*), Debra Paget (*Helene*), David Frankham (*Dr. James*), Scotty Brown (*Servant*).

Three short stories based on the works of the master horror writer, Edgar Allan Poe. All three–"Morella," "The Black Cat," and "The Case of Mr. Valdemar"–feature Price in the starring role. This group of stories was the fourth such release by American International. In "Morella," Price is an embittered widower, living in, of course, a gloomy mansion all alone since the death of his wife some 26 years ago. His daughter Pierce shows up; Price is extremely bitter toward her since he blames her for his wife's death. Pierce, while prowling around the house, finds her mother in a mummified state. In the evening, Gage's spirit awakens and takes over Pierce's body. Hearing the commotion, Price sprints to the room only to find his daughter dead and his wife's body now telling him she has come back to seek revenge. To thwart her, Price drops a candle on the bed and all three die in the fire. In "The Black Cat" Lorre is superb as a drunken loser, who forces his wife to seek safety and comfort in the arms of Price. To get even, Lorre kills them and walls up the bodies of his wife and Price behind a brick wall. But also entombed was the couple's cat and her screeching alerts the authorities. The final story, "The Case of Mr. Valdemar," features Price in a comatose state–not dead–but not alive. Meanwhile, wife Paget has gotten involved with Frankham, but the evil Rathbone who put Price in the spell in the first place wants Paget for himself. He will only take Price out of his misery if she becomes his bride. When she relents, Price becomes lifelike and surrounds Rathbone who is scared to death. Finally, the trance is lifted and Price just becomes liquid around Rathbone's rigid corpse. Rathbone is excellent, but the story is fairly weak. "Morella" is far and away the best told and best done story, and, not surprisingly, it's also the shortest in length.

ph, Floyd Crosby (Panavision, Pathe Color); m, Les Baxter; ed, Anthony Carras; art d, Daniel Haller; set d, Harry Reif; spec eff, Pat Dinga; makeup, Louis La Cava.

Horror   **Cas.**   (PR:C MPAA:NR)

TALES OF THE UNCANNY***   (1932, Ger.) 89m Roto bw (UNHEIMLICHE GESCHICHTEN)

Paul Wegener, Bert Reisfeld, Harald Paulsen, Roma Bahm, Mary Parker, Paul Henkels, Eugen Kloepfer, John Gottowt, Blandine Ebinger, Maria Koppenhoefer.

Wegener played the mad scientist part in a few German silent films and now gets his chance to play one again in this early sound film. This time he wipes out his wife and is sent to an asylum. There he takes control over the other patients and forms a suicide club. TALES OF THE UNCANNY opened up a whole new path for the "expressionist" genre and inspired two more films about the same subject in the next two years. This film was often mistaken for a film done in 1919.

p, Gabriel Pascal; d, Richard Oswald; w, Heinz Goldberg, Eugen Szatmari; ph, Heinrich Gaertner.

Horror   (PR:C MPAA:NR)

TALES THAT WITNESS MADNESS½**

(1973, Brit.) 90m Amicus-World Film Services/PAR c

"Clinic Scenes": Jack Hawkins (*Nicholas*), Donald Pleasence (*Dr. Tremayne*), "Mr. Tiger": Georgia Brown (*Fay Patterson*), Donald Houston (*Sam Patterson*), Russell Lewis (*Paul Patterson*), David Wood (*Tutor*), "Penny Farthing": Suzy Kendall (*Ann/Beatrice*), Peter McEnery (*Timothy Patrick*), Frank Forsyth (*Uncle Albert*), Beth Morris (*Polly*), Neil Kennedy, Richard Connaught (*Moving Men*), "Mel": Joan Collins (*Bella Thompson*), Michael Jayston (*Brian Thompson*), "Luau": Kim Novak (*Auriol Pageant*), Michael Petrovitch (*Kimo*), Mary Tamm (*Ginny Pageant*), Lesley Nunnerley (*Vera*), Leon Lissek (*Keoki*), Zohra Segal (*Malia*).

Four principle characters are in a clinic and all have terrifying stories to tell about why they are there. The clinic is run by wacky Pleasence, who is trying to sway his colleague, Hawkins, to his psychiatric theories. In the first tale, Lewis is a boy who is extremely bothered by his parents' fighting, so he invents an imaginary tiger to kill them. In the second tale, an old bicycle fascinates McEnery, who can travel backward in time with its help. While time-traveling, he assumes the identity of one of his Victorian-era relatives, and he is doomed to assume that man's fate as well. Collins gets hers in the next one as her husband, Jayston, brings home a tree that is more human than plant. Collins tells him that it is either her or his new-found interest, then ensues a life and death struggle. The last story featuring Novak is the worst of the lot. It was her first time on the screen in four years and it shows. She is the literary agent for Petrovitch, who must find a virgin to sacrifice to help his mother's spirit rest in peace. The virgin happens to be Novak's alluring daughter, Tamm. The climax is a luau scene where the guests unknowingly enjoy more than pineapple and roast pig. This was Hawkins' last film; he died of cancer in 1973. Novak, who sank to new lows in the film, replaced the already ailing Rita Hayworth who was dropped from the film after only a few days of shooting.

p, Norman Priggen; d, Freddie Francis; w, Jay Fairbank; ph, Norman Warwick (Eastmancolor); m, Bernard Ebbinghouse; ed, Bernard Gribble; art d, Roy Walker; set d, Michael Almont; makeup, Eric Allwright.

Horror   (PR:O MPAA:R)

TALISMAN, THE½**   (1966) 93m Gillman bw (AKA: THE SAVAGE AMERICAN)

Ned Romero (*The Indian*), Linda Hawkins (*The Woman*), Richard Thies (*Buford*), Jerald Cormier (*Jubilo*), Raymond Brown (*Martineau*), Raymond DeAnda (*Leveque*), Louis Bacigalupi (*Isaac*).

A western drama without a big gun scene, just acts of individual brutality. Romero and his Indian brothers have just wiped out a wagon train with Hawkins as the only survivor. He can't get himself to complete the massacre and takes this as a signal from the Great Spirit in the sky. He decides to become her bodyguard. While escorting her he's attacked by three whites, but she saves his life because she has fallen in love with him. However, she still goes off with her own kind who eventually turn on her. They rape her and she goes back to Romero who swears to avenge this evil act. After finding the men, he doesn't use conventional methods to kill them, rather he buries one up to his head. But he's not finished] He then coats the guy's head with honey to attract ants. The next unfortunate gets strapped to a couple of saplings which, when sprung, tear him in two. The third one he merely tortures, then slowly kills with a rattlesnake.

p,d&w, John Carr; m, Jaime Mendoza-Nava.

Western   (PR:C MPAA:NR)

TALK ABOUT A LADY*½** (1946) 71m COL bw (AKA: DUCHESS OF BROADWAY)

Jinx Falkenburg (*Janie Clark*), Forrest Tucker (*Bart Manners*), Joe Besser (*Roly Q. Entwhistle*), Trudy Marshall (*Toni Marlowe*), Richard Lane (*Duke Randall*), Jimmy Little (*Buffalo*), Frank Sully (*Rocky Jordan*), Jack Davis (*Carleton Vane*), Robert Regent (*Arthur Harrison*), Mira McKinney (*Letitia Harrison*), Robin Raymond (*Peaches Berkeley*), Stan Kenton and his Orchestra.

A tired plot helped or not by Falkenburg's singing. She's a naive, plain ol' country girl who's left a few million dollars along with a popular nightclub. She has to fight off the catty remarks and bitterness of Marshall, a high society gal who thought all the goodies should have gone to her. While the production sails along fairly well, the plot is too old to generate any real excitement. Songs include: "You Gotta Do Watcha Gotta Do," "I Never Had a Dream Come True," "Avocado" (Allan Roberts, Doris Fisher), "A Mist is over the Moon" (Ben Oakland, Oscar Hammerstein II).

p, Michel Kraike; d, George Sherman; w, Richard Weil, Ted Thomas (based on a story by Robert D. Andrews, Barry Trivers); ph, Henry Freulich; ed, James Sweeney; md, Mario Silva; art d, George Brooks; set d, James Crowe.

Musical   (PR:A MPAA:NR)

TALK ABOUT A STRANGER**   (1952) 65m MGM bw

George Murphy (*Robert Fontaine, Sr.*), Nancy Davis (*Marge Fontaine*), Billy Gray (*Robert Fontaine, Jr.*), Lewis Stone (*Mr. Wardlaw*), Kurt Kasznar (*Matlock*), Anna Glomb (*Camille*), Katherine Warren (*Dr. Dorothy Langley*), Teddy Infuhr (*Gregory*), Stanley Andrews (*Mr. Wetzell*), Maude Wallace (*Mrs. Wetzell*), Cosmo Sardo (*Barber*), Jon Gardner, Donald Gordon, Warren Farlow, Wayne Farlow (*Boys*), Gary Stewart (*Boys*), Margaret Bert (*Woman's Voice*), Tudor Owen (*Policeman*), Harry Lauter (*Canavan*), Dan Riss (*Mr. Taylor*), Charles La Torre (*Batastini*), Kathleen Freeman (*Rose*), Burt Mustin (*Mr. McEley*), Ralph Moody (*Short*), Jack Williams (*Truck Driver*), Jack Moore (*Sailor*), William Tannen (*Driggs*), Leslie K. O'Pace (*MacLarnin*), Harry Hines (*Talmadge*), Edward Cassidy (*Soloway*), Virginia Farmer (*Mrs. Campbell*).

Both leading characters had better luck in politics later in their lives. If this movie were shown at election time, it would get plenty of laughs–not because it's a comedy, either. A shady stranger moves next door to Murphy and Davis, a happy couple who are citrus fruit growers. Their boy wants a dog in the worst way and finally gets one. A little while later, the dog is found poisoned to death, and everything points to the new man in town as the villain. It's cleared up with a simple unbelievable explanation which pretty much sums up the entire film. It was director David Bradley's first feature film, he's better known for creating that cult "classic," THEY SAVED HITLER'S BRAIN.

p, Richard Goldstone; d, David Bradley; w, Margaret Fitts (based on the short story "The Enemy" by Charlotte Armstrong); ph, John Alton; m, David Buttolph; ed, Newell P. Kimlin; art d, Cedric Gibbons, Eddie Imazu.

Drama   (PR:A   MPAA:NR)

TALK ABOUT JACQUELINE**   (1942, Brit.) 84m Excelsior/MGM bw

Hugh Williams (*Dr. Michael Thomas*), Carla Lehmann (*Jacqueline Marlow*), Joyce Howard (*June Marlow*), Roland Culver (*Leslie Waddington*), John Warwick (*Donald Clark*), Mary Jerrold (*Aunt Helen*), Guy Middleton (*Capt. Tony Brook*), Martita Hunt (*Colonel's Wife*), Max Adrian (*Lionel*), Antony Holles (*Attendant*), Katie Johnson (*Ethel*), Eileen Peel, Percy Walsh, Ian Fleming, Joan Kemp-Welch, Beatrice Varley, Roland Pertwee, Gerhardt Kempinski.

Sisterly love knows no bounds here. Lehmann has a notorious past, and while on the Riviera looking for more fun, meets Williams. The hapless guy knows nothing of her past, and they fall in love and get married. He's shocked when he sees her name splashed about in a sleazy scandal sheet. To save the marriage, her sister, Howard, tells him it is she, not Lehmann, who is the subject of those dirty stories. But her own love life starts to suffer, and so her elder sibling finally admits all.

p, Marcel Hellman; d, Harold French; w, Roland Pertwee, Marjorie Deans (based on the novel by Katherine Holland); ph, Bernard Knowles, Cyril Knowles.

Comedy   (PR:A   MPAA:NR)

TALK OF A MILLION   (SEE: YOU CAN'T BEAT THE IRISH, 1952, Brit.)

TALK OF HOLLYWOOD, THE*½   (1929) 80m Prudence/Sono Art-World Wide bw

Nat Carr (*J. Pierpont Ginsburg, Film Producer*), Fay Marbe (*Adore Renee*), Hope Sutherland (*Ruth Ginsburg*), Sherline Oliver (*John Applegate, Lawyer*), Edward Le Saint (*Edward Hamilton*), Gilbert Marbe (*Reginald Whitlock*), John Troughton (*Butler*), Al Goodman and his Orchestra, Leonidoff Ballet.

An early talkie that should have had the soundtrack unplugged right after it was made. A mangled story with all kinds of loose ends leaves everyone trying to figure out the plot and why this was even made in the first place. Part of the story is about a film producer (typecast as a Jewish character) who groans and makes nasty remarks about his film venture that went sour. It became a mass of trailers left for everyone to sort out–just like the thing on screen] The film came out of Prudence Pictures which was Excellent Pictures before it went under. The company was saved by Sam Zierler who didn't do anyone a favor.

d, Mark Sandrich; w, Darby Aaronson (based on a story by Nat Carr, Sandrich); ph, Walter Strenge; ed, Russell G. Shields; md, Al Goodman.

Drama   (PR:A   MPAA:NR)

TALK OF THE DEVIL**   (1937, Brit.) 76m British and Dominions/GAU-UA bw

Ricardo Cortez (*Ray Allen*), Sally Eilers (*Ann Marlow*), Basil Sydney (*Stephen Findlay*), Randle Ayrton (*John Findlay*), Frederick Culley (*Alderson*), Charles Carson (*Lord Dymchurch*), Gordon McLeod (*Inspector*), Dennis Cowles (*Philip Couls*), Langley Howard (*Clerk*), Quinton MacPherson (*Angus*), Margaret Rutherford (*Housekeeper*), Moore Marriott (*Dart-Thrower*), Pam Downing, Anne Daniels, Stafford Hilliard, Aubrey Mallalieu, Mac

Callaghan.

Sydney gives new meaning to the role of villain because he's so ruthless and conniving in this film. It is his character that redeems the film in the beginning and makes it move, but when he's done in, the film slips into neutral and just coasts the rest of the way. Ayrton has built up a profitable shipping firm that his brother, who might not actually be his brother, wants. Sydney gets unexpected help in framing the old man from Cortez who is involved with the owner's daughter. Seems that Cortez can impersonate people and does so to help Sydney gain information. To save the firm's name, Ayrton kills himself. To make sure Cortez doesn't talk, Sydney tries to kill him, but Cortez escapes. Cortez once again uses his gift of mimicry to bring Sydney to justice and win back the heart of his love.

p, Jack Raymond; d, Reed; w, Carol Reed, George Barraud, Anthony Kimmins (based on a story by Reed, Kimmins); ph, Francis Carver; ed, Helen Lewis, Merrill White, John Morris; md, Percival McKay; art d, Wilfred Arnold.

Crime Drama   (PR:A   MPAA:NR)

TALK OF THE TOWN****   (1942) 118m COL bw

Cary Grant (*Leopold Dilg*), Jean Arthur (*Nora Shelley*), Ronald Colman (*Michael Lightcap*), Edgar Buchanan (*Sam Yates*), Glenda Farrell (*Regina Bush*), Charles Dingle (*Andrew Holmes*), Emma Dunn (*Mrs. Shelley*), Rex Ingram (*Tilney*), Leonid Kinskey (*Jan Pulaski*), Tom Tyler (*Clyde Bracken*), Don Beddoe (*Chief of Police*), George Watts (*Judge Grunstadt*), Clyde Fillmore (*Sen. James Boyd*), Frank M. Thomas (*District Attorney*), Lloyd Bridges (*Forrester*), Ralph Peters, Max Wagner (*Moving Men*), Pat McVey (*Cop*), Eddie Laughton (*Henry*), Billy Benedict (*Western Union Boy*), Harold "Stubby" Kruger (*Ball Player*), John Tyrrell, George Hickman, Frank Mills, Bud Geary, Holger Bendixen, Joe Garcia, Jay Guedalia, Oscar Hendrian, Dave Harper, Dick Jensen, Robert Keats, Herman Marks, Charles Perry, Al Rhein, Al Seymour, Charles St. George, Victor Travers, Ralph Volkie (*Men*), Maynard Holmes (*Vendor*), Jack Carr (*Usher*), Ralph Dunn, Bill Lally, Edward Hearn (*Sergeants*), Roberta Smith, Dorothy Babb (*School Girls*), Lee Phelps, Al Ferguson (*Detectives*), Edward Coke, Jack Shay, Eddie Bruce (*Reporters*), Ferike Boros (*Mrs. Pulaski*), Jack Gardner (*Cameraman*), William Gould (*Sheriff*), Lee "Lasses" White (*Hound Keeper*), Joe McGuinn (*Jailer*), Dewey Robinson (*Jake*), Georgia Backus, Lelah Tyler (*Women*), Lew Davis, Gino Corrado (*Waiters*), Frank Sully (*Road Cop*), Dan Seymour (*Headwaiter*), Mabel Todd (*Operator*), Lee Prather (*Sergeant at Arms*), Clarence Muse (*Doorkeeper*), Leslie Brooks (*Secretary*), Alan Bridge (*Desk Sergeant*), Joe Cunningham (*McGuire*), Jack Lowe (*Workman*), Robert Walker (*Deputy Sheriff*).

TALK OF THE TOWN is a witty comedy, full of some wonderful *bon mots* that dot the clever dialog, and essayed with zest by Grant, Arthur and Colman. Colman plays a renowned law professor who wants to spend a quiet summer writing while he awaits an appointment to the Supreme Court. He takes lodgings in the home of Arthur, a schoolteacher, but Colman's summer proves to be anything but quiet. Grant, who has escaped jail after being labeled as the man behind a deadly factory fire, has taken refuge in the house as well. Arthur tells the bearded professor that Grant is actually the house gardener, taking great care to protect Grant's secret. Coleman is set in his ways when it comes to legalities, but some discussions with Grant soon change his hard line views. He soon learns the real reason Grant stays at the house. Grant explains he was framed for the arson by a corrupt local government, and what's more, the foreman who supposedly died in the blaze is very much alive. Both men develop an active interest in Arthur, and Colman goes to extreme lengths to impress her, including shaving off his beard. Grant is recaptured and a crazed mob is more than willing to string him up then and there. However Colman comes forth with the not-so-dead foreman, thus clearing Grant of the charges. Colman gets the appointment to the Supreme Court, while Grant ends up winning Arthur's charms. Grant, Arthur, and Colman are a terrific threesome, playing well off of one another in a finely constructed love triangle. Both men want Arthur, yet Colman never lets this take precedence over the justice that must be done. Stevens directs his cast well, handling the double-edged story with grace and style. He originally shot two endings, one with Colman getting Arthur, and the other having Arthur pair with Grant. Both endings were done in preview screenings, and audience pollings found the Grant-Arthur romance to be the more popular among viewers. This was Colman's first film at Columbia since 1937's LOST HORIZON. Much to his delight, he learned that Stevens had arranged it so the actor would not have to deal in the very least with studio chief Harry Cohn during TALK OF THE TOWN's production. At the time Colman had been experiencing some popularity problems at the box office, and said of TALK OF THE TOWN: "It couldn't have come at a more propitious moment." The film was a hit with the public, giving Colman's career a much needed boost.

p&d, George Stevens; w, Irwin Shaw, Sidney Buchman (based on a story by Sidney Harmon, adapted by Dale Van Every); ph, Ted Tetzlaff; m, Frederick Hollander; ed, Otto Meyer; md, Morris Stoloff; art d, Lionel Banks, Rudolph Sternad; cos, Irene; spec eff, Donald Starling.

Comedy   (PR:AA   MPAA:NR)

TALKING BEAR, THE   (SEE: BEAR, THE, 1963, Fr./Ital.)

TALKING FEET*½   (1937, Brit.) 79m United Kingdom Photoplays/Sound City bw

Hazel Ascot (*Hazel Barker*), Jack Barty (*Joe Barker*), Davy Burnaby (*Mr. Shirley*), Enid Stamp-Taylor (*Sylvia Shirley*), John Stuart (*Dr. Roger Hood*), Ernest Butcher (*Thomas*), Edgar Driver (*Titch*), Muriel George (*Mrs. Gumley*), Kenneth Kove (*Lord Cedric Scattery*), Robert English (*Lord Langdale*), Scott Sanders (*Scotty McDonald*), Jennie Gregson (*Mrs. Barker*), Mark Hambourg, Billy Thorburn, Walter Amner, Freddie Watts, John Turnbull, Patch, May Hallatt, Johnnie Schofield, Mark Stone, Duggie Ascot, Vi Kaley, Nora d'Argel, Sydney Monckton, Douglas Burley, Wilfred Roy, David Keir, K.J. Shepherd, Griffiths-Moss, Sonny Farrer and His Band, Scots Kilties Band, Dagenham Girl Pipers, William Heughen, The Corona Babes, The Gordon Ray Girls, Band of the Royal Marines, Minipiano Ensemble of Juveniles, The Variety Proteges.

Ascot is a precocious working class youngster whose dog, Patch, gets injured in an auto accident. Friendly doctor Stuart offers his assistance and Ascot is indebted for life. She and her friends arrange a benefit concert that will help Stuart's hospital raise enough funds to continue operating. Of course the show is a smashing success and the hospital doors stay open.

p, John Barter; d, John Baxter; w, H. Fowler Mear (based on a story by Geoffrey Orme, Jack Francis).

Musical   (PR:A MPAA:NR)

TALL BLOND MAN WITH ONE BLACK SHOE, THE½**
(1973, Fr.) 90m GAU-Gueville-Madeline/Cinema 5 c (LE GRAND BLOND AVEC UNE CHAUSSURE NOIRE)

Pierre Richard (*Francois*), Bernard Blier (*Milan*), Jean Rochefort (*Toulouse*), Mireille Darc (*Christine*), Jean Carmet (*Maurice*), Colette Casel (*Paulette*), Paul Le Person (*Perrache*), Jean Obe (*Botrel*), Robert Castel (*Georghiu*), Robert Caccia (*Mons. Boudart*), Robert Dalban (*Faux Livreur*), Jean Saudray (*Poucet*), Arlette Balkis (*Mme. Boudart*), Yves Robert (*Chef d'Orchestre*).

Infighting at the French Secret Service has resulted in chief Rochefort setting a trap for his ambitious underling, Blier, with innocent concert violinist Richard as the bait. Richard goes through his life, oblivious to the fact that gangs of assassins are out to kill him. Darc is one agent assigned to get close to him, but ends up falling in love with him. The best scene has Richard groggily wandering through his morning routine, oblivious to the two hit men stalking him silently. The two end up killing each other and Richard leaves for work, not knowing a thing. A trivial comedy, to be sure, but one with a few good laughs along the way. Remade in the U.S. in 1985 as THE MAN WITH ONE RED SHOE. Sequel: RETURN OF THE TALL BLOND MAN WITH ONE RED SHOE.

p, Alain Poire, Yves Robert; d, Robert; w, Robert, Francis Veber; ph, Rene Mathelin (Eastmancolor); m, Vladimir Kosma; ed, Ghislaine Desjonqueres.

Comedy   **Cas.**   (PR:C MPAA:PG)

TALL, DARK AND HANDSOME*   (1941) 78m FOX bw

Cesar Romero (*Shep Morrison*), Virginia Gilmore (*Judy*), Charlotte Greenwood (*Winnie*), Milton Berle (*Frosty*), Sheldon Leonard (*Pretty Willie*), Stanley Clements (*Harry*), Frank Jenks (*Puffy*), Barnett Parker (*Quentin*), Marc Lawrence (*Louie*), Paul Hurst (*Biff*), Frank Bruno, Anthony Caruso (*Gunmen*), Marion Martin (*Dawn*), Leon Belasco (*Alfredo*), Charles D. Brown (*District Attorney*), Addison Richards (*Commandant*), George Watts (*Joe*), Stanley Blystone (*Policeman*), Mary Treen (*Martha*), Vicki Lester (*Sales Girl*).

Romero is a super polite and well-dressed crook in Chicago in 1929. He constantly woos Gilmore, who has vowed to fight the temptation of being mixed up with such a bad guy. But Romero isn't all that bad. He takes Clements under his wing and really takes care of the poor people in his area by getting rid of rival Leonard. He and Gilmore then take off for South America to start a new way of living. Berle is there for laughs and Gilmore, when not fighting off Romero's advances, sings a couple of tunes. Remade as LOVE THAT BRUTE.

p, Fred Kohlmar; d, H. Bruce Humberstone; w, Karl Tunberg, Darrell Ware; ph, Ernest Palmer; ed, Allen McNeil; md, Emil Newman; m/l, "Hello Ma, I Done It Again," "Wishful Thinking," Leo Robin, Ralph Rainger (sung by Virginia Gilmore), "I'm Alive and Kickin'," Robin, Rainger (sung by Charlotte Greenwood).

Comedy/Drama   (PR:A MPAA:NR)

TALL HEADLINES   (SEE: FRIGHTENED BRIDE, THE, 1952, Brit.)

TALL IN THE SADDLE*   (1944) 87m RKO bw

John Wayne (*Rocklin*), Ella Raines (*Arly Harolday*), Audrey Long (*Clara Cardell*), George "Gabby" Hayes (*Dave*), Elisabeth Risdon (*Miss Martin*), Ward Bond ("*Judge*" *Garvey*), Don Douglas (*Mr. Harolday*), Russell Wade

(*Clint Harolday*), Frank Puglia (*Juan Tala*), Paul Fix (*Bob Clews*), Harry Woods (*George Clews*), Emory Parnell (*Sheriff Jackson*), Cy Kendall (*Cap the Bartender*), Bob McKenzie (*Doc Riding*), Raymond Hatton (*Zeke*), Russell Simpson (*Pat*), Wheaton Chambers (*Ab Jenkins*), Walter Baldwin (*Stan*), Frank Orth (*Ferdy Davis*), William Desmond, George Chandler, Eddy Waller, Frank Darien, Clem Bevans, Erville Alderson, Russell Hopton.

A hard-hitting, overly plotted John Wayne western which stars the "duke" as a ranch hand who arrives in Santa Inez at the KC ranch. He is to apply for a foreman position, but when he learns that the owner has died and the ranch is now run by Long and her aunt Risdon, he declines, refusing to work for a woman. Later, Long asks for his assistance in retrieving a letter which has fallen into the hands of the town's untrustworthy judge, Bond. The letter is proof that Long is old enough to be the legal owner of the ranch-information that Bond and Risdon want to suppress. Wayne arrives at Bond's office just after he has burned the letter. Wayne is quickly clued in to Bond's character when he finds a deck of marked cards in his desk. A fight breaks out that ends with Bond crashing through a door. Wayne soon is introduced to gutsy ranch owner Raines, but his misogynistic attitude angers her. In revenge, Raines has her stepfather, Douglas, hire Wayne to work on the ranch just so she can have the satisfaction of firing him. As much as she tries, however, she cannot overcome her attraction to him. It turns out that Bond isn't the only corrupt townsperson, just one of many involved in a conspiracy to gain control of the KC ranch. To silence Wayne, a murder is pinned on him-his gun is used to kill Wade, a volatile gambler-causing him to be run out of town by an angry posse. He retreats to the KC ranch, where he overhears a conversation between Long and Risdon. He learns that he is the dead owner's nephew and therefore the rightful heir. Firmly convinced of his innocence, Raines arrives to help Wayne out. She informs him that Douglas, her stepfather, is the real killer and that he has plotted with Risdon to wrestle away control of the ranch. After a final shootout the villains are killed and Long decides to return to her New England home, leaving Wayne and Raines to begin a life together. TALL IN THE SADDLE, while for the most part a typical oater, is interesting in its portrayal of women and their effect on the rugged Wayne. He enters the picture as a callous misogynist but, after being whipped into shape by the frisky Raines (who not only shoots at him, but also throws a knife in his direction), he softens and learns to respect women as people. This, however, wouldn't be believable if it weren't for the fine performance by the beautiful Raines. In another commendable acting job (though a totally familiar one) is Hayes, a stage driver and Wayne's sidekick, who adds some comic relief when the film gets bogged down in its convoluted plot mechanisms. Grossing $4,000,000 (a hefty sum for a grade B western, even if it did star Wayne), TALL IN THE SADDLE was a labor of love for Wayne who liked the script (cowritten by Paul Fix, a friend of Wayne's as well as a supporting player in many of his films, including this one) enough to try to persuade John Ford to direct. Wayne had already appeared in two Ford masterpieces, STAGECOACH (1939) and THE LONG VOYAGE HOME (1940), but this picture would fall far short of those heights.

p, Robert Fellows; d, Edwin L. Marin; w, Michael Hogan, Paul P. Fix (based on a story by Gordon Ray Young); ph, Robert de Grasse; m, Roy Webb; ed, Philip Martin, Jr.; md, Constantin Bakaleinikoff; art d, Albert S. D'Agostino, Ralph Berger; spec eff, Vernon L. Walker.

Western   **Cas.**   (PR:A MPAA:NR)

TALL LIE, THE   (SEE: FOR MEN ONLY, 1952)

TALL MAN RIDING*   (1955) 83m WB c

Randolph Scott (*Larry Madden*), Dorothy Malone (*Corinna Ordway Willard*), Peggie Castle (*Reva, Saloon Singer*), Bill [William] Ching (*Rex Willard*), John Baragrey (*Cibo Pearlo*), Robert Barrat (*Tucker "Tuck" Ordway*), John Dehner (*Ames Luddington, Lawyer*), Paul Richards (*The Peso Kid*), Lane Chandler (*Hap Sutton, Ordway Foreman*), Mickey Simpson (*Deputy Jeff Barkley*), Joe Bassett (*Will*), Charles Watts (*Al, Bartender*), Russ Conway (*Jim Feathergill, U.S. Marshal*), Bill [William] Fawcett (*Andy, Saloon Handyman*), Nolan Leary (*Dr. William Stone*), Mike Ragan, Carl Andre, John Logan, Guy Hearn, Phil Rich, Eva Novak, Buddy Roosevelt, Jack Henderson, Bob Peoples, William Bailey, Patrick Henry, Joe Brooks, Vernon Rich, Bob Stephenson, Dub Taylor, Roger Creed.

Too much talking between the fighting slows down this western. Scott returns to town with vengeance on his mind. He wants to knock off Barrat, who has cheated his way into becoming a cattle baron and wouldn't let Scott marry his daughter. To prevent the wedding, Barrat even had Scott's small ranch burned to the ground. He gets in a few fights while waiting Barrat out, but doesn't even have to kill Barrat to ruin him since Barrat's land is actually public property. Malone, who had been defending her father, finally relents and goes back to Scott, her true love.

p, David Weisbart; d, Lesley Selander; w, Joseph Hoffman (based on the novel by Norman A. Fox); ph, Wilfrid M. Cline (Warner Color); m, Pau Sawtell; ed, Irene Morra; set d, Stanley Fleischer; set d, G.W. Bernsten; cos Moss Mabry; makeup, Gordon Bau.

Western   (PR:A MPAA:NR

TALL MEN, THE***½   (1955) 122m FOX c

Clark Gable *(Ben Allison)*, Jane Russell *(Nella Turner)*, Robert Ryan *(Nathan Stark)*, Cameron Mitchell *(Clint Allison)*, Juan Garcia *(Luis)*, Harry Shannon *(Sam)*, Emile Meyer *(Chickasaw)*, Steven Darrell *(Colonel)*, Will Wright *(Gus the Bartender)*, Robert Adler *(Wrangler)*, Russell Simpson *(Emigrant Man)*, Tom Wilson *(Miner)*, Tom Fadden *(Stable Owner)*, Dan White *(Hotel Clerk)*, Argentina Brunetti *(Maria)*, Doris Kemper *(Mrs. Robbins)*, Carl Harbaugh *(Salesman)*, Post Park *(Stagecoach Driver)*, Gabrile Del Valle *(Man)*, Meyito Pulito, Gilda Fontana *(Spanish Girls)*, Frank Leyva *(Waiter)*, Jack Mather *(Cavalry Lieutenant)*.

Texas brothers Gable and Mitchell, who had ridden with Quantrill's Raiders during the Civil War, head North to Montana in search of gold. Desperate for cash, the men waylay Ryan, a wealthy businessman transporting $20,000. The fast-thinking Ryan turns the robbery to his advantage, however, by offering Gable and Mitchell a chance to be his partners in a cattle drive from Texas to Montana. They accept the offer and Gable is made trail boss. As they head back down to Texas, Gable saves the life of Russell, a young settler whose party was attacked by Indians. A blizzard prevents the pair from continuing their journey and they are forced to seek shelter in a deserted shack. For warmth, Russell and Gable snuggle together under a large blanket, and a romance soon develops. Unfortunately, their relationship is short-lived. Gable wishes only to make enough money to buy a small ranch in Texas and settle down. Russell is more ambitious and desires the finer things in life. Gable's dreams are too small for her and they soon break up. Once in Fort Worth, Russell meets Ryan and decides his obsessive ambition to be one of the most powerful men in the country suits her needs. Ryan and Russell take up together and he insists she accompany the cattle drive back to Montana. This causes friction between Gable and Ryan during the drive. Tensions finally explode when Ryan balks upon learning that the final part of the cattle drive will take them through dangerous Indian territory. Ryan announces his intention to abort the drive and take the loss, but Gable is determined to continue and keeps the cattle moving. Russell begins having doubts about Ryan, and their relationship cools. During the last part of the journey, Mitchell is killed, but Gable stampedes the herd through a narrow canyon and foils the Indians' ambush. Once in Montana, Ryan tries to double-cross Gable but Gable turns the tables on him. Gable returns to camp and discovers that Russell has finally chosen him over Ryan. Shot in CinemaScope and color by cinematographer Leo Tover, THE TALL MEN is a beautiful film to look at and also boasts a good script, solid performances, and typically fine direction from veteran helmsman Walsh. Though the action is supposed to take place in Texas and Montana, Walsh learned that there were not enough longhorn cattle in the area to make a decent herd for the film. The cast and crew were sent to Durango, Mexico, where large herds of longhorn roamed the countryside. Walsh was assisted by a man named Carlos, the governor's son-in-law. Carlos spoke English, was a fan of American movies, and had good connections with the local cattle ranchers. According to Walsh in his autobiography *Each Man in His Time*, after one week of shooting, a swarthy representative of the beef-growers association named Diaz, who wore a pistol on his hip, showed up on the set and demanded more money for the cattle. The governor's son-in-law reminded the man that they had signed a contract which stated a specific price for the cattle. According to Walsh, when this did not faze the cattleman, "...my self-appointed protector jumped in his car and raised more dust between us and the town. When he came back, he was driving a truck with 10 soldiers in it. That was the end of the holdup. The soldiers prodded Diaz into the truck after taking his gun away. 'You can roll your cameras now,' Carlos grinned, 'but I would advise you to get out of town the day you finish the picture.'" The rest of the shooting proceeded smoothly, though director Walsh and his cast enjoyed playing tricks and teasing each other. Walsh roomed with Gable, Ryan roomed with Mitchell and Russell had a house to herself. One night the director borrowed a tame skunk that had been "deodorized" by two young Mexican boys and tossed it in Gable's bedroom. When Gable spotted the creature, he yelled for help and Walsh calmly advised the actor to slowly get out of bed and whistle to the skunk because skunks are afraid of whistling. So Gable stood in the corner whistling "Ol' Man River" and "If I Loved You," while Walsh came over and picked up the little beast. The next day Gable told the entire company how brave Walsh was for removing the animal. "I wouldn't have touched that little bastard for a million dollars," remarked Clark. Somehow, Walsh managed to keep a straight face through the entire affair.

p, William A. Bacher, William B. Hawks; d, Raoul Walsh; w, Sydney Boehm, Frank Nugent (based on the novel by Clay Fisher); ph, Leo Tover (CinemaScope, DeLuxe Color); m, Victor Young; ed, Louis Loeffler; md, Young; art d, Lyle R. Wheeler, Mark-Lee Kirk; set d, Walter M. Scott, Chester Bayhi; cos, Travilla; spec eff, Ray Kellogg; m/l, title song, Ken Darby, "Cancion Mixteca,"Jose Lopez Alaves.

Western   **Cas.**   **(PR:A   MPAA:NR)**

TALL STORY*½   (1960) 91m WB bw

Anthony Perkins *(Ray Blent)*, Jane Fonda *(June Ryder)*, Ray Walston *(Leo Sullivan)*, Marc Connelly *(Charles Osman)*, Anne Jackson *(Myra Sullivan)*, Murray Hamilton *(Coach Hardy)*, Bob Wright *(President Nagel)*, Bart Burns *(D.A. Davis)*, Karl Lukas *(1st D.A. Man)*, Elizabeth Patterson *(Connie)*, Tom

Laughlin *(Fred Jensen)*, Barbara Darrow *(Frieda Jensen)*, Van Williams, Phil Phillips, Ruthie Robinson, Rick Allen.

This was Jane Fonda's screen debut and that is all that makes it memorable. A listless comedy, it is set on a college campus where she is so smitten by basketball player Perkins that she takes the same courses he does and becomes a cheerleader to be near him until he falls for her. Meanwhile, there are some gamblers who want him to shave points and throw a basketball game to the visiting Russian team. But to play he must pass a crucial exam and his whole life rides on this one test. Cheap sex jokes sink this comedy even lower and just try to show that college students have only one thing on their mind--when they are not thinking about sports. It is a bit refreshing, however, to see a young, fresh-faced Perkins tackle a fairly healthy, normal role--just months before he would be typecast forever as a looney playing Norman Bates in PSYCHO.

p&d, Joshua Logan; w, Julius J. Epstein (based on the play by Howard Lindsay, Russel Crouse and the novel The Homecoming Game by Howard Nemerov); ph, Ellsworth Fredericks; m, Cyril J. Mockridge; ed, Philip W. Anderson; cos, Kay Nelson; m/l, title song, Andre Previn, Shelly Manne, Dory Langdon (sung by Bobby Darin).

Comedy   **(PR:C   MPAA:NR)**

TALL STRANGER, THE**   (1957) 81m AA c

Joel McCrea *(Ned Bannon)*, Virginia Mayo *(Ellen)*, Barry Kelley *(Hardy Bishop)*, Michael Ansara *(Zarata)*, Whit Bissell *(Judson)*, James Dobson *(Dud)*, George Neise *(Harper)*, Adam Kennedy *(Red)*, Michael Pate *(Charley)*, Leo Gordon *(Stark)*, Ray Teal *(Cap)*, Philip Phillips *(Will)*, Robert Foulk *(Pagones)*, Jennifer Lea *(Mary)*, George J. Lewis *(Chavez)*, Guy Prescott *(Barrett)*, Ralph Reed *(Murray)*, Mauritz Hugo *(Purcell)*, Ann Morrison *(Mrs. Judson)*, Tom London, Lennie Geer *(Workers)*, Don McGuire, Danny Sands *(Settlers)*.

A typical "adult" western story with a few modern touches such as the use of some cuss words, here and there, along with talk about rape and houses of ill-repute, but the basic story is still the same through the ages. A land baron wants more land and is putting the pressure on some emigrating Confederate homesteaders who have moved north after the Civil War. They enlist the help of Union Army vet McCrea whom they found almost dead after he had been ambushed. The homesteaders happen to be traveling across the land that is ruled by McCrea's half-brother Kelley. McCrea works for peace on both sides, but to no avail. At the same time, Ansara, a local cattle rustler, uses the homesteaders as a cover for his stealing. He also was the one who left McCrea for dead at the beginning of the film. All is settled in the big gun battle at the end with Kelley getting shot so the land falls to McCrea. He then lets the homesteaders stay on the land and starts keeping house himself with Mayo who led a less than pure life before, but like everyone else in the film, gets a second chance to do good.

p, Walter Mirisch; d, Thomas Carr; w, Christopher Knopf (based on a story by Louis L'Amour); ph, Wilfrid Cline (CinemaScope, DeLuxe Color); m, Hans Salter; ed, William Austin; art d, David Milton.

Western   **(PR:A   MPAA:NR)**

TALL T, THE****   (1957) 78m COL c

Randolph Scott *(Pat Brennan)*, Richard Boone *(Usher)*, Maureen O'Sullivan *(Doretta Mims)*, Arthur Hunnicutt *(Ed Rintoon)*, Skip Homeier *(Billy Jack)*, Henry Silva *(Chink)*, John Hubbard *(Willard Mims)*, Robert Burton *(Tenvoorde)*, Robert Anderson *(Jace)*, Fred E. Sherman *(Hank Parker)*, Chris Olsen *(Jeff)*.

Veteran cowboy actor Scott is on the trail again, but this time things are a little more interesting, a little more offbeat than in the standard shoot-em-up. The story contains more suspense than most as Scott is captured by Boone and his thugs. They have also kidnaped newlyweds O'Sullivan and Hubbard. The film moves along at a brisk pace and includes elements of both comedy and drama. Boone and his boys want to rob a stagecoach, but the slimy Hubbard, in an attempt to save himself, tells them that O'Sullivan comes from a wealthy family and it would be easier to get money by holding her for ransom. From there the tension builds as Scott plans to outwit their captors. It finally comes down to just him and Boone with Scott, probably tired of doing this over and over in film after film, doing it one more time before riding off with O'Sullivan. This film has received a fair amount of critical analysis in recent years, particularly in light of the interest paid to "genre" films--those films which seem to represent a certain category without unusual dramatics or production values. Burt Kennedy's script and Budd Boetticher's direction have been applauded in the case of THE TALL T as solid representations of the psychological western which makes use of modern adult themes and which depicts the struggle between good and evil as a complicated one--too complicated, in fact, for a black-and-white presentation. Rather, the viewer is shown how elements outside man's control can influence the struggle and make clear-cut conclusions impossible. In THE TALL T there is Scott as the strong-willed, laconic representative of western man (pre-Eastwood) pitted against an equally strong-minded, laconic villain. They are an evenly matched pair with Boone as the appropriately worthy foe. The struggle between the two is depicted as a delicate balance of power in which Scott, the force of good, is not necessarily stronger–or even better–in all aspects of his life, but merely more wily in the end. THE TALL T, like the Leone westerns to follow, used the American West as the perfect setting for an eternal struggle whose outcome is always a crap shoot.

p, Harry Joe Brown; d, Budd Boetticher; w, Burt Kennedy (based on the stroy "The Captive" by Elmore Leonard); ph, Charles Lawton, Jr. (Technicolor); m, Heinz Roemheld; ed, Al Clark; md, Mischa Bakaleinikoff; art d, George Brooks.

Western   **(PR:A MPAA:NR)**

TALL TARGET, THE**   (1951) 78m MGM bw

Dick Powell (*John Kennedy*), Paula Raymond (*Ginny Beaufort*), Adolphe Menjou (*Col. Caleb Jeffers*), Marshall Thompson (*Lance Beaufort*), Ruby Dee (*Rachel*), Will Geer (*Homer Crowley, Conductor*), Richard Rober (*Lt. Coulter*), Florence Bates (*Mrs. Charlotte Alsop, Novelist*), Victor Kilian (*John K. Gannon*), Katherine Warren (*Mrs. Gibbons*), Leif Erickson (*Stranger*), Peter Brocco (*Fernandina*), Barbara Billingsley (*Young Mother*), Will Wright (*Thomas I. Ogden*), Regis Toomey (*Tim Rielly*), Jeff Richards (*Policeman*), Tom Powers (*Simon G. Stroud*), Leslie Kimmel (*Abraham Lincoln*), James Harrison (*Allan Pinkerton*), Dan Foster (*Dapper Man*).

The bodyguard of newly elected President Lincoln finds out there is a plan to kill his tall boss. Powell lets his superiors know about this, but when they laugh at his thinking and tell him the idea is nonsense, he quits and intensifies his search for the assassins. On a train going to Baltimore, he finds out that one of the would-be killers is also on board. This increases the suspense as Powell tracks him down. Tense moments come as he fights all the assassins one-on-one, and slowly unravels the plot.

p, Richard Goldstone; d, Anthony Mann; w, Art Cohn, George Worthington Yates (based on a story by Yates, Geoffrey Homes); ph, Paul C. Vogel; ed, Newell P. Kimlin; art d, Cedric Gibbons, Eddie Imazu.

Drama   **(PR:A MPAA:NR)**

TALL TEXAN, THE**   (1953) 82m Lippert bw

Lloyd Bridges (*Ben Trask*), Lee J. Cobb (*Capt. Theodore Bess*), Marie Windsor (*Laura Niblett*), Luther Adler (*Josh Tinnen*), Syd Saylor (*Carney*), Samuel Herrick (*Sheriff Chadbourne*), George Steele (*Jaqui*), Dean Train (*Jerome Niblett*).

On the surface this seems to be a psychological character study. But the characters are never fully developed, and questions about their motivations are never answered. A sleazy bunch of gold-seekers discovers a gold deposit on Indian land. Led by Bridges, they strike a deal with the Indians to mine the gold. But one of the group breaks the Indians' trust and the Indians go on the warpath against the group. Finally, only Bridges and Windsor are left, and the film ends abruptly without any clues as to what happens to them. This was Elmo Williams' first shot at directing after working as a film editor on such films as HIGH NOON. His work, and the camera work by Biroc, are better than the slight plot deserves.

p, T.J. Wood, Robert L. Lippert, Jr; d, Elmo Williams; w, Samuel Roecca; ph, Joseph Biroc; m, Bert Schefter; ed, Williams.

Western   **(PR:A MPAA:NR)**

TALL TIMBER   (SEE: BIG TIMBER, 1950)

TALL TIMBERS***½   (1937, Aus.) 85m Cinesound/Associated British Empire bw

Shirley Ann Richards, Frank Leighton, Frank Harvey, Campbell Copelin, Alleen Britten, Joe Valli, Harvey Adams, Ronald Whelan.

A fine Australian drama about two companies fighting over ripe timber land in New South Wales. The companies are entangled because one of the managers is having a clandestine fling with Britten, the sister of one of the other company's overseers. He's also engaged to Richards, the foster daughter of the rival company's owner. The overseer is on the take, meanwhile, but a new man arrives and starts shaking things up. It seems he's the prodigal son of the owner of the timber land. He wins Richard's heart, and helps cause the death of the double-dealing overseer and the two-timing manager. Shirley Ann Richards would later go to Hollywood and–billed as Ann Richards–do such films as RANDOM HARVEST (1942), AN AMERICAN ROMANCE (1944), and THE SEARCHING WIND (1946).

d, Ken G. Hall; w, Capt. Frank Hurley; ph, George Heath; m, W. Hamilton Webber; set d, Eric Thompson.

Drama   **(PR:A MPAA:NR)**

TALL TROUBLE, THE   (SEE: HELL CANYON OUTLAWS, 1957)

TALL WOMEN, THE**   (1967, Aust./Ital./Span.) 101m Danubia Danny Film-L.M. Films/AA c (FRAUEN, DIE DURCH DIE HOLLE GEHEN; DONNE ALLA FRONTIERA; LAS SIETE MAGNIFICAS)

Anne Baxter (*Mary Ann*), Maria Perschy (*Ursula*), Gustavo Rojo (*Gus McIntosh*), Rosella Como (*Katy*), Adriana Ambesi (*Betty*), Perla Cristal (*Perla*), Maria Mahor (*Dorothy*), Crista Linder (*Bridgette*), Luis Prendes (*Pope*), Mara Cruz (*Blanche*), Fernando Hilbeck (*White Cloud*), Alejandra Nilo (*White Cloud's Squaw*), John Clarke (*Col. Howard*), Jorge Rigaud, Valentino Macchi.

European western depicts the bravery of a group of women. Seven women survive an Indian attack led by the ruthless Prendes. Escaping, they find sanctuary in a cave and plot how to survive. Led by Baxter, they decide to push on to Fort Lafayette despite not having guns, horses, or food to help them get across the Arizona desert. At the same time, Rojo is leading an expedition to find the women and he finally succeeds. But they are being watched by Prendes who is getting ready to attack the group once more. Rojo hides the women at an Indian burial ground and leads his men out to meet the Indians. They are all wiped out with the exception of Rojo who crawls back to safety with the women. Once again they start across the desert as Prendes prepares for one final attack. But he is stopped by his leader Hilbeck, who admires the women for their bravery and provides protection for Rojo and the women until they reach the fort.

p, Zeliko Kunkera; d, Rudolf Zehetgruber; w, Mino Roli, Jim Henaghan (based on a script by Mike Ashley); ph, CinemaScope, Eastmancolor); m, Gregario Garcia Segura, Carlo Savina; ed, Antonio Ramirez; art d, Luis Arguello.

Western   **(PR:A MPAA:NR)**

TAM-LIN   (SEE: DEVIL'S WIDOW, THE, 1972)

TAMAHINE**   (1964, Brit.) 85m ABF/MGM c

Nancy Kwan (*Tamahine*), John Fraser (*Richard Poole*), Dennis Price (*Charles Poole, Headmaster*), Coral Browne (*Mme. Becque, Couturier*), Dick Bentley (*Storekeeper*), Derek Nimmo (*Clove*), Justine Lord (*Diana*), Michael Gough (*Cartwright*), Allan Cuthbertson (*Housemaster*), Noel Hood (*Mrs. MacFarlane*), Derek Fowlds (*Bash*), Robin Stewart (*Fiend*), Viola Keats (*Mrs. Spruce*), Howard Marion Crawford (*Maj. Spruce*), Lally Bowers (*Mrs. Cartwright*), Joan Benham (*Mrs. O'Shaugnessy*), Max Kirby (*Mr. O'Shaugnessy*), William Mervyn (*Lord Birchester*), Ian Fleming (*Manservant*), James Fox (*Oliver*), Barbara Cavan, Bee Duffell (*Nuns*), Harry Lockhart (*2nd Young Man*).

Can't decide whether it wants to poke fun at the British education system or send up sex comedies. A beautiful Polynesian girl comes to England after her father dies and his cousin is awarded guardianship. She is so stunning that the male libidos race every time she is seen. All the while she raises men's temperatures, she is completely naive about what she is doing. One scene shows her posing nude for an artist, raising an uproar in the stiff-upper-lipped British community, when, as she sees it, that is what she wore all the time back home. She shines in the athletic competitions, winning almost every event against the boys. She marries her cousin's son Fraser and after several years Fraser becomes headmaster when Price retires to Kwan's native island. Filmed on location in England, Paris, and Bora-Bora.

p, John Bryan; d, Philip Leacock; w, Denis Cannan (based on the novel by Thelma Nicklaus); ph, Geoffrey Unsworth (CinemaScope, Metrocolor); m, Malcolm Arnold; ed, Peter Tanner; art d, Tony Masters; cos, Julie Harris, Guy Laroche; makeup, Neville Smallwood.

Comedy   **(PR:C MPAA:NR)**

TAMANGO**½   (1959, Fr.) 98m Cyclops-SNEG/HR c

Dorothy Dandridge (*Aiche*), Curt Jurgens (*Capt. Reinker*), Jean Servais (*Dr. Corot*), Alex Cressan (*Tamango*), Roger Hanin (*1st Mate Bebe*), Guy Mairesse (*Werner*), Clement Harari (*Cook*), Julien Verdier.

A gripping portrait of life aboard a slave ship in 1830 en route to Cuba from Africa. Jurgens is the ship's captain who takes a black girl, Dandridge, as his mistress in an effort to resolve the conflict he feels in delivering her people into slavery. Tired of Jurgens' lack of affection, Dandridge allies herself with Cressan, a heroic African warrior who is trying to organize a revolt. Not surprisingly, the revolt is quelled and Dandridge gives up her life fighting for its cause. TAMANGO benefits most from director Berry's courage in bringing conflict and racial tension to the screen instead of powdering it with sugary romance. Both French and English-language versions were filmed.

d, John Berry; w, Lee Gold, Tamara Hovey, Berry, Georges Neveaux (based on the novelette by Prosper Merimee); ph, Edmond Sechan (CinemaScope Eastmancolor); ed, Roger Dwyer.

Adventure/Drama   **(PR:C MPAA:NR**

TAMARIND SEED, THE*½ (1974, Brit.) 123m ITC Jewel-Lorimar/AE c

Julie Andrews (*Judith Farrow*), Omar Sharif (*Feodor Sverdlov*), Anthony Quayle (*Jack Loder*), Daniel "Dan" O'Herlihy (*Fergus Stephenson*), Sylvia Syms (*Margaret Stephenson*), Oscar Homolka (*Gen. Golitsyn*), Bryan Marshall (*George MacLeod*), David Baron (*Richard Paterson*), Celia Bannerman (*Rachael Paterson*), Roger Dann (*Col. Moreau*), Sharon Duce (*Sandy Mitchell*), George Mikell (*Maj. Sukalov*), Kate O'Mara (*Anna Skriabina*), Constantin de Goguel (*Dimitri Memenov*), John Sullivan, Terence Plummer, Leslie Crawford (*KGB Agents*), Alexei Jawdokimov (*Igor Kalinin*), Janet Henfry (*Embassy Section Head*).

When Blake Edwards is hot with a film, he's hot, but when he's not, he's not. This time he's not. He directs wife Julie Andrews in a lackluster spy story about a simple clerk who is swept off her feet by dashing Russian Sharif. While they are falling in love under the Caribbean skies, he wants to turn her into a secret agent to help the mother country. But she resists, so he decides to stay with her, which is easier said than done. They have to battle a British agent, who is really a Russian agent. But there is a happy ending: he stays and so does she. Edwards had much better luck with comedies such as "S.O.B." and the "Pink Panther" films.

p, Ken Wales; d&w, Blake Edwards (based on the novel by Evelyn Anthony); ph, Freddie Young; (Panavision, Eastmancolor); m, John Barry; ed, Ernest Walter; art d, Harry Pottle; m/l, "Play It Again," Barry, Don Black (sung by Wilma Reading).

Drama Cas. (PR:C MPAA:PG)

TAMING OF DOROTHY, THE*½ (1950, Brit.) 75m Orlux/EL-UA bw (GB: HER FAVOURITE HUSBAND)

Jean Kent (*Dorothy*), Robert Beatty (*Antonio/Leo*), Margaret Rutherford (*Mrs. Dotherington*), Rona Anderson (*Stellina*), Gordon Harker (*Mr. Dotherington*), Walter Crisham (*Caradottio*), Max Adrian (*Catoni*), Tamara Lees (*Rosana*), Michael Balfour (*Pete*), Jack McNaughton (*El Greco*), Norman Shelley (*Mr. Dobson*), Danny Green (*Angel Face*), Joss Ambler, Mary Hinton, Peter Illing, Jimmy Vientola.

The Brits do such a silly job of playing American gangsters that this almost becomes a laughable satire. It is filled with gangster cliches, spoken with British accents. The plot revolves around a mild-mannered Italian, Beatty, who is often mistaken for an American bad guy. It's bad enough he is always being taken for a gangster, but his wife is so domineering, she should be shot. Leo the gangster decides to use his double to advantage, kidnaping him and taking his place in the family and robbing a bank so the blame falls on Antonio. Leo is caught and Antonio returns to his wife, but now with the same mannerisms of the gangster so as to keep control over his bossy wife. The film keeps moving but corny dialog bogs it down much of the time.

p, John Sutro, Colin Lesslie; d, Mario Soldati; w, Noel Langley, W.F. Templeton (based on the play by Pepine de Felipe); ph, Mario Bava; m, Nino Rota.

Comedy (PR:A MPAA:NR)

TAMING OF THE SHREW, THE**½ (1929) 63m UA bw

Mary Pickford (*Katherine*), Douglas Fairbanks (*Petruchio*), Edwin Maxwell (*Baptista*), Joseph Cawthorn (*Gremio*), Clyde Cook (*Grumio*), Geoffrey Wardwell (*Hortensio*), Dorothy Jordan (*Bianca*), Charles Stevens (*Servant*).

Two early screen stars–Pickford and Fairbanks–pose and preen so much in this Shakespeare classic that it becomes satire. Ripe with physical comedy and plenty of pratfalls by the pair. Pickford falls in the mud with pigs in her bridal gown, and the first time she meets Fairbanks the pair trade insults before tumbling down the stairs. Strictly played for laughs. The film is widely regarded to have the most ludicrous of all credit lines: "Written by William Shakespeare; additional dialog by Samuel Taylor."

d, Samuel Taylor; w, Taylor (based on the play by William Shakespeare); ph, Karl Struss; ed, Allen McNeil; art d, William Cameron Menzies, Laurence Irving.

Comedy Cas. (PR:A MPAA:NR)

TAMING OF THE SHREW, THE***½ (1967, U.S./Ital.) 122m Royal-F.A.I./COL c

Elizabeth Taylor (*Katharina*), Richard Burton (*Petruchio*), Cyril Cusack (*Grumio*), Michael Hordern (*Baptista*), Alfred Lynch (*Tranio*), Alan Webb (*Gremio*), Victor Spinetti (*Hortensio*), Roy Holder (*Biondello*), Mark Dignam (*Vincentio*), Bice Valori (*The Widow*), Natasha Pyne (*Bianca*), Michael York (*Lucentio*), Giancarlo Cobelli (*The Priest*), Vernon Dobtcheff (*Pedant*), Ken Parry (*Tailor*), Anthony Garner (*Haberdasher*), Alberto Bonucci (*Nathaniel*), Gianni Magni (*Curtis*), Lino Capolicchio (*Gregory*), Roberto Antonelli (*Philip*), Tina Perna, Milena Vucotich, Alfred Bianchini, Valentino Bacchi.

A lusty, bawdy version of Shakespeare's rambunctious comedy as helmed by Italian director Zeffirelli, who later went on to make a superb ROMEO AND JULIET. In the late 1500s in Padua, Hordern is a rich merchant with a difficult problem. He has a brace of daughters: sweet, comely, and shy

Pyne, and gorgeous but mean-tempered Taylor. Pyne is being courted by several eligible young men and all of them are stunned when Hordern announces that her hand cannot be taken in marriage by anyone until Taylor has been married off. Since Taylor's reputation as a witch on wheels precedes her by miles, the young men are all in a dither because they can't find anyone stupid enough to marry Taylor. York is a traveling student who sees Pyne, falls madly in love with her, and takes a job in Hordern's household as a tutor just so he can get close to Pyne. Burton arrives in town. He's a ne'er-do-well who makes it clear that he's come to Padua to find himself a rich wife who is too proud to allow her husband to work. The moment he meets Taylor, the sparks fly as she flings epithets his way and even attacks him physically. Burton is the picture of calm, however, and sees something in Taylor that no one else in Padua can see. Then he tells her to prepare for their upcoming wedding. She laughs in his face. But on the appointed date, she is at the church. Burton arrives, drunk and disheveled, and everyone watches with bated breath. The hitching goes off without a hitch and Burton takes Taylor to his tacky home after a long journey on a muddy highway. He tells her that he loves her and that there is no reason why they should have to surround themselves with earthly goods and luxuries as long as they have each other. Now that Taylor has been married, York can move in and he is then revealed to be not the poor student he's claimed as his identity. Instead, Hordern and Pyne learn that he is, in fact, the son of Dignam, a well-known man in the area. When York asks permission to wed Pyne, it is promptly granted. Burton and Taylor are invited to the wedding and everyone there is surprised to see a docile Taylor, totally devoted to her husband and offering all sorts of sage advice to the other women there on how to behave and obey their mates. First made in 1908 by D.W. Griffith for the Biograph Company, two more silent versions followed, then a sound picture with Douglas Fairbanks and Mary Pickford in 1929. (They also shot a silent version in case the newfangled sound gimmick proved a bust.) It was this sound picture that carried the screen credit "with additional dialog by Sam Taylor, who directed the movie. As funny as that may seem, consider the gall of Roman Polanski when he titled his Playboy production "Roman Polanski's MacBeth," to distinguish it from anyone else's. In between the Fairbanks-Pickford version and this one, Cole Porter's musical play "Kiss Me Kate" was made into a fairly successful movie. Zeffirelli, a one-time scenic designer, had staged several Shakespeare plays in Italy, all of which were distinguished by the "look" he gave them, if not the interpretations. He'd wanted Sophia Loren and Marcello Mastroianni for this but when that union failed to transpire, he decided Burton might make a marvelous Petruchio after having seen Burton's version of "Hamlet." When you asked for Burton in those days, you almost automatically got Taylor. The couple put well over $1 million of their own money into the film which began shooting in Rome in late March, 1966, and finished in August. This is a fine motion picture and Shakespeare might have been pleased, though not necessarily proud, of the way some of the scenes were handled. It was chosen to be the official film to open the British Royal Film Festival. Since Burton and Taylor used their own money to help back the picture, they are listed as coproducers. Filmed eight times previously, 1908, 1911, 1914, 1923, 1929, 1953 (as KISS ME, KATE), 1955, 1961.

p, Richard Burton, Elizabeth Taylor, Franco Zeffirelli; d, Zeffirelli; w, Paul Dehn, Suso Cecchi D'Amico, Zeffirelli (based on the play by William Shakespeare); ph, Oswald Morris, Luciano Trasatti (Panavision, Technicolor); m, Nino Rota; ed, Peter Taylor, Carlo Fabianelli; md, Carlo Savina; prod d, John De Cuir; art d, Giuseppe Mariani, Elven Webb; set d, Dario Simoni, Carlo Gervasi; cos, Irene Sharaff, Danilo Donatti; spec eff, Augie Lohman; makeup, Frank LaRue, Ron Berkeley, Alberto De Rossi, Giannetto De Rossi.

Comedy Cas. (PR:A-C MPAA:NR)

TAMING OF THE WEST, THE** (1939) 55m COL bw

Bill Elliott (*Wild Bill Saunders*), Iris Meredith (*Pepper*), Dick Curtis (*Rawhide*), Dub Taylor (*Cannonball*), James Craig (*Handy*), Stanley Brown (*Slim*), Ethan Allen (*Judge Bailey*), Kenneth MacDonald, Victor Wong, Don Beddoe, Charles King, Hank Bell, Irene Herndon, John Tyrell, Lane Chandler, George Morrell, Bob Woodward, Art Mix, Richard Fiske.

Elliott was an established cowboy star by this time, and Columbia Pictures gave him a bigger budget to stop the cattle rustlers with in this one. The cattle rustlers are evil through and through, disposing of sheriffs like disposable razor blades. Elliott's fists get ready to do the talking. Instead of the customary gun battles, Elliott was known for his fisticuffs action and so he uses his knuckles to clean out the bad guys and win the heart of Meredith, who had been the main lady for Charles Starrett in his westerns.

p, Leon Barsha; d, Norman Deming; w, Charles Francis Royal, Robert Lee Johnson (based on a story by Johnson); ph, George Meehan; ed, Otto Meyer.

Western (PR:A MPAA:NR)

TAMING SUTTON'S GAL*½ (1957) 71m Variety/REP bw

John Lupton (*Frank McClary*), Gloria Talbott (*Lou Sutton*), Jack Kelly (*Jugger Phelps*), May Wynn (*Evelyn Phelps*), Verna Felton (*Aunty Sutton*).

No money spent to make this one and it becomes apparent by the opening scene. Lupton goes to the California backwoods to do some hunting but gets into trouble with local tough Kelly. He boards with Talbott and her aunt,

Felton. Wynn takes a shine to the newcomer, but Lupton turns down her advances, which throws her into a jealous rage. In a fit, she kills her husband, but the blame is laid on the newcomer. First he fights with his fists, then proceeds to guns until the truth comes out and he and Talbott can set up shop for ever and ever.

p, William J. O'Sullivan; d, Lesley Selander; w, Thames Williamson, Frederic Louis Fox (based on a story by Williamson); ph, Jack Marta (Naturama); ed, Tony Martinelli; md, Gerald Roberts; art d, Ralph Oberg.

Comedy (PR:A MPAA:NR)

TAMING THE WILD*½ (1937) 55m Ed W. Rote/Victory bw (GB: MADCAP)

Rod La Rocque (*Dick Clayton*), Maxine Doyle (*June Bolton*), Barbara Pepper (*Hazel*), Bryant Washburn (*Graham*), Donald Kerr (*Reporter*), Zella Russell (*Mrs. Bolton*), Reed Howes (*Gus*).

Wooden dialog and misdirected plot about lawyer La Rocque who is trying to keep an eye on whirlwind socialite Doyle. The chase drags on and on. La Rocque saves her from con men who want her money and finally catches her for good at the merciful end.

Sam Katzman; d, Bob Hill; w, Al Martin (based on the story "Shipmates" by Peter B. Kyne); ph, Bill Hyer; ed, Earl Turner.

Drama (PR:A MPAA:NR)

TAMMY (SEE: TAMMY AND THE BACHELOR, 1957)

TAMMY AND THE BACHELOR*** (1957) 89m UNIV c (GB: TAMMY)

Debbie Reynolds (*Tammy Tyree*), Leslie Nielsen (*Peter Brent*), Walter Brennan (*Grandpa*), Mala Powers (*Barbara*), Sidney Blackmer (*Prof. Brent*), Mildred Natwick (*Aunt Renie*), Fay Wray (*Mrs. Brent*), Philip Ober (*Alfred Bissle*), Craig Hill (*Ernie*), Louise Beavers (*Osia*), April Kent (*Tina*).

Reynolds shines as a country girl who saves Nielsen after a plane crash in her backwoods area. The wealthy Nielsen invites her to his plantation. When her irascible grandfather, Brennan, gets himself arrested for selling moonshine, she decides to go. The film focuses on Reynolds being out of place yet her refreshing outlook on life is able to bring all the miserable characters at the plantation out of their shells. Wray is classic as the bent-minded mother, who wants to make the place identical to "Tara" in the movie "GONE WITH THE WIND." But everything blooms under the country girl's touch, including the love between her and Nielsen. This film was one of the top grossers in 1957, and rightfully so. It was also the film that really established Reynolds as a major box-office star. Two sequels followed, TAMMY AND THE DOCTOR and TAMMY TELL ME TRUE as well as a TV series. (See TAMMY series, Index.)

p, Ross Hunter; d, Joseph Pevney; w, Oscar Brodney (based on the novel Tammy Out of Time by Cid Ricketts Sumner); ph, Arthur E. Arling (CinemaScope, Technicolor); m, Frank Skinner; ed, Ted J. Kent; art d, Richard H. Riedel, Bill Newberry; cos, Bill Thomas; spec eff, Clifford Stine; m/l, "Tammy," Jay Livingston, Ray Evans (sung by The Ames Brothers and Debbie Reynolds).

Comedy (PR:A MPAA:NR)

TAMMY AND THE DOCTOR** (1963) 88m Ross Hunter/UNIV c

Sandra Dee (*Tammy Tyree*), Peter Fonda (*Dr. Mark Cheswick*), MacDonald Carey (*Dr. Wayne Bentley*), Beulah Bondi (*Mrs. Call*), Margaret Lindsay (*Rachel Coleman, Head Nurse*), Reginald Owen (*Jason Tripp*), Alice Pearce (*Millie*), Adam West (*Dr. Eric Hassler*), Joan Marshall (*Vera*), Stanley Clements (*Wally Day*), Doodles Weaver (*Traction Patient*), Mitzi Hoag (*Pamela*), Alex Gerry (*Chief of Staff*), Robert Foulk (*Surgeon*), Jill Jackson (*Assistant Surgeon*), Forrest Lewis (*Dr. Crandall*), Sondra Rodgers (*1st Nurse*), Charles Seel (*Dr. Smithers*), Susie Kaye (*Dora*), Paul Nesbitt (*David*).

A rich lady is in the hospital and her naive backwoods companion, Dee, gets a nurse's aide job to take care of her. Her lack of knowledge gets her into trouble with the nurses, but she has a winning way with people. Even tough head nurse Lindsay likes her while Fonda takes a special liking to her. But Fonda's ideas are put on ice when he is warned by his stoic boss, Carey, that any romantic notions about Dee will cost him his job. To complicate the plot, Lindsay is in love with Carey. Dee tries to bring them together, but Lindsay resigns. Dee helps save the old woman's life and Carey admits love for Lindsay, so Fonda and Dee can live happily ever after. This was the third in a series for producer Ross Hunter and probably the worst of the bunch. Fonda's film debut. (See TAMMY series, Index.)

p, Ross Hunter; d, Harry Keller; w, Oscar Brodney (based on characters created by Cid Ricketts Sumner); m, Frank Skinner; ed, Milton Carruth; art d, Alexander Golitzen, George Webb; set d, Howard Bristol; cos, Rosemary Odell; m/l, "Tammy," Jay Livingston, Ray Evans (sung by Sandra Dee); makeup, Bud Westmore, Jack Freeman, Allan Snyder, Jean Mollner.

Comedy (PR:A MPAA:NR)

TAMMY AND THE MILLIONAIRE** (1967) 87m Uni-Bet/UNIV c

Debbie Watson (*Tammy Tarleton*), Frank McGrath (*Uncle Lucius*), Denver Pyle (*Grandpa*), George Furth (*Dwayne Whitt*), Donald Woods (*John Brent*), Dorothy Green (*Lavinia Tate*), David Macklin (*Peter Tate*), Linda Marshall (*Gloria Tate*), Jay Sheffield (*Steven Brent*), Teddy Quinn (*Dewey Maine McKinley*), Bella Bruck (*Sybelline Tate*), Andy Albin (*Mailman*), Craig Hundley (*Billy Joe Morgan*), Roy Roberts (*Gov. Alden*), Jeff York (*Grundy Tate*).

Squeaky-clean Watson becomes a secretary to wealthy Woods who has a very eligible college-aged son. Green is a conniver who wanted her daughter to get the job so she could charm Sheffield. Of course, Sheffield and Watson hit it off, so Green and her daughter do everything possible to make the girl look bad. They even try to get her house taken away for back taxes. But Watson's grandfather and uncle find an old deed that shows not only that they own their house but the land the Tates are on as well. Watson wants no part of her relatives' dirty dealings. Woods secretly pays the money owed, even when Watson's hillbilly relatives ruin a party. Everyone shrugs it off and Watson and Sheffield find eternal happiness. Compiled from three episodes of the TV series.

p, Dick Wesson; d, Leslie Goodwins, Sidney Miller, Ezra Stone; w, George Tibbles (based on the novels Tammy Out of Time and Tammy Tell Me True by Cid Ricketts Sumner); ph, John F. Warren, Robert Wyckoff, Enzo A. Martinelli, Bud Thackery (Pathe Color); m, Jack Marshall; ed, Larry D. Lester; art d, Henry Larrecq, Howard E. Johnson; set d, John McCarthy, Audrey Blasdel, Ralph Sylos; makeup, Bud Westmore.

Comedy (PR:A MPAA:NR)

TAMMY, TELL ME TRUE** (1961) 97m Ross Hunter/UNIV c

Sandra Dee (*Tammy Tyree*), John Gavin (*Tom Freeman*), Charles Drake (*Buford Woodly*), Virginia Grey (*Miss Jenks*), Julia Meade (*Suzanne Rook*), Beulah Bondi (*Mrs. Call*), Cecil Kellaway (*Capt. Joe*), Edgar Buchanan (*Judge Carver*), Gigi Perreau (*Rita*), Juanita Moore (*Della*), Hayden Rorke (*Joshua Welling*), Ward Ramsey (*Caleb Slade*), Henry Corden (*Capt. Armand*), Don Dorrell (*Roger*), Pat McNulty (*Joan*), Taffy Paul (*Kay*), Lowell Brown (*John*), Bill Herrin (*Phil*), Catherine McLeod (*Mrs. Bateman*), Ross Elliott (*Prof. Bateman*), Ned Wever (*Dr. Stach*), Billy Mumy (*Neil Bateman*), Stephanie Powers (*Speech Student*).

Ross Hunter comes up with another story based on the "Tammy" novels by Cid Ricketts Sumner. After rousing success with Debbie Reynolds in the first one, Dee takes the lead in this tear-jerker. Dee is a river-person, sad because her boy friend never writes to her from college. She takes matters into her own hands, floats her boat downriver to the local university, and enrolls. To offset costs she becomes an aide to Bondi (a staple in all the "Tammy" films) and Bondi is so delighted with her new worker, she moves onto the boat and rewards Dee with an expensive necklace. Dee has also caught the eye of handsome Gavin, a teacher on campus. Bondi's selfish niece Meade can't find her rich aunt, so she organizes a search party. She spies Dee with the necklace and has her arrested and her aunt brought up for a sanity hearing. Dee's earnestness comes through and every charge is cleared. With all this going on, she has completely forgotten about her old beau and finds true love in Gavin. (See TAMMY series, Index.)

p, Ross Hunter; d, Harry Keller; w, Oscar Brodney (based on the novel by Cid Ricketts Sumner); ph, Clifford Stine (Eastmancolor); m, Percy Faith; ed, Otto Ludwig; art d, Alexander Golitzen, Alfred Sweeney; set d, Howard Bristol; cos, Rosemary Odell; m/l, title song, Dorothy Squires (sung by Sandra Dee); makeup, Bud Westmore.

Comedy (PR:A MPAA:NR)

TAMPICO* (1944) 75m FOX bw

Edward G. Robinson (*Capt. Bart Manson*), Lynn Bari (*Kathie Hall*), Victor McLaglen (*Fred Adamson*), Robert Bailey (*Watson*), Marc Lawrence (*Valdez*), E.J. Ballentine (*Silhouette Man*), Mona Maris (*Dolores*), Tonio Selwart (*Kruger*), Carl Ekberg (*Mueller*), Roy Roberts (*Crawford*), George Sorel (*Stranger*), Charles Lang (*Naval Officer*), Ralph Byrd (*Quartermaster*), Oscar Hendrian, Paul Kruger, Constantin Romanoff, Louis Hart (*Crew Members*), Antonio Moreno (*Justice of the Peace*), Nestor Paiva (*Naval Commander*), Muni Seroff (*Rodriguez*), Juan Varro (*Photographer*), Ben Erway (*Dr. Brown*), Helen Brown (*Mrs. Kelly*), Martin Garralaga (*Serra*), Margaret Martin (*Proprietor*), David Cota (*Messenger Boy*), Arno Frey (*Navigator*), Chris-Pin Martin (*Waiter*), Trevor Bardette (*Waiter*), Peter Helmers (*Captain*), Otto Reichow (*2nd. Lieutenant*), Ludwig Donath (*Commander*), Rudolph Lindau (*Radio Operator*), Jean Del Val (*Port Pilot*), Hans Von Morhart (*2nd. Officer*), Daniel Ocko (*Immigration Inspector*), Karen Palmer (*Bit*), Martin Black (*Steward*), Margaret Martin (*Proprietor*), Virgil Johanson (*Seaman*).

A WW II film about which the word bomb is most appropriate. Even the glamor added by notables such as Robinson couldn't defuse it. Robinson stars as the skipper of an oil tanker, who picks up survivors, including Bari, whose ship has been sunk by torpedoes in the Gulf of Mexico. As Robinson and Bari engage in a feisty romance, his boat sinks, and she is the prime suspect because no one knows who she really is. In trying to prove her innocence, Robinson discovers that his trustworthy first mate, who didn't want to pick up the survivors, is really a German spy. The highlight is the scenery of Tampico, Mexico.

p, Robert Bassler; d, Lothar Mendes; w, Kenneth Gamet, Fred Niblo, Jr., Richard Macaulay (based on a story by Ladislas Fodor); ph, Charles Clarke; m, David Raksin; ed, Robert Fritch; md, Emil Newman; art d, James Basevi, Albert Hogsett; set d, Thomas Little; cos, Yvonne Wood; spec eff, Fred Sersen.

Drama (PR:A MPAA:NR)

TANGANYIKA** (1954) 80m UNIV c

Van Heflin (John Gale), Ruth Roman (Peggy Merion), Howard Duff (Dan Harder), Jeff Morrow (Abel McCracken), Joe Comadore (Andolo), Noreen Corcoran (Sally Merion), Gregory Marshall (Andy Merion), Naaman Brown (Nukumbi Prisoner), Edward C. Short (Head Porter), Murray Alper (Paul Duffy).

Based on a story by William R. Cox, it stars Heflin as the leader of a safari trying to catch the ruthless Morrow, who is using one of the local evil tribes to control the jungle during the early 1900s when the British ruled East Africa. Roman and Duff also join the hunt, she a schoolteacher and he, Morrow's brother, who leads a good life instead of walking on the criminal side. Plenty of stock jungle footage and a climax in which Heflin deceives Morrow's tribe into thinking they are being bombed on all sides. Morrow also gets his, letting Heflin concentrate on other things--mainly Roman.

p, Albert J. Cohen; d, Andre de Toth; w, William Sackheim, Richard Alan Simmons (based on a story by William R. Cox); ph, Maury Gertsman (Technicolor); ed, Al Clark; cos, Rosemary Odell.

Adventure (PR:A MPAA:NR)

TANGA-TIKA** (1953) 75m Norton-Condon c

Adeline Tetahaimuai (Nenu, Girl), Paul Meoe (Timi, Boy), Alice Swenson (Nenu's Mother), Tumaatura (Timi's Mother), Roger Soui (Chinese Boy), Governor Anzani (Himself), Mayor Poeui (Himself), Capt. Darr (Himself), Ah Fu (Himself).

An artsy attempt to show the slow and tranquil lifestyle enjoyed on Tahiti. Beautiful scenic shots add to the film that featured an all-native cast to make it authentic. Thin story line is about Meoe, a stubborn island man, and the problems he and his girl face as they make their intentions known to get married. The film slows in pace, focusing on the island dances for too long. This effort was by Dwight Long, who had won an Academy Award for a wartime documentary about the men on a Navy carrier titled, "Fighting Lady." He filmed this using 16m Kodachrome (reproduced on 35m Eastmancolor Film), during a two-year stay in Tahiti. It is narrated by George Fenneman while the islanders use their native languages.

p, Arch Monson, Dwight Long; d, Long; w, Charles Tedford Lela Rogers (based on a story by Rogers); ph, Long; m, Les Baxter, Victor Young; ed, Robert Beltcher, Merrill White; m/l, "Tahiti, My Island," Young.

Drama (PR:A MPAA:NR)

TANGIER*½ (1946) 76m UNIV bw

Maria Montez (Rita), Robert Paige (Paul Kenyon), Sabu (Pepe), Preston Foster (Col. Jose Artiego), Louise Allbritton (Dolores), Kent Taylor (Ramon), J. Edward Bromberg (Alec Rocco), Reginald Denny (Fernandez), Charles Judels (Dmitri), Francis McDonald (Sanchez), Erno Verebes (Capt. Cartiaz), Peter George Lynn (Lieutenant), Rebel Randell (Rocco's Girl), Dorothy Lawrence (Maid), James Linn (Servant), Billy Greene (Mike), Phil Garris (Elevator Boy), John Banner (Ferris Wheel Operator), Charles Wagenheim (Hadji), Joe Bernard, Dick Dickinson (Men), Charles Stevens (Juan), Eddie Ryans, Jerry Riggio, Parker Garvie, Wheaton Chambers (Vendors), Billy Snyder (Barker), Margaret Hoffman (Police Matron), Jack Chefe (Hotel Clerk), Abel Pina, Henry Pina, Jerry Pina, Jr, Antonio Pina (Tumbling Act), Bobby Barker (Sergeant), Crystal White (Barber Maid), Murray Parker (Juggler), Roxanne Hilton, Karen Raven (Girls), Pierre Andre, Maurice St. Clair, Crystal White (Dance Doubles).

Cliche-ridden spy film stars Montez, a Spanish dancer, who is looking for the person who killed her brother. Also on the scene is a burned-out journalist, discredited by his colleagues, who needs that big story to regain respect. He's on the trail of a story that involves a large diamond and the murders that surround the stone. Montez catches her man, a Nazi, and he dies in what is probably the most exciting part of the film--an elevator crash. Lightest moment and one that evokes the most reaction is Sabu's version of "She'll Be Comin' Round the Mountain." Set in Tangier, Africa, it should have stayed there.

p, Paul Malvern; d, George Waggner; w, M.M. Musselman, Monty F. Collins (based on a story by Alice D.G. Miller); ph, Woody Bredell; m, Milton Rosen; ed, Edward Curtiss; md, Rosen; art d, John B. Goodman, Sturges D. Carne; set d, Russell A. Gausman, Ted Von Hemert; cos, Travis Banton; ch, Lester Horton; m/l, "Love Me Tonight," Waggner, Gabriel Ruiz, Jose Antonio Zorrill.

Spy Drama (PR:A MPAA:NR)

TANGIER ASSIGNMENT* (1954, Brit.) 64m Rock/New Realm bw

Robert Simmons (Valentine), June Powell (Vicky), Fernando Rey (Inspector).

Secret agent Simmons and cabaret singer Powell travel to Tangier to break up a gun-running ring. The pair are captured at the gang's coastal headquarters, but Powell manages to escape and informs the police of their whereabouts. Standard British programmer which is mercifully short.

p, Cyril Parker; d&w, Ted Leversuch; ph, Stanley Lipinski.

Crime (PR:A MPAA:NR)

TANGIER INCIDENT** (1953) 77m AA bw

George Brent (Steve), Mari Aldon (Millicent), Dorothy Patrick (Nadine), Bert Freed (Kozad), Dan Seymour (Rabat), Dayton Lummis (Henry Morrison), Alix Talton (Olga), John Harmon (Tony), Richard Karlan (Rosnev), Shepard Menken (Kravich), Benny Rubin (Blalu), Mike Ross (Ivan).

Run-of-the-mill spy thriller. Three scientists who have knowledge of atomic power band together to make money from the Communists. American and British intelligent agents must learn to get along and pool their sources. Brent, an American agent, pretends he is in the black market, when in reality he wants to foil the sale of the secrets. Aldon is posing as a wealthy American but she's really working for the Russians and is out to stop Brent. Everyone is a suspect and there is plenty of back-stabbing to keep everyone on their toes and the reels going, but Brent wins and the world is safe once more.

p, Lindsley Parsons; d, Lew Landers; w, George Bricker; ph, William Sickner; ed, Leonard W. Herman; art d, David Milton.

Drama (PR:A MPAA:NR)

TANGLED DESTINIES*** (1932) 64m Like/Mayfair bw

Lloyd Whitlock, Doris Hill, Glenn Tryon, Vera Reynolds, Sidney Bracey, Gene Morgan, Ethel Wales, Syd Saylor, Mona Lindley, James B. Leong, William Burt, Henry Hall, William Humphrey.

One of the few independently made films at the time, and successful to boot. Fine story and energetic acting add up to make this interesting. The drama centers on the passengers of a plane, its two pilots, and horses that seek shelter in a deserted house after the plane is forced down by fog. A shaky electrical system is put to use but the lights flicker and a man is shot. He was carrying some expensive diamonds and being watched over by a detective. The detective grills the passengers, adding to the suspense. The story deepens when it is found that the diamonds are fakes. The killing is solved but not before the audience lays the blame on almost everyone. And this is done without prodding by the director, a stunning effect that is difficult to achieve.

p, Ralph M. Like; d, Frank M. Strayer; w, Edward T. Lowe; ph, Jules Cronjager; ed, Byron Robinson; md, Lee Zahler; art d, Ben Dore.

Drama (PR:A MPAA:NR)

TANGLED EVIDENCE*½ (1934, Brit.) 57m REA/RKO bw

Sam Livesey (Inspector Drayton), Joan Marion (Anne Wilmot), Michael Hogan (Ingram Underhill), Michael Shepley (Gilbert Morfield), Reginald Tate (Ellaby), Dick Francis (Frame), Edgar Norfolk (Dr. Ackland), John Turnbull (Moore), Davina Craig (Faith), Gillian Maude.

Livesey investigates the death of a man involved in the world of the occult, reexamining clues that implicate the innocent Marion, the dead man's niece. He discovers that Marion is indeed innocent and that the man was killed by a person fearful of "the other world."

p, Julius Hagen; d, George A. Cooper; w, H. Fowler Mear (based on the novel by Mrs. Champion de Crespigny).

Crime (PR:A MPAA:NR)

TANGO*½ (1936) 66m CHES-IN bw

Marian Nixon (Treasure McGuire), Chick Chandler (Oliver Huston), Matty Kemp (Tony Carver), Marie Prevost (Betty Barlow), Warren Hymer (Joe Sloan), Herman Bing (Mr. Kluckmeyer), Franklin Pangborn (Oscar), George Meeker (Foster Carver), Virginia Howell (Mrs. Carver), Barbara Bedford (Receptionist), Katherine Sheldon (Mrs. Alman).

Nixon stars as a struggling chorus girl. She falls for Kemp but is rebuffed by his snobbish family, and she is tormented at work by her nasty boss. To make ends meet she tries her luck at waitressing and even modeling for an advertising photographer. Chandler is the good guy, always waiting in the wings, who becomes her buddy through good times and bad.

p, Maury M. Cohen; d, Phil Rosen; w, Arthur T. Horman (based on a novel by Vida Hurst); ph, M.A. Andersen; ed, Roland Reed.

Drama   **(PR:A MPAA:NR)**

TANGO BAR**   (1935) 87m PAR bw

Carlos Gardel (*Ricardo*), Rosita Moreno (*Laura*), Enrique de Rosas (*Comandante*), Tito Lusiardo (*Puccini*), Jose Luis Tortosa (*Capitan*), Collette d'Arville (*Chichita*), Manuel Pelufo (*Manuel Gonzalez*), Susanne Dulier (*La Criada de Laura*), William Gordon (*Mr. Cohen*), Carmen Rodriguez (*Mrs. Cohen*), Jose Nieto (*Inspector*), Juan D'Vega (*Ramos*).

Gardel was a big draw for films in Spain and South America and this was his last screen effort before he died in a plane crash–just a few weeks after the film was done. When he isn't singing, the plot wears awfully thin. He plays a guy in love with a pretty dancer, Moreno, who is running with some bad apples. They turn on her and Gardel comes to the rescue, but not without almost getting in trouble himself. But in the finale, he can sing a happy tune and she can do a happy dance, as their love conquers all. (In Spanish.)

d, John Reinhardt; ph, William Miller; md, Reig Tucci; m/l, Carlos Gardel, Alfredo Le Pera.

Musical   **(PR:A MPAA:NR)**

TANIN NO KAO   (SEE: FACE OF ANOTHER, THE, 1967, Jap.)

TANK BATTALION**   (1958) 80m AIP bw (GB: THE VALLEY OF
                                                                         DEATH)

Don Kelly (*Sgt. Brad Dunne*), Marjorie Hellen (*Alice Brent*), Edward G. Robinson, Jr (*Corbett*), Frank Gorshin (*Skids*), Regina Gleason (*Norma*), Barbara Luna (*Nikko*), Bob Padget (*Collins*), Mark Sheeler (*Capt. Caswell*), Baynes Barrow (*Buck*), Tetsu Komai (*Egg Charlie*), John Trigonis (*Lieutenant*), Don Devlin (*1st Soldier*), Warren Crosby (*2nd Soldier*), Troy Patterson (*Soldier*).

A routine, guns-blazing war story set in Korea. It tells the tale of four fighting men in a tank who are battling behind enemy lines. While fighting the enemy, they also reminisce about their love lives. Kelly's love life is more immediate as he romances nurse Hellen. The tank becomes trapped against a cliff and is hampered by a broken gear box. Robinson becomes the hero as he gets back to camp, gets the part, and fights his way back to the tank to get the boys out of danger.

p, Richard Bernstein; d, Sherman A. Rose; w, Bernstein, George W. Waters (based on a story by Waters); ph, Frederick Gately; m, Dick La Salle; ed, Rose; art d, Rudi Feld.

War Drama   **(PR:A MPAA:NR)**

TANK COMMANDO   (SEE: TANK COMMANDOS, 1959)

TANK COMMANDOS**   (1959) 79m AIP bw (GB: TANK
                                                                      COMMANDO)

Robert Barron (*Lt. Blaine*), Maggie Lawrence (*Jean*), Wally Campo (*Lazzotti*), Donato Farretta (*Diano*), Leo V. Metranga (*Shorty*), Jack Sowards (*Todd*), Anthony Rich (*Sands*), Larry Hudson (*Capt. Praxton*), Maria Monay (*Italian Girl*), Carmen D'Antonio (*Tessie*), David Addis (*Clifton*), Russ Prescott (*Taylor*), Freddy Roberto (*Italian Prisoner*), Jerry Lear (*Bartender*), Fred Gavlin (*German Prisoner*), Joan Connors (*Streetwalker*), Larry Shuttleworth (*GI Sergeant*), Lee Redman (*GI*), Norberto Kermer (*Nazi Sergeant*).

A few good moments help carry this war epic but they aren't enough to lift it from mediocrity. Barron leads a demolition squad to blow up an underwater bridge used by the Germans. The only one knowing the whereabouts of the bridge is a young Italian boy. In between quizzing the kid and leading his men, Barron gets involved with nurse Lawrence while the rest of his men scurry after the local Italian women.

p,d&w, Burt Topper; ph, John Nicholaus, Jr; m, Ronald Stein; ed, Asa Clark; art d, Dan Haller.

War Drama   **(PR:A MPAA:NR)**

TANK FORCE**   (1958, Brit.) 81m Warwick/COL bw (GB: NO TIME
                                                                              TO DIE)

Victor Mature (*Sgt. David Thatcher*), Leo Genn (*Sgt. Kendall*), Bonar Colleano (*Pole*), Luciana Paluzzi (*Carola*), George Coulouris (*Commandant*), Robert Rietty (*Alberto*), Martin Boddey (*S.S. Colonel*), Alfred Burke (*Capt. Ritter*), David Lodge (*Fred Patterson, Australian Sgt. Major*), George Pravda (*Volkswagen Sergeant*), Alan Tilvern (*Silvernio*), Percy Herbert, Kenneth Cope (*English Soldiers*), Maxwell Shaw (*Sheik*), Anne Aubrey (*Girl in Lido*), Andreas Malandrinos (*Cook*), Ernest Walder (*German Corporal*), Sean Kelly (*Bartlett*), Anthony Newley (*Tiger Noakes*), Kenneth Fortesque (*Johnson*).

Mature is the leader of five escapees from an Italian POW camp. As they work their way through the Libyan desert back to friendly territory, the y

get caught by a sheik, who is pro-Nazi. While the sheik contemplates whether or not to turn his new-found prisoners over to the Nazis, Mature leads his men on another escape and wipes out the bad guys.

p, Irving Allen, Albert Broccoli; d, Terence Young; w, Richard Maibaum, Young (based on a story by Merle Miller); ph, Ted Moore (CinemaScope, Technicolor); m, Kenneth V. Jones; ed, Bert Rule; md, Muir Mathieson; art d, John Box; spec eff, Cliff Richardson, Roy Whybrow; makeup, William Lodge, Tom Smith.

War Drama   **(PR:A MPAA:NR)**

TANKS A MILLION**   (1941) 50m UA bw

William Tracy (*Dodo*), James Gleason (*Barkley*), Noah Beery, Jr (*Charlie*), Joe Sawyer (*Sgt. Ames*), Elyse Knox (*Jeanne*), Douglas Fowley (*Capt. Rossmead*), Knox Manning (*Radio Announcer*), Frank Faylen (*Skivic*), Dick Wessel (*Monkman*), Frank Melton (*Cleary*), Harold Goodwin (*Lt. Caldwell*), William Gould (*Maj. Green*), Norman Kerry (*Major*).

This was the first of a series of short films put out by Hal Roach to play on double features. Tracy is a wacky genius inducted into the Army and his superb memory gets him in one slapstick situation after another. He quickly achieves a sergeant's rank but has trouble leading his own group of recruits. He is saved when he steps in to help the colonel, who gets the shakes when making a broadcast. Plenty of canned humor, old stuff that has carried through the decades. Strangest thing is that Tracy doesn't go near a tank, nor is one mentioned in the entire film.

p, Hal Roach; d, Fred Guiol; w, Paul Gerard Smith, Warren Wilson, Edward E. Seabrook; ph, Robert Pittack; ed, Richard Currier; md, Edward Ward; art d, Charles D. Hall; spec eff, Roy Seawright.

Comedy   **(PR:A MPAA:NR)**

TANKS ARE COMING, THE**   (1951) 90m WB bw

Steve Cochran (*Sully*), Philip Carey (*Lt. Rawson*), Mari Aldon (*Patricia Kane*), Paul Picerni (*Danny*), Harry Bellaver (*Lemchek*), James Dobson (*Ike*), George O'Hanlon (*Tucker*), John McGuire (*Col. Matthews*), Robert Boon (*Heinie*), Michael Steele (*Sgt. Joe Davis*).

All superlatives are pulled out by the narrator of this one as he expounds on the efforts of the Third Armored Division's move on the Germans in 1944. Cochran is a rough-and-tumble guy leading his boys into battle after their master sergeant is killed. Lieutenant Carey was supposed to be in charge, but Cochran is a man's man and so the real leader. The boys throw about a few jokes to keep it light, but when the action is tense they can be counted on. It was interspersed with actual war footage for realism. This is like all the other tank films before it.

p, Bryan Foy; d, Lewis Seiler, D. Ross Lederman; w, Robert Hardy Andrews (based on a story by Samuel Fuller); ph, Edwin DuPar, Warren Lynch; m, William Lava; ed, James C. Moore; art d, Leo K. Kuter.

War Drama   **(PR:A MPAA:NR)**

TANNED LEGS**   (1929) 68m RKO bw

June Clyde (*Peggy Reynolds*), Arthur Lake (*Bill*), Sally Blane (*Janet Reynolds*), Allen Kearns (*Roger*), Albert Gran (*Mr. Reynolds*), Edmund Burns (*Clinton Darrow*), Dorothy Revier (*Mrs. Lyons-King*), Ann Pennington (*Tootsie*), Lincoln Stedman (*Pudgy*), Lloyd Hamilton (*Detective*), Nella Walker (*Mrs. Reynolds*).

The title is apt because it's all legs and bathing suits, not much dialog. But it's more interesting to look than listen anyway. Walker and Gran are wife and husband, looking for eternal youth by romancing younger partners. The older sister, Blane (in real life, Loretta Young's sister), falls for a con man who is in cahoots with dad's young lady. Little sis is in love but wants to straighten out the family mess before being really happy. Songs are thrown in to break up the monotony but they don't help much. They include: "You're Responsible," "How Lovely Everything Could Be," "With You, With Me" (Oscar Levant, Sidney Clare).

p, Louis Sarecky; d, Marshall Neilan; w, Tom Geraghty (based on a musical comedy book by Sarecky); ph, George Hull, Leo Tover; ed, Archie Marshek; art d, Max Ree.

Musical   **(PR:A MPAA:NR)**

TANTE ZITA   (SEE: ZITA, 1968, Fr.)

TANYA'S ISLAND**½   (1981, Can.) 82m International Film
                                                      Exchange-Fred Baker c

D.D. Winters (*Tanya*), Richard Sargent (*Lobo*), Mariette Levesque (*Kelly*), Don McCleod (*Blue*).

A fantasy with a twist, which bombed at the box office. A Beauty and the Beast theme about gorgeous model Winters who lives with an abusive artist. His art work gets her dreaming about living on an island where Sargent is still violent but she runs along the beach naked and happy. On the beach she makes friends with an ape that has blue eyes (no wonder the film bombed). Sargent objects to the friendship and locks up her new buddy. The ape escapes and Winters is put in the cage. Sargent and the ape continue their charade until Winters snaps out of her dream. It almost gets humorous as man and ape imitate each other. Included is footage from the film MIGHTY JOE YOUNG. Filmed in Puerto Rico.

p, Pierre Brousseau; d, Alfred Sole; w, Brousseau; ph, Mark Irwin (Film House Color); m, Jean Musy; ed, Michael MacLaverty; art d, Angelo Stea; spec eff, Rick Baker, Rob Bottin; makeup, Bottin.

Fantasy (PR:O MPAA:R)

TAP ROOTS*½ (1948) 109m UNIV c

Van Heflin (*Keith Alexander*), Susan Hayward (*Morna Dabney*), Boris Karloff (*Tishomingo*), Julie London (*Aven Dabney*), Whitfield Connor (*Clay MacIvor*), Ward Bond (*Hoab Dabney*), Richard Long (*Bruce Dabney*), Arthur Shields (*Rev. Kirkland*), Griff Barnett (*Dr. MacIntosh*), Sondra Rodgers (*Shellie*), Ruby Dandridge (*Dabby*), Russell Simpson (*Sam Dabney*), Jack Davis (*Militia Captain*), Gregg Barton (*Captain*), George Hamilton (*Quint*), Jonathan Hale (*Gen. Johnston*), Arthur Space, Kay Medford (*Callers*), William Haade (*Mob Leader*), Harry Cording (*Leader*), Bill Neff, Keith Richards (*Lieutenants*), Dick Dickinson (*Field Hand*), Elmo Lincoln (*Sergeant*), George Lewis, Helen Mowery, William Challee, John James, Hank Worden.

TAP ROOTS is GONE WITH THE WIND with another cast, from another studio, with a good deal less success. The Civil War is brewing and the Lebanon Valley of Mississippi is determined to remain neutral. Bond is the acknowledged leader of the area and appeals to the other landowners who abhor slavery to secede from the secessionist state as an indication of their desire to remain out of the fracas. Bond's friend is Karloff, an Indian, and the two men promise the fearful plantation people that they will strive to keep the Gray army away from their peaceful valley. Bond's family includes Hayward, an independent young woman cut from the same cloth as Scarlett O'Hara, London, and son Long. Karloff and Bond's father, Simpson, had carved a civilization out of the raw land and meant to keep it tranquil. When Mississippi withdraws from the Union, Lebanon Valley withdraws from Mississippi. Heflin is the local newspaper publisher and totally behind the cause of the local neutrals, backing his beliefs with his pen and with the dueling pistols for which he is notorious. Heflin has serious ambitions for Hayward's hand but she is affianced to Connor and a wedding is on the horizon. When Hayward has a horseback-riding accident and becomes partly paralyzed, the wedding plans are put on hold. It's just as well because Connor, while supposedly engaged to Hayward, has been dallying with sister London on the side. He is politically behind the Gray cause so it's no surprise that he intends to fight for the Jefferson Davis group. Connor and London run off to get married when Bond finds Connor's presence and his embracing of slavery too much to take. Hayward remains paralyzed and the doctor, Barnett, can't figure a way to cure her. Bond and Long join with local preacher Shields (it seems that every other part Shields played required him to don the clerical collar), and move around the valley in an attempt to rally the other landowners to their neutral position. Karloff, realizing that the white man's medicine often leaves much to be desired, calls upon the ancient methods of his ancestors and restores Hayward to full mobility. The Lebanon Valley is now in accord and the occupants mean to rebel against any force that attempts to conquer them, Blue or Gray. The Confederates send in an army to straighten out these recalcitrants and that unit is headed by Connor, who has worked his way up in the ranks in no time to become a major. Hayward hurls her beautiful body into the arms of the malevolent major in a futile attempt to delay his attack, but to no avail. A huge battle takes place and Shields is killed almost immediately. Everyone pitches in to fight Connor's forces, even the women. Bond is hurt and Long is killed and it looks as though there is no hope. Then Heflin comes face to face with Connor, his rival for the love of Hayward and now with the added designation of "enemy." Since Heflin has already been established as an ace duelist, you need only one guess to know who wins that mano-a-mano fight in the swamps. Heflin saves the bloodied Bond by taking him to a small cabin in the woods. Hayward arrives and she and Heflin will remain together for their lifetimes. The Johnny Rebs have been driven from the valley by a ferocious counterattack and decide to leave the farmers alone rather than suffer any further losses at the hands of fellow Southerners. TAP ROOTS was shot in the Smoky Mountains of Tennessee and North Carolina to simulate Mississippi. Hayward had wanted to play the role Vivien Leigh eventually won and this was her chance. She handled it well. Lots of steamy sex (as much as they could get away with in those days) between Heflin and Hayward. After playing monsters (FRANKENSTEIN) and Asians (MR. WONG in several of the WONG films), Karloff was now expanding his career with roles as an Indian. He had played "Guyasuta", a Seneca chief, in the Gary Cooper-Paulette Goddard vehicle UNCONQUERED released the previous year.

p, Walter Wanger; d, George Marshall; w, Alan LeMay, Lionel Wiggam (based on the novel by James Street); ph, Lionel Lindon, Winton C. Hoch (Technicolor); m, Frank Skinner; prod d, Alexander Golitzen; art d, Frank A. Richards; set d, Russell A. Gausman, Ruby R. Levitt; cos, Yvonne Wood; makeup, Bud Westmore.

Drama (PR:C MPAA:NR)

TAPS*½ (1981) 119m FOX c

George C. Scott (*Gen. Harlan Bache*), Timothy Hutton (*Brian Moreland*), Ronny Cox (*Col. Kerby*), Sean Penn (*Alex Dwyer*), Tom Cruise (*David Shawn*), Brendan Ward (*Charlie Auden*), Evan Handler (*Edward West*), John P. Navin, Jr (*Derek Mellott*), Billy Van Zandt (*Bug*), Giancarlo Esposito (*J.C. Pierce*), Donald Kimmel (*Billy Harris*), Tim Wahrer (*John Cooper*), Tim Riley (*Hulk*), Jeff Rochlin (*Shovel*), Rusty Jacobs (*Rusty*), Wayne Tippett (*M/Sgt. Kevin Moreland*), Jess Osuna (*Dean Ferris*), Earl Hindman (*Lt. Hanson*), James Handy (*Sheriff*), Steven Ryan (*Marshal*), Michael Longfield (*Deputy*), Jay Gregory (*Interviewer*), Karen Braga (*Woman Announcer*), Ralph Drischell (*Stewart*), Jane Cecil (*Secretary*), Thomas Medearis (*Male Clerk*), Amelia Romano (*Mrs. Malloy*), Sheila Marra (*Lori Cable*), Gary McCleery, Arnie Mazer, L. Michael Craig, Chris Hagan, John Taylor, Eugene Krumenacker, David McGinley, John Faucher, Declan Weir, Ryan Helm, Lou Milione, John McBrearty, Frank Chambers, John Newmuis, Paul Lyons, Tom Hutchinson (*Cadets*), Tom Klunis, Brenda Currin, Elizabeth Perry, Jeanne Fisher, Robena Rogers, Jim Arnett (*Parents*).

A gripping, though verbose, drama about what happens when a military school becomes a military zone. Scott, (who is seldom on screen although top-billed) is the general who runs this military academy. It's in danger of being closed because a rapacious real estate combine wants to knock down the ivy-covered, tradition-laden buildings and erect a community of luxury condominiums on the valuable property (this is one of the most ancient plots in drama). The deal is done and when the real estaters try to move in and shut the place down prior to razing the structures, the students revolt. Led by Hutton, the boys are united into a fighting force and will now demonstrate all they've learned. They take over the armory, which is filled with weaponry and live ammunition, and keep the invaders at bay. The Army is called in to quell this student revolution and the boys continue to fight. One thing leads to another and bullets begin flying, the result being the deaths of many of the teenage students. In the end, the beleaguered force must surrender and the real estate people, amply supplemented by the U.S. Army, win the little war. Penn is sensational as one of the students; he became a star because of this film. Hutton and Cruise also went on to star in many films. Scott's role could have been played by anyone and it seems that he took the job for money alone because it needed a star to make the movie package come to pass. It's a moralizing movie that pits honor, tradition, and duty against money, profits, and disdain for those virtues. Chief of production at Fox at the time was Sherry Lansing. She later quit her position to partner with producer Jaffe in several films, including RACING WITH THE MOON, which starred Penn. This movie was shot at a real school in Valley Forge, Pennsylvania.

p, Stanley R. Jaffe, Howard B. Jaffe; d, Harold Becker; w, Darryl Ponicsan, Robert Mark Kamen, James Lineberger (based on the novel *Father Sky* by Devery Freeman); ph, Owen Roizman (DeLuxe Color); m, Maurice Jarre; ed, Maury Winetrobe; art d, Stan Jolley, Alfred Sweeney.

Drama **Cas.** (PR:C MPAA:PG)

TARANTULA* (1955) 80m UNIV bw

John Agar (*Dr. Matt Hastings*), Mara Corday (*Stephanie Clayton*), Leo G. Carroll (*Prof. Gerald Deemer*), Nestor Paiva (*Sheriff Jack Andrews*), Ross Elliott (*Joe Burch*), Edwin Rand (*Lt. John Nolan*), Raymond Bailey (*Townsend*), Hank Patterson (*Josh*), Bert Holland (*Barney Russell*), Steve Darrell (*Andy Anderson*), Eddie Parker (*Paul Lund*), Clint Eastwood (*1st Pilot*), Jane Howard (*Coed Secretary*), Billy Wayne (*Murphy*), Dee Carroll (*Telephone Operator*), Tom London, Edgar Dearing (*Miners*), James J. Hyland (*Trooper Grayson*), Stuart Wade (*Major*), Vernon Rich (*Ridley*), Bob Nelson, Ray Quinn (*Troopers*), Bing Russell (*Deputy*), Robert R. Stephenson (*Warehouseman*), Don Dillaway (*Jim Bagney*), Bud Wolfe (*Bus Driver*), Jack Stoney (*Helper*), Rusty Wescoatt (*Driver*).

The film THEM enjoyed stunning success in 1954 and gave way to many other insect-gone-rampant films in the following years. TARANTULA is just what it is titled–a spider runs amok on the desert. This well-done film, tension-mounting by just using silence, is about a little spider that Agar has been working with. He has been testing nutrients but the little eight-legged guy gets loose. In the desert the nutrients take full effect and he eats cattle instead of flies. The spider grows and grows, becoming as big as a city block and having a taste for humans. The spider loves to chew on cars and spit them out. The Air Force is called in and napalm is dropped on the spider to burn him to death. We get a brief look at Clint Eastwood at this point. Director Jack Arnold uses the features of the desert to add to the scariness of the film.

p, William Alland; d, Jack Arnold; w, Robert M. Fresco, Martin Berkeley (based on a story by Arnold, Fresco); ph, George Robinson; m, Henry Mancini; ed, William M. Morgan; md, Joseph Gershenson; art d, Alexander Golitzen, Alfred Sweeney; cos, Jay Morley; spec eff, Clifford Stine, David S. Horsley; makeup, Bud Westmore.

Science Fiction **Cas.** (PR:A MPAA:NR)

TARAS BULBA*½   (1962) 123m Hecht-Curtleigh/UA c

Tony Curtis (Andrei Bulba), Yul Brynner (Taras Bulba), Christine Kaufmann (Natalia Dubrov), Sam Wanamaker (Filipenko), Brad Dexter (Shilo), Guy Rolfe (Prince Grigory, Polish Leader), Perry Lopez (Ostap Bulba), George Macready (Governor), Ilka Windish (Sophia Bulba), Vladimir Sokoloff (Old Stepan), Vladimir Irman (Grisha Kubenko), Daniel Ocko (Ivan Mykola), Abraham Sofaer (Abbot), Mickey Finn (Korzh), Richard Rust (Capt. Alex), Ron Weyand (Tymoshevsky), Vitina Marcus (Gypsy Princess), Martine Milner (Redheaded Girl), Chuck Hayward (Dolotov), Syl Lamont (Kimon Kandor), Ellen Davalos (Zina), Marvin Goux (Brother Bartholomew), Jack Raine (Mayor).

TARAS BULBA was doomed to fail from the start. First, producer Harold Hecht wanted to cut costs, so he filmed in Argentina this story about 16th-Century Cossacks. The local gauchos didn't like his order-giving and fought with each other to get on camera more than they fought during the actual filming. Curtis' character became unbelievable due to his heavy Brooklyn accent, and his personal life went awry when he fell for 17-year-old Kaufmann, causing wife-at-the-time Janet Leigh to go home and Curtis followed her, which caused some delays. The story is about a Cossack leader, Brynner, betrayed by some Poles and forced to run. He raises two sons, one of them Curtis, and they follow in their father's footsteps. They go off to invade and Curtis falls in love with Kaufmann, who comes from the wrong side of society. She is captured and he tries to save her even though his ruthless father has taken over the city. He does rescue her, but is killed by his father as a traitor. Brynner then shows some emotion as Kaufmann cries over her dead lover's body. The battle scenes are spectacular. Waxman's musical score is first-rate in the way he builds up his thematic scheme as the various Cossack tribes ride and come together for the climactic battle.

p, Harold Hecht; d, J. Lee Thompson; w, Waldo Salt, Karl Tunberg (based on the story by Nikolai Gogol); ph, Joseph MacDonald (Panavision, Eastmancolor); m, Franz Waxman; ed, William Reynolds, Gene Milford, Eda Warren, Ace and Folmar Blangsted; art d, Edward Carrere; set d, William Calvert; cos, Norman Koch; spec eff, Fred Wolff, Barney Wolff; makeup, Frank McCoy, Emile Levigne, Dan Striepeke.

Drama   (PR:A   MPAA:NR)

TARAS FAMILY, THE   (1946, USSR) 82m Kiev Film
                                               Studios/Artkino bw

Ambrosi Butchma (Taras), Benjamin Zuskin (Dr. Fishman), Daniel Sagal (Stepan), Eugene Ponomarenko (Andrei), Vera Slovina (Nastya), Maria Samosvat (Antonia), Lubov Kartasheva (Efrosinia), Elena Osmyalovskaya (Valya), Nikolai Zimovetz (Vesilek), Luda Lizengevich (Granddaughter), Vadin Zakurenko (Lonka), Mikhail Visotsky (German Head).

More Russian propaganda, this film is a heavy story about Nazi brutality and no holds are bared. It tells the story of a Russian family and how the Nazis want them to reopen a weapons factory. Best part of the film deals with the treatment of Jews, one graphic scene showing a search for hideaways and another sickening scene showing a mass slaughter of people. It never relents in its story on how Russians are fighting against the Teutonic occupation. (In Russian; English subtitles.)

d, Mark Donskoy; w, Boris Gorbatov (based on a novel by Gorbatov); ph, Boris Monastrisky; m, Lev Schwartz; English titles, Charles Clement.

War Drama   (PR:A   MPAA:NR)

TARAWA BEACHHEAD*   (1958) 77m Morningside/COL bw

Kerwin Mathews (Sgt. Tom Sloan), Julie Adams (Ruth Campbell), Ray Danton (Lt. Joel Brady), Karen Sharpe (Paula Nelson), Onslow Stevens (Gen. Nathan Keller), Russell Thorsen (Casey Nelson), Eddie Ryder (Lt. Gideon), John Baer (Johnny Brodzky), Mike Garth (Maj. Westerly), Larry Thor (Col. Kempler), Buddy Lewis (Brodzky), Lee Farr (Sgt. Anderson), Bill Boyett (Ullman), Don Reardon (Greer).

A study in how far a serviceman must respect his commanding officer. Mathews is a Marine through and through, but sees his commander, Danton, kill another soldier during combat. Mathews keeps silent, knowing the higherups would probably believe the word of a superior officer. The tension builds as the two are paired together time and time again, in the service and in their private lives. The lives become more intertwined when Mathews falls for Adams, who is the murdered man's widow, and Danton weds Adams' sister. At the end, Mathews is ready to file charges against Danton. But Danton dies in what appears to be a hero's death. Last scene has a general asking Mathews all about Danton, because he wants to get Danton the Medal of Honor, but Mathews replies: "Nobody knows anybody ... That's a fact." A fine story with excellent character development, a sharp turn from most WW II films.

p, Charles H. Schneer; d, Paul Wendkos; w, Richard Alan Simmons; ph, Henry Freulich; ed, Jerome Thoms; art d, Carl Anderson.

War Drama   (PR:A   MPAA:NR)

TARGET**   (1952) 60m RKO bw

Tim Holt (Tim), Linda Douglas (Marshal Terry), Walter Reed (Conroy), Harry Harvey (Carson), John Hamilton (Bailey), Lane Bradford (Garrett), Riley Hill (Foster), Mike Ragan (Higgins), Richard Martin (Chito Rafferty).

A lady marshal is the only twist in this mediocre western. Douglas comes to Pecos to take over for her ill father and then is helped by Holt and Martin, who have arrived to work for an old buddy. Their buddy, Hamilton, along with the other townsfolk, are being terrorized by the land-hungry Reed and his cronies. Reed is an evil railroad agent ready to make big profits off the scared ranchers. But he never gets the chance because the good guys gun down his men (Holt and Martin rarely miss in this film, probably to save bullets for the next one) and make Pecos safe again.

p, Herman Schlom; d, Stuart Gilmore; w, Norman Houston; ph, J. Roy Hunt; ed, George Shrader; md, C. Bakaleinikoff; art d, Albert S. D'Agostino, Feild Gray.

Western   (PR:A   MPAA:NR)

TARGET EARTH*½   (1954) 74m Abtcon/AA bw

Richard Denning (Frank), Kathleen Crowley (Nora), Virginia Grey (Vicki), Richard Reeves (Jim), Robert Roark (Davis), Mort Marshall (Otis), Arthur Space (General), Whit Bissell (Scientist), Jim Drake (Lieutenant), Steve Pendleton (Colonel), House Peters, Jr (Technician).

Venus sends down an army of robots and they wipe out Chicago, leaving only a few survivors. Denning and Crowley wake up one morning in different parts of the city and find no one is left. They gather the survivors and plot to save Earth. Finally, scientist Bissell finds the robots' weakness: their faceplates can be cracked with supersonic airwaves. Bissell's discovery costs him his life and the lives of the other survivors, except Denning and Crowley. They not only have to get away from the robots that gun down people with death rays, but a crazy Roark who also wants to kill them. Robots are just plain disappointing. The science fiction gangster idea would appear in THE ASTOUNDING SHE-MONSTER and THE DAY THE WORLD ENDED. The 23-year-old Cohen made his producing debut and director Rose would go on to make only two other movies.

p, Herman Cohen; d, Sherman A. Rose; w, William Raynor (based on the novella The Deadly City by Paul W. Fairman); ph, Guy Roe; ed, Rose; spec eff, Dave Koehler.

Science Fiction   Cas.   (PR:A   MPAA:NR)

TARGET FOR SCANDAL   (SEE: WASHINGTON STORY, 1952)

TARGET: HARRY*½   (1980) 85m Corman/ABC c (AKA: HOW TO
                                   MAKE IT; WHAT'S IN IT FOR HARRY?)

Vic Morrow (Harry Black), Suzanne Pleshette (Diane Reed), Victor Buono (Mosul Rashi), Cesar Romero (Lt. George Duval), Stanley Holloway (Jason Carlyle), Charlotte Rampling (Ruth Carlyle), Michael Ansara (Maj. Miles Segora), Katy Fraysse (Lisa Boulez), Christian Barbier (Sulley Boulez), Fikret Hakan (Inspector Devrim), Milton Reid (Kemal), Jack Leonard (Valdez), Ellen Gilbert, Tony Barnum, Joanne Clerc, Kemal Alinoren, Sait Nasifoglu, Michel Carre, Iraz Hatche, Pierre Cannon, Ali Safa, Nan Morris, Julien Faget, Memed Durdu, Horali Kalayji.

Originally scheduled for TV release in 1969, but shelved for 11 years, this limp rehashing of THE MALTESE FALCON has Morrow working as a charter pilot flying Holloway to Istanbul. When Holloway is killed, a valuable valise with priceless engraving plates from the British Treasury is stolen. In the meantime, Morrow gets involved with Pleshette, but soon learns she has a habit of killing people. He turns her in and turns over the plates to the local authorities. Roger Corman directed under the pseudonym of Harry Neill and it's no wonder why. With Corman's style of filmmaking it should have been retitled "How to Make It Cheap." Edited by director Monte Hellman (TWO-LANE BLACKTOP).

p, Gene Corman; d, Harry Neill [Roger Corman]; w, Bob Barbash; ph, Patrice Pouget (DeLuxe Color); m, Les Baxter; ed, Monte Hellman; prod d, Sharon Compton; set d, Edith Moyal; m/l, "What's in It for Harry?" Baxter, Bob Merrill; makeup, Nicole Barbe.

Crime/Drama   (PR:C   MPAA:R)

TARGET HONG KONG½**   (1952) 66m COL bw

Richard Denning (Mike Lassiter), Nancy Gates (Ming Shan), Richard Loo (Fu Chao), Soo Yong (Lao Shan), Ben Astar (Suma), Michael Pate (Dockery Pete Gresham), Philip Ahn (Sin How), Henry Kulky (Dutch Pfeifer), Victor Sen Yung (Johnny Wing), Weaver Levy (Lo Chi), Kam Tong (Tai Ching), Robert W. Lee (Wong Lu Cheh).

Denning is an American mercenary enlisted by some Hong Kong Nationalists. He has just lost $25,000 at the local bar, so the Nationalists recruit him to stop the Communist threat. Gates runs the bar, the Green Dragon, and unwittingly aids the Commies in their efforts to take over Hong Kong. Denning and a couple of buddies help out to expose the plot and get rid of the Communists Naturally, their efforts come not a second too soon, as a bomb floating on a raft was set to blow in the city's sewage system, threatening to wipe out a big chunk of the city. Action is plentiful and the pace is fast enough to hold interest throughout.

p, Wallace MacDonald; d, Fred F. Sears; w, Herbert Purdum; ph, Henry Freulich; ed, Richard Fanti; md, Mischa Bakaleinikoff; art d, Ross Bellah; set d, James Crowe.

Action   **(PR:A   MPAA:NR)**

TARGET IN THE SUN   (SEE: MAN WHO WOULD NOT DIE, THE, 1975)

TARGET UNKNOWN**   (1951) 90m UNIV bw

Mark Stevens (*Capt. Jerome Stevens*), Alex Nicol (*Al Mitchell*), Robert Douglas (*Col. von Broeck*), Don Taylor (*Lt. Webster*), Gig Young (*Capt. Reiner*), Joyce Holden (*Nurse*), Suzanne Dalbert (*Theresa*), Malu Gatica (*French Entertainer*), James Best (*Ralph Phelps*), Richard Carlyle (*Brooklyn*), Steven Geray (*Jean*), John Sands (*Crawford*), Tony Christian (*Gundlach*), James Young (*Russ Johnson*).

The focus is an unusual one--the lengthy questioning of prisoners--but little else is handled differently from other films that have broached the subject. A handful of American fly boys are caught by Nazis in France. Through interrogation after interrogation, the men unwittingly give the enemy enough information to figure that a bombing mission by the Allies is impending. With Dalbert's help, however, an escapee makes it back to friendly ground in time for the Allies to change their plan.

Aubrey Schenck; d, George Sherman; w, Harold Medford (based on the story "Target Unknown" by Medford); ph, Maury Gertsman; ed, Frank Gross; md, Joseph Gershenson; art d, Bernard Herzbrun, Hilyard Brown.

War Drama   **(PR:A   MPAA:NR)**

TARGET ZERO**   (1955) 92m WB bw

Richard Conte (*Lt. Tom Flagler*), Peggie Castle (*Ann Galloway*), Charles Bronson (*Sgt. Vince Gaspari*), Richard Stapley (*Sgt. David Kensemmit*), L.Q. Jones (*Pvt. Felix Zimbalist*), Chuck Connors (*Pvt. Moose*), John Alderson (*Cpl. Devon Enoch*), Terence De Marney (*Pvt. Harry Fontenoy*), John Dennis (*PFC George*), Angela Loo (*Sue*), Abel Fernandez (*Pvt. Geronimo*), Richard Park (*Pvt. Ma Koo Sung*), Don Oreck (*Pvt. Stacey Zorbados*), Strother Martin (*Dan O'Hirons*), Aaron Spelling (*Strangler*), George Chan (*Priest*), Joby Baker (*Soldier*), Leo K. Kuter (*Colonel*), Hal Sheiner (*Marine Officer*).

A group of soldiers, with characterizations to fit all the molds, and three Brits are trapped behind enemy lines in Korea. They work their way to what is supposed to be a friendly outpost, only to find that the rest of their company has been wiped out. They are commanded to stay put and hold the spot for the other companies to push in. They do so with help from the Navy, which swoops in from off shore to keep the North Koreans at a distance. As they fight, the Americans and Brits become buddies. For romance, Castle sets her sights (and succeeds) on snaring rough guy Conte.

p, David Weisbart; d, Harmon Jones; w, Sam Rolfe (based on the story "Bug Out" by James Warner Bellah); ph, Edwin DuPar; m, David Buttolph; ed, Clarence Kolster; art d, Leo K. Kuter; set d, G. W. Berntsen; cos, Moss Mabry.

War Drama   **(PR:A   MPAA:NR)**

TARGETS***½   (1968) 90m Saticoy/PAR c

Boris Karloff (*Byron Orlok*), Tim O'Kelly (*Bobby Thompson*), Nancy Hsueh (*Jenny*), James Brown (*Robert Thompson, Sr.*), Sandy Baron (*Kip Larkin*), Arthur Peterson (*Ed Loughlin*), Mary Jackson (*Charlotte Thompson*), Tanya Morgan (*Ilene Thompson*), Monty Landis (*Marshall Smith*), Peter Bogdanovich (*Sammy Michaels*), Paul Condylis (*Drive-in Manager*), Mark Dennis, Stafford Morgan (*Gunshop Salesmen*), Daniel Ades (*Chauffeur*), Timothy Burns (*Waiter*), Warren White (*Grocery Boy*), Geraldine Baron (*Larkin's Girl*), Gary Kent (*Gas Tank Worker*), Ellie Wood Walker (*Woman on Freeway*), Frank Marshall (*Ticket Boy*), Byron Betz (*Projectionist*), Mike Farrell (*Man in Phone Booth*), Carol Samuels (*Cashier*), Jay Daniel (*Snack Bar Attendant*), James Morris (*Man with Pistol*), Elaine Partnow, Paul Belcher, James Bowie, Anita Poree, Robert Cleaves, Kay Douglas, Raymond Roy, Diana Ashley, Kirk Scott, Susan Douglas.

An unconventional horror picture which draws comparison between the real-life horror of the 1966 Charles Whitman murder spree and the film horrors of movie legend Boris Karloff. TARGETS opens with a film clip from Roger Corman's 1963 THE TERROR. The clip then ends, revealing a screening room occupied by Karloff, Bogdanovich (as the director of THE TERROR), and some film executives. Karloff informs them that he's had enough of horror films and plans to return to his home in England. He is aware that his films no longer frighten people and that the public is only affected by the horrors in the headlines. Describing not only his character but his own career, Karloff states, "The world belongs to the young. Make way for them. Let them have it. I am an anachronism." He walks out of the room and into the street where he winds up in the gunsight of a young man across the street in a gunshop. Inside the shop the man, O'Kelly, pays for

the gun, informing the salesman that he is going hunting for pigs. He then loads the gun into the trunk of his car, which is already spilling over with weapons. O'Kelly, a clean-cut All-American looking fellow in his early twenties, lives in the sterile San Fernando Valley home of his parents, Brown and Jackson, with his plain wife, Morgan. He tries to tell his wife that his head is filled with strange ideas, but she doesn't have time to listen. The following morning, after Brown has left for work, O'Kelly shoots his wife, mother, and a delivery boy who happens by. In the meantime, Bogdanovich is trying to convince Karloff to appear in his next picture--a dramatic picture which wouldn't capitalize on Karloff's fiendish monster image. While watching an early Karloff film on television--THE CRIMINAL CODE (1931)--Bogdanovich and Karloff discuss Howard Hawks (the director of THE CRIMINAL CODE) and get increasingly drunk. Both men pass out drunk. The following morning Bogdanovich wakes up and, seeing Karloff's face, lets out a scream. "I had a nightmare," Bogdanovich explains. "I open my eyes, the first thing I see is Byron Orlok." "Very funny, very funny," Karloff responds. Karloff proceeds to glance into a mirror and also lets out a scream. While Karloff prepares himself for a guest appearance that evening at a drive-in showing of THE TERROR, O'Kelly is preparing himself for a bloodbath. He stocks up on food and ammunition and drives out to an oil storage tank which sits alongside a heavily traveled freeway. He loads his arsenal of weapons and takes aim. In just a few short minutes several motorists have been murdered, their cars veering uncontrollably off the road. A security guard investigates the shooting but is also felled by one of O'Kelly's bullets. Before the police can apprehend O'Kelly, he escapes. He takes refuge in a drive-in, his car blending in with countless other cars. Coincidentally it is the drive-in where Karloff is about to appear. As the night grows darker, O'Kelly hides out behind the screen. Through a small hole in the screen, he takes aim and begins to shoot at the patrons in their cars--while the film is running. A vigilante group lays chase, causing O'Kelly to retreat. He looks up to see Karloff's giant image approaching him on screen. He turns around and sees Karloff, the actor, approaching him. Confused by the presence of two Karloff's, O'Kelly cowers in the corner. Karloff knocks his gun away with a cane and slaps him repeatedly. Reacting to O'Kelly's fear, Karloff comments, "Is this what I was afraid of?" O'Kelly is then taken away by the police as he proudly states "I didn't miss much, did I?", referring to his accuracy at target shooting. Shot on a budget of $130,000 ($22,000 of which went to Karloff), TARGETS is yet another example of what the Roger Corman camp can produce on a good day. Corman, who acted here as executive producer, had Karloff under contract for two more days of filming after finishing up THE TERROR early (which in turn was made on the left-over budget of THE RAVEN). Rather than lose the chance of another Karloff film, Corman called on Bogdanovich to try his hand at directing his first picture. Bogdanovich recalls what Corman told him: "I want you to shoot two days with Karloff. You can shoot 20 minutes in two days...Now I made a picture a few years ago called THE TERROR with Boris, and I want you to take 20 minutes of Boris out of that film. Now you've got 40 minutes of Karloff. Then you can get another bunch of actors and shoot for about 10 days for another 40 minutes and you've got an 80 minute Karloff picture I can release." Bogdanovich had a better idea, however. He dwindled down the 20 minute flood scene of THE TERROR to about two and a half minutes, persuaded Karloff to work for a couple more days than scheduled, and ended up with a 90-minute modern horror story. Where Karloff's horror films were about gruesome monsters with frightening physical attributes, TARGETS was about the--to use Bogdanovich's term--"ghouls next door." O'Kelly is not a square-headed living corpse with bolts in the side of his neck. He is an All-American boy and therefore even more of a threat to his victims. O'Kelly's danger is not apparent. The brilliant finale of TARGETS has both of these horrors--the fiction of Karloff and the immediate danger of O'Kelly--up on the screen together. Down below the audience screams in fright, not at Karloff but at O'Kelly. The murderer of the headlines, O'Kelly, has outscared Karloff. O'Kelly has proven that he is more of a menace to society than Karloff's monsters. While atop the oil tank, O'Kelly picks off people at random--his next target can be anyone. TARGETS is even more potent because it is based, in part, on fact. Two years before the film's release a 25-year-old Texan, Charles Whitman, killed his mother and wife and then barricaded himself atop a tower on the University of Texas campus in Austin. A short while later 46 people had become Whitman's targets, 16 of whom were killed. (Whitman, unlike O'Kelly's character, was shot to death later that day by police.) Because of Whitman, and the assassinations of Robert Kennedy and Martin Luther King, there was a great deal of public outcry for gun control. Paramount (which paid $150,000 for the film) was torn in its decision to release the film. Finally it was decided to market it as a gun control picture with an ad campaign that asked the question, "Why Gun Control?" Not surprisingly, the crowds stayed away and Bogdanovich had to wait until his next picture, THE LAST PICTURE SHOW, to receive any fame. TARGETS was later rereleased, without its anti-gun angle, and eventually garnered critical acclaim. Besides marking Bogdanovich's beginning, TARGETS marked Karloff's finale (he was to die the next year). Karloff, a fine actor who toward the end was tossed into a number of mediocre scripts which never gave him room to act, finally got a chance to play a character close to himself. In TARGETS he is not a fiend, but a hero who disarms the fiend. Though Karloff made four more Mexican "quickies" (none of which he was proud of), he kept referring to TARGETS as his last film--a true sign that he was pleased with the outcome.

p,d&w, Peter Bogdanovich (based on a story by Polly Platt, Bogdanovich);

ph, Laszlo Kovacs (Pathe Color); m, Charles Greene, Brian Stone; ed, Bogdanovich; prod d, Platt; makeup, Scott Hamilton.

Crime   Cas.   (PR:O MPAA:NR)

TARNISHED**   (1950) 60m REP bw

Dorothy Patrick (Lou Jellison), Arthur Franz (Bud Dolliver), Barbara Fuller (Nina), James Lydon (Junior Bunker), Harry Shannon (Kelsey Bunker), Don Beddoe (Curtis Jellison), Byron Barr (Joe Pettigrew), Alex Gerry (Judge Oliver), Hal Price (Jed Gillis), Stephen Chase (Sheriff McBride), Esther Somers (Edna Jellison), Paul E. Burns (Sam Haines), Ethel Wales (Ida Baker), Michael Vallon (Steve Barron).

Small-town thinking is examined in a small-time way, with only short bursts of originality and excitement. Franz returns to his tiny Maine home town from the Marines but is greeted coolly by most natives. Based on his past exploits as a youth, most town folk assume he has just spent the time in jail. Only Patrick stands by him, believing that he has always been a good person. Finally, Franz proves himself worthy of respect by pulling off some heroic deeds to win over the townspeople and Patrick's heart.

p, Sidney Picker; d, Harry Keller; w, John K. Butler (based on the novel Tarnished by Eleanor R. Mayo); ph, John MacBurnie; m, Stanley Wilson; ed, Robert M. Leeds; art d, Frank Arrigo; cos, Adele Palmer.

Drama   (PR:A MPAA:NR)

TARNISHED ANGEL**   (1938) 67m RKO bw

Sally Eilers (Connie Vinson), Lee Bowman (Paul Montgomery), Ann Miller (Violet McMaster), Alma Kruger (Mrs. Stockton), Paul Guilfoyle (Eddie Fox), Jonathan Hale (Detective Cramer), Jack Arnold (Dan Bennett), Cecil Kellaway (Reginald Roland), Janet Dempsey (Jane Thompson), Hamilton MacFadden (Rev. Summers), Byron Foulger (A Cripple), Robert Gleckler (Checkers, Night Club Owner).

Eilers, who is supposed to carry the film, doesn't last for the duration. She is a fake evangelist who not only heals her flock, but fleeces them as well. She herself finds religion when she heals a crippled person. She turns over a new leaf and hits the preaching trail with zest. Many people thought much of the story was based on the life of Aimee Semple McPherson, a Los Angeles evangelist.

p, B.P. Fineman; d, Leslie Goodwins; w, Jo Pagano (based on the story "Miracle Racket" by Saul Elkins); ph, Nicholas Musuraca; ed, Desmond Marquette; md, Frank Tours; art d, Van Nest Polglase; cos, Renie; m/l, "It's the Doctor's Orders," Lew Brown, Sammy Fain.

Drama   (PR:A MPAA:NR)

TARNISHED ANGELS, THE***   (1957) 91m UNIV bw

Rock Hudson (Burke Devlin), Robert Stack (Roger Shumann), Dorothy Malone (LaVerne Shumann), Jack Carson (Jiggs), Robert Middleton (Matt Ord), Alan Reed (Col. Fineman), Alexander Lockwood (Sam Hagood), Chris Olsen (Jack Shumann), Robert J. Wilke (Hank), Troy Donahue (Frank Burnham), William Schallert (Ted Baker), Betty Utey (Dancing Girl), Phil Harvey (Telegraph Editor), Steve Drexel (Young Man), Eugene Borden (Claude Mollet), Stephen Ellis (Mechanic).

This is, perhaps, the best-ever adaptation of a Faulkner novel for the screen, directed with passion and perception by Sirk. An underrated director, Sirk draws forth excellent portrayals from Hudson, Stack, Malone, and Carson in an authentic and stimulating Depression drama of racing pilots and daredevil exploits. Stack arrives in New Orleans in 1932 with his nomadic barnstorming troupe–his wife Malone, a sizzling blonde; his son, Olsen; and his loyal-unto-death mechanic, Carson. They have arrived to participate in an air show and race, with Stack hoping to win the big prize money. But Stack's plane is a relic from the WW I days and he has burned it out barnstorming with his family across America. His sexy wife Malone produces some profit for the gypsies of the air by wing-walking and then parachuting to earth, wearing a dress, of course, so that the updraft will blow her skirt skyward and reveal her attractive legs. Hudson, an idealistic reporter for one of the local newspapers, is assigned to write some features about the air show and he interviews Stack and his family, intrigued by their seemingly irresponsible life style. As he comes to know these people, his initial sarcastic attitude toward them changes to one of respect. Stack had been a famous ace during WW I and he cannot bear to be on the ground, having fallen in love with airplanes as a child. During his early barnstorming days he met and fell in love with Malone and she went off into the sky with him, staying with him ever since. Their son's parentage is in doubt and at one time or another Hudson comes to believe that Carson, not Stack, is the boy's real father, although Olsen believes his father to be Stack. Stack, too, is full of idealism, but he forsakes his scruples to obtain the use of a new, experimental airplane when his own plane breaks down completely. Middleton, a wealthy, dirty old man who lusts after Stack's wife Malone, gives the plane to Stack to race in the air show but it is understood that Stack will send his wife to him for some sexual gratification as part payment for the plane. Malone goes to Middleton, but runs away from him before bedding her curvaceous body next to his obese carcass. Stack, meanwhile, proves himself master of the air until his plane, while turning the last pylon

to win the race, tips the structure with its wing and catches fire. He begins to crash toward the crowds in the reviewing stands, but then aims his ship into a nearby lake, dying a hero's death. Hudson, who has followed Malone's path of humiliation and degradation for the sake of "the flying machine," helps her and Olsen leave town in the end, lending money to her so she can return to the farm where she first met her heroic husband, Stack, and giving her a copy of her favorite book, My Antonia, by Willa Cather. The acting is first-rate here, and the script is outstanding, full of wit, black humor, and sometimes fine poetic monologs, especially lines delivered by Stack when wistfully looking back upon the First World War, and by Hudson when he returns drunk to his newspaper and describes to his cynical editor the lives of the gypsy nomads of the air. Sirk does a marvelous job with his action scenes, all of which appear realistic. Faulkner saw this film and considered it the best picture ever made of his work. The author based much of his story on the exploits of his own brother, Dean Faulkner, who was a barnstorming pilot with Faulkner in the early 1930s and was killed in the skies over Tupelo, Mississippi, while barnstorming farmers for rides in his beat-up airplane.

p, Albert Zugsmith; d, Douglas Sirk; w, George Zuckerman (based on the novel Pylon by William Faulkner); ph, Irving Glassberg (Cinemascope); m, Frank Skinner; ed, Russell F. Schoengarth; md, Joseph Gershenson; art d, Alexander Golitzen, Alfred Sweeney; set d, Russell A. Gausman, Oliver Emert; cos, Bill Thomas; spec eff, Clifford Stine.

Aviation Drama   (PR:C MPAA:NR)

TARNISHED HEROES**   (1961, Brit.) 75m Danziger/WPD bw

Dermot Walsh (Maj. Roy Bell), Anton Rodgers (Don Conyers), Patrick McAlinney (Reilly), Richard Carpenter (Freddy), Maurice Kaufmann (Tom Mason), Max Butterfield (Tony), Brian Peck (Bernie White), Sheila Whittingham (Josette).

A group of army soldiers who favor drunkenness, stealing, and desertion over fighting are drafted to complete a "do-or-die" mission. With Walsh as their commanding officer, the daredevil squad succeeds in destroying a strategic bridge and holding a besieged church.

p, Brian Taylor; d, Ernest Morris; w, Brian Clemens.

War   (PR:A MPAA:NR)

TARNISHED LADY**   (1931) 83m PAR bw (AKA: TARNISHED LADY: A STORY OF A NEW YORK LADY)

Tallulah Bankhead (Nancy Courtney), Clive Brook (Norman Cravath), Phoebe Foster (Germaine Prentiss), Alexander Kirkland (DeWitt Taylor), Osgood Perkins (Ben Sterner), Elizabeth Patterson (Mrs. Courtney), Eric Blore (Jewelry Counter Clerk), Ed Gargan (Man in the Bar).

This was Bankhead's very first sound film but unfortunately the title sums up the film's quality. The husky-voiced actress plays a New York socialite who marries Brook so she can dig her claws into his vast wealth. Foster, Bankhead's chief rival in social circles, is thoroughly dismayed by this union, as is Kirkland, one of Bankhead's former suitors. Bankhead grows bored with the marriage and takes to hanging out in nightclubs, then gets a job of her own. When Wall Street wipes out Brook's fortunes, Bankhead, now with a child to raise, realizes she does indeed love her husband and the two are reunited. This was Cukor's first solo directorial effort (following three codirected films: GRUMPY, VIRTUOUS SIN, and THE ROYAL FAMILY OF BROADWAY) but it shows none of the skill or subtleties he would later develop that made him the quintessential "woman's director." Instead, he delivers a soap opera that differs little from many similar pictures of the era. Bankhead had spent the previous seven years in London theater, where she made headlines for both on and off-stage dramatics. Her reputation as both an acting talent and fiery personality preceded her and with TARNISHED LADY (subtitled A STORY OF A NEW YORK LADY), Paramount hoped to launch another star along the lines of Marlene Dietrich. Bankhead appeared to fit the profile with her striking looks, heavy-lidded eyes, and husky voice. Posters for the film boldly exclaimed: "...the picture producers who brought you Dietrich bring you another woman thrill–Tallulah Bankhead. She enthralled a nation. England's adored American beauty on the screen. Get within range of her radiance–feel the rapturous thrill of her voice, her person!" Publicity material went so far as to suggest theater owners rig up a low-charged sash cord so patrons might have an opportunity to experience Bankhead's "shocking" personality for themselves. Yet for all the studio hype, Bankhead's dynamic qualities failed to ignite the film. Her stage training translated poorly to the camera, lacking compassionate traits that would have rounded out her character in this different medium. Cukor, who admitted the script was hardly refined to begin with, later stated "...I don't think (Bankhead's) quality of excitement ever quite worked on the screen." In her autobiography Tallulah, Bankhead wrote: "Was it any good? In a word, NO!...The picture was made by trial and error. What appeared on the screen showed it." Though shot at Paramount's Astoria studios, TARNISHED LADY required some location shooting in a Harlem nightclub. Bankhead was enraptured with Harlem nightlife and soon became a popular figure among the regulars there. Word of Bankhead's nightly jaunts eventually reached her father, a member of the U.S. House of Representatives. The proper southern gentleman was greatly distressed to hear of his daughter's carousing in New York's famed black sector and sent her a letter expressing his displeasure with her actions.

Bankhead implored producer Wanger to help straighten out relations with her father. Wanger agreed, responding with a telegram which read in part: "I think it is scandalous that her sole trip to Harlem should be so misinterpreted. She was sent there with her director...to see conditions as there was a Harlem nightclub scene in her present picture. But after a visit it was decided atmosphere was too vulgar....I regret the episode should have caused such misrepresentation." Bankhead made a few more pictures in a similar vein for Paramount but not one was able to capture the spark that made her unique. Not until 1944, when she starred in Alfred Hitchcock's LIFEBOAT, were the actress' skills successfully put on film and her true abilities acknowledged.

p, Walter Wanger; d, George Cukor; w, Donald Ogden Stewart (based on his story "New York Lady"); ph, Larry Williams; ed, Barney Rogan.

Drama   (PR:A MPAA:NR)

TARS AND SPARS**   (1946) 88m COL bw

Janet Blair (*Christine Bradley*), Alfred Drake (*Howard Young*), Marc Platt (*Junior Casady*), Jeff Donnell (*Penny McDougal*), Sid Caesar (*Chuck Enders*), Ray Walker (*Lt. Scully*), James Flavin (*Chief Bosun Mate Gurney*).

Another musical set in wartime that has a hilarious Sid Caesar (in his film debut) for comedic relief. The name of the film came from the Coast Guard show called "Tars and Spars" and featuring Victor Mature. Drake can't get to the water, despite being a seaman, but he still manages to end up a hero. This makes Blair think he's a fake and it's up to Caesar to set everything straight. Platt adds some excellent dancing and the songs are better than average. Songs include "Love Is a Merry-Go-Round," "I'm Glad I Waited for You," "Kiss Me Hello, Baby," "He's a Hero," "I Have a Love in Every Port," "I Always Mean to Tell You," "Don't Call Me After the War, Baby," "When I Get to Town," "I Love Eggs" (Jule Styne, Sammy Cahn).

p, Milton H. Bren; d, Alfred D. Green; w, John Jacoby, Sarett Tobias, Decla Dunning (based on a story by Barry Trivers); ph, Joseph Walker; ed, Al Clark; md, M.W. Stoloff; art d, Stephen Goosson, Carl Anderson; ch, Jack Cole.

Musical   (PR:A MPAA:NR)

TARTARS, THE**½   (1962, Ital./Yugo.) 83m Lux Film-Dubrava
                                              Film/MGM c (I TARTARI)

Victor Mature (*Oleg*), Orson Welles (*Burandai*), Folco Lulli (*Togrul*), Liana Orfei (*Helga*), Bella Cortez (*Samia*), Luciano Marin (*Eric*), Arnoldo Foa (*Chu-lung*), Furio Meniconi (*Sigrun*), Pietro Ceccarelli, Renato Terra, Spartaco Nale.

Two big-time American names, Mature and Welles, couldn't add enough luster to this Italian exploitation film. The plot centers on how the evil and ruthless Tartars fought with the mild Vikings in Russia, in medieval times. Mature leads the Vikings while Welles is the bossman for the Tartars. Both have a beautiful woman hostage in the encampments. The film doesn't delve into political differences, focusing instead on the battles and a pair of star-crossed lovers, he a Viking, she a Tartar. Plenty of trite fighting with a muddled climax leaves both Mature and Welles dead, the Viking camp in flames, and both sides whaling away at each other. The only peaceful moment comes between the pair that have gone away unnoticed, taking to the Volga river for a blissful midday cruise. Plenty of action for voyeurs with the treatment of women hostages, but it's obvious Mature and Welles just needed the money.

p, Riccardo Gualino; d, Richard Thorpe, Ferdinando Baldi; w, Sabatino Ciuffini, Ambrogio Molteni, Gaio Fratini, Oreste Palella, Emimmo Salvi, Julian Vroome de Kassel; ph, Amerigo Gengarelli, Elios Vercelloni (Totalscope, Technicolor); m, Renzo Rossellini; ed, Maurizio Lucidi; md, Pierluigi Urbini; art d, Oscar D'Amico, Pasquale D'Alpino; cos, Giovanna Natili; makeup, Renato Bomarsi.

Action   (PR:A MPAA:NR)

TARTU   (SEE: ADVENTURES OF TARTU, 1943, Brit.)

TARZAN AND HIS MATE***½   (1934) 105m MGM bw

Johnny Weissmuller (*Tarzan*), Maureen O'Sullivan (*Jane Parker*), Neil Hamilton (*Harry Holt*), Paul Cavanagh (*Martin Arlington*), Forrester Harvey (*Beamish*), William Stack (*Pierce*), Desmond Roberts (*Van Ness*), Nathan Curry (*Saidi*), Paul Porcasi (*Mons. Gironde*).

The second MGM TARZAN film and sequel to TARZAN THE APE MAN, this picture concentrated, as the title states, on Weissmuller and O'Sullivan. The story, which is as scant as O'Sullivan's dress, picks up where its predecessor left off. The native couple are living together (in "sin") atop the trees when their civilized beau Hamilton returns to the jungle with a greedy ivory hunter, Cavanagh. The search continues for Mutia Escarpment, the elephant burial grounds. Cavanagh injures an elephant with the hope that it will lead them to the grounds. Weissmuller, objecting to the merciless treatment of his animal friends, is shot and left to die. His ape companions rescue him and he regains his health. Hamilton and Cavanagh make it to the burial grounds, where they are devoured along with their bearers by a

herd of lions. Stampeding elephants rescue O'Sullivan before she too becomes lunch, and the jungle lovers are reunited. Most interesting about this entry is its appeal to adults. Weissmuller and O'Sullivan are obviously living an erotic, sexually free existence swinging from the trees. O'Sullivan, who is supposed to be a civilized Londoner (though in Rice's novels, she is from Baltimore and named Jane Porter), has thrown away all inhibitions here. She wears only a skimpy animal skin bra and a lion cloth, which clearly reveals her hip and thigh area. She wears a dress only so others "won't think me immodest," as she says, and sleeps in the nude. One scene, clipped from the film after Legion of Decency protests, has Weissmuller and O'Sullivan (actually a stand- in) in a nude swim that revealed her bare breasts–not a common sight in those days. The first two TARZAN pictures were clearly meant for an adult audience– Tarzan and Jane were not married, freely displayed their bodies, and were almost constantly touching each other. It is not surprising, then, that the Hays Code brought about changes in the following pictures. To appease those who wanted double beds for the pair (a rather unfeasible idea for tree-top living), a jungle house was soon built. The house was complete with walls and a ceiling–so beginning the downfall of the series. Although the first talkie TARZAN was directed by W.S. Van Dyke with Cedric Gibbons as art director, MGM finally gave in to Gibbons' wishes and let him direct. The effort proved less than productive, however, and Gibbons was given the hook after a few weeks (MGM's TARZANS were done slowly and carefully with a large budget and generous shooting schedule). Gibbons was replaced by the more experienced Jack Conway, who directed the majority of the film. (See TARZAN series, Index.)

p, Bernard H. Hyman; d, Cedric Gibbons (uncredited, Jack Conway); w, Howard Emmett Rogers, Leon Gordon (based on the story by J. Kevin McGuinness and the characters created by Edgar Rice Burroughs); ph, Charles Clarke, Clyde De Vinna; ed, Tom Held.

Adventure/Romance   (PR:A-C MPAA:NR)

TARZAN AND THE AMAZONS**½   (1945) 76m RKO bw

Johnny Weissmuller (*Tarzan*), Brenda Joyce (*Jane*), Johnny Sheffield (*Boy*), Henry Stephenson (*Henderson*), Maria Ouspenskaya (*Amazon Queen*), Barton MacLane (*Ballister*), Don Douglas (*Andres*), J.M. Kerrigan (*Splivers*), Shirley O'Hara (*Athena*), Steven Geray (*Brenner*).

Weissmuller is still Tarzan but Joyce is now Jane, in her first appearance in the role. The heroic jungle man protects a group of gold-rich Amazon women from some greedy archaeologists, most of whom get killed for their efforts. Sheffield gets himself in trouble and is nearly killed by the Amazons, but he is luckily spared. A decent, adroitly directed adventure. (See TARZAN series, Index.)

p, Sol Lesser; d, Kurt Neumann; w, Hans Jacoby, Marjorie L. Pfaelzer (based on the characters created by Edgar Rice Burroughs); ph, Archie Stout; ed, Robert O. Crandall; md, Paul Sawtell; art d, Walter Koessler.

Adventure   (PR:A MPAA:NR)

TARZAN AND THE GREAT RIVER**½   (1967, U.S./Switz.) 88m
                                              Banner-Allfin, A.G./PAR c

Mike Henry (*Tarzan*), Jan Murray (*Capt. Sam Bishop*), Manuel Padilla, Jr (*Pepe*), Diana Millay (*Dr. Ann Phillips*), Rafer Johnson (*Chief Barcuna*), Paulo Gracindo (*Professor*).

Henry doesn't match up as Tarzan in this mindless comic bookish series entry. When a friend is murdered by Leopard Men at Tarzan's favorite zoo, he gets a few animals and Jan Murray to help stop a tribal uprising. They kill tribal chief Johnson and leave his Leopard Man cult powerless and unorganized. (See TARZAN series, Index.)

p, Sy Weintraub; d, Robert Day; w, Bob Barbash (based on the story by Barbash, Lewis Reed and on the characters created by Edgar Rice Burroughs); ph, Irving Lippman (Panavision, Eastmancolor); m, William Loose; ed, Anthony Carras, Edward Mann, James Nelson; md, Loose; art d, Herbert Smith; spec eff, Ira Anderson.

Adventure   (PR:A MPAA:G)

TARZAN AND THE GREEN GODDESS*   (1938) 72m
                                              Burroughs-Tarzan/Principal bw

Herman Brix [Bruce Bennett] (*Tarzan*), Ula Holt (*Ula Vale*), Frank Baker (*Maj. Martling*), Dale Walsh (*Alice Martling*), Harry Ernest (*Gordon Hamilton*), Don Castello (*Raglan*), Lewis Sergeant (*George*), Merrill McCormick (*Bouchart*), Jack Mower (*Blade*), Jiggs the Monkey.

Brix (later known as Bruce Bennett), who hopped into the loin cloth in 1935 with THE NEW ADVENTURES OF TARZAN, continues swinging through the trees in this picture, which uses much footage from the 1935 film. A pair of expeditions set out to find the ledgendary "Green Goddess," which leads to fighting between the two groups, one led by Baker and the other by Castello. Poor acting and even poorer direction. (See TARZAN series, Index.)

p, George W. Stout, Ben S. Cohen, Ashton Dearholt, Edgar Rice Burroughs; d, Edward Kull; w, Charles F. Royal (adapted by Royal, Edwin H. Blum, based on the characters created by Burroughs); ph, Ernest F. Smith, Kull.

Adventure   Cas.   (PR:AA MPAA:NR)

TARZAN AND THE HUNTRESS**½   (1947) 72m RKO bw

Johnny Weissmuller (Tarzan), Brenda Joyce (Jane), Johnny Sheffield (Boy), Patricia Morison (Tanya), Barton MacLane (Weir), John Warburton (Marley), Wallace Scott (Smithers), Charles Trowbridge (King Farrod), Maurice Tauzen (Prince Suli), Ted Hecht (Prince Ozira), Mickey Simpson (Monak), Cheta the Monkey.

Weissmuller defends his animal companions when a zoo expedition led by Morison comes into the wilds, looking for new inhabitants for their empty cages. One yell from Tarzan and the elephants come running, chasing the vile hunters all the way back to civilization. Sheffield's last appearance as "Boy", moving on to his role as the adventurous Bomba. (See TARZAN series, Index.)

p, Sol Lesser; d, Kurt Neumann; w, Jerry Gruskin, Rowland Leigh (based on the characters created by Edgar Rice Burroughs); ph, Archie Stout; m, Paul Sawtell; ed, Merrill White; md, Sawtell; art d, McClure Capps.

Adventure   (PR:AA MPAA:NR)

TARZAN AND THE JUNGLE BOY*½   (1968, US/Switz.) 90m
Banner-Allfin,A.G./PAR c

Mike Henry (Tarzan), Rafer Johnson (Nagambi), Alizia Gur (Myrna Claudel), Steven Bond (Erik Brunik), Ron Gans (Ken Matson), Edward Johnson (Buhara).

Not necessarily a bad entry in the series, just an unexciting one. Henry returns as the modernized Tarzan, but he seems to have lost his rapport with the animals. The film lacks much contact in friendly terms or in battles, except for Henry's trusty chimp companion. This time he helps Gur find a lost jungle boy, abandoned in the wilds when his father's plane went down seven years earlier. (See TARZAN series, Index.)

p, Robert Day; d, Robert Gordon; w, Stephen Lord (based on the characters created by Edgar Rice Burroughs); ph, Ozen Sermet (Panavision, Technicolor); m, William Loose; ed, Milton Mann, Reg Browne; md, Loose; art d, Herbert Smith; spec eff, Gabriel Queiroz.

Adventure   (PR:AA MPAA:G)

TARZAN AND THE JUNGLE QUEEN
(SEE: TARZAN'S PERIL, 1951)

TARZAN AND THE LEOPARD WOMAN**½   (1946) 72m RKO bw

Johnny Weissmuller (Tarzan), Brenda Joyce (Jane), Johnny Sheffield (Boy), Acquanetta (Lea), Edgar Barrier (Lazar), Tommy Cook (Kimba), Dennis Hoey (Commissioner), Anthony Caruso (Mongo), George J. Lewis (Corporal), Iris Flores, Helen Gerald, Lillian Molieri, Kay Solinas (Zambesi Maidens), Doris Lloyd (Superintendent), Robert Barron, King Kong Kashey, Marek Windheim, Louis Mercier, Georges Renavent, Cheta the Chimp.

The series by now was getting tired, as was Weissmuller, but thanks to an inventive story, TARZAN AND THE LEOPARD WOMAN has some life to it. When a peaceful tribe is found murdered, seemingly by leopards, Weissmuller looks for clues. He finds Acquanetta, the queen of a deadly secret cult that wears iron claws. Weissmuller, Joyce, and Sheffield are captured and nearly sacrificed, but Cheta saves the day. This one lacks the stock Tarzan ingredients–Weissmuller's jungle yell and a herd of stampeding elephants. (See TARZAN series, Index.)

p, Sol Lesser; d, Kurt Neumann; w, Carroll Young (based on the characters created by Edgar Rice Burroughs); ph, Karl Struss; ed, Robert O. Crandall; md, Paul Sawtell; art d, Lewis Greber; ch, Lester Horton.

Adventure   (PR:AA MPAA:NR)

TARZAN AND THE LOST SAFARI**½
(1957, Brit.) 84m Solar/MGM c

Gordon Scott (Tarzan), Robert Beatty ("Tusker" Hawkins), Yolande Donlan (Gamage Dean), Betta St. John (Diana Penrod), Wilfrid Hyde-White ("Doodles" Fletcher), George Coulouris (Carl Kraski), Peter Arne (Dick Penrod), Orlando Martins (Chief Ogonooro), Cheta the Chimp.

A number of things changed in this series entry–color was used for the first time, Jane was missing, CinemaScope was used, and the picture was actually shot in Africa. Scott turns in a convincing performance as the jungle hero who leads a chartered plane's passengers to safety after a crash. Some of the snooty survivors don't deserve to live, however, especially Beatty, who strikes a deal to exchange human lives for a fortune in ivory. Needless to say, Tarzan nixes that business proposal. (See TARZAN series, Index.)

p, John Croydon; d, Bruce Humberstone; w, Montgomery Pittman, Lillie Hayward (based on the characters created by Edgar Rice Burroughs); ph, C.R. Pennington-Richards, Miki Carter (CinemaScope, Technicolor); m, Clifton Parker; ed, Bill Lewthwaite; md, Louis Levy; art d, Geoffrey Drake; cos, Anna Duse; ch, Harold Holness.

Adventure   (PR:AA MPAA:NR)

TARZAN AND THE MERMAIDS***   (1948) 68m RKO bw

Johnny Weissmuller (Tarzan), Brenda Joyce (Jane), Linda Christian (Mara), John Lanenz (Benji), Fernando Wagner (Varga), Edward Ashley (Commissioner), George Zucco (Palanth), Andrea Palma (Luana), Gustavo Rojo (Tike), Matthew Bolton (British Inspector-General).

Weissmuller spends a great deal of time in Mexican waters, helping Christian and her seaside tribe overthrow the evil leader. He has to defeat an octopus before he can get to the villain, but he eventually frees the people from their high priest's clutches. After 16 years in a loin cloth, Weissmuller made this his final TARZAN appearance, though he did go on to 16 JUNGLE JIM films. The film is aided by Florey's fine direction, Draper's superb camera work, and Tiomkin's score. (See TARZAN series, Index.)

p, Sol Lesser; d, Robert Florey; w, Carroll Young (based on the characters created by Edgar Rice Burroughs); ph, Jack Draper, Gabriel Figueroa, Raul Martinez Solares; m, Dimitri Tiomkin; ed, Merrill White; md, Tiomkin; art d, McClure Capps.

Adventure   (PR:AA MPAA:NR)

TARZAN AND THE SHE-DEVIL*   (1953) 76m RKO bw

Lex Barker (Tarzan), Joyce MacKenzie (Jane), Monique Van Vooren (Lyra), Raymond Burr (Vargo), Tom Conway (Fidel), Robert Bice (Maka), Mike Ross (Selim), Henry Brandon (M'Tara), Michael Grainger (Lavar), Cheta the Chimp.

A boring TARZAN entry that has the ape-man kept as Van Vooren's prisoner for most of the film. She and her ivory hunting friends plan on doing the elephants out of their tusks, but they meet opposition when Tarzan gives his deafening jungle cry. The tusked creatures come running, stomping all over Van Vooren's greedy counterparts. Includes scenes from 1934's WILD CARGO. (See TARZAN series, Index.)

p, Sol Lesser; d, Kurt Neumann; w, Karl Lamb, Carroll Young (based on the characters created by Edgar Rice Burroughs); ph, Karl Struss; ed, Leon Barsha; md, Paul Sawtell; art d, Carroll Clark.

Adventure   (PR:AA MPAA:NR)

TARZAN AND THE SLAVE GIRL**
(1950) 74m RKO bw (AKA: TARZAN AND THE JUNGLE QUEEN)

Lex Barker (Tarzan), Vanessa Brown (Jane), Robert Alda (Neil), Hurd Hatfield (Prince), Arthur Shields (Randini Doctor), Robert Warwick (High Priest), Anthony Caruso (Sengo), Denise Darcel (Lola), Tito Renaldo (Chief's Son), Mary Ellen Kay (Moana), Shirley Ballard, Rosemary Bertrand, Gwen Caldwell, Martha Clemmons, Mona Knox, Josephine Parra, Jackee Waldron (Slave Girls), Cheta the Chimp.

Brown makes her first appearance as Barker's mate in this fair TARZAN outing. A lion-worshipping tribe, the Lionians, kidnaps Brown when their tribe falls ill to a mysterious plague. Barker comes to her rescue but first has to do battle over a pit full of lions. Cheta turns in an exciting performance, as usual, this time playfully exploring a bottle of booze. (See TARZAN series, Index.)

p, Sol Lesser; d, Lee Sholem; w, Hans Jacoby, Arnold Belgard (based on the characters created by Edgar Rice Burroughs); ph, Russell Harlan; m, Paul Sawtell; ed, Christian Nyby; md, Sawtell.

Adventure   (PR:AA MPAA:NR)

TARZAN AND THE VALLEY OF GOLD**   (1966 U.S./Switz.) 90m
Banner-Allfin/AIP c

Mike Henry (Tarzan), Nancy Kovack (Sophia Renault), David Opatoshu (Vinaro), Manuel Padilla, Jr (Ramel), Don Megowan (Mr. Train), Enrique Lucero (Perez), Eduardo Noriega (Talmadge), John Kelly (Voss), Francisco Riquerio (Manco), Frank Brandstetter (Ruiz), Carlos Rivas (Romulo), Jorge Beirute (Rodriquez), Oswald Olvera (Antonio).

Henry's first appearance as the legendary ape-man has him donning a loin cloth and rescuing the young Padilla from the clutches of the evil Opatoshu, who believes the boy can lead him to hidden gold. Henry warns the chieftain of the gold mines about the impending attack by Opatoshu, but the fortune is spared when the mad leader is suffocated by gold dust. A former pro football star, Henry appeared in only three TARZAN entries, calling it quits after a lawsuit and a bite from Dinky the chimp. (See TARZAN series, Index.)

p, Sy Weintraub; d, Robert Day; w, Clair Huffaker (based on the characters created Edgar Rice Burroughs); ph, Irving Lippman (Panavision, Eastmancolor); m, Van Alexander; ed, Frank P. Keller; md, Alexander; art d, Jose Rodriquez Granada; cos, Alfonso Rubio; spec eff, Ira Anderson, Ira Anderson, Jr.; makeup, Roman Juarez, Elvira Oropoeza.

Adventure   (PR:AA MPAA:NR)

TARZAN ESCAPES*** (1936) 95m MGM bw

Johnny Weissmuller *(Tarzan)*, Maureen O'Sullivan *(Jane Parker)*, John Buckler *(Capt. Fry)*, Benita Hume *(Rita Parker)*, William Henry *(Eric Parker)*, Herbert Mundin *(Herbert Henry Rawlins)*, E. E. Clive *(Masters the Resident)*, Darby Jones *(Bomba)*, Cheta the Chimp.

Weissmuller and O'Sullivan appear together in their third TARZAN picture, but this time Jane is wearing a dress (compliments of the Hays Code fashion emporium) and the loving couple are living in a tree house, complete with an elephant-driven elevator. O'Sullivan is tricked into separating from Weissmuller by some dastardly hunters, leaving the ape-man with a sad look on his face. After the usual animal battles and elephant stampedes, the swinging pair are reunited. One shockingly evil scene includes a painful ritual performed by a native tribe, showing victims tied spread-eagled to bent trees. The trees are then released, sending the poor souls flying into various sections of the jungle. Originally titled THE CAPTURE OF TARZAN, this picture was chiefly reshot and re-edited, apparently being too frightening and daring for the pampered audiences. One of the film's three writers, John Farrow, went on to marry O'Sullivan. (See TARZAN series, Index.)

p, Sam Zimbalist; d, Richard Thorpe; w, Cyril Hume, John Farrow, Karl Brown) (based on the characters created by Edgar Rice Burroughs); ph, Leonard Smith; ed, W. Donn Hayes.

Adventure (PR:A MPAA:NR)

TARZAN FINDS A SON!*** (1939) 90m MGM bw

Johnny Weissmuller *(Tarzan)*, Maureen O'Sullivan *(Jane)*, John Sheffield *(Boy)*, Ian Hunter *(Austin Lancing)*, Henry Stephenson *(Sir Thomas Lancing)*, Frieda Inescort *(Mrs. Lancing)*, Henry Wilcoxon *(Mr. Sande)*, Laraine Day *(Mrs. Richard Lancing)*, Morton Lowry *(Richard Lancing)*, Gavin Muir *(Pilot)*.

It was a long three-year wait for audiences who hadn't seen a decent TARZAN adventure since TARZAN ESCAPES (other non-Weissmuller-O'Sullivan cheapies had cropped up in the meantime, but the public knew this one would shine above its competitors). The film has the Tarzan clan growing with the addition of Sheffield, a 5-year-old orphan (the Hays Code wouldn't allow Tarzan and Jane to have their own offspring--remember, they weren't married). It seems that Sheffield's relatives are hoping he's dead, in order to receive a hefty inheritance. When they learn he's living with Weissmuller and O'Sullivan and practicing survival techniques, they aren't pleased. Eventually the jungle family is captured by a wicked tribe. Sheffield escapes, however, calls on the stampeding elephants, and saves the day. Originally this entry had O'Sullivan dying off in the final minutes, heeding to her wishes to break off her six-picture contract. Burroughs, however, wouldn't permit MGM to kill any of his characters, so the ending had to be reshot. MGM coughed up some more cash and O'Sullivan suffered through two more jungle extravaganzas. (See TARZAN series, Index.)

p, Sam Zimbalist; d, Richard Thorpe; w, Cyril Hume (based on the characters created by Edgar Rice Burroughs); ph, Leonard Smith; ed, Frank Sullivan, Gene Ruggiero.

Adventure (PR:AA MPAA:NR)

TARZAN GOES TO INDIA** (1962, U.S./Brit./Switz.) 88m
Banner-Allfin Solar/MGM c

Jock Mahoney *(Tarzan)*, Jai *(The Elephant Boy, Jai)*, Leo Gordon *(Bryce)*, Mark Dana *(O'Hara)*, Feroz Khan *(Ragu Kuma)*, Simi *(Princess Kamara)*, Murad *(Maharajah)*, Jagdish Raaj *(Raaj)*, G. Raghaven *(Chakra)*, Aaron Joseph *(Driver)*, Abas Khan *(Pilot)*, Pehelwan Ameer *(Mooty)*, K. S. Tripathi *(Conservation Officer)*, Peter Cooke *(Foreman)*, Denis Bastian *(Servant)*, Rajendra Presade *(Dutt)*, Gajendra the Elephant.

Mahoney took over the role of the title character after being second billed in TARZAN THE MAGNIFICENT. Here, he ventures to India to aid a herd of elephants about to be swept away by the completion of a dam. The young Jai (a modern version of Sabu) helps Mahoney complete his task and stop the careless plans of contractors Gordon and Dana. Ravi Shankar contributed the score of Indian music. (See TARZAN series, Index.)

p, Sy Weintraub; d, John Guillermin; w, Robert Hardy Andrews, Guillermin (based on the characters created by Edgar Rice Burroughs); ph, Paul Beeson (CinemaScope, Metrocolor); m, Ken Jones, Ravi Shankar, Panchal Jaikishan; ed, Max Benedict; art d, George Provis; spec eff, Roy Whybrow; makeup, Stuart Freeborn.

Adventure (PR:AA MPAA:NR)

TARZAN NO. 22 (SEE: TARZAN AND THE JUNGLE BOY, 1968, U.S./Switz.)

TARZAN '65 (SEE: TARZAN AND THE VALLEY OF GOLD, 1966)

TARZAN '66 (SEE: TARZAN AND THE VALLEY OF GOLD, 1966)

TARZAN, THE APE MAN***½ (1932) 99m MGM bw

Johnny Weissmuller *(Tarzan)*, Neil Hamilton *(Harry Holt)*, Maureen O'Sullivan *(Jane Parker)*, C. Aubrey Smith *(James Parker)*, Doris Lloyd *(Mrs. Cutten)*, Forrester Harvey *(Beamish)*, Ivory Williams *(Riano)*, Cheta the Chimp.

The beginning of a legend occurred when MGM cast Johnny Weissmuller, a 28-year-old swimming champ from the 1924 and 1928 Olympic Games, in the role of Tarzan. The Edgar Rice Burroughs character was a popular one from the days of silents, but this picture was the first sound version. O'Sullivan, her father, Smith, and her boy friend, Hamilton, venture into the wilds of Africa in search of the Elephant's Graveyard, the place where the creatures instinctively go to die. Expecting it to be rich in ivory, the three hire a number of bearers and begin their quest. They experience the gravest of dangers, especially as they try to scale a large mountain and cross narrow paths, thereby sacrificing a luckless member of the journey. The jungle yell of Weissmuller is heard, stirring up the fears and anxieties of the expedition. Before long, O'Sullivan has been taken captive, screaming and kicking, as she is carried into the treetops. Her father and suitor demand that she be returned to safety, threatening to fill Weissmuller with bullets. She is finally released, but she comes to the defense of the ape-man with whom she is slowly falling in love. She is soon swinging through the trees under his arm, clowning around with Cheta (in an amazingly captivating performance), and taking swims with Tarzan. In one of the series' finest moments (as well as cinema's), O'Sullivan laboriously tries to teach Weissmuller to speak. She points to herself and says, "Me." He mimics her and refers to her as "Me." She then points to him and says, "You," and he calls himself "You." Finally the immortal words--"Me Tarzan, You Jane"--are spoken repeatedly as Weissmuller nearly knocks O'Sullivan off her feet. The bond between the two builds until they are captured by a tribe of pygmies. The end looks near as they are lowered into a pit with a giant ape called Zumangani, who at will can crush the life out of men. Cheta is thrown aside like a rag doll, but Tarzan gets enough energy to let out a thundering yell. In moments, a herd of elephants come running to Tarzan's aid, smashing the pygmies and their village with the greatest of ease. Smith rides a wounded elephant to the graveyard, where he dies with the elephant amongst a fortune in ivory. Hamilton returns to England without Smith, O'Sullivan, or the ivory. The first of six MGM Weissmuller-O'Sullivan TARZAN adventures, TARZAN, THE APE MAN, was directed by W. S. Van Dyke. He had shot TRADER HORN, a dismal picture with an abundance of stock Africa footage in 1931. The excellent sequence of pygmies, which on its own has an anthropological value, is ineptly cut together (but not without a certain charm) with the cast, which even walks in front of the stock shots. The animal sequences offer some especially convincing moments, the most skillful being a hippopotamus attack and a pair of alligators chasing a swimming Weissmuller. Although most viewers have become accustomed to (or spoiled by) the technological superiority of RAIDERS OF THE LOST ARK-type jungle adventures, TARZAN still has enough thrills to put most films to shame. The almost nonstop excitement holds up even today, making it one of Hollywood's most memorable adventure films. Filmed previously in 1918, remade in 1959 and 1981. (See TARZAN series, Index.)

p, Irving Thalberg; d, W. S. Van Dyke; w, Cyril Hume, Ivor Novello (based on the characters created by Edgar Rice Burroughs); ph, Harold Rosson, Clyde DeVinna; ed, Ben Lewis, Tom Held; art d, Cedric Gibbons.

Adventure/Romance Cas. (PR:AA MPAA:NR)

TARZAN, THE APE MAN* (1959) 82m MGM c

Dennis [Denny] Miller *(Tarzan)*, Joanna Barnes *(Jane Parker)*, Cesare Danova *(Holt)*, Robert Douglas *(Col. Parker)*, Thomas Yangha *(Riano)*.

MGM scraped the barrel for this remake of the 1932 Weissmuller-O'Sullivan picture, the first in the series made at the studio since 1942. Ex-UCLA basketball jock Miller teams up with Barnes and an excess of shots from previous TARZAN pictures, which are tinted to fit in with the color footage. Except for the 1981 Derek outing, this one is the worst in the series (See TARZAN series, Index.)

p, Al Zimbalist; d, Joseph Newman; w, Robert Hill (based on the characters created by Edgar Rice Burroughs); ph, Paul C. Vogel (Technicolor); m, Shorty Rogers; ed, Gene Ruggiero; art d, Hans Peters, Malcolm Brown; spec eff, Lee LeBlanc, Robert R. Hoag.

Adventure/Romance (PR:A MPAA:NR)

TARZAN, THE APE MAN zero (1981) 112m Svengali-MGM/UA c

Bo Derek *(Jane)*, Richard Harris *(Parker)*, John Phillip Law *(Holt)*, Miles O'Keefe *(Tarzan)*, Akushula Selayah *(Africa)*, Steven Strong *(Ivory King)*, Maxime Philoe *(Riano)*, Leonard Bailey *(Feathers)*, Wilfrid Hyde-White, Laurie Mains, Harold Ayer *(Club Members)*, C.J. the Orangutan.

John and Bo Derek's version of the 1932 classic adventure tale starts off fine enough--over the MGM Leo the Lion logo one hears Tarzan's yell instead of the lion's roar. From there on, however, TARZAN, THE APE MAN is one of the most boring, ugliest looking, abominably acted, and shallowest pieces of drivel ever to pop out of a motion picture camera. Produced by Bo and "directed by" John (who, on a good day, could not direct his wife from screen left to screen right without her screwing it up), TARZAN, THE APE MAN tells the tale of Derek (as Jane) and her father Harris' journey to the legendary Elephant Graveyard. Along the way Harris pretends to be St. Francis and calls wild creatures, shouts embarrassingly dumb philosophies to any one who'll listen, and has an unhealthy attraction for his daughter. Before the final credits, which never seem to come, Bo is stripped and painted white by a crazy tribal leader, hangs out naked with monkeys, and pretends to be a calendar girl on the beach. Amidst this sexual island fantasy is someone named Miles O'Keefe, who plays Tarzan. Equally as dull as John's direction is his wife's acting is his third-rate Hallmark Card photography which always seems to show characters talking in the dark around a campfire. An awful movie. (See TARZAN series, Index.)

p, Bo Derek; d, John Derek; w, Tom Rowe, Gary Goddard (based on the characters created by Edgar Rice Burroughs); ph, John Derek (Metrocolor); m, Perry Botkin; ed, James B. Ling; art d, Alan Roderick-Jones; cos, Patricia Edwards.

Adventure   Cas.   (PR:O MPAA:R)

TARZAN THE FEARLESS**   (1933) 61m Lesser/Principal bw

Buster Crabbe *(Tarzan)*, Jacqueline Wells [Julie Bishop] *(Mary Brooks)*, E. Alyn Warren *(Dr. Brooks)*, Edward Woods *(Bob Hall)*, Philo McCollough *(Jeff Herbert)*, Mathew Betz *(Nick Moran)*, Frank Lackteen *(Abdul)*, Mischa Auer *(Eltar, High Priest)*, Carlotta Monti *(Priestess of Zar)*, Symonia Boniface *(Arab Woman)*, Darby Jones *(Head Bearer)*, Al Kikume *(Warrior)*, George De Normand *(Guard)*.

Sol Lesser, who would go on to produce a number of TARZAN features, came up with a new idea for this Buster Crabbe entry into the series. He strung together the first four episodes of a 12-part serial and released them as a full-length movie. The problem is, TARZAN THE FEARLESS does not end, so unless you hung around the theater for the next eight weeks you would not know how this move wraps up. The start, at least, has Crabbe rescuing a scientist who is captured while on an expedition to find the people of Zar. He saves the scientist, then turns his energies to helping his daughter, Wells, escape the nearly fatal jaws of a crocodile. Made on a shoestring budget with a lion that, according to Crabbe, "didn't have a tooth in his head." (See TARZAN series, Index.)

p, Sol Lesser; d, Robert Hill; w, Basil Dickey, George Plympton, Ford Beebe, Walter Anthony, (based on characters created by Edgar Rice Burroughs); ph, Harry Neumann, Joe Brotherton; m, Sam K. Wineland; ed, Carl Himm.

Adventure   Cas.   (PR:AA MPAA:NR)

TARZAN THE MAGNIFICENT*½   (1960, Brit.) 82m Solar/PAR c

Gordon Scott *(Tarzan)*, Jock Mahoney *(Coy Banton)*, Betta St. John *(Fay Ames)*, John Carradine *(Abel Banton)*, Lionel Jeffries *(Ames)*, Alexandra Stewart *(Laurie)*, Earl Cameron *(Tate)*, Charles Tingwell *(Conway)*, Al Mulock *(Martin Banton)*, Gary Cockrell *(Johnny Banton)*, Ron MacDonnell *(Ethan Banton)*, Harry Baird *(Warrior Leader)*, Christopher Carlos *(Native Chief)*, John Sullivan *(Winters)*, Ewen Solon, Jacqueline Evans, Thomas Duggan, Peter Howell, John Harrison, George Taylor.

Scott dons his Tarzan loin cloth for the fifth and final time in this series entry, which does not include "Jane" or "Boy". Far from magnificent, as the title would have us believe, Scott's adventures teeter on the edge between boredom and mild amusement. Scott's job is to escort criminal Mahoney through the jungle to the police along with an entourage of Britons. When Jeffries' wife falls for Mahoney, Scott realizes that the infighting is worse than the dangers the jungle has to offer. Mahoney's image would change by the next entry, TARZAN GOES TO INDIA when he would become the jungle king. After this followup to TARZAN'S GREATEST ADVENTURE, Scott went to Italy to do Hercules roles and Mahoney became king of the jungle movies. (See TARZAN series, Index.)

p, Sy Weintraub, Harvey Hautin; d, Robert Day; w, Berne Giler, Day (based on characters created by Edgar Rice Burroughs); ph, Ted Scaife (Eastmancolor); m, Ken Jones; ed, Bert Rule; art d, Ray Simm.

Adventure   (PR:A MPAA:NR)

TARZAN TRIUMPHS**½   (1943) 78m RKO bw

Johnny Weissmuller *(Tarzan)*, Johnny Sheffield *(Boy)*, Frances Gifford *(Zandra)*, Stanley Ridges *(Col. von Reichart)*, Sig Rumann *(Sergeant)*, Pedro de Cordoba *(Patriarch)*, Philip Van Zandt *(Bausch)*, Stanley Brown *(Archmet)*, Rex Williams *(Schmidt)*, Otto Reichow, Sven Hugo Borg *(German Soldiers)*, Cheta the Chimp.

Nazi-occupied Africa (no, there was never such a place in reality) is no place for Jane or MGM, so Weissmuller hooked up with RKO and took boy Sheffield with him. They help princess Gifford battle the nasty paratrooper forces from Germany, with Cheta the Chimp letting 'em have it with a Tommy gun. (See TARZAN series, Index.)

p, Sol Lesser; d, William Thiele; w, Carroll Young, Roy Chanslor (based on the story by Young and characters created by Edgar Rice Burroughs); ph,

Harry Wild; m, Paul Sawtell; ed, Hal Kern; md, Constantine Bakaleinikoff; art d, Hans Peters.

Adventure   (PR:AA MPAA:NR)

TARZAN VERSUS I.B.M.   (SEE: ALPHAVILLE, 1965, Fr./Ital.)

TARZANA, THE WILD GIRL*   (1973) 87m Ellman Enterprises c

Ken Clark, Beryl Cunningham, Franca Polesello, Frank Ressel, Andrew Ray, Alfred Thomas.

Trying to hop on that TARZAN bandwagon, this cheapie gives us a female version of the jungle hero. Girl yes, wild no.

p, Glen Hart; d, James Reed; w, Philip Shaw; ph, (Eastmancolor).

Adventure   (PR:O MPAA:R)

TARZANOVA SMRT (SEE: DEATH OF TARZAN, THE, 1968, Czech.)

TARZAN'S DEADLY SILENCE*   (1970) 88m NGP c (AKA: THE DEADLY SILENCE)

Ron Ely *(Tarzan)*, Manuel Padilla, Jr *(Jai)*, Jock Mahoney *(The Colonel)*, Woodrow "Woody" Strode *(Marshak)*, Gregorio Acosta *(Chico)*, Rudolph Charles *(Officer)*, Michelle Nicols *(Ruana)*, Robert DoQui *(Metusa)*, Kenneth William Washington *(Akaba)*, Lupe Garnica *(Boru)*, Jose Chaves *(Okala)*, Virgil Richardson *(Tabor)*.

This TARZAN adventure put former Tarzan Mahoney back into the type of villain role where he started. He plays a power-hungry colonel who threatens Ely's African home with his private army. The ape-man goes mental in this one, using telepathy rather than brawn to subdue a lion. The silence of the title is the result of hand grenades thrown into a river in the mandatory swim scene. The submerged Ely loses one of his keen senses temporarily because of the blasts. Actually two episodes of a television show titled THE DEADLY SILENCE. Scriptwriter Steve Shagan (SAVE THE TIGER) is listed as production executive (See TARZAN series, Index.)

p, Leon Benson; d, Robert L. Friend, Lawrence Dobkin; w, Lee Erwin, Jack A. Robinson, John Considine, Tim Considine (based on characters created by Edgar Rice Burroughs); ph, Abraham Vialla (DeLuxe Color); m, Walter Greene; ed, Gabriel Torres, Edward M. Abroms; md, Greene; art d, Jose Rodriguez Granada; spec eff, Laurencio Cordero.

Adventure   (PR:AA MPAA:G)

TARZAN'S DESERT MYSTERY**   (1943) 70m Principal Artists/RKO bw

Johnny Weissmuller *(Tarzan)*, Johnny Sheffield *(Boy)*, Nancy Kelly *(Connie Bryce)*, Otto Kruger *(Hendrix)*, Joe Sawyer *(Karl)*, Robert Lowery *(Prince Selim)*, Lloyd Corrigan *(Sheik)*, Frank Puglia, Phil Van Zandt, Cheta the Chimp.

The least convincing of Weissmuller's "Tarzan" entries has him fighting Nazis once again, after doing the same in TARZAN'S TRIUMPH. He meets up with an American showgirl, Kelly, a few Arabs, more Nazis than you can shake a stick at, dinosaurs, and a giant spider. If it sounds like a Saturday morning cartoon, that's because it practically is. Judging from the production values in this film, the move from MGM to RKO resulted in some financial belt-tightening for the "Tarzan" series. This picture marked Sheffield's fifth appearance as "Boy." (See TARZAN series, Index.)

p, Sol Lesser; d, William Thiele; w, Edward T. Lowe (based on a story by Carroll Young and on the characters created by Edgar Rice Burroughs); ph, Harry Wild, Russ Harlan; m, Paul Sawtell; ed, Ray Lockert; md, Constantin Bakaleinikoff; art d, Hans Peters, Ralph Berger; set d, Victor Gangelin.

Adventure   (PR:AA MPAA:NR)

TARZAN'S FIGHT FOR LIFE**½   (1958) 86m MGM c

Gordon Scott *(Tarzan)*, Eva Brent *(Jane)*, Rickie Sorensen *(Tantu)*, Jill Jarmyn *(Anne Sturdy)*, James Edwards *(Futa)*, Carl Benton Reid *(Dr. Sturdy)*, Harry Lauter *(Dr. Ken Warwick)*, Woody Strode *(Ramo)*, Roy Glenn *(High Counselor)*, Cheta the Chimp.

A decent Scott entry in the "Tarzan" series which has him battling a wicked witch doctor in the Dark Continent and coming to the aid of physician Reid. Superstition is the greatest enemy for the scientifically minded Reid, who tries to convince the tribe that his treatment works. This was Scott's third starring role as the King of the Jungle. (See TARZAN series, Index.)

p, Sol Lesser; d, Bruce Humberstone; w, Thomas Hal Phillips (based on the characters created by Edgar Rice Burroughs); ph, William Snyder, Miki Carter (Eastmancolor); m, Ernest Gold; ed, Aaron Stell.

Adventure   (PR:AA MPAA:NR)

TARZAN'S GREATEST ADVENTURE***

(1959, Brit.) 88m Solar/PAR c

Gordon Scott (Tarzan), Anthony Quayle (Slade), Sara Shane (Angie), Niall MacGinnis (Kruger), Sean Connery (O'Bannion), Al Mulock (Dino), Scilla Gabel (Toni).

Outside of the Weissmuller films, this Scott entry is, as the title claims, the greatest adventure in the series. Filmed on location in Africa and London, this tale has a group of five diamond scavengers heading up African rivers and making life tough for Scott. Before they can do anything with their fortune, all five (including Quayle and Connery) meet untimely demises. One of the more adult-oriented "Tarzan" films. Directed by John Guillermin, who would return to the jungle in 1976 to helm KING KONG. (See TARZAN series, Index.)

p, Sy Weintraub, Harvey Hayutin; d, John Guillermin; w, Guillermin, Berne Giler (based on the story by Les Crutchfield and the characters by Edgar Rice Burroughs); ph, Ted Scaife, Skeets Kelly (Eastmancolor); m, Douglas Gamley; ed, Bert Rule; art d, Michael Stringer.

Adventure   (PR:AA MPAA:NR)

TARZAN'S HIDDEN JUNGLE**

(1955) 73m RKO bw

Gordon Scott (Tarzan), Vera Miles (Jill Hardy), Peter Van Eyck (Dr. Celliers), Don Beddoe (Johnson), Jester Hairston (Witch Doctor), Rex Ingram (Sukulu Makumwa), Jack Elam (Burger), Charles Fredericks (DeGroot), Richard Reeves (Reeves), Ike Jones (Malenki), Maidie Norman (Suma), Cheta the Chimp, Lucky the Chimp.

This was Scott's first of six "Tarzan" films, but the last for RKO, who put out a total of 12. Scott and his elephants squash (literally) the attempt made by hunter Elam to collect large quantities of animal fat, lion skins, and ivory, as well as lend a helping hand to doctor Van Eyck and nurse Miles. Zippy the Chimp, who you may remember from TV's "Howdy Doody," offers a helping paw. After the film's production, Scott and Miles tied the old matrimonial knot. (See TARZAN series, Index.)

p, Sol Lesser; d, Harold Schuster; w, William Lively (based on the characters by Edgar Rice Burroughs); ph, William Whitley; m, Paul Sawtell; ed, Leon Barsha; art d, William Flannery.

Adventure   (PR:AA MPAA:NR)

TARZAN'S JUNGLE REBELLION*

(1970) 92m NG c

Ron Ely (Tarzan), Manuel Padilla, Jr (Jai), Ulla Stromstedt (Mary), Sam Jaffe (Singleton), William Marshall (Tatakombi), Harry Lauter (Miller), Jason Evers (Ramon), Lloyd Haynes (Matto), Chuck Wood (Sergeant), Cheta the Chimp, Packy the Elephant.

Made up of a couple of episodes spliced together from the television series which aired from 1966-69, this is far from exciting, which is probably why it was on television. People may have watched it then, but given the choice, they opted to stay away from the big screen version. (See TARZAN series, Index.)

p, Steve Shagan; d, William Witney; w, Jackson Gillis (based on the characters created by Edgar Rice Burroughs); ph, Abraham Vialla; ed, Gabriel Torres.

Adventure   (PR:AA MPAA:NR)

TARZAN'S MAGIC FOUNTAIN**

(1949) 73m RKO bw

Lex Barker (Tarzan), Brenda Joyce (Jane), Evelyn Ankers (Gloria James), Albert Dekker (Trask), Charles Drake (Dodd), Alan Napier (Jessup), Henry Kulky (Vredak), Henry Brandon (Siko), Ted Hecht (Pasco), David Bond (Leader), Cheta the Chimp.

The script department was hurting when they hit upon this idea–Joyce is an aviatrix who crash lands in the jungle and discovers a fountain of youth. She lives there for 20 years, never aging, before Barker rescues her and returns her to civilization. This was Barker's first appearance as Tarzan and Joyce's last as Jane. It was the last "Tarzan" adventure filmed while Burroughs was alive and he was reportedly on the set while it was being made. (See TARZAN series, Index.)

p, Sol Lesser; d, Lee Sholem; w, Curt Siodmak, Harry Chandlee (based on the characters created by Edgar Rice Burroughs); ph, Karl Struss; ed, Merrill White; art d, McClure Capps.

Adventure   (PR:AA MPAA:NR)

TARZAN'S NEW YORK ADVENTURE**½

(1942) 70m MGM bw

Johnny Weissmuller (Tarzan), Maureen O'Sullivan (Jane), John Sheffield (Boy), Virginia Grey (Connie Beach), Charles Bickford (Buck Rand), Paul Kelly (Jimmy Shields), Chill Wills (Manchester Mountford), Cyrus W. Kendall (Col. Ralph Sergeant), Russell Hicks (Judge Abbotson), Howard Hickman (Blake Norton), Charles Lane (Gould Beaton), Miles Mander, Matthew Boulton (Portmaster), Milton Kibbee (Doorman), Mantan Moreland (Sam), Anne Jeffreys (Girl), Elmo Lincoln (Roustabout), Cheta the Chimpanzee.

Granted this may seem like a horrible idea for a film, but aren't you really dying to know what Weissmuller looks like in a suit? When Sheffield gets snatched by a show business menace and dragged to the Big Apple, Tarzan, Jane, and Cheta follow along, hoping to rescue him. Before long, however, Weissmuller is hauled into court for not having officially married O'Sullivan or officially adopted Sheffield. He responds to the judge's civil tactics by picking him up and tossing him into the jurybox (Tarzan 1, New York Judicial Branch 0). He also climbs on skyscrapers and jumps from the Brooklyn Bridge into the Hudson. Elmo Lincoln, the screen's first Tarzan, makes a cameo appearance. O'Sullivan bid adieu to Jane with this performance and, devoting herself to family life, didn't return to the screen for six more years. Sources differ on the credit for the role of Portmaster: some listing Matthew Boulton, others citing Miles Mander. (See TARZAN series, Index.)

p, Frederick Stephani; d, Richard Thorpe; w, Myles Connolly, William R. Lipman (based on a story by Connolly and the characters created by Edgar Rice Burroughs); ph, Sidney Wagner; m, David Snell; ed, Gene Ruggiero; md, Snell; art d, Cedric Gibbons; spec eff, Arnold Gillespie, Warren Newcombe.

Adventure   (PR:AA MPAA:NR)

TARZAN'S PERIL**½

(1951) 79m RKO bw (GB: TARZAN AND THE JUNGLE QUEEN)

Lex Barker (Tarzan), Virginia Huston (Jane), George Macready (Radijeck the Gunrunner), Douglas Fowley (Trask, His Accomplice), Glenn Anders (Andrews the Gun Smuggler), Frederick O'Neal (Bulam the Evil Chieftain), Dorothy Dandridge (Queen Melmendi), Alan Napier (Peters), Edward Ashley (Connors), James Moultrie (Nessi), Walter Kingsford (Barney), Cheta the Chimp.

A well-crafted addition to the series, with Barker appearing for the third time as the ape-man. A pair of gunrunners try to make trouble on the Dark Continent by getting the short-tempered Yorango tribe to attack the tolerant, peaceful Ashubas. The villains try to kill Barker when he gets in the way, but they forget that he's king of the jungle and always emerges victorious. The additional location footage, shot in British East Africa, was directed by Phil Brandon and photographed by Jack Whitehead who worked as a special effects cameraman on a few Alfred Hitchcock's British films (THE THIRTY-NINE STEPS, SECRET AGENT, YOUNG AND INNOCENT) while under contract with Gaumont British. He also worked on GOODBYE MR. CHIPS (1939), ODD MAN OUT (1947) and HAMLET (1948) before retiring to the United States. (See TARZAN series, Index.)

p, Sol Lesser; d, Byron Haskin, Phil Brandon; w, Samuel Newman, Francis Swann, John Cousins (based on the characters created by Edgar Rice Burroughs); ph, Karl Struss, Jack Whitehead; m, Michel Michelet; ed, John Murray; art d, John Meehan.

Adventure   (PR:A MPAA:NR)

TARZAN'S REVENGE*

(1938) 70m FOX bw

Glenn Morris (Tarzan), Eleanor Holm (Eleanor), C. Henry Gordon (Ben Alleu Bey), Hedda Hopper (Penny), George Meeker (Nevin), Corbet Morris (Jigger), Joseph Sawyer (Olaf), John Lester Johnson (Koko), George Barbier (Roger).

Olympic decathlon champion Morris gave the audience what they wanted in 1938–another "Tarzan" movie. It had been two years since the last Weissmuller entry and would still be another year before the next. Unfortunately Fox couldn't wait either and cast Morris in the role. His film career was thankfully shortlived. In this one he saves Holm from the evil grip of ruler Gordon, who keeps the girl all to himself in his hidden African fortress. (See TARZAN series, Index.)

p, Sol Lesser; d, D. Ross Lederman; w, Robert Lee Johnston, Jay Vann (based on characters created by Edgar Rice Burroughs); ph, George Meehan; m, Abe Meyer; ed, Gene Milford; md, Hugo Riesenfeld.

Adventure   Cas.   (PR:AA MPAA:NR)

TARZAN'S SAVAGE FURY*½

(1952) 80m RKO bw

Lex Barker (Tarzan), Dorothy Hart (Jane), Patric Knowles (Edwards), Charles Korvin (Rokov), Tommy Carlton (Joey).

Barker is approached by a pair of thieves, disguised as British agents, who request help in reaching the diamond-rich Wazuri region. Barker isn't keen on the idea but relents and guides them, bringing along new Jane, Hart, and a pseudo-Boy, Carlton. Barker soon discovers the crooks' plot and deals the pair some jungle justice. Uninteresting and slowly paced. (See TARZAN series, Index.)

p, Sol Lesser; d, Cyril [Cy] Endfield; w, Cyril Hume, Hans Jacoby, Shirley White (based on the characters created by Edgar Rice Burroughs); ph, Karl Struss; m, Paul Sawtell; ed, Frank Sullivan; art d, Walter Keller.

Adventure   (PR:AA MPAA:NR)

TARZAN'S SECRET TREASURE**½ (1941) 81m MGM b,w

Johnny Weissmuller (Tarzan), Maureen O'Sullivan (Jane), John Sheffield (Boy), Reginald Owen (Prof. Elliott), Barry Fitzgerald (O'Doul), Tom Conway (Medford), Philip Dorn (Vandermeer), Cordell Hickman (Tumbo), Cheta the Chimp.

The official Tarzan clan–Weissmuller, O'Sullivan, and Sheffield–team up again for another action-packed African adventure. This time Weissmuller saves an expedition from the clutches of a savage tribe, only to have the group use O'Sullivan and Sheffield as a way to get their hands on a secret treasure of gold. Weissmuller is not easily buffaloed, however, and rescues his loved ones while showing the expedition who's boss. (See TARZAN series, Index.)

p, B.P. Fineman; d, Richard Thorpe; w, Myles Connolly, Paul Gangelin (based on the characters created by Edgar Rice Burroughs); ph, Clyde De Vinna; ed, Gene Ruggiero; art d, Cedric Gibbon; spec eff, Warren Newcombe.

Adventure (PR:AA MPAA:NR)

TARZAN'S THREE CHALLENGES*** (1963) 92m Banner/MGM c

Jock Mahoney (Tarzan), Woody Strode (Khan/Tarim), Tsuruko Kobayashi (Cho-San), Earl Cameron (Mang), Salah Jamal (Hani), Anthony Chinn (Tor), Robert Hu (Nari), Christopher Carlos (Sechung), Ricky Der (Kashi), Hungry the Baby Elephant.

The "Tarzan" series is given a breath of freshness with a change of locale in the second and final Mahoney starrer. He heads to Thailand (where the film was photographed) to insure that a young heir to the throne is crowned as his father's successor. Strode, the dying ruler's brother, has other plans, however, but is unable to carry them out when Mahoney arrives. The final battle has Mahoney and Strode battling with knives in a net which hangs over a pit of burning coals. (See TARZAN series, Index.)

p, Sy Weintraub; d, Robert Day; w, Berne Giler, Day (based on the characters created by Edgar Rice Burroughs); ph, Ted Scaife (Dyaliscope, Metrocolor); m, Joseph Horovitz; ed, Fred Burnley; prod d, Wilfrid Shingleton; md, Marcus Dods; makeup, Freddie Williamson; spec eff, Cliff Richardson, Roy Whybrow.

Adventure (PR:AA MPAA:NR)

TASK FORCE***½ (1949) 116m WB bw c

Gary Cooper (Jonathan L. Scott), Jane Wyatt (Mary Morgan), Wayne Morris (McKinney), Walter Brennan (Pete Richard), Julie London (Barbara McKinney), Bruce Bennett (McCluskey), Jack Holt (Reeves), Stanley Ridges (Bentley), John Ridgely (Dixie Rankin), Richard Rober (Jack Southern), Art Baker (Sen. Vincent), Moroni Olsen (Ames), Ray Montgomery, Richard A. Paxton (Pilots), Harlan Warde (Timmy), James Holden (Tom Cooper), Rory Mallinson (Jerry Morgan), John Gallaudet (Jennings), Warren Douglas (Winston), Charles Waldron, Jr. (Aide), Robert Rockwell (Lt. Kelley), William Gould (Mr. Secretary), Sally Corner (Mrs. Secretary), Kenneth Tobey (Capt. Williamson), Tetsu Komai (Japanese Representative), Beal Wong (Japanese Naval Attache), Laura Treadwell (Mrs. Ames), Roscoe J. Behan (Ames' Attache), Basil Ruysdael (Admiral), Reed Howes (Officer), Edwin Fowler (Comdr. Price), William Hudson (Lt. Leenhouts), Mary Lawrence (Ruth Rankin), John McGuire (Supply Officer), Charles Sherlock (Capt. Wren), Charles Williams (Luggage Clerk), Brad Evans, Gerard Waller (Midshipmen), Tommy Walker (Lieutenant), Mal Merrihue (Jones), Mickey McCardell (Lindsay), Paul McWilliams (Harrison), Alex Gerry (Chairman), Joe Forte (Presidential Representative).

The saga of naval aviation is told vividly in this fine WW II film which details Cooper's efforts to prove the tactical and strategic effectiveness of carrier-based airplanes to the Navy. The battle begins in 1921 as Cooper and his enthusiastic group of men try to prove to their superiors that planes can be landed on the decks of ships. He and his buddy Brennan make several landings but the dubious top brass only put one carrier into service. Named the Langley, the small ship has a dangerously short 65-foot deck. Still convinced his ideas are valuable to the military, Cooper ventures to the nation's capital to lobby for the construction of bigger and better carriers. There he meets the widow of an old buddy, Wyatt, and the two begin a romance. While at a party, Cooper gets into an argument with a Japanese diplomat over the viability of naval aviation and loses his temper. For insulting the diplomat, Cooper is assigned a desk job in Panama. While he is pushing papers in Panama, the Navy finally builds other carriers and Cooper is assigned to serve on the USS Saratoga. Unfortunately, he is injured during an exercise and spends a long time in the hospital. During his convalescence his and Wyatt's relationship deepens and upon his release they are married. When Pearl Harbor is attacked Cooper is given command of his own aircraft carrier. At Okinawa his ship suffers heavy damage from Kamikaze planes and looks as if it will be lost. Cooper stays at the helm, however, and manages to make it back to the States. The use of aircraft carriers proves to be extremely effective in the Pacific and Cooper is finally vindicated. Graced with a strong cast, professional direction, and lots of stunning color battle footage from WW II (most of the film is black and white), TASK FORCE is an interesting and exciting war film. Cooper is fine as the Navy man who finds he must also play the role of diplomat when trying to persuade the government to make a firm commitment to naval

aviation. Director-writer Daves strikes an interesting contrast between the frustratingly slow bureaucratic machinery which must be appeased before implementing the new technology and the fast, violent, and deadly battles that naval aviation was created for. A word of warning: some television prints may be entirely black and white.

p, Jerry Wald; d&w, Delmer Daves; ph, Robert Burks, Wilfrid M. Cline (color sequence in Technicolor); m, Franz Waxman; ed, Alan Crosland, Jr.; art d, Leo K. Kuter; set d, George James Hopkins; spec eff, Roy Davidson, Edwin Du Par; makeup, Perc Westmore; tech adv, Capt. S.G. Mitchell, USN, Capt. James Dyer, USN.

War (PR:A MPAA:NR)

TASTE FOR WOMEN, A** (1966, Fr./Ital.) 90m Les Films Number One-Francoriz-Feder iz/Comet bw (AIMEZ-VOUS LES FEMMES?)

Sophie Daumier (Violette/Marguerite), Guy Bedos (Jerome Fenouic), Edwige Feuillere (Aunt Flo), Gregoire Aslan (Inspector Rossi), Guido Alberti (Mr. Kouroulis), Roger Blin (Larsen), Gerard Sety (Palmer), Georges Adet (Richter), Maria Rosa Rodrigues (Stripper), Colette Castel (Jeanine Dupellier), Raoul Delfosse (Bargeman), Graziella Granata (Bargeman's Wife), Gordon Felio (Dr. Rotman).

A strange little black comedy which has Bedos discovering a dead body in a restaurant and taking the corpse's hat. He is then mistaken for the dead man by the mysterious Daumier and barely survives a number of attempts on his life. Daumier is found dead, but it may actually be her twin sister who has been killed. Bedos then stumbles on a feud between a gang of cannibals (who are preparing to eat Daumier) and some opium smugglers. Bedos stops the gang-fighting and falls in love with Daumier...or her sister. Scripted by Roman Polanski, which should explain everything.

p, Pierre Kalfon; d, Jean Leon; w, Roman Polanski, Gerard Brach, Leon (based on the book Aimez-Vous Les Femmes? by George Bardawil); ph, Sacha Vierny; m, Ward Swingle; ed, Kenout Peltier; art d, Bernard Evein; m/l, Swingle, Gerard Brach.

Mystery/Comedy (PR:O MPAA:NR)

TASTE OF BLOOD, A zero (1967) 120m Creative Film Enterprises/Ajay c (AKA: THE SECRET OF DR. ALUCARD)

Bill Rogers (John Stone), Elizabeth Wilkinson (Helene Stone), Thomas Wood (Hank Tyson), Otto Schlesinger (Howard Helsing), Eleanor Vaill (Hester), Lawrence Tobin (Detective Crane), Ted Schell (Lord Gold), Sheldon Seymour (Seaman), Dolores Carlos (Sherri Morris), Sidney Jaye (Lawyer), Gail Janis (Vivacious Vivian).

When an American businessman (Rogers) receives a couple of bottles of brandy in the mail, he drinks them and turns into a vampire. He's supposed to receive an inheritance, so he travels to England and throws a pool cue through Schell's heart in revenge for the death of his relative, Count Dracula. Filmed in Miami–a really eerie place to make a vampire film–this is about as bad a horror film as you'll ever see.

p&d, Herschell Gordon Lewis; w, Donald Stanford; ph, Andy Romanoff (Eastmancolor); ed, Richard Brickman; md, Larry Wellington.

Horror (PR:O MPAA:NR)

TASTE OF EXCITEMENT** (1969, Brit.) 99m Trio-Group W/Crispin c

Eva Rienzi (Jane Kerrell), David Buck (Paul Hedley), Peter Vaughan (Inspector Malling), Paul Hubschmid (Hans Beiber), Sophie Hardy (Michela), Kay Walsh (Miss Barrow), Francis Matthews (Mr. Breese), Peter Bowles (Alfredo Guardi), George Pravda (Dr. Forla).

A painter gets himself involved with a girl who is mixed up in a plot to murder a traitor. A bland offering which shows no signs of the excitement that the title promises.

p, William Gell, George Willoughby; d, Don Sharp; w, Brian Carton, Sharp (based on the novel Waiting For A Tiger by Ben Healey).

Crime (PR:C MPAA:NR)

TASTE OF FEAR (SEE: SCREAM OF FEAR, 1961, Brit.)

TASTE OF FLESH, A zero (1967) 73m Mostest/Jerand bw

Cleo Nova (Hannah), Michael Lawrence (Nick), Layla Peters (Bobi), Buck Starr (Frankie), Darlene Bennett (Carol).

A pair of assassins use the apartment of a couple of lesbians as a stakeout, seduce the women, but then botch the murder when one of the would-be killers is himself done away with and his partner made to look like the guilty party. The knife that takes the assassin's life is actually wielded by another visitor to the apartment, a woman who also happens to be the secretary of the politico the boys had come to kill.

p,d&w, Louis Silverman; ph, C. Davis Smith; ed, Silverman.

Crime/Drama (PR:O MPAA:NR)

TASTE OF HELL, A* (1973) 90m Boxoffice International c

John Garwood (*Barry Mann*), Lisa Lorena (*Maria*), William Smith (*Jack Lowell*), Vic Diaz (*Maj. Kuramoto*), Lloyd Kino (*Capt. Seiko*), Angel Buenaventura (*Tomas*), Ruben Rustia (*Mario*).

Garwood is an American soldier in the Philippines who is injured when he and his fellow troops are machine-gunned by a Japanese officer after they've surrendered. Garwood, with his gimpy leg, vows vengeance and at the picture's finale lops off the Japanese officer's head. A uniformly poorly made and acted cheapie.

p, John Garwood; d, Neil Yarema, Basil Bradbury; w, Yarema; ph, Fred Conde (Movielab Color); m, Nester Robles.

War (PR:C MPAA:PG)

TASTE OF HONEY, A**** (1962, Brit.) 100m Woodfall/CD bw

Dora Bryan (*Helen*), Rita Tushingham (*Jo*), Robert Stephens (*Peter*), Murray Melvin (*Geoffrey*), Paul Danquah (*Jimmy*), David Boliver (*Bert*), Moira Kaye (*Doris*), Herbert Smith (*Shoe Shop Proprietor*), Valerie Scarden (*Woman in Shoe Shop*), Rosalie Scase (*Nurse*), Veronica Howard (*Gladys*), Jack Yarker (*Ship's Mate*), Margo Cunningham (*Landlady*), John Harrison (*Cave Attendant*), A. Goodman (*Rag and Bone Man*), Janet Rugg, Sonia Stephens (*Girls on Pier*), Eunice Black (*School Mistress*).

Honest depiction of life in the British working class with an offbeat treatment, superb acting, realistic direction, and a complex script that enlightens the plight of these people. What could have been a sordid story takes on a fresh glow as we are plunged into the life and times of Tushingham, a 17-year-old who lives with her promiscuous, alcoholic mother, Bryan, in various furnished rooms, all of which are underwritten by whomever Bryan is sleeping with at the moment. Tushingham is gawky, not terribly attractive, and desperate to be held. She gets no love whatsoever from Bryan and has a great chasm in her heart that requires filling. Bryan's current lover is Stephens, who has no use or time for her illegitimate child, Tushingham. While Bryan and Stephens do their thing on a short holiday in the seaside town of Blackpool, Tushingham wanders around the docks and meets Danquah, a black sailor on a brief leave on shore. When she realizes that she is a thorn in the side of Bryan and Stephens, she spends the night with Danquah, who is sailing off the next morning. Tushingham arrives home and learns that Stephens and Bryan have impulsively married and that she is really a fifth wheel now. Bryan moves in with Stephens and Tushingham is left alone and must take a room of her own. She secures employment in a shoe store and meets Melvin, a gentle and kind homosexual who is in need of a place to stay. The price of the flat is too much for Tushingham alone so she allows him to help out and be her platonic roommate. Melvin, repeating the role he played in the successful London production of the play, is as lonely as Tushingham and the two find perfect company with each other. Tushingham soon realizes that she carrying Danquah's child. Melvin is elated at the thought of the baby and plunges himself into the surrogate role that Bryan should be playing. He knits baby clothes, he tidies up the residence to await the birth of the child, he does all of the things that a devoted husband would do, and eventually offers to marry Tushingham so the unborn child will have a name. Tushingham declines and becomes increasingly depressed. Melvin is worried about her condition, and tells Bryan what's happening, but Bryan couldn't care less until Stephens abandons her. With no place else to go, Bryan moves in with Melvin and Tushingham. It isn't long before the loud and vicious Bryan asserts herself and, over Tushingham's protests, tosses Melvin back out on the street. Melvin sighs, exits, and walks along the road where he watches a group of children playing. Their joy and unconcern about the worries of the world give him a new smile and he walks off, renewed by what he's seen in these innocent tots. The movie was shot for a pittance on location in Blackpool and on the Salford docks. Delaney was only 19 when she wrote the play which had a long run in the West End as well as on Broadway after first trying out at Stratford-Upon-Avon in May, 1958. Tushingham had been a backstage worker and did a bit in Arnold Wesker's play "The Kitchen" at Liverpool Rep before she answered an advert, walked in, auditioned, and won this plum role. Bryan had spent most of her career as a comedienne in movies since she began in ODD MAN OUT (1946). Casting her in this was an inspired choice as she showed her scope. If you have a sharp ear, you may be able to recognize Johnny Dankworth's theme from SATURDAY NIGHT AND SUNDAY MORNING which was uncredited. Richardson coproduced that film with Harry Saltzman so it can be assumed he had permission for the tune's use. The hit song "A Taste of Honey" had nothing to do with this film. It was written by Ric Marlow and Bobby Scott and traded on the success of the movie, which won Cannes Film Festival Awards for Melvin and Tushingham as well as British Film Academy Awards for Best Picture, Best Actress (Bryan), Best Screenplay (Delaney and Richardson), and Most Promising Actress (Tushingham). Poignant, funny, moody, and never maudlin, it's a picture that haunts the memory.

p&d, Tony Richardson; w, Shelagh Delaney, Richardson (based on the play by Delaney); ph, Walter Lassally; m, John Addison; ed, Anthony Gibbs; md, Addison; art d, Ralph Brinton; cos, Sophie Harris; makeup, George Frost.

Drama Cas. (PR:C MPAA:NR)

TASTE OF HONEY, A SWALLOW OF BRINE! A (SEE: SMELL OF HONEY, A SWALLOW OF BRINE!

TASTE OF HOT LEAD, A (SEE: HOT LEAD, 1951)

TASTE OF MONEY, A** (1960, Brit.) 71m Danziger/UA c

Jean Cadell (*Miss Brill*), Dick Emery (*Morrissey*), Pete Murray (*Dave*), Ralph Michael (*Supt. White*), Donald Eccles (*Joe*), C. Denier Warren (*Tyler*), Robert Raglan (*Simpson*), Christina Gregg (*Ruth White*).

An uninspired comedy about an elderly cashier who engineers a plot to rob the insurance firm that employs her. Cadell, at 76 years of age, turns in a charming performance, but that alone cannot save the picture from mediocrity.

p, Brian Taylor; d, Max Varnel; w, Mark Grantham.

Comedy (PR:A MPAA:NR)

TASTE OF SIN, A* (1983) 84m New-West/Ambassador c

Suzanna Love (*Olivia*), Robert Walker (*Michael Grant*), Jeff Winchester (*Richard*), Bibbe Hansen (*Mother*), Amy Robinson (*Olivia, at Age 6*), Nicholas Love (*G.I.*), Ulli Lommel (*Detective*).

An interesting suspense-murder plot that has a young girl witnessing her prostitute mother's murder by a U.S. GI. Years later the girl grows up to be Love, a married Englander who hears her mother's voice from the grave and, out of guilt, dresses as a hooker, killing anyone she can. She tosses her husband off London Bridge (a favorite spot of hers) and eventually falls in love with Walker, an American working on the bridge's reconstruction. The story jumps ahead four years to Arizona (where London Bridge has been moved), changes Love's identity, gives her a new accent and job (condominium saleslady), and reunites her with Walker. Falling somewhere between Alfred Hitchcock (VERTIGO) and Brian De Palma (OBSESSION), Lommel's film is a superior cheap thriller. Lommel worked in Germany for a number of years, acting in R.W. Fassbinder films, before heading out on his own and directing.

p&d, Ulli Lommel; w, Lommel, John P. Marsh, Ron Norman; ph, Lommel, Jochen Breitenstein, Jon Kranhouse, Dave Sperling, Jorg Walther (Getty Color); m, Joel Goldsmith; ed, Terrell Tannen.

Crime Drama (PR:O MPAA:R)

TASTE THE BLOOD OF DRACULA½** (1970, Brit.) 95m Hammer/WB c

Christopher Lee (*Dracula*), Geoffrey Keen (*William Hargood*), Gwen Watford (*Martha Hargood*), Linda Hayden (*Alice Hargood*), Peter Sallis (*Samuel Paxton*), Isla Blair (*Lucy Paxton*), John Carson (*Jonathan Secker*), Martin Jarvis (*Jeremy Secker*), Anthony Corlan (*Paul Paxton*), Ralph Bates (*Lord Courtley*), Roy Kinnear (*Weller*), Shirley Jaffe (*Hargood's Maid*), Michael Ripper (*Cobb*), Russell Hunter (*Felix*), Reginald Barratt (*Vicar*), Keith Marsh (*Father*), Peter May (*Son*), Maddy [Madeleine] Smith (*Dolly*), Lai Ling (*Chinese Girl*), Malaika Martin (*Snake Girl*).

Lee makes a brief appearance as Dracula for the fourth time for Hammer after being revived in a blood-drinking ceremony led by Bates. Three guests of Bates--who met him at a classy bordello-- beat him to death and become the targets of the vampire. It is the children of the three who actually do the killing, which adds an uneasy eeriness to the picture. One of Hammer's last decent pictures. TV director Sasdy here helmed his first feature film and did a creditable job. The Victorian sets and costumes come a little closer to Stoker's original idea than most of the Hammer Dracula pictures. Player Bates does decadence well; he went on after this, his first featured role, to appear in THE HORROR OF FRANKENSTEIN (1970), LUST FOR A VAMPIRE (1971), DR. JEKYLL AND SISTER HYDE (1971), and others of the ilk. Followed by SCARS OF DRACULA. (See DRACULA series, Index.)

p, Aida Young; d, Peter Sasdy; w, John Elder (based on the character created by Bram Stoker); ph, Arthur Grant (Technicolor); m, James Bernard; ed, Chris Barnes; md, Philip Martell; art d, Scott MacGregor; spec eff, Brian Johncock; makeup, Gerry Fletcher.

Horror (PR:O MPAA:GP)

TATSU½** (1962, Jap.) 115m Toho c (DOBUROKU NO TATSU)

Toshiro Mifune (*Tatsu*), Tatsuya Mihashi, Chikage Awashima, Junko Ikeuchi, Ichiro Arishima, Yoshio Tsuchiya, Sonomi Nakajima, Jun Tazaki, Soji Kiyokawa, Ryosuke Kagawa, Chieko Nakakita, Yoshio Kosugi, Sachio Sakai.

Mifune brings his lovable and violent heroics to a Japanese construction camp where the workers receive pay but are forced by armed guards to work until they drop. A rapport builds between Mifune and a female mess hall worker, who also is the subject of another worker's advances. A duel with axes follows and the girl falls for Mifune, but reveals that she is married. Mifune tells her that he has an escape planned and that he will guarantee her safety as well as her husband's. This one's worth it just to see

Mifune ranting and raving with an axe in his hand. A fun piece from the director of the Oscar-winning SAMURAI (1955).

d, Hiroshi Inagaki; w, Masato Ide, Toshio Yasumi; ph, Kazuo Yamada (Tohoscope, Agfacolor); m, Kan Ishii.

Drama   (PR:C   MPAA:NR)

TATTERED DRESS, THE½**   (1957) 93m UNIV bw

Jeff Chandler (James Gordon Blane), Jeanne Crain (Diane Blane), Jack Carson (Sheriff Nick Hoak), Gail Russell (Carol Morrow), Elaine Stewart (Charleen Reston), George Tobias (Billy Giles), Edward Andrews (Lester Rawlings), Philip Reed (Michael Reston), Edward C. Platt (Ralph Adams), Paul Birch (Frank Mitchell), Alexander Lockwood (Paul Vernon), Edwin Jerome (Judge), William Schallert (Court Clerk), Joseph Granby (2nd Jury Foreman), Frank Scannell (Cal Morrison), Floyd Simmons (Larry Bell), Ziva Shapir (Woman on Train), Marina Orschel, Ingrid Goude (Girls by Pool), Billy Snyder (Rod Staley), Helene Marshall (Newspaper Woman), Charles J. Conrad, John Phillips (Reporters), Forrest Stanley (Hank Bell), Vincent G. Perry, Gordon Morehouse (Poker Players), Jack Shutta (Gas Station Proprietor), Dick Wilson (Foreman of 1st Jury), Clarence Straight (Bailiff), June McCall (Girl at Slot Machine), Robert Malcolm (Elderly Citizen), Todd Ferrell (Timmy), Charles Herbert (Johnny), Napoleon Whiting (Willie, Porter), Freda Jones (Sarah Bell), King Lockwood (Steward), Joseph Gilbert, Arthur Tovey, Danny Dowling, Murray Pollack, Maurice Marks, Mary Bayless, Jack Del Rio, Jeffrey Sayre, Jerry Elliott, Charles E. Perry, Donald Chaffin, Beau Anderson, Richard Dale Clark, Lillian Ten Eyck (People).

A great looking near-film noir which doesn't have much going for it in the dialog department. The basic story line bears a truly remarkable resemblance to a much better film, ANATOMY OF A MURDER (1959). Chandler is a hotshot lawyer known for his ability to get guilty criminals off the hook. He is hired by married couple Stewart and Reed to defend the latter, who is on trial for murdering a bartender who made a pass at Stewart and ripped her dress. The jury finds Reed innocent, but only after Chandler undermines the testimony of sheriff Carson. Carson plans revenge by getting juror Russell to admit that she accepted a bribe from Chandler in return for a vote of not guilty. Things look rough for Chandler until it is proven that Russell is the sheriff's mistress. The finale has Chandler getting his freedom and being reconciled with his wife Crain, while Carson gets gunned down on the courthouse steps by his mistress. Arnold also directed IT CAME FROM OUTER SPACE and THE INCREDIBLE SHRINKING MAN, which should make it obvious that direction was one of this picture's problems.

p, Albert Zugsmith; d, Jack Arnold; w, George Zuckerman; ph, Carl E. Guthrie (CinemaScope); m, Frank Skinner; ed, Edward Curtiss; md, Joseph Gershenson; art d, Alexander Golitzen, Bill Newberry; set d, Russell A. Gausman, John P. Austin; cos, Jay A. Morley, Jr.; spec eff, Clifford Stine.

Crime Drama   (PR:C   MPAA:NR)

TATTOO zero   (1981) 103m FOX c

Bruce Dern (Karl Kinski), Maud Adams (Maddy), Leonard Frey (Halsey), Rikke Borge (Sandra), John Getz (Buddy), Peter Iacangelo (Dubin), Alan Leach (Customer), Cynthia Nixon (Cindy), Trish Doolin (Cheryl), Anthony Mannino (George), Lex Monson (Dudley), Patricia Roe (Doris), Jane Hoffman (Teresa), Robert Burr (Ralph), John Snyder (Hawker), B.J. Cirell, Kevin O'Rourke, Sally-Jane Heit, Gavin Reed, Henry Dibling, Alan Brasington, Anne Anderson, Winnie, John Granger, Sam Schacht, Orlando Dole, Jonathan Hogan, Robert Hitt, Kate McGregor-Stewart, Don Jay, Jack Davidson, E. Katherine Kerr, Daniel Suchar, David Suchar, Shunshin Kan, Richard McGonagle, Harold Mandel, Frank Santos.

This vile, misogynist trash features Dern in yet another psychotic role, this time as a morally obsessed tattoo artist. Dern has phobias about cleanliness as well, and won't speak on a telephone without covering the mouthpiece. He's contracted to do a series of fake tattoos for a fashion campaign, with Adams as one of the models Dern must decorate. She is attracted to this strange individual and accepts his invitation to dinner. After eating, Adams tries to seduce Dern, but he is appalled by her desire for "intercourse." Later, Dern kidnaps Adams and drugs her, then creates an elaborate tattoo which covers her body. Adams is shocked, but the mad Dern pays no attention. He takes off his clothes, revealing his own torso to be covered with tattoos as well. He begins to make love to Adams, who manages to grab the tattooing needle and stab Dern to death. Repulsive and unoriginal, this film is poorly constructed with major gaps in both continuity and character credibility. In a desperate attempt to give Dern's character some motivation, he's given a strange dead mother, and a creepy old house, artifacts that bear more than a passing resemblance to PSYCHO. The music from Alfred Hitchcock's classic shower sequence is also blatantly lifted when Dern first applies the tattooing needle to Adams' flesh. Dern's psychotic characterization is a loathsome creation, recalling his performance as a mad scientist in the low-budget horror film THE INCREDIBLE TWO-HEADED TRANS-PLANT (1971). Though his salary may have increased over the years, Dern's acting range hasn't changed in the least. With only an occasional lapse in casting, the actor with possibly the worst teeth in Hollywood continued to make crazed psychotics his own specialty. TATTOO was the subject of some controversy for an advertising campaign that showed the naked legs of a

woman bound at the ankles. Many feminist organizations protested, with pickets marching in front of theaters that showed the film.

p, Joseph E. Levine, Richard P. Levine; d, Bob Brooks; w, Joyce Bunuel (based on a story by Brooks); ph, Arthur Ornitz, Michael Seresin (Technicolor); m, Barry DeVorzon; ed, Thom Noble; prod d, Stuart Wurtzel.

Drama   Cas.   (PR:O   MPAA:R)

TATTOOED STRANGER, THE*   (1950) 64m RKO bw

John Miles (Detective Tobin), Patricia White (Mary Mahan), Walter Kinsella (Lt. Corrigan), Frank Tweddell (Capt. Lundquist), Rod McLennan (Capt. Gavin), Henry Lasko (Joe Canko), Arthur Jarrett (Johnny Marseille), Jim Boles (Fisher), William Gibberson (Aberfoyle).

Gritty and honest story of police investigation that accurately portrays the seamier sides of law enforcement. Miles is a newly appointed detective who begins searching for the killer of a woman found murdered in Central Park. Her identity is unknown and all Miles has to go on is a tattoo on the corpse's wrist: the emblem of the U.S. Marine Corps. With police lieutenant Kinsella, Miles begins taking small amounts of evidence and methodicaly pieces together what he can. Eventually he is able to forge a link between the murder and a tattooed granite worker. Miles closes in on his man, engaging in a shoot-out amidst a forest of gravestones. For all his work, Miles is rewarded by being assigned as a noninvestigating police officer. Unlike many police films, this is a story that tells it like it is. The film is presented in documentary style, shot on location in the streets of New York. A good cast of non-professional actors adds to this heightened sense of realism. Producer Bonafield and director Montagne originally began with RKO making documentary short subjects. They had created a two-reel short called CRIME LAB, which served as a model for this fictional feature. Using the techniques they learned as documentary filmmakers, Bonafield and Montagne follow Miles' investigation in a similar step-by-step procedure, not allowing any camerawork or motifs of film noir to intrude into the production. By taking their cameras to New York City's underbelly, they present a world no studio could completely and honestly portray. Made for just $124,000, this was an excellent example of what independent filmmakers of the day were capable of, an entertaining and intriguing work that reflects honesty in every shot. Made during the short, unhappy reign of Howard Hughes at RKO, the film was intended as the first of a string of low-budget pictures which were to be made on the East Coast.

p, Jay Bonafield; d, Edward J. Montagne; w, Phil Reisman, Jr.; ph, William Steiner; m, Alan Schulman; ed, David Cooper; md, Herman Fuchs; art d, Sam Corso, William Saulter.

Crime   (PR:O   MPAA:NR)

TAWNY PIPIT½**   (1947, Brit.) 81m Two Cities/UNIV bw

Bernard Miles (Col. Barton-Barrington), Rosamund John (Hazel Broome), Niall MacGinnis (Jimmy Bancroft), Jean Gillie (Nancy Forester), Lucie Mannheim (Russian Sniper), Christopher Steele (Reverend Kingsley), Brefni O'Rorke (Uncle Arthur), George Carney (Whimbrel), Wylie Watson (Croaker), Lionel Watts (Silver), Scott Harold (Shuttleworth), John Salew (Pickering), Marjorie Rhodes (Mrs. Pickering), Ann Wilton (Miss Penyman), Ian Fleming (Schoolmaster), Ernest Butcher (Tommy Fairchild), Grey Blake (Capt. Dawson), Joan Sterndale-Bennett (Rose), Stuart Latham (Cpl. Philpotts), Arthur Burne, Billy Bridget, John Rae, Johnnie Schofield, Katie Johnson, Sam Wilkinson, David Keir, Sydney Benson, Jenny Weaver.

For those of you without vast ornithological knowledge (shame on you) a tawny pipit is a slender little bird which always wags its tail. It's also rather rare, so when a nest of them is found in an English wheat field, the whole community goes batty trying to protect them. Charmingly harmless.

p, Bernard Miles; d&w, Miles, Charles Saunders (based on the story by Miles); ph, Eric Cross, Ray Sturgess; m, Noel Newton-Wood (played by the London Symphony); ed, Douglas Myers; md, Muir Mathieson; art d, Alex Vetchinsky.

Comedy   (PR:A   MPAA:NR)

TAXI!*½**   (1932) 70m WB bw

James Cagney (Matt Nolan), Loretta Young (Sue Riley), George E. Stone (Skeets), Guy Kibbee (Pop Riley), David Landau (Buck Gerard), Ray Cooke (Danny Nolan), Leila Bennett (Ruby), Dorothy Burgess (Marie Costa), Matt McHugh (Joe Silva), George MacFarlane (Father Nulty), Polly Walters (Polly), Nat Pendleton (Truckdriver), Berton Churchill (Judge West), Lee Phelps (Onlooker), George Raft (William "Willie" Kenny), Harry Tenbrook (Cabby), Robert Emmet O'Connor (Cop with Jewish Man), Russ Powell, Eddie Fetherstone (Dance Judges), Ben Taggart (Cop), The Cotton Club Orchestra (Themselves), Hector V. Sarno (Monument Maker), Aggie Herring (Cleaning Woman), Donald Cook, Evalyn Knapp (Movie Stars).

Cagney is a tough taxicab driver whose livelihood is threatened by the growing strength of the monopolistic taxi trust which uses strong-arm tactics to run him off the good cab stands. He gains allies in other independent hacks, including Kibbee, whose taxi is smashed by a truck when he refuses to knuckle under to pressure from the trust. Kibbee goes to jail when he shoots the driver, and not much later Cagney marries his daughter, Young. She tries to restrain him as he battles the bad guys, but when they kill his brother, Cooke, nothing can hold him back. He narrowly avoids several attempts on his life, getting into running gun battles. Finally, he traps the chief villain in a building and when he taunts the man into coming out, the police grab him. Fast-moving and exciting, this film marked the first time Cagney ever danced on screen. When he and Young go to a nightclub, they enter a Peabody contest. They dance well, but not as well as another New York hoofer come west, George Raft. When Raft and his partner win the contest, he taunts Cagney, asking him, "How do you like that, wise guy?" Cagney immediately punches him in the nose. It was at Cagney's insistence that Raft was given his small role, the two men had known each other in New York and Cagney knew that Raft was the best Peabodyer around. Another first for Cagney in this film was his comic speaking of Yiddish with a strong Irish bent as he rescues an old Jewish man from a cop who can't understand anything the man is saying. For the last time he worked with live machine gun bullets being fired at him, a habit of which early directors were quite fond. He had put up with several near misses in THE PUBLIC ENEMY, but while filming one shootout for this film, a stray bullet hit a nail in the backing board above Cagney's head and shot around the studio, finally hitting a coat rack and falling into the pocket of someone's overcoat. All the performances are good, with Cagney at his early pugnacious best and the rest of the Warner's stock company working at their usual high level. The film was fantastically successful and helped considerably in Cagney's rise to become of the biggest stars of the period.

d, Roy Del Ruth; w, Kubec Glasmon, John Bright (based on the play "The Blind Spot" by Kenyon Nicholson); ph, James Van Trees; ed, James Gibbons, Ralph Dawson; md, Leo F. Forbstein; art d, Esdras Hartley; makeup, Perc Westmore.

Crime (PR:A MPAA:NR)

TAXI** (1953) 77m FOX bw

Dan Dailey *(Ed Nielson)*, Constance Smith *(Mary)*, Neva Patterson *(Miss Millard)*, Blanche Yurka *(Mrs. Nielson)*, Kyle MacDonnell *(Dottie)*, Walter Woolf King *(Business Man)*, Anthony Ross *(Mr. Alexander)*, Mark Roberts *(Jim Turner)*, Harry Clark *(Riso)*, Jack Diamond *(Chick)*, Stubby Kaye *(Morris)*, B. S. Pulley *(Amchy)*, Bert Thorn *(Clerk)*, Curtis Cooksey *(Capt. Skavlon)*, Bill Neil *(Pier Guard)*, Frank McNellis *(Ship's Officer)*, Elliott Sullivan *(Delivery Man)*, Hilda Haynes *(Mabel)*, James Little *(Policeman)*, Ann Dere *(Mrs. Albert)*, Geraldine Page *(Florence Albert)*, Rex O'Malley *(Butler)*, Bruno Wick *(Pawnbroker)*, Art Hannes *(Jenkins)*, De Forest Kelley *(Fred)*, Melville Ruick *(George)*, Henry Jones *(Thorndike)*, Ralph Dunn *(Rafferty)*, Betty Buehler *(Frances)*, Virginia Vincent *(Hortense)*, Mario Siletti *(Amato)*, John Kullers *(Cabie)*, Glenn Hardy *(Newscaster)*, Jonathan Hale *(Mr. Barker)*, Al Eben *(Cab Driver)*, John Cassavetes.

Dailey is a New York City cabbie who picks up a fare–young Irish immigrant Smith–and ends up driving around with her for most of the day. The pregnant colleen needs to find her husband or else face deportation. Smith finds the man she's looking for, but she is rejected by him and winds up marrying Dailey. The film debuts for both Geraldine Page and John Cassavetes.

p, Samuel G. Engel; d, Gregory Ratoff; w, D. M. Marshman, Jr., Daniel Fuchs (based on the story "Sans Laisser d'Adresse" by Hans Jacoby, Fred Brady, A lex Joffe, Jean Paul Le Chanois); ph, Milton Krasner; m, Leigh Harline; ed, Hugh S. Fowler; md, Lionel Newman; art d, Lyle Wheeler, Richard Irvine.

Comedy/Drama (PR:A MPAA:NR)

TAXI DRIVER* (1976) 112m Bill/Phillips/COL c

Robert De Niro *(Travis Bickle)*, Cybill Shepherd *(Betsy)*, Jodie Foster *(Iris Steensman)*, Peter Boyle *(Wizard)*, Harvey Keitel *(Sport)*, Albert Brooks *(Tom)*, Leonard Harris *(Charles Palantine)*, Martin Scorsese *(Passenger)*, Diahnne Abbott *(Concession Girl)*, Frank Adu *(Angry Black Man)*, Vic Argo *(Melio)*, Gino Ardito *(Policeman at Rally)*, Garth Avery *(Iris' Friend)*, Harry Cohn *(Cabby in Bellmore)*, Copper Cunningham *(Hooker in Cab)*, Brenda Dickson *(Soap Opera Woman)*, Beau Kayser *(Soap Opera Man)*, Harry Fischler *(Dispatcher)*, Nat Grant *(Stick-up Man)*, Richard Higgs *(Tall Secret Service Man)*, Vic Magnotta *(Secret Service Photographer)*, Robert Maroff *(Mafioso)*, Norman Matlock *(Charlie T)*, Bill Minkin *(Tom's Assistant)*, Murray Moston *(Iris' Time Keeper)*, Harry Northup *(Doughboy)*, Gene Palma *(Street Drummer)*, Carey Poe, Robin Utt *(Campaign Workers)*, Steven Prince *(Easy Andy, Gun Salesman)*, Peter Savage *(The John)*, Robert Shields *(Palantine Aide)*, Ralph Singleton *(TV Interviewer)*, Joe Spinell *(Personnel Officer)*, Maria Turner *(Angry Hooker on Street)*, Devi 'Debbie' Morgan *(Girl at Columbus Circle)*.

De Niro's strong presence in this horrific and often disgusting panorama of violence, street sex, and, at the climax, bloodletting, is the only reason to see TAXI DRIVER. Scorsese, remaking the same old street profile of dirty, big New York, indulges himself in every conceivable perversion and lets loose, irresponsibly enough, the foulest, most offensive dialog in any so-called major film, all in the name of holy "realism," all in honor of presenting life style "authenticity." This much overrated idol built from the slime and

dregs of New York's sewers, leaves no permanent memory, nor one single important scene, other than an overall image of revulsion, and, as such, it is a miserable failure. This is a selfish, arrogant movie, made by a tunnel-visioned director who has mastered the profiling of stereotypes and who cares not whether his audience neither understands what he is profiling nor can even blindly accept the despicable Neanderthalistic characters as real or important. They are not; this is a self-indulgent excursion by Scorsese into the sewers. He is obsessed by the rats feeding on waste, lapping up the vile pus from humanity's open sores and totally unconcerned with how to treat the cancer. To know his main character, taxi driver De Niro, is to meet a sociopath who later goes over the line into homicidal rage, to stare at an illiterate loner for almost two hours and realize within the first few minutes the viewer is staring at an unappealing cretin whose place is in a padded cell and not behind the wheel of a cab, nor up on a screen pretending to create a legitimate demand for anyone's attention. De Niro is a self-styled moralist who keeps a diary and condemns all the human filth in the city which he hates: the hookers, pimps, and killers who infest the streets. He becomes enamored of good girl Shephard who works as a political organizer, she representing decent society, but to her he is but a stumbling, mumbling curiosity. (Actually, he's not at all interesting, only a thick-witted dullard who speaks in a monotone, albeit an *intense* monotone.) He later meets 14-year-old prostitute Foster and decides to free her from her brutal, garbage-mouthed pimp, Keitel (who is about the most offensive creature ever to blot a screen). De Niro buys guns, goes into training, and later marches out to slaughter Keitel, and then into a hotel to shoot down more pimps and low-level mobsters, all to send little Jodie back to the impoverished parents she fled earlier when seeking a new life in the city. De Niro, implausible as it all is, escapes being indicted for mass murder and is hailed as a hero by a society turning with drooling lips and ogling eyes toward vigilantism. It's all so much trash, expensively arranged in Scorsese's unimaginative garbage cans. It's also another load of literary vomit spewed forth by the violence-and-sex-obsessed writer, Schrader, who has never produced (except for RAGING BULL where the violence was justified) one screenplay of worth. TAXI DRIVER appeals to the worst in all humans while fiercely pretending to be significant filmmaking. Posturing film critics fell by the score for Scorsese's con here, terrified of not appearing to be savants and being able to read meaning into the director's mindless, purposeless characters, his pandering, cheap, repulsive dialog, his tawdry and nutty notion of "real life." All achieved here by a brilliant craftsman– and Scorsese is a brilliant *techician*–is a panoply of moronic and psychopathic images that endlessly repeat what everyone knows New York City is overrun by whores and pimps, a dirty wasteland where violence abounds, a city where drugs, guns, and sex are for sale at bargain-basement prices. Big deal. None of the characters is likable or interesting or has one word to say that is memorable (or printable), and that especially includes Scorsese's social- outcast hack driver, although De Niro gives his role a certain amount of one-dimensional fascination, albeit a portrait as inconsistent as a tourniquet twisted back and forth (under Scorsese's rather sadistic hand) to staunch the flow of blood. And there is so much blood in this film that the screen drips it. (This film avoided getting an MPAA "X" and received an "R" because the director was kind enough to tone down the rich red tones of the blood splattered over his scenes to a more respectable brown hue, a moral criterion which only acrocephalics can accept without questioning the idiotic standards of such arbitration, proving once more the incredibility of the MPAA rating system. TAXI DRIVER does not reflect a grain of art, only craft. It does not reflect a problem that is dealt with logically or provide remedies to that problem, but rather says in an anti- intellectual, trigger-happy way that the whole world is nuts and the best way to deal with your hates is to get a gun and kill people, especially bad people. Travis Bickle, Scorsese's apparent alterego, could only be a hero to Caligula or Heinrich Himmler. The whole mess, which is definitely NOT FOR CHILDREN or anyone who has ever had an artistic or intellectual thought, is reminiscent of a bit of doggerel written by Ernest Hemingway in his early days: "I know that monks masturbate at night/That pet cats screw and some girls bite/But what can I do/To set things right?" Why, see TAXI DRIVER, of course.

p, Michael Phillips, Julia Phillips; d, Martin Scorsese; w, Paul Schrader; ph, Michael Chapman (Panavision, Metrocolor); m, Bernard Herrmann; ed, Marcia Lucas, Tom Rolf, Melvin Shapiro; md, Dave Blume, Herrmann; art d, Charles Rosen; set d, Herbert Mulligan; cos, Ruth Morley; spec eff, Tony Parmelee; m/l, "Late for the Sky," Jackson Browne, "Hold Me Close," Keith Addis, Herrmann; makeup, Dick Smith, Irving Buchman.

Crime Cas. (PR:O MPAA:R)

TAXI FOR TOBRUK** (1965, Fr./Span./Ger.) 90m Franco London S.N.E. GAU-Procusa-Continental/Seven Arts bw (UN TAXI POUR TO-BROUK; UN TAXI PARA TOBROUK; TAXI NACH TOBRUK)

Hardy Kruger *(Capt. Ludwig von Stegel)*, Charles Aznavour *(Samuel Goldman)*, Lino Ventura *(Theo)*, German Cobos *(Paolo)*, Maurice Biraud *(Francois)*.

During WW II a group of French commandos returning from a successful raid on a German depot kidnap a German officer and take his patrol car. They set out across blistering North Africa dodging mines along the way and building a strong camaraderie with the German, even though one of them is Jewish. They near their camp, but are attacked by their own troops, who believe them to be the advancing enemy. Only Ventura survives.

p&d, Denys de La Patelliere; w, Rene Havard, Michel Audiard, de La Patelliere); ph, Marcel Grignon (Dyaliscope); m, Georges Garvarentz; ed, Jacqueline Thiedot; art d, Paul-Louis Boutie.

War Drama   **(PR:A MPAA:NR)**

TAXI FOR TWO**   (1929, Brit.) 73m Gainsborough/Woolf and Freedman bw

Mabel Poulton (*Molly*), John Stuart (*Jack Devenish*), Gordon Harker (*Albert*), Renee Clama (*Gladys*), Anne Grey (*Charlotte*), Grace Lane (*Lady Devenish*), Claude Maxten (*The Baron*).

Poulton is an honest girl who finds a missing necklace that belongs to a titled lady, Lane. She returns it, accepts a reward, and buys a taxi with the money. Stuart, the lady's son, becomes infatuated with the girl and hires himself out as a taxidriver. The next logical step is for the pair to fall in love, and fall in love they do. A part-talkie which is a successful charmer, with some interesting interior shots of the famous London department store, Harrods.

p, Michael Balcon; d, Alexander Esway, Denison Clift; w, Esway, Ian Dalrymple, Angus Macphail; ph, Jimmy Wilson.

Comedy/Romance   **(PR:A MPAA:NR)**

TAXI NACH TOBRUK   (SEE: TAXI FOR TOBRUK, 1965, Fr.)

TAXI 13**½   (1928) 64m FBO bw

Chester Conklin (*Angus Mactavish*), Ethel Wales (*Mrs. Mactavish*), Martha Sleeper (*Flora Mactavish*), Hugh Trevor (*Dan Regan*), Lee Moran (*Dennis Moran*), Jerry Miley (*Mason*), Charles Byer (*Berger*).

Conklin is a hard working cab driver trying to support a wife and 10 children with a worn-out old vehicle. He's trying to raise $100 for a down payment on a new cab so he can ease his woes. One day he picks up Miley and Byer, a pair of crooks who plan to use him as a getaway driver after they blow up a safe. Trevor, a cop, surprises the two, who use Conklin's cab to escape. Trevor chases them in another cab but the crooks escape on foot. However, they've left behind a pearl necklace, hidden in the taxi's upholstery. Conklin's daughter, Sleeper, meets Miley and learns the secret of the necklace. She recovers it and with the $5,000 reward her father can buy a new taxi. This mildly amusing comedy is largely silent with a few talking sequences. Conklin, of course, was better known as a second banana for numerous silent comedies, particularly his work with Charlie Chaplin. Serving as editor for the film was Pandro S. Berman who in later years would become a well-known producer.

d, Marshall Neilan; w, George Le Maire, W. Scott Darling (based on a story by Darling); ph, Phil Tannura; ed, Pandro S. Berman.

Comedy   **(PR:AAA MPAA:NR)**

TAXI TO HEAVEN**   (1944, USSR) 70m Central/Artkino bw (AKA: AIR-CHAUFFEUR)

Mikhail Zharov (*Baranov*), Ludmila Tselikovskaya (*Natasha*), Boris Blinov (*The Colonel*), Georgi Spiegel (*Svetlovidov*), B. Grigkov (*Kulikov*), Tamara Govorkova (*Kulikova*), K. Sorokin (*Zadunalsky*), L. Shabaldina (*Marusya*), Boris Shishkin (*Tolya*), Mikhail Kuznetsov (*Copilot*).

A fast-moving Russian musical comedy which stars Tselikovskaya as a young lovely who is the center of attraction for both opera singer Spiegel and courageous pilot Zharov. The latter, though not accepted for military service, performs heroic feats with his transport airplane, including downing an enemy aircraft. Ironically, writer Petrov was killed in an airplane crash shortly after completing the screenplay of this, his final film. Director Rappaport made many light musical comedies both before and after WW II. He was also capable of serious drama, having co-directed PROFESSOR MAMLOCK in 1938; he received his training from G. W. Pabst, for whom he served as assistant on the classic KAMERADSCHAFT in 1931. Producer Ermler was a talented director in his own right. (In Russian; English subtitles.)

p, Frederick Ermler; d, Herbert Rappaport; w, Eugene Petrov [Y. Katayev]; ph, A. Halpern; m, U. Birkukov (with selections from Peter Ilyich Tchaikovsky's "Pique Dame" and Ruggiero Leoncavallo's "Pagliacci"); spec eff, B. Khrennikov, M. Kortkin.

Musical   **(PR:A MPAA:NR)**

TAZA, SON OF COCHISE**½   (1954) 79m UNIV c

Rock Hudson (*Taza*), Barbara Rush (*Oona*), Gregg Palmer (*Capt. Burnett*), Bart Roberts (*Naiche*), Morris Ankrum (*Grey Eagle*), Ian MacDonald (*Geronimo*), Richard H. Cutting (*Cy Hagen*), Joe Sawyer (*Sgt. Hamma*), Robert Burton (*Gen. Crook*), Eugene Iglesias (*Chato*), Lance Fuller (*Lt. Willis*), Brad Jackson (*Lt. Richards*), James Van Horn (*Skinya*), Charles Horvath (*Kocha*), Robert Hoy (*Lobo*), William Leslie (*Cavalry Sergeant*), Dan White (*Tiswin*), Edna Parrish, Seth Bigman (*Indians*), John Kay Hawks (*Soldier*), Barbara Burck (*Bit*), Jeff Chandler (*Cochise*).

An unsuccessful but interesting venture into the western genre from

melodrama king Douglas Sirk. Hudson is cast as the son of a dying indian, Cochise, who--with his father on the deathbed--promises that he will keep the tribe at peace. Hudson's brother, however, wants the tribe to join with the warring Geronimo clan. Again, as in his later films, ALL THAT HEAVEN ALLOWS (1955) and WRITTEN ON THE WIND (1956), Sirk casts Hudson as a character trapped between two factions of society, a favorite theme of the director's. Originally shown in 3-D, so try to excuse some of the gimmicky comin'-at-ya' shots. An early producer stint by former low-budget musical film star Hunter.

p, Ross Hunter; d, Douglas Sirk; w, George Zuckerman, Gerald Grayson Adams (based on the story by Adams); ph, Russell Metty (3-D, Technicolor); m, Frank Skinner; ed, Milton Carruth; art d, Bernard Herzbrun, Emrich Nicholson; set d, Russell A. Gausman, Oliver Emert; cos, Jay A. Morley, Jr.

Western   **(PR:A MPAA:NR)**

TE QUIERO CON LOCURA**   (1935) 74m FOX bw (AKA: I'M CRAZY ABOUT YOU)

Rosita Moreno, Raul Roulien, Enrique de Rosas.

A Spanish-language production from Fox about an heiress, Moreno, who pretends to be crazy in order to disrupt the life her relatives have mapped out for her. While in an elegant sanatorium Moreno falls in love with Roulien. Together they sing and dance and tell jokes constantly, making her world inside the madhouse seem more sane than life on the outside with its wars, fatal accidents, and homicides. (In Spanish.)

d, John J. Boland.

Musical/Comedy   **(PR:A MPAA:NR)**

TEA AND RICE***   (1964, Jap.) 115m Shochiku bw (OCHAZUKE NO AJI; AKA: THE FLAVOR OF GREEN TEA OVER RICE)

Shin Saburi, Michiyo Kogure, Koji Tsuruta, Keiko Tsushima, Kuniko Miyake, Chikage Awashima, Chishu Ryu, Yuko Mochizuki.

Ozu's character study of a modern Japanese married couple trying desperately to hold themselves together as husband and wife. There is a tension between her leisurely life style spent with her friends and his desire for a simpler life. The reconciliation comes over a meal of tea and rice which she despises but eats anyway, in an attempt to adopt her husband's ways. Ozu followed this picture (released in Japan in 1952) with another Ryu vehicle, TOKYO STORY, hailed as the director's masterpiece.

d, Yasujiro Ozu; w, Ozu, Kogo Noda; ph, Yushun Atsuta.

Drama   **(PR:A MPAA:NR)**

TEA AND SYMPATHY***½   (1956) 122m MGM c

Deborah Kerr (*Laura Reynolds*), John Kerr (*Tom Robinson Lee*), Leif Erickson (*Bill Reynolds*), Edward Andrews (*Herb Lee*), Darryl Hickman (*Al*), Norma Crane (*Ellie Martin*), Dean Jones (*Ollie*), Jacqueline de Wit (*Lilly Sears*), Tom Laughlin (*Ralph*), Ralph Votrian (*Steve*), Steven Terrell (*Phil*), Kip King (*Ted*), Jimmy Hayes (*Henry*), Richard Tyler (*Roger*), Don Burnett (*Vic*), Mary Alan Hokanson (*Mary Williams*), Ron Kennedy (*Dick*), Peter Miller (*Pete*), Bob Alexander (*Pat*), Michael Monroe (*Earl*), Byron Kane (*Umpire*), Paul Bryar (*Alex*), Harry Harvey, Jr, Bobby Ellis (*Boys*), Saul Gorss, Dale Van Sickel (*Burly Men*), Peter Leeds (*Headmaster at Bonfire*), Del Erickson (*Ferdie*).

A slightly tamer version of a landmark stage play that dealt with alleged homosexuality and an older woman's desire to prove the machismo of the suspect young man. John Kerr is a married writer with three children who returns to his exclusive prep school in New England for a reunion. He flashes back to his troubled years at the school and what happened to him then. The younger John Kerr is inept at every sport except tennis (which is regarded as a sissy pastime) and this sets him apart from the other boys. He wears his hair long and spends his off-hours in romantic pursuits such as reading and other subjects that the other members of the school scorn. J. Kerr rooms with Hickman, who is slightly embarrassed by J. Kerr's behavior, although Hickman defends him to the others because he knows Kerr is just "different," which doesn't necessarily make him a pervert. Kerr's housemaster is big, hearty Erickson, a smiling boor who emphasizes masculine games for his charges. Erickson is in league with Andrews, J. Kerr's father, who shares the housemaster's feeling that the boy should have his hair cut and make an attempt to get into the mainstream of the school's activities. Kerr is shunned by almost everyone at the school except Hickman and Erickson's wife, Deborah Kerr. She is a sensitive woman who realizes that this lad is in trouble. Further, he sends her memory back to the thought of her late first husband, a boy who volunteered for the army during WW II in order to show everyone that he was fearless. She was an early widow because of that. The other students begin to question J. Kerr's masculinity even further when they see that he knows how to sew, an art they consider specifically feminine. They don't know that he learned it from a nanny he'd been left with as a child and that the ability to sew is actually very handy. The other boys continue ragging him and it appears that he is going to be hazed at a fraternity function. Andrews can't bear the thought that his son is anything but a chip off the old block and encourages him to fight back. Erickson is getting a kick out of what they are doing to the student while his wife is showing concern, thereby causing undue jealousy on Erickson's part. Her job, he tells her, should be limited to the dispensing of tea and sympathy to the boys and he doesn't appreciate her taking this strong an attachment to one boy in particular. Kerr and Kerr become closer and closer as he bares his problems to her and she understands. He has planned a visit to the local hooker, Crane, and she tries to talk him out of it. He wonders if he may be strange and he wants to put that out of his mind and thinks that making love to Crane might be just the ticket. Kerr warns him against the visit so he tries to make love to her instead, but she rejects him. She is a good and faithful wife to Erickson (Lord knows why) and can't handle the student's advances. He goes to see Crane but the affair turns out terribly (this scene was written for the screenplay and didn't appear in the stage version) and he runs away, then attempts to kill himself. When Andrews and Erickson discuss the boy, D. Kerr overhears their conversation and later, she and Erickson have an argument about the way he is. She says that she appreciates the boy's plight and was trying to be more than a house mother to him and that he needed more than just tea and sympathy, he needed love, especially since he received none of that from his father, Andrews. The intimation is given that Erickson is a repressed homosexual and sorely resents the boy for having the guts to live his own life and not conform. The argument comes to a close and it's easy to see that Erickson and D. Kerr have come to a crossroads in their relationship. She leaves and finds the boy wandering through the dense brush. She takes his hand and says "When you speak of this in future years, and you will, be kind." And with that, she leads him down the path of sexuality. The picture should have ended there but, alas, it didn't. Flash back to the present and the news that Kerr's affair with Kerr ruined Erickson's life. That sop to the censors is what allowed the film to be shown in the temple of middle-class morality, Radio City Music Hall. Casting Kerr and Kerr caused confusion, although she pronounces it "Carr," while he chooses the other pronunciation. John Kerr never had the career that he should have had after his success in the play and picture. TEA AND SYMPATHY was his third film after THE COBWEB and GABBY. He later attended law school while appearing in SOUTH PACIFIC, GIRL OF THE NIGHT, THE CROWDED SKY and a few other minor films. He now practices law and is also a member of the Writers Guild. Crane was later seen as Golda in FIDDLER ON THE ROOF. Note Dean Jones, who went on to become Walt Disney's favorite leading man, as well as Tom Laughlin, who went on to become Tom Laughlin's leading man in BILLY JACK. In a small role, note Kip King, who later became one of the country's most successful actors in commercials. Kerr, Kerr, and Erickson all played their parts in the play that opened in September, 1953, and ran for more than 700 performances. The sets for the picture were a rebuild of scenery for FORTY LITTLE MOTHERS, GOOD NEWS, and THE COBWEB, John Kerr's first picture. Since Anderson himself wrote the screenplay (with the censors looking over his shoulder), any bowdlerization must be attributed to him. Still, under such stringent bluenoses, he managed to get his points across. Minnelli's direction was true to the material. The older woman/young boy situation was seen years later in SUMMER OF '42 (1971) and there are some startling similarities between the two. In the latter, a widow loses her young husband in the war and she also says something to the effect that she wishes to be remembered kindly by a young boy, although the youth is not portrayed as a boy doubting his sexual proclivities.

p, Pandro S. Berman; d, Vincente Minnelli; w, Robert Anderson (based on the play by Anderson); ph, John Alton (CinemaScope, Metrocolor); m, Adolph Deutsch; ed, Ferris Webster; art d, William A. Horning, Edward Carfagno; cos, Helen Rose.

Drama   (PR:C-O   MPAA:NR)

TEA FOR TWO*½**   (1950) 98m WB c

Doris Day *(Nanette Carter)*, Gordon MacRae *(Jimmy Smith)*, Gene Nelson *(Tommy Trainor)*, Patrice Wymore *(Beatrice Darcy)*, Eve Arden *(Pauline Hastings)*, Billy De Wolfe *(Larry Blair)*, S. Z. Sakall *(J. Maxwell Bloomhaus)*, Bill Goodwin *(William Early)*, Virginia Gibson *(Mabel Wiley)*, Crawford Kent *(Stevens)*, Mary Eleanor Donahue *(Lynne)*, Johnny McGovern *(Richard)*, Harry Harvey *(Crotchety Man)*, George Baxter *(Backer)*, Herschel Dougherty *(Theater Manager)*, Abe Dinovitch *(Taxi Driver)*, Elizabeth Flournoy *(Secretary)*, Buddy Shaw *(Piano Mover)*, John Hedloe *(Chorus Boy)*, Jack Daley *(Truck Driver)*, Art Gilmore *(Radio Announcer)*.

A delightful musical suggested by the Broadway hit of 1924, "No, No, Nanette," but having an almost all-new screenplay and several new songs. Gentle Sakall is seen telling the story of how Day and MacRae met to their two teenaged children. Flashback to the era of the 1920s and Day is seen as a wealthy heiress with a desire to finance and star in a Broadway show. Her uncle is Sakall and he doesn't have the heart to tell her that she's been wiped out by the Wall Street crash. She tells De Wolfe, the producer, that she's willing to put up the $25 thousand necessary to underwrite the show and when she asks guardian Sakall for the money, he tries to weasel his way out of it. He says that her problem is that she always says "yes" to everyone who asks her for anything. If she is be willing to answer every question for 24 hours with a "no," he will give her the money (which she no longer has). The next day proves to be immensely difficult, with predictable consequences and comedy as Day has to be negative about everything while pal Wymore looks on and can't say anything either in order to satisfy the terms of the deal Day's made with Sakall. When Day completes the requisite 24 hours,

she asks for the money and is stunned to find that she is now poor. Day's attorney, who has some money of his own, puts up the cash. The show that they do is "No, No, Nanette" and it's a hit. Day and MacRae work well together and later appeared as a duo in THE WEST POINT STORY, ON MOONLIGHT BAY, and BY THE LIGHT OF THE SILVERY MOON. Day dances for the first time here with help from Nelson and the energetic choreography of Prinz. Sharp dialog from Clork, peppy dances, and a host of tunes including: "I Know That You Know" (Anne Caldwell, Vincent Youmans, sung by Day, MacRae, later danced by Nelson and Day), "Crazy Rhythm" (Irving Caesar, Roger Wolfe Kahn, Joseph Meyer, danced by Wymore, Nelson), "Charleston" (Cecil Mack, Jimmie Johnson, performed by Billy De Wolfe, Virginia Gibson), "I Only Have Eyes For You" (Harry Warren, Al Dubin, sung by MacRae, danced by Gibson), "Tea For Two" (Caesar, Youmans, sung by Day, MacRae), "I Want to Be Happy" (Caesar, Youmans, sung by Day, MacRae), "Oh Me, Oh My" (Ira Gershwin, Youmans, sung by Day, danced by Nelson) "The Call Of The Sea" (Youmans, Caesar, Otto Harbach), "Do Do Do" (George and Ira Gershwin), "No, No, Nanette" (Youmans, Harbach). On "Oh Me, Oh My," Ira Gershwin used his pseudonym of "Arthur Francis." Excellent band work under the direction of Heindorf. Included in the aggregation were jazz players Buddy Cole, Onest Conley, Manny Vanderhans, Rolly Bundock, Dick Fisher, Ernie Felice, and Dick Anderson. Butler's direction was solid, no-nonsense helming that let the actors do their turns. De Wolfe was very funny, as was Sakall, two of the best second bananas in the movie business. Composer Caesar was a most generous man who opened his own publishing company in New York's famed Brill Building and gave breaks to many aspiring songwriters. He loved songs and loved to sing his own and often entertained at benefits around New York. In his later years, he appeared on David Letterman's TV show to reminisce and delight audiences with his wittiness. During the 1950s, he would speak at Abraham Lincoln High School in Brooklyn, where his sister was a Spanish teacher. Since Lincoln High School turned out such stellar songwriters as Neil Sedaka, Howard Greenfield, and Neil Diamond (to name but a few), Caesar's inspiration to young composers and lyricists continues to be felt, long after his demise.

p, William Jacobs; d, David Butler; w, Harry Clork (based on the musical play "No, No, Nanette" by Frank Mandel, Otto Harbach, Vincent Youmans, Emil Nyitray); ph, Wilfred M. Cline (Technicolor); ed, Irene Morra; md, Ray Heindorf; art d, Douglas Bacon; set d, Lyle B. Reifsnider; cos, Leah Rhodes; ch, LeRoy Prinz.

Musical/Comedy   (PR:A   MPAA:NR)

TEA LEAVES IN THE WIND   (SEE: HATE IN PARADISE, 1938, Brit.)

TEACHER, THE**   (1974) 98m Crown International c (AKA: THE SEDUCTRESS)

Angel Tompkins, Jay North, Anthony James, Marlene Schmidt, Med Flory, Sivi Aberg, Barry Atwater.

Tompkins is the teacher of the title and North (of TV's "Dennis the Menace" fame) is her student. The lessons she teaches, however, are better learned in the bedroom than in the classroom. In the meantime, they are both being threatened by psychotic killer James.

p,d&w, Hikmet Avedis; m, Shorty Rogers; m/l, title song, Sammy Fain, Paul Francis Webster (sung by Jackie Ward).

Drama   (PR:C   MPAA:NR)

TEACHER AND THE MIRACLE, THE**½**   (1961, Ital./Span.) 88m Gladiator-Union/Presi dent bw (IL MAESTRO; EL MAESTRO)

Aldo Fabrizi *(Giovanni Merino)*, Edoardo Nevola *(Antonio)*, Marco Paoletti *(Gabriel)*, Alfredo Mayo *(Principal)*, Mary Lamar *(Teacher)*, Felix Fernandez *(Porter)*, Julio San Juan *(Doctor)*, Jose Calvo *(Chauffeur)*, Julia Caba Alba *(Portress)*.

Having recovered from the loss of his wife, Fabrizi, an aging and popular art school instructor who plans to start his own school, devotes all his energies to his young son. Upon receiving an official letter licensing the opening of the school, the youngster runs to his father with the news, but is struck and killed by a car. Depressed, Fabrizi hands in his resignation, but finds new hope when his class is visited by a new student, young Paoletti. He again learns to enjoy teaching, but is disappointed when Paoletti prepares to leave. Fabrizi tries to find him, but instead notices a statue of the Madonna and Child; the latter bears an exact resemblance to Paoletti. Guaranteed to wrench out a tear or two. (Dubbed into English.)

p&d, Aldo Fabrizi (U.S. version directed by Carol Riethof, Peter Riethof); w, Fabrizi, L. Lucas, J. Gallardo, Mario Amendola; ph, Antonio Macasoli, Manuel Merino; m, Carlo Innocenzi.

Religious Drama   (PR:A   MPAA:NR)

TEACHER'S PET***   (1958) 120m Perlsea/PAR bw

Clark Gable (*Jim Gannon*), Doris Day (*Erica Stone*), Gig Young (*Dr. Hugo Pine*), Mamie Van Doren (*Peggy DeFore*), Nick Adams (*Barney Kovac*), Peter Baldwin (*Harold Miller*), Marion Ross (*Katy Fuller*), Charles Lane (*Roy, Assistant*), Jack Albertson (*Guide*), Florenz Ames (*J. L. Ballentine*), Harry Antrim (*Lloyd Crowley*), Vivian Nathan (*Mrs. Kovac*), Terry Becker (*Mr. Appino*), Elizabeth Harrower (*Clara Dibney*), Margaret Muse (*Miss Gross*), Merritt Smith (*Mr. Cory*), Steffi Sidney (*Book Store Girl*), Cyril Delevanti (*Copy Man*), Norton Mockridge (*Harry*), Sandra Gould (*Tess*), Frank Richards (*Cab Driver*), Army Acherd, Sidney Skolsky, Vernon Scott, Joe Hyams, Paine Knickerbocker, Erskine Johnson, Frank P. Quinn (*Themselves*).

Slightly lengthy newspaper comedy with many fine moments and Young stealing the show from stars Day and Gable, who was 57 at the time and nearing the end of his long career. Gable is a hard-boiled newspaperman in the "Hildy Johnson" style. He thinks that those who learned the business in a college don't know what they are writing about. A professor at a local college has asked him to guest lecture at an evening session and he writes a scathing letter back to the teacher that pulls no punches. When his boss orders him to comply with the professor's wish, he reluctantly drags himself to the class and walks in late, just in time to hear the teacher, Day, giving her comments on the letter he's written. She spares nothing in her remarks and Gable figures he'd better just sit there and shut up and pretend to be a student. Day's late father was a Pulitzer Prize-winning journalist and she uses his work as an example for the class. Day is dating psychologist Young and Gable, who is rapidly falling for Day, must get the rival out of the way. He does it adroitly and Young's farcical performance as the lovelorn suitor is so good that he was nominated for an Oscar for this role. Class continues and Gable shows that he knows what he's doing behind the typewriter so Day tries to get him a job at the local paper and when the publisher calls in his editor and it turns out to be Gable, she is miffed. Then, when Gable learns that one of his own good reporters is, in fact, a former student of Day's, they make up and love rears its head for good. The story doesn't much matter as it has little surprise. The details are what make this film funnier than the plot. Van Doren does a striptease and sweet, virginal Day emulates her in an apple pie fashion that sets Gable's temperature rising. The newspaper office is filled with real-life reporters, many of whom have never before been seen on film, and that's a treat for anyone who knows these men and women, all of whom ham it up. In the end, Gable decides to lecture at Day's classes and they will go home together. The major problem with the film is Gable's overdone performance. Like Paul Newman, who never has learned the delicate art of comedy, Gable mistook mugging for acting and was almost a parody of himself. And yet, 21 years before, he had handled the same light comedy chores in IT HAPPENED ONE NIGHT, winning an Oscar. Admittedly, Gable was better than Newman at the light stuff, but he seemed to be trying too hard here and the insouciance was lost. The movie screamed to be in color and one wonders why they didn't shoot it that way. Joe Lubin, who had written tunes before in Day movies such as PILLOW TALK, wrote two more for this, "Teacher's Pet" and "The Girl Who Invented Rock and Roll." Marion Ross and Jack Albertson show their comedy timing and a good performance is also thrown in by young Nick Adams. It's really a one-joke premise, but the Oscar-nominated script by Fay and Michael Kanin and the amiable acting by most of the cast make this funny enough to watch late at night on TV when the only other movie on is anything by Brian de Palma.

p, William Perlberg; d, George Seaton; w, Fay and Michael Kanin; ph, Haskell Boggs (VistaVision); m, Roy Webb; ed, Alma Macrorie; art d, Hal Pereira, Earl Hedrick; set d, Sam Comer, Robert Benton; cos, Edith Head; spec eff, Farciot Edouart; m/l, Joe Lubin.

Comedy   **(PR:A MPAA:NR)**

TEAHOUSE OF THE AUGUST MOON, THE****

                                             (1956) 123m MGM c

Marlon Brando (*Sakini*), Glenn Ford (*Capt. Fisby*), Machiko Kyo (*Lotus Blossom*), Eddie Albert (*Capt. McLean*), Paul Ford (*Col. Purdy*), Jun Negami (*Mr. Seiko*), Nijiko Kiyokawa (*Miss Higa Jiga*), Mitsuko Sawamura (*Little Girl*), Henry [Harry] Morgan (*Sgt. Gregovich*), Shichizo Takeda (*Ancient Man*), Kichizaemon Saramaru (*Mr. Hokaida*), Frank Tokunaga (*Mr. Omura*), Raynum K. Tsukamoto (*Mr. Oshira*), Minoru Nishida (*Mr. Sumata*), Dansho Miyazaki (*Sumata's Father*), Miyoshi Jingu (*Old Woman on Jeep*), Aya Oyama (*Daughter on Jeep*), Tsuruta Yozan (*Judge*), John Grayson, Roger McGee, Harry Harvey, Jr, Carl Fior (*Soldiers*).

Charming adaptation of the novel and play that shows Brando has a flair for comedy. The picture opens with the same prolog seen on the Broadway stage (done there by David Wayne). Brando is the Okinawan who introduces himself and the other players and tells, with pride, that Okinawa has the honor of being the most subjugated place in history. It has been overrun by the Chinese and the Japanese, and now, the Americans. He smiles and comments: "Okinawa very fortunate. Culture brought to us, not have to leave home for it." The chief of the island is Paul Ford (who replaced Louis Calhern when the veteran actor had a fatal heart attack on location in Japan), a befuddled military man who runs the occupation troops but has no idea what the Okinawans are about. Glenn Ford arrives and Paul Ford (no relation) assigns him to bring civilization to a small village. With Brando

as his official interpreter, Glenn Ford is supposed to start up a women's club, build a schoolhouse, and establish democracy according to the plan sent out by the powers in Washington. Glenn Ford is a pleasant officer with a history of screwing up and he's been just about exiled to Okinawa, where his superiors hope he can do no further damage. Brando sees what kind of officer Glenn Ford is and tries to lead him. The small village doesn't care much for a school. What they desire most is a teahouse and a horde of geishas to woman it. As hard as Glenn Ford tries to establish himself as a fair-but-firm officer, Brando's wily ways make mincemeat of his best-laid plans. The locals bring various presents to Glenn Ford to curry favor with him. The most prominent of these gifts is Kyo. When Glenn Ford says he cannot accept a human being as a gift, Brando explains that to refuse would be a great loss of face for the village. If that happens, they are liable to revolt and their normally pleasant ways will turn dark. The longer he stays, the more easily Glenn Ford is manipulated by Brando. Back at HQ, Paul Ford has begin to suspect something is awry because the messages coming in from the village are strangely non-specific. After a particularly confusing phone call from Glenn Ford, Paul Ford orders service shrink Albert out to the village to examine the man. What Paul Ford doesn't know is that psychiatrist Albert has a hobby; he loves to grow organic foods. Once in the village, Albert soon falls prey to the relaxed life style and enlists the locals in doing his kind of farming. Glenn Ford and Albert are impressed also by the hand-made wares of the area and encourage the villagers to make more and sell them as souvenirs. It doesn't work out and everyone in the village feels awful and will now go home and get loaded. Glenn Ford wants to know what they drink and Brando informs him that they brew a very potent brandy from sweet potatoes. Glenn Ford jumps at the opportunity and gets the villagers working. Soon, the phone is ringing off the hook with constant orders for the brandy from various bases on Okinawa. The teahouse is completed and a great celebration is about to take place. Glenn Ford and Albert will be honored and all is going well until Paul Ford arrives to see for himself what the heck is happening. No sooner does he note the teahouse than he orders Glenn Ford arrested and the lovely teahouse razed. Paul Ford begins to nose around. He's wondering why there is no democracy and how this poor village has been managing to have such a good life style when it seems to have no industry to speak of. Now he thinks that the teahouse must be a bordello and he sends his report in to Washington. The bureaucracy responds in a totally different fashion than Paul Ford had expected. Washington is delighted that the Okinawans have shown such spunk and have embraced the recovery program. Paul Ford gets glum because he feels he's ruined the village's chance to stand on its own. The stills have been destroyed, the teahouse has been demolished, and Paul Ford is very sorry about the whole thing. Brando smiles, explains that the stills exist, they've only been hidden. Further, the teahouse was taken apart in such a manner that it can be rebuilt in no time. And it is. Once that's done, Brando tells the audience in an epilog that the movie is over. Paul Ford had played the role on Broadway more than 1000 times and yet managed to bring a freshness to it for the screen. He was later to do the same kind of role on TV's "You'll Never Get Rich" when he played Sgt. Bilko's (Phil Silver) commanding officer. Kyo spoke no English when she accepted the role. She had previously been seen in GATE OF HELL and RASHOMON. The music was mostly Okinawan and Japanese and that lent authenticity to the affair. Although David Wayne was a marvel in the play (which won the Tony as Best Play that year), he was almost unknown by the movie-going public, so when Brando indicated he wanted the part, he got it. Brando does one of his best roles here, submerging his own powerful personality under layers of makeup. He spent months learning the proper way to move like an Asian. Some of the humor is labored and Glenn Ford overplays a bit but the ultimate result is a charming, though somewhat talky, movie that elevates whimsy to a new high.

p, Jack Cummings; d, Daniel Mann; w, John Patrick (based on the novel by Vern J. Sneider and play by Patrick); ph, John Alton (CinemaScope, Metrocolor); m, Saul Chaplin; ed, Harold F. Kress; md, Chaplin; art d, William A. Horning, Eddie Imazu; ch, Masaya Fujima; m/l, Kikuko Kanai.

Comedy   **(PR:AA MPAA:NR)**

TEAR GAS SQUAD*   (1940) 55m WB bw

Dennis Morgan (*Tommy McCabe*), John Payne (*Bill Morrissey*), Gloria Dickson (*Jerry Sullivan*), George Reeves (*Joe McCabe*), Frank Wilcox (*Sgt. Crump*), Julie Stevens (*Lois*), Harry Shannon (*Lt. Sullivan*), Mary Gordon (*Mrs. Sullivan*), William Gould (*Capt. Henderson*), John Hamilton (*Chief Ferris*), Edgar Buchanan (*Cousin Andy*), Dick Rich (*Cousin Pat*), DeWolf [William] Hopper (*George*).

Having little to do with tear gas, this cheapie casts Morgan as a nightclub piano player who has a thing for a cop's daughter, Dickson. In order to prove that he's no pansy, he joins the police, gets trained by the girl's beau, policeman Payne, gets kicked out, and eventually becomes the hero after saving Payne's life. Of course he gets the girl. Includes that tune that every cop should whistle while on the beat, "I'm an Officer of the Law" (M.K. Jerome, Jack Scholl).

p, Bryan Foy; d, Terry Morse; w, Charles Belden, Don Ryan, Kenneth Gamet (based on their story "The State Cop"); ph, Sid Hickox; ed, Ernest Nims.

Crime/Romance   **(PR:A MPAA:NR)**

TEARS FOR SIMON***   (1957, Brit.) 91m RANK/REP c (GB: LOST)

David Farrar *(Inspector Craig)*, David Knight *(Lee Cochrane)*, Julia Arnall *(Sue Cochrane)*, Anthony Oliver *(Sgt. Lyel)*, Thora Hird *(Kelly's Landlady)*, Eleanor Summerfield *(Sgt. Cook)*, Ann Paige *(Nanny)*, Marjorie Rhodes *(Mrs. Jeffries)*, Anna Turner *(Mrs. Robey)*, Everley Gregg *(Viscountess)*, Meredith Edwards *(Sgt. Davies)*, Irene Prador *(Mitzi)*, Anita Sharp Bolster *(Miss Gill)*, Beverley Brooks *(Pam)*, Brenda Hogan *(Sue's Secretary)*, Joan Sims *(Ice Cream Girl)*, Shirley Anne [Ann] Field *(Girl)*, Eileen Peel *(Henrietta Gay)*, Barbara Shotter *(Mrs. Martin)*, Alma Taylor *(Mrs. Bellamy)*, Robert Brown, Harry Brunning, Fanny Carby, Cyril Chamberlain, Peggyann Clifford, Glenda Davies, Guy Deghy, Michael Ward, Dorothy Gordon, Fred Griffiths, Joan Hickson, Glyn Houston, Ray Jackson, Shirley Jenkins, Freda Bamford, Jack Lambert, Margot Lister, Arthur Lovegrove, William Lucas, Barry McCourmick, Jack McNaughton, Charlotte Mitchell, Hugh Morton, Dandy Nichols, Eileen Peel, Grace Denbigh Russell, Ewen Solon, Marianne Stone, Mike Ward, Ronald Ward, Mona Washbourne, John Welsh, Leonard White, Barbara Windsor, George Woodbridge.

Knight is an official at the U.S. Embassy in London and his wife is Arnall. Paige, the couple's nanny, leaves their 18-month-old baby in a carriage while she goes into a drugstore. When she comes out, the baby is gone. Farrar is the detective assigned to the case, but he has few clues to go on. The torn pages from a novel finally lead him to the baby, and the baby is saved from falling off a cliff. A gripping detective drama.

p, Vivian A. Cox; d, Guy Green; w, Janet Green; ph, Harry Waxman (Eastmancolor); m, Benjamin Frankel; ed, Anne V. Coates; md, Frankel; art d, Cedric Dawe, Harold Pottie.

Drama   **(PR:A   MPAA:NR)**

TEARS OF HAPPINESS*   (1974) 105m Mutual c

Manuel *(Raffi)*, Sosie Kodjian *(Silva)*, S. Sepian *(Son)*, Levon Yergat *(Father)*, Jon Kouzouyan *(Brother)*, Lynne Guthrie *(Lisa)*, Jack D. Boghaossian *(Manager)*, Adam Aivazian *(Artist)*.

Armenian nightclub singer Manuel stars in this tale about his rise to fame and his relationship with his estranged wife and child. Intended for Armenian-speaking communities, this picture's quality is so poor even they would have trouble with it. (In Armenian; English subtitles.)

p, John Kurkjian; d&w, Sarky Mouradian; ph, Gregory Sandor (Eastmancolor); m, Jaime Mendoza; ed, Sergio Murad.

Drama/Musical   **(PR:A   MPAA:NR)**

TECHNIQUE D'UN MEUTRE   (SEE: HIRED KILLER, THE, 1967, Fr./Ital.)

TECKMAN MYSTERY, THE**½   (1955, Brit) 90m Corona/Associated Artists bw

Margaret Leighton *(Helen Teckman)*, John Justin *(Philip Chance)*, Roland Culver *(Inspector Harris)*, Michael Medwin *(Martin Teckman)*, George Coulouris *(Garvin)*, Duncan Lamont *(Inspector Hilton)*, Raymond Huntley *(Maurice Miller)*, Jane Wenham *(Ruth Wade)*, Meier Tzelniker *(John Rice)*, Harry Locke *(Leonard)*, Frances Rowe *(Eileen Miller)*, Barbara Murray *(Girl in Plane)*, Warwick Ashton *(Sgt. Blair)*, Irene Lister *(Waitress)*, Gwen Nelson *(Duty Woman)*, Mary Grant *(BEA Clerk)*, Andrea Malandrinos *(Waiter)*, Dan Cressey *(Drake)*, Peter Taylor *(Leroy)*, Ben Williams, Frank Webster *(Beefeaters)*, Peter Augustine *(Man with Pipe)*, Maurice Lane *(GPO Messenger)*, Mollie Palmer *(Air Hostess)*, Bruce Beeby *(Wallace)*, Gordon Morrison *(Boris)*.

Justin is a biographer working on a book about a pilot who apparently went down during the test flight of a new plane. He falls in love with the dead man's sister, Leighton, discovering that an air of mystery shrouds the man's disappearance. When people involved with the pilot begin dying off, Justin fears for his own life, but Scotland Yardmen Lamont and Culver uncover a plot by a gang of international spies that proves the pilot is alive. His sister proves to be the control of the espionage nest; she comes to an exciting end.

p, Josef Somlo; d, Wendy Toye; w, Francis Durbridge, James Matthews (based on the TV serial "The Teckman Biography" by Durbridge); ph, Jack Hildyard; m, Clifton Parker; ed, Albert Rule; md, Muir Mathieson; prod d, William Kellner.

Mystery   **(PR:A   MPAA:NR)**

TECNICA DI UN OMICIDO   (SEE: HIRED KILLER, THE, 1967, Fr./Ital.)

TEDDY BEAR, THE   (SEE: MY FATHER'S MISTRESS, 1970, Swed.)

TEEN AGE TRAMP   (SEE: THAT KIND OF GIRL, 1963, Brit.)

TEEN KANYA   (SEE: TWO DAUGHTERS, 1963, India)

TEENAGE BAD GIRL**½   (1959, Brit.) 100m Everest/DCA bw (GB: MY TEENAGE DAUGHTER; AKA: BAD GIRL)

Anna Neagle *(Valerie Carr)*, Sylvia Syms *(Janet Carr)*, Norman Wooland *(Hugh Manning)*, Wilfrid Hyde-White *(Sir Joseph)*, Kenneth Haigh *(Tony Ward Black)*, Julia Lockwood *(Poppet Carr)*, Helen Haye *(Aunt Louisa)*, Josephine Fitzgerald *(Aunt Bella)*, Wanda Ventham *(Gina)*, Murray Mayne *(Don)*, Michael Shepley *(Sir Henry)*, Avice Landone *(Barbara)*, Michael Meacham *(Mark)*, Ballard Berkeley *(Magistrate)*, Edie Martin *(Miss Ellis)*, Myrette Morven *(Anne)*, Grizelda Hervey *(Miss Bennett)*, Betty Cooper *(Celia)*, Launce Maraschal *(Senator)*, Diana King, Daphne Cave, Laidman Browne.

Neagle is a war widow who edits a fiction magazine for adolescents. But she's out of touch with the feelings of her own teenage daughter (Syms)-in her first starring role--who falls in with a bad crowd. Neagle tries to stop her daughter from going out on all-night clubs hops, but to no avail. Finally Syms gets in trouble with the police and comes to her senses after spending a week in jail. Hopelessly predictable, but Syms makes this film better than it deserves to be. She has the right amounts of energy and spunk that cut through the moralizing and stereotyped character. Dripping in sentiment, the direction goes for easy and cheap emotional payoffs that are effective on an exploitational level. Ultimately unrealistic and too conventional to be much more than soap opera.

p&d, Herbert Wilcox; w, Felicity Douglas; ph, Max Greene [Mutz Greenbaum]; m, Stanley Black; ed, Bunny Warren.

Drama   **(PR:O   MPAA:NR)**

TEENAGE CAVEMAN**   (1958) 65m Nicholson-Arkoff/AIP bw (GB: OUT OF THE DARKNESS; AKA: PREHISTORIC WORLD)

Robert Vaughn *(The Boy)*, Darrah Marshall *(The Maiden)*, Leslie Bradley *(Symbol Maker)*, Frank De Kova *(The Villain)*, Joseph Hamilton, Marshall Bradford, Robert Shayne, Beach Dickerson, June Jocelyn, Charles P. Thompson, Jonathan Haze *(Members of the Tribe)*.

Vaughn may have been a little too hard on producer-director Corman when he called TEENAGE CAVEMAN "one of the best-worst films of all-time." It's not quite down there with the worst to be considered the best of the bunch (Let's not forget about PLAN 9 FROM OUTER SPACE). In fact TEENAGE CAVEMAN isn't even half bad. Vaughn stars as the title teen, a caveman who inhabits part of the dinosaur-populated wasteland with his "symbol maker" father. He is warned never to go across the river because of an evil monster. Teenagers will be teenagers, however, and Vaughn goes across, finding not a monster but an old man. The old fellow dies and Vaughn finds a book which tells about past civilizations in the 20th Century. A well-conceived cheapie from Corman, which even has its own post-holocaust message--something you don't usually find in his films. Love interest Marshall, as The Maiden, is--appropriately enough--a one-time Miss Teenage America. The prehistoric-reptile shots were picked up from ONE MILLION B.C. Tribesman Dickerson plays four roles in the film.

p&d, Roger Corman; w, R. Wright Campbell; ph, Floyd Crosby (Superama); m, Albert Glasser; ed, Irene Morra; cos, Marjorie Corso.

Science Fiction   **(PR:A   MPAA:NR)**

TEEN-AGE CRIME WAVE*   (1955) 77m Clover/COL bw

Tommy Cook *(Mike Denton)*, Mollie McCart *(Terry Marsh)*, Sue England *(Jane Koberly)*, Frank Griffin *(Ben Grant)*, James Bell *(Tom Grant)*, Kay Riehl *(Sarah Grant)*, Guy Kingsford *(Mr. Koberly)*, Larry Blake *(Sgt. Connors)*, James Ogg *(Al)*, Robert Bice *(Patrolman Smith)*, Kathleen Mulqueen *(Matron)*, Helen Brown *(Mrs. Koberly)*, Sydney Mason *(Bill Salisbury)*, George Cisar *(Man)*.

Cook and McCart are just a couple of fun-loving hooligans who get their kicks on Route 66, until one day crazy Cook blows away the town sheriff. With a car full of delinquents, Cook speeds up one road and down another with the police determined to catch the post-pubescent murderers. They hole up in a farmhouse and later are chased to a mountain observatory where a climactic shootout takes place.

p, Sam Katzman; d, Fred F. Sears; w, Ray Buffum, Harry Essex (based on the story by Buffum); ph, Harry Freulich; m, Mischa Bakaleinikoff; ed, Jerome Thoms; md, Bakaleinikoff; art d, Paul Palmentola.

Crime   **(PR:C   MPAA:NR)**

TEENAGE DELINQUENTS   (SEE: NO TIME TO BE YOUNG, 1957)

TEENAGE DOLL**   (1957) 68m Woolner Bros./AA bw (AKA: THE YOUNG REBELS)

June Kenney *(Barbara)*, Fay Spain *(Hel)*, John Brinkley *(Eddie)*, Collette Jackson *(May)*, Barbara Wilson *(Betty)*, Ziva Rodann *(Squirrel)*, Sandy Smith *(Lorrie)*, Barboura Morris *(Janet)*, Richard Devon *(Dunston)*, Jay Sayer *(Wally)*, Richard Cutting *(Phil)*, Dorothy Neumann *(Estelle)*, Ed

Nelson (*Dutch Doctor*), Bruno Ve Sota.

Kenney is a teen gang member with the Vandalettes who gets herself in hot water when she knifes a girl from a rival gang, The Black Widows. She takes to the streets and hides out with the Vandals, her gang's male counterparts. It all leads up to a big rumble pitting the Vandals and Vandalettes against the Tarantulas and the Black Widows. The film ends with the members of The Black Widows parading back to police cars in a shot composed in such a manner as to reveal the nihilistic elegance of Corman. Plenty of exposed flesh in this one. Vandalette leader Spain went on to play the rustic nubile nymphomaniac in GOD'S LITTLE ACRE, released the following year. And you thought the Jets were cool.

p&d, Roger Corman; w, Charles B. Griffith; ph, Floyd Crosby; m, Walter Greene; ed, Charles Gross; art d, Robert Kinoshita.

Crime Drama   **(PR:O   MPAA:NR)**

TEENAGE FRANKENSTEIN   (SEE: I WAS A TEENAGE FRANKENSTEIN, 1958)

TEENAGE GANG DEBS*   (1966) 77m Jode/CIP Ltd. bw

Diana Conti (*Terry*), Linda Gale (*Angel*), Eileen Scott (*Ellie*), Sandra Kane (*Annie*), Robin Nolan (*Maria*), Linda Cambi (*Shirley*), Sue McManus (*Sally*), Geri Tyler (*Geri*), Joey Naudic (*Nino*), John Batis (*Johnny*), Tom Yourk (*Hawkeye*), Thomas Andrisano (*Piggie*), George Winship (*Slats*), Doug Mitchell (*Burt*), Tom Eldred (*Tony*), Frank Spinella (*Diablo*), Alec Primrose (*Bartender*), Gene Marrin (*Mr. Fiore*), Lyn Kennedy (*Mrs. Fiore*), Janet Banzet (*Rosie*), RPM Motorcycle Club of Brooklyn (*The Rat Pack*).

Conti is a conniving young femme fatale who falls for gang member Naudic and offers him her body if he becomes the leader of his gang. He kills the current leader, makes it appear as if a rival gang is responsible, and then—urged on by Conti—starts a street war. Chains and kn ives and rocks and clubs then grace the faces of all involved, causing the gang debs to get a bit perturbed. They corner Conti, slash her face up, and carve the initials of the former leader in her chest. Shot in Brooklyn, New York Morbid? Yes. Unrealistic? Probably not.

p, Jerry Denby; d, Sande Johnsen; w, Hy Cahl; ph, Harry Petricek; m, Steve Karmen.

Crime Drama   **(PR:O   MPAA:NR)**

TEENAGE LOVERS   (SEE: TOO SOON TO LOVE, 1960)

TEENAGE MILLIONAIRE**   (1961) 84m Ludlow/UA bw-c

Jimmy Clanton (*Bobby Chalmers*), Rocky Graziano (*Rocky*), ZaSu Pitts (*Aunt Theodora*), Diane Jergens (*Bambi*), Joan Tabor (*Adrienne*), Sid Gould (*Sheldon Vale*), Maurice "Doberman" Gosfield (*Ernie*), Eileen O'Neill (*Desidieria*), Jackie Wilson, Chubby Checker, Dion, Bill Black's Combo, Marv Johnson, Vicki Spencer, Jack Larson (*Performers*).

Some deranged casting agent decided to put ZaSu Pitts and Rocky Graziano in the same movie, but somehow it all makes sense. Clanton is the orphaned son of millionaires who is taken care of by his aunt Pitts and her bodyguard Graziano. His mind gets taken over by rock 'n' roll; he cuts his own record and gets it played on the family-owned radio station. Next thing you know everyone's on their feet, dancing to the beat. Clanton's big tune is his own "Green Light," while other performers such as Chubby Checker, Dion, and Jackie Wilson appear. Some sequences filmed in Musicolor which simply looks like tinted gels.

p, Howard B. Kreitsek; d, Lawrence F. Doheny; w, H. B. Cross [Harry Spalding], Doheny; ph, Gordon Avil, Arthur J. Ornitz (part Musicolor); ed, Jack Ruggiero; art d, Rolland M. Brooks, Paul Sylbert, Howard Hollander; set d, Harry Gordon.

Comedy/Musical   **(PR:A   MPAA:NR)**

TEENAGE MONSTER zero   (1958) 65m Marquette-Howco International/Favorite Films bw (AKA: METEOR MONSTER)

Anne Gwynne (*Ruth Cannon*), Gloria Castillo (*Kathy North*), Stuart Wade (*Sheriff Bob*), Gilbert Perkins (*Charles Cannon*), Stephen Parker (*Charles Cannon, as a Boy*), Charles Courtney (*Marv Howell*), Norman Leavitt (*Deputy Ed*), Jim McCullough (*Jim Cannon*), Gaybe Mooradian (*Fred Fox*), Arthur Berkeley (*Man with Burro*), Frank Davis (*Man on Street*).

When a meteor turns Perkins into a crazed hairy killer with a face only a mother could love he is hidden in the cellar by (who else?) his dear old mom, Gwynne. He growls, the police discover him, he kills his own mother. So what? A slow, mega-tedious exploitationer which began production as METEOR MONSTER but changed to TEENAGE MONSTER to cash in on the teen movie craze of the 1950s.

p&d, Jacques Marquette; w, Ray Buffum; ph, Taylor Byars; m, Walter Greene; ed, Irving Schoenberg.

Science Fiction   **(PR:A   MPAA:NR)**

TEENAGE MOTHER zero   (1967) 78m Arrow/Cinemation c

Arlene Sue Farber (*Arlene Taylor*), Frederick Riccio (*Duke Markell*), Julie Ange (*Erica Peterson*), Howard Le May (*Tony Michaels*), George Peters (*Mr. Taylor*).

A worthless waste of precious acetate which has a Swedish sex-education teacher arriving in a small town and teaching high school kids all about the facts of love. She stirs up interest in the youngsters' loins and one girl pretends to get pregnant to trick her beau into marriage. Includes footage of an actual birth, which is simply the film's way of getting away with some taboo material. Gross, the film's creator, gives himself a plug by showing the film's stars going to see a film called GIRL ON A CHAIN GANG, another Gross film. He's not alone in this sort of self-promotion, however; George Roy Hill did it in A LITTLE ROMANCE, Spielberg and Dante did it in GREMLINS, and the New Wave directors had a habit of constantly boosting each other's films in their own.

p, Jerry Gross, Nicholas Demetroules; d&w, Gross (based on a story by Demetroules); ph, George Zimmermann, Richard E. Brooks DeLuxe Color; m, Steve Karmen; ed, Israel Ortiz.

Drama   **(PR:O   MPAA:NR)**

TEENAGE PSYCHO MEETS BLOODY MARY
(SEE: INCREDIBLY STRANGE CREATURES WHO STOPPED LIVING AND BECAME CRAZY MIXED-UP ZOMBIES, 1965)

TEENAGE REBEL**   (1956) 94m FOX bw

Ginger Rogers (*Nancy Fallon*), Michael Rennie (*Jay Fallon*), Mildred Natwick (*Grace Hewitt*), Rusty Swope (*Larry Fallon*), Lili Gentle (*Gloria, Teenager at Races*), Louise Beavers (*Willamay*), Irene Hervey (*Helen McGowan*), John Stephenson (*Eric McGowan*), Betty Lou Keim (*Dodie*), Warren Berlinger (*Dick Hewitt*), Diane Jergens (*Jane Hewitt*), Suzanne Luckey (*Madeleine Johnson*), James O'Rear (*Mr. Heffernan*), Gary Gray (*Freddie*), Pattee Chapman (*Erna*), Wade Dumas (*Airport Porter*), Richard Collier (*Cabdriver*), James Stone (*Pappy Smith*), Sheila James (*Teenager*), Joan Freeman (*Teenager in Malt Shop*), Gene Foley (*Soda Fountain Girl*).

Rogers' teenage daughter comes home after living with her father for a number of years, only to find that she isn't too fond of her new step-dad or step-brother. She soon grows to love her new surroundings, for the first time feeling accepted and loved. Oscar nominations went to the film's art directors, set decorators, and costume designers. Songs: "Cool It, Baby" (Leigh Harline, Carroll Coates); "Dodie" (Ralph Freed, Edmund Goulding).

p, Charles Brackett; d, Edmund Goulding; w, Walter Reisch, Charles Brackett (based on the play "Roomful of Roses" by Edith Sommer); ph, Joe MacDonald (CinemaScope); m, Leigh Harline; ed, William Mace; md, Lionel Newman; art d, Lyle R. Wheeler, Jack Martin Smith; set d, Walter M. Scott, Stuart A. Reiss; cos, Charles Le Maire, Mary Wills; makeup, Ben Nye.

Comedy/Drama   **(PR:A   MPAA:NR)**

TEEN-AGE STRANGLER zero   (1967) 61m Original Six/Ajay c

Bill A. Bloom, Jo Canterbury, John Ensign, Jim Asp, Johnny Haymer, Bill Mills.

A low-budgeter geared to the drive-in crowd which tells the tale of a high school "Bluebeard" killer who terrorizes his community. Filmed in West Virginia in 1964.

p, Clark Davis; d, Bill Posner; w, Davis; ph, Fred Singer.

Horror   **(PR:O   MPAA:NR)**

TEENAGE THUNDER*   (1957) 78M Howco bw

Charles Courtney (*Johnnie Simpson*), Melinda Byron (*Betty Palmer*), Robert Fuller (*Maurie Weston*), Tyler McVey (*Frank Simpson*), Paul Bryar (*Bert Morrison*), Helene Heigh (*Aunt Martha*), Gilbert Perkins (*Sgt. Benson*), Bing Russell (*Used Car Salesman*), Gregory Marshall (*Jimmy Morrison*), Marshall Kent (*Mr. Palmer*), Mona McKinnon (*Sis Palmer*).

Courtney works at Bryar's gas station and tries to convince his father, McVey, that hot rods are "with it." Dad thinks his kid is just another crazy teenager, until he actually takes first place in the big race. Dad proves how proud he is of junior by buying him his own set of wheels. Includes the tune "Teenage Kisses," sung by David Houston.

p, Jacques Marquette; d, Paul Helmick; w, Rudy Makoul; ph, Marquette; m, Walter Greene; ed, Irving Schoenberg; stunts, Frank Huszar.

Drama   **(PR:A   MPAA:NR)**

TEENAGE ZOMBIES zero   (1960) 73m Governor bw

Don Sullivan (*Regg*), Katherine Victor (*Dr. Myra*), Steve Conte (*Whorf*), Paul Pepper (*Skip*), Bri Murphy (*Pam*), Mitzi Albertson (*Julie*), Jay Hawk (*Morrie*), Nan Green (*Dot*), J.L.D. Morrison (*Brandt*), Mike Concannon (*Sheriff*), Chuck Miles (*Ivan*), Don Neely (*Maj. Coleman*).

Teenage water-skiers fall prey to the proverbial mad island doctor and are turned into zombies. Doesn't that sound exciting? And the doctor uses tear gas in his experiments! Not excited yet? Well, throw in a killer gorilla. If that doesn't do it take a rain check on this one.

p&d, Jerry Warren; Jacques Lecotier; ph, Allen Chandler; md, Erich Bromberg; set d, Jack Hoffner; makeup, Jean Morrison.

Horror   **Cas.**   **(PR:C   MPAA:NR)**

TEENAGERS FROM OUTER SPACE zero

(1959) 86m WB bw (GB: THE GARGON TERROR)

David Love (Derek), Dawn Anderson (Betty Morgan), Harvey B. Dunn (Grandpa Morgan), Bryan Grant (Thor), Tom Lockyear (Joe Rogers), King Moody (Captain), Helen Sage (Miss Morse), Frederic Welch (Dr. Brandt), Sonia Torgenson (Swimmer).

Tom Graeff didn't need anyone's help in turning out this piece of teenage blubber about some invading space teenagers (never trust an alien over 30) who come to Earth with the intention of world domination. One creature falls in love with an Earthling woman and blows up his nasty cohorts. The wee little microscopic budget used what appears to be cutouts of lobsters shown in shadows to represent the alien creatures.

p,d,w,ph,ed,md&spec eff, Tom Graeff.

Science Fiction   **(PR:A   MPAA:NR)**

TEENAGERS IN SPACE**½ (1975, USSR) 85m Gorki c (OTROKI VO VSELENNOI)

Misha Yershov, Sasha Grigoriev, Volodya Savin, Volodya Basov, Innokenty Smoktunovsky, Olya Bityukova.

An entertaining Soviet science fiction film which follows the escapades of a group of youngsters who travel to distant planets. A sequel to MOSCOW-CASSIOPEIA, this one has the kids freeing a race of Earthlike people who are controlled by robots.

d, Richard Viktorov; w, Avenir Zak, Isai Kuznetsov; ph, Andrei Kirillov.

Science Fiction/Children's   **(PR:AA   MPAA:NR)**

TEHERAN   (SEE: PLOT TO KILL ROOSEVELT, THE, 1948, Brit.)

TEL AVIV TAXI zero   (1957, Israel) 70m Geva-Frisch/Principal bw

Shy Ophir (The Soldier), Miriam Bergstein-Cohen (The Old Lady), Nathan Cogan (Policeman), Raphael Klatchkin (Old Man), Gilda Doorn Van Steyn (Young Wife), Azaria Rapoport (Husband), Smuel Rodensky (Boss), David Vardi (Rabbi), Joe Carl (Bank Clerk), Bat Ami (Boss's Wife), David Segal (Driver), Mina Cruvi.

An independent comedy made in Israel by 26-year-old American documentarian Frisch which has five travelers stranded when their taxi breaks down. They spend some time in an old house and tell stories in flashbacks. A technical mess with poor acting and even worse comedy. Made both in Hebrew and English versions.

p, Larry Frisch, Izhak Agadati, Mordhay Navon; d&w, Frisch; ph, Leon Nissam; m, Edmond Halpern; ed, Nellie Bagor; md, George Singer; art d, Joe Carl.

Comedy   **(PR:A   MPAA:NR)**

TELEFON***   (1977) 103m MGM/UA c

Charles Bronson (Grigori Borzov), Lee Remick (Barbara), Donald Pleasence (Nicolai Dalchimsky), Tyne Daly (Dorothy Putterman), Alan Badel (Col. Malchenko), Patrick Magee (Gen. Strelsky), Sheree North (Marie Wills), Frank Marth (Harley Sandburg), Helen Page Camp (Emma Stark), Roy Jenson (Doug Stark), Jacqueline Scott (Mrs. Hassler), Ed Bakey (Carl Hassler), John Mitchum (Harry Bascom), Iggie Wolfington (Father Stuart Diller), Kathleen O'Malley (Mrs. Maloney), Ake Lindman (Lt. Alexandrov), Ansa Konen (Dalchimsky's Mother), Hank Brandt (William Enders), John Carter (Stroller), John Hambrick (TV Newsman), Henry Alfaro (TV Reporter), Glenda Wina (TV Anchorwoman), Jim Nolan (Appliance Store Clerk), Burton Gilliam (Gas Station Attendant), Regis J. Cordic (Doctor), George Petrie (Hotel Receptionist), Jeff David (Maitre d'), Carmen Zapata (Nurse), Carl Byrd (Navy Lieutenant), Lew Brown (Petty Officer), Peter Weiss (Radar Operator), Robert Phillips, Cliff Emmich (Highway Patrolmen), Alex Sharp (Martin Callender), Margaret Hall Baron (Airport Clerk), Al Dunlap (Taxi Driver), Sean Moloney (Hot Rod Kid), Ville Veikko Salminen (Russian Steward), Teppo Heiskanen, Mika Levio (Hockey Players), Marlene Hazlett, Thomas M. Runyon, Claudia Butler, Philippe Butler (Tourist Family), Stephanie Ann Rydall, Derek Rydall (Mrs. Wills' Children).

An old line Stalinist opposed to warming U.S.-Soviet relations, KGB man Pleasence begins activating Americans brainwashed 20 years earlier to blow up U.S. defense emplacements when someone reads the Robert Frost

passage "The woods are lovely dark and deep/But I have promises to keep/And miles to go before I sleep" to them over the phone. When the Kremlin, previously unaware of the whole scheme, realizes what a series of bombings at abandoned U.S. installations means, they send crack KGB man Bronson to stop Pleasence. With him is fellow KGB agent Remick, secretly a double agent, and predictably the woman Bronson wants to run away with at the end. The ludicrous relationship between these two spies almost destroys what little credibility the story has, but director Siegel keeps their screen time to a minimum and keeps the story moving. The Russian scenes were shot in Finland, the usual Hollywood substitute for the real thing, which has served the same purpose in films from DR. ZHIVAGO and THE KREMLIN LETTER to GORKY PARK.

p, James B. Harris; d, Don Siegel; w, Peter Hyams, Stirling Silliphant (based on the novel by Walter Wager); ph, Michael Butler (Panavision, Metrocolor); m, Lalo Schifrin; ed, Douglas Stewart; prod d, Ted Haworth; art d, William F. O'Brien; set d, Robert Benton; spec eff, Joe Day; cos, Jane Robinson, Luster Bayless, Edna Taylor; stunts, Paul Baxley.

Spy Drama   **Cas.**   **(PR:C-O   MPAA:PG)**

TELEGIAN, THE   (SEE: SECRET OF THE TELEGIAN, 1961, Jap.)

TELEGRAPH TRAIL, THE*½   (1933) 60m WB-FN bw

John Wayne (John Trent), Marceline Day (Alice Ellis), Frank McHugh (Sgt. Tippy), Otis Harlan (Zeke Keller), Albert J. Smith (Gus Lynch), Yakima Canutt ("High Wolf"), Lafe McKee (Lafe, Oldtimer), Clarence Geldert (Cavalry Commander).

A weak oater, even with Wayne in the cast, which tells the tale of an Army scout who helps some western workers complete the first trancontinental wire line. Of course there's a fellow who doesn't want the telegraph completed because it'll interfere with his unscrupulous business activities. He tries to stir up the redskins against the workers, but fails when Wayne gets tough. Made on the cheap, much of the action footage is taken from the 1926 silent, THE RED RAIDERS.

p, Leon Schlesinger; d, Tenny Wright; w, Kurt Kempler; ph, Ted McCord; ed, William Clemens.

Western   **Cas.**   **(PR:A   MPAA:NR)**

TELEPHONE OPERATOR*   (1938) 61m MON bw

Judith Allen (Helen), Grant Withers (Red), Warren Hymer (Shorty), Alice White (Dottie), Pat Flaherty (Summers), Greta Granstedt (Sylvia), William Haade (Heaver), Ronnie Cosbey, Dorothy Vaughn, Cornelius Keefe.

A couple of telephone line installers fall for a pair of switchboard operators and end up spending a great deal of time with them. It's a flood that brings them together, however, with water rising high. The screenwriters must have been hard-pressed when they came up with this one. Interesting flood scenes were taken from newsreels and there are some well-done miniatures for the flooded interiors.

p, Lon Young; d, Scott Pembroke; w, Scott Darling (based on the story by John Krafft); ph, Gil Warrenton; ed, Russell Schoengarth.

Drama/Adventure   **(PR:A   MPAA:NR)**

TELEVISION SPY*½   (1939) 58m PAR bw

William Henry (Douglas Cameron), Judith Barrett (Gwen Lawson), William Collier, Sr (James Llewellyn), Richard Denning (Dick Randolph), William Eldredge (Boris), Dorothy Tree (Reni Vonich), Anthony Quinn (Forbes), Minor Watson (Burton Lawson), Morgan Conway (Carl Venner), Byron Foulger (William Sheldon), Chester Clute (Harry Payne), Wolfgang Zilzer (Frome), Olaf Hytten (Wagner), Hilda Plowright (Amelia Sheldon), Ottola Nesmith (Caroline Sheldon), Wade Boteler (Police Sergeant), Archie Twitchell [Michael Brandon] (Jim Winton), Clem Wilenchick [Crane Whitley] (Tamley), Monte Vandegrift (Grinton), Charles L. Lane (Adler), Eric Wilton (Edgar), Edward J. Le Saint (Judge), Ivan Miller (Senator), Eugene Jackson (Tommy), Major McBride (Life of Party), Pat West (Bunce), Gloria Williams (Maid).

A complex tale of espionage which has Henry developing a means by which one can send television transmissions across the continent (this was still the 1930s) and becoming the target of a group of international agents. The secret plans leave Henry's hands and end up on the other side of the globe, but eventually everything is squared away. The most interesting aspect in this prophetic story is the long-distance romance carried out between Henry and Barrett, the daughter of the scientist's former partner. The film, instead of ending on the familiar "clinch," has the lovers staring into each other's electronically transmitted eyes.

p, William Le Baron, Edward T. Lowe; d, Edward Dmytryk; w, Horace McCoy, William R. Lipman, Lillie Hayward (based on the story by Endre Bohem); ph, Harry Fischbeck; m, Boris Morros; ed, Anne Bauchens; art d, Hans Dreier, Franz Bachelin.

Spy Drama   **(PR:A   MPAA:NR)**

TELEVISION TALENT** (1937, Brit.) 56m Alexander/Ambassador bw

Richard Goolden (*Prof. Langley*), Polly Ward (*Mary Hilton*), Gene Sheldon (*Herbert Dingle*), Hal Walters (*Steve Bagley*).

Ward and Sheldon take jobs teaching at an acting school, then get their big break when the whole school goes on TV. Ward gets a better job, and Sheldon gets his big opportunity after dropping a weight on the head of a banjo player. Oh, there's a subplot about forgers, too. Despite optimistic title, nothing of interest here.

p, R. Howard Alexander; d&w, Robert Edmunds (based on a story by Alexander).

Comedy   **(PR:A   MPAA:NR)**

TELI SIROKKO   (SEE: WINTER WIND, 1970, Fr./Hung.)

TELL ENGLAND   (SEE: BATTLE OF GALLIPOLI, 1931, Brit.)

TELL IT TO A STAR**   (1945) 67m REP bw

Ruth Terry (*Carol Lambert*), Robert Livingston (*Gene Ritchie*), Alan Mowbray (*Col. Ambrose Morgan*), Franklin Pangborn (*Horace Lovelace*), Isabel Randolph (*Mrs. Arnold Whitmore*), Eddie Marr (*Billy Sheehan*), Adrian Booth (*Mona St. Clair*), Frank Orth (*Augustus T. Goodman*), Tom Dugan (*Ed Smith*), George Chandler (*Al Marx*), Mary McCarty (*Miss Dobson*), William B. Davidson (*Brannigan*), Aurora Miranda (*Specialty*).

Terry is cast as a cigarette girl with singing aspirations who tries to get bandleader Livingston to lend an ear. She doesn't have a puff of success until her uncle Mowbray shows up. He pretends to be a colonel and secures a solo for his niece. Their fraud is found out, but by then it's too late, Livingston's already fallen for her. Songs: "Tell It to a Star" (Shirley Botwin), "Love Me or Leave Me" (Gus Kahn, Walter Donaldson), "You're So Good to Me" (Sammy Cahn, Jule Styne), "A Batucada Corazon" (Ary Barroso, danced by Miranda).

p, Walter H. Goetz; d, Frank McDonald; w, John K. Butler (based on the story by Gerald Drayson Adams, John Krafft); ph, Ernest Miller; ed, Arthur Roberts; md, Lucius Croxton; ch, Aida Broadbent; spec eff, Howard Lydecker.

Musical/Romance   **(PR:A   MPAA:NR)**

TELL IT TO THE JUDGE**½   (1949) 87m COL bw

Rosalind Russell (*Marsha Meredith*), Robert Cummings (*Pete Webb*), Gig Young (*Alexander Darvac*), Marie McDonald (*Ginger Simmons*), Harry Davenport (*Judge MacKenzie Meredith*), Fay Baker (*Valerie Hobson*), Katherine Warren (*Kitty Lawton*), Douglas Dumbrille (*George Ellerby*), Clem Bevans (*Roogle*), Grandon Rhodes (*Ken Craig*), Louise Beavers (*Cleo*), Thurston Hall (*Sen. Caswell*), Jay Novello (*Gancellos*), William "Billy" Newell (*Bartender*), Polly Bailey (*Dumpy Woman*), Bill Lechner (*Elevator Boy*), Harlan Warde (*Pete's Associate*), Herbert Vigran (*Reporter*), Lee Phelps (*Police Sergeant*), Lester Dorr (*Incoming Reporter*), Dorothy Vaughn (*Another Dumpy Woman*), William Bevan (*Winston*), Steven Geray (*Francois*).

A screwball marital comedy which casts Russell as the sassy ex-wife of lawyer Cummings. Every time it seems they will reconcile, dumb blonde McDonald shows up and Cummings drops his jaw. Russell plays hard-to-get by skipping off to the Adirondacks, pretending to be married to Young. Cummings follows and before long the lovebirds are getting remarried. Well-handled and full of laughs, especially for Russell fans.

p, Buddy Adler; d, Norman Foster; w, Nat Perrin, Roland Kibbee (based on the story by Devery Freeman); ph, Joseph Walker; m, Werner R. Heymann; ed, Charles Nelson; md, Morris Stoloff; art d, Carl Anderson; set d, William Kiernan; cos, Jean Louis; makeup, Fred Phillips.

Comedy   **(PR:A   MPAA:NR)**

TELL IT TO THE MARINES   (SEE: HERE COME THE MARINES, 1952)

TELL ME A RIDDLE**½   (1980) 90m Godmother/Filmways c

Melvyn Douglas (*David*), Lila Kedrova (*Eva*), Brooke Adams (*Jeannie*), Lili Valenty (*Mrs. Mays*), Dolores Dorn (*Vivi*), Bob Elross (*Sammy*), Jon Harris (*Mathew*), Zalman King (*Paul*), Winifred Mann (*Hannah*), Peter Owens (*Phil*), Deborah Sussel (*Nancy*), Nora Heflin (*Young Eva*), Peter Coyote (*Young David*), Nora Bendich (*Lisa*).

Kedrova is an aging woman on her deathbed after a 40-year marriage to Douglas, in which neither felt fulfilled. She is unaware that she is terminally ill, but her family persuades her to go on a vacation and visit granddaughter Adams in San Francisco. She realizes many of the things she missed in life. Before dying, she and Douglas reconcile. Directed by Lee Grant in her debut at the helm, and it is a fine job. In a bit part is Peter Coyote as the young Douglas. After adding a couple of years he went on to appear in E.T. and STRANGERS KISS.

p, Mindy Affrime, Rachel Lyon, Susan O'Connell; d, Lee Grant; w, Joyce Eliason, Alev Lytle (based on the novella by Tillie Olsen); ph, Fred Murphy (CFI Color); m, Sheldon Shkolnik; ed, Suzanne Pettit; prod d, Patrizia von Brandenstein.

Drama   **Cas.**   **(PR:A   MPAA:PG)**

TELL ME IN THE SUNLIGHT**   (1967) 82m BRIT/Movie-Rama bw

Steve Cochran (*Dave*), Shary Marshall (*Julie*), Jay Robinson (*Barber*), Dave Bondu (*Alex*), Patricia Wolf (*Chata*), George Hopkins (*Tony*), Rockne Tarkington (*Rocky*), Harry Franklin (*Dr. Franklin*), Hamish MacKay (*Airport Attendant*), Lucille (*Princess Naga*), George Roberts (*Pickpocket*), Jill Walden (*Carol, the Girl in Park*), Oliver Nissick (*Pepe*), Joe Hardy (*Driver*).

Cochran is a merchant seaman who falls in love with stripper Marshall while on shore leave in Nassau. She's got someone else, but after temporarily splitting the pair find their mutual attraction too strong to resist. Made in 1964 under Cochran's direction, the film originally ran over two hours but was cut after Cochran's death aboard his boat in 1965.

p&d, Steve Cochran; w, Cochran, Jo Heims (based on the story by Robert Stevens); ph, Rod Yould; m, Michael Andersen; ed, David Woods; art d, Jerry Sjolander; m/l, title song, Cochran, Franz Steininger, Jack Ackerman (sung by Darlene Paul).

Romance   **(PR:C-O   MPAA:NR)**

TELL ME LIES**   (1968, Brit.) 118m Ronorus/CD bw-c

Mark Jones (*Mark*), Pauline Munro (*Pauline*), Robert Lloyd (*Bob*), Eric Allan, Jeremy Anthony, Noel Collins, John Hussey, Marjie Lawrence, Leon Lissek, Clifford Rose, Hugh Sullivan, Henry Woolf, Mary Allen, Hugh Armstrong, Ian Hogg, Glenda Jackson, Joanne Lindsay, Ursula Mohan, Morgan Sheppard, Barry Stanton, Michael Williams, Kingsley Amis, James Cameron, Peggy Ashcroft, Stokeley Carmichael, Tom Driberg, Reginald Paget, Jacqueline Porcher, Ivor Richards, Hilary Rose, Steven Rose, Paul Scofield, Patrick Wymark, Peregrine Worsthorne.

Pretentious experimental drivel has London actors Jones, Munro, and Lloyd obsessed by a photo of a wounded Vietnamese child and determined to come to some sort of understanding about the whole thing. After attending a series of discussions, including one with black activist Stokeley Carmichael, and putting on a series of skits reenacting various events of the war, they come to the realization they can't understand anything. At one point, one of the characters asks, "How long can you look at this before you lose interest?" The answer is considerably under 118 minutes. Famed theatrical director Brook had some powerful talent at his service here, including many members of Britain's Royal Shakespeare Company. Writer Amis, known for screen comedies such as TAKE A GIRL LIKE YOU (1970) and LUCKY JIM (1957), (from his brilliant comic novel) makes a brief appearance.

p&d, Peter Brook; w, Denis Cannan, Michael Kustow, Michael Scott (based on Cannan's play "US"); ph, Ian Wilson (Eastmancolor); m, Richard Peaslee; ed, Ralph Sheldon; md, Michael Reeves; prod d, Sally Jacobs; m/l, Peaslee, Adrian Mitchell.

Drama   **(PR:O   MPAA:NR)**

TELL ME THAT YOU LOVE ME, JUNIE MOON**
                              (1970) 112m PAR c

Liza Minnelli (*Junie Moon*), Ken Howard (*Arthur*), Robert Moore (*Warren*), James Coco (*Mario*), Kay Thompson (*Miss Gregory*), Fred Williamson (*Beach Boy*), Ben Piazza (*Jesse*), Emily Yancy (*Solana*), Leonard Frey (*Guiles*), Clarisse Taylor (*Minnie*), James Beard (*Sidney Wyner*), Julie Bovasso (*Ramona*), Gina Collens (*Lila*), Barbara Logan (*Mother Moon*), Nancy Marchand (*Nurse Oxford*), Lynn Milgrim (*Nurse Holt*), Ric O. Feldman (*Joebee*), James D. Pasternak (*Artist*), Angelique Pettyjohn (*Melissa*), Anne Revere (*Miss Farber*), Elaine Shore (*Mrs. Wyner*), Guy Sorel (*Dr. Gaines*), Wayne Tippett (*Dr. Miller*), Pete Seeger, Pacific Gas & Electric (*Themselves*), Ulla Bomser, Cynthia Korman, Anne Larson.

Earnest attempt at a comedy/drama about a scarred young woman, a paraplegic homosexual, and an apparent epileptic who decide to throw in their lots together. Sound like fun? It wasn't. Minnelli's face has been badly scarred by Piazza, an ex-boy friend who threw acid at her when she laughed at him for wanting her to undress and make love in a cemetery. Moore was shot in a hunting accident when he made a pass at a friend and now he must spend his life in a wheelchair. Howard was thought to be retarded but it turns out to be an unnamed disease that most closely resembles epilepsy. When the trio meet in a hospital and are released at the same time, they decide to move in together and draw help from each other. Thompson is a wealthy eccentric who rents them a house and Howard gets a job working at a fish market run by Coco. Everything seems to be going along well until Thompson invites her tenants to dinner. In the middle of the evening, she makes Moore an offer. If he is willing to give up his paralysis (Thompson thinks everything is mental) and get up out of his wheelchair and walk, she'll give him a valuable jeweled cross. Naturally, Moore can't walk and Thompson is disappointed in his lack of ability. When Coco gets a call from someone saying that Howard is gay (the caller figures that he must be if he is living with Moore, who is obviously that way), he fires Howard, albeit reluctantly. The three are despondent so the kindly Coco lends them the needed money to take a short holiday at a resort by the sea. Coco has fallen in love with Minnelli and will do anything for her. At the resort, Moore gets around on the back of the social director, Williamson, and later has his first heterosexual experience with Williamson's girl friend, Yancy. Howard declares his love for Minnelli but she fears men since her scarring and keeps him away. He continues his wooing of her and she finally acquiesces. No sooner do they make love than Howard's health begins to deteriorate. He eventually dies of this unnamed ailment in Minnelli's arms and his funeral is attended by only she, Moore, and Coco. To his credit, Preminger never presented these people in a grotesque fashion. There was every attempt to show them as slightly quirky, a trifle neurotic, but striving for normal lives. Howard had been discovered while playing in the Broadway musical "1776." He'd worked before with Moore, who directed "Promises, Promises" for the stage as well as "The Boys in the Band." Moore wanted to work as an actor so he could learn the film medium for his directorial career. Preminger auditioned him and Moore was given the role and did well with it. He later directed Neil Simon plays, then the Simon movie MURDER BY DEATH, THE CHEAP DETECTIVE, and others before dying of AIDS-related complications in 1985. It was while this movie was being shot that Minnelli's mother, Judy Garland, died in Chelsea, London, and the strain on the young actress was enormous and may have even contributed to her excellent portrayal of an emotionally immature woman. After shooting in a New England cemetery, Preminger was sued by a few people who claimed that he had desecrated their relatives' graves. Since Preminger had obtained permission, rather than settle the nuisance suits, he went to court, fought the cases, and won. Songs in the movie include: "Elvira" (written and sung by Pacific Gas And Electric), "Old Devil Time" (written and sung by Pete Seeger), "The Rake," "Work Your Own Show" (Estelle Levitt, Philip Springer). The movie was expensive to do because of several locations, including The Kona Kai hotel on Shelter Island near San Diego, Sequoia National Park, and towns in Massachusetts including Salem, Manchester, Rockport, and Magnolia. Costume design by Talsky, et al, was superior. The movie waffled between comedy and drama and failed to take a stand in either camp, thus causing audiences to be confused and stay away.

p&d, Otto Preminger; w, Marjorie Kellogg (based on her novel); ph, Boris Kaufman (Technicolor); m, Philip Springer, Johann Sebastian Bach; ed, Henry Berman, Dean O. Ball; md, Thomas Z. Shepard; prod d, Lyle Wheeler; set d, Morris Hoffman; cos, Ronald Talsky, Phyllis Garr, Halston; makeup, Charles Schram.

Drama/Comedy   **(PR:A-C   MPAA:GP)**

TELL NO TALES**   (1939) 68m MGM bw

Melvyn Douglas (*Mike Cassidy*), Louise Platt (*Ellen Frazier*), Gene Lockhart (*Arne*), Douglas Dumbrille (*Matt Cooper*), Florence George (*Lorna Travers*), Zeffie Tilbury (*Miss Mary*), Halliwell Hobbes (*Dr. Lovelake*), Harlan Briggs (*Dave Bryant*), Joseph Crehan (*Chalmers*), Addison Richards (*Hollis*), Jean Fenwick (*Mrs. Lovell*), Esther Dale (*Mrs. Haskins*), Gladys Blake (*Myra Haskins*), Hobart Cavanaugh (*Charlie Daggett*), Theresa Harris (*Ruby*), Ernest Whitman (*Elab Giffin*), Mary Gordon (*Mrs. Bryant*), Ray Walker (*Dell*), Ernie Alexander (*Johnson*), Jack Carlton (*Wilson*), Thomas Jackson (*Eddie*), Tom Collins (*Phil Arno*), Oscar O'Shea (*Sam O'Neil*), Frank Orth (*Vic the Bartender*), Roger Imhof (*Taxi Driver*), Claire Dubrey (*Miss Arnold*), Chester Clute (*Manders*), Renie Riano (*Swedish Maid*), Charles D. Brown (*Lt. Brandon*), Norman Willis (*Meves*), Anthony Warde (*Lewis*), Ian Wolfe (*Fritz*), George Noisom (*Office Boy*), E. Alyn Warren (*Janitor*), Pat Flaherty (*Printer*), Fred Kelsey, James C. Morton, Jack Daley, Lee Phelps, Monte Vandergrift (*Cops*), Hilda Haywood, Bess Flowers (*Teachers*), Harry Depp (*Robert E. More*), James Flavin (*Simmons*), Gertrude Sutton (*Gertrude*), Harry Tyler (*Man on Bus*), Brandon Hurst (*Butler*), Everett Brown (*Black Doorman*), Mantan Moreland (*Sporty Black*), Mme. Sul-te-wan (*Alley Cat's Mother*), Florence O'Brien (*Belle*), Rosalie Lincoln (*Girl*), Ruby Elsy (*Woman in Chair*), Thad Jones (*Preacher*), Ben Carter (*Politician*), Phil Tead (*Marty*), James G. Blaine (*Capt. Hendry*), Gladden James (*Male Secretary*), Nick Copeland (*Attendant*), Claire Rochelle (*Girl at Phone*), Ward Wing (*Kammy*), George Magrill (*Alex*), Ben Taggart (*Lieutenant*), John Marlowe (*Pianist*), Heinie Conklin, Billy Engle (*Tramp Comics*), Joseph E. Bernard (*Man*), Sara Haden (*Miss Brandan*).

An episodic tale which casts Douglas as a newspaper editor trying to keep the presses from shutting down on his failing daily. He gets the scoop on a kidnaping case and, after a series of vignettes, eventually winds up falling in the gang's clutches. He saves his skin by crushing the crooks and in the process keeps the ink flowing. Fenton's first feature after directing scores of CRIME DOES NOT PAY shorts.

p, Edward Chodorov; d, Leslie Fenton; w, Lionel Houser (based on the story by Pauline London, Alfred Taylor); ph, Joseph Ruttenberg; m, William Axt; ed, W. Donn Hayes; art d, Cedric Gibbons.

Crime Drama   **(PR:A   MPAA:NR)**

TELL-TALE HEART, THE, 1934   (SEE: BUCKET OF BLOOD, 1934, Brit.)

TELL-TALE HEART, THE**½   (1962, Brit.) 78m
Danziger/Brigadier-Union bw (AKA: THE HIDDEN ROOM OF 1,000 HORRORS)

Laurence Payne (*Edgar Marsh*), Adrienne Corri (*Betty Clare*), Dermot Walsh (*Carl Loomis*), Selma Vaz Dias (*Mrs. Vine*), John Scott (*Inspector*), John Martin (*Police Sergeant*), Annette Carell (*Carl's Landlady*), David Lander (*Jeweler*), Rosemary Rotheray (*Jackie*), Suzanne Fuller (*Dorothy*), Yvonne Buckingham (*Mina*), Richard Bennett (*Mike*), Elizabeth Paget (*Elsie*), Frank Thornton (*Barman*), Joan Peart (*Street Girl*), Nada Beall (*Old Crone*), Graham Ashley (*Neston*), Pamela Plant (*Manageress*), Patsy Smart (*Mrs. Marlow*), Brian Cobby (*Young Man*), Madeline Leon (*Young Woman*), David Courtney.

This version of the creepy Poe tale puts Payne in the role of the dreamy author Marsh who fantasizes that he falls in love with Corri and kills his best friend, Walsh, over her. He hides the body under the floor but can still hear the heart beating. Cutting the heart from the corpse, he buries it in the woods. He awakens from his dream to find Corri moving in next door to him.

p, Edward J. Danziger, Harry Lee Danziger; d, Ernest Morris; w, Brian Clemens, Eldon Howard (based on the story by Edgar Allan Poe); ph, James Wilson; m, Tony Crombie, Bill Le Sage; ed, Derek Parsons; art d, Norman Arnold; set d, Peter Russell.

Horror   **(PR:O   MPAA:NR)**

TELL THEM WILLIE BOY IS HERE***½   (1969) 97m UNIV c

Robert Redford (*Christopher Cooper*), Katharine Ross (*Lola*), Robert Blake (*Willie Boy*), Susan Clark (*Liz Arnold*), Barry Sullivan (*Ray Calvert*), John Vernon (*Hacker*), Charles Aidman (*Benby*), Charles McGraw (*Frank Wilson*), Shelly Novack (*Finney*), Robert Lipton (*Newcombe*), Lloyd Gough (*Dexter*), Ned Romero (*Tom*), John Wheeler (*Newman*), Erik Holland (*Digger*), Garry Walberg (*Dr. Mills*), Jerry Velasco (*Chino*), George Tyne (*Le Marie*), Lee De Broux (*Meathead*), Wayne Sutherlin (*Harry*), Jerome Raphel (*Salesman*), Lou Frizzell (*Station Agent*), John Day (*Sam Wood*), Steve Shemayne (*Johnny Hyde*), John Hudkins (*3rd Man*), Mikel Angel (*Old Mike*), Everett Creach (*Fake Indian*), Johnny Coons (*Clerk*), Stanley Torres (*1st Committee Man*), Kenneth Holzman, Joseph C. Mandel (*Reporters*), Spencer Lyons (*Cody*), Robert Du Laine (*1st Escort*).

A powerful drama masquerading as a western that promises slightly more than it is able to deliver. It's 1909 in Banning, California, and Blake, a Paiute Indian, has been in the white man's world for a while and is now coming home to the reservation on which he grew up. There's a two fold reason for his return; he'd like to see all his old friends and what remains of his family and he would also enjoy rekindling the love he had for Ross. In the past, Ross' father, Angel, had opposed their relationship and now Blake wants to see if he can bypass the parental permission. There's a huge Indian party to celebrate tribal unity and Blake makes a late date with Ross to meet after midnight. When Angel finds that Blake is still interested in Ross, he makes no secret of his hatred for Blake and says he will shoot the youth if he insists on seeing Ross. Clark is an East Coast aristocrat who is the physician attached to the Indian reservation. She is also the superintendent and treats the tribe in a patronizing fashion. That same attitude is applied to Redford, a lawman who comes by. Even though she finds Redford interesting and stirring to her loins, she is also somewhat repulsed by his manners and his lack of Bostonian couth. Since she is a doctor and he is but a pistol-packing sheriff, she finds him far below her aristocratic level, yet the attraction is there. At night, Ross and Blake have their rendezvous in the woods and their sexual coupling is halted when Angel and his sons arrive. There's a battle and Angel is killed by Blake, acting in self-defense. With Angel dead, Ross automatically becomes Blake's "woman" according to this tribe's beliefs. But the crime is murder and Clark tells Redford that he must capture the Indian. Blake and Ross leave immediately and a chase begins. Redford enlists the aid of local rancher Sullivan, who loves the idea of stalking an Indian. Cowhand Lipton and a few others make up the bloodthirsty group who equate Indian hunting with shooting deer. Redford has no axe to grind against Blake and would like to get out of this assignment but he is carried along by the tide of sentiment in the area that demands an eye for an eye. Blake and Ross know the territory better than their pursuers and are able to elude the posse in the wilderness. Redford finally gives up and says that he is taking a job as personal security for President Taft (who was eventually shot), but Sullivan and the others continue chasing the couple. Blake shoots the posse's horses and wounds Sullivan. Then the small town is worried that all of the local Indians will revolt. Add that to the assassination attempt on the President and Redford must return to chasing Blake and Ross, as distasteful as it is to him. Ross is so tired she can no longer continue so she asks to be left behind rather than cause Blake's escape to be thwarted. Her dead body is found the following day and no one knows if she shot herself or if Blake shot her. The chase continues and gets down to a duel between Blake and Redford. Blake knows that Redford is only doing his job and bears him no personal grudge. The men face each other. Blake holds up his rifle but doesn't fire. Redford shoots first and kills Blake, then learns that there was no ammunition in the rifle. He is disgusted by the needless loss of life and requests that Blake be given his tribe's traditional funeral for a chief.

Although the picture is nominally about Blake's character, it is Redford who is the focus as he goes through many changes in emotion and desire, trying to come to terms with what he must do. The entire history of the white man versus the native American is shown in microcosm and too many sociological points are made, so the action is downplayed in favor of the preaching. It was 21 years since writer-director Polonsky's last movie, FORCE OF EVIL. He'd been trapped in the McCarthy "witch hunt" and forced to go underground in order to make his living. Polonsky ghost-wrote many scripts (which he will not reveal) and didn't officially surface until MADIGAN in 1967. WILLIE BOY is beautifully lensed by Hall, and Polonsky took the time to allow the actors to have their moments. Despite this, the movie was not a success, perhaps due to the manner in which the studio held it, then sent it out in a less than tub-thumping fashion. It was completed before BUTCH CASSIDY AND THE SUNDANCE KID but released after DOWNHILL RACER so Redford fans had three different movies to see him in during 1969. Polonsky gave the Indians some literate dialog to speak, perhaps too literate. And Blake, who was a contract player at Universal, was a mistake in the role. He looked right for the part (you may recall that he played "Little Beaver" in the "Red Ryder" movies and was also seen as the young Mexican boy who sold Bogart and the others their winning lottery ticket in THE TREASURE OF THE SIERRA MADRE) but his New Jersey manner of speech shone through. TELL THEM WILLIE BOY IS HERE was shot in Thousand Oaks, California, with the help of the Indian tribes of the Morongo, Pechanga, Los Coyotes, Agua Caliente, Soboba, and Torrez-Martinez peoples. The major problem with the film was that it seemed to be studied, arty, and filled with Polonsky's personal desire to appear meaningful in his return to direction. Nevertheless, it should have had more success than it did. Californians will recognize the Indian tribe named "Morongo" because, as one drives from Los Angeles to Palm Springs, right through the Banning area where this film is set, one of the biggest, brightest neon signs along the highway announces "Morongo Indian Bingo." The tribe has a huge building in which it regularly holds enormous Bingo games with prizes in the thousands of dollars. Although Bingo is outlawed as a commercial enterprise in California, that statute does not include playing the game to raise funds for religious institutions nor if the group running the game is an accredited Indian tribe.

p, Philip A. Waxman; d&w, Abraham Polonsky (based on the book Willie Boy...A Desert Manhunt by Harry Lawton); ph, Conrad Hall (Panavision, Technicolor); m, Dave Grusin; ed, Melvin Shapiro; md, Stanley Wilson; art d, Alexander Golitzen, Henry Bumstead; set d, John McCarthy, Ruby Levitt; cos, Edith Head; stunts, John Daheim; makeup, Bud Westmore.

DRAMA   Cas.   (PR:C   MPAA:M)

TELL YOUR CHILDREN   (SEE: REEFER MADNESS, 1936)

TEMPEST**½   (1932, Ger.) 80m UFA/Leo Brecher bw (STURME DER
                                                                     LEIDENSCHAFT)

Emil Jannings (Gustav Bumke), Anna Sten (Annya), Franz Nicklisch (Willy Prawanzke), Anton Pointner (Ralph Kruschewski, Photographer), Otto Wernicke (Police Commissioner), Trude Hesterberg (Yvonne), Julius Falkenstein (Paul).

Jannings turns in an awesome performance as the successful Bumke, who is brought down through his association with the cold-hearted Sten. When he discovers that she has a lover, he commits murder and then forces himself upon the girl after nearly killing her. The next day, after buttering up to Jannings, Sten informs the police of his crime. A fine job of direction from Siodmak even if the picture is a bit long. Once again Erich Pommer kept a watchful eye over his UFA product.

p, Erich Pommer; d, Robert Siodmak; w, Robert Liebmann, Hans Mueller; ph, Gunther Rittau; m, Friedrich [Frederick] Hollander; ed, Victor Gertler.

Drama   (PR:C   MPAA:NR)

TEMPEST***½   (1958, Ital./Yugo./Fr.) 125m DD-Bosna-Gray/PAR c
                                                                     (AKA: THE TEMPEST)

Silvana Mangano (Masha), Van Heflin (Pugacev), Viveca Lindfors (Catherine II), Geoffrey Horne (Peter Griniev), Robert Keith (Capt. Miranov), Agnes Moorehead (Vassilissa), Oscar Homolka (Savelic), Helmut Dantine (Svabrin), Vittorio Gassman (Prosecutor), Fulvia Franco (Palaska), Finlay Currie (Count Griniev), Laurence Naismith (Maj. Zurin), Aldo Silvani (Pope Gerasim), Nevenka Mikulic (Akulina), Milivoi Zivanovic (Suvorov), Javon Gec (Capt. Dimitri), Niksa Stefanini (Beloborodov), Janez Vrhovec (Sakolov), Claudio Gora (Minister), Maria Cristina Gajoni (Girl), Milivoje Pepovic Mavid (Pugacev Chief), Milutin Jasnik (Bashir Prisoner), Guido Celano (Peasant), Marija Crnobori (Woman on Cart), Tonio Selwart, Dragutin Felba, Pera Obradovic, Mirdo Sreckovic.

An international cast in an exciting adaptation of historical facts as novelized by Pushkin. Horne is an officer who is being punished and sent to the outmost reaches of Russia. He is accompanied by Homolka, his valet and old family retainer. The two men are trekking across the frozen wastes and save the life of Heflin, a Cossack who would have turned into an icicle had they not come in this direction. Heflin later rallies a group of peasants and assumes the identity of the mentally retarded son of Peter the Great, who had been assassinated and disposed of years before. Horne arrives at the fort where he is to be stationed and falls for the commander's daughter, Mangano, but her father, Keith, is not thrilled about Horne's attentions. Nor is Dantine, a traitorous officer who'd hoped to win her hand. Heflin's troops capture the fort and Keith, as a loyalist, is hanged. But since Horne had saved Heflin's life, he spares Horne and Mangano. Horne goes to St. Petersburg and tries to get the High Command to attack the fort but evokes no interest. Further, they wonder how it was that he was spared and think that Horne may be in league with Heflin. Mangano is still being held in the fort and Horne goes back there to save her. By leaving St. Petersburg, he is tagged a deserter. Heflin's men capture Horne but the old debt still hangs over Heflin's head and he realizes that Horne and Mangano are in love so he orders them to be married. Heflin's men are defeated in a huge battle and he and Horne are captured by the forces of the empress, Lindfors. Horne and Heflin are both scheduled to be executed for treason. Mangano attends a palace ball and makes a direct appeal to Lindfors to spare Horne's life. The empress goes to the prison to meet her enemy, Heflin, and she asks if Horne is or isn't a traitor. Heflin assures her that Horne is a loyalist and had no part of the rebellion. Satisfied, Lindfors saves Horne while Heflin loses his head as the lovers are united and the picture concludes. As you can tell by the synopsis, this had nothing whatsoever to do with Shakespeare's play. It was adapted from two Pushkin novels, each of which had some basis in history, although liberties were taken to make the stories meld and be dramatically viable. Shot in Yugoslavia (where the country allowed their soldiers to be used in part payment for distribution rights), France, and Italy, it is a spectacular film and one of the best ever about life in Russia in pre-Soviet times. Many of the same technicians were used who had worked on WAR AND PEACE and their attention to detail makes this a visual delight. A palace at Caserta was used to simulate St. Petersburg and it looked quite authentic, probably because many of the men who designed the Russian royal buildings were, in fact, Italian. Good performances by everyone and a special acknowledgement to Heflin, who was superb in a highly complex role. The sweep of the battle scenes is vast and they often look as good as Altdorfer's famous painting that hangs in Munich's art museum. The love story between Mangano and Horne is a standard sidebar tale and adds nothing to the immensity of the film. Gassman does a small bit as the crown's prosecutor (he later appeared in Paul Mazursky's TEMPEST (1982)) and the rest of the cast comes from the U.S., England, Italy, Yugoslavia and, judging from their names, just about every other country in Eastern Europe. An artistic saga that looked as if it cost $100 million but actually came in for $98 million less than that. De Laurentiis sure knows how to stretch the lira.

p, Dino De Laurentiis; d, Alberto Lattuada; w, Louis Peterson, Lattuada, Ivo Perilli (based on The Captain's Daughter and The Revolt of Pugacev by Alexander Pushkin); ph, Aldo Tonti (Technirama, Technicolor); m, Piero Piccioni; ed, Henry Rust, Otello Colangeli; md, Franco Ferrari; art d, Mario Chiari; cos, Maria De Matteis.

Historical Adventure   (PR:C   MPAA:NR)

TEMPEST**   (1982) 140m COL c

John Cassavetes (Phillip), Gena Rowlands (Antonia), Susan Sarandon (Aretha), Vittorio Gassman (Alonzo), Raul Julia (Kalibanos), Molly Ringwald (Miranda), Sam Robards (Freddy), Paul Stewart (Phillip's Father), Jackie Gayle (Trinc), Anthony Holland (Sebastian), Jerry Hardin (Harry Gondorf), Lucianne Buchanan (Dolores), Vassilis Glezakos (Greek Boat Captain), Sergio Nicolai, Luigi Laezza (Sailors), Paul Mazursky (Terry Bloomfield), Betsy Mazursky (Betsy Bloomfield), Carol Ficatier (Gabrielle), Peter Lombard (Mackenzie), Fred Pasternack (Doctor), Nadine Darling, Nina Kolment (Nurses), Cynthia Harris (Cynthia), Paul Hecht (Paul), Mark Soper (Mark), Murray Grand (Piano Player), John Marolakos (New York Cafe Owner), George Moscaidis (Athens Cafe Owner), Camille Lefko (Guard), Jerry Hewitt (Stuntman), Barry Mitchell (Woody Allen Lookalike), Al Cerullo (Pilot), Sheila Ozden (Belly Dancer), Nicos Mousoullis (Deck Hand), Evanthia Glezakou (Old Woman), Clint Chin (Steward), Stella Nastou (Secretary), Rudy Cherney (Man with Pigeons), Thanasis Pagonis (Waiter).

Disappointing modernistic fantasy-drama that used Shakespeare's comedy as a jumping-off point and then went off into never-never land. Cassavetes is a fiercely independent architect married to Rowlands, an actress. They have a nubile daughter in Ringwald (making her debut) and a neurotic relationship between them. Cassavetes owes a great deal of money to casino boss Gassman and he hates his life in New York so he takes Ringwald to Greece where he meets Sarandon, a singer who lives from hand to mouth as she roams the world. The three move to a bleak Greek island where they encounter Julia, a hermit living on the goats that are his only company. The movie goes into fantasy and everyone in Cassavetes' life (Rowlands, Gassman, Gassman's son (Robards), and Rowlands' producer (Mazursky)) as well as a few others lands on the island when their boat is shipwrecked. The relationship between Cassavetes and Sarandon is celibate so the eventual reconciliation with Rowlands is to be expected. The picture roams all over the place emotionally and never settles into being much of anything. A few funny moments but the whole idea is pretentious, filled with intellectuality that escapes everyone and, in the end, it is a bust. It cost about $13 million and looks excellent. The man who had his eye to the camera was Australian McAlpine and he gave it better treatment than it deserved. Comedian

Jackie Gayle makes an appearance and shows that he's not just another funny face. The best part of the movie is the storm sequence but audiences could get the same effect by watching Midwest tornadoes on the TV news. It goes a long way around to show that having a mid-life crisis is tough.

p&d, Paul Mazursky; w, Mazursky, Leon Capetanos (based on the play "The Tempest" by William Shakespeare); ph, Donald McAlpine (Metrocolor); m, Stomu Yamashta; ed, Donn Cambern; prod d, Pato Guzman; art d, Paul Eads, Gianni Quaranta; set d, Paul Hefferan, Giorgio Desideri; cos, Albert Wolsky; spec eff, Bran Ferren; ch, Gino Landi.

Comedy/Drama **Cas.** **(PR:C-O MPAA:PG)**

TEMPLE DRAKE (SEE: STORY OF TEMPLE DRAKE, 1933)

TEMPLE TOWER*½ (1930) 58m FOX bw

Kenneth MacKenna (*Capt. Hugh "Bulldog" Drummond*), Marceline Day (*Patricia Verney*), Henry B. Walthall (*Blackton*), Cyril Chadwick (*Peter Darrell*), Peter Gawthorne (*Matthews*), Ivan Linow (*Gaspard*), A.B. Lane (*The Nightingale*), Yorke Sherwood (*Constable Muggins*).

MacKenna stars in this sequel to BULLDOG DRUMMOND, but he lacks the verve of his predecessor, Ronald Colman, whose 1929 BULLDOG DRUMMOND was one of his most successful pictures. When MacKenna discovers that a gang of crooks is hiding out in a neighborhood house he sneaks in and scouts around. After a maze of secret passages and tunnels, he finally captures the crooks. (See BULLDOG DRUMMOND series, Index.)

d, Donald Gallagher; w, Llewellyn Hughes (based on the character created by Herman Cyril McNeile); ph, Charles G. Clarke; ed, Clyde Carruth.

Mystery **(PR:A MPAA:NR)**

TEMPO DI MASSACRO (SEE: BRUTE AND THE BEAST, THE, 1968, Ital.)

TEMPORARY WIDOW, THE** (1930, Ger./Brit.) 84m UFA/Wardour bw

Lilian Harvey (*Kitty Kellermann*), Laurence Olivier (*Peter Bille*), Felix Aylmer (*Public Prosecutor*), Frederick Lloyd (*Counsel for the Defense*), Athole Stewart (*President of the Court of Justice*), Fritz Schmuck (*Councillor Hartmann*), Henry Caine (*Councillor Lindberg*), Rene Hubert (*Witness Loiret*), Frank Stanmore (*Witness Kulicke*), Gillian Dean (*Witness Anny Sedal*), Norman Williams (*Auctioneer Kuhnen*), Stanley Lathbury (*Valet John*), Johannes Roth (*Master Mailor*), John Payne (*Old Usher*), Erich Kestin (*Young Usher*), Adolf Schroder (*Soldier*), Danchell E. Hambro (*Foreman of the Jury*), Ida Teater (*Female Juror*), Oswald Skilbeck (*1st Juror*).

This simple German comedy would probably have been completely forgotten had it not had the distinction of being the film in which Olivier made his cinematic debut. Harvey is married to Olivier, a painter who creates futuristic works. His career is going nowhere when suddenly he "drowns" in a boating accident. Harvey is accused of his murder and goes against a jury on the charges. Finally a man confesses to the crime and all charges are cleared. While Harvey dines with her lawyers to celebrate her exoneration, Olivier turns up. He was the confessed murderer, also the putative victim, and now, having shaved his beard, he no longer needs to be missing. He and Harvey had concocted the entire scheme in order to make Olivier a name–and thus sell his paintings. Two versions of this film were simultaneously made by the famed Universum Film Aktiengesellschaft (UFA) studios of Germany, a common practice of the day. One version, in German, featured Willy Fritsch in Olivier's role. Oscar Homolka played a part in the German-language version. This English-language version plays like what it is: a standard programmer. Harvey played the same role in both films and does a good job here, as does Olivier. But the story is slight and one that has an easily predictable outcome. Critics of the day had mixed reactions to the film but most agreed that Olivier was a talented actor with a good future ahead of him. A section of the film was later seen in the compilation film ELSTREE STORY in 1952.

p, Erich Pommer; d, Gustav Ucicky; w, Karl Hartl, Walter Reisch, Benn Levy (based on the play "Hokuspokus" by Curt Goetz); ph, Carl Hoffman, Werner Brandes; prod d, Rohrig and Herlth.

Mystery **(PR:C MPAA:NR)**

TEMPTATION*½ (1935, Brit.) 77m Milofilm/GAU bw

Frances Day (*Antonia Palmay*), Stewart Rome (*Paul Palmay*), Anthony Hankey (*William Parker*), Peggy Simpson (*Piri*), Mickey Brantford (*Johnny*), Lucy Beaumont (*Headmistress*), Billy Watts (*Gus*), C. Denier Warren (*Director*), Effie Atherton (*Vera Hanka*), Molly Hamley-Clifford (*Maresa*), Alfred Rode and His Tzigane Orchestra.

Jealousies flare during the fifth wedding anniversary celebration for Day and Rome when she toys with the idea of returning to the stage. Rome gets angry and runs off, but after some confusion about her being seen with her niece's beau, he returns and everything is resolved. Set in Budapest.

d&w, Max Neufeld (based on the play "Antonia" by Melchior Lengyel).;

Musical Comedy **(PR:A MPAA:NR)**

TEMPTATION** (1936) ??m Micheaux bw

Alfred "Slick" Chester, Ethel Moses, Andrew S. Bishop, Pope Sisters, Bobby Hargreaves and His Kit Kat Club Orchestra, Lillian Fitzgerald, Dot and Dash (*Tap Dancers*), Lorenzo Tucker, Hilda Rogers, Bea Freeman, Taft Rice, Raymond Kallund, Six Sizzlers Orchestra, Larry Seymore.

Moses stars as a model who gets involved with some shady characters and tries her best to go straight. She gets some support from Chester and Bishop and finally finds safety. TEMPTATION stars "The Colored Cagney," Slick Chester; "The Black Valentino," Lorenzo Tucker; "The Negro Harlow", Ethel Moses, and "The Sepia Mae West," Bea Freeman.

d, Oscar Micheaux.;

Drama **(PR:A MPAA:NR)**

TEMPTATION** (1946) 92m International/UNIV bw

Merle Oberon (*Ruby*), George Brent (*Nigel*), Charles Korvin (*Bareudi*), Paul Lukas (*Isaacson*), Lenore Ulric (*Marie*), Arnold Moss (*Ahmed*), Ludwig Stossel (*Dr. Mueller*), Gavin Muir (*Smith-Barrington*), Ilka Gruning (*Frau Mueller*), Robert Capa (*Hamza*), John Eldredge (*Don Gibbs*), Andre Charlot (*Prof. Dupont*), Suzanne Cloutier (*Yvonne Dupont*), Gloria Lloyd (*Jean McCormick*), Mary Young (*Mrs. McCormick*), Aubrey Mather (*Dr. Harding*), Samir Rizkallah (*Abdullah*), Egon Brecher (*Ibrahim*), Reginald Sheffield (*Wickersham*), Fred Essler (*Pepito*), George Humbert (*Mustapha Pasha*), George Carleton (*Mr. McCormick*), Tom Stevenson (*Photographer*), Eddie Abdo (*Egyptian Policeman*), Rouhia Bey (*Oriental Dancer*), Lane Watson (*Guest*), Nick Thompson (*Native Waiter*), George David (*Conductor*), Bobby Hale (*Coachman*), Jean Ransome (*Receptionist*).

Oberon leaves her Egyptologist husband Brent for the more attentive rogue Korvin, but soon realizes that she'd rather play wife than lover. She doesn't come upon this revelation until Korvin, who is financially strapped, comes up with a plot to kill Brent and live off his inheritance. She isn't fond of the idea and kills Korvin instead, doing the same to herself shortly afterwards. The last picture made by International before it joined forces with Universal. A remake of a 1923 Pola Negri vehicle.

p, Edward Small; d, Irving Pichel; w, Robert Thoeren (based on the novel Bella Donna by Robert Hichens and the play by James Bernard Fagan); ph, Lucien Ballard; m, Daniele Amfitheatrof; ed, Ernest Nims; art d, Bernard Herzbrun; set d, Hugh Hunt.

Drama **(PR:A MPAA:NR)**

TEMPTATION* (1962, Fr.) 94m Riviera International-Jean Joannon/Cameo Internatio nal bw (L'ILE DU BOUT DU MONDE)

Magali Noel (*Jane*), Dawn Addams (*Victoria*), Rossana Podesta (*Caterina*), Christian Marquand (*Patrick*).

A war correspondent, Marquand, and three women are washed up on a deserted island when their Red Cross ship returning from Korea is sunk. Passions quickly come into play, with Noel the catalyst. Podesta dies when her patched-up lifeboat, in which she sets off to find help, sinks in a storm, and Addams then tells Marquand that Noel is a psychopath whom she was taking back to the U.S. to face murder charges. When Addams becomes intimate with Marquand, Noel kills her, and, finally, as a passing ship is sighted and Marquand signals to it for help, she jumps from a cliff to her death. Another bleak outing from France.

p&d, Edmond T. Greville; w, Greville, Henri Crouzat, Louis A. Pascal, (based on the novel The Island at the End of the World by Crouzat); ph, Jacques Lemare; m, Charles Aznavour, Marguerite Monnot, Eddie Barclay, Jean-Pierre Landreau; ed, Jean Ravel; art d, Jean Douarinou; cos, Annie Marolt, Majo Brandley, Clo Ramoin; makeup, Marcel Occelli.

Drama **(PR:C MPAA:NR)**

TEMPTATION HARBOR** (1949, Brit.) 91m Associated British/MON bw

Robert Newton (*Bert Mallinson*), Simone Simon (*Camelia*), William Hartnell (*Jim Brown*), Marcel Dalio (*Inspector Dupre*), Margaret Barton (*Betty Mallinson*), Edward Rigby (*Tatem*), Joan Hopkins (*Beryl Brown*), Kathleen Harrison (*Mabel*), Leslie Dwyer (*Reg*), Charles Victor (*Gowshall*), Irene Handl (*Mrs. Gowshall*), Wylie Watson (*Fred*), John Salew (*C.I.D. Inspector*), George Woodbridge (*Frost*), Kathleen Boutall (*Mrs. Frost*), W. G. Fay (*Night Porter*), Edward Lexy (*Stationmaster*), Gladys Henson (*Mrs. Titmuss*), Dave Crowley (*Teddy*).

Newton is a hard-working, honest railroad signalman who one day finds $20,000 in the harbor after witnessing a murder. He decides not to turn the cash over to the police, choosing to leave town with his daughter, Barton, and the gold-digging Simon. They are pursued by the killer, who meets death accidentally at the hands of Newton. Newton finally decides to go to the police and return the money. The first British adaptation of a novel by

Georges Simenon, and far from the last.

p, Victor Skutezky; d, Lance Comfort; w, Skutezky, Frederic Gotfurt, Rodney Ackland (based on the novel Newhaven-Dieppe by Georges Simenon); ph, Otto Heller; m, Mischa Spoliansky; ed, Lito Carruthers; art d, Cedric Dawe; makeup, R. Clark.

Crime Drama   (PR:A MPAA:NR)

TEMPTER, THE**   (1974, Ital./Brit.) 105m Euro
                              International-Lifeguard c

Glenda Jackson (*Sister Geraldine*), Claudio Casinelli (*Rodolfo*), Lisa Harrow (*Emily*), Adolfo Celi (*Father Borelli*), Arnoldo Foa (*Monsignor Bodensky*), Gabriele Lavia (*Principe Ottavio*), Francisco Rabal (*Bishop Marques*).

Jackson stars as a nun who runs a convent which provides shelter for religious exiles. One of her guests is a Fidel Castro sympathizer, while another is a prince who's in love with his own sister. When the group is visited by Casinelli, an energetic young author, the shelter's sense of order is thrown up for grabs. He takes the exiles out on a retreat, temporarily freeing them from their confines, but before long it is obvious that the exiles cannot deal with modern life. Well-crafted on all levels. (In English.)

p, Anis Nohra; d&w, Damiano Damiani; ph, Mario Vulpiani (Eastmancolor); m, Ennio Morricone; ed, Peter Taylor; art d, Umberto Turco.

Religious Drama   (PR:A-C MPAA:NR)

TEMPTER, THE zero   (1978, Ital.) 96m AE c (L'ANTI CRISTO; AKA: ANTICRISTO)

Carla Gravina (*Ippolita*), Mel Ferrer (*Massimo*), Arthur Kennedy (*Bishop*), George Coulouris (*Father Mittner*), Alida Valli (*Irene*), Anita Strindberg (*Gretel*), Mario Scaccia (*Faith Healer*), Umberto Orsini (*Psychiatrist*).

Having no relation to the Italian-British THE TEMPTER, this picture does share the same original European release date (1974) and the musical talents of Ennio Morricone. From there on, however, this obvious EXORCIST ripoff is the exact opposite of director Damiano Damiani's film. Gravina is a 20-year-old paralyzed girl who is possessed by the devil. A priest and a psychiatrist try to help, but she spews up vomit and yells at them, and is finally saved by the priest's efforts. Gravina is even raped by an invisible demon spirit. A tasteless piece of trash which is also poorly dubbed.

p, Edmondo Amati; d, Alberto DeMartino; w, Martino, Vincenzo Mannino, Gianfranco Clerici; ph, Aristide Massaccesi; m, Ennio Morricone; ed, Vincenzo Tomassi; art d, Umberto Bertacca.

Horror   Cas.   (PR:O MPAA:R)

TEMPTRESS, THE**   (1949, Brit.) 85m Bushey/Ambassador bw

Joan Maude (*Lady Clifford*), Arnold Bell (*Dr. Leroy*), Don Stannard (*Derek Clifford*), Shirley Quentin (*Nurse Rowe*), John Stuart (*Sir Charles Clifford*), Ferdy Mayne (*Julian*), Conrad Phillips (*Capt. Green*), Michael Bazalgette, Roy Russell, Richard Leech, John Serret, Rita Varian.

Doctor Bell, obsessed with finding a polio cure, is persuaded by patient Maude to murder her husband in return for half his fortune. The plot is foiled though, when the money all goes to Maude's son, Stannard, who loves Bell's nurse, Quentin. Bell sets out to kill Stannard, but Quentin prevents it and Bell kills himself instead. Depressing but interesting crime story.

p, Gilbert Church; d, Oswald Mitchell; w, Kathleen Butler (based on the novel Juggernaut by Alice Campbell); ph, S. D. Onions.

Crime   (PR:A MPAA:NR)

TEMPTRESS AND THE MONK, THE**   (1963, Jap.) 88m
Nikkatsu/Gaston Hakim Production s International c (BYAKUYA NO
                                    YOJO; AKA: THE TEMPTRESS)

Yumeji Tsukioka (*Temptress*), Ryoji Hayama (*Socho*), Tadashi Kobayashi (*Dwarf*), Ichijiro Oya (*Grandfather*), Jun Hamamura (*Criminal*), Akitake Kono.

Set in the ancient days of Japan, this tale has a monk traveling through the forest and losing his way. He makes it to a house inhabited by the beautiful Tsukioka and her bizarre dwarf husband. She regularly seduces any man who wanders by the house and then changes him into a wild animal. Planning to do the same with her new visitor, she finds herself instead falling in love with him and allowing him to live. Released in Japan in 1958.

p, Masayuki Takaki; d, Eisuke Takizawa; w, Toshio Yasumi, Kyoka Izumi (based on the story by Izumi); ph, Minoru Yokoyama (CinemaScope, Eastmancolor); m, Yutaka Makino; ed, Masanori Tsujii; art d, Takashi Matsuyama.

Drama/Horror   (PR:C MPAA:NR)

10***   (1979) 122m Orion/WB c

Dudley Moore (*George*), Julie Andrews (*Sam*), Bo Derek (*Jenny*), Robert Webber (*Hugh*), Dee Wallace (*Mary Lewis*), Sam Jones (*David*), Brian Dennehy (*Bartender*), Max Showalter (*Reverend*), Rad Daly (*Josh*), Nedra Volz (*Mrs. Kissel*), James Noble (*Fred Miles*), Virginia Kiser (*Ethel Miles*), John Hawker (*Covington*), Deborah Rush (*Dental Assistant*), Don Calfa (*Neighbor*), Walter George Alton (*Larry*), Annette Martin (*Redhead*), John Hancock (*Dr. Croce*), Lorry Goldman (*TV Director*), Arthur Rosenberg (*Pharmacist*), Mari Gorman (*Waitress*), Marcy Hanson, Senilo Tanney, Kitty DeCarlo, Bill Lucking, Owen Sullivan, Debbie White, Laurence Carr, Camila Ashland, Burke Byrnes, Doug Sheehan, J. Victor Lopez, Jon Linton, John Chappell, Art Kassul.

A very funny film that sent Dudley Moore's career soaring while making some telling points about the problems of middle age. Moore is a successful songwriter with four Oscars to his name. He lives in a huge Southern California home, drives a Rolls, and is dissatisfied with his life. He is turning 42 and spending too much time ogling the gorgeous young women who walk the Los Angeles streets. He watches his neighbor (Calfa) through a telescope and sees that the man has a bevy of nude women surrounding him. The fact that his life is passing him by is beginning to gnaw at Moore's innards. This causes pain to his star girl friend, Andrews, who adores him and whose singing voice has been the reason for much of his success. Moore's partner is Webber, who is having his own crisis because he is gay and, as he ages, can no longer attract the same young men he is accustomed to cavorting with. Moore is suffering from a combination of ennui and self-doubt when he sees a limousine go past. In it is Derek, who is on her way to get married to Jones at a Beverly Hills church. This is the girl of his dreams, an "11" on the scale of "10." Moore goes to the church (banging up his Rolls in the process), learns Derek's identity, and finds out where she and Jones are honeymooning in Mexico. Moore flies to the resort at Las Hadas and drowns his sorrows at the bar while a willing Dennehy keeps pouring him drinks. Without hearing Derek say a word, Moore is hopelessly in love with her, peering at her fabulous figure as she romps on the beach with Jones. His fantasies take over and he imagines all sorts of experiences with Derek, then he gets his chance. Jones falls asleep on a surfboard and is drifting out to sea and in danger of losing his life. Moore rents a boat, goes after Jones, and saves the man's life. His deed makes him famous, newspapers herald his bravery and, most importantly, he gets to meet Derek. Jones is redder than a matador's cape and must spend some time in the local hospital to recover. Derek is thankful of Moore's derring-do and asks him to come to her room. Once there, things go better than Moore had ever expected as she admits that she had been watching him at the hotel and thought that he was very sexy, "for an older man." After a dinner together, Derek takes Moore to her room again and proceeds to make a pass at him. But the traditional Moore, who is from another generation, can't handle her open attitude toward sex. This is no sweet, young naive bride who was losing her virginity on the honeymoon. Derek is a woman who has been around...and around...and around. Moore wants romance, soft lights, the chase. Derek just wants sex. Moore walks away from his dream girl and goes back to California where he finally pops the question to his longtime amour, Andrews. Derek became a star due to her part in this film and has failed to achieve any further success, despite several movies that might have been hits if handled by anyone but her indulgent director husband, John Derek. There are several standout comedy bits including one with aging Volz, who keeps allowing gas to escape from her body. Her dog knows that he will be blamed for what's happened and automatically flees whenever Volz lets one go. Moore gets drunk, has a bee sting his nose, burns his feet on the hot beach sand, and has a dream sequence that is uproarious as the strains of Ravel's "Bolero" pound in the background. Moore also played the piano (which he does quite well) in the band that provided the background music. Mancini's music was nominated for an Oscar. The movie made about $40 million, thus qualifying it as the "sleeper" of 1979. Since then, Moore has made one disaster after another, evidently paying more attention to the fees than the scripts. With all of the talk and the waltzing around about sex, Moore and Derek never get to the act but it's still a movie that kids should not see. Webber plays his role with supreme understatement and shows again why he is one of Hollywood's best supporters. Casting Moore opposite Andrews was a mistake as she towers above him and, despite the fact that they are both British, they seem like all they could be is just good friends. But since Andrews was sleeping with director Edwards, who else could he have cast? (Don't be offended. Edwards and Andrews have been happily married for years, since she divorced designer Tony Walton.)

p, Blake Edwards, Tony Adams; d&w, Edwards; ph, Frank Stanley (Panavision, Metrocolor); m, Henry Mancini; ed, Ralph E. Winters; prod d, Rodger Maus; set d, Reg Allen, Jack Stevens; cos, Pat Edwards; spec eff, Fred Cramer; m/l, Carol Bayer Sager, Robert Wells; makeup, Bron Roylance, Ben Nye II; stunts, Dick Crockett.

Comedy   Cas.   (PR:O MPAA:R)

TEN CENTS A DANCE**   (1931) 75m COL bw

Barbara Stanwyck (*Barbara O'Neill*), Ricardo Cortez (*Bradley Carlton*), Monroe Owsley (*Eddie Miller*), Sally Blane (*Molly*), Blanche Frederici (*Mrs. Blanchard*), Phyllis Crane (*Eunice*), Olive Hill (*Mrs. Carlton in Photo*), Victor Potel (*Smith the Sailor*), Al Hill (*Jones the Sailor*), Jack Byron (*Leo*),

Pat Harmon *(Casey the Bouncer)*, Martha Sleeper *(Nancy Clark)*, David Newell *(Ralph Clark)*, Sidney Bracey *(Wilson, Carlton's Butler)*, Harry Todd *(Mr. Carney)*, Aggie Herring *(Mrs. Carney)*, Peggy Doner *(Yvonne)*, James Ford *(Dancer)*, Hal Price *(Doorman)*, Bess Flowers *(Bridge Player)*, Ernie Alexander *(Elevator Operator)*, Abe Lyman and His Band.

Stanwyck is a tough taxi dancer collecting the title fee from sailors and the like while watching out for her naive coworker, Blane. One night wealthy Cortez gives Stanwyck $100, which she turns around and gives to Owsley, an impoverished resident of the same boarding house, with whom Stanwyck has fallen in love. Cortez offers to take Stanwyck to Europe with him but she refuses. Disappointed, Cortez fades into the background as Stanwyck and Owsley are married. The marriage, however, soon turns sour. Owsley turns out to be a wastrel and Stanwyck asks Cortez to give him a job. Owsley promptly embezzles $5,000 from the company and Stanwyck must again go to Cortez, this time to ask him for enough money to replace her husband's theft. Cortez, still in love with Stanwyck, gives her the money without protest. Owsley is angry at his wife's actions and walks out on her. Cortez again offers Stanwyck a trip to Europe so she can be divorced and remarry him, and this time she accepts. Undistinguished melodrama has little more than a decent performance by Stanwyck to recommend it. Both Olive Tell and Harry Todd were cut from the final print before the film's release. This was Lionel Barrymore's third and last directorial outing. Barrymore was already suffering from the arthritis that was eventually to confine him to a wheelchair for the last 15 years of his life. The doctors prescribed drugs to ease the pain but they had the unfortunate side effect of putting the director to sleep, leaving the actors to work out scenes for themselves. Stanwyck later claimed that Barrymore had done all he could under the circumstances and that she simply had to try a little harder. Stanwyck received much better reviews than the film as a whole, and it marked one more stepping stone on her long and tedious road to stardom.

p, Harry Cohn; d, Lionel Barrymore; w, Jo Swerling, Dorothy Howell (based on the song by Richard Rodgers, Lorenz Hart); ph, Ernest Haller, Gil Warrenton; m, Abe Lyman and His Band; ed, Arthur Huffsmith; md, Constantin Bakaleinikoff; art d, Edward Jewell; m/l, "Ten Cents a Dance" Rodgers, Hart.

Romance **(PR:A MPAA:NR)**

TEN CENTS A DANCE** (1945) 60m COL bw

Jane Frazee *(Jeanne Hollis)*, Jimmy Lloyd *(Billy Sparks)*, Robert Scott *(Ted Kimball III)*, Joan Woodbury *(Babe)*, John Calvert *(Breezy Walker)*, George McKay *(Bits)*, Edward Hyans *(Joey)*, Dorothea Kent *(Sadie)*, Carole Mathews *(Marge)*, Muriel Morris *(Glad)*, Pattie Robbins *(Vi)*, Marilyn Johnson *(Mae)*, Jewel McGowan *(Pat)*, Billy Nelson *(Rocky)*.

A harmless and forgettable comedy which has Frazee and Woodbury working in a dance hall setting up scams on innocent folk along with Calvert. They try to make GI's Lloyd and Scott part with their cash in a card game, but wind up in love with the boys instead.

p, Michel Kraike; d, Will Jason; w, Morton Grant; ph, Benjamin Kline; ed, James Sweeney; art d, George Brooks; m/l, "Ten Cents a Dance," Richard Rodgers, Lorenz Hart.

Musical/Comedy **(PR:A MPAA:NR)**

TEN COMMANDMENTS, THE**** (1956) 219m PAR c

Charlton Heston *(Moses)*, Yul Brynner *(Rameses)*, Ann Baxter *(Nefretiri)*, Edward G. Robinson *(Dathan)*, Yvonne De Carlo *(Sephora)*, Debra Paget *(Lilia)*, John Derek *(Joshua)*, Sir Cedric Hardwicke *(Sethi)*, Nina Foch *(Bithiah)*, Martha Scott *(Yochabel)*, Judith Anderson *(Memnet)*, Vincent Price *(Baka)*, John Carradine *(Aaron)*, Eduard Franz *(Jethro)*, Olive Deering *(Miriam)*, Donald Curtis *(Mered)*, Douglas Dumbrille *(Jannes)*, Lawrence Dobkin *(Hur Ben Caleb)*, Frank DeKova *(Abiram)*, H.B. Warner *(Amminadab)*, Henry Wilcoxon *(Pentaur)*, Julia Faye *(Elisheba)*, Lisa Mitchell, Noelle Williams, Joanne Merlin, Pat Richard, Joyce Vanderveen, Diane Hall *(Jethro's Daughters)*, Abbas El Boughdadly *(Rameses' Charioteer)*, Fraser Heston *(Infant Moses)*, Eugene Mazzola *(Rameses' Son)*, John Miljan *(The Blind One)*, Tommy Duran *(Gershom)*, Francis J. McDonald *(Simon)*, Ian Keith *(Rameses I)*, Joan Woodbury *(Korah's Wife)*, Ramsay Hill *(Korah)*, Woody Strode *(King of Ethiopia)*, Dorothy Adams *(Hebrew at Golden Calf/Hebrew Woman at Rameses' Gate/Slave Woman)*, Eric Alden *(High-Ranking Officer/Taskmaster/Slave Man/Officer)*, Henry Brandon *(Commander of the Hosts)*, Touch 'Mike' Connors *(Amalekite Herder)*, Henry Corden *(Sheik of Ezion)*, Edna May Cooper *(Court Lady)*, Kem Dibbs *(Corporal)*, Fred Kohler, Jr. *(Foreman)*, Gail Kobe *(Pretty Slave Girl)*, John Merton, Mena Mohamed *(Architect's Assistants)*, Addison Richards *(Fan Bearer)*, Onslow Stevens *(Lugal)*, Clint Walker *(Sardinian Captain)*, Frank Wilcox *(Wazir)*, Luis Alberni *(Old Hebrew at Moses' House)*, Michael Ansara *(Taskmaster)*, Fred Coby *(Hebrew at Golden Calf/Taskmaster)*, Tony Dante *(Libyan Captain)*, Frankie Darro, Carl Switzer, Edward Earle *(Slaves)*, Franklyn Farnum *(High Official)*, John Hart *(Cretan Ambassador)*, Ed Hinton *(Taskmaster/Flagman)*, Walter Woolf King *(Herald)*, Frank Lackteen *(Old Man Praying/Old Man in Granary/Hebrew at Dathan's Tent/Elder of Joseph/Old Man)*, Emmett Lynn *(Old Slave Man/Hebrew at Golden Calf)*, Stanley Price *(Slave Carrying Load)*, Robert Vaughn *(Spearman/Hebrew at Golden Calf)*, Herb Alpert *(Drum Player)*, Esther Brown *(Princess Tharbis)*, Paul DeRolf *(Eleazar)*, Zeev Bufman *(Hebrew at Golden Calf)*, Kathy Garver *(Child Slave)*, George Melford, Jeane Wood, Lillian Albertson, Joel Ashley, George Baxter, Robert Bice, Peter Coe, J. Stevan Darrell, Matty Fain, Tony George, Gavin Gordon, Kay Hammonf, Peter Hansen, Adeline de Walt Reynolds, Irene Tedrow, Barry Macollum.

It was DeMille's last film and appropriately the master of the biblical epic finished his career with a larger-than-life production, jam-packed with enormous crowd scenes, lavish spectacles, strong willed men and their devoted women, and wide- screen special effects, all orchestrated with dazzling brilliance. For his film, DeMille went to the Old Testament, taking the story of Moses and the Jewish Exodus from Egypt, a tale he had previously filmed in 1923. The film opens as Rameses I (Keith), the Egyptian king who has enslaved the Jewish people, is told that the Deliverer of the Hebrews will soon be born and grow up to free his people. Keith demands all newborn Jewish males to be slaughtered but Scott places her small son in a basket and sends him floating down the river Nile. Foch, Keith's sister, finds the child and brings him up as her own son, naming him Moses. Years pass and the now-adult Moses (Heston) has become a prince. Brynner, Keith's son, is jealous of Heston, knowing that only one of them can succeed Keith. Baxter, an Egyptian princess, also has strong feelings for Heston, openly lusting after the handsome young man. Heston kills Price, an Egyptian builder, just as he is about to kill Derek, a Jewish slave. Robinson, a Hebrew spy for Keith, tells Keith about this and Heston's background is soon revealed. Heston is banished into the desert, where he ends up in the camp of Franz. Heston helps Franz fend off some attackers, and eventually marries Franz's daughter, De Carlo. After several years, Heston again meets Derek, who has now escaped. Derek tells Heston that he is the Hebrew Deliverer, a prophecy the Lord later commands of Heston when he sees a miraculous burning bush. Heston confronts Brynner, who refuses to let the Jews go free. With the might of the Lord behind him Heston causes 10 plagues to fall upon the Egyptians. Brynner refuses to budge until finally all first born Egyptian sons are killed. Brynner allows the Hebrews to leave in a mass exodus, but decides to send his chariots after the freed slaves. Poised on the edge of the Red Sea, Heston raises his arms and the waters divide. As a pillar of fire holds off the Egyptians, the Jews safely make their way through to the opposite side of the great body of water. When the Egyptian soldiers catch up they are drowned as Heston closes the Red Sea in on them. Brynner is left on the shore, stunned at this holocaust. Heston brings his people to Mount Sinai. While he climbs to the top to receive the Lord's commandments, Robinson convinces the others that Heston is misguided. He has them build a Golden Calf to worship, and challenges Heston when he descends from the mountains with God's 10 commandments on stone tablets. Heston angrily smashes the tablets against the Golden Calf, destroying Robinson and those who chose to follow him. As punishment for their disbelief in God's might, the Hebrews are forced to wander 40 years in the desert. Finally, they see the Promised Land. Though Heston does not join them, he lovingly watches as Derek leads the masses across the River Jordan into the land of Israel. With THE TEN COMMANDMENTS, DeMille brings to life the story of Moses on a scale no other filmmaker ever envisioned. Everything here is presented in a grandiose style, yet the fine cast is never overwhelmed by the lavish sweep of this epic. Heston is magnificent as Moses, playing the great prophet as a humble man with a great inner strength. His role is unforgettable, and it is a part with which he will forever be identified with. Brynner, as the evil pharaoh, essays the role with the utmost seriousness, though he occasionally delivers lines a bit tongue-in-cheek. In a cast this large, it was important for DeMille to have a strong ensemble. The supporting players give Heston, Brynner, and their director that strength, and there is hardly a bad performance in the lot. This was Robinson's comeback part after being unfairly blacklisted in the 1950s. Though many encouraged DeMille not to hire Robinson for the role, DeMille felt that the actor had been dealt a severe injustice. Robinson was grateful to the director, writing in his autobiography *All My Yesterdays*: "Cecil B. DeMille returned me to films. Cecil B. DeMille restored my self respect." DeMille's handling of his "cast of thousands" is a sight to behold. The Exodus sequence is a masterful coordination of cast, crew, and camera. DeMille, high above on a crane, shouted orders through a public address system to those gathered below. There were over 12,000 people, plus some 15,000 animals stretched out over three miles. For the climactic chasing of the Jews by chariot, DeMille hired the Egyptian army and had them train for four months so their skills would look realistic on screen. Though much of the film was shot in the studio (on 12 sound stages in Paris and 18 in Hollywood), DeMille did shoot a good deal of footage in the Egyptian deserts in locations thought to be close to the actual sites where the historic events took place. Tragedy nearly struck the project while DeMille was investigating a broken camera. Climbing to the top of a 103-foot ladder, he suddenly experienced a sharp pain in his chest. Forced to descend the ladder himself, DeMille collapsed when he finally reached the ground. He was able to get to a chair, and his doctor, after examining him, told the director he should quit the film if he wanted to live. DeMille would hear nothing of the sort, and the deeply religious man spent that night in intensive prayer. The next day he was back on the set, his energy renewed as if nothing had happened. DeMille chose Heston, in part, because of his strong resemblence to the famed Michaelangelo statue of Moses. DeMille later stated "...my choice was strikingly affirmed when I had a sketch of Chuck in a white beard and compared it to...(the) statue. The resemblance was amazing." Heston took the role with the utmost seriousness. He would do take after take until satisfied with the results, and buried himself in Old Testament readings.

Heston memorized whole sections, and, like Moses did thousands of years before, the actor even walked barefoot through the jagged Mount Sinai rocks. Though the performances and epic nature of the film were unforgettable, THE TEN COMMANDMENTS is well remembered for its Oscar-winning special effects. The most impressive of all was the splitting of the Red Sea. This was achieved by photographing some 300,000 gallons of water being poured into a tank. This footage was then reversed, giving the impression of the great sea parting. Next footage of the Hebrews crossing the dry sea bed was superimposed over this image, creating the uncanny effect. DeMille spent over $13 million on his epic, a figure no one in their right mind expected could possibly be made back. But DeMille proved his detractors wrong and the public loved the film, as THE TEN COMMANDMENTS eventually grossed over $80 million, enjoying several re-releases. "To transfer the Bible to the screen you cannot cheat," DeMille said. "You have to believe." DeMille's vision remains a powerful one. This was the culmination of a life's work, with each element in the massive work meticulously scrutinized by the director. It is testament to both DeMille's love of his subject and his undeniable talent as the master of the epic cinema.

p&d, Cecil B. DeMille; w, Aeneas MacKenzie, Jesse L. Lasky, Jr., Jack Gariss, Fredric M. Frank (based on the novels *The Prince of Egypt* by Dorothy Clarke Wilson, *Pillar of Fire* by the Rev. J.H. Ingraham, *On Eagle's Wings* by the Rev. G.E. Southon, and in accordance with the Holy Scripture, the ancient texts of Josephus, Eusebius, Philo, The Midrash); ph, Loyal Griggs, John Warren, Wallace Kelly, Peverell Marley (VistaVision, Technicolor); m, Elmer Bernstein; ed, Anne Bauchens; art d, Hal Pereira, Walter Tyler, Albert Nozala; set d, Sam Comer, Ray Moyer; cos, Edith Head, Ralph Jester, John Jensen, Dorothy Jeakins, Arnold Friberg; spec eff, John P. Fulton; ch, LeRoy Prinz, Ruth Godfrey; makeup, Wally Westmore, Frank Westmore, Frank McCoy.

Biblical Epic   **Cas.**   **(PR:AA MPAA:NR)**

TEN DAYS IN PARIS   (SEE: MISSING TEN DAYS, 1941, Brit.)

TEN DAYS TO TULARA*   (1958) 77m UA bw

Sterling Hayden (*Scotty*), Grace Raynor (*Teresa*), Rodolfo Hoyos (*Cesar*), Carlos Muzquiz (*Dario*), Tony Caravajal (*Francisco*), Juan Garcia (*Piranha*), Rafael Alcayde (*Colonel*), Felix Gonzales (*Marco*), Jose Pulido (*Capitan*), Major M. Badager (*Copilot Luis*), Milton Bernstein (*Teniente*), Barry Grail (*Medico*), Paco Arenas (*Chris*).

A bad guys film shot in Mexico features Hayden as an independent pilot whose son is taken hostage by crook Hoyos. Hoyos and his gang have $250,000 in gold and they force Hayden to use his plane to make a getaway. The plane crashes and the gang members hop in cars and take off on foot to escape the authorities. They come across a few village ceremonies along the way but there is no real tension built between Hayden and Hoyos. Hayden and Raynor do make eyes at each other, which proves difficult since she is Hoyos' daughter. In gunplay at the finale, Hoyos is shot dead and everything ends well with Hayden reunited with his son.

p, George Sherman, Clarence Eurist; d, Sherman; w, Laurence Mascott; ph, Alex Phillips; m, Lon Adomian; ed, Carlos Savage.

Western   **(PR:A MPAA:NR)**

TEN DAYS' WONDER*½   (1972, Fr.) 101m Les Films La
                              Boetie/Levitt-Pickman c (LA DECADE PRODIGIEUSE)

Orson Welles (*Theo Van Horn*), Marlene Jobert (*Helene Van Horn*), Michel Piccoli (*Paul Regis*), Anthony Perkins (*Charles Van Horn*), Guido Alberti (*Ludovic*), Ermando Casanova (*One-Eyed Old Man*), Mathilde Ceccarelli (*Receptionist*), Eric Frisdal (*Child Charles*), Aline Montovani (*Child Helene No. 1*), Corinne Koeningswarter (*Child Helene No. 2*), Giovanni Sciuto (*Pawnbroker*), Vittorio Sanipoli (*Police Officer*), Fabienne Gaugloff (*Little Girl on Train*), Tsilla Chelton (*Charles' Mother*).

An outlandish and clouded variation on mystery and suspense which is based on an Ellery Queen tale. Divided into 10 days, the film focuses on the wealthy Van Horns–the patriarch Welles, his adopted daughter-wife Jobert, and his adopted son Perkins–and their interaction with Perkins' mentor and former philosophy professor Piccoli. After one of Perkins' amnesiac blackouts, he awakens with blood-covered hands and summons Piccoli. He persuades Piccoli to stay as a guest on the Van Horn estate just in case their are any more blackouts. Before long, Jobert and Perkins admit to Piccoli that they are lovers being blackmailed by someone who has confiscated their love letters. Perkins steals $25,000 from Welles' safe in order to pay off the unknown blackmailer, who a couple of days later again asks for money–this time for the photocopies of the letters. In the meantime, Welles tells the story of how Perkins' parents were struck by lightning and put to rest in a nearby cemetery. Perkins snaps into a crazed state and the following day drives to the cemetery and violates the gravesite. Not surprisingly, Piccoli packs his bags and leaves the Van Horn estate. On his return trip to Paris, however, he has a vision of what Perkins is trying to do– break each and every one of the Ten Commandments. Piccoli telephones Welles and warns him that Perkins may try to murder him–Thou Shalt Not Kill is the last remaining Commandment. Piccoli is wrong, however, and Perkins kills Jobert. In a rage, Perkins then destroys his collection of God

statues, all of them resembling Welles, and jumps from his window. His gruesome death has him impaled on the iron gate below. Piccoli then hands Welles a gun and, in a CITIZEN KANE-style ending, the lights in Welles' room go dim as he kills himself. The thing to "wonder" most about in TEN DAYS' WONDER is just what the heck is going on. The film is filled with obscurities (which only diehard Chabrol fans will bother with) such as the Van Horns all dressing in fashions from 1925. There's also the question of Perkins having God statues which all look just like Welles. Why does Perkins seem more deranged (and as a result downright silly) in this film than in PSYCHO and FEAR STRIKES OUT combined? And, in a question which stumped practically all reviewers, why does Welles' nose appear to be grey? There are undoubtedly many academic answers to the films baroque allusions to Christianity and the Oedipal complex, but none of them can answer why the film plods along as it does. The performances are wholly cliched, the plot unredeemably muddled, and to top it off the English-language dubbing job is incompetent.

p, Andre Genoves; d, Claude Chabrol; w, Paul Gardner, Paul Gegauff, Eugene Archer (based on the novel by Ellery Queen [Frederic Dannay and Manfred B. Lee]; ph, Jean Rabier (Technicolor); m, Pierre Jansen; ed, Jacques Gaillard; md, Andre Girard; art d, Guy Littaye; set d, Guy Maugin; cos, Karl Lagerfeld; m/l, Dominique Zardin.

Drama   **(PR:O MPAA:PG)**

$10 RAISE*   (1935) 70m FOX bw (GB:MR. FAINTHEART)

Edward Everett Horton (*Hubert T. Wilkins*), Karen Morley (*Emily Converse*), Alan Dinehart (*Fuller*), Glen Boles (*Don Bates*), Berton Churchill (*Mr. Bates*), Rosina Lawrence (*Dorothy Converse*), Ray Walker (*Perry*), Frank Melton (*Clark*), William Benedict (*Jimmy*).

Horton is a wimpy bookkeeper bullied by his boss and his girl friend, who doubts his manliness. Tired of working for nothing, he finally gets up the nerve to ask the miserly boss for a raise and prove his worth to his lady. Predictable and basically dumb. This one didn't get a rise out of anyone, let alone a raise for excellent actor Horton, who finally makes it financially big when some land he owns turns out to be worth a fortune.

p, Joseph Engel; d, George Marshall; w, Henry Johnson, Louis Breslow, Lamar Trotti (based on a story by Peter B. Kyne); ph, Harry Jackson; md, Samuel Kaylin.

Drama   **(PR:A MPAA:NR)**

TEN GENTLEMEN FROM WEST POINT**   (1942) 102m FOX bw

George Montgomery (*Dawson*), Maureen O'Hara (*Carolyn Bainbridge*), John Sutton (*Howard Shelton*), Laird Cregar (*Maj. Sam Carter*), John Shepperd [Shepperd Strudwick] (*Henry Clay*), Victor Francen (*Florimond Massey*), Professor of Military Strategy, Harry Davenport (*Bane*), Ward Bond (*Scully*), Douglas Dumbrille (*Gen. William Henry Harrison*), Ralph Byrd (*Maloney*), Joe Brown, Jr (*Benny Havens*), David Bacon (*Shippen*), Esther Dale (*Mrs. Thompson*), Louis Jean Heydt (*Capt Danforth*), Stanley Andrews (*Capt. Sloane*), James Flavin (*Capt. Luddy*), Edna Mae Jones (*Letty*), Charles Trowbridge (*Senate President*), Tully Marshall (*Grandpa*), Edwin Maxwell (*John Randolph*), Uno (*Old Put*), Edward Fielding (*William Eustis*), Morris Ankrum (*Wood*), Selmer Jackson (*Sersen*), Noble Johnson (*Tecumseh*), Edward "Eddie" Dunn (*O'Toole*), Frank Ferguson (*Alden Brown*), Richard Derr, George Holmes, Dick Winslow, Blake Edwards, John Meredith, Anthony Marsh, Dick Hogan, Gordon Wynne, Roger Kirby, Stanley Parlam, Gene Garrick, Malcolm McTaggart, Gene Rizzi, Herbert Patterson, Max Cole, John Whitney, John Hartley, Tom Neal, Don Peters, William Kersen.

West Point was founded in the early 1800s and this story tells the tale of the first class. After Congress commissioned the money to build it, it met fierce political opposition with the opponents maneuvering evil Cregar in charge of the Point. He drives the first class into the ground, leaving just 10 soldiers at the end. One is rural boy Montgomery, who will do anything for his country. The other is rich boy Sutton, at the academy because it is fashionable. Both want the hand of O'Hara, with Montgomery winning her with his straight ways. The young cadets prove themselves to Cregar by repelling an Indian attack and he sees that the academy is a good idea.

p, William Perlberg; d, Henry Hathaway; w, Richard Maibaum, George Seaton (based on a story by Malvin Wald); ph, Leon Shamroy; m, Alfred Newman; ed, James B. Clark; art d, Richard Day, Nathan Juran.

Drama   **Cas.**   **(PR:A MPAA:NR)**

TEN LAPS TO GO*   (1938) 67m States Rights bw

Rex Lease (*Larry Evans*), Muriel Evans (*Norma*), Duncan Renaldo (*DeSylva*), Tom Moore (*Corbett*), Charles Delaney (*Steve*), Marie Prevost (*Elsie*), Yakima Canutt (*Barney*), Edward Davis (*Adams*).

Literally a blurry look at the early days of auto racing. Lease is the cocky driver who gets in an accident with bad guy Renaldo and loses his nerve. Strange things start occurring and Lease is blamed for them. His girl, Evans, doubting him, seemingly is attracted to Renaldo. On the day of the big race Lease finds the people causing the trouble. He takes over driving for Evans father, and wins the race and her hand. Clips from newsreels are used for the long shots in this dreary mess, and the closeups are obvious fakes.

p, Fanchon Royer; d, Elmer Clifton; w, Charles R. Condon (based on a story by William F. Bleecher); ph, Arthur Martinelli; ed, Edward Schroeder.

Drama (PR:A MPAA:NR)

TEN LITTLE INDIANS* (1965, Brit.) 92m Tenlit/Seven Arts bw

Hugh O'Brian (*Hugh Lombard*), Shirley Eaton (*Ann Clyde*), Fabian (*Mike Raven*), Leo Genn (*Gen. Mandrake*), Stanley Holloway (*William Blore*), Wilfrid Hyde-White (*Judge Cannon*), Daliah Lavi (*Ilona Bergen*), Dennis Price (*Dr. Armstrong*), Marianne Hoppe (*Frau Grohmann*), Mario Adorf (*Herr Grohmann*).

Eight people go to a home in the Alps and wait to see who is hosting their party. In a message to the group, the host tells how each is a killer and all will meet their death by the end of the weekend. All start dying with only O'Brian and Eaton left, and they have fallen in love. Still, she kills him and goes back to the house to find Hyde-White, who tells her he is the one responsible for the gathering. He tells how she will be found guilty and how he has poisoned himself to make sure he is dead before the police arrive. Just then O'Brian walks in and, while waiting for the police, they tell the dying Hyde-White how they flushed him out. One variation from the original, AND THEN THERE WERE NONE (1945), was casting the insipid Fabian as a U.S. rock star instead of a prince, as the character formerly was. Film was released with a two-minute murder break to allow the audience to guess the killer.

p, Oliver A. Unger; d, George Pollock; w, Peter Yeldham, Dudley Nichols, Peter Welbeck [Harry Alan Towers] (based on the novel and play *Ten Little Niggers* by Agatha Christie); ph, Ernest Steward; m, Malcolm Lockyer; ed, Peter Boita; md, Lockyer; art d, Frank White.

Mystery Cas. (PR:A MPAA:NR)

TEN LITTLE INDIANS*½ (1975, Ital./Fr./Span./Ger.) 105m Talia-Coralta-Corona-C omeci/AE c (AKA: AND THEN THERE WERE NONE)

Oliver Reed (*Hugh*), Elke Sommer (*Vera*), Stephane Audran (*Ilona*), Charles Aznavour (*Raven*), Richard Attenborough (*Judge*), Gert Frobe (*Blore*), Herbert Lom (*Dr. Armstrong*), Maria Rohm (*Elsa*), Adolfo Celi (*General*), Alberto de Mendoza (*Martino*), Teresa Gimpera, The Voice of Orson Welles.

An uninteresting adaptation of the Agatha Christie mystery Ten Little Niggers, which falls short of the previous British version and can't hold a candle to Rene Clair's 1945 AND THEN THERE WERE NONE. For presumably budgetary reasons the film is set in Iran (ruling out aesthetic reasons) instead of London. That's one strike against it. The script, which has 10 guests as the helpless victims of a mysterious murderer, is almost entirely lacking in suspense. The cast, headed by Reed, seems to be running in slow motion, boasting only worthy performances from Frobe and Aznavour, who manages to get off a tune before being picked off. Again produced by Harry Alan Towers (see TEN LITTLE INDIANS 1965) who couldn't get it right the first time, but at least left the "whodunit break" out of this one.

p, Harry Alan Towers; d, Peter Collinson; w, Enrique Llouet, Erich Krohnke (based on the novel Ten Little Niggers by Agatha Christie); ph, Fernando Arribas (Eastmancolor); m, Bruno Nicolai; ed, John Trumper; set d, Jose Maria Tapiador.

Mystery Cas. (PR:C MPAA:PG)

TEN LITTLE NIGGERS (SEE: AND THEN THERE WERE NONE, 1945)

TEN MINUTE ALIBI** (1935, Brit.) 75m BL-TRA bw

Phillips Holmes (*Colin Derwent*), Aileen Marson (*Betty Findon*), Theo Shall (*Philip Sevilla*), Morton Selten (*Sir Miles Standish*), Charles Hickman (*Sgt. Brace*), Philip Hatfield (*Hunter*), George Merritt (*Inspector Pemper*).

A film version of a hugely successful British play about a man who gets away with murder. A playboy woos a woman away from her fiance, persuading her to go with him to Paris, where they will get married. The enraged fiance learns that the playboy is something else indeed—he is the meanest kind of a gigolo, who robs women, then deserts them. The fiance kills him, and then, by an ingenious trick with a timepiece, convinces the police that he was in his apartment at the time of the murder. This one deserves plaudits.

p, Paul Soskin; d, Bernard Vorhaus; w, Michael Hankinson, Vera Allinson (based on the play by Anthony Armstrong).

Crime (PR:A MPAA:NR)

TEN NIGHTS IN A BARROOM* (1931) 79m Roadshow bw

William Farnum (*Joe Morgan*), Thomas Santschi (*Simon Slade*), Patty Lou Lynd (*Mary Morgan*), Robert Frazer (*Dr. Romaine*), Phyllis Barrington (*Ann Slade*), Rosemary Theby (*Sarah Morgan*), John Darrow (*Frank Slade*), Lionel Belmore (*Bill*), Thomas Jefferson (*Silent Sam*), Frank Leigh (*Harvey Green*), Kathrin Clare Ward (*Grandma Morgan*), Sheila Manners (*June Manners*), Fern Emmett (*Fanny*), Harry Todd (*Sample*), John Uppman (*The Singer*), Daisy Belmore (*The Old Hag*).

A preachy condemnation of whiskey is all this uneventful drama has to offer. A businessman spends his time at a bar while his family waits for him at home, occasionally sending his daughter to fetch him. By the finale he is redeemed and is shown the path to recovery. Roadshow Productions was affiliated with the Women's Christian Temperance Union as well as the American Advancement Society, Department of Prohibition Education. The picture did little more than alienate "wet" communities and cater to the "dry." The subject was very popular in the silent days and was filmed twice in 1903, then again in 1909, 1910, 1911, 1913, 1921, and 1926.

p, L.E. Goetz; d, William O'Connor; w, Norton S. Parker (based on a play by Edwin Waugh); ph, Verne L. Walker; set d, Tec-Art Studios.

Drama (PR:A MPAA:NR)

10 NORTH FREDERICK**½ (1958) 102m FOX bw

Gary Cooper (*Joe Chapin*), Diane Varsi (*Ann Chapin*), Suzy Parker (*Kate Drummond*), Geraldine Fitzgerald (*Edith Chapin*), Tom Tully (*Slattery*), Ray Stricklyn (*Joby*), Philip Ober (*Lloyd Williams*), John Emery (*Paul Donaldson*), Stuart Whitman (*Charley Bongiorno*), Linda Watkins (*Peg Slattery*), Barbara Nichols (*Stella*), Joe McGuinn (*Dr. English*), Jess Kirkpatrick (*Arthur McHenry*), Nolan Leary (*Harry Jackson*), Helen Wallace (*Marion Jackson*), Beverly Jo Morrow (*Waitress*), Buck Class (*Bill*), Rachel Stephens (*Salesgirl*), Bob Adler (*Farmer*), Linc Foster (*Peter*), John Harding (*Robert Hooper*), Dudley Manlove (*Ted Wallace*), Mack Williams (*Gen. Coates*), Vernon Rich (*Board Chairman*), Mary Carroll (*Nurse*), George Davis (*Waiter*), Joey Faye (*Taxi Driver*), Fred Essler (*Hoffman*), Irene Seidner (*Wife*), Melinda Byron (*Hope*), Sean Meany (*Sax Player*), John Indrisano, Michael Pataki, Michael Morelli, Charles Bronson (*Men*).

A confusing movie from a complex book with a performance by Cooper that almost, but not quite, manages to save the story. The picture begins in 1945 with Cooper's funeral, then goes into flashback. Icy Fitzgerald is a woman who has great plans for her quiet husband, Cooper. He's a good man, a gentle man, and he lives in the shadow of his grandfather who had once served as lieutenant governor of the state. Cooper is wealthy, a lawyer, and happy with his comfortable life. Fitzgerald wants more for herself than just being the wife of an attorney. She realizes that the only way she can achieve power is through Cooper so she prods the reluctant man into thinking about a political career. She persuades Cooper to make a large donation to Tully, a bigwig in the party, so he can get a nomination. (We're never told if Tully actually puts the money in the party's coffers or into his own pocket. We do know, however, that he has nothing but disdain for Cooper and his amateurish attempts to get into the arena.) Cooper and Fitzgerald have a daughter, Varsi, who falls in love with and marries musician Whitman, a jazz trumpeter. Fitzgerald is totally against it and tries to break up the marriage. Varsi becomes pregnant and suffers a miscarriage after she and Fitzgerald have an argument. In the background is their son, Stricklyn, who loves his gentleman father and knows exactly what kind of a harridan his mother is. Cooper slips Whitman some money to get out of Varsi's life and the young woman's heart is broken. Cooper didn't want to arrange for the annulment but he was again prodded by shrewish Fitzgerald who is certain she knows what's best for everyone. Tully has been looking for an excuse to get rid of the obligation he owes Cooper for the money donated so he makes sure the press gets wind of what's happened with Varsi. At the same time, Fitzgerald is having an affair and Cooper's life is falling to pieces around him. Varsi has moved to New York (she did the same thing the year before in PEYTON PLACE) and Cooper, hoping to reassemble the shards of his existence, travels there from Pennsylvania to try and patch things up. He meets Varsi's roommate, the gorgeous Parker, and the two of them fall in love and begin a May-December romance. This goes on until Cooper realizes that there is just too much of a chasm between their ages (he was actually 57 and she was 25), so he walks away from their love. Varsi has been opposed from the start as the thought of her wrinkled father and the lithe Parker is too much for her to fathom. Later, Cooper discovers he is suffering from a terminal illness and, just before he dies, Stricklyn brings Varsi home and they reconcile. Back to the present and Stricklyn tells Fitzgerald off as the picture fades out. Parker was excellent, believable, and much more than the model that everyone thought she was. Her career never took off and she married actor Brad Dillman. The novel by O'Hara was not very good and neither was this movie. In an attempt to make Cooper sympathetic, he went beyond vulnerability and into wimpdom. Charles Bronson, who had worked with Cooper in VERA CRUZ and U.S.S TEAKETTLE, turns up in a cameo. Cooper and O'Hara had met 22 years before when O'Hara came to Hollywood (which he disliked) to visit Clifford Odets. While he was in California, as a lark he appeared as an extra in Cooper's triumph THE GENERAL DIED AT DAWN. In a small role with Bronson, see if you can recognize the man who played the Russian representative in ROCKY IV, Michael Pataki.

p, Charles Brackett; d&w, Philip Dunne (based on the novel by John O'Hara); ph, Joe MacDonald (CinemaScope); m, Leigh Harline; ed, David Bretherton; md, Lionel Newman; art d, Lyle R. Wheeler, Addison Hehr; set d, Walter M. Scott, Eli Beneche; cos, Charles LeMaire; spec eff, L.B. Abbott; makeup, Ben Nye.

Drama   Cas.   (PR:A-C MPAA:NR)

10 RILLINGTON PLACE*   (1971, Brit.) 111m
                                        Genesis-Filmways-COL/COL c**

Richard Attenborough (*John Reginald Christie*), Judy Geeson (*Beryl Evans*), John Hurt (*Timothy John Evans*), Pat Heywood (*Mrs. Ethel Christie*), Isobel Black (*Alice*), Miss Riley (*Baby Geraldine*), Phyllis McMahon (*Muriel Eady*), Ray Barron (*Workman Willis*), Douglas Blackwell (*Workman Jones*), Gabrielle Daye (*Mrs. Lynch*), Jimmy Gardner (*Mr. Lynch*), Edward Evans (*Detective Inspector*), Tenniel Evans (*Detective Sergeant*), David Jackson, Jack Carr, George Lee, Richard Coleman (*Constables*), Andre Morell (*Judge Lewis*), Robert Hardy (*Malcolm Morris*), Geoffrey Chater (*Christmas Humpreys*), Basil Dignam, Norman Henry, Edward Burnham (*Medical Board*), Edwin Brown (*Hangman*), Norma Shebbeare (*Woman in Cafe*), Sam Kydd (*Furniture Dealer*), Reg Lye (*Tramp*), Rudolph Walker, Tommy Ansah (*West Indians*), Edward Cast (*Plainclothes Sergeant*), Tony Thawnton (*Desk Sergeant*), Fred Hugh, Art Gross, Howard Lang (*Men in Pub*), Uel Deane (*Irish Tenor*), Margaret Boyd (*Old Lady*).

Attenborough portrays murderer John Reginald Christie, whose actions led to the hanging of an innocent man and the eventual abolition of capital punishment in Britain. The film picks up in 1944, as Attenborough coaxes a young lady into his flat by promising a cure for her bronchitis. Once inside, he renders her unconscious with gas, then rapes and strangles her, burying the body in his back yard. Several years later, Hurt and wife Geeson, along with their baby daughter, move into the building and are charmed by Attenborough, who claims all sorts of medical and legal knowledge. Later Geeson learns she is pregnant and wants an abortion. Hurt loudly kicks her out of the apartment, but relents when Attenborough tells him that he can do the operation. He murders Geeson the same way he killed the earlier victim and tells Hurt she died during the operation. He further tells Hurt that he should go away and leave the child in his care. Numbed by Geeson's death and never too bright, Hurt does as he is told. That same night, the child's cries disturb Attenborough, so he kills her. Hurt goes to Wales, but Geeson's death and his culpability weigh on his mind and he goes to the police and confesses to murdering her. At his trial, Hurt tells the facts, but is condemned by perjured testimony from Attenborough. On a cold March day in 1950, Hurt is hanged. Attenborough's wife learns what has been going on under her own roof and threatens to tell police, but her husband adds her to the tally of victims. He kills several more women, secreting their bodies under the floors and in the walls of his home. Eventually he moves out of the house and the new residents find three of the bodies hidden behind a door. Attenborough is arrested and confesses his crimes (although he always denied killing the child) and is hanged in 1953. Based on the Christie-Evans case, the film is painstakingly accurate, and was shot in the building next door to the one where the actual killings took place. After filming was completed, the entire block, now renamed Ruston Close, was razed and council houses built on the location. Attenborough is excellent as the banal, middle-class killer and Hurt is effective as usual as the man too dim to keep himself from being executed for a crime he didn't commit. The film is somber and frightening, and omits the stylistic flourishes that marred director Fleischer's previous excursion into the world of true crime, THE BOSTON STRANGLER. Character actor Bernard Lee essayed a role as the chief inspector of police in the film–a familiar role for him–but was cut from the final release print. Director Fleischer helmed two other suspense-filled films the same year, THE LAST RUN and SEE NO EVIL.

p, Martin Ransohoff, Leslie Linder; w, Clive Exton (based on the book by Ludovic Kennedy); d, Richard Fleischer; ph, Denys Coop (Eastmancolor); m, John Dankworth; ed, Ernest Walter; md, Dankworth; art d, Maurice Carter; set d, Andrew Campbell; makeup, Stuart Freeborn.

Crime   Cas.   (PR:O MPAA:GP)

TEN SECONDS TO HELL½**   (1959) 93m Seven Arts-Hammer/UA
                                                                    bw**

Jeff Chandler (*Karl Wirtz*), Jack Palance (*Eric Koertner*), Martine Carol (*Margot Hofer*), Robert Cornthwaite (*Loeffler*), Dave Willock (*Tillig*), Wesley Addy (*Sulke*), Jimmy Goodwin (*Globke*), Virginia Baker (*Frau Bauer*), Richard Wattis (*Maj. Haven*), Nancy Lee (*Ruth Sulke*), Charles Nolte (*American Doctor*).

Chandler and Palance play it tough in this WW II drama as members of a German bomb squad. Each member of the squad puts a portion of his pay into a common pool, the last surviving member of the group to collect it all. The squad is decimated one by one until only Palance and Chandler are left. Finally, summoned to deactivate a blockbuster bomb, Chandler tries to rig it so that Palance is blown up–but the reverse happens. The pair falter somewhat in trying to put across German accents, but with a can't-miss formula for suspense the audience is paying more attention to their possible doom. Unfortunately Aldrich's direction favors examination of the bomb

deactivating technique over the development of character.

p, Michael Carreras; d, Robert Aldrich; w, Aldrich, Teddi Sherman (based on the novel The Phoenix by Lawrence P. Bachmann); ph, Ernest Laszlo; m, Kenneth V. Jones; ed, Harry Richardson, James Needs; art d, Ken Adam.

Drama   (PR:A MPAA:NR)

TEN TALL MEN½**   (1951) 97m Norma/COL c**

Burt Lancaster (*Sgt. Mike Kincaid*), Jody Lawrance (*Mahla*), Gilbert Roland (*Cpl. Luis Delgado*), Kieron Moore (*Cpl. Pierre Molier*), George Tobias (*Londos*), John Dehner (*Jardine*), Nick Dennis (*Mouse*), Mike Mazurki (*Roshko*), Gerald Mohr (*Caid Hussin*), Ian MacDonald (*Lustig*), Mari Blanchard (*Marie DeLatour*), Donald Randolph (*Yussif*), Robert Clary (*Mossul*), Henry Rowland (*Kurt*), Michael Pate (*Browning*), Stephen Bekassy (*Lt. Kruger*), Raymond Greenleaf (*Sheik Ben Allal*), Paul Marion (*Eijah*), Henri Letondal (*Administrator*), Philip Van Zandt (*Henri*), Joy Windsor, JoAnn Arnold, Edith Sheets, Diana Dawson, Gwen Caldwell, Helen Reichman (*Ladies in Waiting*), George Khoury (*Aide*), Nick Cravat, Shimen Ruskin (*Disgruntled Riffs*), Carlo Tricoli (*Holy Man*), Tom Conroy (*Chanter/Hussin's Aide*), Alan Ray, Frank Arnold, Ralph Volkie (*Riffs*), Mickey Simpson (*Giant Riff*), Charlita, Rita Conde (*Belles*), Benny Burt (*Beggar*).

In between the successes of JIM THORPE–ALL AMERICAN and THE CRIMSON PIRATE, Lancaster took time out to make this quick adventure which, like THE CRIMSON PIRATE, is an unashamed self-parody. Lancaster is a sergeant in the Foreign Legion. After deliberately disobeying a lieutenant he gets tossed into jail, finding himself in a cell with nine fellow Legionnaires. While imprisoned, Lancaster learns that Riff bandits plan to invade their city. He and the other jailed men volunteer to undertake a mission to thwart the Riffs. For their plan to work the hardy band kidnaps Lawrance, the daughter of a sheik who is set to marry an important member of another Arab clan. The plan succeeds, which stops the two groups from uniting into a larger faction. The Riffs are diverted and all ends peacefully for the Legionnaires. Lancaster was building his reputation as the leading screen athlete of the time and, though minor, this film adds to that lore. He bares his chest in a manly fashion as he romps around on his horse, fights, takes on the Riffs, and even finds time to try to make a little love with Lawrance. The film relies a good deal on near-slapstick comedy, with the Riffs portrayed as the biggest band of buffoons since the Keystone Kops took nightsticks in hand. There are smaller spoofs as well within the broad comedy as in the constant tongue-in-check references to Lancast er by his men as "Sarge." An amazingly good sandstorm (coming just in the nick of time to help Lancaster, naturally) is a highlight, creating a believable Sahara storm on a set thousands of miles from the desert. Made as a diversion between films, TEN TALL MEN did well at the box office and helped to further Lancaster's image.

p, Harold Hecht; d, Willis Goldbeck; w, Roland Kibbee, Frank Davis (based on a story by James Warner Bellah, Goldbeck); ph, William Snyder (Technicolor); ed, William Lyon; md, Morris Stoloff; art d, Carl Anderson.

Adventure/Comedy   (PR:AA MPAA:NR)

10:30 P.M. SUMMER½**   (1966, U.S./Span.) 85m Jorilie-Argos/Lopert c**

Melina Mercouri (*Maria*), Romy Schneider (*Claire*), Peter Finch (*Paul*), Julian Mateos (*Rodrigo Palestra*), Isabel Maria Perez (*Judith*), Beatriz Savon (*Rodrigo's Wife*).

Lesbianism, adultery, and murder are all mixed up in this farrago which attempted to combine the talents of director Dassin and New Wave novelist Duras. Dassin's real-life wife, Mercouri, is cast as the alcoholic wife of Finch, both of whom are traveling through Spain with their daughter and Schneider, who presumably (it is never stated) is Mercouri's lover and the lover also of adulterous Finch (with a child in their entourage]). Along the way Mercouri and Schneider take a shower together, there are some highly erotic lovemaking scenes between Finch and Schneider (imagined by Mercouri or real, the audience never knows), and finally Mercouri befriends a simple Spaniard who has just murdered his wife and her lover, hiding him and promising that the next day she will take him across the border to safety. The next day she finds him dead in his hiding place, and after a bitter argument with Schneider, she leaves her husband and child and sets out on her own. New Wave or Old Hat, it is simply a dull story boringly told and indifferently acted.

p, Jules Dassin, Anatole Litvak; d, Dassin; w, Dassin, Marguerite Duras (based on a novella by Duras); ph, Gabor Pogany (Technicolor); m, Cristobal Halffter; ed, Roger Dwyre; art d, Enrique Alarcon.

Drama   (PR:O MPAA:NR)

TEN THOUSAND BEDROOMS**   (1957) 114m MGM c**

Dean Martin (*Ray Hunter*), Anna Maria Alberghetti (*Nina Martelli*), Eva Bartok (*Maria Martelli*), Dewey Martin (*Mike Clark*), Walter Slezak (*Papa Vittorio Martelli*), Paul Henreid (*Anton*), Jules Munshin (*Arthur*), Marcel Dalio (*Vittorio Cisini*), Evelyn Varden (*Countess Alzani*), Lisa Montell (*Diana Martelli*), Lisa Gaye (*Anna Martelli*), John Archer (*Bob Dudley*), Steve Dunne (*Tom Crandall*), Dean Jones (*Dan*), Monique Van Vooren (*Gir on Main Title).*

Dean Martin's first film without his former partner, Jerry Lewis, TEN THOUSAND BEDROOMS failed to live up to the promise of the title. Martin starred as an easygoing hotel magnate (hence the title) who takes off for Rome to check out a new acquisition. Meantime, he gets involved with the four daughters of Slezak, particularly Bartok, the eldest. Those who thought they'd never miss Lewis were by now begging for him to come back. This brainless entertainment includes the tunes "Ten Thousand Bedrooms," "Money Is a Problem," "You I Love," "Only Trust Your Heart" (Nicholas Brodszky, Sammy Cahn, both sung by Martin and Alberghetti), "The Man Who Plays the Mandolin" (George Fancuilli), "Nisa" (Marilyn Keith, Alan Bergman), "We're Gonna Rock Around the Clock" (Max C. Freedman, Jimmy De Knight, sung by Lisa Gaye), "No One But You" (Jack Lawrence, Brodszky, sung by Gaye).

p, Joe Pasternak; d, Richard Thorpe; w, Laslo Vadnay, Art Cohn, William Ludwig, Leonard Spigelgass; ph, Robert Bronner (CinemaScope, Metrocolor); ed, John McSweeney, Jr.; md, George Stoll; art d, William A. Horning, Randall Duell; cos, Helen Rose.

Musical/Comedy   **(PR:A   MPAA:NR)**

10,000 DOLLARS BLOOD MONEY*½   (1966, Ital.) 97m Zenith/Flora
                          c (10,000 DOLLARI PER UN MASSACRO)

Gary Hudson [Gianni Garko] *(Django)*, Claudio Camaso, Adriana Ambesi, Fernando Sancho, Loredana Nuschiah, Pinuccio Ardia.

A standard spaghetti western which tells the saga of a bounty hunter who turns his back on an offer to aid a rich landowner in getting his daughter back from a kidnaper. Instead he joins up with the criminal but is soon double-crossed, causing him to change his mind about saving the girl.

p, Mino Loy, Luciano Martino; d, Romolo Guerrieri; w, Martino, Franco Fogagnolo, Ernesto Gastaldi, Sauro Scavolini; ph, Frederico Zanni.

Western   **(PR:O   MPAA:NR)**

10 TO MIDNIGHT*   (1983) 101m Y&M-City/Cannon c

Charles Bronson *(Leo Kessler)*, Lisa Eilbacher *(Laurie Kessler)*, Andrew Stevens *(Paul McAnn)*, Gene Davis *(Warren Stacy)*, Geoffrey Lewis *(Dave Dante)*, Wilford Brimley *(Capt. Malone)*, Robert Lyons *(Nathan Zager)*, Bert Williams *(Mr. Johnson)*, Iva Lane *(Bunny)*, Ola Ray *(Ola)*, Kelly Palzis *(Doreen)*, Cosie Costa *(Dudley)*, Paul McCallum *(Lab Technician)*, Jeana Tomasina *(Karen)*, June Gilbert *(Betty)*, Arthur Hansel *(Judge)*, Sam Chew *(Minister)*, Katrina Parish *(Tina)*, Shawn Schepps *(Peg)*, Sydna Scott *(Mrs. Johnson)*, Barbara Pilavin *(Mrs. Byrd)*, Beau Billingslea *(Desk Sergeant)*, James Keane *(Jerry)*, Jerome Thor *(Medical Examiner)*, Breck Costin *(Tim Bailey)*, Carmen Filpi *(Hotel Clerk)*, Deran Sarafian *(Dale Anders)*, Jeane Manson *(Margo)*, Lynette Harrison *(Ticket Girl)*, Neal Fleming *(Young Man)*, John Garwood *(Millikan)*, Shay Duffin *(Nestor)*, Daniel Ades *(Ben Linker)*, Cynthia Reams *(Hooker)*, Kyle Edward Cranston *(Party Intern)*, Patti Tippo *(Party Girl)*, Beth Reinglass, Monica Ekblad *(Office Girls)*.

A disturbing, unpleasant Bronson vigilante picture which has the usual perverted madman killing the usual helpless women. Bronson as a cop is determined to put him away even if it means tampering with the evidence to do so. If it weren't for Bronson this would be a waste.

p, Pancho Kohner, Lance Hool; d, J. Lee Thompson; w, William Roberts; ph, Adam Greenberg (Metrocolor); m, Robert O. Ragland; ed, Peter Lee Thompson; art d, Jim Freiburger; set d, Cecilia Rodarte; cos, Robert Dale, Del Adey-Jones; makeup, Alan Marshall.

Action/Crime   **Cas.**   **(PR:O   MPAA:R)**

10 VIOLENT WOMEN**   (1982) 95m Cinema Features/New
                                        American-Aquarius c

Sherri Vernon *(Samantha)*, Dixie Lauren *(Maggie)*, Georgia Morgan *(Bri Terry)*, Jane Farnsworth *(Madge)*, Ted V. Mikels *(Leo)*, Anne Gaybis *(Vickie)*, Melodie Bell, Christina de Cattani.

Ted V. Mikels, the creator of such memorable bad movies as THE ASTRO-ZOMBIES (1967) and BLOOD ORGY OF THE SHE DEVILS (1973), returns to the scene with this exercise in exploitative cinema. The title women (though there never seems to be more than eight of them) are coal miners who grow tired of laboring in the pits and begin a crime spree. A jewelry store heist comes off perfectly, but their fence (Mikels himself) trades them cocaine for the gems, and when they try to deal that, they are arrested by narcotics agents. In jail they are submitted to the usual indignities found in women-in-prison movies, including the obligatory large, sadistic lesbian guard. Two of the women (Vernon and Lauren) see how bad conditions are and waste no time breaking out. They end up on an Arab sheik's yacht sailing for freedom and happiness. Trash, but thoroughly good-natured trash, and an example of filmmaking not seen since the heyday of New World Pictures.

p&d, Ted V. Mikels; w, Mikels, James Gordon White; ph, Yuval Shousterman (Movielab Color); m, Nicholas Carras; ed, Mikels; prod d, Mike McClusky.

Crime   **(PR:O   MPAA:R)**

TEN WANTED MEN**   (1955) 80m Ranown/COL c

Randolph Scott *(John Stewart)*, Jocelyn Brando *(Corinne Michaels)*, Richard Boone *(Wick Campbell)*, Alfonso Bedoya *(Hermando)*, Donna Martell *(Maria Segura)*, Skip Homeier *(Howie Stewart)*, Clem Bevans *(Tod Grinnel)*, Leo Gordon *(Frank Scavo)*, Minor Watson *(Jason Carr)*, Lester Matthews *(Adam Stewart)*, Tom Powers *(Green)*, Dennis Weaver *(Sheriff Clyde Gibbons)*, Lee Van Cleef *(Al Drucker)*, Kathleen Crowley *(Marva Gibbons)*, Boyd "Red" Morgan *(Red Dawes)*, Denver Pyle *(Dave Weed)*, Francis McDonald *(Warner)*, Pat Collins *(Bartender)*, Louis Jean Heydt *(Tom Baines)*, Paul Maxey, Jack Perrin, Julian Rivero, Carlos Vera, Edna Holland, Reed Howes, Terry Frost, Franklyn Farnum, George Boyce.

A formula oater made by Scott's own production company stars him as a powerful rancher of the Arizona range who makes an attempt to rule the vast area through lawful means. He meets opposition, however, from landowner Boone, who still prefers the power and persuasion of the pistol. A rivalry builds between the two with Scott coming out on top after a climactic fight, in which, unfortunately, the double used for Scott is painfully apparent.

p, Harry Joe Brown; d, Bruce Humberstone; w, Kenneth Gamet (based on the story by Irving Ravetch, Harriet Frank, Jr.); ph, Wilfrid M. Cline (Technicolor); m, Paul Sawtell; ed, Gene Havlick.

Western   **(PR:A-C   MPAA:NR)**

TEN WHO DARED zero   (1960) 92m Disney/BV c

Brian Keith *(William Dunn)*, John Beal *(Maj. John Wesley Powell)*, James Drury *(Walter Powell)*, R.G. Armstrong *(Oramel Howland)*, Ben Johnson *(George Bradley)*, L.Q. Jones *(Billy Hawkins)*, Dan Sheridan *(Jack Sumner)*, David Stollery *(Andrew Hall)*, Stan Jones *(Seneca Howland)*, David Frankham *(Frank Goodman)*, Pat Hogan *(Indian Chief)*, Ray Walker *(McSpadden)*, Jack Bighead *(Ashtishkel)*, Roy Barcroft *(Jim Baker)*, Dawn Little Sky *(Indian Woman)*.

Given the task of teaching school children U.S. history, TEN WHO DARED would be outperformed by flashcards. A very bad movie, it lacks even beautiful locations and good photography (this one has enough zoom shots to sprain an assistant cameraman's wrist). Based on the true-life adventures of one-armed Maj. John Wesley Powell, the tale dwells on his dangerous expedition down the Colorado River in 1869, which only six of his crew survived. Unfortunately, none of the excitement makes it to the screen, nor does any sympathy for the characters. Noteworthy only for being Disney's worst effort.

p, Walt Disney; d, William Beaudine; w, Lawrence Edward Watkin (based on the journal of Maj. John Wesley Powell); ph, Gordon Avil (Technicolor); m, Oliver Wallace; ed, Norman Palmer, Cotton Warburton; art d, Carroll Clark, Hilyard Brown; set d, Emile Kuri; cos, Chuck Keehne; spec eff, Ub Iwerks; m/l, "Ten Who Dared," "Jolly Rovers," "Roll Along," Watkin, Stan Jones; makeup, Pat McNally.

Adventure   **(PR:A   MPAA:NR)**

TENANT, THE***   (1976, Fr.) 124m PAR c (LE LOCATAIRE)

Roman Polanski *(Trelkovsky)*, Isabelle Adjani *(Stella)*, Shelley Winters *(Concierge)*, Melvyn Douglas *(Mr. Zy)*, Jo Ann Fleet *(Mme. Dioz)*, Bernard Fresson *(Scope)*, Lila Kedrova *(Mme. Gaderian)*, Claude Dauphin *(Husband)*, Claude Pieplu *(Neighbor)*, Rufus *(Badar)*, Romain Bouteille *(Simon)*, Jacques Monod *(Cafe Proprietor)*, Patrice Alexandre *(Robert)*, Josiane Balasko *(Viviane)*, Jean Pierre Bagot *(Policeman)*, Michel Blanc *(Scope's Neighbor)*, Jacky Cohen *(Stella's Friend)*, Florence Blot *(Mme. Zy)*, Bernard Donnadieu *(Bar Waiter)*, Alain Frerot *(Beggar)*, Gerard Jugnot *(Office Clerk)*, Raoul Guylad *(Priest)*, Helena Manson *(Head Nurse)*, Arlette Reinerg *(Tramp)*, Eva Ionesco *(Mme. Gaderian's Daughter)*, Gerard Pereira *(Drunk)*, Maite Nahyr *(Lucille)*, Andre Penvern *(Cafe Waiter)*, Dominique Poulange *(Simone Choule)*, Serge Spira *(Philippe)*, Jacques Rosny *(Jean-Claude)*, Vanessa Vaylor *(Martine)*, Francois Viaur *(Police Sergeant)*.

A creepy psychological horror tale starring Polanski as a young Polish office clerk living in Paris. He rents an apartment in a serene building populated by bitter elderly folks who have their eyes on Polanski (or so it seems) from the start. He is told that the previous tenant, named Simone, jumped from the apartment window. He pays a visit to the dying Simone, an unidentifiable person covered head to toe in wrappings. While there, he meets Adjani, an old friend of Simone's. Simone soon lets out a bloodcurdling scream and dies. Polanski and Adjani are bonded by this dreadful experience and nearly become lovers, but drift apart. Meantime, Polanski has increasing difficulty when it comes to pleasing his fellow-tenants–they complain that he makes noise (though we don't see or hear anything) and threaten to "take steps." He grows steadily more interested in Simone–who she was, what she was interested in, why she died, and why she hid a tooth in a crack in the wall. A neighborhood cafe owner insists on serving Polanski hot cocoa and Marlboros (Simone's favorites) when he prefers coffee and Gauloises. His paranoia increases. He is certain he is being watched from across the courtyard (we begin to share his fear since we are able to see the mysterious

Peeping Toms also). In short, he is positive that they, his neighbors, are trying to kill him. He renews his relationship with Adjani, sleeps with her, and tells her he loves her. His paranoia, however, seems less justified as the film progresses–he destroys both his and later Adjani's apartments, creating a great deal of noise, and imagines himself being strangled in his courtyard. He sees himself as Simone and, in the most frightening fashion, begins to act like her and wear her clothes. He buys a wig and makes up his face. He paints his nails. A bloodcurdling scream is again heard. In many ways THE TENANT is REPULSION, with Polanski in the Catherine Deneuve role. The concept of a person's inside world clashing with the outside world until no sense can be made of either is quite apparent. In both cases the result of these two conflicting forces leads to violence. We are never really sure if there is a plot against Polanski (or if strange men are terrorizing Deneuve), but a logical interpretation tells us that he is imagining everything. We can assume that Polanski moved into an apartment previously inhabited by a suicide and then simply began to live that person's life in order to understand why she killed herself. What makes the film so effective, however, is the uneasy feeling that maybe Polanski's character is right– maybe they are trying to kill him. Technically, THE TENANT is superb– Nykvist's stunning camerawork (an incredible electronically operated crane shot opens the film), Sarde's eerie score, and thoroughly convincing performances from each and every performer. Adjani, one of the most beautiful actresses on the screen today, is made to look surprisingly frumpy (forcing her to rely even more on her excellent acting ability) and, believe it, is less attractive than Polanski in drag. Well, not really.

p, Andrew Braunsberg; d, Roman Polanski; w, Polanski, Gerard Brach (based on the novel LE LOCATAIRE CHIMERIQUE by Roland Topor); ph, Sven Nykvist (Panavision, Eastmancolor); m, Phillippe Sarde; ed, Francoise Bonnot; prod d, Pierre Guffroy; md, Hubert Rostaing; art d, Claude Moesching, Albert Rajau; set d, Eric Simon; cos, Jacques Schmidt.

Horror/Drama   **Cas.**   **(PR:O MPAA:R)**

TENCHU!**   (1970, Jap.) 140m Katsu-Fuji Telecasting/Daiei c
(HITOKIRI)

Shintaro Katsu (Izo Okada), Tatsuya Nakadai (Hampeita Takechi), Yukio Mishima (Shimbei Tanaka), Yujiro Ishihara (Ryoma Sakamoto), Mitsuko Baisho (Onimo), Takumi Shinjo (Minakawa), Noberu Nakaya, Tsutomo Shimomoto, Kei Yamamoto.

Set during the mid 1800s, TENCHU! tells the story of a group of political supporters who attempt to restore their emperor to the throne. Nakadai, however, is intent on securing the position for himself, hiring a warrior to reduce his competition. After Nakadai's rise to power, the warrior is placed in a prison where he eventually commits hara-kiri. Yukio Mishima, one of Japan's greatest writers, appears in a supporting role, just one year before he himself was to commit hara-kiri during a political overthrow.

d, Hideo Gosha; w, Shinobu Hashimoto; ph, Fujio Morita (Daiei Scope, Eastmancolor); m, Masaru Sato; art d, Yoshinobu Nishioka.

Historical Drama   **(PR:O MPAA:NR)**

TENDER COMRADE**   (1943) 102m RKO bw

Ginger Rogers (Jo), Robert Ryan (Chris), Ruth Hussey (Barbara), Patricia Collinge (Helen Stacey), Mady Christians (Manya), Kim Hunter (Doris), Jane Darwell (Mrs. Henderson), Mary Forbes (Jo's Mother), Richard Martin (Mike), Richard Gaines (Waldo Pierson), Patti Brill (Western Union Girl), Euline Martin (Baby), Edward Fielding (Doctor), Claire Whitney (Nurse), Donald Davis, Robert Anderson (Boys).

This archetypical WW II film features Rogers in a straight dramatic role as a woman left on the home front when her husband (Ryan) is killed in battle. After giving birth to a son, Rogers realizes she needs to be around others in order to get through her ordeal both financially and emotionally. She moves into a house with some fellow workers at a defense plant, which include Hussey, Collinge, Hunter, and Christians. Each has a similar story of the war's effect on their lives. Hussey worries about her Navy husband and stories she has heard about the affairs military men carry on overseas. Collinge suffers as both her husband and son are off doing their part, while Hunter waits for her new husband to return on a furlough so they can consummate the marriage. Mixed into this soap opera are messages that touch on just about every issue that faced the average American of the day, including the importance of obeying ration laws, the price of freedom, and plenty of old fashioned flag-waving patriotism. The story is told episodically and doesn't miss a trick in attempting to wring tears from the audience. The musical score goes heavy on the string section, milking as much sentiment from a scene as is humanly possible. Each actress gives her all, which only adds to the over-emotionalized feelings. Rogers in particular overacts, spouting lines which are comical in retrospect. Audiences of the day were

hungry for material like this and the film was a box-office success, grossing some $843,000. Dmytryk's direction is overdone, to say the least, emphasizing the gung ho spirit of Trumbo's script to the point of being ridiculous. At the time these two filmmakers thought they were doing their part for the war effort, little realizing that TENDER COMRADE would later come back in ways they never could have imagined. When the two were called before the House Un-American Activities Committee (HUAC) as members of the "Hollywood Ten" this film was used against them in the government's case for their Communist leanings. This well-meaning portrait of women working together in a collective and sharing things equally was interpreted by some Communist witch hunters as out-and-out propaganda cleverly disguised as a woman's drama. Rogers, whom Dmytryk had looked forward to working with, also turned against the two, claiming that what she had perceived to be anti-American sentiments had popped up in her dialog. The experience left Dmytryk a little bitter about the nature of the American way. In his autobiography It's A Hell of a Life But Not a Bad Living he wrote: "Their motto (in TENDER COMRADE) is 'share and share alike,' which sounded quite innocently democratic when we made the film, but which turned up to haunt me a few years later when I was instructed that the real motto of a democracy is 'Get what you can while you can and the devil take the hindmost.'"

p, David Hempstead; d, Edward Dmytryk; w, Dalton Trumbo (based on a story by Trumbo); ph, Russell Metty; m, Leigh Harline; ed, Roland Gross; md, C. Bakaleinikoff; art d, Albert D'Agostino, Carroll Clark; set d, Darrell Silvera, Al Fields; cos, Edith Head, Renie; spec eff, Vernon L. Walker; makeup, Mel Burns.

Drama   **(PR:A MPAA:NR)**

TENDER FLESH*½   (1976) 85m Brut/WB (AKA: WELCOME TO
ARROW BEACH)

Laurence Harvey (Jason Henry), Joanna Pettet (Grace Henry), Stuart Whitman (Deputy Rakes), John Ireland (Sheriff H. "Duke" Bingham), Gloria Leroy (Ginger), David Macklin (Alex Heath), Dody Heath (Felice), Meg Foster (Robbin Stanley), Altovise Gore (Deputy Molly), Elizabeth St. Clair (Head Nurse), Jesse Vint (Hot Rod Driver).

An oddity which stars Harvey (who also acted as executive producer and director) as a war vet who, upon his return to California, finds he has an appetite for human flesh, a fondness shared by his sister, Pettet. Foster is a flower child who stumbles across the cannibalistic pair and goes to the police with her supposedly farfetched tale. The final picture of Harvey's, who starred in ROOM AT THE TOP and BUTTERFIELD 8, is definitely a change of pace. Harvey died of cancer, at age 45, the year TENDER FLESH came out.

p, Jack Cushingham, Steven North; d, Laurence Harvey; w, Wallace C. Bennett, Jack Gross, Jr (based on a story by Bennett); ph, Gerald Perry Finnerman (Eastmancolor); m, Tony Camillo; ed, James Potter; m/l, "Who Can Tell Us Why?" Bert Keyes, George Barrie, Sammy Cahn.

Horror   **(PR:O MPAA:R)**

TENDER HEARTS**   (1955) 78m Haas bw

Hugo Haas (Valentine), Francesca de Scaffa (Jenette), June Hammerstein (June), Jeffrey Stone (Chauffeur), Ken Carlton (Jim), John Vosper (Mr. Hawkins), Tracy Roberts (Mrs. Hawkins), Tony Jochim (Butler), Pat Goldin (Foxie), Sid Melton (Shmoe), Steve Mitchell (Bus Driver).

A kind-hearted beggar, appropriately named Valentine, lives in squalor with his pet pooch, Flip, but finally gives away his furry companion to a wealthy family when he becomes too sick to care for it. One of the better shows of talents from the versatile Haas.

p,d&w, Hugo Haas; ph, Eddie Fitzgerald; m, Ernest Gold; ed, Robert Eisen.

Drama   **(PR:A MPAA:NR)**

TENDER IS THE NIGHT*½**   (1961) 146m FOX c

Jennifer Jones (Nicole Diver), Jason Robards, Jr. (Dick Diver), Joan Fontaine (Baby Warren), Tom Ewell (Abe North), Cesare Danova (Tommy Barban), Jill St. John (Rosemary Hoyt), Paul Lukas (Dr. Dohmler), Bea Benadaret (Mrs. McKisko), Charles Fredericks (Mr. McKisko), Sanford Meisner (Dr. Gregorovious), Mac McWhorter (Colis Clay), Albert Carrier (Louis), Richard De Combray (Francisco), Carole Mathews (Mrs. Hoyt), Alan Napier (Pardo), Leslie Farrell (Topsy Diver), Michael Crisalli (Lanier Diver), Earl Grant (Piano Player), Maurice Dallimore (Sir Charles Golding), Carol Veazie (Mrs. Dunphrey), Arlette Clark (Governess), Marcel de la Brosse (Proprietor), Art Salter (Photographer), Armand Largo (Reporter), Michael Korda (Italian Gentleman), George Clark (Young Roman Aristocrat), Eric Feldary (Headwaiter), Joe La Cava (Bartender), Con Convert (Female Impersonator), Jacques Gallo (Gendarme), Florene Williams (Girl), Tom Hernandez (Nobleman), Vera de Winter, Katherine Berger, Renee Godfrey (Nurses), Orrin Tucker (Musician), Nora Evans (Singer), Bruno Della Santana (Reception Clerk), Jean de Briac (Dr. Faurore), Louis Mercier (Concierge), Jean Bori (Barber), Carl Princi (Assistant Manager), Gilbert Paol (Maitre d'), Linda Hutchins, Maggi Brown, John Richardson (Bits).

Famed author Fitzgerald's semi-autobiographical novel of the woman-induced downfall of a man who once saw a brilliant career in his future, set amidst the decadence of post-WW I Europe–with its many American expatriates–is given a slow, syrupy cinematic treatment here by director King (whose habit was to dwell unduly on noncritical visuals). The story opens at the posh French Riviera villa occupied by affluent young Jones and her husband, Robards. Among their party guests is a beautiful cinema starlet, St. John, to whom Robards takes a fancy. Jones' jealousy at this occurrence brings on a relapse of a mental disorder to which she had once been prey, and she creates an ugly scene. In flashback, the picture shifts to a psychiatric clinic in Zurich, Switzerland, staffed by Robards, who performs his doctoring chores under the friendly supervision of an older physician, Lucas. Remanded to the care of Robards, Jones–whose illness was induced by an early incestuous sexual assault by her father– effects the appropriate emotional transference during her treatment and falls desperately in love with Robards. The latter is under her spell as well, a condition the talented young psychiatrist confesses to his mentor, Lukas. The older doctor warns his coprofessional colleague against marriage to Jones, pointing out that his function–as Robards should well know–is to serve as a crutch for the temporarily disabled, a barrier against another breakdown. Lukas warns that Jones will soon discover Robards to be not a god, not a haven offering respite from emotional turmoil, but merely a frail and fallible human being. Robards disregards the portentous advice and marries Jones. Continuing the type of relationship they had developed for therapeutic reasons at the clinic, Robards accords his bride her every folly, playing a nurturing role through a seemingly endless whirl of high-society socializing. Party follows party–all funded through the none-too-gracious funnel of Fontaine, Jones' older sister and guardian, who holds the purse strings of the family fortune–their lives a hedonistic, empty carousel of pleasure. Finally, the tragic end of besotted Ewell–a once-great Broadway songwriter turned expatriate drunk–in a gratuitous bar brawl brings edification to Robards. He resolves to rejoin the Zurich clinic staff to put some purpose in his dissolute existence. It is too late, though; his support for Jones' chosen path has sapped him of will. He functions as a failure at the clinic, unable to regain his former skills, using alcohol as personal therapy. Leaving Lukas again, he tries to recapture the life style he formerly led with his bride, but he fails even at this. Jones, strengthened in direct proportion to Robards' increasing deterioration, asks him to divorce her so that she might marry her lover. To proud to beg, and too dissolute to battle, he accedes to her request. Rejected by both of the worlds he has explored so fervently, Robards departs, a prodigal returning to the tiny town of his birth in the U.S., hoping to find renewal of spirit. Actress Jones was a little long in the tooth to play this spirited simulation of author Fitzgerald's disturbed wife Zelda; she had not appeared in a picture since A FAREWELL TO ARMS five years previously. Robards plays his role without evidencing the gradual dissolution required of his character, seeming too much in control at all times. The people and the period had been covered before–in the 1957 release of Ernest Hemingway's THE SUN ALSO RISES–which had a lot more *elan* but lacked the period flavor of TENDER IS THE NIGHT. Hurting for cash, Fitzgerald had tried unsuccessfully to peddle his none-too-successful novel (in terms of sales, that is) to Hollywood as early as 1934. With the assistance of a younger, untested writer, Charles Marquis Warren–who was later to become a successful TV writer, originating such series as "Gunsmoke" and "Rawhide"–Fitzgerald prepared his own screen treatment of his novel. He then financed a trip to Hollywood for Warren, who had received $250 for his screen-treatment efforts, and Warren made the rounds of all the major studios trying to sell the concept. Warren had letters of introduction from his better-known peer, saying of him "I haven't believed in anybody so strongly since Ernest Hemingway." All to no avail; the studio moguls were distressed by the theme of incestuous molestation leading to the emotional imbalance of the heroine. Only two studios–RKO and Samuel Goldwyn–nibbled at the bait; Goldwyn's studio writers actually prepared their *own* synopsis of the proposed property and telephoned Fitzgerald to sound him out, but made no firm offer for the film rights. (Fitzgerald and Warren had actually bowdlerized the novel in their own screen treatment, softening the sexuality to better suit the Hollywood formula.) Producer David O. Selznick–a long-time admirer of the author's work–was another who nibbled lightly in 1934, writing to an associate, "I can't get anything out of this synopsis, but I am such a Scott Fitzgerald fan that I hope to be able to read the book." Selznick *did* read the book later, and he loved it. He purchsed the screen rights from Fitzgerald's estate (the author's daughter Scottie was reluctant to sell such rights to filmmakers where her father's presumably autobiographical works were concerned for fear of what Hollywood might do to his memory) and worked on the script with writer Moffat. This was to be the ailing Selznick's final film, his even though he did not himself produce it. Selznick sold the script and the services of his wife Jones to 20th Century-Fox, and prodigiously flooded the director with memos about the project, in which he maintained a sustaining interest. The sale contract called for Selznick to have casting approval as well as final script approval, but the toilers in Fox's fields "$e3ignored my advice, and, in my opinion, ruined the film."

p, Henry T. Weinstein; d, Henry King; w, Ivan Moffat (based on the novel by F. Scott Fitzgerald); ph, Leon Shamroy (CinemaScope, DeLuxe Color); m, Bernard Herrmann; ed, William Reynolds; art d, Jack Martin Smith, Malcolm Brown; set d, Walter M. Scott, Paul S. Fox; cos, Marjorie Best, Pierre Balmain; spec eff, L.B. Abbott, Emil Kosa, Jr.; m/l, title song, Sammy Fain, Paul Francis Webster; makeup, Ben Nye.

Drama Cas. (PR:C MPAA:NR)

TENDER MERCIES**½ (1982) 89m EMI/UNIV c

Robert Duvall *(Mac Sledge)*, Tess Harper *(Rosa Lee)*, Betty Buckley *(Dixie)*, Wilford Brimley *(Harry)*, Ellen Barkin *(Sue Anne)*, Allan Hubbard *(Sonny)*, Lenny Von Dohlen *(Robert)*, Paul Gleason *(Reporter)*, Michael Crabtree *(Lewis Menefee)*, Norman Bennett *(Rev. Hotchkiss)*, Andrew Scott Hollon *(LaRue)*, Rick Murray *(Jake)*, Stephen Funchess *(Bertie)*, Glen Fleming *(Steve)*, James Aaron *(Henry)*, Suzanne Jacobs *(Nurse)*, Jerry Biggs *(Man at Bar)*, Sheila Bird *(Concessionaire)*, Robert E. Blackburn III *(Boy at Dance)*, Eli Cummins *(Doorman)*, Tony Frank *(Man at Motel)*, Pat Minter, Oliver Seal, Berkley H. Garrett *(Men at Dixie's House)*, Helena Humann *(Woman with Groceries)*, Barbara Jones *(Country Woman)*, Jerry Jones *(Country Man)*, Harlan Jordan *(Waiter)*, Robert P. Kelley *(Choirmaster)*, Ray LePere *(Man in Bar)*, Terry Schoolcraft *(Ada, Dixie's Dresser)*, Denise Simek *(Concessionaire)*, Susan Aston, Vicki Neff, Pamela Putnam *(Women at Dance)*, Jerry Abbot, Bobby Hibbitts, Buddie Hrabal, Jerry Matheny, Wayne Milligan *(Country Blues Band)*.

An overrated drama set in Texas, one of the continuing stories of screenwriter Foote's life in the hinterlands. Duvall, who won the Oscar for this role, is a down-and-out singer who has recently broken up with his no-nonsense wife, Buckley, who also earns her living chirping country and western tunes. Duvall does what is expected and gets rip-roaring drunk. He wakes up in a motel-gas station owned by religious Harper, a widow who is raising her son, Hubbard, by herself since her husband was killed fighting in Vietnam. When Harper offers Duvall a job, he stays on and the two fall in love. After he proposes marriage, Harper makes sure that Duvall and Hubbard are properly baptized by local reverend Bennett. Meanwhile, Buckley and her manager Brimley are lurking in the background and Duvall attempts to patch matters up with her as well as with their daughter, Barkin. He also tries to make a comeback (not that he was ever in the class of Waylon Jennings or Willie Nelson) but soon realizes that show business is not for him and that true happiness is right before his eyes in the presence of Harper and Hubbard. It's a spiritual picture, no action, no sex, nothing but lots of talk. If old values are what appeals, you might enjoy TENDER MERCIES. However, it is so out of touch with today that many moments ring falsely. Director Beresford, the Aussie who did so many good films, must have thought he could accomplish what English Michael Apted did with COAL MINER'S DAUGHTER or Czech Milos Forman did with RAGTIME. This is so patently an American story that it needed someone like Texan Robert Benton to handle it. Beresford brought several of his Down Under pals with him; editor Anderson and cinematographer Boyd among them. One song by Bobby Hart and Austin Roberts, "Over You." Foote came back to write the much superior THE TRIP TO BOUNTIFUL in 1985.

p, Philip S. Hobel, Mary-Ann Hobel, Horton Foote, Robert Duvall; d, Bruce Beresford; w, Foote; ph, Russell Boyd (Technicolor); m, George Dreyfus; ed, William Anderson; art d, Jeannine Oppewall; set d, Daniel L. May; cos, Elizabeth McBride; ch, Nick Felix.

Drama Cas. (PR:A-C MPAA:PG)

TENDER SCOUNDREL** (1967, Fr./Ital.) 94m Sud Pacifique-Fono/EM c (TENDER VOYOU, UN AVVENTURIERO A TAHITI)

Jean-Paul Belmondo *(Tony Marechal)*, Nadja Tiller *(Baroness Minna von Strasshofer)*, Mylene Demongeot *(Muriel)*, Robert Morley *(Lord Swift)*, Stefania Sandrelli *(Veronique)*, Maria Pacome *(Germaine)*, Genevieve Page *(Beatrice Dumonceaux)*, Philippe Noiret *(Dumonceaux)*, Jean-Pierre Marielle *(Bob)*, Ellen Bahl *(Josette)*, Micheline Dax *(Marjorie)*, Michele Girardon *(Stranger from the Ritz)*, Paula Dehelly *(Mlle. Aline)*, Peter Carsten *(Capt. Otto Hanz)*, Ivan Desny *(Haberdasher)*, Marcel Dalio *(Veronique's Father)*, Elisabeth Teissier.

A comedy which casts the roguish Belmondo aptly as an irresistible rogue. He constantly finds himself under the pressures of beautiful women who passionately desire him, until one day the dizzy pace of his adventures exhaust him and he decides to give up being a gigolo. Racy and amusing tale of a likable imposter.

p, Paul-Edmond Decharme; d, Jean Becker; w, Albert Simonin, Becker, Daniel Boulanger, Michel Audiard (based on the story by Simonin); ph, Edmond Sechan (Techniscope, Eastmancolor); m, Michel Legrand; ed, Monique Kirsanoff; art d, Georges Wakhevitch.

Comedy (PR:C MPAA:NR)

TENDER TRAP, THE**½ (1955) 110m MGM c

Frank Sinatra *(Charlie Y. Reader)*, Debbie Reynolds *(Julie Gillis)*, David Wayne *(Joe McCall)*, Celeste Holm *(Sylvia Crewes)*, Jarma Lewis *(Jessica Collins)*, Lola Albright *(Poppy Matson)*, Carolyn Jones *(Helen)*, Howard St. John *(Sam Sayers)*, Joey Faye *(Sol Z. Steiner)*, Tom Helmore *(Mr. Loughran)*, Willard Sage *(Director)*, Marc Wilder *(Ballet Actor)*, Jack Boyle *(Audition Dancer)*, James Drury *(Eddie)*, Benny Rubin *(Mr. Wilson)*, Reginald Simpson *(Stage Manager)*, Gil Harman *(TV Announcer)*, Madge Blake *(Society Reporter)*, Wilson Wood *(Elevator Boy)*, Frank Sully, Gordon

Richards (Doormen), Lennie Bremen, Dave White (Cab Drivers).

Moderately amusing adaptation of a hit comedy that shows off Sinatra's comedic ability and introduces a hit tune by Cahn and Van Heusen which should have won the Oscar, but didn't. Wayne, a man from Indiana, has come to visit old pal Sinatra, who is an agent in New York. Married Wayne is astounded to see the line of gorgeous women who jiggle in and out of Sinatra's bachelor life. The women include Albright, Holm, Jones, and Lewis, each one more beautiful and willing than the next. Wayne sees what he's been missing and is further amazed when Sinatra admits that his life is empty and he yearns for the solidity of a happy marriage. Sinatra goes to an audition and meets Reynolds, a virgin who is determined to get married. She is so sure of herself that she's even set the wedding date, although she still hasn't met the man who will walk her down the aisle. Wayne smells a woman who is setting a snare out and tells Sinatra that if he wants to sustain his bachelorhood, he'd wise to jettison Reynolds as this one is serious] Reynolds is a smart cookie and her trap is quite tender. She finally pulls the string and tells Sinatra, whom she's been dating, that she wouldn't consider marrying him until long after he gave up dating Jones, Lewis, Holm, and Albright. Sinatra is astounded when she gives him this ultimatum because he's never said one word about marriage to Reynolds. Time passes and when Sinatra finds that all of the aforementioned are rapidly being picked off, he understands how lonely his life truly is. He's not able to make a decision so he asks both Reynolds and Holm to marry him, on the same evening. Both accept his proposal and he is in hot water. Reynolds finds out what he's done and leaves his apartment in a huff. Sinatra tells the truth to Holm and admits that Reynolds has stolen his heart. Wayne has been watching this and tells Holm that he loves her and would be willing to avoid returning to Indiana if she would accept him. Holm lets him down gently but firmly and Wayne nods and accepts his lot in life and will go back to his home state. Holm exits, gets into the building elevator, and meets Helmore, a charming man. Before they hit the lobby, Helmore asks her out to dinner. That leads to a marriage proposal. Reynolds and Sinatra are both invited to the wedding and when Holm tosses her bridal bouquet to Sinatra, he symbolically gives it to Reynolds. The title of the film eventually came into use among the panderers in New York who referred to their streetwalkers as "tender traps" rather than prostitutes. This was a slick comedy with all the usual scenes, the hangover sequence, the "I thought you meants," and so forth. A very funny bit as career girl Holm does a parody of Reynolds that is devastating. Max Shulman, who co-authored the play's script, was one of the 1950s favorite humorists with a succession of books that were among the funniest written at the time. They included "Barefoot Boy With Cheek," "Sleep Till Noon," and "The Feather Merchants." He later created the TV series "The Many Loves Of Dobie Gillis." His cowriter was Robert Paul Smith who wrote "Where Did You Go? Out! What Did You Do? Nothing!" The screenplay was by the surviving Epstein twin, Julius, who co-wrote CASABLANCA with his brother and Howard Koch. Cahn and Van Heusen's Oscar-nominated title tune became a pop standard but lost that year to "Love is a Many Splendored Thing" from the tear-jerker of the same name. TV's "Virginian," James Drury, is seen in a small role, before he became a huge television star and lost his hair.

p, Lawrence Weingarten; d, Charles Walters; w, Julius J. Epstein (based on the play by Max Shulman, Robert Paul Smith); ph, Paul C. Vogel (CinemaScope, Eastmancolor); m, Jeff Alexander; ed, John Dunning; art d, Cedric Gibbons, Arthur Lonergan; set d, Edwin B. Willis, Jack D. Moore; cos, Helen Rose; m/l, "Love is the Tender Trap," by James Van Heusen, Sammy Cahn, sung by Frank Sinatra; makeup, William Tuttle.

Comedy   (PR:A MPAA:NR)

TENDER WARRIOR, THE   (1971) 77m Safari Films c

Dan Haggerty (Cal), Charles Lee (Sammy), Liston Elkins (Pa Lucas).

Frontier family adventures tend to be pretty harmless pieces of entertainment and THE TENDER WARRIOR is no exception. Haggerty takes on the uncharacteristic role of a mean moonshiner who gives the young Lee a hard time, as the latter and his animal friends–a chimp, lion, bear, and alligator–try to exist in the Okefenokee Swamp in Georgia. Some fascinating footage of wild animals, denizens of the frightening swamp.

p, William Thompson; d, Stewart Raffill; w, Raffill, David Dalie; ph, Gerardo H. Wenziner (Techniscope, Technicolor); m, Kenneth Wannberg; ed, John Shouse.

Adventure   Cas.   (PR:AAA MPAA:G)

TENDER YEARS, THE   (1947) 81m FOX bw

Joe E. Brown (Rev. Will Norris), Richard Lyon (Ted), Noreen Nash (Linda), Charles Drake (Bob), Josephine Hutchinson (Emily), James Millican (Barton), Griff Barnett (Sen. Cooper), Jeanne Gail (Jeanie), Harry V. Cheshire (Sheriff), Blayney Lewis (Frank), Jimmie Dodd (Spike).

After a break from films, comedian Brown returned in a dramatic role as a small town preacher who pulls in the reins on the sport of dog fighting. He takes the side of a youngster who's grown fond of a particular dog, by stealing it and then preparing to stand trial for the crime. Justice prevails, and instead of a trial, for Brown, the court outlaws the cruel sport. The outcome is pleasant enough, but some may turn off the vicious dog-fighting scenes.

p, Edward L. Alperson; d, Harold Schuster; w, Jack Jungmeyer, Jr., Harold Belgard (based on a story by Jungmeyer, Jr.); ph, Henry Freulich; m, Dr. Edward Kilenyi; ed, Richard Farrell; md, Kilenyi; art d, Arthur Lonergan; set d, Robert Priestley.

Drama   (PR:A-C MPAA:NR)

TENDERFOOT, THE½   (1932) 70m FN-WB bw

Joe E. Brown (Peter Jones), Ginger Rogers (Ruth), Lew Cody (Joe Lehman), Vivien Oakland (Miss Martin), Robert Greig (Mack), Spencer Charters (Oscar), Ralph Ince (Dolan), Marion "Peanuts" Byron (Kitty), Douglas Gerrard (Stage Director), Walter Percival (Depot Slicker), Wilfred Lucas (Patterson), George Chandler (Depot Bum), Jill Dennett (Cafe Cashier), Mae Madison (Cafe Maid), John Larkin (Depot Porter), Harry Seymour (Newsstand Proprietor), Zita Moulton, Charlotte Merriam (Actresses), Theodore Lorch, Allan Lane (Actors), Richard Cramer (Racketeer), Joe Barton (The Hebrew), Edith Allen (Tart at Depot), Lee Kohlmar (Waiter).

Joe E. Brown literally goes to town in this fine comedy about a wealthy Texan (Brown) who packs his bags and winds up in New York City. He may be a tenderfoot, but when some gangsters try to get tough with him, he resorts to gunplay and emerges victorious. All his problems start when he buys into a failing Broadway production, falling in love with typist Rogers. After Rogers gets fired, Brown buys out the play and casts his love in the lead role, turning her and the production into a success. Remade in 1937 as DANCE CHARLIE DANCE and again in 1940 as AN ANGEL FROM TEXAS.

p, Ray Griffith; d, Ray Enright; w, Arthur Caesar, Monty Banks, Earl Baldwin (based on the story by Richard Carle, from the play "The Butter And Egg Man" by George S. Kaufman); ph, Gregg Toland; ed, Owen Marks; art d, Esdras Hartley; makeup, Perc Westmore.

Comedy   (PR:A MPAA:NR)

TENDERFOOT GOES WEST, A   (1937) 61m Hoffberg bw

Jack LaRue (Killer Madden), Virginia Carroll (Ann), Russell Gleason (Pike), Joseph Girard (Groth), John Ince (Hal), Ralph Byrd (Steve), Chris-Pin Martin (Stubby), John Merton (Butch), Peewee!!Glenn]iStrange, Ray Turner, Si Jenks.

Gleason is a writer of Western pulp who leaves the big city and ventures into the Old West–the part of the country that made him a success. He quickly finds himself in hot water when he gets mixed up with the villainous LaRue. Gleason is then suspected of a murder even though he obviously is innocent. LaRue comes around and saves the tenderfoot city boy from an early demise at the gallows. A solid piece of oater entertainment.

p&d, Maurice G. O'Neil; ph, Art Reed; ed, Holbrook N. Todd.

Western   (PR:A MPAA:NR)

TENDERLOIN   (1928) 88m WB bw

Dolores Costello (Rose Shannon), Conrad Nagel (Chuck White), Georgie Stone ("Sparrow"), Mitchell Lewis (The Professor), Dan Wolheim ("Lefty"), Pat Hartigan ("The Mug"), Fred Kelsey (Detective Simpson), G. Raymond Nye (Cowles), Evelyn Pierce (Bobbie), Dorothy Vernon (Aunt Molly), John Miljan (Bank Teller).

A melodramatic part-talkie, Curtiz's first, which stars Costello as a cabaret dancer who gets entangled with gangster Nagel. He thinks that she is concealing $50,000 in stolen bills which is his and tries to befriend her in order to learn if she really has it. She insists, truthfully, that she doesn't have the money. Lewis, another thug and a colleague of Nagel's, tries to force the money out of her in a secluded mountain cabin. Before the situation gets ugly, however, Nagel breaks down the door and beats Lewis senseless. Nagel then realizes how much he loves Costello. TENDERLOIN was written by Darryl F. Zanuck under one of his three aliases, Melville Crossman–the name he specifically designated for his classier pictures. He also wrote under two other names, Mark Canfield for melodramas and Gregory Rogers for comedies. This picture is generally regarded to be the first real dialog film, in which the actors actually spoke their characterizations. It also initiated many of the hallmarks of the later Warner Bros. gangster films in cinematographer Mohr's somber shots of mean streets and bleak interiors. Not a critical success at its premiere, the film was re-released with some of the talking sequences cut.

p, Darryl F. Zanuck; d, Michael Curtiz; w, Edward T. Lowe, Jr., Joseph Jackson (based on a story by Melville Crossman [Zanuck]); ph, Hal Mohr; ed, Ralph Dawson.

Crime   (PR:A MPAA:NR)

TENDERLY   (SEE: GIRL WHO COULDN'T SAY NO, 1969)

TENDRE POULET   (SEE: DEAR DETECTIVE, 1978, Fr.)

TENDRE VOYOU   (SEE: TENDER SCOUNDREL, 1967, Fr./Ital.)

TENNESSEE BEAT, THE   (SEE: THAT TENNESSEE BEAT, 1966)

TENNESSEE CHAMP**½   (1954) 72m MGM c

Shelley Winters (*Sarah Wurble*), Keenan Wynn (*Willy Wurble*), Dewey Martin (*Daniel Norson*), Earl Holliman (*Happy Jackfield*), Dave O'Brien (*Luke MacWade*), Charles Buchinsky [Charles Bronson] (*Sixty Jubel*), Yvette Dugay (*Blossom*), Frank Richards (*J.B. Backett*), Jack Kruschen (*Andrews*), Johnny Indrisano (*Referee*), Alvin J. Gordon (*Sam*), Paul Hoffman, Bruno Ve Sota, John Damler (*Poker Players*), William "Billy" Newell (*Ring Announcer*).

Martin plays a young prizefighter from the South who is given his chance by manager Wynn. The future looks good for Martin until he discovers that Wynn is fixing an upcoming match. His disapproval is voiced and along with it his religious and moral upbringing, which finally gets through to Wynn, causing him to rethink his malicious ways. Wynn promotes a fair fight between Martin and a fellow named Charles Buchinsky (who would later change his name to Bronson) for the film's finale, inferring that Martin will find his future in God's corner instead of Wynn's. The story the film is based on, "The Lord in His Corner," had as its main character a black fighter.

p, Sol Baer Fielding; d, Fred M. Wilcox; w, Art Cohn (from the story "The Lord in His Corner" and other stories by Eustace Cockrell); ph, George Folsey (Ansco Color); m, Conrad Salinger; ed, Ben Lewis; m/l, "Weary Blues," Harry Warren, Ralph Blane.

Drama/Comedy   (PR:A   MPAA:NR)

TENNESSEE JOHNSON***   (1942) 103m MGM bw (GB: THE MAN
                                              ON AMERICA'S CONSCIENCE)

Van Heflin (*Andrew Johnson*), Ruth Hussey (*Eliza McCardle*), Lionel Barrymore (*Thad Stevens*), Marjorie Main (*Mrs. Fisher*), Regis Toomey (*McDaniel*), Montagu Love (*Chief Justice Chase*), Porter Hall (*The Weasel*), Charles Dingle (*Sen. Jim Waters*), J. Edward Bromberg (*Coke*), Grant Withers (*Mordecai Milligan*), Alec Craig (*Andrews*), Morris Ankrum (*Jefferson Davis*), Sheldon Leonard (*Atzerodt*), Noah Beery, Sr. (*Sheriff Cass*), Lloyd Corrigan (*Mr. Secretary*), Charles Trowbridge (*Lansbury*), Harry Worth (*John Wilkes Booth*), Robert Warwick (*Maj. Crooks*), Dane Clark (*Wirts*), Robert Emmett O'Connor (*Robinson*), Lee Phelps (*Deputy*), Brandon Hurst, Charles Ray, Harlan Briggs, Hugh Sothern, Frederick Burton, (*Senators*), Allen Pomeroy, Duke York (*Assassins*), Roy Barcroft (*Officer on Crutches*), Ed O'Neill (*Lincoln*), Jack Norton (*Drunk*), Russell Simpson (*Kirby*), Louise Beavers (*Addie*), James Davis, William Roberts, Frank Jaquet, Emmett Vogan, Pat O'Malley (*Reporters*), William Wright (*Alderman*), William F. Davidson (*Vice President Breckenridge*), Russell Hicks (*Emissary*).

The life of Andrew Johnson, the only President ever to face impeachment proceedings by Congress (the motion to oust him failed by one vote), gets the Hollywood treatment in this slightly above-average biography. Heflin is the backwoods boy who flees a cruel tailor to whom he has been apprenticed and finds his way to the town where Hussey is schoolteacher. She teaches him to read and write and soon he is leading a voting rights crusade. When the Civil War erupts, Heflin's loyalties remain with the Union and when Lincoln is re-elected in 1864, Heflin becomes his Vice President. Lincoln is later killed and Heflin succeeds him and faces a great deal of opposition from senators who think he is taking too conciliatory an approach toward the defeated South. His enemies, led by Barrymore, bring assorted trumped-up charges against him but they fail to gather the needed votes and Heflin triumphs. Adequate and reasonably accurate biography takes the usual liberties with the facts, but the film does show more sensitivity to the real issues involved than most films of this nature. Heflin gives a good performance, doing his usual man-of-integrity-under-pressure bit with his usual skill. Hussey is little more than a decorative and useful plot device but Barrymore is quite good as the senator determined to bring Heflin down.

p, J. Walter Ruben; d, William Dieterle; w, John L. Balderston, Wells Root (based on a story by Milton Gunsberg, Alvin Meyers); ph, Harold Rosson; m, Herbert Stothart; ed, Robert J. Kern; art d, Cedric Gibbons; spec eff, Warren Newcombe.

Biography   (PR:A   MPAA:NR)

TENNESSEE'S PARTNER***   (1955) 87m Filmcrest-RKO c

John Payne (*Tennessee*), Ronald Reagan (*Cowpoke*), Rhonda Fleming (*Elizabeth "Duchess" Farnham*), Coleen Gray (*Goldie Slater*), Anthony Caruso (*Turner*), Morris Ankrum (*The Judge*), Chubby Johnson (*Grubstake McNiven*), Leo Gordon (*The Sheriff*), Myron Healey (*Reynolds*), Joe Devlin (*Prendergast*), John Mansfield (*Clifford*), Angie Dickinson (*Girl*).

A quirky western from Allan Dwan which stars Payne as a gambler whose life is saved by Reagan. In return Payne befriends the cowpoke and convinces him that his girl friend, Gray, is nothing but a gold-digging hussie.

By the finale Payne is readying to marry Fleming, the tough operator of a saloon tagged "The Marriage Market," which is little more than a glorified whorehouse. One of Dwan's personal favorites (he was 70 when he made it), and one of his better achievements of the 1950s. Previously filmed for Paramount in 1918 as TENNESSEE'S PARDNER, and again for PRC as THE FLAMING FORTIES in 1924 (the latter starring Harry Carey), this version bears little resemblance to the Bret Harte story it was based upon.

p, Benedict Bogeaus; d, Allan Dwan; w, Milton Krims, D.D. Beauchamp, Graham Baker, Teddi Sherman (based on the story by Bret Harte); ph, John Alton (SuperScope, Technicolor); m, Louis Forbes; ed, James Leicester; art d, Van Nest Polglase; set d, Alfred Spencer; cos, Gwen Wakeling; m/l, "Heart of Gold," Forbes, Dave Franklin.

Western   **Cas.**   (PR:C   MPAA:NR)

TENSION****   (1949) 95m MGM bw

Richard Basehart (*Warren Quimby*), Audrey Totter (*Claire Quimby*), Cyd Charisse (*Mary Chanler*), Barry Sullivan (*Lt. Collier Bonnabel*), Lloyd Gough (*Barney Deager*), Tom D'Andrea (*Freddie*), William Conrad (*Lt. Edgar Gonsales*), Tito Renaldo (*Narco*), Philip Van Zandt (*Lt. Schiavone*), Tommy Walker (*Man at Counter*), Dewey Robinson, Tom Ryan, Jack Davis, Jack Daley (*Men*), Hayward Soo Hoo (*Kid*), Stephen Roberts (*Attendant*), Virginia Brissac (*Mrs. Andrews*), John Indrisano (*Handler*), Ray Bennett (*House Manager*), Kitty McHugh (*Waitress*), John Gallaudet (*Newspaperman*), Peter Brocco (*Technician*), Carl Sklover, Bert Davidson, Mike Morelli (*Reporters*).

A tightly controlled, well-developed thriller of infidelity and murder, TENSION opens with a police detective speaking directly to the audience. Everybody has a breaking point, he explains, stretching a rubber band tighter and tighter until at last it snaps. Like the rubber band, every man can only be pulled so far before he snaps. The story begins with Basehart, a modest pharmacist whose emotions are shattered after learning his wife (Totter) is having an affair with Gough. Basehart decides to murder his rival in an elaborate plan that necessitates taking a completely new identity in order for the pharmacist to have a legitimate alibi. Under this guise Basehart molds the perfect crime, then meets Charisse. He falls in love with her, then decides not to carry out his murderous plans. Basehart goes to Gough's beach house anyway, finding himself inexplicably drawn to the place. To his horror Basehart finds that Gough has been murdered by another and his alter ego is now the prime suspect. Assigned to the case are Sullivan and Conrad, two cops who believe that the unfaithful Totter is actually the anonymous face behind the trigger. The two set a trap for her, exposing Totter as the true killer and clearing Basehart. This is film noir at its best, creating an intriguing story of crime and passion while using the various themes and characterizations of the genre with care and precision. Basehart's essentially good man is driven to the very edges of his sanity, spellbound by a cruel, manipulative woman. Totter has that evil edge to her character and is well contrasted by Charisse, whose beauty and innocence plays off nicely against Totter's cold manipulations. Berry's direction from Rivkin's well-detailed script holds a good command over the material. The dialog is sharp and to the point, living up well to the promise of the title. The film has all the earmarks of James M. Cain and Raymond Chandler's influence on the genre, riveting the viewer by stretching the tension within to the very brink.

p, Robert Sisk; d, John Berry; w, Allen Rivkin (based on a story by John Klorer); ph, Harry Stradling; m, Andre Previn; ed, Albert Akst; art d, Cedric Gibbons, Leonid Vasian; set d, Edwin B. Willis, Jack D. Moore.

Crime   (PR:O   MPAA:NR)

TENSION AT TABLE ROCK**½   (1956) 93m RKO c

Richard Egan (*Wes Tancred*), Dorothy Malone (*Lorna Miller*), Cameron Mitchell (*Sheriff Miller*), Billy Chapin (*Jody*), Royal Dano (*Jameson*), John Dehner (*Hampton*), DeForrest Kelley (*Breck*), Joe DeSantis (*Burrows*), Angie Dickinson (*Cathy*), Paul Richards (*Sam Murdock*), Edward Andrews (*Kirk*).

Egan is unjustly scorned after killing his gang leader, a man the public wrongly perceived as a hero. He is so disliked that a ballad is written about him, "The Ballad of Wes Tancred," which plays wherever he goes. When he comes into Table Rock, he finds that the town's sheriff, Mitchell, is badly in need of some assistance (and courage) in handling a rowdy gang of trailherders. Egan brings peace to the town, but also falls in love with Malone, the sheriff's wife, leaving her and Table Rock at the finale. A moody western that pays more attention to atmosphere than anything else, which isn't necessarily a bad thing.

p, Sam Wiesenthal; d, Charles Marquis Warren; w, Winston Miller (based on the novel Bitter Sage by Frank Gruber); ph, Joseph Biroc (Technicolor); m, Dimitri Tiomkin; ed, Harry Marker, Dean Harrison; md, Tiomkin; art d, Albert S. D'Agostino, John B. Mansbridge; m/l, "The Ballad of Wes Tancred" Josef Myrow, Robert Wells (sung by Eddy Arnold), Tiomkin, Ned Washington.

Western   (PR:A   MPAA:NR)

TENTACLES*   (1977, Ital.) 102m AIP-FOX c

John Huston (*Ned Turner*), Shelley Winters (*Tillie Turner*), Bo Hopkins (*Will Gleason*), Henry Fonda (*Mr. Whitehead*), Delia Baccardo (*Vicky Gleason*), Cesare Danova (*John Corey*), Alan Boyd (*Mike*), Claude Akins (*Capt. Robards*), Sherry Buchanan (*Judy*), Franco Diogene (*Chuck*), Marc Fiorini (*Don*), Helena Makela (*Jane's Mother*), Alessandro Poggi, Roberto Poggi, Giancarlo Nacinelli, Consolato Marciano, Philip Dallas, Leonard C. Lightfoot, John White, William Van Raaphorst, Joanne Van Raaphorst, Patrick Mulvihill, Janet Myers, Kristin M. Brekke, Janet Raycraft, Kenneth Lundeen, Rita Real, Alan Scharf, Ross Gordon, Ronald Shapiro, Joseph Johnson.

The makers of TENTACLES were lucky enough to get Huston, Winters, and Fonda to sign on for this picture; otherwise it would have gotten a "zero" rating without the blink of an eye. A movie with Fonda in it just can't be that bad. Outside of his minor role as an executive and Huston's equally small part as a reporter married to Winters, this exploitative JAWS ripoff is garbage. Hopkins does the best that he can with his role as a marine biologist who trains whales to attack a killer octopus that's been sucking and strangling the town dry. Produced and directed by the same greedy moneymakers who made BEYOND THE DOOR, an EXORCIST Xerox.

p, E.F. Doria; d, Oliver Hellman [Olvidio Assonitis]; w, Jerome Max, Tito Carpi, Steve Carabatsos, Sonia Molteni; ph, Robert D'Ettore (Technicolor); m, S.W. Cipriani; ed, A.J. Curi; art d, M. Spring; cos, N. Hercules; underwater sequences, Nestore Ungaro.

Horror   Cas.   (PR:C MPAA:PG)

TENTH AVENUE ANGEL*   (1948) 74m MGM bw

Margaret O'Brien (*Flavia Mills*), Angela Lansbury (*Susan Bratten*), George Murphy (*Steve Abbott*), Phyllis Thaxter (*Helen Mills*), Warner Anderson (*Joseph Mills*), Rhys Williams (*Blind Mac*), Barry Nelson (*Al Parker*), Connie Gilchrist (*Mrs. Murphy*), Tom Trout (*Daniel Oliver Madson*), Dickie Tyler (*Jimmy Madson*), Henry Blair (*Rad Ardley*), Charles Cane (*Parole Officer*), Richard Lane (*Street Vendor*).

O'Brien is a lovable youngster who lives in one of New York's tenements and tries to better the lives of her neighbors. Her charm works best on a gangster who straightens out his act, but audiences won't fall under her spell so easily. Eighteen months in the making, TENTH AVENUE ANGEL went through a series of versions and cast changes before MGM released it. Made before O'Brien's UNFINISHED DANCE, but released after it.

p, Ralph Wheelwright; d, Roy Rowland; w, Harry Ruskin, Eleanore Griffin (based on a story by Angna Enters and a sketch by Craig Rice); ph, Robert Surtees; m, Rudolph G. Kopp; ed, Ralph E. Winters, George Boemler; art d, Cedric Gibbons, Wade Rubottom; set d, Edwin B. Willis, Mildred Griffiths.

Drama   (PR:A MPAA:NR)

TENTH AVENUE KID**   (1938) 60m REP bw

Bruce Cabot (*Jim "Silk" Loomis*), Beverly Roberts (*Susan*), Tommy Ryan (*Tommy*), Ben Welden (*Dayton*), Horace MacMahon (*Max*), John Wray (*Turner*), Jay Novello (*Hobart*), Charles Wilson (*Commissioner*), Paul Bryar (*Wheeler*), Walter Sande (*Faber*), Ralph Dunn (*Egan*), Julian Petruzzi (*Jerry Simons*), Billy Wayne (*Wacker*), Byron K. Foulger (*Belknap*).

Ryan is a tough 12-year-old orphaned when his dad is gunned down by private eye Cabot, a murder which the youngster sees. Cabot feels responsible for Ryan and befriends him, but also tries to get him to reveal the whereabouts of money stolen by his dad during a bank heist. Naturally, Ryan isn't responsive, but soon comes around after a stint in a reform school.

p, Harry Grey; d, Bernard Vorhaus; w, Gordon Kahn (based on a story by Kahn, Adele Buffington); ph, Ernest Miller; ed, William Morgan.

Crime/Drama   (PR:A MPAA:NR)

TENTH MAN, THE**   (1937, Brit.) 68m ABF/Wardour bw

John Lodge (*George Winter*), Antoinette Cellier (*Catherine Winter*), Athole Stewart (*Lord Etchingham*), Clifford Evans (*Ford*), Iris Hoey (*Lady Etchingham*), Aileen Marson (*Anne Etchingham*), George Graves (*Col. Trent*), Frank Cochrane (*Bennett*), Bruce Lister (*Edward O'Donnell*), Barry Sinclair (*Robert Colby*), Hindle Edgar (*Jason*), Edith Sharpe (*Miss Hobbs*), Antony Holles (*Swalescliffe*), John Harwood (*Morrison*), Aubrey Mallalieu (*Bank Manager*), Mavis Clair (*Dora*), Kathleen Harrison.

An intriguing drama which stars Lodge as a fiercely determined business-man who values success more than anything. He climbs to the top by buying off those he can't win over, until he meets a man who threatens to expose his shady deals, and won't be bought. Lodge kills him, and then finds out that he has struck it rich with a gold mine he thought worthless. Cleverly written from a play by W. Somerset Maugham.

p, Walter C. Mycroft; d, Brian Desmond Hurst; w, Marjorie Deans, Geoffrey Kerr, Dudley Leslie, Jack Davies (based on the play by W. Somerset Maugham); ph, Walter Harvey.

Drama   (PR:A MPAA:NR)

TENTH VICTIM, THE**   (1965, Fr./Ital.) 92m CHAM-CON-Les
Films/EM c (LA DECIMA VITTIMA; LA DIXIEME VICTIME)

Marcello Mastroianni (*Marcello Polletti*), Ursula Andress (*Caroline Mere-dith*), Elsa Martinelli (*Olga*), Salvo Randone (*Professor*), Massimo Serato (*Lawyer*), Evi Rigano (*Victim*), Milo Quesada (*Rudi*), Luce Bonifassy (*Lidia*), Anita Sanders (*Relaxatorium Girl*), Mickey Knox (*Chet*), Richard Arm-strong (*Cole*), Walter Williams (*Martin*), George Wang (*Chinese Assailant*).

A bizarre, pop look at life in the future which stars Mastroianni and Andress as participants in a game of legalized murder known as "Man Hunt," a replacement for violence and war. Andress must kill her tenth victim to achieve the pinnacle of success, and Mastroianni happens to be the chosen one. He also is plotting to kill her, which confuses the situation, especially when they fall in love. Eventually they decide to marry, but are killed by a gunman after the ceremony. Petri created an interesting atmosphere where people kill with double-barreled bras, hang out at a nightery called Club Masoch, and define literature as comic books, all, unfortunately, badly dubbed into English.

p, Carlo Ponti; d, Elio Petri; w, Petri, Ennio Flajano, Tonino Guerra, Giorgio Salvioni (based the on short story "The Seventh Victim" by Robert Sheckley); ph, Gianni di Venanzo (Technicolor); m, Piero Piccioni; ed, Ruggero Mastroianni; art d, Piero Poletto; set d, Giovanni Checchi, Dario Micheli; cos, Giulio Coltellacci; ch, Gino Landi.

ScienceFiction   Cas.   (PR:O MPAA:NR)

TENTING TONIGHT ON THE OLD CAMP GROUND*½
(1943) 59m UNIV bw

Johnny Mack Brown (*Wade Benson*), Tex Ritter (*Bob Courtney*), Fuzzy Knight (*Si Dugan*), Jennifer Holt (*Kay Randolph*), John Elliott (*Talbot*), Earle Hodgins (*Judge Higgins*), Rex Lease (*Zeke Larkin*), Lane Chandler (*Duke Merrick*), Allan Bridge (*Matt Warner*), Dennis Moore (*Ed Randolph*), Tom London (*Pete*), Jimmy Wakely Trio (*Jimmy Wakely, Scotty Harrel, Johnny Bond*), Bud Osborne (*Deputy Snell*), Reed Howes (*Smokey*), Lynton Brent (*Stage Driver*), Hank Worden (*Sleepy Martin*), Ray Jones, George Eldridge.

Not quite the campfire songfest that the title implies, this oater tells the familiar tale of a stagecoach rivalry with Brown leading the honorable forces and Chandler heading up the black hats. Holt is used to keep Brown and his boys from thinking about work, by thinking about her instead. One of the better Brown and Ritter series westerns.

p, Oliver Drake; d, Lewis D. Collins; w, Elizabeth Beecher (based on a story by Harry Fraser); ph, William Sickner; ed, Charles Maynard; md, H.J. Salter; art d, Jack Otterson.

Western   Cas.   (PR:A MPAA:NR)

TEOREMA**   (1969, Ital.) 93m Aetos/CD c (AKA: THEOREM)

Terence Stamp (*Visitor*), Silvana Mangano (*Mother*), Massimo Girotti (*Father*), Anne Wiazemsky (*Daughter*), Laura Betti (*Maid*), Andres Jose Cruz Soublette (*Son*), Alfonso Gatto (*Doctor*), Ninetto Davoli (*Messenger*), Susanna Pasolini (*Old Peasant*), Adele Cambria, Carlo De Mejo, Luigi Barbini, Ivan Scratuglia, Cesare Carboli.

A heavily symbolic and highly intellectual look at the bourgeois milieu and the effect that a mysterious visitor, Stamp, has on one specific family. Into the life of a prominent Milanese family walks Stamp, an angelic looking stranger (something of a godlike figure, though Pasolini acknowledges that he may also represent the Devil), whose spiritual sexuality touches each member of the household in a different way, elevating each to a certain level of grace. He becomes involved with Mangano, the wife; Girotti, the husband; Wiazemsky, their daughter; Cruz, their son; and the housemaid, Betti. Then one day, Stamp leaves as mysteriously as he arrived. The family feels the void and can no longer attain that state of spirituality that Stamp offered, and falls back into the worldliness of the bourgeoisie. Mangano tries to recapture that state by wandering the streets and picking up lovers at random; Wiazemsky enters a catatonic trance and completely withdraws from her society; Cruz becomes an artist whose displeasure with his paintings causes him to urinate on them; and Girotti relinquishes control of the factory he owns to the workers and wanders naked through a vast wasteland. Only Betti, the maid, can survive without Stamp. This is because she, unlike the family that employs her, is from the peasant class and is able to understand Stamp's divinity. Instead of deteriorating, Betti returns to her village, performs miracles for the peasants, and even levitates. For her brilliant performance (the rest of the cast is equally admirable), Betti was awarded the Best Actress Prize at the 1968 Venice Film Festival. The film's release, like so many of Pasolini's films, was shrouded in controversy. The left wing of the Italian Catholics gave the film an award for its "mysticism," while the Catholic Right countered by unleashing a scathing attack on the picture. According to Pasolini (whose self-analysis is usually more confusing than clarifying): "The point of the film is roughly this: a member of the bourgeoisie, whatever he does, is always wrong...anything done by the bourgeoisie, however sincere, profound, and noble it is, is always on the wrong side of the track." Pasolini had hoped to include Orson Welles in the cast, though he didn't make clear whether he would have had Stamp's or Girotti's role. In either case, the mind boggles.

p, Franco Rossellini, Manolo Bolognini; d&w, Pier Paolo Pasolini (based on his novel); ph, Giuseppe Ruzzolini (Movielab); m, Ennio Morricone, "Requiem," Wolfgang Amadeus Mozart; ed, Nino; md, Bruno Nicolai; Baragli; art d, Luciano Puccini; cos, Marcella De Marchis, Roberto Capucci; spec eff, Goffredo Rocchetti.

Religious Drama   (PR:O MPAA:NR)

TERESA***   (1951) 102m MGM bw

Pier Angeli (Teresa), John Ericson (Philip Quas), Patricia Collinge (Philip's Mother), Richard Bishop (Philip's Father), Peggy Ann Garner (Susan), Ralph Meeker (Sgt. Dobbs), Bill Mauldin (Grissom), Ave Ninchi (Teresa's Mother), Edward Binns (Sgt. Brown), Rod Steiger (Frank), Aldo Silvani (Prof. Crocce), Tommy Lewis (Walter), Franco Interlenghi (Mario), Edith Atwater (Mrs. Lawrence), Lewis Cianelli (Cheyenne), William King (Boone), Richard McNamara (G.I. Cook).

Angeli is the title character in the stirring performance of a young Italian girl who marries U.S. GI Ericson during his stay in her village. He suffers through a hospital stay, but eventually gets back on his feet, bringing his new bride with him to the States. They move into his parents' small tenement, causing tensions between their habits and his mother's. A separation follows the arrival of their newborn, but by the finale the whole family is living peacefully. Rod Steiger makes his film debut as a psychiatrist. Based on a story from Alfred Hayes and Stewart Stern which won an Oscar nomination, but unfortunately the story's power didn't translate as well as it could have.

p, Arthur M. Loew; d, Fred Zinnemann; w, Stewart Stern (based on the story by Stern, Alfred Hayes); ph, William J. Miller; m, Louis Applebaum; ed, Frank Sullivan; md, Jack Schaindlin; art d, Leo Kerz.

Drama/Romance   (PR:A MPAA:NR)

TERM OF TRIAL½**   (1962, Brit.) 130m WB bw

Laurence Olivier (Graham Weir), Simone Signoret (Anna Weir), Sarah Miles (Shirley Taylor), Hugh Griffith (O'Hara), Terence Stamp (Mitchell), Roland Culver (Trowman), Frank Pettingell (Ferguson), Thora Hird (Mrs. Taylor), Dudley Foster (Detective Sgt. Kiernan), Norman Bird (Mr. Taylor), Newton Blick (Prosecutor), Allan Cuthbertson (Sylvan-Jones), Nicholas Hannen (Magistrate Sharp), Roy Holder (Thompson), Barbara Ferris (Joan), Rosamund Greenwood (Constance), Lloyd Lamble (Inspector Ullyat), Vanda Godsell (Mrs. Thompson), Earl Cameron (Chard), Clive Colin Bowler (Collins).

Olivier proves that there is one thing he cannot do as he plays a wimp in this contrived drama. Olivier is a spineless schoolteacher working at a difficult education institution. He has been sent there because he was a pacifist and his reward was the toughest facility his superiors could find. Olivier likes to think of himself as a man of principles but those principles have only resulted in scorn and disdain, mostly from his wife, Signoret, who taunts him unmercifully. The school's students are rowdy, unruly, and care little for bettering their northern England lot in life. When teenager Miles asks Olivier to aid her with some tutoring, he is thrilled that at least one of the students is interested in learning something. Olivier's disenchantment with his work has caused him to drink, a fact that is not helped by the presence of the school's bully, Stamp, in his class. Olivier takes some of the students on a field trip to Paris. Miles has, by this time, built an enormous crush on Olivier and when she goes to his hotel room, she offers herself to him. Olivier properly rejects her ploy in as jocular a fashion as he can, without hurting her feelings. He sends her out of his room with a parental slap on her slim behind. Miles is not that easily tossed aside and she goes home and tells her parents, Hird and Bird (which sounds like a silly law firm) that she has been sexually assaulted by Olivier. Hird is up in arms and demands satisfaction, so Olivier goes to trial. It's almost a kangaroo court and he is convicted of the crime, then makes a plea to the courtroom (actually to Miles) and she can't bear it as she knows she has lied. Miles breaks down and admits that she lied about what Olivier supposedly did. The case is set aside and Signoret, in the privacy of their home, twits Olivier for not having seduced the obviously willing Miles. She thinks that he is such a stiff that something like that might have brought him out of his stuffy image. Olivier then lies to Signoret in order to save his marriage and tells her that Miles was speaking the truth, he did take advantage of the teenager. This news delights Signoret as she feels that her mouse has now been magically transformed into a man. Miles makes her debut in this film, the first of many excellent jobs she has done. Stamp also appears for the first time although his role is not nearly as important. His next film was made before this but released afterward. It was BILLY BUDD and he played the lead and became a star. Olivier had already proven he could play kings and princes (RICHARD III and HAMLET) and the defeated types like "Archie Rice" in THE ENTERTAINER, but this role left him stymied. There was little to sink his teeth into as the teacher was a somber person, a moral person, but incredibly dull. Olivier and Miles won awards in 1962 at the Cork (Ireland) Film Festival. Although Signoret was most believable, casting her opposite Olivier seemed all wrong as she was so strong it seemed impossible that he could love that type of woman, given the type of man he was shown to be. The joke at the end doesn't ring true and relegates this movie to just another "kitchen sink" drama, the sort of which were very popular in the early 1960s.

p, James Woolf; d&w, Peter Glenville (based on the novel by James Barlow); ph, Oswald Morris; m, Jean-Michel Demase; ed, James Clark; prod d, Wilfred Shingleton; art d, Antony Woolard; set d, Peter James; cos, Beatrice Dawson; makeup, Ernest Gasser.

Drama   (PR:C MPAA:NR)

TERMINAL ISLAND   (1973) 88m Dimension c

Phyllis Davis (Joy Lang), Don Marshall (A. J. Thomas), Ena Hartman (Carmen Sims), Marta Kristen (Lee Phillips), Barbara Leigh (Bunny Campbell), Sean David Kenney (Bobby Farr), Geoffrey Deuel (Chino), Tom Selleck (Dr. Milford), Ford Clay (Cornell), Clyde Ventura (Julian Dylan), Frank Christi (Teale), Randy Boone, Roger E. Mosley, Jo Morrow, Jim Whitworth, Sandy Ward, Richard Stahl, Albert Cole, Chris Allen, Richard Taylor, Ray Saniger.

Feminist ideology prevails in this violent exploitationer about female prisoners who are carted off to an island prison camp populated by men. Those in charge are ruthless dictators who beat and rape the women, but amongst the prison population is an underground waiting to rebel. The women help with the overthrow and set up a democratic means of existence. Extremely violent but intelligently conceived and directed. Reissued with the rising popularity of TV's "Magnum P.I." stars, Tom Selleck and Roger Mosley.

p, Charles S. Swartz; d, Stephanie Rothman; w, Rothman, Swartz, Jim Barnett; ph, Daniel Lacambre; m, Michael Andres; ed, John O'Connor; art d, Jack Fisk.

Prison Adventure   Cas.   (PR:O MPAA:R)

TERMINAL MAN, THE   (1974) 104m WB c

George Segal (Harry Benson), Joan Hackett (Dr. Janet Ross), Richard A. Dysart (Dr. John Ellis), Jill Clayburgh (Angela Black), Donald Moffat (Dr. Arthur McPherson), Matt Clark (Gerhard), Michael C. Gwynne (Dr. Robert Morris), Normann Burton (Detective Capt. Anders), William Hansen (Dr. Ezra Manon), James Sikking (Ralph Friedman), Ian Wolfe (The Priest), Gene Borkan, Burke Byrnes (Benson's Guards), Jim Antonio (Richards), Jordan Rhodes (Questioner No. 1), Dee Carroll (Night Nurse), Jason Wingreen (Instructor), Steve Kanaly (Edmonds), Fred Sadoff (Police Doctor), Robert Ito (Anesthetist), Victor Argo (Orderly), Lee DeBroux (Reporter), Jack Colvin (Coroner).

An aimless and unexciting science-fiction story about a computer scientist, Segal, who undergoes brain surgery and is transformed into a maniacal murderer. His doctor has connected him to a small computer embedded in his neck, but things short-circuit in his head. Clayburgh, an ex-girlfriend of the robotic Segal, winds up a victim of his killing spree. Based on a novel by Michael Crichton, who had previously written and directed WEST-WORLD, which is far more fun than THE TERMINAL MAN.

p,d&w, Mike Hodges (based on the novel by Michael Crichton); ph, Richard H. Kline (Technicolor); m, Johann Sebastian Bach (played by Glenn Gould); ed, Robert Wolfe; art d, Fred Harpman; set d, Marvin March; cos, Nino Novarese.

Science Fiction   Cas.   (PR:C MPAA:PG)

TERMINAL STATION   (SEE: INDISCRETION OF AN AMERICAN WIFE, 1954 U.S./Ital.)

TERMS OF ENDEARMENT*½**   (1983) 130m PAR c

Debra Winger (Emma Horton), Shirley MacLaine (Aurora Greenway), Jack Nicholson (Garrett Breedlove), Danny DeVito (Vernon Dahlart), Jeff Daniels (Flap Horton), John Lithgow (Sam Burns), Betty King (Rosie), Lisa Hart Carroll (Patsy Clark), Huckleberry Fox (Toddy), Megan Morris (Melanie), Troy Bishop (Tommy), Shane Serwin (Young Tommy Horton), Jennifer Josey (Young Emma Greenway), Tara Yeakey (Baby Melanie), Norman Bennett (Edward Johnson), Kate Charleston (Janice), Tom Wees (Dr. Budge), Paul Menzel (Dr. Maise), F. William Parker (Doctor), Amanda Watkins (Meg), Buddy Gilbert (Dr. Ratcher), David Wohl (Phil), Shelley K. Kielsen, Betty Croissant (Nurses), Charles Beall (Rudyard's Employer), Lelise Folse (Dors), Sharisse Baker (Lee Anne), Judith A. Dickerson (Checkout Girl), Devon O'Brien (Lizbeth), Dana Vance (Victoria), Alexandra O'Karma (Jane), Nancy Mette (Woman at Party), Holly Beth Holmberg (T.J.), Lear Levin (Jack Stern), A. Brooks (Rudyard's Voice), Lanier Whilden (Patsy's Mother), Helen Stauffer (Flap's Secretary), Barbara Balik, Michelle Watkins (Women), John C. Conger (Moving Man), Sandra Newkirk (Mrs. Johnson), Elaine McGown (Herself), Mary Kay Place (Voice of Doris).

Well-made tearjerker that aims for the heart but is essentially a fraudulent movie, distinguished by excellent acting. TV veteran ("Mary Tyler Moore Show," etc.) James Brooks wrote, directed, and coproduced this movie which spreads over a 30-year period in the lives of MacLaine and her doomed daughter, Winger. MacLaine has been widowed early and is raising her daughter, Josey, as best she can. MacLaine is guilty of smother love and the young Josey grows up to be Winger, a headstrong woman who wants to escape the cloying and seemingly unbreakable silver cord between her and her mother. When the child doesn't seem to be breathing, MacLaine climbs into the infant's crib to make sure she's okay. Winger grows up, marries weak college teacher Daniels, and promptly bears three children. MacLaine is not thrilled at the marriage and is even angrier at the thought that she is now a grandmother. Daniels gets a chance to move from Houston to a midwestern university and Winger looks forward to it, if only to get away from MacLaine, who hates Daniels and makes no secret of it. At the new school, Daniels has an affair with student Charleson. It's not long before Winger meets unhappily married banker Lithgow and has an affair with him. All the while, MacLaine is living next to ex-astronaut Nicholson, a bachelor who has no couth to speak of and is far too forward for MacLaine. She has other men she dates including De Vito and Bennett, but Nicholson keeps after her and his unfailing good humor begins to wear her down. After years of being alone, MacLaine finds sexual happiness in the arms of the balding, pot-bellied Nicholson and she sees what she's been missing. Then Winger is discovered to have terminal cancer and the picture abruptly switches from a fast-moving comedy to a reach-for-the-tissue weeper. Winger dies, but not before coming to terms with her mother and her children. Sniffles were heard all over the theater in between the snores. Brooks writes some of the best dialog around as he did for Moore, Ed Asner in "Lou Grant," and all the gang on "Taxi". But sharp dialog is not enough. It's directed in a perfunctory fashion (Brooks had never directed anything before and still won the Oscar for this) and the scenes go on far too long. Brooks also won for the script, MacLaine as Best Actress (she said on TV, "I really deserve this"), Nicholson (who was paid $1 million) as Best Supporting Actor and the movie won as Best Picture. Winger was nominated but lost. Were it not for the wonderful casting, it would have been like any of the thousands of patented TV movies that offer the "disease of the week." A huge success, TERMS OF ENDEARMENT is as manipulative as anything Spielberg ever did. Sentimentality drips from every scene without Nicholson and MacLaine. Their courtship is the highlight of the movie and it deserves a sequel. Lots of laughs, just as many tears, and a general feeling of having one's strings pulled.

p, James L. Brooks, Penney Finkelman, Martin Jurow; w, Brooks (based on the novel by Larry McMurtry); ph, Andrzej Bartkowiak (Metrocolor); m, Michael Gore; ed, Richard Marks, Sidney Wolinsky; prod d, Polly Platt; art d, Harold Michelson; set d, Sandy Veneziano, Tom Pedigo, Anthony Mondell; cos, Kristi Zea, Anthony J. Faso; makeup, Ben Nye, Jr.

Comedy/Drama   **Cas.**   **(PR:A-C MPAA:PG)**

TERRA EM TRANSE   (SEE: EARTH ENTRANCED, 1970, Brazil)

TERRACE, THE*   (1964, Arg.) 90m Internacional/Royal bw (LA
                                          TERRAZA; AKA: THE ROOF GARDEN)

Belita (Belita), Graciela Borges (Claudia), Leonardo Favio (Rodolfo), Marcela Lopez Rey (Vicky), Hector Pellegrini (Alberto), Dora Baret (Valeria), Norberto Suarez (Luis), Enrique Leporace (Horacio), Luis Walmo (Pablo), Mirtha Dubner (Mercedes), Oscar Caballero (Guille), Bernardo Kullock (Gaspar), Fernando Vegal (Father Alfonso), Maria Esther Duckse (Grandmother), Alfredo Tobares (Alberto's Father), Sergio Corona (2nd Floor Tenant), Susana Brunetti (Cuban Woman), Felix Robles (Porter), Pedro Lexalt (Igarzabal).

A disturbing social commentary about a group of youths who rebel and take over the rooftop pool in a Buenos Aires apartment building. They indulge in sex, drinking, and defiance while their elders try to get them to leave. Belita, the 10-year-old granddaughter of the superintendent, is eventually taken hostage by the group. Night falls and the world below becomes less patient with the rebels and storms their private party. It is Belita who suffers, however. She is thrown off the roof and sustains serious, though not fatal, injuries. An existential picture from perhaps the most highly regarded Argentinian director, Torre Nilsson, scripted (as are many of his films) by his wife Guido.

p, German Szulem; d, Leopoldo Torre Nilsson; w, Beatriz Guido; ph, Ignacio Souto; m, Jorge Lopez Ruiz; ed, Juan Sires, Jacinto Cascales; art d, Ricardo Luna, Oscar Lagomarsino; makeup, Kurt Grun.

Drama   **(PR:O MPAA:NR)**

TERRIBLE BEAUTY, A   (SEE: NIGHT FIGHTERS, 1960, Brit.)

TERRIFIED!*   (1963) 81m Bern-Field/Crown bw

Rod Lauren (Ken), Steve Drexel (David), Tracy Olsen (Marge), Stephen Roberts (Wesley Blake), Sherwood Keith (Mr. Hawley), Barbara Luddy (Mrs. Hawley), Denver Pyle (Sheriff), Lee Bradley (Mulligan), Ben Frank (Duell), Danny Welton (Wise Guy Drunk), Michael Fellen (Buzzy), Robert Towers (Joey), Angelo Rossitto.

A bafflingly stupid horror film which was unfortunately the last effort from veteran Lew Landers. Olsen and a couple of college friends investigate the mysterious murders that have been occurring in a ghost town and find an old caretaker impaled in the local cemetery. Olsen goes to get help from the sheriff. In the meantime one of her pals gets buried alive, while the other is knocked unconscious. She is carried off to an abandoned mine shaft by the

killer, who hides his identity under a hood. She is soon rescued by the sheriff, and the killer is discovered to be her former boss, an ex-vaudevillian ventriloquist who is obsessed by a need to protect Olsen.

p, Richard Bernstein; d, Lew Landers; w, Bernstein; ph, Curt Fetters; m, Michael Andersen; ed, Rex Lipton; art d, Rudi Feld; set d, Ted Driscoll; cos, Mickey Sherrard; spec eff, Charles Duncan; makeup, Harry Thomas.

Horror   **(PR:O MPAA:NR)**

TERROR, THE½   (1928) 80m WB bw

May McAvoy (Olga Redmayne), Louise Fazenda (Mrs. Elvery), Edward Everett Horton (Ferdinand Fane), Alec B. Francis (Dr. Redmayne), Matthew Betz (Joe Connors), Holmes Herbert (Goodman), John Miljan (Alfred Katman), Otto Hoffman (Soapy Marks), Joseph W. Girard (Supt. Hallick), Frank Austin (Cotton), Conrad Nagel (Narrator), Carl Stockdale, Reed Howes, Lester Cuneo.

A creative mystery which would simply be average had it not been for a smart use of sound. McAvoy is one of many patrons of an inn terrorized by a hooded figure who plays the organ late at night. Some standard murders occur, but their effect is multiplied by the filmmakers' use of creepy, squeaky sound effects. Before McAvoy can be killed, the murderer is caught and identified as a former bank robber who had framed a pair of fellow cons. The first talkie completely free of subtitles and title cards, and Warner's second all-talkie after LIGHTS OF NEW YORK. The somewhat nutty guest who turns out to be the chief of detectives is played by Horton in one of his first talking roles. He continued to play lovable screwballs throughout his long film career, which continued into the 1970s.

d, Roy Del Ruth; w, Harvey Gates, Joseph Jackson (based on a play by Edgar Wallace); ph, Barney McGill; ed, Thomas Pratt, Jack Killifer.

Mystery   **(PR:A MPAA:NR)**

TERROR, THE**   (1941, Brit.) 63m Alliance bw

Wilfrid Lawson (Mr. Goodman), Bernard Lee (Ferdie Fane), Arthur Wontner (Col. Redmayne), Linden Travers (Mary Redmayne), Henry Oscar (Connor), Alastair Sim (Soapy Marks), Iris Hoey (Mrs. Elvery), Lesley Wareing (Veronica Elvery), Stanley Lathbury (Hawkins), John Turnbull (Inspector Hallick), Richard Murdock (P.C. Lewis), Edward Lexy (Inspector Dobie).

A remake of the 1928 version which again has the malicious crook tagged "The Terror" running loose and killing off folks living in a hostelry. Cleverly written, but the cast and the direction don't quite hold up to mystery standards.

p, Walter C. Mycroft; d, Richard Bird; w, William Freshman (based on the play by Edgar Wallace); ph, Walter Harvey; ed, Lionel Tomlinson.

Mystery   **(PR:A MPAA:NR)**

TERROR, THE* (1963) 81m Filmgroup/AIP c (AKA: LADY OF THE
                                                          SHADOWS)

Jack Nicholson (Lt. Andre Duvalier), Boris Karloff (Baron Von Leppe), Sandra Knight (Helene), Richard [Dick] Miller (Stefan, Baron's Servant), Dorothy Neumann (Old Woman), Jonathan Haze (Gustaf, Servant).

One of the "quickies" that made Roger Corman a legend–this one supposedly shot in only three days, after THE RAVEN finished up ahead of schedule. Nicholson unconvincingly (but who ever said he was trying to convince) portrays a Napoleonic officer who wakes up on the Baltic Coast (really California) and sees the figure of a woman, who then disappears. After seeing her several times, he follows her trail to the castle of Karloff, an elderly baron. It turns out that the baron isn't really the baron, but a man who killed the real baron years ago and took his place. The woman Nicholson has been obsessed with ends up falling apart in his arms as he tries to rescue her, being nothing more than a rotting corpse. And poor Karloff gets swallowed up by his castle which is destroyed by an onslaught of sea water. This destructive finale, filmed on the set of THE RAVEN, ended up in Peter Bogdanovich's TARGETS four years later as a film being shown at a drive-in. Directed only partly by Corman, THE TERROR actually boasts the uncredited directorial assistance of such heavies as Francis Coppola, Monte Hellman, Jack Hill, Dennis Jacob, and Nicholson. Knight, who played Nicholson's crumbling apparition, was his real-life wife at the time.

p&d, Roger Corman (uncredited directorial assistance, Francis Coppola, Monte Hellman, Jack Hill, Dennis Jacob, Jack Nicholson); ph, John Nickolaus (VistaScope, Pathe Color); w, Leo Gordon, Jack Hill; m, Ronald Stein; ed, Stuart O'Brien; art d, Daniel Haller; set d, Harry Reif; cos, Marjorie Corso.

Horror   **Cas.**   **(PR:C MPAA:NR)**

TERROR*   (1979, Brit.) 86m Crown International c

John Nolan *(James)*, Carolyn Courage *(Ann)*, James Aubrey *(Philip)*, Sarah Keller *(Suzy)*, Tricia Walsh *(Viv)*, Glynis Barber *(Carol)*, Michael Craze *(Gary)*, Rosie Collins *(Diane)*, L.E. Mack *(Mad Dolly)*, Chuck Julian, Elaine Ives-Cameron, Patti Love, Mary Maude, William Russell, Peter Craze, Peter Attard, Peter Sproule, Colin Howells, Peter Mayhew, Milton Reid, Mike O'Malley.

Nearly as unexciting as its title, TERROR is nothing more than the usual lunatic-on-the-rampage picture with people getting their heads lopped off, a woman getting pinned to a tree, and a poor sap getting caught in a bear trap. The cause of these unfortunate events is a film-within-the-film which is being made to express the director's feelings about his ancestors having burned a witch at the stake. The film affects the director's cousin Courage so acutely that she goes on a slicing and stabbing binge. Pretty poor.

p, Les Young, Richard Crafter; d, Norman J. Warren; w, David McGillivray (based on a story by Les Young, Moira Young); ph, Young; m, Ivor Slaney; ed, Jim Elderton; art d, Hayden Pearce.

Horror   **Cas.**   **(PR:O MPAA:R)**

TERROR ABOARD**   (1933) 69m PAR bw

John Halliday, Charlie Ruggles, Neil Hamilton, Shirley Grey, Verree Teasdale, Jack LaRue, Leila Bennett, Morgan Wallace, Thomas Jackson, William Janney, Paul Hurst, Stanley Fields, Frank Hagney, Clarence Wilson, Paul Porcasi, Marty Faust, Clem Beauchamp, Peter Hancock, Bobby Dunn.

A homicidal maniac is on board an ocean liner and is killing everyone in sight. A stark whodunit with some colorful murders–a woman is stuck inside a refrigerator, a man is poisoned, one is shot, another stabbed, and finally a boatload of sailors is tossed into the sea where they all meet their watery end.

p, William Le Baron; d, Paul Sloane; w, Manuel Seff, Harvey Thew (based on a story by Robert Presnell); ph, Harry Fischbeck.

Crime   **(PR:A MPAA:NR)**

TERROR AFTER MIDNIGHT**   (1965, Ger.) 82m Roxy-Film/Parade bw (NEUNZIG MINUTEN N ACH MITTERNACHT)

Christine Kaufmann *(Julie)*, Martin Held, Hilde Krahl, Christian Doermer, Karel Stepanek, Bruno Dietrich.

Released in Germany in 1962, this tame crime drama has Kaufmann being abducted by a kidnaper after a love triangle fiasco. A ransom is set, but the girl's father kills the kidnaper before he can collect the money.

d, Jurgen Goslar; ph, Klaus Von Rautenfeld; m, Bert Kaempfert.

Crime/Drama   **(PR:C MPAA:NR)**

TERROR AT BLACK FALLS*   (1962) 76m Meridan/Beckman bw

Peter Mamakos *(Father)*, House Peters, Jr *(Sheriff)*, John Alonzo, Sandra Knight, Gary Gray, Jim Bysel, I. Stanford Jolley, Marshall Bradford, Bill Erwin, Jim Hayward.

A Mexican gunfighter tries to save his son from a lynch mob, but ends up causing the boy's death and getting shot in the hand. He is then sent to jail for four years, and his hand is amputated. When he is released from prison he seeks revenge on the sheriff who put him away by taking eight hostages and threatening to kill one every 10 minutes until he can talk to the sheriff. Thirty minutes later, with three corpses on the ground, the sheriff draws on the Mexican, who in turn goes for his gun with his amputated hand and is killed. An ending so bad it's almost brilliant. In a supporting role is Sandra Knight, who at the time was Mrs. Jack Nicholson.

p&d, Richard C. Sarafian; ph, Floyd Crosby.

Western   **(PR:C MPAA:NR)**

TERROR AT HALFDAY   (SEE: MONSTER A GO-GO, 1965)

TERROR AT MIDNIGHT*½   (1956) 70m REP bw

Scott Brady *(Neal Rickards)*, Joan Vohs *(Susan Lang)*, Frank Faylen *(Fred Hill)*, John Dehner *(Lew Hanlon)*, Virginia Gregg *(Helen)*, Ric Roman *(Sgt. Brazzi)*, John Gallaudet *(George Flynn)*, Kem Dibbs *(Nick Mascotti)*, Percy Helton *(Speegie)*, Francis DeSales *(Lt. Conway)*, John Maxwell *(Capt. Allyson)*.

A lower-rung programmer which has newly promoted police sergeant Brady discovering that his girl friend Vohs is apparently involved in a stolen car ring. She turns out to be innocent, however, and Brady rounds up the real thieves. Uneventful.

d, Franklin Adreon; w, John K. Butler (based on a story by Butler, Irving Shulman); ph, Bud Thackery; m, R. Dale Butts; ed, Tony Martinelli; art d, Walter Keller; cos, Adele Palmer.

Crime Drama   **(PR:A MPAA:NR)**

TERROR BENEATH THE SEA*½   (1966, Jap.) 95m Toei/Teleworld c (KAITEI DAISENSO; AKA: WATER CYBORGS)

Shinichi "Sonny" Chiba, Peggy Neal, Franz Gruber, Gunther Braun, Andrew Hughes, Erik Nielson, Make Daning, Hideo Murata.

A typically stiff Japanese science-fiction picture which seems to go to great pains to achieve a comic book look. This one has a mad scientist in control of an underwater city populated by human beings who have been transformed into CREATURE FROM THE BLACK LAGOON-type creatures. Chiba, who plays a newsman, went on to make his mark in martial arts films billed as "Sonny" Chiba. Director Sato used an American-sounding alias on the the credits in the U.S. version to convince potential audiences that this was not just another cheap Japanese monster movie.

d, Hajime Sato [Terence Ford]; w, M. Fukuishima; ph, K. Shimomura; spec eff, Nobuo Yajima.

Science Fiction   **(PR:C MPAA:NR)**

TERROR BY NIGHT, 1931   (SEE: SECRET WITNESS, 1931)

TERROR BY NIGHT**   (1946) 60m UNIV bw

Basil Rathbone *(Sherlock Holmes)*, Nigel Bruce *(Dr. John H. Watson)*, Alan Mowbray *(Maj. Duncan Bleek)*, Dennis Hoey *(Inspector Lestrade)*, Renee Godfrey *(Vivian Vedder)*, Mary Forbes *(Lady Margaret Carstairs)*, Billy Bevan *(Train Attendant)*, Frederic Worlock *(Prof. Kilbane)*, Leyland Hodgson *(Conductor)*, Geoffrey Steele *(Ronald Carstairs)*, Boyd Davis *(McDonald)*, Janet Murdoch *(Mrs. Shallcross)*, Skelton Knaggs *(Sands)*, Gerald Hamer *(Mr. Shallcross)*, Harry Cording *(Mock, Coffin Maker)*, Charles Knight *(Guard)*, Bobby Wissler *(Mock, Jr.)*.

A standard Holmes entry which this time places him on an express train speeding through the countryside from London to Edinburgh. On board is the owner of the cursed Star of Rhodesia diamond, the kind that kills whoever possesses it. Of course, the owner is killed, as are a couple of others. Holmes gets to the bottom of the case once he discovers that the coffin being transported in the baggage car has a false bottom, creating a secret chamber where the killer had been hiding. Everyone involved turns out an entertaining and admirable performance, but the film has little more to recommend it. A clever casting twist has Alan Mowbray, who had played Scotland Yard detectives in two previous Sherlock Holmes films, as the villain. (See SHERLOCK HOLMES series, Index.)

p&d, Roy William Neill; w, Frank Gruber (based on a story by Sir Arthur Conan Doyle); ph, Maury Gertsman; ed, Saul A. Goodkind; md, Mark Levant; art d, John B. Goodman, Abraham Grossman; set d, Russell A. Gausman, Carl Lawrence.

Mystery   **Cas.**   **(PR:A MPAA:NR)**

TERROR CASTLE   (SEE: HORROR CASTLE, 1963, Ital.)

TERROR CIRCUS   (SEE: BARN OF THE NAKED DEAD, 1974)

TERROR-CREATURES FROM THE GRAVE zero
    (1967, U.S./Ital.) 85m M.B.S.-G.I.A.-International Entertainment/Pacemaker c (CINQUE TOMBE PER UN MEDIUM)

Barbara Steele *(Cleo Hauff)*, Richard Garret [Riccardo Garrone] *(Joseph Morgan)*, Walter Brandt [Walter Brandi] *(Albert Kovaks)*, Marilyn Mitchell *(Corinne Hauff)*, Alfred Rice [Alfredo Rizzo] *(Dr. Nemek)*, Alan Collins [Luciano Pigozzi] *(Kurt)*, Tilde Till *(Louise)*, Ennio Balbo *(Paralytic)*, Steve Robinson, Edward Bell, Rene Wolfe.

Steele finds herself the target of grisly revenge plotted by the husband she murdered. Before his death, he had used his occult powers to resurrect medieval victims of the Black Death so that they would infect his wife with bubonic plague. Steele and her cohorts fall prey to the monsters one by one. Only her daughter, Mitchell, and Mitchell's lover, Brandt, are saved after they are immunized by a sudden rain. This one belongs six feet under, along with the creatures in the title.

p, Frank Merle; d, Ralph Zucker [Massimo Pupillo]; w, Roberto Natale, Romano Migliorini; ph, Carlo Di Palma (Cinepanoramic); m, Aldo Piga; ed, Robert Ardis.

Horror   **(PR:O MPAA:NR)**

TERROR EN EL ESPACIO   (SEE: PLANET OF THE VAMPIRES, 2, 1965, U.S./Ital./Span.)

TERROR EYES*   (1981) 89m Lorimar/RANK c

Leonard Mann, Rachel Ward, Drew Snyder, Joseph R. Sicari, Nicholas Cairis, Karen MacDonald, Annette Miller, Bill McCann, Margo Skinner, Elizabeth Barnitz, Holly Hardman, Meb Boden, Leonard Corman, Belle McDonald, Ed Higgins, William McDonald, Kevin Fennessy, Ed Chalmers,

John Blood, Lisa Allee, Elizabeth Allee, Patricia Pellows, J. J. Wright, Ted Duncan, Patricia Rust, Jane-Leah Bedrick, Wally Hooper, Jr, Kevin King, Nancy Rothman.

A sleazy thriller about a psychotic motorcyclist who cruises around Boston lopping the heads off college girls. Rachel Ward's career took a positive turn after this picture with appearances in SHARKEY'S MACHINE (1981), DEAD MEN DON'T WEAR PLAID (1982), and AGAINST ALL ODDS (1984).

p, Larry Babb, Ruth Avergon; d, Kenneth [Ken] Hughes; w, Avergon; ph, Mark Irwin; m, Brad Fiedel; ed, Robert Reitano; prod d, William F. DeSeta.

Horror   **(PR:O MPAA:NR)**

TERROR FACTOR, THE   (SEE: SCARED TO DEATH, 1981)

TERROR FROM THE SUN   (SEE: HIDEOUS SUN DEMON, THE, 1959)

TERROR FROM THE YEAR 5,000*
    (1958) 66m AIP bw (GB: CAGE OF DOOM; AKA: TERROR FROM 5,-000 A.D.; THE GIRL FROM 5,000 A.D.)

Ward Costello (Robert Hedges), Joyce Holden (Claire Erling), John Stratton (Victor), Frederic Downs (Prof. Howard Erling), Fred Herrick (Angelo), Beatrice Furdeaux (Miss Blake), Jack Diamond (1st Lab Technician), Fred Taylor (2nd Lab Technician), Salome Jens (5,000 A.D. Woman).

Following the 1950s science fiction formula, this alien-comes-to-Earth picture has the visitor transported back to 1958 via a time machine built by some inventive island scientists. She hypnotizes one of the men in order to take him back to the future to restart a human race uncontaminated by radioactivity. Before she can get away, however, she is destroyed by a heroic archaeologist. Includes a clip from AIP's I WAS A TEENAGE FRANKENSTEIN in a movie theater sequence. This picture was the film debut of Salome Jens, whose career would seem to lose its momentum after her fine performance in ANGEL BABY in 1961.

p,d&w, Robert J. Gurney, Jr.; ph, Arthur Florman; ed, Dede Allen; art d, Beatrice Gurney; set d, William Hoffman.

Science Fiction   **(PR:A MPAA:NR)**

TERROR FROM UNDER THE HOUSE**
    (1971, Brit.) 89m Hemisphere c (GB: REVENGE; AKA: INN OF THE FRIGHTENED PEOPLE; AFTER JENNY DIED)

Joan Collins (Carol Radford), James Booth (Jim Radford), Ray Barrett (Harry), Sinead Cusack (Rose), Tom Marshall (Lee Radford), Kenneth Griffith (Seely), Zuleika Robson (Jill Radford), Angus Mackay (Priest), Ronald Clark (Brewery's Driver Mate), Patrick McAlinney (George), Artro Morris (Jacko), Donald Morley (Inspector), Martin Carroll (Undertaker), Richard Holden (Pub Customer), Geoffrey Hughes (Brewery Driver), Basil Lord (Sales Representative), Barry Andrews (Sergeant).

When pub owner Booth's daughter is murdered and the police are unable to come up with enough evidence to convict the suspected culprit, he and a buddy who also lost his daughter take on their own form of revenge. They kidnap the youth they believe is responsible and subject him to various tortures in an effort to get him to confess. But the kid doesn't budge, and when he turns up dead, the tone switches to Booth's guilt at the possibility of having killed the wrong man. A sexual undertone is kept bubbling beneath the surface, with the possibilities for the exploration of complex and important themes. But the script doesn't offer the needed material, and halfway through the picture all interest is lost.

p, George H. Brown; d, Sidney Hayers; w, John Kruse; ph, Ken Hodges (Eastmancolor); ed, Tony Palk; cos, Courtenay Elliott.

Drama   **(PR:C MPAA:NR)**

TERROR HOUSE***½   (1942, Brit.) 79m ABF/Pathe bw (GB: THE NIGHT HAS EYES)

James Mason (Stephen Deremid), Wilfred Lawson (Sturrock), Mary Clare (Mrs. Ranger), Joyce Howard (Marian Ives), Tucker McGuire (Doris), John Fernald (Dr. Barry Randall), Dorothy Black, Amy Daley.

Howard and McGuire are schoolteachers who set out on a walking holiday on the very moors where a friend of theirs, another teacher, vanished the year before. A thunderstorm forces them to seek refuge in the home of Mason, a composer who fought in the Spanish Civil War and who suffers occasional "fits" as a result. He lives a reclusive life out on the moors with just his housekeeper-nurse, Clare, and her unpleasant husband, Lawson, for company. Mason and Howard fall in love, but Mason is afraid that he killed Howard's friend during one of his fits. Things look black for the lovers when Howard discovers a secret room containing a skeleton and a locket that belonged to the missing girl. Fortunately, though, it is revealed that it was Clare and Lawson who killed the girl, using Mason's lapses as a way to keep him under their control. The evil couple flee out onto the fogbound moor but they don't get far, falling victims to quicksand. Melodramatic and sounds-

tage-bound, but the film is still quite effective and eerie. Fog covers almost every exterior and cinematographer Krampf would spend long periods getting the artificial fog at just the right density. The moor set was quite small and for the scene where Clare and Lawson flee into the night, it was necessary to use midgets to give the appearance of the pair being farther away than the actual size of the set would allow. The final film was almost too effective, and after initially getting an "A" rating from the British censor and being booked on the biggest cinema circuit in Britain, the rating was suddenly changed to "H" (for "Horrific"), making it off-limits for anyone under 16 years of age. The big circuits had a policy of showing only "A" films, so the independent cinemas became the big winners, getting an excellent thriller starring the top leading man in Britain at the time.

p, John Argyle; d, Leslie Arliss; w, Argyle, Arliss, Alan Kennington (based on a story by Kennington); ph, Gunther Krampf; m, Charles Williams; art d, Duncan Sutherland.

Horror   **(PR:C MPAA:NR)**

TERROR HOUSE*½   (1972) 90m Red Wolf/Scope III-Far West c
    (AKA: TERROR AT RED WOLF INN; THE FOLKS AT RED WOLF INN)

Linda Gillin (Regina), Arthur Space (Henry), John Neilson (Baby John), Mary Jackson (Evelyn), Michael Macready (Policeman), Earl Parker (Pilot), Janet Wood (Pamela), Margaret Avery (Edwina).

A gruesome cannibalistic parody in which Gillin wins a vacation trip to the Red Wolf Inn, where she is greeted by the retarded Neilson and his grandparents. The nauseated girl soon flees after finding a freezerful of body parts, only to be captured and brought back. The "classy" ending has Neilson and the girl in love, working in the kitchen while Grandpa's grinning, winking head watches approvingly from a nearby shelf.

p, Michael Macready; d, Bud Townsend; w, Allen J. Actors; ph, John McNichol; m, Bill Marx; ed, Al Maguire.

Horror/Parody   **(PR:O MPAA:R/PG)**

TERROR IN A TEXAS TOWN*½   (1958) 80m UA bw

Sterling Hayden (George Hansen), Sebastian Cabot (Ed McNeil), Carol Kelly (Molly), Eugene Martin (Pepe Mirada), Ned Young (Johnny Crale), Victor Millan (Jose Mirada), Ann Varela (Rosa Mirada), Sheb Wooley (Baxter), Fred Kohler, Jr (Weed), Steve Mitchell (Keeno), Marilee Earle (Monsy), Jamie Russell (Johnson), Tyler McVey (Sheriff Stoner), Ted Stanhope (Sven Hansen), Gil Lamb (Barnaby), Frank Ferguson (Holmes), Hank Patterson (Brady).

An offbeat western which casts Hayden as a Swede who returns home from the sea to find that his farmer father has been gunned down by the greedy, murderous Young. It seems that the outlaw wants to buy up everyone's land in order to drill for oil, and if people won't sell, he shoots them. In the fir HIGH NOON-style showdown, Hayden comes armed not with a pair of six-shooters, but with a harpoon, with which he has no trouble dispatching Young. A slow-paced, almost hypnotic western, which relies more on characterization and form than on plot. Sharp-eyed viewers will catch a glimpse of Sheb Wooley, who made the charts in 1958 with his immortal hit, "Purple People Eater."

p, Frank N. Seltzer; d, Joseph H. Lewis; w, Ben L. Perry; ph, Ray Rennahan; m, Gerald Fried; ed, Frank Sullivan, Stefan Arnsten; art d, William Ferrari.

Western   **(PR:A MPAA:NR)**

TERROR IN THE CITY   (SEE: PIE IN THE SKY, 1964)

TERROR IN THE HAUNTED HOUSE
                                (SEE: MY WORLD DIES SCREAMING, 1958)

TERROR IN THE JUNGLE zero   (1968) 84m Torres International/Crown c

Jimmy Angle (Henry Clayton, Jr.), Robert Burns, Fawn Silver, Joan Addis, Ivan Stephen, Lee Childress, Jeanette Rollins, Kris Fasseas, Ben Pfeifer, Cynthia McArthur, Bob Bridges, Lizie Curtis, James C. Gates, Cholita Suray, Fernando Larranga, William Cocklin, Elaine Partnow, Henning Bystron, Chase Cordell, Wayne Douglas, Oliver Howard, Herbert Fink, Mitzie Johnson, Byrd Holland, Faith Christopher, Mario Cagnion, Tania Lish, John Johnston, Chuck Angle, Nichola Krujac, Cherleen Baxter.

Vastly inferior to the serial adventures it tries to imitate, this picture, set in the Peruvian jungles, has the young Angle crash-landing on his way to visit his mother. He is kidnaped by a group of Jivaro Indians who think he is a god, but escapes after his stuffed tiger turns into a real one and kills his captors. Cinematography, editing, and acting are all below par.

p, Enrique Torres Tudela; d, Tom De Simone (Plane sequences), Andy Janzack (Jungle Sequences), Alexander Grattan (Temple Sequences); w, Tudela, Richard Ogilvie; ph, Janzack, Lewis Quinn, Mario Tosi (Pathe Color); m, Les Baxter, Stan Hofman; ed, Alberto Soria, Tom Mosca; cos, Zoraida Geradino; spec eff, Jim P. Nielson; m/l, "Intr-ramy," Robert Ojeda, other songs, Ricky Torres, Jeanette Rollins, The Hypnotics; makeup, John De Heven, Robert Hunter, Art Werner.

Adventure   (PR:A MPAA:GP)

TERROR IN THE MIDNIGHT SUN   (INVASION OF THE ANIMAL PEOPLE, 1962, U.S./Swed.)

TERROR IN THE WAX MUSEUM*½   (1973) 93m Crosby/Cinerama c

Ray Milland (*Harry Flexner*), Broderick Crawford (*Amos Burns*), Elsa Lanchester (*Julia Hawthorn*), Maurice Evans (*Inspector Daniels*), Shani Wallis (*Laurie Mell*), John Carradine (*Claude Dupree*), Louis Hayward (*Tim Fowley*), Patric Knowles (*Southcott, Lawyer*), Mark W. Edwards (*Sgt. Michael Hawks*), Lisa Lu (*Mme. Yang*), Steven Marlo (*Karkov, Handyman*), Nicole Shelby (*Meg*), Ben Wright (*Constable*), Matilda Calnan, Peggy Stewart (*Charwomen*), Don Herbert (*Jack the Ripper*), Judy Wetmore (*Lizzie Borden*), George Farina (*Bluebeard*), Rosa Huerta (*Lucretia Borgia*), Rickie Weir (*Marie Antoinette*), Ben Brown (*Attila The Hun*), Paul Wilson (*Ivan the Terrible*), Ralph Cunningham (*Willie Grossman*), Evelyn Reynolds (*Flower Woman*), Jo Williamson (*Mrs. Borden*), Diane Wahrman (*Girl in Bed*), Don Williamson (*Constable Bolt*), Leslie Thompson (*Constable Parker*).

A familiar wax museum murder picture which boasts a number of horror talents, none of whom is given much to do. As Carradine is preparing to sell his museum to Crawford, which would end the careers of workers Milland and Marlo, he is mysteriously murdered. Lanchester comes in to take charge of the museum, but soon a number of mysterious deaths occur at the hands of wax figures who come to life. As with most horror films of this type, it's always fun to try to catch the "wax figures" breathing. Carradine claimed that this was his 415th film, which would have made him a superhumanly prolific actor, even considering that his career had already spanned more than four decades. The actual count at the time was somewhere in the 150s.

p, Andrew J. Fenady; d, Georg Fenady; w, Jameson Brewer (based on a story by Andrew Fenady); ph, William Jurgensen (DeLuxe Color); m, George Duning; ed, Melvin Shapiro; prod d, Stan Jolley; set d, Carl Biddiscombe; cos, Oscar Rodriguez, Vou Lee Giokaris.

Horror   Cas.   (PR:C MPAA:R/PG)

TERROR IS A MAN**   (1959, U.S./Phil.) 89m Valiant bw (AKA: BLOOD CREATURE)

Francis Lederer (*Dr. Girard*), Greta Thyssen (*Frances Girard*), Richard Derr (*Fitzgerald*), Oscar Keesee (*Walter*), Lilia Duran (*Selene*), Peyton Keesee (*Tiago*), Flory Carlos (*The Man*).

The first of a crop of Filipino horror films which soon began to pop up like weeds. Lederer (who had played in such films as Pabst's PANDORA'S BOX in 1929 and Renoir's DIARY OF A CHAMBERMAID in 1946) is cast as a mad scientist who resides on Blood Island and carries out experiments with the goal of transforming a panther into a man. When a shipwrecked sailor (Derr) washes up on shore, Lederer's wife (Thyssen) falls in love with him. The humanoid panther carries Thyssen off, and when Lederer pursues them, the creature kills him and is himself killed. (Or is he?) Derr and Thyssen begin a new life together. A loose remake of the classic THE ISLAND OF LOST SOULS.

p, Kane Lynn, Eddie Romero; d, Gerry De Leon; w, Harry Paul Harber; ph, Emmanuel I. Rojas; m, Ariston Auelino; art d, Vicente Bonus.

Horror   (PR:C MPAA:NR)

TERROR OF DR. CHANEY, THE   (SEE: MANSION OF THE DOOMED, 1976)

TERROR OF DR. MABUSE, THE**   (1965, Ger.) 88m CCC-Filmkunst/Thunder bw (AKA: THE TESTAMENT OF DR. MABUSE; THE TERROR OF THE MAD DOCTOR.)

Gert Frobe (*Inspector Lohmann*), Helmut Schmid (*Johnny Briggs*), Charles Regnier (*Mortimer*), Senta Berger (*Nelly*), Wolfgang Preiss (*Dr. Mabuse*), Walter Rilla (*Prof. Polland*), Harald Juhnke (*Sgt. Kruger*), Leon Askin (*Floke*), Ann Savo (*Wabble/Heidi*), Claus Tinney (*Jack*), Zeev Berlinski (*Gulliver*), Albert Bessler (*Paragraph Joe*), Arthur Schilski (*Toni*), Alan Dijon, Alon Armand, Rolf Eden.

An unimpressive remake of Fritz Lang's 1933 THE TESTAMENT OF DR. MABUSE which has the mad doctor imprisoned in an insane asylum, hypnotizing Rilla to carry out his evil plans. Frobe investigates a series of crimes similar to those of Preiss and soon finds himself taken prisoner by Rilla who mercilessly tortures him with electro-shock treatments. Released in Germany in 1962.

p, Artur Brauner; d, Werner Klinger; w, Ladislaus Fodor, Robert A. Stemmle (based on the story by Thea von Harbou); ph, Albert Benitz; m, Raimund Rosenberger; ed, Walter Wischniewsky; art d, Helmut Nentwig, Paul Markwitz; cos, Vera Mugge; makeup, Willy Stamm.

Crime   (PR:C MPAA:NR)

TERROR OF FRANKENSTEIN   (SEE: VICTOR FRANKENSTEIN, 1975, Swed./Ireland)

TERROR OF GODZILLA   (SEE: MONSTERS FROM THE UNKNOWN PLANET, 1975, Jap.)

TERROR OF SHEBA   (SEE: PERSECUTION, 1974, Brit.)

TERROR OF THE BLACK MASK*½   (1967, Fr./Ital.) 96m S.N.C.-Romana/EMB c

Pierre Brice (*Don Diego*), Helen Chanel (*Carmencita*), Daniele Vargas, Aldo Bufi-Landi, Carlo Latimer, Gisella Arden, Massimo Serato.

A disguised cavalier who is really a Spanish officer gains entrance into a castle which has just been taken over by a malicious tyrant. Meanwhile, the 17th Century village celebrates the end of the plague with a glorious feast which is made even more glorious when the officer kills the tyrant and weds the former castle owner's orphaned daughter.

d, Umberto Lenzi; w, Gino De Santis, Guido Malatesta, Lenzi (based on a story by De Santis).

Adventure   (PR:A MPAA:NR)

TERROR OF THE BLOODHUNTERS*   (1962) 60m ADP bw

Robert Clarke (*Steven Duval*), Steve Conte (*Dione*), Dorothy Haney (*Marlene*).

Clarke is a controversial French author and painter who is framed and sent to Devil's Island where he is befriended by fellow prisoner Conte and the commandant's daughter, Haney. She helps the two men escape from the island through the rugged Amazon jungle, but Conte is devoured by a jaguar. Haney's fiance, a prison guard, is in pursuit of the escapee, but hits an obstacle when he's captured by Indians. Clarke, the noble fellow that he is, returns to save his pursuer, who in turn arranges his freedom.

p,d&w, Jerry Warren.

Adventure   (PR:A MPAA:NR)

TERROR OF THE HATCHET MEN   (SEE: TERROR OF THE TONGS, THE, 1961, Brit.)

TERROR OF THE MAD DOCTOR, THE   (SEE: TERROR OF DR. MABUSE, THE, 1965, Ger.)

TERROR OF THE TONGS, THE**½   (1961, Brit.) 80m Hammer-Merlin/COL c

Geoffrey Toone (*Capt. Jackson*), Christopher Lee (*Chung King*), Yvonne Monlaur (*Lee*), Marne Maitland (*Beggar*), Brian Worth (*Harcourt*), Ewen Solon (*Tongman Tang How*), Burt Kwouk (*Mr. Ming*), Barbara Brown (*Helena Jackson*), Richard Leech (*Inspector Dean*), Bandana Das Gupta (*Anna*), Michael Hawkins (*Priest*), Marie Burke (*Maya*), Milton Reid (*Tong Guardian*), Charles Lloyd Pack (*Doctor*), Roger Delgado (*Tang How*), Tom Gill (*Beamish*), Eric Young (*Confucius*), Johnny Arlan (*Executioner*).

Lee and his Tong gang of drug-slave traders become the target of seaman Toone, who goes on the rampage when his daughter and servant are murdered by Lee's henchmen. He hooks up with Monlaur, a former slave, and together they incite a riot which destroys Lee and his group of bandits. Violent and gory, but full of action.

p, Kenneth Hyman; d, Anthony Bushell; w, Jimmy Sangster; ph, Arthur Grant (Eastmancolor); m, James Bernard; ed, Eric Boyd-Perkins; prod d, Bernard Robinson; art d, Thomas Goswell; makeup, Roy Ashton, Colin Garde.

Crime/Adventure   (PR:O MPAA:NR)

TERROR OF TINY TOWN, THE*   (1938) 62m COL bw

Billy Curtis (*Pat*), Little Billy (*Haines*), Yvonne Moray, Billy Platt, Johnny Bambary, Charles Becker, Joseph Herbert, Nita Krebs, George Ministeri, Karl Casitzky, Fern McDill, W.H. O'Docharty.

One of the strangest ideas ever put to film, THE TERROR OF TINY TOWN is a stock B-western with one unusual note: the cast, with the exception of a prolog announcer, is comprised entirely of midgets. Buell, who produced the first all-black Western, HARLEM ON THE PRAIRIE (1937), wanted to create another novelty film that would capture the public's attention. The result was the first all-midget movie and, as can be expected, the gimmick peters out long before the film is over. The story itself is standard B-western material. Tiny Town is a peaceful village until the bad guy (played by Little Billy) tries to stir up some ranch wars. He hopes the feuding families will kill each other, thus leaving their land free for him to claim. Curtis, the pint-sized good guy in white, catches on to Little Billy's nefarious schemes and patches up ill feelings the notorious badman has caused. After exposing Little Billy to the townspeople, Curtis meets up with his foe. Little Billy retreats to a log cabin where Curtis puts a final stop to the outlaw's plans by blowing up the cabin with a stick of dynamite. Being a formula western, Curtis also has a girl friend (the virginal Moray), while Little Billy gets his affections from dance-hall girl Krebs. As westerns go, this is about average for plot, character, and production values. However, Buell's use of midgets as novelty items is another story. His cast rides around on Shetland ponies but the hitching posts are just beyond reach. Rough-and-tough cowboys enter the bar by walking *beneath* the swinging doors. Playing on his cast's deformities for laughs, Buell exhibits more cruelty than anything else. The whole point behind this seems to be that midgets unable to reach things and singing in high-pitched voices are hilariously funny. Because Hollywood lacked the number of midgets needed to round out his cast, Buell advertised for actors around the country, promising "Big Salaries for Little People." He finally assembled a cast of 60 whose average height was about 3'8". The film was produced at a cost of $100,000 and was fairly successful at the box office. Buell was inspired by this reception and announced plans for an entire series of midget movies. The first film was to be a retelling of the Paul Bunyan legend with a full-sized actor in the lead role. Fortunately, these plans never came to fruition.

p, Jed Buell; d, Sam Newfield; w, Fred Myton, Clarence Marks (based on a story by Myton); ph, Mack Stengler; ed, Martin G. Cohn, Richard G. Wray; art d, Fred Preble; m/l, "I Wanna Make Love to You," "The Wedding of Jack and Jill," Lew Porter.

Western   **Cas.**   **(PR:A MPAA:NR)**

TERROR ON A TRAIN*½   (1953) 72m MGM bw (GB: TIME BOMB)

Glenn Ford *(Peter Lyncourt)*, Anne Vernon *(Janine Lyncourt)*, Maurice Denham *(Jim Warrilow)*, Harcourt Williams *(Vicar)*, Victor Maddern *(Saboteur)*, Harold Warrender *(Sir Evelyn Jordan)*, John Horsley *(Constable Charles Baron)*, Campbell Singer *(Inspector Branson)*, Bill Fraser *(Constable J. Reed)*, Herbert C. Walton *(Old Charlie)*, Martin Wyldeck *(Sgt. Collins)*, Harry Locke *(Train Fireman)*, Frank Atkinson *(Guard)*, Ernest Butcher *(Martindale)*, Ada Reeve *(Old Lady)*, Arthur Hambling, Sam Kydd.

A bomb, located aboard a freight train, threatens the lives of many people as well as the fate of a naval shipyard until Ford, a demolitions expert, is called in to disarm the thing in a race against the clock. A routine effort which only carries tension because of the time element. Performances do reveal, however, the right amount of uneasiness.

p, Richard Goldstone; d, Ted Tetzlaff; w, Kem Bennett (based on his novel *Death at Attention*); ph, F. A. Young; m, John Addison; ed, Robert Watts, Frank Clarke; art d, Alfred Junge.

Drama   **(PR:A MPAA:NR)**

TERROR ON BLOOD ISLAND   (SEE: BRIDES OF BLOOD, 1968)

TERROR ON TIPTOE*½   (1936, Brit.) 58m MB/New Realm bw

Bernard Nedell *(Clive Morell)*, Mabel Poulton *(Poppy)*, Jasper Maskeleyne *(Vivian)*, Stella Bonheur *(Mrs. Morell)*, Joe Hayman *(Sol Hyman)*, Victor Fairley *(Dr. Strauss)*.

A routine crime mystery starring Poulton, who works as a double for a popular Hollywood actress. After nearly falling victim to a bullet fired from the gun of an unseen assassin, Poulton finds help from an American detective, Nedell, and together they defeat the killer. Notable only for the rare talkie appearance of popular silent star Poulton.

p, Reginald Fogwell, Nell Emerald; d, Louis Renoir; w, Fenn Sherie, Ingram d'Abbes (based on the play "Shadow Man" by Sherie, d'Abbes); ph, Geoffrey Faithfull.

Crime   **(PR:A MPAA:NR)**

TERROR ON TOUR zero   (1980) 88m IFD-Four Feathers/Tour Features c

Rick Styles *(Fred)*, Chip Greenman *(Ralph)*, Rich Pemberton *(Henry)*, Dave Galluzzo *(Cherry)*, Larry Thomasof *(Tim)*, Jeff Morgan *(Herb)*, Dave Thompson *(Jeff)*, Lisa Rodriguez *(Jane)*, John Green *(Lt. Lambert)*, Sylvia Wright *(Carol)*, Lindy Leah *(Nancy)*.

A hard-rock band known as the Clowns wear makeup (a la Kiss), play music, are surrounded by drugged-out groupies, and get involved in a string of murders. It seems that someone has been donning their makeup and killing off prostitutes. The premise may have promise if intelligently executed, but TERROR ON TOUR is simply trash. The filmmakers don't even attempt to show a tour, much less a crowd, only occasionally showing a few cheering extras. Made for the video shelves without even attempting a theatrical release, apparently so as to avoid embarrassment.

p, Sandy Cobe; d, Don Edmonds; w, Dell Lekus; ph, James Roberson (United Color); m, The Names; ed, Bob Ernst; art d & set d, Verkina Flower; spec eff, Charlie Spurgeon; spec eff makeup, Jack Petty; stunts, Edmonds.

Horror   **Cas.**   **(PR:O MPAA:NR)**

TERROR SHIP**   (1954, Brit.) 72m Merton Park/Anglo-Amalgamated bw (GB:DANGEROUS VOYAGE)

William Lundigan *(Peter Duncan)*, Naomi Chance *(Joan Drew)*, Vincent Ball *(John Drew)*, Jean Lodge *(Vivian Bolton)*, Kenneth Henry *(Inspector Neal)*, Richard Stewart *(Sgt. French)*, John Warwick *(Carter)*, Beresford Egan *(Hartnell)*, Frank Littlewood, Armand Guinle, Peter Bathurst, Stanley Van Beers, Oliver Johnston, Hugh Morton, Michael Ingrams, Frank Henderson.

When an empty yacht is spotted drifting at sea, three people board it and, surmising that the ship was used for smuggling, they search the vessel but find nothing. Soon they begin to develop radiation burns on their arms which leads to the discovery of stolen uranium hidden in the ship's mast. They summon the police, but before they arrive the uranium thieves return and during an open-sea chase the yacht explodes, killing the criminals. An interesting premise ineptly handled.

p, W. H. Williams; d, Vernon Sewell; w, Julia Ward; ph, Jo [Joe] Ambor.

Crime   **(PR:A MPAA:NR)**

TERROR STREET*   (1953) 83m Hammer/Lippert bw (GB: THIRTY-SIX HOURS)

Dan Duryea *(Bill Rogers)*, Elsy Albiin *(Katie)*, Ann Gudrun *(Jenny)*, Eric Pohlmann *(Slauson)*, John Chandos *(Neville Hart)*, Kenneth Griffith *(Henry)*, Harold Lang *(Harry)*, Jane Carr *(Sister Helen-Clair)*, Michael Golden *(Inspector Kevin)*, Marianne Stone *(Pam)*, Lee Patterson *(Joe)*, John Wynn, Russell Napier, Jacqueline Mackenzie, John Warren, Stephen Vercoe, Robert Henderson, Gabrielle Blunt, Sheila Berry, Cleo Rose, Christine Adrian, Robert O'Neal, Angela Glynne, Richard Ford, Kenneth Brown.

A dull innocent-man-accused-of-murder programmer which has U.S. Air Force pilot Duryea returning to his home in Britain on a 36-hour pass. He discovers that his wife has been murdered by a gang of blackmailers, and he's been set up to take the rap, so he must flee the police while gathering evidence.

p, Anthony Hinds; d, Montgomery Tully; w, Steve Fisher (based on his story); ph, Jimmy Harvey; m, Ivor Slaney; ed, James Needs; art d, J. Elder Wills.

Crime   **Cas.**   **(PR:A MPAA:NR)**

TERROR STRIKES, THE   (SEE: WAR OF THE COLOSSAL BEAST 1958)

TERROR TRAIL**   (1933) 62m UNIV bw

Tom Mix *(Tom Munroe)*, Naomi Judge *(Norma Laird)*, Arthur Rankin *(Little Casino)*, Raymond Hatton *(Lucky Dawson)*, Francis J. McDonald *(Tad McPherson)*, Robert Kortman *(Tim McPherson)*, John St. Polis *(Col. Charles Ormsby)*, Francis Brownlee *(Sheriff Judell)*, Harry Tenbrook *(Deputy Sheriff)*, Lafe McKee *(Shay)*, W.J. Holmes *(Dr. Wilson)*, Hank Bell *(Smith)*, Leonard Trainer *(Jones)*, Jim Corey *(Henry)*, Jay Wilsey [Buffalo Bill, Jr.] *(Prisoner)*, Tony, Jr. the Horse.

A standard oater which has Mix drawing his gun and clenching his fists in an effort to end an outlaw gang's doings. His adventure ends with him winning the girl (Judge) as everyone has come to expect.

d, Armand Schaefer; w, Jack Cunningham (based on the story "Riders of Terror Trail" by Grant Taylor); ph, Dan Clarke.

Western   **(PR:A MPAA:NR)**

TERROR TRAIN**   (1980, Can.) 97m Astral Bellevue Pathe/FOX c (AKA: TRAIN OF TERROR)

Ben Johnson *(Carne)*, Jamie Lee Curtis *(Alana)*, Hart Bochner *(Doc)*, David Copperfield *(The Magician)*, Derek MacKinnon *(Kenny Hampson)*, Sandee Currie *(Mitchy)*, Timothy Webber *(Mo)*, Anthony Sherwood *(Jackson)*, Howard Busgang *(Ed)*, Steve Michaels *(Brakeman)*, Greg Swanson *(Class President)*, D.D. Winters *(Merry)*, Joy Boushel *(Pet)*, Victor Knight *(Engineer)*.

Better than most in the slice-n-dice genre, TERROR TRAIN can boast decent performances by Johnson and Scream Queen Curtis, as well as photography from Alcott (BARRY LYNDON) and direction from Spottiswoode (UNDER FIRE). The script follows the fright essentials to a tee–a disturbed student terrorizes a train full of partying college kids and kills them off one by one in an assortment of gory, gruesome techniques. The killer, who dons various outfits, is a hypersensitive med student who goes off his rocker after a nasty fraternity hazing. Magician Copperfield also makes an appearance.

p, Harold Greenberg; d, Roger Spottiswoode; w, T.Y. Drake; ph, John Alcott (DeLuxe Color); additional ph, Rene Verzier, Peter Benison, Al Smith; m, John Mills-Cockell; ed, Anne Henderson; prod d, Glenn Bydwell; art d, Guy Comtois.

Horror   **Cas.**   **(PR:O MPAA:R)**

TERRORE NELLO SPAZIO   (SEE: PLANET OF THE VAMPIRES, 1965, U.S./Ital./Span.)

TERRORISTS, THE*   (1975, Brit.) 97m Lion/FOX c (GB: RANSOM)

Sean Connery (Nils Tahlvik), Ian McShane (Petrie), Norman Bristow (Capt. Denver), John Cording (Bert), Isabel Dean (Mrs. Palmer), William Fox (Ferris), Richard Hampton (Joe), Robert Harris (Palmer), Harry Landis (Lookout Pilot), Preston Lockwood (Hislop), James Maxwell (Bernhard), John Quentin (Shepherd), Jeffry Wickham (Barnes), Sven Aune (2nd Pilot), Knut Hansson (Matson), Kaare Kroppan (Donner), Alf Malland (Police Inspector), Noeste Schwab (Female Housekeeper), Kare Wicklund (Male Housekeeper), Knut Wigert (Poison), Froeydis Damslora, Inger Heidal, Brita Rogde (Air Hostesses).

Connery stars as a Scandinavian government agent who is called in to settle a hostage crisis. A group of gunmen have hijacked a plane and are keeping the passengers at gunpoint until the government releases some political prisoners. It becomes a tense battle of wits, but when it nearly looks settled–with the terrorists heading out of the country–Connery blows them all away. There is no attempt to explore any of the reasons behind the attack, or what is going on in the terrorizers' minds, thus reducing the picture to a pile of cliches. If anything, THE TERRORISTS has a superb "look" to it, thanks to Nykvist's expertise.

p, Peter Rawley; d, Casper Wrede; w, Paul Wheeler; ph, Sven Nykvist (DeLuxe Color); m, Jerry Goldsmith; ed, Thelma Connell; art d, Sven Wickman.

Action   (PR:C   MPAA:PG)

TERRORNAUTS, THE*½   (1967, Brit.) 75m Amicus/EM c

Simon Oates (Dr. Joe Burke), Zena Marshall (Sandy Lund), Charles Hawtrey (Joshua Yellowlees), Patricia Hayes (Mrs. Jones), Stanley Meadows (Ben Keller), Max Adrian (Dr. Henry Shore), Frank Barry (Burke as a Child), Richard Carpenter (Danny), Leonard Cracknell (Nick), Robert Jewell (Robot Operator), Frank Forsyth (Uncle), Andre Maranne (Gendarme).

Oates is a British astronomer who in his efforts to contact alien beings gets more than he bargained for. The building he's working in, as well as its inhabitants, is beamed across the galaxy to another planet. They are exposed to a savage race that was formerly a civilized colony. The symbolism seems clear: here's what could happen to our dear planet Earth if we're not careful. Second-rate special effects and tame direction don't add up to much for this run-of-the-galaxy science fiction venture.

p, Max J. Rosenberg, Milton Subotsky; d, Montgomery Tully; w, John Brunner (based on the novel The Wailing Asteroid by Murray Leinster); ph, Geoffrey Faithfull (Pathe Color); m, Elisabeth Lutyens; ed, Peter Musgrave; prod d, Bill Constable; art d, Scott Slimon; set d, Andrew Low; cos, Eileen Welch; spec eff, Ernest Fletcher; makeup, Dore Hamilton.

Science Fiction   (PR:A   MPAA:NR)

TERRORS ON HORSEBACK**   (1946) 55m PRC bw

Buster Crabbe (Billy Carson), Al "Fuzzy" St. John (Fuzzy), Patti McCarty (Roxie), I. Stanford Jolley (Grant Barlow), Kermit Maynard (Wagner), Henry Hall (Doc Jones), Karl Hackett (Ed Sperling), Marin Sais (Mrs. Bartlett), Budd Buster (Sheriff Bartlett), Steve Darrell (Jim Austin), Steve Clark (Cliff Adams), George Chesebro, Frank Ellis, Jack Kirk, Lane Bradford.

Crabbe and St. John team up again in this lukewarm screen fodder. Here they come across a stagecoach filled with nothing but dead passengers. They set out to find the killers and their trail leads to the usual outlaw gang who crumble when the law-abiding pair start shooting. A standard oater except for the lack of a romantic subplot. The viewer can be thankful for small things. (See: BILLY CARSON series, Index.)

p, Sigmund Neufeld; d, Sam Newfield; w, George Milton (based on his story); ph, Jack Greenhalgh; ed, Holbrook N. Todd; md, Lee Zahler.

Western   (PR:A   MPAA:NR)

TESEO CONTRO IL MINOTAURO   (SEE: MINOTAUR, THE, 1961, Ital.)

TESHA**   (1929, Brit.) 87m BI-Burlington/Wardour bw

Maria Corda (Tesha), Jameson Thomas (Robert Dobree), Paul Cavanagh (Lenane), Mickey Brantford (Simpson), Clifford Heatherley (Doctor), Daisy Campbell, Espinosa, Bunty Fosse, Boris Ranevsky.

Corda stars as a Russian ballerina who marries a shell-shocked veteran of WW I, but bears the child of his best friend in this film adaptation of a popular novel of the 1920s by Countess Barcynska. Originally made as a silent in 1928, the film was re-released the next year with a soundtrack added.

p&d, Victor Saville; w, Saville, Walter C. Mycroft (based on the novel by Countess Barcynska); ph, Werner Brandes.

Romance   (PR:A   MPAA:NR)

TESS***   (1980, Fr./Brit.) 170m Renn-Burrill/COL c

Nastassia Kinski (Tess Durbeyfield), Leigh Lawson (Alec d'Urberville), Peter Firth (Angel Clare), John Collin (John Durbeyfield), David Markham (Rev. Mr. Clare), Rosemary Martin (Mrs. Durbeyfield), Richard Pearson (Vicar of Marlott), Carolyn Pickles (Marian), Pascale de Boysson (Mrs. Clare), Tony Church (Parson Tringham), John Bett (Felix Clare), Tom Chadbon (Cuthbert Clare), Sylvia Coleridge (Mrs. d'Urberville), Caroline Embling (Retty), Arielle Dombasle (Mercy Chant), Brigid Erin Bates, Jeanne Biras (Girls in Meadow), Peter Benson (Religious Fanatic), Josine Comellas (Mrs. Crick), Patsy Smart (Housekeeper), Graham Weston (Constable).

Polanski's delicate, visually rich adaptation of Thomas Hardy's classic novel places the supremely photogenic Kinski in the title role. A peasant girl, Kinski, is sent to the estate of the wealthy d'Urberville family by her desperate father after he learns that his family is distantly related. It turns out, however, that the d'Urbervilles are not the d'Urbervilles after all, but a family who simply bought the noble family's name. Lawson, the cocky young master of the household, takes Kinski as his lover after feeding her ripe red strawberries. (Kinski's feasting on the fruit may be one of cinema's classic moments.) She soon returns home, disillusioned and pregnant. The baby dies and Kinski finds work on a dairy farm where she falls in love with Firth. Their romance leads to a marriage which ends abruptly on their wedding night when an outraged Firth refuses to accept news of her past. He leaves her and once again she must struggle alone. She returns to Lawson and the d'Urbervilles after her father's death forces her to find some sort of financial compensation. When Firth returns to find Kinski living in a lavish house as Lawson's lover, his desire for his wife is rekindled. Kinski lashes out at Lawson and fatally stabs him. She and Firth spend a final idyllic evening together before fleeing to Stonehenge with the police hot on their trail. Visually the film is a masterwork, capturing in amazing detail the scenery and atmosphere of old England–a surprising achievement considering the film was shot in France. The film's chief drawback, however, is its lack of vitality, making it seem very cautious and reserved rather than passionate and emotional as Hardy intended for his tale of ruin and disenchantment. TESS was awarded Oscars for Best Cinematography (the film was begun by Geoffrey Unsworth who died midpoint and completed with no noticeable loss of texture by Ghislain Cloquet), Best Costume Design, and Best Art Direction.

p, Claude Berri; d, Roman Polanski; w, Polanski, Gerard Brach, John Brownjohn (based on the novel Tess of the d'Urbervilles by Thomas Hardy); ph, Geoffrey Unsworth, Ghislain Cloquet (Panavision, Eastmancolor); m, Philippe Sarde; ed, Alastair McIntyre, Tom Priestly; prod d, Pierre Guffroy; art d, Jack Stephens; cos, Anthony Powell; ch, Sue Lefton.

Drama   Cas.   (PR:A-C   MPAA:PG)

TESS OF THE STORM COUNTRY**½   (1932) 80m FOX bw

Janet Gaynor (Tess Howland), Charles Farrell (Frederick Garfield, Jr.), Dudley Digges (Capt. Howland), June Clyde (Teola Garfield), George Meeker (Dan Taylor), Edward Pawley (Ben Letts), Claude Gillingwater (Frederick Garfield, Sr.), Matty Kemp (Dillon), De Witt Jennings (Game Warden), Louise Carter (Mrs. Garfield), Bruce Warren (Jim), Sara Padden (Old Martha), Eleanor Hunt, Marjorie Peterson, Peppy the Monkey.

Gaynor is cast as the fiery, seafaring daughter of sea captain Digges. Both live as squatters on the land of stodgy old Gillingwater. Their house burns to the ground, Digges is wrongly accused of a crime and sent to prison, and Gaynor is mistakenly believed to be an unwed mother. This last bit of news causes her to lose her beau, Gillingwater's son Farrell, whom she earlier saved from drowning. The discrepancies are cleared up by the finale and Gaynor marries Farrell. An average script which is saved by some fine performances, especially Gaynor's plucky Tess.

d, Alfred Santell; w, S.N. Behrman, Sonya Levien, Rupert Hughes (based on the dramatization by Hughes of the novel by Grace Miller White); ph, Hal Mohr; cos, David Cox.

Drama   (PR:A   MPAA:NR)

TESS OF THE STORM COUNTRY**   (1961) 84m FOX bw

Diane Baker (Tess MacLean), Jack Ging (Peter Graves), Lee Philips (Eric Thorson), Archie Duncan (Hamish MacLean), Nancy Valentine (Teola Graves), Bert Remsen (Mike Foley), Wallace Ford (Fred Thorson), Grandon Rhodes (Mr. Foley), Robert F. Simon (Mr. Graves).

An updated version of the Grace Miller White novel which made it to the screen three times before–with Mary Pickford in 1914 and 1922 and again with Janet Gaynor in 1932. This time Baker gives an effervescent performance as the tough title character who finds herself in the middle of a conflict when she moves to Pennsylvania Dutch country. She's on the side of a group of Mennonite farmers who sold land to a powerful chemical company and who now regret the sale because of the pollution that resulted. In the middle of all the feuding, Baker finds herself falling in love with Mennonite Ging and eventually overcoming the prejudices his people have against her. The film is made worthwhile by James Wong Howe's superlative photography and by evocative location shots in and around Sonora, Calif.

p, Everett Chambers; d, Paul Guilfoyle; w, Charles Land (based on the dramatization by Rupert Hughes of the novel by Grace Miller White); ph, James Wong Howe (CinemaScope, DeLuxe Color); m, Paul Sawtell, Bert Shefter; ed, Eddy Dutko; art d, John Mansbridge.

Drama   **(PR:A MPAA:NR)**

TEST OF PILOT PIRX, THE   (1978, Pol./USSR) 104m
Zespoly/Tallinnfilm c (DOZNANIYE PILOTA PIRKSA; AKA: TEST PILOT PIRX)

Sergiusz Desnitsky, Boleslaw Abart, Vladimir Ivashov, Alexandr Kaidanovsky, Tyno Saar, Zbigniew Lesien.

An uninspired science-fiction tale which somehow won top honors (the Golden Asteroid) at Trieste's Sci-Fi Fest. It tells a typical tale of humans and robots who look like humans. They travel together into space on a mission organized by an electronics company. The robots are given more responsibilities than the humans who are cursed with such nasty habits as emotions and irrational actions and choices. The crew's captain is pitted against a robot whom he ultimately destroys in a battle of decision-making. Lame art direction and sets don't help matters, as they did for Andrei Tarkovsky's SOLARIS which was also based on a story by Stanislaw Lem, Poland's top sci-fi author.

d, Marek Piestrak; w, Piestrak, Vladimir Valutski (based on the story "Inquiry" by Stanislaw Lem); ph, Janusz Pavlovski.

Science Fiction   **(PR:C MPAA:NR)**

TEST PILOT**   (1938) 118m MGM bw

Clark Gable *(Jim Lane),* Myrna Loy *(Ann Barton),* Spencer Tracy *(Gunner Sloane),* Lionel Barrymore *(Howard B. Drake),* Samuel S. Hinds *(Gen. Ross),* Arthur Aylesworth *(Frank Barton),* Claudia Coleman *(Mrs. Barton),* Gloria Holden *(Mrs. Benson),* Louis Jean Heydt *(Benson),* Ted Pearson *(Joe),* Marjorie Main *(Landlady),* Gregory Gaye *(Grant),* Virginia Grey *(Sarah),* Priscilla Lawson *(Mabel),* Dudley Clements *(Mr. Brown),* Henry Roquemore *(Fat Man),* Byron Foulger *(Designer),* Frank Jaquet *(Motor Expert),* Roger Converse *(Advertising Man),* Dorothy Vaughan *(Fat Woman),* Billy Engle *(Little Man),* Brent Sargent *(Movie Leading Man),* Mary Howard *(Movie Leading Woman),* Gladden James *(Interne),* Douglas McPhail *(Singing Pilot in Cafe),* Forbes Murray, Richard Tucker, Don Douglas, Hudson Shotwell, James Flavin, Hooper Atchley, Dick Winslow, Ray Walker, Frank Sully *(Pilots in Cafe),* Tom O'Grady *(Bartender),* Syd Saylor *(Bus Leader),* Jack Mack, Wally Maher *(Mechanics),* Richard Kipling, Arthur Stuart Hull *(Floorwalkers),* Charlie Sullivan, Ernie Alexander, Buddy Messinger *(Field Mechanics),* Nick Copeland, Donald Kerr *(Drake Mechanics),* Tom Rutherford, James Donlan, Phillip Terry *(Photographers),* Robert Fiske, Jack Cheatham *(Attendants),* Alonzo Price *(Weatherman),* Mitchell Ingraham, Frank DuFrane, Cyril Ring *(N.A.A. Officials),* Lester Dorr, Charles Waldron, Jr., Garry Owen *(Pilots),* Bobby Caldwell, Marilyn Spinner, Tommy Tucker *(Benson Children),* William O'Brien *(Waiter),* Martin Spellman, Knowlton Levenick, Ralph Gilliam, Dix Davis *(Kids),* Fay Holden, Lulumae Bohrman, Estella Ettaire *(Salesladies),* Ken Barton *(Announcer).*

One of the best aviation dramas ever made, TEST PILOT sparkles with a great cast and sprightly direction by Fleming, a "man's director" who made a "man's film" but had the good sense to throw in a great female, Loy. Gable is one of the world's most renowned test pilots, working for plane manufacturer Barrymore. While testing the company's new plane, "The Bullet," Gable is forced to land in a Kansas cornfield because of engine trouble and there meets farm girl Loy. He stays for breakfast and falls in love with the girl while his plane is away being repaired. Gable invites Loy to go off with him and she does, flying to Pittsburgh, where they are married. Gable asks for a week's vacation to honeymoon, but the cranky boss refuses, telling him that he wants his new plane back and in good shape. Gable quits and he–along with Tracy, his devoted mechanic, and Loy–goes on a drinking honeymoon. Then Gable goes off on his own and Tracy tracks him down, sobers him up, and returns him to a wife who by now is having second thoughts about staying with her new hubby. Gable patches things up with Barrymore and settles down a bit. He and Loy begin to enjoy domestic life. Tracy, however, knows what to expect and sees Loy grow more and more apprehensive about Gable's test piloting, anxiously watching him take up experimental planes and risking his life. Gable calls the sky "that lady all dressed in blue," and it is soon obvious that he deeply enjoys putting his life on the line. Loy cannot bear to watch the tests anymore and begins to stay home, where she becomes a nervous wreck. As she later tells Gable, "I am dead until you come down. Is he alive? Like a clock ticking...still alive...still alive...still alive." Hinds, a U.S. Army general, wants Gable to test the Army's new B-17 bomber (which would later become the workhorse of the Air Corps during WW II), and he accepts the challenge, but the mission terrifies Loy. She is on the verge of a crackup by the time Gable and Tracy–the mechanic going along as copilot–climb into the bomber. Gable pushes the plane beyond its expected limits and keeps going, trying to reach 30,000 feet. The bomber, however, cannot take the pressure and it gives out, plummeting earthward in a screaming uncontrollable nosedive. Gable and

Tracy battle the controls fiercely but the dozens of sandbags, used for ballast in the back of the plane, break loose and come crashing into the cabin, pinioning the men against the controls. Both are desperately throwing sandbags out the window and trying to pull up the plane at the same time. Just before the plane crashes nose first into the earth, Gable manages to yank up the controls and pull the plane level, but it's a losing struggle and the plane crashes anyway. By the time Gable manages to pull away the dozens of sandbags from Tracy, he finds his dear friend dying, the life crushed out of him. He drags Tracy's body away from the plane just as its gasoline tanks explode and holds his friend closely in the wilderness. Battered, his face scarred, his arm broken, Gable returns to Loy, believing she has left him over not being able to endure his dangerous profession. He tells her tearfully of Tracy's death and is about to go when Loy throws her arms around him. Gable says he is through with flying and that he will never test another plane, but his rehabilitation comes about when Hinds and Drake–with Loy for Gable's good–enlist him in the Army Air Corps, where he becomes a flight instructor. Gable is shown two years later instructing new pilots and then ordering them into the air, sticking a piece of chewing gum onto one plane for good luck, the very gesture Tracy has performed throughout the film, sticking a piece of gum to every plane Gable takes into the air. As the Air Corps trainees take flight, Gable steps off the field and joins his wife Loy. Their little boy looks skyward with his mother and father, smiling, as Gable complains about not being up there with his boys, but down on the ground, which delights his devoted wife Loy. It was during the production of this film that Tracy gave Gable the sobriquet for which he would be forever known. Trying to drive into the MGM lot one morning, Tracy's car was blocked by scores of screaming female movie fans, all demanding that Gable sign their pictures of him. Tracy beeped his horn, but the fans took one look and ignored him. Finally, the frustrated Tracy stood up in his convertible and shouted at Gable: "Long live the king! And now...let's get inside and go to work!" The prop department found out about the incident and made Gable a cardboard crown lined with rabbit's fur. Then Ed Sullivan heard of the incident and conducted a nationwide poll to find out who really were the king and queen of Hollywood. The fans universally elected Gable and Loy. Mantz, who was in charge of the exciting aerial scenes in TEST PILOT (and who was later killed doing the same thing during the production of THE FLIGHT OF THE PHOENIX), became Gable's good friend and he and Gable and Ray Moore, Gable's stand-in for stunts, became drinking buddies. When Tracy learned that he was not invited to a Catalina Island party the three men went to, Tracy went on a 24-hour bender, so hung over the next day he refused to have makeup put on his face before his scenes. When he saw the day's rushes he shouted to the makeup man: "How come you can't make me look as good as Gable?" Tracy took his frustration out at having to perform another supporting role in a Gable film by stretching out his death scene so that Gable, holding him, finally shouted: "God's sake, Spence, die, will you?" TEST PILOT was a box-office smash, with stunning aerial photography unmatched to this day.

p, Louis D. Lighton; d, Victor Fleming; w, Vincent Lawrence, Waldemar Young, (uncredited) Howard Hawks (based on a story by Frank Wead); ph, Ray June; m, Franz Waxman; ed, Tom Held; art d, Cedric Gibbons, John Detlie; set d, Edwin B. Willis; cos, Dolly Tree; spec eff, Arnold Gillespie, Donald Jahraus; makeup, Jack Dawn; aerial ph, Paul Mantz, Ray Moore.

Aviation Drama   **(PR:A MPAA:NR)**

TESTAMENT½**   (1983) 90m Entertainment Events-American Playhouse/PAR c

Jane Alexander *(Carol Wetherly),* William Devane *(Tom Wetherly),* Ross Harris *(Brad Wetherly),* Roxana Zal *(Mary Liz Wetherly),* Lukas Haas *(Scottie Wetherly),* Philip Anglim *(Hollis),* Lilia Skala *(Fania),* Leon Ames *(Henry Abhart),* Lurene Tuttle *(Rosemary Abhart),* Rebecca DeMornay *(Cathy Pitkin),* Kevin Costner *(Phil Pitkin),* Mako *(Mike),* Mico Olmos *(Larry),* Gerry Murillo *(Hiroshi),* J. Brennan Smith *(Billdocker),* Lesley Woods *(Lady Mayor),* Wayne Heffley *(Police Chief),* William Schilling *(Pharmacist),* David Nichols *(Worried Man),* Gary Bayer *(Angry Man),* Martin Rudy *(Dr. Jenson),* Jamie Abbott *(Boy Mayor),* Rocky Krakoff *(Pied Piper),* Rachel Gudmundson *(Nancy),* Keri Houlihan *(Lisa),* Pauline Lomas *(Woman),* Clete Roberts *(Newscaster),* Jess Wayne *(Man in Line).*

After enduring the trivialities of modern everyday American family life that plague the first 20 minutes of this picture, one is almost ashamed to admit he can hardly wait for the bomb to drop. The opening segment (pre-holocaust) is an attempt to present a typical family from Hamlin, Calif. Alexander and Devane are an average couple who bicker, joke, and make love, while their children go through the various motions of growing up and calling each other names (Mary Elizabeth is tagged Mary Lizard). One fine day Devane goes off to work and never comes back. The effects of nearby nuclear explosions are felt via an overexposed screen. The post-holocaust portion of the picture, unfortunately, is nearly as trivial as the beginning. A meeting is called at the local church where various authorities deliver carefully scripted statements, but a fundamental feeling of doom clouds the proceedings. As the picture progresses and living conditions deteriorate, people begin to die, looting occurs, and Alexander's family relies on memories to carry them through. With the use of Super 8 footage, we get bits and pieces of the past–shots of Devane (who is assumed dead), of the dead children (all but Harris have gone), and of the happy times they all shared. Nearly giving up, Alexander, Harris, and Murillo (a retarded friend) attempt suicide by locking themselves in the garage with the car motor running, but find that their will to live is too strong. The picture ends with the three survivors wishing for a future which includes memories of the good times and bad, over a Super 8 of the entire family in happier days. TESTAMENT is a film one really wants to like, mainly because of the powerful statement it makes, but it just isn't that compelling. Much of the film's meaning is conveyed through watching the characters think, or feel miserable, or remember their past...and remembering is not a very cinematic action. At the same time, some scenes are truly magical, such as Harris and Alexander dancing to The Beatles' "All My Loving," followed by Super 8 flashbacks of the same dance. Even if TESTAMENT is top-heavy with symbolism (the children's version of "The Pied Piper of Hamelin" is horrid), the intentions of director Littman (a commendable debut) are enough to warrant a positive response. A restrained picture which never resorts to the sensationalism of the TV film THE DAY AFTER. Alexander, in the role of the sturdy though faltering mother, received a well-deserved Oscar nomination. Hers is simply one of a number of exceptional performances. Also featured are Philip Anglim, Broadway's "Elephant Man,"- 'Rebecca DeMornay of RISKY BUSINESS, and little Lukas Haas of WITNESS. Originally produced to be shown on PBS' program "American Playhouse,"

p, Jonathan Bernstein, Lynne Littman; d, Littman; w, John Sacret Young (based on the story "The Last Testament" by Carol Amen); ph, Steven Poster (CFI Color); m, James Horner; ed, Suzanne Pettit; prod d, David Nichols; art d, Linda Pearl; set d, Waldimar Kalinowski; cos, Julie Weiss.

Drama   Cas.   (PR:A MPAA:PG)

TESTAMENT OF DR. MABUSE, THE*½**   (1943, Ger.) 122m
        Nero-Constantine-Deutsche Universal/Janus bw (DAS TESTAMENT
        DES DR. MABUSE; LE TESTAMENT DU DR. MABUSE; AKA: TH E
        LAST WILL OF DR. MABUSE, CRIMES OF DR. MABUSE)

Rudolf Klein-Rogge (*Dr. Mabuse*), Oskar Beregi (*Prof. Dr. Baum, Director of Insane Asylum*), Karl Meixner (*Hofmeister*), Theodor Loos (*Dr. Kramm, Dr. Baum's Assistant*), Otto Wernicke (*Commissioner Karl Lohmann [German Version Only]*), Klaus Pohl (*Muller, Lohmann's Assistant*), Wera Liessem (*Lilli*), Gustav Diesel (*Kent*), Camilla Spira (*Juwelen-Anna*), Rudolph Schundler (*Hardy*), Theo Lingen (*Hardy's Friend*), Paul Oskar Hocker (*Bredow*), Paul Henckels (*Lithographer*), Georg John (*Baum's Servant*), Ludwig Stossel (*Employee*), Hadrian M. Netto, Paul Bernd, Henry Pless, A.E. Licho, Gerhard Bienert, Josef Damen, Karl Platen, Paul Rehkopf, Franz Stein, Eduard Wesener, Bruno Ziener, Heinrich Gotho, Michael von Newlinski, Anna Goltz, Heinrich Gretler, French Version Only: Jim Gerald (*Commissioner Karl Lohmann*), Thomy Bourdelle, Maurice Maillot, Monique Rolland, Rene Ferte, Daniel Mendaille, Raymond Cordy, Ginette Gaubert, Sylvie de Pedrillo, Merminod, Georges Tourreil, George Paulais, Jacques Ehrem, Lily Rezillot.

A hauntingly suspenseful sequel to director Lang's 1922 silent DR. MABUSE, THE GAMBLER, this entry was originally filmed in 1932 but did not get U.S. release until 11 years later (under its less familiar title THE LAST WILL OF DR. MABUSE). Reprising his role as the mad Dr. Mabuse is Klein-Rogge who appears at the start of this film just where he was last seen–in a cell in an insane asylum (in response to the length of time between his filming the previous picture and the sequel Lang said, "I had left Mabuse in an insane asylum at the end of the last film and I didn't know how to get him out"). Beregi stars as the director of the asylum, whose mind is soon controlled by Klein-Rogge. When Klein-Rogge dies, Beregi becomes possessed with the dead doctor's spirit and is compelled to carry out Klein-Rogge's master plan of destroying the state through stealing, violence, murder, and destruction–all of which have been detailed in journals written while Klein-Rogge was imprisoned. Beregi engineers these acts of chaos, but manages to lead a double life and retain his position at the asylum. On the trail of Beregi's mysterious gang is police inspector Wernicke (whom audiences had come to know already in Lang's previous film M, in which he also played a character named Lohmann) who, with information supplied by former detective Meixner, is able to put a lid on the anti-state terrorist activities. After an explosives attack on a chemical factory, Beregi flees the site by car. He is finally apprehended and driven crazy after seeing a ghastly apparition of Klein-Rogge. The end has Beregi being returned to the asylum, this time as an inmate rather than the director. Intertwined into this story is the tale of two lovers–Diesel, a member of Beregi's gang, and his sweetheart, Liessem. Diesel, who is trying to separate himself from the gang's activities (and therefore unable to ally himself with the police), manages to prove the connection between Klein-Rogge's plans and the chaos occurring in Berlin. It is then that Beregi's double life is exposed. What makes THE TESTAMENT OF DR. MABUSE such a marvel is Lang's mastery of sound and visuals. While the film as a whole is a lesser achievement than the previous M, it still contains a number of scenes which can be held to be on the same level. From the very opening Lang's brilliance at creating a tense atmosphere is clearly apparent. A man is seen walking through an extremely forbidding warehouse. He is unknown to the audience, as is the setting. Frightened, he makes his way across the floor, protecting his ears from a thundering drone which echoes throughout. Two more men enter the scene and discover the third man's presence. He escapes but is nearly obliterated by a piece of stonework which crashes down from overhead. He reaches the safety of the street (or so he thinks) only to have

his path blocked by a group of dangerous-looking thugs. As he doubles back he narrowly escapes a barrel which falls from a truck and then explodes. He hurries to a telephone to inform inspector Wernicke of his discovery–that the warehouse is where the gang is counterfeiting banknotes (the thundering sound being that of the printing press)–only to be silenced by the thugs when they catch up with him. The most frightening aspect of this scene is its mystery–one never knows who is attacking the man (who, we learn from his phone call, is Meixner) so how can one fight back? It is this aspect (among others) that led to the belief that Lang was making an anti-Nazi film in THE TESTAMENT OF DR. MABUSE. In 1943, at the film's New York opening, Lang announced, "This film meant to show Hitler's terror methods as in parable. The slogans and beliefs of the Third Reich were placed in the mouths of criminals. By these means I hoped to expose those doctrines behind which there lurked the intention to destroy everything a people holds dear" (from Lotte Eisner's *Fritz Lang*). The attack on Naziism, however, seems to have been created more in hindsight than during the actual production. Lang was, after all, a German in the U.S. trying to work and survive amidst a growing outrage against the German people. By calling THE TESTAMENT OF DR. MABUSE anti-Hitler, Lang allied himself with American sentiment. If THE TESTAMENT OF DR. MABUSE was indeed anti-Nazi (and it can clearly be viewed as such, though it is Lang's original intention that is questioned here) it is surprising that Hitler had Goebbels (then Minister of Propaganda) invite Lang to head the Nazi film board (Filmprufstelle). During Goebbels' and Lang's meeting, Lang also learned that THE TESTAMENT OF DR. MABUSE was going to be banned, not because of anti-Nazi messages, but because, in the words of Goebbels (cited in Eisner's book from *Dr. Goebbels* by Karina Niehoff and Boris von Bonesholm), "I shall ban this film...because it proves that a group of men who are determined to the last...could succeed in overturning any government by brute force." Realizing what a commitment to the Nazis meant, Lang "agreed" to Goebbels' offer and then left his office. Lang was also concerned that the new regime would discover that his mother, Paula Schlesinger, was Jewish–though she was raised an Austrian Catholic. In Lang's words, "The interview lasted from noon to 2:30 by which time the banks had already closed and I could not withdraw any money. I had just enough at home to buy a ticket to Paris, and I arrived practically penniless at the Gare du Nord." Before leaving, however, Lang divorced his wife and long-time scenarist Thea von Harbou who was already a member of the Nazi party and wished to stay behind in Germany. THE TESTAMENT OF DR. MABUSE was scheduled to open at the Ufa Palast on March 23, 1933 (nearly two months after Hitler assumed power). It was pulled and replaced by the pro-Nazi BLUTENDES DEUTSCHLAND (BLEEDING GERMANY) which in turn was replaced by DER CHORAL VON LEUTHEN. Although the Nazis had banned Lang's film, they had failed (thankfully) to destroy it. Seymour Nebenzal, the picture's executive producer, managed to smuggle out of Germany both the German and French versions of the film (they were filmed simultaneously with variants in casting). The German version received its World premiere in, of all places, Hungary in May of 1933. The French version, however, was yet unedited– this work was completed by Luther Wolf whom Lang would not meet until 1943. It was in this year that the U.S. finally saw the film, under the title THE LAST WILL OF DR. MABUSE. It was based on a French adaptation of von Harbou's script by Rene-Sti and subtitled by Herman G. Weinberg. These additional "contributors" no doubt altered the film to some extent, possibly with even more of an anti-Nazi slant in response to the climate of the day. Whatever political stance THE TESTAMENT OF DR. MABUSE holds, it is still a classic example of Lang's talent and a superb psychological thriller. Followed by THE THOUSAND EYES OF DR. MABUSE in 1960.

p&d, Fritz Lang; w, Lang, Thea von Harbou [French version only, A. Rene-Sti] (based on the characters from the novel by Norbert Jacques); ph, Fritz Arno Wagner, Karl Vash; m, Hans Erdmann; prod d, Karl Vollbrecht, Emile Hasler; art d, Vollbrecht, Hasler.

Crime   (PR:C MPAA:NR)

TESTAMENT OF DR. MABUSE, THE (1965) (SEE: TERROR OF DR.
                                                    MABUSE, THE, 1965, Ger.)

TESTAMENT OF ORPHEUS, THE***   (1962, Fr.) 79m Editions
        Cinegraphiques/Films Around the World-Brandon bw-c (LE TESTA-
                                                    MENT D'ORPHEE)

Jean Cocteau (*Himself, the Poet*), Edouard Dermit (*Cegeste*), Jean-Pierre Leaud (*The Schoolboy*), Henri Cremieux (*The Professor*), Francoise Christophe (*The Nurse*), Maria Casares (*The Princess*), Francois Perier (*Heurtebise*), Yul Brynner (*The Court Usher*), Daniel Gelin (*The Intern*), Nicole Courcel (*The Young Mother*), Jean Marais (*Oedipus*), Claudine Auger (*Minerva*), Georges Chretelain, Michele Lemoigne (*The Lovers*), Philippe Juzau (*1st Man-Horse*), Daniel Moossmann (*2nd Man-Horse*), Alice Sapritch, Marie-Josephe Yoyotte (*Gypsies*), Henry Torres (*The Master of Ceremonies*), Michele Comte (*The Little Girl*), Alec Weisweiller (*The Confused Lady*), Philippe (*Gustave*), Guy Dute (*1st Man-Dog*), Jean-Claude Petit (*2nd Man-Dog*), Alice Heyliger (*Isolde*), Brigitte Morissan (*Antigone*), Pablo Picasso, Jacqueline Roque [Jacqueline Picasso], Luis-Miguel Dominguin, Lucia Bose, Serge Lifar, Charles Aznavour, Francoise Arnoul, Francoise Sagan, Roger Vadim, Annette Stroyberg, Brigitte Bardot (*Themselves*), Michael Goodliffe (*English Narrator*).

Poet/filmmaker/sculptor/painter Jean Cocteau bade his fond farewell to the cinema with this free-flowing, spirited collection of images and scenes which include characters from his past films and a gathering of personal friends and admirers. The cast reads like a who's who of French artists. What there is of a story travels the same ground as Cocteau's earlier THE BLOOD OF A POET (1930) and ORPHEUS (1949), bringing his cinematic career (which is difficult to separate from his other talents) full circle. For fans of Cocteau, everything in this picture stikes a familiar chord–a poet lives, must die, is resurrected, and must die again to qualify for immortality. Cocteau again employs some of the most inventive and beautiful photographic manipulations ever done in films, including the reverse motion techniques which never fail to bring a smile to his devotees. Included in this homage, of sorts, to Cocteau's career are Picasso, Aznavour, and bullfighter Dominguin–all friends of the filmmaker. Also making appearances are familiar faces from ORPHEUS, including Marais, Casares, Dermit, Perier, and Cremieux. Francois Truffaut, in honor of one of his masters, assisted with the production and financing of the picture. A pure, personal poem from one of the greats.

p, Jean Thuillier, d&w, Jean Cocteau; ph, Roland Pontoiseau; m, Georges Auric, Martial Solal, (Christoph Gluck, George Frederik Handel, Johann Sebastian Bach, Richard Wagner); ed, Marie-Josephe Yoyotte; art d, Pierre Guffroy; cos & sculptures, Janine Janet; English subtitles, Charles Frank.

Drama   **Cas.**   **(PR:C   MPAA:NR)**

TESTIGO PARA UN CRIMEN   (SEE: VIOLATED LOVE, 1966, Arg.)

TEUFEL IN SEIDE   (SEE: DEVIL IN SILK, 1968, Ger.)

TEVYA**½   (1939) 93m Rutenberg and Everett Yiddish Film Library of the America n Jewish Historical Society bw

Maurice Schwartz *(Tevya)*, Miriam Riselle *(Chave)*, Rebecca Weintraub *(Golde)*, Paula Lubelska *(Zeitel)*, Leon Liebgold *(Fedia)*, Vicki Marcus *(Shloimele)*, Perle Marcus *(Surele)*, Julius Adler *(Priest)*, David Makarenke *(Mikita)*, Helen Grossman *(Mikita's Wife)*, Morris Strassberg *(Starasta)*, Louis Weissberg *(Starshina)*, Al Harris *(Zazulia)*, Boez Young *(Uradnik)*.

Sholem Aleichem's stories about the Russian-Jewish milkman Tevya are probably best known for the musical FIDDLER ON THE ROOF. However, Tevya's story had been adapted for stage and film once before. This version had been a popular vehicle in the Yiddish Theater in New York City and its star, Schwartz, had made the role his own long before Zero Mostel or Topol. Schwartz also adapted the play for the screen and directed a charming film. The story involves a crisis within Schwartz's family when his daughter, Riselle, falls under the charms of the goy next door (Liebgold). It's bad enough that Liebgold's a gentile, but he also reads secular writers like Gorky. Riselle naturally takes this up as well, much to her father's dismay. Schwartz fills his character with an abundance of wit and bitter sarcasm. Though one might find him to be a stereotypical Jewish father, the characterization is realistic and emphatically human. This was shot in Long Island, but its recreation of a Ukranian shetl is remarkable. Despite some overacting (Riselle in particular) TEVYA is one of the best of the Yiddish films produced in this country. It boasted the highest budget for a Yiddish film and every penny is on the screen. The re-creation of a world long gone is well worth seeing as an historical document in addition to being an enjoyable entertainment. In 1978, some 39 years after the film's debut, TEVYA was restored by Sharon Puucker Rivo and Henry Felt and premiered once more in New York City. (In Yiddish; English subtitles.)

p, Henry Ziskin; d&w, Maurice Schwartz (based on the play by Sholem Aleichem); ph, Larry Williams; m, Sholem Secunda; ed, Sam Citron; English titles, Leon Crystal.

Drama/Comedy   **(PR:A   MPAA:NR)**

TEX***   (1982) 103m Disney/BV c

Matt Dillon *(Tex McCormick)*, Jim Metzler *(Mason McCormick)*, Meg Tilly *(Jamie Collins)*, Bill McKinney *(Pop McCormick)*, Frances Lee McCain *(Mrs. Johnson)*, Ben Johnson *(Cole Collins)*, Emilio Estevez *(Johnny Collins)*, Phil Brock *(Lem Peters)*, Jack Thibeau *(Coach Jackson)*, Zeljko Ivanek *(Hitchhiker)*, Tom Virtue *(Bob Collins)*, Pamela Ludwig *(Connie)*, Jeff Fleury *(Roger)*, Suzanne Costallos *(Fortune Teller)*, Marilyn Redfield *(Ms. Carlson)*, Mark Arnott *(Kelly)*, Jill Clark *(Marcie)*, Sheryl Briedel *(Lisa)*, Lisa Mirkin *(Shelly)*, Rod Jones *(Doctor)*, Richard Krause *(Ride Operator)*, Don Harral *(Doctor in Hospital)*, Janine Burns *(Nurse)*, Mark Huebner *(Orderly)*, Ron Thulin *(Anchorman)*, Mary Simons *(Mrs. Germanie)*, Francine Ringold *(Reporter)*, Darren Cates, Wayne Dorris, Adam Hubbard *(Kids)*, Robin Winters *(Girl on Bike)*, Lance Parkhill *(Boy)*, Mike Coats *(Dave)*, Charlie Haas *(Lee)*, Larry Stallsworth *(Patrolman)*, Scott Smith, Eric Beckstrom *(Bikers)*, S.E. Hinton *(Mrs. Barnes)*, Coralie Hunter *(Lukie)*.

Dillon takes his urban toughness to Oklahoma as a young farmboy raised by his elder brother when his mother dies and his father wanders away. The pitfalls of growing up are examined with honesty as the film probes such subjects as sex, boozing, and fighting–three areas the Disney folks have stayed clear of in the past. Dillon, though occasionally annoying, turns in a

decent performance, as does brother Metzler, and the unrelentingly adorable Tilly (THE BIG CHILL, PSYCHO II, AGNES OF GOD) as his girl friend. Based on a teen novel by S.E. Hinton (who also appears in the film). If you're keeping score, Dillon's been in three Hinton adaptations (THE OUTSIDERS, RUMBLEFISH) and Estevez has been in three (THE OUTSIDERS, THAT WAS THEN, THIS IS NOW).

p, Tim Zinnemann; d, Tim Hunter; w, Hunter, Charlie Haas (based on the novel by S.E. Hinton); ph, Ric Waite (Technicolor); m, Pino Donaggio; ed, Howard Smith; md, Natale Massara; prod d, Jack T. Collis; art d, John B. Mansbridge.

Drama   **Cas.**   **(PR:A   MPAA:PG)**

TEX RIDES WITH THE BOY SCOUTS*   (1937) 57m GN bw

Tex Ritter *(Tex)*, Marjorie Reynolds *(Norma)*, Horace Murphy *(Stubby)*, Karl Hackett *(Kemp)*, Edward Cassidy *(Sheriff)*, Tim Davis *(Tommie)*, Snub Pollard *(Pee Wee)*, Charles King *(Stark)*, Philip Ahn *(Sing Fong)*, Tommy Bupp *(Buzzy)*, Lynton Brent *(Pete)*, Heber Snow [Hank Worden], Forrest Taylor, White Flash the Horse.

A weak oater which has Ritter hunting down some outlaws who knocked off a bullion shipment. He gets a helping hand from a Boy Scout troop, certainly a novel twist on an old theme. The climactic chase scene has Ritter pursuing the gang, who've decided to take the gold and make a run for the border. Thanks to Ritter's sharpshooting, the outlaws are stopped short of their destination. Released with the official seal of the Boy Scouts of America.

p, Edward F. Finney; d, Ray Taylor; w, Edmond Kelso (based on a story by Kelso, Lindsley Parsons); ph, Gus Peterson; ed, Frederick Bain; md, Frank Sanucci.

Western   **Cas.**   **(PR:A   MPAA:NR)**

TEX TAKES A HOLIDAY*   (1932) 68m Argosy/FD c

Wallace MacDonald, Virginia Brown Faire, Ben Corbett, Olin Francis, George Chesebro, James Dillon, Claude Peyton, George Gerwing, Jack Perrin, Sheldon Lewis.

A sub-standard horse opry which casts MacDonald as the proverbial mysterious stranger who blows into the Lone Star state causing everyone to sit up and take notice. What really catches one's eye, however, is the amazingly bad color (it was in its infancy) that severely hampers the visuals.

d, Alvin J. Neitz; w, Allan James, Robert Walker (based on a story by Walker); ph, Otto Himm (Multicolor).

Western   **(PR:A   MPAA:NR)**

TEXAN, THE***   (1930) 72m PAR bw

Gary Cooper *(Enrique "Quico" , The Llano Kid)*, Fay Wray *(Consuelo)*, Emma Dunn *(Senora Ibarra)*, Oscar Apfel *(Thacker)*, James Marcus *(John Brown)*, Donald Reed *(Nick Ibarra)*, Soledad Jiminez *(The Duenna)*, Veda Buckland *(Mary the Nurse)*, Cesar Vanoni *(Pasquale)*, Edwin J. Brady *(Henry)*, Enrique Acosta *(Sixto)*, Romualdo Tirado *(Cabman)*, Russell 'Russ' Columbo *(Singing Cowboy at Campfire)*.

In 1885, Cooper, an infamous bandit known as the Llano Kid, rides into a small town policed by Marcus, a sheriff obsessed with the Bible. The brash bandit soon enters into a game of poker at the local saloon and finds himself faced with a cheating opponent. Cooper is forced to kill the gambler in self-defense and beat it out of town on the next train to Galveston. On board he meets Apfel, a rather shady character who has been hired by wealthy Mexican aristocrat Dunn to find her long-lost son who disappeared when he was 10 years old. Dunn has offered a $1,000 reward if Apfel can find the boy, now a young man. Certain he can bilk the old woman out of her estate, Apfel convinces Cooper–who speaks Spanish and looks Latin–to pose as Dunn's son. Coached by Apfel, Cooper fools the old woman with ease. At the same time, Cooper begins to fall in love with his "niece," Wray. As the two grow close, Cooper learns that the man he killed at the poker game was Dunn's real son and he decides to back out of the plot. Determined to get Dunn's money, Apfel forms a gang of thugs to attack the ranch and steal the fortune. Meanwhile, sheriff Marcus has finally caught up to Cooper at Dunn's ranch. Cooper asks that Marcus not arrest him until after nightfall so that he can help defend Dunn from Apfel's forces. During the battle, Cooper is wounded and Apfel is killed. Impressed with Cooper's obvious commitment to Dunn and Wray, Marcus lets the bandit go and claims that Marcus' body is that of the Llano Kid. Based on an O. Henry short story entitled "The Double-Dyed Deceiver," THE TEXAN was given an impressive production by Paramount and was rewarded with strong box-office receipts. After his success in THE VIRGINIAN (1929), Cooper found himself to be a hot property at Paramount and the studio began placing him in starring roles. The additional responsibility and exposure was good for Cooper and he began to establish himself as an actor of high caliber. THE TEXAN marked the third romantic teaming of Cooper and Wray (a fourth film, PARAMOUNT ON PARADE in 1930, was just a variety revue designed to show off the studio's stable of stars, the first two being: LEGION OF THE CONDEMNED and THE FIRST KISS (both in 1928). While the pair played well together, the team wasn't very popular with the public and they made only one more film together, ONE SUNDAY AFTERNOON (1933). Director Cromwell's assistant was Henry Hathaway–still two years from directing his first feature–but who would later direct Cooper in seven films, including: THE LIVES OF A BENGAL LANCER (1935) and SOULS AT SEA (1937). THE TEXAN was remade by Paramount in 1939 as THE LLANO KID, starring Tito Guizar in the title role.

d, John Cromwell; w, Daniel N. Rubin, Oliver H.P. Garrett (based on the story "The Double-Dyed Deceiver" by O. Henry); ph, Victor Milner; ed, Verna Willis; m/l, "Chico," "To Hold You" L. Wolfe Gilbert, Abel Baer.

Western   **(PR:A   MPAA:NR)**

TEXAN MEETS CALAMITY JANE, THE*   (1950) 71m COL c

Evelyn Ankers (Calamity Jane), James Ellison (Gordon Hastings), Lee "Lasses" White (Colorado Charley), Ruth Whitney (Cecelia Mullen), Jack Ingram (Matt Baker), Frank Pharr (Sheriff Atwood), Sally Weidman (Emmy Stokes), Ferrell Lester (Rollo), Rudy De Saxe (Herbert), Paul Barney (Dave), Ronald Marriott (Nick), Walter Strand (Carlos), Hugh Hooker (Sam), Bill Orisman (Shotgun Messenger), Lou W. Pierce (Elmer), Elmer Herzberg (Henry the Whistler), Ray Jones.

An easily forgettable western which casts Ankers as the proprietress of a gambling hall. She nearly loses the business to a shady crook, but Texas lawyer Ellison puts up a legal battle to help her stay in charge.

p,d&w, Andre Lamb; ph, Karl Struss (Cinecolor); m, Rudy De Saxe; ed, George McGuire; art d, David Milton.

Western   **(PR:A   MPAA:NR)**

TEXANS, THE**½   (1938) 92m PAR bw

Joan Bennett (Ivy Preston), Randolph Scott (Kirk Jordan), May Robson (Granna), Walter Brennan (Chuckawalla, Foreman), Robert Cummings (Capt. Alan San ford), Raymond Hatton (Cal Tuttle), Robert Barrat (Isaiah Middlebrack), Harvey Stephens (Lt. David Nichols), Francis Ford (Uncle Dud), Chris-Pin Martin (Juan Rodriguez), Anna Demetrio (Rosita Rodriguez), Clarence Wilson (Sam Ross), Jack Moore (Slim), Richard Tucker (Gen. Corbett), Edward Gargan (Sgt. Grady), Otis Harlan (Henry), Spencer Charters (Chairman), Archie Twitchell (Cpl. Thompson), William Haade (Sgt. Cahill), Irving Bacon (Pvt. Chilina), William B. Davidson (Mr. Jessup, Railroad Man), Bill Roberts (Mustang), Richard Denning (Cpl. Parker), John Eckert, Slim Hightower, Scoop Martin, Whitey Sovern, Slim Talbot (Cowboys), Jimmie Kilgannon, Edwin John Brady, Carl Harbaugh, Dutch Hendrian (Union Soldiers), Oscar Smith (Black Soldier), Jack Perrin (Private Soldier), Ernie Adams, Edward J. LeSaint, James Quinn (Confederate Soldiers), Harry Woods (Cavalry Officer), Wheeler Oakman (U.S. Captain), Everett Brown (Man with Watches), Margaret McWade (Middle-Aged Lady), Vera Steadman, Virginia Jennings (Women On Street), James Kelso (Snorer), J. Manley Head (Fanatic), Philip Morris (Fen), James Burtis (Swenson), Esther Howard (Madame), James T. Mack, Lon Poff (Moody Citizens), John Qualen (Swede), Kay Whitehead (Stella), Ralph Remley (Town Lawyer), Pat West (Real Estate Man), Laurie Lane, Helaine Moler (Girls), Francis MacDonald.

Set during the post-Civil War Reconstruction period, THE TEXANS tells the saga of trail boss Scott and his efforts to drive a herd of 10,000 cattle to Kansas. He runs into every obstacle possible including a blizzard, prairie blazes, and angry Indians. Also worked into the plot is Bennett's plan to smuggle ammunition to Mexico in the hopes of stirring up a second war combining the forces of the South and the Mexicans against the North. The film combines the script of a B-western with the budget and promotion of a major production. It's a remake of the 1924 silent NORTH OF '36.

p, Lucien Hubbard; d, James Hogan; w, Bertrand Millhauser, Paul Sloane, William Wister Haines (based on the story "North of '36" by Emerson Hough); ph, Theodor Sparkuhl; ed, LeRoy Stone; m/l, "Silver on the Sage," Leo Robin, Ralph Rainger.

Western   **(PR:A   MPAA:NR)**

TEXANS NEVER CRY**   (1951) 66m COL bw

Gene Autry (Himself), Pat Buttram (Pecos Bates), Mary Castle (Rita Bagley), Russ Hayden (Steve Diamond), Gail Davis (Nancy Carter), Richard Powers (Tracy Wyatt), Don Harvey (Blackie Knight), Roy Gordon (Frank Bagley), Michael Ragan (Rip Braydon), Frank Fenton (Capt. Weldon), Harry Mackin (Bill Ross), Harry Tyler (Dan Carter), Richard Flato (Carlos Corbal), I. Stanford Jolley (Red), Duke York (Baker), Roy Butler (Sheriff Weems), Minerva Urecal (Martha Carter), Sandy Sanders (Bart Thomas), John R. McKee (Ed Durham), Champion the Horse.

Texas lawman Autry restores order when he foils a plot by Powers to make his fortune via phony Mexican lottery tickets. After smacking the villains around with a few well-placed punches, Autry still has enough energy to warble some tunes.

p, Armand Schaefer; d, Frank McDonald; w, Norman S. Hall; ph, William Bradford; ed, James Sweeney; md, Mischa Bakaleinikoff.

Western   **(PR:A   MPAA:NR)**

TEXAS***½   (1941) 93m COL bw

William Holden (Dan Thomas), Glenn Ford (Tod Ramsey), Claire Trevor ("Mike" King), George Bancroft (Windy Miller), Edgar Buchanan (Doc Thorpe), Don Beddoe (Sheriff), Andrew Tombes (), Addison Richards (Matt Laskan), Edmund MacDonald (Comstock), Joseph Crehan (Dusty King), Willard Robertson (Wilson), Patrick Moriarty (Matthews), Edmund Cobb (Blaire), Raymond Hatton (Judge), Ralph Peters (Deputy), Lyle Latell (Dutch Henry, Boxer), Duke York (Wise Guy), James Flavin (Announcer), Carleton Young, Jack Ingram (Henchmen), Ethan Laidlaw (Henry's Handler), William Gould (Cattle Buyer).

Holden and Ford are a pair of Confederate veterans wandering the Texas prairies after the Civil War. They first run into trouble when Holden accepts a challenge to fight the bare knuckles boxing champion of the town to keep the two of them out of jail for vagrancy and the fight soon degenerates into a wild melee involving most of the town. Later they see robbers hold up a stagecoach and they rob the robbers, but the sheriff takes them for the first set of thieves and they again narrowly escape. The two friends then lose track of each other and only meet much later, after Ford has taken a job on the ranch run by Trevor and her father, Crehan, and Holden has turned outlaw, joining a gang of rustlers headed by Buchanan, who doubles as the town dentist. Ford is assigned to drive the herd to the railhead at Abilene and Holden is ordered to steal them. Heightening their rivalry is the fact that both men are in love with Trevor, although she only has eyes for Holden. Holden doublecrosses Buchanan and the gang and helps Ford get the cattle through, but when they try to get back to Texas Holden is killed by the pursuing outlaws. Fast-moving and quite entertaining, TEXAS marks Columbia's attempt to make a lightweight and funny western after its bloated paean to the pioneer spirit, ARIZONA, went belly-up at the box office the year before. All of the supporting performances are good, especially Buchanan as the dentist and outlaw chieftain, a performance close to his own heart as he had been a dentist before he turned to acting. Holden and Ford had long been rivals of a sort as they rose to stardom through the Columbia stock company and director Marshall used this fact to get better performances out of them, as well as to make them do their own stunts. He would approach each actor separately and tell him the other had already agreed to do the stunt, and the other would of course agree. At one point he used this trick to get them to swim their horses across a lake. The two asked a stunt man if swimming a horse was dangerous and he told them it was very dangerous, saying that if the horse rolled over it could kick them to death under water. The two were stuck with doing the stunt, though, and after receiving some instructions from the stunt man, they managed to pull it off safely. The two men became fast friends after that, although their professional rivalry would continue all their lives.

p, Sam Bischoff; d, George Marshall; w, Horace McCoy, Lewis Meltzer, Michael Blankfort (based on a story by Meltzer, Blankfort); ph, George Meehan (Sepia Color); ed, William Lyon; md, M.W. Stoloff; art d, Lionel Banks.

Western   **(PR:A   MPAA:NR)**

TEXAS ACROSS THE RIVER**   (1966) 101m UNIV c

Dean Martin (Sam Hollis), Alain Delon (Don Andrea Baldasar), Rosemary Forsyth (Phoebe Ann Taylor), Joey Bishop (Kronk), Tina Marquand (Lonetta), Peter Graves (Capt. Stimpson), Michael Ansara (Chief Iron Jacket), Linden Chiles (Yellow Knife), Andrew Prine (Lt. Sibley), Stuart Anderson (Yancy Cottle), Roy Barcroft (Cy Morton), George Wallace (Floyd Willet), Don Beddoe (Mr. Naylor), Kelly Thordsen (Turkey Shoot Boss), Nora Marlowe (Emma), John Harmon (Gabe Hutchins), Dick [Richard] Farnsworth (Medicine Man).

Delon is a Spanish nobleman who flees his wife-to-be and the law after being wrongly accused of murder. He hooks up with gun runner Martin and his Indian sidekick Bishop. Indian attacks and oil wells supply most of the chuckles, eventually leading up to romance for all involved. It's nothing but the usual from Martin and Bishop, who just don't belong in westerns. The Kingston Trio sings the title tune.

p, Harry Keller; d, Michael Gordon; w, Wells Root, Harold Greene, Ben Star, (uncredited, John Gay); ph, Russell Metty (TechniScope, Technicolor); m, DeVol; ed, Gene Milford; md, Joseph Gershenson; art d, Alexander Golitzen, William D. DeCinces; set d, John McCarthy, James S. Redd; cos, Vincent Dee; Rosemary Odell, Helen Colvig; m/l, "Texas Across the River," Sammy Cahn, James Van Heusen (sung by the Kingston Trio); makeup, Bud Westmore; stunts, Robert Buzz Henry.

Western/Comedy   **(PR:A   MPAA:NR)**

TEXAS BAD MAN**½   (1932) 63m UNIV bw

Tom Mix, Lucille Powers, Fred Kohler, Edward J. LeSaint, Willard Robertson, Richard Alexander, Capt. C.E. Anderson, Lynton Brent, Franklyn Farnum, Joseph Girard, Bob Milash, Buck Moulton, James Burtis, Slim Cole, Boothe Howard, Frances Sayles, Richard Sumner, Theodore Lorch, George Magrill, Bud Osborne, Tony the Horse.

Mix covers up his sheriff's badge and dons a black hat in order to finagle his way into Kohler's band of outlaws. Once in the crook's good graces, Mix explodes the whole gang and brings them to justice.

p, Carl Laemmle, Jr.; d, Edward Laemmle; w, Jack Cunningham; ph, Dan Clark.

Western   **(PR:A   MPAA:NR)**

TEXAS BAD MAN**   (1953) 62m AA bw

Wayne Morris (Walt), Frank Ferguson (Gil), Elaine Riley (Lois), Sheb Wooley (Mack), Denver Pyle (Tench), Myron Healey (Jackson), Mort Mills (Bartender), Nelson Leigh (Bradley).

Morris is pitted against a thieving gang led by his unscrupulous father, Ferguson, who wants to get his hands on the gold in a local mine. It's a tough battle, since dad taught Morris everything he knows, but in the end the lawman prevails. Despite the Oedipal innuendoes, the film is a routine programmer.

p, Vincent M. Fennelly; d, Lewis D. Collins; w, Joseph F. Poland; ph, Gil Warrenton; m, Raoul Kraushaar; ed, Sam Fields.

Western   **(PR:A   MPAA:NR)**

TEXAS, BROOKLYN AND HEAVEN**
                    (1948) 76m UA bw (GB: THE GIRL FROM TEXAS)

Guy Madison (Eddie Tayloe), Diana Lynn (Perry Dunklin), James Dunn (Mike), Lionel Stander (The Bellhop), Florence Bates (Mandy), Michael Chekhov (Gaboolian), Margaret Hamilton (Ruby Cheever), Moyna Magill (Pearl Cheever), Irene Ryan (Opal Cheever), Colin Campbell (MacWirther), Clem Bevans (Capt. Bjorn), William Frawley (The Agent), Alvin Hammer (Bernie), Roscoe Karns (Carmody), Erskine Sanford (Dr. Dunson), John Gallaudet (McGonical), James Burke (Policeman), Guy Wilkerson (Thibault), Audie Murphy (Copy Boy), Tom Dugan (Bartender), Jesse White (Customer), Frank Scannell (Barker), Dewey Robinson (Sergeant), Ralph Peters (Cop On Phone), Herb Vigran (Man in Subway), Jody Gilbert (Lady), Mary Treen (Wife), Charles Williams (Reporter).

This aimless tale follows a Texan who meets up with a gal who longs to see Brooklyn and a spinster pickpocket on his way to the big city. Once there they visit Coney Island, see the sights, and do some riding at a horse stable before heading home to the range. The story is told in flashbacks, which doesn't make for too much excitement. Attempts at comedy produce few laughs.

p, Robert S. Golden; d, William Castle; w, Lewis Meltzer (based on the story "Eddie and the Archangel Mike" by Barry Benefield); ph, William C. Mellor; ed, James Newcom; md, Emil Newman; art d, Jerome Pycha, Jr.; set d, George Sawley; m/l, "Texas, Brooklyn and Heaven," Ervin Drake, Jimmy Shirl; makeup, Mel Burns.

Romance   **(PR:A   MPAA:NR)**

TEXAS BUDDIES*½   (1932) 57m TIF/World Wide bw

Bob Steele, Nancy Drexel, George ["Gabby"] Hayes, Francis McDonald, Harry Semels, Dick Dickinson, Slade Harulbert, William Dyer.

An interesting variation on the oater casts Steele as a former military flyer who uses his plane to round up outlaws. It's a new idea, but suffers from lame execution. Hayes' comic relief is overpowering.

p, Trem Carr; d&w, Robert N. Bradbury.

Western   **(PR:A   MPAA:NR)**

TEXAS CARNIVAL**   (1951) 77m MGM c

Esther Williams (Debbie Telford), Red Skelton (Cornie Quinell), Howard Keel (Slim Shelby), Ann Miller (Sunshine Jackson), Paula Raymond (Marilla Sabinas), Keenan Wynn (Dan Sabinas), Tom Tully (Sheriff Jackson), Glenn Strange (Tex Hodgkins), Dick Wessel, Donald MacBride (Concessionaires), Marjorie Wood (Mrs. Gaytes), Hans Conried (Hotel Clerk), Thurston Hall (Mr. Gaytes), Duke Johnson (Juggler), Wilson Wood (Bell Boy), Michael Dugan (Card Player), Doug Carter (Cab Driver), Earle Hodgins (Doorman), Gil Patrick (Assistant Clerk), Rhea Mitchell (Dealer), Emmett Lynn (Cook), Bess Flowers, Jack Daley, Fred Santley (People in Lobby), Joe Roach, Manuel Petroff, Robert Fortier, William Lundy, Alex Goudovitch (Specialty Dancers), Foy Willing and His Orchestra, Red Norvo Trio.

Skelton and Williams are a pair of carnival performers who make their meager wages by putting the latter in a dunk tank and letting the former toss balls at the target. Skelton gets mistaken for millionaire oil tycoon Wynn and lives the life of luxury for a short while. There's nothing new or interesting about this one, with Williams swimming only once, in a dream sequence. Songs include "It's Dynamite" (sung by Ann Miller), "Whoa! Emma," "Young Folks Should Get Married," "Carnie's Pitch" (Dorothy Fields, Harry Warren), "Clap Your Hands," "Deep in the Heart of Texas" (June Hershey, Don Swander), "Schnaps" (Maurice Vandair).

p, Jack Cummings; d, Charles Walters; w, Dorothy Kingsley (based on a story by Kingsley, George Wells); ph, Robert Planck (Technicolor); ed, Adrienne Fazan; md, David Rose; art d, Cedric Gibbons, William Ferrari; set d, Edwin B. Willis, Keough Gleason; cos, Helen Rose; spec eff, A. Arnold

Gillespie, Warren Newcombe; ch, Hermes Pan; makeup, William Tuttle.

Musical   **(PR:A   MPAA:NR)**

TEXAS CHAIN SAW MASSACRE, THE***   (1974) 83m
                                     Vortex-Henkel-Hooper/Bryanston c

Marilyn Burns (Sally), Allen Danziger (Jerry), Paul A. Partain (Franklin), William Vail (Kirk), Teri McMinn (Pam), Edwin Neal (Hitchhiker), Jim Siedow (Old Man), Gunnar Hansen (Leatherface), John Dugan (Grandfather), Jerry Lorenz (Pickup Driver).

Though its exploitation title suggests that THE TEXAS CHAIN SAW MASSACRE is just another mindless gore film, it is in fact an intelligent, absorbing and deeply disturbing horror film that is nearly bloodless in its depiction of violence. Using the age-old technique of suggestion, combined with a gritty, well executed (no pun intended) visual style, the film seems much bloodier than it actually is. Disturbed by news reports that vandals have been violating a remote Texas cemetery where her grandfather is buried, Burns and her wheelchair-bound brother, Partain, gather up some of their friends and take the family van to see if her grandfather's grave is still intact. While in the area they decide to visit the old farmhouse where grandpa lived. On the road, the group picks up a strange young man who soon proves to be more than a bit crazy. The man explains that he and his father and brother have been laid off from their jobs as slaughterhouse workers because new technology has replaced the old sledgehammer method of killing cattle. When the man's babbling becomes too much for the group, they stop the van and eject the hitchhiker. When they finally get to grandpa's farmhouse, Vail and McMinn become bored with Burns and Partain's childhood reminiscences and wander off to nearby a farmhouse. Vail goes inside and is surprised by a large man (Hansen) wearing what looks like the skin from a human face as a mask. The man pulls out a hammer, hits Vail over the head and drags the body into the bowels of the house. McMinn also enters the house and discovers that it is filled with grisly items made from human and animal skin and bones. Chairs, soup bowls, and hanging decorations constructed from human materials horrify McMinn, but before she has a chance to escape, she becomes the next victim. After other members of the party are done in, we learn that the crazies are the young hitchhiker's unemployed slaughterhouse family, including their ancient grandfather. (Grandma and the family dog, both dead, are stored in the attic–fairly well preserved. Eventually all the youths are dead but Burns, who is kidnaped by the sick clan and invited to join the family for "dinner." Before the family has a chance to kill her, Burns escapes and Hansen chases after her with his chainsaw running. She makes it to the highway and is helped by a truckdriver. As she leaps into the back of the pick-up, Burns looks back to see a frustrated Hansen crazily spinning his chainsaw in the air with no one to kill. Obviously based on real-life Wisconsin farmer Ed Gein (whose grotesque exploits also inspired Hitchcock's PSYCHO) THE TEXAS CHAIN SAW MASSACRE is one of the best examples of the "horror of the family" sub-genre that sprang up with PSYCHO (and which even has roots in Raoul Walsh's gangster film WHITE HEAT where the relationship between Cody and his Ma is amazingly similar to that of Norman and Mrs. Bates in PSYCHO). This subject matter takes the American family–a traditionally wholesome, positive force–and examines the dark side, the side that is claustrophobic, stifling and incestuous. These films avoid the urban environment and instead are set in remote areas (TEXAS CHAIN SAW), small towns (PSYCHO), or with families living a nomadic existence (WHITE HEAT), all of which ensures that they represent a minority of society that cannot survive under close scrutiny from normal, healthy outsiders. These films are deeply disturbing and they are meant to be. The best of the horror genre does not exist just to "scare" people (a mindless sensibility all too common among producers and audiences), but to examine the darker impulses, the fears, taboos, and repressed desires found in human beings, and to purge them from our collective subconscious.

p&d, Tobe Hooper; w, Kim Henkel, Hooper; ph, Daniel Pearl (CFI Color); m, Hooper, Wayne Bell; ed, Sallye Richardson, Larry Carroll; art d, Robert A. Burns; m/l, Roger Bartlett & Friends, Timberline Rose, Arkey Blue, Los Cyclones.

Horror   **Cas.**   **(PR:O   MPAA:R)**

TEXAS CITY*½   (1952) 55m Silvermine/MON bw

Johnny Mack Brown (Johnny), Jimmy Ellison (Jim Kirby), Lois Hall (Lois), Lorna Thayer (Aunt Harriet), Lane Bradford (Hank), Marshall J. Reed (Varnell), Terry L. Frost (Crag), Pierce Lyden (Markham), Lennie [Bud] Osborne (Birk), John Hart (1st Sergeant), Stanley Price (2nd Sergeant), Lyle Talbot (Hamilton).

Instead of outshooting a gang of gold robbers, Brown outwits them in this less-than-exciting oater. Cast as a U.S. Marshal, Brown learns that an insider has let out information of the shipment's arrival and puts him and the thieves behind bars. The cliche-crammed dialog makes the film seem longer than it is.

p, Vincent M. Fennelly; d, Lewis Collins; w, Joseph Poland; ph, Ernest Miller; ed, Sam Fields; md, Raoul Kraushaar.

Western   **(PR:A   MPAA:NR)**

TEXAS CYCLONE** (1932) 63m COL bw

Tim McCoy (*Pecos Grant*), Wheeler Oakman (*Utah Becker*), Shirley Grey (*Helena Rawlins*), James Farley (*Webb Oliver*), Walter Brennan (*Lew Collins*), John Wayne (*Steve Pickett*), Harry Cording (*Jake Farwell*), Wallace MacDonald (*Nick Lawlor*), Vernon Dent (*Hefty*), Mary Gordon (*Kate*).

McCoy is cast as the stranger who rides into Stampede, a quiet western town, only to find himself treated like a long-lost friend. He soon learns that the townsfolk believe him to be a rancher who disappeared five years previously, and had been presumed dead. Even the "dead" man's wife is convinced McCoy is her husband. After a knock on the head, McCoy's memory is restored and he realizes that he really is the missing rancher.

p, Irving Briskin; d, D. Ross Lederman; w, Randall Faye (based on a story by William Colt MacDonald); ph, Benjamin Kline; ed, Otto Meyer.

Western (PR:A MPAA:NR)

TEXAS DESPERADOS (SEE: DRIFT FENCE, 1936)

TEXAS DYNAMO*½ (1950) 54m COL bw (GB: SUSPECTED)

Charles Starrett (*Steve Drake/The Durango Kid/Gunman*), Smiley Burnette (*Himself*), Lois Hall (*Julia Beck*), Jock O'Mahoney (*Bill Beck*), John Dehner (*Stanton*), Greg Barton (*Luke*), George Chesebro (*Kroger*), Emil Sitka (*Turkey*), Fred Sears (*Hawkins*), Marshall Reed, Lane Bradford, Slim Duncan.

This is a thoroughly confusing oater which instead of casting Starrett in the usual dual lead, has him play three parts. As Drake he calls on a friend to help bring in a gang of outlaws, who in turn want to capture Starrett's other personality, the Durango Kid. When his pal gets killed, Starrett adopts his identity and finally ends the gang's reign. (See DURANGO KID series, Index).

p, Colbert Clark; d, Ray Nazarro; w, Barry Shipman; ph, Fayte Browne; ed, Paul Borofsky; art d, Charles Clague.

Western (PR:A MPAA:NR)

TEXAS GUN FIGHTER*½ (1932) 63m Quadruple/TIF bw

Ken Maynard, Sheila Mannors, Harry Woods, James Mason, Bob Fleming, Edgar Lewis, Lloyd Ingraham, Jack Rockwell, Frank Ellis, Jack Ward, Roy Bucko, Buck Bucko, Bud McClure, Bob Burns, "Tarzan.".

Maynard leaves his gang behind when he gets into an argument over an injured member's inclusion in a bank haul. He takes the side of the law, getting a sheriff's position, but finally falls prey to the gang he walked out on. A chase ensues, but Maynard emerges victorious after a shootout.

p, Phil Goldstone; d, Phil Rosen; w, Bennett Cohen; ph, Jackson Rose; ed, Jerry Webb.

Western Cas. (PR:A MPAA:NR)

TEXAS KID, THE** (1944) 56m MON bw

Johnny Mack Brown (*Nevada*), Raymond Hatton (*Sandy*), Marshall Reed (*Texas Kid*), Shirley Patterson (*Nancy*), Robert Fiske (*Naylor*), Edmund Cobb (*Scully*), Lynton Brent (*Jess*), Bud Osborne (*Steve*), Kermit Maynard (*Alex*), John Judd (*Roy*), Cyrus Ring (*Atwood*), Stanley Price (*Ed*), Charles King, George J. Lewis.

Reed takes the title character from outlaw surroundings to the side of the law when he lends a hand to U.S. Marshals Brown and Hatton. They team up to crush outlaws whose stagecoach holdups are nearly sinking the local landowners and ranchers. The movie has a little romance and a little comedy, but not enough of either to heighten interest.

p, Scott R. Dunlap; d, Lambert Hillyer; w, Jess Bowers (based on a story by Lynton W. Brent); ph, Harry Neumann; ed, Carl Pierson.

Western (PR:A MPAA:NR)

TEXAS KID (SEE: TEXICAN, THE, 1966)

TEXAS KID, OUTLAW (SEE: KID FROM TEXAS, THE, 1950)

TEXAS LADY** (1955) 86m RKO c

Claudette Colbert (*Prudence Webb*), Barry Sullivan (*Chris Mooney*), Greg Walcott (*Jess Foley*), James Bell (*Cass Gower*), Horace MacMahon (*Stringy Winfield*), Ray Collins (*Ralston*), Walter Sande (*Sturdy*), Don Haggerty (*Sheriff Herndon*), Douglas Fowley (*Clay Ballard*), Harry Tyler (*Choate*), John Litel (*Mead Moore*), Alexander Campbell (*Judge Herzog*), Celia Lovsky (*Mrs. Gantz*), LeRoy Johnson (*Rancher*), Florenz Ames (*Wilson*), Kathleen Mulqueen (*Nanny Winfield*), Robert Lynn (*Rev. Callander*), Grandon Rhodes, Bruce Payne, George Brand, Raymond Greenleaf.

Colbert is a tough newspaper owner who takes every opportunity to slam the crooked ways of cattle barons Collins and Sande. Sullivan comes to town hoping to get vengeance on Colbert because she blamed him for her father's

suicide. But he falls in love with her instead and helps out in her fight for law and order.

p, Nat Holt; d, Tim Whelan; w, Horace McCoy; ph, Ray Rennahan (Superscope, Technicolor); m, Paul Sawtell; ed, Richard Farrell; art d, William Ross; m/l, "Texas Lady,"Sawtell, Johnnie Mann (sung and played by Les Paul, Mary Ford).

Western Cas. (PR:A MPAA:NR)

TEXAS LAWMEN** (1951) 54m Frontier/MON bw (AKA: LONE STAR LAWMAN)

Johnny Mack Brown (*Johnny*), Jimmy Ellison (*Sheriff Tod*), I. Stanford Jolley (*Bart Morrow*), Lee Roberts (*Steve Morrow*), Lane Bradford (*Mason*), Marshall Reed (*Potter*), John Hart, Lyle Talbot, Pierce Lyden, Stanley Price, Terry Frost.

Brown is a U.S. marshal who asks for help from sheriff Ellison in bringing in the latter's bandit father and brother. Ellison is torn between blood and his badge, but finally chooses to use his expertise on the side of the law. Oddly, no women appear in this story focusing on family relationships.

p, Vincent M. Fennelly; d, Lewis Collins; w, Joseph Poland (based on a story by Myron Healey); ph, Ernest Miller; ed, Sammy Fields.

Western (PR:A MPAA:NR)

TEXAS LIGHTNING** (1981) 93m Film Ventures International c

Cameron Mitchell, Channing Mitchell, Maureen McCormick, Peter Jason, Danone Camden, J.L. Clark.

Father and son truck drivers Mitchell and Mitchell spend their free time at a roughneck cowboy bar in this little-seen effort. Not totally pointless and inconsequential, but close.

p, Jim Sotos; d&w, Gary Graver.

Drama Cas. (PR:O MPAA:R)

TEXAS MAN HUNT** (1942) 60m PRC bw

Bill "Cowboy Rambler" Boyd (*Himself*), Art Davis (*Himself*), Lee Powell (*Lee Clark*), Julie Duncan (*Carol Price*), Dennis Moore (*Jim Rogers*), Frank Hagney (*Jensen*), Karl Hackett (*Paul Clay*), Frank Ellis (*Hank Smith*), Arno Frey (*Otto Reuther*), Eddie Phillips (*Nate Winters*), Kenne Duncan.

Boyd (not to be confused with William "Hopalong" Boyd or William "Stage" Boyd) and Davis are a pair of cowboy radio gossip columnists known as the "Winchells of the Prairie." When their items begin hitting close to a gang of saboteurs led by Hagney, Hackett, and enemy spy Frey, the three plan to murder the snoops. Sheriff Powell saves the duo, then goes on to break up the whole ring. Frey meets his end in a buckboard full of TNT. Okay Poverty Row western directed by the astoundingly prolific Newfield under one of his many pseudonyms. Includes the song "When I Had My Pony On The Range."

p, Sigmund Neufeld; d, Peter Stewart [Sam Newfield]; w, William Lively; ph, Jack Greenhalgh; m, Johnny Lange, Lew Porter; ed, Holbrook N. Todd.

Western (PR:A MPAA:NR)

TEXAS MARSHAL, THE** (1941) 58m PRC bw

Tim McCoy (*Tim Rand*), Kay Leslie (*Margery*), Karl Hackett (*Moore*), Edward Piel, Sr (*Adams*), Charles King (*Titus*), Dave O'Brien (*Buzz*), Budd Buster (*Henderson*), John Elliott (*Gorham*), Wilson Edwards (*Announcer*), Byron Vance (*Deputy*), Frank Ellis, Art Davis and His Rhythm Riders.

McCoy shows off his trigger finger as he rounds up a gang of gold-hungry outlaws who are killing anyone in their way. The culprits nearly carry out their evil plans by disguising themselves as a "League of Patriots," but they can't fool McCoy. The movie differs from other singing cowboy films in that it is the feature character rather than the hero who does the crooning.

p, Sigmund Neufeld; d, Peter Stewart [Sam Newfield]; w, William Lively; ph, Jack Greenhalgh; ed, Holbrook N. Todd; m/l, "West is Always Ready," "Riding Down the Texas Trail," Johnny Lange, Lew Porter (sung by Art Davis and His Rhythm Riders).

Western (PR:A MPAA:NR)

TEXAS MASQUERADE**½ (1944) 59m UA bw

William Boyd (*Hopalong Cassidy*), Andy Clyde (*California Carlson*), Jimmy Rogers (*Himself*), Mady Correll (*Virginia Curtis*), Don Costello (*Ace Maxson*), Russell Simpson (*J.K. Trimble*), Nelson Leigh (*James Corwin*), Francis McDonald (*Sam Nolan*), J. Farrell MacDonald (*John Martindale*), June Pickerell (*Mrs. Martindale*), John Merton (*Jeff*), Pierce Lyden (*Al*), Robert McKenzie (*Rowbottom*), Bill Hunter (*Sykes*), George Morrell (*Old-timer*).

An ample amount of flying fists and whizzing bullets livens up this standard series entry starring Boyd in his usual role. Here he sets his sights on a gang of bandits who are trying to illegally secure all the ranches in the area. (See HOPALONG CASSIDY series, Index).

p, Harry A. Sherman; d, George Archainbaud; w, Norman Houston, Jack Lait, Jr. (based on the characters created by Clarence E. Mulford); ph, Russell Harlan; ed, Walter Hannemann; art d, Ralph Berger.

Western   **(PR:A   MPAA:NR)**

TEXAS PIONEERS**   (1932) 54m MON bw (GB: THE BLOOD BROTHER)

Bill Cody, Andy Shuford, Sheila Mannors, Harry Allen, Frank Lackteen, Ann Ross, John Elliott, LeRoy Mason, Iron Eyes Cody, Chief Standing Bear, Hank Bell.

An army officer gets himself demoted in order to fight beside his men as they fend off an Indian attack. It seems that someone has been tipping off the soldiers to false train robberies, leaving the fort wide open to Indian attacks. Standard material fills this feature notable only for its quantity of extras, about 100 playing Indians and almost as many in the cavalry.

p, Trem Carr; d, Harry Fraser; w, Wellyn Totman (based on a story by Fraser); ph, Faxon Dean.

Western   **(PR:A   MPAA:NR)**

TEXAS RANGER, THE**½   (1931) 65m Beverly/COL bw

Buck Jones, Carmelita Geraghty, Harry Woods, Ed Brady, Nelson McDowell, Billy Bletcher, Harry Todd, Budd Fine, Bert Woodruff, Edward Piel, Sr, Blackie Whitford, Lew Meehan, Silver the Horse.

Jones comes to the aid of gal rancher Geraghty who has become a vigilante in an effort to get back her stolen property. Jones first poses as an outlaw, but when he realizes her good intentions he reveals his true identity. There's some humor along the way.

p, Sol Lesser; d, D. Ross Lederman; w, Forrest Sheldon; ph, Teddy Tetzlaff; ed, Gene Milford.

Western   **(PR:A   MPAA:NR)**

TEXAS RANGERS, THE**½   (1936) 95m PAR bw

Fred MacMurray (Jim Hawkins), Jack Oakie (Wahoo Jones), Jean Parker (Amanda Bailey), Lloyd Nolan (Sam McGee), Edward Ellis (Maj. Bailey), Bennie Bartlett (David), Frank Shannon (Capt. Stafford), Frank Cordell (Ranger Ditson), Richard Carle (Casper Johnson), Jed Prouty (Prosecuting Attorney), Fred Kohler Sr (Higgins), George ["Gabby"] Hayes (Judge), Elena Martinez (Maria), Kathryn Bates (School Teacher), Rhea Mitchell (Passenger), Lloyd A. Saunders, Homer Farra, Ray Burgess, Hank Bell, Jack Montgomery, Howard Joslin, Joe Dominguez, Joseph Rickman, Frank Ellis, Bill Gillis, Neal Hart, Cecil Kellogg, Frank Cordell (Rangers), Gayne Whitman (Announcer), Bobby Caldwell (Boy in Coach), Dell Henderson (Citizen), Stanley Andrews (Henchman), William Strauss (Juror), Irving Bacon (David's Father).

The Texas Rangers are glorified in this classier-than-usual western, released during the Lone Star state's centennial celebration. MacMurray and Oakie are a couple of bandits who switch over to the side of the law, but are soon asked to bring in Nolan, a fellow gang member. MacMurray refuses but Oakie accepts, only to get killed in the fight. MacMurray finally realizes it is necessary to chase down Nolan, if only to avenge the death of Oakie. A sequel, THE TEXAS RANGERS RIDE AGAIN, followed in 1940. The picture was remade as THE STREETS OF LAREDO in 1949 with William Holden, Macdonald Carey, and William Bendix.

p&d, King Vidor; w, Louis Stevens (based on a story by Vidor, Elizabeth Hill Vidor, based on data in the book The Texas Rangers by Walter Prescott Webb); ph, Edward Cronjager; md, Boris Morros; art d, Bernard Herzbrun, Hans Dreier; m/l, Phil Boutelje, Jack Scholl, Sam Coslow.

Western   **(PR:A   MPAA:NR)**

TEXAS RANGERS, THE**½   (1951) 68m COL c

George Montgomery (Johnny Carver), Gale Storm (Helen Fenton), Jerome Courtland (Danny Bonner), Noah Beery, Jr (Buff Smith), William Bishop (Sam Bass), John Litel (Maj. John D. Jones), Douglas Kennedy (Dave Rudabaugh), John Dehner (John Wesley Hardin), Ian MacDonald (The Sundance Kid), John Doucette (Butch Cassidy), Jock O'Mahoney (Duke Fisher), Joseph Fallon (Jimmy), Myron Healey (Capt. June Peak), Julian Rivero (Pecos Palmer), Trevor Bardette (Telegraph Operator), Stanley Andrews (Marshal Goree), Edward Earle (Banker Lowden).

The beginnings of the legendary Texas Rangers are portrayed in a gritty, realistic manner as Montgomery, the fastest gun in the West, leads his men in pursuit of Bishop's notorious Sam Bass gang. Montgomery has been given the choice of finishing out a life prison term or taking off on this mission, with the guarantee that he get Bishop. He succeeds, and along the way fills the Sundance Kid (MacDonald) with holes since he was the one responsible for his prison stint in the first place.

p, Edward Small; d, Phil Karlson; w, Richard Schayer (based on a story by Frank Gruber); ph, Ellis W. Carter (Super Cinecolor); ed, Al Clark; md, Mischa Bakaleinikoff; art d, Harold MacArthur.

Western   **(PR:A   MPAA:NR)**

TEXAS RANGERS RIDE AGAIN**½   (1940) 68m PAR bw

Ellen Drew (Ellen "Slats" Dangerfield), John Howard (Jim Kingston), Akim Tamiroff (Mio Pio), May Robson (Cecilia Dangerfield), Broderick Crawford (Mace Townsley), Charley Grapewin (Ben Caldwalder), William Duncan (Capt. Inglis), Anthony Quinn (Joe Yuma), Harvey Stephens (Ranger Blair), Eva Puig (Maria), Edward Pawley (Palo Pete), Eddie Foy, Jr (Mandolin), Joseph Crehan (Johnson), Jim Pierce (Highboots), Monte Blue (Slide Along), Stanley Price (Nevers), Tom Tyler (Ranger Gilpin), Donald Curtis (Ranger Stafford), Eddie Acuff (Stenographer), Robert Ryan (Eddie), Ruth Rogers (Girl), Gordon Jones (Announcer), Harold Goodwin (Comstock), John Miljan (Carter Dangerfield), Franklin Parker (Gas Station Attendant), Chuck Hamilton (Truck Driver), Charles Lane (Train Passenger), Henry Roquemore (Conductor), Paul Kruger (Laborer), Jack Perrin (Radio Technician), John "Skins" Miller (Station Attendant).

Pretending to be out of work cowpokes, Howard and Crawford turn up at the White Sage ranch, at the secret request of owner Robson. She has the feeling that her workers, led by foreman Quinn, are commandeering her cattle, killing them, and shipping them off to market on the sly. Unfortunately for the two Rangers, they get assigned to work on the other side of the ranch, but eventually discover Quinn's tactics. Before long, order is restored as the Rangers crush the racket, paving the way for range romance with Howard pairing off with Drew, Robson's niece, and Robson rekindling an old affair with veteran Ranger Grapewin. This is billed as a sequel to the 1936 film THE TEXAS RANGERS, but shares only the Ranger characters and nothing more.

p, Edward T. Lowe; d, James Hogan; w, William R. Lipman, Horace McCoy; ph, Archie Stout; ed, Arthur Schmidt; md, Boris Morros; art d, Hans Dreier, Earl Hedrick.

Western   **(PR:A   MPAA:NR)**

TEXAS ROAD AGENT   (SEE: ROAD AGENT, 1941)

TEXAS ROSE   (SEE: RETURN OF JACK SLADE, THE, 1955)

TEXAS SERENADE   (SEE: OLD CORRAL, THE, 1937)

TEXAS STAGECOACH**½   (1940) 59m COL bw (GB: TWO ROADS)

Charles Starrett (Larry Kincaid), Iris Meredith (Jean Harper), Bob Nolan (Bob), Dick Curtis (Shoshone Larsen), Edward J. LeSaint (Jim Kincaid), Kenneth MacDonald (John Appleby), Harry Cording (Clancy), Francis Walker (Jug Wilson), George Becinita, Don Beddoe, Fred Burns, Lillian Lawrence, Eddie Laughton, George Chesebro, George Morrell, Blackie Whiteford, Pat Brady, Tim Spencer, The Sons of the Pioneers.

This clever oater has Starrett up against the nasty ways of banker Curtis, who lends money to a pair of rival stagecoach companies but then forces foreclosure upon them. With Starrett's assistance the companies band together and fight the evil banker. Cast members wrote the songs.

p, Leon Barsha; d, Joseph H. Lewis; w, Fred Myton; ph, George Meehan; ed, Charles Nelson; m/l, "Roll On with the Texas Express," "In My Tumble-Down Home," Bob Nolan, Tim Spencer (sung by Sons of the Pioneers).

Western   **(PR:A   MPAA:NR)**

TEXAS STAMPEDE**   (1939) 57m COL bw

Charles Starrett (Tom Randall), Iris Meredith (Joan Cameron), Fred Kohler, Jr (Wayne Cameron), Lee Prather (Jeff Cameron), Raphael [Ray] Bennett (Zack Avery), Blackjack Ward (Abe Avery), Hank Bell (Hank), Edmund Cobb (Hobbs), Eddie Hearn (Owens), Ed Coxen (Seth), Bob Nolan (Bob), The Sons Of The Pioneers, Blackie Whiteford, Charles Brinley, Ernie Adams.

Starrett faces some difficult times while trying to calm the emotions of ranchers who are upset over water rights, but by the finale brings harmony to the valley. He also gets himself a gal in the form of Meredith, the daughter of cattle baron Kohler. Much of the dialog is interchangeable with lines from dozens of other westerns.

p, Harry Decker; d, Sam Nelson; w, Charles Francis Royal (based on the story "The Dawn Trail" by Forrest Sheldon); ph, Lucien Ballard; md, M.W. Stoloff.

Western   **(PR:A   MPAA:NR)**

TEXAS TERROR**½ (1935) 58m Lone Star/MON bw

John Wayne (John Higgins), Lucile Brown (Beth Matthews), LeRoy Mason (Joe Dickson), George Hayes (Sheriff Williams), Buffalo Bill, Jr (Blackie), Bert Dillard (Red), Lloyd Ingraham (Dan), Yakima Canutt, Bobby Nelson, Fern Emmett, John Ince, Henry Rocquemore, Jack Duffy.

After wrongly believing that he accidentally killed his friend, sheriff Wayne turns in his badge and lives the life of a prospector. When his dead pal's sister (Brown) is attacked by bandits, he investigates and finds evidence that Mason actually killed his friend. Relieved of the guilt that had been plaguing him, he focuses on a new start with Browne.

p, Paul Malvern; d&w, Robert N. Bradbury; ph, Archie Stout; ed, Carl Pierson.

Western (PR:A MPAA:NR)

TEXAS TERRORS* (1940) 57m REP bw

Don "Red" Barry (Bob Milbourne), Julie Duncan (Jane Bennett), Arthur Loft (Blake), Al St. John (Frosty), Eddy Waller (Judge Bennett), William Ruhl (Ashley), Ann Pennington (Dancer), Sammy McKim (Bob as Boy), Reed Howes (Ed), Robert Fiske (Barker), Fred "Snowflake" Toones (Snowflake), Jimmy Wakely and his "Roughriders", Hal Taliaferro, Edmund Cobb, Al Haskell, Jack Kirk, Ruth Robinson, Blackjack Ward.

Barry plays a lawyer out to avenge the murders of his parents, who were killed by a claim jumper when he was just a tot. Duncan plays the romantic interest. Pretty dull for a Barry oater.

p&d, George Sherman; w, Doris Schroeder, Anthony Coldeway; ph, John MacBurnie; m, Cy Feuer; ed, Tony Martinelli.

Western Cas. (PR:A MPAA:NR)

TEXAS TO BATAAN* (1942) 56m MON bw (GB: THE LONG, LONG TRAIL)

John King (Dusty), Dave Sharpe (Davy), Max Terhune (Alibi), Marjorie Manners (Dallas), Budd Buster (Tad), Kenne Duncan (Capt. Anders), Escolastico Baucin (Cookie), Frank Ellis (Richards), Carl Mathews (Engel), Guy Kingsford (Miller), Steve Clark (Conroy), Al Ferguson (Tuillax), Tom Steele (Lamac), Tex Palmer (Grob).

Wartime oater which sees the Range Busters traveling to the Philippines in order to deliver a shipment of livestock to the Army. Once there, they discover a Japanese spy masquerading as a Filipino cook. They put an end to his insidious schemes, managing at the same time to stop a similar plot in the U.S. (See RANGE BUSTERS series, Index.)

p, George W. Weeks; d, Robert Tansey; w, Arthur Hoerl; ph, Robert Cline; ed, Roy Claire; md, Frank Sanucci; m/l, "Me and My Pony," "Goodbye Old Paint," John King.

Western Cas. (PR:A MPAA:NR)

TEXAS TORNADO** (1934) 60m Kent/FD bw

Lane Chandler, Buddy Roosevelt, Doris Hill, Robert Gale, Yakima Canutt, Ben Corbett, Edward Hearn, Bart Carre, Mike Brand, Fred Burns, J. Frank Glendon, Pat Healy, Wes Warner, "Raven.".

Big city gangsters travel West to try their hand at rustling cattle. Chandler plays a Texas Ranger out to stop them, despite the fact that they have machine guns at their disposal. This particular film rises above the seven others in Chandler's Western series.

p,d&w, Oliver Drake; ph, James Diamond; ed, S. Roy Luby.

Western (PR:A MPAA:NR)

TEXAS TRAIL** (1937) 58m PAR bw

William Boyd (Hopalong Cassidy), George ["Gabby"] Hayes (Windy Halliday), Russell Hayden (Lucky Jenkins), Judith Allen (Barbara Allen), Alexander Cross (Black Jack Carson), Robert Kortman (Hawks), Billy King (Boots), Rafael [Ray] Bennett (Brad), Karl Hackett (Maj. McCready), Jack Rockwell (Shorty), Philo McCullough (Jordan), John Beach (Smokey), John Judd (Lieutenant), Ben Corbett (Orderly), Clyde Kinney (Courier), Leo MacMahon (Corporal), Earle Hodgins.

Boyd is assigned the task of turning his Bar 20 boys into Rough Riders to gather more horses for the U.S. Army, which needs the ponies in the Spanish-American War. Of course, there's a gang of crooks out to sabotage the project and the usual battles ensue. Solid acting helps to create a believable plot. (See HOPALONG CASSIDY series, Index.)

p, Harry Sherman; d, David Selman; w, Jack O'Donnell, Jack Mersereau, Harrison Jacobs (based on a story by Clarence E. Mulford); ph, Russell Harlan; ed, Robert Warwick; art d, Lewis Rachmil.

Western (PR:A MPAA:NR)

TEXAS WILDCATS** (1939) 57m Victory bw

Tim McCoy (Carson), Joan Barclay (Molly), Ben Corbett (Magpie), Forrest Taylor (Burrows), Ted Adams (Reno), Avando Renaldo (Rita), Bob Terry (Mort), Dave O'Brien (Arden), Frank Ellis (Al), Reed Howes (Ace), Slim Whitaker (Durkin), George Morrell, Carl Mathews.

McCoy plays a masked Robin Hood of the plains who helps weary settlers when their land is grabbed by nasty villains. As such a villain, Taylor wants to do away with do-gooder McCoy, so he offers a hefty reward for his capture–dead or alive. Taylor is moved to do this because he has learned of a lucrative gold vein on the property of innocent homesteader O'Brien. Not only does Taylor offer a reward for McCoy's head, but he tries to get his son to marry O'Brien's daughter so he can have legal access to the property. He doesn't get very far.

p, Sam Katzman; d, Sam Newfield; w, George H. Plympton; ph, Marcel Picard; ed, Holbrook N. Todd.

Western (PR:A MPAA:NR)

TEXICAN, THE* (1966, U.S./Span.) 86m M.C.R.-Balcazar/COL c

Audie Murphy (Jess Carlin), Broderick Crawford (Luke Starr), Diana Lorys (Kit O'Neal), Aldo Sambrell (Gil), Antonio Casas (Frank Brady), Anthony Molino (Harv), Juan Antonio Peral (Eb), Helga Genth (Maria Banta), Luz Marquez (Sandy Adams), Jorge Rigaud (Mitch), Luis Induni (U.S. Marshal), Martha May (Elena), Victor Vilanova (Roy Carlin), Carlos Hurtado (Tobe), Victor Israel (Station Master), Jose Maria Pinillo (Miguel), Cesar Osinaga (Bounty Hunter), Gerard Tichy (Thompson), Vincente Soler (Dr. Miller), Juan Carlos Torres (Townsman), Oscar del Campo (Guitar Player), Manuel Quintana (Gunslinger), Carlos Miguel Sola, Angel Lombardi (Poker Players), A. Malla (Mexican Boy).

Dreary, uneventful western which sees framed-but-on-the-lam Murphy (who still can't act) come out of hiding in Mexico. His objective is to track down corrupt saloon keeper Crawford, who not only set Murphy up in the first place, but then murdered his brother, a newspaperman, for trying to expose the scheme. Murphy gets his man and also finds love in the arms of dancehall girl Lorys.

p, John C. Champion, Bruce Balaban; d, Lesley Selander; w, Champion, Jose Antonio de la Loma; ph, Francis Marin (Techniscope, Technicolor); m, Nico Fidenco; ed, Teresa Alcocer; md, Robby Poitevin; art d, John Soler; cos, Ralph Borque; spec eff, Tony Molina; makeup, Rod Gurrucharri.

Western (PR:A MPAA:NR)

THANK EVANS*½ (1938, Brit.) 78m WB/FN bw

Max Miller (Evans), Hal Walters (Nobby), Polly Ward (Rosie), Albert Whelan (Sgt. Challoner), John Carol (Harry), Robert Rendel (Lord Claverley), Glen Alyn (Brenda), Freddie Watts (Mulcay), Harvey Braban (Inspector Pine), Aubrey Mallalieu (Magistrate), Charlotte Leigh, Ian MacLean, George Pughe, Charles Wade.

Another Edgar Wallace adaptation, this time comedy as opposed to mystery, focuses on a down-on-his-luck race track tout (Miller). In return for a favor, he comes to the rescue of a lord who's being fleeced by an evil trainer.

p, Irving Asher; d, Roy William Neill; w, Austin Melford, John Dighton, John Meehan, Jr. (based on the novel Good Evans by Edgar Wallace); ph, Basil Emmott.

Comedy (PR:A MPAA:NR)

THANK GOD IT'S FRIDAY zero (1978) 100m Motown-Casablanca/COL c

Donna Summer (Nicole Sims), Valerie Landsburg (Frannie), Terri Nunn (Jeannie), Chick Vennera (Marv Gomez), Ray Vitte (Bobby Speed), Mark Lonow (Dave), Andrea Howard (Sue), Jeff Goldblum (Tony), Robin Menker (Maddy), Debra Winger (Jennifer), John Freidrich (Ken), Paul Jabara (Carl), Marya Small (Jackie), Chuck Sacci (Gus), Hilary Beane (Shirley), DeWayne Jessie (Floyd), The Commodores (Themselves).

At the end of the 1970s, Hollywood suddenly decided to revive the expensive, extravagant musical (CAN'T STOP THE MUSIC was another modern classic of the genre). Unfortunately, the inspiration seems to have come from the worst, most inane musicals of Monogram and Republic studios. THANK GOD IT'S FRIDAY is basically an excuse to parade a variety of fleetingly popular 1970s disco acts across the screen. The "plot" follows a variety of dull characters through one night spent at a "hip" Disco. That's it. Oh yes, and it was also singer Donna Summer's film debut. Songs include: "After Dark" (Simon & Sabrina Soussan); "Find My Way" (J. Melfi); "It's Serious" (Gregory Johnson, Larry Blackman); "Let's Make a Deal" (Michael Smith); "Romeo and Juliet" (Alec Costadinos); "You're the Reason I Feel Like Dancing" (H. Johnson); "From Here to Eternity" (Giorgio Moroder, Pete Bellotte); "Dance All Night" (Willie Hutch); "Love Masterpiece" (H. Davis, J. Powell, A. Posey); "I'm Here Again" (B. Sutton, M. Sutton, Kathy Wakefield); "Disco Queen" (Paul Jabara); "Trapped in a Stairway" (Jabara, Bob Esty); "Thank God It's Friday"; "You are the Most Precious Thing in My Life" (A.R. Costadinos); "I Wanna Dance" (P. Bellote);

"Meco's Theme" (Harold Wheeler); "Floyd's Theme" (D. St. Nicklaus); "Down to Lovetown" (Don Daniels, Michael Sutton, Kathy Wakefield); "Lovin', Livin', and Givin'" "Do You Want the Real Thing," "You Can Always Tell a Lady by the Company She Keeps" (Esty, D.C. LaRue).

p, Rob Cohen; d, Robert Klane; w, Barry Armyan Bernstein; ph, James Crabe (Metrocolor); m, Paul Jabara; ed, Richard Halsey; prod d, Tom H. John; set d, Jeff Haley; cos, Betsy Jones, Michael Kaplan, Jack Angel, Kathy O'Rear, Paula Cain; stunts, Phil Adams.

Musical   Cas.   (PR:C MPAA:PG)

THANK HEAVEN FOR SMALL FAVORS½**
(1965, Fr.) 84m Le Film d'Art-A.T.I.L.A./International Classics bw (DEO GRATIAS, UN DROLE DE PAROISSIEN; AKA: THE FUNNY PARISH-IONER; HEAVEN SENT)

Bourvil (Georges Lachesnaye), Francis Blanche (Chief Inspector Cucherat), Jean Poiret (Raoul), Jean Yonnel (Lachesnaye Pere), Jean Tissier (Inspector Bridoux), Jean Galland (Bishop), Veronique Nordey (Francoise), Marcel Peres (Raillargaud), Solange Certain (Juliette), Denise Peronne (Aunt Claire), Bernard Lavalette (Prefect of Police), Roger Legris.

A moderately funny French comedy starring Bourvil as a member of an aristocratic French family that refuses to work, despite the fact that they are tearing up the estate's floorboards for firewood to keep themselves warm. Seeking solace in the Catholic church, Bourvil sits in a pew awaiting divine guidance. When he hears coins dropping into the collection plate, he assumes God means for him to take the money. Bourvil boosts the collection and then ventures from church to church, amassing a small fortune in religious donations. Eventually church officials, with help from the local police, catch up to Bourvil and make him return the money. He gives back half, invests the rest, and flees the country.

p, Henri Diamant-Berger, Jerome Goulven; d, Jean-Pierre Mocky; w, Michel Servin, Alain Moury, Mocky; ph, L.H. Burel; m, Joseph Kosma; ed, Marguerite Renoir; art d, Pierre Tyberghein.

Comedy   (PR:A MPAA:NR)

THANK YOU ALL VERY MUCH*   (1969, Brit.) 106m Palomar-Amicus/COL c (GB: A TOUCH OF LOVE)

Sandy Dennis (Rosamund Stacey), Ian McKellen (George), Eleanor Bron (Lydia), John Standing (Roger), Michael Coles (Joe), Rachel Kempson (Sister Harvey), Peggy Thorpe-Bates (Mrs. Stacey), Kenneth Benda (Mr. Stacey), Sarah Whalley (Octavia), Shelagh Fraser (Miss Guernsey), Deborah Stanford (Beatrice), Margaret Tyzack (Sister Bennett), Roger Hammond (Mike), Maurice Denham (Dr. Prothero).

Dennis stars as a graduate student who is seduced by TV announcer McKellen and becomes pregnant. Despite the advice of her friends, Dennis decides to have the baby, though she keeps her pregnancy a secret from McKellen and her parents. Eventually she gives birth to a daughter, but the baby has a heart condition and must have a tricky operation. The surgery is successful, and Dennis goes on to earn her doctorate while raising the child. One day, more than a year after her daughter's birth, Dennis bumps into McKellen again and invites him to her home. He accepts, but when he sees that she has a child, he makes a feeble excuse and leaves quickly, never learning that he is the father. Deciding that she is better off alone, Dennis lets him go. This well-written, understated drama paints vivid portraits of its characters and is enhanced by fine performances from Dennis and McKellen.

p, Max J. Rosenberg, Milton Subotsky; d, Waris Hussein; w, Margaret Drabble (based on her novel The Millstone); ph, Peter Suschitzky II (Eastmancolor); m, Michael Dress; ed, Bill Blunden; md, Dress; prod d, Bernard Sarron; art d, Tony Curtis; makeup, Bob Lawrence.

Drama   (PR:C MPAA:M/PG)

THANK YOU, AUNT*   (1969, Ital.) 93m Doria G. Film/AE bw (GRAZIE, ZIA; AKA: COME PLAY WITH ME)

Lisa Gastoni (Lea), Lou Castel (Alvise), Gabriele Ferzetti (Stefano), Luisa De Santis, Nicoletta Rizzi, Massimo Sarchielli, Anita Dreyer.

A fresh perspective on disaffected youth in the nuclear era, this first film directed by the 24-year-old Samperi is a story of social and sexual frustration, filled with rich political allegories. Seventeen-year-old Castel–unlike many of his contemporaries, neither complacent striver nor destructive radical–has reached his accord with this world he never made by retreating behind a psychosomatically induced paralysis. Confined to an electric wheelchair, this scion of affluence works cruel mind-games on the propinquitous. His parents travel, leaving him in the care of his youthful aunt, Gastoni, who's a doctor, on her country estate. The clever cripple deliberately alienates all her many visitors, and–playing on her nurturing instincts–wrests her attention from her philosophically leftist lover, Ferzetti. Isolated now with his aunt, he implements a strategy to make her completely subordinate to his will, physically as well as emotionally, despite his impotence. The troubled youth arouses Gastoni sexually, but denies her fulfillment, sustaining both her tension and her concentration with his

marvelous manipulations. Immersed in his mystique, she grants him the release he seeks: final release, through the agency of a lethal injection. A finely crafted film, with many turns and twists, and with superb performances by the principals. Writer-director Samperi apparently made his peace with society after this film; his later MALIZIA (1974) and LOVERS AND OTHER RELATIVES (1976) were flat-out comedies, even though they dealt with some of the same elements (notably youthful desire, impotence, sexual fetishes, and vengeance).

p, Enzo Doria; d, Salvatore Samperi; w, Sergio Bazzini, Pier Giuseppe Murgia, Samperi (based on a story by Samperi); ph, Aldo Scavarda; m, Ennio Morricone; ed, Alessandro Giselli; md, Bruno Nicolai; art d, Giorgio Mecchia Maddalena.

Drama   (PR:O MPAA:NR)

THANK YOU, JEEVES*   (1936) 57m FOX bw (AKA: THANK YOU, MR. JEEVES)

Arthur Treacher (Jeeves), Virginia Field (Marjorie Lowman), David Niven (Bertie Wooster), Lester Matthews (Elliott Manville), Colin Tapley (Tom Brock), John Graham Spacey (Jack Stone), Ernie Stanton (Mr. Snelling), Gene Reynolds (Bobby Smith), Douglas Walton (Edward McDermott), Willie Best (Drowsy), Paul McVey (Mr. Brown), Colin Kenny (Crook), Jimmie Aubrey (Cab Driver), Joe North (Butler), Dorothy Phillips (Mrs. Brown), Ed Dearing (Motor Cop).

The first of 20th Century-Fox's short-lived series of mysteries based on the classic P.G. Wodehouse characters (they only made one more, STEP LIVELY, JEEVES) sees the inspired casting of Treacher as Jeeves and Niven as his bumbling master. Treacher mistakes some enemy spies out to get aeronautical secrets for government agents, but he soon learns the truth and teams up with Niven to capture the crooks. Good cast, lousy script.

p, Sol M. Wurtzel; d, Arthur Greville Collins; w, Joseph Hoffman, Stephen Gross (based on the story by P.G. Wodehouse); ph, Barney McGill; ed, Nick DeMaggio; md, Samuel Kaylin; cos, Herschel.

Comedy/Mystery   (PR:A MPAA:NR)

THANK YOU, MR. MOTO½**   (1937) 66m FOX bw

Peter Lorre (Mr. Moto), Thomas Beck (Tom Nelson), Pauline Frederick (Mme. Chung), Jayne Regan (Eleanor Joyce), Sidney Blackmer (Eric Koerger), Sig Rumann (Col. Tchernov), John Carradine (Pereira), William von Brincken (Schneider), Nedda Harrigan (Mme. Tchernov), Philip Ahn (Prince Chung), John Bleifer (Ivan), James Leong (Officer).

The second film in the MR. MOTO series and one of the best has Lorre once again starring as the diminutive international detective. This time he's hot on the trail of a series of Chinese scrolls that, when pieced together, will reveal the hidden tomb of Genghis Khan with all its treasures. Of course several unscrupulous characters are also after the ancient scrolls, including Blackmer and his gang of cutthroats, who kill Frederick in the course of their quest. Eventually Lorre catches up with the killers, shoots Blackmer and burns the scrolls so that no one will ever disturb the resting place of Genghis Khan. Good production values, a fine supporting cast, and a very fast (though at times confusing) pace really keeps things rolling along at an enjoyable clip. (See MR. MOTO series, Index.)

p, Sol M. Wurtzel; d, Norman Foster; w, Foster, Willis Cooper (based on a story by John P. Marquand); ph, Virgil Miller; ed, Irene Morra, Nick De Maggio; md, Samuel Kaylin; art d, Bernard Herzbrun, Albert Hogsett; cos, Herschel.

Mystery   (PR:A MPAA:NR)

THANK YOUR LUCKY STARS*½**   (1943) 127m WB bw

Eddie Cantor (Joe Sampson/Himself), Joan Leslie (Pat Dixon), Dennis Morgan (Tommy Randolph), Dinah Shore (Herself), S.Z. Sakall (Dr. Schlenna), Edward Everett Horton (Farnsworth), Ruth Donnelly (Nurse Hamilton), Joyce Reynolds (Girl with Book), Richard Lane (Barney Jackson), Don Wilson (Himself), Henry Armetta (Angelo), Willie Best (Soldier), Humphrey Bogart, Jack Carson, Bette Davis, Olivia de Havilland, Errol Flynn, John Garfield, Alan Hale, Ida Lupino, Ann Sheridan, Alexis Smith, George Tobias, Spike Jones and His City Slickers (Specialties), Frank Faylen (Sailor), Creighton Hale, Jack Mower (Engineers), Noble Johnson (Charlie the Indian), Ed Gargan (Doorman), Billy Benedict (Bus Boy), Hank Mann (Assistant Photographer), Don Barclay (Pete), Stanley Clements, James Copedge (Boys), Leah Baird, Joan Matthews, Phyllis Godfrey, Lillian West, Morgan Brown, George French (Bus Passengers), Joe De Rita (Milquetoast Type), Eleanor Counts (Sailor's Girl Friend), Charles Soldani, J.W. Cody (Indians), Harry Pilcer (Man in Broadcasting Station), Mike Mazurki (Olaf), Bennie Bartlett (Page Boy), Marjorie Hoshelle, Anne O'Neal (Maids), Jerry Mandy (Chef), Betty Farrington (Assistant Chef), William Haade (Butler), Lou Marcelle (Commentator), Mary Treen (Fan), Juanita Stark (Secretary), Paul Harvey (Dr. Kirby), Bert Gordon (Patient), David Butler, Mark Hellinger (Themselves), Billy Wayne (Chauffeur), Howard Mitchell, James Flavin (Policemen), Dick Rich (Fred), Ralph Dunn (Marty), James Burke (Bill the Intern Guard), Frank Mayo (Dr. Wheaton), Angi O. Poulos (Waiter), Boyd Irwin (Man), Helen O'Hara (Show Girl), "Ice Cold

Katie Number": Hattie McDaniel (*Gossip*), Rita Christiani (*Ice Cold Katie*), Jess Lee Brooks (*Justice*), Ford, Harris, and Jones (*Trio*), Matthew Jones (*Gambler*), "Errol Flynn Number": Monte Blue (*Bartender*), Art Foster, Fred Kelsey, Elmer Ballard, Buster Wiles, Howard Davies, Tudor Williams, Alan Cook, Fred McEvoy, Bobby Hale, Will Stanton, Charles Irwin, David Thursby, Henry Ibling, Earl Hunsaker, Hubert Hend, Dudley Kuzello, Ted Billings (*Pub Characters*), "Bette Davis Number": Jack Norton (*Drunk*), Henri DeSoto (*Maitre d'Hotel*), Dick Elliott, Dick Earle (*Customers*), Harry Adams (*Doorman*), Sam Adams (*Bartender*), Conrad Wiedell (*Jitterbug*), Charles Francis, Harry Bailey (*Bald-headed Men*), Joan Winfield (*Cigarette Girl*), Nancy Worth, Sylvia Opert (*Hatcheck Girls*), "The Lucky Stars": Harriette Haddon, Harriett Olsen, Joy Barlowe, Nancy Worth, Janet Barrett, Dorothy Schoemer, Dorothy Dayton, Lucille LaMarr, Mary Landa, Sylvia Opert (*The Lucky Stars*), "Humphrey Bogart Sequence": Matt McHugh (*Fireman*), "Ann Sheridan Number": Georgia Lee Settle, Virginia Patton (*Girls*), "Good Neighbor Number": Igor DeNavrotsky (*Dancer*), Brandon Hurst (*Cab Driver*), Angelita Mari (*Duenna*), Lynne Baggett (*Miss Latin America*), Mary Landa (*Miss Spain*).

During WW II the Hollywood community did everything it could to support the war effort, both overseas and on the home front. Every major studio, beginning with Paramount's STAR SPANGLED RHYTHM in 1942, produced a showcase musical featuring their star contract players. THANK YOUR LUCKY STARS was the Warner Bros. effort, giving audiences an unusual opportunity to see some of the studio's biggest names performing in song-and-dance numbers. The flimsy story which holds this all together involves Sakall and Horton as two producers trying to stage a Cavalcade of Stars. They sit in on Cantor's radio show in hopes of finding new talent, and like what they see in Shore (making her film debut). Though Sakall and Horton want the talented singer, they hope to avoid getting Cantor involved with their show. Meanwhile, Lane, a phony show-biz agent, gets Cantor to sign an equally phony contract for Morgan, a singer, to appear on the popular radio show. Lane collects 60 bucks as a commission from the ever enthusiastic young man. Before he can slip away, though, Lane is confronted by Leslie, a struggling songwriter, who has also been gypped by the reprehensible representative. She follows Lane onto a bus that gives tourists a tour of the stars' homes. Driving the bus is a Cantor look-alike (Cantor, of course, in a dual role) who can't get a job in pictures because he bears too strong a resemblance to the star. The congenial bus driver takes Leslie out to Gower Gulch, the area he lives in with other out-of-work actors. (In reality Gower Gulch never existed. They filmed these sequences around Sunset Boulevard and Gower Street, an area where many actors from the Poverty Row studios would hang out after working hours.) Morgan lives there as well, and is celebrating his seeming success. Sakall and Horton continue to put together their show, but Cantor, who has been put in charge of the entertainment, is proving to be an egocentric headache. When Morgan learns Lane has cheated him, Leslie comes up with a plan to help both the singer and the bus driver. Three actors from Gower Gulch, dressed as Indians, approach Cantor, explaining he's been named an honorary Indian chief, and *Life* magazine wants to do a photo spread on it. Cantor is taken hostage, while his bus driver look-alike is given a haircut and sheds his glasses. He is sent to the theater, where-taken to be Cantor-he promises Sakall and Horton to stop trying to run things if they'll allow Morgan to sing on the show. The two producers wearily agree, and the show is a success. Before the big finale, Morgan, Leslie, and the Cantor double learn the real Cantor has escaped, and is on his way to the theater. Horton arrives with a telegram from none other than studio head Jack L. Warner, offering Morgan a movie contract. Cantor finally arrives, dressed in Indian garb, and madder than a wet cat. He demands something be done, but his double, who has convinced everyone he is the real Eddie Cantor, declares this strangely clothed man to be an impostor. Cantor is tossed out, and the show is a success. As expected, the plot is as light and fluffy as a souffle. What it lacks in substance it makes up for in energy, but the real heart and soul of this film are the musical numbers featuring such unlikely names as Errol Flynn and John Garfield. The stars were paid $50,000 for their respective cameo appearances, which sums were subsequently turned over to the Hollywood Canteen for the war effort, though according to Flynn, Warners was not exactly on the up-and-up in donating money to the Canteen. "What Warner Brothers had told us," he wrote in *My Wicked, Wicked Ways*, "was: since it was their distribution, they were getting a big chunk of the proceeds out of the bottom drawer-through distribution." Flynn's number, "That's What You Jolly Well Get," has the famous swashbuckler playing a Cockney sailor who enters a London pub, where he sings about his obviously phony exploits on the field of battle. The patrons join in with Flynn, going along with his story, until at last he is royally tossed out. Flynn proves himself to be a talented song-and-dance man with this number, parodying himself while giving a lively performance. Reportedly, he originally had not been scheduled to do the film, until the star implored Jack Warner to give him a chance. Though Flynn's number is obvious in intent, many war-minded citizens in both America and England were offended by the routine, feeling patriotism was hardly a subject for lampooning. Flynn was going through personal turmoil at the time with his infamous rape case. Two days after he completed filming the sequence, the trial (at which he was eventually acquitted) began. Davis' number, "They're Either Too Young or Too Old," is the story of a woman whose love has entered the army. The sequence was shot with multiple cameras so retakes would be unnecessary. On the day of shooting Davis' dance partner, Conrad Weidell, appeared on set, terrified of appearing with an actress of Davis' stature. Davis looked at the nervous,

sweat-soaked man, then told him: "Just forget who I am and do it!" Davis, who remained fond of this Academy Award-nominated number, recalled in the book *Mother Goddam* by Whitney Stine, "'The song' was Frank Loesser's first big hit. It was the top song on the 'Lucky Strike Hit Parade'...for almost a year. I have sung it many times professionally since. It was fun to be identified with a song hit-a new experience for me." De Havilland, Lupino, and Tobias appear in one of the lesser numbers, a reprise of one of Shore's songs, "The Dreamer." While Lupino and Tobias did their own singing, de Havilland had her voice dubbed by singer Lynn Martin. In order to disguise the lip synch, de Havilland chewed gum during the sequence so no one would notice if she missed mouthing a few words. Garfield, doing "Blues in the Night" by Harold Arlen and Johnny Mercer, attempted to do the song as a tough-guy parody, mostly talking his way through the number. A real treat is the mad musician Spike Jones and his band, the City Slickers, performing a frenzied version of "Otchichornia" as the "Hotcha Cornia." Other numbers include: "Ridin' for a Fall" (sung by Morgan, Leslie), "We're Staying Home Tonight" (sung by Cantor), "Goin' North" (sung by Jack Carson, Alan Hale), "Love Isn't Born, It's Made" (sung by Ann Sheridan, verse spoken by Joyce Reynolds), "No You, No Me" (sung by Morgan, Leslie), "The Dreamer" (sung by Shore), "Ice Cold Katie" (sung by Hattie McDaniel, Willie Best, Jesse Lee Brooks, Rita Christina, chorus), "How Sweet You Are" (sung by Shore), "Good Night, Good Neighbhor" (sung by Morgan, chorus, Alexis Smith), "Finale" (sung by entire cast), and the title song, "Thank Your Lucky Stars" (sung by Shore).

p, Mark Hellinger; d, David Butler; w, Norman Panama, Melvin Frank, James V. Kern (based on a story by Everett Freeman, Arthur Schwartz); ph, Arthur Edeson; ed, Irene Morra; md, Leo F. Forbstein; art d, Anton Grot, Leo K. Kuter; set d, Walter F. Tilford; cos, Milo Anderson; spec eff, H.F. Koenekamp; ch, LeRoy Prinz; m/l, Schwartz, Frank Loesser; makeup, Perc Westmore.

Musical (PR:A MPAA:NR)

THANK YOUR STARS (SEE: SHOOT THE WORKS, 1934)

THANKS A MILLION*** (1935) 85m FOX bw

Dick Powell (*Eric Land*), Ann Dvorak (*Sally Mason*), Fred Allen (*Ned Lyman*), Patsy Kelly (*Phoebe Mason*), Raymond Walburn (*Judge Culliman*), David Rubinoff (*Orchestra Leader*), Benny Baker (*Tammany*), Andrew Tombes (*Mr. Grass*), Alan Dinehart (*Mr. Kruger*), Paul Harvey (*Maxwell*), Edwin Maxwell (*Mr. Casey*), Margaret Irving (*Mrs. Kruger*), Charles Richman (*Gov. Wildman*), Charles Adler, James V. Kern, Billy Mann, George Kelly (*The Yacht Club Boys*), Russell Hicks (*Mr. Bradley*), Paul Whiteman and His King's Men with Ramona Rubinoff.

A fast-paced, funny musical satire on politics stars Powell as the lead in a group of traveling singers and introduces the now-classic song "Happy Days Are Here Again" (the late Hubert Humphrey's favorite, now widely used as a theme by the Democrats). Allen, as Powell's wiley manager, makes a successful transition here from radio to movies but sadly never fully exploited it later on. The story has Allen pushing Powell into becoming a candidate for the governor of Pennsylvania when the party hopeful turns out to be a hopeless drunk. Though Powell has absolutely no interest or experience in politics, the party loves him because he has a dynamic personality and is good with crowds. Unfortunately all this politicking ruins his relationship with Dvorak, and eventually Powell is fed up with the charade. When he learns that powerful members of the party are nothing more than crooks, he blows the whistle on their activities and, to everyone's surprise, wins the election. To prove to Dvorak that he still loves her, he quits his office, only to find that the voters, and even Dvorak, want him to stay. A well-written, funny, and insightful script by Nunnally Johnson, combined with good performances from Powell and especially Allen make for an entertaining film. Remade in 1946 as IF I'M LUCKY. Songs include: "Thanks a Million," "I'm Sitting High on a Hilltop," "I've Got a Pocketful of Sunshine" (Gus Kahn, Arthur Johnston, sung by Powell), "Sugar Plum" (Kahn, Johnston, sung by Dvorak, Kelly), "New O'leans" (Kahn, Johnston, sung by Whiteman's King's Men and Ramona), "Sing, Brother," "The Square Deal Party" (Kahn, Johnston), "Happy Days Are Here Again" (Jack Yellen, Milton Ager), "NRA-ABC" (sung by the Yacht Club Boys).

p, Darryl F. Zanuck; d, Roy Del Ruth; w, Nunnally Johnson (based on a story by Melville Crossman [Zanuck]); ph, Peverell Marley; ed, William Lambert; md, Arthur Lange; art d, Jack Otterson.

Musical/Comedy Cas. (PR:A MPAA:NR)

THANKS FOR EVERYTHING**½ (1938) 70m FOX bw

Adolphe Menjou (*J.B. Harcourt*), Jack Oakie (*Brady*), Jack Haley (*Henry Smith*), Arleen Whelan (*Madge Raines*), Binnie Barnes (*Kay Swift*), George Barbier (*Joe Raines*), Warren Hymer (*Marine Sergeant*), Gregory Gaye (*Ambassador*), Andrew Tombes (*Mayor*), Renie Riano (*Mrs. Sweeney*), Jan Duggan (*Miss Twitchell*), Charles Trowbridge (*Draft Doctor*), Frank Sully (*Lem Slininger*), Gary Breckner (*Announcer*), Paul Hurst (*Guard*), James Flavin, Ed Dearing (*Policemen*), Charles Lane (*Dr. Olson*).

Menjou and Oakie play a pair of advertising men who produce a radio contest offering $25,000 for the perfect "Average Man." Plainville, Missouri grocery clerk Haley wins the prize, and the dubious honor of having his taste in clothes, food, cars, etc., held as representative of the country. Menjou and Oakie exploit this for all it's worth and merchandise Haley as much as they can. Trouble arises when Haley falls in love with small-town girl Whelan, who sees that her beau is being taken advantage of and takes action to put a stop to the advertising men's ever-increasing demands.

p, Darryl F. Zanuck; d, William A. Seiter; w, Harry Tugend, Curtis Kenyon, Art Arthur (based on a story by Gilbert Wright); ph, Lucien Andriot; ed, Robert Simpson; md, Louis Silvers; art d, Bernard Herzbrun, Mark-Lee Kirk; m/l, "Thanks for Ev'rything," Mack Gordon, Harry Revel (sung by Tony Martin).

Comedy (PR:A MPAA:NR)

THANKS FOR LISTENING* (1937) 60m Conn bw (GB: PARTLY CONFIDENTIAL)

Pinky Tomlin (Homer), Maxine Doyle (Toots), Aileen Pringle (Lulu), Claire Rochelle (Trixie), Henry Roquemore (Peter), Rafael Storm (Maurice), George Lloyd (Champ), Three Brian Sisters (Irene, Mary, Sally), Beryl Wallace (Gloria), Eliot Jones (Gabriel).

Tomlin plays a hayseed who is duped by big-time con woman Pringle and her gang into playing the patsy in a number of scams. Eventually Tomlin wisens up and returns to his duck farm. Songs include: "The Love Bug Will Bite You," "I Like to Make Music," "In the Name of Love" (Tomlin, Connie Lee, sung by Tomlin).

p, Maurice Conn; d, Marshall Neilan; w, John B. Clymer; ph, Jack Greenhalgh; ed, Martin G. Cohn; md, Connie Lee; m/l, Pinky Tomlin, Lee, Al Heath, Buddy LaRoux.

Comedy (PR:A MPAA:NR)

THANKS FOR THE MEMORY** (1938) 77m PAR bw

Bob Hope (Steve Merrick), Shirley Ross (Anne Merrick), Charles Butterworth (Biney), Otto Kruger (Gil Morrell), Hedda Hopper (Polly Griscom), Laura Hope Crews (Mrs. Kent), Emma Dunn (Mrs. Platt), Roscoe Karns (George Kent), Eddie "Rochester" Anderson (Janitor), Ed Gargan (Flanahan), Jack Norton (Bert Monroe), Patricia "Honey Chile" Wilder (Luella), William Collier, Sr (Mr. Platt), Jack Chapin (Messenger), Barney Dean (Kelly), Pat West, Vernon Dent (Refuse Men), Johnny Morris (Newsboy).

Seeing how popular the sequence where Hope and Ross sing "Thanks For The Memory" was with audiences watching THE BIG BROADCAST OF 1938, Paramount threw together this quick "sequel" to capitalize on the situation. The film, however, is a bit stale. Hope is a frustrated author who stays home and takes care of the house while trying to write his novel. Ross plays the wife, who leaves the house in the morning and goes to work. This odd (for 1938) arrangement soon leads to a break-up, but eventually the couple is reunited. Hope and Ross sing "Two Sleepy People" (Ralph Rainger, Leo Robin) in addition to "Thanks for the Memory" (Hoagy Carmichael, Frank Loesser).

p, Mel Shauer; d, George Archainbaud; w, Lynn Starling (based on the play "Up Pops the Devil" by Albert Hackett, Frances Goodrich); ph, Karl Struss; ed, Alma Macrorie; md, Boris Morros; art d, Hans Dreier, Franz Bachelin.

Comedy (PR:A MPAA:NR)

THANOS AND DESPINA** (1970, Fr./Gr.) 96m Lenox/Grove Press bw (LES PATRES DU DE SORDRE)

Olga Carlatos (Despina), George Dialegmenos (Thanos), Lambros Tsangas (Yankos), Elli Xanthaki (Katina), Theo Karousos (Vlahopoulos), Dimos Starenios (Karavidas), Yannis Arghyris (Haralambos), N. Naneris (Pericles), Maria Kostandarou (Loula), Djolly Garbi (Mme. Vlahopoulos), Nassos Kedrakas (Papadimas).

A Greek variation of "Romeo and Juliet" stars Carlatos and Dialegmenos as two young lovers fleeing an arranged marriage which would force a man she can't stand on Carlatos. The pair steal supplies and flee into the mountains, but they are soon located by the girl's father and her jilted suitor. A fight ensues between Dialegmenos and the suitor in which the latter is killed. Faced with an unhappy future, the lovers then commit suicide by leaping off the mountain.

p, Dimos Theos, A. Lappas; d, Nico Papatakis; w, Papatakis (based on a story by Jean Vauthier, Papatakis); ph, Jean Boffety, Christian Guillouet; m, Pierre Barbaud.

Drama (PR:C MPAA:NR)

THARK** (1932, Brit.) 79m British and Dominions/Woolf and Freedman bw

Tom Walls (Sir Hector Benbow), Ralph Lynn (Ronald Gamble), Mary Brough (Mrs. Todd), Robertson Hare (Hook), Claude Hulbert (Lionel Todd), Joan Brierley (Cherry Buck), Gordon James (Death), Evelyn Bostock (Kitty Stratton), Beryl de Querton (Lady Benbow), Marjorie Corbett (Warner).

Walls, Lynn, and Bostock sell Thark Manor to Brough who, on her first

night, hears eerie sounds and deems the house to be haunted. The three salespersons then agree to spend a night in the house, fending off the thrills and chills in a highly humorous manner.

p, Herbert Wilcox; d, Tom Walls; w, Ben Travers (based on a play by Travers); ph, F. A. Young.

Comedy (PR:A MPAA:NR)

THAT BRENNAN GIRL*½ (1946) 95m REP bw

James Dunn (Denny Reagan), Mona Freeman (Ziggy Brennan), William Marshall (Mart Neilson), June Duprez (Natalie Brennan), Frank Jenks (Joe), Dorothy Vaughan (Mrs. Reagan), Charles Arnt (Fred), Rosalind Ivan (Mrs. Merryman), Fay Helm (Helen), Bill Kennedy (Arthur), Connie Leon (Miss Jane), Edythe Elliott (Miss Unity), Sarah Padden (Mrs. Graves), Jean Stevens (Dottie), Lucien Littlefield (The Florist), Marian Martin (Natalie's Girl Friend).

Freeman plays an unhappy young woman who was raised by her thoughtless mother to take what she wanted out of life without regard for others. While this approach brings her material gain, she is unlucky in romance until she reforms her outlook.

p&d, Alfred Santell; w, Doris Anderson (based on a story by Adela Rogers St. Johns); ph, Jack Marta; m, George Antheil; ed, Arthur Roberts; md, Cy Feuer; art d, James Sullivan; cos, Adele Palmer; spec eff, Howard Lydecker, Theodore Lydecker.

Drama (PR:A MPAA:NR)

THAT CERTAIN AGE½** (1938) 95m UNIV bw

Deanna Durbin (Alice Fullerton), Melvyn Douglas (Vincent Bullitt), Jackie Cooper (Ken), Irene Rich (Mrs. Fullerton), Nancy Carroll (Grace Bristow), John Halliday (Mr. Fullerton), Jack Searl (Tony), Juanita Quigley (The Pest), Peggy Stewart (Mary Lee), Charles Coleman (Stephens), Grant Mitchell (Jeweler), Claire DuBrey (Horsewoman), Helen Greco (Girl), Lon McCallister (Billy), Buddy Pepper, Vondell Darr (Friends), Leonard Sues (Orchestra Leader), Bess Flowers, Ed Mortimer (Guests), Ruth Weston (Admirer), David Oliver (Farmer), Russell Hicks (Scout Leader), Troop 536 Boy Scouts of Los Angeles (Themselves).

Durbin jilts local boy friend Cooper after she develops a strong crush on her parents' houseguest, Douglas, who is a worldly news correspondent working on articles for her father's newspaper. While Douglas does not take advantage of Durbin's attentions, he is amused by her company, and uses the situation to avoid boring social gatherings. Eventually Durbin realizes the silliness of her infatuation and returns to Cooper. Songs include: "That Certain Age," "You're as Pretty as a Picture," "Be a Good Scout," "Has Anybody Ever Told You Before?" (Jimmy McHugh, Harold Adamson), Juliet's Waltz Song (from Charles Gounod's "Romeo and Juliet"), Les Filles De Cadiz (Alfred de Musset, Leo Delibes).

p, Joe Pasternak; d, Edward Ludwig; w, Bruce Manning, Charles Brackett, Billy Wilder (based on a story by F. Hugh Herbert); ph, Joseph Valentine; ed, Bernard W. Burton; md, Charles Previn; art d, Jack Otterson; cos, Vera West; makeup, Bill Ely.

Musical/Comedy (PR:A MPAA:NR)

THAT CERTAIN FEELING* (1956) 103m PAR c

Bob Hope (Francis X. Dignan), Eva Marie Saint (Dunreath Henry), George Sanders (Larry Larkin), Pearl Bailey (Gussie, Maid), David Lewis (Joe Wickes), Al Capp (Himself), Jerry Mathers (Norman Taylor), Herbert Rudley (Doctor), Florenz Ames (Sen. Winston), Richard Shannon (Cab Driver), Valerie Allen, Jacqueline Beer, Jeanette Miller (Models), Herbert Vigran, Paul Dubov (TV Directors), Jeff Hayden (TV Technician), Emory Parnell, Douglas Wood (Senators), Lawrence Dobkin, Sid Tomack, Eric Alden, Jan Bradley, Jack Pepper, Jack Lomas, Richard Keene, Joseph Kerr.

Silly Hope comedy starring "Ol' Ski Nose" as a bumbling artist who "ghosts" famed cartoonist Sanders strip because the master has lost his touch. Unfortunately for Hope, his ex-wife, Saint, is engaged to Sanders. With the help of Sanders' maid, Bailey, and a young boy, Mathers, Hope and Saint are reunited. The players look bored, especially Sanders (but then, he always looked bored), and the jokes are infantile. Look for a few of Hope's children as Mathers' playmates. Songs include: "That Certain Feeling" (George and Ira Gershwin), "Hit the Road to Dreamland" (Johnny Mercer, Harold Arlen), "Zing Went the Strings of My Heart" (James F. Hanley).

p&d, Norman Panama, Melvin Frank; w, Panama, Frank, I. A. L. Diamond, William Altman (based on the play "The King of Hearts" by Jean Kerr, Eleanor Brooke); ph, Loyal Griggs (VistaVision, Technicolor); m, Joseph J. Lilley; ed, Tom McAdoo; md, Lilley; art d, Hal Pereira, Henry Bumstead; cos, Edith Head; ch, Nick Castle.

Comedy (PR:A MPAA:NR)

THAT CERTAIN SOMETHING**   (1941, Aus.) 90m Argossy/RKO bw

Megan Edwards (*Patsy O'Connell*), Thelma Grigg (*Miss Hemingway*), Georgie Sterling (*Blanche Wright*), Howard Craven (*Jimmie Jones*), Lou Vernon (*Robert Gimble*), Charles Kilburn (*Alan Burke*), Arundel Nixon (*Announcer*), Ronald Morse (*Marcel Dubois*), Marshall Crosby (*Stephen Appleby*), Leslie Victor (*Maurice Appleby*), Joe Lawman (*Bill Lake*).

Early Australian film detailing an American movie director's efforts to make a film "down under".

d&w, Clarence Badger; ph, Frank Coffey.

Drama   (PR:A   MPAA:NR)

THAT CERTAIN WOMAN**½   (1937) 91m WB bw

Bette Davis (*Mary Donnell*), Henry Fonda (*Jack Merrick*), Ian Hunter (*Lloyd Rogers*), Anita Louise (*Flip*), Donald Crisp (*Mr. Merrick, Sr.*), Hugh O'Connell (*Virgil Whitaker*), Katherine Alexander (*Mrs. Rogers*), Mary Phillips (*Amy*), Minor Watson (*Tilden*), Ben Welden (*Harry Aqueilli*), Sidney Toler (*Neely*), Charles Trowbridge (*Dr. James*), Norman Willis (*Fred*), Herbert Rawlinson (*Dr. Hartman*), Tim Henning (*Kenyon*), Dwane Day (*Jackie*), John Hamilton (*American*), Georges Renavent (*Frenchman*), Barry Noble Downing (*Little Boy*), Andre Rouseyrol (*French Boy*), Cliff Saum (*Bus Conductor*), Rosalind Marquis (*Hatcheck Girl*), Roger Davis (*Waiter*), Claudia Simmons (*Switchboard Girl*), Forbes Murray, Emmett Vogan (*Men*), Donn Downen, Jr (*Elevator Man*), Richard Jack (*Page Boy*), Frank Darien (*Night Porter*), Loia Cheaney (*Secretary*), Frank Faylen, Willard Parker, Granville Owen, Paddy O'Flynn, Mike Lally, Charles Sherlock, Philip Waldron, Ted Thompson (*Reporters*), Bernice Pilot (*Maid*), Etta McDaniel (*Cook*), Jack Ryan (*Baggage Man*), Andre Cheron (*Concierge*).

Undistinguished weeper in the genre of STELLA DALLAS and CONFESSION that indicated Davis' star position at Warners when she demanded who would play opposite her. Ed Goulding wrote and directed this remake of THE TRESPASSER which he made in 1929 with Gloria Swanson. Davis was the teenage bride of a bootlegger and when he was cut down by a hail of machine gun bullets, she decided that it was time for her to try and find a better life. She signs on as secretary to unhappily married Hunter, an attorney who loves her but strives valiantly to keep business and pleasure separated. Hunter's most important client is Crisp, whose playboy son, Fonda, spends his time between the bars of cafe society and the watering spots of Europe. When he returns home from his latest trip abroad, he meets and falls for Davis and she agrees to marry him. They elope but Crisp is appalled by Fonda's choice of a wife. He'd hoped his son would wed someone more of their caste. Crisp has the honeymooners trailed and pushes hard to get the marriage set aside by annulment. Fonda, who has no income of his own, is totally beholden to his father and thus acquiesces at once. Davis loves Fonda dearly but understands the position he's in and agrees to the split, then takes her old job at Hunter's office. Soon she discovers that the honeymoon left her pregnant. She gives birth to Day and swears Hunter to secrecy about the father of the boy. Fonda finally marries a woman, Louise, of whom Crisp approves. Fonda's marital luck continues poorly as Louise is almost fatally injured in an automobile accident after a few days of marriage. Hunter falls ill with some unnamed fever. He is taken to the hospital and it looks as though he will expire momentarily but he struggles out of his hospital bed and trudges to Davis' residence where he gives up the ghost. Before breathing his last, Hunter admits to Davis that he has adored her from the instant they met. Knowing her situation, he has written a new will which leaves Davis and Day enough money so she needn't ever struggle again. When the terms of his will are published, his widow, Alexander, wrongly suggests that Day is Hunter's illegitimate son. Fonda's wife is still bedridden and holding on when he learns of Davis' motherhood and the terms of Hunter's will, which Alexander is trying to overturn. Fonda comes to Davis, she tells him he is the boy's real father. Crisp goes into action once he knows that he has a grandson. He starts proceedings to take Day away from Davis on the unfair grounds that she is an unfit mother (this plot turn is a convenience as there is no court which might find the loving Davis unfit). Davis thinks she won't be able to keep her son under the legal onslaughts being prepared by Crisp so she offers Day to Fonda and Louise for adoption. After giving Day to the couple, Davis goes to Europe and lives in a lonely fashion on the money she received from Hunter's will. As you might imagine, the injured Louise finally dies and Fonda leaves after the funeral to go to Europe and find Davis. She's located in a sylvan location, Fonda professes his love for her, and the match that began a little over an hour before is now again ignited. Early in her teens, Davis worked as a bit player in a stock company where Fonda played the leads. She had a puppy love crush on him but he was so busy memorizing his roles that he paid her little attention. When her star rose at Warners, she was able to insist on whomever she wished and she chose Fonda for JEZEBEL and this. Fonda was three years older but didn't get his break in films until THE FARMER TAKES A WIFE in 1935, while Davis had already been in movies since 1931's BAD SISTER. In an interview with Johnny Carson in 1986, Davis admitted that she was a maiden when she was married for the first time and her New England upbringing didn't allow her to have affairs without benefit of clergy. If she had it to do all over again, she would have wished to have been born later to take advantage of more modern traditions. Knowing that about Davis makes one realize how good an actress she was because so many of the roles she played were in direct contrast to her deep-seated conserva-

tive Yankee life.

p, Robert Lord; d&w, Edmund Goulding (based on the screenplay THE TRESPASSER by Goulding); ph, Ernest Haller; m, Max Steiner; ed, Jack Killifer; md, Leo F. Forbstein; art d, Max Parker; cos, Orry-Kelly.

Drama   (PR:A-C   MPAA:NR)

THAT CHAMPIONSHIP SEASON**   (1982) 110m Cannon c

Bruce Dern (*George Sitkowski*), Stacy Keach (*James Daley*), Robert Mitchum (*Coach Delaney*), Martin Sheen (*Tom Daley*), Paul Sorvino (*Phil Romano*), Arthur Franz (*Macken*), Michael Bernosky (*Jacks*), James M. Langan (*Cooney*), Joseph Kelly (*Malley*), Tony Santaniello (*Marelli*), William G. McAndrew (*Harrison*), Barry Weiner (*Sharmen*), Edward Cunningham (*Newspaper Editor*), Robert E. Schlesinger (*Nelson*), George Lowry (*Zookeeper*), Jim Sparkman (*Heckler*).

The Pulitzer Prize play adapted and directed by the playwright makes the mistake of being too kind to the stage material and forgetting the fact that this was supposed to be a movie. Very talky and too long. It's been 20 years since the local basketball team won the high school championship. The coach, Mitchum, and four of the five starting players get together for a reunion to celebrate the great moment they shared two decades before. It all begins affably enough as the men surround their coach. The former players are Dern, who is currently embroiled in a serious reelection bid for his job as mayor of Scranton, Pennsylva nia. Keach is his campaign manager and totally subservient to Dern, Sheen is an alcoholic writer who hasn't been back to town for a few years, and Sorvino is the hale businessman who has become very successful using underhanded methods. As the picture unreels, we get a chance to examine each man more closely. The friendly exteriors are soon corroded by the drinks they consume and bitterness, envy, and anger start to appear. Mitchum tries to keep them from going for each other's throats and mouths sports cliches to calm them. He's a dead-pan mother hen and delivers his lines with so little emotion that audiences outsnored the sound track in places. (Compare that to the riveting job done by Charles Durning in the stage version and one can see how far Mitchum had fallen.) The other men seem to have been characters sent into a computer and programmed mechanically, so every sort of dramatic plot and counterplot spewed from the printer. It's contrived and far too stagy and would have been effective if someone else had written the adaptation and directed it because Miller couldn't bear to cut or alter a thing (or so it seemed). Good technical work and an apt score by Conti, but the fireworks which exploded on stage never happen on the screen. Sorvino is excellent, Sheen isn't, Dern plays a part not unlike the role he did in SMILE. The big problem is Mitchum, as it has been in the latter part of his life. It's just fine to have a lot of words in a movie, if those words are brilliant, make points, cause laughter or tears. In THAT CHAMPIONSHIP SEASON, all they are are words. Ex-basketball players may enjoy it but anyone who has ever been on a court will wonder how such a short group could win a state championship. The one player missing, the man they refer to as Martin, must have been eight feet tall...that's the only explanation. Abusive language and a few racist remarks make this a poor choice for children, or adults.

p, Menahem Golan, Yoram Globus; d&w, Jason Miller (based on his play); ph, John Bailey (Metrocolor); m, Bill Conti; ed, Richard Halsey; prod d, Ward Preston; cos, Ron Talsky.

Drama   Cas.   (PR:O   MPAA:R)

THAT COLD DAY IN THE PARK**   (1969, U.S./Can.) 113m
Factor-Altman-Mirell/Commonw ealth United Entertainment c

Sandy Dennis (*Frances Austen*), Michael Burns (*Boy*), Susanne Benton (*Nina*), Luana Anders (*Sylvie*), John Garfield, Jr (*Nick*), Edward Greenhalgh, Frank Wade, Lloyd Berry, Alicia Ammon, Rae Brown, Michael Murphy.

Before director Robert Altman went on to gain fame for films like M*A*S*H and NASHVILLE, and infamy for films like BUFFALO BILL AND THE INDIANS and QUINTET, he directed this grim, uneven film starring Dennis as a wealthy, lonely, spinster approaching middle age who finds a mysterious young man, Burns, sitting on a park bench in the rain. She invites him in and he accepts without a word. She assumes he is a mute and lets him spend the night. A strange relationship develops between the two, with Dennis pampering Burns, barely being able to conceal her sexual desires in contrast to his silent, uncaring acceptance. Eventually Dennis goes to offer herself to him but he has sneaked out of the apartment. Enraged, she waits until he returns and then locks him in, keeping him prisoner. Burns finally speaks and yells that he never asked for her help and doesn't need it. Not wanting to lose him, Dennis hires a prostitute for his pleasure. He makes love to the hooker, but in the heat of passion, Dennis invades the room and stabs the girl to death. Horrified, Burns sits helplessly as a totally insane Dennis passionately hugs him.

p, Donald Factor, Leon Mirell; d, Robert Altman; w, Gillian Freeman (based on the novel by Richard Miles); ph, Laszlo Kovacs (Eastmancolor); m, Johnny Mandel; ed, Danford B. Greene; art d, Leon Ericksen.

Drama   Cas.   (PR:O   MPAA:R)

THAT DANGEROUS AGE   (SEE: IF THIS BE SIN, 1949, Brit.)

THAT DARN CAT***   (1965) 116m Disney/BV c

Hayley Mills (Patti Randall), Dean Jones (Zeke Kelso), Dorothy Provine (Ingrid Randall), Roddy McDowall (Gregory Benson), Neville Brand (Dan), Elsa Lanchester (Mrs. MacDougall), William Demarest (Mr. MacDougall), Frank Gorshin (Iggy), Richard Eastham (Supervisor Newton), Grayson Hall (Margaret Miller), Ed Wynn (Mr. Hofstedder), Tom Lowell (Canoe), Richard Deacon (Drive-in Manager), Iris Adrian (Landlady), Liam Sullivan (Graham), Don Dorrell (Spires), Gene Blakely (Cahill), Karl Held (Kelly), Ben Lessy (Candy Man), Larry J. Blake (Police Officer).

An entertaining Disney film about a Siamese cat owned by Mills and Provine leading FBI agent Jones on a wild chase to find the kidnape rs of bank teller Hall, who was snatched during a hold-up. Hall had managed to scratch the letters HEL (she didn't have time to add the "P") on the back of her watch and attach it to the cat's collar with the hope that someone would see it and rescue her. After running into a series of funny slapstick situations while following the cat on its nocturnal wanderings, Jones finds the robbers' hideout and brings them to justice. Silly stuff, but with a good supporting cast of Lanchester, Demarest, and McDowall as nosy neighbors, Wynn as a helpful jeweler, and Brand and Gorshin as the robbers, it's a lot of fun.

p, Bill Walsh, Ron Miller; d, Robert Stevenson; w, Gordon Gordon, Mildred Gordon, Walsh (based on the novel Undercover Cat by Gordon and Mildred Gordon); ph, Edward Colman (Technicolor); m, Bob Brunner; ed, Cotton Warburton; art d, Carroll Clark, William H. Tuntke; set d, Emile Kuri, Hal Gausman; spec eff, Eustace Lycett; m/l, "That Darn Cat," Richard M. and Robert B. Sherman (sung by Bobby Darin) makeup, Pat McNalley, La Rue Matheron.

Comedy   Cas.   (PR:AAA MPAA:G)

THAT FORSYTE WOMAN***   (1949) 114m MGM c (GB: THE
                                                      FORSYTE SAGA)

Errol Flynn (Soames Forsyte), Greer Garson (Irene Forsyte), Walter Pidgeon (Young Jolyon Forsyte), Robert Young (Philip Bosinney), Janet Leigh (June Forsyte), Harry Davenport (Old Jolyon Forsyte), Stanley Logan (Swithin Forsyte), Lumsden Hare (Roger Forsyte), Aubrey Mather (James Forsyte), Matt Moore (Timothy Forsyte), Florence Auer (Ann Forsyte Hayman), Marjorie Eaton (Hester Forsyte), Evelyn Beresford (Mrs. Taylor), Gerald Oliver Smith (Beveridge), Richard Lupino (Chester Forsyte), Wilson Wood (Eric Forsyte), Gabrielle Windsor (Jennie), Renee Mercer (Martha), Nina Ross (Louise), Constance Cavendish (Alice Forsyte), Charles McNaughton (Attendant), Wallis Clark (Cabby), Isabel Randolph (Mrs. Winthrop), Tim Hawkins (Freddie), Olaf Hytten (Assistant), Reginald Sheffield (Mr. McLean), Frank Baker (Lord Dunstable), Jean Ransome (Amelia), William Eddritt (Waiter), Leonard Carey (Butler), Morgan Farley (Bookseller), John Sheffield, Norman Rainey (Footmen), Herbert Evans (M.C.'s Voice), James Aubrey (Cabby), Billy Bevan (Porter), David Dunbar (Driver), Colin Kenny (Constable), Leyland Hodgson (Detective), Rolfe Sedan (Official), Andre Charlot (Director Braval), Lilian Bond (Maid), Blanche Franke, Jack Chefe, Olga Nina Borget, Albert Petit (Guests), Jimmy Hawkins (Gerald), Gloria Gordon (Girl).

Expensive Victorian drama based on the first book in Galsworthy's trilogy is heavy going, despite luxurious mounting and a few good performances. Pidgeon is the artist son of a prominent family in England. His decision to turn to the world of art has made him an outcast in their eyes. Pidgeon's daughter is Leigh, who has been raised by the family when Pidgeon's wife died. The family has kept Leigh from Pidgeon and taken over her upbringing stringently. The Victorian attitudes of the family have affected everyone in the younger generation. Pidgeon's cousin is Flynn, a conservative type who went against the clan's wishes and married Garson, a seductive redheaded piano teacher. Garson is not nearly on the social level of the family and they objected strenuously to Flynn's taking her hand but he is so in love with her that he bypassed their tradition of marrying to enhance position. Garson and Leigh become friends and Leigh asks Garson to be of assistance in her desire to marry Young, an architect with an insouciant attitude that rankles the hidebound family. Garson uses her influence and the family accepts Young and his intentions to marry Leigh. But after meeting Garson, Young is not so sure he wants Leigh. Garson is gorgeous, bright, and a rich, robust woman, more to Young's liking than the naive Leigh. But she is also married to Flynn, a major problem. Flynn hires Young to design a home for them and Garson and Young are thrown together by the business of the architect working with the client. Even though Garson is starting to lose her passion for Flynn, she keeps Young at arm's length because he is engaged to Leigh and she can't bear to be the "other woman." Garson realizes she must put a damper on Young's passion for her so she travels to his residence to confront him with that refusal. Her appearance at his place is seen by Leigh, who suspects that they are having an affair. Leigh goes to Flynn and emotionally tells him what she thinks is transpiring. When Garson gets home, Flynn verbally lashes her, then has a message sent to Young to come to their home. Young arrives, Flynn accuses him of dallying with Garson, and there is an argument which culminates when Young admits that he loves Garson. Garson has left the house and gone back to Young's place where she meets Pidgeon, who came to Young's

apartment to chastise him for the manner in which he has been treating Leigh. Flynn arrives at Young's and tells Garson and Pidgeon that Young has been killed in an accident when he fell beneath the wheels of a wagon on the foggy streets of London. Garson is devastated and will not accompany Flynn back to their home. She wants nothing more to do with him and lets him know that in no uncertain terms. Time passes and the picture ends with Garson and Pidgeon married and living in glorious happiness in Paris. Many years after this, the entire story was told in a BBC-TV series that was far superior to the movie because it had the time to penetrate everyone's motivations and not worry about having to cram a lot of plot into under two hours. The role of the patriarch was played by Harry Davenport, who died shortly thereafter at the age of 83, with more than 76 years in the acting profession to cite on his resume. The movie had been scheduled as a 1933 picture for MGM's David Selznick but it took this long to get before the cameras. Flynn was a contract actor at Warners at the time and was borrowed for this production as a trade for William Powell, who appeared in WB's LIFE WITH FATHER. Flynn was paged for the Pidgeon or Young role but felt he wanted to expand his image by choosing the less flashy part of the apparently cuckolded husband. He did well but audiences were accustomed to seeing Flynn wielding a saber or a six-gun and the picture did not catch fire at the box office, although it did turn a bit of a profit. The director was Compton Bennett, who was making his U.S. debut after THE SEVENTH VEIL and three other smaller British pictures. Former editor Bennett also directed KING SOLOMON'S MINES.

p, Leon Gordon; d, Compton Bennett; w, Jan Lustig, Ivan Tors, James B. Williams, Arthur Wimperis (based on the novel A Man of Property from the trilogy The Forsyte Saga by John Galsworthy); ph, Joseph Ruttenberg (Technicolor); m, Bronislau Kaper; art d, Cedric Gibbons, Daniel B. Cathcart; set d, Edwin B. Willis, Jack D. Moore; cos, Walter Plunkett, Valles; makeup, Jack Dawn.

Drama   (PR:A-C MPAA:NR)

THAT FUNNY FEELING**   (1965) 93m UNIV c

Sandra Dee (Joan Howell), Bobby Darin (Tom Milford), Donald O'Connor (Harvey Granson), Nina Talbot (Audrey), Larry Storch (Luther), James Westerfield (Officer Brokaw), Leo G. Carroll (O'Shea), Gregory Shannon (Lennie), Robert Strauss (Bartender), Ben Lessy (2nd Bartender), Frank Killmond (Mr. Scruggs), Benny Rubin (Taxi Driver), Reta Shaw, Nora Marlowe, Kathleen Freeman, Minerva Urecal (Women at Phone Booth), Arte Johnson (Paul), Aki Hara (Hatacki), Don Haggerty, Larry Blake (Policemen), Herb Vigran, Jordan Whitfield.

Dee plays a struggling actress who works as a maid to pay the bills. One of her clients is rich and powerful publisher Darin (her husband in real life). The pair fall in love after bumping into each other several times around New York without realizing that they also have a professional relationship. Embarrassed to take Darin home to her tiny apartment, she instead brings him to his own large and opulent apartment (thinking that her employer is away on business) and pretends it is hers. Darin realizes that she is his housekeeper but stays silent, allowing her to continue the deception. His business trip was canceled, and he can't go home because it would mean revealing his identity to Dee, so Darin moves in with his partner, O'Connor. Eventually each party learns the identity of the other but remains silent about the knowledge, until things get out of hand when Dee plays a prank on Darin (she has his old girl friends dress as prostitutes and throws a wild party at his apartment) and they all end up in jail.

p, Harry Keller; d, Richard Thorpe; w, David R. Schwartz (based on a story by Norman Barasch, Carroll Moore); ph, Clifford Stine (Technicolor); m, Bobby Darin; ed, Gene Milford; art d, Alexander Golitzen, George Webb; set d, John McCarthy, Julia Heron; m/l, title song, Darin (sung by Darin); makeup, Bud Westmore.

Comedy/Romance   (PR:C MPAA:NR)

THAT GANG OF MINE*½   (1940) 62m MON bw

Bobby Jordan (Danny Dolan), Leo Gorcey (Muggs Maloney), Clarence Muse (Ben), Dave O'Brien (Knuckles Dolan), Joyce Bryant (Louise), Donald Haines (Skinny), David Gorcey (Peewee), Sunshine Sammy Morrison (Scruno), Eugene Francis (Algernon "Algy" Wilkes), Milton Kibbee (Conrad Wilkes), Hazel Keener (Mrs. Wilkes), Richard R. Terry (Blackie Towne), Wilbur Mack (Nick Buffalo).

A weak Bowery Boys effort about Gorcey who is an aspiring jockey despite the teasing he gets from the other gang members. When the gang discover Muse, a poor black man who owns a racehorse, they convince him to let Gorcey ride the steed in a big race. Muse agrees, but the boys must raise the money for the entry fees themselves. The gang gets the dough from Francis' father Kibbee, but he insists that a different jockey ride the horse because Gorcey has proven himself talentless as a jockey. Though Gorcey's feelings are hurt, he agrees to relinquish the saddle so that Muse and Kibbee will get their investments back. (See BOWERY BOYS series, Index.)

p, Sam Katzman; d, Joseph H. Lewis; w, William Lively (based on a story by Alan Whitman); ph, Robert Cline, Harvey Gould; ed, Carl Pierson; md, Lew Porter; set d, Fred Preble.

Comedy   (PR:A MPAA:NR)

THAT GIRL FROM BEVERLY HILLS
                (SEE: CORPSE OF BEVERLY HILLS, THE, 1965, Ger.)

THAT GIRL FROM COLLEGE   (SEE: SORORITY HOUSE, 1939)

THAT GIRL FROM PARIS***   (1937) 110m RKO bw

Lily Pons (*Nikki Martin*), Gene Raymond (*Windy McLean*), Jack Oakie (*Whammo*), Herman Bing (*Hammacher*), Lucille Ball (*Claire Williams*), Mischa Auer (*Butch*), Frank Jenks (*Laughing Boy*), Patricia Wilder (*Coat Room Girl*), Vinton Haworth (*Reporter*), Gregory Gaye (*Paul De Vry*), Ferdinand Gottschalk (*Uncle*), Rafaela Ottiano (*Marie*), Harry Jans (*Purser*), Landers Stevens (*Ship's Captain*), Edward Price (*Photographer*), Alec Craig (*Justice of the Peace*), Michael Mark, Louis Mercier, Richard Carle (*Bits*), Pat Hartigan, Willard Robertson (*Immigration Officers*), Ferdinand Munier (*Mayor*), Edgar Dearing (*Ship's Officer*).

French operatic star Lily Pons, RKO's answer to Columbia's Grace Moore, is appropriately cast as a French opera star in this joyful musical farce. While in the U.S., a jealous suitor's failure to secure her a passport causes her to hide from immigration officials. She hooks up with McLean's Wildcats, a swing band led by Raymond, who is unaware of her success as a coloratura soprano opera singer. It's not long before Pons and Raymond fall in love, plan marriage, and return to New York where Pons has a date at the Met. Includes a number of musical numbers, including "Una Voce Poco Fa" (from Gioacchino Antonio Rossini's "The Barber of Seville"), a swing version of "The Blue Danube" (Johann Strauss), "Love and Learn," "The Call to Arms," "Seal It with a Kiss," "My Nephew from Nice," "Moon Face" (Arthur Schwartz, Edward Heyman), "Tarantella" (Panofka). Remade in 1942 as FOUR JACKS AND A JILL with June Havoc in Pons' "Jill" role. A 33-year-old Jimmy Dorsey appeared, uncredited, as one of the jazz musicians in Raymond's band, in this, the biggest hit of Pons' brief movie career. She married conductor Andre Kostelanetz the year after THAT GIRL FROM PARIS came out.

p, Pandro S. Berman; d, Leigh Jason; w, P.J. Wolfson, Dorothy Yost, Joseph A. Fields (based on a story by Jane Murfin, suggested by a magazine story by J. Carey Wonderly), ph, J. Roy Hunt; m, Nathaniel Shilkret, Andre Kostelanetz; ed, William Morgan; md, Shilkret, Kostelanetz; art d, Van Nest Polglase; set d, Darrell Silvera; cos, Edward Stevenson.

Musical/Comedy   **(PR:A   MPAA:NR)**

THAT HAGEN GIRL zero   (1947) 83m WB bw

Ronald Reagan (*Tom Bates*), Shirley Temple (*Mary Hagen*), Rory Calhoun (*Ken Freneau*), Lois Maxwell (*Julia Kane*), Dorothy Peterson (*Minta Hagen*), Charles Kemper (*Jim Hagen*), Conrad Janis (*Dewey Coons*), Penny Edwards (*Christine Delaney*), Jean Porter (*Sharon Bailey*), Nella Walker (*Molly Freneau*), Harry Davenport (*Judge Merrivale*), Winifred Harris (*Selma Delaney*), Moroni Olsen (*Trenton Gateley*), Frank Conroy (*Dr. Stone*), Kathryn Card (*Miss Grover*), Douglas Kennedy (*Herb*), Barbara Brown (*Lorna Gateley*), Tom Fadden (*Village Loafer*), Jane Hamilton (*Widow Bailey*), William B. Davidson (*Mr. Bowman*), Kyle MacDonnell (*Grace Gateley*), William Edmunds (*Corey the Chauffeur*), Virginia Farmer (*Millie Corey*), Constance Purdy (*Ruth Laverty*), Lois Austin (*Kate Hillston*), Sarah Edwards (*Charlotte Miller*), Claire Meade (*Liza Bingham*), Helen Wallace (*Rose Halliday*), Milton Parsons (*Station Agent*), Gracile LaVinder (*Nurse Boswell*), Boyd Irwin (*Rev. Sparling*), Jack Smart, Jack Mower (*Men in Drugstore*), Gu y Wilkerson (*Link Spencer*), Ray Montgomery, Kathryn Kane, Robert Palmer, Ray Klinge, Billy Henderson, Jessica Jordan, Rhoda Williams (*College Students*), Florence Allen, Ed Russell (*School Board Members*), Anthony Warde, Paul Weber (*Slickers*), Billy Roy (*Boy*).

Not only an oddity from the casting of future politicos Reagan and Temple in the same film, but a true mutant due to its rotten script and nearly incomprehensible resolution. Reagan himself despised the experience and did all he could to get out of doing the film because this was one time he *knew* the movie was going to be an embarrassment before the cameras rolled. Supposedly a condemnation of the rumor-mongering activities in small-town America, THAT HAGEN GIRL stars Temple (in her first role as a "young lady") as the adopted daughter of Peterson and Kemper who has had to grow up with suspicions that she is the illegitimate daughter of successful young lawyer Reagan, who fled town soon after she was born. Temple has become accustomed to the cold stares and secret whispers, but when she becomes a teenager, the rumors prove too much for her boy friend, Calhoun, and he dumps her. Enter Reagan, who has returned to town from Washington. Reagan is a lady's man and strikes up a romance with Maxwell, Temple's teacher and only true friend. The rumor mill is soon out of control with the townsfolk remarking about what a nice "family" Reagan, Maxwell, and Temple make when they go on outings together. Temple has had enough of this dirty talk and tries to commit suicide by throwing herself into a lake. Reagan happens by and saves her life, and this incident proves to Maxwell that it is really Temple Reagan is in love with and not her. In an embarrassing exchange of dialog, Maxwell points outs Reagan's pedophilic obsession with Temple (it's all very wholesome of course—almost "cute"!) and darned if all the parties involved don't agree! Bearing in mind that the film was produced in the 1940s, the potentially incestuous nature of this relationship is dealt with rather swiftly and it is soon discovered that

Temple came from an orphanage in Illinois (why *someone* didn't bother trying to discover this little tidbit when Temple was a child is anybody's guess), once and for all proving that she's not Reagan's illegitimate daughter (whew!). The conclusion is Reagan and Temple boarding a train and waving good-bye to the snotty little town. Did they marry? Did Reagan adopt her? Not even the President of the United States knows for sure.

p, Alex Gottlieb; d, Peter Godfrey; w, Charles Hoffman (based on the novel by Edith Roberts); ph, Karl Freund; m, Franz Waxman; ed, David Weisbart; md, Leo F. Forbstein; art d, Stanley Fleischer; set d, Lyle B. Reifsnider; cos, Travilla; spec eff, William McGann, Wesley Anderson.

Drama   **(PR:A-C   MPAA:NR)**

THAT HAMILTON WOMAN**½   (1941) 128m UA bw (GB: LADY HAMILTON)

Vivien Leigh (*Emma Hart Hamilton*), Laurence Olivier (*Lord Horatio Nelson*), Alan Mowbray (*Sir William Hamilton*), Sara Allgood (*Mrs. Cadogan-Lyon*), Gladys Cooper (*Lady Nelson*), Henry Wilcoxon (*Capt. Hardy*), Heather Angel (*Street Girl*), Halliwell Hobbes (*Rev. Nelson*), Gilbert Emery (*Lord Spencer*), Miles Mander (*Lord Keith*), Ronald Sinclair (*Josiah*), Luis Alberni (*King of Naples*), Norma Drury (*Queen of Naples*), Georges Renavent (*Hotel Manager*), Leonard Carey (*Orderly*), Alec Craig (*Gendarme*), Juliette Compton (*Lady Spencer*), Olaf Hytten (*Gavin*), Guy Kingsford (*Capt. Troubridge*), George Davis.

A slatternly, penniless, drunken old crone–played by Leigh–is consigned to the lock-up on charges of thievery and assault. There, she relates the story of her life to a young streetwalker cellmate, played by the inappropriately named Angel. The tale unfolds in flashback (with Leigh narrating in voice-over). The young, vibrant, naive–but sexually experienced–Leigh arrives at the Court of Naples in 1786 fully expecting to wed the nephew of the British ambassador, Mowbray. Discovering that she has been deceived and discarded by her rascally former lover, she rebounds from her initial depression and her appealing piquancy endear her to the ambassador himself. She becomes Mowbray's mistress, and later, his bride. Seven years pass, with Leigh's childishly enthusiastic ways endearing her to the court. Lord Nelson, the British naval hero–played by Olivier–is dispatched to Naples to plead for safe haven and resupply privileges for British naval vessels, a strategic device deemed necessary in the war against Napoleon. Mowbray and Olivier lay their case before the King of Naples, Alberni, to no effect; the troubled king, his fiefdom near revolt, seeks neutrality. Leigh befriends Olivier and uses her influence with the queen, Drury–the real power behind the throne–to gain the long-sought advantage needed by the English fleet. Olivier and Leigh become ever closer during his tenure in Naples. Olivier departs with the fleet for Egypt, where he is victorious against the Napoleonic forces in the famed Battle of the Nile. Wounded, Olivier returns to Naples to recuperate, having lost an arm and an eye in the conflict. The breathlessly waiting Leigh is shocked: "They told me of your victories, but not of the price you paid." The two fall ever more deeply in love as she helps him recover; stoical, patriotic Mowbray bears his young wife's infidelity unflinchingly, knowing of Olivier's value to his country's cause. The word of this illicit romance filters back to England, where the tongues of the gossips wave like the flags of the victory parades upon the hero's return. Revolution overturns the Neapolitan throne, and Olivier evacuates to England in the company of his married mistress, who is now carrying his child. There, Olivier confronts his stern-visaged wife, Cooper, and requests a divorce. Cooper states that as long as she lives, she will be his wife. Cooper retires to Olivier's country estate. Olivier and Leigh, still friendly with Leigh's now-ailing husband, Mowbray, set up housekeeping. With the course of the war going badly for England, Leigh determines to sacrifice her domestic happiness for her country's good, and persuades Olivier to return to his command of the fleet. Olivier engages the fleet of Napoleon at the Battle of Trafalgar and, in victory, is mortally wounded. His trusted captain, Wilcoxon, arrives at Leigh's country home–where she has secluded herself to await her lover's return–with the news of his heroic demise. And so begins Leigh's denigration and fall, her transformation into the old slattern, who finishes her tale in an epilog. England was enmeshed in WW II when THAT HAMILTON WOMAN was made. Producer Korda had journeyed to the U.S. where filmmaking facilities were more readily available than in his war-torn adopted country, England. Hungarian-born Korda got the idea for the picture during a train trip from New York City to Hollywood as he whiled away the travel time reading a book on naval history by Adm. William Mahan. Leigh and Olivier, married for almost a year, were in New York with their unsuccessful stage production of "Romeo and Juliet." They had invested heavily in the play, and were losing their shirts on it. They were both delighted to team up with Korda on the film. Korda was happy to get his two leading players, who were bound to lend marquee magic to the movie; Leigh had achieved great popularity with the stunning GONE WITH THE WIND the previous year. Nearly broke himself, Korda needed all the help he could get. The exigencies forced Korda into the unusual position–for him–of being forced to make a movie quickly, one without lavish sets such as had characterized his other recent films. Screenwriter Sherriff journeyed from England to join his co-writer Reisch, and the film–like CASABLANCA–was written while shooting was going on. The budget considerations forced the filmmakers to concentrate on humanity rather than epic battle scenes, as were customary in the producer's oeuvre. Model shots and relatively low-cost sets had to be used. The production was completed in only six weeks, an unheard-of time for a Korda film. Britain was at war at the time (the U.S. was still holding on to its tenuous neutrality), and–like the Soviet film ALEXANDER NEVSKY–the movie carries a political message: "We must fight those who want to dictate to the world," says Mowbray. The screenwriters altered history greatly, to the film's detriment at the box office. Britons have long liked Perfidious Albion's heroes to be rascals; Robin Hood, Prince Hal, and the piratical Sir Francis Drake seem more to their liking than such truth-telling U.S. pantheoned figures as George Washington and Honest Abe. Raunchy, cuckolding, adulterous Admiral Lord Nelson was certainly cast in the English heroic mold, and audiences might legitimately have expected more than the very few, very muted references to the sexual proclivities of the historical figures portrayed in the picture. Reviewers of the time expressed their disappointment; they had anticipated more titillation from the man who made THE PRIVATE LIFE OF HENRY VIII. THAT HAMILTON WOMAN was the favorite film of Britain's great wartime prime minister, Winston Churchill. Churchill's introduction to the movie began even before production started. The prime minister had cabled Korda the day following the announcement that a film about Lord Nelson was to be made; Churchill suggested a title for the film. Many more cables were to follow. Security-conscious, Korda kept the cables a secret, but he was later told by Churchill, "I *meant* them to be used; I sent them to put your stock up." A shame; Korda could have used the cash. Korda had unanticipated censor trouble with this film. He had deliberately distorted history by having the adulteress end her days a withered, penniless hag in the finest tradition of Hollywood comeuppance for sinners, but the concurrent writing and filming meant that he was unable to supply a script to the chief censor of the time, Joseph Breen, until after the picture had been shot. The film *had* to meet the Production Code of the time; otherwise, it would have been refused by the great majority of exhibitors in the U.S. Breen's dictates forced Korda to add a new scene–which Korda later cut from the film–in which Olivier is lectured by his wheelchair-bound father, Hobbes–"What you are doing is wrong . . . . I beg of you to see no more of this woman." Olivier expresses contrition, but replies that he is simply too weak to give her up. The theme was first treated in a British silent, NELSON (1927). For a far more accurate historical account, see THE NELSON AFFAIR (1973).

p&d, Alexander Korda; w, Walter Reisch, R.C. Sherriff; ph, Rudolph Mate; m, Miklos Rozsa; ed, William Hornbeck; prod d, Vincent Korda; md, Rozsa; set d, Julia Heron; cos, Rene Hubert; spec eff, Lawrence Butler; makeup, Blagoe Srephanoff.

Historical Drama   **Cas.**   **(PR:A   MPAA:NR)**

THAT HOUSE IN THE OUTSKIRTS½
(1980, Span.) 101m Kalender c (AQUELLA CASA EN LAS AFUERAS)

Javier Escriva (*Joaquin*), Silvia Aguilar (*Nieves*), Alida Valli (*Isabel*), Mara Goyanes, Carmen Maura.

Spooky Spanish suspense film starring Aguilar as a young girl from the provinces whose husband, Escriva, rents a beautiful home in the outskirts of Madrid where she can relax during the last three months of her pregnancy. When the couple approaches the house, Aguilar is horrified to discover that it is the same place where she had an illegal abortion five years before (she never told her husband). Though the clandestine abortion clinic is no longer operating from the house, Aguilar is apprehensive. The upstairs tenant, Valli, turns out to be the former abortionist's aide, and is now a psychopath who keeps all of the abortion supplies, including jars containing fetuses, in the attic. Eventually Valli snaps and tries to destroy both the house and Aguilar, but the pregnant woman survives.

d, Eugenio Martin; w, Manuel Summers, Antonio Cuevas, Jose G. Castrillo, Eduardo Alvarez, Martin, Manuel Matji; ph, Manuel Rojas (Eastmancolor); m, Carmelo Bernaola; ed, Pablo G. del Amo; set d, Jose Maria Alarcon.

Suspense   **(PR:C-O   MPAA:NR)**

THAT I MAY LIVE   (1937) 70m FOX bw

Rochelle Hudson (*Irene Howard*), Robert Kent (*Dick Mannion*), J. Edward Bromberg (*Tex Shapiro*), Jack La Rue (*Charlie*), Frank Conroy (*Pop*), Fred Kelsey (*Abner Jenkins*), George Cooper (*Mack*), DeWitt Jennings (*Chief of Police*), Russell Simpson (*Bish Plivens*), William Benedict (*Kurt Plivens*).

Kent plays a young man who was conned into helping criminals crack a safe, a crime for which he took the rap. Three years later, Kent is released from prison, to find the same crooks forcing him into more criminal acts. Kent having outlived his usefulness to the gang, they kill a cop during a robbery and frame him for the killing. Kent flees with waitress Hudson, and the pair hooks up with a kind peddler, Bromberg, who befriends them and eventually clears Kent.

p, Sol M. Wurtzel; d, Allan Dwan; w, Ben Markson, William Conselman; ph, Robert Planck; md, Samuel Kaylin; cos, Herschel.

Crime   **(PR:A   MPAA:NR)**

THAT KIND OF GIRL   (SEE: MODELS, INC., 1952)

THAT KIND OF GIRL zero   (1963, Brit.) 78m
Animated-Tekli/Topaz-IA bw (AKA: TEEN AGE TRAMP)

Margaret-Rose Keil (*Eva*), David Weston (*Keith Murray*), Linda Marlowe (*Janet Bates*), Peter Burton (*Elliot Collier*), Frank Jarvis (*Max*), Sylvia Kay (*Mrs. Millar*), David Davenport (*Mr. Millar*), Stephen Stocker (*Nicholas*), Charles Houston (*Ted*), Max Faulkner (*Johnson*), Patricia Mort (*Barbara*), Martin Wyldeck (*Bates*), John Wood (*Doctor*).

The horrors of venereal disease are illustrated in this film that introduces Austrian harlot Keil into a small, tightly knit British community and then follows the havoc that her promiscuous ways cause. During the course of the film Keil seduces an engaged man, inadvertently causing his fiancee to relent and have relations with him before marriage, resulting in an early pregnancy; gets raped by a boy friend who is jealous of her other affairs; and contracts venereal disease, which panics the rest of the community. In the end, the engaged couple marry and Keil's boy friend is arrested for making obscene phone calls.

p, Robert Hartford-Davis; d, Gerry O'Hara; w, Jan Read; ph, Peter Newbrook; m, Malcolm Mitchell; ed, Derek York; md, Mitchell; art d, William Brodie.

Drama   **(PR:O   MPAA:NR)**

THAT KIND OF WOMAN**   (1959) 92m Ponti-Girosi/PAR c

Sophia Loren (*Kay*), Tab Hunter (*Red*), George Sanders (*The Man*), Jack Warden (*Kelly*), Barbara Nichols (*Jane*), Keenan Wynn (*Harry Corwin*).

A ridiculously cliched soap opera which stars Loren as a woman kept by millionaire Sanders to help him influence those in power at the Pentagon. She is escorted, along with friend Nichols, on a Miami-to-New York train trip by Sanders' aide Wynn. Along the way she meets a group of GIs and becomes especially fond of one of them, Hunter. Although she spends the night with him, the following morning, when the train pulls into the station, she unemotionally says goodbye. Hunter, however, refuses to give up on Loren and persuades her to stay with him. Torn between a life of luxury with Sanders (who finally proposes to her) and a life of true love with Hunter, she agrees to stay with the latter. What starts out with the promise of a real relationship soon falls apart at the seams when Loren is confronted with the supposedly difficult choice. Very little rings true in the picture except for the Nichols character–a loose girl who loves anyone she can to satisfy her insecurity–who, unfortunately, isn't given enough screen time. This was supposed to be the film that turned Loren into a big American success, but then again the same was said about THE PRIDE AND THE PASSION, BOY ON A DOLPHIN, LEGEND OF THE LOST (all 1957), and HOUSEBOAT (1958). Loren did manage to get some good reviews of her acting, but that is only because her costar, Hunter, was far from the ranks of a Cary Grant, Alan Ladd, or John Wayne (all previous U.S. costars). Director Lumet made an effort to reduce the gloss that is usually associated with Loren's films by shooting on location in New York City, but after numerous disagreements with Ponti and a nasty editing job in Hollywood, THAT KIND OF WOMAN emerged on the same wretched level as most of Loren's pictures.

p, Carlo Ponti; d, Sidney Lumet; w, Walter Bernstein (based on a story by Robert Lowry); ph, Boris Kaufman (VistaVision); m, Daniele Amphitheatrof; ed, Howard Smith; md, Van Cleave; art d, Hal Pereira, Roland Anderson; cos, Edith Head.

Romance   **(PR:C   MPAA:NR)**

THAT LADY**   (1955, Brit.) 100m Atlanta/FOX c

Olivia de Havilland (*Ana de Mendoza*), Gilbert Roland (*Antonio Perez*), Paul Scofield (*Philip II*), Francoise Rosay (*Bernadina*), Dennis Price (*Mateo Vasquez*), Anthony Dawson (*Don Inigo*), Robert Harris (*Cardinal*), Peter Illing (*Diego*), Jose Nieto (*Don Escovedo*), Christopher Lee (*Captain*), Andy Shine (*Fernando*), Angel Peralta.

This lavish historical drama is visually stunning but unfortunately becomes so bogged down in dialog that the film is unfulfilling as a whole. Based in truth, this features de Havilland as Ana de Mendoza, the Princess of Eboli in Spain of 1580. The beautiful and enticing woman wears a patch over her right eye, having lost it years before in a duel over the king, Scofield's, honor. She has since become a loyal and dear friend of Scofield. He in turn has become sexually passionate about the woman, though these feelings are not returned. Instead she has married one of Scofield's ministers, with whom she has had a son. At the story's opening de Havilland is now widowed but still a close confidante of the king. Roland is a commoner whom Scofield wishes to make his first secretary. He asks de Havilland for help in training this man for high office but is dismayed when teacher and pupil fall in love. Outraged by jealousy, Scofield has Roland placed under arrest on a bogus murder charge. He then orders de Havilland to leave Madrid but the haughty lady refuses. Scofield then has her imprisoned as well, first in a jail cell and then in a closely watched house arrest. Roland manages to escape from his confinement, then sneaksin to see his beloved. The princess is overjoyed to see Roland once more but insists he leave the country to insure his safety, taking de Havilland's son along as well. De Havilland becomes depressed over this course of events and her physical health begins to deteriorate along with her mental well-being. Shortly before she passes away word reaches de Havilland that Roland and her son are safe. Upon her death Scofield plunges into mourning, realizing that the suffering he caused de Havilland was cruel and extreme. The story had first been produced on Broadway in 1949 with Katharine Cornell in the lead role. It was hardly a noteworthy production, yet producers must have felt this true-life story of royal intrigue had the makings of an intelligent and racy drama that would be greatly enhanced by shooting in Spanish castles of the era. This was true to an extent, for the scenery and actual 16th-Century locations give this a fine realistic feeling. Costuming also pays close attention to period detail with some very colorful garb. However, the potentially exciting story was overwritten, with long stretches of boredom in a relatively short 100 minutes. The result is a series of staged set pieces which hold none of the zeal the story demands. Scofield made his film debut with this role and is impressive in the part. He overcomes the talky script, delivering a good character study of a man tortured by his inner feelings. This was de Havilland's first film in three years and she injects her character with the lively yet sad personality demanded. Her performance commands attention and, like Scofield, de Havilland is able to rise above the script troubles. But these two performances are not enough to conquer the inherent problems of the production and stand out only as two jewels amidst a pile of simple polished rocks. In a minor role is Lee, later the star of many British horror films. The studio advertised this film with the tag line "England had its Amber...America had its Scarlett... But you'll never forget the woman of Spain marked for all time as THAT LADY." THAT LADY never capitalizes on the fiery nature of its heroine, resulting in a beautiful but disappointingly shallow film.

p, Sy Bartlett; d, Terence Young; w, Anthony Veiller, Bartlett (based on a play by Kate O'Brien); ph, Robert Krasker (CinemaScope, Eastmancolor); m, John Addison; ed, Raymond Poulton; md, Addison; art d, Frank White.

Drama   (PR:C   MPAA:NR)

THAT LADY IN ERMINE**½   (1948) 89m FOX bw

Betty Grable (Francesca/Angelina), Douglas Fairbanks, Jr (Col. Ladislas Karolyi Teglash/The Duke), Cesar Romero (Mario), Walter Abel (Maj. Horvath/Benvenuto), Reginald Gardiner (Alberto), Harry Davenport (Luigi), Virginia Campbell (Theresa), Edmund MacDonald (Capt. Novak), David Bond (Gabor), Harry Cording, Belle Mitchell, Mary Bear, Jack George, John Parrish, Mayo Newhall (Ancestors), Whit Bissell (Guilio), Lester Allen (Jester), Harry Carter, Thayer Roberts, Don Haggerty (Staff Officers), Duke York (Sergeant), Francis Pierlot (Priest), Joe Haworth (Soldier), Ray Hyke (Albert's Knight).

Though this film is listed in his filmography as his last, Ernst Lubitsch only directed eight days-worth of shooting before he died of a heart attack on November 30, 1947. Otto Preminger was called in to finish the film, but took no credit and allowed Lubitsch to stand as director. Unfortunately, Lubitsch probably wouldn't want credit in his filmography, because THAT LADY IN ERMINE is definitely not a Lubitsch film. Just a period piece musical, Fairbanks, Jr., stars in it as a 19th-Century European army officer who takes over a castle to house his tired men. There he meets and falls in love with the castle's owner, Grable. Seeking to rid herself of this nuisance, Grable dreams of her great-great-grandmother, who found herself in the same situation 200 years ago. Her grandmother advises that Grable pretend to fall in love with Fairbanks, Jr., and then kill him. After all, it worked for her. Grable awakens and sets out to do as her dream advised, but she actually does fall in love with Fairbanks, Jr., and decides not to kill him. Though the production was lavish, the film has no life and remains an exercise in trite and contrived plotting. Songs include: "OOOh What I'll Do to That Wild Hungarian," "This Is the Moment," "There's Something About Midnight," "The Melody Has to Be Right," "Jester's Song" (Leo Robin, Frederick Hollander).

p, Ernst Lubitsch; d, Lubitsch, Otto Preminger; w, Samson Raphaelson (based on an operetta by Rudolph Schanzer, Ernest Welisch); ph, Leon Shamroy (Technicolor); ed, Dorothy Spencer; md, Alfred Newman; art d, Lyle Wheeler, J. Russell Spencer; set d, Thomas Little, Walter M. Scott; cos, Rene Hubert; spec eff; Fred Sersen; ch, Hermes Pan.

Musical   (PR:A   MPAA:NR)

THAT LUCKY TOUCH*   (1975, Brit.) 93m Gloria-RANK/AA c

Roger Moore (Michael Scott), Susannah York (Julia Richardson), Shelley Winters (Diane Steedeman), Lee J. Cobb (Lt. Gen. Henry Steedeman), Jean-Pierre Cassel (Leo Devivia), Raf Vallone (Gen. Antonio Peruzzi), Sydne Rome (Sophie), Donald Sinden (Gen. Armstrong), Michael Shannon (Lt. Davis), Alfred Hoffman (Berckman), Aubrey Woods (Viscount L'Ardey), Timothy Carlton (Tank Commander), Fabian Cevellos (Paul, Photographer), Vincent Hall (David Richardson), Julie Dawn Cole (Tina Steedman), Merelina Kendall (Antoinette), Taki Emmanuel (Arab Sheik), Michael Green (Young Arab), Sultan Lalani (Ambassador), Jamila Massey (Ambassador's Wife), Marianne Stone, Linda Gray, Leonard Kavanaugh, Mercia Mansfield, Bonnie Hurren, David Enders (Party Guests), Franco Derossa (Italian Sergeant), Donna Todd (Neighbor).

Dull, dim-witted comedy starring Moore as a playboy arms dealer trying to

sell weapons to the NATO forces during war games, despite the interference of feminist, pacifist reporter York who is covering the military activities for the Washington Post. Of course they hate each other. Of course they fall in love. Believe it or not, William Friedkin's similar DEAL OF THE CENTURY is better (by a hair).

p, Dimitri de Grunwald; d, Christopher Miles; w, John Briley (based on an idea by Moss Hart); ph, Douglas Slocombe (Technicolor); m, John Scott; prod d, Tony Masters; art d, Jack Maxsted.

Comedy   (PR:A-C   MPAA:PG)

THAT MAD MR. JONES   (SEE: FULLER BRUSH MAN, THE, 1948)

THAT MAN BOLT zero   (1973) 102m UNIV c (AKA: TO KILL A DRAGON; THUNDERBOLT)

Fred Williamson (Jefferson Bolt), Byron Webster (Griffiths), Miko Mayama (Dominique), Teresa Graves (Samantha), Satoshi Nakamura (Kumada), John Orchard (Carter), Jack Ging (Connie), Ken Kazama (Spider), Vassili Lambrinos (DeVargas).

Rotten and unforgivably dull (and if it's dull, what's the point?) black exploitation film starring Williamson as a kung fu expert being chased around the world by a government agent (exactly which government is never really made clear) for no apparent reason. Basically an excuse for lots of bedroom scenes and kung fu fights. A word to the wise: whenever you see two directors credited on a trashy film (or in fact, almost any film) stay away; it means the film has big problems.

p, Bernard Schwartz; d, Henry Levin, David Lowell Rich; w, Quentin Werty, Charles Johnson; ph, Gerald Perry Finnerman (Technicolor); m, Charles Bernstein; ed, Carl Pingitore, Robert F. Shugrue; art d, Alexander Golitzen; set d, Chester R. Bayhi.

Drama   (PR:O   MPAA:R)

THAT MAN FLINTSTONE   (SEE: MAN CALLED FLINTSTONE, THE, 1966)

THAT MAN FROM RIO***   (1964, Fr./Ital.) 114m Ariane-Artistes Associes-Dear/Lopert c (L'HOMME DE RIO; L'UOMO DI RIO)

Jean-Paul Belmondo (Adrien Dufourquet), Francoise Dorleac (Agnes), Jean Servais (Prof. Catalan, Museum Curator), Simone Renant (Lola), Milton Ribeiro (Tupac), Ubiracy de Oliveira (Sir Winston, Bootblack), Adolpho Celi (Senor De Castro, Industrialist), Daniel Ceccaldi, Roger Dumas, Sabu do Brasil.

A wacky adventure yarn which begins with French Air Force pilot Belmondo on an eight-day pass to see his girl friend Dorleac in Paris. Unfortunately Belmondo arrives just in time to see his girl kidnaped by South American Indians who are trying to get a hold of a set of valuable statues that when assembled will point the way to an Amazon treasure. Dorleac is taken because her late father had led an expedition in the area and the Indians suspect she knows where the statues are. After a lengthy series of misadventures in the jungle, Belmondo and Dorleac eventually escape and return to Paris just in time for Belmondo to return to his unit. Belmondo, as always, is a delight.

p, Alexandre Mnouchkine, Georges Dancigers; d, Philippe de Broca; w, Jean-Paul Rappeneau, Ariane Mnouchkine, Daniel Boulanger, de Broca; ph, Edmond Sechan (Eastmancolor); m, Georges Delerue; ed, Laurence Mery, Francoise Javet; spec eff, Gil Delamare.

Comedy/Adventure   (PR:A   MPAA:NR)

THAT MAN FROM TANGIER**   (1953) 88m Elemsee Overseas/UA bw

Nils Asther (Henri), Roland Young (George), Nancy Coleman (Mary Ellen), Margaret Wycherly (Mrs. Sanders).

Uneventful romantic comedy starring Coleman as a rowdy, spoiled sophisticate who awakes after an all-night drunk to discover she's married. The husband soon disappears and Coleman is distressed to learn that the man had been using a stolen passport to pose as rich dandy Asther. Desperate to save face with her family, Coleman tracks Asther down and begs him to pretend that he's married her, just for a little while until her grandmother, Wycherly, is satisfied. Wouldn't you know it, by the end of the picture those crazy kids really do fall in love.

p&d, Robert Elwyn; w, John Meehan, Jr.; ph, Don Malkames; m, Elizabeth Firestone.

Romance   (PR:A   MPAA:NR)

THAT MAN GEORGE!**   (1967, Fr./Ital./Span.) 90m Europazur-Benito Perojo-Atlantis-Jolly/AA c (L'HOMME DE MARRAKECH; LOS SAQUEADORES DEL DOMINGO; AKA; OUR MAN IN MARRAKESH)

George Hamilton (George), Claudine Auger (Lila), Alberto de Mendoza (Travis), Daniel Ivernel (Vibert), Tiberio Murgia (Jose), Jorge Rigaud, Giacoma Furia, Renato Baldini, Roberto Camardiel.

Hamilton stars as a member of a criminal gang that plans and successfully executes the robbery of an armored van transporting a shipment of gold through the Moroccan desert. Soon after the robbery, however, trouble brews among the gang members, and two end up dead. Hamilton and Auger flee with the gold, leaving survivor Ivernel determined to get revenge and the goods. Eventually Ivernel corners the lovers and demands his share. Hamilton, who has gotten fed up with the chase, offers to give him all the gold because now he only cares for Auger. Auger, however, doesn't quite feel that way and she takes off with Ivernel and the gold. In the end, the police catch up with the couple and they are killed, leaving Hamilton to seek new adventures.

p, Claude Giroux; d, Jacques Deray; w, Henri Lanoe, Jose Giovanni, Suzanne Arduini, Deray (based on the novel The Heisters by Robert Page Jones); ph, Henri Raichi (Eastmancolor); m, Alain Goraguer; ed, Paul Cayatte; art d, Eduardo Torre de la Fuente.

Adventure/Crime   (PR:A-C MPAA:NR)

THAT MAN IN ISTANBUL**   (1966, Fr./Ital./Span.) 117m
E.D.I.C.-C.C.M.-Isasi/COL c (L'HOMME D'ISTAMBUL; COLPO GROSSO
A GALATA: BRIDGE; ESTAMBUL 65)

Horst Buchholz (Tony Maecenas), Sylva Koscina (Kenny), Mario Adorf (Bill), Perette Pradier (Elisabeth), Klaus Kinski (Schenck), Alvaro de Luna (Bogo), Gustavo Re (Brain), Georges Rigaud (CIA Chief), Christiane Maybach (Josette), Gerard Tichy (Hansi), Agustin Gonzales (Gunther), Rocha (Chinese), Angel Picazo (Inspector Mallouk), Umberto Raho (Prof. Pendergast), Henri Cogan, Luis Induni, Marta Flores.

Buchholz plays an international playboy with a penchant for living dangerously who is hired by sexy FBI agent Koscina to rescue an atomic scientist from the clutches of an evil cabal who seek to control the world. If that isn't enough, a gang of Chinese agents are also trying to get their hands on the scientist. Unruffled by any of this, Buchholz uses his vast knowledge of Istanbul to carry out his mission.

p&d, Antonio Isasi Isasmendi; w, George Simonelli [Giovanni Simonelli], Nat Wachberger, Isasmendi, Luis Comeron, Jorge Illa (English dialog by Lewis Howard); ph, Juan Gelpi (Techniscope, Technicolor); m, Georges Garvarentz; ed, Juan Palleja; art d, Jean Alberto [Juan Alberto Soler]; makeup, Praxedes Martinez, Carmen Menchaca.

Adventure   (PR:A-C MPAA:NR)

THAT MAN MR. JONES   (SEE: FULLER BRUSH MAN, 1949)

THAT MAN'S HERE AGAIN*½   (1937) 69m FN-WB bw

Hugh Herbert (Thomas J. Jesse), Mary Maguire (Nancy Lee), Tom Brown (Jimmy Whalen), Joseph King (Mr. Murdock), Teddy Hart (Bud), Arthur Aylesworth (Johnson), Dorothy Vaughan (Mrs. Matthews), Tetsu Komai (Wong).

Dull romance starring Herbert as a rich eccentric living in a ritzy apartment house who cleverly pushes elevator operator Brown and chambermaid Maguire into a romantic entanglement that both had been too shy to initiate. An almost unrecognizable remake of the 1929 film YOUNG NOWHERES.

p, Bryan Foy; d, Louis King; w, Lillie Hayward (based on the story "Young Nowheres" by Ida A.R. Wylie); ph, Warren Lynch; ed, Harold McLernon.

Romance   (PR:A MPAA:NR)

THAT MIDNIGHT KISS**   (1949) 96m MGM c

Kathryn Grayson (Prudence Budell), Jose Iturbi (Himself), Ethel Barrymore (Abigail Budell), Mario Lanza (Johnny Donnetti), Keenan Wynn (Artie Glenson), J. Carroll Naish (Papa Donnetti), Jules Munshin (Michael Pemberton), Thomas Gomez (Guido Betelli), Marjorie Reynolds (Mary), Arthur Treacher (Hutchins), Mimi Aguglia (Mama Donnetti), Amparo Iturbi (Herself), Bridget Carr (Donna), Amparo Ballester (Rosina), Ann Codee (Mme. Bouget), Edward Earle (Jason), George Meader (Paul), Sheila Stein (Peanuts).

A colorful, musical, and partially biographical tale of Mario Lanza, who made his debut in this box-office winner. Barrymore is a rich Philadelphia dowager who once had plans for a career in opera. Her granddaughter is Grayson and Barrymore hopes to vicariously live her frustrations out through the comely young woman. Barrymore is putting up the money for a local opera company and has hired Jose Iturbi (as himself) to helm the orchestra. Grayson meets jolly truck driver Lanza and is impressed by his voice so she prevails on Iturbi to give the tenor a listen. Gomez is the tenor who has been engaged to help in Grayson's operatic debut. He is past his prime and his temperamental tantrums cause him to walk out on the company before the opening. They need another tenor to replace him and, in a moment right out of 42ND STREET (and a hundred other films), Lanza

is asked to step in. Then he and Grayson have a lovers' spat and he walks out. Opening night rolls around and Lanza comes back to triumph with Grayson after having been given some sage advice by his father, Naish. A thin plot and lots of music from various classical as well as popular writers. Grayson and Lanza duet on "They Didn't Believe Me" Jerome Kern, Herbert Reynolds), and Grayson sings the (new) tune "I Know, I Know, I Know" (Bob Russell, Bronislau Kaper). Naish sings the old classic "Three O'Clock in the Morning" (Julian Robledo, Dorothy Terriss), as well as "Santa Lucia" (Teodoro Cottrau). Keenan Wynn leads a quartet in "Down Among the Sheltering Palms" (Abe Olman, James Brockman). Frederick Chopin's "Revolutionary Etude" is played by Jose and Amparo Iturbi. Jose Iturbi also plays for Grayson on Giuseppe Verdi's "Cara Nome" from the opera "Rigoletto." Verdi also wrote "Celeste Aida" from his opera "Aida," which Lanza sings. Lanza is accompanied by Jose Iturbi on Gaetano Donizetti's "Una Furtiva Lacrima" from his opera "L'Elisir D'Amore." Iturbi plays segments from Peter Mitch Tschaikowsky's "Piano Concerto Number 1" and Franz Liszt's "Piano Concerto In E Flat." Lanza sings Pietro Mascagni's "Mama Mia Che Vo Sape" from the opera "Cavaliera Rusticana" and teams with Grayson on the theme from Tschaikowsky's "Fifth Symphony" with some sappy lyrics by the producer. Lanza burst into national prominence with this movie. He was an average Joe with a sensational voice and he took the country by storm. Note that there are two women with the name of "Amparo" in this film. How many movies can make that statement?

p, Joe Pasternak; d, Norman Taurog; w, Bruce Manning, Tamara Hovey; ph, Robert Surtees; ed, Gene Ruggiero; md, Charles Previn; art d, Cedric Gibbons, Preston Ames; cos, Helen Rose.

Musical/Romance   (PR:A MPAA:NR)

THAT NAVY SPIRIT   (SEE: HOLD 'EM NAVY, 1937)

THAT NAZTY NUISANCE*½   (1943) 50m Hal Roach/UA bw

Bobby Watson (Hitler), Joe Devlin (Mussolini), Johnny Arthur (Suki Yaki), Jean Porter (Kela), Ian Keith (Chief), Henry Victor (Von Popoff), Emory Parnell (Spence), Frank Faylen (Benson), Ed "Strangler" Lewis (Guard), Abe "King Kong" Kashey (2nd Guard), Rex Evans (Goering), Charles Rogers (Goebbels), Wedgewood Nowell (Himmler).

Silly wartime comedy starring Watson, Devlin, and Arthur as Hitler, Mussolini, and a fictitious Japanese ruler called Suki Yaki. They travel to a mythical country known as Norom to sign a treaty with the country's ruler, Keith. One day the crew of a torpedoed American merchant marine vessel washes up onshore, and the boys are determined to defeat Hitler and his allies. Lame comedy with a healthy dose of wartime ethnic slurs against Germans, Italians, and Japanese.

p&d, Glenn Tryon; w, Earle Snell, Clarence Marks; ph, Robert Pittack; m, Edward Ward; ed, Bert Jordan; art d, Charles D. Hall.

Comedy/War   (PR:A MPAA:NR)

THAT NIGHT**   (1957) 88m Galahad-RKO/UNIV bw

John Beal (Chris Bowden), Augusta Dabney (Maggie Bowden), Malcolm Brodrick (Tommy Bowden), Dennis Kohler (Chrissie Bowden), Beverly Lunsford (Betsy Bowden), Shepperd Strudwick (Dr. Bernard Fischer), Rosemary Murphy (Nurse Chornis), Bill Darrid (Dr. Perroni), Joe Julian (Mr. Rosalie).

While not exactly blockbuster entertainment, THAT NIGHT is a straightforward account of a Madison Avenue advertising executive, Beal, who suffers a heart attack and must adjust his life style if he hopes to recover. The film details the events leading up to the attack, the trip to the hospital, the measures taken to save Beal's life, and then the changes Beal must make to prevent a recurrence. The crisis brings Beal and his wife Dabney to a new plateau in their relationship, which leads to their accepting a slower pace and toning down their expectations. Interesting, honest, and well-acted.

p, Himan Brown; d, John Newland; w, Robert Wallace, Jack Rowles (based on their story and TV drama "The Long Way Home"); ph, Maurice Hartzband; m, Mario Nascimbene; ed, David Cooper; md, Nascimbene; art d, Mel Bourne.

Drama   (PR:A MPAA:NR)

THAT NIGHT IN LONDON   (SEE: OVERNIGHT, 1933, Brit.)

THAT NIGHT IN RIO**   (1941) 90m FOX c

Alice Faye (Baroness Cecilia Duarte), Don Ameche (Larry Martin/Baron Duarte), Carmen Miranda (Carmen), S. Z. Sakall (Arthur Penna), J. Carrol Naish (Machado), Curt Bois (Felicio Salles), Leonid Kinskey (Pierre Dufont), Banda Da Lua (Carmen Miranda's Orchestra), Frank Puglia (Pedro, the Valet), Maria Montez (Inez), Georges Renavent (Ambassador), Eddy Conrad (Alfonso), Fortunio Bonanova (Pereira, the Headwaiter), Flores Brothers (Specialty Singers), Lillian Porter (Luiza, the Maid), Fred Malatesta (Butler), Alberto Morin (Eca, the Pilot), Fredrik Vogeding (Trader), Jean Del Val (Man), Charles de Ravenne (Page Boy), Gino Corrado

(Clerk), Eugene Borden *(Official at Airport)*, Andre Cuyas *(Waiter)*, George Bookasta *(Bell Boy)*, Mary Ann Hyde, Vivian Mason, Barbara Lynn, Jean O'Donnell *(Secretaries)*, Bettye Avery, Bunny Hartley, Marion Rosamond, Mary Joyce Walsh, Lillian Eggers, Roseanne Murray, Poppy Wilde, Dorothy Dearing, Bonnie Bannon, Monica Bannister *(Models)*.

A bright, splashy, and well-produced remake of FOLIES BERGERE (1935) with Ameche and Miranda stealing the film from everyone else. As in the earlier Maurice Chevalier movie, the story is about an entertainer who is a ringer for a well-known businessman. The setting has been changed from Paris to Rio de Janeiro and there are new songs, but the plot is a virtual duplicate of the original. Since Ameche plays both roles, we'll refer to him as "Don" when he plays the performer. Faye is married to wealthy financier Ameche. They are on the town in Rio and come to see the latest star, Don, who is working at the local hot spot. When Don does a devastating impression of the well-known Ameche, Bonanova, the club's manager, is worried that the entertainer may have insulted the financier. Ameche and Faye assure the nervous boniface that no umbrage was taken and insist on meeting Don. Backstage, Ameche encounters Miranda, a former girl friend. She is fooled into thinking that Ameche is Don and launches into one of her fractured English tirades because she and Don are now lovers and she's annoyed about something. Ameche explains that he and Don are mirror images but don't even know each other. When Miranda learns the reality, she apologizes profusely and Ameche asks if she would like to come to a fete he is tossing for ambassador Renavent the next night. She says thanks, but no thanks. Faye meets Don and can't get over the similarity between this performer and her husband. She makes him do his mimicry again and watches him closely. Ameche owns an airline and it's in trouble so he must leave to straighten out the problem. He has to raise some money to cover cash that he's taken from his own bank. If he can't get the money, he will be ruined. Naish is Ameche's rival in big business and suspects what Ameche has done and that he's left Rio to get the needed cruzeiros. Ameche's associates Kinskey, Sakall, and Bois hire Don to masquerade as Ameche at the stock exchange. Ameche owns 51 percent of the airline and Don, getting into his impersonation, makes the mistake of buying the other 49 percent of the airline's stock in Ameche's name. Don and Faye attend Renavent's party and she now knows that the man on her arm is not her husband, but she plays the scenes as though he is, and Don is not aware that she is onto him. Miranda exhibits fiery jealousy when she finds out that Don is at the party without her. She makes a shambles of his dressing room at Bonanova's club, then races to the party for a confrontation. Miranda finds Don in the mansion's library and gives him a piece of her mind. Faye walks in and Don covers the situation by saying that Miranda has generously agreed to do a show for the people at the party. Later, Naish approaches Don and wants to talk business. He knows that Ameche speaks French so he begins chatting in that language to keep their conversation a secret. But Don doesn't speak a word of French and has to fake it in a very funny sequence. Ameche comes home having failed in his quest for the money. He thinks that Faye doesn't know the reality of who Don is, so he gets rid of Don, tells the servants to keep mum, and takes Faye to bed. Faye isn't sure if this man is Don or Ameche but she sleeps with him anyhow. In the morning, the servants tell her that Ameche's plane has only just now arrived and this throws Faye into a tizzy. With whom did she sleep last night? Was it Don or Ameche? If it was Don, her marriage is ruined. Don later tells her that it was her own husband and she is mightily relieved. Ameche is still in trouble and it looks as though he will lose his airline. He's talking with Kinskey, Bois, and Sakall when Naish walks in with a check. He wants to buy the airline (thus bailing Ameche out of trouble) because of the brilliant way in which Don responded to his French conversation at the party the night before. Ameche is amazed, accepts the check, says a silent prayer of thanks to Don and leaves his office to share the good news with wife Faye. Faye feels that Ameche may be engaging in romantic shenanigans so she hires Don to be her lover (a scene that was cut from the U.S. version but retained for Europe) and Ameche realizes that Faye is a terrific wife and decides to give up his roving in her favor. Miranda and Don get back together and the picture winds up with both couples happy again. This was the sixth and final pairing for Faye and Ameche, a successful series of movies for Fox. Miranda was in her second movie and her first that required her to act as anyone other than Miranda. She was hysterical and her energy fairly poured off the screen. She only made 14 movies before having a fatal heart attack in 1955 at the age of 46. Although technically a musical, there weren't that many songs in the picture. Harry Warren and Mack Gordon (who had also written the tunes for Miranda's debut film DOWN ARGENTINE WAY) contributed "I-Yi-Yi-Yi (I Like You Very Much)" (performed by Miranda), "Chica Chica Boom Chick" (Miranda), "The Baron Is in Conference" (Ameche), "Boa Noite" (Ameche, Faye), and "They Met in Rio" (Faye). The Portuguese tune "Cae Cae" (written by Roberto Martins) is also heard. Pan's choreography for the "Chica Chica Boom Chic" number is spectacular. Miranda's own band and the Flores Brothers are featured in specialties. Miranda, who playe d Argentines, Mexicans, and Brazilians, was actually born in Portugal and made five movies in Brazil before coming to Broadway where she was the star of "Streets of Paris" in 1939. THAT NIGHT IN RIO successfully skirted the Production Code with some risque dialog and a ticklish situation in the plot. It should go right over the heads of children because the whole affair is heavily cloaked in subtlety. Still... Later made again as ON THE RIVIERA (1951) with Danny Kaye in the dual role.

p, Fred Kohlmar; d, Irving Cummings; w, George Seaton, Bess Meredyth,

Hal Long, Samuel Hoffenstein, Jessie Ernst (based on a play by Rudolph Lothar, Hans Adler); ph, Leon Shamroy, Ray Rennahan (Technicolor); ed, Walter Thompson; md, Alfred Newman; art d, Richard Day, Joseph C. Wright; set d, Thomas Little; cos, Travis Banton; ch, Hermes Pan; m/l, Harry Warren, Mack Gordon, Roberto Martins.

Musical Comedy Cas. (PR:A-C MPAA:NR)

THAT NIGHT WITH YOU** (1945) 84m UNIV bw

Franchot Tone *(Paul Renaud)*, Susanna Foster *(Penny)*, David Bruce *(Johnny)*, Louise Allbritton *(Sheila Morgan)*, Jacqueline De Wit *(Blossom Drake)*, Buster Keaton *(Sam, the Short Order Cook)*, Irene Ryan *(Prudence)*, Howard Freeman *(Wilbur)*, Barbara Sears *(Clarissa)*, Tony N. [Anthony[Caruso *(Tenor)*, Julian Rivero *(Concertina Player)*, Teddy Infuhr *(Bingo)*, Janet Ann Gallow *(Orphan Girl)*, Thomas [Tom] Fadden *(Milkman)*, Arthur Miles, Margaret Pert, Sandra Orans, Dulce Daye, Virginia Eagels, Mary Benoit, Belle Mitchell.

Contrived musical comedy starring Foster as an ambitious young singer who becomes so desperate to get a break on Broadway that she confronts producer Tone and announces that she's the offspring of his one-day marriage to De Wit years ago. Surprisingly, Tone greets the news with enthusiasm and soon puts his "daughter" on Broadway. Potential trouble arises when Miss De Wit arrives, but she goes along with the deception in order to fool Tone for her own reasons. In the end all works out happily. Songs include: "Once Upon a Dream" (Jack Brooks, Hans J. Salter), "Market Place", "Shadows", "Largo Al Factotum" (from Rossini's Barber of Seville).

p, Michael Fessier, Ernesto Pagano; d, William A. Seiter; w, Fessier, Pagano (based on a story by Arnold Belgard); ph, Charles L. Van Enger; ed, Fred R. Feitshans, Jr.; md, H.J. Salter; art d, John B. Goodman, Martin Obzina; cos, Vera West; spec eff, John P. Fulton; ch, Leslie Horton, George Moro, Louis DaPron.

Musical (PR:A MPAA:NR)

THAT OBSCURE OBJECT OF DESIRE***½ (1977, Fr./Span.) 100m Greenwich-Galaxie-In cine/First Artists c (CET OBSCUR OBJET DU DESIR)

Fernando Rey *(Mathieu)*, Carole Bouquet, Angela Molina *(Conchita)*, Julien Bertheau *(Judge)*, Milena Vukotic *(Traveler)*, Andre Weber *(Valet)*, Pieral *(Psychologist)*, Maria Asquerino, Ellen Bahl, Valerie Blanco, Auguste Carriere, Jacques Debary, Antonio Duque, Andre Lacombe, Lita Lluch-Piero, Annie Monange, Jean Claude Montalbam, Bernard Musson, Muni, Isabelle Rattier, David Rocha, Isabelle Sadoyan, Juan Santamaria.

The final film from the 77-year-old Luis Bunuel which caps a career that began in 1929 with the surrealist short UN CHIEN ANDALOU. This time he is as ambiguous as ever, casting two women–the graceful Bouquet and the saucy Molina–in the role of Conchita, a beautiful but elusive Spanish girl who becomes the center of obsession for Rey, an upstanding French businessman. Having lived as a widower for seven years, Rey still looks upon love and sex in a moralistic way, priding himself on his ability to count on one hand the number of occasions in which he had sex with a woman he didn't love. When he sees Conchita, however, his mind overflows with thoughts of her. Conchita leaves for Switzerland, but Rey arranges (through Conchita's mother) to have her brought back to Paris to serve as his maid. When he finally manages to get her into bed, she is dressed in such an impenetrable outfit (a chastity belt of sorts) that Rey is unable to satisfy his uncontrollable sexual urge. Conchita insists that she is a virgin, although she prances around with a boy she calls a lover. Conchita makes a habit of leaving Rey, and Rey habitually follows, until a terrorist bombing ends the film. This straightforward tale of obsessive love is colored with the always amazing Bunuelian touches. Rey's story is framed by a train trip in which he tells his fellow passengers of Conchita–a French official, a woman and her teenage daughter, and a dwarf psychologist. Also prevalent throughout the picture is a rash of bombings by a terrorist group which calls itself The Revolutionary Army of the Infant Jesus. The most fascinating aspect of THAT OBSCURE OBJECT OF DESIRE is the character of Conchita, who is exactly what the title promises. Conchita is, in fact, so obscure that Bunuel chose to cast two actresses in her role. (LAST TANGO IN PARIS star Maria Schneider was originally cast to play Conchita, by herself, but was replaced early in the shooting.) It is logical to him that since Conchita varies so much in her feelings for Rey (first she professes her love and then she leaves him) that she should vary also in her physical appearance. The most memorable sequence has Bouquet's Conchita walking into her bathroom and coming out as Molina. Rey, a Bunuel favorite (he appeared in VIRIDIANA [1961!, TRISTANA [1970!, and THE DISCREET CHARM OF THE BOURGEOISIE [1972!), perfectly portrays the perverse, tortured businessman so central to Bunuel's work. Those used to his Spanish accent, however, will be shocked to hear a Parisian one, his voice being dubbed by actor Michel Piccoli. Based on a 19th-Century novel by eroticist Pierre Louys, THAT OBSCURE OBJECT OF DESIRE has roots in a 1929 film directed by Jacques de Baroncelli entitled LA FEMME ET LE PANTIN, as well as in Josef von Sternberg's THE DEVIL IS A WOMAN (1935), and Julien Duvivier's THE FEMALE (1960). THAT OBSCURE OBJECT OF DESIRE, nominated for a Foreign Film Oscar and a Best Adapted Screenplay Oscar, is not so much a film to be understood but to be savored. (In French; English subtitles.)

p, Serge Silberman; d, Luis Bunuel; w, Bunuel, Jean-Claude Carriere (based on the novel *La Femme et la Pantin* by Pierre Louys); ph, Edmond Richard (Eastmancolor); ed, Helene Plemiannikov; art d, Pierre Guffroy.

Drama   **Cas.**   **(PR:O   MPAA:R)**

THAT OTHER WOMAN**   (1942) 75m FOX bw

Virginia Gilmore *(Emily)*, James Ellison *(Henry Summers)*, Dan Duryea *(Ralph)*, Janice Carter *(Constance Powell)*, Alma Kruger *(Grandma)*, Bud McCaleister *(George)*, Minerva Urecal *(Mrs. MacReady)*, Charles Arnt *(Bailey)*, Charles Halton *(Smith)*, Charles Trowbridge *(Linkletter)*, Frank Pershing *(Lauderback)*, George Melford *(Zineschwich)*, Paul Fix *(Tough Guy)*, Syd Saylor *(Tramp)*, Henry Roquemore *(Clerk)*, Leon Belasco *(Walter)*.

Gilmore plays a dippy secretary who devises a scheme to win the love of her boss, Ellison. She begins sending strange letters to Ellison under an assumed name, and when she introduces her frustrated fiance Duryea, Ellison mistakes him for a dangerous criminal and assumes the letters were death threats. After a series of comedic chases, Ellison realizes he loves Gilmore.

p, Walter Morosco; d, Ray McCarey; w, Jack Jungmeyer, Jr.; ph, Joseph MacDonald; ed, J. Watson Webb, Jr.; md, Cyril J. Mockridge; art d, Richard Day, Nathan Juran.

Comedy/Romance   **(PR:A   MPAA:NR)**

THAT RIVIERA TOUCH**   (1968, Brit.) 98m RANK/CD c

Eric Morecambe *(Eric)*, Ernie Wise *(Ernie)*, Suzanne Lloyd *(Claudette)*, Paul Stassino *(Le Pirate)*, Armand Mestral *(Inspector Duval)*, George Eugeniou *(Marcel)*, George Pastell *(Ali)*, Peter Jeffrey *(Mauron)*, Gerald Lawson *(Coco)*, Michael Forrest *(Pierre)*, Clive Cazes *(Renard)*, Steven Scott *(Gaston)*, Paul Danquah *(Hassim)*.

A routine comedy which was the second theatrical outing for British TV comedians Morecambe and Wise. Out for a holiday on the Riviera, the boys wind up involved with a gang of jewel thieves and infatuated with sultry gang-moll Lloyd. Eventually it dawns on Morecambe and Wise that they've been duped, and after a series of slapstick episodes involving water skis and a helicopter, the boys escape and the police capture the crooks.

p, Hugh Stewart; d, Cliff Owen; w, Sidney C. Green, Richard M. Hills, Peter Blackmore; ph, Otto Heller (Eastmancolor); m, Ron Goodwin; ed, Gerry Hambling; art d, John Blezard; set d, Arthur Taksen; cos, Anna Duse.

Comedy   **(PR:A   MPAA:NR)**

THAT SINKING FEELING***   (1979, Brit.) 82m Minor Miracle Film
                                                                          Cooperative/Samuel Goldwyn c

Robert Buchanan *(Ronnie)*, John Hughes *(Vic)*, Billy Greenlees *(Wal)*, Douglas Sannachan *(Simmy)*, Alan Love *(Alec)*, Danny Benson *(Policeman)*, Eddie Burt *(Van Driver)*, Tom Mannion *(Doctor)*, Eric Joseph *(The Wee Man)*, Janette Rankin *(Mary)*, Derek Miller *(Bobbie)*, Gordon John Sinclair *(Andy)*, Drew Burnt *(Pete)*, James Ramsey *(Alan)*, Gerry Clark *(Watchman)*, Kim Masterton, Margaret Adams *(Gang Girls)*, Margaret McTear *(Ward Nurse)*, Anne Graham *(Computer Nurse)*, David Scott *(Hi-Fi Salesman)*, Alex Mackenzie *(Tramp)*, Richard DeMarco *(Himself)*, Tony Whitemore *(Boy in Daimler)*.

Early comedy by Scottish director Bill Forsyth (GREGORY'S GIRL, LOCAL HERO) which follows the goofy exploits of a gang of unemployed youths who steal and try to sell a shipment of stainless steel sinks. Of course the boys have a bit of trouble unloading their loot, and the film details their increasingly frustrated efforts to turn a sticky situation into a profitable one. Great performances from nonprofessionals, directed with Forsyth's usual insightful wit, though some viewers may have trouble deciphering the Scottish accents.

p,d&w, Bill Forsyth; ph, Michael Coulter (Fujicolor Negative); m, Colin Tully; ed, John Gow; prod d & cos, Adrienne Atkinson.

Comedy   **Cas.**   **(PR:A   MPAA:PG)**

THAT SPLENDID NOVEMBER*   (1971, Ital./Fr.) 93m
                    Adelphia-Artistes Associes/UA c (UN BELLISSIMA NOVEMBRE)

Gina Lollobrigida *(Cettina)*, Gabriele Ferzetti *(Biagio)*, Andre Laurence *(Sasa)*, Paolo Turco *(Nino)*, Isabella Savona *(Giulietta)*, Margareta Lozano *(Amalia)*, Pasquale Fortunato *(Umberto)*, Corrado Gaipa *(Uncle Alfio)*, Ileana Rigano *(Rosario)*, Grazia di Marza *(Assunta)*, Jean Maucorps *(Mimi)*, Franco Abbinia *(Enzo)*, Ettore Ribotta *(Concetto)*, Maria di Benedetto *(Aunt Tecla)*, Vanni Castellani *(Turiddu)*, Amalia Troiani *(Aunt Maria)*, Maria Rosa Amato *(Juzza)*, Giuseppe Naso *(Uncle Nicola)*.

Another aggravating Italian sex drama that was produced in 1968, but wasn't released in the U.S. until 1971 because the stateside distributors didn't know what to do with it. The plot follows the sexual exploits of a large Sicilian family whose patriarch expounds on the virtues of self-control, but who, along with the rest of the family, runs the gamut of debauchery.

p&d, Mauro Bolognini; w, Lucia Dridi Demby, Antonio Altoviti, Ennio de Concini, Henry Vaughn (based on a novel by Ercole Patti); ph, Armando Nannuzzi (Eastmancolor); m, Ennio Morricone; ed, Roberto Perpigani; art d, Vanni Castellani; cos, Cesare Rovatti, M. Teresa Stefanelli [Gina Lollobrigida]; makeup, Mauro Gavazzi.

Drama   **(PR:C-O   MPAA:GP)**

THAT SUMMER**   (1979, Brit.) 94m COL c

Ray Winstone *(Steve)*, Tony London *(Jimmy)*, Emily Moore *(Carole)*, Julie Shipley *(Angie)*, Jon Morrison *(Tam)*, Andrew Byatt *(Georgie)*, Ewan Stewart *(Stu)*, David Daker *(Pub Landlord)*, Jo Rowbottom *(Pub Landlady)*, John Judd *(Swimming Coach)*, John Junkin *(Mr. Swales)*, Stephanie Cole *(Mrs. Mainwaring)*, Nick Donnelly *(Detective)*.

Dull British drama starring Winstone as a teenager just released from reform school who travels to a seaside resort with three friends, Shipley, Moore, and London, for a summer of fun in the sun. Unfortunately a gang of Scottish thugs arrives and causes some trouble, but eventually Winstone proves his honor and wins the girl.

p, Davina Belling, Clive Parsons; d, Harley Cokliss; w, Janey Preger (based on a story by Tony Attard); ph, David Watkin; m, Ray Russell; ed, Michael Bradsell; art d, Tim Hutchinson.

Drama   **(PR:A-C   MPAA:NR)**

THAT TENDER AGE   (SEE: ADOLESCENTS, THE, 1967, Can.)

THAT TENDER TOUCH*   (1969) 88m Artisan/World Premiere c

Sue Bernard *(Terry Manning)*, Bee Tompkins *(Marsha Prentis)*, Rick Cooper *(Ken Manning)*, Phae Dera *(Wendy Barrett)*, Margaret Read *(Dodie)*, Victoria Hale *(Jane)*, Richard St. John *(Paul Barrett)*, Tania Lemani *(Irene Barrett)*, Roger Helfond *(Jim)*, Joe Castagna *(Joe)*.

Bernard plays a young orphan who, as a reaction to an attempted rape, becomes involved in a lesbian relationship with older woman Tompkins. One day Bernard meets Cooper, as a sensitive young man who proves to her that not all men are rapists. Bernard breaks with Tompkins and marries Cooper without telling him about the affair. The women meet again at a party and Tompkins tries to revive the relationship, but Bernard will have none of it. Faced with a lonely future, Tompkins drowns herself in a swimming pool.

p,d&w, Russel Vincent; ph, Robert Caramico (Berkey-Pathe Color); m, Hans Haller; ed, Maurice Wright; m/l, Haller, David Saxon.

Drama   **(PR:O   MPAA:R)**

THAT TENNESSEE BEAT*½   (1966) 84m Lippert/FOX c (AKA: THE
                                                                          TENNESSEE BEAT)

Sharon De Bord *(Opal Nelson)*, Earl Richards *(Jim Birdsell)*, Dolores Faith *(Belle Scofield)*, Minnie Pearl *(Rev. Rose Conley)*, Merle Travis *(Larry Scofield)*, Jim Reader *(Matt Nelson)*, Cecil Scaife *(Dan Birdsell)*, Rink Hardin *(Wally Cooper)*, Lightnin' Chance *(Sheriff)*, Sam Tarpley *(Ticket Seller)*, Buddy Mize *(Hoodlum Leader)*, Ed Livingston *(Hoodlum)*, Ernest Keller *(Announcer)*, Maurice Dembsky *(Doorman)*, The Statler Brothers, Boots Randolph, Stoney Mountain Cloggers, Peter Drake *(Guest Stars)*.

Aspiring country singer Richards steals some money to pay for a trip to Nashville in the hope that he will be discovered and become a star. En route he is jumped by some hoods who take his stolen money, leaving him penniless. A friendly brother-and-sister singing team, Reader and De Bord, take Richards under their wing, reform his thieving ways, and eventually help him fulfill his dream and become a country music star.

p&d, Richard Brill; w, Paul Schneider; ph, Jack Steeley (DeLuxe Color); ed, Ace Herman, Carl Pierson; set d, Bill Gernert; md, Tommy Hill; m/l, title song, Merle Travis (sung by Travis), "I'm Sorry" Merle Travis (su ng by Earl Richards).

Drama   **(PR:A   MPAA:NR)**

THAT THEY MAY LIVE   (SEE: J'ACCUSE, 1939, Fr.)

THAT TOUCH OF MINK***½   (1962) 99m Granley-Arwin-Nob
                                                                          Hill/UNIV c

Cary Grant *(Philip Shayne)*, Doris Day *(Cathy Timberlake)*, Gig Young *(Roger)*, Audrey Meadows *(Connie)*, Alan Hewitt *(Dr. Gruber)*, John Astin *(Beasley)*, Richard Sargent *(Young Man)*, Joey Faye *(Short Man)*, John Fiedler *(Mr. Smith)*, Willard Sage *(Hodges)*, Jack Livesey *(Dr. Richardson)*, John McKee *(Collins, Chauffeur)*, Laurie Mitchell *(Showgirl)*, June Ericson *(Millie)*, Laiola Wendorff *(Mrs. Golden)*, Roger Maris *(Himself)*, Mickey Mantle *(Himself)*, Yogi Berra *(Himself)*, Art Passarella *(Umpire)*, Dorothy Abbott *(Stewardess)*, Ralph Manza *(Taxi Driver)*, William Landeau *(Leonard)*, Kathryn Givney *(Mrs. Haskell)*, Alice Backes *(Miriam)*, Richard Deacon *(Mr. Miller)*, Fred Essler *(Mr. Golden)*, Helen Brown *(Mrs. Farnum)*, Nelson Olmsted *(Mr. Hackett)*, Clegg Hoyt *(Truck Driver)*, Isabella Albonico *(Lisa)*, Billy Greene *(Al)*, Melora Conway *(Miss Farrell)*, Yvonne Peattie

(Fashion Consultant), Russ Bender *(Williams)*, Jon Silo *(Mario)*, Tyler McVey *(Doorman)*, Jan Burrell *(Miss Jones)*, Louise Arthur *(Woman)*, John Morley *(Man)*, Edna Bennett *(Mrs. Wilson)*, Sally Hughes *(Secretary)*, William Gleason *(Hotel Manager)*, Rosalind Roberts *(Stewardess)*, Cathie Merchant *(Irene)*, Barbara Collentine *(Mrs. Smith)*, Jack Rice *(Customer in Automat)*, Suzanne Barton, Bette Woods, Doris Lynn *(Models)*, George Simmons *(Bellboy)*.

A bouncy comedy from the fertile mind of Stanley Shapiro, who also contributed to PILLOW TALK and LOVER COME BACK. Shapiro and co-author Monaster have come up with a thin plot but scads of very funny dialog enhanced by Grant, Day, and Young in excellent performances. Day is out of work in New York and about to cash her unemployment check when Grant's passing limousine splashes her with mud. Grant is one of those corporate raiders who has spent his life gobbling up companies and neglecting his personal life (Humphrey Bogart did the same role in SABRINA). Day walks into the local automat (a restaurant which no longer exists in New York; it featured compartments filled with food. A person would slip the money into a slot, the glass door could then be slid up, and a salad or sandwich retrieved) and Grant sends Young, his tippling financial advisor, into the restaurant to offer Day money for her muddied dress. Day's roommate is Meadows (in an Eve Arden-like role as the wisecracker) and she and Young tell Day to give Grant what for if she is so indignant at him. Day marches into Grant's fabulous office and her wrath is soon assuaged by Grant's incomparable suavity. When Grant has to make a business trip to Maryland, he invites her to join him and she agrees. Thus begins a whirlwind journey as he takes her to Philadelphia for drinks, to the U.N. where he gives a speech, then down to Baltimore for dinner and a game between the Yankees and the Orioles. (Seen briefly are Mickey Mantle, Roger Maris, and Yogi Berra as themselves.) This cat-and-mouse game has to end eventually and it does when Grant asks the aging virgin if she'd like to go to Bermuda with him. The lady both protest at first but when Grant plies her with lavish clothing (designed by Rosemary Odell) and a full-length mink coat, Day changes her blonde mind and agrees to go to Bermuda with him. As night begins to approach, Day realizes that this is nothing out of Plato; Grant wants to take Richmond here and there and there is no getting away from it. Day breaks out in a rash and Grant has to spend the night playing cards. The romantic trip becomes a disaster. She feels awful about what's happened and wants another chance. Prior to their next date, Day begins to drink to relax herself and falls off a terrace. Grant feels that the whole affair has been a waste of time and he won't call her anymore. Day is frustrated and wants to make Grant jealous so she asks Young for his help. Young arranges a motel tryst with Astin, an unemployment clerk with a lecherous ogle in his eye. Then Young notifies Grant so he can rescue Day from this fate. Once Day is out of Astin's clutches, Grant realizes that she is the woman for him. He proposes marriage and the two of them are wed, then fly to Bermuda to consummate their union. Once they arrive at the island paradise, lifetime bachelor Grant gets so nervous about being married that he breaks out in the same skin rash Day suffered from earlier. Most of the jokes are verbal rather than slapstick and the film whips along like a Formula One car under Mann's capable direction of the Oscar-nominated script. The only problem was that 58-year-old Grant and 38-year-old Day were getting slightly too long in the tooth for this kind of "will she or won't she?" plot complication. Astin was excellent, appearing in his second movie after WEST SIDE STORY. Right after this, he teamed with Marty Ingels in his first TV series, "I'm Dickens, He's Fenster."

p, Martin Melcher, Stanley Shapiro; d, Delbert Mann; w, Shapiro, Nate Monaster; ph, Russell Metty (Panavision, Eastmancolor); m, George Duning; ed, Ted J. Kent; art d, Alexander Golitzen, Robert Clatworthy; set d, George Milo; cos, Norman Norell, Rosemary Odell; makeup, Bud Westmore.

Comedy   **Cas.**   **(PR:C   MPAA:NR)**

THAT UNCERTAIN FEELING**½   (1941) 84m UA bw

Merle Oberon *(Jill Baker)*, Melvyn Douglas *(Larry Baker)*, Burgess Meredith *(Sebastian)*, Alan Mowbray *(Dr. Vengard)*, Olive Blakeney *(Margie Stallings)*, Harry Davenport *(Attorney Jones)*, Eve Arden *(Sally)*, Sig Rumann *(Mr. Kofka)*, Richard Carle *(Butler)*, Mary Currier *(Maid)*, Jean Fenwick *(Nurse)*.

In this remake of his 1925 silent feature KISS ME AGAIN, director Lubitsch pairs Douglas and Oberon as a seemingly happily married couple. Douglas is an insurance man who loves his job and home life, not realizing that Oberon is bored to tears. Douglas is also negligent in showing Oberon some amorous attention, which subconsciously causes Oberon to hiccup in the middle of the night. After visiting a psychiatrist (Mowbray), Oberon gets to the root of her problem. As she's trying to warm up Douglas, Meredith, an eccentric piano player, moves into their home and is soon pitching woo to Oberon. Douglas discovers what's going on behind his back and the trio all end up squabbling in a lawyer's office about a divorce. This film has its moments but on the whole is rather disappointing. Lubitsch's pacing is too slow for the humor, though there are a few moments when the famed "Lubitsch Touch" stand out. One particularly enjoyable sequence has Oberon trying to trap a nonexistent woman in Douglas' hotel room. The cast certainly lends the film some charm, but overall this remake is an unsatisfying effort. Meredith enjoyed working on the production and years later recalled, "I don't know when I had a better time in my whole career

than during that period." Of Lubitsch, Meredith said, "He was very psychic. I'd fall down laughing because right away he'd improvise, in the middle of a scene he was doing for me, some very personal thing about my life, with his big cigar in his mouth, and he knew I'd come over and say, 'How did you know about that?' and he'd say, 'I have ways of knowing.' " Heymann's music earned an Oscar nomination.

p&d, Ernst Lubitsch; w, Donald Ogden Stewart, Walter Reisch (based on the play "Divorcons" by Victorien Sardou, Emile de Najac); ph, George Barnes; m, Werner Heymann; ed, William Shea; art d, Alexander Golitzen; cos, Irene.

Comedy   **(PR:A   MPAA:NR)**

THAT WAY WITH WOMEN**   (1947) 84m WB bw

Dane Clark *(Greg Wilson)*, Martha Vickers *(Marcia Alden)*, Sydney Greenstreet *(James P. Alden)*, Alan Hale *(Herman Brinker)*, Craig Stevens *(Carter Andrews)*, Barbara Brown *(Minerva Alden)*, Don McGuire *(Slade)*, John Ridgely *(Sam)*, Dick [Richard] Erdman *(Eddie)*, Herbert Anderson *(Melvyn Pfeiffer)*, Howard Freeman *(Dr. Harvey)*, Ian Wolfe *(L.B. Crandall)*, Olaf Hytten *(Davis)*, Joe Devlin *(Desk Sergeant)*, Charles Arnt *(Harry Miller)*, Suzi Crandall *(1st Party Girl)*, Janet Murdoch *(Alice Green)*, Creighton Hale *(Briggs)*, Philo McCullough *(Hawkins)*, Jack Mower *(Deacon)*, Jane Harker *(Angela)*, Monte Blue *(MacPherson)*.

Dull remake of THE MILLIONAIRE starring Greenstreet as the benevolent tycoon who has retired from the automobile business and moved on to making people happy. Despite his doctor's warnings, Greenstreet buys into a small gas station with struggling entrepreneur Clark and together the men fight off various threats, including gangsters. Between battles, Greenstreet finds time to spark a romance between Clark and Vickers. The original version of the film, made in 1931 with George Arliss in the role of the millionaire, was a big hit with depression audiences. This version was much less successful. It had been rewritten to make the young couple, rather than the millionaire, the focus of the picture, and the idea of meeting a benevolent millionaire held much less fascination for the more affluent postwar audiences.

p, Charles Hoffman; d, Frederick de Cordova; w, Leo Townsend, Francis Swann (based on a story by Earl Derr Biggers); ph, Ted McCord; m, Frederick Hollander; ed, Folmer Blangsted; md, Leo F. Forbstein; art d, Leo E. Kuter; set d, Fred M. MacLean; cos, Leah Rhodes; spec eff, William McGann, H. F. Koenekamp.

Drama   **(PR:A   MPAA:NR)**

THAT WOMAN**   (1968, Ger.) 83m Globe bw (BERLIN IST EINE SUNDE WELT)

Eva Renzi *(Alexandra Borovski)*, Harald Leipnitz *(Siegbert Lahner)*, Paul Hubschmid *(Joachim Steigenwald, Architect)*, Umberto Orsini *(Timo)*, Elga Stass *(Hildchen Volker)*, Narziss Sokatscheff *(Bogdan)*, Hans-Joachim Ketzlin *(Henry)*, Rudolf Schundler *(Doctor)*, Oestergard *(Fashion Designer)*, Ricci *(Nightclub Operator)*, Zellermayer *(Hotelier)*, Christian Doermer, Susanne Korda.

Highlypaid, much-adored fashion model Renzi wants a steady, traditional relationship with a strong, caring man, but she can't seem to find one while she bed-hops from creep to creep. She pauses with rich businessman Leipnitz, a potential candidate for marital bliss, but he too proves incompatible, so Renzi moves on to an uncertain future.

p,d&w, Will Tremper; ph, Wolfgang Luhrse; m, Peter Thomas; ed, Ursula Mohrle.

Drama   **(PR:C-O   MPAA:R)**

THAT WOMAN OPPOSITE   (SEE: CITY AFTER MIDNIGHT, 1957, Brit.)

THAT WONDERFUL URGE***   (1948) 82m FOX bw

Tyrone Power *(Thomas Jefferson Tyler)*, Gene Tierney *(Sara Farley)*, Reginald Gardiner *(Count Andre de Guyon)*, Arleen Whelan *(Jessica Woods)*, Lucile Watson *(Aunt Cornelia Farley)*, Gene Lockhart *(Judge Parker)*, Lloyd Gough *(Duffy)*, Porter Hall *(Attorney Ketchell)*, Richard Gaines *(Whitson)*, Taylor Holmes *(Attorney Rice)*, Chill Wills *(Justice of the Peace Homer Beggs)*, Hope Emerson *(Mrs. Riley, Housekeeper)*, Frank Ferguson *(Findlay)*, Charles Arnt *(Mr. Bissell)*, Francis Pierlot *(Barret)*, Joe Haworth *(Ski Patrolman)*, John Butler *(Process Server)*, Charles Woolf *(Joe the Copy Boy)*, Hal K. Dawson *(Passerby)*, Norman Phillips *(Western Union Messenger)*, Mickey Simpson, Robert Foulk *(Workmen)*, Edwin Randolph *(Waiter)*, Gertrude Michael *(Mrs. Whitson)*, Norman Leavitt *(Grocery Clerk)*, Isabel Randolph *(Mrs. Vickers)*, Forbes Murray *(Butler)*, Wilson Wood *(Court Clerk)*, Perry Ivins *(Fisher)*, Al Bridge *(Conovan)*, Robert B. [Bob] Williams *(Special Policeman)*, David Newell, Charles Tannen, Jack Gargan, Bob McCord, Don Kohler *(Reporters)*, Marjorie Wood *(Woman)*, David Thursby, Frank O'Connor *(Bailiffs)*, Eddie Parks *(Artist)*, Bess Flowers *(Party Guest)*, Harry Tyler *(Counterman)*, Percy Helton *(Drunk)*, Eula Guy *(Mrs. Beggs)*, Charles Hamilton *(Chauffeur)*, Mike Kilian *(Policeman)*.

Power's last attempt at comedy is a remake of a movie he made 12 years before, LOVE IS NEWS. The same story also served as the book for the musical SWEET ROSIE O'GRADY in 1943. Power is again the newspaper reporter who has written a series of smarmy articles about the Doris Duke-type heiress played by Gene Tierney (Loretta Young did the part in the original), who has led a life filled with incidents. Tierney accompanies her aunt, Watson, and European count Gardiner to Sun Valley, Idaho, where they are on a brief vacation. (Fox boss Darryl F. Zanuck liked Sun Valley and used it some years before as the locale for SUN VALLEY SERENADE). Since Tierney has no idea what Power looks like, he uses a false name and takes her to a cabin where he tells her that he's a local reporter who is eager to help her clear her name. If she'll tell him the truth about her life, he'll make certain that those scurrilous articles which have been written will be refuted. As Power spends time with Tierney, love happens. He leaves for New York and that's when she learns his true identity. Tierney is livid and when she returns to Manhattan, she tells the panting members of the Fourth Estate that she and Power are married and that she has given him a great deal of money. That headline hits all the newspapers except Power's, thus sending his city editor Gough into a rage. He fires Power for holding out that information and allowing all of the other papers to scoop him on the story. Power is out and the only way he can get his job back is to talk Tierney into confessing that she has told a lie. But she won't do that and says turnabout is fair play and now he knows how it feels to be on public display. Power thinks the only way he can disprove Tierney's claim of marriage is for him to actually get married. He proposes to coworker Whelan and she accepts. They get to the license bureau and are prepared to sign the necessary papers when Tierney arrives and accuses Power of bigamy. Power is in a pickle and decides to play it out all the way. There's a society party that Tierney and Gardiner are attending and Power arrives playing the role of the jealous husband. Later, Tierney says she is willing to tell Gough the truth now, rather than have more problems with Power. The two are on their way to the newspaper when Tierney gets Power embroiled in a battle with some tough teamsters. While he's trying to get out of that, Tierney eludes him. Power appeals to Gough and convinces him that the whole thing was a ruse on Tierney's part, so the editor backs Power and a libel suit is filed against Tierney. She doesn't know this when she arrives at the paper's office to tell Gough the truth. She walks in, is handed a summons, and her response to that is to allow the trial to take place. In Lockhart's court, Power is depicted as a cad. During a break, Power asks judge Lockhart if there is any way that the jurist can help this "marriage" stay put. Lockhart suggests that he consummate the union. Power races for Tierney's house, tells her that he really loves her, and their troubles dissolve in a clinch. Power was better in this version than in the original. The extra years not only added wrinkles, they added strength and courage of conviction and he played his part in a far more adult fashion. Tierney was beautiful and talented and this was her best comedy performance.

p, Fred Kohlmar; d, Robert B. Sinclair; w, Jay Dratler (based on the story "Love Is News" by William R. Lipman, Frederick Stephani); ph, Charles C. Clarke; m, Cyril J. Mockridge; ed, Louis Loeffler; md, Lionel Newman; art d, Lyle Wheeler, George Davis; set d, Thomas Little, Walter M. Scott; cos, Oleg Cassini, Fred A. Picard; spec eff, Fred Sersen; makeup, Ben Nye, Allen Snyder.

Comedy (PR:A MPAA:NR)

THAT'LL BE THE DAY*** (1974, Brit.) Goodtimes Enterprises/EMI c

David Essex *(Jim MacLaine)*, Ringo Starr *(Mike)*, Rosemary Leach *(Mrs. MacLaine)*, James Booth *(Mr. MacLaine)*, Billy Fury *(Stormy Tempest)*, Keith Moon *(J.D. Clover)*, Rosalind Ayres *(Jeanette)*, Robert Lindsay *(Terry)*, Beth Morris *(Jean)*, James Ottaway *(Granddad)*, Verna Harvey *(Wendy)*, Erin Geraghty *(Joan)*, Deborah Watling *(Sandra)*, Patti Love *(Sandra's Friend)*, Daphne Oxenford *(Mrs. Sutcliffe)*, Bernard Severn *(Sutcliffe)*, Kim Braden *(Charlotte)*, Johnny Shannon *(Jack)*, Susan Holderness, Sally Watts *(Girls in Coffee Shop)*, Karl Howman *(Johnny)*, Brenda Bruce *(Doreen)*, Alan Foss *(Teacher)*, Patsy Blower *(Young Girl at Fair)*, Sara Clee *(Girl with Baby)*, Sacha Puttnam *(Young Jim)*.

A surprisingly adept rock 'n' roll youth film set in the late 1950s starring real life rocker David Essex (his big hit was "Rock On") as an alienated, working-class youth who goes through his rights of passage. Ex-Beatle Starr is fine as Essex's buddy. Insightful, well-written and acted, THAT'LL BE THE DAY is an honest, realistic youth anthem that soon spawned a sequel, STARDUST, which is just as good.

p, Sanford Lieberson, David Puttnam; d, Claude Whatham; w, Ray Connolly (based on his story); ph, Peter Suschitzky (Technicolor); ed, Michael Bradsell; art d, Brian Morris.

Drama Cas. (PR:C MPAA:PG)

THAT'S A GOOD GIRL* (1933, Brit.) 83m British & Dominions/UA bw

Jack Buchanan *(Jack Barrow)*, Elsie Randolph *(Joy Dean)*, Dorothy Hyson *(Moya Malone)*, Garry Marsh *(Francis Moray)*, Vera Pearce *(Sunya Berata)*, William Kendall *(Timothy)*, Kate Cutler *(Helen Malone)*, Frank Stanmore *(Malone)*, Antony Holles *(Canzone)*.

Director/actor Buchanan stars in this musical comedy set in the south of

France. The plot revolves around his efforts to get himself out of the poorhouse by arranging for his cousin to marry a wealthy friend. Slight, but the perfect vehicle for the sophisticated comic antics of Buchanan who epitomized the British song-and-dance man of the era. Here he must interact with a variety of stock British characters, and enjoys the affections of an attractive woman detective played by Randolph. One gets the feeling Fred Astaire could have also handled the part nicely in a U.S. version.

p, Herbert Wilcox; d, Jack Buchanan; w, Douglas Furber, Buchanan, Donovan Pedelty (based on the play by Furber); ph, F.A. Young; cos, Eileen Idare Ltd., Norman Hartnell.

Musical/Comedy (PR:A MPAA:NR)

THAT'S GRATITUDE* (1934) 67m COL bw

Frank Craven *(Bob Grant)*, Mary Carlisle *(Dora Maxwell)*, Arthur Byron *(Thomas Maxwell)*, John Buckler *(Clayton Lorimer)*, Sheila Mannors *(Delia Maxwell)*, Charles Sabin *(William North)*, Helen Ware *(Mrs. Maxwell)*, Blythe Daley *(Nora)*, Franklin Pangborn, Johnny Sheehan.

Insipid comedy starring Craven as the leader of a musical comedy troupe. He meets wealthy man Byron in a bar and cures his illness with a drink of booze. Grateful for his new-found health, Byron invites Craven to spend some time at his mansion. When the troupe goes bust, Craven takes the man up on his offer and invades the house, quickly wearing out his welcome. Accompanied by Byron's nice-but-homely daughter Carlisle, Craven leaves the Byron house for greener pastures. Recognizing that her singing voice is marvelous, but her face leaves something to be desired, Craven takes the girl to a plastic surgeon and has her transformed into a beauty. Her career takes off, much to the delight of Craven, but then he's shocked to learn that she has abandoned him for the handsome tenor in the show. And THAT'S GRATITUDE for you.

p, Brian Foy; d&w, Frank Craven (based on his story); ph, Henry Freulich; ed, Arthur Hilton.

Musical/Comedy (PR:A MPAA:NR)

THAT'S MY BABY*½ (1944) 68m REP bw

Richard Arlen *(Tim Jones)*, Ellen Drew *(Betty Moody)*, Leonid Kinskey *(Dr. Svatzky)*, Richard Bailey *(Hilton Payne)*, Minor Watson *(R.P. Moody)*, Marjorie Manners *(Miss Wilson)*, Madeline Grey *(Hettie Moody)*, Alex Callam *(Dr. Calloway)*, P.J. Kelly *(Barber)*, Billy Benedict *(Office Boy)*, Jack Chefe *(Waiter)*, Mike Riley, Freddie Fisher, Isabelita, Gene Rodgers, Peggy and Peanuts, Frank Mitchell, Lyle Latell, Alphonse Berge, Doris Duane, Aida Kuznetzoff, Chuy Reyes, Al Mardo, Pigmeat Markham.

Strange brew of animation, live-action, seriousness, and music sees engaged couple Arlen and Drew struggling with the problem of snapping her father, Watson, out of a deep depression. "Popeye" animator Dave Fleischer created the cartoons.

p, Walter Colmes; d, William Berke; w, Nicholas Barrows, William Tunberg (based on a story by Irving Wallace); ph, Robert Pittack; ed, Robert Jahns; , md, Jay Chernis; art d, Frank Dexter.

Drama (PR:A MPAA:NR)

THAT'S MY BOY*½ (1932) 71m COL bw

Richard Cromwell *(Tommy)*, Dorothy Jordan *(Dorothy)*, Mae Marsh *(Mom)*, Arthur Stone *(Pop)*, Douglas Dumbrille *(Adams)*, Lucien Littlefield *(Uncle Louie)*, Leon Waycoff [Ames] *(Al Williams)*, Russell Saunders *(Pinkie)*, Sumner Getchell *(Carl)*, Otis Harlan *(Mayor)*, Dutch Hendrian *(Hap)*, Elbridge Anderson *(1st Student)*, Crilly Butler *(2nd Student)*, Douglas Haig *(Tommy as a Boy)*.

Typical college football yarn starring Cromwell as a studious and honest young student working his way through school while becoming the star player on the football team. Since actor Cromwell was no giant, the script shows the lightweight proving his pigskin prowess by hot-footing it all over the field. To make some extra money, Cromwell foolishly becomes involved in a phoney stock-selling scheme that threatens to destroy his career. Luckily the kid wises up and pays back every dime he inadvertently bilked out of hapless investors before going on to win the big game in the inevitable "final minutes."

d, Roy William Neill; w, Norman Krasna (based on the novel by Francis Wallace); ph, Joseph August; ed, Jack Dennis; cos, Robert Kalloch.

Drama (PR:A MPAA:NR)

THAT'S MY BOY** (1951) 98m PAR bw

Dean Martin *(Bill Baker)*, Jerry Lewis *("Junior" Jackson)*, Ruth Hussey *(Ann Jackson)*, Eddie Mayehoff *("Jarring Jack" Jackson)*, Marion Marshall *(Terry Howard)*, Polly Bergen *(Betty Hunter)*, Hugh Sanders *(Coach Wheeler)*, John McIntire *(Benjamin Green, Psychiatrist)*, Francis Pierlot *(Henry Baker)*, Lillian Randolph *(May, Maid)*, Selmer Jackson *(Doc Hunter)*, Tom Harmon *(Sports Announcer)*.

The genuine laughs are few and far between in this ho-hum Martin and

Lewis comedy which sees the boys involved in college football antics. Lewis plays the nebbish son of wealthy college alumnus Mayehoff who pushes his talentless son into playing football for his old team Ridgeville. Realizing that Lewis needs some special training to avoid being slaughtered, Mayehoff hires high school pigskin star and Lewis teammate Martin for the tutoring. Lewis, of course, goes through the usual spastic struggles until finally, during the proverbial final minutes of the season's big game, he is confident enough to go out and win the battle for Ridgeville. The usual spattering of songs was kept to a minimum.

p, Hal B. Wallis; d, Hal Walker; w, Cy Howard (based on his story); ph, Lee Garmes; m, Leigh Harline; ed, Warren Low; art d, Hal Pereira, Franz Bachelin; cos, Edith Head; m/l, "I'm in the Mood for Love" Jimmy McHugh, Dorothy Fields (sung by Dean Martin), "Ridgeville Fight Song" Jay Livingston, Ray Evans, "Ballin' the Jack" Chris Smith, Jim Burris.

Comedy (PR:A MPAA:NR)

THAT'S MY GAL*½ (1947) 66m REP c

Lynne Roberts (Natalie Adams), Donald Barry (Benny Novak), Pinky Lee (Harry Coleman), Frank Jenks (Louie Koblentz), Edward Gargan (Mike), Judy Clark (Helen McBride), Paul Stanton (Governor Thompson), John Hamilton (Assemblyman McBride), Ray Walker (Danny Malone), Marian Martin (Pepper), Elmer Jerome (Joshua Perkins), George Carleton (Judge), Jan Savitt and His Top Hatters, Isabelita, Guadalajara Trio, Four Step Brothers, St. Clair & Vilova, Dolores & Don Graham.

Lame musical which sees a gang of clever swindlers raise a bunch of money from a group of foolish investors. It seems the investors are infatuated with show biz and so agree to back a stinko musical revue that will most certainly bomb, leaving the crooks with a nice wad of dough. Unfortunately for them, one of the investors dies and his estate's executrix, Roberts, makes sure the show will be a hit. Songs include: "That's My Girl," "The Music in My Heart Is You," "Take It Away" (Jack Elliott), "For You and Me," "Sentimental," "Hitchhike to Happiness" (Kim Gannon, Walter Kent), and "720 in the Books" (Jan Savitt).

p, Armand Schaefer; d, George Blair; w, Joseph Hoffman (based on a story by Frances Hyland, Bernard Feins); ph, Bud Thackery (Trucolor); ed, Arthur Roberts; md, Morton Scott; art d, Frank Arrigo.

Musical (PR:A MPAA:NR)

THAT'S MY MAN (1947) 104m REP bw

Don Ameche (Joe Grange), Catherine McLeod (Ronnie), Roscoe Karns (Toby Gleeton), John Ridgely (Ramsey), Kitty Irish (Kitty), Joe Frisco (Willie Wagonstatter), Gregory Marshall (Richard), Dorothy Adams (Millie), Frankie Darro (Jockey), Hampton J. Scott (Sam), John Miljan (Secretary), William B. Davidson (Monte), Joe Hernandez (Race Track Announcer), Gallant Man the Horse.

Ameche plays a professional gambler who lets his obsession nearly ruin his life. Seeing a chance to make some big dough, Ameche buys a sickly colt, nurses it back to health, and then trains it until it promises to win big at the track. Placing a small fortune on the horse's head, Ameche wins a bundle, but the money doesn't please his wife, McLeod, who feels her husband has ignored his family duties. She leaves him, and his gambling luck ends. In the end he is left with nothing but his horse. Seeking to win just one more big bet, Ameche takes the nag out of retirement and runs him. The horse wins, Ameche is back on his feet financially, and he forsakes gambling to the delight of McLeod, who returns to him.

p&d, Frank Borzage; w, Steve Fisher, Bradley King (based on their story); ph, Tony Gaudio; m, Hans J. Salter; ed, Richard L. Van Enger; md, Cy Fever; art d, James Sullivan, Frank Arrigo; set d, John McCarthy, Jr.; spec eff, Howard Lydecker, Theodore Lydecker.

Drama (PR:A MPAA:NR)

THAT'S MY STORY* (1937) 62m UNIV bw

Claudia Morgan (Janet Marlowe), William Lundigan (Fields), Eddie Garr (Jenks), Hobart Cavanaugh (Sheriff Otis), Ralph Morgan (Carter), Bernadene Hayes (Bonnie Rand), Charles Wilson (Cummings), Harlan Briggs (Sheriff Allen), Edward Gargan (John), Charles Trowbridge (Martin), Murray Alper (Blackie), Jerry Mandy (Eddie).

Another dim-witted newspaper story sees Lundigan as a hot-dog newshound on thin ice with his editor when he decides to get an exclusive interview with a prominent gangster's moll by getting himself thrown in jail with her. He succeeds and begins the interview, but quickly learns that the woman he is interviewing, Morgan, is also a reporter who had pulled the same stunt he did. Of course, they fall in love.

p, Robert Presnell; d, Sidney Salkow; w, Barry Trivers (based on the story "Scoop" by Van Terrys Perlman); ph, Elwood Bredell; ed, Maurice Wright.

Drama (PR:A MPAA:NR)

THAT'S MY UNCLE* (1935, Brit.) 58m Twickenham/UNIV bw

Mark Daly (Walter Frisbee), Richard Cooper (Arthur Twindle), Betty Astell (Maudie), Margaret Yarde (Mrs. Frisbee), Michael Shepley (Charlie Cookson), Wally Patch (Splinty Woods), David Horne (Col. Marlowe), Hope Davy (Betty Marlowe), Ralph Truman (Monty), Colin Lesslie, Gladys Hamer.

Daly is a moralistic chap who stumbles through life with a wife who relentlessly henpecks him. His life takes an exciting turn when a gang of crooks plant a stolen wallet on him and then try to get it back. The job becomes a challenge for the crooks when Daly takes a job as a butler. Not very funny and overlong at 58 minutes.

p, Julius Hagen; d, George Pearson; w, Michael Barringer (based on the play "The Iron Woman" by Frederick Jackson).

Comedy (PR:A MPAA:NR)

THAT'S MY WIFE½** (1933, Brit.) 67m BL bw

Claud Allister (Archie Trevor), Frank Pettingell (Josiah Crump), Betty Astell (Lillian Harbottle), Davy Burnaby (Maj. Harbottle), Helga Moray (Queenie Sleeman), Hal Walters (Bertie Griggs), Thomas Weguelin (Mr. Sleeman), Jack Vyvyan (Sam Griggs), John Morley.

Allister plays the nephew of a rich Yorkshire manufacturer, Pettingell, and saves the manufacturer's hide from scandal after he flirts with the wife of a crotchety major. Pettingell mistakenly believes Allister to be a lawyer when actually he is the manager of a beauty parlor. These mixups lead to Pettingell and Allister reaping financial benefits from a successful invention. Bright comedy richly performed by all hands.

p, Herbert Smith; d, Leslie Hiscott; w, Michael Barringer (based on a story by William C. Stone).

Comedy (PR:A MPAA:NR)

THAT'S RIGHT--YOU'RE WRONG** (1939) 91m RKO bw

Kay Kyser (Kay), Adolphe Menjou (Stacey Delmore), May Robson (Grandma), Lucille Ball (Sandra Sand), Dennis O'Keefe (Chuck Deems), Edward Everett Horton (Tom Village), Roscoe Karns (Mal Stamp), Moroni Olsen (J.D. Forbes), Hobart Cavanaugh (Dwight Cook), Ginny Simms (Ginny), Harry Babbitt (Harry), Sully Mason (Sully), Ish Kabibble (Ish), Dorothy Lovett (Miss Cosgrave), Lillian West (Miss Brighton), Denis Tankard (Thomas), Fred Othman, Erskine Johnson, Sheilah Graham, Hedda Hopper, Jimmy Starr, Feg Murray (Themselves), Stephen Chase, Forbes Murray, Vinton Haworth (Producers), Charles Judels (Luigi, the Makeup Man), Horace McMahon, Elliott Sullivan (Hoods), Kathryn Adams (Elizabeth), Jane Goude, Effie Parnell, Charles Doehrer, Kay Kyser's Band.

The first in a series of films featuring popular radio band leader Kay Kyser and his band. The thin plot sees the boys travel to Hollywood to be in their first movie (life imitating art? or vice versa?) and becoming quickly frustrated when bumbling screenwriters Horton and Cavanaugh can't think of a thing to put them in. Things look grim for the band until starlet Ball falls in love with band manager O'Keefe and insists that the band be included in her next movie. Yes, and it's a big hit. Songs include: "I'm Fit to Be Tied" (Walter Donaldson), "Scatterbrain" (Johnny Burke, Frankie Masters, Kahn Keene, Carl Bean), "Little Red Fox" (James Kern, Hy Heath, Johnny Lange, Lew Porter), "The Answer Is Love" (Charles Newman, Sammy Stept), "Chatterbox" (Jerome Brainin, Allan Roberts; sung by Ginny Simms, Harry Babbitt), "Happy Birthday to Love" (Dave Franklin).

p&d, David Butler; w, William Conselman, James V. Kern (based on a story by Butler, Conselman); ph, Russell Metty; ed, Irene Morra; art d, Van Nest Polglase; cos, Edward Stevenson; spec eff, Vernon L. Walker.

Musical (PR:A MPAA:NR)

THAT'S THE SPIRIT½** (1945) 93m UNIV bw

Peggy Ryan (Sheila), Jack Oakie (Steve), June Vincent (Libby), Gene Lockhart (Jasper, Banker), Johnny Coy (Martin, Jr.), Andy Devine (Martin, Theater Manager), Arthur Treacher (Masters, Butler), Irene Ryan (Bilson, Maid), Buster Keaton (L.M.), Victoria Horne (Patience), Edith Barrett (Abigail).

A slightly goofy musical which stars Oakie as a hoofer, dead for nearly 18 years, who returns to Earth as an angel to help his young daughter, Peggy Ryan, fulfill her ambition to become a singer, despite the protestations of her grandfather, Lockhart, who doesn't want to see another entertainer in the family. Buster Keaton has a cameo as the guy who handles complaints in Heaven. Songs include: "Oh, Oh, Oh," "Fellow with a Flute" (Inez James, Sidney Miller), "Evenin' Star," "No Matter Where You Are" (Jack Brooks, Hans J. Salter), "Nola" (Felix Arndt), "How Come You Do Me Like You Do?" (Roy Bergere, Gene Austin; sung by Johnny Coy), "Baby, Won't You Please Come Home?" (Clarence Williams, Charles Warfield; sung by Irene Ryan), "Bugle Call Rag" (J. Hubert Blake, Carey Morgan), "Ja-Da" (Bob Carleton), "Do You Ever Think of Me?" (Earl Burnett, John Cooper, Harry D. Kerr).

p, Michael Fessier, Ernest Pagano; d, Charles Lamont; w, Fessier, Pagano; ph, Charles Van Enger; ed, Fred R. Feitshans, Jr.; md, Hans J. Salter; art d, John B. Goodman, Richard H. Reidel; cos, Vera West; spec eff, John P. Fulton; ch, Carlos Romero.

Musical/Comedy   **(PR:A   MPAA:NR)**

THAT'S THE TICKET*½   (1940, Brit.) 63m WB bw

Sid Field (*Ben Baker*), Hal Walters (*Nosey*), Betty Lynne (*Fifi*), Gus McNaughton (*Milkbar Monty*), Gordon McLeod (*Ferdinand*), Charles Castella (*The Bull*), Gibb McLaughlin (*The Count*), Ian Maclean (*Hercule*), Ernest Sefton (*Marchand*).

Field and Walters play two drifters who bounce from one job to another. One fateful night they happen to land jobs in the hatcheck room of a posh nightclub and wind up with valuable wartime blueprints that were hidden in a top hat by spies. A chase for the goods ensues which sees the boys slapsticking their way to the conclusion where the papers arrive in safe hands.

p, A.M. Salomon; d, Redd Davis; w, Jack Henley, John Dighton, Frank Richardson; ph, Basil Emmott.

Comedy   **(PR:A   MPAA:NR)**

THAT'S THE WAY OF THE WORLD**
                  (1975) 100m UA-Marvin c (AKA: SHINING STAR)

Harvey Keitel (*Coleman Buckmaster*), Ed Nelson (*Carlton James*), Cynthia Bostick (*Velour Page*), Bert Parks (*Franklyn Page*), Jimmy Boyd (*Gary Page*), Michael Dante (*Mike Lemongello*), Maurice White (*Early*), Ron Gorton (*Warren*), Valerie Shepherd (*Ellen*), Herb Towner (*Player*), Francesca Di Sapio (*Amanda*), Charles MacGregor (*Mantan*), Fred Versacci (*Ferrara*), Murray Moston (*Buck's Father*), Mike Richards (*Norman*), Chuck Stepney (*Johnny*), Linda Fields (*Annabel*), Nick La Padula (*Al*), Steve Shore (*The Kid*), Murray the "K" (*Big John*), Vi Higgenson (*Wonder Woman*), Frankie Crocker (*Himself*), Dick Stewart (*Mel*), Ramon Feliciano (*Busboy*), Aubrey De Souza (*Chauffeur*), Jerry Rush (*TV Interviewer*), John Powers (*The Greek*), Leonard Smith (*Bouncer*), John Haney (*Engineer*), Doris Troy (*Pianist*), Barbara Engel (*Secretary*), Andrew Blau (*TV Director*), Earth, Wind and Fire.

Badly produced expose of the music industry which stars Keitel as an ambitious young record executive who sees a black-oriented band (played by the members of Earth, Wind and Fire) as the next big thing and tries to promote them, but is quashed by the mobster types who run the company. The powerbrokers would rather see Keitel put his energies behind an insipid all-white family group featuring Parks, Bostick, and Boyd, so they force him to do so. While the subject matter regarding the wholesale packaging of homogenized music is important and topical, the film is very low budget and hardly survives its sloppy presentation.

p&d, Sig Shore; w, Robert Lipsyte (based on his story); ph, Alan Metzger (Movielab Color); m, Maurice White, Earth, Wind and Fire; ed, Bruce Wittkin.

Drama   **Cas.**   **(PR:C   MPAA:PG)**

THEATRE OF BLOOD***   (1973, Brit.) 104m UA c

Vincent Price (*Edward Lionheart*), Diana Rigg (*Edwina Lionheart*), Ian Hendry (*Peregrine Devlin*), Harry Andrews (*Trevor Dickman*), Coral Browne (*Miss Chloe Moon*), Robert Coote (*Oliver Larding*), Jack Hawkins (*Solomon Psaltery*), Michael Hordern (*George Maxwell*), Arthur Lowe (*Horace Sprout*), Robert Morley (*Meredith Merridew*), Dennis Price (*Hector Snipe*), Diana Dors (*Mrs. Psaltery*), Joan Hickson (*Mrs. Sprout*), Renee Asherson (*Mrs. Maxwell*), Madeline Smith (*Rosemary*), Milo O'Shea (*Inspector Boot*), Eric Sykes (*Sgt. Dogge*), Brigid Eric Bates (*Agnes*), Tony Calvin (*Police Photographer*), Bunny Reed, Peter Thornton (*Policemen*), Tutte Lemkow, Jack Maguire, Joyce Graeme, John Gilpin, Eric Francis, Sally Gilmore, Stanley Bates, Declan Mulholland (*Meths Drinkers*).

Hysterically funny, at times sick, but always entertaining black comedy starring Price as an aging Shakespearean actor who goes off the deep end when eight British critics prevent him from being voted Best Actor of the Year. Seeking revenge, the now-insane thespian, aided by his lovely and equally mad daughter Rigg, sets about killing the eight critics in eight different, diabolical ways derived from Shakespeare's plays. Deaths include: the pound-of-flesh trick; drowning in wine; force-feeding of two ground-up pet poodles; a spear through the chest; being dragged by a horse; etc. While a bit grotesque at times, THEATRE OF BLOOD is presented with a charming tongue-in-cheek sensibility that really makes all the carnage entertaining. Price obviously relishes his role.

p, John Kohn, Stanley Mann; d, Douglas Hickox; w, Anthony Greville-Bell; ph, Wolfgang Suschitzky (DeLuxe Color); m, Michael J. Lewis; ed, Malcolm Cooke; prod d, Michael Seymour; set d, Ann Mollo; cos, Michael Baldwin; spec eff, John Stearns; ch, Tutte Lemkow; stunts, Terry York.

Horror   **Cas.**   **(PR:O   MPAA:R)**

THEATRE OF DEATH**   (1967, Brit.) 91m Pennea/Hemisphere c
                                                              (AKA: BLOOD FIEND)

Christopher Lee (*Philippe Darvas*), Lelia Goldoni (*Dani Cirreaux*), Julian Glover (*Charles Marquis*), Evelyn Laye (*Mme. Angele*), Jenny Till (*Nicole Chapel*), Ivor Dean (*Inspector Michaeud*).

Lee stars as a mysterious, supposedly violent operator of a Grand Guignol playhouse in Paris who is suspected of murdering a number of people in a vampire-like manner. A decent thriller which also provides a good look at the little-seen workings of a Grand Guignol theater.

p, Michael Smedley-Astin, William Gell; d, Samuel Gallu; w, Ellis Kadison, Roger Marshall (based on a story by Kadison); ph, Gilbert Taylor (Techniscope, Technicolor).

Horror   **Cas.**   **(PR:C-O   MPAA:NR)**

THEATRE ROYAL, 1930 (SEE: ROYAL FAMILIES OF BROADWAY,
                                                                     THE, 1930)

THEATRE ROYAL***   (1943, Brit.) 101m BN/Anglo-American bw

Bud Flanagan (*Bob Parker*), Chesney Allen (*Gordon Maxwell*), Peggy Dexter (*Connie Webster*), Lydia Sherwood (*Claudia Brent*), Horace Kenney (*George*), Marjorie Rhodes (*Agnes*), Finlay Currie (*Clement J. Earle*), Owen Reynolds (*Harding*), Maire O'Neill (*Mrs. Cope*), Gwen Catley (*Singer*), Buddy Flanagan (*Callboy*), Jack Melford, Charles Mortimer, Ben Williams, Jimmy Skidmore, Ted Heath, George Shearing (*Themselves*), Jiver Hutchinson, Victor Feldman and His Orchestra.

Flanagan, the prop man at the financially strapped Theatre Royal, organizes some entertainers from among the talented staff for a big revue to save the theater from being sold out to a rival. The show is such a success in rehearsals that solid backing is won and Allen, the owner of the theater, offers Flanagan a partnership.

p&d, John Baxter; w, Bud Flanagan, Austin Melford, Geoffrey Orme; ph, Jimmy Wilson.

Comedy   **(PR:A   MPAA:NR)**

THEIR BIG MOMENT*½   (1934) 68m RKO bw (GB: AFTERWARDS)

ZaSu Pitts (*Tillie Whim*), Slim Summerville (*Bill*), Julie Haydon (*Mrs. Fay Harley*), Ralph Morgan (*Dr. Portman*), William Gaxton (*La Salle, Magician*), Bruce Cabot (*Lane Franklyn*), Kay Johnson (*Mrs. Eve Farrington*), Tamara Geva (*Mme. Lottie Marvo*), J. Huntley Gordon (*John Farrington*), Edward Brady.

Silly, badly directed comedy thriller starring Pitts and Summerville as assistants to stage magician Gaxton. One day Gaxton's medium quits, so when an important gig comes up the magician drafts Pitts into service as his new psychic. The job takes the trio to a spooky house where the sister of a rich widow is trying to break the hold a bogus doctor has on her sibling. The obsessed sister believes that her late husband is contacting her from the grave. Pitts performs a seance, and to everyone's surprise, she *does* possess psychic powers that tell her that the woman's husband didn't die in an accident. The intrepid trio then dig out enough evidence to uncover the scheme and prove that the doctor was trying to bilk the woman out of her fortune.

d, James Cruze; w, Arthur Caesar, Marion Dix (based on a story by Walter Hackett); ph, Harold Wenstrom; ed, William Hamilton.

Mystery/Comedy   **(PR:A   MPAA:NR)**

THEIR NIGHT OUT**   (1933, Brit.) 74m BI/Wardour bw

Claude Hulbert (*Jimmy Oliphant*), Renee Houston (*Maggie Oliphant*), Gus McNaughton (*Fred Simpson*), Binnie Barnes (*Lola*), Jimmy Godden (*Archibald Bunting*), Amy Veness (*Gertrude Bunting*), Judy Kelly (*Betty Oliphant*), Ben Welden (*Crook*), Hal Gordon (*Sgt. Bert Simpson*), Marie Ault (*Cook*).

A comedy about Hulbert, a junior partner of a business firm, who takes Houston, a Scottish buyer, out to dinner and they both get comically drunk. Hulbert gets his wallet lifted, is mistaken for a jewel thief, and before long is mixed up in a web of criminal violence.

p,d&w, Harry Hughes (based on a play by George Arthurs, Arthur Miller); ph, Walter Harvey.

Comedy   **(PR:A   MPAA:NR)**

THEIR OWN DESIRE**½   (1929) 65m MGM bw

Norma Shearer (*Lally*), Belle Bennett (*Harriet Marlett*), Lewis Stone (*Mr. Marlett*), Robert Montgomery (*Jack*), Helen Millard (*Beth*), Cecil Cunningham (*Aunt Caroline*), Henry Herbert (*Uncle Nate*), Mary Doran (*Susan*), June Nash (*Mildred*).

Shearer is a young woman whose novelist father, Stone, is having an affair with another woman, Millard. She decides to take her mother, Bennett, on a vacation and they travel to a resort. There Shearer meets Montgomery and the two fall in love. They make wedding plans, then Shearer discovers that Montgomery's mother is the very woman with whom her father is having an affair. She calls off the marriage and the pair decide to take a final farewell boat ride. A storm comes up suddenly and the boat is missing. Stone and Millard join in the search and after the young lovers are found the old lovers decide for the good of all concerned to call off their relationship. Stone returns to Bennett and Shearer and Montgomery are free to marry. Not a very interesting film nowadays, despite Shearer at her loveliest moving through an awesome string of silk pajamas, swimsuits, polo outfits, and evening gowns. Shearer had become one of the first silent stars to make a hit in talkies with her performances in THE TRIAL OF MARY DUGAN and THE LAST OF MRS. CHEYNEY (both 1929), but this overblown melodrama nearly dropped her back into the ranks. Montgomery's career, however, got a big boost from being paired with Shearer and he went on to become one of the most reliable leading men in Hollywood during the 1930s and 1940s.

d, E. Mason Hopper; w, James Grant Forbes (based on the novel by Sarita Fuller); ph, William Daniels; m, Fred Fisher, Reggie Montgomery, George Ward; ed, Harry Reynolds; art d, Cedric Gibbons; cos, Adrian; m/l, "Blue Is the Night," Fisher.

Drama   **(PR:A MPAA:NR)**

THEIR SECRET AFFAIR   (SEE: TOP SECRET AFFAIR, 1957)

THELMA JORDAN   (SEE: FILE ON THELMA JORDAN, THE, 1950)

THEM!*½   (1954) 93m WB bw

James Whitmore (Sgt. Ben Peterson), Edmund Gwenn (Dr. Harold Medford), Joan Weldon (Dr. Patricia Medford), James Arness (Robert Graham), Onslow Stevens (Brig. Gen. O'Brien), Sean McClory (Maj. Kibbee), Chris Drake (Officer Ed Blackburn), Sandy Descher (Little Girl), Mary Ann Hokanson (Mrs. Lodge), Don Shelton (Captain of Troopers), Fess Parker (Crotty), Olin Howlin (Jensen), William Schallert (Ambulance Attendant), Leonard Nimoy (Sergeant), Dub Taylor (Watchman), Ann Doran (Psychiatrist), Frederick J. Foote (Dixon), Robert Scott Correll (Jerry), Richard Bellis (Mike), Joel Smith (Ben's Driver), Cliff Ferre (Lab Man), Matthew McCue (Gramps), Joe Forte (Coroner Putnam), Wally Duffy (Airman), Fred Shellac (Attendant), Norman Field (General), Otis Garth (Admiral), John Maxwell (Dr. Grant), Janet Stewart (WAVE), Dick Wessel (Cop), Russell Gage (Coroner), Robert Berger (Sutton), John Beradino (Ryan), Dorothy Green (Matron), Dean Cromer (M.P. Sergeant), Lawrence Dobkin (Engineer), Chad Mallory (Loader), Gayle Kellogg (Gunner), Victor Sutherland (Senator), Charles Perry (Soldier), Warren Mace (Radio Operator), Jack Perrin (Army Officer), John Close (Pilot's Voice), Marshall Bradford, Waldron Boyle (Doctors), Willis Bouchey, Alexander Campbell (Officials), Harry Tyler, Oscar Blanke (Inmates), Eddie Dew, James Cardwell (Officers), Walter Coy, Booth Colman (Reporters), Hubert Kerns, Royden Clark (Jeep Drivers), Charles Meredith, Richard Deacon.

The best of the giant monster movies that sprang up during the 1950s which all had their roots in the concerns that arose from the advent of the nuclear age. Whitmore and Drake, two New Mexico state troopers patrolling the desert, happen across a trailer home that has been opened like a sardine can and gutted. Inside is a little girl who is nearly catatonic from fear. All she can utter is the word, "Them!" As the mystery deepens, FBI man Arness, scientist Gwenn and his daughter Weldon (a scientist in her own right), are called in to help in the investigation. Eventually they learn that secret atomic testing in the area had sent deadly radiation into the ground and spawned a giant colony of ants that have grown to nearly 20 feet long. Realizing that if the queen is able to mate, the world may be overrun by the giant creatures, Whitmore and company hurriedly work to locate the nest and destroy it. They trace the creatures to the Los Angeles drainage system (perhaps the best use of an overly photographed location, and armed with large flame-throwers, the humans succeed in destroying the monstrous ants, but not before Whitmore makes the ultimate sacrifice. Though the description sounds silly and a bit camp, THEM! pulls it off quite convincingly. The giant ants do look a bit phony, but they are never on screen long enough to become bothersome. In fact, the image of dozens of giant ants sitting in their underground nest is unforgettable. There was no stop-motion animation used in THEM!. Instead, two actual-sized models were constructed by prop man Dick Smith (one entire ant, and another front section for closeups). Special effects supervisor Ayers was nominated for an Academy Award for his work on the film. The film is produced and performed with such seriousness that one becomes engrossed in the machinations of dealing with such creatures and forgets about plausibility. THEM! was a smash at the box office (it was Warner Brothers' highest grossing film of 1954) and inspired countless imitations, all of which were inferior to the original.

p, David Weishart; d, Gordon Douglas; w, Ted Sherdeman, Russell Hughes; (based on a story by George Worthing Yates); ph, Sid Hickox; m, Bronislau Kaper; ed, Thomas Reilly; md, Ray Heindorf; art d, Stanley Fleischer; set d, G.W. Bernstein; cos, Edith Head; spec eff, Ralph Ayres, William Mueller, Francis J. Scheid; makeup, Gordon Bau.

Science Fiction   **Cas.**   **(PR:C MPAA:NR)**

THEM NICE AMERICANS**   (1958, Brit.) 62m Chelsea/BUT bw

Bonar Colleano (Joe), Vera Day (Ann Adams), Renee Houston (Mrs. Adams), Sheldon Lawrence (Johnny), Basil Dignam (Inspector Adams), Patti Morgan (Lady Theodora), Michael Wade (Billy Adams), Ryck Ryden (Butch), Gilbert Winfield (Captain), Ron Gilliland, Ronald Brand, Bill Edwards, Robert Edwards, Chuck Keyser, John Evans, John Stacy, Jan Kent, Marian Collins, Anthony Wilson, Denis Gilmore.

Lawrence, an American soldier, falls in love with Day. Her father (Dignam) hates Yanks and opposes his daughter's affair. Colleano, as Lawrence's best friend, tries to improve relations between the two men but it is only when Day's little brother wanders into a minefield and Lawrence rescues him that the crusty old dad allows the relationship to continue. Okay comedy with slightly more appeal for Americans than the usual British offering of this type.

p, Anthony Young, Richard Griffith; d, Young; w, Gilbert Winfield; ph, Ernie Palmer.

Comedy   **(PR:A MPAA:NR)**

THEN THERE WERE THREE*½   (1961) 74m Alexandra/Parade bw

Frank Latimore (Lt. Willotsky), Alex Nicol (Sam McLease), Barry Cahill (Sgt. Travers), Sidney Clute (Ben Harvey), Frank Gregory (Harry Miller), Michael Billingsley (T.I. Ellis), Frederick R. Clark (Calhoun), Paola Falchi (Giovanna), Brendan Fitzgerald, Gerard Herter, Kurt Polter, Richard Bull.

Dull WW II drama which sees six GIs who have become separated from their outfits in Italy join together to find their way to safety. Along the way they pick up Nicol (also the producer/director), who unbeknownst to them, is actually a Nazi spy with orders to kill a prominent underground leader. The soldiers are picked off one by one as a result of Nicol's evildoing and eventually only four reach the resistance fighters. Nicol captures the leader of the partisans, but he is foiled by the three remaining GIs and forced to run toward the German troops, who mistake him for an American and gun him down.

p&d, Alex Nicol; w, Frank Gregory, Allan Lurie (based on a story by Lurie); ph, Gastone Di Giovanni; m, Tarcisio Fusco; ed, Manuel Del Campo.

War   **(PR:A-C MPAA:NR)**

THEODORA GOES WILD**½   (1936) 94m COL bw

Irene Dunne (Theodora Lynn), Melvyn Douglas (Michael Grant), Thomas Mitchell (Jed Waterbury), Thurston Hall (Arthur Stevenson), Rosalind Keith (Adelaide Perry), Spring Byington (Rebecca Perry), Elizabeth Risdon (Aunt Mary), Margaret McWade (Aunt Elsie), Nana Bryant (Ethel Stevenson), Henry Kolker (Jonathan Grant), Leona Maricle (Agnes Grant), Robert Greig (Uncle John), Frederick Burton (Gov. Wyatt), Mary Forbes (Mrs. Wyatt), Grace Hayle (Mrs. Cobb), Sarah Edwards (Mrs. Moffat), Mary MacLaren (Mrs. Wilson), Wilfred Hari (Toki), Laura Treadwell (Mrs. Grant), Corbet Morris (Artist), Ben F. Hendricks (Taxi Driver), Frank Sully (Clarence), James T. Mack (Minister), William "Billy" Benedict (Henry), Carolyn Lee Bourland (Baby), Paul Barrett (Adelaide's Husband), Leora Thatcher (Miss Baldwin), Billy Wayne, Harold Goodwin, Jack Hatfield (Photographers), Harry Harvey, Don Brodie, Eddie Fetherstone, Ed Hart, Lee Phelps, Sherry Hall, Ralph Malone, Beatrice Curtis (Reporters), Maurice Brierre (Waiter), Sven Borg (Bartender), Dennis O'Keefe (Man), Rex Moore (Newsboy), Georgia Cooper, Jane Keckley, Jessie Perry, Noel Bates, Betty Farrington, Stella Adams, Isabelle LaMal, Georgia O'Dell, Dorothy Vernon (Women).

Dunne's first starring comedy role after several weepers was good enough to secure her an Oscar nomination, her second after the 1931 CIMARRON. Dunne is a New England woman who writes a steamy best seller about the morals of a sleepy little town that lies north of New York. The book takes off and she decides to see the big city for herself. Once she arrives in Manhattan she meets Douglas, the ultra-sophisticated artist who did the illustrations for her book. Her escapades begin, as she is the proverbial "fish out of water" in New York. The nature of the quaint and hard-bitten Yankees from her village is examined vis-a-vis the sharp Big Apple types and the conclusion drawn is that there are nuts in both places. The idea was to produce a screwball comedy on the style of some of Capra's Columbia pictures, but this movie had the wrong Riskin (Everett, rather than Capra's long-time associate-screenwriter, Robert Riskin) and it just wasn't wacky enough, despite a valiant try by Dunne to breathe life into Buchman's pedestrian script. Director Boleslawski, the Polish stage director who cut his teeth with the Moscow Arts Theatre, made a few better movies than this, most notably CLIVE OF INDIA, THE PAINTED VEIL, and LES MISERABLES, which he directed in succession in 1934-35. Buchman followed this movie by writing MR. SMITH GOES TO WASHINGTON for Capra (and getting an Oscar nomination), then winning the coveted statue for his screenplay of HERE COMES MR. JORDAN. In this film, there are all the predictable situations with the foregone results. The story of a writer who exposed small town life was done again later in SITTING PRETTY and was actually done by author Grace Metalious when she wrote the enormous hit known as PEYTON PLACE. Both films are better than this one.

p, Everett Riskin; d, Richard Boleslawski; w, Sidney Buchman (based on a story by Mary E. McCarthy); ph, Joseph Walker; m, Morris Stoloff; ed, Otto Meyer; md, Stoloff; art d, Stephen Goosson; cos, Bernard Newman.

Comedy   **(PR:A MPAA:NR)**

THEOREM   (SEE: TEOREMA, 1968, Ital.)

THERE AIN'T NO JUSTICE*   (1939, Brit.) 83m Ealing-CAPAD/ABF
                                                                                                              bw

Jimmy Hanley (Tommy Mutch), Edward Rigby (Pa Mutch), Mary Clare (Ma Mutch), Phyllis Stanley (Elsie Mutch), Edward Chapman (Sammy Sanders), Jill Furse (Connie Fletcher), Richard Ainley (Billy Frost), Gus McNaughton (Alfie Norton), Nan Hopkins (Dot Ducrow), Sue Gawthorne (Mrs. Frost), Michael Hogarth (Frank Fox), Michael Wilding (Len Charteris), Richard Norris (Stan), Al Millen (Perce), Mike Johnson, Patsy Hagate, Bombardier Billy Wells.

Hanley plays an auto mechanic who discovers he has a talent for boxing. Wanting to earn quick money so he can marry his sweetheart, Hanley goes into the ring. Unfortunately he hooks up with a crooked promoter who tries to force him to take a dive. Knowing that the odds will be lopsided if it's rumored that the fight is fixed, Hanley has his father bet big on him and knocks the intended victor onto the canvas.

d, Penrose Tennyson; w, Tennyson, Sergei Nolbandov, James Curtis (based on the novel by Curtis); ph, Mutz Greenbaum [Max Greene]; m, Ernest Irving; ed, Ray Pitt; art d, Wilfred Shingleton.

Drama   **(PR:A MPAA:NR)**

THERE GOES KELLY*   (1945) 61m MON bw

Jackie Moran (Jimmy), Wanda McKay (Anne), Sidney Miller (Sammy), Ralph Sanford (Marty), Dewey Robinson (Delaney), Jan Wiley (Rita), Anthony Warde (Farrel), Harry Depp (Hastings), George Eldredge (Quigley), Edward Emerson (Martin), John Gilbreath (Tex), Pat Gleason (Pringle), Don Kerr (Bowers), Charlie Jordon (Wallis), Terry Frost (Stevens), Ralph Linn (Norris), Gladys Blake (Stella).

Inept murder mystery starring Moran and Miller as two obnoxious page boys at a radio station who are determined to make the receptionist, who sings, a star. When the star vocalist on a popular show is bumped off, the boys push their protege in front of the mike and then run off to solve the k illing. She's a hit, and they solve the murder, naturally.

p, William Strohbach; d, Phil Karlstein [Karlson]; w, Edmond Kelso, Tim Ryan; ph, William Sickner; ed, Richard Currier; md, Edward J. Kay; art d, E.R. Hickson, Dave Milton; set d, Vin Taylor.

Mystery   **(PR:A MPAA:NR)**

THERE GOES MY GIRL**   (1937) 74m RKO bw

Gene Raymond (Jerry Martin, Reporter), Ann Sothern (Connie Taylor, Reporter), Gordon Jones (Dunn), Richard Lane (T. J. "Tim" Whalen, Editor), Frank Jenks (Tate), Bradley Page (Joe Rethburn), Joan Woodbury (Margot Whitney), Marla Shelton (Mrs. Grace Andrews), Alec Craig (Bum), Joseph Crehan (Sgt. Wood), William Corson (Dan Curtis), Maxine Jennings (Actress), Clyde Dilson (Actor), Charles Coleman (Faraday), George Davis (Waiter), Irving Bacon, Edgar Dearing (Cops), Roy James, Harry Worth, Chester Clute, Dorothy Vaughn.

More newspaper hijinks, this time starring Lane as the unscrupulous but appealing managing editor who will stop at nothing to ruin the marriage of his star reporter, Sothern, to rival newsman Raymond. Predictable climax sees Sothern abandon Raymond at the altar when she sees a chance for a big scoop. Watch HIS GIRL FRIDAY 15 times instead.

p, William Sistrom; d, Ben Holmes; w, Harry Segall (based on the story "Women Are Poison" by George Beck); ph, Joseph H. August; ed, Desmond Marquette; spec eff, Vernon L. Walker.

Comedy   **(PR:A MPAA:NR)**

THERE GOES MY HEART½**   (1938) 81m UA bw

Fredric March (Bill Spencer), Virginia Bruce (Joan Butterfield), Patsy Kelly (Peggy O'Brien), Alan Mowbray (Penny E. Pennypepper), Nancy Carroll (Dorothy Moore), Eugene Pallette (Mr. Stevens the Editor), Claude Gillingwater (Cyrus Butterfield), Etienne Girardot (Hinckley the Secretary), Arthur Lake (Flash Fisher), Robert Armstrong (Detective O'Brien), Irving Bacon (Mr. Dobbs the Floorwalker), Irving Pichel (Mr. Gorman the Attorney), Syd Saylor (Robinson), J. Farrell MacDonald (Officer), Marjorie Main (Irate Customer), Mary Field (Mrs. Crud), Harry Langdon (Minister), Greta Granstedt (The Maid).

A pale imitation of several movies, most notably IT HAPPENED ONE NIGHT (1934) and NOTHING SACRED (1937) with a little bit of LOVE IS NEWS (1937) thrown in for bad measure. Bruce is a wealthy heiress, the granddaughter of department store mogul Gillingwater, who keeps a tight rein on her. When Gillingwater goes off to Europe on a business trip, Bruce tells her yacht captain to leave the South of France area and steam for New

York right away. The idea of taking this relatively small ship across the Atlantic is big news and New York newspaper editor Pallette deploys March, his top man, to be waiting at the dock when Bruce arrives. March and his photographer Lake get to the pier as the boat is waiting to clear customs and quarantine. Lake meets Bruce and she spots him as a newsman right away, so she tells him that she is the maid and that her maid, Granstedt, is the heiress. Lake falls for it and Bruce uses the device to get away. When March begins to interview Granstedt, he realizes that he's been fooled. He runs after Bruce and sees just a quick glimpse of her as she escapes. Bruce is one of those very rich people who doesn't ever know how much money she has in the bank or in her pocketbook (there is always someone else around to fork over cash when she needs it). She's enjoying the feeling of being one of the "People" of the city. Bruce enters a cafeteria, uses her final coins to buy a cup of coffee, and meets Kelly (who was about 35 pounds thinner than she was in her last movie and looked wonderful), a wisecracking department store clerk with a heart of gold. Kelly feels sorry for Bruce (not knowing her real identity). Knowing how it is to be out of money and have no place to live, she invites Bruce to bunk with her and her roommate, Carroll, until she can land a job. Carroll meets Bruce, hates her at first sight, resents the fact that Kelly has brought home a third person to live in the cramped flat, and retaliates by gathering her small wardrobe and other gear and exiting in a huff. Kelly helps Bruce get a job at the large department store owned by Bruce's grandfather. Bruce is working in cookwear, Kelly demonstrates weight-reducing equipment, and Carroll sells perfume. When Carroll's beau, Bacon, indicates more than a floorwalker's interest in Bruce, Carroll gets yet more irritated. Meanwhile, March--frustrated by missing Bruce at the docks--decides to write a story about the plight of struggling salesclerks compared with the posh existence of such society damsels as Bruce. He goes to the department store and spots Bruce immediately, then uses Kelly's introduction to meet her. Bruce finds March attractive; they go out and have dinner, then go ice-skating. (There's a very funny sequence here as an unbilled acrobatic skater does a drunk routine on the ice.) Carroll discovers Bruce's true identity and tells Gillingwater about it. Gillingwater's men go looking for Bruce in the store but she's at home with Kelly, who tells her that she must leave right away or risk being discovered. Bruce phones March and he takes her to a shack he keeps as a retreat on a small island near the city. They fall in love while hiding out, causing March to decide against writing the expose on the heiress. Pallette wants the story but March tears it into little pieces and quits the paper. Pallette and his staff patch and tape the strips of paper together and the story is printed, causing embarrassment to Bruce. Gillingwater, who has been worried sick about Bruce's disappearance, contacts Pallette and demands to know where she is. Pallette has a hunch Bruce might be with March at the shack and gives the old man the location. With Lake leading Gillingwater and his aides, they arrive at the island. Bruce has seen the story and is livid. March, carrying a marriage license for them, doesn't know that his story was printed. When he gets there, Bruce reads him off and leaves with Gillingwater, not allowing March a word to explain what must have happened. Kelly knows that the two love each other and can't bear the thought of them apart so she and her boy friend, Mowbray, send each of them a telegram requesting that they meet at the shack. Bruce and March arrive simultaneously. The reconciliation is effected and a minister, Langdon, walks in and says that he would be delighted to make the two of them into one as the movie fades. Harry Langdon hadn't been seen in a feature for about six years and does a neat turn as the baby-faced minister. Carroll, who had co starred with March seven years before in THE NIGHT ANGEL, was in her penultimate film at the early age of 34. She began her film career in 1927's LADIES MUST DRESS and was Oscar-nominated for THE DEVIL'S HOLIDAY in 1930, losing to Norma Shearer for THE DIVORCEE. March was wrong for the part and he knew it. His performance showed it as he went through the motions of playing a Cary Grant-type role. Kelly is by far the comedy highlight and her scene as she demonstrates the vibrating weight-loss machine is a riot. There are several amusing moments in the movie, all of which would have been funnier if we hadn't seen the basic story before. "The newsman and the heiress" had been used so often that it was already a tired premise back in 1938, and no amount of excellent direction by McLeod could save it. The story, such as it was, had been written by Broadway columnist Ed Sullivan, who later hosted one of the most successful TV variety shows in history and gave the first big break to scores of performers who would later light up the show business world. Hatley's music was nominated for an Oscar.

p, Hal Roach; d, Norman Z. McLeod; w, Eddie Moran, Jack Jevne (based on a story by Ed Sullivan); ph, Norbert Brodine; m, Marvin Hatley; ed, William Terhune; md, Hatley; art d, Charles D. Hall; spec eff, Roy Seawright.

Comedy   **(PR:A MPAA:NR)**

THERE GOES SUSIE   (SEE: SCANDALS OF PARIS, 1934, Brit.)

THERE GOES THE BRIDE*½   (1933, Brit.) 75m Gainsborough/GAU
                                                                                                              bw

Owen Nares (Max), Jessie Matthews (Annette Marquand), Carol Goodner (Cora), Charles Carson (Mons. Marquand), Barbara Everest (Mme. Marquand), Basil Radford (Rudolph), Winifred Oughton (Housekeeper), Jerry Verno (Clark, the Chauffeur), Jack Morrison (Alphonse), Roland Culver (Jacques), Max Kirby (Pierre), Gordon McLeod (Mons. Duchaine), Lawrence

Hanray (*Police Chief*), George Zucco (*Prosecutor*).

Matthews plays a young girl who flees her home to avoid an unwanted, prearranged marriage. On the train to Paris she meets a dashing young man whom she eventually marries after a series of barely funny screwball situations.

p, Michael Balcon; d, Albert de Courville; w, Fred Raymond, Noel Gray, W.P. Lipscomb (based on a story by Herman Kosterlitz [Henry Koster], Wolfgang Wilhelm); ph, Alex Bryce; m, Raymond, Gray.

Comedy (PR:A MPAA:NR)

THERE GOES THE BRIDE zero (1980, Brit.) 88m Vanguard c

Tom Smothers (*Timothy Westerby*), Twiggy (*Polly*), Martin Balsam (*Mr. Babcock*), Sylvia Syms (*Ursula Westerby*), Michael Whitney (*Bill Shorter*), Geoffrey Sumner (*Gerald Drimond*), Graham Stark (*Rossi, Italian Waiter*), Hermione Baddeley (*Daphne Drimond*), Toria Fuller (*Judy Westerby*), Margot Moser (*Mrs. Babcock*), John Terry (*Nicholas Babcock*), Jim Backus (*Mr. Perkins*), Phil Silvers (*Psychiatrist*), Broderick Crawford (*Gas Station Attendant*), Gonzales Gonzales (*Mr. Ramirez*), Carmen Zapata (*Mrs. Ramirez*), Steve Franken (*Church Organist*).

Unfunny low-budget comedy which sees a horribly miscast Smothers as the father of bride Fuller. Dad bumps his head on the wedding day and is convinced he's romancing 1920s model Twiggy (whom he had seen in an old photograph), but only he can see her. This, of course, causes havoc at the wedding until Smothers comes to and realizes it was all just a fantasy. The film does have a few funny moments, but none of them are intentional.

p, Ray Cooney, Martin Schute; d, Terence Marcel; w, Cooney, Marcel, John Chapman (based on the play by Cooney); ph, James Devis (Rank Film Laboratories Color); m, Harry Robinson; ed, Alan Jones; prod d, Peter Mullin; art d, John Siddall; ch, Gilliam Gregory.

Comedy (PR:C MPAA:PG)

THERE GOES THE GROOM** (1937) 64m RKO bw

Ann Sothern (*Betty Russell*), Burgess Meredith (*Dick Mathews*), Mary Boland (*Mrs. Russell*), Onslow Stevens (*Dr. Becker*), William Brisbane (*Potter Russell*), Louise Henry (*Janet Russell*), Roger Imhof (*Hank*), Sumner Getchell (*Billy Rapp*), George Irving (*Yacht Captain*), Leona Roberts (*Martha*), Adrian Morris (*Eddie, Intern*).

Burgess Meredith followed his very serious movie debut in WINTERSET with this light comedy. He plays a fresh-out-of-college lad who abandons civilization hoping to strike it rich in the gold fields of Alaska. After a long absence, he returns home to sweep former girl friend Henry off her feet. She's not too interested anymore, until her momma hears the boy's stinking rich. By this time Henry's turn-around is too late, because her younger sister, Sothern, has picked up where she left off. The family explodes in an uproar when the siblings battle for Meredith's attentions. Imhof, Meredith's gold-mining buddy from Alaska, chases his pal around trying to preserve his sense of perspective. In the end, the good sister gets her man.

p, Albert Lewis; d, Joseph Santley; w, S.K. Lauren, Dorothy Yost, Harold Kussell (based on a story by David Garth); ph, Milton Krasner; ed, Jack Hively.

Comedy (PR:A MPAA:NR)

THERE IS ANOTHER SUN (SEE: WALL OF DEATH, 1950, Brit.)

THERE IS NO 13** (1977) 91m Bill and Margaret Features/Film Ventures c

Mark Damon (*George Thomas*), Margaret Markov (*No.11*), Harvey Lembeck (*Older George*), Jean Jennings (*No.12*), Lee Moore (*Dr. Honneycutt*), Reuben Schafer (*Mr. A*), Bonnie Inch (*Rosie*).

An interesting low-budget film starring Damon as a young soldier in Vietnam who spends his time in battle reminiscing about his life and loves. The title is derived from Damon's recollection of his 12 love affairs, the end of the film preventing the possibility of a 13th.

p, Robert Boggs, William Sachs, Alan N. Harris; d&w, Sachs; ph, Ralf Bode (Eastmancolor); m, Riz Ortolani; ed, George T. Norris.

War (PR:O MPAA:R)

THERE IS STILL ROOM IN HELL*½
(1963, Ger.) 90m Theumer/Sam Lake bw (IN DER HOLLE IST NOCH PLATZ; AKA: STILL ROOM IN HELL)

Barbara Valentin (*Janet*), Paul Glawion (*Ismail*), Hermann Nehlsen (*Dexter*), Fikret Hakan (*Hassan*), Maria Vincent, Sadri Alisik.

A vicious drama about drug runners starring Glawion as a Turkish dealer and Hakan as his partner, who double-cross powerful American suppliers and find themselves in trouble with hit man Nehlsen but in love with his mysterious agent, Valentin. After a series of flip-flops, betrayals and double-dealing all the drug runners are killed and only Valentin survives.

p&d, Ernst Ritter von Theumer; w, Theo Gallehr; ph, Ali Ismir; m, Frank Dallone.

Crime (PR:C-O MPAA:NR)

THERE WAS A CROOKED MAN** (1962, Brit.) 90m Knightsbridge/Lopert-UA bw

Norman Wisdom (*Davy Cooper*), Alfred Marks (*Adolf Carter*), Andrew Cruickshank (*McKillup*), Reginald Beckwith (*Station Master*), Susannah York (*Ellen*), Jean Clarke (*Freda*), Timothy Bateson (*Flash Dan*), Paul Whitsun-Jones (*Restaurant Gentleman*), Fred Griffiths (*Taxi Driver*), Ann Heffernan (*Hospital Sister*), Rosalind Knight (*Nurse*), Reed De Rouen (*Dutchman*), Brian Oulton (*Ashton*), Percy Herbert (*Prison Warden*), Edna Petrie (*Woman at Assembly Hall*), Jack May (*Police Sergeant*), Ronald Fraser (*Gen. Cummins*), Ed Devereaux (*American Colonel*), Sam Kydd (*Foreman*), Redmond Phillips (*Padre*), Fred Haggerty, Eddie Boyce, Totti Truman-Taylor, William Hutt, John Barrard, John Kidd.

British comedy starring Wisdom as a likeable sap whose expertise in demolition involves him with a gang of crooks who pose as doctors and burrow into a large bank from the hospital next door. After successfully blowing the safe and grabbing the money, the cops arrive and arrest Wisdom, and the other gang members escape. Five years later Wisdom is released from prison and wants to go straight. Taking a job in a small seaside town, Wisdom soon realizes that the owner of much of the town, Cruickshank, is cheating the locals by selling shares in the town's future. Seeking to rid the town of the hustler, Wisdom calls his former gang into service and they pose as American soldiers expressing an interest in building a missile base in the town. Cruickshank wants a piece of the action and he buys back the land he sold. Wisdom then puts his demolition skills to work and blows up all of Cruickshank's land. The real American Army, who are embarrassed at the con game, volunteer to build a new town on the land. The townsfolk praise Wisdom as a hero while watching him being dragged off by the police.

p, Albert Fennell, John Bryan; d, Stuart Burge; w, Reuben Ship (based on the play "The Odd Legend of Schultz" by James Bridie); ph, Arthur Ibbetson; m, Kenneth V. Jones; ed, Peter Hunt; art d, Charles Bishop; set d, Roger Ramsdell; makeup, Harry Frampton, Dick Bonnor-Moris.

Comedy (PR:A MPAA:NR)

THERE WAS A CROOKED MAN** (1970) 126m WB c

Kirk Douglas (*Paris Pitman, Jr.*), Henry Fonda (*Woodward Lopeman*), Hume Cronyn (*Dudley Whinner*), Warren Oates (*Floyd Moon*), Burgess Meredith (*The Missouri Kid*), John Randolph (*Cyrus McNutt*), Arthur O'Connell (*Mr. Lomax*), Martin Gabel (*Warden Le Goff*), Michael Blodgett (*Coy Cavendish*), Claudia McNeil (*Madam*), Alan Hale, Jr (*Tobaccy*), Victor French (*Whiskey*), Lee Grant (*Mrs. Bullard*), C. K. Yang (*Ah-Ping Woo*), Pamela Hensley (*Edwina*), Bert Freed (*Skinner*), Barbara Rhoades (*Miss Jessie Brundidge*), J. Edward McKinley (*Governor*), Gene Evans (*Col. Wolff*), Jeanne Cooper (*Prostitute*), Ann Doran, Byron Foulger, Paul Newlan, Karl Lukas, Larry D. Mann, Paul Prokop, Bart Burns.

Douglas leads a gang that robs half a million dollars from O'Connell. The only survivor of the gang, Douglas ties up the loot in a pair of ladies' bloomers and drops it into a rattlesnake pit for safekeeping. Later the depressed O'Connell visits the local brothel. Since he doesn't have any money, the madam lets him look through a peephole at another client enjoying the company of two of the girls. He recognizes the man as the one who robbed him and soon Douglas has been arrested by sheriff Fonda and shipped off to the territorial prison. There Douglas soon establishes himself as top dog and when the warden, Gabel, finds out about the still-hidden loot, he offers to let him escape in return for a share. Before their scheme can succeed, Gabel is killed by a Chinese prisoner during a brawl. The new warden is Fonda, walking with a limp now after being shot by Oates, also a prisoner. Fonda is a reformer; he tries to work with Douglas to improve conditions at the prison while the convict is using the privileges Fonda has given him to plan a breakout with Oates, with confidence men and homosexual couple Cronyn and Randolph, and with Meredith, a former outlaw terror turned into a fearful old man by decades in stir. Fonda invites the governor for an inspection and Douglas uses the opportunity to escape. He double-crosses all his cohorts and escapes alone, with a betrayed and angry Fonda in pursuit. Douglas reaches the snake pit and uses his pistol to shoot the rattlers. Then he wraps his arm in his jacket and reaches down to retrieve the bloomers. When he unties them, though, a snake springs out and bites him on the neck. Within minutes Douglas is dead. Fonda arrives shortly thereafter and throws Douglas' body over the saddle of his horse and, with the money, heads back to the prison. When he arrives near the gates he contemplates the place, then the money, and after slapping the horse carrying Douglas toward the prison he rides off toward Mexico with the loot. One of the most cynical and bitterly funny westerns ever made, written by the same team that wrote BONNIE AND CLYDE (1967), Benton and Newman. They had written the script at the suggestion of Warner Bros. production chief Kenneth Hyman and titled it "Hell." The script was toned down and rewritten several times, but was constantly rejected. Mankiewicz finally saw one of the drafts, asked for a rewrite, and when shown the first script exclaimed, "Jesus, m'boys, this is what I was talking about. Why didn't you show this to me in the first place?" The biggest problem the writers and the director had was charting and explaining Fonda's change of heart as he gradually takes on a number of the characteristics of his nemesis, Douglas. The fact that the film had to be kept down around two hours in length is the reason a number of written scenes that make this transformation explicable are missing, including a scene between Fonda and Lee Grant that originally went on for some time but was reduced to three mostly meaningless lines in the final release. Most of the criticism leveled at the film resulted from this unexpected character switch. Douglas himself later said of the film "...the switch–his almost taking on my identity–was...brilliant, but it started too late in the picture." In other areas, though, the film was more successful. Meredith is terrific as the Missouri Kid, grown old in prison and growing marijuana in his cell. In the scene where he's asked to join the escape plot he changes from an old man ("You don't want an old coot like me") to the outlaw terror he once was ("Look, pissant, this is the Missouri Kid you're talking to") in the space of a single scene. When the time comes for him to escape, though, Meredith refuses, afraid to leave the prison that has for too long been his home. The details of the prison, built out in the California desert at a cost of $300,000, are perfect, evidence of the extensive research done by Benton and Newman. Mankiewicz ordered that none of the horse manure be cleaned off the set, saying, "My western is going to be the first that has h— s— in every scene." Despite these charms, though, the film proved too bitter for the public to swallow and it was only slightly successful at the box office.

p&d, Joseph L. Mankiewicz; w, David Newman, Robert Benton (based on the story "Prison Story" by Newman, Benton); ph, Harry Stradling, Jr. (Panavision, Technicolor); m, Charles Strouse; ed, Gene Milford; art d, Edward Carrere; set d, Keogh Gleason; cos, Anna Hill Johnstone; spec eff, John Barton; stunts, Roger Creed; makeup, Perc Westmore; m/l, title song, Strouse, Lee Adams (sung by Trini Lopez).

Western   Cas.   (PR:C MPAA:R)

THERE WAS A YOUNG LADY** (1953, Brit.) 84m Nettlefold/But bw

Michael Denison (David Walsh), Dulcie Gray (Elizabeth Foster), Sydney Tafler (Johnny), Bill Owen (Joe), Geraldine McEwen (Irene), Charles Farrell (Arthur), Robert Adair (Basher), Bill Shine (Duke of Chiddingford), Kenneth Connor (Countryman), Tommy Duggan (Weatherspoon), Marcel Poncin, Basil Dignam, Ben Williams, Janet Butler, Gerald Rex.

Gray, a secretary for a diamond merchant, is fired by new boss Denison (Gray's real-life husband) for her too efficient ways. Kidnaped by a gang of thieves out to get the diamonds, she quickly ingratiates herself into their ranks and gets them organized. Then she slips a message to Denison and he comes to her rescue. Decent comedy slightly better than average, with Gray at her brightest.

p, Ernest G. Roy, A.R. Rawlinson; d&w, Lawrence Huntington (based on a radio serial by Vernon Harris, John Jowett); ph, Gerald Gibbs.

Comedy   (PR:A MPAA:NR)

THERE WAS A YOUNG MAN* (1937, Brit.) 63m FOX British bw

Oliver Wakefield (George Peabody), Nancy O'Neil (Barbara Blake), Clifford Heatherley (Wallop), Robert Nainby (Vicar), Molly Hamley Clifford (Mrs. Blake), Eric Hales (Vernon), Brian Buchel (Prince Bunkhadin), John Laurie (Stranger), Syd Crossley (Slim), Patric Curwen, Peter Popp, Bouncer the Dog.

Just plain bad little comedy has Wakefield mistaken for an heir, entangled in a land swindle, and chased by a gang of orientals who want the holy bone he has somehow obtained, which they consider sacred.

p&d, Albert Parker; w, David Evans (based on a story by Dudley Clark); ph, Stanley Grant.

Comedy   (PR:A MPAA:NR)

THERE WAS AN OLD COUPLE*** (1967, USSR) 103m
Mosfilm/Artkino bw (ZHILIBYLI STARIK SO STARUKHOV; AKA: THE COUPLE)

Ivan Marin (The Old Man, Gusakov), Vera Kuznetsova (The Old Woman, Gusakova), Lyudmila Maksamova (Nina), Grigoriy Martynyuk (Valentin), Galina Polskikh (Galya), Anatoliy Yabbarov (Sectarian), V. Kolpakov (Paramedic), Nikolay Kryuchkov (Director of the Sovkhoz), Nikolay Sergeyev (Accountant), Gyuli Chokhonelidze (Engineer), Lenochka Derzhavina (Irochka), O. Amalina, R. Aristarkhova, N. Barmin, Yu Volkov, V. Vyshkovskiy, M. Drozdovskaya, L. Kadrov, V. Kazanskiy, G. Krasheninnikov, M. Lukach, V. Markin, A. Fyodorinov, O. Fomichyova, N. Khlibko, O. Shtoda.

A fine Soviet drama about an elderly Russian couple who travel to live with their needy daughter after their farm burns down. When they arrive at their daughter's tiny cabin they are shocked to discover that she has left her husband and small child to run off with a married man. The parents stay to help their alcoholic son-in-law through his crisis. Eventually the old man and his wife become solid members of their new community, and a new young lady who has always been fond of the son-in-law and his child joins them. The old couple's daughter returns after being dumped by her lover. Though

it is very difficult for all concerned, the old man sends his daughter away because they have built a new life without her. This was released in the U.S.S.R. in 1965 as a two-part film of 140 minutes.

d, Grigoriy Chukhray; w, Yuliy Dunskiy, Valeri Fried; ph, Sergei Poluyanov; m, Aleksandra Pakhmutova; art d, Boris Nemechek; m/l, L. Oshanin, Yu. Danilovich.

Drama   (PR:A MPAA:NR)

THERE'S A GIRL IN MY HEART** (1949) 79m AA bw

Lee Bowman (Terrence Dowd), Elyse Knox (Claire Adamson), Gloria Jean (Ruth Kroner), Peggy Ryan (Sally Mullin), Lon Chaney, Jr (John Colton), Ludwig Donath (Joseph Kroner, Music Teacher), Ray McDonald (Danny Kroner), Joel Marson (Dr. Henlein), Richard Lane (Sgt. Mullin), Irene Ryan (Mrs. Mullin), Lanny Simpson (Lennie), Paul Guilfoyle (Father Callaghan), Iris Adrian (Lulu), Kay Anne Nelson (Carol Anne), Martin Garralaga (Luigi), Lee Tong Foo (Charlie Li), Robert Emmett Keane (Capt. Blake).

Just another 1890s musical, this one starring Bowman as a hustling, successful property developer who tries to swindle young widow Knox out of her plot of valuable land which sits next to reluctant partner Chaney's music hall. Despite the fact that his plans will leave dozens homeless, Bowman puts the scheme into motion until he suddenly falls in love with Knox and gives up his ambitious moneymaking idea. Songs include: "There's a Girl in My Heart" (Arthur Dreifuss, Robert Bilder), "The Roller Skating Song," "Be Careful of the Tidal Wave," "We Are the Main Attraction," "Any Old Street" (Bilder), "A Bicycle Built for Two (Daisy Bell)" (Harry Dacre), "After the Ball" (Charles K. Harris).

p&d, Arthur Dreifuss; w, Arthur Hoerl, John Eugene Hasty; ph, Phillip Tannura; m, Herschel Burke Gilbert; ed, Richard Currier, Olive Hoffman; art d, Danny Hall; ch, Louis Da Pron.

Musical   (PR:A MPAA:NR)

THERE'S A GIRL IN MY SOUP½** (1970, Brit.) 94m Ascot/COL c

Peter Sellers (Robert Danvers), Goldie Hawn (Marion), Tony Britton (Andrew Hunter), Nicky Henson (Jimmy), John Comer (John), Diana Dors (John's Wife), Gabrielle Drake (Julia Halforde-Smythe), Geraldine Sherman (Caroline), Judy Campbell (Lady Heather), Nicola Pagett (Clare), Christopher Cazenove (Nigel), Robin Parkinson, Roy Skelton (Reporters), Caroline Seymour (Nigel's Girl Friend), Raf De La Torre (Mons. Le Guestier), Constantin De Goguel (Michel Le Guestier), Thorley Walters (Manager of Carlton Hotel), Georges Lambert (Floor Waiter), Andre Charise (Concierge), John Serret (Elevator Operator), Avril Angers (Woman in Elevator), Ruth Trouncer (Gilly), Lance Percival, Mark Dignam, Eric Barker (Guests at Wedding Reception), Francoise Pascal (Paola), Marianne Stone (Reporter at Airport), Margaret Lacey (Autograph Hunter).

A funny, sexy romp that was daring for its day but could later be seen on late-night TV with nary a snip in the action. Sellers is the libidinous star of a television cooking show, making him sort of a combination of Casanova and "The Galloping Gourmet." Not a set of wiggling hips escapes his leer. When he spots a young bride changing out of her wedding dress and into her street clothes, he uses his charm to get to her before the groom does. Hawn is a young American who has just battled with her British lover, Henson, because he has an eye rivaled only by Sellers' in the roving department. Hawn and Henson have a free relationship but she can't handle the fact that he runs around behind her back. Sellers invites Hawn to his sumptuous flat, an apartment devoted solely to seduction, not unlike the residences in UNDER THE YUM YUM TREE (1963) or LOVER COME BACK (1961). Sellers turns on his Don Juan ways and attempts to seduce her in an almost Victorian fashion, with flourishes and grandiose verbal statements. Hawn laughs in his face and bluntly suggests that he and she sleep with each other. Sellers is taken aback by her up-front effrontery but falls madly in love with her fresh ways. The following day, Hawn moves in; then it's off to France for a tour of the Riviera, followed by a wine-tasting journey through the chauteaus. Back in London, Sellers asks for Hawn's hand in marriage but she declines, saying that she's spoken to Henson; he's promised to cease cheating and he needs her. Sellers is crushed by her decision. Despondency doesn't last long, though, as he brightens up when an interesting secretary finds him attractive. His jealous doorman, Comer, watches the parade of birds flocking to Sellers' roost and he takes it out on his shrewish wife, Dors (an odd casting choice, but she does well with it). Sellers ultimately realizes that he's not getting any younger but he can remain as old as he feels, and he feels good when he's with young women. Sellers underplays well, doing his best work since I LOVE YOU, ALICE B. TOKLAS (1968). Based on the play by Frisby which was a hit in London before coming to the U.S. for a year with Barbara Ferris as the girl and Gig Young as the lecher. Hawn had just won a Supporting Actress Oscar for CACTUS FLOWER, and this was a pretty good follow-up, although it didn't make too much of a dent at the box office. It's really a TV movie with movie star names.

p, M. J. Frankovich, John Boulting; d, Roy Boulting; w, Terence Frisby, Peter Kortner (based on the play by Frisby); ph, Harry Waxman (Eastmancolor); m, Mike D'Abo; ed, Martin Charles; art d, John Howell; set d, Patrick McLoughlin; cos, Vangie Harrison; m/l, "Miss Me in the Morning,"

"Arabella Cinderella," Mike D'Abo, Nicki Chinn, "The Lady's in Love," "It's Gotta Be Now," D'Abo; makeup, Eric Allwright, John O'Gorman.

Comedy   **Cas.**   **(PR:C   MPAA:R)**

THERE'S ALWAYS A THURSDAY**½   (1957, Brit.) 62m Associated Film Sound Industries/RANK bw

Charles Victor (*George Potter*), Marjorie Rhodes (*Marjorie Potter*), Frances Day (*Vera Clanton*), Patrick Holt (*Middleton*), Jill Ireland (*Jennifer*), Bruce Seton (*James Pelley*), Ewen Solon (*Inspector Bradley*), Lloyd Lamble (*Sgt. Bolton*), Glen Alyn (*Mrs. Middleton*), Alex MacIntosh (*TV Interviewer*), Richard Thorp (*Dennis*), Lance George (*Mr. Bristow*), Deirdre Mayne (*Miss Morton*), Howard Green (*Head Waiter*), Peter Fontain (*Detective Constable Carter*), Geoff Goodhart (*Commissionaire*), Reginald Hearne (*Bannister*), Martin Boddey (*Sergeant*), Alexander Field (*Tramp*), Robert Raglan (*Crosby*), Yvonne Savage (*Receptionist*), Margaret Rowe (*Margaret*), Yvette Davis (*Miss Hewson*), Andrea Malandrinos.

Well-crafted little comedy has Victor a meek bank clerk sent by his boss to deliver blackmail money to voluptuous Day. When his brother-in-law sees him leaving her house, he spreads the rumor that Victor is quite the ladies' man, bringing him to the attention of a racy undergarment manufacturing concern which offers him a directorship. Good performance by Victor and intelligent script lift this one above the ranks.

p, Guido Coen; d, Charles Saunders; w, Brandon Fleming; ph, Brendan Stafford.

Comedy   **(PR:A   MPAA:NR)**

THERE'S ALWAYS A WOMAN***   (1938) 82m COL bw

Joan Blondell (*Sally Reardon*), Melvyn Douglas (*William Reardon*), Mary Astor (*Lola Fraser*), Frances Drake (*Anne Calhoun*), Jerome Cowan (*Nick Shane*), Robert Paige (*Jerry Marlowe*), Thurston Hall (*District Attorney*), Pierre Watkin (*Mr. Ketterling*), Walter Kingsford (*Grigson*), Lester Matthews (*Walter Fraser*), Rita Hayworth (*Ketterling's Secretary*), Wade Boteler (*Sam, Radio Car Driver*), Arthur Loft (*Radio Patrolman*), William H. Strauss (*Rent Collector*), Marek Windheim (*Head Waiter*), Bud Jamison (*Jim, Bartender*), George Davis (*Waiter*), Robert Emmett Keane (*City Editor*), John Gallaudet (*Reporter*), Eddie Fetherston (*Photographer*), Josef De Stefani (*Cigar Stand Clerk*), Ted Oliver (*Cop*), George Morgan (*Officer Fogarty*), Tom Dugan (*Detective Flannigan*), Bud Geary (*District Attorney's Assistant*), Billy Benedict (*Bellhop*), Lee Phelps (*Police Broadcaster*), Eddie Dunn, George McKay (*Cops*).

Columbia decided to copy the success of MGM with that studio's THIN MAN series by creating their own comic detective couple. Douglas and Blondell are the sleuths, but business has been lousy so Douglas has taken back his old job as an investigator with the district attorney's office. Blondell is sitting in the empty office when Astor enters, plunks three hundred dollars on the desk, and asks that Douglas take her case. Blondell's eyes grow large looking at the money and she decides to look into the matter herself. Of course her sleuthing gets her into trouble, including being charged with murder and given the third-degree. In the film's funniest scene, it is the policemen who eventually crack, while Blondell continues to sit in the harsh light, smiling cheerfully and apparently oblivious to the whole thing. In the end, Douglas helps unravel the mystery, proving Astor and Cowan the killers, and the way is paved for the sequel that came the same year (THERE'S THAT WOMAN AGAIN). The script was surprisingly good, largely due to the uncredited efforts of Ryskind, Sayre, and Rapp. The teaming of Blondell and Douglas worked quite well, and it was possibly the fact that Blondell was replaced by Virginia Bruce in the sequel that accounts for the aspiring series dying an early death. Rita Hayworth had a fairly substantial role in the film as originally shot, playing a secretary in the district attorney's office who spies for Blondell, but thinking they were launching a series, the Columbia executives didn't want any characters who would be missed in subsequent installments so they cut Hayworth's part down to a half-minute of screen time.

p, William Perlberg; d, Alexander Hall; w, Gladys Lehman (Joel Sayre, Philip Rapp, Morrie Ryskind, uncredited) (based on a short story by Wilson Collison); ph, Henry Freulich; ed, Viola Lawrence; md, Morris Stoloff; art d, Stephen Goosson, Lionel Banks; cos, Robert Kalloch.

Crime-Comedy   **(PR:A   MPAA:NR)**

THERE'S ALWAYS TOMORROW
(SEE: ALWAYS TOMORROW, 1934)

THERE'S ALWAYS TOMORROW***½   (1956) 84m UNIV bw

Barbara Stanwyck (*Norma Miller*), Fred MacMurray (*Clifford Groves*), Joan Bennett (*Marion Groves*), Pat Crowley (*Ann*), William Reynolds (*Vinnie Groves*), Gigi Perreau (*Ellen Groves*), Race Gentry (*Bob*), Myrna Hansen (*Ruth*), Judy Nugent (*Frankie Groves*), Jane Darwell (*Mrs. Rogers*), Paul Smith (*Bellboy*), Jane Howard (*Flower Girl*), Helen Kleeb (*Miss Walker*), Frances Mercer (*Ruth Doran*), Sheila Bromley (*Woman from Pasadena*), Louise Lorimer (*Chic Lady with Dog*), Dorothy Bruce (*Sales Manager*), Hermine Sterler, Fred Nurney (*Tourists*), Hal Smith (*Bartender*),

James Rawley (*Foreman*), Jack Lomas (*Pianist*), Jean Byron (*Saleswoman*), Bert Holland (*Clerk*), Carlyle Mitchell (*Mr. Carl*), Mack Williams (*Norma's Hotel Clerk*), Richard Mayer (*Customer*), Pat Meller (*Groom*), Vonne Lester (*Junior Executive*), Lorelei Vitek (*Bit*), June Clayworth, Ross Hunter.

Another of director Sirk's melodramatic and bitter attacks on the values of American middle-class life in the 1950s. This one stars MacMurray as a middle-aged milquetoast who lives in his claustrophobic home with his token wife, Bennett, and their three self-absorbed children. When not confined to his boring home life (where he is practically ignored by Bennett and the children), he spends his days at a toy manufacturing company. From his desk job, he okays production of a new robot toy, "Rex," which walks and talks, spouting such statements as "Push me and steer me wherever you can," a statement which clearly defines MacMurray's position. He finds new hope, however, when he is reunited with an old flame, Stanwyck. Although their reunion begins innocently enough, MacMurray's teenage son, Reynolds, becomes determined to catch his father in a spot, preferring to think the worst instead of listening to a truthful explanation. Reynolds (like the character he played in Sirk's previous film, ALL THAT HEAVEN ALLOWS) is a childish brat who refuses to allow his father (or mother in the case of ALL THAT HEAVEN ALLOWS) a life other than that of material provider. MacMurray is looking for a way out, however, and entertains thoughts of running off with Stanwyck. The interference of the children brings about a change in Stanwyck's mind and she decides that MacMurray should stay with his family. Like the robot,"Rex", MacMurray is "pushed and steered" back into his home, depressed by the fact that he cannot go back to the days of his youth and fearful of the tomorrow that holds no hope. It should come as no surprise that a film with a view this bleak should draw less-than-enthusiastic reviews, especially during the supposedly idyllic 1950s. Sirk's view was even darker than what appeared on the screen. The ending he filmed has MacMurray's robot marching across a table top—making a final connection between MacMurray and "Rex." His original intention (which was deemed too grim) had "Rex" reaching the edge of the desk and toppling to the ground. After crashing to the floor, the robot would struggle through a few final kicks before the end credits rolled up. Light is shed onto this finale in an interview Sirk gave to Michael Stern (printed in his book Douglas Sirk): "In tragedy the life always ends. By being dead, the hero is at the same time rescued from life's troubles. In melodrama, he lives on–in an unhappy happy end." Filmed previously under the same title in 1934.

p, Ross Hunter; d, Douglas Sirk; w, Bernard C. Schoenfeld (based on a story by Ursula Parrott); ph, Russell Metty; m, Herman Stein, Heinz Roemheld; ed, William M. Morgan; md, Joseph Gershenson; art d, Alexander Golitzen, Eric Orbom; set d, Russell A. Guasman, Julia Heron; cos, Jay Morley, Jr.

Drama   **(PR:A   MPAA:NR)**

THERE'S ALWAYS VANILLA*½   (1972) 91m Latent Image/Cambist c (AKA: THE AFFAIR)

Ray Laine (*Chris Bradley*), Judith Streiner (*Lynn*), Johanna Lawrence (*Terri Terrific*), Richard Ricci (*Television Producer*), Roger McGovern (*Mr. Bradley*), Ron Jaye, Bob Wilson, Louise Sahene, Christopher Priore, Robert Trow, Bryson Randolph, Thomas Ashwell, George Kosana, Bob Stevens, Dorrit Chase, Helen Tumpson, Donald Neeld, Bill Hinzman, Val Stanley, Vincent Survinski, Eleanor Schirra, Jack Dutch, Mike Marracino, Lee Hartman, Al Croft, Roger Ray, Ken Peters, Elsie Doughty, Richard France, Nat Carter.

Having recently received his discharge from the Army, Laine decides to become a drifter and make some money at everything from pimping to guitar playing. He finds himself back in his home town, Pittsburgh, and he visits his father. Dad wants his son to abandon his new lifestyle and join him in the family baby food business but Laine refuses. On the street Laine meets a beautiful young woman, Streiner, and soon he has charmed her into letting him live with her. Streiner works as a model in television commercials and it is her income that supports them while Laine claims to be working on a novel based on his life. Though for a time their life together is a pleasant escape (lovemaking, pot-smoking, rock 'n' roll), eventually Streiner starts to resent having to support Laine and she motivates him to find a steady job. Using his wits and charm, Laine manages to land a position in an advertising agency, but when he is given an Army account he quits. Meanwhile, Streiner learns she is pregnant and, without telling Laine, she plans an abortion. When the time comes she changes her mind and opts to return to her home town and marry her childhood sweetheart, who has agreed to raise the child as his own. The relationship shattered, Laine moves in with his father who tells him that of all life's exotic flavors one can always choose vanilla. THERE'S ALWAYS VANILLA is the first of only a handful of non-horror films directed by the dean of modern American horrors, George Romero (the others being the marginally horrific JACK's WIFE, 1972, and the vastly underrated KNIGHTRIDERS, 1981). After making the powerful and controversial NIGHT OF THE LIVING DEAD (1968), Romero feared being pegged as a horror director and launched immediately into this GRADUATE-inspired romance written by Ricci. By Romero's own admission the film was a disaster and shouldn't have been made at all. It is quite obvious that the director's heart just wasn't in it. Romero is a very passionate filmmaker and when that passion transfers to the screen it creates some incredible films, but the script wasn't his (he has written all his best films) and the subject matter was too derivative for any true creativity. In fact, it seems as if Romero's main interest was in the visuals. Still smarting from negative criticism of the grainy black and white photography in NIGHT OF THE LIVING DEAD (which only adds to the overall power of the film), Romero was determined to make a slick Hollywood-style film in gorgeous color and he did the photography himself. THERE'S ALWAYS VANILLA does look nice, but it is a misfired exercise that the director has stated "doesn't count" when one evaluates the films of George A. Romero.

p, Russell W. Streiner, John A. Russo; d, George A. Romero; w, Rudolph J. Ricci; ph, Romero; m, Steve Gorn, Jim Drake, Mike Marracino, Barefoot in Athens; ed, Romero; cos, Carol Muldoon; m/l, "Wild Mountain Thyme," "Wild and Wooly Years," by Frank Joseph (sung by Joseph).

Drama   **(PR:C   MPAA:R)**

THERE'S MAGIC IN MUSIC**   (1941) 80m PAR bw (AKA: THE
                                                              HARD-BOILED CANARY)

Allan Jones (*Michael Maddy*), Susanna Foster (*Toodles La Verne*), Margaret Lindsay (*Sylvia Worth*), Lynne Overman (*George Thomas*), Grace Bradley (*Madie Duvalie*), William Collier, Sr (*Dr. Joseph E. Maddy*), Heimo Haitto, William Chapman, Dolly Loehr [Diana Lynn], Irra Petina, Richard Bonelli, Patricia Travers, Deems Taylor, Richard Hageman, Tandy MacKenzie, Baby Mary Ruth (*Themselves*), Fay Helm (*Miss Wilson*), Esther Dale (*Miss Clark*), Fred Hoose (*Mr. Stevens*), Ottola Nesmith (*Mrs. Stevens*), Bertram Marburgh (*Mr. Myers*), Ruth Robinson (*Mrs. Myers*), Hobart Cavanaugh (*Announcer*), Ruth Rogers (*Receptionist*), Bert Roach (*Cop*), Charles Bimbo (*Bum*), Emmett Vogan (*Stokes*), Russ Coller (*Elevator Boy*), Astrid Allwyn, Rosella Towne, Jean Porter, Elena Verdugo, Adele Horner (*Girls*).

Dull musical detailing the trials and tribulations of managing the famed National Music Camp for young artists. The camp, located in Interlochen, Michigan, is run by handsome crooner Jones. Young burlesque performer Foster is discovered by Jones and brought to the music camp. She rebels against the strict routine of the camp, but soon becomes a devotee. An unfavorable newspaper story scares away the backers of the camp and Foster gives a charity performance to help save it. Arias from Bizet's "Carmen," Gounod's "Faust," and Tovani's "Rienzi Overture" are performed, among others.

p&d, Andrew L. Stone; w, Frederick Jackson (based on a story by Stone, Robert Lively, idea by Ann Ronell); ph, Theodor Sparkuhl; ed, James Smith; md, Phil Boutelje; art d, Hans Dreier, Earl Hedrick; m/l, "Fireflies on Parade," Ronell.

Musical   **(PR:A   MPAA:NR)**

THERE'S NO BUSINESS LIKE SHOW BUSINESS*½**
                                                              (1954) 117m FOX c

Ethel Merman (*Molly Donahue*), Donald O'Connor (*Tim Donahue*), Marilyn Monroe (*Vicky*), Dan Dailey (*Terrance Donahue*), Johnny Ray (*Steve Donahue*), Mitzi Gaynor (*Katy Donahue*), Richard Eastham (*Lew Harris*), Hugh O'Brian (*Charles Gibbs*), Frank McHugh (*Eddie Duggan*), Rhys Williams (*Father Dineen*), Lee Patrick (*Marge*), Chick Chandler (*Harry*), Eve Miller (*Hatcheck Girl*), Robin Raymond (*Lillian Sawyer*), Lyle Talbot (*Stage Manager*), George Melford (*Stage Doorman*), Alvy Moore (*Katy's Boy Friend*), Henry Slate (*Dance Director*), Gavin Gordon (*Geoffrey*), Nolan Leary (*Archbishop*), Mimi Gibson (*Katy at Age 4*), Linda Lowell (*Katy at Age 8*), John Potter (*Steve at Age 2*), Jimmy Baird (*Steve at Age 6*), Billy Chapin (*Steve at Age 10*), Neal McCaskill (*Tim at Age 2*), Donald Gamble (*Tim at Age 6*), Charlotte Austin (*Lorna*), John Doucette (*Stage Manager*), Isabelle Dwan (*Sophie Tucker*), Donald Kerr (*Bobby Clark*).

An entertaining musical packed with tunes by Irving Berlin, THERE'S NO BUSINESS LIKE SHOW BUSINESS tells the fictional story of Merman and Dailey, two vaudeville performers who incorporate their growing brood into the act. Eventually their son Ray leaves the stage to become a priest, leaving the remaining two children, O'Connor and Gaynor, to continue in the family profession. O'Connor meets Monroe, a nightclub hatcheck girl with aspirations toward a singing career. He hears her sing, then runs into Monroe again when the family act is booked on the same bill with her at a Florida hotel. He persuades his family to do a different number, leaving room for Monroe to sing the enticing song "Heat Wave." Merman grows angry with the intrusion Monroe has made on a once stable act. When Monroe gets a part on Broadway, she persuades O'Connor and Gaynor to join her in this new show. Without their children, Merman and Dailey work as a duet, continuing to please audiences. While rehearsing for the Broadway opening, Gaynor meets the show's lyric writer, O'Brian. O'Connor, in the meantime, has fallen for Monroe but is convinced she is secretly involved with Eastham, the show's producer. The jealous O'Connor gets inebriated on opening night and ends up in a car wreck. He's rushed to the hospital, but in the best of show biz traditions, he's replaced by Merman. Dailey goes to see O'Connor, who has suffered only minor injuries. He angrily chews out his son for his unprofessional behavior, then hits O'Connor in anger, and storms out. He later returns to the hospital with Merman, but O'Connor has left and no one knows his whereabouts. Dailey grows depressed, which eventually causes him to leave the stage. Merman is ever the trouper, though, and continues to perform in the show despite her dislike for Monroe. Gaynor marries O'Brian, while Merman asks Dailey to perform in a benefit

for the Actor's Fund at the soon-to-be leveled Hippodrome Theater. Though Dailey turns down his wife's request, Gaynor decides to use the benefit to force a reconciliation between Merman and Monroe. Monroe explains that she has loved O'Connor all along and was never involved with Eastham. Merman accepts this as the truth, healing the long festering wounds. Ray shows up backstage, in his new position as an Army chaplain, as Merman is about to go on with her number. After she begins, Merman spies O'Connor standing backstage in a Navy uniform. Dailey joins his family, and the reunited clan, along with Monroe, take to the boards to sing a rousing rendition of "There's No Business Like Show Business." This is packed with every vaudeville cliche and stereotype the movies have ever conjured up, yet presented in a fresh and colorful manner that gives the film a warm glow. Merman naturally is a standout performer, but this is a lively cast that never allows the *tour de force* singer to dominate. Monroe, who reportedly felt intimidated at working with such strong musical comedy talents as Merman and O'Connor, is funny and sexy all at once, providing some nice bubble to the frothy story. Her romance with O'Connor works nicely, though Merman thought otherwise. "With all due respect to Marilyn," Merman wrote in her autobiography, "nobody could understand this combination. Mitzi and Donald would have made much more sense, but Marilyn was just too much glamour for Donald. It was like Eddie Fisher and Elizabeth Taylor in real life." Vaudeville entertainer Bobby Clark is portrayed in the film (by Kerr), yet he is mistakenly decked out in a raccoon coat, the garb normally associated with his partner, Paul McCullough. One of the highlights in the many musical numbers is each member of the family taking different turns (and accents) in a goofy and rousing version of "Alexander's Ragtime Band." The CinemaScope process is well employed, filling the screen with boisterous and colorful musical numbers. Filling out the wonderful Berlin songs are: "When the Midnight Choo Choo Leaves for Alabam" (sung by Merman, Dailey, Gaynor, O'Connor), "Let's Have Another Cup of Coffee" (sung by Merman), "Play a Simple Melody" (sung by Merman, Dailey), "After You Get What You Want You Don't Want It" (sung by Monroe), "You'd Be Surprised" (sung by Dailey), "A Sailor's Not a Sailor" (sung by Merman, Gaynor), "A Pretty Girl is Like a Melody" (sung by Merman, Dailey), "Lazy" (sung by Gaynor, O'Connor, Monroe), "If You Believe Me" (sung by Ray), "A Man Chases a Girl Until She Catches Him" (sung by O'Connor), "Marie."

p, Sol C. Siegel; d, Walter Lang; w, Phoebe Ephron, Henry Ephron (based on a story by Lamar Trotti); ph, Leon Shamroy (CinemaScope, DeLuxe Color); m, Irving Berlin; ed, Robert Simpson; md, Alfred Newman, Lionel Newman; art d, Lyle Wheeler, John De Cuir; spec eff, Ray Kellogg; ch, Robert Alton; m/l, Irving Berlin.

Musical   **Cas.**   **(PR:A   MPAA:NR)**

THERE'S NO PLACE BY SPACE   (SEE: HOLD ON!, 1965)

THERE'S ONE BORN EVERY MINUTE**½**   (1942) 60m UNIV bw

Hugh Herbert (*Lemuel P. Twine/Abner Twine/Col. Claudius Zebediah Twine*), Peggy Moran (*Helen Barbara Twine*), Tom Brown (*Jimmie Hanagan*), Guy Kibbee (*Lester Cadwalader, Sr.*), Catharine Doucet (*Minerva Twine*), Edgar Kennedy (*Mayor Moe Carson*), Scott Jorden [William Henry] (*Lester Cadwalader, Jr.*), Gus Schilling (*Prof. Asa Quisenberry*), Charles Halton (*Trumbull*), Elizabeth Taylor (*Gloria Twine*), Renie Riano (*Aphrodite Phipps*), Carl "Alfalfa" Switzer (*Junior Twine*), Jack Arnold [Vinton Haworth] (*Photographer*), Ralph Brooks (*Man at Meeting*), Frankie Van (*Busboy Brawler*), Melville Ruick (*Radio Announcer at Election*), Barbara Brown (*Club Woman*), Claire Whitney (*Mrs. Barstow*), Harlan Briggs (*Luke Simpson the Grocer*), Jack Gardner, Ted Oliver (*Reporters*), Bess Flowers (*Luncheon Extra*), Nell O'Day (*Antoinette*), Maude Eburne (*Agatha*).

A seemingly forgotten film, THERE'S ONE BORN EVERY MINUTE sports a 9-year-old Elizabeth Taylor in her movie debut. She plays the bratty sister of equally bratty OUR GANG alumnus Alfalfa Switzer, both children of bumbling pudding manufacturer Herbert. Herbert is drafted into his town's mayoral race by the village bosses, who want to deal with someone manageable. To boost the popularity of his pudding, Herbert declares that it contains the vital, little-known vitamin "Z," and sales skyrocket along with his political campaign. When it is revealed vitamin Z is a hoax, the town bosses try to dump Herbert and expose him as a fraud, but the scrappy pudding seller turns the tables and reveals them as the crooks. Herbert wins the election, despite his pudding scandal. While Herbert is fine in the role, the film lacks real punch due to the contrived situations and rather tame lunacy. Suspected at one time as being a discarded project for W.C. Fields (the title certainly belongs alongside NEVER GIVE A SUCKER AN EVEN BREAK and YOU CAN'T CHEAT AN HONEST MAN, and the plot and character names beg for Fields' participation), THERE'S ONE BORN EVERY MINUTE leaves one wondering whether the material would have been funnier if Fields had been the star instead of Herbert. The film apparently wasn't considered too memorable by its stars, either. When asked during an interview what it had been like to work with Taylor, Moran (who had a lead role) responded, "I never worked with Elizabeth Taylor. Your information is wrong." In Taylor's 1964 autobiography, she refers to the film only by its working title, "Man or Mouse."

p, Ken Goldsmith; d, Harold Young; w, Robert B. Hunt, Brenda Weisberg (based on the story "Man or Mouse" by Hunt); ph, John W. Boyle; ed, Maurice Wright; md, H.J. Salter; art d, Jack Otterson; cos, Vera West.

Comedy   (PR:A MPAA:NR)

THERE'S SOMETHING ABOUT A SOLDIER*½ (1943) 81m COL bw

Tom Neal (Wally Williams), Evelyn Keyes (Carol Harkness), Bruce Bennett (Frank Mallov), John Hubbard (Michael Crocker), Jeff Donnell (Jean Burton), Frank Sully (Alex Grybinski), Lewis Wilson (Bolivar Jefferson), Robert Stanford (George Edwards), Jonathan Hale (Gen. Sommerton), Hugh Beaumont (Lt. Martin), Kane Richmond (Sgt. Cummings), Douglass Drake (Burroughs), Craig Woods (Jonesy).

Neal plays the usual rebellious, wisecracking tough guy who joins Officer Candidate School and has to be slapped down before picking himself up off the ground and becoming a man. Girl friend Keyes and North African campaign veteran Bennett are the ones who put Neal on the road to manhood.

p, Samuel Bischoff; d, Alfred E. Green; w, Horace McCoy, Barry Trivers; ph, Philip Tannura, George Meehan; ed, Richard Fantl; md, M.W. Stoloff; art d, Lionel Banks.

Drama   (PR:A MPAA:NR)

THERE'S SOMETHING FUNNY GOING ON
(SEE: MAIDEN FOR A PRINCE, A, 1967, Fr./Ital.)

THERE'S THAT WOMAN AGAIN**
(1938) 70m COL bw (GB: WHAT A WOMAN)

Melvyn Douglas (Bill Reardon), Virginia Bruce (Sally Reardon), Margaret Lindsay (Mrs. Nacelle), Stanley Ridges (Tony Croy), Gordon Oliver (Charles Crenshaw), Tom Dugan (Flannigan), Don Beddoe (Johnson), Jonathan Hale (Rolfe Davis), Pierre Watkin (Mr. Nacelle), Paul Harvey (Stone), Marc Lawrence (Stevens), Charles Wilson (Police Captain), Don Barry, Jack Hatfield (Bellboys), Harry Burns (Shoe Shop Proprietor), Helen Lynd (Pearl), Georgette Rhodes, Lillian Yarbo (Attendants), Vivien Oakland (Large Woman), William Newell (Waiter), Gladys Blake (Fran), Pat Flaherty (Husky Gent), Dick Curtis (Subway Guard), June Gittelson (Fat Woman), Lucille Lund (Receptionist), John Dilson (Coroner's Deputy), Eric Mayne (Bearded Man), Maurice Costello, Russell Heustis (Headwaiters), Lola Jensen (Hat Check Girl), Frank Hall Crayne, Charles McMurphy (Detectives), Mantan Moreland (Porter), George Turner (Delivery Boy), Lee Shumway (Policeman), Nell Craig, Lillian West (Women), Allen Fox (Taxi Driver), Larry Wheat (Clerk).

This sequel to THERE'S ALWAYS A WOMAN retained director Hall and debonair star Douglas but this time Bruce replaced Joan Blondell in the role of Douglas' wife and she simply couldn't muster the skills of her predecessor. The Mr.-and-Mrs. team of private detectives is this time trailing some stolen jewels. While looking into the robbery, a pair of murders, including that of a diamond merchant, crop up. In the film's funniest scene, the erstwhile Bruce accidentally is caught in the shower of one of the suspects, making for a few good moments. However, the picture is no THE THIN MAN and ultimately rings hollow in its attempt to be a light, charming murder mystery. Things are just a little too cute for their own good and the story is filled with too many implausibilities. Douglas and Bruce have little trouble finding the clues they need or getting into seemingly locked doors, making for an easy, predictable chain of events. Though Douglas gives this one of his usual gentlemanly humorous performances, Bruce overdoes it trying to re-create Blondell's performance. Though she has some funny moments, Bruce doesn't remain consistent. Bogged down with cliches and forced demeanor that passes off as engaging, this sequel is a poor follow-up to a clever effort.

p, B. B. Kahane; d, Alexander Hall; w, Philip G. Epstein, James Edward Grant, Ken Englund (based on a play by Gladys Lehman, Wilson Collison); ph, Joseph Walker; ed, Viola Lawrence; md, Morris W. Stoloff; art d, Lionel Banks; set d, Babs Johnstone.

Comedy/Mystery   (PR:AA MPAA:NR)

THERESE***   (1963, Fr.) 107m Filmel/Pathe Contemporary bw
(THERESE DESQUEYROUX)

Emmanuelle Riva (Therese Desqueyroux), Philippe Noiret (Bernard Desqueyroux), Edith Scob (Anne de la Trave), Sami Frey (Jean Azevedo), Renee Devillers (Mme. de la Trave), Richard Saint-Bris (Hector de la Trave), Lucien Nat (Jerome Larroque), Helene Dieudonne (Aunt Clara), Jeanne Perez (Balionte), Jacques Monod (Duros), Jean-Jacques Remy (Specialist).

Georges Franju's incredibly faithful adaptation of Francois Mauriac's novel about a woman, Riva, who feels trapped in her marriage to the pompous French upper-class Noiret. In order to escape from her country chateau life, Riva poisons Noiret with arsenic, but the dosage isn't lethal. Instead of jail, Riva is allowed to return home when Noiret refuses to file charges against her. Noiret devises his own prison for Riva and locks her in a room, allowing her only cigarettes and wine to sustain life. She rapidly deteriorates and when her friends are shocked at her appearance during a social gathering he allows Riva to leave for Paris. Riva is finally free, leaving behind Noiret who still cannot understand why she tried to kill him. Riva, who was so compelling in HIROSHIMA MON AMOUR (1959), again turns in a tortured

performance, receiving a Best Actress award at the Venice Film Fest. Special credit must also go to the direction of Franju for capturing the spirit of the novel, to the adaptation by Mauriac and his son Claude, and to the refined piano score of Maurice Jarre. THERESE so impressed the Cannes Festival jury that it was cited "for the successful arrangement of special effects, color, and sound in a discerning montage." (In French; English subtitles.)

p, Eugene Lepicier; d, Georges Franju; w, Francois Mauriac, Claude Mauriac, Franju (based on the novel Therese Desqueyroux by Francois Mauriac); ph, Christian Matras; m, Maurice Jarre; ed, Gilbert Natot; art d, Jacques Chalvet; cos, Lola Prussac.

Drama   (PR:O MPAA:NR)

THERESE AND ISABELLE**   (1968, U.S./Ger.) 118m
Amsterdam-Berolina/Audubon Films bw (THERESE UND ISABELL)

Essy Persson (Therese), Anna Gael (Isabelle), Barbara Laage (Therese's Mother), Anne Vernon (Mlle. Le Blanc), Maurice Teynac (Mons. Martin), Remy Longa (Pierre), Simone Paris (The Madame), Suzanne Marchellier (Mlle. Germain), Nathalie Nort (Renee), Darcy Pullian (Agnes), Martine Leclerc (Martine), Bernadette Stern (Francoise), Serge Geraert, Edith Ploquin, Alexander Kobes.

A fairly sensitive, if somewhat exploitative drama about a young woman's foray into a lesbian relationship. Told in a flashback triggered by a visit to her old school, Persson recalls being sent away to school by an indifferent mother, recently married to a man who dislikes children. Painfully lonely, Persson relies on fellow female student Gael for solace. After both young woman engage in brutal sexual relations with men, they look to each other for sexual fulfillment. At one point the affair begins to get ugly, and before the women can straighten things out, Gael is removed from the school by her mother. Shaken and saddened by the memories of her lesbian lover, Persson returns to her fiance. (In French; English subtitles.)

p&d, Radley H. Metzger; w, Jesse Vogel (based on the novel Therese et Isabelle by Violette Leduc); ph, Hans Jura (Ultrascope); m, Georges Auric; ed, Humphrey Wood; makeup, Marie-Madeleine Paris.

Drama   **Cas.**   (PR:O MPAA:NR)

THERESE DESQUEYROUX   (SEE: THERESE, 1963, Fr.)

THERESE UND ISABELL   (SEE: THERESE AND ISABELLE, 1968,
U.S./Ger.)

THESE ARE THE DAMNED***   (1965, Brit.) 77m
Hammer-Swallow/COL bw (GB: THE DAMNED)

Macdonald Carey (Simon Wells), Shirley Ann Field (Joan), Viveca Lindfors (Freya Neilson, Sculptress), Alexander Knox (Bernard, Scientist), Oliver Reed (King), Walter Gotell (Maj. Holland), James Villiers (Capt. Gregory), Thomas Kempinski (Ted), Kenneth Cope (Sid), Brian Oulton (Mr. Dingle), Barbara Everest (Miss Lamont), Alan McClelland (Mr. Stuart), James Maxwell (Mr. Talbot), Rachel Clay (Victoria), Caroline Sheldon (Elizabeth), Rebecca Dignam (Anne), Siobhan Taylor (Mary), Nicholas Clay (Richard), Kit Williams (Henry), Christopher Witty (William), David Palmer (George), John Thompson (Charles), David Gregory, Anthony Valentine, Larry Martyn, Leon Garcia, Jeremy Phillips (Teddy-boys), Edward Harvey, Neil Wilson, Fiona Duncan, Tommy Trinder, Victor Gorf.

One of the best British science-fiction films and one of the most controversial. THESE ARE THE DAMNED was made in 1961, butchered by its producers, and not released in England until 1963, eventually finding its way to American shores in 1965. The story concerns a young American, Carey, who, while visiting the English seaside, meets and falls in love with Field, the sister of sadistic and lecherous motorcycle gang leader Reed. Reed despises the American and this rivalry for his sister's affections bring his own incestuous feelings for her bubbling to the surface. Eventually the couple are driven away by Reed and they take refuge in a cave under a nearby military base. There, they discover a group of children living in the cave, who are cold to the touch. The children are the result of an experiment conducted by scientist Knox, who seeks to develop a race of humans capable of surviving an atomic blast. Unfortunately, the children have all become radioactive during the experiment and unwittingly kill anyone who comes in unguarded contact with them. Seeing the children as surrogates for the family they will never be allowed to have (if Reed has anything to say about it), Carey and Field free the youngsters and are unknowingly subjected to massive doses of radiation. The climax sees the scientist and the military recapturing the children as a lone helicopter hovers over the young couple (who have drifted out to sea in a small boat), waiting for them to die. Unrelentingly grim and haunting, the film was directed by American expatriate Losey, who fled the U.S. because of his declared Marxist beliefs. The film won the Golden Asteroid at the 1964 Trieste Festival of Science Fiction Films.

p, Anthony Hinds; d, Joseph Losey; w, Evan Jones (based on the novel The Children of Light by Henry Lionel Lawrence); ph, Arthur Grant (Hammerscope); m, James Bernard; ed, Reginald Mills; md, John Hollingsworth; prod d, Bernard Robinson; art d, Don Mingaye; cos, Mollie Arbuthnot; m/l, "Black Leather Rock," James Bernard, Evan Jones.

Science Fiction (PR:C MPAA:NR)

THESE CHARMING PEOPLE*½   (1931, Brit.) 82m PAR bw

Cyril Maude (*Col. Crawford*), Godfrey Tearle (*James Berridge*), Nora Swinburne (*Julia Berridge*), Ann Todd (*Pamela Crawford*), Anthony Ireland (*Geoffrey Allen*), Cyril Raymond (*Miles Winter*), C.V. France (*Minx*), Billy Shine (*Ulysses Wiggins*), Vincent Holman, Minnie Rayner.

British colonel Maude becomes very distressed when he learns that his daughter Swinburne plans to leave her boring and unattentive husband Tearle, a shipbuilder, for a fling with his male secretary. When it is learned that the latter is actually the son of Maude's butler, Maude decides this affair will never do, chases his daughter to Paris, and ends the relationship. Despite the fact that this was the first film Paramount studios produced in England, the movie is typically British and dull.

p, Walter Morosco; d, Louis Mercanton; w, Hugh Perceval, Irving Howard (based on the play "Dear Father" by Michael Arlen).

Drama (PR:A MPAA:NR)

THESE DANGEROUS YEARS (SEE: DANGEROUS YOUTH, 1958, Brit.)

THESE GLAMOUR GIRLS**   (1939) 78m MGM bw

Lew Ayres (*Philip S. Griswold*), Lana Turner (*Jane Thomas*), Tom Brown (*Homer Ten Eyck*), Richard Carlson (*Joe*), Jane Bryan (*Carol Christy*), Anita Louise (*Daphne Graves*), Marsha Hunt (*Betty Ainsbridge*), Ann Rutherford (*Mary Rose Wilston*), Mary Beth Hughes (*Ann Van Reichton*), Owen Davis, Jr (*Greg Smith*), Ernest Truex (*Alumnus*), Sumner Getchell (*"Blimpy"*), Peter [Lind] Hayes (*Skel Lorimer*), Don Castle (*Jack*), Tom Collins (*Tommy Torgler*), Henry Kolker (*Mr. Griswold*), Dennie Moore (*Mavis*), Mary Forbes (*Mrs. Van Reichton*), Nella Walker (*Mrs. Graves*), Robert Emmett Keane (*Mr. Wilston*), Tom Kennedy, James Pierce (*Bouncers*), Gladys Blake (*Cashier*), John Kelly (*Sailor*), Dave Oliver (*Cabby*), Lee Bennett, Rod Bacon, Russell Wade (*College Boys*), Arthur Q. Bryan (*Dance Customer*).

A forgettable college comedy-drama that served as Lana Turner's first leading role. First published as a story in Cosmopolitan, it's a purported satire of the snobbish Ivy League types who shun anyone outside their small circle of friends. Ayres, Carlson, Brown, and Davis are the undergrads. One night, while out on the town and in his cups, Ayres meets dime-a-dance girl Turner and invites her up to his school for the annual party weekend. When he recovers his senses, he's forgotten that he extended the invitation. The weekend begins and Turner arrives, only to be told by Ayres that it might be better if she departed quickly because the other girls–Rutherford, Hughes, Louise, et al–will make mincemeat out of her and cut her dead. Turner shrugs; she's already there, and not about to go home. True to Ayres' prediction, the snobs gang up on Turner, but she is sharper than they are and tells the crowd off in strong words. The parties commence and Turner goes to every one of them, winning hearts along the way. At one party, she performs a wild dance and her personality is so refreshing to all the boys that she is soon the belle of all the balls. At the conclusion, Ayres has finally awakened to the fact that the debutantes are empty-headed twittes and that Turner is the woman for him. In between the comedy, there's an uncalled-for dramatic moment when 23-year-old Hunt, a recent widow and former prom queen, takes her own life because she can't find a guy. Peter Lind Hayes stands out as he does the dance with Turner. Good dialog in the script, and Turner shows a flair for comedy, but almost everyone else is a stick and the production bears little resemblance to reality. Contract player Rutherford, who was Andy Hardy's girl friend, is wasted in a small role.

p, Sam Zimbalist; d, S. Sylvan Simon; w, Jane Hall, Marion Parsonnet (based on a magazine story by Hall); ph, Alfred Gilks; m, Edward Ward, David Snell; ed, Harold F. Kress; art d, Cedric Gibbons, Harry McAfee; set d, Edwin B. Willis; cos, Dolly Tree; m/l, "Loveliness," Ward, Bob Wright, Chet Forrest.

Comedy/Drama (PR:A MPAA:NR)

THESE THIRTY YEARS**   (1934) 60m Industrial/Caravel bw

K. Elmo Lowe (*Dave Haines*), Frances Lee (*Mae Lercombe*), Robert Strange (*Jed Travers*), Donald MacDonald (*Sam Bailey*), Robert T. Haines (*The Colonel*), Frederick Forrester (*Doc Anderson*), Alice John (*Mrs. Haines*), Jimmie Barry (*Bill Tibbets*), David Morris (*Robert Haines*), Helen Wynn (*Ann Bailey*).

The early 20th Century is reviewed in this obscure independent film from New York. Lowe is a man convinced of the worth of Henry Ford's newfangled automobile, and he becomes a successful businessman selling them. His son, Morris, though, grows up rich and spoiled and wants nothing to do with new car sales, preferring to play the booming stock market. Of course the stock market crash wipes him out and he returns to the family business, having seen the error of his ways. Interesting performances by a cast of Broadway actors lost in poor production values.

d&w, Dave Pincus (based on a story by James Creelman, Phil Strong); ph, Jules Sindic.

Drama (PR:A MPAA:NR)

THESE THOUSAND HILLS***   (1959) 96m FOX c

Don Murray (*Lat Evans*), Richard Egan (*Jehu*), Lee Remick (*Callie*), Patricia Owens (*Joyce*), Stuart Whitman (*Tom Ping*), Albert Dekker (*Conrad*), Harold J. Stone (*Ram Butler*), Royal Dano (*Carmichael*), Jean Willes (*Jen*), Douglas Fowley (*Whitney*), Fuzzy Knight (*Sally the Cook*), Robert Alder (*Godwin*), Barbara Morrison (*Miss Fran*), Ned Wever (*Gorham*), Ken Renard (*Happy*), Steve Darrell (*McLean*), Tom Greenway (*Chanault*), Frank Lavier (*Little Runner*), Nelson Leigh (*Brother Van*), Ben Wright (*Frenchy*), Jesse Kirkpatrick (*Strain*), John Epper (*Swede*).

A fine, thoughtful western stars Murray as an ambitious cowboy who borrows money from dance hall floozy Remick to buy a ranch and make a new life. Unfortunately he abandons all his seedier friends and enters into a loveless marriage with banker Dekker's niece Owens in order to better his position in the community. Murray goes so far as to allow a posse led by Egan to hang his old riding buddy Whitman, rather than ruffle the feathers of any of his new-found society friends. Eventually Murray must abandon his pretensions and become his old self when Egan goes after Remick. Murray is nearly killed by Egan, but Remick once again comes to his rescue and shoots the villain. An interesting character study, the film is filled with good performances.

p, David Weisbart; d, Richard Fleischer; w, Alfred Hayes (based on the novel *These Thousand Hills* by A.B. Guthrie, Jr.); ph, Charles G. Clarke (CinemaScope, DeLuxe Color); m, Leigh Harline; ed, Hugh S. Fowler; art d, Lyle R. Wheeler, Herman A. Blumenthal; m/l, "These Thousand Hills," Ned Washington, Harry Warren (sung by Randy Sparks).

Western (PR:A MPAA:NR)

THESE THREE****   (1936) 93m UA bw

Miriam Hopkins (*Martha Dobie*), Merle Oberon (*Karen Wright*), Joel McCrea (*Dr. Joseph Cardin*), Catherine Doucet (*Mrs. Lily Mortar*), Alma Kruger (*Mrs. Tilford*), Bonita Granville (*Mary Tilford*), Marcia Mae Jones (*Rosalie Wells*), Carmencita Johnson (*Evelyn*), Mary Ann Durkin (*Joyce Walton*), Margaret Hamilton (*Agatha*), Mary Louise Cooper (*Helen Burton*), Walter Brennan (*Taxi Driver*), Frank McGlynn, Anya Taranda, Jerry Larkin.

Censors forced Lillian Hellman to tone down the lesbian theme in her play "The Children's Hour" but she came up with a screenplay solution that made this picture even better than the hit play, which was still running when the movie was released. Granville, in an Oscar-nominated role, is a mean, vicious girl who is censured by the teachers at the posh private school she attends. The school is run by college friends Oberon and Hopkins and is located in a large New England home which has been inherited. Oberon is the warm and loving one of the two while Hopkins is the austere yankee type. Oberon is in love with the local doctor, McCrea, who shares her passion but maintains a close friendship with Hopkins. When Granville gets into trouble with the stern teachers, she retaliates by making up lies about them, saying that Hopkins and McCrea had been "carrying on" in a bedroom near where the students had been sleeping. She tells this to her grandmother, Kruger, who knows that Granville is a compulsive liar but believes her anyhow, especially after the lie is corroborated by Jones, a 9-year-old whom Granville has enlisted to support the fabricated story. Jones had stolen a watch and Granville knows about it so she uses blackmail to get Jones to back her up. Heavy dramatic scenes as charges and countercharges are hurled. When Hopkins breaks down Jones, who confesses that the whole thing was a lie, Kruger is forced to apologize, but the school has been ruined by what's happened. A happy ending is tacked on. McCrea has gone to Vienna and when Oberon learns through Kruger that Granville has been lying, she goes to Austria to join him. All indications of the incipient lesbianism have been deleted from this version, which uses a love triangle as the fulcrum around which the story seesaws. While the play was on Broadway for over 600 performances, Goldwyn thought he might be able to take advantage of the notoriety of Hellman's first stage effort by getting the movie out to the theaters. He'd purchased the rights for $50,000 but the Production Code people insisted he remove much of what made the play such a sensation. Goldwyn was true to the author and hired her to make the alterations. More than 25 years later, the movie was made again under the original title, with Hopkins in another role and Wyler again directing. Even though that picture retained the play's theme, it didn't work as well as this one. In both cases, the major flaw of the story was in believing a character like Granville (it was Karen Balkin in the remake), who had been established as one of the rottenest kids ever seen on any screen. This was Goldwyn's and Wyler's first of eight collaborations, some of which remain as classics to this day. Wyler here worked with Toland for the first time; he would continue their association for many years. Toland died at 44 after having photographed almost half of Goldwyn's filmic output (as well as his memorable work on CITIZEN KANE). The stage presentation starred Katherine Emery, Robert Keith, and Anne Revere, with Florence McGee as the brat. Despite Granville's superb acting, she was beaten out for the Best Supporting Actress Oscar by Gale Sondergaard for her work in ANTHONY

ADVERSE. Often, Academy voters will bypass a youngster in favor of an older person because they figure the young one has many more opportunities to win the award in years to come. Other than MAID OF SALEM (1937), Granville never did get another chance at bat. She eventually married millionaire Jack Wrather and became a producer. Her work in THESE THREE was a revelation for the audiences who were accustomed to seeing sweet little girls like Shirley Temple. Remade as THE CHILDREN'S HOUR in 1961.

p, Samuel Goldwyn; d, William Wyler; w, Lillian Hellman (based on her play "The Children's Hour"); ph, Gregg Toland; m, Alfred Newman; ed, Daniel Mandell; art d, Richard Day; cos, Omar Kiam.

Drama   **Cas.**   **(PR:C MPAA:NR)**

THESE WILDER YEARS***   (1956) 91m MGM bw

James Cagney (*Steve Bradford*), Barbara Stanwyck (*Ann Dempster*), Walter Pidgeon (*James Rayburn*), Betty Lou Keim (*Suzie*), Don Dubbins (*Mark*), Edward Andrews (*Mr. Spottsford*), Basil Ruysdael (*Judge*), Grandon Rhodes (*Roy Oliphant*), Will Wright (*Old Cab Driver*), Lewis Martin (*Dr. Miller*), Dorothy Adams (*Aunt Martha*), Dean Jones (*Hardware Clerk*), Herb Vigran (*Traffic Cop*), Ruth Lee (*Miss Finch*), Matt Moore (*Gateman*), Jack Kenny (*Chauffeur*), Harry Tyler (*Doorman*), Luana Lee (*Stenographer*), William Forrest (*Blount*), John Maxwell, Emmett Vogan, Charles Evans (*Board of Directors*), Michael Landon (*Boy in Poolroom*), Leon Tyler (*Student Secretary*), Sid Tomack (*Jess the Bartender*), Russ Whitney (*Hotel Clerk*), Audrey Swanson (*Saleslady*), Jimmy Hayes (*Young Reporter*), Tom Laughlin (*Football Player*), Bob Alden (*Bellhop*), Jimmy Ogg (*Ad Lib Boy*), Nesdon Booth, Ricky McGough, Louis Towers, Mary Alan Hokanson, Marc Platt, Mary Lawrence, Elizabeth Flournoy, Charles Herbert, Kathleen Mulqueen, Burt Mustin, Russell Simpson, Bruce Irwin, Charles Tannen, Billy Wayne, Lillian Powell, Edna Holland, Ralph Neff, Lois Kimbrell, Frank Connor, Eleanor Grumer, Byron Amidon, Janet Lake, Don Burnett.

Having forsaken the notion of a wife and family in order to concentrate on making his fortune in the steel industry, middle-aged multimillionaire Cagney begins to feel the loneliness that is sure to mark his old age. To circumvent the inevitable, he launches a search for his illegitimate son whom had been given up for adoption 20 years before. At the adoption agency Cagney meets Stanwyck, the woman in charge of the institution. Stanwyck is familiar with the case, and refuses to help Cagney track down his son because it would violate the boy's privacy. Cagney and Stanwyck are attracted to each other, but this does not stop her from standing firm, nor he from suing the agency for information regarding the whereabouts of his son. With the help of his lawyer, Pidgeon, Cagney continues his search while preparing for a legal battle. Cagney loses in court, but his relationship with Stanwyck has taught him that his son's right to live his life without outside interference is more important than Cagney's desire to suddenly become a father. Eventually Cagney does track down his son, Dubbins, and follows him to a bowling alley where he learns that the young man is very happy and content living with his foster parents. Realizing it would be a mistake to force a reconciliation, Cagney turns his attention to Keim, a 16 year-old girl pregnant with an illegitimate child who has turned to Stanwyck for help. Instead of seeing the girl give up her baby, Cagney adopts Keim–becoming a father and grandfather at the same time. Though THESE WILDER YEARS is really nothing more than a sudsy tearjerker, the performances by Cagney and Stanwyck give the film a special quality it would not have had otherwise. Ironically, the film marked the long-delayed pairing of the two stars, an event which almost took place back in 1931 when Stanwyck and Cagney were slated to star in NIGHT NURSE. By the time shooting was to commence, however, Cagney had been catapulted into super-stardom in PUBLIC ENEMY and the relatively small supporting role went to another young actor on the lot, Clark Gable. THESE WILDER YEARS seemed to be in trouble from the start. Originally titled *All Our Yesterdays*, the film was to have starred Debbie Reynolds as the young unwed mother. When this deal failed to gel, the title was changed to *Somewhere I'll Find Him* with Susan Strasberg cast as the girl and Helen Hayes in the part of the adoption agency mistress. This also fell through, and Myrna Loy was offered the Hayes role. Loy wasn't available so finally the studio opted for Stanwyck and Cagney in the leads with Keim as the girl. The title was changed again to *The Wilder Years*, and again to *The Wild Years*, until eventually a hybrid of the last two titles, THESE WILDER YEARS was chosen. Not only did the studio have trouble selecting lead players, but the director was changed from John Sturges to Roy Rowland. During all this confusion, someone forgot to take a close look at the script. The film is filled with tired situations, dull dialog, and downright maudlin sentiment, but somehow Cagney and Stanwyck made it work through sheer professionalism and experience. The two actors enjoyed and respected each other's talent and even treated the crew to an impromptu dance routine with steps learned during their vaudeville days in New York during the 1920s.

p, Jules Schermer; d, Roy Rowland; w, Frank Fenton (based on a story by Ralph Wheelwright); ph, George J. Folsey; m, Jeff Alexander; ed, Ben Lewis; art d, Cedric Gibbons, Preston Ames; set d, Edwin B. Willis, Edward G. Boyle; cos, Helen Rose; makeup, William Tuttle.

Drama   **(PR:C MPAA:NR)**

THESEUS AGAINST THE MINOTAUR

(SEE: MINOTAUR, THE, 1961, Ital.)

THEY ALL COME OUT**½   (1939) 70m MGM bw

Rita Johnson (*Kitty*), Tom Neal (*Joe Z. Cameron*), Bernard Nedell (*Clyde Madigan/Reno*), Edward Gargan (*George Jacklin/Bugs*), John Gallaudet (*Albert Crane/Groper*), Addison Richards (*Warden in Atlanta*), Frank M. Thomas (*Superintendent in Chillicothe*), George Tobias ("*Sloppy Joe*"), Ann Shoemaker (*Dr. Ellen Hollis*), Charles Lane (*Psychiatrist*).

Masterful horror and film noir director Jacques Tourneur (CAT PEOPLE, I WALKED WITH A ZOMBIE, OUT OF THE PAST) made his feature film debut with THEY ALL COME OUT, which was originally part of MGM's CRIME DOES NOT PAY series of two-reelers (a number of which Tourneur directed), but was eventually expanded into a feature-length film. Neal stars as the getaway driver for a gang of thieves led by Nedell who is eventually captured along with his fellow gang members and thrown in prison. From there the film shifts to a near-documentary style showing the rehabilitation offered to interested prisoners. Neal and gang moll Johnson decide to make a go of the straight and narrow, while tough-guy Nedell forsakes reform and remains a hood. The couple's good behavior earns them an early parole and they leave prison with crime far behind them. While the movie is basically just another crime melodrama, Tourneur brings his flair for visuals and handling actors into play, nudging this prison picture up a notch or two.

p, Jack Chertok; d, Jacques Tourneur; w, John C. Higgins; ph, Clyde DeVinna, Paul C. Vogel; ed, Ralph E. Goldstein.

Crime   **(PR:A MPAA:NR)**

THEY ALL DIED LAUGHING   (SEE: JOLLY BAD FELLOW, A, 1964, Brit.)

THEY ALL KISSED THE BRIDE***½   (1942) 85m bw

Joan Crawford (*Margaret J. Drew*), Melvyn Douglas (*Michael Holmes*), Roland Young (*Marsh*), Billie Burke (*Mrs. Drew*), Allen Jenkins (*Johnny Johnson*), Andrew Tombes (*Crane*), Helen Parrish (*Vivian Drew*), Emory Parnell (*Mahony*), Mary Treen (*Susie Johnson*), Nydia Westman (*Secretary*), Ivan Simpson (*Dr. Cassell*), Roger Clark (*Stephen Pettingill*), Gordon Jones (*Taxi Driver*), Edward Gargan (*Private Policeman*), Larry Parks (*Joe Krim*), Tom Dugan (*Callahan*), John Dilson (*Man*), Charles Miller, George Pembroke, Wyndham Standing (*Department Heads*), Shirley Patterson (*Receptionist*), Douglas Wood (*Hoover*), Boyd Irwin (*Endore*), Frank Dawson (*Nolan*), Ann Doran (*Maid*), Alma Carroll (*Bridesmaid*), Charles Coleman (*Butler*), Father Neal Dodd (*Minister*), Ralph Sanford (*Detective*), Wheaton Chambers, Arthur Stuart Hull, Richard Kipling, Hal Cooke, John Merkyl (*Board Members*), Dale Van Sickel (*Marine*), Polly Bailey (*Irish Woman*), Walter Merrill, Terrance Ray, Harry Strang, Charles Sullivan, Frank Marlowe, Ernie Adams, Lyle Latell, Ralph Peters (*Truck Drivers*), Charles Lane, Kitty Kelly (*Spotters*), Tom Lincir, Rosalie Miller (*Dance Specialties*), George McKay (*Announcer*), Norman Willis (*Cop*), Charles Halton (*Doctor*).

A witty script, crisp direction, and bubbly performances all contribute to a fun movie which was originally slated for Carole Lombard but was given to Crawford when Lombard died in a tragic airplane accident while returning from a war bond selling trip to the Midwest in January, 1942. Crawford is splendid as the tough businesswoman who is devoted to her work and has little time to smile. Her father, a trucking czar, dies and, as the oldest daughter, she takes over the company. Her dad was tough, but a pussycat next to what she does, whipping the firm into shipshape and relentlessly giving everyone–including her mother, Burke, playing her usual flighty type–a hard time. The younger sister is Parrish; Crawford is trying to maneuver her into a marriage of convenience that would be based on money, rather than love. The men on the board of directors and the many truck drivers in her employ are all cowed by her ruthlessness. Enter Douglas, a newspaperman who is privy to some inside information and uses it to write a series of editorial blasts against Crawford and the way she runs her business. When Douglas and Crawford meet (and she thinks he's someone else) he finds her attractive and reckons he might be able to thaw out this ice princess. Douglas explains that these truck drivers who work for her aren't just faceless numbers, they are real human beings with wants and desires, and they are also men who care about what they do. She would be wise to get to know them better. Always striving to improve her knowledge, Crawford attends a truck drivers' dance and winds up doing the "Lindy Hop" with one of her employees, Jenkins. Douglas has a secondary method to his friendliness. He wants to keep writing about Crawford and enlists garrulous Jenkins into revealing other information about the company and the way the men feel about their comely employer. At the same time, Crawford is learning that there is more to life than assets and liabilities and ledgers and profit-and-loss statements. Douglas is his usual buoyant self and Crawford begins to fall in love with him, melting in the rays of his sunny personality. The change is for the better and she starts to mellow, stops sacking people, starts dressing in a feminine fashion, begins to listen to the needs of both family and hired help and, in the end, winds up with Douglas. Some very funny sight gags include the one where Crawford's knees buckle when she is in the presence of a man she loves (a genetic throwback that happened to Burke when she met her husband). Many funny lines, but some of them are so dated that one might wince at them now. What will keep this picture from ever being seen on Tokyo TV is a line Crawford quips. She says: "When I want a sneak, I'll get the best and hire a Jap." Audiences roared at that in 1942, as it was only 6 months after the attack at Pearl Harbor. Later, it seemed of questionable taste and was cut from some showings on TV, lest the country that sent us most of the television sets be offended.

p, Edward Kaufman; d, Alexander Hall; w, P. J. Wolfson, Andrew P. Solt, Henry Altimus (based on the story by Gina Kaus, Solt); ph, Joseph Walker; m, Werner R. Heymann; ed, Viola Lawrence; md, Morris W. Stoloff; art d, Lionel Banks, Cary Odell; cos, Irene.

Comedy (PR:A-C MPAA:NR)

THEY ALL LAUGHED*** (1981) 115m Time-Life Films-Moon/FOX-UA Classics c

Audrey Hepburn (*Angela Niotes*), Ben Gazzara (*John Russo*), John Ritter (*Charles Rutledge*), Colleen Camp (*Christy Miller*), Patti Hansen (*Deborah "Sam" Wilson*), Dorothy Stratten (*Dolores Martin*), George Morfogen (*Leon Leondopolous*), Blaine Novak (*Arthur Brodsky*), Sean Ferrer (*Jose*), Linda MacEwen (*Amy Lester*), Glenn Scarpelli (*Michael Niotes*), Vassily Lambrinos (*Stavros Niotes*), Antonia Bogdanovich (*Stefania Russo*), Alexandra Bogdanovich (*Georgina Russo*), Sheila Stodden (*Barbara Jo*), Lisa Dunsheath (*Tulips*), Joyce Hyser (*Sylvia*), Elizabeth Pena (*Rita*), Riccardo Bertoni (*Martin*), Shawn Casey (*Laura*), Earl Poole Ball, Jo-El Sonnier, Eric Kaz, Ken Kosek, Larry Campbell, Lincoln Schleifer, John Sholle, Brigitte Catapano, Parris Bruckner, Vivien Landau, Lillian Silverstone, Steve Cole, Steven Fromewick, Tzi Ma, William Craft, William DeNino, Kelly Donnally, Linda Ray, Andrea Weber, Spike Spigener, Nick Micskey, Robert Hawes, Michael McGifford, Vittorio Tiburz, Alex MacArthur, George Cardini, Robert Skilling, Kennely Noble, Anthony Paige, Violetta Landek, Brandy Roven, Joan Lauren, Debora Lass, Noel King, Don Marino, John Murray, Sharon Spits, Marty Greene, Harry Matson, Brett Smrz, Brian Smrz, Alex Stevens, Victoria Van Der Kloot.

This light-hearted maze of romance is set against a detective background as a vehicle for the characters to pursue one another. The well-composed Gazzara, the bumbling Ritter (who looks remarkably like director Bogdanovich), and the ultra-hip Novak all are employed by a detective agency and become romantically involved with the women they are shadowing. Gazzara charms his way into the bed of Hepburn, whose husband has hired the detective to keep a watchful eye over her. In the meantime, Gazzara hits it off famously with tough and sexy cab driver Hansen. Inter-cut with Gazzara's frolicking is Ritter and Novak trailing the vivacious Stratten, whose jealous husband wants to know her every move. By the finale Gazzara has lost Hepburn but retains the consolation of Hansen, whom he affectionately calls "Sam," and Ritter has overcome his shyness and won over Stratten. The film has been praised by many for its breezy, carefree style (compared somewhat flippantly to that of Hawks) but what it gains in lightness of tone it loses in a weak, hard-to-grasp structure. As lovable as the characters and their situations are, one is never quite sure where the film is leading; in fact it never feels as if the story has actually begun. THEY ALL LAUGHED spent nearly a year on the shelf and would have been seen by almost no one (as it is very few have yet seen the film) had Bogdanovich not bought back the film from Fox and distributed himself. It is unfortunate that the chief interest of the film lies in the presence of former Playboy magazine playmate Stratten, who was killed before the film's release. The circumstances surrounding her death were frighteningly similar to those that Bogdanovich sets up in his film, where Stratten is pursued by Ritter while evading the watchful eye of her jealous husband. In real life Stratten was having an affair with Bogdanovich during the filming of THEY ALL LAUGHED and was being trailed by a detective hired by her husband Paul Snider. Her story has become a favorite of the press, implicating Playboy head Hugh Hefner, Bogdanovich (who published a piece of romanticized sleaziness about Stratten, *The Killing Of The Unicorn*), and Snider, who became infamous in Paul Schraeder's STAR 80.

p, George Morfogen, Blaine Novak; d&w, Peter Bogdanovich; ph, Robby Muller (DeLuxe Color); m, Douglas Dilge; ed, Scott Vickrey; art d, Kert Lundell; set d, Joe "Peppy" Bird.

Romance Comedy **Cas.** (PR:A MPAA:PG)

THEY ARE GUILTY (SEE: ARE THESE OUR PARENTS?, 1944)

THEY ARE NOT ANGELS**½ (1948, Fr.) 130m Pathe/Siritzky International bw

Pierre Blanchar (*Ferane*), Raymond Bussieres (*Paname*), Jean Wall (*Ben Sassein*), Christian Bertola (*Lt. de Carrizy*), Rene Lefevre (*Baptiste*), Jeanne Crispin (*Berthe Servais*), Pierre Louis (*Drobel*), Charles Moulin (*Le Gorille*), Mouloudji (*Le Canaque*), Henri Nassiet (*Bouvier*), Nic Vogel (*Veran*), Andrieux (*Brizeux*), Daphne Courtney (*June*), John Howard (*Willy*), Pamela Sterling (*Molly*), Charles Rolfe (*Marc Intyre*).

Well done, but unspectacular French WW II film sees the invasion of France by 400 English paratroopers who aim to strike and weaken Hitler's troops ahead of D-Day. Great detail is given to the training of the troops and the planning of the invasion, which leads to the second half of the film - the

British paratroopers teaming up with the French commandos to battle the Nazis. It was one of the first war films produced by the French since the end of the war. (In French, English subtitles.)

d, Alexandre Esway; w, Joseph Kessel; ph, Nicolas Hayer; m, Maurice Thieret; English titles, Charles Clements.

War (PR:A MPAA:NR)

THEY ASKED FOR IT*½ (1939) 61m UNIV bw

William Lundigan (*Steve Lewis*), Joy Hodges (*Mary Lou Carroll*), Michael Whalen (*Howard Adams*), Isabel Jewell (*Molly Herkimer*), Lyle Talbot (*Marty Collins*), Thomas Beck (*Dr. Peter Sparks*), Spencer Charters (*Chief Lawson*), James Bush (*Tucker Tyler*), Charles Halton (*Dr. Tyler*), Edward McWade ("*Pi*" *Kelly*).

Lundigan plays the owner/editor of a small town newspaper who teams up with two of his old college buddies, Whalen and Beck, to investigate the mysterious death of an old man who lived on the outskirts of town. While the coroner claims it is a case of alcoholism, the news hounds suspect murder. Their suspicions seem confirmed when the man's daughter confesses she murdered her father, but it is soon proven that she lied. Eventually, Lundigan and company discover that the man was indeed killed by a gang of silk thieves who were using his barn as a hideout.

p, Max Goden; d, Frank McDonald; w, Arthur T. Horman (based on a story by James B. Lowell, Lester Fuller); ph, Stanley Cortez; ed, Phillip Cahn.

Crime (PR:A MPAA:NR)

THEY CALL HER ONE EYE zero (1974, Swed.) 89m United Producers/AIP c

Christina Lindberg (*Frigga*), Heinz Hopf (*Tony*), Despina Tomazani (*Lesbian*).

Totally obnoxious and vile action film starring Lindberg as a young victim of white slavery who is raped, mutilated (hence the vision problem) and beaten throughout most of this dubbed film, just so she can rehabilitate herself physically and return to affect her own tortures on those who did her wrong. Really depraved stuff from Sweden.

p, Bo A. Vibenius; d, Alex Fridolinski; w, Fridolinski, Vibenius; ph, (Movielab Color).

Crime (PR:O MPAA:R)

THEY CALL IT SIN*½ (1932) 68m FN-WB bw (GB: WAY OF LIFE, THE)

Loretta Young (*Marion Cullen*), George Brent (*Dr. Tony Travers*), David Manners (*James Decker*), Louis Calhern (*Ford Humphries*), Una Merkel (*Dixie*), Joseph Cawthorne (*Mr. Hollister*), Helen Vinson (*Enid Hollister*), Nella Walker (*Mrs. Hollister*), Mike Marito (*Mato*), Erville Alderson (*Timothy Cullen*), Elizabeth Patterson (*Mrs. Cullen*).

It's the old story about the innocent country girl who comes to the big city and finds her knight in shining armor. Young plays the kid from Kansas who makes her way to the Big Apple, thinking she can find stardom via the chorus line. She is pursued by a married man, and her producer, Calhern. Doctor Brent, who also is taken by Young, makes sure she has someone to turn to after she overcomes her growing pains.

p, Hal Wallis; d, Thornton Freeland; w, Lillie Hayward, Howard J. Green (based on the novel by Alberta Stedman Eagan); ph, James Van Trees; ed, James Gibbons; art d, Jack Okey.

Drama (PR:A MPAA:NR)

THEY CALL ME BRUCE zero (1982) 88m Film Ventures International c (AKA: A FISTFUL OF CHOPSTICKS)

Johnny Yune (*Bruce*), Ralph Mauro (*Freddy*), Pam Huntington (*Anita*), Margaux Hemingway (*Karmen*), Tony Brande (*Boss of Bosses*), Bill Capizzi (*Lil Pete*), Martin Azarow (*Big Al*).

A brainless martial-arts comedy with Yune as a cook who is mistaken for Bruce Lee. He cooks for the mob, and unwittingly delivers drugs for them while fighting off kung-fu adversaries.

p&d, Elliott Hong; w, Hong, David Randolph, Johnny Yune, Tim Clawson; ph, Robert Roth (TVC Color); m, Tommy Vig.

Comedy **Cas.** (PR:C MPAA:PG)

THEY CALL ME MISTER TIBBS**½ (1970) 108m Mirisch/UA c

Sidney Poitier (*Virgil Tibbs*), Martin Landau (*Rev. Logan Sharpe*), Barbara McNair (*Valerie Tibbs*), Anthony Zerbe (*Rice Weedon*), Jeff Corey (*Capt. Marden*), David Sheiner (*Herbert Kenner*), Juano Hernandez (*Mealie*), Norma Crane (*Marge Garfield*), Edward Asner (*Woody Garfield*), Ted Gehring (*Sgt. Deutsch*), Beverly Todd (*Puff*), Linda Towne (*Joy Sturges*), George Spell (*Andrew Tibbs*), Wanda Spell (*Ginger Tibbs*), Garry Walberg (*Medical Examiner*).

The second in the series of three films built around the exploits of tough city cop Virgil Tibbs (the first being IN THE HEAT OF THE NIGHT with THE ORGANIZATION to follow) has Poitier, in the title role, investigating the violent murder of a prostitute. The prime suspect is Poitier's close friend, activist priest Landau. The detective does not want to believe Landau is involved in the slaying, but since he was the last person seen with the girl, he is not above suspicion. Investigating all the suspects, including the girl's pimp and any other people associated with the hooker, Poitier encounters several threats against his own life. But the guilty party turns out to be the man he least wanted to see convicted of the crime, Landau. Being the law-abiding cop Poitier is, he must arrest the priest, even though Landau is in the middle of a fight to pass a bill which would clean up the city government. Incidents from Poitier's domestic life are juxtaposed against his professional one in an attempt to give him a more well-rounded character. He comes off looking very much like an angel, though one hardened by many earthly experiences. Probably the most human moment is the scene in which Poitier catches his 11-year-old son smoking. He sits down with the lad and has him light up a giant cigar, talking with him as he would to a buddy at the local bar. After puffing on the cigar the kid gets drastically sick, but be sure won't be tempted to smoke again. Other than this sequence, Poitier's character isn't fleshed out much; Landau, on the other hand, gives an intense and well-rounded portrayal of the guilt-ridden priest whose Roman collar doesn't keep him from being victimized by his own sexual desires. Poitier was allowed to direct several scenes in which he did not appear. This may not be the cause of the shaky direction, but it does suggest that Douglas was not interested in the job.

p, Herbert Hirschman; d, Gordon Douglas; w, Alan R. Trustman, James R. Webb (based on a story by Trustman and on the character created by John Ball); ph, Gerald Finnerman (DeLuxe Color); m, Quincy Jones; ed, Bud Molin; prod d, Clifford Yates, James F. McGuire; art d, Addison F. Hehr; set d, Edward G. Boyle; spec eff, Justus Gibbs; makeup, Mark Reedall, Al Fleming.

**Crime/Drama			Cas.			(PR:C MPAA:GP)**

THEY CALL ME ROBERT**½** (1967, USSR) 91m Lenfilm bw (YEVO ZOVUT ROBERT; AKA: HIS NAME IS ROBERT; HE WAS CALLED ROBERT; CALL ME ROBERT)

Oleg Strizhenov, Marianna Vertinskaya, Vladimir Pobol, Mikhail Pugovkin, Yuri Tolubeyev, D. Dranizin, N. Mamaeva.

A robot named Robert, which is an exact replica of its inventor, suddenly finds itself set loose in human society. Robert soon discovers that it takes more than logic to get along in the world.

d, Ilya Olshvanger; w, Lev Kuklin, Yuri Printsev; ph, Edgar Shtyrtskober.

**Fantasy/Comedy					(PR:A MPAA:NR)**

THEY CALL ME TRINITY**** (1971, Ital.) 109m West Film/AE c (LO CHIAMAVANO TRINITA)

Terence Hill [Mario Girotti] (Trinity), Bud Spencer [Carlo Pedersoli] (Bambino), Farley Granger (Maj. Harriman), Steffen Zacharias (Jonathan), Dan Sturkie (Tobias), Gisela Hahn (Sarah), Elena Pedemonte (Judith), Ezio Marano (Weasel), Luciano Rossi (Timid), Michele Spadaro (Peone), Remo Capitani (Mezcal).

A Spaghetti Western with a humorous bent features a lackadaisical sheriff and his sidekick half-brother, Spencer and Hill respectively, in a town totally under the domination of Granger (known mainly for his role in STRANGERS ON A TRAIN). When a Mormon group wanders through town, the two are actually forced into service to protect these people from becoming the prey of a gang of Mexican bandits. The slow pace conflicts with the slapstick comedy routines, bogging the picture down at times, though it is at least an interesting effort. This was the first in a series of which the sequel was entitled TRINITY IS STILL MY NAME. (In English.)

p, Italo Zingarelli; d&w, E.B. Clucher [Enzo Barboni]; ph, Aldo Giordani (Techniscope, Technichrome); m, Franco Micalizzi; ed, Giampiero Giunti; art d, Enzo Bulgarelli; spec eff, S. Chiusi.

**Western/Comedy			Cas.			(PR:A MPAA:G)**

THEY CAME BY NIGHT*½** 				(1940, Brit.) 73m FOX bw

Will Fyffe (James Fothergill), Phyllis Calvert (Sally), Anthony Hulme (Sgt. Tolley), George Merritt (Inspector Metcalfe), John Glyn Jones (Llewellyn Jones), Athole Stewart (Lord Netherley), Cees Laseur (Vollaire), Kathleen Harrison (Mrs. Lightbody), Wally Patch (Bugsie), Hal Walters (Hopkins), Kuda Bux (Ali), Sylvia St. Claire (Claire), Peter Gawthorne (Commissionaire), Leo Britt, Sam Kydd, Pat Williams.

Fyffe is a jeweler who becomes entangled with a group of thieves in an effort to aid Scotland Yard. Also hoping to get revenge against the hoods responsible for his brother's death, he joins the gang and leads the police to the crooks. Fyffe and Calvert give interesting performances, but the lame script and flawed production values are just impossible to overcome.

p, Edward Black; d, Harry Lachman; w, Frank Launder, Michael Hogan, Sidney Gilliat, Roland Pertwee (based on the play by Barre Lyndon); ph,

Jack Cox; ed, R.E. Dearing.

**Crime						(PR:A MPAA:NR)**

THEY CAME FROM BEYOND SPACE*½**
					(1967, Brit.) 85m Amicus/EM c

Robert Hutton (Dr. Curtis Temple), Jennifer Jayne (Lee Mason), Zia Mohyeddin (Farge), Bernard Kay (Richard Arden), Michael Gough (Monj), Geoffrey Wallace (Allan Mullane), Maurice Good (Stilwell), Luanshiya Greer (Girl Attendant), John Harvey (Bill Trethowan), Diana King (Mrs. Trethowan), Paul Bacon (Rogers), Christopher Banks (Doctor on Street), Dermot Cathie (Peterson), Norman Claridge (Dr. Andrews), James Donnelly (Guard), Frank Forsyth (Blake), Leonard Grahame (McCabe), Michael Hawkins (Williams), Jack Lambert (Doctor in Office), Robin Parkinson (Maitland), Edward Rees (Bank Manager), Katy Wild (Girl in Street), Kenneth Kendall (TV Commentator).

An interesting idea that didn't take to the screen very well, has aliens invading Earth in order to gain assistance in repairing their ship that has crashed on the moon. They accomplish this by taking over peoples' minds, then sending them to work as virtual slaves. But Hutton remains immune to this treatment because of the metal disk in his head. Being the responsible scientist he is, he goes about sorting out the mess, taking a spaceship to the moon and convincing the invaders that a more democratic means of repairing their ship can be achieved. A real disappointment which takes a good book, The Gods Hate Kansas, and does a horrid job of translating it to the screen. A bit more effort in the effects and direction department could have salvaged things.

p, Max J. Rosenberg, Milton Subotsky; d, Freddie Francis; w, Subotsky (based on the novel The Gods Hate Kansas by Joseph Millard); ph, Norman Warwick (Eastmancolor; m, James Stevens; ed, Peter Musgrave; prod d, Bill Constable; art d, Don Mingaye, Scott Slimon; spec eff, Bowie Films; makeup, Bunty Phillips.

**Science Fiction					(PR:A MPAA:NR)**

THEY CAME FROM WITHIN*½** (1976, Can.) 88m AIP c (AKA: THE PARASITE MURDERS; FRISSONS; SHIVERS)

Paul Hampton (Roger St. Luc), Joe Silver (Rollo Linsky), Lynn Lowry (Forsythe), Alan Migicovsky (Nicholas Tudor), Susan Petrie (Janine Tudor), Barbara Steele (Betts), Ronald Mlodzik (Merrick).

Highly touted as one of Canadian horror director David Cronenberg's masterpieces by his followers, THEY CAME FROM WITHIN has an interesting, albeit disturbing, premise which is executed sloppily with little attention paid to balance, character development, or compassion. The entire film is a sick little essay on sexuality. A research scientist who specializes in parasites develops an aphrodisiac parasite with an active veneral disease component that enters a patient's body and turns him into a sex fiend. (Why he does this is never really made clear motivationally–a problem in the vast majority of Cronenberg's films.) The mad doctor then implants one of the parasites into the body of his teenage mistress. However, the teenager happens to be fairly promiscuous, and soon the parasite has spread to most of the residents of a modern, self-sufficient high-rise, turning everyone into crazed, libidinous maniacs. While Cronenberg paints a grim, disturbing portrait of modern sexuality (every sexual taboo in the book is depicted as a breeding ground for the parasites) his criticism of the modern lifestyle (if indeed that is what he is saying) is not balanced with any representation of a normal, healthy sexual relationship. Cronenberg's world is entirely populated by amoral, sexually degenerate characters with absolutely no redeeming qualities that would move an audience to sympathize with their plight. Therefore, the viewer must play the uncomfortable role of voyeur.

p, Ivan Reitman; d&w, David Cronenberg; ph, Robert Saad (Movielab Color); ed, Patrick Dodd; spec eff & makeup, Joe Blasco.

**Horror						(PR:O MPAA:R)**

THEY CAME TO A CITY**½** 			(1944, Brit.) 78m EAL bw

John Clements (Joe Dinmore), Googie Withers (Alice), Raymond Huntley (Malcolm Stritton), Renee Gadd (Mrs. Stritton), A.E. Matthews (Sir George Gedney), Mabel Terry-Lewis (Lady Loxfield), Ada Reeve (Mrs. Batley), Norman Shelley (Cudworth), Frances Rowe (Philippa Loxfield), Ralph Michael, Brenda Bruce (Couple on Hillside), J. B. Priestley (Himself).

A screen adaptation of a successful play was hardly changed at all in terms of script and original players. This is all for the best as it is mainly a story of ideas and how people face adapting to a different sort of life in an "ideal" city. The story deals with a select and varied group of people about to become inhabitants of a new city, one which will be quite different from the one they have grown accustomed to. As they get ready to embark on this new experience, their thoughts and the ideals they hold dear are brought under intense scrutiny.

p, Michael Balcon; d, Basil Dearden; w, Dearden, Sidney Cole (based on the play by J. B. Priestley); ph, Stan Pavey; m, Scriabin; ed, Michael Truman; art d, Michael Relph.

**Fantasy						(PR:A MPAA:NR)**

THEY CAME TO BLOW UP AMERICA**½   (1943) 73m FOX bw

George Sanders (*Carl Steelman*), Anna Sten (*Frau Reiker*), Ward Bond (*Craig*), Dennis Hoey (*Col. Taeger*), Sig Ruman (*Dr. Herman Baumer*), Ludwig Stossel (*Julius Steelman*), Robert Barrat (*Capt. Kranz*), Poldy Dur (*Helga Lorenz*), Ralph Byrd (*Heinrich Burkhardt*), Elsa Janssen (*Mrs. Henrietta Steelman*), Rex Williams (*Eichner*), Charles McGraw (*Zellerbach*), Sven Hugo Borg (*Cmdr. Houser*), Kurt Katch (*Schonzeit*), Otto Reichow (*Fritz*), Andre Charlot (*Zugholtz*), Arno Frey (*Kranz's Aide*), Sam Wren (*Jones*), Etta McDaniel (*Theresa*), Peter Michael (*Gertzer*), Dick Hogan (*Coast Guardsman*), Lisa Golm (*Saleslady*), Wolfgang Zilzer (*Schlegel*), Egon Brecher (*Kirschner*), Walter O. Stahl (*Col. Taeger's Aide*), Charles Tannen (*Smith*), Eula Guy (*Anne the Nurse*), Lane Chandler (*Reynolds*), Torben Meyer (*Gottwald*), George Lynn (*Herman*), Henry Guttmann (*Fiertag*), Sigurd Tor (*Holtzfeld*), Walter Sande (*Boatswain's Mate*), John Epper (*Dispatch Rider*), Bob Stephenson (*Sentry*), Fred Nurney (*Ernest Teiker*), Jack Lorentz (*Marine Sentry*), John Mylong (*German Officer*), Ruth Brady (*Secretary*), Frederick Giermann, William Yetter, John Banner (*Gestapo*), Pierre Watkin, Forbes Murray (*Diplomats*), Frederick Brunn, Albert d'Arno (*German Soldiers*), Arthur Space, Brice Warren, Hugh Prosser (*FBI Men*).

An intriguing WW II drama which has Sanders infiltrate the Nazi espionage efforts in order to discover the identities of spies working in the U.S. An American FBI agent born in Germany, Sanders assumes the identity of a dead spy, allowing himself to make contact with Nazi intelligence officials. He narrowly escapes death when his real identity is discovered just as he exits a German sub and lands on American soil. There he must appear in a drawn-out court case in which the various spies are convicted. Told almost entirely in flashback, using the courtroom as the continuity device. The plot forces Sanders to retain German identity until the air is totally clear. Though this flashback method is not really called for in this type of material, it helps lend an atmosphere of realism to situations which are at times hard to swallow. Another suave performance by Sanders, and solid direction are big pluses.

p, Lee Marcus; d, Edward Ludwig; w, Audrey Wisberg (based on a story by Michael Jacoby); ph, Lucien Andriot; m, Hugo W. Friedhofer; ed, Nick De Maggio; md, Emil Newman; art d, James Basen; John Ewing; set d, Thomas Little; spec eff, Fred Sersen.

Spy Drama   (PR:A   MPAA:NR)

THEY CAME TO CORDURA***½   (1959) 123m COL c

Gary Cooper (*Maj. Thomas Thorn*), Rita Hayworth (*Adelaide Geary*), Van Heflin (*Sgt. John Chawk*), Tab Hunter (*Lt. William Fowler*), Richard Conte (*Cpl. Milo Trubee*), Michael Callan (*Pvt. Andrew Hetherington*), Dick York (*Pvt. Renziehausen*), Robert Keith (*Col. Rogers*), Carlos Romero (*Arreaga*), James Bannon (*Capt. Raltz*), Edward Platt (*Col. DeRose*), Maurice Jara (*Mexican Federale*), Sam Buffington, Arthur Hanson (*Correspondents*), Wendell Hoyt (*Cavalry Soldier*).

Cooper made one of his last performances in this adaptation of a best-selling novel. As an officer during the punitive expedition against Pancho Villa into Mexico in 1916, he has a moment of hesitation in battle and is branded a coward, but his commanding officer, Keith, is eager for promotion to general so he assigns Cooper to duty researching and writing up awards, one of which he expects to receive himself in return for not sending Cooper packing in disgrace. Furthermore, the Army is eager to come up with some heroes to boost award writing for America's imminent involvement in WW I. Cooper, though, has different ideas and he picks five men who displayed courage above and beyond the call of duty during an assault on a house occupied by some of Villa's men to be nominated for the Congressional Medal of Honor. As he brings them back to base, Cooper tries to fathom what made these men heroes and himself a coward. When he arrives at headquarters, Keith, angry at Cooper for not nominating him for a medal, orders the major to accompany the group to the rear area base at Cordura. It is clear from his tone that he expects them all to die in the desert during the long trek. Along with them is Hayworth, the daughter of a disgraced U.S. senator and the owner of the hacienda where Villa's men were holed up; she is to be taken back for trial as a traitor. As they travel through the awesomely forbidding desert, Cooper still probing for the spark of heroism in these men, all order begins to break down. The heroes all begin to show their worst sides and Cooper his real strength. Heflin turns out to be a wanted murderer who joined the Army seeking anonymity and is willing to kill Cooper to keep his picture out of the papers. Young lieutenant Hunter doesn't want the award because he thinks it will ruin his Army career by intimidating colleagues. Cooper is reduced to keeping the mutinous group together at gunpoint after Conte and Heflin try to rape Hayworth, but when Cooper is falling asleep and Heflin is just waiting to kill him, Hayworth gives herself to the sergeant to give Cooper a chance to rest. Eventually Cooper is reduced to pulling a railroad handcar with all the men riding on it up a hill. He falls down on his face and the men ridicule him, but then they look over the hill and see Cordura and realize that Cooper has brought them through. A film painful to watch because of the way it revels in humiliating its aging star. Cooper was in frail health during shooting and the masochistic agony he brings to the part especially when he pulls the railroad car from the end of a long rope, is hard to bear. The film certainly had promising material [a novel written by a man who had performed the same award-writing function as Cooper, but during WW II] the intelligent film

that director Rossen made was raped in the cutting room and flopped with the public. Rossen bought back his own film and planned to recut it the way he had originally intended, but he died before his plans could be realized. The shooting went far over budget and far over schedule when the first desert location chosen, St. George, Utah, had a record-setting cold snap. They then moved to Las Vegas and filmed outside of town, reshooting almost everything from the first location. Certainly not a particularly good movie, but it somehow has a power thanks to Cooper, clearly too old and too sick for his role, but pulling it off anyway. Together with a couple of other performances, those of Hunter and Heflin, the film manages to keep from falling apart completely. The film ended up losing more than $5 million.

p, William Goetz; d, Robert Rossen; w, Ivan Moffat, Rossen (based on the novel by Glendon Swarthout); ph, Burnett Guffey (CinemaScope, Eastmancolor by Pathe); m, Elie Siegmeister; ed, William A. Lyon; md, Morris W. Stoloff; art d, Cary Odell; set d, Frank A. Tuttle; cos, Tom Dawson, Jean Louis; m/l, "They Came to Cordura," James Van Heusen, Sammy Cahn; tech adv, Col. Paul Davidson, USA (Ret.); makeup, Clay Campbell.

Drama   (PR:C-O   MPAA:NR)

THEY CAME TO ROB LAS VEGAS*   (1969, Fr./Ital./Span./Ger.) 129m Isasi Producciones Cinematograficas-Capitole-Eichberg-Franca/WB-Seven Arts c (LES HOMMES DE LAS VEGAS; RADIOGRAFIA D'UN COLPO D'ORO; LAS VEGAS 500 MILLONES: AN EINEM FREITAG IN LAS VEGAS)

Gary Lockwood (*Tony Vincenzo*), Elke Sommer (*Anne*), Lee J. Cobb (*Skorsky*), Jack Palance (*Douglas*), Georges Geret (*Leroy*), Gustavo Re (*Salvatore*), Daniel Martin (*Merino*), Jean Servais (*Gino Vincenzo*), Roger Hanin (*The Boss*), Maurizio Arena (*Clark*), Armand Mestral (*Mass*), Fabrizio Capucci (*Cooper*), Enrique Avila (*Baxter*), Rossella Bergamonti, Gerard Tichy, Ruben Rojo.

Lockwood plans to rob an armored truck owned by casino owner Cobb to avenge the death of his brother, who was killed while attempting a similiar caper. He pulls off the scheme with help from Cobb's secretary (Sommer). But he soon learns that government agents are after the same truck because it's being used to smuggle goods into Mexico. A burdensome script is further hampered by weak performances.

p, Nat Wachsberger; d, Antonio Isasi [Isamendi] w, Isasi, Jo Eisinger, Luis Comeron, Jorge Illa, Giovanni Simonelli (based on the novel *Les Hommes de Las Vegas* by Andre Lay); ph, Juan Gelpi (Techniscope, Technicolor); m, Georges Garvarentz; ed, Elena Jaumandreu, Emilio Rodriguez Oses; art d, Antonio Cortes, Juan Alberto Soler; spec eff, Antonio Baquero.

Crime   (PR:O   MPAA:R)

THEY CAN'T HANG ME**   (1955, Brit.) 75m Vandyke/IF-BL bw

Terence Morgan (*Inspector Brown*), Yolande Donlan (*Jill*), Andre Morell (*Robert Pitt*), Ursula Howells (*Antonia Pitt*), Anthony Oliver (*Newcome*), Reginald Beckwith (*Harold*), Guido Lorraine (*Piotr Revsky*), Basil Dignam (*Riddle*), Raymond Rollett (*Sir Robert Rosper*), Fred Johnson, Arnold Marle, John Maxwell, Nigel Sharpe, Barry Lowe, Diana Lambert, Cyril Renison, Petra Davies, Arthur Lovegrove, Michael Godfrey, Guy Mills.

Sporadically intriguing spy drama has Morell a murderer scheduled to hang who offers to identify the leaders of a spy ring in return for a commuted sentence. Detective Morgan gets on the case and unravels the conspiracy by himself, then visits the useless Morell one last time before he goes to the gallows. Slightly more interesting than the normal run of British spy films, thanks to an unusually intelligent script.

p, Roger Proudlock; d, Val Guest; w, Guest, Val Valentine (based on a novel by Leonard Mosley); ph, Michael Brandt.

Spy Drama   (PR:A   MPAA:NR)

THEY DARE NOT LOVE*½   (1941) 75m COL bw

George Brent (*Prince Kurt von Rotenberg*), Martha Scott (*Marta Keller*), Paul Lukas (*Baron von Helsing*), Egon Brecher (*Prof. Keller*), Roman Bohnen (*Baron Shafter*), Edgar Barrier (*Capt. Wilhelm Ehrhardt*), Kay Linaker (*Barbara Murdock*), Frank Reicher (*Captain*).

Brent falls for Austrian Scott during their attempt to flee from the Germans. En route to Czechoslovakia, they are separated. Brent plays the noble lover when he offers himself to the Nazis as a prisoner in exchange for the release of seven men, among them Scott's fiance. Brent and Scott reunite, marry and look forward to a bright future. An overabundance of anti-Nazi propaganda gets in the way of plot development and dramatic intent, and characterizations are stereotyped.

p, Samuel Bischoff; d, James Whale; w, Charles Bennett, Ernest Vajda (based on a story by James Edward Grant); ph, Franz F. Planer; ed, Al Clark; md, Morris W. Stoloff.

War Drama   (PR:A   MPAA:NR)

THEY DIDN'T KNOW* (1936, Brit.) 67m BL/MGM bw

Eve Gray *(Cutie)*, Leslie Perrins *(Duval)*, Kenneth Villiers *(Basil Conway)*, Hope Davy *(Ursula)*, John Deverell *(Lord Budmarsh)*, Diana Beaumont *(Pamela Budmarsh)*, C. Denier Warren *(Padre)*, Patrick Ludlow *(Charles Rockway)*, Maidie Hope *(Lady Charfield)*, Fred Withers, A. Scott-Gaddy, Hal Walters.

Vapid comedy centering on a couple about to marry but each being secretly blackmailed by their former loves, who turn out to be estranged husband and wife. By the end all do know, and this innocuous thing mercifully comes to a halt.

p&d, Herbert Smith; w, Brock Williams; ph, Geoffrey Faithfull.

Comedy **(PR:A MPAA:NR)**

THEY DIED WITH THEIR BOOTS ON**** (1942) 140m WB bw

Errol Flynn *(George Armstrong Custer)*, Olivia de Havilland *(Elizabeth Bacon Custer)*, Arthur Kennedy *(Ned Sharp, Jr.)*, Charles Grapewin *(California Joe)*, Gene Lockhart *(Samuel Bacon)*, Anthony Quinn *(Crazy Horse)*, Stanley Ridges *(Maj. Romolus Taipe)*, John Litel *(Gen. Phil Sheridan)*, Walter Hampden *(Sen. Sharp)*, Sydney Greenstreet *(Gen. Winfield Scott)*, Regis Toomey *(Fitzhugh Lee)*, Hattie McDaniel *(Callie)*, G.P. Huntley, Jr. *(Lt. Butler)*, Frank Wilcox *(Capt. Webb)*, Joseph Sawyer *(Sgt. Doolittle)*, Minor Watson *(Sen. Smith)*, Gig Young *(Lt. Roberts)*, John Ridgley *(2nd Lt. Davis)*, Joseph Crehan *(President Grant)*, Aileen Pringle *(Mrs. Sharp)*, Anna Q. Nilsson *(Mrs. Taipe)*, Harry Lewis *(Youth)*, Tod Andrews *(Cadet Brown)*, William Hopper *(Frazier)*, Selmer Jackson *(Capt. McCook)*, Pat McVey *(Jones)*, Renie Riano Minerva Urecal, Virginia Sale *(Nurses)*, Vera Lewis *(Head Nurse)*, Frank Orth, Ray Teal *(Barflies)*, Spencer Charters, Hobart Bosworth *(Clergyman)*, Irving Bacon *(Salesman)*, Roy Barcroft, Dick French, Marty Faust, Bob Perry, Paul Kruger, Steve Darrell *(Officers)*, Lane Chandler, Ed Parker *(Sentries)*, Ed Keane *(Congressman)*, Francis Ford *(Veteran)*, Frank Ferguson *(Grant's Secretary)*, Herbert Heywood *(Newsman)*, Harry Strang, Max Hoffman, Jr., Frank Mayo *(Orderlies)*, Walter Brooke *(Rosser)*, Eddie Acuff *(Cpl. Smith)*, Sam McDaniel *(Waiter)*, Virginia Brissac *(Woman)*, Walter Baldwin *(Settler)*, George Reed *(Charles)*, William Forrest *(Adjutant)*, James Seay *(Lt. Walsh)*, George Eldredge *(Capt. Riley)*, John Hamilton *(Colonel)*, Dick Wessell *(Staff Sgt. Brown)*, Weldon Heyburn *(Staff Officer)*, Russell Hicks *(Colonel of 1st Michigan)*, Victor Zimmerman *(Colonel of 5th Michigan)*, Ian MacDonald *(Soldier)*, Sol Gorss, Addison Richards *(Adjutants)*, Jack Mower *(Telegrapher)*, Alberta Gary *(Jane the Kitchen Maid)*, Annabelle Jones *(Maid)*, Hugh Sothern *(Maj. Smith)*, Arthur Loft *(Tillaman)*, Carl Harbaugh *(Sergeant)*, G. Pat Collins *(Corporal)*, Joe Devlin, Fred Kelsey, Wade Crosby *(Bartenders)*, Joseph King *(Chairman)*.

Every schoolboy in America knew that Errol Flynn would some day don buckskin and play the legendary Gen. George Armstrong Custer, even Flynn himself. And though others have essayed the role, no one else but Flynn has ever captured the color, panache, and verve of this controversial hero of the Civil War and the far plains where he and 225 troopers of his old 7th Cavalry died with their boots on along the Little Big Horn River on June 25, 1876. Director Walsh creates a rousing and often stirring film here, with a pace as fast as the many charges on horseback the dashing Flynn leads. The picture does not conform to historical facts and, in many instances, goes far afield to keep Custer's legend intact, but for adventure and excitement there's little that can match this production. Flynn is shown as a brash young cadet at West Point who excels at horsemanship and weaponry but whose antics and lack of study habits keep him close to the bottom of the class. Vexing him is rich man's son Kennedy who resents the boyish pranks Flynn is always playing and the two become mortal enemies. While doing punishment duty for one of his pranks, marching back and forth between two points, Flynn is approached by the beautiful de Havilland who asks directions to the commandant's headquarters. He cannot answer her since is not allowed to speak when on guard duty and, after her repeated requests for directions go unanswered, de Havilland upbraids Flynn for being "the rudest young man I have ever met." She and he later meet and fall in love, but before they can wed the Civil War erupts, and Flynn is commissioned a second lieutenant and given an early graduation so he can join his regiment on the battlefield. Shortly after joining his Michigan brigade, Flynn, through a clerical error, is promoted to the rank of brigadier general. (This, of course, is nothing more than Hollywood hokum, although Custer did become one of the youngest generals in the Union Army in the Civil War, being promoted through the ranks in a swift period of time due to the attrition rate of officers being killed and wounded and because he proved early on to have excellent leadership qualities.) As a new general, Flynn has his tailor make a resplendent uniform of his own design and he appears peacock proud on the battlefield. At Gettysburg he leads several charges, using up one regiment after another until smashing through the Confederate lines and winning the day. Following the war, reduced in rank to captain, Flynn returns home to de Havilland, whom he has married. He tries to settle down, but he is restless and yearns for a new command. Through her family–members of which are high-placed in Washington–de Havilland manages to get Flynn a new post through General Sheridan (Litel), then commanding the U.S. Army. He is sent to Fort Lincoln, Nebraska, to command the 7th Cavalry. He finds the post a shambles and his troopers drunken idlers. As Flynn and his wife settle in at the post, Flynn begins to put the 7th Cavalry into shape, ordering drills, patrols, and inspections, and inspiring the men to become "the best cavalry unit in the West." Flynn even bestows upon the 7th Cavalry his favorite marching and drinking song, "Gary Owen." Before long the 7th is the most renowned Army unit facing the hostile plains Indians, not the least of whom is Quinn, playing Chief Crazy Horse, one of the most powerful leaders of the Sioux tribe. Flynn tries to keep the peace with the Indians but Kennedy, who had been a cadet at West Point and had been kicked out of the post for his radical ideas, has remained Flynn's enemy over the years, and is his undoing. When some dignitaries visit the post and the troops are paraded, the cavalrymen ride by yelling and falling off their horses, most of them having gotten drunk at Kennedy's saloon earlier. Flynn is suspended from his command and later learns that Kennedy's father and others have encouraged gold-seekers to invade the Black Hills, the sacred burial grounds of the Sioux, thus violating their agreement with Washington that these lands would remain exclusive Indian lands. Flynn rightly concludes that the gold rush has been planned by Kennedy, his father Hampden, and Ridges, in a scheme to send prospectors by the thousands into the Black Hills. This will cause the government to send in troops to the area to protect them and thereby open the land for the railroad owned by Hampden, Ridges, and others. The scheme works. Thousands of foolish gold-seekers rush into the Black Hills and are killed by the Sioux. The cavalry is ordered to go into the area and subdue the angry Indians. In a desperate move to regain his command before the 7th Cavalry rides into the field, Flynn goes to Washington and barges in on President Grant, demanding that his command be restored to him. Though Grant, played by Crehan, tells Flynn that he dislikes him for making accusatory statements against his administration, he reluctantly gives Flynn back his command of the 7th, after Flynn appeals to him as a soldier. Flynn rushes back to Fort Lincoln, and, in a touching farewell scene with de Havilland, leaves on a campaign against the Sioux, taking his command deep into Sioux country. He has abducted the scoundrel Kennedy, letting him out of a wagon on the eve of battle. When Kennedy asks where he is, Flynn tells him that he's a few miles from "the banks of the Little Big Horn River." He tells Kennedy that he has his choice, either try to ride back through country now swarming with Indians or ride with the 7th Cavalry. "But where is the regiment going?" asks the incredulous Kennedy. "To hell or to glory," Flynn replies. "It depends upon your point of view." The next day, Flynn follows a band of Sioux braves and is led into an ambush, with thousands of Indians converging upon his command from four sides. He orders the men to fight on foot and the hundreds of troopers form a rough circle with Flynn at the center, two pistols in hand, hatless, his long, golden hair streaming in the breeze next to the flapping guidon. Again and again the waves of Indians come charging against the completely outnumbered soldiers, thinning their ranks until only a few remain, including Flynn. Then in one massive, sweeping charge led by Quinn, the Indians crash forward. Flynn waits for them with saber in hand and by the time the great horde of savages rushes by and over the spot, Flynn is dead with every last member of his command, including Kennedy; it is Custer's Last Stand and Flynn and the 7th Cavalry are now legend. De Havilland, in the final scenes, accompanied by Sheridan (Litel), goes to Washington and exposes the corrupt officials and the land-grabbing scheme engineered by Hampden and Ridges, causing their resignation. She offers proof sent to her by Flynn on the eve of battle which proves to be the undoing of his enemies. Litel shows de Havilland out of the Washington office, saying: "Come, my dear, your soldier won his last battle." Though historically inaccurate, THEY DIED WITH THEIR BOOTS ON still provides a sprawling, exciting epic where huge masses of men are moved about in the Civil War scenes and, particularly, in the final Indian battle, with great skill by Walsh. The director proves his ability to execute enormously difficult scenes with apparent ease. One of the most spectacular scenes in any western film is where Flynn's regiment–seen at a distance of many miles from atop a high ridge–gallops straight into the trap and–seen from many more miles distant–the Indians, enormous hordes of them galloping forward on horseback, are shown dashing forth from four different directions. The sweeping panoramic shot is breathtaking and fearsome. All the exteriors for the film were shot about 40 miles north of Los Angeles in a wide valley that could easily pass for the plains of Nebraska-Dakota. Walsh had bad luck in getting real Sioux Indians to play the parts of the attacking savages. Only 16 real Sioux Indians answered his call to the reservation at Fort Yates, North Dakota. He was forced to use hundreds of Filipino extras, and those Caucasians employed as Indians were kept far in the background, with the 16 Sioux Indians used in closeups again and again. Walsh used more than 1,000 extras in this mighty epic, one of the factors that caused the budget to soar beyond $2 million, the biggest budget Walsh had been given up to that time. Dozens of extras who were also stuntmen were injured in horse falls, so many that the studio had to send a field hospital up to the location site to handle the daily injuries, with doctors and nurses–along with veterinarians–attending the scores of riders and horses hobbling in for treatment after battle scenes. Walsh kept calling the studio and demanding that more extras be sent to him, which caused Jack Warner to get nervous. He feared someone would get killed. Someone did–in fact, three men were killed during the filming of this wild actioner. The first fell from a horse and broke his neck; another stuntman had a heart attack. The third, actor Jack Budlong, insisted on using a real saber to lead a cavalry attack across a bridge supposedly under artillery fire. As Budlong dashed forward with his men, an explosive charge beneath the bridge went off prematurely and blew the actor and his horse straight upward. Budlong's saber came down point upward, wedged in some splintered wood of the bridge, and Budlong fell on top of it, running himself through. This was one of the first films that showed considerable sympathy to the plight of the Indian, which had much to do with Walsh. He later stated: "Most westerns had depicted the Indian as a painted, vicious savage. In THEY DIED WITH THEIR BOOTS ON I tried to show him as an individual who only turned violent when his rights as defined by treaty were violated by white men." The original director of this film, Michael Curtiz, was not suitable to Flynn, who had made too many films with the mad Hungarian and had grown to hate his bullying, often sadistic ways, as exemplified in the SEA HAWK. When Jack Warner told Flynn he was going have Curtiz make THEY DIED WITH THEIR BOOTS ON, the actor said he would break his contract before working again with Curtiz. Walsh was then brought in and the actor and director, both kindred spirits in more ways than tippling, got along famously. They produced, in this film, the most exciting and action-packed picture of the decade for the studio. De Havilland is also a standout in this, her eighth and last film with Flynn. Her final scene with Flynn is exquisitely touching. She knows he is going off to his death but they bid farewell graciously, without emotional breakdown. Flynn breaks his watch on purpose and gives her half of it, his picture inside, keeping the other containing her picture, and she sees him doing it, knowing he knows he won't come back. "Walking through life with you, ma'am, has been a very gracious thing," Flynn tells her and leaves. She *then* collapses. When the normally super-critical Jack Warner saw the film, he said that de Havilland had played her role "impeccably." He added: "This is one of Flynn's best. If Custer really died like that history should applaud him." He did, according to Sitting Bull, the Sioux medicine man who witnessed the massacre and said that Custer "stood like a sheaf of corn with all the ears fallen around him." However, much of this so-called biography was sheer fiction. On the other hand, the profile offered in the failed western spoof LITTLE BIG MAN is only absurd. Custer never took drink in his life, was never out of the Army, and had commanded the 7th Cavalry for seven years until he led it to "hell or to glory, depending upon your point of view."

p, Hal B. Wallis; d, Raoul Walsh; w, Wally Klein, Aeneas MacKenzie; ph, Bert Glennon; m, Max Steiner; ed, William Holmes; md, Leo F. Forbstein; art d, John Hughes; cos, Milo Anderson; makeup, Perc Westmore.

Western/Biography   Cas.   (PR:A   MPAA:NR)

THEY DON'T WEAR PAJAMAS AT ROSIE'S
(SEE: FIRST TIME, THE, 1969)

THEY DRIVE BY NIGHT*½   (1938, Brit.) 84m WB-FN bw

Emlyn Williams (*Shorty Matthews*), Ernest Thesiger (*Walter Hoover*), Anna Konstam (*Molly O'Neill*), Allan Jeayes (*Wally Mason*), Antony Holles (*Murray*), Ronald Shiner (*Charlie*), Yolande Terrell (*Marge*), Julie Barrie (*Pauline*), Kitty de Legh (*Mrs. Mason*), George Merritt, Billy [William] Hartnell, Jennie Hartley, Joe Cunningham.

Another malevolently delightful appearance by Thesiger marks this superior and rarely seen British thriller directed by Arthur Woods, whose potentially important career was cut short by his death while serving in the Army during WW II. The film opens as a petty crook, Williams, is released from prison. He drifts back to the London underworld where he chats with his old cohorts to see if there are any good "jobs" available. Williams pays a visit to one of his old girl friends, but he finds her lying very still on her bed. He goes to wake the girl, but to his horror, finds that she has been strangled with a silk stocking. Panic-stricken, Williams flees the apartment and is spotted by the nosy landlady. Fearing he will be caught and accused of murder, Williams begins hitchhiking out of town and grabs a ride from Jeayes, a friendly trucker. While at a truck stop, Williams runs into another former girl friend, Konstam, who is hitchhiking back to London. A close friend of the dead girl, when she hears news of the murder, Konstam believes Williams is innocent. The pair head off in opposite directions, but intersect again when Williams and Jeayes rescue Konstam from the clutches of a truck driver about to force himself on her. The thwarted villain gets revenge by telling the police of Williams whereabouts, forcing the fugitive and Konstam to flee back to the urban jungle of London. Williams hides out in a deserted mansion while Konstam goes back to her job as a dance-hall girl in the hopes of hearing a few clues as to the identity of their friend's murderer. At the club Konstam meets Thesiger, a rather eccentric amateur detective and criminologist. He takes a liking to Konstam and follows her home when she gets off work. While Williams eats the food Konstam has brought him, he listens to her explain how Thesiger may help them find the killer. Suddenly she screams in terror and we see Thesiger peering maniacally through the window. Williams manages to capture Thesiger and knock him out. Inside the house, Thesiger comes to and appears to be his friendly self. Happy to meet the man wrongly accused of murder, Thesiger promises to help the couple prove Williams' innocence. The odd man suggests that they move their hideout to his own house, as the police would be less likely to look there. The plan is agreed to and the couple soon find themselves Thesiger's guests. Venturing about the house, Williams discovers that Thesiger keeps a scrapbook of newspaper clippings pertaining to several strangulation murders, including the one of which he is suspected. Meanwhile, Konstam discovers a drawer full of silk stockings and other grisly souvenirs of the murders. Before she can alert Williams to her discovery, Thesiger, with wild, murderous hate in his eyes, tries to strangle Konstam with a silk stocking. Williams hears the struggle and once

again manages to capture Thesiger before he gets too far. Having caught the real killer, Williams has cleared his name and they leave the prison just as Thesiger is about to be executed for his crimes. THEY DRIVE BY NIGHT is a superbly atmospheric film that uses darkness, fog, and almost constant rain to give the audience the chills. Thesiger is magnificent as the crazed killer who can alternate between friendly, harmless charm and dank, deadly evil in a split second. The film was never distributed in America because Warner Bros. borrowed the title and truck-driving milieu for another film starring George Raft and Humphrey Bogart which was released the same year. Perhaps the British thriller was lost somewhere in the shuffle, because no one saw fit to retitle it and release it in the U.S.

p, Jerome Jackson; d, Arthur Woods; w, Derek Twist (based on the novel by James Curtis); ph, Basil Emmott.

Crime   (PR:C   MPAA:NR)

THEY DRIVE BY NIGHT**   (1940) 93m WB bw (GB: ROAD TO FRISCO)

George Raft (*Joe Fabrini*), Ann Sheridan (*Cassie Hartley*), Ida Lupino (*Lana Carlsen*), Humphrey Bogart (*Paul Fabrini*), Gale Page (*Pearl Fabrini*), Alan Hale (*Ed J. Carlsen*), Roscoe Karns (*Irish McGurn*), John Litel (*Harry McNamara*), Henry O'Neill (*District Attorney*), George Tobias (*George Rondolos*), Charles Halton (*Farnsworth*), Joyce Compton (*Sue Carter*), John Ridgeley (*Hank Dawson*), Paul Hurst (*Pete Haig*), Charles Wilson (*Mike Williams*), Norman Willis (*Neves*), George Lloyd (*Barney*), Lillian Yarbo (*Chloe*), Eddy Chandler (*Truck Driver*), Pedro Regas (*Mexican Helper*), Frank Faylen, Ralph Sanford, Sol Gorss, Michael Harvey, Eddie Featherston, Alan Davis, Dick Wessel, Al Hill, Charles Sullivan, Eddie Acuff, Pat Flaherty, Mike Lally, Don Turner, Ralph Lynn, Charles Sherlock, Frank Mayo, Dutch Hendrian (*Drivers*), George Haywood (*Policeman*), Claire James (*Party Guest*), Marie Blake (*Waitress*), Vera Lewis (*Landlady*), Frank Wilcox, J. Anthony Hughes (*Reporters*), Joe Devlin (*Fatso*), William Haade (*Tough Driver*), Phyllis Hamilton (*Stenographer*), Jack Mower (*Deputy*), Carl Harbaugh (*Mechanic*), Mack Gray (*Mike*), Richard Clayton (*Young Man*), Max Wagner (*Sweeney the Driver*), Demetrius Emanuel (*Waiter*), Dorothy Vaughan, Brenda Fowler (*Matrons*), Billy Wayne, Matt McHugh (*Electricians*), Howard Hickman (*Judge*), Wilfred Lucas (*Bailiff*).

A cult classic today, and one of the best Road movies ever to emerge from a major studio in the period. Raft and Bogart are brothers and truckers who have split away from the large company run by Hale and bought their own truck to work as independents. The first half of the film details their rise as they drive all night sometimes, skimp on needed repairs, and struggle to keep their fledgeling concern afloat. Bogart is married to Page, and she resents his neglect of her in favor of the business. One night, when the men are pulled over at a roadside diner, they meet waitress Sheridan. She's got a sharp tongue in her mouth and a mane of red hair and Raft is almost instantly attracted to her. He tells her, "I always have liked redheads." She tells him, "Red means stop." Raft shoots back with, "I'm color blind." Later the two men stop to pick up a hitchhiker and it turns out to be Sheridan, who has quit her job in the face of her boss' continued advances. Raft sets her up with a room in a boarding house. Shyly, he makes some romantic comments, which she turns away without being discouraging. Bogart falls asleep at the wheel of the truck one night and loses his arm in the subsequent accident. Raft is forced to take a job with Hale as traffic manager, and there Lupino, Hale's venomous wife, sets her sights on him. He spurns her, refusing to fool around with the boss' wife. She decides then to get rid of her husband, leaving him drunk and unconscious in the car while she closes the door and leaves the engine running. She offers to share the company she has inherited with Raft, but still he refuses her. She explodes, screaming at Raft: "You're not marrying that cheap redhead..-...you're mine and I'm hanging on to you....I committed murder to get you." She goes to the police and tells them that Raft forced her to kill her husband and Raft is quickly arrested and charged. Sheridan comes to jail and pleads with Lupino to tell the truth, but Lupino tells her that she will take Raft with her wherever she goes. Things go badly for Raft in court with circumstantial evidence implicating him and the testimony of his friends doing nothing to clear him. Lupino takes the stand and her story crumbles under cross-examination when Raft gives her a long, hard look, and he is quickly acquitted. Lupino is hauled off to the penitentiary, and as she sees the gates she becomes completely unhinged. Raft takes over the trucking company and installs Bogart as traffic manager as he and Sheridan plan for a life together. A loose remake of BORDERTOWN (in which Bette Davis leaves husband Eugene Pallette in a running car in the garage in order to win Paul Muni), THEY DRIVE BY NIGHT could have been another routine item but for the incredibly forceful performance of Lupino and Raft's smooth depiction of the tough trucker. Bogart, still wallowing in the lull in his career between the time THE PETRIFIED FOREST established him as a serious actor and the time HIGH SIERRA would finally make him a star for the rest of his career, is very good, especially when he is embittered by the loss of his arm. Walsh's direction is as forceful and vigorous as always and the film is among his very best. During the shooting of the film, the experience Raft gained as the driver of bootleg liquor shipments while working for his childhood chum, gangster Owney Madden, came in handy as Raft drove a truck with Bogart and Sheridan aboard down a steep California mountain. Suddenly the brakes failed and Raft was forced to control the careening truck as it hurtled down the twisting road. Finally he spotted an embankment that had been pushed up by a bulldozer and guided the truck into it, slowing it finally to a full stop. Badly shaken, Bogart climbed from the truck and thanked Raft. Raft later recalled thinking to himself: "Don't thank me, write a letter to Owney Madden or Feets Edson." Today the film is frequently revived via repertory theater showings, television broadcasts, and videocassette rentals, and remains one of the most enduring films of Raft's and Walsh's careers.

p, Mark Hellinger; d, Raoul Walsh; w, Jerry Wald, Richard Macaulay (based on the novel *The Long Haul* by A.I. Bezzerides); ph, Arthur Edeson; ed, Oliver S. Garretson, Thomas Richards; md, Adolph Deutsch; art d, John Hughes; cos, Milo Anderson; spec eff, Byron Haskin, H.F. Koenekamp, James Gibbons, John Holden, Edwin B. DuPar; makeup, Perc Westmore.

Drama   Cas.   (PR:A-C MPAA:NR)

THEY FLEW ALONE (SEE: WINGS AND THE WOMAN, 1942, Brit.)

THEY GAVE HIM A GUN*   (1937) 93m MGM bw

Spencer Tracy *(Fred Willis)*, Gladys George *(Rose Duffy)*, Franchot Tone *(Jimmy Davis)*, Edgar Dearing *(Sgt. Meadowlark)*, Mary Lou Treen *(Saxe)*, Cliff Edwards *(Laro)*, Charles Trowbridge *(Judge)*, Joseph Sawyer *(Doyle)*, George Chandler *(Taxi Driver)*, Gavin Gordon *(Captain)*, Ernest Whitman *(Roustabout)*, Nita Pike, Joan Woodbury *(French Girls)*.

During WW I, Tone, a shy and frightened clerk, and Tracy, a circus barker, become friends and comrades. The two vie for the affections of George, but Tracy eventually steps aside and after he is captured in battle by the Germans, Tone marries her. Tone also finally overcomes his fear of battle and becomes a decorated hero. After the war Tone finds it impossible to overcome the indoctrination and training that turned him into a killer and he becomes a gangster. He and Tracy encounter each other years later after George has found out the truth about her husband's occupation and she and Tracy, now the owner of his own circus, try to get Tone out of the rackets, but to no avail. Finally in desperation George turns her husband in to the police and Tone goes to jail. George is forced to take a job in Tracy's circus to make ends meet and when Tone later breaks out of jail he assumes she and Tracy are having an affair. He confronts Tracy with a gun and threatens to kill him, but Tracy takes the gun away from him and tells him that it's the only thing that gives him courage. Tone realizes what he has become and flees into the night, only to be cut down by police bullets. A little too melodramatic, especially in its convenient and neat ending (Tone is killed by his old Army gunnery instructor, now turned cop). The performances are mostly good, with Tracy doing his patented best friend bit and actually ending up with the girl. The battle scenes were filmed on the same fields that had been painstakingly cultivated for THE GOOD EARTH. Tracy was constantly being pulled off the set of this film to return to the set of CAPTAINS COURAGEOUS for pickup shots. Although far from a significant film in the career of Tracy, it did garner good reviews and did respectable business at the box office.

p, Harry Rapf; d, W.S. Van Dyke II; w, Cyril Hume, Richard Maibaum, Maurice Rapf (based on the novel by William Joyce Cowen); ph, Harold Rosson; ed, Ben Lewis; art d, Cedric Gibbons, Harry McAfee; set d, Edwin B. Willis; spec eff, Slavko Vorkapich.

Drama   (PR:A MPAA:NR)

THEY GOT ME COVERED**   (1943) 95m Goldwyn/RKO bw

Bob Hope *(Robert Kittredge)*, Dorothy Lamour *(Christina Hill)*, Lenore Aubert *(Mrs. Margo Vanescu)*, Otto Preminger *(Otto Fauscheim)*, Eduardo Ciannelli *(Baldanacco)*, Marion Martin *(Gloria the "Glow Girl")*, Donald Meek *(Little Old Man)*, Phyllis Ruth *(Sally)*, Philip Ahn *(Nichimuro)*, Donald MacBride *(Norman Mason)*, Mary Treen *(Helen)*, Bettye Avery *(Mildred Smith)*, Margaret Hayes *(Lucille)*, Mary Byrne *(Laura)*, William Yetter *(Holtz)*, Henry Guttman *(Faber)*, Florence Bates *(Gypsy Woman)*, Walter Catlett *(Hotel Manager)*, John Abbott *(Gregory Vanescu)*, Frank Sully *(Red)*, Wolfgang Zilzer *(Gross)*, Nino Pipitone *(Testori)*, George Chandler *(Smith)*, Stanley Clements *(Office Boy)*, Don Brodie *(Joe McGirk)*, Arnold Stang *(Drug Store Boy)*, Etta McDaniel *(Georgia)*, Hugh Prosser *(Captain)*, Donald Kerr *(Stage Manager)*, Doris Day *(Beautiful Girl in Sheet)*, Lane Chandler, Dick Keene *(Reporters)*, Edward Gargan, Ralph Dunn *(Cops)*, Lou Lubin *(Bellboy)*, Harry C. Bradley *(Hotel Waiter)*, Ferike Boros *(Laughing Woman)*, Pat Lane *(Ballet Dancer)*, Jack Carr *(Comedian)*, Bill O'Leary *(Tramp)*, Peggy Lynn *(Burlesque Actress)*, Lillian Castle *(Wardrobe Woman)*, Anne O'Neal *(Woman Patron)*, Hans Schumm *(Schmidt)*, Henry Victor *(Straeger)*, Vic Mazetti, Tom Mazetti, John Sinclair, Gil Perkins *(Nazis)*, George Sherwood *(Reporter)*, Byron Shores *(FBI Man)*, Charles Legneur *(Passenger in Plane)*, Joe Devlin *(Mussolini)*, Kam Tong *(Hawara)*, Willie Fung *(Laundry Man)*, Greta Meyer *(Katrina)*, Walter Soderling, Lyle Latell, John Mather, Ray Turner, Stanley Price, Shimen Ruskin, Robert O. Davis.

Without the talent of Bob Hope this picture would be one dull thud. It has very forced situations, a yarn that makes absolutely no sense, and not much acting from the other members of the cast. But Hope is magnificent as a WWII war correspondent fired for forgetting to announce that Hitler has invaded Russia. He then goes about trying to prove himself a worthy

reporter by uncovering a Nazi spy ring. And the way he goes about doing so is quite bizarre to say the least, taking him from impersonations of Veronica Lake to posing as a wax mannequin, and a few other things that only Hope can do without looking totally ridiculous. The film--its title was that of Hope's paperback biography, a best-seller at three million copies-- represented a change of pace for producer Goldwyn, who had previously specialized in romantic dramas. Basically a remake of 1942's MY FAVOR- ITE BLONDE, a box-office smash, its director was Butler, who had previously directed Hope and Lamour--with Bing Crosby--in one of the best of the ROAD series pictures (see Index), THE ROAD TO MOROCCO (1942). In-gags abound in the film; Crosby was brought into it off camera, singing his classic theme, "Where the Blue of the Night Meets the Gold of the Day," every time Hope opens his musical cigarette case. Preminger, in his second year of portraying Nazis in Hollywood, proved himself capable on either side of the camera in his role as the chief of the bad guys. Singer Doris Day, later a star, had an early bit part, as did Diana Lynn in one of the first films in which she used that screen pseudonym (she'd used her real name, Dolly Loehr, in earlier bits).

p, Samuel Goldwyn; d, David Butler; w, Harry Kurnitz (based on a story by Leonard Q. Ross, Leonard Spigelgass); ph, Rudolph Mate; m, Leigh Harline; ed, Daniel Mandell; md, C. Bakaleinikoff; art d, Perry Ferguson; cos, Adrian; spec eff, Ray Binger; m/l, "Palsy Walsy," Johnny Mercer, Harold Arlen.

Comedy   (PR:A MPAA:NR)

THEY HAD TO SEE PARIS½   (1929) 96m FOX bw

Will Rogers *(Pike Peters)*, Irene Rich *(Mrs. Peters)*, Marguerite Churchill *(Opal Peters)*, Owen Davis, Jr *(Ross Peters)*, Fifi D'Orsay *(Claudine)*, Ivan Lebedeff *(Marquis De Brissac)*, Marcelle Corday *(Marquise De Brissac)*, Theodore Lodi *(Grand Duke Makiall)*, Rex Bell *(Clark McCurdy)*, Christiane Yves *(Fleurie)*, Edgar Kennedy *(Ed Eggers)*, Bob Kerr *(Tupper)*, Marcia Manon *(Miss Mason)*, Andre Cheron *(Valet)*, Gregory Gay *(Prince Ordinsky)*, Mr. Persian Pussy *(Claudine's Kitty)*.

The first sound picture to feature Will Rogers, and although he appeared in several silents, none offered him the chance to display what this great American folk hero was most popular for, his wit. There is plenty on display in this farce about an Oklahoman who suddenly finds himself a very wealthy man when oil is discovered on his property. On the insistence of his wife, Rich, he and the family head for Paris, buy a large chateau, and try to adapt to a new lifestyle. Though Rich has a ball playing at being a socialite, Rogers finds the new climate exceedingly tiresome and longs for his simple life back in the good old U.S. The film--which was also released in a silent version, with titles by Wilbur J. Morse, Jr., for theaters that had not yet converted to sound--was unanimously rated among the top 10 of 1929 by critics of the time. Background shooting was done in Rogers' real adoptive home town, Claremore, Oklahoma.

d, Frank Borzage; w, Sonya Levien, Owen Davis, Sr. (based on the novel by Homer Croy); ph, Chester Lyons, Al Brick; m, Con Conrad, Sidney Mitchell, Archie Gottler; ed, Margaret V. Clancey; art d, Harry Oliver; cos, Sophie Wachner; ch, Bernard Steele; m/l, "I Could Do it for You," Conrad, Mitchell, Gottler.

Comedy   (PR:A MPAA:NR)

THEY JUST HAD TO GET MARRIED*½   (1933) 69m UNIV bw

Slim Summerville *(Sam Sutton)*, ZaSu Pitts *(Molly Hull)*, Roland Young *(Hillary Hume)*, Verree Teasdale *(Lola Montrose)*, Fifi D'Orsay *(Marie)*, C. Aubrey Smith *(Aubrey Hampton)*, Robert Grieg *(Radcliffe)*, David Landau *(Montrose)*, Elizabeth Patterson *(Lizzie)*, Wallis Clark *(Fairchilds)*, Vivien Oakland *(Mrs. Fairchilds)*, Cora Sue Collins *(Rosalie Fairchilds)*, David Leo Tillotson *(Wilmot Fairchilds)*, William Burress *(Bradford)*, Louise Mackin- tosh *(Mrs. Bradford)*, Bertram Marburg *(Langley)*, Virginia Howell *(Mrs. Langley)*, James Donlan *(Clerk)*, Henry Armetta *(Tony)*.

Pitts and Summerville are up to the antics customary to them when they appear together, here they play maid and butler to a very wealthy man who dies, leaving his entire estate to the pair. This gives them the chance to marry, but the lifestyle of the rich isn't quite up their alley. They have to lose all their money and suffer a breakup before they can finally get together as a regular couple. Done in routine fashion from a script that is filled with holes, but this doesn't matter as the main attraction is to see Pitts and Summerville in action.

d, Edward Ludwig; w, Gladys Lehman, H.M. Walker, Clarence Marks [Uncredited: Preston Sturges] (based on a play by Cyril Harcourt); ph, Edward Snyder; ed, Ted Kent; makeup, Jack P. Pierce.

Comedy   (PR:A MPAA:NR)

THEY KNEW MR. KNIGHT*   (1945, Brit.) 93m G.H.W./GFD bw

Mervyn Johns *(Tom Blake)*, Nora Swinburne *(Celia Blake)*, Alfred Drayton *(Mr. Knight)*, Joyce Howard *(Freda Blake)*, Joan Greenwood *(Ruth Blake)*, Olive Sloane *(Mrs. Knight)*, Joan Maude *(Carrie Porritt)*, Peter Hammond *(Douglas Knight)*, Marie Ault *(Grandma Knight)*, Frederick Cooper *(Ed- ward Knight)*, Grace Arnold *(Isabel Knight)*, Kenneth Kove *(Coggie Selby)*, Frederick Burtwell *(Mr. Berry)*, Winifred Oughton, Tarva Penna, Patric

Curwen, Muriel Aked, Anthony Holles, Gordon Begg, Ian Fleming, Sheila Raynor, Pat Stevens, Doyley John.

A domestic drama about a simple man, Johns, who suddenly finds himself wealthy with the aid of successful speculator Drayton. Just as suddenly, Johns is ruined financially when it is revealed that Drayton and he have invested in fraudulent securities. Unable to accommodate a return to a lesser lifestyle, Johns commits forgery and is imprisoned. Drayton, also ruined kills himself. Johns' daughter pulls the family out of its penury by marrying a wealthy socialite. Lackluster writing and unsympathetic characters make this a dull drama.

p, James B. Sloan; d, Norman Walker; w, Walker, Victor MacClure (based on the novel by Dorothy Whipple); ph, Erwin Hillier.

Drama　　　　　　　　　　　　　　　　　　　　　**(PR:A   MPAA:NR)**

THEY KNEW WHAT THEY WANTED***½　　　(1940) 96m RKO bw

Carole Lombard (Amy), Charles Laughton (Tony), William Gargan (Joe), Harry Carey (Doctor), Frank Fay (Father McKee), Joe Bernard (R.F.D.), Janet Fox (Mildred), Lee Tung-Foo (Ah Gee), Karl Malden (Red), Victor Kilian (Photographer), Effie Anderson (Nurse), Paul Lepere (Hired Hand), Marie Blake, Millicent Green, Grace Lenard, Patricia Oakley (Waitresses), Bobby Barber, Nestor Paiva (Pals at Table), Antonio Filauri (Customer), Joe Sully (Father of Family), Ricca Allen (Mrs. Thing), Tom Ewell (New Hired Hand), The Pina Troupe (Themselves).

Lombard is a waitress in San Francisco whose life is going nowhere quickly. She begins a correspondence with an Italian vineyard owner, and, after he sends her a picture of himself, she accepts his proposal of marriage. The picture, however, is not of her fiance, but of his handsome hired man, Gargan. Lombard is shocked and upset when she learns that she is engaged to marry Laughton, a fat, boisterous, unattractive fellow. On the eve of their wedding, Laughton falls and breaks both legs. The wedding delayed while he recovers, Lombard nurses him, but her resentment of him grows daily. She becomes involved in an affair with Gargan, who seduces her, then tells her he won't marry her because he doesn't "owe no man nothing–or no woman." Lombard is pregnant by Gargan, and shortly afterward he and Lombard argue and he leaves her for good. Laughton, who has always loved her, forgives her transgression and she realizes that she loves him too. She goes away to have the child, but clearly she will return to Laughton. Lombard shows the dramatic range she was too infrequently able to exercise. Laughton, on the other hand, is as hammy and overbearing as usual, his portrayal of the Italian immigrant just short of insulting with his pidgin English, greasy hair, and ridiculous mannerisms. Gargan is only adequate and Fay (Barbara Stanwyck's first husband and an alcoholic) is downright bad. Among the supporting players only veteran Carey, as a kindly country doctor, is good. Karl Malden makes his screen debut in a small role. The story had its first incarnation as a play, in which Amy is married to Tony before she goes to bed with Joe, but the Breen Office (the successor to the Hays Office) would only allow the story on the screen if the sin were seduction, not adultery. Twice before, in 1928 and 1930, the story had been filmed in bowdlerized versions (THE SECRET HOUR and A LADY IN LOVE) under the strictures of censorship, which removed any real point from it. It was only after years of negotiations with the Breen Office that the story was allowed to be filmed under its own title and mostly intact.

p, Erich Pommer; d, Garson Kanin; w, Robert Ardrey (based on the play by Sidney Howard); ph, Harry Stradling; m, Alfred Newman; ed, John Sturges; art d, Van Nest Polglase; set d, Darrell Silvera; cos, Edward Stevenson; spec eff, Vernon L. Walker.

Drama　　　　　　　　**Cas.**　　　　　　　　**(PR:C   MPAA:NR)**

THEY LEARNED ABOUT WOMEN**　　　(1930) 72m MGM bw

Joseph T. Schenck (Jack), Gus Van (Jerry), Bessie Love (Mary), Mary Doran (Daisy), J.C. Nugent (Stafford), Benny Rubin (Sam), Tom Dugan (Tim), Eddie Gribbon (Brennan), Francis X. Bushman, Jr (Haskins).

Schenck and Van are professional baseball players who give up the bat for the footlights, becoming vaudeville singers. Love is the dancer who offers herself to one, although she really loves the other. Another woman enters the scene and almost breaks up the singing duo, but they both end up leaving the stage and returning to baseball in time to play in the World Series and Love ends up with her true love. Adequate musical entertainment, remade in 1949 as TAKE ME OUT TO THE BALL GAME. Includes the songs: "Dougherty Is the Name" (by Joseph T. Schenck, Gus Van), "Harlem Madness," "He's That Kind of a Pal," "Ain't You Baby?","A Man of My Own," "Does My Baby Love," "There'll Never Be Another Mary," "Ten Sweet Mammas" (Jack Yellen, Milton Ager).

d, Jack Conway, Sam Wood; w, Sarah Y. Mason, Arthur "Bugs" Baer (based on a story by A.P. Younger); ph, Leonard Smith; ed, James McKay, Tom Held; art d, Cedric Gibbons; cos, David Cox; ch, Sammy Lee.

Musical　　　　　　　　　　　　　　　　　　**(PR:A   MPAA:NR)**

THEY LIVE BY NIGHT****　　　(1949) 95m RKO bw (GB: THE TWISTED ROAD; AKA: YOUR RED WAGON)

Cathy O'Donnell (Keechie), Farley Granger (Bowie), Howard Da Silva (Chickamaw), Jay C. Flippen (T-Dub), Helen Craig (Mattie), Will Wright (Mobley), Marie Bryant (Singer), Ian Wolfe (Hawkins), William Phipps (Young Farmer), Harry Harvey (Hagenheimer), Regan Callais (Young Wife), Frank Marlowe (Mattie's Husband), Jim Nolan (Schreiber), Charles Meredith (Commissioner Hubbell), J. Louis Johnson (Porter), Myra Marsh (Mrs. Schaeffer), Tom Kennedy (Cop-Bumper Gag), Stanley Prager (Short Order Man), Suzi Crandall (Lulu), Fred Graham (Motorcycle Cop), Lewis Charles (Parking Lot Attendant), Dan Foster (Groom), Marilyn Mercer (Bride), Jimmy Dobson (Boy at Parking Lot), Lynn Whitney (Waitress), N. L. Hitch (Bus Driver), Carmen Morales (Mother), Ralph Dunn (Policeman), Paul Bakanas, Mickey Simpson (Shadows), Boyd Davis (Herman), Kate Lawson (Tillie), Guy Beach (Plumber), Byron Foulger (Lambert), Teddy Infuhr (Alvin), Gail Davis (Girl at Parking Lot), Curt Conway (Man in Tuxedo), Chester Jones (Waiter in Nightclub), Douglas Williams (Drunk), Helen Crozier (Nurse), Jimmy Moss (Boy), Erskine Sanford (Doctor), Frank Ferguson (Bum), Eula Guy (Mrs. Havilland), Will Lee (Jeweler), Russ Whitman, Jane Allen (People).

The energetic first film by director Ray, THEY LIVE BY NIGHT tells the tragic story of two doomed lovers–Granger and O'Donnell–who live a short fast life together before they are torn apart by the fate of the criminal world. At the film's opening, Granger and O'Donnell are seen kissing. Over the picture comes the words "This boy...and this girl...were never properly introduced to the world we live in." In this folksy manner, the saga of Keechie and Bowie (as their characters are called) hits the screen. Granger, a decent enough youngster whose greatest crime is his naivete, joins a prison break engineered by Da Silva and Flippen, two callous criminals who have no place in their hearts for Granger's innocence. They simply take him along because they need a third hand for a bank job. An auto accident caused by Da Silva ends up injuring Granger, who recovers in a dark hideout. He is nursed to health by O'Donnell, a young woman who quickly falls in love with Granger, sensing that he is not like his two counterparts. Granger returns O'Donnell's affections and the two cannot keep their hands off each other. To legally seal their romance the pair marry in the dilapidated office of a justice of the peace. Granger is not strong enough to say no to Da Silva's offer of another bank job. It's not long before Flippen is killed and Da Silva has angrily gone off on his own. Soon Da Silva is killed, leaving Granger the last of the gang still to be sought by police. The young fugitive wants nothing more than a quiet home for himself and his wife, but his fate has been sealed. Granger is informed on by Craig, the sister of Flippen, who cooperates with the police in order to get her husband out of prison. Before Granger can get far he is gunned down by police. Alone and pregnant, O'Donnell is left to live on her own. More than the standard cops-and-robbers tale, THEY LIVE BY NIGHT is a depression-era saga about lovers on the run. Entangled in a situation they cannot escape–one over which they have absolutely no control they love to the fullest, only to be tragically separated. Based on the novel Thieves Like Us by Edward Anderson (which was later filmed by Robert Altman under that title), THEY LIVE BY NIGHT owes an equal debt to the Bonnie and Clyde myth which, while bearing no resemblance whatsoever to the film, has permeated the cinema's image of lovers on the run. It's an image which can also be seen in 1949's GUN CRAZY and the 1937 Fritz Lang picture YOU ONLY LIVE ONCE. Having read the novel on a recommendation by producer Houseman, Ray began the task of adapting the story. After finishing a 124-page treatment, Schnee (who had just completed work on Howard Hawks' RED RIVER) was called upon to pen the screenplay. The choice of director was still unsettled when Houseman suggested to RKO production head Dore Schary that Ray be given a chance. Ray undertook the project with an undying enthusiasm for creating his own personal style. From the very start of the film this is apparent. After Granger and O'Donnell exchange their kiss at the opening, a getaway car carrying the three criminals is seen traveling down a dusty road, pursued by police. Rather than shoot with a standard camera set-up, Ray demanded that the scene be photographed from a helicopter. A highly unorthodox idea (today it can be readily seen in television and has become an overused shot), the helicopter shot met with strong opposition–that is, until everyone saw just how remarkably the shot turned out. Not only did it open the film with a burst of unharnessed activity, but thematically it represented godlike fate looking down on Granger and relentlessly pursuing him. A finished cut of the film was finally shown to Schary, who suggested that the title be changed to YOUR RED WAGON, a ridiculous title which comes from a song in the film. Unfortunately, the film's release fell victim to a studio shake-up which resulted in Schary being replaced by Howard Hughes. The film gathered a goodly amount of dust on some studio shelf, during which Ray had completed and released two other films–A WOMAN'S SECRET and KNOCK ON ANY DOOR. A year after its 1947 completion date it was shown in England as THEY LIVE BY NIGHT (its original U.S. title was to have been THE TWISTED ROAD), before finally hitting U.S. screens under that title.

p, John Houseman; d, Nicholas Ray; w, Charles Schnee, Ray (based on the novel Thieves Like Us by Edward Anderson); ph, George E. Diskant; m, Leigh Harline (uncredited, Woody Guthrie); ed, Sherman Todd; md, Constantin Bakaleinikoff; art d, Albert S. D'Agostino, Al Herman; set d, Darrell Silvera, Maurice Yates; spec eff, Russell A. Cully; m/l, "Your Red Wagon", Richard M. Jones, Don Raye, Gene DePaul, sung by Marie Bryant;

makeup, Gordon Bau.

Crime   Cas.   (PR:C   MPAA:NR)

THEY LIVE IN FEAR**   (1944) 65m COL bw

Otto Kruger, Clifford Severn, Pat Parrish, Jimmy Carpenter, Erwin Kalser,
Danny Jackson, Jimmy Zaner, Jimmy Clark, Danny Desmond, Billy
Benedict, Kay Dowd, Eileen McClory, Douglas Wood, Frederick Giermann.

A refugee who has fled Nazi oppression and come to America worries about
the safety of his family left behind. Occasionally effective wartime propaganda.

p, Jack Fier; d, Josef Berne; w, Michael L. Simmons, Sam Ornitz (based on
a story by Wilfred Pettitt); ph, George Meehan; ed, James Sweeney; art d,
Lionel Banks, Carl Anderson.

Drama   (PR:A   MPAA:NR)

THEY LOVE AS THEY PLEASE
                        (SEE: GREENWICH VILLAGE STORY, 1963)

THEY LOVED LIFE   (SEE: KANAL, 1961, Pol.)

THEY MADE HER A SPY**   (1939) 69m RKO Radio bw

Sally Eilers (Irene Eaton), Allen Lane (James Huntley), Frank M. Thomas
(Col. Shaw), Fritz Leiber (Dr. Krull), Larry Blake (Ben Dawson), Charles
Halton (Beldon), Theodore von Eltz (Page), Pierre Watkin (Col. Wilson),
Addison Richards (Everett Brock), Louis J. Heydt (Gillian), Spencer
Charters (Lucius), Alec Craig (Canby), Leona Roberts (Ella), Roger Hunt.

A patriotic espionage tale about a pretty young woman, Eilers, who joins the
U.S. Army Intelligence Corps in order to avenge the death of her brother.
With the help of cub reporter Lane, she uncovers clues that lead to a spy
ring headed by Leiber. A climactic chase climaxes atop the Washington Monument, ending with Leiber jumping to his death. Not quite as patriotic as the
spy chase atop the Statue of Liberty in Hitchcock's SABOTEUR (1942), but
it'll do. Although some sources credit Garson Kanin with the screenplay, it
was his brother Michael who penned it.

p, Robert Sisk; d, Jack Hively; w, Michael Kanin, Joe Pagano (based on a
story by Lionel Houser, George Bricker); ph, Nicholas Musuraca; ed, Harry
Marker; Roy Webb; cos, Edward Stevenson.

Spy Drama   (PR:A   MPAA:NR)

THEY MADE ME A CRIMINAL***   (1939) 92m WB bw

John Garfield (Johnny Bradfield/"Jack Dorney"), Gloria Dickson (Peggy),
Claude Rains (Detective Monty Phelan), Ann Sheridan (Goldie), May Robson
(Gramma), Billy Halop (Tommy), Bobby Jordan (Angel), Leo Gorcey (Spit),
Huntz Hall (Dippy), Gabriel Dell (T.B.), Bernard Punsley (Milty), Robert
Gleckler (Doc Ward), John Ridgely (Charlie Magee), Barbara Pepper
(Budgie), William B. Davidson (Inspector Ennis), Ward Bond (Lenihan,
Fight Promoter), Robert Strange (Malvin, Lawyer), Louis Jean Heydt
(Smith), Ronald Sinclair (J. Douglas Williamson), Frank Riggi (Gaspar
Rutchek), Cliff Clark (Rutchek's Manager), Dick Wessel (Collucci), Ray-
mond Brown (Sheriff), Sam Hayes (Fight Announcer), Irving Bacon (Speed
the Gas Station Attendant), Sam McDaniel (Splash), Bert Roach (Hen-
dricks), Dorothy Varden (Woman), Eddy Chandler, Hal Craig (Detectives),
Jack Austin, Frank Meredith (Cops), Richard Bond, Nat Carr (Reporters),
Arthur Houseman (Drunk), Elliott Sullivan (Hoodlum), Tom Dugan, Frank
Mayo, Cliff Saum (Men), Al Lloyd, John Sheehan (Men), Leyland Hodgson (Mr.
Williamson), Doris Lloyd (Mrs. Williamson), Stuart Holmes (Timekeeper),
Bob Perry (Cawley), Nat Carr (Haskell), Clem Bevans (Ticket Taker), Jack
Wise (Ticketman).

Seeking to capitalize on the sensation made by their new young actor
Garfield in FOUR DAUGHTERS (1938), Warner Bros. immediately cast him
in this remake of the 1933 boxing-crime drama THE LIFE OF JIMMY
DOLAN. Garfield plays a recently crowned world champion boxer whose
public image is that of a kind, gentle, clean-cut kid who is devoted to his
mother. In reality Garfield is a cynical, heavy-drinking womanizer who
hasn't given so much as a thought to his mother in years. One morning the
boxer awakes from a drunken stupor to learn from the newspaper that he
has murdered a reporter and then been killed in a fiery car crash. His seedy
lawyer advises him to stay "dead" and beat it out of town. Rains, the
detective assigned to the case, suspects that Garfield is alive and becomes
obsessed with finding him. Hitching rides on boxcars, Garfield travels to
Arizona where he wanders onto a date farm owned and operated by the
elderly Robson. The farm serves as a rehabilitation center for a group of
boys from the slums of New York (Halop, Jordan, Gorcey, Hall, Dell, and
Punsley) and they are supervised by Dickson, the sister of Halop, who has
been made their legal guardian. Garfield introduces himself under an
assumed name and offers to help out on the farm because he feels empathy
for the boys. Noticing that the farm would be a valuable place for motor
travelers to stop for gasoline, Garfield suggests that they have a pump
installed with which to make extra money. To pay for the gas pump, Garfield
offers to box an up-and-coming fighter. The stunt will earn Garfield $500 per

round. The plan hits a snag, however, when Garfield spots detective Rains
buying a ticket for the bout. Knowing that his unique boxing stance will
reveal his true identity, Garfield calls the fight off. The disappointment of
the boys proves to be too much for Garfield and he decides to go through
with the fight after all. Garfield holds his own against the challenger for
three rounds, but in the fourth he is defeated. As expected, Rains arrives to
arrest Garfield and the boxer turns himself in. Seeing that Garfield has
rejected his shadowy lifestyle and sacrificed his freedom to help out Dickson
and her charges, Rains decides to let Garfield stay "dead" and allow him to
return to the farm. THEY MADE ME A CRIMINAL begins with Garfield
once again playing the fatalistic, cynical, tough-guy from the slums, but his
personality undergoes a change during the course of the film and by the
conclusion he has attained a minor state of grace. By seeing himself in the
faces of the troubled youngsters, Garfield is able to identify his problems and
work to eradicate them from the boys and himself. Formerly self-centered,
arrogant, and uncaring, Garfield finds that he is able to teach others, be
dependable, and make sacrifices. Garfield handles the role admirably, able
to convey the conflicting emotions churning inside the fugitive boxer.
Surprisingly, the film was directed by Busby Berkeley, who had made his
name as a choreographer-director of extravagantly staged musicals like
FOOTLIGHT PARADE (1933), FOURTY-SECOND STREET (1933), GOLD-
DIGGERS OF 1933, GOLDDIGGERS OF 1935, and HOLLYWOOD HOTEL
(1937) among others. Berkeley became tired of musicals--as had the public
and the critics by the late 1930s--and was urging the studio to let him direct
something different. With only one film left under his contract, Warners
decided to take what they considered a chance and assigned Berkeley the
new Garfield picture. Berkeley directed the film in the trademark Warners
style: gritty, fast-paced, and sometimes brutally realistic. Transferring his
choreographic talents from the stage to the boxing ring, Berkeley created
some vivid fight scenes that wouldn't be outdone until Garfield's magnum
opus BODY AND SOUL in 1947 (which was also photographed by the great
James Wong Howe). As an acknowledgement to his musical past, director
Berkeley added a small joke to the film which sees Hall playfully croon "By
a Waterfall"(Sammy Fain, Irving Kahal) to the showering Garfield. The
tune was a hit song from the film FOOTLIGHT PARADE, which Berkeley
choreographed.

p, Jack L. Warner, Hal B. Wallis; d, Busby Berkeley; w, Sid Herzig (based
on the book by Bertram Millhauser, Beulah Marie Dix); ph, James Wong
Howe; m, Max Steiner; ed, Jack Killifer; md, Leo F. Forbstein; art d, Anton
Grot; cos, Milo Anderson.

Drama   Cas.   (PR:A   MPAA:NR)

THEY MADE ME A CRIMINAL   (SEE: I BECAME A CRIMINAL,
                                                              1947)

THEY MADE ME A FUGITIVE   (SEE: I BECAME A CRIMINAL,
                                                       1947, Brit.)

THEY MADE ME A KILLER*   (1946) 64m Pine-Thomas/PAR bw

Robert Lowery (Tom Durling), Barbara Britton (June Reynolds), Frank
Albertson (Al), Lola Lane (Betty), James Bush (Frank Chance), Edmund
McDonald (Jack Chance), Byron Barr (Steve Reynolds), Elisabeth Risdon
(Ma), Ralph Sanford (Roach), John Harmon (Lafferty), Paul Harvey
(District Attorney).

An escaped convict, Lowery, and the sister of a man killed in a bank holdup,
Britton, join forces to take a cross-country jaunt in search of the gang of
hoodlums who have framed Lowery. Thoroughly unbelievable, aimed solely
at arousing a few thrills through an abundance of action.

p, William Pine, William C. Thomas; d, Thomas; w, Geoffrey Homes,
Winston Miller, Kae Salkow (based on a story by Owen Francis); ph, Fred
Jackman, Jr.; m, Alexander Laszlo; ed, Henry Adams, Howard Smith; art
d, F. Paul Sylos, set d, Glenn Thompson.

Crime   (PR:A   MPAA:NR)

THEY MEET AGAIN*½   (1941) 69m RKO bw

Jean Hersholt (Dr. Paul Christian), Dorothy Lovett (Judy Price), Robert
Baldwin (Roy Davis), Maude Eburne (Mrs. Hastings), Neil Hamilton (Robert
Webster), Anne Bennett (Janie Webster), Leon Tyler (Messenger), Frank
Melton, Barton Yarborough, Arthur Hoyt, John Dilson, Milton Kibbee, Gus
Glassmire, Patsy Lee Parsons, Meredith Howard.

The final episode in the adventures of the kindly country doctor, has
Hersholt using his intuition and good sense to help out an innocent man
convicted of embezzlement. Operating on the feeling that the man is not
guilty, and not liking the depressed state of his girl friend, Hersholt puts
together enough clues to clear the man's name. Not a very exciting ending
for the old doctor. Songs include: "When Love is New" (Jack Owens, Claude
Sweeten), "In the Make Believe Land of Dreams," "Get Alive" (Owens),
"The Rhythm is Red an' White an' Blue" (David Gregory, Al Moss). (See DR.
CHRISTIAN SERIES, Index.)

p, William Stephens; d, Erle C. Kenton; w, Peter Milne, Maurice Leo (based
on the story by Milne); ed, Alexander Troffey; md, C. Bakaleinikoff.

Drama   **Cas.**   **(PR:A MPAA:NR)**

THEY MET AT MIDNIGHT   (SEE: PICADILLY INCIDENT, 1948)

THEY MET IN A TAXI**   (1936) 69m COL bw

Chester Morris *(Jimmy)*, Fay Wray *(Mary)*, Lionel Stander *(Fingers, Pickpocket)*, Raymond Walburn *(Mr. Clifton)*, Henry Mollison *(Mr. Stewart)*, Kenneth Harlan *(Mr. Andrews)*, Ann Merrill *(Edna Fletcher)*, Ward Bond *(Policeman)*, Frank Melton *(Specks)*.

Model Wray is innocently involved in the theft of a pearl necklace from the household of the society woman for whom she is modeling a wedding dress. The pearls latched to the underside of her dress, she escapes a number of accusations to find safety in the cab of Morris. A romance soon develops between the couple as he harbors her from the law, and with the aid of a few pals they try to figure out the robbery scheme. A pleasant farce that's weak in plot development, but that does a good job in delivering laughs through characterizations and situations.

p, Howard J. Green; d, Alfred E. Green; w, Green (based on the story by Octavus Roy Cohen); ph, James Van Trees; ed, Gene Milford.

Comedy   **(PR:A MPAA:NR)**

THEY MET IN ARGENTINA*½   (1941) 77m RKO bw

Maureen O'Hara *(Lolita)*, James Ellison *(Tim Kelly)*, Alberto Vila *(Alberto Delmonte)*, Buddy Ebsen *(Duke Ferrel)*, Robert Barrat *(Don Enrique)*, Joseph Buloff *(Santiago)*, Diosa Costello *(Panchita)*, Victoria Cordova *(Nina Maria)*, Antonio Moreno *(Don Carlos)*, Robert Middlemass *(George Hastings)*, Chester Clute *(Hastings' Secretary)*, Carlos Barbe *(Nicanor)*, Francisco Maran *(Don Ramon)*, Fortunio Bonanova *(Pedro)*, Luis Alberni *(Don Frutos)*, George Lewis *(Reporter)*, Paul Ellis.

A dismal effort at trying to make a film that would appeal to both South American and U.S. audiences. Hardly anyone cared too much for it as it barely made half of the $500 thousand sunk into it. Yarn centers around the efforts of Ellison, as a representative of a Texas oil baron, to secure a prize Argentine race horse; instead, he winds up falling for the horse-owner's daughter, O'Hara. The result is turbulent romance and a headache for the audience. Vila, a popular star in Argentina, was relegated to a small, subordinate role, which may have been a serious mistake as far as South American reception was concerned. Choreographer Veloz–of the well-known cinematic dance team of Veloz and Yolanda–should have stuck to performing. Producer Brock, who bore much of the credit for the successful south-of-the-border film FLYING DOWN TO RIO (1933)–the first film to pair Fred Astaire and Ginger Rogers–never again worked for RKO after this flop. The film was plagued with production problems; codirector Hively had to fill in for the originally assigned Goodwins, who became ill after production began. That a South American market existed for U.S.-made pictures was certain; Walt Disney's four-part cartoon feature SALUDOS AMIGOS (1943) beat GONE WITH THE WIND (1939) as Argentina's biggest box-office winner only two seasons after this one. Three-fourths of all the films shown in Argentina were imports from the U.S. during 1941. RKO was dilatory in its approach to this potential market; of the eight big studios, it was tied with United Artists for the fewest releases screened in Mexico, for example. Financial mogul Nelson Rockefeller, the power behind the scenes at RKO during this period, was determined to open up the market; he had many other interests in the region, and had gotten himself appointed "Coordinator of Commercial and Cultural Relations Between [sic! the American Republi cs." This film with probably the worst of Rodgers and Hart's musical offerings, was neither commercially nor culturally acceptable. Songs include "Carefree Carretero," "You've Got the Best of Me," "Amarillo," "Cutting the Cane," "Never Go to Argentina," "Lolita," "North America Meets South America," "Simpatica" (Richard Rodgers, Lorenz Hart).

p, Lou Brock; d, Leslie Goodwins, Jack Hively; w, Jerry Cady (based on a story by Brock, Harold Daniels); ph, J. Roy Hunt; m, Richard Rodgers, Lorenz Hart; ed, Desmond Marquette; md, Lud Gluskin; ch, Frank Veloz; spec eff, Vernon L. Walker.

Musical   **(PR:A MPAA:NR)**

THEY MET IN BOMBAY***   (1941) 86m MGM bw

Clark Gable *(Gerald Meldrick)*, Rosalind Russell *(Anya Von Duren)*, Peter Lorre *(Capt. Chang)*, Jessie Ralph *(Duchess of Beltravers)*, Reginald Owen *(General)*, Matthew Boulton *(Inspector Cressney)*, Leslie Vincent *(Lt. Ashley)*, Eduardo Ciannelli *(Hotel Manager)*, Jay Novello *(Bolo)*, Rosina Galli *(Carmencita)*, Luis Alberni *(Maitre d'Hotel)*, Adelaide Whytal *(Old Lady)*, Harry North *(Clerk)*, Nanette Vallon *(Beauty Operator)*, Lilyan Irene *(Duchess' Maid)*, James B. Leong *(Third Mate)*, Duke Chan *(Radio Operator)*, Chester Gan *(Woo Ling Woo)*, Eric Lonsdale, David Clyde, David Thursby *(Sergeants)*, Stephen Chase, Cornelius Keefe *(Officers)*, Key Luke *(Mr. Toy)*, Roland Got *(Young Foo Sing)*, Lee Tung-Foo *(Elder Foo Sing)*, Harry Cording *(Corporal)*, Judith Wood *(Nurse)*, Philip Ahn, Richard Loo *(Japanese Officers)*, Alan Ladd *(British Soldier)*.

A likable adventure romp which begins in India and then takes off to China,

showcasing some glorious locations as well as its two big box-office stars. Gable is in Bombay posing as an insurance detective for Lloyd's of London, while Russell is pretending to be a friend of the royal family. In actuality, both are jewel thieves intent on stealing a priceless diamond necklace belonging to duchess Ralph. When Gable realizes Russell's plan he allows her to do the dirty work, while planning to snatch the stolen goods from her later on. Russell, however, is aware of his plan, and the pair decide to make their getaway together. They hop a freighter captained by the unscrupulous Lorre, who informs on them in order to receive a hefty reward. Before Scotland Yard inspector Boulton can track them down, however, Gable and Russell escape to Hong Kong. Gable and Russell have a difficult time selling the necklace, however, and are soon desperate for money. Gable steals a British officer's uniform and concocts a scheme to confiscate funds from a crooked Chinese merchant. While dressed as a British officer, Gable is rallied into an emergency operation to evacuate British and Chinese citizens from a village recently invaded by the Japanese. Gable performs heroically and is rewarded with the Victoria Cross. After rushing off to wed Russell, Gable turns himself in, agrees to serve his punishment, and then promises to reenlist. A fine studio entry which manages to successfully mix romance, adventure, comedy, and the then- necessary patriotism into one picture, resulting in a delightful audience pleaser. Although the story falters somewhat by the halfway point, THEY MET IN BOMBAY is definitely worth a look, if only for Gable and Russell. If one looks closely, Alan Ladd can be spotted in one of his numerous pre-THIS GUN FOR HIRE bit parts.

p, Hunt Stromberg; d, Clarence Brown; w, Edwin Justus Mayer, Anita Loos, Leon Gordon (based on a story by John Kafka); ph, William Daniels; m, Herbert Stothart; ed, Blanche Sewell; art d, Cedric Gibbons; spec eff, Warren Newcombe.

Comedy/Adventure   **(PR:A MPAA:NR)**

THEY MET IN THE DARK**   (1945, Brit.) 94m I.P.-Excelsior/English Films bw

James Mason *(Comdr. Richard Heritage)*, Joyce Howard *(Laura Verity)*, Tom Walls *(Christopher Child)*, Phyllis Stanley *(Lily Bernard)*, Edward Rigby *(Mansel)*, Ronald Ward *(Carter)*, David Farrar *(Comdr. Lippinscott)*, Karel Stepanek *(Riccardo)*, Betty Warren *(Fay)*, Walter Crisham *(Charlie)*, George Robey *(Pawnbroker)*, Peggy Dexter *(Bobby)*, Ronald Chesney *(Max, Harmonica Player)*, Finlay Currie *(Merchant Captain)*, Brefni O'Rorke *(Inspector Burrows)*, Jeanne de Casalis *(Lady with Dog)*, Patricia Medina *(Mary, Manicurist)*, Eric Mason *(Benson, Illusionist)*, Herbert Lomas *(Van Driver)*, Charles Victor *(Pub Owner)*, Robert Sansom *(Petty Officer Grant)*, Alvar Lidell *(Boothby, Radio Announcer)*, Ian Fleming.

As a naval commander, Mason has the wool pulled over his eyes by a pretty girl who is actually working in collusion with a group of Nazi spies. Mason inadvertently reveals the sailing dates of warships, resulting in a major mishap at sea and the commander losing his post. This leads Mason to try to find the girl responsible, hoping to discover who is behind the scheme. But the girl turns up dead, leaving few clues. With the aid of Howard, Mason is able to track a Nazi spy ring to a theatrical agency. Capable performances in a story that offers little new. Editing chores went to Terence Fisher, who would later make his biggest claim to fame as a director for Hammer studios. Stanley sings one song, "Toddle Along" (Ben Frankel, Moira Heath).

p, Marcel Hellman; d, Karel Lamac; w, Anatole de Grunwald, Miles Malleson, Basil Bartlett, Victor McClure, James Seymour (based on the novel *"The Vanished Corpse"* by Anthony Gilbert); ph, Otto Heller; m, Ben Frankel; ed, Terence Fisher; art d, Norman Arnold.

Spy Drama/Mystery   **(PR:A MPAA:NR)**

THEY MET ON SKIS*½   (1940, Fr.) 75m C.L. Import bw

Wissia Dina *(Helene)*, Henri Presles *(Michel)*, Charpin *(Uncle Justin)*, Assia *(Ginette)*, Max Derly *(Barsac)*, Mila Parely *(Nicole)*, Marcel Mouloudji *(Pierrot)*, Louis Agnel, The Women's Team of the Paris Ski Club.

The owner of an inn in the French Alps falls for the daughter of his chief competitor in this overly familiar romantic tale. Highlights come from some of the excellent skiing sequences, in which actual professionals and capable amateurs grace the slopes with their skills. (In French; English subtitles.)

p&d, Henri Sokal; w, Fred Schiller; ph, Otto Heller, Adrien Porchet, Albert Benitz.

Drama   **(PR:A MPAA:NR)**

THEY MIGHT BE GIANTS**½   (1971) 91m UNIV c

Joanne Woodward *(Dr. Mildred Watson)*, George C. Scott *(Justin Playfair/ Sherlock Holmes)*, Jack Gilford *(Wilbur Peabody)*, Lester Rawlins *(Blevins Playfair)*, Rue McClanahan *(Daisy)*, Ron Weyland *(Dr. Strauss)*, Kitty Winn *(Grace)*, Peter Fredericks *(Her Boy Friend)*, Sudie Bond *(Maud)*, Jenny Egan *(Miss Finch)*, Theresa Merritt *(Peggy)*, Al Lewis *(Messenger)*, Oliver Clark *(Mr. Small)*, Jane Hoffman, Dorothy Greener *(Telephone Operators)*, M. Emmet Walsh, Louis Zorich *(Sanitation Men)*, Michael McGuire *(Telephone Guard)*, Eugene Roche *(Policeman)*, James Tolkan *(Mr. Brown)*, Jacques Sandulescu *(His Driver)*, Worthington Miner *(Mr. Bagg)*, Frances Fuller *(Mrs. Bagg)*, Matthew Cowles *(Teenage Boy)*, Candy Azzara *(Teenage Girl)*,

John McCurry (Police Lieutenant), Tony Capodilupo (Chief), F. Murray Abraham (Usher), Staats Cotsworth (Winthrop), Paul Benedict (Chestnut Vendor), Ralph Clanton (Store Manager), Ted Beniades (Cab Driver).

A strange movie that doesn't seem to know what it wants to be. Sentimental, biting, satirical, whimsical, and self-righteous, it begins with a romp at high speed then goes straight into a hole from which it never extricates itself. Scott is an aging, recently widowed judge who has gone off the deep end. His mind snapped beyond repair, he believes that he is actually Sherlock Holmes, so he dresses, speaks, and comports himself like Doyle's famed detective in a Deerstalker. His brother is Rawlins, a cad who is being blackmailed and would like to see Scott shut up in an institution so he can get his hands on the money in Scott's estate. Scott is taken to a clinic and meets Woodward, whose name just happens to be "Watson." When Scott uses Holmesian logic to correctly assess the problems of one of her patients, she is impressed. Clark is a short, fat man who thinks he is Rudolph Valentino but is unable to speak. Scott reckons that Clark won't talk because Valentino was, after all, a star of silent pictures. Clark is thrilled that someone understands and as he leaves, Scott tells him to pass on regards to Vilma Banky. Woodward goes along with Scott's mental condition and aids him in his "work" just as her long-ago relative, also a doctor, helped Sherlock. Scott's brother has left a blackmail note lying around which mentions "twenty grand" and Scott feels that it's a clue which will help him trap his long-time enemy, the heinous Professor Moriarty. He takes the note literally and he and Woodward go downtown to No. 20 Grand Street. That begins a chase that is only missing the wild geese. They travel through Manhattan, visit an aged couple (Miner and Fuller) who have not come out of their home since before WW II, sneak into a telephone company switchboard office, visit a library and meet Gilford, an aged keeper of the books who dreams of being "The Scarlet Pimpernel," then on to a movie house on 42nd Street where Scott engages in conversation with the flotsam who make the theater their home as they watch movies that Hoot Gibson wouldn't have liked. Rawlins' blackmailer tracks Scott all the while, hoping to get enough on him to have him committed once and for all. Scott keeps telling Woodward that he can darn near smell Moriarty and that they are getting closer. Woodward makes dinner for Scott at her place and shots ring out and almost kill Scott. Ahah! It must be the professor. Late in the movie, Scott and Woodward are joined by all the nuts they've met earlier and they form a hardy band. It seems that the whole group shares a paranoia and each has another identity. There's a huge supermarket they all march into and Scott takes the manager's microphone and announces outlandish prices on items, setting off a frantic race for the food by the store's customers. By this time, instead of Scott being "cured," Woodward has entered into Scott's world and is just as crazy as he is. The two stand in Central Park at night and walk toward a tunnel. They hear the clop of horses' hooves in the tunnel and Scott is convinced that Moriarty approaches, but before anything is completed, the screen fades to white and the ponderous statement that "the human heart can see what is hidden to the eyes, and the heart knows things that the mind does not begin to understand" flashes on. Whatever it means, it's as enigmatic as most of this disappointing movie. Goldman did the screenplay from his stage play that never did make it to New York. The supermarket sequence was cut from the theatrical prints, then restored for the TV showings. It's a lot of nonsense cloaked in platitudes. Scott is funny, Woodward is a good foil, the peripheral characters are all well-drawn from the reality of the populace in New York and yet the picture doesn't hold together. AMADEUS Oscar winner F. Murray Abraham does a bit, as does famed TV producer Worthington Miner. Shortly after this, Theresa Merritt (Peggy) was hired to play the lead in TV's "That's My Mama" after having been seen in this movie by one of your editors, Ross, who developed that series for ABC.

p, John Foreman, (uncredited, Paul Newman); d, Anthony Harvey; w, James Goldman (based on his play); ph, Victor J. Kemper (DeLuxe Color); m, John Barry; ed, Gerald Greenberg; prod d, John Robert Lloyd; set d, Herbert Mulligan; cos, Ann Roth, Fern Buchner; makeup, Vince Callaghan.

Comedy/Drama   **Cas.**   **(PR:A MPAA:G)**

THEY NEVER COME BACK*½   (1932) 67m Weiss Bros./Artclass bw

Regis Toomey (Nolan), Dorothy Sebastian (Adele), Gertrude Astor (Kate), Earle Foxe (Filmore), Greta Granstedt (Mary Nolan), Eddie Woods (Ralph), George Byron (Donovan), James J. Jeffries (Referee), Little Billy (M.C.).

Toomey plays a boxer who meets with an early retirement when he breaks his arm in the ring. He doesn't stay idle but becomes a bouncer in Foxe's nightclub which stars inappropriately innocent hoochie-koochie dancer Sebastian, only to become the victim of an envious guy who is jealous of Toomey's success with Sebastian. Light entertainment that rests on the heavy-handed action as Toomey, needing money to get Sebastian out of a jam, reenters the ring despite his crippled south paw, Jeffries, world heavyweight boxing champion from 1899 through his initial retirement in 1905, plays the referee.

d, Fred Newmeyer; w, Arthur Hoerl, Sherman Lowe (based on the story by Hoerl); ph, James Diamond.

Drama   **Cas.**   **(PR:A MPAA:NR)**

THEY ONLY KILL THEIR MASTERS*½   (1972) 97m MGM c

James Garner (Police Chief Abel Marsh), Katharine Ross (Kate), Hal Holbrook (Dr. Watkins, Veterinarian), Harry Guardino (Capt. Streeter, Sheriff), June Allyson (Mrs. Watkins), Christopher Connelly (John, Cop), Tom Ewell (Walter, Cop), Peter Lawford (Lee Campbell), Edmund O'Brien (George, Liquor Store Owner), Arthur O'Connell (Ernie, Cafeteria Owner), Ann Rutherford (Gloria, Police Secretary), Art Metrano (Malcolm), Harry Basch (Mayor), Jenifer Shaw (Diana), Jason Wingreen (Mallory), Robert Nichols (Doctor), Norma Connolly (Mrs. DeCamp), David Westberg (State Trooper), Lee Pulford (Jenny Campbell), Roy Applegate (Harry), Alma Lenor Beltran (Rosa), Murphy the Dog.

A Doberman pinscher is accused as the killer of its owner, a recently divorced woman who aroused a lot of community wrath because of her wild ways. The investigation by Garner soon shows that the girl was actually drowned, his sleuthing turning up the real reasons for the murder. The film features cameo appearances in wildly anti-type roles by a number of 1940s MGM stars. A good part of the picture was filmed on MGM's old lot number two, home of the Hardy family in the old days (see HARDY FAMILY series, Index). One of the roles went to Ann Rutherford, who had been Mickey Rooney's long-time girl friend Polly Benedict in so many films of that series; studio publicists distributed pre-release photographs of her standing under a banner that read "Welcome Home Polly." The real shocker was the casting of Allyson, the one-time prototype cute/pert casting type, as a bisexual killer.

p, William Belasco; d, James Goldstone; w, Lane Slate; ph, Michel Hugo (Metrocolor); m, Perry Botkin, Jr.; ed, Edward A. Biery; art d, Lawrence G. Paull; set d, Philip Abramson; cos, Arnold M. Lipin; makeup, Charles Schram; dog trainer, Karl Miller.

Crime/Mystery   **(PR:C MPAA:PG)**

THEY PASS THIS WAY   (SEE: FOUR FACES WEST, 1948)

THEY RAID BY NIGHT*   (1942) 80m PRC bw

Lyle Talbot (Capt. Robert Owen), June Duprez (Inga), Victor Varconi (Oberst von Ritter), George Neise (Lt. Falken), Charles Rogers (Harry), Paul Baratoff (Gen. Heden), Leslie Dennison (Capt. Deane), Crane Whitley (Doctor), Sven Hugo Borg (Dalberg), Eric Wilton (Gen. Lloyd), Pierce Lyden (Braun), John Beck (Beggar), William Kellogg (Sentry), Robert C. Fisher (Von Memel), Sigfrid Tor (German Lieutenant), Brian O'Hara (Lammet).

A sad looking attempt to try to get the blood going by showing a bunch of commandos in action, here flying into Norway to rescue a Norwegian general from the grip of the Nazis. Twist has one of the ex-girl friends of a commando now working for the enemy; she does her best to get back at her old flame but it's not enough to stop the stalwart heroes. The "Poverty-Row" Producers Releasing Corporation had recently been absorbed by the Pathe Corporation whose moguls had decided that, after a long hiatus, they wanted to get back into picture production and distribution. WW II offered exploitation opportunities; the small company cranked out 10 such war-related films in a short period of time, rivaling the patriotic efforts of some of the major studios in quantity if not in quality. The industry was into conservation of necessary wartime materials, and a cost ceiling of $5,000 dollars for new materials had been imposed on individual movie sets. This would have appeared to favor the low-budget fast-film specialists such as PRC, but the majors responded by reusing their old sets effectively at a time when shortages forced the companies to sterilize and recycle even the hairpins of the stars.

p, Dixon R. Harwin; d, Spencer Gordon Bennett; w, Jack Natteford; ph, Gilbert Warrenton; m, David Chudnow; ed, Charles Henkel; art d, Glenn T. Thompson.

War   **(PR:A MPAA:NR)**

THEY RAN FOR THEIR LIVES*½   (1968) 92m Masterpiece/Color Vision c

John Payne (Bob Martin), Luana Patten (Barbara Collins), John Carradine (Laslow), Bravo (Bob's Dog), Scott Brady, Jim Davis, Anthony Eisley.

Gangsters fight it out in the desert with Payne and his dog after chasing Patten in order to obtain an oil document that belonged to her late father. The heat and Payne's wit are more than the hoodlums can handle, leaving only Carradine–the sleazy partner of the dead man– to contend with. He too is no match for Payne's trusty German shepherd. Payne, who had retired from the screen following HIDDEN FEAR (1957), briefly returned to films for this low-budget dog picture which he also directed. He then dropped out again. Patten, a one-time Walt Disney child star, also retired after this career-killing effort.

p, Samuel Ray Calabrese; d, John Payne; w, Monroe Manning; ph, Ross Kelsay (Eastmancolor); ed, Thor Brooks; m/l, "They Ran for Their Lives," The Knickerbockers; stunts, Boyd Stockman.

Adventure/Drama   **(PR:A MPAA:NR)**

THEY RODE WEST** (1954) 84m COL c

Robert Francis *(Dr. Allen Seward)*, Donna Reed *(Laurie MacKaye)*, May Wynn *(Manyi-ten)*, Phil Carey *(Capt. Peter Blake)*, Onslow Stevens *(Col. Ethan Waters)*, Peggy Converse *(Mrs. Walters)*, Roy Roberts *(Sgt. Creever)*, Jack Kelly *(Lt. Raymond)*, Stuart Randall *(Satanta)*, Eugene Iglesias *(Red Leaf)*, Frank DeKova *(Isatai)*, John War Eagle *(Chief Quanah)*, Ralph Dumke *(Dr. Gibson)*, Julia Montoya *(Maria)*, James Best *(Lt. Finlay)*, George Keymas *(Torquay)*, Maurice Jara *(Spotted Wolf)*.

Given the job of medical officer at a western fort in which his predecessors did little to prove the worth of their profession, Francis shows himself to be a capable doctor and slowly wins the faith of the residents. But his liberal mindedness soon works against him as he uses his skills for members of the local Kiowa tribe. The hardened soldiers stop trusting him, apparently rightly so when the Kiowa join a band of Comanches to invade the fort. But Francis' tactics prove the best medicine when he ends the raids by helping the Kiowa once again. Strong characterizations and capable direction keep the plot from becoming too bogged down. Low-budget director Karlson, who did most of his work for Universal Pictures, here ventures into John Ford's territory very capably. He demonstrates the meticulous attention to detail that gained him a cult following among some cinema addicts. Leading players Francis and Wynn had appeared in THE CAINE MUTINY (1954); this was only the second film for both. The handsome, muscular blond-haired Francis died the year following the film's release at the age of 25.

p, Lewis J. Rachmil; d, Phil Karlson; w, DeVallon Scott, Frank Nugent (based on the story by Leo Katcher); ph, Charles Lawton, Jr. (Technicolor); m, Paul Sawtell; ed, Henry Batista.

Western (PR:A MPAA:NR)

THEY SAVED HITLER'S BRAIN zero (1964) 74m San-S/Crown

International bw (AKA: MADMEN OF MANDORAS, THE RETURN OF MR. H.)

Walter Stocker *(Phil Daly)*, Audrey Caire *(Kathy Daly)*, Carlos Rivas *(Camine)*, John Holland *(John Coleman)*, Dani Lynn *(Suzanne)*, Marshall Reed *(Frank Dvorak)*, Nestor Paiva *(Police Chief Alaniz)*, Scott Peters *(David Garrick)*, Pedro Regas *(Padua)*, Keith Dahle *(Tom Sharon)*, Bill Freed *(Mr. H.)*, Hap Holmwood, Dick McHale, Chuck Beston.

One of the all-time worst. THEY SAVED HITLER'S BRAIN has a mighty cult reputation, but the film is so slow, convoluted, and badly acted that it is nearly unwatchable, regardless of the unintentional comedy value (the best moments all involve Der Fuhrer's severed noggin, which is only on screen briefly). The plot, created by taking old footage from a 1950s espionage melodrama and combining it with new footage that appears to have been shot somewhere in the Philippines, details Caire's search for her neurobiologist father who has disappeared along with her sister. Caire gets her husband, Stocker, to fly her to Mandoras to search for her family, and it is only a matter of time until they discover a bunch of Nazis (formerly of the Third Reich high command) who are taking orders from Hitler's severed head, which is connected to a mechanical box. The evil gang plans to take over the world once again by using a deadly nerve gas dubbed "Nerve Gas G." From here on the film is one big mess of plot and counterplot involving mistaken identity, assassination, uprisings, and blackmail, until the Nazis and Mr. H's head are destroyed. The only scene worth suffering through is the flashback where we are treated to the operation which detached Der Fuhrer's head from his lifeless body.

p, Carl Edwards; d, David Bradley; w, Richard Miles, Steve Bennett (based on a story by Bennett); ph, Stanley Cortez; ed, Leon Selditz; art d, Frank Sylos; makeup, Maurice Seiderman.

Science Fiction Cas. (PR:C MPAA:NR)

THEY SHALL HAVE MUSIC** (1939) 105m Goldwyn/UA bw (GB: MELODY OF YOUTH; AKA: RAGGED ANGELS)

Jascha Heifetz *(Himself)*, Joel McCrea *(Peter McCarthy)*, Walter Brennan *(Prof. Lawson)*, Andrea Leeds *(Ann Lawson)*, Gene Reynolds *(Frankie)*, Terry Kilburn *(Dominick)*, Tommy Kelly *(Willie)*, Chuck Stubbs *(Fever Jones)*, Walter Tetley *(Rocks Mulligan)*, Alfred Newman *(Musical Director)*, Jacqueline Nash [Gale Sherwood] *(Betty)*, Mary Ruth *(Susie)*, Arthur Hohl *(Ed Miller)*, Marjorie Main *(Jane Miller)*, Porter Hall *(Mr. Flower)*, Paul Harvey *(Heifetz's Manager)*, John St. Polis *(Menken)*, Alex Schonberg *(Davis)*, Frank Jaquet *(Mr. Morgan)*, Perry Ivins *(Mr. Wallace)*, Dorothy Christie *(Young Woman)*, Paul Stanton *(Inspector Johnson)*, Charles Coleman *(Heifetz's Butler)*, Arthur Aylesworth, John Hamilton *(Detectives)*, Virginia Brissac *(Willie's Mother)*, James Flavin *(Police Sergeant)*, Wade Boteler *(Police Lieutenant)*, J. Farrell MacDonald *(Police Chief)*, Roger Imhof, Louis Mason *(Deputies)*, Marjorie Wood *(Mother)*, Emmett Vogan *(Police Chief's Aide)*, Lee Phelps *(Policeman in Auditorium)*, Jessie Arnold *(Woman in Alley)*, Mrs. Willard Louis, Dulce Daye *(Women in Line)*, Bryant Washburn, Jr *(Usher)*, Dolly Loehr [Diana Lynn] *(Girl at Piano)*, Zero *(Sucker the Dog)*, Alan Edwards, John Kelly, Emory Parnell, Effie Anderson, Stanley Blystone, Wyndham Standing, Ethan Laidlaw, The Peter Meremblum California Junior Symphony Orchestra.

The youthful, ragged Reynolds–later to become a celebrated producer of TV shows–finds a Carnegie Hall concert ticket on the sidewalk and decides, for a lark, to use it. Listening to famed violinist Heifetz, the near-delinquent slum kid becomes entranced by the thought of a music career. He enrolls in Brennan's underfinanced inner-city music school to receive free instruction. Seeing that the school is near the end of its rope, he enlists the assistance of his streetwise pals to implore Heifetz to help save it. A benefit concert does the trick. Ill-educated producer Goldwyn, though best known for the musical-spectacular Girls who assumed his name, strove mightily to impose culture on the great unwashed. His THE GOLDWYN FOLLIES the year previously mixed popular and classical music, but Goldwyn wanted to try his hand at an all-classical film, featuring his good friend Heifetz. The violinist's busy concert schedule forced Goldwyn to film Heifetz' solos well before the long-delayed screenplay was completed. Heifetz was paid $70,000 for this four-week stint on the soundstage. The screenplay finally approved had a tangled history; arguments about credits ensued, and Von Cube was later credited with the original story while Lawson got the screenplay credit. One critic described the plot line as "The Dead End Kids In Music School," but it didn't much matter; the important thing was the music. Adolphe Menjou had originally been slated for the Brennan part, and Margot Stevenson for the part of his daughter, actually played by Leeds. McCrea had been cast at the outset in an undemanding role as the love interest for Leeds. Little five-year-old Dolly Loehr (later Diana Lynn) played a piano solo. Ten-year-old operatic singer Jacqueline Nash (later, as Gale Sherwood, the singing partner of Nelson Eddy in nightclubs) sang two arias. Heifetz was called in again during production to demonstrate his ineptitude at acting and to film a few more musical pieces, at an added fee of $50,000. The latter were directed by an uncredited William Wyler. After the film's premiere, *The New York Times* was highly critical. Publisher Arthur Sulzberger–a personal friend of Heifetz, who had attended the premiere in the company of his good friend–ordered that a gentler review be written for later editions of the newspaper. Two separate advertising campaigns were launched to promote the film: one, featuring Heifetz, for the highbrows, and another, featuring the slum-dweller plot, for the plebians. Box office returns may have suffered somewhat through audience confusion with the British film SHE SHALL HAVE MUSIC (1935). THEY SHALL HAVE MUSIC was re-released with emphasis on the non-musical story in 1945 under the title RAGGED ANGELS. Violin pieces played by Heifetz include "Rondo Capriccioso" (Camille Saint-Saens), "Hora Staccato" (Dinicu, Heifetz), "Estrellita" (Ponce, Heifetz), "Melody" (Peter Ilyich Tchaikovsky), and–accompanied by Mer emblum's group–the third movement of "Concerto in E Minor for Violin and Orchestra" (Felix Mendelssohn). Little pianist Loehr plays "Waltz in D Flat, Opus 64, No. 1 (The Minute Waltz)" (Frederic Chopin). Nash sings "Cara Nome" (Giuseppe Verdi) and "Casta Diva" (Vincenzo Bellini). Peter Meremblum's youthful orchestra renders "Italian Symphony" (Mendelssohn), selections from "The Barber of Seville" (Giacchimo Antonio Rossini), and "Eine Kleine Nachtmusik" (Wolfgang Amadeus Mozart).

p, Samuel Goldwyn, Robert Riskin; d, Archie Mayo; w, Irmgard von Cube, John Howard Lawson, Robert Presnell, Anthony Veiller (based on the novel by Charles L. Clifford); ph, Gregg Toland; ed, Sherman Todd; md, Alfred Newman; art d, James Basevi.

Musical/Drama (PR:A MPAA:NR)

THEY SHOOT HORSES, DON'T THEY?***½ (1969) 129m Palomar/ABC-Cinerama c

Jane Fonda *(Gloria Beatty)*, Michael Sarrazin *(Robert Syverton)*, Susannah York *(Alice)*, Gig Young *(Rocky)*, Red Buttons *(Sailor)*, Bonnie Bedelia *(Ruby)*, Bruce Dern *(James)*, Michael Conrad *(Rollo)*, Al Lewis *(Turkey)*, Robert Fields *(Joel)*, Severn Darden *(Cecil)*, Allyn Ann Mclerie *(Shirl)*, Jacquelyn Hyde *(Jackie)*, Felice Orlandi *(Mario)*, Art Metrano *(Max)*, Gail Billings *(Lillian)*, Maxine Greene *(Agnes)*, Paul Mantee *(Jiggs)*, Madge Kennedy *(Mrs. Layden)*, Mary Gregory *(Nurse)*, Robert Dunlap *(College Boy)*, Tim Herbert *(Doctor)*, Tom McFadden, Noble "Kid" Chissell *(Trainers)*, Philo McCullough *(Audience Extra)*, Marilyn Hassett *(Girl)*, Teddy Buckner, Hugh Bell, Harold Land, Teddy Edwards, Hadley Coliman, Thurman Green, Les Robertson, Ronnell Bright, Ike Isaacs, Joe Harris *(House Band)*, Bobby Hutcherson *(Band Leader)*.

An allegorical, socially conscious response to the injustices of the Depression era, THEY SHOOT HORSES, DON'T THEY? has managed to surface from the late 1960s, unlike so many other films of that period, without appearing the least bit dated. Preparing the audience for an inevitable ending, the film begins with Sarrazin standing trial for murder, the details of which are purposely vague. The scene then switches to the 1930s in Chicago's famous Aragon Ballroom where a dance marathon is about to get under way. Among the contestants is Fonda, an independent, disagreeable loner who seems to enjoy lashing out at those around her, whose original partner has dropped out only to be replaced by Sarrazin, a drifter with no real desire to partake in the decadent escapade. Also wearing numbers on their backs are Bedelia, a pregnant farm girl; her husband Dern; a sailor and veteran marathoner Buttons, who suffers from heart trouble but still continues to pound the dance floor; and a Jean Harlowesque aspiring actress, York, who hopes to be discovered while dancing in the spotlight. As the master of ceremonies is a sweaty, unshaven Young whose job it is to keep the audience content and the dancers dancing. Everyone's reason for participating is simple–three meals a day and a chance at winning the $1,500 prize, a promising reward in the days of record unemployment and bread lines. As the marathon wears on, dancers begins to drop, passing out on the dance floor, collapsing in a state of mental decay, leaving their numbed, disqualified partners alone on the dance floor. As the weak are crushed by the sadistic Young, who goads his dancers to self-destruction, the strong continue to fight, week after painstaking week. When a gown of York's is stolen, suspicions arise and eat away at the mental well-being of the marathoners. Fonda, who believes that Sarrazin and York have become involved, finds herself a new partner, Fields. However, when Fields is offered a job, he leaves the competition. Again Fonda must find a new partner and this time it is Buttons. To thrill the audience, who impatiently wait for the marathoners to collapse, Young makes the dancers race around the dance floor like horses on a track, causing all three of the remaining couples to drop out. (Photographed with a frenzied camera technique, this scene was, in part, shot by the director, who achieved such mobility by traveling along the dance floor while wearing roller skates.) Unable to withstand any further torture, Buttons is stricken with a heart attack, but that doesn't prevent Fonda from carrying him on her back. Fonda, near the breaking point, reunites with former partner Sarrazin. In order to please his audience, Young asks Fonda and Sarrazin to marry on the dance floor. When the marathoners refuse, Young exposes the fraud of the marathon, admits to stealing York's dress himself to create a scandal, and then refuses to give away the $1,500 in prize money. Having fought for 62 days on the dance floor without emerging the victor, Fonda collapses into depression. With a gun in her hand she struggles with the thought of suicide, but cannot find the courage or energy to pull the trigger. When she asks Sarrazin to do it, he fulfills her wish. Asked by the police why he killed her, Sarazzin replies, in keeping with the allusion of the marathoners as weakening horses with no hope for recovery, "They shoot horses, don't they?" Although it is at times heavy-handed and self-consciously allegorical, THEY SHOOT HORSES, DON'T THEY? is a *tour de force* of acting. Fonda, best known at the time as Roger Vadim's wife and the sex toy of BARBARELLA, here gets her first chance to prove herself as a serious, dramatic actress. For bringing such gritty, sweaty, hopeless, self-degradation to the screen, Fonda received universal praise, as well as an Oscar nomination for Best Actress–one of a total of nine nominations for the picture. Gig Young, the only one to win the prized statuette, for Best Supporting Actor, is superb in the role most remembered for his authentic delivery of the words "yowsa, yowsa, yowsa," which represented a sharp switch from his usual *bon vivant* casting. Other categories in which the film was nominated were Best Director (Pollack), Supporting Actress (York), Adapted Screenplay, Art Direction and Set Decoration, Editing, Music, and Costume Design. Based on a critically hailed (though largely unread) 1935 novel by Horace McCoy, THEY SHOOT HORSE, DON'T THEY? was kicked around as a film project for some time before it landed in Pollack's hands. The novel became a great success in Paris, where Jean-Paul Sartre, Simone de Beauvoir, Andre Gide, and Andre Malraux hailed it as a great existential masterpiece. First purchased by Charles Chaplin, the rights to the book wound up in Winkler's and Chartoff's hands in 1966 with Pollack working as screenwriter on the project, which was to have been directed by his coscreenwriter James Poe. The soundtrack is filled with a number of songs from the period– including a few written by the picture's musical director, lyricist John Green–adding an atmosphere of authenticity. The songs include: "Easy Come, Easy Go," "I Cover the Waterfront," "Out of Nowhere" (Edward Heyman, John Green), "Coquette" (Gus Kahn, Carmen Lombardo, Green), "Sweet Sue– Just You" (Will J. Harris, Victor Young), "I'm Yours" (E. Y. Harburg), "Brother, Can You Spare a Dime" (Harburg, Jay Gorney), "Paradise" (Gordon Clifford, Nacio Herb Brown), "The Japanese Sandman" (Raymond B. Egan, Richard A. Whiting), "Between the Devil and the Deep Blue Sea" (Ted Koehler, Harold Arlen), "The Best Things in Life Are Free" (B.G. De Sylva, Lew Brown, Ray Henderon), "California, Here I Come" (Al Jolsen, De Sylva, Joseph Meyer), "Body and Soul" (Heyman, Robert Sour, Frank Eyton, Green), "I Found a Million Dollar Baby" (Billy Rose, Mort Dixon, Harry Warren), and "By the Beautiful Sea." The film also makes a few allusions to movies: at one point Young introduces as a member of the audience, director Mervyn LeRoy; another time Sarrazin describes a scene played by John Cromwell and Anita Louise, and a poster for GRAND HOTEL and a Barbara Stanwyck advertisement appear in the background. Busby Berkeley and Ruby Keeler were to have appeared in cameos but were deleted from the release print.

p, Irwin Winkler, Robert Chartoff, Sydney Pollack; d, Pollack; w, James Poe, Robert E. Thompson (based on the novel by Horace McCoy); ph, Philip H. Lathrop (Panavision, DeLuxe Color); m, John Green; ed, Frederic Steinkamp; prod d, Harry Horner; md, Green, Albert Woodbury; set d, Frank McKelvy; cos, Donfeld; spec eff, Blondie Anderson; ch, Tom Panko; makeup, Frank McCoy, Maggie O'Connor.

Drama   Cas.   (PR:O MPAA:M)

THEY WANTED PEACE*½   (1940, USSR) 73m Tbilisi/Amkino bw
                                          (AKA: GREAT DAWN)

F. Bagaschvili (*Gudushauri*), Tamara Makarova (*Svetlana*), A. Smirnova (*Her Mother*), K. Miuffko (*Vladimir Lenin*), M. Gelovani (*Joseph Stalin*), G. Sagaradze (*Tseretell*), D. Ivanov (*Panasiuk*), V. Matov (*Erslov*), M. Chikhladze (*Col. Mikeladze*), I. Perestiani (*The General*), S. Gambashidze (*"Diplomat" Karoumidze*), G. Shavgulidze (*Pavel Gudushauri*), N. Chkeidze (*His Mother*).

A piece of communist propaganda that shows the efforts of the early party leaders to combat the horrors of the Czarist regime. Originally released shortly after Stalin had made ties with Hitler, which would be broken soon enough, making the material less effective in light of what this pact represented. Originally released in the Soviet Union in 1937, this film was one of many to portray then-contemporary political figures in fictionalized terms. Soviet filmmakers had hesitated to do this until urged on by Stalin, who had desperately wanted a film to commemorate the 20th anniversary of the October revolution. LENIN IN OCTOBER (1937) broke the ice, and others quickly followed. The tyrannical Stalin favored actor Gelovani's portrayal of him; Gelovani was to enact the same role in more than 20 pictures. (In Russian; English subtitles.)

d&w, M. Chiaureli (based on a story by Chiaureli, C. Tsagarell); m, I. Gokleli.

Historical Drama   (PR:A MPAA:NR)

THEY WANTED TO MARRY   (1937) 60m RKO bw

Betty Furness (*Sheila Hunter*), Gordon Jones (*Jim Tyler*), E. E. Clive (*Stiles, the Butler*), Patsy Lee Parsons (*Patsy Hunter*), Henry Kolker (*Mr. Hunter*), Charles Wilson (*Managing Editor*), William "Billy" Benedict (*Office Boy*), Diana Gibson (*Helen Hunter*), Frank M. Thomas (*Detective*).

Newspaper photographer Jones, assigned to cover a society wedding, falls for Furness, the bride's younger sister. The romance is opposed by Kolker, the father of the girls, on grounds of sheer snobbery. The lovelorn lensman is forced to take on a more "respectable" profession as an advertising copywriter, with ludicrous results, but all comes out well in the end. Jones, a former football player, ordinarily handled supporting roles; this was his big shot at stardom. He and Furness worked well together thanks, in part, to the realistic dialog penned by co-scripter Yawitz, a one-time newspaper columnist. Landers–who had made his feature film debut as director under his real name, Louis Friedlander, two years before with THE RAVEN starring Boris Karloff and Bela Lugosi–here proves his abil ity to handle light comedy.

p, Zion Myers; d, Lew Landers [Louis Friedlander]; w, Paul Yawitz, Ethel Borden (based on a story by Larry Bachmann and Darwin L. Teilhet); ph, Russell Metty; ed, Desmond Marquette; art d, Van Nest Polglase; cos, Edward Stevenson.

Comedy   (PR:A MPAA:NR)

THEY WENT THAT-A-WAY AND THAT-A-WAY*
                    (1978) 95m International Picture Show c

Tim Conway (*Dewey*), Chuck McCann (*Wallace*), Richard Kiel (*Duke*), Dub Taylor (*Warden Warden*), Reni Santoni (*Billy Jo*), Lenny Montana (*Brick*), Ben Jones (*Lugs*), Timothy Blake (*Margie Dell*), Hank Worden (*Butch*).

It's very sad to see the extent to which capable comic talents like Conway and McCann must fall in order to find work. With the exception of a few impersonations by Conway and the well-done interplay between the two stars, this picture is nothing new with slapstick routines that audiences have seen numerous times since the heydays of Hollywood comedians. The inane plot lacks cohesion, and has Conway and McCann posing as convicts who go undercover investigating missing money. The only money lost is that sunk into this production.

p, Lang Elliott; d, Edward Montagne, Stuart E. McGowan; w, Tim Conway; ph, Jacques Haitkin; m, Michael Leonard.

Comedy   Cas.   (PR:C MPAA:PG)

THEY WERE EXPENDABLE***   (1945) 135m MGM bw

Robert Montgomery (*Lt. John Brickley*), John Wayne (*Lt. J.G. "Rusty" Ryan*), Donna Reed (*2nd Lt. Sandy Davyss*), Jack Holt (*Gen. Martin*), Ward Bond (*"Boots" Mulcahy, C.B.M.*), Marshall Thompson (*Ens. Snake Gardner*), Paul Langton (*Ens. Andy Andrews*), Leon Ames (*Maj. James Morton*), Arthur Walsh (*Seaman Jones 1c*), Donald Curtis (*Lt. J.G. "Shorty" Long*), Cameron Mitchell (*Ens. George Cross*), Jeff York (*Ens. "Lefty" Tony Aiken*), Murray Alper (*"Slug" Mahan, T.M. 1c*), Harry Tenbrook (*"Cookie" Squarehead Larsen SC 2c*), Jack Pennick (*"Doc, Storekeeper*), Alex Havier (*Benny Lacoco . . . Steward 3c*), Charles Trowbridge (*Adm. Blackwell*), Bruce Kellogg (*Lt. Elder Tompkins, M.M. 2c*), Louis Jean Heydt (*Capt. Ohio Carter*), Robert Barrat (*Gen. Douglas MacArthur*), Russell Simpson (*Dad Knowland*), Vernon Steele (*Army Doctor at Corregidor*), Trina Lowe (*Gardner's Girl Friend*), Robert Shelby Randall, Art Foster, Larry Dods, Jack Stoney, Duke Green, Stubby Kruger, Phil Schumacher, Maj. Frank Pershing, Joey Ray, Dan Borzage, William Neff, Del Hill, Bill Barnum, Ted Lundigan, Michael Kirby, William McKeever Riley (*Boat Crew Members*), Frank McGrath (*Slim*), Sammy Stein (*Sammy*), Blake Edwards (*Gunner*), Ernest Seftig, Stephen Barclay, Franklin Parker (*Navy Officers*), Robert Emmett O'Connor (*Bartender at Silver Dollar*), Leslie Sketchley (*Marine Orderly*), Phillip Ahn (*Army Orderly*), Pacita Tod-Tod (*Filipino Girl Singer*), Robert Homans (*Bartender at Manila Hotel*), William B. Davidson (*Hotel Manager*), Jack Cheatham (*Commander*), Forbes Murray (*Navy Captain*), Emmett Vogan (*Navy Doctor*), Sherry Hall (*Marine Major*), Alan Bridge (*Lt. Colonel*), Jack Luden (*Naval Air Captain*), Jon Gilbreath (*Sub Commander*), Marjorie Davies, Eve March (*Nurses*), Karl Miller, Len Stanford, George Bruggeman,

Reginald Simpson, James Carlisle, Dutch Schlikenmeyer, Tony Carson, Jack Lorenz, Brad Towne, Charles Calhoun, Leonard Mellin, Frank Donahue, Dan Quigg, Clifford Rathjen, Dick Karl, Jack Lee, Wedgewood Nowell, Dick Thorne, Leonard Fisher, John Roy, Michael Kostrick, Jimmy Magrill, George Magrill, Sam Simone, Paul Kruger, Bruce Carruthers, Jack Semple, Roy Thomas, Bob Thom, Larry Steers, Gary Delmar *(Personnel in Admiral's Office)*, Eleanor Vogel, Leota Lorraine, Almeda Fowler, Betty Blythe, Jane Crowley *(Officers' Wives)*, Charles Murray, Jr. *(Jeep Driver)*, Margaret Morton *(Bartender's Wife)*, George Economides, Michael Economides, Roque Yberra, Jr., Nino Pipitone, Jr. *(Bartender's Children)*, Ralph Soncuya *(Filipino Orderly)*, Vincent Isla *(Filipino Schoolteacher)*, Max Ong *(Mayor of Cebu)*, William Neff *(Sub Skipper)*, Jim Farley *(Mate)*, Ernest Dominguez, Henry Mirelez *(Filipino Boys)*, Lee Tung Foo *(Bartender)*, Tom Tyler *(Captain of Airport)*, Bill Wilkerson *(Sgt. Smith)*, John Carlyle *(Lt. James)*, Mary Jane French *(Lost Nurse)*, Patrick Davis *(Pilot)*, Roger Cole, Fred Beckner, Jack Ross, Brent Shugar, Kermit Maynard, Bill Donahue, Frank Eldridge, Jack Carrington, Hansel Warner, Charles Ferguson, Jack Trent, Robert Strong, Jon Eppers, Bill Nind, Don Lewis *(Officers at Airport)*, William 'Merrill' McCormick *(Wounded Officer at Airport)*, Jack Mower *(Officer)*.

This superb WW II film is directed passionately by Ford. The picture not only shows the pain, loneliness, and sacrifice of war–in this case the Americans in the Philippines doomed to Japanese conquest–but effectively captures the mystique of heroism. Everything about this film is heroic, and movingly depicted, right from the first scenes which show Montgomery, Wayne, and others maneuvering their PT boats for admiral Trowbridge and other ranking Navy men watching them skim the waters of Manila Bay in late 1941. Trowbridge later tells Montgomery that his boats "maneuver beautifully," but he prefers something more substantial like a battleship. The PT squadron (motor torpedo boats, equipped with torpedoes and machine guns, having high-speed capabilities) is assigned routine duties and Wayne, who yearns for more adventuresome duty, decides to resign from Montgomery's command, requesting a transfer. In fact, while all the officers of the command attend a formal dinner dance at one of Manila's best restaurants that night, Wayne is still filling out transfer papers at the bar. News of the Japanese sneak attack at Pearl Harbor interrupts the festivities, however, and Wayne tears up the papers and all report for duty. Montgomery has a hard time seeing Trowbridge in order to get specific orders for his command as the top Navy brass hold frantic war conferences, but he is finally told to have one boat patrol Manila Bay and have another boat stand by for courier duty. Again Wayne explodes at being assigned unimportant duties, kicking a bucket at the PT headquarters when hearing the news. Montgomery asks him, "Does that help?" Roars Wayne, "Yes!" The PT base is attacked by Japanese planes and Montgomery saves his boats by having them race out into the Bay, but when they return they find the base in a smoking shambles and they must move their site of operations to a more secluded base. In their first encounter with the enemy, Wayne injures his hand while trying to maneuver his boat and this injury worsens so that his arm becomes infected. Before the boats pull out for another sortie with an approaching enemy cruiser, Montgomery orders Wayne to sick bay in Corregidor, the island fortress squatting in Manila Bay. He goes reluctantly and proves to be a troublesome patient for the Army nurses stationed there, particularly Reed, who has problems with him from the first moment when she tells him to take off his pants and pops a thermometer in his mouth. He tells her he outranks her and she tells him that he outranks no one in the hospital. Heydt, an airman in the next bed, tells Wayne that he had better do as he is told. When physician Steele inspects Wayne's wound, he tells him that had he waited another day he would have lost the arm. While Wayne recuperates he watches in admiration as the nurses and doctors slave away, saving countless lives of servicemen wheeled into the operating areas, a night-and-day flow. When the casualty rate ebbs, a dance is scheduled and Wayne is asked to attend by Reed. "Listen, sister," he tells her gruffly, "I don't dance, and I can't take time to learn. All I want is to get out of here." She takes the rebuff wordlessly and joins several other nurses–all exhausted and wearing medical overalls, slowly walking down one of the dimly lit tunnels of Corregidor–some of them smoking cigarettes, the smoke curling over their shoulders as they almost stagger in their fatigue. (This scene captures the hopelessness of the situation in the surrounded Philippines, one where the defenders refused to shirk their duties and drained themselves of strength.) One of the nurses says to a very tolerant Reed, who is emotionally involved with Wayne in spite of his brusque manner, "How is tall, dark, and obnoxious?" Reed says nothing. She knows how Wayne is. Wayne watches the nurses disappear down the gloomy corridor, and tells Heydt that the women do not impress him "all uglied up in those potato sacks!" Wayne does attend the dance, however, and grows fond of Reed when they talk of their homes in the States. Montgomery shows up asking Reed if her patient can be released and she tries to convince him that Wayne is too seriously injured to go back to duty, but her motives are obviously selfish, and Wayne is released as fit for duty. The squadron goes back into action, most of their forays against the enemy never seen up close, only their awesome weapons, scores of strafing planes, huge cruisers seen mostly at night in silhouettes, an invisible enemy Ford makes more terrifying by their lack of physical identity. That the war in the Philippines is lost is made evident when Trowbridge tells Montgomery: "Listen, son...you and I are professionals. If the manager says, 'Sacrifice,' we lay down a bunt and let somebody else hit the home runs. Our job is to lay down that sacrifice. That's what we were trained for and that's what we'll do." The sacrifice is one of attrition, where Montgomery loses his men and boats in one battle after another. The battle scenes are no less than spectacularly beautiful in their composition, the little PT boats slashing across the water, spray and explosions from enemy gunfire engulfing them as they let loose their defiant torpedoes to sink the enemy ships, their crew members blazing away with machine guns. Reed, who is reassigned to a field hospital on Bataan, arrives at the hardscrabble PT base one night to have dinner with Wayne and the other officers. They share their meager food, putting together what is, for them, an elegant dinner. Then word comes that the end on Bataan and Corregidor is nearing and that all the top brass have been ordered to leave the doomed islands. Montgomery is told that his four remaining PT boats must ferry the top admirals and generals to islands in the south where planes will fly them to Australia. The high-ranking officers arrive by Navy launch at the PT base where all is ready for departure. Wayne tries desperately to reach Reed by phone and he does, telling her he has new orders and won't be seeing her for a long time, unable to tell her just where he is going. He is cut off in mid-sentence as the phone lines are taken over by generals conferring on Bataan. His romance with Reed is as forlorn as the American-Filipino cause. The haggard but still feisty PT boat crews stand at attention as the Navy launch disgorges its important passengers. The men see a nurse and a little boy being helped from the launch, then a woman, the boy's mother, then a general wearing a trench coat, crushed hat with its bill adorned with heavy insignia, sunglasses, and from his mouth juts a corncob pipe. It's General of the Armies Douglas MacArthur, the great hero of the Philippines (Barrat). He walks with great dignity down the dock as the Navy men stiffen with pride at having the honor to ferry him and his family out of danger. (This scene, with Barrat marching the whole length of the dock while "The Battle Hymn of the Republic" is played, is one of the most magnificently moving ever put into any war film, and makes the image of MacArthur larger than life–which he was in real life, anyway.) Barrat goes to the control deck of Montgomery's PT boat and looks outward to sea, then lowers his head. In that gesture the whole Philippine campaign is capsulized, signifying MacArthur's profound regret, sorrow, and tragedy at having to leave his post. But there is no sense of defeat here, because Ford manages to show the general as utterly heroic, a symbol of courage, an icon for freedom. Brief comic relief is interjected when one of the younger sailors leans forward and begs Barrat to autograph his cap, which the general does, while seasoned veteran Bond raises his arms in helpless wonder at the audacity of his young charge. The boats roar off and take their precious cargo south to a remote island. There the army takes over the remaining PT boat while ordering Montgomery and Wayne and two of their young ensigns, Thompson and Mitchell, to fly to Australia and organize another PT squadron. The little boats, it has been decided, have proved their immeasurable worth in the war. Montgomery says a moving farewell to his men, telling Bond and other veterans to "look after the kids." Then Bond, hobbling down the road on a crutch, leads the Navy men down the road to join the Army troops in their jungle fighting against the ever-advancing Japanese troops. The Army itself is a bedraggled and exhausted lot of men, typified in one brief scene as Wayne and Montgomery squat on a roadway. They watch troops march by, men whose faces can hardly be seen, hidden by their tilted pie-shaped helmets. As they file past, the music swells in a strange plaintive burst that sounds almost like a cry of anguish. Wayne and Montgomery then go to a small airfield where hundreds of men wait. One plane, however–not the two planes expected–lands and air control officer Tyler begins to read off the names of the lucky men who will be leaving. This is obviously the last plane from the Philippines. Those who will remain will stay to fight and die or be captured by a savage enemy. At the last minute, after Montgomery and Wayne are on board the plane, Wayne says he is getting off, that he has "business to attend to," and it is clear from his earlier remarks to Heydt–who has been waiting for the plane, too–that he means to find Reed. But Montgomery calls after Wayne: "Who are you working for? Yourself?" It is a call to duty, and Wayne turns at the plane's door, then takes his seat. "I guess I forgot," he tells Montgomery. The plane takes off as the remaining men on the field stand away from the prop washes of the whining motors, then drift backward and slip like specters into the surrounding jungle. They are ghosts now, dead men, left behind to face an enemy they cannot hope to defeat. In the words of the title, they were expendable. The plane takes off and roars over the jungle and then begins to head out to sea, flying right over a tiny knot of men struggling down the beach: Bond and the remaining crew members of the PT boats. Bond and the men look up at the fast-disappearing plane and Bond grins, happy at the thought that Montgomery and Wayne have gone to safety, gone to Australia to continue the fight, gone to life. Ford keeps his camera on the plane as it slices skyward, showing the jungle, a lighthouse, and the sea beneath it as the film ends.

Ford packed one poignant and powerful scene after another into this tremendous film (one which he later claimed he never saw completely edited and one he was ordered to do by the Navy). His portrait of restrained courage seen in Reed's quiet dinner with the gracious PT boat officers while enlisted men, who have crawled beneath the hut where they are dining, sing romantic songs. (This Ford would repeat in RIO GRANDE and other films.) It is seen in the determination of an old man, Simpson, who repairs Wayne's boat at his broken-down shipyard in the backwaters of Mindinao, then waits stoically with gun in hand for the Japanese to close in on him after the Navy men leave. Here, in Ford's shot of Simpson–alone on the steps of the house he has lived in for decades–a gun, a jug, and a loyal dog at his side, the director's favorite tune, "Red River Valley," is played in the background to signify the heartland of America, the source of the courage, extended thousands of miles away into the exotic unwelcoming jungles of the Philippines. Montgomery is outstanding as the leader of the PT squadron, a man of quiet resolve who takes and carries out orders he doesn't always agree with, executing those orders with unflagging determination. He is as secure and as dependable as the island fortress of Corregidor, "The Rock," as it was known, while Wayne represents the unbounded spirit of the American fighting man who refuses to give up, full of fight, unable to ever really believe that that fight is lost. The rest of the cast is superb, with Ford using stalwart stock players such as Bond, Simpson, Tenbrook, and Pennick to great advantage. Tenbrook is the cook of the outfit who had once served on the battleship *Arizona* and he keeps looking for the great ship "with her stacks blowing smoke and her 16-inch guns firing salvos" to steam to the rescue of the Philippines, unwilling to accept the fact that his beloved *Arizona* lies at the bottom of Pearl Harbor and is now only a memory. Much of this film suggests the memories of the Americans for their far- away homeland, a place they will not see again and, as these briefly nostalgic scenes are shown by Ford, painful evocative feeling is created and sustained throughout the film. For these children of America, the first to serve, are the most courageous, the purest, the most cherished, and they are lost. Yet everywhere in the film Ford shows a fighting spirit that states clearly that the war will not be lost, that it will be won with people like those in the Philippines and it will be won because of them and their willingness to sacrifice their lives for the sake of freedom. The fire and the life of the characters shown in this masterpiece film came from only one man, Ford. MGM executive Jim McGuinness was put in charge of the project after the studio purchased White's best-selling book about the heroic PT boat captain, John Bulkeley, who, along with three of his officers, received the Congressional Medal of Honor for taking MacArthur and his family and staff out of the doomed Philippines. McGuinness had to pull strings to get Ford out of the Navy Photographic Field Unit where he was serving to have him direct the film. (Montgomery, ironically, had commanded some PT boats during the war himself, and was later in charge of a destroyer during the Normandy landings.) Ford, who had been filming documentaries for the Navy since Pearl Harbor, insisted that his $225,000 salary for making the film go to the Navy to build a shelter home for those men of his service. (Ford lost 13 men from his unit while covering the war; he held the rank of captain throughout the war.) McGuinness had to talk Ford into doing the film, finally telling the master that (as quoted in *Pappy* by Dan Ford): "This isn't another war movie. The story of John Bulkeley and this PT squadron is part of America's heroic tradition. It's like the Alamo or Valley Forge. It would be like re-creating a great moment of history while it's still fresh in people's minds. it would be available for our youth, generation after generation." Ford had recently won an Oscar for his documentary DECEMBER 7TH and wanted to continue making documentaries until the war was over. Later, Bulkeley–then serving in England–was ushered into Ford's London hotel room to meet him and when Ford learned who he was, he jumped out of bed, absolutely naked, to salute the Medal of Honor winner. He and Bulkeley were later side by side during the Normandy invasion and after growing to like the personable Navy officer, Ford returned to Hollywood, called McGuinness, and told him he would produce and direct THEY WERE EXPENDABLE. He cast every actor in the film, rewriting Wead's script to make provisions for Bond–who had been injured in an auto accident–so that this great character actor could appear on camera with crutches, the only way Bond could move around. Wayne, Ford's erstwhile leading man, poker companion, and drinking partner, later stated that the director "was awfully intense on that picture and working with more concentration than I had ever seen. I think he was really out to achieve something." The film, which began shooting on Ford's fiftieth birthday, was done on location, mostly at Key Biscayne, Florida, where the sultry jungle-like coves and waterways easily passed for the exotic Philippines. Navy brass scrutinized the production and marveled at Ford's energy to get his scenes done promptly while manipulating the PT boats the Navy made available to him. Several high-ranking Navy officers were present when the MacArthur scene was made. They made some disparaging comments about the general before the shooting began but, as Wayne later stated: "When the scene started and the guy who was playing MacArthur (Barrat) walked out and Danny Borzage was there with his little music box, you could see the look in their eyes change. Jack had created such a sense of awe that even among these Navy men there was a feeling of respect for the man." This scene and many others, coupled to the plaintive tune "Marquita" to suggest the Latin-based Philippines–a tune which runs throughout the great score by Stothart–helped to create the deep feeling of loss Ford wanted. Ford doted on Montgomery who, Wayne later claimed, "was his pet in that picture," because they had both served in the Navy. Ford and Wayne were at odds in the film, with the director calling the actor "a big oaf, clumsy," and that he "moved like an ox." In one scene, the technicians forgot to replace the glass windshield of Wayne's boat with plexiglass, and when a Japanese plane strafes the boat–the technicians fired ball bearings at the boat to simulate bullets– the glass smashed and flew into Wayne's face. The actor exploded, grabbed a hammer, and ran after the technicians. Ford jumped up and barred his path, shouting: "No, you don't. They're my crew!" Roared Wayne: "Your crew, dammit, they're my eyes!" The two men stared at each other for several minutes, fists clenched, almost coming to blows before tempers cooled. Ford became so energetic in directing this film that he fell from a scaffold while overseeing a battle scene and broke his leg. Montgomery stepped in and finished directing the last two weeks of the picture. Later, Ford told Peter Bogdanovich (in *John Ford*): "Any war *I* was in–we always *won*....I despise these happy endings with a kiss at the finish. I've never done that. Of course they were glorious in defeat in the Philippines–they kept on fighting." But beyond the lost battles in the Philippines, Ford captured the essential loneliness of the serviceman and their selfless service, an attitude best summed up by Wayne when, instead of reading from the Bible over two of his best veterans who have been killed, he recites lines from Stevenson's "Requiem": "Home is the sailor/Home from the Sea/And the hunter home from the hill." This superlative film was not without its share of post-production problems. Bulkeley's real- life second-in-command, Lt. Robert Balling Kelly–whose life is essayed by Wayne–thought he had been unfairly depicted and sued MGM. He was given $3,000. Reed's part, supposedly based on the life of military nurse Lt. Beulah Greenwalt, caused the studio much more serious damage. Greenwalt sued and won $290,000. MGM realized great profits from this film which Ford continued to like and dislike for the rest of his life–wavering as to his loyalties toward a film that, more than any other Fordian projects, serves as a symbol of team effort–both on the screen and behind it. This was grimly evident on-screen when the PT-boat officers go to the Corregidor hospital to visit Langton, who is dying of wounds, all of them pretending that he is only superficially injured and will be back with them before long. Langton knows they are just making small talk and the extent of his mortal wounds but he, too, is a team player and goes along with the scenario, later telling Montgomery, "Nice act you boys put on." Bulkeley, whose heroic command Ford took such pains to portray, would go on to become a high-ranking Navy officer. When Castro took over Cuba in 1959, and ordered the water supply cut to the U.S. base at Guantanamo, it was Bulkeley who quickly developed a new water system.

p, John Ford; d, Ford, (uncredited) Robert Montgomery; w, Frank W. Wead (based on the book by William L. White); ph, Joseph H. August; m, Herbert Stothart; ed, Frank E. Hull, Douglass Biggs; art d, Cedric Gibbons, Malcolm F. Brown; set d, Edwin B. Willis, Ralph S. Hurst; spec eff, A. Arnold Gillespie; m/l, "To the End of the World," Earl Brent, Stothart.

War Drama **(PR:A MPAA:NR)**

THEY WERE FIVE*** (1938, Fr.) 78m Arys/Lenauer bw (LA BELLE EQUIPE)

Jean Gabin *(Jeannot)*, Charles Vanel *(Charlot)*, Raymond Aimos *(Tintin)*, Viviane Romance *(Gina)*, Marcelle Geniat *(Grandmother)*, Raymond Cordy *(Drunkard)*, Jacques Baumer *(Mons. Jubette)*, Charpin *(Gendarme)*, Raphael Medina *(Marie)*, Micheline Cheirel *(Huguette)*, Robert Lynen *(Rene)*, Charles Granval *(Proprietor)*, Charles Dorat *(Jacques)*, Robert Ozanne *(Patron)*, Vincent Hyapa *(Photographer)*.

A populist French story about five unemployed Parisians who win the lottery, pool their earnings, and purchase a rundown chateau. Before long, however, their ideal business venture begins to dissolve. One of the men leaves after falling in love with another's sweetheart. A second man, a foreigner, is pressured to leave when there are problems with his papers. A third is killed after falling from the chateau's roof. Only two men are left–Gabin and Vanel–and their relationship is strained because Gabin is in love with Vanel's lovely wife, Romance. In the "happy" ending supplied for the U.S. release (which also played in some theaters in France at its original running time of 94 minutes), Gabin and Vanel realize that their friendship and the chateau is more important than the woman who has come between them. The "tragic" finale that the U.S. didn't get to see (it played only in France's "upper-class" theaters) had Romance filling Vanel's head with suspicions that Gabin was responsible for the disappearance of the other three. When Vanel confronts Gabin on the chateau's opening day, Gabin retaliates by shooting Vanel. Gabin is then arrested. A compelling tale of relationships which is built around three strikingly realistic characters. Not surprisingly, Jean Renoir wanted to direct this film as his follow-up to THE CRIME OF MONSIEUR LANGE (1936). (In French; English subtitles.)

p, M. Aryss-Nissotti; d, Julien Duvivier; w, Duvivier, Charles Spaak; ph, Jules Kruger, Marc Fossard; m, Maurice Yvain; ed, Marthe Poncin; art d, Jacques Krauss.

Drama **(PR:A MPAA:NR)**

THEY WERE NOT DIVIDED** (1951, Brit.) 91m TC/UA-RANK bw

Edward Underdown *(Philip)*, Ralph Clanton *(David)*, Helen Cherry *(Wilhelmina)*, Stella Andrews *(Jane)*, Michael Brennan *(Smoke O'Connor)*, Michael Trubshawe *(Maj. Bushy Noble)*, John Wynn *(45 Jones)*, Desmond Llewellyn *(77 Jones)*, Rufus Cruickshank *(Sgt. Dean)*, Estelle Brody *(Correspondent)*, Christopher Lee *(Lewis)*, R.S.M. Brittain *(Himself)*, Anthony Dawson, Ian Murray, Rupert Gerard, Robert Ayres, Peter Burton, Charles Perry.

The plight of two soldiers in the tank corps during WW II, one British and one American, covering a five year span from the time they are recruited until their death in the battle at Ardennes. Emphasis is placed more on the men's personal lives and the interaction between the other soldiers, than upon actual battle scenes. Although the pace lags, a number of interesting caricatures are provided, including one of the most nasty top-sergeants on the screen.

p, Herbert Smith; d&w, Terence Young; ph, Harry Waxman; m, Lambert

Williamson; ed, Ralph Kemplen, Vera Campbell; md, Muir Mathieson.

War/Drama   **(PR:A   MPAA:NR)**

THEY WERE SISTERS½   (1945, Brit.) 110m Gainsborough/UNIV
bw

Phyllis Calvert (*Lucy*), James Mason (*Geoffrey*), Hugh Sinclair (*Terry*), Anne Crawford (*Vera*), Peter Murray Hill (*William*), Dulcie Gray (*Charlotte*), Barrie Livesey (*Brian*), Pamela Kellino (*Margaret*), Ann Stephens (*Judith*), Helen Stephens (*Sarah*), John Gilpin (*Stephen*), Brian Nissen (*John*), David Horne (*Mr. Field*), Brefni O'Rourke (*Coroner*), Roland Pertwee (*Sir Hamish Nair*), Amy Veness (*Mrs. Pursley*), Thorley Walters (*Channing*), Joss Ambler (*Blakemore*), Roy Russell (*Lethbridge*), Edie Martin (*Cook*), Dora Sevening (*Janet*), Helen Goss (*Webster*).

Three sisters, Calvert, Crawford, and Gray, become involved in marriages which over the years develop into three very different types of relationships. Calvert makes out the best with a marriage to a man who has some human compassion, and bases their marriage on understanding. Crawford soon grows tired of her overly affectionate hubby and has a string of affairs. But Gray winds up with a total monster in Mason, an overbearing sadist who has literally taken away his wife's freedom, forcing her to become an alcoholic. When her sister attempts to get help for her, but fails because Mason becomes aware of the appointment, Gray commits suicide by throwing herself in front of a truck. A perfect role for Mason who outwardly appears as a thoroughly likable and normal person, but in brief moments displays the real personality behind the mask.

p, Harold Huth; d, Arthur Crabtree; w, Roland Pertwee, Katherine Strueby (based on the novel by Dorothy Whipple); ph, Jack Cox; m, Louis Levy; ed, Charles Knott; art d, David Rawnsley; cos, Yvonne Caffin.

Drama   **(PR:A   MPAA:NR)**

THEY WERE SO YOUNG**   (1955) 80m Corona/Lippert bw

Scott Brady (*Lanning*), Raymond Burr (*Coltos*), Johanna Matz (*Eve*), Ingrid Stenn (*Connie*), Gisela Fackeldey (*Lanzowa*), Kurt Meisel (*Pasquale*), Katherina Mayberg (*Felicia*), Eduard Linkers (*Albert*), Gordon Howard (*Garza*), Elizabeth Tanney (*Emily*), Erica Beer (*Elise*), Hanita Hallan (*Lena*), Hannelore Axman (*Vincenta*), William Trenk-Trebitsch (*Bulanos*), Pero Alexander (*Manuel*), Joseph Dahmen (*Doctor*), Gert Froebe (*Lobos*).

A German model goes to Brazil under the auspices of modeling for a top fashion house. But she soon discovers that her beauty is wanted for duties beyond that of showing off clothes, so the girl tries to break out of the racket. Given assistance by Brady, the girl is given temporary asylum at the estate of Brady's boss. But a twist has this man as the behind-the-scenes owner of the setup the model is trying to get out of. Shot in Berlin and Italy which pose as Brazil locations, and quite effectively so. Filmed in English and German versions.

p&d, Kurt Neumann; w, Felix Luetzkendorf, Neumann (based on the idea by Jacques Companeez); ph, Ekkehard Kyrath; m, Michael Jary; ed, Eva Kroll; md, Jary; art d, Hans Sohnle.

Drama   **(PR:A   MPAA:NR)**

THEY WERE TEN**   (1961, Israel) 105m Orb-Scopus/George Schwartz-Arthur Sachson-Film Representations bw (HEM HAYU ASAR)

Ninette Linar (*Manyah*), Oded Teomi (*Yosef*), Leo Filler (*Zalman*), Yosef Safra (*Shimon*), Yosef Zur (*Berl*), Gavriel Dagan (*Mirkin*), Israel Rubinshik (*Avraham*), Nissim Azikri (*Asher*), Amnon Kahanovitsh (*Shmulik*), Itzhak Bareket (*Yoel*), Yehuda Gabbai (*Dr. Weiss*), Shlomit Kaplansky (*Mrs. Weiss*), Yosef Bashi (*Jamal*), Moshe Kedem (*Sheikh Mustafa*), Moshe Yaari (*Turkish Officer*), Abu Attef, Eytan Priver.

Touching story about early immigrants to Galilee, from Russia, who manage to overcome numerous hardships, from the harsh climate, Arab neighbors and within themselves, to form a settlement. Much of the drama centers around a young couple's marriage as they settle into this new land.

p&d, Baruch Dienar; w, Gavriel Dagan, Dienar, Menachem Shuval (based on a story by Dienar); ph, Lionel Banes; m, Gari Bertini; ed, Helga Cranston.

Drama   **(PR:A   MPAA:NR)**

THEY WHO DARE½   (1954, Brit.) 100m Mayflower/BL c

Dirk Bogarde (*Lt. Graham*), Denholm Elliott (*Sgt. Corcoran*), Akim Tamiroff (*Capt. George One*), Gerard Oury (*Capt. George Two*), Eric Pohlmann (*Capt. Papadopoulos*), Alec Mango (*Patroklis*), Kay Callard (*Nightclub Singer*), Russell Enoch [William Russell] (*Lt. Poole*), Lisa Gastoni (*George-Two's Girl Friend*), Sam Kydd (*Marine Boyd*), Peter Burton (*Marine Barrett*), David Peel (*Sgt. Evans*), Michael Mellinger (*Toplis*), Anthea Leigh (*Marika*), Eileen Way (*Greek Woman*).

A neatly concocted script detailing the experiences of six British Commandos and four Greek soldiers given the assignment of blowing up airfields on a Mediterranean island, in order to allow for a greater attack to take place. Much of the action centers on their contending with crossing the rugged

terrain and remaining out of sight from possible enemy sightings. A gripping and suspenseful effort, in which director Milestone threw away the script upon arrival, having Bogarde improvise as they went along.

p, Maxwell Setton, Aubrey Baring; d, Lewis Milestone; w, Robert Westerby; ph, Wilkie Cooper (Technicolor); m, Robert Gill; ed, V. Sagovsky; art d, Don Ashton.

War   **(PR:A   MPAA:NR)**

THEY WON'T BELIEVE ME*½   (1947) 95m RKO bw

Robert Young (*Larry Ballentine*), Susan Hayward (*Verna Carlson*), Jane Greer (*Janice Bell*), Rita Johnson (*Gretta Ballentine*), Tom Powers (*Trenton*), George Tyne (*Lt. Carr*), Don Beddoe (*Thomason*), Frank Ferguson (*Cahill*), Harry Harvey (*Judge Fletcher*), Wilton Graff (*Patrick Gold*), Janet Shaw (*Susan Haines*), Glen Knight (*Parking Lot Attendant*), Anthony Caruso (*Tough Patient*), George Sherwood (*Highway Cop*), Perc Launders (*Police Stenographer*), Bryon Foulger (*Mortician*), Hector Sarno (*Nick*), Carl Kent (*Chauffeur*), Lee Frederick (*Detective*), Elena Warren (*Mrs. Bowman*), Herbert Heywood (*Sheriff*), Lillian Bronson (*Mrs. Hines*), Paul Maxey (*Mr. Bowman*), Jean Andren (*Maid*), Martin Wilkins (*Sailor*), Dot Farley (*Emma*), Milton Parsons (*Court Clerk*), Lee Phelps (*Baliff*), Frank Pharr (*Patrick Collins*), Bert LeBaron (*Joe Pots*), Ellen Corby (*Screaming Woman*), Bertha Ledbetter (*Mrs. Oaks*), Polly Bailey (*Untidy Woman*), Matthew McHugh (*Tiny Old Man*), Bob Pepper (*Officer Guarding Larry*), Ira Buck Woods (*Waiter*), Charles Flynn (*Masseur*), Freddie Graham (*Deputy Sheriff*), Irene Tedrow (*1st Woman*), Bob Thom (*Hotel Clerk*), Lida Durova (*Girl at Newsstand*), Jack Gargan, Ivan Browning (*Bartenders*), Mme. Borget (*Mrs. Roberts*), Alben Roberling (*Headwaiter*), George Morrell (*Rancher*), Harry Strang (*Ryan*), Bud Wolfe (*Driver*), Sol Gorss (*Gus*), Helen Dickson (*Woman*), Lovyss Bradley (*Miss Jorday*), Harry D'Arcy (*Fisherman*), Harry Gillespie (*Waiter*), Netta Packer (*Spinster*), Jack Rice (*Tour Conductor*), Ann Cornwall.

Young, well cast against type, plays a man charged with the murder of his wife. On the witness stand Young's story is related in flashback. A broker on Wall Street, Young is married to Johnson, a wealthy woman he uses for her money. He meets Greer, a young writer, and the two begin a short affair. Greer wants to end it and goes to Montreal but Young claims he will divorce his wife and follow her. Johnson learns of her husband's indiscretion and, in an effort to save their marriage, buys Young a brokerage firm in Los Angeles. This effort backfires, though, when Young begins an affair with Hayward, his partner's secretary. The partner (Powers) is angered by this, as is Johnson. She tries to stop this second affair by buying her husband a remote ranch but this is to no avail. Young empties his wife's bank account and prepares to run off with his paramour, but Hayward changes her mind. The two decide to return the money to the bank but en route their car crashes. Hayward is killed, her body burned beyond recognition. Young learns the police believe the corpse is his wife's. On returning home, he finds Johnson dead, having committed suicide after reading her husband's farewell note. He dumps the body in a lake, then heads to Jamaica where he starts to drink Johnson's fortune away. He ends up reuniting with Greer and the two return to Los Angeles. Greer learns of Johnson's and Hayward's deaths and tells Powers. Johnson's body is found, now decomposed beyond recognition as well, and Powers mistakenly identifies it as Hayward's corpse. Young is immediately suspect and arrested for murder. The film flashes back to the trial as the jury files in to deliver the verdict. Young goes out of control and tries to escape through the window but is killed by police. When order is restored the jury delivers its ironic verdict of "not guilty." Young's fans were perturbed that the normally wholesome actor would play such a loathsome character but his performance here is excellent. He delivers an honest portrait that helps the unusual plot twists work well. Hayward is sensual as the other woman, while Johnson and Greer also give fine performances. Latimer's screenplay is well plotted, helmed by Pichel's strong direction. Pichel was best at directing tearjerk romances but here displays a good sense of *film noir* with moody photography and suspenseful pacing. Though certainly not in the same league with DOUBLE INDEMNITY (a film THEY WON'T BELIEVE ME clearly takes its cue from), this is an engrossing crime story. Producer Harrison had previously worked with Alfred Hitchcock.

p, Joan Harrison; d, Irving Pichel; w, Jonathan Latimer (based on a story by Gordon McDonell); ph, Harry J. Wild; m, Roy Webb; ed, Elmo Williams; md, Constantin Bakaleinikoff; art d, Albert S. D'Agostino, Robert Boyle; set d, Darrell Silvera, William Magginetti; cos, Edward Stevenson; spec eff, Russell A. Cully; makeup, Gordon Bau.

Crime Drama   **Cas.**   **(PR:C   MPAA:NR)**

THEY WON'T FORGET**   (1937) 95m WB bw

Claude Rains (*Andrew J. Griffin*), Gloria Dickson (*Sybil Hale*), Edward Norris (*Robert Paerry Hale*), Otto Kruger (*Michael Gleason*), Allyn Joslyn (*William P. Brock*), Lana Turner (*Mary Clay*), Linda Perry (*Imogene Mayfield*), Elisha Cook, Jr. (*Joe Turner*), Cy Kendall (*Detective Laneart*), Clinton Rosemond (*Tump Redwine*), E. Alyn Warren (*Carlyle P. Buxton*), Elisabeth Risdon (*Mrs. Dale*), Clifford Soubier (*Jim Timberlake*), Granville Bates (*Pindar*), Ann Shoemaker (*Mrs. Mountford*), Paul Everton (*Gov. Thomas Mountford*), Donald Briggs (*Harmon Drake*), Sybil Harris (*Mrs.*

Clay), Eddie Acuff *(Fred the Soda Jerk)*, Frank Faylen *(Bill Price)*, Raymond Brown *(Foster)*, Leonard Mudie *(Judge Moore)*, Trevor Bardette *(Shattock Clay)*, Elliott Sullivan *(Luther Clay)*, Wilmer Hines *(Ransome Clay)*, John Dilson *(Briggs the Detective)*, Harry Davenport, Edward McWade, Harry Beresford *(Veterans)*, Thomas Jackson, George Lloyd *(Detectives)*, Earl Dwire *(Jury Foreman)*, Peter Potter 'Bill Moore', John Ridgely, Jerry Fletcher *(Boys in Poolroom)*, Robert Cumming, Sr. *(Whippel the Banker)*, I. Stanford Jolley, Henry Hall *(Courtroom Extras)*, Tom Wilson *(Farmer)*, Forbes Murray *(Doughty the Publisher)*, Tom Brower, Harry Hollingsworth *(Turnkeys)*.

Turner, a secretary-to-be, attends a school in the Southern town of her birth learning dictation and touch-typing technique from young Northerner Norris, a recent arrival. The class ends and Turner progresses to a local soda fountain for refreshments (a scene redolent of the untrue tale spread about her "discovery" for films), then back out into the street, where a Confederate Day parade is in progress. The camera tracks Turner's sweatered progress, catching the cadence of "Dixie" blaring from a nearby marching band, catching her figure from every angle, her bosom jouncing contrapuntally to the strains of the Rebel anthem. She returns to the deserted classroom to retrieve her misplaced vanity case–she has earlier told her teacher that "I don't feel dressed without my lipstick"–when she hears the scary sound of footsteps in the hallway. Her face in closeup contorts with fear as the film dissolves to a metaphorical musket blast signifying the start of the Confederate Day celebration. Black school janitor Rosmond finds Turner's battered body and alerts authorities to the murder. District attorney Rains has long sought a lever that will lift him to political prominence. Rather than seeking the most obvious suspect in the crime, Rosmond, he decides to try to convict outlander Norris, the teacher. "Anyone can convict a Negro in the South," states the ambitious Rains, who wants a better challenge than Rosmond might afford him. Cynical newspaper reporter Joslyn needles Rains, but helps him make his case against the accused Yankee by discovering that Turner had a crush on her teacher. Norris is also discovered to have been in the school area at the time of the murder. Forensic investigation proves that Norris has a bloodstain on his jacket, a stain that Norris insists is his own blood, one incurred when his barber's razor slipped. The news media make much of the story both North and South. While the local press whips up rage in the Southern citizens, a crusading New York newspaper sends attorney Kruger and detective Kendall South to help make a case for the defense. This "Damn Yankee" interference simply serves as a further incitement to the courtroom mob during Norris' trial. Unmoved by the obvious lies of the prosecution's well-coached witnesses, the prejudiced jury convicts Norris of the crime; he is sentenced to death. The state's governor, Everton, appalled by the apparent injustice, commutes his sentence to life in prison. As Norris is escorted to prison by railroad, a howling, vindictive mob of bigots led by the brothers of the dead girl–Bardette, Sullivan, and Hines–block the train's passage, enter a baggage car, and drag the terrified, handcuffed Norris from its bowels as a speeding cross-bound train hurtles by, its mail hook–in closeup–snatching a mail pouch from its pole in as startling a metaphor for a lynching as has been seen on-screen. When the lynched Norris' widow, Dickson, denounces Rains for his duplicitous actions, reporter Joslyn is jarred into reconsidering the case. "I wonder if he really did it," muses Joslyn to the district attorney. "I wonder," responds Rains. Chiefly known now as the picture which introduced Turner to cinema audiences (she'd done bits before, but had never gotten billing), this film–which followed close on the heels of Fritz Lang's famed lynch-mob film FURY (1936)–was touted by some critics of the time as one of the few true cinema classics; the National Board of Review cited it one of the 10 best of the year. The screenplay closely follows its source, author Greene's novel *Death in the Deep South*, which was based on a true incident that occurred in Atlanta in 1915; Greene, then a reporter for the Atlanta *Journal*, had covered the story, which later so obsessed him that he checked into the Waldorf-Astoria hotel in New York and wrote his novel in three weeks' time. The real incident involved the lynch-mob murder of Leo M. Frank, a Northern Jew who traveled South to manage a pencil factory where a 14-year-old girl, Mary Phagan, was murdered. The innocent Frank was held and convicted of the rape-murder despite a barrage of contradictory evidence through the offices of an ambitious county solicitor general who was goaded on in his mission by rabid racist newspaper publisher Tom Watson ("We can lynch a nigger any time, but when do we get a chance to hang a Yankee Jew?" he is reported to have said to associates). Watson founded a secret society "The Knights of Mary Phagan," which later became "The Knights of the Ku Klux Klan" under the leadership of local bigot William Simmons. The hilltop site of Franks' lynching was established as a shrine for the organization by Simmons (who, in a remarkable demonstration of the cinema's power, formed his revived Klan when–just after Franks' trial–he witnessed a screening of D.W. Griffith's famed film THE BIRTH OF A NATION in a local theater). Watson's nemesis was Harold Ross–then a reporter for the Atlanta *Journal*, like author Greene, and later to found *The New Yorker*– who reported the case both fairly and passionately. Georgia's governor of the time, John M. Slaton, was persecuted by mobs after commuting the innocent Franks' death sentence (the crime had been committed by Jim Conley, a black roustabout in the factory, who confessed his involvement later to a number of people). Gov. Slaton was hounded out of the state with his family as a result of his even-handed, brave decision. The sixth-billed Turner–who appears only in the first few minutes of the film– nonetheless makes a vivid impression as the fresh-faced, quickly blossoming adolescent

victim. Her face was blazoned from publicity posters and newspaper advertisements, captioned "16 years old . . . discovered in Hollywood High school 'sic' . . . signed to do live role of high school girl!" In a later interview, director LeRoy stated that Turner's soon-famous sweater was his idea. "When Lana walked down the street," said LeRoy, "her bosom seemed to move in a rhythm all its own." The director's 75-foot tracking shot of Turner's sensual strut established in every viewer's mind that the unseen crime was sex-related without in any way risking the wrath of the censors; the actress' character may have been violated, but the Production Code was not. Rains, as the prosecutor, seems somewhat out of place among the rednecks in the courtroom; his British suavity ill-suits the setting. Even so, this remarkable actor–who never gave a bad screen performance–is eminently believable in his role: scheming and devious, but perceptive about his own character. Kruger, the only other well-known leading player in the cast, is solid as the Northern attorney. Dickson, in her screen debut, had been recruited from a Los Angeles Federal Theater Project. Joslyn had worked on the stage in New York; he was to become a fine second lead and character actor following this initial screen performance. Norris had been a contract player for MGM for a few years, but had been little utilized by the studio. Director LeRoy's Warner Bros. contract expired with this picture. He signed on with MGM. Turner–who had been under a personal contract with LeRoy–followed his lead and signed with the same studio the following year. In retrospect, it seems surprising that the anti-Semitism which marked the real occurrence on which the picture was based never entered the story. Apparently, the time was not yet ripe for such a cinematic theme; Hollywood, with its great number of Jewish industry leaders, didn't want to make waves.

p&d, Mervyn LeRoy; w, Robert Rossen, Aben Kandel (based on the novel *Death in the Deep South* by Ward Greene); ph, Arthur Edeson; m, Adolph Deutsch; ed, Thomas Richards; md, Leo F. Forbstein; art d, Robert Haas.

Drama   **Cas.**   **(PR:C   MPAA:NR)**

THEY'RE A WEIRD MOB**½   (1966, Aus.) 109m Williamson-Powell
                                             International/British Empire c

Walter Chiari *(Nino Culotta)*, Clare Dunne *(Kay Kelly)*, Chips Rafferty *(Harry Kelly)*, Alida Chelli *(Giuliana)*, Ed Devereaux *(Joe)*, Slim de Grey *(Pat)*, John Meillon *(Dennis)*, Charles Little *(Jimmy)*, Anne Haddy *(Barmaid)*, Jack Allen *(Fat Man in Bar)*, Red Moore *(Texture Man)*, Ray Hartley *(Newsboy)*, Muriel Steinbeck *(Mrs. Kelly)*, Gloria Dawn *(Mrs. Chapman)*, Tony Bonner *(Lifesaver)*, Alan Lander *(Charlie)*, Judith Arthy *(Dixie)*, Keith Petersen *(Drunk Man on Ferry)*, Jeanne Dryman *(Betty)*, Gita Rivera *(Maria)*, Doreen Warburton *(Edie)*, Barry Creyton, Noel Brophy, Graham Kennedy.

A pleasant farce which has Chiari leaving his native Italy to become a journalist for his brother's small Sidney paper. But when he gets to Australia, he discovers that no paper exists, as the brother has walked out with the initial investments. Being a man of honor, Chiari vows to pay back the money to Dunne, the lass who is the victim of his brother's unscrupulousness. He gets a job as a bricklayer and attempts to romance Dunne, only to be met with rebuff after rebuff. Performances are varied and the direction is overly forced in parts, but overall a good piece of light entertainment.

p&d, Michael Powell; w, Richard Imrie, Emeric Pressburger (based on the novel by John O'Grady, Nino Culotta); ph, Arthur Grant (Eastmancolor); m, Laurence Leonard, Alan Boustead; ed, Gerald Turney-Smith; md, Leonard; art d, Dennis Gentle; m/l, "Big Country," "In This Man's Country" (Reen Devereaux), "I Kiss You, You Kiss Me" (Walter Chiari), "Cretan Dance" (Mikis Theodorakis).

Comedy   **(PR:A   MPAA:NR)**

THEY'RE OFF   (SEE: STRAIGHT, PLACE AND SHOW, 1938)

THIEF, THE***   (1952) 85m Fran/UA bw

Ray Milland *(Allan Fields)*, Martin Gabel *(Mr. Bleek)*, Rita Gam *(The Girl)*, Harry Bronson *(Harris)*, John McKutcheon *(Dr. Linstrum)*, Rita Vale *(Miss Philips)*, Rex O'Malley *(Beal)*, Joe Conlin *(Walters)*.

An unusual if not altogether successful film with the gimmick of being entirely nonverbal–not silent, mind you, the film does have sound effects, music, and some narration–but none of the characters speak. Milland is an American nuclear physicist working for the Atomic Energy Commission who is persuaded by enemy agents to steal secrets and pass them to the Russians. He narrowly escapes being caught as he photographs documents one day, but his luck ends when one of the links in the chain of spies transferring the microfilm out of the country is killed and a roll of film is found in his hand. The FBI starts to investigate everyone at the AEC as a routine measure and the spy ring sends a telegram to Milland telling him to get out and leave the country. The FBI traces the telegram and discovers it came from a false name and address. Milland flees to New York and proceeds to Grand Central Station, where he picks up a suitcase from a locker along with a set of instructions telling him to go to a cheap rooming house in a bad part of town. There he receives instructions to meet a woman atop the Empire State Building to receive his false passport and tickets. He is tailed to this rendezvous by an FBI agent and when the agent starts up a ladder at the top of the building to come after Milland, the aspiring defector steps on the agent's hand and causes him to fall to the sidewalk and his death. When Milland leaves the building he has to pass by the body and is obviously rattled by the sight. In his shabby room that night he cries. Later, as he goes to the ship that will spirit him across the Iron Curtain, he stops and discards his false papers and waits outside FBI headquarters to turn himself in. The film ends confined by its own conceit, that of telling the whole story without dialog. While the effect is startling in the early stages, it bogs down in the middle as events happen, but no one can speak to explain their motivations. What turns Milland into a traitor? The audience never finds out. The film does work on a number of levels, though, as a thriller, as a bleak *film noir* with a protagonist caught up in events he'd never dreamed would happen when he made his first step into the netherworld of espionage, and as a fascinating exercise in nonverbal story telling rarely seen since the advent of the talkie. Milland is very good and occasionally magnificent, especially when he breaks down after killing the FBI agent. Gam, in her film debut as Milland's seductive neighbor at the boarding house, is also memorable. The technical aspects are superb, especially the somber photography and the almost documentary style of direction. One of the best spy films to come out of the Red scare of the early 1950s.

p, Clarence Greene; d, Russell Rouse; w, Greene, Rouse; ph, Sam Leavitt; m, Herschel Burke Gilbert; ed, Chester Schaeffer; prod d, Joseph St. Amand.

Spy Drama   **(PR:C MPAA:NR)**

THIEF*½   (1981) 122m UA c (GB: VIOLENT STREETS)

James Caan *(Frank)*, Tuesday Weld *(Jessie)*, Willie Nelson *(Okla)*, James Belushi *(Barry)*, Robert Prosky *(Leo)*, Tom Signorelli *(Attaglia)*, Dennis Farina *(Carl)*, Nick Nickeas *(Nick)*, W.R. [Bill] Brown *(Mitch)*, Norm Tobin *(Guido)*, John Santucci *(Urizzi)*, Gavin MacFayden *(Boreksco)*, Chuck Adamson *(Ancell)*, Sam Cirone *(Martello)*, Spero Anast *(Bukowski)*, Walter Scott *(D. Simpson)*, Sam T. Louis *(Large Detective in Suit)*, William La Valley *(Joseph)*, Lora Staley *(Paula)*, Hal Frank *(Joe Gags)*, Del Close, Bruce Young, John Kapelos *(Mechanics)*, Mike Genovese *(Green Mill Bartender)*, Joan Lazzerini *(Attaglia's Receptionist)*, Beverly Somerman *(Secretary)*, Enrica R. Cannataro *(Plating Salesman)*, Donna J. Fenton, Mary Louise Wade *(Waitresses)*, William L. Peterson *(Katz & Jammer Bartender)*, Nancy Santucci *(Hojo Waitress)*, Nathan Davis *(Grossman)*, Thomas O. Erhart, Jr *(Judge)*, Fredric Stone *(Garner)*, Robert J. Kuper *(Bailiff)*, Joene Hanhardt *(Recorder)*, Marge Kolitsky *(Mrs. Knowles)*, J.J. Saunders *(Doctor)*, Susan McCormick *(Nurse)*, Karen Bercovici *(Ruthie)*, Michael Paul Chan *(Waiter)*, Tom Howard, Richard Karie *(Salesmen)*, Patti Ross *(Marie)*, Margot Charlior *(Rosa)*, Oscar DiLorenzo *(Customer at Green Mill)*.

A steady rain lends an unreal, shimmering aura to the canyon-like alleys of the urban jungle. A man, La Valley, sits in an expensive American car parked behind a building. He listens to a blinking police scanner. Inside the building another man, Belushi, monitors a variety of electronic systems designed to bypass alarms. In front of a vault stands Caan. Gloved, goggled, and wearing workmen's overalls, he places a large drill over the lock of the vault and holds it there using a giant magnet. Caan drills through the locks, opens the vault, and discards thousands of less valuable jewels until he finds what he is looking for–a specific drawer of diamonds. Caan is a professional thief, and one of the best in the business. The next morning, Caan stops by the used car lot he owns to check on business. Caan also owns a bar, The Green Mill. While there, he receives a call from Belushi, who tells him that the man fencing the diamonds has been killed and their money is gone. Caan finds out who bought the diamonds and confronts the buyer in his business offices. The buyer, Signorelli, pleads ignorance of the entire situation. Not a man to be trifled with, Caan immediately pulls his .45 automatic and pokes it in Signorelli's face. Signorelli agrees to set up a meeting between Caan and his boss to take place that night. Later in the day Caan visits his mentor, Nelson, who is still serving time in prison. Nelson tells Caan that the doctors have informed him that he has a severe heart ailment and will die soon. Nelson asks Caan to get him out of prison because he doesn't want to die behind bars. That night at the meeting– which is held outdoors–Caan meets big-time mobster Prosky. Prosky pays Caan his money, and then offers him a job. The mob is well aware of Caan's work and would like to borrow his talents for a few big jobs. Caan refuses and states he is the master of his own destiny. Prosky takes the news with a smile and tells Caan to think it over. Later that night, Caan picks up the woman he has been dating, Weld, and takes her out for some coffee. In an effort to stabilize his life and realize his dream of a home, wife, and family, Caan offers to pull one last big score and quit if she will marry him. He shows her a postcard he made while in prison with pictures cut from magazines that represent what he wants out of life. Having once been on the wrong side of the law herself, she agrees to marry him, but she cannot have children. Caan decides they will adopt. Wanting to score quickly, Caan calls Prosky and agrees to his deal. The mobster wants Caan to crack a high-security vault in Los Angeles that is filled with diamonds. Special tools are needed to burn the vault open, so Caan visits an old friend at a steel mill who can make a huge thermal torch to do the job. In the meantime, Belushi is in Los Angeles figuring out how to crack the six alarm systems in the building. In the weeks that precede the robbery, Caan and Weld go to an adoption agency and are refused a child because of his prison record. Having nowhere else to turn, Caan accepts Prosky's offer to illegally buy a baby for him. Two crooked detectives, Santucci and Adamson, also appear and try to shake Caan down for a percentage of his profits. He

defiantly refuses and even manages to shake their sophisticated surveillance. Caan manages to bribe a judge into letting Nelson out of prison, but Nelson dies of heart trouble soon after. Sad, but content that he fulfilled his obligation to his friend, Caan says goodbye to Weld and the baby and goes off to California to do the job. The robbery is performed flawlessly and Prosky is very pleased with the results. When Caan goes to Prosky's house to get paid however, he finds only a small percentage of his fee is given to him in cash. Prosky laughs and says, "That's the cash part," informing Caan that the rest of his money has been invested in several shopping malls around the country. "I take care of my people," the mobster states. Caan doesn't care to be part of the "family" and informs Prosky that he wants the rest of his money in cash. He did his job and now it is time to move on. "I thought we had this good thing here," Prosky says, and then tells Caan he has a new job set up for him. Caan refuses and threatens Prosky's life if he isn't paid what is owed him. That night Prosky's chief enforcer, Farina, and three other men beat up Belushi at the used car dealership. As Caan walks in, Belushi tries to warn him, but Caan is hit in the back of the head with the butt of a rifle. Belushi attempts to escape but is shotgunned. When Caan awakens he is on the floor of Prosky's electroplating plant. Belushi's dead body sits on the edge of an acid bath. Prosky and his men stand over him. Prosky tells Caan that he will be working for him exclusively. "I own you...I bought you your house, your kid, businesses...I own a paper on your whole life. I'll wipe out your whole family. People will be eatin' 'em for lunch tomorrow in their burgers and not even know it. You're workin' for me until you are burned out, busted, or dead. Got it?" The mobsters dump Belushi's body into the acid and Caan is sent home. Caan, a man incapable of allowing himself to be used, decides to give it all up and stop pretending he can have a normal life. He gives Weld a huge sum of money and tells her to take the kid and get lost. He then blows up his house and his bar and sets fire to his used car lot. He takes the postcard representing his dream life and throws it in the gutter. Caan then breaks into Prosky's house, and with military precision kills Prosky, Signorelli, Farina, and another bodyguard in a bloody gun battle. Emerging from the carnage with only a shoulder wound, Caan walks off into the night and disappears. THIEF was ex-Chicagoan Michael Mann's feature film directorial debut and it was a stunner. Mann had previously directed the highly acclaimed made-for-TV prison film THE JERICHO MILE, which was praised for its realism. Shooting almost entirely on the streets of Chicago, Mann demonstrates a savvy understanding of the effect casting, location, costumes, music (a superior score by Tangerine Dream), and visuals can have on an audience. The film is slickly shot with great emphasis on wet streets, neon lights, and steel-blue colors. Mann meticulously details the procedures Caan goes through to rob a safe and it is fascinating to watch. The picture is loosely based on a book entitled The Home Invaders, a veritable textbook of robbery written by real-life thief Frank Hohimer (still in prison at the time). Mann hired several former thieves and cops as technical advisors on the film and many of them also played parts in the film. Santucci, a former master-thief who advised Mann on the technical aspects of safecracking, was cast as one of the corrupt cops. His partner in the film, Adamson, once was a detective. Farina, who plays Prosky's chief enforcer, is a Chicago police officer who frequently takes time off to act (a promising actor, the large, mustached cop has since appeared on Mann's television series "Miami Vice" and played Chuck Norris' partner in CODE OF SILENCE). Having grown up in Chicago, Mann knew how to use the city to best advantage. The bar Caan owns in the film, The Green Mill, is one of the city's oldest and most colorful watering holes, which once served as a stopping place for the likes of Charlie Chaplin, William S. Hart, and Wallace Beery when Essanay Studios reigned during the silent days. Years later, "Machine Gun" Jack McGurn, a member of Al Capone's gang, earned 25% worth of interest in the bar when comedian-singer Joe E. Lewis tried to quit The Green Mill and perform elsewhere. As a favor to the owner of the bar, the mobster's men attacked Lewis in his hotel room and slit his throat (he survived). To this day, patrons of The Green Mill can ask the bartender for a look at the frayed scrapbook kept under the bar which details the historic events surrounding it. A large section is devoted to the shooting of THIEF. The performances Mann got from Caan, Prosky, Belushi, and Weld are nothing less than terrific. Caan has his best role since THE GODFATHER here and he holds the film together with cool intensity. Jim Belushi, brother of John, is a revelation, showing he can handle straight dramatic roles with aplomb. Perhaps best of all is Prosky, who steals the film by underplaying the role of the powerful mob chieftan. Alternating between jovial friendliness and brutal, cold-hearted cruelty, Prosky seems to embody the essence of real-life gangsters, who need not yell and harangue to prove their power. It is a detailed, multi-leveled performance (nowhere else have we seen a mob chieftan sitting in his living room reading the newspaper while absent-mindedly wiggling his stocking feet on the coffee table) and Prosky succeeds brilliantly. Mann would go on to direct the disappointing, completely incoherent horror film THE KEEP, but then come back with the phenomenally successful TV series "Miami Vice," where he continues the visual experiments he started in THIEF. This film is brutally realistic in its street language and violence, so more sensitive viewers should be warned.

p, Jerry Bruckheimer, Ronnie Caan; d&w, Michael Mann (based on the book *The Home Invaders* by Frank Hohimer); ph, Donald Thorin (Technicolor); m, Tangerine Dream; ed, Dov Hoenig; prod d, Mel Bourne; art d, Mary Dodson.

Crime   **Cas.**   **(PR:O MPAA:R)**

THIEF OF BAGHDAD, THE***** (1940, Brit.) 106m LFP/UA c

Conrad Veidt *(Jaffar)*, Sabu *(Abu)*, June Duprez *(Princess)*, John Justin *(Ahmad)*, Rex Ingram *(Djinni)*, Miles Malleson *(Sultan)*, Morton Selten *(King)*, Mary Morris *(Halima)*, Bruce Winston *(Merchant)*, Hay Petrie *(Astrologer)*, Roy Emerton *(Jailer)*, Allan Jeayes *(Storyteller)*, Adelaide Hall *(Singer)*, Miki Hood, David Sharpe.

There is no doubt that this film is *the* best fantasy film ever made, with astounding special effects and wonderful performances by Veidt, Sabu, Justin, and Duprez. A host of different directors worked on this marvelous and inventive Arabian Nights spectacle, all under the meticulous eye of producer Korda. This film and THE FOUR FEATHERS (1939) were the two most important films Korda would produce in a lifetime of great filmic achievements. Every frame of this film is magical and exciting. Many incidents from Arabian Nights fables were assembled for this exquisite picture, beginning with Sabu– stealing food in the marketplace of Baghdad, a colorful gamin who leaps along rooftops and scurries through the bazaar–only to be arrested and thrown into a dungeon for his minor offenses. The city is ruled by a goodhearted prince, Justin. The prince's grand vizier, Veidt, is utterly evil. Behind Justin's back, Veidt oppresses the people. He overthrows Justin and places him in the same dungeon that contains Sabu. The inventive little thief works up a plan whereby they both escape and flee to the exotic city of Basra. There–now wearing rags, rather than his customary raiment–Justin learns the art of thievery from Sabu, though he is an unwilling pupil. As the two filch their supper in Basra's bazaar, horsemen ride forth. They force the citizens to bow, shielding their faces so they will be unable to view the beautiful countenance of Duprez, princess of the city. Secretly, Justin peeks. Smitten by her stunning appearance, he vows that he will see her once more. Against Sabu's cautions, Justin scales the palace wall and enters the royal garden, where he climbs a tree. Duprez strolls through the garden singing a lyrical love song. She looks into a pool and sees Justin's reflected face. He tells her he is a genie and she speaks to him. Justin tells her of his love for her and she responds in kind, but the illusion is dispersed when guards appear and Justin jumps from the tree, escaping. Justin later learns that his hated enemy, Veidt, covets Duprez himself, and has been busy plying her senile father, Malleson–the king of Basra–with magical toys, bargaining for Malleson's luscious daughter. The toy-obsessed old man has promised Duprez that he will not yield to Veidt's importunities, but he changes his mind when the evil vizier presents him with a mechanical winged horse that flies about the enormous rooms of the palace and out over the city. "I must have it, I must have it," drools Malleson, who then agrees that Duprez can become Veidt's spouse. Malleson then mounts the steed and–cackling with delight–rides into the air and over the city. While Malleson is in mid-flight, the wicked Veidt uses his magic to destroy the horse, dashing the senile king to his death. When Justin and Sabu attempt to interfere with Veidt's plan to abduct Duprez, the wicked vizier turns Sabu into a dog and makes Justin a blind beggar. The prince is next seen begging in the streets of Basra with his "dog" at his side. Discovering the fate that has befallen the man she loves, Duprez promises to wed Veidt if he will revoke his curse. Justin and Sabu are returned to their former forms, but the prince is in agony. "What good are my eyes if I cannot see her," he cries. Justin and Sabu learn that Veidt plans to take Duprez back to Baghdad on his huge ship. Acquiring a small sailboat, the two take up the pursuit, but the evil Veidt sees their approach. He causes an enormous storm to come from nowhere and engulf the little craft. Following the storm, Sabu finds himself on a wide, sunny beach, with Justin nowhere to be seen. The boy discovers an ancient bottle stuck in the sand. He rubs the bottle, attempting to discern its contents, then uncorks it. Out of the bottle shoots a huge plume of smoke which rises hundreds of feet, then forms into a giant genie, Ingram, whose laughter seems to shake the land on which he stands. Ingram tells Sabu that "King Solomon imprisoned me in that bottle 3,000 years ago," and now he is free. He looks down at Sabu, prepared to crush the young thief as one might an ant, but the clever youth tricks him by challenging Ingram to prove he's a real genie through going back into the bottle. That trick accomplished, Sabu renews Ingram's captivity by replacing the cork in the bottle. Only when Ingram agrees to grant Sabu three wishes does the thief release the genie. Ingram patronizes the little trickster, who ponders about his prospective wishes, and then tricks *him* into making the first of the three, one for a frying pan containing sizzling sausages. "To hear is to obey, little master of the universe," booms Ingram, who lowers his hand to reveal the requested provender. As Sabu nibbles at the sausages, he considers his options, then makes another wish: that he might see his friend Justin. Ingram grants the wish by taking Sabu to the "All-Seeing Eye" housed high in the Tibetan mountains. In a spectacular sequence, Sabu is seen flying through the air over continents and oceans while grasping Ingram's pigtail. Arriving at a huge monastery, the genie deposits Sabu on the stairs leading into the cavernous place and tells him he must obtain the "All-Seeing Eye" on his own. He pushes the thief through the doors, and Sabu finds himself in an enormous hall, a giant Shiva- like statue before him, at the peak of which radiates–set in the many-armed statue's forehead–the coveted "All-Seeing Eye." Sabu starts to climb the statue–which is guarded by arrow- shooting little green men–and narrowly evades death during the incredible ascent, imperiled also by an enormous spider. He manages to pluck the eye from the idol's forehead, then returns to the waiting Ingram, who–tricking the lad into his third wish–deposits Sabu on the side of a high cliff, from which there appears to be no escape. Laughing so hard he almost causes the canyon in which he stands to crumble, Ingram then declares himself free of his promised bondage and goes soaring away, howling hysterically. Holding the "All-Seeing Eye," Sabu peers into the glowing gem and sees Justin, now a prisoner of the evil Veidt and condemned to die, while almond-eyed Duprez is to wed the sinister vizier. Frustrated about not being able to assist his friend, Sabu hurls the crystal to the canyon floor. Its destruction shatters the canyon itself, which, collapsing, propels the thief into a whirling void. He finds himself in an outer world beyond the planet, one peopled by all the wise old men of the East, all waiting to travel to Paradise on a magic flying carpet. They are to protect themselves during this impending journey with a golden bow and arrow, one which, when aimed, never misses its mark. Apologizing for his kleptomania to the wisest of these sages, Sabu steps on the magic carpet, grabs the golden bow and arrow, and orders the rug to take him to Baghdad. There, Veidt is about to execute Justin, ridding himself of the man to whom Duprez has given her heart. Anticipating that the prince's demise will increase Duprez's willingness to more readily accept his own lascivious embrace, the evil vizier orders the executioner to swing his axe. Before this can occur, Sabu appears on the magic carpet and sends a golden arrow into the headsman, saving Justin at the last moment. The evil vizier– seeing that all is lost–mounts his mechanical steed and attempts to flee by riding skyward, but Sabu shoots another golden arrow, which finds its mark and kills him. Like his victim Malleson before him, Veidt crashes to earth, dead. Justin and Duprez are united, and the prince regains his throne, promising the populace a fair and happy reign and making Sabu his new grand vizier. The irascible youth wants no part of politics, however, and is soon off on his stolen magic carpet seeking new adventures. Douglas Fairbanks, Sr. had made a spectacular film in his own THE THIEF OF BAGHDAD in 1924, but that silent film bore little real resemblance to this Korda super-spectacular of 1940. (The two remakes that followed are pale, cheap imitations.) Korda involved himself directly with this production after discovering that his contracted director, Berger–who had made some important early talkies, including THE VAGABOND KING (1930) and the Dutch version of PYGMALION (1937)–had gotten bogged down and displayed no flair whatsoever for fantasy and spectacle (being basically a director of intimate parlor-room pictures). The producer brought in Whelan and Powell to oversee the action scenes. The shooting ground on for two years and WW II intervened, preventing Korda from using desired locations in Egypt and Arabia. He later finished the film in Hollywood and had his brother Zoltan and renowned designer Menzies direct the final scenes in the Grand Canyon and the Painted Desert. Although six directors worked on the picture, it is amazing to see that it all works, and works wonderfully, with no apparent breaks in the transitional scenes. THE THIEF OF BAGHDAD retains a consistent appearance of grandeur; its pace flows so evenly that it might well have been directed by one man. Essentially, it really was: by Korda himself. The producer also employed his genius of a set-designing brother, Vincent, whose marvelous creations seem *truly* out of this world. He brought composer Rozsa in to create the rich, romantic, dynamic score. This great producer originally wanted Vivien Leigh to play the much-put-upon princess, but Leigh left for America to visit her true love Laurence Olivier, then appearing in producer David O. Selznick's WUTHERING HEIGHTS. Once in the U.S., Leigh herself was "discovered" by Selznick, and went into GONE WITH THE WIND and history. Bereft of his chosen leading lady, Korda signed the sultry Duprez, a stunning beauty whose pretty face was enhanced by the rich hues of the Technicolor process then in use. Jon Hall was the producer's first choice for the part of the prince, but the actor was unavailable. The producer cast Justin in the role mostly because he resembled Hall, and Korda thought Hall looked like a prince. He was right. Justin, with his soft, melodious voice, was perfect in the part. Korda's favorite actors, Veidt and Sabu, are both splendid in their respective roles, and the rest of the cast comprises enchanting character players such as the chinless, blustering Malleson and the stentorian, towering Ingram (who had played "De Lawd" in GREEN PASTURES). The film won Oscars for art direction, color photography, and special effects. THE THIEF OF BAGHDAD remains to this day one of the most dazzling fantasies ever created for the screen.

p, Alexander Korda; d, Ludwig Berger, Michael Powell, Tim Whelan, Zoltan Korda, William Cameron Menzies, Alexander Korda; w, Lajos Biro, Miles Malleson; ph, Georges Perinal, Osmond Borrodaile (Technicolor); m, Miklos Rozsa; ed, William Hornbeck, Charles Crichton; prod d, Vincent Korda; md, Muir Mathieson; cos, Oliver Messel, John Armstrong, Marcel Vertes; spec eff, Lawrence Butler, Tom Howard, Johnny Mills.

Fantasy **Cas.** **(PR:AAA MPAA:NR)**

THIEF OF BAGHDAD, THE** (1961, Ital./Fr.) 90m Titanus-C.C.F. Lux/MGM c (IL LADRO DI BAGDAD; LE VOLEUR DE BAGDAD)

Steve Reeves *(Karim)*, Georgia Moll *(Amina)*, Arturo Dominici *(Prince Osman)*, Edy Vessel *(Kadeejah)*, Georges Chamarat *(Magician)*, Antonio Battistella, Daniele Vargas, Fanfulla, Giancarlo Zarfati, Rosario Borelli, Eduardo Bergamo, Luigi Visconti, Gina Mascetti, Antonio Rosmino, Ignazio Dolce, Mohammed Agrebi, Joudi Mohammed Jamil, Franco Cobianchi, Anita Todesco, Walter Grant, Mario Passante, Chignone.

In a somewhat modernized version of THE ARABIAN NIGHTS, Reeves plays the thief who falls in love with the beautiful daughter of a sultan. She is also loved by the evil Dominici, who attempts to win the princess with the aid of a magic love potion. But because she is really in love with Reeves, the potion turns to poison and the girl falls gravely ill. The only thing that can save her is a blue rose that grows beyond the mystical Seven Gates. Reeves takes off after the rose, along with Dominici and several other suitors. His adventures include crossing a plain of boiling lava, outwitting the temptress Vessel, and surviving a sudden flood. He finally finds the blue rose and brings it back to the princess. The sultan is eternally grateful to Reeves and makes him the king of Baghdad. Previous versions in 1924 and 1940 were vastly superior to this.

p, Bruno Vailati; d, Arthur Lubin; w, Augusto Frassineti, Filippo Sanjust, Vailati; ph, Tonino Delli Colli (CinemaScope, Eastmancolor); m, Carlo Rustichelli; ed, Gene Ruggiero; art d, Flavio Mogherini; set d, Massimo Tavazzi; cos, Georges Benda; spec eff, Tom Howard; ch, Paul Steffen; makeup, Romolo De Martino.

Fantasy	Cas.	(PR:A MPAA:NR)

THIEF OF DAMASCUS*½ (1952) 78m COL c

Paul Henreid (*Abu Andar*), John Sutton (*Khalid*), Jeff Donnell. (*Sheherazade*), Lon Chaney, Jr (*Sinbad*), Elena Verdugo (*Neela*), Robert Clary (*Aladdin*), Edward Colmans (*Sultan Raudah*), Nelson Leigh (*Ben Jammal*), Philip Van Zandt (*Ali Baba*), Leonard Penn (*Habayah*), Larry Stewart (*Hassan*), Robert Conte (*Horse Trader*).

The medieval city of Damascus is the setting for this exercise in pure escapism, in which Henreid plays a debunked general who joins forces with Aladdin (Clary), Sinbad (Chaney), and Ali Baba (Zandt) to save it from the hands of invaders. Little attempt is made at authenticity, that not being one of the goals of the filmmakers as much as providing for feather weight entertainment. Footage was lifted from JOAN OF ARC and reused here.

p, Sam Katzman; d, Will Jason; w, Robert E. Kent; ph, Ellis W. Carter (Technicolor); m, Mischa Bakaleinikoff; ed, William Lyon; art d, Paul Palmentola.

Adventure	(PR:A MPAA:NR)

THIEF OF PARIS, THE*** (1967, Fr./Ital.) 119m NEF-Artistes Associes-Compagnia Cinematografica Montoro/Lopert c (LE VOLEUR)

Jean-Paul Belmondo (*Georges Randal*), Genevieve Bujold (*Charlotte*), Marie Dubois (*Genevieve*), Francoise Fabian (*Ida*), Julien Guiomar (*Lamargelle*), Paul Le Person (*Roger La Honte*), Martine Sarcey (*Renee*), Marlene Jobert (*Broussaille*), Bernadette Lafont (*Marguerite*), Madeleine Damien (*Marie Jeanne*), Christian Lude (*Uncle Randal*), Fernand Guiot (*Van Der Busch*), Jacqueline Staup (*Mrs. Van Der Busch*), Marc Dudicourt (*Antoine*), Charles Denner (*Cannonier*), Christian de Tiliere (*Armand*), Jacques David (*The Robbed Man*), Roger Crouzet (*Mouratet*), Jacques Debary (*Courbassol*), Paul Vally (*The Solicitor*), Nane Germon (*Mrs. Voisin*), Jean Champion (*Owner of the Hotel de la Biche*), Odette Piquet (*His Wife*), Irene Daix (*Old English Maid*), Julien Loisel (*Mr. de Montareuil*), Dario Meschi (*Owner of the Hotel du Roi Salomon*), Maurice Auzel (*Marcel*), Jacques Gheusi (*Prof. Boileau*), Pierre Etaix (*Pickpocket*), Monique Melinand, Nicole Chollet, Gabriel Gobin, Duncan Elliott.

Known mainly for its charming look at Paris at the end of the last century, this Malle feature centers on the escapades of a young man who turns to thievery in order to get his vengeance. He discovers that he likes stealing so much he continues swiping expensive jewels until he becomes quite wealthy. Belmondo plays the young man tricked by his uncle out of a fortune, who then robs the jewels from the suitor of his cousin Bujold, because he doesn't want to see her married to anyone else. Once this is done, he continues on his path of crime, using his flirtatious manner to full advantage. With growing political instability in France, Belmondo goes to England, and is eventually joined by Bujold upon the death of her father. Light-hearted and lacking in pretentions.

p&d, Louis Malle; w, Malle, Jean-Claude Carriere (based on the story by Georges Darien); ph, Henri Decae (DeLuxe Color); ed, Henri Lanoe; art d, Jacques Saulnier; cos, Ghislain Uhry.

Comedy/Drama	(PR:A MPAA:NR)

THIEF OF VENICE, THE**½ (1952) 91m FOX bw

Maria Montez (*Tina*), Paul Christian (*Alfiere Lorenzo Contarini*), Massimo Serato (*Scarpa the Inquisitor*), Faye Marlowe (*Francesca Disani*), Aldo Silvani (*Capt. Von Sturm*), Louis Saltamerenda (*Alfredo*), Guido Celano (*Polo*), Humbert Sacripanti (*Durro*), Camillo Pilotto (*Adm. Disani*), Ferdinand Tamberlani (*Lombardi*), Liana Del Balzo (*Duenna*), Paul Stoppa (*Marco*), Mario Tosi (*Mario*), Vinicio Sofia (*Grazzi*), Leon Renoir (*Sharp Eye*).

A costume drama set in the Middle Ages of Venice in which Christian plays a navy officer who takes to thieving in order to get the money together to stand up against the crafty political aims of Serato. Montez plays the tavern keeper who originally overhears Serato's scheming, and with the backing of a number of freed slaves, gives Christian the needed backing to see that Serato is brought to justice. The authentic costumes, as well as the actual background of Venice, help to create the appropriate atmosphere. This was the last film appearance of Montez who died in 1951 at the age of 33.

p, Robert Haggiag; d, John Brahm; w, Jesse L. Lasky, Jr. (based on a story by Michael Pertwee); ph, Anchise Brizzi; m, Alessandro Cicognini; ed, Terry Morse, Renzo Lucidi; art d, Otto Scotti, Louis Scacciandoci.

Adventure	(PR:A MPAA:NR)

THIEF WHO CAME TO DINNER, THE** (1973) 105m Tandem/WB c

Ryan O'Neal (*Webster*), Jacqueline Bisset (*Laura*), Warren Oates (*Dave Reilly*), Jill Clayburgh (*Jackie*), Charles Cioffi (*Henderling*), Ned Beatty (*Deams*), Austin Pendleton (*Zukovsky, Chess Editor*), Gregory Sierra (*Dynamite*), Michael Murphy (*Ted*), John Hillerman (*Laxker, Realtor*), Alan Oppenheimer (*Insurance Agent*), Margaret Fairchild (*Mrs. Donner*), Jack Manning (*Tom*), Richard O'Brien (*Sgt. Del Conte*), George Morfogen (*Rivera*).

An unimpressive picture about a computer brain, O'Neal, who becomes a successful jewel thief when things begin to get a little dull at his job. He gets himself invited to high society parties where his capers take place, while at the same time finds himself falling in love with high society girl, Bisset. Oates plays an insurance detective who knows O'Neal is the real thief, but is unable to prove it. A poorly paced picture with a needlessly complicated plot.

p&d, Bud Yorkin; w, Walter Hill (based on the novel by Terence Lore Smith); ph, Philip Lathrop (DeLuxe Color); m, Henry Mancini; ed, John C. Horger; prod d, Polly Platt; art d, Platt; set d, Audrey A. Blasdel.

Comedy	Cas.	(PR:A MPAA:PG)

THIEVES*½ (1977) 103m Brut/PAR c

Marlo Thomas (*Sally Cramer*), Charles Grodin (*Martin Cramer*), Irwin Corey (*Joe Kaminsky*), Hector Elizondo (*Man Below*), Mercedes McCambridge (*Street Lady*), John McMartin (*Gordon*), Gary Merrill (*Street Man*), Ann Wedgeworth (*Nancy*), Larry Scott (*Carlton*), Bob Fosse (*Mr. Day*), Norman Matlock (*Mr. Night*), Ian Martin (*Devlin*), Janet Colazzo (*Marianna*), Ken Kimmins (*Stanley*), Santos Morales (*Perez*), MacIntryre Dixon (*Passenger*), Bill Lazarus (*Officer Miranda*), Alice Drummond (*Mrs. Ramsey*), Zvee Scooler (*Old Man*), Craig Barrie (*Sheriff*), Victor Le Guillow (*Julio*), Lee Wallace (*Harry*), Jess Osuna (*Gilbey*), Joan Kaye (*Flo*).

Unsuccessful attempt to transfer a popular play to the screen stars Thomas and Grodin as a New York couple who find themselves drifting apart. Grodin is successful as the head of a private school and can't understand Thomas' need to continue teaching on the Lower East Side where they both grew up. After each has an affair, they find that they are lonely for each other, but when they return to their luxury apartment they wind up getting into another argument. Angry, Grodin whips out a gun Thomas' father has given him for protection and shoots three shots into the air. As the police sirens close in, Thomas realizes that Grodin is still the zany man she fell in love with, and the two are reunited. Look for a brief appearance by director Bob Fosse.

p, George Barrie; d, John Berry, Al Viola; w, Herb Gardner (based on the play by Gardner); ph, Arthur J. Ornitz, Andrew Lazlo; m, Jule Styne, Mike Miller, Shel Silverstein; ed, Craig McKay; prod d, John Robert Lloyd; art d, Robert Gundlach; set d, George De Titta; cos, Albert Wolsky; makeup, Robert Laden, Tom Case.

Comedy	(PR:A MPAA:PG)

THIEVES FALL OUT**½ (1941) 72m WB-FN/WB bw

Eddie Albert (*Eddie Barnes*), Joan Leslie (*Mary Mathews*), Jane Darwell (*Grandma Allen*), Alan Hale (*Robert Barnes*), William T. Orr (*George Formsby*), John Litel (*Tim Gordon*), Minna Gombell (*Ella Barnes*), Anthony Quinn (*Chic Collins*), Edward Brophy (*Rork*), Hobart Cavanaugh (*David Tipton*), Vaughan Glaser (*Charles Matthews*), Nana Bryant (*Martha Matthews*), Frank Faylen (*Pick*), Edward Gargan (*Kane*), William B. Davidson (*Harry Eckles*), Tom Kennedy (*Cab Driver*), Etta McDaniel (*Blossom*), Ann Edmonds (*Secretary*), Jack Wise (*Janitor*), Cliff Clark (*Policeman*), Walter Soderling (*Justice of the Peace*).

Entertaining, undemanding picture about gangsters and a witty grandmother who shows a tough hood just what she's made of. Darwell stars as the grandmother to Albert, a tenderfooted kid who wants to marry his sweetheart, Leslie, but can't get the needed dough to start a household. So granny suggests he use his expected inheritance to get a loan. He does better than this by selling it to hood Cavanaugh for a hefty sum, who turns right around and jacks up the interest price for Quinn. Quinn then tries to force Albert's father to buy the inheritance back. He eventually resorts to the kidnaping of Darwell. The hoods get more than they bargained for with Darwell who uses the imagination inspired by dozens of radio shows to totally turn the tables on Quinn. He winds up giving the inheritance back without receiving a single cent. No one except Darwell has much to do in this picture, and those performances revolve around the little old lady. For the most part, this works out all right, with Darwell being a delight to watch as she shows a deft usage of the gangster slang.

p, Edmund Grainger; d, Ray Enright; w, Charles Grayson, Ben Markson (based on the play "Thirty Days Hath September" by Irving Gaumont, Jack

Sobel); ph, Sid Hickox; m, Heinz Roemheld; ed, Clarence Kolster.

Comedy   (PR:A MPAA:NR)

THIEVES' HIGHWAY***   (1949) 94m FOX bw

Richard Conte *(Nick Garcos)*, Valentina Cortesa *(Rica)*, Lee J. Cobb *(Mike Figlia)*, Barbara Lawrence *(Polly Faber)*, Jack Oakie *(Slob)*, Millard Mitchell *(Ed)*, Joseph Pevney *(Pete)*, Morris Carnovsky *(Yanko Garcos)*, Tamara Shayne *(Parthena Garcos)*, Kasia Orzazewski *(Mrs. Polansky)*, Norbert Schiller *(Polansky)*, Hope Emerson *(Midgren)*, George Tyne *(Charles)*, Edwin Max *(Dave)*, David Clarke *(Mitch)*, Walter Baldwin *(Riley)*, David Opatoshu *(Frenchy)*, Ann Morrison *(Mable)*, Percy Helton *(Proprietor)*, Maurice Samuels *(Mario)*, Saul Martell *(Stukas)*, Holland Chamberlain *(Mr. Faber)*, Irene Tedrow *(Mrs. Faber)*, Al Eben *(Newman)*, Joe Haworth *(Inspector)*, Dick Wessel *(Cab Driver)*, Frank Kreig *(Clerk)*, Mario Sletti *(Pietro)*, Robert Bice *(Announcer)*, Frank Richards *(Pig)*, Roy Damron *(Motor Policeman)*, Ted Jordan, John Merton *(State Highway Policemen)*.

This was to be Dassin's last film in America for over a decade, as a victim of the House Un-American Activities he was labeled a communist and forced to work in Europe. Unlike many of the blacklisted filmmakers, Dassin was able to continue making films, his talent actually developing when given the freedom from the Hollywood system. Effectively using the hilly terrain of San Francisco and the surrounding countryside, THIEVES' HIGHWAY is the story of a vengeance-minded GI who returns home from the war to discover that his father has lost the use of both his legs as a result of a feud with Cobb. As the son, Conte had originally planned on taking the small amount of savings he had from the war to marry the pretty, but very shallow, Lawrence. Instead he buys a truck to become involved in the same racket as his father, and thus deals directly with the crooked Cobb. This money is soon lost, and Lawrence decides that there is no use in hanging around for Conte. With a truckload of apples, and the assistance of his buddy Mitchell, Conte plans to deliver a load to the door of Cobb. He arrives to have the produce manager use the prostitute Cortesa to lure him to her den, while Cobb takes advantage of the truckload of apples. Cortesa soon reveals her own distaste for Cobb, warning her new lover that he has been set in a trap. When Conte goes back to confront Cobb, he finds another trap set up by a couple of henchmen. Eventually Conte does get his vengeance on Cobb, after the henchmen discover that their boss has also been cheating him. A major focus of this picture is the changes in which Conte goes through as a result of his confrontation with Cobb. Coming back from the war a clean-cut soldier, ready to make a go at an honest living and marry the all-American girl of every soldier's dream, instead he finds himself enmeshed in the world of hoods. The American dream is quickly destroyed, and what is revealed is a much more real world. This is probably best expressed in the photography, in which everything is shown in a distorted fashion. Only the flat of Cortesa is photographed in a straightforward manner, revealing the truth in the relations Conte has with her as opposed to with Lawrence. Along with this highly visualized style, Dassin has effectively paced the movement of the plot to create a hard hitting drama.

p, Robert Bassler; d, Jules Dassin; w, A.I. Bezzerides (based on the novel *Thieves' Market* by Bezzerides); ph, Norbert Brodine; m, Alfred Newman; ed, Nick De Maggio; md, Lionel Newman; art d, Lyle Wheeler, Chester Gore; set d, Thomas Little, Fred J. Rode; cos, Kay Nelson; spec eff, Fred Sersen; makeup, Ben Nye.

Crime/Drama   (PR:C MPAA:NR)

THIEVES' HOLIDAY   (SEE: SCANDAL IN PARIS, 1946)

THIEVES LIKE US***½   (1974) 123m UA c

Keith Carradine *(Bowie)*, Shelly Duvall *(Keechie)*, John Schuck *(Chicamaw)*, Bert Remsen *(T-Dub)*, Louise Fletcher *(Mattie)*, Ann Latham *(Lula)*, Tom Skerritt *(Dee Mobley)*, Al Scott *(Capt. Stammers)*, John Roper *(Jasbo)*, Mary Waits *(Noel)*, Rodney Lee, Jr *(James Mattingly)*, William Watters *(Alvin)*, Joan Tewkesbury *(Lady in Train Station)*, Edward Fisher, Josephine Bennett, Howard Warner *(Bank Hostages)*, Eleanor Matthews *(Mrs. Stammers)*, Pam Warner *(Woman in Accident)*, Suzanne Majure *(Coca-Cola Girl)*, Walter Cooper, Lloyd Jones *(Sheriffs)*.

A well-done remake of THEY LIVE BY NIGHT that's slightly long but unusually free of Altman's customary indulgences. A 1930s crime story with humor and humanity, THIEVES LIKE US owes more than a passing nod to BONNIE AND CLYDE and BADLANDS in theme and treatment. Young killer-crook Carradine escapes from a Mississippi jail with older, hard-bitten criminals Remsen and Schuck. After a brief respite, they return to the only way they know to make a living, robbing banks. Carradine's girl friend is Skerritt's daughter, Duvall, and she becomes part of the team as they go on a Depression rampage, thus joining Dillinger, Nelson, Ma Barker, and all the others who plied their trades by asking bank tellers to cash "This is a Stick-Up" notes. The three men are all armed and dangerous but not very good at what they do and that incompetency eventually catches up with them. The title is drawn from the trio's theory that everyone is a thief in one way or another and big businesses, like banks, are just as guilty of criminal activity as they are. The fact that Carradine, Schuck, and Remsen kill people as part of their daily labors never enters into their thinking. After a few thefts, Carradine intends to leave the bank robbing industry and move

to Mexico with Duvall, where he hopes he can find some serenity. Remsen has a fling with Latham, which proves his undoing. The robbers are celebrated in the press and feared by the towns and chased by the cops who begin moving closer. Remsen is erased by the law, the psychotic Schuck is nabbed, and Carradine and Duvall continue on the run until they hide out at the house of Remsen's sister-in-law Fletcher. (This is Fletcher's film debut. The fact that she was married to producer Bick may have had some influence on her casting). Carradine tries to get Schuck out of jail and succeeds, then the men quarrel and he leaves Schuck and returns to Fletcher's house where the cops are waiting. While Fletcher holds the screaming, pregnant Duvall, Carradine is mowed down by the cops. Duvall later has the baby and moves off to find a new beginning. Unlike BONNIE AND CLYDE, there is a real love story between Carradine and Duvall and it comes across. The music and background sounds were supplied by John Dunning, who is credited for "radio research." He provided radio shows like "Gangbusters," "The Heart Of Gold," remote band broadcasts, and an actual "Romeo And Juliet" dramatization which is heard while Duvall and Carradine are making love. Most of the killings are referred to, rather than seen, so this is a character study more than a violence film. The executive producer was George Litto, who used to be Altman's agent and was making his bow in production. Litto was later responsible for a few of De Palma's debacles. Remsen, who is one of Altman's stock company, has another career as one of the most respected casting directors in Hollywood. Coscreenwriter Tewkesbury makes a cameo.

p, Jerry Bick; d, Robert Altman; w, Calder Willingham, Joan Tewkesbury, Altman (based on the novel by Edward Anderson); ph, Jean Boffety; ed, Lou Lombardo; visual cons, Jack De Govia, Scott Bushnell.

Crime Drama   **Cas.**   (PR:C MPAA:R)

THIN AIR   (SEE: BODY STEALERS, THE, 1969, Brit.)

THIN ICE***½   (1937) 78m FOX bw (GB: LOVELY TO LOOK AT)

Sonja Henie *(Lili Heiser)*, Tyrone Power *(Prince Rudolph)*, Arthur Treacher *(Nottingham)*, Raymond Walburn *(Uncle Dornic)*, Joan Davis *(Orchestra Leader)*, Alan Hale *(Baron)*, Sig Rumann *(Prime Minister)*, Melville Cooper *(Krantz)*, Maurice Cass *(Count)*, George Givot *(Alex)*, Torben Meyer *(Chauffeur)*, Leah Ray *(Singer)*, Egon Brecher *(Janitor)*, George Davis *(Waiter)*, Lon Chaney, Jr *(American Reporter)*, Rudolph Anders *(German Reporter)*, Pat Somerset *(English Reporter)*, Nino Bellini *(Italian Reporter)*, Eugene Borden *(French Reporter)*, Albert Pollet *(Waiter)*, Frank Puglia *(Porter)*, Georges Renavent *(Headwaiter)*, Zola de Crott *(Chambermaid)*, Bert Sprotte *(Farmer)*, Elsa Janssen *(Woman)*, Greta Meyer *(Martha)*, Alberto Morin *(Attendant)*, Alphonse Martell, Walter Bonn *(Officers of Prime Minister)*, Christian Rub *(Man)*, Iva Stewart, Dorothy Jones, June Storey, June Gale, Clarice Sherry, June Wilkins, Monica Bannister, Bonnie Bannon, Pauline Craig, Ruth Hart, Wanda Perry, Doris Davenport, Diane Cook, Margaret Lyman *(Members of Girl's Band)*.

Fun-filled musical love story featuring Henie in her second film. An old theme that turned into a smash hit due to a fine score, a sharp script, and Henie's incomparable ice skating. Power is a European prince who arrives at an Alpine resort with his whole entourage in tow. The purpose of his visit is to conduct some very delicate negotiations regarding the neutrality of his country in the light of the problems taking place in Europe. Power is bored by all the machinations and decides to have some fun on his own so he goes up on the slopes for a bit of shussing. While doing some passable slaloms, he meets Henie, the Swiss ice skating teacher at a small lodge. Power doesn't let on that he's of royal lineage and instead claims to be a newspaper reporter (a role Power played in many films). They fall in love at once but she doesn't know his true identity despite the fact that everyone else does. She is besieged by diplomats and other toadies and they hand her all sorts of gifts, hoping that she will use her influence on Power. Henie's uncle is Walburn, and Hale and Cass, two men who want to get to Power, slip Walburn some money to be their liaison between Henie and Power. Inadvertantly, it appears that Walburn is the person responsible for cooking up a phony romance between Henie and Power and when Hale and Cass think that Walburn has taken them, they demand their money back. The prime minister of Power's country arrives. This is Rumann and he is there because it seems that what should have been finished in a day or so has gone long past the usual time. Rumann is annoyed that Power has been wasting valuable hours with a common skater, setting rumors racing across the continent. Power says that they are not rumors and he wants to prove that they are true. He is madly in love with Henie and asks for her hand and a wedding to end all weddings is planned as the movie fades out. It's a typical "Cinderella" story and the same sort of basis has been used for many movies, including THE PRINCE AND THE SHOWGIRL. The major difference between this film and countless others like it is that we get a chance to see the Olympic champion Henie do her stuff. She was just as good a negotiator as she was on the ice and when Zanuck wanted to team her with Power (they were dating at the time) she used her edge to get Zanuck to give her so much money that she became the highest paid actress in 1937, earning more than $200,000. Henie was also a good comedienne, something that emerged in later movies. Here, the comedy was handled by Fox's resident funny lady, Joan Davis, who played the role of the band leader at the hotel. Davis sang the Harry Revel-Mack Gordon tune, "I'm Olga from the Volga" and "My Swiss Hillbilly" (Lew Pollack and Sidney Mitchell).

Pollack and Mitchell also wrote "My Secret Love Affair" and "Over Night" both of which were performed by the band singer, Leah Ray. Henie's ice skating was breathtaking. She was a virtuoso, a ballerina on skates and riveted one's eyes whenever she was on screen. Her much-publicized affair with Power eventually ended and he married actress Annabella in 1939, which lasted through 1948. Henie only made 12 films in the U.S. but parlayed her wages into an enormous fortune.

p, Raymond Griffith; d, Sidney Lanfield; w, Boris Ingster, Milton Sperling (based on the play "Der Komet" by Attila Obok); ph, Robert Planck, Edward Cronjager; ed, Robert Simpson; md, Louis Silvers; art d, Marklee Kirk; set d, Thomas Little; cos, Royer; ch, Harry Losee; m/l, Mack Gordon, Harry Revel, Lew Pollack, Sidney D. Mitchell.

Musical Comedy/Romance   **(PR:A MPAA:NR)**

THIN LINE, THE*   (1967, Jap.) 102m Toho bw (ONNA NO NAKANI IRU TANIN)

Keiju Kobayashi, Michiyo Aratama, Tatsuya Mihashi, Akiko Wakabayashi, Daisuke Kato, Mitsuko Krusabue.

A man's guilt over the accidental murder of his best friend's wife (they were lovers and he accidentally kills her in the heat of passion), almost forces him to confess to the murder. But his wife is more concerned about the family honor so she poisons him. A highly structured, dark film that reveals the hypocrisy in bourgeois Japan, where honor has more relevance than love. Claude Chabrol would examine similar themes and content in his JUST BEFORE NIGHTFALL (1971).

p, Sanezumi Fujimoto, Masakatsu Kaneko; d, Mikio Naruse; w, Toshiro Ide; ph, Yasumichi Fukuzawa (Tohoscope); m, Hikaru Hayashi.

Drama   **(PR:C MPAA:NR)**

THIN MAN, THE**   (1934) 93m MGM bw

William Powell (*Nick Charles*), Myrna Loy (*Nora Charles*), Maureen O'Sullivan (*Dorothy Wynant*), Nat Pendleton (*Lt. John Guild*), Minna Gombell (*Mimi Wynant*), Porter Hall (*MacCauley*), Henry Wadsworth (*Tommy*), William Henry (*Gilbert Wynant*), Harold Huber (*Nunheim*), Cesar Romero (*Chris Jorgenson*), Natalie Moorhead (*Julia Wolf*), Edward Brophy (*Joe Morelli*), Thomas Jackson, Creighton Hale, Phil Tead, Nick Copeland, Dink Templeton (*Reporters*), Ruth Channing (*Mrs. Jorgenson*), Edward Ellis (*Clyde Wynant*), Gertrude Short (*Marion*), Clay Clement (*Quinn*), Cyril Thornton (*Tanner*), Robert E. Homans (*Bill the Detective*), Raymond Brown (*Dr. Walton*), Douglas Fowley, Sherry Hall (*Taxi Drivers*), Polly Bailey, Dixie Laughton (*Janitresses*), Arthur Belasco, Ed Hearn, Garry Owen (*Detectives*), Fred Malatesta (*Headwaiter*), Rolfe Sedan, Leo White (*Waiters*), Walter Long (*Stutsy Burke*), Kenneth Gibson (*Apartment Clerk*), Tui Lorraine (*Stenographer*), Bert Roach (*Foster*), Huey White (*Tefler*), Ben Taggart (*Police Captain*), Charles Williams (*Fight Manager*), John Larkin (*Porter*), Harry Tenbrook (*Guest*), Pat Flaherty (*Cop/Fighter*).

Probably the best-loved detective film ever made, and certainly one of the most popular, THE THIN MAN reteamed Powell and Loy, who had shown their onscreen chemistry the year before in MANHATTAN MELODRAMA. As Nick Charles, Powell is a retired detective who has married wealthy Loy and now intends to devote himself to looking after her business interests and doing some serious drinking. They travel to New York for the holidays, and there O'Sullivan asks him to help her find her missing father, Ellis. He is an inventor who some months before told O'Sullivan that he was going into seclusion to work on a new project, but that he would return in time to attend her wedding. That event is drawing near and there is no word from Ellis, so she has contacted Powell, whose reputation precedes him. Powell is not anxious to ruin his happy retirement from sleuthing, but Loy, eager for some excitement, prods him into it. Before long Ellis' secretary (Moorhead) is murdered and when Ellis' watch chain is found in her hand, detective Pendleton immediately assumes that the missing man is the murderer. Not long after that Powell pays a visit to the inventor's workshop along with his wire-haired fox terrier, Asta. The dog begins sniffing around the floor and Powell digs, soon uncovering a badly decomposed and unrecognizable body. Other clues found with the corpse, later confirmed by X-rays of the body, reveal that the body is that of Ellis. Powell, still not knowing exactly who the killer is, invites all the suspects to his home for a dinner party. There he starts to explain the mystery, asking each suspect questions and carefully noting their responses. Finally he forces the murderer, Hall, Ellis' lawyer, to confess, drawing the whole story about how he and Moorhead had stolen a fortune in bonds from Ellis' safe, then murdered him when he found out. Hall later killed Moorhead when Powell started sniffing around the case to keep her quiet and throw suspicion on the dead man. The story is strictly programmer material, but what makes THE THIN MAN an enduring film today is the interplay between Powell and Loy, one of the first *happily* married couples ever to flicker on a screen. The repartee they shoot back and forth is priceless, such as in one scene the morning after a gunman had broken into their suite and superficially wounded Powell before being subdued and hauled away. As they read the morning papers about the event, Powell says, "I'm a hero, I was shot twice in the *Tribune*." Loy: "I read you were shot five times in the tabloids." "It's not true. He didn't come anywhere near my tabloids," Powell snaps back. The pair proved so popular that they were teamed no less than 12 times

during their careers, six of the pairings coming in the THIN MAN series, which would continue with increasingly diminishing success for 13 years. Louis B. Mayer did not think that the two would go over and tried to give the part of Nora to Laura LaPlante, but director Van Dyke, who had directed the pair's first effort, MANHATTAN MELODRAMA, insisted and Mayer relented. The film was shot in an amazingly short time, somewhere between 12 and 18 days (sources differ) and on a small budget. The film became one of the biggest successes of the year and was favored to win an Oscar for Powell (he ended up losing it to Clark Gable in another sleeper film of the year, IT HAPPENED ONE NIGHT). Almost as important as Powell and Loy to the series was their dog, Asta. Loy later recalled: "He was a wire-hair terrier and they were not popular at all at the time. His name was really Skippy and he was highly trained to do all of his tricks for a little squeaky mouse and a biscuit. He'd do anything for that reward. But the minute his scenes were over, it was definitely *verboten* to hug him or have any further contact with him off the set." He set off a national craze for the breed which led to a sharp decline in the standards for the type as "puppy mills" began breeding them as quickly as they could to keep up with demand (much the same way that the German shepherd breed had nearly been ruined by the RIN-TIN-TIN series). It was later said that Asta was the best known dog in the nation, with Franklin Roosevelt's Scottish Terrier Fala a close second. Although Loy and Powell seemed the perfect couple on screen, they actually had little more than a professional relationship, and Loy soon began to grow tired of her "perfect wife" role, although she was contractually forced to continue the series long after she had lost all interest in the part. Her weariness with the role shows in the later installments. At its peak (the first three films), Nick and Nora Charles, as played by Powell and Loy, were the finest thing going on the screen, setting a style for husband and wife detective teams still powerful today.

p, Hunt Stromberg; d, W.S. Van Dyke; w, Albert Hackett, Frances Goodrich (based on the novel by Dashiell Hammett); ph, James Wong Howe; ed, Robert J. Kern; md, Dr. William Axt; art d, Cedric Gibbons, David Townsend, Edwin B. Willis; cos, Dolly Tree.

Crime/Comedy   **Cas.**   **(PR:A MPAA:NR)**

THIN MAN GOES HOME, THE½   (1944) 100m MGM bw

William Powell (*Nick Charles*), Myrna Loy (*Nora Charles*), Lucile Watson (*Mrs. Charles*), Gloria DeHaven (*Laura Ronson*), Anne Revere (*Crazy Mary*), Harry Davenport (*Dr. Charles*), Helen Vinson (*Helena Draque*), Lloyd Corrigan (*Bruce Clayworth*), Donald Meek (*Willie Crump*), Edward Brophy (*Brogam*), Leon Ames (*Edgar Draque*), Paul Langton (*Tom Clayworth*), Donald MacBride (*Chief MacGregory*), Minor Watson (*Sam Ronson*), Anita Bolster (*Hilda*), Charles Halton (*Tatum*), Morris Ankrum (*Willoughby*), Nora Cecil (*Miss Peavy*), Wally Cassell (*Bill Burns*), Arthur Hohl (*Charlie*), Anthony Warde (*Captain*), Bill Smith, Lucille Brown (*Skating Act*), Mickey Harris (*Contortionist*), Rex Evans (*Fat Man*), Harry Hayden (*Conductor*), Connie Gilchrist (*Woman with Baby*), Robert Emmett O'Connor (*Baggage Man*), Dick Botiller (*Big Man's Companion*), John Wengraf (*Big Man*), Ralph Brooks (*Tom Burton*), Jane Green (*Housekeeper*), Irving Bacon (*Tom the Proprietor*), Virginia Sale (*Tom's Wife*), Garry Owen (*Pool Player*), Saul Gorss (*Bartender*), Bert May (*Sailor*), Chester Clute (*Drunk*), Clarence Muse (*Porter*), Tom Fadden, Joseph Greene, Sarah Edwards, Frank Jaquet (*Train Passengers*), Oliver Blake (*Reporter*), Don Wilson (*Masseur*), Etta McDaniel (*Ronson's Maid*), Tom Dugan (*Slugs*), Ed Gargan (*Mickey*), Thomas Dillon, Bill Hunter (*Officers*), Marjorie Wood (*Montage Shot Mother*), Catherine McLeod (*Montage Shot Daughter*), Clancy Cooper (*Butcher*), Joe Yule (*Barber*), Robert E. Homans (*Railroad Clerk*), Lee Phelps (*Cop*), Helyn Eby Rock, Jean Acker (*Tarts*), Mike Mazurki, Mitchell Lewis, Ray Teal (*Men*).

The fifth, and penultimate, entry in the THIN MAN series finds Powell and Loy somewhat under form as they swear off the booze when they go to Powell's home town for a family reunion. His sleuthing reputation follows him even to this sleepy community and he is soon approached by a young man obviously distraught about something. Before he can speak, though, he is shot down by an unknown assailant. Powell takes up the investigation and learns from an old friend, Corrigan, that the victim was a painter of landscapes. He further learns that some of the paintings were sold by an art dealer to a mysterious couple new in town. Powell suspects that there are spies involved, probably out to steal the plans for a secret new type of propeller under development at a nearby defense plant. As his investigation proceeds, Powell puts a number of prominent citizens under an unpleasant light and they threaten to withdraw funding from the hospital his doctor father is building if he doesn't lay off the case. Powell's father, Davenport, is unconcerned about this threat and tells his son to go on with his detecting. Powell learns that the victim's mother is a local eccentric named "Crazy Mary" who lives in a shack outside of town. When he goes to see her, he finds her murdered, but also finds a sketch that confirms his suspicions. He calls all the suspects together in his usual fashion and reconstructs the case until he reveals that there is indeed a spy ring operating in town, and the mysterious couple buying the paintings, Vinson and Ames, are part of it. But it is Corrigan, who had been helping the investigation so he could keep a leash on it, that is the spymaster. Perhaps the new sobriety of Nick and Nora were to blame for the flatness of this installment, or perhaps it was the way Nora's IQ, once a match for Nick's, seemed to have fallen through the floor since the earlier films, or the fact that Woody Van Dyke, who had helmed all the series to this point, was dead. Loy had not acted in three years, being kept busy with her war work and her marriage, and some of the chemistry that she and Powell once had was definitely gone. On the plus side, though, audiences were happy to be rid of little Nick, Jr., and the inevitable cloying cuteness he always brought, and the performances of the MGM stock company of character actors were fine as always, particularly Watson and Davenport as Nick's parents. The film was a big hit at the box office, and although the series would produce one more episode, the fizz was definitely gone.

p, Everett Riskin; d, Richard Thorpe; w, Robert Riskin, Dwight Taylor, Harry Kurnitz (based on characters created by Dashiell Hammett); ph, Karl Freund; m, David Snell; ed, Ralph E. Winters; art d, Cedric Gibbons, Edward Carfagno; set d, Edwin B. Willis.

Crime **(PR:A MPAA:NR)**

THIN RED LINE, THE½** (1964) 99m Philip Yordan-Security-A.C.E./AA bw

Keir Dullea *(Pvt. Doll)*, Jack Warden *(1st Sgt. Welsh)*, James Philbrook *(Col. Tall)*, Ray Daley *(Capt. Stone)*, Bob Kanter *(Fife)*, Merlyn Yordan *(Judy)*, Kieron Moore *(Lt. Band)*, Jim Gillen *(Capt. Gaff)*, Steve Rowland *(Pvt. Mazzi)*, Stephen Levy *(Staff Sgt. Stack)*, Mark Johnson *(Medic)*, Edward King, Jack Gaskins, Graham Sumner, Charles Stalnaker, Gary Lasdun, Jeffrey O'Kelly, Joe Collins, Thomas Freeman, Ted Macauley, Howard Hagen, Bill Barrett, Thomas Entwhistle, Francis Deale, Gonzalo Largo, Russ Stoddard, Evaristo Falco, Ben Tatar, John Clarke, Stan Nelson, Solomon Silva, Bill Christmas, Frank Koomen, Harold Core.

Filmed on location in Spain, this adaption of the James Jones novel takes place during the invasion of Guadalcanal in WW II. Dullea is a private who does not want to die in the conflict and pilfers a pistol for extra protection in case of any unforseen danger. Warden is Dullea's sergeant, a man whose life has been permanently scarred by war, leaving him a bitter and sadistic man. He quickly develops ill feelings towards Dullea and an animosity builds between the two. After Dullea kills a Japanese soldier, the young man is horrified, an attitude that further irks Warden. The next day, after dreaming of his wife back home, Dullea wipes out an enemy machine gun nest. Though his peers admire the private's courage, Warden sees through this and suspects that Dullea is actually beginning to feel the same sadistic thrill towards war that the older man does. However, the rift between them still remains, even though the pair must work together to clear a dangerous gorge of explosive mines. As the operation is carried out, the American troops are surprised by an enemy raid. Though only a few members of the platoon are left, the remaining Americans try to capture a group of caves that the Japanese machinegunners use as hideouts. These caves sit atop a cliff that Dullea is forced to climb to gain access to the desired position. Once there, the private discovers that the caves form an elaborate maze. Eventually his comrades join him but once more are attacked by the Japanese. Warden throws himself into the line of fire to save Dullea, and in the end, dies in the arms of the young man he so despised. Dullea and Warden are well-matched opposites. The younger man bears a keen intensity fueled by his will to survive, while Warden displays a more laidback nature, hardened by his experiences in the military. Marton's direction handles the material well, pumping the needed energy into battle sequences that accurately capture the mayhem and brutality of war. The film falters, though, in trying to do too much in too short of a running time. In adapting Jones' novel for the screen, whole scenes from the book have been neatly compacted, which causes occasional confusion. Motivations are often just touched on without any probing into the psychology of men at war. The result is a good, though not entirely satisfactory, account of two men's journey through hell.

p, Sidney Harmon; d, Andrew Marton; w, Bernard Gordon (based on the novel by James Jones); ph, Manuel Berenguer; m, Malcolm Arnold; ed, Derek Parsons; md, Arnold; art d, Jose Alguero; spec eff, Ron Ballanger, Pat Carr; makeup, Emilio Puyol.

War **(PR:O MPAA:NR)**

THING, THE***** (1951) 87m Winchester/RKO bw (AKA: THE THING FROM ANOTHER WORLD)

Kenneth Tobey *(Capt. Pat Hendry)*, James Arness *(The Thing)*, Margaret Sheridan *(Nikki Nicholson)*, Robert Cornthwaite *(Dr. Arthur Carrington)*, Douglas Spencer *(Ned "Scotty" Scott)*, James Young *(Lt. Ed Dykes)*, Dewey Martin *(Bob, the Crew Chief)*, Robert Nichols *(Lt. Ken Erickson)*, William Self *(Sgt. Barnes)*, Eduard Franz *(Dr. Stern)*, John Dierkes *(Dr. Chapman)*, Sally Creighton *(Mrs. Chapman)*, Paul Frees *(Dr. Vorrhees)*, George Fenneman *(Redding)*, David McMann *(Gen. Fogerty)*, Billy Curtis *(The Thing While Shrinking)*, Everett Glass *(Prof. Wilson)*, Tom Steele *(Stuntman)*, Norbert Schiller *(Dr. Laurenz)*, Edmund Breon *(Dr. Ambrose)*, William Neff *(Olson)*, Lee Tung Foo, Walter Ng *(Cooks)*, Robert Stevenson *(Capt. Smith)*, Robert Gutknecht *(Cpl. Hauser)*, Robert Bray *(Captain)*, Ted Cooper, Allan Ray *(Lieutenants)*, Nicholas Byron *(Ted Richards)*.

One of the greatest science-fiction films ever made, THE THING was produced by Howard Hawks and supposedly directed by his editor on RED RIVER, Christian Nyby. Anyone familiar with the Hawks' films will immediately recognize that the director's style, themes, and handling of actors dominate THE THING, and that Nyby's participation was that of an apprentice observing the master. Set in the sub-zero environment of the North Pole, the film follows an Air Force captain, Tobey, as he and his crew fly to Polar Expedition Six–a group of scientists led by Cornthwaite who are studying arctic conditions–to investigate reports that a flying craft of some sort has crashed into the ice. At the base camp Tobey finds an old flame, Sheridan, who is working as Cornthwaite's secretary. Sheridan is a tough woman in the Hawksian mold and the romantic banter between her and Tobey is a joy to watch. When Tobey meets with Cornthwaite, he is shown pictures of the strange object as it streaked across the sky. A party is organized to investigate the crash site and when they arrive they discover that the object has sunk into the ice and has been frozen. The soldiers, scientists, and Spencer, a journalist, fan out to determine the shape of the object. When they all take their places at the edge of the object, they have formed a perfect circle. Always looking for a catchy buzzword that will make good copy for the folks back home, Spencer breathlessly exclaims, "A flying saucer!" The men decide to melt the ship out of the ice by detonating thermite bombs around it, but the plan goes awry and the ship is destroyed. Gravely disappointed, the men head back for their plane only to discover something else frozen in the ice–an alien. Using axes, they cut out a block of ice encasing the extraterrestrial corpse and bring it back to the base camp. While the soldiers and scientists debate over what to do with the creature, the ice melts and the thing (Arness) breaks free of its prison–very much alive. The soldier assigned to guard the thing shoots it several times, but the bullets have no effect and it escapes from the room and runs out into the bitter cold. Soldiers and scientists crowd around the windows to get a glimpse of the creature and they watch as Arness is attacked by the sled dogs. The giant creature (it's eight feet tall) takes on three dogs at once and kills them all. It then disappears into the blizzard. Tobey sends men out to investigate and they find the severed forearm of the thing that one of the dogs managed to bite off. When Cornthwaite examines the limb he discovers that it possesess no flesh or blood. It is a vegetable of some sort. From the hands fall seedpods and Cornthwaite marvels at the creature's ability to reproduce without "pain or pleasure as we know it." When the severed hand begins to move on its own, the scientists surmise that it draws nourishment from blood. Tobey prepares a search party for the thing and Cornthwaite, who is convinced the being is superior to humans in every way, begs the military man not to harm the alien. Tobey agrees, if it can be done without costing lives. While the soldiers are out in the icy wasteland, the scientists discover that the thing has broken a hole in the base greenhouse and is using it to bring his prey (this time it's the dogs, but the thing's tastes will soon escalate) there to feed. Cornwaithe assigns his men to keep watch in the greenhouse for when the thing returns. Tobey and his party return empty-handed, but they are soon called to action by the screams of one of the scientists, Franz, heralding the return of the thing to the greenhouse. Franz tells Tobey that he and two others were in the greenhouse when the thing returned. It immediately grabbed the two others and killed them, hanging their bodies upside-down from the rafters to drain their blood as if they were slaughtered cattle. Tobey runs to the door of the greenhouse and opens it– only to find himself staring right into the eyes of the thing. He swiftly closes the door, but the thing's arm (it has grown a new one) gets caught in the door and the jamb is ripped apart as the thing retracts its arm. Tobey secures the doors and then turns his attention to Cornthwaite, now convinced that the scientist is insane. Cornthwaite protests that he has been trying to learn more about the creature and he shows Tobey the pods that have grown from the seeds found in the thing's hand. Fed with bottles of blood plasma, the seeds have grown quite large in a matter of hours. Stunned and angered by the scientist's foolishness, Tobey restricts Cornthwaite and the others to their lab. He then brainstorms with his men for a way to kill the creature. When Tobey wonders, "What do you do with a vegetable?" Sheridan immediately responds, "Boil it, stew it, bake it, fry it." The men decide to try and fry the beast by setting it on fire. Using a geiger counter (the thing is a bit radioactive as well), the men determine that the thing has left the greenhouse and is now about to enter the base camp through a door in the radio room. The soldiers fill buckets with kerosene and shut off the lights. The thing forces the door open and is briefly silhouetted in the doorway. It takes a few steps forward and is doused with kerosene. One of the soldiers shoots a flare gun into the alien's chest and the monster bursts into flames. The heat does not affect it, however, and it continues to make its way through the room. More kerosene is thrown on the thing and it finally dashes over to a window, throws itself through, and runs off into the night–still in flames. The trick seemed to work, but instead of burning the whole base down, they decide to try and electrocute the thing. The soldiers rig a metal grate in the corridor and hook it to a generator. The thing returns and the men try to lure it towards them. Cornthwaite runs up and trys to reason with the monster, telling it that he wants to be friends, but he is answered by a violent swipe of the arm which sends him across the room. As the thing approaches, it walks to the side of the metal grate, thwarting the electrocution plan. One of the soldiers slides an ax down the corridor toward the monster and the thing nimbly sidesteps the object–but lands on the grate. The soldiers kick on the juice and the thing screams in pain as it is electrocuted. The thing shrinks in size until it is nothing more than a smoking lump of coal. The men reassemble the radio room and reporter Spencer is allowed to send out his story: "One of the world's greatest battles was fought and won today by the human race. Here on top of the world, a handful of American soldiers met the first invasion from another planet. Now, before I bring you the details of the battle, I bring you a warning...to everyone listening to the sound of my voice. Tell the world. Tell this to everyone wherever they are: 'Watch the skies! Watch everywhere. Keep on looking. Watch the skies!'" THE THING was based rather loosely on a science-fiction story by John W. Campbell, Jr. (it was first published under his pseudonym, Don A. Stuart) in which the alien had the ability to change its shape at will, causing havoc among the soldiers who begin to suspect *each other* of harboring the monster (John Carpenter's remake of THE THING in 1982 stuck closer to this story line but the film turned out to be a massive disappointment). Lederer's screenplay (rumor has it that frequent Lederer-Hawks collaborator Ben Hecht had a hand in it as well) streamlines the narrative and allows Hawks to concentrate on the human interaction in the face of crisis. Where the original story (and Carpenter's remake) is a pantheon to paranoia among comrades, Hawks' film revels in the interworkings of a hardened group of professionals capable of handling any crisis if they stick together. Tobey is the leader of the group and the star of the film, but the characters operate as an ensemble and no one is really given much solo screen time. Their unity is what the film is about (with the point beautifully emphasized visually when they assemble to make the circle on the ice), and anyone familiar with Hawks' work will know that it is a theme that runs throughout most of his films. While the film is frequently stunning on a visual level, THE THING is a symphony for the ears as well, with Hawks' patented overlapping dialog with the protagonists snappily going about their work, asking each other questions, and providing quick, succinct responses. Whereas it is the very nature of the science-fiction film to be filled with long, ponderous explanations of the rather incredible things presented, Hawks manages to handle the same material in a wholly realistic and entertaining manner sprinkled with doses of light humor. THE THING also draws the line that would mark most science-fiction films of the 1950s, the conflict between the military and science. Although Cornthwaite is shown in a bad light, Hawks still has compassion for the character. Cornthwaite believes the invader to be a superior being and is sympathetic to it because he sees it as an extension of himself–high intellect devoid of emotion, feeling, or pain, the perfect scientist (although the viewer sees it as a violent, rampaging monster which demonstrates little intelligence, only strong survival instincts). The scientist's intentions are valid and noble–of course, studying the thing would yield valuable information–but his intellectual concerns begin to take over his rational sensibilities and lives are lost because of it. Hawks is a much more practical man–sometimes the price of knowledge is too high. If the survival of the group is threatened, the choice is clear: the group (i.e. society) must survive. In a genre where elaborate special effects are required (and expected), THE THING is sweet simplicity. Much like a horror film, the monster (played by James Arness who would later be Sheriff Matt Dillon in TV's "Gunsmoke") is only glimpsed in shadows and darkness, thus making the imagination fill in the terrifying details. Harlan's cinematography and Tiomkin's eerie electronic score (he used a theramin) provide enough chills to satisfy any horror fan. No ray-guns, strange costumes, or futuristic inventions are needed here; even the spaceship is only suggested–never seen. The fact that the alien closely resembles a man heightens the sense of personal (human) struggle that is a cornerstone of all good drama. Those who still doubt that this is Hawks' film need only look at production stills that show Hawks very much in control of the actors, and examine Nyby's directorial filmography. There was a five-year gap between THE THING and Nyby's next film, HELL ON DEVIL'S ISLAND, which is odd for a "hot" director (THE THING garnered critical raves and was a big hit at the box office). None of Nyby's subsequent films even came close to the brilliance of THE THING, leaving one to assume that Hawks granted his friend Nyby directorial credit as a favor so that the editor could begin a new career.

p, Howard Hawks; d, Christian Nyby, (uncredited) Hawks; w, Charles Lederer (based on the story "Who Goes There," by John Wood Campbell, Jr. 'Don A. Stuart'); ph, Russell Harlan; m, Dimitri Tiomkin; ed, Roland Gross; md, Tiomkin; art d, Albert D'Agostino, John J. Hughes; set d, Darrell Silvera, William Stevens; spec eff, Donald Stewart, Linwood Dunn; stunts, Tom Steele; makeup, Lee Greenway.

Science Fiction   Cas.   (PR:C   MPAA:NR)

THING, THE**   (1982) 108m UNIV c

Kurt Russell (*MacReady*), A. Wilford Brimley (*Blair*), T.K. Carter (*Nauls*), David Clennon (*Palmer*), Keith David (*Childs*), Richard Dysart (*Dr. Copper*), Charles Hallahan (*Norris*), Peter Maloney (*Bennings*), Richard Masur (*Clark*), Donald Moffat (*Garry*), Joel Polis (*Fuchs*), Thomas Waites (*Windows*), Norbert Weisser (*Norwegian*), Larry Franco (*Norwegian Passenger with Rifle*), Nate Irwin (*Helicopter Pilot*), William Zeman (*Pilot*), Anthony Cecere, Kent Hays, Larry Holt, Melvin Jones, Eric Mansker, Denver Mattson, Clint Rowe, Ken Strain, Rock Walker, Jerry Wills.

A major disappointment. Horror director John Carpenter let the special effects run amok (literally) in this remake of the 1951 science fiction classic THE THING, and they ooze over everything else in the film. The plot is pared down to the essentials: a group of American scientists in the Antarctic find the frozen remains of an alien, which they soon thaw out. The only problem is that the alien is not dead and it springs back to life, taking on the form of any living being that suits its purpose (dogs, men, etc.) in order to feed. This boils the film down to a weak examination of paranoia (who is human and who is not?) among the survivors. The cast is superb, but unfortunately they are not allowed to show their stuff because their

characters are nothing more than fodder for the effects and their performances are limited to standing around grimacing at the gore in a series of dull reaction shots. Russell once again sleepwalks through his role (he did the same in ESCAPE FROM NEW YORK), and the ending of the film is unsatisfying and ambiguous. The effects are absolutely fantastic, complicated, and grotesque but the film ultimately fails because it is more an exercise in technology than an essay in human terror.

p, David Foster, Lawrence Turman; d, John Carpenter; w, Bill Lancaster (based on the story "Who Goes There?" by John W. Campbell, Jr.); ph, Dean Cundey (Panavision, Technicolor); m, Ennio Morricone; ed, Todd Ramsay; prod d, John J. Lloyd; art d, Henry Larrecq, set d, John Dwyer, Graeme Murray; spec eff, Roy Arbogast, Albert Whitlock, Leroy Routly, Michael A. Clifford; makeup, Rob Bottin.

Science Fiction   Cas.   (PR:O   MPAA:R)

THING THAT CAME FROM ANOTHER WORLD, THE
                                                    (SEE: THING, THE, 1951)

THING THAT COULDN'T DIE, THE*   (1958) 69m UNIV bw

William Reynolds (*Gordon Hawthorne*), Andra Martin (*Linda Madison*), Jeffrey Stone (*Hank Huston*), Carolyn Kearney (*Jessica Burns*), Peggy Converse (*Aunt Flavia McIntire*), Robin Hughes (*Gideon Drew*), James Anderson (*Boyd Abercrombie*), Charles Horvath (*Mike*), Forrest Lewis (*Ash*).

Something is missing in this creepy story about a girl who uncovers the head and then the body of a man who was beheaded by Sir Francis Drake in the 16th century. The atmosphere is eerie enough, with a soundtrack that helps heighten this aspect. As the young girl who accidently uncovers the thing while playing with a divining rod, Kearney has the right aura of innocence. But once this monster is put together, so to say, there is just no place for the plot to go. It just dies.

p&d, Will Cowan; w, David Duncan; ph, Russell Metty, Clifford Stine; ed, Edward Curtiss; md, Joseph Gershenson; art d, Alexander Golitzen, Eric Orbom; cos, Bill Thomas.

Horror   (PR:C   MPAA:NR)

THING WITH TWO HEADS, THE**   (1972) 93m Saber/AIP c

Ray Milland (*Dr. Maxwell Kirshner*), Rosey Grier (*Jack Moss*), Don Marshall (*Dr. Fred Williams*), Roger Perry (*Dr. Philip Desmond*), Kathy Baumann (*Nurse Patricia*), Chelsea Brown (*Lila*), John Dullaghan (*Thomas*), John Bliss (*Dr. Donald Smith*), Rick Baker (*Gorilla*), Lee Frost (*Sgt. Hacker*), Dick Whittington (*TV Newscaster*), William Smith (*Hysterical Condemned Man*), Tommy Cook (*Chaplain*), Bruce Kimball (*Police Lieutenant*), Jane Kellem (*Miss Mullen*), Lee Frost (*Sgt. Hacker*), Wes Bishop (*Dr. Smith*), Roger Gentry (*Police Sergeant*), Britt Nilsson (*Nurse*), Phil Hoover (*Policeman*), Rod Steele (*Medical Salesman*), Michael Viner (*Prison Guard*), Jerry Butler, George E. Carey, Albert Zugsmith (*Guest Performers*).

Racist scientist Milland is dying of cancer. He figures the only way to defeat the disease is stitch his own head next to someone else's and conduct some bizarre two-headed experiments with a gorilla (created by Hollywood makeup whiz Baker). When he slips into a coma, Milland has quite a surprise in store when he is stitched onto the shoulders of ex-pro football player Grier, a wrongly condemned convict who volunteered for the experiment to save his life. When he wakes up Milland and his traveling companion run around fighting for control of the body by screaming racist remarks and punching each other in their respective heads. Directed by a 1960s adult film veteran with much of the same production team of the highly inferior THE INCREDIBLE TWO-HEADED TRANSPLANT, THE THING WITH TWO HEADS somehow overcomes its inherent stupidity with some zippy direction and Baker's excellent makeup jobs. Best of all is the rapport between Milland and Grier. The two make this inane material work with an unusual comic chemistry that really fits.

p, Wes Bishop; d, Lee Frost; w, Frost, Bishop, James Gordon White (based on a story by Frost, Bishop); ph, Jack Steely (DeLuxe Color); m, Robert O. Ragland; ed, Ed Forsyth; m/l, "Oh Happy Day" (performed by the Mike Curb Congregation), "A Prayer," David Angel, Porter Jordan (sung by Jerry Butler), "The Thing Theme (Police Chase)," Jordan (performed by Jordan); stunts, Bud Elkins, Paul Nuckles; makeup, Rick Baker; creative makeup design, Dan Striepeke, Gail Brown, Tom Burman, Charles Schram, James White, Pete Peterson.

Horror   (PR:C   MPAA:PG)

THING WITHOUT A FACE, A   (SEE: PYRO, 1964, US/Span.)

THINGS ARE LOOKING UP**½   (1934, Brit.) 78m GAU bw

Cicely Courtneidge (*Cicely/Bertha Fytte*), Max Miller (*Joey*), William Gargan (*Van Guard*), Mary Lawson (*Mary Fytte*), Dick Henderson (*Mr. Money*), Dick Henderson, Jr (*Money, Jr.*), Mark Lester (*Chairman*), Henrietta Watson (*Miss MacTavish*), Cicely Oates (*Miss Crabbe*), Judy Kelly (*Opal*), Danny Green (*Big Black Fox*), Wyn Weaver (*Governor*), Alma Taylor (*Schoolmistress*), Suzanne Lenglen (*Herself*), D. Hay Plumb, Charles Mortimer, Vivian Leigh.

Courtneidge plays a double role in this quite good comedy, as a teacher in a private girls' school and as her twin, a circus trick rider who assumes her sister's place when the former elopes with a wrestler. She is a great success in her new position and has been raised to headmistress before her sister returns. Vivian Leigh (she had not yet changed the spelling of her first name) makes her film debut here as a schoolgirl with only one line, but a number of closeups. She tried out for the part mostly on a lark, but enjoyed the experience of acting so much that she began to devote more of her energies that way.

p, Michael Balcon; d, Albert de Courville; w, Stafford Dickens, Con West (based on a story by de Courville, Daisy Fisher); ph, Glen MacWilliams.

Comedy   (PR:A   MPAA:NR)

THINGS ARE TOUGH ALL OVER zero
                                    (1982) 90m C&C Brown/COL c

Richard "Cheech" Marin (Himself/Mr. Slyman), Tommy Chong (Himself/Prince Habib), Michael Aragon (Cheech's Double), Toni Attell (Cocktail Waitress), Mike Bacarella (Cop), Billy Beck (Pop), Don Bovingloh (Maitre d'), Richard Calhoun (Drummer), Jennifer Condos (Bass), John Corona (St. Louis Biker), David Couwlier (Man with Tongue), Shelby Fiddis, Rikki Marin (French Girls), Aaron Freeman (Cop), Mike Friedman (Car Rental), Evelyn Guerrero (Donna), Maya Harman (Belly Dancer), Vanaghan S. Housepian (Henchman), Lance Kinsey (Plastic Surgeon), Irvin Koszewski (Chong's Double), Janice Ladik (Mom in Laundromat), Jay Lawson (Gas Station Attendant), Senta Moses (Kid), Dorothy Newmann (Mom), John Paragon, Sandy Weintraub (Red Carpet Men), Shabazz Perez (Man with Toupee), Gregory Polcyn (Busboy), Ben Powers (Pimp), Ernest Rayford III, John Tisdale (Car Wash Attendants), John Steadman (Oldtimer), Rip Taylor (Himself), George Wallace (The Champ), Ruby Wax (Patron), Diana Wild (Waitress), Farouk A. Zurond (Chauffeur).

Cheech and Chong play dual roles as wealthy Arabs and the two buffoons the Middle Easterners hire to drive a limousine stuffed with a secret cache of money. The two chauffeurs don't know about the money, of course, and end up losing it along the road between Chicago and Las Vegas. The thin plot line is nothing more than a clothesline for the drug-inspired duo to hang their dirty-underwear humor on. The jokes tossed into this cesspool involve Cheech and Chong in drag, herpes, and an S & M porno adventure featuring the comedians' real life spouses Fiddis and Marin. Peroxided comedian Taylor shows up to toss confetti and spout a few of his witless one-liners. Avildsen, who had previously worked as an editor for the pair's earlier films, takes over the director's chair from Chong and proves himself to be just as incompetent as his predecessor. Things must be tough in the movie business if bile like this gets fobbed off as comedy. Apart from a peyote button popped by Chong, the film is free of hallucinogens, a first for the nominally comical drug duo, who had at least an excuse of being stoned in their previous cinematic ventures.

p, Howard Brown; d, Thomas K. Avildsen; w, "Cheech" Marin, Thomas Chong; ph, Bobby Byrne (Panavision, Metrocolor); m, Gaye Delorme; ed, Dennis Dolan; prod d, Richard Tom Sawyer; set d, Gary Moreno; m/l, Delorme.

Comedy   Cas.   (PR:O   MPAA:R)

THINGS HAPPEN AT NIGHT* (1948, Brit.) 79m Tudor-Alliance/REN bw

Gordon Harker (Joe Harris), Alfred Drayton (Wilfred Prescott), Robertson Hare (Vincent Ebury), Olga Lindo (Hilda Prescott), Gwyneth Vaughan (Audrey Prescott), Garry Marsh (Spencer), Wylie Watson (Watson), Joan Young (Mrs. Venning), Beatrice Campbell (Joyce Prescott), Grace Denbigh-Russell (Miss Handcock), Judith Warden (Mrs. Fortescue), June Elvin (Miss Minter), Knox Crichton (Himself), Eric Micklewood (Nobby Ebury), Charles Doe (Bill), Michael Callin (Mac), George Bryden (Freddie Simpson), Eric Robinson (Himself), L. Franks (Midget), Marilyn Williams (Singer), Ernest Borrow, Esme Lewis, Lillian Stanley, Peter Reynolds, Patricia Owens.

Drayton's house and family are plagued by a poltergeist, so he asks insurance investigator Harker to come and investigate. With help from scientist Marsh he discovers that the malign spirit is residing in Vaughan, Drayton's youngest daughter. But it soon switches to Harker as comic complications pile on. Flat comedy with a number of stars well past their prime.

p, A.R. Shipman, James Carter; d, Francis Searle; w, St. John Legh Clowes (based on the play "The Poltergeist" by Frank Harvey); ph, Leslie Rowson; m, George Melachrino; ed, Eily Boland; art d, Harry Moore.

Comedy   (PR:A   MPAA:NR)

THINGS OF LIFE, THE***   (1970, Fr./Ital./Switz.) 90m Lira Fida Sonocam/COL c (LES CHOSES DE LA VIE)

Michel Piccoli (Pierre), Romy Schneider (Helene), Lea Massari (Catherine), Gerard Lartigau (Bertrand), Jean Bouise (Francois), Boby Lapointe (Driver of the Pig Truck), Herve Sand (Truckdriver), Henri Nassiet (Pierre's

Father), Marcelle Arnold (Helene's Mother), Roger Crouzet (Promoter), Jean-Pierre Zola (Helene's Father), Betty Beckers, Dominique Zardi (Hitchhikers), Gabrielle Doulcet (Guitte), Jacques Richard (Nurse), Claude Confortes (Doctor), Jerry Brouer (Suitor), Jean Gras (Building Site Foreman), Marie-Pierre Casey (Postmistress), Gerard Streiff (Motorcyclist), Max Amyl (Priest), Isabelle Saroyan (Nurse), M. Carmet (Paul), Raoul Delpard (Ambulance Man), Loudiche (Intern), Christian Bertola (Surgeon), Beram, Luigi (Policemen), Karine Jeantet (Telephonist), Mme. Blome, Mme. Duval (Customers at the Post Office).

Schneider, a young woman having an affair with older architect Piccoli, does not understand why her lover will not give up things from his past life. Piccoli still has feelings for his estranged wife (Massari) and his son and father. He evades Schneider's request that they vacation together by promising his son (Bouise) that they shall go sailing together. Schneider confronts him at a party she throws, demanding he make a choice about the future. Piccoli goes on a business trip to Rennes and writes to his lover from there. The letter explains how they must end their affair but Piccoli changes his mind and does not mail the letter. He is killed in an auto accident though and Massari finds the letter in his coat pocket, destroying the document before Schneider arrives at the hospital.

p, Roland Girard, Jean Bolvary; d, Claude Sautet; w, Paul Guimard, Jean-Loup Dabadie, Sautet (based on the novel Les Choses de la Vie by Paul Guimard); ph, Jean Boffety (Eastmancolor); m, Philippe Sarde; ed, Jacqueline Thiedot; art d, Andre Piltant; makeup, Irene Servet.

Drama   (PR:C   MPAA:GP)

THINGS TO COME****   (1936, Brit.) 113m LFP/UA bw

Raymond Massey (John Cabal/Oswald Cabal), Edward Chapman (Pippa Passworthy/Raymond Passworthy), Ralph Richardson (The Boss), Margaretta Scott (Roxana/Rowena), Cedric Hardwicke (Theotocopulos), Maurice Braddell (Dr. Harding), Sophie Stewart (Mrs. Cabal), Derrick de Marney (Richard Gordon), Ann Todd (Mary Gordon), Pearl Argyle (Catherine Cabal), Kenneth Villiers (Maurice Passworthy), Ivan Brandt (Morden Mitani), Anne McLaren (The Child), John Clements (The Airman), Abraham Sofaer (The Jew), Patricia Hilliard (Janet Gordon), Charles Carson (Great Grandfather), Patrick Barr (World Transport Official), Anthony Holles (Simon Burton), Allan Jeayes (Mr. Cabal), Pickles Livingston (Horrie Passworthy), George Sanders (Pilot), Paul O'Brien.

Not since Fritz Lang's METROPOLIS had there been a science fiction film of such epic scope and vision as was to be found in Alexander Korda's production of H.G. Wells' 1933 essay on the future The Shape of Things to Come. The story begins in the year 1940 and is set in an urban metropolis known as Everytown. It is Christmas time and the celebration is tempered by the fear of another world war. As Massey holds a discussion on the nature of war with his friends Chapman and Braddell, scores of bombers are flying over the English channel to drop bombs on Everytown. Soon the war is on and Massey, a pilot, is called to duty. The war drags on for decades and the devastation is immense. By 1966 a strange disease has gripped the land and those who have survived the destruction are now being killed by the lethal illness. In 1970, the disease has run its course, having elminated half of the world's population. The ruins of Everytown are now run by Richardson, a vagabond killer who has set himself up as ruler and sends a private army to do battle with other survivors who live in the nearby hills. Richardson's dream is to fix his fleet of airplanes so that he can broaden his domination and secure oil-rich territories. One day the silence is broken by the drone of a modern aircraft. The strange looking plane lands and from it emerges Massey, much older now, wearing a jet-black spacesuit and an enormous glass helmet. Massey announces that he is a representative of "Wings over the World" an organization of scientists and engineers determined to end war and build a new civilization based on technology. Richardson sees Massey as a threat to his fiefdom and has him imprisoned, sneering at him with the line, "What do you think of that, Mr. 'Wings over the World'?" His incarceration does not last long, for a fleet of planes sent by "Wings over the World" soon arrives and drops bombs containing the "gas of peace," a harmless gas which causes all the citizens of Everytown to lose consciousness. Inexplicably, only Richardson dies from the gas and Massey finds it appropriate that such a savage anachronism perish before the building of a new world. What follows is a lengthy montage sequence showing the rebuilding of Everytown. Giant digging machines plow their way under the earth where the new, entirely self-suffcient city will be constructed. Artificial sunlight is perfected, as are people-moving machines, television, and communications. By the year 2036, Everytown is a temple of new technology and man turns his attention to the stars. Massey's great-grandson (also played by Massey) is the ruler of the new Everytown, and he finds himself having to cope with a revolt led by Hardwicke, an artist who feels that the new society has forsaken human values for technology. The focus of Hardwicke's hatred is a giant space cannon Massey has constructed for the purpose of launching a rocket to colonize the moon. Massey's own daughter, Argyle, and her boy friend Villiers, the son of Massey's friend Chapman, volunteer to be the first to travel to the moon. Though Chapman has reservations about his son's participation in the event, the decision is made for them when Hardwicke's minions revolt and head for the space cannon intent on destroying it. Villiers and Argyle race for the spacecraft and they are launched in the nick of time. The film ends as Massey and

Chapman stare into space confident that mankind's true destiny lies somewhere in the vast reaches of the universe. Eager to have Wells' participation in the project, producer Korda approached the great author and offered him the chance to write the screenplay for the film. Two years and four drafts later, with considerable help from Korda, writer Lajos Biro, and director Menzies, the script was completed. Wells was allowed to wander around the set during production and he influenced every detail of the film from the look of the costumes and set design to the blocking of the actors. Everything that THINGS TO COME is, its strengths and considerable weaknesses, is directly attributable to Wells. While the epic scope of the film and its predictions and vision of the future are impressive, the human element is sorely lacking. Wells was a product of the Victorian age and the dialog in his script is very stilted and uninteresting. There is little interaction among characters and everyone makes speeches. Massey found the dialog nearly impossible to handle and it is a tribute to his skill as an actor that the speeches play as well as they do. Though the film fails as a human drama, it succeeds impressively in the scenes of devastation and reconstruction–a purely visual experience. Korda's brother Vincent was in charge of the production design and he plundered every new concept in architecture, industry, furniture, and clothing design for the Everytown of 2036. Famed Hungarian futurist Laszlo Moholy-Nagy was hired to contribute his vision, but his designs where scrapped as being too impractical. Wells, of course, had final approval on everything but eventually he grew frustrated with the filmmaking process and admitted he knew little about making movies: "Many of the sequences which slipped easily from my pen when I wrote the scenario were extremely difficult to screen and some were impossible," he would later write. Though he stayed on the set and observed the shooting, his only tampering later on was to adjust the costumes on attractive female extras so they looked just right. Director Menzies, himself one of the most influential art directors in the history of motion pictures, was the perfect choice to direct the film (though Lewis Milestone was signed on at one time). Though his skill at directing actors was negligible (considering the written-in-stone dialog he was saddled with it really didn't matter), Menzies possessed a true feel for design and he knew how to photograph it. Perhaps the most significant contribution to the film is the musical score by Arthur Bliss. At Wells' insistence, Bliss was brought in before production started and he composed parts of the score based on the script and Wells' suggestions (the author felt that the music should be incorporated into the filmmaking process from the beginning, instead of after the filming was completed). The result was that some scenes were shot with the music already in mind, thus the score was wholly integrated with the visuals. Bliss' work on the film proved so popular with critics and the public that his music for THINGS TO COME was the first movie score to be recorded commercially and sold in record stores. When it was all over Korda had spent over $1.5 million on THINGS TO COME, an incredible sum for the time and the most money he had ever spent on a single production. The film failed to ignite the box offices worldwide, but it eventually made money. The original release print in Britain ran 130 minutes, but the running time was cut for release in the U.S. (there are several different versions of the film now in distribution running the gamut from 96m, 100m, 113m, to 130m). Despite its flaws, THINGS TO COME is a truly epic work which continually fascinates, if only for the contributions of H.G. Wells.

p, Alexander Korda; d, William Cameron Menzies; w, H.G. Wells, Lajos Biro (based on the book *The Shape of Things to Come* by Wells); ph, Georges Perinal; m, Sir Arthur Bliss; ed, Charles Crichton, Francis Lyon; prod d, Vincent Korda; md, Muir Mathieson; cos, John Armstrong, Rene Hubert, Marchioness of Queensbury; spec eff, Ned Mann, Lawrence Butler, Edward Cohen, Harry Zech, Wally Vaevers, Ross Jacklin; astronomical adviser, Nigel Tangye.

Science Fiction   **Cas.**   **(PR:C   MPAA:NR)**

THINK DIRTY zero   (1970, Brit.) 94m BL c (GB: EVERY HOME
                                                                SHOULD HAVE ONE)

Marty Feldman (*Teddy*), Shelley Berman (*Nat Kaplan*), Judy Cornwell (*Liz*), Julie Ege (*Inga Giltenberg*), Patrick Cargill (*Wallace Truefit, M.P.*), Jack Watson (*McLaughlin*), Patience Collier (*Mrs. Levin*), Penelope Keith (*Lotte von Gelbstein*), Dinsdale Landen (*Rev. Mellish*), John McKelvey (*Col. Belper*), Annabel Leventon (*Chandler's Secretary*), Moray Watson (*Chandler*), Sarah Badel (*Joanna Snow*), Michael Bates (*Magistrate*), Roland Curram (*Headwaiter*), Dave Lee (*Ern*), Hy Hazell (*Mrs. Kaplan*), David Hutchinson (*Stockbroker*), Judy Huxtable (*Dracula's Victim*), John Wells (*Tolworth*).

Offensive, dumb, leering comedy from Feldman, a man with a permanently fixed dumb, offensive leer. Here he is an advertising agency worker who dreams up a series of sexy commercials for a line of frozen porridge.

p, Ned Sherrin; d, Jim Clark; w, Marty Feldman, Barry Took, Denis Norden (based on a story by Milton Shulman, Herbert Kretzmer); ph, Ken Hodges (Eastmancolor); m, John Cameron; ed, Ralph Sheldon; art d, Roy Stannard; cos, Daphne Dare; m/l, Sherrin; Caryl Brahms; animation & titles, Richard Williams.

Comedy   **Cas.**   **(PR:O   MPAA:NR)**

THINK FAST, MR. MOTO***   (1937) 66m FOX bw

Peter Lorre (*Mr. Moto*), Virginia Field (*Gloria Danton*), Thomas Beck (*Bob Hitchings*), Sig Rumann (*Nicholas Marloff*), Murray Kinnell (*Mr. Joseph Wilkie*), Lotus Long (*Lela Liu*), John Rogers (*Carson, Ship's Steward*), George Cooper (*Muggs Blake*), J. Carrol Naish (*Adram*), George Hassell (*Mr. Hitchings*), Dick Alexander (*Doorman*), Frederick Vogeding (*Curio Dealer*).

Japanese detective Lorre is trailing some smugglers. He boards the ship Marco Polo on a course for the Far East and comes to know Beck, the son of the liner's owner, who is delivering a letter to Kinnell. The latter is his father's branch manager in Shanghai and the letter tells Kinnell to be on the lookout for contraband. But no such voyage is complete without intrigue which arrives in the form of Field and Rogers. The pair have been hired by Rumann to foil Beck's mission. Field romances him. Lorre kills Rogers and, on arriving in Shanghai, infiltrates the smuggler's gang. In the nightclub where Field sings Lorre is recognized as a policeman and is shot. However, he is wearing a bulletproof vest and fights off the gang. Kinnell is arrested as the mastermind of the group and all ends happily. This was the first of Lorre's Mr. Moto series; eight of the Moto films were made over the next two years. This was intended as a one-shot film. Lorre's characterization here was highly engaging. The character was taken from a fictional series in the "Saturday Evening Post" which had been inspired by a real-life Japanese detective. Some called the Moto series better than the Charlie Chan films and for good reason. The script here is witty and enjoyable, directed with good pace and well-acted by the ensemble. This was an unusual character departure for Lorre which he handled with ease. (See MR. MOTO Series, Index.)

p, Sol M. Wurtzel; d, Norman Foster; w, Foster, Howard Ellis Smith (based on the novel by John P. Marquand); ph, Harry Jackson; m, Samuel Kaylin; ed, Alex Troffey; md, Kaylin; art d, Lewis Creber; cos, Herschel; m/l, Sidney Clare, Harry Akst.

Mystery   **(PR:A   MPAA:NR)**

THIRD ALARM, THE**   (1930) 79m TIF bw

Anita Louise (*Milly Morton*), James Hall (*Dan*), Paul Hurst (*Beauty*), Jean Hersholt (*Dad Morton*), Hobart Bosworth (*Captain*), Mary Doran (*Neeta*), Dot Farley (*Woman Barber*), Nita Martan (*Mamie*), Georgie Billings (*Jimmy Morton*), Walter Perry (*Uncle*), Aileen Manning (*Orphanage Matron*), Joseph Girard, Franklyn Farnum, Tom London, Charlotte Merriam.

When a firefighter is killed, his children are sent to an orphanage despite the offer from two firefighters to look after the girl and her younger brother. When the orphanage they are sent to catches on fire, the fire company rushes to the scene and finds the children. One of the firemen weds the girl, who is now of marrying age, and the other takes another girl as his bride. An average programmer though not much different than similarly storied silent films of a few years earlier.

d, Emory Johnson; w, Frances Hyland, John F. "Jack" Natteford (based on a story by Emilie Johnson); ph, Max Dupont; art d, George Sawley; set d, Ralph De Lacy.

Drama   **(PR:A   MPAA:NR)**

THIRD ALIBI, THE½**   (1961, Brit.) 68m Eternal/GN bw

Laurence Payne (*Norman Martell*), Patricia Dainton (*Helen Martell*), Jane Griffiths (*Peggy Hill*), Edward Underdown (*Dr. Murdoch*), John Arnatt (*Supt. Ross*), Humphrey Lestocq (*Producer*), Lucy Griffiths (*Miss Potter*), Cleo Laine (*Singer*).

Tight little thriller, made on a small budget, has Payne conspiring with pregnant mistress Griffiths to murder his wife, who is also her sister. Twist ending has things not quite working out to plan, which is a powerful shock to the audience.

p, Maurice J. Wilson; d, Montgomery Tully; w, Wilson (based on the play "Moment Of Blindness" by Pip and Jane Baker); m/l, "Now and Then," Don Banks, David Dearlove (sung by Cleo Laine).

Crime   **(PR:A   MPAA:NR)**

THIRD CLUE, THE*½   (1934, Brit.) 72m FOX British bw

Basil Sydney (*Reinhardt/James Conway*), Molly Lamont (*Rosemary Clayton*), Robert Cochran (*Peter Kerrigan*), Alfred Sangster (*Rupert Clayton*), C.M. Hallard (*Gabriel Wells*), Raymond Lovell (*Robinson*), Frank Atkinson (*Lefty*), Ernest Sefton (*Newman*), Ian Fleming (*Mark Clayton*), Quinton McPherson (*Reuben*), Eric Fawcett (*Jack Tully*), Bruce Lister (*Derek Clayton*), Mabel Terry-Lewis, Adela Mavis, Noel Dainton, Rani Waller.

Convoluted crime drama which details the efforts of rival criminals to locate a cache of stolen jewels. The crooks use all manner of tricks and disguises to outwit the competition and eventually the loot is traced to a spooky old house. Routine low-budget thrills.

p, Ernest Garside; d, Albert Parker; w, Michael Barringer, Lance Sieveking, Frank Atkinson (based on the novel *The Shakespeare Murders* by Neil Gordon); ph, Alex Bryce.

Crime   (PR:A   MPAA:NR)

THIRD DAY, THE½**   (1965) 119m WD c

George Peppard (*Steve Mallory*), Elizabeth Ashley (*Alexandria Mallory*), Roddy McDowall (*Oliver Parsons*), Arthur O'Connell (*Dr. Wheeler*), Mona Washbourne (*Catherine Parsons*), Herbert Marshall (*Austin Parsons*), Robert Webber (*Dom Guardiano*), Charles Drake (*Lawrence Conway*), Sally Kellerman (*Holly Mitchell*), Arte Johnson (*Lester Aldrich*), Bill Walker (*Logan*), Vincent Gardenia (*Preston*), Janine Gray (*Totti*).

Peppard is involved in an automobile crash-up alongside a river. He loses all memory, but over the course of the next three days things come back to him in a big way. His wife (Ashley) wants to leave him and his cousin (McDowall) expects Peppard to sell him the family china manufacturing business. Problems are compounded when he learns that Kellerman, a cocktail waitress married to Johnson (good in a pre-"Laugh-In" appearance), was killed in the accident. Johnson and McDowall try to frame Peppard for the death and he is arrested. Johnson kidnaps Ashley and threatens revenge for his wife's death. But Peppard is helped by his aunt (Washbourne) in escaping just in time to save his wife. It is revealed that Kellerman drowned herself and Johnson is arrested. Despite some turgid moments in the script, the ensemble of THE THIRD DAY works well together making for a not-too-bad melodrama. The direction covers some of the script's problems with some success, taking the story at a good pace.

p&d, Jack Smight; w, Burton Wohl, Robert Presnell, Jr. (based on the novel by Joseph Hayes); ph, Robert Surtees (Panavision, Technicolor); m, Percy Faith; ed, Stefan Arnsten; art d, Edward Carrere; set d, Ralph S. Hurst; cos, Donald Brooks; m/l, "Love Me Now," Jay Livingston, Ray Evans, Faith (sung by Arte Johnson); makeup, Gordon Bau.

Drama   (PR:C   MPAA:NR)

THIRD FINGER, LEFT HAND**   (1940) 96m MGM bw

Myrna Loy (*Margot Sherwood Merrick*), Melvyn Douglas (*Jeff Thompson*), Lee Bowman (*Philip Booth*), Bonita Granville (*Vicky Sherwood*), Raymond Walburn (*Mark Sherwood*), Felix Bressart (*August Winkel*), Donald Meek (*Mr. Flandrin*), Sidney Blackmer (*Hughie Wheeler*), Ernest Whitman (*Sam*), Ann Morriss (*Beth Hampshire*), Edna Holland (*Miss Lawton*), Jean Fenwick (*Miss Carruthers*), William Halligan (*Ralph Russell*), Marjorie Gateson (*Mrs. Russell*), Halliwell Hobbes (*Burton*), Howard Lang (*Rev. Johnson*), Florence Shirley (*Agnes*), Olive Blakeney (*Louise*), Jeff Corey (*Johann*), Greta Grandstedt (*Selma*), Mira McKinney (*Miss Dell*), Marvin Stephens (*Marton*), Harry Tyler (*Martin*), Dick Paxton (*Messenger Boy*), Ray Cooke, Milton Kibbee (*Stewards*), Tim Ryan (*Mate*), Jimmy Conlin (*Ernest*), Jane Goude (*Emma*), Milton Parsons (*Photographer*), Joe Yule (*Waiter*), Philip Sleeman (*Headwaiter*), May McAvoy (*Girl Operator*), Forbes Murray (*Wilbur*), Lloyd Whitlock (*Herbert*), Jack Mulhall (*Guide*), Andrew Tombes (*Mr. Kelland*), Grace Hayle (*Mrs. Kelland*), Frank McGlynn (*Rev. Holmes*), Rita Quigley (*Elvira Kelland*), Frederick Burton (*Mr. Thompson*), Leila McIntyre (*Mrs. Thompson*), Ray Teal (*Cameraman*), John Butler (*Telegrapher*), Ken Christy (*Pullman Conductor*), Ed Cecil (*Train Conductor*), Ann Marsters, Barbara Bedford, Christina Teague, Dorothy Vernon, Alice Keating (*Women at Railroad Station*), Art Belasco, Frank O'Connor, John Webb Dillon, Ernie Alexander, Sid D'Albrook, Art Berry, Sr, Maurice Costello, Dick Rush, Cyril Ring, John Ince (*Men at Railroad Station*), Joe Whitehead (*Barney*), Helen Dickson, Gertrude Simpson (*Women in Berths*), Walter Soderling (*Man in Berth*).

Loy is a no-nonsense editor of a women's fashion magazine. She wears a gold band on her ring finger, despite her single status, to protect her from male clients, salesmen, and possibly jealous wives. Of course this simple ring is not enough to stop one man, the ever-on-the-prowl Douglas. He plays a portrait artist who tries to woo the stodgy businesswoman with little success. But the inevitable happens and romance blossoms and Loy is suddenly faced with the problem of explaining her wedding ring. THIRD FINGER, LEFT HAND was made at the height of Loy's popularity with the American public and she does a good comic job here. Unfortunately the story is ever so routine, hampered by poor dialog and badly constructed scenes. Despite the mess Loy overcomes the script problems and Douglas is his usual charming self. The direction is adequate though hampered by the script.

p, John W. Considine, Jr.; d, Robert Z. Leonard; w, Lionel Houser; ph, George Folsey; m, David Snell; ed, Elmo Veron.

Comedy   (PR:A   MPAA:NR)

THIRD KEY, THE***   (1957, Brit.) 96m EAL/RANK bw (GB: LONG ARM, THE)

Jack Hawkins (*Supt. Tom Halliday*), Dorothy Alison (*Mary Halliday*), Michael Brooke, Jr (*Tony Halliday*), John Stratton (*Sgt. Ward*), Geoffrey Keen (*Supt. Malcolm*), Newton Blick (*Comdr. Harris*), Ralph Truman (*Col. Blenkinsop*), Joss Ambler (*Shipping Officer Cashier*), Sydney Tafler (*Stone*), Richard Leech (*Night Watchman*), Meredith Edwards (*Thomas*), Ian Bannen (*Workman*), Maureen Davis (*His Wife*), George Rose (*Informer*), Glyn Houston (*Detective Sgt.*), Nicholas Parsons (*Police Constable Bates*), Alec McCowen (*Surgeon*), Ursula Howells (*Mrs. Elliot*), John Welsh (*Estate

Agent), Gillian Webb (*Housewife*), Maureen Delaney (*Daily Help*), Harry Locke (*Secondhand Dealer*), William Mervyn (*Festival Hall Manager*), Harold Goodwin (*Somerset House Official*), Sam Kydd, Stratford Johns (*Constables*), John Warwick, Barry Keegan, Warwick Ashton, David Davies, Julie Milton, Jameson Clark.

Hawkins stars as a police detective patiently sorting through the scant clues left which remain after a mysterious robbery has left a safe empty. As Hawkins investigates, the robberies continue and the detective notes that all the safes were of the same make. Checking the employee records of the safe manufacturing company, Hawkins learns that the only possible suspect has been dead for quite some time. When a workman trying to stop his getaway is killed by the robber, the stakes get even higher. Hawkins continues to dig and eventually reveals that the man, Leech, is not dead at all, and, in fact, fooled police who arrived at his first robbery by posing as a nightwatchman. The detective sets a trap for Leech at the London Festival Hall, and in an exciting climax justice is served. An unsensational, but solid crime thriller that counterpoints Hawkins' dedicated investigation with the domestic situation at his dreary middle-class home. This was the last film Ealing Studios produced in their own facilities.

p, Tom Morahan; d, Charles Frend; w, Janet Green, Robert Barr, Dorothy and Campbell Christie (based on the story "The Long Arm" by Barr); ph, Gordon Dines; m, Gerbrand Schurmann; ed, Gordon Stone; art d, Edward Carrick.

Crime   (PR:A   MPAA:NR)

THIRD LOVER, THE***   (1963, Fr./Ital.) 85m Rome-Paris Films-Lux/Atlantic bw (L'OEIL DU MALIN)

Jacques Charrier (*Albin Mercier*), Stephane Audran (*Helene Hartmann*), Walther Reyer (*Andreas Hartmann*), Daniel Boulanger, Badri (*Policemen*).

Charrier, a minor French writer, is befriended by the more successful author Reyer and his wife, Audran. They take Charrier into their Bavarian villa so he can work on a series of stories about Germany but slowly he becomes obsessed with the couple's happiness and plots to overpower and destroy it. When Reyer goes away on business, Charrier tries to seduce Audran. She rejects him and Charrien discovers that she has a secret lover. He takes photographs of the two and hands them over to Reyer on his return. Reyer ends up stabbing his wife and calls the police. Charrier is overwhelmed with guilt, knowing it was he who was responsible for the killing and tries to persuade a cynical public that this was the truth. Chabrol, the most obviously Alfred Hitchcock-inspired member of the French New Wave provides some interesting touches in this drama, often showing characters' visions through the camera lens and then turning it directly at the audience.

p, Carlo Ponti, Georges de Beauregard; d, Claude Chabrol; w, Chabrol, Martial Matthieu; ph, Jean Rabier; m, Pierre Jansen; ed, Jacques Gaillard.

Drama   (PR:O   MPAA:NR)

THIRD MAN, THE***   (1950, Brit.) 104m LFP/Korda-Selznick Releasing Organization bw

Joseph Cotten (*Holly Martins*), Orson Welles (*Harry Lime*), Alida Valli (*Anna Schmidt*), Trevor Howard (*Maj. Calloway*), Paul Hoerbiger (*Porter*), Ernst Deutsch (*Baron Kurtz*), Erich Ponto (*Dr. Winkel*), Siegfried Breuer (*Popescu*), Bernard Lee (*Sgt. Paine*), Geoffrey Keen (*British Policeman*), Hedwig Bleibtreu (*Anna's "Old Woman"*), Annie Rosar (*Porter's Wife*), Herbert Halbik (*Hansel*), Alexis Chesnakov (*Brodsky*), Wilfrid Hyde-White (*Crabbin*), Paul Hardtmuth (*Hall Porter*), Nelly Arno (*Kurtz's Mother*), Jenny Werner (*Winkel's Maid*), Leo Bieber (*Barman at Casanova*), Frederick Schreicher (*Hansel's Father*), Paul Smith (*M.P.*), Martin Boddey (*Man*), Erich Pohlmann, Geoffrey Wade, Thomas Gallagher, Walter Hortner, Martin Miller, Rona Grahame, Holga Walrow, Harry Belcher, Michael Connor, Lilly Khan 'Kann'.

A gripping and beautifully structured picture from the British film industry, THE THIRD MAN is a tour de force for director Reed, one which has left lasting memories in the minds of every moviegoer who has seen it. The enigmatic Harry Lime, an eerie, frantic chase through the sewers of Vienna, and the haunting music of a zither, are the legendary ingredients of this stellar *film noir* entry. Cotten arrives in a bleak postwar Vienna. He is a writer of pulp western novels and has been promised a job by old friend Welles. But Cotten is no sooner in his hotel room than he learns that his dear friend Welles is dead, killed in an accident and, in fact, his body is about to be lowered into a grave within the hour. He attends the funeral, stunned. Standing near the grave is a beautiful girl, Valli, who is weeping. Following the brief funeral, Cotten is stopped by Howard who asks him if he wants a lift back to his hotel. Cotten accepts the ride and the two men go to a bar where Howard begins to pump Cotten for information about Welles, saying that he was a crook and a murderer. Howard, a member of British Intelligence, so infuriates Cotten that he takes a poke at the agent. When Howard leaves, Cotten vows to carry on his own investigation into Welles' background and clear him of the crimes Howard insists Welles committed. He finds Deutsch, an impoverished nobleman, who tells him he witnessed Welles' death, that Welles crossed a street and simply didn't look where he was going and a truck struck him. He learns that Breuer, a friend of Welles', picked him up after the accident and carried him to the square where he died of his injuries. Cotten learns from Deutsch that the girl at the funeral, Valli, knew Welles and works at a nearby theater. Valli, still in shock over Welles' death, agrees to talk to Cotten when he shows up and she tells him that one of Welles' own drivers actually ran him over, but the man was found innocent in a quick investigation that day. She adds that Welles' own doctor, who happened to be on his way to see Welles at the time, spotted him lying in the square and pronounced him dead. Cotten is baffled, saying: "I don't get this. All of them there....his own driver knocking him over. His own doctor passing by. No strangers there at all?" Replies Valli, "I wondered about it a hundred times– if it was really an accident." Cotten and Valli go to Welles' apartment and learn from the porter, Hoerbiger, that he witnessed three men carry the body away–Deutsch, Breuer, and a third man he could not recognize. "You don't mean the doctor?" asks Cotten. The porter shakes his head: "No, he came later. I didn't recognize him 'the third man'." The porter has apparently talked too much; he is found dead the next day, murdered. Then two thugs try to beat up Cotten but he escapes from them by running into some bombed-out buildings, relics of WW II, and manages to find Valli's apartment. There he tells her he is mystified by events and while he is trying to work out the puzzle, he realizes that he has fallen in love with this beautiful woman. Cotten makes a weak advance but Valli is not interested. He leaves and, as he steps outside, he sees a figure standing in a dark doorway, noticing a man's shoes that quickly recede into the shadows. An apartment light flashes on nearby and illuminates the doorway. Cotten, to his amazement, sees the smiling face of Welles staring at him. Before Cotten can reach Welles, a car going down the street blocks his path and by the time Cotten crosses the street he finds the doorway empty. Cotten goes to Howard to tell him that he has just seen a man who is supposed to be dead, Welles. The British agent orders Welles' coffin disinterred and the body of a police informant who had testified against Welles is found inside. Now Cotten knows that Welles is the third man he has been searching for. Howard explains to Cotten that Welles is corrupt through and through, that he is a black marketeer who has been selling illegally obtained, diluted, but much needed penicillin, and its use, he graphically demonstrates, has caused the deaths of many sick children. Cotten agrees to help Howard trap his monstrous friend. He secretly meets with Welles in the Prater, a deserted amusement park, and they talk on a moving Ferris wheel. Cotten is full of disgust for Welles, asking him, "Have you ever seen one of your victims?" Welles peers down from the swaying Ferris wheel car which is now high in the air and says: "Would you really feel any pity if one of those dots stopped moving forever? If I offered you 20,000 pounds for every dot that stops, would you really, old man, tell me to keep my money? Or would you calculate how many dots you could afford to spare? Free of income tax, old man." Welles tells him he has a gun and that he could shoot Cotten easily, now that they are at the very top of the Ferris wheel, and that no one would bother to look for a bullet hole in a corpse that would be crushed after falling from such a great altitude. Cotten is unmoved by the threat, telling Welles that "they dug up your coffin." Welles realizes that his charade is over but he does not shoot Cotten. The car starts downward and Welles tells his friend that if he goes into business with him he will become rich. He asks Cotten to think it over. When the car gets to the bottom, Welles steps out, then turns to Cotten and says smugly: After all, it's not that awful. You know what the fellow said: 'In Italy for 30 years under the Borgias they had warfare, terror, murder, bloodshed. They produced Michelangelo, Leonardo da Vinci, and the Renaissance. In Switzerland they had brotherly love, 500 years of democracy and peace. And what did that produce? The cuckoo clock.' So long, Holly." Howard, at his wit's end to capture drug dealer Welles, arrests Valli, threatening to revoke her passport and turn her over to the Russians. Cotten tells Howard that if he leaves the girl alone, he will set up a trap for Welles so Howard and his men can arrest him. Welles meets with Cotten at a cafe but Valli, incensed over Cotten's betrayal and still in love with Welles, tries to warn the drug dealer. Welles leaps to his feet and begins to flee but it's too late. Police are everywhere. Pulling aside a manhole cover, Welles drops into the Vienna sewer system, cavernous tunnels through which he begins to run. The police of four nations–American, French, British, Austrian–chase the fugitive through the tunnels, exchanging gunfire with him. The police and Welles play a running cat-and-mouse game in these subterranean passages with lights playing upon the sweating ancient tunnel walls and glimmering on the dark waters through which the police splash. (This is an astounding visual sequence captured impactfully by cameraman Krasker who deservedly won an Oscar for his work.) A policeman closes in on Welles and he shoots the cop, who shoots back. Welles is wounded and staggers up an iron spiral staircase to a manhole cover. Reed, in an ironic, telling closeup, shows Welles' fingers curling through the holes of the manhole cover, trying desperately to push it up, but a tire from a parked car sits on it, keeping it down. Welles slips back down the stairs to meet in the tunnel his old friend Cotten. Welles looks at Cotten with a baleful expression, one that speaks of friendship, old times, memories, anything that will allow him the mercy of escape. Cotten's expression is cold as ice. All he can think about are those children Welles' has killed with his doctored drugs. Cotten pulls for a gun and shoots and kills Welles. Now there is a second funeral for Welles, who is really dead this time. Howard drives Cotten away from the funeral and, as they go down a bleak tree-lined roadway, they pass Valli, who has also attended the funeral and is on foot. "One can't just leave," Cotten tells Howard and has the agent stop his Jeep. Cotten gets out and waits for Valli to catch up to him. But Valli does not go to Cotten, as expected. She pretends he does not exist as she walks wordlessly by him without a glance, without a murmur. In this last scene she shows her utter contempt for Cotten and her love for Welles, despite the fact that he was a monster. It is one of the most downbeat endings ever in an overall murky but totally absorbing film. Reed, through Krasker's cleverly tilted camera–offering unusual angles and shadowy images–produces here a classic *film noir* picture, one that provides one chilling moment after another. Reed further enhanced this stimulating offbeat film by having only a single stringed instrument heard throughout, one that increased the tension by its rapid playing, the then unheard-of zither, played by Anton Karas. Following the success of this film, zither music swept the U.S. and Europe and its popularity would not diminish for years. THE THIRD MAN began with some scribbled notes. Reed and author Greene had just enjoyed a huge success with THE FALLEN IDOL and were planning another film together when producer Alexander Korda joined them for dinner. The trouble was that Greene said he had no story for another film, but he did have a notation, or an idea, which he had written down on the back of an envelope. He pulled it forth and read what he had scribbled: "I had paid my farewell to Harry a week ago, when his coffin was lowered into the ground. So it was, with some incredulity that I saw him pass by, without a hint of recognition, amongst the host of strangers in the Strand." With only these few words, Korda assigned Greene to write an original screenplay and the author went off to Italy. In eight weeks he had produced THE THIRD MAN. (It is interesting to note that the basic premise here, one where a man is presumed dead, having arranged for his own death to further his criminal pursuits, is a device used effectively by Eric Ambler in his novel *A Coffin for Dimitrios*, later turned into the superb film, THE MASK OF DIMITRIOS.) Nothing of the script was changed except the ending. Reed wanted Valli to ignore Cotten at the end instead of going into his arms as Greene originally intended, thinking this a much more effective finish. Greene agreed and the ending was changed to one that jarred the public and critics alike, who lavished justifiable praise on the movie. The subtle little touches Reed introduced into the film, shot in five weeks in Vienna, such as repeatedly showing Welles' cat as an extension of the sinister drug-trafficker, gave many levels of meaning to an already powerful film. The strange camera angles were selected purposely by the director who wanted "to suggest that something crooked was going on," and "to make the audience uncomfortable" as Cotten certainly becomes when learning the truth about his friend. Korda and coproducer David O. Selznick clashed with Reed when Selznick insisted that Noel Coward, of all people, play the drug pusher but Reed begged for Welles and was lucky enough to get him. Welles' performance is riveting, the very embodiment of suavity and evil. Howard is as dependable as a terrier and Cotten is superb as the duped friend. Valli is beautiful and mysterious as the woman loving the wrong man.

p, David O. Selznick, Alexander Korda, Carol Reed; d, Reed; w, Graham Greene; ph, Robert Krasker; m, Anton Karas; ed, Oswald Hafenrichter; prod d, Vincent Korda, Joseph Bato; John Hawkesworth; set d, Dario Simoni.

Crime Drama **Cas.** **(PR:C MPAA:NR)**

THIRD MAN ON THE MOUNTAIN****
(1959) 107m Disney/BV c (AKA: BANNER IN THE SKY)

Michael Rennie *(Capt. John Winter)*, James MacArthur *(Rudi Matt)*, Janet Munro *(Lizbeth Hempel)*, James Donald *(Franz Lerner)*, Herbert Lom *(Emil Saxo, Guide)*, Laurence Naismith *(Teo Zurbriggen)*, Lee Patterson *(Klaus Wesselhoft)*, Walter Fitzgerald *(Herr Hempel)*, Nora Swinburne *(Frau Mott)*, Ferdy Mayne *(Andreas)*, James Ramsey Ullmann, Helen Hayes *(Tourists)*.

This story of youth finding itself is an exciting, well-filmed picture set against the backdrop of the Matterhorn (called the Citadel here). MacArthur is a young boy whose father was killed while climbing the mountain and he is determined to complete the unfinished ascent. His youthful exuberance at first shames him with a party led by Rennie, then his mother and uncle forbid him to climb anymore. With the help of Munro and Naismith, Donald helps MacArthur with his studies and the lad soon is mastering the art. The most important thing he learns is to never endanger his fellow climbers, a lesson he puts to good use later when he saves Rennie during an ascent. THIRD MAN ON THE MOUNTAIN is a fine film for children, giving a message about courage and self-supports without ever becoming heavy-handed. The breathtaking photography of the Alps locations is well used under a sure-handed direction. The cast is uniformly excellent with MacArthur carrying the meat of the story with confidence. Walt Disney fell in love with Switzerland and spared no expense on this film. The Alps locations proved to be of some problems to the filmmakers. Unfamiliar with the intricacies of mountain climbing, a local was hired to consult them on the film's accuracy and work as a double for the more dangerous moments. The cast was taught the fundamentals of mountain climbing, which MacArthur took to with great ease. He later gave the production crew and insurance company assigned to the film quite a fright when he snuck off one day to actually climb the Matterhorn by himself. His real life mother, Hayes, makes a cameo appearance as a tourist as does Ullman, the author of the novel that was the basis for the film. This was later shown on TV's "Wonderful World of Disney" under the title BANNER IN THE SKY.

p, William H. Anderson; d, Ken Annakin; w, Eleanore Griffin (based on the novel *Banner in the Sky* by James Ramsey Ullman); ph, Harry Waxman (Technicolor); m, William Alwyn; ed, Peter Boita; prod d, John Howell; ch,

Mme. Derivaz; m/l, "Climb the Mountain," Franklyn Marks, By Dunham, "Good Night Valais," G. Haenni, Tom Adair.

Drama   (PR:A MPAA:NR)

THIRD OF A MAN**   (1962) 82m Phoenix/UA bw

Simon Oakland (Doon), James Drury (Emmet Spile), Jan Shepard (Helen Detweiler), Whit Bissell (Dr. Maxwell), Jimmy Gaines (Leroy Spile), Lyda Stevens, Lee Sabinson, Marshall Reed, James Maloney, Josip Elic, Norma Connolly, Robert Fresco, Bob Roberts, Stuart Nisbet, Mary Ann Dighton, Bill Stevens, Jim Cook, Robert Coogan, Sky Hixon, Phyllis Coughlin.

Gaines is the illegitimate son of Drury and Shepard. Shepard will not marry the man because of his violent streak and she is raising the boy. The family secret is Oakland, Drury's mute brother confined to an insane asylum. Oakland is terrified of water and escapes after a guard turns a hose on him. He meets Gaines and the two develop a friendship. Oakland overcomes his fear of water when he saves the boy from drowning. He carries the boy in his arms. But the posse looking for the escapee think he has harmed the child and he is returned to the hospital after a beating. Gaines runs away to join his uncle and Drury follows. The boy locks Drury in a room with some patients and Drury comes to realize that these people mean him no harm. He promises to visit his brother the next day and Oakland says "tomorrow," the first word he has spoken in years. The drama tries to be meaningful but never goes beyond shallow emotions and characterizations. There are too many cliches and stereotypes for this to be successful. Oakland's attempts to inject some sympathy into his character is undercut by seeming homages to FRANKENSTEIN, a wholly inappropriate idea.

p, Robert Lewin, William Redlin; d&w, Lewin (based on an idea by Lewin, Allan Grant); ph, Vilis Lapenieks; m, Samuel Matlovsky; ed, Frederic Knudtson; art d, Paul Mathison; makeup, George Mitchell.

Drama   (PR:C MPAA:NR)

THIRD PARTY RISK   (SEE: DEADLY MANTIS, THE, 1957)

THIRD ROAD, THE   (SEE: 7TH DAWN, THE, 1964, US/Brit.)

THIRD SECRET, THE**½   (1964, Brit.) 103m Hubris/FOX bw

Stephen Boyd (Alex Stedman), Jack Hawkins (Sir Frederick Belline), Richard Attenborough (Alfred Price-Gorham), Diane Cilento (Anne Tanner), Pamela Franklin (Catherine Whitset), Paul Rogers (Dr. Milton Gillen), Alan Webb (Alden Hoving), Rachel Kempson (Mildred Hoving), Peter Sallis (Lawrence Jacks), Patience Collier (Mrs. Pelton), Freda Jackson (Mrs. Bales), Judi Dench (Miss Humphries), Peter Copley (Dr. Leo Whitset), Nigel Davenport (Lew Harding), Charles Lloyd Pack (Dermot McHenry), Barbara Hicks (Police Secretary), Ronald Leigh-Hunt (Police Officer), Geoffrey Adams (Floor Manager), James Maxwell (Mark), Gerald Case (Mr. Bickes), Sarah Brackett (Nurse), Neal Arden (Mr. Morgan).

When a noted psychiatrist is found dead of a supposedly self-inflicted gunshot wound, his patient, Boyd, a TV commentator, suspects foul play. He obtains a list of patients from Franklin, the dead man's 14-year-old daughter. He visits each one in his search for the murderer, but finds only that each person has a secret life known only to the psychiatrist. He stumbles across the files on another patient, who turns out to be Franklin. She confesses to the murder, claiming her father was about to send her to an institution to be treated for her schizophrenia. The crime is re-enacted and Franklin stabs Boyd. He recovers and visits her at the institution, promising to remain her friend. The episodic, talky drama has some moments that overcome the script deficiencies, but the film tends to be too pretentious and deliberately vague. The performances are adequate, with Franklin particularly good as the troubled young girl. An additional sequence featuring Patricia Neal was filmed but subsequently cut from the final version.

p, Robert L. Joseph; d, Charles Crichton; w, Joseph; ph, Douglas Slocombe (CinemaScope); m, Richard Arnell; ed, Frederick Wilson; prod d, Tom Morahan; md, Arnell; makeup, Ken MacKay.

Drama   (PR:C MPAA:NR)

THIRD STRING, THE*½   (1932, Brit.) 65m Welsh-Pearson/GAU bw

Sandy Powell (Ginger Dick), Kay Hammond (Hebe Tucker), Mark Daly (Pete Russett), Alf Goddard (Bill Lumm), Charles Paton (Sam Small), Sydney Fairbrother (Miss Peabody), Pollie Emery (Mrs. Chip), James Knight (Webson).

Powell is a sailor on leave who finds himself forced to pose as a champion boxer from Australia to win the love of beautiful barmaid Hammond. This masquerade leads to Powell having to fight a real boxer, Goddard, who just happens to be Hammond's old flame. Sympathetic to the seaman's plight, Goddard agrees to let Powell win, but after the fight Hammond rejects them both and runs off with the bar owner.

p, George Pearson, T. A. Welsh; d, Pearson; w, Pearson, James Reardon, A. R. Rawlinson (based on a story by W. W. Jacobs).

Comedy   (PR:A MPAA:NR)

THIRD TIME LUCKY**½   (1931, Brit.) 85m Gainsborough/Woolfe and Freedman bw

Bobby Howes (Rev. Arthur Fear), Gordon Harker (Meggitt), Dorothy Boyd (Jennifer), Garry Marsh (Crowther), Henry Mollison (Crofts), Gibb McLaughlin (Charlie), Clare Greet (Mrs. Scratton), Margaret Yarde (Mrs. Clutterbuck), Viola Compton (Mrs. Starkey), Marie Ault (Mrs. Midge), Alexander Field (Snoopy), Harry Terry (Gregg), Peter Godfrey (Gus), Matthew Boulton (Inspector), Gunner Moir, Henry Latimer, Willie Graham.

Howes is a sheepish clerk who must overcome his timidity and defend his ward, Boyd, who is being blackmailed by a former lover. It's not an easy task but Howes finally gets the blackmail letters back.

p, Michael Balcon; d, Walter Forde; w, Angus Macphail (based on the play by Arnold Ridley); ph, William Shenton.

Comedy   (PR:A MPAA:NR)

THIRD TIME LUCKY**   (1950, Brit.) 91m Alliance-Kenilworth/Pentagon bw

Glynis Johns (Joan), Dermot Walsh (Lucky), Charles Goldner (Flash), Harcourt Williams (Doc), Yvonne Owen (Peggy), Helen Haye (Old Lady), John Stuart (Inspector), Harold Berens (Young Waiter), Ballard Berkeley (Bertram), Sebastian Cabot (Benny), Millicent Wolf (Matron), Bruce Walker, Marianne Deeming, Jean Short, Michael Hordern, Edna Kaye, Jack Tottenham, Tom Block.

Average British programmer details the life of professional gambler Walsh. He takes up with Johns, a naive young girl, who serves as his good luck charm. Eventually his rival takes a liking to her and Walsh ends up getting shot in the back. He realizes that gambling is a foolish life and Johns waits for her man to recover. Watch for an early appearance by Cabot.

p, Mario Zampi; d, Gordon Parry; w, Gerald Butler (based on the novel They Cracked Her Glass Slipper by Butler); ph, Cedric Williams, Peter Newbrook; m, Stanley Black; ed, Giulio Zampi; art d, Ivan King.

Drama   (PR:A MPAA:NR)

THIRD VISITOR, THE*½   (1951, Brit.) 85m Eros bw

Sonia Dresdel (Steffy Millington), Guy Middleton (Inspector Mallory), Hubert Gregg (Jack Kurton), Colin Gordon (Bill Millington), Karel Stepanek (Richard Carling), Eleanor Summerfield (Vera Kurton), John Slater (James Oliver), Cyril Smith (Horton), Michael Martin-Harvey (Hewson).

Dresdel is wrongly accused of murder when crooked crime boss Stepanek is found dead. Police inspector Middleton, however, is not convinced of her guilt and sets out to find the real killer. Eventually Stepanek turns up alive, having killed a former partner and passed the corpse off as his own. A thoroughly unbelievable caper.

p, Ernest Gartside; d, Maurice Elvey; w, Gerald Anstruther, David Evans (based on the play by Anstruther); ph, Stephen Dade.

Crime   (PR:A MPAA:NR)

THIRD VOICE, THE***   (1960) 80m FOX bw

Edmond O'Brien (The Voice), Julie London (Corey Scott), Laraine Day (Marian Forbes), Olga San Juan (Blonde Prostitute), George Eldredge (Judge Kendall), Tom Hernandez (Desk Clerk, Hotel Bahia), Abel Franco (Police Inspector), Edward Colmans (Carreras), Tom Daly (Tourist at Bar), Ralph Brooks (Harris Chapman), Lucile Curtis (Mrs. Kendall), Shirley O'Hara (Carreras' Secretary), Raoul De Leon (Bank Official), Sylvia Rey (Cashier, Hotel Miramar), George Trevino (Capt. Campos), Eddie Le Baron (Carlos the Cab Driver), Alberto Monte (Photographer), John Garrett (Bank Clerk), Francisco Ortega (Bank Cashier), Rouque Ybarra, Ruben Moreno (Fishermen), Henry Delgardo (Clerk), Hotel Palacio, Andre Oropeza (Clerk, Hotel Miramar), Robert Hernandez (Bellhop), Francis Ravel (Waiter), Manuel Serrano (Headwaiter), Mario Armenta (Orchestra Leader).

Day is the former secretary and current mistress of a wealthy businessman. She hires O'Brien to kill him and assume her lover's identity so they can share his wealth. O'Brien wants all the money for himself, though, and comes close to killing Day. London, a woman O'Brien picks up, is actually the fiancee of the man Day have murdered, and the police arrive to arrest the two. THE THIRD VOICE is an interesting suspense film which is let down by its all too conventional ending. The body of the film draws out the crime nicely with good plotting and some fine camerawork. The characterizations are quite adept with O'Brien giving a fine tour de force performance.

p, Maury Dexter, Hubert Cornfield; d&w, Cornfield (based on the novel All the Way by Charles Williams); ph, Ernest Haller (CinemaScope); m, Johnny Mandel; ed, John A. Bushelman.

Suspense   (PR:O MPAA:NR)

THIRD WALKER, THE**   (1978, Can.) 83m
Simon-Quadrant-Wychwood c

Colleen Dewhurst (Kate MacLean), William Shatner (Munro MacLean),
Frank Moore (James MacLean), Monique Mercure (Marie Blanchard),
Tony Meyer (Etienne Blanchard), David Meyer (Andrew MacLean), Andree
Pelletier (Laura), Simon Rankin (Etienne as a Boy), Andrew Rankin
(Andrew as a Boy), Darren DiFonzo (James as a Boy), Diane LeBlanc (The
Nun), Marshall McLuhan (Voice of the Judge).

This interesting idea is unfortunately marred by confused direction, though
the story often holds great interest. Twins get mixed up at birth, resulting
in one woman taking home her child and a stranger's, while another woman
takes home the second twin. Twenty-eight years later the twins meet at their
father's funeral, become friends, and plan their lives together, leaving the
non-twin an outsider. The raising of the twins is told in flashback by a nun
(LeBlanc) in a muddled fashion that detracts from the narrative. Motivations are sometimes slim, though the characterizations, particularly by
Shatner and Dewhurst, are quite effective. Listen for the voice of noted
media theorist McLuhan as a judge. The film was the first directoral effort
of his daughter, who was an identical twin herself.

p, Teri McLuhan, Brian Winston; d, McLuhan; w, Robert Thom, (based on
a story by McLuhan); ph, Robert Fiore; m, Paul Hoffert; ed, Ulla Ryghe; art
d, William McCrow.

Drama   (PR:C   MPAA:NR)

THIRST**   (1979, Aus.) 98m F.G. Film/Greater Union/New Line
Cinema c

Chantal Contouri (Kate Davis), David Hemmings (Dr. Fraser), Henry Silva
(Dr. Gauss), Max Phipps (Hodge), Shirley Cameron (Mrs. Barker), Rod
Mullinar (Derek), Robert Thompson (Sean), Walter Pym (Dichter), Rosie
Sturgess (Lori), Lulu Pinkus (Nurse), Amanda Muggleton (Martha).

This grisly story has an unusually classy production. Beautiful Contouri is
a businesswoman kidnaped by a secret organization called the Hyma
Brotherhood. The group believe themselves to be superior to the rest of the
human race because of their favorite beverage: human blood derived from
victims and packaged in milk-type cartons. Contouri has the dubious honor
of being asked to join this elite group. THIRST unfortunately avoids the
black comedy inherent in the material, with an all too serious direction that
hurts the overall film. The script is full of holes no amount of direction or
editing can cover. However, it is redeemed by its look, which is of the highest
quality. Special effects are fine and there are some nice atmospheric location
settings that heighten the mood.

p, Antony I. Ginnane; d, Rod Hardy; w, John Pinkney (based on his "Instant
Terror" stories); ph, Vincent Monton (Panavision, Eastmancolor); m, Brian
May; ed, Phil Reid; art d, Jon Dowding, Jill Eden; spec eff, Conrad Rothman;
stunts, Grant Page.

Horror   **Cas.**   (PR:O   MPAA:R)

THIRSTY DEAD, THE zero   (1975) 90m International Amusements c
(AKA: THE BLOOD CULT OF SHANGRI-LA)

John Considine, Jennifer Billingsley, Judith McConnell, Fredricka Meyers,
Tani Guthrie.

Considine is a young jungle dweller with an unusual penchant: he needs sexy
women for his bizarre blood rituals and so he kidnaps young lovelies for this
purpose. Unbelievably, the women fight each other to see who will be his
lucky lady. Made on a zero budget in the Philippines, this laughable horror
film features a canoe trip in the sewers of Manila.

p, Wesley E. Depue; d, Terry Becker; w, Charles Dennis; ph, (Movielab
Color).

Horror   **Cas.**   (PR:O   MPAA:PG)

THIRTEEN, THE***   (1937, USSR) 86m Mosfilm/Artkino bw

Ivan Novoseltsev (The Commander), Helen Kuzmina (His Wife), Alexander
Chistyakov (The Geologist), Arsen Fait (Lieutenant Colonel), Olya Kuznet-
sov (Akchurin), Andrei Dolinin (Timoshkin), Pyotr Masokha (Sviridenko),
David Zolts (Lakoev), Vassily Kulakov (Balandin), Sergei Krilov (Zhurba),
Alexander Repinov (Muradov), Andrei Kuliev (Bakhtiulin), Nikolai Kriuch-
kov (Gusev).

A well done Russian style LOST PATROL (1934) has a group of Russian
army cavalrymen, the commander's wife, and a geologist lost in the desert
after a battle. They take refuge in an abandoned fort and some Soviet
enemies, two hundred strong, attack them in search of water. Just when all
appears to be lost, a cavalry troop rides up to save the day. Though a simple
story, THE THIRTEEN is well crafted with an exciting story and some
excellent performances. Director Romm, given the job of filming this
excellent story on a meager budget in the Karakam Desert, had to contend
with more than a shortage of money before it was finished, because the
terrible desert heat crippled much of his crew. His splendid work did not go
unnoticed by Soviet big shots. When Premier Josef Stalin ordered a movie
made to commemorate the 20th anniversary of the October Revolution,

Romm was called upon to direct it although he had only made two pictures
previously. Given a script (LENIN IN OCTOBER), in August, 1937, and
constantly being prodded from above, he finished filming in November,
three months later, setting an example for efficiency and economy other
Russian directors would find it hard to emulate although they were
henceforth ordered to. The basic plot for the picture was reworked by
American screenwriters John Howard Lawson and Zoltan Korda for the
Humphrey Bogart-starring film SAHARA (1943). This also served as a basis
for the Broderick Crawford Film LAST OF THE COMANCHES (1953). (In
Russian; English subtitles).

d, Mikhail Romm; w, Ivan Prut, Romm; ph, Boris Volchek; m, Antoll
Alexandrov.

Drama   (PR:A   MPAA:NR)

13   (SEE: EYE OF THE DEVIL, 1967, Brit.)

13 EAST STREET**½   (1952, Brit.) 71m Tempean/Eros bw

Patrick Holt (Gerald Blake), Sandra Dorne (Judy), Robert Ayres (Larry
Conn), Sonia Holm (Joan), Dora Bryan (Valerie), Michael Balfour (Joey
Long), Michael Brennan (George Mack), Hector MacGregor, Alan Judd,
Michael Ward, Alan Gordon, Harry Fowler.

A British programmer which follows every crime expectation in the book,
but still is entertaining. Holt is a detective who goes undercover to break up
a gang of thieves. The gang discovers his identity and plots to kill him after
the next robbery. Luckily for him, the police intervene, save his life, and
smash the ring. 13 EAST STREET is just more proof that cliches are cliches
because they work so well.

p, Robert S. Baker, Monty Berman; d, Baker; w, John Gilling (based on a
story by Baker); ph, Berman.

Crime   (PR:A   MPAA:NR)

13 EAST STREET   (SEE: 13 WEST STREET, 1962)

THIRTEEN FIGHTING MEN**   (1960) 69m FOX bw

Grant Williams (Forrest), Brad Dexter (Maj. Boyd), Carole Mathews
(Carole), Robert Dix (Lt. Wilcox), Richard Garland (Prescott), Richard Crane
(Loomis), Rayford Barnes (Sgt. Yates), John Erwin (Cpl. McLean), Bob
Palmer (Pvt. Jensen), Rex Holman (Root), John Merrick (Lee), Mark
Hickman (Sgt. Mason), Walter Reed (Col. Jeffers), I. Stanford Jolley (Pvt.
Ebb), Ford Dunhill (Pvt. Harper), Mauritz Hugo (Ives), Stephen Ferry (Sgt.
Wade), Brad Harris (Pvt. Fowler), Fred Kohler, Jr (Corey), Earl Holmes (2nd
Soldier), Dick Jeffries (Jimmy), Ted Knight (Samuel), Bill Browne (Pvt.
Connors), Jerry Mobley (Sentry).

A troop of Union soldiers, led by Williams, is transporting a gold shipment
shortly after the end of the Civil War. Some Confederates under the
command of Dexter are after the gold to help them make new starts when
they return to their war-ravaged homes. Williams' troops are demoralized,
knowing they are protecting what they can't have, and Dexter must keep
his men from turning into outlaws. Potentially an interesting psychological
western but the treatment is only on the most simplest of terms. The
characterizations are stereotypes and plenty of shooting and action fill up
the time. Strictly by the book.

p, Jack Leewood; d, Harry Gerstad; w, Robert Hammer, Jack Thomas; ph,
Walter Strenge (CinemaScope); m, Irving Gertz; ed, John Bushelman.

Western   (PR:C   MPAA:NR)

THIRTEEN FRIGHTENED GIRLS*   (1963) 89m COL c (AKA: THE
CANDY WEB)

Kathy Dunn (Candace Hull), Murray Hamilton (Wally Sanders), Joyce
Taylor (Soldier), Hugh Marlowe (John Hull), Khigh Dhiegh (Kang), Charlie
Briggs (Mike), Norma Varden (Miss Pittford), Garth Benton (Peter Van
Hagen), Lynne Sue Moon (Mai-Ling), Maria Cristina Servera (Argentina),
Janet Mary Prance (Australia), Penny Anne Mills (Canada), Alexandra L.
Bastedo (England), Ariane Glaser (France), Ilona Schutze (Germany), Anna
Baj (Italy), Aiko Sakamoto (Japan), Judy Pace (Liberia), Luz Gloria Hervias
(Mexico), Marie-Louise Bielke (Sweden), Ignacia Farias Luque (Venezuela),
Emil Sitka (Ludwig), Jon Alvar (Fernando), Walter Rode (Kagenescu), Gina
Trikonis (Russia).

Idiotic spy film aimed at juveniles features Dunn as a daughter of an
American diplomat on a holiday in London. She stumbles onto a political
murder and informs Hamilton, a CIA man she has a schoolgirl crush on.
Through her father's connections, Dunn has access to many foreign
embassies and she becomes known in the espionage world as "Kitten," a
hunted agent. Hamilton finds this out and goes to the Swiss boarding school
she attends to save her from disaster. Noted low-budget filmmaker Castle
held an international search to find the stars for this film (and expand his
distribution outlets) but he needn't have gone to the trouble. His direction
is usually bad and the screaming gaggle of girls he "discovered" get on one's
nerves after a bit. This may have been the only teeny-bop espionage film in

movie history.

p&d, William Castle; w, Robert Dillon (based on a story by Otis L. Guernsey, Jr.); ph, Gordon Avil (Eastmancolor); m, Van Alexander; ed, Edwin Bryant; art d, Don Ament; set d, William Kiernan; cos, Lanz; makeup, Ben Lane, Joseph DiBella.

Spy Drama/Adventure (PR:A MPAA:NR)

THIRTEEN GHOSTS**½ (1960) 85m COL bw-c

Charles Herbert (*Buck Zorba*), Jo Morrow (*Medea Zorba*), Martin Milner (*Ben Rush, Lawyer*), Rosemary De Camp (*Hilda Zorba*), Donald Woods (*Cyrus Zorba*), Margaret Hamilton (*Elaine Zacharides, Housekeeper*), John Van Dreelen (*E. Van Allen*).

A fun film about 12 ghosts who inhabit an old house. Woods and De Camp are the parents and Herbert and Morrow the children comprising the nice family that moves in. The ghosts want to add another member to their clan. Who will it be? Hamilton is featured as an unusual housekeeper and Milner is a local nasty guy. The acting is quietly professional, with the cast never making more out of their roles than what they are. The audience draw was one of producer-director Castle's nifty gimmicks, called "Illusion-O," a pair of red and blue colored glasses. During the color ghost sequences audiences could see the spirits only by using the red "Ghost Viewer" side and remove them with the blue "Ghost Remover."

p&d, William Castle; w, Robb White; ph, Joseph Biroc (Eastmancolor); m, Von Dexter; ed, Edwin Bryant; art d, Cary Odell.

Horror (PR:A MPAA:NR)

THIRTEEN HOURS BY AIR**½ (1936) 77m PAR bw

Fred MacMurray (*Jack Gordon*), Joan Bennett (*Felice Rollins*), ZaSu Pitts (*Mina Harkins*), Alan Baxter (*Curtis Palmer*), Fred Keating (*Gregorie Stephani*), Brian Donlevy (*Dr. Evarts*), John Howard (*Freddie Scott*), Adrienne Marden (*Ann McKenna*), Ruth Donnelly (*Vi Johnson*), Bennie Bartlett (*Waldemar Pitt III*), Grace Bradley (*Trixie La Brey*), Dean Jagger (*Hap Waller*), Jack Mulhall (*Horace Lander*), Granville Bates (*Pop Andrews*), Arthur Singley (*Pete Stevens*), Clyde Dilson (*Fat Rickhauser*), Mildred Stone (*Ruth Bradford*), Henry Arthur (*Assistant Clerk*), Ed Schaefer (*Harry*), Dennis O'Keefe (*Baker the Copilot*), Bruce Warren (*Tex Doyle*), John Huettner (*Copilot*), Gertrude Short, Marie Prevost (*Waitresses*).

A pre-AIRPORT disaster film has Lothario pilot MacMurray guiding his commercial airplane through a blinding snowstorm while a gangster terrorizes the passengers. He handles the job well, winning the heart of socialite Bennett in the process. Though strictly programmer material this has a nice balance between comedy and drama (the gangster is stopped by a kid with a squirt gun!) with some good dialog and performances.

p, E. Lloyd Sheldon; d, Mitchell Leisen; w, Bogart Rogers, Kenyon Nicholson (based on the story "Wild Wings" by Rogers, Frank Mitchell Dazey); ph, Theodore Sparkuhl; ed, Doane Harrison; art d, Hans Dreier, John B. Goodman; set d, A.E. Freudeman; spec eff, Gordon Jennings, Farciot Edouart.

Drama/Comedy (PR:A MPAA:NR)

THIRTEEN LEAD SOLDIERS**½ (1948) 64m FOX bw

Tom Conway (*Bulldog Drummond*), Maria Palmer (*Estelle*), Helen Westcott (*Cynthia*), John Newland (*Algy*), William Stelling (*Seymour*), William Stelling (*Coleman*), Gordon Richards (*Inspector McIver*), Harry Cording (*Vane*), John Goldsworthy (*Steadman*), William Edmunds (*Collier*).

This entry in the minor "Bulldog Drummond" series finds detective Conway on the trail of a set of lead Soldiers. It seems these toy men were made 900 years ago by King Harold of the Normans and are the key to a bounty of loot. In order to fool two groups chasing after the money, Conway claims to have two of the soldiers. He's able to nab the bad guys and turns them over to the police. The direction is well paced, giving this a good suspenseful air for a programmer. Acting is fine and production values are pretty standard. (See: BULLDOG DRUMMOND series, Index.)

p, Bernard Small, Ben Pivar; d, Frank McDonald; w, Irving Elman (based on an or iginal story by "Sapper"); ph, George Robinson; ed, Saul A. Goodkind; md, Milton Rosen; art d, Walter Koessler.

Crime (PR:A MPAA:NR)

13 MEN AND A GUN*** (1938, Brit.) 64m TC-Pisorno/British Independent bw

Arthur Wontner (*Captain*), Clifford Evans (*Jorg*), Howard Marion-Crawford (*Kramer*), Allan Jeayes (*Gen. Vloty*), Gibb McLaughlin (*Col. Vlatin*), Wally Patch (*Hans*), Scott Harold (*Ludwig*), Donald Gray (*Johann*), Bernard Miles (*Schultz*), Andre Morell (*Kroty*), John Kevan (*Peder*), Kenneth Warrington, Frank Henderson, Herbert Cameron, Oscar Paterson, Roy Russell, R. Van Boolen, Joe Cunningham, Noel Dainton.

An intense war drama, set in 1914 Austria on the Russo-Austrian front,

about 13 soldiers who are members of a secret gun crew. They are the only men who know the gun's location and when the Russians destroy it one of the men is suspected of informing. The identity of the traitor is not known so the Austrian commander orders the entire gun crew shot. Before this can happen, however, the traitor is located and the lives of the other 12 are saved. Shot in Italy in both English and Italian versions.

p&d, Mario Zampi; w, Basil Dillon, Kathleen Connors (based on the story by Giovanni Forzano); ph, Albertelli.

War (PR:A MPAA:NR)

13 NUNS (SEE: REVENGE OF THE SHOGUN WOMEN, 1982, Taiwan)

13 RUE MADELEINE***½ (1946) 95m FOX bw

James Cagney (*Bob Sharkey*), Annabella (*Suzanne de Bouchard*), Richard Conte (*Bill O'Connell*), Frank Latimore (*Jeff Lassiter*), Walter Abel (*Charles Gibson*), Melville Cooper (*Pappy Simpson*), Sam Jaffe (*Mayor Galimard*), Marcel Rousseau (*Duclois*), Everett G. Marshall (*Emile*), Blanche Yurka (*Mme. Thillot*), Peter Von Zerneck (*Karl*), Alfred Linder (*Hans Feinkl*), Judith Lowry (*Peasant Lady*), Richard Gordon, Walter Greaza (*Psychiatrists*), Ben Low (*Hotel Clerk*), Roland Belanger (*Joseph*), James Craven, Edward Cooper (*RAF Officers*), Alexander Kirkland (*Briefing Officer*), Donald Randolph (*LaRoche*), John Morre, Leslie Barrie, Charles Campbell (*Psychiatrists-Instructors*), Red Buttons, Peter Gowland (*Dispatchers*), Otto Simanek (*German Staff Officer*), Mario Gang, Henry Rowland, Martin Brandt, Fred Nurney, Julius Carmer, Albert D'Arno, Dick Wessel, Frederic Brunn, Arno Frey (*German Officers*), Frank De Langton (*Athletic Instructor*), Robert Morgan (*Telegraph Instructor*), Roland Winters (*van Duyval*), Harold Young (*Tailor*), William Syran (*Detective Inspector, Submarine Plant*), Reginald Mason (*Communications Chief*), Sally McMarrow (*Chief Operator*), Durant Rice, William Mendrek (*Men*), Coby Neal (*Flier*), Karl Malden (*Flight Sergeant*), Otto Reichow (*German Soldier*), Jean Val (*French Peasant*), Reed Hadley (*Narrator*), James Craven (*English Announcer--Voice Only*).

This tense WW II thriller was Henry Hathaway's follow-up to his successful semi-documentary spy thriller HOUSE ON 92ND STREET. Cagney is the training officer for a group of American agents preparing to serve in occupied Europe for Operations-77 (a thinly veiled copy of the OSS, which withdrew its endorsement for the film after the producers argued with legendary spymaster "Wild Bill" Donovan). He knows that of his students is a German agent, and must determine which one it is before he can do too much damage to the organization. Training is rigorous, and includes radio-telegraphy, psychological training, and exhausting physical exercise. During the training, two agent trainees become close friends, Conte and Latimore. They are given a final test of their skills when they are ordered to infiltrate an American submarine factory and steal the plans for a new torpedo detonator. They are almost caught by factory security, but Conte pulls a forged card from his pocket that identifies him as a security agent himself and he walks off with Latimore supposedly under arrest. Back at the training school, Cagney is now convinced that Conte is the German agent, but he has plans to use him. He tells Conte that he will be parachuted into France to prepare the way for the Allied invasion of Holland. He hopes that as soon as Conte reaches the ground he will immediately return to his superiors at the Gestapo and give them this misleading information. In case he doesn't, Cagney tells Latimore what he suspects and that he must kill Conte if he doesn't do as planned. On the plane bound for occupied territory, Conte senses the change in Latimore's attitude, and as his friend is about to jump out of the plane, he quickly and surreptitiously slices his ripcord with a razor. When Cagney finds out what happened, he goes to France himself, planning to kill Conte. He is captured and taken to the Paris Gestapo headquarters at the title address where he is tortured to make him reveal the truth about the invasion plans. Allied command knows Cagney will crack eventually, as any man will, so they order a bombing mission to destroy the entire building and Cagney with it. As the bombs begin to fall and Conte looks around at him at the crumbling room, Cagney starts to laugh maniacally and triumphantly and they go to their deaths together. The first half of the film, detailing the training procedures, was the most documentary-oriented and the best. The second half, in which a Cagney starting to show his age competes with young men like Conte, doesn't work nearly so well. Cagney didn't have much interest in making this film, preferring to develop projects for his own production company, but he was having trouble getting THE TIME OF YOUR LIFE off the ground and the $300,000 he received was too good to pass up. Conte is excellent as the double agent, cold and efficient as he kills Latimore without hesitation and even blocks a bullet meant for him by pulling another German officer in front of him. The film proved quite successful and gave Cagney the freedom he wanted. Unfortunately, THE TIME OF YOUR LIFE was not successful, and Cagney was quickly forced back to the studios for work.

p, Louis De Rochemont; d, Henry Hathaway; w, John Monks, Jr., Sy Bartlett; ph, Norbert Brodine; m, Alfred Newman; ed, Harmon Jones; md, David Buttolph; art d, James Basevi, Maurice Ransford; set d, Thomas Little; cos, Rene Hubert; spec eff, Fred Sersen; makeup, Ben Nye.

Spy Drama (PR:A-C MPAA:NR)

THIRTEEN WEST STREET** (1962) 80m Ladd Enterprises/COL bw

Alan Ladd (*Walt Sherill*), Rod Steiger (*Detective Sgt. Koleski*), Michael Callan (*Chuck Landry*), Dolores Dorn (*Tracey Sherill*), Kenneth MacKenna (*Paul Logan*), Margaret Hayes (*Mrs. Landry*), Stanley Adams (*Finney*), Chris Robinson (*Everett*), Jeanne Cooper (*Mrs. Quinn*), Arnold Merritt (*Bill*), Mark Slade (*Tommy*), Henry Beckman (*Joe Bradford*), Clegg Hoyt (*Noddy*), Jordan Gerler (*Jack*), Robert Cleaves (*Doctor*), Bernie Hamilton (*Negro*), Pepe Hern (*Mexican*), Frank Gerstle (*Mr. Johnson*), Ted Knight (*Baldwin*), Olan Soule.

For one of his final films, Ladd portrays a man of violence in the darkened city streets. Here, he plays an aerospace engineer attacked by a gang of toughs on his way home from work one evening. He quickly recovers from his injuries but becomes exasperated when the cop assigned to the case (Steiger) is too slow in rounding up suspects. Ladd takes the law into his own hands, beginning his own investigation. His single-minded zealousness forces him to lose his job, but the investigation continues until Ladd starts to make progress. Callan, a rich young punk who led the attack, hears about this and when one of his fellow gang members commits suicide, the boy decides to take out a little revenge. He breaks into Ladd's home and terrorizes his wife (Dorn). When the private detective Ladd had hired to trace the boys dies Ladd goes over the edge. He breaks into the home of Callan's socialite mother and attacks the boy, coming within moments of killing him with his bare hands. However, Ladd's sensibilities catch up with him and he realizes this is no different from the original attack. Ladd turns the boy over to Steiger, leaving the authorities to handle the crime. This is a film of mixed quality. The direction grabs the story and carefully mounts the violent tension to the climactic finish with intelligence and skill. Unlike other vigilante films, this is not a clearcut case of "us versus them," but a statement about the capabilities of violence within all men. Ladd's performance, however, was not one of his best. Though he still maintained a strong screen presence, his portrayal was less than convincing. Gone was the crisp style that had made his name in the 1940s, replaced with an almost tired performance that doesn't quite fit the character. Still, the film's film noir style works well with the story. It may not be Ladd's best, but it works well on its own level.

p, William Bloom; d, Philip Leacock; w, Bernard C. Schoenfeld, Robert Presnell, Jr. (based on the novel *The Tiger Among Us* by Leigh Brackett); ph, Charles Lawton, Jr.; m, George Duning; ed, Al Clark; art d, Walter Holscher; set d, Darrell Silvera; cos, Israel Berne, Pat Page; makeup, Ben Lane.

Drama   (PR:O   MPAA:NR)

THIRTEEN WOMEN** (1932) 74m RKO bw

Ricardo Cortez (*Sgt. Barry Clive*), Irene Dunne (*Laura Stanhope*), Myrna Loy (*Ursula Georgi*), Jill Esmond (*Jo Turner*), Florence Eldredge (*Grace Coombs*), Kay Johnson (*Helen Dawson*), Julie Haydon (*Mary*), Harriet Hagman (*May Raskob*), Mary Duncan (*June Raskob*), Peg Entwistle (*Hazel*), Elsie Prescott (*Nan*), Wally Albright (*Bobby Stanhope*), C. Henry Gordon (*Swami Yogadachi*), Ed Pawley (*Burns, Chauffeur*), Blanche Frederici (*Miss Kirsten*), Marjorie Gateson (*Martha*), Phyllis Fraser (*12th Woman*), Betty Furness (*13th Woman*), Audrey Scott, Aloha Porter (*Equestriennes*), Clayton Behee, Eddie Viera, Eddie DeComa, Buster Bartell (*Trapeze Acts*), Teddy Mangean (*Wire Walker*), Cliff Herbert (*Circus Act*), Lee Phelps (*Conductor*), Edward LeSaint (*Police Chief*), Leon Ames, Kenneth Thomson, Clarence Geldert, Violet Seaton, Louis Natheaux, Oscar Smith, Allan Pomeroy.

Loy is a half Japanese-half Indian woman forced to leave a college sorority because of 12 racist members. She sets up a plan for revenge using Gordon, an astrologer, to assist her. He comes up with terrifying horoscopes for the assorted victims that frightens the women into doing terrible things. One kills herself while another murders her husband. The terror continues until Gordon predicts a tragic ending for Loy. She forces him into leaping in front of a subway train through an "evil eye" trick, but his prophecy comes true. After trying to kill Dunne's son with poisoned candy, she arouses suspicion from police detective Cortez. He follows her to a train station where she plans to do away with Dunne once and for all, but instead meets her own death fleeing from Cortez. Loy is overwhelming in her role, and there are some moments of interesting terror, but ultimately this ends up with an implausible, poorly done direction.

p, David O. Selznick; d, George Archainbaud; w, Bartlett Cormack, Samuel Ornitz (based on the novel by Tiffany Thayer); ph, Leo Tover; ed, Buddy Kimball.

Drama/Suspense   (PR:C   MPAA:NR)

THIRTEENTH CANDLE, THE*½ (1933, Brit.) 68m WB-FN bw

Isobel Elsom (*Lady Sylvia Meeton*), Arthur Maude (*Sir Charles Meeton*), Gibb McLaughlin (*Capt. Blythe*), Joyce Kirby (*Marie*), Louis Hayward (*Paul Marriott*), Louis Goodrich (*Tarrant*), D.A. Clarke-Smith (*Blades*), Winifred Oughton (*Pettit*), Claude Fleming (*Sgt. Harris*), Charles Childerstone (*Inspector Hart*), Eric Hales, Hilliard Vox.

Thirteen is an unlucky number in this mystery about a village squire who is murdered in his house during a dinner party. All the clues point to his wife, Elsom, but McLaughlin, a friend of the accused, proves that the family chauffeur is the guilty one. The title refers to the 13th candle of the chandelier which triggered a dagger to be sent into the squire.

p, Irving Asher; d, John Daumery; w, Brock Williams.

Crime/Mystery   (PR:A   MPAA:NR)

THIRTEENTH CHAIR, THE** (1930) 71m MGM bw

Conrad Nagel (*Richard Crosby*), Lelia Hyams (*Helen O'Neill*), Margaret Wycherly (*Mme. Rosalie La Grange*), Helen Millard (*Mary Eastwood*), Holmes Herbert (*Sir Roscoe Crosby*), Mary Forbes (*Lady Crosby*), Bela Lugosi (*Inspector Delzante*), John Davidson (*Edward Wales*), Charles Quartermaine (*Dr. Philip Mason*), Moon Carroll (*Helen Trent*), Cyril Chadwick (*Brandon Trent*), Bertram Johns (*Howard Standish*), Gretchen Holland (*Grace Standish*), Frank Leigh (*Prof. Feringeea*), Clarence Geldert (*Commissioner Grimshaw*), Lal Chand Mehra (*Chotee*), Joel McCrea.

The second filmed version of this popular Broadway play (a silent version was made in 1919) is notable as the first collaboration between director Browning and Lugosi, the team that would gain much success with DRACULA in just two years. Wycherly recreates her Broadway role for this version, playing a medium who's really just a kindhearted fake. She takes in Hyams, a young runaway. A murderer is on the loose and Hyams is blamed for the killings. Wycherly stages a seance and exposes the killer, freeing Hyams from any guilt. Lugosi is the inspector investigating the crime. The players read their lines in overblown English accents (the story takes place in India), which sounded bad in 1930 and have not aged well with time.

p&d, Tod Browning; w, Elliot Clawson (based on the play by Bayard Veiller); ph, Merritt B. Gersted; ed, Harry Reynolds; titles, Joe Farnham.

Mystery   (PR:A   MPAA:NR)

THIRTEENTH CHAIR, THE** (1937) 66m MGM bw

Dame May Whitty (*Mme. Rosalie La Grange*), Madge Evans (*Helen O'Neill*), Lewis Stone (*Inspector Marney*), Elissa Landi (*Helen Trent*), Thomas Beck (*Dick Crosby*), Henry Daniell (*John Wales*), Janet Beecher (*Lady Crosby*), Ralph Forbes (*Lionel Trent*), Holmes Herbert (*Sir Roscoe Crosby*), Heather Thatcher (*Mary Eastwood*), Charles Trowbridge (*Dr. Mason*), Robert Coote (*Stanish*), Elsa Buchanan (*Miss Stanish*), Lal Chand Mehra (*Prof. Feringeea*), Neil Fitzgerald (*Constable*), Louis Vincenot (*Chotee*), Matthew Boulton (*Commissioner Grimshaw*).

Third filmed version of the Broadway show is a pretty dull affair enlivened only by Whitty's good performance. All the hokum of mediums are exposed in this, as Whitty helps Stone investigate a murder. The best scenes involve Whitty leading a seance, otherwise this is a ho-hum mystery. Herbert repeated his role from the 1930 film here, that starred Bela Lugosi.

p, J.J. Cohn; d, George B. Seitz; w, Marion Parsonnet (based on a play by Bayard Veiller); ph, Charles Clarke; m, David Snell; ed, W. Donn Hayes; art d, Cedric Gibbons.

Mystery   (PR:A   MPAA:NR)

THIRTEENTH GUEST, THE**½ (1932) 69m MON bw (GB: LADY BEWARE)

Ginger Rogers (*Marie Morgan/Lela*), Lyle Talbot (*Phil Winston*), J. Farrell MacDonald (*Capt. Ryan*), James C. Eagles (*Harold "Bud" Morgan*), Eddie Phillips (*Thor Jensen*), Erville Alderson (*John Adams*), Robert Klein (*John Barksdale*), Crauford Kent (*Dr. Sherwood*), Frances Rich (*Marjorie Thornton*), Ethel Wales (*Aunt Joan Thornton*), Paul Hurst (*Detective Grump*), William B. Davidson (*Capt. Brown*), Phillips Smalley (*Uncle Dick Thornton*), Tom London (*Detective Carter*), Harry Tenbrook (*Cabby*), John Ince (*John Morgan*), Allan Cavan (*Uncle Wayne Seymour*), Alan Bridge (*Policeman*), Henry Hall (*Sergeant, Jailer*), Tiny Sandford (*Mike, Jailer*), Kit Guard, Lynton Brent (*Prisoners*), Adrienne Dore (*Winston's Date*), Charles Meacham (*Marie's Father*), Isobel LeMall (*Marie's Mother*), Robert Klein (*John Barksdale, Lawyer*), Bobby Burns (*Photographer*).

In what was Rogers' second feature (and her first melodrama), the young starlet found herself deep in trouble. It's 13 years after a dinner party where all 13 guests were shocked when the host suddenly died. Now everyone who was there is back and a hooded killer is determined that none of them shall survive. Though only average as thrillers go, this was better than many programmer mysteries went. Performances are good with a direction that handles the unusual story well. Because of Rogers' popularity, in later years this film was re-released several times. It was later remade as THE MYSTERY OF THE THIRTEENTH GUEST.

p, M.H. Hoffman; d, Albert Ray; w, Frances Hyland, Arthur Hoerl, Armitage Trail (based on the novel by Trail); ph, Harry Neumann, Tom Galligan; ed, Leete R. Brown; art d, Gene Hornbostel.

Mystery   Cas.   (PR:A   MPAA:NR)

13TH HOUR, THE*½   (1947) 65m COL bw

Richard Dix, Karen Morley, Mark Dennis, John Kellogg, Bernardene Hayes, Jim Bannon, Regis Toomey, Nancy Saunders, Lillian Wells, Michael Towne, Anthony Warde, Jack Carrington, Charles Jordan, Ernie Adams, Selmer Jackson, Pat O'Malley, Cliff Clark, Ed Park.

Dix is the head of a trucking firm framed for murder by a jealous rival. Dix has difficulty proving his innocence but at the last minute is able to uncloak the real culprit. The final film for Richard "The Jaw" Dix after 97 films.

p, Rudolph Flothow; d, William Clemens; w, Edward Bock, Raymond L. Schrock (based on a story by Leslie Edgley); ph, Vincent Farrar; m, Wilbur Hatch; ed, Dwight Caldwell; md, Misha Bakaleinikoff; art d, Hans Radon; set d, Albert Richard.

Crime Drama   **(PR:A MPAA:NR)**

THIRTEENTH LETTER, THE***   (1951) 85m FOX bw

Linda Darnell (*Denise*), Charles Boyer (*Dr. Laurent*), Michael Rennie (*Dr. Pearson*), Constance Smith (*Cora Laurent*), Francoise Rosay (*Mrs. Sims*), Judith Evelyn (*Sister Marie*), Guy Sorel (*Robert Helier*), June Hedin (*Rochelle*), Camille Ducharme (*Fredette*), Paul Guevremont (*Postman*), George Alexander (*Dr. Fletcher*), J. Leo Cagnon (*Dr. Helier*), Ovila Legare (*Mayor*), Wilford Davidson, Arthur Groulx, Sheila Coonan, L.P. Herbert, Odie Lemire, Gilles Pelletier, C. Bosvier, J.L. Roux, Blanche Gauthier, Jerry Rowan, Louis Roux, Eleanor Stuart, Lucie Boitres (*Townspeople*), Jacques Auger (*Priest*), Patrick O'Moore, Robin Hughes (*Interns*), Stanley Mann, Vernon Steele (*Officers*).

In a small town in French Canada, Smith, the wife of doctor Boyer, receives a letter accusing her of having an affair with young doctor Rennie. Soon more poison pen letters begin to appear, all signed with the mysterious pseudonym "Raven," and soon everyone in town begins to suspect everyone else. One letter informs a shell-shocked veteran that he is dying of cancer and the distraught man commits suicide. Suspicion falls on a nurse, who is imprisoned, but the letters continue to come, one falling out of the choir loft while everyone is at church. Boyer assumes control of the investigation and analyzes the handwriting of everyone in the choir, but he is unable to determine the culprit. Finally it is Rennie who learns the identity of "The Raven." It is Smith, who wrote the first letter when the aloof Rennie failed to notice her attraction to him. The real villain, though, is Boyer, who discovered his wife's action and forced her to continue to write the letters in order to prove some strange theory of his about "insanity of two." As Boyer himself writes a final letter, the vengeful mother of the suicidal veteran slips up behind him and slits the good doctor's throat from ear to ear. While not nearly so good as the original, Henri-George Clouzot's THE RAVEN (LE CORBEAU), Preminger's film does have some power and a great deal of suspense. Boyer returned to the screen after a three-year absence, no longer as a romantic idol, but rather as a character actor, a career almost as satisfying as his earlier one. His own and the other leads are also convincingly done, especially Rennie's idealistic but solitary doctor and Darnell's clubfooted would-be seductress. For most of the lesser roles, Preminger cast unknowns, most of whom do a creditable job.

p&d, Otto Preminger; w, Howard Koch (based on the story and screenplay "Le Corbeau" by Louis Chavance); ph, Joseph LaShelle; m, Alex North; ed, Louis Loeffler; md, Lionel Newman; art d, Lyle Wheeler, Maurice Ransford; set d, Thomas Little, Walter M. Scott; cos, Edward Stevenson; spec eff, Fred Sersen; makeup, Ben Nye.

Drama   **(PR:C MPAA:NR)**

THIRTEENTH MAN, THE**   (1937) 70m MON bw

Weldon Heyburn (*Swifty Taylor*), Inez Courtney (*Julie Walters*), Selmer Jackson (*Baldwin*), Milburn Stone (*Jimmy Moran*), Matty Fain (*Louie Cristy*), Robert E. Homans (*Lt. O'Hara*), Eadie Adams (*Stella Leroy*), Grace Durkin (*Alice Bryant*), Sidney D. Albrook (*Legs Henderson*).

When a local crusading district attorney is killed by a poison dart, newspaperman Stone looks into the murder. He, too, is killed so gossip columnist Heyburn takes over the story. He ends up finding the killer–his own boss, publisher Jackson–and marrying his secretary, Courtney, as well. The direction is at a nice quick pace but the photography leaves a little to be desired. Actor Stone's first featured film when he was still practically a juvenile. He later went on to win an Emmy award for his 20-season characterization as "Doc Adams" on TV's "Gunsmoke." Courtney, who played comic-pal parts to many femme leads, here handles the femme-lead spot well herself.

p, Lon Young; d, William Nigh; w, John Krafft; ph, Paul Ivano; ed, Russell Schoengarth.

Mystery   **Cas.**   **(PR:A MPAA:NR)**

--30--*** (1959) 96m Mark VII/WB bw (GB: DEADLINE MIDNIGHT)

Jack Webb (*Sam Gatlin*), William Conrad (*Jim Bathgate*), David Nelson (*Earl Collins*), Whitney Blake (*Peggy Gatlin*), Louise Lorimer (*Bernice Valentine*), James Bell (*Ben Quinn*), Nancy Valentine (*Jan Price*), Joe Flynn (*Hy Shapiro*), Richard Bakalyan (*Carl Thompson*), Dick Whittinghill (*Fred*

Kendall*), John Nolan (*Ron Danton*), Donna Sue Needham (*Lucille Greghauser*).

Interesting feature directed by and starring Webb as the managing editor of a newspaper working the late shift on a more or less typical Thursday night. Conrad is the crusty city editor, Lorimer the dowager rewrite-woman who has seen it all and remained above it, and Nelson the much put-upon copy boy. The film starts as Webb arrives in the city room late after his regular visit to the graves of his first wife and child. He is having trouble with his new wife who wants to adopt a child, something Webb just can't bring himself to do. As the night goes on, two news items come into prominence: the first concerns a little girl who wanders into the city's storm drains and becomes lost as a storm begins to fill the sewers; the second is the story of an attempt by Air Force pilots to set a new record flying from Hawaii to Washington, D.C., Lorimer's grandson among the fliers. The whole office holds its breath as the search for the girl continues while the waters rise and as the planes disappear. Eventually the girl is found and the story is the headline, but the plane story is less happy, and the planes are discovered to have crashed with no survivors. Lorimer is visibly distressed and Webb tells her to go home, but she insists on writing up the story of her grandson's death before going. Webb comes to some sort of conclusions about life and death during the course of the evening's events and tells his wife that he no longer opposes adopting a child. Well-done newspaper story has the usual faults of Webb's films–dialog staccato to the point of silliness and a directorial style serviceable at best, but it works here, especially in the later scenes as the whole staff gets down to the real work of getting the paper out. Conrad is very good as the city editor and Lorimer gives a convincing performance as a woman whose job is more important than her emotions. One of the most accurate and most memorable newspaper films ever made, and one of Webb's best productions.

p&d, Jack Webb; w, William Bowers; ph, Edward Colman; m, Ray Heindorf; ed, Robert M. Leeds; art d, Feild Gray, Gibson Holley; m/l, "Boy," Don Ralke, William Bowers, sung by David Nelson.

Drama   **(PR:A-C MPAA:NR)**

THIRTY-DAY PRINCESS**½   (1934) 74m PAR bw

Sylvia Sidney (*Nancy Lane/Princess Catterina Theodora Margerita Zizzi*), Cary Grant (*Porter Madison III*), Edward Arnold (*Richard Gresham*), Henry Stephenson (*King Anatole XII*), Vincent Barnett (*Count Nicholaus*), Edgar Norton (*Baron Passeria*), Ray Walker (*Dan Kirk*), Lucien Littlefield (*Parker*), Robert McWade (*Managing Editor*), George Baxter (*Donald Spottswood*), Eleanor Wesselhoeft (*Mrs. Schmidt the Landlady*), Frederic Sullivan, William Augustin (*Detectives*), Ed Dearing (*Tim the Policeman at Mrs. Schmidt's*), Bruce Warren (*Spottswood's Friend*), William Arnold (*City Editor*), J. Merrill Holmes (*Radio Man at Boat*), Dick Rush (*Sergeant of Police*), Jean Chatburn (*Blonde*), Maj. Sam Harris (*Court Officer*), Marguerite Namara (*Lady in Waiting*), Thorner Monk (*Gresham's Butler*), Skippy (*The Wire-Haired Terrier Dog*).

A combination of "Cinderella" and "The Prisoner Of Zenda," this is a pleasant comedy with a few moments of exceptional dialog from the typewriters of Preston Sturges and several others. Sidney plays a dual role as the princess of a middle European country and a New York struggling actress. When Sidney (we'll use that name when referring to the princess) comes to the U.S. to secure backing for her country's bond issue, she contracts a case of the mumps and has to be put in bed immediately. Arnold is the Manhattan banker behind the bonds and stands to lose a huge commission if this falls through. Sidney is scheduled for several public appearances in front of various potential investors and so a substitute has to be found. (A similar plot was used in FOLIES BERGERE and countless other movies.) Arnold knows that in a city the size of New York there must be some woman who can be pressed into service. Sylvia, an actress who is one step away from welfare, is found and hired to be Sidney until the latter's mumps disappear. Grant publishes New York's most important newspaper and knows the real reason why the princess has come. Although the official press release is that she's here on a goodwill mission, Grant suspects Arnold's motives and knows that the man is not to be trusted. Further, Grant is an America-first type who abhors anyone not home-grown. When Grant meets Sylvia, he is at once entranced by her and his reservations about foreigners begin to crumble. Grant falls in love with Sylvia, but thinking she is a princess, he keeps his attentions on the highest level and never admits how he feels. Sylvia is falling in love with Grant but he is so important in the press that she can't come clean. When Sidney's European boy friend Barnett arrives, he becomes insanely jealous of the goo-goo eyes being made by the two. A few plot turns for good comedic value and, after a month, Sidney's jaws abate and she can again resume her position as princess. Grant is stunned to think that he believed Sylvia but that's set aside when he realizes that he does love her and that he can marry her. This plot is so old that it must have been found written in cuneiform somewhere. Yet Grant's sincerity and Sidney's charm manage to carry it off. Barnett is a smasher as the suitor and gets huge laughs in an unaccustomed role.

p, B.P. Schulberg; d, Marion Gering; w, Sam Hellman, Edwin Justus Mayer, Preston Sturges, Frank Partos (based on the story by Clarence Buddington Kelland); ph, Leon Shamroy; ed, June Loring; art d, Hans Dreier.

Comedy   **(PR:A MPAA:NR)**

THIRTY DAYS (SEE: SILVER LINING, 1932)

THIRTY FOOT BRIDE OF CANDY ROCK, THE** (1959) 75m D.R.B./COL bw

Lou Costello *(Artie Pinsetter)*, Dorothy Provine *(Emmy Lou Raven)*, Gale Gordon *(Raven)*, Jimmy Conlin *(Magruder)*, Charles Lane *(Standard Bates)*, Robert Burton *(First General)*, Will Wright *(Pentagon General)*, Lenny Kent *(Sergeant)*, Ruth Perrott *(Aunt May)*, Peter Leeds *(Bill Burton)*, Bobby Barber, Joey Faye, Doodles Weaver, Jack Rice, Russell Trent, Joe Greene *(Boosters)*, Robert Nichols *(Bank Manager)*, Veola Vonn *(Jackie Delaney)*, Jack Straw *(Pilot)*.

Costello made this, his only film without long-time partner Bud Abbott, after his bitter splitup with his straight man. The picture is basically a one-joke one, the theme being that "size isn't everything," with the sexually suggestive subject muted sufficiently to make it suitable for younger audiences. Mixing science fiction with domestic farce, much like its precursor THE ATTACK OF THE 50-FOOT WOMAN (1958), the plot line deals with independent garbage collector Costello's invention of a time machine (Conlin) crafted from bits of junk. When girl friend Provine wanders into a canyon known as "Dinosaur Springs," strange forces cause her to grow to the title height. Costello attempts to explain her plight to her father, Gordon, the town's capitalist despot, who controls all local industries save for Costello's minuscule enterprise. Misconstruing Costello's reference to Provine's "increased size," Gordon forces the confused Costello to marry his monstrous daughter. Ultimately, the time machine– which shares its creator's confusion–sets things right, but only after the town is mistakenly terrorized and military forces are called into action. The basic comedy idea by Rabin and Block is expressed in the difficulties experienced by the loving but size-mismatched newlyweds during their initial domestic days. The picture was advertised as being lensed in "Wonderama" and "Mattascope," which appear to be nothing more than conventional matte processes. Fairly funny and, without the services of Abbott, less frantically paced than most Costello vehicles. Costello died shortly before the film's release.

p, Lewis J. Rachmil; d, Sidney Miller; w, Rowland Barber, Arthur Ross (based on a story by Lawrence L. Goldman from an idea by Jack Rabin, Irving Block); ph, Frank G. Carson; m, Raoul Kraushaar; ed, Al Clark; md, Kraushaar; art d, William Flannery; spec eff, Rabin, Block, Louis DeWitt.

Comedy **(PR:AAA MPAA:NR)**

30 IS A DANGEROUS AGE, CYNTHIA*½** (1968, Brit.) 85 COL c

Dudley Moore *(Rupert Street)*, Eddie Foy, Jr *(Oscar)*, Suzy Kendall *(Louise Hammond)*, John Bird *(Herbert Greenslade)*, Duncan MacRae *(Jock McCue)*, Patricia Routledge *(Mrs. Woolley)*, Peter Bayliss *(Victor)*, John Wells *(Hon. Gavin Hopton)*, Harry Towb *(Mr. Woolley)*, Jonathan Routh *(Capt. Gore-Taylor)*, Ted Dicks *(Horst Cohen, Jr.)*, Nicky Henson *(Paul)*, Clive Dunn *(Doctor)*, Frank Thornton *(Registrar)*, Derek Farr *(TV Announcer)*, Michael MacLiammoir *(Irish Storyteller)*, Dudley Moore Trio.

A virtual Dudley Moore festival as he stars, wrote the score, cowrote the script, and even conducted his own trio (Moore is a superb pianist), playing the background music. Moore is going through an age crisis as he teeters on the brink of 30. (He later did it again when he was supposedly 42 in the movie 10). His ambition is to be married and to write a smash musical before he reaches that age. The only problem is that he is working so hard at the nightclub owned by MacRae that he has no time to write and even less to find a suitable mate. MacRae runs his club like an army camp and even makes the employees line up for fingernail inspection before they can go to work. Moore is so determined to get married that he takes out a marriage license but leaves the name of the bride empty because he still hasn't found anyone. (A similar character was seen in THE TENDER TRAP when Debbie Reynolds already had her wedding date set, with no man to march her down the aisle until she nailed Sinatra.) Moore lives at a boarding house overseen by Routledge and is thrilled when Kendall, an art student, moves in. He sets his sights on the beauteous artist and pays no attention to the fact that she already has a boy friend in Henson. Kendall and Henson come to see Moore play piano in MacRae's club and there is a battle between the diminuitive Moore and the larger Henson which results in Moore's arm being broken. This delights Moore's agent, Bayliss, because it will give the composer a chance to work on his musical. Moore's friend is Foy, who takes him to Dublin where he can have some peace and get to work on the musical. But Moore finds no inspiration until he meets MacLiammoir, a story-teller who provides Moore with the needed plot for the musical. Kendall has gone north to Birmingham after battling with Henson. Moore writes furiously, finishes his opus, then travels south to Birmingham to locate Kendall. He doesn't know it but he is being tailed by private eye Bird, who's been hired by Bayliss to bring Moore back to London. Once Moore finds Kendall, he admits that the marriage license he carries has been in his possession since long before they met. Nevertheless, she finds him attractive and decides to marry him. The musical is staged (with a takeoff on the Radio City Musical Hall's leggy "Rockettes" and some brilliant parodies of pieces by Amadeus Wolfgang Mozart, Ludwig von Beethoven, Johann Sebastian Bach, and Moore even does some of the singing) and is a hit. It's all unbelievable that so much could take place in two weeks (it requires about six weeks of rehearsal to mount a musical), but there are so many gags and Moore is so ingenuous that logic is tossed out and nobody minds. Moore was married to Kendall for a time, then married actress Tuesday Weld and divorced her. His long-time romance with much taller Susan Anton occurred when both appeared on a TV awards show, "The American Movie Awards, and were introduced at the after-show party at Chasen's restaurant by one of your editors, Ross.

p, Walter Shenson; d, Joseph McGrath; w, Dudley Moore, McGrath, John Wells; ph, Billy Williams; m, Moore; ed, Bill Blunden; art d, Brian Eatwell; cos, Bermans of London; makeup, Cliff Sharpe.

Comedy/Musical **Cas.** **(PR:A-C MPAA:NR)**

39 STEPS, THE***** (1935, Brit.) 85m GAU/GFD bw

Madeleine Carroll *(Pamela)*, Robert Donat *(Richard Hannay)*, Lucie Mannheim *(Miss Smith/Annabella)*, Godfrey Tearle *(Prof. Jordan)*, Peggy Ashcroft *(Margaret, Crofter's Wife)*, John Laurie *(John Crofter)*, Helen Haye *(Mrs. Jordan)*, Wylie Watson *(Mr. Memory)*, Frank Cellier *(Sheriff Watson)*, Peggy Simpson *(Young Maid)*, Gus McNaughton, Jerry Vernon *(Two Voyagers)*, Miles Malleson *(Director of the Palladium)*.

For those who love a grand spy mystery, a wild chase, and a harrowing portrait of an innocent man struggling to prove his innocence while the world turns inexplicably against him, THE 39 STEPS is ideal. Donat is the innocent man, a Canadian rancher on vacation in London. He goes to the London Palladium and enjoys some vaudeville acts, one of which is Mr. Memory, essayed by Watson. The audience is challenged by Watson to stump him on any question concerning facts he has programmed to his photographic memory and he does a remarkable job of answering the oddball queries voiced from members of the audience such as "What causes Pip in poultry?" Suddenly, a shot rings out and the audience panics, everyone running for the exits, including an especially terrified young woman, Mannheim. She begs Donat to help her and he gallantly takes her back to his apartment where she confides her secrets to him. She is a British spy who is on the trail of a masterspy who has valuable military secrets he plans to smuggle out of the country. Mannheim doesn't know the identity of the masterspy, she says, but she does know that he is missing the little finger on his right hand, severed at the first joint, and then she cryptically mentions something about "The 39 Steps," but refuses to go on for fear of involving him further. Donat takes all of this in stride, not really believing Mannheim for a moment. His disbelief changes to horror some hours later when Mannheim, whom he has allowed to stay the night (in another room) staggers into his room and falls forward, a knife buried in her back. She tells him with her dying words that his own life is now in danger and he must flee. Donat takes from her dead hand a map of Scotland which has a circle drawn around a village. Peering outside, Donat sees several men loitering about, staring up at the windows of his apartment. He grabs his coat and hat and dashes downstairs, seeing a milkman entering the foyer, making his deliveries. He tells the milkman that he is escaping from a love nest, that the "old boy" came home unexpectedly and the milkman, appreciating the predicament he's in, allows Donat to disguise himself in his white delivery jacket and carry out the empty bottles to the delivery wagon to avoid detection, for a little cash, of course. Donat completely hoodwinks the men outside and later gets on a train headed for Scotland. In his compartment are two men, McNaughton and Vernon, salesmen who eye him suspiciously. They talk incessantly about cricket and the new corset line they are expected to sell. When the train stops at Edinburgh, Donat gets off and buys a newspaper in the station which is crawling with police. Getting back into his compartment, Donat learns that he is being sought everywhere as the prime suspect in the Mannheim killing. Police have concluded, since Mannheim was found murdered in his rented flat, that he is the logical killer, and he has reaffirmed his guilt by fleeing. The train pulls out of the station and Donat sees that detectives are searching the compartments one by one. Desperately, Donat works his way down the cars ahead of the detectives, but when police show up at the other end of a car he finds himself trapped. He goes into a compartment where a beautiful blonde, Carroll, is reading a book, and sits down next to her. Donat takes her in his arms and tells her that the police are looking for him for a crime he did not commit, begging her not to give him away. When detectives reach the compartment, Donat clutches the startled Carroll and kisses her passionately. A detective looks in on the couple and is about to leave, believing the pair to be lovers, but Carroll breaks away from Donat's hold and says to the detective, "I believe this is the man you are looking for." With that Donat leaps up and out of the compartment, hanging on the side of the still moving train, clinging to windows and handrails, working himself down the car. The train comes to a stop at the orders of police just as it begins to cross the huge Firth of Forth Bridge, one of the engineering marvels of Scotland. Donat makes his precarious way under the bridge, so that he is clinging to the underpining girders as police frantically search the bridge for him. The train then begins to move and Donat escapes, hurrying across the barren Scottish highlands until he comes to small farm. He asks the farmer, Laurie, if he can put him up for the night and offers him a substantial sum. The farmer squints at him and says, "Can ye eat the herring?" Donat tells him he's so hungry he can eat just about anything. Laurie's young, pretty wife, Ashcroft, serves dinner and later chats with Donat who tells her she is attractive and should get into the city, and that she would look good in some of the newly designed dresses being shown in the Edinburgh shops. She is obviously dominated by the cruel Laurie for she quivers in fear whenever the farmer appears. Donat sleeps that night in a tumble bed but at dawn

Ashcroft awakens him, telling him that detectives are outside and that she knows he is the man they are seeking and that her mercenary husband, who has heard about the reward on Donat's head, will probably sell him out. Ashcroft gives Donat one of her husband's old coats and he kisses her hand before fleeing. Laurie enters the house to find Donat but sees he is gone, then confronts his wife, slapping her. Donat is chased along the highlands by the police who even use a helicopter (an early variation thereof) to track him down, but he eludes his pursuers by taking refuge in a great house on a hill where a party is going on. The genial owner, Tearle, takes him in, gives him a drink, and makes him feel comfortable. To the gentle host, a professor, Donat pours out his story and that of Mannheim's, stating that he believes she spoke the truth about the spies and the spymaster, describing how, as Mannheim said, he is missing a little finger at the first joint. Tearle holds up his hand, smiling, and says: "You mean this hand don't you?" He is missing the little finger of his right hand at the first joint and Donat's mouth drops open. He has run straight to the spymaster. When Donat makes a move, Tearle pulls a gun and shoots him. Donat falls to the floor and Tearle goes to get men to remove his body. But when he comes back, Donat is gone. He is shown explaining the whole thing to the local police commissioner in the town. Donat shows the commissioner a Bible which had been tucked away in the old coat Ashcroft gave him, one which absorbed the bullet Tearle fired at him. He tells the commissioner that Tearle is a spymaster and is about to take military secrets out of the country and the commissioner promises that he will look into the matter immediately. There is a knock at the door and the commissioner opens it with a sigh of relief, greeting Scotland Yard detectives. He complains that it took them long enough to answer his call while he "had to keep company with a murderer!" The detectives rush Donat but he smashes a window and escapes to the street, the detectives in hot pursuit. They rush down the crowded street and past a Salvation Army band with marchers behind it. The camera sweeps along with the marchers to show the enterprising Donat with them, marching along, singing their triumphant psalm. He slips out of the line of marching people and into a hall where a political meeting is going on, surprised to discover that he is mistaken for the guest speaker who is long overdue. He stands up when called to the platform and gives an impassioned speech for one of the local politicians running for office, a speech packed with gibberish and gobbldeygook but one which is so moving in a plea for the common man victimized by society (and here he's really talking about himself) that the bored voters come to life and cheer him, begging *him* to be their candidate. Just then Carroll, the beautiful blonde from the train, arrives with the real guest speaker and once she spots Donat on the platform, she calls the Scotland Yard detectives who run in from the street and arrest Donat just as he leaves the stage. They insist Carroll come with them to report Donat's exploits with her on the train, and when she refuses, they pull her into the car and handcuff her to Donat. The car zooms out of the town, heading for another community but Carroll tells them that they are going the wrong way. Donat then realizes that the men are not detectives at all but spies in the employ of the insidious Tearle. When the car stops on a bridge to wait for a herd of sheep to get out of the way, Donat seizes his opportunity and leaps from the car, dragging Carroll with him. He takes her under the bridge and through a gully, to cross the mist- enshrouded moors, covering her mouth with his hand so she will not scream for help. When they finally elude their pursuers and sit down to rest, Carroll tells Donat that she suspects the detectives were not real but she still distrusts him. They make their way to a small inn and, hiding the handcuffs, Donat asks for a room. At first the proprietor refuses, saying that they are booked up, but his wife takes a look at the pair and orders her husband to give them a room, quietly pointing out to him that Donat and Carroll are obviously a "couple of runaways in love," and they should be helped. She even prepares sandwiches and milk for them, taking it to their room as they stand in front of a fire. When she leaves, the two sit down and munch awkwardly on their sandwiches, working around the handcuffs. Carroll complains that her stockings are all wet. Donat suggests that she remove them. Since he is handcuffed to her, he asks, as she bares her legs to the garter line, if he "can be of any assistance," his hand dragged along the line of her leg as she removes the stockings. (This was quite a daring scene for the day and especially daring in that the stunningly beautiful but decidedly prudish Carroll had never before shown so much of her voluptuous body in any film and never would again.) They hang up the stockings to dry before the fireplace and then try to get some sleep, Carroll lying uncomfortably next to Donat on the bed. He jocularly tells her that she has every reason to be afraid, that he comes from a long line of notorious murderers, so infamous that one of his ancestors was reproduced as a wax figure for Madame Tussaud's Museum. Jokes Donat, "Can't mistake him as you go in, red whiskers and a harelip, and that lady is the story of my life, poor orphan boy who never had a chance." Exhausted, he falls asleep and Carroll works her hand free of the handcuff, going out into the hall to look down from a balcony overlooking the registration desk. She is about to call out to the innkeeper when two of the fake detectives rush inside and demand to know where Donat and Carroll are. Then, with the innkeeper gone for a moment, they make a call which Carroll overhears, realizing that the detectives are fake and are working for a secret organization called "The 39 Steps." The innkeeper's wife tells the pursuers that the young couple is not there. She believes she is protecting the runaway lovers. Carroll goes back into the room, looks down lovingly at Donat, knowing him now to be innocent, then curls up on a small couch at the foot of the bed. He is surprised to see her there in the morning, free of the cuffs and that she has not fled. She tells him that she now believes him and mentions the phony detectives who talked about the "The 39 Steps" organization and that they are picking up someone at the Palladium. As Donat rushes to the hall, Carroll goes to the police, telling them the whole story but officials refuse to believe her. All they want is Donat and she tells him she has no idea where he might be. The police follow her when she leaves, right to the London Palladium where Donat sits in the audience, finally realizing that it's Mr. Memory with his photographic recall that the spies are taking out of the country. After Carroll joins him, Donat spots Tearle motioning to Watson. He jumps up from the audience when Watson comes on stage and asks, "What are The 39 Steps?" Instinctively, the little performer answers that "The 39 Steps is an organization of spies collecting information on behalf of the foreign office of–" A shot rings out; Tearle has shot Watson, mortally wounding him. Tearle jumps from his box seat onto the stage and injures his leg. Trying to hobble away, police swarm in on him from all sides, capturing him as the curtain quickly closes. (This scene is almost an exact duplication of the assassination of Lincoln as shown in D.W. Griffith's BIRTH OF A NATION, when actor (later director) Raoul Walsh shoots Edwin Hanneberry, playing Lincoln, and it is obviously Hitchcock's private little bow to the master filmmaker, Griffith.) As Tearle is taken into custody, Watson is helped off the stage and there, for the police, at Donat's urging, rattles off a long, involved mathematical formula for a military engine, one that Tearle had Watson commit to memory. Behind the dying Watson, a line of unconcerned chorines kick their legs high in the air, almost indifferent to the little man bleeding to death in the wings. (Here is Hitchcock, in this little scene, at his most cynical, not only parading the cliche that the show must go on, but stating that the world doesn't care too much about its humanity.) Watson dies after spewing forth the secret and Donat is free to go off with his lady love Carroll. This film was the thriller that established Hitchcock as a masterpiece maker in the mystery-spy genre and the film is jam-packed with his inventive techniques. When the landlady finds Mannheim's corpse at the beginning of the film, she lets out a piercing scream that immediately blends with the screech of a train whistle, allowing Hitchcock to cut to the train station where Donat is boarding the train. His casting here is as brilliant as his astounding camera setups and hair-raising scenes, matching the suave, handsome, and intellectual Donat to the blonde, intelligent, and detached Carroll. Here he matches sound and visual techniques perfectly, "What I like about THE 39 STEPS," Hitchcock once stated, "were the sudden switches and the jumping from one situation to another with such rapidity. Donat leaping out of the police station with half of a handcuff on, and immediately walking into a Salvation Army band, darting down an alleyway into a room. 'Thank God, you've come, Mr. So-and-So,' they say and put him on to a platform. A girl comes along with two men, takes him into a car to the police station, but it's not really to the police station...You know, the rapidity of the switches, that's the great thing about it." The herd of 60 sheep Hitchcock brought onto the set–the entire film was shot inside Lime Grove Studio on the Gaumont lot–caused the director no end of problems. The animals literally ate up his sets. Hitchcock was up to his usual pranks in the production. Carroll and Donat had never met until the first day of shooting and Hitchcock promptly locked them up with handcuffs to get them used to the idea, then disappeared for the whole day, returning to face angry stars. "I just wanted to see how you would cope with it all," he said to them. "You'll have to in the film, you know." Of the astonishingly beautiful leading lady, Hitchcock was to later comment: "I suppose the first blonde who was a real Hitchcock type was Madeleine Carroll. The English woman or the North German or the Swedish can look like a schoolmarm, but boy, when they get going these women are quite astonishing." Donat was a kindred spirit but in one scene with Ashcroft he fell to giggling with her and Hitchcock, after five takes, quelled the outburst by smashing a lamp with his fist. The giggling stopped.

p, Michael Balcon, Ivor Montagu; d, Alfred Hitchcock; w, Charles Bennett, Alma Reville, Ian Hay (based on the novel by John Buchan); ph, Bernard Knowles; m, Louis Levy; ed, Derek Twist; prod d, Otto Wendorff, Albert Jullion; cos, J. Strassner; spec eff, Jack Whitehead.

Spy Drama **Cas.** **(PR:A MPAA:NR)**

THIRTY NINE STEPS, THE** (1960, Brit.) 93m RANK/FOX c

Kenneth More *(Richard Hannay)*, Taina Elg *(Fisher)*, Brenda de Banzie *(Nellie Lumsden)*, Barry Jones *(Prof. Logan)*, Reginald Beckwith *(Lumsden)*, Faith Brook *(Nannie)*, Michael Goodliffe *(Brown)*, James Hayter *(Mr. Memory)*, Duncan Lamont *(Kennedy)*, Jameson Clark *(McDougal)*, Andrew Cruikshank *(Sheriff)*, Leslie Dwyer *(Milkman)*, Betty Henderson *(Mrs. McDougal)*, Joan Hickson *(Miss Dobson)*, Sidney James *(Perce)*, Brian Oulton *(Mr. Pringle)*, Sam Kydd *(Dining Steward)*, John Richardson, Michael Brennan.

This is a remake in every sense of the term. Scene for scene, this version of Hitchcock's great mystery takes the same plot and nearly duplicates the original on every point. Thus it remains uninspired and rather flat despite the addition of color. More and Elg are the saving grace of the film: their coupling is engaging and fun, giving some good life to their respective roles. Released in Britain in 1959. A third version followed in 1978.

p, Betty E. Box; d, Ralph Thomas; w, Frank Harvey (based on the novel by John Buchan); ph, Ernest Steward (CinemaScope, Eastmancolor); m, Clifton Parker; ed, Alfred Roome; cos, Yvonne Caffin.

Mystery **Cas.** **(PR:C MPAA:NR)**

THIRTY NINE STEPS, THE½** (1978, Brit.) 102m RANK/International Picture Show c

Robert Powell *(Hannay)*, David Warner *(Appleton)*, Eric Porter *(Lomas)*, Karen Dotrice *(Alex)*, John Mills *(Scudder)*, George Baker *(Sir Walter Bullivant)*, Ronald Pickup *(Bayliss)*, Donald Pickering *(Marshall)*, Timothy West *(Porton)*, Miles Anderson *(David)*, Andrew Keir *(Lord Rohan)*, Robert Flemyng *(Magistrate)*, William Squire *(Harkness)*, Paul McDowell *(McLean)*, David Collings *(Tillotson)*, John Normington *(Fletcher)*, John Welsh *(Lord Belthane)*, Edward De Souza *(Woodville)*, Tony Steedman *(Admiral)*, John Grieve *(Police Constable Forbes)*, Andrew Downie *(Stewart)*, Donald Bisset *(Renfrew)*, Derek Anders *(Donald)*, Oliver Maquire *(Martins)*, Joan Henley *(Lady Nettleship)*, Prentis Hancock *(Perryman)*, Leo Dolan *(Milkman)*, James Garbutt *(Miller)*, Artro Morris *(The Scott)*, Robert Gillespie *(Crombie)*, Raymond Young *(Guide)*, Paul Jerricho *(Police Constable Scott)*, Michael Bilton *(Vicar)*.

The third version of this mystery story differs from the earlier two in that this is a more faithful adaptation of the original novel. Powell and Dotrice are all right, though nothing terrific, as the couple running across the Scottish Highlands, nicely lensed with some good location shooting. The new ending, with Powell dangling from the minute hand of Big Ben is a letdown, more reminiscent of Harold Lloyd's SAFETY LAST than thriller material. Some good support comes from Warner as the villain, and the film does capture the WW I era with nice feeling. There's a lot of energy in this picture that makes it fun in its own way.

p, Greg Smith; d, Don Sharp; w, Michael Robson (based on the novel by John Buchan); ph, John Coquillion; m, Ed Welch; ed, Eric Boyd-Perkins; prod d, Harry Pottle.

Thriller (PR:C MPAA:PG)

THIRTY SECONDS OVER TOKYO**** (1944) 138m MGM bw

Spencer Tracy *(Lt. Col. James H. Doolittle)*, Van Johnson *(Capt. Ted W. Lawson)*, Robert Walker *(David Thatcher)*, Phyllis Thaxter *(Ellen Jones Lawson)*, Tim Murdock *(Dean Davenport)*, Scott McKay *(Davey Jones)*, Gordon McDonald *(Bob Clever)*, Don DeFore *(Charles McClure)*, Robert Mitchum *(Bob Gray)*, John R. Reilly *(Shorty Manch)*, Horace 'Stephen' McNally *(Doc White)*, Donald Curtis *(Lt. Randall)*, Louis Jean Heydt *(Lt. Miller)*, William Phillips *(Don Smith)*, Douglas Cowan *(Brick Holstrom)*, Paul Langton *(Capt. Ski York)*, Leon Ames *(Lt. Jurika)*, Moroni Olsen *(General)*, Benson Fong *(Young Chung)*, Dr. Hsin Kung Chuan Chi *(Old Chung)*, Myrna Dell, Peggy Maley, Hazel Brooks, Elaine Shepard, Kay Williams *(Girls in Officer's Club)*, Dorothy Ruth Morris *(Jane)*, Ann Shoemaker *(Mrs. Parker)*, Alan Napier *(Mr. Parker)*, Wah Lee *(Foo Ling)*, Ching Wah Lee *(Guerrilla Charlie)*, Jacqueline White *(Emmy York)*, Jack McClendon *(Dick Joyce)*, John Kellogg *(Pilot)*, Peter Varney *(Spike Henderson)*, Steve Brodie *(M.P.)*, Morris Ankrum *(Capt. Halsey)*, Selena Royle *(Mrs. Jones)*, Harry Hayden *(Judge)*, Blake Edwards *(2nd Officer)*, Will Walls *(Hoss Wyler)*, Jay Norris *(Hallmark)*, Robert Bice *(Jig White)*, Bill Williams *(Bud Felton)*, Wally Cassell *(Sailor)*.

In 1942, 131 days after the Japanese bombing of Pearl Harbor that brought the U.S. into WW II, an American force retaliated, bombing the major Japanese cities of Tokyo and Yokohama. This picture is a quasi-documentary re-creation of that event, as authored by one of the survivors of the raid, Ted Lawson (played by Johnson). Army Air Corps captain Johnson is informed that he is to be one of the fliers to perform a dangerous top-secret mission, a retaliatory surprise attack on Japan. Island bases near the target being unavailable–and in-flight refueling techniques undeveloped–a dangerous, untried tactic must be employed: for the first time in history, twin-engined bombers will take off from the deck of an aircraft carrier. Since the large aircraft can't land on a carrier deck, after the attack they must attempt to make it to mainland China–then occupied by enemy forces–to land, and make their way back as best they can. Tracy–as Lt. Col. Doolittle–will lead the mission. He visits the assembled airmen to explain the dangers of the near-kamikaze assault and tells the fliers that if any of them want to drop out, they may do so without fear of besmirching their service records. Weeks of preparation and training take place before the aircraft and their crews are finally loaded aboard the *USS Hornet*. Following a final shipboard briefing by Tracy, the fliers man their twin-engine Mitchell bombers. The China Sea is choppy, and an impending storm forces the planes to catapult from the flight deck ahead of schedule, led by the aircraft piloted by Tracy. The remainder of the film follows the adventures of Johnson's crew only, the men who man the "Ruptured Duck." Hurtling from the aircraft carrier in Tracy's bomber's wake, pilot Johnson, copilot Murdock, navigator DeFore, gunner-mechanic Walker, and other crewmen, including Mitchum (playing his last minor character part; he was to go on to greater things)–head for Japan. The strategy calls for the aircraft to fly at low altitude in the hope that they will be mistaken for Japanese bombers returning from a mission. The plan succeeds beyond the wildest dreams of its planners; Japanese are seen waving at the aircraft in friendly fashion as they speed inland. The low- flying, unopposed aircraft crews find their targets easily and drop their deadly cargoes, raining destruction on two of the enemy's major industrial centers. The jubilant crews now face the difficult part of the mission: the ill-planned return. Forced to crash-land the "Ruptured Duck" off the coast of China, pilot Johnson is injured. Helped by Walker and other crewmen, he manages to make the shoreline, where the survivors are greeted by friendly Chinese. Sheltered by these new-found friends, the crewmen manage to evade capture by the occupying Japanese forces. Johnson's injured leg gets gangrenous and requires amputation. It is severed below the knee by primitive means with the help of the locals, who later thoughtlessly present the one-legged survivor with a gift of a pair of slippers. When the injured Johnson recovers enough to be able to travel–albeit with difficulty and pain–he and the other survivors are helped to Allied lines by Chinese guerrillas. Reunited with his commander, Tracy, who has also made it home, the thankful, wheelchair-ridden Johnson sees his bride Thaxter enter his hospital room. Forgetful of his missing limb, the excited airman rises from his wheelchair and falls flat on his face. A well-made war film, THIRTY SECONDS OVER TOKYO was sufficiently true to its topic to cause all the principals in the real-life situation to give their approval for the use of their actual names for the picture. Released two-and- half years after the actual event, to a public weary of seeing John Wayne cradling a machine gun in his arms to decimate the enemy, the studio had serious reservations about the picture's acceptance. The movie moguls needn't have worried; the verisimilitudinous picture was well received by both critics and the public. In its initial release, it grossed $4.5 million in domestic rentals alone. Tracy gives a sterling performance as Doolittle in what is, basically, a cameo part. The actor was initially loath to accept the role, feeling that he was being stereotyped as a war hero (A GUY NAMED JOE, 1943, and THE SEVENTH CROSS, 1944), and he was hesitant about simulating a *real* war hero such as Doolittle. He took the part partly in order to boost the budding career of his friend, Johnson, knowing that his name on the marquee would add to public interest in the picture. This was Johnson's first important dramatic part, and the boyish actor handled it well. Phlegmatic actor Mitchum had just signed a new contract with RKO and was on loan-out. Viewing Mitchum's test for his part, director LeRoy reportedly told the actor, "You're either the lousiest actor in the world or the best. I can't make up my mind which." When the picture was re-released in 1955, new screen credits were shot, with Mitchum's name coming ahead of the title–along with Tracy's and Johnson's–to replace that of the deceased Robert Walker, an honor ill-merited by the small role Mitchum played in the picture. In the ancillary love story– mandatory for the studio's 1940s formula–Thaxter makes her film debut as Johnson's wife. Her work was appealing enough to gain her a contract with the studio. She was to work again with Johnson in WEEKEND AT THE WALDORF (1945), and with Tracy in THE SEA OF GRASS (1947). The picture also marked the screen debut of Steve Brodie. In small roles were future director Blake Edwards and Kay Williams, later the wife of Clark Gable. Screenwriter Trumbo wisely elected not to attempt to alter the limited perspective of coauthor Lawson's memoir by including more of the details of the famous raid. In the actual event, all of the 16 bombers that participated made it to China, although three men died in crashes. Eleven other men were captured by the Japanese, who executed three of them. Doolittle was 45 years old at the time. He had earlier made his mark as a pilot when he made the first coast-to-coast flight to take place during a single day in 1922, when he was only 25. The scene depicting the approach to Tokyo from the nose pod of Johnson's bomber was later reused, appearing behind the opening credits of MIDWAY (1976). It was the best thing about that picture. THIRTY SECONDS OVER TOKYO was number eight in the National Board of Review's list of ten best. It received an Oscar for Best Special Effects.

p, Sam Zimbalist; d, Mervyn LeRoy; w, Dalton Trumbo (based on the book by Capt. Ted W. Lawson, Robert Considine); ph, Harold Rosson, Robert Surtees; m, Herbert Stothart; ed, Frank Sullivan; art d, Cedric Gibbons, Paul Groesse; set d, Edwin B. Willis, Ralph S. Hurst; spec eff, A. Arnold Gillespie, Warren Newcombe, Donald Jahraus; m/l, "Sweetheart of All My Dreams" (Art Fitch, Kay Fitch, Bert Lowe), "Wonderful One" (Dorothy Terris, Paul Whiteman, Ferde Grofe).

War (PR:A MPAA:NR)

THIRTY-SIX HOURS (SEE: TERROR STREET, 1953)

36 HOURS*** (1965) 115m Perlberg-Seaton-Cherokee/MGM bw

James Garner *(Maj. Jefferson Pike)*, Rod Taylor *(Maj. Walter Gerber, Psychiatrist)*, Eva Marie Saint *(Anna Hedler)*, Werner Peters *(Otto Schack)*, Alan Napier *(Col. Peter MacLean)*, Celia Lovsky *(Elsa)*, John Banner *(Ernst)*, Ed Gilbert *(Capt. Abbott)*, Russell Thorson *(Gen. Allison)*, Oscar Beregi *(Lt. Col. Ostermann)*, Sig Rumann *(German Guard)*, Karl Held *(Cpl. Kenter)*, Martin Kosleck *(Kraatz)*, Majorie Bennett *(Charwoman)*, Henry Rowland, Otto Reichow *(German Soldiers)*, Hilda Plowright *(German Agent)*, Walter Friedel *(Denker)*, Joseph Mell *(Lemke)*, John Gilgreen *(Lt. Busch)*, Joe de Reda, Jeffrey Morris *(GIs)*, Mike Stroka, Chris Anders *(German Officers)*, Kurt Lander *(German Sergeant)*, James Doohan *(Bishop)*, Erick Micklewood *(British Officer)*, Richard Peel *(Dudley)*, Roy Eason *(Reynolds)*, Leslie Bradley *(British Announcer)*, Louis Sarrano *(Portuguese Official)*, Luis Delgado *(Lieutenant)*, Harold Dyrenforth *(Maj. Gen. Ungerland)*, Danny Klega *(German Lieutenant)*, Walter Janowitz *(Dr. Metzler)*, Charles Hradilac *(Dr. Kleiner)*, Rudolph Anders *(Dr. Winterstein)*, Norbert Schiller *(Dr. Wittelbach)*, John Dennis *(M.P. Guard)*, Barry Macollum *(Bartender)*, Roy Jenson *(Soldier)*, John Hart *(Perkins)*, Howard Curtis *(Dutton)*, Owen McGiveney *(Elderly Man)*, Henry dar Boggia, Rolfe Sedan *(Frenchmen)*, Kort Falkenberg *(Radio Voice)*, George Dee *(French Informer)*, Werner Reichow, Paul Busch *(Germans)*, Chic Masi *(Waiter)*, Charles

Bastian (Swiss Soldier), Horst Ebersberg (Swiss Officer).

Garner, an American intelligence agent during WW II, is abducted by Nazi forces and drugged shortly before D-day. He knows every detail about the proposed allied landings and the Germans are determined to get it out of him. The enemy agents take him to Bavaria where they have set up an elaborate hoax. Upon awakening Garner finds himself in what is seemingly an American hospital in 1950. All the papers are carrying that date and he even has a "wife." The war apparently is over and a psychiatrist wants to talk to Garner about his long bout of amnesia. The doctor, Taylor, in an interesting job of casting, is really a German officer who has the title time to get information from Garner before resorting to torture. Garner begins to discuss the Normandy Invasion but soon catches on to the German scheme. He then engages in a mental game of cat-and-mouse with Taylor and Peters, an agent of the Gestapo. Along with Saint, his "wife," Garner goes for more questioning. Taylor falls out of favor with the Nazis for the plan's failure and, after helping Garner and Saint escape, he kills himself. D-day begins and Peters, enraged at the deception, follows Garner and Saint to the Swiss border. However, he's shot by a guard and the two are safe. Garner returns to London, assured that he'll reunite with Saint after the war. The implausible plot is intriguing, with some good performances by the cast that make it work. The pace is fine, with some genuine moments of suspense that work well within the story's framework. Toward the end things bog down, and the final chase is all too conventional, but this doesn't detract from the overall effect.

p, William Perlberg; d&w, George Seaton (based on a story by Carl K. Hittleman, Luis H. Vance and on "Beware of the Dog" by Roald Dahl); ph, Philip H. Lathrop (Panavision); m, Dimitri Tiomkin; ed, Adrienne Fazan; art d, George W. Davis, Edward Carfagno; set d, Henry Grace, Frank McKelvy; cos, Edith Head; makeup, William Tuttle, Stan Smith.

War/Suspense   (PR:C   MPAA:NR)

THIRTY SIX HOURS TO KILL**½

(1936) 65m FOX bw (AKA: THIRTY SIX HOURS TO LIVE)

Brian Donlevy (Frank Evers), Gloria Stuart (Anne Marvis), Douglas Fowley (Duke Benson), Isabel Jewell (Jeanie Benson), Stepin Fetchit (Flash), Julius Tannen (Dr. Borden), Warren Hymer (Hazy), Romaine Callender (Simpkins), James Burke (Doyle), Jonathan Hale (Conductor), Gloria Mitzi Carpenter (Gertrude), Charles Lane (Rickert).

After legally winning $150,000 in a sweepstakes, gangster Fowley has some problems collecting his prize. Seems the law wants him, which makes his winnings a little difficult to pick up. Donlevy is the G-man after the gangster and Stuart a journalist who falls in love with him during the course of the action. Some swift direction and clever dialog make this an interesting and funny outing. However the comedy scenes involving Fetchit have lost what little humor they had to start with, coming off as typical Hollywood racism today.

p, Sol M. Wurtzel; d, Eugene Forde; w, Lou Breslow, John Patrick (based on a story by W.R. Burnett); ph, Arthur Miller; ed, Louis Loeffler; md, Samuel Kaylin; cos, Herschel.

Crime   (PR:A   MPAA:NR)

THIRTY SIX HOURS TO LIVE
(SEE: THIRTY SIX HOURS TO KILL, 1936)

THIS ABOVE ALL***½
(1942) 110m FOX bw

Tyrone Power (Clive Briggs), Joan Fontaine (Prudence Cathaway), Thomas Mitchell (Monty), Henry Stephenson (Gen. Cathaway), Nigel Bruce (Ramsbottom), Gladys Cooper (Iris), Philip Merivale (Dr. Roger Cathaway), Sara Allgood (Waitress in Tea Room), Alexander Knox (Rector), Queenie Leonard (Violet Worthing), Melville Cooper (Wilbur), Jill Esmond (Nurse Emily), Arthur Shields (Chaplain), Dennis Hoey (Parsons), Miles Mander (Major), Rhys Williams (Sergeant), John Abbott (Joe), Carol Curtis-Brown (Maid), Holmes Herbert (Dr. Mathias), Denis Green (Dr. Ferris), Thomas Louden (Vicar), Mary Forbes (Vicar's Wife), Forrester Harvey (Proprietor), Harold de Becker (Conductor), Jessica Newcombe (Matron), Billy Bevan (Farmer), Aubrey Mather, Lumsden Hare (Headwaiters), Heather Thatcher, Jean Prescott (Nurses), Brenda Forbes (Mae the Singer), Doris Lloyd (Woman Sergeant), Rita Page, Clare Verdera (WAAF Corporals), Joyce Wynn, Valerie Cole, Stephanie Insall, Dorothy Daniels de Becker (WAAFs), Alan Edmiston (Porter), Virginia McDowall (Girl), Olaf Hytten (Proprietor), Morton Lowry (Soldier in Underground Club), Wyndham Standing (Doctor), Alec Craig (Conductor), Anita Bolster, May Beatty (Customers), Mary Field (Maid), Cyril Thornton (Station Master), Leonard Carey, Val Stanton (Policeman), Colin Campbell (Man), Will Stanton (Bartender), Herbert Clifton (Secretary), Andy Clyde (Fireman).

A solid dramatic flag-waver featuring superb acting and an excellent adaptation of a best-selling novel. Fontaine was just coming off her Oscar for SUSPICION when she costarred with Power in this war-time saga that took an Oscar for Art-Set Decoration, was nominated for Cinematography, Editing, and Best Sound, and yet was overlooked in all other departments. Fontaine is the daughter of wealthy Merivale, a London Harley Street surgeon of great repute. The war is on the horizon and Fontaine volunteers

for the WAAFs over the objections of her doughty aunt, Cooper, who thinks that if her niece is going to fight, she should at least enter as an officer. But Fontaine wants to go in at the bottom and attends training camp as a private. While there, she is fixed up with Power, who is not in the service. Power is a bitter man, a lower-class young man who feels that the upper crust rules England and saving their lives is hardly worth losing his. Power has no idea that Fontaine is an aristocrat when they begin dating and though they are of vastly different backgrounds, she finds herself attracted to him and accepts when he asks her to spend a weekend at the sea. When they arrive at the tiny hotel run by Bruce, Fontaine questions him about why he is not in uniform but he is reluctant to answer. She learns the truth from Mitchell, a war pal of Power's. It seems that Power had been one of the men at Dunkirk, was hurt in the crossfire, and was placed on a recuperation status. The time for him to return to duty has now passed and Power is about to be branded a deserter. When Fontaine appeals to Power's patriotism, he responds by walking out on her, avoiding any further confrontation on the subject. Power walks around the area trying to avoid any human contact. He crosses some private property and is hurt in a battle with the landowner. Seeking some sort of attention, Power winds up at the tiny church of Knox, who gives him balm, surcease, and some good advice. Power decides that it's time he quit turning away from the war. He phones Fontaine and they make a date to meet in London. Just as he's about to leave for the big city, Power is captured by military troops led by Mander. When major Mander sees Power's history and how he was hurt at Dunkirk, he allows Power a three-hour respite to say farewell to Fontaine. There's an air raid and Power, who was on his way to Fontaine, shows his bravery by rescuing a trapped woman and her family. In the process, he is hurt by debris and has his head crushed. Fontaine knows that he's not the kind of man who would stand her up and she senses that something dire might have happened. With the aid of Merivale, they search the city and find Power in mortal danger from a brain injury. Merivale does the surgery and it seems as though it may have been a success but Merivale warns Fontaine that Power may never be the same, only time will tell. Fontaine waits patiently at his bedside and helps him through the crisis. After he is totally recovered, Power has changed his mind about the way he feels regarding the upper classes. He and Fontaine marry and his faith in England is restored. A stirring movie that was just right for the time, THIS ABOVE ALL made lots of money for the studio and spoke volumes about patriotism without ever sounding preachy. The title is from Shakespeare's speech for Polonius in "Hamlet," and reads: "This above all...to thine own self be true." Power entered service in August, 1942, after first repeating his role in THIS ABOVE ALL on radio opposite Barbara Stanwyck on "Lux Radio Theatre."

p, Darryl F. Zanuck; d, Anatole Litvak; w, R. G. Sherriff (based on the novel by Eric Knight); ph, Arthur Miller; m, Alfred Newman; ed, Walter Thompson; art d, Richard Day, Joseph C. Wright; set d, Thomas Little; cos, Gwen Wakeling.

War Drama   **Cas.**   (PR:A   MPAA:NR)

THIS ACTING BUSINESS*½
(1933, Brit.) 54m WB-FN bw

Hugh Williams (Hugh), Wendy Barrie (Joyce), Donald Calthrop (Milton Stafford), Violet Farebrother (Mary Kean), Marie Wright (Mrs. Dooley), Charles Paton (Ward), Janaice Adair, Henry B. Longhurst.

A sappy comedy about two young lovers, both active in that "acting business," who marry against their parents' wishes. When they both appear in a play together arguments flare and it seems as if their parents were right. But, lo and behold, Barrie, the young wife, gets pregnant and the pair are reconciled. A fine example of mindless entertainment.

p, Irving Asher; d, John Daumery.

Comedy/Romance   (PR:A   MPAA:NR)

THIS ANGRY AGE**
(1958, Ital./Fr.) 111m COL c (LA DIGA SUL PACIFICO; AKA: THE SEA WALL)

Anthony Perkins (Joseph Dufresne), Silvana Mangano (Suzanne Dufresne), Richard Conte (Michael), Jo Van Fleet (Mme. Dufresne), Nehemiah Persoff (Albert), Yvonne Sanson (Carmen), Alida Valli (Claude), Chu Shao Chuan (Caporal), Guidio Celano (Bart).

A coproduction that utilizes several talents from many countries to no avail as it tells a muddled story with the varied styles of acting clashing. Van Fleet is a widow operating a large rice plantation in Indochina (Vietnam, presumably) that is in danger of being swallowed by the angry sea. She has two children, Perkins and Mangano (why one speaks with an Italian accent can only be attributed to the fact that she is the producer's wife). They are struggling to make this farm profitable when Conte, a government agent, arrives and attempts to get them off their land. That idea is soon tossed aside when he meets and falls for Mangano. At the same time, Perkins leaves the farm and goes to Bangkok when he can't handle all the pressure put on him by his forceful mother. While there, he meets Valli at a movie house and has a drinking evening with her. Persoff is another landowner who would like to buy out Van Fleet's interest, and take over the rice paddies and Mangano at the same time. The wall that keeps the sea out is damaged and Van Fleet and Mangano have to go to Bangkok to raise money. Then Mangano and brother Perkins have a few sequences that bring them up against the Asian mentality. At the same time their behavior toward each other seems lots closer than a brother-sister act, but that is more implied than indicated. The two do a sensuous dance and Perkins sings "One Kiss Away from Heaven" by Sam Coslow and A. Romeo. Other songs included, for no good reason, are "Uh Huh," by Billy Dawn and Leroy Kirkland, "Only You," by Ram and Rand, and "Ya Ya Ya," by Alvy West. In the end, Van Fleet dies, Mangano winds up with Conte, and Perkins goes back to the plantation to rebuild the sea wall after a flood (the only truly exciting scene) damages the area. There is far more atmosphere than plot and virtually no cinematic activity other than the lovingly photographed vistas of Thailand. Made with actors from the U.S., France, Italy, and Thailand, directed by a Frenchman from a script by himself and an American, and produced by an Italian in Thailand and at studios in Italy, this is a true coproduction, a broth that suffers from too many cooks.

p, Dino De Laurentiis; d, Rene Clement; w, Irwin Shaw, Clement (based on the novel *Sea Wall* by Marguerite Duras); ph, Otello Martelli (Technirama, Technicolor); m, Nino Rota; ed, Leo Catozzo; md, Franco Ferrara; art d, Mario Chiari; cos, Maria De Matteis; ch, Roye Dodge.

Drama   (PR:C MPAA:NR)

THIS COULD BE THE NIGHT**½   (1957) 103m MGM bw

Jean Simmons (*Anne Leeds*), Paul Douglas (*Rocco*), Anthony Franciosa (*Tony Armotti*), Julie Wilson (*Ivy Corlane*), Neile Adams (*Patsy St. Clair*), Joan Blondell (*Crystal St. Clair*), J. Carrol Naish (*Leon, Cook*), Rafael Campos (*Hussein Mohammed*), ZaSu Pitts (*Mrs. Shea*), Tom Helmore (*Stowe Devlin*), Murvyn Vye (*Waxie London*), Vaughn Taylor (*Ziggy Dawlt*), Frank Ferguson (*Mr. Shea*), William Ogden Joyce (*Bruce Cameron*), James Todd (*Mr. Hallerby*), Ray Anthony and his Orchestra (*Themselves*), John Harding (*Eduardo*), Percy Helton (*Charlie, Bookmaker*), Richard Collier (*Homer*), Edna Holland (*Teacher*), Betty Uitti (*Sexy Girl*), Lew Smith (*Waiter*), June Blair, Nita Talbot (*Chorus Girls*), Harry Hines, Gregg Martell, Matty Fain (*Guests*), Archie Savage, Andrew Robinson, Walter Davis (*Archie Savage Trio*).

A lesser GUYS AND DOLLS has Douglas and Franciosa (in his first film) as two small-time gangsters who run a Broadway nightclub. They fill the club with stock characters, trying to make of it a home away from home for it's denizens. Simmons is a schoolteacher doubling as a secretary who provides romance for Franciosa when she goes to work at the club. This is a film full of good cheer and good performances. It never quite makes it on its own footing but ends up a sweet, slightly naive little film. Songs include: "This Could Be the Night," "Hustlin' News Gal," "I Got It Bad," (Duke Ellington, Paul Francis Webster), "I'm Gonna Live Till I Die" (Al Hoffman, Walter Kent, Mann Curtis), "Taking a Chance on Love" (John Latouche, Ted Fetter, Vernon Duke), "Trumpet Boogie," "Mamba Combo," "Blue Moon" (Richard Rodgers, Lorenz Hart), "Dream Dancing" (Cole Porter), "The Tender Trap" (Sammy Cahn, Jimmy Van Heusen).

p, Joe Pasternak; d, Robert Wise; w, Isobel Lennart (based on short stories by Cordelia Baird Gross); ph, Russell Harlan (CinemaScope); ed, George Boemler; md, George Stoll; ch, Jack Baker.

Musical   (PR:AA MPAA:NR)

THIS DAY AND AGE**½   (1933) 86m PAR bw

Charles Bickford (*Garrett*), Judith Allen (*Gay Merrick*), Richard Cromwell (*Steve Smith*), Harry Green (*Herman*), Eddie Nugent (*Don Merrick*), Ben Alexander (*Morry Dover*), Oscar Rudolph (*Gus*), Billy Gilbert (*Manager of Nightclub*), Lester Arnold (*Sam Weber*), Fuzzy Knight (*Max*), Wade Boteler-Sheriff, Bradley Page (*Toledo*), Harry C. Bradley (*Mr. Smith*), Louise Carter (*Mrs. Smith*), Guy Usher (*Chief of Police*), Charles Middleton (*District Attorney*), Warner Richmond (*Defense Attorney*), Arthur Vinton (*Little Fellow*), Nella Walker (*Little Fellow's Mother*), Mickey Daniels (*Mosher*), Samuel S. Hinds (*Mayor*), Donald Barry (*Young Man*), Michael Stuart (*Billy Anderson*), George Barbier (*Judge McGuire*), Onest Conly (*George Harris*), Howard Lang (*City Editor*).

Hoodlum chieftan Bickford, expanding his protection-racket extortion empire, attempts to exact an "insurance" payment from a little tailor-presser who has lovingly labored over the garments of his good friends, the boys from a nearby high school. When the tailor refuses to pay the requisite "premium," the gangster murders him as a lesson for other tailors who might exhibit similar resistance. In the same city, local councilmen have ordained "Boys' Week," and a day has been set aside for the city's youngsters to temporarily hold the reins of government. In their capacities as city officials for the day, working alongside their elected and appointed adult counterparts, the boys bear witness to the ease with which mobster Bickford– who has high-placed associates–evades just punishment for the murder of their late sartorial assistant. Banding together, the youths decide that civic duty requires that they themselves must bring the hoodlum to the bar of justice. They institute a quest for clues and evidence solid enough to convict the crime lord unequivocally. When the boys approach success, Bickford has one of them shot and killed. Pressing a girl friend, Allen, into service, the vengeful lads use her to assist them in the thug's abduction. They take the snarling criminal to an abandoned brickyard, where they convene a kangaroo court, each of the youths reprising his city-government role. When sullen Bickford refuses their importunities that he confess to his crimes, the lads third-degree him, finally lowering the criminal on a rope

into a brickyard pit filled with rats (Bickford's nightmarish nemesis). As the broken-willed, terrified gangster shouts out the litany of his many crimes, his hoodlum associates discover his whereabouts and prepare to take the place by force of arms. As they begin their attack, police–alerted by Allen–storm the brickyard and capture the entire gang. A broken man, Bickford is brought to justice. Two of the grateful boys, both enamored of Allen, join her in the car she has stolen in order to bring the police to the scene. At the film's ironic conclusion, the three comrades are arrested by police for Grand Theft, Auto. Director DeMille's only gangster-genre talking picture followed hard on the heels of his Biblical epic THE SIGN OF THE CROSS. The theme itself was not entirely novel to the great man and his associates, however; his very first part-talkie, THE GODLESS GIRL (1929), carried some very similar situations. (The youth-in-prison picture similarly pitted young people against evildoing adults.) DeMille may have been influenced somewhat by Fritz Lang's film M, released two years previously; the kangaroo-court trial in the brickyard bears remarkable resemblances to Lang's council of cutthroats sitting in judgment on Peter Lorre's child-murderer. DeMille habitually raced out such small quickies as THIS DAY AND AGE shortly after completing one of his many magnum opuses.

p&d, Cecil B. DeMille; w, Bartlett Cormack; ph, J. Peverell Marley; m, Howard Jackson, L.W. Gilbert, Abel Baer; ed, Anne Bauchens.

Crime/Drama   (PR:A MPAA:NR)

THIS EARTH IS MINE**   (1959) 125m Vintage/UNIV c

Rock Hudson (*John Rambeau*), Jean Simmons (*Elizabeth Rambeau*), Dorothy McGuire (*Martha Fairon*), Claude Rains (*Philippe Rambeau*), Kent Smith (*Francis Fairon*), Anna Lee (*Charlotte Rambeau*), Cindy Robbins (*Buz*), Ken Scott (*Luigi*), Francis Bethencourt (*Andre Swann*), Stacey Graham (*Monica*), Augusta Merighi (*Mrs. Griffanti*), Peter Chong (*Chu*), Jack Mather (*Dietrick*), Ben Astar (*Yakowitz*), Alberto Morin (*Petucci*), Penny Santon (*Mrs. Petucci*), Emory Parnell (*Berke*), Lionel Ames (*Nate Forster*), Dan White (*Judge Gruber*), Geraldine Wall (*Maria*), Lawrence Ung (*David*), Ford Dunhill (*Tim Rambeau*), Jean Blake (*Suzanne*), George De Normand (*Ronald Fairon*), Janelle Richards (*Cousin*), Tammy Windsor (*Clarissa*), Philip Tonge (*Dr. Stone*), Alexander Lockwood (*Dr. Regis*), Torben Meyer (*Hugo*), Josephine Parra (*Juanita*), Adonis De Milo (*Mamoulian*), Cecil Weston (*Rambeau Friend*), Gino De Agustino (*Porter*), Ethel Sway, Olga Nina Borget, Paul King, Emma Palmese, Thomas Murray.

Two generations of wine vintners in California's Napa Valley battle during the Prohibition era. Rains is the older man who believes in his craft, while his grandson, Hudson, is in the business solely to make money and wants to cut the family in on the thriving bootlegging business. When his cousin Simmons arrives from England, the two have an affair but she is unsure of Hudson. Unfortunately the film meanders from these two main plot lines into various subplots involving a pregnant worker whose child is perhaps fathered by Hudson, and anti-Semitic and anti-Italian themes. The end result is a rambling film that never finds focus, delivered in an epic wide-screen presentation. The location shooting is beautiful and Hudson gives a good performance, but the film lacks cohesiveness. It's another example of "big" not always meaning "better."

p, Casey Robinson, Claude Heilman; d, Henry King; w, Robinson (based on the novel *The Cup and the Sword* by Alice Tisdale Hobart); ph, Winton C. Hoch, Russell Metty (CinemaScope, Technicolor); m, Hugo Friedhofer; ed, Ted J. Kent; art d, Alexander Golitzen, George W. Davis; set d, Russell A. Gausman, Ruby R. Levitt, Oliver Emert; cos, Bill Thomas; m/l, "This Earth Is Mine" (Sammy Cahn, James Van Heusen, sung by Don Cornell).

Drama   (PR:O MPAA:NR)

THIS ENGLAND*   (1941, Brit.) 84m BN-Anglo American/World bw
(AKA: OUR HERITAGE)

Emlyn Williams (*Appleyard*), John Clements (*John Rokeby*), Constance Cummings (*Ann*), Frank Pettingell, Esmond Knight, Roland Culver, Morland Graham, Leslie French, Martin Walker, Ronald Ward, James Harcourt, Walter Fitzgerald, Charles Victor, Roddy McDowall, Norman Wooland, David Keir, Robert Warwick, A.E. Matthews, Dennis Wyndham, Kynaston Reeves, Judy Ross, Leslie French, Andrea Troubridge, William Humphries.

Cummings is an American journalist who, on a visit to England, is told the history of a village by town squire Clements. We see British freedom fighters during the Norman conquest, the Spanish Armada, the Napoleonic Wars, WW I, and the air attacks on England in 1940. It served as a morale booster in 1941, but now serves only as a historical document of a people's eternal fight for freedom.

p, John Corfield; d, David Macdonald; w, Emlyn Williams (based on the story by A.R. Rawlinson, Bridget Boland); ph, Mutz Greenbaum [Max Greene].

Historical Drama   (PR:A MPAA:NR)

THIS GREEN HELL***   (1936, Brit.) 71m RKO bw

Edward Rigby (*Dan Foyle*), Sybil Grove (*Mrs. Foyle*), Richard Dolman (*Andy*), Roxie Russell (*Peggy Foyle*), John Singer (*Billy Foyle*), Billy Watts (*Barton*), Norman Pierce (*Willington*), Quinton McPherson.

An inventive comedy about a sheepish clerk, Rigby, who loses his memory when injured in a train wreck. His personality takes a radical turn and he believes that he is the heroic explorer of the bedtime stories he tells his son. His exploits are published and he becomes a highly successful author. He finally regains his memory but is no longer the sheepish clerk he was, but the author he became.

p,d&w, Randall Faye.

Comedy   (PR:A   MPAA:NR)

THIS GUN FOR HIRE****   (1942) 80m PAR bw

Veronica Lake (*Ellen Graham*), Robert Preston (*Michael Crane*), Laird Cregar (*Willard Gates*), Alan Ladd (*Philip Raven*), Tully Marshall (*Alvin Bewster*), Mikhail Rasumny (*Slukey*), Marc Lawrence (*Tommy*), Pamela Blake (*Annie*), Harry Shannon (*Steve Finnerty*), Frank Ferguson (*Albert Baker*), Bernadene Hayes (*Baker's Secretary*), James Farley (*Night Watchman*), Virita Campbell (*Crippled Girl*), Roger Imhof (*Sen. Burnett*), Victor Kilian (*Brewster's Secretary*), Olin Howland (*Blair Fletcher*), Emmett Vogan (*Charlie*), Chester Clute (*Mr. Stewart*), Charles Arnt (*Will Gates*), Virginia Farmer (*Woman in Shop*), Clem Bevans (*Scissor Grinder*), Harry Hayden (*Restaurant Manager*), Tim Ryan (*Weems the Guard*), Yvonne De Carlo (*Show Girl*), Ed Stanley (*Police Captain*), Eddy Chandler (*Foreman*), Phil Tead (*Machinist*), Charles R. Moore (*Dining Car Waiter*), Pat O'Malley (*Conductor*), Katherine Booth (*Waitress*), Sarah Padden (*Mrs. Mason*), Louise La Planche (*Dancer*), Richard Webb (*Young Man*), Francis Morris (*Receptionist*), Cyril Ring (*Waiter*), Lora Lee (*Girl in Car*), William Cabanne (*Laundry Truck Driver*), Patricia Farr (*Ruby*), Charles C. Wilson (*Police Captain*), Mary Davenport (*Salesgirl*), Earle Dewey (*Mr. Collins*), Lynda Grey (*Gates' Secretary*), Dick Rush (*Lt. Clark*), Elliott Sullivan (*Officer Glennon*), Don Barclay (*Piano Player*), John Sheehan (*Keever*), Alan Speer (*Frog*), Frad Walburn (*Walt*), Robert Winkler (*Jimmie*), Dickie Moore (*Young Raven in Cut Dream Sequence*), Hermine Sterler (*Raven's Aunt in Cut Dream Sequence*), Josephine the Monkey.

Although Ladd had been acting in minor roles in Hollywood for a few years, it took the role of icy, professional killer Philip Raven to turn him into the superstar that so many audiences would come to love and admire. Opening in a run-down boarding house, Ladd awakens with a glazed look and proceeds to get himself ready for his day's work, just like anyone else, except that he's got a gun in his hand. He seems gentle enough, pouring milk for a pet cat, but when a young maid comes in to clean and whisks away the cat, something inside him clicks. He beats her, ripping her dress in her process. With his gun packed away in his briefcase, Ladd cooly calls on his victim, Ferguson, filling him with lead. When Ferguson's girl friend, who wasn't meant to be there, realizes what's happened she retreats into another room. Unable to let her live, the callous Ladd fires a few shots through the door. As the bullets splinter the wood, the girl's body is heard falling to the floor with a thud. Putting his gun away, Ladd leaves the apartment, but at the bottom of the stairs spots a little crippled girl playing with a ball. Unsure whether or not she heard the gunshots, Ladd decides to play it safe. Being a professional killer and feeling no guilt in killing a child, he reaches for his gun as the girl's ball bounces down the steps and lands at Ladd's feet. The girl innocently asks for her ball back, convincing him that she is harmless. He puts his gun back and returns the girl's ball. Ladd heads off for a meeting with Cregar, a snide fat man who adores candy mints and abhors violence. Cregar, a fifth columnist who is working for Marshall in a plot to sell poison gas to the enemy, is intrigued by Ladd's quiet, undisturbed demeanor. "How do you feel when you're doing a job like this?," Cregar inquires curiously, while continuing to stuff his mouth full of mints. Ladd's response is scary and simple: "I feel fine." Ladd then accepts his pay–$1,000 in $10 bills. Ladd soon discovers that he has been double-crossed by Cregar, who has paid him in marked bills and then reported the money to the police as being stolen in a robbery. Ladd stops at a dress shop on his way home to buy a new dress for the maid, paying the saleslady with one of the tens. The saleslady recognizes the bill's serial number and informs the police. Ladd manages to sneak away after hiding in the boarding house phone booth in an ingenious little scene where he is faced with forcing a caller to keep his cover. In the meantime, a Los Angeles detective, Preston, who is trying to track down Marshall and his gang, has talked his girl friend, Lake, into auditioning for a singing job in Cregar's nightclub. Lake, hiding behind her alluring peek-a-boo hairstyle, delivers a number called "Now You See It" (Frank Loesser, Jacques Press), with a routine of such staggeringly ridiculous proportions that it is impossible to take seriously. Singing her song (her voice dubbed by Martha Mears), Lake performs a number of magic tricks (taught her by magician Jan Grippo), making things appear and disappear with sleight of hand while trying to retain her aura of sexiness. She manages to impress Cregar who hires her on the spot and tells her to take the next train to his club. By chance, Ladd is also on the train, sitting next to her. Knowing his money is worthless, he performs a little sleight of hand himself and lifts a bill from Lake's handbag while she's asleep. She catches him and confronts him, but seems attracted to his distant personality. When Cregar, who is also on the train, spots the two sitting together, he wrongly assumes

that they are working together. At the next stop the train is searched for Ladd, though he can be identified only by a malformed wrist. He manages to slip away, taking Lake with him. Having made their escape, Ladd drags Lake into an abandoned building and plans to eliminate her when someone comes. Lake eventually makes her way to Cregar's club, but the suspicious fat man also wants to get rid of her. He invites her to his estate, has her bound and stuffed in a closet, and leaves the actual killing to his chauffeur, Lawrence. Ladd, however, arrives on time and confronts Cregar with evidence, Lake's discarded purse, that the girl has been there. Cregar manages to get away, Ladd batters Lawrence and brutally pushes him down a flight of wooden stairs before finding Lake and helping her get to safety. They then head back to the club to get Cregar, finding Preston as well. Ladd fends them off with his gun and escapes with Lake in tow. Lake, however, leaves a trail of magic cards for Preston to follow. Ladd and Lake scale a small wall (which Lake dusts with her compact for Preston to follow) and take refuge in a large, echoing generator room. Ladd is shocked to hear that the police have found them so quickly and the pair must again make a run for it. They wind up in a cold, damp railway building in the middle of a dark, desolate, foggy freight yard. It is nighttime and as long as the fog holds out they are safe. Ladd begins to open up to her, even though he vowed earlier that he would keep from "going soft." He tells her how he is haunted by nightmares of his first murder–an aunt who abused him–"I picked up a knife, and I let her have it–in the throat. They put a label on me, 'Killer,' and sent me to reform school,' and they beat me there, too." To Ladd's surprise, his story doesn't scare Lake, and for the first time in his life he has found someone who doesn't label him "killer." When a cat wanders into the building, Ladd picks it up and warmly caresses it, claiming, "Cat's bring luck." Its purring, however, is too loud and may give them away. He tries to silence the cat, but in his intensity, strangles the life out of it. "I killed it, I killed my luck." Lake tries to teach Ladd that he doesn't have to kill, and Ladd truly seems intent on starting anew. Lake agrees to help Ladd escape (partly because she cares for him, partly because he will lead her to Marshall), dons his raincoat, hides her hair under his hat, and makes a break for a nearby train. The police, who have surrounded the freight yard, chase her, allowing Ladd to slip away. When confronted by a policeman, Ladd forgets his conversation with Lake and resorts to his old method as he kills the cop. Ladd eventually makes it to Marshall's heavily secured office building complex. He tricks a guard and manages to sneak through security, hiding behind a bizarrely disfiguring gas mask, into Marshall's office. Taking off his mask, Ladd locks the large office doors from the inside, confronting the elderly, decaying, wheelchair-bound Marshall and the nervous Cregar. Ladd forces Marshall to sign a confession admitting his guilt in selling the poison gas to the enemy, Marshall then kills Cregar before being killed by Ladd. Police manage to break down the doors as Preston enters through the window, lowering himself from above. Lake tries to prevent any more killing, but Preston guns Ladd down. Ladd, with a smile trying to break through his emotionless exterior, dies with his head on Lake's lap, knowing that he has helped her–the only person to show him any compassion–and, the entire country, as well. Although it is slowed by two sub-par musical numbers and never fully develops Lake's or Preston's characters, THIS GUN FOR HIRE is an outstanding *film noir* entry, which presents one of the most disturbed (and disturbing) killers ever to cross the screen. Ladd is scary because he doesn't care, he is a killing machine hired out by who ever will pay. He has no moral qualms about who he kills, nor any sense of national pride. Since he has already killed a family member, killing any one else comes easily, especially once one is labeled 'Killer,' as he is. It is only when someone takes the time to break through the emotional fortress which he has built around himself, does Ladd begin to care. The most amazing aspect of THIS GUN FOR HIRE is that millions of moviegoers began their love affairs with Ladd–the women identifying with Lake's intrigue and attempt to unravel the mystery of the murderous Raven, and the men seeing themselves as the quiet one who tries to keep from "going soft." Director Tuttle has originally intended to cast Preston in the lead role, when he decided to hunt for an unknown. Essentially a B picture, everyone figured THIS GUN FOR HIRE would be long-forgotten in less than a year's time, even though it was based on a novel by Graham Greene (significantly, in terms of film history, combining the British elements of mystery and espionage with the generic elements of American *film noir*). The blonde-haired Ladd was soon thereafter introduced to Tuttle who felt the 28-year-old actor looked like someone who would say, "Tennis, anyone?, " elaborating that "He'd be perfect for a part like that, but this script needs someone who can play a cold-blooded killer and still come off sympathetical-ly." Contracted at $300 per week, Ladd underwent screen tests, and even had his hair dyed black in keeping with his character name, Raven. Though the film was conceived as a Lake-Preston vehicle, it soon became quite apparent that the studio had something with Ladd, reworking the script during production to favor the actor. The film became, in more ways than one, the Alan Ladd story–with all attention being paid to him and his role. The film's romantic angle was soon tossed away, Preston reduced to a plot device, and not even a kiss between Ladd and Lake. Still, however, they became one of Hollywood's hottest and most bankable love teams, with three more pictures following–THE GLASS KEY, THE BLUE DAHLIA, and SAIGON. (Interestingly, Ladd never again played a killer, a role in which the public would not, paradoxically, accept him again, thereby setting him apart from previous tough guys like James Cagney and Humphrey Bogart.) THIS GUN FOR HIRE was originally to have begun with a dream of Ladd's in which we saw him as a young boy (played by Dickie Jones) murder his aunt and guardian (Hermine Sterler) after she attacks him and injures his wrist. This rather morbid beginning was omitted, however, and the film began, instead, with his awaking from the dream. THIS GUN FOR HIRE was remade in 1957 in the James Cagney directed SHORT CUT TO HELL. Plans for a 1972 remake starring (gulp!) Sammy Davis, Jr. were fortunately squelched.

p, Richard M. Blumenthal; d, Frank Tuttle; w, Albert Maltz, W.R. Burnett (based on the novel *A Gun For Sale* by Graham Greene); ph, John Seitz; m, David Buttolph; ed, Archie Marshek; art d, Hans Dreier; m/l, "Now You See It," "I've Got You," Frank Loesser, Jacques Press, sung by Martha Mears.

Crime   **Cas.**   **(PR:C-O MPAA:NR)**

THIS HAPPY BREED*½   (1944, Brit.) 110m Two
                                      Cities/Prestige-UNIV c

Robert Newton (*Frank Gibbons*), Celia Johnson (*Ethel Gibbons*), John Mills (*Billy Mitchell*), Kay Walsh (*Queenie Gibbons*), Stanley Holloway (*Bob Mitchell*), Amy Veness (*Mrs. Flint*), Alison Leggart (*Aunt Sylvia*), Eileen Erskine (*Vi*), John Blythe (*Reg*), Guy Verney (*Sam Ledbetter*), Merle Tottenham (*Edie*), Betty Fleetwood (*Phyllis*), Laurence Olivier (*Narrator*).

A cavalcade of British life between "The war to end all wars" and the war they said would never happen. Based on Noel Coward's hit play (in which he also starred), it was one of the top moneymakers in 1944 England but it took three more years until it reached the U.S. Olivier narrates the episodic story of one family that lives in a small row house, totally indistinguishable from all the other houses surrounding it. They are an average working-class family led by Newton, as the father, Johnson as the mother with two children, Blythe and Walsh (Walsh just happened to be married to director Lean at the time). WW I is ending and Newton, who has served four years in the army, is coming home to take Johnson and the children away from the home they've occupied with Johnson's mother, Veness, and her sister, Leggart. The whole group moves into a larger residence in Clapham and looks forward to a happy life. Snatches of scenes establish everyone staking out their areas in the house. Veness and Leggart are always battling and Leggart, who is a spinster, finds that she has to make up for her lack of a husband and family by volunteering for just about every committee and charity group around. Most of the time, it's just to get out of the house and away from the sharp tongue of Veness. Time passes and the children are growing and getting more independent. Newton, in a performance that is remarkably understated when one is familiar with his usual scene-stealing tactics, tends his garden and watches his brood. The famous General Strike occurs and Blythe is right in the middle of it, coming home one evening badly bruised and cut for his having been at the scene of the riots. Walsh takes a job in a fashionable beauty salon in London's posh West End, in the hopes of bettering her lot. She's been dating Mills, the sailor son of Holloway who lives next door, and it is just assumed that they will eventually wed. At the same time, Blythe is engaged to Fleetwood and a wedding is on the horizon. The applecart is overturned when Walsh runs off with a married man and the family is crushed. Blythe and Fleetwood are married but tragedy strikes when both are killed in an auto crash and the news is given to the family in one of the most memorable scenes in British cinema. Walsh walks into the parlor, tells Veness what's happened, and the grandmother exits. Newton and Johnson are in Newton's prized garden outside. Walsh walks through the French doors to the garden and the screen is empty of people for a long moment as she informs her parents of the deaths off-screen. The time passing is brief but excruciating, then Newton and Johnson walk silently into the room, sit down, and say nothing. A superior and subtle bit of direction. Walsh eventually marries Mills and they have a child. Mills is shipped to sea and Walsh goes off to visit him in the Far East and entrusts the child to Newton and Johnson. The house that held so much happiness and sadness is now far too large for the couple and they opt for a small flat. Newton and Johnson take one last look around their home, he mentions that he's glad they are together, and they walk out. The camera stays inside, roves around the empty house for a last look at the rooms where people once lived. Dissolve to a high overhead shot of the row of houses, each remarkably alike, to prove the point that this is but one home and that each of these unimpressive houses had their own story to tell and it just happened that No. 17 Sycamore Road was chosen as the focal point for this particular tale. The play was a hit and so was the movie. Coward and Lean codirected IN WHICH WE SERVE and Coward was impressed enough by Lean to hand him the film rights for BRIEF ENCOUNTER and BLITHE SPIRIT as well. This was Lean's first direction on his own and he was partnered in a company with cinematographer Neame (who later became a producer and director) and Havelock-Allan. In 1944, there were almost no color cameras in England but somehow they managed to find one of them for this film, although the color is muted and not nearly as stark as the process used in the U.S. at the time. A charming movie, with many tears and many moments of warmth, and although the action takes place mainly in the house, there is never a feeling of claustrophobia. Newton was excellent, and Johnson, who could look glamorous when the part called for it, was deliberately dressed dowdily and de-glamorized in order to make this work. Johnson was only six years older than Walsh and 13 years older than Blythe but managed to pull off the age deception well. The movie was released by Eagle-Lion in 1944, then by the combo of Prestige Pictures-Universal in 1947.

p, Noel Coward, Anthony Havelock-Allan; d, David Lean; w, Lean, Ronald

Neame, Havelock-Allan (uncredited, Coward) from Coward's play; ph, Neame (Technicolor); m, Coward, Muir Mathieson; ed, Jack Harris; art d, C.P.Norman; md, Muir Mathieson; m/l, "Broadway Melody," Nacio Herb Brown, Arthur Freed (sung by Charles King) from the movie BROADWAY MELODY.

Drama   **(PR:A MPAA:NR)**

THIS HAPPY FEELING*½   (1958) 92m UNIV c

Debbie Reynolds (*Janet Blake*), Curt Jurgens (*Preston Mitchell*), John Saxon (*Bill Tremaine*), Alexis Smith (*Nita Hollaway*), Mary Astor (*Mrs. Tremaine*), Estelle Winwood (*Mrs. Early*), Troy Donahue (*Tony Manza*), Hayden Rorke (*Mr. Booth*), Gloria Holden (*Mrs. Dover*), Alex Gerry (*Mr. Dover*), Joe Flynn (*Dr. McCafferty*), Alexander Campbell (*Briggs*), Clem Fuller (*George*).

This early Edwards-directed comedy shows occasional sparks of things to come in his slapstick PINK PANTHER films, but for the most part is routine comic escapism featuring Reynolds (hot with success from the very similar TAMMY AND THE BACHELOR from the year before) as a young woman who arrives at Jurgens' horse breeding farm. He's a retired movie star who is more than a little surprised when Reynolds tries to fire up a romance with him, causing complications with his love, Smith. Eventually Reynolds changes her sights to next-door neighbor Saxon. The performances are good but, alas, the script is much too light for such a strong cast.

p, Ross Hunter; d&w, Blake Edwards (based on the play "For Love or Money" by F. Hugh Herbert); ph, Arthur E. Arling (CinemaScope, Eastmancolor); m, Frank Skinner; ed, Milton Carruth; md, Joseph Gershenson; art d, Alexander Golitzen, Richard Riedel; spec eff, Clifford Stine.

Comedy   **(PR:A MPAA:NR)**

THIS IMMORAL AGE   (SEE: SQUARE ROOT OF ZERO, THE, 1964)

THIS IS A HIJACK zero   (1973) 90m Fanfare c

Adam Roarke (*Mike Christie*), Neville Brand (*Dominic*), Jay Robinson (*Simon Scott*), Lynn Borden (*Diane*), Milt Kamen (*Phillips*), John Alderman (*Latimer*), Sandy Balson (*Mrs. Phillips*), Sam Chew (*Pierce*), Don Pedro Colley (*Champ*), Dub Taylor (*Sheriff Gordon*), Carol Lawson (*Mrs. Pierce*), Jackie Giroux (*Scott's Girl*), Barney Phillips (*Banker*), Patricia Winters (*Latimer's Girl*).

A cheapie ground out to cash in on the early wave of air piracies in America. Roarke hijacks a plane his boss Robinson is on. It seems Roarke has piled up massive debts by gambling and wants ransom money to pay them off. The film runs roughshod through the silly, inane story with more ham to be found here than in a butcher shop. The direction is shamefully amateurish.

p, Paul Lewis; d, Barry Pollack; ph, Bruce Logan (DeLuxe Color); m, Charles Alden; ed, Peter Parasheles; art d, Vincent Cresciman; set d, Ingrid Grunewald.

Drama   **Cas.**   **(PR:C MPAA:PG)**

THIS IS ELVIS*½   (1982) 101m WB c-bw

David Scott (*Elvis at 18*), Paul Boensch III (*Elvis at 10*), Johnny Harra (*Elvis at 42*), Lawrence Koller (*Vernon Presley*), Rhonda Lyn (*Priscilla Presley*), Debbie Edge (*Gladys Presley*), Larry Raspberry (*Dewey Phillips*), Furry Lewis (*Bluesman*), Liz Robinson (*Minnie Mae Presley*), Dana MacKay (*Elvis at 35*), Knox Phillips (*Sam Phillips*), Cheryl Needham (*Linda Thompson*), Andrea Cyrill (*Ginger Alden*), Jerry Phillips (*Bill Black*), Emory Smith (*Scotty Moore*), Narration: Ral Donner (*Elvis*), Joe Esposito (*Himself*), Linda Thompson (*Herself*), Lisha Sweetnam (*Priscilla*), Virginia Kiser (*Gladys*), Michael Tomack (*Vernon Presley*).

This pseudo-documentary of the king of rock 'n' roll combines an unusual combination of film clips and so-called dramatic reconstructions of Presley's life. At times it is fascinating, at other times it is pure Memphis cornpone. After his death, Presley took on the status of an American myth, a point that underscores this entire work. That such a film would even be put together says a great deal about the greedy nature of the entertainment business as well as the idol worshipping fans who turned out to see THIS IS ELVIS.

p,d&w, Malcolm Leo, Andrew Solt; ph, Gil Hubbs (Technicolor); m, Walter Scharf; ed, Bud Friedgen, Glenn Farr.

Biography   **Cas.**   **(PR:A MPAA:PG)**

THIS IS HEAVEN**   (1929) 90m Goldwyn/UA bw

Vilma Banky (*Eva Petrie*), James Hall (*James Stackpoole*), Fritzi Ridgeway (*Mamie Chase*), Lucien Littlefield (*Frank Chase*), Richard Tucker (*E. D. Wallace*).

Banky is a recent arrival in the U.S. from Hungary. Taken in by her uncle (Littlefield), she gets a job as a waitress and one day sees and falls in love with Hall, a millionaire. Believing him to be a chauffeur (probably because of the chauffeur's hat he is wearing) and when they are married not long afterwards, she insists that he buy a taxi and go into business for himself. Littlefield, though, gambles away the cab money and Banky is compelled to borrow money from her cousin Ridgeway's rich lover. Hall finally reveals his wealth and Banky is swept up in a new love for her adopted country. Silly romantic comedy with talking sequences is mostly a holdout from the silents. With the advent of sound, Banky was restricted by her accent to roles such as this in her first talking picture. She retired from the screen shortly afterward.

d, Alfred Santell; w, Hope Loring, George Marion, Jr. (based on a story by Arthur Mantell); ph, George Barnes, Gregg Toland; m, Hugo Riesenfeld; ed, Viola Lawrence; m/l, "This Is Heaven," Jack Yellen, Harry Akst.

Comedy   (PR:A   MPAA:NR)

THIS IS MY AFFAIR½**   (1937) 99m FOX bw (GB: HIS AFFAIR)

Robert Taylor (*Lt. Richard L. Perry*), Barbara Stanwyck (*Lil Duryea*), Victor McLaglen (*Jock Ramsey*), Brian Donlevy (*Batiste Duryea*), Sidney Blackmer (*President Theodore Roosevelt*), John Carradine (*Ed*), Alan Dinehart (*Doc Keller*), Douglas Fowley (*Alec*), Sig Rumann (*Gus the Boatman*), Robert McWade (*Adm. George Dewey*), Frank Conroy (*President William McKinley*), Marjorie Weaver (*Miss Blackburn*), Douglas Wood (*Henry V. Maxwell the Bank Examiner*), J.C. Nugent (*Ernie*), Tyler Brooke (*Specialty*), Willard Robertson (*George Andrews*), De Witt Jennings (*Bradley Wallace, Secret Service*), Joseph Crehan (*Priest*), Dale Van Sickel (*Officer at Ball*), Tom London (*Alec's Pal*), Frank Moran (*Guard*), Lynn Bari, June Gale (*Girls with Keller*), Ethan Laidlaw (*Barfly*), Walter James (*Friend*), Ruth Gillette (*Blonde*), Edward Piel, Sr (*Secretary Hayes*), John Quillan (*Page Boy*), Lee Shumway (*Secret Service Man*), Ben Taggart (*Police Captain*), John Lester Johnson, W.S. McDunnough, Arthur Rankin, Paul Hurst, Jonathan Hale, James Donlan, Rice & Cady, Monte Vandergrift, Davison Clark, James Flavin, June Terry, Ralf Harolde, Emmett Vogan, Antonio Filauri, Mary Young, June Cole.

A combination crime-love story and semi-musical set against some true facts, THIS IS MY AFFAIR was the second teaming for off-screen lovers Taylor and Stanwyck. The results may or may not have been what caused them to wait 27 years until they worked together again in THE NIGHT WALKER. Set in the early years of the 20th Century, Taylor is seen as a young navy man who had served heroically at Manila under McWade (as Adm. Dewey). There is a gang of bank robbers who have been terrorizing the Midwest by using several modern methods. They appear to have been able to bypass security systems, have ways of obtaining bank keys, and seem to take whatever they want whenever and wherever they want. This series of robberies is causing the populace to wonder if banks are safe and money is being withdrawn and stuffed back into the mattresses from whence it came. The President himself, Conroy (as the ill-fated McKinley), arranges to have Taylor resign his commission and disappear, then emerge again as another person with no history, the reason being that Taylor has been secretly handed the role of breaking up this bank robbery gang. The only person who knows about it is the president. Now undercover, Taylor arrives in Minnesota where he begins hanging around with nefarious types. He soon meets Stanwyck, a singer in a saloon owned by McLaglen, who is the leader of the bank robbers. McLaglen's sidekick is Donlevy, the half-brother of Stanwyck. Taylor uses Stanwyck to worm his way into the bank robbers' confidence and he is soon accepted. He is bothered by the fact that he is falling in love with Stanwyck but his duty to his country is more important to him so he continues his plan to expose the crooks. Taylor becomes one of the mob and goes on a job with them. They don't know that he's anonymously tipped off the authorities so when they are all captured, he is one of them and he assumes he can get out by calling upon Conroy. The entire group is sentenced to be executed, and that includes Taylor, because McKinley is assassinated by crazed anarchist Leon Czolgosz at the Pan-American Exposition on September 6th, 1901, in Buffalo, New York. (The wounds were not dressed correctly and McKinley lived eight more days until dying of gangrene.) Blackmer (as Teddy Roosevelt) takes over the reins of the nation and Stanwyck has to make a direct appeal to him in order to get Taylor out of the shadow of the gallows. By this time, Taylor has the names of the higher-ups who have been providing McLaglen with the information on the banks but it may be too late. Stanwyck has to use all sorts of wiles to get to the closely guarded Blackmer but she is desperately in love with Taylor and just manages to catch Blackmer's ear. Taylor is released once Blackmer hears the truth and the two lovers wind up in a clinch at the fadeout. Zanuck was in charge of production at the studio and used his pen name of "Melville Crossman" to supply the story, which had some basis in fact. Since DFZ was so busy, the film was actually produced by Ken Macgowan, who received "associate producer" credit on the picture. There really was no novel by the name of *The McKinley Case* that we could uncover. Franchot Tone and Alice Faye were the first choices, then Don Ameche was announced. Taylor was under contract to MGM and must have been on a loan-out. He and Stanwyck married two years after this. Despite having once been a chorus girl in the "Ziegfeld Follies" and other stage reviews, Stanwyck never had much of a singing voice. She was coached by composer Jule Styne in the singing of the Mack Gordon, Harry Revel tunes, which included: "I Hum a Waltz," "Fill It Up," and "Put Down Your Glasses, Pick Up Your Girl." Blackmer's portrayal of Roosevelt was so well done and his face was so well disguised that he submerged his personality entirely and darn near became the "Bully Boy" president. A well-made picture with an authentic period feel about it.

p, Darryl F. Zanuck; d, William S. Seiter; w, Allen Rivkin, Lamar Trotti (based on the novel *The McKinley Case* by Melville Crossman); ph, Robert Planck; ed, Allen McNeil; md, Arthur Lange; art d, Rudolph Sternad; set d, Thomas Little; cos, Royer; ch, Jack Haskell.

Historical Crime/Romance   (PR:A   MPAA:NR)

THIS IS MY LOVE½*   (1954) 91m RKO c

Linda Darnell (*Vida*), Rick Jason (*Glenn*), Dan Duryea (*Murray*), Faith Domergue (*Evelyn*), Hal Baylor (*Eddie*), Connie Russell (*Herself*), Jerry Mathers (*David Myer*), Susie Mathers (*Shirley Myer*), Mary Young (*Mrs. Timberly*), William Hopper (*District Attorney*), Stuart Randall (*Investigator*), Kam Tong (*Harry*), Judd Holdren (*Dr. Raines*), Carl Switzer (*Customer*).

Darnell is a would-be writer who lives in a world of her own. Her sister, Domergue, is married to Duryea, a man confined to a wheelchair after an accident. When Darnell brings home her new beau, Jason, Domergue wants him for her own. She tricks Darnell into giving her husband poison in place of his medicine, thus conveniently getting rid of both of them. The plan works and Darnell is arrested for murder. But Jason finally rejects Domergue and she walks through the rain to confess to the police. Some fine production values in this potboiler but its seamy aspects discolor and it plays too casually with audience emotions. Watch for an appearance of ex-child star Carl Switzer, long grown out of his starring days in the "Our Gang" comedies.

p, Hugh Brooke; d, Stuart Heisler; w, Hagar Wilde, Brooke (based on the story "Fear Has Black Wings" by Brooke); ph, Ray June (Pathe Color); m, Franz Waxman; ed, Otto Ludwig; m/l, "This Is My Love" (Waxman, Brooke).

Drama   (PR:O   MPAA:NR)

THIS IS MY STREET½**   (1964, Brit.) 94m Warner-Pathe bw

Ian Hendry (*Harry King*), June Ritchie (*Margery Graham*), Avice Landone (*Lily*), Meredith Edwards (*Steve*), Madge Ryan (*Kitty*), John Hurt (*Charlie*), Annette Andre (*Jinny*), Philippa Gail (*Maureen*), Mike Pratt (*Sid Graham*), Tom Adams (*Paul*), Hilda Fenemore (*Doris*), Susan Burnet (*Phyllis*), Robert Bruce (*Mark*), John Bluthal (*Joe*), Carl Bernard (*Fred*), Patrick Cargill (*Rinsome*), Margo Johns (*Isabel*), Derek Francis (*Fingus*), Ursula Hirst (*Molly*), Sheraton Blount (*Gindy*), Margaret Boyd.

After moving into a boarding house, Hendry tries to seduce Ritchie, the woman who lives next door with her daughter and husband. She ignores Hendry's advances but finally gives in after he helps find her daughter, who has become lost. Bored with Ritchie, he next turns his attentions to her educated sister, Andre. The two plan to marry but Ritchie stops this with a failed suicide attempt and a note baring all she knows about the man. The smooth direction covers over the ugly plot of a mean little womanizer seducing women trapped in the sordid surroundings of London squalor. Hendry and Ritchie exude an interesting chemistry together and the movie spins right along while they are on the screen.

p, Peter Rogers, Jack Hanbury; d, Sidney Hayers; w, Bill MacIlwraith (based on the novel by Nan Maynard); ph, Alan Hume; m, Eric Rogers; ed, Roger Cherrill.

Drama   (PR:O   MPAA:NR)

THIS IS NOT A TEST zero   (1962) 72m Modern bw

Seamon Glass, Mary Morlass, Thayer Roberts, Aubrey Martin.

An inept science-fiction picture which takes a stab at making a social statement. A policeman setting up a roadblock for a killer hears a report of an impending atom bomb attack. A group of passing travelers takes refuge in the back of their van, while the trooper is left outside. The bomb drops, the trooper dies, and the people inside the van emerge alive. Fortunately this one has been seen by next to no one.

p, Frederic Gadette, Murray De'Atley; d, Gadette; w, Peter Abenheim, Betty Laskey, Gadette; ph, Brick Marquard; m, Greig McRitchie; ed, Hal Dennis.

Science Fiction/Drama   (PR:A   MPAA:NR)

THIS IS THE ARMY*   (1943) 120m WB c

Irving Berlin (*Himself*), George Murphy (*Jerry Jones*), Joan Leslie (*Eileen Dibble*), George Tobias (*Maxie Stoloff*), Alan Hale (*Sgt. McGee*), Charles Butterworth (*Eddie Dibble*), Rosemary DeCamp (*Ethel*), Dolores Costello (*Mrs. Davidson*), Una Merkel (*Rose Dibble*), Stanley Ridges (*Maj. Davidson*), Ruth Donnelly (*Mrs. O'Brien*), Dorothy Peterson (*Mrs. Nelson*), Kate Smith (*Herself*), Frances Langford (*Cafe Singer*), Gertrude Niesen (*Singer*), Ronald Reagan (*Johnny Jones*), Joe Louis (*Himself*), Alan Anderson, Ezra Stone, Tom D'Andrea, James Burrell, Ross Elliott, Alan Manson, John Prince Mendes, Julie Oshins, Earl Oxford, Robert Shanley, Philip Truex, James MacColl, Ralph Magelssen, Tileston Perry, Joe Cook, Jr, Larry Weeks, The Allon Trio [Geno Erbisti, Angelo Buono, Louis Bednarcik] (*Soldiers*), Robert Shenley (*Ted Nelson*), Herbert Anderson (*Danny Davidson*), Sgt. Fisher (*Blake Nelson*), Victor Moore, Ernest Truex (*Fathers of Soldiers*), Jackie

Brown (*Mike Nelson*), Patsy Moran (*Marie Twardofsky*), James Conlin (*Doorman*), Ilka Gruning (*Mrs. Twardofsky*), Irving Bacon (*Waiter*), Murray Alper (*Soldier*), Pierre Watkin (*Stranger*), Frank Coghlan, Jr, Dick Crane, Arthur Space, Arthur Foster, Jimmy Butler, Ross Ford, Gayle de Camp, John Daheim, Alan Pomeroy, John James (*Soldiers at Camp Cook*), Henry Jones (*Soldier-Singer*), Doodles Weaver (*Soldier on Cot*), Leah Baird (*Old Timer's Wife*), Warner Anderson (*Sports Announcer*), Jack Young (*Franklin D. Roosevelt*), Sidney Robin, William Roerich, Dick Bernie, John Draper, Richard Irving, Fred Kelly, Hank Henry, J. P. Mandes, Gene Berg, Arthur Steiner, Belmonte Cristiani, Pinkie Mitchell.

A star-studded musical salute to the American Army soldier filled with Irving Berlin's songs, good acting, and a morale-boosting sense of patriotism that radiates in every frame. Taken from Berlin's stage play which opened July 4th, 1942, it also uses some of Berlin's earlier musical "Yip Yip Yaphank" and combines the two. Murphy (later to be a senator from California) is seen as a big-time Broadway star at the beginning of WW I. He's drafted into the service, given the job of putting on a big show, does his bit and, when the show ends, the cast and crew go off to fight in Europe. Years pass and Murphy is now a producer with a son, Reagan (later governor of California, then president), who is drafted for service in WW II and given the same job his father had; create a show for the men in khaki. Reagan manages to write a terrific show as well as marry his sweetheart, Leslie. The show is toured around the country and at the final performance, before the boys go to war, Berlin (as himself) comes on stage in Washington to sing. Two other parent-offspring tales are interwoven. Tobias is the father of Oshins and Butterworth is seen as Leslie's dad. Hale is the career sarge who spans the wars and appears in both shows. (Note: Actor Ernest Truex's real son, Philip, is seen as his real son.) The plot is just barely enough to hang the musical numbers on but it's the tunes that count more than the story here. Michael Curtiz directed it in a breezy fashion that was similar to the stage plays from whence it sprung. Berlin wrote the score and the book of the stage show and put it all together although the producer's credit was "Uncle Sam" in the Broadway Playbill. Berlin used his clout to get the Army to lend him more than 300 soldiers for the stage show when he promised that he would donate more than a million dollars from the show's receipts to a relief fund for the families the boys left behind. After Broadway, the show went on the road and took in many more millions, all of which were donated. Warners Bros. bought the rights to the play and the picture took in another $2 million, mainly because the soldiers worked for their regular pay and the actors did it for minimums, then donated those back to the relief fund. Audiences knew where the money was going so it almost became a neighborhood patriotic event to go see the movie. You could have fun and support the war effort at the same time. Berlin's songs include: "Your Country and My Country" (performed by Gertrude Niesen in a recruiting rally sequence), "My Sweetie" (sung and danced by Murphy), "Poor Little Me, I'm On K.P." (performed by Tobias), "We're On Our Way to France" (Murphy, Tobias, Hale, Soldiers), "God Bless America" (Kate Smith, who else?) "What Does He Look Like?" (sung by Frances Langford, the one new ditty composed by Berlin for the movie), "This is the Army, Mr. Jones" (performed by Col. Sidney Robin, Pfc. Henry Jones, Cpl. William Roerich, other soldiers), "I'm Gettin' Tired So I Can Sleep" (sung by Staff Sgt. James Burrell), "Mandy" (performed by Cpl. Ralph Magelssen, Sgt. Richard Irving (who later went to Hollywood to be a writer-producer), Sgt. Fred Kelly (Gene's brother), and other soldiers in a minstrel sequence), "Ladies of the Chorus" (performed by Hale and soldiers), "That's What the Well-Dressed Man in Harlem Will Wear" (performed by James Cross, Pvt. William Wyckoff, Harlem Dance Group with Sgt. Joe Louis punching a boxing bag in rhythm), "How About a Cheer for the Navy?" (soldiers), "I Left My Heart at the Stage Door Canteen" (sung by Sgt. Earl Oxford around a sketch featuring Pvt. James McColl as Alfred Lunt, Cpl. Tileston Perry as Lynn Fontanne, Sgt. Alan Manson as Jane Cowl), "With My Head in the Clouds" (Sgt. Robert Shanley), "American Eagles" (Shanley and company in an elaborate production), "Oh, How I Hate to Get Up in the Morning" (sung by Berlin, Soldiers), "This Time is the Last Time" (Shanley and everyone else), and "The Army's Made a Man Out of Me" (performed by Master Sgt. Ezra Stone, Sgt. Phil Truex, Sgt. Julie Oshins). Stone, who had been a well-known radio actor ("Henry Aldrich" among others) came home after the war to become a successful television director. Almost everyone concerned with the picture was involved with the service, including screenwriter Claude Binyon, who was a captain at the time. Since a great deal had to do with authenticity, Lt. Col. Frank McCabe was hired as technical advisor. In small roles, note Victor Moore and Henry Jones. Reagan had a splendid time coming back to his home studio, not that he was busy fighting the war. Actually, Reagan's job during WW II was making service training films, a far cry from some of the other actors who went to war and actually saw combat. The movie cost almost $1 ½ million to make but looks like five times that amount. Anyone interested in knowing how the country felt during those dark days before the D-Day attack in 1944 would be wise to watch THIS IS THE ARMY. It's a splendid movie on all counts. Murphy was only nine years older than his "son" Reagan. Good specialty acts in the show-within-the-show are done by Pfc. Joe Cook, Jr., Pfc. Hank Henry (who later became a burlesque comic and sidekick to Frank Sinatra in a few films), Cpl. Larry Weeks, and Sgt. John Mendes. Irving Berlin is the essence of the American dream. Born in Siberia in 1888, Berlin came to the U.S., mastered the language, worked as a singing waiter in Coney Island, and had his first hit song published when he was 19. At the age of 23, he wrote "Alexander's Ragtime Band" and went on to write more than 1000 songs.

A shy man, he resisted the pleas of the brothers Warner to appear in this movie. He finally agreed but made it clear that he was not doing it for them, he was doing it for the boys in service. The U.S. gave him the Medal Of Merit for his work on the stage and screen versions of THIS IS THE ARMY. His deep sincerity about his adopted land can best be summed up in his classic "God Bless America," for which he won the Congressional Gold Medal. Berlin writes in the difficult key of F Sharp (he must be the only composer who does that) but had a piano made that could transpose to other keys. He's had a few of those pianos and one is now owned by actor/writer/director Sidney Miller, who worked with Donald O'Connor for so many years. For the last several decades of his life, Berlin remained in seclusion in his Sutton Place residence in New York. Like the Statue of Liberty, he is a national treasure. Heindorf's musical arrangements won an Oscar.

p, Jack L. Warner, Hal B. Wallis; d, Michael Curtiz; w, Casey Robinson, Claude Binyon (based on the play by Irving Berlin); ph, Bert Glennon, Sol Polito (Technicolor); ed, George Amy; md, Leo F. Forbstein, Frank Heath (Ray Heindorf, arrangements); art d, John Koenig, John Hughes; cos, Orry-Kelly; spec eff, Jack Cosgrove; ch, LeRoy Prinz, Robert Sidney; m/l, Berlin.

Musical/Comedy   **Cas.**   **(PR:AA   MPAA:NR)**

THIS IS THE LIFE*   (1933, Brit.) 78m BL bw

Gordon Harker (*Albert Tuttle*), Binnie Hale (*Sarah Tuttle*), Betty Astell (*Edna Wynne*), Ray Milland (*Bob Travers*), Jack Barty (*Bert Scroggins*), Charles Heslop (*Mr. Diggs*), Percy Parsons (*Lefty Finn*), Ben Welden (*Two Gun Mullins*), Norma Whalley (*Miss Vavasour*), Julian Royce (*Bronson*), Percival Mackey and His Band.

Harker and Hale are a pair of teahouse proprietors who inherit a great deal of money from their uncle. They step into high society and live it up in London. Before long they are involved with a gang of Chicago gangsters, led by Welden. Harker and Hale break up the gang's wrongdoings, but in the process discover that their inheritance money was acquired through illegal methods. Reduced to their middle-class means, they return to the teahouse and find that it has been turned into a fashionable roadhouse. Harker and Hale deliver a rendition of "Il Trovatore" from Giuseppe Verdi's opera of the same name.

p, Herbert Smith; d, Albert de Courville; w, Clifford Grey, R.P. Weston, Bert Lee (based on a story by Grey).

Comedy   **(PR:A   MPAA:NR)**

THIS IS THE LIFE½**   (1935) 63m FOX bw

Jane Withers (*Geraldine Revier*), John McGuire (*Michael Grant*), Sally Blane (*Helen Davis*), Sidney Toler (*Prof. Breckenridge*), Gloria Roy (*Diane Revier*), Gordon Westcott (*Ed Revier*), Francis Ford (*Sticky*), Emma Dunn (*Mrs. Davis*), Del Henderson, Robert Graves, Selmer Jackson, Nick Lucas, Fritzi Brunette, Jayne Hovig, Harry C. Bradley.

In a plot too nasty for Shirley Temple, child star Withers plays a singing and dancing orphan (an abundant commodity in 1930s films) who's taken advantage of by an unscrupulous vaudeville couple. Tired of being used by the couple, she dresses like a boy and runs off, meeting McGuire. He's wanted by the police but Withers helps hide him. Eventually he is caught but is proven innocent at the end. Withers is a natural, giving this minor feature real charm. An enjoyable entry in the "singing and dancing orphan" genre.

p, Joseph Engel; d, Marshall Neilan; w, Lamar Trotti, Arthur Horman (based on a story by Gene Towne, Graham Baker, Lou Breslow, Sid Brod); ph, Daniel Clark; ed, Fred Allen; m/l, "Gotta New Kind of Rhythm," "Sandy and Me," Sidney Clare, Sammy Stept.

Musical   **(PR:A   MPAA:NR)**

THIS IS THE LIFE½**   (1944) 85m UNIV bw

Donald O'Connor (*Jimmy Plum*), Susanna Foster (*Angela*), Peggy Ryan (*Sally McGuire*), Louise Allbritton (*Harriet*), Patric Knowles (*Hilary Jarret*), Dorothy Peterson (*Aunt Betsy*), Jonathan Hale (*Dr. Plum*), Eddie Quillan (*Gus*), Otto Hoffman (*Oscar*), Frank Jenks (*Eddie*), Frank Puglia (*Music Teacher*), Maurice Marsac (*Leon*), Virginia Brissac (*Mrs. Tiggett*), Mantan Moreland, Martha Vickers, Ray Eberle and his Orchestra, Bobby Brooks Quartet.

Light fare for O'Connor features him as a soldier in love with Foster, but she has a schoolgirl crush on the much older Knowles, whom she follows to New York City. O'Connor follows in turn and runs into Albritton, Knowles' ex-wife, who still loves him and O'Connor maneuvers the two back together and wins Foster for himself. O'Connor is not as peppy as usual, but works well under the lively direction. This was adapted from a stage play by Sinclair Lewis and KING KONG star Fay Wray, and not too surprisingly on Wray's part, since her first husband was screenwriter Robert Riskin, and her second playwright-screenwriter John Monk Saunders, and she has written several plays herself. Songs include: "Gremlin Walk," "It's the Girl," "Yippee-I-Vot" (Inez James, Sidney Miller), "With a Song in My Heart" (Richard Rodgers, Lorenz Hart), "All or Nothing at All" (Jack Lawrence,

Arthur Altman), "You're a Lallapalooza" (Bill Grage, Grace Shannon), "At Sundown" (Walter Donaldson), "L'Amour Toujours L'Amour" (Rudolph Friml, Catherine Chisholm Cushing).

p, Bernard W. Burton; d, Felix Feist; w, Wanda Tuchock (based on the play "Angela is 22" by Sinclair Lewis, Fay Wray); ph, Hal Mohr; ed, Ray Snyder; md, Charles Previn; art d, John B. Goodman; spec eff, John P. Fulton; ch, Louis Da Pron.

Musical (PR:A MPAA:NR)

THIS IS THE NIGHT****   (1932) 78m PAR bw

Lily Damita (Germaine), Charlie Ruggles (Bunny West), Roland Young (Gerald Grey), Thelma Todd (Claire), Cary Grant (Stephen), Irving Bacon (Jacques), Claire Dodd (Chou-Chou), Davison Clark (Studio Official).

This blithe comedy marked Grant's film debut, a charming and engaging romp that maintains a fresh air from first frame to the last. Taken from the 1925 Broadway comedy "Naughty Cinderella", the film opens with Todd off in gay Paree making time with rich bachelor Young. While escorting her to a party, Young catches Todd's long dress in a car door and the garment is torn from the woman. A cry breaks out that "Madame has lost her skirt!" This turns into a joyful song that suddenly sweeps the city, springs up from the streets, on the radio, and even from the top of the Eiffel Tower! Unperturbed, Todd merely wraps herself in her long fur coat and heads back home with her lover. En route she tells Young that her husband (Grant) is back home in Los Angeles competing in the Olympics as a javelin thrower. The two are naturally more than a little surprised then when they arrive at home to find Grant, javelins in tow, waiting for his wife. At that moment Young's friend Ruggles arrives at the flat, bearing two tickets to Venice meant for the lovers. Young, frightened by the potential of a sharply pointed javelin in a jealous champion's hands, quickly explains that he, too, is married and suggests that both couples take a holiday to Venice. Of course this puts the previously happy bachelor in the rather awkward position of having to obtain a wife on extremely short notice. Ruggles helps out by hiring Damita, a movie extra in need of some cash, to pose as Young's wife for the trip. While in Venice Damita's winsome charms prove much too tantalizing for any of the men to resist. First Grant begins paying attention to her, which causes the green-eyed monster to flare up in both Todd and Damita's "husband." Ruggles is enraptured with her as well, which adds to the increasingly tangled love knot. Young confronts his friend and the two engage in an animated (and quickly inebriated) conversation. After expressing affection for one another as chums Ruggles offers to help out Young by taking Damita off of his friend's hands. Young is outraged by this and their chat quickly erupts into a war of words with Ruggles exclaiming that his friend is "the menace of Venice!" Damita, frustrated at being the center of so much attention, decides to leave Venice altogether. But Young comes to realize that he cannot go on without this woman, so he catches up with her and proposes marriage. Damita finally agrees while Todd decides she really does love Grant after all and returns to her husband. Ruggles, left to himself and a bottle, laments that he is alone while his would-be love and Young "gloating in a fondola." The comedy here clearly shows the influences of Ernst Lubitsch and Rene Clair. Like the former director the war between the sexes is dealt with in a sophisticated manner, waltzing in and out of situations amidst the characters with concise skill. The sexual tension between the principals is always held in tight rein, and the film sparkles with witty dialog. The "Madame Has Lost Her Skirt" number clearly takes its cue from Clair and is one of the film's most enjoyable flourishes in both style and comedy. The number becomes a running gag throughout the story, enjoyable each time without growing a bit stale. Of course none of this could be accomplished without a skilled cast and strong direction. Tuttle's helming is excellent, perhaps the best job in his varied career. Though the story is thin he is able to move the farce along at a delightful pace, never allowing story or stylization to conflict with one another. The ensemble could not be a finer one. Each player works well as a separate unit within the whole, creating genuine tensions of love and sex with marvelously funny results. Grant received fifth billing here but did not escape the notice of the critics, the majority of whom predicted a bright future for the handsome and witty young actor. Though it would still be a few years before he came to the forefront as a leading man, he shows a marvelous talent in his characterization that would blossom into legend.

d, Frank Tuttle; w, Avery Hopwood, George Marion, Jr. (based on the play "Naughty Cinderella" by Hopwood, adapted from "Pouche" by Rene Peter, Henri Falk); ph, Victor Milner; m, Ralph Rainger; m/l, "This is the Night," Sam Coslow, Rainger, "Madame Has Lost Her Dress," "Tonight is All a Dream," George Marion, Jr., Rainger.

Comedy (PR:A MPAA:NR)

THIS ISLAND EARTH***   (1955) 87m UNIV c

Jeff Morrow (Exeter), Faith Domergue (Dr. Ruth Adams), Rex Reason (Cal Meacham), Russell Johnson (Steve Carlson), Lance Fuller (Brack), Robert Nichols (Joe Wilson), Douglas Spencer (Monitor), Karl Lindt (Dr. Adolph Engelborger), Eddie Parker, Regis Parton (Mutants), Olan Soule (1st Reporter), Richard Deacon (Pilot), Robert B. Williams (Webb), Mark Hamilton (Metalunan), Coleman Francis (Expressman), Spencer Chan, Lizalotta Valesca (Scientists), Edward Ingram, Jack Byron (Photographers), Guy

Edward Hearn, Les Spears (Reporters), Bart Roberts.

A landmark science-fiction film, this is an intelligent interplanetary epic filled with beautifully crafted designs and marvelous special effects. A futuristic TV/telephone device is sent to Earth from the planet Metaluna. Scientist Reason puts together the device and soon finds himself hostage in a secluded mansion in Georgia to Morrow, a Mozart-loving agent from Metaluna. He tries to escape with the help of Domergue, but they are caught and placed in a state of suspended animation. Morrow takes them to Metaluna in his flying saucer in hopes that they will help him restore his war-ravaged homeland with a new source of atomic energy. Reason and Domergue face a host of outer space dangers before returning home with Morrow's help. The story is run-of-the-mill science fiction but the real beauty of the film is in its effects and art work. THIS ISLAND EARTH set new standards with its wondrous shots of spaceships and intergalactic battles, and the makeup is a sight to behold. The famous mutant with the exposed cranium cost the producers $24,000 and showed every penny spent in the final effect. This feature undoubtedly benefitted from the unbilled codirection of 1950s science fiction master Arnold.

p, William Alland; d, Joseph Newman, Jack Arnold; w, Franklin Coen, Edward G. O'Callaghan (based on the novel by Raymond F. Jones); ph, Clifford Stine (Technicolor); m, Herman Stein; ed, Virgil Vogel; md, Joseph Gershenson; art d, Alexander Golitzen, Richard H. Riedel; set d, Russell A. Gausman, Julia Heron; spec eff, Charles Baker, Stine, Stanley Horsley; makeup, Bud Westmore; mutant design, Millicent Patrick.

Science Fiction Cas. (PR:A MPAA:NR)

THIS LAND IS MINE***½   (1943) 103m RKO bw

Charles Laughton (Arthur Lory), Maureen O'Hara (Louise Martin), George Sanders (George Lambert), Walter Slezak (Maj. Erich von Keller), Kent Smith (Paul Martin), Una O'Connor (Mrs. Emma Lory), Philip Merivale (Prof. Sorel), Thurston Hall (Mayor Henry Manville), George Coulouris (Prosecuting Attorney), Nancy Gates (Julie Grant), Ivan Simpson (Judge), John Donat (Edmund Lorraine), Frank Alten (Lt. Schwartz), Leo Bulgakov (Little Man), Wheaton Chambers (Mr. Lorraine), Cecil Weston (Mrs. Lorraine), Louis Donath (German Captain), Lillian O'Malley (Woman In Street), Gordon Clark (Lieutenant), Hans Moebus (German Chauffeur), Jack Martin (German Captain), Gabriel Lenoff, Philip Ahlm (German Lieutenants), Albert d'Arno, Rudolph Myzet, Lester Sharpe, Sven Borg, Nick Vehr, Russell Hoyt, Walter Thiele (German Soldiers), Louis Arno, Bob Stevenson, Hans Schumm, John Banner, George Sorel (German Sergeants), Ferdinand Schumann-Heink (Karl), Gus Taillon (Newsman), Bill Yetter (Otto), the German Soldier, Edward McNamara (Policeman), Otto Hoffman (Printer), Hans von Morhart (Soldier Who Gets Slapped), John Dilson (Mayor's Secretary), Ernest Grooney (Priest), George MacQuarrie (Chief of Police), Tommy Bond (Julian), John Rice, Jack Shea (Burly Cops), Ida Shoemaker (Woman in Street), Oscar Loraine (Clerk), Joan Barclay (Young Woman), Mildred Hardy, Margaret Fealy (Old Woman), Linda Ann Bieber (Emily), Lloyd Ingraham (Paper Man in Street), Terrellyne Johnson (Girl), Hallene Hall (Woman at Window), Mary Stuart (Photo Double), Casey Johnson (Boy), George Carleton (Jury Foreman), Hal Malone (Bit in Courtroom), Henry Roquemore (Butcher).

Set "Somewhere in Europe" (though clearly representative of Jean Renoir's French homeland) THIS LAND IS MINE stars Laughton as a cowardly schoolteacher who whimpers during air raids and can only be comforted by his overly possessive mother, O'Connor. Laughton prefers to keep a low profile and go about his business unnoticed until his mentor, Merivale, lights a patriotic spark in him. Aware of his cowardice, he turns to fellow school teacher O'Hara, who is sympathetic to his fears. She, however, is also sympathetic to the cause of the Resistance. When her brother, Smith, bombs a German officer's car she is forced to lie for him, as is Laughton who is inadvertently involved in the questioning. As much as he tries to remain neutral, Laughton finds himself increasingly sympathetic to the Resistance movement. This grows stronger when Merivale is carted away from the school by soldiers. As Laughton whimpers, Merivale simply tells him, "dignity, Lory, dignity" and places him in charge of running the school. Laughton soon arouses suspicion and is hauled off by German soldiers to be imprisoned as a "hostage," which means he will soon be executed if no one confesses to the bombing. To save her son, O'Connor informs on Smith to Sanders, a lifelong friend and a high-ranking railroad official who is a collaborator. Sanders, in turn, passes this information on, furious with his own hypocritical lack of loyalty to his French countrymen. Before Smith can be caught, a guilt-stricken Sanders warns him that he informed. It is too late, however, and Smith is gunned down in the train yard by German soldiers. The following day Laughton is released, unaware of his mother's actions or even that Smith has been killed. He pays a visit to O'Hara who is filled with hatred for him, and only then does he realize that the price of his freedom was Smith's death. Laughton then stands up to his mother and scolds her for her self-serving attitude. He marches off to Sanders' office to confirm his mother's story, but when he arrives he finds Sanders dead, a victim of suicide brought on by his guilt. Laughton innocently picks up the gun and by doing so implicates himself as the murderer. A trial follows and the prosecution seems to have an easy case of cold-blooded murder. When Laughton is finally allowed to make a speech he, in his innocent and thoughtful manner, condemns Sanders for being a collaborationist, as well as the mayor and the entire Vichy judicial system. The court adjourns and Laughton is returned to his cell, where he is visited by German commandant Slezak. Slezak guarantees Laughton his freedom by promising that a suicide note penned by Sanders will turn up, thereby proving that no murder was committed. In exchange, Laughton will quietly live out his days as a school teacher in support of the Vichy government. Laughton seems to agree to the terms, but the following day in court he continues his speech. He tells the courtroom that Slezak unjustly arranged for his freedom, that French patriots are innocently being killed, and that every collaborationist who supports the Vichy government is responsible for these deaths. He also makes one final proclamation–that he is in love with O'Hara. The following day, while in his classroom reading to his students from "A Declaration of the Rights of Man," Laughton is hauled away by German soldiers to be executed. It was Renoir's desire to create a film "made uniquely for America, to suggest to the Americans that daily life in an occupied country was not as simple as some might assume." Although some critics (the most vicious being French) consider THIS LAND IS MINE preachy and overly talky, it must be praised for its understanding of humanity. Instead of painting the Germans as mighty evildoers and the French people as innocent victims, Renoir took a more daring and honest approach. He implicates his countrymen as being partly responsible for the Occupation. Afraid of the consequences, many French citizens collaborated with the Germans to ensure that they remain immune from punishment, as well as ensuring that their orderly lives would not be shattered by the occupying forces. Renoir avoided propagandistic cliches and took into consideration human nature. Human nature, however, is not what people look for when creating war heroes and patriotic inspiration, hence the negative reaction from the French. Although long considered as a propaganda film THIS LAND IS MINE is more correctly seen as anti-propagandistic. There is no black and white, no good and evil. There is only gray and an understanding of the frailty of human nature.

p, Jean Renoir, Dudley Nichols; d, Renoir; w, Nichols; ph, Frank Redman; m, Lothar Perl; ed, Frederic Knudtson; md, Constantin Bakaleinikoff; prod d, Eugene Lourie; art d, Albert S. D'Agostino, Walter E. Keller; set d, Darrell Silvera, Al Fields; cos, Renie; spec eff, Vernon L. Walker.

War Drama   Cas.   (PR:A   MPAA:NR)

THIS LOVE OF OURS½   (1945) 90m UNIV bw

Merle Oberon (Karin Touzac), Charles Korvin (Michel Touzac), Claude Rains (Joseph Targel), Carl Esmond (Uncle Robert), Sue England (Susette Touzac), Jess Barker (Chadwick), Harry Davenport (Dr. Jerry Wilkerson), Ralph Morgan (Dr. Lane), Fritz Leiber (Dr. Bailey), Helen Thimig (Tucker), Ferike Boros (Housekeeper), Howard Freeman (Dr. Barnes), Selmer Jackson (Dr. Melnik), Dave Willock (Dr. David Dailey), Ann Codee (Anna), Andre Charlot (Mons. Flambertin), Doris Merrick (Vivian), William Edmunds (Jose, Chauffeur-Butler), Barbara Bates (Mrs. Dailey), Leon Tyler (Ross), Cora Witherspoon (Woman), Maris Wrixon (Evelyn), Robert Raison (Call Boy), Evelyn Falke (Nanette), Joanie Bell (Susette as a Small Child), Beatrice Roberts (Surgical Nurse), Daun Kennedy (Receptionist), Jane Adams, Kathleen O'Malley, Jean Trent, Joan Shawlee, Karen Randall, Kerry Vaughn (Chorus Girls), Frank Arnold (Mons. Labrot), Loulette Sablon (Nurse), Ralph Littlefield (Comic), George Davis (Character Man), Constance Purdy (Character Woman), Simone La Brousse (Mme. Rigaud), Irving Greines, Peter Miles, Billy Ward, Diane Miller, Kay Smith, Robert Cole, Vicki Benedict, Olivia West (Children), Andre Marsauden (Dr. Fessier), Georges Renavent (Dr. Lebreton), Jacques Catelain (Dr. Robichaux), Eve Garrick, Nanette Vallon, Francesca Waskowitz (Guests), Rosita Marstini (Mme. Flambertin), Marcelle Corday (Woman), Adrienne D'Ambricourt (Mme. Rocheville), Ian Wolfe (Dr. Straus), Tony Ellis (Anesthetist), Nolan Leary (Waiter), Vangie Beilby (Irish Mother), Louise Long (Stout Woman), Richard Ryen (Chabon), Cyril Delevanti (Man Secretary), Herbert Heywood (Gardener), Joel Fluellen (Porter), Ruth Brennan (Maid), Pearl Early (Cook), Bobby Dillon, Dickie Love, Bonnie Henjum, Hugh Maguire, Pamela Peyton, Mickey Kuhn, Sewell Shurtz, Loretta Cunningham, Eleanor Taylor, Ian Bernard, Edna Mae Wonacott, Jane Eckland (Youngsters).

Only in Hollywood could a psychological drama by the playwright Luigi Pirandello be taken apart and put together again as a romantic star vehicle. "As Before, Better Than Ever" had been filmed in 1932 with Greta Garbo under the title AS YOU DESIRE ME which had carefully played with the mental and emotional themes of the play. THIS LOVE OF OURS plays up the romance of the story, running roughshod over deeper meanings. Oberon is an assistant to Rains, a Chicago cafe artist. A medical convention is being held in that town and Oberon runs into handsome Korvin, a noted scientist who had been her husband 15 years before. She tries to kill herself over the reencounter but Korvin saves her life in surgery. While recovering, Korvin explains to Oberon that they have a 10-year-old daughter who needs her love. The story flashes back to Europe where Oberon is the star of a traveling show. She sprains her ankle and Korvin, then an intern, mends her. She remains in Paris and marries Korvin, and they have a daughter. But neighborhood gossips say Oberon is fooling around with another man. Korvin believes the rumors despite her denials and he leaves, taking the child with him. Korvin later discovers his error and tries to find his wife. Eventually he moves to America and knows nothing of Oberon's whereabouts until this fateful meeting. She still loves him but is understandably wary because of his desertion. However, her mother instincts overwhelm

her and against Rains' advice she returns as Korvin's "second wife." The little girl, now age 10, believes her mother to be dead and keeps a shrine in her honor. She resents Oberon's presence and refuses to call her "mother." Rains enters to give some sage advice and the film winds down to a predictable ending with Bell accepting Oberon and all forgiven between husband and wife. The story is hardly different from any of a number of 1940s "women" pictures but the production is so handsome it really doesn't matter. A budget of $2 million went into the film and it is evident in every frame. The direction obviously knows a tear-jerker formula and stays with it, and the music is likewise weepy. Oberon gives her role a classy feel, teaming well with Korvin. THIS LOVE OF OURS is not close to Pirandello's intentions, but on its own soap opera level it's great fun. The story was filmed again as NEVER SAY GOODBYE in 1956.

p, Howard Benedict; d, William Dieterle; w, Bruce Manning, John Klorer, Leonard Lee (based on the play "Come Prima Meglio de Prima" ["As Before, Better Than Before"] by Luigi Pirandello); ph, Lucien Ballard; m, H.J. Salter; ed, Frank Gross; art d, John B. Goodman, Robert Clatworthy; set d, Russell A. Gausman, Oliver Emert; cos, Vera West, Travis Banton.

Drama   (PR:C   MPAA:NR)

THIS MAD WORLD**   (1930) 70m MGM bw

Kay Johnson (Victoria), Basil Rathbone (Paul), Louise Dresser (Pauline), Veda Buckland (Anna), Louis Natheaux (Emile).

Rathbone is a French secret agent in WW I who ventures behind enemy lines into Alsace-Lorraine on a mission and to visit his mother, Dresser. While staying at his mother's inn, Rathbone falls in love with Johnson, the wife of a German general, and the two carry on a passionate romance. Their bond is broken, however, when Rathbone admits that he was responsible for the death of her nephew. In an act of vengeance, Johnson informs on Rathbone and he is executed by the Germans. Johnson then commits suicide. Dresser accepts the death of her son stoically and makes plans to carry out his mission. A gloomy picture which was far from uplifting for a Depression era audience.

d, William De Mille; w, Clara Beranger, Arthur Caesar (based on the play "Terre Inhumaine, Drame en Trois Actes" by Francois de Curel); ph, Peverell Marley, Hal Rosson; ed, Anne Bauchens; art d, Cedric Gibbons; cos, Adrian.

War Drama   (PR:C   MPAA:NR)

THIS MADDING CROWD**½   (1964, Jap.) 101m Tokyo Eiga/Toho International c (AOBE KA MONOGATARI)

Hisaya Morishige (Professor), Eijiro Tono (Grandpa Yoshi), Sachiko Hidari (Osei), Nobuko Otowa (Kimino), Frankie Sakai (Goro), Meiko Nakamura (1st Bride), Junko Ikeuchi (2nd Bride).

In order to write about older fashions and customs, Morishige goes to a small fishing village near Tokyo. There he observes the local people in their everyday life, including a former alcoholic who cares for his disabled spouse; a frustrated and confused newlywed whose wife will not sleep with him; a head-to-head confrontation between a mother and her beggar daughter; and a man who lives aboard a boat and remembers his younger days and the girl he loved. A telling look at Japanese village life and customs.

p, Ichiro Sato, Hideyuki Shiino; d, Yuzo Kawashima; w, Kaneto Shindo (based on a novel by Shugoro Yamamoto); ph, Kozo Okazaki.

Comedy/Drama   (PR:C   MPAA:NR)

THIS MAN CAN'T DIE**   (1970, Ital.) 90m Mercurio/Fine-Capital c

Guy Madison (Martin Benson), Peter Martell (Tony Guy), Rik Battaglia (Vic Graham), Lucienne Bridou (Susy Benson), Steve Merrich (Daniel Benson), Rosalba Neri (Jenny Benson), John Bartha (Melin).

Madison and Martell are adventurers who pose as gun runners to infiltrate an illegal operation. Madison's brother Merrich comes home to find his parents murdered and his sister, Neri, now mute after a brutal rape. Merrich and his other sister, Bridou, find one of the intruders lying unconscious and they hold him hostage, hoping he'll reveal his accomplices. Madison finds out about the crime from an old girl friend and returns home. He discovers that the hostage is his pal Martell, who reveals that Battaglia, a rejected beau of Bridou and a powerful local store owner, is behind the crime. Madison finds the man and kills him in a shootout.

p, Gino Rossi; d, Gianfranco Baldanello; w, Luigi Emmanuele, Gino Mangini (based on a story by Emmanuele); ph, Claudio Cirillo; m, Amedeo Tommasi; ed, Alberto Gallitti; set d, Giorgio Giovannini; cos, Maria Luisa Panaro; spec eff, CI-PA-ROMA; makeup, Giuseppe Peruzzi.

Western   (PR:O   MPAA:M/PG)

THIS MAN IN PARIS**½   (1939, Brit.) 86m Pinebrook/PAR bw

Barry K. Barnes (Simon Drake), Valerie Hobson (Pat Drake), Alastair Sim (Macgregor), Jacques Max Michel (Emile Beranger), Mona Goya (Torch Bernal), Edward Lexy (Holly), Garry Marsh (Sgt. Bright), Anthony Shaw

(Gen. Craysham), Cyril Chamberlain (Swindon), Charles Oliver (Gaston), Paul Sheridan (Reception Clerk), Michael Rennie, Billy Watts.

Stylish Barnes is a top crime reporter for a Fleet Street daily. He goes to Paris on the trail of a banknote forger, accompanied by his wife, ladylike Hobson. Though he thinks she's a nuisance and the two always fight, Hobson proves to be adept at solving the crime herself. This well done, clever comedy was a follow-up film to THIS MAN IS NEWS, a British attempt to duplicate America's THIN MAN. However, this second film proved to be the last effort along that line. Hobson is excellent in her role, though Barnes isn't quite the character he tries to be. Sim provides good comic support in another one of his eccentric specialties. Director MacDonald wins huzzahs for another entertaining middle-bracket crime story.

p, Anthony Havelock-Allen; d, David MacDonald; w, Allan MacKinnon, Roger MacDougall; ph, Henry Harris.

Comedy/Mystery (PR:A MPAA:NR)

THIS MAN IS DANGEROUS (SEE: PATIENT VANISHES, THE 1947, Brit.)

THIS MAN IS MINE**½ (1934) 76m RKO bw

Irene Dunne (Toni Dunlap), Ralph Bellamy (Jim Dunlap), Constance Cummings (Fran Harper), Kay Johnson (Bee McCrea), Charles Starrett (Jud McCrea), Sidney Blackmer (Mort Holmes), Louis Mason (Slim), Vivian Tobin (Rita).

Dunne is happily married to Bellamy. However their "ideal" marriage is threatened when Cummings, Dunne's sister, sets her eyes on Bellamy and tries to destroy the marriage. Dunne wins, of course, and all ends happily. This sappy soap is a cut above others of its ilk thanks to the direction and handsome production values. The players do well in their roles, though Bellamy is too sugary sweet. Starrett, in a supporting role here, would soon move on to stardom in cowboy films.

p, Pandro S. Berman; d, John Cromwell; w, Jane Murfin (based on the play "Love Flies in the Window" by Anne Morrison Chapin); ph, David Abel; m, Max Steiner; ed, William Morgan; md, Steiner; art d, Van Nest Polglase, Carroll Clark.

Drama (PR:A MPAA:NR)

THIS MAN IS MINE**½ (1946 Brit.) 103m COL British bw

Tom Walls (Philip Ferguson), Glynis Johns (Millie), Jeanne de Casalis (Mrs. Ferguson), Hugh McDermott (Bill Mackenzie), Nova Pilbeam (Phoebe Ferguson), Barry Morse (Ronnie), Rosalyn Boulter (Brenda Ferguson), Ambrosine Philpotts (Lady Daubney), Mary Merrall (Mrs. Jarvis), Agnes Lauchlan (Cook), Bernard Lee (James Nicholls), Charles Victor (Hijacker), Peter Gawthorne (Businessman), King Whyte, Bryan Herbert, Leslie Dwyer, Charles Farrell, John Coyle, Natalie Lynn, Johnnie Schofield, Mai Bacon, Paul Carpenter, Olwen Brookes, Capt. Bob Farnon and the Canadian Army Orchestra.

At Christmas, 1946, McDermott is at home enjoying his holiday in Canada. He receives a telegram from "the Fergusons" and in a flashback remembers the Christmas he spent with this family. It is 1942 and McDermott is a soldier in the Canadian army. He's taken as a holiday guest by this British family and soon finds himself being chased by both the daughter (Pilbeam) and the former maid, now in uniform herself, the husky heroine Johns. In the end Johns wins and she is seen preparing Christmas dinner in McDermott's Canadian home. This is a charming little comedy directed by the irrepressible Frenchman Marcel Varnel, full of good cheer and many funny moments and, surprisingly, it has aged well.

p&d, Marcel Varnel; w, Doreen Montgomery, Norman Lee, Nicholas Phipps, Reginald Beckwith, Mabel Constanduros, Val Valentine, David Evans (based on the play "A Soldier for Christmas" by Beckwith); ph, Phil Grindrod.

Comedy (PR:A MPAA:NR)

THIS MAN IS NEWS**½ (1939, Brit.) 63m Pinebrook/PAR bw

Barry K. Barnes (Simon Drake), Valerie Hobson (Pat Drake), Alastair Sim (Macgregor), John Warwick (Johnnie Clayton), Garry Marsh (Sgt. Bright), Edward Lexy (Inspector Hollis), Kenneth Buckley (Ken Marquis), Philip Leaver ("Harelip" Murphy), James Birrie (Doyle), David Keir (Brown), Tom Gill (Brown, Jr.), Jack Vyvyan (Fireman), Billy Watts.

The first British attempt to duplicate the success of THE THIN MAN. Barnes is a reporter fired by editor Sim. He had neglected an assignment after receiving a tip on a supposed front-page story. But soon a man connected with the phony tip is dead and Barnes finds himself looking into the London underworld. Accompanying him is his wife, Hobson, a wisecracking and smart lady who can solve crimes herself. Though Barnes and Hobson never amount to another William Powell or Myrna Loy, they handle the assignment with humor and great style. The film is directed with energy and the dialog helps keep the brisk pace along. This is the first screenwriting credit for Basil Dearden, who would go on to do many stories, both

serious and topical, in association with noted British producer and art director Michael Relph. (Sequel: THIS MAN IN PARIS, 1939)

p, Anthony Havelock-Allan; d, David MacDonald; w, Allan MacKinnon, Roger MacDougal, Basil Dearden (story by MacDougal and MacKinnon); ph, Henry Harris; ed, Reginald Beck; md, Percival Mackey.

Comedy-Mystery (PR:A MPAA:NR)

THIS MAN MUST DIE***½ (1970, Fr./Ital.) 115m Les Films La Boetie-Rizzoli/AA c (QUE LA BETE MEURE; UCCIDERO UN UOMO)

Michael Duchaussoy (Charles Thenier), Caroline Cellier (Helene Lanson), Jean Yanne (Paul Decourt), Anouk Ferjac (Anna), Marc DiNapoli (Philippe Decourt), Maurice Pialat (Police Inspector), Guy Marly (Jacques Ferrand), Lorraine Rainer (Anna Ferrand), Stephane Di Napoli (Michel Thenier), Louise Chevalier (Mme. Levenes), Dominique Zardi (Policewoman), Jean-Louis Maury (Peasant/Charles' Friend), Raymone, Michel Charrel, France Girard, Bernard Papineau, Robert Rondo, Jacques Masson, Georges Charrier.

When Duchaussoy's son is killed by a hit-and-run driver the quiet author of children's books can think only of revenge. He begins a search, recording each step he takes in his diary. First he meets a farmer who tells Duchaussoy that on the day of the accident he saw a damaged sports car with TV personality Cellier as the passenger. Duchaussoy travels to Paris and meets Cellier. Soon the two are having an affair and Duchaussoy learns that her brother-in-law (Yanne) runs an auto repair shop. Yanne becomes Duchaussoy's prime suspect and he and Cellier spend a weekend at his home. Duchaussoy takes an immediate dislike to Yanne, but grows close to his son, Marc DiNapoli, who confides to the author that he plans to kill his father. Duchaussoy then takes Yanne out on a sailboat to drown him under the guise of an accident. However, Yanne pulls a pistol on the man, saying he's read the diary and knows everything and that the police will know that his death is not an accident. Duchaussoy leaves Paris with Cellier but on the way out of town they learn Yanne has been poisoned. Duchaussoy is arrested because of his incriminating diary, but Marc DiNapoli confesses all and the author is released. Duchaussoy then writes a false confession, boards his boat, and sails off. One of Chabrol's best films.

p, Andre Genoves; d, Claude Chabrol; w, Chabrol, Paul Gegauff (based on the novel The Beast Must Die by Nicholas Blake); ph, Jean Rabier (Eastmancolor); m, Pierre Jansen; ed, Jacques Gaillard; md, Andre Girard; art d, Guy Littaye; m/l, "Vier Ernste Gesange," Johannes Brahms (sung by Kathleen Ferrier).

Drama/Suspense Cas. (PR:O MPAA:GP)

THIS MAN REUTER (SEE: DISPATCH FROM REUTERS, A, 1940)

THIS MAN'S NAVY**½ (1945) 100m MGM bw

Wallace Beery (Ned Trumpet), Tom Drake (Jess Weaver), James Gleason (Jimmy Shannon), Jan Clayton (Cathey Cortland), Selena Royle (Maude Weaver), Noah Beery, Sr (Joe Hodum), Henry O'Neill (Lt. Comdr. Roger Graystone), Steve Brodie (Tim Shannon), George Chandler (Bert Bland), Donald Curtis (Operations Officer), Arthur Walsh (Cadet Rayshek), Will Fowler (David), Richard Crockett (Sparks), Paul Cavanagh (Sir Anthony Tivall), Donald Curtis (Operations Officer), Connie Weiler (WAVE), Dick Rich (Shore Patrolman), John Kellogg (Junior Pilot), Blake Edwards (Flier), Bruce Kellogg, George Ramsey (Pilots), Henry Daniels, Jr (Crew Member), Carlyle Blackwell, Jr, Bob Lowell (Mechanics).

Some good performances pick up this otherwise ordinary wartime story about Wallace Beery as a blowhard chief pilot of a Navy blimp who talks on and on about his imaginary son and his fighting accomplishments. Gleason is his pal who doesn't believe it, but when Beery befriends widow Royle and her son Drake, Beery suddenly has a ready-made family. The boy is quite sick but on recovering enters the Army and sinks a submarine from a blimp. Gleason is convinced and Beery takes Royle as a bride. Some good direction and interesting footage of blimps in action as well.

p, Samuel Marx; d, William A. Wellman; w, Borden Chase [uncredited], John Twist, Hugh Allen, Allen Rivkin (based on a story by Chase from an idea by Comdr. Herman E. Halland, USN); ph, Sidney Wagner; m, Nathaniel Shilkret; ed, Irvine Warburton; art d, Cedric Gibbons, Howard Campbell; set d, Edwin B. Willis, Glen Barner; spec eff, A. Arnold Gillespie, Donald Jahraus.

War/Comedy (PR:AA MPAA:NR)

THIS MARRIAGE BUSINESS** (1938) 70m RKO bw

Victor Moore (Jud), Allan Lane (Bill), Vicki Lester (Nancy), Cecil Kellaway (Hardy), Jack Carson (Candid), Richard Lane (Joe), Kay Sutton (Bella), Paul Guilfoyle (Frankie), Jack Arnold (Lloyd), Frank M. Thomas (Frisbee), Leona Roberts (Mrs. Platt), George Irving (Madden).

Moore, cast in a comedy below his talents, plays a marriage license clerk in a small town. In over 20 years not one of his happy couplings has ever ended in divorce, a fact seized upon by journalist Lane. Lane's publicity results in a slew of matrimonial-minded couples to his office. Lane then promotes

Moore for the mayor's office under the nickname "Lucky License." The opposition tries to frame him with scantily clad girls and the like, and goes so far as to jail him for murder, but all turns out well in the end. The players and direction are fine, but the story is weak. Lester, who played Moore's daughter and Lane's sweetie, took her professional name from Janet Gaynor's character in A STAR IS BORN.

p, Cliff Reid; d, Christy Cabanne; w, Gladys Atwater, J. Robert Bren (based on a story by Alex Ruben, Mel Riddle); ph, Joseph H. August; ed, Harry Marker.

Comedy   (PR:A   MPAA:NR)

THIS MODERN AGE**½   (1931) 76m MGM bw

Joan Crawford (*Valentine Winters*), Pauline Frederick (*Diane Winters*), Neil Hamilton (*Bob Blake*), Monroe Owsley (*Tony*), Hobart Bosworth (*Mr. Blake*), Emma Dunn (*Mrs. Blake*), Albert Conti (*Andre de Graignon*), Adrienne d'Ambricourt (*Marie*), Marcelle Corday (*Alyce*), Marjorie Rambeau, Sandra Ravel, Armand Kaliz.

Aimed directly at the heartstrings of its intended female audience, this features Crawford as an American socialite who has grown up in her father's home after her parents' divorce years before. Now the young woman is off to Paris where she is to see her mother (Frederick) after their long-time separation. What Crawford does not know is that her high-living mother is the mistress of Conti, a rich Frenchman who is passed off to the girl as a mere friend of the family. While in Paris Crawford decides to sample the *risque* life for herself. She takes up with Owsley, a young drunkard for whom fast cars and rumpled tuxedos are simple daily pleasures. While the two are out driving Owsley accidentally causes their automobile to flip over. This is witnessed by Hamilton, a handsome Harvard football star, who rescues the hapless pair. As Crawford and Hamilton become better acquainted their friendship blossoms into amour. Hamilton, eager to marry Crawford, brings his conservative, wealthy parents—Bosworth and Dunn—to meet the mother of his intended. The meeting proves to be a trying one, for Owsley—accompanied by some fellow inebriates—bursts into the room. To compound this social *faux pas*, Conti arrives, and his relationship with Frederick is made all too clear. Bosworth and Dunn, rife with indignation, demand Hamilton break off his romance with Crawford. The pair then storm out. This leads to a tear-inducing heart-to-heart talk between Crawford and Frederick that ties a stronger bond between child and parent. Hamilton, bound by love, ignores his parents' wishes and returns once more to the side of his true love. The reunited pair run off together as Frederick reassesses her life. She comes to realize that her affair with Conti is doing her no good and brings the relationship to a conclusion. THIS MODERN AGE is a story that pours on the melodramatics like thick maple syrup onto waffles. Almost every emotional turn is a major revelation or a crisis for the principals involved. Crawford, her hair dyed blonde for the part, gives her role all the high-handed emotions that she was famous for throughout her career. Though Frederick's talents are clearly above the part, she too gives this some histrionic acting that brings added life to the tawdry story. Grinde emphasizes this in his direction with zeal, bubbling all the elements of soap opera together in a decidedly non-subtle manner. The comedy sequences involving Owsley have a better flair, coming off with a more natural feeling than the serious moments. All in all it's entertaining enough, occasionally crossing the border into good campy fun.

d, Nicholas Grinde; w, Sylvia Thalberg, Frank Butler, John Meehan (based on the story "Girls Together" by Mildred Cram); ph, Charles Rosher; ed, William LeVanway; cos, Adrian.

Drama   (PR:A-C   MPAA:NR)

THIS OTHER EDEN**   (1959, Brit.) 80m Emmett Dalton/RF bw

Audrey Dalton (*Maire McRoarty*), Leslie Phillips (*Crispin Brown*), Niall MacGinnis (*Devereaux*), Geoffrey Golden (*McRoarty*), Norman Rodway (*Conor Heaphy*), Milo O'Shea (*Pat Tweedy*), Harry Brogan (*Clannery*), Eddie Golden (*Sgt. Grilly*), Ria Mooney, Isobel Couser, Gerald Sullivan, Paul Farrell, Hilton Edwards, Philip O'Flynn.

A comedy set in 1945 Ireland with the IRA as a backdrop. The townsfolk plan to build a monument to a rebel killed in the 1920s and Phillips, the son of the British colonel who killed the rebel, opposes its construction. Rodway, the rebel's son, destroys the newly unveiled statue and places the blame on Phillips. The townsfolk prepare to lynch the vandal but Rodway's confession prevents that. An unlikely subject for a comedy which is slanted in favor of the British.

p, Alec C. Snowden; d, Muriel Box; w, Patrick Kirwan, Blanaid Irvine (based on the play by Louis d'Alton); ph, Gerald Gibbs.

Comedy   (PR:A   MPAA:NR)

THIS PROPERTY IS CONDEMNED**½   (1966) 110m Seven Arts-Ray Stark/PAR c

Natalie Wood (*Alva Starr*), Robert Redford (*Owen Legate*), Charles Bronson (*J.J. Nichols*), Kate Reid (*Hazel Starr*), Mary Badham (*Willie Starr*), Alan Baxter (*Knopke*), Robert Blake (*Sidney*), John Harding (*Johnson*), Dabney Coleman (*Salesman*), Ray Hemphill (*Jimmy Bell*), Brett Pearson (*Charlie*

Steinkamp), Jon Provost (*Tom*), Quentin Sondergaard (*Hank*), Michael Steen (*Max*), Bruce Watson (*Lindsay Tate*), Bob Random (*Tiny*), Nick Stuart (*Railroad Conductor*).

Two kids (Badham and Provost) are sitting at a railway station. In flashback Badham relates to her companion the sordid tale of her much admired, deceased sister. In a Depression-ravaged town in rural Mississippi Reid runs a boarding house. Her daughter, Wood, is a beautiful young girl madly in love with Redford, a stranger from New Orleans staying at the house. He's in town to lay off some railroad workers but is beaten up by five of them. He plans to leave town after this and take Wood with him. However, Reid fools Redford into thinking that Wood is engaged to Harding, a wealthy middle-aged man Reid would rather see her daughter with. Redford leaves without Wood and when she hears why she gets drunk and marries Bronson, her mother's violent, mean lover, out of spite. Realizing her mistake, Wood follows Redford to New Orleans the day after the wedding. But her mother catches up to them and reveals to Redford that Wood has married Bronson, destroying her daughter's happiness and will to live. Wood ends up becoming the town slut, eventually dying from tuberculosis. Years later, as the film returns to the two 13-year-olds, all Badham can see is the romance behind her sister's life. THIS PROPERTY CONDEMNED is a film wracked by many problems, but it somehow survived to become an interesting potboiler. The seamy sexual story is taken from a play by Tennessee Williams, a short one-act originally intended for Elizabeth Taylor with her on-again, off-again husband Richard Burton to direct. This fell through and the property went through 12 different screenwriters until a script emerged from Coppola, Coe, and Sommer. Williams, disgusted with the final version, demanded his that name be removed from the project. This request was not granted, though his name was de-emphasized in the ad campaign. After a search for directors, Pollack was finally chosen. Wood, who had enjoyed working with Redford before (reportedly because of his reputation of not putting the make on actresses he worked with), demanded the fledgling star once more. Problems were plentiful on the set. As filming continued, Pollack's dissatisfaction with the script grew, forcing him to cut and change things quite often. Redford resented the role executive producer Stark played, often making intrusions onto the set and wanting changes of his own. Bronson felt his role should have been expanded and the triangle between he, Redford, and Wood given more emphasis. The director chose otherwise though, emphasizing Wood's character and leaving Bronson's confrontations with his co-star mostly silent looks. Problems also arose on the location shooting as the Mississippi town of Bay St. Louis didn't care for the filmmakers or their subject. A petition drive was started to drive them from their streets but this was unsuccessful. All in all, the resulting film was a mixture of good and bad, with some wonderful cinematography by the great cameraman Howe. The script is riddled with obvious problems but the acting is terrific. Wood takes her trashy part and gives it higher quality than what was probably intended. Redford gives her good support in what was his fourth film (he would follow this with BAREFOOT IN THE PARK and his career would take off).

p, John Houseman; d, Sydney Pollack; w, Francis Ford Coppola, Fred Coe, Edith Sommer (based on the play by Tennessee Williams); ph, James Wong Howe (Technicolor); m, Kenyon Hopkins; ed, Adrienne Fazan; art d, Hal Pereira, Stephen Grimes, Phil Jeffries; set d, William Kiernan; cos, Edith Head, Ann Landers; spec eff, Paul Lerpae; m/l, "Wish Me a Rainbow," Jay Livingston, Ray Evans; makeup, Wally Westmore.

Drama   (PR:O   MPAA:NR)

THIS REBEL AGE   (SEE: BEAT GENERATION, THE, 1959)

THIS REBEL BREED*½   (1960) 90m WB bw (AKA: THREE SHADES OF LOVE; LOLA'S MISTAKE)

Rita Moreno (*Lola*), Mark Damon (*Frank*), Gerald Mohr (*Lt. Brooks*), Jay Novello (*Papa*), Eugene Martin (*Rudy*), Tom Gilson (*Muscles*), Richard Rust (*Buck*), Douglas Hume (*Don*), Richard Laurier (*Manuel*), Don Eitner (*Jimmy*), Diane [Dyan] Cannon (*Wiggles*), Kenny Miller (*Winnie*), Al Freeman (*Satchel*), Charles Franc (*Scratch*), Ike Jones, Shirley Falls, Stevie Perry, Hari Rhodes.

Two police academy cadets (Damon and Hume) are assigned to go undercover at a local high school to investigate drug traffic. Damon is half-black, half-Latino, which makes him a good candidate for this assignment in the racially mixed school. He meets Moreno, a student who has lost her boy friend in a gang fight. Meanwhile, the gangs rule the school with their dope dealings, knife fights, and terror tactics against innocents. THIS REBEL BREED has a naive air that is wholly unacceptable. Pushers peddle their wares on 6-year-olds and Damon is obviously wearing makeup so the audience will know he is black. Moments like these draw laughs. Moreno gives a fine performance and the next year would again play a street girl and win an Oscar for Best Actress in WEST SIDE STORY. This was Cannon's second film and she was still using her real middle name of Diane.

p, William Rowland; d, Richard L. Bare; w, Morris Lee Green (based on the story "All God's Children" by Rowland and Irma Berk); ph, Monroe Askins; m, David Rose; ed, Tony Martinelli.

Drama   (PR:O   MPAA:NR)

THIS RECKLESS AGE*½   (1932) 80m PAR bw

Charles "Buddy" Rogers (*Bradley Ingals*), Richard Bennett (*Donald Ingals*), Peggy Shannon (*Mary Burke*), Charles Ruggles (*Goliath Whitney*), Frances Dee (*Lois Ingals*), Frances Starr (*Eunice Ingals*), Maude Eburne (*Rhoda*), David Landau (*Matthew Daggett*), Reginald Barlow (*Lester Bell*), Mary Carlisle (*Cassandra Phelps*), Allen Vincent ("*Pig*" *Van Dyke*), George Pearce (*John Burke*), Grady Sutton ("*Stepladder*" *Schultz*), Harry Templeton (*Monk Turner*), Leonard Carey (*Braithwaite*).

Some things never change, like generation gap conflicts. This comedy deals with the problems some nice parents face when their kids misbehave. After coming home from college, Rogers surprises his parents (Starr and Bennett) with his new fangled ideas. Shannon and Dee play two contrasting young ladies, one fairly conventional and the other a flapper type with mixed emotions about her life style. The story is simple and full of script weaknesses, but it is told with liveliness by the cast and is amusingly directed. There's a sense of fun to this, strained though it may be.

d, Frank Tuttle; w, Joseph L. Mankiewicz, Tuttle (based on the play "The Goose Hangs High" by Lewis Beach); ph, Henry Sharp.

Comedy   (PR:A MPAA:NR)

THIS SAVAGE LAND*½   (1969) 97m Universal
Television-NBC/UNIV c (AKA: THE ROAD WEST)

Barry Sullivan (*Ben Pride*), Brenda Scott (*Midge Pride*), Andrew Prine (*Timothy Pride*), Kelly Corcoran (*Kip Pride*), Katherine Squire (*Grandma*), Charles Seel (*Grandpa*), Kathryn Hays (*Elizabeth*), Roy Roberts (*Elizabeth's Father*), John Drew Barrymore (*Stacey*), Glenn Corbett (*Chance*), George C. Scott (*Jud Barker*).

Shortly after the Civil War, widower Sullivan takes his parents and children from their Ohio home to Lawrence, Kansas. They build a home but suffer from a harrassing gang of ex-Confederates led by Scott. While Sullivan is away the gang attacks the family, burning one of their wagons and wounding Sullivan's father, Seel. Afraid to return home, Sullivan asks Hays, the daughter of a local doctor, to help him. Once more the gang attacks, this time killing Hays' father and Seel. Sullivan falls for Hays along the way and has her move into his home. However the gang returns, this time kidnaping Hays and Sullivan's daughter, Scott, in hopes they can provide medical help. Sullivan, his son, Prine, and Hays' brother, Corbett, ride in and rescue the ladies at the end. Originally shown on NBC television as a two-part episode of "The Road West" series in 1966 before its theatrical release three years later.

p, James McAdams; d, Vincent McEveety; w, Richard Fielder; ph, Ray Flin (Technicolor); m, Leonard Rosenman; ed, Richard Belding; art d, Russell Kimball; set d, John McCarthy, John M. Dwyer; makeup, Bud Westmore.

Western   (PR:A MPAA:G)

THIS SIDE OF HEAVEN*½   (1934) 76m MGM bw

Lionel Barrymore (*Martin Turner*), Fay Bainter (*Francene Turner*), Mae Clarke (*Jane Turner*), Tom Brown (*Seth Turner*), Mary Carlisle (*Peggy Turner*), Una Merkel (*Birdie, Servant*), Onslow Stevens (*Walter Hamilton*), Henry Wadsworth (*Hal Jennings*), Eddie Nugent (*Vance Patterson*), C. Henry Gordon (*William Barnes*), Dickie Moore (*Freddie*), Edwin Maxwell (*Sawyer*), Richard Tucker (*Producer*), Claire Du Brey (*Miss Blair*), Sumner Getchell (*Gus*), Nell O'Day (*Secretary*), Herbert Prior (*Grouch*), Edward J. LeSaint (*Minister*), Phil Tead (*Radio Announcer*), Lee Phelps (*Policeman*), Paddy O'Flynn (*Taxi Driver*), Geneva Mitchell, Ailene Carlyle (*Nurses*), Paul Stanton, Theodore Von Eltz (*Doctors*), Nell Craig (*Nurse Attendant*), Bobby Watson (*Interior Decorator*), Dawn O'Day [Anne Shirley] (*Flower Girl*), Charles Williams (*Reporter*), James Durkin (*Raymond*), Charles Giblyn (*Harvey*), Mickey Daniels (*Stinky Bliss*), Ed Norris (*Upper Classman*), Billy Taft (*School Boy*), Niles Welch (*Druggist*), Stanley Taylor (*Intern*).

Barrymore plays the head of a large family who becomes mixed up in some underhanded financial dealings. His wife, Bainter, is a budding writer who has just sold a story to a motion picture company, so he covers his guilty feelings with a pretense of happiness. His eldest daughter's fiance is an auditor for Barrymore's company who discovers the errors in the books and knows Barrymore's in for some big trouble. He is abandoned by the daughter, who decides she must stick with her father after the fiance becomes embarrassed over Barrymoore's misdeeds. Meanwhile his younger daughter elopes but returns to be with her family during the crisis. The youngest son is denied membership into a fraternity and, driving in a highly emotional state, crashes and is sent to the hospital. Barrymore ingests poison so he won't embarrass his family with a public scandal, and is hospitalized as well. But the clan sticks by him. A cut and dried melodrama made realistic by the quality of the acting. The film did quite well at the box office, particularly with the family audiences it was aimed at.

p, John Considine, Jr; d, William K. Howard; w, Zelda Sears, Eve Greene, Florence Ryerson, Edgar Allan Woolf (based on the novel *It Happened One Day* by Marjorie B. Paradise); ph, Hal Rosson; ed, Frank Hull.

Drama   (PR:AA MPAA:NR)

THIS SIDE OF THE LAW**   (1950) 74m WB bw

Viveca Lindfors (*Evelyn*), Kent Smith (*David Cummins*), Janis Paige (*Nadine Taylor*), Robert Douglas (*Philip Cagle*), John Alvin (*Calder Taylor*), Monte Blue (*The Sheriff*), Frances Morris (*Miss Roberts*), Nita Talbot.

When smooth-talking lawyer Douglas talks Smith into impersonating a missing millionaire, the poverty-stricken man finds himself in trouble. He immediately finds himself with a hateful wife and brother, as well as an amorous sister-in-law. Smith discovers that Douglas' plot also involves murder in order to collect a lot of cash. Smith manages to escape after a struggle with the crooked lawyer, and exposes the entire plan. The cast is capable, but the story is unconvincing, with a directorial style that confuses rather than builds suspense.

p, Saul Elkins; d, Richard L. Bare; w, Russell Hughes (based on a story by Richard Sale); ph, Carl Guthrie; m, William Lava; ed, Frank Magee.

Suspense   (PR:C MPAA:NR)

THIS SPECIAL FRIENDSHIP**   (1967, Fr.) 99m Pro Ge Fi-C.C.F.
Lux/Pathe bw (LES AMITIES PARTICULIERES)

Francis Lacombrade (*Georges de Sarre*), Didier Haudepin (*Alexandre Motier*), Lucien Nat (*The Father Superior*), Louis Seigner (*Father Lauzon*), Michel Bouquet (*Father Trennes*), Francois Leccia (*Lucien Rouvere*).

At a French parochial school in the early 1930s, Lacombrade, a sixteen-year-old young man, becomes close friends with his fellow student, Leccia. After finding a love letter from another boy to Leccia, Lacombrade turns the note over to Nat, the Father Superior. A scandal is raised, forcing the note's author to leave, though Leccia is allowed to remain at the school. Soon Lacombrade finds himself in a similar predicament, for he is attracted to a younger student at the school, Haudepin. With the encouragement of Leccia, the two boys begin to meet in secret. Bouquet, a younger priest, begins to suspect something but Lacombrade tries to stop him by telling Nat that Bouquet has been carrying on with some students. Bouquet is caught with a boy and fired from his position, but before going he has a talk with Lacombrade about passing judgments on others. Soon after, Lacombrade and Haudepin are caught together by Seigner, Lacombrade's father confessor. He threatens the two with expulsion unless they give up their relationship. Lacombrade agrees to this but H.audepin prefers expulsion to losing his friend. He is emotionally crushed by Lacombrade's rejection and commits suicide by jumping in front of the train that was to take him home.

p, Christine Gouze-Renal; d, Jean Delannoy; w, Jean Aurenche, Pierre Bost (based on *Les Amities Particulieres* by Roger Peyrefitte); ph, Christian Matras; m, Jean Prodromides; ed, Louisette Hautecoeur; art d, Rene Renoux.

Drama   **Cas.**   (PR:O MPAA:NR)

THIS SPORTING AGE*½   (1932) 67m COL bw

Jack Holt (*Capt. John Steele*), Evalyn Knapp (*Mickey Steele*), Hardie Albright (*Johnny Raeburn*), Walter Byron (*Charles Morrell*), J. Farrell MacDonald (*Jerry O'Day*), Ruth Weston (*Mrs. Rita Duncan*), Nora Lane (*Mrs. Wainleigh*), Shirley Palmer (*Ann Erskine*), Hal Price (*Surgeon*).

Melodramatic soaper starring Holt as an Army captain whose fanatical devotion to polo gets him into trouble when he goes after another polo player, Byron, after the latter has compromised the former's daughter, Knapp. Holt is so enraged at the news, that he causes Byron to suffer a fatal accident on the playing field, which is deemed manslaughter, and then a price must be paid on the scales of justice.

d, Andrew W. Bennison, A. F. Erickson; w, Dudley Nichols (based on a story by J. K. McGuinness); ph, Teddy Tetzlaff; ed, Maurice Wright.

Drama   (PR:A MPAA:NR)

THIS SPORTING LIFE**½   (1963, Brit.) 129m Independent
Artists/CD bw

Richard Harris (*Frank Machin*), Rachel Roberts (*Mrs. Hammond*), Alan Badel (*Weaver*), William Hartnell (*Johnson*), Colin Blakely (*Maurice Braithwaite*), Vanda Godsell (*Mrs. Weaver*), Arthur Lowe (*Slomer*), Anne Cunningham (*Judith*), Jack Watson (*Len Miller*), Harry Markham (*Wade*), George Sewell (*Jeff*), Leonard Rossiter (*Phillips*), Frank Windsor (*Dentist*), Peter Duguid (*Doctor*), Wallas Eaton (*Waiter*), Anthony Woodruff (*Head Waiter*), Katherine Parr (*Mrs. Farrer*), Bernadette Benson (*Lynda*), Andrew Nolan (*Ian*), Michael Logan (*Riley*), Murray Evans (*Hooker*), Tom Clegg (*Gower*), John Gill (*Cameron*), Ken Traill (*Trainer*).

Harris plays a former coal miner who wishes to better his lot in life and joins the world of professional rugby, quickly establishing himself as one of the sport's most violent and aggressive competitors. He rents a room in Roberts' boarding house and tries to impress the lonely widow with his skills. She cares little for this egocentric roughneck, preferring to dwell on her late husband's memory, a man rumored to have committed suicide at his factory job. She eventually is sexually attracted to him and the two begin a physical relationship. For Roberts the affair is only physical and she remains emotionally detached. Harris' fame grows and with it comes money, which he spends quite freely. He begins flaunting Roberts as his mistress but, at the wedding of one of Harris' teammates, she becomes overwhelmed by her pent-up feelings. She begins to fight with Harris, which leads to more angry confrontations between them. Harris leaves her but soon realizes that he can't live without her. He learns that Roberts has suffered a brain hemorrhage and is in a coma. He visits her and tries to show that he is capable of emotion. However, Roberts dies and Harris returns to the world where he is accepted for what he is–a violent rugby player. Anderson's first directorial effort after a successful career in documentary filmmaking is nothing short of a tour-de-force. He combines his documentary background with a good sense of story telling in this unique and powerful film. The characters are not pretty people, but they are real. Harris and Roberts are strong leads, building a smoldering passion that holds the viewer's attention tightly. Both received well-deserved Oscar nominations for their performances. One of the best of England's "Angry Young Man" films.

p, Karel Reisz; d, Lindsay Anderson; w, David Storey (based on the novel *This Sporting Life* by Storey); ph, Denys Coop; m, Roberto Gerhard; ed, Peter Taylor; md, Jacques-Louis Monod; art d, Alan Withy; set d, Peter Lamont; cos, Sophie Devine; makeup, Bob Lawrence.

Drama   **Cas.**   **(PR:O   MPAA:NR)**

THIS STRANGE PASSION TORMENTS   (SEE: EL, 1955, Mex.)

THIS STUFF'LL KILL YA! zero   (1971) 100m Ultima c

Jeffrey Allen (*Roscoe Boone*), Tim Holt (*Clark*), Gloria King (*Elsie*), Ray Sager (*Grady*), Erich Bradly (*Sam*), Terence McCarthy (*Carter*), Ronna Riddle (*Lynn*), Larry Drake (*Bubba*), John Garner (*Turnip*), Bill Mays (*Policeman*), Lee Danser (*Zeke*), Pamela Polsgrove (*Maryellen*), Doffy Candler (*Beau*), Skip Nicholson (*Lawyer Grimes*), Carol Merrell (*Bubba's Nurse*), Pamela Bloomfield (*Marcia*), Debbie Gardiner (*Janet*).

An abysmal moonshiner picture about a preacher, Allen, who promotes free love and hard drinking. He enlists McCarthy to help him with his illegal distillery, but the pair meet opposition from the FBI and many of the townsfolk. A rash of religious murders (people are stoned to death and crucified) is committed by Sager, a deranged fanatic, who is trying to help the preacher. McCarthy and Sager eventually wind up fighting and the latter gets his head blown off by his own shotgun. Another repugnant H.G. Lewis entry which was, unfortunately, the last picture for Tim Holt. After appearing in some of Hollywood's finest pictures, STAGECOACH (1939), THE MAGNIFICENT AMBERSONS (1942), MY DARLING CLEMENTINE (1946), and his memorable role in THE TREASURE OF SIERRA MADRE (1948), Holt came out of retirement that had lasted 14 years to suffer the indignity of THIS STUFF'LL KILL YA!

p,d&w, Herschell Gordon Lewis; ph, Alex Ameri, Daniel P. Krogh (Eastmancolor); m, Sheldon Seymour; ed, Eskandar Ameripoor; m/l, Seymour.

Crime   **(PR:O   MPAA:GP)**

THIS, THAT AND THE OTHER*   (1970, Brit.) 85m Dorak/Paul Mart
                                             c (GB: A PROMISE OF BED)

Victor Spinetti (*George*), Vanessa Howard (*Barbara*), Vanda Hudson (*Susan Stress*), John Bird (*Harold*), Peter Kinsley (*Wilbur*), Roy Brannigan (*Jeffrey*), Alexandra Bastedo (*Angie*), Christopher Mitchell (*Carl*), Sue Cole (*Jo*), Robin Courbet (*Jimmy*), Dennis Waterman (*Photographer*), Gordon Sterne (*Producer*), Yutte Stensgaard (*Taxi Girl*), Angie Grant (*Flower Girl*), Cleo Goldstein (*Hands Girl*), Michel Durant (*Playboy*), Larry Taylor (*Policeman*), Valerie Leon (*Bath Girl*), Heather Barber (*Exposure Girl*), Sheila Ruskin (*Snake Girl*), Siobhan Taylor (*Party Girl*), Bill Jarvis, Gregory Reid (*Guests*).

Spinetti, a British comic actor who appeared in both major Beatle films– A HARD DAY'S NIGHT (1964) and HELP] (1965)–stars in this lame sex comedy as a suicidal bloke whose life is inadvertently saved by Howard, a voluptuous party-loving blonde. Intertwined with this tale are a couple of others. Hudson seduces the teenage son of a producer, only to find that his father isn't a producer at all. The other story has taxi driver Bird dreaming of a fantasy world populated by sunbathers and stripteasers. An all-around sophomoric picture.

p, Stanley Long; d, Derek Ford; w, Derek Ford, Donald Ford; ph, Long (Eastmancolor); ed, Glyn Byles.

Comedy   **(PR:O   MPAA:NR)**

THIS THING CALLED LOVE**   (1929) 72m Pathe bw-c

Edmund Lowe (*Robert Collings*), Constance Bennett (*Ann Marvin*), Roscoe Karns (*Harry Bertrand*), ZaSu Pitts (*Clara Bertrand*), Carmelita Geraghty (*Alverez Guerra*), John Roche (*DeWitt*), Stuart Erwin (*Fred*), Ruth Taylor (*Dolly*), Wilson Benge (*Dumary*), Adele Watson (*Secretary*), Jean Harlow (*Bit*).

When Lowe returns from Peru with a large sum of money, he's anxious to find a wife and settle down. He's about to buy a house but accompanies the real estate agent home for dinner and discovers what married life is *really* like. Nevertheless, he still wants a wife for his new home and comes up with an arrangement with the agent's sister-in-law, Bennett. They agree to a 1929

version of an open marriage, with Bennett merely managing the house but not sleeping with Lowe, and each partner being free to see whomever they please. Of course, they eventually fall in love with each other, though neither will admit it. Both go to elaborate extremes to make the other jealous. In the end they agree to try a real marriage. This early comedy is predictable, telegraphing its jokes ahead of time and holding nothing in the way of surprises. Blonde bombshell Jean Harlow is seen in a very early bit role. Originally, the film contained a three-minute color sequence.

p, Ralph Block; d, Paul L. Stein; w, Horace Jackson (based on the play by Edwin Burke); ph, Norbert Brodine (bw and Technicolor), ed, Doane Harrison; art d, Edward Jewell; cos, Gwen Wakeling.

Comedy   **(PR:C   MPAA:NR)**

THIS THING CALLED LOVE***
          (1940) 98m COL bw (GB: MARRIED BUT SINGLE)

Rosalind Russell (*Ann Winters*), Melvyn Douglas (*Tice Collins*), Binnie Barnes (*Charlotte Campbell*), Allyn Joslyn (*Harry Bertrand*), Gloria Dickson (*Florence Bertrand*), Lee J. Cobb (*Julio Diestro*), Gloria Holden (*Genevieve Hooper*), Paul McGrath (*Gordon Daniels*), Leona Maricle (*Ruth Howland*), Don Beddoe (*Tom Howland*), Rosina Galli (*Mrs. Diestro*), Sig Arno (*Arno*).

Russell and Douglas play a pair of newlyweds who have a problem with sex. The problem is he wants to and she doesn't. Russell feels that a three-month celibacy period should come first, but Douglas, ever the charmer, tries to wear her down. Eventually his little schemes work but he still must wait a bit longer as he's contracted poison oak] This adult comedy was directed gracefully, handling the sensitive material nicely. Occasionally repetitive, the result is a funny, well-acted sex comedy. By today's standards it's fairly mild, with a good deal of innocent charm, but it was scandalous enough in 1940 to be banned by the Legion of Decency.

p, William Perlberg; d, Alexander Hall; w, George Seaton, Ken Englund, P. J. Wolfson (based on the play by Edwin Burke); ph, Joseph Walker; m, Werner Heymann; ed, Viola Lawrence; md, M. W. Stoloff; art d, Lionel Banks; cos, Irene.

Comedy   **(PR:O   MPAA:NR)**

THIS TIME FOR KEEPS*   (1942) 73m MGM bw

Ann Rutherford (*Katherine White*), Robert Sterling (*Lee White*), Virginia Weidler (*Harriett Bryant*), Guy Kibbee (*Harry Bryant*), Irene Rich (*Mrs. Bryant*), Henry O'Neill (*Arthur Freeman*), Dorothy Morris (*Edith Bryant*), Richard Crane (*Eustace Andrews*), Connie Gilchrist (*Miss Nichols*), Joseph Strauch, Jr (*Milton*), Tim Ryan (*Prof. Diz*), John "Buddy" Williams (*Porter*), Ken Christy (*Conductor*), Ava Gardner (*Girl in Car*), George Noisom (*Caddy*), Robert Emmett Keane (*Mr. Reiner*), Frank Hagney (*Linesman*), Doris Day (*Freeman's Secretary*), Bess Flowers (*Saleslady*), Babe London (*Fat Lady*), Regina Wallace (*Mrs. Lornow*).

This simplistic and poorly done film is the old story of the newlywed husband who goes to work for his father-in-law. Sterling plays the husband, Rutherford the wife, and Kibbee the nasty man who won't give his son-in-law an even break. Despite Sterling and Rutherford's chemistry, this predictable and thin story goes nowhere. The film was the second and last in an attempted series featuring part of the same cast. Watch for early screen appearances by Ava Gardner and Doris Day.

p, Samuel Marx; d, Charles Riesner; w, Muriel Roy Bolton, Rian James, Harry Ruskin (based on characters created by Herman J. Mankiewicz); ph, Charles Lewton; ed, Frederick Y. Smith.

Comedy   **(PR:A   MPAA:NR)**

THIS TIME FOR KEEPS**   (1947) 105m MGM c

Esther Williams (*Nora Cambaretti*), Lauritz Melchior (*Hans Herald*), Jimmy Durante (*Ferdi Farro*), Johnnie Johnston (*Dick Johnson*), Xavier Cugat (*Himself*), Dame May Whitty (*Grandma*), Sharon McManus (*Deborah*), Dick Simmons (*Gordon Coome*), Mary Stuart (*Frances*), Ludwig Stossel (*Peter*), Dorothy Porter (*Merle*), Tommy Wonder (*Himself*), Nella Walker (*Mrs. Allenbury*), Holmes Herbert (*Norman*), William Tannen, Robert Strickland, Kenneth Tobey, Don Garner (*Soldiers*), Herbert Heywood (*Doorman*), Nan Bennett (*Luci LeRoy*), Esther Dale (*Mrs. Fields*), Duncan Richardson (*Duncan*), Chris Drake (*Soldier at Pool*), Anne Francis, Richard Terry (*Bobby-Soxers*), Harry Tyler (*Bartender*).

MGM's musical factory couldn't always produce something terrific as this film shows. The story is the familiar one of boy meets girl as opera singer Melchior brings his son, Johnston, to Mackinac Island. There Johnston meets Williams, the star of the "aquacaper." Durante provides some comic moments as her piano-playing bodyguard and Whitty plays Williams' grandmother. Noted bandleader Cugat plays himself, providing several musical numbers with his orchestra. Though the production is colorful and glossy, and the choreography is by Stanley Donen, the film on the whole seems flat, with none of the liveliness a musical needs to succeed. Durante gets to do his famous "Inka Dinka Do" (Durante, Ben Ryan). Other songs include: "M'Appari" from *Martha* (Friedrich von Flotow–sung by Lauritz Melchior), "La Donna E Mobile" from *Rigoletto* (Giuseppe Verdi–sung by

Melchior), "You Are So Easy to Love" (Cole Porter–sung by Melchior), "The Man Who Found the Lost Chord," "A Little Bit of This and A Little Bit of That" (Durante–sung by Durante), "Chiquita Banana" (Leonard Mackenzie, Garth Montgomery, William Wirges), "No Wonder They Fall in Love," "Ten Percent Off" (Ralph Freed, Sammy Fain), "Why Don't They Let Me Sing a Love Song," "Little Big Shot" (Benny Davis, Harry Akst), "I Love to Dance" (Freed, Burton Lane), and "When It's Lilac Time on Mackinac Island" (Leslie Kirk).

p, Joseph Pasternak; d, Richard Thorpe; w, Gladys Lehman (based on a story by Erwin Gelsey, Lorraine Fielding); ph, Karl Freund (Technicolor); m, Georgie Stoll; ed, John Dunning; md, Stoll; art d, Cedric Gibbons, Randall Duell; set d, Edwin B. Willis, Henry W. Grace; spec eff, A. Arnold Gillespie; ch, Stanley Donen.

Musical   (PR:AAA MPAA:NR)

THIS WAS A WOMAN**   (1949, Brit.) 102m Excelsior/FOX bw

Sonia Dresdel (Sylvia Russell), Walter Fitzgerald (Arthur Russell), Emrys Jones (Terry Russell), Barbara White (Fenella Russell), Julian Dallas (Valentine Christie), Cyril Raymond (Austin Penrose), Marjorie Rhodes (Mrs. Holmes), Celia Lipton (Effie), Lesley Osmond (Sally), Kynaston Reeves (Dr. Morrison), Joan Hickson (Miss Johnson), Clive Morton (Company Director), Percy Walsh (Professor of Music), Noel Howlett (Chief Surgeon).

A psychotic woman who craves power (Dresdel) takes out her problems on her family in humiliating and devastating ways. Her daughter, White, is married to a doctor but Dresdel doesn't approve and ruins the marriage. Dresdel then decides to take on another man for herself and poisons her husband. Jones plays the son she is infinitely proud of for his medical research, but he catches on to his mother's ways and calls the police. Eventually Dresdel is convicted of murder but declared insane and sent to an institution. Though the film has an interesting plot, the stagey presentation hurts the final product. Dresdel is a tour de force but depends on too many mannerisms from her performance of the stage version.

p, Marcel Hellman; d, Tim Whelan; w, Val Valentine (based on the play by Joan Morgan); ph, Gunther Krampf, Hal Britten; m, Mischa Spoliansky; ed, E.B. Jarvis; art d, Andrew Mazzei, Ivan King.

Drama   (PR:O MPAA:NR)

THIS WAS PARIS**   (1942, Brit.) 77m WB bw (AKA: SO THIS WAS PARIS)

Ann Dvorak (Anne Morgan), Ben Lyon (Butch), Griffith Jones (Bill Hamilton), Robert Morley (Van Der Stuyl), Harold Huth (De La Vague), Mary Maguire (Blossom Leroy), Harry Welchman (Forsyth), Frederick Burtwell (Entwhistle), Miles Malleson (Watson), Bernard Miles (Propaganda Officer), Vera Bogetti (Mme. Florien), Marian Spencer (Lady Muriel), Hay Petrie (Popinard), Billy Holland, Harry McElhone.

A well-made but completely hollow war film starring Dvorak as an American ambulance driver in war-torn France. She's unwittingly being used by the Nazis. Jones plays a British Intelligence man who rescues her from the enemy and Lyon provides support as the sterotypical hard-driven war correspondant. The film is well photographed and directed, but neither of these factors can cover the empty headed script, making this a less than average war film.

p, Max Milder; d, John Harlow; w, Brock Williams, Edward Dryhurst (based on a story by Gordon Wellesley, Basil Woon); ph, Basil Emmott; ed, Les Norman.

Drama   (PR:C MPAA:NR)

THIS WAY PLEASE**   (1937) 72m PAR bw

Charles "Buddy" Rogers (Brad Morgan), Betty Grable (Jane Morrow), Ned Sparks (Inky Wells), Jim Jordan, Marian Jordan (Fibber McGee and Molly), Porter Hall (S.J. Crawford), Lee Bowman (Stu Randall), Cecil Cunningham (Miss Eberhardt), Wally Vernon (Bumps), Romo Vincent (Trumps), Jerry Bergen (Mumps), Rufe Davis (Sound Effects Man), Mary Livingstone (Maxine Barry), Ellen Drew (Chorus Girl), Akim Tamiroff.

A simple behind-the-scenes show biz story starring Rogers as the master of ceremonies at a local movie house. Live vaudeville-type acts perform there between films, and Grable, in an early starring role, wants to get on the stage and perform. Instead, she's quickly handed a flashlight to become an usherette with Livingston (Jack Benny's wife in real life). Popular radio comics Jim and Marian Jordan provide some laughs as their Fibber McGee and Molly characters but the real fun is Davis. He's the broadcasting sound effects man, and he steals the show with his one-man bit. Otherwise, it's a routine musical programmer. Songs include "Is It Love or Is It Infatuation?" (Sam Coslow, Frederick Hollander), "This Way Home," "Delighted to Meet You," "What This Country Needs is Voom Voom" (Al Siegel, Sam Coslow), "I'm the Sound Effects Man" (George Gray).

p, Mel Shauer; d, Robert Florey; w, Grant Garrett, Seena Owen, Howard J. Green (based on a story by Maxwell Shane, Bill Thomas); ph, Harry Fischbeck; ed, Anna Bauchens; md, Boris Morros; art d, Hans Dreier, Jack Otterson; cos, Edith Head; ch, LeRoy Prinz.

Musical   (PR:AA MPAA:NR)

THIS WEEK OF GRACE**½   (1933, Brit.) 92m REA/RKO bw

Gracie Fields (Grace Milroy), Henry Kendall (Lord Clive Swinford), John Stuart (Henry Baring), Frank Pettingell (Mr. Milroy), Minnie Rayner (Mrs. Milroy), Douglas Wakefield (Joe Milroy), Vivian Foster (Vicar), Marjorie Brooks (Pearl Forrester), Helen Haye (Lady Warmington), Nina Boucicault (Duchess Of Swinford), Lawrence Hanray.

A working-class charmer about an unemployed girl, Fields, who is given control of a duchess' estate when it is discovered that it has been mismanaged. Fields doesn't have much of a business mind but she has more common sense than anyone around her. Funny, bright, and uplifting.

p, Julius Hagen; d, Maurice Elvey; w, H. Fowler Mear, Jack Marks (based on a story by Maurice Braddell, Nell Emerald); ph, Sydney Blythe.

Comedy   (PR:A MPAA:NR)

THIS WINE OF LOVE**   (1948, Ital.) 75m Prora/Superfilm bw (L'ELISIR D'AMORE)

Nelly Corradi (Adina), Loretta Di Lelio (Giannetta), Tito Gobbi (Belcore), Gino Sinimberghi (Nemorino), Italo Tajo (Dulcamara), Milton Cross.

This adaption of the Donizetti comic opera features Corradi as a young coquette who enjoys teasing the local boys. Sinimberghi is the young man who worships the girl and is finally united with her after medicineman Tajo concocts a powerful love potion. The American version featured an unneeded commentary by Milton Cross at the film's beginning. It should have been left out as the delightful talents of the players are all that's needed to convey the story. Watch for an appearance by the noted opera talent Gobbi. The film was shot without sound with the voices dubbed later, occasionally with less than successful results. (In Italian; English subtitles.)

d, Mario Costa; w, Costa, R. Castelli, Aldo Caiva, P. Salvucci, R. J'Acurio Ristori, E. Natale, Libero Petrazzi, Antonio Leonardi (based on the opera by Gaetano Donizetti); ph, Mario Bava; ed, Otello Colangelli; md, Guiseppe Morelli.

Opera   (PR:AA MPAA:NR)

THIS WOMAN IS DANGEROUS**½   (1952) 100m WB bw

Joan Crawford (Beth Austin), Dennis Morgan (Dr. Ben Halleck), David Brian (Matt Jackson), Richard Webb (Franklin), Mari Alden (Ann Jackson), Philip Carey (Will Jackson), Ian MacDonald (Joe Grossland), Katherine Warren (Admitting Nurse), George Chandler (Dr. Ryan), William Challee (Ned Shaw), Sherry Jackson (Susan Halleck), Douglas Fowley (Club Manager), Harry Lauter (Trooper), Karen Hale (Nurse), Charles Sullivan (Attendant), Jean Carry (Technician), Dick Bartell (Waiter), Mary Alan Hokanson (Prison Doctor), Eileen Stevens (Chambermaid), Dee Carroll (Telephone Operator), Kenneth Patterson (Oculist), Harry Tyler (Mike), Gladys Blake (Hairdresser), Cecil Weston (Prison Matron).

A strange amalgam of crime and soap opera which served as Crawford's final film under her Warners contract. She is the stylish leader of a gang of thieves. Her brains are what makes the band function but her beauty and body are what turns on the gang's killer, Brian. The group successfully robs a gambling parlor in New Orleans and she now has enough money to pay for a hospital stay. Crawford's eyesight has been dimming and she travels to a hospital far away from Louisiana to have some exploratory eye surgery. Brian is a jealous lover and a man who always wants to be in action but he agrees to cease and desist his robbery work until after she has recovered from her medical problem. The FBI, in the person of Webb, gets a clue to Crawford's location and tracks her to the hospital where her opthamologist is Morgan. As is often the case, patient falls in love with physician and vice versa. During her overlong stay in the hospital, Morgan and Crawford find much to care for about the other. Brian is still hiding out with his brother, Carey, and Carey's wife, Aldon. Brian suspects that Crawford is malingering in the medical facility but he can't show his face so he hires a private detective, MacDonald, to find out what's happening. Crawford has decided to give up her life of crime but she fears Morgan will be hurt by her past and may even be in danger from Brian so she tells him that she doesn't love him, in the hope that he will get out of her life in order to save his own. Crawford attempts to contact Brian, as she senses what the crazed man may do to Morgan. Morgan is in the operating theater in the midst of surgery when Brian comes in, armed and dangerous. MacDonald has reported what's going on and Brian means to rub out the doctor. Just as Brian is taking a bead on Morgan, Webb and his FBI men get there in time to stop him. Since Crawford is apparently reformed, she will be given a short term in the womens' slammer and Morgan will, no doubt, be standing outside the gate when she is released. A little bit of DARK VICTORY and I WANT TO LIVE at the same time.

p, Robert Sisk; d, Felix Feist; w, Geoffrey Homes, George W. Yates (based on the story "Stab of Pain" by Bernard Girard); ph, Ted McCord, m, David Buttolph; ed, James C. Moore; art d, Leo K. Kuter; cos, Sheila O'Brien.

Crime/Romance   (PR:A-C MPAA:NR)

THIS WOMAN IS MINE   (SEE: 18 MINUTES, 1935, Brit.)

THIS WOMAN IS MINE*   (1941) 91m UNIV bw

Franchot Tone *(Robert Stevens)*, John Carroll *(Ovide de Montigny)*, Walter Brennan *(Capt. Jonathan Thorn)*, Carol Bruce *(Julie Morgan)*, Nigel Bruce *(Duncan MacDougall)*, Paul Hurst *(2nd Mate Mumford)*, Frank Conroy *(1st Mate Fox)*, Leo G. Carroll *(Angus McKay)*, Abner Biberman *(Lamazie)*, Sig Rumann *(John Jacob Astor)*, Morris Ankrum *(Roussel)*, Louis Mercier *(LaFantasie)*, Philip Charbert *(Franchere)*, Ignacio Saenz *(Matouna)*, Ray Beltram *(Chief Nakoomis)*, Charles Judels *(Cafe Proprietor)*.

Brennan plays the captain of a schooner filled with trappers and traders bound for a fur-trapping expedition in Oregon. Those on board include Bruce, Frenchman John Carroll, Tone, and stowaway Carol Bruce. All the men vie for her affections during the two-year voyage, but she eventually falls in love with Tone. The group survives several adventures during the voyage, and are attacked by Indians upon their arrival. During the seige, Brennan is forced to blow up his ship as the others make their way to shore. Though the cast contains many well-known and interesting actors, the weak script, with its series of uninteresting events that never seem to pull together, makes this film tedious.

p&d, Frank Lloyd; w, Seton I. Miller, Frederick Jackson (based on the novel *I, James Lewis* by Gilbert W. Gabriel); ph, Milton Krasner; ed, Edward Curtiss; cos, Vera West; spec eff, John P. Fulton; m/l, Bernie Grossman, Charles Previn, Richard Hageman.

Drama   (PR:A MPAA:NR)

THIS'LL MAKE YOU WHISTLE**   (1938, Brit.) 78m Wilcox/C&M bw

Jack Buchanan *(Bill Hoppings)*, Elsie Randolph *(Bobbie Rivers)*, Jean Gillie *(Joan Longhurst)*, William Kendall *(Reggie Benson)*, David Hutcheson *(Archie Codrington)*, Maidie Hope *(Mrs. Longhurst)*, Antony Holles *(Sebastian Venables)*, Marjorie Brooks *(Laura Buxton)*, Bunty Pain *(Betty)*, Miki Hood *(Clarice)*, Scott Harrold *(Gendarme)*, Irene Vere *(Mrs. Crimp)*.

On the French Riviera, playboy Buchanan wants to get rid of his fiancee's *(Randolph)* guardian. To shock her out of the job, Buchanan poses as a ne'er-do-well forger. This slight musical comedy was based on a popular London musical that had been a vehicle for Buchanan. He repeats his stage role here, as do most of the original cast, and their performances cover up the story's weaknesses with some success.

p&d, Herbert Wilcox; w, Guy Bolton, Paul Thompson (based on the play by Bolton and Thompson); ph, F.A. Young; m/l, Sigler, Goodhart, and Hoffman.

Musical/Comedy   (PR:A MPAA:NR)

THISTLEDOWN*   (1938, Brit.) 79m WB-FN bw

Aino Bergo *(Therese Glenloch)*, Keith Falkner *(Sir Ian Glenloch)*, Athole Stewart *(Duke of Invergower)*, Sharon Lynne *(Ivy Winter)*, Bruce Lister *(Lord James Dunfoyle)*, Ian Maclean *(Rossini)*, Amy Veness *(Mary Glenloch)*, Vera Bogetti *(Simmonds)*, Gordon McLeod *(Gallagher)*, Jack Lambert, Herbert Leslie, Richard Lownes.

A weak musical set in Scotland about an opera singer, Bergo, who marries a lord, Falkner. She is soon disenchanted with her lonely life on his estate and considers resuming the operatic career. When Falkner accuses her of carrying on with a neighboring landowner, Bergo packs up her bags and returns to the stage. She makes her fortune, while Falkner hits a patch of hard times. Bergo purchases Falkner's estate and the pair is reunited.

p, Irving Asher; d, Arthur Woods; w, Brock Williams (based on a story by John Meehan, Jr., J.O.C. Orton); ph, Basil Emmott.

Musical/Romance   (PR:A MPAA:NR)

THOMAS CROWN AFFAIR, THE**   (1968) 102m
Mirisch-Simkoe-Solar/UA c (AKA: THOMAS CROWN AND COMPANY; THE CROWN CAPER)

Steve McQueen *(Thomas Crown)*, Faye Dunaway *(Vicky Anderson)*, Paul Burke *(Eddy Malone)*, Jack Weston *(Erwin Weaver)*, Biff McGuire *(Sandy)*, Yaphet Kotto *(Carl)*, Todd Martin *(Benjy)*, Sam Melville *(Dave)*, Addison Powell *(Abe)*, Sidney Armus *(Arnie)*, Jon Shank *(Curley)*, Allen Emerson *(Don)*, Harry Cooper *(Ernie)*, John Silver *(Bert)*, Astrid Heeren *(Gwen)*, Carol Corbett *(Miss Sullivan)*, John Orchard *(John)*, Gordon Pinsent *(Jamie MacDonald)*, Patrick Horgan *(Danny)*, Peg Shirley *(Honey Weaver)*, Leonard Caron *(Jimmy Weaver)*, Ted Gehring *(Marvin)*, Nora Marlowe *(Marcie)*, Judy Pace *(Pretty Girl)*, Tom Rosqui *(Private Detective)*, Michael Shillo *(Swiss Banker)*, Carole Kelly *(Motel Girl)*, Nikita Knatz *(Sketch Artist)*, Charles Lampkin, James Rawley, Paul Verdier *(Elevator Operators)*, Victor Creatore, Paul Rhone *(Cash Room Guards)*, Richard Bull *(Booth Guard)*, Patty Regan *(Girl in Elevator)*.

A very expensive caper picture that drowned in its own artiness, using multi-images, cinematic tricks, and other pretentious film gimmicks, all of which detracted from the story. Set and partially filmed in Boston, it's the tale of a self-made millionaire, McQueen, who decides that he has been a member of the Establishment long enough and now wants to part company.

With the help of aides who never actually meet him, McQueen arranges a brilliant bank robbery that nets millions. McQueen pays off his assistants (most notable is Weston; the others are Kotto, Martin, Silver, Cooper, Armus, Shank, Emerson, and Powell), then banks the residue, almost \$3 million, in Switzerland. The bank is insured and the company pays off the loss, then assigns its number one investigator, Dunaway, to the case. She is working in league with police officer Burke and, through a gut instinct that is totally unbelievable, she picks McQueen as the most likely suspect (audiences groaned at this jump of logic). Dunaway moves in on McQueen and the two recognize each other as the enemy. In an artsy sequence, Jewison sends his camera around the two (the way it was done in A MAN AND A WOMAN) as they fall in love after a chess game that is a parody of the eating sequence in TOM JONES. Dunaway is completely ga-ga over McQueen and thinks she can get him off without a prison sentence if he gives back the money he took. The chances of that are slim to none and McQueen wants to see if she really loves him or is using her body as part of her investigation. McQueen says he's about to pull off another caper and wants her to meet him in a local cemetery after the job's done. She shows up there with Burke and the money is in a garbage can. Now, McQueen's Rolls-Royce arrives and she thinks it's him. But no; it's a boy from Western Union with a telegram that tells her to either bring the money or keep his Rolls. Dunaway begins to cry and looks up to see an airplane overhead. It's bound for Rio and McQueen is seated aboard it contemplating the rest of his life. Split-screen techniques, which were all the rage after having been seen to great advantage at the 1964 World's Fair, are used time and again. The Bergman's song, "The Windmills of Your Mind," written with Legrand, won an Oscar and Legrand was nominated for his music. The supervising film editor was Hal Ashby, who also was associate producer. Walter Hill--who later became a writer/director--was one of the assistant directors on this and, thankfully, picked up none of Jewison's bad ideas. Trustman was a practicing attorney when he wrote the script; he has since written several more films. McQueen is charming, reads his lines well, and shows that he isn't just another short actor with an interesting face. Watching it in the 1980s, one can sense the era in which it was filmed, as many other movies made the mistake of placing technique over characterization in that time.

p&d, Norman Jewison; w, Alan R. Trustman; ph, Haskell Wexler (DeLuxe Color); m, Michel Legrand; ed, Hal Ashby, Ralph Winters, Byron Brandt; art d, Robert Boyle; set d, Edward G. Boyle; cos, Ron Postal, Theadora Van Runkle, Alan Levine; spec eff, Pablo Ferro Films; m/l, "The Windmills of Your Mind," Legrand, Alan Bergman, Marilyn Bergman (sung by Noel Harrison); makeup, Del Armstrong.

Crime Drama   **Cas.**   (PR:C MPAA:R)

THOMASINE AND BUSHROD**½   (1974) 93m COL c

Max Julien *(Bushrod)*, Vonetta McGee *(Thomasine)*, George Murdock *(Bogardie)*, Glynn Turman *(Jomo)*, Juanita Moore *(Pecolia)*, Joel Fluellen *(Nathaniel)*, Jackson D. Kane *(Adolph)*, Bud Conlan *(Mr. Tyler)*, Kip Allen *(Jenkins)*, Ben Zeller *(Scruggs)*, Herb Robins *(Dodson)*, Harry Luck *(Sheriff)*, Jason Bernard *(Seldon)*, Paul Barby *(Teller)*, Scott Britt *(Frank)*, Geno Silva *(Taffy)*, John Gill *(Card Dealer)*, Dave Burleson *(Card Player)*, James Sargeant *(Farley)*, Leigh Potter, Tedi Altice *(Washerwomen)*, Charles Gaines *(Bank Customer)*, Katy Martin *(Mrs. Tyler)*, Patricia Milner *(Mrs. Carter)*, Brad Woolley *(Ricky)*, Lilybell Crawford *(Lady in Bank)*, Max Cisneros *(Kane)*, Neil Davis *(Barber)*, Raleigh Gardenhire *(Renegade)*.

Set in the New Mexico of 1912-1915, THOMASINE AND BUSHROD details the exploits of a fictional black "Bonnie and Clyde"-type duo. Julien and McGee, the title characters, race through the Southwest in their ancient jalopies, shooting lawmen and sharing the riches with poor blacks, whites, and Indians alike. One avenging sheriff, Murdock, is determined to bring the pair in and pursues them relentlessly. Although there's a heavy dose of exploitative violence (director Parks, Jr. also delivered SUPERFLY, 1972) Julien and McGee offset it with two superb performances of characters with real emotions. Lucien Ballard's exceptional photography and Dale Beldin's production design wonderfully capture the vibrant atmosphere of New Mexico in the 1910s.

p, Harvey Bernhard, Max Julien; d, Gordon Parks, Jr.; w, Julien; ph, Lucien Ballard (Metrocolor); m, Coleridge-Taylor Perkinson; ed, Frank C. Decot; cos, Andra Lilly; prod d, Dale Beldin; m/l, title song, Arthur Lee (sung by Lee).

Crime Drama   (PR:O MPAA:PG)

THOROUGHBRED*   (1932, Brit.) 64m EPC bw

John F. Argyle *(Edward Foster)*, Margaret Delane *(Eleanor Halliford)*, James Benton *(Smithy)*, Jack Marriott *(Henry Hamilton)*, Thomas Moss *(David Foster)*.

Amnesiac victim Benton is about to lose the love of his life, Delane, to the son of her guardian. A horse racing accident restores Benton's memory, however, and he becomes the man he used to be--a wealthy racehorse trainer. An overly melodramatic tale which was filmed silent and later had sound added.

p, John F. Argyle; d, Charles Barnett; w, Argyle.

Drama   (PR:A MPAA:NR)

THOROUGHBRED*½   (1936, Aus.) 78m Cinesound/British Empire
Films bw

Helen Twelvetrees, Frank Leighton, John Longden, Nellie Barnes.

Some gangsters try to muscle in on the Australian racing scene. They try
to kill the favored horse in the Melbourne Cup and manage to shoot one of
the racing ponies from the stands during the climactic finale. A poorly
produced feature with a muddled plot saved by its well done climax.
Twelvetrees (that was really her name carried on from her first marriage)
steals the acting honors, and certainly deserved her trip down under to
make the picture.

d, Ken G. Hall; w, Edmond Seward; ph, George Heath.

Crime   (PR:C   MPAA:NR)

THOROUGHBRED, THE**   (1930) 57m TIF bw

Wesley Barry (Tod Taylor), Nancy Dover (Colleen Riley), Pauline Garon
(Margie), Larry Steers (Drake), Robert E. Homans (Riley), Walter Perry
(Donovan), Onest Conly (Ham), Mildred Washington (Purple), Mme. Sul-Te-
Wan (Sacharine).

Barry is a jockey who finds himself in the middle of a rivalry between two
horse owners. A romance starts between Barry and Dover, the daughter of
one of the owners, but Barry gets entangled with Garon, a come-on girl for
a shifty gambler. The gambling debts begin piling high and to pay them off
Barry must throw a race. He chooses, instead, to be honest, wins the race,
and luckily had his debts paid off by Dover's father.

d, Richard Thorpe; w, John Francis Natteford; ph, Max Dupont; ed, Clarence
Kolster; set d, Ralph De Lacy.

Drama   (PR:A   MPAA:NR)

THOROUGHBREDS**   (1945) 56m REP bw

Tom Neal (Rusty Curtis), Adele Mara (Sally Crandall), Roger Pryor (Harold
Matthews), Paul Harvey (John Crandall), Gene Garrick (Jack Martin),
Doodles Weaver (Pvt. Mulrooney), Eddie Hall (Dapper), Tom London (Pop),
Charles Sullivan (Nails), Alan Edwards (Maj. Lane), Sam Bernard (Pete),
Buddy Gorman (Roberts), John Crawford, Jack Gardner, Robert Strange,
Dick Bartell, Timothy Mahen, Nolan Leary, Michael Owen, Howard
Mitchell, Harrison Greene, Kenne Duncan.

Cavalry sergeant Neal is released from the Army at the same time his
beloved horse is sold to Mara, a rich society woman, to run in steeplechases.
Neal is initially hired to train the horse, but is able to stop some gamblers
who want the steed kept out of an important race. When the regular jockey
can't ride, Neal takes over, winning both the race and Mara's affections.
Routine material from Republic. With that B studio's usual high standards
in production values.

p, Lester Sharpe; d, George Blair; w, Wellyn Totman; ph, William Bradford;
ed, Ralph Dixon; art d, Fred Ritter.

Drama   (PR:AA   MPAA:NR)

THOROUGHBREDS DON'T CRY**½   (1937) 80m MGM bw

Judy Garland (Cricket West), Mickey Rooney (Tim Donahue), Sophie
Tucker (Mother Ralph), C. Aubrey Smith (Sir Peter Calverton), Ronald
Sinclair (Roger Calverton), Forrester Harvey (Wilkins), Helen Troy (Hilda),
Charles D. Brown (Click Donahue), Frankie Darro (Dink Reid), Henry
Kolker (Doc Godfrey).

Garland's first star billing and her first of many movies with Rooney is a
predictable race horse story with a couple of tunes tossed in to liven up the
hokum plot. Young Sinclair (who was 14 at the time and whom the studio
was grooming to take the parts Freddie Bartholomew was having to bypass
as his voice became deeper) arrives in the U.S. with his crusty grandpa,
Smith. They own a race horse and want to put it on American tracks and
make a killing. Smith meets jockey Rooney (who was 17 at the time) and
gives him the riding whip of a famous jockey as a present. There's an
important race at Santa Anita in California and Smith needs a jockey.
Rooney accepts the mount and feels that this is a winning horse that he can
take to the finish line ahead of the pack. Rooney's father is a nogoodnick
gambler, Brown, who lies that he is ill and needs some expensive medical
care. The only way he can earn the five grand needed for the doctors is to
know the outcome of a race ahead of time. Since his son is racing in the big
handicap event, he prevails on Rooney to throw the race. Brown will tell his
gambler pals to bet against Smith's and Sinclair's horse and they will give
him enough money in return to have his physical problems attended to.
Rooney lives at a boarding house for jockeys which is run by Tucker (in a
non-singing role), with Garland as her niece preparing food, dusting
furniture, making beds, etc. The two youngsters are close friends and
whenever Rooney is despairing, she is always there to lend him a word of
encouragement. The race is run and Rooney deliberately pulls the horse
back so it loses. Aged Smith drops dead of a heart attack at that and
Rooney's shoulders slump with guilt. Another race is coming up and Sinclair
doesn't have enough money for the entry fee so Rooney asks Brown to give
him $1 thousand dollars to take care of the animal, pay the fee, and have

a few bucks left over, as Sinclair is now broke and stranded in the U.S.
Brown won't hear of it and Rooney is forced to steal the money from his
father. Once Brown finds out the money has been taken, that rat finks on
his own son to the track officials and says that Rooney made the Handicap
into a boat race. The track management decides that Rooney must be barred
from riding. With no money to get a jockey, there is only one other person
who can do it, Sinclair. He dons the silks, runs the race and wins, and
Rooney, Garland, and the others cheer him on. Garland sings two tunes by
Arthur Freed and Nacio Herb Brown, "Got a New Pair of Shoes" and "Sun
Showers" (which was cut from some prints). This was the second time
Garland had played a relative of Tucker. In BROADWAY MELODY OF
1938, Judy was Sophie's daughter. Given Rooney's stature, it was only
natural that he play a jockey or an ex-jockey in years to come and he did
it many times, most notably in NATIONAL VELVET, STABLEMATES, and
THE BLACK STALLION.

p, Harry Rapf; d, Alfred E. Green; w, Lawrence Hazard (based on a story
by Eleanore Griffin, J. Walter Ruben); ph, Leonard Smith; ed, Elmo Vernon;
md, William Axt; cos, Dolly Tree; m/l, Arthur Freed, Nacio Herb Brown.

Comedy/Drama   (PR:AA   MPAA:NR)

THOROUGHLY MODERN MILLIE***   (1967) 138m UNIV c

Julie Andrews (Millie Dillmount), Mary Tyler Moore (Dorothy Brown),
Carol Channing (Muzzy Van Hossmere), James Fox (Jimmy Smith),
Beatrice Lillie (Mrs. Meers), John Gavin (Trevor Graydon), Jack Soo (1st
Oriental), Pat Morita (2nd Oriental), Philip Ahn (Tea), Cavada Humphrey
(Miss Flannery), Anthony Dexter (Juarez), Lou Nova (Cruncher), Michael
St. Clair (Baron Richter), Albert Carrier (Adrian), Victor Rogers (Gregory
Huntley), Lisabeth Hush (Judith Tremaine), Herbie Faye (Taxi Driver),
Ann Dee (Singer), Benny Rubin (Waiter), Buddy Schwab (Dorothy's Dance
Partner), Jay Thompson (Pianist), Todd Mason (Male Pedestrian), Mae
Clarke (Woman in the Office).

This charming spoof of the 1920s and film conventions unfortunately runs
out of steam just before it ends. Out-of-towner Andrews is introduced in a
marvelous opening sequence shedding her stodgy curls and dress for the
more sophisticated big-city flapper look. Her goal is to find a good job with
a handsome and wealthy boss, then marry her employer for a happy ending.
On her way back to the women's hotel she lives in, Andrews runs into the
virginal Moore, who is also a newcomer to New York. Moore checks into the
hotel where she catches the eye of Lillie, the hotel's clerk and secret operator
of a white-slavery gang. She wants Moore for the nefarious outfit and plots
to get the innocent young lady. At a dance held at the hotel, Lillie spikes
Moore's drink, but during a mix-up, Lillie ends up drinking the potion. Also
attending the dance is Fox, an eager young man who forces his attentions
on Andrews. They make up a new dance, then take a spin in a shiny red
roadster Fox has borrowed from his employer. After a necking session in
which Andrews insists she is a "modern," the two promise to see each other
again. The next day Andrews applies for a job at an insurance company run
by Gavin. Gavin is the handsomest of men, complete with a stunning profile
and pipe (a parody of Gavin's popular ads for Arrow Shirts). Andrews falls
for him immediately. Despite her efforts to attract his attention, Gavin
succumbs to Moore's charms. Andrews, Moore, and Fox fly in a biplane to
the Long Island estate of Channing, an eccentric and wealthy widow. There,
at a weekend-long party, Andrews is crushed when she sees Moore sneaking
into Fox's room. Though angered, Andrews later forgives Fox when he goes
to elaborate lengths to apologize. Moore, Gavin, and Andrews go out to a
vaudeville show where Channing is the surprise star attraction. Lillie, in the
meantime, is determined to get Moore in her clutches. She finally kidnaps
Moore and tells Andrews the missing girl has suddenly left town. Andrews
discovers the truth and, with Gavin and Fox, plots to rescue Moore. Fox is
decked out in drag and checks into the hotel, catching Lillie's attention as
another potential victim. However Lillie soon learns what is going on and
knocks out Gavin with a doped-up dart. Fox is kidnaped by her Oriental
henchmen (Soo and Morita, both unrecognizable in this mutual early
appearance) and Andrews follows them to Chinatown. She finds the white
slavers have holed up in a firecracker factory. Amidst explosions and chaos,
Andrews is able to rescue her friends and the group heads to Channing's
estate. They are closely followed by Lillie, Soo, and Morita, but the evil three
are put down thanks to Channing's handy physical prowess. Later that
night, Andrews once again ventures to Fox's room and sees Moore sneak in.
She is doubly crushed when Channing sneaks in as well. Andrews barges
into the room and there learns the truth about this trio. Channing is
stepmother to Moore and Fox and sent them out in the world to seek suitable
partners who weren't out after their inheritance. All ends happily as
Andrews marries Fox, and Moore is coupled with Gavin. THOROUGHLY
MODERN MILLIE is an enjoyable feature, sparked with energy from its
lively and enthusiastic cast. Andrews is a comic delight, combining both
sophisticated and naive elements for a strong characterization. Moore is
charming, as is Channing, who steals every scene she's in with astonishing
ease. This is a film studded with marvelous little moments, such as an
elevator that only works when its occupants tap dance. There's also a sense
of fun for the medium itself, employing many silent-film techniques within
the proceedings. Andrews periodically comments on the action by looking
directly into the camera, then a title card with her thoughts appears.
Vignettes and clever use of dissolves also add to the film's charm. Fox's
character is an obvious reference to the earnest, all-American fellow that

Harold Lloyd perfected in silent comedy. Complete with Lloyd-type glasses, there is even a quick reference to the great comedian's best known film (SAFETY LAST) when Fox scales a building to get to Andrews. Hill's direction is snappy, with a good feel for self-parody, but unfortunately the hectic pacing slips away from him at the end. By the time Moore is rescued, the climactic chase has turned into a routine slapstick chase that carries on far too long. The film does suffer from excessive running time. Something this frothy doesn't need to run over two hours. This was originally released as a road show, complete with intermission and inflated ticket prices, and blown up to 70 mm for some theaters. Conceived as a straight comedy without music, Andrews became enamored of the project, seeing it as "the last chance I'd have to do the ingenue. After all, when you're thirty-one, how many more chances can you have?" Andrews enjoyed working on the production, even coming in to help her co-stars on days she wasn't needed on set. At one point she came in to read her off-camera lines for Channing to react to, rather than leave this work to a stand-in. Andrews knew this would make Channing's performance better, something for which Channing was grateful. Still, Andrews was not completely satisfied with the final results. "I wish they had cut just twenty minutes and not made it a road show. It wasn't planned as a road show, and I think it was blown up too far out of proportion from its original conception." The star implored the studio to cut a number she sings at a Jewish wedding, citing it as unnecessary to plot development. Studio executives thought otherwise, and the number stayed. Despite Andrews' complaints, THOROUGHLY MODERN MILLIE was both a critical and a box-office success, reaping over $30 million and becoming Universal's biggest money maker for the time. It made Andrews the number one box-office attraction of 1967 and garnished seven Oscar nominations including Best Art Direction and Best Supporting Actress for Channing. Bernstein took home an Oscar for Best Original Score. The songs, mixing 1920s tunes with new songs, include: "Thoroughly Modern Millie" (Jimmy Van Heusen, Sammy Cahn, performed by Andrews), "The Tapioca" (Van Heusen, Cahn, performed by Andrews and Fox), "Jimmy" (Jay Thompson, performed by Andrews), "The Jewish Wedding Song (Trinkt Le Chaim)" (Sylvia Neufeld, performed by Andrews), "Baby Face" (Benny Davis, Harry Akst, performed by Andrews), "Do It Again" (Buddy De Sylva, George Gershwin, performed by Channing), "Poor Butterfly" (John Golden, Raymond Hubbell, performed by Andrews), "Rose of Washington Square" (James Hanley, Ballard MacDonald, performed by Dee), "I Can't Believe That You're in Love With Me" (Jimmy McHugh, Clarence Gaskill), "I'm Sitting On Top of the World" (Sam M. Lewis, Joe Young, Ray Henderson), "Stumbling" (Zez Confrey, performed by Andrews, Moore), "Japanese Sandman" (Ray Egan, Richard A. Whiting, performed by Soo, Morita), "Charmaine" (Erno Rapee, Lew Pollack), "Jazz Baby" (standard, performed by Channing).

p, Ross Hunter; d, George Roy Hill; w, Richard Morris; ph, Russell Metty (Technicolor); m, Elmer Bernstein; ed, Stuart Gilmore; md, Andre Previn; art d, Alexander Golitzen, George C. Webb; set d, Howard Bristol; cos, Jean Louis. ch, Joe Layton; makeup, Bud Westmore.

Musical   **Cas.**   **(PR:A MPAA:NR)**

THOSE CALLOWAYS***   (1964) 131m Disney/BV c

Brian Keith (Cam Calloway), Vera Miles (Liddy Calloway), Brandon de Wilde (Bucky Calloway), Walter Brennan (Alf Simes), Ed Wynn (Ed Parker), Linda Evans (Bridie Mellot), Philip Abbott (Dell Fraser), John Larkin (Jim Mellot), Parley Baer (Doane Shattuck), Frank De Kova (Nigosh), Roy Roberts (E.J. Fletcher), John Qualen (Ernie Evans), Tom Skerritt (Whit Turner), Paul Hartman (Charley Evans), Russell Collins (Nat Perkins), John Davis Chandler (Ollie Gibbons), Chet Stratton (Phil Petrie), Renee Godfrey (Sarah Mellot), Frank Ferguson (Doctor).

Keith plays an Irish trapper raised by the Micmac Indians. He and wife Miles and their 19-year-old son, De Wilde, live in Swiftwater, Maine. He hopes to begin a sanctuary for the enormous flocks of geese that fly through that small town each autumn. Keith spends a year's worth of trapping money on land for the sanctuary and consequently can't make his mortgage payments on the family home. They are evicted and move near the lake where their friends help them build a new home. A major problem arises when Abbott, a traveling salesman, decides he can make some good money by turning the area into a haven for goose hunters. He pretends to be a conservationist and gives Keith money for corn to feed the geese, which would lure the geese to Swiftwater consistently. De Wilde learns of Abbott's plans and tells his father who confronts the schemer. Keith is shot in a struggle, but the townspeople rally around him, petitioning the government to back his plan. A town meeting is held and, after much emotional arguing, it's decided that Abbott and his partners should leave the area. The next day Brennan, the town crier, brings this news to Keith, and the family realizes that his dream is going to come true. THOSE CALLOWAYS is moving film, presented in a mature manner without the naivete and sentimentality that marred the later Disney live-action features. Though the cynical viewer might find it too warm-hearted, the film contains strong performances, particularly from Keith, but also from the supporting players. Brennan and Wynn provide some comedy relief. The film's lengthy running time and distracting subplots, such as De Wilde's discovering his manhood, are a hindrance, but the score and the Vermont locations overcome these minor problems. A money loser for Disney, but in the process he personally won faith in director Tokar and screenwriter Pelletier, assigning them to work

on another film of his, FOLLOW ME, BOYS (1966).

p, Winston Hibler, Walt Disney; d, Norman Tokar; w, Louis Pelletier (based on the novel *Swiftwater* by Paul Annixter); ph, Edward Colman (Technicolor); m, Max Steiner; ed, Grant K. Smith; art d, Carroll Clark, John B. Mansbridge; set d, Emile Kuri, Hal Gausman; cos, Bill Thomas; spec eff, Eustace Lycett; m/l, "Angel," Steiner, Jay Livingston, Ray Evans, "The Cabin Raising Song," "Rhyme-Around," Richard M. Sherman, Robert B. Sherman; makeup, Pat McNalley.

Drama   **(PR:AA MPAA:NR)**

THOSE DARING YOUNG MEN IN THEIR JAUNTY JALOPIES*½
(1969, Fr./Brit./ Ital.) 122m Dino De Laurentiis-Marianne-Basil Keys/ PAR c (QUEI TEMERARI SULLE LORO PAZZE, SCATENATE, SCAL-CINATE CARRIOLE, GB: MONTE CARLO OR BUST!)

Tony Curtis (Chester Schofield), Susan Hampshire (Betty), Terry-Thomas (Sir Cuthbert Ware-Armitage), Eric Sykes (Perkins), Gert Frobe (Willi Schickel/Horst Muller), Peer Schmidt (Otto), Peter Cook (Maj. Digby Dawlish), Dudley Moore (Lt. Kit Barrington), Walter Chiari (Angelo Pincelli), Lando Buzzanca (Marcello Agosti), Jack Hawkins (Count Levino-vitch), Mireille Darc (Marie-Claude), Marie Dubois (Pascale), Nicoletta Machiavelli (Dominique), Bourvil (Mons. Vendredi [Mons. Dupont]), Jacques Duby (Motorcycle Gendarme), Hattie Jacques (Lady Journalist), Derren Nesbitt (Waleska), Nicholas Phipps (Golfer), William Rushton (John O'Groats Official), Michael Trubshawe (German Rally Official), Richard Wattis (Golf Club Secretary), Walter Williams (German Customs Official), Joe Wadham, Roy Scammel, Dinny Powell, Frank Henson, Mark Boyle, Bockie Taylor, Geoff Silk (Driving Team).

Despite a huge budget, an international cast, and an intercontinental setting this comedy about a 1,500 mile, five-country Monte Carlo auto rally quickly becomes tedious, with only intermittent spots of humor. This quasi-sequel to THOSE MAGNIFICENT MEN IN THEIR FLYING MACHINES (with a bit of THE GREAT RACE thrown in as well) has men competing in the international auto race held in the early 1920s. Curtis is a gambler who co-owns a British auto factory with Thomas, thanks to a handy poker game with Thomas' father. They have entered the race on the condition that whichever of the pair wins gets to keep the factory. They constantly try to fool each other along the road, doing every dirty trick imaginable to win. Curtis meets cutie Hampshire along the way and there's much comic intrigue, most of it falling flat. Some stereotyped nonsense about feminists is thrown in, with a few car smashups and accidents as well. Thomas loses the factory when a tire blows out and Hampshire ends up pushing Curtis' car across the finish line. The best moments were provided by Cook and Moore as a pair of kooky British racers. This duo was originally part of the famous BBC "Goon Show" and were a hysterical partnership in the 1960s. As in their wonderful comic adventure, BEDAZZLED (1967), the two comics are great fun to watch. Otherwise THOSE DARING YOUNG MEN... is a tiresome, overblown mess that proves once more that comedy relies more on character than crazy situations to work.

p, Ken Annakin; d, Annakin, Sam Itzkovitch; w, Annakin, Jack Davis; ph, Gabor Pogany, Walter Wottitz, Bert Palmgren (Panavision, Technicolor); m, Ron Goodwin; ed, Peter Taylor; prod d, Ted Haworth; art d, Elven Webb, Boris Juraga, Marc Fredrix, Erik Bjork; set d, Dario Simoni; cos, John Furness, Orietta Nasalli Rocca; spec eff, Dick Parker, m/l, "Monte Carlo or Bust," Ron Goodwin (sung by Jimmy Durante); makeup, Amato Garbini.

Comedy   **(PR:A MPAA:G)**

THOSE DIRTY DOGS*   (1974, U.S./Ital./Span.) 89m
                                          Horse-Plata/Cinema Financial of America c

Stephen Boyd (Chadwell), Johnny Garko (Korano), Howard Ross (Younger), Simon Andrew (Angelo Sanchez), Harry Baird (Washington Smith), There-sa Gompers (Miss Adams), Daniel Vargas (Gen. Mueller).

When some Mexican revolutionaries start raiding towns in the Southwest, Boyd and two companions are sent by the government to stop them. Bounty hunter Garko joins them and after a customary gun fight the bandits are handily done away with. Idiotic script and inept direction, plus a cast that is woefully untalented doom this juvenile attempt to make a movie.

d, Guiseppe Rosati; w, Carl Veo, Henry Lovet, Rosati; ph, Godfrey Pacheco (Eastmancolor); m, Nick Fidenco; ed, Robert Colan; set d, Angel Arzuaga.

Western   **(PR:C MPAA:PG)**

THOSE ENDEARING YOUNG CHARMS**   (1945) 81m RKO bw

Robert Young (Hank), Laraine Day (Helen), Ann Harding (Mrs. Brandt), Marc Cramer (Capt. Larry Stowe), Anne Jeffreys (Suzanne), Glenn Vernon (Young Sailor), Norma Varden (Haughty Floor Lady), Lawrence Tierney (Ted, Pilot), Vera Marshe (Dot), Bill Williams (Jerry), Larry Burke (Singer), Edmund Glover, Robert Clarke (Operations Officers), Johnny Strong, Paul Brinkman, George Holmes (Pilots), Jimmy Jordan (Bellhop), Tommy Dugan (Waiter), Barbara Slater (Girl), John Vosper (Drunk), Georges Renavent (Maitre D'Hotel), Eddy Hart (Bus Conductor), Larry McGrath (Cabby), Tom Dillon (Traffic Cop), Dorothy Vaughn (Matron), George Anderson, Dewey Robinson (Doormen), Aina Constant (Miss Glamour), Florence Wix (Custom-

er), Catherine Wallace, Elizabeth Williams, Margaret Farrell, Helen Dickson *(Women).*

When young Army man Williams introduces his soldier pal Young to girl friend Day it's love at first sight for Day, but Young only sees her as some mild amusement. Gradually he reforms his caddish ways and ends up marrying the girl. This light nonsense, based on a play, is over talkative and lacks sincerity. There are some moments of charm that the unevenness of the cast works against the production, resulting in a hit-and-miss romantic comedy. Williams was being promoted strongly by RKO, which hoped he would go on to leading roles. However, he was fated to play few leads, and mostly second leads in low budget films in what became a long movie career.

p, Bert Granet; d, Lewis Allen; w, Jerome Chodorov (based on the play by Edward Chodorov); ph, Ted Tetzlaff; m, Roy Webb; ed, Roland Gross; md, C. Bakaleinikoff; art d, Albert S. D'Agostino, Walter E. Keller; set d, Darrell Silvera, John Sturtevant; spec eff, Vernon L. Walker.

Comedy   **Cas.**   **(PR:A   MPAA:MR)**

THOSE FANTASTIC FLYING FOOLS**   (1967, Brit) 95m Jules Verne/AIP c (GB: JULES VERNE'S ROCKET TO THE MOON; AKA: BLAST-OFF)

Burl Ives *(Phineas T. Barnum),* Troy Donahue *(Gaylord Sullivan),* Gert Frobe *(Prof. von Bulow),* Hermione Gingold *(Angelica),* Custodian of the Wayward Girls' Home, Lionel Jeffries *(Sir Charles Dillworthy),* Daliah Lavi *(Madelaine),* Dennis Price *(Duke of Barset),* Stratford Johns *(Warrant Officer),* Graham Stark *(Grundle),* Terry Thomas *(Capt. Sir Harry Washington-Smythe),* Jimmy Clitheroe *(Gen. Tom Thumb),* Joachim Teege *(Bulgeroff),* Joan Sterndale-Bennett *(The Queen),* Renate von Holt *(Anna),* Edward De Souza *(Henri),* Judy Cornwell *(Electra),* Derek Francis *(Puddleby),* Allan Cuthbertson *(Scotland Yard Man).*

Combining elements of Jules Verne's stories with the legend of P.T. Barnum, this slight science fiction comedy has some high spots but fails to maintain them. When his circus burns down, Ives decides to send the reluctant Clitheroe (the ever-present "comedy midget") on a rocket to the moon. This attracts the attention of spies around the world. Frobe is a German scientist who has invented the device, and Jeffries the man who designed the final craft. There is just one flaw with the spaceship: there is no way for it to make a return trip from the moon. Donahue, in yet another forgettable appearance, is a balloonist who claims his rockets can make return trips. Numerous subplots involving spies and sabotage pad out the rest of the film, most of it having no relation to Jules Verne. The finale finds the rocket landing in Tzarist Russia and the cast assuming that the Russians beat them to the moon. The pre-credit opening is very funny, setting up a promise for good entertainment that is never delivered. Despite some quality names in the cast, nobody stands out in this uninspired work.

p, Harry Alan Towers; d, Don Sharp; w, Dave Freeman (based on a story by Peter Welbeck [Towers] from the writings of Jules Verne); ph, Reg Wyer (Panavision/Eastmancolor); m, Patrick John Scott; ed, Ann Chegwidden; art d, Frank White; set d, Frank Graves; cos, Carl Toms; spec eff, Les Bowie, Pat Moore; m/l, "We Must Always Trust the Stranger," Ron Goodwin.

Science Fiction/Comedy   **(PR:AAA   MPAA:NR)**

THOSE HIGH GREY WALLS***   (1939) 81m COL bw

Walter Connolly *(Dr. MacAuley),* Onslow Stevens *(Dr. Norton),* Paul Fix *(Nightingale),* Bernard Nedell *(Redlands),* Iris Meredith *(Mary MacAuley),* Oscar O'Shea *(Warden),* Nicholas Soussanin *(Lindy),* Don Beddoe *(Jockey).*

Prison drama features Connolly as a doctor who ends up in the pen after treating a convict whom he had delivered as a baby. Once inside, Connolly tries to get onto the medical staff of the prison but is prevented from doing so by the staff doctor, Stevens. After a prisoner's visiting wife goes into labor, Connolly is brought in to assist Stevens, who comes to accept his fellow medic. A prison break, in which Connolly is mistakenly implicated is thwarted, and he is paroled. Stevens and Connolly give good performances, and both receive excellent support from Nedell as the man behind the prison break. Directed with smart efficiency, this is an effective, well-done B film.

p, B. B. Kahane; d, Charles Vidor; w, Lewis Meltzer (based on a story by William A. Ullman, Jr.); ph, John Stumar; ed, Gene Milford.

Drama   **(PR:C   MPAA:NR)**

THOSE KIDS FROM TOWN**   (1942, Brit.) 82m BN/Anglo American bw

Shirley Lenner *(Liz Burns),* Jeanne de Casalis *(Sheila),* Percy Marmont *(Earl),* D.J. Williams *(Butler),* Maire O'Neill *(Housekeeper),* Charles Victor *(Vicar),* Angela Glynne *(Maud Burns),* George Cole *(Charlie),* Harry Fowler *(Ern),* Olive Sloane *(Vicar's Wife),* Sydney King *(Donald),* Bransby Williams *(Uncle Sid),* Ronald Shiner *(Mr. Burns),* Josephine Wilson *(Mrs. Burns),* A. Bromley Davenport *(Egworth).*

A couple of Cockney youngsters, Cole and Fowler, are given refuge from the war in the country home of earl Marmont. The initial differences nearly send everything awry between the two boys and the earl but by the finale Marmont has learned some valuable lessons from Cole and Fowler.

p, Richard Vernon; d, Lance Comfort; w, Adrian Arlington (based on his novel *These Our Strangers*); ph, Jimmy Wilson.

Comedy   **(PR:A   MPAA:NR)**

THOSE LIPS, THOSE EYES***   (1980) 107m UA c

Frank Langella *(Harry Crystal),* Glynnis O'Connor *(Ramona),* Thomas Hulce *(Artie Shoemaker),* Kevin McCarthy *(Mickey Bellinger),* Jerry Stiller *(Mr. Shoemaker),* Herbert Berghof *(Dr. Julius Fuldauer),* Joseph Maher *(Fibby Geyer),* George Morfogen *(Sherman Spratt),* Marshall Colt *(Cooky),* Anthony Mannino *(D'Angeli),* Rose Arrick *(Mrs. Shoemaker),* William Robertson *(Mr. Henry),* Steve Levitt *(Westervelt),* Mandy Stumpf *(Loomis),* Mark Keyloun *(Hlavacek),* Steve Nevil *(Stage Manager),* Dan Siretta *(Larry),* Jordan Charney *(Professor),* David Adams, Cheryl Armstrong, Providence Hollander, David O. Frazier, Don Kost, Chiara Peacock, J. Clayton Conroy, F. L. Schmidlapp, Frank Picard, Mel Pittenger, Susan Berlin, Heidi Albrecht, Nanci Glass, Jodi Moccia, Frank Hruby.

A charming little romantic comedy set against the background of summer stock theater features Hulce (later to score very big in AMADEUS) as a pre-med student who takes a part-time job at an outdoor Ohio theater. Hired as a prop boy, he proves incompetent and is taken to task by stage director Morfogen. However, the theater's star, Langella, a minor character actor who harbors pipe dreams of Broadway, takes a liking to Hulce and protects him from Morfogen. With the older man's help, Hulce begins a romance with a chorus dancer played with vigor by O'Connor. The film has an earnestness that makes it enchanting. The leads are well cast and are guided by fine direction. This film about small-time theater never saw a wide box-office release.

p, Steven-Charles Jaffe, Michael Pressman; d, Pressman; w, David Shaber; ph, Bobby Byrne (Technicolor); m, Michael Small; ed, Millie Moore; prod d, Walter Scott Herndon; set d, Blake Russell, Cloudia; ch, Dan Siretta.

Comedy   **Cas.**   **(PR:O   MPAA:R)**

THOSE MAGNIFICENT MEN IN THEIR FLYING MACHINES; OR HOW I FLEW FROM LONDON TO PARIS IN 25 HOURS AND 11 MINUTES***½   (1965, Brit.) 133m FOX c (AKA: THOSE MAGNIFICENT MEN IN THEIR FLYING MACHINES)

Stuart Whitman *(Orvil Newton),* Sarah Miles *(Patricia Rawnsley),* James Fox *(Richard Mays),* Alberto Sordi *(Count Emilio Ponticelli),* Robert Morley *(Lord Rawnsley),* Gert Frobe *(Col. Manfred von Holstein),* Jean-Pierre Cassel *(Pierre Dubois),* Eric Sykes *(Courtney),* Terry-Thomas *(Sir Percival Ware-Armitage),* Irina Demick *(Brigitte/Ingrid/Marlene/Francoise/Yvette/Betty),* Tony Hancock *(Harry Popperwell, an Inventor),* Benny Hill *(Fire Chief Perkins),* Yujiro Ishihara *(Yamamoto),* Flora Robson *(Mother Superior),* Karl Michael Vogler *(Capt. Rupelstrasse),* Sam Wanamaker *(George Gruber),* Eric Barker *(French Postman),* Fred Emney *(Elderly Col. Willie),* Gordon Jackson *(McDougal, a Pilot),* Davy Kaye *(Jean),* Pierre's Chief Mechanic, John Le Mesurier *(French Painter),* Jeremy Lloyd *(Lt. Parsons, a Pilot),* Zena Marshall *(Sophia Ponticelli),* Millicent Martin *(Airline Hostess),* Eric Pohlmann *(Italian Mayor),* Marjorie Rhodes *(The Waitress in the Old Mill Cafe),* Norman Rossington *(Assistant Fire Chief),* William Rushton *(Tremayne Gascoyne),* Jimmy Thompson *(The Photographer in the Old Mill Cafe),* Michael Trubshawe *(Niven, Lord Rawnsley's Aide),* Red Skelton *(The Neanderthal Man),* Gerald Campion *(2nd Fireman),* Graham Stark *(3rd Fireman),* Maurice Denham *(Trawler Skipper),* Robin Chapman *(Postman),* Ronnie Stevens *(R.A.C. Officer),* Steve Plytas *(Continental Journalist),* Ferdy Mayne *(French Official),* Bill Nagy *(American Journalist),* James Robertson Justice *(Narrator),* Cicely Courtneidge *(Muriel).*

A rip-roaring flying adventure about early pilots in an English Channel race that runs out of jokes before it runs out of time. Lots of laughs spread out over too many minutes but fun nevertheless. The time is 1910 and Morley, a press lord, seeks to prove that Great Britain is number one in the air as well as being the gem of the ocean. He puts up 10,000 pounds as a prize and invites the very best pilots from all over the world to compete in an air race from London to Paris. All sorts of dandy planes arrive such as Bleriots, Bristols, Avros, Demoiselles, tri-planes, bi-planes, the lot. Although the race is open to anyone, Morley is rooting for his daughter's (Miles) fiance, Fox, who is serving in the Royal Navy as a lieutenant. The field is crowded with contenders including Sordi, an Italian count traveling with his huge brood, led by his wife, Marshall. Others in the race are Frobe, a parody of a Prussian who will die before he allows anyone else to win; Cassel, a Frenchman who is followed by a sextet of women all played by Demick; Terry-Thomas, a villainous Brit who will stop at nothing in his quest for the prize; Ishihara, a Japanese who never betrays his emotions, and American barnstormer Whitman, who spots Miles and decides that she is the woman for him, much to the dismay of Fox and Morley. The race starts and mishaps occur instantly. Terry-Thomas has been at work and one of the planes can only fly in reverse so it goes off toward Scotland. This one is piloted by Hancock, a British inventor, and it soon disappears. Ishihara's plane goes down before it barely has a chance to rise, more of Terry-Thomas's tomfoolery. Frobe goes down in a pile of mud after having a duel in the air with Cassel, complete with balloons and huge blunderbusses. Both men crash and are unhurt. After completing his labors, Terry-Thomas flies across the Channel under cover of darkness and makes the mistake of landing his plane on a moving train just as it approaches a tunnel and wipes him out. Little by little, the competitors are winnowed until the three remaining are Whitman, Fox, and Sordi. While racing for the finish, Sordi's plane suddenly catches on fire, the result of Terry-Thomas's doings, and Whitman forgoes the prize by effecting a daring mid-air rescue of Sordi. Fox crosses the line and Morley is delighted. Fox is one of the old-line British with stiff upper lip and good moral fiber wrapped around his spine so he offers half the prize to Whitman because he saw the heroism of the American flier. By this time, Miles has decided which of the competitors has won her heart. She opts for Whitman as the picture ends. Good, clean fun in the genre of IT'S A MAD MAD MAD MAD WORLD and THE GREAT RACE. The real stars of the movie are the airships and the paces they are put through. Fast and furious action, good cinematography, okay dialog (which was good enough to get Annakin and Davies an Oscar nomination), fine costumes (which won the British Film Award), and a host of some of the funniest men in movies such as Skelton, Hill, Hancock, Terry-Thomas, and Sordi. Filmed in Great Britain and France with the very authentic technical supervision being handled by Commodore Allen Wheeler. Director Annakin's career has been up and down more than some of these planes. Ups include SWISS FAMILY ROBINSON and PAPER TIGER. Downs outnumber those with the nadir of his career being the TV movie THE PIRATE which was one of 1978's embarrassments.

p, Stan Margulies; d, Ken Annakin; second unit d, Don Sharp; w, Jack Davies, Annakin; ph, Christopher Challis (Todd-AO, DeLuxe Color); m, Ron Goodwin; ed, Gordon Stone, Anne V. Coates; prod d, Tom Morahan; md, Goodman; art d, Jim Morahan; set d, Arthur Taksen; cos, Osbert Lancaster, Dinah Greet; spec eff, Richard Parker, Ron Ballanger; makeup, William Partleton, Stuart Freeborn; anim, Ralph Ayres; title design, Ronald Searle.

Comedy   Cas.   (PR:A   MPAA:G)

THOSE PEOPLE NEXT DOOR*   (1952, Brit.) 77m Film Studios
                                                        Manchester/Eros bw

Jack Warner (Sam Twigg), Charles Victor (Joe Higgins), Marjorie Rhodes (Mary Twigg), Gladys Henson (Emma Higgins), Garry Marsh (Sir Andrew Stevens), Jimmy James (Drunk), Patricia Cutts (Anne Twigg), Peter Forbes-Robertson (Victor Stevens), Anthony Newley (Bob Twigg), Norah Gaussen [Gorsen], Grace Arnold, Geoffrey Sumner.

A working-class girl, Cutts, falls for an RAF officer, Forbes-Robertson, much to the consternation of their class-conscious parents. When Forbes-Robertson is reportedly shot down, both sets of parents are brought together. The flier, of course, hasn't been killed and everyone lives happily ever after.

p, Tom Blakeley; d, John Harlow; w, uncredited (based on the play "Wearing The Pants" by Zelda Davees); ph, Roy Fogwell.

Comedy   (PR:A   MPAA:NR)

THOSE REDHEADS FROM SEATTLE½**   (1953) 90m PAR c

Rhonda Fleming (Kathie Edmonds), Gene Barry (Johnny Kisco), Agnes Moorehead (Mrs. Edmonds), Guy Mitchell (Joe Keenan), Teresa Brewer (Pat Edmonds), Kay Bell (Neil Edmonds), Bill Pullen (Rev. Petrie), John Kellogg (Mike Yurkil), Frank Wilcox (Vance Edmonds), Jean Parker (Liz), Roscoe Ates (Dan Taylor), Michael Ross (Mack Donahue), Walter Reed (Whitey Marks), Ed Rand (Jacobs), Cynthia Bell (Connie Edmonds).

A lightweight 3-D musical about a mother (Moorehead) who takes daughters Fleming, Brewer, Bell, and Bell to the Yukon to meet their father (Wilcox), who has joined the gold rush. Upon arriving they learn he's been killed, and the women are forced to find work to make ends meet. Naturally, they find romance in the frozen North as well. The story was innocuous but entertaining. The direction and performances are fine, numbers including "Baby Baby Baby" (Mack David, Jerry Livingston, sung by Teresa Brewer) and "I Guess It Was You All the Time" (Johnny Mercer, Hoagy Carmichael, sung by Brewer, Guy Mitchell) fill out the time. This film has the unique distinction of being the first 3-D musical. Other songs include "Mr. Banjo Man" (Jay Livingston, Ray Evans, sung by Brewer), "Chic-a-Boom" (Bob Merrill, sung by Mitchell), and "Take Back Your Gold" (M.H. Rosenfeld, Louis W. Pritzkow, sung by Cynthia and Kay Bell).

p, William H. Pine, William C. Thomas; d, Lewis R. Foster; w, Foster, Geoffrey Homes, George Worthing Yates; ph, Lionel Lindon (3-D, Technicolor); m, Leo Shuken, Sidney Cutner; ed, Archie Marshek; ch, Jack Baker.

Musical   (PR:AA   MPAA:NR)

THOSE THREE FRENCH GIRLS*½   (1930) 72m MGM bw

Fifi D'Orsay (Charmaine), Reginald Denny (Larry), Cliff Edwards (Owly), Yola d'Avril (Diane), Sandra Ravel (Madelon), George Grossmith (Earl of Ippleton), Edward Brophy (Yank), Peter Gawthorne (Parker), Polly Moran.

A series of loosely connected episodes comprises this minor musical. D'Orsay, d'Avril and Ravel are the title characters who wear cute French smocks and run around the countryside. There's little plot to speak of, and a few moments of comedy that come too far apart. The film would have been better if it had stripped the padding and been released as a musical short.

The cast provides a good serving of energy; D'Orsay was still kicking her heels in 1972, when she appeared in the Broadway musical "Follies."

d, Harry Beaumont; w, Sylvia Thalberg, Frank Butler, P.G. Wodehouse (based on a story by Arthur Freed, Dale Van Every); ph, Merritt B. Gerstad; ed, George Hively; art d, Cedric Gibbons; cos, Rene Hubert; ch, Sammy Lee; m/l, "You're Simply Delish," "Six Poor Mortals," Joseph Meyer, Arthur Freed.

Musical   (PR:A   MPAA:NR)

THOSE WE LOVE½**   (1932) 76m KBS/World Wide bw

Mary Astor (May), Kenneth MacKenna (Fred), Lilyan Tashman (Valerie), Hale Hamilton (Blake), Tommy Conlon (Ricky), Earle Foxe (Bert Parker), Forrester Harvey (Jake), Virginia Sale (Bertha), Pat O'Malley (Daley), Harvey Clark (Mr. Hart), Cecil Cunningham (Mrs. Henry Abbott), Edwin Maxwell (Marshall).

This early 1930s woman's picture was better than most of its ilk, thanks to the good work of the cast. A wandering husband, played by MacKenna, is cheating on wife Astor by having an affair with Tashman. Conlon is the 13-year-old son who ultimately confronts his father about the affair. The story ends with MacKenna breaking it off to regain his son's respect. Though the story starts slowly, once it gets going the drama works well. The cast is sensitively directed, and Astor gives an effective performance, although Tashman overacts.

d, Robert Florey; w, F. Hugh Herbert (based on the play by S. K. Lauren, George Abbott); ph, Arthur Edeson; m, Val Burton; ed, Rose Loewinger; art d, Ralph De Lacey.

Drama   (PR:C   MPAA:NR)

THOSE WERE THE DAYS*   (1934, Brit.) 80m BIP/Wardour bw

Will Hay (Brutus Poskett), Iris Hoey (Agatha Poskett), Angela Baddeley (Charlotte), Claud Allister (Capt. Horace Vale), George Graves (Col. Alexander Lukyn), John Mills (Bobby), Jane Carr (Minnie Taylor), Marguerite Allan (Eve Douglas), H.F. Maltby (Mr. Bullamy), Lawrence Hanray (Wormington), Syd Crossley (Wyke), Wally Patch (Inspector Briggs), Jimmy Godden (Pat Maloney), Jimmy Hanley (Boy), Lily Morris, Harry Bedford, Gaston and Andree, G.H. Elliott, Sam Curtis, Frank Boston and Betty, Ian Wilson, Charles Hayes.

Music hall star Will Hay made his first entry on the screen with this energetic adaptation of the popular stage play. Hay stars as a very proper magistrate who is married to Hoey, a woman he thinks is much younger than she is. To keep her age from him, Hoey dresses her 20-year-old son, Mills, as a much younger boy. After a riotous music hall party, Hay discovers the truth about his family, accepting them as they are. An early performance for Mills who was, surprisingly, 26 years old in this picture and trying very hard to look younger.

p, Walter C. Mycroft; d, Thomas Bentley; w, Fred Thompson, Frank Miller, Frank Launder, Jack Jordan (based on the play "The Magistrate" by Arthur Wing Pinero); ph, Otto Kanturek.

Comedy   (PR:A   MPAA:NR)

THOSE WERE THE DAYS*   (1940) 74m PAR bw (GB: GOOD OLD
                                     SCHOOLDAYS; AKA: AT GOOD OLD SIWASH)

William Holden (P.J. "Petey" Simmons), Bonita Granville (Martha Scroggs), Ezra Stone (Alexander "Allie" Bangs), Judith Barrett (Mirabel Allstairs), Vaughan Glaser (Judge Malachi Scroggs), Lucien Littlefield (Prof. Sillicocks), Richard Denning (Briggs), Phillip Terry (Ranson), Tom Rutherford (Sam Byers), Aldrich Bowker (Judge Squire Jennings), James Seay (Andrews), Douglas Kennedy (Allen), John Laird (Saunders), John Hartley (Whipple), Robert Scott (Allison), Gaylord [Steve] Pendleton (Connie Mathews), Alan Ladd (Keg Rearick), James Dodd (Evans), Wilda Bennett (Miss Chickering), Cyril Ring (Mr. Sanford), Kitty Kelly (Mrs. Sanford), John Marston (Mr. Holland), Dora Clemant (Mrs. Holland), Frank Coghlan, Jr (Chick Struthers), Wanda McKay (Miss Clair), Janet Waldo (Miss Willowboughy), Jean Phillips, Kay Stewart, Kathleen McCormack, Paula de Cardo, Audrey Maynard (Girls), Harry Bradley (Conductor), Stanley Mack (Court Clerk), Rod Cameron (Bartlett), Edgar Dearing (Policeman), Joyce Mathews (Telephone Operator), Ruth Rogers (Secretary).

Holden receives top billing (in what was only his fourth picture) for the first time in this film, which casts Holden as a man looking back on his college days at the turn of the century. A regular ladies' man who draws the wrath of all but his steadfast and loyal roommate Stone, Holden commits one too many pranks and finds himself facing judge Glaser in the courtroom. Holden is granted a week's continuance in an effort to find witnesses who will attest to his innocence. He learns that Granville is the judge's daughter and proceeds to woo her to get himself off the hook. Granville discovers Holden's scheme and, though she is hurt, helps him out anyway. Glaser lets Holden off on the condition he never see his daughter again. But, of course, Holden's fallen for her. He follows her everywhere, but Granville ignores him. In a desperate move, Holden ties her to a chair. He professes his true feelings and finally convinces Granville he is sincere. Glaser finds the couple and, in a fit of anger, has Holden tossed in jail. His fellow students rally behind the rogue's cause and riot in front of the jail, which finally causes Glaser to give in. The film ends some 36 years later, with Holden and Granville recounting the story at an anniversary party. Holden is wonderful in the role, giving a strong, comic performance. Only 22 when this was made, he showed an amazing range of emotion. Though the story is lightweight, the direction is breezy and fun, giving it ample energy. The film was based on the popular stories by Fitch and shot on location at Knox College in Galesburg, Illinois, the original site of the famed Lincoln-Douglas debates. Watch for an early appearance by Alan Ladd in his pre *film noir* days.

p&d, J. Theodore Reed; w, Don Hartman (based on the "Siwash" stories by George Fitch); ph, Victor Milner; ed, William Shea; md, Victor Young; art d, Hans Dreier, Robert Usher; m/l, Frank Loesser.

Comedy   **(PR:A MPAA:NR)**

THOSE WERE THE HAPPY TIMES   (SEE: STAR!, 1968)

THOSE WHO DANCE**   (1930) 65m WB bw

Monte Blue (*Dan Hogan*), Lila Lee (*Nora Brady*), William Boyd (*"Diamond Joe" Jennings*), Betty Compson (*Kitty*), William Janney (*Tim Brady*), Wilfred Lucas (*"Big Ben" Benson*), Cornelius Keefe (*Pat Hogan*), DeWitt Jennings (*Capt. O'Brien*), Gino Corrado (*Tony*), Bob Perry (*Bartender*), Charles McAvoy (*Prison Guard*), Kernan Cripps (*Detective*), Richard Cramer (*Steve Daley*), Harry Semels, Nick Thompson, Frank Mills, Lew Meehan (*Hoods*).

This typical gangster melodrama, featuring a talented cast, has Blue as an undercover cop who infiltrates a gang to find out who did in his younger brother. Lee is the sister of the man who's been framed for the murder. Though direction is uninspired, the talented cast played the hokey story for what it's worth. Boyd, who played a gangster here, went on to star as "Hopalong Cassidy." This is a remake of a 1924 silent film.

d, William Beaudine; w, Joseph Jackson (based on a story by George Kibbe Turner); ph, Sid Hickox; ed, George Amy.

Crime   **(PR:A MPAA:NR)**

THOSE WHO LOVE*½   (1929, Brit.) 87m BIP/FN-Pathe bw

Blanche Adele (*Mary/Lorna*), William Freshman (*David Mellor*), Lawson Butt (*Joe*), Carol Goodner (*Anne*), Hannah Jones (*Babe*), Dino Galvani (*Frenchman*).

Freshman is an author whose fiancee, Adele, dies sending him into a tailspin of depression. He finds hope, however, when he meets a prostitute (also played by Adele) who strangely resembles his dead sweetheart. A slow-moving tale with a theme of obsessive love that unfortunately fails to hold much interest. Filmed silent, then turned into a part-talkie.

d, Manning Haynes; w, Lydia Hayward (based on the novel *Mary Was Love* by Guy Fletcher).

Drama/Romance   **(PR:A MPAA:NR)**

THOU SHALT NOT KILL*   (1939) 67m REP bw

Charles Bickford (*Rev. Chris*), Owen Davis, Jr (*Allen Stevens*), Doris Day (*Mary Olsen*), Paul Guilfoyle (*Gordon Mavis*), Granville Bates (*Mr. Miller*), Charles Waldron (*Father O'Reilly*), Sheila Bromley (*Julie*), George Chandler (*Johnny*), Charles Middleton (*Lars Olsen*), Emmett Vogan (*District Attorney*), Leona Roberts (*Mrs. Stevens*), Ethel May Halls (*Mrs. Olsen*), Edmund Elton (*Dr. Holmes*), Elsie Prescott (*Mrs. Kron*).

A young minister, played by Bickford, tries to reform Davis, who has been convicted of murder and sent to prison. However, another man reveals to Bickford during confession that he's the real killer. The potential for good drama never was realized due to a hackneyed script and uninspired direction, which stifled the actors.

p, Robert North; d, John H. Auer; w, Robert Presnell (based on a story by George Carleton Brown); ph, Jack Marta; ed, Ernest Nims; cos, Adele Palmer.

Drama   **(PR:A MPAA:NR)**

THOUSAND AND ONE NIGHTS, A***   (1945) 92m COL c

Cornel Wilde (*Aladdin*), Evelyn Keyes (*The Genie*), Phil Silvers (*Abdullah*), Adele Jergens (*Princess Armina*), Dusty Anderson (*Novira*), Dennis Hoey (*Sultan Kamar Al-Kir/Prince Hadji*), Philip Van Zandt (*Grand Wazir Abu-Hassan*), Gus Schilling (*Jafar*), Nestor Paiva (*Kahim*), Rex Ingram (*Giant*), Richard Hale (*Kofir the Sorcerer*), Carole Mathews, Pat Parrish, Shelley Winters (*Handmaidens*), Vivian Mason (*Exotic Girl*), Trevor Bardette (*Hasson*), Dick Botiller (*Ramud*), Cy Kendall (*Auctioneer*), Charles LaTorre (*Innkeeper*), Frank Lackteen, Murray Leonard (*Camel Drivers*), Mari Jinishian (*Dancer*), Frank Scannell, Patric Desmond (*Retainers*), John Abbott (*Ali the Tailor*).

A clever, self-parodying version of the Aladdin tales has Wilde trying to win

the heart of princess Jergens. Nothing goes right for him until he discovers the magic lamp that houses genie Keyes. She in turn falls for her new master and successfully thwarts his would-be royal romance. There are some wonderful comic moments provided by the cast and a script that contains some unusual twists. Ingram reprises his genie role from THE THIEF OF BAGDAD. Silvers has some wonderful comic turns, pre-dating his "Sergeant Bilko" television series. The lively direction presents this film with tongue firmly placed in cheek.

p, Samuel Bischoff; d, Alfred E. Green; w, Richard English, Jack Henley, Wilfred H. Pettitt (based on a story by Pettitt); ph, Ray Rennahan (Technicolor); m, Marlin Skiles; ed, Gene Havlick; md, Morris W. Stoloff; art d, Stephen Goosson, Rudolph Sternad; set d, Frank Tuttle; cos, Jean Louis; spec eff, Lawrence W. Butler.

Comedy   **(PR:A MPAA:NR)**

THOUSAND CLOWNS, A***   (1965) 117m UA bw

Jason Robards, Jr (*Murray Burns*), Barbara Harris (*Sandra*), Martin Balsam (*Arnold Burns*), Barry Gordon (*Nick*), Gene Saks (*Leo*), William Daniels (*Albert*).

A wonderful comedy-drama about a man who eschews conformity at every juncture and lives his life marching to a drummer only he can hear. Robards is an out-of-work writer who quit his last job writing a kiddie TV show known as "Chuckles the Chipmunk" when he could no longer stand the gaff. It's been five months since he earned any money and he needs cash to help support his nephew, Gordon, a bright 12-year-old whom his sister dropped off one afternoon seven years ago, then vanished. Gordon is illegitimate and, after living with Robards this long, more like a son than a nephew. The relationship between them is warm, loving, and respectful. Robards has never legally adopted Gordon so a social worker, Harris, comes by to see if she can straighten out the situation. With her is Daniels, a prissy man who is a by-the-book social worker. Unless Robards can prove that he has a real job, they are going to have to take Gordon out of the ratty apartment and give him a foster home. Harris and Robards become romantically attached, something social workers are supposed to avoid at all costs. Daniels, upon seeing the entanglement, orders Harris to leave this particular case. No longer attached, she can pursue her feelings about Robards and she and Gordon prevail on Robards to seek employment through his agent brother, Balsam. Robards reluctantly goes on a few job interviews but his disdainful attitude toward TV writing in general causes him to remain jobless. Realizing that he has to do something fast, Robards swallows his pride and goes back to his former boss, Saks, and asks for his old job back. Saks is a dreadful man who hates children, Gordon in particular because the boy sees right through his toothy grin. Saks is delighted to welcome Robards back into the fold. Later, when Robards tells Harris and Gordon what he's done, the boy is almost in tears because it means giving up his principles and becoming one of the "dead people" (the conformists). Robards tries to explain that he has to do it if they are to stay together. Harris moves in and starts to clean up the cluttered apartment and the picture ends as free wheeling Robards joins the hordes of rush hour people racing to get to work before the time clock punches them in late. The movie was a forerunner of many movies to come because it examined independence at a time when the status of the country was quo. Touching, often hysterically funny, with superb performances by everyone, especially the young Gordon who read lines like a seasoned pro. Saks, who is also a well-known stage and film director, is sensational as the grotesque "Chuckles" and actually more powerful than Balsam, who won the Best Supporting Actor Oscar for his role. The picture, Walker's music, and Gardner's script were also nominated. Gardner is one of the more than 40 members of the Writers Guild who all attended the same school in Coney Island, Abraham Lincoln High. (He won the Tony in 1986 for his new play "I'm Not Rappaport.") Fred Coe directs without a flaw. The 1962 play had nearly the same cast. The title song was a collaboration between saxophonist Gerry Mulligan and his wife, actress Judy Holliday who died at 43 before the picture was released.

p&d, Fred Coe; w, Herb Gardner (based on his play); ph, Arthur J. Ornitz; m, Don Walker; ed, Ralph Rosenblum; set d, Herbert Mulligan, George De Titta; cos, Ruth Morley; makeup, Irving Buchman; m/l, title song, Judy Holliday, Gerry Mulligan (sung by Rita Gardner), "Yes Sir, That's My Baby," Walter Donaldson, Gus Kahn (sung by Jason Robards, Jr.); makeup, Ruth Morley.

Comedy   **Cas.**   **(PR:A-C MPAA:NR)**

THOUSAND CRANES*   (1969, Jap.) Daiei c (SEMBAZURU)

Mikijiro Hira (*Kikuji Mitani*), Ayako Wakao (*Mrs. Ota*), Eiko Azusa (*Fumiko*), Machiko Kyo (*Chikako Kurimoto*), Yoko Nawikawa (*Yukiko Inamura*), Eiji Funakoshi.

Hira remembers via flashbacks his father's two lovers and the bitterness he now feels toward them. As a boy he meets Kyo, the first lover, with whom his father's affair is brief. He later becomes involved with Wakao, a widow. After his father's death he is invited to a tea ceremony by Kyo. There he meets Nawikawa, whom Kyo wants him to marry. He is surprised to find Wakao there, knowing of the jealousy that existed between his father's two lovers. She is accompanied by her daughter, Azusa. Embarrassed by Kyo's presumption, Hira is nevertheless attracted to Nawikawa. He speaks with

Wakao after the tea ceremony and realizes she can't distinguish him from his father. They go to a nearby inn and make love. However, she is crushed when Hira says he doesn't want to marry Nawikawa and commits suicide. Kyo destroys Hira's romances by constantly belittling him and his lovers. Asuza leaves, and Hira is left alone.

d, Yasuzo Masumura; w, Kaneto Shindo (based on the novel *Sembazuru* by Yasunari Kawabata); ph, Setsuo Kobayashi (Daiei Scope, Eastmancolor); m, Hikaru Hayashi; art d, Tomoo Shimogawara.

Drama   (PR:O MPAA:NR)

THOUSAND EYES OF DR. MABUSE, THE* ½**
(1960, Fr./Ital./Ger.) 103m CCC-Filmkuns t-CEI Incom-Criterion/Ajay bw (DIE TAUSEND AUGEN DES DR. MABUSE; IL DIABOLICO DR. MABUSE; LE DIABOLIQUE DOCTEUR MABUSE; AKA: EYE OF EVIL; THE SHADOW VERSUS THE THOUSAND EYES OF DR. MABUSE)

Dawn Addams (*Marion Menil*), Peter Van Eyck (*Henry B. Travers*), Gert Frobe (*Commissioner Krauss*), Wolfgang Preiss [Lupo Prezzo] (*Jordan/Cornelius*), Werner Peters (*Hieronymous P. Mistelzweig*), Andrea Checchi (*Inspector Berg*), Reinhard Kolldehoff (*The Clubfoot*), Howard Vernon ("*No. 12*"), Jean-Jacques Delbo (*Deiner the Servant*), Christiane Maybach (*Pretty Blonde*), David Cameron (*Parker, Travers' Secretary*), Nico Pepe (*Hotel Manager*), Werner Buttler ("*No. 11*"), Linda Sini (*Corinna*), Rolf Moebius (*Police Officer*), Bruno W. Pantel (*Reporter*), Marie-Luise Nagel, Albert Bessler.

Noted German director Lang returned to his native land to make his last film, a fine, low-budget sequel to his pre-war films dealing with the notorious Dr. Mabuse, DR. MABUSE DER SPIELER (1922) and DAS TESTAMENT DES DR. MABUSE (1933). Lang had fled Germany after Hitler, impressed with Lang's METROPOLIS, offered him a position as the official Nazi filmmaker. (Lang expected the offer to be a trap, and feared the Nazis would stumble upon information revealing his mother's Jewish background.) He went to France, where he directed one film. In 1934 he was signed by producer David O. Selznick in London to a one-picture deal with MGM. He sailed to the U.S., and became a citizen in 1935. Using an actual Nazi blueprint on how to bug a hotel for inspiration, Lang fashioned a story about a series of strange murders in Berlin's fictional Hotel Luxor. Authorities come to believe the man behind the crimes may be someone who believes he is a reincarnation of the evil Dr. Mabuse. Van Eyck is an American millionaire who saves Addams from killing herself at the Luxor, and the two become involved in the investigation. Frobe (later of GOLDFINGER) is the police commissioner who thinks that either Preiss or Peters is the killer. The former is a supposedly blind clairvoyant, and the latter an insurance salesman. Lang fills his eerie tale with a tightly controlled mise-en-scene, a world of hidden cameras, two-way mirrors and mistaken impressions. Addams is hypnotized by Prezzo (a pseudonym for Preiss). With the same actor playing two roles, Lang further confuses the audience and thus heightens the tale's frightening disorientation. This film which was dubbed into English for American release, is pure cinema, using camera angle, shot composition and lighting to achieve an overwhelming power that stays long after the final reel goes through the projector. Five sequels followed in light of this film's enormous popularity: IM STAHLNETZ DES DR. MABUSE (1961), DIE UNSICHTBAREN KRALLEN DES DR. MABUSE (1961), SCOTLAND YARD JAGT DR. MABUSE (1963), DAS TESTAMENT DES DR. MABUSE (1962), and DIES TODESSTRAHLEN DES DR. MABUSE (1964). (See DR MABUSE series, Index.)

p&d, Fritz Lang; w, Lang, Heinz Oskar Wuttig (based on an idea by Jan Fethke, from a character created by Norbert Jacques); ph, Karl Lob; m, Bert Grund, Gerhard Becker; ed, Walter Wischniewsky, Waltraute Wischniewsky; art d, Erich Kettelhut, Johannes Ott; cos, Ina Stein; makeup, Heinz Stamm.

Crime/Horror   (PR:O MPAA:NR)

THOUSAND PLANE RAID, THE   (SEE: 1,000 PLANE RAID, THE, 1969)

THOUSANDS CHEER* ½**   (1943) 126m MGM c

Kathryn Grayson (*Kathryn Jones*), Gene Kelly (*Eddie Marsh*), Mary Astor (*Hyllary Jones*), Jose Iturbi (*Himself*), John Boles (*Col. Jones*), Dick Simmons (*Capt. Avery*), Ben Blue (*Chuck*), Frank Jenks (*Sgt. Koslack*), Frank Sully (*Alan*), Wally Cassell (*Jack*), Ben Lessy (*Silent Monk*), Frances Rafferty (*Marie*), Odette Myrtil (*Mama Corbino*), Will Kaufman (*Papa Corbino*), Lionel Barrymore (*Announcer*), Mickey Rooney, Judy Garland, Red Skelton, Eleanor Powell, Ann Sothern, Lucille Ball, Virginia O'Brien, Lena Horne, Marsha Hunt, Marilyn Maxwell, Donna Reed, Margaret O'Brien, June Allyson, Gloria DeHaven, Sara Haden, Frank Morgan, Kay Kyser and His Orchestra, Bob Crosby and His Orchestra, Chorus of United Nations, Benny Carter and Orchestra, Don Loper, Maxine Barrat (*Guest Stars*), Sig Arno (*Uncle Algy*), Connie Gilchrist (*Taxicab Driver*), Bea Nigro (*Woman*), Daisy Buford (*Maid*), Pierre Watkin (*Alex*), Peggy Remington, Ed Mortimer (*Guests*), Ray Teal (*Ringmaster*), Carl Saxe (*Sergeant Major*), Bryant Washburn, Jr (*Lt. Col. Brand*), Harry Strang (*Capt. Haines*), James Millican (*Sgt. Carrington Major*), William Tannen (*Prison Sergeant*), Flo-

rence Turner (*Mother at Station*), Linda Landi (*Polish Girl at Station*), Eileen Coghlan, Eve Whitney, Aileen Haley, Betty Jaynes, Natalie Draper (*Girls at Station*), Myron Healey, Cliff Danielson, James Warren, Don Taylor (*Soldiers at Station*), Paul Speer (*Specialty Dancer*), Marta Linden (*Skit Nurse*), John Conte (*Skit Doctor*).

During WW II, every major studio shot at least one movie using all their stars in a flag-waving extravaganza. Warner Bros. produced THIS IS THE ARMY and HOLLYWOOD CANTEEN, Sol Lesser made STAGE DOOR CANTEEN, Paramount did STAR SPANGLED RHYTHM, and MGM presented this. The Louis B. Mayer axiom that MGM had "more stars than there are in heaven" was proven true by this huge movie, which had nothing at all to do with the Irving Berlin musical "As Thousands Cheer," produced on the stage in 1933. Grayson is an opera singer living on an Army base with her father, Boles, a colonel. Although she is spending a promising career warbling arias, she is spending the duration of the war as her dad's housekeeper ever since her mother, Astor, has departed. Astor and Boles have been estranged for some time and Grayson feels sorry for her father so she foregoes any attempts at stepping out on her own. While Grayson is at a railway station, she is spotted by Kelly, who doesn't know her, but he musters up the courage to kiss her because he is by himself and feels awful that there's no one at the station to greet him upon his arrival. He has no idea that she is the daughter of commandant Boles and when he learns that, he is miffed because he is a natural rebel against military domination and Grayson represents that in his mind. Kelly is an ex-circus high flyer and is accustomed to being the center of attention. He'd like to get a transfer to the Air Corps and is told that if he wants it bad enough, he'll make up with Grayson and she might be able to use her influence to convince her father to recommend the transfer. Kelly decides to take their advice and, at first, he's playing up to her for selfish reasons. Then it dawns on him that Grayson is terrific and he begins to fall in love with her. Boles doesn't like the idea of his daughter and Kelly so he asks Astor how she would handle it. Kelly squires Grayson to meet the people with whom he did his trapeze work, Kaufman and Myrtil, and she is surprised to learn that Kelly was a star under the Big Top. Astor arrives and tries to convince Grayson that Kelly is not the marrying kind. By this time, Grayson has planned a huge show for the servicemen and is in contact with many big stars who are promising to perform. Astor wants Grayson to leave the base and return to their home in New York. Kelly fears that Grayson may do that and leaves his post to run into Boles' office to speak on behalf of his love for Grayson. Deserting his post results in his being sent to his barracks and ordered to remain there. The show is about to be produced and Kaufman and Myrtil are part of the entertainment. They prevail on Boles to allow Kelly out of confinement so they can do their act with him. Boles consents and the three perform and Kelly, who has been a loner always battling against authority, now has the meaning and importance of teamwork impressed on his psyche. Just as Astor begins to convince Grayson to return to New York, the big show ends and the entire camp is ordered to report for immediate shipping to the war zone. The final sequence has Grayson, Astor, and Boles waving "ta-ta" to Kelly. With all the songs and production numbers, there was hardly any time for any plot at all and it's a wonder they managed to cram this much into the two hour running time. Rooney is the M.C. of the camp show and gets to do an hysterical impression of Lionel Barrymore and Clark Gable from TEST PILOT (Gable was unable to appear in the film because he was away in service). Frank Morgan plays a lecherous man impersonating a Navy Doctor as he examines the forms of Lucille Ball, Marsha Hunt, and Anne Sothern while John Conte acts as his sketch assistant. Red Skelton plays a soda jerk who turns green as he watches little Margaret O'Brien eat mounds of ice cream. Each of those comedy bits is a standout and there are many others. Songs from various writers include: "The Joint Is Really Jumpin' in Carnegie Hall" (Roger Edens, Ralph Blane, Hugh Martin, sung by Judy Garland and accompanied by Jose Iturbi in his first Hollywood movie), "Tico Tico" (Zequinha Abreu, danced by Don Loper, Maxine Barrett), "Honeysuckle Rose" (Fats Waller, Andy Razaf, sung by Lena Horne), "In a Little Spanish Town" (Mabel Wayne, Joe Young, Sam M. Lewis, sung by Virginia O'Brien), "Daybreak" (Ferde Grofe, Harold Adamson, sung by Kathryn Grayson), "Three Letters in the Mailbox" (Walter Jurmann, Paul Francis Webster, sung by Grayson), "Let There Be Music" (Earl Brent, E.Y. Harburg, sung by Grayson), "The United Nations on the March" (Dimitri Shostakovich with Harburg, Harold Rome, and Herbert Stothart, sung by Grayson), "Sempre Libera" (from "Aida" by Giuseppe) Verdi, sung by Grayson), "I Dug a Ditch in Wichita" (Ralph Freed, Burton Lane, Lew Brown, performed by Ben Lessy and the company, reprised by Kay Kyser's orchestra with Harry Babbitt singing). Gene Kelly did a creative "Mop Dance" to "Wichita" and "Let Me Call You Sweetheart" (Leo Friedman, Beth S. Whitson). Other tunes were "I'm Lost, You're Lost," and "Why Don't We Try?" (Walter Ruick), "Just as Long as I Know Katie's Waitin'" (Lew Brown, George R. Brown), "Why Should I?" (Arthur Freed, Nacio Herb Brown), "American Patrol" (E.H. Meacham), "Columbia, the Gem of the Ocean" (traditional), and "Yankee Doodle" (traditional). June Allyson and Gloria DeHaven chime in with O'Brien on "Spanish Town" for a few bars while Bob Crosby and His BobCats back them up. Benny Carter led the band behind Horne. Good color, excellent technical credits, first-rate production values–just what one might expect from the Culver City lot.

p, Joe Pasternak; d, George Sidney; w, Paul Jarrico, Richard Collins (based on their story "Private Miss Jones"); ph, George Folsey (Technicolor); m, Herbert Stothart; ed, George Boemler; md, Stothart; art d, Cedric Gibbons,

Daniel B. Cathcart; set d, Edwin B. Willis, Jacques Mesereau; cos, Irene.

Musical   **(PR:A MPAA:NR)**

THREADS*   (1932, Brit.) 76m Samuelson/UA bw

Lawrence Anderson (John Osborne Wynn), Dorothy Fane (Amelia Wynn), Gerald Rawlinson (Arthur), Wendy Barrie (Olive Wynn), Ben Webster (Lord Grantham), Irene Rooke (Lady Grantham), Walter Piers (Col. Packinder), Leslie Cole (James), Aileen Despard (Chloe), Pat Reid (Parsons), Clifford Cobbe (Jefferson Jordan).

A standard British programmer which stars Anderson as a man wrongly imprisoned for murder. He is released after 17 years only to find that his son is engaged to the daughter of the judge who sentenced him. Needless to say, he is opposed to their wedding. Anderson's wife arranges for the young lovers' elopement, however, and the pair run away together. By the finale Anderson's daughter, Barrie, manages to bring the family together and mend all past wounds.

p, Gordon Craig; d, G.B. Samuelson; w, Frank Stayton (based on his play).

Drama   **(PR:A MPAA:NR)**

THREAT, THE***   (1949) 66m RKO bw

Michael O'Shea (Williams), Virginia Grey (Carol), Charles McGraw (Kluger), Julie Bishop (Ann), Frank Conroy (Mac), Robert Shayne (Murphy), Anthony Caruso (Nick), Don McGuire (Joe Turner), Frank Richards (Lefty), Michael McHale (Jensen).

Despite its B budget, THE THREAT is an exciting, tightly controlled film that never lets the audience down. McGraw is a vicious killer who busts out of prison and is determined to get even with everyone responsible for his conviction. He kidnaps O'Shea, the cop who arrested him; Conroy, the district attorney who convicted him; and Grey, the nightclub singer McGraw is convinced ratted on him in the first place. Shayne is the cop who must stop McGraw and rescue the hostages. The film becomes a violent cat-and-mouse game between the principals, with tension that never lets up. The performances are excellent. McGraw is the quintessential psychotic, drawing his character well and making him terrifyingly believable. The direction pays close attention to all details, from police investigations to the tense confrontations. It's films like this that the French New Wave rightfully recognized as true cinema.

p, Hugh King; d, Felix E. Feist; w, King, Dick Irving Hyland (based on a story by King); ph, Harry J. Wild; m, Paul Sawtell; ed, Samuel E. Beetley; md, C. Bakaleinikoff; art d, Albert S. D'Agostino, Charles F. Pyke; set d, Darrell Silvera, William Stevens; makeup, William Phillips.

Crime   **Cas.**   **(PR:O MPAA:NR)**

THREAT, THE**   (1960) 66m WB bw

Robert Knapp (Steve Keenan), Linda Lawson (Gerri), Lisabeth Hush (Sandy), James Seay (Harry Keenan), Mary Castle (Laura), Barney Phillips (Lucky), Richard S. Cowl (Chessner), Lew Brown (Smiley), Art Lewis (Mousie), Tom Gilson (Junior), Emile Meyer (Duncan), Nicholas King.

Knapp is a cop with a reputation for being sadistic when dealing with thugs. He kills an important underworld figure who resists arrest and then spends the rest of the film being pursued by someone trying to avenge the gangster's death. Though the direction is competent enough, the script takes a few unbelievable story twists that only confuse the viewer as to the film's direction and intent. Is this a psychological story or just a mystery? No one seems to know and neither will the viewer, in what is just another routine cop film. A good jazz score helps set the mood.

p&d, Charles R. Rondeau; w, Jo Heims; ph, Edward Cronjager; m, Ronald Stein; ed, Howard Epstein.

Crime   **(PR:O MPAA:NR)**

THREE*   (1967, Yugo.) 79m Avala Film/Impact Films bw (TRI)

Bata Zivojinovic [Velimir Zivojinovic] (Milos), Ali Raner (Man), Senka Veletanlic-Petrovic (Girl), Voja Miric (Partisan), Slobodan Perovic, Mica Tomic.

Zivojinovic is a young Yugoslav who tries to escape from the Nazis during WW II. While waiting for a train among a crowd of refugees, a man with no identification papers is suspected of wrongdoing, and the crowd demands that three soldiers arrest him. Zivojinovic tries to intervene, but the the man is shot. Suddenly the dead man's wife appears and proclaims his innocence. In a second vignette, Zivojinovic is chased by the Germans into a swamp after he takes part in a resistance raid. There he meets another man in hiding. Knowing the Nazis are looking for only one fugitive, the man sacrifices himself so that Zivojinovic can escape. In the final episode, the war is ending and Zivojinovic is now an officer in Yugoslav army. He must pass an execution order on citizens accused of collaborating with the enemy. One is a woman to whom he is attracted, but Zivojinovic carries out the order anyway.

d, Aleksandar Petrovic; w, Antonije Isakovic, Petrovic (based on the book

Paprat I Vatra by Isakovic); ph, Tomislav Pinter; ed, Mila Milanovic.

War Drama   **(PR:C MPAA:NR)**

THREE*   (1969, Brit.) 105m Obelisk/UA c

Charlotte Rampling (Marty), Robie Porter (Bert), Sam Waterston (Taylor), Pascale Roberts (Claude), Edina Ronay (Liz), Gillian Hills (Ann), Mario Cotone (Silvano), Patrizia Giammei (Gloria).

A pleasant film about a menage a trois has Porter and Waterston playing a pair of friends who take a battered car and tour Europe. They meet many women but are both attracted to Rampling, an English girl. The two friends make a pact, vowing to keep the relationship with her on a platonic level. Porter meets Roberts and goes off with her for a time while Waterston gradually finds himself growing attracted to Rampling. He keeps the pact in mind though and resists all temptations. When Porter returns, he immediately has an affair with Rampling which causes a break in the friendship with Waterston. The latter leaves Rampling and Porter, crushed but with a newfound feeling of maturity. There is a certain naive charm to this film, based on a fine short story by Shaw. The actors are completely natural, making their characters and the film believable and often touching. The direction has an easy-going style that never has to rely on heavy-handed symbolism to make a point. Interesting and highly enjoyable.

p, Bruce Becker; d&w, James Salter (based on the story "Then There Were Three" by Irwin Shaw); ph, Etienne Becker (Eastmancolor); m, Laurence Rosenthal; ed, Edward Nielson.

Drama   **(PR:O MPAA:M/PG)**

THREE BAD MEN IN THE HIDDEN FORTRESS
                  (SEE: HIDDEN FORTRESS, THE, 1959, Jap.)

THREE BAD SISTERS*½   (1956) 76m Bel-Air/UA bw

Maria English (Vicki), Kathleen Hughes (Valerie), Sara Shane (Lorna), John Bromfield (Jim Norton), Jess Barker (George Gurney), Madge Kennedy (Aunt Martha), Tony George (Tony Cadiz), Patsy Nayfack (Mary), Eric Wilton (Wilson), Brett Halsey (Carlos), Marlene Felton (Nadine).

This turgid potboiler features the three worst sisters since Macbeth stumbled on the witches in the woods. When their father is killed in a plane crash, Hughes immediately starts in on English and Shane so that she can inherit the estate for herself. First she disfigures English who ends up killing herself after seeing her new looks. Then Hughes engages Bromfield, the pilot of the plane her father died on, to help destroy sister no. 2. In return for a cut of the estate, Bromfield agrees to help drive Shane mad, but ends up falling for her instead. The two marry and Hughes makes certain that she'll get some sadistic revenge. In the final scene, Hughes tells Shane that her husband is carrying on a torrid affair with her. Shane is about to leap off a cliff when Hughes and Bromfield are killed fighting over the control of a moving car. Though the plot holds plenty of juice, the presentation is dull with an ambling direction that shows no feel for the material at all. This is the sort of film that demands hot treatment and the trio of actresses try their best. However the direction, coupled with a less than steamy script, never gives them a chance.

p, Howard W. Koch; d, Gilbert L. Kay; w, Gerald Drayson Adams; ph, Lester Shorr; m, Paul Dunlap; ed, John F. Schreyer; md, Dunlap; cos, Wesley V. Jefferies.

Drama   **(PR:C MPAA:NR)**

THREE BITES OF THE APPLE*½   (1967) 98m MGM c

David McCallum (Stanley Thrumm), Sylva Koscina (Carla Moretti), Tammy Grimes (Angela Sparrow), Harvey Korman (Harvey Tomlinson), Domenico Modugno (Remo Romano), Aldo Fabrizi (The Doctor), Avril Angers (Gladys Tomlinson), Claude Aliotti (Teddy Farnum), Freda Bamford (Gussie Hagstrom), Arthur Hewlett (Alfred Guffy), Alison Fraser (Peg Farnum), Cardew Robinson (Bernhard Hagstrom), Ann Lancaster (Winifred Batterly), John Sharp (Joe Batterly), Maureen Pryor (Birdie Guffy), Edra Gale (The Yodeler), Mirella Maravidi (Francesca Bianchini), Riccardo Garrone (Croupier).

When McCallum, a mild mannered tour guide, wins a grand sum of money on a Riviera casino, he's faced with either taking it all back to England and paying taxes on it or investing it in Switzerland. McCallum opts for the latter, all the while being monitored by Koscina, a woman who wants a taste of the cash herself. From there it's a supposedly madcap chase across Europe as Koscina enlists the aid of her ex-husband to get the money while McCallum tries to transport it in secret and place it in a Swiss bank account. The result is a no-joke comedy that looks more like a travelog than feature filmmaking. There's plenty of scenery to look at, most quite nicely photographed, but that's about it. McCallum, of the popular T.V. series "The Man from U.N.C.L.E.," merely goes through the motions. Audiences were smart, for this is one tour few bothered taking on its release.

p&d, Alvin Ganzer; w, George Wells; ph, Gabor Pogany (Panavision, Metrocolor); m, Eddy Manson; ed, Norman Savage; art d, Elliot Scott; set d, Arrigo Breschi; cos, Pino Lancetti; m/l, "In the Garden–Under the Tree,"

Paul Francis Webster, David McCallum (sung by McCallum), "Carla," Mario Castellacci, Domenico Modugno; makeup, Amato Garbini.

Comedy   (PR:A   MPAA:NR)

THREE BLIND MICE***   (1938) 75m FOX bw

Loretta Young (Pamela Charters), Joel McCrea (Van Smith), David Niven (Steve Harrington), Stuart Erwin (Mike Brophy), Marjorie Weaver (Moira Charters), Pauline Moore (Elizabeth Charters), Binnie Barnes (Miriam), Jane Darwell (Mrs. Killian), Leonid Kinskey (Young Man), Spencer Charters (Hendricks), Franklin Pangborn (Clerk), Herb Heywood (Workman), Ben Hendricks (Bartender), Elisha Cook, Jr (Boy), Lillian Porter (Girl), Antonio Filauri (Maitre d'Hotel), Alex Pollard (Butler), Iva Stewart (Cigarette Girl).

In a plot right out of any good GOLDDIGGERS flick Young, along with sisters Weaver and Moore, head off from the flatlands of Kansas to the rich valleys of California in search of rich husband material. Young pretends to be an important socialite with her two sisters completing the ruse posing as her staff. She meets McCrea, an apparently wealthy young man, and it's true love for Young. It turns out McCrea is just as poor as she, but Cupid doesn't know beans when it comes to dollar signs and love triumphs. Moore gets the ever delightful Niven and Weaver scores a jackpot by marrying the seemingly poor, but actually quite wealthy, bartender Erwin. This is a delightful comedy, well scripted and directed with a sense of fun. The players are clearly enjoying themselves making the most they can out of the good material. The easily adaptable plot later turned up in two remakes: MOON OVER MIAMI (1941) and THREE LITTLE GIRLS IN BLUE (1946).

p, Raymond Griffith; d, William A. Seiter; w, Brown Holmes, Lynn Starling (based on a play by Stephen Powys); ph, Ernest Palmer; ed, James B. Morley; md, Arthur Lange; cos, Gwen Wakeling; m/l, Lew Pollack, Sidney D. Mitchell.

Comedy   (PR:A   MPAA:NR)

THREE BLONDES IN HIS LIFE*   (1961) 86m Cinema Associates bw

Jock Mahoney (Duke Wallace), Greta Thyssen (Helen Fortner), Tony [Anthony] Dexter (Richard Rogers), Jesse White (Ed Kelly), Valerie Porter (Martha Carr), Elaine Edwards (Lois Collins).

Mahoney is a private eye in this predictable whodunit which gets him involved with a trio of blondes, Thyssen, Edwards, and Porter, while trying to uncover the mystery behind a colleague's murder.

p, George Moskov; d, Leon Chooluck; w, Moskov; ph, Ernest Haller; ed, Maurice Wright; art d, Theobald Hotsoppie

Crime   (PR:C   MPAA:NR)

THREE BRAVE MEN**½   (1957) 88m FOX bw

Ray Milland (Joe Di Marco), Ernest Borgnine (Bernie Goldsmith), Frank Lovejoy (Capt. Winfield), Nina Foch (Lt. McCoy), Dean Jagger (Rogers), Virginia Christine (Helen Goldsmith), Edward Andrews (Maj. Jensen), Frank Faylen (Enos Warren), Diane Jergens (Shirley Goldsmith), Warren Berlinger (Harry Goldsmith), Andrew Duggan (Browning), Joseph Wiseman (Jim Barron), James Westerfield (O'Reilly), Richard Anderson (Lt. Horton), Olive Blakeney (Miss Scott), Robert Burton (Dietz), Jason Wingreen (Perry), Ray Montgomery (Sanford), Sandy Descher (Alice), Patty Ann Gerrity (Ruthie), Jonathan Hole (Gibbons), Barbara Gould (Susie), Fern Barry (Miss Howell), Lee Roberts (Investigator), Selmer Jackson (Retired Admiral), John Close (Photographer), Keith Vincent (East), Tom Daly (Sherrod), Juanita Close (Bernie's Secretary), Edith Claire (Dietz's Secretary), Walter Woolf (Adm. Mason), Gene O'Donnell (Washington Correspondent), Carleton Young (Board Chairman), Joseph McGuinn (Gaddis), Samuel Colt (Funston), Bill Hughes, Leonard Graves, Helen Mayon, Tom Daley.

Borgnine is a Navy Security employee who gets discharged with a feeble excuse and hires himself a lawyer, Milland. Communist affiliations are uncovered but in the most innocent of degrees–subscribing to a Commie-owned publication and joining a Commie-inspired study group. With the help of the Assistant Secretary of the Navy, Jagger, Borgnine is returned to duty (with back pay!) in light of his longtime faithful service and community involvement. Based on the actual case involving Abraham Chasanow which appeared in a series of Pulitzer Prize winning articles.

p, Herbert B. Swope, Jr.; d&w, Philip Dunne (based on articles by Anthony Lewis); ph, Charles G. Clarke (CinemaScope); m, Hans Salter; ed, David Brotherton; art d, Lyle R. Wheeler, Mark-Lee Kirk; cos, Adele Balcan; spec eff, Ray Kellogg.

Drama   (PR:A   MPAA:NR)

THREE BROADWAY GIRLS   (SEE: GREEKS HAD A WORD FOR THEM, 1932)

THREE BROTHERS   (SEE: SIDE STREET, 1929)

THREE BROTHERS***   (1982, Ital.) 113m Iter Film-GAU-Artificial Eye/New World c

Philippe Noiret (Raffaele Giuranna), Charles Vanel (Donato Giuranna), Michele Placido (Nicola Giuranna), Vittorio Mezzogiorno (Rocco Giuranna/Young Donato), Andrea Ferreol (Raffaele's Wife), Maddalena Crippa (Giovanna), Sara Tafuri (Rosaria), Marta Zoffoli (Marta, the Little Girl), Tino Schipinzi (Raffaele's Friend), Simonetta Stefanelli (Young Donato's Wife), Pietro Biondi (1st Judge), Ferdinando Greco (2nd Judge), Accursio DiLeo (1st Friend at Bar), Cosimo Milone (Raffaele's Son), Luigi Infantino (2nd Friend at Bar), Gina Pontrelli (The Brother's Mother), Girolamo Marzano (Nicola's Friend), Ferdinando Murolo (Friend at Bar), Maria Antonia Capotorto (Post Office Clerk), Francesco Capotorto, Cristofaro Chiapparino (Friends at Bar).

After a long separation, three brothers–a teacher, magistrate, and factory worker–return to the small Italian village of their youth to attend their mother's funeral. With their father (Vanel) still alive, reminiscence occurs, but is accompanied with flared emotions. At times the film is powerful, though often painfully slow.

p, Georgio Nocell, Antonio Macri; d&w, Francesco Rosi (based on the story "The Third Son" by A. Platonov); ph, Pasqualino DeSantis (Technicolor); m, Piero Piccioni; ed, Ruggero Mastroianni; art d, Andrea Crisanti; m/l, Pino Daniele.

Drama   Cas.   (PR:C   MPAA:PG)

THREE CABALLEROS, THE****   (1944) 70m Disney/RKO c

Aurora Miranda, Carmen Molina, Dora Luz, Nestor Amarale, Almirante, Trio Calaveras, Ascencio Del Rio Trio, Padua Hill Players and the voices of Sterling Holloway, Clarence Nash (Donald Duck), Jose Oliveira (Joe Carioca), Joaquin Garay (Panchito), Fred Shields, Frank Graham.

A smashing followup to SALUDOS AMIGOS, this is one of the most dazzling achievements of the cartoon genre and the use of drawn figures with live action has never been seen to better advantage. Donald Duck is delivered three presents on his birthday, which falls on Friday the 13th. He opens the first and discovers that it's a movie projector. He puts the film on the projector and we are plunged into the story of a penguin who became sick and tired of the cold at the bottom of the world and wanted to live in the tropics. Pablo the Penguin declares his feelings in a charming segment narrated by Holloway who says "a blanket of fog rolled in" and that's exactly what the eye sees, a blanket made of fog. Pablo gets into a little boat and keeps bouncing off the map lines on the screen. Of the segments, this first one is whimsical but nowhere near the brilliance of what follows. The second half of the bird sequence shows a little Mexican boy finding a donkey with wings which he enters in a race and incurs the wrath of the crowd when they discover the donkey has an edge. (In the film, the name of the beast is the "Flying Burrito" which may, or may not, have been where the rock group got its name.) Donald finishes watching his films, then opens his next present, a large book. The moment he opens it, up pops Joe Carioca (from SALUDOS AMIGOS). He takes Donald on a tour of Brazil (after singing "Baia" by Ary Barroso) by smashing the duck on the head so he shrinks to a tiny size and can step inside the picture book. Then it's off on one of the fastest-moving cartoon sequences ever devised as they get on a train and travel to Brazil where Donald meets and falls in love with Aurora Miranda (Carmen's sister) in a huge production number that is as elaborate as anything Busby Berkeley ever choreographed except that the stars are a live woman and a duck. After this huge number, Donald and Joe get out of the book and go on their last adventure into Mexico. It's one of the most creative uses of animation ever as Donald gets into the sound track (represented by a moving line). Donald and Joe are joined by a rooster named Panchito and go on a breakneck trip around Mexico that includes a quick history of the country, the Christmas traditions of the pinata, a fiesta, jaunts to Acapulco, Veracruz, and Patzcuaro. They cavort with beautiful women in bathing suits, dance with animated plants as well as with famed terp Carmen Molina, who does her trademark "Jesusita" number from the state of Chihuahua. Donald even gets into a bullfight that winds up with fireworks. Writing about the hundreds of animation gags is truly impossible. There is so much happening on screen that any synopsis will fall far short. Disney used many Latino composers for the score which also included "You Belong to My Heart" (Augustin Lara, Ray Gilbert, sung by Dora Luz), "The Three Caballeros" (Gilbert, Manuel Esperon, sung by Donald Duck [Clarence Nash], Joe Carioca [Jose Oliveira], Panchito [Joaquin Garay], "Os Quindins De Yaya" (Barroso, Ervin Drake), and "Mexico" (Charles Wolcott, Gilbert). This is a fast (71 minute) and funny picture that is a must for anyone or any age. A hit when released, the studio waited three decades before sending it out again, then cut it down and offered a badly edited version that did no justice to the geniuses who made the original. In SALUDOS AMIGOS, Disney concentrated on South America. Here, he wisely stays closer to home for much of the movie and the Mexican government loved it. Watching Saturday morning cartoons in the 1980s, then looking at something as visually delicious as this makes one realize just how good the Disney animators were.

p, Norman Ferguson; d, Ferguson, Clyde Geronimi, Jack Kinney, Bill

Roberts, Harold Young; w, Homer Brightman, Ernest Terrazzas, Ted Sears, Bill Peet, Ralph Wright, Roy Williams, William Cottrell, Del Connell, James Bodrero; ph, Ray Rennahan (Technicolor); ed, John Haliday; md, Charles Wolcott, Paul J. Smith, Edward H. Plumb; art d, Richard F. Irvine; ch, Billy Daniels, Aloysio Oliveira, Carmelita Maracci; anim, Ward Kimball, Eric Larson, Fred Moore, John Lounsbery, Les Clark, Milt Kahl, Hal King, Franklin Thomas, Harvey Toombs, Bob Carlson, John Sibley, Bill Justice, Oliver M. Johnston, Jr., Milt Neil, Marvin Woodward, John Patterson; spec eff anim, Joshua Meador, George Rowley, Edwin Aardal, John McManus; backgrounds, Albert Dempster, Art Riley, Ray Huffine, Don Douglass, Claude Coats.

Animated Feature/Fantasy/
Musical   Cas.   **(PR:AAA MPAA:G)**

THREE CAME HOME**   (1950) 106m FOX bw

Claudette Colbert *(Agnes Keith)*, Patric Knowles *(Harry Keith)*, Florence Desmond *(Betty Sommers)*, Sessue Hayakawa *(Col. Suga)*, Sylvia Andrew *(Henrietta)*, Mark Keuning *(George)*, Phyllis Morris *(Sister Rose)*, Howard Chuman *(Lt. Nekata)*, Drue Mallory, Virginia Keley, Mimi Heyworth, Helen Westcott *(Women Prisoners)*, Taka Iwashaiki *(Japanese Captain)*, Devi Dja *(Ah Yin)*, Leslie Thomas *(Wet Man)*, John Burton *(Elderly Resident)*, James Yanari *(1st Lieutenant)*, George Leigh *(Australian Prisoner of War)*, Li Sun *(Wilfred)*, Duncan Richardson *(English Boy)*, Melinda Plowman *(English Girl)*, Lee MacGregor *(Sailor)*, Masaji "Butch" Yamamota *(Japanese Sergeant)*, Pat Whyte *(Englishman)*, David Matsushama *(Evil Guard)*, Alex Fraser *(Dr. Bandy)*, Frank Kobata *(Japanese Non-Com)*, Al Saijo *(Japanese Boat Pilot)*, Jim Hagimori *(Japanese Sea Captain)*, Patricia O'Callaghan *(English Woman)*, Ken Kurosa, Giro Murashami *(Orderlies)*, Leonard Willey *(Governor General)*, Harry Martin, Pat O'Moore, Clarke Gordon, Douglas Walton, Robin Hughes, John Mantley, James Logan *(Australian POWS)*, Campbell Copelin, Leslie Denison *(English Radio Announcers)*.

This is a powerful and moving picture that examines life in a Japanese POW camp from a woman's point of view. Colbert plays American writer Agnes Newton Keith, who is married to British administrator Knowles. They live in the East Indian islands, and shortly after the outbreak of WW II, are arrested along with other noncombatants, then imprisoned in a concentration camp. Life in the camp is harsh as the prisoners are subjected to inhumane conditions. They are given paltry food rations, as well as beatings and other humiliations. Colbert refuses to lose her spirit and at one point crawls beneath barbed wire in order to spend a few minutes with her husband. She is later beaten by the Japanese, who will go to any lengths to draw forth a prisoner's confession. Hayakawa is the U.S.-educated Japanese colonel who runs the camp. He is a man torn up inside, struggling between his obedience to orders and the dictates of his conscience. The prisoners, including children, manage to build some semblance of life for themselves as they struggle to maintain a daily existence. However conditions in the camp worsen and many of the inmates die. Eventually the camp is liberated but those remaining are only shadows of their former selves. Based on Keith's autobiography, this film intricately develops the relationships between characters. Colbert is stunning in the lead, delivering an honest portrait of Keith's three-year struggle. Hayakawa, a former silent-film actor, is charged with mixed emotions, creating a character of high intensity. Fighting with his own feelings towards the inmates, Hayakawa builds an unusual relationship with Colbert, well handling his mixture of kindness and cruelty. In the end, knowing that his family was obliterated by the atomic bomb, Hayakawa comes to a strange peace within himself as he reaches out to the imprisoned children under his command. A fine film in all departments.

p, Nunnally Johnson; d, Jean Negulesco; w, Johnson (based on a book by Agnes Newton Keith); ph, Milton Krasner; m, Hugo Friedhofer; ed, Dorothy Spencer; md, Lionel Newman; art d, Lyle Wheeler, Leland Fuller; set d, Thomas Little, Fred J. Rode.

War   **(PR:O MPAA:NR)**

THREE CAME TO KILL*   (1960) 71m Premium Pictures/UA bw

Cameron Mitchell *(Marty Brill)*, John Lupton *(Hal Parker)*, Lyn Thomas *(June Parker)*, Steve Brodie *(Dave Harris)*, Paul Langton, Jan Arvan, Logan Field, King Calder, Jean Ingram, Tom McKee, Ron Foster, Jack Kenney, Shep Sanders, Cecil Weston, Frank Lackteen.

Professional assassins led by Mitchell invade flight controller Lupton's home and hold his family hostage in their attempt to assassinate a visiting Middle Eastern premier. Their plan is to have Lupton broadcast a coded message that will tell them which of the airplanes taking off from a Los Angeles airport is the premier's; they will then blast the plane with an incendiary bullet. Lupton must decide whether to save wife Thomas or to further international relations in this choppily edited thriller redolent of so many others.

p, Robert E. Kent; d, Edward L. Cahn; w, James B. Gordon (based on a story by Orville H. Hampton); ph, Maury Gertsman; m, Bert Shefter, Paul Sawtell; ed, Grant Whytock; art d, William Glasgow.

Crime   **(PR:C MPAA:NR)**

THREE CARD MONTE**   (1978, Can.) 91m Regenthall Saguenay c

Richard Gabourie *(Busher)*, Chris Langevin *(Toby)*, Lynne Cavanagh *(Nicki)*, Valerie Waburton *(Clorissa)*, John Rutter *(Walker)*, Tony Sheer *(Ryan)*, Sean McCann *(Car Salesman)*.

An all-too-familiar approach to the tale of a gambling drifter, Gabourie, who is on the run from a gang of thugs, and the 12-year-old boy he lets accompany him. An honest attempt which fails because of a shabby script and the amateurish acting of a nonprofessional cast. First-time director Rose's efforts brought THREE CARD MONTE 11 Canadian Film Award nominations, but that's not saying much when the country's top director is David Cronenberg.

d, Les Rose; w, Richard Gabourie; ph, Henry Fiks; m, Jim Caverhill, Paul Zaza; ed, Ron Wisman.

Drama   **(PR:C MPAA:NR)**

THREE CASES OF MURDER*** (1955, Brit.) 99m Wessex Associated
                                                            Artists bw

"In the Picture": Alan Badel *(Mr. X)*, Hugh Pryse *(Jarvis)*, John Salew *(Mr. Rooke)*, Leueen MacGrath *(Woman in the House)*, Eddie Byrne *(Snyder)*, Ann Hanslip *(The Girl)*, Harry Welchman *(Connoisseur)*, John Gregson *(Edgar Curtain)*, Elizabeth Sellars *(Elizabeth Grange)*, Jack Lambert *(Inspector Acheson)*, Philip Dale *(Sgt. Mallot)*, Colette Wilde *(Jane)*, Christina Forrest *(Susan)*, Maurice Kaufmann *(Pemberton)*, Alan Badel *(Owen)*, Helen Cherry *(Lady Mountdrago)*, Peter Burton *(Under Secretary for Foreign Affairs)*, Arthur Wontner *(Leader of the House)*, John Humphrey *(Private Secretary)*, David Horne *(Sir James)*, Andre Morell *(Dr. Audlin)*, Zena Marshall *(Beautiful Blonde)*, Evelyn Hall *(Lady Connemara)*.

A trio of gripping murder stories, each of which is fast-moving and admirably scripted. The first, "In the Picture", takes an art museum guide to a spooky old house which appears in one of the paintings, greeting him with a deranged taxidermist. "You Killed Elizabeth" is a straightforward crime whodunit about a pair of school chums both in love with the same girl. When she turns up dead, it's apparent that one of them is guilty. The best and final episode, "Lord Mountdrago", stars Orson Welles as the title character and is based on a story by W. Somerset Maugham. Welles destroys the career of a fellow Parliament member and is haunted by thoughts of retaliation.

p, Ian Dalrymple, Alexander Paal, Hugh Perceval; "In the Picture": d, Wendy Toye; w, Donald Wilson (based on a story by Roderick Wilkinson); "You Killed Elizabeth": d, David Eady; w, Sidney Carroll (based on a story by Brett Halliday); "Lord Mountdrago": d, George More O'Ferrell; w, Dalrymple (based on a story by W. Somerset Maugham); all sequences: ph, Georges Perinal; m, Doreen Carwithen; ed, Gerald Turney-Smith; md, Muir Mathieson; prod d, Paul Sheriff.

Crime   **(PR:A MPAA:NR)**

THREE CHEERS FOR LOVE*½   (1936) 65m PAR bw

Eleanore Whitney *(Skippy Dormant)*, Robert Cummings *(Jimmy Tuttle)*, William Frawley *(Milton Shakespeare)*, Roscoe Karns *(Doc Wilson)*, John Halliday *(Charles Dormant)*, Elizabeth Patterson *(Wilma Chester)*, Grace Bradley *(Eve Bronson)*, Olympe Bradna *(Frenchy)*, Louis DaPron *(Elmer)*, Veda Ann Borg *(Consuelo Dormant)*, Billy Lee *(Johnny)*, Irving Bacon *(Rider)*, Si Wells *(Winton)*.

Whitney is sent to an East Coast finishing school which, unknown to her, is run by an unemployed stage troupe. The chorus girls pose as students, and the rest of the show acts as faculty, but soon all are found out. When Whitney's Hollywood-producer father comes to see her "school" performance he is so delighted he signs them all to contracts. An interesting opportunity to see the ever-youthful Cummings as a song-and-dance man during this second year of his film career. The funniest expression in an otherwise pallid show-business screenplay is the motto of Halliday's Miracle movie studio: "If It's a Good Picture It's a Miracle." This picture was no miracle. Songs include: "Where Is My Heart?," "The Swing Tap," "Tap Your Feet," "Long Ago and Far Away" (Ralph Rainger, Leo Robin), "Learn to Be Lovely."

p, A. M. Botsford, M. A. Shauer; d, Ray McCarey; w, Barry Trivers (based on a story by George Marion, Jr.); ph, Harry Fischbeck; ed, Edward Dmytryk; ch, Danny Dare; m/l, Ralph Rainger, Leo Robin, Mack Gordon, Harry Revel.

Musical   **(PR:A MPAA:NR)**

THREE CHEERS FOR THE IRISH½**   (1940) 100m FN-WB bw

Priscilla Lane *(Maureen Casey)*, Thomas Mitchell *(Peter Casey)*, Dennis Morgan *(Angus Ferguson)*, Alan Hale *(Gallagher)*, Virginia Grey *(Patricia Casey)*, Irene Hervey *(Heloise Casey)*, William Lundigan *(Dennis Flaherty)*, Frank Jenks *(Ed McKean)*, Henry Armetta *(Tony)*, Morgan Conway *(Joe Niklas)*, Alec Craig *(Callagan)*, J. M. Kerrigan *(Scanlon)*, Cliff Clark *(Mars)*, William B. Davidson *(Police Commissioner)*, Joe King *(Police Captain)*, Ed Gargan *(Policeman)*, Walter Miller *(Sergeant)*, William Gould *(Desk Sergeant)*, Wade Boteler *(Lieutenant)*.

A homey Irish drama which casts Morgan as a young Scotsman who not only plans to marry Mitchell's daughter Lane, but also is intent on taking the job vacated by retired policeman Mitchell. Filled with typically Irish scenes of brogue-heavy dialog, hard-drinking Irishmen, and country romance. Veteran Italian stereotype Armetta steals all his scenes as the vendor who loses apples to the police in this multi-ethnic movie. Better than average thanks to a witty script. Includes the ditty "Dear Old Donegal."

p, Samuel Bischoff; d, Lloyd Bacon; w, Richard Macauley, Jerry Wald; ph, Charles Rosher; ed, William Holmes; cos, Milo Anderson.

Drama   (PR:A   MPAA:NR)

THREE COCKEYED SAILORS**½   (1940, Brit.) 86m EAL/ABF bw
(GB: SAILORS THREE)

Tommy Trinder (*Tommy Taylor*), Claude Hulbert (*Admiral*), Michael Wilding (*Johnny*), Carla Lehmann (*Jane*), Jeanne de Casalis (*Mrs. Pilkington*), James Hayter (*Hans*), Henry Hewitt (*Prof. Pilkington*), John Laurie (*McNab*), Harold Warrender (*Mate*), John Glyn Jones (*Best Man*), Julien Vedey (*Resident*), Manning Whiley (*German Commander*), Robert Rendel (*Captain*), Allan Jeayes (*Commander*), Alec Clunes (*Pilot*), Derek Elphinstone (*Observer*), Danny Green (*Night Club Bouncer*), E.V.H. Emmett (*Newsreel Commentator*), Brian Fitzpatrick, Eric Clavering, Hans [John] Wengraf, Victor Fairley, Olaf Olsen, Jonny Bloor.

Three WW II drunken British sailors in a South American port mistake a German battleship for their own and board it. To the credit of the Royal Navy, the sauced trio manage to capture the ship and the Germans on board. A funny comedy from the propagandistic Ealing studios.

p, Culley Forde; d, Walter Forde; w, Angus Macphail, John Dighton, Austin Melford; ph, Gunther Krampf; ed, Ray Pitt; md, Ernest Irving; art d, Wilfred Shingleton.

War/Comedy   (PR:A   MPAA:NR)

THREE COINS IN THE FOUNTAIN***   (1954) 101m FOX c

Clifton Webb (*Shadwell*), Dorothy McGuire (*Miss Francis*), Jean Peters (*Anita*), Louis Jourdan (*Prince Dino Di Cessi*), Maggie McNamara (*Maria*), Rossano Brazzi (*Georgio*), Maggie McNamara (*Maria*), Kathryn Givney (*Mrs. Burgoyne*), Cathleen Nesbitt (*Principessa*), Vincent Padula (*Dr. Martinelli*), Mario Siletti (*Bartender*), Alberto Morin (*Waiter*), Dino Bolognese (*Headwaiter*), Tony De Mario (*Venice Waiter*), Jack Mattis (*Consulate Clerk*), Willard Waterman (*Mr. Hoyt*), Zachary Yaconelli (*Ticket Agent*), Celia Lovsky (*Baroness*), Larry Arnold (*Waiter*), Select Restaurant, Renata Vanni (*Anna*), Grazia Narciso (*Louisa the Maid*), Gino Corrado (*Butler*), Iphigenie Castiglioni, Norma Varden (*Women*), Merry Anders (*Girl*), Charles La Torre (*Chauffeur*), Maurice Brierre (*Butler*).

A pleasant boy-meets-girl story (times three) that is more distinguished for the photography and the title song than for the predictable plot. This was the first CinemaScope picture ever made on location, and Rome and Venice never looked better. Peters, McGuire, and McNamara are a trio of American women living in Rome in a posh apartment. A legend states that if you throw a coin in the Fountain of Trevi and you want to come back to the Eternal City, your wish will be granted. McNamara is coming to work as a secretary and meets Italian prince Jourdan, whose mother, Nesbitt, is watching out that some gold digger doesn't snap him up. McNamara is naive but also sharp in some ways and eventually captures Jourdan as her own. McGuire is a quiet older woman who works as the secretary to Webb, an American writer who prefers living in Rome. She finally convinces Webb that she should be his life's companion and the final scene between the two, as she goes wading in the Trevi Fountain, is a lovely moment. Peters is a high-powered executive type who has had it with the board rooms and now wants to find a simpler existence. She falls for Brazzi–a wolf who haunts the Via Veneto–and by the time the movie is over, he's donned sheep's clothing, for real. That's about it for the story. There are the customary romantic complications but the conclusion is as easy to spot as an elephant at a mouse picnic. A few sexy (for the time) lines of dialog but a general feeling of traditional romance coated the tales. The same director, Negulesco, handled another movie about a trio of women on the make, HOW TO MARRY A MILLIONAIRE. The title song, crooned unbilled by Frank Sinatra, won the Oscar for Sammy Cahn and Jule Styne. Cinematographer Krasner also took an Oscar and the movie was nominated as Best Picture. It was later remade, sort of, as THE PLEASURE SEEKERS with Negulesco again directing. When producer Siegel acquired the Secondari novel, he asked Cahn if it were possible to write a tune using the words "Three Coins in the Fountain," which was hardly the usual sort of title for a tune. Cahn shrugged and is quoted as having said, "Hey, Sol, It makes no difference. I can write a song called "EH!" if you want it bad enough." The quote may be apocryphal, but Cahn is one of the wittiest men in movies, and chances are he said it or, at least, something like it. As for the movie itself, the best capsule description would be that it was a travelog with kissing.

p, Sol C. Siegel; d, Jean Negulesco; w, John Patrick (based on the novel by John H. Secondari); ph, Milton Krasner (CinemaScope, DeLuxe Color); m, Victor Young; ed, William Reynolds; art d, Lyle Wheeler, John De Cuir; cos, Dorothy Jeakins; m/l, title song, Jule Styne, Sammy Cahn (sung by Frank Sinatra).

Romance   Cas.   (PR:C   MPAA:NR)

THREE COMRADES****   (1938) 100m MGM bw

Robert Taylor (*Erich Lohkamp*), Margaret Sullavan (*Pat Hollmann*), Franchot Tone (*Otto Koster*), Robert Young (*Gottfried Lenz*), Guy Kibbee (*Alfons*), Lionel Atwill (*Franz Breuer*), Henry Hull (*Dr. Heinrich Becker*), George Zucco (*Dr. Plauten*), Charley Grapewin (*Local Doctor*), Monty Woolley (*Dr. Jaffe*), Spencer Charters (*Herr Schultz*), Sarah Padden (*Frau Schultz*), Ferdinand Munier (*Burgomaster*), Morgan Wallace (*Owner of Wrecked Car*), Priscilla Lawson (*Frau Brunner*), Esther Muir (*Frau Schmidt*), Walter Bonn (*Adjutant*), Edward McWade (*Major Domo*), Henry Brandon (*Man with Patch*), George Chandler, Ralph Bushman, Donald Haines (*Comics*), Claire McDowell (*Frau Zalewska*), Marjorie Main (*Old Woman*), Mitchell Lewis (*Boris*), E. Alyn Warren (*Bookstore Owner*), Ricca Allen (*Housekeeper*), Roger Converse (*Becker's Assistant*), Jessie Arnold (*Nurse*), Barbara Bedford (*Rita*), Alva Kellogg (*Singer*), Norman Willis (*Vogt Men*), William Haade (*Vogt Men*), Leonard Penn (*Tony*), Harvey Clark (*Bald-Headed Man*), George Offerman, Jr. (*Adolph*).

The flip side of the era covered by F. Scott Fitzgerald and Ernest Hemingway in the respective novels *Tender is the Night* and *The Sun Also Rises*–both later also brought to the screen–was author Remarque's international best-seller, here presented with a stellar cast and literary giant Fitzgerald as co-scripter. The scene is post-WW I Germany, a time and place of want, where pfennigs were useful only as paperweights and marks were borne to the marketplace by the wheelbarrow-load to be exchanged for a beefsteak. Three returning German soldiers– Taylor, Tone, and Young–are among the many war-wearied, newly homeless, nearly hopeless young men who travel from the trenches of France to their war-ravaged homeland. Prewar friends, the three reunite and decide to try to find a future in the prospectively emergent automobile market in the new republic to be. Pooling their meager resources, they set up a repair shop. Working with bits and pieces of salvaged wrecks, they put together an automobile of their own–which they affectionately dub "Heinrich"–and then proceed to scramble for business in the intensely competitive field. Motoring on a highway, the three engage in an informal race with the owner of a shiny new automobile, Atwill. Victorious, they stop for provender at an old mill which has been converted into an inn. There the vanquished Atwill joins them, saying "You wiped me off the map!" Admiring their scrapheap amalgam, Atwill introduces them to his motoring companion, the lovely Sullavan, and the travelers dine together. Taylor persuades Sullavan to give him her telephone number. He renews the acquaintance the following day, visiting her in the elegant apartment in which the absent Atwill had established the impoverished beauty, once a child of wealth. Sullavan ultimately forms the final member of what has now become a quartet of comrades. Reluctant to marry Taylor due to the tuberculosis which has ravaged her lungs (she had only recently emerged, uncured, from a sanitarium), Sullavan is at last persuaded by Taylor's two best friends to live what life is left her to the fullest. She and Taylor wed amidst the ominous setting of a Germany in dark transition, reeking with political unrest. The politicized Young is killed in a street riot; Sullavan, refusing treatment for her malady, hastens her own demise. The end sees survivors Tone and Taylor, joined by the spirits of their late companions (in double exposure), facing a most uncertain future. Sullavan is superb in this bleak drama, her throaty voice and striking appearance projecting at their very best (she was to get an Oscar nomination for her role, and was named the year's best actress by the New York Film Critics' association. Sullavan had been a bit difficult during filming; subscribing to a long-standing superstition, she refused to work until a rainfall occurred. She also protested that some of co-scripter Fitzgerald's dialog was literally unspeakable. Producer Mankiewicz agreed with his star and, with the help of other studio writers, rewrote and excised much of the script, to Fitzgerald's great disgruntlement. The bristling author–already angry about having had to work with a co-scripter–later came to refer to the producer as "Monkeybitch" for his temerity in modifying the labors of a perfectionist. In truth, Mankiewicz was himself a talented screenwriter, one who understood far better than the imperiously proud novelist the basic elements of a good visual presentation. The producer later stated "I . . . have been attacked as if I had spit on the American flag because . . . I rewrote some dialog by . . . Fitzgerald . . . . It was very literary, novelistic dialog that lacked all the qualities required for screen dialog. The latter must be 'spoken.' Scott Fitzgerald wrote very bad spoken dialog." The talented but hard-drinking Fitzgerald also wrote an incredibly hokey montage in the script: when Taylor telephones Sullavan for the first time, the central switchboard is seen in cutaway being operated by a winged angel, the call routed through St. Peter–robed and bearded–and, the connection made, the operator altering, becoming an obviously lustful satyr. Other scenes were cut from the film for less obvious reasons, including several which related to the upcoming Nazi domination of Germany. Some scenes were removed because of objections by the Breen Office–the industry's self-censorship group–and others were removed as a result of studio chief Louis B. Mayer's reluctance to offend the Germans lest he lose the export market. Although he continued to write screenplays–indeed, was signed by the studio at the enormously high salary (for the time) of $1,250 weekly—this was to be Fitzgerald's only *credited* screenwriting assignment. Taylor is unconvincing in his role, one that he had not wanted to play. Cinemogul Mayer had to persuade the actor that the part would lend him prestige and help to erase the pretty-boy image he had developed over the course of his career. The picture–though well directed by romance-drama specialist Borzage–is overlong, and only partly redeemed by Sullavan's splendid performance.

p, Joseph L. Mankiewicz; d, Frank Borzage; w, F. Scott Fitzgerald, Edward Paramore (based on the novel by Erich Maria Remarque); ph, Joseph Ruttenberg; m, Franz Waxman; ed, Frank Sullivan; art d, Cedric Gibbons, Paul Grosse; set d, Edwin B. Willis; m/l, "Ragtime College Jazz," "Mighty Forest," "Comrade Song," "How Can I Leave Thee," Chet Forrest, Waxman, Bob Wright.

Drama   **(PR:A   MPAA:NR)**

THREE CORNERED FATE*½   (1954, Brit.) 75m Danzigers/PAR bw

Ron Randell, Joyce Heron, Mark Dignam, Ian Whittaker, Maureen Swanson, Derek Bond, Joan Schofield, Jean Aubrey, Anthony Snell, Josephine Douglas, Helen Goss.

A trilogy of poorly handled tales of death. The first has a women trying to save her poisoned husband and son. The problem is that she only has enough antidote to save one of them. The second tale is of a stage producer and his fiancee whose idyllic life is upset when a jealous dancer comes between them. The fiancee then tries to kill the dancer but is inadvertently killed himself. The final story is about a young girl who falls in love with her music teacher. She hides herself in a chest of his and almost suffocates. All three episodes have possibilities but none deliver what is promised.

p, Edward J. Danziger, Harry Lee Danziger; d, David Macdonald; w, Paul Tabori, James Eastwood, Kate Barlay; ph, Jack Cox.

Drama   **(PR:A   MPAA:NR)**

THREE-CORNERED MOON***   (1933) 77m PAR bw

Claudette Colbert (Elizabeth Rimplegar), Richard Arlen (Dr. Alan Stevens), Mary Boland (Nellie Rimplegar), Wallace Ford (Kenneth Rimplegar), Lyda Roberti (Jenny), Tom Brown (Eddie Rimplegar), Joan Marsh (Kitty), Hardie Albright (Ronald), William Bakewell (Douglas Rimplegar), Sam Hardy (Hawkins), Nick Thompson (Apple Peddler), John M. Sullivan (Briggs), Fred Santley (Clerk), Margaret Armstrong (Mrs. Johnson), Charlotte Merriam (Gracie), Joseph Sawyer (Swimming Pool Director), Leonid Kinskey (Interpreter), George Le Guerre (Call Boy), Jack Clark (Stage Director/Joe Willis), Elliott Nugent (Broker), Clara Blandick (Landlady), Edward Gargan (Mike), Sam Godfrey (Albert).

A wildly funny domestic comedy which is often credited with being the first to portray a screwball family. Boland is mom Rimplegar, who makes the mistake of losing the family fortune on worthless mining stock during the Great Depression. Cooped up in a Brooklyn home which they can't sell, the Rimplegars–Colbert, the bright daughter; Ford, the law student; Bakewell, the aspiring actor–endlessly get on each other's nerves. Colbert, slated to marry struggling writer Albright, instead weds doctor Arlen and gets the family out of its predicament. Full of laughs and knee-slapping situations.

p, B. P. Schulberg; d, Elliott Nugent; w, S. K. Lauren, Ray Harris (based on a play by Gertrude Tonkonogy); ph, Leon Shamroy; cos, Travis Banton; m/l, Leo Robin, Ralph Rainger.

Comedy   **(PR:A   MPAA:NR)**

THREE CRAZY LEGIONNAIRES, THE
(SEE: THREE LEGIONNAIRES, THE, 1936)

THREE CROOKED MEN**   (1958, Brit.) 71m Danzigers/PAR bw

Gordon Jackson (Don Wescott), Sarah Lawson (May Wescott), Warren Mitchell (Prinn), Philip Saville (Seppy), Michael Mellinger (Vince), Eric Pohlmann (Masters), Kenneth Edwards (Inspector Wheeler), Arnold Bell (Mr. Brady), Alex Gallier, Michael Allinson, Peter Bathurst, Len Sharp, Frank Sieman, Noel Dyson.

A trio of crooks breaks into Jackson's store with the intent of robbing a neighboring bank by entering through the shared wall. Jackson unexpectedly returns to his store and is held captive by the crooks. When passerby Mitchell attempts to help Jackson, he, too, is captured. The police intervene and round up the crooks, but not without first mistaking Jackson and Mitchell for the culprits.

p, Edward J. Danziger, Harry Lee Danziger; d, Ernest Morris; w, Brian Clemens, Eldon Howard; ph, Jimmy Wilson.

Crime   **(PR:A   MPAA:NR)**

THREE DARING DAUGHTERS**½   (1948) 115m MGM c (GB: THE BIRDS AND THE BEES)

Jeanette MacDonald (Louise Rayton Morgan), Jose Iturbi (Himself), Jane Powell (Tess Morgan), Edward Arnold (Robert Nelson), Harry Davenport (Dr. Cannon), Moyna MacGill (Mrs. Smith), Mary Eleanor Donahue (Alix Morgan), Ann E. Todd (Ilka Morgan), Tom Helmore (Michael Pemberton), Kathryn Card (Jonesy), Amparo Iturbi (Herself), Larry Adler (Himself), Dorothy Porter (Specialty Singer), Thurston Hall (Mr. Howard), Nan

Bennett (Toney Tiger), Charles Coleman, Ian Wolfe (Butlers), Stephen Hero (Ribs), Leon Belasco (Ship's Orchestra Leader), Virginia Brissac (Miss Drake), Frank Pershing, Bill Lewin, Thomas E. Breen (Stewards), William Forrest (Ship's Captain), Joanee Wayne (Telephone Operator), Don Avalier (Headwaiter), Diane Lee Stewart, Dorita Pallais, Nina Bara, Phyllis Gaffeo, Conchita Lamus (Singers), Jack Lipson (Fat Man on Street), Anita Aros, Estellita Zarco, Connie Mintoya, Aldana Rios (Telephone Operators), Wheaton Chambers (Stage Manager), Ed Peil, Sr (Waiter), Joan Valerie (Hostess), Brick Sullivan (Taxi Driver), Amparo Ballester (Cigarette Girl), David Cota (Cuban Bellboy).

Deserted by her foreign-correspondent husband, and subsequently divorced, the multiparous MacDonald supports herself and her three daughters as editor of a high-fashion magazine. When she faints and almost misses oldest daughter Powell's graduation ceremony, MacDonald is counseled by her boss, Hall, and a doctor, Davenport, to take a vacation cruise by herself. Daughters Powell, Donahue, and Todd enthusiastically agree, conspiring to return their errant father to the scene during this maternal hiatus. The siblings go to visit newspaper publisher Arnold, "the 13th richest man in the world," and charm him into agreeing to return the rascal, who is in his employ. Meanwhile, mother MacDonald has met and married concert pianist Iturbi in a shipboard romance. The espoused pair agree that they will break the news of their nuptials gently to MacDonald's brood upon their return to New York City. On his initial visit to MacDonald's posh penthouse apartment, Iturbi inadvertently finds himself solo with the siblings. He gulls them into thinking he is auditioning Powell for a singing career. Ultimately, the girls discover that Iturbi is their new foster father and drive a wedge between him and his bride. With the help of little Donahue and millionaire Arnold, Iturbi and MacDonald are reunited, and make their peace with MacDonald's other two daughters. Producer Pasternak convinced MacDonald to return to the screen for this, her next-to-last film, after a four-year absence. In plot construction, the picture reprises Pasternak's first production effort, Universal's THREE SMART GIRLS (1937), which made a star of Deanna Durbin. Wilcox's direction is well-paced and the film has some witty dialog. The main thing is the music, though. MacDonald was in good voice, and Powell matched her in range and talent. Iturbi did well at the keyboard, especially in the piano duets with his real-life sister Amparo. Classical harmonica player Adler was a standout. Critics of the time thought that young Donahue and Todd (who used a middle initial to distinguish herself from the British actress) sang fairly well, apparently failing to realize that their voices had been dubbed by, respectively, Beverly Jean Garbo and Pat Hyatt. Outstanding in support roles were Card as MacDonald's acerbic housekeeper and MacGill–actress Angela Lansbury's mother–as her talkative, name-dropping, celebrity collector shipboard acquaintance. The movie made money despite being termed "morally objectionable" by the Catholic Legion of Decency, which held that it "tended to justify as well as accept the respectability of divorce." The seemingly endless cavalcade of musical numbers and songs includes: "Route 66" (Bobby Troup), "The Dickey Bird Song" (Sammy Fain, Howard Dietz), "Alma Mater" (Georgie Stoll, Billy Katz), "Fleurette" (Victor Herbert, Ralph Freed), "Passepied" (Leo Delibes, Princess Anna Eristoff), "Where There's Love" (Earl Brent, based on the waltz from "Der Rosenkavalier" by Richard Strauss), "Ritual Fire Dance (El Amor Brujo)" (Manuel De Falla), "You Made Me Love You" (Joseph McCarthy, James V. Monaco), "Happy Birthday" (Patty Smith Hill, Mildred J. Hill), "Je Veux Vivre" (Gounod, from "Romeo And Juliet"), "Liebestraum" (Franz Liszt), "Hungarian Fantasy" (Liszt), "Sweethearts" (Victor Herbert, Bob Wright, Chet Forrest), "Allegro Appassionato, Opus 10" (Saint-Saens), "Springtide, Opus 43, no. 6" (Edvard Grieg, Earl Brent), Mozart's "Piano Sonata No. 11 in A," Tchaikovsky's "Fourth Symphony," Enesco's "Rumanian Rhapsody."

p, Joe Pasternak; d, Fred M. Wilcox; w, Albert Mannheimer, Frederick Kohner, Sonya Levien, John Meehan (based on the play "The Bees and the Flowers" by Kohner and Albert Manning); ph, Ray June (Technicolor); ed, Adrienne Fazan; md, George Stoll; art d, Cedric Gibbons, Preston Ames; set d, Edwin B. Willis, Arthur Krams; cos, Irene, Shirley Barker; makeup, Jack Dawn.

Musical   **(PR:A   MPAA:NR)**

THREE DAYS AND A CHILD   (SEE: NOT MINE TO LOVE, 1969, Israel)

THREE DAYS OF THE CONDOR***½
(1975) 117m PAR-Wildwood/PAR c

Robert Redford (Joe Turner), Faye Dunaway (Kathy Hale), Cliff Robertson (Higgins), Max von Sydow (Joubert), John Houseman (Mr. Wabash), Addison Powell (Atwood), Walter McGinn (Sam Barber), Tina Chen (Janice), Michael Kane (Wicks), Don McHenry (Dr. Lappe), Michael Miller (Fowler), Jess Osuna (Mitchell), Dino Narizzano (Thomas), Helen Stenborg (Mrs. Russell), Patrick Gorman (Martin), Hansford Rowe, Jr (Jennings), Carlin Glynn (Mae Barber), Hank Garrett (Mailman), Arthur French (Messenger), Jay Devlin (Tall Thin Man), Frank Savino (Jimmy), Robert Phalen (Newberry), John Randolph Jones (Beefy Man), Garrison Phillips (Hutton), Lee Steele (Heidegger), Ed Crowley (Ordinance Man), John Connell (TV Reporter), Norman Bush (Alice Lieutenant), James Keane (Store Clerk), Ed Setrakian (Customer), Myron Natwick, Michael Prince (Civilians), Carol Gustafson (Landlady), Sal Schillizi (Locksmith), David Bowman (Telephone

Worker), Eileen Gordon *(CIA Receptionist)*, Robert Dahdah *(Santa Claus)*, Steve Bonino, Jennifer Rose, David Allen, Glenn Ferguson, Paul Dwyer *(Kids)*, Marian Swan, Dorothi Fox *(Nurses)*, Ernest Harden, Jr *(Teenager)*, Harmon Williams *(CIA Agent)*.

A CIA thriller that grossed more than $20 million and again proved the point that "we have met the enemy, and he is *us*!" Redford is the bookish and bespectacled reader for what appears to be the Literary Historical Society but is really a CIA front in a brownstone in Manhattan. Redford and his coworkers spend their time reading plots of mysteries and synopsizing them to see if they can use any of the fictitious plots and ploys in CIA operations so that life can imitate art. Redford has made a discovery in some data and he thinks it may be important but is told by his superiors that he's wrong. He goes out to get lunch for the others (it's his turn) and while he's picking up the food, killers armed with automatic weapons enter the building and massacre everyone there. Redford fears that he may be next so he goes to a phone booth away from the bloody site and calls headquarters, identifying himself by his code name, "Condor." The man in charge in New York is Robertson. He tells Redford to wait at the Ansonia Hotel, where he will be taken in out of the "cold." Redford is jumpy and not sure that his life is safe so Robertson says that Redford's pal, McGinn, will be there to verify that the agent, Kane, is a legitimate representative for "The Company." McGinn and Kane arrive in the alley behind the venerable hotel and all seems well until Kane pulls a gun and tries to shoot Redford, killing McGinn in the process. Redford shoots and wounds Kane, then flees. He knows that his own apartment is unsafe and he has nowhere to turn. Redford enters a clothing store and tries to lose himself, looking over his shoulder at every turn. In the store, he meets photographer Dunaway, a woman who specializes in grim, bleak pictures like the late Diane Arbus. Redford kidnaps her (although she is more fascinated than frightened by this) and they go to her residence. Simultaneously, Robertson is talking with his bosses, including Houseman, and they all try to fathom why the workers were killed and why Redford was spared, only to have shot Kane and killed his pal McGinn. No one can figure out this turn of events but after the meeting, we are given the opportunity to see that CIA man Powell is not what he appears to be as he contacts von Sydow, the contract killer who oversaw the multiple slayings earlier. Powell says that Redford and Kane must be eliminated and the stoical von Sydow accepts the assignment. In Dunaway's apartment, Redford believes he can't trust her, so he ties and gags the photographer (she is still not offering more than token resistance) in order for him to be able to leave the place and pay a call on the widow of McGinn, Glynn. Von Sydow's brilliant mind has foreseen Redford's decision to see the widow and he is at the building. When Redford gets into an elevator after talking to the bereaved woman, von Sydow is in there with him. Redford smells "professional" on von Sydow and escapes from him when other people are in the lobby. He races away in Dunaway's auto, but not before von Sydow notes the license plates. From there, it's easy for von Sydow to trace Redford's whereabouts. Redford returns to the apartment and he and Dunaway make love. The next morning, Garrett, posing as a mailman, comes to deliver a package. Redford spots the man's shoes as not being standard Post Office wear and there's a pitched battle that wrecks the apartment. It ends when Redford kills Garrett. (In real life, that would have been unlikely as Garrett's character is that of a trained killer and Redford's that of an intellectual. Garrett, by the way, is a one-time professional boxer who fought under his real name, Hank Greenberg, in and around New York before becoming an actor.) Redford peruses Garrett's pockets and finds a slip of paper connecting Kane to this. But where is Kane? He's disappeared as effectively as Redford. Redford thinks that the only way he can get to the bottom of things is by going to the source, Robertson. Enlisting Dunaway's assistance, he goes to Robertson's office and uses a ruse to get him out of the building and down to the street where he is forced into Dunaway's car by the gun in Redford's fist. Robertson claims he knows nothing of the killings other than he thinks they have something to do with the fact that one of the many novels they were analyzing at the cover facility was translated into two languages, Dutch and Arabic, and no other tongues. This makes no sense to Redford, who then suggests that Robertson ask Kane why he took a shot at him. Robertson admits that Kane is dead. Robertson says that Kane and von Sydow were in some sort of alliance, perhaps working for the other side. Garrett's body also produced a hotel key. Redford traces von Sydow to the hotel, gets into the inn's switchboard, and taps von Sydow's phone as the man is speaking to Powell in Washington. Redford has no idea of who Powell is or why von Sydow is in contact with him. Redford leaves Dunaway and travels to Washington, breaks into Powell's home, and forces the latter to tell the truth. Powell is a CIA man who has been operating his own undercover unit inside "The Company" with an eye toward helping the U.S. in its relations with the OPEC countries. This was not an authorized activity and when Redford's early inquiry looked as though it would break open the illegal unit, the entire section, including Redford, had to be "terminated with extreme prejudice." After Powell spills the beans, von Sydow appears and kills Powell, explaining that he now works for the CIA (they hired him away from Powell). Redford expects to be shot next, but von Sydow won't do it; he has no orders to do that, and he is not a craven killer, just an employee. Von Sydow is downright pleasant as he and Redford talk about what's happened. Redford can't believe the calm of this killer and asks him if he will now stay in the U.S. Von Sydow shakes his head; he much prefers Europe and the old ways, rather than the plastic and chrome of the U.S. Then he gives Redford a lift from Powell's suburban mansion into the city. Von Sydow wonders if Redford might be

interested in staying with the CIA in a more active capacity. The trail of bodies Redford's left behind indicates that he might have a penchant for "wet work" (which is what the private-sector killers refer to when discussing anything that requires blood to be shed). Redford doesn't think so, and von Sydow warns him that he is marked for death. It'll happen when he least expects it. Someone he trusts will ask him to get into a car. It will all seem honest enough, but the next thing he knows, he'll be garrotted or injected or shot. Back in New York, Redford contacts Robertson (who says he is thrilled to hear from him and that now everything is just fine and he can go back to his old job) and asks for a meeting. Redford is on a New York street and Robertson arrives in a car with a couple of other guys, smiling and friendly, just as von Sydow predicted. Redford tells Robertson to get out of the car and take a walk with him. Robertson has no choice. They stroll along and Redford says that he's given the entire story to the *New York Times*. Robertson is disappointed by that and thinks Redford may have done himself and his country a disservice by compromising the CIA. Redford says he had to do it and Robertson leaves him with the lingering warning that the newspaper just may *not* print it. Based on the novel "Six Days of the Condor" (Hollywood is always trying to undercut), it's basically an Alfred Hitchcock movie in that "an innocent man is accused of a crime he doesn't commit, finds woman who thinks he's guilty, ultimately convinces her he isn't, then must get to another man who can clear him but that man turns out to be the brains behind the plot." (We have just given you the basic story of at least eight Hitchcock movies plus this one.) Writer Semple did the first draft which was rewritten by Rayfiel, who had worked with director Pollack and Redford on JEREMIAH JOHNSON and THE WAY WE WERE, receiving a credit on neither. Redford was preparing ALL THE PRESIDENT'S MEN while shooting this picture, but the division of his time didn't seem to hurt his solid performance. While the film was being made, there was some question as to the authenticity of the plot, but suddenly a raft of sensational news items began coming out of Washington regarding illegal wiretaps, surveillance, and killings motivated by political expediency. The movie became more and more believable. THREE DAYS OF THE CONDOR is a technically excellent movie that purports to "say" something but is, in the end, a "gee whiz" chase film with a distinguished cast that elevates it above the status of programmer. Blood and foul language give it a questionable rating for anyone under the age of consent.

p, Stanley Schneider; d, Sydney Pollack; w, Lorenzo Semple, Jr., David Rayfiel (based on the novel *Six Days of the Condor* by James Grady); ph, Owen Roizman (Panavision, Technicolor); m, Dave Grusin; ed, Frederick Steinkamp, Don Guidice; prod d, Stephen Grimes; art d, Gene Rudolf; set d, George De Titta; cos, Joseph C. Aulisi; spec eff, Augie Lohman.

Drama   **Cas.**   **(PR:C-O   MPAA:R)**

THREE DAYS OF VIKTOR TSCHERNIKOFF**
                (1968, USSR) 115m Central Studio Maxim Gorki Production bw

S. Koralkow *(Victor Tschernikoff)*, W. Wladimirowa, A. Tschernow, G. Saibulin, D. Tschukowski, L. Prysonow.

Three days in the life of title character Koralkow are examined as we see him go about his daily routine as a Moscow factory worker. He eventually gets himself in trouble with the law, much to the consternation of his mother. Overlong and hampered by worker slogans, but Koralkow's performance is exceptional.

d, Mark Ossepijan; w, J. Grigorojew; ph, M. Jakowitsch; m, A. Rybnikow.

Drama   **(PR:C   MPAA:NR)**

THREE DESPERATE MEN**   (1951) 71m Lippert bw

Preston Foster *(Tom Denton)*, Jim Davis *(Fred Denton)*, Virginia Grey *(Laura Brock)*, Ross Latimer *(Matt Denton)*, William Haade *(Bill Devlin)*, Monte Blue *(Pete Coleman)*, Sid Melton *(Connors)*, Rory Mallinson *(Ed Larkin)*, John Brown *(Fairwether)*, Margaret Seddon *(Mrs. Denton)*, House Peters, Jr *(Dick Cable)*, Anthony Jochim *(Farmer)*, Joel Newfield *(George Denton)*, Lee Bennett *(Dick Patten)*, Steve Belmont *(Jones)*, Carol Henry *(Deputy Smith)*, Kermit Maynard *(Guard)*, Bert Dillard *(Hangman)*, Bill Bailey *(Buckboard Driver)*, Milton Kibbee *(Cashier)*, Gene Randall *(Clerk)*.

Foster, Davis, and Latimer are the three men of the title, all brothers, who are running from the law. After one is framed for a murder and robbery he didn't commit and tossed in jail, the other two free him and begin a rampage of robbery and murder. The law finally catches up to them in their hometown, slaughtering the trio.

p, Sigmund Neufeld; d, Sam Newfield; w, Orville Hampton; ph, Jack Greenhalgh; m, Albert Glasser; ed, Carl Pierson; md, Glasser.

Crime   **(PR:A   MPAA:NR)**

THREE DOLLS FROM HONG KONG*½   (1966, Jap.) 98m Toho c
        (ONEICHAN MAKARI TORU; AKA: THREE DOLLS GO TO HONG
                                                            KONG)

Reiko Dan *(Punch)*, Sonomi Nakajima *(Pinch)*, Noriko Shigeyama *(Senti)*, Tatsuya Ebara *(Tatsuo Maebara)*, Akira Kubo *(Hiroshi Kubota)*, Shinji Yamada *(Hideo Kiyokawa)*.

In this comedy, Dan plays a reporter for a weekly magazine whose best friend, Shigeyama, is a dancer. Dan helps her obtain a booking for an international tour whose first play date is in Hong Kong. Just before they are due to leave, they are joined by their wealthy friend, Nakajima, who plans to travel with them, even though she has no passport or ticket. They hide Nakajima in their suitcase and smuggle her past customs. While in Hong Kong, they are approached by a Chinese man who passes himself off as a wealthy gentleman, when in reality he is only a wealthy man's secretary. He promises to help them in Hong Kong, but they soon find out his true identity when they discover that Shigeyama's promoter has vanished with all her money. During Shigeyama's performance, she is spotted by the secretary's boss, who propositions her after the show and invites her to become his 13th concubine. Dan comes to the rescue of her dancer friend by threatening the wealthy man with exposure in her magazine unl ess he allows his son to marry the woman he loves, a nightclub singer. Ending has the three friends returning to Japan after their parents have notified the authorities that they are missing. Originally released in 1959.

p, Sanezumi Fujimoto; d, Toshio Sugie; w, Ryozo Kasahara; ph, Taiichi Kankura (Tohoscope, Eastmancolor); m, Yoshiyuki Kozu.

Comedy   **(PR:C MPAA:NR)**

THREE DOLLS GO TO HONG KONG
      (SEE: THREE DOLLS FROM HONG KONG, 1966, Jap.)

THREE FABLES OF LOVE**   (1963, Fr./Ital./Span.) 76m Madeleine Franco London-Ajace Cinematografica-Hispamer/Janus bw (LES QUATRES VERITES; LE QUATTRO VERITA; LAS CUATRO VERDADES)

"The Tortoise and the Hare": Monica Vitti (Madeleine), Sylva Koscina (Mia), Rossano Brazzi (Leo), Alessandro Blasetti, Gianrico Tedeschi, "The Fox and the Crow": Michel Serrault (Mr. Crow, [Albert]), Jean Poiret (Mr. Fox, [Marcel]), Anna Karina (Colombe), "Two Pigeons": Leslie Caron (Annie), Charles Aznavour (Charles), Raymond Bussieres.

A trilogy of romantic tales, the first ("The Tortoise and the Hare") of which stars Vitti as a wife determined to get her husband back, upsetting his vacation with his mistress to do so. The second episode, "The Fox and the Crow," has Karina as the object of her neighbor's love, who hopes to take her away from her husband and succeeds while at a picnic. "Two Pigeons" has Caron preparing to leave on a vacation when she gets herself locked in her room. Aznavour attempts to help her out but gets himself locked in also, paving the way for a weekend love affair between the two. A fourth episode, "La Mort et le Bucheron," was originally included.

p, Gilbert de Goldschmidt; w, (based on an idea by Frederic Grendel, Herve Bromberger); m, Georges Garvarentz, Charles Aznavour; "The Tortoise and the Hare": d, Alessandro Blasetti; w, Suso Cecchi D'Amico, Blasetti (based on the fable "Le Lievre et la Tortue" by Jean de La Fontaine); ph, Carl o Di Palma; ed, Nino Baragli; "The Fox and the Crow": d, Bromberger; w, Grendel, Bromberger (based on the fable "Le Corbeau et le Renard" by de La Fontaine); ph, Jacques Mercanton; ed, Borys Lewin; "Two Pigeons": d&w, Rene Clair; (based on the fable "Les Deux Pigeons": by de La Fontaine); ph, Armand Thirard; ed, Denise Natot; art d, Leom Barsacq.

Romance   **(PR:C MPAA:NR)**

THREE FACES EAST**½   (1930) 71m WB bw

Constance Bennett (Frances Hawtree/Z-1), Erich von Stroheim (Valdar/Schiller Blecher), Anthony Bushell (Capt. Arthur Chamberlain), William Courtenay (Mr. Yates), Crauford Kent (Gen. Hewlett), Charlotte Walker (Lady Catherine Chamberlain), William Holden (Sir Winston Chamberlain), William von Bricken (Capt. Kugler), Ulrich Haupt (Colonel), Paul Panzer ("Kirsch" the Decoy).

A remake of the 1926 silent, THREE FACES EAST cast von Stroheim as a German spy living as a butler in the English household of Holden. His cover is blown by Bennett, a British spy who is sent to stop his operation, eventually shooting him in the back. This was only Stroheim's second acting role after his demise as a director, appearing previously in THE GREAT GABBO. With this picture, however, Stroheim was given the okay to suggest changes in the script, an idea that tasted bitter in the mouths of director Del Ruth and star Bennett. Both wanted nothing to do with the one-time great director, with Bennett loudly voicing her protests and screaming for mouthwash after shooting kissing scenes with Stroheim. While the dislike for Stroheim was growing stronger, prospects for directorial work still lingered, but only the botched WALKING DOWN BROADWAY/HELLO SISTER! would make it to the screen. Filmed again in 1940 as BRITISH INTELLIGENCE starring Boris Karloff.

p, Darryl F. Zanuck; d, Roy Del Ruth; w, Oliver H.P. Garrett, Arthur Caesar (based on the play by Anthony Paul Kelly); ph, Chick McGill; ed, William Holmes.

Spy Drama   **(PR:A MPAA:NR)**

THREE FACES OF A WOMAN**   (1965, Ital.) 120m DD c (I TRE VOLTI)

"The Screen Test": Soraya (Princess Soraya), Ivano Davoli (Reporter), Giorgio Sartarelli (Photographer), Piero Tosi (Designer), Ralph Serpe (American Producer), "Famous Lovers": Soraya (Linda), Richard Harris (Robert), Esmeralda Ruspoli (Hedda), Jose de Villalonga (Rudolph), "Latin Lover": Soraya (Mrs. Melville), Alberto Sordi (Armando Tucci), Goffredo Alessandrini (Agency Manager), Renato Tagliani, Alberto Giubilo (TV Reporters).

Former empress Soraya is cast in three episodes, the first, "The Screen Test," being viewed as a prolog to the other two. Directed by Antonioni, it presents a view of Soraya on the night of her screen test for this picture. Reportedly, however, "The Screen Test" was struck from the release print and the negative destroyed. "Famous Lovers" casts Soraya as a married woman having an affair with a struggling writer, Harris. The final episode has her playing an executive on a trip to Rome, who is entertained by Sordi, a gigolo hired by her travel agency.

"The Screen Test": d&w, Michelangelo Antonioni; ph, Carlo Di Palma (Techniscope, Technicolor); ed, Eraldo da Roma; "Famous Lovers": d, Mauro Bolognini; w, Tullio Pinelli, Clive Exton; ph, Otello Martelli (Techniscope, Technicolor); ed, Nino Baragli; "Latin Lover": d, Franco Indovina; w, Indovina, Alberto Sordi, Rodolfo Sonego; ph, Martelli (Techniscope, Technicolor); ed, Baragli.

Drama   **(PR:C MPAA:NR)**

THREE FACES OF EVE, THE***½   (1957) 91m FOX bw

Joanne Woodward (Eve), David Wayne (Ralph White), Lee J. Cobb (Dr. Luther), Edwin Jerome (Dr. Day), Alena Murray (Secretary), Nancy Kulp (Mrs. Black), Douglas Spencer (Mr. Black), Terry Ann Ross (Bonnie), Ken Scott (Earl), Mimi Gibson (Eve, Age 8), , Alistair Cooke (Narrator).

Joanne Woodward's Oscar-winning performance was a tour de force as she had to play three different people, with enough separation in the characterizations to make the audience believe she was a woman with a trio of personalities bubbling inside her. Woodward is married to Wayne, an insensitive clod. She is emotionally disturbed, has headaches, forgets things, and decides she needs the professional help of a psychiatrist, although Wayne thinks she's faking it. At first, Cobb, the doctor, gives her the usual answers about getting more rest, trying to calm down, etc. Woodward goes home to Wayne and her daughter, Ross, but her mental woes continue. She returns to Cobb's office later, this time with a new personality. Instead of the unsure housewife, she is suddenly a sexual, loose woman with an attitude of total irresponsibility. She denies being the mother of Ross and lives for hedonistic pleasure. Wayne is rapidly getting disgusted with Woodward but Cobb is intrigued as he sees the two women almost side by side, the personalities switching while she's in his presence. Eventually, a third person emerges and this one seems to be a combination of the other two in that she is a well-balanced woman who speaks in a different pattern. Whereas the first two talk in a southern dialect, this one sounds as though she went to Wesleyan or Cornell and graduated summa cum laude. Cobb uses hypnotic techniques on Woodward and is able to conjure up each "face" by merely suggesting that she step forward. When Wayne leaves Woodward the drab housewife attempts to kill herself, but is saved when her second persona comes out and rescues her. Cobb continues his probing and learns that when she was just eight years old (played by Gibson) her mother, Kulp, made the little child kiss her late grandmother good-bye just before the old woman was buried. That incident affected Woodward's mind in a way that is never quite explained. Cobb's analysis bears fruit and Woodward is cured, then goes off to marry her new beau, Scott. It's an interesting psychological tale that is not without humor, much of which is supplied by the witty narration of Cooke. Professionals in the field may find it more intriguing than a lay audience. Another film, LIZZIE, came out just prior to this one but did not have the benefit of Woodward's talents. Years later, Sally Field did the TV movie SYBIL in which she had even more personalities. (In TV, bigger is better.) Based on a true story, as documented by the psychiatrists who treated the woman in real life. Although there are several other actors in the movie, it's basically a two-character piece between Woodward and Cobb, and would have probably made a very good play. Cinematically, it's lacking on several levels. Wayne, a marvelous actor, was apparently directed to play his role for laughs in order to take the edge off Woodward's dramatics. The mixture of styles works against the ultimate outcome.

p,d&w, Nunnally Johnson (based on a book by Corbett H. Thigpen, M.D., H ervey M. Cleckley, M.D.); ph, Stanley Cortez; m, Robert Emmett Dolan; ed, Marjorie Fowler; art d, Lyle Wheeler, Herman A. Blumenthal; set d, Walter M. Scott, Eli Benneche; cos, Renie.

Drama   **Cas.**   **(PR:A-C MPAA:NR)**

THREE FACES OF SIN*½   (1963, Fr./Ital.) 95m Films Caravelle-S.N.E. GAU-Ultra Este-Cameo International bw (LE PUITS AUX TROIS VERITES; IL POZZO DELLE TRE VERITA; AKA: TROIS VERITES; THREE SINNERS)

Michele Morgan (Renee Plege), Jean-Claude Brialy (Laurent), Catherine Spaak (Daniele Plege), Scilla Gabel (Rossana), Franco Fabrizi (Guerbois),

Michel Etcheverry (Inspector), Jacques-Henri Duval (Man), Alberto Farnese, Milton Reid, Marco Tulli.

Brialy is a self-centered painter who gets involved first with an antique dealer, Morgan, then marries her daughter. He then drops both for a stripper. His wife, Spaak, is found dead after a violent argument has broken out between her and Brialy, causing both him and her mother to feel responsible, even though the police list her death as a suicide.

p, Irenee Leriche; d, Francoise Villiers; w, Remo Forlani, Henri Jeanson, Jean Canolle, Villiers (based on the novel by Jean Jacques Gautier); ph, Jacques Robin; m, Maurice Jarre; ed, Christian Gaudin; art d, Francois de Lamothe.

Drama (PR:O MPAA:NR)

THREE FACES WEST½ (1940) 79m REP bw (AKA: THE REFUGEE)

John Wayne (John Phillips), Charles Coburn (Dr. Braun), Sigrid Gurie (Leni Braun), Spencer Charters (Dr. "Nunk" Atterbury, Veterinarian), Roland Varno (Dr. Eric Von Scherer), Trevor Bardette (Clem Higgins), Helen MacKellar (Mrs. Welles), Sonny Bupp (Billy Welles), Wade Boteler (Harris), Russell Simpson (Minister), Charles Waldron (Dr. Thorpe), Wendell Niles (Radio Announcer), Dewey Robinson (Bartender).

An interesting John Wayne picture which has him falling in love with Gurie, the daughter of Coburn, a Viennese surgeon. Coburn and Gurie have come to the States to set up a practice, choosing a Dust Bowl community as their home. Gurie turns down Wayne's proposal of marriage, explaining that she is still in love with the memory of Varno, her Austrian lover who died for her. When she receives word that Varno is still alive and is coming to the States, she arranges a trip to Oregon to meet him. He is not the same man she loved, however, spouting off Nazi doctrines and wishing for her to come back to the fatherland. She returns to the Dust Bowl instead, marries Wayne, and helps her father set up a new community in Oregon.

p, Sol C. Siegel; d, Bernard Vorhaus; w, F. Hugh Herbert, Joseph Moncure March, Samuel Ornitz, Doris Anderson; ph, John Alton; m, Victor Young; ed, William Morgan; art d, John Victor MacKay; cos, Adele Palmer.

Western/Romance Cas. (PR:A MPAA:NR)

THREE FOR BEDROOM C* (1952) 74m Brenco/WB c

Gloria Swanson (Ann Haven), James Warren (Oli J. Thrumm), Fred Clark (Johnny Piz er), Hans Conried (Jack Bleck), Steve Brodie (Conde Marlow), Janine Perreau (Barbara), Ernest Anderson (Fred Johnson), Margaret Dumont (Mrs. Hawthorne).

Pure malarkey. And made even more malarkeian by the fact that Swanson had just come off one of her greatest roles in SUNSET BOULEVARD. This was a dreadful selection for the 52-year-old star as a follow-up to her "Norma Desmond" role. Swanson is again a movie star. She's going from New York to Hollywood aboard a cross-country train with her young daughter, Perreau, a precocious child who should have been gagged. The studio wants Swanson back right away to star in a film that she doesn't much care about. She and Perreau have no train reservation and inadvertently occupy the compartment assigned to Warren, a Harvard professor who is shy and scholarly and specializes in biochemistry. Warren gets on board in Chicago and there is no other compartment available. Also on the train are Conried, the studio's nervous press agent and Clark, Swanson's long-suffering agent. Brodie plays a part not unlike the rage of the day, Marlon Brando. Swanson manages to convince Warren that she and Perreau need the compartment and he sleeps in a jerry-built bed in the train car's men's room. Margaret Dumont is also around, but without the antics of the Marx Brothers, she hardly registers. After a very few ordinary complications, Warren and Swanson wind up in a clinch by the time they reach Pasadena. Swanson herself designed the clothes she wore and they are as bad as the rest of the movie. The story came from a novel by a renowned musical figure, the man who ran Columbia Records for many years and was responsible for many hit albums, Lieberson. Photographed in a process known as "Natural Color" which did nothing for the movie. The only real humor is strictly "inside show business" stuff as Conried and Clark manage to snap off a few good gags that won't be understood by anyone east of Burbank. Warren was discovered by Swanson when she met him in an art gallery in Los Angeles and was taken by him, although she denied this later. After this film laid an egg, Swanson returned to New York and the stage, appearing in "Nina" with David Niven.

p, Edward L. Alperson, Jr.; d&w, Milton H. Bren (based on the novel by Goddard Lieberson); ph, Ernest Laszlo (Natural Color); m, Heinz Roemheld; ed, Arthur Hilton; cos, Swanson.

Comedy (PR:A MPAA:NR)

THREE FOR JAMIE DAWN* (1956) 81 ½m AA bw

Laraine Day (Sue), Ricardo Montalban (Tom), Richard Carlson (Random), June Havoc (Lorrie), Maria Palmer (Julia), Eduard Franz (Karek), Regis Toomey (Murph), Scotty Beckett (Gordon), Herb Vigran (Robbins), Marilyn Simms (Jamie Dawn), Dorothy Adams (Helen March).

When a wealthy socialite kills her boy friend, she hires the shadiest lawyer

in town, Carlson, as her defense. To insure a vote of not guilty, Carlson buys off three of the jurors, all of whom have their reasons for betraying justice. Before the verdict is read, the three jurors, bothered by their consciences, side with the others and convict the girl.

p, Hayes Goetz; d, Thomas Carr; w, John Klempner; ph, Duke Green; m, Walter Scharf; ed, Richard Cahoon; art d, David Milton.

Crime Drama (PR:A MPAA:NR)

THREE FOR THE SHOW*½ (1955) 93m COL c

Betty Grable (Julie), Marge Champion (Gwen Howard), Gower Champion (Vernon Lowndes), Jack Lemmon (Marty Stewart), Myron McCormick (Mike Hudson), Paul Harvey (Col. Wharton), Robert Bice (Sgt. O'Hallihan), Hal K. Dawson (Theater Treasurer), Charlotte Lawrence (Girl), Willard Waterman (Moderator), Gene Wesson (Reporter), Aileen Carlyle (Mother), Rudy Lee (Boy), Eugene Borden (Costume Designer).

This musical reworking of TOO MANY HUSBANDS (1940), adapted from a play by W. Somerset Maugham, features Grable as a top singer and dancer who's been widowed by WW II. She marries her late husband's song-writing partner, Gower Champion, but the new marriage is thrown for a loop when Lemmon, her first husband, unexpectedly arrives home very much alive and eager to see Grable. Grable is now in a pickle over which man to take because she loves them both. Unable to make up her mind, Grable sets up house with both men while Marge Champion, her best friend (and Gower Champion's real-life spouse), patiently sits it out, preparing to comfort whichever man loses Grable's affections. The film wastes a potentially charming premise with a rather clumsy telling. The story is simplistic and predictable, but these weaknesses are punched up by some lively dance numbers. Cole's choreography has some exciting moments with originality and spice in his work. The Champions, two of the best dancers ever to hit Broadway and the silver screen, do a wonderful piece to George and Ira Gershwin's beautiful song "Someone to Watch Over Me," while Grable works her magic with an all-male harem in a delightful dream sequence. Such moments aren't enough, though, and Lemmon (who made his film musical debut with this) seems lost in it all. He later remarked (as quoted in the book Lemmon by Don Widener): "I just wasn't that wild about the movie or the part...There's not much to say about it; it was a Hollywood musical." Others did have something to say about THREE FOR THE SHOW. The Roman Catholic Legion of Decency found the film's treatment of polygamy too flippant and gave the film its "C" (for condemned) rating. After a few cuts the Legion saw fit to rerate the film, raising it to a "B" (some parts morally objectionable). The songs include: "Which One?" (Lester Lee, Ned Washington, sung by M. Champion), "Down Boy!" (Hoagy Carmichael, Harold Adamson, sung by Grable, Lemmon, G. Champion), "I've Been Kissed Before" (Bob Russell, Lee, sung by Grable), "I've Got a Crush on You" (George Gershwin, Ira Gershwin, sung by Lemmon, Grable), "How Come You Like Me Like You Do?" (Gene Austin, Roy Bergere, sung by Grable), "Swan Lake" (excerpt from Tchaikovsky ballet), "The Homecoming" (danced by Lemmon, G. Champion), "Three for the Show" (danced by Grable, G. Champion, Lemmon).

p, Jonie Taps; d, H.C. Potter; w, Edward Hope, Leonard Stern (based on the play "Too Many Husbands" by W. Somerset Maugham); ph, Arthur Arling (CinemaScope, Technicolor); m, George Duning; ed, Viola Lawrence; md, Morris Stoloff; art d, Walter Holscher; set d, William Kiernan; cos, Jean Louis; ch, Jack Cole.

Musical (PR:A MPAA:NR)

THREE GIRLS ABOUT TOWN* (1941) 71m COL bw

Joan Blondell (Hope Banner), Robert Benchley (Wilburforse Paddle), John Howard (Tommy Hopkins), Binnie Barnes (Faith Banner), Janet Blair (Charity Banner), Hugh O'Connell (Chief of Police), Paul Harvey (Fred Chambers), Frank McGlynn (Josephus Wiegal), Eric Blore (Charlemagne), Una O'Connor (Maggie O'Callahan), Almira Sessions (Tessie Conarchy), Dorothy Vaughan (Mrs. McDougall), Walter Soderling (Charlie), Ben Taggart (Doorman), Chester Clute, Eddie Laughton, Dick Elliott (Magicians), Charles Lane (Mortician), Bess Flowers (Mortician's Wife), Minna Phillips (Martha), Alec Craig (Samuel), Larry Parks, Ray Walker, Bruce Bennett, Lloyd Bridges, John Tyrrell, Lester Dorr (Reporters), William "Billy" Newell (Laundry Man), George Hickman (Bellhop), Arthur Aylesworth, Arthur Loft, Harrison Greene (Poker Players), Vera Lewis, Jessie Arnold, Sarah Edwards, Barbara Brown (Clubwomen).

A wacky comedy which has two hotel hostesses who are sisters and their other sister getting involved in a murder case when a corpse shows up in the hotel during convention time. Blondell lets reporter Howard in on their secret, allowing him to get an exclusive. Howard, in turn, thanks Blondell by marrying her.

p, Samuel Bischoff; d, Leigh Jason; w, Richard Carroll; ph, Franz F. Planer; ed, Charles Nelson; md, Morris W. Stoloff; art d, Lionel Banks.

Comedy (PR:A MPAA:NR)

THREE GIRLS LOST*½   (1931) 72m FOX bw

Loretta Young (Noreen McMann), John Wayne (Gordon Wales), Lew Cody (William Marriott), Joyce Compton (Edna Best), Joan Marsh (Marcia Tallant), Kathrin Clare Ward (Mrs. McGree), Paul Fix (Tony), Bert Roach.

Three girls leave their small towns for Chicago with two of them turning out okay, but Marsh ending up with riff-raff. She gets mixed up with a racketeer only to have the other girls lend a hand. Nothing special here.

p, A.L. Rockett; d, Sidney Lanfield; w, Bradley King (based on a story by Robert D. Andrews); ph, L. William O'Connell; ed, Ralph Dietrich.

Drama   **(PR:A   MPAA:NR)**

THREE GODFATHERS**½   (1936) 82m MGM bw (AKA: MIRACLE IN THE SAND)

Chester Morris (Bob), Lewis Stone (Doc), Walter Brennan (Gus), Irene Hervey (Molly), Sidney Toler (Prof. Snape), Dorothy Tree (Blackie), Roger Imhof (Sheriff), Willard Robertson (Rev. McLane), Robert Livingston (Frank), John Sheehan (Ed), Victor Potel (Buck), Helen Brown (Mrs. Marshall), Joseph Marievsky (Pedero), Jean Kirchner (The Baby), Harvey Clark (Marcus Treen), Virginia Brissac (Mrs. McLane).

Three bandits make their way through the desert, after knocking off the New Jerusalem Bank, where they stumble upon a covered wagon. Inside is a newborn baby and its dying mother. They risk their own lives and their stolen fortune to bring the baby back to safety, with Morris the one who actually does the deed while the others, too weak to go on, stay behind. This picture was the third remake (out of four) of the Peter B. Kyne story, with its "Three Wise Men" parallel. Hervey went on to become the wife of one singing star, Allan Jones, and was the mother to another, Jack Jones.

p, Joseph L. Mankiewicz; d, Richard Boleslawski; w, Edward E. Paramore, Jr., Manuel Seff (based on the story by Peter B. Kyne); ph, Joseph Ruttenberg; m, Dr. William Axt; ed, Frank Sullivan; cos, Dolly Tree.

Western   **(PR:A   MPAA:NR)**

THREE GODFATHERS, THE*****   (1948) 106m Argosy/MGM c

John Wayne (Robert Marmaduke Hightower), Pedro Armendariz (Pedro "Pete" Roca Fuerte), Harry Carey, Jr. (William Kearney "The Abilene Kid"), Ward Bond (Perley "Buck" Sweet), Mildred Natwick (The Mother), Charles Halton (Mr. Latham), Jane Darwell (Miss Florie), Mae Marsh (Mrs. Perley Sweet), Guy Kibbee (Judge), Dorothy Ford (Ruby Latham), Ben Johnson, Michael Dugan, Don Summers (Members of Posse), Fred Libby (Deputy Sheriff "Curly"), Hank Worden (Deputy Sheriff), Jack Pennick (Luke, Train Conductor), Francis Ford (Drunken Old-Timer at Bar), Richard Hageman (Saloon Pianist), Cliff Lyons (Guard at Mojave Tanks).

Overshadowed by Ford's cavalry pictures (WAGON MASTER would soon suffer the same fate), THREE GODFATHERS is a wonderful, heartfelt western about a bad man redeemed through love and sacrifice that served as a tribute to Ford's mentor and friend, actor Harry Carey, who had succumbed to cancer the year before. One of the most oft-told tales in western genre history, the film follows a trio of bad men, led by Wayne, as they ride into the town of Welcome (the citizens have recently changed the name of the town–the original was Tarantula) with designs on robbing the bank. None of the outlaws are particularly evil, they have just wandered onto a bad path and have no motivation for changing their ways. Armendariz is a Mexican who has stolen everything he owns and Carey, Jr. (son of Harry Carey) is a young gunslinger with little experience. Wayne and his boys stop and chat with a citizen of Welcome out tending his garden, Bond, but they realize their mistake when the man pins on his tin star revealing that he's the sheriff. The outlaws decide to go through with the robbery anyway, but on their escape Carey is wounded in the shoulder and another bullet hits their water bag. Because their escape route takes them right into the desert, the bullet to the water is the greater wound. Bond organizes a posse (Johnson, Dugan, and Summers) and takes off after the outlaws, knowing that they'll head for the railroad's water tanks. Bond and his men beat them to it, forcing the outlaws to head for another water supply known as Terrapin Tanks. A savage sandstorm kicks up, forcing the outlaws to tether their horses and sit tight until it is over. When the winds calm down, the men are horrified to discover that their horses have gotten loose and disappeared. The men must continue on foot, and Wayne is selected to scout ahead when they approach Terrapin Tanks to see if the posse has beaten them there. When Wayne returns he has a tale of woe. Some greenhorn and his wife found the watering hole a bit dry so the idiot dynamited the hole and destroyed it. He wandered off leaving his wife behind and now there is one slight problem, the woman is about to give birth. Wayne concludes his story with a near-hysterical, "I'm a tough bird, an awful tough old bird, but I'm not goin' back in there!" Armendariz, who has eight children scattered throughout Mexico, has been present at births and handles the delivery of the baby. The woman, Natwick, knows she is dying and begs the three men to save her baby. Wayne vows that they will and Natwick dies confident her child will grow up to be as fine a man as the men who raised him (she never knew they were outlaws). Carey finds a book on baby care and the men refer to it for advice. "...the best and surest way of feeding the baby," Carey reads aloud, "is the one which Nature has provided." "Well that's out!" Wayne quickly responds. While Wayne and

Armendariz feed and change the infant, Carey peruses a Bible left among Natwick's possessions. The young outlaw is struck when he realizes that they have been given a mission similar to the three wise men. Knowing that the town of New Jerusalem, Arizona, is nearby, Carey tells the men they should follow the brightest star as a guide. His wound worsening and gripped with the knowledge that he won't survive the trek, Carey carries the child for as long as he can because his comrades will have to go it alone soon. Exhausted and weak from loss of blood, Carey dies while saying a childhood prayer. Armendariz carries the child next but tragedy strikes him as well. He steps into a gopher hole, and rather than fall forward on the child, he twists his body around and falls in a sitting position breaking his leg. Knowing he cannot go on, Wayne leaves his friend a gun and continues on. The trek begins to take it's toll on Wayne. He begins to resent the biblical similarities in the situation and throws the Bible into the sand. He is immediately overcome by guilt and retrieves the holy book. Wayne begins to sing a favorite song of Carey's,"The Streets of Laredo," and he hallucinates the voices of Carey and Armendariz joining in. The voices of his comrades push Wayne forward and he becomes more determined than ever to complete his mission. Eventually Wayne and the baby stumble into the town of New Jerusalem and the strains of "Holy Night" float from a nearby saloon. It is Christmas Eve. Delirious, Wayne shouts: "Merry Christmas to all!" and then collapses. We next see Wayne arguing with Bond over custody of the child. Bond offers to adopt the baby and drop the charges against Wayne if the outlaw will sign the custody papers. Wayne refuses and decides to face the judge and take over custody of the child when he is released from prison. Bond is sensitive to Wayne's vow to the baby's mother and agrees to take care of the infant until Wayne gets out. The judge, Kibbee, makes note of Wayne's sacrifice for the child and gives the outlaw a minimum sentence of one year and one day. The community thinks he's a hero and the citizens bid him a farewell as he is taken off to jail. Ford first filmed this story in 1919 as MARKED MEN with Harry Carey. Carey had appeared in the very first version of the story also titled THREE GODFATHERS in 1916. The story was remade again in 1929 as HELL'S HEROES, and again in 1936 as THREE GODFATHERS. Harry Carey was Ford's mentor–the man who encouraged him to make movies–and when he died Ford set out to enshrine his memory forever in movie history. The THREE GODFATHERS, Ford's first color film, begins as a silhouetted cowboy (stuntman Cliff Lyons who bore a great resemblance to Carey) astride "Sonny," Carey's favorite horse, rides to the top of a hill and pushes his hat back on his head. The words: "Dedicated to Harry Carey, a bright star in the early western sky" appear. In addition to the dedication, Ford set out to make Carey's son, known to friends and family as "Dobie" because his hair color resembled that of an adobe hut, a movie star. Although Dobie had been in four previous pictures and been given "introducing" billing in every one of them (including in Howard Hawks' RED RIVER–his father's last film) Ford was determined to introduce the kid to the public again. When young Carey protested to Wayne that it was unnecessary, Wayne responded, "It gives the Old Man pleasure to do it, makes him feel he's carrying on a tradition." The film's shooting was a bit harrowing for young Carey because he had grown up knowing the cantankerous Ford as "Uncle Jack." Before shooting commenced Ford warned the youngster, "You're gonna hate my guts before this picture is over." The film was shot in Death Valley and Ford enjoyed rankling Carey by grousing that he should have gotten Audie Murphy for the part every time Carey did something wrong. This made the boy try harder and as the actor later confessed in Dan Ford's biography of his grandfather Pappy: "I was always self-concious and never really comfortable with him off the set, but I was completely relaxed in front of the camera....He gave me tremendous confidence, and I was never more at ease." When the shooting was over and Carey realized what Ford had been trying to do with him as an actor, he caught the director in the parking lot and thanked him: "You said before we started the picture that I was going to hate you when it was over. But I don't hate you. I love you." Carey remembered that Ford seemed embarassed and didn't know what to say so: "He just grunted and drove off."

p, John Ford, Merian C. Cooper; d, Ford; w, Laurence Stallings, Frank S. Nugent (based on the story by Peter B. Kyne); ph, Winton C. Hoch (Technicolor); m, Richard Hageman; ed, Jack Murray; art d, James Basevi; set d, Joe Kish.

Western   **Cas.**   **(PR:A   MPAA:NR)**

THREE GUNS FOR TEXAS*   (1968) 99m UNIV c

Neville Brand (Reese Bennett), Peter Brown (Chad Cooper), William Smith (Joe Riley), Martin Milner (MacMillan), Philip Carey (Capt. Parmalee), Albert Salmi (Cleetus Grogan), Cliff Osmond (Running Antelope), Michael Conrad (Willy G. Tinney), Shelley Morrison (Linda Little Trees), John Abbott, Richard Devon, Ralph Manza, Dub Taylor.

The Texas Rangers try to bring peace to Laredo but meet opposition from a bitter widowed Indian squaw. She offers her support, however, after falling in love with one of the Rangers, and this leads to a truce between the Indians and the Rangers. Together the two factions successfully lead an attack on a bandit gang. Originally this picture ran on NBC-TV as three episodes of Laredo–"Yahoo," "Jinx," and "No Bugles– One Drum." It should have stayed on TV.

p, Richard Irving; d, David Lowell Rich, Paul Stanley, Earl Bellamy; w, John D. Black; ph, Andrew Jackson, Lionel Lindon (Technicolor); m, Russ

Garcia; ed, Richard G. Wray; art d, Howard E, Johnson, Russell Kimball, Lloyd S. Papez; set d, John McCarthy, James M. Walters, Sr., Robert C. Bradfield, Claire P. Brown; makeup, Bud Westmore.

Western   **(PR:A   MPAA:G)**

THREE GUYS NAMED MIKE**½   (1951) 90m MGM bw

Jane Wyman *(Marcy Lewis)*, Van Johnson *(Michael Lawrence)*, Howard Keel *(Mike Jamison)*, Barry Sullivan *(Mike Tracy)*, Phyllis Kirk *(Kathy Hunter)*, Anne Sargent *(Jan Baker)*, Jeff Donnell *(Alice Raymond)*, Herbert Heyes *(Scott Bellamy)*, Robert Sherwood *(Benson)*, Don McGuire *(MacWade Parker)*, Barbara Billingsley *(Ann White)*, Hugh Sanders *(Mr. Williams)*, John Maxwell *(Dr. Matthew Hardy)*, Lewis Martin *(C.R. Smith)*, Ethel "Pug" Wells *(Herself)*, Sydney Mason *(Osgood)*, Percy Helton *(Hawkins)*, Dan Foster *(Rogers)*, Jack Shea *(Nashville Passenger Agent)*, King Mojave *(Passenger Agent)*, Arthur Space *(Clerk)*, Matt Moore *(Mr. Tannen)*, Mae Clarke *(Convair Passenger)*, Jack Gargan *(Mr. Rogers)*.

Wyman is a rookie stewardess who makes more than enough mistakes while trying to learn the ropes. In the meantime, she is getting the eye from a trio of Mikes–Johnson, an aspiring scientist-bartender; Keel, a pilot; and Sullivan, an ad man. Humorous romance placed against a relatively realistic American Airlines-sponsored backdrop.

p, Armand Deutsch; d, Charles Walters; w, Sidney Sheldon (based on the story by Ruth Brooks Flippen, from suggestions made by Ethel "Pug" Wells); ph, Paul C. Vogel; m, Bronislau Kaper; ed, Irvine Warburton; art d, Cedric Gibbons, William Ferrari.

Romantic Comedy   **(PR:A   MPAA:NR)**

THREE HATS FOR LISA**½   (1965, Brit.) 99m Seven Hills/
                                              WB-Pathe c

Joe Brown *(Johnny Howjego)*, Sophie Hardy *(Lisa Milan)*, Sidney James *(Sid Marks)*, Una Stubbs *(Flora)*, Peter Bowles *(Sammy)*, Seymour Green *(Signor Molfino)*, Josephine Blake *(Miss Penny)*, Jeremy Lloyd *(Guards Officer)*, Michael Brennan *(Police Sergeant)*, Eric Barker *(Station Sergeant)*, Dave Nelson.

A group of young Britons meet Hardy, their favorite Italian film star, and take her around town for the day. To keep her happy, they must satisfy her desire to steal hats for her collection. The targeted heads are a policeman with his helmet, a businessman with a bowler, and a guard with a bearskin. Filled with a number of lively tunes and capturing some of the same spirit as seen in ON THE TOWN and ROMAN HOLIDAY. The picture-postcard London scenery is a plus.

p, Jack Hanbury; d, Sidney Hayers; w, Leslie Bricusse, Talbot Rothwell (based on the story by Bricusse); ph, Alan Hume (Eastmancolor); m, Eric Rogers, Bricusse; ed, Tristam Cones; ch, Gillian Lynne.

Musical   **(PR:A   MPAA:NR)**

THREE HEARTS FOR JULIA*½   (1943) 89m MGM bw

Ann Sothern *(Julia Seabrook)*, Melvyn Douglas *(Jeff Seabrook)*, Lee Bowman *(David Torrance)*, Felix Bressart *(Mr. Anton Ottaway)*, Reginald Owen *(John Girard)*, Richard Ainley *(Philip Barrows)*, Marta Linden *(May Elton)*, Jacqueline White *(Kay)*, Kay Medford *(Thelma)*, Ann Richards *(Clara)*, Elvia Allman *(Miss Stickney)*, Marietta Canty *(Mattie)*, Charles La Torre *(Bureau Clerk)*, Marek Windheim *(Perfume Clerk)*, Bill Lally *(Customs Man)*, William Tannen, Rudolph Cameron, Hooper Atchley, Art Belasco, George Lollier, Anthony Warde, Estelle Etterre *(Reporters)*, Phyllis Cook *(Western Union Girl)*, Oscar O'Shea *(Doorman)*, Frank Faylen *(Meek Gateman)*, Dick Rich *(Mug Attendant)*, Joe Yule *(Cab Driver)*, Fred Rapport, Bill Dill *(Waiters)*, Dick Elliott *(Smith)*, Ernie Alexander *(Johnson)*, Russell Gleason *(Jones)*, Max Willenz *(Bartender)*, Nell Craig *(Maid)*, Howard Hickman *(Mr. Doran)*, James Warren *(Program Vendor)*, Bert Hicks *(Usher)*, Russell Hicks *(Col. Martin)*, Hans Von Morhart, John Van Eyck, Curt Furberg, Nicholas Vehr, Jack Deery *(Nazis)*, Dick Wessel *(Soldier)*, Mary Field, Eve Whitney, Marie Windsor, Mary Benoit, Natalie Draper *(Musicians)*.

Douglas returns from his job as a foreign war correspondent to find that his wife has taken up with Bowman and funneled all her attentions to her musical career. It's an effort for Douglas to win her back but he finally succeeds after she finishes running around with a women's symphony that performs for USO shows.

p, John W. Considine, Jr.; d, Richard Thorpe; w, Lionel Houser; ph, George Folsey; m, Herbert Stothart; ed, Irvine Warburton; art d, Cedric Gibbons, Howard Campbell; set d, Edwin B. Willis, Helen Conway; cos, Irene.

Romance/Musical   **(PR:A   MPAA:NR)**

THREE HOURS**½   (1944, Fr.) 85m J.H. Hoffberg bw

Jean-Pierre Aumont *(Paul Marchand)*, Betty Bovy *(Mrs. Marchand)*, E. Delmont *(Mr. Marchand)*, Corinne Luchaire *(Marie)*, Almos *(Jean)*, Roger Legris *(Auguste)*.

Aumont is a French soldier on a troop train that gets stalled for three hours near his hometown. He takes off to see his girl friend, who hasn't written in some time. When he gets home he learns that his mother kicked the orphaned girl out of her home. But before he leaves on the train, the lovers are reunited. After this film, Aumont himself took up arms with the French Army. Originally shot in France in 1940. (In French; English subtitles.)

p, Arnold Pressburger; d, Leonide Moguy; w, Marcel Achard (based on the story by Jacques Companez, Michel Deligne); ph, Robert Lefebvre, Andre Germann; m, Arthur Honegger, Henry Verdun; English titles, Charles Clement.

War/Romance   **(PR:A   MPAA:NR)**

THREE HOURS TO KILL***   (1954) 77m COL c

Dana Andrews *(Jim Guthrie)*, Donna Reed *(Laurie Mastin)*, Dianne Foster *(Chris Plumber)*, Stephen Elliott *(Ben East)*, Richard Coogan *(Niles Hendricks)*, Laurence Hugo *(Marty Lasswell)*, James Westerfield *(Sam Minor)*, Richard Webb *(Carter Mastin)*, Carolyn Jones *(Polly)*, Charlotte Fletcher *(Betty)*, Whit Bissell *(Deke)*, Felipe Turich *(Esteban)*, Arthur Fox *(Little Carter)*, Francis McDonald *(Vince)*, Frank Hagney *(Cass)*, Paul E. Burns *(Albert, Drunk)*, Julian Rivero *(Dominquez)*, Robert A. Paquin *(Storekeeper)*, Elsie Baker *(Woman)*, Reed Howes *(Bits)*, Ada Adams *(Bits)*, Edward Earle *(Rancher)*, Buddy Roosevelt *(Drunk)*, Hank Mann *(Man)*, Syd Saylor *(Townsman)*.

Andrews turns in a delightfully tough performance as a cowboy wrongly accused of killing his former fiancee's brother. An angry lynch mob strings him up but, rather than killing him, it lets him loose to prove his innocence. With his noose-scarred neck he turns cold-blooded and hunts down the real killer, who happens to be one of the few sympathetic characters in the entire town. The film benefits from Werker's sure directorial hand and leathery tone.

p, Harry Joe Brown; d, Alfred Werker; w, Richard Alan Simmons, Roy Huggins, Maxwell Shane (based on the story by Alex Gottlieb); ph, Charles Lawton, Jr. (Technicolor); m, Paul Sawtell; ed, Gene Havlick; art d, George Brooks.

Western   **(PR:A   MPAA:NR)**

365 NIGHTS IN HOLLYWOOD**½   (1934) 74m FOX bw

James Dunn *(Jimmy Dale)*, Alice Faye *(Alice Perkins)*, Frank Mitchell *(Percy)*, Jack Durant *(Clarence)*, John Qualen *(Prof. Ellenbogen)*, John Bradford *(Adrian Almont)*, Frank Melton *(Frank Young)*, Grant Mitchell *(J. Walter Delmar)*, Ray Cooke *(Assistant Director)*, Addison Richards *(Assistant District Attorney)*, Arthur Housman *(Drunk)*, Tyler Brooke, Paul McVey, Dick Whiting, Ben Hall, James Conlin, Frank Sully, Al Klein.

From Peoria to Hollywood comes Faye, seeking a career in the movies. Along with her icemen friends Frank Mitchell and Durant, she enrolls in a fraudulent acting school run by Grant Mitchell and Bradford. Wealthy Melton turns up looking for a place to invest some money and G. Mitchell, smelling an opportunity, persuades him to finance a film starring Faye, on the stipulation that should production stop for any reason, the money would be his. Stacking odds in his favor, Mitchell hires alcoholic has-been director Dunn to helm the film. Dunn sees this as his last chance to save his declining career and works hard to make the film good. G. Mitchell isn't through yet, though. He has Bradford take Faye up to a remote cabin and there he drinks until he passes out, leaving Faye stranded. Dunn, who has fallen in love with Faye, is desperate, both for her safety and for the future of his career. In the nick of time F. Mitchell and Durant, her icemen friends who have returned to that calling, find her and deliver her back to the studio. The big production number is filmed, Bradford and G. Mitchell go to jail, and the film becomes a big hit. A mediocre, cliche-ridden script is nearly turned into something good by the direction of Marshall and the performance of Faye, but their efforts aren't enough and the film sinks in a quagmire of boredom interrupted by the idiotic clowning of F. Mitchell and J. Durant. The production numbers are only fair, and go on too long. The lead was originally to go to Lilian Harvey, but she was replaced by rising star Faye, in her fourth screen appearance. Faye's first big break also came at Harvey's expense, when she replaced Harvey on Broadway in "George White's Scandals" and was spotted and signed by a 20th Century-Fox talent scout.

p, Sol Wurtzel; d, George Marshall; w, William Conselman, Henry Johnson (based on a book of short stories by Jimmie Starr); ph, Harry Jackson; m, Richard Whiting; md, Samuel Kaylin; cos, Royer; ch, Sammy Lee; m/l, "My Future Star," "Yes to You," Whiting, Sidney Clare.

Comedy   **(PR:A   MPAA:NR)**

300 SPARTANS, THE* (1962) 108m FOX c (AKA: LION OF SPARTA)

Richard Egan *(King Leonidas of Sparta)*, Ralph Richardson *(Themistocles of Athens)*, Diane Baker *(Ellas)*, Barry Coe *(Phylon)*, David Farrar *(Xerxes)*, Donald Houston *(Hydarnes)*, Anna Synodinou *(Gorgo)*, Kieron Moore *(Ephialtes)*, John Crawford *(Agathon)*, Robert Brown *(Pentheus)*, Laurence Naismith *(1st Delegate)*, Anne Wakefield *(Artemisia)*, Ivan Triesault *(Demaratus)*, Charles Fawcett *(Mogistias)*, Michael Nikolinakos *(Myron)*, Sandro Giglio *(Xenathon)*, Anna Raftopoulou *(Toris)*, Dimos Starenios

(Samos), George Moutsios, Nicholas Papakonstantinou, John G. Contes, Marietta Flematomas.

An overlong spectacle that tells how a band of only 300 Spartans fended off an army of thousands in the Battle of Thermopylae in 480 B.C. The filmmakers were more concerned with the immenseness of battle than with historic credibility or story, though amid all the excess Richardson's performance (given the feebleness of the script) shines through. Not much better than the Italian muscleman imports.

p, Rudolph Mate, George St. George; d, Mate; w, St. George (based on the original story material by Ugo Liberatore, Remigio Del Grosso, Giovanni D'Eramo, Gian Paolo Callegari); ph, Geoffrey Unsworth (CinemaScope, DeLuxe Color); m, Manos Hadjidakis; ed, Jerome Webb; art d, Arrigo Equini; set d, Carlo Gentili, Enzo Constantini; spec eff, Fred Etcheberry; cos, Ginette Devaud; makeup, George Frost, Amato Garbini; tech advisor, Paul Nord, Cleanthis Damianos.

Historical Adventure　　　　　　　　　**(PR:A　MPAA:NR)**

300 YEAR WEEKEND zero　　　　(1971) 84m ABC Cinerama c

Michael Tolan *(Dr. Marshall)*, Sharon Laughlin *(Nancy)*, Roy Cooper *(Hal)*, Gabriel Dell *(Wynter)*, M'el Dowd *(Carole)*, Bernard Ward *(Rockne)*, Dorothy Lyman *(Jean)*, William Devane *(Tom)*, James Congdon *(Dr. Roland)*, Carole Demas *(Joy)*.

An overacted melodrama about a doctor who spends 24 hours in a clinic with its patients. Each character has his or her own story to tell, about their fathers, mothers, or spouses who don't understand them, and how they've turned instead to drugs. They all reveal something "moving" about their personal lives, enough to make viewers rebel unless, of course, they're just as troubled as the people on the screen.

p&d, Victor Stoloff; w, Stoloff, William Devane, Jerome Alden; ph, Joseph Brun (Metrocolor); m, Gilber Fuller; art d, Trevor Williams.

Drama　　　　　　　　　　　　　　　**(PR:C　MPAA:GP)**

THREE HUSBANDS**½　　　　　(1950) 79m Gloria UA bw

Eve Arden *(Lucille McCabe)*, Ruth Warrick *(Jane Evans)*, Vanessa Brown *(Mary Whittaker)*, Howard da Silva *(Dan McCabe)*, Shepperd Strudwick *(Arthur Evans)*, Robert Karnes *(Kenneth Whittaker)*, Emlyn Williams *(Maxwell Bard)*, Billie Burke *(Mrs. Whittaker)*, Louise Erickson *(Matilda Clegg)*, Jonathan Hale *(Mr. Wurdeman)*, Jane Darwell *(Mrs. Wurdeman)*, Benson Fong *(George, Butler)*, Frank Cady *(Elevator Operator)*, Dorothy Wolbert *(Cleaning Woman)*, Ralph Peters *(Policeman)*, Martha Mitrovich *(Secretary)*, Jill Kraft *(Receptionist)*, Jerry Hausner *(Bartender)*, Dorothy Vaughn *(Maid)*, John Dierkes *(Warden)*, Alvin Hammer *(Seedy Little Man)*, Richard Flato *(Waiter)*, William Simpson *(Barry)*, Maurice Marsac *(Frenchman)*, Gay Gayle *(French Girl)*, Stanley Prager *(Sharpy)*.

An engaging comedy told in flashback about a man, Williams, who dies and leaves three letters in his will. Addressed to the husbands of the women he had affairs with, the letters inspire some amusing reactions out of the three. Vera Caspary, who cowrote the script for THREE HUSBANDS, also adapted a similar story for the reverse of this film called LETTER TO THREE WIVES (1949).

p, I.G. Goldsmith; d, Irving Reis; w, Vera Caspary, Edward Eliscu (based on Caspary's story); ph, Frank [Franz F.] Planer; m, Herschel Burke Gilbert; ed, Louis H. Sackin; art d, Rudolph Sternad; m/l, "Poor Chap," Gilbert, Eliscu (sung by Emlyn Williams, Eve Arden).

Comedy　　　　　　**Cas.**　　　　　　**(PR:A　MPAA:NR)**

THREE IN EDEN　　　　　　(SEE: ISLE OF FURY, 1936)

THREE IN ONE**½　　　　(1956, Aus.) 90m Tradition bw

John McCallum, Edmund Allison, Jerome Levy, Leonard Thiele, Joan Landor, Brian Viary.

A trilogy from Australia shot in the famed neo-realist style made famous by the Italians at the close of WW II with such films as OPEN CITY and PAISAN. The first story follows a group of miners who are left with the body of a stranger who has died in their town. Despite the fact that no one knows who the dead man is, the miners stage an impressive funeral. The second tale takes place while Australia is in the throes of an economic depression. A fiercely proud worker is forced to steal wood from a greedy landowner so that his friends won't freeze on a bitterly cold night. The third and final episode sees a young couple finally make the decision to marry despite their worries about money and security. An obscure and valuable film for those interested in neo-realism.

d, Cecil Holmes; w, Rex Reinit (based on stories by Henry Lawson, Frank Hardy, Ralph Peterson); ph, Ross Wood; ed, Raymond Hanson.

Drama　　　　　　　　　　　　　　　**(PR:A　MPAA:NR)**

THREE IN THE ATTIC*½　　　　(1968) 90m AIP-Hermes/AIP c

Christopher Jones *(Paxton Quigley)*, Yvette Mimieux *(Tobey Clinton)*, Judy Pace *(Eulice)*, Maggie Thrett *(Jan)*, Nan Martin *(Dean Nazarin)*, Reva Rose *(Selma)*, John Beck *(Jake)*, Richard Derr *(Mr. Clinton)*, Eve McVeagh *(Mrs. Clinton)*, Honey Alden *(Flo)*, Tom Ahearne *(Wilfred)*.

Jones is a campus Casanova who falls head over heels for Mimieux but refuses to admit he's in love. He starts shacking up with a couple of swinging female hippies, one black and one Jewish. They and Mimieux unite and lock Jones in an attic, where they take turns having sex with him. Finally, his physical strength gives out, and he agrees to remain faithful to Mimieux. A stupid sex fantasy geared to the sexploitation crowd. Stephen Yafa, who wrote the screenplay, originally titled "Paxton Quigley's Had the Course," disassociated himself from the film.

p&d, Richard Wilson; w, Stephen H. Yafa; ph, J. Burgi Contner (Pathe Color); m, Chad Stuart; ed, Richard C. Meyer, Eve Newman; md, Al Simms; prod d, William Creber; cos, Fern Vollner; m/l, "Paxton Quigley's Had the Course," Stuart, Jeremy Clyde (sung by Chad and Jeremy); makeup, Ted Coodley.

Comedy/Drama　　　　　**Cas.**　　　　　**(PR:O　MPAA:R)**

THREE IN THE CELLAR　　　　(SEE: UP IN THE CELLAR, 1970)

THREE IN THE SADDLE**　　　　(1945) 61M PRC bw

Tex Ritter, Dave O'Brien, Guy Wilkerson, Lorraine Miller, Charles King, Edward Howard, Edward Cassidy, Bud Osborne, Frank Ellis.

Ritter and his upstanding pals come to the aid of a defenseless woman rancher who is being pressured by the notorious head of a stagecoach empire into selling her land. The Texas Rangers clean up the town, depose the villainous leader, and restore stolen properties to their rightful owners. (See TEXAS RANGERS series, Index.)

p, Arthur Alexander; d, Harry Fraser; w, Elmer Clifton; ph, Robert Cline; ed, Holbrook N. Todd; md, Lee Zahler; set d, Harry Reif; m/l, Frank Harford, Tex Ritter, Ernest Tubb.

Western　　　　　　**Cas.**　　　　　　**(PR:A　MPAA:NR)**

THREE INTO TWO WON'T GO****　　　　(1969, Brit.) 93m UNIV c

Rod Steiger *(Steve Howard)*, Claire Bloom *(Frances Howard)*, Judy Geeson *(Ella Patterson)*, Peggy Ashcroft *(Belle)*, Paul Rogers *(Jack Roberts)*, Lynn Farleigh *(Janet)*, Elizabeth Spriggs *(Marcia)*, Sheila Allen *(Beth)*.

An intelligent drama with elements of mystery; audiences may find their perspectives shifting about the central question: who is victim, who is victimizer? Steiger is a salesman who feels trapped in a love-starved, childless marriage to Bloom, a schoolteacher. While on the road, Steiger picks up Geeson, a 19-year-old hitchhiker. The two end up at a hotel owned by Steiger's friend, Rogers. After they make love, Steiger discovers a notebook of Geeson's in which she has rated all her lovers. Her encounter with Steiger is also detailed and the salesman is ranked as one of her best lovers. Eventually Steiger heads home to Bloom while Geeson decides to remain at the hotel as an employee. On his arrival at his newly purchased suburban house, Steiger finds his wife still in the process of unpacking their belongings. He finds the atmosphere stifling and once more leaves for Geeson's company. They make love again; then Steiger goes on a sales call. In the meantime, Geeson takes off for Steiger's home to confront his wife. She tells Bloom that she was forced to leave her job at the hotel because of Rogers' attempts to seduce her. Bloom offers Geeson the guest bedroom. Steiger returns to Rogers' hotel to find that Geeson has taken some of his money, leaving him only a farewell note. Again he returns to his new home and is angered to find Geeson there. He is further enraged when the girl announces that she may be pregnant. After she threatens him with the possibility of aborting the unborn child Steiger agrees to Geeson's demand that he leave Bloom. Bloom confronts her husband, offering to adopt the baby, but Steiger tells her of his decision. However, Geeson is not around after the two have planned their departure so the depressed Steiger finds solace in alcohol. Once more he returns to Bloom, this time finding her with her mother (Ashcroft), whom Steiger dislikes, and with Geeson. Geeson now explains that she is not pregnant. Steiger violently argues with his wife and mother-in-law, who respond by walking out. Geeson rejects him as well, leaving Steiger to his suitcase. Much goes unsaid in this drama. The strain between the principals has the biting sting of realism. Issues are in shades of gray rather than straight black and white. The multiple aspect of each personality is explored without reference to moral superiority. Steiger's character is both a self-centered oaf and a man searching for his own identity. Bloom's is a sad figure--due to her repressive mother and her husband's infidelities--yet, in her own way, the very force behind Steiger's behavior. Dialog seems authentic, including the awkward pauses and bursts of unintended anger that one finds in everyday conversation. Hall, an internationally acclaimed theatrical director, holds this fine cast under a tight rein while making the most of his settings. The house becomes symbolic of Steiger's and Bloom's marriage, a place possibly full of hope for new life or, anomalously, a hollow, loveless shell that no amount of decoration can cover. Hall builds his film on small moments, achieving a whole that is disturbing, sad, and thoroughly honest. Originally released at 93 minutes, some extra footage was shot by the studio and edited into the television version of this film. The results are not nearly as satisfying as Hall's original work. At the time this film was made Steiger and Bloom were off-screen husband and wife. Steiger was a leading proponent of the "Method" school of acting and the American actor was able to blend in well with the otherwise all-British cast. His approach to character development proved to be much different than–though just as effective as–that of his English counterparts. At first, Steiger's unfamiliar style of creating character was highly upsetting to Hall. In his drunken confrontation with Bloom and Ashcroft, Steiger initially played the role in a hammy, boisterous manner. In her autobiography, *Limelight and After*, Bloom recalled that "the English contingent...were dumbstruck. He'd was all over the place, no control, no sense, just spewing out of a scene." Hall, worried that the scene would be destroyed, consulted Bloom but she could offer him no help. But with each succeeding take, Steiger's characterization smoothed out the rough edges, gradually bringing his part into a believable and energetic performance infused with realism. Though the opposite of Bloom's approach to a characterization, she recalled that her husband's style made her realize "...that you could as well start from the top and work your way down, as start from the most minimal twitchings and stirrings and keep grafting onto it." The clashes in acting styles never appear on screen within the tight-knit ensemble and the result is a deeply humanistic picture of relationships with all their pock marks bared.

p, Julian Blaustein; d, Peter Hall; w, Edna O'Brien (based on a novel by Andrea Newman); ph, Walter Lassally (Technicolor); m, Francis Lai; ed, Alan Osbiston; md, Christian Gaubert; art d, Peter Murton; set d, Bryan Graves; cos, Ruth Myers; makeup, Michael Morris.

Drama   (PR:O   MPAA:R)

3 IS A FAMILY½   (1944) 81m UA bw

Marjorie Reynolds (*Kitty Mitchell*), Charlie Ruggles (*Sam Whitaker*), Fay Bainter (*Frances Whitaker*), Helen Broderick (*Irma Dalrymple*), Arthur Lake (*Archie Whitaker*), Hattie McDaniel (*Maid*), Jeff Donnell (*Hazel Whitaker*), John Philliber (*Dr. Bartell*), Walter Catlett (*Barney Meeker*), Clarence Kolb (*Mr. Steele*), Elsa Janssen (*Adelaide*), Renie Riano (*Genevieve*), Warren Hymer (*Coolie*), Clyde Fillmore (*Mr. Spencer*), Christian Rub (*Bell Boy*), Donna and Elissa Lambertson (*Susan and Patty Whitaker*), William Terry (*Joe Franklin*), Cheryl Walker (*Marian Franklin*), Fred Brady (*Gene Mitchell*), Margaret Early (*Steel's Daughter*).

Ruggles is an unaggressive husband whose financial wheeling and dealing isn't providing enough capital to live well. Wife Bainter decides to take control and enter the working world herself, assigning Ruggles the job of house husband. After a series of silly situations, Ruggles finally reasserts himself and once again takes hold of the family finances.

p, Sol Lesser; d, Edward Ludwig; w, Harry Chandlee, Marjorie L. Pfaelzer (based on a play by Phoebe Ephron, Henry Ephron); ph, Charles Lawton, Jr.; m, Werner R. Heymann; ed, Robert Crandall; prod d, Phil Paradise, J. Patrick; md, Charles Previn; art d, Al Ybarra.

Comedy   (PR:A   MPAA:NR)

THREE KIDS AND A QUEEN**   (1935) 87m UNIV bw (GB: THE BAXTER MILLIONS)

May Robson (*Mary Jane Baxter*), Frankie Darro (*Blackie*), Charlotte Henry (*Julia*), William "Billy" Benedict (*Flash*), Billy Burrud (*Doc*), Henry Armetta (*Tony Orsatti, Barber*), Herman Bing (*Walter*), Lillian Harmer (*Elmira*), John Miljan ("*Boss*" *Benton*), Lawrence Grant (*Wilfred Edgar*), Hedda Hopper (*Mrs. Cummings*), Hale Hamilton (*Ralph*), Noel Madison (*Stanley*), Tom Dugan (*Bill*), Henry Kolker (*Crippets*), Frank McHugh, Irving Pichel, Emmett Vogan.

An enjoyable piece of pure entertainment, which makes no attempt to do anything but provide a little escapism. Robson is the "queen" of the title, though in reality she is an elderly recluse. When she is erroneously believed to be kidnaped, she goes along with the scheme to collect the $50,000 reward so that she can help a needy family. Filled with a cast of cute kids, including the 6-year-old Burrud.

p, Ben Verschleiser; d, Edward Ludwig; w, Barry Trivers, Samuel Ornitz (based on the story by Harry Poppe, Chester Beecroft, Mary Marlind); ph, George Robinson; ed, Byron Robinson.

Comedy   (PR:A   MPAA:NR)

THREE LEGIONNAIRES, THE*   (1937) 65m GEN bw (GB: THREE CRAZY LEGIONNAIRES)

Robert Armstrong (*Chuck*), Lyle Talbot (*Jimmy*), Fifi D'Orsay (*Olga*), Anne Nagel (*Sonia*), Donald Meek (*U.S. Grant*), Stanley Fields (*Stavinski*), Maurice Black (*Aide*), Leonid Snegoff (*Innkeeper*), Man Mountain Dean (*Ivan*).

The misleading title to this lame programmer probably should have been "Two Soldiers," because that's what it's really about. Armstrong and Talbot are a pair of American Army buddies in Russia who get themselves into a

series of bungling escapades while trying to lead a crusade against the government. The third person of the title is Meek, a scientist who calls himself "General Grant" in the hopes of mixing up the Bolsheviks. None of them is even in the legion.

p, Robert E. Welsh; d, Hamilton MacFadden; w, George Waggner, Carl Harbaugh (based on the story by Waggner); ph, Ira Morgan; ed, Finn Ulbach.

War/Comedy   (PR:A   MPAA:NR)

THREE LITTLE GIRLS IN BLUE*   (1946) 90m FOX c

June Haver (*Pam*), George Montgomery (*Van Damm Smith*), Vivian Blaine (*Liz*), Celeste Holm (*Miriam*), Vera-Ellen (*Myra*), Frank Latimore (*Steve*), Charles Smith (*Mike*), Charles Halton (*Hoskins*), Ruby Dandridge (*Mammy*), Thurston Hall (*Colonel*), Clinton Rosemond (*Ben*), William Forrest, Jr (*Head Clerk*), Theresa Harris (*Maid*), Eddie Acuff (*Josh*), Al Murphy (*Bartender*), Robert Neury (*Headwaiter*), Coleen Gray (*Girl*), Robert "Smoky" Whitfield (*Sam*), Jesse Graves (*Headwaiter*), Don Garner (*Boy on Beach*).

Haver, Blaine, and Vera-Ellen try to sell themselves as three society women in Atlantic City but all wake up to unpleasant surprises-- being that money can't buy love. After belting out a few tunes and strolling about the lavishly designed Boardwalk in the equally impressive costumes, the three all fall in love without concern for bank balances. Haver pairs up with empty-pocketed Montgomery, Vera-Ellen ends up with waiter Smith, and Blaine hooks Latimore, the only wealthy one of the bunch. Vera-Ellen's singing was dubbed by Carol Stewart, Montgomery's by Ben Gage and Smith's by Del Porter. Josef Myrow, Mack Gordon songs include the title number (sung by June Haver, Vera-Ellen, Vivian Blaine), "You Make Me Feel So Young" (sung by Vera-Ellen, Charles Smith), "On the Boardwalk in Atlantic City" (sung by Haver, Vera-Ellen, Blaine), "Somewhere in the Night" (sung by Blaine), "I Feel Like Mike" (sung by Vera-Ellen), "A Farmer's Life Is a Very Merry Life" (sung by Haver, Vera-Ellen, Blaine), "Oh My Love" and "Always a Lady" (sung by Celeste Holm), as well as "If You Can't Get a Girl in the Springtime" (Bert Kalmar, Harry Tierney).

p, Mack Gordon; d, H. Bruce Humberstone; w, Valentine Davis, Brown Holmes, Lynn p, Mack Gordon; d, H. Bruce Humberstone; w, Valentine Davis, Brown Holmes, Lynn Starling, Robert Ellis, Helen Logan (based on the play "Three Blind Mice" by Stephen Powys); ph, Ernest Palmer (Technicolor); m, Josef Myrow, Gordon; ed, Barbara McLean; md, Alfred Newman; art d, Lyle Wheeler, Joseph C. Wright; cos, Bonnie Cashin; ch, Seymour Felix, Babe Pearce.

Musical   (PR:A   MPAA:NR)

THREE LITTLE SISTERS**½   (1944) 69m REP bw

Mary Lee (*Sue Scott*), Ruth Terry (*Hallie Scott*), Cheryl Walker (*Lily Scott*), William Terry (*Pvt. Robert Mason*), Jackie Moran (*Chad Jones*), Charles Arnt (*Ezra Larkin*), Frank Jenks (*Pvt. "Rosey" Rownan*), William Shirley (*Pvt. Ferguson*), Tom Fadden (*Ambrose Pepperdine*), Tom London (*Twitchell*), Milt Kibbee (*Tom Scott*), Addison Richards (*Col. Flemming*), Lillian Randolph (*Mabel*), Sam "Deacon" McDaniel (*Benjy*), Forrest Taylor (*Mayor Thatcher*).

A sentimental tale about a GI who falls for a girl he's never seen after writing to her and hearing about the luxurious life she leads. The girl, Lee, is really confined to a wheelchair and her two sisters barely make enough money to get by as scrub-girls. When the GI arrives, the girls switch identities and pretend to be socialites. Without knowing Lee's true identity he falls for her and, even after the truth comes out, stays by her side.

p, Harry Grey; d, Joseph Santley; w, Olive Cooper (based on a story by Maurice Clark, Cooper); ph, Reggie Lanning; ed, Fred Allen; md, Morton Scott; art d, Gano Chittenden; cos, Adele Palmer; m/l, "Don't Forget the Little Girl Back Home," "Sweet Dreams Sweetheart" Kim Gannon, Walter Ke nt (sung by Mary Lee, Ruth Terry).

Romance   (PR:A   MPAA:NR)

THREE LITTLE WORDS**   (1950) 102m MGM c

Fred Astaire (*Bert Kalmar*), Red Skelton (*Harry Ruby*), Vera-Ellen (*Jessie Brown Kalmar*), Arlene Dahl (*Eileen Percy*), Keenan Wynn (*Charlie Kope*), Gale Robbins (*Terry Lordel*), Gloria DeHaven (*Mrs. Carter DeHaven*), Phil Regan (*Himself*), Harry Shannon (*Clanahan*), Debbie Reynolds (*Helen Kane*), Paul Harvey (*Al Masters*), Carleton Carpenter (*Dan Healy*), George Metkovich (*Al Schacht*), Harry Mendoza (*Mendoza the Great*), Billy Gray (*Boy*), Pat Flaherty (*Coach*), Pierre Watkin (*Philip Goodman*), Syd Saylor (*Barker*), Elzie Emanuel (*Black Boy*), Sherry Hall (*Pianist*), Pat Williams (*Assistant*), Charles Wagenheim (*Waiter*), Tony Taylor (*Kid*), Phyllis Kennedy (*Mother*), Donald Kerr (*Stage Manager*), Beverly Michaels (*Francesca Ladovan*), Bert Davidson, William Tannen (*Photographers*), George Sherwood (*Director*), Harry Barris (*Guest Piano Player*), Alex Gerry (*Marty Collister*), Helen Kane (*Singing Voice of Debbie Reynolds*), Anita Ellis (*Singing Voice of Vera-Ellen*).

An utter delight, this biographical musical portrays the lives of the famed composing team of Bert Kalmar (Astaire) and Harry Ruby (Skelton). Astaire is a song-and-dance man on the vaudeville circuit who harbors a secret hope of becoming a magician. After injuring his knee, Astaire's dancing days are over and eventually he takes to writing song lyrics. Skelton plays the piano at a Coney Island honky-tonk and also writes lyrics, though he, too, has other career plans. He hopes to play baseball, but eventually Skelton meets Astaire and a songwriting team is born. The two go on to write numerous hits for both Broadway and the movies, though a misunderstanding ends the partnership. Vera-Ellen, Astaire's wife, and Skelton's spouse Dahl finally bring the two men back together for a happy, if somewhat fictionalized, conclusion. For the most part, though, this movie sticks to the facts and never fails to entertain. Astaire is his usual charming self, and dances a couple numbers with Vera-Ellen. Skelton gives one of the best performances of his career, playing down from his usual slapstick. The two performers worked well together, and Skelton had great respect for Astaire's talents, though he wasn't above a practical joke on the set. In Bob Thomas' book *Astaire, The Man, The Dancer*, Skelton reminisced: "Fred is not a prude by any means, but he is pretty conservative. When we were making THREE LITTLE WORDS, *Playboy* magazine was just becoming popular, and in those times nude centerfolds were something new and sensational. I had the prop guy go down to the studio newsstand and buy up as many *Playboys* as he could find. When Fred was at lunch, we pinned the centerfolds all over Fred's dressing room. When Fred came back from lunch, he sat down at his dressing room mirror. As he always did before he went to work, he was thinking intently about what he was going to do. Then he looked up and saw the pictures on the wall. Immediately he said, 'Why that red-headed son of a bitch!'" The film is sparked by some wonderful supporting players, particularly Vera-Ellen and Dahl as the wives. Appearing as themselves in cameo roles are Regan and Mendoza, and Ruby himself served as technical advisor. Gloria DeHaven portrayed her own mother, Mrs. Carter DeHaven. Reynolds made her third film appearance here as Helen Kane, the legendary "Boop-Boop-a-Doop" girl, performing Kalmar, Ruby, and Herb Stothart's comical "I Wanna Be Loved By You." Though Reynolds gave it her all, it was actually Kane herself who provided the dubbed-in voice. Other numbers include: "Who's Sorry Now?" (Kalmar, Ruby, Ted Snyder, sung by Gloria DeHaven), "Three Little Words" (Kalmar, Ruby, sung by Astaire, Skelton, Vera-Ellen dubbed by Anita Ellis), "I Love You So Much" (Kalmar, Ruby, sung by Dahl, male chorus), "She's Mine, All Mine" (Kalmar, Ruby), "So-Long, Oo-Long" (Kalmar, Ruby, sung by Astaire, Skelton), Groucho Marx's unforgettable theme song "Hooray for Captain Spaulding" (Kalmar, Ruby, sung by Astaire, Skelton), "Up In the Clouds" (Kalmar, Ruby), "All Alone Monday" (Kalmar, Ruby, sung by Robbins), "Where Did You Get That Girl?" (Kalmar, Ruby, Harry Puck, sung by Astaire, Vera-Ellen dubbed by Ellis), "My Sunny Tennessee" (Kalmar, Ruby, Herman Ruby, sung by Astaire, Skelton), "Come On Papa" (Ruby, Edgar Leslie, sung by Vera-Ellen dubbed by Ellis, chorus), "You Are My Lucky Star" (Arthur Freed, Nacio Herb Brown, sung by Regan), "Thinking of You" (Kalmar, Ruby), and "Mr. and Mrs. Hoofer at Home" (Kalmar, Ruby, danced by Astaire, Vera-Ellen).

p, Jack Cummings; d, Richard Thorpe; w, George Wells (based on the lives and songs of Bert Kalmar and Harry Ruby); ph, Harry Jackson (Technicolor); ed, Ben Lewis; md, Andre Previn; art d, Cedric Gibbons, Urie McCleary; ch, Hermes Pan.

Musical   **(PR:AA MPAA:NR)**

THREE LIVE GHOSTS*½   (1929) 87m UA bw

Beryl Mercer (*Mrs. Gubbins*), Hilda Vaughn (*Peggy Woofers*), Harry Stubbs (*Bolton*), Joan Bennett (*Rose Gordon*), Nancy Price (*Alice*), Charles McNaughton (*Jimmie Gubbins*), Robert Montgomery (*William Foster*), Claud Allister (*Spoofy*), Arthur Clayton (*Paymaster*), Tenen Holtz (*Crockery Man*), Shayle Gardner (*Briggs*), Jack Cooper (*Benson*), Jocelyn Lee (*Lady Leicester*).

An overly talky and stagey comedy about three soldiers who return home to find the government and war department have listed them as casualties. Things get difficult when one of the boys' mother, Mercer, tries to turn an American soldier over to the authorities. A slow-moving picture that likes to hear itself talk.

p, Max Marcin; d, Thornton Freeland; w, Helen Hallet, Marcin (based on the story by Sally Winters, and on the play by Frederic Stewart Isham, Marcin); ph, Robert H. Planck; ed, Robert Kern.

Comedy   **(PR:A MPAA:NR)**

THREE LIVE GHOSTS*½   (1935) 70m MGM bw

Richard Arlen, Beryl Mercer, Claude Allister, Charles McNaughton, Cecelia Parker, Dudley Digges, Nydia Westman, Jonathan Hale, Lillian Cooper, Robert Grieg.

Previously filmed in 1929, THREE LIVE GHOSTS stars Arlen, Allister and McNaughton as three war buddies who return home to find that they have been listed as dead. A weak transformation from a stage play which has McNaughton and Allister reprising their roles from the 1929 film, as well as casting Mercer again as one of the boys' mothers.

p, John W. Considine, Jr.; d, H. Bruce Humberstone; w, C. Gardner Sullivan (based on the play by Frederick S. Isham, Max Marcin); ph, Chester Lyons,

James Wong Howe; ed, Tom Held; cos, Dolly Tree.

Comedy/Drama   **(PR:A MPAA:NR)**

THREE LIVES OF THOMASINA, THE***   (1963, U.S./Brit.) 87m
                                                     Disney/BV c

Patrick McGoohan (*Andrew MacDhui*), Susan Hampshire (*Lori MacGregor*), Karen Dotrice (*Mary MacDhui*), Laurence Naismith (*Rev. Angus Peddie*), Jean Anderson (*Mrs. MacKenzie*), Wilfrid Brambell (*Willie Bannock*), Finlay Currie (*Grandpa Stirling*), Vincent Winter (*Hughie Stirling*), Denis Gilmore (*Jamie McNab*), Ewan Roberts (*Constable McQuarrie*), Oliver Johnston (*Mr. Dobbie*), Francis De Wolff (*Targu*), Charles Carson (*Doctor*), Nora Nicholson (*Old Lady*), Jack Stewart (*Birnie*), Matthew Garber (*Geordie*), Elspeth March (*The Voice of Thomasina*), Alex Mackenzie, Ruth Dunning, Gwen Nelson, Thomasina the Cat.

A charming tale of a young girl, Dotrice, and her cat, Thomasina, who together survive life-threatening situations. Dotrice lives in turn-of-the-century Scotland with her veterinarian father, McGoohan, who orders the family cat killed when it is diagnosed as having tetanus. Miraculously the cat is saved by the mysterious Hampshire, who is thought by the children to be a witch, and spends much of her time tending to animals in the forest. As the cat is about to be buried, Hampshire brings it back to life, but not before the feline ventures through cat heaven, complete with cat goddesses and sparkling stars. After chasing Thomasina outside during a thunderstorm, Dotrice contracts pneumonia and is near death. Upon Hampshire's advice, McGoohan brings her Thomasina, restoring her will to live. A thoroughly enjoyable children's film, which will leave the kids in awe and begging for their very own Thomasina.

p, Hugh Attwooll; d, Don Chaffey; w, Robert Westerby (based on the novel *Thomasina, the Cat Who Thought She Was God* by Paul Gallico); ph, Paul Beeson (Technicolor); m, Paul J. Smith; ed, Gordon Stone; md, Eric Rogers; art d, Michael Stringer; set d, Vernon Dixon; cos, Margaret Furse; spec eff, Ub Iwerks, Jim Fetherolf; m/l, "Thomasina" Terry Gilkyson; makeup, Harry Frampton; animal trainer, Jimmy Chipperfield.

Children's Film/Fantasy   **(PR:AAA MPAA:NR)**

THREE LOVES HAS NANCY**½   (1938) 69m MGM bw

Janet Gaynor (*Nancy Briggs*), Robert Montgomery (*Malcolm Niles*), Franchot Tone (*Robert Hansen*), Guy Kibbee (*Pa Briggs*), Claire Dodd (*Vivian Herford*), Reginald Owen (*William, Valet*), Cora Witherspoon (*Mrs. Herford*), Emma Dunn (*Mrs. Briggs*), Charley Grapewin (*Grandpa Briggs*), Lester Matthews (*Dr. Alonzo Z. Stewart*), Grady Sutton (*George*), Edgar Dearing (*Conductor*), Charles Lane (*Manager of Cleaning Establishment*), Greta Meyer (*Mrs. Swanson*), Priscilla Lawson (*Gertie*), Sarah Edwards (*Chairwoman*), Grace Hayle, Marie Blake, Elise Cavanna, Carol Tevis (*Women*), Etta McDaniel (*Mammy*), Eddie Kane (*Steward*), Sam McDaniel (*Waiter*), Lester Dorr (*Newsstand Man*), James B. Carson (*Waiter*), George Chandler (*Baggage Master*), Tom O'Grady (*Bartender*), Harold Miller, David Newell, David Alison Horsley, Cyril Ring, Jack Donaldson (*Men at Party*), Cecille Thurlow, Barbara Salisbury, Jenifer Gray, Bonnie Bannon (*Girls at Party*), Louis Natheaux (*Promoter*), Grant Withers (*Jack*), Kane Richmond, James Flavin (*Jack's Friends*), Matt McHugh (*Traveling Salesman*).

A festival of screwball antics fills the screen in this zany romantic comedy, which has innocent, small-town native Gaynor paying a visit to the Big Apple. There she becomes the object of novelist Montgomery's desires, as well as publisher Tone's. Guaranteed to tickle a rib or two...or three...or even a whole slab.

p, Norman Krasna; d, Richard Thorpe; w, Bella Spewack, Sam Spewack, George Oppenheimer, David Hertz (based on the story by Lee Loeb, Mort Braus); ph, William Daniels; m, Dr. William Axt; ed, Frederick Y. Smith; cos, Adrian.

Romance/Comedy   **(PR:A MPAA:NR)**

THREE MARRIED MEN**   (1936) 66m PAR bw

Lynne Overman (*Jeff Mullins*), William Frawley (*Bill Mullins*), Roscoe Karns (*Peter Cary*), Mary Brian (*Jennie Mullins*), George Barbier (*Mr. Cary*), Marjorie Gateson (*Clara*), Bennie Bartlett (*Percy Mullins*), Cora Sue Collins (*Sue Cary*), Mabel Colcord (*Mrs. Mullins*), Betty Ross Clark (*Annie*), Gail Sheridan (*Rose Cary*), Donald Meek (*Mr. Frisbee*).

Fear of marriage is given the comic treatment when country boy Karns readies to marry Brian, much to the dismay of both their families. Karns soon is victimized by Brian's two married brothers– Frawley and Overman– who try to convince the shaky groom not to go on with the ceremony.

p, Arthur Hornblow, Jr.; d, Eddie Buzzell; w, Dorothy Parker, Alan Campbell (based on the story by Owen Davis, Sr.); ph, Edward Cronjager.

Comedy   **(PR:A MPAA:NR)**

THREE MAXIMS, THE   (SEE: SHOW GOES ON, THE, 1938, Brit.)

THREE MEN AND A GIRL, 1938   (SEE: KENTUCKY MOONSHINE, 1938)

THREE MEN AND A GIRL, 1949, Brit.
(SEE: GAY ADVENTURE, THE, 1949, Brit.)

THREE MEN FROM TEXAS***   (1940) 70m PAR bw

William Boyd (*Hopalong Cassidy*), Russell Hayden (*Lucky Jenkins*), Andy Clyde (*California*), Morris Ankrum (*Morgan*), Morgan Wallace (*Andrews*), Thornton Edwards (*Pico*), Esther Estrella (*Paquita*), Davison Clark (*Thompson*), Dick Curtis (*Gardner*), Glenn Strange, Neyle Marx, Robert Burns, Jim Corey, George Morrell, George Lollier, Frank McCarroll, Lucio Villegas.

One of the finest Hopalong Cassidy entries has Boyd and Hayden teaming as Texas Rangers to put a stop to Ankrum's illegal plan to control the Mexican border. This entry is boosted above many of the others, thanks to the comic relief of Clyde and the witty dialog he is given. An outstanding musical score by Young further elevates this oater to stardom.

p, Harry Sherman; d, Lesley Selander; w, Norton S. Parker (based on the characters created by Clarence E. Mulford); ph, Russell Harlan; m, Victor Young; ed, Sherman A. Rose, Carroll Lewis; art d, Lewis A. Rachmil.

Western   **(PR:A   MPAA:NR)**

THREE MEN IN A BOAT*½   (1933, Brit.) 60m Associated Talking Pictures/ABF bw

William Austin (*Harris*), Edmond Breon (*George*), Billy Milton (*Jimmy*), Davy Burnaby (*Sir Henry Harland*), Iris March (*Peggy*), Griffith Humphreys (*Sergeant*), Stephen Ewart (*Doctor*), Victor Stanley (*Cockney*), Frank Bertram (*Fisherman*), Sam Wilkinson (*Police Constable*), Winifred Evans (*Lady Harland*).

A trivial comedy about three Englishmen who travel along the Thames in a boat, getting themselves into a series of predicaments along the way. Two of the men have slapstick personalities while the third plays the straight man and winds up falling in love with a young lovely. This poor outing marked an early effort of top silent director Cutts on his way to the top again after being temporarily eclipsed by the advent of sound.

p, Basil Dean; d, Graham Cutts; w, D.B. Wyndham-Lewis, Reginald Purdell (based on the novel by Jerome K. Jerome); ph, Robert Martin.

Comedy   **(PR:A   MPAA:NR)**

THREE MEN IN A BOAT**   (1958, Brit.) 84m Romulus/Valiant c

Laurence Harvey (*George*), Jimmy Edwards (*Harris*), David Tomlinson (*J*), Shirley Eaton (*Sophie Clutterbuck*), Jill Ireland (*Bluebell Porterhouse*), Lisa Gastoni (*Primrose Porterhouse*), Martita Hunt (*Mrs. Willis*), Campbell Cotts (*Ambrose Porterhouse*), Joan Haythorne (*Mrs. Porterhouse*), Adrienne Corri (*Clara Willis*), Noelle Middleton (*Ethelbertha*), Charles Lloyd Pack (*Mr. Quilp*), Robertson Hare (*Photographer*), A.E. Matthews (*Crabtree, 1st Old Gentleman*), Miles Malleson (*Baskcomb, 2nd Old Gentleman*), Ernest Thesiger (*3rd Old Gentleman*), Pat Lanski (*Woman Pianist*), Christian Duvaliex (*Man Pianist*), Mark Hashfield (*Bowler*), Graham Curnow (*Captain*), Stuart Saunders (*Dad at Regatta*), Margaret St. Barbe West (*Mum at Regatta*), Shane Cordell (*Girl Lover*), Norman Rossington (*Boy Lover*), Oswald Laurence (*Cocky Young Man*), Angela Krefeld (*Girl Friend*), Frank Atkinson (*Lockkeeper*), Rhett Ward (*Man in Dinghy*), Margot Lister (*Lady Walker*), George Woodbridge (*Policeman*), Esma Cannon (*Meek Woman*), Toke Townley (*Meek Man*), Peggy Ann Taylor (*Gertrude*), Michael Barber (*Harold*), Julia Nelson (*Mother with Baby*), Martyn Garrett (*Baby*), Barbara Archer (*Pretty Girl*), Judith Warden (*Large Woman*), Harold Goodwin (*Mazekeeper*), Pauline Winter (*1st Woman at Picnic*), Sheila Raynor (*2nd Woman at Picnic*), Carl Bernard (*Tall Man in Maze*), Leslie Weston (*Baker*), Neta the Dog.

A remake of the dated 1933 film which again displays a trio of goons traveling the Thames on a two-week holiday. They meet three young ladies on the shore, but seem to get in just as much trouble on land, running into Hampton Court maze, for example, as on water. Either way, the script doesn't hold water and neither should have the boat. It was only the second picture for London-born Ireland, a one-time ballet dancer who made her screen debut the year before, as a dancer in ROSALIE. She acquitted herself well before the cameras and won special mention in this dim-witted attempt at farce.

p, Jack Clayton; d, Ken Annakin; w, Hubert Gregg, Vernon Harris (based on the novel by Jerome K. Jerome); ph, Eric Cross (CinemaScope, Eastmancolor); m, John Addison; ed, Ralph Kemplen; art d, John Howell; cos, Peter Rice.

Comedy   **(PR:A   MPAA:NR)**

THREE MEN IN WHITE*½   (1944) 85m MGM bw

Lionel Barrymore (*Dr. Leonard Gillespie*), Van Johnson (*Dr. Randall Adams*), Marilyn Maxwell (*Ruth Edley*), Keye Luke (*Dr. Lee Wong How*), Ava Gardner (*Jean Brown*), Alma Kruger (*Molly Byrd*), Rags Ragland (*Hobart Genet*), Nell Craig (*Nurse Parker*), Walter Kingsford (*Dr. Walter Carew*), George H. Reed (*Conover*), Patricia Barker (*Mary Jones*), Sam McDaniel (*Black Phone Operator*), Billy Cummings (*Boy on Street*), Addison Richards (*Mr. Brown*), George Chandler (*Attendant*), Byron Foulger (*Technician*).

A weak entry in the "Dr. Gillespie" series, with the astute wheel chair-bound Barrymore having to decide on a new assistant. In order to base his decision on medical talent, he gives the two prospects--Johnson and Luke--a case to tend to. One gets to treat a woman's "incurable" arthritis, while the other must treat a young boy's allergy to sugar. Marilyn Maxwell and Ava Gardner lend their talents brightly and winningly to the proceedings. (See: DR. GILLEPSIE series, Index.)

d, Willis Goldbeck; w, Martin Berkeley, Harry Ruskin (based on the characters created by Max Brand); ph, Ray June; m, Nathaniel Shilkret; ed, George Hively; art d, Cedric Gibbons, Harry McAfee; set d, Edwin B. Willis; cos, Irene.

Drama   **(PR:A   MPAA:NR)**

THREE MEN ON A HORSE***   (1936) 88m FN-WB bw

Frank McHugh (*Erwin Trowbridge*), Joan Blondell (*Mabel*), Carol Hughes (*Audrey Trowbridge*), Allen Jenkins (*Charley*), Guy Kibbee (*Mr. Carver*), Sam Levene (*Patsy*), Teddy Hart (*Frankie*), Edgar Kennedy (*Harry*), Paul Harvey (*Clarence Dobbins*), Margaret Irving (*Gloria*), George Chandler (*Al*), Harry Davenport (*William*), Eddie "Rochester" Anderson (*Moses*), Virginia Sale (*Chambermaid*), Charles Lane (*Cleaner*), Mickey Daniels (*Delivery Boy*), Cliff Saum (*Bus Conductor*), Harry Hayden (*Man on Bus*), Tola Nesmith (*Head Nurse*), Eily Malyon (*Nurse*), Edith Craig, Irene Colman (*Woman Bettors*), John Sheehan, Pat West (*Male Bettors*), Ted Bliss (*Radio Announcer*).

A lively comedy which more than successfully makes the transition from Broadway stage play to the screen thanks to the talents of director LeRoy and star McHugh. The film follows the exploits of McHugh, a writer of greeting cards, who is referred to throughout as "Oiwin," a bastardization of his real name, Erwin. It is soon discovered that McHugh has the remarkable talent of predicting horse races. Bettors Levene, Hart, and Kennedy are quite aware of the financial reward that McHugh's talents offer, and before long the thoroughbred prophet is abducted and forced to pick the winners. While he is holed up in a hotel room, his cranky boss, Kibbee, desperately tries to get him back to work before the Mother's Day greeting card crunch. Kibbee tries all he can, even raising McHugh's salary, but his release comes only after his captors break an unbreakable rule–bringing McHugh to the racetrack. To test McHugh's predictions, his captors force him to bet on his own tip, thereby rendering his talents useless. It's all a great deal of fun, albeit wholly unbelievable, but with McHugh's gift for farce and Blondell's role as a "Film Fun" covergirl, THREE MEN ON A HORSE is a pleasure. However, if it's horseracing scenes you're looking for this film doesn't have much to offer. The publicity photo doesn't even include a real horse (nor does it include three men), but a wooden one on top of which sit McHugh, Blondell and Hughes.

p, Sam Bischoff; d, Mervyn LeRoy; w, Laird Doyle (based on the play by John Cecil Holm, George Abbott); ph, Sol Polito; ed, Ralph Dawson; md, Leo F. Forbstein; art d, Robert Haas.

Comedy   **(PR:A   MPAA:NR)**

THREE MEN TO DESTROY**   (1980, Fr.) 90m Adel-Antenne 2/UGC c
(TROIS HOMMES A ABATTRE)

Alain Delon (*Michel Gerfaut*), Dalila DiLazzaro (*Bea*), Pierre Dux (*Emmerich*), Michel Auclair (*Leprince*), Simone Renant (*Mme. Gerfaut*).

Delon gives a wooden performance as a professional gambler who accidentally lends a hand to a gangster's enemy. He is soon targeted for death or mutilation by a ruthless bunch of killers, but goes on the rampage after his friend is killed by the gang. His luck runs out by the finale and he is killed by Dux, who has been on his trail all along. Every action cliche is thrown into the soup in this dismal movie.

p, Alain Delon; d, Jacques Deray; w, Deray, Christopher Frank (based on the novel by Jean-Patrick Manchette); ph, Jean Tournier; m, Claude Bolling; ed, I. Garcia de Herreros; art d, Jacques Brizzio.

Crime Drama   **(PR:O   MPAA:NR)**

THREE MESQUITEERS, THE**½   (1936) 61m REP bw

Robert Livingston (*Stony Brooke*), Ray Corrigan (*Tucson Smith*), Syd Saylor (*Lullaby Joslin*), Kay Hughes (*Marian*), J.P. McGowan (*Brack*), Al Bridge (*Olin*), Frank Yaconelli (*Pete*), John Merton (*Bull*), Jean Marvey (*Bob*), Milburn Stone (*John*), Duke York (*Chuck*), Nena Quartaro (*Rosita*), Allen Connor (*Milt*), Stanley Blystone.

The first entry in the THREE MESQUITEERS series has Livingston and Corrigan being discharged from an Army hospital and riding out West to become homesteaders. They are confronted with the slam-bang ways of western living, however, and soon band together with cattlemen and destroy an outlaw gang. The pair then team up with the motorcycle riding Saylor and venture off into the wilderness in the hope of bringing justice to the outlaw West. (See THREE MESQUITEERS series, Index.)

p, Nat Levine; d, Ray Taylor; w, Jack Natteford (based on the story by Charles Condon from an idea by William Colt MacDonald); ph, William P. Nobles; m, Harry Grey; ed, William Thompson, Murray Seldeen.

Western   **Cas.**   **(PR:A MPAA:NR)**

THREE MOVES TO FREEDOM**½   (1960, Ger.) 104m RANK bw
(SCHACHNOVELLE; AKA: THE ROYAL GAME)

Curt Jurgens (*Werner von Basil*), Claire Bloom (*Irene Andreny*), Jorg Felmy (*Hans Berger*), Mario Adorf (*Mirko Centowic*), Albert Lieven (*Hartmann*), Alan Gifford (*Mac Iver*), Dietmar Schonherr (*Rabbi*), Karel Stepanek (*Baranow*), Wolfgang Wahl (*Moonface*), Rudolf Forster (*Hotel Manager*), Albert Bressler (*Scientist*), Jan Hendriks (*1st Officer*), Harald Maresch (*Ballet Master*).

Jurgens plays an art thief who smuggles great works out of the country in order for a church to reap the profits, and Bloom plays a ballerina. Told chiefly in flashbacks, it concerns itself with the effect that Nazi brainwashing has on a healthy mind.

p, Luggi Waldleitner; d, Gerd Oswald; w, Harold Medford, Oswald (based on the novel *The Royal Game* by Stefan Zweig); ph, Gunther Senftleben; m, Hans-Martin Majewski; ed, K.M. Eckstein.

Drama   **(PR:A MPAA:NR)**

THREE MUSKETEERS, THE**½   (1935) 90m RKO bw

Walter Abel (*D'Artagnan*), Paul Lukas (*Athos*), Margot Grahame (*Milady de Winter*), Heather Angel (*Constance*), Ian Keith (*de Rochefort*), Moroni Olsen (*Porthos*), Onslow Stevens (*Aramis*), Rosamond Pinchot (*Queen Anne*), Ralph Forbes (*Duke of Buckingham*), Lumsden Hare (*de Treville*), Miles Mander (*King Louis XIII*), Nigel de Brulier (*Cardinal Richelieu*), John Qualen (*Planchet, D'Artagnan's Servant*), Murray Kinnell (*Bernajou*), Wade Boteler (*Peylerand*), Stanley Blystone (*Villand*), Ralph Faulkner (*Jussac, Richelieu's Soldier*).

A tame version of the Dumas, classic which had previously been filmed silently in 1921 with Douglas Fairbanks. Originally this was to have been directed by John Ford with Francis Lederer in the starring role; instead, Abel is miscast in his first opportunity off the Broadway stage, and Lee woefully misdirects a swashbuckler that has every right to a spirited production from all hands.

p, Cliff Reid; d, Rowland V. Lee; w, Dudley Nichols, Lee (based on the novel by Alexandre Dumas); ph, Peverell Marley; m, Max Steiner; ed, George Hively; cos, Walter Plunkett; spec eff, Vernon L. Walker.

Adventure   **(PR:A MPAA:NR)**

THREE MUSKETEERS, THE**½   (1939) 73m FOX bw (GB: THE
SINGING MUSKETEER)

Don Ameche (*D'Artagnan*), Ritz Brothers (*Three Lackeys*), Binnie Barnes (*Milady De Winter*), Lionel Atwill (*De Rochefort*), Gloria Stuart (*Queen*), Pauline Moore (*Lady Constance*), Joseph Schildkraut (*King*), John Carradine (*Naveau*), Miles Mander (*Cardinal Richelieu*), Douglas Dumbrille (*Athos*), John King (*Aramis*), Russell Hicks (*Porthos*), Gregory Gaye (*Vitray*), Lester Matthews (*Duke of Buckingham*), Egon Brecher (*Landlord*), Moroni Olsen (*Bailiff*), Georges Renavent (*Capt. Fageon*), Montague Shaw (*Ship Captain*), Jean Parry, Fredrik Vogeding (*Guards*).

Director Allan Dwan had some fun with Dumas' original by turning the swashbuckling D'Artagnan into a singing D'Artagnan played with jubilation by Ameche. His fearless "musketeers" were the funny Ritz Brothers, phonys all, who had to struggle to get the laughs. It's fun but lacking as a true swashbuckler. Songs include: "My Lady," "Song of the Musketeers," "Voila," "Chicken Soup" (Samuel Pokrass, Walter Bullock).

p, Raymond Griffith; d, Allan Dwan; w, M.M. Musselman, William A. Drake, Sam Hellman, Sid Kuller, Ray Golden (based on characters created by Alexandre Dumas); ph, Peverell Marley; ed, Jack Dennis; md, David Buttolph; cos, Royer.

Adventure/Comedy   **(PR:A MPAA:NR)**

THREE MUSKETEERS, THE****   (1948) 126m MGM c

Lana Turner (*Milady Countess Charlotte de Winter*), Gene Kelly (*D'Artagnan*), June Allyson (*Constance Bonacieux*), Van Heflin (*Robert Athos*), Angela Lansbury (*Queen Anne*), Frank Morgan (*King Louis XIII*), Vincent Price (*Richelieu the Prime Minister*), Keenan Wynn (*Planchet*), John Sutton (*George, Duke of Buckingham*), Gig Young (*Porthos*), Robert Coote (*Aramis*), Reginald Owen (*De Treville*), Ian Kieth (*De Rochefort*), Patricia

Medina (*Kitty*), Richard Stapley (*Albert*), Byron Foulger (*Bonacieux*), Sol Gross (*Jussac*), Robert Warwick (*D'Artagnan, Sr.*), Marie Windsor (*Dark-Eyed Lady-in-Waiting*), Ruth Robinson (*Mother of D'Artagnan*), Tom Tyler (*Traveler*), Fred Coby, Leonard Penn (*Musketeers*), Kirk Alyn, John Holland (*Friends of Aramis*), Francis McDonald (*Fisherman*), Reginald Sheffield (*Subaltern*), Wilson Benge, Alec Harford (*Valets*), Harry Wilson (*Kidnaper*), Mickey Simpson (*Executioner*), Frank Hagney (*Executioner of Lyons*), William Edmunds (*Landlord*), Irene Seidner (*Landlord's Wife*), Paul Maxey (*Major Domo*), Arthur Hohl (*Dragon Rouge Host*), Gil Perkins (*Guard*), Albert Morin (*Bazin*), Norman Leavitt (*Mousqueton*), William "Bill" Phillips (*Grimaud*), Richard Simmons (*Count DeWardes*).

This is a rollicking version of the oft-filmed Dumas classic, with Kelly essaying the role of D'Artagnan in a marvelous style. The film opens as Kelly leaves his country home for Paris to join the famed Musketeers. After some misadventures with nobleman Keith, Kelly finally makes it to Paris. There he again spies Keith and runs after him, but Kelly ends up knocking into Heflin, a member of the Musketeers. Along with his fellow musketeers Young and Coote, Heflin challenges Kelly to a duel. When Kelly later meets the trio, he offers to take them all on at once. Heflin fights Kelly single-handedly, and finds the young man to be handy with his sword. The duel is interrupted by some of Price's guards. Price has outlawed dueling, but with their "one for all and all for one" spirit, the musketeers and Kelly easily defeat the guards. Now one of the band, Kelly joins the others in serving their king, Morgan. Price is trying to overthrow Morgan's reign and uses his mistress, Turner, to help his nefarious plans. After learning that the queen, Lansbury, is dallying with Sutton, a duke, Price and Turner work to bring disgrace to Lansbury's name. They learn Lansbury has given a necklace to Sutton. Allyson overhears the two plotting, and tells Kelly, who is now the subject of her affections. Kelly in turn has fallen for Turner and is broken-hearted to hear the news. He and the other musketeers set out to retrieve the necklace so Price cannot disgrace the queen, but they must fend off Price's guards before accomplishing their mission. The necklace soon finds its way back to Lansbury's hands, and Price is forced to clam up. Turner ends up losing her head as punishment, and the brave Kelly has his revenge with Keith. Kelly is sheer delight, taking to the swashbuckling story with enormous zest. His acrobatics are a sight to behold, a marvelous extension of Kelly's much loved dancing skills. This was Kelly's favorite role of his nonmusical films, and he had hoped his performance here would convince MGM to let him do a musical version of "Cyrano de Bergerac," a dream that never saw fruition. The supporting cast was marvelous, taking the comedy in good spirits. Morgan gives a wonderful portrayal of King Louis XIII. This was Turner's first Technicolor film, something MGM loudly heralded in its ad campaign. Turner originally did not want the role, and accepted a studio suspension rather than take what she considered to be a secondary part. Eventually she relented, though at one point Alida Valli was considered for the part. The photography is wonderful, capturing the colorful aspects of the yarn with a marvelous use of hues that earned cinematographer Planck an Oscar nomination. Price as the infamous Cardinal Richelieu, had the religious aspects of his character toned down by the studio. MGM feared a backlash if a man of the cloth was portrayed in an unfavorable light, so the character became more of a political figure. MGM hired Jean Heremans, a Belgian fencing champion, to teach Kelly his fance swordplay for the film. Heremans worked as fencing instructor for the Los Angeles Athletic club, a position held previously by Henry J. Uyttenhove. Ironically, Uyttenhove was the Belgian fencing master who had taught the same skills to Douglas Fairbanks, Sr. for his version of THE THREE MUSKETEERS IN 1921.

p, Pandro S. Berman; d, George Sidney; w, Robert Ardrey (based on the novel by Alexandre Dumas, pere); ph, Robert Planck (Technicolor); m, Herbert Stothart; ed, Robert J. Kern, George Boemler; art d, Cedric Gibbons, Malcolm Brown; set d, Edwin B. Willis, Henry W. Grace; cos, Walter Plunkett; spec eff, Warren Newcombe.

Action/Adventure/Comedy   **Cas.**   **(PR:C MPAA:NR)**

THREE MUSKETEERS, THE****   (1974, Panama) 105m FOX c

Oliver Reed (*Athos*), Raquel Welch (*Constance*), Richard Chamberlain (*Aramis*), Michael York (*D'Artagnan*), Frank Finlay (*Porthos*), Christopher Lee (*Rochefort*), Jean-Pierre Cassel (*Louis XIII*), Geraldine Chaplin (*Anne of Austria*), Simon Ward (*Duke of Buckingham*), Faye Dunaway (*Milady*), Charlton Heston (*Cardinal Richelieu*), Spike Milligan (*Mons. Bonacieux*), Roy Kinnear (*Planchet*), Michael Gothard (*Felton*), Sybil Danning (*Eugenie*), Gitty Djamal (*Beatrice*), Nicole Calfan (*Kitty*), Georges Wilson (*Treville*), Angel Del Pozo (*Jussac*), Rodney Bewes (*Richelieu's Spy*), Ben Aris (*1st Musketeer*), Joss Ackland (*D'Artagnan's Father*), Gretchen Franklyn (*D'Artagnan's Mother*), Francis De Wolff (*Captain*), William Hobbs (*Swordsman at Inn*).

Although technically a Panamanian production, it was actually shot in England with an international cast. The oft-told tale by Dumas is told once again in, perhaps, the best of the films about the four men who were known as THE THREE MUSKETEERS (people forget that Di'Artagnan was apart from A thos, Aramis, and Porthos). This one sticks closely to the story but with some added high-jinks that are all to the good. York is a happy rustic youth, schooled at swordsmanship but not politically motivated, as was everyone else in those days. He's a country boy, a bit of a bumbler, but with such high spirits that he is instantly lovable. He would like to become part of the Musketeers, the leaders of whom are Reed, Chamberlain, and Finlay, a trio more intrigued by cleavage and cash than by any sort of loyalty to their king, Cassel, who is, at best, an idiot. Cassel's wife is Chaplin, a duplicitous queen who is having a royal fling with Ward, a peer of England. She gives Ward an expensive necklace as a token of their "friendship" and that news is relayed to the evil cardinal, Heston, who intends to tell the word that Chaplin is an adulteress. His desire to reveal her duplicity is not out of any Catholic morality; rather, it's because he wants to be the power behind Cassel's throne and if he eliminates Chaplin, he'll be up there with the boss. There's a large gala coming up and Heston, aware that Chaplin has given the necklace to Ward, tells Cassel to have Chaplin wear it to show off to the nation. Cassel orders Chaplin to wear the necklace and now she has to get it back from Ward before the grand ball. At the same time, Heston sends adventuress Dunaway off to England to see if she can bring back two of the necklace's jewels as evidence that Chaplin has given it to Ward. Meanwhile, the trio of Reed, Finlay, and Chamberlain is exercising its penchant for wenches and swordplay and just having a good time. York meets and falls for Welch, Chaplin's best friend and lady-in-waiting. She is on to Heston's plot and tells York about it in the hope that something can be done to save the honor of Chaplin. York tells the three Musketeers. Can they head off Dunaway before she gets to Ward and takes the gems? Lee is in league with Heston and while the Musketeers race toward the sea, they are attacked by Lee's men and seem to have been killed in the battle. The only one who escapes is York and he continues on toward England, guilt-ridden that he was the reason for the demise of Reed, Chamberlain, and Finlay. Dunaway has already gotten to Ward and taken the two gems, returned to France, and presented the diamonds to Heston, who cackles happily at what he has planned. Knowing Cassel is insisting that Chaplin wear the necklace, Heston sits back and waits for the fireworks. York gets to Ward, who examines the necklace and sees that there are, indeed, two stones missing. When Ward is told why, he quickly calls for an artisan to make two fake baubles and insert them into the necklace. York takes the intact necklace (and no one, save a master, could tell the difference or discern which diamonds are real and which aren't) and races for France. He gets to the palace on the night of the large ball and is elated to see that Finlay, Chamberlain, and Reed are alive. They slip the necklace to Chaplin. She is thrilled that her honor has not been besmirched, and she glides into the ballroom wearing the necklace, causing Heston to utter miscellaneous curses under his breath. For his heroic journey, York is rewarded and made a Musketeer, which has been his dream since childhood. In the past, the story by Dumas had been so trifled with by filmers that it seldom resembled what he'd written. Here, writer Fraser and director Lester went back to the original and hewed closely to the source material, proving that Dumas was right. A funny screenplay, some good slapstick, moments of real drama and menace all combine to make this a movie bonbon that satisfies the cinematic taste buds. There's not one false moment, no cheap jokes (like what Gene Wilder or Mel Brooks do when going back in history) and a wonderful period feel in the decor and costumes. The producer, Salkind, paid the cast for one picture but shot two at the same time without telling them. This was accomplished by saying it was a long script and that it would eventually be cut. The cast was having a fine time under Lester; they were in a marvelous location; and no one minded that the shooting schedule seemed inordinately long. Later, Salkind brought out the sequel, THE FOUR MUSKETEERS, and the cast banded together to sue the producer for more wages. They were awarded a considerable sum, though not nearly as much as if they'd been hired to make two movies. Salkind allegedly attempted the same trick with SUPERMAN and SUPERMAN II. Despite the glowing reviews, the movie did not knock them over at the box office, although it turned a tidy profit after all the receipts were counted.

p, Michael Alexander, Ilya Salkind; d, Richard Lester; w, George MacDonald Fraser (based on the novel by Alexandre Dumas); ph, David Watkins (Panavision, DeLuxe Color); m, Michel Legrand; ed, John Victor Smith; cos, Yvonne Blake, Ron Talsky.

Historical Comedy/Drama   Cas.   (PR:C   MPAA:PG)

THREE NIGHTS OF LOVE½   (1969, Ital.) 112m Jolly/Magna c
(TRE NOTTI D'AMORE)

"Fatebenefratelli": Catherine Spaak (Ghiga), John Phillip Law (Fra Felice), "La vedova": Spaak (Giselle), Renato Salvatori (Nicola), Aldo Puglisi, "La Moglie Bambina": Spaak (Cirilla), Enrico Maria Salerno (Giuliano), Diletta D'Andrea (Gabriella).

Three amusing stories starring versatile and stylish Spaak are told in this episodic film. In the first, cast with Law, she is a call girl brought to a hospital after a car accident, and put into a cast up to her neck. She attempts to compromise a young man who is preparing to take his final vows for the priesthood, and he, in turn, tries to save her soul. At the end, she has joined the brother's order, and he has left the church. In the second episode she is a widow who transports her husband's body back to Sicily, unaware that he was a Mafioso. She becomes friends with his allies until she learns that they are the ones who killed him. The final episode has her cast as a young bride to a middle-aged man who has many emotional problems. She suggests he take another woman as a lover, and then learns that he already has. Released in Italy in 1964.

p, Silvio Clementelli; d, Luigi Comencini ("Fatebenefratelli"), Renato Castellani ("La vedova"), Franco Rossi ("La Mogli Bambina"); w, Marcello Fondato, Franco Castellano, Pipolo, Massimo Franciosa; ph, Mario Montuori, Roberto Gerardi (Techniscope, Technicolor); m, Giuseppe Fusco, Carlo Rustichelli, Piero Piccioni; ed, Renato Cinquini, Iolanda Benvenuti, Giorgio Serralonga; cos, Piero Gherardi.

Comedy/Drama   (PR:O   MPAA:NR)

THREE NUTS IN SEARCH OF A BOLT*   (1964) 80m Harlequin
International bw-c

Mamie Van Doren (Saxie Symbol), Tommy Noonan (Tommy), Ziva Rodann (Dr. Myra Von), Paul Gilbert (Joe Lynch), John Cronin (Bruce Bernard), Peter Howard (Dr. Otis Salverson), T.C. Jones (Henry), Charles Irving (R.L. Katz), Alvy Moore (Sutter T. Finley), Robert Kenneally (Lennie), Marjorie Bennett (Mrs. Berkley-Kent), Arthur Gould-Porter (Mr. Blyth), Pat O'Moore (Edwards), Jennie Lee (Miss Griswald), Jimmy Cross (Drunk), Curt Mercer (1st Crook), Richard Normoyle (2nd Crook), Frank Kreig (Bartender), Pat Noone (Miss Frisbee), Kathy Waniata (School Teacher), Phil Arnold (Television Technician).

A nudie comedy which casts Noonan (as the bolt?) who agrees to help out a trio of nuts–Van Doren, Gilbert, and Cronin–who need psychiatric advice but can't afford it. The idea is that unemployed actor Noonan can act out all three personalities in one session before a psychiatrist and get all the information they need for one-third the price. His zany performance is caught on the doctor's closed-circuit TV to other doctors around the world, and somehow breaks out into a nationwide telecast. A Hollywood producer sees the nutty goings on and buys the screen rights to the "show" for $100,000, putting the three nuts and wacky Noonan on easy street. Principle nudie segments are of stripper Van Doren, who bumps and grinds her delicious torso in a torrid strip at one point, and when she takes a beer bath. Rodann, as the doctor, displays a few French postcard shots of her beauty herself. These segments, basically, are what THREE NUTS IN SEARCH OF A BOLT is all about. Includes the anthem "I Used To Be a Stripper Down on Main, Now I'm the Main Attraction on the Strip" (Pony Sherrell, Phil Moody). Noonan previously made PROMISES, PROMISES with Jayne Mansfield, and before that starred with Marilyn Monroe in GENTLEMEN PREFER BLONDES. Art director Carroll Ballard went on to direct THE BLACK STALLION.

p, Tommy Noonan, Ian McGlashan; d, Noonan; w, Noonan, McGlashan; ph, Fouad Said (Eastmancolor); m, Phil Moody; ed, Bill Martin; art d, Carroll Ballard; ch, Ward Ellis.

Comedy   (PR:O   MPAA:NR)

THREE OF A KIND**   (1936) 68m Invincible bw

Chick Chandler (Jerry Bassett), Evalyn Knapp (Barbara Penfield), Berton Churchill ("Con" Cornelius), Patricia Farr (Prudence Cornelius), Richard Carle (F. Thorndyke Penfield), Bradley Page (Rodney Randall), Lew Kelly (Sgt. Cogarty), Pat West ("Beef" Smith), Bryant Washburn (Mr. Grimwood), Harry C. Bradley (Mr. Fash), John Dilson (Doc Adams), Billy Gilbert (The Tailor).

A modest comedy about romance and deception among three men who each try to pull one over on the other. Churchill, appropriately cast as "Con" Cornelius, steals the show with his impersonation of a feisty owner of a mythical tobacco plantation. Not exactly bewitching, but acceptable nonetheless.

p, Maury M. Cohen; d, Phil Rosen; w, Arthur T. Horman; ph, M.A. Andersen; ed, Roland D. Reed.

Romance/Comedy   (PR:A   MPAA:NR)

THREE ON A COUCH zero   (1966) 109m COL c

Jerry Lewis (Christopher Pride/Warren/Ringo/Rutherford/Heather), Janet Leigh (Dr. Elizabeth Acord), Mary Ann Mobley (Susan Manning), Gila Golan (Anna Jacque), Leslie Parrish (Mary Lou Mauve), James Best (Dr. Ben Mizer), Kathleen Freeman (Murphy), Buddy Lester (Drunk), Renzo Cesana (Ambassador), Fritz Feld (Attache), Jesslyn Fax, Renie Riano, Scatman Crothers.

Again Lewis takes on multiple roles (five!) as in his brilliant THE NUTTY PROFESSOR (1963), but this time he bombs. He plays an artist commissioned to paint in Paris who wants to take his psychiatrist-girl friend Leigh along and celebrate their honeymoon. She, however, has three man-hating patients who can't do without her. Lewis disguises himself as a variety of people and becomes each of their boy friends. His charade is finally discovered and he nearly loses Leigh, but she is convinced by her now-cured patients to take the vacation. After a long stretch with Paramount, this was Lewis' first effort for Columbia and though the film did turn a profit, there were some embarrassingly lame ad schemes to help it do so–the kind Frank Tashlin would make fun of in WILL SUCCESS SPOIL ROCK HUNTER? Since the number three was in the title, Columbia sponsored a number of contests having to do with the number, and even let triplets into the theater for free, far from a financial risk, however, considering the mathematical improbability of triplets. Another "bright idea" was to start a "We Hate

Men" fan club. To enjoy this film one must be a Jerry Lewis fan to the death, a close friend or a relative of Mr. Lewis, and be French. Three beauties with little acting ability were chosen by Lewis to play the man-hating trio in the picture. They were former Miss America, Mary Ann Mobley, Gila Golan, a former Miss Israel, and Parrish, a former NBC "Color Girl" the network used to promote the wonders to be seen on color TV. All got plenty of screen time in which to display their talents, but none seem to have had that spark that clicked, and film moguls remained indifferent to them. The picture was a disaster critically for Lewis but did manage to gross more than $2.5 million, for a fair profit.

p&d, Jerry Lewis; w, Bob Ross, Samuel Taylor (based on the story by Arne Sultan, Marvin Worth); ph, W. Wallace Kelley, Robert Bronner (Pathe Color); m, Louis Y. Brown; ed, Russel Wiles; art d, Leo K. Kuter; set d, Howard Bristol; cos, Moss Mabry; m/l, "A Now and a Later Love" Louis Y. Brown (sung by Danny Costello); makeup, Ben Lane, Jack Stone.

Comedy   (PR:A MPAA:NR)

THREE ON A HONEYMOON*   (1934) 65m FOX bw

Sally Eilers (Joan Foster), ZaSu Pitts (Alice Mudge), Henrietta Crosman ("Ma" Gillespie), Charles Starrett (Dick Charlton), Irene Hervey (Millicent Wells), John Mack Brown (Chuck Wells), Russell Simpson (Ezra MacDuff), Cornelius Keefe (Phil Lang), Howard Lally, Wini Shaw.

A boring comedy about a spoiled rich kid who happens to be the daughter of the owner of a steamship line. Before long she's fallen in love, as has just about everyone else on this archaic love boat. Nothing of interest here except the appearance of two top B-western stars, Starrett and Brown, without the ten-gallon hats and cowboy boots.

p, John Stone; d, James Tinling; w, Edward T. Lowe, Jr., Douglas Doty, George Wright, Raymond Van Sickle (based on the novel Promenade Deck by Ishbel Ross); ph, Joseph Valentine; Arthur Arling; ed, Alex Troffey; md, Samuel Kaylin; cos, Royer; ch, Dave Gould.

Comedy/Romance   (PR:A MPAA:NR)

THREE ON A MATCH***   (1932) 64m FN-WB bw

Joan Blondell (Mary Keaton), Warren William (Henry Kirkwood), Ann Dvorak (Vivian Revere), Bette Davis (Ruth Westcott), Lyle Talbot (Mike Loftus), Humphrey Bogart (Harve the Mug), Patricia Ellis (Linda), Sheila Terry (Naomi), Grant Mitchell (Principal Gilmore), Glenda Farrell (Reformatory Girl), Frankie Darro (Bobby), Clara Blandick (Mrs. Keaton), Hale Hamilton (Defense Attorney), Dick Brandon (Horace), Junior Johnson (Max), Dawn O'Day 'Anne Shirley' (Vivian as a Child), Virginia Davis (Mary as a Child), Betty Carse (Ruth as a Child), Buster Phelps (Junior), John Marston (Randall), Edward Arnold (Ace), Allen Jenkins (Dick), Sidney Miller (Willie Goldberg), Herman Bing (Prof. Irving Finklestein), Jack LaRue, Stanley Price (Mugs), Spencer Charters (Street Cleaner), Hardie Albright (Lawyer), Ann Brody (Mrs. Goldberg), Mary Doran (Prisoner), Blanche Frederici (Miss Blazer, Teacher), Selmer Jackson (Voice of Radio Announcer), Harry Seymour (Jerry Carter).

Paced with lightning speed, this compact 64-minute gangster melodrama brings together Blondell, Dvorak, and Davis as former schoolmates who have a reunion after more than 10 years. Blondell, after spending time in reform school, is a stage actress; Dvorak is a superior high-society woman who is married to lawyer William; and the intelligent Davis is a stenographer. Meeting in a restaurant, the women light their cigarettes from the same match, defying the superstition that the last person to use the match will be the first to die. Later, they meet at a bon voyage party for Dvorak, who is preparing to embark on a cruise with her son, Phelps. Blondell brings along as her date, Talbot, a tough underworld figure whose raw energy appeals to Dvorak. Instead of leaving on the cruise, she runs off with Talbot out of a perverse boredom with her society ways. William enlists the help of Blondell in finding his wife and son and along the way falls in love with her. When Williams finds that Dvorak has taken up with Talbot, he divorces her and regains custody of Phelps, employing Davis as his nanny. Later, when William's marriage to Blondell is announced, Dvorak falls into a depressed state and resorts to drink and drugs. Meanwhile, Talbot is deep over his head in gambling debts and tries unsuccessfully to blackmail William. He then hires mobster Bogart (referred to simply as "The Mug") and his two henchmen, Jenkins and LaRue, to kidnap Phelps. When it looks as if William will not pay the ransom, Dvorak fears that her son will be killed and tries to interfere, but is too drugged up to do any good. She also is taken prisoner by the kidnapers. As a morbid last resort, Dvorak scribbles a message in lipstick on her nightgown and jumps from the hideout's window, alerting the police to his location. She is killed, but the police manage to save the boy from the same fate. LeRoy skillfully crams a great deal of plot into 64 minutes, avoiding the pitfalls that would turn this into a 120-minute soap opera in lesser hands. Still, LeRoy creates three-dimensional characters instead of resorting to the cardboard cutouts which usually hamper a melodrama of this short length. THREE ON A MATCH not only brings life to its characters but also to the era of the 1920s. That decade is given a classic, nostalgic treatment (although it had ended just two years previously) in a year-by-year montage constructed of newsreel footage, headlines, fashions, and music. THREE ON A MATCH also provided Humphrey Bogart with his first gangster role after playing a succession of pretty-boy

roles. He would return to Warners four years later (costarring with Davis) as the full-fledged gangster Duke Mantee in THE PETRIFIED FOREST. For some ridiculous reason, the studio's publicity people decided to undermine the realistic nature of THREE ON A MATCH with an idiotic puzzle-game in which the audience was expected to match together the faces of the film's female stars--Blondell, Davis, Dvorak--with those of the male stars--William, Talbot, Bogart. THREE ON A MATCH was remade as the routine BROADWAY MUSKETEERS in 1938.

p, Samuel Bischoff; d, Mervyn LeRoy; w, Lucien Hubbard, Kubec Glasmon, John Bright (based on a story by Glasmon, Bright); ph, Sol Polito; ed, Ray Curtis; md, Leo F. Forbstein; art d, Robert Haas.

Drama   (PR:C MPAA:NR)

THREE ON A SPREE*   (1961, Brit.) 83m Caralan & Dador/UA bw

Jack Watling (Michael Brewster), Carole Lesley (Susan), Renee Houston (Mrs. Gray), John Slater (Sid Johnson), Colin Gordon (Mitchell), John Salew (Mr. Monkton), Julian Orchard (Walker), Libby Morris (Trixie), Cardew Robinson (Micki), Ernest Clark (Col. Drew), Ronald Adam (Judge), June Cunningham (Rosie), Jeanne Moody (Barbara Drew), Marne Maitland (Eastern Gentleman), Hugh Morton (Grant), Gertan Klauber (Joe), Ruth Lee (Receptionist), John Vivyan (Big Louis).

Yet another version of BREWSTER'S MILLIONS, but this time hiding its identity under a different title. Here Watling is the lucky fellow who must spend money in order to make it. Previously filmed in 1921, 1935, 1945, and recently in 1985.

p, George Fowler; d, Sidney J. Furie; w, Siegfried Herzig, Charles Rogers, Wilkie Mahoney, James Kelly, Peter Miller (based on the novel Brewster's Millions by George Barr McCutcheon and the play "Brewster's Millions; a Comedy in Four Acts" by Winchell Smith, Byron Ongley); ph, Stephen Dade; ed, A.H. Rule; md, Philip Martell; art d, John Blezard; cos, Jackie Cummins; makeup, Scott Fletcher.

Comedy   (PR:A MPAA:NR)

THREE ON A TICKET**½   (1947) 64m PRC bw

Hugh Beaumont (Michael Shayne), Cheryl Walker (Phyllis Hamilton), Paul Bryar (Tim Rourke), Ralph Dunn (Pete Rafferty), Louise Currie (Helen Brinstead), Gavin Gordon (Pearson), Charles Quigley (Kurt Leroy), Douglas Fowley (Mace Morgan), Noel Cravat (Trigger), Charles King, Sr (Drunk), Brooks Benedict (Jim Lacy).

A nifty little Michael Shayne detective picture with Beaumont in the lead role. He and a gang of crooks are all franticly searching for a railway locker ticket which has been ripped into thirds and distributed. The owner of the ticket will then be able to open the locker, which is filled with the results of a bank heist. Fast-moving and keenly directed. (See MICHAEL SHAYNE series, Index.)

p, Sigmund Neufeld; d, Sam Newfield; w, Fred Myton (based on a story by Brett Halliday [Davis Dresser]); ph, Jack Greenhalgh; m, Emil Cadkin; ed, Holbrook N. Todd; md, Dick Carruth; set d, Elias H. Reif.

Crime   (PR:A MPAA:NR)

THREE ON THE TRAIL**   (1936) 67m PAR bw

William Boyd (Hopalong Cassidy), Jimmy Ellison (Johnny Nelson), Onslow Stevens (Pecos Kane), Muriel Evans (Mary Stevens), George "Gabby" Hayes (Windy), Claude King (J.P. Ridley), William Duncan (Buck Peters), Clara Kimball Young (Rose Peters), Ernie Adams (Idaho), Ted Adams (Jim Trask), John St. Polis (Sam Corwin), Al Hill (Kit Thorpe), John Rutherford (Lewis), Lita Cortez (Conchita), Lew Meehan, Artie Ortego, Franklyn Farnum.

Boyd is back in his familiar Hopalong role as he tries to bust a gang which splits its efforts between cattle rustling and coach robbing. Unfortunately, Boyd gets no help from the corrupt sheriff, but, fortunately, he doesn't need it. (See HOPALONG CASSIDY series, Index.)

p, Harry Sherman; d, Howard Bretherton; w, Doris Schroeder, Vernon Smith (based on the book Bar 20 Three; Relating a Series of Startling and Strenuous Adventures in the Cow Town of Mesquite... by Clarence Edward Mulford); ph, Archie Stout; ed, Edward Schroeder.

Western   (PR:A MPAA:NR)

THREE OUTLAWS, THE**   (1956) 74m Associated bw

Neville Brand, Alan Hale, Jr, Bruce Bennett, Jose Gonzales, Jeanne Carmen, Rudolfo Hoyos, Robert Tafur, Lillian Molderi, Robert Christopher, Vincent Padula, Henry Escalante, Bill Henry, Jonathan Hale, Stanley Andrews.

Solid "B" western which sees three American crooks run into Mexico and deposit their loot in a bank. The men then settle in a small village and look forward to a relaxed retirement. Unfortunately the bank is robbed by bandits and the gringos are forced to strap on their guns and give chase.

p, Sigmund Neufeld; d, Sam Newfield; w, Orville Hampton.

Western   (PR:A MPAA:NR)

THREE PENNY OPERA**   (1963, Fr./Ger.) 83m C.E.C./EM c (DIE
                                                        DREIGROSCHENOPER)

Sammy Davis, Jr (*Ballad Singer*), Curd [Curt] Jurgens (*Macheath*), June
Ritchie (*Polly Peachum*), Hildegarde Neff (*Pirate Jenny*), Marlene Warrlich
(*Lucy Brown*), Lino Ventura (*Tiger Brown*), Gert Frobe (*J.J. Peachum*), Hi
lde Hildebrandt (*Mrs. Celia Peachum*), Walter Giller (*Beggar Filch*), Hans
W. Hamacher (*Constable Smith*), Henning Schluter (*Rev. Kimball*), Hans
Reiser (*A Guide*), Siegfried Wischnewski (*Money Matthew*), Walter Feuch-
tenberg (*Hook-Finger Jacob*), Stanislav Ledinek (*Robert the Saw*), Martin
Berliner (*Wally the Weeper*), Max Strassberg (*Ed*), Stefan Wigger (*Jimmy*),
Robert Manuel, Jurgen Feindt (*Hangmen*), Adeline Wagner (*Suky Tawdry*),
Erna Haffner, Clessia Wade, Jacqueline Pierreux (*Prostitutes*).

A tolerable version of the Bertolt Brecht-Kurt Weill opera which seems to
defy an expert transformation to the screen, especially after G.W. Pabst's
minor attempt. This time Sammy Davis, Jr. takes over the role of the ballad
singer, while Jurgens is Mack the Knife. The story, a simple one, has
Jurgens proposing to marry Ritchie, and follows the ruckus that action
raises on the beggar-populated streets. Stick to the 1931 version, THE
THREEPENNY OPERA.

p, Kurt Ulrich; d, Wolfgang Staudte; w, Staudte, Gunter Weisenborn, Marc
Blitzstein (based on the opera by Bertolt Brecht, Kurt Weill, from the opera
"Beggar's Opera" by John Gay); ph, Roger Fellous (Franscope, Eastmancol-
or); m, Kurt Weill; ed, Wolfgang Wehrum; md, Peter Sandloff; set d, Hein
Heckroth; ch, Dick Price; cos, Hein Heckroth, Heinz Willeg; m/l, Weill,
Brecht, (English lyrics) Blitzstein, Eric Bentley.

Musical   **Cas.**   (PR:A MPAA:NR)

THREE RASCALS IN THE HIDDEN FORTRESS
                              (SEE: HIDDEN FORTRESS, THE, 1959, Jap.)

THREE RING CIRCUS**   (1954) 103m PAR c (AKA: JERRICO, THE
                                                        WONDER CLOWN)

Dean Martin (*Pete Nelson*), Jerry Lewis (*Jerry Hotchkiss*), Joanne Dru (*Jill
Brent*), Zsa Zsa Gabor (*Saadia*), Wallace Ford (*Sam Morley*), Sig Ruman
(*Schlitz*), Gene Sheldon (*Puffo*), Nick Cravat (*Timmy*), Elsa Lanchester
(*Bearded Lady*), Douglas Fowley (*Payroll Official*), Sue Casey (*Snake
Charmer*), Mary L. Orosco (*Fat Lady*), Frederick E. Wolfe (*Giant*), Phil Van
Zandt (*Johnny*), Ralph Peters (*Chef*), Chick Chandler (*Pitchman*), Kathleen
Freeman, Robert McKibbon, Neil Levitt, Al Hill, Robert LeRoy Diamond,
George E. Stone, Lester Dorr, Donald Kerr, James Davies, Louis Michael
Lettieri, Sandy Descher, Billy Curtis, Harry Monty, Milton A. Dickinson,
Bobby Kay, Sonny Vallie, Robert Locke Lorraine, John Minshull, Joe
Evans, George Boyce.

Lewis and Martin are up to their antics under the big top, with Dean as the
straight man who becomes a trapeze "assistant," and Lewis, not surprisingly, as the clown. It all builds up to romance for Martin, silliness for Lewis,
and smiles for the children who are on the receiving end of a big benefit
performance. The best sequence has Lewis trying to shave bearded lady Elsa
Lanchester.

p, Hal B. Wallis; d, Joseph Pevney; w, Don McGuire; ph, Loyal Griggs
(VistaVision, Technicolor); m, Walter Scharf; ed, Warren Low; cos, Edith
Head; ch, Nick Castle; m/l, "It's a Big, Wide, Wonderful World," John Rox
(sung by Dean Martin), "Hey Punchinello," Jay Livingston, Ray Evans
(sung by Martin, Jerry Lewis).

Comedy   (PR:A MPAA:NR)

THREE ROGUES**   (1931) 70m FOX bw (AKA: NOT EXACTLY
                                                        GENTLEMEN)

Victor McLaglen (*Bull Stanley*), Fay Wray (*Lee Carlton*), Lew Cody (*Ace
Beaudry*), Eddie Gribbon (*Bronco Dawson*), Robert Warwick (*Layne Hunt-
er*), Franklyn Farnum (*Nelson*), David Worth (*Bruce*), Carol Wines (*Bull's
Girl*), Joyce Compton (*Ace's Girl*), Louise Huntington (*Bronco's Girl*), James
Farley (*Marshall Dunn*).

Wray is the subject of three men's affections in the Wild West when they
discover she has a map which tells the location of a gold mine. All
three–McLaglen, the bank robber; Cody, the card cheat; and Gribbon, the
rustler–plan to propose to Wray on the premise that a husband and a wife
must share their belongings, i.e., the map. All three strike out, however,
when true love Farnum takes her away. A remake of the silent THREE BAD
MEN.

d, Benjamin Stoloff; w, William Conselman, Dudley Nichols, Emmett Flynn
(based on the novel *Over the Border* by Herman Whitaker); ph, Daniel Clark;
ed, Clyde Carruth.

Western   (PR:A MPAA:NR)

THREE RUSSIAN GIRLS*½   (1943) 80m UA bw (GB: SHE WHO
                                                        DARES)

Anna Sten (*Natasha*), Kent Smith (*John Hill*), Mimi Forsaythe (*Tamara*),
Alexander Granach (*Maj. Braginski*), Kathy Frye (*Chijik*), Paul Guilfoyle
(*Trishin*), Kane Richmond (*Sergei*), Manart Kippen (*Doctor*), Jack Gardner
(*Misha*), Marcia Lenack (*Shoora*), Mary Herriot (*Zina*), Anna Marie Stewart
(*Olga*), Dorothy Gray (*Manya*), Feodor Chaliapin (*Terkin*).

Sten is a Russian nurse on the front lines during WW II who tends to an
injured American, Smith, the victim of a plane crash. In the midst of the
fighting and the injuries, the pair become attracted to each other, but
nothing ever really comes of the romance. By the end of the picture, they
part and resume their duties. Based on the Soviet feature GIRL FROM
LENINGRAD, this was the sort of wartime fare that was meant to bring us
closer to our Russian allies.

p, Gregor Rabinovitch; d, Fedor Ozep, Henry Kesler; w, Aben Kandel, Dan
James, Maurice Clark, Victor Trivas (based on the film GIRL FROM
LENINGRAD); ph, John Mescall; m, W. Frank Harling; ed, S.K. Winston,
Gregg Tallas; art d, Frank Sylos, Eugene Lourie; spec eff, Frank Hills.

War/Romance   (PR:A MPAA:NR)

THREE SAILORS AND A GIRL**   (1953) 95m WB c

Jane Powell (*Penny Weston*), Gordon MacRae (*Choir Boy Jones*), Gene
Nelson (*Twitch*), Sam Levene (*Joe Woods*), George Givot (*Rossi*), Veda Ann
Borg (*Faye Foss*), Archer MacDonald (*Webster*), Raymond Greenleaf (*Mor-
row*), Henry Slate (*A Sailor*), Jack E. Leonard (*Parky*), Burt Lancaster
(*Marine*), Mickey Simpson (*Guard*), Elizabeth Flournoy (*Secretary*), Phil
Van Zandt (*Garage Owner*), Wayne Taylor (*Bellhop*), Al Hill (*Sign Painter*),
Guy E. Hearn (*Workman*), Grandon Rhodes (*George Abbott*), David Bond
(*Moss Hart*), Alex Gerry (*Ira Gershwin*), Frank Scannell (*Boxoffice Man*),
Roy Engel (*Walter Kerr*), Herald-Tribune Critic, Claire Meade, Dick
Simmons, John Parrish, Everett Glass, Bob Carson (*Clients*), Cliff Ferre,
Paul Burke (*Actors*), Murray Alper, Ed Hinton (*Marines*), John Crawford,
Dennis Dengate (*Shore Patrolmen*), Merv Griffin, Arthur Walsh, Jack
Larson, Michael Pierce, King Donovan (*Sailors*), Bess Flowers, Harold
Miller (*Indignant Patrons*).

A trio of sailors and a young singer (no lies from the title this time) join
together with a struggling producer to bring a stage flop to Broadway
where, of course, it becomes the hottest show in town. "The Butter And Egg
Man," the George S. Kaufman play on which this bit of pure, unabashed
escapism is based, served as the inspiration for four other films: THE
BUTTER AND EGG MAN (1928), THE TENDERFOOT (1932), DANCE,
CHARLIE, DANCE (1937), and AN ANGEL FROM TEXAS (1940). Look for
TV talk show host Merv Griffin in the midst of all the singing and dancing.
Sammy Fain, Sammy Cahn songs include "Home Is Where the Heart Is"
(sung by Jane Powell, Gordon MacRae, Gene Nelson), "Kiss Me or I'll
Scream," "Face to Face" (sung by Powell), "There Must Be a Reason,"
"When It's Love," "My Heart Is a Singing Heart" (sung by Powell, MacRae),
"The Lately Song" (sung by Jack E. Leonard, Powell, MacRae, Nelson),
"Show Me a Happy Woman And I'll Show You a Miserable Man," (sung by
Leonard, Powell), "You're But Oh So Right," "I Got Butterflies," "The Five
Senses," "I Made Myself a Promise."

p, Sammy Cahn; d, Roy Del Ruth; w, Roland Kibbee, Devery Freeman
(based on the play "The Butter And Egg Man" by George S. Kaufman); ph,
Carl Guthrie (Technicolor); ed, Owen Marks; md, Ray Heindorf; art d, Leo
K. Kuter; ch, LeRoy Prinz, Gene Nelson.

Musical   (PR:A MPAA:NR)

THREE SECRETS**½   (1950) 98m United States/WB bw

Eleanor Parker (*Susan Chase*), Patricia Neal (*Phyllis Horn*), Ruth Roman
(*Ann Lawrence*), Frank Lovejoy (*Bob Duffy*), Leif Erickson (*Bill Chase*), Ted
de Corsia (*Del Prince*), Edmon Ryan (*Hardin*), Larry Keating (*Mark
Harrison*), Katherine Warren (*Mrs. Connors*), Arthur Franz (*Paul Radin*),
Duncan Richardson (*Johnny*).

An interesting story about a 5-year-old boy who survives a private plane
crash which kills his foster parents. Dealing evocatively with the attempt
to rescue him, the film also presents segments involving three women, each
of whom believes the boy is her own, all having given up a son to adoption
five years earlier. For the most part the picture works, due to sharp
direction by Robert Wise, but the flashback construction becomes disturbing.

p, Milton Sperling; d, Robert Wise; w, Martin Rackin, Gina Kaus (based on
the story "Rock Bottom" by Rackin, Kaus); ph, Sid Hickox; m, David
Buttolph; ed, Thomas Reilly; art d, Charles Clarke; cos, Lea Rhodes.

Drama   (PR:A MPAA:NR)

THREE SHADES OF LOVE   (SEE: THIS REBEL BREED, 1960)

THREE SILENT MEN**   (1940, Brit.) 72m BUT bw

Sebastian Shaw (*Sir James Quentin*), Derrick de Marney (*Capt. John Mellish*), Patricia Roc (*Pat Quentin*), Arthur Hambling (*Ginger Brown*), Meinhart Maur (*Karl Zaroff*), John Turnbull (*Inspector Gill*), Peter Gawthorne (*Gen. Bullington*), Andre Morell (*Klein*), Cameron Hall, Jack Vyvyan, Scott Harrold, Cynthia Stock, Basil Cunard, F.B.J. Sharp, Charles Oliver, Hugh Dempster, Ian Fleming, Billy Watts, Kay Lewis, Marjorie Taylor, Barbara Lott.

Pacifist surgeon Shaw operates on the inventor of a terrible new weapon, but the next day the patient is found dead from an excess of ether and naturally Shaw is the prime suspect. His daughter (Roc) and her boy friend succeed in proving him innocent. Badly written, though the suspense makes it entertaining.

p, F.W. Baker; d, Daniel Birt; w, Dudley Leslie, John Byrd; (based on a novel by E.P. Thorne); ph, Geoffrey Faithfull.

Crime   **(PR:A   MPAA:NR)**

THREE SINNERS   (SEE: THREE FACES OF SIN, 1963, Fr./Ital.)

THREE SISTERS, THE**   (1930) 77m FOX bw

Louise Dresser (*Marta*), Tom Patricola (*Tony*), Kenneth MacKenna (*Count d'Amati*), Joyce Compton (*Carlotta*), June Collyer (*Elena*), Addie McPhail (*Antonia*), Clifford Saum (*Pasquale*), Paul Porcasi (*Rinaldi*), John Sainpolis (*Judge*), Sidney De Grey (*Tito*), Herman Bing (*Von Kosch*).

Of the title's three sisters, one dies during childbirth, one marries and prospers in the States, while the third does quite well with a musician in Vienna. Meanwhile, their mother, alone in Italy, has resorted to an unrewarded life of labor. The daughters soon discover that the money they've been sending her has been pocketed by a third party. The situation is remedied when the girls and their husbands take a trip to Italy and give their mother enough cash to live comfortably. Songs include "Italian Kisses," L. Wolfe Gilbert, Abel Baer; "Lonely Feet," "Hand in Hand," "Keep Smiling," "Won't Dance," "Roll on Rolling Road," "What Good are Words," "You Are Doing Very Well," Jerome Kern, Oscar Hammerstein II.

d, Paul Sloane; w, George Brooks, James K. McGuiness (based on a story by Brooks, Marion Orth); ph, L.W. O'Connell).

Drama   **(PR:A   MPAA:NR)**

THREE SISTERS, THE**   (1969, USSR) 112m Mosfilm/Brandon bw
                                                  (TRI SESTRY)

Lyubov Sokolova (*Olga*), Margarita Volodina (*Masha*), Tatyana Malchenko (*Irina*), Leonid Gubanov (*Andrei*), Alla Larionova (*Natalya*), Lev Ivanov (*Vershinin*), Leonid Gallis (*Kulygin*), Konstantin Sorokin (*Chebutykin*), Oleg Strizhenov (*Tuzenbakh*), Vladimir Druzhnikov (*Solyony*), L. Konstantinova, P. Vinnik, V. Stepanov, Boris Smirnov, N. Lubko, G. Dudarev.

A depressing Chekhov adaptation from Russian director Samsanov about three sisters who lead a dreary life of suffering in a garrison town, longing only to return to Moscow. Instead of getting better, their lives get worse when their brother marries and lets his wife manage the family funds. Before long the family is deep in debt, fire destroys the town, and the love affairs of the girls end as the troops pull out. The finale has them all wondering if their lives will ever improve. Released in Russia in 1964.

d&w, Samson Samsanov (based on the play by Anton Pavlovich Chekhov); ph, Fyodor Dobronravov; m, Vasiliy Dekhteryov; art d, Sergey Voronkov, I. Novoderezhkin.

Drama   **(PR:C   MPAA:NR)**

THREE SISTERS***½   (1974, Brit.) 165m Alan Clore-BL/American
                                                  Film Theatre c

Jeanne Watts (*Olga*), Joan Plowright (*Masha*), Louise Purnell (*Irina*), Derek Jacobi (*Andrei*), Sheila Reid (*Natasha*), Kenneth Mackinesh (*Kulighin*), Daphne Heard (*Anfissa*), Harry Lomax (*Ferrapont*), Judy Wilson (*Serving Maid*), Mary Griffiths (*Housemaid*), Ronald Pickup (*Tusenbach*), Laurence Olivier (*Chebutikin*), Frank Wylie (*Maj. Vassili Vassilich Solloni*), Alan Bates (*Col. Vershinin*), Richard Kay (*Lt. Fedotik*), David Belcher (*Lt. Bode*), George Selway (*Orderly*), David Munro, Alan Adams, Robert Walker (*Officers*).

There are many problems in adapting theatrical works to cinema. While one does not want to destroy the essence of a play, theater and film are different mediums and require different approaches. With this in mind, Olivier's adaption of Chekov's "Three Sisters" successfully overcomes the problems of filming a play without losing any of the work's theatrical aspects. The story opens in turn-of-the-century Russia. Three sisters–Watts, Plowright, and Purnell–along with brother Jacobi dream of leaving their small town in the countryside so they might return to the sophisticated atmosphere of their beloved Moscow. During a celebration for Purnell's patron saint, the siblings are joined in the festivities by Olivier, an aging doctor and long-time friend of the family. Also present are members of the army stationed nearby including Purnell's would-be suitor Wylie and a similarly inclined baron,

Pickup. Soon Bates–the new battery commander–arrives and finally Plowright's husband husband, Mackintosh. ackintosh. The little party grows by one when Reid, a naive local girl, arrives. Two years go by and Reid is now married to Jacobi. He is a member of the town council and unhappy with his lot. Plowright has fallen in love with Bates despite her own marriage and her lover's union with a sickly wife. Wylie and Pickup still carry a torch for Purnell and both express their feelings, though it is apparent she cares little for either man. After a destructive fire Reid quarrels with her husband's sisters. Life in their little community further breaks down when the respected Olivier turns up drunk. Watts has a discussion with Purnell and suggests to her sister that she wed Pickup. Though Purnell finally agrees, this decision is made moot when Wylie kills his rival suitor in a duel. Meanwhile Plowright's life falls apart when the military unit–including her lover Bates–is transferred to another town. She is left to the cold comfort of her husband while Watts sums up the trials and tribulations her family has undergone, expressing hope despite the suffering they have all experienced. Rather than open up the play for a more realistic perspective, Olivier wisely maintains an air of theatricality within the film, using semi-realistic settings which would ordinarily only be seen on stage. Having directed the play at the Old Vic for the National Theatre, Olivier retains much of what he did on stage with his cast, leaving the camera to observe rather than impose itself on the action. While in some cases this technique wears thin, as in the film version of MY FAIR LADY and Volker Schlondorff's television version of "Death of a Salesman," the idea of theater is retained under the medium of cinema. The cast is clearly familiar with the work and performs Chekov's play with the precision it demands. There is always a certain difficulty in translating works from one language to another, but none of the original rhythms or feelings are lost in this English-language production. The film fails only where Olivier takes a cinematic diversion from his material in opening scenes of a train, as well as a dream sequence. These moments–which on their own are fine–detract from Olivier's intent to present this as a filmed play rather than a motion picture. In taking this production from stage to screen Olivier made a few changes in the cast in order to make it a bigger box office attraction. Most notable were the addition of Bates as Vershinin and Olivier himself as the old doctor Chebutikin. Released through the auspices of the American Film Theatre project, this was the first of that series that was independently produced. Originally released in England in 1970, THREE SISTERS waited until 1974 for its first American screening. It was well worth the wait. Though Chekov has been often imitated (particularly noticeable in Woody Allen's somber film INTERIORS), the drama and imagery he conjures up is unique within the world of theater. This version of THREE SISTERS, though flawed, is an important rendition of this master playwright's work. While directing the stage version, Olivier let his beard grow and kept the whiskers for his role in the film. "It saves me an hour in the makeup chair each morning and I use the time to work out the day's scenes," he was quoted as saying.

p, John Goldstone; d, Laurence Olivier, John Sichel; w, Moura Budberg (based on the play by Anton Chekhov); ph, Geoffrey Unsworth (Eastmancolor); m, Sir William Walton, Derek Hudson, Gary Hughes; ed, Jack Harris; md, Marc Wilkinson; prod d, Josef Svoboda; art d, Bill Hutchinson; cos, Beatrice Dawson; makeup, Bob Lawrence, Philip Leakey.

Drama   **(PR:C   MPAA:G)**

THREE SISTERS, THE**   (1977) 166m Actors Studio Theatre/NTA c

Gerald Hiken (*Andrei*), Shelley Winters (*Natalya*), Geraldine Page (*Olga*), Kim Stanley (*Masha*), Sandy Dennis (*Irina*), Albert Paulsen (*Kulygin*), Kevin McCarthy (*Vershinin*), James Olson (*Baron Tuzenbach*), Robert Loggia (*Solyony*), Luther Adler (*Chebutikin*), John Harkins (*Fedotik*), David Paulsen (*Roday*), Salem Ludwig (*Ferapont*), Tamara Daykarhanova (*Anfisa*).

Chekhov's classic is badly bungled in this production, a videotape-to-film record of the Actor's Studio 1966 production directed by Lee Strasberg. The fine cast seem to be going off in all directions at once. An excellent film for criticizing Method Acting.

p, Ely Landau; d, Paul Bogart (original stage production directed by Lee Strasberg); w, Anton Chekhov (English translation by Randall Jarrel).

Drama   **(PR:A   MPAA:NR)**

THREE SMART GIRLS***   (1937) 86m UNIV bw

Deanna Durbin (*Penny Craig*), Binnie Barnes (*Donna Lyons*), Alice Brady (*Mrs. Lyons*), Ray Milland (*Lord Michael Stuart*), Charles Winninger (*Judson Craig*), Mischa Auer (*Count Arisztid*), Nan Grey (*Joan Craig*), Barbara Read (*Kay Craig*), Ernest Cossart (*Binns the Butler*), Hobart Cavanaugh (*Wilbur Lamb*), John King (*Bill Evans*), Lucile Watson (*Trudel*), Nella Walker (*Dorothy Craig*), Dennis O'Keefe (*Club Extra*), Gladden James (*Waiter*), Wade Boteler, John Hamilton (*Sergeants*), Lane Chandler (*Cop*), Charles Coleman (*Butler*), Franklin Pangborn (*Jeweler*), Albert Conti (*Count's Friend*), Selmer Jackson.

In her film debut, 14-year-old singing sensation Deanna Durbin was cast as one of three sisters who try to keep their father from marrying a golddigger. By the picture's finale two of the sisters have found themselves prospective husbands, and their father has reconciled with their mother, leaving Durbin single, but thoroughly content with everyone's new found happiness. Producer Pasternak and director Koster had both worked for Universal's European branch in Germany, and when that operation was discontinued, Carl Laemmle, the studio's chief, brought them to Hollywood. THREE SMART GIRLS spawned two sequels, THREE SMART GIRLS GROW UP (1939) and HERS TO HOLD (1943), both of which starred Durbin, and one remake, THREE DARING DAUGHTERS (1948), produced by MGM, with Jane Powell in the Durbin role. Songs: "My Heart Is Singing," "Someone To Care For Me" (Gus Kahn, Walter Jurmann, Bronislaw Kaper, sung by Deanna Durbin), "Il Bacio" (Luigi Arditi, sung by Durbin).

p, Joseph Pasternak; d, Henry Koster [Herman Kosterlitz]; w, Adele Comandini, Austin Parker (based on the story by Comandini); ph, Joseph Valentine; ed, Ted J. Kent; md, Charles Previn; art d&cos, John Harkrider.

Comedy/Romance/Musical   (PR:AA MPAA:NR)

THREE SMART GIRLS GROW UP***   (1939) 90m UNIV bw

Deanna Durbin (Penny "Mouse" Craig), Charles Winninger (Judson Craig), Nan Grey (Joan Craig), Helen Parrish (Kay Craig), Robert Cummings (Harry Loren), William Lundigan (Richard Watkins), Ernest Cossart (Binns, Butler), Nella Walker (Mrs. Dorothy Craig), Felix Bressart (Penny's Music Teacher).

A sprightly sequel to THREE SMART GIRLS (1937), this picture became one of the years top-grossing films and netted Durbin one of her biggest hits, "Because." Again she can't keep herself from meddling in the love lives of her siblings and steps in when both her sisters fall for the same fella. Of course, she works out all the kinks by turning on her girlish charm. Grey is along again as one of the sisters, but Parrish has replaced Barbara Read in the role of the third sister.

p, Joe Pasternak; d, Henry Koster [Herman Kosterlitz]; w, Bruce Manning, Felix Jackson; ph, Joe Valentine; ed, Ted J. Kent; md, Charles Previn; cos, Vera West; m/l, "Because," Edward Teschemacher, Guy D'Hardelot (sung by Deanna Durbin), "The Last Rose of Summer," Thomas Moore, Richard Alfred Milliken (sung by Durbin).

Comedy/Romance   (PR:A MPAA:NR)

THREE SONS*   (1939) 72m RKO bw

Edward Ellis (Daniel Pardway), William Gargan (Thane Pardway), Kent Taylor (Gene Pardway), J. Edward Bromberg (Abe Ullman), Katherine Alexander (Abigail Pardway), Virginia Vale [Dorothy Howe] (Phoebe Pardway), Robert Stanton [Kirby Grant] (Bert Pardway), Dick Hogan (Freddie Pardway), Grady Sutton (Grimson), Adele Pearce (Mamie), Alexander D'Arcy (Phoebe's Husband), Barbara Pepper (Viola).

Ellis plays a department store owner who built his business up from the ashes of the Chicago Fire, only to find that none of his children wants to take over the operation. He is heartbroken and tries every way he can to convince them, finally handing out shares of the company stock but with only the youngest son taking heed. When this was originally filmed in 1933 as SWEEPINGS, Lionel Barrymore starred in the Ellis role. Gargan, who plays Ellis' brother in THREE SONS, portrayed one of the sons in the earlier version. Vale and Stanton made their entree into the movies via Jesse L. Lasky's broadcast talent search, "Gateway to Hollywood," and Stanton gets a chance to exercise his singing voice in this film on "Tootin' Down to Tennessee."

p, Robert Sisk; d, Jack Hively; w, John Twist (based on the novel Sweepings by Lester Cohen); ph, Russell Metty; m, Roy Webb; ed, Theron Warth; cos, Edward Stevenson.

Drama   (PR:A MPAA:NR)

THREE SONS O'GUNS**   (1941) 65m FN-WB bw

Wayne Morris (Charley Patterson), Marjorie Rambeau (Aunt Lottie), Irene Rich (Margaret Patterson), Tom Brown (Eddie), William T. Orr (Kenneth), Susan Peters (Mary Tyler), Moroni Olsen (Philip Talbot), Barbara Pepper (Francie), John Kelly (Buffalo Bill Oxenstern), Fritz Feld (Blotievkin), Charles D. Waldron (Henry Gresham), Charles Halton (Haddock), Florence Shirley (Mrs. Tyler), William B. Davidson (Baxter), Frank M. Thomas (Reynolds), Alexis Smith.

A minor comedy about a trio of sons raised by mother Rich and aunt Rambeau who turn out to be unruly brats with no intention of enlisting in the Army. Rambeau tells them a thing or two about patriotism and sends all three into a uniform. Released four months before the Japanese bombing of Pearl Harbor, this film's concern with patriotism and conscription mirrors the increasing awareness of the need for preparedness that was being felt in certain quarters in the U.S. at the time. Observations about its historical context aside, the best thing about this picture is its title.

p, William Jacobs; d, Ben Stoloff; w, Fred Niblo, Jr. (based on his story "Mother's Boys"); ph, Arthur Todd; ed, Terry Morse.

Comedy   (PR:A MPAA:NR)

THREE SPARE WIVES*   (1962, Brit.) 70m Danziger/UA bw

Robin Hunter (George Pittock), Susan Stephen (Susan Pittock), John Hewer (Rupert Duff-Cooper), Barbara Leake (Mrs. Hornsby), Ferdy Mayne (Hazim Bey), Gale Sheridan (O'Hara), Dani Seper (Blini), Golda Casimir (Fatima).

Hunter inherits three wives when his Arabic uncle dies, making for great difficulty with both his wife and the British Foreign Office. Stupid little comedy with nothing to recommend it.

p, Ralph Goddard; d, Ernest Morris; w, Eldon Howard (based on a play by Talbot Rothwell).

Comedy   (PR:A MPAA:NR)

THREE STEPS IN THE DARK*   (1953, Brit.) 60m Corsair/AB-Pathe
bw

Greta Gynt (Sophy Burgoyne), Hugh Sinclair (Philip Burgoyne), Sarah Lawson (Dorothy), Helene Cordet (Esme), Elwyn Brook-Jones (Wilbrahim), John Van Eyssen (Henry Burgoyne), Nicholas Hannen (Arnold Burgoyne), Alistair Hunter (Inspector Forbes), Katie Johnson (Mrs. Riddle), Alan Robinson, Neil Hallett, Raymond Young.

Wretched big-scary-house mystery with Hannen announcing a change in his will and then promptly getting murdered. Nice niece Gynt, a writer of mystery novels, solves the murder in the usual fashion. Very low budget and very dull.

p, Harold Richmond; d, Daniel Birt; w, Brock Williams (based on a story by Roger East); ph, Hone Glendinning.

Crime   (PR:A MPAA:NR)

THREE STEPS NORTH*   (1951) 85m UA bw

Lloyd Bridges (Frank Keeler), Lea Padovani (Elena Ravezza), Aldo Fabrizi (Pietro), William C. Tubbs (Jack Conway), Dino Galvani (Massina), Adriano Ambrogi (Baldori), Gianna Rizzo (The Greek), John Fostini (Vince), Peggy Doro (Mrs. Day), Adam Genette (Policeman Falzone).

A misguided and contrived programmer which stars Bridges as an American GI in Italy who manages to stash away a fortune before being apprehended by the authorities and put behind bars. After doing his time, he goes back to his hidden loot, only to find that someone else has gotten their paws on it. A number of people get mixed up in its disappearance, including his former girl, Padovani; a cemetery caretaker, Fabrizi; and a U.S. gangster, Tubbs. Bridges then discovers it was Fabrizzi who uncovered the cash and spent it on a new chapel. Far from compelling.

p&d, W. Lee Wilder; w, Lester Fuller (based on a story by Robert Harari); ph, Aldo Giordani; ed, Ruth Totz; md, Roman Vlad; art d, Gastone Medin; set d, Kromberg.

Drama   (PR:A MPAA:NR)

THREE STOOGES GO AROUND THE WORLD IN A DAZE, THE*
(1963) 94m Normandy/COL bw

Moe Howard, Larry Fine, Joe De Rita (The Three Stooges), Jay Sheffield (Phileas Fogg III), Joan Freeman (Amelia), Walter Burke (Lory Filch), Peter Forster (Vickers Cavendish), Maurice Dallimore (Crotchet), Richard Devon (Maharajah), Antony Eustrel (Kandu), Iau Kea (Itchi Kitchi), Robert Kino (Charlie Okuma), Phil Arnold (Referee), Murray Alper (Gus), Don Lamond (Bill), Jack Greening (McPherson), Emil Sitka (Butler), Geoffrey A. Maurer (Timmy), Ramsay Hill (Gatesby), Colin Campbell (Willoughy), Michael St. Clair (1st Mate), Ron Whelan (Harry).

You have to be a real fan to sit through 94 minutes of Stooge comedy, but, then again, their biggest audience hasn't made it through second grade yet and can probably outgrow a pair of pants in the time it takes to watch this picture. Moe, Larry, and Joe (replacing the late Shemp Howard) embark on a world-wide journey with the great-grandson of Phileas Fogg a la AROUND THE WORLD IN 80 DAYS. Fogg III (Sheffield) wagers that he and his Stooge servants can make the same trip his great-grandfather made, claiming that his elderly relative was swindled in his attempt. Crime and attempted murder clouds Sheffield's voyage, but in the end he and the Stooges are successful.

p&d, Norman Maurer; w, Elwood Ullman (based on a story by Maurer); ph, Irving Lippman; m, Paul Dunlap; ed, Edwin Bryant; art d, Don Ament; set d, James M. Crowe; cos, Ted Tetrick, Grace Kuhn; spec eff, Richard Albain; makeup, Joe DiBella.

Adventure/Comedy   (PR:AA MPAA:NR)

THREE STOOGES IN ORBIT, THE*   (1962) 87m Normandy/COL bw

Moe Howard, Larry Fine, "Curly Joe" De Rita (The Three Stooges), Carol Christensen (Carol), Edson Stroll (Capt. Tom Andrews), Emil Sitka (Prof. Danforth), George Neise (Ogg), Rayford Barnes (Zogg), Norman Leavitt (Williams), Peter Dawson (Chairman), Peter Brocco (Dr. Appleby), Don Lamond (Col. Smithers), Thomas Glynn (George Galveston), Maurice Manson (Mr. Lansing), Jean Charney (WAF Sergeant),

Duane Ament (*Personnel Clerk*), Bill Dyer (*Col. Lane*), Roy Engel (*Welby*), Jane Wald (*Bathing Girl*), Cheerio Meredith (*Tooth Paste Old Maid*).

Moe, Larry, and Joe star as themselves in this science fiction farce which has a pair of Martians trying to steal an all-powerful submarine-tank-rocket military weapon. As the Martians are flying away with it, the Stooges hang on and force it to crash land in a television studio. They should have stayed in orbit.

p, Norman Maurer; d, Edward Bernds; w, Elwood Ullman (based on a story by Maurer); ph, William F. Whitley; m, Paul Dunlap; ed, Edwin Bryant; art d, Don Ament; set d, Richard Mansfield; cos, Ted Tetrick, Pat Page; makeup, Frank McCoy.

Comedy/ScienceFiction　　　　　**(PR:AA　MPAA:NR)**

THREE STOOGES MEET HERCULES, THE*

(1962) 89m Normandy/COL bw

Moe Howard, Larry Fine, "Curly Joe" De Rita (*The Three Stooges*), Vicki Trickett (*Diane Quigley*), Quinn Redeker (*Schuyler Davis*), George N. Neise (*Ralph Dimsal/Odius*), Samson Burke (*Hercules*), Mike McKeever (*Ajax*), Marlin McKeever (*Argo*), Emil Sitka (*Shepherd*), Hal Smith (*Thesus*), John Cliff (*Ulysses*), Lewis Charles (*Achilles*), Barbara Hines (*Anita*), Terry Huntington (*Hecuba*), Diana Piper (*Helen*), Gregg Martell (*Simon*), Gene Roth (*Captain*), Edward Foster (*Freddie*), Cecil Elliott (*Matron*), Rusty Wescoatt (*Philo*), Don Lamond (*Narrator*).

The self-explanatory title tells what happens when the Three Stooges hop in a time machine and are transported to Ithaca, Greece, in 961 B.C. The usual slapstick comedy of the Stooges is carried out with the trio dressed in sandals and togas; otherwise, it's the same "N'Yuk-N'Yuk-N'Yukking" you can catch on television reruns. Former professional football players and real-time twins, Mike and Marlin McKeever, are along for the ride, playing a Siamese twin cyclops.

p, Norman Maurer; d, Edward Bernds; w, Elwood Ullman; ph, Charles S. Welborn; m, Paul Dunlap; ed, Edwin Bryant; art d, Don Ament; set d, William Calvert.

Comedy　　　　Cas.　　　　**(PR:AA　MPAA:NR)**

THREE STOOGES VS. THE WONDER WOMEN*

(1975, Ital./Chi.) 105m Shaw Bros. c

Yueh Hua (*Chang*), Karen Yeh (*May May Wong*), Nick Jordan (*Aru*), Mark Hannibal (*Mug*), Malisa Longo (*Mila*), Genie Woods (*Akela*), Riccardo Pizzuti (*Philones*), Kirsten Gilles (*High Priestess*).

A group of comic warriors–the Chinese Yueh, the white Jordan, and the black Hannibal–battle Amazon forces and try to churn up a few laughs along the way. After seeing this picture, you'll be begging for THE THREE STOOGES MEET HERCULES...with the *real* Stooges, who conk each other on the noggin a heck of a lot better than these pseudo-stooges.

d, Al Bradley (Alfonso Brescia); w, Aldo Crudo, Brescia; ph, Fausto Rossi; ed, Liliana Serra.

Comedy　　　　　**(PR:C　MPAA:NR)**

THREE STRANGERS**½

(1946) 92m WB-FN bw

Sydney Greenstreet (*Arbutney*), Geraldine Fitzgerald (*Crystal*), Peter Lorre (*Johnny West*), Joan Lorring (*Icy*), Robert Shayne (*Fallon*), Marjorie Riordan (*Janet*), Arthur Shields (*Prosecutor*), Rosalind Ivan (*Lady Rhea*), John Alvin (*Junior Clerk*), Peter Whitney (*Gabby*), Alan Napier (*Shackleford*), Clifford Brooke (*Senior Clerk*), Doris Lloyd (*Mrs. Proctor*), Stanley Logan (*Maj. Beach*), Holmes Herbert, Ian Wolfe, Connie Leon, Colin Kenny, Olaf Hytten, Eric Wilton, Keith Hitchcock, Leslie Denison, Leyland Hodgson, Alec Craig, Reginald Sheffield, Benny Burt.

The menacing duo of Greenstreet and Lorre was teamed together again by Warner Bros. under the helm of director Negulesco who had made his debut with the team in the superior THE MASK OF DIMITRIOS (1944). Set in shadowy London, THREE STRANGERS begins on the eve of the Chinese New Year. Three strangers–shady lawyer Greenstreet; Lorre, an alcoholic, small-time hood; and Fitzgerald, a woman separated from her straying husband–meet on the street and eventually make their way to Fitzgerald's apartment. There she shows them the statuette of Kwan Yin, a Chinese idol. Legend has it that at midnight on the New Year, the idol will open its eyes and grant a wish to three strangers. Greenstreet would like to be admitted into an exclusive barrister's club; Lorre would like to open his own tavern; and Fitzgerald would like to get back together with her husband. Just at midnight, however, the candle lighting the room goes out and the trio cannot see whether Kwan Yin has opened her eyes. To stave off the disappointment, Lorre produces a sweepstakes ticket he has purchased and allows the other two to buy into it (they sign the ticket with the pseudonym "Kwan Yin")–maybe they'll get lucky. Bad luck, however, is all that follows. Greenstreet learns that he is about to be revealed as an embezzler and contemplates committing suicide. Lorre is framed for the murder of a policeman and it looks as if he'll hang. Fitzgerald's husband has fallen in love with another woman and won't be coming back. Once again, luck plays a factor and Lorre is set free by the dying confession of the real murderer.

Greenstreet tries to sell his share of the sweepstakes ticket and use the money to replace that which he embezzled, but Fitzgerald puts up a fight. There is a struggle and the crazed Greenstreet kills the woman by bashing her on the head with the statuette of the Chinese goddess. Just as the murder is committed, it is revealed that the sweepstakes ticket is a winner and now worth 30,000 pounds. The killing drives Greenstreet's frail sanity over the edge and he is hopelessly insane. Lorre, who holds the valuable ticket, decides it is much too dangerous a thing to collect on (because it will tie him into Fitzgerald's murder), so he burns it in the hope that his life will return to normal. Screenwriter Huston came up with the idea for THREE STRANGERS in 1936 after he had bought a strange statuette in London which he decided was Burmese in origin. He went to visit a friend and as he relates in his autobiography: "Somebody present had a sheet of Irish Sweepstakes tickets, and it was proposed that we sign with a pseudonym. 'Burmese' sounded like a good pseudonym to me, so I took some tickets jointly and some singly, and signed them 'Burmese.' " The day's events inspired Huston to write the story which would become THREE STRANGERS. Author Huston's odd story appears to have been a portent of things to come; his initial directorial effort, Dashiell Hammett's novel *The Maltese Falcon*, also dealt with a mysterious statuette, and introduced the duo of Lorre and Greenstreet. British director Alfred Hitchcock was interested in Huston's story and wanted to direct it, but studio head Michael Balcon wasn't so enthusiastic and the project never materialized. When Huston returned to the U.S. he worked on the screenplay with Howard Koch for Warner Bros. (British author John Collier is said to have had a hand in the screenplay as well, but he is not credited) and it sat on the shelf until after WW II. By this time Huston had become a director in his own right and had created the team of Greenstreet and Lorre in THE MALTESE FALCON (1941). He had intended to star Humphrey Bogart, Greenstreet, and Mary Astor as the "Three Strangers," but he soon went off to war and the project eventually went into other hands. Greenstreet and Lorre proved such a popular duo that they were teamed up several times in both supporting and starring roles. Huston's mysterious, gripping, and ironic script was finally filmed in 1945 under the direction of Negulesco, who conveyed the moments of suspense and terror with considerable flair. The actors all have a field day with the delicious situation and dialog, with Lorre the real standout, and he even gets to go off with his girlfriend, Lorring, at the end! As is the case with most of the Greenstreet-Lorre team-ups, this is great fun.

p, Wolfgang Reinhardt; d, Jean Negulesco; w, John Huston, Howard Koch (based on the story "Three Men and a Girl" by Huston); ph, Arthur Edeson; m, Adolph Deutsch; ed, George Amy; md, Leo F. Forbstein; art d, Ted Smith; spec eff, Edwin DuPar.

Drama　　　　　**(PR:A-C　MPAA:NR)**

THREE STRIPES IN THE SUN* (1955) 93m COL bw (GB: GENTLE SERGEANT, THE)

Aldo Ray (*Hugh O'Reilly*), Phil Carey (*Colonel*), Dick York (*Cpl. Neeby Muhlendorf*), Mitsuko Kimura (*Yuko*), Chuck Connors (*Idaho*), Camille Janclaire (*Sister Genevieve*), Henry Okawa (*Father Yoshida*), Tatsuo Saito (*Konoya*), Chiyaki (*Chiyaki*), Sgt. Demetrios (*Himself*), Sgt. Romaniello (*Himself*), L Tamaki (*Mr. Ohta*), Lt. Col. Mike Davis (*Maj. Rochelle*), Lt. Thomas Brazil (*Himself*), Takeshi Kamikubo (*Kanno*), Tamao Nakamura (*Satsumi*), Teruko Omi (*Yuko's Mother*), Kamiko Tachibana (*Yuko's Sister*).

Ray is a lifer in the U.S. Army, stationed in the Far East and slowly but surely becoming fond of the village children. He starts to help the orphans by gathering up army food for them, eventually emptying his own pockets in order to feed and shelter the kids. He also earns the love and respect of Kimura, who first serves as his interpreter and then becomes his wife. An interesting picture coming out of post-war sentiments, it has Jap-hater Ray softening to the point of sacrifice for the children of those people his soldiers have killed. The story is taken from the experiences of Master Sergeant Hugh O'Reilly, who acted as the technical adviser for the film.

p, Fred Kohlmar; d, Richard Murphy; w, Murphy, Albert Duffy (based on the *New Yorker* magazine article "The Gentle Wolfhound" by E.J. Kahn, Jr.); ph, Burnett Guffey; m, George Duning; ed, Charles Nelson; md, Morris Stoloff; art d, Carl Anderson.

Drama/Romance　　　　　**(PR:A　MPAA:NR)**

THREE SUNDAYS TO LIVE* (1957, Brit.) 71m Danziger's/UA bw

Kieron Moore (*Frank Martin*), Jane Griffiths (*Judy Allen*), Sandra Dorne (*Ruth Chapman*), Basil Dignam (*Davitt*), Hay Ayer (*Al Murray*), John Stone (*Detective*), John Longden (*Warder*), Ferdy Mayne (*Davis*), Norman Mitchell (*Police Sergeant*), Mona Washbourne.

Moore, the conductor of a dance band, is sentenced to death for a murder he didn't commit. He breaks jail and sets out with girl friend Griffiths to find the only witness who can clear him. They find her, but she is murdered and Moore manages to trick the killer into thinking he has killed the wrong woman. When the murderer comes back to try again, they trap him. Badly written and performed, without a single entertaining facet.

p, Edward J. and Harry Lee Danziger; d, Ernest Morris; w, Brian Clemens; ph, Jimmy Wilson.

Crime　　　　　**(PR:A　MPAA:NR)**

THREE TALES OF CHEKHOV   (1961, USSR) 76 m Mosfilm c/bw

"Aniouta": Klavdia Blokhina (*Aniouta*), Anatoli Adoskine (*Klotchkov*), Eugueni Eustigneev (*Painter*), "A Vengeance": Mikhail Yanchine (*Touramov*), Ludmilla Kasatkina (*Wife*), Gueorgui Vitsine (*Degtiarev*), Anastasia Guerguievaskia (*Woman*), "Vanka": Sacha Barsov (*Vanka*), Nikolai Plotnikov (*Aliakine*), Nikolai Nikitine (*Nikititch*).

A Chekhov trilogy from a trio of Soviet directors. "A Vengeance," the only color episode in the batch, tells the tale of an aging man, married to a lovely young woman, who tries to get revenge on a friend. "Aniouta" delves into the human misery that surrounds the existence of a group of hotel boarders, while "Vanka" centers on a singular character in the throes of depression–a slave tormented by his employers.

d, Marie Andjaparidze ("Aniouta"), Irina Poplavaskaia ("A Vengeance"), Edouard Botcharov ("Vanka"); w, Andjaparidze ("Aniouta"), Grigori Koltounov ("A Vengeance"), Geunrikh Oganissian ("Vanka") (all episodes based on short stories by Anton Pavlovich Chekhov); ph, Nicolai Olonovski (Sovcolor), Piotr Emelianov, Piotr Kataev, Joseph Martov; ed, V. Dorman, S. Popov, K. Gordon.

Drama   (PR:A   MPAA:NR)

3:10 TO YUMA*½**   (l957) 92m COL bw

Van Heflin (*Dan Evans*), Glenn Ford (*Ben Wade*), Felicia Farr (*Emmy*), Leora Dana (*Alice Evans*), Henry Jones (*Alex Potter*), Richard Jaeckel (*Charlie Prince*), Robert Emhardt (*Mr. Butterfield*), Sheridan Comerate (*Bob Moons*), George Mitchell (*Bartender*), Robert Ellenstein (*Ernie Collins*), Ford Rainey (*Marshal*), Barry Curtis (*Mathew*), Jerry Hartleben (*Mark*).

This fine western opens with Heflin as a rancher whose family is suffering from the devastating effects of a long drought. Heflin needs $200 to build a well, then learns he can obtain the money as a reward for delivering Ford, a notorious outlaw now in the hands of the law, to the state prison in Yuma, Arizona. Though this will put Heflin in great personal danger, the peaceful man accepts this assignment, knowing what the money will mean to his family. Heflin and Ford hole up in a small hotel in another town while waiting for the train to Yuma. The outlaw begins toying with Heflin's mind, talking in a friendly manner to his escort about his job and financial situation. Playing psychological games, Ford tries to convince Heflin to take $10,000 to look the other way while he escapes. Heflin finds himself in a quandary, knowing that he desperately needs the money, yet being bound by his word to carry out the job. Ford's gang, led by Jaeckel, discovers where their leader is hidden and set out to rescue him. The town officials abandon Heflin, rather than put themselves in danger, leaving the troubled rancher alone and isolated from help in facing off with the outlaws. Ford ends up assisting Heflin, helping his captor onto the 3:10 to Yuma, explaining: "...I owed you that." Heflin has come through the ordeal, body and integrity intact, and, as if in answer to this baptism by fire, the skies burst forth with rain, putting an end to the drought. Much like HIGH NOON, this film deals with a man alone after town officials have passed on their duties, leaving him to face both his adversaries and his conscience. Daves' direction is gritty, confining much of the story to the small hotel room, with a hard-hitting use of close-up. His outdoor sequences are equally good, particularly the portrait of a land desperate for water. Heflin is superior in the role with his intense portrait of a man caught between personal needs and social duties. Ford is equally good, mixing amiable feelings with monstrous qualities. This is a landmark western, redefining what the genre was capable of doing, and is one of Daves' best works.

p, David Heilwell; d, Delmer Daves; w, Halsted Welles (based on the story by Elmore Leonard); ph, Charles Lawton, Jr.; m, George Duning; ed, Al Clark; md, M.W. Stoloff; art d, Frank Hotaling; cos, Jean Louis; m/l, "3:10 to Yuma," Duning, Ned Washington (sung by Frankie Laine).

Western   Cas.   (PR:O MPAA:NR)

THREE TEXAS STEERS*½   (1939) 59m REP bw (GB: DANGER RIDES THE RANGE)

John Wayne (*Stony Brooke*), Ray Corrigan (*Tucson Smith*), Max Terhune (*Lullaby Joslin*), Carole Landis (*Nancy Evans*), Ralph Graves (*George Ward*), Roscoe Ates (*Sheriff Brown*), Collette Lyons (*Lillian*), Billy Curtis (*Hercules*), Ted Adams (*Steve*), Stanley Blystone (*Rankin*), David Sharpe (*Tony*), Ethan Laidlaw (*Morgan*), Lew Kelly (*Postman*), John Merton (*Mike Abbott*), Dave Willock (*Hotel Clerk*), Ted Mapes, Naba the Gorilla (*Willie*).

While not up to par with the rest of the series, THREE TEXAS STEERS still provides a few chuckles, even if they're not all intentional. Landis, the femme owner of a circus, inherits a plot of land which the government wants for a water improvement project. The shifty Graves, Landis' manager, tries to get the land for himself, but his plan is foiled by Wayne and his fellow Mesquiteers. This was ventriloquist Terhune's final appearance in the series, which accounts for the excessive footage of him and his sawdust dummy. The circus fire scenes are courtesy of CIRCUS GIRL (1937). (See THREE MESQUITEERS series, Index.)

p, William Berke; d, George Sherman; w, Betty Burbridge, Stanley Roberts; (based on the characters created by William Colt MacDonald); ph, Ernest Miller; m, William Lava; ed, Tony Martinelli.

Western   (PR:A   MPAA:NR)

THREE THE HARD WAY½**   (1974) 93m Three C's Service/AA c

Jim Brown (*Jimmy Lait*), Fred Williamson (*Jagger Daniels*), Jim Kelly (*Mr. Keyes*), Sheila Frazier (*Wendy Kane*), Jay Robinson (*Monroe Feather*), Charles McGregor (*Charley*), Howard Platt (*Keep*), Richard Angarola (*Dr. Fortrero*), David Chow (*Link*), Marian Collier (*Eva*), Junero Jennings (*House*), Alex Rocco (*Lt. DiNisco*), Corbin Bernsen (*Boy*), Renie Radich (*Girl*), Janice Carroll (*Nurse*), Angelyn Chester (*Chicago Girl*), Norman Evans (*NY Cop*), Pamela Serpe (*Countess*), Marie O'Henry (*Princess*), Irene Tsu (*Empress*), Robert Cleaves (*Doctor*), Roberta Collins (*Lait's Secretary*), Lance Taylor (*Pool Player*), Jeanie Bell (*Polly*), Victor Brandt, Mario Roccuzzo, Don Gazzaniga (*Guards*), the Impressions: Fred Cash, Sam Gooden, Ralph Johnson, Reggie Torian.

An all-star blaxploitation cast–Brown, Williamson, and Kelly–star in this well-directed actioner. The hard-hitting trio work together in stopping a fascist, all-white sect that is bent on ridding Los Angeles, Detroit, and Washington of their black population. Their method is to pollute the water supply with a drug that affects only blacks. Far-fetched and a bit comic-bookish, but filled with all you'd want from the genre and then some. One of two pictures Lucien Ballard shot for Parks, Jr. at the end of his long career, which began with Sternberg in 1934. The other Parks-Ballard collaboration was THOMASINE AND BUSHROD, 1974.

p, Herry Bernsen; d, Gordon Parks, Jr.; w, Eric Bercovici, Jerry Ludwig; ph, Lucien Ballard (DeLuxe Color); m, Richard Tufo; ed, Robert Swink; spec eff, Joe Lombardi; m/l, Tufo, Lowrell Simon (performed by the Impressions); stunts, Hal Needham.

Crime   Cas.   (PR:O   MPAA:R)

3,000 A.D.   (SEE: CAPTIVE WOMEN, 1952)

THREE TO GO½**   (1971, Aus.) 90m Australian Commonwealth Film Unit bw

"Michael": Matthew Burton (*Michael*), Grahame Bond (*Grahame*), Peter Colville (*Trantor*), Georgina West (*Georgina*), "Judy": Judy Morris (*Judy*), Serge Lazareff (*Mike*), Mary Anne Severne (*Margaret*), "Toula": Rina Ioannou (*Toula*), Erica Crowne (*Assimina*), Andrew Pappas (*Stavros*).

A trilogy about Australia's youth which marks the first fiction feature film to be produced by that country's Commonwealth Film Unit, which has gone on to make quite an impact. The most interesting aspect of THREE TO GO is the chance it provides to see an early short (each episode runs approximately 30 minutes) from Peter Weir, who has gone on to become the most respected of Australia's new breed, directing PICNIC AT HANGING ROCK, THE LAST WAVE, and WITNESS. His episode, "Michael," concerns a young office worker affected by a film on guerrilla warfare who becomes attracted to the hippie lifestyle. "Judy," the next sketch, deals with a 20-year-old girl who wants to leave her small-town heritage behind and head for the city. "Toula" tells the story of a young Greek girl who is locked into her parents' ways, while she would rather be living like her Australian peers.

p, Gil Brealey; d&w, Peter Weir ("Michael"), Brian Hannant ("Judy"), Oliver Howes ("Toula"); ph, Kerry Brown; m, The Cleves ("Michael"), Grahame Bond, Rory O'Donoghue ("Judy"), Wolfgang Amadeus Mozart ("Toula"); ed, Wayne Le Clos.

Drama   (PR:A-C MPAA:NR)

THREE TOUGH GUYS   (1974, U.S./Ital.) 92m DD/PAR c

Lino Ventura (*Father Charlie*), Isaac Hayes (*Lee Stevens*), Fred Williamson (*Joe Snake*), Paula Kelly (*Fay Collins*), William Berger (*Capt. Ryan*), Luciano Salce (*Bishop*), Vittorio Sanipoli (*Mike Petralia*), Jacques Herlin (*Tequila*), Jess Hahn (*Bartender*), Lorella De Luca (*Anne Lombardo*), Thurman E. Scott (*Tony Red*), Mario Erpichini (*Gene*), Guido Leontini (*Sgt. Sam*), Joel Cory (*Truckdriver*), Dutchell Smith (*Streetwalker*), Ira Rogers (*Lou*), Margot Novick (*Prostitute*), Tommy Brubaker (*Hood*), Buddy Stein (*Cab Driver*), Max Klevin (*Huge Man*), Walt Scott (*Petralia's Man*), Frank Grimaldi (*Blinky*), Emanuele Spatafora (*Joe Bell*), Hans Jung Bluth (*Mechanic*).

An Italian-American coproduction which brings Ventura together with Hayes and Williamson in the blaxploitationer. Ventura is a former man of God who is determined to get to the bottom of a string of machine-gun murders in the hope of clearing an innocent friend's name. Ventura sure doesn't act like he has spent time in a religious order, as he and his partner Hayes smash heads and nearly kill people before they finally put the finger on Williamson. Most of the actors had to be dubbed into English, which becomes annoying after about the first 30 seconds. This was the fifth film appearance for Hayes, best known as musician and composer. He played the title role in TRUCK TURNER, also released in 1974.

p, Dino De Laurentiis; d, Duccio Tessari; w, Luciano Vincenzoni, Nicola Badalucco; ph, Aldo Tonti (Technicolor); m, Isaac Hayes; ed, Mario Morra, Richard Marks; art d, Francesco Bronzi.

Action/Crime   (PR:C MPAA:PG)

THREE VIOLENT PEOPLE½   (1956) 100m PAR c

Charlton Heston (*Colt Saunders*), Anne Baxter (*Lorna Hunter Saunders*), Gilbert Roland (*Innocencio, Foreman*), Tom Tryon (*Cinch Saunders*), Forrest Tucker (*Cable, Deputy Commissioner*), Bruce Bennett (*Harrison*), Elaine Stritch (*Ruby LaSalle*), Barton MacLane (*Yates*), Peter Hansen (*Lt. Marr*), John Harmon (*Massey*), Ross Bagdasarian (*Asuncion*), Bobby Blake (*Rafael*), Jameel Farah (*Pedro*), Leo Castillo (*Luis*), Don Devlin (*Juan*), Raymond Greenleaf (*Carleton*), Roy Engel, Don Dunning (*Carpetbaggers*), Argentina Brunetti (*Maria*), Ernestine Wade (*Maid*), Paul Levitt (*Bartender*), Robert Arthur (*One-Legged Confederate Soldier*), Kenneth MacDonald (*Croupier*).

The title's three violent people–former Confederate soldier Heston; former prostitute and wife of Heston Baxter; and Heston's one-armed brother, Tryon–find themselves battling each other and moneygrabbing carpetbaggers. Heston and Baxter marry after knowing little or nothing about each other, and return to his Bar-S ranch which has been run by Mexican ranch foreman Roland and his sons. Conflicts arise when Tryon demands his portion of the ranch, in gold, and tries to convince Heston to sell to any Northerner who wants it. Heston's world is further upset when he discovers Baxter was once a hooker and is now pregnant with his child. He gives her enough money to live on and asks her to leave. However, after a plot to kill Heston has been foiled, he and Baxter stay together to run the ranch with Roland, but Tryon gets killed in a gunbattle with government troops. Interesting mainly in respect to THE TEN COMMANDMENTS, which saw Heston and Baxter in two considerably more pious roles.

p, Hugh Brown; d, Rudolph Mate; w, James Edward Grant (based on a story by Leonard Praskins, Barney Slater); ph, Loyal Griggs (VistaVision, Technicolor); m, Walter Scharf; ed, Alma Macrorie; md, Scharf; art d, Hal Pereira, Earl Hedrick; cos, Edith Head; spec eff, John P. Fulton, Farciot Edouart; m/l, "Un Momento," Mack David, Martita.

Western   (PR:A MPAA:NR)

THREE WARRIORS**   (1977) 109m Fantasy Films c

McKee "Kiko" Red Wing (*Michael*), Charles White Eagle (*Grandfather*), Randy Quaid (*Quentin Hammond*), Lois Red Elk (*Mother*).

Average family entertainment about a 13-year-old Indian boy who is forced to return to the reservation to see his "dying" grandfather. The boy has a strong dislike for his new surroundings but is soon won over by his grandfather's kindness. Before you know it the boy is skillfully shooting a bow and arrow and showing off the best redskin prowess. Quaid, who got an Oscar nomination as Best Supporting Actor for his work in THE LAST DETAIL as the befuddled, court-martialed sailor, is the only known name in a cast otherwise comprising native American amateurs. Producer Zaentz–who, with Michael Douglas, coproduced ONE FLEW OVER THE CUCKOO'S NEST (1975)–must have liked the land of the author of that film, Ken Kesey; this one makes the most of the Oregon wilderness scenery.

p, Saul Zaentz, Sy Gomberg; d, Keith Merrill; w, Gomberg; ph, Bruce Surtees.

Adventure   Cas.   (PR:A MPAA:G)

THREE-WAY SPLIT* (1970) 76m Green Dolphin/Preferred
                                                    Enterprises c

Peter Owen, Donov Franchetti.

Action and exploitation go hand-in-hand in this lame tale about a group of demented crooks who pull a robbery in Las Vegas, and on the way seduce a few ladies.

p, Dave Ackerman; d, Charles Nizet

Crime   (PR:O MPAA:NR)

THREE WEEKS OF LOVE*   (1965) 75m Westminster-Polimer c

Lane Nakano (*Ken Okimura*), Tamiko Aya (*Sumi*), Tony Russel (*Bud*), Tatsuo Saito (*Mr. Yasuda*), Roland Ray (*Captain*), Joe Yue (*Joe Young*), Miyako Morita (*Mrs. Young*), Keiko Doi (*Sumi's Sister*), Reiko Okada (*Sumi's Friend*), Lucille Soong (*Girl in Hong Kong*), Kiyono Sasaki (*Sumi's Mother*).

A well-meaning portrayal of Japanese customs and traditions which ultimately looks like a travelog, complete with excessive narration. The story, which is merely an excuse to show off the beautiful scenery, has a nisei seaman falling in love with a Japanese nightclub hostess, but unable to marry her because of strong devotion to archaic customs. Lensed in Hong Kong and Japan. Producer/director Brusseau's first feature film, one that betrays his metier as a documentarist.

p&d, William E. Brusseau; w, Harry Brown (based on a story by Brusseau); ph, Junichi Segawa (CinemaScope, Eastmancolor); m, Calvin Jackson, Ralph Carmichael; ed, Warren Adams; art d, Totetsu Hirakawa; ch, Don Yaka.

Romance   (PR:A MPAA:NR)

THREE WEIRD SISTERS, THE**   (1948, Brit.) 82m BN/Pathe bw

Nancy Price (*Gertrude Morgan-Vaughan*), Mary Clare (*Maude Morgan-Vaughan*), Mary Merrall (*Isobel Morgan-Vaughan*), Nova Pilbeam (*Claire Prentiss*), Anthony Hulme (*David Davies*), Raymond Lovell (*Owen Morgan-Vaughan*), Elwyn Brook-Jones (*Thomas*), Edward Rigby (*Waldo*), Hugh Griffith (*Mabli Hughes*), Marie Ault (*Beattie*), David Davies (*Police Sergeant*), Hugh Pryse (*Minister*), Lloyd Pearson (*Solicitor*), Doreen Richards (*Mrs. Probart*), Bartlett Mullins (*Dispenser*), Frank Crawshaw (*Bank Manager*), Frank Dunlop (*Ben*), Elizabeth Maude (*Olwen Harries*), Belinda Marshall (*Mrs. Bevan*), D.J. Tawe-Jones (*Dying Workman*), Wilfred Boyle (*Solicitor's Clerk*), Lionel Gadsden, John Humphries (*Welsh Workmen*), Ursula Granville (*Welsh Woman*), Ethel Beal, Dora Levis, Helen Lee, Elizabeth Allen (*Old Welsh Women*).

Macbeth's fantasy comes to fruition in this tale about three deranged elderly sisters who run their large mansion with the help of an equally bizarre man and his mother. In order to inherit enough cash to live comfortably they plot to kill their half-brother Lovell, but of course the plan is foiled. Dylan Thomas contributed to the scripting. Birt does well in his first feature-film directorial effort, cowritten by his wife, Louise.

p, Louis H. Jackson; d, Dan Birt; w, Louise Birt, David Evans, Dylan Thomas (based on the novel *The Case of the Three Weird Sisters* by Charlotte Armstrong); ph, Ernest Palmer, Morlay Grant; ed, Monica Kimick.

Crime   Cas.   (PR:A MPAA:NR)

THREE WHO LOVED*½   (1931) 72m RKO bw

Betty Compson, Conrad Nagel, Robert Ames, Robert Emmett O'Connor, Bodil Rosing, Dickie Moore, Fred Santley.

Compson is a Swedish girl who comes to America at the request of her bankteller boy friend Nagel. Nagel's coworker Ames soon has his eyes on the thick-accented svenska flicka, but that is soon ended when he is sent to prison after Nagel steals $10,000 out of his bank till. After a few years have passed, Nagel and Compson are living a life of luxury with their young son in a plush mansion. Ames, however, has escaped from jail with the intention of getting revenge on his "friend." He is gunned down by the police before he gets his chance; eaten away by his own guilt, Nagel confesses to his old crime. Compson dutifully promises to be waiting for him when he's through with his prison term.

p, Bertram Millhauser; d, George Archainbaud; w, Beulah Marie Dix (based on a story by Martin Flavin); ph, Nick Musuraca.

Drama   (PR:A MPAA:NR)

THREE WISE FOOLS**   (1946) 90m MGM bw

Margaret O'Brien (*Sheila O'Monohan*), Lionel Barrymore (*Dr. Richard Gaunght*), Lewis Stone (*Judge Thomas Trumbull*), Edward Arnold (*Theodore Findley*), Thomas Mitchell (*Terence Aloysius O'Davern*), Ray Collins (*Judge Watson*), Jane Darwell (*Sister Mary Brigid*), Charles Dingle (*Paul Badger*), Harry Davenport (*The Ancient*), Henry O'Neill (*Horace Appleby*), Cyd Charisse (*Rena Fairchild*), Warner Anderson (*The O'Monohan*), Billy Curtis (*Dugan*).

A strong cast and the youthful exuberance of O'Brien help this mediocre venture from falling to the wayside. Amidst fairy tales of leprechaun spells, O'Brien helps bring cheer into the lives of three crotchety old men after they've realised they no longer have any friends. Previously filmed as a 1923 silent.

p, William H. Wright; d, Edward Buzzell; w, John McDermott, James O'Hanlon (based on the play by Austin Strong); ph, Harold Rosson; m, Bronislau Kaper; ed, Gene Ruggiero; art d, Cedric Gibbons, Edward Imazu; set d, Edwin B. Willis, Hugh Hunt; cos, Valles.

Drama/Fantasy   (PR:A MPAA:NR)

THREE WISE GIRLS**   (1932) 68m COL bw

Jean Harlow (*Cassie Barnes*), Mae Clarke (*Gladys Kane*), Walter Byron (*Jerry Dexter*), Marie Prevost (*Dot*), Andy Devine (*Chauffeur*), Natalie Moorhead (*Ruth*), Jameson Thomas (*Arthur Phelps*), Lucy Beaumont (*Cassie's Mother*), Katherine C. Ward (*Mrs. Kane*), Robert Dudley (*Lem*), Marcia Harris (*Landlady*), Walter Miller (*Manager of Store*), Armand Kaliz (*Andre*).

A weak attempt at an urban comedy marked Harlow's final picture for the Gower Street lot. After this, she moved to MGM. Even in 1932, the story of three girls in the big city and the machinations in which they become embroiled was old hat. Harlow is a straight young woman from a small town. When she tires of life in the slow lane and hears that her old friend Clarke is having a swell time in Manhattan, Harlow exits Hicksville and hies for Gotham. She moves in with Prevost, who addresses envelopes for a living. Harlow gets a job but when her boss gets fresh, she quits and hires on as a model in the same couturier store as Clarke. While there, Harlow encounters wealthy man-about-town Byron and falls hard for the scoundrel.

It turns out that the cad is already married. He claims he's about to ask his wife for a divorce but Harlow doesn't buy his blah-blah and tells him to find another patsy. Clarke is seeing Thomas, another married man who has been keeping her in a Park Avenue pad, supplied with all the accouterments that the standard mistress should have. When Thomas, a banker, begins yawning, he decides that it would be better to go back to his wife. This causes Clarke to take the suicide's way out of life. Meanwhile, Prevost has fallen in love with lovable Devine, a chauffeur, and when Byron is true to his word and gets his spouse to agree to a split, he contacts Prevost and Devine because he doesn't know where Harlow has gone. She's back in the small town where it all began. Byron, Devine, and Prevost arrive in the little burg and he manages to convince her that he really is leaving his wife (in real life, they seldom do) and she believes him and promises to stay by his side until the judge awards the ex her alimony and they can get married. A few scenes with scanty clothes on the models, some mild comedy from Prevost, and a moral that comes out and slugs one in the jaw (when Clarke kills herself after having cavorted with married Thomas). Strictly for Harlow buffs.

d, William Beaudine; w, Agnes C. Johnson, Robert Riskin (based on the story "Blonde Baby" by Wilson Collison); ph, Teddy Tetzlaff; ed, Jack Dennis.

Drama   (PR:A   MPAA:NR)

THREE WISE GUYS, THE*   (1936) 73m MGM bw

Robert Young (Joe Hatcher), Betty Furness (Clarabelle Brooks), Raymond Walburn (Doc Brown), Thurston Hall (Old Man Hatcher), Bruce Cabot (Blackie Swanson), Donald Meek (Gribble), Herman Bing (Baumgarten), Harvey Stephens (Ambersham), Harry Tyler (Yegg), Pat West (Bartender), Edward Hearn (Cop), Alexander Melesh (Waiter), Clay Clement (Manager of Mangin's), Buddy Messenger (Elevator Operator).

Damon Runyon's coined-language version of the same nativity play done as a western by John Ford (THREE GODFATHERS, 1948, and the silent MARKED MEN, 1919), and done again by many other directors, features a young Young as a rich boy disinherited and abjured by his father when he marries socially unacceptable Broadway babe Furness. After Young squanders the remnants of his cash on an extended round-the-world honeymoon, gold digger Furness discovers that she truly loves the lad. Pursued by confidence-man Cabot and his two tough-talking cronies, all convinced that Furness double-crossed them in a scam, the now-indigent couple seek refuge in a barn. Their pursuers arrive to find the lone and very pregnant Furness on the straw amidst the cattle. They assist with the delivery of her infant on a cold, snowy Christmas. Their hearts softened by the birth, they contribute some cash to get the falsely accused Young released from the local jail in a town called--what else? Bethlehem.

p, Harry Rapf; d, George B. Seitz; w, Elmer Harris (based on the story by Damon Runyon); ph, Jackson Rose; m, Dr. William Axt; ed, Frank E. Hull; art d, Cedric Gibbons, Eddie Imazu; set d, Edwin B. Willis; cos, Dolly Tree.

Romance   (PR:A   MPAA:NR)

THREE WITNESSES*   (1935, Brit.) 68m Twickenham/UNIV bw

Henry Kendall (Leslie Trent), Eve Gray (Margaret Truscott), Sebastian Shaw (Roger Truscott), Garry Marsh (Charles Rowton), Richard Cooper (Claude Pember), Geraldine Fitzgerald (Diane Morton), Noel Dryden (Cyril Truscott), Ralph Truman (Mr. Bellman), Gladys Hamer (Mrs. Bellman), Gerald Hamer, Henry Woolston.

Kendall is a solicitor investigating the death of his fiancee's brother. He eventually proves his own partner to be the killer, but too late, as most of the audience will have fallen asleep long before.

p, Julius Hagen; d, Leslie Hiscott; w, Michael Barringer (based on the novel by S. Fowler Wright).

Crime   (PR:A   MPAA:NR)

THREE WOMEN*   (1977) 122m Lion's Gate/FOX c

Shelley Duvall (Millie Lammoreaux), Sissy Spacek (Pinky Rose), Janice Rule (Willie Hart), Robert Fortier (Edgar Hart), Ruth Nelson (Mrs. Rose), John Cromwell (Mr. Rose), Sierra Pecheur (Mr. Bunweill), Craig Richard Nelson (Dr. Maas), Maysie Hoy (Doris), Belita Moreno (Alcira), Leslie Ann Hudson (Polly), Patricia Ann Hudson (Peggy), Beverly Ross (Deidre), John Davey (Dr. Norton).

One of Altman's better pictures, although it still suggests that he believes an enigma is more important than a beginning, middle, and end. Spacek arrives at a California desert community where she is to work at an old-age center that specializes in rehabilitation from arthritis for the senior citizens. She's from a small town in Texas and very naive in the ways of Southern California. There are several other women there but Spacek hits it off immediately with Duvall, who is also a Lone Star State native. Duvall thinks of herself as a sexpot but everyone around her thinks she's a nerd, though that's not noticed by Spacek, who hangs on Duvall's blouse tails. Duvall would like to meet a nice guy so she makes it her business to eat lunch only where she can converse with the residents and interns at the hospital cafeteria. She also lives in a "singles" apartment complex and spends her nights drinking beer at a motorcycle bar. Spacek moves in with Duvall and

is taken by the oddities of the place in which she now lives. There is a small Western town built behind the apartment complex and both the town and residential section are heavily decorated with weird paintings by Rule, the silent, pregnant wife of the place's owner, Fortier. He's a one-time movie stunt man, a drunk, and a man who attends to his six guns more than he does his wife. Rule's paintings are all strange, vaguely sexual, and somewhat eerie. Spacek and Duvall hit it off right away, a fact Duvall records in her secret diary. Time passes and Spacek begins borrowing Duvall's clothes, using the same expressions, and generally aping Duvall. She even looks at Duvall's diary. Duvall plans a party for some men and asks Spacek to help prepare the food, but the young girl is totally unable to handle things. Then the men don't arrive and Duvall storms out, leaving Spacek alone in the apartment with various kinds of chip dip, spreads, cheap wine, and plastic glasses. Later that night, Duvall brings home Fortier, who is roaring drunk. Spacek feels awful that Duvall and Fortier are together, especially since Rule is sitting at home with a baby growing inside her, so Spacek leaps into the swimming pool in an apparent suicide attempt. She's rescued by Rule and taken to the hospital, where Duvall remains at her side until she recovers. Duvall has greeting cards sent to Spacek, then phones the girl's parents, Cromwell and Nelson, to come to California. They are old and look more like her grandparents and Spacek, who is evidently now suffering from a mental problem, won't even admit that they are her folks. Spacek is released and returns to the apartment and the roles change. Before, Spacek was the puppy dog who followed Duvall around. Now, Duvall attends Spacek's every wish. Duvall goes to work every day and Spacek uses the empty afternoons to dally with Fortier, who also gives her pistol-shooting lessons at his Dodge City complex. Spacek is growing stronger, more dominant. She takes Duvall's car and uses it without asking. She also starts to keep her own diary. A strange metamorphosis is happening but, despite her new confidence, Spacek is still a young, scared girl. After a nightmare, Spacek crawls into bed with Duvall (in a sisterly, rather than lesbian fashion) and Fortier arrives, drunk and whooping. Rule is in labor. Duvall and Spacek rush to Rule's side and Duvall tells Spacek to find a physician. Fortier is too drunk to move and Spacek is frozen on the spot at what she sees. (It's like the scene in GONE WITH THE WIND when Butterfly McQueen stands rigid as she admits that she doesn't know anything about "birthing babies.") Rule delivers a stillborn son and Duvall blames Spacek for not having been able to rout and find a doctor. Spacek accepts the guilt. Then Fortier dies mysteriously in a gunshot accident (although it might seem that these women did him in). Spacek goes back to being a child, Duvall takes over the management of the place and seems somewhat like Rule, while Rule finally comes out of her shell but seems content to sit in the shadow of Duvall, who has become the man of the house and business. Altman supposedly based his script on a dream he had while his wife was in surgery. The story is often incomprehensible, the cinematic techniques are film-school, but the acting is first-rate. Altman fans will tell you that it is multi-layered with meaning, metaphor, and allegory. Choose to believe that if you wish. No question that it's inventive and different from most movies (the notable exception being Ingmar Bergman's PERSONA, which it resembles), but so was the explosive weapon dropped on Japan by the "Enola Gay" in 1945. Filmed in the Palm Springs area.

p,d&w, Robert Altman; ph, Chuck Rosher (Panavision, DeLuxe Color); m, Gerald Busby; ed, Dennis Hill; art d, James D. Vance; spec eff, Modern Film Effects; makeup, Monty Westmore; visual consultant, J. Allen Highfill.

Drama   (PR:C   MPAA:PG)

THREE WORLDS OF GULLIVER, THE½**   (1960, Brit.) 98m
                     Morningside/COL c (AKA: THE WORLDS OF GULLIVER)

Kerwin Mathews (Dr. Lemuel Gulliver), Jo Morrow (Gwendolyn), June Thorburn (Elizabeth), Lee Patterson (Reldresal), Gregoire Aslan (King Brobdingnag), Basil Sydney (Emperor of Lilliput), Charles Lloyd Pack (Makovan), Martin Benson (Flimnap), Mary Ellis (Queen Brobdingnag), Peter Bull (Lord Bermogg), Alec Mango (Galbet), Sherri Alberoni (Glumdal-clitch), Marian Spencer (Empress of Lilliput).

Mathews plays Gulliver in this Ray Harryhausen live/animation feature which explores the lands of Lilliput and Brobdingnag (the third world is England). Miniature people are seen dwarfed by giant people and animals with the same technique and skills as the previous SEVENTH VOYAGE OF SINBAD, which also starred Mathews. The tempo is boosted along by a fine Bernard Herrmann score. Segments of Swift's caustic work remain sharp, despite cutting the three additional worlds of the novel and adding romantic interest Thorburn to the story line.

p, Charles H. Schneer; d, Jack Sher; w, Arthur Ross, Sher (based on Jonathan Swift's novel Gulliver's Travels); ph, Wilkie Cooper (Superdyna-mation, Eastmancolor); m, Bernard Herrmann; ed, Raymond Poulton; md, Herrman; art d, Gil Parrendo, Derek Barrington; cos, Eleanor Abbey; spec eff, Ray Harryhausen; m/l, Ned Washington, George Duning.

Fantasy/Adventure   (PR:AAA   MPAA:NR)

THREE YOUNG TEXANS**   (1954) 77m Panoramic/FOX c

Mitzi Gaynor (Rusty Blair), Keefe Brasselle (Tony Ballew), Jeffrey Hunter (Johnny Colt), Harvey Stephens (Jim Colt), Dan Riss (Sheriff Carter), Michael Ansara (Apache Joe), Aaron Spelling (Catur), Morris Ankrum (Jeff

Blair), Frank Wilcox *(Bill McAdoo)*, Helen Wallace *(Mrs. Colt)*, John Harmon *(Thorpe)*, Alex Montoya *(Tomas)*, Vivian Marshall *(Saloon Singer)*.

Hunter helps his dad, Stephens, out of a bind when a gang of blackmailers approach the old man and try to force him to pull off a train robbery. To save his dad from danger, Hunter knocks off the train himself and hides the cash, but it is later found by the malevolent Brasselle. Hunter tries to relocate the money while dodging the sheriff, and eventually it turns up, clearing his own name and saving his father from an early demise. Brasselle and the bad blackmailers pay the customary price for their villainy in a succession of shoot-outs.

p, Leonard Goldstein; d, Henry Levin; w, Gerald Drayson Adams (based on a story by William MacLeod Raine); ph, Harold Lipstein (Technicolor); ed, William Murphy; md, Lionel Newman; cos, Travilla; m/l, "Just Let Me Love You," Newman, Eliot Daniel.

Western/Drama   **(PR:A   MPAA:NR)**

THREEPENNY OPERA, THE* **   (1931, Ger./U.S.) 113m Nero Film AG-Tobis Klangfilm-WB bw (DIE DREIGROSCHENOPER; L'OPERA DE QUAT'SOUS; BEGGARS' OPERA)

German: Rudolf Forster *(Mackie Messer)*, Carola Neher *(Polly)*, Reinhold Schunzel *(Tiger Brown)*, Fritz Rasp *(Peachum)*, Valeska Gert *(Mrs. Peachum)*, Lotte Lenya *(Jenny)*, Hermann Thimig *(Vicar)*, Ernst Busch *(Street-Singer)*, Vladimir Sokolov *(Smith)*, Paul Kemp, Gustav Puttjer, Oskar Hocker, Kraft Raschig *(Mackie's Gang)*, Herbert Grunbaum *(Filch)*, French: Albert Prejean *(Mackie Messer)*, Florelle *(Polly)*, Jack Henley *(Tiger Brown)*, Gaston Modot *(Peachum)*, Jane Markem *(Mrs. Peachum)*, Margo Lion *(Jenny)*, Antonin Artaud, Vladimir Sokolov, Merminod *(Mackie's Gang)*.

While not as revered today as the Brecht play or the Weill songs, Pabst's film version of "The Threepenny Opera" is still a fine example of pre-Hitler German filmmaking. In the German version (a French version exists with a different cast, while the planned English version was never completed), Forster plays the infamous "Mackie Messer," or "Mack the Knife," an underworld gangster of the 1890s whose territory is London. A dashing and respected criminal, Forster, is best of friends with the corrupt police chief, Schunzel. After meeting Neher Forster decides to marry her. In a dusty underground warehouse, Forster's wedding is planned–the room is lavishly prepared with goods stolen from London's top shops. A crowd of beggars and thieves attend, as does Schunzel. Neher, however, is the daughter of Rasp, the king of the beggars, who strongly opposes the marriage. He puts pressure on Schunzel to send Forster to the gallows. If Schunzel does not heed Rasp's wishes, then a revolt will be organized by the beggars to disrupt the upcoming coronation of the queen. Although Schunzel wants to stand by Forster, he is forced to prevent the beggars' revolt. With help from Lenya, a prostitute that Forster once loved, Schunzel is able to bring about Forster's arrest. While Forster is behind bars, Neher takes charge of the underworld criminals and continues her husband's banking scheme. Suspicious of Schunzel and Forster, Rasp mobilizes the beggars. Together with the criminals as associates, Neher opens a bank, subscribing to the theory that legalized stealing is more profitable than the usual means of robbery. When Rasp hears of his daughter's entrepreneurial outing, he tries to get involved. The beggars, however, go ahead with their riot, while Forster escapes–with help from the remorseful Lenya–from prison. Rasp and Schunzel both emerge from the coronation disturbance as ruined men, but Forster takes the pair on as partners in the bank. The foundation for their banking empire has been laid. Based on the John Gay satire of 1728, "The Beggar's Opera," this film lacks the punch that made the Brecht-Weill collaboration so potent when it hit the stage in 1928. The sting of social criticism is lessened here and instead emphasis is placed more on dramatics. In fact, Brecht was so disappointed with Pabst's perception of the play, that he ended his collaboratory efforts on the screenplay. He then brought a lawsuit against the production company which tied up the film's German distribution. The lawsuit, however, had far less effect than the Nazi rise to power. The negatives and all prints were confiscated and destroyed. The film did find an audience in France, where the picture was highly acclaimed. London was less impressed with the cutthroat image that pervaded and banned the picture after only a single showing. It was thought that the German print had vanished until 1960, when film distributor Thomas J. Brandon located it–after a decade of hunting–and reconstructed a version. Although there is a noticeable absence of some of Weill's tunes–"Ballad of Sexual Dependency," "The Ballad for the Hangman," and "The Tango Ballad"–the film does open and close with the Ernst Busch rendition of "Moritat," a song which became a huge pop music hit in 1957 for Bobby Darin titled "Mack the Knife." Also prominently featured is "Pirate Jenny" (Brecht-Weill) which is delivered by Lenya. Not only did she appear in the film, but Lenya (Weill's wife) stayed with the theatrical production for a number of years. What the film lacks in Brechtian qualities, it makes up for in the aesthetics of Pabst. Having previously exposed the seedier side of London in PANDORA'S BOX (1929, silent), Pabst once again brings it to the screen in a unique mixture of realism and expressionism. He takes great care in bringing forth the textures of London's underworld–one populated by the lowest of low-lifes–both in his visuals and (although sound films were still a new form) his soundtrack. In THE THREEPENNY OPERA, Pabst has succeeded in making the characters and their surroundings appear as one, not merely mirroring the London of the 1890s, but recreating a richer, more cinematic

one. (In German; English subtitles.)

p, Seymour Nebenzahl; d, Georg Wilhelm Pabst; w, Leo Lania, Bela Balasz, Ladislaus Vajda, Solange Bussi, Andre Mauprey, Ninon Steinhoff (based on the play by Bertolt Brecht, adapted from John Gay's satire "The Beggar's Opera"); ph, Fritz Arno Wagner; m, Kurt Weill; ed, Hans Oser, Henri Rust; prod d, Andrei Andreiev.

Musical/Drama   **Cas.**   **(PR:O   MPAA:NR)**

THREE'S A CROWD*½   (1945) 58m REP bw

Pamela Blake [Adele Pearce] *(Diane Whipple)*, Charles Gordon *(Jeffrey Locke)*, Gertrude Michael *(Sophie Whipple)*, Pierre Watkin *(Marcus Pett)*, Virginia Brissac *(Cary Whipple)*, Ted Hecht *(Jacob Walte)*, Grady Sutton *(Willy Devaney)*, Tom London *(Grayson)*, Roland Varno *(Ronald Drew)*, Anne O'Neal *(Mamie)*, Bud Geary *(Detective)*, Nanette Vallon *(Mme. Francine)*.

A standard whodunit with newlyweds Blake and Gordon both accused of murder when the lady's previous fellow gets killed. Selander's direction is apt, but you've seen all this before with a better script and a more engrossing cast. Another of the studio's meritorious efforts to suffer from a no-name cast (except for the character-part stalwarts). Blake had changed her name a few years previously in the hope that this might get her a fresh start, but her career wasn't helped by her screen pseudonym. Gordon revivified four years later in THE BLACK BOOK (1949), then faded back into obscurity.

p, Walter H. Goetz; d, Lesley Selander; w, Dane Lussier based on the novel Hasty Wedding by Mignon G. Eberhart; ph, William Bradford; ed, Tony Martinelli; md, Richard Cherwin; art d, Russell Kimball.

Mystery   **(PR:A   MPAA:NR)**

THREE'S COMPANY*   (1953, Brit.) 78m BL bw

Basil Sydney, Elizabeth Sellars, George Benson, Douglas Fairbanks, Jr, Constance Cummings.

An anthology of stories culled from the "Douglas Fairbanks Presents" TV series and edited together for theatrical release in Britain. In the first story, surgeon Sydney is forced to operate on someone his own daughter has shot. In the second, Benson innocently becomes involved in murder, and in the third episode Fairbanks, Jr., and wife Cummings buy a haunted house that soon adds another victim to its total. Of universally low quality.

p, Douglas Fairbanks, Jr.; d, Terence Fisher, Charles Saunders; w, Richard Alan Simmons, Larry Marcus, John Cresswell; ph, Jimmy Wilson, Brendan Stafford.

Drama   **(PR:A   MPAA:NR)**

THREES, MENAGE A TROIS*   (1968) 61m C.I.T./I.R.M.I. bw

Jane Lako *(Marilyn)*, John D. White, Suzanne Greco.

A senseless melodrama about a couple living in an open marriage with Lako having an affair with a Czechoslovakian spy. When he is deported, she becomes distraught, gets drunk, seduces her husband, kills him, then kills herself. Deep, isn't it?

p, Sven Erikson; d, Jan Anders; ed, Jack Miles; art d, Miles.

Drama   **(PR:O   MPAA:NR)**

THRESHOLD½**   (1983, Can.) 97m Paragon/FOX c

Donald Sutherland *(Dr. Thomas Vrain)*, Jeff Goldblum *(Dr. Aldo Gehring)*, Allan Nicholls *(Dr. Basil Rents)*, Sharon Acker *(Tilla Vrain)*, Jana Stinson *(Sally Vrain)*, Jessica Steen *(Tracy Vrain)*, Mavor Moore *(Usher)*, Mare Winningham *(Carol Severance)*, Lally Cadeau *(Anita)*, John Marley *(Edgar Fine)*, Michael Lerner *(Henry DeVici)*, Marilyn Gardner *(Vivian)*, Bob Warner *(Rex)*, Robert Joy *(David Art)*, Barbara Gordon *(Wanda)*, Jonathan Welsh *(Pleatman)*, Ray Stancer *(Simone)*, Jan Muzynski *(Diamond)*, Marcia Brunne *(Marcia)*, Dr. Darrell Walsh *(Roger)*, Bob Hannah, Steve Ballantine *(Motorcyclists)*, Richard Blackburn *(Cutter)*, Maureen McRae *(Bonnie)*, Paul Hecht *(Fallaci)*, Carol Berry *(Cathy)*, Valeria Elia *(Announcer)*, Michael C. Gwynne *(Jay)*, Murray Westgate *(Host)*, Robert Goodier *(Elegant Man)*, Elza Pickthorne *(His Wife)*, Ara Hovan *(Arab)*, Kate Trotter *(Ms. Anderson)*, Ken James *(Severance)*, Deborah Turnbull *(Mrs. Severance)*, Margaret Edgar *(Secretary)*, Stan Lesk *(Attendant)*, Jack Messinger, Barry Flatman *(Newsmen)*, Harvey Chao *(Cameraman)*, Dennis Hayes *(Keene)*, Ian Orr *(Willimer)*, Gordon Jocelyn *(Shack)*, Harry Gulkin *(Jawit)*, James Loxley *(Headwaiter)*, Kenny Wells *(Engineer)*.

Released in the U.S. two years after its Canadian premiere, THRESHOLD predates the artificial heart-transplant mania which swept the country in the early 1980s. Sutherland is the doctor who performs the surgery, throwing his hospital's board up in arms; Goldblum is the heart's inventor who wallows in the media attention he receives; and Winningham is the recipient who has trouble dealing with not being totally human. As with any picture that treads "new technology" waters it eventually becomes outdated. Sutherland turns in a commanding performance as the doctor with an iron will and solid hand, benefitting from an engrossing script and able direction. American distributors ignored the film until Barney Clark's real-life artificial heart operation provided free advertising.

p, Jon Slan, Michael Burns; d, Richard Pearce; w, James Salter; ph, Michael Brault; m, Micky Erbe, Maribeth Solomon; ed, Susan Martin; prod d, Anne Pritchard; art d, Jackie Field; cos, Sharon Purdy.

Drama   **Cas.**   **(PR:C MPAA:PG)**

THRILL HUNTER, THE**   (1933) 60m COL bw

Buck Jones, Dorothy Revier, Arthur Rankin, Robert Ellis, Edward J. LeSaint, Frank LaRue, Al Smith, Harry Semels, Eddie Kane, John Ince, Alf James, Harry Todd, Willie Fung.

A Buck Jones entry which is only a western because Jones is in it. The story is a standard piece of entertainment about a fellow who lies excessively and is overheard by members of a movie company, who then hire him to put his money where his blabbing mouth is. In the process he wrecks a countless number of cars and even manages to crack up a plane while performing stuntwork. He loses his job but comes through in the end and manages to win over Revier.

p, Irving Briskin; d, George B. Seitz; w, Harry O. Hoyt; ph, Ted Tetzlaff; ed, Gene Milford.

Western/Comedy   **(PR:A MPAA:NR)**

THRILL KILLERS, THE* (1965) 69m Hollywood Star bw (AKA: THE MONSTERS ARE LOOSE; THE MANIACS ARE LOOSE)

Cash Flagg [Ray Dennis Steckler] (Mort Click), Liz Renay (Liz Saxon), Brick Bardo (Joe Saxon), Carolyn Brandt, Ron Burr (Murdered Lovers), Gary Kent (Gary), Herb Robins (Herbie), Keith O'Brien (Keith), Laura Benedict (Linda), Erina Enyo (Erina Devore), Atlas King (Dennis Kesdekian), Titus Moede (Motorcycle Cop), George J. Morgan (Producer).

An oddity which stars Flagg as a psychotic killer who kills a businessman, King, and then a prostitute, Enyo, while in the meantime three mental patients have escaped and are beheading people. It all ties together (somehow) as Flagg and one of the head-choppers are captured. It was a lot more fun if you saw it in the theater. At the opening run, there was not only a prolog by a real (yeah, sure) hypnotist, but also a few goons running up and down the aisles with fake axes trying to scare the audience. We were supposed to believe we were hypnotized by a spinning wheel on the screen into thinking the maniacs were really jumping out from the screen. Renay is one of the few believable players as the runaway wife of savior Bardo. In later years, she was to become the senior partner in a mother-daughter ecdysiast team.

p, George J. Morgan; d, Ray Dennis Steckler; w, Steckler, Gene Pollock; ph, Joseph V. Mascelli; m, Henry Price; ed, Austin McKinney; art d, Tom Scherman.

Horror   **(PR:O MPAA:NR)**

THRILL OF A LIFETIME**   (1937) 73m PAR bw

The Yacht Club Boys (Jimmy, Charlie, Kelly, Red), Judy Canova (Judy Lovelee), Ben Blue (Skipper), Eleanore Whitney (Betty Jane), Johnny Downs (Stanley), Betty Grable (Gwen), Leif Erickson (Howdy Nelson), Larry ["Buster"] Crabbe (Don), Zeke Canova (Himself), Anne Canova (Herself), Tommy Wonder (Billy), Franklin Pangborn (Mr. Williams), June Schafter (Receptionist), Howard M. Mitchell (Business Man), Si Jenks (Messenger Boy), The Fanchonettes and specialty by Dorothy Lamour, Marie Burton, Paula DeCardo, Norah Gale, Harriette Haddon, Lola Jensen, Gwen Kenyon, Joyce Matthews (The Girls), Billy Daniels, Bill Roberts, Frank Abel, Lee Bennett, Carlyle Blackwell, Jr, Bob Parrish (The Boys).

Silly musical starring Erickson as the manager of "Camp Romance," a retreat where people go to fine-hone their romantic skills. Grable plays Erickson's secretary, who is in love with her boss, but hides her beauty behind an unappealing hairdo and thick glasses. While Erickson puts the finishing touches on a musical he has written, Grable decides to get her man and miraculously transforms herself into a real looker to get the boss's attention. In the end she gets her man, Erickson sees his musical performed, and the audience is treated to tunes sung by The Yacht Club Boys, Judy Canova, and Dorothy Lamour (in a cameo appearance). Songs include: "Keeno, Screeno and You", "I'll Follow My Baby", "Thrill of a Lifetime", "Paris in Swing", "Sweetheart Time" (Sam Coslow, Frederick Hollander), "It's Been a Whole Year", "If We Could Run the Country for a Day" (The Yacht Club Boys).

p, Fanchon Roger; d, George Archainbaud; w, Seena Owen, Grant Garrett, Paul Gerard Smith (based on a story by Owen, Garrett), ph, William C. Mellor; ed, Doane Harrison; md, Boris Morros; art d, Hans Dreier, Franz Bachelin; ch, LeRoy Prinz, Carlos Romero.

Musical   **(PR:A MPAA:NR)**

THRILL OF A ROMANCE**½   (1945) 105m MGM c

Esther Williams (Cynthia Glenn), Van Johnson (Maj. Thomas Milvaine), Frances Gifford (Maude Bancroft), Henry Travers (Hobart Glenn), Spring Byington (Nona Glenn), Lauritz Melchior (Nils Knudsen), Carleton G. Young (Robert G. Delbar), Helene Stanley (Susan), Donald Curtis (K.O. Karny), Jerry Scott (Lyonel), Billy House (Dr. Tove), Ethel Griffies (Mrs. Fenway), Vince Barnett (Oscar), Fernando Alvarado (Julio), Joan Fay Macoboy (Betty), Carli Elinor (Gypsy Orchestra Leader), Thurston Hall (J.P. Bancroft), King Sisters (Specialty), Alex Novinsky, Stuart Holmes (Chess Players), Pierre Watkin (Tycoon), Tim Murdock (Naval Ensign), Jean Porter Brick (Ga-Ga Bride), Frank Ferguson, Selmer Jackson (Hotel Clerks), Robert Emmett O'Connor (Mr. Vemmering), Dagmar Oakland (Guest at Reception), Tom Brannigan (Johnny), Arno Frey (Headwaiter), Dick Earle (Mr. Carter), Virginia Brissac (Secretary), Jack Baxley (Detective), Ray Goulding (Dance Extra), Art Buehler (Chauffeur), Tony Coppala (Waiter), Jack Shea (Donald Curtis' Diving Double), Ruth Nurmi (Esther Williams' Diving Double), Henry Daniels, Jr, Douglas Cowan, Fulton Burley, Wally Boag, Phil Hanna, Joe Sullivan (Canadian Fliers), Tommy Dorsey, Xavier Cugat and Their Orchestras.

Army Air Corps hero Johnson takes a vacation in the Sierra Nevadas and falls in love with sprightly swimmer Williams at a mountain lodge. Things get a bit shaky in between Williams' dips in the lodge's pool when Johnson learns that she is a newlywed, but that problem is solved when her boring husband is suddenly called off to Washington on business. Wagnerian tenor Melchior, who plays a chaperone, made his film debut here. Songs include: "Please Don't Say No, Say Maybe" (Ralph Freed, Sammy Fain, sung by Melchior), "I Should Care" (Sammy Cahn, Axel Stordahl, Paul Weston, sung by Robert Allen), "Lonely Night" (George Stoll, Richard Connell), "Vive L'Amour" (Stoll, Ralph Blane, Kay Thompson), "Schubert's Serenade," "The Thrill Of A Romance."

p, Joe Pasternak; d, Richard Thorpe; w, Richard Connell, Gladys Lehman; ph, Harry Stradling; m&md, Georgie Stoll; ed, George Boemler; art d, Cedric Gibbons, Hans Peters; cos, Irene.

Musical   **(PR:A MPAA:NR)**

THRILL OF BRAZIL, THE**   (1946) 91m COL bw

Evelyn Keyes (Vicki Dean), Keenan Wynn (Steve Farraugh), Ann Miller (Linda Lorens), Allyn Joslyn (John Harbour), Tito Guizar (Himself), Veloz and Yolanda (Themselves), Felix Bressart (Ludwig Kriegspeil), Sid Tomack (Irkie Bowers), Eugene Borden (Luiz), Enric Madriguera Orchestra, George J. Lewis (Bartender), Pat Lane (Stage Manager), Eddie Parkes (Little Man), Antonio Filauri (Cafe Manager), Robert Conte (Waiter), Nino Bellini (Pedrina), Martin Garralaga (Alberto), Fred Godoy (Head Waiter), Leon Lenoir (Night Clerk), John Laurenz (Hotel Clerk), Alex Montoya (Car Driver), Frank Yaconelli (Photographer), Antonio Roux (Porter), Paul Monte (Ticket Taker), Jamiel Hasson, Manuel Paris, Joe Dominguez (Policemen), Mary Meade, Norma Brown, Helen Chapman, Diane Mumby, Jasmin Jenks, Peggy Maley, Doris Houck, Nita Mathews, Cornelia Kirwin, Daun Kennedy (Show Girls), J. Emanuel Vanderhauf (Primitive Drummer), Edward Lynn, Onset [Tom-Tom] Conley (Specialty Dancers), John Fostini, George Mendoza, Nina Bara.

A less-than-thrilling musical starring Wynn as a Broadway producer in Brazil who attempts to prevent his ex-wife, Keyes from marrying toothpaste magnate Joslyn. Though the story line is paper thin, the discomfiture of looking is greatly relieved by some of the best tap dancing Miller has ever done, and another chance to glimpse the wonderful dancing team of Veloz and Yolanda. Songs include: "A Man is a Brother to a Mule" (sung by Miller), "Thrill of Brazil," "CopaCabana," "The Custom House," "That's Good Enough for Me," "My Sleepy Guitar," (Doris Fisher, Allan Roberts), "Silhouette Samba," "Linda Mujer (You Never Say Yes and You Never Say No)," "Minute Samba," "Mucho Dinero."

p, Sidney Biddell; d, S. Sylvan Simon; w, Allen Rivkin, Harry Clork, Devery Freeman; ph, Charles Lawton, Jr.; ed, Charles Nelson; md, Leo Arnaud; art d, Stephen Goosson, Van Nest Polglase, A. Leslie Thomas; set d, James M. Crowe, Robert Priestley; cos, Jean Louis; ch, Eugene Loring, Nick Castle, Jack Cole; m/l, Allan Roberts, Doris Fisher, Raphael Duchesne, Enric Madriguera, Albert Gamse.

Musical   **(PR:A MPAA:NR)**

THRILL OF IT ALL, THE***   (1963) 108M UNIV c

Doris Day (Beverly Boyer), James Garner (Dr. Gerald Boyer), Arlene Francis (Mrs. Fraleigh), Edward Andrews (Gardiner Fraleigh), Reginald Owen (Old Tom Fraleigh), ZaSu Pitts (Olivia, Maid), Elliott Reid (Mike Palmer), Kym Karath (Maggie Boyer), Brian Nash (Andy Boyer), Lucy Landau (Mrs. Goethe), Paul Hartman (Dr. Taylor), Hayden Rorke (Billings, "Yes Man"), Alex Gerry (Stokely), Robert Gallager (Van Camp), Anne Newman (Miss Thompson), Burt Mustin (Butler), Hedley Mattingly (Chauffeur), Robert Strauss, Len Feinrib, Maurice Gosfield (Truck Drivers), William Bramley (Driver), Pamela Curran (Starlet), Herbie Faye (Man), Lenny Kent (Cabbie), John Alderman (Mr. Caputo), Alice Pearce (Woman in Car), Carl Reiner.

Another in a surprisingly good series of romantic comedies starring Doris Day from producers Ross Hunter and Martin Melcher. This one, scripted by

Carl Reiner, sees Day as the average American housewife. She is married to successful gynecologist Garner and stays home to raise their two children. When one of Garner's patients, Francis, hears Day enthusiastically rave about her new shopping discovery, "Happy Soap," a product that happens to be produced by Francis' father-in-law, Owen, she takes Day to meet the old man and he is thrilled by her freshness, honesty, and candor, and signs her to an $80,000 contract to appear in television commercials as the "Happy Soap" lady. Day is a big success and soon much of her time is spent with advertising executives instead of with her family. Husband Garner is upset at these developments, the last straw being when he drives his convertible into a freshly dug swimming pool that had not been in his backyard when he left in the morning. Frustrated, he throws dozens of boxes of "Happy Soap" into the pool and, by morning, the whole house is encased in bubbles. Eventually Garner hits upon a plan to bring Day back home. He, too, acts as though he is too busy to be concerned with their home life, and this unsettles Day to the point that she gives up advertising and returns home. Sixty-five year old ZaSu Pitts, who played the family maid, died of cancer soon after shooting was completed, bringing to an end her long and illustrious career in movies.

p, Ross Hunter, Martin Melcher; d, Norman Jewison; w, Carl Reiner (based on a story by Reiner, Larry Gelbart); ph, Russell Metty (Eastmancolor); m, De Vol; ed, Milton Carruth, md, Joseph Gershenson; art d, Alexander Golitzen, Robert Boyle; set d, Howard Bristol; cos, Jean Louis; m/l, "The Thrill of it All," Arnold Schwarzwald, Frederick Herbert.

Comedy (PR:A MPAA:NR)

THRILL OF YOUTH zero (1932) 63m CHES/IN bw

June Clyde, Allen Vincent, Dorothy Peterson, Matty Kemp, George Irving, Ethel Clayton, Lucy Beaumont, Tom Ricketts, Caryl Lincoln, Bryant Washburn.

Exploitation drama condemned by critics at the time of release because it was the type of film that could damage the moral tone of the industry. In a tale of a broken family, Dad runs around with a married woman while his two sons take girls into their bedrooms. Dad doesn't seem to mind, and even serves the drinks. He brings his married lover, his son, and his son's girl friend up to the family cabin for a weekend of lovemaking. Bizarre, to say the least, for the early 1930s.

p, George R. Batcheleir; d, Richard Thorpe; w, Edward T. Lowe; ph, M.A. Anderson; ed, Vera Wade.

Drama (PR:C (MPAA:NR)

THRILL SEEKERS (SEE: GUTTER GIRLS)

THRONE OF BLOOD**** (1961, Jap.) Brandon Films bw
KUMONOSUJO, KUMONOSU-DJO; AKA: COBWEB CASTLE; THE
CASTLE OF THE SPIDER'S WEB)

Toshiro Mifune (*Taketoki Washizu*), Isuzu Yamada (*Asaji, His Wife*), Takashi Shimura (*Noriyasu Odagura*), Minoru Chiaki (*Yoshaki Miki*), Akira Kubo (*Yoshiteru, His Son*), Takamaru Sasaki (*Kuniharu Tsuzuki*), Yoichi Tachikawa (*Kunimaru, His Son*), Chieko Naniwa (*Witch*).

THRONE OF BLOOD is a truly remarkable film in which beauty, terror, and mood have been brought forth with haunting power. Japanese master Akira Kurosawa fulfilled a long-time ambition and brought Shakespeare's "Macbeth" to Japanese audiences with brilliant results. To make the plot relevant to the Japanese, Kurosawa set the film in feudal Japan and the transposition of cultures is surprisingly successful, with all the plot elements still intact. After putting down a mutinous rebellion for their warlord, warriors Mifune and Chiaki are called to the main castle for an audience with the sovereign. While riding through the dense and foggy forest that protects the warlord's castle, the warriors encounter a mysterious and eerie old woman bathed in white light and mist. When questioned, the woman prophesies that Mifune will be given command of a castle and soon become warlord, but his reign will be brief and his throne will be occupied by Chiaki's son thereafter. Thinking the old woman ridiculous but amusing, the warriors continue their journey. At a ceremony honoring their bravery, Mifune is indeed given command of a castle, fulfilling part of the old woman's prophesy–a fact that is not lost on either of the men. Once in command of his own castle, Mifune's ambitions begin to get the best of him and are fueled by his evil, conniving wife, Yamada, who urges her husband to assassinate the warlord and take his throne. Soon the perfect opportunity arrives and Mifune frames another warrior for the death of the warlord, takes over the throne, and begins to wage a war against the innocent dupe. Soon it becomes obvious to the other warrior sects in his domain that Mifune is in fact the guilty party, and crazed with fear and paranoia, Mifune has his old friend Chiaki murdered. Seeking revenge, Chiaki's son, Kubo, bands together with the other suspicious members of the clan to attack Mifune and take back the fortress. Sensing he is going to be defeated, Mifune frantically rides into the forest for another audience with the old woman. She cackles and tells him that he cannot be defeated unless the forest itself moves against him. Reassured, Mifune returns to the castle and gives an impassioned speech to his soldiers in which he tells them of the old woman's prophecies. Mifune's men are confident as they watch the rival forces gather

in the woods and prepare to attack. The next morning however, the soldiers are thrown into a panic when the trees of the forest begin moving slowly toward the castle in the morning mist (the rival armies had cut down the trees and used them as shields). Mifune tries to stop his fleeing men only to find that to save themselves they would rather kill him and surrender. The now mad warlord goes to his doom amidst a hail of arrows fired by his own men. It is a stunning finale to a stunning film. THRONE OF BLOOD is filled with unforgettable, haunting imagery. Beauty and terror are combined in such a way that one can never forget the tragedy that unfolds before their eyes. In THRONE OF BLOOD, Kurosawa departs from his usual (very Western) fluid camera-style and fast-paced editing and instead gets his inspiration from the classic Noh theater tradition. While the visuals are gorgeous to look at, the compositions are static and stage-like, especially in the scenes between Mifune and Yamada, and they concentrate on the emotional moment as it hangs in the air–unaltered by editing or camera movement. The visual (and acting) styles work marvelously with this material, but unfortunately the film is somewhat cold and detached, containing little of the exhilarating passion to be found in Kurosawa's other work. (In Japanese; English subtitles.)

p, Akira Kurosawa, Sojiro Motoki; d, Kurosawa; w, Hideo Oguni, Shinobu Hashimoto, Ryuzo Kikushima, Kurosawa (based on the play "Macbeth" by William Shakespeare); ph, Asaichi Nakai (Tohoscope); m, Masaru Sato; ed, Kurosawa; art d, Yoshiro Muraki, Kohei Ezaki; English subtitles, Donald Richie.

Drama Cas. (PR:O MPAA:NR)

THROUGH A GLASS DARKLY** (1962, Swed.) 91m Janus bw
(SASOM I EN SPEGEL)

Harriet Andersson (*Karin the Daughter*), Gunnar Bjornstrand (*David the Father*), Max von Sydow (*Martin the Husband*), Lars Passgard (*Minus the Brother*).

The first in Bergman's trilogy of films examining man's futile search for God (the other two: WINTER LIGHT, 1962, and THE SILENCE, 1963.) sees Andersson as a young schizophrenic woman recently released from a mental institution who spends the summer with her family in an isolated cabin on the Baltic coast. Her father, Bjornstrand, is a writer who studies his disturbed daughter with a cold, intellectual detachment that only makes her condition worse. Her husband, von Sydow, is a doctor, but finds himself unable to assist Andersson in her recovery. Passgard, Andersson's brother, is a youth on the verge of sexual awakening and he, too, is occupied with his own troubled thoughts and emotions. Soon Andersson is suffering from seizures, during which she hears voices from the walls telling her not to fear, God will come and save her. Her madness deepening, Andersson seduces her brother, an event that leaves him stricken with silence. Distressed that the voices' promise of God's salvation has not come true, Andersson has a violent breakdown, forcing her father and husband to restrain her until an ambulance arrives to take her away. Once Andersson is sent back to the institution, the men realize they should not put their hopes in the hands of an uncaring (or in fact, nonexistent) God, and instead take it upon themselves to love, because love is the only true salvation. The usual fine performances from Bergman's regulars combined with a script not as ponderous as much of the director's other works earned THROUGH A GLASS DARKLY an Academy Award for Best Foreign Film of 1961.

p, Allan Ekelund; d&w, Ingmar Bergman; ph, Sven Nykvist; m, Johann Sebastian Bach; ed, Ulla Ryghe; art d, P.A. Lundgren; cos, Mago; music, "Suite No. 2 in D Minor for Violincello," Johann Sebastian Bach.

Drama (PR:O MPAA:NR)

THROUGH DAYS AND MONTHS½** (1969 Jap.) 98m Shochiku c
(Jap: HI MO TSUKI MO)

Shima Iwashita (*Matsuko*), Masayuki Mori (*Her Father*), Yoshiko Kuga (*Her Mother*), Jin Nakayama (*Munehiro*), Koji Ishizaka (*Koji*), Mayumi Ozora.

Melancholy Japanese drama starring Iwashita as a lonely young woman who lives with her aging father, Mori. One day Iwashita meets her former lover, Nakayama, whom she still loves although he is now married. Nakayama, though suffering from a debilitating illness, tells Iwashita that he still loves her and wishes to resume their relationship. Ishizaka, Nakayama's brother, makes matters worse by expressing his desire for Iwashita also. Her problems seem to be solved for her when Iwashita's father dies and Nakayama commits suicide (due to depression over his illness), leaving Ishizaka for her to love. However, due to this series of personal catastrophes, Iwashita decides that she can no longer become emotionally involved with life. Another exploration of a young girl's attempt to cope with life by director Nakamura (A WOMAN'S LIFE).

d, Noboru Nakamura; w, Yuzuru Hirose (based on the novel *Hi Mo Tsuki Mo* by Yasunari Kawabata); ph, Hiroshi Takemura (Shochiku GrandScope, Eastmancolor); m, Masao Yagi; art d, Yutaka Yokoyama.

Drama (PR:AC MPAA:NR)

THROUGH DIFFERENT EYES (SEE: THRU DIFFERENT EYES, 1943)

THROUGH HELL TO GLORY (SEE: JET ATTACK, 1958)

THROUGH THE STORM (SEE: PRAIRIE SCHOONERS, 1940)

THROWBACK, THE** (1935) 60m UNIV bw

Buck Jones (Buck Saunders), Muriel Evans (Muriel Fergus), Eddie Phillips (Milt Fergus), George ["Gabby"] Hayes (Ford Cruze), Byrant Washburn (Jack Thorpe), Allan Ramsay (Buck as a Boy), Margaret Davis (Muriel as a Girl), Bobby Nelson, Mickey Martin, Paul Fix, Frank LaRue, Earl Pingree, Bob Walker, Charles K. French, Silver the Horse.

Back when our hero was just a boy (played by Ramsay), Buck suffered alienation in his Oklahoma town when the citizens came to believe that his father was a cattle rustler. Eventually young Buck leaves town, but years later returns as an adult and sets out to clear his father's name. Story avoids the usual cliche stuff of westerns, and all concerned turn in a fine job. Evans handles a charming romantic angle in great style.

p, Buck Jones; d, Ray Taylor; w, Frances Guihan (based on a story by Cherry Wilson); ph, Allen Thompson, H. Kirkpatrick; ed, Bernard Loftus.

Western (PR:A MPAA:NR)

THRU DIFFERENT EYES** (1929) 67m FOX bw

Mary Duncan (Viola Manning), Edmund Lowe (Harvey Manning), Warner Baxter (Jack Winfield), Natalie Moorhead (Frances Thornton), Earle Foxe (Howard Thornton), Donald Gallagher (Spencer), Florence Lake (Myrtle), Sylvia Sidney (Valerie Briand), Purnell Pratt (Marston, District Attorney), Selmer Johnson (King, Defense Attorney), Dolores Johnson (Anna), Nigel de Brulier (Maynard), Lola Salvi (Maid), Stepin Fetchit (Janitor), DeWitt Jennings (Paducah), Arthur Stone (Crane), George Lamont (Traynor), Natalie Warfield (Aline Craig), Jack Jordan, Marian Spitzer, Stanley Blystone, Stuart Erwin (Reporters).

A spicy early talkie saddled with a dull visual sense and a hackneyed script sees a complicated flashback structure as the only point of interest. During a murder trial, different viewpoints as to the exact events the night of the killing are enacted. The prosecution sees vampish wife Duncan cleverly getting her husband, Lowe, out of the house so that she may greet her lover, Baxter. When Lowe returns unexpectedly, catching his wife dressed in a scanty nightgown with her arms around Baxter, a struggle ensues, leaving Baxter dead. The defense, however, sees the crime another way. In its version, Baxter is hopelessly in love with Duncan, who, due to her loyalty to Lowe, drives the obsessed Baxter to suicide. The truth, of course, isn't even close to the prosecution and defense versions. Shocked into a confession when Lowe is convicted of murder, Duncan announces that she killed Baxter because he had deserted her and left her with a child years ago. A loose remake of this material was released under the same title in 1942.

d, John Blystone; w, Tom Barry, Milton Herbert Gropper (based on a story by Gropper, Edna Sherry); ph, Ernest Palmer, Al Brick; ed, Louis Loeffler; cos, Sophie Wachner.

Crime (PR:A MPAA:NR)

THRU DIFFERENT EYES** (1942) 64m FOX bw

Frank Craven (Steve Pettijohn), Mary Howard (Constance Gardner), Donald Woods (Ted Farnsworth), June Walker (Margie), Vivian Blaine (Sue Boardman), George Holmes (Harry Beach), Jerome Cowan (Jim Gardner), Charles Lane (Mott), James Flavin (Thomas), Ruth Warren (Julia), Pat O. Malley (Coroner), Selmer Jackson (Chaplain), Charles D. Waldren (Dr. Whittier), Irving Bacon (Stu Johnson).

Owing nothing more than its title and inspiration to the 1929 version, THRU DIFFERENT EYES stars Craven as a seasoned district attorney lecturing a group of law students on the risks of accepting circumstantial evidence. He relates the tale of a murder that his young assistant was tried and convicted for. While circumstantial evidence made it look as though the man would hang, Craven's wife had a hunch the man was innocent and personally waged a campaign to find the real killer. A relaxed and interesting little walk through the maze of justice.

p, Sol M. Wurtzel; d, Thomas Z. Loring; w, Samuel G. Engel; ph, Charles Clarke; ed, Louis Loeffler; md, Emil Newman; art d, Richard Day, Chester Gore.

Crime (PR:A MPAA:NR)

THUMB TRIPPING** (1972) 94m AE c

Michael Burns (Gary), Meg Foster (Chay), Mariana Hill (Lynn), Burke Burns (Jack), Mike Conrad (Diesel), Bruce Dern (Smitty), Larry Hankin (Simp), Joyce Van Patten (Mother), Ed Greenburg (Ed), Eric Butler (Eric).

Archaic hippie "road picture" starring Burns and Foster as two happy-go-lucky flower children who hitchhike in the beautiful Big Sur-Monterey area of California. Along the way they meet a variety of eccentric characters including Conrad, a truck driver who develops a passion for Foster; Van Patten, a dull-witted parent searching for her runaway daughter; Greenberg and Butler, two bikers; and Dern, once again playing a dangerous nut. After these encounters, with the audience numb from the ghastly parade of sub-humanity lurking out there, the two youngsters tire of each other and go their separate ways. This one is so dated it deserves to vanish in last night's dusk.

p, Irwin Winkler, Robert Chartoff; d, Quentin Masters; w, Don Mitchell (based on a novel by Mitchell); ph, Harry Stradling, Jr. (DeLuxe Color); m, Bob Thompson; ed, Gene Fowler, Jr.; cos, Lambert Marks; m/l, "I Am Moving," (sung by Friends of Distinction).

Drama (PR:O MPAA:R)

THUMBELINA*** (1970) 62m Cinetron/R&S Film Enterprises c

Shay Garner, Pat Morell, Bob O'Connell, Heather Grinter, Mike Yuenger, Sue Cable.

A well done live action version of Hans Christian Andersen's beloved fairy tale involving witches, royalty, magic, and kidnaping. As always, in Andersen's tales, mature wisdom and gay whimsy combine to invest the story with wonderful symbolic significance.

p&d, Barry Mahon (based on "Tommelise" by Hans Christian Andersen); ph, Bill Tobin; set d, Thelma Raniero, Guy Brugger; m/l, George Linsenmann, Ralph Falco; makeup, Tom Brumberger.

Fantasy (PR:AAA MPAA:G)

THUMBS UP** (1943) 67m REP bw

Brenda Joyce (Louise Latimer), Richard Fraser (Douglas Heath), Elsa Lanchester (Emmy Finch), Arthur Margetson (Bert Lawrence), J. Pat O'Malley (Sam Keats), Queenie Leonard (Janie Brooke), Molly Lamont (Welfare Supervisor), Gertrude Niesen (Herself), George Byron (Foreman), Charles Irwin (Ray Irwin), Andre Charlot (E.E. Cartwright), The Hot Shots.

Wartime musical starring Joyce as a plucky singer in a run-down London nightclub determined to become a star. When her producer-fiance Margetson and his partner decide to recruit new talent from the war factories, Joyce gets a job in an airplane plant in order to be "discovered." There she meets dashing RAF officer Fraser and the couple fall in love. The plan causes more trouble than it's worth because when her roommate, Lanchester, and fellow plant workers, including Fraser, discover that Joyce joined the war effort just to further her singing career, she is ostracized. Eventually Joyce manages to persuade the cast that she is not such a bad person after all. Songs include: "From Here On," "Love is a Corny Thing" (by Sammy Cahn, Jule Styne; sung by Joyce), "Who are the British?" (by Cahn, Styne; sung by Niesen), "Thumbs Up" (by Jaffe, O'Brien, and Lee; sung by Joyce), and "Zing Went the Strings of My Heart" (by James Hanley).

p, Albert J. Cohen; d, Joseph Santley; w, Frank Gill, Jr. (based on a story by Ray Golden, Henry Moritz); ph, Ernest Miller; ed, Thomas Richards; md, Walter Scharf; art d, Russell Kimball.

Musical (PR:A MPAA:NR)

THUNDER ACROSS THE PACIFIC (SEE: WILD BLUE YONDER, THE, 1951)

THUNDER AFLOAT**½ (1939) 94m MGM bw

Wallace Beery (Jon Thorson), Chester Morris ("Rocky" Blake), Virginia Grey (Susan Thorson), Douglas Dumbrille (District Commander), Carl Esmond (U-Boat Captain), Clem Bevans ("Cap" Finch), Jun Qualen (Milt), Regis Toomey (Ives), Henry Victor (German U-Boat Captain), Addison Richards (Adm. Ross), Hans Joby (U-Boat Petty Officer), Henry Hunter (Ens. Dyer), Jonathan Hale (Adm. Girard), Charles Lane (Capt. Sabin), Phillip Terry (Lt. West), Wade Boteler, Leon Ames (Recruiting Officer), Harry Strang (Sailor), Frank Faylen (Petty Officer), Leigh De Lacy (Mrs. Gill), Don Castle, Larry McGrath (Radio Operators), Roger Moore (Orderly), Howard Hickman (Surgeon), Milton Kibbee, Philip Morris (Fishermen), Walter Thiele (Young German Sailor), Bud Fine (Survivor), Claire McDowell (Nurse), Wolfram Von Bock (German Officer), Charles Johnson (Signal Man).

What was originally intended as a plain old WW I adventure film turned into a topical propaganda piece when Adolf Hitler unleashed the German U-boats in the Atlantic once again in preparation for WW II. Beery stars as a tough tugboat captain who joins the Navy after his boat is sunk by the German submarines. To his surprise, Beery's commanding officer is his hated tugboat rival Morris. This of course, leads to Beery violating his orders and foolishly setting out on his own to capture a sub. When he returns to the fleet, Morris busts him down to seaman and gives him shore duty. Eventually Morris relents and gives Beery active duty on a mission, but soon the former tugboat captain is captured by the Germans. Beery does not give up hope however and he cleverly taps a signal on the hull of the U-boat to warn Morris and his men of the sub's location so that they can capture it.

p, J. Walter Ruben; d, George B. Seitz; w, Wells Root, Comdr. Harvey Haislip (based on a story by Ralph Wheelwright, Haislip); ph, John F. Seitz; m, Edward Ward, David Snell; ed, Frank E. Hull; art d, Cedric Gibbons, Urie McCleary; set d, Edwin B. Willis; cos, Dolly Tree, Valles.

War　　　　　　　　　　　　　　　　**(PR:A　MPAA:NR)**

THUNDER ALLEY*½　　　　　　　　(1967) 90m AIP c

Annette Funicello (*Francie Madsen*), Fabian (*Tommy Callahan*), Diane McBain (*Annie Blaine*), Warren Berlinger (*Eddie Sands*), Jan Murray (*Pete Madsen*), Stanley Adams (*Mac Lunsford*), Maureen Arthur (*Babe*), Michael T. Mikler (*Harry Wise*), Michael Bell (*Leroy*), Kip King (*Dom*), Sandy Reed (*Announcer*), Sammy Shore, Baynes Barron, Michael Dugan, Band without a Name.

Fabian plays a stock car driver who must retire after suffering a blackout while driving which caused the death of another racer. Fabian takes the demeaning job of staging phony crashes and spinouts at a "Thrill Circus" run by cheap promoter Murray. Among those racing cars in Murray's track are his own daughter, Funicello (oh sure) and her beau, Berlinger. The bored Fabian trains Berlinger to race professionally and the kid actually wins his first race. Seeing a new sugar-daddy, Fabian's old girl friend, McBain, zeros in on Berlinger, much to Funicello's dismay. This leads to some tension between Fabian and his protege, but as luck would have it, the pair are entered as partners in an important 500-mile race. While zooming along at top speeds, Fabian begins to have another blackout and realizes that his fainting spells are caused by his guilt over the childhood accident in which he ran his brother over with a go-cart. Filled with a new sense of understanding, Fabian snaps out of his malaise and drives with confidence. But Berlinger has plans of his own, and he cuts off Fabian to try to take first place. This foolish move spells doom for the inexperienced racer. He loses control of his vehicle and crashes into the wall. Fabian wins the trophy and Funicello while Berlinger goes to the hospital. Pretty funny (albeit unintentionally) stuff directed by Richard Rush whose next picture HELLS ANGELS ON WHEELS became a biker classic, and who eventually would get some respect by directing THE STUNT MAN.

p, Burt Topper; d, Richard Rush; w, Sy Salkowitz; ph, Monroe Askins (Panavision, Pathe Color); ed, Ronald Sinclair, Kenneth Crane; art d, Daniel Haller; set d, Harry Reif; cos, Richard Bruno, Ray Phelps, Connie Anderson; spec eff, Joe Zomar; m/l, "When You Get What You Want," Guy Hemric, Jerry Styner (sung by Annette Funicello); makeup, Gus Norin.

Drama　　　　　　　　　　　　　　**(PR:A　MPAA:NR)**

THUNDER AND LIGHTNING½**　　　　(1977) 93m FOX c

David Carradine (*Harley Thomas*), Kate Jackson (*Nancy Sue Hunnicutt*), Roger C. Carmel (*Ralph Junior Hunnicutt*), Sterling Holloway (*Hobe Carpenter*), Ed Barth (*Rudi Volpone*), Ron Feinberg (*Bubba*), George Murdock (*Jake Summers*), Pat Cranshaw (*Taylor*), Charles Napier (*Jim Bob*), Hope Pomerance (*Mrs. Hunnicutt*), Malcolm Jones (*Rainey*), Charles Willeford (*Bartender*), Christopher Raynolds (*Scooter*), Claude Jones (*Carl*), Emilio Rivera (*Honeydew Driver*).

Pretty good crash-and-burn epic starring Carradine as a Florida moonshine runner who enters into an informal competition with his girl friend's father, Carmel, a fellow moonshiner. The men stage a contest to see who can produce more moonshine and then transport it from their distillery without the law or the mob capturing them. TV's "Charlie's Angels" alumnus Jackson plays Carradine's girl friend. Worth a look for the car and boat chases through the Everglades.

p, Roger Corman; d, Corey Allen; w, William Hjortsberg; ph, James Pergola (DeLuxe Color); m, Andy Stein; ed, Anthony Redman; cos, Dyke Davis; spec eff, J.B. Jones; makeup, Guy Del Russo; stunts, Joie Chitwood, Jr.

Adventure　　　　　　**Cas.**　　　　**(PR:C　MPAA:PG)**

THUNDER AT THE BORDER**　　　　(1966, Ger./Yugo.) 94m
　　　　　　　　　　Rialto/Preben Philipsen/Jadran/COL c (WINNETOU UND SEIN
　　　　　　　　　　FREUND; OLD FIREHAND)

Rod Cameron, Pierre Brice, Todd Armstrong, Marie Versini, Harald Leipnitz, Nadia Gray.

A shift in this series of European westerns based on the novels of Karl May features Cameron as the great white hero (replacing Lex Barker and Stewart Granger) who rides the plains with his noble Indian friend Winnetou, played by Brice. The two heroes agree to defend a small Mexican village from a gang of bandits led by Leipnitz (a la THE SEVEN SAMURAI, or THE MAGNIFICENT SEVEN). What is really different about this entry in the series is the shift of locale from May's lush mountains and forests, to the deserts which distinguished the then-popular Italian westerns.

p, Horst Wendlandt; d, Alfred Vohrer; w, David Dereszke, C.B. Taylor, Harald G. Petersson; ph, Karl Lob.

Western　　　　　　　　　　　　　**(PR:A　MPAA:NR)**

THUNDER BAY**　　　　　　　　(1953) 103m UNIV c

James Stewart (*Steve Martin*), Joanne Dru (*Stella Rigaud*), Gilbert Roland (*Teche Bossier*), Dan Duryea (*Johnny Gambi*), Marcia Henderson (*Francesca Rigaud*), Robert Monet (*Phillipe Bayard*), Jay C. Flippen (*Kermit MacDonald*), Antonio Moreno (*Dominique Rigaud*), Henry [Harry] Morgan (*Rawlings*), Fortunio Bonanova (*Sheriff Antoine Chighizola*), Mario Siletti (*Louis Chighizola*), Antonio Filauri (*Joe Sephalu*), Frank Chase (*Radio Technician*), Allen Pinson, Dale Van Sickel, Ted Mapes (*Oil Men*), Ben Welden, Jean Hartelle, Jack Tesler, Adrine Champagne, Donald Green (*Fishermen*), Laurie Vining (*Technician*), Emanuel Russo (*Radio Man*).

Stewart, who had by 1953 appeared in three Mann-directed westerns (WINCHESTER '73, BEND OF THE RIVER, and THE NAKED SPUR), heads for the Louisiana coastal town of Port Felicity in this vibrantly colored wide-screen adventure tale. Stewart and Duryea team up as a pair of daring oil riggers who are convinced there is "black gold" at the bottom of the Gulf of Mexico. The wealthy Flippen decides to gamble on their hunch and financially supports Stewart's construction of a stormproof oil platform. The Port Felicity villagers are far less enthusiastic about Stewart and Duryea's venture. The town relies on shrimp fishing and the local fishermen are already in the midst of hard times. The disruption caused by the drilling isn't going to improve their plight. Tensions come to a breaking point when two daughters–Dru and Henderson–of a fisherman, Moreno, fall for, respectively, Stewart and Duryea. The villagers grow increasingly impatient and angry, finally forming a mob which plans to destroy the rig. Meanwhile, Stewart and Duryea are battling the elements, as well as a financial crisis. Monet, the jealous fiance of Henderson, sets out to dynamite the rig. A hurricane brews, however, and Monet dies before any damage is done. Just when it appears that time has run out, Stewart and Duryea strike it rich. Not only does oil gush into the sky, but they discover a nighttime shrimp bed which appeases the villagers. The finale has the oil company and the shrimp fishermen making amends, and Stewart and Duryea paired off with, respectively, Dru and Henderson. THUNDER BAY marked Universal's foray into the wide-screen battle of the day, adding to its expansive 43x24½ foot screen a new three-speaker stereophonic sound system. Unfortunately many of the new films of the day fell victim to technical advances which overshadowed or completely forgot about storytelling and direction.

p, Aaron Rosenberg; d, Anthony Mann; w, Gil Doud, John Michael Hayes (based on a story by Michael Hayes from an idea by George W. George, George F. Slavin); ph, William Daniels (Technicolor); m, Frank Skinner; ed, Russell Schoengarth; art d, Alexander Golitzen, Richard H. Riedel; cos, Rosemary Odell; m/l, "Gue Gue Solingaie," (arranged by Milton Rosen; sung by Robert Monet).

Adventure　　　　　　　　　　　　**(PR:A　MPAA:NR)**

THUNDER BELOW*½　　　　　　　(1932) 67m PAR bw

Tallulah Bankhead (*Susan*), Charles Bickford (*Walt*), Paul Lukas (*Ken*), Eugene Pallette (*Horner*), Ralph Forbes (*Davis*), Leslie Fenton (*Webb*), James Finlayson (*Scotty*), Edward Van Sloan (*Doctor*), Mona Rico (*Pajarita*), Carlos Salazar (*Chato*), Enrique Acosta (*Pacheo*), Gabry Rivas (*Delapena*).

Overwrought Bankhead vehicle set in the oil fields of Central America which sees our heroine as the bored wife of oil rigger Bickford. Bankhead loves Bickford's best pal Lukas, but the busy hubby doesn't realize it. When Bickford goes blind (a bit symbolic eh?), Bankhead shifts her attentions to a third man, Forbes. Lukas, who has gotten fed up with Bankhead's fickle philandering, tells her to return to Bickford. Eventually Bankhead can no longer live with her indiscretions so she throws herself off a cliff.

d, Richard Wallace; w, Josephine Lovett, Sidney Buchman (based on the novel by Thomas Rourke); ph, Charles Lang.

Drama　　　　　　　　　　　　　　**(PR:A　MPAA:NR)**

THUNDER BIRDS½**　　　　　　　(1942) 78m FOX c

Gene Tierney (*Kay Saunders*), Preston Foster (*Steve Britt*), John Sutton (*Peter Stackhouse*), Jack Holt (*Col. McDonald*), Dame May Whitty (*Lady Stackhouse*), George Barbier (*Gramps*), Richard Haydn (*George Lockwood*), Reginald Denny (*Barratt*), Ted North (*Cadet Hackzell*), Janis Carter (*Blonde*), Archie Got, Lawrence Ung (*Chinese Cadets*), Montague Shaw (*Doctor*), Nana Bryant (*Mrs. Blake*), Iris Adrian (*Saleswoman*), Viola Moore (*Nurse*), Connie Leon (*Ellen*), Walter Tetley (*Messenger*), Billy McGuire, Richard Woodruff (*English Cadets*), Joyce Compton (*Saleswoman*), Bess Flowers (*Nurse*), Peter Lawford (*British Cadet*), Selmer Jackson (*Man*), Charles Tannen (*Recording*), Harry Strang (*Forest Ranger*), John Gunther (*Special Commentary*).

In the opening months of U.S. involvement in WW II, Foster is a flight instructor–a WW I veteran– teaching an international group of pilot trainees at a remote base in the Arizona desert. He is in love with Tierney, the daughter of a nearby rancher, but has a rival for her affections in the person of one of his students, Britisher Sutton. Sutton is stricken with nausea whenever he goes up and is in danger of washing out, but Foster pays special attention to him despite rivalry off the base. Sutton makes the grade, graduating as a combat pilot and winning Tierney. Foster remains in the desert, dutifully turning out more pilots for the war effort. Not one of director Wellman's more memorable efforts, this is one of two films he was forced to accept without question under the terms of a contract he signed with Darryl F. Zanuck at 20th Century-Fox that allowed the director to make his coveted OX-BOW INCIDENT, but bound him to the studio for five years. The film's flying sequences are excellent– as one would expect from a director whose best work was usually aviation-related–but there's a minimum of flying here, little more than establishing shots, and far too much time is spent on the romantic triangle, the resolution of which is obvious from the outset. Perhaps the most interesting moment in the film comes when Foster sits down with Sutton to give him a pep talk and tells the young flier that he had known Sutton's father during WW I. He pulls a picture of Sutton's father out of his wallet and shows it to the young man. The photo is actually Wellman himself from that war, posing in front of one of his planes in a heavy fur coat. When Sutton visits his grandmother, Whitty, she has a large portrait of Wellman over her mantel. Competent performances, decent direction, and attractive color photography helped a little, but the film was mostly a routine maudlin wartime romance and it was far from successful.

p, Lamar Trotti; d, William A. Wellman; w, Trotti (based on a story by Melville Crossman [Darryl F. Zanuck]); ph, Ernest Palmer (Technicolor), m, David Buttolph; ed, Walter Thompson; art d, Richard Day, James Basevi; cos, Dolly Tree; stunts, Paul Mantz.

Drama　　　　　　　　　　　　　　　　　　　　**(PR:A　MPAA:NR)**

THUNDER IN CAROLINA*½　　　(1960) 92m Darlington/Howco c

Rory Calhoun (Mitch Cooper), Alan Hale, Jr (Buddy Schaeffer), Connie Hines (Rene York), John [Race] Gentry (Les York), Ed McGrath (Reichert), Troyanne Ross (Kay Hill), Helen Downey (Eve Mason), Van Casey (Stoogie), Tripplie Wisecup (Myrtle Webb), Carey Loftin (Tommy Webb), Billie Langston (Peaches), Ann Stevens (Singer), George Rembert, Jr (Junior Thorsen), Olwen Roney (Motel Manager), Richard Taylor (Higgins), William Sprott (Roy Greenleaf), Wes Stone (Deputy), Rev. Thomas M. Godbold (Minister), Ray Melton (Announcer "Southern 500"), Raymond Caddell (Dirt Track Announcer), Edith Scott (Maid), Carolyn Melton ("Miss Southern 500"), Joe Weatherly, Buck Baker, Curtis Turner, Neil Castles, Joe Caspolich, Shep Langdon, Joe Eubanks (Grand National Race Drivers).

Yet another stockcar racing film set in the South. Calhoun plays a former stockcar driver who was forced to retire after a nasty crash that left his leg permanently injured. Left with nothing much to do, Calhoun takes young garage owner Gentry under his wing and teaches the eager mechanic how to race. Gentry soon becomes obsessed with racing and practically forces his beautiful wife Hines into Calhoun's arms after he (Gentry) has become smitten with a racetrack groupie. Realizing that he has made a mistake, Calhoun cooks up a plan to snap Gentry back to reality, and reunite him with his wife.

p, J. Francis White; d, Paul Helmick; w, Alexander Richards; ph, Joseph Brun (Eastmancolor); m, Walter Green; ed, Rex Lipton.

Sports Drama　　　　　　　　　　　　　　　　　**(PR:A　MPAA:NR)**

THUNDER IN DIXIE*　　　　　　(1965) 76m Willpat/MPI bw

Harry Millard (Mickey Arnold), Judy Lewis (Lili Arnold), Nancy Berg (Karen Hallet), Mike Bradford (Ticker Welsh), Ted Erwin (Ben Forrest), Richard Kuss (Link Duggan), Pat McAndrew (Rachel), Herb Rodgers (Motel Manager), Barry Darval (Himself), Sheri Benet (Herself), Bob Wills (Track Announcer), Johnny Carlson (Spotter), George Brenholtz (Bartender), Richard Petty.

Stupid stock car racing movie set during Atlanta's "Dixie 400" and starring Bradford as a racer obsessed with avenging the death of his fiancee who he believes was killed because of fellow racer Millard's thoughtlessness. Bradford plans to get Millard during the big race, despite the protestations of his new girl friend, Berg, and Millard's wife, Lewis. During the race Bradford's recklessness causes an accident which lands him in the hospital, leaving the way clear for Millard to win the race. A stay in intensive care seems to have sapped the vengeful blood from Bradford's veins and he makes his peace with Millard.

p&d, William T. Naud; w, George Baxt; ph, Thomas E. Spalding; m, Elliot Lawrence; md, Lawrence; art d, Chris Bottomly, Jim Johnson, Carl Hillman; m/l, "Maybe Tomorrow" (sung by Barry Darval).

Sports Drama　　　　　　　　　　　　　　　　　**(PR:A　MPAA:NR)**

THUNDER IN GOD'S COUNTRY*　　(1951) 67m REP bw

Rex Allen (Himself), Mary Ellen Kay (Dell Stafford), Buddy Ebsen (Happy Hooper), Ian MacDonald (Smitty), Paul Harvey (Carson Masterson), Harry Lauter (Tim Gallery), John Doucette (Slack Breedon), Harry Cheshire (Mayor Larkin), John Ridgely (Bill Stafford), Frank Ferguson (Bates), Wilson Wood (Johnson), Koko the Horse.

Modern-day western starring Allen as a wandering artist accompanied by his sidekick Ebsen into Hidden Valley where they decide to stop crooked gambler MacDonald's plans to build a new Las Vegas in the area. MacDonald, of course, would get a large share of the proceeds, but Allen is able to spoil the plot and expose the gambler as a criminal.

p, Melville Tucker; d, George Blair; w, Arthur E. Orloff; ph, John MacBurnie; m, Stanley Wilson; ed, Harold Minter; art d, Frank Hotaling; m/l, "Mollie Darling," "John Henry" (sung by Rex Allen), "Melody of the Plains," Irving Beriau, Leonard M. Sive (sung by Allen).

Western　　　　　　　　**Cas.**　　　　　**(PR:A　MPAA:NR)**

THUNDER IN THE BLOOD**　　　　(1962, Fr.) 95m Florida Films-Compagnie Generale Cinematographique/Seven Continents bw (COLERE FROIDE; AKA: THE WARM BODY)

Estella Blain (Catherine), Harold Kay (Roland), Pierre-Jean Vaillard (Girardier), Jean-Marie Fertey (Alex), Pierre Fromont (Christian Lambert), Liliane Brousse (Georgina), Michel Nastorg, Jean-Paul Thomas, Guy Henry, Jean Barrez.

French crime melodrama starring Fertey as a crazed, alcoholic novelist who writes trashy detective thrillers to support the opulent lifestyle to which his wife, Blain, has become accustomed. Bored with her husband's drinking and fits of jealousy, Blain takes wealthy art collector, Fromont as a lover. Unfortunately Fromont's underworld dealings appear to catch up with him and he is murdered. Kay, a police inspector, investigates the case and eventually comes to the conclusion that Fertey is the killer. Under duress, Fertey confesses to the crime and tries to kill his wife as well, but he stumbles and falls off a roof to his death.

d, Andre Haguet, Jean-Paul Sassy; w, Haguet; ph, Lucien Joulin; m, Marcel Stern; ed, Maurice Serien; art d, Jean-Roland Quignon.

Crime　　　　　　　　　　　　　　　　　　　　**(PR:C　MPAA:NR)**

THUNDER IN THE CITY**　　　　(1937, Brit.) 76m Atlantic/COL bw

Edward G. Robinson (Dan Armstrong), Luli Deste (Lady Patricia), Nigel Bruce (The Duke of Glenavon), Constance Collier (The Duchess of Glenavon), Ralph Richardson (Henry Graham Manningdale), Annie Esmond (Lady Challoner), Arthur Wontner (Sir Peter Challoner), Elizabeth Inglis (Dolly), Cyril Raymond (James), Nancy Burne (Edna), Billy Bray (Bill), James Carew (Snyderling), Everley Gregg (Millie), Elliott Nugent (Casey), Terence De Marney (Reporter), Roland Drew (Frank).

Robinson is an American publicist and salesman whose employers find his high-pressure techniques a little too intense. He is sent to London to watch the more sedate way of doing business there. He meets some titled distant relatives, Wontner and Esmond, who invite him to their estate for the weekend. There he meets another aristocratic pair, Bruce and Collier, and their daughter Deste. Also spending the weekend is Richardson, a successful stockbroker. Bruce and Collier have lost most of their fortune and their only asset of any value is an unexploited mine in Rhodesia containing "Magnelite." Richardson offers to help them develop the mine in return for Deste's hand in marriage. Robinson steps in and–using his American methods–sets up a company with Bruce as chairman. He sells enough stock to provide capital to begin working the mine. Richardson doesn't give up easily, though; he takes over patents on the only process by which the metal can be refined. Robinson is forced by this maneuver to surrender his shares in the company to Richardson. Dejected, he prepares for a flight back to U.S. At the airport, a crowd of friends thank him and see him off. Deste rejects Richardson and flies to U.S. with Robinson. Robinson was loaned out by Warner Bros. for this film and he went willingly, happy to be away from the socially significant material that was Warner's stock-in-trade. When he arrived in London and saw the script, he told the producers what he thought of it, namely that it was "obvious, predictable, on the nose, flat, frequently silly." He was surprised when they agreed. A few days later Robinson was wandering about London when he spotted an old friend, co-author of the story and playwright Robert Sherwood. Over tea the actor persuaded Sherwood to do write the script and the writer turned it into a fairly witty satire. But the Sherwood script and a good cast were not enough and the film died at the box office. It was not a total loss, though, as it was during Robinson's stay in London that he began building the art collection that was to become his great passion.

p, Alexander Esway, Akos Tolnay; d, Marion Gering; w, Tolnay, Aben Kandel, Robert Sherwood, Walter Hackett (based on a story by Sherwood, Kandel); ph, Al Eilks; ed, Arthur Hilton.

Comedy　　　　　　　　**Cas.**　　　　　**(PR:A　MPAA:NR)**

THUNDER IN THE DESERT**　　　　(1938) 56m REP bw

Bob Steele (Radford), Louise Stanley (Betty), Don Barclay (Rusty), Ed Brady (Reno), Charles King (Harris), Horace Murphy (Sheriff), Steve Clark (Andrews), Lew Meehan (Mike), Ernie Adams, Richard Cramer (Tramps), Budd Buster (Oscar), Sherry Tansey.

Steele inherits a ranch from his murdered uncle. With help from his sidekick Barclay, Steele tries to find his uncle's killer.

p, A.W. Hackel; d, Sam Newfield; w, George H. Plympton; ph, Robert Cline; ed, S. Roy Luby.

Western　　　　　　　　　　　　　　　　　　　　**(PR:A　MPAA:NR)**

THUNDER IN THE DUST (SEE: SUNDOWNERS, THE, 1950)

THUNDER IN THE EAST (SEE: BATTLE, THE, 1934, Brit./Fr.)

THUNDER IN THE EAST* (1953) 97m PAR bw

Alan Ladd (*Steve Gibbs*), Deborah Kerr (*Joan Willoughby*), Charles Boyer (*Singh*), Corinne Calvet (*Lizette Damon*), Cecil Kellaway (*Dr. Willoughby*), Mark Cavell (*Moti Lal*), John Abbott (*Nitra Puta*), Philip Bourneuf (*Newab Khan*), John Williams (*Gen. Harrison*), Charlie Lung (*Maharajah*), Leonard Carey (*Dr. Paling*), Nelson Welch (*Norton*), Queenie Leonard (*Miss Huggins*), George J. Lewis (*Bartender*), Aram Katcher (*Servant*), Joh n Davidson (*Hotel Clerk*), Trevor Ward (*Mr. Darcy Thompson*), Bruce Payne (*Harpoole*), Maeve MacMurrough (*Mrs. Harrison*), Margaret Brewster (*Mrs. Corbett*), Arthur Gould Porter (*Mr. Corbett*), Robert Ben Ali (*Habibbudin*).

In the turmoil of India after independence, a rebel army under the command of Bourneuf pillages the countryside, moving toward the city of Ghandahar. Pilot-adventurer Ladd, seeing an opportunity to make some fast money, flies a planeload of arms to the threatened city. He tries to sell the weapons to Boyer, the prime minister of Ghandahar and chief advisor to the Maharajah, but finds Boyer to be a pacifist who thinks he can negotiate with Bourneuf. Ladd casually mentions that Bourneuf might be a more willing buyer for the guns and Boyer immediately orders them confiscated. Waiting to see what develops, Ladd meets several members of the old British colonial establishment who have stayed past their time, including Kerr, the blind daughter of missionary Kellaway. She and Ladd fall in love, but she is repulsed when he offers to fly the Britishers to safety for an exorbitant fee. Bourneuf and his army arrive and surround the city, destroying Ladd's plane. Boyer goes out to try to negotiate, but Bourneuf has his hand cut off and sends him back. When Bourneuf begins shelling the city, Ladd and the Britishers seek protection in the palace. There he and Kerr are reconciled and married by her father. The rebels storm the palace but the still pacifistic (if one-handed) Boyer won't allow the guns to be used. It is only when he sees Cavell, a young boy who has been following Ladd around, killed that he breaks out the machine guns and side by side he and Ladd mow down the attacking hordes. Ladd is good as usual, playing the sort of cynical hero he perfected in the 1940s, but the rest of the cast is wasted due to a wordy script and slack direction. Unusually dark for its time, and with a very depressing view of the political situation in India, the film was completed in 1951, but on request of the U.S. State Department it was held up for two years before being released in U.S. and was never released in India or Pakistan. Calvet, though feature-billed, has very little to do in her role as a French expatriate who tries to buy her way out of the beleaguered city using sexual favors. Boyer is fine in his part as the gentle pacifist. Interestingly, he had played a Japanese naval officer in THE BATTLE (1934), a French-made film which was re-released with the title THUNDER IN THE EAST.

p, Everett Riskin; d, Charles Vidor; w, Jo Swerling, George Tabori, Frederick Hazlitt Brennan (based on the novel *Rage of the Vulture* by Alan Moorehead); ph, Lee Garmes, Everett Douglas; m, Hugo Friedhofer.

Adventure (PR:A MPAA:NR)

THUNDER IN THE NIGHT*½ (1935) 67m FOX bw

Edmund Lowe (*Capt. Torok*), Karen Morley (*Madelaine*), Paul Cavanagh (*Count Alvinczy*), Una O'Connor (*Julie*), Gene Lockhart (*Gabor*), John Qualen (*Porter*), Russell Hicks (*Police Prefect*), Arthur Edmund Carew (*Prof. Omega*), Bodil Rosing (*Lisa*), Gloria Roy (*Katherine Szabo*), Cornelius Keefe (*Paul Szegedy*), Polly Ann Young, Herman Bing.

Overly plotty murder mystery set in Budapest and starring Lowe as a clever police inspector out to stop a blackmailer who threatens to destroy the career of his friend, newly appointed diplomat Cavanagh. When the blackmailer turns up dead, Cavanagh is under suspicion, so Lowe tries to clear his friend's name.

p, John Stone; d, George Archainbaud; w, Frances Hyland, Eugene Solow (based on the play "A Woman Lies" by Ladislaus Fodor); ph, Bert Glennon; m, Samuel Kaylin; cos, Helen A. Myron.

Mystery (PR:A MPAA:NR)

THUNDER IN THE PINES* (1949) 61m Lippert/Screen Guild bw

George Reeves (*Jeff Collins*), Ralph Byrd (*Boomer Benson*), Greg McClure (*Hammerhead Hogan*), Michael Whalen (*Pete*), Denise Darcel (*Yvette*), Marian Martin (*Pearl*), Lyle Talbot (*Nick*), Vince Barnett (*Bernard*), Roscoe Ates (*Whiskers*), Tom Kennedy (*Station Master*).

A rugged outdoors adventure film starring Reeves and Byrd as two logging buddies who send away for a mail-order bride and are shocked to discover they both requested the same woman, the lovely Darcel. Their boss, Talbot, who also owns the local saloon, offers a hefty bonus to the man who can cut down the most trees. To solve the sticky marital situation, the friends agree that the man who cuts down the most timber and collects the bonus can marry Darcel. Unfortunately, while Reeves and Byrd are swinging axes, Darcel gets bored and wanders into the welcome arms of Talbot. Talbot's discarded girl friend, Martin, decides to get revenge by exposing him as a card cheat. With this information in hand, Reeves and Byrd play Talbot in

a game of poker with the stakes being everything he owns. They win, kick the bum out, and unite to run an honest town.

p, William Stephens; d, Robert Edwards; w, Maurice Tombragel (based on a story by Jo Pagano); ph, Carl Berger (Sepiatone); m, Lucien Cailliet; ed, Norman Cerf; md, David Chudnow.

Western (PR:A MPAA:NR)

THUNDER IN THE SUN*½ (1959) 81m Seven Arts-Carrollton/PAR c

Susan Hayward (*Gabrielle Dauphin*), Jeff Chandler (*Lon Bennett*), Jacques Bergerac (*Pepe Dauphin*), Blanche Yurka (*Louise Dauphin*), Carl Esmond (*Andre Dauphin*), Fortunio Bonanova (*Fernando Christophe*), Bertrand Castelli (*Edmond Duquette*), Veda Ann Borg (*Marie*), Pedro de Cordoba (*Gabrielle's Dance Partner*), Felix Locher (*Danielle*).

Disappointing Hayward vehicle that slips, fairly often, into the realm of unintentional comedy, mainly because of Hayward's ludicrous Basque accent. Set in the Old West of 1847, Hayward plays the wife of Basque leader Esmond whose mission is to guide his people to California territory where they will plant grapevines and start wineries. Though their marriage was arranged long ago and Hayward feels no passion for her husband, she remains faithful to Esmond despite the romantic attentions of brother-in-law Bergerac and hired scout Chandler. When Esmond is killed in an accident involving Chandler, Hayward agrees to comply with Basque tradition and marry her husband's brother. After a series of hardships including brush fires and Indian attacks, Bergerac realizes that Hayward loves Chandler and he rides off leaving her to decide her own fate. Eventually the wagon train reaches its destination and Hayward, disgusted by her mindless devotion to the "cause" without regard to the many lives lost on the trail, pulls a freshly planted vine out of the ground. Chandler calms her down, replants the vine, and assures her that they have finally won the battle.

p, Clarence Greene; d, Russell Rouse; w, Rouse, Stewart Stern (based on a story by Guy Trosper, James Hill); ph, Stanley Cortez (Eastmancolor); m, Cyril Mockridge; ed, Chester Schaeffer; art d, Boris Leven; cos, Charles LeMaire; ch, Pedro de Cordoba; m/l, "Mon Petit," Mockridge, Ned Washington (sung by Jacques Bergerac).

Western (PR:A MPAA:NR)

THUNDER IN THE VALLEY (SEE: BOB, SON OF BATTLE, 1947)

THUNDER ISLAND** (1963) 65m Associated Producers/FOX bw

Gene Nelson (*Billy Poole*), Fay Spain (*Helen Dodge*), Brian Kelly (*Vincent Dodge*), Miriam Colon (*Anita Chavez*), Art Bedard (*Ramon Alou*), Antonio Torres Martino (*Col. Cepeda*), Esther Sandoval (*Rena*), Jose de San Anton (*Antonio Perez*), Evelyn Kaufman (*Jo Dodge*), Stephanie Rifkinson (*Linda Perez*), Axel Anderson.

A fairly routine programmer that boasts the screenwriting talents of a young Jack Nicholson (he co-authored the screenplay with Don Devlin). The story centers on the activities of professional assassin Nelson, who is hired by a group of nationalists to kill the exiled ruler of a South American country, now living in the Caribbean. The cold-blooded Nelson waylays one-time advertising executive Kelly and his wife Spain and forces them to take him to the dictator's retreat in their boat. Keeping Spain as a hostage, Nelson botches the assassination attempt on the dictator and soon finds himself running from the deposed ruler's men and from Kelly. Eventually Nelson is killed by Kelly and Spain is rescued. Shot on location in Puerto Rico, making good use of famed El Morro Castle in a final chase sequence.

p&d, Jack Leewood; w, Don Devlin, Jack Nicholson; ph, John Nickolaus, Jr. (CinemaScope); m, Paul Sawtell, Bert Shefter; ed, Jodie Copelan; makeup, Bob Mark.

Drama (PR:A-C MPAA:NR)

THUNDER MOUNTAIN½** (1935) 68m Atherton/FOX bw

George O'Brien (*Kal Emerson*), Barbara Fritchie (*Sydney Blair*), Frances Grant (*Nugget*), Morgan Wallace (*Rand Levitt*), George F. Hayes (*Foley*), Edward J. LeSaint (*Samuel Blair*), Dean Benton (*Steve Sloan*), William Norton Bailey (*Cliff Borden*).

Loosely based on a Zane Grey story, THUNDER MOUNTAIN sees its action take place in the scenic tall timber territory. O'Brien plays a rugged prospector who legally stakes a claim on gold-rich ground, but then gets double-crossed by dishonest saloonkeeper Wallace. Eventually O'Brien catches up with the swindler and the crook takes a nose-dive off the mountain during a fist fight. This was the fourth in the series of seven high-budget westerns starring O'Brien made by independent Atherton for release by 20th Century-Fox. The star considered these films to be among his best.

p, Sol Lesser; d, David Howard; w, Dan Jarrett, Don Swift (based on a novel by Zane Grey); ph, Frank B. Good; ed, Robert Crandall.

Western (PR:A MPAA:NR)

THUNDER MOUNTAIN**   (1947) 60m RKO bw

Tim Holt (*Marvin Hayden*), Martha Hyer (*Ellen Jorth*), Richard Martin (*Chito Rafferty*), Steve Brodie (*Chick Jorth*), Virginia Owen (*Ginger Kelly*), Harry Woods (*Trimble Carson*), Jason Robards, Sr (*James Gardner*), Robert Clarke (*Lee Jorth*), Richard Powers [Tom Keene] (*Johnny Blue*), Harry Harvey (*Sheriff Bagley*).

Based on Zane Grey's novel in title only, this version of THUNDER MOUNTAIN is really a loose remake of TO THE LAST MAN, which had been made before; once in 1923, and again in 1933. Holt plays the returning son who arrives back at the homestead after college only to find that an old family feud has been reignited. After a bit of digging, Holt discovers that the fighting is being fueled by a gang of ambitious crooks trying to drive the farmers off their land because the government intends to build a dam there and pay a high price for the privilege. With the help of girl friend Hyer (who happens to be a daughter of the rival family), Holt exposes the crooks and reunites the families. This western Romeo-Juliet tale was originally to have been released with a title which more closely resembled its origin, "To the Last Man." Another film company had scheduled a feature titled "The Last Man," so to avoid confusion the producer selected another title from author Grey's lengthy litany. He needn't have bothered; the competitive title was never released.

p, Herman Schlom; d, Lew Landers; w, Norman Houston (based on the novel *To the Last Man* by Zane Grey); ph, Jack MacKenzie; m, Paul Sawtell; ed, Philip Martin; md, C. Bakaleinikoff; art d, Albert S. D'Agostino, Charles F. Pyke.

Western   (PR:A   MPAA:NR)

THUNDER MOUNTAIN, 1964   (SEE: SHEPHERD OF THE HILLS, THE, 1964)

THUNDER OF DRUMS, A**½   (1961) 97m Enders/MGM c

Richard Boone (*Capt. Stephen Maddocks*), George Hamilton (*Lt. Curtis McQuade*), Luana Patten (*Tracey Hamilton*), Arthur O'Connell (*Sgt. Rodermill*), Charles Bronson (*Trooper Hanna*), Richard Chamberlain (*Lt. Porter*), Duane Eddy (*Trooper Eddy*), James Douglas (*Lt. Gresham*), Tammy Marihugh (*Laurie*), Carole Wells (*Camden Yates*), Slim Pickens (*Trooper Erschick*), Clem Harvey (*Trooper Denton*), Casey Tibbs (*Trooper Baker*), Irene Tedrow (*Mrs. Scarborough*), Marjorie Bennett (*Mrs. Yates*), J. Edward McKinley (*Capt. Alan Scarborough*).

A routine cavalry picture is redeemed somewhat by a decent cast of character actors. Hamilton plays the naive young officer assigned to serve under brutal and rough captain Boone. The two get off on a bad footing and Hamilton only complicates his situation by trying to rekindle an old romance with Patten, who is living on the base to be close to her fiance, Douglas. When it is discovered that Douglas has been killed by Indians while out on patrol, Hamilton suspects the lieutenant lost his life due to his lack of concentration, stemming from the stormy romantic situation that Hamilton fostered. Feeling rotten about the whole affair, Hamilton volunteers to be used as a decoy in a plan devised by Boone to bring the violent Apaches out in the open. The trick works and the Apaches are routed, but the cost is high and many men die, including Boone's only true friend, O'Connell. Hamilton returns to the fort a hardened soldier and bids Patten goodbye as she boards the stagecoach headed back east. Bronson has a strong secondary part as a hard-drinking, womanizing trooper; Chamberlain, who went on to greater things, made his feature-film debut in this first effort of producer Enders. Screenwriter Bellah's cavalry stories were filmed by John Ford for his remarkable trilogy FORT APACHE (1948), SHE WORE A YELLOW RIBBON (1949), and RIO GRANDE (1950). Director Newman is no Ford. Songs–written and sung by trooper Eddy–include "Water from a Bad Well" and "Ballad of Camden Yates."

p, Robert J. Enders; d, Joseph M. Newman; w, James Warner Bellah; ph, William W. Spencer (CinemaScope, Metrocolor); m, Harry Sukman; ed, Ferris Webster; art d, George W. Davis, Gabriel Scognamillo; set d, Henry Grace, Jack Mills; cos, Kitty Mager.

Western   (PR:A-C   MPAA:NR)

THUNDER ON THE HILL***   (1951) 84m UNIV bw (GB: BONAVENTURE)

Claudette Colbert (*Sister Mary Bonaventure*), Ann Blyth (*Valerie Carns*), Robert Douglas (*Dr. Jeffrey*), Anne Crawford (*Isabel Jeffreys*), Philip Friend (*Sidney Kingham*), Gladys Cooper (*Mother Superior*), Michael Pate (*Willie*), John Abbott (*Abel Harmer*), Connie Gilchrist (*Sister Josephine*), Gavin Muir (*Melling*), Phyllis Stanley (*Nurse Phillips*), Norma Varden (*Pierce*), Valerie Cardew (*Nurse Colby*), Queenie Leonard (*Mrs. Smithson*), Patrick O'Moore (*Mr. Smithson*).

A fine Douglas Sirk melodrama starring Colbert as a nun at an English convent who becomes convinced that convicted murderess Blyth did not kill her brother. Working against the gallows, Colbert sets out to prove Blyth innocent and eventually exposes local doctor Douglas as the killer who poisoned Blyth's brother in a fit of jealousy due to the younger man's attentions to his wife. Much of the action takes place during a violent flood

that forces the townsfolk to seek refuge in the convent. Sirk successfully uses the raging outdoor elements to comment on the equally stormy emotions of the characters. Minor, but nonetheless fascinating, Sirk. British actress Crawford, as the slatternly wife of killer Douglas, made her U.S. screen debut here.

p, Michel Kraike; d, Douglas Sirk; w, Oscar Saul, Andrew Solt (based on the play "Bonaventure" by Charlotte Hastings); ph, William Daniels; m, Hans J. Salter; ed, Ted J. Kent; art d, Bernard Herzbrun, Nathan Juran; set d, Russell A. Gausman, John Austin; cos, Bill Thomas.

Drama   (PR:A   MPAA:NR)

THUNDER ON THE TRAIL   (SEE: THUNDERING TRAIL, THE, 1951)

THUNDER OVER ARIZONA**   (1956) 75m REP c

Skip Homeier, Kristine Miller, George Macready, Wallace Ford, Jack Elam, Nacho Galindo, Gregory Walcott, George Keymas, John Doucette, John Compton, Bob Swan, Julian Rivero, Francis McDonald.

Mediocre western has a small town going up for grabs when the mother lode of silver is discovered there. The mayor wants it all for himself, but Homeier stands in his way. Immediately forgettable, but a pleasant time-waster.

p&d, Joseph Kane; w, Sloan Nibley; ph, Bud Thackery (Naturama, Trucolor); m, R. Dale Butts; ed, Tony Martinelli; md, Butts; art d, Walter Keller; cos, Adele Palmer.

Western   (PR:A   MPAA:NR)

THUNDER OVER HAWAII   (SEE: NAKED PARADISE, 1957)

THUNDER OVER SANGOLAND**   (1955) 73m Arrow/Lippert bw

Jon Hall, Ray Montgomery, Marjorie Lord, House Peters, Jr, Myron Healey, Nick Stewart, Frank Richards, James Edwards, Louise Franklin.

A famous American doctor comes to the African jungle to help Lord and her missionary brother stop a pair of prospectors who are trying to foment tribal war as a way of driving white colonists away from a mine they have secretly located. Mediocre adventure that never grabs audience attention.

p, Rudolph C. Flothow; d, Sam Newfield; w, Sherman L. Lowe.

Adventure   (PR:A   MPAA:NR)

THUNDER OVER TANGIER*   (1957, Brit.) 66m Sunset Palisades/REP bw (GB: MAN FROM TANGIER)

Robert Hutton (*Chuck Collins*), Lisa Gastoni (*Michele*), Martin Benson (*Voss*), Derek Sydney (*Darracq*), Jack Allen (*Rex*), Leonard Sachs (*Heinrich*), Robert Raglan (*Inspector Meredith*), Harold Berens (*Sammy*), Emerton Court (*Armstrong*), Richard Shaw (*Johnny*), Michael Balfour (*Spade*), Frank Forsyth (*Sgt. Irons*), Reginald Hearne (*Walters*), Fred Lake (*Hotel Porter*), Alex Gallier (*Max*), Marianne Stone (*Woman in Hotel*), Adeeb Assaly (*Lean Arab*), James Lomas (*Fat Man*), Frank Singuineau (*Montez*), Ronald Clark (*Coster*), Victor Beaumont (*Film Director*).

Hutton is a movie stuntman who somehow becomes entangled with a gang of passport forgers preying on displaced persons in post-WWII Algeria. They try to frame him for the murder of the man who stole the plates, but he teams with Gastoni, a displaced person being blackmailed by the gang, to clear his name and put an end to the criminal empire. Poorly plotted crime drama has attractive Gastoni, but not much else.

p, W. G. Chalmers; d, Lance Comfort; w, P. Manning O'Brine; ph, Geoffrey Faithfull; ed, Peter Mayhew; md, Wilfred Burns.

Crime   (PR:A   MPAA:NR)

THUNDER OVER TEXAS**   (1934) 61m Beacon bw

[Guinn] "Big Boy" Williams (*Ted Wright*), Marion Shilling (*Helen Mason*), Helen Westcott (*Tiny*), Claude Peyton (*Bruce Laird*), Philo McCullough (*Tom Collier*), Robert McKenzie (*Judge Blake*), Tiny Skelton (*Tiny*), Dick Botiller, Jack Kirk, Hank Bell.

Cowpoke Williams rides the plains in this first of his westerns for Beacon Productions. When youngster Skelton is left an orphan and then kidnaped after her father is killed in a holdup, Williams and schoolteacher Shilling set out to find the culprits. The crook turns out to be none other than local banker Peyton, who staged the robbery in order to obtain important papers pertaining to the upcoming railroad, and Williams soon sees that justice is served. This was the first western directed by Edgar Ulmer (THE BLACK CAT) who was known for darker, more disturbing material. Ulmer directed under a pseudonym from a story written by his wife because he didn't want his regular studio, Universal, to discover that he was moonlighting. Ulmer only directed one other western, THE NAKED DAWN (1955), and it is vastly superior to this.

p, Max and Arthur Alexander; d, John Warner [Edgar G. Ulmer]; w, Eddie Granemann (based on a story by Sherle Castle [Mrs. Edgar G. Ulmer]; ph,

Harry Forbes; ed, George Merrick.

Western   (PR:A MPAA:NR)

THUNDER OVER THE PLAINS**½   (1953) 82m WB c

Randolph Scott (Capt. David Porter), Lex Barker (Capt. Bill Hodges), Phyllis Kirk (Norah), Charles McGraw (Ben Westman), Henry Hull (Lt. Col. Chandler), Elisha Cook, Jr (Standish), Hugh Sanders (Balfour), Lane Chandler (Faraday), James Brown (Conrad), Fess Parker (Kirby), Richard Benjamin (Sgt. Shaw), Mark Dana (Lt. Williams), Jack Woody (Henley), Trevor Bardette (Walter Morgan), Frank Matts (Jurgens), Steve Darrell (McAvoy), Earle Hodgins (Auctioneer), John Carson, Monte Montague, Carl Andre, Charles Horvath, John McKee, Gail Robinson, Boyd Morgan, Gayle Kellogg.

Texas, 1869. Scott, a Texan and former Confederate soldier, is now wearing the Union uniform and has been assigned to guard the carpetbaggers and swindlers from the angry locals who would like to lynch them. While Scott has great distaste for his assignment, he is a good soldier and performs his duty. He begins to have doubts when McGraw, a Texas patriot, appears unfairly to have been charged with murder by fellow officer Barker, the darling of Yankee commander Hull. Eventually Scott gets to the bottom of the mess, straightens things out, and kicks the bums back North. While the script does some amazingly contrived somersaults, Andre de Toth's crisp direction nearly pulls it off.

p, David Weisbart; d, Andre de Toth; w, Russell Hughes; ph, Bert Glennon (Warner Color); m, David Buttolph; ed, James Moore; art d, Stanley Fleischer; cos, Moss Mabry.

Western   (PR:A MPAA:NR)

THUNDER OVER THE PRAIRIE**   (1941) 61m COL bw

Charles Starrett (Dr. Steven Monroe), Cliff "Ukelele Ike" Edwards (Bones Malloy), Eileen O'Hearn (Nona Mandan), Stanley Brown (Roy Mandan), Danny Mummert (Timmy), David Sharpe (Clay Mandan), Joe McGuinn (Hartley), Donald Curtis (Taylor), Ted Adams (Dave Wheeler), Jack Rockwell (Clayton), Budd Buster (Judge Merryweather), Horace B. Carpenter, Cal [Carl] Shrum and His Rhythm Rangers.

The third and last of cowboy star Starrett's three fairly bizarre oaters that feature our hero as a brave frontier doctor out to cure the sick in the wild West. Starrett leaves his graduate studies in the East to fulfill his ambition of offering his services to the needy in the western territories. After curing the poor settlers of a variety of ills, Starrett takes time out to clear a young Indian–and former medical student–of a murder charge drummed up by a crooked construction firm that is abusing its Indian labor.

p, William Berke; d, Lambert Hillyer; w, Betty Burbridge (based on a story by James L. Rubel); ph, Benjamin Kline; ed, Burton Kramer; m/l, Cal Shrum, Billy Hughes.

Western   (PR:A MPAA:NR)

THUNDER PASS,   (SEE: THUNDER TRAIL, 1937)

THUNDER PASS**   (1954) 76m William F. Broidy/Lippert bw

Dane Clark, Dorothy Patrick, Andy Devine, Raymond Burr, John Carradine, Mary Ellen Kay, Raymond Hatton, Nestor Paiva, Charles Fredericks, Tom Hubbard, Rick Vallin, Tommy Cook, Paul McGuire, Elizabeth Harrower, Gordon Wynne.

Hostile Indians are threatening a wagon train, but Army officer Clark steps into the breach and leads the settlers to safety. A routine story handled routinely.

p, Robert A. Nunes; d, Frank McDonald; w, Tom Hubbard, Fred Eggers (based on a story by George Van Marter); m, Edward Kay.

Western   (PR:A MPAA:NR)

THUNDER RIVER FEUD*½   (1942) 56m MON bw

Ray Corrigan (Crash), John King (Dusty), Max Terhune (Alibi), Jan Wiley (Maybelle), Jack H. Holmes (Pembroke), Rick Anderson (Colonel), Carleton Young (Grover), George Chesebro (Taggart), Carl Mathews (Tex), Budd Buster (Sheriff), Ted Mapes (Buck), Steve Clark (Shorty), Dick Cramer, Tex Palmer, Hal Price.

Corrigan, King, and Terhune (dummy in tow) ride to the rescue of a pair of ranchers unwittingly being conned into a range war by a group of crooks hoping the parties will slaughter each other, leaving the land for the bad guys to exploit. Another entry in the RANGE BUSTERS series (see Index) featuring Corrigan as the fighter, King as the songster, and Terhune as the frontier ventriloquist.

p, George W. Weeks; d, S. Roy Luby; w, John Vlahos, Earle Snell (based on a story by Snell); ph, Robert Cline; ed, Roy Claire; md, Frank Sanucci; m/l, "What a Wonderful Day," Jean George.

Western   Cas.   (PR:A MPAA:NR)

THUNDER ROAD***   (1958) 92m DRM/UA bw

Robert Mitchum (Lucas "Luke" Doolin), Gene Barry (Troy Barrett), Jacques Aubuchon (Carl Kogan), Keely Smith (Francie Wymore), Trevor Bardette (Vernon Doolin), Sandra Knight (Roxanna Ledbetter), Jim [James] Mitchum (Robin Doolin), Betsy Holt (Mary Barrett), Francis Koon (Sarah Doolin), Randy Sparks (Singer/Guitarist), Mitch Ryan (Jed Moultrie), Peter Breck (Stacey Gouge), Peter Hornsby (Lucky), Jerry Hardin (Niles Penland), Robert Porterfield (Preacher).

One of the earliest, and by far the best, of the moonshine-running films starring Robert Mitchum who not only wrote the original story, produced, and starred, but also wrote the theme song "Whippoorwill" which he later recorded and turned into a radio hit. If that isn't enough, Bob's 16-year-old son Jim made his movie debut playing his dad's brother] The fairly simple story line is a southern slice of life which sees Mitchum, Sr. coming home to Tennessee from the "police action" in Korea to take over operation of the family moonshine still. Worried that his kid brother, Mitchum, Jr., might get tangled up in the dangerous business, Mitchum, Sr. tries to discourage the rowdy youth from getting involved in the moonshine wars. Soon powerful mobster Aubuchon wants in on the elder Mitchum's action, and when his offers to buy out the operation are rudely rebuffed, the hoodlum sends some of his boys over to kill one of the family's truckdrivers. Adding to Mitchum's troubles is Barry, a federal agent out to smash the moonshine trade. Mitchum, Sr. avenges his driver by beating up Aubuchon. This leads to all-out war between the mob and Mitchum. Eventually Mitchum, Sr. is captured by Aubuchon, but he is rescued by his brother. At this point, Barry steps in and arrests Aubuchon. Still dead-set on ending the moonshine business, Barry sets out after Mitchum, Sr. and after a thrilling car chase through the backwoods, Mitchum, Sr. meets his end when his car speeds out of control and hits a power transformer which electrocutes him. Footage of the exciting crash was used in the weird THEY SAVED HITLER'S BRAIN (1963). Popular vocalist Smith, with her unusual mannerisms and unique appearance, was an inspired choice as the love interest. Newcomer Knight, the secondary love interest, had her first featured role. The former wife of actor Jack Nicholson, Knight matriculated from this into low-budget horror films such as FRANKENSTEIN'S DAUGHTER (1959) and BLOOD BATH (1966). In 1975, young James Mitchum starred in a picture, MOONRUNNERS, with much the same theme as this moonshine-running bench mark. A minor cult classic and one of Mitchum's more interesting (and bizzare) efforts.

p, Robert Mitchum [uncredited]; d, Arthur Ripley; w, James Atlee Phillips, Walter Wise (based on a story by Mitchum); ph, Alan Stensvold, David Ettinson; m, Jack Marshall; ed, Harry Marker; spec eff, Jack Lannan, Lester Swartz; m/l, "Whippoorwill," Mitchum, Don Raye (sung by Keely Smith); makeup, Carly Taylor.

Crime   Cas.   (PR:C MPAA:NR)

THUNDER ROCK***½   (1944, Brit.) 90m Charter/MGM-EFI bw

Michael Redgrave (David Charleston), Barbara Mullen (Ellen Kirby), James Mason (Streeter), Lilli Palmer (Melanie Kurtz), Finlay Currie (Capt. Joshua), Frederick Valk (Dr. Kurtz), Frederick Cooper (Ted Briggs), Sybilla Binder (Anne-Marie), Jean Shepeard (Mrs. Briggs), Barry Morse (Robert), George Carney (Harry), Miles Malleson (Chairman of Directors), Bryan Herbert (Planning), James Pirrie (New Pilot), A. E. Matthews (Mr. Kirby), Olive Sloane (Woman Director), Tommy Duggan, Tony Quinn (Office Clerks), Harold Anstruther (British Consul), Alfred Sangster (Director), Gerhard Hinze [Gerard Heinz], Andrea Malandrinos.

A well-developed and unique fantasy, this film features Redgrave as a writer living in England shortly before WW II. He grows disillusioned with the political climate in Europe, eventually deciding the only way to avoid the rising tide of fascism is to leave his homeland altogether. Mason is a close friend who attempts to dissuade Redgrave from leaving but this is to no avail. The writer leaves England, heading off to Canada. There he attains a job working as keeper of a lighthouse known as Thunder Rock. Here Redgrave slowly builds himself a psychological bastion from the outside world. He finds a ship's log from a steamer that had gone down in the waters near Thunder Rock in 1849. This book lists the names of passengers who had drowned in the tragedy. To further bolster his security inside the lighthouse Redgrave begins imagining what the lives of these people had been like. His delusions take an unusual twist when the specters of these victims begin interacting with him. Gradually Redgrave learns these apparitions had died while fleeing problems of injustice similar to those he is convinced will conquer Europe. Finding his isolation penetrated from within, Redgrave desperately tries to rid himself of the ghosts. They will not easily be dismissed, though, and Redgrave finds inspiration in their stories, eventually coming to realize that he must be part of the struggle against tyranny at home. The message here is hardly covert, yet thanks to the sensitive treatment, the cry to stand up for one's beliefs never becomes heavy handed or preachy. Rather, the film approaches its underlying theme with grace and care, developing it within the unusual story. Redgrave is marvelous as the man caught between the world he has fled and the world he has conjured, re-creating his stage role in a sensitive portrait. The special effects here are second to none, creating a group of specters within the lighthouse that have cinematic magic all their own. These elements integrate into something very special, delivering an important message within a sensitively handled and artistic production. Released in England in 1942, THUNDER ROCK had its U.S. premiere two years later.

p, John Boulting; d, Roy Boulting; w, Jeffrey Dell, Bernard Miles (based on the play by Robert Ardrey); ph, Mutz Greenbaum; m, Hans May; ed, Roy Boulting; art d, Duncan Sutherland; cos, Honoris Plesch.

Drama/Fantasy (PR:A MPAA:NR)

THUNDER TOWN*½ (1946) 57m PRC bw

Bob Steele (Jim Brandon), Syd Saylor (Utah McGirk), Ellen Hall (Betty Morgan), Bud Geary (Chuck Wilson), Charles King (Bill Rankin), Edward Howard (Dunc Rankin), Steve Clark (Sheriff Matt Warner), Bud Osborne (Henry Carson), Jimmy Aubrey (Peter Collins), Pascale Perry.

Steele, wrongly convicted of an armed robbery, returns to his home town after being paroled from prison to find the villains who framed him and to clear his name. After more than a few fist fights, Steele eventually proves his innocence with a newly discovered ballistic test. This is one of a series of four B westerns with Saylor as comic sidekick to hero Steele. The four pictures (the last of which had Steele with a mustache, an unheard-of thing for a cowboy hero, such hirsuteness being connected to villainy in the B westerns; Steele grew it for his upcoming role in THE BIG SLEEP that same year) were Steele's last as a star; with 119 starring parts behind him, he segued into support roles.

p, Arthur Alexander; d, Harry Fraser; w, James Oliver; ph, Robert Cline; md, Lee Zahler; ed, Roy Livingston; set d, E. H. Reif.

Western (PR:A MPAA:NR)

THUNDER TRAIL**½ (1937) 56m PAR bw (AKA: THUNDER PASS)

Gilbert Roland (Arizona Dick Ames), Marsha Hunt (Amy Morgan), Charles Bickford (Lee Tate), Monte Blue (Jeff Graves), James Craig (Bob Ames), J. Carroll Naish (Rafael Lopez), Barlowe Borland (Jim Morgan), Billy Lee (Bob Ames as a Child), William Duncan (John Ames), Gene Reynolds (Richard Ames at 14), Edward Coxen (Martin), Vester Pegg (Lee), Earl Askam (Flinty), Bob Clark, Frank Cordell, Slim Hightower, Pardner Jones, Cecil Kellogg, Jack Moore, Guy Schultz, Ed Warren, Tommy Coats, Alan Burk, Danny Morgan (Cowboys), Carol Halloway, Gertrude Simpson, Mary Foy (Women), Jack Daley (Bartender), Lee Shumway, Ray Hanford (Miners), Hank Bell (Barfly).

A fine low-budget western starring Roland and Craig as brothers who are separated after the villainous Bickford kills their father and then kidnaps Craig to raise as his own son. Roland sets out on a lengthy search for Bickford, and years later he encounters the killer trying to run helpless farmer Blue and his daughter Hunt off their land. The wandering cowboy comes to the aid of the farmers, romances Hunt, and eventually wreaks his revenge on Bickford. Good cast, intelligent script, and solid direction. Composer Morros based his fine score on George Antheil's brilliant music for Cecil B. DeMille's THE PLAINSMAN, released by Paramount a year previously. The studio was undergoing major trauma at the time of production; its long-time president, Adolph Zukor, lost his battle with other bigwigs and got kicked upstairs to a position of industry impotence as chairman of the board.

d, Charles Barton; w, Robert Yost, Stuart Anthony (based on the novel Arizona Ames by Zane Grey); ph, Karl Struss; m, Boris Morros, George Antheil; ed, John Link.

Western (PR:A MPAA:NR)

THUNDERBALL**½ (1965, Brit.) 130m Eon/UA c

Sean Connery (James Bond), Claudine Auger (Domino Derval), Adolfo Celi (Emilio Largo), Luciana Paluzzi (Fiona Volpe), Rik Van Nutter (Felix Leiter), Bernard Lee ("M"), Martine Beswick (Paula Caplan), Guy Doleman (Count Lippe), Molly Peters (Patricia Fearing), Desmond Llewelyn ("Q"), Lois Maxwell (Moneypenny), Roland Culver (Foreign Secretary), Earl Cameron (Pinder), Paul Stassino (Maj. Derval), Rose Alba (Mme. Boitier), Philip Locke (Vargas), George Pravda (Kutze), Michael Brennan (Janni), Leonard Sachs (Group Captain), Edward Underdown (Air Vice Marshall), Reginald Beckwith (Kenniston), Bill Cummings (Quist), Maryse Guy Mitsouko (Mlle. La Porte), Bob Simmons (Jacques Boitier), Evelyn Boren (Domino Double), Frank Cousins, Harold Sanderson (Bond Doubles).

Distressingly dull entry in the James Bond series (No. 4) sees Connery out to stop the evil machinations of SPECTRE number two man Celi, who has stolen a nuclear armed NATO aircraft, hidden it in the Bahamas (underwater), and then threatened to nuke a location somewhere in Britain or the U.S. As the film plods along, Connery discovers the beautiful Auger, sister of the doomed jet pilot and mistress of Celi. She, of course, doesn't realize that her lover is responsible for her brother's death, but Connery soon convinces her that Celi and his henchmen aren't quite kosher (the man has dozens of sharks in his swimming pool, for gosh sakes!). After lots of tedious underwater sequences that only tend to confuse the action, Connery eventually locates the downed plane and calls in the American aquaparatroops (attired in bright orange neoprene) who dive in to participate in a numbingly long underwater battle sequence with dozens of SPECTRE scuba

divers (dressed in black neoprene, naturally), all brandishing underwater spearguns. When it is all over, Celi escapes and reveals his yacht to be a disguised hydrofoil. The cool villain jettisons the "yacht" part of the boat (which turns into a heavily armed float manned by dozens of foolishly loyal SPECTRE lackey, who attempt to fight off the U.S. Navy), and then speeds off with Connery desperately clinging to the side. Eventually Connery boards the boat and fights it out hand-to-hand with Celi, which sends the hydrofoil zipping crazily toward some rocks. Finally Auger appears from below, kills Celi, and Connery manages to grab his girl and abandon ship before the hydrofoil hits the rocks and explodes. Producers Albert R. "Cubby" Broccoli and Harry Saltzman engaged in a lengthy and expensive legal battle with Kevin McClory, a renegade producer who bought the rights to screen THUNDERBALL and intended to produce a Bond epic on his own. McClory won in the courts, but when it became apparent to him that his film would most certainly wind up a turkey without Broccoli and Saltzman's assistance (they had Connery on contract), he approached the veteran Bond team for negotiations. The three struck a deal which gave McClory the producer credit and a percentage of the profits. Broccoli was not happy with the arrangement, but it was worth it just to be able to keep inferior Bond films off the market. Unfortunately, THUNDERBALL proved vastly inferior to their three previous efforts. Apparently Connery himself felt the film was a wasted effort, for he remade it in 1983 as NEVER SAY NEVER AGAIN, returning to the screen as James Bond for the first time in 12 years. It wasn't any better the second time around. Despite its shortcomings, the film was an enormous financial success, the top moneymaker of 1966, grossing more than any other in the series. During the hunt for a suitable actress to play the part of Domino, a number of then relatively unknown players were considered. Auger won out over the first three on the list: Julie Christie, Raquel Welch, and Faye Dunaway. Welch had actually contracted to play the part, but executive producer Broccoli reluctantly released her as a favor to 20th Century-Fox production head Richard Zanuck, who wanted her for FANTASTIC VOYAGE (1966). (See JAMES BOND series, Index.)

p, Kevin McClory; d, Terence Young; w, Richard Maibaum, John Hopkins (based on the characters created by Ian Fleming and the story by McClory, Jack Whittingham, Fleming); ph, Ted Moore, underwater ph, Lamar Boren (Panavision, Technicolor); m, John Barry; ed, Peter Hunt; md, Barry; prod d, Ken Adam; art d, Peter Murton; set d, Freda Pearson; cos, Anthony Mendleson; spec eff, John Stears; m/l, "Thunderball," Barry, Don Black (sung by Tom Jones); stunts, Bob Simmons.

Adventure/Spy Cas. (PR:A-C MPAA:GP)

THUNDERBIRD 6** (1968, Brit.) 90m A.P. Films-Century 21/UA c

Voices: Peter Dyneley (Jeff Tracy), Christine Finn (Tin-Tin), Keith Alexander (Black Phantom/John Tracy), Jeremy Wilkin (Virgil Tracy/Hogarth), Gary Files (Foster/Lane), John Carson (Foster 2), Sylvia Anderson (Lady Penelope Creighton-Ward), David Graham (Brains/Gordon/Parker), Matt Zimmerman (Alan Tracy), Geoffrey Keen (Controller), Shane Rimmer (Scott Tracy).

The second theatrical film inspired by the popular British television series "Thunderbirds" which details the 21st-Century adventures of a group of puppets known as International Rescue, who fly amazing spaceships. In this drama, the heroes find themselves battling the evil renegades of New World Aircraft Corporation, who kidnap Lady Penelope and company in order to learn more about International Rescue.

p&w, Gerry and Sylvia Anderson; d, David Lane; ph, Harry Oakes (Techniscope Technicolor); m, Barry Gray; art d, Bob Bell; spec eff, Derek Meddings; model design, Ray Brown; puppet manipulator, Wanda Webb.

Science Fiction Cas. (PR:A MPAA:G)

THUNDERBIRDS**½ (1952) 98m REP bw

John Derek (Gil Hackett), John Barrymore, Jr (Tom McCreery), Mona Freeman (Lt. Ellen Henderson), Gene Evans (Mike Braggart), Eileen Christy (Mary Caldwell), Ward Bond (Sgt. Logan), Barton MacLane (Sgt. Durkee), Wally Cassell (Pfc. Sam Jacobs), Ben Cooper (Calvin Jones), Robert Neil (Keith Watson), Slim Pickens (Pvt. Wes Shelby), Armando Silvestre (Cpl. Ralph Mogay), Benny Baker (Pvt. Charles Klassen), Norman Budd (Pvt. Lou Radtke), Mae Clarke (Mrs. Jones), Sam McKim (Cpl. Ray Hanford), Allene Roberts (Mrs. Ray Hanford), Richard Simmons (Capt. Norton), Walter Reed (Lt. Hammond), Suzanne Dalbert (Marie Etienne), Barbara Pepper (Mrs. Mike Braggart), Pepe Hern (Pvt. Jim Lastchance), Victor Millan (Pvt. Joe Lastchance).

Routine military training film starring Derek and Barrymore, Jr. as two young recruits of the Oklahoma National Guard who are called into active service in 1940 and eventually shipped to Europe. The film follows the buddies as they battle their way through Salerno, Anzio, and Cassino, into the south of France and, eventually, Germany. A contrived plot twist sees crusty old veteran Bond (who steals the movie from his younger counterparts) revealing himself to be the long-thought-dead father of Barrymore, Jr.

p&d, John H. Auer; w, Mary C. McCall, Jr. (based on a story by Kenneth Gamet); ph, Reggie Lanning; m, Victor Young; ed, Richard L. Van Enger; art d, Frank Hotaling; set d, John McCarthy, Jr., Otto Siegel.

War   (PR:A MPAA:NR)

THUNDERBIRDS ARE GO**½ (1968, Brit.) 94m Century 21-A.P./UA
c

Voices: Sylvia Anderson (*Lady Penelope Creighton-Ward*), Ray Barrett (*John Tracy/The Hood/Controller at Glenn Field*), Alexander Davion (*Greg Martin*), Peter Dyneley (*Jeff Tracy*), Christine Finn (*Tin-Tin*), David Graham (*Brains/Gordon Tracy/Parker*), Paul Maxwell (*Paul Travers*), Neil McCallum (*Dr. Pierce*), Bob Monkhouse (*Brad Newman*), Shane Rimmer (*Scott Tracy*), Charles Tingwell (*Dr. Grant/Public Relations Officer/Angry Young Man*), Jeremy Wilkin (*Virgil Tracy/President of Exploration Center*), Matt Zimmerman (*Alan Tracy/Messenger*).

The first feature film inspired by the British television series "Thunderbirds" which was created by the husband-and-wife team of Sylvia and Gerry Anderson (Sylvia also supplied the voice of Lady Penelope). Utilizing sophisticated marionettes shot in a process called "Supermarionation," the Thunderbirds–a group of heroes in the 21st century–who pilot their spaceships for an organization known as International Rescue. In this adventure, the Thunderbirds go to the rescue of the first manned space flight to Mars, which has been delayed because of sabotage. When the astronauts arrive on Mars, they are faced with deadly Martian rock serpents. The group manages to complete its mission but on the return flight their radio communications go dead, making a crash landing on Earth unavoidable. Luckily the members of International Rescue send a Thunderbird plane to the injured ship and manage to separate the rescue pod containing the crew members and guide it safely back home. The Shadows sing "Lady Penelope;" Cliff Richard, backed by the group, sings "Shooting Star." A sequel, THUNDERBIRD 6, followed.

p, Sylvia Anderson; d, David Lane; w, Gerry and Sylvia Anderson; ph, Paddy Seale (Techniscope, Technicolor); m, Barry Gray; ed, Len Walter; art d, Bob Bell, Grenville Knott; spec eff, Derek Meddings; m/l, The Shadows; model design, Ray Brown; puppet manipulation, Christine Glanville, Mary Turner.

Science Fiction   Cas.   (PR:A MPAA:NR)

THUNDERBOLT***   (1929) 91m FP-PAR bw

George Bancroft (*"Thunderbolt" Jim Lang*), Fay Wray (*Mary/ "Ritzy"*), Richard Arlen (*Bob Morgan*), Tully Marshall (*Warden*), Eugenie Besserer (*Mrs. Morgan*), James Spottswood (*"Snapper" O'Shea*), Fred Kohler, Sr. (*"Bad Al" Friedberg*), Robert Elliott (*Prison Chaplain*), E.H. Calvert (*District Attorney McKay*), George Irving (*Mr. Corwin, Bank Officer*), Mike Donlin (*Kentucky Sampson*), S.S. Stewart (*Convict*), William L. Thorne (*Police Inspector*), King Tut the Dog.

Serving as more proof that Josef von Sternberg did make fine films before THE BLUE ANGEL, THUNDERBOLT is a bizarre gangster picture which is as much a romance as a thriller. Bancroft stars as the title character, a hard-edged bank robber with a dedicated following of underworld cronies. Like all good mobsters, Bancroft has a soft spot for a special girl, namely Wray. She, however, serves as a catalyst for trouble when she falls for a young banker, Arlen, and asks Bancroft's permission to go straight. Before long, Bancroft has fouled up and gone to prison where he sits on death row, Wray has devoted herself to Arlen, and Arlen has lost his job because of his association with Wray. Rather than lose his girl, Bancroft vows to kill anyone who steps between them. Bancroft shows no mercy while awaiting his execution and has his henchmen frame Arlen for a murder and bank robbery. Arlen also finds himself on death row, in a cell opposite Bancroft's. Wray expresses her devotion for all the prison to see by convincing the warden to let her and Arlen marry on death row. Bancroft is moved by this show of love and, at the eleventh hour, on his way to the electric chair, he admits to the frame-up and clears Arlen of any wrongdoing. Arlen and Wray are then free to start anew outside the walls of the prison. Released in both sound and silent versions (though the 81-minute silent with titles by Joseph Mankiewicz, was barely shown), THUNDERBOLT was another of those films produced during that transition period when audiences expected to hear their actors speak. Essentially a visual director, Sternberg continued to put his energies into composition and visual atmosphere. Still, the sound techniques and experiments of THUNDERBOLT are far in advance of most other films of the day. Sternberg would later write in his autobiography, *Fun in a Chinese Laundry*, that "to be correctly and effectively used, sound had to bring to the image a quality other than what the lens included, a quality out of the range of the image. Sound had to counterpoint or compensate the image, add to it–not subtract from it." It is this that he attempts in THUNDERBOLT. Even Sternberg's use of music is unconventional, choosing not to rely on a lush score to enhance (or as he would view it, "subtract from") the beauty of the image. This was Sternberg's first sound picture and, for the most part, its sound innovations went ignored. As Sternberg remembers, only German director Ludwig Berger (best known for his co- directorial effort on the 1940 THIEF OF BAGHDAD) noticed, sending a telegram which read: "Saw your THUNDERBOLT and congratulate you with all my heart. It is the first rounded out and artistically elaborated sound film. Bravo." Starting the following year with THE BLUE ANGEL, however, Sternberg would begin an unbroken streak of critically acclaimed films that would continue until 1936's CRIME AND PUNISHMENT. Includes the songs "Thinkin' About My Baby" (Sam Coslow), "Broken Hearted," and "Rock-a-bye-baby" (both Negro spirituals). Bancroft, star of

four Sternberg pictures, received his (and THUNDERBOLT'S) only Oscar nomination for his work on this film.

p, B.P. Fineman; d, Josef von Sternberg; w, Jules Furthman, Herman J. Mankiewicz (based on a story by Jules Furthman, Charles Furthman); ph, Henry Gerrard; ed, Helen Lewis; art d, Hans Dreier.

Crime/Romance   (PR:A MPAA:NR)

THUNDERBOLT zero   (1936) 55m Regal bw

Lobo the Marvel Dog (*Thunderbolt*), Kane Richmond, Bobby Nelson, Lafe McKee, Wally West, Frank Ellis, George Morrell, Jack Kirk, Hank Bell, Bob McKenzie, Frank Hagney, Barney Furey.

Yet another of Hollywood's lame super-dog films, this time Lobo the Marvel Dog pants his way through this bloody mess which sees the robbery of an express office, the aftermath of which leaves four corpses (one burned to death). Luckily Lobo and his master, child star Nelson, solve the crimes and bring the killers to justice. Inexcusably lurid story that unfolds in the shoddiest filmmaking imaginable.

p, Samuel S. Krellberg; d, Stuart Paton; w, Jack T.O. Gevne [Jack Jevne].

Crime   (PR:A-C MPAA:NR)

THUNDERBOLT AND LIGHTFOOT***½

                                       (1974) 114m Malpaso/UA c

Clint Eastwood (*John "Thunderbolt" Doherty*), Jeff Bridges (*Lightfoot*), Geoffrey Lewis (*Goody*), Catherine Bach (*Melody*), Gary Busey (*Curly*), George Kennedy (*Red Leary*), Jack Dodson (*Vault Manager*), Gene Elman, Lila Teigh (*Tourists*), Burton Gilliam (*Welder*), Roy Jenson (*Dunlop*), Claudia Lennear (*Secretary*), Bill McKinney (*Crazy Driver*), Vic Tayback (*Mario*), Dub Taylor (*Gas Station Attendant*), Gregory Walcott (*Used Car Salesman*), Erica Hagen (*Waitress*), Virginia Baker, Stuart Nisbet (*Couple at Gas Station*), Alvin Childress (*Janitor*), Irene K. Cooper (*Cashier*), Cliff Emmich (*Fat Man*), June Fairchild (*Gloria*), Ted Foulkes (*Little Boy*), Karen Lamm (*Girl on Motorcycle*), Luanne Roberts (*Suburban Housewife*), Titos Vandis (*Counterman*).

Before the disastrous HEAVEN'S GATE and YEAR OF THE DRAGON, and before the success of THE DEER HUNTER, intermittently brilliant director Michael Cimino directed his marvelous first film, THUNDERBOLT AND LIGHTFOOT. Eastwood, whose production company produced the film, had become impressed with Cimino after Cimino co-authored the screenplay for another Eastwood vehicle, MAGNUM FORCE (1973). The film is a crisp, well-written, witty, tough, superbly cast movie sporting some stunning landscapes and a fine core of performances (Bridges earned an Academy Award nomination as Best Supporting Actor). Young drifter Bridges hooks up with ex-thief Eastwood, who has been on the lam from his former partners for several years because they believe he set him up and took off with the loot from a government vault they robbed in Montana. The two remaining members of his gang, Kennedy, a sadistic war buddy of Eastwood, and Lewis, a likable dimwit, are in pursuit of revenge and hot on Eastwood's tail. The thief, therefore, reluctantly strikes up a friendship with Bridges to escape. Bridges admires Eastwood and wants to prove himself worthy of his friendship, so the crazy kid takes part in the dangerous maneuvering. Eventually Kennedy and Lewis corner the pair and prepare to kill them. Eastwood convinces Kennedy he has no idea where the money is (it was hidden behind the blackboard of an old schoolhouse that no longer exists) and their lives are spared. With nothing better to do, Bridges convinces the group it should rob the same vault, the same way, all these years later because no one would suspect another attempt (they shot their way into the vault with a Howitzer cannon). After some elaborate planning, the four men successfully execute the robbery, but their getaway goes awry and Lewis is killed. Kennedy panics and becomes angry, knocks out Eastwood, severely beats Bridges (Kennedy always seemed jealous of Bridges' and Eastwood's relationship) and takes off with the loot. The police chase Kennedy through the streets at high speeds, and the thief ends up crashing his car into a department store and getting his throat ripped out by the store's vicious Doberman guard dogs. Meanwhile, Eastwood and Bridges manage to escape, though it is obvious that Bridges was severely wounded by Kennedy. The two friends wander down the lonely Montana roads until Eastwood spots the old schoolhouse where the original loot was stashed (the building was moved after being declared a historical monument). The two find the money and Eastwood buys Bridges his dream car, a white Cadillac convertible. As the pair drive through the beautiful Montana mountains, Bridges bravely tries to joke with Eastwood. He eventually dies, leaving Eastwood rich, but friendless. THUNDERBOLT AND LIGHTFOOT is a multifaceted caper film told in fine detail with richly developed characters. Eastwood is nearly overshadowed by Bridges, Kennedy, and Lewis, who brings great depth to his weak-willed, somewhat stupid, character without resorting to cliches. Here, as well as in THE DEER HUNTER, Cimino's main characters–Eastwood and DeNiro–seem detached from their peers and unmoved by their environment, until events beyond their control force them to realize what it was they had. It is only then that they experience a melancholy sense of loss. Cimino's first two films succeed because he allows well-drawn *characters* to affect the audience, not the *epic scale* of the production. When Cimino's obsessions with American icons and institutions (the land, the church, the law) override his sense of character, his films fail. The epic, breathtaking qualities in much of HEAVEN'S GATE crumbled due to the hollowness of the people in it. The same is true in THE YEAR OF THE DRAGON. All of the script's preaching about honesty, valor, and noble crusades becomes hollow because the characters involved just don't ring true. The power of THUNDERBOLT AND LIGHTFOOT and THE DEER HUNTER stems from their eloquent, complex, honest characters, and Cimino would do well to return to what he does best.

p, Robert Daley; d&w, Michael Cimino; ph, Frank Stanley (Panavision, DeLuxe Color); m, Dee Barton; ed, Ferris Webster; art d, Tambi Larsen; set d, James Berkey; spec eff, Sam Bedig; stunts, m/l, Paul Williams; stunts, Buddy Van Horn; titles, Wayne Fitzgerald.

Crime   Cas.   **(PR:O   MPAA:R)**

THUNDERCLOUD   (SEE: COLT .45, 1950)

THUNDERHEAD—SON OF FLICKA **   (1945) 78m FOX bw

Roddy McDowall (Ken McLaughlin), Preston Foster (Rob McLaughlin), Rita Johnson (Nelle), James Bell (Gus), Diana Hale (Hildy), Carleton Young (Maj. Harris), Ralph Sanford (Mr. Sargent), Robert Filmer (Tim), Alan Bridge (Dr. Hicks).

This follow-up to MY FRIEND FLICKA (1943) is every bit as entertaining as the original, an enjoyable and engaging tale that is perfect family viewing. McDowall, returning from the original film along with Foster, Johnson, and Bell, is trying to break in Thunderhead, the title horse. The all-white colt is trained for racing, and McDowell enters him in competition. At a county race it appears Thunderhead is going to win when the animal suddenly pulls a tendon. McDowell is content to use Thunderhead riding around his father's ranch, but trouble brews when an albino horse--who had sired Thunderhead--goes wild. The horse causes trouble for all the ranchers of the valley by stealing mares, but eventually it is challenged by Thunderhead. The brave colt saves McDowall, then takes on the albino. The two horses engage in a terrific fight, with Thunderhead defeating his renegade father. McDowall's horse returns to his master, but shows a desire to live free on the range. Though heartbroken, McDowall understands what is best for his friend and allows the horse to go free. The film is well acted, though the players are really secondary to the real stars of the film: the horses and the beautiful Utah locations. The scenery is lushly photographed, with vivid color that captures the beauty of the western landscapes. Thunderhead is amazing, as are the other horses, a credit to the talents of their trainer. The story is well told, and McDowall has some fine moments in this heart-warming tale.

p, Robert Bassler; d, Louis King; w, Dwight Cummins, Dorothy Yost (based on a novel by Mary O'Hara); ph, Charles Clarke (Technicolor); m, Cyril J. Mockridge; ed, Nick De Maggio; md, Emil Newman; art d, Lyle Little, Fred J. Rode.

Drama   **(PR:AAA   MPAA:NR)**

THUNDERHOOF*   (1948) 77m COL bw

Preston Foster (Scotty Mason), Mary Stuart (Margarita), William Bishop (The Kid), Thunderhoof the Horse.

An unusual, fascinating low-budget western starring Foster as a middle-aged rancher who dreams of setting up a successful horse ranch in Texas. His much-younger wife, Stuart, begins to feel trapped in their relationship and questions her love for Foster. Her doubts are strengthened by Bishop, Foster's troublesome adopted son, who attempts to seduce his stepmother during the trio's obsessive search for a beautiful black-and-white wild stallion. On the trail, Foster captures the horse but breaks his leg. The return to the ranch is a tense one, aggravated by Foster's injury, the unruly horse, and the lack of food. The group finds a deserted farmhouse containing supplies. Holed up together, tempers flare again when Foster apparently ignores Bishop's attentiveness to Stuart. The group leaves the farmhouse upon learning it had been evacuated when typhoid was discovered in the water supply. The horse escapes, and Foster gets into a fight with Bishop. Bishop knocks the older man down a ravine and leaves him for dead. Surprisingly, the horse returns and saves Foster. Meanwhile, Bishop reveals he drank some contaminated water and dies of typhoid, leaving Stuart stranded in the desert. While wandering, Stuart hears the thundering hoofbeats of the wild horse and thinks it's her imagination. Foster then arrives and saves her.

p, Ted Richmond; d, Phil Karlson; w, Hal Smith, Kenneth Gamet; ph, Henry Freulich; m, Mischa Bakaleinikoff; ed, Jerome Thoms; art d, Walter Holscher.

Western   **(PR:A   MPAA:NR)**

THUNDERING CARAVANS   (1952) 54m REP bw

Allan "Rocky" Lane (Himself), Eddy Waller (Nugget Clark), Mona Knox (Alice Scott), Roy Barcroft (Ed Brill), Isabel Randolph (Deborah Cranston), Richard Crane (Dan Reed), Bill Henry (Bert Cranston), Edward Clark (Tom), Pierre Watkin (Head Marshal), Stanley Andrews (Henry Scott), Boyd "Red" Morgan (Joe), Black Jack the Stallion.

U.S. Marshal Lane rides to the rescue of beleaguered sheriff Waller, who is desperately trying to solve a series of gold ore robberies. Meanwhile, he contends with constant harassment from villainous newspaper publisher Randolph in the press. Lane discovers that Randolph is waging her print crusade against Waller so that her brother, Henry, will be elected sheriff. This information in hand, Lane sets things straight and insures Waller's job.

p, Rudy Ralston; d, Harry Keller; w, M. Coates Webster; ph, John MacBurnie; m, Stanley Wilson; ed, Harold Minter; art d, Frank Hotaling; set d, John McCarthy, Jr., John Redd.

Western   **(PR:A   MPAA:NR)**

THUNDERING FRONTIER*   (1940) 57m COL bw

Charles Starrett (Jim Filmore), Iris Meredith (Norma Belknap), Raphael [Ray] Bennett (Ed Filmore), Alex Callam ("Square Deal" Scottie), Carl Stockdale (Andrew Belknap), Fred Burns (Hank Loomis), Bob Nolan (Bob), John Tyrrell (Mac), Francis Walker (Stub), John Dilson (Carter Filmore), Pat Brady, The Sons of the Pioneers, Blackie Whiteford.

Uneventful Starrett film that features the hero and his men sitting around singing hillbilly tunes when they should be after Bennett and his gang of killers, who have been shooting residents, blowing up supply trains, and robbing payrolls. Eventually Starrett and his boys put aside their artistic pursuits and catch the baddies.

d, D. Ross Lederman; w, Paul Franklin; ph, George Meehan; ed, Arthur Seid; m/l, Bob Nolan, Tim Spencer.

Western   **(PR:A   MPAA:NR)**

THUNDERING GUN SLINGERS*½   (1944) 59m PRC bw

Buster Crabbe (Billy Carson), Al [Fuzzy] St. John (Fuzzy Jones), Frances Gladwin (Bab Halliday), Karl Hackett (Jeff Halliday), Charles King (Steve Kirby), Jack Ingram (Vic), Kermit Maynard (Ed), Budd Buster (Sheriff), George Chesebro (Dave).

Cowboy Crabbe sets out to avenge his honest uncle, who was run off his land by a gang of crooks out to gather up all the property in the area for a cheap price. Western fans will find it dull, except for the usual funny stuff produced by St. John from behind his whiskers. (See BILLY CARSON series, Index.)

p, Sigmund Neufeld; d, Sam Newfield; w, Fred Myton; ph, Robert Cline; ed, Holbrook N. Todd.

Western   Cas.   **(PR:A   MPAA:NR)**

THUNDERING HERD, THE½**   (1934) 57m PAR bw (AKA: IN THE DAYS OF THE THUNDERING HERD)

Randolph Scott (Tom Doan), Judith Allen (Milly Fayre), Larry "Buster" Crabbe (Bill Hatch), Noah Beery, Sr (Randall Jett), Raymond Hatton (Jude Pilchuck), Blanche Frederici (Mrs. Jett), Harry Carey (Clark Sprague), Monte Blue (Joe), Barton MacLane (Pruitt), Al Bridge (Catlee), Dick Rush (Middlewest), Frank Rice (Blacksmith), Buck Connors (Buffalo Hunter), Charles McMurphy (Andrews).

Better than average Zane Grey inspired oater starring Scott as a brave buffalo hunter out to stop loathsome villain Beery, who has been stirring up trouble between the white settlers and the Indians so that he can steal a fortune in buffalo hides. To complicate matters, Scott is in love with Beery's daughter Allen, Cecil B. DeMille's great star discovery of the year before. A good cast and swift direction by Henry Hathaway make this worth a look. Heavy doses of stock footage of the same material from from the 1925 silent version (which also featured Beery and Hatton) do not get in the way at all. Chief among these was a beautifully staged stampede of massed covered wagons going across a frozen lake, by the great silent director William Kerrigan Howard, who later in his career was deprecated as being a slick, commercial director, but who nevertheless made many grand actioner westerns full of dramatic tension. Allen, alas, after in a inauspicious debut in THIS DAY AND AGE (1933) wound up in low-bud get westerns and dramas.

p, Harold Hurley; d, Henry Hathaway; w, Jack Cunningham, Mary Flannery (based on the novel by Zane Grey); ph, Ben Reynolds; art d, Earl Hedrick.

Western   **(PR:A   MPAA:NR)**

THUNDERING HOOFS*½   (1941) 60m RKO bw

Tim Holt (Bill), Ray Whitley (Smokey), Les "Lasses" White (Whopper), Luana Walters (Nancy), Archie Twitchell (Farley), Gordon DeMain (Underwood), Charles Phipps (Kellogg), Monte Montague (Slick), Joe Bernard (Hank), Frank Fanning (Adams), Fred Scott (Dode), Frank Ellis (Carver), Bob Kortman, Lloyd Ingraham.

Holt plays the son of a stageline owner who discovers crooked lawyer Twitchell's scheme to use his father as a fall guy in evil attempt to drive rival stage operator Walters and her father out of business. After acquiring the rival stage line, Twitchell plans to drive Holt's dad out as well. Needless to say, Holt puts a stop to it.

p, Bert Gilroy; d, Lesley Selander; w, Paul Franklin; ph, J. Roy Hunt; ed, Frederic Knudtson; m/l, "Thundering Hoofs," "Ramble On," "As Along the Trail I Ride," Fred Rose, Ray Whitley.

**Western								(PR:A MPAA:NR)**

**THUNDERING JETS*					(1958) 73m FOX bw**

Rex Reason (Capt. Morley), Dick Foran (Lt. Col. Spalding), Audrey Dalton (Susan Blair), Robert Dix (Lt. Erskine), Lee Farr (Capt. Murphy), Barry Coe (Capt. Davis), Buck Class (Maj. Geron), John Douglas (Kurt Weber), Robert Conrad (Lt. Kiley), Sid Melton (Sgt. Stone), Gregg Palmer (Capt. Dexter), Lionel Ames (Capt. Anderson), Dick Monahan (1st Mechanic), Maudie Prickett (Mrs. Blocher), Jimmie Smith (Long), Bill Bradley (1st Student), Robert Rothwell (2nd Mechanic), Kevin Enright (Saunders), Walter Kent (Pianist), Tom Walton (Vocalist), Ronald Foster (Control Tower Sergeant), Kenneth Edwards (2nd Student).

Frustrated Air Force hero Reason takes his anger out on his students after he is pulled from active service and sent to Edwards Air Force Base to train recruits in the art of flying jets. Bored with his job and paranoid that his pretty young girl friend, Dalton, will be stolen away from him by one of these upstarts, Reason proves himself to be a spiteful, petty, and mean instructor. Luckily, he realizes the importance of his job when he is forced to save the life of one of his brighter students, Class, who loses his nerve while in air and threatens to crash the jet, and there is a subsequent surprise party and "bravos" from the other students.

p, Jack Leewood; d, Helmut Dantine; w, James Landis; ph, John Nicholaus, Jr. (RegalScope); m, Irving Gertz; ed, Frank Baldridge; art d, John Mansbridge.

**Drama								(PR:A MPAA:NR)**

**THUNDERING TRAIL, THE*	(1951) 55m REA bw (GB: THUNDER ON THE TRAIL)**

Lash LaRue (U.S. Marshal), Al St. John (Fuzzy Q. Jones), Sally Anglim (Betty-Jo), Archie Twitchell (Tom Emery), Ray Bennett (Ed West), Reed Howes (Schaeffer), John Cason (Conway), Clarke Stevens (Clarke), George Chesebro (Jones), Jim Martin (Clinton), Cliff Taylor (Moore), Bud Osborne (Stage Driver), Mary Lou Webb (Miss Smith), Sue Hussey (Sue), Ray Broome (Bartender).

When the newly elected governor of the territory needs a bodyguard for his trip from his ranch to the capital, LaRue takes the job in this lightweight outing. On the trail he must battle the likes of Bennett and his cut-throat gang who make several attempts on the governor's life.

p&d, Ron Ormond; w, Alexander White; ph, Ernest Miller; ed, Hugh Winn.

**Western				Cas.				(PR:A MPAA:NR)**

THUNDERING TRAILS					(1943) 56m REP bw**

Bob Steele, Tom Tyler, Jimmie Dodd, Nell O'Day, Sam Flint, Karl Hackett, Charles Miller, John James, Forrest Taylor, Ed Cassidy, Forbes Murray, Reed Howes, Bud Geary, Budd Buster, Vince Barnett, Lane Bradford, Cactus Mack, Edwin Parker, Al Taylor, Art Mix, Jack O'Shea.

Routine series entry has the Mesquiteers riding to the rescue of the brother of one of them, who is innocently involved with outlaws. Fans of the B western should find this one up to standard, others beware. (See THREE MESQUITEERS series, Index.)

p, Louis Gray; d, John English; w, Norman S. Hall, Robert Yost (based on a story by Yost, based on characters created by William Colt MacDonald); ph, Reggie Lanning; m, Mort Glickman; ed, William Thompson; art d, Russell Kimball.

**Western								(PR:A MPAA:NR)**

THUNDERING WEST, THE				(1939) 56m COL bw**

Charles Starrett (Dale), Iris Meredith (Helen), Hank Bell (Tucson), Dick Curtis (Wolf), Bob Nolan (Bob), Robert Fiske (Barkeep), Edward J. Le Saint (Judge), Hal Taliaferro (Kendall), Blackie Whiteford, Art Mix, Edmund Cobb, Ed Piel, Sr, Slim Whitaker, Steve Clark, Fred Burns, Clem Horton, Sons of the Pioneers.

Reluctant outlaw Starrett is surprised to find himself suddenly yanked from his villainous cronies and set up as sheriff of a small town. He is soon faced with protecting a gold shipment from the very men he used to ride with.

d, Sam Nelson; w, Bennett R. Cohen; ph, Lucien Ballard; ed, William Lyon; m/l, "Tumbling Tumbleweed," Bob Nolan.

**Western								(PR:A MPAA:NR)**

**THUNDERING WHEELS			(SEE: THUNDER IN DIXIE, 1965)**

THUNDERSTORM				(1934, USSR) 78m Soyuzfilm/Amkino bw**

Alla Tarasova (Katherine), Varvara Massalitinova (Kabanova), I.P. Tschouvelev (Tikhon), I.P. Zaroubina (Barbara), M.M. Tarkhanov (Saveli Dikoy), M.I. Jaroff (Vania Koudriash), Mikhail Zharov (Boris).

A gloomy but polished Russian melodrama starring Tarasova as the wife trapped in her husband's family of vile, religious zealots ruled by a strong and domineering mother. Seeking a refuge, Tarasova falls into an affair with a dashing young man that ends in tragedy when she drowns herself in a river rather than face the music. This is one of the heavily theatrical and stickily sentimental films produced in early 1934, a time which thereafter became known as "the guilty period" in Russian cinema of the 1930s.

d&w, Vladimir Petrov; ph, Vyacheslav Gardanov; m, Vladimir Shcherba-chov; set d, Nikolai Suvorov.

**Drama								(PR:A MPAA:NR)**

THUNDERSTORM					(1956) 81m Hemisphere/AA bw**

Carlos Thompson (Diego Martinez), Linda Christian (Maria Ramon), Charles Korvin (Pablo Gardia), Gary Thorne (Miguel Gardia), Tito Junco (Toro), Erica Vaal (Juana), Catherina Ferraz (Mrs. Martinez), Marco Davo (Padre Flores), Fleixes De Pomes (Domingo Ribas), Nestor M. Neana (Lalo), Carlos Diaz Mendoza (Pedro), Julia Caba Alba (Senora Hidalgo), Isabel De Pomes (Senora Alvarez), Conchita Bautista (Margo), Amalia Iglesias (Dolores), Manuel San Roman (Manuel Hidego).

Set in a small fishing town on the coast of Spain, THUNDERSTORM stars Thompson as a lonely fisherman who rescues the beautiful Christian from drowning in the sea. The fisherman soon falls in love with his find, but the village's mayor, Korvin, and his son, Thorne, are also quite taken with Christian's beauty and cause trouble for Thompson. Seeing that her presence will only bring disaster, Christian abandons the town and sets sail by herself. Wisecracking former actress Binnie Barnes, who produced this arty little number, can take credit for her support of an unusual subject, well handled by all involved.

p, Binnie Barnes; d, John Guillermin; w, Daniel Mainwaring (based on a story by George St. George); ph, Manuel Berenguer; m, Paul Misraki; ed, Lee Doig; md, Misraki.

**Drama								(PR:A MPAA:NR)**

THURSDAY'S CHILD				(1943, Brit.) 81m ABF/Pathe bw**

Sally Ann Howes (Fennis Wilson), Wilfrid Lawson (Frank Wilson), Kathleen O'Regan (Ellen Wilson), Eileen Bennett (Phoebe Wilson), Stewart Granger (David Penley), Marianne Davis (Gloria Dewey), Gerhardt Kempinski (Rudi Kaufmann), Felix Aylmer (Mr. Keith), Margaret Yarde (Mrs. Chard), Vera Bogetti (Mme. Felicia), Percy Walsh (Charles Lennox), Ronald Shiner (Joe), Pat Aherne (Lance Sheridan), Michael Allen, Margaret Drummond, Antony Holles, Terry Randall.

Howes is a little girl who becomes a child star in the movies, only to have her family crumble under the strain. Her mother begins paying so much attention to her little star that the older sister leaves home and the father soon follows her. After Howes earns a bundle of money for one part, she drops out of show business and uses the money to finance a first-class education at a private boarding school. A fair script wasted by lackluster direction and performances.

p, John Argyle; d, Rodney Ackland; w, Donald Macardle, Ackland (based on the novel by Macardle); ph, Desmond Dickinson.

**Drama								(PR:A MPAA:NR)**

**THY NEIGHBOR'S WIFE*½				(1953) 77m FOX bw**

Cleo Moore, Hugo Haas, Ken Carlton, Kathleen Hughes, Tony Jochim, Tom Fadden, Darr Smith, Oscar O'Shea, Tom Wilson, Roy Engels, Bob Knapp, Joe Duval, Henry Corden.

Another somber romantic epic from one of the only true low-budget "auteurs," producer-director-writer-star Hugo Haas. This time Haas tackles a period piece set in a 19th Century Moravian village. He plays an aging and ruthless judge whose beautiful wife, Moore, has a fling with her former beau, Carlton. Soon Carlton's uncle turns up murdered and Haas is quick to suspect Carlton as the killer. Unfortunately, the village idiot confesses to the murder before Carlton can be convicted. Haas kills the man so that the lover will hang. Too bad for Haas that his wife has seen him kill the real murderer, and he is forced to kill her as well. In the end, Haas is the one who goes to the gallows. A less than stunning drama.

p,d&w, Hugo Haas (based on a novelette "The Peasant Judge" by Oskar Jellinek); ph, Paul Ivano; ed, Merrill White, Albert Shaff; md, Adolph Heller; art d, Martin Obzina.

**Drama								(PR:C MPAA:NR)**

TIARA TAHITI**½ (1962, Brit.) 100m Rank/Zenith c

James Mason (*Capt. Brett Almsley*), John Mills (*Lt. Col. Clifford Southey*), Claude Dauphin (*Henri Farengue*), Herbert Lom (*Chong Sing*), Rosenda Monteros (*Belle Annie*), Jacques Marin (*Marcel Desmoulins, French Policeman*), Libby Morris (*Adele Franklin*), Madge Ryan (*Millie Brooks*), Gary Cockrell (*Joey*), Peter Barkworth (*Lt. David Harper*), Roy Kinnear (*Capt. Tom Enderby*).

Young WW II officer Mason is shocked when he learns that the commanding officer of his new unit is none other than Mills, an arrogant, self-important man who used to work as a clerk in Mason's father's firm. Mills goes to great lengths to hide this news from his men, and Mason, using his commander's paranoia against him, begins to erode Mills' authority with the regiment. Learning that Mason is dealing in black market goods, Mills has his rival arrested and court-martialed. Mason flees to Tahiti where he settles down with beautiful native girl Monteros. Years later, after the war ends, Mills arrives in Tahiti a wealthy businessman scouting locations for a tourist hotel he plans to build. When the two meet, a fight ensues and Mills knocks out Mason. Local villain Lom, who wants Monteros for himself, attempts to have Mason killed and tries to frame Mills, but the plan fails and Mason is then hospitalized. Mills is arrested for attempted murder, but Mason learns the truth and nobly clears Mills on the condition that he leave Tahiti, never to return. Deft, taut, and polished.

p, Ivan Foxwell; d, William T. Kotcheff; w, Geoffrey Cotterell, Foxwell, Mordecai Richler (based on the novel by Cotterell); ph, Otto Heller (Eastmancolor); m, Philip Green; ed, Anthony Gibbs; art d, Alex Vetchinsky; set d, Arthur Taksen; cos, Yvonne Caffin; m/l, "Tiara Tahiti," Green, Norman Newell (sung by Danny Street); makeup, Ernest Gasser.

Drama Cas. (PR:A MPAA:NR)

...TICK...TICK...TICK...**½ (1970) 96m MGM c

Jim Brown (*Jimmy Price*), George Kennedy (*John Little*), Fredric March (*Mayor Jeff Parks*), Lynn Carlin (*Julia Little*), Don Stroud (*Bengy Springer*), Janet MacLaughlin (*Mary Price*), Richard Elkins (*Bradford Wilkes*), Clifton James (*D.J. Rankin*), Bob Random (*John Braddock*), Mills Watson (*Deputy Joe Warren*), Bernie Casey (*George Harley*), Anthony James (*H.C. Tolbert*), Dub Taylor (*Junior*), Ernest Anderson (*Homer*), Karl Swanson (*Braddock, Sr.*), Barry Cahill (*Bob Braddock*), Anne Whitfield (*Mrs. Dawes*), Bill Walker (*John Sawyer*), Dan Frazer (*Ira Jackson*), Leonard O. Smith (*Fred Price*), Renny Roker (*Shoeshine Boy*), Roy E. Glenn, Sr (*The Drunk*), George Cisar (*Barber*), Paulene Myers (*Mrs. Harley*), Dino Washington (*Randy Harley*), Calvin Brown (*Harrison Harley*), Beverly Taylor (*Sara Jean*).

March, even at age 72, shines above the rest of the cast as the mayor of a small southern town in this weak racial drama. Kennedy plays the tough-but-honorable sheriff who retires, opening his office for an election. The newly elected sheriff happens to be a black man, Brown, and both men anticipate the transfer of power to be a shaky one. Though Kennedy is no bleeding-heart liberal, he swears to assist Brown in handling the wary locals if need be. Brown shows his even-handedness by arresting both black and whites if they have broken the law. The town stays in a very uneasy holding pattern until Brown makes the mistake of arresting a young white man from another town for killing a small child in a hit-and-run accident. The jailed boy's father, a powerful man from the next county, organizes a white mob to get his son out of jail by force. With the help of March and Kennedy, Brown is able to mobilize the townsfolk and turn back the hostile whites. While the filmmakers' hearts are in the right place, the film has the feel of a bandwagon effort designed to capitalize on the success of films like GUESS WHO'S COMING TO DINNER? and IN THE HEAT OF THE NIGHT. Thanks to March, the picture carries a certain class that would otherwise be missing.

p, Ralph Nelson, James Lee Barrett; d, Nelson; w, Barrett; ph, Loyal Griggs (Panavision, Metrocolor); m, Jerry Styner; ed, Alex Beaton; md, Mike Curb; art d, George W. Davis, William Glasgow; set d, Robert R. Benton, Don Greenwood, Jr.; m/l, "Set Yourself Free," Willis Hoover, "All That Keeps Ya Goin'," "Walk Unashamed," "What Does It Take," Jim Glaser, "Woman Woman," Glaser, Jimmy Payne, "Gentle on My Mind," "Why Do You Do Me Like You Do?" John Hartford, "California Girl and the Tennessee Square," Jack Clement, "Where Has All the Love Gone?" Glaser, "Home Is Where the Hurt Is," Arthur Ownes Owens (all sung by Tompall and the Glaser Brothers).

Drama (PR:A MPAA:G)

TICKET OF LEAVE* (1936, Brit.) 69m British & Dominions/PAR bw

Dorothy Boyd (*Lillian Walters*), John Clements (*Lucky Fisher*), George Merritt (*Inspector Black*), Max Kirby (*Goodman*), Wally Patch (*Sgt. Knott*), Enid Lindsay (*Edith Groves*), Neil More (*Sir Richard Groves*), Molly Hamley-Clifford (*Old Rose*).

Clements is a professional burglar who is caught one night by Boyd as he is pilfering her apartment. She turns out to be a thief too, and the pair team up to steal a necklace. The heist comes off, but the two find themselves in love and decide to go straight and return the necklace. This proves a much more difficult escapade. Lightweight crime comedy of little interest.

p, Anthony Havelock-Allen; d, Michael Hankinson; w, Margaret McDonell (based on a story by Hankinson, Vera Allinson); ph, Francis Carver.

Crime (PR:A MPAA:NR)

TICKET OF LEAVE MAN, THE* (1937, Brit.) 71m George King/MGM bw

Tod Slaughter (*Tiger Dalton*), Marjorie Taylor (*May Edwards*), John Warwick (*Bob Brierly*), Robert Adair (*Hawkshaw*), Frank Cochran (*Melter Moss*), Peter Gawthorne (*Joshua Gibson*), Jenny Lynn (*Mrs. Willoughby*), Arthur Payne (*Sam Willoughby*), Norman Pierce.

Slaughter stars in another of the lurid melodramas that were his specialty, here playing the head of an organization allegedly intended to help ex-convicts return to the straight and narrow, but actually a front for organizing them into a criminal syndicate. One former prisoner who tries to go straight gets a job in a bank but is blackmailed by Slaughter into robbing the safe. His girl friend gets word to the police and a chase across a graveyard comes to an abrupt end when Slaughter falls into an open grave and succumbs to a broken neck. Not very good in any objective sense, but good fun for those who savor trash.

p&d, George King; w, H. F. Maltby, A. R. Rawlinson (based on a play by Tom Taylor).

Crime Cas. (PR:A MPAA:NR)

TICKET TO CRIME*½ (1934) 67m Beacon bw

Ralph Graves (*Clay Holt*), Lois Wilson (*Mrs. Purdy*), Lola Lane (*Peggy Cummings*), James Burke (*Detective Lt. McGinnis*), Charles Ray (*Courtney Mallory*), Edward Earle (*Mr. Purdy*), Hy Hoover (*Jerry Papolas*), John Elliott (*Mr. Davidson*).

Routine murder mystery starring Graves as an ex-cop turned private eye who runs into old ally Burke, a local police detective, while investigating a murder which saw the theft of a string of pearls and $50,000 in cash. Some friendly competitive banter develops between the investigators while they set about solving the mystery.

p, Max Alexander; d, Lewis D. Collins; w, Jack Neville, Charles A. Logue (based on a story by Carroll John Daly); ph, Gilbert Warrenton.

Mystery (PR:A MPAA:NR)

TICKET TO HEAVEN*** (1981) 107m UA c

Nick Mancuso (*David*), Saul Rubinek (*Larry*), Meg Foster (*Ingrid*), Kim Cattrall (*Ruthie*), R.H. Thompson (*Linc Strunk*), Jennifer Dale (*Lisa*), Guy Bond (*Eric*), Dixie Seatle (*Sarah*), Paul Soles (*Morley*), Harvey Atkin (*Mr. Stone*), Robert Joy (*Patrick*), Stephen Markle (*Karl*), Timothy Weber (*Greg*), Patrick Brymer (*Dr. Dryer*), Marcia Diamond (*Esther*), Michael Zelnicker (*Danny*), Denise Naples (*Bonnie*), Angelo Rizacos (*Paul*), Cindy Girling (*Buffy*), Gina Dick (*Sandy*), Christopher Britton (*Simon*), Margot Dionne, Claire Pimpare, Lynne Kolber, Lyn Harvey, Josh Freed (*Sharing Group*), Candace O'Connor (*Ginny*), Michael Wincott (*Gerry*), Doris Petrie (*Mrs. Foster*), David Main (*Businessman*), Les Rubie (*Short Order Cook*), Sandra Gies (*Airport Bookseller*), Susan Hannon (*Nanny at Mansion*), Marie Lynn Hammond (*Singer at Mansion*), Paul Booth, Charlie Gray, Brian Leonard, Ron Nigrini, Craig Stephens, Grant Slater (*Musicians*).

Fascinating, well-acted examination of the power of religious cults and the methods they employ to attract new members. Mancuso is outstanding as the vulnerable youth who seeks solace and comfort in a cult after having a messy breakup with his girl friend. The film details Mancuso's conversion (i.e., brainwashing) to the cult's beliefs and his parents' efforts to locate him. When he is found he is taken away from the influence of the cult members, but it is then a long and painful process to deprogram Mancuso and bring him back to normalcy.

p, Vivienne Leebosh; d, Ralph L. Thomas; w, Thomas, Anne Cameron (based on the book *Moonwebs* by Josh Freed); ph, Richard Leiterman; m, Micky Erbe, Maribeth Solomon; ed, Ron Wisman; prod d, Susan Longmire; art d, Jill Scott; cos, Lynda Kemp.

Drama Cas. (PR:C MPAA:PG)

TICKET TO PARADISE*½ (1936) 70m REP bw

Roger Pryor (*Terry Dodd*), Wendy Barrie (*Jane Forbes*), Claude Gillingwater (*Mr. Forbes*), Andrew Tombes (*Nirney*), Luis Alberni (*Dr. Munson*), E.E. Clive (*Barkins, Butler*), John Sheehan (*Taxi Driver*), Theodore Von Eltz (*Small*), Russell Hicks (*Colton*), Earle Hodgins (*Cab Starter*), Grace Hale (*Minnie Dawson*), Harry Woods (*Dawson*), Charles Lane (*Shyster*), Herbert Rawlinson (*Townsend*), Gavin Gordon (*Tony*), Harry Harvey (*Spotter*), Duke Yorke (*Milkman*), Eric Mayne (*Dr. Eckstrom*), Bud Jamison (*Taxi Dispatcher*), Harrison Greene (*Merry-Go-Round Man*), Stanley Fields (*Kelly*), Wallace Gregory (*Intern*), Fern Emmett, Eleanor Huntley (*Nurses*).

Amnesia victim Pryor runs off with the lovely young Barrie and the girl's father hires detective Tombes to track down the runaways. Throw evil gangster nightclub owner Fields into the fray and the result is a less-than-fresh screwball comedy that was promptly forgotten.

p, Nat Levine; d, Aubrey Scotto; w, Jack Natteford, Nathaniel West, Ray Harris (based on a story by David Silverstein); ph, Ernest Miller; ed, Albert C. Clark; md, Harry Grey.

Comedy   **(PR:A MPAA:NR)**

TICKET TO PARADISE*   (1961, Brit.) 61m Bayford/Eros bw

Emrys Jones (*Jack Watson*), Patricia Dainton (*Mary Rillston*), Vanda Hudson (*Gina*), Denis Shaw (*Giuseppe*), Claire Gordon (*Sybil*), Maureen Davis (*Betty*), Raymond Rollett (*Higginbottom*).

Each thinking the other outrageously rich, travel agent Jones and tourist Dainton fall in love in Italy, then find out the truth about each other. Dumb romance of little value except as an excellent example of how to make a film nobody will care about.

p, Charles A. Leeds, Francis Searle; d, Searle; w, Brock Williams (based on a story by Max Kester).

Romance   **(PR:A MPAA:NR)**

TICKET TO TOMAHAWK**½   (1950) 90m FOX c

Dan Dailey (*Johnny Behind-the-Deuces*), Anne Baxter (*Kit Dodge, Jr.*), Rory Calhoun (*Dakota, Gunman*), Walter Brennan (*Terence Sweeney, Engineer*), Charles Kemper (*Chuckity, Deputy*), Connie Gilchrist (*Mme. Adelaide*), Arthur Hunnicutt (*Sad Eyes*), Will Wright (*Dodge, U. S. Marshal*), Chief Yowlachie (*Pawnee*), Victor Sen Yung (*Long Time, Laundryman*), Mauritz Hugo (*Dawson*), Raymond Greenleaf (*Mayor*), Harry Carter (*Charley*), Harry Seymour (*Velvet Fingers*), Robert Adler (*Bat*), Lee MacGregor (*Gilo*), Raymond Bond (*Station Master*), Charlie Stevens (*Trancos*), Chief Thundercloud (*Crooked Knife*), Marion Marshall (*Annie*), Joyce MacKenzie (*Ruby*), Marilyn Monroe (*Clara*), Barbara Smith (*Julie*), Jack Elam (*Fargo*), Paul Harvey (*Mr. Bishop*), John War Eagle (*Lone Eagle*), Shooting Star (*Crazy Dog*), Herbert Heywood (*Old Timer*), William Self (*Telegrapher*), Guy Wilkerson (*Dr. Brink*), Edward Clark (*Jet*), Olin Howlin (*Conductor*).

Lighthearted western comedy starring Calhoun as a gunslinger hired by stagecoach owner Hugo to halt the oncoming railroad by any means available because his business will be ruined if the train makes it to Colorado. The clever Calhoun uses everything from Indians, holdup men, and dance hall girls (a young Marilyn Monroe among them) to thwart the iron horse, but the train workers prove braver than Calhoun expected. Led by female sharpshooter Baxter, with help from ambitious salesman Dailey, the train people eventually defeat the bad guys and see their efforts pay off when the railroad company establishes a franchise in Tomahawk. Fast, lively, with a good cast and a lush Technicolor production. Monroe's part in her fourth film was minor but extremely decorative, the review in Variety calling her group of dance hall girls "a comely quartet of terpers." Along with Dailey, they performed a number called "Oh, What a Forward Young Man You Are" (Ken Darby, John Read). "A Ticket to Tomahawk" was another tune in the movie.

p, Robert Bassler; d, Richard Sale; w, Mary Loos, Sale; ph, Harry Jackson (Technicolor); m, Cyril J. Mockridge; ed, Harmon Jones; md, Lionel Newman; art d, Lyle Wheeler, George W. Davis.

Western/Comedy   **Cas.**   **(PR:A MPAA:NR)**

TICKLE ME**   (1965) 90m AA c

Elvis Presley (*Lonnie Beale*), Julie Adams (*Vera Radford*), Jocelyn Lane (*Pam Merritt*), Jack Mullaney (*Stanley Potter*), Merry Anders (*Estelle Penfield*), Bill Williams (*Deputy Sturdivant*), Edward Faulkner (*Brad Bentley*), Connie Gilchrist (*Hilda*), Barbara Werle (*Barbara*), John Dennis (*Adolph the Chef*), Grady Sutton (*Mr. Dabney*), Allison Hayes (*Mabel*), Inez Pedroza (*Ophelia*), Lilyan Chauvin (*Ronnie*), Angela Greene (*Donna*), Louie Elias (*Jerry the Groom*), Robert Hoy (*Henry the Gardener*), Dorothy Konrad (*Mrs. Dabney*), Eve Bruce (*Pat*), Francine York (*Mildred*), Laurie Burton (*Janet*), Linda Rogers (*Clair Kinnamon*), Ann Morell (*Sibyl*), Jean Ingram (*Evelyn*), Jackie Russell (*Gloria*), Peggy Ward (*Dot*), Dorian Brown (*Polly*).

Just another lackluster Elvis movie, but this time written by screenwriters Ullman and Bernds who wrote many of the Three Stooges features (this alone was enough to doom this Elvis effort). Presley plays a crooning rodeo rider who finds himself in an exclusive female dude ranch and beauty spa populated with gorgeous fashion model-types. Naturally, Elvis wants to stick around for a while so he fast-talks owner-operator Adams into hiring him as a handyman, much to the dismay of swimming instructor Faulkner, who doesn't dig the competition. When one of the guests, the lovely Lane, learns that her grandfather has left her the instructions to a stash of gold located in the ghost town of Silverado, several attempts to kidnap her are made. Lane, of course, falls in love with Elvis, but when she sees him kissing Adams she dumps him and refuses to listen to his protestations of innocence. Fed up, Elvis returns to the rodeo circuit and tries to forget the whole thing. Unfortunately he is dragged back into the fray when Lane ventures into Silverado in search of the gold and winds up in trouble. Eventually, Elvis exposes the local sheriff and most of the male employees at the dude ranch as crooks who are after Lane's treasure, so Elvis captures them, finds the

gold, and marries Lane. Songs include "(It's a) Long, Lonely Highway," "Night Rider" (Doc Pomus, Mort Shuman) "It Feels So Right" (Ben Weisman, Fred Wise), "Dirty, Dirty Feeling" (Jerry Lieber, Mike Stoller), "(Such an) Easy Question" (Otis Blackwell, Winfield Scott), "Put the Blame on Me" (Norman Blagman, Kathleen G. Twomey, Wise), "I'm Yours" (Don Robertson, Hal Blair), "I Feel that I've Known You Forever" (Pomus, Alan Jeffreys), "Slowly but Surely" (Sid Wayne, Weisman).

p, Ben Schwalb; d, Norman Taurog; w, Elwood Ullman, Edward Bernds; ph, Loyal Griggs (Panavision, DeLuxe Color); ed, Archie Marshek; md, Walter Scharf; art d, Hal Pereira, Arthur Lonergan; set d, Arthur Krams; cos, Leah Rhodes; ch, David Winters; makeup, Frank Westmore.

Musical   **Cas.**   **(PR:A MPAA:NR)**

TICKLED PINK   (SEE: MAGIC SPECTACLES, 1961)

TICKLISH AFFAIR, A**   (1963) 88m Euterpe/MGM c

Shirley Jones (*Amy Martin*), Gig Young (*Comdr. Key Weedon*), Red Buttons (*Flight Officer Simon Shelley*), Carolyn Jones (*Tandy Martin*), Edgar Buchanan (*Gramps Martin*), Eddie Applegate (*Yeoman Corker Bell*), Edward Platt (*Capt. Haven Hitchcock*), Billy Mumy (*Alex Martin*), Bryan Russell (*Luke Martin*), Robert Foulk (*Policeman*), Milton Frome (*Fireman*), Peter Robbins (*Grover Martin*).

Weak romantic comedy starring Young as a dashing Navy commander who spots an SOS coming from the shore off San Diego Bay and goes to investigate. What he finds is rowdy youngster Robbins, who was given a signal light to play with by his uncle, Buttons, a commercial airplane pilot. This chance meeting throws Young and Robbins' widowed mother, Jones, into a romance. While Jones is quite taken with Young, she declines his offers of marriage because she wants her children (there are two more in addition to Robbins) to have a normal home life–not a Navy brat's. The boys, like Young, are disappointed, so when their uncle arrives with some weather balloons to play with, Robbins sails himself across San Diego Bay knowing that Young will come to his rescue. Young does just that, and, seeing his devotion to the boys, and they to him, Jones agrees to marry the sailor.

p, Joe Pasternak; d, George Sidney; w, Ruth Brooks Flippen (based on the story "Moon Walk" by Barbara Luther); ph, Milton Krasner (Panavision, Metrocolor); m, George Stoll; ed, John McSweeney, Jr.; art d, George W. Davis, Edward Carfagno; set d, Henry Grace, Keogh Gleason; spec eff, J. McMillan Johnson; m/l, "Love Is a Ticklish Affair," Stoll, Robert Van Eps, Harold Adamson (sung by Jack Jones).

Romance/Comedy   **(PR:A MPAA:NR)**

TI-CUL TOUGAS**   (1977, Can.) 83m ACPAV/Nu-Image c

Claude Maher (*Ti-Cul Tougas*), Micheline Lanctot (*Odette*), Gilbert Sicotte (*Martin*), Suzanne Garceau (*Gilberte*).

Dull character study starring Maher as a pathetic thief who steals $5,000 from a Canadian marching band and flees across the border into the U.S. accompanied by his giddy girl friend, Lanctot, and a rather characterless couple, Sicotte and Garceau. Some bleak Canadian scenery is livelier than any of the performers. (In French; English subtitles.)

d&w, Jean-Guy Noel; ph, Francois Beachemin; m, Georges Langford; ed, Marthe de la Chevrotiere; art d, Fernand Durand; cos, Mickie Hamilton.

Drama   **(PR:C MPAA:NR)**

TIDAL WAVE, 1939   (SEE: S.O.S. TIDAL WAVE, 1939)

TIDAL WAVE*   (1975, U.S./Jap.) 81m Toho/New World c (NIPPON CHIUBOTSU; AKA: THE SUBMERSION OF JAPAN; JAPAN SINKS)

Lorne Greene (*Warren Richards*), Keiji Kobayashi (*Dr. Tanaka Tadokoro*), Rhonda Leigh Hopkins (*Fran*), Hiroshi Fujioka (*Toshio Onoda*), Tetsuro Tamba (*Prime Minister Yamato*), Ayumi Ishida (*Reiko*), Shogo Shimada (*Prince Watari*), John Fujioka (*Narita*), Andrew Hughs (*Australian Prime Minister*), Nobuo Nakamura (*Australian Ambassador*), Tadao Nakamura, Yusuke Takita, Isao Natsuyagi, Hideaki Nitani, Marvin Miller, Susan Sennett, Ralph James, Phil Roth, Cliff Pellow, Joseph J. Dante.

Shot in Japan as THE SUBMERSION OF JAPAN in 1973 and released as a two-and-a-half hour disaster epic, the film showed scientists discovering that the island was sinking and would be destroyed in less than two years. The rest of the movie details the elaborate evacuation plans and soap opera-like subplots involving various characters. The film was very popular in Japan at the time, and, knowing how to ruin a good thing when he sees it, New World chief Roger Corman bought the American distribution rights, shaved off over an hour of the running time, inserted ludicrous new footage featuring Lorne Greene, and released the resulting dubbed-in mess in drive-ins across the country.

p, Tomoyuki Tanaka; d, Shiro Moritani, Andrew Meyer; w, Shinobu Hashimoto (based on a story by Sakyo Komatsu); ph, Hiroshi Murai (Panavision, Metrocolor), Daisaka Kimura, Eric Saarinen; m, Masaru Sato;

art d, Yoshiro Muraki; English dialog, Andrew Meyer.

Drama   **Cas.**   **(PR:A-C   MPAA:PG)**

TIERRA BRUTAL   (SEE: SAVAGE GUNS, THE, 1961, U.S./Span.)

TIFFANY JONES**   (1976) 90m Cineworld c

Anouska Hempel (*Tiffany Jones*), Ray Brooks, Eric Pohlmann, Martin
Benson, Susan Sneers.

Silly exploitation film has Hempel a super-agent trying to save her life and
her secrets from hordes of villains who would like to take both. For fans of
bad movies only.

p&d, Pete Walker; w, Alfred Shaughnessy; m, Cyril Ornadel.

Spy Drama   **Cas.**   **(PR:O   MPAA:R)**

TIGER AMONG US, THE   (SEE: 13 WEST STREET, 1962)

TIGER AND THE FLAME, THE**½   (1955, India) 97m UA c

Mehtab (*Rani Lakshmibal*), Sohrab Modi (*Rajguru*), Mubarak (*Raja
Gangadhar Rao*), Ulhas (*Ghulam Ghaus Khan*), Ramsingh (*Sadashiv Rao*),
Sapru (*Gen. Sir Hugh Rose*), Baby Shika (*Manu*), Anil Kishore (*Lt. Henry
Dowker*), Gloria Gasper (*Doris Dowker*), Kamalakant (*Moropant*), Michael
Shea (*Maj. Ellis*), Marconi (*Col. Sleeman*), Nayampalli (*Panditji*), Shakila
(*Kashi*).

The first Indian film shot entirely in Technicolor stars Mehtab as a young
queen who was destined at the age of nine to someday organize and lead the
overthrow of the British. When she is old enough, Mehtab weds an elderly
Raja and is sent to school to learn military tactics. Finally the time is right
and Mehtab leads a bloody battle against the British imperialists, but in the
end, she is defeated and killed. The cameraman, Ernest Haller, is an
American who was quite active in the Indian cinema.

p&d, Sohrab M. Modi; w, Geza Herczeg, Pandit Sudershan, Adi F. Keeka
(based on a story and research by Pandit S.R. Dube); ph, Ernest Haller
(Technicolor); m, Vasant Desai; ed, P. Bhalchander, D. Shridhankar; cos,
Kanu Desai; m/l, Pandit Radheshyam; ch, Mme. Simkie, Vinod Chopra.

Drama   **(PR:A-C   MPAA:NR)**

TIGER AND THE PUSSYCAT, THE**½   (1967, U.S., Ital.) 105m
                                                  Fair-EM/EM c (IL TIGRE)

Vittorio Gassman (*Francesco Vincenzini*), Ann-Margret (*Carolina*), Eleanor
Parker (*Esperia*), Caterina Boratto (*Delia*), Eleonora Brown (*Luisella*),
Antonella Steni (*Pinella*), Fiorenzo Fiorentini (*Tazio*), Giambattista Salerno
(*Luca*), Jacques Herlin (*Monsignor*), Luigi Vannucchi (*Company President*),
Ivan Scratuglia, Nino Segurini, Egidio Casolari.

Aging businessman Gassman seeks to revitalize his life and he soon falls into
an affair with flirtatious American art student Ann-Margret, who is
studying in Rome. Although Ann-Margret has already driven Gassman's
son to the brink of suicide, the middleaged man becomes obsessed with her
beauty, energy, and youth. Gassman destroys his reputation because of the
affair and he foolishly agrees to leave his wife and go to Paris with the girl.
He writes a farewell note to his wife and goes to the train station, but at the
last minute realizes the stupidity of the situation and returns to his wife,
who is forgiving enough to take him back. (In English.)

p, Mario Cecchi Gori; d, Dino Risi; w, Agenore Incrocci, Furio Scarpelli
(based on a story by Incrocci, Scarpelli, Risi); ph, Sandro D'Eva (Eastmancol-
or); m, Fred Bongusto; ed, Marcello Malvestiti; art d, Luciano Ricceri; set
d&cos, Ezio Altieri; English dialog, John Douglas.

Comedy/Drama   **(PR:A-C   MPAA:NR)**

TIGER BAY*   (1933, Brit.) 70m Wyndham/ABF bw

Anna May Wong (*Lui Chang*), Henry Victor (*Olaf*), Rene Ray (*Letty*),
Lawrence Grossmith (*Whistling Rufus*), Victor Garland (*Michael*), Ben
Soutten (*Stumpy*), Margaret Yarde (*Fay*), Wally Patch (*Wally*), Ernest Jay
(*Alf*), Brian Buchel (*Tony*).

Wong is a Chinese woman with an English girl as a ward operating a
restaurant in Wales. A Swedish criminal mastermind kidnaps the girl and
Wong, with the help of an Englishman, finds and kills the Swede before
turning the gun on herself. A serious essay in foreign relations it ain't.

p, Bray Wyndham; d, J. Elder Wills; w, John Quin (based on a story by Wills,
Eric Ansell); ph, Robert Martin.

Crime   **(PR:A   MPAA:NR)**

TIGER BAY*½   (1959, Brit.) 105m Independent
                                              Artists/RANK-Continental bw

John Mills (*Supt. Graham*), Horst Buchholz (*Korchinsky*), Hayley Mills
(*Gillie*), Yvonne Mitchell (*Anya*), Megs Jenkins (*Mrs. Phillips*), Anthony
Dawson (*Barclay*), George Selway (*Detective Sgt. Harvey*), Shari (*Christine*),

George Pastell (*Poloma Captain*), Marne Maitland (*Dr. Das*), Paul Stassino
(*1st Officer*), Meredith Edwards (*Police Constable George Williams*), Ma-
rianne Stone (*Mrs. Williams*), Rachel Thomas (*Mrs. Parry*), Brian Hammond
(*Dai Parry*), Kenneth Griffith (*Choirmaster*), E. Eynon Evans (*Mr. Morgan*),
Christopher Rhodes (*Inspector Bridges*), Edward Cast (*Detective Constable
Thomas*), David Davies (*Desk Sergeant*).

When Buchholz, a Polish sailor, takes leave from his ship docked in Cardiff
he returns to visit his girl friend Mitchell, who lives in the dock section of
town known as Tiger Bay. On his arrival he is outraged to find that Mitchell
is now living with another man. The angered seaman shoots Mitchell with
a handgun, killing his one-time mistress. The noise of their argument has
attracted the attention of 12-year-old Hayley Mills, a lonely tomboy who
witnesses the murder through a mail slot. She gets hold of the murder
weapon, convinced that having a gun will make her more popular with her
peers when they play cowboys and Indians. When police catch up to her the
precocious youngster is confronted by a detective, played by Hayley's
reallife father John Mills. However, she only frustrates him by telling him
a convincing string of lies. Eventually Buchholz catches up with Hayley in
a church attic and kidnaps her, hoping to keep her quiet until he can leave
the country. The two build up a surprisingly close relationship while in
hiding and Hayley offers to help Buchholz make his escape. After he leaves
Hayley is once more under the eye of John Mills, who takes her aboard a
Venezuelan ship with which Buchholz has signed up. John hopes to catch
the killer before he leaves British territorial waters, but Hayley will not go
against her friend and refuses to identify him. Buchholz appears to be home
free, but when Hayley falls off the ship, the Polish seaman dives in the water
to save his friend. In doing so he reveals himself and is arrested for
Mitchell's murder. The film operates on several levels, creating a thriller of
varying tensions tinged with a warm, humanistic relationship as well. At the
very center is the friendship between Hayley Mills and Buchholz. His
interest in the girl grows from a desperate need to keep his crime a secret
into genuine affection. Likewise, Hayley sees this first as a chance to be
popular with playmates, then as an exciting adventure, before she too
develops a shared feeling with the sailor. As the nature of their relationship
changes, so does the tenseness between the two, developed naturally and
changing audiences' expectations with subtlety and poignancy. This marked
Hayley's film debut; she gives quite a performance for an actress of any age.
Her face registers a gamut of emotions, never once letting an unnatural
feeling show. Critics and studios alike were highly impressed with her
ability and Hayley was awarded a special prize at the 1959 Berlin Film
Festival. It was also on the basis of this film that she was signed up by the
Walt Disney studios, for whom she would make the beloved POLLYANNA
the following year. Thompson's direction is exacting, drawing out the
humanistic qualities of the story while never forgetting that this is also a
crime film, a genre that itself carries a certain set of expectations. His ability
to combine the thriller elements with the story of a young girl's lonely search
for attention and love is a highly accomplished effort, an intelligent vision
marked with wisdom and insight.

p, John Hawkesworth; d, J. Lee Thompson; w, Hawkesworth, Shelley Smith
(based on the novel *Rodolphe et le Revolver* by Noel Calef); ph, Eric Cross;
m, Laurie Johnson; ed, Sidney Hayers; art d, Edward Carrick.

Crime/Drama   **Cas.**   **(PR:A   MPAA:NR)**

TIGER BY THE TAIL, 1958   (SEE: CROSSUP, 1958)

TIGER BY THE TAIL**   (1970) 99m United/COM c

Christopher George (*Steve Michaelis*), Tippi Hedren (*Rita Armstrong*),
Dean Jagger (*Top Polk*), John Dehner (*Sheriff Chancey Jones*), Charo
(*Darlita*), Lloyd Bochner (*Del Ware*), Glenda Farrell (*Sarah Harvey*), Alan
Hale, [Jr.] (*Billy Jack Whitehorn*), Skip Homeier (*Deputy Sheriff Laswell*),
R.G. Armstrong (*Ben Holmes*), Dennis Patrick (*Frank Michaelis*), Martin
Ashe (*Jimmy-San Ricketts*), Frank Babich (*Reporter*), Marilyn Devin (*Julie
Foster*), Ray Martell (*Garcia*), Burt Mustin (*Tom Dugger*), Fernando Pereira
(*Mendoza*), Olga Velez (*Candita*), Della Young, Tricia Young (*Bikini Girls*),
The Mescalero Apache Horn Dancers, Meredith Neal and the Boot Heel
Boys.

Routine crime drama helped somewhat by a decent cast of character
players. Vietnam vet George returns home to find his brother, who was the
principal shareholder in a successful California racetrack, has been murdered by two Mexicans during a robbery. It appears to George that the
robbery was a coverup for the murder, which must have been ordered by
a rival shareholder. After a bit of digging, George forces a confession out of
shareholder Bochner, but Bochner soon turns up dead. Accompanied by old
flame Hedren, George reveals the sheriff, Dehner, to be behind the scheme
and kills him in a struggle for his gun. With all the shareholders eliminated,
George takes over control of the racetrack.

p, Francis D. Lyon; d, R.G. Springsteen; w, Charles A. Wallace; ph, Alan
Stensvold; m, Joe Greene; ed, Terry O. Morse; cos, Laura Rosser; m/l, "Let's
Drink, Friends," Xavier Cugat, Charo (sung by Charo).

Crime   **(PR:C   MPAA:GP)**

TIGER FANGS*½   (1943) 57m PRC bw

Frank Buck (*Himself*), June Duprez (*Linda MacCardle, Biologist*), Duncan Renaldo (*Peter Jeremy*), Howard Banks (*Tom Clayton*), J. Farrell MacDonald (*Geoffrey MacCardle*), J. Alex Havier (*Ali*), Arno Frey (*Dr. Lang*), Dan Seymour (*Henry Gratz*), Pedro Regas (*Takko*).

Real-life big game hunter Frank Buck hacks his way through dense underbrush once again in this WW II jungle drama, a little fatter than he was in JACARE–KILLER OF THE AMAZON the year before. When insidious Nazis travel to the rubber-rich areas of the Malay jungle to drug tigers into becoming crazed man-eaters to ruin rubber plant production by eating the workers, Buck, joined by MacDonald, Renaldo, and Duprez, enters the fray and defeats the scum. Highly unlikely, but exciting for the children.

p, Jack Schwartz; d, Sam Newfield; w, Arthur St. Claire; ph, Ira Morgan; ed, George M. Merrick; m, Lee Zahler; art d, Paul Palmentola.

Adventure/War   **Cas.**   **(PR:A   MPAA:NR)**

TIGER FLIGHT*   (1965, Jap.) 104m Toho c (KYOMO WARE OZORANI ARI)

Tatsuya Mihashi, Makoto Sato, Yosuke Natsuki, Takashi Inagaki.

Tedious Oriental offering has a squadron of hotshot pilots, whose sole interest is breaking the sound barrier, whipped into shape by a new commander. Not likely to be of interest to anyone.

p, Tomoyuki Tanaka; d, Kengo Furusawa.

Drama   **(PR:A   MPAA:NR)**

TIGER GIRL**   (1955, USSR) 98m Leninfilm/Artkino c

Lena Kasatkina (*Lena*), Peter Kadochnikov (*Fyodor Yermolayev*), Rolan Bykov (*Petya Mokin*), P. Sukhanov (*Circus Manager*), K. Sorokin (*Bookkeeper*), G. Bogdanova-Chestnokova (*His Wife*), N. Urgant (*His Daughter*), Boris Elder (*Telegin*), T. Peltser (*Lena's Mother*), A. Orlov (*Lena's Father*), S. Filippov (*Almazov*), V. Korolkevich (*Magician*).

Russian circus story starring Kasatkina as the darling of the big top, a tiger trainer, who is loved by both a sailor, who wants her to give up the circus, and a daredevil motorcyclist. In the end the motorcyclist wins her love. A flat visual style makes this only interesting for the romance, and that is too heavily sentimental.

d, Alexander Ivanovsky, N. Kosheverova; w, K. Mints, E. Pomeshchikov; ph, A. Dudko (Sovcolor); m, M. Weinberg.

Drama   **(PR:A   MPAA:NR)**

TIGER IN THE SKY   (SEE: MCCONNELL STORY, THE, 1955)

TIGER IN THE SMOKE**½   (1956, Brit.) 94m Rank bw

Donald Sinden (*Geoffrey Levett*), Muriel Pavlow (*Meg Elgin*), Tony Wright (*Jack Havoc*), Bernard Miles (*Tiddy Doll*), Alec Clunes (*Assistant Commissioner Oates*), Laurence Naismith (*Canon Avril*), Christopher Rhodes (*Chief Inspector Luke*), Charles Victor (*Will Talisman*), Thomas Heathcote (*Rolly Gripper*), Sam Kydd (*Tom Gripper*), Kenneth Griffith (*Crutches*), Gerald Harper (*Duds Morrison*), Wensley Pithey (*Detective Sgt. Pickett*), Stanley Rose (*Uncle*), Stratford Johns (*Police Constable Perkins*), Brian Wilde (*Trumps*), Hilda Barry (*Mrs. Talisman*), Beatrice Varley (*Mrs. Cash*).

British caper film stars Wright as a killer who escapes prison and travels to the French seashore where he has learned of a buried treasure somewhere in the mansion owned by widow Pavlow. Pavlow, who is about to marry Sinden to fill the void in her life, begins receiving photographs of her dead husband in the mail, implying that he is alive. Upset, she goes to the police with the pictures, and they tie the evidence to Wright. The cops return to the mansion just in time to watch Wright dash from the estate clutching the treasure, a priceless statue of the Madonna. Wright is cornered by the law and he learns that though the statue is valuable, it is of no use to a thief because he has nowhere to fence it.

p, Leslie Parkyn; d, Roy Baker; w, Anthony Pelissier (based on the novel by Margery Allingham); ph, Geoffrey Unsworth; m, Malcolm Arnold; ed, John D. Guthridge.

Crime   **(PR:A   MPAA:NR)**

TIGER MAKES OUT, THE**   (1967) 94m COL c

Eli Wallach (*Ben Harris*), Anne Jackson (*Gloria Fiske*), Bob Dishy (*Jerry Fiske*), John Harkins (*Leo*), Ruth White (*Mrs. Kelly, Landlady*), Roland Wood (*Mr. Kelly*), Rae Allen (*Beverly*), Sudie Bond (*Miss Lane*), David Burns (*Mr. Ratner*), Jack Fletcher (*Pawnbroker*), Bibi Osterwald (*Mrs. Ratner*), Charles Nelson Reilly (*Registrar*), Frances Sternhagen (*Lady on Bus*), Elizabeth Wilson (*Receptionist*), Kim August (*Toni Songbird*), Alice Beardsley (*Kentucky Neighbor*), Mariclare Costello (*Rosi*), David Doyle (*Housing Clerk*), Dustin Hoffman (*Hap*), Michele Kesten (*Waitress*), Remak Ramsey (*Housing Guard*), Sherman Raskin (*Red Schwartzkopf*), James Luisi (*Pete

Copolla*), John Ryan (*Toni's Escort*), Edgar Stehli (*Old Man*), Oren Stevens (*Policeman*).

Wacky but overlong adaptation of Murray Schisgal's one-act play "The Tiger," starring Wallach as a frustrated New York mailman who decides to strike out against the injustice in society. He goes on rampage, terrorizes his eccentric husband-and-wife landlords (who have been bilking him) and the city housing authority, and finally kidnaps a suburban housewife, Jackson, and holes up in the apartment that the husband and wife landlord pair give him to atone for their bilking him. Wallach gets a surprise when he learns that Jackson feels the same way he does about life, and the two strike up a close friendship. He releases Jackson but follows her to her home because he wants to be near her. Wallach climbs into her bedroom window, but is routed by her wife-baiting husband who gives chase. The tired Wallach returns to his apartment building where he is greeted by his landlords, who invite him in to eat fried chicken and watch television. Wallach figures that this is as good a solution to life's problems as any, so he joins them. A fitfully amusing comedy, also notable as one of Dustin Hoffman's first film performances, in which he was cast as one of a pair of beatnik lovers.

p, George Justin; d, Arthur Hiller; w, Murray Schisgal (based on a play by Schisgal); ph, Arthur J. Ornitz (Eastmancolor); m, Milton "Shorty" Rogers; ed, Robert C. Jones; prod d, Paul Sylbert; set d, John Godfrey; cos, Anthea Sylbert; m/l, "The Tiger Makes Out," Rogers, Diane Hilderbrand; makeup, Martin Bell.

Comedy   **(PR:A-C   MPAA:NR)**

TIGER MAN   (SEE: LADY AND THE MONSTER, THE, 1944)

TIGER OF BENGAL   (SEE: JOURNEY TO THE LOST CITY, 1960, Ger./Fr./Ital.)

TIGER OF ESCHNAPUR, THE   (SEE: JOURNEY TO THE LOST CITY, 1960, Ger./Fr./Ital.)

TIGER OF THE SEVEN SEAS**   (1964, Fr./Ital.) 90m Liber-Euro/EM c (LE TIGRE DES MERS; LA TIGRE DEI SETTE MARI)

Gianna Maria Canale (*Consuelo*), Anthony Steel (*William*), Maria Grazia Spina (*Anna da Cordoba*), Ernesto Calindri (*Inigo da Cordoba*), Andrea Aureli (*Laura*), Carlo Ninchi (*Robert*), John Kitzmiller (*Turpentine*), Carlo Pisacane, Pasquale De Filippo, Renato Izzo, Renato Giomini.

Italian pirate adventure starring dark beauty Canale as the rambunctious daughter of a retired pirate captain who takes over her father's command after defeating her lover, Steel, in a duel (he lets her win). A disgruntled pirate, Ninchi, murders Canale's father and frames Steel. Steel takes off and a vengeful Canale gives chase. She catches up to him, he tells her he is innocent, and vows to capture Ninchi himself, but Steel is captured by Ninchi's men and tortured. Canale comes to the rescue, kills Ninchi, and frees her lover. Dashing tale of a formidable and resolute woman. This was the sequel to QUEEN OF THE PIRATES.

p, Ottavio Poggi; d, Luigi Capuano; w, Arpad De Riso, Capuano, Poggi (based on a story by Nino Battiferri); ph, Alvaro Mancori (Totalscope, Eastmancolor); m, Carlo Rustichelli; ed, Renato Cinquini; art d, Ernesto Kromberg, Amedeo Mellone; cos, Giancarlo Bartolini Salimbeni.

Adventure   **(PR:A   MPAA:NR)**

TIGER ROSE**   (1930) 63m WB bw

Monte Blue (*Sgt. Devlin*), Lupe Velez (*Rose*), H.B. Warner (*Dr. Cusick*), Tully Marshall (*Hector McCollins*), Grant Withers (*Bruce*), Gaston Glass (*Pierre*), Bull Montana (*Joe*), Rin Tin Tin (*Scotty*), Slim Summerville (*Heine*), Louis Mercier (*Frenchie*), Gordon Magee (*Hainey*), Heinie Conklin (*Gus*), Leslie Sketchley (*Mounted Police Officer*), Fred MacMurray (*Rancher*), Cy Clegg, Chief Yowlache, Georgia Mazetti, Emil Chautard.

Remake of a 1923 romantic adventure melodrama starring Velez as a fiery lovely who drives both Northwest Mountie Blue and railway worker Withers wild. She picks Withers and he decides to take her away to the big city, but soon finds that all the men she drove nuts don't want her to leave. Withers kills a man while trying to escape, and Blue gives chase to the pair. The action winds up at the rapids as Withers and Velez barely escape with their lives. In the end, Blue nobly lets the lovers go. Rin-Tin-Tin runs around barking and wagging his tail.

d, George Fitzmaurice; w, Harvey Thew, Gordon Rigby, De Leon Anthony (based on the play by Willard Mack); ph, Tony Gaudio; ed, Thomas Pratt; m/l, "The Day You Fall in Love," Ned Washington, Herb Magidson, Michael Cleary.

Adventure   **(PR:A   MPAA:NR)**

TIGER SHARK***½   (1932) 80m FN-WB bw

Edward G. Robinson (*Mike Mascarena*), Richard Arlen (*Pipes Boley*), Zita Johann (*Quita Silva*), Leila Bennett (*Muggsey, Barber*), Vince Barnett (*Engineer*), J. Carrol Naish (*Tony*), William Ricciardi (*Manuel Silva*), Edwin

Maxwell (Doctor).

An excellent, overlooked story about a tuna fisherman that owed some of its heritage to Moby Dick and that JAWS may have been drawn from, whether they realized it or not. By his own admission, Robinson is the "best fisherman in the ocean." He is ugly, not lovable, and yet he thinks he is God's gift to women. Instead of moaning in his beer about the face God gave him, he celebrates it and even dares his lady barber, Bennett, to make him look good. On a tuna fishing trip, he saves the life of his best friend, Arlen, and loses his own hand to a huge shark in the process. One of his pals is also swallowed by the sea and it is this man's daughter, Johann, whom Robinson loves. Robinson's hand is replaced by a hook and he worries that he will be rejected by heaven because he will not go to his reward in the same "whole" body with which he began. Johann is so struck by her father's death that she almost commits suicide and is saved by Robinson. Although he is noisy and a blowhard, Robinson is also a kind man and Johann senses that, so when he asks to marry her, she accepts, more out of affection than love. Arlen is not so sure that Johann is the woman for Robinson and thinks that she might be after him for his money. The wedding takes place and when Robinson invites his pal to dance with his wife, he doesn't notice the hesitation of Arlen. They dance and it's clear to the audience, in a subtle fashion, that these two are sexually attracted to each other. Arlen loves his friend so much that he tries to stay away from Johann. The men go out to sea and Arlen becomes ill and has to be nursed back to health on land at Robinson's house. Arlen sees what's happening and wants to leave, but he is torn between his passion for Johann and his camaraderie with Robinson. Robinson catches the two in a clinch and his eyes narrow. He takes Arlen on his boat and wants revenge. He knocks Arlen out, puts him in a small open boat, and tosses a harpoon through the boat's bottom with the intention of sinking the vessel with the unconscious Arlen aboard. A huge shark comes his way and Robinson launches another harpoon at the beast, but the rope catches around his foot and he is pulled into the water by the harpooned shark. One of these sharks has already taken Robinson's hand, and now this man-eater takes the rest of him. Arlen is rescued and the bloodied Robinson dies in Johann's arms with Arlen looking on. The best part of this picture is that it never stoops to triangular steamy sex. All the scenes are subtle, the moods are muted, the moments are understated. Hawks did a fine directorial job and the movie holds up 50 years later. Proof is that in the spring of 1984, the Parisian movie show "Cine Club" featured this as their Friday Night Movie. TIGER SHARK never gets melodramatic and stays almost matter-of-fact as it presents the characters and their problems, intercutting the story with some superb tuna-fishing documentary footage that captures the life of the men who go down to the sea in ships. Robinson uses a Portuguese accent that never slips. Barnett is around for the little bit of comedy that leavens the drama.

p, Ray Griffiths; d, Howard Hawks; w, Wells Root (based on the story "Tuna" by Houston Branch); ph, Tony Gaudio; m, Leo F. Forbstein; ed, Thomas Pratt; art d, Jack Okey; cos, Orry-Kelly; marine supervision, Capt. Guy Silva.

Drama (PR:A-C MPAA:NR)

TIGER WALKS, A** (1964) 91m Disney/BV c

Brian Keith (Sheriff Pete Williams), Vera Miles (Dorothy Williams), Pamela Franklin (Julie Williams), Sabu (Ram Singh), Kevin Corcoran (Tom Hadley), Peter Brown (Vern Goodman), Edward Andrews (Governor), Una Merkel (Mrs. Watkins), Arthur Hunnicutt (Lewis), Connie Gilchrist (Lewis' Wife), Theodore Marcuse (Josef Pietz), Merry Anders (Betty Collins), Frank McHugh (Bill Watkins), Doodles Weaver (Bob Evans), Frank Aletter (Joe Riley), Jack Albertson (Sam Grant), Donald May (Capt. Anderson), Robert Shayne (Governor's Adviser), Hal Peary (Uncle Harry), Ivor Francis (Mr. Wilson), Michael Fox, Richard O'Brien, Rajah the Bengal Tiger.

A fairly disturbing Disney film starring Franklin as a 12-year-old girl, the daughter of local sheriff Keith, who wages a one-tot campaign to save the life of a savage tiger that has escaped its circus and killed its trainer. After getting some television exposure, children from all over the country send money to help the tiger. This upsets the governor and his cronies because an election is coming up, and the adults expect him to kill the beast. Disaster strikes when a nervous National Guardsman mistakenly shoots a farmer who was running toward him to announce that the tiger was on his property. Eventually Keith attains the help of Sabu (in his last movie), a circus employee, and they capture the tiger alive. Succumbing to pressure, the governor allows the tiger to be placed in a zoo. Aside from the fact that the little girl defends a vicious tiger, the film shows a distinctly disturbing view of small-town life in the U.S. Except for Keith and Sabu, every adult in the film is portrayed as weak, stupid, mean, or corrupt. This may be the norm for the world of Steven Spielberg and his proteges (BACK TO THE FUTURE, GREMLINS), but for Disney it is a real, and unwelcome surprise.

p, Walt Disney, Bill Anderson; d, Norman Tokar; w, Lowell S. Hawley (based on a novel by Ian Niall); ph, William Snyder (Technicolor); m, Buddy Baker; ed, Grant K. Smith; md, Bob Brunner; art d, Carroll Clark, Marvin Aubrey Davis; set d, Emile Kuri, Frank R. McKelvy; cos, Chuck Keehne, Gertrude Casey; makeup, Pat McNalley.

Drama (PR:C MPAA:NR)

TIGER WOMAN, THE*½ (1945) 57m REP bw

Adele Mara (Sharon Winslow), Kane Richmond (Jerry Devery), Richard Fraser (Stephen Mason), Peggy Stewart (Phyllis Carrington), Cy Kendall (Inspector Leggett), Beverly Loyd (Constance Grey), Gregory Gay (Joe Sapphire), John Kelly (Sylvester), Addison Richards (Mr. White), Donia Bussey (Rosie Gargan), Frank Reicher (Coroner), Garry Owen (Bartender).

Evil nightclub vamp Mara kills her husband for the insurance money, and then does the same to her lover. Too bad for her, private eye Richmond figures out what she's up to and eventually weasels a confession out of her before she has a chance to kill him. Routine programmer.

p, Dorell and Stewart E. McGowan; d, Phillip Ford; w, George Carleton Brown (based on the radio play by John A. Dunkel); ph, Ernest Miller; ed, Fred Allen; md, Richard Cherwin; art d, Frank Hotaling; spec eff, Howard and Theodore Lydecker.

Crime (PR:A MPAA:NR)

TIGHT LITTLE ISLAND*** (1949, Brit.) 81m EAL/UNIV bw (GB: WHISKY GALORE)

Basil Radford (Capt. Paul Waggett), Catherine Lacey (Mrs. Waggett), Bruce Seton (Sgt. Odd), Joan Greenwood (Peggy Macroon), Gordon Jackson (George Campbell), Wylie Watson (Joseph Macroon), Gabrielle Blunt (Catriona Macroon), Jean Cadell (Mrs. Campbell), James Robertson Justice (Dr. MacLaren), Morland Graham (The Biffer), Duncan Macrae (Angus MacCormac), Compton Mackenzie (Capt. Buncher), John Gregson (Sammy MacConrum), James Woodburn (Roderick MacRuire), James Anderson (Old Hector), Jameson Clark (Constable Macrae), Mary McNeil (Mrs. MacCormac), Norman MacOwan (Capt. MacPhee), Alistair Hunter (Capt. MacKechnie), Henry Mollison (Mr. Farquharson), Frank Webster (1st Mate), Finlay Currie (Narrator), A.E. Matthews (Col. Linsey-Woolsey).

Authority, and not the Nazis, is the enemy in this wartime Ealing comedy. During WW II an island community in the Outer Hebrides finds its whiskey stock has evaporated. Fate intervenes, stranding a cargo ship laden with the sought-after commodity just off shore. But water isn't the only thing keeping the islanders from the booze; the local Home Guard, commanded by priggish Englishman Radford, presents a much more bothersome obstacle. And because this treasure ship has arrived on the sabbath, the "pious" island folk must also wait 24 hours before undertaking to liberate the ship's hold. In the finest Ealing tradition of circumventing authority while satirically poking holes in it, the thirsty Scotsmen outwit the Home Guard and get their hands on the much-desired cargo. Novelist and coscreenwriter Mackenzie found the inspiration for the book on which the film is based in the real-life wreck of a cargo ship (which contained some 50,000 cases of whiskey) off the Isle of Eriskay in 1941, and the "rescue" efforts by locals. This was the first feature directed by Mackendrick, who had worked for the studio as a screenwriter. The original title, WHISKY GALORE, was reputedly changed for U.S. distribution because of objections to the inclusion of the word "whisky" in the title.

p, Michael Balcon; d, Alexander Mackendrick; w, Compton Mackenzie, Angus Macphail (based on the novel Whisky Galore by Mackenzie); ph, Gerald Gibbs, Chick Waterson; m, Ernest Irving; ed, Joseph Sterling; art d, Jim Morahan.

Comedy **Cas.** (PR: MPAA:NR)

TIGHT SHOES**½ (1941) 68m Mayfair/UNIV bw

John Howard (Jimmy Rupert), Binnie Barnes (Sybil Ash), Broderick Crawford (Speedy Miller), Anne Gwynne (Ruth), Leo Carrillo (Amalfi), Samuel S. Hinds (Horace Grover, "the Brain"), Shemp Howard (Okay), Richard Lane (Allan McGrath), Sarah Padden (Mrs. Rupert), Ed Gargan (Blooch), Selmer Jackson (District Attorney), Robert Emmett O'Connor (Beebe), Tom Dugan (Professor D).

Amusing adaptation of a Damon Runyon story starring Crawford as a brutish, corrupt ward heeler who has big feet and buys a pair of tight shoes from shoe salesman Howard. Deciding that the shoe store would be a good front for his gambling den, Crawford buys the store and kicks Howard out in the street. Angry, Howard follows the advice of his girl friend, Gwynne, and crusading city editor, Lane, and vows to expose the crooked Crawford. This leads to Crawford being pushed off his pedestal and being stripped of his power by his bosses. The corrupt politicians, and Crawford's floozy, Barnes, latch onto Howard and the new-found power goes to his head. Luckily, Gwynne brings Howard to his senses, and they get married. Good cast has fun with Runyon's patented New Yorkese.

p, Jules Levey; d, Albert S. Rogell; w, Leonard Spigelgass, Art Arthur (based on the story by Damon Runyon); ph, Elwood Bredell; ed, Otto Ludwig; md, H.J. Salter; art d, Jack Otterson.

Comedy (PR:A MPAA:NR)

TIGHT SKIRTS (SEE: TIGHT SKIRTS, LOOSE PLEASURES, 1966, Fr.)

TIGHT SKIRTS, LOOSE PLEASURES** (1966, Fr.) 84m Comptoir Francais du Film-Roal/ Times c (L'AMOUR A LA CHAINE; AKA: TIGHT SKIRTS; CHAINWORK LOVE; LOOSE PLEASURES)

Valeria Ciangottini (*Catherine*), Jean Yanne (*Pornotropos*), Jacques Destoop (*Paul*), Perrette Pradier (*Corinne*), Jean-Marie Fertey (*Thanatos*), Jean-Pierre Janssen, Jean-Paul Janssen (*Twins*), Anne-Marie Coffinet (*Juliette*), Maria Rosa Rodrigues (*Barbara*), Amarande (*Melanie*), Max Montavon (*Photographer*), Roger Fradet (*Doudou*), Alain Raffael (*Raffa*), Jean Dalmain (*Catherine's Father*), Hella Petri (*Thais*), Lisette Le Bon (*Impresario*), Annie Duroc (*Prostitute*), Jean Roger Caussimon (*Priest*), Roger Karl (*Old Man*), Jean Degrave.

Exploitative drama starring Ciangottini as a young woman who becomes a prostitute after a messy love affair. She soon falls in with vicious vice-lord Yanne, who beats her when she moves to another brothel. Aided by Destoop, a handsome public relations man investigating the death of his elderly boss in her room, she tries to escape Yanne and his brother, Fertey a brutal killer. She is captured by the hoods, and Destoop is able to rescue her after Fertey accidentally kills Yanne.

d, Claude de Givray; w, de Givray, Bernard Revon; ph, Roger Fellous (CinemaScope); m, Georges Delerve; ed, Pierre Geran, Jean-Marie Gimel; makeup, Danielle Thevenot.

Crime (PR:O MPAA:NR)

TIGHT SPOT***½ (1955) 97m COL bw

Ginger Rogers (*Sherry Conley*), Edward G. Robinson (*Lloyd Hallett*), Brian Keith (*Vince Striker*), Lucy Marlow (*Prison Girl*), Lorne Greene (*Benjamin Costain*), Katherine Anderson (*Mrs. Willoughby*), Allen Nourse (*Marvin Rickles*), Peter Leeds (*Fred Packer*), Doyle O'Dell (*Mississippi Mac*), Eve McVeagh (*Clara Moran*), Helen Wallace (*Warden*), Frank Gerstle (*Jim Hornsby*), Gloria Ann Simpson (*Miss Masters*), Robert Shield (*Carlyle*), Norman Keats (*Arny*), Kathryn Grant (*Girl Honeymooner*), Ed "Skipper" McNally (*Harris*), Erik Paige, Tom Greenway, Kevin Enright (*Men*), John Marshall (*Detective*), Will J. White, Patrick Miller (*Plainclothesmen*), Tom de Graffenried (*Doctor*), Joseph Hamilton (*Judge*), Alan Reynolds (*Bailiff*), Alfred Linder (*Tonelli*), John Larch, Ed Hinton (*Detectives*), Bob Hopkins (*TV Salesman*), Robert Nichols (*Boy Honeymooner*), Kenneth N. Mayer, Dean Cromer (*Policemen*).

An intelligent and gritty crime story, TIGHT SPOT opens as Rogers, a model wrongly put behind bars, is released into the custody of Robinson, a U.S. attorney. Rogers is considered a key witness in the trial of Greene, a well-known and ruthless gangster. Rogers does not wish to testify, seeing that none of the other potential witnesses lived long enough to tell their stories in court. Robinson hopes she will change her mind, and to that end books Rogers into a nice hotel room. Rogers remains adamant, but does grow attracted to her police bodyguard, Keith. Anderson, a policewoman who also watches after Rogers, is killed by one of Greene's anonymous hit men. Robinson learns that Keith is actually in Greene's employ as well. He rushes to the hotel to save Rogers, and ends up dead after an explosive gunfight. Rogers, shaken by the killings, realizes what she must do and bravely testifies against Greene, telling the judge she is a racket buster by profession. This is one of Rogers' best roles, again showing audiences that her range went well beyond the famous musicals with Fred Astaire. She gives a well-rounded portrait, showing both the tough and tender sides of her character. Karlson's direction is to the point, guiding the story succinctly without indulging in any extraneous directoral flourishes that would impose on it. Keith and Greene both provide good support, and Robinson is excellent, though the esteemed actor thought little of the role. In his autobiography *All My Yesterdays*, Robinson categorized TIGHT SPOT as a film from "...the 'B' picture phase of my career as a movie star--or former movie star, if that's a better way of putting it, or has- been, if that's still a better way...In TIGHT SPOT Ginger Rogers was the star."

p, Lewis J. Rachmil; d, Phil Karlson; w, William Bowers (based on the play "Dead Pigeon" by Lenard Kantor); ph, Burnett Guffey; m, George Duning; ed, Viola Lawrence; md, Morris W. Stoloff; art d, Carl Anderson; cos, Jean Louis.

Crime Drama (PR:O MPAA:NR)

TIJUANA STORY, THE* (1957) 72m COL bw

Rodolfo Acosta (*Manuel Acosta Mesa*), James Darren (*Mitch*), Robert McQueeney (*Eddie March*), Jean Willes (*Liz March*), Joy Stoner (*Linda Alvarez*), Paul Newlan (*Peron Diaz*), George E. Stone (*Pino*), Michael Fox (*Reuben Galindo*), Robert Blake (*Enrique Acosta Mesa*), William Fawcett (*Alberto Rodriguez*), Ric Vallin (*Ricardo*), Ralph Valencia (*Paul Acosta Mesa*), Susan Seaforth (*Alma Acosta Mesa*), William Tannen (*Miguel Fuentes*), Susan Ridgeway (*Lupe*), Paul Coates (*Narrator*).

Acosta stars in this hackneyed crime drama based on a real-life incident of a Mexican newspaperman who wages a one-man press war against a powerful crime syndicate led by Newlan. After Acosta digs up the names of influential politicians involved in Newlan's illegal activities, the mob boss has Acosta assassinated. This foolish move incenses the local population and Acosta's son, Blake, picks up the crusade. Now, aided by the people, Blake ensures that justice triumphs by cleaning out the rogues. Narrator Coates is the real-life newspaperman who dug up the dirt against the criminals, and he would probably have been the first to say that the "cleanup" accomplished very little in the long run.

p, Sam Katzman; d, Leslie Kardos; w, Lou Morheim; ph, Benjamin H. Kline; ed, Edwin Bryant; md, Mischa Bakaleinikoff; art d, Paul Palmentola.

Crime (PR:A MPAA:NR)

TIKI TIKI***½ (1971, Can.) 71m Potterton-Commonwealth-United c

Voices: Barrie Baldaro, Peter Cullan, Joan Stuart, Gayle Claitman, J. Shepard.

An offbeat and thoroughly enjoyable mixture of live action and animation comprise this children's feature that's just as much fun for adults as well. Footage from a Soviet children's feature, DR. ABOLIT, comprises the live-action sequences. It tells the story of a doctor who blasts off with a duo of monkeys. They're on the run from some pirates and trying to rescue a colony of monkey children as well. Integrated with this are some delightfully loopy animated sequences involving a Hollywood producer. He's everything a hip, smarmy moviemaker should be, with the added advantage of being a monkey trying to produce "the first all-people picture" in the biz. It's a wonderful spoof of the Hollywood life full of throw-away lines and inside movie gags (the studio head, fondly referred to as "K . K.", is none other than King Kong.

d, Gerald Potterton; w, Potterton, Martin Hornstein, J. Chorodov; ph, Claude Lapierre; m, Jerry Blatt, L. Burnstein; ed, Peter Hearn.

Animation/Comedy (PR:AAA MPAA:NR)

TIKO AND THE SHARK**½ (1966, U.S./Ital./Fr.) 88m Titanus-P.C.M.-MGM-S.N.P.C.- S.G.C./MGM c (TI-KOYO E IL SUO PRESCACANE; TI-KOYO ET SON REQUIN; AKA: TIKOYO AND HIS SHARK)

Marlene Among (*Diana*), Al Kauwe (*Ti-koyo*), Denis Pouira (*Ti-koyo as a Child*), Diane Samsoi (*Diana as a Child*), Roau (*Cocoyo*).

Beautifully photographed South Seas drama starring Kauwe as a young Polynesian island boy who finds a baby shark and raises it as a pet with the help of his girl friend Among. When the shark grows up, Kauwe returns it to the deep waters, fearing he will never see his pet again. Ten years later, progress comes to the small island and the natives are being driven out. Among's brother becomes one of the driving forces behind the organized fisheries that are now dotting the landscape, and he sends his sister to the U.S. to be educated. Kauwe now earns a living diving for pearls and one day his pet shark returns to him as a protector. His happiness is destroyed, however, when the monopoly behind the fisheries begins burning down the natives' homes and running them out. When Among returns from the U.S., Kauwe convinces her to leave the island with him, and the pair, along with the shark, set sail for destinations unknown.

p, Goffredo Lombardo; d, Folco Quilici; w, Augusto Frassineti, Quilici, Ottavio Alessi, Giorgio Prosperi, Franco Prosperi (based on a story by Italo Calvino from a novel by Clement Richer); ph, Pier Lidovico Pavoni (Eastmancolor), Masino Manunza (underwater ph); m, Francesco De Masi; ed, Mario Serandrei; cos, Nadia Vitali.

Drama (PR:A MPAA:NR)

TIKOYO AND HIS SHARK (SEE: TIKO AND THE SHARK, 1966, U.S./Ital./Fr.)

'TIL WE MEET AGAIN*** (1940) 99m WB bw

Merle Oberon (*Joan Ames*), George Brent (*Dan Hardesty*), Pat O'Brien (*Steve Burke*), Geraldine Fitzgerald (*Bonnie Coburn*), Binnie Barnes (*Countess de Vaubert*), Frank McHugh (*Achilles Peddicord*), Eric Blore (*Sir Harold Landamuir*), George Reeves (*Jimmy Coburn*), Henry O'Neill (*Dr. Cameron*), Frank Wilcox (*Assistant Purser*), Doris Lloyd (*Louise the Maid*), John Ridgely (*Junior Officer*), Marjorie Gateson (*Mrs. Hestor*), Regis Toomey (*Freddy*), William Halligan (*Barman*), Victor Kilian (*McGillis*), Wade Boteler (*Stoddard*), Charles Sherlock (*Master-at-Arms*), Frank Orth (*Bartender*), Maris Wrixon, Jane Gilbert, Mary Anderson (*Girls*), Chester Gan (*Hong Kong Policeman*), Frank Mayo, William Hopper (*Men*), Hal Brazealeo (*Lemmy*), Sol Gorss (*Sailor*), Mary MacLaren (*Woman*), Jeffrey Sayre, Jack Mower (*Stewards*), Grace Hayle (*Fussy Woman Passenger*), Lynn Merrick (*Her Daughter*), David Tillotson (*Boy*), Nat Carr, David Newell (*Assistant Pursers*), Ed Keane (*Officer*), William Gould (*Chief of Police*), Robert Homans (*Dock Policeman*), Robert Elliott, Edwin Parker (*Detectives*), Walter Miller (*American Bartender*), Frank Puglia, George Regas (*Mexican Bartenders*).

This remake of 1932's ONE WAY PASSAGE (which starred William Powell and Kay Francis) is an unabashed weeper that yanks mercilessly at the heartstrings of the audience. However, thanks to the fine casting of Oberon and Brent, as well as a number of entertaining supporting roles, 'TIL WE MEET AGAIN proves to be an effective melodrama. Oberon and Brent star as a pair of lovers who fall in love while on a transatlantic ocean cruise. What they keep secret from each other is that neither of them has long to live. Brent is a captive criminal being transported to San Quentin for a ride in the electric chair, while Oberon is inflicted with a fatal heart condition. Luckily for the lovers, Brent's captor, police officer O'Brien, is understanding and allows them a certain amount of freedom and privacy. In addition to keeping an eye on Brent, O'Brien has been eyeing Fitzgerald, a tourist who is sympathetic to the lovers' plight. Brent gets his chance at freedom, only to learn Oberon's secret. Surrendering to fate, Brent returns to the ship with Oberon. The downbeat finale has both Oberon and Brent meeting their maker where they will no doubt "meet again." The chief difference between this version and its predecessor is length. Where ONE WAY PASSAGE needed only 69 minutes to tell its story, 'TIL WE MEET AGAIN stretched it out another 30 minutes. Most of the padding occurs in the romance between O'Brien and Fitzgerald, which is only barely touched in the original. Jack Warner had originally hoped to get Bette Davis in the picture but Davis' merciless schedule (and her strong dislike for Warner) forced her to take a four-month vacation instead.

p, Jack L. Warner, Hal B. Wallis; d, Edmund Goulding; w, Warren Duff (based on a story by Robert Lord); ph, Tony Gaudio; ed, Ralph Dawson; md, Leo F. Forbstein; cos, Orry-Kelly; spec eff, Byron Hasken.

Romance   (PR:A MPAA:NR)

TILL DEATH*   (1978) 80m Cougar c

Keith Atkinson, Bert Freed, Belinda Balaski, Marshall Reed, Jonathan Cole, Keith Walker.

A numbingly slow and dull tale of the supernatural starring Balaski and Atkinson as bride and groom, just married, who are involved in a terrible car accident while on their honeymoon. Balaski is killed and Atkinson is injured so severely that several months of hospitalization are required. Upon his recovery, Atkinson visits his wife's tomb. Soon after his arrival, Balaski rises from the grave and attempts to seduce him into joining her on the dark side. Shot in 1972 but unreleased until 1978, TILL DEATH-apparently concerns the overwhelming power of love and what it can accomplish-in reality the film is a ghoulish affair which exploits necrophilia.

p&d, Walter Stocker; w, Gregory Dana; ph, G. Smart, J. Steeley; m, Chick Rains, J.E. Norman; spec eff, Roger George; makeup, Jerry Soucie.

Horror   (PR:C-O MPAA:PG)

TILL DEATH DO US PART   (SEE: ALF 'N' FAMILY, 1968, Brit.)

TILL MARRIAGE DO US PART**   (1979, Ital.) 110m Dean
Cinematografica/Franklin Med ia c (DIO MIO, COME SONO CADUTA IN BASSO; AKA: HOW LOW CAN YOU FALL?)

Laura Antonelli (Eugenia), Alberto Lionello (Raimondo), Michele Placido (Pantasso), Jean Rochefort (Henry), Karin Schubert (Evelyn).

Another in the series of Italian sex farces starring the international sex-symbol Laura Antonelli. This one sees two newlyweds, Antonelli and Lionello, discover that they are actually brother and sister. Luckily, this is revealed before the marriage is consummated, forcing the frustrated pair to seek satisfaction elsewhere. Lionello begins to read the erotic novels of Gabriele D'Annunzio voraciously, while Antonelli finds refuge in the Bible. Eventually she can no longer stand it and falls into an affair with the chauffeur. Fed up, Lionello joins the army and goes off to war where he is killed, leaving Antonelli to her chauffeur. Made and released abroad more than five years before its American release.

p, Pio Angeletti, Adriano de Micheli; d, Luigi Comencini; w, Comencini, Ivo Perilli; ph, Tonino delle Colli (Technicolor); m, Fiorenzo Carpi; ed, Nino Baragli; art d, Dante Ferretti.

Comedy   **Cas.**   (PR:O MPAA:R)

TILL THE CLOUDS ROLL BY*   (1946) 120m MGM c

Robert Walker (Jerome Kern), Judy Garland (Marilyn Miller), Lucille Bremer (Sally), Joan Wells (Sally as a Girl), Van Heflin (James I. Hessler), Paul Langton (Oscar Hammerstein II), Dorothy Patrick (Mrs. Jerome Kern), Mary Nash (Mrs. Muller), Harry Hayden (Charles Frohman), Paul Maxey (Victor Herbert), Rex Evans (Cecil Keller), William "Bill" Phillips (Hennessey), Dinah Shore (Julie Sanderson), Van Johnson (Band Leader), June Allyson, Angela Lansbury, Ray McDonald (Guest Performers), Maurice Kelly, Cyd Charisse, Gower Champion (Dance Specialties), Ray Teal (Orchestra Conductor), Wilde Twins (Specialty), Showboat Number: William Halligan (Capt. Andy), Tony Martin (Ravenal), Kathryn Grayson (Magnolia), Virginia O'Brien (Ellie), Lena Horne (Julie), Caleb Peterson (Joe), Bruce Cowling (Steve), Frank Sinatra, Johnny Johnston (Finale), Herschel Graham, Fred Hueston, Dick Earle, Larry Steers, Reed Howes, Hazard Newsberry, Ed Elby, Lee Smith, Larry Williams, James Plato, Leonard Mellen, James Darrell, Tony Merlo, Charles Madrin, Charles Griffin (Opening Night Critics), Byron Foulger (Frohman's Secretary), Lee Phelps,

Ralph Dunn (Moving Men), Lucille Casey, Mary Jane French, Beryl McCutcheon, Alice Wallace, Irene Veron, Gloria Joy Arden, Mickey Malloy, Alma Carroll, Wesley Brent (Showgirls), George Peters, Harry Denny, Bob McLean, Frank McClure, George Murray, John Alban, Lee Bennett (Stage Door Johnnies), Jean Andren (Secretary), John Albright (Call Boy), Margaret Bert (Maid), Herbert Heywood (Stagehand), Thomas Louden (Rural Postman), Ann Codee (Miss Laroche), James Finlayson (Candy Vendor), Elspeth Dudgeon, Margaret Bert (Maids), Lilyan Irene (Barmaid), Tom Stevenson (Genius), Penny Parker (Punch and Judy Operator), Robert Emmett O'Connor (Clerk), Stanley Andrews (Doctor), Russell Hicks (Motion Picture Producer), William Forrest (Motion Picture Director), Arnaut Brothers (Bird Act), Jim Grey, Douglas Wright (Bull Clown), Louis Manley (Swivel Chair Lady), Don Wayson, Howard Mitchell (Detectives), Sally Forrest, Mary Hatcher (Chorus Girls).

A movie that bore as much resemblance to the truth as Cole Porter's purported biography NIGHT AND DAY or the story of Rodgers and Hart, WORDS AND MUSIC. Colorful and tuneful, but Jerome Kern's life was evidently free of drama. Walker is Kern. It's the night that "Showboat" is to open and before he goes to the theater, he orders his driver to take him back to his old Manhattan brownstone. That sets his memory reeling back from that night, December 27, 1927, to his youth as a struggling songwriter. Walker needs someone to help with arrangements and meets Heflin (who may have been giving a loose portrayal of Kern's real arranger, Frank Sadler), who becomes his pal and orchestrator. Heflin sees that this beardless youth has serious talent and takes him under his wing. When Hayden, a Broadway producer, makes the blanket statement that no good songs are written in the U.S., and that the best composers come from England, Walker decides to journey to Blighty and establish himself there. Once in England, Walker writes a hit, then another, then another, and when Hayden asks him to write the music for a new show, Walker realizes that going to England was the right move. In London, Walker meets Patrick; they fall in love and wedding bells are on the horizon until Walker has to race back to the U.S. to write a show. Back in New York, Walker's star soars and he eventually returns to London to marry Patrick. Smooth sailing for several years (with the one jarring note being that Hayden goes down on the Lusitania) with hit after hit. Meanwhile, Heflin's health is precarious and getting weaker by the minute. Heflin's daughter is Bremer and Walker promises to give her a part in his new show. But things don't work out and Walker is forced to use someone else in the role, Garland (as Marilyn Miller). Bremer is crushed by what's happened and won't listen to any explanations so she runs off down South, causing the already weak Heflin to become even sicker with fear that some harm may have come to Bremer. Heflin dies and Kern is distraught and devotes himself to locating Bremer, foregoing all of his work and even his relationship with those around him in an attempt to assuage his guilt over what's transpired. Walker finally finds Bremer in a Tennessee nightclub and tries to salve her ruffled feathers. But Bremer is made of strong stuff and says she can make it on her own, thank you, and would prefer that she do it that way rather than call in old favors. Walker is relieved at seeing that Bremer is a tough cookie. He returns to New York, plunges himself into his latest labors with collaborator Langton (as Oscar Hammerstein II), and they adapt Edna Ferber's "Showboat" into a smashing success, bringing the picture back to where it began. Kern died while they were shooting the movie. He would have been proud of the manner in which they used his songs but might have wondered whose story they were trying to tell. The movie was a great hit, mainly due to the star-studded cast and the high-gloss productions given to Kern's superior tunes. The script went through many hands, including the uncredited contributions of Fred F. Finklehoffe, Lemuel Ayers, John Lee Mahin, and Hans Willheim. Whorf directed most of the proceedings, with the exceptions being Vincente Minnelli's handling of the scenes starring his wife, Garland, and the finale, which was helmed by George Sidney. Kay Thompson handled the vocal arrangements, and the excellent orchestrations were cleffed by Ted Duncan, Wally Heglin, Leo Shuken, Robert Franklyn, and Sidney Cutner. All the melodies were by Kern. Songs include a mini-version of "Showboat" (lyrics by Oscar Hammerstein II) featuring Kathryn Grayson and Tony Martin singing "Make Believe," the chorus singing "Cotton Blossom," Lena Horne tearing out your heart with "Can't Help Lovin' Dat Man," Caleb Peterson's version of "Ol' Man River," Martin again on "Who Cares if My Boat Goes Upstream?" and a funny rendition of "Life Upon the Wicked Stage" by Virginia O'Brien. June Allyson and Ray McDonald sang "Till the Clouds Roll By" (lyrics by P.G. Wodehouse, creator of the books about "Jeeves"), Ed Laska wrote the lyrics for "Howja Like to Spoon with Me?" (Kern's first big hit, performed by Angela Lansbury), Dinah Shore sang "The Last Time I Saw Paris" (lyrics by Hammerstein) and "They Didn't Believe Me" (lyrics by Herbert Reynolds), Van Johnson and Lucille Bremer did "I Won't Dance" (lyrics by Otto Harbach, Hammerstein). Hammerstein also wrote the lyrics for Lena Horne's rendition of "Why Was I Born?" and collaborated with Harbach again on "Who?" (sung by Garland), and "Sunny" (danced by Garland, sung by the chorus). Hammerstein also wrote the words for "All the Things You Are" (sung by Martin) and "One More Dance" (sung by Bremer). Harbach contributed the words for "Smoke Gets in Your Eyes" (sung by Cyd Charisse and Gower Champion, making his movie debut), "Yesterdays" (chorus), and "She Didn't Say Yes," (performed by the Wilde Twins). Garland sang Buddy De Sylva's lyrics on "Look for the Silver Lining," June Allyson and Wodehouse's words on "Leave It to Jane" and "Cleopatterer," Grayson sang Ira Gershwin's sentiments on "Long Ago and Far Away," while O'Brien did "A Fine Romance" (lyrics by Dorothy

Fields). Wodehouse also wrote "The Land Where The Good Songs Go" (performed by Bremer) and instrumentals on "Kalua" and "Polka" from the "Mark Twain Suite." The finale featured Frank Sinatra reprising "Ol' Man River." Cut from the film were "Dearly Beloved," "I've Told Ev'ry Little Star," "Lovely to Look At," "The Song Is You," "Bill," and "D' Ye Love Me?" Background songs by Kern and his various lyricists were "I Dream Too Much," "Cat and the Fiddle," "Crickets Are Calling," "In the Egern of the Tegern Sea," words by Wodehouse and Guy Bolton. Other tunes used under action were "The Touch of Your Hand," "'Twas Not So Long Ago," "Go Little Boat," "You Never Knew About Me," "You Are Love," "La Jeunne Fille," "Siren's Song," "Sun Shines Brighter," "Pal Like You," "Passionate Pilgrim." Kern shared Best Song Oscars for "The Way You Look Tonight" and "The Last Time I Saw Paris." All in all, an overblown picture that would have made a terrific record album, or two. Walker was ingenuous and the acting was okay but if the glorious Kern-els of music had been taken away, it would have been a huge yawn.

p, Arthur Freed; d, Richard Whorf; w, Myles Connolly, Jean Holloway (based on the life and music of Jerome Kern, story by Guy Bolton, adapted by George Wells); ph, Harry Stradling, George J. Folsey (Technicolor); m, Conrad Salinger, Lennie Hayton, Roger Edens; ed, Albert Akst; md, Hayton; art d, Cedric Gibbons, Daniel B. Cathcart; set d, Edwin B. Willis, Richard Pefferle; cos, Irene, Helen Rose, Valles; spec eff, Warren Newcombe; ch, Robert Alton; makeup, Jack Dawn.

Musical/Biography   **Cas.**   **(PR:AA MPAA:NR)**

TILL THE END OF TIME***   (1946) 105m RKO bw

Dorothy McGuire *(Pat Ruscomb)*, Guy Madison *(Cliff Harper)*, Robert Mitchum *(William Tabeshaw)*, Bill Williams *(Perry Kincheloe)*, Tom Tully *(C.W. Harper)*, William Gargan *(Sgt. Gunny Watrous)*, Jean Porter *(Helen Ingersoll)*, Johnny Sands *(Tommy Hendricks)*, Loren Tindall *(Pinky)*, Ruth Nelson *(Amy Harper)*, Harry Von Zell *(Scuffy)*, Selena Royle *(Mrs. Kincheloe)*, Richard Benedict *(Boy from Idaho)*, Dickie Tyler *(Jimmy Kincheloe)*, Stan Johnson *(Capt. Jack Winthrop)*, Billy Newell *(Warrant Officer)*, Lee Slater *(Burton)*, Robert Lowell *(Epstein)*, Peter Varney *(Franks)*, George Burnett *(Gilman)*, Bill Barnum *(Jackson)*, Richard Slattery *(Captain)*, Harry Hayden *(Ed Tompkins)*, Mary Worth *(Mrs. Tompkins)*, Tim Ryan *(Steve Sumpter)*, Ellen Corby *(Mrs. Sumpter)*, Margaret Wells *(Mrs. Ingersoll)*, Fred Howard *(Zeke Ingersoll)*, Teddy Infuhr *(Freddie Stewart)*, Blake Edwards *(Foreman)*, Paul Birch *(Serviceman)*, Jack Parker *(Collector)*, Drew Alan *(Marine)*, John S. Roberts, Anthony Marsh, John Bailey, Michael Kostrick *(Interviewers)*, Stubby Kruger *(Practical Life Guard)*, Eddie Craven *(Waiter)*, William Forrest *(Detective Lieutenant)*.

A post-WW II drama that would have been more effective if the U.S. had not seen THE BEST YEARS OF OUR LIVES. It suffered by comparison but had enough stuff to make it ring the cash registers as it featured three of the newer heart throbs, Williams, Madison, and Mitchum, a trio of ex-servicemen come home to a world at peace. Mitchum was injured in the war and now has a steel plate in his head which provides him with a dull pain and a need to drink. Madison is Mitchum's best pal, a small-town boy whose parents, Tully and Nelson, would like him to marry and settle down right away. The third member of the group is Williams, who has been crippled as a result of war injuries. Williams had the desire of becoming a pugilist before the war and can now only dream of it. Nelson and Tully apply pressure on Madison, while his neighbor, Porter, makes no bones about wanting to marry him, so Madison goes off on a drunken toot with Mitchum. Madison had met McGuire early on and when they meet again, she urges him to stop wasting time and seek employment. Since he has fallen in love with McGuire, he takes her advice but soon is having hassles with his immediate superior. McGuire is a war widow and understands that there is a period of adjustment for any serviceman so she won't agree to become Madison's wife until he has proven that he has the stuff to stick it out in his job. Mitchum and Madison meet in a tavern and Mitchum is in pain from the steel plate. He should really be inside a medical facility but he resists that out of pride, even though he has no money and is hurting. Williams is now wearing artificial limbs and managing to see what sunniness is in his life. Of the three, his attitude is, by far, the best and most realistic. They meet a group of racial bigots who are essentially a Klan-like group claiming to be veterans. What follows is the most famous scene in the movie as the pals have a huge battle with the bigots and even Williams gets in his licks. Later, while their wounds are being tended in a hospital, Madison finally gets closer to Nelson and Tully. Mitchum decides that he has to buy that ranch he's always dreamed of in New Mexico (he had lost his mustering-out pay on a trip to Las Vegas and was understandably depressed) and Williams is content to make the best of what life has to offer. Mitchum's portrayal of the cowboy is one of his best before he fell into the bad habits that he showed in later years. The trio was united out of RKO's budget-films department, but only Mitchum stepped up in class. Williams made several B movies, married actress Barbara Hale ("Della Street" on TV's "Perry Mason"), and they are the parents of William Katt, who starred in a couple of movies and one TV series. Williams' real name is Herman Katt. Madison, born Robert Moseley, starred in the TV series "Wild Bill Hickok" and then went to Europe where he made several movies. This picture did better than anyone thought it might and was surely helped by the success of the theme song. Based on Chopin's "Polonaise In A Flat Major," it was a huge recording hit for Perry Como and publicized the movie.

p, Dore Schary; d, Edward Dmytryk; w, Allen Rivkin (based on the novel *They Dream of Home* by Niven Busch); ph, Harry J. Wild; m, Leigh Harline; ed, Harry Gerstad; md, C. Bakaleinikoff; art d, Albert S. D'Agostino, Jack Okey; set d, Darrel Silvera, William Stevens; m/l, title song, Buddy Kaye, Ted Mossman (based on Chopin's "Polonaise in A Flat Major"), sung by Perry Como.

Post War Drama   **Cas.**   **(PR:A-C MPAA:NR)**

TILL TOMORROW COMES**½**   (1962, Jap.) 113m Toho bw (ASU ARU KAGIRI; ASHITA ARU KAGIRI)

Kyoko Kagawa, Yuriko Hoshi, Shuji Sano, Junko Ikeuchi, Kumi Mizuno, Haruko Sugimura, Tsutomo Yamazaki, Nobuko Otowa, Takashi Inagaki.

Sensitive Japanese melodrama about a young girl who is born blind in 1941, just as her father is sent off to war. Seeking a cure for the girl's blindness, her mother approaches a local doctor, who agrees to perform the surgery, but he, too, is called off to the military before the operation can be arranged. Years later, the doctor performs the operation, but it is a failure and the girl resigns herself to her condition. Eventually the girl falls in love with a blind boy and the two make a life together.

p, Ichiro Sato, Ken-ichiro Tsunoda; d, Shiro Toyoda; w, Toshio Yazumi; ph, Kozo Okazaki (Tohoscope); m, Hikaru Hayashi.

Drama   **(PR:C MPAA:NR)**

TILL WE MEET AGAIN**½**   (1936) 72m PAR bw (AKA: FORGOTTEN FACES)

Herbert Marshall *(Alan Barclay)*, Gertrude Michael *(Elsa Durany)*, Lionel Atwill *(Ludwig)*, Rod LaRocque *(Carl Schrottle)*, Guy Bates Post *(Capt. Minton)*, Vallejo Gantner *(Vogel)*, Torben Meyer *(Kraus)*, Julia Faye *(Nurse)*, Egon Brecher *(Schultz)*, Spencer Charters, Frank Reicher, Colin Tapley, Colin Kenny.

Surprisingly well-done WW I spy thriller that came at the end of a cycle for these popular melodramas. Marshall plays an English actor and Michael a German actress who meet and fall in love in 1914. When the war tears their countries, and them, apart, they both wind up as spies for their homelands. Of course, they run into each other as enemies, but those old feelings return, and with the help of sympathetic master-spy, Atwill, they flee to Holland and are married.

p, Albert Lewis; d, Robert Florey; w, Edwin Justus Meyer, Brian Marlow, Alfred Davis, Morton Barteaux (based on the play "The Last Curtain" by Davis); ph, Victor Milner; ed, Richard Currier.

Romance/War   **(PR:A MPAA:NR)**

TILL WE MEET AGAIN***   (1944) 88m PAR bw

Ray Milland *(John)*, Barbara Britton *(Sister Clothilde)*, Walter Slezak *(Vitrey the Mayor)*, Lucille Watson *(Mother Superior)*, Konstantin Shayne *(Maj. Krupp)*, Vladimir Sokoloff *(Cabeau, Gardener)*, Marguerite D'Alvarez *(Mme. Sarroux)*, Mona Freeman *(Elise)*, William Edmunds *(Henri Maret)*, George Davis *(Gaston the Waiter)*, Peter Helmers *(Examiner)*, John Wengraf *(Gestapo Chief)*, Mira McKinney *(Portress)*, Tala Birell *(Mme. Bouchard)*, Buddy Gorman *(Messenger)*, Dawn Bender *(Francoise)*, Eilene Janssen *(Yvonne)*, Henry Sharp *(Andre)*, Alfred Paix, Eugene Borden *(Refugees)*, Muni Seroff *(Jacques)*, Philip Van Zandt *(Lieutenant)*, Georges Renavent *(Gabriel)*, Diane Dubois, Janet Gallow, Nils Rich, Sharon McManus, Mary Thomas, Diana Martin, Yvette Duguay *(Orphans)*, Byron Nelson, Don Cadell, Hans Furberg, Robert Stevenson *(German Soldiers)*, Frances Sandford, Iris Lancaster *(Girls in Restaurant)*, Nina Borget *(Jeannette)*, George Sorel *(Gendarme)*, Marcelle Corday *(Elderly Waitress)*, Francis McDonald *(Driver of the Cart)*, Crane Whitley *(Man with Silver)*.

Another forbidden-love-during-the-tensions-of-WW II film, this one stars Milland as an American pilot who crashes in France and must get to the underground before the Nazis can capture him. He is helped by a naive young nun (Britton) who, despite her calling to the Lord, and the fact that Milland is happily married and says so frequently, falls in love with the stranded pilot. Once they hook up with the underground, she agrees to pose as his "wife" so that he may transport secret documents from the French freedom fighters to London. In the end, Britton sacrifices herself to save Milland, and she is captured by the Nazis, who plan to ship her off to a German whorehouse for active duty. Rather than see her suffer a fate worse than death, French Mayor Slezak kills Britton.

p, David Lewis; d, Frank Borzage; w, Lenore Coffee (based on the play by Alfred Maury); ph, Theodor Sparkuhl, Farciot Edourat; m, David Buttolph; ed, Elmo Veron; art d, Hans Dreier, Robert Usher; set d, Ray Moyer; spec eff, Gordon Jennings.

War   **(PR:A MPAA:NR)**

TILLIE AND GUS***   (1933) 58m PAR bw

W.C. Fields (*Augustus Q. Winterbottom*), Alison Skipworth (*Tillie Winterbottom*), Ronald LeRoy "Baby LeRoy" Overacker (*The "King" Sheridan*), Jacqueline Wells [Julie Bishop] (*Mary Blake Sheridan*), Clifford Jones [Phillip Trent] (*Tom Sheridan*), Clarence Wilson (*Phineas Pratt, Executor*), George Barbier (*Capt. Fogg*), Barton MacLane (*Commissioner McLennan*), Edgar Kennedy (*Judge Elmer, "Old Naked-Skull"*), Robert McKenzie (*Defense Attorney*), Master Williams (*High Card Harrington*), William Irving (*Man in Tall Silk Hat*), Ivan Linow (*The Swede*), Lon Poff, James Burke, Ferris Taylor (*Jurors*), Frank Hagney (*Jury Foreman*), Lew Kelly (*Sourdough, Hotel Manager*), John "Blackie" Whiteford (*Man at Bar*), Harry Dunkinson (*Bartender*), Irving Bacon (*Nosy Extra at Gambling Table*), Billy Engle (*Sailor*), Herbert Evans (*Butler*), Brooks Benedict (*Mr. Black*), Walter C. Percival (*Mr. Green*), Cyril Ring (*Mr. White*), Ted Stanhope (*Telegraph Clerk*), Ed Brady (*Barfly*), Harry Schultz (*Kibitzer*), Jerry Jerome (*Customer*), Frank O'Connor (*Reporter*), Eddie Baker (*Race Judge*), Maurice Black (*Bit*).

Watching W.C. Fields is like eating Chinese food. Even when the food is just so-so, it's still pretty good. This movie was just so-so, but Fields' and Skipworth's performance made up for the shortcomings. Wells and Jones are a young married couple being bilked by attorney Wilson. Wells' father died and left her an inheritance but Wilson's legal shenanigans have dissipated the money until all they now own is a riverboat. Wilson also owns a riverboat and would like to get his hands on the couple's vessel so he can control a ferry concession. He tells them that he will erase all their debts (they really have none) if they will sign over their boat. Wells and Jones would like to keep the boat because they have nothing else to their name. Fields and Skipworth are married but not living together. Ostensibly missionaries, they parted company long ago and have since found other fish to fry. She has been running a bar and house of ill repute in the Far East while he's been cheating at cards in Alaska. She is in financial trouble, having lost her holdings in a crap game, and he is about to be ridden out of the Alaskan territory on a rail for having too many aces up his sleeve. They are both notified about the will and make their respective ways to the small town, thinking they might be able to grab some of the inheritance. When they meet at a train station, their first response is to draw guns on each other. Old arguments are soon settled and the two decide that they'd better keep up their missionary pretense. After a card game on the train with some yokels, they get to town and soon size up Wilson's chicanery. Fields and Skipworth feel for the young couple and arrange a winner-take-all race between the old scow and Wilson's newer and faster riverboat. Fields pulls some tricks of his own by tying Wilson's boat to the dock. The race begins and the old boat gets a lead, then Wilson's boat pulls away part of the dock and steams after it. Several tricks from both sides occur, including fireworks and various bits of sabotage. The boat with Fields as captain wins and this captures a valuable ferry franchise which Wilson wanted. Wilson eventually confesses that he used duplicity to ravage the inheritance and he will return the money. (This is done only after Fields has dunked the man in the water and has him hooked by the neck.) Wells and Jones are thrilled at regaining some of their lost money and cede part of their booty to Fields and Skipworth. The final scene has Fields and Skipworth happily strolling to the home of the young couple as they sing the traditional "Bringing in the Sheaves." Although supposedly set partly in Singapore and Alaska, the film was an obvious studio job. The location work was done at Malibu Lake and the director, Martin, was helming his first and only feature film. Baby LeRoy appears in his premiere picture with Fields and they actually got along fairly well, a situation which would alter as they worked together. Fields was always a tight man with a buck and deliberately created havoc on a few nights so the shooting went past midnight. Many of the cast and crew couldn't figure out why Fields seemed to be lousing up his lines. They didn't know that his contract called for an additional payment of $800 every time the shooting went past midnight. Fields was 54 when he made this and Skipworth was 70, although Fields had led such a dissolute life that the difference in their ages hardly showed. She and Fields had already appeared together in a segment of the episodic IF I HAD A MILLION and would reunite on SIX OF A KIND the following year.

p, Douglas MacLean; d, Francis Martin; w, Walter De Leon, Martin (based on a story by Rupert Hughes); ph, Benjamin Reynolds; art d, Hans Dreier, Harry Oliver.

Comedy   (PR:A   MPAA:NR)

TILLIE THE TOILER*½   (1941) 67m COL bw

Kay Harris (*Tillie Jones*), William Tracy (*Mac*), George Watts (*Simpkins*), Daphne Pollard (*Mumsy*), Jack Arnold (*Whipple*), Marjorie Reynolds (*Bubbles*), Bennie Bartlett (*Glennie*), Stanley Brown (*Ted Williams*), Ernest Truex (*George Winkler*), Franklin Pangborn (*Perry Tweedale*), Sylvia Field (*Teacher*), Edward Gargan (*Policeman*), Harry Tyler (*Pop*).

The first in a series of programmers based on the comic strip character created by Russ Westover. Harris, who was discovered by the studio for this role, plays Tillie, a flighty gal who lands a job in her boy friend Tracy's office as a steno girl. She soon turns the business upside down, but in the end manages to right all her wrongs and impress the boss. The story was first presented on the screen in the silent TILLIE THE TOILER (1927), with Marion Davies in the Harris role.

p, Robert Sparks; d, Sidney Salkow; w, Karen DeWolf, Francis Martin (based on a story by Karen DeWolf, from the comic strip created by Russ Westover); ph, Henry Freulich, Phillip Tannura; ed, Gene Milford; art d, Lionel Banks; cos, Monica.

Comedy   (PR:A   MPAA:NR)

TILLY OF BLOOMSBURY**   (1931, Brit.) 70m STER bw

Sydney Howard (*Samuel Stillbottle, Butler*), Phyllis Konstam (*Tilly Welwyn*), Richard Bird (*Dick Mainwaring*), Edward Chapman (*Percy Welwyn*), Ellis Jeffreys (*Lady Marion Mainwaring*), Marie Wright (*Mrs. Banks*), Mabel Russell (*Mrs. Welwyn*), H.R. Hignett (*Lucius Welwyn*), Ena Grossmith (*Amelia Welwyn*), Sebastian Smith (*Abel Mainwaring*), Leila Page (*Sylvia*), Olwen Roose (*Constance Damery*).

Typical British comedy of manners starring Bird as a rich boy who falls in love with the daughter of a boarding-house keeper. Once exposed to the life style of the "other half", Bird learns that they're not so bad and decides to take his girl down to the family country house for the weekend. This, of course, sends Bird's mother, Jeffreys, into a predictable tailspin, but in the end, true love triumphs. This was the second film version of Ian Hay's play; it was preceded by a version done in 1921 and followed by one released in 1940.

p&d, Jack Raymond; w, W.P. Limpscomb (based on the stage play by Ian Hay); ph, F.A. Young; ed, T. Dickinson; art d, Clifford Pember.

Comedy   (PR:A   MPAA:NR)

TILLY OF BLOOMSBURY*½   (1940, Brit.) 83m Hammersmith/RKO bw

Sydney Howard (*Samuel Stillbottle*), Jean Gillie (*Tilly Welwyn*), Henry Oscar (*Lucius Welwyn*), Athene Seyler (*Mrs. Banks*), Michael Wilding (*Percy Welwyn*), Kathleen Harrison (*Mrs. Welwyn*), Athole Stewart (*Abel Mainwaring*), Michael Denison (*Dick Mainwaring*), Martita Hunt (*Lady Marion Mainwaring*), Joy Frankau (*Amelia Mainwaring*), Eve Shelley (*Diana*), Ian Fleming, Lloyd Pearson, Mavis Raeburn, Hendry White, Ben Williams, Charles Hersee, Reg Mankin.

British actor Sydney Howard liked playing a butler mixed up with a rich boy who finds love in the arms of a lowly boarding-house gal so much that he did it twice: once in the 1931 version of TILLY OF BLOOMSBURY, and then again, nine years later, in this film. There was, however, no improvement over the earlier effort, just different faces (except for Howard's). Both pictures were remakes of a 1921 silent.

p, Kurt Sternberg, A. Barr Smith; d, Leslie Hiscott; w, Nils Holstius, Jack Marks (based on the play by Ian Hay); ph, Bernard Browne.

Comedy   (PR:A   MPAA:NR)

TILT**   (1979) 111m Melvin Simon/WB c

Brooke Shields (*Tilt*), Ken Marshall (*Neil Gallagher*), Charles Durning (*The Whale*), John Crawford (*Mickey*), Harvey Lewis (*Henry Bertolino*), Robert Brian Berger (*Replay*), Geoffrey Lewis (*Truck Driver*), Gregory Walcott (*Mr. Davenport*), Helen Boll (*Mrs. Davenport*).

Dull Shields film which producer-director-cowriter Rudy Durand waited 10 years to make (?!). The story revolves around skillful pinball players and the only interesting thing about it is the fairly remarkable point-of-view shots from inside the pinball machine. Shields stars as an expert pinball player who hooks up with aspiring rock star Marshall and joins him on a cross-country adventure, seeking fame and fortune. Eventually the pair enter an intense game of high-stakes pinball with bar owner and pinball champ Durning. While some of the pinball scenes manage to generate some excitement, most of the film is slow and dull, with little wit and lots of bad performances–except for Durning, who, as usual, is superb.

p&d, Rudy Durand; w, Durand, Donald Cammell (based on a story by Durand); ph, Richard Kline (Technicolor); m, Lee Holdridge; ed, Bob Wyman, Don Guidice; prod d, Ned Parsons.

Drama   Cas.   (PR:C   MPAA:PG)

TIM**½   (1981, Aus.) 90m Pisces/Satori c

Piper Laurie (*Mary Horton*), Mel Gibson (*Tim Melville*), Alwyn Kurts (*Ron Melville*), Pat Evison (*Emily Melville*), Peter Gwynne (*Tom Ainsley*), Deborah Kennedy (*Dawn Melville*), David Foster (*Mick Harrington*), Margo Lee (*Mrs. Harrington*), James Condon (*Mr. Harrington*), Michael Caulfield (*John Martinson*), Brenda Senders (*Mrs. Parker*), Brian Barrie (*Dr. Perkins*), Kevin Leslie (*Curly Campbell*), Louise Pago (*Secretary*), Arthur Faynes (*Ambulance Attendant*), Geoff Usher (*Minister*), Sheila McGuire-Taylor (*Marriage Celebrant*), Alan Penny (*Storekeeper Thompson*), Catherine Bray (*Mrs. Martinson*), Doris Goddard (*Barmaid Maudie*).

The ultimate fantasy film for females in love with hunk Mel Gibson. Laurie plays a middle-aged woman who takes gorgeous young retarded man Gibson under her wing and teaches him how to function in the world. While his sexy looks and engaging manner definitely attract Laurie's lust, she manages to repress it through the film as she instructs the dim Gibson in reading. His parents eventually learn to trust the benevolent woman, and, of course, the audience alternately pants and sobs. The manipulation notwithstanding, Gibson is quite good as the young retarded man and it is a nice change of pace from his MAD MAX persona. TIM is based on a novel by the author of *The Thorn Birds*, Colleen McCullough.

p,d&w, Michael Pate (based on a novel by Colleen McCullough); ph, Paul Onorato; m, Eric Jupp; ed, David Stiven; art d, John Carroll; cos, Pat Forster.

Drama   **Cas.**   **(PR:C MPAA:NR)**

TIM DRISCOLL'S DONKEY**   (1955, Brit.) 59m Bushey-Children's Film Foundation/BL bw

David Coote (*Tim Driscoll*), John Kelly (*Mike Driscoll*), Hugh Latimer (*Mr. Marshall*), Peggy Marshall (*Mrs. Riordan*), Carole Lorimer (*Sheila Riordan*), Anthony Green (*Pat Reilly*), Shay Gordon (*Mr. Sullivan*).

Sappy kiddie affair starring Coote as a young orphan who lives and works on his grandfather's farm in Ireland raising donkeys. One day Coote's very own pet donkey named Patchy is sold by accident and shipped to England. The plucky lad leaves the farm and tracks down his favorite beast of burden. The boy then manages to enter a donkey race and rides Patchy to victory, with the ownership of the beast being his reward. An uninteresting and poorly put together film that will not hold the attention of even the most undiscriminating child.

p, Gilbert Church; d, Terry Bishop; w, Bishop, Patricia Latham (based on a story by Mary Cathcart Borer); ph, S.D. Onions.

Children's Film   **(PR:AA MPAA:NR)**

TIMBER**   (1942) 58m UNIV bw

Leo Carrillo (*Quebec*), Andy Devine (*Arizona*), Dan Dailey, Jr (*Kansas*), Marjorie Lord (*Yvette Lacour*), Edmund MacDonald (*Pierre Lacour*), Wade Boteler (*Dan Crowley*), Nestor Paiva (*Jules Fabian*), Paul E. Burns (*Pop Turner*), James Seay (*Joe Radway*), Jean Phillips (*Ann Barrows*), William Hall (*Bill Cormack*), Walter Sande (*Sandy*).

Usual wartime nonsense starring Carrillo as a timber-mill boss and Devine as a wood-crew foreman who join undercover agent Dailey in his battle to stop evil Nazi agents from destroying timber shipments vital to the war effort. Lord turns in a credible performance as the distaff love interest. This film brought together two actors who would later be among the best-known TV western sidekicks: Devine, who was Jingle B. Jones to Guy Madison's "Wild Bill Hickok," and Leo Carrillo, Pancho to Duncan Renaldo's "Cisco Kid."

p, Ben Pivar; d, Christy Cabanne; w, Griffin Jay (based on a story by Larry Rhine, Ben Chapman); ph, Jack McKenzie; ed, Otto Ludwig.

Drama   **(PR:A MPAA:NR)**

TIMBER FURY*½   (1950) 63m Jack Schwarz/EL bw

David Bruce (*Jim*), Laura Lee (*Phyllis*), Nicia Di Bruno (*Yvonne*), Sam Flint (*Henry Wilson*), George Slocum (*McCabe*), Lee Phelps (*Sheriff*), Gilbert Frye (*Pete*), Paul Hoffman (*Spike*), Spencer Chan (*Chung*), Zoro the Wonder Dog.

A timber war between rival logging firms pads out the action in this woodsy drama. Bruce stars as a bright young engineer who is hired by the "good" timber firm to figure out a way to transport the logs down river despite the efforts of an evil, rival timber firm to stop them. Aided by clever canine Zoro the Wonder Dog, Bruce manages to defeat villain Slocum and get the timber to market on time.

p&d, Bernard B. Ray; w, Michael Hansen (based on the short story "Retribution" by James Oliver Curwood); ph, Elmer Dyer; md, Ralph Stanley; art d, McClure Davis; m/l, "Blue in Love Again," "My Baby and Me" (sung by Nicia Di Bruno).

Adventure   **(PR:A MPAA:NR)**

TIMBER QUEEN*½   (1944) 66m PAR bw

Richard Arlen (*Russ*), Mary Beth Hughes (*Elaine*), June Havoc (*Lil*), Sheldon Leonard (*Smacksie*), George E. Stone (*Squirrel*), Dick Purcell (*Milt*), Tony Hughes (*Talbot*), Edmund MacDonald (*Birdsell*), Bill [William] Haade (*Rawson*), Clancy Cooper (*Barney*), Dewey Robinson (*Wenzel*), Horace McMahon (*Rodney*), Jimmy Ames (*Strudel*).

Another timberland adventure, this time starring Arlen as a returned WW II vet, discharged due to an injury. He comes to the rescue of Hughes, the widow of one of his war buddies, who is embroiled in a battle to keep her sawmill from the evil clutches of the gangsters who are trying to force her out of business. In order to save the business, Arlen and Hughes must cut and deliver a huge load of timber on time, despite the interference of the evildoers.

p, William Pine, William Thomas; d, Frank McDonald; w, Maxwell Shane, Edward T. Lowe; ph, Fred Jackman, Jr.; m, Willy Stahl; ed, Howard Smith; art d, F. Paul Sylos.

Drama   **(PR:A MPAA:NR)**

TIMBER STAMPEDE**   (1939) 59m RKO bw

George O'Brien (*Scott*), Chill Wills (*Whopper*), Marjorie Reynolds (*Anne, Reporter*), Morgan Wallace (*Dunlap*), Robert Fiske (*Matt*), Guy Usher (*Jones*), Earl Dwire (*Henry*), Frank Hagney (*Champ*), Robert "Bob" Burns (*Sheriff*), Monte Montague (*Jake*), Bud Osborne (*Brady*), William Benedict, Tom London, Elmo Lincoln, Bob Kortman, Ben Corbett, Cactus Mack, Hank Worden.

O'Brien plays a noble and heroic rancher who fights to stop a group of land grabbers from ruining valuable timberland. The property-hungry badmen claim they intend to build a railroad; O'Brien knows better. Naive New York newspaper reporter Reynolds is duped by the villains into launching a print campaign extolling the virtues of the project, but in the end, O'Brien manages to turn her head, and she strikes out against the land despoilers, falling in love with the rancher in the process. While all of O'Brien's earlier westerns for RKO had been moneymakers, this one failed to return a profit.

p, Bert Gilroy; d, David Howard; w, Morton Grant (based on stories by Bernard McConville, Paul Franklin); ed, Frederic Knudtson.

Western   **(PR:A MPAA:NR)**

TIMBER TERRORS*½   (1935) 59m Stage and Screen bw (GB: MORTON OF THE MOUNTED)

John Preston, Marla Bratton, James Sheridan [Sherry Tansey], William Desmond, Tiny Skelton, Fred Parker, Harold Berquest, Tom London, Harry Beery, Tex Jones, "Captain" King of the Dogs, "Dynamite" the Wonder Horse.

A determined Mountie risks life and limb in an effort to capture the cruel killers who murdered his partner. Typical Northwest woods adventure with emphasis on canine and equine escapades.

p,d&w, Robert Emmett [Tansey].;

Western   **(PR:A MPAA:NR)**

TIMBER TRAIL, THE**   (1948) 67m REP c

Monte Hale (*Himself*), Lynne Roberts (*Alice Baker*), James Burke (*Jed Baker*), Roy Barcroft (*Bart*), Francis Ford (*Ralph Baker*), Robert Emmett Keane (*Jordon Weatherbee*), Steve Darrell (*Sheriff*), Fred Graham (*Frank*), Wade Crosby (*Walt*), Eddie Acuff (*Telegraph Operator*), Foy Willing and the Riders of the Purple Sage.

Hale plays a friendly cowboy who makes a brief stop in a town run by outlaws to help Roberts, the daughter of a stagecoach operator who is being driven out of business by an evil banker and his hoods. The badmen do not take kindly to Hale's heroics so they frame him, throw him in jail, and beat the daylights out of him. Never fear, Hale pulls himself up, brushes himself off, and brings the baddies before the law.

p, Melville Tucker; d, Philip Ford; w, Bob Williams; ph, Reggie Lanning (TruColor); ed, Tony Martinelli; md, Mort Glickman; art d, Frank Hotaling; set d, John McCarthy, Jr., Charles Thompson; spec eff, Howard Lydecker, Theodore Lydecker; m/l, Tim Spencer, Ned Washington, Phil Ohman.

Western   **(PR:A MPAA:NR)**

TIMBER WAR*½   (1936) 55m Ambassador bw

Kermit Maynard (*Jim Dolan*), Lucille Lund (*Sally Martin*), Lawrence Gray (*Larry Keene*), Robert Warwick (*Ferguson*), Wheeler Oakman (*Murdock*), Lloyd Ingraham (*O'Leary*), Roger Williams (*Bowan*), George Morrell, James Pierce, Patricia Royal, Rocky the Horse.

Maynard gets involved in a battle between lumber companies when fire threatens the woodlands. By assuming the role of Gray, the careless owner of one company, Maynard gets into the fray and punches his way out.

p, Maurice Conn, Sigmund Neufeld; d, Sam Newfield; w, Joseph O'Donnell, Barry Berenges (based on a story by James Oliver Curwood); ph, Jack Greenhalgh; ed, Richard Wray.

Western   **(PR:A MPAA:NR)**

TIMBERJACK*   (1955) 94m REP bw

Sterling Hayden (*Tim Chipman*), Vera Ralston (*Lynne Tilton*), David Brian (*Croft Brunner*), Adolphe Menjou (*Swiftwater Tilton*), Hoagy Carmichael (*Jingles*), Chill Wills (*Steve Rilka*), Jim Davis (*Poole*), Howard Petrie (*Axe-Handle Ole*), Ian MacDonald (*Pauquette*), Elisha Cook, Jr (*Punky*), Karl Davis (*Red Bush*), Wally Cassell (*Veazie*), Tex Terry (*Charley*), George Marshall (*Fireman*).

A tiring tale about two feuding families in the woods of western Montana. Hayden in one camp has seen Brian kill his father and vows to seek his vengeance. But a well-meaning saloon girl, Ralston, tries to talk him out of the idea. She changes her tune when Brian kills her own father. Even the scenic photography of the Northern woods and the appearance of Hoagy

Carmichael, as the saloon pianist, can not overcome the triteness of this script.

p, Herbert J. Yates; d, Joseph Kane; w, Allen Rivkin (based on the novel by Dan Cushman); ph, Jack Marta (TruColor); m, Victor Young; ed, Richard L. Van Enger; art d, Frank Arrigo; set d, John McCarthy, Jr., George Milo; cos, Adele Palmer; ch, Jack Baker; m/l, "He's Dead but He Won't Lie Down," Johnny Mercer, Hoagy Carmichael, "Timberjack," Ned Washington, Victor Young.

Western   **(PR:A   MPAA:NR)**

TIMBUCTOO**   (1933, Brit.) 72m BIP/Wardour bw

Henry Kendall (*Benedict Tichbourne*), Margot Grahame (*Elizabeth*), Victor Stanley (*Henry*), Rama Tahe (*Native Girl*), Emily Fitzroy (*Aunt Agatha*), Jean Cadell (*Wilhelmina*), Una O'Connor (*Myrtle*), Hubert Harben (*Uncle George*), Edward Ashley Cooper (*Steven*).

Kendall has a row with his fiancee and takes off for a safari in Timbuctoo with his valet Stanley. His sweetheart is grief-stricken and travels to Timbuctoo to meet him. A simple comedy with actual desert photography incorporated from producer-director Summers' documentary ACROSS THE SAHARA.

p, Walter Summers; d, Summers, Arthur Woods; w, Summers (based on the anonymous book *Africa Dances*); ph, James Wilson.

Comedy   **(PR:A   MPAA:NR)**

TIMBUKTU**   (1959) 91m Imperial/UA bw

Victor Mature (*Mike Conway*), Yvonne De Carlo (*Natalie Dufort*), George Dolenz (*Col. Dufort*), John Dehner (*Emir*), Marcia Henderson (*Jeanne Marat*), Robert Clarke (*Capt. Girard*), James Foxx (*Lt. Marat*), Paul Wexler (*Suleyman*), Leonard Mudie (*Mohamet Adani*), Willard Sage (*Maj. Leroux*), Mark Dana (*Capt. Rimbaud*), Larry Perron (*Dagana*), Steve Darrell (*Nazir*), Larry Chance (*Ahmed*), Allan Pinson (*Sgt. Trooper*).

Set in the Sudan, members of the French Foreign Legion battle natives who are tired of the invaders. Mature plays an American trader who helps the French and steals De Carlo from her husband, the commander of the fort. Much of the plot concerns efforts to use a Moslem holy man, stereotypically depicted by Mudie, to quiet the rebels. To do so they must trek across the desert to the city of Timbuktu. Director Tourneur was out of place with this type of stuff. Producer Small dropped his name from the credits.

p, Edward Small; d, Jacques Tourneur; w, Anthony Veiller, Paul Dudley; ph, Maury Gertsman; m, Gerald Fried; ed, Grant Whytock; art d, Bill Glasgow; set d, Darrell Silvera; cos, Elva Martien; spec eff, Joe Zomar, Alex Weldon; makeup, Layne Britton.

Adventure/Drama   **(PR:A   MPAA:NR)**

TIME AFTER TIME***   (1979, Brit.) 112m WB-Orion c

Malcolm McDowell (*Herbert G. Wells*), David Warner (*Dr. John Lesley Stevenson*), Mary Steenburgen (*Amy Robbins*), Charles Cioffi (*Lt. Mitchell*), Laurie Main (*Inspector Gregson*), Andonia Katsaros (*Mrs. Turner*), Patti D'Arbanville (*Shirley*), Keith McConnell (*Harding*), Geraldine Baron (*Carol*), James Garrett (*Edwards*), Byron Webster (*McKay*), Leo Lewis (*Richardson*), Joseph Maher (*Adams*), Kent Williams (*Assistant*), Bob Shaw (*Bank Officer*), Karin Mary Shea (*Jenny*), Ray Reinhardt (*Jeweler*), Michael Evans (*Sergeant*), Stu Klitsner (*Clergyman*), Nicholas Shields (*Diner*), Larry J. Blake (*Guard*), Read Morgan (*Booking Cop*), Bill Bradley (*Pawnbroker*), Rita Conde (*Maid*), Shelley Hack (*Docent*), Clete Roberts (*Newscaster*), Gail Hyatt (*Woman Cop*), Jim Haynie, Wayne Storm, John Colton, Earl Nichols, Glenn Carlson (*Cops*), Gene Hartline (*Cab Driver*), Shirley Marchant (*Dolores*), James Cranna (*Man*), Antonie Becker (*Nurse*), Clement St. George (*Bobby*), Hilda Haynes (*2nd Nurse*), Corey Feldman (*Boy at Museum*), Mike Gainey (*London Bobby*), Daniel Leegant (*Man on Street*), Liz Roberson, Regina Waldron (*Women*), Anthony Gordon, Lou Felder, Doug Morrisson (*Men*).

This entertaining and imaginative work opens in Victorian London. From a point-of-view shot, the notorious killer Jack the Ripper stalks and murders a prostitute. Later that evening, at the home of noted writer H.G. Wells (McDowell), friends gather and McDowell tells them of his new invention. Warner, a surgeon, arrives late, then McDowell begins his lecture. He takes his friends to the cellar, where he has built a machine capable of traveling backward and forward in time. Though the group scoffs, McDowell is insistent that the machine will work. The police arrive, saying the Ripper has been seen in the neighborhood. They investigate Warner's medical bag and find his blood-stained gloves, pinpointing the good doctor as the crazed murderer. A search of the house turns up nothing, but after the police leave McDowell discovers Warner has escaped, using the time machine. The machine returns and McDowell learns Warner has traveled to November 5, 1979. McDowell grabs some jewels and money, then boards the machine to begin his search for Warner. Through a fantastical combination of sound and images, McDowell travels through the 20th Century and finally wakes up in an H.G. Wells exhibit in a San Francisco museum. McDowell quickly adjusts to the modern world, then goes to various banks to exchange his

English currency for American money. At the Bank of London he meets Steenburgen, an airhead teller who is immediately attracted to this strangely dressed man. She exchanges his money, then McDowell questions her about Warner. Steenburgen tells McDowell she directed him to a nearby hotel. McDowell takes a cab to the hotel, where he confronts Warner in his room. Warner refuses McDowell's pleas to return to Victorian London, exclaiming that now he is "home." Rather than the Utopian society McDowell had predicted for the future, the 20th Century is an era of materialism and violence. Warner proves this by switching on the television set and McDowell is shocked by the violent images that emanate from the tube. Warner flees the room and McDowell gives chase. Warner is hit by a car and taken to the hospital, where McDowell is told a man fitting the killer's description has died of internal injuries. McDowell makes a date with Steenburgen, and the two quickly fall in love. Meanwhile, Warner is far from dead and begins an all new killing spree. McDowell goes to the police, giving his name as "Sherlock Holmes," and tells them he knows who San Francisco's mysterious killer is. The police don't buy his story, frustrating McDowell. Later Warner returns to the Bank of London to exchange more money and learns Steenburgen has led McDowell to him. Warner threatens Steenburgen, who later confronts McDowell, demanding something be done. McDowell tells her the truth, which of course Steenburgen cannot believe. McDowell proves it to her by taking her into the time machine after the museum has closed. They voyage two days into the future (which takes only a quarter of a second), and Steenburgen finds a newspaper with an article stating she is the killer's latest victim. McDowell and Steenburgen go back to stop this, but are unable to prevent Warner from killing another woman. Steenburgen takes too much Valium and falls asleep in her apartment, while the police arrest McDowell as the killer. Knowing Warner is on his way to kill Steenburgen, McDowell makes a deal with his interrogators. He confesses to the killings in return for a patrol car being sent to Steenburgen's apartment. When the police arrive they find a bloodbath has taken place. McDowell is released but later finds Warner holding Steenburgen hostage. The dead woman was a friend Steenburgen had invited over for supper who mistakenly walked in on the killer. McDowell gives Warner the key to start the time machine in hopes of getting Steenburgen free, but the killer takes his hostage with him to the museum. McDowell grabs a car and drives in pursuit. At the Wells exhibit, Warner catches his watch chain on the machine, and in the confusion Steenburgen escapes. Warner prepares his voyage but McDowell sends him into infinity by pulling a protective device from the ship's side. McDowell persuades Steenburgen to return to Victorian London with him, and together they travel back in time. This well-crafted blend of fiction and history is a unique adventure that rarely fails to engage viewers with its inventive plotting and excellent special effects. McDowell is marvelous as the free-thinking Victorian who suddenly is confronted with the future. His sense of wonderment and horror at what the future offers works well, making this one of McDowell's better performances. Steenburgen, in her first major role, seems appropriately cast as the slightly daft bank teller, though her acting skills don't match McDowell's. Her characterization is too bland, never giving the part the energy it needs. And her voice is something similar to a cat screech. However, there is a good chemistry between the two, which extended off screen as well. McDowell and Steenburgen fell in love while making TIME AFTER TIME and were later married. Meyer makes a fine directorial debut, pacing the film nicely with a good sense for suspense, despite some obvious holes in the script. Meyer couldn't have been more qualified to take on this project. A few years earlier he had conquered the best seller lists with his original Sherlock Holmes novel *The Seven Per Cent Solution*, in which the great detective matched wits with none other than Sigmund Freud. After writing the script for the movie version of his book, Meyer proposed TIME AFTER TIME to the executives at Warner Bros. Based on his previous success in mixing fiction and fact, the project was approved and Meyer was given the opportunity to direct. Though an engaging and clever work, some of the language and blood-stained sequences make this inappropriate for younger viewers.

p, Herb Jaffe; d&w, Nicholas Meyer (based on a story by Karl Alexander, Steve Hayes); ph, Paul Lohmann (Panavision, Metrocolor); m, Miklos Rozsa; ed, Donn Cambern; prod d, Edward C. Carfagno; set d, Barbara Knieger; cos, Sal Anthony, Yvonne Kubis; spec eff, Larry Fuentes, Jim Blount; stunts, Everett Creach, Larry Duran, Gadie David, Brad Eide; makeup, Lynn Reynolds.

Science Fiction/Drama   **Cas.**   **(PR:O   MPAA:PG)**

TIME AND THE TOUCH, THE*½   (1962) 110m N.V. Productions bw

Vicki Cummins (*Elizabeth*), Xavier Marc (*Aristeo*), Tito Guizar (*Max*).

Cummins plays an elderly widow, living in Mexico, who takes up with teen-ager Marc when he rescues her from a drunken slob who is making advances to her. She had been married to a much older man and had lived a sheltered life. Now that her husband has died, she finds herself unaccustomed to handling many situations. When Marc makes a pass at her, she jumps into the affair. One of the problems with the film is that the actors always look as if they are playing a role. A worthy attempt that fails.

d, Benito Alezraki; w, Alezraki, Emilio Carballido; ph, Walter Reuter; m, Carlos Mabarek, Enrico Cabiati.

Drama   **(PR:C   MPAA:NR)**

TIME BANDITS* *** (1981, Brit.) 110m Handmade Films/AE c

John Cleese (*Robin Hood*), Sean Connery (*King Agamemnon*), Shelley Duvall (*Pansy*), Katherine Helmond (*Mrs. Ogre*), Ian Holm (*Napoleon*), Michael Palin (*Vincent*), Ralph Richardson (*Supreme Being*), Peter Vaughan (*Ogre*), David Warner (*Evil Genius*), David Rappaport (*Randall*), Kenny Baker (*Fidget*), Jack Purvis (*Wally*), Mike Edmunds (*Og*), Malcolm Dixon (*Strutter*), Tiny Ross (*Vermin*), Craig Warnock (*Kevin*), David Baker (*Kevin's Father*), Sheila Fearn (*Kevin's Mother*), Jim Broadbent (*Compere*), John Young (*Reginald*), Myrtle Devenish (*Beryl*), Brian Bowes (*Stunt Knight/Hussar*), Leon Lissek (*1st Refugee*), Terence Bayler (*Lucien*), Preston Lockwood (*Neguy*), Charles McKeown (*Theater Manager*), David Leland (*Puppeteer*), John Hughman (*The Great Rumbozo*), Derrick O'Connor (*Robber Leader*), Peter Jonfield (*Arm Wrestler*), Derek Deadman (*Robert*), Jerold Wells (*Benson*), Roger Frost (*Cartwright*), Martin Carroll (*Baxi Brazilia III*), Marcus Powell (*Horse Flesh*), Winston Dennis (*Bull-Headed Warrior*), Del Baker (*Greek Fighting Warrior*), Juliette James (*Greek Queen*), Ian Muir (*Giant*), Mark Holmes (*Troll Father*), Andrew MacLachlan (*Fireman*), Chris Grant (*Voice of TV Announcer*), Tony Jay (*Voice of Supreme Being*), Edwin Finn (*Supreme Being's Face*), Neil McCarthy (*2nd Robber*), Declan Mulholland (*3rd Robber*), Frances De La Tour (*Salvation Army Major*).

Gilliam and Palin from Monty Python's Flying Circus masterminded this madcapped journey through history, in which the tot Warnock is whisked out of his home by six mischievous dwarfs holding a map that reveals gaps in the universe. They travel throughout history encountering the likes of Cleese in a rendition of Robin Hood, Connery as a mystical Greek warrior, and Holm as Napoleon. Also prominent is Sir Ralph Richardson as the mastermind behind the structure of the universe, a great depiction that has him dressed in a business suit. Beneath all the merriment is the message that the media, primarily television, are doing a good job of destroying human imagination. Delivered in the customary mayhem-like manner of Python features, resulting in an onslaught of clever witticisms and slapstick.

p&d, Terry Gilliam; w, Michael Palin, Gilliam; ph, Peter Biziou (Technicolor); m, Mike Moran; ed, Julian Doyle; prod d, Millie Burns; art d, Norman Garwood; m/l, George Harrison.

Comedy **Cas.** **(PR:A-C MPAA:PG)**

TIME BOMB, 1953 (SEE: TERROR ON A TRAIN, 1953)

TIME BOMB½ (1961, Fr./Ital.) 92m Le Groupe des Quatre-Da. Ma./AA bw (LE VENT SE LEVE; IL VENTO SI ALZA)

Curt Jurgens (*Eric Mullen*), Mylene Demongeot (*Catherine*), Alain Saury (*Michel*), Paul Mercey (*Cook*), Robert Porte (*Steward*), Daniel Sorano (*Mathias*), Jean Daurand (*Pepere*), Gabriel Gobin (*Aubriand*), Andre Dalibert (*Carminati*), Jess Hahn (*Chewing-Gum*), Raymond Loyer (*Laurent*), Jim Gerald (*Drunk*), Pierre Collet, Guy Dakar, Jean-Jacques Lecot, Henri Maik, Pierre Paulet, Jean Murat, Claire Guibert (*crew*).

As the captain of a freighter belonging to a family with money problems, Jurgens gets involved in a plot to blow up the ship to collect the insurance money. The plan is to sail to what is believed to be an active minefield and let the bombs do their work. Before Jurgens leaves Hamburg, he places a time bomb in the ship's hold set to go off when it reaches the alleged minefield. But this creates problems. One worker is trapped when a boiler burns up, forcing Jurgens to disconnect the bomb. And he is happy to do it because he never fully approved of the scheme. He then sails back to Hamburg to discover that part of the family never liked the plan either. This film concentrates on the guilt that accompanies making a less-than-honest choice.

p, Raymond Froment; d, Yves Ciampi; w, Jacques-Laurent Bost, Ciampi, Henri-Francois Rey (based on a story by Jean-Charles Tacchella); ph, Armand Thirard; m, Henri Crolla, Andre Hodeir; ed, Georges Alepee; art d, Roger Briaucourt; cos, Pierre Balmain, Jeannine Germes-Vergne, Yvette Bonnay; makeup, Alexandre Marcus.

Drama **(PR:A MPAA:NR)**

TIME FLIES** ** (1944, Brit.) 88m Gainsborough/GFD bw

Tommy Handley (*Tommy*), Evelyn Dall (*Susie Barton*), George Moon (*Bill Barton*), Felix Aylmer (*Professor*), Moore Marriott (*Soothsayer*), Graham Moffatt (*His Nephew*), John Salew (*William Shakespeare*), Leslie Bradley (*Walter Raleigh*), Olga Lindo (*Queen Elizabeth*), Roy Emerton (*Capt. John Smith*), Iris Lang (*Princess Pocahontas*), Stephane Grappelly (*Troubadour*), Peter Murray, Lloyd Pearson, Vincent Holman, Paul Morton, Nicholas Stuart, Tommy Duggan, Sydney Young, Noel Dainton, Glyn Rowlands, Brooks Turner, Wallace Bosco.

A crazed inventor, Aylmer, and his sidekick valet, Handley, become part of the Elizabethan era when their time machine actually works. A well-tuned script takes full advantages of the possibilities for comedy, but radio star Handley is a bit of a disappointment, looking sourly out of place on the screen.

p, Edward Black; d, Walter Forde; w, Howard Irving Young, J.O.C. Orton, Ted Kavanagh; ph, Basil Emmott.

Fantasy/Comedy **(PR:A MPAA:NR)**

TIME FOR ACTION (SEE: TIP ON A DEAD JOCKEY, 1957)

TIME FOR DYING, A* *** (1971) 87m Fipco/Etoile Distribution c

Richard Lapp (*Cass Bunning*), Anne Randall (*Nellie Winters*), Audie Murphy (*Jesse James*), Victor Jory (*Judge Roy Bean*), Beatrice Kay (*Mamie*), Bob Random (*Billy Pimple*), Peter Brocco (*Ed*), Burt Mustin (*Seth*).

A return to feature films after nearly 10 years during which time director Boetticher devoted himself to a documentary on the matador Arruza. This is an offbeat western that explores the myth of the western hero. A young farm boy, Lapp, comes off the farm and into the land of killers and lawlessness. His goal is to make something of himself through his gunhandling ability, and he attempts to do so as a bounty hunter. Unfortunately he is no match for a psychotic gunman, giving Lapp an early burial. But before the lad is gunned down, he encounters several of the legendary heroes of the West; the first being Jory as Judge Roy Bean, who is depicted as a drunken sentimentalist. He later runs into Audie Murphy, in his last screen role, as Jesse James, who stops the boy long enough to give him some much needed advice. Though A TIME FOR DYING is loaded with violence, it takes a decidedly humanistic perspective toward the western genre, showing how a kid seeks to become a hero when he has yet to know anything about how the world works. This is especially relevant to modern society where the heroes from movies and TV are role models both the young and not so young emulate.

p, Audie Murphy; d&w, Budd Boetticher; ph, Lucien Ballard (DeLuxe Color); m, Harry Belts; ed, Harry Knapp; art d, Leslie Thomas.

Western **(PR:C MPAA:NR)**

TIME FOR GIVING, A (SEE: GENERATION, 1969)

TIME FOR HEROS, A (SEE: HELL WITH HEROS, THE, 1968)

TIME FOR KILLING, A½ (1967) 83m Sage/COL c (GB: THE LONG RIDE HOME)

Glenn Ford (*Maj. Charles Wolcott*), George Hamilton (*Capt. Dorrit Bentley*), Inger Stevens (*Emily Biddle*), Paul Petersen (*Blue Lake*), Timothy Carey (*Billy Cat*), Kenneth Tobey (*Sgt. Cleehan*), Max Baer (*Sgt. Luther Liskell*), Todd Armstrong (*Lt. Prudessing*), Duke Hobbie (*Lt. Frist*), Dean Stanton (*Sgt. Dan Way*), Richard X. Slattery (*Cpl. Paddy Darling*), Harrison J. Ford (*Lt. Shaffer*), Kay E. Kuter (*Owelson*), Dick Miller (*Zollicoffer*), Emile Meyer (*Col. Harries*), Marshall Reed (*Stedner*), James Davidson (*Little Mo*), Charlie Briggs (*Sgt. Kettlinger*), Craig Curtis (*Bagnef*), Jay Ripley (*Lovingwood*), Dean Goodhill (*Bruce*).

This tale of confrontations between Union and Confederate troops at the close of the Civil War is a gritty western, desolate in its outlook and with often numbing violence. In Fort Hawkes, Utah a group of rebel soldiers is held captive by the Union. A guard is killed by one of the Confederates in an attempt to escape, but he is captured before making his getaway. The southerner is sentenced to die and after he insults a commanding Union officer it is decided that his executioners will be a group of black orderlies, untrained in marksmanship. The doomed young man is shot repeatedly by the squad, yet they cannot kill him. Finally Glenn Ford, a Union major, enters to put the poor man out of his misery. Hamilton, leader of the captured Southern forces, is enraged over the treatment of his soldier and with the help of his remaining troops is able to escape by blowing up Fort Hawkes. Hamilton and his men later kill a group of Union soldiers and take Stevens--a missionary and Ford's fiancee--as a hostage. Ford and a group of Union soldiers go out to rescue her not knowing that the confederates plan an ambush. Hamilton learns that General Lee has surrendered to General Grant at Appomattox. Keeping this news from his men, Hamilton tells Stevens before he savagely rapes and beats her. Hamilton then takes his men to the Arizona-Mexico border, hoping Stevens will send Ford after them for revenge without telling him of the war's end. Things go exactly as Hamilton has planned as Ford confronts the man in an abandoned mission. The battle is vicious and Hamilton is mortally injured. Before dying he is able to tell Ford of the North's victory and Stevens' knowledge of this. After Hamilt on dies, his rival, stunned by the needless events, returns home with his men. Behind them follows Stevens, herself shaken by the happenings. The script is somewhat overwritten but this problem is overcome by careful, studied direction. Karlson makes the most of the rivalry between North and South embodied in the two men, creating tension that builds into the final bloody confrontation. His camera dwells on the violence without mercy and while not gratuitous, the intensity lingers well past a comfortable point for the viewer. Glenn Ford is fine in his stoic role but the film suffers from weaker secondary characters intended as comic relief. Baer, better remembered as the idiotic Jethro from the television show "The Beverly Hillbillies", is little more than an extension of that image in his role as a rebel soldier ready to fire on sight. Also in minor parts of company soldiers are Harrison Ford, later an Oscar nominee for his role in the 1985 film WITNESS, and cult favorite Harry Dean Stanton, here under the name "Dean Stanton." Shot on location in Utah's Zion National Park and the Glen

Canyon National Recreation Area along the Arizona-Utah border, the film's original director was Roger Corman, but a few weeks into the production the job was taken over by Karlson. Also replaced after the initial production work was the film's original editor Monte Hellman, director of such fine films as THE SHOOTING and TWO-LANE BLACKTOP.

p, Harry Joe Brown; d, Phil Karlson; w, Halsted Welles (based on the novel *The Southern Blade* Nelson Wolford, Shirley Wolford); ph, Kenneth Peach (Panavision, Pathe Color); m, Van Alexander, Mundell Lowe; ed, George White; md, Lowe; art d, Daniel Heller; set d, Jack Ahern; m/l, "The Long Ride Home" Ned Washington, Alexander (sung by Eddy Arnold); makeup, Ben Lane.

Western   (PR:A   MPAA:A)

TIME FOR LOVING, A**   (1971, Brit.) 104m London Screen Plays c
                               (AKA: PARIS WAS MADE FOR LOVERS)

Joanna Shimkus, Mel Ferrer, Britt Ekland, Philippe Noiret, Lila Kedrova, Robert Dhery, Michael Burns.

This film chronicles a series of romantic interludes, all of which take place in the same Parisian apartment. It tries to be a sort of British version of PLAZA SUITE (1971) but the comedy is just too thin to sustain laughs. Ferrer, best remembered as LILI's (1953) disabled puppeteer, served as producer in addition to his featured role.

p, Mel Ferrer; d, Christopher Miles; w, Jean Anouilh; ph, Andreas Winding; m, Michel Legrand; prod d, Theo Meurisse.

Comedy   (PR:A-C   MPAA:NR)

TIME GENTLEMEN PLEASE!**½   (1953, Brit.) 79m Group
                                    3/Mayer-Kingsley bw

Eddie Byrne (*Dan Dance*), Hermione Baddeley (*Emma Stebbins*), Raymond Lovell (*Sir Digby Montague*), Jane Barrett (*Sally*), Dora Bryan (*Peggy Stebbins*), Robert Brown (*Bill Jordan*), Marjorie Rhodes (*Miss Mouncey*), Thora Hird (*Alice Crouch*), Ivor Barnard (*Timothy Crouch*), Sidney James (*Eric Hace*), Edie Martin (*Mary Wade*), Sydney Tafler (*Joseph Spink*), Joan Young (*Mrs. Round*), Marianne Stone (*Mrs. Pincer*), Patrick McAlinney (*Reverend Soater*), Peter Jones (*Lionel Batts*), Ian Carmichael (*PRO*), Julian d'Albie, Nigel Clarke, Henry Longhurst, Peter Swanwick, Thomas Gallagher, Freda Bamford, Brian Roper, Harry Herbert, Jack May, Toke Townley, Tristram Rawson, Donovan Winter, Sheila Aza, Julie Millan, Michael Edmunds, Cora Bennett, Audrey Noble, Virginia Winter, Neil Gemmell, Helen Boursnell.

A witty comedy about an Irishman, Byrne, living in a small English village, who sets the rest of the community on their heels with his unwillingness to work. The town is about to be the recipient of a visit by the prime minister, who is making the trip just to reward the place for having almost total employment, the only holdout in this respect being the feisty Byrne. Though nearly everyone in the village, especially the hypocritical members of the city council, harasses the poor man, he gains a friend in a new clergyman. When the councilmen force the free-spirited indigent into the local poorhouse, where he is the only occupant, the vicar discovers that he becomes entitled thereby to a grant of a substantial sum of money to be paid out of the village treasury. This results in the entire council being swept out of office; a new council is established with Byrne as its chairman. The townsfolk then find him employment appropriate to his capabilities as a mattress tester in a furniture factory. Fine performances by Abbey Theatre player Byrne and a great supporting cast. Another of the taut comedies made in Britain with government money under the auspices of Group 3, headed by famed documentarist Grierson.

p, John Grierson, Herbert Mason; d, Lewis Gilbert; w, Peter Blackmore, Val Guest (based on the novel *Nothing To Lose* by R. J. Minney); ph, Wilkie Cooper; m, John Addison.

Comedy   (PR:A   MPAA:NR)

TIME IN THE SUN, A*½   (1970, Swed.) 104m Europa/UNIV bw
                              (PRINSESSAN; AKA: THE PRINCESS)

Grynet Molvig ("*Princess*"), Lars Passgard (*Gunnar*), Monica Nielsen (*Pirjo*), Birgitta Valberg (*Doctor*), Thor Lyndthal (*Obstetrician*), Heinz Spira (*Chum*), Axel Duberg (*Clergyman*).

A boring Swedish drama about a woman dying of a dreadful disease who overcomes her illness when she falls in love with a journalist. Every bit of sentiment is pulled as the couple marry, have a child, than slowly watch the woman become totally healthy. (In Swedish; English subtitles.)

d, Ake Falck; w, Falck, Lars Widding (based on the novel *Prinsessan* by Gunnar Mattsson); ph, Mac Ahlberg, Ralph Evers; m, Harry Arnold. (English Titles: Noelle Gillmor).

Drama   (PR:O   MPAA:R)

TIME IS MY ENEMY**   (1957, Brit.) 64m Vandyke/REP bw

Dennis Price (*Martin Radley*), Renee Asherson (*Barbara Everton*), Susan Shaw (*Evelyn Gower*), Patrick Barr (*John Everton*), Bonar Colleano (*Roommate*), Duncan Lamont (*Inspector Charles Wayne*), Brenda Hogan (*Diana*), Alfie Bass (*Ernie Gordon*), Agnes Lauchlan (*Aunt Laura*), William Franklyn (*Peter Thompson*), Bruce Beeby, Mavis Villiers, Barbara Grayley, Dandy Nichols, Nigel Neilson, Neil Wilson, Alastair Hunter, Erik Chitty, Audrey Hessey, Ian Wilson.

Price tries to cover up a murder he committed by framing his ex-wife, Asherson. He goads her into firing a gun loaded with blanks at him so that she will confess to the murder of the man she thinks he is, the man he had killed. Police inspector Lamont puts the pieces of the puzzle together and proves that Price is the guilty one. Too routine in dialog to lift it in any memorable way.

p, Roger Proudlock; d, Don Chaffey; w, Allan Mackinnon (based on the play "Second Chance" by Ella Adkins); ph, Geoffrey Faithfull; ed, Sam Simmonds; art d, Bert Davey.

Crime   (PR:A   MPAA:NR)

TIME LIMIT****   (1957) 96m Heath/UA bw

Richard Widmark (*Col. William Edwards*), Richard Basehart (*Maj. Harry Cargill*), Dolores Michaels (*Cpl. Jean Evans*), June Lockhart (*Mrs. Cargill*), Carl Benton Reid (*Gen. Connors*), Martin Balsam (*Sgt. Baker*), Rip Torn (*Lt. George Miller*), Alan Dexter (*Mike*), Yale Wexler (*Capt. Joe Connors*), Manning Ross (*Lt. Harvey*), Kaie Deei (*Col. Kim*), Skip McNally (*Poleska*), Joe di Reda (*Gus*), Kenneth Alton (*Boxer*), James Douglas (*Steve*), Jack Webster (*Lt. Harper*).

This compelling courtroom drama features Basehart as an army major on trial for collaborating with the enemy while he was captive in Korea. The former prisoner-of-war readily admits his guilt in such acts as broadcasting anti-American sentiments for his captors. Widmark is the Army colonel investigating the case, suspicious as to why Basehart--an essentially good man--would break so readily. The truth is slowly revealed, then finally brought into the open by Torn, a young lieutenant who tells the court Basehart's real motivation. In order to save the lives of 16 fellow POW's following the execution of an informer, Basehart had been forced to cooperate with the North Koreans; a secret the man has carried for the entire trial. This raises a moral issue that has no easy answer: is Basehart a traitor despite his good intentions? Such themes run through the film. Morality comes in varied shades of gray in the damning process, with answers coming in a tortured and agonizing process for both accused and the accuser. This journey into the conflict between humanism and duty is an excellent examination, performed and directed with intensity. Basehart and Widmark are superb in their characterizations, two men in a face-off of disturbing ideas. Directed by actor Malden, the film is a tightly structured piece that forces its audience to think about the difficult issues it raises. He makes excellent use of his cast, wringing out emotion without bathos and adding flashback sequences to Korea at crucial moments. Denker adapted the script from a play he co-wrote with Ralph Berkey, constructing the story like a series of Chinese boxes, revealing information slowly until the emotional climax. TIME LIMIT is not an easy film to take, but certainly is important in the issues it raises and the sensitive manner with which they are handled.

p, Richard Widmark, William Reynolds; d, Karl Malden; w, Henry Denker (based on the play by Denker, Ralph Berkey); ph, Sam Leavitt; m, Fred Steiner; ed, Aaron Stell; md, Steiner; art d, Serge Krizman; cos, Henry West.

Drama   (PR:C   MPAA:NR)

TIME LOCK**   (1959, Brit.) 73m Romulus-Beaconsfield/Distributors bw

Robert Beatty (*Peter Dawson*), Betty McDowall (*Lucille Walker*), Vincent Winter (*Steven Walker*), Lee Patterson (*Colin Walker*), Sandra Francis (*Evelyn Webb*), Alan Gifford (*George Foster*), Robert Ayres (*Inspector Andrews*), Victor Wood (*Howard Zeeder*), Jack Cunningham (*Max Jarvis*), Peter Mannering (*Dr. Foy*), Gordon Tanner (*Dr. Hewitson*), Larry Cross (*Reporter*), John Paul (*Foreman*), Donald Ewer (*Bank Customer*), Murray Kash, Sean Connery (*Welders*), Roland Brand, David Williams (*Police Officers*).

A young boy is accidentally locked inside a bank vault which is set to remain locked for another 63 hours, setting the stage for a number of experts to figure how to get the child out. Meanwhile the boy's parents look on in terror at the thought that their child may soon be dead, in the airless chamber, the clock constantly ticking away. Acetylene torches fail, but vault expert Beatty turns the tide and retrieves the child, unconscious but alive. Filmed in England but set in Canada, with some Canadian actors lending authenticity.

p, Peter Rogers; d, Gerald Thomas; w, Rogers (based on a television script by Arthur Hailey); ph, Peter Hennessy; m, Stanley Black; ed, John Trumper; art d, Norman Arnold.

Drama   (PR:A   MPAA:NR)

TIME LOST AND TIME REMEMBERED½**   (1966, Brit.) 91m
Partisan-Rank/CD bw (GB: I WAS HAPPY HERE)

Sarah Miles (Cass), Cyril Cusack (Hogan), Julian Glover (Dr. Matthew Langdon), Sean Caffrey (Colin Foley), Marie Kean (Barkeeper), Eve Belton (Kate), Cardew Robinson (Gravedigger).

Miles is an Irish girl who takes off for the city lights of London. She leaves expecting her fisherman boy friend, Caffrey, to follow her, but that never happens. Lonely and desperate, she ends up in a bad marriage with a boorish young doctor, Glover. At Christmas she goes back to her home town to find that Caffrey is engaged. She also discovers that she has changed more than the town has. Glover arrives to bring her back to London but she elects to stay even though all her dreams have been shattered. Slow in pace, with beautiful photography and fine acting, this is a well-told tale of disenchantment and resignation. Partly financed by the British government through the National Film Finance Corporation in an effort to encourage independent productions.

p, Roy Millichip; d, Desmond Davis; w, Davis, Edna O'Brien (based on the story "A Woman by the Seaside" by O'Brien); ph, Manny Wynn; m, John Addison; ed, Brian Smedley-Aston; art d, Tony Woollard; makeup, Richard Mills.

Drama   (PR:A   MPAA:NR)

TIME MACHINE, THE**   (1960; Brit./U.S.) 103m Galaxy/MGM c

Rod Taylor (George), Alan Young (David Filby/James Filby), Yvette Mimieux (Weena), Sebastian Cabot (Dr. Philip Hillyer), Tom Helmore (Anthony Bridewell), Whit Bissell (Walter Kemp), Doris Lloyd (Mrs. Watchell), Paul Frees (Voice of the History Machine), Bob Barran (Eloi Man).

A smashing science-fiction adaptation of H. G. Wells' novel that has more creativity in every frame than most latter-day rip-offs Have in the entire movie. Rod Taylor is a turn-of-the-century inventor. The action begins on the final day of the last century and shoots forward, making brief stops for the two World Wars, a third–atomic–conflagration, and then into an era circa the year 800,000. Back in the Victorian era, Taylor's friends (Bissell, Helmore, Cabot) fear for his sanity as he talks about his latest invention, a time machine. It looks like a buggy without the horse and they are convinced that he is unsound. His only believer is Young, a Scotsman. (Young plays three roles, as the Scot, the son of the Scot, and the son when he is ancient). Taylor sits in his little machine with red velvet upholstery, sets it forward, and we can see time pass by the way the clothing changes on the mannequin in the window across the road from Taylor's home. While this machine travels in time, it does not travel in space, so all of the action takes place in the general area where Taylor's home stands in England. Taylor zips forward to the Great War and encounters Young, who doesn't seem to have aged. Then he realizes that Young is the son of the man who was his friend years before. Taylor visits his home, now deserted and abandoned, and decides to go even further into the future. He visits the time of the Second World War, then is startled to learn that the Earth was almost destroyed in an atomic battle in 1966 (since this movie was made in 1959/60 and the "Cold War" was freezing relationships between the East and West, this was an added bit of gloom) and finally sets his time-gear for a distant age. Upon arriving in the year 802,701, give or take a month, Taylor learns that humanity has been divided into two distinctly different tribes. Beneath the earth is a tribe of cannibals known as Morlocks. These creatures are mutated and occupy a high-tech world underground. Above the ground is a group of blonde, happy but vacant people, who spend most of their time milling around and procreating. The entire reason for their existence is to act as a human herd for the Morlocks to dine upon. This tribe is known as the Eloi and they have no leader, no organization, no abilities. They have become so bovine that they march herd-like whenever they hear the sirens that signify it's time for them to be eaten. Taylor can't believe how the human race has altered. He meets Mimieux, falls in love with her, and stirs up the Eloi until they revolt against the Morlocks. Taylor then returns to 1900, picks up three books which he wants to use to educate the Eloi, and returns with them to the future. Now, the question is: what three books would a person choose to effect an educational process on people who have no idea of what books are? That is never answered. The dour vision of Wells has been changed in the movie. The novel had Mimieux's character killed and the Taylor character continuing until the end of time. It's too bad that no sequels were made. Any number of time travel movies have been done since but few of them can hold a candle to this. Producer/director Pal, who was born in Hungary, came to the U.S. and produced and directed a series of puppet shorts using stop motion which were known as "Puppetoons." In the 1950s, he turned to feature films as a producer and special-effects person. His effects were always first-rate and he won (or shared) Oscars for his work on this film, DESTINATION MOON, WHEN WORLDS COLLIDE, and THE WAR OF THE WORLDS. In 1943, he received a special Oscar for his "Puppetoons" technique. Although the acting was uniformly good, the performances took second place to the effects. When one realizes the small budget on a film like this next to the inflated costs of many other science-fiction movies, it's easy to see why Pal was so revered. Every dollar he spent looked like ten dollars on the screen. The pace of the picture flagged in a few scenes but that was because the other scenes were so swift and forceful by comparison. A fine musical score by jazz composer Russ Garcia.

Some of the more grotesque effects might cause nightmares in small children.

p&d, George Pal; w, David Duncan (based on the novel by H. G. Wells); ph, Paul C. Vogel (Metrocolor); m, Russell Garcia; ed, George Tomasini; art d, George W. Davis, William Ferrari; set d, Henry Grace, Keogh Gleason; spec eff, Gene Warren, Tim Baer, Wah Chang; makeup, William Tuttle.

Fantasy   Cas.   (PR:A   MPAA:G)

TIME OF DESIRE, THE*   (1957, Swed.) 81m Europa/Janus bw

Barbro Larsson (Lilly Lilja), Margaretha Lawler (Ragni Lilja), George Fant (The Father), Berger Malmsten (Algot Wiberg), Marianne Lofgren (Maid), Nils Hallberg (Nils), Ingemar Pallin (Pastor).

A slow-moving, pastoral picture with some steamy sexuality in the Swedish style, this deals with an extended farm family headed by Fant. The males of the household spend the long, cold nights pursuing the nubile household helpers, while Fant's daughters Larsson and Lawler develop a sexual interest in one another. Their bucolic idyll is interrupted by Malmsten, new to the community, with whom Lawler has a brief, unsatisfactory fling. These goings-on are punctuated by glimpses of the customary Swedish hellfire-and-damnation pastor pontificating about sin and salvation. Delivered of Malmsten's child, Lawler resumes her relationship with her sister. The final scene has the two, with the infant, driving past preacher Pallin, who looks upon them bemusedly.

d&w, Egil Holmsen (based on a story by Arthur Lundquist); ph, Ingvar Borild; m, Harry Arnold.

Drama   (PR:O   MPAA:NR)

TIME OF HIS LIFE, THE*   (1955, Brit.) 74m Shaftesbury/REN bw

Richard Hearne (Charles Pastry), Ellen Pollock (Lady Florence), Richard Wattis (Edgar), Robert Moreton (Humphrey), Frederick Leister (Sir John), Peter Sinclair (Kane), John Downing (Simon), Anne Smith (Penelope), Darcy Conyers (Morgan), Yvonne Hearne (Guest), Arthur Hewlett, Andrea Troubridge, Neil Wilson, Alan Whittaker, Edgar Driver, Jessica Cairns, Peggyann Clifford.

A harmless comedy about a socially upstanding young woman, Pollock, who is embarrassed by her jailbird father, Hearne. She tries to have him shipped off to Australia to avoid a scandal. When that fails she locks him in her attic, but that, too, proves unsuccessful. The situation is resolved when Hearne gets a job as the governor's handyman. A simple picture with likable characters.

p, Elizabeth Hiscott, W.A. Smith; d, Leslie Hiscott; w, Leslie Hiscott, Richard Hearne (based on the story by Leslie Hiscott, Brock Williams); ph, Kenneth Talbot.

Comedy   (PR:A   MPAA:NR)

TIME OF INDIFFERENCE*   (1965, Fr./Ital.) 84m C.C.F. Lux-Ultra Film-Vides/CD bw (GLI INDIFFERENTI; LES DEUX RIVALES)

Rod Steiger (Leo), Claudia Cardinale (Carla Ardengo), Shelley Winters (Lisa), Paulette Goddard (Maria Grazia Ardengo), Tomas Milian (Michele Ardengo).

Steiger plays an opportunist trying to take advantage of a wealthy aristocrat, Goddard, who is too lost within her decaying world to notice Steiger's wooing of her daughter Cardinale. Adapted from the novel by Alberto Moravia, an attempt is made to show a dying society unable to grasp the changing world. Even though director Maselli has an excellent cast, he doesn't have the ability to effectively bring these themes to the screen; this is more up the alley of Luchino Visconti.

p, Franco Cristaldi; d, Francesco Maselli; w, Maselli, Suso Cecchi D'Amico (based on the novel Gli Indifferenti by Alberto Moravia); ph, Gianni Di Venanzo; m, Giovanni Fusco; ed, Ruggero Mastroianni; art d, Luigi Scaccianoce; cos, Marcel Escoffier.

Drama   (PR:A   MPAA:NR)

TIME OF RETURN, THE   (SEE: MURIEL, 1963, Fr./Ital.)

TIME OF ROSES**   (1970, Fin.) 90m Filminor/Cinema Dimensions bw (RUUSUJEN AIKA)

Ritva Vespa (Saara), Arto Tuominen (Raimo), Tarja Markus (Anu), Eero Keskitalo, Kalle Holmberg, Eila Pelikonen, Unto Salminen.

An Orwellian view of the future and of the impact of the mass media on history. Tuominen, a 21st-century historian/filmmaker, produces a TV picture dealing with the 1970s. His film, a drama distorted by the political perspective of his own time, deals with the life of shopgirl Vespa–who also plays Tuominen's contemporary girl friend–who dies in an automobile accident (or was it suicide?). Some of Tuominen's employees are radicals who secretly despise his view of the past. A fascinating subject, one of a series of filmic social criticisms from director Jarva, his country's leading filmmaker.

p&d, Risto Jarva; w, Jarva, Peter von Bagh, Jaakko Pakkasvirta; ph, Antti Peippo; m, Otto Donner; spec eff, Anssi Blomstedt, Erkki Kurenniemi.

Fantasy/Drama   (PR:C   MPAA:NR)

TIME OF THE HEATHEN*½   (1962) 75m Emshwiller/Lion
                                                          International bw

John Heffernan (Gaunt), Stewart Heller (Ted), Barry Collins (Jesse), Orville Steward (Link), Ethel Ayler (Marie), Nathaniel White (Cal), Dan Goulding.

A bible-toting drifter, Heffernan, happens upon the rape-murder of a black woman, Ayler, by farm boy Heller. The latter's father, Steward, attempts to pin the crime on the stranger, and urges Heller to shoot both Heffernan and another witness, Ayler's mute son Collins. The intended victims escape, pursued by the father and son and by sheriff White. Confronted in some woods, Heffernan kills Heller, and is later wounded by Steward. Delirious, the injured Heffernan relives his past in flashback, revealing himself as one of the airplane crew to drop the atom bomb on Hiroshima. The mute boy brings a doctor, who states his intention to turn Heffernan in. Heffernan and the boy embrace just as Steward shoots the former. This first feature picture by writer/director Kass suffers from its attempt to cover too much ground.

p, Calvin Floyd; d&w, Peter Kass; ph, Ed Emshwiller; m, Lejaren A'Hiller, Jr.; ed, Emshwiller, Kass; md, Robert Gray.

Drama   (PR:C   MPAA:NR)

TIME OF THE WOLVES**½   (1970, Fr.) 105m Lira-Paris
                                           Cannes-Seven/Fernand Rivers c (TEMPS DES LOUPS)

Robert Hossein (Dillinger), Charles Aznavour (Inspecteur), Virna Lisi (Stella), Genevieve Thenier (Girl), Albert Minsky (Hood), Marcel Bozzuffi (Sidekick), Roger Coggio (Innkeeper).

An old Hollywood gangster yarn given modern-day French stylishness, with Hossein as a hardened criminal edging on insanity, with the responsibility for his capture going to childhood friend Aznavour (SHOOT THE PIANO PLAYER, 1962). Concentration is mainly on the psychological aspects of Hossein's personality, hinting at the events which have made him become a criminal. Lisi plays a girl who passingly meets Hossein and immediately takes a genuine liking to him. (In French.)

d, Sergio Gobbi; w, Gobbi, Andre Tabet; ph, Daniel Diot (Eastmancolor); m, Georges Gavarentz; ed, Gabriel Rongier.

Crime/Drama   (PR:O   MPAA:NR)

TIME OF THEIR LIVES, THE**½
                (1946) 82m UNIV bw (AKA: THE GHOST STEPS OUT)

Bud Abbott (Cuthbert/Dr. Greenway), Lou Costello (Horatio Prim), Marjorie Reynolds (Melody Allen), Binnie Barnes (Mildred Prescott), John Shelton (Sheldon Gage), Jess Barker (Tom Danbury), Gale Sondergaard (Emily), Robert Barrat (Maj. Putnam), Donald MacBride (Lt. Mason), Anne Gillis (Nora), Lynne Baggett (June Prescott), William Hall (Connors), Rex Lease (Sgt. Makepeace), Selmer Jackson (Curator), Vernon Downing (Leigh), Marjorie Eaton (Bessie), George Carlton, Wheaton Chambers (Guards), Myron Healey, Kirk Alyn, Scott Thomson, John Crawford (Dandies), Harry Woolman (Motorcycle Rider), Harry Brown (2nd Sergeant), Walter Baldwin (Bates), Boyd Irwin (Cranwell).

A large mansion where many congregate serves as the setting for this mildly funny outing in which Costello is a ghost who was wrongfully shot as a traitor during the Revolutionary War. He is joined in this plight by beauteous ghost Reynolds, the two unable to leave Earth for a better place until their innocence is proven. In a dual role, Abbott is a psychologist visiting the mansion, who strangely resembles one of the men responsible for the ghosts' long-ago deaths. For a change, Costello has a chance to get his licks in on Abbott, by using his invisible presence to play numerous tricks on his usual pal. Likewise, most of the gags in this film are derived from the fact that Costello and Reynolds cannot be seen. The best of these is probably when Costello drives a car around the mansion. One of the boys' better outings. (See ABBOTT AND COSTELLO series, Index.)

p, Val Burton; d, Charles Barton; w, Burton, Walter De Leon, Bradford Ropes, John Grant; ph, Charles Van Enger; m, Milton Rosen; ed, Phillip Cahn; md, Rosen; art d, Jack Otterson, Richard H. Reidel; spec eff, D.S. Hursley, Jerome Ash.

Comedy   (PR:AAA   MPAA:NR)

TIME OF YOUR LIFE, THE**½   (1948) 109m UA bw

James Cagney (Joe), William Bendix (Nick), Wayne Morris (Tom), Jeanne Cagney (Kitty Duval), Broderick Crawford (Policeman), Ward Bond (McCarthy), James Barton (Kit Carson), Paul Draper (Harry), Gale Page (Mary L), James Lydon (Dudley), Richard Erdman (Willie), Pedro De Cordoba (Arab), Reginald Beane (Wesley), Tom Powers (Blick), John "Skins" Miller (Drunk), Natalie Schafer (Society Lady), Howard Freeman (Society Gentleman), Renie Riano (Blind Date), Lanny Rees (Newsboy), Nanette

Parks (Girl in Love), Grazia Marciso (Nick's Mother), Claire Carleton ("Killer"), Gladys Blake (Sidekick), Marlene Aames (Nick's Daughter), Moy Ming (Cook), Donald Kerr (Bookie), Ann Cameron (B Girl), Floyd Walters (Sailor), Eddie Borden (Salvation Army Man), Rena Case (Salvation Army Woman).

This warm and engaging adaptation of Saroyan's superlative comedy represents a labor of love by James Cagney and his brother, producer William Cagney. The film, set in a San Francisco waterfront saloon, is told in a helter skelter fashion, as Cagney (who remains seated through almost the entire picture) functions as the calm, controlling eye of the human hurricane that whirls on the screen. Cagney is a barroom philosopher, endlessly drinking expensive champagne as he indulges in his own peculiarities. He enjoys listening to old records as he sits on his roost, sending out Morris, an earnest, mildly retarded young man, on various errands. Morris continually runs out to help Cagney–betting on horses, picking up children's toys, and buying gum that this good friend loves to chew in big wads. Bendix, a member of the original Broadway cast, is the bartender, slightly perturbed by Cagney though he willingly puts up with the man. He even falls for a Cagney con job by hiring Draper to dance part- time at the saloon. Cagney's real-life sister Jeanne is a down- on-her-luck streetwalker who harbors a self-mocking sense of humor. By the film's end, Cagney has given her life some hope by fixing her up with Morris. Barton plays "Kit Carson," a quintessential old-timer, whom Cagney constantly prods into telling stories about the Wild West. In the end the world inside the saloon is nearly upset by Tom Powers (ironically, this actor bears the same name as the punk criminal Cagney played in his 1931 breakthrough film, THE PUBLIC ENEMY), but Cagney at last rises from his chair to defend his terrain and friends. He beats up Powers, and this unique world is once again in harmony. The story's message–encouraging people to live out their dreams– is simple but told in an engaging milieu that never fails to captivate viewers. Though he only comes up from his chair at the end, Cagney's performance is a delight. He controls the world from his seat and is clearly more at home there than anywhere else. The supporting cast is marvelous, an eclectic and enjoyable bunch that keeps the film moving along at a bouncy pace. Potter's direction allows the material to flow freely, giving his cast every opportunity to excel without letting the camera call attention to itself. This was the third film Cagney did in conjunction with his brother William. The first two (JOHNNY COME LATELY, 1943, and BLOOD ON THE SUN, 1945) had not done well at the box office, so the Cagney brothers were determined to find a script of quality that would also be popular with filmgoers. Cagney grew interested in Saroyan's play, which had won both the New York Critic's Circle Award for Best Play, as well as the 1940 Pulitzer Prize (an award that Saroyan refused to accept). Cagney purchased the screen rights for $150,000, then called up Saroyan to arrange a meeting to discuss the proposed film. The two met at the Players, a New York City club, and Cagney, in his book Cagney by Cagney, recalled that Saroyan "...had jet-black hair in high pompadour, a complexion white as bleached parchment, and strong, dark, protruding eyes." Later the two men were interrupted by Allan Reagan, a friend of Cagney's who delighted in sharing obscure tunes with the actor. After pointing at Saroyan, Reagan jokingly sang a jingoistic ditty, which greatly disturbed the writer. "After Allan left," Cagney recalled, "I asked Bill what disturbed him so much. 'I thought he was accusing me of being un-American,' he said. It's fascinating that Saroyan, a man who wrote so many good comedies, apparently confines his sense of humor to his writings." Cagney handpicked his cast, and was delighted to get Barton to play Kit Carson. Cagney felt Barton's own career was as colorful as the character he was playing, and casting the ex-vaudevillian in this role proved to be a perfect match. The cast rehearsed the script for two weeks before any shooting was begun, blocking the entire film for the cameras. However, Potter later changed his mind on some of these setups, which ended up costing the production more money, angering Cagney. The film followed the play almost to the letter, including Saroyan's original ending in which Powers' character is killed. Though the killing took place off-screen, preview audiences reacted negatively to this. At a cost of $300,000, Cagney had the ending reshot, substituting the brawl between himself and Powers, inflating the film's overall budget to $2 million. Despite this significant change, Saroyan himself was delighted with the results. He sent Cagney a letter of congratulation which read in part: "...I think you have made one of the most original and entertaining movies I have seen. Furthermore, I have no intention of pretending that it's my fault that you have made such a film, for I think the truth of the matter is this: that you and your associates have expertly edited and translated into the medium of the motion picture a most difficult and almost unmanageable body of material. I send you congratulations, profound thanks and all good wishes." Despite Saroyan's praises, the film proved to be another failed effort for the Cagney brothers. THE TIME OF YOUR LIFE was unpopular with filmgoers, losing $500,000 at the box office. It was the only Cagney picture ever to lose money, and though the actor was proud of his artistic achievement, he remained disappointed that this never caught on with the public.

p, William Cagney; d, H.C. Potter; w, Nathaniel Curtis (based on the play by William Saroyan); ph, James Wong Howe; m, Carmen Dragon, Reginald Beane; ed, Walter Hannemann, Truman K. Wood; art d, Wiard Ihnen; set d, A. Roland Fields; cos, Courtney Haslam; makeup, Otis Malcolm.

Comedy/Drama   (PR:A-C   MPAA:NR)

TIME OUT FOR LOVE**½   (1963, Ital./Fr.) 91m Films
Pomereu-International Productions-PEG Produzione/Zenith International
bw (LES GRANDES PERSONNES; AKA: FIVE DAY LOVER)

Jean Seberg (Ann), Micheline Presle (Michele), Maurice Ronet (Philippe), Francoise Prevost (Gladys), Annibale Ninchi (Dr. Severin), Fernando Bruno (Bucchieri).

An American girl, Seberg, living in Paris, discovers that the city of love and romance does not always live up to this ideal as she becomes friends with a group of people who first offer her closeness, than sourly reject her. She starts a brief affair with racing driver Ronet, discovering aspects about him that his old lover, the suicidal Presle, did not understand. This growing attachment to Ronet brings Seberg further apart from Presle, until she is eventually dumped by her lover, Ronet returning to the arms of Presle.

p, Bertrand Javal, Yvon Guezel; d, Jean Valere; w, Valere, Roger Nimier (based on the novel Histoire d'un Amour by Nimier); ph, Raoul Coutard; m, Germaine Tailleferre; ed, Leonide Azar; art d, Bernard Evein.

Drama   **(PR:A   MPAA:NR)**

TIME OUT FOR MURDER*½   (1938) 60m FOX bw

Gloria Stuart (Margie Ross), Michael Whalen (Barney), Chick Chandler (Snapper), Douglas Fowley (Dutch Moran), Robert Kellard (Johnny Martin), Jane Darwell (Polly), Jean Rogers (Helen Thomas), June Gale (Muriel), Ruth Hussey (Peggy Norton), Cliff Clark (Capt. Collins), Peter Lynn (Blackie), Edward Marr (Eddie), Lester Matthews (Phillip Gregory).

A pair of witless newspaper people, Whalen as the reporter and Chandler as his sidekick photographer, turn detective to clear an innocent man, Kellard, from a charge of murder. For added effect, bill-collector Stuart, who previously spent most of her time trying to get Whalen to pay his bills, gets into the act. The obvious culprit was right in front of their noses all along. The racy dialog is substantially superior to the story line in this film, which the studio intended as a pilot for a series featuring reporter Whalen and comic photographer Chandler. Only one picture with the pair followed, WHILE NEW YORK SLEEPS, in the same year. Director Humberstone and writer Cady had ample series experience with their earlier CHARLIE CHAN pictures (see Index).

p, Howard J. Green; d, H. Bruce Humberstone; w, Jerry Cady (based on the story "Meridian 7-1212" by Irving Reis); ph, Virgil Miller; ed, Jack Murray; md, Samuel Kaylin.

Comedy/Mystery   **(PR:A   MPAA:NR)**

TIME OUT FOR RHYTHM*   (1941) 74m COL bw

Ann Miller (Kitty Brown), Rudy Vallee (Daniel Collins), Rosemary Lane (Frances Lewis), Allen Jenkins (Off-Beat Davis), Joan Merrill (Herself), Richard Lane (Mike Armstrong), Stanley Andrews (James Anderson), The Three Stooges, Brenda & Cobina, Six Hits and A Miss, Eddie Durant's Rhumba Orchestra, Glen Gray and His Casa Loma Band.

Vallee and Richard Lane–aided by pal Jenkins–start a theatrical booking agency, but their partnership nearly founders when Lane's old sweetheart, Rosemary Lane, ends her marriage and tries to get back into show business. The female Lane importunes the male Lane to replace singer Merrill with herself on an important television show, and he agrees to do so, to Vallee's disgust. Meanwhile, Vallee has discovered a fresh singing/dancing talent in Rosemary Lane's maid, Miller; he grooms her for stardom, which finally dooms his partnership with Richard Lane. The latter purchases a nightclub in which to star his singing sweetheart Rosemary Lane. When a big-time talent scout arrives to witness Vallee's show, Vallee begs Rosemary Lane to let him use the new nightclub as a showcase. She agrees, but only if she can star. When her fiance finds that her career means more to her than marriage, he forbids her that perquisite. Miller is pressed into service as a substitute star and proves a hit; everybody ends up with a Hollywood contract. The Three Stooges and the comic radio team of Brenda and Cobina wander about in slapstick cameos in this slim story which appears to be a studio effort to get an A picture on a B budget. Musical numbers include: "Did Anyone Ever Tell You?" "Boogie Woogie Man," "Time Out For Rhythm," "Twiddlin' My Thumbs," "Obviously the Gentleman Prefers to Dance," "As If You Didn't Know," "The Rio De Janeiro," and "Shows How Wrong a Gal Can Be" (Sammy Cahn, Saul Chaplin).

p, Irving Starr; d, Sidney Salkow; w, Edmund L. Hartmann, Bert Lawrence, Bert Granet (based on the play by Alex Ruben); ph, Franz F. Planer; ed, Arthur Seid; md, M. W. Stoloff; art d, Lionel Banks; cos, Saltern; ch, LeRoy Prinz; m/l, Sammy Cahn, Saul Chaplin.

Musical   **(PR:A   MPAA:NR)**

TIME OUT FOR ROMANCE**   (1937) 72m FOX bw

Claire Trevor (Barbara Blanchard), Michael Whalen (Bob Reynolds), Joan Davis (Midge Dooley), Chick Chandler (Ted Dooley), Douglas Fowley (Roy Webster), Bennie Bartlett (Orville Healy), William Griffith (Ambrose Healy), William Demarest (Willoughby Sproggs), Lelah Tyler (Cora Sproggs), Andrew Tombes (James Blanchard), Georgia Caine (Vera Blanchard), Vernon Steele (Count Michael Montaine), Inez Courtney (Mabel), George

Chandler (Simpson), Fred Kelsey (Policeman), Pop Byron (Jailer), Guy Usher (Chief of Police), Dick French, Lee Phelps, George Riley, Franklin Parker (Reporters), Paul McVey (Ship's Officer), Syd Saylor (Truck Driver), Jack Norton, Eddie Kane, Harrison Greene, Larry Wheat (Crapshooters), Grover Liggon, Hal Craig (Motor Cops), Harry Watson (Messenger).

Light-hearted comedy that has Trevor as the rich girl escaping the altar. When she discovers her fiance's true nature, and his mercenary motivation for marrying her, she hightails to the road, where she meets recreational-vehicle driver Whalen. True love soon develops. The cement to this affair is added when Whalen is temporarily sent to jail after unknowingly being framed as a thief. Fast-moving direction of a very capable cast makes this picture work.

p, Milton Feld; d, Malcolm St. Clair; w, Lou Breslow, John Patrick (based on a story by Eleanore Griffin, William Rankin); ph, Robert Planck; ed, Al De Gaetano; md, Samuel Kaylin.

Comedy   **(PR:A   MPAA:NR)**

TIME OUT OF MIND*½   (1947) 88m UNIV bw

Phyllis Calvert (Kate Fernald), Robert Hutton (Christopher Fortune), Ella Raines (Rissa Fortune), Eddie Albert (Jake Bullard), Leo G. Carroll (Capt. Fortune), Helena Carter (Dora Drake), John Abbott (Max Lieberman), Henry Stephenson (Wellington Drake), Olive Blakeney (Mrs. Fernald), Janet Shaw (Penny), Emil Rameau (Alfred Stern), Samuel S. Hinds (Dr. Weber), Lilian Fontaine (Aunt Melinda), Houseley Stevenson (George), Maudie Prickett (Annie), Harry Shannon (Capt. Rogers), Taylor Holmes.

A listless story about the son of a New England sea captain who would rather spend his life making music than drifting across the Seven Seas. The lad, played by Hutton, is given the impetus to achieve his goal, against the wishes of father Carroll, through the pushings of Calvert, maid in the New England household. This was Calvert's first role in a U.S. production. Her character, like all the others in this film, was not the type that audiences could really sink their teeth into. This is mainly the fault of the director, who has the material and the talent, but not the ability to create the needed chemistry.

p&d, Robert Siodmak; w, Abem Finkel, Arnold Phillips (based on the novel by Rachel Field); ph, Maury Gertsman; m, Miklos Rozsa, Mario Castelnuovo-Tedesco; ed, Ted J. Kent; art d, Bernard Herzbrun, John F. DeCuir.

Drama   **(PR:A   MPAA:NR)**

TIME SLIP**½   (1981, Jap.) 139m Toei c (SENGOKU JIEITAI)

Sonny Chiba (Lt. Iba), Isao Natsuki (Samurai Leader), Miyuki Ono (Village Girl), Nana Okada (Modern Girl).

Japanese soldiers suddenly find themselves back in the 16th Century, the modern men are forced to do battle with dozens of sword-waving samurai before they even realize that they've entered into some sort of time slip. The leader, Chiba, thinks that there may be a chance to be sent back to modern days if they upset history enough to be rejected to the future. But this doesn't take, paving for the unusual ending that the soldiers never return to the present. Some of the battle scenes are quite breathtaking, performed in a very dancelike manner.

p, Haruki Kadokawa; d, Kosei Saito; w, Toshio Kaneda (based on a story by Ryo Hanmura); ph, Iwao Isayama; m, Kentaro Haneda; spec eff, Hiyoshi Suzuki; ch, Sonny Chiba.

Fantasy/Adventure   **(PR:C   MPAA:NR)**

TIME, THE PLACE AND THE GIRL, THE**   (1929) 70m WB bw

Grant Withers (Jim Crane), Betty Compson (Doris Ward), Gertrude Olmstead (Mae Ellis), James R. Kirkwood (Professor), Vivian Oakland (Mrs. Davis), Gretchen Hartman (Mrs. Winters), Irene Haisman (Mrs. Parks), John Davidson (Peter Ward), Gerald King (Radio Announcer), Bert Roach (Butter and Egg Man).

Egotist Withers, a one-time college football star, had paid little attention to former coed Olmstead when both attended their alma mater. When they meet again as employees in an investment house, he begins to take notice of her. Better at passing a ball than he is at peddling a bond, he is about to be fired from his job when his boss notices that he has a way with the ladies. He is pressed into service selling bad bonds to flirtatious females, his boss planning to use him as the fall guy when the swindle is exposed. Olmstead apprises him of the plan, and he reimburses the gullible girls with money he gets by cozening his boss' own wife with the fake bonds. This pleasant musical play employed Western Electric's Vitaphone sound-on-disc system in its talkie release; it was simultaneously released in a shorter non-musical silent version for theaters which lacked the playback equipment. Songs include "I Wonder Who's Kissing Her Now" (Frank Adams, Will Hough, Joe Howard), "Collegiate" (Mo Jaffe, Nat Bonx); "Doin' the Raccoon" (Raymond Klages, J. Fred Coots, Herb Magidson); "Fashionette" (Robert King, Jack Glogan); "Jack and Jill" (Larry Spier, Sam Coslow); "How Many Times" (Irving Berlin); "Everything I Do I Do for You" (Al Sherman); "If You Could Care" (E. Ray Goetz, Arthur Wimperis, Herman Darewski).

d, Howard Bretherton; w, Robert Lord (based on the musical play by Frank R. Adams, Joseph E. Howard, Will Hough); ph, John Stumar; m, Louis Silvers; ed, Jack Killifer.

Comedy　　　　　(PR:A　MPAA:NR)

TIME, THE PLACE AND THE GIRL, THE**　　(1946) 105m WB c

Dennis Morgan (*Steven Ross*), Jack Carson (*Jeff Howard*), Janis Paige (*Sue Jackson*), Martha Vickers (*Victoria Cassel*), S. Z. Sakall (*Ladislaus Cassel*), Alan Hale (*John Braden*), Angela Greene (*Elaine Winters*), Donald Woods (*Martin Drew*), Florence Bates (*Mme. Lucia Cassel*), Carmen Cavallaro Orchestra, Condos Brothers, Chandra Kaly and His Dancers.

The effort by Morgan and Carson to stage a Broadway musical against the wishes of ancient opera star Bates is the tired-and-true plot around which some decent musical numbers, brilliant settings and costumes, and a sufficient number of laughs is built. Morgan eventually gets to see the show through, given help by Bates' husband Sakall as well as by her granddaughter, Vickers, a budding star in her own right. Not at all the same plot as the fine 1929 film with the same title from Warner Bros., but this one made good money at the box office despite its hackneyed screenplay. Songs include: "A Gal in Calico," "A Rainy Night in Rio," "Oh but I Do," "Through a Thousand Dreams," "A Solid Citizen of the Solid South," and "I Happened to Walk Down First Street."

p, Alex Gottlieb; d, David Butler; w, Francis Swann, Agnes Christine Johnston, Lynn Starling (based on the story by Leonard Lee); ph, William V. Skall, Arthur Edeson (Technicolor); ed, Irene Morra; ch, LeRoy Prinz; m/l, Arthur Schwartz, Leo Robin.

Musical　　　　　(PR:A　MPAA:NR)

TIME TO DIE, A**　　(1983) 91m Almi bw (AKA: SEVEN GRAVES FOR ROGAN)

Edward Albert, Jr (*Michael Rogan*), Rod Taylor (*Bailey*), Rex Harrison (*Von Osten*), Linn Stokke (*Dora*), Raf Vallone (*Genco Bari*), Cor Van Rijn (*Vrost*), Lucie Visser (*Mrs. Rogan*).

A revenge picture based on a story by *The Godfather* author Mario Puzo about a WW II veteran, Albert, who hunts down the men who killed his wife, one of whom is now a top German official. An average revenge tale hampered by a deadening script.

p, Charles Lee; d, Matt Cimber; w, John Goff, Cimber, William Russell (based on a story by Mario Puzo); ph, Eddy van der Enden, Tom Denove (CFI Color); m, Robert O. Ragland, Ennio Morricone; ed, Byron Brandt, Fred Chulack; art d, Frank Rosen, John Thompson.

Crime Drama　　　Cas.　　(PR:O　MPAA:R)

TIME TO KILL**　　(1942) 61m FOX bw

Lloyd Nolan (*Michael Shayne*), Heather Angel (*Merle*), Doris Merrick (*Linda Conquest*), Ralph Byrd (*Louis Venter*), Richard Lane (*Lt. Breeze*), Morris Ankrum (*Alex Morny*), Sheila Bromley (*Lois Morny*), Ethel Griffies (*Mrs. Murdock*), James Seay (*Leslie Murdock*), Ted Hecht (*Phillips*), William Pawley (*Hench*), Syd Saylor (*Postman*), Lester Sharpe (*Washburn*), Charles Williams (*Dental Assistant*), LeRoy Mason (*Headwaiter*), Phyllis Kennedy (*Ena*), Paul Guilfoyle (*Manager*), Helen Flint (*Marge*), Bruce Wong (*Houseboy*).

The last entry in the MICHAEL SHAYNE series in which Nolan plays the private eye, here given the job of retrieving an expensive coin which rightfully belongs to dowager Griffies. From this point on Nolan sleuths his way through three murders until he tracks down both the coin and the killer. The last and probably the best of Nolan's appearances as Shayne, largely because of the superior story supplied by author Chandler, whose plot was mixed with Halliday's hero. Remade in 1947 as THE BRASHER DOUBLOON. (See MICHAEL SHAYNE series, Index.)

p, Sol. M. Wurtzel; d, Herbert I. Leeds; w, Clarence Upson Young (based on the novel *The High Window* by Raymond Chandler, and on a character created by Brett Halliday); ph, Charles Clarke; m, Emil Newman; ed, Alfred Day; art d, Richard Day, Chester Gore.

Mystery/Crime　　　　(PR:A　MPAA:NR)

TIME TO KILL, A**　　(1955, Brit.) 65m Fortress/AB-Pathe bw

Jack Watling (*Dennis Willows*), Rona Anderson (*Sallie Harbord*), John Horsley (*Peter Hastings*), Russell Napier (*Inspector Simmons*), Keneth Kent (*Dr. Cole*), Mary Jones (*Florence Cole*), Alastair Hunter (*Sgt. Thorpe*), Joan Hickson (*Miss Edinger*), John le Mesurier (*Phineas*), June Ashley (*Madeline*), Edward Frency, Arthur Gross.

A convoluted thriller about a playboy chemist, Horsley, whose mistress, Ashley, is poisoned. Naturally Horsley is blamed for her death, though he swears he is innocent. His fiancee, Anderson, comes to his aid, determined to get him released from prison. Her investigations uncover a blackmail scheme Ashley was a victim of, engineered by news reporter Watling. A TIME TO KILL is not bad if one has nothing but time to waste.

p, Clive Nicholas, Fred Swann; d, Charles Saunders; w, Doreen Montgomery; ph, James Wilson.

Crime　　　　　(PR:A　MPAA:NR)

TIME TO LOVE AND A TIME TO DIE, A**½　　(1958) 133m UNIV c

John Gavin (*Ernest Graeber*), Lilo Pulver (*Elizabeth Kruse*), Jock Mahoney (*Immerman*), Don DeFore (*Boettcher*), Keenan Wynn (*Reuter*), Erich Maria Remarque (*Pohlmann*), Dieter Borsche (*Capt. Rahe*), Barbara Rutting (*Woman Guerrilla*), Thayer David (*Oscar Binding*), Charles Regnier (*Joseph*), Dorothea Wieck (*Frau Lieser*), Kurt Meisel (*Heini*), Agnes Windeck (*Frau Witte*), Clancy Cooper (*Sauer*), John Van Dreelen (*Political Officer*), Klaus Kinski (*Gestapo Lieutenant*), Alice Treff (*Frau Langer*), Alexander Engel (*Warden*), Dana J. Hutton [Jim Hutton] (*Hirschland*), Wolf Harnisch (*Sgt. Muecke*), Karl-Ludwig Lindt (*Dr. Karl Fresenburg*), Lisa Helwig (*Frau Kleinert*).

A long apology for the German side in WW II, this fails to stir any sympathy for the so-called patriots who were against Hitler's policies. Casting obvious Americans in the German roles causes any believability to crumble. German soldier Gavin is fighting on the Russian front in 1944 and gets a furlough. He returns to his small village to find that his home has been razed and his parents have disappeared. He falls in love with Pulver. They get married and spend their first days together running from cellar to bombed-out rubble, from one home to another, stealing their moments together as they solidify their love. Along the way, Gavin deals with chief Nazi David, a man who is shown to have some semblance of humanity as he is willing to share his black-market booty with Gavin. After a long honeymoon, Gavin returns to war. With a letter from his wife in his hand that tells him that he's to be a father, Gavin is shot and killed back on the Russian front in a finale not unlike ALL QUIET ON THE WESTERN FRONT, another Remarque story. The fact that the Nazis were the most inhuman enemies in history is glossed over in favor of the theory that "War is Hell" for soldiers on both sides. Shot on location in Germany amid the real ruins, it never touched the hearts of audiences, who recalled the events of just 13 years before. Remarque does an effective cameo as a high-school teacher who is suspected of being anti-Hitler. Wieck had starred in MAEDCHEN IN UNIFORM, the 1931 German film about the goings-on at a strict girls' school. In a small early role, note Klaus Kinski, before he began to look very weird. Kinski, who was born in what was once Poland, wisely changed his name from his original moniker, Claus Gunther Nakszynski. Gavin was being pushed hard by the studio to be another Rock Hudson. After serving as president of the Screen Actors Guild (the same position once held by Ronald Reagan), Gavin tried his hand at public service in later years and became Ronald Reagan's Ambassador to Mexico. The mixture of accents works against the movie and it was nowhere nearly as effective as THE YOUNG LIONS, a movie on the same subject.

p, Robert Arthur; d, Douglas Sirk; w, Orin Jannings (based on the novel by Erich Maria Remarque); ph, Russell Metty (CinemaScope, Eastmancolor); m, Miklos Rozsa; ed, Ted J. Kent; art d, Alexander Golitzen, Alfred Sweeney; set d, Russell A. Gausman; cos, Bill Thomas; spec eff, Clifford Stine, "Whitey" McMahan.

War Drama　　　　(PR:A-C　MPAA:NR)

TIME TO REMEMBER*½　　(1962, Brit.) 58m Merton Park/Anglo-Amalgamated bw

Yvonne Monlaur (*Suzanne*), Harry H. Corbett (*Jack Burgess*), Ernest Rietty (*Victor*), Ernest Clark (*Cracknell*), David Lodge (*Jumbo Johnson*), Ray Barrett (*Sammy*), Genine Graham (*Mrs. Johnson*), Patricia Mort (*Vera*), Jack Watson (*Inspector Bolam*).

A real estate agent gets involved in a search for a jewel thief's hidden cache. He, however, must compete with the thief's widow and her fellow criminals. Screenplay by Arthur LaBern (whose story was the basis for FRENZY, 1972) from a story by Edgar Wallace.

p, Jack Greenwood; d, Charles Jarrett; w, Arthur LaBern (based on the novel *The Man Who Bought London* by Edgar Wallace).

Crime　　　　　(PR:A　MPAA:NR)

TIME TO SING, A*½　　(1968) 91m Four Leaf/MGM c

Hank Williams, Jr (*Grady Dodd*), Shelley Fabares (*Amy Carter*), Ed Begley (*Kermit Dodd*), Charles Robinson (*"Shifty" Barker*), D'Urville Martin (*Luke Harper*), Donald Woods (*Vernon W. Carter*), Clara Ward (*Clara*), Harold Ayer (*Dr. Cartwright*), Dick Haynes, Gene Gentry (*M.C.s*), The X-L's (*Themselves*).

A dull and tiring tale about a musician-songwriter, in this case Hank Williams, Jr., who goes against the wishes of the uncle who raised him and devotes his life to music. It seems that somewhere back in the mysterious past his mother was also a singer, and died when running off with another musician. This is revealed to the young Williams, along with the knowledge that there is a lot of money to be made if you can strum a few chords and sing with a slight tremble in your voice. Songs include: "The Humming Bird," "It's All Over but the Crying," "Rock in My Shoe" (Hank Williams, Jr.), "A Man is on His Own" (John Scoggins, Williams, Jr.), "Money Can't

Buy Happiness," "Old Before My Time" (Steve Karliski), "Next Time I Say Goodbye, I'm Leaving" (Larry Kusik, Eddie Snyder), and "A Time to Sing" (Scoggins).

p, Sam Katzman; d, Arthur Dreifuss; w, Robert E. Kent, Orville H. Hampton; ph, John F. Warren (Panavision Metrocolor); m, Fred Karger; ed, Ben Lewis; art d, George W. Davis, Leroy Coleman; set d, Henry Grace, Charles S. Thompson; makeup, William Tuttle.

Musical/Drama   **(PR:A   MPAA:G)**

TIME TRAP   (SEE: TIME TRAVELERS, THE, 1964)

TIME TRAVELERS, THE½   (1964) 83m Dobil Productions/AIP c
                                                      (AKA: TIME TRAP)

Preston Foster (*Dr. Erik von Steiner*), Philip Carey (*Steve Connors*), Merry Anders (*Carol White*), John Hoyt (*Varno*), Dennis Patrick (*Councilman Willard*), Joan Woodbury (*Gadra*), Dolores Wells (*Reena*), Steve Franken (*Danny McKee*), Gloria Leslie (*Councilwoman*), Peter Strudwick (*Deviant*), Margaret Seldeen, Forrest J. Ackerman (*Technicians*).

The old H.G. Wells theme of being able to travel to the future through a time machine is given a pretty good, as well as relevant, treatment here. The plot concerns a group of scientists from the 1960s who accidentally stumble 107 years into the future when Franken falls into a time portal and the researching doctor, Foster, and two of his students try to rescue him. They are transported to a time when nuclear war has almost totally destroyed the human race, except for a handful who live underground and are desperately trying to construct a spaceship which will take them to a place where they can start a new civilization. Offshoots of the human race, who have mutated into horrible creatures, continually attack their human counterparts, and destroy the ship the humans were trying to build. Foster and company then try to flee back to the year 1964, but encounter a trap that has them stuck in a time circle forever. Though the themes are basically reworkings of similar ones, the picture has a certain energy which comes through in the production. The inexpensive special effects are really quite creative. Remade in 1967 as JOURNEY TO THE CENTER OF TIME.

p, William Redlin; d&w, Ib Melchior (based on a story by Melchior, David Hewitt); ph, William (Vilmos) Zsigmond (Pathe Color); m, Richard LaSalle; ed, Harold J. Dennis; art d, Ray Storey; spec eff, Hewitt; makeup, Mark Shegoff.

Fantasy   **(PR:A   MPAA:NR)**

TIME WALKER½   (1982) 83m Villard-Wescom/New World c

Ben Murphy (*Doug McCadden*), Nina Axelrod (*Susy Fuller*), Kevin Brophy (*Peter*), James Karen (*Wendell Rossmore*), Robert Random (*Parker*), Austin Stoker (*Dr. Ken Melrose*), Clint Young (*Willoughby*), Shari Belafonte-Harper (*Linda*), Antoinette Bower (*Dr. Hayworth*), Jason Williams (*Jeff*), Jack Olson (*Ankh Venaris, Mummy*), Melissa Prophet, Sam Chew, Gerard Prendergast.

Young professor Murphy brings Pharaoh Tutankhamen's sarcophagus to his campus and has it X-rayed. Accidental overexposure to the radiation revivifies the alien creature within, which had killed the Pharaoh eons ago. The linen-swathed creature, whose touch kills humans, is infuriated by a student's theft of the transmitter crystals it needs to return to its home planet. It goes on a killing rampage, with green-filtered footage representing its point of view. The technical aspects of the film are as dated as the genre in this hackneyed presentation, which differs from its older brethren only in that the bandaged alien moves at a high rate of speed, rather than doddering along like a conventional movie mummy. It might be more aptly titled "E.T., the Bandaged Killer."

p, Dimitri Villard, Jason Williams; d, Tom Kennedy; w, Karen Levitt, Tom Friedman; ph, Robbie Greenberg (DeLuxe Color); m, Richard Band; ed, Joseph Yanuzzi; art d, R.A. Burns, Joe Garrity; animation, January Nordman; makeup, Sue Dolph.

Fantasy/Horror   **(PR:A   MPAA:PG)**

TIME WITHOUT PITY½ (1957, Brit.) 88m Harlequin/Eros-Astor bw

Michael Redgrave (*David Graham*), Ann Todd (*Honor Stanford*), Leo McKern (*Robert Stanford*), Peter Cushing (*Jeremy Clayton*), Alec McCowen (*Alec Graham*), Renee Houston (*Mrs. Harker*), Paul Daneman (*Brian Stanford*), Lois Maxwell (*Vicky Harker*), Richard Wordsworth (*Maxwell*), George Devine (*Barnes*), Joan Plowright (*Agnes Cole*), Ernest Clark (*Under-Secretary*), Peter Copley (*Padre*), Hugh Moxey (*Prison Governor*), Julian Somers (*1st Warder*), John Chandos (*1st Journalist*), Dickie Henderson, Jr (*The Comedian*), Richard Leech (*Proprietor of Espresso Bar*), Christina Lubicz (*Jenny Cole*).

Redgrave is a desperate alcoholic in the process of drying out when he discovers that his son, McCowen, is about to be executed for a crime he didn't commit. The police have enough evidence to damn McCowen ten times over, but still Redgrave isn't convinced of his boy's guilt. With only 24 hours to act, he carefully probes the evidence, which leads him to the site of the murder–the home of McKern, an automobile magnate. Redgrave

learns that his son had been living there along with McKern's wife, Todd, a neurotic who loved McCowen. Eventually Redgrave is able to prove his son's innocence in a confrontation with McKern. Having discovered that McKern is the real murderer, Redgrave forces the killer to shoot him, thereby sacrificing himself in place of his son. Losey makes a fine directorial choice at the start of the film by showing the audience that McCowen is innocent. The suspense is thereby shifted from "Is he guilty?" to "Will he be saved from execution?" Aside from making an anti-capital punishment case (which the film does indirectly), TIME WITHOUT PITY makes a case about men and the families they destroy. As Losey stated in Tom Milne's *Losey On Losey*, "I was talking about men who are tyrants in their families or in their businesses, about human beings who walk over other people to make fortunes, about people who go along with hypocrisies which they dress up in all sorts of trappings.... It was also about a father and son, about the condemnations of a man who was hopelessly sick as an alcoholic, and what makes him so, what makes him irresponsible."

p, John Arnold, Anthony Simmons; d, Joseph Losey; w, Ben Barzman (based on the play "Someone Waiting" by Emlyn Williams); ph, Freddie Francis; m, Tristram Cary; ed, Alan Osbiston; md, Marcus Dods; prod d, Reece Pemberton; art d, Bernard Sarron.

Crime   **(PR:C   MPAA:NR)**

TIMERIDER½   (1983) 93m Jensen-Farley c (AKA: THE
                                           ADVENTURE OF LYLE SWANN)

Fred Ward (*Lyle Swann*), Belinda Bauer (*Clair Cygne*), Peter Coyote (*Porter Reese*), Ed Lauter (*Padre*), Richard Masur (*Claude Dorsett*), Tracey Walter (*Carl Dorsett*), L.Q. Jones (*Ben Potter*), Chris Mulkey (*Daniels*), Macon McCalman (*Dr. Sam*), Jonathan Bahnks (*Jesse*), Laurie O'Brien (*Terry*), William Dear, Susan Dear (*Technicians*), Bruce Gordon (*Earl*), Ben Zeller (*Jack Peoples*), Tommy Leyba (*Manuel*), Ernie Quintana (*Zapata*), Miguel Sandoval (*Emil*), Reginald Johnson (*George*), Philip L. Mead (*Wally*), Manny Smith (*Devil Man*), Ray Valdez (*Man in Crowd*), Bob Dunbar (*Pilot*), Sam Chadwyck, Rusty Dillen, Joseph V. DiPrima, Audie Edmundson, Buddy Edmundson, Raleigh Gardenhire, Christopher Garrett, Steven Hartley, Luke Jones, Curtis Plagge (*Outlaws*).

What would happen to the Old West if a motorcycle were to appear on the dusty plains along with the horses? This is the question that the makers of this light independent must have asked themselves before undertaking this project. Whether or not their estimate is correct one will never know, but at least it provides for some enjoyable entertainment. Ward plays the modern biker who rides through a time warp to suddenly find himself involved with a gang of outlaws. The outlaw leader, Coyote, sees the motorbike as being an extreme asset to his trade. Former rock singer Nesmith acted as executive producer, and also provided the score and coauthored the script.

p, Harry Gittes; d, William Dear; w, Dear, Michael Nesmith; ph, Larry Pizer (Movielab Color); m, Nesmith; ed, Suzanne Pettit, Kim Secrist, R.J. Kizer; art d, Linda Pearl; set d, Kevin Hughes; cos, Jack Buehler.

Western/Science Fiction   **Cas.**   **(PR:C   MPAA:PG)**

TIMES GONE BY½   (1953, Ital.) 106m Cines/I.F.E. bw (ALTRI
                                                                  TEMPI)

"The Excelsior Ball": danced by Alba Arnova, Carlo Mazzone, Ballet of the Teatro dell 'Opera of Rome; "The Old Book Stand": Aldo Fabrizi (*Vendor*), Mario Riva (*Client*), Enzo Staiola (*Boy*), "Less Than a Day": Andrea Checchi (*The Lover*), Alba Arnova (*His Mistress*), "A Question of Property": Arnoldo Foa (*1st Farmer*), Folco Lulli (*2nd Farmer*), "The Idyll": Maurizio di Nardo (*Boy*), Geraldina Parrinello (*Girl*), Paolo Stoppa (*Father*), Rina Morelli (*Mother*), "A Pot-Pourri of Songs": Elio Pandolfi (*Boy*), Barbara Florian (*Girl*), Dina Perbellini, Oscar Andriani, Clelia Fiamma, Pietro de Falco (*Singers*), "The Vise": Amedeo Nazzari (*He*), Elisa Cegani (*She*), Rolando Lupi (*Other Man*), "The Trial of Frine": Gina Lollobrigida (*Frine*), Vittorio De Sica (*Her Lawyer*).

A conglomeration of short stories meant to depict a time in Italy's history when things were quite a bit simpler. All these tales deal with love and desire in some aspect or other, ranging from a boy and a girl getting their first taste of romance, to an adulterous affair, to a fight between two farmers for a hunk of "fertilizer." Though all these stories are graced with a certain level of charm, the most prominent and striking is THE TRIAL OF FRINE in which Lollobrigida plays the town whore being put on trial for exceeding questioned boundaries. De Sica is the lawyer who sways the jury by pointing out that physical beauty is a law unto itself.

p, Carlo Civallero; d, Alessandro Blasetti; w, uncredited (based on short stories by Camillo Boito, Renato Fucini, Guido Nobili, Luigi Pirandello, Eduardo Scarfoglio, and others); ph, Carlo Montuori, Gabor Pogany; m, Alessandro Cicognini; ed, Mario Serandrei.

Drama   **(PR:C   MPAA:NR)**

TIMES SQUARE**   (1929) 78m Lumas/Gotham bw

Alice Day (Elaine Smith), Arthur Lubin (Russ Glover/Benjamin Lederwitski), Emil Chautard (David Lederwitski), Ann Brady (Sarah Lederwitski), John Miljan (Dick Barclay), Arthur Housman (Lon Roberts), Joseph Swickard (Prof. Carrillo), Natalie Joyce (Lida), Eddie Kane (Nat Ross).

Lubin is a young musician from a family of serious composers who decides to take a less respectable Tin Pan Alley job. He falls in love with secretary Day and changes his name from Lederwitski, a name associated with class musicianship, to Glover. He then takes a job in a small-time cafe banging out honkytonk piano. One day he absentmindedly scribbles a masterpiece of music on a menu in the cafe. The cafe violinist takes the composition to a music publisher and from there it is read by Lubin's father, Chautard, a famed music publisher. Chautard, impressed with the idea of meeting a young virtuoso, ventures to the cafe where he is shocked and overjoyed to learn that it is his son who has composed the piece, and they have a tearful reunion.

p, Harold Shumate; d, Joseph C. Boyle; w, Adele Buffington, Shumate (based on a story by Norma Houston); ph, Ray June; ed, Donn Hayes.

Drama   (PR:A MPAA:NR)

TIMES SQUARE*½   (1980) 111m Butterfly Valley N.V.-RSO Films/AFD c

Tim Curry (Johnny Laguardia), Trini Alvarado (Pamela Pearl), Robin Johnson (Nicky Marotta), Peter Coffield (David Pearl), Herbert Berghof (Dr. Huber), David Marguilies (Dr. Zymabsky), Anna Maria Horsford (Rosie Washington), Michael Margotta (JoJo), J.C. Quinn (Simon), Miguel Pinero (Roberto), Ronald "Smokey" Stevens (Heavy), Tiger Haynes (Andy), Billy Mernit, Paul Sass, Artie Weinstein, Tim Choate, Elizabeth Pena, Kathy Lojac, Susan Merson, George Morfogen, Charles Blackwell, Bill Anagnos, Tammas J. Hamilton, Franklyn Scott, Jane Solar, Victoria Vanderkloot, Steve W. James, Jay Acovone, Alice Spivak, Calvin Ander, Peter Iacangelo, Michael Riney.

A shallow attempt to show the plight of kids on the streets of New York. Two teen-age girls, one the daughter of Park Avenue types, the other her tough talking lower, class buddy, leave home to lead a life of destruction near Times Square. All they do is break things and cause trouble. Perhaps they are devotees of punk, a phenomenon that was taking hold in America at that time, of breaking with the old to make room for the new. Though this theme is never considered directly. They eventually turn to music, which gets them off the streets at least. Also involved is Tim Curry (the transsexual from THE ROCKY HORROR PICTURE SHOW) as a late night disc jockey, a sort of messiah of modern music. He is not at all bad in this role. An overabundance of loud modern music accompanies the images. The music serves no other purpose than providing atmosphere, as if the grittiness of the streets were not enough. Director Moyle would be wise to go back to film school and learn something about developing perspective and shot continuity.

p, Robert Stigwood, Jacob Brackman; d, Alan Moyle; w, Brackman (based on a story by Moyle, Leanne Unger); ph, James A. Contner (DeLuxe Color); ed, Tom Priestley; prod d, Stuart Wurtzel; set d, Leslie Bloom; cos, Robert de Mora.

Drama   **Cas.**   (PR:0 MPAA:R)

TIMES SQUARE LADY**   (1935) 69m MGM bw

Robert Taylor (Steve Gordon), Virginia Bruce (Toni Bradley), Helen Twelvetrees (Margo Heath), Isabel Jewell (Babe Sweeney), Nat Pendleton (Mack), Pinky Tomlin (Pinky), Henry Kolker (Adam Fielding, Attorney), Raymond Hatton (Slim Kennedy), Jack LaRue (Jack Kramer), Robert Elliott (Brick Culver), Fred Kohler (Dutch Meyers), Russell Hopton (Ed).

Bruce is the daughter of a wealthy Broadway producer, who leaves her a fortune, including the nightclub of which Taylor is the manager. But attorney Kolker seeks to steal her assets. He enlists Taylor in his dastardly scheme. But once Taylor gets to know Bruce, he cannot go through with the plan, something that upsets Kolker. A fairly routine production, with Taylor getting his first lead role and the camera taking as much advantage of him as possible.

p, Lucien Hubbard; d, George B. Seitz; w, Albert Cohen, Robert Shannon; ph, Lester White; ed, Hugh Wynn; m/l, "The Object of My Affection," Pinky Tomlin (sung by Tomlin), "What's the Reason I'm Not Pleasing You" (sung by Tomlin).

Drama   (PR:A MPAA:NR)

TIMES SQUARE PLAYBOY*½   (1936) 62m WB bw (GB: HIS BEST MAN)

Warren William (Vic Arnold), June Travis (Beth Calhoun), Barton MacLane (Casey), Gene Lockhart (P.H. Bancroft), Kathleen Lockhart (Lottie Bancroft), Dick Purcell (Wally Calhoun), Craig Reynolds (Joe Roberts), Granville Bates (Mr. Calhoun), Dorothy Vaughan (Mrs. Calhoun).

Overly forced and talky version of the George M. Cohan play, in which the country bumpkin comes to the big city to attend the wedding of his old friend. Lockhart plays the idiot friend who promptly puts his foot in his mouth and almost ruins William's marriage. Too bad he did not silence the rest of the cast.

p, Bryan Foy; d, William McGann; w, Roy Chanslor (based on the play "The Home Towners" by George M. Cohan); ph, L. William O'Connell; ed, Jack Killifer; m/l, "Lookin' for Trouble," M.K. Jerome, Joan Jasmyn (sung by June Travis).

Comedy   (PR:A MPAA:NR)

TIMESLIP   (SEE: ATOMIC MAN, THE, 1955, Brit.)

TIMETABLE½**   (1956) 79m UA bw

Mark Stevens (Charlie), King Calder (Joe), Felicia Farr (Linda), Marianne Stewart (Wife), Wesley Addy (Brucker), Alan Reed (Wolfe), Jack Klugman (Frankie), John Marley (Bobik), Rodolfo Hoyos (Lt. Castro).

Tightly woven yarn in which insurance investigator Stevens finds the daily routine of the office and the confines of his cozy home unbearable. Making a complete switch, he takes to the other side of the law, becoming the target of a one-time dear friend, railroad cop Calder, who doesn't want to accept the fact that he must bring the cold wrath of justice down on his buddy. Performances are all solid, and director Stevens makes good use of the potential beneath each character. Only problem seems to be with the scripter, who was unable to effectively tie all the elements together.

p&d, Mark Stevens; w, Aben Kandel (based on the story by Robert Angus); ph, Charles Van Enger; m, Walter Scharf; ed, Kenneth Crane; md, Walter Scharf; art d, William H. Tuntke; m/l, "Salud Felicidad y Amor," Scharf, Jack Brooks.

Crime/Drama   (PR:A MPAA:NR)

TIMOTHY'S QUEST*½   (1936) 65m PAR bw

Dickie Moore (Timothy), Virginia Weidler (Samantha Tarbox), Eleanore Whitney (Martha), Tom Keene (David Masters), Elizabeth Patterson (Vilda Cummins), Samuel S. Hinds (Rev. Fellows), Esther Dale (Hitty Tarbox), Bennie Bartlett (Jimmy), J.M. Kerrigan (Dr. Cudd), Irene Franklin (Flossie Cudd), Sally Martin (Gay), Jack Clifford (Ed the Tramp), John Kelly (Herb), Raymond Hatton ("Jabe" Doolittle), Ralph Remley (Joe), Robert Perry (Bartender), Otto Fries (Timid Tenor), Irving Bacon (Henry the Drunken Wagon Driver), Clarence H. Wilson (Mr. Simpson), Tempe Pigott (Mrs. Simpson), George Guhl (Policeman), John Kelley (Herb), Lew Kelly (Sheriff).

Fatuous story which has Moore and impish Weidler as young orphans who find a place in the heart of ice-cold spinster Patterson. It all attempts to evoke a few tears, with the scripters piling cliche upon cliche in a very irritating manner. Molasses runs faster than this bit of fluff, and tastes better. Good work by many of the cast is a shameful waste.

p, Harold Hurley; d, Charles Barton; w, Virginia Van Upp, Dore Schary, Gilbert Pratt (based on the novel by Kate Douglas Wiggin); ph, Harry Fishbeck; ed, Jack Dennis; art d, Hans Dreier, Robert Odell.

Drama   (PR:A MPA:NR)

TIN DRUM, THE*½**   (1979, Ger./Fr./Yugo./Pol.) 142m Artemis-Hallelujah-Argos/N ew World c (DIE BLECHTROMMEL)

David Bennent (Oskar Matzerath), Mario Adorf (Alfred Matzerath), Angela Winkler (Agnes Matzerath), Daniel Olbrychski (Jan Bronski), Katharina Tahlback (Maria), Charles Aznavour (Sigismund Markus), Heinz Bennent (Greff), Andrea Ferreol (Lina Greff), Fritz Hakl (Bebra, Midget), Mariella Oliveri (Raswitha Raguna), Tina Engel (The Young Anna Kollaiczek), Berta Drews (The Old Anna Kollaiczek), Roland Beubner (Joseph Kollaiczek), Ernst Jacobi (Gauleiter Lobsack), Werner Rehm (Scheffler the Baker), Ilse Page (Gretchen Scheffler), Kate Jaenicke (Mother Truczinski), Wigand Witting (Herbert Truczinski), Schugger-Leo (Marek Walczewski), Wolcech Pszoniak (Faingold), Otto Sander (Meyn the Musician), Karl-Heinz Titelbach (Felix), Bruno Thost (Cpl. Lankes), Gerda Blisse (Miss Spollenhauer), Joachim Hackethal (Father Wiehnke), Zygmunt Huebner (Dr. Michon), Mieczyslaw Czechowicz (Kobyella), Emil Feist, Herbert Behrent (Circus Performers).

Winner of the Academy Award for Best Foreign Film and cowinner of the grand prize at the Cannes Film Festival (along with APOCALYPSE NOW) THE TIN DRUM is a wholly original work; a combination of surreal images and straightforward storytelling. Bennent is born to a German rural family of the 1920s. Disgusted with the behavior of adults, he decides on his third birthday (for which he has received a beloved tin drum) not to grow any more. He stages an accident as a ruse to explain his small stature in the years to come. Bennent is taken to a doctor but when they attempt to take away his tin drum the boy accidentally discovers a hidden talent: his piercing scream will shatter glass. Bennent continues to observe the events and hypocritical behavior of the adults, beating out a constant tattoo on his tin drum to control the world around him. In what is the film's best sequence, the boy hides out beneath a stand and uses his pounding rhythm to reduce a Nazi rally to utter chaos. He also uses his scream to destroy windows after observing his mother (Winkler) in a torrid lovemaking session with his uncle (and probable father), Olbrychski. Bennent is taken to the circus where he meets Hakl, a performing midget. Hakl is impressed with Bennent's skills and advises the boy that their kind must look out for one another. On a family outing at the beach, Winkler is appalled when she sees a man catching eels with a horse's head. She is compelled to eat only raw fish and ends up killing herself. Bennent is left only with his brutish father (Adorf) who hires 16-year-old Tahlbach as a housemaid. She also becomes Bennent's first love, though Adorf makes her his mistress. The girl ends up pregnant and marries Adorf, though Bennent is convinced the child is his. Once more the boy–who is now growing in age though not stature–runs into Hakl, who manages a troupe of performing midgets. Bennent joins them and falls in love with Oliveri, a beautiful member of the group. Eventually she is killed and Bennent returns home to war-torn Germany. The Russians are taking over and the family hides out in a cellar. Adorf is killed thanks to Bennent's treachery, and the boy/man decides at the funeral that it's time for him to grow. He deliberately falls into the grave, thus creating a physical ruse as he did at age three. The film ends as Bennent, Tahlbach, and their son are deported, leaving Bennent's old grandmother Drews alone in the potato fields. THE TIN DRUM is a film rich with black humor and is a decidedly bitter look at the German people. Like many directors of the New German Cinema group, Schlondorff takes a hard look at the causes behind Germany's problems and at how the Nazis succeeded in achieving power thanks to the complacency of the people. Only Bennent, in his singularly demented view, is the voice of reason. "Once there was a credulous people who believed in Santa Claus, but Santa Claus turned out to be the gas man!" he says at one point. Schlondorff creates a nightmarish world, filmed in a mostly naturalistic style with some inventive and disturbing images mixed in. We first meet Bennent as a babe in the womb, curled up and reluctant to leave. The birth sequence is filmed entirely from his point of view, a remarkable example of coordination of actors and camera. At the heart of the film is Bennent himself. Rather than cast a midget in the role, Schlondorff chose a 12-year-old boy whose own growth had been stunted. The director picked Bennent because of his eyes and one cannot leave the film without understanding why. Bennent's wide blue eyes are haunting and fierce, carrying a hypnotic quality all their own. He also proves to be a highly accomplished actor, pulling off the difficult role of Oskar and all his perverseness, while singularly carrying on the episodic story. Bennent is backed by an excellent ensemble. There is not a weak performance in the lot. Aznavour, the French singer who had also appeared in Francois Truffaut's SHOOT THE PIANO PLAYER, turns in a performance brimming with pathos as the Jewish shopkeeper in love with Bennent's mother. THE TIN DRUM is taken from the noted novel by German writer Gunter Grass. Grass originally had the novel published in 1959 and was approached numerous times for a film version. Producer Seitz's offer finally convinced the author to let his story be filmed and Grass supplied some additional dialog to the completed screenplay. THE TIN DRUM covers the first two thirds of the novel (Schlondorff proposed making a sequel from the final third at a later date) and ranked as the single most expensive product ion in German filmmaking. Though it maintains a strong tone throughout, one wishes that Schlondorff would have made more use of Bennent's running commentary. The child provides a narration for most of the story but strangely has nothing to say at the end. It leaves the viewer with a feeling of something unfinished, which detracts from an otherwise fine job of filmmaking. (In German; English subtitles.)

p, Franz Seitz, Anatole Dauman; d, Volker Schlondorff; w, Seitz, Schlondorff, Jean-Claude Carriere, Gunter Grass (based on the novel *The Tin Drum* by Grass); ph, Igor Luther (Eastmancolor); m, Friedrich Meyer, Maurice Jarre; ed, Suzanne Baron; prod d, Nicos Perakis; art d, Perakis; spec eff, Georges Jaconelli.

Drama   **Cas.**   **(PR:O   MPAA:R)**

TIN GIRL, THE**   (1970, Ital.) 95m Scetr Films c (LA RAGAZZA DI LATTA; AKA: THE GIRL OF TIN)

Roberto Antonelli, Sydne Rome, Elena Persiani, Umberto D'Orsi, Adriano Amidei Migliano.

Set sometime in the future, Antonelli plays an executive of the Smack Corp. who spies a beautiful girl which releases a fantasy world in his heart and mind. He soon discovers that the girl is nothing but an android and a product of the company he works for. A one-joke story that takes 95 minutes to unwind, and then one finds that the joke is pointless.

p&d, Marcello Aliprandi; w, Aliprandi, Fernando Imbert; ph, Gastone de Giovanni.

Fantasy   **(PR:A   MPAA:NR)**

TIN GODS*½   (1932, Brit.) 52m BIP/Pathe bw

Frank Cellier (*Maj. Drake*), Dorothy Bartlam (*Daphne Drake*), Peter Evan Thomas (*Robert Staveley*), Frank Royde (*Cheng Chi Lung*), Ben Welden (*Cyrus P. Schroeder*), Alexander Field (*Lane*), Margaret Damer (*Mrs. Drake*), Ruth Maitland (*Mrs. Schroeder*), Athol Fleming (*Padre*).

A tedious picture about a group of Chinese pirates-terrorists who take over a passenger ship, demand a hefty ransom, and order the death of major

Cellier. Their attempt fails, thanks to the heroics of a marine rescue squad.

p&d, F.W. Kramer; w, Edgar G. Middleton (based on his play).

Drama   **(PR:A   MPAA:NR)**

TIN MAN**   (1983) 95m Goldfarb/Thomas-Biston & Westcom c

Timothy Bottoms, Deana Jurgens, John Philip Law, Troy Donahue.

Bottoms, an auto mechanic born deaf, tinkers in his workshop and invents a computer that serves as his ears and tongue. His speech therapist is very enthusiastic about the invention and introduces Bottoms to some computer salesmen. Unfortunately, the salesmen only want to exploit Bottoms' invention, forcing him to take action against them. The silly premise isn't helped by the inept script or lackluster direction.

p&d, John G. Thomas; w, Bishop Holiday; ph, Virgil Harper; m, Holiday.

Drama   **Cas.**   **(PR:A   MPAA:NR)**

TIN PAN ALLEY**½   (1940) 92m FOX bw

Alice Faye (*Katie Blane*), Betty Grable (*Lily Blane*), Jack Oakie (*Harry Calhoun*), John Payne (*Skeets Harrigan*), Allen Jenkins (*Sgt. Casey*), Esther Ralston (*Nora Bayes*), Harold Nicholas, Bayard Nicholas (*Dance Specialty*), Ben Carter (*Boy*), John Loder (*Reggie Carstair*), Elisha Cook, Jr. (*Joe Cadd*), Fred Keating (*Harvey Raymond*), Billy Gilbert (*Sheik*), Lillian Porter (*Telephone Operator*), Brian Sisters (*Specialty*), Robert Brothers (*Specialty*), Princess Vanessa Ammon (*Specialty*), Tyler Brooke (*Bert Melville*), Hal K. Dawson (*Hotel Clerk*), William B. Davidson (*Hotel Manager*), Lionel Pape (*Lord Stanley*), Billy Bevan (*Doorman*), Dewey Robinson (*Dumb Guy*), Robert Emmett Keane (*Manager*), John Sheehan (*Announcer*), George Watts (*Mike Buckner*), Jack Roper (*Nick Palerno*), James Flavin (*Sergeant*), Franklyn Farnum (*Man in Audience*), Harry Strang (*Doughboy*).

Oakie and Payne are a pair of songsmiths who need to sell a tune so they can pay their rent. They meet Faye and Grable, singing sisters, who push the song for the writers. Later Faye has dinner with Oakie and Payne, where they hear Cook playing one of his songs. Using money provided by Faye, Oakie and Payne make a deal with Cook for this tune and it soon becomes a hit. Grable gets a part in a show, so Faye goes to work for Oakie and Payne at their new Tin Pan Alley offices. Their music business thrives as Faye continues to plug songs for the pair. Then Payne finds a song he is sure will be the company's biggest seller. Instead of using Faye to introduce the tune, Payne gets Ralston, a big name singer, to sing the song at an important benefit. Faye goes to London to join her sister after this snub, and the two become big stars. Meanwhile, back at Tin Pan Alley, Payne turns down a war song by Cook, convinced that it won't sell. WW I is declared and Oakie and Payne's music business goes into a decline, so they decide to enlist in the army. The two are sent to England, where they hope to reunite with Faye and Grable. Payne and Oakie go AWOL to see the girls perform in their hit show, then say a final goodbye at a pier before being shipped off to the front. Oakie goofs around and falls into the water where he is hit by inspiration. The plunge–where the non-swimming Oakie frantically calls out "K-K-K-Katie!"–leads to lyrics for a song he has unsuccessfully tried to finish. Finally "the war to end all wars" is over, reuniting Faye and Payne as the victorious soldiers parade down the streets of New York City. Full of wonderful old tunes, this is an entertaining musical brimming with energy. Payne and Faye play well off one another, while Oakie and Grable provide good support in their secondary roles. Lang's direction moves the story along at a breezy pace. The film is full of some fine production numbers, as well as an entertaining dance routine by the Nicholas Brothers. "The Sheik of Araby," the movie's big production number, had to be cut down after complaints by the Hays Office that an abundance of unneeded female flesh was displayed in the sequence. Originally this was to feature Faye with Tyrone Power and Don Ameche, as a follow-up to their successful ALEXANDER'S RAGTIME BAND (1938), but these plans fell through. Eventually Oakie and Payne were cast. The Payne-Faye team worked sufficiently well in this, their first teaming, to be cast together three more times (Don Ameche was paired with Faye six times to Payne's four). A new part was written for rising star Grable. Studio executives had been impressed with her performance in DOWN ARGENTINE WAY earlier that year, and were eager to showcase her talents (ironically, Faye had been replaced by Grable as the star of DOWN ARGENTINE WAY after Faye came down with appendicitis). The period look of the film is excellent, from sets to costumes, and musical director Newman won an Oscar for Best Score. Ralston, once known as the "American Venus," made her last major appearance with this picture, which was remade in 1950 as I'LL GET BY. The songs include: "The Sheik of Araby" (Harry B. Smith, Francis Wheeler, Ted Snyder), "You Say the Sweetest Things, Baby" (Mack Gordon, Harry Warren), "America I Love You" (Edgar Leslie, Archie Gottler), "Goodbye Broadway, Hello France" (Francis Riesner, Benny Davis, Billy Baskette), "K-K-K-Katy" (Geoffrey O'Hara), "Moonlight Bay" (Edward Madden, Percy Wenrich), "Honeysuckle Rose" (Andy Razaf, Thomas "Fats" Waller), "Moonlight And Roses" (Ben Black, Neil Moret, Edwin H. Lemare). Cut from the film was a musical number involving a flivver, "Get Out and Get Under," another period classic.

p, Kenneth MacGowan; d, Walter Lang; w, Robert Ellis, Helen Logan (based on a story by Pamela Harris); ph, Leon Shamroy; ed, Walter Thompson; md,

Alfred Newman; art d, Richard Day, Joseph C. Wright; set d, Thomas Little; cos, Travis Banton; ch, Seymour Felix.

Musical   Cas.   (PR:A   MPAA:NR)

TIN STAR, THE***   (1957) 93m PAR bw

Henry Fonda (*Morg Hickman*), Anthony Perkins (*Sheriff Ben Owens*), Betsy Palmer (*Nona Mayfield*), Michael Ray (*Kip Mayfield*), Neville Brand (*Bart Bogardus*), John McIntire (*Dr. McCord*), Mary Webster (*Millie Parker*), Peter Baldwin (*Zeke McGaffey*), Richard Shannon (*Buck Henderson*), Lee Van Cleef (*Ed McGaffey*), James Bell (*Judge Thatcher*), Howard Petrie (*Harvey King*), Russell Simpson (*Clem Hall*), Hal K. Dawson (*Andy Miller*), Jack Kenney (*Sam Hodges*), Mickey Finn (*McCall*), Frank Cady (*Abe Pickett*), Bob Kenaston (*Hardman*), Allen Gettel (*Sloan*), Frank Cordell (*Posse Member*), Tim Sullivan (*Virgil Hough*), Frank McGrath (*Jim Clark*).

A tale of the old West that concentrates on character and the interaction between individuals. Fonda plays the bounty hunter, also a former sheriff, who rides into town, a body lying over his horse, to collect a reward. The representative of law in town is young Perkins, a tenderfoot who has yet to learn his job. After Fonda gets Perkins out of one jam after another, the two strike up a friendship, the elder man acting as teacher and advisor to the sheriff until he is able to muster the confidence needed for his job. The reason Fonda quit his job of sheriff was the apathy he found among the people of the town he protected. This attitude exists for Perkins, and is what links the pair. Chief among their adversaries is Brand, who is quick with a gun and who takes the law into his own hands when a posse is formed to hunt down two murderers. It is Perkins' overcoming of Brand that solidifies his position as sheriff. This was a perfect role for aloof Fonda. From his initial ride into town, carrying the dead body on his horse–the people flocking into the street to stare–he ignores the townsfolk as a loner is meant to do, a man embittered by experience but performing what is necessary to carry on honorably.

p, William Perlberg, George Seaton; d, Anthony Mann; w, Dudley Nichols (based on the story "The Tin Badge" by Barney Slater, Joel Kane); ph, Loyal Griggs (VistaVision); m, Elmer Bernstein; ed, Alma Macrorie; art d, Hal Pereira, Joseph MacMillan Johnson; cos, Edith Head.

Western   Cas.   (PR:A   MPAA:NR)

TINDER BOX, THE½**   (1968, E. Ger.) 81m DEFA/Childhood Productions c (DAS FEUERZEUG; AKA: TINDERBOX)

Rolf Ludwig, Bella Waldritter, Hannes Fischer, Anna-Maria Besendahl, Detlev Heinze, Barbara Mehlan, Rolf Defrank, Heinz Schubert, Hans Fiebrandt, Senta Bonacker, Fritz Schlegel.

A screen adaptation of the lovely Hans Christian Andersen fairy tale about a soldier who performs an errand for a witch, which is to retrieve a tinderbox from a cave. Instead of giving her the box, the soldier keeps it, using its powers to marry a beautiful princess and become king of the land.

p, William L. Snyder; d, Siegfried Hartmann; w, Hartmann, Anneliese Kocialek, Fred Rodrian (based on the story "Fyrtojet" by Hans Christian Andersen); ph, Erich Gusko (Agfacolor); m, Siegfried Bethmann; art d, Hans Poppe.

Fantasy   (PR:AA   MPAA:NR)

TINGLER, THE½**   (1959) 80m COL bw

Vincent Price (*Dr. William Chapin*), Judith Evelyn (*Mrs. Higgins*), Darryl Hickman (*David Morris*), Patricia Cutts (*Isabel Chapin*), Pamela Lincoln (*Lucy Stevens*), Philip Coolidge (*Ollie Higgins*).

Perhaps the most noted film for the imaginative gimmicks that producer-director Castle used to give people a thrill. In this one, he hooked up Army surplus vibrating motors to the backs of some theater seats to send tingles up the audience's spines while they were watching the show. If that did not produce shrieks, then a "plant" in the theater would faint and would be carried out to the lobby by ushers. But this thriller is frightening enough in its own right not to have to resort to antics like those. Price is a scientist who believes screaming releases tensions that would otherwise kill people. A deaf mute theater operator dies and Price discovers that the cause of her death was an insect that attaches itself to a person's spinal cords and can only be killed if the victim screams. The insect gets loose in a theater, and the rigged-up motors go into action. On the whole, an effectively paced and conceived project, and more proof of Castle's talent as a master of entertainment.

p&d, William Castle; w, Robb White; ph, Wilfrid M. Cline; m, Van Dexter; ed, Chester W. Schaeffer; art d, Phil Bennett.

Horror   (PR:C   MPAA:NR)

TINKER*½**   (1949, Brit.) 70m Citizen/Eros bw

Derek Smith (*Tinker*).

Maudlin melodrama starring Smith as a young gypsy who runs away from home and winds up in a mining town. There he is taught to read and write,

while making many friends among the miners. Smith's new-found happiness is short-lived, however, when it appears to the miners that he has committed a theft. Panicked, Smith leaves the mining camp. During his wanderings the gypsy boy nearly drowns, but his friends from the mining camp save his life and invite him back. Producer-writer-director Marshall, who was married to his cowriter-producer Brilliant, studied filmmaking under Sergei Eisenstein in the 1930s. He would later translate the great Soviet director's autobiography *Immoral Memories* into English, but unfortunately his films display none of the skills or intelligence his mentor possessed.

p, Herbert P.J. Marshall, Alfredda Brilliant; d, Marshall; w, Marshall, Brilliant; ph, Gunther Krampf.

Drama   (PR:AA   MPAA:NR)

TINTORERA...BLOODY WATERS*   (1977, Brit./Mex.) 91m Hemdale Leisure-Conacine/Unit ed Film Distribution c (AKA: TINTORERA; TINTORERA...TIGER SHARK)

Susan George (*Gabriella*), Hugo Stiglitz (*Esteban*), Andres Garcia (*Miguel*), Fiona Lewis, Jennifer Ashley.

George finds herself the object of the attentions of two adventurers who aren't satisfied with the pleasures she provides, but further their drive for excitement by taking on a very hungry and a very large shark. As trite as they come.

p, Gerald Green; d, Rene Cardona, Jr.; w, Ramon Bravo; m, Basil Poledouris.

Adventure   Cas.   (PR:O   MPAA:R)

TIOGA KID, THE*½**   (1948) 54m PRC/EL bw

Eddie Dean (*Eddie/Tioga Kid*), Roscoe Ates (*Soapy*), Jennifer Holt (*Jenny*), Dennis Moore (*Morino*), Lee Bennett (*Tucson*), Bill [William] Fawcett (*Tennessee*), Eddie Parker (*Clem*), Bob Woodward (*Trigger*), Louis J. Corbett (*Sam*), Terry Frost (*Ranger Captain*), Tex Palmer, Andy Parker and the Plainsmen, Flash the Horse.

Dean takes on two roles, that of a Texas Ranger and an outlaw who goes by the name of "The Tioga Kid." As the former, Dean brings a band of horse rustlers to justice after they make off with a federal payroll. His counterpart is busy trying to do some rustling of his own, much to the dismay of the heavies who already have the area sewn up. Some fresh western scenics help make this palatable. Andy Parker and the Plainsmen serve up three cowboy tunes amongst the shooting and fisticuffs.

p, Jerry Thomas; d, Ray Taylor; w, Ed Earl Repp; ph, Ernie Miller; ed, Hugh Winn; m/l, Eddie Dean, Johnny Bond, Pete Gates, Lewis Porter, Robert Tansey.

Western   (PR:A   MPAA:NR)

TIP ON A DEAD JOCKEY*½**   (1957) 98m MGM bw (GB: TIME FOR ACTION)

Robert Taylor (*Lloyd Tredman*), Dorothy Malone (*Phyllis Tredman*), Gia Scala (*Paquita Heldon*), Martin Gabel (*Bert Smith*), Marcel Dalio (*Toto del Aro*), Jack Lord (*Jimmy Heldon*), Joyce Jameson (*Sue Fan Finley*).

Taylor is a pilot and veteran of WW II haunted by memories of the pilots he inadvertently sent to their deaths during that war. He lives as an expatriate in Madrid and is in the midst of divorcing wife Malone despite her desperate attempts to hold their marriage together. He loses all his money when a horse he bets on throws its jockey, killing him. This, along with wanting to help his financially strapped war buddy Lord, leads to his agreeing to participate in a currency smuggling scheme masterminded by Gabel. Taylor and sidekick Dalio evade various authorities in a long chase, but when they discover that their contraband includes narcotics they turn it all over to the authorities and send the police after Gabel. All this action puts some of the old spirit back in Taylor; he is reconciled with Malone and goes back to his prewar occupation as an airline pilot. Competently written and directed, the film is nonetheless tedious when Taylor wallows in self-pity as Malone tries to hold their marriage together. It is only when the smuggling scheme and subsequent chase enter the film that any real excitement is generated, but these come too late in the story to redeem it by themselves. Taylor contributes his usual performance, adequately showing the world pressing down on him, but that wasn't enough either. Malone is good, but hasn't much to do, and the rest of the cast is only competent.

p, Edwin H. Knopf; d, Richard Thorpe; w, Charles Lederer (based on a story by Irwin Shaw); ph, George J. Folsey (CinemaScope); m, Miklos Rozsa; ed, Ben Lewis; art d, William A. Horning, Hans Peters; cos, Helen Rose; m/l, "You Found Me and I Found You," P.G. Wodehouse, Jerome Kern.

Crime   (PR:A-C   MPAA:NR)

TIP-OFF, THE**   (1931) 70m RKO-Pathe bw (GB: LOOKING FOR TROUBLE)

Eddie Quillan (*Tommy Jordan*), Robert Armstrong (*Kayo McClure*), Ginger Rogers (*Baby Face*), Joan Peers (*Edna Moreno*), Ralf Harolde (*Nick Vatelli*),

Charles Sellon (*Pop Jackson*), Mike Donlin (*Swanky Jones*), Ernie Adams (*Slug McGee*), JackHerrick (*Joe*), Cupid Ainsworth (*Miss Waddums*), Frank Darien (*Edna's Uncle*), Luis Alberni (*Searno, Roadhouse Manager*), Ivan Linow (*Kayo's Sparring Partner*), Dorothy Granger (*Hat Check Girl*), James Burtis (*Men's Room Patron*), Harry Wilson (*Hood*), Charles Sullivan (*Chuck the Bouncer*).

Quillan plays a "little mister innocence" guy who becomes involved with the mob when he attempts to cut in on the kingpin's girl, Peers. His saving grace is in the friendship he strikes up with thick-skinned but good-hearted boxer Armstrong, who has a sweetheart in the engaging and exuberant Rogers. Armstrong not only saves Quillan but saves this picture as well. His performance and the interplay between him and Rogers make for some entertaining situations in this smart-paced story. This was Rogers' first picture for RKO-Pathe after she won a release from her contract at Paramount, which had done little for her career.

p, Charles R. Rogers; d, Albert Rogell; w, Earl Baldwin (based on the story by George Kibbe Turner); ph, Edward Snyder; ed, Charles Craft; md, Arthur Lange; art d, Carroll Clark; cos, Gwen Wakeling.

Comedy   **(PR:A MPAA:NR)**

TIP-OFF GIRLS**½   (1938) 64m PAR bw

Lloyd Nolan (*Bob Anders*), Mary Carlisle (*Marjorie Rogers*), J. Carroll Naish (*Joseph Valkus*), Harvey Stephens (*Jason Baardue*), Roscoe Karns (*Tom Benson*), Larry "Buster" Crabbe (*Red Deegan*), Anthony Quinn (*Marty*), Benny Baker (*Scott*), Evelyn Brent (*Rena Terry*), Irving Bacon (*Sam*), Gertrude Short (*"Boots" Milburn*), Archie Twitchell [Michael Branden] (*Hensler*), Barlowe Borland (*Blacky*), Pierre Watkin (*George Murkil*), John Hart, Harry Templeton, Vic Demourelle, Jr, Jack Pennick, Ethan Laidlaw, Stanley King (*Drivers*), Stanley Price (*Louis*), Phillip Warren (*Steve*), Wade Boteler (*Pete*), John Patterson (*Jim*), Frank Austin (*Gus*), Richard E. Allen (*Police Lieutenant*), Stanley Andrews (*Police Sergeant*), Oscar "Dutch" Hendrian (*Hijacker*), Barbara Jackson (*Nurse*), Joyce Mathews (*Tessie*), Ruth Rogers, Laurie Lane, Margaret Randell, Cheryl Walker (*Waitresses*).

Nolan and Karns play federal agents investigating a number of truck hijackings along state highways. The plaintiff, Naish, who asks for assistance in the first place, is actually the man behind the gang staging the robberies, and goes to the police as a decoy. The G-Men go under cover and posing as truck drivers hijack one of the gang's trucks, impress the crooks, and work their way into the gang. An extremely well-paced job. The title refers to women on the highways who flag down the trucks to be victimized.

p, Edward T. Lowe; d, Louis King; w, Maxwell Shane, Robert Yost, Stuart Anthony; ph, Theodor Sparkuhl; m, Boris Morros; ed, Ellsworth Hoagland; art d, Hans Dreier, Robert Odell.

Crime   **(PR:A MPAA:NR)**

TIRE AU FLANC   (SEE: ARMY GAME, THE, 1963, Fr.)

TIREZ SUR LE PIANISTE   (SEE: SHOOT THE PIANO PLAYER, 1962, Fr.)

'TIS A PITY SHE'S A WHORE*½   (1973, Ital.) 102m Clesi/Euro International c (ADDIO, FRATELLO CRUDELE)

Charlotte Rampling (*Annabella*), Oliver Tobias (*Giovanni*), Fabio Testi (*Soranzo*), Antonio Falsi (*Bonaventura*), Rick Battaglia, Angela Luce, Rino Imperio.

A costume drama set in Renaissance Italy centering around the incestuous relationship between Rampling and her brother, Tobias. Her pregnancy puts a quick end to the affair, with the family marrying her off to Testi. Upon discovery of Rampling's pregnancy, her husband goes into a fury, threatening to kill all of his in-laws. The highpoints of this picture are the incredibly beautiful staging given full power through Storaro's photography, accompanied by the equally beautiful score by Morricone. Strange to find such magnificent efforts in photography, design, and music against the background to a violent film about abnormal people, with bloodletting a high point of the story, based on Ford's 17th-Century drama.

p, Silvio Clementelli; d, Giuseppe Patroni Griffi; w, Griffi, Alfio Valdarnini, Carlo Carunchio (based on the play by John Ford); ph, Vittorio Storaro (Technicolor); m, Ennio Morricone; ed, Kim Arcalli; art d, Mario Ceroli.

Drama   **(PR:O MPAA:R)**

TISH**½   (1942) 84m MGM bw

Marjorie Main (*Letitia Carberry*), ZaSu Pitts (*Aggie Pilkington*), Aline MacMahon (*Lizzie Wilkins*), Lee Bowman (*Charlie Sands*), Guy Kibbee (*Judge Bowser*), Susan Peters (*Cora Edwards*), Richard Quine (*Ted Bowser*), Virginia Grey (*Katherine Bowser*), Al Shean (*Rev. Ostermaier*), Ruby Danbridge (*Violet*), Gerald Oliver Smith (*Butler*), Sam Ash, King Baggott (*Men on Street*), Margaret Bert (*Mrs. Phelps*), Jessie Arnold (*Woman on Street*), Jenny Mac, Nora Cecil, Gertrude Hoffmann (*Spinsters*), Kathryn Sheldon (*Acidulous Spinster*), George Humbert (*Italian*), Robert Emmett

O'Connor (*Game Warden*), Arthur Space (*Court Clerk*), Howard Hickman (*Mr. Kelbridge*), William Farnum (*Gardener*), Rudy Wissler (*Newsboy*), Byron Shores (*Dr. McRegan*).

The busybody of a small town, Main, tries to run everybody's life, including playing matchmaker for love affairs she sees as perfect. She attempts to match her nephew with Peters, but discovers that he is only interested in the daughter of Main's archenemy, judge Kibbee. Peters as well has eyes only for another of the judge's brood, Quine, whom she secretly marries. Quine goes to war and Peters dies soon after childbirth without telling anyone who the father was. Main gets the bright idea of saying the baby is hers, which nobody believes. The son turns up alive at the finale and announces his parenthood, and the village goes back to sleep. Ridiculous in the main and a waste of talent, although the pretty misses Peters and Grey do far more than the script asks.

p, Orville O. Dull; d, S. Sylvan Simon; w, Harry Ruskin, Annalee Whitmore Jacoby, Thomas Seller (based on stories by Mary Roberts Rinehart); ph, Paul Vogel; ed, Robert J. Kern; art d, Cedric Gibbons.

Comedy   **(PR:A MPAA:NR)**

TITANIC***½   (1953) 98m FOX bw

Clifton Webb (*Richard Sturges*), Barbara Stanwyck (*Julia Sturges*), Robert Wagner (*Giff Rogers*), Audrey Dalton (*Annette Sturges*), Thelma Ritter (*Mrs. Maude Young*), Brian Aherne (*Capt. E.J. Smith*), Richard Basehart (*George Healey*), Allyn Joslyn (*Earl Meeker*), James Todd (*Sandy Comstock*), William Johnstone (*John Jacob Astor*), Charles FitzSimons (*Chief Officer Wilde*), Barry Bernard (*1st Officer Murdock*), Harper Carter (*Norman Sturges*), Edmund Purdom (*2nd Officer Lightoller*), Camillo Guercio (*Mr. Guggenheim*), Antony Eustrel (*Sanderson*), Alan Marston (*Quartermaster*), James Lilburn (*Devlin*), Christopher Severn (*Messenger*), Frances Bergen (*Madeleine, Mrs. John Jacob Astor*), Guy Standing, Jr. (*George D. Widener*), Hellen Van Tuyl (*Mrs. Straus*), Roy Gordon (*Isidor Straus*), Marta Mitrovich (*Mrs. Uzcadam*), Ivis Goulding (*Emma*), Dennis Fraser (*Bride*), Ashley Cowan (*Phillips*), Lehmer 'Lee' Graham (*Symons*), Merry Anders, Gloria Gordon, Melinda Markey (*College Girls*), Ronald F. Hagerty, Conrad Feia, Richard West (*College Boys*), Mae Marsh (*Woman*), William Cottrell, Owen McGiveney, Donald Chaffin, Ralph Grosh, Michael Ferris, John Fraser (*Stewards*), David Hoffman (*Tailor*), Gordon Richards (*Manager*), Elizabeth Flournoy (*Woman with Baby*), Robin Hughes (*Junior Officer*), Robin Camp (*Messenger Boy*), Pat Aherne David Thursby (*Seamen*), Pat O'Moore (*Relief Man*), John Costello, Nick Coster, Camillo Guercio, Antony Eustrel, Alan Marston, Michael Hadlow, Ivan Hayes, Robin Sanders Clark, Herbert Deans, John Dodsworth, Charles Keane, Salvador Baguez, Eugene Borden, Alberto Morin, Richard Peel, Harry Cording, Joan Hayes, Bert Stevens, Duke Seba, Joyce Newhart, George Boyce.

The *Titanic* disaster of April 15, 1912 has been filmed several times, and this time the tragedy gets the full Hollywood melodrama treatment. Stanwyck is the mother of two children and the wife of Webb, whom she is deserting because of his snobbish, socialite ways, taking her children back to America with her to keep them from their father's corrupting influence. Webb manages to get passage on the ship by buying the third-class tickets of a Basque family and persuading them to catch another ship. He and Stanwyck have a number of confrontations on board before she lays the big truth on him to drive him away once and for all: her son, Carter, is not his child. While this story has been developing, other subplots are developed. Wagner is a young college student returning home who falls in love with Dalton, Stanwyck's daughter. Basehart is a priest defrocked for alcoholism. The ship's captain, Aherne, is pushing for a record crossing-time, and is ignoring warnings of icebergs in the area. Finally the inevitable disaster strikes the "unsinkable" ship, and an underwater spur on an iceberg tears a long hole in the side of the ship (when the wreck was finally located and explored in 1986, it was discovered that, in fact, rivets had popped and plates separated, rather than a hole being torn in the plate steel). For a time the passengers are unaware of the danger, but before long the ship begins to list and the passengers start for the lifeboats, only to discover that there are entirely too few to hold all the passengers. Webb sees Stanwyck and his children to a boat, then goes about helping other passengers. When he locates a friend and asks him to help, the man asks if the situation is that serious. "We could be having sand for supper," Webb replies, his upper lip growing stiff. Captain Aherne goes to the engine room to ask the chief stoker to keep the engine running as long as possible to keep power up for the lights and wireless. "I suppose you know you may not get out of here," Aherne tells the brawny, sweaty stoker. With infinite calm and resignation, the man quietly answers back, "Well, that's the way it is sometimes." Back up on deck, young Carter abandons his place on the lifeboat in favor of a young mother and her baby, then goes to find his father, who, of course, wants nothing to do with him anymore since he isn't his son. One lifeboat becomes tangled in the ropes as it is lowered and Wagner climbs down the rope to free it. After the boat is safely in the water, though, Wagner is unable to climb back aboard and falls into the icy waters, only to be pulled out by Dalton and Stanwyck onto their boat (a too convenient way to get the juvenile lead to survive the disaster without looking like a coward). One woman in the boat is revealed to be a man. Webb accepts his son as a brave person worthy of his name and the two hold hands as the ship goes down, the band playing "Nearer My God to Thee." Despite a too melodramatic main story, the film is quite effective in conveying the tragedy, the panic, and the calm of the *Titanic* sinking. A 20-foot-long model of the ship was built and the scenes of the sinking are a tour de force of special effects. Even the actors were affected by the magnitude of the tragedy they were re-creating. Stanwyck later said: "The night we were filming the scene of the dying ship in the outdoor tank at Twentieth Century-Fox, it was bitter cold. I was 47 feet up in a lifeboat swinging on the davits. The water below was agitated into a heaving, rolling mass and it was thick with other lifeboats full of woman and children. I looked down and thought: if one of these ropes snaps now, it's good-bye for you. Then I looked up at the faces lining the rail, those left behind to die with the ship. I thought of the men and women who had been through this thing. We were re-creating an actual tragedy and I burst into tears. I shook with great racking sobs and couldn't stop." The story and screenplay by Charles Brackett, Walter Reisch, and Richard Breen won the Oscar that year.

p, Charles Brackett; d, Jean Negulesco; w, Brackett, Walter Reisch, Richard Breen; ph, Joe MacDonald; m, Sol Kaplan; ed, Louis Loeffler; md, Lionel Newman; art d, Lyle Wheeler, Maurice Ransford; set d, Stuart Reiss; cos, Dorothy Jeakins; spec eff, Ray Kellogg; ch, Robert Alton; tech adv, Commodore Sir Gordon Illingworth (ret.).

Drama   **Cas.**   **(PR:A-C   MPAA:NR)**

TITFIELD THUNDERBOLT, THE**½

(1953, Brit.) 84m EAL/UNIV c

Stanley Holloway (*Valentine*), George Relph (*Rev. Weech*), Naunton Wayne (*Blakeworth*), John Gregson (*Gordon*), Godfrey Tearle (*The Bishop*), Hugh Griffith (*Dan*), Gabrielle Brune (*Joan*), Sidney James (*Hawkins*), Reginald Beckwith (*Coggett*), Edie Martin (*Emily*), Michael Trubshawe (*Ruddock*), Jack McGowran (*Vernon Crump*), Ewan Roberts (*Alec Pearce*), Herbert C. Walton (*Seth*), John Rudling (*Clegg, Ministry Inspector*), Nancy O'Neil (*Mrs. Blakeworth*), Frank Atkinson (*Police Sergeant*), Campbell Singer, Wensley Pithey, Harold Alford, Ted Burbidge, Frank Green.

The closing of a railway line by the government, which hopes to substitute a bus line for the rails, arouses the town of Titfield, and the citizens open the battle by taking over the train themselves. The bus company officials surreptitiously wreck the train one night, ruining the villagers' enterprise. But wait! The wily inhabitants bring out an old engine, The Thunderbolt, from the village museum and make a triumphant run for it, winning the government's blessing to continue in business. Rich in laughs, and equally rich in rustic scenery with full color lensing.

p, Michael Truman; d, Charles Crichton; w, T.E.B. Clarke; ph, Douglas Slocombe (Technicolor); m, Georges Auric; ed, Seth Holt; art d, C.P. Norman; cos, Anthony Mendleson.

Comedy   **(PR:A   MPAA:NR)**

TITLE SHOT*

(1982, Can.) 96m Regenthall/Cinepax c

Tony Curtis (*Frank Renzetti*), Richard Gabourie (*Blake*), Susan Hogan (*Sylvia*), Allan Royal (*Dunlop*), Robert Delbert (*Rufus Taylor*), Natsuko Ohama (*Terry*), Jack Duffy (*Mr. Green*), Sean McCann (*Lt. Grace*), Taborah Johnson (*Connie Rose*), Robert O'Ree (*Iggy*), Dennis Strong (*Eddie*).

A poorly acted, poorly scripted, and poorly conceived project which has Curtis involved in a Mafia plot to kill the heavyweight champion boxer during a boxing match, with Gabourie as a tough cop on his tail. Not worth a shot at all.

p, Bob Iveson; d, Les Rose; w, John Saxton (from a story by Richard Gabourie); ph, Henry Fiks; m, Paul James Zaza; ed, Ronald Sanders; art d, Karen Bromley.

Crime   **Cas.**   **(PR:C   MPAA:R)**

TO ALL A GOODNIGHT zero

(1980) 84m IRC-IWC and Four Features c

Buck West (*Weird Ralph*), Sam Shamshak (*Polansky*), Katherine Herington (*Mrs. Jensen*), Jennifer Runyon, Forrest Swanson, Linda Gentile, William Lauer, J. Bridges.

Another entry in the disturbingly fertile series of "psycho-killer Santa Claus" films which include BLACK CHRISTMAS (1974), YOU BETTER WATCH OUT (1980), SILENT NIGHT, DEADLY NIGHT (1984) and even one episode in TALES OF THE CRYPT (1972) entitled "All Through The House" (note the clever yuletide titles). This one takes place at the swanky Calvin Finishing School for Girls as the students prepare for Christmas break. Unfortunately the holiday is spoiled for five of the students when the crazed parents of a girl who was killed on campus two Christmases before dress up as Santa and slaughter them (the parents hold the coeds responsible for their daughter's death). By the time it's over most of the girls and several bystanders have been dispatched in a variety of bloody ways (by a crossbow, an ax, and even an airplane propeller) leaving the audience to ponder why they have wasted nearly an hour and a half to witness this inane carnage when they could be out wandering the mall.

p, Sandy Cobe; d, David Hess; w, Alex Rebar; ph, B. Godsey; m, Rich Tufo; prod d, Joe Garrity; makeup, Mark Shostrum, Miles Liptak.

Horror   **Cas.**   **(PR:O   MPAA:R)**

TO BE A CROOK**½

(1967, Fr.) 93m Films de la Pleiade-Les Films Treize/International-Comet bw (UNE FILLE ET DES FUSILS)

Jean-Pierre Kalfon (*Jean-Pierre*), Amidou Ben Messoud (*Amidou*), Pierre Barouth (*Pierrot*), Jacques Portet (*Jacques*), Janine Magnan (*Martine*), Annette Karsenti (*Stand-in*), Yane Barry (*Cafe Owner*), Gerard Sire (*Reporter's Voice*), Pierre Bourdon.

Claude Lelouch chose a theme not too dissimilar from that of Godard's BREATHLESS–restless youth's romanticism with the image of the U.S. movie gangster. Here the theme is treated much more light heartedly as four young men quit their jobs to turn to crime, but they are totally inept, fumbling even the simplest caper. One of these is the attempted kidnaping of a movie star, which winds up with them taking the actress' stand-in instead. The movie company agrees to pay to have the actress returned, in this way keeping the affair quiet. However, at the arranged meeting place one of the men spots a police officer and immediately panics, firing his gun. Two different endings were devised for this film. In the French version, the four men wind up shooting each other, while the American release has the four lying down as if dead, than jumping up and laughing. A decidedly different impact and meaning results from these changes.

p&d, Claude Lelouch; w, Lelouch, Pierre Uytterhoeven; ph, Jean Collomb; m, Pierre Vassiliu; ed, Lelouch, Claude Barrois.

Crime/Comedy   **(PR:A   MPAA:NR)**

TO BE A LADY*½

(1934, Brit.) 68m British and Dominions/PAR British bw

Dorothy Bouchier (*Diana Whitcombe*), Bruce Lister (*Jerry Dean*), Vera Boggetti (*Countess Delavel*), Charles Cullum (*Dudley Chalfont*), Ena Moon (*Annette*), Florence Vie (*Mrs. Jubb*), Tony de Lungo (*Manager*), Pat Ronald.

Unbelievable contrivances mar this romancer about a country girl, Bouchier, who comes to the city and falls in love with musician Lister. She gets arrested for innocently wearing a stolen dress, while Lister is nearly killed in a car wreck. If that's not enough, Cullum, the man Bouchier planned to marry, reunites the two young lovers. Only for gullible audiences.

p&d, George King; w, Violet Powell (based on a story by C.H. Nicholson).

Drama   **(PR:A   MPAA:NR)**

TO BE A MAN

(SEE: CRY OF BATTLE, 1963)

TO BE FREE*½

(1972) 82m Emerson/Magarac c (AKA: IMAGO; HOW NOW, SWEET JESUS?)

Barbara Douglas (*Carole*), Morgan Evans (*Dr. Keith*), Victoria Wales (*Althea*), Dick Decoit (*Bruce*), Jenie Jackson (*Molly*), Robert Webb (*Dr. O'Donnell*), Peter Cord (*Peter*), Paul Hernandez (*Rehan*), Bubby Arett (*Mr. Dobbs*), Najila (*Barbara*).

Douglas plays a young woman who has trouble coming to terms with sex–it seems that she gets ill whenever she is about to confront it. A wild party at the end of the film explodes across the screen and comes mighty close to calling for an "X" rating, but sensitivity and charm help save it. A sincere attempt by a young producer to show the stultifying effects of frigidity, it lacks the maturity in handling to make it effective.

p,d&w, Ned Bosnick; ph, Gregory Sandor; m, Lalo Schifrin.

Drama   **(PR:O   MPAA:R)**

TO BE OR NOT TO BE*****

(1942) 99m UA bw

Carole Lombard (*Maria Tura*), Jack Benny (*Joseph Tura*), Robert Stack (*Lt. Stanislav Sobinski*), Felix Bressart (*Greenberg*), Lionel Atwill (*Rawitch*), Stanley Ridges (*Prof. Alexander Siletsky*), Sig Rumann (*Col. Ehrhardt*), Tom Dugan (*Bronski*), Charles Halton (*Dobosh*), Peter Caldwell (*Wilhelm Kunze*), Helmut Dantine, Otto Reichow (*Copilots*), Miles Mander (*Maj. Cunningham*), George Lynn (*Actor-Adjutant*), Henry Victor (*Capt. Schultz*), Maude Eburne (*Anna the Maid*), Armand Wright (*Makeup Man*), Erno Verebes (*Stage Manager*), Halliwell Hobbes (*Gen. Armstrong*), Leslie Dennison (*Captain*), Frank Reicher (*Polish Official*), Wolfgang Zilzer (*Man in Bookstore*), Olaf Hytten (*Polonius in Warsaw*), Charles Irwin, Leyland Hodgson (*Reporters*), Edgar Licho (*Prompter*), Robert O. Davis (*Gestapo Sergeant*), Roland Varno (*Pilot*), Maurice Murphy, Gene Rizzi, Paul Barrett, John Kellogg (*R.A.F. Flyers*), Sven-Hugo Borg (*German Soldier*), Alec Craig, James Finlayson (*Scottish Farmers*).

A masterpiece of satire and one of the more controversial films of its day, TO BE OR NOT TO BE is a brilliant example of how comedy can be as equally effective at raising social and political awareness as a serious propaganda film, and yet still provide a great entertainment to its audience. The film begins in Poland, 1939, with a narrator describing the scene as "the man with the little mustache...Adolf Hitler" appears walking down the streets. The narrator, confused, asks why Hitler is "in Warsaw when the two countries are still at peace...and all by himself," as a crowd of curious Poles watches the dumbfounded Fuhrer. The scene then shifts to a Polish theater rehearsal with Benny starring in a satire of the Nazis. "Heil Hitler," Benny exclaims as Hitler, played by Dugan, walks into the room, sheepishly answering, "Heil, myself." The theater director is outraged at Dugan's ad-libbing, and accuses the actor of not playing Hitler correctly ("I just can't smell Hitler in him," he gripes), and of not even looking like him, at which point Dugan, still in costume, walks out into the street, answering the question of why Hitler is in Germany, alone, in 1939. Benny, one of the top theater actors in Germany, and his wife Lombard, a national institution in Warsaw, are the stars of the theater company. One specific Pole, Stack, a young aviator, is madly in love with Lombard, sending her flowers night after night. She responds to a note of his, telling him to meet her during the show in her dressing room. While Benny is on-stage performing "Hamlet" (the troupe's anti-Nazi satire was censored), Stack makes his move for Lombard's dressing room–causing a disruption as he leaves his second row seat right after Benny begins his "To be or not to be" soliloquy. Stack's virility and his military bravery impresses Lombard. After exchanging a few romantic glances, the embarrassed Stack asks her for a date, telling her, "I never met an actress," drawing a glassy-eyed, loving response from Lombard, "Lieutenant, this is the first time I ever met a man who could drop three tons of dynamite in two minutes." The following night Stack returns and again walks out on Benny's soliloquy, further enraging the tremendously vain actor. His vanity is hushed by the news of Germany's invasion of Poland. Stack is called to duty, leaving Lombard with the promise that he'll return. In England, Stack and his fellow fighters in the Polish squadron of the RAF are bidding farewell to their much-loved mentor, professor Ridges, who confides to them that he is on a secret mission to Warsaw. Stack becomes suspicious, however, when he asks Ridges to deliver a message to Lombard, and the professor claims to have never heard of the famous singer. Stack reports this to his superiors who order him to fly to Warsaw and stop Ridges from keeping an appointment with Nazi colonel Rumann, an appointment which will destroy the Warsaw underground. Stack arrives at Lombard's empty apartment, while in the meantime, Lombard is brought to Nazi headquarters for a meeting with Ridges. The professor gives her Stack's message– "To be or not to be"–which he interprets as being a top secret coded message instead of the innocent declaration of love that it really is. He then tries to convince Lombard to choose allegiance to the Nazis, as well as to have dinner later with him. Lombard returns home to find Stack in Benny's robe and slippers, and Benny thoroughly confused and infuriated. The more she tries to explain, the less Benny understands and the more he searches for an explanation, "I think a husband is entitled to an inkling" he whines. Lombard tells Stack that the meeting between Ridges and the colonel is set for the following morning. Their only chance, they decide, is for Lombard to kill Ridges at dinner that evening. Naturally, Benny objects: "Wait a minute, I'll decide with whom my wife is going to have dinner, and who she's going to kill." Benny then turns on Stack, defending his own national honor: "First you walk out on my soliloquy, then you walk into my slippers, now you question my patriotism. I love my country and I love my slippers." Benny, honorably, decides to kill Ridges, adding, "and after I kill him, I hope you'll be kind enough to tell me what it was all about." With the help of his theater troupe, Benny turns their building into Nazi headquarters and Benny, donning a Nazi outfit, plays the colonel. In the meantime, Lombard is back in Ridges' room, supposedly awaiting his return but actually planting a faked suicide note signed by Ridges. Ridges catches on to Benny's game, however, when the actor becomes too interested in the Nazi's budding romance with Lombard. While trying to escape, Ridges is killed. Benny must still return to the real Nazi headquarters and get a duplicate set of secret papers from Ridges' hotel room, this time disguising himself as Ridges. At the hotel he meets up with Lombard and is whisked away by a Nazi officer who is assigned to take him to a meeting with the colonel–this time the real colonel, played by Rumann. Rumann is a likable idiot who faithfully adheres to Nazi beliefs but makes countless, damaging errors in the process, blaming all his mistakes on his assistant, Victor. Benny is eventually found out when the real Ridges is found dead. Benny is locked in a room with the corpse, while outside Rumann and his cronies await Benny's response. Benny ingeniously cuts off Ridges beard and glues on a fake. He then accuses Rumann of murdering his duplicate, coercing Rumann into pulling the fake beard off of the corpse, thereby proving Benny's tale. Benny is found out, however, by Rumann's superior. The theater troupe than concocts a plan to rescue Benny, in which they again disguise Dugan as Hitler. They pull off their deception, convince everyone of their legitimacy, and escape via airplane to England. On the plane, Dugan tests his disguise by ordering a couple of German soldiers to jump from the plane without parachutes. They obediently reply, "Ja, mein Fuhrer." In England, Benny is given his chance to play Hamlet on the legitimate stage, but again at the "To be or not to be" line of the soliloquy a young naval officer gets up from his seat and leaves. As Charles Chaplin did with THE GREAT DICTATOR, Lubitsch tried to attack the Nazi regime and its easily lampooned leader with a sharply pointed comedy. The Nazis are made to look like complete cartoonish fools, though not without the capability of ruthlessly murdering an opposition. The Poles on the other hand, while often making many mistakes in their plots, are brave patriots who are fighting for their land–people to which "To be or not to be" refers to the country's existence as well as to Shakespeare. Released in 1942, in the midst of America's involvement in WW II, TO BE OR NOT TO BE drew a great deal of criticism by detractors who felt that Lubitsch, a German (though he left long before Hitler's rise to power) was somehow making fun of the Poles. One specific line stood alone in the battlefield of criticism–a Nazi official upon viewing Benny's bloodless performance as "Hamlet," remarks "What he did to Shakespeare, we are now doing to Poland." Even Lubitsh's own cast and crew felt the line was tasteless, requesting that it be deleted. Lubitsch, however, refused–the line just got too many laughs, which, after all, is what pleased Lubitsch the most. Lubitsch was forced to defend himself in a letter to the New York Times: "Why do audiences laugh during TO BE OR NOT TO BE, and at times very heartily? Aren't they aware of what happened to Poland? Did I try to make them look at the Polish background through those rose-colored glasses? Nothing of the kind. I went out of my way to remind them of the destruction of the Nazi conquest, of the terror regime of the Gestapo...Do I minimize their danger because I refrained from the most obvious methods in their characterization? Is whipping and flogging the only way of expressing terrorism? No, the American audience don't laugh at those Nazis because they underestimate their menace, but because they are happy to see this new order and its ideology being ridiculed." TO BE OR NOT TO BE is also remembered as the last screen appearance for the lovely Carole Lombard who, just after the film's completion, was killed in a plane crash while on tour selling war bonds. Rather than take a train, Lombard chose to travel more quickly through the air, hurrying back to Hollywood for a spot on Jack Benny's radio show.

p&d, Ernst Lubitsch; w, Edwin Justus Mayer (based on a story by Lubitsch, Melchior Lengyel); ph, Rudolph Mate; m, Miklos Rozsa; ed, Dorothy Spencer; prod d, Vincent Korda; md, Werner Heyman; set d, Julia Heron; cos, Irene; spec eff, Lawrence Butler; makeup, Gordon Bau.

War/Drama/Comedy **Cas.** **(PR:A MPAA:NR)**

TO BE OR NOT TO BE½** (1983) 108m Brooksfilms/FOX c

Mel Brooks *(Frederick Bronski)*, Anne Bancroft *(Anna Bronski)*, Tim Matheson *(Lt. Andre Sobinski)*, Charles Durning *(Col. Erhardt)*, Jose Ferrer *(Prof. Siletski)*, Christopher Lloyd *(Capt. Schultz)*, James Haake and Scamp *(Sasha and Mutki)*, George Gaynes *(Ravitch)*, George Wyner *(Ratkowski)*, Jack Riley *(Dobish)*, Lewis J. Stadlen *(Lupinski)*, Ronny Graham *(Sondheim)*, Estelle Reiner *(Gruba)*, Zale Kessler *(Bieler)*, Earl Boen *(Dr. Boyarski)*, Ivor Barry *(Gen. Hobbs)*, William Glover *(Maj. Cunningham)*, John Francis *(British Intelligence Aide)*, Raymond Skipp *(RAF Flight Sergeant)*, Marley Sims *(Rifka)*, Larry Rosenberg *(Rifka's Husband)*, Max Brooks *(Rifka's Son)*, Henry Kaiser *(Gestapo Officer)*, Henry Brandon *(Nazi Officer)*, Milt Jamin *(Gestapo Soldier)*, George Caldwell *(Gestapo Guard)*, Wolf Muser *(Desk Sergeant)*, Lee E. Stevens *(2nd Nazi Officer)*, Roy Goldman *(Hitler)*, Robert Goldberg *(Hitler Adjutant)*, John McKinney *(Elite Guard Officer)*, Eda Reiss Merin *(Frightened Jewish Woman)*, Manny Kleinmuntz *(Husband of Jewish Woman)*, Phil Adams *(Airport Sentry)*, Curt Lowens *(Airport Officer)*, Ron Diamond *(Pub Bartender)*, Gillian Eaton *(Pub Barmaid)*, Paddi Edwards *(Pub Waitress)*, Winnie McCarthy *(Picadilly Usherette)*, Terence Marsh *(Startled British Officer)*, Leeyan Granger, Sandra Gray, Lainie Manning, Antonette Yuskis, Clare Culhane, Stephanie Wingate *(Ladies)*, Robin Haynes, Ron Kuhlman, John Otrin, Blane Savage, Joey Sheck *(Polish Fliers)*, Scott Beach *(Narrator)*, Dieter Curt, Howard Goodwin, Paul Ratliff, Ian Bruce, John Frayer, Edward J. Heim, Spencer Henderson, George Jayne, Bill K. Richards, Neil J. Schwartz, Tucker Smith, Ted Sprague.

It seems as though Mel Brooks is most successful with his odd humor when applying it to works that have already been performed in the film format (YOUNG FRANKENSTEIN and THE TWELVE CHAIRS). TO BE OR NOT TO BE, originally done by Ernst Lubitsch in 1942, fits into this pattern. This may be because Brooks' skill in capturing farcical humor far outweighs his storytelling ability. Brooks and real-life wife Bancroft star for the first time together, both involved in the theater during the Nazi occupation of Poland in WW II. Through a mishap, resistance fighter Matheson (who is also carrying on an affair with Bancroft) gets Bancroft, and thus Brooks, involved with the Polish Resistance. Consequently, an evil German is led to believe that these theater people are part of the Resistance and must be removed, lays himself open to the pranks of Brooks and crew as they attempt to save their skins and those of the rest of the Polish Resistance. Everything is played for laughs, with Brooks his funniest in impersonations of Nazis, particularly a witty rendition of Hitler. Other than these moments, his appearances on screen are a bit obnoxious. Luckily, Bancroft makes up for her husband's problems. Songs include "Ladies," "A Little Peace" (Mel Brooks, Ronnie Graham), "Sweet Georgia Brown" (Ben Bernie, Maceo Pinkard, Kenneth Casey (sung in Polish by Brooks, Bancroft).

p, Mel Brooks; d, Alan Johnson; w, Thomas Meehan, Ronny Graham p, Mel Brooks; d, Alan Johnson; w, Thomas Meehan, Ronny Graham (based on the film by Ernst Lubitsch, written by Edwin Justus Mayer); ph, Gerald Hirschfeld (DeLuxe Color); m, John Morris; ed, Alan Balsam; prod d, Terence Marsh; art d, J. Dennis Washington; set d, Craig Edgar, Joseph E. Hubbard; cos, Albert Wolsky; ch, Charlene Painter.

Comedy **Cas.** **(PR:C MPAA:PG)**

TO BEAT THE BAND*½ (1935) 68m RKO bw

Hugh Herbert *(Hugo Twist)*, Helen Broderick *(Freeda MacCreery, Attorney)*, Roger Pryor *(Larry Barry)*, Fred Keating *(Fred Carson)*, Eric Blore *(Hawkins, Butler)*, Phyllis Brooks *(Rowena)*, Evelyn Poe *(Barbara Shelby)*,

Johnny Mercer (*Member of the Band*), Ray Mayer (*McCory*), Joy Hodges (*Girls' Band Leader*), Sonny Lamont (*Dancer*), Ronald Graham (*Singer*), Torben Meyer (*Headwaiter*), The Original California Collegians, The Fred Keating Orchestra.

The dismal conception for this film has affianced Herbert trying to figure out a way to secure the fortune of his rich aunt, who has left a clause in her will leaving her money to the young man if he marries a widow. He only has three days to accomplish this feat, paving the route for some ridiculous comedy routines. Songs include: "Eeny-Meeny-Miney-Mo," "I Saw Her At Eight O'Clock," "If You Were Mine," "Meet Miss America," "Santa Claus Came in the Spring" (Johnny Mercer, Matt Malneck).

p, Zion Myers; d, Ben Stoloff; w, Rian James (based on the story by George Marion, Jr.); ph, Nick Musuraca; m, Matt Malneck; ed, George Crone, Ted Cheesman; cos, Walter Plunkett.

Musical/Comedy   (PR:A MPAA:NR)

TO BED OR NOT TO BED   (SEE: DEVIL, THE, 1963, Ital.)

TO BEGIN AGAIN**   (1982, Span.) 92m Nickel Odeon/FOX c
(VOLVER A EMPEZAR)

Antonio Ferrandis (*Albajara*), Encarna Paso (*Elena*), Jose Bodalo (*Roxiu*), Agustin Gonzalez (*Gervasio Losada*), Pablo Hoyos (*Ernesto*), Marta Fernandez Muro (*Carolina*), Pablo del Hoyo (*Sabino*).

Ferrandis is a Nobel prize-winning professor returning to his home town in Spain. There he is reunited with Paso, an old love of many years before. The two had been parted during the Spanish Civil War and now their romance begins to rekindle. To complicate matters further Ferrandis is dying of an ever-handy movie terminal illness. It's soap opera material pure and simple and all right on that level though hardly a memorable film. Surprisingly it won an Oscar as the Best Foreign Film of 1983. (In Spanish; English subtitles.)

p&d, Jose Luis Garci; w, Garci, Angel Llorente; ph, Manuel Rojas (Eastmancolor); m, Johann Pachelbel, Cole Porter; ed, Miguel G. Sinde; prod d, Gil Parrondo; art d, Parrondo.

Drama   (PR:C MPAA:PG)

TO CATCH A SPY   (SEE: CATCH ME A SPY, 1971, Brit./Fr.)

TO CATCH A THIEF*   (1936, Brit.) 66m GS Enterprises/RKO bw

John Garrick (*John*), Mary Lawson (*Anne*), H.F. Maltby (*Sir Herbert Condine*), John Wood (*Bill Lowther*), Vincent Holman (*Galloway*), Eliot Makeham (*Secretary*), Max Adrian (*Salesman*), Gordon McLeod (*Detective*), Bryan Powley, Ralph Teasdale, Billy Shine, Michael Ripper, Brian Herbert, Norman Pierce.

Worthless comedy features Garrick as the inventor of a device designed to stop car thieves. Unfortunately, the car is kept in a friend's garage which is also being used as the hideout for a gang of the auto heisters. Garrick manages to trap them all and the owner of an automobile factory purchases the device.

p, A. George Smith; d, Maclean Rogers; w, Kathleen Butler, H.F. Maltby (based on a play by Margaret and Gordon MacDonnell); ph, Geoffrey Faithfull.

Comedy   (PR:A MPAA:NR)

TO CATCH A THIEF****   (1955) 103m PAR c

Cary Grant (*John Robie, alias "The Cat, Mr. Smith, Mr. Burns*), Grace Kelly (*Frances Stevens*), Jessie Royce Landis (*Mrs. Jessie Stevens*), John Williams (*H.H. Hughson*), Charles Vanel (*Bertani*), Brigitte Auber (*Danielle Foussard*), Jean Martinelli (*Foussard*), Georgette Anys (*Germaine*), Roland Lessaffre (*Jean Hebey*), Rene Blancard (*Commissioner Lepic*), Wee Willie Davis (*Big Man in Kitchen*), Dominque Davray (*Antoinette*), Edward Manouk (*Kitchen Help*), Russell Gaige (*Mr. Sanford*), Marie Stoddard (*Mrs. Stanford*), Paul "Tiny" Newlan (*Vegetable Man in Kitchen*), Lewis Charles (*Man with Milk in Kitchen*), Aimee Torriani (*Woman in Kitchen*), John Alderson, Frank Chelland (*Chefs*), Don Megowan, Bela Kovacs, Guy De Vestel, George Adrian, Alberto Morin (*Detectives*), Leonard Penn, Michael Hadlow (*Monaco Policemen*), Margaret Brewster (*Cold Cream Woman*), Adele St. Maur (*Woman with Bird Cage on Bus*), Eugene Borden (*French Waiter*), Philip Van Zandt (*Jewelry Clerk*), Steven Geray (*Desk Clerk*), Albert Pollet, George Paris, George A. Nardelli, Manuel Paris, Louis Mercier (*Croupiers*), Gladys Holland (*Elegant French Woman*), Ed Le Baron, Barry Norton (*Frenchmen*), Jeanne Lafayette, Loulette Sablon, Nina Borget (*Frenchwomen*), Alfred Hitchcock (*Man Seated Next to Grant on Bus*), Otto F. Schulze, Martha Bamattre, Cosmos Sardo.

Lushly photographed along the French Riviera, this Hitchcock romantic comedy stars Grant as a former professional thief, known through France as "the Cat," who, after serving heroically as part of the French Resistance, gets a parole under the eyes of the law. He lives a quiet, luxurious life tucked away in his mountainside home until he becomes the suspect in a recent rash

of robberies, patterned exactly after his famous style. Grant is believed guilty by everyone from the police to his former cohorts in the Resistance to his teenage French girl friend, Auber, the perky daughter and former partner of another cat burglar, Martinelli. Grant's only choice in proving his innocence is to find the copycat burglar, a plan which involves staking out the rooftops of the rich as if he himself were planning the heist. Helping Grant is Williams, a very proper insurance salesman from London, whose company is taking a beating due to the recent robberies. What Grant wants from Williams is a list of the wealthiest people on the Riviera and the value of their jewelry. Williams is, at first, hesitant until Grant convinces him that everyone has a bit of the criminal inside them, whether it means stealing professionally or just taking hotel ashtrays and cheating on the company's expense account. "You don't have to spend every day of your life proving your honesty," Grant tells Williams, "but I do." Williams gives him the list, at the top of which is Stevens, a fearless, uncompromising woman who refuses to oblige William's wish of putting her jewelry in a safe. Grant is invited to her hotel room for a meal, which is also attended by her beautiful, but quiet, daughter Kelly. Grant takes no interest in Kelly until he escorts her to her room at the end of the night, and she kisses him passionately before slowly closing the door in his face. The following day, Williams insists on Grant accompanying her to the beach. Instead, Grant runs into Auber and swims out to a raft for a rendezvous, only to have Kelly follow. Kelly and Auber exchange barbs while Grant, confused and embarrassed, simply whimpers. Later, Kelly insists that Grant accompany her on a picnic, though when Grant realizes they are being shadowed by two detectives, a hair-raising chase through the winding mountain roads ensues. (This scene is a rather eerie foreshadowing of Kelly's actual death which occurred in 1982 when her car crashed in Monaco.) Having eluded their pursuers, Kelly and Grant start their picnic--a scene which is filled with double-entendre dialog such as Kelly opening a basket full of chicken and asking Grant, "Do you want a leg or a breast?"-- which ends in a romantic clinch. Kelly confronts Grant with his true identity--that of "the Cat"--and seems to be aroused just at the thought of his burgling. She is convinced that Grant is guilty and, excited by the thought of stealing, offers to work as his partner, telling him "The 'cat' has a new kitten. When do we start?" The relationship between the two grows increasingly more intense during a nighttime interlude in Kelly's hotel room as fireworks colorfully burst over the Mediterranean outside of their window. Taunting Grant, Kelly pulls him onto the couch, begging him to steal her sparkling necklace. "You know as well as I do this necklace is imitation," Grant claims. Kelly's red hot response, "But I'm not," convinces Grant and the two embrace in an explosive kiss which is intercut with the equally explosive fireworks outside. The following morning, when Kelly awakens, she finds that a thief has entered and stolen her mother's jewels. Believing Grant guilty she calls the police, but Grant is able to make his getaway. Grant still tries to convince her with a plan to unmask the real thief at a costume ball attended by the greatest wealth on the Riviera. With the help of Williams, Grant is able to slip away and, in a rooftop chase, catches Auber, who proves to be the copycat "Cat." With his innocence clearly proven, Grant returns to the quiet of his home with Kelly at his side...and the promise of mother coming along to live there as well. Shot on location in France (the film's opening shot tells us, "If you love life you'll love France"), TO CATCH A THIEF was referred to by Hitchcock as being "a lightweight" story, and is a throwback to the comedy that used to fill many of his British pictures. Casting Kelly in her third consecutive Hitchcock role--after DIAL M FOR MURDER and REAR WINDOW--the director chose to divert his attentions away from the suspenseful intensity of those films to concentrate on a less serious travelog of a comedy and romance--the usual murder element watered down to simple burglary. Here, Hitchcock's interest is in playfully exposing Kelly's flaming sexuality and Grant's cool charm, all of which is done in a rather schoolboyish manner as if Hitchcock is reveling in the naughtiness of what he is showing us. If not a great Hitchcock suspenser (if a suspenser at all), TO CATCH A THIEF is, at least, a display of Hitchcock's sense of humor and joy of using witty double entendres--the title itself being the best of all, the French police are trying to catch a thief (Grant), Grant is trying to catch a thief (Auber), while Kelly is trying to catch (in a different sense than the law) a thief (Grant) as well. It is on this film, while shooting in Monaco, that Kelly met Prince Ranier--the man who soon married her and made her Princess Grace. TO CATCH A THIEF, as has come to be expected of Hitchcock's films, performed superbly at the box office, and again was noticed at Oscar time, chiefly for its brilliant Technicolor visuals. It won in the Best Cinematography catagory (Burks), and received nominations for Best Art Direction-Set Decoration (Pereira, Johnson, Comer, Krams), Best Costume Design (Head).

p&d, Alfred Hitchcock; w, John Michael Hayes (based on the novel by David Dodge); ph, Robert Burks (VistaVision, Technicolor); m, Lyn Murray; ed, George Tomasini; art d, Hal Periera, Joseph MacMillan Johnson; set d, Sam Comer, Arthur Krams; cos, Edith Head; spec eff, John P. Fulton; spec ph eff, Farciot Edouart.

Crime/Romantic Comedy   **Cas.**   (PR:C MPAA:NR)

TO COMMIT A MURDER**   (1970, Fr./Ital./Ger.) 91m Gaumont International-S.N.E. Gaumont-Eichberg-Franca/Cinerama c (PEAU D'ESPION; CONGIURA DI SPIE; DER GRAUSAME JOB)

Louis Jourdan (*Charles Beaulieu*), Senta Berger (*Gertrud*), Edmond O'Brien

(Sphax), Bernard Blier *(Rhome)*, Fabrizio Capucci *(Cecil)*, Giuseppe Addobbati *(Moranez)*, Maurice Garrel *(Banck)*, Gamil Ratib *(Belloum)*, Patricia Scott *(Scandinavian Girl)*, Anna Gael *(Kiki)*, Charles Millot *(Poker Player)*, Gerhard Bohrmann, Peter Martin Urcel, Jean Rupert.

Writer Jourdan is seduced by Berger, than finds himself involved with government agents who talk him into helping them thwart Berger's husband in his plan to kidnap a nuclear scientist and take him to China. A clever suspense yarn that keeps one guessing who are the good and who are the bad guys.

p, Alain Poire; d, Edouard Molinaro; w, Molinaro, Jacques Robert (based on the story by Robert); ph, Raymond LeMoigne (Eastmancolor); m, Jose Berghmans; ed, Robert, Monique Isnardon; art d, Robert Clavel, Oliver Girard.

Drama							(PR:C MPAA:M/PG)

TO DOROTHY, A SON	(SEE: CASH ON DELIVERY, 1956, Brit.)

TO EACH HIS OWN**						(1946) 122m PAR bw

Olivia de Havilland *(Miss Josephine Norris)*, John Lund *(Capt. Bart Cosgrove/Gregory Piersen)*, Mary Anderson *(Corinna Piersen)*, Roland Culver *(Lord Desham)*, Phillip Terry *(Alex Piersen)*, Bill Goodwin *(Mac Tilton)*, Virginia Welles *(Liz Lorimer)*, Victoria Horne *(Daisy Gingras)*, Griff Barnett *(Mr. Norris)*, Alma Macrorie *(Belle Ingham)*, Bill Ward *(Griggsy at Age 5 ½)*, Frank Faylen *(Babe)*, Arthur Loft *(Mr. Clinton)*, Willard Robertson *(Dr. Hunt)*, Virginia Farmer *(Mrs. Clinton)*, Doris Lloyd *(Miss Pringle)*, Clyde Cook *(Mr. Harkett)*, Ida Moore *(Miss Claflin)*, Mary Young *(Mrs. Nix)*, Chester Clute *(Clarence Ingham)*, Crane Whitley *(Police Captain)*, Leyland Hodgson *(Porter at Reindeer Club)*, Reginald Sheffield *(Headwaiter)*, Will Stanton *(Funny Little Waiter)*, Gladys Blake *(Lorena)*, William Hunter, Jack Clifford *(Policemen)*, Clara Reid *(Ida)*, Jack Rogers *(Cockney Taxi Driver)*, James Millican *(Lt. Flyer)*, Almeda Fowler *(Sara)*, Anthony Ellis *(Messenger Boy)*, Gloria Williams *(Woman)*, Beverly Thompson, Lucy Knoch *(WACs)*, Harlan Briggs *(Dr. McLaughlin)*, Billy Gray *(Billy Ingham)*, Gary Gray *(Casey Ingham)*.

What might have been a trite soap opera is elevated to the status of superior emotional drama through a wise script, sensitive direction, and an Oscar-winning performance by de Havilland, her first and the first for an actress at Paramount. Covering 27 years in the life and times of a woman who loved not wisely or well, it begins during the blitz on London. Middle-aged de Havilland is an air raid warden and marches her beat with confidante Culver, a peer of the realm and another warden. Between the wars, de Havilland made a fortune in the cosmetics business and spent so much time working that there was not a moment for love in her life. When she learns that a handsome U.S. pilot, Lund, is in town, her thoughts flash back to an earlier time in her life. As a young woman in a small town in the U.S., she meets a good-looking pilot (also played by Lund), spends a passionate few hours with him, and falls in love. He goes off to fight on the continent and leaves her pregnant. When he dies in the service, she gives birth in another town so as not to embarrass her druggist father, Barnett. After a struggle, she gives her son up for adoption to Anderson and Terry. She regrets having done that quickly but has no recourse, so she plunges herself into her work. When she has some money, she begins plying the young boy, Ward, with toys and affection and manages to get custody of him, but he wants to go back to Anderson, whom he thinks is his real mother. She eventually allows Ward to return to Anderson, then goes to London. Years later, Lund (the son) comes to call on de Havilland because Anderson has suggested he look her up while he's in London. She asks him to stay at her posh flat and doesn't reveal their true relationship. Lund is properly deferential to this contemporary of his "mother" and shows her the greatest respect as de Havilland aches to hug him. Lund is in love with and hoping to marry Welles. Culver learns the whole story and how de Havilland wishes she could do more for Lund. Culver helps the young lovers get together and hints enough times about de Havilland for Lund to finally realize why this older woman has been so generous and doting with him. Welles and Lund are married and de Havilland is invited, and the most touching moment occurs when Lund approaches de Havilland while the wedding band is playing and says, "I believe this is our dance, Mother." Lund was making his film debut after impressing on the Broadway stage. An interesting sidelight is that de Havilland hadn't worked for two years. She'd been on suspension from Warner Bros. and was trying to break a contract which they claimed included all of her suspension time. She sued the studio successfully and the result was a law that limited studios to a seven-year agreement with an actor, with no clause regarding suspensions. That became known as "The de Havilland Decision" and other actors have thanked her ever since. Leisen and de Havilland had worked together in HOLD BACK THE DAWN and when she asked for him to direct, he passed on it at first, then was convinced when the studio gave him script approval as well as several other concessions. It was sentimental but never bathetic and the reality was present in every scene so it didn't fall into the sudsy morass of so many other "women's" pictures. Leisen knew that de Havilland had given a star performance and on the wrap day gifted her with a bracelet that featured a mini-Oscar. His prophecy was on the money and she took the Oscar home at the next awards' ceremony. Brackett's story was nominated for a statuette, but that was it from the Academy. Audiences loved it and credit

must be given to the studio for attempting a "soft" picture at the time. No one expected it to do as well as it did. Good editing by Macrorie, and Victor Young's music kept the mood swings right on target. Miss de Havilland's winning of the Oscar was a surprise to many who had placed their bets on the formidable quartet of losers in 1946. They were Celia Johnson for BRIEF ENCOUNTER, Jane Wyman in THE YEARLING, Jennifer Jones for DUEL IN THE SUN, and Rosalind Russell as SISTER KENNY.

p, Charles Brackett; d, Mitchell Leisen; w, Brackett, Jacques Thery (based on a story by Brackett); ph, Daniel L. Fapp; m, Victor Young; ed, Alma Macrorie; art d, Hans Dreier, Roland Anderson; set d, Sam Comer, James M. Walters; cos, Edith Head; spec eff, Gordon Jennings, Farciot Edouart.

Drama							(PR:A-C MPAA:NR)

TO ELVIS WITH LOVE	(SEE: TOUCHED BY LOVE, 1980)

TO FIND A MAN**		(1972) 90m Rastar/COL c (AKA: THE BOY NEXT DOOR; SEX AND THE TEENAGER)

Pamela Sue Martin *(Rosalind McCarthy)*, Darren O'Connor *(Andy Morrison)*, Lloyd Bridges *(Frank McCarthy)*, Phyllis Newman *(Betty McCarthy)*, Tom Ewell *(Dr. Hargrave)*, Tom Bosley *(Mr. Katchaturian)*, Miles Chapin *(Pete)*, Schell Rasten *(Rick)*, Antonia Rey *(Modesta)*, Susan Tully *(Rosalind's Friend)*.

The platonic friendship between two high school youths is explored in this modest effort, centering on the attempts to get the girl, Martin, an abortion. Her young male friend, O'Connor, offers the girl his support and tries to find her a doctor. She is grateful, but spoiled child that she is, she finds trouble in expressing her thanks. At times funny, at other times touching, this is an uncommon look at teenage friendship, and it is refreshing.

p, Irving Pincus; d, Buzz Kulik; w, Arnold Schulman (based on the novel by S.J. Wilson); ph, Andrew Lazlo; m, David Shire; ed, Rita Roland; prod d, Peter Dohanos; set d, Alan Hicks; cos, Ruth Morley; makeup, Bob Laden.

Drama							(PR:A MPAA:GP)

TO HAVE AND HAVE NOT**					(1944) 100m WB bw

Humphrey Bogart *(Harry Morgan)*, Walter Brennan *(Eddie)*, Lauren Bacall *(Marie Browning)*, Dolores Moran *(Helene De Bursac)*, Hoagy Carmichael *(Cricket)*, Walter Molnar *(Paul De Bursac)*, Sheldon Leonard *(Lt. Coyo)*, Marcel Dalio *(Gerard)*, Walter Sande *(Johnson)*, Dan Seymour *(Capt. M. Renard)*, Aldo Nadi *(Bodyguard)*, Paul Marion *(Beauclerc)*, Pat West *(Bartender)*, Sir Lancelot *(Horatio)*, Eugene Borden *(Quartermaster)*, Elzie Emanuel, Harold Garrison *(Black Urchins)*, Major Fred Farrell *(Headwaiter)*, Pedro Regas *(Civilian)*, Adrienne d'Ambricourt, Marguerita Sylva *(Cashiers)*, Margaret Hathaway, Louise Clark, Suzette Harbin, Gussie Morris, Kanza Omar, Margaret Savage *(Waitresses)*, Emmett Smith *(Emil the Bartender)*, Maurice Marsac, Fred Dosch, George Suzanne, Louis Mercier, Crane Whitley *(DeGaullists)*, Hal Kelly *(Detective)*, Jean de Briac *(Gendarme)*, Chef Joseph Milani *(Chef)*, Oscar Lorraine *(Bartender)*, Ron Rondell *(Naval Ensign)*, Audrey Armstrong *(Dancer)*, Marcel de la Brosse *(Sailor)*, Edith Wilson *(Black Woman)*, Patricia Shay *(Mrs. Beauclerc)*, Janette Gras *(Rosalie)*, Jack Chefe *(Guide)*, George Sorel *(French Officer)*, Roger Valmy, Keith Lawrence, Jack Passin *(Flirtatious Frenchmen)*, Alphonse Dubois, James Burross, Milton Shockley, Jack Winslowe, Frank Johnson.

The dialog was sharp, the direction first-rate, the acting superb, but TO HAVE AND HAVE NOT undoubtedly is best remembered for the romance of Bogart and Bacall, both on the screen and off. Warner Brothers wanted another CASABLANCA, and in many ways Bogart's character here resembles his classic portrait of Rick Blaine. It is WW II and France has just fallen to the Nazi occupation. Bogart, living on the island of Martinique, is the owner of a cabin cruiser, the *Queen Conch*, on which he takes wealthy customers out on fishing trips. Working with him is Brennan, a not too bright alcoholic, whose amiable demeanor charms almost anybody. Sande, Bogart's current customer, loses some expensive tackle on a run and the disgusted captain brings him back to port. Sande claims to have no money, but promises to go to the bank in the morning to get some cash. Bogart is approached by Dalio, the owner of the hotel where Bogart lives. Dalio, a deGaullist fighting for a free France, asks Bogart for his services to help smuggle one of the underground movement's top leaders into Martinique. Bogart, who cares little for politics, turns down Dalio and refuses to discuss the matter. Returning to his room at the hotel, Bogart notices a newcomer across the hall. It is, of course, Bacall, who shoots him a sultry glance, then, in a husky, and o-so-sexy voice, asks: "Anybody got a match?" Bogart is intrigued, and gives Bacall a book of matches. Later, in the hotel bar, Bogart tries to collect from Sande. Bacall steals Sande's wallet, which proves to hold enough traveler's checks to pay Bogart and then some. The Vichy police stage a raid on the hotel, and Sande is killed by a stray bullet just as he is about to sign the traveler's checks. Bogart and Bacall are brought into police headquarters for questioning, and what little money he has is confiscated. The two return to the hotel and go to Bogart's room. Bogart at first is unreceptive to her overt sexual advances, and finally Bacall kisses him. At last Bogart warms up and Bacall tells him: "It's even better when you help." Bacall leaves, but later returns, asking Bogart for help in getting off the island. She starts to go, then, before she exits through the door, Bacall turns to Bogart, and utters some of the most unforgettable lines ever emitted by a screen siren: "You don't have to say anything or do anything. Maybe just whistle. You know how to whistle, don't you Steve? You just put your lips together and blow." The sultry woman disappears through the doorway, then Bogart responds by letting out a long wolf whistle. Bogart, in order to help Bacall get back to the U.S., agrees to make the dangerous run for the underground movement. He gets an advance and buys Bacall a plane ticket. Though Bogart has ordered Brennan not to go out on this run, Brennan has sneaked aboard. Bogart pilots the *Queen Conch* out into the waters, where he picks up Molnar and his wife Moran. On the way back, Bogart encounters a Vichy patrol boat and Molnar is badly wounded in the crossfire. Bogart manages to get him back to the hotel, where Molnar is hidden in the basement, but is surprised to find that Bacall has decided to remain, singing to bar patrons while Carmichael plays the piano. Bogart, with Bacall as his nurse, patches up Molnar's wounds, while Moran passes out from the sight of her husband's blood. Bogart has Bacall pack her things, as they will be leaving for Martinique shortly. However Bogart cannot find Brennan, and will not leave without his alcoholic friend. Leonard and Seymour, members of the Vichy police, enter Bogart's room, telling him they are holding Brennan hostage. They promise to withhold any alcohol from Brennan, setting off unbearable D.T.'s. Bogart kills one of Seymour's bodyguards, then forces him to call police headquarters, telling Seymour to give the order to free Brennan. Dalio and members of the underground watch the police while Bogart, Bacall, and Brennan prepare to leave. Bogart tells Bacall she doesn't have to go if she doesn't want to. Bacall is game though, ready to join up with Bogart and Brennan. As they prepare to leave the hotel, Carmichael asks Bacall if she is happy. She fires back: "What do you think?" As Carmichael plays a Latin American style number on his piano, Bacall exits with the men, swaying her hips in a sultry manner, with a sly smile planted firmly on her face. TO HAVE AND HAVE NOT is an immensely entertaining film, stylish and with a great deal of intended humor. The film was the result of a argument between director Hawks and novelist Ernest Hemingway. On a fishing trip in Florida with the author, Hawks tried to convince Hemingway he should come out to Hollywood to work on a screenplay. Hemingway refused, and Hawks responded with the bold statement that he could make a film out of Hemingway's worst book. Hemingway, angered by this challenge, asked Hawks: "What is my worst book?" "That goddamned piece of junk called *To Have and Have Not*," Hawks shot back. When Hemingway claimed the novel could never be filmed, and Hawks responded with another insult: "Okay, I'll get Faulkner to do it. He can write better than you can anyway." Hemingway's original story took place in Cuba and the Florida Keys, and was set in the 1930s. The Bogart character was less heroic, a married man with children, who is forced to run booze and men on his boat when his financial situation becomes desperate. Hawks kept the title and the character, then threw out the Hemingway story. Faulkner, upon receiving Hawks' outline for the new story, helped to expand it while Furthman provided the body of the script. (One report claimed that the American Affairs Committee, headed by Nelson Rockefeller, suggested the production change the locale from Florida to Martinique so the film would not offend Latin American countries.) Next was casting. Bogart seemed perfect for the part of Harry Morgan, but who was fiery enough to play opposite him? Hawks took a chance on an unknown talent named Betty Bacall, a beautiful 18-year-old New York model who was virtually unknown in Hollywood. Hawks had become interested in Bacall after his wife spotted her on the cover of Vogue. Bacall had received some interest from other movie companies, but realizing that Hawks was probably her best bet, she signed with the director, rather than risk being swallowed up by the anonymous studio system. It was a wise move, to say the least. By her 19th birthday, Hawks had decided to cast her in TO HAVE AND HAVE NOT. He introduced her to her costar Bogart, an undistinguished meeting where the famous actor told Bacall: "I've just seen your test. We'll have a lot of fun together." Among the first things Hawks did was change Bacall's first name from Betty to Lauren, convinced the latter moniker had more appeal. He also told her to work on lowering her voice, telling her "...there is nothing more unattractive than screeching. I want you to train your voice in such a way that...your voice will remain low." As she recalled in her autobiography, *By Myself*: "I found a spot on Mulholland Drive and proceeded to read *The Robe* aloud, keeping my voice lower and louder than normal. If anyone had ever passed by, they would have found me a candidate for an asylum. Who sat on mountaintops in cars reading books aloud to the canyons? Who did? I did!" To help further develop the character, Hawks had Bacall work with a well seasoned chorus girl nicknamed "Stuttering Sam." In the film Bogart and Bacall refer to each other as "Steve" and "Slim," the pet names Hawks and his wife had for one another. While shooting the scene where she first meets Bogart, Bacall was so nervous she could bearly stop from trembling. "By the end of the third or fourth take," Bacall wrote, "I realized that one way to hold my trembling head still was to keep it down, chin low, almost to my chest, and eyes up at Bogart. It worked, and turned out to be the beginning of 'The Look.' " This "Look" immediately became a film classic, with a seductive quality that smoldered from the screen. Bacall's famous "whistle" sequence had originally been part of her screentest made with actor John Ridgely. Hawks loved the scene but was hard pressed as how to work it into the film. He turned to Faulkner, who found a simple solution. Hawks recalled: "He said: 'If we put those people in a hotel corridor where nobody else is around, then I think we can make that scene work.' So we did. I wrote the line, but he wrote the

stuff that led up to it." (Quoted from *Hawks on Hawks* by Joseph McBride.) TO HAVE AND HAVE NOT contains a great deal of humor, not only in the repertee between Bogart and Bacall, but also from Brennan's comical portrayal of the amiable rummy. Brennan's dimwitted honesty is charming and highly engaging. He constantly asks people he meets: "Was you ever bit by a dead bee?" Most choose to dismiss him, but when Bacall responds with a serious (albeit tounge-in-cheek) response, Brennan immediately takes a liking to her. Bacall has a wonderful chemistry with Carmichael in their scenes at the piano, and practically glows with an erotic aura as she sings. Many accounts claim that her voice was dubbed by Andy Williams of all people, but according to Bacall, she recorded her numbers, then lip-synched on the set. Hawks settled the controversy himself, telling McBride: "We had a hell of a time trying to find a girl to sing with as low a voice as Bacall's. So I got Andy Williams, and we took all the music he recorded and let Bacall mouth it to his singing. But she was singing at the same time, and I thought she sounded better than Andy Williams. So we went back and did the whole thing over again. It was all her singing." Of course the heart of TO HAVE AND HAVE NOT is the romantic electricity generated between Bogart and Bacall throughout the film. It was important for the two to be believed as lovers, but this on-screen romance worked well beyond anybody's expectations. Three weeks into the production, Bogart stopped off in Bacall's dressing room, and as the two were joking around he suddenly stopped, leaned over and kissed her. It was the begining of an off-screen love story that would captivate Hollywood's filmmaking community as well as the American public. As it became obvious the two stars were becoming involved, Hawks took Bacall aside, telling her that the 45 year old star was simply using this innocent 19-year-old to escape for awhile from his unhappy marriage. "When the picture's over, he'll forget all about it...," Hawks told Bacall. "You're throwing away a chance anyone would give their right arm for. I'm not going to put up with it. I tell you I'll just send you to Monogram. I'll wash my hands of you." Of course this was an empty threat, and there were some suggestions that Hawks used the off-screen affair to heighten the on-screen romance. Bogart didn't forget Bacall and the two were married the next year. Hawks went to one preview screening for the film, but soon left the theater for the comfort of a nearby bar. When he came back, Hawks was confronted by Jack Warner, head of the studio. "Where the hell have you been?" demanded Warner. "Out having some drinks," replied Hawks. "How's it going?" "Just great." Warner asked him, "Why did you leave?" "I knew when they laughed at that thing," Hawks responded, "they were going to laugh at the whole thing." Hawks had every reason to remain confident, for the film was both a critical and box office success. TO HAVE AND HAVE NOT's three songs are: "How Little We Know" (Hoagy Carmichael, Johnny Mercer), "Hong Kong Blues" (Carmichael, Stanley Adams), "Am I Blue?" (Harry Akst, Grant Clarke). This was remade twice, first as THE BREAKING POINT in 1950, the as THE GUN RUNNERS in 1958.

p&d, Howard Hawks; w, Jules Furthman, William Faulkner (based on the novel by Ernest Hemingway); ph, Sidney Hickox; m, Franz Waxman (uncredited); ed, Christian Nyby; md, Leo F. Forbstein; art d, Charles Novi; set d, Casey Roberts; cos, Milo Anderson; spec eff, Roy Davidson.

Drama   Cas.   **(PR:A-C MPAA:NR)**

TO HAVE AND TO HOLD**   (1951, Brit.) 63m Hammer/Exclusive bw

Avis Scott *(June de Winter)*, Patrick Barr *(Brian Harding)*, Robert Ayres *(Max)*, Eunice Gayson *(Peggy Harding)*, Ellen Pollock *(Roberta)*, Richard Warner *(Cyril)*, Harry Fine *(Robert)*, Peter Neil.

Barr is crippled when he falls from a horse and he learns that he will live only a short time. He devotes himself to caring for his wife and daughter and encouraging his wife's affection for another man. Strange melodrama not especially believable, but well acted.

p, Anthony Hinds; d, Godfrey Grayson; w, Reginald Long (based on a play by Lionel Brown); ph, James Harvey; m, Frank Spencer; ed, Jimmy Needs.

Drama   **(PR:A MPAA:NR)**

TO HAVE AND TO HOLD*½   (1963, Brit.) 71m Merton Park/AA bw

Ray Barrett *(Sgt. Henry Fraser)*, Katharine Blake *(Claudia Lyon)*, Nigel Stock *(George Lyon)*, William Hartnell *(Inspector Roberts)*, Patricia Bredin *(Lucy)*, Noel Travarthen *(Blake)*, Richard Clarke *(Charles Wagner)*.

Vaguely entertaining variation on DOUBLE INDEMNITY has Barrett a police sergeant who falls in love with Blake. She coaxes him into cooperating in her plan to murder her husband for his insurance money. Yet another of the seemingly endless string of Edgar Wallace films made by Merton Park in the early 1960s.

p, Jack Greenwood; d, Herbert Wise; w, John Sansom (based on the novel *The Breaking Point* by Edgar Wallace).

Crime   **(PR:A MPAA:NR)**

TO HELL AND BACK***   (1955) 106m UNIV c

Audie Murphy (*Himself*), Marshall Thompson (*Johnson*), Jack Kelly (*Kerrigan*), Charles Drake (*Brandon*), Paul Picerni (*Valentino*), Gregg Palmer (*Lt. Manning*), David Janssen (*Lt. Lee*), Richard Castle (*Kovak*), Paul Langton (*Col. Howe*), Bruce Cowling (*Capt. Marks*), Julian Upton (*Steiner*), Denver Pyle (*Thompson*), Felix Noriego (*Swope*), Art Aragon (*Sanchez*), Brett Halsey (*Saunders*), Tommy Hart (*Klasky*), Anthony Garcen (*Lt. Burns*), Gordon Gebert (*Audie as a Boy*), Mary Field (*Mrs. Murphy*), Howard Wright (*Mr. Houston*), Edna Holland (*Mrs. Houston*), Anabel Shaw (*Helen*), Susan Kohner (*Maria*), Maria Costi (*Julia*), Didi Ramati (*Carla*), Barbara James (*Cleopatra*), Joey Costaretta (*Vincenti*), Rand Brooks (*Lt. Harris*), Nan Boardman (*Maria's Mother*), Henry Kulky (*Stack*), John Pickard (*M.P.*), Ashley Cowan (*Scottish Soldier*), Don Kennedy (*Marine Recruit Sergeant*), Ralph Sanford (*Chief Petty Officer*), Howard Price (*Truck Driver*), Alexander Campbell (*Rector*), Rankin Mansfield (*Dr. Snyder*), Madge Meredith (*Corinne*), Mort Mills (*Soldier*), John Bryant (*Jim*).

Murphy was America's most decorated soldier of WW II, gathering more than 20 medals, including the Congressional Medal of Honor, while fighting through North Africa, Italy, France, Germany, and Austria. When he returned to the U.S. his fame brought him to the attention of Hollywood, which starred him in a number of B westerns throughout the late 1940s and early 1950s. (Other war heroes who became actors after the war include Neville Brand and John Agar.) After several years of quickie oaters, Murphy proved he really could act in John Huston's RED BADGE OF COURAGE (1951) and finally in 1955 he starred in the film adaptation of his own best-selling autobiography. The film traces Murphy from his hardworking origins as the son of Texas sharecroppers, to his rejection by both the Marines and the Navy for being too short, and his acceptance by the Army, where he rises through the ranks to lieutenant and company commander, killing some 240 of the enemy in the process. The script is loaded with cliches and the direction is lackluster at best, but the battle scenes are exciting and Murphy does a fairly good job in the role he was literally born to play.

p, Aaron Rosenberg; d, Jesse Hibbs; w, Gil Doud (based on the autobiography *To Hell and Back* by Audie Murphy); ph, Maury Gertsman (CinemaScope, Technicolor); ed, Edward Curtiss; md, Joseph Gershenson; art d, Alexander Golitzen, Robert Clatworthy.

War/Biography   (PR:A-C   MPAA:NR)

TO KILL A CLOWN**   (1972) 104m FOX c

Alan Alda (*Maj. Ritchie*), Blythe Danner (*Lily Frischer*), Heath Lamberts (*Timothy Frischer*), Eric Clavering (*Stanley*).

Bickering couple Danner and Lamberts are stranded on an island off the New England coast with only psychotic Vietnam veteran Alda to terrorize them. Pallid story plus bad direction make this one easy to miss.

p, Teddy B. Sills; d, George Bloomfield; w, Bloomfield, I.C. Rapoport (based on the story "Master of the Hounds" by Algis Budrys); ph, Walter Lassally; m, Richard Hill, John Hawkins; ed, Ralph Kemplen; art d, Trevor Williams; m/l, "With My Eyes," sung by Georgie Fame.

Drama   **Cas.**   (PR:C-O   MPAA:R)

TO KILL A MOCKINGBIRD****   (1962) 129m UNIV bw

Gregory Peck (*Atticus Finch*), Mary Badham (*Jean Louise "Scout" Finch*), Phillip Alford (*Jem Finch*), John Megna (*Dill Harris*), Frank Overton (*Sheriff Heck Tate*), Rosemary Murphy (*Miss Maudie Atkinson*), Ruth White (*Mrs. Dubose*), Brock Peters (*Tom Robinson*), Estelle Evans (*Calpurnia*), Paul Fix (*Judge Taylor*), Collin Wilcox (*Mayella Violet Ewell*), James Anderson (*Bob Ewell*), Alice Ghostley (*Stephanie Crawford*), Robert Duvall (*Arthur "Boo" Radley*), William Windom (*Gilmer*), Crehan Denton (*Walter Cunningham*), Richard Hale (*Mr. Radley*), Steve Condit (*Walter Cunningham, Jr.*), Bill Walker (*Rev. Sykes*), Hugh Sanders (*Dr. Reynolds*), Pauline Myers (*Jessie*), Jester Hairston (*Spence Robinson*), Jamie Forster (*Hiram Townsend*), Nancy Marshall (*School Teacher*), Kim Hamilton (*Helen Robinson*), Kelly Thordsen (*Burly Man*), Kim Hector (*Cecil Jacobs*), David Crawford (*Tom Robinson, Jr.*), Guy Wilkerson (*Jury Foreman*), Charles Fredericks (*Court Clerk*), Jay Sullivan (*Court Reporter*), Barry Seltzer (*School Boy*), Dan White, Tex Armstrong (*Men*), Kim Stanley (*Narrator*).

A hauntingly nostalgic portrayal of childhood mischief set in the racially divided 1930s town of Macomb County, Alabama. Peck, as Atticus Finch, plays an uncorruptible man of his word, a respected lawyer who has been left, by the death of his wife, to raise his two children, 10-year-old Alford and the tomboyish 6-year-old Badham. During the summer in the dusty, hot town, Alford and Badham, in their worn overalls and bare feet, find ways to occupy the day–rolling each other down the street in a tire, or playing in a treehouse. What occupies them the most, however, is the creaky wooden house where Boo Radley–a crazed young boy who, as neighborhood lore goes, is chained to his bed by his father– lives, but has never been seen, at least by the children. With a precocious visiting neighbor, Megna, the children daringly sneak onto the Radley porch in the hopes of glimpsing the elusive Boo. Even more frightening to the children than Boo is his father, Hale, a venomous old man who won't hesitate to shoot at the children if

they're in his yard. While the children play their games, Peck becomes involved in a heated social issue when he agrees to represent a black family man, Peters, accused of raping and beating a young white girl, Wilcox. A number of townspeople, led by Anderson, the victim's father, and Denton, try to pressure Peck into stepping down from the case, but Peck cannot be swayed from his duty to justice. Alford and Badham also feel the pressure from fellow school children who call Peck a "nigger lover," fighting words for the tough Badham who has a habit of beating up on the neighborhood boys. When the trial finally comes, Alford and Badham sit in the courtroom balcony with the black friends and family of Peters. Peck, with dignity and eloquence, defends his client, clearly proving that Peters is innocent of attacking Wilcox and that it is her father, Anderson, who beat her. The prejudiced jury, however, hands down a guilty verdict, which Peck plans to appeal. Before he can do so, however, Peters is gunned down while supposedly trying to escape. Although Peters was found guilty, Anderson still is filled with hate for Peck and is determined to retaliate. One evening, after a school gathering, Alford and Badham, who has lost her dress and must wear a giant ham costume home, walk home through the woods, but hear the sound of someone following them. Suddenly, the children are attacked; Alford is thrown unconscious to the ground, while Badham struggles to stand upright and get out of her cumbersome costume. A mysterious, unseen person intervenes and wrestles the attacker away from Badham, who watches through her costume. Alford is then carried by the person to the safety of the Finch household. By the time Badham gets home, she finds Alford safely asleep in his bedroom, his arm in a cast, and the doctor just leaving. The sheriff, Overton, then arrives to inform Peck that Anderson has been found stabbed to death and to question Badham about the identity of the man who helped her. She points to a man standing quietly behind the shadow of the bedroom door, Boo Radley (Duvall)–a ghostly, frightened young man who seems to prefer the shadow of the door and appears helpless otherwise. Badham–who no longer fears Boo as some sort of monster–takes Boo out to the front porch where they sit quietly and tenderly on the porch swing. Although Peck seems ready to defend Boo for the murder of Anderson, the sheriff refuses to bring that much attention to the clearly unfit boy and fabricates a story that Anderson accidentally killed himself by falling on his own knife. Badham explains to her father that it would be a sin to subject Boo to a courtroom scene, just as it "is a sin to kill a mockingbird," as Peck earlier warned his children about killing a creature as harmless and pleasant as the mockingbird. Based on the semi-autobiographical, Pulitzer Prize- winning Harper Lee novel of 1960, TO KILL A MOCKINGBIRD beautifully captures the aura and feel of the small southern town and the people who inhabit it, especially in the portrayal of the children. Badham, a 9-year old who had never acted before, is truly charming as the tough little sister who tries to keep pace with her brother, but must finally come into her own as a girl and wear a dress, however embarrassing it is to her. Alford, also in his first role and then 13 years old, is nearly as superb in a role which is less developed than Badham's. (The film is narrated by a grown-up Badham in the voice of Kim Stanley, which, along with the film's semi-autobiographical nature, explains the favoritism towards Badham's character.) Rounding out the child performers is Megna, a youngster with stage experience in the Broadway production of "All the Way Home," whose character of "Dill" is based on author Truman Capote, a childhood friend of Harper Lee's. Amidst the scene-stealing capabilities of the children stands Peck, whose acting virtuosity and solid persona prevents him from being enveloped by Badham and Alford. Stating that "MOCKINGBIRD is still my favorite film, without any question," Peck was able to draw on his childhood to better relate to the children's characters, through whose eyes the film is seen: "I felt I could climb into Atticus' shoes without any play-acting, that I could be him. And I felt that I knew those two children. My own childhood was very much like that. It was not in the true South, it was in Southern California, but it was nevertheless a small town where we ran around barefooted in the summertime and lived in trees and rolled down the street curled up in an old rubber tire." The film (which was scripted by Foote, since Lee was busy at work on another novel) so wonderfully followed the spirit of Lee's novel that it prompted the author to remark, "I can only say that I am a happy author. They have made my story into a beautiful and moving motion picture. I am very proud and grateful." The picture, which opened in 1962 to qualify for Oscar time, though it didn't receive a wide release until February of the following year, was warmly received by audiences who responded not only to the nostalgic feelings the film culled from viewers, but to the heroic image portrayed by Peck, who here made himself an exemplary pattern for citizenship and fatherhood. TO KILL A MOCKINGBIRD was well rewarded by the Academy who gave statuettes to Peck for Best Actor, Foote for Best Adapted Screenplay, Golitzen, Bumstead, and Emert for Art Direction and Set Decoration, and nominations for Best Picture (losing to that year's big winner LAWRENCE OF ARABIA), Best Supporting Actress: Badham, Best Director: Mulligan, and Best Black-and-White Cinematography: Harlan. Also receiving a nomination, and deserving of special mention, is the superb score by Elmer Bernstein, which is as responsible for the atmosphere of TO KILL A MOCKINGBIRD as any other element of the film. The delicate, magical melody which is first quietly delivered on the piano, followed by woodwinds, and finally the swelling of a string section, perfectly conveys the fragility of the childhood memories that are so important to the film. A perfect compliment to the visuals, Bernstein's score is not only effective as a soundtrack, but can also stand alone as a an example of classical American folk music.

p, Alan J. Pakula; d, Robert Mulligan; w, Horton Foote (based on the novel by Harper Lee); ph, Russell Harlan; m, Elmer Bernstein; ed, Aaron Stell; md, Bernstein; art d, Alexander Golitzen, Henry Bumstead; set d, Oliver Emert; cos, Rosemary Odell, Viola Thompson; makeup, Bud Westmore.

Drama   **Cas.**   **(PR:C   MPAA:NR)**

TO KILL OR TO DIE*   (1973, Ital.) 98m CBA (IL MIO NOME E SHANGHAI JOE)

Chen Lee, Carla Romanelli, Klaus Kinski, Katsutoshi Mikuriya, Giacomo Rossi Stuart, Gordon Mitchell.

Martial arts master Lee discovers the problems of trying to live in the American West, being Oriental. Lee eventually breaks loose with his fancy footwork and speedy hands, and turns on the boss who has had him herding peons across the border for sale as slaves. Tedious and too loaded with tricks to be believed.

p, Renato Angiolini, Roberto Bessi; d, Mario Caiano; w, Caiano, Fabrizio Trifone Trecca; ph, Guglielmo Mancori.

Western   **(PR:C   MPAA:NR)**

TO LIVE   (SEE: IKIRU, 1960, Jap.)

TO LIVE IN PEACE*   (1947, Ital.) 90m Lux-Pao/Times bw

Aldo Fabrizi (Uncle Tigna), Gar Moore (Ronald), Mirello Monti (Silvia), John Kitzmiller (Joe), Heinrich Bode (Hans), Ave Ninchi (Corinna), Ernesto Almirante (The Grandfather), Nando Bruno (Political Secretary), Aldo Silvani (The Doctor), Gino Cavalieri (The Priest), Piero Palermini (Franco), Franco Serpilli (Citto).

A small isolated Italian village suddenly finds itself involved in WW II when two American soldiers escape their Nazi captors to take refuge there. The men are given shelter by the family of Fabrizi, while the townspeople are torn in their sentiment for protecting the soldiers and their fear of Nazi retribution if discovered. This fear is given fuel by a young Nazi who comes to monitor the village. Though Fabrizi does his best to hide the Americans, one of them, a black soldier, comes face to face with the Nazi while both are wildly drunk. Instead of fighting, they continue with their merriment. Offering suspense, comedy, and drama, TO LIVE IN PEACE avoids the stereotypes in the portrayals of the black and the Nazi, with both drawn as full human beings. (In Italian; English subtitles)

p, Carlo Ponti; d, Luigi Zampa; w, Suso Cecchi D'Amico, Aldo Fabrizi, Piero Tellini; ph, Carlo Montuori; m, Nino Rota; English titles, Armando Macaluso.

Drama/War   **(PR:A   MPAA:NR)**

TO LOVE*   (1964, Swed.) 90m Sandrews/Prominent-L.&N bw (ATT ALSKA)

Harriet Andersson (Louise), Zbigniew Cybulski (Fredrik), Isa Quensel (Marta), Thomas Svanfeldt (Jakob), Jane Friedmann (Nora), Nils Eklund (The Priest), Jan-Erik Lindqvist (The Speaker), the Eje Thelin Quintet.

An intense look into the changes a woman undergoes after spending 10 years married to a man who offered her virtually no sexual pleasure, and then suddenly finds herself involved with a man who is just the opposite. When the husband dies, Andersson meets an exuberant, gay Pole, Cybulski, with whom she starts an affair. She goes through a period of rediscovering herself and becomes a much happier woman.

p, Rune Waldekranz; d&w, Jorn Donner; ph, Sven Nykvist; m, Bo Nilsson; ed, Lennart Wallen; md, Stig Westerberg, Eje Thelin; art d, Jan Boleslaw; cos, Mago.

Drama   **(PR:O   MPAA:NR)**

TO MARY--WITH LOVE**   (1936) 87m FOX bw

Warner Baxter (Jock Wallace), Myrna Loy (Mary Wallace), Ian Hunter (Bill Hallam), Jean Dixon (Irene), Pat Somerset (Sloan Potter), Claire Trevor (Kitty Brant), Helen Brown (Switchboard Nurse), Wedgewood Nowell, Harold Forshay (Doctors), Franklin Pangborn, Tyler Brooks (Guests), Paul Hurst (Drunk), Arthur Aylesworth (Bartender), Florence Lake (Salesgirl), Edward Cooper (Butler), Margaret Fielding, Ruth Clifford (Nurses).

Ten years in the married life of Baxter and Loy are traced against newsreel footage of events that were occuring in the world of the time. The dates are 1925 (Jimmy Walker elected mayor of New York) to 1935 (depths of the Depression). Both have extramarital flings along the way as Baxter climbs high in the business world, but their marriage eventually is saved by the intervention of Loy's sometime lover Hunter. An interesting cavalcade of events certainly, but lacking a point, bitter or otherwise, to tie the principals to the flash of newsreels going by.

p Kenneth Macgowan; d, John Cromwell; w, Richard Sherman, Howard Ellis Smith (based on a short story by Sherman); ph, Sidney Wagner; md, Louis Silvers; ed, Ralph Dietrich; art d, Mark-Lee Kirk; cos, Royer.

Drama   **(PR:A   MPAA:NR)**

TO OBLIGE A LADY*   (1931, Brit.) 70m BL bw

Maisie Gay (Mrs. Harris), Warwick Ward (George Pinder), Mary Newland (Betty Pinder), Haddon Mason (John Prendergast), James Carew (Sir Henry Markham), Annie Esmond (Mrs. Higgins), Gladys Jennings, Gladys Hamer.

Ward and Newland try to find a cook at the last minute for a dinner in which they hope to gain the blessings of the rich uncle and a $25,000-a-year job for Ward. But the whole thing turns into a flop, both for the couple and the people who sit through this unfunny mess.

p, S.W. Smith; d, Manning Haynes; w, Edgar Wallace; m/l, "What Love Means to Girls Like Me," sung by Maisie Gay.

Comedy   **(PR:A   MPAA:NR)**

TO PARIS WITH LOVE*½   (1955, Brit.) 78m TC/CD bw

Alec Guinness (Col. Sir Edgar Fraser), Odile Versois (Lisette Marconnet), Vernon Gray (Jon Fraser), Jacques Francois (Victor de Colville), Elina Labourdette (Sylvia Gilbert), Austin Trevor (Leon de Colville), Claude Romain (Georges Duprez), Maureen Davis (Suzanne de Colville), Jacques Brunius (Aristide Marconnet), Pamela Stirling (Mme. Marconnet), Mollie Hartley Milburn (Mme. Alvarez), Michael Anthony (Pierre), Andre Mikhelson (Head Porter), Jacques Cey (Night Porter), Nicholas Bruce (Night Clerk), Toni Frost (Vendeuse), George Lafaye Company and Claude Collier (Cabaret Act).

A flawed yet still charming comedy features Guinness as a retired British officer who takes off for Paris in a Rolls Royce with his son Gray. The baronet is convinced Gray has led too sheltered a life style and it's high time for him to experience some of the charms that Parisian women have to offer. On the other hand, Gray feels that his father has been living by himself for much too long on his Scottish estate. Convinced that female companionship would perk up Guinness, Gray decides to spend this holiday finding the right female counterpart for his father. Guinness meets Versois, an enticing redhead, daughter of cab driver Brunius. The old man is convinced she will be perfect for his son. In the meantime Gray finds Labourdette, an older woman more suited for Guinness, and tries to fix her up with his widowed father. This leads to complications as partners switch amidst the quartet. Eventually the entanglements work out, though not as Guinness had originally intended. Versois decides she'd rather be with her childhood sweetheart than with Gray, but the lad is hardly crushed by this. He's found a woman his own age which, of course, leads to a happy denouement. This light romantic comedy has its moments but never quite reaches the appropriate level of sophistication. The screenplay develops in a predictable manner. What makes this work is Guinness' delightful performance. He takes the twists within the story in good comic stride, handling every moment with care even when his talents are clearly much better than the material. A trifle perhaps, but certainly an entertaining one.

p, Antony Darnborough; d, Robert Hamer; w, Robert Buckner; ph, Reginald Wyer (Technicolor); m, Edwin Astley; ed, Anne V. Coates; md, Astley; art d, Maurice Carter; cos, Yvonne Caffin.

Comedy   **Cas.**   **(PR:A   MPAA:NR)**

TO PLEASE A LADY*½   (1950) 91m MGM bw (AKA: RED HOT WHEELS)

Clark Gable (Mike Brannan), Barbara Stanwyck (Regina Forbes), Adolphe Menjou (Gregg), Will Geer (Jack Mackay), Roland Winters (Dwight Barrington), William C. McGaw (Joie Chitwood), Lela Bliss (Regina's Secretary), Emory Parnell (Mr. Wendall), Frank Jenks (Newark Press Agent), Helen Spring (Janie), Bill Hickman, Lew Smith (Mike's Mechanics), Ted Husing (Indianapolis Announcer), Richard W. Joy (TV Voice), William Welsh (Sports Announcer), John McGuire (Newark Referee), Lee Phelps (Steward), Dominic "Pee Wee" Distarce, Henry Banks, Johnny Parsons, Johnny Tolan (Ad Lib Drivers), Al Hill (Steward), Raymond H. Brown (Newark Announcer), Joe Garson (Joe Youghal), John Gallaudet (IMRA Promoter), Hal K. Dawson (IMRA Manager), Billy Newell (Hank Harmon), Byron Foulger (Shoe Fitter), Arthur Loew, Jr (Studio Production Man), Marilyn Rich, Frank Hyers, Tom Hanlon, Dick Simmons, Marcel de la Brosse, Carlotta Monti, Ernest Ohman, Jean Ransome, Holmes Herbert, Anne O'Neal, Jerry Hausner, Tim Ryan, Cecil Green, Jack McGrath, Cay Forrester.

Fast cars and romance mix in this yarn which stars Gable as a notorious midget race car driver. On the track Gable draws more boos than cheers from the crowds, who won't forgive him for a crash he once caused which resulted in another driver's death. A hard-edged columnist, Stanwyck, decides to give Gable a fair shake and interview him. Gable, however, wants nothing to do with her. Stanwyck stays to see the race and witnesses another fatal crash caused by Gable. Convinced that he is a callous individual with no respect for life, she condemns him in her column. She wields enough power to get him barred from the race circuit. Gable takes up stunt-car performing in a sideshow and manages to save enough cash to buy a full-sized racer. Before the race Gable and Stanwyck meet, but instead of despising each other, they fall in love. Gable then heads out to the racetrack for the big race, but while letting another driver pass he crashes. Gable survives the wreck and Stanwyck is now convinced that he has redeemed himself. Although the title of the picture is TO PLEASE A LADY, the most memorable moments of the film occur on the race track. Photographed at the Indianapolis Speedway, the twelve-minute finale brims with the excitement that is absent from the dialog. Gable and Stanwyck do their best with the script but most of their interchanges fall flat. The most electric moment between the pair occurs when Gable, by now attracted to Stanwyck, slaps her face. Instead of running off, Stanwyck stays, proving both her love for Gable and her ability to take what he dishes out. Twenty years previously Stanwyck took another slap from Gable in the picture NIGHT NURSE. In response to a meager box office showing, MGM re-released TO PLEASE A LADY under the more graphic title RED HOT WHEELS.

p&d, Clarence Brown; w, Barre Lyndon, Marge Decker; ph, Harold Rosson; m, Bronislau Kaper; ed, Robert J. Kern; art d, Cedric Gibbons, James Basevi; set d, Edwin B. Willis, Jack Bonar, Ralph S. Hurst; cos, Helen Rose; spec eff, A. Arnold Gillespie, Warren Newcombe; makeup, Bob Ewing, William J. Tuttle; technical advisers, Wilbur Shaw, Babe Stapp.

Sports Drama/Romance (PR:A MPAA:NR)

TO SIR, WITH LOVE*** (1967, Brit.) 105m James Clavell/COL c

Sidney Poitier (*Mark Thackeray*), Christian Roberts (*Denham*), Judy Geeson (*Pamela Dare*), Suzy Kendall (*Gillian Blanchard*), Lulu [Marie Lawrie] (*Barbara Pegg*), Faith Brook (*Mrs. Evans*), Geoffrey Bayldon (*Weston*), Edward Burnham (*Florian*), Gareth Robinson (*Tich*), Grahame Charles (*Fernman*), Roger Shepherd (*Buckley*), Patricia Routledge (*Clinty*), Mona Bruce (*Jose Dawes*), Fiona Duncan (*Miss Phillips*), Christopher Chittell (*Potter*), Marianne Stone (*Gert*), Rita Webb (*Mrs. Joseph*), Cyril Shaps (*Mr. Pinkus*), Adrienne Posta (*Moira Jackson*), Peter Attard (*Ingham*), Anthony Villaroel (*Seales*), Ann Bell (*Mrs. Dare*), Fred Griffiths, Dervis Ward, Sally Cann, Albert Lampert, Chitra Neogy, Elna Pearl, Stewart Bevan, Carla Challoner, Joseph Cuby, Lynne Sue Moon, Jane Peach, Michael Des Barres, Margaret Heald, Ellison Kemp, Donita Shawe, Richard Willson, Sally Gosselin, Kevin Hubbard, Howard Knight, Stephen Whittaker, The Mindbenders.

A sentimental picture which stars Poitier as an engineer from British Guiana who, because he is black, cannot find work in his field. He accepts a teaching position in a slummy high school in London's East End. He quickly learns that he signed on for more than he bargained for–the students are poorly educated, viciously rebellious, and downright crude to those in authority. Rather than end up like the previous string of instructors–who have given up on the students–Poitier tries an unorthodox method. Instead of relying on textbooks, Poitier teaches from experience. His belief is that the students must be treated like adults in order for them to behave as such. They are products of an East End society which impresses upon them certain roles–the boys must be tough, the girls must be subordinate. Poitier tries to break down these societal barriers. He teaches his class–boys and girls alike–how to cook, how to act respectfully as gentlemen and ladies, and how to be considerate of others. He even arranges for the class to take a field trip to a museum where, in a montage composed of still photographs (the sequence was directed by George White) they gawk at the enormous skeletons of dinosaurs. Gradually Poitier gains the students' trust and respect. They soon take to calling him "Sir," more out of affection than authority. One girl–Geeson, a dreamy blonde–develops a crush on Poitier and stands by his side in the hope that he will reciprocate. Rather than take advantage of her, Poitier gently lets her down. Others are less responsive. One cynical instructor, Bayldon, strongly disapproves of Poitier's methods and sways the school into forbidding any further field trips. Poitier's main opposition comes from Roberts, a young tough who defies all rules and tries to turn his classmates against the teacher. When a gym instructor's callousness results in an injury to a student, Roberts comes to the latter's defense and physically threatens the teacher. Poitier is called to the scene. He reprimands Roberts, but to no effect. Roberts prefers to settle the argument with a fight. Poitier straps on a pair of boxing gloves and, to everyone's surprise, delivers a healthy blow to Roberts' gut. With the semester coming to a close, the students dread the thought of losing "Sir" to an engineering job. During an end-of-the-semester dance, Poitier is given a gift by the class representative, Lulu, who also sings "To Sir, With Love" for him. Poitier is driven to tears of joy by the gesture and retreats to the solitude of his classroom. The quiet is broken by a rowdy teenage couple barging into the room. They have been assigned to "Sir's" class and seem to look forward to giving him a hard time. Poitier then tears up a letter informing him of an engineering job, planning instead to remain as a teacher. What makes TO SIR, WITH LOVE such an enjoyable film is the mythic nature of "Sir." He manages to come across as a real person, while embodying everything there is to know about morality, respect, and integrity. "Sir" is heroic yet human at the same time, and because of his care and understanding, he is able to redeem a group of children who would otherwise end up at the bottom of the social heap. As charming as TO SIR, WITH LOVE is, it does suffer from some excessive simplicity–real life hoodlums just aren't converted to the good life so easily, even with someone like "Sir." Surprisingly (in relation to the rest of Poitier's career), TO SIR, WITH LOVE pays little attention to racial issues. Although it occasionally enters into the story, Poitier is never considered a black man, just a teacher who happens to be black. The film's success baffled Columbia executives who just didn't know how to market it. In an attempt to learn why people

liked the film so much, they even handed out questionnaires–a method which proved fruitless. One factor in the film's popularity and its sustaining charm is the tuneful title song, which was a top hit for Lulu and is heard throughout the film. TO SIR, WITH LOVE went on to become the eighth largest grosser of the year, raking in $7.2 million.

p,d&w, James Clavell (based on the novel by E.R. Braithwaite); ph, Paul Beeson (Technicolor); m, Ron Grainer; ed, Peter Thornton; md, Philip Martell; art d, Tony Woollard; set d, Ian Whittaker; m/l, title song, Don Black, Marc London (sung by Lulu), "It's Getting Harder All the Time," Charles Albertine, Ben Raleigh, "Off and Running," Carole Bayer, Toni Wine, "Stealing My Love from Me," London (sung by The Mindbenders); makeup, Jill Carpenter.

Drama **Cas.** (PR:A MPAA:NR)

TO THE DEVIL A DAUGHTER** (1976, Brit./Ger.) 92m Hammer-Terra/EMI c

Richard Widmark (*John Verney*), Christopher Lee (*Father Michael Raynor*), Honor Blackman (*Anna Fountain*), Denholm Elliott (*Henry Beddows*), Michael Goodliffe (*George de Grass*), Nastassja Kinski (*Catherine Beddows*), Eva-Marie Meineke (*Eveline de Grass*), Anthony Valentine (*David*), Derek Francis (*Bishop*), Isabella Telezynska (*Margaret*), Constantin de Goguel (*Kollde*), Anna Bentinck (*Isabel*), Irene Prador (*German Matron*), Petra Peters (*Sister Helle*), William Ridoutt (*Airport Porter*), Brian Wilde (*Room Attendant*), Howard Goorney (*Critic*), Frances De La Tour (*Salvation Army Major*), Zoe Hendry, Lindy Benson, Jo Peters, Bobby Sparrow (*Girls*).

As a writer of books dealing in the occult, Widmark is given the chance to put some of his knowledge to work as he pursues Lee, a priest turned Satan who seeks a woman to bring his child into the world. Lee puts under his spell a young nun, Kinski in one of her first roles, whose father requests the aide of Widmark to save her. An appropriately eerie atmosphere is maintained through all the supernatural doings, with a perfect performance by Lee as the demonic priest. But the development of the plot and suspense are thwarted by placing too much emphasis on the mystery of the occult.

p, Roy Skeggs; d, Peter Sykes; w, Chris Wicking (based on the novel by Dennis Wheatley); ph, David Watkin (Technicolor); m, Paul Glass; ed, John Trumper; art d, Don Picton; Spec eff, Les Bowie; makeup, Eric Allright, George Blackler.

Horror **Cas.** (PR:O MPAA:R)

TO THE ENDS OF THE EARTH*** (1948) 109m COL bw

Dick Powell (*Michael Barrows*), Signe Hasso (*Ann Grant*), Maylia (*Shu Pan Wu*), Ludwig Donath (*Nicolas Sokim*), Vladimir Sokoloff (*Lum Chi Chow*), Edgar Barrier (*Grieg*), John Hoyt (*Bennett*), Marcel Journet (*Commissioner Lariesier*), Luis Van Rooten (*Alberto Berado*), Fritz Leiber (*Binda Sha*), Vernon Steele (*Commissioner Hadley*), Peter Virgo (*Mahmoud*), Lou Krugman (*Commissioner Amar Hassam*), Eddie Lee (*Chian Soo*), Ivan Triesault (*Naftalie Vrandstadter*), Leon Lenoir (*Hernando*), Peter Chong (*Joe*), George Volk (*Cassidy*), Robert Malcolm (*Clark*), Commissioner Harry J. Anslinger (*Himself*).

An engrossing, globetrotting semi-documentary on the evils of narcotics pushers, specifically those who try smuggling opium onto U.S. shores. Powell is a government man investigating a plot to spread the use and addiction of opium throughout the world. He finds his first clue along the West Coast where a Japanese crew of an unchartered ship is drawing some attention. Before Powell can catch up with them they reach the safety of international waters, leaving behind 100 opium plantation slaves floating face down in the water. Powell follows the clues to Shanghai where he locates the gang, but he is unable to hang the murders on them. He does, however, discover that Hasso, while acting as governess to the orphaned Maylia, is engineering the gang's moves. After a stop in Egypt, where the plantations are located, Powell travels to Cuba, the site of the next opium shipment. Some brilliant deductions and lucky guesswork prove correct for Powell who is able to crack the operation after a high-speed boat chase along the New Jersey coast. As it turns out, Hasso is an innocent figure whose strings are being pulled by the guilty Maylia. The chief factor in the film's success as an adventure picture is the realistic documentary approach. With a hefty (for the time) $2 million budget no expenses were spared in achieving realism. The film also had the support of the U.S. Treasury Department whose head at the time, Harry J. Anslinger, even makes an appearance. Director Stevenson managed to receive permission to film a session of the narcotics control commission at work at the United Nations council at Lake Success, New York, location of UN headquarters from 1946 to 1951. None of this could have been shown, however, had the Motion Picture Association not eased its rigid anti-drug Production Code regulations, which prohibited any themes regarding narcotics.

p, Sidney Buchman; d, Robert Stevenson; w, Jay Richard Kennedy; ph, Burnett Guffey; ed, William Lyon; md, M.W. Stoloff; art d, Stephen Goosson, Cary Odell.

Crime (PR:A-C MPAA:NR)

TO THE LAST MAN** (1933) 61m PAR bw

Randolph Scott (*Lynn Hayden*), Esther Ralston (*Ellen Colby*), Buster Crabbe (*Bill Hayden*), Jack LaRue (*Jim Daggs*), Noah Beery, Sr (*Jed Colby*), Barton MacLane (*Neil Standing*), Muriel Kirkland (*Molly Hayden*), Fuzzy Knight (*Jeff Morley*), Gail Patrick (*Ann Hayden Standing*), Egon Brecher (*Mark Hayden*), James Eagles (*Ely Bruce*), Eugenie Besserer (*Granny Spelvin*), Harlan Knight (*Grandpa Spelvin*), John Peter Richmond [Carradine] (*Pete Garon*), Harry Cording (*Harry Malone*), Erville Alderson (*Judge*), James Burke (*Sheriff*), Jay Ward (*Lynn Hayden as a Child*), Rosita Butler (*Ann Hayden as a Child*), Cullen Johnson (*Bill Hayden as a Child*), Russell Powell (*Greaves*), Delmar Watson (*Tad Standing*), Shirley Temple (*Mary Standing*).

Decent oater about a feud between two families. Starting back in the hills of Kentucky and continuing on the plains of the West, members of one of the families take to cattle rustling. A romance between Scott and Ralston develops amidst this tension, but Scott brings the rustlers to justice, then sets about marrying Ralston, an event which will hopefully bring peace to the families. Five-year- old Shirley Temple made an appearance in her second screen outing.

p, Harold Hurley; d, Henry Hathaway; w, Jack Cunningham (based on the novel by Zane Grey); ph, Ben Reynolds; art d, Earl Hedrick.

Western (PR:A MPAA:NR)

TO THE SHORES OF HELL** (1966) 82m Robert Patrick/Crown International c

Marshall Thompson (*Maj. Greg Donahue*), Kiva Lawrence (*Mary*), Richard Jordahl (*Father Jacques Bourget*), Robert Dornan (*Dr. Gary Donahue*), Jeff Pearl (*Mic Phin*), Richard Arlen (*Brig. Gen. F.W. Ramgate*), Dick O'Neill (*Maj. Fred Howard*), Freeman Lusk (*Capt. Lusk*), Bill Bierd (*Sgt. Bill Gagreski*), Marvin Yim (*Maj. Toang*).

A marine, Thompson, infiltrates the territory of the Viet Cong to rescue his brother, Dornan, a doctor being held captive and forced to treat wounded Viet Cong. Thompson is given the aid of a priest, a native, and another soldier on the mission. These heroes don't make it, as a rescue helicopter saves the two brothers just in the nick of time.

p&d, Will Zens; w, Zens, Robert McFadden; ph, Leif Rise (Techniscope, Technicolor); m, William Schaefer; ed, Michael David; spec eff, Harry Woolman.

War (PR:A MPAA:NR)

TO THE SHORES OF TRIPOLI*** (1942) 86m FOX c

John Payne (*Chris Winters*), Maureen O'Hara (*2nd Lt. Mary Carter*), Randolph Scott (*Dixie Smith*), Nancy Kelly (*Helene*), William Tracy (*Johnny*), Maxie Rosenbloom (*Okay*), Henry [Harry] Morgan (*Mouthy*), Edmund MacDonald (*Butch*), Russell Hicks (*Maj. Wilson*), Minor Watson (*Capt. Winters*), Ted North (*Bill Grady*), Frank Orth (*Barber*), Iris Adrian (*Blonde*), Alan Hale, Jr (*Tom Hall*), Basil Walker (*Joe*), Charles Tannen (*Swifty*), Stanley Andrews (*Doctor*), Richard Lane (*Lieutenant*), Gordon Jones, Gaylord [Steve] Pendleton, Anthony Nace (*Corporals*), Robert Conway (*Ensign*), Elena Verdugo (*Dancer Specialty*), James C. Morton (*Bartender*), Esther Estrella, Marissa Flores (*Spanish Girls*), Frank Coghlan, Jr (*Bellboy*), William Haade (*Truck Driver*), Walter Sande (*Pharmacist's Mate*), James Flavin (*Warden*), Hugh Beaumont (*Orderly*), Hillary Brooke, Patricia Farr (*Girls*), Margaret Early (*Susie*), Byron Shores (*Captain*), Knox Manning (*Newscaster*), Charles Brokaw, Jack Arnold [Vinton Haworth] (*Officers*), Harry Strang (*Chief Petty Officer*), Chester Gan (*Chinaman*), Pat McVey (*Radio Operator*), Frank Sully (*Truck Driver*), Joseph Crehan (*Uncle Bob*), John Hamilton (*Gen. Gordon*).

An effective flag-waver which put the Marine Corps in the spotlight and was made with the full cooperation of that branch of the U.S. armed services. Payne is an arrogant lad awaiting a cushy job in Washington, D.C., which his girl friend, Kelly, is supposed to land him. In the meantime, he decides to sign up with the Marines. His smart-mouthed attitude doesn't get him very far, however, when confronted by granite-tough drill sergeant Scott. It's not long before Payne eyes a beautiful Navy nurse, O'Hara, and is destined to fall in love with her. The strict regulations of the Marines humble Payne and he learns to accept his stay in the service with seriousness. He redeems himself in Scott's eyes when he saves the sergeant from a mishap during target practice. When Payne receives word that a job has been found for him in Washington, he readies himself to leave. Before he can say his goodbyes, however, Pearl Harbor is attacked and Payne is struck by a wave of patriotism. Although it seems cliched today, TO THE SHORES OF TRIPOLI did the job in 1942 when patriotic cliches were the most effective way to lure young men into battle. To help their cause the Marine Corps allowed the studio use of its base in San Diego and access to the Pacific Fleet. The film is perhaps best remembered as O'Hara's first film in color–marking the audience's first opportunity to see the shimmering red hair that became her trademark. In 1950, O'Hara and Payne made it past the *shores* of Tripoli and appeared in a picture entitled, simply, TRIPOLI.

p, Darryl F. Zanuck; d, Bruce Humberstone; w, Lamar Trotti (based on a story by Steve Fisher); ph, Edward Cronjager, William Skall, Harry Jackson (Technicolor); m, Alfred Newman; ed, Allen McNeil; cos, Gwen Wakeling.

War Drama (PR:A MPAA:NR)

TO THE VICTOR**½ (1938, Brit.) 78m Gainsborough/GB bw (GB: OWD BOB)

Will Fyffe (*Adam McAdam*), John Loder (*David Moore*), Margaret Lockwood (*Jeannie McAdam*), Graham Moffatt (*Tammas*), Moore Marriott (*Samuel*), Wilfred Walter (*Thwaites*), Eliot Mason (*Mrs. Winthrop*), A. Bromley Davenport (*Magistrate*), H. F. Maltby (*Sgt. Musgrave*), Edmund Breon (*Lord Meredale*), Wally Patch, Alf Goddard (*Bookies*).

Fyffe is an old Scottish farmer who is constantly fighting with his neighbors. He lives on his sheep farm with his daughter Lockwood and his faithful companion sheepdog, Black Wull. Loder plays a young farmer who moves in next door with his own dog, Owd Bob. Loder and Lockwood take an immediate liking to one another, but problems arise when Fyffe and Loder enter their dogs in sheepdog trials. Loder wins and Fyffe, who has bet all he owns on his Black Wull, is left bankrupt. To add to his problems, Black Wull is discovered to be a sheep killer. Loder and Lockwood marry and take care of the old man, who is given a new pup to raise. An amiable, routine British programmer with some good performances and a nice use of the country locations. Part of the film's plot was later lifted for THUNDER IN THE VALLEY (1947).

p, Edward Black; d, Robert Stevenson; w, J. B. Williams, Michael Hogan (based on a novel by Alfred Olivant); ph, Jack Cox; ed, R. E. Dearing; md, Louis Levy.

Drama (PR:A MPAA:NR)

TO THE VICTOR** (1948) 100m WB bw

Dennis Morgan (*Paul*), Viveca Lindfors (*Christine*), Victor Francen (*Capt. Beauvals*), Bruce Bennett (*Henderson*), Dorothy Malone (*Miriam*), Tom D'Andrea (*Gus*), Eduardo Ciannelli (*Firago*), Douglas Kennedy (*Steve*), Joseph Buloff (*Bolyanov*), William Conrad (*Farnsworth*), Luis van Rooten (*Geran*), Konstantin Shayne (*Pablo*), Anthony Caruso (*Mikki*), Joanee Wayne (*Gabby*), John Banner (*Lestrac*), Henry Rowland (*Zinzer*), Felipe Turich (*Victor*).

Set in post-WW II Paris, where a rampant black market exists and citizens are hunting down those who supported the Nazis. American black marketeer Morgan offers shelter to Lindfors, a woman whose husband is on trial as a Nazi collaborator, but she will not testify against him, so a killer henchman of her husband's stalks the streets whose aim is to silence her. The pair fall in love and undergo a change of heart. Morgan decides to go straight and Lindfors decides to give evidence that will jail her husband. The direction by Daves manages to pace things out well enough to make for an entertaining outing. Filmed on location in France. An auspicious introduction of darkly beautiful Lindfors to the U.S. filmgoing public.

p, Jerry Wald; d, Delmer Daves; w, Richard Brooks; ph, Robert Burks; m, David Buttolph; ed, Folmar Blangsted; md, Leo F. Forbstein; art d, Leo K. Kuter; cos, Milo Anderson; spec eff, Marcel Grignon.

Drama (PR:A MPAA:NR)

TO TRAP A SPY*½ (1966) 92m Arena/MGM c

Robert Vaughan (*Napoleon Solo*), David McCallum (*Illya Kuryakin*), Luciana Paluzzi (*Angela*), Patricia Crowley (*Elaine May Donaldson*), Fritz Weaver (*Vulcan*), Will Kuluva (*Mr. Allison*), William Marshall (*Ashumen*), Ivan Dixon (*Soumarin*), Victoria Shaw (*Gracie Ladovan*), Miguel Landa (*Lancer*), Eric Berry (*Alfred Ghist*), Mario Siletti (*Del Floria*), Rupert Crosse (*Nobuk*).

The original pilot for TV's "The Man From U.N.C.L.E." with a few extra feet of footage tacked on to allow for commercial release. This added footage does absolutely nothing to develop the plot, rather it gives Vaughan a chance to indulge in some of his super-stud-spy antics. It's really not needed at all. An organization called W.A.S.P. attempts to take control of an African republic by killing off its president and his top aides, but Vaughan, aided by simple housewife Crowley, puts an end to the scheme. The pilot was shot in color but shown in black-and-white on TV. This was one of several theatrical releases culled from the television series. Another of the films made up of these expanded series episodes, THE SPY WITH MY FACE, was also released in 1966.

p, Sam Rolfe; d, Don Medford; w, Rolfe; ph, Joseph Biroc (Metrocolor); m, Jerry Goldsmith; ed, Henry Berman; art d, George W. Davis, Merrill Pye; set d, Henry Grace, Frank McKelvy.

Spy/Drama (PR:A MPAA:NR)

TO WHAT RED HELL** (1929, Brit.) 100m Strand-Twickenham/TIF bw

Sybil Thorndike (*Mrs. Fairfield*), John Hamilton (*Harold Fairfield*), Bramwell Fletcher (*Jim Nolan*), Jillian Sande (*Eleanor Dunham*), Janice Adair (*Madge Barton*), Arthur Pusey (*George Hope*), Athole Stewart (*Mr. Fairfield*), Drusilla Wills (*Mrs. Ellis*), Wyn Weaver (*Dr. Barton*), Matthew Boulton (*Inspector Jackson*), Sara Allgood.

Grim little drama has Hamilton an epileptic who kills a prostitute during a seizure. Hidden and protected by his mother, Thorndike, he finally confesses and commits suicide just before the victim's boy friend is to be hanged for the crime. More interesting than good, the film began production as a silent, then all the footage was thrown out and production began again as a talkie.

p, Julius Hagen; d, Edwin Greenwood; w, Leslie Hiscott (based on a play by Percy Robinson); ph, Basil Emmott.

Crime **(PR:A MPAA:NR)**

TOAST OF NEW ORLEANS, THE*** (1950) 97m MGM c

Kathryn Grayson *(Suzette Micheline)*, Mario Lanza *(Pepe Abellard Duvalle)*, David Niven *(Jacques Riboudeaux)*, J. Carroll Naish *(Nicky Duvalle)*, James Mitchell *(Pierre)*, Richard Hageman *(Maestro P. Trellini)*, Clinton Sundberg *(Oscar)*, Sig Arno *(Mayor)*, Rita Moreno *(Tina)*, Romo Vincent *(Manuelo)*, George Davis *(Stooge)*, Marietta Canty *(Angelique)*, Alex Gerry *(Headwaiter)*, Wallis Clark *(Mr. O'Neill)*, Paul Frees *(Narrator)*, Henry Corden, Nick Thompson *(Fishermen)*, Mary Benoit *(Woman)*, Betty Daniels, Louise Bates *(Dowagers)*, Leon Belasco *(Orchestra Leader)*, Fred Essler *(Emile)*, Nino Pipitone *(Store Keeper)*, Eduard Moreno, Dino Bolognese, Guy DeVestal *(Waiters)*.

Capitalizing on the successful teaming of Lanza and Grayson in THAT MIDNIGHT KISS, the studio rushed this into production. It's a virtual carbon of the first, with a few minor alterations and the plus factor of Niven, who took third billing below the aforementioned couple. It's 1905 in New Orleans and Lanza is a rough-and-ready fisherman. The time has come for the traditional "Blessing of the Fleet" and Lanza can't keep his eyes off Grayson, an opera diva who is the guest of honor at the annual rite. Lanza is piloting his uncle Naish's boat and doesn't keep his eyes on the water, preferring to watch Grayson. That causes him to misnavigate. These fishing people are superstitious and Lanza is no exception. By missing the "Blessing," he thinks he has put the ship in danger and his worst fears are realized when a freak storm sends the boat to the locker of Davey Jones. Lanza meets Grayson later at a fete and they duet together. Her manager is Niven, who runs her opera company and takes more than just a business interest in Grayson. The moment Niven's trained ear hears the glorious Lanza tenor, he approaches Lanza with the idea that the young man give up hauling fish in favor of exercising his lungs to music. Lanza is not sure he is qualified but the thought of working closely with the comely Grayson appeals to him, and since he feels responsible for having destroyed Naish's boat, he wants to earn enough money to purchase a new one. Lanza begins to work seriously on his music. At the same time, he tries to move in on Grayson, but she keeps him at arm's length. Lanza becomes increasingly blue at her rejections and decides to quit opera before he has given it a chance to embrace him. While she appreciates his voice, Grayson finds Lanza to be a bit of a boor and apparently far too crude for her. Niven intercedes and gives Lanza some lessons in couth while he continues his voice work. Even with his new-found suavity, Grayson still keeps him at romantic bay. Then he realizes that she does love him, but because he is a real person and not a foppish dandy. While they are singing an aria from "Madame Butterfly," Lanza finally gets the idea and sweeps Grayson off her feet, to no one's surprise. This was an even bigger hit than THAT MIDNIGHT KISS, with several operatic arias as well as a good score by Sammy Cahn and Nicholas Brodszky which included the Oscar-nominated "Be My Love" (sung by Lanza and Grayson), "Tina Lina" (Lanza, then reprised as a dance), "I'll Never Love You," "The Toast of New Orleans," "Song of the Bayou," and "Boom Biddy Boom Boom." Classical snatches were: "Je Suis Titania," from Ambroise Thomas' "Mignon," "M'Appari" from Fredrich von Flotow's "Martha," Georges Bizet's "Flower Song" from "Carmen," "Brindisi" from "La Traviata" by Giuseppe Verdi, "O Paradiso" from Amilcare Ponchielli's "La Gioconda," plus the love duet from "Madame Butterfly" by Giacomo Puccini. Niven had just decided to free-lance and accepted this supporting role that did nothing for his career. What little comedy there is in the movie was provided by Naish, in one of his many Italian roles (he was actually Irish), Sig Arno, and Clinton Sundberg. In a small role, note Rita Moreno, long before she made her mark on Broadway and everywhere else. She was 19 at the time and had already appeared in a few movies, including A MEDAL FOR BENNY and SO YOUNG, SO BAD. Special kudos for sharp editing from Ruggiero, who had to cram all of the musical numbers as well as the story into a tight 96 minutes.

p, Joe Pasternak; d, Norman Taurog; w, Sy Gomberg, George Wells; ph, William Snyder (Technicolor); ed, Gene Ruggiero; md, George Stoll, Johnny Green; art d, Cedric Gibbons, Daniel B. Cathcart; cos, Helen Rose, Walter Plunkett; ch, Eugene Loring.

Musical **(PR:A MPAA:NR)**

TOAST OF NEW YORK, THE*½** (1937) 109m RKO bw

Edward Arnold *(Jim Fisk)*, Cary Grant *(Nick Boyd)*, Frances Farmer *(Josie Mansfield)*, Jack Oakie *(Luke)*, Donald Meek *(Daniel Drew)*, Thelma Leeds *(Fleurique)*, Clarence Kolb *(Cornelius Vanderbilt)*, Robert McClung *(Bellhop)*, Dudley Clements *(Collins)*, Marie Marks *(Check Room Girl)*, Ginger Connolly *(Call Boy)*, Joseph De Stefani *(Headwaiter)*, George Offerman, Jr. *(Usher)*, Lloyd Ingraham, Ted Thompson, Jack Luden, Reed Howes, Wally Dean, Jay Eaton *(Men in Restaurant)*, Fred Lee *(Bostonian in Restaurant)*, Crauford Kent, Otto Hoffman, Winter Hall, Frank Darien, Earl Dwire *(Board of Directors)*, George Cleveland *(Secretary)*, Ben Hall, James Finlayson, Frank Swales, Foy Van Dolsen *(Inventors)*, Lon Poff, Frank Hammond *(Mountaineers)*, Nelson McDowell, Clem Bevans *(Panhandlers)*, Maxine Hicks *(Mother)*, Daisy Bufford *(Maid)*, Stanley Blystone *(Sheriff)*, Jack Kenny, Chris Frank *(Deputy Sheriffs)*, Frank Rasmussen *(Clerk)*, Robert Dudley *(Janitor)*, Mary Gordon *(Charwoman)*, Dewey Robinson *(Beefy Dolan)*, Reginald Barlow *(Hotel Proprietor)*, Stanley Fields *(Top Sergeant)*, Jack Egan, Charles Doherty, Mike Jeffries, Lynton Brent, Max Wagner, Jack Carson, Eddie Hart, Bentley Hewlett *(Reporters)*, Homer Dickinson *(Toastmaster)*, Margaret Morris, Isabel La Mal *(Women)*, Pete Gerrard, Ed Heim *(Painters)*, Sidney Bracy *(Waiter)*, William Gould, Don Brodie, Tom Brewer, Bradley Page *(Bits)*, Francis Tilton *(Artist)*, Oscar Apfel *(Wallack)*, George Irving, James Barnes, William Jeffrey, Walter Murray, Robert Brister, Tom O'Grady, Jack Mulhall, Hal Craig, William Lemuels, Billy Arnold, James Carlyle *(Brokers)*, Gavin Gordon *(Southern Major)*, Edward Piel, Sr., Malcolm Graham, Gladden James *(Gentlemen)*, Allan Cavan, Clarence Harvey, Lionel Belmore, Tom Ricketts *(Board of Directors)*, Edward Le Saint *(President of the Board)*, Harvey Clark, Frank Hall Crane *(Tailors)*, Russell Hicks *(Lawyer)*, Nick Thompson *(Italian Driver)*, Frank Mills, Russ Powell, Ethan Laidlaw *(Mugs)*, Joyce Compton, Virginia Carroll *(Southern Girls)*, Al Greer, Tyrone Brereton *(Southern Crackers)*, Frank Hemphill *(Stage Hand)*, Tom Chatterton, John Marshall *(Fisk Brokers)*, Emile Durelle, Larry Steers, J. C. "Jack" Fowler, Cameron Smith *(Buyers)*, Ernest Shield *(Clerk)*, Jerry Storm *(Little Broker)*, William Worthington *(Judge)*, John Maurice Sullivan *(President of Exchange)*, James Quinn *(News Butcher)*, Tom Coleman *(Sergeant)*, Dick Kipling *(Southerner)*, Billy Gilbert *(Portrait Photographer)*.

An entertaining though thoroughly distorted biography of carpetbagger-turned-millionaire "Jubilee Jim" Fisk, which gives star Arnold a wonderful opportunity to display his solid acting ability. The film opens in the midst of the Civil War as Arnold travels through the south turning a nice profit as a medicine- show impresario. Helping him along are two business partners and friends–Oakie, who sets up an office in the north, and Grant, who remains down south. At a higher risk and for greater financial gain, Arnold concocts a scheme to smuggle cotton out of the south and send it north for a magnificent profit. Years later, at the end of the war, Arnold and Grant return to Oakie, with grandiose plans for spending their huge profits. Oakie, however, has invested all the money in Confederate bonds which are now–after the South's surrender–completely worthless. Not to be defeated, Arnold decides to use the bonds as a tool to bluff his way out of financial ruin and into the pockets of big business. After befriending an unscrupulous millionaire, Meek, Arnold and Grant are made directors of the Erie Railroad. From that vantage point Arnold is able to hook industrial magnate Cornelius Vanderbilt (played by Kolb) into trying to buy out Erie's stock. Arnold, in order to amass his own personal wealth, simply runs off, as needed, additional phony stock. (The real- life Jim Fisk was quoted as saying "If this printing press don't break down, I'll be damned if I don't give the old hog 'Vanderbilt' all he wants of Erie.") Kolb just keeps buying, until he finally realizes he's been duped. The fabulously wealthy crooks leave New York and retreat to the Taylor Hotel in New Jersey, which they fortify and dub "Fort Taylor". While hiding out at Fort Taylor, Grant falls in love with Arnold's mistress, a young showgirl played by Farmer. In the meantime, Kolb presses charges against Arnold and the story reaches the press. Eventually, however, Arnold becomes something of a hero–the little man being attacked by the all-powerful magnate. While Grant stays behind the scenes, Arnold lives the high-life, showering his mistress with jewels and fine clothes, and even buying her Pike's Opera House. Arnold finally goes too far when he tries to corner the gold market, resulting in the tragic day of financial ruin known as Black Friday, September 24, 1869. This causes a division between Arnold and Grant, the latter taking sides with Kolb. When an angry mob–those who realize Arnold is responsible for their financial destruction–storms Fort Taylor, bullets fly and Arnold lies dead. Grant and Farmer are then free to carry on their romance without fear or guilt. Budgeted at a hefty $1,072,000, THE TOAST OF NEW YORK didn't show the profit that RKO had hoped for, resulting in over a half-million dollar loss. It wasn't for lack of talent, however, boasting the atmospheric direction of Lee, the talented pen of Dudley Nichols, and a fine cast from leads to supporting players. This was a reprise of a familiar characterization for the corpulent Arnold, who was so often cast as a wealthy schemer, as in DIAMOND JIM (1935); this part fits him like his own skin. Grant performed admirably in a rather commonplace role. His career had just begun to take off towards superstar status with TOPPER, released one month earlier, and would soon escalate even higher with THE AWFUL TRUTH, BRINGING UP BABY, and HOLIDAY in 1938. Grant managed to bring the proper debonair charm to his character which, although the credits are deceptive, is based on a combination of Fisk's aide and close confidant Ned Stokes and business partner Jay Gould. Not surprisingly, Hollywood altered the facts of Jim Fisk's celebrated life and death to fit its framework. Portraying Fisk as a likable, roly-poly socialite is only partly correct. While he was a well-known backer of stage shows and opera in New York, and flashed his wealth for all to see and admire, "Jubilee Jim" Fisk was also a ruthless and corrupt businessman who ruined countless lives and fortunes in order to strengthen his own. What THE TOAST OF NEW YORK leaves out is Fisk's wining-and-dining of President Ulysses S. Grant in hope of cornering the gold market, the bribery of a White House aide to obtain information on the gold reserve, and the bribery of countless Tammany Hall officials (including the infamous Senator William Marcy "Boss" Tweed) to vote in his favor. In addition to his political and financial corruption, Fisk also was an adulterous cheat who deserted his wife for the younger, more beautiful Josie Mansfield, a divorcee with a past in music halls and brothels. Upon their first meeting, Mansfield and the reportedly irresistible Stokes fell in love. When Fisk learned that he had lost his adored Mansfield, he immediately accused Stokes of embezzlement and brought charges against him. Later that day, January 6, 1872, after also being indicted for blackmail, Stokes grabbed his revolver and raced to Fisk's hotel, where he gunned down "Jubilee Jim." Stokes was later tried for manslaughter and sentenced to six years in Sing Sing. Mansfield, who promised to await his release, soon afterwards left for Europe with a new lover, never again seeing Stokes. Included are a couple of songs sung by Francis Farmer, "The First Time I Saw," "Ooh, La, La" (Nathaniel Shilkret, Allie Wrubel) and "Temptation Waltz" (Shilkret, L. Wolfe Gilbert).

p, Edward Small; d, Rowland V. Lee; w, Dudley Nichols, John Twist, Joel Sayre (based on *The Book of Daniel Drew* by Bouck White and the story "Robber Barons" by Matthew Josephson); ph, Peverell Marley; ed, George Hively, Samuel Beetley; md, Nathaniel Shilkret; art d, Van Nest Polglase; cos, Edward Stevenson; spec eff, Vernon L. Walker; m/l, Shilkret, Allie Wrubel, L. Wolfe Gilbert.

Biography   **Cas.**   **(PR:A   MPAA:NR)**

TOAST OF THE LEGION   (SEE: KISS ME AGAIN, 1931)

TOAST TO LOVE*   (1951, Mex.) 82m Promesa bw

Irina Baronova *(Yolanda Petrova)*, David Silva *(Julio Castro)*, Miguel Arenas *(Don Carlos)*, Leon Greanin *(Papa Niko)*, Alberto Galan *(Father Pablo)*, Lucy Delgado *(Anita)*, Jose Morcillo *(Secretary of War)*, Herman Vera *(Prison Warden)*, Crox Alvarado, Ricardo Adalid *(Cadets)*.

While in Mexico with her touring dance company, Russian ballerina Baronova becomes the object of desire for both elderly statesman Arenas and young soldier Silva. The former will intercede to prevent Baronova's parents from being packed off to Siberia, but only if she marries him. Reluctantly, she does, not only spurning the love of the cadet she really cares for, but also turning him over to the authorities when he joins a rebellious group after being shattered by her rejection. Things get worse–much worse–but it doesn't matter because the whole series of events proves to be nothing more than a bad dream brought on by a letter informing her of her parents' impending exile. The statesman steps in to save the day. However, nothing can save this picture, burdened by some exceptionally poor performances and trite direction. It features excerpts from "Sleeping Beauty," "Swan Lake" (Peter Ilich Tchaikovsky), and "La Fille Ma Gardee" (Hertel). (In Spanish; English subtitles.)

p, Manuel Reachi; d, Arman Chelieu; w, Chelieu, A. Anthony Davis; ed, George Grone, Antonio Bustos.

Drama   **(PR:A   MPAA:NR)**

TOBACCO ROAD**   (1941) 84m FOX bw

Charley Grapewin *(Jeeter Lester)*, Marjorie Rambeau *(Sister Bessie)*, Gene Tierney *(Ellie May Lester)*, William Tracy *(Duke Lester)*, Elizabeth Patterson *(Ada Lester)*, Dana Andrews *(Dr. Tim)*, Slim Summerville *(Henry Peabody)*, Ward Bond *(Lov Bensey)*, Grant Mitchell *(George Payne)*, Zeffie Tilbury *(Grandma Lester)*, Russell Simpson *(Sheriff)*, Spencer Charters, George Chandler *(Employee)*, Irving Bacon *(Teller)*, Harry Tyler *(Auto Salesman)*, Charles Halton *(Mayor)*, Jack Pennick *(Deputy Sheriff)*, Dorothy Adams *(Payne's Secretary)*, Francis Ford *(Vagabond)*, John "Skins" Miller *(Garage Attendant)*, Charles Halton *(Mayor)*.

A twisted and humorous antithesis to the usual "Fordian" style of family bonding and love of the land, TOBACCO ROAD is a beautifully photographed examination of life among the "poor white trash" of Georgia's Tobacco Road area during the Depression. One of three Nunnally Johnson-scripted Ford films– following the PRISONER OF SHARK ISLAND (1936) and THE GRAPES OF WRATH (1940)–TOBACCO ROAD takes the long-running Kirkland play, which opened in 1933, and the popular Caldwell novel and turns them into a story, albeit strangely distorted, of individualism and integrity. As the film opens with the apocalyptic statement, "All that they were, and all that they had, is gone with the wind and the dust," the mood is a sombre one, a character study of man battered by the elements. But Ford, not to be that easily pigeon-holed, plays much of the film for laughs. Ford has diminished the sexual atmosphere that was present in the play between the characters of Ellie May and Lov Bensey, and instead concentrates on the amiability and frivolity of the Jeeter Lester character, played with unbounding energy by Grapewin. Grapewin and Patterson play husband and wife, trying to keep their family together, while also trying to raise the necessary $100 to pay that month's bills. Grapewin has little or no success with either. Grandmother Tilbury just gets up and leaves one day, walking into the forest, presumably to die, and is never seen again. Tracy, the rambunctious son, is more concerned with getting his car, blowing its horn, and making a wreck of it after one day, than he is with helping his

father in daily affairs. It is this car, however, that brings the family together, all of them admiring its design, fondling the chassis, testing the hood. This unity, however, is short-lived. Tracy goes so far as to taunt, mercilessly, his parents, reveling in the idea that they cannot make ends meet and will probably be forced off their land by creditors. Meanwhile, daughter Tierney is more concerned with making passes at neighbor Bond. The one person who has the chance to get Grapewin out of his dire financial straits is sister Rambeau, who instead carelessly spends every last cent of her money. Nearly everyone in the picture is stricken with sloth, refusing to work the land or even plant the necessary vegetables, chosing instead to steal. By the finale, the family unit is nonexistent, but Grapewin has succeeded in finding the funds to stay afloat. Amidst all the deception, carelessness, and laziness, Grapewin has somehow managed to emerge, thanks to his levity, from Tobacco Road with his dignity and individualism still in tact. Truly a combination of Ford's pictorial skills and Johnson's character sketches (which can be seen in the classic John Renoir portrait of the South, THE SOUTHERNER, to which he, and William Faulkner, contributed), TOBACCO ROAD is an oddity in Ford's career–a career in which one has come to expect family values, the love of the land, a work ethic, honesty, and a serious tone. Instead, however, these qualities are parodied, and the result, while unorthodox, is highly unjoyable, making TOBACCO ROAD perhaps Ford's most underrated achievement. Photographed by Arthur C. Miller, the man responsible for the breathtaking visuals of HOW GREEN WAS MY VALLEY (for which he won an Oscar), TOBACCO ROAD is, if nothing else, a marvel to look at. Further illustrating the change that this film represented for Ford, Miller has said of the director: "After working with him for some time, I realized what an impossible task it was to describe his work, because when John Ford made a picture, he could not be compared even to himself from one day to the next. He was one hundred per cent unpredictable and had no special method or formula."

p, Darryl F. Zanuck; d, John Ford; w, Nunnally Johnson (based on the play by Jack Kirkland and the novel by Erskine Caldwell); ph, Arthur C. Miller; ed, Barbara McLean; m, David Buttolph; art d, Richard Day, James Basevi; set d, Thomas Little.

Drama   **Cas.**   **(PR:A   MPAA:NR)**

TOBOR THE GREAT**   (1954) 77m Dudley/REP bw

Charles Drake *(Dr. Ralph Harrison)*, Karin Booth *(Janice Roberts)*, Billy Chapin *(Gadge Roberts)*, Taylor Holmes *(Dr. Nordstrom)*, Steven Geray *(Man with Glasses)*, Henry Kulky *(Paul)*, Franz Roehn *(Karl)*, Hal Baylor *(Max)*, Alan Reynolds *(Gilligan)*, Peter Brocco *(Dr. Gustav)*, Norman Field *(Commissioner)*, Robert Shayne *(1st General)*, Lyle Talbot *(Admiral)*, Emmett Vogan *(1st Congressman)*, William Schallert *(Johnston)*, Helen Winston *(Secretary)*, Jack Daly, Maury Hill *(Scientists)*.

An 11-year-old kid becomes closely attached to the robot (unimaginatively named "Tobor", or robot spelled backwards) invented by his grandfather, Holmes. Though most of the plot concerns the relationship between the boy, the inventor, and the robot, this robot has feelings. Some anti-communist propaganda seeped its way in when Holmes and Chapin were captured by communists. Of course "Tobor" managed to rescue them, only to be rewarded with an eternal existence in space, for fear the thing might become a menace. Aimed solely at arousing sentiment.

p, Richard Goldstone; d, Lee Sholem; w, Goldstone, Phillip MacDonald (based on a story by Carl Dudley); ph, John L. Russell, Jr.; m, Howard Jackson; ed, Basil Wrangell.

Fantasy   **Cas.**   **(PR:AA   MPAA:NR)**

TOBRUK½**   (1966) 107m Gibraltar/UNIV c

Rock Hudson *(Maj. Donald Craig)*, George Peppard *(Capt. Kurt Bergman)*, Nigel Green *(Col. John Harker)*, Guy Stockwell *(Lt. Max Mohnfeld)*, Jack Watson *(Sgt.-Maj.Tyne)*, Norman Rossington *(Alfie)*, Percy Herbert *(Dolan)*, Liam Redmond *(Henry Portman)*, Heidy Hunt *(Cheryl Portman)*, Leo Gordon *(Sgt. Krug)*, Robert Wolders *(Cpl. Bruckner)*, Anthony Ashdown *(Lt. Boyden)*, Curt Lowens *(German Colonel)*, Henry Rico Cattani *(Cpl. Stuhler)*, Peter Coe *(Tuareg Chieftain)*, Lawrence Montaigne *(Italian Officer)*, Robert Hoy *(British Corporal)*, Phil Adams *(S.I.G. Bocker)*, Ronnie R. Rondell *(S.I.G. Schell)*, Lee Faulkner, Fritz Fard, Joe Sargent.

Action-filled WW II drama finds Hudson in command of a small special force whose mission is to cross the Libyan desert and destroy the fuel depot at Tobruk, thus slowing the advance of Rommel's Afrika Korps on the Suez Canal. The detachment of 90 men is made up of German-born Jews and British commandos; the former pose as Nazis, the latter as prisoners of war being transported through Axis territory by them. En route, the brave column uses cunning to outwit the German and Italian contingents they encounter. They also discover that a traitor is in their midst. Hudson and fellow British officer Green suspect the Palestinian commander, Peppard (Stockwell is actually the turncoat), but despite the internal conflict, they pull together to successfully complete their mission–though only four men survive. This well-paced, tension-filled effort was produced at a cost of a about $6 million. Yuma, Arizona, and El Centro, California, stood in for the North African desert. The screenplay was written by actor-writer Gordon, who also plays a small role.

p, Gene Corman; d, Arthur Hiller; w, Leo V. Gordon; ph, Russell Harlan, (aerial ph) Nelson Tyler, (Techniscope, Technicolor); m, Bronsilau Kaper; ed, Robert C. Jones; art d, Alexander Golitzen, Henry Bumstead; set d, John McCarthy, Oliver Emert; makeup, Bud Westmore; stunts, John Daheim.

War (PR:A MPAA:NR)

TOBY TYLER*** (1960) 96m Disney/BV c

Kevin Corcoran (*Toby Tyler*), Henry Calvin (*Ben Cotter*), Gene Sheldon (*Sam Treat*), Bob Sweeney (*Harry Tupper*), Richard Eastham (*Col. Sam Castle*), James Drury (*Jim Weaver*), Barbara Beaird (*Mlle. Jeanette*), Dennis Joel (*Mons. Ajax*), Edith Evanson (*Aunt Olive*), Tom Fadden (*Uncle Daniel*), Ollie Wallace (*Bandleader*), Mr. Stubbs (*Himself*), The Flying Viennas, The Jungleland Elephants, The Marquis Family, The Ringling Brothers Clowns: "Eddie Spaghetti" Emerson, Abe "Korky" Goldstein, Duke Johnson, and Harry Johnson.

Another one of those Disney pictures that is beyond the limitations of time, having as much relevance today or 20 years from now as it did when first released back in 1960. The subject matter is every kid's dream (and probably that of many adults): running away from home to join the circus. Little Corcoran goes through a period of rejection at the farm home of his aunt and uncle; for relief, he hooks up with the traveling circus, getting a job as an assistant to somewhat dishonest Sweeney, the concession stand operator. He is brought into the exotic world of the circus, with all its eccentric characters, its excitement, and wild animals. Corcoran even gets a chance to become a hero when called upon to perform a horseback trick. By the end, the tot discovers that his family really does care about him, and has, in fact, been trying to contact him, but because Sweeney did not want to lose the money he was getting for Corcoran (a finder's fee), he never gave the boy his letters. Corcoran returns to the farm, having grown through his experiences with the circus. A little wiser, he has learned that it takes all types of people to make up the world-a world he has encountered in microcosm in the circus. Juvenile star Corcoran had already earned a considerable following for his work in such Disney pictures as THE SHAGGY DOG and OLD YELLER, and picked up a nickname, "Moochie," as a result of his role in a Disney TV serial. His lovable chimpanzee companion in TOBY TYLER, Mr. Stubbs, was spotted first by Disney while doing a send up of Jack Benny's violin playing on the comedian's television program. Among the other casting innovations for this picture was the screen "introduction" of Ollie Wallace as the circus bandleader–Wallace had been a longtime contributor to Disney films as a composer and conductor.

p, Bill Walsh; d, Charles Barton; w, Walsh, Lillie Hayward (based on the novel boy James Otis Kaler); ph, William Snyder (Technicolor); m, Buddy Baker; ed, Stanley Johnson; art d, Carroll Clark, I. Stanford Jolley; set d, Emile Kuri, Fred MacLean; cos, Chuck Keehne, Gertrude Casey; spec eff, Ub Iwerks; m/l, "Biddle-Dee-Dee," Diane Lampert, Richard Loring; makeup, Pat McNalley.

Drama **Cas.** (PR:AAA MPAA:NR)

TODAY* (1930) 80m Majestic bw

Conrad Nagel (*Fred Warner*), Catherine Dale Owen (*Eve Warner*), Sarah Padden (*Emma Warner*), John Maurice Sullivan (*Henry Warner*), Judith Vosselli (*Marian Garland*), Julia Swayne Gordon (*Mrs. Farrington*), William Bailey (*Gregory*), Edna Marion (*Gloria Vernon*), Robert Thornby (*Telka*), Drew Demarest (*Pierre*).

A very poor adaptation of a play that hit the New York stage in 1913, this film presents Nagel as a man who goes broke playing the stock market–an experience that was not unfamiliar to Americans at the time when this picture was released. Owen, Nagel's wife, doesn't adapt easily to the changes in their financial situation, and after initially trying to soldier through, gives up and falls in with bad company. All of which leads to her being shot by her husband; however, she awakes to discover it was all just a bad dream. By taking the easy way out, this picture disappoints in a big way.

d, William Nigh; w, Seton I. Miller, Abraham Schomer, George Broadhurst (based on the play by Schmomer, Broadhurst); ph, James [Wong] Howe; art d, Albert D'Agostino.

Drama (PR:A MPAA:NR)

TODAY I HANG** (1942) 67m PRC bw

Walter Wolf [Woolf] King (*Jim O'Brien*), Mona Barrie (*Martha Courtney*), William Farnum (*Warden Burke*), Harry Woods (*Henry Courtney*), James Craven (*Joseph Rand*), Michael Raffetto (*Roger Lanning*), Sam Bernard (*Slick Pheeney*), Robert Fiske (*Detective Johnson*), Paul Scardon (*Hobbs*).

King plays a man framed with a murder rap and destined to hang, but Barrie and company do everything possible to make sure that his fate is different. The stay in jail puts King in contact with an interesting assortment of characters, not the least of whom is likable warden Farnum. Woods and Craven, who have managed to get their hands on a stolen necklace, provide plenty of evil scheming.

p, George R. Batcheller; d, Oliver Drake, George Merrick; w, Drake; ph, Edward Lindin; ed, Charles Hankel.

Crime/Drama (PR:A MPAA:NR)

TODAY IT'S ME...TOMORROW YOU!**½ (1968, Ital.) 95m
P.A.C./Splendid c (OGGI A ME DOMANI A TE!)

Montgomery Ford [Brett Halsey], Bud Spencer [Carlo Pedersoli], William Berger, Wayde Preston, Tatsuya Nakadai.

Halsey, an Indian, has been falsely accused of his wife's murder. Accompanied by a bunch of gunslingers, he goes searching for the man who has done him wrong. Exceptional cinematography and a script aimed at efficiency make this an above-average spaghetti western.

p, Franco Cucca; d, Tonino Cervi; w, Cervi, Dario Argento; ph, Sergio d'Offizi.

Western (PR:C MPAA:NR)

TODAY WE LIVE**½ (1933) 113m MGM bw

Joan Crawford (*Diana Boyce-Smith*), Gary Cooper (*Richard Bogard*), Robert Young (*Claude*), Franchot Tone (*Ronnie Boyce-Smith*), Roscoe Karns (*McGinnis*), Louise Closser Hale (*Applegate*), Rollo Lloyd (*Major*), Hilda Vaughn (*Eleanor*).

A star cast, a great director, and William Faulkner's original story fail to raise this above an ordinary triangle love story set against WW I. Crawford, a British woman devoted to hedonism, is having a fling with Young, a fellow officer of Crawford's brother, Tone. The two men serve together in the Royal Navy and are best pals. Crawford believes that Young may be the man of her dreams but she has to alter her opinions when Cooper enters the picture. He's an American stude student and her heart flutters when she meets him. Cooper joins the U.S. Air Corps, goes off to fly in the battle over France, and the news comes back that he's been killed. Crawford is destroyed, but Young is still waiting in the wings, so she returns to him and they rekindle their affair. Although Tone is her brother, when Crawford and Young have some squabbles, Tone supports Young because he feels that Crawford is not being aboveboard with Young. Crawford's life is beginning to fall apart. Her father had died at the start of the picture, and now the man she loves has supposedly been killed. Young and Tone are running a torpedo boat in the Atlantic and Crawford works with an ambulance corps so she can be closer to Tone and Young. Cooper comes back, the news of his death having been greatly exaggerated. When he sees that Crawford is now living unmarried with Young, he is shocked. The airman and the sailors have a spirited rivalry between them, and Cooper eventually takes Tone and Young up in the air for a hair-raising ride. Then Tone asks Cooper to come to sea with him on one of their raids. The boat only has one torpedo and requires the captain to launch the missile from up close, then turn 180 degrees and hightail it out of there. Cooper sees that sea duty is just as dangerous as what he does in the wild blue yonder. Young loses his vision in a battle and both he and Tone decide that Cooper is the one man who can bring Crawford happiness. But Cooper has volunteered for a suicide mission that requires him to attack a German ship on his own. Before Cooper can fly out on the mission, Tone and Young take their boat to sea and ram the enemy ship with their torpedo. They lose their lives in the process and Cooper returns to earth and Crawford. They are reunited in love but both understand what Tone and Young did in order to secure their love for each other. Cooper was loaned by Paramount, and Tone arrived from New York's Group Theatre. Two years after this, Crawford and Tone were married for four stormy years. The Faulkner story had no women in it so the Crawford character was purely the imagination of the scripters. Terrific aerial photography on the order of HELL'S ANGELS, also directed by Hawks, who was coming off SCARFACE when he did this. While Tone and Young make some attempt at British accents, Crawford doesn't, and the result is unbalanced, which is sort of what happened when Robert Redford refused to even try an accent in OUT OF AFRICA.

p&d, Howard Hawks; w, Edith Fitzgerald, Dwight Taylor, William Faulkner (based on the story "Turn About" by Faulkner); ph, Oliver T. Marsh; ed, Edward Curtis; art d, Cedric Gibbons; cos, Adrian.

Drama (PR:C MPAA:NR)

TODAY WE LIVE, 1963 (SEE: DAY AND THE HOUR, THE, 1963, Fr.)

TODD KILLINGS, THE* (1971) 93m NG c (AKA: A DANGEROUS FRIEND; SKIPPER)

Robert F. Lyons (*Skipper Todd*), Richard Thomas (*Billy Roy*), Belinda Montgomery (*Roberta*), Barbara Bel Geddes (*Mrs. Todd*), Sherry Miles (*Amata*), Joyce Ames (*Haddie*), Holly Near (*Norma*), James Broderick (*Sam Goodman*), Gloria Grahame (*Mrs. Roy*), Fay Spain (*Mrs. Mack*), Edward Asner (*Fred Reardon*), Michael Conrad (*Detective Shaw*), Guy Wilkerson (*Elderly Man*), Sugar Ray Robinson (*Police Officer*), Meg Foster, Mike Rupert, Billy Bowles, Jason Wingreen, Forrest Lewis, Georgene Barnes, Sherry Lynn Diamant, Tanis Montgomery, Clete Roberts, Morgan Sterne, George Murdock, Harry Lauter, Eddie Firestone, Eve Brent, William Lucking, Frank Webb, Sandy Brown Wyeth, Robert Williamson, Jack Riley, Barbara Mallory.

Lyons plays a severely disturbed 23-year-old "teenager" who possesses a strange power (much of it sexual) over a bunch of teens in a small California town. In between his hanging out with his young followers, he kills one of his dates, an action which forces him to commit two more murders to cover his trail. However, justice prevails in the end in this film which attempts to delve into the psychology of youth, but winds up as a long list of cliches. The only question it raises is why actors like Grahame, Bel Geddes, and Asner would ever appear in trash like this. It was originally to have been produced and directed by Abby Mann, who also contributed the original, uncredited screenplay, but a disagreement with the studio resulted in his departure from the project, which turned out to be the last film produced by National General.

p&d, Barry Shear; w, Dennis Murphy, Joel Oliansky (based on a story by Mann Rubin); ph, Harold E. Stine (Panavision, Technicolor); m, Leonard Rosenman; ed, Walter Thompson; art d, Arthur Lonergan; set d, James Payne; makeup, Jack P. Wilson.

Horror/Drama (PR:O MPAA:R)

TOGETHER**½ (1956, Brit.) 52m British Film Institute/Connoisseur bw

Michael Andrews, Eduardo Paolozzi, Valy, Denis Richardson, Cecilia May.

A depressing experimental tale, heavily and darkly poetic, about a pair of mute dockworkers from London's East End who fall in love and live together in their silent world. One is accidentally killed by some cruel and insensitive young people and ends up floating helplessly down the river. A commendable effort by 25-year old director Mazzetti, a British Film Institute student, which received praise at the Cannes Film Festival.

d, Lorenza Mazzetti; w, Denis Horn; ph, Walter Lassally; m, Daniele Paris; ed, Lindsay Anderson.

Drama (PR:A MPAA:NR)

TOGETHER AGAIN*** (1944) 93m COL bw

Irene Dunne (Anne Crandall), Charles Boyer (George Corday), Charles Coburn (Jonathan Crandall, Sr.), Mona Freeman (Diana Crandall), Jerome Courtland (Gilbert Parker), Elizabeth Patterson (Jessie), Charles Dingle (Morton Buchanan), Walter Baldwin (Witherspoon), Fern Emmett (Lillian), Frank Puglia (Leonardo), Janis Carter (Miss Thorn), Adele Jergens (Gloria LaVerne), Edwin Mills (Potter Kid), Virginia Sale (Secretary), Jessie Arnold, Isabel Withers, Virginia Brissac (Women), Sam Flint, Ferris Taylor, Fred Howard, Charles Marsh (Men), Carole Mathews, Shelley Winters, Adelle Roberts, Ann Loos (Girls), Carl "Alfalfa" Switzer (Elevator Boy), Jimmy Lloyd (Master of Ceremonies), Rafael Storm (Artist), Nina Mae McKinney (Maid), Ralph Dunn, James Flavin (Policemen), Constance Purdy, Jody Gilbert (Fat Women), Wally Rose (News Cameraman), Charles Arnt (Clerk), Paul Burns, Milton Kibbee (Workmen), Nora Cecil (Woman at Recital), Dudley Dickerson (Porter), Hobart Cavanaugh (Perc Mather), Jimmy Carpenter, Billy Lord, Bobby Alden (Newsboys), Billy Newell (Cab Driver).

An endearing comedy which stars Dunne as the mayor of a small Vermont town who inherited her position five years earlier upon the death of her husband. She retains the position more out of family honor than political aspirations. She soon becomes the target of a cupid's arrow shot by her father-in-law, Coburn. When lightning strikes a statue of Dunne's dead husband and knocks off its head, Coburn takes this as a sign to find his daughter-in-law another husband. He sends her off to New York to hire a sculptor, Boyer, and hopefully fall in love. At Dunne's first meeting with Boyer, the sculptor, thinking she is one of his models, asks her to take off her clothes. Not surprisingly, she is offended and returns to Vermont. He follows and agrees to sculpt the statue. Romance soon blossoms between the pair, but not without complications. Dunne's daughter, Freeman, mistakenly assumes Boyer is in love with her, while Dunne makes a pitch for Freeman's teenage boy friend, Courtland. When Courtland finally works up the courage to kiss Dunne, the entire situation goes haywire. By the finale Dunne and Boyer are rightfully paired as are Freeman and Courtland. TOGETHER AGAIN doesn't take itself too seriously, nor does it make any attempts at social relevance. What results is a lightweight dose of fun and humor.

p, Virginia Van Upp; d, Charles Vidor; w, Van Upp, F. Hugh Herbert (based on a story by Stanley Russell, Herbert Biberman); ph, Joseph Walker; m, Werner R. Heymann; ed, Otto Meyer; md, M.W. Stoloff; art d, Stephen Goosson, Van Nest Polglase; set d, Ray Babcock; cos, Jean Louis.

Comedy (PR:A MPAA:NR)

TOGETHER BROTHERS*** (1974) 94m FOX c

Ahmad Nurradin (H.J.), Anthony Wilson (Tommy), Nelson Sims (A.P.), Kenneth Bell (Mau Mau), Owen Pace (Monk), Kim Dorsey (Gri Gri), Ed Bernard (Mr. Kool), Lincoln Kilpatrick (Billy Most), Glynn Turman (Dr. Johnson), Richard Yniguez (Vega), Mwako Cumbuka (Strokes McGee), Frances Williams (Mama Wes), Craig Campfield (Maria), Bessie Griffin (Rev. Brown), Lynne Holmes (Sugar), Danny Big Black (Armstrong), Gloria Calomee (Alice Martin), Charles Lemons (Matthew), Joe Zapata (Chicano), Leah Ward (Clutie), William Dagg (Desk Officer), Roberta Ester (Nurse),

Ernest Boyd (Harry), John Jennings (Policeman), Lane Mitchell (Dude), Angela Gibbs (Francine), Howard Picard (Police Detective).

When a well-liked police officer, Bernard, is murdered, the 15-year-old leader of a Galveston, Texas, gang made up of blacks and Chicanos gathers his buddies to track down the deranged killer. The only witness is the gang leader's 5-year-old brother, and while the killer tries to point the gang out of the way, the other boys are able to gain enough clues to see that murderer is put behind bars. Bril Brilliant performances by young, inexperienced actors help make this picture work: Nurradin as the gang leader and Wilson as his younger brother are particularly effective, infusing the story with an energetic intensity. Songs include: "Somebody's Gonna Off the Man," "Honey, Can't Ya See" (Barry White, Gene Page, sung by White), "People of Tomorrow are the Children of Today," (White, Page, sung by The Love Unlimited Orchestra).

p, Robert L. Rosen; d, William A. Graham; w, Jack De Witt, Joe Greene (based on a story by De Witt); ph, Philip Lanthrop, Charles Rosher (DeLuxe Color); m, Barry White; ed, Stanley E. Johnson; cos, Raymond H. Summers.

Drama (PR:C MPAA:PG)

TOGETHER FOR DAYS*½ (1972) 84m TFD/Olas c (AKA: BLACK CREAM)

Clifton Davis (Gus), Lois Chiles (Shelley), Northern Calloway (Calvin), Leonard Jackson (Phil), Gisela Caldwell (Karen), Woodie King (Jerry), Liz Wright (Miriam), Ben Jones (Douglas), Andrea Frye (Sister Sonji), Gilbert Lewis (Big Bubba), Sam Jackson (Stan), Brooke Clift (Officer Hanratty), Sherman Perkins (Officer Murchinson), Scott Childress (1st Policeman), Michael Hatfield (2nd Policeman), Emmanuel Hall (Reporter), J.E. Nation (Museum Guard), Dennis Henry (1st Sponsor), Robert Hill (2nd Sponsor), Eileen Gordon (Party Hostess), Frank Hines (Shelley's Dance Partner), Brad Blaisdell (Hippie), Georgia Allen (Gus' Mother), Mimi Honce (Wig Lady).

A love affair between a black male and a white female is at the center of this independently produced feature. The problems that arise for them are due primarily to the intolerant reactions of blacks to their interracial romance, and though this exploration of black bigotry is an interesting switch, it isn't enough to carry the film. Wallowing in banal dialog, all of the characters appear unflatteringly and are worthy of little interest. The woman, played by Chiles, is made to look so subservient that her mate, Davis, comes off looking repulsively macho. Neither performance has much sparkle, nor do any of the others offered.

p, Robert S. Buchanan; d, Michael Shultz; w, William B. Branch (based on a story by Lindsay Smith); ph, Donald H. Hudgins (DeLuxe Color); m, Coleridge-Taylor Perkinson; ed, Marshall M. Borden; art d, Carlton Moulette.

Drama (PR:C MPAA:PG)

TOGETHER IN PARIS (SEE: PARIS WHEN IT SIZZLES, 1964)

TOGETHER WE LIVE*½ (1935) 70m COL bw

Willard Mack (Hank), Ben Lyon (Max), Esther Ralston (Jenny), Sheila Mannors (Mary), Hobart Bosworth (Col. Dickenson), Wera Engels (Sonia), Charles Sabin (George), William Bakewell (Billy), Claude Gillingwater (Dick), William V. Mong (Johnny), Richard Carle (Charlie), Lou Tellegen (Bischofsky), Carlyle Moore, Jr (Arthur).

A San Francisco family is torn apart by a general strike in this film which places the blame squarely on Red agitators. Patriarch Mack is a dyed-in-the-wool American patriot, but his two oldest boys get mixed up with Communists. Tensions rise and violence erupts before a group of Civil War veterans gives the Reds their comeuppance. Scripter, director, and star Mack died shortly after the production was completed, delaying the film's release.

d&w, Willard Mack; ph, Roy Overbaugh; ed, Arthur Hilton.

Drama (PR:A MPAA:NR)

TOILERS OF THE SEA*½ (1936, Brit.) 83m Beaumont/COL bw

Cyril McLaglen (Gilliatt), Mary Lawson (Deruchette), Ian Colin (Peter Caudray), Andrews Engelmann (Capt. Clubin), Walter Sondes (Rataine), Wilson Coleman (Lethierry), William Dewhurst (Landois).

A pallid film adaptation of Victor Hugo's violently melodramatic novel about the captain of the first steamship, played here by Engelmann. He jumps ship for personal gain and leaves McLaglen in command. Some picturesque Channel Islands locations are the best part of this otherwise heartless film, and poetically so, for it was to these islands that author Victor Hugo fled in exile for 18 years after protesting the restoration of the Second Empire in France in 1851.

p, L.C. Beaumont; d, Selwyn Jepson, Ted Fox; w, Jepson (based on the novel Toilers of the Sea by Victor Hugo); ph, D.P. Cooper.

Adventure (PR:A MPAA:NR)

TOKYO AFTER DARK**   (1959) 80m Nacriema/PAR bw

Michi Kobi (Sumi), Richard Long (Sgt. Robert Douglas), Lawrence Dobkin (Maj. Bradley), Paul Dubov (Jesse Bronson), Teru Shimada (Sen-Sei), Robert Okazaki (Store Proprietor), Carlyle Mitchell (Mr. Johnson), Frank Kumagai (Nakamura), John Brinkley (2nd GI), Edo Mito (Kojima), Lowell Brown (1st GI), Don Keigo Takeuchi (Toshio), Jerry Adler (Sgt. Williams), Butch Yamamoto (Priest), Nobu McCarthy.

Based on an actual event, this picture presents Long as an American soldier stationed in Japan who has taken a sincere interest in that country's culture, even taking a Japanese fiancee. His behavior varies greatly from the usual bullheaded antics of the troops stationed in Japan, but when he accidentally shoots and kills a Japanese youth, Long becomes the center of controversy. The Japanese use him as an example of the cruel actions the American soldiers are known for, leaving Long in a rather sticky situation. Though the premise has the makings of an intriguing story, the film soon becomes a boring discussion of what Long plans to do. The problem is he doesn't do anything; he just talks about it, which doesn't make for very interesting viewing.

p, Norman T. Herman, Marvin Segal; d, Herman; w, Herman, Segal; ph, William Marguilies; m, Alexander Courage; ed, Robert Lawrence.

Drama   **(PR:A   MPAA:NR)**

TOKYO FILE 212*½   (1951) 84m RKO bw

Florence Marly (Steffi Novac), Robert Peyton [Lee Frederick] (Jim Carter), Katsu kaika Haida (Taro), Reiko Otani (Taro's Girl), Tatsuo Saito (Taro's Father), Satoshi Nakamura (Oyama), Suisei Matsui (Joe), Byron Michie (Jeffrey), Hoirachiro Okawa, Jun Tazaki, Dekao Yokoo, Hideto Hayabusa, Gen Shimizu, Maj. Richard W.N. Childs, USAR, Cpl. Stuart Zimmerly, USA, Pvt. James Lyons, USA, Lt. Richard Finiels, USA.

Though a colorful atmosphere is created through the photography of the backstreets and nightspots of Tokyo, the lack of a concrete story keeps this picture from being anything but moderate entertainment. The plot concerns U.S. agent Peyton's efforts to curb communist activities in Japan during the Korean War. Unfortunately, this film doesn't amount to much beyond the beautifully captured setting.

p, George Breakston, Dorrell McGowan; d&w, Dorrell and Stuart McGowan (based on a story by Breakston); ph, Herman Schopp, m, Albert Glasser; ed, Martin G. Cohn; art d, Seigo Shindo; m/l, "Oyedo Boogie," Yasuo Shimizu, Shizuo Yoshikawa (performed by Ichimaru and the Tainosuke Mochizuki Band).

Spy Drama   **(PR:A   MPAA:NR)**

TOKYO JOE**   (1949) 88m Santana/COL bw

Humphrey Bogart (Joe Barrett), Alexander Knox (Mark Landis), Florence Marly (Trina), Sessue Hayakawa (Baron Kimura), Jerome Courtland (Danny), Gordon Jones (Idaho), Teru Shimada (Ito), Hideo Mori (Kanda), Charles Meredith (Gen. Ireton), Rhys Williams (Col. Dahlgren), Lora Lee Michel (Anya), Kyoko Kama (Nani-San), Gene Gondo (Kamikaze), Harold Goodwin (Maj. Loomis), James Cardwell (MP Captain), Frank Kumagai (Truck Driver), Tetsu Komai (Takenobu), Otto Han (Hara), Yosan Tsuruta (Goro).

Bogart is a former Air Corps hero who returns to Tokyo years after deserting his wife Marly, mistakenly believing her to have died in a Japanese concentration camp. When he arrives at "Tokyo Joe's," the bar he used to co-own with Shimada, that Marly is alive, remarried to lawyer Knox, and living with a 7- year-old daughter, Michel. He tracks Marly and her husband down, learns that Michel is really his daughter, and becomes determined to win back his ex-wife's love. He enters a business deal with former Japanese secret service head Hayakawa, in which he is to run an airline franchise that ships goods across the border. Bogart is actually forced into the deal when Hayakawa threatens to reveal the fact that Marly made wartime propaganda broadcasts. Marly, however, insists she got involved with the broadcasts only to save the life of her child. When Bogart learns that part of the airplane shipment is three Japanese war criminals, he tries to back out. Hayakawa, however, takes Michel as a hostage in order to guarantee safe passage for the criminals. Before Bogart can safely land the plane, the criminals hijack it and fly on to another airport, but are apprehended by alert military police. Since the criminals are arrested, Bogart fears for the life of Michel. He tracks his daughter to Hayakawa's cellar hideout and, after a highly charged judo match with bodyguard Mori, he winds up in a shootout with Hayakawa. He is shot in the back by the abductor, but manages to fill Hayakawa with lead before breathing his last breath. In sacrificing his life, Bogart saves the life of his child. The second of four pictures produced by Bogart's Santana company and released by Columbia, TOKYO JOE failed to live up to the expectations of many critics. His harshest detractors even stated that TOKYO JOE would have been nothing but an overlooked B picture without Bogart's involvement, a criticism that could also be leveled at CASABLANCA. Although compelling and well-crafted, it was on par with neither the previous Santana film, KNOCK ON ANY DOOR, nor the following one, IN A LONELY PLACE, chiefly because it lacked a director with the talent of Nicholas Ray at the helm. Practically the entire list of technical credits remained unchanged,

however, from Anthiel's provocative score to Peterson's art direction and Louis' costumes, with the only new face being cameraman Lawton, who supplied some superb low-key compositions.

p, Robert Lord; d, Stuart Heisler; w, Cyril Hume, Bertram Millhauser, Walter Doniger (based on a story by Steve Fisher); ph, Charles Lawton, Jr.; m, George Antheil; ed, Viola Lawrence; md, Morris W. Stoloff; art d, Robert Peterson; set d, James Crowe; cos, Jean Louis; m/l, "These Foolish Things (Remind Me of You)," Jack Strachy, Harry Link, Holt Marvell 'Eric Maschwitz'; makeup, Clay Campbell.

Drama   **(PR:A   MPAA:NR)**

TOKYO ROSE**   (1945) 69m PAR bw

Lotus Long (Tokyo Rose), Byron Barr (Pete Sherman), Osa Massen (Greta Swanson), Don Douglas (Timothy O'Brien), Richard Loo (Col. Suzuki), Keye Luke (Charlie Otani), Grace Lem (Soon Hee), Leslie Fong (Wong), H.T. Tsiang (Caung Yu), Larry Young (Jack Martin), William Challee (Mike Koyak), Chris Drake (Frank), James Millican (Al Wilson), Al Ruiz (Mel), Blake Edwards (Joe).

Barr plays a prisoner of war who is selected to be interviewed by the infamous Tokyo Rose (Long), the dangerously seductive voice that many WW II veterans will never forget. Given the opportunity, Barr makes a shambles of her broadcast studio and escapes with the aid of an Irish journalist. Determined to revenge the death of one of his brothers in arms (Rose is indirectly to blame), Barr decides to kidnap the broadcaster. With the aid of members of the Tokyo underground, he goes about accomplishing this task. Though it suffers in development and believability, this is a well-paced, well-handled film.

p, William H. Pine, William C. Thomas; d, Lew Landers; w, Geoffrey Homes, Maxwell Shane (based on the idea by Whitman Chambers); ph, Fred Jackman, Jr.; m, Rudy Schrager; ed, Henry Adams, Howard Smith; art d, F. Paul Sylos; set d, Glenn Thompson.

War   **(PR:A   MPAA:NR)**

TOKYO STORY**   (1972, Jap.) 136m Shochiku-Ofuna/New Yorker bw (TOKYO MONOGATARI)

Chishu Ryu (Shukishi Hirayama), Chiyeko Higashiyama (Tomi Hirayama), So Yamamura (Koichi), Kuniko Miyake (Fumiko), Haruko Sugimura (Shige Kaneko), Nobuo Nakamura (Kurazo Kaneko), Kyoko Kagawa (Kyoko), Setsuko Hara (Noriko), Shiro Osaka (Keiso), Eijiro Tono (Sanpei Numata), Teruko Nagaoka (Yone Hattori), Zen Murase (Minoru), Mitsuhiro Mori (Isamu), Hisao Toake (Osamu Hattori), Toyoko Takahashi (Shukichi Hirayama's Neighbor), Mutsuko Sakura (Patron of The Oden Restaurant), Toru Abe (Railroad Employee), Sachiko Mitani (Noriko's Neighbor), Junko Anan (Beauty Salon Assistant), Yoshiko Togawa, Ryoko Mizuki (Beauty Salon Clients).

Of Yasujiro Ozu's 53 films, only a handful have received U.S. release and 34 of these were silents directed before 1936, many of which have been destroyed. TOKYO STORY, released in Japan in 1953, did not receive its U.S. release until 19 years later, and is the finest of Ozu's pictures to be sent to Western audiences. It concerns itself with Ozu's favorite theme--the family. Ryu and Higashiyama are an elderly couple who live in Onomichi, a small town near Hiroshima. With their youngest daughter Kagawa, they travel to Tokyo to visit the rest of their family--their son Yamamura, a doctor, and their daughter, Sugimura, a beauty salon operator. The children are too busy to meet with their parents so they send them to a resort. After a sleepless night in the noisy resort, the parents decide to return to Tokyo. Before leaving, however, Higashiyama spends a night with her son's widow, Hara, and Ryu visits some old drinking buddies. Hara, unlike Higashiyama's own children, extends her friendship to the saddened old woman. The next morning Ryu and Higashiyama terminate their visit and board a train home. They are forced to stop when Higashiyama becomes ill. She is brought to the nearby home of her youngest son, Osaka, where she dies. The entire family comes to her funeral and after a short while return to their own lives. Only Hara stays on, consoling Ryu who accepts his wife's death and the loneliness that must follow. Like so many of Ozu's films there is practically no camera movement, no flashy editing, and only a few camera angles that rise above the knee-high, or tatami level. This is not because Ozu doesn't care about visuals but because he is paying reverence to the characters and their story. Not surprisingly, Ozu is often called "boring" by Western audiences who want their car crashes and gun blasts in lethal doses, but for those audiences who want to experience Japanese culture, Ozu's films are a must. If, as some people say, a destroyed France could be rebuilt from the films of Jean Renoir, then Japanese culture could be recreated from the work of Ozu.

p, Takeshi Yamamoto; d, Yasujiro Ozu; w, Ozu, Kogo Noda; ph, Yuhara Atsuta; m, Takanori Saito; ed, Yoshiyasu Hamamura; prod d, Tatsuo Hamada, Itsuo Takahashi; art d, Hamada, Takahashi; cos, Taizo Saito.

Drama   **(PR:A   MPAA:NR)**

TOL'ABLE DAVID**   (1930) 65m COL bw

Richard Cromwell (*David Kinemon*), Noah Beery, Sr (*Luke*), Joan Peers (*Esther Hatburn*), Henry B. Walthall (*Amos Hatburn*), George Duryea [Tom Keene] (*Alan Kinemon*), Edmund Breese (*Hunter Kinemon*), Barbara Bedford (*Rose Kinemon*), Helen Ware (*Mrs. Kinemon*), Harlan E. Knight (*Iska*), Peter Richmond [John Carradine] (*Buzzard*), James Bradbury, Sr (*Galt*), Richard Carlyle (*Doctor*).

Except for the addition of sound, this thin remake of the 1922 First National silent of the same name departed little from the original. In fact, being an action picture, the addition of voices hampered more than helped the unwinding of the story. Cromwell, in his first "real" screen role (he had worked as an extra on KING OF JAZZ), plays the youngest member of a hillbilly family that is feuding with an unruly bunch known as the Hatburns. Though warned to keep out of the proceedings, Cromwell shows his stuff when he has to retrieve a U.S. Mail bag that has been pilfered by the Hatburns. Columbia mounted something of a publicity campaign touting Cromwell's screen debut, making the dubious claim that he was discovered hanging around the studio. Conjecture had it that his appearance at Columbia had more to do with a bit of media manipulation cooked up by the studio and a journalist. Nevertheless, Cromwell turned in a credible performance.

d, John Blystone; w, Benjamin Glazer (based on the story by Joseph Hergesheimer); ph, Ted Tetzlaff; ed, Glen Wheeler; art d, Edward Jewell.

Drama   (PR:A   MPAA:NR)

TOLL OF THE DESERT*   (1936) 58m COMM bw

Fred Kohler, Jr (*Bill Carsos*), Betty Mack (*Jean*), Roger Williams (*Tom Collins*), Ted Adams (*Tegue*), Edward Cassidy (*Dr. Streeter*), Tom London (*Joe Carson*), John Elliott, Earl Dwire (*Gangsters*), George Chesebro ("*One Eye*"), Billy Steuer (*Gangster*), Blackie Whiteford, Blackjack Ward, Iron Eyes Cody, Herman Hack, Budd Buster, Ace Cain.

Kohler plays a lawman who must bring to justice Williams, the father who left him at the age of four and is now the head of a ruthless gang. Kohler does some neat stunts, but the rest of the acting is just dreadful. The script and direction are little better.

p, William Berke; d, Lester Williams [William Berke]; w, Miller Easton (based on a story by Allen Hall); ph, Robert Cline; ed, Arthur A. Brooks.

Western   (PR:A   MPAA:NR)

TOM*   (1973) 83m Challenge/Four Star International c (AKA: MOTHERS, FATHERS AND LOVERS; THE AMERICAN LOVE THING)

Greydon Clark (*Jim*), Tom Johnigarn (*Makimba*), Aldo Ray (*Lt. Stans*), Jock Mahoney (*Sgt. Berry*), Jacquin Cole (*Nancy*), Bambi Allen (*Bobbie*), Pamela Corbett (*Tina*), Fred Scott (*Mr. Washington*), Carl Craig (*Willie*).

Director, writer, and star Clark must at least get some credit for trying to make a meaningful piece of film. The only problem is he obviously knew nothing about filmmaking, including plot development, setting up shots, or conveying a sense of realism to his actors. Apparently he managed to get enough money together to make a film, and with it took up issues such as Vietnam vets, racial relations, and romance. The result is a total catastrophe.

p, Mardi Rustam, Robert Brown; d, Greydon Clark; w, Clark, Alvin L. Fast; ph, Louis Horvath (Eastmancolor); ed, Earl Watson, Jr.; m/l, "Tom," Sheldon Lee.

Drama   (PR:O   MPAA:R)

TOM BROWN OF CULVER**½   (1932) 82m UNIV bw

Tom Brown (*Tom Brown*), H.B. Warner (*Dr. Henry Brown*), Slim Summerville (*Elmer "Slim" Whitman*), Richard Cromwell (*Bob Randolph III*), Ben Alexander (*Cpl. John Clarke*), Sidney Toler (*Maj. Wharton*), Russell Hopton (*Legion Doctor*), Andy Devine (*Mac the Call Boy*), Willard Robertson (*Capt. White*), Norman Phillips, Jr (*Ernest Carruthers*), Tyrone Power, Jr (*Donald MacKenzie*), Kit Guard (*K.O. Mooney the Boxer*), Betty Blythe (*Dolores Delight*), Frank Hagney (*Fight Manager*), Eugene Pallette (*Deaf Diner*), Lew Kelly (*Daffy Diner*), Phil Dunham (*Counterman*), Kit Wain, Dick Winslow, Marty Roubert, Matty Roubert (*Cadets*), Alan Ladd, The Personnel of Culver Military Academy Units of Indiana.

A touching story about the transformation of Brown from an unruly kid into an outstanding cadet at Culver Military Academy. He believes (as everyone else does) that his father died a war hero, and the American Legion puts him through military school. However, his father turns out not to be a dead but a deserter. This knowledge almost shatters the young boy, but the support of his pals from the academy helps him to get back on his feet and to accomplish the feat of getting his dad an honorable discharge. The development of the plot gets bogged down in the routines of the school, but the performances by the young actors are nonromanticized, making these scenes seem very realistic. This was the first time the face of Hollywood idol Tyrone Power was to grace the screen; he is seen here in a minor role as one

of the upper-classmen cadets. This film was remade by Universal as SPIRIT OF CULVER (1939).

p, Carl Laemmle, Jr.; d, William Wyler; w, Tom Buckingham, Clarence Marks (based on the story by George Green, Dale Van Every); ph, Charles Stumar; ed, Frank Gross.

Drama   (PR:AA   MPAA:NR)

TOM BROWN'S SCHOOL DAYS**   (1940) 86M The Play's The Thing/RKO bw (AKA: ADVENTURES AT RUGBY)

Sir Cedric Hardwicke (*Dr. Thomas Arnold*), Freddie Bartholomew (*East*), Jimmy Lydon (*Tom Brown*), Josephine Hutchinson (*Mrs. Arnold*), Billy Halop (*Flashman*), Polly Moran (*Sally*), Hughie Green (*Walker*), Ernest Cossart (*Squire Brown*), Alec Craig (*Old Thomas*), Gale Storm (*Effie*), Barlowe Borland (*Old Grimes*), Forrester Harvey (*Coachman*), Leonard Willey (*Farmer Jenkins*), Ian Fulton (*Old Brooke*), Charles Smith (*Digges*), Dick Chandler (*Tadpole*), Paul Matthews (*Leyton*), John Collum (*Sidney*), Harry Duff (*Westcott*).

An uneventful adaptation of the childhood classic that was never really good movie material to begin with. Lydon plays the young lad forced to leave his comfortable home to attend a school filled with ruthless hooligans. He manages to make a few friendships and learns to defend himself, getting through to the point where he's almost a well-disciplined young man. Hardwicke is the schoolmaster with the unflattering task of maintaining order and developing a sense of respect in the boys. He goes by the philosophy of sparing the rod, which has unbelievable (in a literal sense) results. TOM BROWN'S SCHOOL DAYS was remade in 1951, and previously filmed in 1914.

p, Gene Towne, Graham Baker; d, Robert Stevenson; w, Walter Ferris, Frank Cavett, Towne, Baker, Stevenson (based on the novel by Thomas Hughes); ph, Nicholas Musuraca; m, Anthony Collins; ed, William Hamilton; art d, Van Nest Polglase; spec eff, Vernon L. Walker.

Drama   Cas.   (PR:AA   MPAA:NR)

TOM BROWN'S SCHOOLDAYS**   (1951, Brit.) 93m Talisman/UA bw

John Howard Davies (*Tom Brown*), Robert Newton (*Dr. Arnold*), Diana Wynyard (*Mrs. Arnold*), Hermione Baddeley (*Sally Harrowell*), Kathleen Byron (*Mrs. Brown*), James Hayter (*Old Thomas*), John Charlesworth (*East*), John Forrest (*Flashman*), Michael Hordern (*Wilkes*), Max Bygraves (*Coach Guard*), Francis de Wolff (*Squire Brown*), Amy Veness (*Mrs. Wixie*), Brian Worth (*Judd*), Rachel Gurney (*Mrs. Arthur*), Michael Brennan (*Black Bart*), Neil North (*Diggs*), Glyn Dearman (*Arthur*), Ben Aris (*Tadpole*), Geoffrey Goodheart, Michael Ward, Peter Madden, Anthony Doonan, Peter Scott, Robin Dowell, John Campbell, Gabriel Woolf, Roland Dallas, David Jenks, Derek Stephens.

Saccharine screen version of the Thomas Hughes classic, with the emphasis placed upon the battles between new boy at the school, Davies, and the brute he must contend with, Forrest. A new headmaster is also introduced, portrayed by Newton. He deals with problems in a manner the boys are not very accustomed to; that is, he treats his students as human beings instead of as untrained animals. Davies is almost too likable in the lead role, while his counterpart is likewise almost too nasty, but this helps to play up the heavy dramatics. This film is a remake of TOM BROWN'S SCHOOL DAYS (1940).

p, Brian Desmond Hurst; d, Gordon Parry; w, Noel Langley (based on the novel by Thomas Hughes); ph, C. Pennington-Richards, Raymond Sturgess; m, Richard Addinsell; ed, Kenneth Heeley-Ray; md, Muir Mathieson; art d, Frederick Pusey.

Drama   (PR:AA   MPAA:NR)

TOM, DICK AND HARRY***½   (1941) 86m RKO bw

Ginger Rogers (*Janie*), George Murphy (*Tom*), Alan Marshal (*Dick Hamilton*), Burgess Meredith (*Harry*), Joe Cunningham (*Pop*), Jane Seymour (*Ma*), Leonore Lonergan (*Babs*), Vicki Lester (*Paula*), Phil Silvers (*Ice Cream Man*), Betty Breckenridge (*Gertrude*), Sid Skolsky (*Announcer*), Edna Holland (*Miss Schlom*), Gus Glassmire (*Music Store Proprietor*), Netta Packer (*Salesclerk*), Sarah Edwards (*Mrs. Burton*), Ellen Lowe (*Matron*), William Halligan (*Mr. Burton*), Joe Bernard (*Judge*), Gertrude Short (*Bridge Matron*), Edward Colebrook (*Stalled Car Driver*), Gayle Mellott (*Brenda*), Dorothy Lloyd (*Gypsy Oracle*), Berry Kroeger (*Boy Lead*), Lurene Tuttle (*Girl Lead*), Knox Manning (*Radio Announcer*), William Alland (*Newsreel Announcer*), Jack Briggs (*Boy*), Maurice Brierre (*French Waiter*), Jane Patten, Theodore Ramsey, Tommy Seidel, Jane Woodworth.

A charming comedy-fantasy that served as Rogers' follow-up to her Oscar for KITTY FOYLE and was distinguished by an Oscar-nominated script, sharp direction, and a bubbly, joyous feeling. Rogers is a dizzy telephone operator who is being courted by three men and can't make up her mind who to choose. She dreams of marrying a millionaire but succumbs to the advances of Murphy, a sharp automobile salesman. Before they can tie the knot, she falls for Meredith, a happy-go-lucky man with a gift of gab, so she also accepts his offer to marry. Then she meets millionaire Marshal and he goes head over heels for her and makes a marriage proposal. Engaged to this trio, Rogers realizes she has to make a decision, but she can't bear to say no to any of them. Rogers has daydreams about the way it might be with each of her suitors (the fantasy shots are excellent and very funny) and eventually settles for Meredith. Murphy came over from MGM and Marshal had been the exclusive property of David O. Selznick. Both men do well but Meredith's sympathetic charm sways Rogers and the audience and he steals every scene in which he appears. Producer Sisk, who had made the RKO budget unit into a tremendous success, left the studio and moved to Paramount after this picture, one of his best. This also was the last film for Rogers under her long-term contract. Director Kanin had worked with Rogers on BACHELOR MOTHER and they had a good relationship, which showed on screen. There are some uncomfortable coy moments by Rogers, but that's a nit-pick. In a small role as the newsreel announcer, note Bill Alland, who was the newspaper reporter tracking Kane's life in CITIZEN KANE. This story was used again in a 1956 musical with Jane Powell starring as THE GIRL MOST LIKELY. In his third movie, Phil Silvers scores as an obnoxious ice cream salesman.

p, Robert Sisk; d, Garson Kanin; w, Paul Jarrico; ph, Merrit Gerstad; m, Roy Webb; ed, John Sturges; art d, Van Nest Polglase, Mark Lee Kirk; set d, Darrell Silvera; cos, Renie; spec eff, Vernon L. Walker; m/l "Tom Collins," Webb, Gene Rose; makeup, Mel Burns.

Comedy **Cas.** **(PR:A MPAA:NR)**

TOM HORN*½** (1980) 98m First Artists-Solar/WB c

Steve McQueen *(Tom Horn)*, Linda Evans *(Glendolene Kimmel)*, Richard Farnsworth *(John Coble)*, Billy Green Bush *(Joe Belle)*, Slim Pickens *(Sam Creedmore)*, Peter Canon *(Assistant Prosecutor)*, Elisha Cook *(Stable Hand)*, Roy Jenson *(Mendenhour)*, James Kline *(Arlo Chance)*, Geoffrey Lewis *(Walter Stoll)*, Harry Northrup *(Burke)*, Steve Oliver *(Gentleman Jim Corbett)*, Bill Thurman *(Ora Haley)*, Bert Williams *(Judge)*, Bobby Bass *(Corbett's Bodyguard)*, Mickey Jones *(Brown's Hole Rustler)*, B.J. Ward *(Cattle Baron)*, Richard Kennedy *(John Cleveland)*, Larry Strawbridge *(MacGregor)*.

A realistically photographed tale which brings the legend of infamous western killer Tom Horn to the screen. Born in 1861 in Missouri, Horn soon gained fame as the man who negotiated the surrender of Apache chief Geronimo. He also served as one of Teddy Roosevelt's Rough Riders and as a Pinkerton detective who single-handedly captured the notorious Hole-in-the-Wall outlaw Peg Leg Watson. His life soon took a wrong turn, however, when he hired himself out to some Cheyenne, Wyoming, cattle barons who were determined to put an end to their range wars. It is at this point in Horn's life that McQueen chose to begin his film. McQueen (without the elegant Tom Horn mustache) is a cowboy stuck in the transition period from the Old West to the modern, industrialized, mechanized West. No longer interested in working for the Pinkertons, McQueen heads for Cheyenne and meets rancher Farnsworth. McQueen accepts an offer to end the interference caused by local rustlers and homesteaders. McQueen acts far more violently than Farnsworth and his fellow ranchers had intended, killing excessive numbers of people with a bloodthirsty vengeance. When he proves to be nothing but a troublesome embarrassment for the ranchers, they arrange to have him framed for the murder of a teenage boy. McQueen insists that he is innocent but, at the urging of local politicians, he is sent to the gallows. Although TOM HORN strays from the facts somewhat, the film still has a sense of realism. Rather than film the actual facts of Tom Horn's life, McQueen (as the film's executive producer) chose to bring the legend to the screen. Instead of painting Horn as a western hero, the gunslinger is portrayed more as a old timer who is destroyed by his inability to adapt to the "New West." As in other films which deal with this transition (Sam Peckinpah's masterful RIDE THE HIGH COUNTRY, 1961, THE SHOOTIST, 1976, and THE GREY FOX, 1983, which starred Farnsworth) one can't help but be impressed by the gunslinger's fight to retain old values and a sense of nostalgic individuality. McQueen's Horn is a murderer and does deserve to be hanged according to the laws of the "New West," but he is still subscribing to the laws of the Old West. Not surprisingly, TOM HORN struck out at the box office, as did all westerns of that period, with the possible exception of the Clint Eastwood vehicle THE OUTLAW JOSEY WALES (1976). Although TOM HORN is riddled with script and technical problems, it failed not because of them but because of audience disinterest in the western genre. The film's production history alone would be enough to sink most films. McQueen, who headed the First Artists company, had originally intended for his second self-produced feature (his first was AN ENEMY OF THE PEOPLE, from the Henrik Ibsen play) to be a version of Harold Pinter's play "Old Times." After a series of disagreements, McQueen decided to adapt Will Henry's novel *I, Tom Horn*, but that idea was abandoned in favor of a script based on Horn's memoirs which were penned while in prison. In the meantime, David Carradine and Robert Redford has also become interested in the legend of Tom Horn. Carradine's project eventually became the made-for-TV film MR. HORN, which costarred Richard Widmark and Karen Black. Redford, rather than battle another big box-office name, dropped out of the running. McQueen's first choice as director was Don Siegel, whose exceptional talents would surely have made TOM HORN a great film. Siegel, however, was soon replaced by Elliott Silverstein (CAT BALLOU, 1965, and A MAN CALLED HORSE, 1970). Silverstein, too, pulled out and was replaced by James Guercio (whose only other credit is ELECTRA GLIDE IN BLUE, 1973). By this time, McQueen had dropped out as producer in favor of becoming executive producer and replaced himself with Fred Weintraub. After only 10 days of shooting, Guercio became the third former director of TOM HORN, being replaced by McQueen himself. It wasn't long, however, before director number five replaced McQueen. This time the man behind the helm was the practically unknown William Wiard, whose chief claim to fame had been a succession of intolerable made- for-TV films--THE GIRL, THE GOLD WATCH AND EVERYTHING, SKI LIFT TO DEATH, HELP WANTED: MALE, and a number of episodes of the "Rockford Files"--hardly the qualifications that a director of Don Siegel's stature could have brought to the film. TOM HORN also went through three screenwriters before McQueen settled on Shrake, working closely with him on the final draft. The most memorable aspect of the film, however, is not the direction or the screenplay, but the stupendous photography by John Alonzo. He beautifully captures the turn-of-the-century atmosphere that pervaded the Old West down to the last detail, with the help of art director Hobbs, set decorator Simpson, and costumer Bayless. Describing McQueen's authentic western attire, Bayless is quoted in William F. Nolan's biography *McQueen*: "We worked out his chaps-and-suspenders look. Scruffy, but real. And no fancy gun rig, just a Colt jammed into his belt at belly level the way a lot of the old westerners used to do it...We studied a great many photographs of the era, and followed the basic styles." Shot on location in Mescal and Nogales, Arizona, and in the San Rafael Valley.

p, Fred Weintraub; d, William Wiard; w, Thomas McGuane, Bud Shrake (based on *Life of Tom Horn, Government Scout and Interpreter* by Tom Horn); ph, John Alonzo (Panavision, Technicolor); m, Ernest Gold; ed, George Grenville; art d, Ron Hobbs; set d, Rick Simpson; cos, Luster Bayless.

Western **Cas.** **(PR:O MPAA:R)**

TOM JONES***** (1963, Brit.) 131m Woodfall/Lopert c

Albert Finney *(Tom Jones)*, Susannah York *(Sophie Western)*, Hugh Griffith *(Squire Western)*, Edith Evans *(Miss Western)*, Joan Greenwood *(Lady Bellaston)*, Diane Cilento *(Molly Seagrim)*, George Devine *(Squire Allworthy)*, David Tomlinson *(Lord Fellamar)*, Joyce Redman *(Mrs. Waters/ Jenny Jones)*, George A. Cooper *(Fitzpatrick)*, Rosalind Atkinson *(Mrs. Miller)*, Angela Baddeley *(Mrs. Wilkins)*, Peter Bull *(Thwackum)*, James Jackson *(Mr. Seagrim)*, Rachel Kempson *(Bridget Allworthy)*, Wilfrid Lawson *(Black George)*, Rosalind Knight *(Mrs. Fitzpatrick)*, Jack MacGowran *(Partridge)*, John Moffatt *(Square)*, Patsy Rowlands *(Honour)*, David Warner *(Blifil)*, Redmond Phillips *(Lawyer Dowling)*, Mark Dignam *(Lieutenant)*, Avis Bunnage *(Landlady at George Inn)*, Lynn Redgrave *(Susan)*, Jack Stewart *(MacLachlan)*, Michael Brennan *(The Jailor at Newgate)*, Michael MacLiammoir *(Narrator)*, Freda Jackson *(Mrs. Seagrim)*, James Cairncross *(Parson Supple)*, Julian Glover *(Northerton)*.

A lusty, bawdy, and rollicking comedic adaptation of Fielding's sprawling novel that justly won four Oscars as Best Picture, for Best Screenplay, Best Direction, and Best Score, and was nominated for six other Academy Awards. It begins in the West Country of England and uses a series of silent film devices (undercranking, titles, various cinematic wipes) to establish the tone of the picture at once. Devine is a local squire who finds an abandoned baby in his bed. He assumes that the child must be the result of a coupling between his unwed servants, Redman and MacGowran. Devine fires the two and plans to raise the boy as his own, a playmate for his son, Warner. Flash forward and the child has grown up to be Finney, a manly and popular young fellow with no trace of guile in his nature but an underlying glint in his eye. Finney spends a great deal of his time trifling with many distaff members, including Cilento, the local slut. He dearly loves the prim, chaste York who is the daughter of wealthy Griffith, an old lecher, a hypocrite, and an incurable rakehell. Finney's roisterings cause York's aunt, Evans, to push her to marry Warner, a sleaze who is twice the cad Griffith is. Warner secretly envies Finney's happy-go-lucky ways and his effortless abilities at attracting the opposite sex. It would appear that York and Warner will be wed, but she balks and tells one and all that Finney is the man for her. Warner is publicly embarrassed at having been thus rejected and enlists his avaricious teachers, Moffat and Bull, to help him heap abuse on Finney and accuse him of a crime he didn't commit. Devine believes that bad rap and sends Finney off to London in shame. Finney takes it with a shrug and goes toward the big city. On his trip, he meets Redman, now using another name, and the two of them engage in one of the most famous scenes in movies as they sit across from each other, devouring meat and fish and vegetables in an orgy of passion prior to jumping into bed to fulfill their wanton desires. (The fact that she may or may not be his mother is implied in the undercurrent of the hysterical sequence.) Once in London, Finney meets Greenwood, a peeress, and he adjusts his style of lovemaking to meet her more refined needs. At the same time, she attempts to teach him some of the gentlemanly ways he'll need in order to succeed in London. Back in the West Country, York is pining away for the love of Finney and leaves the area with Knight, a cousin trapped in a bad marriage to Cooper. Once there, Tomlinson puts a move on York and Cooper arrives, convinced our lad has done the deed with Knight. There's a battle between Finney and the husband who thinks he's been cuckolded, and Cooper is hurt in the fracas. Warner, still smarting over York's rejection, frames Finney on a robbery rap and he is placed in the shadows of the noose. Just before they slip the rope around his neck, Warner is shown to be the perpetrator of the phony charges. Innocent, Finney is welcomed back into Devine's arms and now the youth learns that Redman wasn't his mother after all. It was Devine's late sister, Kempson, who bore the lad, thus making Finney his blood nephew. The picture concludes with Finney and York look forward to their marriage. Cutting down and molding Fielding's huge 1749 episodic novel was a gargantuan task and while screenwriter Osborne, who was well known for his sense of social realism in LOOK BACK IN ANGER and other works, may have seemed like an odd choice, he more than succeeded with his writing. Richardson and Osborne had both come from the "kitchen sink" school of British movies and a Restoration comedy was an odd dish for their plates at first glance. Not to worry. Their work was superior and, besides winning U.S. Academy Awards, they also took British Film Academy Awards for Best Film, Best British Film, and Best Screenplay. Purists balked at Richardson's use of stop-motion photography, freeze frames, actors giving asides to the camera, and a host of other techniques from the Keystone Kops era. They were wrong because, as anachronistic as it seemed, the techniques worked for the overall movie. It's silly, warm, touching, funny and, in the end, was an enormous success with audiences around the world. Several set pieces stand out in memory: a huge stag hunt at the estate of Griffith; the Georges Feydeau-type bedroom farce at the inn; but, most of all, the famous Redman-Finney scene which, while it shows nothing sexual–just two people staring into each others' eyes as they rip food apart and stuff it in their faces–remains among the most erotic few minutes in cinema. Finney was appearing on the Broadway stage in "Luther" when this was released in New York and people who attended both the play and the film were struck by his chameleon ability to submerge himself in either role. The attitude of the movie was always tongue-in-cheek but never satirical. It was fun from the first frame, when the style was set in a re-creation of an old melodrama with title cards, frantic spinet music, and a close-up of the baby, with a supercilious narrator (MacLiammoir) telling us: "Tom Jones, of whom the opinion of all was that he was born to be hanged." From that moment we are plunged into the tale and the sly direction, such as when Finney puts his cap over the camera lens before he beds down Redman, never intrudes. The fact that such an historical epic should have been such a popular winner was annoying to intellectuals who decried the alterations in Fielding. What it actually did was set millions to reading the author's work and Fielding became a best seller again, more than two centuries after the book was published. Oscar nominations were given to Finney, Griffith, Cilento, Redman, and Evans. A 1917 silent version also exists.

p&d, Tony Richardson; w, John Osborne (based on the novel by Henry Fielding); ph, Walter Lassally (Eastmancolor); m, John Addison; ed, Antony Gibbs; md, Addison; prod d, Ralph Brinton; art d, Ted Marshall; set d, Josie MacAvin; cos, John McCorry; makeup, Alex Garfath.

Historical Comedy/Adventure Cas.   **(PR:O MPAA:NR)**

TOM SAWYER***   (1930) 85M PAR bw

Jackie Coogan (Tom Sawyer), Junior Durkin (Huckleberry Finn), Mitzi Green (Becky Thatcher), Lucien Littlefield (Teacher), Tully Marshall (Muff Potter), Clara Blandick (Aunt Polly), Mary Jane Irving (Mary), Ethel Wales (Mrs. Harper), Jackie Searl (Sid), Dick Winslow (Joe Harper), Jane Darwell (Widow Douglass), Charles Stevens (Injun Joe), Charles Sellon (Minister), Lon Puff (Judge Thatcher).

A remake of the 1917 silent version of Samuel Clemens' classic, this succeeds on several levels, not the least of which was casting teenager Coogan in the lead. Coogan lives with his aunt, Blandick, and yearns to be out of school and getting into mischief. His best pal is Durkin and the two boys dream of a life away from the small Missouri town. Green is the little girl who tags along (this role was larger in the film than in the book). All of the famous scenes are handled well, such as Coogan and Durkin listening to themselves being eulogized when it's thought that they have drowned in the Mississippi, the moment when Coogan uses his brains to convince some other boys to whitewash the fence he has been assigned to, and the fright when they are menaced in the denouement by Stevens. The following year, Paramount made HUCKLEBERRY FINN with the same cast and then a budget film called TOM SAWYER, DETECTIVE in 1938. Durkin was excellent and had a promising career in front of him that was tragically cut short when he and Coogan's father were both killed in an automobile accident in 1935. The story of Tom and Huck was also made in 1937 as THE ADVENTURES OF TOM SAWYER, again in a Roumanian-French production in 1969 under the same title, then musically in 1973, as well as a straight telling of the tale on TV in 1973. Tom and Huck remain two of the most durable lads in literature and Huck's story served as the basis for the Tony Award-winning musical "Big River" on Broadway in the 1980s. Blandick made a career out of playing aunts and will best be recalled for an "auntie" role as "Em" in THE WIZARD OF OZ.

p, Louis D. Lighton; d, John Cromwell; w, Sam Mintz, Grover Jones, William Slavens McNutt (based on The Adventures of Tom Sawyer by Mark Twain); ph, Charles Lang; ed, Alyson Shaffer; art d, Bernard Herzbrun, Robert O'Dell.

Historical Comedy   **(PR:AAA MPAA:NR)**

TOM SAWYER, 1938 (SEE: ADVENTURES OF TOM SAWYER, THE, 1938)

TOM SAWYER**½   (1973) 100m Reader's Digest/UA c

Johnny Whitaker (Tom Sawyer), Celeste Holm (Aunt Polly), Warren Oates (Muff Potter), Jeff East (Huckleberry Finn), Jodie Foster (Becky Thatcher), Lucille Benson (Widder Douglas), Henry Jones (Mister Dobbins), Noah Keen (Judge Thatcher), Dub Taylor (Clayton), Richard Eastham (Doc Robinson), Sandy Kenyon (Constable Clemens), Joshua Hill Lewis (Cousin Sidney), Susan Joyce (Cousin Mary), Steve Hogg (Ben Rogers), Sean Summers (Billy Fisher), Kevin Jefferson (Joe Jefferson), Page Williams (Saloon Girl), Kunu Hank (Injun Joe), James A. Kuhn (Blacksmith), Mark Lynch (Prosecuting Attorney), Jonathan Taylor (Small Boy), Anne Voss (Girl).

A musical version marks the fourth time around for Twain's most famous novel. Bathed in nostalgia, with good songs, it still manages to fail due to Taylor's uninspired direction. It's the same tale as the other three movies but with a lilting score by the Sherman brothers, who also provided the screenplay. The problem is that there is no edge to the story and the menace never feels real because the Reader's Digest people, who co-financed this film, seemed so intent on providing family entertainment that the reality went right out of the project. Shot entirely on location in Missouri, it had a young Missouri boy, East, making his debut as Huck Finn, and the fact that he was an amateur never entered into matters as he more than managed to hold his own with TV veteran Whitaker ("Family Affair"). Perhaps the addition of the tunes was not a good idea, as they slowed down the narrative. The Sherman's songs include: "River Song" (sung on the sound track by Charley Pride), "Gratification" (sung by Whitaker, as he convinces the other boys to whitewash the fence for him), "Tom Sawyer" (sung by Celeste Holm as Whitaker's aunt), "Freebootin" (sung by Whitaker and East as they celebrate the joy of doing nothing at all), "Aunt Polly's Soliloquy" (sung by Holm), plus "If'n I Was God," "A Man's Gotta Be What He's Born to Be," "How Come?" and "Hannibal, Mo." Jeffries was nominated for an Oscar for his excellent production design, as were Donfeld's costumes, the Sherman's score and John Williams for his musical direction. Despite the tepid quality of the movie, it more than doubled its $2,500,000 cost in film rentals on the first release. Foster was only 10 years old and appearing in her third film, after having done several TV appearances for Disney. The sequel to this, HUCKLEBERRY FINN (1974), was not nearly as good.

p, Arthur P. Jacobs; d, Don Taylor; w, Robert B. Sherman, Richard M. Sherman (based on The Adventures of Tom Sawyer by Mark Twain); ph, Frank Stanley (Panavision, DeLuxe Color); m, Richard Sherman, Robert Sherman; ed, Marion Rothman; md, John Williams; prod d, Phillip Jefferies; set d, Robert DeVestel; cos, Donfeld; ch, Danny Daniels.

Musical/Historical Comedy   Cas.   **(PR:AAA MPAA:G)**

TOM SAWYER, DETECTIVE**½   (1939) 68m PAR bw

Billy Cook (Tom Sawyer), Donald O'Connor (Huckleberry Finn), Porter Hall (Uncle Silas), Phillip Warren (Jeff Rutledge), Janet Waldo (Ruth Phelps), Elisabeth Risdon (Aunt Sally), William Haade (Jupiter Dunlap/Jake Dunlap), Edward J. Pawley (Brace Dunlap), Clem Bevans (Sheriff Slocum), Raymond Hatton (Judge Tyler), Howard Mitchell (Prosecutor), Stanley Price (Clayton), Harry Worth (Dixon), Clara Blandick (Aunt Polly), Si Jenks (Farmer Sikes), Etta McDaniel (Tulip), Oscar Smith (Curfew), Monte Blue (Sheriff Walker), Foy Van Dolson (Alex Cooper).

The famous Mark Twain characters are up to their usual antics along the river, taking a little time off to go to school and help clear a preacher from a murder rap. A very plodding picture that takes far too much time to develop characters who are commonly known to start with. Some bright spots emerge in the casting, but the actors remain thwarted through incompetent handling.

d, Louis King; w, Lewis Foster, Robert Yost, Stuart Anthony (based on the characters created by Mark Twain); ph, Ted Tetzlaff; ed, Ellsworth Hoagland.

Drama/Mystery   **(PR:A MPAA:NR)**

TOM THUMB**½   (1958, Brit./U.S.) 92m Galaxy/MGM c

Russ Tamblyn (Tom Thumb), Alan Young (Woody the Piper), Terry-Thomas (Ivan), Peter Sellers (Tony), Jessie Matthews (Anna), June Thorburn (The Forest Queen), Bernard Miles (Jonathan), Ian Wallace (The Cobbler), Peter Butterworth (Kapellmeister), Stan Freberg (Voice of Noveltoon Puppets), Peter Bull (The Town Crier), Barbara Ferris (Voice of Thumbelina), Stan Freberg (Voice of Yawning Man), Dal McKennon (Voice of Con-fu-shon), Norma Zimmer (Singing Voice of Anna).

A lot of effort went into providing a realistic and entertaining--for adults as well as children--adaptation of the famous Grimm fairy tale. Unfortunately concentration was almost totally on the visuals and the song-and-dance routines, leaving out the true basis for good filmmaking, a well-developed script and the ensuing interaction between the characters. Tamblyn is a charmer as the five-inch tot to woodcutter Miles; he jumps about with unyielding grace and brings joy to just about everyone's heart. But

Terry-Thomas and Sellers see his small size as useful for their own unsavory schemes. Their attempts to take this little ball of energy from the woodcutter's cottage to a life of evil eventually fail, but not until a number of songs and forced humorous episodes are delivered. The special effects are quite good in providing the illusion of the small boy's world; in fact good enough to receive an Academy Award. The songs are likewise of high caliber, but without these two factors TOM THUMB would be a dull adaptation of a great fairy tale. Songs include: "The Yawning Song," "Tom Thumb's Tune," "Talented Shoes," "After All These Years," and "Are You a Dream?"

p&d, George Pal; w, Ladislas Foder (based on a story by The Brothers Grimm); ph, Georges Perinal (Eastmancolor); m, Douglas Gamley, Ken Jones; ed, Frank Clarke; md, Muir Mathieson; ch, Alex Romero; m/l, Peggy Lee, Fred Spielman, Janice Torre, Kermit Goell.

Fantasy   **Cas.**   **(PR:AAA MPAA:G)**

TOM THUMB*   (1967, Mex.) 79m Clasa Films Mundiales/Childhood Productions c (PULG ARCITO)

Maria Elena Marques (*Fairy Princess*), Jose Elias Moreno (*Ogre*), Cesareo Quesada (*Tom Thumb*), Paquito Fernandez, Rafael Banquells, Pablo Jorge Nava, Angel Arturo Limon, Gonzalo Carmona, Eduardo Rodriguez, Manuel Donde, Nora Veyran.

A Mexican version of the famed folk tale which strays far from its origins. Little Quesada and his six brothers stray into a forest to help their father with his woodcutting work. There, they are accosted by an ogre, Moreno, who looks upon them as lunch. Escaping his clutches, they find themselves at his home, occupied by his ugly wife and seven dirty daughters. Quesada persuades the girls to wash up and, thus transformed, they become little ladies, persuading their mother to give the boys a magic wand. The wand changes the mother into a beautiful princess and the cannibalistic ogre into a vegetarian gentleman. Suitable for teaching children about what's next to godliness, the film was released in Mexico in 1958. A ridiculously dubbed English-language version was released in the U.S. nine years later.

p, Armando Orive Alba; d, Rene Cardona; w, Cardona, Adolfo Torres Portillo (based on the story "Le Petit Pouce" by Charles Perrault); ph, Jose Ortiz Ramos (Eastmancolor); m, Raul Lavista; ed, Jorge Bustos; set d, Roberto Silva.

Fantasy   **(PR:A MPAA:NR)**

TOMAHAWK*   (1951) 82m UNIV c (GB: BATTLE OF POWDER RIVER)

Van Heflin (*Jim Bridger*), Yvonne De Carlo (*Julie Madden*), Preston Foster (*Col. Carrington*), Jack Oakie (*Sol Beckworth*), Alex Nicol (*Lt. Rob Dancy*), Tom Tully (*Dan Costello*), Ann Doran (*Mrs. Carrington*), Rock Hudson (*Burt Hanna*), Susan Cabot (*Monahseetah*), Arthur Space (*Capt. Fetterman*), Stuart Randall (*Sgt. Newell*), John Peters (*Pvt. Osborne*), Russell Conway (*Maj. Horton*), Raymond Montgomery (*Blair Streeter*), Dave Sharpe (*Pvt. Parr*), David H. Miller (*Capt. Ten Eyck*), John War Eagle (*Red Cloud*), Regis Toomey (*Smith*), Sheila Darcy (*Woman*), James A. Hermstad, Robert J. T. Simpson, Abner George, Archie N. MacVicar, Floyd Sparks, Edward Tullis, Adiel F. Wahl (*Men*), Chief American Horse, Chief Bad Bear (*Indians*).

A more sympathetic treatment of Indians than normal for pictures of this era, the blame for unwarranted slaughter falling on prejudice from both sides. Heflin plays a scout in a Dakota fort, where he tries to convince the officers in charge that there is a way to settle their problems with the Sioux other than through bloodshed. But the tactics used by Nicol–kill as many Indians as possible–are more then Heflin can contend with. After a small band of cavalry is wiped out (known in the history books as the Fetterman Massacre) there seems to be one obvious outcome. Attempts at drawing sympathy for the Sioux include depicting the plight of Cabot, the maiden who is left alone after all her people are mercilessly killed. Nicol's first starring role.

p, Leonard Goldstein; d, George Sherman; w, Silvia Richards, Maurice Geraghty (based on a story by Daniel Jarrett); ph, Charles P. Boyle (Technicolor); m, Hans J. Salter; ed, Danny B. Landres; art d, Bernard Herzbrun, Richard H. Riedel.

Western   **(PR:A MPAA:NR)**

TOMAHAWK AND THE CROSS, THE
    (SEE: PILLARS OF THE SKY, 1956)

TOMAHAWK TRAIL, THE, 1950   (SEE: IROQUOIS TRAIL, THE, 1950)

TOMAHAWK TRAIL*   (1957) 60m Bel-Air/UA bw (GB: MARK OF THE APACHE)

Chuck Connors (*Sgt. Wade McCoy*), John Smith (*Pvt. Reynolds*), Susan Cummings (*Ellen Carter*), Lisa Montell (*Tula*), George Neise (*Lt. Jonathan Davenport*), Robert Knapp (*Pvt. Barrow*), Eddie Little (*Johnny Dogwood*), Frederick Ford (*Pvt. Macy*), [Harry] Dean Stanton (*Pvt. Miller*).

Renegade Apaches make things tough for a cavalry outpost. First, they steal all the horses of a column, which must make its way back to the fort by foot. Once there, they discover the entire population dead from an Indian attack. This leaves Neise, an unseasoned West Point graduate, in control. But he just doesn't know how to handle the trouble, so up steps Connors, the tough sergeant who at least knows which way is up.

p, Howard W. Koch; d, Robert Parry [Lesley Selander]; w, David Chandler; ph, William Margulies; m, Les Baxter; ed, John F. Schreyer, John A. Bushelman.

Western   **(PR:A MPAA:NR)**

TOMB OF LIGEIA, THE*   (1965, Brit.) 80m Alta Vista/AIP c (AKA: TOMB OF THE CAT)

Vincent Price (*Verden Fell*), Elizabeth Shepherd (*Lady Ligeia Fell/Lady Rowena Trevanion*), John Westbrook (*Christopher Gough*), Oliver Johnston (*Kenrick*), Derek Francis (*Lord Trevanion*), Richard Vernon (*Dr. Vivian*), Ronald Adam (*Parson*), Frank Thornton (*Peperel*), Denis Gilmore (*Livery Boy*), Penelope Lee.

Director Corman meets Poe again, but the results don't measure up to the quality of the earlier MASQUE OF THE RED DEATH. Price plays the country gentleman whose rather mysterious wife passes on, leaving poor Vincent in a transfixed state thinking that his dead wife's spirit will always be around. He preserves the body, and isn't beyond necrophilia, which exists even when he takes on new wife Shepherd, the exact replica of the first one. The girl soon discovers Price's fixation on the earlier wife, but can't convince her husband that he's only been put under a spell. Though it does have its moments, this is not a very convincing or suspenseful film. Price goes through his role as if he really were hypnotized; he's pretty stiff to say the least.

p&d, Roger Corman; w, Robert Towne (based on the story "Ligeia" by Edgar Allan Poe); ph, Arthur Grant (Colorscope, Pathe Color); m, Kenneth V. Jones; ed, Alfred Cox; md, Jones; art d, Colin Southcott; spec eff, Ted Samuels; makeup, George Blackler.

Horror   **(PR:C MPAA:NR)**

TOMB OF THE CAT   (SEE: TOMB OF LIGEIA, THE, 1965, Brit.)

TOMB OF THE LIVING DEAD   (SEE: MAD DOCTOR OF BLOOD ISLAND, THE, 1969)

TOMB OF THE UNDEAD*   (1972) 59m Millenium c

Duncan McLeod, John Dennis, John Dullaghan, Lee Frost, Lewis Sterling, Marland Procktor, Susan Charney.

A bunch of zombies, one-time convicts, are up to their usual antics of preying on the living. A ridiculous picture that doesn't come up with a good way for raising the things from the dead; formaldehyde on their dead bodies acts as the reactor. From there it's all downhill.

p, H. A. Milton; d&w, John Hayes; ph, Phil Kenneally.

Horror   **(PR:O MPAA:NR)**

TOMB OF TORTURE*   (1966, Ital.) 88m Virginia/Trans-Lux bw (AKA: METEMPSYCOSE)

Annie Albert (*Anna Darnell/Countess Irene*), Thony Maky [Adriano Mikahtoni] (*Dr. Darnell*), Mark Marian [Marco Mariani] (*George Dickson*), Elizabeth Queen [Flora Caroselli] (*Countess Elizabeth*), William Gray, Bernard Bly, Emy Eko, Terry Thompson, Fred Pizzot, Antonio Boccacci.

Albert is a young woman who is haunted by recurring fantasies that she is a countess who was killed 20 years earlier. She is helped by a caring journalist who takes her to the decrepit castle where the murder took place. She falls into a trance and wanders into a torture chamber run by the countess' former butler who believes Albert to be the dead woman. Watching this picture is about all the torture most of us can handle.

p, Frank Campitelli; d, Anthony Kristye [Antonio Boccacci]; w, Kristye, Johnny Seemonell [Giovanni Simonelli]; ph, William Grace, Campitelli; m, Armando Sciascia; ed, Jean-Pierre Grasset, Gaby Vital.

Horror   **(PR:O MPAA:NR)**

TOMBOY*   (1940) 70m MON bw

Marcia Mae Jones (*Pat*), Jackie Moran (*Steve*), Grant Withers (*Kelly*), Charlotte Wynters (*Frances*), George Cleveland (*Matt*), Marvin Stephens (*Harry*), Clara Blandick (*Martha*), Gene Morgan (*1st Tramp*).

A harmless tale of young love which travels the familiar path of a city girl (Jones) who comes to the country and falls head over heels for a down-to-earth country boy (Moran). Their romance blooms even in the midst of a storm of objections from the boy's crotchety uncle, but by the finale all is well.

p, William T. Lackey; d, Robert McGowan; w, Dorothy Reid, Marion Orth;

ph, Harry Neumann; ed, Russell Schoengarth.

Romance   Cas.   (PR:A MPAA:NR)

TOMBOY AND THE CHAMP*½   (1961) 92m Signal/UNIV c

Candy Moore (*Tommy Jo*), Ben Johnson (*Uncle Jim*), Jesse White (*Windy Skiles*), Jess Kirkpatrick (*Model T. Parson*), Christine Smith (*Aunt Sarah*), Paul Bernath (*Jaspar Stockton*), Norman Sherry (*Fowler Stockton*), John Carpenter (*Fred Anderson*), Wally Phillips (*Hi Fi Club Announcer*), Ralph Fischer (*4-H Club President*), Larry Hickie (*Curly Cone*), Rex Allen, Casey Tibbs, Jerry Naill (*Themselves*), Champy the Bull.

A teen-age ranch girl from Texas wins a prize at the county fair–a calf. She raises the animal and it helps her through a battle with polio. The animal is entered in the Chicago International Exposition where it takes the top prize, much to the youngster's delight. Her mood turns sour, however, when it is learned that the winning livestock are auctioned off and ultimately wind up in the slaughterhouse. A meat-packer with a heart of gold comes to the girl's aid and ensures the animal's safety. Popular Chicago radio host Wally Phillips has a minor role as, of course, an announcer. Okay for kids, but there's something a bit strange about the whole premise. Songs: "Get Ready with the Ribbon, Judge," "Who Says Animals Don't Cry" (Tommy Reynolds, William Lightfoot), "Barbecue Rock" (Elsie Pierce Wilkes).

p, Tommy Reynolds, William Lightfoot; d, Francis D. Lyon; w, Virginia M. Cooke (based on the story by Reynolds, Lightfoot); ph, William H. Clothier (Eastmancolor); m, Richard Shores; ed, William B. Murphy.

Drama   (PR:A MPAA:NR)

TOMBS OF HORROR   (SEE: CASTLE OF BLOOD, 1964, Fr./Ital.)

TOMBSTONE CANYON**½   (1932) 62m KBS/World Wide bw

Ken Maynard (*Ken Mason*), Cecilia Parker (*Jenny Lee*), Lafe McKee (*Col. Lee*), Sheldon Lewis (*The Phantom*), Frank Brownlee (*Alf Sykes*), Jack Clifford (*Henchman*), George Gerwing (*Clem*), Edward Piel, Sr, Jack Clifford, George Chesebro (*Henchman*), Bob Burns (*Sheriff*), Jack Kirk, Merrill McCormack, Bud McClure, Tarzan the Horse.

A fast-moving oater which has Maynard receiving more assistance than usual from femme Parker and trusty horse Tarzan in their attempts to unmask a phantom murderer who is plaguing the range, and who proves to be Maynard's father. The volatile Maynard had argued with Carl Laemmle, Jr.–the head of his usual studio, Universal–and filmed this one at Tiffany Studios using his customary Universal production crew. The histrionics and self-applied makeup of Lewis, who played The Phantom, suffice to put him in the same league as the senior Lon Chaney in this outstanding performance. Burns, who played the sheriff, later became a popular radio and movie comedian; when the film was reissued, Burns was showcased as a costar, his name occupying the position usually accorded that of Tarzan, Maynard's horse.

p, Irving Starr; d, Alan James [Alvin J. Neitz]; w, Claude Rister, Earle Snell; ph, Ted McCord; md, Val Burton; art d, Ralph M. DeLacy; set d, Eddie Boyle; cos, Elizabeth Coleman.

Western   (PR:A MPAA:NR)

TOMBSTONE TERROR*½   (1935) 58m Supreme/William Steiner bw

Bob Steele, George ["Gabby"] Hayes, Kay McCoy, Earl Dwire, John Elliott, Hortense Petro, Ann Howard, Nancy DeShon, Frank McCarroll, Artie Ortego, George Morrell, Herman Hack.

Steele and Hayes team up again to fight the bad guys in this second-rate western which has Steele being mistaken for a criminal. Another Bob Steele picture directed by his father, Robert N. Bradbury.

p, A.W. Hackel; d&w, Robert N. Bradbury.

Western   (PR:A MPAA:NR)

TOMBSTONE, THE TOWN TOO TOUGH TO DIE**½
                                       (1942) 79m PAR bw

Richard Dix (*Wyatt Earp*), Kent Taylor (*Doc Holliday*), Edgar Buchanan (*Curly Bill Brocius*), Frances Clifford (*Ruth Grant*), Don Castle (*Johnny Duane*), Clem Bevans (*Tadpole*), Victor Jory (*Ike Clanton*), Rex Bell (*Virgil Earp*), Charles Halton (*Dan Crane*), Harvey Stephens (*Morgan Earp*), Chris-Pin Martin (*Chris*), Dick Curtis (*Frank McLowery*), Paul Sutton (*Tom McLowery*), Donald Curtis (*Phineas Clanton*), Wallis Clark (*Ed Schieffelin*), James Ferrara (*Billy Clanton*).

An exciting but historically inaccurate western tale which once again brings the legendary town of Tombstone, Arizona, to the screen. Dix admirably portrays Earp, a brave gunslinger who settles in the town and is soon deputized as a U.S. marshall, assisting sheriff Halton in cleaning up Tombstone. When local baddie Buchanan (as Curly Bill Brocius) accidentally kills a child in a gun battle on the street, Dix accepts the sheriff's badge. With the help of his brothers, Bell and Stephens, and dentist-gunslinger Taylor (as Doc Holliday), Dix confronts Buchanan and his gang. Dix learns

that the gang is working in cahoots with Halton and he manages to pin a stagecoach robbery on them. The rivalry between Earp and the outlaws finally comes to a head when guns smoke and bullets fly outside the O.K. Corral, felling the bad men and leaving Tombstone a law-abiding town. While the film manages to bend and twist the reality of what occurred at the O.K. Corral, it still proves to be a fast-paced entertainment. Dix comes across superbly as Earp (his first acclaimed role since 1931's CIMARRON), but as deputy Doc Holliday Taylor leaves much to be desired, coming nowhere near the sickly, drunken, mean-tempered gunfighter that he really was.

p, Harry Sherman; d, William McGann; w, Albert Shelby LeVino, Edward E. Paramore (based on the book Tombstone: *The Toughest Town in Arizona* by Walter Noble Burns); ph, Russell Harlan; ed, Carroll Lewis.

Western   (PR:A MPAA:NR)

TOMCAT, THE*   (1968, Brit.) 79m Tigon-Global/Joseph Brenner bw
                                       (GB: MINI WEEKEND)

Anthony Trent (*Tom*), Liza Rogers (*Sandra*), Veronica Lang (*Jenny*), Connie Frazer (*Tom's Mother*), Vicky Hodge (*1st Dream Sequence*), Jane MacIntosh (*Supermarket Girl*), Patti Bryant, Avril Gaynor (*Girls in Cafe Sequence*), Rosalind Elliot, Kathleen Southern (*Girls in Tube Sequence*), Maria Hauffer, Lucy Swain (*Girls in Boutique Sequence*), Eve Aubrey (*Old Hag*), Anna Palk (*Girl in Tiles Club and Cinema*), Karen Leslie (*Girl in Pub*), Nina Dwyer (*Girl on Bus*), Valerie Stanton (*Girl in Barbershop*).

Trent is trapped in a relationship with a conservative girl friend, but prefers to carry on a fantasy life which is more sexually fulfilling. He hangs around London's West End looking for someone to fit the bill, finding himself imagining sexual situations with the girls he sees on the street.

p, Tony Tenser; d, Georges Robin; w, Robin, Tenser; ph, Stanley A. Long; m, De Wolfe; ed, Roy Nevill; art d, Tony Curtis.

Comedy   (PR:O MPAA:NR)

TOMMY*½   (1975, Brit.) 111m COL c

Ann-Margret (*Nora Walker Hobbs*), Oliver Reed (*Frank Hobbs*), Roger Daltrey (*Tommy Walker*), Elton John (*Pinball Wizard*), Eric Clapton (*Preacher*), Keith Moon (*Uncle Ernie*), Jack Nicholson (*Specialist*), Robert Powell (*Capt. Walker*), Paul Nicholas (*Cousin Kevin*), Tina Turner (*Acid Queen*), Barry Winch (*Young Tommy*), Victoria Russell (*Sally Simpson*), Arthur Brown (*Priest*), Ben Aris (*Rev. Simpson*), Mary Holland (*Mrs. Simpson*), Jennifer Baker, Susan Baker, Imogen Claire (*Nurses*), Juliet King, Gillian King (*Handmaidens*), Peter Townshend, John Entwistle, Keith Moon, Roger Daltrey (*The Who*).

Who fans watch out: Ken Russell has applied his rococo meanderings to the rock opera written by Pete Townshend, ruining not only the visuals but the fine score. With its beginnings as a 1969 album by The Who, one of rock music's most successful, enduring, and ear-blistering bands, TOMMY went on to become a stage smash in England. Then Russell, with his taste for the flamboyant and meaningless, added a little Ann-Margret and Oliver Reed, cast lead singer Daltrey in the title role, and wasted a number of talents in useless cameos. The story, told entirely in song, centers on Daltrey, a "deaf, dumb, and blind boy" who enters his own little world after the death of his father. His mother (Ann-Margret) and stepfather (Reed) bring him to Nicholson for treatment, but nothing seems to help. The panacea turns out to be pinball. Daltrey beats The Pinball Wizard (Elton John) at his own game, getting the high score because he "plays by sense of smell." Eventually Daltrey breaks free and starts life anew. The Who drummer Moon is a highlight as the perverted Holiday Camp counsellor Uncle Ernie; rock guitarist Clapton continues his role as a god; Turner explodes as the Acid Queen, but comes and goes with little explanation; and Townshend, the brains behind it all, rightly is disgusted by the whole thing. His music is mauled by the vocals of Ann-Margret, Reed, and Nicholson, who can't sing a note among them. Daltrey, however, went on to work again with Russell, starring in another rock fiasco, LISZTOMANIA. One scene in TOMMY has a television screen spewing forth a flood of champagne and beans, which seems to parallel the extravagant gaseous drudge that spews forth from the movie screen. For die-hard Who fans it may hold a few moments, but otherwise forget it. Producer Robert Stigwood went on to ruin a Beatles album in SERGEANT PEPPER'S LONELY HEARTS CLUB BAND just three years later. A special multi-track sound system for theaters was developed for TOMMY by John Mosely, who, as chief audio engineer for the U.S. recording company Audio Fidelity, had guided the first disk record released in the then-new vertical/lateral stereophonic system in 1958. Songs include "Underture," "Captain Walker Didn't Come Home," "It's a Boy," "'51 is Going to Be a Good Year," "What About the Boy?" "The Amazing Journey," "Christmas," "See Me, Feel Me," "Eyesight to the Blind," "The Acid Queen," "Do You Think It's All Right?" "Cousin Kevin," "Fiddle About," "Sparks," "Pinball Wizard," "Today It Rained Champagne," "There's a Doctor," "Go to the Mirror (The Specialist)," "Tommy Can You Hear Me?" "Smash the Mirror," "I'm Free," "Miracle Cure (including "Extra, Extra")," "Sensation," "Sally Simpson," "Welcome," "Deceived," "Tommy's Holiday Camp," "We're Not Gonna Take It," "Listening to You" (Peter Townshend, John Entwistle, Keith Moon).

p, Robert Stigwood, Ken Russell; d&w, Russell (based on the musical drama by Peter Townshend, John Entwistle, Keith Moon); ph, Dick Bush, Ronnie Taylor, Robin Lehman (Metrocolor); m, Townshend, Roger Daltrey, Entwistle, Moon; ed, Stuart Baird; md, Townshend; art d, John Clark; set d, Paul Dufficey, Ian Whittaker; cos, Shirley Russell; ch, Gillian Gregory; makeup, George Blackler, Peter Robb-King.

Musical   **Cas.**   **(PR:C   MPAA:PG)**

TOMMY STEELE STORY, THE
            (SEE: ROCK AROUND THE WORLD, 1957, Brit.)

TOMMY THE TOREADOR**   (1960, Brit.) 90m Fanfare/WB-Pathe c

Tommy Steele (*Tommy Tomkins*), Janet Munro (*Amanda*), Sidney James (*Cadena, Impresario*), Bernard Cribbins (*Paco*), Noel Purcell (*Captain*), Virgilio Texera (*Parilla, Bullfighter*), Pepe Nieto (*Inspector Quintero*), Ferdy Mayne (*Lopez*), Harold Kasket (*Jose*), Kenneth Williams (*Vice-Consul*), Eric Sykes (*Martin*), Manolo Blazquez (*Matador*), Francis de Wolff (*Hotel Proprietor*), Tutte Lemkow (*Bootblack*), Warren Mitchell (*Waiter*), Charles Gray (*Gomez*), Andrea Malandrinos, Jose Valero, Edwin Richfield, Pilarin San Clemente, Michel Andel Rodriguez.

Popular singer Steele is cast as a young seafarer who winds up in Spain and gets tricked into being a bullfighter for a day. Not much of a story but a lot of Steele and his tunes. Included are "Tommy the Toreador" and "Little White Bull" (Lionel Bart, Michael Pratt, Jimmy Bennett).

p, George H. Brown; d, John Paddy Carstairs; w, Nicholas Phipps, Sid Colin, Talbot Rothwell (based on a story by Brown, Patrick Kirwan); ph, Gilbert Taylor (Technicolor); m, Stanley Black; ed, Peter Bezencenet.

Comedy/Musical   **(PR:A   MPAA:NR)**

TOMORROW***½   (1972) 103m Filmgroup bw

Robert Duvall (*Jackson Fentry*), Olga Bellin (*Sarah Eubanks*), Sudie Bond (*Mrs. Hulie*), Richard McConnell (*Isham Russell*), Peter Masterson (*Lawyer Douglas*), William Hawley (*Papa Fentry*), James Franks (*Preacher Whitehead*), Johnny Mask (*Boy*), Dick Dougherty, Effie Green, Ken Lindley, R. M. Weaver, Billy Summerford, Thomas C. Coggin.

Duvall turns in one of his many virtuoso performances as a helpful, quiet farmer in early 1900s Mississippi. He takes in an abandoned pregnant girl, falls in love with her, and helps her through the birth of her child. He marries her, only to have her die just minutes after the vows are exchanged. After raising the child for a few years, Duvall again suffers a loss as his wife's kin come for the kid. Beautifully scripted by Horton Foote who creates a realistic atmosphere of the era. Duvall and Foote were teamed again in 1983's TENDER MERCIES, which brought Oscars to both. Screenwriter Foote first did this story in 1960 for TV's "Playhouse 90." In 1968, he rewrote it as an off-Broadway play starring the two leads of the film, Duvall and Bellin (the stage-actress wife of coproducer Roebling, himself a stage actor). A first production effort for the team of Roebling and Pearlman, the latter a one-time publicist for Columbia.

p, Paul Roebling, Gilbert Pearlman; d, Joseph Anthony; w, Horton Foote (based on a story by William Faulkner); ph, Allan Green; m, Irwin Stahl; ed, Reva Schlesinger.

Drama/Romance   **Cas.**   **(PR:C   MPAA:G)**

TOMORROW AND TOMORROW**½   (1932) 80m PAR bw

Ruth Chatterton (*Eve Redman*), Robert Ames (*Gail Redman*), Paul Lukas (*Dr. Nicholas Faber*), Harold Minjir (*Samuel Gillespie*), Tad Alexander (*Christian Redman*), Walter Walker (*Dr. Walter Burke*), Arthur Pierson (*Spike*), Margaret Armstrong (*Miss Frazer*), Winter Hall (*President Adee*).

Chatterton goes outside her marriage when her husband, Ames, refuses-of is unable-to father a child. She finds Lukas, a Viennese brain surgeon, has an affair with him, and gets herself pregnant. She makes both men believe it is Ames' child, until years later when the boy falls from a horse. He is taken to Lukas, who saves the boy's life. Chatterton tells the doctor the truth, but decides to remain with her husband rather than returning to Lukas. Playwright Barry's dramadidn't work nearly as well on screen as his high-society comedies such as THE PHILADELPHIA STORY (1940), but good dialog and fine performances help to salvage this picture. Ames died before the film was released. It was Chatterton's last picture for Paramount; she was in transit to Warner Bros.

d, Richard Wallace; w, Josephine Lovett (based on the play by Philip Barry); ph, Charles Lang.

Drama   **(PR:A   MPAA:NR)**

TOMORROW AT MIDNIGHT   (SEE: FOR LOVE OR MONEY, 1939)

TOMORROW AT SEVEN**   (1933) 62m Jefferson/RKO bw

Chester Morris (*Neil Broderick*), Vivienne Osborne (*Martha Winters*), Frank McHugh (*Clancy*), Allen Jenkins (*Dugan*), Henry Stephenson (*Drake*), Grant Mitchell (*Winters*), Charles Middleton (*Simons*), Oscar Apfel (*Marsden*), Cornelius Keefe (*Henderson*), Edward J. Le Saint (*Coroner*), Virginia Howell (*Mrs. Quincey*), Gus Robinson (*Pompey*).

Morris is a mystery writer on the trail of a killer known only as the Ace of Spades. Using a playing card to call on his victims, the killer warns them that they will be killed off at a precise moment, and sure enough they are. Osborne is the daughter of one of the victims who lends a hand in Morris' investigations. McHugh and Jenkins handle the comedy well as two bumbling detectives. The producers borrowed talented director Enright from Warner Bros. and picked up the rest of the crew from World Wide Pictures, which had just gone under. RKO thought well enough of this independent production to give it the full promotional treatment the studio ordinarily reserved for its A pictures.

p, Joseph I. Schnitzer, Samuel Zierler; d, Ray Enright; w, Ralph Spence; ph, Charles Schoenbaum; ed, Rose Loewenger; art d, Edward Jewell.

Mystery   **Cas.**   **(PR:A   MPAA:NR)**

TOMORROW AT TEN**½   (1964, Brit.) 80m Mancunian/Governor bw

John Gregson (*Inspector Parnell*), Robert Shaw (*Marlow*), Alec Clunes (*Anthony Chester*), Alan Wheatley (*Bewley*), Kenneth Cope (*Sgt. Grey*), Ernest Clark (*Dr. Towers*), Piers Bishop (*Jonathan*), Helen Cherry (*Robbie*), William Hartnell (*Freddy*), Betty McDowall (*Mrs. Parnell*), Harry Fowler (*Smiley*), Renee Houston (*Mrs. Maddox*), Noel Howlett (*Specialist*), Bernadette Woodman, Marguerite McCourt (*Nurses*), Ray Smith (*Briggs*), John Dunbar (*Henry*).

Shaw kidnaps the young son (Bishop) of millionaire Clunes, locking him in a remote house with a time bomb, which is hidden in a doll. Shaw pays a visit to Clunes' mansion, demands the ransom, and then promises to cable where the boy is while on a flight to South America. A fight breaks out and Shaw is killed, without telling where he has hidden the child. The police rush to try to find him by 10 o'clock the following morning, the scheduled time of the explosion. Just minutes after the deadline they find him, the boy having deactivated the bomb by immersing the toy in water.

p, Tom Blakeley; d, Lance Comfort; w, Peter Millar, James Kelly; ph, Basil Emmott; m, Bernie Fenton; ed, John Trumper; md, Fenton; art d, Jack Shampan.

Crime   **(PR:A   MPAA:NR)**

TOMORROW IS ANOTHER DAY**   (1951) 90m WB bw

Ruth Roman (*Catherine*), Steve Cochran (*Bill Clark*), Lurene Tuttle (*Mrs. Dawson*), Ray Teal (*Mr. Dawson*), Morris Ankrum (*Hugh Wagner*), John Kellogg (*Monroe*), Lee Patrick (*Janet Higgins*), Hugh Sanders (*Conover*), Stuart Randall (*Frank Higgins*), Bobby Hyatt (*Johnny*), Harry Antrim (*Warden*), Walter Sande (*Sheriff*).

A cliche-ridden tale of a pair of fugitive lovers, Roman and Cochran, who pack their bags after the former shoots detective Sanders. Cochran, just released from prison after serving 18 years for killing his father, wrongly believes he did the shooting after Roman tries to pull one over on him. They are pursued by the police and finally caught, only to hear that Sanders cleared their name by admitting the killing was in self-defense. Warner Bros. doctored the ridiculous finale after the press preview. The original ending had the pair brought in after someone informed on them in order to receive a $1,000 reward. The district attorney failed to make a case against them, and then they were cleared by Sanders' confession. Either way the ending seems contrived, as does most of the beginning and the middle.

p, Henry Blanke; d, Felix Feist; w, Art Cohn, Guy Endore (based on the story "Spring Kill" by Endore); ph, Robert Burks; m, Daniele Amfitheatrof; ed, Alan Crosland, Jr.; md, Ray Heindorf; art d, Charles H. Clarke.

Crime Drama   **(PR:A   MPAA:NR)**

TOMORROW IS FOREVER**   (1946) 105m International/RKO bw

Claudette Colbert (*Elizabeth MacDonald Hamilton*), Orson Welles (*John MacDonald/Erich Kessler*), George Brent (*Larry Hamilton*), Lucile Watson (*Aunt Jessie*), Richard Long (*Drew*), Natalie Wood (*Margaret*), Sonny Howe (*Brian*), John Wengraf (*Dr. Ludwig*), Ian Wolfe (*Norton*), Douglas Wood (*Charles Hamilton*), Joyce MacKenzie (*Cherry*), Tom Wirick (*Pudge*), Henry Hastings (*Butler*), Lane Watson (*Hamilton's Secretary*), Michael Ward (*Baby Drew*), Jesse Graves (*Servant*), Lois Austin (*Receptionist*), Anne Loos (*Freckle-Faced Nurse*), Irving Pichel (*Commentator's Voice*), Thomas Louden (*Englishman on Ship*), Charles D. Brown (*Immigration Officer*), Milton Kibbee (*Postman*), Ann Howard, Marguerite Campbell, Betty Greco, Bobby Brooks, Barbara Bletcher (*Girl Friends*), Libby Taylor (*Maid*), Lane Chandler (*Technician*), Boyd Irwin (*Dr. Callan*), Evan Thomas (*Ship Doctor*), Buster Phelps, Frank Wyrick, Bill Dyer (*Fraternity Boys*), Helen Gerald, Nena Ruth (*Girls*), Jessie Grayson (*Servant*).

Tired variation on an old theme produced under David Lewis' International

Pictures banner. Not much to recommend here other than the debut of 6-year-old Wood and a host of superior costumes from Jean Louis. It starts around the time of WW I as Colbert and Welles are wed. The call to arms comes and Welles goes to do battle with the forces of the Kaiser. He is scarred horribly, becomes lame, and chooses to be reported as "dead" rather than face his wife and new son as a crippled, ugly man. Settling in Austria, Welles takes on a new identity and Colbert, thinking herself a widow, marries Brent and lives happily, bearing another child, Wood, and enjoying her second chance at joy. Brent runs a plant that manufactures chemicals and as luck (and plot contrivance) would have it, he hires Welles to come to the U.S. from Austria. Despite his long beard, his limp, and an attempt to disguise himself, it isn't many moments before Colbert realizes who he is. She is having her own woes with son Long, who wants nothing more than to join the Air Force and fly off to fight the new version of the Germans. With Welles knowing that Colbert knows who he is and aware of his feelings toward the son he never knew, there is every opportunity for emotional highlights in the film, but they are missed and the movie becomes a series of climaxes without enough motivation. Slow-moving, yawnable, with some restraint shown by Welles, who could have eaten everyone up in this role but didn't. Director Pichel moved the actors around as though they'd all just awakened from a nap. He also used his own voice as that of the commentator. There was nothing actually wrong with the movie but there weren't too many things which were right, either. A fine cast is wasted in a trifling story.

p, David Lewis; d, Irving Pichel; w, Lenore Coffee (based on the novel by Gwen Bristow); ph, Joseph Valentine; m, Max Steiner; ed, Ernest Nims; md, Lou Forbes; art d, Wiard B. Ihnen; cos, Jean Louis; m/l, "Tomorrow Is Forever," Steiner, Charles Tobias.

Drama   (PR:A MPAA:NR)

TOMORROW IS MY TURN**   (1962, Fr./Ital./Ger.) 117m Franco London-Gibe-Jonia-UFA/ Showcorporation bw (LE PASSAGE DU RHIN; JENSEITS DES RHEINS; IL PASSAGGIO DEL RENO)

Charles Aznavour (Roger), Nicole Courcel (Florence), Georges Riviere (Jean), Cordula Trantow (Helga), Jean Marchat (Delmas), Betty Schneider (Alice), Georges Chamarat (Baker), Michel Etcheverry (Ludovic), Lotte Ledl (Lotte), Nerio Bernardi (Rodier), Benno Hoffmann (Otto), Colette Regis (Baker's Wife), David Tonnelli (Barman), Alfred Schieske (Fritz Kessler), Ruth Hausmeister (Frau Kessler), Oscar Albrecht (Burgomaster), Arne Madin, Henri Lambert, Serge Frederic, Albert Remy, Bernard Musson, Konrad Mayerhoff.

Aznavour and Riviere are French soldiers who are captured during WW II and ordered to help farm a German family's land. Riviere tricks Trantow, the farmer's daughter, into helping him escape, while Aznavour becomes increasingly more fond of the girl and stays behind. By time the war ends, Riviere has become a successful journalist and Aznavour has returned to his wife, whom he no longer loves and who no longer loves him. He decides to go back to Trantow. Following suit, Riviere returns to Courcel, the mistress he deserted after she slept with a Gestapo agent to save him from being arrested.

d, Andre Cayatte; w, Cayatte, Armand Jammot, Maurice Auberge (adapted by Cayatte, Pascal Jardin from the idea by Jammot); ph, Roger Fellous; m, Louiguy; ed, Borys Lewin, Alix Paturel; art d, Robert Clavel.

War Drama   (PR:C MPAA:NR)

TOMORROW NEVER COMES*½   (1978, Brit./Can.) 107m Anglo-Canadian/RANK c

Oliver Reed (Wilson), Susan George (Janie), Raymond Burr (Burke), John Ireland (Captain), Stephen McHattie (Frank), Donald Pleasence (Dr. Todd), Paul Koslo (Willy), Cec Linder (Milton), Richard Donat (Ray), Dolores Etienne (Hilde), Sammy Snyder (Joey), Jane Eastwood (Lois), Mario De Iorio (Doug), Stephen Mendel (Vic), Walter Massey (Sergeant), Earl Pennington (1st Waiter), Jack Fisher (Hotel Manager), John Osborne (Robert Lynn).

An undistinguished cop drama about a peaceful lieutenant (Reed) and a violent police chief (Burr) who are trying to resolve a hostage crisis. McHattie is a good guy-turned-homicidal nut who shoots a cop and holds his former girl friend (George) at gunpoint. Psychology and philosophy are batted around until McHattie gives up, but unexpectedly is greeted with gunfire ordered by Burr. An easily forgettable police picture.

p, Julian Melzack, Michael Klinger; d, Peter Collinson; w, David Pursall, Jack Seddon, Sydney Banks; ph, Francois Protat (Eastmancolor); ed, John Shirley; art d, Michael Proulx; set d, Norman Sarrazin; m/l, "Alone Am I," sung by Matt Monroe; stunts, Jerome Tiberghien.

Crime Drama   (PR:O MPAA:PG)

TOMORROW THE WORLD**½   (1944) 86m UA bw

Fredric March (Mike Frame), Betty Field (Leona Richards), Agnes Moorehead (Jessie), Skippy Homeier (Emil Bruckner), Joan Carroll (Pat Frame), Edit Angold (Frieda), Rudy Wissler (Stan), Boots Brown (Ray), Marvin Davis (Dennis), Patsy Ann Thompson (Millie), Mary Newton (School Principal), Tom Fadden (Mailman).

A fascinating wartime film that takes a thoroughly indoctrinated Hitler Youth member and drops him into Main Street America, where he recruits followers and preaches hate. The son of a prominent anti-Nazi who dies in a concentration camp, Homeier is brought over to the U.S. by his only living relative, uncle March, a professor in a small college town. Immediately he goes about trying to break up March's impending marriage to the part-Jewish Field, befriending a Chinese boy at school he believes is a Japanese ally, and fostering unrest among the students. March tries reason and tolerance, but Homeier only twists it to his own ends while trying to sneak a peek at the secret plans March is working on for the war effort. Eventually he is driven to attack Carroll, March's daughter, and he goes into hiding as the whole neighborhood, tired of his monkeyshines, searches for him. Caught, he repents and seems headed for a new life as a normal American boy. Homeier repeats his role from the successful Broadway play, and although his performance is a bit broad for the movie screen, he still conveys the poisonous nature of his indoctrination with frightening effectiveness. The other performances are good but March is almost ridiculously low-key for most of the film, seemingly blind to Homeier's activities. Homeier's sudden seeing of the light of democracy was much criticized as too unmotivated and sudden. The film was successful, though, partly because of its message that Nazis could be rehabilitated to an American way of life. Homeier would later shorten his first name to Skip and have a long if undistinguished career in Hollywood, but he would never make as big an impression as he does in his film debut here.

p, Lester Cowan; d, Leslie Fenton; w, Ring Lardner, Jr., Leopold Atlas (based on the play by James Gow, Armand D'Usseau); ph, Henry Sharp; ed, Anne Bauchens; art d, James Sullivan.

Drama   (PR:A MPAA:NR)

TOMORROW WE LIVE*   (1936, Brit.) 72m Conquest/ABF bw

Godfrey Tearle (Sir Charles Hendra), Haidee Wright (Mrs. Gill), Renee Gadd (Patricia Gordon), Sebastian Shaw (Eric Morton), Eliot Makeham (Henry Blossom), Thea Holme (Mary Leighton), George Carney (Mr. Taylor), Rosalind Atkinson (Mrs. Taylor), Jessica Black (Mrs. Carter), Fred Withers (Mr. Carter), Cyril Raymond (George Warner), Alfred Wellesley, Hugh Ardale, Juliet Mansell, Judith Nelmes, R.W. Steele.

Longtime stage star Tearle is a financier on the verge of bankruptcy who invites a dozen suicidal failures to his house for dinner, then presents each with a check for them to try to start again. All but one take advantage of the offer, and Tearle manages to persuade her not to kill herself, either. He finds that the experience has given him new hope, too, and he goes back to rebuilding his fortune. Silly drama roughly stolen from IF I HAD A MILLION (1932), but on a lower budget.

p, Clayton Hutton; d&w, Manning H. Haynes.

Drama   (PR:C MPAA:NR)

TOMORROW WE LIVE**½   (1942) 66m PRC bw

Ricardo Cortez (The Ghost), Jean Parker (Julie Bronson), Emmett Lynn (Pop Bronson), William Marshall (Lt. Bob Ford), Roseanne Stevens (Melba), Ray Miller, Frank S. Hagney, Rex Lease, Jack Ingram, Barbara Slater, Jane Hale.

Another fascinating programmer from the master of the B picture, director Edgar G. Ulmer. Cortez, a master criminal with the ability to control the will of others, ensnares an aging ex-con, Lynn, and forces him to commit crimes. Lynn's daughter, Parker, learns of Cortez's scheme and with the help of her boy friend she breaks the evil man's spell over her father. His mind cleared, Lynn confronts Cortez and a vicious fight ensues which kills both men. Once again Ulmer takes the standard programmer plot line and manipulates it into a very watchable, interesting film by bringing to the fore his skill in composition of images, lighting, and editing. Ulmer embraces the narrow economic margins of his budgets, uses this handicap to his advantage, and then transforms the routine into the extraordinary.

p, Seymour Nebenzal; d, Edgar G. Ulmer; w, Bart Lytton; ph, Jack Greenhalgh; m, Leo Erodody; ed, Dan Milner.

Crime   (PR:A MPAA:NR)

TOMORROW WE LIVE, 1942, Brit.   (SEE: AT DAWN WE DIE, 1943, Brit.)

TOMORROW'S YOUTH*   (1935) 63m MON bw

Dickie Moore, John Miljan, Gloria Shea, Martha Sleeper, Jane Darwell, Franklin Pangborn, Paul Hurst, Barbara Bedford, Harry C. Bradley, Niles Welch, Edward J. Le Saint.

Little Moore is shaken by the divorce of his parents, but everything works out for the best. Maudlin melodrama, but one it seems every generation must contend with.

d, Charles Lamont; w, Harry Sauber, Gene Whitney, Robert Meller; ph, Jack Mackenzie; ed, Carl Pierson.

Drama (PR:A MPAA:NR)

TONI***½ (1968, Fr.) 90m Films d'Aujourd'hui/Pathe Contemporary
bw

Charles Blavette *(Antonio "Toni" Canova),* Celia Montalvan *(Josepha),* Jenny Helia *(Marie),* Edouard Delmont *(Fernand),* Andrex *(Gaby),* Andre Kovachevitch *(Sebastian),* Max Dalban *(Albert),* Paul Bozzi *(Jacques Bozzi the Guitarist),* Jacques Levert [Jacques Mortier].

Released in Paris in 1935, TONI has often been called the first "neorealist" film, preceding Luchino Visconti's OSSESSIONE by seven years. (Interestingly, Visconti's influence dates to TONI, on which he was one of Renoir's assistants.) It is based on a news item from police files about a group of people in the small town of Les Martigues. To capture authenticity, Renoir brought his crew to the town, used the townsfolk as characters, and brought the news story to the screen. It centers on the life of an Italian laborer, Blavette, who falls in love with his landlady, Helia, and then with a Spanish woman, Montalvan. He gets permission from Montalvan's father to marry, but is stopped when he discovers that a sleazy foreman has raped his future bride. The foreman marries Montalvan, but she is persuaded to run away, taking all his money with her. While trying to leave, she accidentally kills her husband, a crime which Blavette takes the blame for when he is caught burying the body. Blavette tries to escape but is killed, unaware that Montalvan has admitted guilt in the murder. An impressive precursor to THE RULES OF THE GAME in its portrayal of male-female relationships, TONI is far from perfect, riddled with numerous technical weaknesses and a seemingly improvised mise-en-scene, but still a wonderful show of talent.

p, Pierre Gault; d, Jean Renoir; w, Renoir, Carl Einstein (based on material gathered by Jacques Levert [Mortier]; ph, Claude Renoir; m, Paul Bozzi; ed, Marguerite Renoir, Suzanne de Troye; set d, Leon Bourelly, Marius Brauquier.

Crime Drama/Romance **Cas.** (PR:C MPAA:NR)

TONIGHT A TOWN DIES** (1961, Pol.) 92m Film Polski bw (DZIS
NOCY UMRZE MIASTO)

Andrezej Lapicki, Beata Tyszkiewicz, Danuta Szaflarski, Barbara Krafft *(Kraftowna).*

A dark look at war-torn Poland which centers on the efforts of a Polish prisoner, Lapicki, to escape Gestapo agents. While on a prison train en route to the concentration camp in Dachau, Lapicki escapes and takes refuge in Dresden, only to see the city destroyed by bombs from American planes. Behind the sincerity of this film is the experience of director Rybkowski, who himself was a prisoner of the Nazis during the war.

d, Jan Rybkowski; w, Rybkowski, Leon Kruczkowski; ph, Boguslaw Lambach.

War Drama (PR:C MPAA:NR)

TONIGHT AND EVERY NIGHT*** (1945) 92m COL c

Rita Hayworth *(Rosalind "Roz" Bruce),* Lee Bowman *(Paul Lundy),* Janet Blair *(Judy Kane),* Marc Platt *(Tommy Lawson),* Leslie Brooks *(Angela),* Professor Lamberti *(The Great Waldo),* Dusty Anderson *(Toni),* Stephen Crane *(Leslie Wiggins),* Jim Bannon *(Life Photographer),* Florence Bates *(May Tolliver),* Ernest Cossart *(Sam Royce),* Philip Merivale *(Rev. Gerald Lundy),* Patrick O'Moore *(David Long),* Gavin Muir *(Group Captain),* Shelley Winters *(Bubbles),* Marilyn Johnson *(Pamela),* Mildred Law *(Frenchie),* Elizabeth Inglise *(Joan),* Aminta Dyne *(Mrs. Peabody),* Joy Harrington *(Mrs. Good),* Ann Codee *(Annette),* Cecil Stewart *(Bert),* Dagmar Oakland, Victor Travers, Charles Meakin *(Jolly Trio),* Gary Bruce, Fred Graff *(American Soldiers),* Edward Cooper, William Lawrence *(Waiters),* David Thursby *(Scotch Soldier),* Jeanne Bates *(WAC),* Robert Williams *(U.S. CPO),* John Bleifer *(Russian Sailor),* Adele Jergens *(Show Girl),* Tom Bryson, Nigel Horton *(English Sailors),* Donald Dewar *(Boy),* P.J. Kelly, Keith Hitchcock *(ARP Men),* Charles McNaughton *(Peters),* Stuart Nedd *(Petty Officer),* Russell Burroughs *(Orderly),* George Kirby *(Father),* John Heath, Tony Marsh *(British Sailors),* Dick Woodruff, Richard Deane *(British Soldiers),* Wilson Benge *(News Vendor),* Nelson Leigh *(British Army Officer),* C. Montague Shaw *(Old Bobby),* Alec Craig *(Englishman),* Dave Clyde *(Police Sergeant),* Queenie Leonard *(Cockney Woman),* Sheilah Roberts *(Barmaid),* Frank Leigh *(Air Warden),* Richard Haydin *(Specialty).*

Interesting musical drama about a British music hall that never stopped presenting their shows, despite the Nazi bombings and a host of other problems. The story opted for a downbeat ending in keeping with reality but wartime audiences wanted something happy and the picture didn't do the kind of business expected. A writer from *Life* magazine interviews the ancient stage manager who flashes back to an earlier time when Hayworth and Blair starred in the show going on at the theater known as the Music Box (it was actually the Windmill Theatre in Old Windmill Street, Soho, London). Several musical sequences are seen as a romance develops between Hayworth and Bowman, an RAF pilot, and a secondary love story between Blair and a dancer, Platt. A chorus of three charwomen are seen intermittently commenting on the proceedings as sort of an English-Greek chorus. In the end, Blair and Platt are sadly killed by Nazi bombs, and Hayworth,

as much as she loves Bowman, decides to stay at her post and sing and dance for the soldiers, sailors, and airmen who treasure the entertainment. The story is ordinary enough but the film will be best recalled for the creativity of the productions, one of which must have inspired Woody Allen to write and direct THE PURPLE ROSE OF CAIRO. In that routine, a black-and-white newsreel is projected on the music hall's movie screen as Blair (and, later in the film, Hayworth) stands in front of it and performs "live." She then turns and asks the people on screen to step out and join her. One by one, the black-and-white characters come forward and are subtly transformed into living, breathing color, then join in the musical presentation, in the same way that the character came off the screen in Allen's film. It was based on a minor success of a play called "Heart of a City" but there were many alterations in order to make it work for the screen. None of the tunes was much to sing about, which was odd because they were written by two of the best in the business, Jule Styne and Sammy Cahn. Their songs included: "Cry and You Cry Alone" (sung by Hayworth, Platt), "What Does an English Girl Think of a Yank?" (Hayworth), "Anywhere" (Blair), "The Boy I Left Behind" (Blair, Hayworth), "You Excite Me" (Hayworth), "Tonight And Every Night" (Hayworth, Blair). Hayworth's singing was actually done by Martha Mears. "Anywhere" was nominated for an Oscar but lost out to "It Might As Well Be Spring" from STATE FAIR (written by Richard Rodgers and Oscar Hammerstein II). The excellent scoring was by Morris Stoloff and Marlin Skiles, who were also nominated but lost to Georgie Stoll for ANCHORS AWEIGH] The dialog was quite adult and the fact that Hayworth and Bowman were so obviously attracted sexually was a bit racy for the time. To keep the censors happy, a character was brought in who is Bowman's minister-father (Merivale), and he asks Hayworth for her hand on behalf of his son, a silly addition added to placate the blue noses. In a small role, note Shelley Winters in her ninth movie at the age of 23 and her second in a row with Hayworth, having just completed COVER GIRL. One very strange comedic routine called for Platt, who had been discovered in "Oklahoma!" on Broadway, to mime and dance to a radio broadcast of a Hitler harangue.

p&d, Victor Saville; w, Lesser Samuels, Abem Finkel (based on the play "Heart of the City" by Lesley Storm); ph, Rudy Mate (Technicolor); m, Jule Styne; ed, Viola Lawrence; md, Morris Stoloff, Jack Cole; art d, Stephen Goosson, Rudolph Sternad, Lionel Banks; set d, Frank Tuttle; cos, Jean Louis, Marcel Vertes; spec eff, Lawrence W. Butler; ch, Jack Cole, Val Rasset; makeup, Clay Campbell.

Musical (PR:A MPAA:NR)

TONIGHT AT 8:30*** (1953, Brit.) 85m British Film Makers/CD
(GB: MEET ME TONIGHT) c

"Ways and Means": Valerie Hobson *(Stella Cartwright),* Nigel Patrick *(Toby Cartwright),* Jack Warner *(Murdoch),* Jessie Royce Landis *(Olive),* Michael Trubshawe *(Chaps),* Mary Jerrold *(Nanny),* Yvonne Furneaux *(Elena),* "Red Peppers": Kay Walsh *(Lily Pepper),* Ted Ray *(George Pepper),* Martita Hunt *(Mabel Grace),* Frank Pettingell *(Mr. Edwards),* Bill Fraser *(Bert Bentley),* Frank's Fox Terriers, Young China Troupe, "Fumed Oak": Stanley Holloway *(Henry Gow),* Betty Ann Davies *(Doris Gow),* Mary Merrall *(Grandma Rockett),* Dorothy Gordon *(Elsie).*

Three of Noel Coward's playlets comprise this charming feature. In "Ways and Means" Hobson and Patrick are a pair of con artists merrily scamming their way along the French Riviera. "Red Peppers" has Walsh and Ray playing a pair of music hall entertainers who constantly argue. They manage to band together when faced with mutual threats and end up causing a riot at the theater. Finally, in "Fumed Oak" the ever-marvelous Holloway plays a man who finally gives up his nagging family for a more sedate life in the South Seas.

p, Anthony Havelock-Allan; d, Anthony Pelissier; w, Noel Coward (based on his stage playlets); ph, Desmond Dickinson (Technicolor); m/l, Coward.

Comedy (PR:A MPAA:NR)

TONIGHT AT TWELVE** (1929) 78m UNIV bw

Madge Bellamy *(Jane Eldridge),* George Lewis *(Tony Keith),* Robert Ellis *(Jack Keith),* Madeline Seymour *(Alice Keith),* Margaret Livingston *(Nan Stoddard),* Donald Douglas *(Tom Stoddard),* Vera Reynolds *(Barbara Warren),* Hallam Cooley *(Bill Warren),* Josephine Brown *(Dora Eldridge),* Norman Trevor *(Prof. Eldridge),* Mary Doran *(Mary, Maid),* Louise Carver *(Ellen),* Nick Thompson *(Joe).*

Romance takes a confusing turn when married masher Ellis finds not one, not two, but three local ladies to have fun with, while his wife and family are at home. His skin is saved when his son admits that a discovered love note is his and not dad's. The son pays the price and loses his girl, but ends up with the woman who really loved him all along.

p&d, Harry A. Pollard; w, Matt Taylor, Pollard (based on the play by Owen Davis); ph, Jerome Ash; ed, Maurice Pivar; titles, Owen Davis.

Drama/Comedy (PR:A MPAA:NR)

TONIGHT FOR SURE zero   (1962) 69m Searchlight/Premier-Sam
Lake-Kino c

Don Kenney, Karl Schanzer, Virginia Gordon, Marli Renfro, Sandy Silver,
Linda Gibson, Pat Brooks, Linda Lightfoot.

Francis Ford Coppola's first film, which doesn't mean it's automatically
good. TONIGHT FOR SURE was directed by the 22-year-old filmmaker
before he hooked up with Rogers Corman and made his first official film,
DEMENTIA 13 (1963). This picture is a nudie western (not graphic,
however, and no worse than most "R" rated pictures) about a pair of dirty
old men who sneak into a burlesque house and rig the electricity supply to
go out at midnight. Pretending to be members of the League Against Nudity,
the two men actually lead a comic life of perversions, one peeking at women
with a telescope, the other imagining he's seeing naked women everywhere.
The film experienced a short revival in 1982 but its only purpose is a
cinematically historic one. Carmen Coppola, who also scored the NAPOLE-
ON revival, contributes an especially annoying score. Needless to say,
Coppola refuses to recognize TONIGHT FOR SURE as a skeleton in his
closet.

p,d&w, Francis Coppola; ph, Jack Hill (Eastmancolor); m&md, Carmen
Coppola; set d, Albert Locatelli, Barbara Cooper.

Comedy   **Cas.**   **(PR:O MPAA:NR)**

TONIGHT IS OURS**   (1933) 75m PAR bw

Claudette Colbert (*Princess Nadya*), Fredric March (*Sabien Pastal*), Alison
Skipworth (*Grand Duchess Emilie*), Paul Cavanaugh (*Prince Keri*), Arthur
Byron (*Gen. Krish*), Ethel Griffies (*Zana*), Clay Clement (*Seminoff*), Warbur-
ton Gamble (*Alex*), Edwin Maxwell (*Mob Leader*).

A minor Noel Coward play is turned into a tedious movie that should have
been a musical. It's the typical Cinderfella story that's been seen all too often
before and required the light touch of Ernst Lubitsch or someone of that ilk
to make it work. Set in Paris, it's the familiar tale of the princess of a
mythical country (Colbert) who meets a commoner, March, falls in love with
him, and goes against the wishes of everyone who wants her to marry a man
of her own station, Cavanaugh. While Colbert and March are having their
romance in Paris, Colbert's father and brother are slain by revolutionaries
and she must race back to her *mittel*-European land to take over the throne.
Just prior to coming to Paris, Colbert had been due to marry Gamble, who
turned out to have slightly weird ideas of how to spend their wedding night,
wishing her to masquerade as a slave so he could dominate her. Meeting
March is a breath of fresh air and she reluctantly leaves him to lead her
land. March follows her to the small country and saves her life when an
assassin takes aim. Then, in a twist that only a musical comedy plot would
allow, the revolutionaries decide that Colbert would make a good ruler so
they establish a constitutional monarchy, approving March as their queen's
consort when they discover that he is a commoner and one of them. Very
talky, with little of Coward's wit to help matters. It's amiable enough and
with sharper words it might have had some impact but it's defeated by the
tedious script, and all the gaiety and bubbliness of the actors can't save the
movie from a monotony of heavy pacing. Mitchell Leisen, who went on to
helm some of the best of this genre, was Walker's associate director, an odd
credit. Usually, there is the director and his (or her) assistants. Calling
Leisen "associate director" must have meant that he was the only person
on the set who would associate with Walker.

d, Stuart Walker; w, Edwin Justus Mayer (based on the play "The Queen
Was in the Parlor" by Noel Coward); ph, Karl Struss; cos, Travis Banton.

Comedy   **(PR:A MPAA:NR)**

TONIGHT OR NEVER**   (1931) 80m Feature/UA bw

Gloria Swanson (*Nella Vago*), Melvyn Douglas (*The Unknown Gentleman*),
Ferdinand Gottschalk (*Rudig*), Robert Greig (*The Butler*), Greta Meyer
(*The Maid*), Warburton Gamble (*Count Albert von Gronac*), Alison Skip-
worth (*The Marchesa*), Boris Karloff (*The Waiter*).

Melvyn Douglas went from the stage to the screen in this adaptation of the
play in which he starred with his wife, Helen Gahagan. Swanson played the
Gahagan part in an attempt to staunch the downward sweep of her
popularity. It didn't help. Swanson (at age 33) plays a young opera singer
who is making her first major appearance at a Venetian opera house. The
critics are less than rapt and her teacher-lover, Gottschalk, says that while
she has the technique, she lacks the passion and fire that separates a singer
from a diva. While in Venice, Swanson is shadowed by the handsome March,
who she suspects is a professional gigolo being kept by a marchesa,
Skipworth. Swanson wants to know more about March so she goes to his
apartment and makes believe it was all an error. They spend the night
together amorously and the following day her voice takes on a new timbre,
the result of an affair that was more or less suggested by Gottschalk, who
is sort of engaged to Swanson. Swanson gets a contract with the Metropolitan Opera and breaks off her engagement with the faithful Gottschalk.
Swanson throws caution to the wind and chases March, even though he is
spending a great deal of time with Skipworth, who he says is his aunt. At
the conclusion, March admits that he has been in Europe trying to scout
good talent for the U.S. stage and that the contract with the Metropolitan
was arranged by him. Further, Skipworth is, in reality, his aunt. Swanson

is thrilled to learn the truth and renews her singing with vigor, basking in
the glow of her new affair with March. The play had been produced by
Broadway impresario David Belasco, his final show before his death.
Douglas was making his film debut in the same role he did on the stage.
Gottschalk, Grieg, Gamble, and Meyer were also featured in the play. This
was Douglas' only film for Goldwyn. In a comic role, note Boris Karloff, who
showed that he had a sly way with humor. Swanson's film career had been
sliding after WHAT A WIDOW] and INDISCREET and this movie did
nothing to halt that.

p, Samuel Goldwyn; d, Mervyn LeRoy; w, Ernest Vajda, Frederic Hatton,
Fanny Hatton (based on the play by Lili Hatvany); ph, Gregg Toland; m,
Alfred Newman; ed, Grant Wytock; md, Newman; art d, Willy Pogany; cos,
Chanel.

Comedy   **(PR:A-C MPAA:NR)**

TONIGHT THE SKIRTS FLY*½   (1956, Fr.) 90m Vox/Imperial c (CE
SOIR LES JUPONS V OLENT)

Sophie Desmarets, Jean Chevrier, Brigitte Auber, Anne Vernon, Philipe
Nicaud, Nadine Tellier, Ginette Pigeon.

An uneventful tale of episodic construction which centers on the love life of
a young girl in Paris. Directed by Russian emigre Kirsanoff, who made his
mark in France's silent days, TONIGHT THE SKIRTS FLY is a mediocre
commercial picture notable only for its being the first to display the
widescreen process of Dyaliscope.

d, Dimitri Kirsanoff; w, Jean Marsan, Claude Desailly; ph, Roger Fellous
(Dyaliscope, Agfacolor); ed, Monique Kirsanoff.

Drama   **(PR:C MPAA:NR)**

TONIGHT WE RAID CALAIS½**   (1943) 70m FOX bw

Annabella (*Odette Bonnard*), John Sutton (*Geoffrey Carter*), Lee J. Cobb
(*Mons. Bonnard*), Beulah Bondi (*Mme. Bonnard*), Blanche Yurka (*Widow
Grelieu*), Howard da Silva (*Sgt. Block*), Marcel Dalio (*Jacques Grandet*), Ann
Codee (*Mme. Grandet*), Nigel de Brulier (*Danton*), Robert Lewis (*Maurice
Bonnard*), Richard Derr (*Captain*), Leslie Denison (*Capt. Baird*), Billy
Edmunds (*Bell Ringer*), Lester Matthews (*Maj. West*), Reginald Sheffield
(*Commander*), John Banner (*Kurz*), Leslie Vincent (*English Pilot*), Robert
O. Davis, George Lynn (*Lieutenants*).

Sutton is a British officer on a mission to sneak behind German lines and
light up a munitions plant so the RAF can locate and destroy it. He gets some
help from Frenchwoman Annabella, who starts out hating the British but
grows to accept them and Sutton. A quick pace and Ballard's sharp
photography help speed this one to a highly satisfactory conclusion.

p, Andre Daven; d, John Brahm; w, Waldo Salt (based on a story by L.
Willinger, Rohama Lee); ph, Lucien Ballard; m, Emil Newman, Cyril J.
Mockridge; ed, Allen McNeil; art d, Richard Day, Russell Spencer.

War   **(PR:A MPAA:NR)**

TONIGHT WE SING½**   (1953) 109m FOX c

David Wayne (*Sol Hurok*), Ezio Pinza (*Feodor Chaliapin*), Roberta Peters
(*Elsa Valdine*), Tamara Toumanova (*Anna Pavlova*), Anne Bancroft (*Emma
Hurok*), Isaac Stern (*Eugene Ysaye*), Byron Palmer (*Gregory Lawrence*),
Oscar Karlweis (*Benjamin Golder*), Mikhail Rasumny (*Nicolai*), Steven
Geray (*Prager*), Walter Woolf King (*Gritti*), Serge Perrault (*Allbrecht*), John
Meek (*Sol Hurok at Age 10*), Eda Reys Merin (*Mrs. Golder*), Russell Cantor
(*Eddie Golder*), Alex Zakin (*Eugene Ysaye's Accompanist*), Alex Steinart
(*Conductor*), Oscar Beregi (*Dr. Markoff*), Leo Mostovoy (*Petlukoff*), Ray
Largay (*Charles Dillingham*), Wolfgang Fraenkel (*Jules Massenet*).

A dull story but some wonderful classical music moments in this biography
of impresario Sol Hurok, who knew early that his greatest talent was in
recognizing the talents of other people. It's hardly more than a raison d'etre
for presenting the excellent artistes. Wayne is Hurok and we soon learn that
he loves music but can't do a thing about it. He thinks that the average Joe
would like to hear classical music as much as the intellectual with season
tickets at the Met. With the aid and encouragement of his wife, Bancroft,
he begins his career, not knowing of the crazed and temperamental
characters with whom he must deal. A few moments of comedy as Pinza is
seen as the Russian basso, Chaliapin, a man with a passion for practical
jokes. Several of the impresario's more famous clients are portrayed and,
while there is nothing wrong with any of the acting, it's not a particularly
exciting story, just straight ahead with a few setbacks but not enough to
make it dramatically interesting. Musical pieces include: "Madame Butterfly" (the love duet by Giacomo Puccini, sung by Peters and Palmer, whose
voice was looped by Jan Peerce), "Le Cygne" (by Camille Saint-Saens,
danced by Toumanova as Anna Pavlova), "Vous Qui Faites L'Endormie"
(from "Faust" by Charles Francois Gounod, sung by Palmer, Pinza),
"Sempre Libera" (from Giuseppe Verdi's "La Traviata," sung by Peters),
"Qu' Attendez-Vouz Encore" (also from "Faust," sung by Palmer, Pinza),
"Andante Le Triste Vero" (from "Madame Butterfly," sung by Palmer),
"Addio Fiorito Asil" (from "Faust," sung by Palmer), "Mattinata" (by
Ruggiero Leoncavallo, sung by Palmer). Stern, as the famed violinist

Eugene Ysaye, played "Valse Caprice in E Flat" by Anton Rubinstein. Toumanova danced in "Valse Caprice," "Dragonfly," "Pas De Deux," and "The Swan." Stern played Felix Mendelssohn's Violin Concerto (first and final movements) and "Processional" from Modest Moussorgky's "Boris Goudonov" was also featured. All technical credits were good and special plaudits to Ken Darby for his vocal direction. Music lovers will enjoy this more than movie lovers. The producer was George Jessel, who had a secondary career as a filmmaker and was the man behind a few notable movies, such as NIGHTMARE ALLEY, THE DOLLY SISTERS, DANCING IN THE DARK, and many others.

p, George Jessel; d, Mitchell Leisen; w, Harry Kurnitz, George Oppenheimer (based on a book by Sol Hurok, Ruth Goode); ph, Leon Shamroy (Technicolor); ed, Dorothy Spencer; md, Alfred Newman; art d, Lyle Wheeler, George W. Davis; cos, Renie; ch, David Lichine.

Musical/Biography   **(PR:A   MPAA:NR)**

TONIGHT'S THE NIGHT* (1932, Brit.) 74m BIP/Wardour bw (AKA: TONIGHT'S THE NIGHT–PASS IT ON)

Leslie Fuller (Bill Smithers), Amy Veness (Emily Smithers), Charles Farrell (Williams), Frank Perfitt (Maj. Allington), Syd Crossley (Warder Jackson), Hal Walters (Alf Hawkins), Hal Gordon (Smiler), Betty Fields (Miss Winterbottom), Rene Ray (Rose Smithers), Monty Banks (Convict), Lola Harvey, Syd Courtenay, Mike Johnson.

Fuller works for a loan company and is imprisoned for embezzlement when some of the money turns up missing. In jail he is locked up with a criminal who tells him that it was he who stole the money, unaware of his cellmate's identity. Fuller escapes and proves his innocence. Mediocre comedy has some good moments, most of them straight dramatic bits.

p&d, Monty Banks; w, Syd Courtenay, Leslie Arliss (based on a story by Courtenay, Lola Harvey).

Comedy   **(PR:A   MPAA:NR)**

TONIGHT'S THE NIGHT* (1954, Brit.) 88m ABF/Pathe c (GB: HAPPY EVER AFTER; AKA: O'LEARY NIGHT)

David Niven (Jasper O'Leary), Yvonne De Carlo (Serena McGlusky), Barry Fitzgerald (Thady O'Heggarty), George Cole (Terence), A.E. Matthews (Gen. O'Leary), Noelle Middleton (Kathy McGlusky), Robert Urquhart (Dr. Michael Flynn), Michael Shepley (Maj. McGlusky), Joseph Tomelty (Dooley), Eddie Byrne (Lannigan), Liam Redmond (Regan), Anthony Nicholls (Solicitor), James Mageean, Patrick McAlinney, Brian O'Higgins, Patrick Westwood, Fred Johnson, Ronan O'Casey, Michael Martin-Harvey, Denis Martin, Bill Shine, Harry Hutchinson, Tommy Duggan.

When Matthews is killed in a fall from a horse, nephew Niven comes to Ireland to inherit the estate. He makes enemies of the villagers by collecting debts verbally canceled by his uncle, evicting an old tenant whose meager rent the uncle had never bothered to collect, and putting an end to poaching. The villagers draw lots to see who's going to dispatch the upstart, but before any of their schemes can succeed a new will is found that sends Niven packing. Hilarious comedy with a sterling cast.

p&d, Mario Zampi; w, Jack Davies, Michael Pertwee, L.A.G. Strong; ph, Stanley Pavey (Technicolor); m, Stanley Black; ed, Kathleen Connors; art d, Ivan King; m/l, "My Heart Is Irish," Michael Carr.

Comedy   **(PR:A   MPAA:NR)**

TONIO KROGER* (1968, Fr./Ger.) 90m Mondex-Procinex-Thalia/Pathe Contemporary bw

Jean-Claude Brialy (Tonio Kroger), Nadja Tiller (Lisaweta Iwanowna), Werner Hinz (Consul Kroger), Anaid Iplicjian (Frau Kroger), Rudolf Forster (Herr Seehaase), Walter Giller (Merchant), Theo Lingen (Knaak), Adeline Wagner (Women), Beppo Brem (Adalbert Prantl), Rosemarie Lucke (Inge Holm), Elisabeth Klettenhauer (Girl), Mathieu Carriere (Young Tonio Kroger), Gert Frobe (Policeman Peterson), Gunther Luders, Valso Holm.

A look at an artist's conflict with his bourgeois world which stars Brialy as a young author who wanders through Europe discussing isolation, modern life, and artistry. At one point he becomes strongly attracted to Tiller, but instead of a relationship he continues his travels. The film also presents the all-too-German conflict between the warm Mediterranean world and the cold Nordic one as the young writer tries to find himself. Erika Mann, who cowrote the screenplay, is Mann's daughter but apparently knew nothing about her father's aims in TONIO KROGER, a novel which many critics have contended was modeled after the great Danish work Niels Lynne by J.P. Jacobsen. (English subtitles.)

d, Rolf Thiele; w, Erika Mann, Ennio Flajano (based on the novel by Thomas Mann); ph, Wolf Wirth; m, Rolf Wilhelm.

Drama   **Cas.**   **(PR:C   MPAA:NR)**

TONKA**½ (1958) 97m Disney/BV c (AKA: A HORSE NAMED COMANCHE)

Sal Mineo (White Bull), Philip Carey (Capt. Miles Keogh), Jerome Courtland (Lt. Henry Nowlan), Rafael Campos (Strong Bear), H.M. Wynant (Yellow Bull), Joy Page (Prairie Flower), Britt Lomond (Gen. George Armstrong Custer), Herbert Rudley (Capt. Benteen), Sydney Smith (Gen. Alfred Howe Terry), John War Eagle (Sitting Bull), Gregg Martell (Cpl. Korn), Slim Pickens (Ace), Robert "Buzz" Henry (Lt. Crittenden).

Sal Mineo puts his Plato role aside from REBEL WITHOUT A CAUSE and is here cast as a young Indian brave from the Sioux tribe. He finds and tames a wild horse which he names Tonka, only to have it taken away by a vicious cousin who joyfully beats it. It is eventually sold to the cavalry where it is taken into the custody of Carey, a decent captain who tags the horse Comanche. To be near his horse, Mineo sneaks into the fort and is captured. When Carey learns why Mineo was there he sets him free, recognizing their common love for the horse. Carey rides the horse into battle with Custer against Sitting Bull's army and, along with every other cavalry member, gets killed, leaving only Tonka alive. Mineo is made an honorary cavalry soldier and put in charge of the horse. Contrived and implausible, TONKA does succeed in portraying the Indians as humans with real emotions, as opposed to the villainous redskin usually seen on the screen–making it an educational film for children, more than an entertaining one for adults. The casting of Mineo in the lead role is superb, but unfortunately the film shifts its center of focus to the cavalry at mid-point, forgetting about Mineo. The film was shot on location at the Warm Springs Indian Reservation in Oregon, with many of the men and women on the Reservation used in the film and to help make the sets.

p, James Pratt; d, Lewis R. Foster; w, Foster, Lillie Hayward (based on the novel Comanche by David Appel); ph, Loyal Griggs (Technicolor); m, Oliver Wallace; ed, H. Ellsworth Hoagland; art d, Robert E. Smith; set d, Emile Kuri, Oliver Emert; cos, Chuck Keehne, Gertrude Casey; m/l, "Tonka" by Gil George, George Bruns; makeup, Pat McNalley.

Adventure   **(PR:AAA   MPAA:NR)**

TONS OF MONEY*½ (1931, Brit.) 97m British and Dominions/GAU bw

Ralph Lynn (Aubrey Allington), Yvonne Arnaud (Louise Allington), Mary Brough (Benita Mullet), Robertson Hare (Chesterman), Gordon James (George Maitland), Madge Saunders (Jane Everard), Philip Hewland (Henry), Willie Warde (Giles), John Turnbull (Sprules), Peggy Douglas (Simpson).

A stale screen version of a British play about a down-and-out inventor who hits upon a scheme and has to pose as his missing cousin. Nothing here but an occasional chuckle, especially when the missing cousin comes on the scene and is proved a phony, and then another "real" cousin appears.

p, Herbert Wilcox; d, Tom Walls; w, Wilcox, Ralph Lynn (based on the play by Will Evans, Arthur Valentine); ph, F.A. Young.

Comedy   **(PR:A   MPAA:NR)**

TONS OF TROUBLE**½ (1956, Brit.) 77m Shaftesbury/REN bw

Richard Hearne (Mr. Pastry), William Hartnell (Bert), Austin Trevor (Sir Hervey Shaw), Joan Marion (Angela Shaw), Robert Moreton (Jevons), Ralph Truman (Inspector Bridger), Ronald Adam (Psychiatrist), Junia Crawford (Diana Little), Tony Quinn (Cracknell), John Stuart (Doctor), Yvonne Hearne.

Hearne is an oddball caretaker in charge of two apartment boilers he's lovingly dubbed "Mavis" and "Ethel." This unusual affection leads him into some unexpected problems and he's fired from his job. Meanwhile, a wealthy man needs Hearne as the key to an important deal. The handyman is found just in time to save both the business man and "Ethel" who is about ready to explode. Surprisingly, this offbeat story works with some good humor, the elements mixing with effectiveness.

p, Elizabeth Hiscott, Richard Hearne; d, Leslie Hiscott; w, Leslie Hiscott, Hearne (based on the story by John Barrow); ph, Norman Warwick.

Comedy   **(PR:AA   MPAA:NR)**

TONTO BASIN OUTLAWS* (1941) 60m MON bw

Ray "Crash" Corrigan (Crash), John King (Dusty), Max Terhune (Alibi), Jan Wiley (Jane), Tristram Coffin (Miller), Edmund Cobb (Stark), Ted Mapes (Ricks), Art Fowler (Brown), Carl Mathews (Ed), Reed Howes (Captain), Rex Lease (Editor), Edward Peil, Sr (Photographer), Budd Buster (Stage Driver), Tex Palmer, Hank Bell, Denver Dixon, Jim Corey.

Corrigan, King, and Terhune are Wyoming cowpokes who join forces with Teddy Roosevelt's Rough Riders, only to end up back in the prairies fighting a gang of rustlers who are putting the finger on government cattle. Corrigan goes under cover and digs up proof that Coffin is the man behind the caper. Standard oater fare. (See RANGE BUSTERS series, Index.)

p, George W. Weeks; d, S. Roy Luby; w, John Vlahos (based on the story by Earle Snell); ph, Robert Cline; m, Frank Sanucci; ed, Roy Claire; m/l, "Cabin of My Dreams," sung by John King.

Western   Cas.   **(PR:A   MPAA:NR)**

TONY DRAWS A HORSE½**   (1951, Brit.) 90m RANK/FA bw

Cecil Parker (*Dr. Howard Fleming*), Anne Crawford (*Clare Fleming*), Derek Bond (*Tim Shields*), Barbara Murray (*Joan Parsons*), Mervyn Johns (*Alfred Parsons*), Barbara Everest (*Mrs. Parsons*), Edward Rigby (*Grandpa*), Dandy Nichols (*Mrs. Smith*), Ann Smith (*Ann*), Susan Dudley (*Susan*), Anthony Lang (*Tony Fleming*), Marjorie Gresley (*Mrs. Carey Brown*), Kynaston Reeves (*Dr. Bletchley*), David Hurst (*Ivan*), Gabrielle Blunt (*Grace*), Harold Richmond, Michael Ward.

An engaging, if uneven, comedy about a doctor and his psychiatrist wife who are thrown into a tizzy when their 8-year-old son draws a picture of a horse which is anatomically correct on his father's consulting room door. Dad thinks he should get a whacking while mom, who believes her boy should behave as he likes, thinks he should be rewarded. The parents split over the incident with the missus taking off to France with her sister's fiance. A reunion follows shortly and everything wraps up for the better.

p, Brock Williams; d, John Paddy Carstairs; w, Williams (based on the play by Lesley Storm); ph, Jack Hildyard; m, Bretton Byrd; ed, Gerald Thomas; md, Byrd; art d, Bernard Robinson; cos, Abbey.

Comedy   **(PR:A-C   MPAA:NR)**

TONY ROME*   (1967) 110m Arcola-Millfield/FOX c

Frank Sinatra (*Tony Rome*), Jill St. John (*Ann Archer*), Richard Conte (*Lt. Dave Santini*), Sue Lyon (*Diana Kosterman Pines*), Gena Rowlands (*Rita Neilson Kosterman*), Simon Oakland (*Rudolph Kosterman*), Jeffrey Lynn (*Adam Boyd*), Lloyd Bochner (*Vic Rood*), Robert J. Wilke (*Ralph Turpin*), Virginia Vincent (*Sally Bullock*), Joan Shawlee (*Fat Candy*), Richard Krisher (*Donald Pines*), Lloyd Gough (*Jules Langley*), Babe Hart (*Oscar*), Templeton Fox (*Mrs. Schuyler*), Rocky Graziano (*Packy*), Elizabeth Fraser (*Irma*), Shecky Greene (*Catleg*), Jeanne Cooper (*Lorna*), Harry Davis (*Ruyter*), Stanley Ralph Ross (*Sam Boyd*), Buzz Henry (*Nimmo*), Deanna Lund (*Georgia McKay*), Michael Romanoff (*Sal, Maitre d'Hotel*), Tiffany Bolling (*Photo Girl*), Joe E. Ross (*Bartender*), Jilly Rizzo (*Card Player*).

This entertaining private-eye story features Sinatra in his very first hard-boiled detective role. The complex plot finds Sinatra living a Travis McGee kind of life on his boat in Miami. He gets a small fee for squiring Lyon, a blotto teenager, out of a motel which is operated by his one-time associate, Wilke. Lyon is an heiress to a huge fortune owned by her father, builder Oakland. Sinatra brings the reluctant young woman back to the family estate (a real mansion that was once owned by a radio magnate). Lyon has taken heavily to the bottle and Oakland wants to know why, especially since she's just married Krisher recently and should be happy. Oakland's wife is Lyon's stepmother and she, Rowlands, gives Sinatra some extra money if he's willing to divulge whatever he learns to her before he tells Oakland. Sinatra begins to investigate and finds out that Lyon has lost a valuable diamond bauble. He is roughed up by some hoodlums but makes his way to a huge house in the Coconut Grove area where he is set upon by a moronic oaf, Ross, who is the behemoth brother of Lynn. Later, Sinatra learns that Wilke has been killed. Sinatra meets St. John, a sexy divorcee, and they team up to investigate further. They discover that Lyon has been giving money to her real mother, the drunken Cooper. She's apparently been taking Rowlands' valuable jewelry and selling it, replacing the gems with paste. The money has been handed over to Cooper. Sinatra prowls around Miami and meets the dregs of humanity. They include homosexual drug dealer Bochner, who is the local peddler feeding the habit of junkie Vincent. He also meets curvaceous Lund, who turns out to be the gay lover of heavyset Shawlee. Davis is the jeweler who has been making the imitations and when he is drowned in a bathtub, it seems that the last link has been broken. All the while, Sinatra–who is an ex-cop in Miami–is followed around by police lieutenant Conte, who resents the fact that Sinatra seems to be one step ahead of him. There's an attempt to kill Oakland and Sinatra finally gets near the bottom of things when he finds that Wilke was killed by Henry, murderer who was once married to Rowlands. It turns out that Henry and Rowlands were never fully divorced when she married Oakland and he has been blackmailing her. So it wasn't Lyon who was switching the jewelry, it was Rowlands herself. Henry dies because of injuries he got when skirmishing with Wilke, and now we learn that Lynn, who was also married to Cooper, tried to kill Oakland so Lyon could be the beneficiary of Oakland's money. Sinatra goes back to the old house occupied by Lynn and his huge brother, Ross. After Sinatra beats up the gargantuan Ross, he arrests Lynn and associate Greene. At the conclusion, Sinatra and St. John talk about going away together but she opts for returning to her former husband and a life that will be considerably duller but somewhat more quiet. This paved the way for the sequel, LADY IN CEMENT (1968). A very confusing story with far too many characters and therefore not enough room to develop anyone past a blur. Breen wrote the screenplay, then died, and novelist Albert, who wrote the original book, came in to handle the rewrite. The killer was played by comedian Shecky Greene who mentions his role in the movie in his act and the fact that he had a skirmish with two bodyguards who had been assigned to watch over Sinatra. (These were men hired by the company, not by Old Blue Eyes.)

When the two toughs were belting Greene, he recalls that: "Frank Sinatra saved my life. The men were rapping me, he walked over and said, "That's enough!" In shooting the first battle with Ross (who had never done a fight scene) and Sinatra, they were choreographed by stunt coordinator Henry (who also played Nimmo) and Ross zigged when he should have zagged and had his nose cracked by a Sinatra punch. Sinatra was very solicitous and apologized profusely, thinking he had hurt the 230-pound Ross, but Ross assured him that it took a lot more than a left hook from a 160-pound actor to bother him. Sinatra laughed, pushed Ross to the padded floor, and the two men began laughing and rolling on the ground. Director Douglas let the cameras roll and it became part of the fight scene. Prior to the fight, Ross had been told that Sinatra liked to do his own fights and stunts and that it was okay to kick, punch, and gouge the star, but hands must never be laid on his tenuous hairpiece. Ross had been a TV writer at Fox doing one "Batman" episode after another and when Albert–who shared a floor in the Lasky building at the studio–asked if Ross would like to be in the movie, Ross jumped at the chance without ever reading the script. He asked "Batman" producer Howie Horwitz if he could leave the lot. Horwitz agreed on the proviso that Ross write an entire "Batman" script while he was on location in Miami. Ross spent his days acting and his nights pounding a rented typewriter. Sinatra occupied a suite on the same floor and heard the clackety-clack of the Smith-Corona late at night. He took Ross aside at dinner to admit that he respects the writer more than any other person in the movie business. He also admitted that he is envious of writers who have the ability to sit by themselves for days, without the need of outside stimulation, because "you guys are never alone." Sinatra would stay up all night, either singing at the Fontainebleau Hotel, or just partying. And yet, when shooting began at the civilized hour of 10 each morning, he always knew his lines. He hated to do more than one "take," and pity the actor who blew his lines due to lack of preparation because Sinatra was always prepared and seldom, if ever, made a mistake. He enjoyed playing a detective so much that he went on to make more films in the genre, including THE DETECTIVE (1968) and THE FIRST DEADLY SIN (1980). Sinatra likes to help out his pals so he asked famed restaurateur Mike Romanoff to do a bit, as well as boxer Rocky Graziano. Deanna Lund was discovered in this film and went on to star in a Fox TV series, "Lost In Space." Ross had not known what his part would be and was hired at 280 pounds. Thinking that he would look grotesque to all his friends, he went on a crash diet and came to Miami at 230 pounds, infuriating producer Rosenberg who hired him *because* he was so fat at the time of the audition. Ross was then offered a role in THE DETECTIVE if he'd "beef up" for the part, but after having dieted so strenuously, Ross declined rather than get fat again.

p, Aaron Rosenberg; d, Gordon Douglas; w, Richard Breen (based on the novel *Miami Mayhem* by Marvin H. Albert); ph, Joseph Biroc (Panavision, DeLuxe Color); m, Billy May; ed, Robert Simpson; md, May; art d, Jack Martin Smith, James Roth; set d, Walter M. Scott, Warren Welch; cos, Moss Mabry, Elinor Simmons, Malcolm Starr; makeup, Ben Nye; m/l, Title Song, Lee Hazlewood, sung by Nancy Sinatra, "Something Here Inside Me," "Hard Times," May, Randy Newman.

Detective Mystery   Cas.   **(PR:C   MPAA:NR)**

TOO BAD SHE'S BAD**   (1954, Ital.) 96m Documento/Gala bw

Sophia Loren (*Lina*), Vittorio De Sica (*Stroppiani*), Marcello Mastroianni (*Paolo*), Umberto Melnati (*Man Whose Wallet Is Stolen*), Margherita Bagni (*His Wife*), Walter Bartoletti (*Brunetto*), Mario Passante (*The Commissioner*), Memmo Carotenuto (*Cesare, Garage Boss*), Giacomo Furia (*Luigi*), Lina Furia (*His Wife*), Mario Scaccia (*Man Whose Bag Is Stolen*), Wanda Benedetti (*His Wife*), Vittorio Braschi (*The Fence*), Manlio Busoni (*The Journalist*), Michael Simone (*Toto*), Mauro Sacripante (*Peppino*), Giulio Galli (*Night Watchman*), Charles Stacy (*English Tourist*), Maria Britnewa (*His Wife*).

The first teaming of Loren, Mastroianni, and De Sica is a lighthearted little farce which sees Mastroianni as a handsome cab driver who picks up Loren and her three male companions who are on their way to the beach. When they get to their destination, Loren encourages the cabbie to join in the fun and before he knows it his fares are trying to steal his cab. He captures Loren and takes her to the police station, but her endlessly chattering explanation of the event takes Mastroianni by surprise and he begins to wonder whether or not he overreacted. To further confuse things, Mastroianni meets Loren's father, De Sica, and is so impressed with the man's obvious integrity that he realizes that Loren cannot possibly have meant to rob him. He accompanies the father and daughter out of the police station and suddenly begins noticing that both of them are crooks, filching anything they can get their hands on by pretending to be an honorable old man and his sweet, beautiful daughter. At home, there are several more family members who also join in on the "business" of conning, robbing, and cheating. Mastroianni once again tries to have them all arrested, but De Sica and Loren are too clever and they again bamboozle the police into believing that it is Mastroianni who is the suspicious one. Determined to rid society of this menace, Mastroianni decides to marry Loren and force her to go straight. Typically inane Italian comedy brightened somewhat by the rapport between the lead performers. De Sica nearly steals the show as the Fagin-like patriarch of the criminal brood.

d, Allessandro Blasetti; w, Alessandro Continenza, Suso Cecchi d'Amico,

Ennio Flaiano (based on a story by Alberto Moravia); ph, Aldo Giordani; m, Allessandro Cicognini; ed, Mario Serandrei; art d, Mario Chiari.

Comedy   (PR:C MPAA:NR)

TOO BUSY TO WORK½**   (1932) 70m FOX bw

Will Rogers (Jubilo), Marian Nixon (Rose), Dick Powell (Dan Hardy), Frederick Burton (Judge Hardy), Constantine Romanoff (Axel), Douglas Cosgrove (Sheriff), Louise Beavers (Mammy), Jack O'Hara (Under Sheriff), Charles B. Middleton (Chief of Police), Bert Hanlon (Pete).

A charming Rogers outing which stars him as a hobo intent on finding the man (Burton) who ran off with his wife and daughter years ago when Rogers went off to war. He finally gets a clue to their whereabouts after witnessing a bank heist which involved (innocently) Burton's son. He soon finds himself working in the Burton's home as a handyman and witnesses Powell's devotion to his daughter. With his wife dead and his daughter unaware that he is her father and obviously living a wholesome life, Rogers goes about straightening out her love life and tending to his wife's grave, without revealing his identity. After he is content with the situation, he returns to a life on the road. A remake of a 1919 Rogers vehicle, JUBILO.

d, John G. Blystone; w, Barry Conners, Philip Klein (based on the story "Jubilo" by Ben Ames Williams); ph, Charles G. Clarke; ed, Alexander Troffey; art d, Max Parker; cos, Earl Luick.

Drama   (PR:A MPAA:NR)

TOO BUSY TO WORK**   (1939) 65m FOX bw

Jed Prouty (John Jones/Mayor), Spring Byington (Mrs. John Jones), Ken Howell (Jack Jones), George Ernest (Roger Jones), June Carlson (Lucy Jones), Florence Roberts (Granny Jones), Billy Mahan (Bobby Jones), Joan Davis (Lolly), Chick Chandler (Cracker McGurk), Marjorie Gateson (Mrs. Randolph Russell), Andrew Tombes (Wilbur Wentworth), Marvin Stephens (Tommy McGuire), Irving Bacon (Gilligan), Helen Ericson (Betty, the Mayor's Secretary), Harold Goodwin (Raymond), Hooper Atchley (Charlie Carter), Sherry Hall (Anbruster), George Melford (Dugan), Eddie Acuff (Stage Manager), Edwin Stanley (Frazier), Jack Green (Policeman).

Confusion rises to comic proportions when the head of the Jones family, Prouty, begins neglecting his drugstore duties in favor of his mayoral duties. The ladies of the household, tired of doing his work, decide to take it easy and give him a dose of his own medicine. This series entry features a new member to the clan in Davis, a visiting cousin. (See JONES FAMILY series, Index.)

p, John Stone; d, Otto Brower; w, Robert Ellis, Helen Logan, Stanley Rauh (based on the plays "The Torchbearers" by George Kelly and "Your Uncle Dudley" by Howard Lindsay, Bertrand Robinson); ph, Edward Cronjager; ed, Fred Allen; md, Samuel Kaylin.

Comedy   (PR:A MPAA:NR)

TOO DANGEROUS TO LIVE**   (1939, Brit.) 74m FN-WB bw

Sebastian Shaw (Jacques Leclerc), Anna Konstam (Lou), Reginald Tate (Collins), Greta Gynt (Marjorie), Ronald Adam (Murbridge/Wills), Edward Lexy (Inspector Cardby), Ian MacLean (Saunders), Henry Caine (Selford), George Relph (Manners), Tonie Edgar Bruce (Mrs. Herbert), Torin Thatcher (Burton), Billy [William] Hartnell.

An entertaining crime picture which tells of a member of the French police, handsome Shaw, who infiltrates a gang of European jewel thieves by posing as an expert crook himself. Nothing new here, but it is swiftly paced enough to hold interest. And the cast is excellent.

p, Jerome Jackson; d, Anthony Hankey, Leslie Norman; w, Paul Gangelin, Connery Chappell, Leslie Arliss (based on the novel Crime Unlimited by David Hume); ph, Basil Emmott.

Crime   (PR:A MPAA:NR)

TOO DANGEROUS TO LOVE (SEE: PERFECT STRANGERS, 1950)

TOO HOT TO HANDLE***   (1938) 105m MGM bw

Clark Gable (Chris Hunter), Myrna Loy (Alma Harding), Walter Pidgeon (Bill Dennis), Walter Connolly (Gabby MacArthur), Leo Carrillo (Joselito), Virginia Weidler (Hulda Harding), Henry Kolker (Pearly Todd), Marjorie Main (Miss Wayne), Robert Emmett Keane (Foreign Editor), Johnny Hines (Parsons), Betty Ross Clarke (Mrs. Harding), Gregory Gaye (Popoff), Aileen Pringle (Mrs. MacArthur), Richard Loo (Charlie), Willie Fung (Willie), Josephine Whittell ("Fake" Mrs. Harding), Patsy O'Connor ("Fake" Hulda Harding), Al Shean (Gumpel), Walter Miller (Flyer), James Flavin (Young Reporter), Lane Chandler (Cameraman), Edwin Parker (Coast Guard Attendant), Frank Faylen (Assistant Dubber), Nell Craig (Todd's Secretary), Cyril Ring (Cameraman).

Fast-paced action picture that takes great liberties with the way it really is in the world of newsreel photographers. Gable and Loy were already the top male and female stars of Hollywood's national polls and had just come off

a far superior picture, TEST PILOT, but the sizzle from that carried over and this one made more money than it may have deserved. Loy is an Amelia Earhart-type aviatrix whose brother, Hines, has been lost in the dense Amazon jungles of the South American interior. She appeals to rival newsreel men Gable and Pidgeon to help her locate Hines, who has been missing for about a year. Both agree for two reasons: it's a good story and Loy is so attractive. They go to Brazil and, in a tiny village, they spot a local native who wears Hines' wristwatch. With the help of Carrillo, Gable's assistant, they learn that the native is part of a voodoo sect (we always thought voodoo was unique to Haiti) that has Hines in captivity and are now seeking a white woman to complete their voodoo incantations. Loy is so eager to find her brother that she will do anything. Gable and Carrillo quickly take the native in a canoe and head for the village of the people who are holding Hines. Once there, Gable and Carrillo sneak into the village where they see Hines, looking more dead than alive. In order to divert their attention, Gable projects some newsreels on the side of a smooth cliff. (Why he is carrying projection and sound equipment with him is never explained.) Gable himself is in the newsreels and the superstitious natives think he is the personification of magic when he steps out of the underbrush in the mustached flesh. Gable gets to the side of Hines, who is close to death from starvation and other travails. Later, Loy and Pidgeon arrive. By this time, Gable is wearing the outlandish mask of a native shaman. He directs Loy and Pidgeon to carry Hines to their seaplane. Meanwhile, Carrillo is shooting footage of the action. Gable is then exposed by the native he'd met earlier in the village. Loy, Pidgeon, and Hines are safely aboard the seaplane and taxiing for a take-off when Gable and Carrillo jump into a small boat, row to the plane, and grab onto the tail. Pidgeon doesn't realize that it's Gable and Carrillo, as they are covered with voodoo warpaint, so he fires at them and they are forced to let go of the plane. Loy and Pidgeon return to New York with Hines. Pidgeon is shocked to discover that Gable has already been there and his footage of what happened is now in theaters across the U.S.; he has been scooped badly. Gable is already on another assignment and Loy, who is now in love with him, leaves Pidgeon to join Gable. The picture actually begins to fall apart once they are in South America because the first 30 minutes is a hysterically witty satire of how newsreel people set up "managed news" stories. In order to please the boss, Connolly, Gable and Carrillo are seen arranging phony bombing raids in China, shooting "orphans," and taking pictures of model airplanes crashing which pass for real. The story was by Hammond, an employee of a newsreel company; the screenplay was co-written by Stallings, a man who also did the same thing for a while. They knew of what they wrote, but went far afield in several ways to show how fraudulent the "news" can be at times. Conway directed at a Hawksian clip which almost made up for the silly transitions and the plot holes.

p, Lawrence Weingarten; d, Jack Conway; w, Laurence Stallings, John Lee Mahin (based on a story by Len Hammond); ph, Harold Rosson; m, Franz Waxman; ed, Frank Sullivan; spec eff, Arnold Gillespie; cos, Dolly Tree.

Adventure   **Cas.**   (PR:A-C MPAA:NR)

TOO HOT TO HANDLE*   (1961, Brit.) 105m ABF-Wigmore/Topaz c
                                  (AKA: PLAYGIRL AFTER DARK)

Jayne Mansfield (Midnight Franklin), Leo Genn (Johnny Solo), Karl Boehm (Robert Jouvel), Danik Patisson (Lilliane Decker), Christopher Lee (Novak), Kai Fischer (Cynthia), Patrick Holt (Inspector West), Martin Boddey (Mr. Arpels), Sheldon Lawrence (Diamonds Dinelli), Barbara Windsor (Pony Tail), John Salew (Moeller), Tom Bowman (Flash Gordon), Ian Fleming (Pawnbroker), Penny Morrell (Terry), Katherine Keeton (Melody), Susan Denny (Marjorie), Judy Bruce (Maureen), Elizabeth Wilson (Jacky), Shari Khan (Jungle), Bill McGuffie (Piano Player), Michael Balfour (Tour Guide), Larry Taylor (Mouth), June Elvin (Hostess), Morton Lowry (Dinelli's Driver), Martin Sterndale (Editor), Harry Lane (Muscles), Robin Chapman (Priest), Monica Marshall, Toni Palmer, Lou Eather, Brian Tucker, Boyd MacKenzie, Ken Martyne (Dancers).

An embarrassingly seamy British crime drama about a French journalist, Boehm, who is working on a story about the lurid underground striptease clubs in London's Soho district. He meets and talks with Genn, the owner of the Pink Flamingo, and his girl friend and star singer, Mansfield. Genn is involved in a blackmail plot which ends in his getting beaten and a decoy of his being killed. He plots revenge on a rival club owner who is behind the goings-on, but is stopped by Mansfield, who informs on him rather than have him get deeper into trouble. Pretty dumb, though it is fun to watch Jayne in a sequined see-through dress.

p, Phil C. Samuel; d, Terence Young; w, Herbert Kretzmer (based on the story by Harry Lee); ph, Otto Heller (Eastmancolor); m, Eric Spear; ed, Lito Carruthers; art d, Alan Withy; ch, Pamela Davis; cos, Dolly Tree.

Crime Drama   (PR:C MPAA:NR)

TOO LATE BLUES**½**   (1962) 100m PAR bw

Bobby Darin (John "Ghost" Wakefield), Stella Stevens (Jess Polanski), Cliff Carnell (Charlie), Seymour Cassel (Red), Bill Stafford (Shelly), Richard Chambers (Pete), Nick Dennis (Nick), Rupert Crosse (Baby Jackson), Everett Chambers (Benny Flowers), Vincent Edwards (Tommy), Alan Hopkins (Skipper), Val Avery (Frielobe), James Joyce (Reno), Marilyn Clark (The

Countess), Allyson Ames *(Billie Gray)*, June Wilkinson *(Girl at Bar)*, Mario Gallo.

John Cassavetes' first Hollywood film stars Darin as a jazz musician who loses his girl friend after not sticking up for himself in a barroom brawl. His band goes on the skids, playing music for scant audiences in parks and an orphanage. He finally gets back on the right track with both his music and his former girl friend, who has since become a hooker. Interesting mainly for its jazz atmosphere and Darin's nonsinging performance. Features the tunes: "Sax Raises its Ugly Head," "Look Inward Angel," "The Rim Shot Heard 'Round the World," "Benny Splits While Jimmy Rowles," "Bass Canard," "Move Over" and "Drum Talk" (David Raksin), plus "A Song After Sundown," "When Your Time Comes," "Samba Do Cabeza Vermelha," "Danzon Del Galante," "Ciudad De Mexico."

p&d, John Cassavetes; w, Cassavetes, Richard Carr; ph, Lionel Lindon; m, David Raksin; ed, Frank Bracht; art d, Tambi Larsen; cos, Edith Head.

Musical/Drama   **(PR:C   MPAA:NR)**

TOO LATE FOR TEARS***   (1949) 99m UA bw

Lizabeth Scott *(Jane Palmer)*, Don DeFore *(Don Blake)*, Dan Duryea *(Danny Fuller)*, Arthur Kennedy *(Alan Palmer)*, Kristine Miller *(Kathy Palmer)*, Barry Kelley *(Lt. Breach)*, Denver Pyle *(Youth)*, Virginia Mullen *(Woman)*, Richard Irving *(1st Bindlestiff)*, George K. Mann *(Texan)*, Harry Vejar *(Teniente)*, June Storey *(Girl)*, Jimmy Ames *(Fat Man)*, Jim Nolan *(Parker)*, John Butler *(Little Man)*, Smokie Whitfield *(Pete)*, William Halop *(Boat Attendant)*, Jimmie Dodd *(2nd Bindlestiff)*, David Clarke *(Sharber)*, Denny O'Morrison, Jack Shea, Charles Flynn, Robert Kellard, Robert Bice, George Backus *(Policemen)*, John Mansfield *(Carlos)*, Garry Owen *(Officer at Switchboard)*, Gregg Barton *(Clerk, Missing Persons Bureau)*, William O. Wayne *(Gas Station Attendant)*, Patricia Wallace *(Woman)*, Perry Ivins *(Attendant at Stand)*, Alex Montoya *(Customs Officer)*, Robert Neff *(Man in Black Car)*, Renee Donatt *(Young Girl)*, Carl Thompson *(Young Boy)*.

Engrossing crime story opens in Los Angeles as Kennedy and wife Scott are driving their convertible to a party. The two are in the midst of a heated argument and accidentally go off the road. For safety's sake the auto's lights are blinked. Another car driving by interprets this as a prearranged signal and a bag is tossed from it into Kennedy's car. This mysterious bag contains $60,000 which Kennedy wants to hand over to the cops. Scott is insistent that they keep the loot. Her husband finally gives in and the money is hidden in a luggage stand at a local train station. Later Scott is visited at home by Duryea, a sleazy private detective who demands the money be handed over to him. Scott will not give up the cash so easily, however, and the two decide to split it. Scott realizes Kennedy would never agree to this, so rather than lose out on her share she kills her spouse. After hiding the claim check for the money in a drawer, Scott calls the police, reporting Kennedy as a missing person. She also tells Miller, Kennedy's sister, of the disappearance. Soon afterwards DeFore comes to visit Scott, claiming to be a friend of Kennedy's from their days together in the military. In reality, DeFore is the brother of Scott's first husband and is convinced Scott murdered the man some time ago and wants to prove it for himself. DeFore finds Miller and tells her who he really is. Miller in turn is beginning to suspect Scott is behind her brother's departure. She shows DeFore the claim ticket she has found in Kennedy's drawer, a place he normally kept a gun. Scott catches on to Miller and decides to kill her, sending Duryea out for poison. He can't bring himself to do this and first gets drunk. Meanwhile, Scott learns who DeFore really is. She confronts DeFore and Miller with gun in hand, taking the claim ticket the two possess. Scott then goes to Duryea's motel room where she hides out. Though the detective has fallen in love with her, Scott murders the man with the very poison she sent him out for. The $60,000 now in hand, Scott flees to Mexico, pursued by DeFore and the police. To escape, Scott slips from a balcony to her death below, money coming down like autumn leaves behind her. As the money-hungry woman without a conscience, Scott is terrific, seductive as Ulysses' sirens and just as destructive to the men who draws into her web. Duryea gives her good support, a weakling counterpart to an overpowering personality. Shot on location in the streets of Los Angeles, the film makes effective use of its setting, and the somewhat talky script develops its mood and themes quite nicely.

p, Hunt Stromberg; d, Byron Haskin; w, Roy Huggins (based on his novel serialized in *The Saturday Evening Post*); ph, William Mellor; m, Dale Butts; ed, Harry Keller; md, Morton Scott; art d, James Sullivan; set d, John McCarthy, Jr., Charles Thompson; cos, Adele Palmer; spec eff, Howard Lydecker, Theodore Lydecker; makeup, Bob Mark.

Crime   **(PR:O   MPAA:NR)**

TOO LATE THE HERO***   (1970) 133m ABC-Palomar Associates and
                                                   Aldrich/Cinerama c (AKA: SUICIDE RUN)

Michael Caine *(Pvt. Tosh Hearne)*, Cliff Robertson *(Lt. Lawson)*, Ian Bannen *(Pvt. Thornton)*, Harry andrews *(Lt. Col. Thompson)*, Denholm Elliott *(Capt. Hornsby)*, Ronald Fraser *(Pvt. Campbell)*, Lance Percival *(Cpl. McLean)*, Percy Herbert *(Sgt. Johnstone)*, Henry Fonda *(Capt. Nolan)*, Ken Takakura *(Maj. Yamaguchi)*, Patrick Jordan *(Sergeant Major)*, Sam Kydd *(Color Sergeant)*, William Beckley *(Pvt. Currie)*, Martin Horsey *(Pvt. Griffiths)*, Harvey Jason *(Signalman Scott)*, Don Knight *(Pvt. Connolly)*, Roger Newman *(Pvt. Riddle)*, Michael Parsons *(Pvt. Rafferty)*, Sean MacDuff *(Pvt.*

Rogers), Frank Webb *(Ensign)*.

Aldrich's vain attempt to get the same sort of box-office bonanza he'd reaped with the 1967 hit THE DIRTY DOZEN comes off only adequately. Shot on location in the Philippines with an all-star cast, it's a tale of bravery and cowardice in a dissimilar group of men. It's the nadir of the second World War and the Japanese are ensconced on a Michener-type island in the New Hebrides where they have an observation base. Their presence is a thorn in the side of the Allied forces because they are able to watch the shipping in the area and order air strikes. The problem is: how to get them out of there? Robertson is a gold-bricking U.S. Navy lieutenant who is doing his best to stay out of harm's way. Because of his ability to speak Japanese, Robertson is recruited--against his will--to be part of what may be a suicide mission to knock out the Japanese outpost. His immediate boss, Fonda (in a pre-title cameo of just a few lines) orders Robertson into the thick of things. The leader of the Brits is Elliot, a wishy-washy type who shows bare signs of intelligence. Almost instantly, three of the British commandos are killed in a trap laid by the Japanese. Caine is a cockney who doesn't like Robertson but the two men share the belief that Elliot is ill-suited to be their boss. The band makes its way to the Japanese encampment. Robertson is ordered to go inside the radio hut, but refuses. Elliott shows his bravery by going inside and destroying the radio gear. He then dies in a hail of bullets. The Japanese begin chasing Robertson, Caine, and the remaining members of the group. Takakura, the head of the Japanese pursuers, offers the men their lives if they will surrender. Fraser and two others give up, but Takakura kills Fraser because the British commando had lopped off a dead Japanese soldier's finger in order to steal a ring. Caine and Robertson trap Takakura and kill him, then race through the jungle toward their own lines. They are almost safe when gunshots kill Robertson. Caine reports the American's heroism to Andrews as the picture ends. Good second-unit direction by one-time actor Oscar Rudolph, who also directed Robertson in an episode of TV's "Batman" a year or so before. Robertson was quite annoyed at Aldrich because the director would not allow the actor to come back to Hollywood for 48 hours. Robertson had been nominated as Best Actor for CHARLY and was a long shot so Aldrich felt it was hardly worth losing Robertson for two days of shooting. Robertson did, in fact, win the Oscar and it had to be accepted by a surrogate on his behalf. Robertson's agent had agreed to allow the actor to do the film without Robertson himself reading the script. When Robertson saw that his role was not nearly as witty as the lines given to Caine and the others, he called upon a screenwriter friend, Stanley Ralph Ross, who had written the "Batman" episodes and had also ghosted the TV movie Robertson made with his wife, Dina Merrill (THE SUNSHINE PATRIOT). Ross added some humor to Robertson's copy of the script and Robertson was able to convince Aldrich, while on the set, that these were off-the-cuff lines that Robertson had come up with himself. Robertson's complaint about the script was that the American character was bland by comparison to the others and he felt that something had to be done. Since Ross and Robertson had worked together before, Ross did the alterations as a favor. And that's how movies sometimes get made. A great deal of money was spent on making this picture and all of the production values are there, but the feeling of *deja vu* is all through the film. Too violent for the youngsters.

p&d, Robert Aldrich; w, Aldrich, Lukas Heller (based on a story by Aldrich, Robert Sherman); ph, Joseph Biroc (Metrocolor); m, Gerald Fried; ed, Michael Luciano; art d, James Dowell Vance; set d, John W. Brown; spec eff, Henry Millar, Jr.; makeup, William Turner, Jack Stone.

War   **Cas.**   **(PR:C   MPAA:GP)**

TOO MANY BLONDES*   (1941) 60m UNIV bw

Rudy Vallee *(Dick Kerrigan)*, Helen Parrish *(Virginia Kerrigan)*, Lon Chaney, Jr *(Marvin Gimble)*, Jerome Cowan *(Ted Bronson)*, Shemp Howard *(Hotel Manager)*, Iris Adrian *(Hortense)*, Eddie Quillan *(Wally Pelton)*, Irving Bacon *(Twitchell)*, Jeanne Kelly [Jean Brooks] *(Angie)*, Paco Moreno *(Garvanza)*, Gus Schilling *(Elevator Operator)*, Dorothy Lee *(Lorene)*, Carmela and Jose Cansino *(Dancers)*, Dinorah Rego *(Singer)*, Elaine Morley *(Sophie Doltz)*, Charles Trowbridge *(Barton)*, Catherine Winter *(Salesgirl)*, Marek Windheim *(Manuel)*, Humberto Herpera and His Orchestra.

A mindless programmer which stars Vallee and Parrish as a married pair of radio entertainers whose romance is on the rocks when a blonde makes a play for Vallee. Parrish threatens divorce, then heads south of the border to make it official, but before she can they happily reunite. Includes the songs: "Whistle Your Tunes to a Bluebird," "Don't Mind If I Do," "Let's Love Again" (Everett Carter, Milton Rosen), "The Man on the Flying Trapeze" (George Leybourne, Alfred Lee, arranged by Walter O'Keefe).

p, Joseph G. Sanford; d, Thornton Freeland; w, Maxwell Shane, Louis S. Kaye (based on the story by Shane); ph, Milton Krasner; ed, Bernard W. Burton; cos, Vera West.

Musical   **(PR:A   MPAA:NR)**

TOO MANY CHEFS   (SEE: WHO IS KILLING THE GREAT CHEFS
                                                           OF EUROPE, 1978, US, Ger.)

TOO MANY COOKS*½   (1931) 77m RKO bw

Bert Wheeler (*Al Bennett*), Dorothy Lee (*Alice Cook*), Sharon Lynn (*Ella Mayer*), Roscoe Ates (*Wilson*), Robert McWade (*Uncle George*), Hallam Cooley (*Frank Andrews*), Florence Roberts (*Mrs. Cook*), Clifford Dempsey (*Mr. Cook*), George Chandler (*Cousin Ned*), Ruth Weston.

An uninspired little romancer mixed with comedy that stars Wheeler (without his usual partner, Bob Woolsey) and Lee as lovers who are trying to make it in spite of the interference of their families. With the constant pestering of the 13-strong clan the relationship is spoiled, only to be patched up by the finale.

p, Douglas MacLean; d, William Seiter; w, Jane Murfin, Frank Craven (based on the play by Craven); ph, Nick Musuraca.

Comedy/Romance   (PR:A   MPAA:NR)

TOO MANY CROOKS**½   (1959, Brit.) 87m RANK/Lopert bw

Terry-Thomas (*Billy Gordon*), George Cole (*Fingers*), Brenda De Banzie (*Lucy*), Bernard Bresslaw (*Snowdrop*), Sidney James (*Sid*), Joe Melia (*Whisper*), Vera Day (*Charmaine*), Delphi Lawrence (*Beryl, Secretary*), John Le Mesurier (*Magistrate*), Sydney Tafler (*Solicitor*), Rosalie Ashley (*Angela*), Nicholas Parsons (*Tommy*), Vilma Ann Leslie (*Girl Journalist*), Edie Martin (*Gordon's Mother*), Tutte Lemkow (*Swarthy Man*), John Stuart (*Inspector Jensen*), Terry Scott (*Fire Policeman Smith*).

A comic crook caper which centers on a consistently unsuccessful gang that botches every robbery attempt they make. They finally hit on the idea of kidnaping the daughter of millionaire Terry-Thomas. Again they err and wind up with the man's naughty wife, whom he couldn't care less about losing. Finding this as an opportunity to devote more time to his mistress, he refuses to meet the kidnapers' demands. Naturally the wife is infuriated and assists the crooks in their attempt to rob him. The humor is spotty but when it works it is hysterical. Raves go to Terry-Thomas for producing some riotous comic moments.

p, Mario Zampi, Giulio Zampi; d, Mario Zampi; w, Michael Pertwee (based on the story by Jean Nery, Christiane Rochefort); ph, Stanley Pavey; m, Stanley Black; ed, Mill Lewthwaite.

Comedy   (PR:A   MPAA:NR)

TOO MANY GIRLS**½   (1940) 85m RKO bw

Lucille Ball (*Connie Casey*), Richard Carlson (*Clint Kelly*), Ann Miller (*Pepe*), Eddie Bracken (*Jojo Jordan*), Frances Langford (*Eileen Eilers*), Desi Arnaz (*Manuelito*), Hal LeRoy (*Al Terwilliger*), Libby Bennett (*Tallulah Lou*), Harry Shannon (*Mr. Casey*), Douglas Walton (*Beverly Waverly*), Chester Clute (*Lister*), Midge Martin (*Tiny Person*), Ivy Scott (*Mrs. Tewksbury*), Byron Shores (*Sheriff Andaluz*), Van Johnson (*Boy No. 41*), John Benton (*Boy*), Janet Lavis, Anna Mae Tessle, Amarilla Morris, Vera Fern, Mildred Law, Ellen Johnson (*Coeds*), Michael Alvarez (*Joe*), Sethma Williams (*Marie*), Averell Harris (*Detective*), Tommy Graham (*Hawker*), Grady Sutton (*Football Coach*), Homer Dickinson (*Butler*), Iron Eyes Cody, Jay Silverheels (*Indians*), Chief John Big Tree (*Chief*), Pamela Blake (*Student*).

A fast-paced musical comedy full of peppy performances and musical numbers. Ball is an heiress who takes a shot at campus life accompanied by a quartet of bodyguards, all of whom are topnotch football players. Though they've been instructed to stay out of the huddle, the four decide to show their talents on the field and bring the sad-looking team to victory. Ann Miller dances up a storm and Arnaz, getting a big push as the new Cuban conga sensation, delivered a tune called "Spic and Spanish." Ball must have liked Arnaz's drumming as much as the audience, for they married shortly after the film was completed. Other musical numbers include: "Heroes in the Fall," "Pottawatomie," "'Cause We All Got Cake," "Love Never Went to College," "Look Out," "I Didn't Know What Time It Was," "The Conga," and "You're Nearer" (Richard Rodgers, Lorenz Hart).

p, George Abbott, Harry Edington; d, Abbott; w, John Twist (based on the stage musical by George Marion, Jr., Richard Rodgers, Lorenz Hart); ph, Frank Redman; m, Rodgers, Hart; ed, William Hamilton; art d, Van Nest Polglase; cos, Edward Stevenson; spec eff, Vernon L. Walker; ch, LeRoy Prinz.

Musical   (PR:A   MPAA:NR)

TOO MANY HUSBANDS*½   (1938, Brit.) 59m Liberty bw

Jack Melford (*Stephen Brinkway*), Iris Baker (*Clare Brinkway*), Geoffrey Sumner (*Capt. Corrie*), Philip Leaver (*Francois*), David Baxter (*Le Fletange*), Brian Oulton (*Pottleby*), Suzanne Lyle (*Ruth*), Carol Rees, Eileen Gerald, Archie Jackson, Robert Field, Monte DeLisle.

Melford is a con man who has a chance to start his life over when a plane he was scheduled to be on crashes. Presumed dead, the swindler changes his identity and prepares elaborate plans to make a killing in Monte Carlo. On arrival Melford is unexpectedly greeted by wife Baker, posing as a countess. Baker thwarts her husband's plans and makes him promise to go straight. An unfunny and confusing so-called comedy that rarely scores on any level.

p,d&w, Ivar Campbell (based on the play "Mirabelle" by Guy Pelham

Bolton).

Comedy   (PR:AA   MPAA:NR)

TOO MANY HUSBANDS***   (1940) 84m COL bw (GB: MY TWO HUSBANDS)

Jean Arthur (*Vicky Lowndes*), Fred MacMurray (*Bill Cardew*), Melvyn Douglas (*Henry Lowndes*), Harry Davenport (*George*), Dorothy Peterson (*Gertrude Houlihan*), Melville Cooper (*Peter, Butler*), Edgar Buchanan (*McDermott*), Tom Dugan (*Sullivan*), Garry Owen (*Sign Painter*), Lee White (*Mailman*), Mary Treen (*Emma*), William Brisbane (*Lawyer*), Sam McDaniel (*Porter*), Ralph Peters (*Cab Driver*), Walter Soderling (*Customer*), Jerry Fletcher (*Man*), Jacques Vanaire (*Headwaiter*), Dave Willock (*Elevator Operator*).

Arthur finds herself in the position of having one excess husband when she marries Douglas after receiving word that her first husband, MacMurray, drowned in a shipwreck. Her marriage to Douglas is cut short when MacMurray returns, having safely made it to an island from which he was rescued. Comic tensions flare when both husbands vie for Arthur's affections. After the two men are fed up with her love for attention, they both leave and become friends. A court ruling finally declares that Arthur's marriage to MacMurray is still legally binding. Remade as THREE FOR THE SHOW.

p&d, Wesley Ruggles; w, Claude Binyon (based on the play "Home And Beauty" by W. Somerset Maugham); ph, Joseph Walker; m, Frederick Hollander; ed, Otto Meyer, William Lyon; md, M.W. Stoloff; art d, Lionel Banks; cos, Irene.

Comedy   (PR:A   MPAA:NR)

TOO MANY MILLIONS**   (1934, Brit.) 57m WB bw

Betty Compton (*Anne*), John Garrick (*Bill*), Viola Keats (*Viola*), Athole Stewart (*Mr. Olcott*), James Carew (*Mr. Worthing*), Martita Hunt (*Mrs. Pilcher*), Phyllis Stanley (*Tamara*), Sybil Grove (*Mrs. Runcorn*), Bruce Belfrage, Eileen Culshaw, Vincent Lawson.

To escape from the constant annoyances of the press, millionairess Compton switches places with her maid. While under the domestic guise she meets Garrick, a starving artist, and falls madly in love. When faced with a choice between all her money and the man she loves, Compton's choice is all too easy as the couple ends up in wedded bliss. Average comedy outing with too slow a pacing to create anything memorable.

p, Irving Asher; d, Harold Young; w, Brock Williams.

Comedy   (PR:A   MPAA:NR)

TOO MANY PARENTS**½   (1936) 73m PAR bw

Buster Phelps (*Clinton Meadows*), George Ernest (*Phillip Stewart*), Billy Lee (*Billy Miller*), Howard C. Hickman (*Col. Colman*), Porter Hall (*Mrs. Saunders*), Colin Tapley (*Miller*), Frances Farmer (*Sally Colman*), Henry Travers (*Wilkins*), Lester Matthews (*Mark Stewart*), Douglas Scott (*Morton Downing*), Jonathan Hale (*Judge*), Mabel Forrest (*Clinton's Mother*), Lillian West (*Clinton's Stepmother*), Frank Mayo (*Clinton's Stepfather*), Bradley Metcalfe (*Cadet Williams*), Lois Kent (*Morton's Sister*), Sherwood Bailey, Sylvia Breamer, Doris Lloyd, Carl "Alfalfa" Switzer, Anne Grey, Henry Roquemore, Jack Norton, Callen Jader.

A well-intentioned tale of a group of boys in a military academy, some of whom have little or no family life outside the school's walls. One such youngster, Ernest, goes through a traumatic time in the school, feeling the neglect of his father. The finale has the boy taking a suicidal canoe ride over a dam which would have been fatal had it not been for his suddenly wiser father's unexpected intervention. Frances Farmer appears in a minor role as the sympathetic daughter of the academy's colonel.

p, A. M. Botsford; d, Robert F. McGowan; w, Virginia Van Upp, Doris Malloy (based on the story by George Templeton, Jesse Lynch Williams); ph, Karl Struss; ed, Edward Dmytryk.

Drama   (PR:A   MPAA:NR)

TOO MANY THIEVES**   (1968) 100m Filmways/MGM c

Peter Falk, Joanna Barnes, Britt Ekland, Nehemiah Persoff, David Carradine, George Couand Elaine Stritch, Ludwig Donath.

When some priceless Macedonian treasures are swiped, enter lawyer Falk to get to the bottom of things. Falk spends a good deal of time dodging more bad guys than in the average film, but that is because this is just two episodes of his "Trials of O'Brien" television show edited together and dumped quickly into the theaters. Plenty of dead bodies pile up along the way but with little excitement en route.

p, Richard Simons; d, Abner Biberman; w, George Bellak.

Crime/Action   (PR:A   MPAA:NR)

TOO MANY WINNERS**   (1947) 61m PRC bw

Hugh Beaumont *(Michael Shayne)*, Trudy Marshall *(Phyllis Hamilton)*, Ralph Dunn *(Rafferty)*, Claire Carleton *(Mayme Martin)*, Charles Mitchell *(Tim Rourke)*, John Hamilton *(Payson)*, Grandon Rhodes *(Hardeman)*, Ben Welden *(Madden)*, Byron Foulger *(Edwards)*, Jean Andren *(Mrs. Edwards)*, George Meader *(Clarence)*, Frank Hagney *(Joe)*, Maurice B. Mozelle *(Punk)*.

Beaumont is cast in the role of private eye Michael Shayne, who this time tries to take a vacation from crime. He and his secretary Marshall plan on some duck hunting, but instead find a race track manager involved in a counterfeiting scheme. After a few dangerous situations Beaumont cracks the case and resumes his vacation. The Michael Shayne character had been originated on film by Lloyd Nolan in a series he played in from 20th Century-Fox some years previously. Poverty-row studio PRC had never before made a series outside the B-western vein; they started this one as part of a product upgrading strategy. (See MICHAEL SHAYNE series, Index.)

p, John Sutherland; d, William Beaudine; w, Sutherland (adapted by Fred Myton, Scott Darling, based on characters and original story by Brett Halliday); ph, Jack Greenhalgh; m, Alvin Levin; ed, Harry Reynolds; art d, Tommy Thompson.

Crime   (PR:A   MPAA:NR)

TOO MANY WIVES**   (1933, Brit.) 58m WB bw

Nora Swinburne *(Hilary Wildeley)*, Jack Hobbs *(John Wildeley)*, Viola Keats *(Sally)*, Claud Fleming *(Baron von Schlossen)*, Alf Goddard *(Jeff)*, John Turnbull, Charles Paton.

Just before he has to entertain an important client, businessman Hobbs suffers a personal setback when his wife runs out on him. Forced to put up a front to entertain his foreign-born client, Hobbs gets his maid Keats to pose as his wife. The ruse runs into difficulties when the important client's secretary turns out to be none other than Hobbs' estranged spouse. Unbelievable complications make an unfunny comedy.

p, Irving Asher; d, George King; w, W. Scott Darling.

Comedy   (PR:A   MPAA:NR)

TOO MANY WIVES**   (1937) 61m RKO bw

John Morley *(Barry Trent)*, Anne Shirley *(Winifred Jackson)*, Gene Lockhart *(Her Father)*, Dudley Clements *(Horatio Mansfield)*, Barbara Pepper *(Angela Brown, His Secretary)*, Frank Melton *(Clabby Holden)*, Charles Coleman *(Rogers)*, Dot Farley *(Mrs. Potts)*, Jack Carson *(Hodges)*, George Irving *(Mr. Otto)*.

Heiress Shirley and the downtrodden Morley fall in love in this mixed-up, bungled, over-plotted comedy which catches them in a scheme which includes a nonexistent wife and a missing stamp worth a fortune. Not worth the effort.

p, William Sistrom; d, Ben Holmes; w, Dorothy Yost, Lois Eby, John Grey (based on a story by Richard English); ph, Nick Musuraca; ed, Desmond Marquette; art d, Van Nest Polglase; cos, Stevenson.

Comedy   (PR:A   MPAA:NR)

TOO MANY WOMEN, 1931   (SEE: GOD'S GIFT TO WOMEN, 1931)

TOO MANY WOMEN*   (1942) 63m PRC bw

Neil Hamilton, June Lang, Joyce Compton, Barbara Read, Fred Sherman, Marlo Dwyer, Kate McKenna, Maurice Cass, Matt McHugh, Harry Holman, George Davis, Pat Gleason, Tom Herbert, Bertram Marburgh, Dora Clement.

A predictable comedy about a man who pretends to be extremely wealthy. His riches attract hordes of women and before long he finds himself engaged to three of them. His troubles multiply when his true fiancee arrives. The other three soon learn that he has no money and leave him. It's addle-headed films like this that gave PRC its "Poverty Row" tag.

p&d, Bernard B. Ray; w, Eddie M. Davis; ph, Jack Greenhalgh; ed, Carl Himm; md, Clarence C. Wheeler; art d, Fred Preble.

Comedy   (PR:A   MPAA:NR)

TOO MUCH BEEF*½   (1936) 60m Colony/GN bw

Rex Bell, Connie Bergen, Horace Murphy, Forrest Taylor, Lloyd Ingraham, Peggy O'Connell, Vincent Dennis, George Ball, Jimmy Aubrey, Jack Cowell, Fred Burns, Steve Clark, Jack Kirk, Dennis Meadows [Dennis Moore], Frank Ellis.

Singing cowboy Rex Allen stars in this oater as a lawman who acts as a mediator between two rival ranch owners. Filled with the usual thrills and gunplay, as well as an inordinate amount of livestock.

p, Max Alexander, Arthur Alexander; d, Robert Hill; w, Rock Hawley [Robert Hill] (based on the story by William Colt MacDonald); ph, Harry Forbes.

Western   (PR:A   MPAA:NR)

TOO MUCH HARMONY**   (1933) 76m PAR bw

Bing Crosby *(Eddie Bronson)*, Jack Oakie *(Benny Day)*, Judith Allen *(Ruth Brown)*, Skeets Gallagher *(Johnny Dixon)*, Harry Green *(Max Merlin)*, Lilyan Tashman *(Lucille Watson)*, Ned Sparks *(Lem Spawn)*, Kitty Kelly *(Patsy Dugan)*, Grace Bradley *(Verne La Mont)*, Anna Demetrio *(Mrs. Galloti)*, Evelyn Oakie *(Mrs. Day)*, Billy Bevan *(Stage Director)*, Shirley Grey *(Lilyan)*, Henry Armetta *(Gallotti)*, Dell Henderson, Cyril Ring, Sammy Cohen.

An old-fashioned backstage show-biz yarn that bears more than a passing resemblance to CLOSE HARMONY (1929), a talkie which was co-directed by Sutherland with titles written by Mankiewicz. Crosby is a New York stage personality who finds himself stuck in a tiny Ohio town. While there, he meets a terrific comedy team in Oakie and Gallagher, plus young Judith Allen, a looker if there ever was one. He helps Allen get her chance at Broadway stardom and she succeeds in that, as well as nabbing Der Bingle out of the clutches of naughty Tashman. Green scores as a noisy, cantankerous Broadway producer; Sparks contributes some funnies as a man who despises actors and Oakie's real-life mother, Evelyn Oakie, shows where her son got his talent. Coslow and Johnston wrote some undistinguished numbers which include Crosby's singing of "Thanks" and "Black Moonlight" (a sequence that has a bevy of chorus beauties change colors from white to black and back to white). Other songs include: "Cradle Me With A Ha-Cha Lullaby," "Two Aristocrats," "Buckin' the Wind," "The Day You Came Along," and "Boo Boo Boo." Some charm, a few funny lines, but little else to recommend it other than Crosby's personal magnetism. Allen disappeared from the screen quickly after this. The role called for a chirper but it was obvious that she didn't have it in the vocal department as the singing voice did not match her speaking voice, whether in tone, timbre, or lip movements.

p, William Le Baron; d, A. Edward Sutherland; w, Harry Ruskin (based on a story by Joseph L. Mankiewicz); ph, Theodore Starkuhl; m/l, Arthur Johnston, Sam Coslow.

Musical/Comedy   (PR:A   MPAA:NR)

TOO MUCH FOR ONE MAN   (SEE: CLIMAX, THE, 1967, Fr./Ital.)

TOO MUCH, TOO SOON**   (1958) 121m WB bw

Dorothy Malone *(Diana Barrymore)*, Errol Flynn *(John Barrymore)*, Efrem Zimbalist, Jr *(Vincent Bryant)*, Ray Danton *(John Howard)*, Neva Patterson *(Michael Strange)*, Murray Hamilton *(Charlie Snow)*, Martin Milner *(Lincoln Forrester)*, John Dennis *(Walter Gerhardt)*, Edward Kemmer *(Robert Wilcox)*, Robert Ellenstein *(Gerold Frank)*, Kathleen Freeman *(Miss Magruder)*, John Doucette *(Crowley)*, Michael Mark *(Patterson)*, Francis DeSales, Jay Jostyn *(Imperial Pictures Executives)*, Herb Ellis, Louis Quinn *(Assistants)*, Robert S. Carson *(Associate)*, Paul Bryar *(Bill)*, Sid Tomack *(Harry/Dick Harrison, Swimming Companion)*, Jack Lomas, Larry Blake *(Reporters)*, Don Hayden *(Theater Manager)*, James Elsegood *(Diana's Tango Partner)*, Bess Flowers, Charles Evans *(Guests)*, Lyn Osborn *(Man)*, Nesdon Booth *(Spectator)*, Jack Rice *(Druggist)*, Gail Bonney *(Nurse)*.

A truncated cinematic version of Diana Barrymore's tell-all autobiography which leaves out too much and doesn't end soon enough. Malone does well as the star-crossed young woman who was the offspring of John Barrymore (played with puffiness by Flynn) and socialite Blanche Oelrichs (Patterson), who wrote poetry under the name of Michael Strange. It is a depressing tale that shows the young daughter seeking affection but having a pair of parents who are too busy to offer her anything in the emotion department. This causes her to take a trio of husbands. The first is Zimbalist (representing actor Bramwell Fletcher), a nice enough chap who can't handle her drinking. Then she teams up with Danton, perhaps the most sadistic and vicious heel she could have met. Danton plays it to the hilt and is so good at making us despise him that audiences hated him for three pictures after this one. Her last husband is Kemmer (playing actor Robert Wilcox), a man who has sworn off the bottle, for a while. The episodic tale takes us through Malone's degradation as she attempts to make a career of acting. They sort of indicate that she only appeared in one film and was a dismal failure, but that's not true. Barrymore herself made three films in 1942 alone, when she was 21 years old. They were EAGLE SQUADRON, BETWEEN US GIRLS, and NIGHTMARE. In 1942, she appeared in FRONTIER BADMEN and FIRED WIFE. In 1944, she was in LADIES COURAGEOUS. The movie further glosses over her amorous adventures with several men and doesn't touch upon the stage success she had on the road with "Cat on a Hot Tin Roof." Flynn had come back to Warner Bros. to make this movie, his contract having lapsed in 1954 when he made his last movie for the Burbank lot, THE MASTER OF BALLANTRAE. Flynn and Barrymore had been drinking buddies until Barrymore died in 1942 at the age of 62. He was able to pull off the impersonation in a couple of scenes, mainly due to the excellent makeup and hair styling. Barrymore was drunk many times in his life and so was Flynn and it is alleged that Flynn was indeed zonked when he shot the scenes of Barrymore under the influence. There was a moment when Flynn might have been able to bring off the role. Flynn is aboard his yacht, drunk, and begins a Shakespearean monolog as the lights from another boat hit his yacht and make the deck seem to be a stage. But Flynn, who was a better actor than usually credited, was nowhere near the bard interpreter that Barrymore was and the scene falls flat. Bad editing, old stock shots, lethargic direction, and documentary-style cinematography all work against the picture. Flynn died the following year at the age of 50 after having made two more films, THE ROOTS OF HEAVEN and CUBAN REBEL GIRLS, which he narrated, co-produced, and wrote. In small roles, note radio's "Mr. District Attorney" Jay Jostyn and funnyman Louis Quinn (Roscoe on "77 Sunset Strip" with Zimbalist). The frankness of the story makes it ill-suited for children.

p, Henry Blanke; d, Art Napoleon; w, Napoleon, Jo Napoleon (based on the book by Diana Barrymore, Gerold Frank); ph, Nick Musuraca, Carl Guthrie; m, Ernest Gold; ed, Owen Marks; art d, John Beckman; set d, George James Hopkins; cos, Orry-Kelly; makeup, Gordon Bau.

Biography (PR:C MPAA:NR)

TOO SOON TO LOVE** (1960) 85m Dynasty/UNIV bw (GB: TEENAGE LOVERS); AKA HIGH SC HOOL HONEYMOON)

Jennifer West (Cathy Taylor), Richard Evans (Jim Mills), Warren Parker (Mr. Taylor), Ralph Manza (Hughie Wineman), Jack Nicholson (Buddy), Jacqueline Schwab (Irene), Billie Bird (Mrs. Jefferson), William Keen (The Doctor).

West and Evans are a pair of young lovers who start their downhill slide into romance by getting arrested for necking in public. Ignoring the warnings of their parents, the pair finds themselves in a real bind when West discovers that she is pregnant. They first try an illegal abortion but are turned off by the sleaziness, turning then to a real doctor. In order to pay the medical bill Evans steals $500, but meets objection from West, who fails in an attempt to commit suicide. Nicholson makes an early appearance, as does writer-director Richard Rush (THE STUNT MAN, 1980) who produced this picture independently and then sold it to Universal. A first filmic effort for the two young stars.

p&d, Richard Rush; w, Rush, Laszlo Gorog; ph, William Thompson; m, Ronald Stein; ed, Stefan Arnstein; art d, Victor Ramos.

Drama (PR:C MPAA:NR)

TOO TOUGH TO KILL*½ (1935) 58m COL bw

Victor Jory (John O'Hara), Sally O'Neil (Ann Miller), Thurston Hall (Whitney), Johnny Arthur (Willie Dent), Robert Gleckler (Bill Andersson), George McKay (Nick Pollack), Robert Middlemass (Hubbel), Dewey Robinson (Shane), Ward Bond (Danny).

When progress on the construction of a tunnel is delayed, engineer Jory is sent into the mountains to insure that it is completed on time. With the help of news girl O'Neil and her cameraman Arthur, he cleans up on recalcitrant crew members, getting rid of the troublemakers. They also uncover a plot to kill Jory, but are successful in preventing bloodshed.

d, D. Ross Lederman; w, Lester Cole, J. Griffin Jay (based on a story by Robert D. Speers); ph, George Meehan; ed, Gene Milford.

Drama (PR:A MPAA:NR)

TOO YOUNG TO KISS** (1951) 91m MGM bw

June Allyson (Cynthia Potter), Van Johnson (Eric Wainwright), Gig Young (John Tirsen), Paula Corday (Denise Dorcet), Kathryn Givney (Miss Benson), Larry Keating (Danny Butler), Hans Conried (Mr. Sparrow), Esther Dale (Mrs. Boykin), Jonathan Cott (Photographer), Antonio Filauri (Veloti), Jo Gilbert (Gloria), Alexander Steinert (Conductor), Bob Jellison (Sparrow's Assistant), Lisa Ferraday (Nina Marescu), Teddy Infuhr (Jeffrey), Ruthelma Stevens (Jeffrey's Mother), Albert Morin (East Indian), Ludwig Stossel (German Accompanist), Betty Farrington, Elizabeth Fournoy, Grace Hayle (Women), Josephine Whittell (Mrs. Fullerton), George McDonald (Boy in Drugstore), Erno Verebes (Headwaiter), Peter Brocco (Waiter), Everett Glass (Druggist), Jack Gargan (Paul the Chauffeur), Jimmy Ames (Cab Driver), Robert Strong, Larry Harmon, Roger Moore (Photographers), Ray Walker (Reporter), Matt Moore (Charles), Bob Stephenson (Stagehand), John McKee (Motorcycle Officer), John Maxwell (Detective), Larry Harmon (Conductor).

An implausible but entertaining comedy which casts the 34-year-old Allyson as a struggling concert pianist who tries her darndest to audition with impresario Johnson. Rebuffed, she resorts to disguising herself as a 14-year-old bobby-soxer complete with braces and a pigeon-toed walk in order to appear to be a child prodigy. Johnson falls for her trick and maintains a healthy, fatherly care for the girl, much to the dismay of Allyson. When he notices her fondness for a drink and a cigarette he begins to feel like more than a protector. Her real identity is eventually revealed and romance blooms. The joke wears thin after a while as with any film gimmick, but Allyson is able to carry it off.

p, Sam Zimbalist; d, Robert Z. Leonard; w, Frances Goodrich, Albert Hackett (based on a story by Everett Freeman); ph, Joseph Ruttenberg; ed, Conrad A. Nervig; md, Johnny Green; art d, Cedric Gibbons, Paul Groesse; cos, Helen Rose.

Comedy (PR:A MPAA:NR)

TOO YOUNG TO KNOW** (1945) 86m WB bw

Joan Leslie (Sally Sawyer), Robert Hutton (Ira Enright), Dolores Moran (Patsy O'Brien), Harry Davenport (Judge Boller), Rosemary DeCamp (Mrs. Enright), Barbara Brown (Mrs. Wellman), Robert Lowell (Johnny Cole), Arthur Shields (Mr. Enright), Craig Stevens (Maj. Bruce), Don McGuire (Lt. Yates), Dick [Richard] Erdman (Tommy), Robert Arthur (Jimmy), Johnny Miles (Lt. Beal), Larry Thompson (Transport Pilot), Dorothy Malone (Mary), Angela Greene, Ramsey Ames, Betty Brodel, Pat Clark, John Compton, John Sheridan, Sid Chatton, Larry Rio (Party Guests).

A wartime romance which pairs Leslie and Hutton as young lovers who marry as teenagers before Hutton goes off to battle. After a three-year stint knocking Japanese planes out of the sky, Hutton hears word that his wife has left him and given away the son he didn't even know he had. He arranges for a trip home and with the help of a kindly judge is reconciled with Leslie and the little one. Emotion overshadows intelligence on this one. Director De Cordova's debut in the position (he had done dialog directing and had worked on stage plays); he matriculated to a long career as a TV talk show director. This was actress Malone's first film for Warner Bros.

p, William Jacobs; d, Frederick de Cordova; w, Jo Pagano (based on a story by Harlan Ware); ph, Carl Guthrie; m, Heinz Roemheld; ed, Folmer Blangsted; md, Leo F. Forbstein; art d, Stanley Fleischer; spec eff, Edwin Du Par.

Romance (PR:A MPAA:NR)

TOO YOUNG TO LOVE*½ (1960, Brit.) 88m Beaconsfield-Welbeck/RANK bw

Thomas Mitchell (Judge Bentley), Pauline Hahn (Elizabeth Collins), Joan Miller (Mrs. Collins), Austin Willis (Mr. Collins), Vivian Matalon (Larry Webster), Sheila Gallagher (Ruby Lockwood), Jess Conrad (Peter Martin), Miki Iveria (Mrs. Martin), Alan Gifford (Mr. Elliott), Cec Linder (Mr. Brill), Bessie Love (Mrs. Busch), Cal McCord (Owens), Robert Henderson (Keller-er), Charles Farrell (Waiting Room Man), Ilona Ference (Miss Porter), Roma Miller (Records Clerk), Bill O'Connor (Court Attendant), Bee Duffell (Society Matron), Robert Desmond (1st Sailor), Tom Gerrard (2nd Sailor), Ian Hughes, Margaret Griffin, Michael Bell, Eric Hewitson, Larry Martyn, Nicholas Evans, Malcolm Knight.

Mitchell does all he can to keep this picture from failing but that's not enough. He is cast as a judge hearing the case of young Hahn, a decent New York kid caught up in a web of circumstances. We see her life in flashbacks which include an abortion after a fling with a sailor, and an arrest after being caught in bed with a man more than twice her age. Hurt mainly by its excess of courtroom scenes.

p, Herbert Smith; d, Muriel Box; w, Muriel Box, Sydney Box (based on the play "Pick-up Girl" by Elsa Shelley); ph, Gerald Gibbs; m, Bruce Montgomery; ed, Jean Barker.

Drama (PR:C MPAA:NR)

TOO YOUNG TO MARRY*½ (1931) 67m FN/WB bw (AKA: BROKEN DISHES)

Loretta Young (Elaine Bumpstead), Grant Withers (Bill Clark), O. P. Heggie (Cyrus Bumpstead), Emma Dunn (Mrs. Bumpstead), J. Farrell MacDonald (Rev. Mr. Stump), Lloyd Neal (Sam Green), Richard Tucker (Chester Armstrong), Virginia Sale (Myra Bumpstead), Aileen Carlisle (Mabel Bumpstead).

An uneventful small-town drama about a sheepish man who finally stands up to his domineering wife, Dunn, and children, with only daughter Young sticking up for him. At first the family is baffled by this sudden show of strength but soon learns to respect him when he gives his consent for Young to marry grocerboy Withers against the wishes of Dunn. Remade in 1936 as LOVE BEGINS AT TWENTY and again in 1940 as CALLING ALL HUSBANDS. Based on the play "Broken Dishes," in which Bette Davis appeared on Broadway.

d, Mervyn LeRoy; w, Francis Edwards Faragoh (based on the Martin Flavin play "Broken Dishes"); ph, Sid Hickox; ed, John Rollins; md, Leo F. Forbstein.

Drama/Comedy (PR:A MPAA:NR)

TOO YOUNG, TOO IMMORAL! zero (1962) 89m Raymond A. Phelan/Rialto bw

John Francis (Mr. Claude), Larry Healey (Joseph), Raymond A. Phelan (Tony Brooks), Donald Shumway (Henry), Taylor Mead (Scribbles), Donald Ratka (Gene Brooks), Susan Ashley (Mary Boyd), Brenda DeNaut (Leeta).

Too pathetic to pay much attention to, this New York underground drug addiction picture tells the tale of a kid hooked on heroin as narrated by his brother. When the junkie mysteriously dies, his brother discovers that the head pusher, an old man in a wheelchair with a Rolls Royce, had him killed when he tried to kick the habit. By the finale vengeance is taken and the culprits are bumped off. This one's as amateurish as they come.

p,d,w&ph, Raymond A. Phelan; m, Bob Vinas, Joe Boppo, Kenny Harris; ed, Phelan.

Drama   (PR:O MPAA:NR)

TOOLBOX MURDERS, THE zero   (1978) 93m Cal-Am c

Cameron Mitchell (*Kingsley*), Pamelyn Ferdin (*Laurie*), Wesley Eure (*Kent*), Nicholas Beauvy (*Joey Ballard*), Aneta Corsaut (*JoAnn Ballard*), Tim Donnelly (*Detective Jamison*), Faith McSwain, Marciee Drake, Mariane Walter, Kelly Nichols (*Victims*), Evelyn Guerrero (*Butch*).

A sick piece of trash with appeal only to those who are or should be locked up. Mitchell is a deranged building superintendent who kills off his victims with an array of tools–a hammer, drill, screwdriver, and a nail gun–while singing "Sometimes I Feel Like A Motherless Child." The filmmakers then try to redeem themselves by telling us that he is getting revenge for the death of his daughter. Sadly deranged.

p, Tony Didio; d, Dennis Donnelly; w, Robert Easter, Ann N. Kindberg; ph, Gary Graver (EFI Color); m, George Deaton; ed, Skip Lusk.

Horror   Cas.   (PR:O MPAA:R)

TOOMORROW*   (1970, Brit.) 95m Lowndes-Sweet Music/RANK c

Olivia Newton-John (*Olivia*), Benny Thomas (*Benny*), Vic Cooper (*Vic*), Karl Chambers (*Karl*), Roy Dotrice (*John Williams*), Imogen Hassall (*Amy*), Tracey Crisp (*Suzanne Gilmore*), Maria O'Brien (*Francoise*), Lynda Westover (*Jenny*), Margaret Nolan (*Johnson*), Roy Marsden (*Alpha*), Carl Rigg (*Matthew*), Student Harry, Sam Apple Pie.

An innocent but mindless science-fiction tale about a group of Chelsea youngsters who finance their schooling by playing in a pop band. They invent something called a "tonalizer" which arouses the interest of something named an "Alphoid." The alien whisks away the teens and has them play their music in the hope of bringing about universal harmony. Only of interest to see a young Newton-John before she made a fool of herself in GREASE. Coproduced by Don Kirshner, best known as the vibrant host of television's "Rock Concert".

p, Harry Saltzman, Don Kirshner; d&w, Val Guest; ph, Dick Bush (Panavision, Technicolor); m, Hugo Montenegro; prod d, Michael Stringer; art d, Ernest Archer, Bert Davey; cos, Ronald Paterson; spec eff, John Stears; m/l, Richie Adams, Mark Barkan.

Science-Fiction/Musical   (PR:A MPAA:NR)

TOOTSIE**   (1982) 116m COL c

Dustin Hoffman (*Michael Dorsey/Dorothy Michaels*), Jessica Lange (*Julie*), Teri Garr (*Sandy*), Dabney Coleman (*Ron*), Charles Durning (*Les*), Bill Murray (*Jeff*), Sydney Pollack (*George Fields*), George Gaynes (*John Van Horn*), Geena Davis (*April*), Doris Belack (*Rita*), Ellen Foley (*Jacqui*), Peter Gatto (*Rick*), Lynne Thigpen (*Jo*), Ronald L. Schwary (*Phil Weintraub*), Debra Mooney (*Mrs. Mallory*), Amy Lawrence (*Amy*), Kenny Sinclair (*Boy*), Susan Merson (*Page*), Michael Ryan, James Carruthers (*Middle-Aged Men*), Robert D. Wilson (*Stage Hand*), Estelle Getty (*Middle-Aged Woman*), Christine Ebersole (*Linda*), Bernie Pollack, Sam Stoneburner (*Actors*), Marjorie Lovett (*Salesgirl*), Willy Switkes (*Man at Cab*), Gregory Camillucci (*Maitre d'*), Barbara Spiegel (*Billie*), Tony Craig (*Joel*), Walter Cline (*Bartender*), Suzanne von Schaack (*Party Girl*), Anne Shropshire (*Mrs. Crawley*), Pamela Lincoln (*Secretary*), Mary Donnet (*Receptionist*), Bernie Passeltiner (*Mac*), Mallory Jones, Patti Cohane (*Girls*), Murray Schisgal (*Party Guest*), Greg Gorman (*Photographer*), Anne Prager (*Acting Student*), John Carpenter, Bob Levine (*Actors*), Richard Whiting (*Priest*), Tom Mardirosian, Jim Jansen (*Stage Managers*), Richard Wirth (*Mel*), Gavin Reed (*Director*), Annie Korzen, Ibbits Warriner, Lois de Banzie, Stephen C. Prutting, Carole Holland (*Autograph Hounds*).

A very funny movie about a man who pretends to be a woman in order to secure employment as an actor-actress. Hoffman is a stage actor with the reputation of being difficult. His agent is director Pollack, a man who suggests that Hoffman seek therapy in order to gain a better attitude. Hoffman's best friend is Murray and his girl friend is Garr. Hoffman is trying to make ends meet by taking various jobs when he hears about an audition at a local New York soap opera directed by Coleman. The part calls for a mature woman and Hoffman decides to dress in drag and try out for the role. Wonder of wonders, he gets it. His rise to fame is almost instant and he begins to shape the scripts in a way he feels his distaff character would approve. The ratings soar and Hoffman becomes famous, although no one knows what he's doing. Garr is a nervous, neurotic type who wants to spend more time with Hoffman, but he's busy working and can't tell her. She wonders if he has another girl friend or if he is, in fact, gay. While working on the soap, the leading male actor is Gaynes (in a brilliant performance) who evidently tries to sleep with every actress who works on the program. The scene in which he attempts to seduce Hoffman is side-splitting. Hoffman finds himself falling in love with the female star of the show, Lange, a single mother who is dating Coleman. Lange and Hoffman become girl friends and she invites Hoffman up to the farm where she grew up and where her father,

Durning, now lives. Durning falls for Hoffman and the farcical scenes are many. Meanwhile, Hoffman has to share a bed with Lange and painfully maintain his distance. Later, Hoffman comes on subtly to Lange and she suspects that he is a lesbian. After playing this out to the nth degree, Hoffman must eventually reveal his true identity because he can't carry off the charade any longer. He does this during a live scene on the soap opera where he rips off his wig and shows the loyal audience that his character is a man. In order to make that work, he departs from the script (driving director Coleman crazy) and changes the whole nature of the show's thrust. Later, Hoffman admits the truth to Durning and, in the finale, Hoffman and Lange are united, after she first tells him that she hates him for what he did. Since the beginning of literature, there have been plays that featured men in women's clothing. Shakespeare used the device often; there was "Charley's Aunt" and, in later years, one of the funniest films ever had Jack Lemmon and Tony Curtis as female musicians in SOME LIKE IT HOT. This time, the emphasis is not on how poorly the men pull it off (or even how well female impersonators do their job, as in LA CAGE AUX FOLLES or how well Julie Andrews played a man in VICTOR, VICTORIA) but on how well Hoffman does as the woman. Anyone with any perception would notice that she is a he, but the suspension of disbelief is handled perfectly and it never descends into gay jokes or anything even close to that. Every single actor and actress comes off well under Pollack's direction and it had been his best picture until OUT OF AFRICA swept the Oscars. If given the choice of Pollack films, watch this one. Pollack had been an actor and a drama coach and his acting in the film is excellent, limning the typical Broadway agent with a sharp delineation. This was Hoffman's followup to KRAMER VS. KRAMER and the wise guys were scratching their heads when they heard what the subject matter was, never dreaming that the creative team could make it work. A huge box office success that was also a hit with the critics, TOOTSIE trod the fine line between comedy and drama and provided the audience with a cast of people one could care about. Hoffman, Garr, Lange, Coleman, and all the others have seldom been better. The story was cowritten by Gelbart (who became a multimillionaire for having developed TV's M*A*S*H) and one-time actor Don McGuire, who left the thespian world (he was in PRIDE OF THE MARINES, HUMORESQUE, and THE FULLER BRUSH MAN) to try his luck at writing and directing and eventually ran the "Hennessey" TV series. Gelbart and Playwright Murray Shisgal (LUV) did the screenplay and Schisgal also did a cameo as a party guest. Although nobody will own up to it, our sources allege that Elaine May did some surgery and additional dialog on the script, a task she has performed without credit on many movies. TOOTSIE was nominated for an Oscar for Best Picture but lost out to Gandhi. Lange won the Award for Best Supporting Actress, beating out Garr, who was also nominated for her work in TOOTSIE. Other nominations from the Academy included Hoffman for Best Actor, Schisgal, McGuire, and Gelbart for Best Screenplay, Roizman for Best Cinematography, Fredric and William Steinkamp for Best Editing, and the hit song "It Might Be You" (Alan and Marilyn Bergman, Dave Grusin, sung by Stephen Bishop).

p, Sydney Pollack, Dick Richards; d, Pollack; w, Larry Gelbart, Murray Schisgal (uncredited, Elaine May, based on a story by Don McGuire, Gelbart); ph, Owen Roizman (Panavision, Technicolor); m, Dave Grusin; ed, Fredric Steinkamp, William Steinkamp; prod d, Peter Larkin; set d, Tom Tonery; cos, Ruth Morley; makeup, Dorothy Pearl, George Masters.

Comedy   Cas.   (PR:C MPAA:PG)

TOP BANANA*½   (1954) UA c

Phil Silvers (*Jerry Biffle*), Rose Marie (*Betty Dillon*), Danny Scholl (*Cliff Lane*), Judy Lynn (*Sally Peters*), Jack Albertson (*Vic Davis*), Johnny Coy (*Tommy Phelps*), Joey Faye (*Pinky*), Herbie Faye (*Moe*), Walter Dare Wahl (*Walter*), Bradford Hatton (*Mr. Parker*), Dick Dana (*Danny*), Johnny Trama (*Little Man*), Gloria Smith, George Marci (*Featured Dancers*), Carolyn Anderson, Marcia Mann, Kaye Gordon, Iris Burton, Mickey Barton, Mara Lynn, Vito Durante, Bill Joyce, Walter Koremin, Nikki Cellini, Charles Zulkeski, Sammy Steen (*Dancers*), Lee Whitney, Dee Harless, Kathy Collins, Gloria Wallace, Arlen Stuart, Patti Shafter, Joyce Stansell, Emmaline Henry, Candy Montgomery, Dave Gard, Pat Welch, Ed Whitman, Dell Hanley, Wayne MacIntyre, Hank Roberts, Tommy Ryan, Dean Campbell (*Singers*).

A photographed version of the Broadway musical that breaks all the cinematic rules and still manages to provide fine entertainment. Rather than "open" the story, they shot this on what appeared to be a stage like New York's Winter Garden theater, where the play dwelt, and just let the cameras roll and allowed the many fine comics to have their moments. Silvers is a manic-depressive, egotistical TV comedy star who more than a little resembles Uncle Miltie (Milton Berle) at the height of his career. When his ratings begin to droop, Silvers is ordered to add some young people as a love interest on his show. He hires Judy Lynn, a sales clerk, and Danny Scholl. Silvers finds himself falling for Lynn but she is going moon-eyes over Scholl. The usual complications occur with Albertson, as Silvers' harried aide, trying to smooth matters over. In the end, the lovers get together and the TV ratings soar. (An odd fact is that while Berle was at the top on NBC, he was knocked out of the public's eye by "You'll Never Get Rich" on CBS, starring Phil Silvers.) It's a long burlesque sketch with many of the best low-comedy faces in the business, like Joey and Herbie Faye, the marvelous Walter Dare Wahl, and Johnny Trama. One of the dancers was Emmaline

Henry, who later starred with John Astin and Marty Ingels on TV's "I'm Dickens, He's Fenster." Hy Kraft wrote the book for the play and Gene Towne did what little film adaptation was needed. Mercer, who usually only wrote lyrics, did the music as well. The songs included: "If You Want to Be a Top Banana," "My Home Is in My Shoes," "I Fought Every Step of the Way," "A Word a Day," "Sans Souci," "Only if You're in Love," and "The Man of the Year This Week." Ron Sinclair and Ron Fletcher are credited with the dances in different places and we can't tell you which is correct. If you find out, let us know. The term "Top Banana" refers to the number-one comedian while his stooges are called "second bananas" and where the expression came from may be the water-filled bladder-like club that comedians used to hit each other over the head way back when. The lack of any true motion picture values hurts the picture somewhat as it appears to be an old-fashioned TV kinescope but Silvers has such energy that he transcends any production problems. A lot of fun and squeaky clean.

p, Albert Zugsmith, Ben Peskay; d, Alfred E. Green; w, Gene Towne (based on the musical by Hy Kraft, Johnny Mercer); ph, William Bradford (Color Corporation of America); md, Harold Hastings, Albert Glasser; ch, Ron Fletcher or Ronald Sinclair; m/l, Mercer.

Musical/Comedy   **(PR:A   MPAA:NR)**

TOP FLOOR GIRL*½   (1959, Brit.) 71m Danziger/PAR bw

Kay Callard (Connie), Neil Hallett (Dave), Robert Raikes (Bob), Maurice Kaufmann (Peter Farnite), Brian Nissen (Stevens, Jr.), Diana Chesney (Miss Prentice), Elizabeth Fraser (Mabel), Arnold Bell (Stevens, Sr.), Robert Dorning, William Hodge, Mark Singleton, Terence Cooper, Vilma Ann Leslie, Ian Wilson, Norah Gordon, Totti Truman Taylor, Olive Kirby, Jan Holden, Hal Osmond, Pauline Arden, Hilary Tindall, Derek Prentice.

A familiar tale of an unscrupulous clerk, Callard, who will do anything to climb to the top. To ensure her success she gets herself engaged to the son of her wealthiest client. Before the marriage, however, she has a change of heart and falls in love with a small-time executive.

p, Edward J. Danziger, Harry Lee Danziger; d, Max Varnel; w, Brian Clemens, Eldon Howard; ph, Jimmy Wilson.

Romance/Drama   **(PR:A   MPAA:NR)**

TOP GUN½**   (1955) 73m Fame/UA bw

Sterling Hayden (Rick Martin), William Bishop (Canby Judd), Karen Booth (Laura), James Millican (Bat Davis), Regis Toomey (O'Hara), Hugh Sanders (Marsh), John Dehner (Quentin), Rod Taylor (Sutter), William "Bill" Phillips (Hank), Dick Reeves (Willetts), Denver Pyle.

A passable western which offers no surprises in its HIGH NOON-like characteristics. Hayden is the West's top gunman who returns to his former home town in order to warn of a raid by Dehner and his gang. The townsfolk want nothing to do with the loner, however, and end up imprisoning him on false charges. His girl friend, Booth, comes to his aid and gets him released in time to put up a battle against Dehner. Things look bad for Hayden until Booth herself picks up a gun and saves her loved one's life and the town's fortune. It may be cliched but at least the cliches are well-executed. Character actor Millican, here a kindly sheriff, died before the film's release.

p, Edward Small; d, Ray Nazarro; w, Richard Schayer, Steve Fisher (based on a story by Fisher); ph, Lester White; m, Irving Gertz; ed, Dwight Caldwell, Henry Adams; md, Gertz; art d, Frank Sylos.

Western   **(PR:A-C   MPAA:NR)**

TOP HAT**   (1935) 101m RKO bw

Fred Astaire (Jerry Travers), Ginger Rogers (Dale Tremont), Edward Everett Horton (Horace Hardwick), Helen Broderick (Madge Hardwick), Erik Rhodes (Alberto Beddini), Eric Blore (Bates, Butler), Lucille Ball (Flower Clerk), Leonard Mudie (Flower Salesman), Donald Meek (Curate), Florence Roberts (Curate's Wife), Edgar Norton (Hotel Manager, London), Gino Corrado (Hotel Manager, Venice), Peter Hobbes (Call Boy), Frank Mills (Lido Waiter), Tom Ricketts (Thackeray Club Waiter), Dennis O'Keefe (Elevator Passenger), Ben Holmes, Nick Thompson, Tom Costello, John Impolito, Genaro Spagnoli, Rita Rozelle, Phyllis Coghlan, Charles Hall.

This was the fourth pairing of Astaire and Rogers, and the first to have a screenplay written with their talents specifically in mind. It couldn't have been a better match. TOP HAT is the quintessential Astaire and Rogers musical, complete with silly plot, romance, dapper outfits, art deco sets, and, of course, plenty of wonderful songs and dance numbers. The film opens in London, though the real setting of TOP HAT is that mythical Hollywood concoction: Fred and Ginger Land. Astaire is an American dancer, newly arrived in London, and waiting at the Thackeray Club for his agent, Horton. Club rules strictly forbid any noise, even the crackling of a newspaper. When Horton finally picks up his man, Astaire bids adieu by tapping out a quick buck and wing, much to the chagrin of club members. While practicing some steps in Horton's hotel room for a new show, Astaire unknowingly wakes up the occupant of the room immediately below: Rogers. Rogers is angered and goes up to Horton's room to complain. There she confronts Astaire, who immediately falls in love with the beautiful woman. Astaire explains himself

by saying he sometimes just breaks out in fancy footwork as he suffers from "St. Vitus' Dance." Rogers returns to her room, while Astaire spreads sand from a fire bucket on his floor, lulling her to sleep with a soft-shoe number from above. Astaire begins sending flowers to Rogers' room (bought at a flower shop where young RKO starlet Ball can briefly be seen as a clerk), putting the posies on Horton's tab. When Rogers hires a hansom for a ride through London, she is surprised–but not displeased–to discover Astaire is driving the rig. He takes her to a gazebo, and, as it begins to rain, Astaire sings to her "Isn't This a Lovely Day (to Be Caught in the Rain)?" Astaire does some fancy footwork, and is surprised by Rogers' ability to match him step for step. Though she still doesn't know Astaire's name, Rogers is also falling in love. Back at the hotel, Rogers receives a letter from her friend Broderick, who is Horton's wife. In a case of mistaken identity, Rogers comes to believe Astaire is Broderick's husband. She slaps Astaire, then storms out of the hotel with her Italian dress designer, Rhodes. They leave for Venice, where Rogers intends to join Broderick. Horton, who is constantly befuddled, convinces himself that Rogers is out to create a scandal and ruin Astaire's new show. To protect his man, Horton sends his faithful butler, Blore, after Rogers to keep an eye on her. Astaire's show opens and he performs the number "Top Hat, White Tie and Tails." The show, naturally, is a big hit, but Astaire couldn't care less and flies off to Venice (in stock footage left over from the 1933 film FLYING DOWN TO RIO) with a reluctant Horton so he can chase Rogers. Astaire still tries to woo Rogers, who remains convinced he is Broderick's husband. She tells her friend that her husband has been flirting with her mercilessly, and Broderick responds by giving Horton a black eye. Astaire meets Rogers again, and the two dance "Cheek to Cheek." He asks her to marry him, and Rogers again responds with a slap. She decides her only course is to marry Rhodes. Eventually Broderick discovers the mix-up, and sets out to right things. She and Horton take Rhodes out for a ride on a boat, conveniently running out of gas, while Astaire straightens everything out with Rogers in a gondola. It turns out that Rhodes and Rogers had been married by a disguised Blore, so their marriage was never legal. Astaire and Rogers are now free to wed, and dance off to happiness. TOP HAT is an effervescent musical that was the perfect panacea for Depression-era audiences. The lighthearted plot (a virtual reworking of THE GAY DIVORCEE) is played with a good sense of whimsy. Astaire is dapper as can be, and Rogers is marvelous. Yet what really makes this work is the wonderful supporting cast. With the exception of Broderick (a stage comedienne here making her feature-film debut), the leading players had all appeared together in THE GAY DIVORCEE, with its remarkably similar mistaken-identity plot. Broderick–and Blore and Rhodes, as well–had appeared on stage with Astaire on Broadway; the four formed a comfortable ensemble. Character actors Meek and Roberts, who appear in the credits, were cut from the release print. Horton and Rhodes were two of the best character actors around, and TOP HAT gave them every opportunity to show why. Horton is delightful in his oft-confused role, while Rhodes' Italian caricature hits just the right notes of parody. Italian officials were highly offended by the character, though, and banned TOP HAT, along with THE GAY DIVORCEE (wherein Rhodes played a similar character) in their country for some time. Of course, the real highlights of the film are the wonderful dance numbers. "Top Hat, White Tie and Tails" is Astaire's big solo number. The sequence contains a clever bit of business in which Astaire "shoots" at the male chorus using his cane as a gun, with his tapping feet providing the gun blasts. This choreography had been an original idea of the great dancer's, one he had used before in the 1930 Broadway show, "Smiles." Though the show was a flop, Astaire remained fond of the idea and asked director Sandrich if he could resurrect it for the screen. In re-creating the work, Astaire demanded perfection. Thirteen canes were made for rehearsals and filming, and Astaire took to breaking one every time something went wrong. "He would take that cane and he would break it across his knee, just like that, and, of course, we were all shocked because we knew we only had 13 canes," recalled a production secretary. "It was a good thing we had that 13th cane because that was the take we printed." Paying a visit to the set during the shooting of the number was Astaire's fellow screen dancer James Cagney. After two takes, Astaire wanted to try the routine just once more, but Cagney took him aside, whispering to Astaire, "Don't shoot it again, kid–you got it on the second take. You'll never top that one." "I insisted on one more," Astaire recalled in his autobiography, "but Jimmy was right. Next morning when I saw the rushes, that second take was the one." "Cheek to Cheek" is perhaps the most famous of all the Astaire and Rogers duets, and for good reason. The number opens with the two gliding around the floor. Then, as the melody switches, they burst into some exuberant moves that sparkle with energy and imagination. Astaire's and Rogers' talents as a team were never better showcased, but creating the number proved to be a dancer's nightmare. Rogers' gown was literally covered with ostrich feathers. Astaire's wife Phyllis (who had some difficulty in pronouncing the letter "r") took one look at Rogers, then remarked to set visitor David Niven, "she looks like a wooster." During the rehearsal feathers flew off the dress like snow, and Astaire grew angry as they caused him to sneeze. During the next day's shooting, the problem still had not been remedied and Astaire angrily left the set after the feathers continued to get in the way of the dancing. After some heated exchanges, dress designer Bernard Newman agreed to sew the feathers in place. The third day of shooting went off without a hitch, but Astaire had learned his lesson well. After this experience, he personally inspected the dresses of all his on-screen dance partners, making sure there would be nothing in their design to get in the way of the choreography. Berlin's music was superb, and every one of his five songs for TOP HAT was a hit. On the September 28, 1935, broadcast of the popular radio show "Your Hit Parade," Berlin scored a coup as all five were lodged firmly in the top 15 songs of the week nationwide. The other two numbers include Astaire's opening solo "No Strings," and the grand finale, "The Piccolino," a production number that required over 125 hours of rehearsal. The producers had great faith in Berlin's talents, creating the film around his songs. The gazebo sequence was originally written to take place in a zoo, but this was quickly changed to fit the song's lyrics. The music generally received critics' kudos. Berlin was unable to write musical notation (he wrote his using a special piano that transposed keys for him), and some of the credit should have gone to the (uncredited) orchestrator, Edward Powell. Though this is one of Astaire's best-loved roles, he initially was unhappy with the script. In a furious handwritten note to producer Berman, Astaire expressed his displeasure with his character. The letter read (in part): "I am cast as a *straight juvenile* and a rather cocky and arrogant one at that–a sort of objectionable young man without charm or sympathy or humor .... After I go to the Lido—I dissolve into practically *nothing*–it seems saying or doing nothing at all interesting or humorous..." Changes were made to suit the star, though his complaints about being slapped twice by Rogers during the film's course were ignored. One sequence, in which Blore argues with an Italian policeman, was cut from some prints. TOP HAT, which cost RKO only $620,000 to produce, was an astounding hit with the public, bringing in over $3 million at the box office. It was the second biggest film gross of 1935 (after MUTINY ON THE BOUNTY) and proved to be the studio's biggest moneymaker of the decade. Both Astaire and Berlin got a percentage of the profits as well, which amounted to a tidy sum for each man. Though the picture won no Oscars, it did receive nominations for Best Picture, Best Art Direction, Best Choreography, and Best Song for "Cheek to Cheek."

p, Pandro S. Berman; d, Mark Sandrich; w, Dwight Taylor, Allan Scott (based on the musical "The Gay Divorcee" by Dwight Taylor, Cole Porter from the play "The Girl Who Dared" by Alexander Farago, Aladar Laszlo); ph, David Abel, Vernon L. Walker; ed, William Hamilton; md, Max Steiner; art d, Van Nest Polglase, Carroll Clark; set d, Thomas Little; cos, Bernard Newman; spec eff, Walker; ch, Fred Astaire, Hermes Pan; makeup, Mel Burns.

Musical/Romance   **Cas.**   **(PR:A MPAA:NR)**

TOP JOB   (SEE: GRAND SLAM, 1968, Ital./Span./Ger.)

TOP MAN*   (1943) 83m UNIV bw (GB: MAN OF THE FAMILY)

Donald O'Connor (*Don Warren*), Susanna Foster (*Connie Allen*), Lillian Gish (*Beth Warren*), Richard Dix (*Tom Warren*), Peggy Ryan (*Jan Warren*), Anne Gwynne (*Pat Warren*), Noah Beery, Jr (*Ed Thompson*), Samuel S. Hinds (*Fairchild*), Louise Beavers (*Cleo, Maid*), Dickie Love (*Tommy*), Marcia Mae Jones (*Erna*), David Holt (*Archie*), Barbara Brown (*Mrs. Fairchild*), Count Basie and His Orchestra, Borrah Minnevitch and His Harmonica Rascals, Bobby Brooks Quartet, Martha Vickers.

A lively musical which is typical of those that sprang up during WW II. O'Connor becomes man of the house when dad Dix gets called up for duty. To boost morale, O'Connor gathers up his sisters and classmates and puts on a show in a local factory. He even gets Count Basie to show up. Songs include: "Wrap Your Troubles In Dreams" (Ted Koehler, Harry Barris, Billy Moll); "Basie Boogie" (Count Basie); "Dream Lover" (Clifford Grey, Victor Schertzinger); "Dark Eyes," "Jurame," "The Road Song," and "Romany Life" (adapted by Inez James, Buddy Pepper).

p, Milton Schwarzwald, Bernard W. Burton; d, Charles Lamont; w, Zachary Gold (based on a story by Ken Goldsmith); ph, Hal Mohr; m, Charles Previn; ed, Paul Landres; md, Previn; art d, John Goodman; ch, Louis Da Pron.

Musical   **(PR:A MPAA:NR)**

TOP O' THE MORNING*   (1949) 100m PAR bw

Bing Crosby (*Joe Mulqueen*), Ann Blyth (*Conn McNaughton*), Barry Fitzgerald (*Officer Briany McNaughton*), Hume Cronyn (*Hughie Devine*), Eileen Crowe (*Biddy O'Devlin*), John McIntire (*Inspector Fallon*), Tudor Owen (*Cormac Gillespie*), Jimmy Hunt (*Pearse O'Neill*), Morgan Farley (*Edwin Livesley*), John Eldredge (*E. L. Larkin*), John "Skins" Miller (*Dowdler*), John Costello (*Village Gossip*), Dick Ryan (*Clark O'Ryan*), Bernard Cauley, Paul Connelly, John O'Brien (*Boys*), Gus Taillon (*Caretaker*), Mary Field (*Maid*).

The third time is often charmed when actors team up. This time it is charmless as Crosby and Fitzgerald get involved in some hokum that is so Irish you can smell the corned beef and cabbage coming off the screen. The Blarney Stone has been stolen and since it's insured by a U.S. company, the company sends its ace investigator, Crosby, over to Erin to help find the monument. He arrives in the small town and meets Fitzgerald, the crusty local constable, and his ineffectual assistant, Cronyn. The tourist business has fallen off in the small village because the rock of garrulousness is the only reason to visit the place. Eventually, the criminal is caught and the stone is returned. Along the way, Crosby falls in love with Fitzgerald's comely daughter, Blyth. Only four original songs, so it doesn't quite qualify

as a musical. The tunes by Johnny Burke and James Van Heusen include: "Top o' the Morning," "You're in Love With Someone," "The Donovans," and "Oh, 'tis Sweet to Think." The old chestnut "When Irish Eyes are Smiling" (Chauncy Olcott, Ernest Ball, George Graff, Jr.) is tossed in, just in case you weren't sure about where the action was taking place. Sentimental, slow, and too sweet for human consumption, this marked the final pairing of Crosby and Fitzgerald. In later years, Cronyn was sometimes confused with actor Harry Morgan (whose real name is Henry Morgan but he had to change it because of the other actor with the same name). Morgan told your editors that he was stopped on the street once and asked: "Say, aren't you that actor who was in BRUTE FORCE? You're...you're...right, your name is Human Crone." It's true, we swear it.

p, Robert L. Welch; d, David Miller; w, Edmund Beloin, Richard Breen; ph, Lionel Lindon; ed, Arthur Schmidt; md, Robert Emmett Dolan; art d, Hans Dreier, Henry Bumstead; set d, Sam Comer, Emile Kuri; cos, Mary Kay Dodson; ch, Eddie Prinz; m/l, James Van Heusen, Johnny Burke, Chauncey Olcott, George Graff, Jr., Ernest R. Ball; makeup, Wally Westmore.

Comedy/Musical   **(PR:A MPAA:NR)**

TOP OF THE BILL   (SEE: FANNY FOLEY HERSELF, 1931)

TOP OF THE FORM*   (1953, Brit.) 75m British Film Makers/GFD bw

Ronald Shiner (*Ronnie Fortescue*), Harry Fowler (*Albert*), Alfie Bass (*Artie Jones*), Jacqueline Pierreux (*Yvette*), Anthony Newley (*Percy*), Mary Jerrold (*Mrs. Bagshott*), Richard Wattis (*Willoughby-Gore*), Howard Marion-Crawford (*Dickson*), Roland Curram (*Terence*), Terence Mitchell (*Clarence*), Gerald Campion (*Pugley*), Oscar Quitak (*Septimus*), Kynaston Reeves (*The Dean*), Martin Benson (*Cliquet*), Eddie Sutch, Ronnie Corbett, Marcel Poncin, Ina de la Haye.

An entertaining comedy about a bookie, Shiner, who inadvertantly winds up as the head of a boys' school. Much to his surprise he discovers that his pupils are quite knowledgeable at gambling. He takes them on a trip to Paris where they all get entangled in a plot to steal the Mona Lisa. After the usual zany mishaps, Shiner and his students save the smiling Da Vinci from greedy hands. Look for a 23-year-old Ronnie Corbett, the costar of BBC-TV's "The Two Ronnies," in a bit part as a student. A remake of the 1937 British film WHERE THERE'S A WILL.

p, Paul Soskin; d, John Paddy Carstairs; w, Carstairs, Patrick Kirwan, Ted Willis, Val Guest, Leslie Arliss, Marriot Edgar (based on a story by Anthony Kimmins); ph, Ernest Steward.

Comedy   **(PR:A MPAA:NR)**

TOP OF THE HEAP*   (1972) 83m Fanfare-St. John Unlimited/Fanfare c

Christopher St. John (*George Lattimer*), Paula Kelly (*Black Chick, Singer*), Florence St. Peter (*Viola Lattimer*), Leonard Kuras (*Bobby Gelman*), Patrick McVey (*Tim Cassidy*), John Alderson (*Capt. Walsh*), Ingeborg Sorenson (*Nurse Swenson*), Allen Garfield [Goorwitz] (*Taxi Driver*), Ron Douglas (*Hip Passenger*), Almeria Quinn (*Valerie Lattimer*), Beatrice Webster (*George's Mother*), Essie McSwine (*African Dancer*), Jerry Jones (*Club Owner*), Willie Harris (*Bouncer*), Tiger Joe Marsh (*Man with Knife*), John McMurtry (*Dope Dealer*), Raymond O'Keefe (*Bus Driver*), Brian Cutler (*Rookie Policeman*), Hedgemon Lewis, Kenneth Norton (*Men in Bar*), Oamu King, Ji-Tu Cumbuka (*Pot Peddlers*), Marilyn Wirt (*Nurse*), Angela Seymour (*Young Hooker*), Joe Tornatore (*Policeman*), Ann Mason (*Walsh's Secretary*), Maria Lennard, Mayrita Varna, Dan Roth, Arnold Dover (*Reporters*), June Fairchild (*Balloon Thrower*), Cliff Emmich (*Hard-Hat*), Pamela Whorf (*Girl Rioter*), Richard M. Dixon (*The President*).

An interesting black exploitation film which combines the reality of police work with a number of fantasies with which St. John, one of the few black men on the police force, fills his empty existence. Despised by many of his coworkers and most of the street people, St. John resorts to scenes in which he pretends to be the first black astronaut or an explorer in Africa. Eventually he gets gunned down, ending the picture with a crack of harsh reality. St. John, who made his name in SHAFT (1971), was brought to court over a dispute on this film's writing credit. The suit filed argues that the Fanfare corporation hired Larry Bischof and Joe Greene as writers, but the credits list only St. John.

p,d&w, Christopher St. John; ph, Richard Kelley (Metrocolor); m, J. J. Johnson; ed, Mike Pozen; art d, Norman Houle; set d, Robert Signorelli; cos, Eddie Marks; spec eff, Tim Smyth; makeup, Maurice Stein.

Crime   **(PR:O MPAA:R)**

TOP OF THE TOWN*   (1937) 86m UNIV bw

George Murphy (*Ted Lane*), Hugh Herbert (*Hubert*), Gregory Ratoff (*J. J. Stone*), Ella Logan (*Dorine*), Gertrude Niesen (*Gilda Norman*), The Three Sailors [Jason, Robson, Blue] (*Themselves*), Henry Armetta (*Maestro Bacciagalluppi*), Mischa Auer (*Hamlet*), Doris Nolan (*Diana Borden*), Samuel S. Hinds (*Henry Borden*), Claude Gillingwater (*William Borden*),

Ernest Cossart (*Augustus Borden*), Richard Carle (*Edwin Borden*), Ray Mayer (*Roger*), Joyce Compton (*Beulah*), Peggy Ryan (*Herself*), Jack Smart (*Beaton*), Gerald Oliver Smith (*Borden Executive*), Carolyn Mason, Juanita Field, Mary Daair (*Girls*), The Californian Collegians, The Four Esquires.

TOP OF THE TOWN is a musical that just sits there without offering anything of value or having anyone pay much notice to it. The razor-thin plot has Manhattan heiress Nolan planning a ballet in the Moonbeam Room, a ballroom 100 stories off the ground. The audience is dreadfully bored, however, until Murphy saves the day by kicking up a storm with the sound of swing. The wall-to-wall collection of tunes includes "Blame It on the Rhumba," "Where Are You?" "Jamboree," "Top of the Town," "I Feel That Foolish Feeling Coming On," "There's No Two Ways About It," "Fireman Save My Child" (Harold Adamson, Jimmy McHugh). Some of the specialty acts include Auer doing a forgettable bit from "Hamlet," The Three Sailors doing a giraffe impersonation, Mayer doing a comic routine at the piano, and Ryan (in her preteen debut) doing a dance number.

p, Lou Brock; d, Ralph Murphy; w, Brown Holmes, Charles Grayson (based on the story by Brock); ph, Joe Valentine; md, Charles Previn.

Musical   (PR:A   MPAA:NR)

TOP OF THE WORLD**   (1955) 90m Landmark/UA bw

Dale Robertson (*Maj. Lee Gannon*), Evelyn Keyes (*Virgie Rayne*), Frank Lovejoy (*Maj. Cantrell*), Nancy Gates (*Lt. Mary Ross*), Paul Fix (*Maj. French*), Robert Arthur (*Lt. Skippy McGuire*), Peter Hansen (*Capt. Cochrane*), Nick Dennis (*Sgt. Cappi*), Russell Conway (*Col. Nelson*), William Shallert (*Capt. Harding*), Peter Bourne (*Lt. Johnson*), David McMahon (*Brownie the Bartender*), Marya Marco (*Koora*).

Action and romance are combined with an arctic setting as Robertson, an angered and aging WW II pilot, is sent to Alaska to help Lovejoy set up a weather post. Lovejoy's in love with nightclub owner Keyes, but officer Gates is in love with Lovejoy. Robertson, however, is still bitter over his recent divorce from, you'll never guess, Keyes. Mildly entertaining.

p, Michael Baird, Lewis R. Foster; d, Foster; w, John D. Klorer, N. Richard Nash; ph, Harry Wild, William Clothier; m, Albert Glasser; ed, Robert Ford; md, Glasser; art d, Wiard Ihnen.

Action/Romance   (PR:A   MPAA:NR)

TOP SECRET   (SEE: MR. POTTS GOES TO MOSCOW, 1953, Brit.)

TOP SECRET AFFAIR**½   (1957) 100m WB bw (GB: THEIR
                                                              SECRET AFFAIR)

Kirk Douglas (*Maj. Gen. Melville Goodwin*), Susan Hayward (*Dottie Peale*), Paul Stewart (*Bentley*), Jim Backus (*Col. Gooch*), John Cromwell (*Gen. Grimshaw*), Michael Fox (*Lotzie*), Frank Gerstle (*Sgt. Kruger*), Roland Winters (*Sen. Burwick*), A. E. Gould-Porter (*Butler*), Charles Lane (*Bill Hadley*), Edna Holland (*Myrna Maynard*), Ivan Triesault (*German Field Marshal*), Lee Choon Wha (*Korean Dignitary*), Franco Corsaro (*Armande*), Lyn Osborn (*Stumpy*), Patti Gallagher (*Girl*), Sid Chatton (*Drunk at Table*), Jonathan Hale (*Mr. Jones*), Charles Meredith (*Personage*), James Flavin (*Man*), Hal Dawson, Hugh Lawrence, Richard Cutting (*Reporters*).

Warner Bros. bought Marquand's book "Melville Goodwin, U.S.A.," then dispensed with it entirely and had a new screenplay written. It didn't help. Originally tailored as a film for Humphrey Bogart and Lauren Bacall, that was jettisoned when Bogie fell ill–terminally–and two unlikely comedy actors, Douglas and Hayward, were tapped for the leads. Hayward is a Clare Luce type who runs a magazine like *Time* or *Newsweek*. She is behind a civilian for an important diplomatic job and when she learns that Douglas, a general, has gotten the nod, she is irate and decides to use her publishing power to wreak some havoc. Her aim is to discredit Douglas so she invites him and public relations officer Backus out to her posh Long Island estate for what she says is an interview. Fox is a photographer and she hires him to snap some shots under cover as she inveigles Douglas to do silly things. Later, they begin touring the nightclubs and she tries to get Douglas tipsy, but fails. They go to a jazz club and she gets Douglas to sing with the group. Douglas is finally catching on that something is awry here. He goes back to her house without her. She arrives later, has had too much to drink, and almost drowns in her pool, but he saves her when she falls off the diving board. They kiss and sparks fly. In the morning, she admits that she is entranced by him and the article that was to be damning will now praise him. Douglas appreciates that but senses that she is after him and tells her that his life is the Army and that the only woman he ever felt anything for turned out to be a spy, whom he had shot. Hayward is livid; since hell hath no fury like a woman scorned, she plans to print the terrible article about Douglas. She sends it in for publishing and Douglas now realizes that he loves her and returns to the mansion to declare as much. But he's waited too long and the article comes out. Douglas must now face a Senate committee and Hayward feels awful about what she's done. She plans to flee the U.S. on a convenient vacation but she gets a summons from the Senate to appear in front of it. She is interrogated, admits that what was written was not true but there is one thing that is true– that Douglas did, in fact, know a spy and may have inadvertently blabbed something to her. Now we learn that Douglas did have a relationship with the late spy but it was

because he was told by his superiors to do that. His job was to give the spy erroneous information regarding the Korean police action. Once that's taken care of, Hayward and Douglas are free to have an affair that will surely lead to marriage. A few farcical scenes are all the comedy mustered in this feeble attempt at a Cary Grant/Doris Day movie. Neither Douglas nor Hayward is able to bring off the delicacy of the situations. Paul Stewart scores as Hayward's assistant. It's not that he gets the best lines, it's merely that he knows what to do with them. The head of the Senate group is Roland Winters, who was still going strong in 1986 when he was elected president of the Player's Club, in Edwin Booth's town house on Gramercy Park in New York. This attempt at building a souffle falls flatter than an omelet. The supporting cast was far better than the leads or the script and that is a problem that generally results in red ink at the box office, which is precisely what happened to TOP SECRET AFFAIR.

p, Martin Rackin; d, H. C. Potter; w, Roland Kibbee, Allan Scott (based on characters from the novel *Melville Goodwin, U.S.A.* by John P. Marquand); ph, Stanley Cortez; m, Roy Webb; ed, Folmar Blangsted; art d, Malcolm Bert; set d, William Wallace; cos, Charles LeMaire; makeup, Gordon Bau.

Comedy   (PR:A   MPAA:NR)

TOP SENSATION   (SEE: SEDUCERS, THE, 1970, Ital.)

TOP SERGEANT**   (1942) 66m UNIV bw

Leo Carrillo (*Franchy Devereaux*), Andy Devine (*Andy Jarrett*), Don Terry (*Dick Manson*), Elyse Knox (*Helen Gray*), Don Porter (*Al Bennett*), Addison Richards (*Col. Gray*), Bradley Page (*Tony Gribaldi*), Gene Garrick (*Jack Manson*), Alan Hale, Jr (*Cruston*), Roy Harris (*Roy*), Richard Davies (*Phil*), Emmett Vogan (*Prosecuting Officer*).

A dash of western and a pinch of war are tossed into this chase picture about a group of WW II noncommissioned officers who get mixed up with the apprehension of a trio of bank robbers. Two of the tobbers are killed and the final one is chased down until caught.

p, Ben Pivar; d, Christy Cabanne; w, Maxwell Shane, Griffin Jay (based on a story by Larry Rhine, Ben Chapman); ph, George Robinson; ed, Milton Carruth; md, H. J. Salter; art d, Jack Otterson.

Crime   (PR:A   MPAA:NR)

TOP SERGEANT MULLIGAN*   (1941) 70m MON bw

Nat Pendleton (*Mulligan*), Carol Hughes (*Avis*), Sterling Holloway (*Snark*), Marjorie Reynolds (*Gail*), Frank Faylen (*Dolan*), Charles Hall (*Doolittle*), Tom Neal (*Don*), Betty Blythe (*Mrs. Lewis*), Dick Elliott (*Mr. Lewis*), Maynard Holmes (*Briggs*), Wonderful Smith (*Himself*).

A pair of drug salesmen join the Army in the hope of dodging a tax collector, only to find that he's their sergeant. They go through the picture getting in and out of dumb situations while trying to keep their noses clean. Includes the ditty "$21 a Day–Once a Month." Redolent of some of the work of Stan Laurel and Oliver Hardy, but Faylen and Hall lack the talent of their illustrious predecessors.

p, Lindsley Parsons; d, Jean Yarbrough; w, Edmond Kelso; ph, Mack Stengler; ed, Jack Oglivie; m/l, Felix Bernard, Ray Klages.

Comedy   (PR:A   MPAA:NR)

TOP SPEED***   (1930) 80m FN-WB bw

Joe E. Brown (*Elmer Peters*), Bernice Claire (*Virginia Rollins*), Jack Whiting (*Gerald Brooks*), Frank McHugh (*Tad Jordan*), Laura Lee (*Babs Green*), Rita Flynn (*Daisy*), Edmund Breese (*Spencer Colgate*), Wade Boteler (*Sheriff*), Cyril Ring (*Vincent Colgate*), Edwin Maxwell (*J. W. Rollins*), Billy Bletcher (*Ipps*), Al Hill (*Briggs*).

Brown is an unsatisfied office clerk who adds some excitement to his life when he pretends to be a millionaire, borrows his girl friend's father's speedboat, and is the first to cross the finish line in a big race. It's all done on a slapstick level which is sure to draw a laugh out of most viewers. For its time, the dialog is rather risque; on release, the film risked censorship by the six states that then had review committees, each following its own set of guidelines (Pennsylvania had the most rigid rules, its censors barring even films which were permitted to play everywhere else). At its premiere, the picture featured the use of an early wide-screen process for the boat-race sequence. Includes some fine race footage as well as the following tunes: "Goodness Gracious," "I'll Know and She'll Know," "Keep Your Undershirt On," "What Would I Care," "Sweeter than You" (Bert Kalmar, Harry Ruby), "As Long as I Have You and You Have Me" (Al Dubin, Joe Burke), "Reaching for the Moon" (Irving Berlin).

d, Mervyn LeRoy; w, Humphrey Pearson, Henry McCarty (based on the play by Bert Kalmar, Harry Ruby, Guy Bolton); ph, Sid Hickox; ed, Harold Young; md, Erno Rapee; art d, Anton Grot; ch, Larry Ceballos.

Musical Comedy   (PR:A   MPAA:NR)

TOPAZ*½** (1969, Brit.) 126m UNIV c

John Forsythe (*Michael Nordstrom*), Frederick Stafford (*Andre Devereaux*), Dany Robin (*Nicole Devereaux*), John Vernon (*Rico Parra*), Karin Dor (*Juanita de Cordoba*), Michel Piccoli (*Jacques Granville*), Philippe Noiret (*Henri Jarre*), Claude Jade (*Michele Picard*), Michel Subor (*Francois Picard*), Roscoe Lee Browne (*Philippe Dubois*), Per-Axel Arosenius (*Boris Kusenov*), Edmon Ryan (*McKittreck*), Sonja Kolthoff (*Mrs. Kusenov*), Tina Hedstrom (*Tamara Kusenov*), John Van Dreelen (*Claude Martin*), Don Randolph (*Luis Uribe*), Roberto Contreras (*Munoz*), Carlos Rivas (*Hernandez*), Lewis Charles (*Mr. Mendoza*), Anna Navarro (*Mrs. Mendoza*), John Roper (*Thomas*), George Skaff (*Rene D'Arcy*), Roger Til (*Jean Chabrier*), Sandor Szabo (*Emile Redon*), Alfred Hitchcock (*Man in Wheelchair*), Lew Brown.

An espionage story that takes the cameras to Cuba, Denmark, New York, Virginia, and several other places, TOPAZ is based on the true-life exploits of French spy Philippe de Vosjoli. The film fails to fire up as much suspense as many of Hitchcock's fictional intrigues. With no stars to speak of, the movie had to get all its attention from the star status of the director, and consequently did not fare all that well at the box office. Stafford is a French spy who is helping the Central Intelligence Agency. The USSR is busy in Cuba and the U.S. wants to know exactly what they are up to in the year 1962. It's apparent that the Russians have someone supplying them with classified secrets from NATO and Stafford's assignment is to uncover the culprit. Arosenius, wife Kolthoff, and daughter Hedstrom defect from the Soviet embassy in Denmark and fly to the U.S. with the aid of Forsythe, an agent for the CIA. When Arosenius tells the Americans about what the Russkies are up to in Cuba (missiles being sent and placed in position), Forsythe gets in touch with cool Stafford and asks him to look into matters. Stafford enlists the aid of Browne, a spy with the cover job of florist. Browne learns of–and weasels his way into–a cadre of visiting Cubans who hang out at New York's Hotel Theresa. (Note: There really was a Hotel Theresa but it was torn down before the picture began shooting so they had to build a replica of it.) Browne manages to get some important information out of the Cubans and gives it to Stafford, who then travels to Havana where his girl friend, Dor, an anti-Castro person, orders her house workers to help Stafford. Two of her loyal staff are Charles and Navarro, who go up the side of a mountain masquerading as picnickers. While there, they shoot photos of Russian long-range missiles being unloaded from ships posing as freighters, not military vessels. When some local seagulls come after their food refuse, this is spotted and the two are arrested, just after stuffing the exposed roll of film in the remains of a chicken. Navarro and Charles are tortured and don't talk. Dor has another lover besides Stafford. It's Vernon, a man close to Castro. Vernon thinks that Stafford is not what he seems to be and orders him tossed out of the island country. Just as Stafford is leaving, Dor hands him a small book of romantic verse, which appears to be a token of her affection for him. However, inside the book is the film taken by Charles and Navarro (with a little chicken fat around the edges, no doubt). When Vernon learns that Dor has done that, he shoots and kills her. Stafford gets to the U.S., drops off the film, and returns to France where he learns that the leak in the French intelligence unit is his friend Piccoli, a spy who is also the lover of Stafford's wife, Robin. When Piccoli is accused of his treason, he kills himself. The name "TOPAZ" refers to the code name of the French ring of spies and has nothing to do with a gem, which this picture was not. Hitchcock's cameo appearance takes place when he is seen in a wheelchair, which was only fitting, as the little round man preferred directing from a seated position rather than risk the varicose veins that so many of his compatriots had criss-crossing their legs. Plenty of plot twists but they are not as motivated as we've become accustomed to in a Hitchcock film. They were never really certain of how to end this film and it is reported that three different endings were shot and tacked on the picture before they settled on the one mentioned above. One of the endings had a mano-a-mano duel in a huge stadium. The two combatants were Piccoli and Stafford, with a referee to handle the arbitrations and the "ready, aim, fire." Just before they shoot, a singer uses a high-powered rifle to kill Piccoli and Stafford shrugs it off by saying that the spy must have outlived his usefulness. Another ending had Piccoli going off to Russia while Robin and Stafford were on their way to the U.S. for a holiday. Two other endings may have been shot, but these have disappeared. Excellent location shooting and the budget of more than $4 million was up there on the screen. Hitchcock has had far better luck with fictional stories than with real ones, such as this. While several of his movies had some basis in fact (a newspaper item, a story told by a friend), the one where he hewed closest to the facts was THE WRONG MAN, which also was not a success. TOPAZ was a novelized version of the scandals which rocked France in the early 1960s and, like Robert Ludlum's novels of intrigue, was perhaps too cerebral to make a great movie. Hitchcock would make two more films, FRENZY and FAMILY PLOT, before his death in 1980.

p&d, Alfred Hitchcock; w, Samuel Taylor (based on the novel by Leon Uris); ph, Jack Hildyard (Technicolor); m, Maurice Jarre; ed, William Ziegler; prod d, Henry Bumstead; md, Jarre; set d, John Austin; cos, Edith Head; spec eff, Albert Whitlock; makeup, Bud Westmore, Leonard Engelman.

Spy Drama **Cas.** **(PR:C MPAA:M/PG)**

TOPAZE*½** (1933) 78m RKO bw

John Barrymore (*Auguste Topaze*), Myrna Loy (*Coco*), Albert Conti (*Henri*), Luis Alberni (*Dr. Bomb*), Reginald Mason (*Baron de Latour-Latour*), Jobyna Howland (*Baroness de Latour-Latour*), Jackie Searle (*Charlemagne de Latour-Latour*), Frank Reicher (*Dr. Stegg*).

An ultra-sophisticated comedy-drama that was a success with the critics and the public and showed off John Barrymore in a totally new light. Loy was on loan from MGM for THE ANIMAL KINGDOM and this and her performance was radiant in her underplaying. Based on a play by Marcel Pagnol, TOPAZE begins as Barrymore, a shy, timid French schoolteacher, attempts to cram some learning into his charges at a private school. The bane of his existence is rotten kid Searle, son of baron Mason and baroness Howland. Searle causes so much trouble in Barrymore's life that Howland insists the beloved teacher be fired. Meanwhile, Mason is having an affair with Loy and keeping her in a superb Parisian apartment. Mason owns a large chemical company that makes bottled water and is trying to elicit the endorsement of Alberni, a well-known chemist, for his new water, which is little more than tap water in a bright bottle. Now out of a job, Barrymore applies for employment with Mason and Mason soon realizes that Barrymore is apparently a boob. Since the man does hold a degree as a professor, Mason decides to name his sparkling water "Topaze" after the ex-teacher and the water becomes a success. Barrymore is busily experimenting in a huge laboratory they've given him and he thinks that the water they are selling is what he's perfected (a concoction totally free of bacteria and pure as fresh snow). When he learns that he's been duped, Barrymore rebels. The metamorphosis of the mouse to the man is slow and intriguing. Mason goes out with Loy and Barrymore for lunch and meets his own wife, Howland, but assures her that Loy is Barrymore's lover, not his. Barrymore becomes increasingly confident, changes his manner of clothing, his manner of speech and, in the end, winds up with Loy, who finds him increasingly attractive. When Barrymore demands a large piece of the company, Mason has no choice but to give it to him and Barrymore becomes a tycoon, with a staff to do his bidding (including the formerly recalcitrant Alberni). The ultimate irony is when he is invited back to the school from which he was fired and asked to present the award for best student to Searle. Barrymore, no longer cowed by his ex-employer at the school, delivers a stinging speech denouncing favoritism (obviously aimed at Searle) and gives the award to all of the students. Although the picture is brief at 78 minutes, the opening classroom sequence with the students takes up nearly 20 minutes, all in one room. It is so well done and the revelation of how this man thinks is so perfectly depicted that it never seems stagy or uncinematic. Barrymore had played one grandiose part after another and his last movie before this was as Prince Youssoupoff in RASPUTIN AND THE EMPRESS. So the role here was quite unlike anything audiences had come to expect from Barrymore and he demonstrated far more depth than in his more flamboyant films. Despite the fact that this movie was made more than a half century ago, it is still fresh and fulfilling and all one need do is substitute the name "Perrier" or "Evian" and the story of the sparkling water would be up to date. (That's not to say those two brands are anything but terrific. We only use them as an example.) This was the second version of Pagnol's play, but the first in English. They had done it before in 1932 and it was made again in 1936 and 1952. The mistress-lover relationship between Loy and Mason was explicit, not hinted at. The studio attempted to release the film again in 1936 but the Breen Office (run by Joseph Breen, the movie censor) refused to give it a certificate because of the lack of moral values in the promiscuous liaison between Mason and Loy. What's odd is that this 1933 movie, which was a box office hit as well as one of the best films cited by the National Board of Review, was suddenly too hot for the public three years later. It was in 1934 that the censorship began and the change in content was almost overnight. Movies prior to 1934 had some meat in them and even some racy moments. From the onset of Breen until late in the 1950s, it was all white bread and mayonnaise if you wanted to get the seal of approval. TOPAZE is not often seen in revival houses but can sometimes be found on pay cable TV services in the uncut state. Stay home and watch it.

p, David O. Selznick; d, Harry d'Abbadie d'Arrast; w, Ben Hecht (adapted by Benn W. Levy from the play by Marcel Pagnol); ph, Lucien Andriot; m, Max Steiner; ed, William Hamilton.

Comedy/Drama **(PR:C MPAA:NR)**

TOPAZE** (1935, Fr.) 92m Joinville/PAR bw

Louis Jouvet (*Auguste Topaze*), Edwige Feuilliere (*Coco*), Pauley, Simone Heliard, Marcel Vallee, Maurice Remy.

Jouvet and Feuilliere take on the roles played by John Barrymore and Myrna Loy in this remake of the Marcel Pagnol play, one of the most popular on the French stage. Feuilliere delivers an admirable performance as the mistress of a tycoon who becomes fond of a sheepish inventor, Jouvet. Truer to the original than its predecessor but not as well acted. One of three adaptations of Pagnol plays to be released with the advent of sound, TOPAZE was the only one filmed without the consent of the author. Pagnol was so offended by Paramount's having brought in another writer to redo his dialog that he became a film producer himself. He formed his own company to film his next few features, including FANNY, filmed in 1932, as was this version of TOPAZE.

d, Louis Gasnier; w, Leopold Marchand (based on the play by Marcel Pagnol).

Drama (PR:A MPAA:NR)

TOPEKA½ (1953) 69m Westwood/AA bw

Wild "Bill" Elliott (*Jim Levering*), Phyllis Coates (*Marian Harrison*), Rick Vallin (*Ray Hammond*), John James (*Marv Ronsom*), Denver Pyle (*Jonas Bailey*), Dick Crockett (*Will Peters*), Harry Lauter (*Mack Wilson*), Dale Van Sickel (*Jake Manning*), Ted Mapes (*Cully*), Fuzzy Knight (*Pop Harrison*), I. Stanford Jolley (*Doctor*), Michael Colgan, Michael Vallon, Edward Clark, Henry Rowland.

A gripping western tale in which outlaw Elliott is hired by helpless townspeople to help them defend themselves against a gang of bandits. Elliott rounds up his former gang to lend a hand, putting down the attack. He very nearly turns evil again and takes over the town for his own benefit, but is tamed by the love of Coates. Interestingly photographed, with a moody use of crane shots. TOPEKA is part of the series of westerns Elliott did for Allied Artists after leaving Republic.

p, Vincent M. Fennelly; d, Thomas Carr; w, Milton M. Raison; ph, Ernest Miller (Sepiatone); m, Raoul Kraushaar; ed, Sam Fields.

Western (PR:A MPAA:NR)

TOPEKA TERROR, THE** (1945) 55m REP bw

Allan Lane (*Chad Stevens*), Linda Stirling (*Jane Hardy*), Roy Barcroft (*Ben Jode*), Earle Hodgins (*Don Quizote*), Twinkle Watts (*Midge Hardy*), Bud Geary (*Clyde Flint*), Frank Jacquet (*Trent Parker*), Jack Kirk (*Mr. Green*), Tom London (*William Hardy*), Eve Novak (*Mrs. Green*), Hank Bell (*Stage Driver*), Bob Wilke (*Townsman*), Monte Hale, Jess Cavan, Fred Graham.

Set in 1893, THE TOPEKA TERROR tells the story of greedy, manipulative land-grabber Barcroft who tries to buy up the developing Cherokee Strip during the Homesteaders' era. Barcroft victimizes a number of honest, hard-working settlers by recording false claims in the name of his own henchmen. When London and his two daughters, Stirling and Watts, are cheated, they receive a helping hand from Lane, a kindly federal agent, and Hodgins, a lawyer who fights for the people. With the law on their side, the cheated townspeople are able to take their revenge on Barcroft.

p, Stephen Auer; d, Howard Bretherton; w, Patricia Harper, Norman S. Hall (based on a story by Harper); ph, Bud Thackery; ed, Charles Craft; md, Richard Cherwin; art d, Frank J. Arrigo. set d, Charles Thompson.

Western (PR:A MPAA:NR)

TOPKAPI*** (1964) 120m Filmways/UA c

Melina Mercouri (*Elizabeth Lipp*), Peter Ustinov (*Arthur Simpson*), Maximilian Schell (*William Walter*), Robert Morley (*Cedric Page*), Akim Tamiroff (*Geven*), Gilles Segal (*Giulio*), Jess Hahn (*Fischer*), Titos Vandis (*Harback*), Ege Ernart (*Maj. Tufan*), Senih Orkan, Ahmet Danyal Topatan (*Shadows*), Joseph Dassin (*Josef*), Amy Dalby (*Nanny*), Despo Diamantidou (*Voula*).

Jules Dassin went back to his hit RIFIFI and spoofed it with this delightful, fast-moving tale of a caper peopled with some of the most delightful types ever assembled on one screen. Locationed in Istanbul and Greece, TOPKAPI is a movie marshmallow that wrings out every cinematic trick, counterpointed with dialog that's sparkling, witty, and pungent. Mercouri (Dassin's real-life wife) is an unreconstituted sexpot whose lover is Schell. The two want to steal a priceless dagger from the heavily secured museum in Istanbul known as Topkapi. To pull off the job, they enlist the aid of some compatriots. Morley is an addled but brilliant British inventor and expert in electronics and burglar alarms, Segal is a mute acrobat who could climb a sheer wall with his fingernails, Hahn is a muscular lout. While in Kavala, Greece, the gang hires Ustinov, a low-life con-man, to drive an expensive car across the border into Turkey. Ustinov doesn't know that the car contains weapons and gear for the robbery and when he is stopped at the border, one of the Turkish police (Ernart) thinks that this may be part of some terrorist ploy. Rather than arrest Ustinov, whom the cops soon realize is a dupe, they ask him to infiltrate the group who've hired him and to report on what they are up to. Ustinov arrives in Turkey and delivers the goods (some bombs, a high-powered rifle) to the gang's villa. The daring robbery is carefully calculated. Hahn will hold a rope and lower Segal through a window. The floor of the museum has wires all through it so a single step will set off the alarm. But Segal will hang from the rope, reach down and take the dagger without ever touching the floor. Meanwhile, at the gang's sumptuous mansion, the alcoholic cook, Tamiroff, believes that Mercouri and the others are Soviet agents and he passes this on to Ustinov, who still doesn't know about the robbery. Ustinov informs Enart. The robbery is about to take place when Tamiroff accidentally hurts Hahn's powerful hand by crushing it in a doorway. With the strongman immobilized, Ustinov is pressed into service to be the man holding the rope, a job for which the paunchy Brit is unsuited. The robbery goes off well, in a long sequence that shows every detail of how they do it (not unlike the silent robbery in RIFIFI). Once the dagger is lifted and the group has avoided capture by Enart, they arrange to have the jeweled dagger smuggled out of the country. But a bird flies in through the

still-open window of the museum, lands on the floor, triggers the alarm and the theft is discovered. The gang members are apprehended and tossed in the clink but their spirit is still strong as Mercouri begins telling the others about her plot to steal the Russian crown jewels from the impenetrable Kremlin. It was based on a little-known book and adapted beautifully by screenwriter Danischewsky. Mercouri is the only woman of any consequence in the movie and she has a marvelous time surrounded by all the men. In any other year, she might have merited an Oscar nomination, but 1964 was the moment for Julie Andrews in MARY POPPINS. Ustinov won a Best Supporting Oscar for his work and deserved it. Ustinov keeps all of his numerous awards in a glass case in his bathroom and when a producer thought that it was sacrilege to place kudos in such a room, Ustinov explained that its's the only location in his residence where he can think about his own exploits without seeming to be egotistical. A fun movie with lots of laughs, a bit of the aforementioned RIFIFI, a smidgeon of BEAT THE DEVIL, and a lot of its own originality. Not to be missed.

p&d, Jules Dassin; w, Monja Danischewsky (based on the novel *The Light of Day* by Eric Ambler); ph, Henri Alekan (Technicolor); m, Manos Hadjidakis; ed, Roger Dwyre; art d, Max Douy; set d, Andre Labussiere; cos, Denny Vachlioti.

Comedy/Adventure Cas. (PR:A-C MPAA:NR)

TOPPER*** (1937) 98m MGM bw

Constance Bennett (*Marion Kerby*), Cary Grant (*George Kerby*), Roland Young (*Cosmo Topper*), Billie Burke (*Henrietta Topper*), Alan Mowbray (*Wilkins*), Eugene Pallette (*Casey*), Arthur Lake (*Elevator Boy*), Hedda Hopper (*Mrs. Stuyvesant*), Virginia Sale (*Miss Johnson*), Theodore Von Eltz (*Hotel Manager*), J. Farrell MacDonald (*Policeman*), Elaine Shepard (*Secretary*), Doodles Weaver, Si Jenks (*Rustics*), Three Hits and a Miss (*Themselves*), Donna Dax (*Hat Check Girl at Rainbow Nightclub*), Hoagy Carmichael (*Bill the Piano Player*), Claire Windsor, Betty Blythe (*Ladies*).

Low-budget comedy producer Hal Roach, who had made a fortune off of Laurel and Hardy shorts, finally decided to risk a big-budget, feature-length sophisticated comedy and came up with a winner that would spawn two sequels, a television series and a made-for-TV remake. Grant and Bennett play a young, wealthy, happy-go-lucky married couple whose main pursuit in life is having a good time. Though they are the chief stockholders in a bank run by the dour, seemingly morose Young, Grant and Bennett's minds are on anything but business (Grant doodles during board meetings and tries to write his name upside down and backward). One night, while they drive recklessly in their big car at high speeds while drunk, they hit a tree and are killed. Their spirits walk out of the wreck and the couple is dismayed to discover that they have not ascended to the heavens but are still on Earth, albeit in a rather astral form (they can turn invisible at will). The couple decide that they will probably be trapped on Earth forever unless they redeem their frivolous life style by doing something of value. After a short debate, it is decided that they will teach their bank president how to enjoy life. The ghostly couple go to Young's home and observe how he is totally dominated by his shrewish wife, Burke. They appear before him and he cannot believe his eyes. He tries to point out his visitors to Burke, but only he can see them. Young's crash course in fast living begins and the ghosts get him into all sorts of predicaments that he must take the blame for because no one else can see the real culprits. With each embarrassing incident, however (getting drunk, being involved in brawls, going to jail, etc.), Young becomes less and less afraid to take risks and begins to have some confidence in himself. Burke, who at first violently resists the change that has suddenly overcome her husband, eventually softens because she realizes that they have not had fun together in years. When Young is slightly injured in yet another car crash involving Grant and Bennett, Burke welcomes her husband home and vows to try to be more understanding. Having done their good deed, Grant and Bennett are finally allowed to ascend. Based loosely on the novel *The Jovial Ghosts* by Thorne Smith, TOPPER is an extremely enjoyable comedy which uses special effects perfected in Universal's horror film THE INVISIBLE MAN (1933) for comedic effect. Special effects supervisor Seawright used every trick in the book to make Grant and Bennett appear and disappear and to make objects appear to move by themselves (with help from the invisible hands of Grant and Bennett of course). The key to the film's success is the performance of Young. Since it is he who must deal with these mischievous apparitions through the entirety of the film, Young's performance had to be flawless- and it is. The actor was quite skillful at contorting his body so that it appeared invisible hands were doing things like hustling him about to and fro, helping him home when drunk, and even straightening out his disheveled appearance in court. The impressive aspect of the performance is that while Young must concentrate on performing the correct physical moves, he also has to react to the ghosts (begging them to leave him alone) and the humans around him (so that he doesn't look like a lunatic). It is a multileveled performance where Young juggles several things at once. Luckily, the actor's peers recognized the considerable skill he employed and nominated him for Best Supporting Actor (he lost to Joseph Schildkraut in THE LIFE OF EMILE ZOLA). Young almost never appeared in TOPPER at all. Hal Roach originally wanted W.C. Fields for the role of Cosmo Topper, and Jean Harlow for Marion Kerby. Both were unavailable at the time (Harlow died a month before the film's release) and the roles went to Young and Bennett. Bennett, who had played an endless series of harlots and was losing her power at the box office, took a chance with a new kind of role and it proved popular. Grant, who was Roach's choice all along for the role of George Kerby, was skittish of appearing in a ghost story, but the director convinced him that the material would make a great screwball comedy (the $50,000 Grant was paid might have helped him make up his mind). TOPPER was a hit at the box office and Roach tried to regroup for a sequel to be released in 1939. Grant, who had risen to superstardom in TOPPER, TOAST OF NEW YORK, THE AWFUL TRUTH, and BRINGING UP BABY, declined to participate (though the car-crash scene from the original film is reprised), but Bennett, Young, and Burke returned. In 1986 TOPPER was subjected to the controversial "colorization" process that enables videotapes of black and white films to be transformed into color via electronic technology. The results are hardly satisfying—the colors are bland, muted, and poorly chosen and executed, which detracts from the film's impact instead of enhancing it—and the colorized version should be avoided.

p, Hal Roach; d, Norman Z. McLeod; w, Jack Jevne, Eric Hatch, Eddie Moran (based on the novel *The Jovial Ghosts* by Thorne Smith); ph, Norbert Brodine; m, Edward Powell, Hugo Friedhofer; ed, William Terhune; md, Marvin Hatley; art d, Arthur Rouce; set d, W.L. Stevens; cos, Samuel Lange, Irene, Howard Schraps; spec eff, Roy Seawright; m/l, "Old Man Moon," Hoagy Carmichael.

Comedy   **Cas.**   **(PR:A   MPAA:NR)**

TOPPER RETURNS***   (1941) 85m UA bw

Joan Blondell (*Gail Richards*), Roland Young (*Cosmo Topper*), Carole Landis (*Ann Carrington*), Billie Burke (*Mrs. Topper*), Dennis O'Keefe (*Bob*), Patsy Kelly (*Emily the Maid*), H.B. Warner (*Mr. Carrington*), Eddie "Rochester" Anderson (*Chauffeur*), George Zucco (*Dr. Jeris*), Donald MacBride (*Sgt. Roberts*), Rafaela Ottiano (*Lillian*), Trevor Bardette (*Rama*).

The third and final installment in the "Topper" series (the first two being TOPPER in 1937 and TOPPER TAKES A TRIP in 1939) sees Young, the unassuming family man who has had some bizarre dealings with ghosts, become an amateur detective hot on the trail of a murderer. When Blondell is murdered by mistake by a mysterious hooded killer, her spirit seeks out Young and begs him to help her find the culprit. It seems that the killer meant to kill Blondell's friend, Landis, but grabbed her by mistake. Blondell surmises that if Young can find the killer, he may save Landis' life. Young rises to the challenge, but his chauffeur, Anderson, isn't so enthusiastic. The investigation takes them to the creepy old house where Blondell was murdered and we are treated to the standard series of sliding panels, secret passageways, strange noises, trap doors, and the like before the killer is uncovered. This is the weakest entry in the series, but the film is still great fun. Cameraman Brodine infuses the visuals with an appropriately sinister style, and the set design is what one might expect from an "old dark house" chiller. Perhaps the only drawback is the now-annoying bug-eyed, "feets-do-your-duty" humor assigned to Anderson (a classy performer who played Jack Benny's smart-aleck, long-suffering chauffeur on radio, in films, and on television) whenever ghosts are mentioned. Blondell uses her voice more than her body here—she's invisible through much of the film—and does an acceptable job replacing Constance Bennett who had played ghost Marion Kerby in the first two films. From here the "Topper" saga would leave the movie houses and move to television where Leo G. Carroll would take over as Cosmo Topper in the 1950s. The original film was remade for television in 1979 starring Kate Jackson and Andrew Stevens as the ghostly Kerbys and Jack Warden as Cosmo.

p, Hal Roach; d, Roy Del Ruth; w, Jonathan Latimer, Gordon Douglas, Paul Gerard Smith (based on characters created by Thorne Smith); ph, Norbert Brodine; ed, James Newcom; spec eff, Roy Seabright.

Comedy/Mystery   **Cas.**   **(PR:A   MPAA:NR)**

TOPPER TAKES A TRIP***½   (1939) 85m Hal Roach/UA bw

Constance Bennett (*Marion Kerby*), Roland Young (*Cosmo Topper*), Billie Burke (*Clara Topper*), Alan Mowbray (*Wilkins*), Verree Teasdale (*Nancy Parkhurst*), Franklin Pangborn (*Louis*), Alexander D'Arcy (*Baron de Rossi*), Paul Hurst (*Bartender*), Eddy Conrad (*Jailer*), Spencer Charters (*Judge Wilson*), Irving Pichel (*Prosecutor*), Paul Everton (*Defender*), Duke York (*Gorgan*), Leon Belasco (*Bellboy*), Georges Renavent (*Magistrate*), George Humbert, Alphonse Martell (*Waiters*), James Morton (*Bailiff*), Torben Meyer (*Doorman*), George Davis (*Porter*), Armand Kaliz (*Clerk*), Cary Grant (*George Kerby--in Scenes from TOPPER*), Skippy the Dog (*Mr. Atlas*).

This follow-up to the surprisingly successful TOPPER, picks up where the last film left off. After reestablishing the auto accident that killed the drunken Cary Grant and Constance Bennett in the first film and turned them into ghosts having to perform a good deed before they are allowed into heaven, the action shifts to Young, who has chased his wife Burke to Paris where she is trying to get a divorce. Burke spotted Young and the ghostly Bennett in his room together and immediately assumed that her henpecked husband had finally taken up with another woman. Unable to explain that Bennett is only a ghost, Young is forced to fast-talk Burke into a reconciliation. Having performed his good deed, Grant disappears entirely from this sequel, leaving Bennett and their dog (Skippy), who was also killed in the wreck, to bail Young out of this marital mess. Several floating martinis later, Bennett manages to reconcile the couple, and having done

her good deed, floats off to rejoin her husband. The trick photography by Roy Seawright is as amusing as it is amazing. Cushions that deflate when invisible figures sit on them, cigarettes being smoked in mid-air, and pencils writing notes by themselves are all executed with skill. Perhaps the most creative and funny invisibility tricks are those involving the dog. It seems that poor little Skippy forgets to turn his tail invisible at times, and audiences are treated to the sight of a disembodied puff of hair wagging furiously in midair, and the feisty little ghost also has a penchant for attacking ankles, and the sight of men struggling to pull their legs free from an invisible hound is simply hilarious. There would be a third TOPPER film entitled TOPPER RETURNS, which would then be followed by a television show in the 1950s and a made-for-TV remake in 1979.

p, Hal Roach; d, Norman Z. McLeod; w, Eddie Moran, Jack Jevne, Corey Ford (based on the novel by Thorne Smith); ph, Norbert Brodine; ed, William Terhune; art d, Charles D. Hall; spec eff, Roy Seawright.

Comedy   **Cas.**   **(PR:A   MPAA:NR)**

TOPS IS THE LIMIT   (SEE: ANYTHING GOES, 1936)

TOPSY-TURVY JOURNEY**   (1970, Jap.) 93m Shochiku c
                                                            (GYAKUTEN RYOKO)

Frankie Sakai (*Goichi Hasegawa*), Chieko Baisho (*Sakura*), Kensaku Morita (*Shinsaku*), Kumi Hayase (*Ayako*), Tomomi Sato (*Kaori*), Arihiro Fujimura (*Mitsui*), Toru Yuri (*Arao*), Chocho Miyako (*Mine*), Junzaburo Ban (*Daikichi Yashiro*), Utako Kyo, Keisuke Ko, Zaizu Ichiro, Hiroshi Minami, Bonta Sesshi, Harumi Miyako.

Sakai is cast as a love-stricken train conductor who enrolls in a cooking class because he is infatuated with the instructor, Sato. Baisho, who in turn loves Sakai, also enrolls in the class in order to keep Sakai away from Sato. After a number of comic escapades, including a dose of laxative snuck into Sakai's picnic basket, Sato agrees to marry Sakai, but only on her terms. She asks him to quit the railroad, which, after much turmoil, he agrees to. Sato backs out, however, and Baisho ends up in the conductor's arms.

p, Kiyoshi Shimazu; d, Shoji Segawa; w, Kazuo Funabashi; ph, T. Takaha; m, Taku Izumi; art d, Masao Kumagi.

Romance/Comedy   **(PR:A   MPAA:NR)**

TORA-SAN PART 2*½   (1970, Jap.) 93m Shochiku c (ZOKU OTOKOWA TSURAIYO; AKA; TORA-SAN'S CHERISHED MOTHER; AM I TRYING PART II)

Kiyoshi Atsumi (*Torajiro "Tora" Kuruma*), Shin Morikawa (*Ryuzo*), Chieko Misaki (*Tsune*), Gin Maeda (*Hiroshi Suwa*), Chieko Baisho (*Sakura*), Eijiro Tono (*Sampo Tsubouchi*), Orie Sato (*Natsuko*), Tsutomu Yamazaki (*Dr. Fujimura*), Chocho Miyako (*Okiku*), Shoko Kazemi, Hiroaki Tsukasa, Hisao Dadayu, Gajiro Sato, Keiroku Sato.

A Japanese comedy which is the sequel to OTOKOWA TSURAIYO, a film which wasn't released in the U.S. Atsumi stars as a mobster who gets himself involved in ridiculous situations while paying visits to important people in his life—his uncle, a teacher, a former schoolmate, and his mother, whom he discovers is the owner of a whore house. This is all bit tough to make sense out of if you haven't seen the first part.

d, Yoji Yamada; w, Yamada, Shun'ichi Kobayashi, Akira Miyazaki (based on a story by Yamada); ph, Tetsuo Takaba; m, Naozumi Yamamoto; ed, Iwao Ishii.

Comedy   **(PR:C   MPAA:NR)**

TORA-SAN'S CHERISHED MOTHER
                                (SEE: TORA-SAN PART 2, 1970, Jap.)

TORA! TORA! TORA!*½   (1970, U.S./Jap.) 143m FOX c

Martin Balsam (*Adm. Husband E. Kimmel*), Soh Yamamura (*Adm. Isoroku Yamamoto*), Jason Robards, Jr. (*Gen. Walter C. Short*), Joseph Cotten (*Henry L. Stimson*), Tatsuya Mihashi (*Comdr. Minoru Genda*), E.G. Marshall (*Lt. Col. Rufus S. Bratton*), Takahiro Tamura (*Lt. Comdr. Fuchida*), James Whitmore (*Adm. William F. Halsey*), Eijiro Tono (*Adm. Chuichi Nagumo*), Wesley Addy (*Lt. Comdr. Alvin D. Kramer*), Shogo Shimada (*Ambassador Kichisaburo Nomura*), Frank Aletter (*Lt. Comdr. Thomas*), Koreya Senda (*Prince Fumimaro Konoye*), Leon Ames (*Frank Knox*), Junya Usami (*Adm. Zengo Yoshida*), Richard Anderson (*Capt. John Earle*), Kazuo Kitamura (*Foreign Minister Yosuke Matuoka*), Keith Andes (*Gen. George C. Marshall*), Edward Andrews (*Adm. Harold R. Stark*), Neville Brand (*Lt. Kaminsky*), Leora Dana (*Mrs. Kramer*), Asao Uchida (*Gen. Hideki Tojo*), George Macready (*Cordell Hull*), Norman Alden (*Maj. Truman Landon*), Walter Brooke (*Capt. Theodore S. Wilkinson*), Rick Cooper (*Lt. George Welch*), Elven Havard (*Doris Miller*), June Dayton (*Miss Ray Cave*), Jeff Donnell (*Cornelius*), Richard Erdman (*Col. Edward F. French*), Jerry Fogel (*Lt. Comdr. William W. Outerbridge*), Shunichi Nakamura (*Kameto Kiroji-ma*), Carl Reindel (*Lt. Kenneth Taylor*), Edmon Ryan (*Rear Adm. Patrick N.L. Bellinger*), Hisao Toake (*Saburo Kurusu*), Susumu Fujita, Bontaro Miyake, Ichiro Reuzaki, Kazuko Ichikawa, Hank Jones, Karl Lukas, Ron

Masak, Kan Nihonyanagi, Toshio Hosokawa.

The Japanese sneak attack that plunged the U.S. into WW II is lavishly and accurately, if not very enthrallingly, brought to the screen in this Japanese-U.S. coproduction. The machinations of the Japanese high command as they prepare to further their expansionist aims by destroying the main American naval base in the Pacific are contrasted with the U.S. government and military establishment going about their peacetime business, with only a few individuals suspicious that the Japanese aren't sincere in their willingness to negotiate. The Japanese fleet sets sail for Hawaii and U.S. naval intelligence intercepts that order but is unable to decode it. Marshall is an officer of naval intelligence who comes to the conclusion, based a a number of reports, that the Japanese are going to attack Pearl Harbor on Sunday, November 30, and the whole base is put on a sort of half-hearted alert. When the attack doesn't come the base lapses back into its normal state. Meanwhile, negotiations have broken down between the Japanese and U.S., and the Japanese ambassador is transmitted an ultimatum he is to deliver to the secretary of state a half-hour before the attack is scheduled to begin, so that the Americans will have time to reject it and the Japanese attack will seem a regular act of war. Decoding problems and a painfully slow typist throw off the schedule and the message is not delivered until the attack is only minutes away. New radar equipment in Hawaii picks up the attacking waves of planes but considers them only an expected flight of American bombers. When the attack begins, the U.S. Pacific Fleet is caught almost entirely unaware in their sleepy Sunday morning routine and the ships are devastated, along with the airplanes on the surrounding fields. The Japanese consider their attack only a limited success, though, because the American aircraft carriers, the main Japanese objective, are out of port at the time. As the film ends, Adm. Yamamoto (Yamamura), opponent but mastermind of the attack, sadly reflects on the awesome retaliation to come. The first half of this movie, as the Japanese plot in Japanese and Americans scratch their heads in apprehension, is static and deadly dull. Its reflection of the real events is incomplete and inaccurate and it simply consists of people talking. This goes on for 79 minutes, the length of many better movies. Then there is an intermission followed by 65 more minutes that largely consist of the actual attack. When the attack does finally come, it is spectacular, involving dozens of planes refurbished to look like Japanese fighters, dive bombers, and torpedo planes (these planes, incidentally, were all sold after the production and still frequently show up in the market-place). A full-size mock- up of the Japanese flagship was built on poles on a Japanese beach. Hundreds of extras were used. But with all the grand spectacle the attack even becomes boring after a while. (How many times can one see planes swoop down and drop bombs on ships without it getting tedious?) The film was the result of years of negotiation between Japanese and American investors. In the end, two different films were made; a Japanese film showing the Japanese side, and an American film doing the same for their side. The two films were then edited together in two different versions, one for each nation. It all ended up costing over $25 million and failed miserably at the box office in the U.S., but was a great success in Japan, although it still took several years before the studio made back its money (partly by selling the battle footage to other filmmakers, some of it appearing in MIDWAY, 1976, and in MACARTHUR, 1977). The performances come and go with such speed that no one is ever given much of a chance to develop a character. Indeed, its rare to see most of the characters more than twice in the course of the proceedings. Despite these flaws, TORA! TORA! TORA! is probably as accurate a film ever to be made about the events the led the United States into WW II, but it is unlikely anyone would ever want to try anyway.

p, Elmo Williams; d, Richard Fleischer (U.S.), Toshio Masuda, Kinji Fukasaku (Japan); w, Larry Forrester, Hideo Oguni, Ryuzo Kikushima (based on *Tora] Tora] Tora]* by Gordon W. Prange and *The Broken Seal* by Ladislas Farago); ph, Charles F. Wheeler (U.S.), Shinsaku Himeda, Masamichi Sato, Osami Furuya (Japan) (Panavision, DeLuxe Color); m, Jerry Goldsmith; ed, James E. Newcom, Pembroke J. Herring, Inoue Chikaya; art d, Jack Martin Smith, Richard Day, Yoshiro Muraki, Taizo Kawashima; set d, Walter M. Scott, Norman Rockett; spec eff, L.B. Abbott, Art Cruickshank; makeup, Dan Striepeke; aerial ph, Vision Photography Inc.; tech adv, Kameo Sonokawa, Kurnaoshuke Isoda, Shizuo Takada, Tsuyoshi Saka.

War　　　　　　　　**Cas.**　　　　　　**(PR:C MPAA:G)**

TORCH, THE**　　　　(1950) 90m EL bw (GB: BANDIT GENERAL)

Paulette Goddard (*Maria Dolores*), Pedro Armendariz (*Jose Juan Reyes*), Gilbert Roland (*Father Sierra*), Walter Reed (*Dr. Robert Stanley*), Julio Villareal (*Don Carlos Penafiel*), Carlos Musquiz (*Fidel Bernal*), Margarito Luna (*Capt. Bocanegra*), Jose I. Torvay (*Capt. Quinones*), Garcia Pena (*Don Apolinio*), Antonia Kaneem (*Adelita*).

An average romance which has a touch of comedy in its portrayal of a Mexican town overrun by revolutionary Armendariz and his men. Many of the townsfolk don't like the general, while others do their best to please him. Armendariz falls in love with Goddard, the daughter of the village's richest man, and eventually proves to her that he's worthy of her. Sharp photography helps the weak script. This was a remake of ENAMORADA (1946), a Mexican production which was also directed by Fernandez.

p, Bert Granet; d, Emilio Fernandez; w, Inigo de Martino Noriega,

Fernandez; ph, Gabriel Figueroa; m, Antonio Diaz Conde; ed, Charles L. Kimball; md, Diaz Conde; art d, Manuel Fontanals.

Romance　　　　　　**Cas.**　　　　　　**(PR:A MPAA:NR)**

TORCH SINGER**　　(1933) 70m PAR bw (GB: BROADWAY SINGER)

Claudette Colbert (*Sally Trent/Mimi Benton*), Ricardo Cortez (*Tony Cummings*), David Manners (*Michael Gardner*), Lyda Roberti (*Dora*), Baby LeRoy (*Bobbie*), Florence Roberts (*Mother Angelica*), Shirley Ann Christensen (*Baby Sally*), Cora Sue Collins (*Little Sally*), Ethel Griffies (*Martha Alden*), Helen Jerome Eddy (*Miss Spaulding*), Mildred Washington (*Carry*), Charles Grapewin (*Mr. Judson*), Albert Conti (*Carlotti*), Virginia Hammond (*Mrs. Judson*), Kathleen Burke (*Sobbing Girl*), Davison Clark (*Detective*), Edward J. LeSaint (*Doctor*), Bobby Arnst (*The Blonde*), William B. Davidson (*Jarrett*), Burke Davison.

Colbert belts out a few tunes as a club singer who doubles as the host of a children's radio show. Her fondness for the kiddies comes after she gave away her child because she lacked a husband. She longs to see her kid again, spending a good portion of the film on her search, which eventually leads to Baby LeRoy. Songs: "Don't Be a Cry Baby," "Give Me Liberty or Give Me Love," "It's a Long Dark Night," "The Torch Singer" (Ralph Rainger, Leo Robin, sung by Claudette Colbert).

p, Albert Lewis; d, Alexander Hall, George Somnes; w, Lynn Starling, Lenore Coffee (based on the play "Mike" by Grace Perkins); ph, Karl Struss; cos, Travis Banton.

Musical　　　　　　　　　　　**(PR:A MPAA:NR)**

TORCH SONG**½　　　　　　　　(1953) 90m MGM c

Joan Crawford (*Jenny Stewart*), Michael Wilding (*Tye Graham*), Gig Young (*Cliff Willard*), Marjorie Rambeau (*Mrs. Stewart*), Henry 'Harry' Morgan (*Joe Denner*), Dorothy Patrick (*Martha*), James Todd (*Philip Norton*), Eugene Loring (*Gene the Dance Director*), Paul Guilfoyle (*Monty Rolfe*), Benny Rubin (*Charlie Maylor*), Peter Chong (*Peter*), Maidie Norman (*Anne*), Nancy Gates (*Celia Stewart*), Chris Warfield (*Chuck Peters*), Rudy Render (*Party Singer*), Charles Walters (*Ralph Ellis*), John Rosser (*Chauffeur*), Norma Jean Salina (*Margaret*), Reginald Simpson (*Cab Driver*), Adolph Deutsch (*Conductor*), Mimi Gibson (*Susie*), Mitchell Lewis (*Bill the Doorman*), Peggy King (*Cora*).

A backstage love story with music that marked Crawford's return to MGM after a 10-year hiatus. Crawford is a Broadway musical star who has tossed aside her private life in favor of a career that has made her a star. Not unlike Margo Channing in ALL ABOUT EVE, she is so dedicated to her work that her neurotic compulsions about perfection have caused her to become a lonely woman shunned by her fellows in the theater. Her regular arranger quits in a huff and she needs a new man at the 88 so blind pianist Wilding is hired to temporarily substitute. Wilding lost his vision during the war and will not kowtow to Crawford's imperious demands. The two are at odds often and loudly. He won't put up with the way she misinterprets various songs and he politely but firmly tells her. (Crawford's singing was dubbed by India Adams in a voice so husky that you could have pulled a dog sled with it.) Wilding also chastises her for the way she speaks to other people. Crawford is not accustomed to anyone criticizing her but she sits still for it from Wilding. Crawford would love to have a man of her own but there doesn't seem to be anyone in her life who is strong enough to deal with her. She's seeing Young, a drinker who is hanging on as part of her professional coterie, but he is far from satisfying her needs. Crawford goes to see her mother, Rambeau, and begins perusing an old scrapbook of reviews that Rambeau (Oscar nominated for Best Supporting Actress) has kept over the years. She reads one glowing rave and discovers that it was written by Wilding, before he lost his vision in WW II. He was a substitute critic and wrote a superior notice about her in one of her first appearances. Meanwhile, Patrick, a pal, has begun to fall in love with the gentle, genial Wilding, thus raising Crawford's ire. Wilding keeps the memory of Crawford's face in his mind and is still in love with her and because he has never laid his eyes on Patrick, there is no way he can love her. Crawford finally realizes that Wilding does love her, in a way that no other man has ever loved her, and she and he wind up together at the fade out as she lets down the moat surrounding her emotional fortress and allows Wilding to walk in and touch her heart. Four songs from various sources, including one of the most inept production numbers ever shot: "Two-Faced Woman" (Howard Dietz, Arthur Schwartz) was originally intended as a piece for Cyd Charisse in THE BANDWAGON and when it was not used, they kept the orchestral tracks and put it into this film. "Tenderly" was written by Jack Lawrence and Walter Gross, who also did the piano work for Wilding; "You Won't Forget Me" was written by Fred Spielman and Kermit Goell, and Rodgers and Hart contributed their perennial "Blue Moon." "Follow Me" was written by musical director Adolph Deutsch and sung by Rudy Render. All of the other tunes were "sung" by Crawford. Director Walters, a former choreographer (DUBARRY WAS A LADY, ZIEGFELD FOLLIES, etc.) dances with Crawford for a brief moment. The movie was coproduced by Sidney Franklin, Jr., son of the well-known producer-director who toiled at MGM for many years and was best known for having directed THE GOOD EARTH. There were four Sidney Franklins in the public eye. The aforementioned MGM person, the actor who played in many Hollywood silent films until his death in 1931, the "Bullfighter from Brooklyn" who also acted in many films until he passed away in 1976, and the man who coproduced this film. Sidney Franklin, Jr. eventually gave up show business and in 1986 was spending half the year living in northern California and the other half on a large houseboat in the river Seine in Paris.

p, Henry Berman, Sidney Franklin, Jr.; d, Charles Walters; w, John Michael Hayes, Jan Lustig (based on the story "Why Should I Cry?" by I.A.R. Wylie); ph, Robert Planck (Technicolor); m, Adolph Deutsch; ed, Albert Akst; md, Deutsch; art d, Cedric Gibbons, Preston Ames; cos, Helen Rose; ch, Charles Walters.

Drama   (PR:A   MPAA:NR)

TORCHY BLANE IN CHINATOWN*½   (1938) 59m WB bw

Glenda Farrell (Torchy Blane), Barton MacLane (Steve McBride), Tom Kennedy (Gahagan), Patric Knowles (Condon), Henry O'Neill (Baldwin), James Stephenson (Mansfield), Janet Shaw (Janet), Anderson Lawlor (Fitzhugh), Frank Shannon (McTavish), George Guhl (Desk Sgt. Graves), Richard Bond (Staunton), Eddy Chandler (Capt. McDonald).

A weak series entry which puts Farrell and MacLane in a Chinese atmosphere amongst murderers, extortionists, and jade smugglers. The femme news reporter gets to the bottom of the case when she discovers that the murders were faked, dealing out the necessary punishment to the culprits. Beaudine failed to enliven the standard TORCHY cliches enough to hold interest. (See TORCHY BLANE series, Index.)

p, Bryan Foy; d, William Beaudine; w, George Bricker (based on the story "The Purple Hieroglyph" by Will F. Jenkins, Murray Leinster); ph, Warren Lynch; ed, Frederick Richards; cos, Howard Shoup.

Crime   (PR:A   MPAA:NR)

TORCHY BLANE IN PANAMA**   (1938) 58m FN-WB bw (GB: TROUBLE IN PANAMA)

Lola Lane (Torchy Blane), Paul Kelly (Steve McBride), Tom Kennedy (Gahagan), Anthony Averill (Crafton), Larry Williams (Bill Canby), Betty Compson (Kitty), Hugh O'Connell (Skinner), James Conlon (Botkin), Joe Cunningham (Maxie), Frank Shannon (Capt. McTavish), Eric Stanley (Capt. McDonald), John Ridgely (Sparks), George Guhl (Desk Sgt. Graves), George Regas (Gomez), James Nolan (Ship's Officer), Jack Mower (Ship's Officer Nelson), John Harron (Aviator).

After a New York City bank robbery in which a teller is killed, female reporter Lane follows her clues all the way to Panama. She manages to get onto an ocean liner while it's at sea, which is no small feat in itself. Once on board, she is able to finger the guilty party. The fifth in the series, this picture has Lane and Kelly taking over for Glenda Farrell and Barton MacLane. The regulars were back, however, by TORCHY GETS HER MAN, but not for long. (See TORCHY BLANE series, Index.)

p, Bryan Foy; d, William Clemens; w, George Bricker (based on a story by AnthonyColdeway and the characters by Frederick Nebel); ph, Tony Gaudio; ed, Thomas Pratt.

Crime   (PR:A   MPAA:NR)

TORCHY BLANE RUNS FOR MAYOR
(SEE: TORCHY RUNS FOR MAYOR, 1939)

TORCHY BLANE, THE ADVENTUROUS BLONDE
(SEE: ADVENTUROUS BLONDE, 1937)

TORCHY GETS HER MAN**   (1938) 62m WB bw

Glenda Farrell (Torchy Blane), Barton MacLane (Steve McBride), Tom Kennedy (Gahagan), Willard Robertson ($100 Bailey), George Guhl (Desk Sgt. Graves), John Ridgely (Bugs), Tommy Jackson (Gloomy), Frank Reicher (Professor), Edward Raquello (Gonzales), Ed Keane (Stoneham), Frank Shannon (Capt. McTavish), Joe Cunningham (Maxie), Herbert Rawlinson (Brennan), John Harron (Wilkins), Lola Cheaney (Moll), Greta Meyer (Mrs. Schmidt), Cliff Saum (O'Brien), Nat Carr (Schmidt).

More mindless comic-book romping as Farrell, the super news gal, tries to bust open a counterfeiting racket run, unknown to her, by Robertson. The gang's leader throws Farrell off the trail by pretending to be a federal agent investigating the crooks, requesting that she not print any information that could blow his cover. She soon catches on to his scheme and brings about the gang's capture. (See TORCHY BLANE series, Index.)

p, Bryan Foy; d, William Beaudine; w, Albert DeMond (based on the story "Torchy Finds Out" by DeMond and the characters created by Frederick Nebel); ph, Arthur Todd, Warren Lynch; ed, Harold McLernon; cos, Howard Shoup.

Crime   (PR:A   MPAA:NR)

TORCHY PLAYS WITH DYNAMITE**   (1939) 59m WB bw

Jane Wyman (Torchy Blane), Allen Jenkins (Lt. Steve McBride), Tom Kennedy (Gahagan), Sheila Bromley ("Jackie" McGuire), Joe Cunningham (Maxie), Eddie Marr (Denver Eddie), Edgar Dearing (Jim Simmons), Frank Shannon (Inspector McTavish), Bruce MacFarlane (Bugsie), George Lloyd (Harp), Aldrich Bowker (Police Court Judge), John Ridgely (1st Reporter), Larry Williams (2nd Reporter), John Harron (Motorcycle Cop), Cliff Clark (Kelly), Tiny Roebuck ("The Bone Crusher"), Pat Flaherty (The "Crusher's" Handler), Creighton Hale (Hotel Clerk), Nat Carr (Book Store Clerk), Ruth Robinson (Head Matron), Frank Moran (Handler), John "Skins" Miller (Taxi Driver), John Sheehan (Desk Sgt. O'Toole), Dudley Dickerson, Mme. Sul-te-wan (Negroes), Ralph Sanford, Jack Mower (Officers), William Gould (Fire Chief), Frank Mayo (Detective), Cliff Saum (Bailiff), Sol Gross (Court Attendant), Lois Cheaney, Kate Lawson, Jessie Perry (Guards), Jack Richardson (Taxi Driver), Bess Meyers (Night Matron), Vera Lewis (Landlady), Charles Sullivan (Charlie), Glen Cavendar (Landlord), Harry Hollingsworth (Officer), Eddy Chandler (Announcer), Bob Perry (Referee).

Wyman dealt the death blow to the "Torchy Blane" series, causing it to fizzle from the screens after going through three different Torchys in a year and a half's time. In the final entry, Wyman gains a gang moll's confidence by getting herself tossed in the slammer for an 11-month stretch. Her plan works and she is able to capture bank robber Marr after being led to him by his gal. (See TORCHY BLANE series, Index.)

p, Bryan Foy; d, Noel Smith; w, Earle Snell, Charles Belden (based on the story "Dead or Alive" by Scott Littleton and the characters created by Frederick Nebel); ph, Arthur L. Todd; ed, Harold McLernon.

Crime   (PR:A   MPAA:NR)

TORCHY RUNS FOR MAYOR**
(1939) 58m WB bw (AKA: TORCHY BLANE RUNS FOR MAYOR)

Glenda Farrell (Torchy Blane), Barton MacLane (Lt. Steve McBride), Tom Kennedy (Gahagan), John Miljan (Dr. Dolan), Frank Shannon (Capt. McTavish), Joe Cunningham (Maxie), George Guhl (Desk Sgt. Graves), Joe Downing (O'Brien), Irving Bacon (Hogarth Ward), John Butler (Chuck Ball), Charles Richman (Mayor), John Harron (Dibble), Walter Fenner (Skinner), Millard Vincent (Reynolds), Joe Devlin (Stone).

There are no surprises in this series entry, as Farrell, the glamorous star-newslady, exposes the corrupt inner workings of city politics but can't find anyone to print them. She finally gets them to press, but can't come up with a candidate to challenge the incumbent mayor in the upcoming election. As the title so neatly points out, Farrell then runs for the office and wins. (See TORCHY BLANE series, Index.)

d, Ray McCarey; w, Earle Snell (based on an idea by Irving Rubine and characters created by Frederick Nebel); ph, Warren Lynch; ed, Everett Dodd.

Crime   (PR:A   MPAA:NR)

TORMENT***½   (1947, Swed.) 95m Svensk Filmindustri/Oxford bw (HETS; GB FRENZY)

Stig Jarrel (Caligula), Alf Kjellin (Jan-Erick Widgren), Mai Zetterling (Bertha), Olof Winnerstrand (Headmaster), Gosta Cederlund (Pippi), Hugo Bjorne (Doctor), Stig Olin (Sandman), Olav Riego (Mr. Widgren), Marta Arbin (Mrs. Widgren), Jan Molander (Petterson), Anders Nystrom (Widgren), Nils Dahlgren (Police Officer).

One of the most popular Swedish films of its day, TORMENT (released in Sweden in 1944) is hailed by many as Sjoberg's masterpiece. It was also the first script written by the 26-year-old Ingmar Bergman and the film which brought Zetterling international attention. It tells the story of a pair of young lovers, Kjellin and Zetterling, who are pitted against the wicked Jarrel, a college professor. Zetterling refuses to be completely open with her love, causing Kjellin to suspect that someone else is involved. He soon discovers who that other person is when he finds Zetterling dead one day, with Jarrel hiding in the hallway. Kjellin loudly accuses his professor of being responsible for the girl's death, but lacks the power that Jarrel has. The student soon finds himself unable to finish his schooling, while the professor continues unscathed. Some time later, teacher and student meet again, but now Jarrel is alone and helpless. Unable to forget the past, Kjellin turns his back on the man and walks away. While the picture is somewhat dated today, it does carry with it a certain innocence, a quality which has considerably diminished in Bergman's own films. Jarrel's character of the professor, here tagged "Caligula," was consciously modeled after the infamous Nazi Heinrich Himmler in the hope of identifying him with a most despicable evil. (In Swedish; English subtitles.)

d, Alf Sjoberg; w, Ingmar Bergman; ph, Martin Bodin; m, Hilding Rosenberg; ed, Oscar Rosander; md, Erik Tuxen; art d, Arne Akermark.

Drama   (PR:A   MPAA:NR)

TORMENT, 1950, Brit.   (SEE: PAPER GALLOWS, 1950, Brit.)

TORMENTED*   (1960) 75m AA bw

Richard Carlson (*Tom Stewart*), Susan Gordon (*Sandy*), Juli Reding (*Vi Mason*), Lugene Sanders (*Meg*), Joseph Turkel (*Nick*), Lillian Adams (*Real Estate Broker*), Gene Roth (*Lunch Stand Operator*), Vera Marshe (*Mother*), Harry Fleer (*Father*), Merritt Stone (*Clergyman*).

A bizarre little horror film from Bert I. Gordon which has pianist Carlson giving his mistress a push from the top of his lighthouse. Parts of her body come back to haunt him and ruin his upcoming marriage. So bad, it's good. Producer-director Gordon contributed the story and collaborated on the special effects; his daughter Susan also appears.

p, Bert I. Gordon, Joe Steinberg; d, Gordon; w, George Worthing Yates (based on a story by Gordon); ph, Ernest Laszlo; m, Albert Glasser, Calvin Jackson; md, Glasser; spec eff, Bert and Flora Gordon; m/l, "Tormented," Glasser, Lewis Meltzer (sung by Margie Rayburn).

Horror   (PR:C MPAA:NR)

TORMENTED, THE zero   (1978, Ital.) 79m Tiberia/21st Century c
(AKA: EERIE MIDNIGHT HORROR SHOW, THE SEXORCISTS)

Stella Carnacina, Chris Avram, Lucretia Love, Ivan Rassimov, Gabriele Tinti, Luigi Pistilli.

When an Italian art student steals the statue of a crucified man from her church, she is surprised to find that he's come to life and has nothing but sex on his mind.

p, Justin Reid; d, Mario Gariazzo.

Horror   (PR:O MPAA:R)

TORN CURTAIN*   (1966) 126m UNIV c

Paul Newman (*Prof. Michael Armstrong*), Julie Andrews (*Sarah Sherman*), Lila Kedrova (*Countess Kuchinska*), Hansjorg Felmy (*Heinrich Gerhard*), Tamara Toumanova (*Ballerina*), Ludwig Donath (*Prof. Gustav Lindt*), Wolfgang Kieling (*Hermann Gromek*), Gunter Strack (*Prof. Karl Manfred*), David Opatoshu (*Mr. Jacobi*), Gisela Fischer (*Dr. Koska*), Mort Mills (*Farmer*), Carolyn Conwell (*Farmer's Wife*), Arthur Gould-Porter (*Freddy*), Gloria Gorvin (*Fraulein Mann*), Erik Holland (*Hotel Travel Clerk*), Hedley Mattingly (*Airline Official*), Norbert Schiller (*Gutman*), Peter Bourne (*Olaf Hengstrom*), Peter Lorr (*Taxi Driver*), Frank Aberschal (*Factory Manager*), Charles H. Radilac (*Jacoby*), Alfred Hitchcock (*Man Holding Baby in Hotel Lobby*).

Hitchcock's 50th film was based on an original idea by him which he gave to scripter Brian Moore for realization. It was not a success perhaps due, in part, to the clash between Hitchcock and Newman which marred the proceedings. The two men had totally different styles and it was evident from the first frame. Newman is a nuclear physicist at a convention in Denmark. He defects from the West to the East, a move which becomes a cause celebre. Newman's assistant-girl friend is Andrews and although she believes he is a patriot, she can't understand why he has chosen to join the enemy. The two of them go to East Germany where Newman wants to meet with Donath, the leading scientist in the field. It isn't long before Andrews understands that Newman is a patriot and has faked his defection to glean some information from either Newman or Andrews, who just didn't catch fire in this pairing. Newman gets Donath to reveal the information in a ploy in which the two men have a brain duel and Donath foolishly lets the secret out. Once that takes place, Newman and Andrews must get out of East Germany and the chase begins. Kedrova, a peeress of what once was Imperial Poland, will help them flee if they can help her get a visa to enter the U.S. They are pursued and wind up in a crowded theater where Toumanova is giving a ballet performance (her first time on screen in 12 years). The theater is teeming with Russian police seeking to nab the two (didn't we see this in THE 39 STEPS?) and Newman gets to safety by yelling "fire" and setting the patrons in a panic. (How the English word "fire" would stampede a German audience is beyond our ken.) The CIA helps get Newman and Andrews out of the theater by hiding them in large costume baskets which are then taken to a ship bound for Sweden. The Russians are on to this, board the ship, and demand that the baskets be opened. When they are told that's impossible, the Reds open fire and riddle the baskets with bullets. Naturally, they are the wrong baskets. Newman and Andrews jump the ship and swim to safety, finding themselves in Stockholm. The picture ends as the two are bundling under a blanket. Nothing works here, least of all Newman. What was needed was a light touch, a tongue firmly in cheek, but Newman (who should know by now that he has no flair for comedy) elected to be serious. Not that Moore's script gave him anything funny to say but a superior farceur might have made something resembling a silk purse out of the sow's ear. One very shocking and brutal scene as Newman has to murder Keiling, his Soviet watchdog. He stabs the man, chokes him, and finally gasses him in the kitchen stove of a farmhouse. Hitchcock maintained that he put that in just to show how difficult it is to kill a human being. The movie was almost totally done at Universal City in the San Fernando Valley, with the East German farm being shot at Camarillo, California. Other locations included the airport in Van Nuys, the USC campus in downtown Los Angeles, and the

water scenes shot at Long Beach. One technical error was seen when Newman and Andrews are supposedly atop a hill but the top of the shot reveals that it's not the sky at all in the background, rather a cyclorama. This is noted easily when one sees, for an instant, the top of the painted drop and the various lights dangling from the overhead walkways. Addison's music didn't help and one wonders if Hitchcock and his usual composer, Bernard Herrmann, hadn't fallen out shortly before. The secondary actors were far more interesting than either Newman or Andrews, who just didn't catch fire in this pairing. Hitchcock enjoys scenes in theaters or in large crowds and used them often, as in THE MAN WHO KNEW TOO MUCH, STAGE FRIGHT, and STRANGERS ON A TRAIN. TORN CURTAIN felt like a recycled story that had been done before, perhaps not as well, but it still had a deja vu aura.

p&d, Alfred Hitchcock; w, Brian Moore (based on a story by Moore); ph, John F. Warren (Technicolor); m, John Addison; ed, Bud Hoffman; prod d, Hein Heckroth; art d, Frank Arrigo; set d, George Milo; cos, Edith Head; makeup, Jack Barron.

Spy   Cas.   (PR:C MPAA:NR)

TORNADO   (1943) 83m PAR bw

Chester Morris (*Pete Ramsey*), Nancy Kelly (*Victory Kane*), Bill Henry (*Bob Ramsey*), Joe Sawyer (*Charlie Boswell*), Gwen Kenyon (*Sally Vlochek*), Marie McDonald (*Diana Linden*), Morgan Conway (*Gary Linden*), Frank Reicher (*Old Man Linden*), Nestor Paiva (*Big Joe Vlochek*).

Illinois coal miner Morris falls in love with showgirl Kelly, eventually marrying her secretly, and, with her prodding, rising to the position of shaft superintendent. She inherits some land and he forms a new company to mine the property. That situation is taken care of by a killer tornado that kills both Kelly and Conway.

p, William H. Pine, William C. Thomas; d, William Berke; w, Maxwell Shane (based on a story by John Guedel); ph, Fred Jackman, Jr.; ed, William Zeigler; art d, F. Paul Sylos; m/l, "I'm Afraid of You," "There Goes My Dream," Ralph Freed, Frederick Hollander, Frank Loesser (sung by Nancy Kelly).

Drama   (PR:A MPAA:NR)

TORNADO RANGE   (1948) 56m PRC/EL bw

Eddie Dean (*Eddie*), Roscoe Ates (*Soapy*), Jennifer Holt (*Mary*), George Chesebro (*Lance*), Brad Slaven (*Jebby*), Marshall Reed (*Wilson*), Terry Frost (*Thayer*), Lane Bradford (*Thorne*), Russell Arms (*Dorgan*), Steve Clark (*Pop*), Hank Bell, Jack Hendricks, Ray Jones, Andy Parker and The Plainsmen: Paul Smith, George Bamby, Earl Murphy, Charles Morgan, Copper the Horse.

The usual oater ingredients fill this tale of a ranchers vs. homesteaders war which is resolved by the presence of U.S. Land Office employee Dean. Ates, his sidekick, tries to introduce some humor into the proceedings. Dean rides Copper in this one, the third of his regular movie mounts, who follows in the hoofprints of Flash and White Cloud.

p, Jerry Thomas; d, Ray Taylor; w, William Lively; ph, James Brown, Jr.; m, Walter Greene; ed, Joseph Gluck; m/l, Eddie Dean, Curt Massey, Alan Massey.

Western   (PR:A MPAA:NR)

TORPEDO ALLEY½   (1953) 84m AA bw

Mark Stevens (*Bingham*), Dorothy Malone (*Susan*), Charles Winninger (*Peabody*), Bill Williams (*Graham*), Douglas Kennedy (*Gates*), James Millican (*Heywood*), Bill Henry (*Instructor*), James Seay (*Skipper*), Robert Rose (*Anniston*), John Alvin (*Professor*), Carleton Young (*Psychiatrist*), Ralph Sanford (*Hedley*), Ralph Reed (*Lookout*), Carl Christian (*Happy*), John Close (*Turk*), Keith Larson, William Schallert, Ross Thompson, Richard Garland.

Stevens is a former Navy pilot who is disturbed by the fact that he was responsible for the deaths of two fellow crew members when he ditched his plane into the Pacific. When WW II ends, he foregoes civilian life and joins a submarine crew, falling in love with nurse Malone in the process. It turns out, however, that Malone is the girl friend of Kennedy, who was an officer on the sub that rescued Stevens after his plane crash. Stevens learns to deal with the guilt that accompanied the death of his crew, and by the finale, ends up with Malone. A great deal of attention is paid to the submarines, turning this more into a naval homage than a romance.

p, Lindsley Parsons; d, Lew Landers; w, Sam Roeca, Warren Douglas; ph, William Sickner; ed, W. Donn Hayes; art d, David Milton.

War Drama   (PR:A MPAA:NR)

TORPEDO BAY   (1964, Ital./Fr.) 78m
Galatea-Panorama/B.L.C.-BL-Albion bw (FINCHE DURA LA TEMPES-
TA; BETA SOM)

James Mason (*Capt. Blayne*), Lilli Palmer (*Lygia da Silva*), Gabriele Ferzetti

(Leonardi), Geoffrey Keen (English Intelligence Officer Hodges), Alberto Lupo (Magri), Renato De Carmine (Ghedini), Valeria Fabrizi (Susanne), Daniele Vargas (Brauzzi), Andrew Keir (O'Brien), Andrea Checchi (Micheluzzi), Gabriele Tinti, Jeremy Burnham, Davide Montemuri, Gaia Germani, Mimmo Poli, Paul Muller, Luigi Visconti, Aldo Pini.

During WW II Ferzetti tries to steer his Italian submarine through enemy waters. Mason is the British commander who must seek out and destroy Ferzetti's craft. The Italian manages to get the submarine into international waters and is given permission to remain there for two weeks. Mason also holes up in this Tangiers port in order to keep his eye on the enemy. The two, through a tenative truce, build up a mutual respect, though Keen, an intelligence officer, wants the Italians to either remain in a neutral position or have their ship destroyed. Using Palmer, Ferzetti's lover, Keen tries to influence Ferzetti's position. Ferzetti accuses Palmer of spying and leaves port. Mason follows in his ship but is sunk by the man he has grown to respect. The film falters with its bare-bones scripting that emphasizes the Ferzetti-Palmer romance more than needed. It also plays the message about the common humanities of opposing sides with all the subtlety of a sledgehammer on fine china. As usual with the lesser films of his career, it is Mason's gentlemanly performance that overcomes the inadequacies of the production, making for a mildly engaging work.

p, Bruno Vailati; d, Charles Frend, Vailati; w, Frend, Vailati, Pino Belli, Alberto Ca'zorzi, Augusto Frassineti, Jack Wittingham; ph, Gabor Pagany; m, Roberto Nicolosi; ed, Giancarlo Cappelli; art d, Georgio Giovanini; cos, Giorgio Desideri.

War Drama   (PR:C   MPAA:NR)

TORPEDO BOAT*   (1942) 69m PAR bw

Richard Arlen (Skimmer Barnes), Jean Parker (Grace Holman), Mary Carlisle (Jane Townsend), Phil Terry (Tommy Whelan), Dick Purcell (Ralph Andrews), Ralph Sanford (Hector Bobry), William Haade (Riveter), Oscar O'Shea (Captain Mike), Robert Middlemass (Mr. Townsend).

The title vessel is the real star of this programmer about the pair who are responsible for its invention–Arlen and Terry. Romance comes to the shipyard, however, as nightclub singer Parker makes eyes at Terry and marries him, much to the chagrin of Arlen. The latter lucks out when Terry gets killed and Parker turns to him for comfort. Far from convincing, especially when it comes to the shabbily built torpedo boat.

p. William Pine, William Thomas; d, John Rawlins; w, Maxwell Shane (based on a story by Aaron Gottlieb); ph, Fred Jackman, Jr., ed, William Ziegler.

Drama/Romance   (PR:A   MPAA:NR)

TORPEDO RUN½   (1958) 98m MGM c

Glenn Ford (Lt. Comdr. Barney Doyle), Ernest Borgnine (Lt. Archer Sloan), Diane Brewster (Jane Doyle), Dean Jones (Lt. Jake "Fuzz" Foley), L.Q. Jones ("Hash" Benson), Philip Ober (Adm. Samuel Setton), Richard Carlyle (Comdr. Don Adams), Fredd Wayne (Orville "Goldy" Goldstein), Don Keefer (Ensign Ron Milligan), Robert Hardy (Lt. Redley), Paul Picerni (Lt. Burl Fisher).

Ford is a submarine commander whose obsession is to sink a certain Japanese aircraft carrier. Earlier in the war he had stalked the carrier, but it was screening itself with a transport carrying more than a thousand American prisoners from the Philippines to Tokyo, Ford's wife and daughter among them. When he finally launched his torpedoes, he missed the carrier and sank the transport. Borgnine is Ford's executive officer and best friend who has passed up his own command to stay with Ford. As the chase of the carrier goes on, Ford driving the crew to the breaking point, he and Borgnine have a falling out. Eventually the ship is found, Borgnine and Ford make up, and the carrier is sent to the bottom. The sub, though, is badly damaged and the crew has to make a dangerous escape from the doomed vessel using Momsen lungs. Utterly routine submarine drama that manages to hit on most of the cliches peculiar to this subgenre (no pun intended). Ford gives an adequate performance but he just isn't convincing as a man who has accidentally sent his wife and child to the bottom of the ocean and is out to make the enemy pay. Borgnine is better, and one wishes that he had accepted his own command and that we were watching a movie about him rather than about Ford. The rest of the cast is only competent. The wide-screen photography adds nothing to the claustrophobic interiors and only manages to make the exterior shots of the submarine and aircraft carrier look like the models they are.

p, Edmund Grainger; d, Joseph Pevney; w, Richard Sale, William Wister Haines (based on stories by Sale); ph, George J. Folsey (CinemaScope, Metrocolor); ed, Gene Ruggiero; art d, William A. Horning, Malcolm Brown; spec eff, A. Arnold Gillespie.

War Drama   (PR:A-C   MPAA:NR)

TORPEDOED!*   (1939) 66m Film Alliance bw (GB: OUR FIGHTING
                                                                                NAVY)

H.B. Warner (Mr. Brent, British Consul General), Robert Douglas (Capt. Markham, H.M.S. "Audacious"), Richard Cromwell (Lt. Bill Armstrong),

Hazel Terry (Pamela Brent), Noah Beery, Sr (President), Esme Percy (Da Costa, Rebel Commandant), Frederick Culley (Admiral), Henry Victor (Enricquo, Rebel Gunner Officer), Richard Ainley (Lieutenant), Binkie Stuart (Jennifer), Julie Suedo (Juanita).

Warner is the British consul for an unnamed South American country governed by Beery, its childish, naive president. Revolution breaks out and Warner's daughter, Terry, is kidnaped. Leave it to Douglas, a heroic navy man, to save the day. This is a well-acted programmer with plenty of action, not all of it that exciting. It certainly was released at an oppor tune moment for the British Royal Navy, whose future financial support was hinging on a proposed tax hike. This film slyly shows how the common man helps support the Navy's efforts to protect the British Empire around the world, a handy bit of propaganda. The British Navy's first onscreen launching took place in the film BORN TO GLORY (1935).

p, Herbert Wilcox; d, Norman Walker; w, Gerald Elliott, Harrison Owens (based on the story by "Bartimeus" [Capt. L. da Costa Ricci], Guy Cameron Pollock, Lt. Cmdr. H. T. Bishop); ph, Claude Friese-Greene; m, Noel Gay; ed, Winifred Cooper; md, Geraldo; art d, L. P. Williams; cos, Morris Angel.

War/Action   (PR:C   MPAA:NR)

TORRID ZONE**   (1940) 88m WB bw

James Cagney (Nick Butler), Pat O'Brien (Steve Case), Ann Sheridan (Lee Donley), Andy Devine (Wally Davis), Helen Vinson (Gloria Anderson), George Tobias (Rosario), Jerome Cowan (Bob Anderson), George Reeves (Sancho), Victor Kilian (Carlos), Frank Puglia (Rodriguez), John Ridgely (Gardiner), Grady Sutton (Sam the Secretary), George Humbert (Hotel Manager), Paul Porcasi (Garcia the Hotel Bar Proprietor), Frank Yaconelli (Lopez), Paul HurstDaniels, Jack Mower (Schaeffer), Frank Mayo (McNamara), Dick Botiller (Hernandez), Elvira Sanchez (Rita), Paul Renay (Jose), Rafael Corio (Man), George Regas (Sergeant), Trevor Bardette, Ernesto Piedra (Policeman), Don Orlando (Employee), Manuel Lopez (Chico), Joe Cominguez (Manuel), Joe Molinas (Native), Tony Paton (Charley), Max Blum, Betty Sanko, Victor Sabuni.

In a seamy seaport nightclub in a Central American banana republic, newly booked singer Sheridan–wearing a shimmering sequined gown–sexily croons a tune to local patrons and then, cheating, relieves them of their pesos at poker. Most of the campesinos in the club are employed by the Baldwin Fruit Company, whose boss–O'Brien–has been watching the illicit activity from the bar. To protect his eagerly influenced employees, O'Brien orders her to leave town on the next boat back to the upper 48, and to ensure her compliance he has her tossed in the local calaboose. Departing for the lockup, Sheridan quips to O'Brien, "The stork that brought you must have been a vulture." In the jail cell adjacent to Sheridan's is the famed bandido, Tobias, awaiting his execution by firing squad. Befriending the clever devil, Sheridan helps him pass his few remaining hours on earth, playing cards with him through the bars. Tobias, grateful for her company, presents her with his ring as a remembrance. When the outlaw manages to cleverly evade the firing squad and make good his escape, Sheridan yells out, "Hurray for our side!" On the morrow, the good-bad girl is escorted to a departing steamboat by O'Brien himself, who wants to personally witness the departure of the disruptive Sheridan. Annoyed by an amorous guard aboard the vessel, Sheridan is protected by devil-may-care Cagney–with a mustache–who knocks the bounder into the briny with a single punch. Cagney, a plantation foreman for O'Brien's company, had made the mistake of messing with the boss'–O'Brien's wife–and as a consequence is heading back to his native city, Chicago. The cocky little ladies' man makes a play for Sheridan, thinking to turn his trip into a pleasure cruise. The crafty O'Brien, however, had another motive for his dockside appearance; having shucked his faithless wife, O'Brien wants Cagney to go back to work, this time managing a troubled plantation in an area threatened by Tobias' revolutionists. Promised a substantial bonus if he succeeds in bringing in the banana crop, Cagney accepts the assignment. He finds an additional bonus at the plantation in the person of Vinson, the attractive wife of the previous plantation foreman. Their romantic idyll is interrupted by incursions of Tobias' revolutionists, by disaffection among the workers, and–most critically–by the arrival of Sheridan, who has escaped from the ship and, pursued by police, has made her way to the plantation. Vinson greets the new arrival with little enthusiasm, but reluctantly offers to put her up. Says Sheridan, "Don't strain yourself. I can always sleep in a tree." In one of her few successful ripostes against her wisecracking rival, Vinson responds, "Heredity." Cagney plans to take Vinson back to Chicago with him, but his plans are spoiled when the bandit, Tobias, gains the upper hand in a battle. Tobias orders Cagney to marry his good friend Sheridan, who is pretending she was wounded in the fight. Cagney–knowing he is being victimized by a ruse–agrees, apparently reluctantly. Tobias gives the plantation–which he regards as rightfully his to give–to the couple as a wedding present. When Tobias departs, tough-guy Cagney unceremoniously dumps the "wounded" Sheridan out of her cot and joins her on the floor in the clinch that finishes the picture. This wonderfully witty romp with its sexually suggestive dialog teamed its two male stars again in their old familiar friendly-enemies rapport, roles in which they always appeared to revel. The parts were so familiar to them that Cagney's brother, associate producer William, wrote to studio production chief Hal Wallis, saying ". . . this is just the type of story that made Cagney want to leave the studio upon the expiration of his last contract".... TORRID ZONE is what has been known for so long as a typical Cagney vehicle and that is just the reason he would refuse to do it...." The part was offered to George Raft, but Cagney finally *did* agree to play it–and play it he did, with great gusto. O'Brien does his usual brusque, entertaining, hard-nosed scoundrel role with his customary aplomb. The actor had recently gone to New York for the premiere of THE FIGHTING 69TH and had been invited to attend President Franklin D. Roosevelt's birthday ball. A crew member had asked O'Brien to speak to the president on his behalf, explaining that he was about to lose his home. With a nudge from his wife Eloise, O'Brien *did* plead the worker's case. On the set of TORRID ZONE, the actor was pleased to be thanked by the grateful grip, who had received a personal reassurance from the president, as recounted in the actor's biography, *The Wind at My Back*. Sheridan here achieves what many viewed as impossible: she steals the picture from its two male leads. In her second starring role, Sheridan proves herself the wisecracking peer of such great quipsters as Carole Lombard. The actress–who, according to Erroll Flynn in *his* autobiography, *My Wicked, Wicked Ways*, got her big break in pictures as a payoff for certain services rendered to Flynn and his actor pals–had been widely hyped by the studio as "The 'Oomph' Girl." An in-joke reference to the studio publicity occurs as the closing line of the picture, as Cagney, breaking from the clinch to catch his breath, says, "You and your fourteen-carat oomph." Tobias is terrific as the comical *bandido* with a heart. The picture was shot in 41 days, with sets constructed on the studio's 30-acre annex. A full 5 acres were used to create a seaport set, a jungle, and a banana grove (950 real banana trees were planted). Director Keighley–who had spent 30 years acting and directing on stage before joining the studio in 1932–worked his players well in this picture, which has been called an amalgam of RED DUST and THE FRONT PAGE, but the real credit for this witty adventure film must go to the writers and the selective, talented producer, Hellinger. There's nothing serious here, only sheer entertainment.

p, Mark Hellinger; d, William Keighley; w, Richard Macaulay, Jerry Wald; ph, James Wong Howe; m, Adolph Deutsch; ed, Jack Killifer; md, Leo F. Forbstein; art d, Ted Smith; set d, Edward Thorne; cos, Howard Shoup; spec eff, Byron Haskin, H.F. Koenekamp; m/l, "Mi Caballero," M.K. Jerome, Jack Scholl; tech adv, John Mari; makeup, Perc Westmore.

Adventure/Romance   **(PR:A MPAA:NR)**

TORSO*   (1974, Ital.) 90m CHAM/Joseph Brenner c (I CORPI PRESENTANO TRACCE DI VIOLENZA CARNALE)

Suzy Kendall *(Jane)*, Tina Aumont *(Dani)*, Luc Meranda *(Roberto)*, John Richardson *(Franz)*, Robert Bisacco *(Stefano)*, Angela Covello *(Katia)*, Carla Brait *(Ursula)*, Cristina Airoldi *(Carol)*, Patricia Adiutori *(Flo)*.

Beautiful young college girls are terrorized by a hooded rapist-killer who gets his kicks by dismembering his victims with saws. It's pretty sick and very boring, but at least the technical end is up to par. Aumont is the daughter of Maria Montez, star of such pictures as ARABIAN NIGHTS (1942) and ALI BABA AND THE FORTY THIEVES (1944). The Italian title of this one translates as "The Bodies Presented Traces of Carnal Violence"–perhaps a bit of an understatement when we're talking about women with their limbs hacked off. (Dubbed in English.)

p, Carlo Ponti, Antonio Cervi; d, Sergio Martino; w, Ernesto Gastaldi, Martino; ph, Giancarlo Ferrando (Technicolor).

Horror   **Cas.**   **(PR:O MPAA:R)**

TORSO MURDER MYSTERY, THE**½**   (1940, Brit.) 70m Rialto/Arthur Ziehm, Inc. bw (GB: TRAITOR SPY)

Bruce Cabot *(Healey Beyersdorf)*, Marta Labarr *(Freyda Beyersdorf)*, Tamara Desni *(Marie Dufreyene)*, Romilly Lunge *(Beverley Blake)*, Edward Lexy *(Inspector Barnard)*, Cyril Smith *(Sgt. Trotter)*, Percy Walsh *(Lemnel)*, Eve Lynd *(Florrie McGowan)*, Alexander Field *(Yorky Meane)*, Peter Gawthorne *(Commissioner)*, Fritz [Frederick] Valk, Hilary Pritchard, Davina Craig, Vincent Holman, Anthony Shaw, Bernard Jukes, Nino Rossi, Rosarita, Ken Johnson's West Indian Band.

Cabot is a double agent who steals secret British plans for a new submarine-hunting patrol boat. He tries to sell it to the Germans, but they beat him up. His wife, Labarr, burns the plans just as police arrive on the scene. The Germans are arrested and the house is set on fire. Cabot shoots Labarr, then dies in the fire. Fast-moving if not especially credible spy action drama.

p, John Argyle; d, Walter Summers; w, Summers, Argyle, Jan Van Lusil, Ralph Gilbert Bettinson (based on a novel by T.C.H. Jacobs).

Spy Drama   **(PR:C MPAA:NR)**

TORTILLA FLAT***   (1942) 105m MGM bw

Spencer Tracy *(Pilon)*, Hedy Lamarr *(Dolores "Sweets" Ramirez)*, John Garfield *(Danny)*, Frank Morgan *(The Pirate)*, Akim Tamiroff *(Pablo)*, Sheldon Leonard *(Tito Ralph)*, John Qualen *(Jose Maria Corcoran)*, Donald Meek *(Paul D. Cummings)*, Connie Gilchrist *(Mrs. Torrelli)*, Allen Jenkins *(Portagee Joe)*, Henry O'Neill *(Father Ramon)*, Mercedes Ruffino *(Mrs. Marellis)*, Nina Campana *(Senora Teresina Cortez)*, Arthur Space *(Mr.*

Brown), Betty Wells *(Cesca)*, Harry Burns *(Torrelli)*, Louis Jean Heydt *(Young Doctor)*, Willie Fung *(Chin Kee)*, Roque Ybarra *(Alfredo)*, Tim Ryan *(Rupert Hogan)*, Charles Judels *(Joe Machado)*, Yvette Duguay *(Little Girl)*, Tito Renaldo *(Boy)*, Harry Strang, Walter Sande *(Firemen)*, Jack Carr *(Owner)*, Shirley Warde *(Nurse)*, Emmett Vogan *(Doctor)*, Bob O'Conor, George Magrill *(Cannery Workers)*, Fleeta, Hobo, Pumpkin, Scooter, Fluff *(Pirate's Dogs)*.

This superlative adaption of Steinbeck's novel features Tracy and Tamiroff as two *paisanos* constantly in search of a free meal in their home of Monterey, California. Garfield is another resident, an eager young man who considers himself to be wealthy after inheriting from his grandfather two houses located on Tortilla Flat. Proud of his new status, Garfield allows Tracy and his friends to move into one of the homes, keeping the other for himself. He then begins courting Lamarr, a beautiful young lady who works in the local cannery, yet she will have nothing to do with him. Morgan is a newcomer to town, arriving with his dogs and what Tracy believes to be a good sum of money. Planning to steal the loot for himself, Tracy invites the newcomer to move into Garfield's home. Morgan tells Tracy he is thinking of burying his fortune, but Tracy insists this is not a safe thing to do. Morgan agrees, and much to Tracy's surprise, the aimiable dog lover entrusts the would-be thief with his money. Morgan tells Tracy to keep a careful watch on the money, for he intends to use it to buy golden candlesticks in honor of St. Francis, the patron saint of animals. Morgan is convinced his prayers to the beloved saint had cured one of his dogs when it was ill, and now he wants to honor his benefactor. Later, one of Garfield's houses burns to the ground. Garfield gets into a fight with Lamarr, who has also seen some romantic interest from Tracy. Garfield gets drunk, then ends up getting hurt in a fight. Lamarr is angred with Tracy, blaming him for Garfield's troubles. Tracy prays for his friend's speedy recovery, then decides to help Garfield win Lamarr over. Eventually Garfield recovers and marries Lamarr, while Tracy manages to raise enough money for Garfield to buy a fishing boat. Tracy decides that Garfield's becoming a property owner was the cause of all the trouble between the friends, so after the young marrieds leave, a match quickly dispatches of the second house. TORTILLA FLAT is an affectionate tale, told with sensitivity and a wonderfully offbeat sense of humor. Steinbeck's characters are engaging, well treated by the talents of this ensemble and Fleming's caring direction. Lamarr is excellent (she considered this the best of all her roles), a level-headed, spunky woman who refuses to settle for anything she doesn't want. Her relationship with Garfield, sparked with both attraction and suspicion, is realistic and honest, a rarity for so many screen romances. Garfield as the earnest Danny gives his heart to the role, a memorable characterization that complements Lamarr. Tracy's lovable rogue and Morgan as the religious man add to the film's cast of colorful characters. Morgan received a well- deserved Oscar nomination as Best Supporting Actor, though he lost that year to Van Heflin in JOHNNY EAGER. Fleming captures the nuances and ambience of life in this small town, a sincere effort that guides the performers with care through the material. MGM built an entire village over three acres of land especially for the film. Garfield dearly wanted to do the picture and eventually Warner Bros. agreed to loan him to MGM. Louis B. Mayer, MGM's head, also liked the idea of Garfield in the role, and, according to one account, the powerful mogul was not above some unorthodox pressuring to get his man. Mayer reportedly threatened to expose Warner Bros. for not making good on their pledges to certain charitable groups unless Garfield was allowed to make the film. Garfield enjoyed working at MGM and hoped to make more films there, though this would not come to be for some time. While on set, Garfield found himself the victim of Fleming's rather unusual sense of humor. "For Christ's sake, Garfield," the director shouted during the actor's first scene, "you have to do better than that. I fought like hell to get you in this picture, so don't make me look like a fool." When Garfield asked what exactly the director wanted, Fleming retorted: "You want me to tell you how to act, Garfield?" Hell, I don't know how to act, and I'd be making more money if I did. You're the actor, you have the reputation; now I just want you to be better." As Tracy laughed to himself off camera, Fleming continued, telling Garfield how he should play opposite Lamarr. "She's not what you'd call unoutclassable," Fleming explained to Garfield, "...Be better than you were the first time, but worse than the second." Eventually Garfield caught on to Fleming's joking around, and he gave the director the best performance he could muster. TORTILLA FLATS was highly praised by the critics of the time, many of whom recognized it for the masterpiece it was. However, the public was less receptive. The film's laid-back setting and simple-minded characters were not what a war-minded American public wanted to see, so MGM tried spicing up the film with an ad campaign that read: "It's the gay paradise on the Pacific....It's warming as the California sun...heady as spring wine...romantic as the tinkle of a guitar in the moonlight." It didn't work, as the film failed to generate much excitement at the box office. Five years before TORTILLA FLAT was made, Paramount had considered filming the story as a musical, featuring George Raft though this, like so many Hollywood projects, never made it to the cameras.

p, Sam Zimbalist; d, Victor Fleming; w, John Lee Mahin, Benjamin Glaser (based on the novel by John Steinbeck); ph, Karl Freund; m, Franz Waxman; ed, James E. Newsom; art d, Cedric Gibbons, Paul Groesse; set d, Edwin B. Willis; cos, Robert Kalloch, Gile Steele; spec eff, Warren Newcombe; m/l, "Oh How I Love a Wedding," "Ai, Paisano" (based on Mexican folk song melody), Waxman, Frank Loesser; makeup, Jack Dawn.

Drama   (PR:A   MPAA:NR)

TORTURE CHAMBER OF DR. SADISM, THE
(SEE: BLOOD DEMON, THE, 1967, Ger.)

TORTURE DUNGEON zero   (1970) 80m Constitution/Mishkin c

Jeremy Brooks (Norman, Duke of Norwich), Susan Cassidy (Heather McGregor), Patricia Dillon (Lady Jane), Donna Whitfield (Lady Agatha), Haal Borske (Alfred), Maggie Rogen (Margaret), Neil Flanagan (Peter the Eye), Richard Mason (Ivan), George Box, Patricia Garvey, Dan Lyra, Helen Adams, Robert Fricelle.

This example of "torture filmmaking" bores the audience to death with unconvincing medieval sets and a lame tale about a crazed duke who attempts to kill off and mutilate all the heirs to his kingdom's throne. nclusion At the picture's conclusion, he comes to a violent end and the rightful ruler assumes her royal birthright. This was filmed on Staten Island, a poor substitute indeed for the England of yore.

p, William Mishkin; d, Andy Milligan; w, Milligan, John Borske; ph, Milligan; set d, James Fox; cos, Raffine; makeup, Walter Terry.

Horror   (PR:O   MPAA:R)

TORTURE GARDEN**½   (1968, Brit.) 92m Amicus/COL c

Jack Palance (Ronald Wyatt), Burgess Meredith (Dr. Diabolo), Beverly Adams (Carla Hayes), Peter Cushing (Lancelot Canning), Barbara Ewing (Dorothy Endicott), Michael Bryant (Colin Williams), Maurice Denham (Colin's Uncle), John Standing (Leo Winston), Robert Hutton (Bruce Benton), John Phillips (Eddie Storm), Michael Ripper (Gordon Roberts), Bernard Kay (Dr. Heim), Catherine Finn (Nurse Parker), Ursula Howells (Miss Chambers), Niall MacGinnis (Doctor), Timothy Bateson (Fairground Barker), David Bauer (Mike Charles), Nicole Shelby (Millie), Clytie Jessop (Atropos), Michael Hawkins (Constable), Hedger Wallace (Edgar Allan Poe), Frank Forsyth (Tramp), Roy Stephens, Geoffrey Wallace, James Copeland, Norman Claridge, Roy Goldfrey, Barry Lowe.

Four Robert Bloch-penned horror stories are bookended by Burgess Meredith as a carnival barker who can give patrons a glimpse into the future. He has an audience of five people, four of whom have their fates revealed. The first episode concerns a young playboy who falls under the spell of a cat and is thereby forced to kill people so the hungry feline can eat their heads. The second has a rising movie hopeful falling in love with a famous star, only to discover that he is a robot. She, too, is turned into a robot and gains great fame. In the third, and worst episode, a female reporter falls in love with a concert pianist. Their relationship is cut short, however, when the piano, controlled by the pianist's mother's spirit, kills the girl out of jealousy. The final story has Palance as a collector of Edgar Allan Poe paraphernalia who kills fellow collector Cushing in an attempt to acquire some rare manuscripts. Poe himself then comes to life and convinces Palance to set the house ablaze. The fifth member of Meredith's audience refuses to have his future looked into and stabs the barker, causing the other four to flee in fear. After they've gone, Meredith reveals that it's just part of the gag. Ultimately, the film is marred by the uneven quality of the episodes.

p, Max J. Rosenberg, Milton Subotsky; d, Freddie Francis; w, Robert Bloch (based on his stories "Enoch," "Terror Over Hollywood," "Mr. Steinway," "The Man Who Collected Poe"); ph, Norman Warwick (Technicolor); m, Don Banks, James Bernard; ed, Peter Elliott; prod d, Bill Constable; art d, Don Mingaye, Scott Slimon; set d, Andrew Low; cos, Evelyn Gibbs; makeup, Jill Carpenter.

Horror   Cas.   (PR:O   MPAA:NR)

TORTURE ME KISS ME*   (1970) 75m Black Mercedes/Jerand bw

Linda Boyce (Madelaine), Elaine Seagal (Pepi), Frank MacIntosh (Count Henri de Prave), Blaine Quincy (Max von Hildebrandt), Christine Cybelle (Ilsa Schneider), Wendy Wood (Marianne Duval), Nick Dundas (Lt. Jaeger), Alf Geisler (The Priest), Jan Saint (Erick the Torture Master).

A sadomasochistic war drama about a Nazi colonel who is sent to France with his secretary in order to kill a Resistance leader. Along the way, Frenchwomen are whipped by a torture master, and the men who come to their aid are killed. Eventually the colonel kills his own secretary after suspecting her of collaborating with the French, but is himself gunned down by a French loyalist disguised as a Nazi.

p&d, David R. Friedberg; m/l, "The Merry Widow Waltz," Franz Lehar.

War Drama   (PR:O   MPAA:NR)

TORTURE SHIP*½   (1939) 57m PDC bw

Lyle Talbot (Lt. Bob Bennett), Irving Pichel (Dr. Herbert Stander), Jacqueline Wells [Julie Bishop] (Joan Martel), Sheila Bromley (Mary Slavish), Anthony Averill (Dirk), Eddie Holden (Ole Olson), Russell Hopton (Harry), Wheeler Oakman (Ritter), Leander de Cordova (Ezra), Dmitri Alexis (Murano), Skelton Knaggs (Jesse), Adia Kuznetzoff (Krantz), Stanley

Blystone (Briggs), Julian Madison (Paul), William Chapman (Bill), Fred Walton (Fred).

Talbot operates a ship which is used by a crazed doctor (Pichel) to transport a group of prisoners to a remote island. The doctor has helped the criminals escape in order to test out a medical theory on them. He believes that all violence is caused by glandular dysfunctions, but has a tough time convincing the prisoners to go under the knife. He is killed and Talbot takes control, helping Wells prove her innocence, which leads to a romantic fling between the pair. Poorly scripted and cast.

d, Victor Halperin; w, George Sayre based on the story "A Thousand Deaths" by Jack London); ph , Jack Greenhalgh; m, David Chudnow; ed, Holbrook N. Todd; art d, Fred Preble.

Drama   (PR:A   MPAA:NR)

TOTO AND THE POACHERS*½   (1958, Brit.) 50m World
Safari/Children's Film Foundation c

John Aloisi (Toto), Mpigano (Baaba), Shabani Hamisi (Shabani), David Betts (Warden), Obago (Poacher), Anso Shaibu, Kiplagat.

Variation of "The Boy who Cried Wolf" set in Africa has little Aloisi a habitual liar who sees some suspicious looking characters hanging around the village but is unable to convince anyone. When an elephant is found killed, though, the adults take him seriously and he helps them capture the poachers. Undiscriminating children might like it, but few others.

p, Henry Geddes; d, Brian Salt; w, Salt, John Coquillon, Michael Johns; ph, Coquillon (Eastmancolor).

Children   (PR:AA   MPAA:NR)

TOTO IN THE MOON*½   (1957, Ital./Span.) 90m
Maxima-Variety-Montfluor bw (TOTO NELIA LUNA)

Toto (Himself), Ugo Tognazzi (Achille), Sylva Koscina, Luciano Salce, Sandro Milo, Giancamo Furia.

In what sounds like THE WIZARD OF OZ revisited, TOTO IN THE MOON follows the comic adventures of Italian comedian Toto as he and Tognazzi get involved in the space race. Their efforts are hampered by alien creatures who clone the pair in an attempt to keep Earthlings on Earth. One of the least successful pictures for Toto, whose real name is Antonio De Curtis. The film features an early screen appearance by Koscina.

p, Mario Cecchi Gori; d, Stefano Steno; w, Steno, Alessandro Continenza; ph, Marco Scarpelli.

ScienceFiction/Comedy   (PR:A   MPAA:NR)

TOTO, VITTORIO E LA DOTTORESSA
(SEE: LADY DOCTOR, THE, 1963, Fr./Ital./Span.)

TOUCH, THE*   (1971, U.S./Swed.) 112m ABC-Persona-Cinematograph
A.B./Cinerama (BE RORINGEN)

Bibi Andersson (Karin Vergerus), Elliott Gould (David Kovac), Max von Sydow (Andreas Vergerus), Sheila Reid (Sara Kovac), Staffan Hallerstram (Anders Vergerus), Maria Nolgard (Agnes Vergerus), Barbro Hiort af Ornas (Karin's Mother), Ake Lindstrom (Doctor), Mimmi Wahlander (Nurse), Elsa Ebbesen (Hospital Matron), Karin Nilsson, Anna von Rosen (Family Neighbors), Margareta Bystrom (Vergerus' Secretary), Alain Simon (Museum Curator), Per Sjostrand (Museum Curator), Aino Taube (Woman on Staircase), Ann-Christin Lobraten (Museum Worker), Carol Zavis (BEA Air Hostess), Dennis Gotobed (British Immigration Officer), Bengt Ottekil (London Bellboy), Erik Nyhlen (Archaeologist).

If you see only one Bergman movie in your life, don't let this be it. His first film in English, THE TOUCH marks a move to a more simplistic style of drama, steering away from symbolic explanations of the inexplicable, and ending up at perhaps the lowest point in his career. The story is an uncomplicated one–Andersson and von Sydow are content in their marriage but nothing more. When Gould, the wandering Jew, enters Andersson's life, she begins yearning for a freedom that she no longer has. Though Andersson is attracted to Gould, she is left indecisive about her situation, torn between her two worlds. The film is not harmed by the fact that the story has been told countless times before (familiarity with a subject rarely works against it), but by the embarrassing presence of Gould in a role which clearly is not suited to him. Especially disturbing is his dialog (perhaps due to an unfamiliarity on Bergman's part), which seems out of place and awkward. As expected of Andersson, she turns in a beautiful performance, delivering more in a single glance than in the entire part written for Gould.

p,d&w, Ingmar Bergman; ph, Sven Nykvist; m, Jan Johansson; ed, Siv Kanalv-Lundgren; prod d, P.A. Lundgren; cos, Mago; makeup, Borje Lundh, Cilla Drott, Bengt Ottekil.

Drama   Cas.   (PR:O   MPAA:R)

TOUCH AND GO (1955) (SEE: LIGHT TOUCH, THE, 1955, Brit.)

TOUCH AND GO*½ (1980, Aus.) 92m Mutiny/Great Union c

Wendy Hughes (*Eva Gilmour*), Chantal Contouri (*Fiona Latham*), Carmen Duncan (*Millicent Hoffman*), Jeanie Drynan (*Gina Tesoriero*), Liddy Clark (*Helen Preston*), Christine Amor (*Sue Fullerton*), Jon English (*Frank Butterfield*), John Bluthal (*Anatole Sushinsky*), Brian Blain (*George Latham*), Vince Martin (*Steve Godfrey*), Barbara Stephens (*Julia Henderson*), Pamela Norman (*Miss Pringle*), Cynthia Cooper (*Daphne Sushinsky*), Beryl Cheers (*Housewife*).

Very little happens out of the ordinary in this thin comedy about three lovely ladies who resort to burglary to keep the local kindergarten afloat. Their idea is to empty out the local seaside resorts of their profits, and to that end they enlist another three lovely ladies to help. Handsome production values give this almost-ran a certain charm, and there is scenic excitement in some of the physical layouts.

p, John Pellatt; d, Peter Maxwell; w, Peter Yeldham (based on a story by Maxwell, Yeldham); ph, John McLean (Eastmancolor); ed, Sara Bennett, Paul Maxwell.

Comedy/Crime   Cas.   (PR:C MPAA:NR)

TOUCH ME NOT** (1974, Brit.) 84m Atlas c (GB: THE HUNTED)

Lee Remick, Michael Hinz, Ivan Desny, Jose Caffarel, Ingrid Garbo.

Hinz plays an industrial spy who wants information on Desny. He goes to Remick, a neurotic secretary, and uses her to get to her boss. A thriller with few thrills. One of many movies American born Remick made and continues to make in England after her marriage to British director William Gowans in 1970.

Thriller   Cas.   (PR:C MPAA:PG)

TOUCH OF CLASS, A**** (1973, Brit.) 105m Brut/AE c

George Segal (*Steve Blackburn*), Glenda Jackson (*Vicki Allessio*), Paul Sorvino (*Walter Menkes*), Hildegard Neil (*Gloria Blackburn*), Cec Linder (*Wendell Thompson*), K. Callan (*Patty Menkes*), Mary Barclay (*Martha Thompson*), Michael Elwyn (*Cecil*), Nadim Sawalha (*Night Hotel Manager*), Ian Thompson (*Derek*), Eve Karpf (*Miss Ramos*), David De Keyser (*Dr. Alvarez*), Gaye Brown (*Dora French*), Samantha Weyson (*Josie Blackburn*), Michael McVey (*Billy Blackburn*), Edward Kemp (*Michael Allessio*), Lisa Vanderpump (*Julia Allessio*), Donald Hewlett (*Spencer Birdsall*), John Sterland, David Healy (*Americans*).

Joseph E. Levine, the man who brought us THE GRADUATE, THE LION IN WINTER, CARNAL KNOWLEDGE, and many more, picked a winner when he elected to "present" this very funny film about infidelity in London. It was nominated for Best Picture, Best Song, Best Script, and Best Music, and Jackson won the Oscar as Best Actress in a field that included Ellen Burstyn, Marsha Mason, Joanne Woodward, and Barbra Streisand that year. Segal is an American insurance executive living in London with wife Neil and children Weyson and McVey. He's playing softball in the regular Sunday game near the Albert Memorial in Hyde Park one Sunday when he meets Jackson, a divorcee with two children of her own, Kemp and Vanderpump. They meet again later when racing after the same cab in a London downpour. Taking this as an omen, Segal asks Jackson to have lunch and they learn about each other. She is a fashion artist who goes to Paris, copies the latest creations, and sells them to New York garment firms who knock them off at discount prices. Segal finds Jackson attractive and suggests that they have a tryst in Spain, a week of sangria and lust. He is very surprised when she agrees. But their plans are immediately thrown for a loop when Neil and the kids return to England before their scheduled arrival. Segal tells Neil that he has to take a "business trip" to Spain and she wants to go along with him. He manages to convince her it would be best if she remained in London and put the house in order and looked after their children. He'll only be gone a few days and she can handle that, can't she? She reluctantly agrees to stay. Segal and Jackson get to Heathrow Airport for their jet to Spain and he runs into Sorvino, a heavyset producer of semi-porno and exploitation pictures. Sorvino is to be on the same plane bound for Spain and is delighted to see Segal and wants to talk with him throughout the flight. This causes Jackson to have to change her seat and sit somewhere else on the plane. They land at Malaga, where Segal has booked a large, comfortable car for the drive to the resort. To shed himself of Sorvino, he gives his rented car to the producer and he and Jackson wind up with a tiny automobile that doesn't work well. The clutch is bad, the seats are cramped, and it is like being in a rolling sardine can. After considerable problems, they get to the resort hotel and immediately go to their room, looking forward to fulfilling their passion for each other. But the hours in the tiny car and his overeager attitude cause Segal to have a back spasm and he can't move at all so the night goes by unsullied. In the morning, Segal's back is finally in place and the two make love. He is hurt when she admits that the earth didn't move for her and all it was "very nice," nothing more. They have a loud argument and he exits. He runs into Sorvino and his wife, Callan, and agrees to have dinner with them that evening. Meantime, Callan has been shopping at the local marketplace, meets

Jackson, and invites her to the same dinner. Jackson and Segal pretend to meet at the meal and the scene is fraught with underlying tension, which expansive Sorvino can't quite fathom. Later, the two return to their room and the argument erupts again, this time even more violently as items of furniture are flung. Their words are bitter, angry, and insults fly fast and furiously. They begin to physically wrestle with each other and the touch of bodies causes them to laugh, then begin to make love. A montage follows and we can see that they are totally committed to each other, very much in love, and unusually happy. Sorvino learns about the affair and warns Segal about continuing it. The vacation ends and Jackson and Segal return to London where they rent a flat in an area just off Shaftesbury Avenue, near the famed Dumpling Inn restaurant. They maintain their affair but it's not quite the same and Segal finds that being a husband and father and keeping his job going is taking a toll on his relationship with Jackson. He decides to call it off and sends her a wire to that effect. Then he changes his mind and tries to abort the telegram but it has already been sent. Jackson gets the wire at the apartment and packs her gear right away, then exits. Segal arrives a few moments later, finds the telegram, then looks out the window into Jerrod Street and spots Jackson waiting for a public bus. The rain is pouring down, reminiscent of their first meeting. All he has to do is open the window and call her name. But he doesn't...and the picture ends. The company behind the picture was Brut Productions, part of the Brut cosmetics firm headed by George Barrie. Barrie always fancied himself a composer and cowrote the film's Oscar-nominated song (lyrics by Sammy Cahn), "All That Love Went to Waste," as well as two other tunes. The scuttlebutt around Hollywood is that he only financed the movie so he could write the songs for it. It was filmed in Spain and London, and interiors were at Lee Studios in London. The picture did quite well at the box office and, while not a comedy classic, turned out to be a fine example of professionals at work. Segal is charming but everyone knew he could play comedy. The big surprise was Jackson's impeccable comic timing, which some likened to Katharine Hepburn. The softball scene at the start of the film was authentic and featured many of the expatriate Americans who lived in London at the time and played regularly. Some of the men who used to play on Summer Sundays (the game was run by producer Arthur Lewis because he owned the bases and bats) were screenwriter Larry Gelbart, producer Peter Katz (DON'T LOOK NOW), producer Si Litvinoff (A CLOCKWORK ORANGE), stage producer Alex Cohen, CBS executive Stu Witt, and screenwriter Stanley Ralph Ross. From time to time, Englishmen would join in and actor David Hemmings would show up to play and be cheered on by his lady, Gayle Hunnicutt. Many of the men in the game in the film were the actual players. Frank was not nominated for his direction but he should have been. Despite the subject matter, it was handled with such good taste that it only merited a PG rating, a tribute to Frank and his cowriter, Jack Rose. Later, George Barrie would team up with Frank's former partner, Norman Panama, and produce I WILL, I WILL...FOR NOW with less than spectacular results.

p&d, Melvin Frank; w, Frank, Jack Rose; ph, Austin Dempster (Panavision, Technicolor); m, John Cameron; ed, Bill Butler; prod d, Terry Marsh; art d, Alan Tompkins; set d, Peter Howitt; cos, Ruth Myers; m/l, "I Always Knew," Cameron, Sammy Cahn; "She Loves Me, She Told Me So Last Night," Melvin Frank, Marvin Frank (sung by George Segal, Glenda Jackson), "All that Love Went to Waste," "Nudge Me Every Morning," "A Touch of Class," George Barrie, Cahn; makeup, Tony Sforzini.

Comedy   Cas.   (PR:C MPAA:PG)

TOUCH OF DEATH*½ (1962, Brit.) 58m Helion/Planet bw

William Lucas (*Pete Mellor*), David Sumner (*Len Williams*), Ray Barrett (*Maxwell*), Jan Waters (*Jackie*), Frank Coda (*Sgt. Byrne*), Roberta Tovey (*Pam*), Geoffrey Denton (*Baxter*).

A gang of thieves steal bundles of money specially rigged to poison them. Not knowing what is happening, they force their way onto a houseboat and make the girl there hide them. Briefly interesting premise deteriorates quickly into routine hideout tension melodrama.

p, Lewis Linzee; d, Lance Comfort; w, Lyn Fairhurst (based on a story by Aubrey Cash, Wilfred Josephs).

Crime   (PR:A MPAA:NR)

TOUCH OF EVIL***** (1958) 95m UNIV bw

Charlton Heston (*Ramon Miguel "Mike" Vargas*), Janet Leigh (*Susan Vargas*), Orson Welles (*Hank Quinlan*), Joseph Calleia (*Pete Menzies*), Akim Tamiroff (*"Uncle Joe" Grandi*), Valentin De Vargas (*Pancho*), Ray Collins (*District Attorney Adair*), Dennis Weaver (*Motel Clerk*), Joanna Moore (*Marcia Linnekar*), Mort Mills (*Schwartz*), Marlene Dietrich (*Tanya*), Victor Millan (*Manolo Sanchez*), Lalo Rios (*Risto*), Michael Sargent (*Pretty Boy*), Mercedes McCambridge (*Gang Leader*), Joseph Cotten (*Detective*), Zsa Zsa Gabor (*Owner of Strip Joint*), Phil Harvey (*Blaine*), Joi Lansing (*Blonde*), Harry Shannon (*Gould*), Rusty Westcoatt (*Casey*), Wayne Taylor, Ken Miller, Raymond Rodriguez (*Gang Members*), Arlene McQuade (*Ginnie*), Domenick Delgarde (*Lackey*), Joe Basulto (*Young Delinquent*), Jennie Dias (*Jackie*), Yolanda Bojorquez (*Bobbie*), Eleanor Dorado (*Lia*), Keenan Wynn (*Man*).

Already famous for directing perhaps the greatest film ever made, CITIZEN

KANE, Welles opens TOUCH OF EVIL with what may be the greatest single shot ever put on film. In a spectacular crane shot, the first scene (over which opening credits are printed) begins with the closeup of an explosive device being attached to the back of a car. The ticking is heard as Mancini's pulsating score builds tension. The camera pulls up and away, showing the car parked in a seedy area of town–Los Robles, an undesirable spot nuzzled along the U.S.-Mexico border. Night has fallen, the streets are dirty, and a sense of decadence permeates the visuals. As the camera reaches up into the sky, looking down, we see a man–the big boss of Los Robles, Rudy Lanniker–and his floozy girl friend get into the doomed car and drive off through the streets. The camera travels along until it spots Heston, a Mexican lawman, driving along with Leigh, his blonde bride, on their way across the border for a honeymoon. The camera travels with them to the border crossing checkpoint, where they answer a few simple questions and nuzzle romantically like the newlyweds they are. After over three minutes of unbroken tension, floating, fluid camerawork, the incessant rhythms of the score, and the ticking of the bomb, an explosion rips through the air (as Welles' name comes up on the credits), light flickering against the lovers' faces. Heston runs across the border to the ball of fire, as the film finally cuts to the mangled shards of what was once an automobile, now engulfed in roaring flames. A witness comments, "An hour ago Rudy Lanniker had this town in his pocket, now you can strain him through a sieve." Into this bravura opening steps the inimitable Welles–a monsterous, unshaven, fat man who darkens the screen with his presence as he eclipses the frame with his black cloaked mass–who practically rolls out of his car into the commotion. Gurgling his dialog as he chomps on a cigar, Welles, an offensive, prejudiced, American detective, examines the scene, as Heston, forgetting about his honeymoon, offers to be of whatever assistance he can. Before long, Welles has a suspect, Millan, a young Mexican who is involved with Linnekar's daughter, Moore. Meanwhile, Leigh is lured by a gang of Mexicans to Tamiroff, a leader of a drug ring, who warns Leigh and her husband not to get involved. Not to be swayed, Heston accompanies Welles to Millan's apartment for questioning and is shocked to discover that Welles has planted false evidence, dynamite, in a shoebox that Heston previously noticed was empty. Determined to topple this globular sponsor of corruption, Heston tries to prove Welles' guilt, but can find no one to listen. "What are you trying to do," Heston is asked by Calleia, a defender of Welles, "Ruin him?" In the process of the investigation Welles' motives, and his dislike of Mexicans, is revealed. As a rookie cop, Welles' wife was brutally murdered by a half-breed, but unable to prove the man's guilt, the killer went free. To assure that no other criminals beat justice, Welles has made a habit of planting evidence on those suspects whose guilt he was sure of. While Heston does his footwork, Leigh remains behind in a seedy motel run by a greasy, sexually repressed delinquent, Weaver, who ogles the blonde. Together, Welles and Tamiroff plot to frame Heston through his wife. Leigh is imprisoned in her motel room, where a demented gang of leather-jacketed motorcyclists, including the psychopathic McCambridge who revels in the sadism of their assault, taunt, molest, and drug the frightened blonde in a strange ritual of sex and violence. (The motel and the perversion of Weaver is something of a precursor to the scenes Leigh would play opposite Tony Perkins in PSYCHO.) Leigh is then left in a Mexican brothel where Welles chokes the life out of Tamiroff, who Welles fears may weaken and inform the police of his plot. Tamiroff's lifeless corpse is then suspended over Leigh, who lies, drugged, in bed. Heston finally catches up with his wife in a police jail cell where she is charged with possession of drugs, prostitution, and the murder of Tamiroff. Outraged that Welles should try to frame his wife, Heston puts down his policeman's badge and decides to fight as a husband. Meantime, Welles has paid a visit to a brothel run by Dietrich, a dark madam and former lover of Welles', who, after chiding the fat man for his addiction to candy bars (a substitute for liquor), warns him, with the aid of tarot cards, that his "future is all used up." Welles' future is indeed over, having made a fatal mistake when killing Tamiroff by forgetting his cane in the room. (It is this cane that Welles' character is clearly identified with–perhaps a subtle joke by director Welles on the Kane character with which he is most identified.) Heston becomes allied with Calleia and the pair work together to ruin Welles. Calleia agrees to be wired with a microphone for a conversation with Welles, while Heston follows the pair with a tape recorder. Calleia gets Welles to admit his guilt as the pair walk through the desolation and filth of a section of canals in town. When Welles realizes that he is being set up he shoots Calleia and confronts Heston. Before Welles can kill again, however, Calleia, still barely alive, fires a fatal shot that pierces the blubber of Welles, sending him flailing into the shallow canal where, like a beached whale, he floats belly up. A small crowd gathers as Heston receives word that Millan has confessed and that Welles was right all along about his guilt. Described as a "great detective but a lousy cop," the dead Welles floats in the mire that suits him so well, as Dietrich delivers her simple eulogy: "He was some kind of man. What does it matter what you say about people?" Directing his first film in America since 1948's MACBETH, Welles was originally just supposed to act in TOUCH OF EVIL. The misunderstanding that led to this bizarre and twisted masterpiece began when Heston read a script based on the novel Badge of Evil. Hearing that Welles was involved, and assuming that his involvement meant actor *and* director, Heston told producer Zugsmith that he would love to do the project. Rather than lose Heston, Zugsmith managed to get Universal to agree to let Welles direct, on the condition that he could also rewrite–Welles would receive a healthy $150,000 for his acting talents, but would write and direct for free. Since the plot was basically that of a B-movie crime meller,

Universal thought Welles could be restrained. To keep an eye on Hollywood's *enfant terrible*, Universal sent studio "spies" to watch over the director and report his progress. Aware that he was under a watchful eye, Welles worked furiously on his first scene (the interrogation of Millan), finishing it with amazing speed. By the end of day one, he was two days ahead of schedule, completing a phenomenal 11 pages of script (where one-third of that is considered impressive). Having appeased his detractors, Welles commented, "Okay, now that we've taken care of the front office we'll go ahead and make our picture." The majority of the photgraphy was then moved to Venice, California, then a rundown suburb of Los Angeles, and completed during evening hours in order to keep nosy executives away. Receiving positive responses from the studio, Welles was confident that he had a success on his hands on a par with his 1947 picture THE LADY FROM SHANGHAI. The problems came soon afterwards in the editing stages. Confused by the complex narrative and the delineation of the structure, Universal asked that it be recut, replacing editor Vogel with Stell. Still convinced that the studio was pleased with TOUCH OF EVIL, Welles went to South America to begin work on his DON QUIXOTE. In a situation that mirrored his MAGNIFICENT AMBERSONS ordeal (Welles left for South America to begin work on JOURNEY INTO FEAR before completing the editing), Welles returned to find TOUCH OF EVIL completely recut, and the studio demanding additional shooting to connect the supposedly haphazard structure. Over Welles' objections, Universal brought in Harry Keller, whose contribution is negligable in that he shot only half a day's worth of closeups. Welles balked, saying TOUCH OF EVIL was no longer his film and was destroyed when its U.S. release proved unimpressive. As usual, however, with Welles, European critics raved about this decadent piece of cinematic poetry, awarding it the international prize at the 1958 Brussell's World Fair, where he proudly accepted the honor without mention of the supposed chop-job done by Universal. If the post-production problems were not enough, TOUCH OF EVIL had a few problems on the set as well, curiously ranking it perhaps the only film in history in which two of the three leads–Welles and Leigh–had serious arm injuries. Leigh, who had broken her left arm just before production began, was fitted with a cast that was set at a 135-degree angle instead of the normal 90-degree angle in order to more easily hide it from the camera. In some scenes, however, disguising the arm proved impossible and the cast had to be cut for the shooting and then reset. Welles also suffered some injuries when, while location scouting one evening, he fell into a canal, spraining his arm, wrist, ankle, and bruising his face, thereby forcing him to wear a splint while off-camera. TOUCH OF EVIL was filled with unbilled cameos that included Marlene Dietrich (who agreed to play the part on one day's notice–a shock to the studio executives who never knew she was cast), Zsa Zsa Gabor, Mercedes McCambridge, Joseph Cotten, and Keenan Wynn. Although it was long believed that the 95-minute version was all that existed, a 105-minute version has also been reported.

p, Albert Zugsmith; d, Orson Welles, (uncredited) Harry Keller; w, Welles (based on the novel *Badge of Evil* by Whit Masterson); ph, Russell Metty; m, Henry Mancini; ed, Virgil W. Vogel, Aaron Stell; md, Joseph Gershenson; art d, Alexander Golitzen, Robert Clatworthy; set d, Russell A. Gausman, John P. Austin; cos, Bill Thomas.

Crime   **(PR:C   MPAA:NR)**

TOUCH OF FLESH, THE**   (1960) 76m Today Theatre/Amity-States Rights bw

Jeanne Rainer (*Joan Denton*), Ted Marshall (*Ed Mercer*), Charles Martin (*Dr. Denton*), Sue Ellis (*Vikky*), Stephen Wesley (*George Brown*), Tony Morris (*Tom Daly*), Robert J. Cannon (*Sam Ingram*), Josie Hascall (*Miss Hannah*).

Obscure exploitation item has Rainer the spoiled girl from the richest family in town getting pregnant by Marshall, who was raised in an orphanage. She wants an abortion and he wants to get married. When her father (Martin) finds out what has been going on, he has the boy jailed and there he is beaten up by the sadistic police sergeant who used to enjoy beating up Marshall at the orphanage. A good girl out on parole (Ellis) gets Marshall a lawyer, and the attorney convinces Martin that the boy's intentions are strictly honorable. But it is too late. Marshall has broken out of jail. Rainer panics and takes her father's gun. She finds Marshall back at the orphanage and forces him at gunpoint to go with her into the adjoining swamp, where the angry townspeople find them. Events climax in the inevitable violent resolution. Not quite so bad as it sounds, but close.

p&d, R. John Hugh; w, Nancy S. Camp; ph, Charles T. O'Rork; md, Harry Glass; songs, "Desert Inn," "Revenge."

Drama   **(PR:C   MPAA:NR)**

TOUCH OF HELL, A   (SEE: IMMORAL CHARGE, 1962, Brit.)

TOUCH OF HER FLESH, THE zero (1967) 78m Rivamarsh/American Film Distributing bw (AKA: WAY OUT LOVE, THE TOUCH OF HER LIFE)

Suzanne Marre, Angelique, Robert West, Vivian Del Rio, Marie Lamont, Sally Farb, David Boxwell, Rit Dexter.

A demented tale about a man driven crazy by an adulterous wife, who vows to kill all women. He kills a go-go dancer with darts, prostitutes with crossbows, his wife with a buzz saw, and nearly kills his wife's lesbian lover before she clubs him and shoots him through the heart with a crossbow. Vile mixture of natural and lesbian lust that could appeal only to lonely, crippled minds.

p, Julian Marsh, Anna Riva; d, Marsh; ph, Riva; m, Robin Aden; ed, Marsh.

Crime   **(PR:O MPAA:NR)**

TOUCH OF HER LIFE, THE (SEE: TOUCH OF HER FLESH, THE, 1967)

TOUCH OF LARCENY, A**½**   (1960 Brit.) 91m Foxwell/PAR bw

James Mason (*Comdr. Max Easton*), George Sanders (*Sir Charles Holland*), Vera Miles (*Virginia Killain*), Oliver Johnston (*Minister*), Robert Flemyng (*Larkin*), William Kendall (*Tom*), Duncan Lamont, Gordon Harris (*Special Branch Men*), Harry Andrews (*Capt. Graham*), Peter Barkworth (*Sub Lt. Brown*), Rachel Gurney (*Clare Holland*), Martin Stephens (*Her Son*), Waveney Lee (*Her Daughter*).

A whimsical comedy which features Mason as a rakehell former submarine captain who has been brought in from active service to handle a desk job. His exploits under the sea and under the bed covers are well known to everyone, and when he meets old pal Sanders, his eyes go whirling at the sight of Sanders' fiancee, American widow Miles. Sanders is very rich and it soon becomes evident to Mason that he must become rich so he concocts a fantastic scheme to garner wealth in a hurry. His plan is to appear to have defected, allow the scurrilous newspapers to besmirch his good name, then sue the pants off the press. Mason leaves a trail of what seems to be indications that he has sold out to the Russians, then arranges to get stranded on an uninhabitable island. He is rescued from the island and subjected to serious interrogation by the men of the Special Branch but he manages to convince them that he is not a defector. Later, Mason arrives at Miles' residence and the two are together when Sanders enters. He sees that Mason and Miles are very much in love and does the decent thing by exiting. A charming, witty film, filled with delicious situations and bon mots.

p, Ivan Foxwell; d, Guy Hamilton; w, Roger MacDougall, Paul Winterton, Foxwell, Hamilton (based on the novel *The Megstone Plot* by Andrew Garve); ph, John Wilcox; m, Philip Green; ed, Alan Osbiston; art d, Elliot Scott; cos, Edith Head.

Comedy   **(PR:A MPAA:NR)**

TOUCH OF LOVE, A (SEE: THANK YOU ALL VERY MUCH, 1969, Brit.)

TOUCH OF SATAN, THE*   (1971) 87m Futurama/Dundee c (AKA: THE TOUCH OF MELISSA, NIGHT OF THE DEMON, CURSE OF MELISSA)

Emby Mellay, Michael Berry, Lee Amber, Yvonne Winslow, Jeanne Gerson.

An engrossing but not too gross tale of a man who stays in pretty, young Mellay's farmhouse after losing his way in the woods. It turns out that she is really a 127-year-old witch, and he has fallen in love with her.

p, George E. Carey; d, Don Henderson; w, James E. McLarty.

Horror   **Cas.**   **(PR:O MPAA:PG)**

TOUCH OF THE MOON, A*   (1936, Brit.) 67m GS Greenspan and Seligman/RKO bw

John Garrick (*Martin Barnaby*), Dorothy Boyd (*Mona Dupare*), Joyce Bland (*Mrs. Fairclough*), David Horne (*Col. Plattner*), Max Adrian (*Francis Leverton*), Aubrey Mallalieu (*Mr. Dupare*), W.T. Ellwanger (*Garfield*), Wally Patch (*Police Constable*), Michael Ripper, Vincent Holman.

Pointless comedy has Garrick an alcoholic who bets a drinking companion that he can flag down the next woman in a motorcar and persuade her to dance with him by the roadside. As it happens, the next woman driver is running away from her rich American fiance, an elderly gent she would rather do without. Garrick not only dances with her, he marries her and gives up drinking.

p, A. George Smith; d, Maclean Rogers; w, Kathleen Butler, H.F. Maltby (based on a play by Cyril Campion); ph, Geoffrey Faithfull.

Comedy   **(PR:A MPAA:NR)**

TOUCH OF THE OTHER, A*   (1970, Brit.) 92m Global/Queensway c

Kenneth Cope (*Delger*), Shirley-Ann Field (*Elaine*), Helen Francois (*Wendy*), Timothy Craven (*Webber*), Vasco Koulolia (*Hughes*), Noel Davis (*Max Ronieau*), Renny Lister (*Sheila*), Gypsy Kemp (*Shirley*), Paul Stassino (*Connely*).

A tired crime picture about a detective who is framed for the murder of a friend. His connections in the crime world help him out and a prostitute tries to prove that he is innocent.

p, Leslie Berens, Arnold Louis Miller, Sheila Miller; d, Arnold Louis Miller; w, Frank Wyman.

Crime   **(PR:O MPAA:NR)**

TOUCH OF THE SUN, A*   (1956, Brit.) 80m Raystro/Eros bw

Frankie Howerd (*William Darling*), Ruby Murray (*Ruby*), Dennis Price (*Hatchard*), Dorothy Bromiley (*Rose*), Katherine Kath (*Lucienne*), Gordon Harker (*Sid*), Reginald Beckwith (*Hardcastle*), Pierre Dudan (*Louis*), Colin Gordon (*Cecil Flick*), Richard Wattis (*Purchase*), Alfie Bass (*May*), Naomi Chance (*Miss Lovejoy*), Willoughby Goddard, Miriam Karlin, Esma Cannon, Edna Morris, Ian Whittaker, Brian Summers, Lee Young, George Margo, Ann George, Jed Brown, Lucy Griffiths, Evelyn Roberts, John Vere.

Howerd is a hotel porter who inherits a small fortune and, unwilling to simply quit his job, wreaks havoc on the establishment and is fired. After some time on the French Riviera he gets bored, so he buys the hotel he was fired from and begins operating it himself. Looking for backers, he disguises the hotel staff as wealthy guests to impress the potential backers when they come to see the place firsthand. Another broad comic mess of the type that seems funny only to the English.

p, Raymond Stross; d, Gordon Parry; w, Alfred Shaughnessy; ph, Arthur Grant.

Comedy   **(PR:A MPAA:NR)**

TOUCH WHITE, TOUCH BLACK
                (SEE: VIOLENT ONES, THE, 1967)

TOUCHDOWN!**½**   (1931) 79m PAR bw (GB: PLAYING THE GAME)

Richard Arlen (*Dan Curtis*), Peggy Shannon (*Mary Gehring*), Jack Oakie (*Babe Barton*), Regis Toomey (*Tom Hussey*), George Barbier (*Jerome Gehring*), J. Farrell MacDonald (*Pop Stewart*), George Irving (*President Baker*), Charles D. Brown (*Harrigan*), Charles Starrett (*Paul Gehring*), Jim Thorpe, Howard Jones, Russ Saunders, Morley Drury, Jesse Hibbs, Nate Barrager, Tom Lieb, Roy Riegels, Manfred Vezie, Herman Brix [Bruce Bennett], Harry Edelson, Cecil Hoff, Marger Aspit, George Dye.

Arlen stars as a tough football coach who'll stop at nothing to bring his team to victory, even if it means turning the players against him. He loses the respect of the team when he sends in an injured player, putting him in the hospital as a result, but also winning the game. Later in the season, Arlen is put in the same situation but has by now learned his lesson. The team loses but at least the players can walk off the field.

d, Norman McLeod; w, William Slavens McNutt, Grover Jones (based on the novel *Stadium* by Francis Wallace); ph, Arthur Todd.

Sports Drama   **(PR:A MPAA:NR)**

TOUCHDOWN, ARMY**   (1938) 60m PAR bw (GB: GENERALS OF TOMORROW)

John Howard (*Brandon Culpepper*), Robert Cummings (*Jimmy Howell*), Mary Carlisle (*Toni Denby*), Owen Davis, Jr (*Kirk Reynolds*), William Frawley (*Jack Heffernan*), Benny Baker (*Dick Mycroft*), Minor Watson (*Col. Denby*), Raymond Hatton (*Bob Haskins*).

The 1938 football season got off to a start with this West Point sports picture starring Cummings as a new cadet whose talent on the field far outweighs his talent on tests. Not extremely well-liked due to his sure-fire anti-disciplinary, anti-upperclassmen attitude, Cummings saves the game when he prevents his teammate, Howard, from running the wrong way with the ball and scoring points for the opponent (see TOUCHDOWN], 1931). On par with the rest of the gridiron films.

p, Edward T. Lowe; d, Kurt Neumann; w, Lloyd Corrigan, Erwin Gelsey; ph, Victor Milner; ed, Arthur Schmidt; md, Boris Morros.

Sports Drama   **(PR:A MPAA:NR)**

TOUCHE PAS A LA FEMME BLANCHE!
                (SEE: DON'T TOUCH WHITE WOMEN, 1974, Fr.)

TOUCHED**   (1983) 93m Wildwoods Partners-Lorimar c

Robert Hays (*Daniel*), Kathleen Beller (*Jennifer*), Ned Beatty (*Herbie*), Gilbert Lewis (*Ernie*), Lyle Kessler (*Timothy*), Farnham Scott (*Thomas*), Meg Myles (*Jennifer's Mother*), Mady Kaplan (*Arlene*), E. Brian Dean (*Dr. Willoughby*), Victoria Boothby (*Adele*).

A well-meaning but emotionless picture about a pair of youngsters who escape from a mental institution and start life anew. Hays gets out first, landing himself a job in a carnival dunk tank. He then returns to get Beller released, followed by their attempts to set up a normal household. Lewis poses a threat when he tries to break up what the pair have created by sending them back to the institution, but he fails.

p, Dirk Petersmann, Barclay Lottimer; d, John Flynn; w, Lyle Kessler; ph, Fred Murphy (Technicolor); m, Shirley Walker; ed, Harry Keramidas; prod d, Patricia von Brandenstein.

Drama/Romance   **Cas.**   **(PR:C MPAA:R)**

TOUCHED BY LOVE**½   (1980) 95m Rastar/COL c (AKA: TO ELVIS, WITH LOVE)

Deborah Raffin *(Lena Canada)*, Diane Lane *(Karen)*, Michael Learned *(Dr. Bell)*, John Amos *(Tony)*, Christina Raines *(Amy)*, Mary Wickes *(Margaret)*, Clu Gulagher *(Don Fielder)*, Twyla Volkins *(Monica)*, Children and Teachers from the Dr. Gordon Townsend School of Calgary, Canada.

Good account of how nurse Raffin, working at a home for cerebral palsy cases, takes on the job of pulling one withdrawn patient (Lane) out of her shell. Slowly she succeeds, then encourages the girl to write a letter to her idol, Elvis Presley. He responds and they begin a correspondence that brings great happiness to Lane until the disease claims her life. Nicely underplayed performances help a lot, but the film ultimately falls victim to mawkish handling. Based on a true story by Lena Canada.

p, Michael Viner; d, Gus Trikonis; w, Hesper Anderson (based on the story "To Elvis, with Love" by Lena Canada); ph, Richard H. Kline (Metrocolor); m, John Barry; ed, Fred Chulack; art d, Claudio Guzman; set d, Ray Molyneaux; cos, Moss Mabry.

Drama   **Cas.**   **(PR:A MPAA:PG)**

TOUGH AS THEY COME*½   (1942) 61m UNIV bw

Billy Halop *(Tommy Clark)*, Huntz Hall *(Pig)*, Bernard Punsley *(Ape)*, Gabriel Dell *(String)*, Helen Parrish *(Ann Wilson)*, Paul Kelly *(Ben Stevens)*, Ann Gillis *(Frankie Taylor)*, Virginia Brissac *(Mrs. Clark)*, John Gallaudet *(Mike Taylor)*, Jimmy Butler *(Gene Bennett)*, Mala Powers *(Esther)*, Giselle Werbiseck *(Ma)*, Clarence Muse *(Eddie)*, Theresa Harris *(Eddie's Wife)*, John Eldredge *(Rogers)*, James Flavin *(Process Server)*, George Offerman, Jr *(Dave)*, Antonio Filauri *(Fruit Vendor)*, Dick Hogan *(Jim Bond)*, Frank Faylen *(Collector)*.

Halop is an ambitious law student who takes a job with a crooked finance company that makes him the scrooge of the neighborhood. He wants to romance the wealthy Parrish but he also has local girl Gillis on his tail. One of his jobs with the sleazy company has him repossess the cab driven by Gillis' father. His "Little Tough Guy" buddies try to stop him but to no avail. Halop finally realizes that his work is hurting his people, so he decides with his friends to expose the company to the authorities. A couple of scrapes later, he gets the evidence he needs along with the heart of Parrish. Also along the way he forms a credit union for the people. (See BOWERY BOYS series, Index.)

p, Ken Goldsmith; d, William Nigh; w, Lewis Amster, Albert Bein; ph, Elwood Bredell; ed, Bernard W. Burton; md, Hans J. Salter; art d, Jack Otterson; cos, Vera West.

Drama   **(PR:A MPAA:NR)**

TOUGH ASSIGNMENT*   (1949) 64m Lippert bw

Don Barry *(Dan Reilly)*, Marjorie Steele *(Margie Reilly)*, Steve Brodie *(Morgan)*, Marc Lawrence *(Vince)*, Ben Welden *(Sniffy)*, Iris Adrian *(Gloria)*, Michael Whalen *(Hutchinson)*, Sid Melton *(Herman)*, Frank Richards *(Steve)*, Fred Kohler, Jr *(Grant)*, John Cason *(Joe)*, Stanley Andrews *(Patterson)*, Hugh Simpson *(Ted)*, Leander de Cordova *(Mr. Schultz)*, Edith Angold *(Mrs. Schultz)*, Stanley Price *(Foster)*, Gayle Kellogg, Jack Geddes *(Ranchers)*, Dewey Robinson *(Customer)*, J. Farrell MacDonald.

Slow-moving crime story has Barry and Steele as a husband and wife who are a reporter and photographer respectively. They are after bad guy Brodie, who runs a rustling operation that forces stolen beef on ma-and-pa shop owners. To track them down, Barry and Steele join the crooks to learn their secrets. Their cover gets blown but the police arrive on the scene before the crooks can do the pair in.

p, Carl K. Hittleman; d, William Beaudine; w, Milton Luban (based on a story by Hittleman); m, Albert Glasser; ed, Harry Gerstad; art d, Frank P. Sylos.

Crime   **(PR:A MPAA:NR)**

TOUGH ENOUGH*   (1983) 107m American Cinema/FOX c

Dennis Quaid *(Art Long)*, Carlene Watkins *(Caroline Long)*, Stan Shaw *(P.T. Coolidge)*, Pam Grier *(Myra)*, Warren Oates *(James Neese)*, Bruce McGill *(Tony Fallon)*, Wilford Brimley *(Bill Long)*, Fran Ryan *(Gert Long)*, Christopher Norris *(Christopher Long)*, Terra Perry *(Wet T-Shirt Girl)*, Big

John Hamilton *(Big John)*, Steve Ward *(Heckler)*, Susann Benn *(Girl in Torryson's)*, Mark Edson *(Janitor)*, Steve "Monk" Miller *(Tigran)*, Jimmy Nickerson *(Jackhammer Malamud)*, Rodger Kieschnick *(Gregor Samsa)*, Preston Salisbury *(Ike Kennedy)*, Darryl Poafbybitty *(Mad Dog Redfeather)*, Tino Zaragosa *(Mando Chandovar)*, Charles Griffin *(Ft. Worth Fan)*, Cloryce Miller *(Cowardly Fighter)*, Ernest Lee Smith *(Truman Wall)*, Eli Cummins *(Gay Bob)*, Murray Sutherland *(Mad Scotsman)*, Tody Smith *(Charley Compton)*, Bennie Moore *(Lionel Trilling)*, Jackie Kallen *(Detroit Corner Girl)*, Michael Brown *(TV Show Host)*, Darlene O'Hara *(Mrs. Wall)*, Domenico Seminara *(Maitre D')*, John McKee *(Detroit Fan)*, Pat Reilly, John Hyden *(Ft. Worth Referees)*, Doug Lord, Bob Watson *(Detroit Referees)*, Cindy Judy, Susanne Hasty, Kathy Lynch *(Ring Girls)*.

Mr. T rose to popularity through the trash sport of "tough man" contests, but the film about the ghastly fad was a dud. Quaid has a wife and child and his career as a country singer has hit bottom. He's always been a good fighter, so he decides to cash in on the contests. Quaid smiles through his part, seeming to know that he won't ever experience defeat, which leaves no suspense in the story line. Oates is his manager and wants the boy to go all the way to the nationals so he can ride on his coattails.

p, William S. Gilmore; d, Richard O. Fleischer; w, John Leone; ph, James A. Contner (Panavision,Technicolor); m, Michael Lloyd, Steve Wax; ed, Dann Cahn; prod d, Bill Kenney; set d, Floyd Smith; cos, Clifford Capone.

Drama   **Cas.**   **(PR:C MPAA:PG)**

TOUGH GUY***   (1936) 76m MGM bw

Jackie Cooper *(Freddie)*, Joseph Calleia *(Joe)*, Rin Tin Tin, Jr *(Duke the Dog)*, Harvey Stephens *(Chief Davison)*, Jean Hersholt *(Doctor)*, Edward Pawley *(Tony)*, Mischa Auer *(Chi)*, Robert Warwick *(Vincent)*.

A good story and fast mover about the love a boy has for his dog, focusing around the adventures of Cooper, Calleia, and Rin Tin Tin, Jr. Cooper's rich father hates the dog, so the boy runs away and falls in with some gangsters. After a series of dangerous situations, Cooper and the dog find themselves with gang leader Calleia hiding in the woods from not only the cops but the other gang members who want Cooper to collect the reward his father has put up for his return. As Cooper, who was a sheltered little boy at the beginning of the film, starts getting tougher, mobster Calleia softens up and actually saves him from the gang.

p, Harry Rapf; d, Chester M. Franklin; w, Florence Ryerson, Edgar Allan Woolf; ph, Leonard Smith; ed, James E. Newcomb.

Drama   **(PR:A MPAA:NR)**

TOUGH KID*   (1939) 61m MON bw

Frankie Darro, Dick Purcell, Judith Allen, Lillian Elliott, Don Rowan, William Ruhl, Lew Kelly, Ralph Peters, Max Marx, Jean Joyce, Cliff Howell, Joe Lynch, Wilbur Mack, Joseph Girard.

Basically a moronic story about tough juvenile delinquents, with poor production values and mediocrity all around. Darro is the "brains" of a family and sees his older brother, boxer Purcell, falling in with the wrong crowd. He has to save him against the gang's machinations, which include a phony doctor's report on Purcell's girl friend, forcing him to borrow money to cure her, and then throw some fights to repay what he owes. Little entertainment here.

p, Scott R. Dunlap; d, Howard Bretherton; w, Wellyn Totman (based on a story by Brenda Weisberg); ph, Harry Newman [Neumann]; ed, Russell Schoengarth.

Drama   **(PR:A MPAA:NR)**

TOUGH TO HANDLE*   (1937) 58m Syndicate bw

Frankie Darro *(Mike)*, Kane Richmond *(Ed)*, Phyllis Fraser *(Gloria)*, Harry Worth *(Franko)*, Johnstone White *(Reggie)*, Lorraine Hayes *(Clara)*, Burr Caruth *(Grandpa)*, Bill Hunter *(Barney)*, Jack Ingram *(Spike)*, Harry Anderson *(Bud)*, Stanley Price *(Jake)*, Lee Phelps *(Editor)*.

Slapped-together drama is slipshod on all accounts. Darro is a newsboy who teams with reporter Richmond to break up a racket run by Worth. Worth is cheating sweepstakes winners, while also running a sleazy nightclub where Darro's sister, Fraser, sings. When Darro's grandfather is killed, Darro gets involved because the gangsters want the grandfather's lucky ticket the boy now holds. But Darro and Richmond battle it out with the bad guys in some of the most laughable, poorly made fight scenes ever filmed, with the two finally prevailing over the entire gang.

p, Maurice Conn; d, Roy Luby; w, Sherman L. Lowe, Jack Neville (based on a story by Peter B. Kyne); ph, Jack Greenhalgh; ed, Martin Cohn.

Drama   **(PR:A MPAA:NR)**

TOUGHER THEY COME, THE*   (1950) 69m COL c

Wayne Morris *(Bill Shaw)*, Preston Foster *(Joe MacKinley)*, Kay Buckley *(Helen)*, William Bishop *(Gus Williams)*, Frank McHugh *(Gig Rafferty)*,

Gloria Henry (*Rattle Rafferty*), Mary Castle (*Flo*), Joseph Crehan (*Thompson*), Frank O'Connor (*Mike Shepard*), Al Thompson (*Tom*), Alan [Al] Bridge (*Jensen*).

Morris and Foster are loggers and Foster inherits a lumber camp, which helps him lure Buckley into marriage, because now she thinks he is rich. However, the camp is plagued by troubles. A corporation makes an attempt to buy him out, and Foster mulls over the offer because of his wife's nagging about having to live in the woods and attempts by Bishop, his foreman but secretly in the employ of the corporation, to sabotage the camp. Morris, who had gone into the fishing business, comes back on the scene and during a forest fire he and Foster catch the crooks feeding the flames along with camp cook McHugh and McHugh's daughter Henry. Foster's wife at first flirts with Morris but she realizes her love for her husband when she saves him from the fire, and sparks fly between Morris and Henry.

p, Wallace MacDonald; d, Ray Nazarro; w, George Bricker; ph, Philip Tannura; m, Ross DiMaggio; ed, Aaron Stell; art d, Victor Greene.

Action/Drama　　　　　　　　　　　(PR:A　MPAA:NR)

TOUGHEST GUN IN TOMBSTONE*　　　　　(1958) 72m UA bw

George Montgomery (*Matt Sloane*), Beverly Tyler (*Beverly Cooper*), Don Beddoe (*David Cooper*), Jim Davis (*Johnny Ringo*), Scotty Morrow (*Terry Sloane*), Harry Lauter (*Barger*), Charles Wagenheim (*Beasley*), Jack Kenny (*Purdy*), John Merrick (*Ranger Burgess*), Al Wyatt (*Olmstead*), Joey Ray (*Hellman*), Gerald Milton (*Ike Clanton*), Lane Bradford (*Bill*), Gregg Barton (*Leslie*), Hank Worden (*Liveryman*), Tex Terry (*Stage Driver*), Charles Hayes (*Shotgun Guard*), Kathleen Mulqueen (*Mrs. Oliver*), Rudolfo Hoyos (*Col. Emilio*), Alex Montoya (*Sergeant*), Rico Alaniz (*Fernandez*), Jack Carr (*Telegraph Operator*), William Forrest (*Governor*), Harry Strang (*Dr. MacAvoy*), Mary Newton (*Mrs. Beasley*), Gloria Rhodes (*Girl*).

Every time an action scene builds in this one it disappointingly lets down. Montgomery is a U.S. marshal who goes undercover to solve the rustling operation run by Milton. As Tombstone goes wild with drinking and killing, Montgomery not only must track down the rustlers but save his son, who is being chased by the killers of his mother in the belief that the boy saw who pulled the trigger. As Montgomery makes his rounds, a narrative is needlessly added to the story telling the back-ground of the fight between the U.S. marshal and the crooks. Finally Montgomery gets his posse and the men who killed his wife to tone down wide-open Tombstone.

p, Robert E. Kent; d, Earl Bellamy; w, Orville Hampton; ph, Kenneth Peach, Sr.; m, Paul Dunlap; ed, Grant Whytock; art d, William Glasgow.

Western　　　　　　　　　　　　　(PR:A　MPAA:NR)

TOUGHEST MAN ALIVE**　　　　　　　(1955) 72m AA bw

Dane Clark (*Lee*), Lita Milan (*Lida*), Anthony Caruso (*Gore*), Ross Elliott (*York*), Myrna Dell (*Nancy*), Thomas Browne Henry (*Dolphin*), Paul Levitt (*Don*), John Eldredge (*Ingo Widmer*), Dehl Berti (*Salvador*), Richard Karlan (*Morgan*), Syd Saylor (*Proprietor*), Jonathan Seymour (*Agency Chief*), Don Mathers (*Bank Manager*).

Good actioner about gun smugglers supplying U.S. ammunition to Central American countries and Clark's efforts to stop them. Clark is a U.S. agent posing as top smuggler Caruso to find out all aspects of the gang's activities. Milan is the young revolutionary taken in by the rhetoric of her leader to pose as a singer while she seeks guns for an uprising in her own country. As Clark works, the real Caruso shows up, tipping the bad guys off that Clark is not one of them. But the authorities show up in the nick of time to save Clark and smash the operation.

p, William F. Broidy; d, Sidney Salkow; w, Steve Fisher; ph, John Martin; m, Edward J. Kay; ed, Chandler House; m/l, "I Hear a Rhapsody," George Fragos, Jack Baker, and Dick Gasparre, "You Walk By," Ben Raleigh and Bernie Wayne (sung by Lita Milan).

Action/Drama　　　　　　　　　　　(PR:A　MPAA:NR)

TOUGHEST MAN IN ARIZONA**　　　　　(1952) 90m REP c

Vaughn Monroe (*Matt Landry*), Joan Leslie (*Mary Kimber*), Edgar Buchanan (*Jim Hadlock*), Victor Jory (*Frank Girard*), Jean Parker (*Della*), Henry [Harry] Morgan (*Verne Kimber*), Ian MacDonald (*Steve Girard*), Lee MacGregor (*Jerry Girard*), Diana Christian (*Joan Landry*), Bobby Hyatt (*Davey Billings*), Charlita (*Senorita*), Nadene Ashdown (*Jesse Billings*), Francis Ford (*Hanchette*), Paul Hurst (*Dalton*), John Doucette.

This was singer Monroe's second attempt at a western and he turns in a good performance. In between the three songs he sings, he plays a U.S. marshal leading the survivors of an Indian attack back to Tombstone, the roughest town in Arizona. Along with them is Jory, who sold the warring Indians the guns in the first place. After he gets them all to safety, Jory escapes and Monroe has to search him out again, leading to a six-gun chase and excitement in tracking him down.

p, Sidney Picker; d, R.G. Springsteen; w, John K. Butler; ph, Reggie Lanning (Trucolor); m, R. Dale Butts; ed, Richard L. Van Enger; art d, Frank Hotaling; set d, John McCarthy, Jr.

Western　　　　　　　　　　　　　(PR:A　MPAA:NR)

TOURIST TRAP, THE zero　　　(1979) 85m Band Compass-Manson c

Chuck Connors (*Slausen*), Jon Van Ness (*Jerry*), Jocelyn Jones (*Molly*), Robin Sherwood (*Eileen*), Tanya Roberts (*Becky*), Keith McDermott (*Woody*), Dawn Jeffory (*Tina*), Shailar Coby (*Davey*).

Connors is a weirdo with strange powers to make things come alive, most specifically the mannequins in the strange little vacation spot he runs. Four college kids accidentally come to the place and spend the rest of the time eluding dummies that come to life, as well as Connors. It never really tells how the dummies came to life but they are everywhere in this bizarre mistake.

p, J. Larry Carroll; d, David Schmoeller; w, Schmoeller, Carroll; ph, Nicholas Von Sternberg (Metrcolor); m, Pino Donnaggio; ed, Ted Nicolaou; art d, Robert Burns; set d, Amanda Flick; spec eff, Rich Helmer.

Horror　　　　　　　　Cas.　　　　　(PR:C　MPAA:PG)

TOUT VA BIEN½**　　　　　(1973, Fr.) 95m Lido-Empire/New Yorker c

Jane Fonda (*She*), Yves Montand (*He*), Vittorio Caprioli (*Factory Manager*), Jean Pignol (*Delegate*), Pierre Ondry (*Frederic*), Ilizabeth Chauvin (*Genevieve*), Eric Chartier (*Lucien*), Yves Gabrielli (*Leon*).

Jean-Luc Godard's most commercial film since WEEKEND (1967) and his strongest attempt to bring political thought into popular film. In order to deliver his message of "class struggle" Godard signed two famous actors–Jane Fonda and Yves Montand–both one-time espousers of leftist viewpoints. The plot of TOUT VA BIEN is insignificant and exists only to satisfy the audience–or, as Godard says in the film, to provide "a story for those who shouldn't still need one." Fonda is an American news reporter living in Paris with her husband, Montand, a former "New Wave" film director (not unlike Godard) who has turned to directing commercials. They pay a visit to a sausage factory and find themselves in the middle of a work stoppage. The workers spout Maoist slogans and read political speeches into the cameras while taking over the factory's corporate offices. The plant manager is locked in his office and not even allowed to go to the bathroom. TOUT VA BIEN ends without neatly tying up the narrative, letting "each individual create his own history." TOUT VA BIEN is different from Godard's other political films (WIND FROM THE EAST, 1969; SEE YOU AT MAO, 1969; or VLADIMIR ET ROSA, 1971, to name a few). It received a commercial release (many of his other political films were shown only to workers and students), had two "movie stars," and even received financial backing from Paramount (which opted not to distribute). It can boast stylistic camera work and set design instead of the usual hand-held graininess that trademarks his other political pictures. The most impressive visual is the multileveled cutaway of the office building which allows a view of all the offices at the same time. TOUT VA BIEN is an important step in bringing anti-bourgeoise cinema to the masses, but as with most of Godard's films of the 1970s it favors words over actions. (In French; English subtitles.)

p, Jean-Pierre Rassam; d&w, Jean-Luc Godard, Jean-Pierre Gorin; ph, Armand Marco; ed, Kernout Peitier; set d, Jacques Dugied.

Drama　　　　　　　　　　　　　(PR:C　MPAA:NR)

TOVARICH***　　　　　　　　　(1937) 94m WB bw

Claudette Colbert (*Grand Duchess Tatiana Petrovna*), Charles Boyer (*Prince Mikail Alexandrovitch Ouratieff*), Basil Rathbone (*Gorotchenko*), Anita Louise (*Helen Dupont*), Melville Cooper (*Charles Dupont*), Isabel Jeans (*Fernande Dupont*), Maurice Murphy (*Georges Dupont*), Morris Carnovsky (*Chauffourier-Dufieff*), Gregory Gaye (*Gen. Count Brekenski*), Montagu Love (*Mons. Courtois*), Renie Riano (*Mme. Courtois*), Fritz Feld (*Martelleau*), May Boley (*Louise, Cook*), Victor Kilian (*Gendarme*), Clifford Soubier (*Grocer*), Heather Thatcher (*Lady Corrigan*), Curt Bois (*Alphonso*), Ferdinand Munier (*Mons. Van Hemart*), Doris Lloyd (*Mme. Chauffourier-Dufieff*), Grace Hayle (*Mme. Van Hemart*), Christian Rub (*Trombone Player*), Tommy Bupp, Jerry Tucker, Delmer Watson (*Urchins*), Torben Meyer (*Servant*), Alphonse Martell (*Hairdresser*), Leo White (*Assistant Hairdresser*).

This enjoyable comedy of manners and politics features Colbert and Boyer as two members of the Russian monarchy who had fled to Paris after the Bolshevik revolution. Before leaving, Boyer had been entrusted by the Czar with a fortune, which comes to billions of dollars worth of French francs. The money now sits in a bank, for Boyer and Colbert do not want to spend a single centime. Instead, the former royal couple now live in utter poverty. To make ends meet, they swallow hard and take jobs as servants, working in the home of Cooper, an extremely wealthy man. Cooper and his wife, Jeans, throw a fancy party, and among the invited guests is Rathbone, a high-ranking Soviet official. Rathbone takes one look at the help, and exposes their secret. Now Cooper and Jeans are thrown into a real dilemma: do they treat Boyer and Colbert like servants, or dispense of their services and treat the couple like royalty? Boyer and Colbert are furious, with a deep-seated anger directed at Rathbone. Not only has he exposed the pair, he had also participated in a sadistic interrogation of Boyer before he and Colbert fled Russia. Rathbone now asks Boyer for the Czar's fortune to help Russia, lest the government have to give up some valuable oil fields to foreign interests. Boyer at first refuses, but Colbert, insisting that the money will help the Russian people, eventually talks him into it. The couple realize what good servants they are, and Cooper invites them to remain in his employ. TOVARICH (the Russian word for "comrade") is a clever comedy, with some charming moments nestled in the satirical situation. Boyer dispenses with his well-known French accent for that of a Russian, ironically playing a Russian exiled in France. It's slightly schizophrenic but Boyer's talents make the unusual combination work. Boyer was initially unhappy with this idea. "He is a Russian, and I am French!" the actor raved. "Furthermore, they are in Paris. It would be idiotic for me to play a Russian around people who are supposed to be French." Litvak's direction shows a good comic flair, though he is no stylist in the Ernest Lubitsch vein. Litvak's delays on the set cost the production a good sum. He insisted on expensive camera setups for minor scenes, then demanded his own editor, Henri Rust, be used for the cutting. Litvak had been pushed by agent Charles Feldman, as a terrific European prodigy. Feldman managed to persuade studio boss Jack Warner, and he, in turn, pushed Litvak onto producer Lord. Because of Feldman's terrific con job, Lord was not allowed to meet Litvak until production was to begin. In addition, Lord wanted to work on the script, but Warner forbade him. Eventually Litvak began work on the film, and as the problems mounted, his reputation fell. Other problems rose between costars Colbert and Boyer when it came to flattering their respective egos. Colbert was insistent that the left side of her face was her most photogenic, and demanded camera angles to flatter this aspect. Boyer also felt that *his* left side was his best, thus creating the ultimate Hollywood filmmaker's nightmare. Somehow, between Litvak's excesses and the costars quibbles, TOVARICH worked; an enjoyable, if not terribly memorable comedy.

p, Robert Lord; d, Anatole Litvak; w, Casey Robinson, Robert E. Sherwood (based on the play by Jacques Deval); ph, Charles Lang; m, Max Steiner; ed, Henri Rust; md, Leo F. Forbstein; art d, Anton Grot; m/l, Samuel Pokrass.

Comedy   (PR:AA MPAA:NR)

TOWARD THE UNKNOWN*   (1956) 115m Toluca/WB c (GB: BRINK OF HELL)

William Holden (*Maj. Lincoln Bond*), Lloyd Nolan (*Brig. Gen. Bill Banner*), Virginia Leith (*Connie Mitchell*), Charles McGraw (*Col. "Mickey" McKee*), Murray Hamilton (*Maj. "Bromo" Lee*), Paul Fix (*Maj. Gen. Bryan Shelby*), L. Q. Jones (*Lt. Sweeney*), James Garner (*Maj. Joe Craven*), Karen Steele (*Polly Craven*), Bartlett Robinson (*Sen. Black*), Malcolm Atterbury (*Hank*), Ralph Moody (*H. G. Gilbert*), Maura Murphy (*Mrs. Sarah McKee*), Carol Kelly (*Debby*), Robert Hover, Les Johnson, Rad Fulton (*Pilots*), Jean Willes (*Carmen*), Nelson Leigh (*Chaplain*), Will White (*Air Police Sergeant*), William Henry (*Air Police Captain*), Don Harvey (*Bartender*), Cathy Ferrara (*Lucy Craven*), Jon Provost (*Joe Craven, Jr.*), Autumn Russel (*Harriet*), Bob Stratton (*Jim*), Maj. James Wilson (*Chase Pilot*), John Day (*Stranger*).

A technically oriented aerial thriller which stars Holden as a test pilot at Edwards Air Force base in California. Holden's strong desire to sit in the cockpit meets with some opposition from general Nolan. Holden was a prisoner during the Korean War and cracked under the pressure of brainwashing. Nolan now fears that Holden will again crack, but this time during the crucial test of the experimental Bell X-2 rocket plane. Nolan's position is swayed by his secretary-girl friend Leith, who was romantically involved with Holden before he was taken prisoner. Holden calms Nolan's fears and proves himself more than capable, especially when he gets Nolan out of a tight situation. Holden has more confidence in the air, however, than on the ground, and is hesitant about becoming involved again with Leith. Nolan, sensing that he is losing Leith, attempts to prove himself in the air by making the final test on the X-2. Fearing that Nolan cannot handle the job, Holden is forced to tell him that his pride may result not only in his death but in death of the X-2 testing operation. Nolan backs off and Holden takes the plane up, successfully surviving the rigorous testing. Nolan decides to accept a transfer, leaving Leith behind to finish what she had started with Holden. Superbly photographed and with aerobatics by the USAF Thunderbirds, TOWARD THE UNKNOWN has a real air of authenticity, fully capturing the dangerous and victorious atmosphere of Edwards Air Force Base during its most exciting period. Following the pattern of many Hollywood stars (Alan Ladd, John Wayne, Burt Lancaster), Holden formed his own independent company, Toluca, for the production of this film. Holden, however, was not as business-minded as some of his peers and dissolved the company after TOWARD THE UNKNOWN was completed.

p&d, Mervyn LeRoy; w, Beirne Lay, Jr.; ph, Hal Rosson (WarnerScope, Warner Color); m, Paul Baron; ed, William Ziegler; art d, John Beckman; cos, Moss Mabry; spec eff, Leo E. Kuter; m/l, Robert Crawford; special aerobatics, the USAF Thunderbirds.

Drama   (PR:A MPAA:NR)

TOWER OF EVIL, 1972 (SEE: HORROR ON SNAPE ISLAND, 1972)

TOWER OF EVIL, 1981   (SEE: BEYOND THE FOG, 1981, Brit.)

TOWER OF LONDON*   (1939) 92m UNIV bw

Basil Rathbone (*Richard III*), Boris Karloff (*Mord the Executioner*), Barbara O'Neil (*Queen Elizabeth*), Ian Hunter (*Edward IV*), Vincent Price (*Duke of Clarence*), Nan Grey (*Lady Alice Barton*), John Sutton (*John Wyatt*), Leo G. Carroll (*Lord Hastings*), Miles Mander (*Henry VI*), Lionel Belmore (*Beacon Chiruegeon*), Rose Hobart (*Anne Neville*), Ralph Forbes (*Henry Tudor*), Frances Robinson (*Duchess Isobel*), Ernest Cossart (*Tom Clink*), G. P. Huntley (*Prince of Wales*), John Rodion (*Lord DeVere*), Ronald Sinclair (*Prince Edward*), Donnie Dunagan (*Prince Richard as a Child*), John Herbert-Bond (*Young Prince Richard*), Walter Tetley (*Chimney Sweep*), Georgia Caine (*Dowager Duchess*), Ivan Simpson (*Retainer*), Nigel De Brulier (*Archbishop, St. John's Chapel*), Holmes Herbert, Charles Miller (*Councilmen*), Venecia Severn, Yvonne Severn (*Princesses*), Louise Brien, Jean Fenwick (*Ladies in Waiting*), Michael Mark (*Servant to Henry VI*), C. Montague Shaw (*Major Domo*), Don Stewart (*Bunch*), Reginald Barlow (*Sheriff at Execution*), Robert Greig (*Father Olmstead*), Ivo Henderson (*Haberdeer*), Charles Peck (*Page Boy*), Harry Cording (*Tyrell-Assassin*), Jack C. Smith (*Forrest, Assassin*), Colin Kenny, Arthur Stenning (*Soldiers*), Evelyn Selbie (*Beggar Woman*), Denis Tankard, Dave Thursby (*Beggars*), Claire Whitney (*Civilian Woman*), Ernie Adams (*Prisoner Begging for Water*), Russ Powell (*Sexton-Bell Ringer*), Ann Todd (*Queen Elizabeth's Daughter*).

A classic thriller that paired two great names in horror--Rathbone and Karloff. Set in the 15th Century, it focuses on various torture methods as Rathbone takes care of the people who are in his way to the throne. Karloff is excellent as the club-footed executioner who takes orders from the evil Rathbone. Each death is done in a brutal way. A couple get their heads graphically chopped off while Price is drowned in a vat of Malmsey wine. The movie was considered extremely violent for the time and some torture scenes had to be cut before it could be released. The story, as bloody as it was, was based on historical fact. Price, then a relative newcomer to the screen, tells the story of his drowning scene which almost became a real thing. It seems that he was directed to dive in to a vat of wine (actually a soft drink), sink to the bottom and hold on to an iron bar for a count of 10, and resurface. By that time the shot would have been made. However, while he was at the bottom of the vat he heard the alarming sound of axes striking the vat, and when he came up learned that the lid had become stuck and the crew had to pound on it to loosen it.

p&d, Rowland V. Lee; w, Robert N. Lee; ph, George Robinson; m, Frank Skinner; ed, Edward Curtiss; md, Charles Previn; art d, Jack Otterson; set d, Russell Gausman; cos, Vera West; makeup, Jack P. Pierce.

Horror   (PR:A MPAA:NR)

TOWER OF LONDON**   (1962) 79m Admiral/UA bw

Vincent Price (*Richard of Gloucester*), Michael Pate (*Sir Ratcliffe*), Joan Freeman (*Lady Margaret*), Robert Brown (*Sir Justin*), Justice Watson (*Edward IV*), Sarah Selby (*Queen*), Richard McCauly (*Clarence*), Eugene Martin (*Edward V*), Sandra Knight (*Mistress Shore, Nursemaid*), Richard Hale (*Tyrus*), Donald Losby (*Prince Richard*), Bruce Gordon (*Earl of Buckingham*), Joan Camden (*Anne*), Sara Taft (*Richard of Gloucester's Mother*).

A pallid remake of the 1939 classic that paired Basil Rathbone and Boris Karloff. Price, who had been drowned by Karloff in a wine vat, the first time, now takes the starring role of the man who will stop at nothing to ascend to the throne of England in the 15th Century. He likes to torture all of his victims. He kills a woman who is in charge of watching over the king's sons and, with each murder, grows madder. Finally, in a battle with the queen's army and Price's, Price sees the ghosts of all his past victims and, completely deranged, falls off his horse onto the battle ax of a dead soldier. Historical nonsense, and virtually tame this time around.

p, Gene Corman; d, Roger Corman; w, Leo V. Gordon, F. Amos Powell, James B. Gordon (based on the story by Gordon, Powell); ph, Arch R. Dalzell; m, Michael Andersen; ed, Ronald Sinclair; art d, Daniel Haller.

Horror   Cas.   (PR:A MPAA:NR)

TOWER OF TERROR, THE*   (1942, Brit.) 62m ABF/MON bw

Wilfrid Lawson (*Wolfe Kristan*), Movita (*Marie Durand*), Michael Rennie (*Anthony Hale*), Morland Graham (*Kleber*), John Longden (*The German Naval Commander*), George Woodbridge (*Jurgens*), Richard George (*Capt. Borkmann*), Edward Sinclair (*Fletcher*), Charles Rolfe (*Albers*), Eric Clavering (*Riemers*), J. Victor Weske (*Peters*), Olive Sloane (*Florist*).

Lawson is a demented German who runs a deserted lighthouse. Movita escapes from a concentration camp and swims to the lighthouse, where she is rescued by Lawson, who thinks she is the image of the wife he had killed 16 years earlier and buried on the lighthouse grounds. He immediately plots to do the same to Movita, but Rennie comes on the scene seeking information on the fortifications of the lighthouse, and Lawson is enraged. The pair fight and Lawson tumbles into his wife's grave that he had already dug up, allowing Movita and Rennie to escape the Germans and return to London. Little to recommend here in this badly acted, implausible B.

p, John Argyle; d, Lawrence Huntington; w, Argyle, John Reinhart (based on a story by Reinhart); ph, Bryan Langley; M.E. Benson; ed, Flora Newton.

Drama   (PR:A MPAA:NR)

TOWER OF TERROR, 1971   (SEE: ASSAULT, 1971, Brit.)

TOWERING INFERNO, THE**   (1974) 165m FOX-WB c

Steve McQueen (*Fire Chief Michael O'Hallorhan*), Paul Newman (*Doug Roberts*), William Holden (*Jim Duncan*), Faye Dunaway (*Susan Franklin*), Fred Astaire (*Harlee Claiborne*), Susan Blakely (*Patty Simmons*), Richard Chamberlain (*Roger Simmons*), Jennifer Jones (*Lisolette Mueller*), O. J. Simpson (*Security Chief Jernigan*), Robert Vaughn (*Sen. Gary Parker*), Robert Wagner (*Dan Bigelow*), Susan Flannery (*Lorrie*), Sheila Mathews (*Paula Ramsay*), Normann Burton (*Will Giddings, Construction Chief*), Jack Collins (*Mayor Robert Ramsay*), Don Gordon (*Kappy*), Felton Perry (*Scott*), Gregory Sierra (*Carlos*), Ernie Orsatti (*Mark, Fireman*), Carol McEvoy (*Mrs. Albright, Deaf Mute*), Michael Lookinland, Carlena Gower (*Albright Children*), Olan Soule (*Engineer*), John Crawford (*Callahan*), Dabney Coleman (*Assistant Fire Chief*), Malcolm Atterbury (*Jeweler*), Lt.Comdr. Norman Hicks, Lt.J.G. Thomas Karnahan (*Pilots*), Scott Newman (*Fireman*), Dave Sharpe (*Stunts*), Norman Grabowski, Erik Nelson, Art Ballinger, Elizabeth Rogers, Ann Leicester, Paul Comi, Patrick Culliton, William H. Bassett, Ross Elliott.

Irwin Allen, a master producer of mediocrities who scored big with THE POSEIDON ADVENTURE two years previously, scored big again with another disaster film, with some help from a big-name cast. Architect Newman and builder Holden together have built the world's largest skyscraper in San Francisco, called the Glass Tower. During the grand-opening party for the building they find out the wiring system is substand-ard and a fire breaks out in a storeroom, which Holden at first ignores. The fire erupts into something major and the fire department is finally called in and panic results all around as people try to escape the blazing tower. As everyone tries to save his neck, superior special effects please all as they show the outside and inside of the burning building. To finally put out the fire, the building's water tanks are blown up and everyone agrees in the end that very tall buildings are too much of a fire risk to be constructed. The picture did wonderfully well at the box office.

p, Irwin Allen; d, John Guillermin, Allen; w, Stirling Silliphant (based on the novels *The Tower* by Richard Martin Stern and *The Glass Inferno* by Thomas N. Scortia, Frank M. Robinson); ph, Fred Koenekamp, Joseph Biroc [aerials, Jim Freeman] (Panavision, DeLuxe Color); m, John Williams; ed, Harold F. Kress, Carl Kress; prod d, William Creber; art d, Ward Preston; set d, Raphael Bretton; cos, Paul Zastupnevich; spec eff, A. D. Flowers, Logan Frazee, L. B. Abbott; m/l, "We May Never Love Like This Again," Al Kasha, Joel Hirschhorn (sung by Maureen McGovern); stunts, Paul Stader.

Drama/Adventure   **Cas.**   (PR:C MPAA:PG)

TOWING*   (1978) 85m Sibling/United International-Condor c (AKA: FUN GIRLS; WHO STOLE MY WHEELS)

Jennifer Ashley (*Jean*), Sue Lyon (*Lynn*), Bobby DiCicco (*Tony*), Joe Mantegna (*Chris*), J. J. Johnston (*Butch*), Audry Neenan (*Irate Lady*), Steve Kampman (*Irate Man*), Don DePollo (*Pizza Man*), Nan Mason (*Nan*), Mike Nusbaum (*Phil*), Susanne Smith (*Lois*), Jake Stockwell (*Tow Truck Driver*), Lee Stein (*Mayor*), Sandy Halpin (*Waitress*), Bob Wallace (*News Reporter*).

The city of Chicago is well-known for towing operations that sting unwitting visitors, literally holding their cars for ransom. This bad comedy tries to tell the story of how a couple of barmaids try to break up one such ring. In between tasteless sex jokes and plain poor acting, the story just wanders on with no real direction. Opening shots get some laughs, showing how nothing, even an ambulance or a television truck, can escape the tower's hook. The only other good thing about the film is that it was made for under $1 million by a group of unknowns, most of whom stayed that way after this was released.

p, Frederick A. Smith; d&w, Maura Smith; ph, Hal Schullman; m, Martin Rubinstein ; ed, Bernard F. Caputo.

Comedy   (PR:C MPAA:PG)

TOWN CALLED BASTARD, A   (SEE: TOWN CALLED HELL, A, 1971, Span.)

TOWN CALLED HELL, A*   (1971, Span./Brit.) 95m
Benmar-Zurbano/Scotia International c (AKA: A TOWN CALLED BAS-TARD)

Robert Shaw (*Town Priest*), Stella Stevens (*Alvira*), Martin Landau (*The Colonel*), Telly Savalas (*Don Carlos*), Michael Craig (*Paco*), Fernando Rey (*Old Blind Farmer*), Dudley Sutton (*Spectre*), Al Lettieri (*La Bomba*), Aldo Sambrelli (*Colebra*), Paloma Cela (*Paloma*), Maribel Hidalgo (*La Perla*), Cass Martin (*Jose*), Antonio Mayans (*Manuel*), Tito Garcia (*Malombre*), Tony Cyrus (*Sanchez*), Adolfo Thous (*Mendoza*), Elizabeth Sands (*Carmine*), Felipe Solano (*Eduardo*), Luis Rivera (*Pedro*), Howard Hagan (*1st Ameri-can*), John Clark (*Quiet American*), Bruce Fischer (*Miguel*), Nilda Alvarez (*Old Mother*), Charlie Bravo (*Juan*), Chris Huertas (*Gonzales*), Georges Rigaud (*Gato*), Stefano Charelli (*Young Boy*).

Some of the folks such as Stevens and Savalas probably hope this never comes out again. Crudely made and poorly acted because the film tries to espouse too much philosophy while shooting at everything in sight. Shaw is a priest, once a revolutionary, who now sleeps with a woman and tries to gain insight into life. He lives in the town run by a ruthless Mexican bandit, who lets nothing get in his way to get what he wants. Stevens shows up in a hearse and declares that the hearse is for her husband's killer when she finds who that is. Take a wild guess who. Despite the obvious inspiration, this isn't up to Sergio Leone at all.

p, S. Benjamin Fisz; d, Robert Parrish; w, Richard Aubrey; ph, Manuel Berenguer (Franscope, Technicolor); m, Waldo De Los Rios; ed, Bert Bates; md, De Los Rios; art d, Julio Molina; set d, German Quejido; cos, Ossie Clark, Alice Pollack, Charles Simminger; spec eff, Manuel Baquero.

Western   **Cas.**   (PR:O MPAA:R)

TOWN LIKE ALICE, A**½**   (1958, Brit.) 107m RANK bw (AKA: RAPE OF MALAYA)

Virginia McKenna (*Jean Paget*), Peter Finch (*Joe Harman*), Takagi (*Japa-nese Sergeant*), Tran Van Khe (*Capt. Sugaya*), Jean Anderson (*Miss Horsefall*), Marie Lohr (*Mrs. Dudley Frost*), Maureen Swanson (*Ellen*), Renee Houston (*Ebbey*), Nora Nicholson (*Mrs. Frith*), John Fabian (*Mr. Holland*), Vincent Ball (*Ben*), Tim Turner (*British Sergeant*), Vu Ngoc Tuan (*Capt. Yanata*), Yamada (*Capt. Takata*), Nakamishi (*Capt. Nishi*), Ikada (*Kemptei, Sergeant*), Geoffrey Keen (*Solicitor*), Eileen Moore (*Mrs. Hol-land*), Cameron Moore (*Freddy*), Margaret Eaden (*Jane*), Geoffrey Hawkins (*Robin*), Peter John (*Timothy*), Domenic Lieven (*Michael Rhodes*), Jane White (*Brenda*), June Shaw, Armine Sandford, Mary Allen, Virginia Clay, Bay White, Philippa Morgan, Dorothy Moss, Gwenda Ewen, Josephine Miller, Edwina Carroll, Sanny Bin Hussein, Charles Marshall, Meg Bucking-ham.

A dark story based on Nevil Shute's novel that tells the story of a group of women and children forced to march through Malaya by the Japanese in WW II. As the women keep moving on, Finch, an Australian POW, and McKenna become friends. He tells her he will get the women a chicken for the next day's meal but is caught and is sentenced to be crucified. During the pair's friendship, Finch has told McKenna about his home town–Alice Springs–and McKenna keeps dreaming about it to keep herself going. The group leaves Finch crucified but learns later he was taken to a hospital so he is still alive. After the war, McKenna goes to Alice Springs and the couple is reunited. A depressing tale, as it shows people dying along the roadside, and the ruthless Japanese having no compassion whatsoever for their prisoners. Finch and McKenna add a few brighter spots as their friendship develops. It was filmed mostly in Australia and Malaya. The two leading players won British Film Awards for Best Actress and Best Actor in 1956, the year of its British release.

p, Joseph Janni; d, Jack Lee; w, W. P. Lipscomb, Richard Mason (based on the novel by Nevil Shute); ph, Geoffrey Unsworth; m, Matyas Seiber; ed, Sidney Hayers; art d, Alex Vetchinsky.

War Drama   (PR:A MPAA:NR)

TOWN ON TRIAL***   (1957, Brit.) 95m Marksman/COL bw

Charles Coburn (*Dr. John Fenner*), John Mills (*Supt. Mike Halloran*), Barbara Bates (*Elizabeth Fenner*), Derek Farr (*Mark Roper*), Alex McCow-en (*Peter Crowley*), Elizabeth Seal (*Fiona Dixon*), Geoffrey Keen (*Mr. Dixon*), Margaretta Scott (*Helen Dixon*), Fay Compton (*Mrs. Crowley*), Meredith Edwards (*Sgt. Rogers*), Harry Locke (*Sgt. Beale*), Maureen Connell (*Mary Roper*), Magda Miller (*Molly Stevens*), David Quitak (*David*), Dandy Nichols (*Mrs. Wilson*), Raymond Huntley (*Dr. Reese*), Harry Fowler, Newton Blick, Oscar Quitak, Trottie Truman Taylor, Grace Arnold.

Gripping murder mystery begins when Miller, a village woman of loose morals, is found strangled on the property of an elite social club. There are several likely suspects so Mills, a Scotland Yard detective, is called in to solve the case. First on his list is Farr, a blackmailer with a concocted war record. He is employed by the club's secretary and was also the father of Miller's unborn child. Another likely suspect is Coburn, a Canadian doctor who had left his native land in a rush, which causes some curiosity. Also on Mills' list is Keen, the town's mayor. This causes quite a row and distrust of the detective among the locals, who cared little for the man to start with. Mills' last suspect is McGowen, a quiet young man with a history of mental problems. That McGowen had also loved the dead woman is another factor which raises the investigator's suspicions. Before the case is solved Keen's daughter Seal is found strangled in a similar fashion, her corpse found in the trunk of Coburn's automobile. Finally Mills discovers that McGowen is dangerously unbalanced and is the man behind the violent deaths. Mills traps him in a clever scheme and the film ends with a chase in the steeple of a local church. The thrills are effectively drawn out within the story, making the most of the several threads Mills must follow. Twist after twist keeps the viewer constantly guessing as to the identity of the guilty party. Mills leads the tight ensemble with a fine performance, under a direction that clearly shows the feeling for a good murder mystery.

p, Maxwell Setton; d, John Guillermin; w, Robert Westerby, Ken Hughes; ph, Basil Emmott; m, Tristram Cary, Paul Brousse; ed, Max Benedict; md, Henry Varse, Michael Terr; art d, Daniel Hallo.

Crime   (PR:C MPAA:NR)

TOWN TAMER** (1965) 89m A.C. Lyles/PAR c

Dana Andrews (Tom Rosser), Terry Moore (Susan Tavenner), Pat O'Brien (Judge Murcott), Lon Chaney, Jr (Mayor Leach), Bruce Cabot (Riley Condor), Lyle Bettger (Lee Ring), Coleen Gray (Carol Rosser), Barton MacLane (James Fenimore Fell), Richard Arlen (Dr. Kent), Richard Jaeckel (Honsinger), Philip Carey (Sim Akins), DeForest Kelley (Guy Tavenner), Sonny Tufts (Carmichael), Roger Torrey (Flon), James Brown (Davis), Richard Webb (Kevin), Jeanne Cagney (Mary), Donald Barry (Deputy), Robert Ivers (Vagrant), Bob Steele (Vigilante), Dale Van Sickel, Dinny Powell, Frank Gruber.

Andrews is a hired gun out to get revenge for the killing of his wife committed by Bettger and Cabot. After a two-year search, he finds them as a sheriff and saloon keeper, respectively, which gives them total control of their town. As Andrews keeps his guns drawn and going, killing everyone that moves, he finally gets the pair– and with them the respect of the townspeople for freeing the place from their control. Bodies are plentiful in the climax; so many died, it seemed they would all run out of bullets. Jaeckel almost steals the entire film as a deputy with a deep sadistic streak. One of director Selander's best westerns, though hindered by a formula plot. Long-time cowboy star Bob Steele has a small part, as does writer Gruber.

p, A. C. Lyles; d, Lesley Selander; w, Frank Gruber (based on his novel); ph, W. Wallace Kelley (Techniscope, Technicolor); m, Jimmie Haskell; ed, George Gittens; art d, Hal Pereira, Al Roelofs; set d, Claude Carpenter; m/l, Haskell, By Dunham.

Western (PR:A MPAA:NR)

TOWN THAT CRIED TERROR, THE (SEE: MANIAC!, 1977)

TOWN THAT DREADED SUNDOWN, THE* (1977) 90M AIP c

Ben Johnson (Capt. J.D. Morales), Andrew Prine (Deputy Norman Ramsey), Dawn Wells (Helen Reed), Jimmy Clem (Sgt. Mal Griffin), Charles B. Pierce (Patrolman A. C. Benson), Cindy Butler (Peggy Loomis), Earl E. Smith (Dr. Kress), Christine Ellsworth (Linda Mae Jenkins), Mike Hackworth (Sammy Fuller), Jim Citty (Police Chief R. J. Sullivan), Robert Aquino (Sheriff Otis Barker), Misty West (Emma Lou Cook), Rick Hildreth (Buddy Turner), Steve Lyons (Roy Allen), Bud Davis (The Phantom Killer), Joe Catalanatto (Eddie LeDoux), Roy Lee Brown (Rainbow Johnson), Jason Darnell (Gus Wells), Mike Downs, Bill Dietz, Carolyn Moreland (Reporters), Michael Brown (Police Officer), Woody Woodman (FBI Agent), James B. McAdams (Sheriff's Deputy), John Stroud (Dr. Preston Hickson), Mason Andres (Rev. Harden), Richard Green (High School Principal), Dorothy Darlene Orr (Dispatcher), Don Adkins (Suspect), Vern Stierman (Narrator).

Producer-director Charles B. Pierce did well with the thriller THE LEGEND OF BOGGY CREEK (1972) and hit it big in the southern markets with this story about a berserk killer terrorizing the border town of Texarkana. The killer murdered five people back in 1946 and was never caught. There are no clues. The film recounts the story in documentary style, with breaks for narration. Johnson leads an inept group in the chase as the townspeople start going nuts trying to pinpoint who is guilty. A few screams and not much else.

p&d, Charles B. Pierce; w, Earl E. Smith; ph, Jim Roberson (Movielab Color); m, Jaime Mendoza-Nava; ed, Tom Boutross; art d, Myrl Teeter, Grant Sinclair; cos, Bonnie Langfliff, Karen Jones; spec eff, Joe Catalanatto; makeup, Cheri Johnston; stunts, Bud Davis.

Horror Cas. (PR:O MPAA:R)

TOWN WENT WILD, THE* (1945) 77m Roth-Greene-Rouse/PRC bw

Freddie Bartholomew (David Conway), James Lydon (Bob Harrison), Edward Everett Horton (Everett Conway), Tom Tully (Henry Harrison), Jill Browning (Carol Harrison), Minna Gombell (Marian Harrison), Ruth Lee (Lucille Conway), Roberta Smith (Millie Walker), Maude Eburne (Judge Bingle), Charles Halton (Mr. Tweedle), Ferris Taylor (Mr. Walker), Jimmy Conlin (Justice of the Peace), Monte Collins (The Public Defender), Charles Middleton (The District Attorney), Fred Burton (Dr. Hendricks), Will Wright (Judge Schrank), Emmett Lynn (The Watchman), Dorothy Vaughn (Nurse Reeves), Olin Howlin.

A slow start and slow end produce few laughs for this "comedy." Tully and Horton are feuding neighbors. Each has a son and one has a daughter, too. The son of one and daughter of the other fall in love, of course, against their families' wishes. Planning their wedding and getting all the legal paperwork done, it turns out they might just be brother and sister. Everything is resolved, the non-incestuous pair can marry, and the fighting fathers become buddies.

p, Bernard R. Roth, Clarence Greene, Russell Rouse; d, Ralph Murphy; w, Roth, Greene, Rouse; ph, Phillip Tannura; ed, Thomas Neff; md, Davis Chudnow; art d, George Van Marter; cos, Karlice.

Comedy (PR:A MPAA:NR)

TOWN WITHOUT PITY**½ (1961, Ger./Switz./U.S.) 112m Mirisch-Gloria- Osweg/UA bw(STADT OHNE MITLEID; VILLE SANS PITIE; AKA: SHOCKER)

Kirk Douglas (Maj. Steve Garrett), E.G. Marshall (Maj. Jerome Pakenham), Christine Kaufmann (Karin Steinhof), Robert Blake (Jim), Richard Jaeckel (Bidie), Frank Sutton (Chuck), Mal Sondock (Joey), Barbara Rutting (Inge Koerner), Hans Nielson (Herr Steinhof), Karin Hardt (Frau Steinhof), Ingrid van Bergen (Trude), Gerhart Lippert (Frank Borgmann), Eleanore van Hoogstraten (Frau Borgmann), Max Haufler (Dr. Urban), Siegfried Schurenberg (Burgermeister), Rose Renee Roth (Frau Kulig), Alan Gifford (Gen. Stafford), Fred Durr, Robert Shankland, Joe Valerio, Gerd Vespermann, Gernot Duda, Dean Jackson, Ted Turner, Lynn Randall, Cecilie Gelers, Stefan Schnabel.

A courtroom drama with intense underlying social messages spread throughout, TOWN WITHOUT PITY bites off more than it can chew as it simultaneously attempts to preach against capital punishment, uncover the prejudices in a small Teutonic town, and jab at the boorish louts who occupied Germany after the war. The small burg of Neustadt is the setting. A quartet of American soldiers, Sutton, Blake, Sondock, and Jaeckel, are spending a drunken afternoon in the woods outside the city. Meanwhile, teenage Kaufmann is wearing a brief bikini and having a brief date with her boy friend, young Lippert. She'd like to make love to him but he is inexperienced and tentative. She chides him for his immaturity and Lippert leaves. The four soldiers arrive and, in their stupor, move in on the curvaceous Kaufmann. Later, her father, Nielsen, contacts the town's burgermeister, Schurenberg, and the two men make a formal complaint against the soldiers for rape. Nielsen wants the four soldiers to get the death penalty and is told that the only way that could happen is if Kaufmann takes the witness stand and personally identifies the rapists. Blake, Jaeckel, Sutton, and Sondock are apprehended and a trial is prepared. To handle their defense, Douglas, a major who is an attorney, is brought in. He travels around Neustadt to gather evidence for the case and is not welcomed. While perambulating, he is approached by Rutting, a reporter. She is looking for a sensational angle for a story and is impressed by Douglas' apparent desire to see justice done. Douglas visits Kaufmann's parents, Nielsen and Hardt, and explains that he will be forced to question Kaufmann and that this might be psychologically harmful to the girl. Nielsen is irate, insists that the trial go on. Douglas talks to whatever neighbors he can and discovers that Kaufmann is hardly the naive young thing she seems to be. Matter of fact, she is a nymphet who is given to undressing in front of open windows in order to titillate passersby. At the trial, Douglas cross-examines some of the prissy villagers and extracts information about Kaufmann's provocative ways. Lippert's mother, van Hoogstraten, tells the court that she never approved of Kaufmann because the young girl was far too seductive toward her son. Kaufmann is called to be a witness and Douglas' questions are pointed, cruel, and destructive to the case of Marshall, the prosecutor. Douglas elicits information to the effect that Kaufmann had been naked in the woods, in an attempt to arouse Lippert, and was in that bare state when the soldiers arrived. Kaufmann falls apart on the stand and cannot finish her testimony. The soldiers are given terms in prison rather than the death penalty. Afterward, Douglas is preparing to leave the town when he learns that Kaufmann, who has been chastised by the bluenoses of the town, has killed herself. Douglas exits the small village after being shunned by friends and foes alike. There doesn't seem to be much point to the story, rather just an incident that could have been covered in a one-hour TV drama. Gene Pitney recorded the title song (which became a hit), and it was used so many times in the picture that the tune eventually began to rankle the ears. It received an Oscar nomination for its composers, Dimitri Tiomkin and Ned Washington, but lost that year to "Moon River." Shot in the south of France and in the German villages of Bamberg and Forcheim, it was released in Germany as STADT OHNE MITLEID, in Switzerland as VILLE SANS PITIE and was also known, in some areas, as SHOCKER, which it wasn't.

p&d, Gottfried Reinhardt; w, Silvia Reinhardt, Georg Hurdalek (based on the novel The Verdict by Manfred Gregor, adapted by Jan Lustig); ph, Kurt Hasse; m, Dimitri Tiomkin; ed, Walter Boos, Hermann Haller; art d, Rolf Zehetbauer; set d, Friedhelm Boehm, Werner Achmann, Zehetbauer; cos, Lilo Hagen; makeup, Albert Nagel, Irmgard Forster.

Drama (PR:C-O MPAA:NR)

TOXI** (1952, Ger.) 79m Fone-Film/Allianz Film bw

Elfie Fiegert (Toxi), Paul Bildt (Grossvater Rose), Johanna Hafer (Grossmutter Helene), Ingeborg Korner (Herta Rose), Carola Hohn (Charlotte Jenrich), Wilfried Seyferth (Theodor Jenrich), Sylvia Hermann (Ilse), Karin Purschke (Susi), Elisabeth Flickenschildt (Tante Wally), Rainer Penkert (Robert Peters), Ernst Waldow (Ubelhack), Erikav Thellmann (Frau Ubelhack), W. Maertens (Krim-Inspector Plaukart), Lotte Brackebusch (Frau Berstel), Al Hoosman (James R. Spencer), Gustel Busch (Anna), Julia Fjorsen (Fanny), Katharina Brauren (Vorsteherin), Gertrude Prey (Fursorgeschwester), Ursula V. Bose (Krankenschwester).

A touching story about a little girl, the product of a German mother and a black U.S. serviceman, who has been left in Germany after her mother dies and her father goes back to the U.S. Fiegert is the 6-year-old left behind with the family of the mother's former employer whose father does not want the child. Fiegert is taken to the local orphanage but the family's grandfather brings the child back. Racial issues arise and she is finally given to the orphanage once again. Finally the family realizes she does belong and takes her back. Such occurrences were a real problem in Germany, but the issue is skimmed over here for the most part, focusing more on the cute Fiegert.

d, R.A. Stemmle; w, Stemmle, Peter Francke, Maria Osten-Sacken; ph, Igor Oberberg; ed, Alice Ludwig.

Drama   (PR:A   MPAA:NR)

TOY, THE*   (1982) 99m Rastar/COL c

Richard Pryor (*Jack Brown*), Jackie Gleason (*U.S. Bates*), Ned Beatty (*Mr. Morehouse*), Scott Schwartz (*Eric Bates*), Teresa Ganzel (*Fancy Bates*), Wilfrid Hyde-White (*Barkley*), Annazette Chase (*Angela*), Tony King (*Clifford*), Don Hood (*O'Brien*), Karen Leslie- Lyttle (*Fraulein*), Virginia Capers (*Ruby Simpson*), B.J. Hopper (*Geffran*), Linda McCann (*Honey Russell*), Ray Spruell (*Sen. Newcomb*), Stocker Fontelieu (*District Attorney Russell*), Stuart Baker- Bergen (*Aerobics Class Leader*), Elbert Andre Patrick (*Jack's Neighbor*), Orwin Harvey (*Grand Dragon*), Jim Clancy (*Clancy*), Davis Hotard (*Eugene Russel*), Debra Cole (*Terry Gay*), Marilyn Gleason (*Mrs. Newcomb*), Steve Kahan, Paul Tuerpe (*State Troopers*), Jim Beyer, Tot Beyer (*Klan Demonstrators*), Robert M. Stevens (*Drunk in Jail*), Sally Birdsong (*Morehouse's Secretary*), Louis Weinberg (*Chauffeur*), Lucy Campbell Rowland (*Bates' Secretary*), Robert Cherry (*Man in Carwash*), Robert Adams, Mark Bennett, John R. Wilson (*Store Executives*), Robert Costley, Robert Earle, Pauline Barcelona, Juan Coleman, Valerian Smith (*Poker Players*), Annie McGuire, Beverly Tagge, George Howard, Helen Howard (*Party Guests*), Bill Holliday, J.D. Martin, James Roddy (*Police*), Delana Renay Cole, Lewis Baker, LaMonica Matthews, Bruce Langley, Dawnis Kaye Smith, Santos Swing, Willie Swing (*Ruby's Children*).

A dreadful remake of the French farce LE JOUET (1976) that was ill-conceived, poorly written, overly directed, and filled with sophomoric attempts at humor. Only Pryor's personal energy manages to save this from the refuse heap of movies. Schwartz is a spoiled brat 9-year-old who goes to boarding school and sees his multimillionaire father, Gleason, once a year. Gleason is an oil man with little time for fatherhood so he showers Schwartz with trinkets rather than sincere parental affection. While visiting a toy store, Schwartz spots Pryor, an unemployed news reporter in deep financial trouble, and tells his father that he wants Pryor as his "toy." Gleason makes the offer and Pryor accepts, becoming Schwartz's personal plaything. Several terrible jokes later, a few dollops of sentimentality are lathered on as Pryor tells the snotnose kid that he has to earn someone's friendship, not buy it. There are pies tossed, people pushed in a swimming pool, an encounter with the KKK, some smarmy sex jokes with Schwartz's German governess, Leslie-Lyttle, and nary a genuine laugh, except when Pryor's elan is demonstrated. It's a one-joke premise, not unlike the tale of the billionaire Arabian oilman who took his young son to Disneyland and when he asked the lad what he wanted, the boy said he'd like a "Mickey Mouse outfit," so the father bought the son the William Morris Agency.

p, Phil Feldman; d, Richard Donner; w, Carol Sobieski (based on the film LE JOUET by Francis Veber); ph Laszlo Kovacs (DeLuxe Color); m Patrick Williams; ed, Richard Harris, Michael A. Stevenson; prod d, Charles Rosen; cos, Moss Mabry.

Comedy   **Cas.**   (PR:C   MPAA:PG)

TOY TIGER**   (1956) 88m Christie/UNIV c

Jeff Chandler (*Rick Todd*), Laraine Day (*Gwen Taylor*), Tim Hovey (*Timmie Harkinson*), Cecil Kellaway (*James Fusenot*), Richard Haydn (*John Fusenot*), David Janssen (*Larry Tripps*), Judson Pratt (*Mike Wyman*), Butch Bernard (*"Owly" Kimmel*), Brad Morrow (*Freddy Doobin*), Jacqueline de Wit (*Edna, Gwen's Secretary*), Mary Field (*Miss Elsie, Woman at Shop*), Robert Anderson (*State Trooper*).

A cute comedy that appeals to family tastes. Hovey is lonely in boarding school, a school he was put in by his widowed mother, advertising executive Day. But Hovey brags to his classmates about the exploits of his imagined father, who, he tells everyone, is still alive. Chandler plays a high-powered fellow executive of Day's agency who is sent out to find and recruit a wayward artist, who now works for the school in upstate New York. Hovey gets Chandler to assume the role of his father to save his pride with his school buddies. At the same time, Chandler runs into Day and the romance begins, with Chandler totally unaware at first that she is the boy's mother. Everything ends up predictably and everyone goes home happy as scene-stealing Hovey gets a new father. The film is a version of the 1938 movie MAD ABOUT MUSIC that starred Deanna Durbin in the cute moppet role.

p, Howard Christie; d, Jerry Hopper; w, Ted Sherdeman (suggested by a story by Frederick Kohner, Marcella Burke); ph, George Robinson (Technicolor); ed, Milton Carruth; md, Joseph Gershenson; art d, Alexander Golitzen, Richard H. Riedel; cos, Rosemary Odell.

Comedy   (PR:AA   MPAA:NR)

TOY WIFE, THE**   (1938) 95m MGM bw (GB: FROU-FROU)

Luise Rainer (*Gilberta Brigard*), Melvyn Douglas (*Georges Sartoris*), Robert Young (*Andre Vallaire*), Barbara O'Neil (*Louise Brigard*), H. B. Warner (*Victor Brigard*), Alma Kruger (*Mme. Vallaire*), Libby Taylor (*Suzanne*), Theresa Harris (*Pick*), Walter Kingsford (*Judge Rondell*), Clinton Rosemond (*Pompey*), Clarence Muse (*Brutus*), Leonard Penn (*Gaston Vincent*), Margaret Irving (*Mme. DeCambri*), Ann Perl (*Georgie*), Rafaela Ottiano (*Felicianne*), Beulah Hall Jones (*Sophie*), George H. Reed (*Gabriel*), Madam Sul-te-wan (*Eve*), Hal Le Seuer, Douglas McPhail (*Brothers*), Tom Rutherfurd (*Jacques*), Alberto Moran (*Emile*), Edward Keane (*Auctioneer*), D'Arcy Corrigan (*Actor*), Natalie Garson (*Woman in Spanish Costume*), George Regas (*Man in Court*), Charles Albin (*Priest*), Esther Muir (*Blonde Woman*), Priscilla Lawson (*Dark Woman*), Brent Sargent (*Young Man*), Marguerite Whitten (*Rose*), Billy McClain (*Orchestra Leader*), George Humbert (*Organ Grinder*), Henry Roquemore (*Proprietor of Toy Shop*), Robert Spindele (*Italian Boy*), Barbara Bedford (*Woman in Doctor's Office*), Ruby Elzy (*Woman at Fruit Stand*), Myrtle Anderson (*Therese*), Willa Curtis (*Marguerite*), Gertrude Saunders (*Yellow Marie*), Violet McDowell (*Brown Marie*), Cora Lang (*Yvonne*), Irene Allen (*Agatha*), Olive Ball, Geneva Williams, Mary Luster, Edna Franklin, Charles Andrews, Ernest Wilson, Henry Thomas, Louise Robinson, Fannie Washington (*Servants*).

A costume drama of morals and manners in Louisiana in the last century, THE TOY WIFE is much ado about nothing. Rainer, who was the only woman to ever win two consecutive Oscars, is a 16-year- old who has just come back to Louisiana after a trip to France. O'Neil is her sister and engaged to Douglas while Young is courting Rainer. It would seem that Young and Rainer might be a good pair but Rainer has the warmies for Douglas, despite Young's ardor. She steals Douglas away, marries him, they have a son, and she is ensconced in the task of supervising their plantation and being a mother. She is not up to it, however, and Douglas asks O'Neil to help manage the slaves. Later, Rainer takes up again with Young and leaves Douglas to run off with Young to New York. When they return to New Orleans, there's a duel between Douglas and Young and the latter is slain. Rainer gets her comeuppance by catching one of those movie diseases. She dies, but not before having secured the love of her son, Douglas, and O'Neil. Old- fashioned, with none of the style of CAMILLE (which is emulated to a point), or the fire of GONE WITH THE WIND, which it also resembled. Screenwriter Akins had written the scripts for CAMILLE and ZAZA and one couldn't help but notice the similarities. The sets came from other films like OPERATOR 13, and the smell of mothballs was all over the costumes. Cooper, the producer, was better known for KING KONG and would that he could have instilled some of the excitement of that film into this one.

p, Merian C. Cooper; d, Richard Thorpe; w, Zoe Akins; ph, Oliver T. Marsh; m, Edward Ward; ed, Elmo Vernon; art d, Cedric Gibbons.

Historical Drama   (PR:A-C   MPAA:NR)

TOYGRABBERS, THE   (SEE: UP YOUR TEDDY BEAR, 1970)

TOYS ARE NOT FOR CHILDREN*   (1972) 85m SHB/Maron c

Marcia Forbes (*Jamie Godard*), Fran Warren (*Edna Godard*), Peter Lightstone (*Phillip Godard*), Harlan Cary Poe (*Charlie Belmond*), Evelyn Kingsley (*Pearl Valdi*), Luis Arroyo (*Eddie*), Tiberia Mitri (*Jamie as a Girl*), Jack Cobb (*The John*), N. J. Osrag (*Max*), Sally Moore (*Elderly Neighbor*), Ronnie Kahn, Irene Signoretti, Sallee St. Aubin, Madelyn Killeen.

A movie that tries to be deep-thinking but just ends up too depressing. A supposed study in psychology that watches young Forbes grow up to be a hooker, and why. She has been controlled by her domineering mother since her whoremonger father deserted them when Forbes was a child. The mother, a man-hater, keeps telling the little girl her daddy liked the company of streetwalkers. It gets weird for the sicko set as she turns to prostitution and has her clients call her "baby" as she calls them "daddy" to fulfill the roles she never had. As bad as that is, a hooker friend attempts a lesbian relationship that Forbes rejects. For revenge, the woman sets up Forbes to bed her own father. When her dad finds out he just romped with his own flesh and blood, he freaks and the end comes mercifully with predictable results. Apparently, the producers made up their minds not to try to fill in the picture with sexually explicit scenes and go for an X rating, although that may have been their original intent. Actress Forbes was the wife of Cannon films president Chris Dewey who, in a publicity release for the picture, claimed that he wanted his wife to give up her acting career. He might well have persuaded her sooner.

p, Stanley H. Brasloff, Samuel M. Chartock; d, Brasloff; w, Macs McAree (based on a story by Brasloff); m, Cathy Lynn; ed, Jerry Siegel; md, Jacques Urbant; m/l, title song and "Lonely Am I," Lynn.

Drama   (PR:O   MPAA:R)

TOYS IN THE ATTIC**½   (1963) 88m Mirisch-Claude/UA bw

Dean Martin (*Julian Berniers*), Geraldine Page (*Carrie Berniers*), Yvette Mimieux (*Lily Prine Berniers*), Wendy Hiller (*Anna Berniers*), Gene Tierney (*Albertine Prine*), Nan Martin (*Charlotte Warkins*), Larry Gates (*Cyrus Warkins*), Frank Silvera (*Henry*), Charles Lampkin (*Gus*).

New Orleans was the site of many of Lillian Hellman's works. In this, she again scratches the underbelly of the Crescent City and comes up with a spiteful slash at chicanery in the Deep South. Neuroses seem to be the most popular export (after Barq's Root Beer and Cajun-Creole cuisine) and there are plenty of them here. Based on her 1960 Broadway play, Hellman spins the yarn of lazy Martin, who goes back to New Orleans with his child-bride, Mimieux, and is welcomed with open arms by his unmarried sisters, Hiller and Page. They live in genteel poverty and hope that Martin will help them. He tells his siblings that his once- prosperous shoe factory in Illinois has gone bankrupt but he managed to save money and he proves it by giving them both some expensive trinkets, as well as purchasing two tickets to Europe so they can have "The Grand Tour." Page loves her brother dearly, perhaps a bit too dearly, and her adoration borders on incest. Hiller is more objective and wonders how it is that Martin managed to extract money and if those gains have been ill- gotten. Martin will not divulge the source of his money and both sisters become curious. Mimieux thinks that Martin may be dating a woman behind her back, a fact Martin denies. Mimieux's mother, Tierney, is a well-to-do woman who is having an affair with her black chauffeur, Silvera. The two of them visit Martin while Mimieux and Page eavesdrop and hear Martin talking about a real estate scam wherein Martin bilked Gates, the husband of Nan Martin, who was one of Dean Martin's former mistresses. Page doesn't like Mimieux and would like to see her out of the way. She convinces the naive Mimieux to call Gates and reveal Dean Martin's duplicity. Then Martin and Martin are ambushed by toughs employed by Gates and their money is taken. Later, Dean Martin is licking his wounds when he returns to the family house. At first, he thinks that it was Mimieux who betrayed him, then he realizes that Mimieux was only a tool of Page's. He walks out on Page to try and find Mimieux. At the same time, Hiller is disgusted with her sister and exits simultaneously, leaving an angry Page behind to sink in the emotional morass she has manufactured. Lurid, talky, with hints at miscegenation, the aforementioned incest, and several other doings, the movie was softened considerably from the raw stage presentation, perhaps with the thought that mass audiences couldn't take the reality of what was on Broadway. This was another typical Hollywood decision made at the expense of the intelligence of the rest of the country. Page was brilliant and Hiller, in a less showy role, was excellent. Dean Martin was much better than anyone expected and showed he had a range beyond crooning and acting as a foil for Jerry Lewis.

p, Walter Mirisch; d, George Roy Hill; w, James Poe (based on the play by Lillian Hellman); ph, Joseph F. Biroc (Panavision); m, George Duning; ed, Stuart Gilmore, Marshall M. Borden; art d, Cary Odell; set d, Victor Gangelin; cos, Bill Thomas; makeup, Frank Prehoda, Loren Cosand.

Drama   (PR:C MPAA:NR)

TRACK OF THE CAT***   (1954) 102m Wayne-Fellows/WB c

Robert Mitchum (*Curt Bridges*), Teresa Wright (*Grace Bridges*), Diana Lynn (*Gwen Williams*), Tab Hunter (*Harold "Hal" Bridges*), Beulah Bondi (*Ma Bridges*), Philip Tonge (*Pa Bridges*), William Hopper (*Arthur*), Carl "Alfalfa" Switzer (*Joe Sam*).

A bleak, moody, slow, somewhat pretentious, but nonetheless fascinating filmic experiment in style from director Wellman and cinematographer Clothier. Adapted from a novel by Walter Van Tilburg Clark (author of THE OX-BOW INCIDENT, which Wellman had brought to the screen), the story is a stark psychological drama set on a snowbound ranch in northern California and involves only a handful of characters. To emphasize the bleak nature of the story, Wellman had Clothier photograph the film in color, but the set, clothing, horses, and props were either black or white. Only the flesh tone of the performers, the blue sky, Mitchum's red mackinaw, and actress Lynn's yellow scarf show color. Trapped by the heavy snow is the Bridges family, which is firmly in the warped grasp of matriarch Bondi. Bondi's cold domineering manner has driven her weakling husband Tonge to the bottle, her daughter, Wright, to bitter spinsterhood, while her sons Mitchum, Hopper, and Hunter range from arrogance (Mitchum) to quiet sensitivity (Hopper). Also on hand is Lynn, a young neighbor girl who is anxious to marry Hunter. Feeling that he has sacrificed the most for the family ranch, Mitchum lets it be known that he intends to control the family, including the affections of Lynn. Contrasted with the dangers inside the house is an external threat: a vicious black panther that has been killing the family's cattle. Mitchum and Hopper venture out to kill the beast, but Hopper is killed after Mitchum leaves to get more rations. The family is beside itself with grief, and Wright coldy bemoans the fact that it was Hopper who was killed and not Mitchum. Sensing that the panther is a threat to his authority over the family, Mitchum immediately departs on a quest to kill the hated animal. After a silence of several days, the youngest brother, Hunter, goes off in search of Mitchum. Hunter finds his brother's horse and a supply of rations and learns that Mitchum had lost his food, panicked, and headed toward the ranch on foot. In blind desperation, Mitchum plunged headlong over a cliff to his death. Hunter takes up the quest for the panther, and in a final confrontation he manges to find and kill the animal. Having proven himself, Hunter confidently returns to claim Lynn as his own. The panther is never seen in the film and remains a dark, shadowy representation of the evil that resides in the family. Mitchum is consumed and destroyed by the dark impulses that the cat represents, as if he was killed chasing himself. Hunter survives and is made whole by his ability to face the evil and to destroy it before it destroys him. While Wellman and Clothier's experiments

with color and CinemaScope composition are admirable and interesting, the film suffers from its ponderous pace and heavy use of symbolism. Mitchum and Bondi give outstanding performances, despite the fact that Miss Bondi and director Wellman clashed frequently on the set. Perhaps the strangest performance is that of former "Little Rascal" Switzer, who plays a 100-year-old Indian. Wellman was able to make this bizarre film based on the tremendous success of his previous film, THE HIGH AND THE MIGHTY, starring John Wayne. Wayne's company had produced the film, and the star was so thrilled with the critical and financial success of THE HIGH AND THE MIGHTY that he told Wellman he could "film the phone book" if he wanted to at his expense. Taking the Duke at his word, Wellman resurrected his long-standing wish to shoot a color film in black and white using only sparse highlights of color. Though TRACK OF THE CAT befuddled most critics of the day and Wellman later stated in his autobiography that it was: "...a flop artistically, financially and Wellmanly," the film remains an interesting, if flawed, curio well worth attention.

p, John Wayne, Robert Fellows; d, William A. Wellman; w, A.I. Bezzerides (based on the novel by Walter Van Tilburg Clark); ph, William H. Clothier (CinemaScope, Warner Color); m, Roy Webb; ed, Fred MacDowell; art d, Al Ybarra; set d, Ralph Hurst; cos, Gwen Wakeling; makeup, Gordon Bau, George Bau.

Western/Drama   (PR:C MPAA:NR)

TRACK OF THE MOONBEAST zero   (1976) 90m Cinema
                                                        Shares/Lizard c

Chase Cordell (*Paul Carson*), Donna Leigh Drake (*Kathy Nolan*), Gregorio Sala (*Johnny Longbow*), Francine Kessler (*Janet Price*), Joe Blasco (*The Monster*), Patrick Wright, Crawford MacCallum, Fred McCaffrey, Timothy Wayne Brown, Alan Swain, Jeanne Swain, Tim Butler.

Just when you think you've seen it all, along comes this would-be bit of camp. A nice-guy minerslogist gets hit in the head by a piece of a meteor which causes him to go through some severe personality changes. Specifically, the man is turned into a giant lizard. The idea is ripe with chances for humor but the production is bogged down with classic examples of inept filmmaking. Story suffers from a slow development and the low-class production values are a further distraction. The only thing horror fanatics might want to take a look at is the lizard makeup created by Baker (who would go on to create the Oscar winning makeup for AN AMERICAN WEREWOLF IN LONDON).

d, Dick Ashe; ph, E.S. Wood; m, Bob Orpin; makeup, Rick Baker, Joe Blasco.

Horror/Science Fiction   (PR:C-O MPAA:NR)

TRACK OF THE VAMPIRE   (SEE: BLOOD BATH, 1966)

TRACK OF THUNDER*   (1967) 83m Ambassador/UA c

Tom Kirk (*Bobby Goodwin*), Ray Stricklyn (*Gary Regal*), H. M. Wynant (*Maxwell Carstairs*), Brenda Benet (*Shelley Newman*), Faith Domergue (*Mrs. Goodwin*), Majel Barrett (*Georgia Clark*), Chet Stratton (*Mr. Regal*), James Dobson (*Bowser Smith*), Paul Crabtree (*Mr. Bigelow*), Sam Tarpley (*Col. Lee*), Bob Stewart, Chuck Doughty, Maurice Dembsky, Don Gregory, Leslie Jameson, Carol Doughty, Bob Smith, Horace Wood, Ed Livingston.

Big with the stock car racing fans, this independently made film tells the tale of a couple of hotshot driving "good ol' boys" who battle it out on the track night after night for the checkered flag. While the track publicity people claim the pair hate each other, they're actually friends until they set eyes on the same girl, Benet. Then they become real nasty enemies. And it gets worse as Kirk's mother marries Stricklyn's father. Finally, Benet makes her choice so one can retire to the farm while the other goes on to racing glory. Overdramatization gives it laughs it doesn't want and the two racers are too old to be battling like jealous high-school kids over a girl.

p, E. Stanley Williamson; d, Joe Kane; w, Maurice J. Hill; ph, Alan Stensvold (Techniscope, Technicolor); ed, Verna Fields; md, John Caper, Jr.

Action/Drama   (PR:A MPAA:NR)

TRACK THE MAN DOWN**   (1956, Brit.) 75m REP bw

Kent Taylor (*Don Ford*), Petula Clark (*June Dennis*), Renee Houston (*Pat Sherwood*), Walter Rilla (*Austin Melford*), George Rose (*Rick Lambert*), Mary Mackenzie (*Mrs. Norman*), Kenneth Griffith (*Ken Orwell*), Ursula Howells (*Mary Dennis*), Lloyd Lamble (*Inspector Barnet*), John Sanger, Bartlett Mullins, Frank Atkinson, John Welsh, Iris Vandeleur, Mona Lilian, Brian Franklin, Jack Lambert, Hugh Cameron, Eric Lander, Ted Palmer, Ned Hood, Charles Lloyd Pack, Arthur Lane, Michael Balfour, Michael Golden, Graeme Ashley.

When Rose two-times his pals at a dog track, he takes his ill-gotten gains and tosses them into a suitcase. He gives this to his girl friend Howells, who passes it to her sister Clark. Clark boards a bus to take the money to the seashore but she arouses the suspicions of Taylor, a reporter taking the same coach. Rose manages to catch up with Clark and Taylor, but so do the cops, bringing all to a legal conclusion. Poorly paced with a bad story construction, this actually is funny if one doesn't take it too seriously. It is one of the last films Clark made before leaving the movies and becoming a successful pop singer in the 1960s.

p, William N. Boyle; d, R.G. Springsteen; w, Paul Erickson, Kenneth R. Hayles; ph, Basil Emmett; m, Lambert Williamson; ed, John Seabourne; md, Williamson; art d, John Stoll.

Crime (PR:A MPAA:NR)

TRACKDOWN zero (1976) 98m Essanness/UA c

Jim Mitchum (*Jim Calhoun*), Karen Lamm (*Betsy Calhoun*), Anne Archer (*Barbara*), Erik Estrada (*Chucho*), Cathy Lee Crosby (*Lynn Strong*), Vince Cannon (*Johnny Dee*), John Kerry (*Sgt. Miller*), Roberto Rodriguez (*Feo*), Ernie Wheelwright (*Rosey*), Zitto Kazann (*Curtain*), Elizabeth Chauvet (*Billie*), Rafael Lopez (*Barba*), Gilbert De La Pena (*Chino*), Joe La Due (*Ben*), Ray Sharkey (*Flash*), James R. Parkes (*Joe Andrews*), Frederick Rule (*Nadine*), Don Reed (*Flora*), Tony Burton (*Zelda*), Lanny Gustavson (*Cowboy*), Leslie Simms (*Juvenile Officer*), Jim Stathis (*Young Doctor*), Larry Gabriel (*Fat Counterman*), Robert Forward (*Lawyer*), Simmy Bow (*Counterman*), Gus Peters (*Panhandler*), John Rayner (*Doctor*), Junero Jennings (*Parking Attendant*), Dick De Cott (*Police Officer*), Russell Shannon (*Traffic Cop*), Joe Tornatore (*Heavy*), Evelyn Guerrero (*Social Worker*), Rebecca Winters (*Hysterical Girl*).

Poor little country girl Lamm gets sucked up into the low-life side of Los Angeles and it's up to her lackluster cowboy big brother (Mitchum) to find her. Mitchum sleepwalks through the streets of L.A. in cowboy gear, fighting all the sleazy elements and people who couldn't care less about another's life. Graphic violence doesn't add anything nor does the nudity except to earn the "R" rating that might attract a few fools tc see this.

p, Bernard Schwartz; d, Richard T. Heffron; w, Paul Edwards (based on a story by Ivan Nagy); ph, Gene Polito (Panavision, Deluxe Color); m, Charles Bernstein; ed, Anthony De Marco; md, John Caper, Jr.; art d, Vincent M. Cresciman; set d, Robert Bradfield; spec eff, Greg Auer; makeup, Mike Westmore; stunts, Eddy Donno.

Thriller (PR:O MPAA:R)

TRACKS* (1977) 90m Trio c

Dennis Hopper (*Sergeant*), Taryn Power (*Stephanie*), Dean Stockwell (*Mark*), Topo Swope (*Chloe*), Michael Emil (*Emile*), Zack Norman (*Gene*), Alfred Ryder (*Man*).

Stark reality mingled with paranoid fantasies in this film about a Vietnam veter an accompanying a fallen friend's body across the U.S. for a proper burial give it an uneasy feeling. Hopper is the vet who experiences flashbacks on the train trip and imagines some of the passengers as people out to get him. He meets up with willful Power (Tyrone Power's daughter) who provides him with the understanding he needs to exorcise the demons within him. Film ends on a depressing note as Hopper won't help a radical in need so Power Leaves him at the end of his journey. The final sight is a symbolic one of Hopper, all alone, burying his friend because the man also has no family waiting for him.

p, Howard Zucker, Irving Cohen, Ted Shapiro; d&w, Henry Jaglom; ph, Paul Glickman ; ed, George Folsey, Jr.

Drama **Cas.** (PR:O MPAA:NR)

TRADE WINDS* (1938) 93m UA bw

Frederic March (*Sam Wye*), Joan Bennett (*Kay Kerrigan*), Ralph Bellamy (*Ben Blodgett*), Ann Sothern (*Jean Livingstone*), Sidney Blackmer (*Thomas Bruhme II*), Thomas Mitchell (*Commissioner Blackton*), Robert Elliott (*Capt. George Faulkiner*), Richard Tucker (*John Johnson*), Joyce Compton (*Mrs. Johnson*), Patricia Farr (*Peggy*), Wilma Francis (*Judy*), Phyllis Barry (*Ruth*), Dorothy Tree (*Clara*), Kay Linaker (*Grace*), Dorothy Comingore (*Ann*), Walter Byron (*Bob*), Wilson Benge (*Martin the Butler*), Harry Paine (*Captain*), Hooper Atchley, Lee Phelps, Franklin Parker, John Webb Dillon, Dick Rush, Jack Baxley (*Detective Squad*), Mrs. Sojin (*Patron*), Princess Luana, Marie de Forest (*Hawaiian Hairdressers*), Beryl Wallace, Paulita Arvizu (*Hawaiian Girls*), Aiko Magara (*Proprietress of Tea House*), Suzanne Kaaren (*Russian Girl*), Gloria Youngblood (*Jinrickisha Girl*), Lotus Liu (*Shanghai Clerk*), Ethelreda Leopold (*Ethel*), Dick Botiller (*Bombay Carriage Driver*), Charlie Williams (*Reporter Jones*), Tom Quinn (*Reporter*), Betty Roadman (*Matron*), Harry Barris (*Pianist*), Cyril Ring, Brooks Benedict (*Party Guests*), Art Baker (*Voices of Various Radio 'Police' Announcers*), Harry Bernard (*Sound Man*), Beal Wong (*Shanghai Cigarette Customer*).

Sharp dialog from the acid pen of Dorothy Parker highlights this lighthearted chase along the rim of Asia. Bennett is a young pianist in San Francisco who sets out for revenge when her sister commits suicide over a man. She goes out to shoot him and when he falls down dead she fakes her own suicide and takes off for the other side of the world, with detectives March and Bellamy in pursuit. Stopping in Honolulu she has her hair dyed brunette (a change that made her look strikingly like Hedy Lamarr, and that was so

well received she kept her hair dark for the rest of her career) before taking off again for Japan, China, Singapore, Bombay, and the tiny chain of Laccadive Islands in the Indian Ocean. By the time March catches up to her, he has fallen desperately in love with her and he helps prove that it wasn't Bennett, but another jilted lover who had shot the cad at the opening. Mostly the film was an excuse for Garnett to use a quantity of stock footage he had shot on a long voyage through the same waters. As the director pointed out in his autobiography, "How often do you get a chance to take your own boat around the world, tax deductible?" March is his usual easy- going self, and Bellamy is adequate as his slightly dim sidekick, but it is Bennett, a revelation in dark hair, and Sothern, whose character here would be turned into the MAISIE series and make her a star, who really carry the picture, thanks to the acerbic and fast-paced script. The film was a great success, revitalizing the careers of Bennett and Sothern, and enhanced the reputations of everyone involved.

p, Walter Wanger; d, Tay Garnett; w, Dorothy Parker, Alan Campbell, Frank R. Adams (based on a story by Garnett); ph, Rudolph Mate; m, Alfred Newman; ed, Dorothy Spencer, Otho Lovering, Walt Reynolds; md, Newman; art d, Alexander Toluboff, Alexander Golitzen; cos, Irene, Helen Taylor.

Crime/Comedy (PR:A MPAA:NR)

TRADER HORN* (1931) 123m MGM bw

Harry Carey (*Trader Horn*), Edwina Booth (*Nina Trend*), Duncan Renaldo (*Peru*), Mutia Omoolu (*Rencharo*), Olive Fuller Golden/Olive Carey (*Edith Trend*), C. Aubrey Smith (*Trader*).

The first time Hollywood brought its cameras to the Dark Continent was for this adventure film that was probably more dangerous for the film crew than it was for the characters in the story. Carey is a trader in Africa, plying the rivers in his canoe and swapping with the natives. Traveling with him is young Renaldo, the son of an old partner. They meet Golden, a missionary who is heading for the dangerous country up river to look for her long-missing daughter in the area of a waterfall where her husband had been killed 20 years before. Carey and Renaldo try to warn her about the dangers, but she is adamant. A few days later the two men find themselves at the waterfall and there discover the mutilated body of Golden. Carey decides to go after the girl himself and he and Renaldo set out into the bush. They are quickly captured and taken to a native village where the savages prepare to inflict a horrible death on them. A white woman (Booth) emerges from the crowd and orders that the two men be tied upside down to crosses and set afire. Then she changes her mind and orders them released. Carey realizes that she is the sought-after captive, now a goddess among these people. She decides to escape with the two men and they narrowly elude pursuing natives as well as the hazards of the jungle. Their trusty native guide, Omoolu, lays down his life to help the others escape to safety. Now there is trouble as Carey and Renaldo have both fallen in love with Booth. Carey, though, concedes her to Renaldo, telling the young man, "I'll still be beholdin' the wonders of a jungle that'll never grow old before your eyes, the way a woman does." Irving Thalberg was the man responsible for this near disaster, having read the original novel and become convinced it would make a great picture. He got Louis B. Mayer's support and then approached Wallace Beery with the lead. The actor did not relish the opportunity to film in Africa and turned him down. Thalberg then went to Carey, who had once commanded $2,500 a week but was now having trouble finding work at any price, and who needed money badly now after a dam break and flood all but destroyed his ranch. Thalberg offered him $600 a week and the actor took it. Booth got the part of the white goddess after a major talent hunt. In 1929 the cast and crew set sail for Africa, where they filmed for months. Disasters happened one after another. The truck carrying all the sound equipment fell off the road and into the river. Insects, snakes, and larger animals tormented the crew, and hostile natives threatened them. Director Van Dyke kept comfortably numb the whole time thanks to the cases of gin he had brought along. They sent the footage ahead when they left Africa and Mayer was shocked at the hodgepodge of useless footage that was all he had to show for his huge investment. When the ship docked at New York, telegrams were waiting telling the whole cast and crew that they had been fired and the project scrapped. Some at MGM didn't think the whole thing was a washout and they convinced Thalberg and Mayer to cut together what they could and then shoot some more footage on sets or in Mexico. For another year the crew worked secretly, for fear the public would find out the whole thing hadn't been shot in Africa. The film was a major success when it came out and was nominated for an Academy Award for Best Picture. Much has been written about the fate of Booth, most of it false. Rumors sprang up that she had contracted a rare disease on location in Africa, either a result of the malarial environment or witchcraft, and had died, either in Africa or in the U.S. after a prolonged illness. Other reports indicated that she went mad in the jungles. The facts are that she did, indeed, contract a disease while filming, but she did not die of it and she later sued the studio and won heavy damages against them. At last report she was still alive in Hollywood, working for the Mormon church and refusing interviews. It was many years before the studios would venture into Africa again. TRADER HORN was remade in 1973.

d, W.S. Van Dyke II; w, Richard Schayer, Cyril Hume, Dale Van Every, John Thomas Neville (based on the novel by Alfred Aloysius Horn, Ethelreda Lewis); ph, Clyde De Vinna; ed, Ben Lewis.

Adventure   (PR:C MPAA:NR)

TRADER HORN* (1973) 105m MGM c

Rod Taylor (*Trader Horn*), Anne Heywood (*Nicole*), Jean Sorel (*Emil*), Don Knight (*Col. Sinclair*), Ed Bernard (*Apaque*), Stack Pierce (*Malugi*), Caro Kenyatta (*Umbopa*), Robert Miller Driscoll (*Alfredo Rozas*), Erik Holland (*Medford*), King Solomon III (*Red Sun*), Willie Harris (*Blue Star*), Oliver Givens (*Dancer*), Curt Lowens (*Schmidt*), John Siegfried (*German Officer*).

A poor, cliche-ridden remake of the 1931 classic. Taylor, with Sorel and Heywood, is trying to get away from German troops in Africa during WW I. As they start the journey, every predictable thing that could happen to them in Africa does: wild-eyed attacks from natives, wild beasts, and getting caught in the crossfire of the German and British armies. Much of the trouble they get into is shown through film footage used in earlier movies, but these clips were better in the original films they were used in. The whole continent of Africa got a bad rap by being associated with this picture, which was filmed nowhere near it.

p, Lewis J. Rachmil; d, Reza S. Badiyi; w, William Norton, Edward p, Lewis J. Rachmil; d, Reza S. Badiyi; w, William Norton, Edward Harper (based on a story by Harper and characters created by Ethelreda Lewis); ph, Ronald W. Browne (Metrocolor); m, Shelly Manne; ed, George Folsey, Jr.; art d, Jan Van Tamelen; set d, Fred R. Price.

Adventure/Drama   (PR:A MPAA:PG)

TRADER HORNEE zero (1970) 105m Trader Film Ventures/Entertainment Ventures c

Buddy Pantsari (*Hamilton Hornee*), Elisabeth Monica (*Jane Sommers*), John Alderman (*Max Matthews*), Christine Murray (*Doris Matthews*), Deek Sills (*Algona*), Lisa Grant (*Tender Lee*), Sir Brandon Duffy (*Kenya Adler*), Fletcher Davies (*Stanley Livingston*), Neal Henderson (*Mr. Allen*), Andrew Herbert (*Colin Carruthers-Carstairs*), Debbie Douglas (*Prentice as a Child*), Ed Rogers (*Witch Doctor*), Ben Cadlett (*Ben*), Chuck Wells (*Warrior*), The Meshpoka (*Themselves*), Bill Babcock (*Barroom Tough*), Dave Friedman (*Barroom Bum*).

The ee's are silent in Pantsari's character name and so should have been the entire film. Or better yet, not made at all. Pantsari is sent to find a missing child, kidnaped in Africa 15 years ago. The child, if found, is in line to inherit a million-dollar estate. With Pantsari are two of the family's conniving cousins, who will get the money if the child is not found, and Davies, who is after a great white gorilla. Pantsari hires an old drunk, Duffy, as their guide and he takes them right to a vicious African tribe, ruled by guess who? The lost child, who now gets her money. Also along the way, it is discovered the white ape is really a Nazi in an ape suit in hiding. Sills, the woman who runs the tribe, talks Pantsari into staying in Africa with her. They all should have been boiled and eaten for dinner.

p, David F. Friedman, William Allen Castleman; d, Tsanusdi; w, Friedman; ph, Paul Hipp (Eastmancolor); ed, Bob Freeman; md, Billy Allen, William Loose; art d, Lee Fischer; cos, Fischer; ch, Rene Jensen; makeup, Ron Kinney.

Comedy   (PR:O MPAA:R)

TRADING PLACES*½** (1983) 106m PAR c

Dan Aykroyd (*Louis Winthorpe III*), Eddie Murphy (*Billy Ray Valentine*), Ralph Bellamy (*Randolph Duke*), Don Ameche (*Mortimer Duke*), Denholm Elliott (*Coleman*), Kristin Holby (*Penelope Witherspoon*), Paul Gleason (*Clarence Beeks*), Jamie Lee Curtis (*Ophelia*), Alfred Drake (*President of Exchange*), Bo Diddley (*Pawnbroker*), Frank Oz (*Corrupt Cop*), James Belusha (*Harvey*), Al Franken, Tom Davis (*Baggage Handlers*), Jim Gallagher, Bonnie Behrend, Jim Newell, Richard D. Fisher, Jr., Anthony DiSabantino, Sunnie Merrill, Mary St. John, David Schwartz, Maurice Woods, Bonnie Tremenal (*D&D Employees*), Tom Degidon, Alan Dellay, Ray D'Amore, Herb Peterson, Walt Gorney, William Magerman, Florence Anglin, Bobra Suiter, Sue Dugan, B. Constance Barry (*Duke Domestics*), P. Jay Sidney (*Heritage Club Doorman*), Avon Long (*Ezra*), Tom Mardirosian (*Officer Pantuzzi*), Charles Brown (*Officer Reynolds*), Robert Curtis-Brown (*Todd*), Nicholas Guest (*Harry*), John Bedford-Lloyd (*Andrew*), Tony Sherer (*Philip*), Robert Earl Jones (*Attendant*), Robert E. Lee, Eddie Jones, John McCurry, Peter Hock (*Cops*), Clint Smith (*Doo Rag Lenny*), Ron Taylor (*Big Black Guy*), James D. Turner (*Even Bigger Black Guy*), Giancarlo Esposito, Steve Hofvendahl (*Cellmates*), James Eckhouse (*Guard*), Gwyllum Evans (*President of Heritage Club*), Michele Mais, Barra Kahn (*Hookers*), Bill Cobbs (*Bartender*), Joshua Daniels (*Party Goer*), Jacques Sandulescu (*Creepy Man*), W.B. Brydon (*Bank Manager*), Margaret H. Flynn (*D&D Receptionist*), Kelly Curtis (*Muffy*), Tracy K. Shaffer (*Constance*), Susan Fallender (*Bunny*), Lucianne Buchanan (*President's Mistress*), Paul Garcia, Jed Gillin (*Junior Executives*), Jimmy Raitt (*Ophelia's Client*), Kate Taylor (*Duke's Secretary*), Philip Bosco (*Doctor*), Bill Boggs (*Newscaster*), Deborah Reagan (*Harvey's Girl Friend*), Don McLeod (*Gorilla*), Stephan Stucker (*Station

Master), Richard Hunt (*Wilson*), Paul Austin, John Randolph Jones, Jack Davidson, Bernie McInerney (*Traders*), Maurice D. Copeland (*Secretary of Agriculture*), Ralph Clanton, Bryan Clark (*Officials*), Gary Klar, Afemo Omilami (*Longshoremen*), Shelly Chee Chee Hall (*Monica*), Donna Palmer (*Gladys*), Barry Dennen (*Demitri*).

Director John Landis has been known to often go overboard in his desire for laughter and this time he has kept a tight rein on his usual proclivities to manufacture a fine comedy with a few gratuitous foul words that gives it the "R" rating. The movie owes more than a passing nod to Mark Twain's *The Prince and the Pauper* as street wise guy Murphy and upscale yuppie Aykroyd are forced to switch positions in life by the whim of two rich brothers, Ameche and Bellamy, who make a one dollar bet about the nature of heredity versus environment and proceed to pay the price for their playing with other persons' lives. Aykroyd works for the two brothers, as conniving a pair as anyone who ever planned a coup against the king. He has a butler, Elliott, and a fiancee, Holby, both of whom are equally predictable in their stuffed shirt (or blouse) ways. Murphy is a street hustler who earns a living by pretending to be blind and lame. Ameche and Bellamy argue that if Murphy had been given the same opportunities as Aykroyd, would he respond in the same fashion? Conversely, if the privileges of rank and birth were removed from Aykroyd's life, would he become a street-wise punk? Ameche and Bellamy arrange for Aykroyd to be framed for a crime he did not commit, then they welcome Murphy into their fold and he is treated like a young prince. (If the similarity to Twain's story hasn't emerged by now, it never will.) Murphy proves that his years in back alleys have stood him in good stead and he begins coming up with all sorts of fresh ideas. There is great fun watching the rise of Murphy and the fall of Aykroyd but the best moments occur when the two boys team up to overthrow the empire of Ameche and Bellamy, thereby giving the aged duo the chance to be hoist on their own petards. Aykroyd meets and falls for Curtis and his formerly unsympathetic characterization turns lovable when he is faced with his plight. Once he and Murphy unite to thwart a business coup planned by Ameche and Bellamy, the picture ends. Although it tends to rely heavily on slapstick in the second half, the movie does provide a goodly share of laughs and seeing Ameche again, after a screen absence of more than a dozen years since THE BOATNIKS, was a pleasure. He was later hired by Ron Howard for COCOON and won the Best Supporting Oscar. Director Landis can be very good or very bad. This is one of his very good movies, despite overtones of racism that had no business being in the story. It appears that he and the writers were attempting to raise the social consciousness of the country with their work but that never happened. Instead, all they did was make millions laugh, which should have been enough reward for anyone. All the four-letter words and the casual sexual references seemed out of place in what might have been classified as a "screwball comedy" of the 1930s.

p, Aaron Russo; d, John Landis; w, Timothy Harris, Herschel Weingrod; ph, Robert Paynter (Metrocolor); m, Elmer Bernstein; ed, Malcolm Campbell; prod d, Gene Rudolf; set d, George DeTitta, Sr., George DeTitta, Jr.; cos, Deborah Nadoolman.

Comedy   **Cas.**   (PR:C-O MPAA:R)

TRAFFIC** (1972, Fr.) 89m Corona/COL c (TRAFIC)

Jacques Tati (*Mons. Hulot*), Maria Kimberly (*Maria the Public Relations Girl*), Marcel Fravel (*Truck Driver*), Honore Bostel (*Managing Director of ALTRA*), Tony Kneppers (*Dutch Garage Proprietor*), Francois Maisongrosse (*Francois*), Franco Ressel, Mario Zanuelli.

Jacques Tati's fifth picture in 25 years (his fourth, PLAYTIME, was not released until 1973), TRAFFIC is a collection of sight gags concerning the modern problem of automobile overpopulation. Tati again plays himself in this English-dubbed outing-the rain-coated, pipe-smoking eccentric-though now he has invented an ultra-modern camping vehicle. With Kimberly, the public relations girl of his firm, he plans to take his new car from Paris to an Amsterdam auto show. Kimberly takes off first in her red convertible sports car, followed by a station wagon full of props (fake birch trees) and then Tati in a truck which houses his camper. The truck first gets a flat tire which Tati changes on the shoulder of the road, nearly being hit by passing traffic. He then runs out of gas. When he doesn't show up at the car show, Kimberly doubles back and looks for him. She helps him out of his mess but gets him into another by speeding through a customs check. Tati is detained by customs officials who demand to know everything about his camper. A demonstration of the camper's modern devices includes an electric shaver which is hidden in the steering wheel and a front grill which also doubles as a cooking grill. By now Tati has missed the opening of the auto show. Adding further to his misadventures is a chain of car crashes which rivals Jean-Luc Godard's WEEKEND (1967). Tati doesn't get to the show until everyone else has left, though a few stragglers take interest in his vehicle. He leaves with Kimberly in tow, choosing to take the train back to Paris instead of dodging traffic. Any plot synopsis of a Tati picture proves to be fruitless since what is most important are the visual gags. So vital are the visuals that Tati rarely uses dialog, thereby negating the need for subtitles. One of the picture's funniest moments is Tati's attempt to climb the vines that cling to a house, pulling them down in the process. Instead of stopping there, however, he yanks them back up and winds up hanging upside down by his foot, refusing to give in and yell for help. Many of the film's brightest moments do not even include Tati (it was his wish that he would eventually be only a minor character in his films). One gag has Kimberly thinking that her dog has been crushed by the back wheel of her sports car. She is unaware that a group of mischievous passersby simply put one of their coats (which is made from the same fur as the dog) under the wheel. Other brilliant bits are created through montage--various people are seen picking their noses while waiting for traffic to advance; or a connection is made between the car a person drives and their physical appearance; or a connection between the person and the movement of their windshield wipers. Tati's films are unlike those of Charlie Chaplin in that Chaplin's style is a personal one that depends on emotional response, whereas Tati's is one of distancing and commenting on modernization. And again Tati's insights into modern life make for one of the freshest and funniest pictures to hit the screen in years.

p, Robert Dorfmann; d, Jacques Tati; w, Tati, Jacques LaGrange; ph, Marcel Weiss, Edouard van den Enden (Eastmancolor); m, Charles Dumont; ed, Maurice Laumain, Sophie Tatischeff [Tati]; md, Bernard Gerard; art d, Adrien de Rooy.

Comedy   **Cas.**   **(PR:AAA   MPAA:G)**

TRAFFIC IN CRIME**   (1946) 56m REP bw

Kane Richmond (Sam Wire), Adele Mara (Silk), Anne Nagel (Ann Marlowe), Wilton Graff (Nick Cantrell), Roy Barcroft (Tip Hogan), Arthur Loft (Murphy), Wade Crosby (Dumbo), Dick Curtis (Jake Schultz), Harry V. Cheshire (Dan Marlowe), Bob Wilke (Hogan's Driver), Charles Sullivan (Cab Driver).

Plot is stretched a little bit in this small-time crime film about an undercover policeman trying to break up not one, but two, gambling rings in a small West Coast community. Richmond is the undercover cop assigned to the case and, in the end, he not only gets the two factions to knock each other off, but to take care of the cops on the take also. The plot line appears to have been lifted whole from Dashiell Hammett's brilliant novel "Red Harvest."

p, Donald H. Brown; d, Lesley Selander; w, David Lang (based on a story by Leslie Turner White); ph, Bud Thackery; ed, Les Orlebeck; md, Mort Glickman; art d, Gano Chittenden.

Crime Thriller   **(PR:A   MPAA:NR)**

TRAGEDY AT MIDNIGHT, A**   (1942) 69M REP bw

John Howard (Greg Sherman), Margaret Lindsay (Beth Sherman), Roscoe Karns (Cassidy), Mona Barrie (Mrs. Wilton), Keye Luke (Ah Foo), Hobart Cavanaugh (Mr. Miller), Paul Harvey (Landeck), Lillian Bond (Lola), Miles Mander (Dr. Wilton), William "Billy" Newell (Swanson), Wendell Niles (Announcer), Archie Twitchell (Henry Carney).

Howard and Lindsay are a married pair who like to solve murders that stymie the police. He even has a popular radio show on which he solves contemporary crimes while the cops fume. Everything falls into their laps as they use a friend's apartment only to find a girl murdered there. They take off just as the police arrive and, while dodging the cops, fight good-naturedly and start finding the real killer. Finale has him a step ahead of the cops, broadcasting the crime's solution and all the background of the case on his radio show. An apparent attempt by the small studio to rip off the popular THIN MAN series (see Index).

p, Robert North, d, Joseph Santley; w, Isabel Dawn (based on a story by Hal Hudson, Sam Duncan); ph, Ernest Miller; m, Cy Feuer; ed, Murray Seldeen, Edward Mann; art d, John Victor Macray.

Mystery   **(PR:A   MPAA:NR)**

TRAGEDY OF A RIDICULOUS MAN, THE**½
(1982, Ital.) 118m Ladd/WB c

Ugo Tognazzi (Primo), Anouk Aimee (Barbara), Laura Morante (Laura), Victor Cavallo (Adelfo), Olimpia Carlisi (Chiromant), Vittorio Caprioli (Marshal), Renato Salvatori (Colonel), Riki Tognazzi (Giovanni), Don Backy (Crossing Keeper), Cosimo Cinieri (Magistrate), Margherita Chiari, Gaetano Ferrari, Gianni Migliavacca, Ennio Ferrari, Franco Trevisi, Pietro Longari Ponzoni.

Bertolucci barely tops his previous effort, LUNA (1979), in this father-son drama set in the Italian countryside amidst a backdrop of terrorism. Tognazzi is cast as a cheese manufacturer who suffers through the disappearance of his son, unsure (as is the audience) whether or not he has been kidnaped. As usual with Bertolucci the film's style and bravura camerawork are clearly in the forefront, but the politics and social commentary never quite find their place.

p, Giovanni Bertolucci; d&w, Bernardo Bertolucci; ph, Carlo DiPalma (Technicolor); m, Ennio Morricone; ed,) Gabriella Cristani; prod d, Gianni Silvestri; cos, Lina Taviani.

Drama   **(PR:A   MPAA:PG)**

TRAIL BEYOND, THE**   (1934) 55m Lone Star/MON bw

John Wayne (Rod Drew), Noah Beery, Sr (George Newsome), Noah Beery, Jr (Wabi), Verna Hillie (Felice Newsome), Iris Lancaster (Marie), Robert Frazer (Jules LaRocque), Earl Dwire (Benoit), Eddie Parker (Ryan the Mountie), James Marcus, Reed Howes, Artie Ortego.

Wayne, in an early role, is searching the West for a girl and trying-- at the same time--to help Beery find a gold mine that is rightfully his. Turns out bad guy Frazer has his hands on both and it is up to Wayne to foil his plans of evil. With some help from his guns and his fists, Wayne handily accomplishes both. The film is a remake of THE WOLF HUNTERS (1926), which was remade again in 1949. Writer Parsons produced the later version, but mercifully had no hand in the writing. This was the first of the Wayne-starring series westerns made by Monogram in which studio-employed hacks failed to write the screenplay, a mistake in this case.

p, Paul Malvern; d, Robert N. Bradbury; w, Lindsley Parsons (based on the novel The Wolf Hunters by James Oliver Curwood); ph, Archie Stout; ed, Charles Hunt; art d, E.R. Hickson.

Western   **Cas.**   **(PR:A   MPAA:NR)**

TRAIL BLAZERS, THE**   (1940) 58M REP bw

Robert Livingston (Stony Brooke), Bob Steele (Tucson Smith), Rufe Davis (Lullaby Joslin), Pauline Moore (Marcia), Weldon Heyburn (Jeff Bradley), Carroll Nye (Jim Chapman), Tom Chatterton (Maj. Kelton), Si Jenks (The Dentist), Mary Field (Alice Chapman), John Merton (Mason), Rex Lease (Reynolds), Robert Blair (Fowler), Barry Hays, Pascale Perry, Harry Strang.

Old cowboy story with just a slight twist, because not only are the bad guys battling the honest folks of Fort Dodge, but also technology. Bad guys don't want the telegraph coming into their territory, because news of their exploits will now travel faster and bring out the U.S. Cavalry that much faster after them. But the bad guys don't fight the townspeople, they do battle with a small Cavalry troop sent out to protect the telegraph's progress. This was part of the THREE MESQUITEERS series (see Index), with Livingston, Steele, and Davis holding down the leads as the undercover men responsible for bringing the new form of communication into town no matter what the obstacles.

p, Harry Grey; d, George Sherman; w, Barry Shipman (based on characters created by William Colt MacDonald and a story by Earle Snell); ph, William Nobles; m, Cy Feuer; ed, Tony Martinelli.

Western   **(PR:A   MPAA:NR)**

TRAIL DRIVE, THE**   (1934) 60m UNIV bw

Key Maynard, Cecilia Parker, William Gould, Wally Wales [Hal Taliaferro], Ben Corbett, Lafe McKee, Alan [AP] Bridge, Bob Kortman, Frank Rice, Fern Emmett, Jack Rockwell, Slim Whitaker, Frank Ellis, Hank Bell, Edward Coxen, Bob Reeves, Art Mix, Jack Kirk, Buck Bucko, Roy Bucko, Bud McClure, "Tarzan" the Horse.

Photography-wise, this is one of Maynard's better westerns, but acting-wise, one of his more lame. Maynard leads a cattle drive with the men being paid in scrip. He gets the beef there on time but the rancher backs down on payment, so it's up to Maynard to collect in cold hard cash. He does, of course, with fists flying.

p, Ken Maynard; d&w, Alan James; ph, Ted McCord.

Western   **Cas.**   **(PR:A   MPAA:NR)**

TRAIL DUST**   (1936) 77m PAR bw

William Boyd (Hopalong Cassidy), James Ellison (Johnny Nelson), George ["Gabby"] Hayes (Windy), Stephen Morris [Morris Ankrum] (Text), Gwynne Shipman (Beth), Britt Wood (Lanky), Earl Askam (Red), John Beach (Hank), Ted Adams (Wilson), Al St. John (Al), Kenneth Harlan (Officer), Dick Dickinson, Al Bridge, Tom Halligan, Dan Wolheim, Harold Daniels, John Elliott, George Chesebro, Emmett Day, Robert Drew.

Boyd, Ellison, and sidekick Hayes battle an unscrupulous cattle combine that wants to stop a cattle drive before it can reach the drought-stricken North and they win out with fast guns. Good laughs are provided when Ellison attempts to sing. Note the presence of Al "Fuzzy" St. John as one of the bad guys before he matriculated into comic-sidekick roles. The eighth in the series of HOPALONG CASSIDY westerns (see Index).

p, Harry Sherman; d, Nate Watt; w, Al Martin (based on a story by Clarence E. Mulford); ph, Archie Stout; m, Charles Bradshaw; ed, Robert Warwick.

Western   **(PR:A   MPAA:NR)**

TRAIL GUIDE*½   (1952) 60m RKO bw

Tim Holt (Tim), Linda Douglas [Mary Jo Tarola] (Peg), Frank Wilcox (Regan), Robert Sherwood (Kenny), John Pickard (Dawson), Kenneth MacDonald (Wheeler), Wendy Waldron (Mary), Patricia Wright (Katie), Tom London (Old Timer), John Merton (Dale), Richard Martin (Chito Rafferty), Mauritz Hugo.

One of a series of films that never really caught on with the public. Typical western shoot-'em-up has Holt and sidekick Martin leading a group of farmer immigrants across the West to the so-called promised land. After battling the elements and Indians, they arrive at their destination only to find the cattlemen not wanting anyone to fence off the area. Holt and Martin are set up on murder charges and almost strung up. The two finally break free and get the goods on the real killers and establish the new families. A side plot had Douglas, whose brother has been killed by the ranchers, going after Holt and Martin, with Holt finally winning her heart along with her trust. Each of the Holt films lost money but the series continued to be made. This one lost a total of $20,000 when it came out and it's not difficult to see why.

p, Herman Schlom; d, Lesley Selander; w, Arthur E. Orloff (based on a story by William Lively); ph, Nicholas Musuraca; ed, Samuel E. Beetley; md, C. Bakaleinikoff; art d, Albert S. D'Agostino, Carroll Clark.

Western   **(PR:A MPAA:NR)**

TRAIL OF KIT CARSON**   (1945) 57m REP bw

Allan "Rocky" Lane, Helen Talbot, Tom London, Twinkle Watts, Roy Barcroft, Kenne Duncan, Jack Kirk, Bud Geary, Tom Dugan, George Chesebro, Bob Wilke, Freddie Chapman, Dickie Dillon, Herman Hack, John Carpenter, Henry Wills, Tom Steele.

Lane is the title character who is investigating circumstances surrounding his partner's death. It all appears to be accidental but things are not always what they seem, are they? Routine western fare for the cowboy hero.

p, Stephen Auer; d, Lesley Selander; w, Jack Natteford, Albert DeMond (based on a story by Natteford); ph, Bud Thackery; ed, Ralph Dixon; md, Richard Cherwin; art d, Fred A. Ritter; set d, George Milo; spec eff, Howard Lydecker, Theodore Lydecker.

Western   **(PR:A MPAA:NR)**

TRAIL OF ROBIN HOOD**½   (1950) 67m REP c

Roy Rogers (*Himself*), Penny Edwards (*Toby Aldridge*), Gordon Jones (*Splinters McGonigle, Blacksmith*), Jack Holt (*Himself*), Emory Parnell (*J. Corwin Aldridge*), Clifton Young (*Mitch McCall, Foreman*), James Magill (*Murtagh*), Carol Nugent (*Sis McGonigle*), Edward Cassidy (*Sheriff Duffy*), Rex Allen, Allan "Rocky" Lane, Monte Hale, William Farnum, Tom Tyler, Ray "Crash" Corrigan, Kermit Maynard, Tom Keene, George Chesebro, Foy Willing and the Riders of the Purple Sage (*Guest Stars*), Trigger the Horse.

Rogers always made sure the cowboy story line never got stale and this pleasing yarn is one of his best and the last done in color. Retired B-western star Holt is a great guy who sells Christmas trees at cost to families of poor kids. However, a big tree corporation comes in and starts paying off the woodcutters to drive the prices up and Holt out of business. Roy arrives and with the aid of a host of other screen cowboy friends he gets Holt's business back on its feet and the trees into the kids' houses in time for a Merry Christmas for all. The film had appearances by a host of cowboy stars including Rex Allen. A highlight of the film occurs when longtime western bad-guy Chesebro, shunned by the other old-time players, states: "...I've been a villain in Jack Holt's movies for 20 years; now I'd like to be on the right side for a change." Rogers sings out, appropriately, "Ev'ry Day Is Christmas in the West" and "Get a Christmas Tree for Johnny." The Riders croon "Home Town Jubilee."

p, Edward J. White; d, William Witney; w, Gerald Geraghty; ph, John MacBurnie (Trucolor); m, Nathan Scott; ed, Tony Martinelli; art d, Frank Arrigo; set d, John McCarthy, Jr., James Redd; cos, Adele Palmer; spec eff, Howard Lydecker, Theodore Lydecker; m/l, Jack Elliott, Foy Willing.

Western   **Cas.**   **(PR:A MPAA:NR)**

TRAIL OF TERROR**   (1935) 59m Supreme bw

Bob Steele, Beth Marion, Forrest Taylor, Charles King, Lloyd Ingraham, Frank Lyman, Jr, Charles K. French, Richard Cramer, Nancy DeShon.

In order to infiltrate a gang of outlaws, government agent Steele must go under cover. Once he's part of their team, Steele's able to get the information he needs. Ordinary story, extraordinary star, average out to middling entertainment.

p, A.W. Hackel; d&w, Robert N. Bradbury.

Western   **Cas.**   **(PR:AA MPAA:NR)**

TRAIL OF TERROR**   (1944) 63m Stern-Alexander/PRC bw

Dave "Tex" O'Brien (*Tex Wyatt/Curly Wyatt*), Jim Newill (*Jim Steele*), Guy Wilkerson (*Panhandle Perkins*), Patricia Knox (*Belle Blaine*), Jack Ingram (*Nevada Simmons*), I. Stanford Jolley (*Hank*), Budd Buster (*Monte*), Kenne Duncan (*Sam*), Frank Ellis (*Joe*), Robert Hill (*Capt. Curtis*), Dan White, Jimmy Aubrey, Rose Plummer, Tom Smith, Artie Ortego.

A western in a highbrow mode. O'Brien plays twin brothers, one of whom is killed by a gang to which he belonged. O'Brien is now Tex Wyatt, Texas Ranger, who joins the gang himself to break it up. They accept him, as does

his late brother's girl friend Knox, until his old buddies inadvertently reveal his identity. The big clash is staged with the Texas Rangers winning and also recovering some of the money the gang had stolen from stagecoach robberies. (See TEXAS RANGERS series, Index.)

p, Alfred Stern, Arthur Alexander; d&w, Oliver Drake; ph, Ira Morgan; m, Lee Zahler; ed, Charles Henkel, Jr.; art d, Fred Preble; m/l, Dave Tex O'Brien, Jim Newill.

Western   **(PR:A MPAA:NR)**

TRAIL OF THE LONESOME PINE, THE***½   (1936) 102m PAR c

Sylvia Sidney (*June Tolliver*), Fred MacMurray (*Jack Hale*), Henry Fonda (*Dave Tolliver*), Fred Stone (*Judd Tolliver*), Nigel Bruce (*Mr. Thurber*), Beulah Bondi (*Melissa*), Robert Barrat (*Buck Falin*), Spanky McFarland (*Buddy*), Fuzzy Knight (*Tater*), Otto Fries (*Corsey*), Samuel S. Hinds (*Sheriff*), Alan Baxter, Margaret Armstrong, Ricca Allen (*Tollivers*), Fern Emmett (*Lena*), Richard Carle (*Ezra*), Henry Brandon (*Wade Falin*), Philip Barker (*Merd Falin*), Bob Kortman (*Gorley Falin*), Charlotte Wynters (*Jack Hale's Sister*), Frank Rice (*Zeke*), Hilda Vaughn (*Gaptown Teacher*), Charles Middleton (*Blacksmith*), Clara Blandick (*Landlady*), Russ Powell (*Storekeeper*), Irving Bacon (*Mailman*), John Larkin (*Ebony*), Frank McGlynn, Sr. (*Preacher*), Lowell Drew (*Bartender*), Lee Phelps (*Taylor*), Jack Curtis (*Store Clerk*), Betty Farrington (*Louisville Teacher*), Jim Burke (*Leader*), John Beck, Fred Burns, Jim Welch, Hank Bell, Bud Geary, Ed LeSaint (*Tolliver Clan*), Bill McCormick, Jim Corey (*Falin Clan*), Norman Willis (*Old Dave in Prolog*), George Ernest (*Dave at Age 10*), Powell Clayton (*Dave at Age 5*), Tuffy the Dog.

First a novel in 1908, then a stage play, then two silent movie productions in 1916 and 1923. THE TRAIL OF THE LONESOME PINE became the first outdoor Technicolor three-strip film as well as Fonda's first movie in color. Set in the backwoods of Kentucky in the early years of the 20th Century, it's the story of feudin' and fussin' mountain people. Two clans have been battling for years and the movie begins as one family, led by Barrat, is firing at the cabin of the Stone family, just as Bondi is giving birth to the daughter who will mature to be Sidney. The feud has been going on so long that no one seems to quite recall what started it. Time passes and Sidney grows up under the watchful eye of her brother, Fonda. The railroad decides to come into the area and MacMurray is one of the engineers. Fonda is almost killed in a fight with the rival clan, and MacMurray saves his life, for which Fonda is much obliged, but that doesn't alter the fact that Fonda doesn't much cotton to the moon-eyed way MacMurray is looking at sister Sidney. Fonda is of a mind to keep his sister away from city slickers such as MacMurray and feels she would be better off in love with a local mountain type, someone who knows the territory and appreciates the way they like to live. More time passes and the sleepy area begins to bustle. The advent of the railroad has brought new prosperity. MacMurray arranges for Sidney to be accepted in a school far away from the mountains, in Louisville. Fonda is angered that his beloved sister will be leaving and lets MacMurray know that. The two men get into a fist fight but then combine their talents to fend off the Barrat clan, who have launched an onslaught on the railroad camp. The workers are frightened for their lives and leave the area in a shambles. Younger brother McFarland is killed in the battle and when Sidney returns from school in Louisville, she calls for a blood bath. MacMurray is unaccustomed to this kind of behavior and attempts to inject a modicum of sanity into the proceedings, thereby angering Sidney. Fonda is beginning to realize that this feud must cease and he tries to make peace by offering to meet Barrat, shake hands, and come out tranquil. Barrat accepts and the time is set for the ritual handshake. Just before that happens, Fonda is shot by one of the rival clan. Barrat can't believe what's happened and pays a visit to the Stone house to express his sorrow as Fonda lies in bed, moments away from dying. Fonda bids Stone and Barrat to shake hands, then watches as Sidney and MacMurray move in close to each other and Fonda is able to die happy. Often poignant, lots of action, well-photographed, and even musically scored with four songs, this is a slice of Americana that proved successful at the box office and is well remembered by those who saw it first time around. C.B. DeMille's version starred Charlotte Walker in the Sidney role (1916), while Mary Miles Minter played the part in the 1923 version, directed by Charles Maigne. McFarland was only eight years old and already a veteran of several "Our Gang" shorts and showed that he could do other things beyond his work in the kiddie comedies. Years later, Al Capp admitted that he'd based his famed "Li'l Abner" character on Fonda's role in this and collectors of comic book lore will recognize some of Capp's early drawings as looking quite similar to Fonda, before he beefed up the mountain boy. Since the story is set in a distinct period, watching it today is just as pleasurable as it was back in the 1930s because there is no feeling of the material being dated. As an itinerant rover, Fuzzy Knight does a fine job acting and warbling the tunes. The songs were "A Melody from the Sky" (nominated for Best Song Oscar), "Stack O' Lee Blues" (which may have been "Stagger Lee"), and "When It's Twilight on the Trail" (all by Sidney Mitchell and Lou Alter), plus Harry Carroll's "Trail of the Lonesome Pine."

p, Walter Wanger; d, Henry Hathaway; w, Grover Jones, Harvey Thew, Horace McCoy (based on the novel by John Fox, Jr.); ph, Howard Greene, Robert C. Bruce (Technicolor); ed, Robert Bischoff; md, Boris Morros; art d, Hans Dreier.

Outdoor Drama   **(PR:A-C MPAA:NR)**

TRAIL OF THE PINK PANTHER, THE*

(1982) 97m Titan-MGM/UA c

Peter Sellers (*Inspector Clouseau*), David Niven (*Sir Charles Litton*), Herbert Lom (*Dreyfus*), Richard Mulligan (*Clouseau Sr.*), Joanna Lumley (*Marie Jouvet*), Capucine (*Lady Litton*), Robert Loggia (*Bruno*), Harvey Korman (*Prof. Balls*), Burt Kwouk (*Cato*), Graham Stark (*Hercule*), Peter Arne (*Col. Bufoni*), Andre Maranne (*Francois*), Ronald Fraser (*Dr. Longet*), Leonard Rossiter (*Quinlan*), Marne Maitland (*Commissioner Lasorde*), Dudley Sutton, Harold Kasket, Liz Smith, Danny Schiller, Denise Crosby, William Hootkins, Kathleen St. John, Harold Berens, Daniel Peacock, Lucca Mezzofanti, Madlena Nedeva, Arthur Howard, Weston Gavin, Marc Smith, John Cassady, Gary Whelan, Joe Praml, Christopher Reich.

A great outpouring of greed must have been the motivation for this stitched-together pastiche of out-takes and old sequences from previous "Panther" movies, as Peter Sellers was already dead two years or so when this was issued. It's a combination of CITIZEN KANE and "This Is Your Life" as Edwards found several sequences, edited them together (and fooled nobody, as Sellers seemed to age, then grow younger, depending on which scene we saw), and hoped to wring the last few dollars out of the public. The famed bauble known as "The Pink Panther" is back in the museum where it all began. It's stolen once more and Sellers is again assigned to capture it. Lom is seen as Sellers' boss, twisting and turning in the psychiatric office of his doctor, Fraser. Several unrelated scenes of Sellers at work and suddenly his plane is reported "missing," thus sparking TV newshen Lumley to go out and interview all of the people who touched the inspector's life. She meets Niven (who looked terrible as he was suffering from "Lou Gehrig's disease" that was to take his life), Kwouk, Stark, Capucine, and others. She also meets the inspector's father, Mulligan, in her quest for a TV profile on the detective. At the end of the film, Edwards promises yet another "Panther" film, the inept picture that starred Ted Wass, and audiences groaned. It was idea whose time had come and gone. In this film, it was patently obvious that a stand-in was used, that an actor was brought in to dub the voice, that the whole thing was cheap exploitation of the memory of a man who had convulsed audiences for years. Making this film was a denigration of Sellers and put the entire affair into the same bucket of worms as the death merchants who flocked to make all of those Bruce Lee ripoff pictures. We would have given it no stars whatsoever except for the fact that, while the master is at work, there are laughs galore. They should have left well enough alone. Shame on Blake Edwards and everyone else associated with this.

p, Blake Edwards, Tony Adams; d, Edwards; w, Frank Waldman, Tom Waldman, Blake Edwards, Geoffrey Edwards (based on a story by Blake Edwards and characters created by David H. DePatie, Friz Freleng); ph, Dick Bush (Panavision, Technicolor); m, Henry Mancini; ed, Alan Jones; prod d, Peter Mullins; art d, Tim Hutchinson, Alan Tomkins, John Siddall; set d, Jack Stephens; cos, Patricia Edwards.

Comedy   **Cas.**   **(PR:C   MPAA:PG)**

TRAIL OF THE SILVER SPURS*

(1941) 57 m MON bw

Ray Corrigan (*"Crash"*), John King (*"Dusty"*), Max Terhune (*"Alibi"*), I. Stanford Jolley (*Jingler*), Dorothy Short (*Nancy*), Milburn Morante (*Nordick*), George Chesebro (*Wilson*), Eddie Dean (*Stoner*), Kermit Maynard, Frank Ellis, Carl Mathews, Steve Clark.

Story tells the tale of a supposed ghost town with just one old man left in it because he still thinks there is gold around. First, fool's gold is found, sparking a renewal in the town; then the real thing is discovered. A group of cowboys arrive and the old man conjures up ghosts to keep people away. Using the old man's bag of tricks the three heroes round up a couple of villains and the old coot is, finally, a rich and happy old man. (See RANGE BUSTERS series, Index.)

p, George W. Weeks; d, S. Roy Luby; w, Earle Snell (based on a story by Elmer Clifton); ph, Robert Cline; ed, Roy Claire; md, Frank Sanucci; m/l, Lew Porter, Johnnie Lange.

Western   **(PR:A   MPAA:NR)**

TRAIL OF THE VIGILANTES**

(1940) 75m UNIV bw

Franchot Tone (*"Kansas" Tim Mason*), Warren William (*Mark Dawson*), Broderick Crawford (*Swanee*), Andy Devine (*Meadows*), Mischa Auer (*Dmitri Bolo*), Porter Hall (*Sheriff Corley*), Peggy Moran (*Barbara Thornton*), Samuel S. Hinds (*George Preston*), Charles Trowbridge (*John Thornton*), Paul Fix (*Lefty*), Harry Cording (*Phil*), Max Wagner (*Joe*), Earle Hodgins, Hank Bell.

A no-frills western that pokes a little fun at its own genre. Tone is a rookie newspaperman from back East sent out to help stop William's protection-racket gang. He gets help from Crawford and Devine along with Russian Auer and the foursome gets into one scrape after another. Straight-up laughs combined with gunplay give it a strange mix. Tone gets some genuine laughs at the beginning with his first-time exploits on a horse. The film also marked Tone's return to movies after he had left Hollywood to pursue a Broadway career. Moran almost steals the film as a wild rancher's daughter, who will stop at nothing to get her hands on Tone. The film was intended to be a standard western, but veteran director Dwan knew better than to

follow the original script; he had it doctored into parody in a one-day rewrite session.

p&d, Allan Dwan; w, Harold Shumate; ph, Joseph Valentine, Milton Krasner; ed, Edward Curtiss; art d, Jack Otterson; cos, Vera West.

Western   **(PR:A   MPAA:NR)**

TRAIL OF THE YUKON*

(1949) 67m MON bw

Kirby Grant (*Bob McDonald*), Suzanne Dalbert (*Marie*), Bill Edwards (*Jim Blaine*), Dan Seymour (*Duval*), William Forrest (*Dawson*), Anthony Warde (*Muskeg*), Maynard Holmes (*Buck*), Jay Silverheels (*Poleon*), Iris Adrian (*Paula*), Guy Beach (*Matt Blaine*), Stanley Andrews (*Rogers*), Dick Elliott (*Sullivan*), Bill Kennedy (*Constable*), Harrison Hearne (*Bank Teller*), Peter Mamakos (*Rand*), Burt Wenland, Alan [Al] Bridge, Wally Walker, Wilbur Mack, Chinook the Wonder Dog.

Chinook the Wonder Dog, in a film debut, is better than the three main characters of the film in performing such heroic tasks as knocking the guns out of bad men's hands, untying people who have been kidnaped, and other great deeds of derring-do. A slow-moving tale about Mountie Grant and reformed crook Edwards, who join forces to catch some thieves. Edwards joins Grant, who was chasing him in the first place for a bank robbery, but he saves himself a jail sentence and goes straight to help Grant and his puppy. They finally uncover the real plot as a banker is behind all the shenanigans to gyp stockholders in a mining town. Plenty of shooting and chases, but not on horses, rather in canoes. The Yukon territory provides some great background scenery. Unfortunately, it is stock footage for the most part, and ill-matched to the rest of the film. The dog is the real star. Grant, hindered by an injury which forces him to use a cane, manages to get the redeemed Edwards and the beauteous Dalbert together with the aid of the pooch. He also sings one number, "A Shantyman's Life," which has nothing to do with the story line.

p, Lindsley Parsons; d, William X. Crowley; w, Oliver Drake (based on the novel *The Gold Hunters* by James Oliver Curwood); ph, William Sickner; ed, Ace Herman; md, Edward J. Kay; art d, Dave Milton.

Adventure   **(PR:A   MPAA:NR)**

TRAIL OF VENGEANCE**

(1937) 58m REP bw

Johnny Mack Brown (*Dude Ramsey*), Iris Meredith (*Jean Warner*), Warner Richmond (*Link Carson*), Karl Hackett (*Mart Pierson*), Earle Hodgins (*Buck Andrews*), Frank LaRue (*Tilden*), Frank Ellis (*Red Cassidy*), Lew Meehan (*Bill O'Donnell*), Frank Ball (*Steve Warner*), Dick Curtis (*Cartwright*), Jim Corey, Horace Murphy, Dick Cramer, Steve Clark, Budd Buster, Jack C. Smith, Jack Kirk, Francis Walker, Tex Palmer.

Brown is perfectly suited for his role as a rough cowboy stalking down the killer of his brother. He waltzes in during a brutal range war and his reputation as a gunslinger has both sides wanting his services. But he would rather find who did in his brother and it comes down to him and Richmond, who also fits the bad-guy role perfectly. Brown did many films for Republic Studios and this one is considered one of his better efforts.

p, A. W. Hackel; d, Sam Newfield; w, George Plympton, Fred Myton (based on a story by E. B. Mann); ph, Bert Longenecker; ed, S. Roy Luby, Tom Neff.

Western   **(PR:A   MPAA:NR)**

TRAIL RIDERS***

(1942) 55m MON bw (GB: OVERLAND TRAIL)

John King (*Dusty*), David Sharpe (*Davy*), Max Terhune (*Alibi*), Evelyn Finley (*Mary*), Forrest Taylor (*Rand*), Lynton Brent (*Jeff*), Charles King (*Cole*), Kermit Maynard (*Ace*), John Curtis (*Tiny*), Steve Clark (*Marshal Hammond*), Kenne Duncan (*Hammond, Jr.*), Frank LaRue (*Banker*), Bud Osborne, Tex Palmer, Dick Cramer, Frank Ellis, Mickey Harrison.

After a bank is robbed and Duncan is killed, Clark sends for the heroic Range Busters to nab the gang responsible. King, one of the town's leading citizens and head of a vigilante group, disapproves of this and runs the three cowboy heroes out of town. Little does anyone realize that King is actually the man behind the bank robbery and murder. Once this is learned a trap is set for the man and all ends happily. Typical Monogram western. (See RANGE BUSTERS series, Index.)

p, George W. Weeks; d, Robert Tansey; w, Frances Kavanaugh; ph, Robert Cline; ed, Roy Claire; md, Frank Sanucci.

Western   **Cas.**   **(PR:AA   MPAA:NR)**

TRAIL STREET***

(1947) 84m RKO bw

Randolph Scott (*Bat Masterson*), Robert Ryan (*Allen Harper*), Anne Jeffreys (*Ruby Stone*), George "Gabby" Hayes (*Billy Jones/Brandyhead Jones*), Madge Meredith (*Susan Pritchett*), Steve Brodie (*Logan Maury*), Billy House (*Carmody*), Virginia Sale (*Hannah*), Harry Woods (*Lance Larkin*), Jason Robards, Sr (*Jason*), Elena Warren (*Mrs. Brown*), Betty Hill (*Dance Hall Girl*), Al Murphy (*Dealer*), Ernie Adams (*Eben Bowen*), Kit Guard (*Drunk*), Guy Beach (*Doc Evans*), Jessie Arnold (*Jason's Wife*), Chris Willowbird (*Indian*), Frank McGlynn, Jr (*Tim McKeon*), Sarah Padden

(*Mrs. Ferguson*), Stanley Andrews (*Ferguson*), Forrest Taylor (*Dave*), Sy Jenks (*Charlie Thorne, Publisher*), Lew Harvey (*Heavy*), Paul Dunn, Donald Olson, Eugene Perrson (*Boys*), Roy Butler, Frank Austin, Carl Wester, Sam Lufkin, Joe Brockman (*Farmers*), Larry McGrath, Warren Jackson, Billy Vincent, Howard McCrorey, Glen McCarthy (*Henchmen*).

Scott protrays western legend Bat Masterson, notoriously fast with his guns. He is called into Liberal, Kansas, where the bad guys have the run of the town and are trying to get rid of the law-abiding farmers. With the ranchers-against-farmers battle raging, Scott helps out land agent Ryan. They plot and shoot everything in sight, finally cleaning things up so the farmers can grow their wheat in peace. Hayes adds the comedic touch with tall tales of Texas grasshoppers and other bits and pieces of advice. A box-office success, the film brought in a profit of $365,000.

p, Nat Holt; d, Ray Enright; w, Norman Houston, Gene Lewis (based on the novel *Golden Horizon* by William Corcoran); ph, J. Roy Hunt; m, Paul Sawtell; ed, Lyle Boyer; md, Constantin Bakaleinikoff; art d, Albert S. D'Agostino, Ralph Berger; set d, Darrell Silvera, John Sturtivant; spec eff, Russell A. Cully; m/l, "You May Not Remember," Ben Oakland, George Jessel; "You're Not the Only Pebble on the Beach," Stanley Carter, Harry Braisted (both sung by Anne Jeffreys).

Western   **Cas.**   **(PR:A   MPAA:NR)**

TRAIL TO GUNSIGHT**   (1944) 58m UNIV bw

Eddie Dew (*Dan Creede*), Maris Wrixon (*Mary Wagner*), Lyle Talbot (*Bill Hollister*), Fuzzy Knight (*Horatius*), Ray Whitley (*Barton*), Buzz Henry (*Tim Wagner*), Marie Austin (*Clementine*), Sarah Padden (*Ma Wagner*), Glenn Strange (*Duke Ellis*), Ray Bennett (*Bert Nelson*), Charles Morton (*Reb Tanner*), Forrest Taylor (*Sheriff*), Terry Frost, Jack Clifford, Henry Wills, Ezra Paulette, Len Giles, Charley Quirt (*Bar-6 Cowboys*).

When a man is killed, the blame is pinned on an innocent cowboy. He spends the next hour going after the real killer, using all the made-to-order B western devices at his disposal. Nothing unusual to be found here.

p, Oliver Drake; d, Vernon Keays; w, Bennett Cohen, Patricia Harper (based on a story by Jay Karth); ph, Maury Gertsman; ed, Russell Schoengarth; md, Paul Sawtell; art d, John B. Goodman, Abraham Grossman.

Western   **(PR:AA   MPAA:NR)**

TRAIL TO SAN ANTONE**   (1947) 67m REP bw

Gene Autry (*Himself*), Peggy Stewart (*Kit Barlow*), Sterling Holloway (*Droopy Stearns*), William Henry (*Rick Malloy*), John Duncan (*Ted Malloy*), Tristram Coffin (*Cal Young*), Dorothy Vaughan (*The "Commodore"*), Edward Keane (*Sheriff Jones*), Ralph Peters (*Sam*), Cass County Boys, Champion the Horse.

Instead of concerning himself with traditional western troubles, Autry is found at the racetrack trying to straighten things out. He wants to help a crippled jockey so he can ride Autry's main horse for the big race. The bad guy isn't a man, but a wild stallion that takes off with the speedy mare. Autry goes in search of the horses and, with a little help from technology, finds the horses by flying over the fields. In one of the more unbelievable moments of any film, he lassoes the mare from the airplane. He gets the horse back, the jockey gets over his crippling injury, and Autry plunks his guitar a little more.

p, Armand Schaefer; d, John English; w, Jack Natteford, Luci Ford; ph, William Bradford; m, Joseph Dubin; ed, Charles Craft; md, Morton Scott; art d, Gano Chittenden; cos, Adele Palmer; m/l, Deuce Spriggens, Sid Robin, Joe Burke, Marty Symes, Spade Cooley, Cindy Walker, Gene Autry.

Western   **(PR:A   MPAA:NR)**

TRAIL TO VENGEANCE**   (1945) 58m UNIV bw (GB: VENGEANCE)

Kirby Grant (*Jeff*), Poni [Jane] Adams (*Dorothy*), Fuzzy Knight (*Hungry*), Tom Fadden (*Horace Glumm*), John Kelly (*Bully*), Frank Jaquet (*Foster Felton*), Stanley Andrews (*Sheriff*), Walter Baldwin (*Jackson*), Roy Brent (*Sanders*), Pierce Lyden (*Sam*), Dan White (*1st Thug*), Beatrice Gray (*Alice*), William Sundholm (*Clergyman*), Carey Loftin.

While trying to root out the man who killed his brother, rancher Grant runs afoul of a corrupt banker and his thugs who are working to seize his land. As it turns out the land-grabbers are also responsible for the murder of Grant's brother. Luckily, the heroic rancher straightens everything out by the fade.

p&d, Wallace W. Fox; w, Robert Williams; ph, Maury Gertsman; ed, Russell Schoengarth; md, Mark Levant; art d, John B. Goodman, Abraham Grossman; set d, Russell A. Gausman, Ralph Warrington.

Western   **(PR:A   MPAA:NR)**

TRAILIN' TROUBLE, 1930   (SEE: TRAILING TROUBLE, 1930)

TRAILIN' TROUBLE, 1937   (SEE: TRAILING TROUBLE, 1937)

TRAILIN' WEST*   (1936) 56m FN-WB bw (GB: ON SECRET SERVICE)

Dick Foran (*Lt. Rod Colton*), Paula Stone (*Lucy Blake*), Gordon [Bill] Elliott (*Jefferson Duane*), Addison Richards (*Curley Thorne*), Robert Barrat (*President Abraham Lincoln*), Joseph Crehan (*Col. Douglas*), Fred Lawrence (*Lt. Dale*), Eddie Shubert (*Happy*), Henry Otho (*Hawk*), Stuart Holmes (*Edwin H. Stanton*), Cliff Saum (*Jim*), Milton Kibbee (*Bandit*), Carlyle Moore, Jr (*Hotel Clerk*), Jim Thorpe, Edwin Stanley, Bud Osborne, Glenn Strange, Gene Alsace [Rocky Cameron], Tom Wilson.

There is plenty of action here, but Foran just walks through his part as a secret agent on assignment from President Lincoln. His assignment, should he accept it, is to put an end to the activities of a group of renegades. With guns spitting and fists flying, Foran tracks them down in the predictable finish and has enough time to romance dance-hall girl Stone along the way.

p, Bryan Foy; d, Noel Smith; w, Anthony Coldeway (based on the story "On Secret Service" by Coldeway); ph, Sidney Hickox, Ted McCord; ed, Frank McGee; m/l, "Moonlight Valley," "Drums of Glory," M.K. Jerome, Jack Scholl.

Western   **(PR:A   MPAA:NR)**

TRAILING DOUBLE TROUBLE*   (1940) 56m MON bw

Ray Corrigan (*Crash*), John King (*Dusty*), Max Terhune (*Alibi*), Lita Conway (*Marian Horne*), Nancy Louise King (*Baby*), Roy Barcroft (*Jim Moreland*), Forrest Taylor (*Sheriff*), Tom London, William Kellogg, Carl Mathews, Kenne Duncan, Dick Cramer, Tex Felker, Jimmy Wakely and His Rough Riders.

The second film in the "Range Buster" series that should have been stopped after this was made. The three boys, Corrigan, King, and Terhune, come across a murder that an attorney masterminded to clear the way for a big gravel contract. The dead rancher's baby girl is now under the attorney's guardianship, which gives him the legal wherewithal to carry out his evil scheme, so the boys kidnap the child to prevent the contract from going through. A couple of good brawls ensue, one in a saloon, the other at an isolated hideout. Ultimately, justice triumphs. Terhume provides what laughs there are with his ventriloquist antics. (See RANGE BUSTER, series, Index.)

p, George W. Weeks; d, S. Roy Luby; w, Oliver Drake (based on a story by George Plympton); ph, Edward Linden; ed, Roy Claire; md, Frank Sanucci; m/l, "Under Western Skies," Lew Porter, Johnny Lange (performed by Jimmy Wakely and his Rough Riders).

Western   **(PR:A   MPAA:NR)**

TRAILING THE KILLER***   (1932) 64m B. F. Zejdman/World Wide bw

Francis McDonald (*Pierre*), Heinie Conklin (*Windy*), Jose de la Cruz (*Pedro*), Peter Rigas (*Manuel*), Caesar the Wolf Dog (*Lobo*), Tom London.

Animals are the stars of this excellent film as they take on very human characteristics. Caesar the wolf dog is accused of being a killer by the humans. But the best moments of the film are with Caesar and his family, particularly those showing the puppies acting just like children: fighting with each other, being frightened, and learning about their surroundings. The story builds as Caesar fights a rattlesnake to protect his family. The final confrontation with the real killer, a mountain lion, is terrific, with Caesar redeeming himself and more.

d, Herman C. Raymaker; w, Jackson Richards.

Adventure   **(PR:A   MPAA:NR)**

TRAILING TROUBLE*   (1930) 57M UNIV bw

Hoot Gibson (*Ed King*), Margaret Quimby (*Molly*), William McCall (*Father*), Peter Morrison (*Buck Saunders*), Olive Young (*Ming Toy*), Bob Perry.

Gibson's reputation wasn't helped with this hodgepodge that suffered from lack of direction. He leads a cattle drive to the city but while there is relieved of the money he had received for the beef. That doesn't help him in his battle with Morrison for the heart of Quimby. But along the way, he helps a Chinese girl, and, in turn, she somehow comes up with the money to save him. In one final act of love, Gibson drops in Quimby's backyard by jumping out of an airplane. He should have jumped when he saw the script.

p, Hoot Gibson; d, Arthur Rosson; w, Rosson, Harold Tarshis (based on the story "Hand 'Em Over" by Rosson); ph, Harry Neumann; ed, Gilmore Walker.

Western   **(PR:A   MPAA:NR)**

TRAILING TROUBLE* (1937) 58M Condor/GN bw

Ken Maynard (*Friendly Fielding*), Lona Andre (*Patience Blair*), Roger Williams (*Crocker*), Grace Woods (*Mrs. Dunn*), Fred Burns (*Sheriff*), Vince Barnett, Phil Dunham, Edward Cassidy, Horace B. Carpenter, Marin Sais, Tex Palmer, Tarzan the Horse.

Much too slow for a typical Maynard western, this film finds him playing a nice guy who is mistakenly identified as bad guy Blackie, a known gunslinger. The good-hearted Maynard is anything but a quick-draw troublemaker, but he does get into some action (guns and fists, the standard fare) by saving the ranch and cattle herd owned by Andre, who has no parents to look after her. Clearly, not one of Maynard's better films and best forgotten.

p, M.K. Hoffman; d, Arthur Rosson; w, Philip Graham White.

Western **Cas.** **(PR:A MPAA:NR)**

TRAIL'S END* (1949) 55m MON bw

Johnny Mack Brown (*Johnny*), Max Terhune (*Alibi*), Kay Morley (*Laurie*), Douglas Evans (*Porter*), Zon Murray (*Kettering*), Myron Healey (*Drake*), Keith Richards (*Bill*), George Chesebro (*Stuart*), William Norton Bailey (*Sheriff*), Carol Henry (*Rocky*), Boyd Stockman (*Idaho*), Eddie Majors (*Luke*).

As Monogram churned out Brown picture after Brown picture, the quality began to suffer so much that by the time they got to this picture, they even recycled music used in his earlier films. Brown is again his typical good, clean cowboy. This time, with assistance from Terhune, he helps Morley fend off the bad guys who want her ranch because they know that gold is on the land.

p, Barney A. Sarecky; d, Lambert Hillyer; w, J. Benton Cheney; ph, Harry Neumann; ed, John C. Fuller; md, Edward Kay.

Western **(PR:A MPAA:NR)**

TRAILS OF DANGER* (1930) 63m National Players/Big Four bw (AKA: TRAILS OF PERIL)

Wally Wales [Hal Taliaferro] (*Bob Bartlett*), Virginia Brown Faire (*Mary Martin*), Jack Perrin (*Sheriff Johnson*), Frank Ellis (*Butch Coleson*), Lew Meehan (*Joe Fenton*), Joe Rickson (*U.S. Marshal Bartlett*), Bobby Dunn (*Shorty*), Buck Conners (*John Martin*), Pete Morrison (*Tom Weld*), Hank Bell (*Hank*).

A cheap, quickly made western with Wales as an ex-soldier accused being a stagecoach robber, because he is in possession of the real crook's horse. Wales escapes the law and its posse, catching the thief on his own and getting a $10,000 reward for his efforts. Wales and Faire sleep throught the romantic scenes.

p, F.E. Douglas; d&w, Alvin J. Heitz (based on a story by Neitz, Henry Taylor); ph, William Nobles; ed, Ethel Davey.

Western **(PR:A MPAA:NR)**

TRAILS OF PERIL (SEE: TRAILS OF DANGER, 1930)

TRAILS OF THE WILD* (1935) 61m Ambassador-Syndicate bw

Kermit Maynard (*McKenna*), Billie Seward (*Jane*), Fuzzy Knight (*Windy*), Monte Blue (*Doyle*), Theodor Von Eltz (*Kincaid*), Matthew Betz (*Hunt*), Robert Frazer (*Stacey*), Wheeler Oakman (*Hardy*), Charles Delaney (*Brent*), John Elliott (*Mason*), Frank Rice (*Missouri*), Roger Williams (*Hammond*), Dick Curtis (*Roper*), Rocky the Horse.

Maynard, of the famous Maynard brothers who starred in westerns, goes north this time to play the role of a Canadian Mountie. He and Knight go about their assignment–to get rid of the riffraff on Ghost Mountain–like a couple of western heroes, using their fists and guns to do all the work. Along the way, Maynard finds a murderer, saves a kidnaped miner, and wins the heart of the same miner's daughter, Seward. To cap it off, they discover that there is actually gold within the mountain. Oh boy.

p, Sigmund Neufeld, Maurice Conn; d, Sam Newfield; w, Joseph O'Donnell (based on the story "Caryl of the Mountains" by James Oliver Curwood); ph, Jack Greenhalgh; ed, Jack [John] English.

Action **(PR:A MPAA:NR)**

TRAIN, THE**** (1965, Fr./Ital./U.S.) 140m Les Productions Artistes-Ariane-Dear/UA bw(LE TRAIN; IL TRENO)

Burt Lancaster (*Labiche*), Paul Scofield (*Col. von Waldheim*), Jeanne Moreau (*Christine*), Michel Simon (*Papa Boule*), Suzanne Flon (*Miss Villard*), Wolfgang Preiss (*Herren*), Richard Munch (*Von Lubitz*), Albert Remy (*Didont*), Charles Millot (*Pesquet*), Jacques Marin (*Jacques*), Paul Bonifas (*Spinet*), Jean Bouchaud (*Schmidt*), Donald O'Brien (*Schwartz*), Jean-Pierre Zola (*Octave*), Art Brauss (*Pilzer*), Jean-Claude Bercq (*Major*), Howard Vernon (*Dietrich*), Bernard La Jarrige (*Bernard*), Louis Falavigna (*Railroad Worker*), Daniel Lecourtois (*Priest*), Richard Bailey (*Sgt. Grote*), Christian Fuin (*Robert*), Elmo Kindermann (*Ordnance Officer*), Roger

Lumont (*Engineer Officer*), Gerard Buhr (*Corporal*), Christian Remy (*Tauber*), Max From (*Gestapo Officer*), Jean-Jacques Lecomte (*Lieutenant of Retreating Convoy*), Jacques Blot (*Hubert*), Wolfgang Saure, Victor Beaumont, Christian Remy (*Tauber*).

A superior WW II film which provides enough edge-of-the-seat action to satisfy fans of cinematic thrills, THE TRAIN also poses a rather serious philosophical question: Is the preservation of art worth a human life? Set in France in the summer of 1944, the film begins as a German general, Scofield, is ordered by the Wehrmacht to gather up the art works of the Jeu de Paume Museum-- some of the world's masterpieces--and ship them on a train to Germany. The Nazis are in retreat and they are grabbing what they can as they run. Flon, the curator of the museum, gets word of the plan to the French Resistance and they try to convince Lancaster, the railway inspector, to try and save the priceless works of art. Lancaster's main concern is with sabotaging Nazi armament trains, and refuses to risk his people's lives for a few paintings. Others in the yard feel differently, however, and an old engineer, Simon, who has been like a father to Lancaster, purposely ruins the engines of a train to delay the shipment of the artwork. Scofield has the old man executed, and to ensure the success of the shipment, he forces Lancaster to take Simon's place. The shock of seeing his mentor gunned down, combined with the influence of the local hotel-keeper, Moreau, finally convinces Lancaster that the art works are worth saving. Because of his detailed knowledge of the railway system, Lancaster concocts an elaborate plan to fool Scofield and the Nazis on the train into thinking that they have passed into Germany. Lancaster uses the members of the Resistance to get ahead of the train and hang phony signs at the stations along the way to indicate that the train is moving east toward Germany instead of the circular route through France that Lancaster is heading. The train comes full circle and arrives back at the station it had departed from. Lancaster arranges an accident to occur in the station that will cripple the train engine. When Scofield realizes the truth, the nearly deranged general takes innocent French civilians hostage and threatens to kill them if the train isn't fixed and back on its way to Germany. Lancaster works desperately to fix the engine while trying to think of another plan to stop their progress. As Scofield becomes more and more obsessed with the art work, Lancaster becomes more determined to stop him. By morning the train is once again ready to roll, and Scofield has all the hostages loaded onto the train as insurance. As the train approaches Germany, the Nazis can see their comrades retreating from the alley and the sight makes the troops nervous. Lancaster finally makes his move and has the train derailed. Chaos erupts, people are injured, the artwork is dumped out of the railroad cars and onto the tracks. Scofield has his troops slaughter the hostages. The retreating Nazi troops roar by during the carnage and Scofield's men throw down their weapons and join them. Scofield is left alone to face Lancaster amidst the ruined train, dead bodies, and scattered artwork. Lancaster shoots and kills Scofield and walks off, leaving the whole insane mess behind him. THE TRAIN was originally to be directed by Arthur Penn, but after two weeks of shooting the director had some severe disagreements with Lancaster and producer Bricken and he left the production. Associate producer Bernard Farrell tried his hand at the helm, but when that proved unwise, Lancaster called Frankenheimer, whom he had just worked with on SEVEN DAYS IN MAY (they had also teamed up on THE YOUNG SAVAGES and THE BIRDMAN OF ALCATRAZ). Frankenheimer was reluctant to get involved in another project so soon after SEVEN DAYS IN MAY, but the lure of a trip to Europe made the decision for him. The new director read the script on the plane and thought it "almost appalling" and when he arrived in France he immediately rewrote it with writers Ned Young and Howard Infell (whose work went uncredited). The film was shot entirely on location in France and Frankenheimer employed several cameras shooting simultaneously so that the action with the trains would be captured from several different angles with as few takes as possible. Real locomotives were used through the entire film and no miniatures or models were used at any time. During one of the crash sequences, Frankenheimer had seven cameras focused on the event–six manned and one on remote buried in the ground near the track. The train was supposed to be moving at only seven miles an hour, but the French engineer brought the train in too fast. As the director recalled in an interview: "I suddenly realized, my God, he's going much too fast...it was up to about 15 miles an hour and thundering down right at us. It got up to around 25, and as quickly as possible I hauled the cameramen out...physically hauled them out. The train went flying off the track, ran over every camera we had, demolishing six of them...it was just awful. And the only camera that recorded the accident was that little camera that was buried." Much of the film was shot at Normandy and the weather became so unsuitable that the production was shut down for several months while the crew waited for Spring. Visually the film is stunning with its gray, foggy atmosphere and stark black and white photography. Frankenheimer's camera placement perfectly captures the massive trains from every conceivable angle and the machinations of the locomotives are directly contrasted with the chess game played out between Lancaster and Scofield. The acting in the film is superb, with Scofield taking top honors as the obsessed Nazi general. Veteran French character actor Simon nearly steals the film as the determined old engineer, and Lancaster and Moreau have several memorable scenes together (though the French actress was quite impatient with Lancaster's "method" acting). All the various delays, accidents, and hardships on the production eventually paid off for THE TRAIN is a thrilling, suspenseful and intelligent war film that raises some hard questions regarding the value of art and life.

p, Jules Bricken; d, John Frankenheimer; w, Franklin Coen, Frank Davis, Walter Bernstein, (French version) Albert Husson (based on the novel *Le Front de l'Art* by Rose Valland); ph, Jean Tournier, Walter Wottitz; m, Maurice Jarre; ed, David Bretherton, Gabriel Rongier; prod d, Willy Holt; md, Jarre: cos, Jean Zay; spec eff, Lee Zavitz; makeup, Georges Bauban.

War   **Cas.**   **(PR:C   MPAA:NR)**

TRAIN GOES EAST, THE*   (1949, USSR) 83m Mosfilm/Artkino c

Lydia Dranovskaya *(Sokolova)*, Leonid Gallis *(Lavrentyev)*, M. Yarotskaya *(Zahkarova)*, M. Vorobyev *(Berezin)*, K. Sorokin *(Train Superintendent)*, V. Liubimov *(Plant Manager)*.

Almost a Soviet version of IT HAPPENED ONE NIGHT, this picture has Dranovskaya and Gallis as a pair of Russians who meet at the end of WW II at a train station as both prepare to make the long journey to Vladivostok. They travel together, getting themselves in many comedic situations, including some that take pokes at bureaucrats and factory managers, and fall in love in the process. As they travel, each thinks the other is married, and that hinders their relationship. They ultimately clear up that misunderstanding and can proceed together happily ever after. In one good scene, Gallis tries to undress in a cramped upper bunk; in another, Dranovskaya takes over a train station's microphone so she can tell an old lady that her train has arrived. At one point, the two are late returning to the train, miss it, and are forced to continue their journey by hitchhiking rides on everything from a horse and wagon to an airplane–all of which only adds to their love for each other. The film features some interesting color footage of Siberian scenery. (In Russian; English subtitles.)

d, Yuri Raizman; w, L. Malughin; ph, L. Geleya, A. Koltsaty (Magicolor); m, Tikhon Khrennikov; English titles, Nicholas Napoli.

Romance/Comedy   **(PR:A   MPAA:NR)**

TRAIN GOES TO KIEV, THE   (1961, USSR) 92m Dovzhenko/Artkino c (GODY MOLODYYE; AKA: AGE OF YOUTH)

Svetlana Zhivankova *(Natasha)*, Viktor Rudoy *(Sergey)*, V. Kulik *(Volodya)*, Aleksandr Khvylya *(Dneprov-Zadunayskiy)*, Ye. Mashkara *(Natasha's Mother)*, M. Yakovchenko *(Uncle Vasya)*, A. Sova *(Director of "Palace of Culture")*, G. Sklyanskiy *(Kolya)*, G. Aladov, L. Anfilova, I. Bondar, G. Gnennaya, V. Draga, F. Dubrovskiy, V. Zinovyev, M. Ivanova, D. Kadnikov, A. Kalaberdin, I. Kuznovich, M. Muravyov, O. Nozhkina, L. Okrent, N. Panasyev, R. Starik, S. Sibel, A. Sumarokov, A. Kharyakov, Yu. Tsupko, S. Shkurat.

A cheery romp from the Soviet Union about a pretty young dance student in Kiev, Zhivankova, and the two boys who fall in love with her. Zhivankova must travel by train to audition for a theater school, but does so disguised as a boy. It takes a while for her suitors to realize that she is in fact a girl, but the perceptive lads at length come around. The picture is filled with singing and dancing, polkas, waltzes, folk tunes, and marches, as the trio of jubilant youngsters head through the city and into the countryside. A free-and-easy tale with a smattering of songs, which isn't normally expected of Soviet films.

d, Aleksey Mishurin; w, A. Shaykevich (based on a story by A. Pereguda); ph, A. Gerasimov; m, Platon Mayboroda; ed, Ye. Gerasimov; set d, G. Prokopets; cos, A. Chepurko; spec eff, L. Shtifanov, V. Deminskiy; ch, A. Berdovskiy; m/l, A. Malyshko; makeup, A. Dubchak, N. Zelenskaya.

Musical/Comedy   **(PR:A   MPAA:NR)**

TRAIN OF EVENTS*   (1952, Brit.) 88m EAL/Film Arts bw

"The Engine Driver": Jack Warner *(Jim Hadcastle)*, Gladys Henson *(Mrs. Hardcastle)*, Susan Shaw *(Doris Hardcastle)*, Patric Doonan *(Ron Stacey)*, Miles Malleson *(Timekeeper)*, Philip Dale *(Hardcastle's Fireman)*, Leslie Phillips *(Stacey's Fireman)*, "The Prisoner-of-War": Joan Dowling *(Ella)*, Laurence Payne *(Richard)*, Olga Lindo *(Mrs. Bailey)*, "The Composer": Valerie Hobson *(Stella)*, John Clements *(Raymond Hillary)*, Irina Baronova *(Irina)*, John Gregson *(Malcolm)*, Gwen Cherrell *(Charmian)*, Jacqueline Byrne *(TV Announcer)*, "The Actor": Peter Finch *(Phillip)*, Mary Morris *(Louise)*, Laurence Naismith *(Joe Hunt)*, Doris Yorke *(Mrs. Hunt)*, Michael Hordern, Charles Morgan *(Plainclothesmen)*, Guy Verney *(Producer)*, Mark Dignam *(Bolingbroke)*, Philip Ashley, Bryan Coleman, Henry Hewitt, Lyndon Brook *(Actors)*, Wylie Watson, Arthur Hambling, Percy Walsh, Will Ambro, Neal Arden, Thelma Grigg, Dennis Webb, Johnnie Schofield.

Divided into four distinct sections, this film surveys the impact a London train crash has on several passengers. "The Engine Driver" focuses on a driver who is making his last run before an awaited promotion. The accident in which the train is involved is the fault of his daughter's boy friend. In "The Actor" Peter Finch is a thespian leaving for America with a case containing the body of his wife, who he has murdered because she was sleeping around. The police are ready to nab him when the crash occurs and he is killed. The last of the grim tales (the predominant mood of the film is very somber indeed), "The Prisoner of War," tells of an unloved orphan girl who is helping a German POW escape, having obtained a ticket to Canada for him. But with all the havoc caused by the crash, he steals off, unaware that his ticket to freedom has been lifted by the wind from the dead orphan's

open handbag. "The Composer," the only bright story, is about a conductor-composer with a wandering eye who tells his latest lover that their affair is over because she had muffed a note at the orchestra's last concert. Surviving the crash, she attempts to get even with him at the next performance, making eyes at a violinist, but the conductor is too busy preparing for his next conquest to really notice. The film ends on an upbeat note; the old engine driver cycles off from the railroad yard on his way to his new job.

p, Michael Balcon; d, Sidney Cole ("The Engine Driver"), Basil Dearden ("The Prisoner of War," "The Actor"), Charles Crichton ("The Composer"); w, Dearden, T.E.B. Clarke, Ronald Millar, Angus Macphail; ph, Lionel Banes, Gordon Dines, Chic Waterson, Paul Beeson; m, Leslie Bridgewater; ed, Bernard Gribble; art d, Malcolm Baker-Smith, Jim Morahan.

Drama   **(PR:A   MPAA:NR)**

TRAIN RIDE TO HOLLYWOOD*½   (1975) 85m Billy Jack/Taylor-Laughlin c (AKA: NIGHT TRAIN)

Bloodstone "Charles" Love, Willis Draffen, Harry Williams, Charles McCormick] *(The Sinceres)*, Michael Payne *(Black Producer/Eric Van Johnson)*, Pete Gonneau *(Assistant Producer)*, Don Dandridge *(Porter)*, Guy Marks, Jay Lawrence, Phyllis E. Davis, Jay Robinson, Roberta Collins, John Myhers, Elliot Robins, Ann Willis, Peter Ratray, Bill Oberlin, Tracy Reed, Gerri Reddick, Jessamine Milner, Burt Mustin, Jack DeLeon, Whitey Hughes, Jimmy Lennon.

A comedy that doesn't provoke many laughs, that evens tries to be campy but with no luck. Harry Williams gets a knock on his head and goes to la-la land where he dreams he and the group are taking a train to Hollywood where Gable is king. All the old-time big names are there–Humphrey Bogart, Jean Harlow, Nelson Eddy and Jeannette MacDonald. The group knocks around Hollywood as the film goes from one bit to another, searching for that elusive funny piece. Even the people imitating the dead stars aren't that good. The whole film was better left dead.

p, Gordon A. Webb; d, Charles Rondeau; w, Dan Gordon; ph, Al Francis; m, Pip Williams; ed, Jim Heckert; art d, Phil Jefferies; set d, Ray Molyneaux; m/l, Bloodstone.

Comedy   **(PR:A   MPAA:G)**

TRAIN ROBBERS, THE½**   (1973) 92m Batjac/WB c

John Wayne *(Lane)*, Ann-Margret *(Mrs. Lowe)*, Rod Taylor *(Grady)*, Ben Johnson *(Wil Jesse)*, Christopher George *(Calhoun)*, Bobby Vinton *(Ben Young)*, Jerry Gatlin *(Sam Turner)*, Richardo Montalban *(Pinkerton Man)*.

One of many films late in Wayne's career where the actor simply rested on his legendary image, this is a lackluster production that never amounts to much. The Duke plays a veteran of the Civil War hired by Ann-Margret to clear her late husband of a crime he had committed years before. The man had stolen $500,000 in gold and hidden the loot somewhere in Mexico. Ann-Margret tells Wayne the secret location and promises him $50,000 that Wells Fargo is offering as reward for the gold. She intends to return the rest to the bank, thus restoring honor to the family name for her son. Wayne hires Taylor and Johnson, two other war veterans, to go along with him. Also joining up are ex-bank robber Vinton and gunslingers George and Gatlin. After crossing the border into Mexico the men are surprised to find themselves being followed by a group of 20 armed riders, along with Montalban, a mysterious loner with a cigar constantly between his lips. After finding the gold hidden in the boiler of an empty train, Wayne's party is attacked by the armed men. Ann-Margret surprises everyone with her ability in using a shotgun and finally the attack is staved off. The group returns home but is ambushed by the remaining gang members who have been lying in wait for them. Using dynamite, Wayne and his cohorts stop the outlaws once more, blowing up much of the town as well. The next day Ann-Margret boards a train so she can take the gold to the bank. She is touched when Wayne gives up his reward as a gift for her son but the Duke quickly learns that he's the one who's been touched. Montalban arrives, telling Wayne that he is a Pinkerton agent who has been keeping his eye on Ann-Margret's activities. It seems she is a saloon girl who found out about the gold at the original thief's deathbed, then concocted an elaborate scheme about her "widowhood" and a nonexistent son in order to get her hands on the loot. Angered by having wool pulled over their collective eyes, Wayne's band rides after the departing train, a justified robbery in mind. This is a simple western in every sense of the term. Characters are easily identifiable archetypes with Wayne at centerstage playing his good-guy role. He's not helped much by director Kennedy. Working from his own script, this has none of the feel Kennedy gave to the westerns he wrote for Wayne and director Budd Boetticher. Shot in Durango, Mexico, the film looks like a commercial for tourism, with lots of pretty, unspoiled pictures of the scenery and the men silhouetted against the sky. Released at a time when the western was undergoing some radical changes thanks to films by Sergio Leone and Sam Peckinpah, THE TRAIN ROBBERS harkens back to the old style westerns Wayne helped make famous. What's lacking is substance and style.

p, Michael Wayne; d&w, Burt Kennedy; ph, William H. Clothier (Panavision, Technicolor); m, Dominic Frontiere; ed, Frank Santillo; art d, Alfred Sweeney; cos, Luster Bayless; spec eff, Howard Jensen; makeup, David Grayson, Joe Dibella, George Masters; stunts, Cliff Lyons.

Western   **Cas.**   **(PR:A   MPAA:PG)**

TRAIN ROBBERY CONFIDENTIAL**   (1965, Braz.) 105m Herbert Richers/Times bw (ASSALTO AO TREM PAGADOR; TIAO MEDONHO)

Eliezer Gomes *(Tiao Medonho)*, Reginaldo Faria *(Grilo Peru)*, Grande Otelo *(Cachaca)*, Atila Iorio *(Tonho)*, Miguel Rosemberg *(Edgar)*, Kele *(Lino)*, Helena Ignez *(Marta)*, Luiza Maranhao *(Zulmira)*, Ruth de Souza *(Judith)*, Dirce Migliaccio *(Edgar's Wife)*, Jorge Doria *(Delegado)*, Miguel Angelo *(Miguel Gordinho)*, A. Fregolente, Oswaldo Louzada, Wilson Grey, Mozael Silveira.

A train is robbed in Brazil by a gang led by Gomes. To avoid being under suspicion, they decide to spend only a little of the loot at a time. But it becomes difficult to hide their new-found wealth. All had lived in poverty and now stand out in the old neighborhood, raising the eyebrows of neighbors and local police. Faria doesn't follow the spending pact and is killed by Gomes. The police track them down and kill ringleader Gomes. His wife gives the money back and goes back with her kids to the poor life they had before.

p, Roberto Farias, Herbert Richers; d, Farias; w, Farias, Luiz Carlos Barreto, Alinor Azevedo; ph, Amleto Daisse; m, Remo Usai; ed, Rafael Justo; art d, Alexandre Horvath, Pierino Massenzi.

Crime Drama   **(PR:A   MPAA:NR)**

TRAIN TO ALCATRAZ**   (1948) 60m REP bw

Donald Barry *(Forbes)*, Janet Martin *(Beatrice)*, William Phipps *(Tommy Calligan)*, Roy Barcroft *(Grady)*, June Storey *(Virginia)*, Jane Darwell *(Aunt Ella)*, Milburn Stone *(Bart Kanin)*, Chester Clute *(Conductor)*, Ralph Dunn *(U.S. Marshal)*, Richard Irving *(Anders)*, John Alvin *(Nick)*, Michael Carr *(Marty)*, Marc Krah *(Mahaffey)*, Denver Pyle *(Hutchins)*, Iron Eyes Cody *(Geronimo)*, Kenneth MacDonald *(Reeves)*, Harry Harvey *(George)*, Steven Baron *(Edgar)*, Bob Stone *(Hollister)*, Don Haggerty *(Billings)*, John A. Doucette *(McHenry)*.

Told with touches of flashback, a group of prisoners headed Told with touches of flashback, a group of prisoners headed to the "Rock" plan a big escape. Barry leads the group. Phipps is on the train, too, but he was framed. He even strikes up an on-board romance with Martin (not a convict). Phipps gets cleared by the authorities before it is over, but the other cons die when they try the big breakout.

p, Lou Brock; d, Philip Ford; w, Gerald Geraghty; ph, Reggie Lanning; ed, HaroldMinter; md, Morton Scott; art d, Fred A. Ritter; cos, Adele Palmer.

Drama   **(PR:A   MPAA:NR)**

TRAIN TO TOMBSTONE zero   (1950) 56m Lippert bw

Don Barry *(Len Howard)*, Robert Lowery *(Staley)*, Wally Vernon *(Gulliver)*, Tom Neal *(Dr. Willoughby)*, Judith Allen *(Belle)*, Minna Phillips *(Abbie)*, Barbara Stanley *(Doris)*, Nan Leslie *(Marie)*, Claude Stroud *(Brown)*, Ed Cassidy *(Conductor)*, Bill Kennedy.

A pitiful attempt at a western about a train on its way to Tombstone. One passenger has plans to rob $250,000 from the baggage car, but that never really develops. Hilarious moments occur, even if unintentionally, during Indian attacks when the same poor guy keeps falling off his horse. Barry leads the passengers in defending themselves against the savages. They all had to defend their careers after this came out.

p&d, William Berke; w, Victor West, Orville Hampton (based on a story by Don Barry); ph, Ernest Miller; m, Albert Glasser; ed, Carl Pierson; md, Glasser; art d, Fred Treble.

Western   **(PR:A   MPAA:NR)**

TRAIN 2419   (SEE: RETURN OF CASEY JONES, 1933)

TRAINED TO KILL   (SEE: NO MERCY MAN, THE, 1975)

TRAITOR, THE*   (1936) 60m Puritan bw

Tim McCoy *(Tim Vallance)*, Frances Grant *(Mary Allen)*, Karl Hackett *(Ranger Captain)*, Jack Rockwell *(Smoky)*, Pedro Regas *(Moreno)*, Frank Melton *(Jimmy)*, Dick Curtis *(Morgan)*, Dick Bottilier *(Remos)*, Wally Wales [Hal Taliaferro] *(Hunk)*, Ed Cobb *(Joe)*, Wally West *(Bud)*, Tina Menard *(Maria)*, Soledad Jiminez *(Juana)*, J. Frank Glendon *(Big George)*, Frank McCarroll.

A western set in modern times, this was McCoy's last film for the Puritan studios. He is a Texas Ranger who is forced to give up his badge (he does this on purpose) so he can go under cover to break up Glendon's illegal activity. After he gets Glendon, he runs into more trouble because no one knows he was working under cover except one person and that person is dead. Some of the boys preferred horses, while other cowboys preferred the

ones with four wheels to get around in.

p, Sigmund Neufeld, Leslie Simmonds; d, Sam Newfield; w, John Thomas Neville; ph, Jack Greenhalgh; ed, Joseph O'Donnell.

Western   **Cas.**   **(PR:A   MPAA:NR)**

TRAITOR, THE, 1957   (SEE: ACCURSED, THE, 1957, Brit.)

TRAITOR SPY   (SEE: TORSO MURDER MYSTERY, THE, 1939, Brit.)

TRAITOR WITHIN, THE*½   (1942) 62m REP bw

Donald M. Barry *(Sam Starr)*, Jean Parker *(Molly)*, George Cleveland *(Pop Betts)*, Ralph Morgan *(John Scott Ryder)*, Jessica Newcombe *(Mrs. Ryder)*, Bradley Page *(Al McGonigle)*, Dick Wessel *(Otis)*, Emmett Vogan *(Carter)*, Edward Keane *(Davis)*, Eddie Acuff *(Tommy)*, Sam McDaniel *(Melrose)*, Eddie Johnson *(Louie)*, Marjorie Cooley *(June)*.

A blackmailing truck driver, not a war spy, is the focus of this okay film. Barry is the not-too-bright driver who romances Parker. Parker lives with her father (Cleveland) who constantly sounds off on how he, not the town mayor, captured a handful of Germans during WW I. Parker meets a German who is now an American citizen and learns that the old man's story is true. She gets Barry to bring this up to the mayor and blackmail him into giving Barry a new truck and other goodies or Barry will tell the real story and end the mayor's good life. Parker also tells the opposition party, and, faced with scandal, the mayor kills himself. Barry gets in trouble then, and all the money-grabbing politicians are tossed in the slammer.

p, Armand Schaefer; d, Frank McDonald; w, Jack Townley (based on a story by Charles G. Booth); ph, Bud Thackery; ed, Charles Craft; md, Morton Scott; art d, Russell Kimball.

Drama   **(PR:A   MPAA:NR)**

TRAITORS*   (1957, Jap.) 90m Toei c

Utaemon Ichikawa, Hizuru Takachiho, Eitaro Shindo.

A type of western, Japanese style--no guns blasting, but plenty of sword-clanging. Ichikawa is the hero of the tale, a samurai sent to Okinawa to make sure things are going smoothly and to prevent trouble. Along the way he gets into fights but always takes care of the bad guys, sometimes a bunch at a time. Sometimes he takes on so many (shades of Bruce Lee) that the results provoke laughter more than anything else.

p, Hiroshi Okawa; d, Sadatsugu Matsuda; w, Yushitake Hisa; ph, Shintaro Kawasaki ; m, Shiro Fukai.

Action   **(PR:A   MPAA:NR)**

TRAITORS, THE, 1958, Brit.   (SEE: ACCURSED, THE, 1958, Brit.)

TRAITORS, THE*   (1963, Brit.) 71m Ello/UNIV bw

Patrick Allen *(John Lane)*, Jacqueline Ellis *(Mary)*, James Maxwell *(Ray Ellis)*, Zena Walker *(Annette Lane)*, Ewan Roberts *(Col. Burlinson)*, Jeffrey Segal *(Dr. Lindt)*, Anne Padwick *(Mrs. Lindt)*, Harold Goodwin *(Edwards)*, John Brown *(Mason)*, Sean Lynch *(Porter)*, Jack May *(Burton)*, Mark Singleton *(Venner)*, A.J. Brown, Reed De Rouen, Michael Corcoran, Robert Raglan, Henry De Bray, Frank Wilson Taylor, Victor Platt, Anton Rodgers, Sheldon Lawrence, Fanny Carby, Arthur Barclay, Mike Martin.

So many spies and double defectors it's hard to keep track without a scorecard. A British agent and a NATO man are trying to break up a Communist spy ring. A roll of microfilm, deemed top secret, is found after an airplane crash. Maxwell and Allen enter a world of double-crossing spies, finally closing in on Lynch and Segal as the masterminds who obtain information for the Communists.

p, Jim O'Connolly; d, Robert Tronson; w, J. Levy, J.P. O'Connolly; ph, Michael Reed; m, Johnny Douglas; ed, Peter Boita; art d, Bert Davey; makeup, Geoffrey Rodway.

Spy Drama   **(PR:A   MPAA:NR)**

TRAITOR'S GATE**   (1966, Brit./Ger.) 80m Summit-Rialto/COL bw
                    (DAS VERRATERTOR)

Albert Lieven *(Trayne)*, Gary Raymond *(Graham/Lt. Dick Lee-Carnaby)*, Margot Trooger *(Dinah Pauling)*, Catherina von Schell *(Hope Joyner)*, Eddi Arent *(Hector)*, Klaus Kinski *(Kinski)*, Anthony James *(John)*, Tim Barrett *(Lloyd)*, Heinz Bernard *(Martin)*, Dave Birks *(Spider)*, Edward Underdown *(Inspector Gray)*, Alec Ross *(Sgt. Carter)*, Julie Mendez *(Stripper)*, Peter Porteous *(Kelly)*, Katy Wild *(Mary)*, Harry Baird *(Mate on Tramp Steamer)*, Joe Ritchie *(News Vendor)*, Frank Sieman *(Yeoman Warden Guide)*, Frank Forsyth *(Chief Yeoman Warden)*, Caron Gardner *(Blonde)*, Maurice Good *(King)*, Robert Hunter *(Captain)*, Marianne Stone *(Cashier at Dandy Club)*, Hedger Wallace *(Detective Sgt. Alexander)*, Beresford Williams *(Warden)*.

Based on the novel The Traitor's Gate by Edgar Wallace, a business executive wants to rob the Tower of London. To get the crown jewels, he kidnaps the guard and replaces him with an escaped convict who bears an uncanny resemblance to the watchman. Everything goes as planned as the businessman crosses up the thief by sending him off with a set of phony jewels that contains a bomb. However, the businessman's secretary finds out about the plan and goes to the authorities. Her boss is arrested, the convict is shot and captured, and the jewels are returned for safekeeping.

p, Ted Lloyd; d, Freddie Francis; w, John Samson (based on a novel by Edgar Wall ace); ph, Denys Coop; m, Peter Thomas; ed, Oswald Hafenrichter; art d, Tony Inglis; makeup, Jill Carpenter.

Crime Drama (PR:A MPAA:NR)

TRAMP, TRAMP, TRAMP** (1942) 68m COL bw

Jackie Gleason (*Hank*), Jack Durant (*Jed*), Florence Rice (*Pam Martin*), Bruce Bennett (*Tommy Lydel*), Hallene Hill (*Granny*), Billy Curtis (*Midget*), Mabel Todd (*Vivian*), Forrest Tucker (*Blond Bomber*), James Seay (*Biggie Waldron*), John Tyrrell (*Lefty*), John Harmon (*Mousey*), Eddie Foster (*Blackie*), Al Hill (*Tim*), Borrah Minevitch, Harmonica Rascals (*Themselves*), Heinie Conklin (*Soldier*), Kenneth MacDonald, Eddie Kane (*Doctors*), William Gould (*Colonel*), Chuck Morrison (*Colonel's Guard*), Herbert Rawlinson (*Ex-Soldier Commander*), Bud Jamison (*Fat Man*), Glenn Turnbull (*Tall Man*), James Millican (*Draftee*), John Dilson (*Judge Smith*), Harry Strang, George Turner, Lloyd Bridges, Eddie Laughton, Walter Sande, Bud Geary (*Guards*).

Uninspired film with poor attempts at getting laughs. Pity would be more appropriate. It's a feeble try at Abbott and Costello humor with Gleason carrying the sorry burden. He and Durant are barbers who see business decline because their customers are being drafted into WW I. They try to enlist but to no avail, and form a home guard unit. A group of killers on the run use the guard as a hiding place. There are couple of mishaps along the way and everyone goes home. Thankfully.

p, Wallace MacDonald; d, Charles Barton; w, Harry Rebuas, Ned Dandy (based on a story by Shannon Day, Hal Braham, Marian Grant); ph, John Stumar; ed, William Lyon.

Comedy (PR:A MPAA:NR)

TRAMPLERS, THE zero (1966, Ital.) 105m Anna Maria Chretien/EM
c (GLI UOMINI DAL PASSO PESANTE)

Joseph Cotten (*Temple Cordeen*), Gordon Scott (*Lon Cordeen*), James Mitchum (*Hoby Cordeen*), Ilaria Occhini (*Edith Wickett*), Franco Nero (*Charley Garvey*), Emma Vannoni (*Bess Cordeen*), Georges Lycan (*Longfellow Wiley*), Muriel Franklin (*Alice Cordeen*), Aldo Cecconi (*Jim Hennessy*), Franco Balducci (*Pete Wiley*), Claudio Gora (*Fred Wickett*), Romano Puppo (*Paine Cordeen*), Dario Michaelis (*Bert Cordeen*), Ivan Scratuglia (*Adrian Cordeen*), Carla Calo (*Mrs. Temple Cordeen*), Dino Desmond (*Sheriff*), Silla Bettini (*Hogan*), Edith Peters (*Emma*), Emil Jordan, Giovanni Cianfriglia, Virgilio Ponti.

Three name American actors–Cotten, Scott, and Mitchum–don't add anything to this Italian western that was actually filmed in Argentina. Cotten stars as the head of an old Southern family split in its views after the Civil War. The old man is set in his ways, even about forcing the women of the family to eat upstairs. The sons leave with their sister and her husband and go west with some cattle. The family guns it out, brother against brother. One shooting scene is so ludicrous it defies all imagination: two guys battle hundred upon hundreds without ever reloading their guns, and the filmmakers even stooped to using some of the footage of men being killed twice during the same 10-minute sequence. At the end only one family member is alive. Too bad.

p, Alvaro Mancori, Albert Band; d, Band, Anthony Wileys [Mario Sequi]; w, Ugo Liberatore, Band (based on the novel *The Guns of North Texas* by Will Cook); ph, Mancori (Eastmancolor); m, Angelo Francesco Lavagnino; ed, Maurizio Lucidi; art d, Peppino Ranieri; set d, Camillo Del Signore; cos, Sergio Selli.

Western (PR:C MPAA:NR)

TRANSATLANTIC**½ (1931) 78m FOX bw

Edmund Lowe (*Monty Greer*), Lois Moran (*Judy Kramer*), John Halliday (*Henry Graham*), Greta Nissen (*Sigrid Carline*), Jean Hersholt (*Rudolph Kramer*), Myrna Loy (*Kay Graham*), Earle Fox (*Handsome*), Billy Bevan (*Hudgins*), Ruth Donnelly (*Burbank*), Goodee Montgomery (*Peters*), Jesse De Vorska (*Buyer*), Rosalie Roy (*Bride*), Claude King (*Captain*), Crauford Kent (*1st Officer*), Henry Sedley, Louis Natheaux, Bob Montgomery.

Excellent character development about a diverse group of people on an ocean liner and how their lives become intertwined. Lowe is a gambler, on the run from some bad guys, who is also looking after the interests of Moran. Halliday is a straight banker who gets involved with dancer Nissen, but goes back to his wife, Loy, at the end. Lowe, in the meantime, is dodging bullets–in one good scene he is on the run in the engine room. But he escapes and when the ship reaches his destination, he thinks he is scot-free. Not really, since the British authorites are there watching him closely. Bevan is on the screen too much as the deck steward throwing out wisecracks, but

he can't come up with anything funny enough to help the film.

d, William K. Howard; w, Guy Bolton, Lynn Starling (based on a story by Bolton); ph, James Wong Howe; art d, Gordon Wiles.

Comedy/Drama (PR:A MPAA:NR)

TRANSATLANTIC*½ (1961, Brit.) 63m Danziger/UA bw

Pete Murray (*Robert Stanton*), June Thorburn (*Judy*), Malou Pantera (*Gina*), Bill Nagy (*Fabroni*), Neil Hallatt (*Evans*), Jack Melford (*Capt. Brady*), Sheldon Lawrence (*Capt. Ives*), Robert Ayres (*Hotchkiss*), Anthony Oliver (*Wentworth*).

An oft-tread crime tale about a search for murderous diamond thieves who destroyed a plane with a time bomb. On their trail is a determined FBI agent and the vengeful sister of the plane's dead pilot. A bottom-rung British programmer briskly directed by Danziger thriller veteran Morris.

p, Brian Taylor; d, Ernest Morris; w, Brian Clemens, James Eastwood.

Crime (PR:A MPAA:NR)

TRANSATLANTIC MERRY-GO-ROUND**½
(1934) 90m Reliance/UA bw

Gene Raymond (*Jimmy Brett*), Sid Silvers (*Shortie*), Jack Benny (*Chad Denby*), Nancy Carroll (*Sally Marsh*), Sydney Howard (*Dan Campbell, Drunk*), Sidney Blackmer (*Lee Lothar*), Ralph Morgan (*Herbert Rosson*), Shirley Grey (*Anya Rosson*), Robert Elliott (*Inspector McKinney*), Sam Hardy (*Jack Summers*), William ["Stage"] Boyd (*Joe Saunders*), Carlyle Moore (*Ned Marsh*), Frank Parker, Mitzi Green, Jean Sargent, Lee Phelps, Syd Saylor, Rex Weber, The Boswell Sisters, The Jimmy Grier Orchestra.

Everything was thrown into this musical set on a transatlantic ocean liner: drama, comedy, satire, thrills. The characters involved are an ex-convict, a cheating wife who doesn't know that her husband is also on the ship, a crook, and two petty gamblers. All cross paths along the way, which provides chuckles galore. Plenty of big names and zany incidents. Songs incude: "It Was Sweet of You" (Sidney Clare, Richard A. Whiting, sung by Frank Parker), "Rock and Roll" (Whiting, Parker, performed by The Boswell Sisters, Jean Sargent), "Moon over Monte Carlo," "Oh Leo, It's Love" (Whiting, Parker), "If I Had a Million Dollars" (Johnny Mercer, Matt Malneck, sung by The Boswell Sisters).

p, Edward Small; d, Benjamin Stoloff; w, Harry W. Conn, Joseph Moncure March (based on a story by Leon Gordon); ph, Ted Tetzlaff; ed, Grant Whytock, H. T. Fritch; md, Alfred Newman; art d, John Ducasse Schulze; cos, Gwen Wakeling; ch, Sammy Lee, Larry Ceballos.

Musical (PR:A MPAA:NR)

TRANSATLANTIC TROUBLE (SEE: TAKE IT FROM ME, 1937, Brit.)

TRANSATLANTIC TUNNEL*** (1935, Brit.) 94m GAU bw (GB: THE TUNNEL)

Richard Dix (*McAllan*), Leslie Banks (*Robbie*), Madge Evans (*Ruth McAllan*), Helen Vinson (*Varlia*), C. Aubrey Smith (*Lloyd*), Basil Sydney (*Mostyn*), Henry Oscar (*Grellier*), Hilda Trevelyan (*Mary*), Cyril Raymond (*Harriman*), Jimmy Hanley (*Geoffrey*), Walter Huston (*President of the U.S.*), George Arliss (*Prime Minister of England*), Hilda Trevelyn (*Mary*).

Set in the future, the plot deals with an undersea tunnel being constructed beneath the Atlantic Ocean which would connect England and the U.S. Despite the time the film was made, the special effects lend reality to the effort, showing how air locks shut down critical sections of the tunnel during a disaster, how people are trapped inside forever, and other troubles faced during construction. The process is shown to an attentive public via worldwide TV and some scenes–such as those showing survivors of an undersea disaster and their relatives grieving at a hospital–are starkly realistic. Dix is the designer of the tunnel, who gets to keep in touch with his family only through TV or a telephone. Banks provides a willing shoulder for Dix's wife. A futuristic disaster movie with some very real touches. Huston had gone from Hollywood to London to make a film about Cecil John Rhodes, the British financier and administrator in South Africa, but found the picture delayed. To fill the time, he played the small role of President of the U.S. in THE TUNNEL (a remake of a German film named TOONEL).

p, Michael Balcon; d, Maurice Elvey; w, Kurt Siodmak, L. DuGarde Peach, Clemence Dane (based on the novel by H. Kellermann); ph, Gunther Krampf; ed, Charles Frend.

Science Fiction **Cas.** (PR:A MPAA:NR)

TRANSCONTINENT EXPRESS (SEE: ROCK ISLAND TRAIL, 1950)

TRANS-EUROP-EXPRESS***   (1968, Fr.) 105m Como Films/Trans
American bw

Jean-Louis Trintignant (*Elias/Himself*), Marie-France Pisier (*Eva*), Charles
Millot (*Franck*), Christian Barbier (*Lorentz*), Nadine Verdier (*Hotel Maid*),
Clo Vanesco (*Cabaret Singer*), Daniel Emilfork (*Phony Policeman*), Henri
Lambert (*Inspector*), Alain Robbe-Grillet (*Jean the Director*), Catherine
Robbe-Grillet (*Lucette*), Gerard Palaprat (*Le Petit Mathieu*), Samy Halfon
(*Marc*), Virginie Vignon (*Suitcase Salesgirl*), Salkin, Ariane Sapriel, Rezy
Norbert, Raoul Guylad, Paul Louyet, Prima Symphony.

The second film from novelist-screenwriter (LAST YEAR AT MARIEN-
BAD) Alain Robbe-Grillet which, as expected, has a narrative line so
complex that a slide rule may come in handy. At its most basic, TRANS-
EUROP-EXPRESS is about a train trip from Paris to Antwerp on which
Robbe-Grillet and his wife are passengers. Also on board but in a different
space and time is gangster Trintignant, who also plays himself, an actor in
a film titled TRANS-EUROP-EXPRESS which Robbe-Grillet and his wife
are planning to film. Robbe-Grillet takes great liberties with narrative form,
commenting on the action and even cutting out portions seen earlier in the
film, all in a humorous manner. The title itself is a play on literary allusions,
with "Transes" being the name of a detective story included in the film,
"Europe" being an adult magazine a character buys, and "L'Express" being
a popular French magazine. (In French; English subtitles.)

p, Samy Halfon; d&w, Alain Robbe-Grillet; ph, Willy Kurant; m, Michel
Fano, excerpts from "LaTraviata" by Giuseppe Verdi; ed, Bob Wade; m/l,
Clo Vanesco; English titles, Noelle Gillmor.

Drama/Crime   (PR:O   MPAA:NR)

TRANSGRESSION**   (1931) 72m RKO bw

Kay Francis (*Elsie Maury*), Paul Cavanagh (*Robert Maury*), Ricardo Cortez
(*Don Arturo*), Nance O'Neal (*Honora Maury*), John St. Polis (*Serafin*),
Adrienne d'Ambricourt (*Julie*), Cissy Fitzgerald (*Countess Longueval*),
Doris Lloyd (*Paula Vrain*), Augustino Borgato (*Carlos*).

A hard-to-believe story about an unfaithful wife and a forgiving husband
which doesn't make the grade called entertainment. Francis is a bored wife
who takes off with Spanish lover Cortez to find excitement. She writes a
letter to her husband explaining why she did it and, while mailing the letter,
learns that Cortez is involved with a peasant girl. That girl's father shoots
Cortez and Francis realizes that she has no yen for this kind of life. She
hurries back to intercept the letter, but a blackmail plot is dragged in
suddenly and the story sags to an embarrassing, confessional ending when
Francis tells all to her husband and is taken back by him. A 1924 version
of the story, filmed by Paramount and called THE NEXT CORNER, also had
Cortez in the same role he played in this version.

p, William LeBaron; d, Herbert Brenon; w, Elizabeth Meehan, Benn W. Levy
(based on the novel by Kate Jordan); ph, Leo Tover.

Drama   (PR:A   MPAA:NR)

TRANSIENT LADY**   (1935) 69m UNIV bw

Gene Raymond (*Carey Marshall*), Henry Hull (*Sen. Hamp Baxter*), Frances
Drake (*Dale Cameron*), June Clayworth (*Pat Warren*), Clark Williams
(*Chris Blake*), Douglas Fowley (*Matt*), Frederick Burton (*Maj. Marshall*),
Edward Ellis (*Nick Kiley*), Clifford Jones (*Fred Baxter*), Helen Lowell (*Eva*),
Clara Blandick.

An ice skating show comes to a small town in the South and problems crop
up. Nice guy Hull runs the town but his brother (Jones), knowing his older
sibling will take care of him, leads the town's gang of thugs. They go to a
skating rink, cause trouble, and are kicked out. They come back for revenge
and Jones is killed by Ellis, who owns the rink. Ellis leaves the scene and
the blame falls on fancy skater Williams. Lawyer Raymond, who has eyes
for Williams' partner, Drake, gets him free in a jury trial. Just when a lynch
mob is ready to take care of Williams, Ellis confesses to the murder and with
that the angry crowd cools off and goes home. Raymond weds Drake instead
of long-time fiancee Clayworth. Some redeemable action, but the courtroom
scenes go on too long.

p, Julius Bernheim; d, Eddie Buzzell; w, Arthur Caesar, Harvey Thew,
Buzzell based on a story by Octavus Roy Cohen); ph, Charles Stumar; ed,
Maurice Wright.

Drama   (PR:A   MPAA:NR)

TRANSPORT FROM PARADISE**   (1967, Czech.) 94m Barrandov
Ceskoslovensky/Impact bw (TRANSPORT Z RAJE)

Zdenek Stepanek (*Lowenbach*), Cestmir Randa (*Marmulstaub*), Ilja Prachar
(*Moric Herz*), Jaroslav Rauser (*Von Holler*), Jiri Vrstala (*Binde*), Ladislav
Pesek (*Roubicek*), Valtr Taub (*Spiegel*), Vlastimil Brodsky (*Mukl*), josef
Abrham (*Datel*), Josef Vinklar (*Vagus*), Jaroslav Rozsival (*A Smith*), Vaclav
Lohnisky (*Man at the Smithy*), Jirina Stepnickova (*Feinerova*), Martin
Gregor (*Geron*), Jindrich Narenta (*Gen. Knecht*), Jiri Nemecek (*Vlastimil
Fiala*), Juraj Herz (*Mylord*), Vladimir Linka, Emanuel Kovarik, Vaclav
Vondracek, Frantisek Nemee (*Dany*), Helga Cockova (*Liza*), Vladimir
Navratil, Stefan Bulejko, Zdenek Braunschlager, Vladimir Hrabanek

(*Zrzek*), Rudolf Cortez, Zdenek Jelinek (*SS Men*), Frantisek Loring (*Dutch-
Speaking Man*), Marta Richterova (*Anna*), Jan Smid (*Stepan*), Ladislav
Potmesil (*Kuzle*), Miroslav Svoboda (*Mayer*), Zlatomir Vacek, Fred Bulin,
Anny Frey, Maurice Orion.

The underlying tensions of a loosely run prisoner camp of Jews is studied.
The Nazis run the camp in a small ghetto section of Germany which contains
no gas chambers. The prisoners seem almost content, running the camp
operations and small businesses in it. But there is always the fear of being
shipped out to another camp—which means certain death. The chairman of
the Council of Jewish Elders will not sign a sheet shipping off some of the
Jews because he knows the shipment is destined for Auschwitz. The
Germans get rid of him and find someone who will sign the order. A group
is rounded up, not realizing where they are headed, so they actually save
places in the train for loved ones and finally, in the last poignant scene, get
aboard the train and go on to death. A grim, sad reminder of an
unforgettable human ordeal.

d, Zbynek Brynych; w, Arnost Lustig, Brynych; ph, Jan Curik; m, Jiri
Sternwald; ed, Miroslav Hajek; art d, Jaroslav Brabenec, Karel Skvor.

Drama   (PR:A   MPAA:NR)

TRAP, THE**   (1947) 68m MON bw (GB: MURDER AT MALIBU
BEACH)

Sidney Toler (*Charlie Chan*), Mantan Moreland (*Birmingham Brown,
Chan's Chauffeur*), Victor Sen Young (*Jimmy Chan*), Tanis Chandler
(*Adelaide Brandt, Press Agent*), Larry Blake (*Rick Daniels, Press Agent*), Kirk Alyn (*Sgt.
Reynolds, State Police*), Rita Quigley (*Clementine*), Anne Nagel (*Marcia*),
Helen Gerald (*Ruby*), Howard Negley (*Cole King, Impresario*), Lois Austin
(*Mrs. Thorn*), Barbara Jean Wong (*San Toy*), Minerva Urecal (*Mrs. Weebles,
Housekeeper*), Margaret Brayton (*Madge Mudge*), Bettie Best (*Winifred*),
Jan Bryant (*Lois*), Walden Boyle (*Doc Brandt, Physiotherapist*).

Super-detective Charlie Chan comes to the aid of a fearful actress whose
fellow thespians are getting killed off. Clues are gathered at the Malibu
beach house where the murders took place and the killer is finally tracked
down. After 22 Charlie Chan films THE TRAP was to be Sidney Toler's final
one. He died later that year and was replaced by Roland Winters, who
stumbled through a handful of mysteries in the series. (See CHARLIE
CHAN series, Index.)

p, James S. Burkett; d, Howard Bretherton; w, Miriam Kissinger; ph, James
Brown; ed, Ace Herman; md, Edward J. Kay; art d, David Milton.

Mystery   (PR:A   MPAA:NR)

TRAP, THE*   (1959) 82m Parkwood-Heath/PAR c (GB: THE BAITED
TRAP)

Richard Widmark (*Ralph Anderson*), Lee J. Cobb (*Victor Massonetti*), Tina
Louise (*Linda Anderson*), Earl Holliman (*Tippy Anderson*), Carl Benton
Reid (*Sheriff Anderson*), Lorne Greene (*Mr. Davis*), Peter Baldwin (*Mellon*),
Chuck Wassil (*1st Policeman*), Richard Shannon (*Len Karger*), Carl Mil-
letaire (*Joey*), Walter Coy.

A big-name cast, with much overacting, this becomes almost a comedy
instead of a crime drama. Widmark has been tossed out of a small town by
his father, the sheriff, because he broke some small law as a youth. He is
now helping him mend when his leg is caught in a trap. But she realizes this
off from the rest of the world. Cobb is all set to leave soon via an airplane
that is supposed to land near the town. Widmark goes along with Cobb until
Reid, Widmark's father, is murdered by Cobb's gang. Then Widmark sets
out to jail Cobb. He looks to his drunk brother Holliman to help, but
Holliman has no backbone, just a gorgeous wife in Louise, who used to be
Widmark's flame. And those two have the sparks flying again. Of course,
Widmark gets his man, and his woman.

p, Norman Panama, Melvin Frank; d, Panama; w, Richard Alan Simmons,
Panama; ph, Daniel L. Fapp (Technicolor); ed, Everett Douglas.

Crime Drama   (PR:A   MPAA:NR)

TRAP, THE**   (1967, Can./Brit.) 106m Parallel/CD c (L'AVENTURE
SAUVAGE)

Rita Tushingham (*Eve*), Oliver Reed (*Jean La Bete*), Rex Sevenoaks (*The
Trader*), Barbara Chilcott (*Trader's Wife*), Linda Goranson (*Trader's Daugh-
ter*), Blain Fairman (*Clerk*), Walter Marsh (*Preacher*), Jo Golland (*Baptiste*),
Jon Granik (*No Name*), Merv Campone (*Yellow Dog*), Reginald McReynolds
(*Captain*).

Set in the Canadian wilderness of the 19th Century, Reed, a trapper, comes
back to civilization after three years with furs and the idea of finding a wife.
He has missed the auction of buying a cast-off woman, so he takes a trader's
housekeeper, a mute named Eve. She serves him well, taking care of him,
even helping him mend when his leg is caught in a trap. But she realizes this
life is not for her, so after she amputates his leg she takes off back to the
settlement. He awakens and discovers he really loved her. Meanwhile, she
is set to marry the clerk of the trader but on the big day she doesn't show
up. She has headed back into the woods with Reed.

p, George H, Brown; d, Sidney Hayers; w, David Osborn; ph, Robert Krasker (Panavision, Eastmancolor); m, Ron Goodwin; ed, Tristam Cones; art d, Harry White; cos, Margaret Furse.

Adventure   **(PR:A   MPAA:NR)**

TRAP DOOR, THE**   (1980) 70m B-Movies c

John Ahearn (Jeremy), Colen Fitzgibbon (Movie Actress), Mary Lou Fogarty (Ms. Hanimex), Robin Harvey (Secretary), Jenny Holzer (Ms. Fist), Gary Indiana (Judge), Dany Johnson (Girl Friend), Richard Prince (Dickie), Marcia Resnick (Bird Woman), Bill Rice (Fuller Brush Man), Jack Smith (Dr. Shrinkelstein), Robin Winters (Movie Actor).

The last Super-8 effort from husband and wife experimental team Scott B. and Beth B., a pair of art school dropouts. Made on a budget of less than $5,000, THE TRAP DOOR tells of the unemployed Ahearn's effort to find some stability in his life, creating a disturbing, oppressive world. This nightmarish life brings Ahearn in contact with a number of exotic characters, each wrapped up in their own selves. Eventually Ahearn is knocked over the head by Smith (a director of many fine American underground films in the 1960s) and robbed. For those interested in experimental art school films, Beth B. and Scott B. will impress. Those who prefer narrative filmmaking, however, should steer clear. In defense of their work, Scott B. is quoted as saying, "Our reason for dealing with Super-8 is that it's important that people who are not part of the industry, who are not part of the power structure or the economic elite, can make films that do get released."

p,d,w&ph, Beth B., Scott B.; m, Bob Mason, Beth B., Scott B.

Drama   **(PR:O   MPAA:NR)**

TRAPEZE*   (1932, Ger.) 80m Harmonie bw (SALTO MORTALE)

Anna Sten (Marina), Reinhold Bernt (Jim), Adolf Wohlbrueck [Anton Walbrook] (Robby), Otto Wallburg (Press Agent), Curt Gerron (Grimby)

This first German talkie by E.A. Dupont also brought German screen star Sten to the attention of the American public. Too bad she couldn't have picked a better-paced film to work in to help her cause. Story centers on a circus with a girl acrobat and two lion feeders. One of them and Sten work out a dangerous trapeze act that has the other man pulling a lever to make it work. The first pair fall in love and marry and then the husband fluffs a trick and breaks a leg. The other steps in and Sten changes allegiances. This angers the husband who doesn't pull the lever, sending the pair to a certain death. In a gripping and taut sequence, the pair barely save themselves. (In German; English subtitles.)

d, E.A. Dupont; w, Rudolf Katscher, Egon Eis (based on a story by Alfred Machard); ph, Friedel Behn-Grund, Akos Farkas; m, Arthur Guttman, Walter Jurmann.

Drama   **(PR:A   MPAA:NR)**

TRAPEZE***½   (1956) 105m Susan/UA c

Burt Lancaster (Mike Ribble), Tony Curtis (Tino Orsini), Gina Lollobrigida (Lola), Katy Jurado (Rosa), Thomas Gomez (Bouglione), Johnny Puleo (Max the Dwarf), Minor Watson (John Ringling North), Gerard Landry (Chikki), Jean-Pierre Kerrien (Otto), Sidney James (Snake Charmer), Gabrielle Fontan (Old Woman), Pierre Tabard (Paul), Gamil Ratab (Stefan), Michel Thomas (Ringmaster), The Gimma Boys (Circus Family Children), Edward Hagopian, Eddie Ward, Sally Marlowe, Fay Alexander, Willy Krause, Betty Codreano, The Arriolas, Mme. Felco Cipriano, The Codreanos, Simpion Bouglione, Zavatta, Mylos, Lulu and Tonio.

Despite some stiff acting and a ponderous script, this was a smash at the box office, if only for the fact that audiences got to see former circus man Lancaster in a milieu he loved and playing against the immensely attractive Lollobrigida and the handsome Curtis. Lancaster is a lame acrobat who is famed for having done the impossible, a "triple" off the trapeze before having the accident that caused his limp. Two somersaults in mid-air were commonplace but the "triple" was what every high flyer dreamed of. He's working as a rigger for a Parisian circus when Curtis arrives, eager to meet Lancaster and learn from him. Curtis is the son of a former circus man who'd been friends with Lancaster, and Curtis thinks that he could do the "triple" if Lancaster were willing to educate him and to be his "catcher." Knowing how dangerous the stunt is, Lancaster does everything he can to discourage Curtis. The circus is owned by Gomez, who would love to have some enormous starring act to help business. After a while, Curtis wears Lancaster down and the older man decides that he might recapture his own glory by helping Curtis achieve the feat. The two men become very close, then Lollobrigida enters. She's a scheming member of a tumbling act who is unsatisfied with staying on the ground and would like to have the fame and the fortune that trapeze artists merit. She begins using her wiles on Lancaster, but he has no interest so she turns to the more naive Curtis, despite the fact that she is in love with Lancaster. That's about it for the story, except that the high-wire work is so exciting and Reed's direction of

the "triple" is breathtaking, and all of that more than compensates for the shortcomings of the remainder of the movie. Seen briefly is Johnny Puleo, the little person who served for so many years as one of the "Harmonica Rascals" with Borah Minevitch. The ambience of circus life is well limned and one can almost smell the elephants.

p, James Hill; d, Carol Reed; w, James R. Webb, Liam O'Brien (based on the novel The Killing Frost by Max Catto); ph, Robert Krasker (CinemaScope, DeLuxe Color); m, Malcolm Arnold; ed, Bert Bates; art d, Rino Mondellini; spec eff, R.J. Lannan.

Drama   **Cas.**   **(PR:A-C   MPAA:NR)**

TRAPP FAMILY, THE*   (1961, Ger.) 106m Divina/Fox c

Ruth Leuwerik (Maria von Trapp), Hans Holt (Baron von Trapp), Josef Meinrad (Dr. Wassner), Maria Holst (Countess), Friedrich Domin (Gruber), Hilde von Stolz (Baroness Mathilde), Michael Ande, Ursula Wolff, Angelika Werth, Knut Mahlke, Monika Wolf, Ursula Ettrich, Monika Ettrich (Children), A.D. Edel.

This dubbed story was told much better with the later and classic Julie Andrews' musical, "The Sound of Music." This one tells about free spirit Leuwerik who is sent to take care of the Baron and his seven musically inclined children. She is shocked at how rigid their discipline is, so she induces them to play games and enjoy life for what it is. This doesn't sit well with the Baron, who is ready to fire her when he hears the children singing. He changes his mind and also falls for her, but she must go back to the convent from where she came to renounce her vows. The kids take their act on the road and attract large crowds. The Nazis come in and ruin everything and confiscate the Baron's money, so the family goes to the U.S. There, the singing doesn't get noticed at first, but gradually a following builds up. They decide the U.S. is for them and buy a farm in Vermont and stay.

p, Wolfgang Reinhardt, Utz Utermann; d, Wolfgang Liebeneiner; w, George Hurdalek, Lee Kresel (based on material provided by Baroness Maria von Trapp); ph, Werner Krien (Eastmancolor); m, Franz Grothe; ed, Margot von Schleffen, Salvatore Billitteri; set d, Robert Herlth, Gottfried Will; cos, Brigitte Scholz; makeup, Charlotte Schmidt-Kersten, Franz Mayrhofer.

Drama   **(PR:A   MPAA:NR)**

TRAPPED*   (1931) 63m Hollywood Syndicate/Big Four bw

Nick Stuart, Priscilla Dean, Nena Quartero, Tom Santschi.

Typical bad-guys-rob-bank movie. Then the story cuts to a nightclub to confuse us and back to the mobsters killing each other. When that is done, the policeman marries a nightclub singer and a driver for the gang marries her daughter. Confusing and not worth even a dime.

d, Bruce Mitchell; w, Jackson Parks, Edith Brown.

Crime   **(PR:A   MPAA:NR)**

TRAPPED***   (1937) 58m COL bw

Charles Starrett (Haley), Peggy Stratford (Adele), Robert Middlemass (Rothert), Allan Sears (Cal), Ted Oliver (Ike), Lew Meehan (Morse), Edward Piel, Sr (Bill), Jack Rockwell (Tom), Edward J. Le Saint (Doctor), Francis Sayles (John), Art Mix.

One of Starrett's best westerns. Fast-moving effort by director Leon Barsha in his first directing effort after working as an editor. Starrett gets home just as his brother is breathing his last breath, shot by rustlers. Starrett takes after them and comes across rustler Middlemass, who is faking paralysis below the waist. Starrett wants to get revenge on Middlemass but has second thoughts about it when he becomes involved with Stratford, his niece. Lots of fists flying and gunplay as Starrett gets his man and the girl after some heavy-duty thinking along with some heavy-duty fighting.

p, Harry Decker; d, Leon Barsha; w, John Rathmell (based on a story by Claude Rister); ph, Allen G. Seigler; ed, William Lyon.

Western   **(PR:A   MPAA:NR)**

TRAPPED**   (1949) 78m EL bw

Lloyd Bridges (Stewart), John Hoyt (Downey), Barbara Payton (Laurie), James Todd (Sylvester), Russ Conway (Gunby), Bert Conway (Mantz), Tom Noonan, Ruth Robinson, Rory Mallinson, Mack Williams, Stephen Chase, Henry [Harry] Antrim, Ken Christy, Renny McEvoy, Bob Karnes, Alex Davidoff, Sid Kane.

Story about how the Secret Service breaks up a counterfeiting ring. They infiltrate the gang, using Bridges, an ex-counterfeiter let out of jail to help in the case. He leads them to the gang, which is using his old plates, and just when the gang is to be rounded up, the mob finds out that Hoyt is a government agent. Suspenseful and well-paced yarn with believable incidents and story.

p, Bryan Foy; d, Richard Fleischer; w, Earl Felton, George Zuckerman; ph, Guy Roe; m, Sol Kaplan; ed, Alfred DeGaetano; md, Irving Friedman; art d, Frank Durlauf. set d, Armor Marlowe; spec eff, Roy W. Seawright;

makeup, Ern Westmore.

Drama Cas. (PR:A MPAA:NR)

TRAPPED BY BOSTON BLACKIE** (1948) 67m COL bw

Chester Morris (*Boston Blackie*), June Vincent (*Doris Bradley*), Richard Lane (*Inspector Farraday*), Patricia White (*Joan Howell*), Edward Norris (*Igor Borio*), George E. Stone (*Runt*), Frank Sully (*Sgt. Matthews*), Fay Baker (*Sandra Doray*), William Forrest (*Mr. Carter*), Sarah Selby (*Mrs. Carter*), Mary Currier (*Mrs. Kenyon*), Pierre Watkin (*Dunn*), Ben Welden (*Louis*), Abigail Adams (*Receptionist*), Ray Harper (*Clerk*).

The 13th in a series put out by Columbia in the "Boston Blackie" cycle. Morris and his amiable runt buddy, Stone, are in charge of guarding some priceless jewelry that is then stolen, with all the evidence pointing to them as the culprits. The film follows formula as they hunt the real thieves. Morris and Stone put on disguises, once as an older couple, and that is so old hat in the series that the story sags a bit. (See BOSTON BLACKIE series, Index.)

p, Rudolph C. Flothow; d, Seymour Friedman; w, Maurice Tombragel (based on a story by Charles Marion, Edward Bock from characters created by Jack Boyle); ph, Philip Tannura; ed, Dwight Caldwell; md, Mischa Bakaleinikoff; art d, George Brooks; set d, Louis Diage.

Mystery (PR:A MPAA:NR)

TRAPPED BY G-MEN*½ (1937) 63m COL bw (AKA: THE RIVER OF MISSING MEN)

Jack Holt (*Bill Donovan/Martin Galloway*), Wynne Gibson (*Alice*), C. Henry Gordon (*Kligcur*), Jack La Rue (*Drake*), Edward Brophy (*Lefty*), William Pawley (*Grady*), Arthur Hohl (*Blackie*), Robert Emmett O'Connor (*Jim*), William Bakewell (*Dick*), Eleanor Stewart (*Nancy*), Charles Lane (*Fingers*), Frank Darien (*Dad Higbee*), Lucien Prival (*Franzy*), Richard Tucker (*Conover*), George Cleveland, Wallis Clark.

The FBI poses Holt as a crook, getting in with a gang member, and then breaking out of prison to find out where the gang hides. Holt is tested each step of the way and passes each test with his fists. As expected, the gang discovers he is a G-man and Holt is forced to fight his way out. One bad chase scene, with Holt and the gang members canoeing over perilous rapids, strains credulity to the breaking point.

p, Larry Darmour; d, Lewis D. Collins; w, Tom Kilpatrick (based on a story by Bernard McConville); ph, James S. Brown, Jr.; ed, Dwight Caldwell.

Crime Drama (PR:A MPAA:NR)

TRAPPED BY TELEVISION*½ (1936) 63m COL bw

Mary Astor (*Bobby Blake*), Lyle Talbot (*Fred Dennis*), Nat Pendleton (*Rocky*), Joyce Compton (*Mae*), Thurston Hall (*Curtis*), Henry Mollison (*Thornton*), Wyrley Birch (*Turner*), Robert Strange (*Standish*), Marc Lawrence (*Griffin*).

Turtle-paced drama about an inventor who is fiddling with television and how a mob wants in on the action. As Talbot dallies in the lab, the gang approaches a radio station, offering the plans for an outrageous sum of money. Astor and Talbot are the romantic interests but they are unbelievable as a team. The story starts agonizingly slow but builds to a spanking good climax as the television whiz takes care of everyone.

p, Ben Pivar; d, Del Lord; w, Lee Loeb, Harold Buchman (based on a story by Sherman Lowe, Al Martin); ph, Allen G. Seigler; ed, James Sweeney.

Drama (PR:A MPAA:NR)

TRAPPED BY THE TERROR* (1949, Brit.) 56m Merton Park/GFD bw

James Kenney (*Philip Dupois*), Colin Stephens (*Maurice*), Valerie Carlton (*Marie*), Ian Colin (*Count Dupis*), Louise Gainsborough (*Countess Dupis*), Alastair Bannerman (*Marcel*), John Longdon (*Pierre*), Martin Benson (*Governor*).

An amateurish production set in France during the French Revolution. A young boy from England sees his count and countess parents carted away to prison. He enlists the aid of some former servants and the children of a friendly baker to help them escape. Some indiscriminate children viewers may identify with the young hero, but most will find the story silly and unbelievable.

p, Frank Hoare; d, Cecil Musk; w, Sherard Powell, Mary Cathcart Borer (based on a story by Ian Grundy); ph, A.T. Dinsdale.

Children's Film/Historical (PR:AAA MPAA:NR)

TRAPPED BY WIRELESS (SEE: YOU MAY BE NEXT, 1936)

TRAPPED IN A SUBMARINE**½ (1931, Brit.) 63m British International/Wardour bw (GB: MEN LIKE THESE)

John Batten, James Enstone, Edward Gee, John Hunt, Sydney Seaward, Syd Crossley, James Peachey, Athol Fleming, Lesley Wareing, Valentine White, James Watts, Chang Fat, Wang Wong.

An early piece of naval heroism from British history is brought to the screen in this nearly plotless picture. Crew members of the submarine *Poseidon*, after being struck by a cargo ship in Chinese waters, bravely make good their escape. English motion picture critics were invited to suggest titles for the film after the original title--which was too close to reality--had to be scrapped due to the reluctance of the British Admiralty to publicize the embarrassing event.

p, Walter C. Mycroft; d, Walter Summers; w, Summers, Mycroft; ph, Jack Parker, Horace Wheddon.

Historical Drama (PR:A MPAA:NR)

TRAPPED IN TANGIERS* (1960, Ital./Span.) 77m Cervi/FOX bw (AGGUATO A TANGERI)

Edmund Purdom (*John Milwood*), Genevieve Page (*Mary Bolevasco*), Gino Cervi (*Professor Bolevasco*), Jose Guardiola, Felix De Franco, Antonio Molino, Enrique Pelayo, Mario Moreno, Amparo Rivelles, Luis Pena.

A poorly put-together drama about drug smuggling. Purdom is the Interpol agent sent to Tangiers to find some drug smugglers and gain information on them. He and Page make eyes at each other and it turns out her stepfather, Cervi, is the head of the whole operation and also a leading citizen of the town. After Purdom battles Page's father and his henchmen, the father is killed and now the two can enjoy life happily forever. One of Purdom's few non-costume historical-epic roles during his fall from early big-budget films when he became a world traveler. The picture, featuring an international cast, typified the ill-dubbed offerings that 20th Century-Fox picked up for distribution at very low cost during the period. The producer is the son of actor Cervi, who plays the chief villain. Director/co-scripter Freda, a visual stylist, has something of a cult following.

p, Antonio Cervi; d, Riccardo Freda; w, Alessandro Continenza, Vittorio Petrilli, Paolo Spinola, Freda; ph, Gabor Pogany (Supercinescope); m, Lilio Luttazzi; m/l, "The Last Phone Call," Edward Brody (sung by Gin Maureen).

Crime Drama (PR:A MPAA:NR)

TRAPPED IN THE SKY** (1939) 61m COL bw

Jack Holt (*Major*), Ralph Morgan (*Col. Whalen*), Paul Everton (*Gen. Mooyp*), Katherine De Mille (*Carol Rayder*), C. Henry Gordon (*Fornay*), Sidney Blackmer (*Mann*), Ivan Lebedeff (*Dure*), Regis Toomey (*Lt. Gray*), Holmes Herbert (*Fielding*), Guy D'Ennery (*Henry*).

Despite its obviously low budget, the film gets everything for its money. It deals with the building of a secret, noiseless plane that foreign agents want to get their hands on. The inventor wants to sell the plans to other countries but they can only get them if the plane tests out a failure. On the first flight, the sabotaged plane crashes and the pilot is killed. His superior, Holt, takes the blame in a scheme that gets him court-martialed to gain the confidence of the foreign agents. They fall for it and Holt rounds them up. One good sequence has Holt flying with the inventor when an explosion occurs. Dangling finish doesn't really tell what happened to the traitorous inventor or whether the government ever did purchase the plane.

p, Larry Darmour; d, Lewis D. Collins; w, Eric Taylor, Gordon Rigby (based on a story by Taylor); ph, James S. Brown, Jr.; ed, Dwight Caldwell.

Action/Aviation Drama (PR:A MPAA:NR)

TRAQUENARDS (SEE: EROTIQUE, 1969, Fr.)

TRAUMA*½ (1962) 93m Artist XVI/Parade bw

John Conte (*Warren Clyner*), Lynn Bari (*Helen Garrison*), Lorrie Richards (*Emmaline Garrison*), David Garner (*Craig Schoonover*), Warren Kemmerling (*Luther*), William Bissell (*Thaddeus Hall*), Bond Blackman (*Robert*), William Justine, Roy Lennert (*Treasury Agents*), Renee Mason (*Carla*), Robert Totten (*Gas Station Attendant*), Afred Chafe (*Police Officer*), Ruby Borner (*Maid*).

This confusing psychological drama deals with newlywed Richards who, suffering amnesia, returns with her husband Conte to her old family home. Her mental condition is the result of her shock at having seen her aunt--one-time lover of her new husband--murdered by an unknown assailant in the family swimming pool. Befriending Garner, the nephew of caretaker Kemmerling, she explores the estate with him; her memory of past events returns as a result and she inquires about the whereabouts of her late aunt's--Bari's--retarded son, who--unknown to anyone--was fathered by Kemmerling. Are you with us so far? In an unrelated subplot, Conte is arrested for fraud, clearing the way for Richards' romance with Garner. Kemmerling reprises an earlier crime by attempting to drown Richards in the swimming pool, but he is interrupted by Garner and conveniently has a fatal heart attack. With his dying breath, he attempts to unravel the complex plot: he had killed the retardate, who was a homicidal maniac, and then had drowned witness Bari. A first film appearance for Richards and one of the last for Bari, the only well-known name in the cast, this was also the first effort of the independent producing company. Having exhausted several plots in this one picture, the producers apparently felt no need to make another.

p, Joseph Cranston; d&w, Robert Malcolm Young; ph, Jacques Marquette; m, Buddy Collette; ed, Harold J. Dennis; md, Collette.

Horror   **(PR:C   MPAA:NR)**

TRAUMSTADT   (SEE: DREAM TOWN, 1973, Ger.)

TRAVELING EXECUTIONER, THE*   (1970) 95m Solitaire/MGM c

Stacy Keach (*Jonas Candide*), Marianna Hill (*Gundred Herzallerliebst*), Bud Cort (*Jimmy*), Graham Jarvis (*Doc Prittle*), James J. Sloyan (*Piquant*), M. Emmet Walsh (*Warden Brodski*), John Bottoms (*Lawyer*), Ford Rainey (*Stanley Mae*), James Greene (*Gravey Combs*), Sammy Reese (*Priest*), Stefan Gierasch (*Willy Herzallerliebst*), Logan Ramsey (*La Follette*), Charles Tyner (*Virgil*), William Mims (*Lynn*), Val Avery (*Jake*), Walter Barnes (*Sheriff*), Charlie Briggs (*Zak*), Paul Gauntt (*Jeremy*), Claire Brennen (*Woman Passerby*), Scottie MacGregor (*Alice Thorn*), Tony Fraser (*1st Child*), Martine Fraser (*2nd Child*), Lorna Thayer (*Madam*), Pat Patterson (*Roscoe*).

A different type of story. Keach is excellent as an executioner for hire who travels around the country in 1918 with his own electric chair performing executions for $100 per customer. In Alabama, he has to kill Hill and her brother Gierasch. He fries the brother but the girl beds Keach in order to put off her execution. The love-struck Keach tries to get prison doctor Jarvis to help him fake the execution. The doctor puts up a steep price tag and when Keach is turned down for a loan at the bank, he murders a guard and frees Hill. She takes off on him anyway when he returns to claim his equipment. Both are caught; her execution commuted, she gets a life sentence and Keach is executed by his idiot assistant Cort, who electrocutes not only Keach but the chair as well, making it into a bonfire. This black comedy was the fourth to be made under the aegis of a new production administrative staff at MGM headed by Herbert F. Solow. Novice screenwriter Bateson was a student at the University of Southern California when he whipped up this macabre froth. The picture premiered in Montgomery, Alabama, where locations were shot.

p&d, Jack Smight; w, Garrie Bateson; ph, Phillip Lathrop (Panavision, Metrocolor); m, Jerry Goldsmith; ed, Neil Travis; art d, George W. Davis, Edward Carfagno; set d, Robert R. Benton, Keogh Gleason; makeup, Fred Williams.

Comedy   **(PR:O   MPAA:R)**

TRAVELING HUSBANDS*   (1931) 73m RKO bw

Evelyn Brent (*Ruby*), Frank Albertson (*Barry*), Constance Cummings (*Ellen Wilson*), Hugh Herbert (*Hymie*), Carl Miller (*Ben*), Frank McHugh (*Pinkie*), Spencer Charters (*Joe*), Dorothy Peterson (*Martha*), Purnell Pratt (*J. C. Wilson*), Gwen Lee (*Mabel*), Rita La Roy (*Vera*), Lucille Williams (*Daisy*), Tom Francis (*Walter*), Stanley Fields (*Dan*).

Salacious salesmen convene in a hotel suite with a group of call girls. Young drummer Albertson, flat broke, can't get to first base with a sales prospect's attractive but mercenary daughter, Cummings, who gets involved with star salesman Miller in the adjacent hotel room. She screams as the raunchy representative lustfully pursues her, and the partying neighbors burst into the room. In the ensuing confusion, party girl Brent shoots one of the salesmen, recognizing him as the man who initiated her into her calling. Albertson becomes the prime suspect, but is saved when Brent confesses that she is the one who wounded the rotter. The Hays Office, with its stern Code, was established a year before this racy picture was released, but it hadn't quite kicked in yet. One song, "There's a Sob in My Heart" (Max Steiner, Humphrey Pearson).

p, William LeBaron; d, Paul Sloane; w, Humphrey Pearson; ph, Leo Tover.

Crime/Comedy   **(PR:O   MPAA:NR)**

TRAVELING LADY   (SEE: BABY THE RAIN MUST FALL, 1965)

TRAVELING SALESLADY, THE½   (1935) 64m FN bw

Joan Blondell (*Angela Twitchell*), William Gargan (*Pat O'Connor*), Glenda Farrell (*Claudette Ruggles*), Hugh Herbert (*Elmer Niles*), Grant Mitchell (*Rufus K. Twitchell*), Ruth Donnelly (*Millicent Twitchell*), Al Shean (*Schmidt*), Johnny Arthur (*Melton*), Mary Treen (*Miss Wells*), ert Roach (*Harry*), Joseph Crehan (*Murdock*), James Donlan (*McNeill*), Harry Holman (*O'Connor, Sr.*), Carroll Nye (*Burroughs*), Selmer Jackson (*Scovil*), Gordon "Bill" Elliott (*Freddie*), Milton Kibbee (*Stenographer*), Frances Lee (*Secretary*), Bill May (*Announcer*), Hattie McDaniel (*Black Woman*), Harry Seymour (*Buyer*), Olive Jones (*Miss Henry*), Gertrude Sutton (*Secretary*), Ferdinand Schumann-Heink (*Clerk*).

Blondell plays the rambunctious daughter of conservative toothpaste

manufacturer Mitchell. Irked by his backwardness in business, she teams with his rival and with nutty inventor Herbert and markets a new brand, "Cocktail Toothpaste," which tastes like whiskey in the morning, martini before dinner, and champagne just before bedtime. Sales zoom, sparked by radio advertising, and daddy learns his lesson. Sharp dialog and good comic performances all around.

p, Sam Bischoff; d, Ray Enright; w, F. Hugh Herbert, Manuel Seff, Benny Rubin (based on a story by Frank Howard Clark); ph, George Barnes; ed, Owen Marks; md, Leo F. Forbstein; art d, Anton Grot, Arthur Gruenbarger; cos, Orry-Kelly.

Comedy   **(PR:A   MPAA:NR)**

TRAVELING SALESWOMAN**   (1950) 75m COL bw

Joan Davis (*Mabel King*), Andy Devine (*Waldo*), Adele Jergens (*Lilly*), Joe Sawyer (*Cactus Jack*), Dean Riesner (*Tom*), John Cason (*Fred*), Chief Thundercloud (*Running Deer*), Harry Hayden (*J. L. King*), Charles Halton (*Clumhill*), Minerva Urecal (*Mrs. Owen*), Eddy Waller (*Mr. Owen*), Teddy Infuhr (*Homer*), Robert Cherry (*Simon*), William "Billy" Newell (*Bartender*), Harry Woods (*Jenkins*), Ethan Laidlaw (*Mike*), Harry Tyler (*Jasper North*), Alan [Al] Bridge (*P. Carter*), Gertrude Charre (*Squaw*), Emmett Lynn (*Desert Rat*), Stanley Andrews (*Banker*), George Chesebro (*Horseman*), Heinie Conklin (*Man*), Chief Yowlachie (*Sam*), Bill Wilkerson (*Tony*), Nick Thompson (*Indian Itch*), George McDonald (*Bob*), Fred Aldrich (*Cow Puncher*), Louis Mason (*Livery Stable Man*), Jessie Arnold (*Lady Customer*), Bob Wilke (*Loser*).

Davis stars in this lighthearted comedy selling soap to save daddy's plant. To make some sales, she heads out West with drip boy friend Devine following her to keep her out of trouble and keep an eye on her interests. All types of trouble follow her including getting involved in an Indian war. Call this one a washout. Songs include "Every Baby Needs a Daddy," "He Died with His Boots On" (Allan Roberts, Lester Lee).

p, Tony Owen; d, Charles F. Riesner; w, Howard Dimsdale; ph, George B. Diskant; ed, Viola Lawrence; md, Mischa Bakaleinikoff; art d, Carl Anderson; set d, George Montgomery; cos, Jean Louis; spec eff, Fred Wolff; makeup, Bob Meading.

Comedy   **(PR:A   MPAA:NR)**

TRAVELLER'S JOY**   (1951, Brit.) 78m Gainsborough/GFD bw

Googie Withers (*Bumble Pelham*), John McCallum (*Reggie Pelham*), Yolande Donlan (*Lil Fowler*), Maurice Denham (*Fowler*), Colin Gordon (*Tony Wright*), Gerard Heinz (*Helstrom*), Geoffrey Sumner (*Lord Tilbrook*), Peter Illing (*Tilsen*), Dora Bryan (*Eva*), Anthony Forwood (*Mick Rafferty*), Sandra Dorne, Eric Pohlmann.

Based on a successful play that ran for two years in London's West End, the picture tells the tale of a divorced couple stranded in Sweden without money and their efforts to get some cash to get back home. Almost too fluffy to be believable with all the expected comic situations occurring. Withers and McCallum run around like chickens with their heads cut off, and eventually come back together with enough money to return home. No one really missed them in the first place.

p, Anthony Darnborough; d, Ralph Thomas; w, Allan Mackinnon, Bernard Quayle (based on the play by Arthur Macrae); ph, Jack Cox; m, Arthur Wilkinson; ed, Jean Barker; cos, Julie Harris.

Comedy   **(PR:A   MPAA:NR)**

TRAVELS WITH ANITA   (SEE: LOVERS AND LIARS, 1981, Ital.)

TRAVELS WITH MY AUNT**   (1972, Brit.) 109m MGM c

Maggie Smith (*Aunt Augusta*), Alec McCowen (*Henry Pulling*), Lou Gossett (*Wordsworth*), Robert Stephens (*Visconti*), Cindy Williams (*Tooley*), Robert Flemyng (*Crowder*), Jose Luis Lopez Vazquez (*Mons. Dambreuse*), Raymond Gerome (*Mario*), Daniel Emilfork (*Hakim*), Corinne Marchand (*Louise*), John Hamill (*Crowder's Man*), David Swift (*Detective*), Bernard Holley (*Bobby*), Valerie White (*Mme. Dambreuse*), Antonio Pica (*Elegant Man*), Alex Savage (*Minister*), Olive Behrendt (*Madame in Messagero*), Nora Norman (*Stripper*), Aldo Sanbrell (*Hakim's Assistant*), Charlie Bravo (*Policeman*), Cass Martin (*Boat Skipper*), Javier Escriva (*Dancer in Messagero*), William Layton Art Expert, Julio Pena (*Mons. Alexandre*).

Madness runs rampant in this adaptation of Graham Greene's best-selling novel. McCowen is an English banker who meets Smith, a classic red-haired example of an older British eccentric, while attending the cremation of his mother's remains. Smith claims to be McCowen's aunt and says the ashes he now holds in an urn are not his mother's. McCowen escorts his newly discovered relative back to her apartment which is flamboyantly decorated. Waiting for them is Gossett, Smith's current lover. After their arrival, Smith receives a package which holds a finger supposedly removed from the hand of Stephens, the true passion of her heart, and an enclosed note informs her that unless she pays a $100,000 ransom the two will again be reunited, though not in one piece. Mc Cowen, a rather boring man, thinks the atmosphere at Smith's home is a little hectic and heads back to his place in the suburbs. When the police pay a call on him, McCowen is surprised to find that Gossett had removed the ashes from inside the urn and replaced them with marijuana. The law lets him go but McCowen hears from Smith, who wants her nephew to travel with her to Paris. There he will join Gossett's company with his aunt. McCowen agrees, not realizing that Smith is also using him to help pay off Stephens' ransom by illegally smuggling foreign money out of England to Turkey. The two board the famed Orient Express where McCowen meets Williams, a young American hippie who takes a liking to the Englishman. she gets her stodgy new companion to join her in smoking some dope, then engages him in uninhibited sex. When the train stops in Milan Smith receives a bouquet of flowers along with an ear that seemingly belongs to her missing lover. Gerome, the flower bearer, proves to be Smith's son whom she had by Stephens, a fact that shocks McCowen. Arriving at the Turkish border McCowen gets another unpleasant surprise when officials discover Smith's smuggling plot, and the two are sent back to Paris. McCowen, whose personality is beginning to show some signs of life for all he's been through thus far, suggests that Smith go to another of her lovers in order to obtain the ransom cash. The plan involves Vazquez, a wealthy Frenchman who drops dead of a heart attack in Smith's hotel suite. A valiant attempt is made to blackmail the man's widow, but she is impervious to their threats. Smith decides to sell an important portrait of herself to raise the money, then informs McCowen that he is not her nephew. Like Gerome, McCowen is a son of hers, fathered by Stephens as well. After the portrait is sold the two rejoin Gossett and take a fishing boat to Africa where they are scheduled to pay off the ransom. The cash is handed over and Stephens appears, nary a hair out of place, to say nothing of fingers and ears. It has all been an elaborate plot to dupe Smith out of her money but thanks to her now wily nephew/son the plan has been foiled. It seems McCowen had only handed the kidnapers a small amount of the ransom money as the whole thing seemed suspicious to him from the start. McCowen now wants to use the money to buy back the painting for Smith. She has other plans for the cash, however, and tells McCowen the money would be better spent continuing their travels. One coin flip later and it's off to Nepal as the pair decide it's high time to reunite with Williams. At the core of TRAVELS WITH MY AUNT is Smith's wildly histrionic and occasionally hammy performance. She sweeps and swirls like a hurricane, picking up everything that comes in her path, as McCowen remains an uneasy eye within her storm. Though she is clearly enjoying the role there are moments when her eccentricity is pushed too far and it drains the character of believability. Her energy is wonderful, but not when it leaps into the realm of overacting. McCowen handles his strait-laced role well, with Gossett and Williams providing delightful performances in their smaller parts. This is a film alive with color, brimming with setting and costumes that match the flamboyant central character. Costume designer Powell was awarded an Oscar for his work on the film. Condensing Greene's novel into a workable screenplay was not entirely successful. Some moments are glossed over, others fly by all too rapidly in a valiant attempt to cram in as much of the book as possible with in the 109-minute running time. While it doesn't always succeed, the spirit is there often enough to cover the rapid-fire plot development. Cukor gives this a sort of tongue-in-cheek direction; at this point in his career his heyday was long past and the film is no match for some of his earlier successes. Like its central character, it is unusual, unexpected, and not entirely what it projects itself to be yet it is entertaining. The role of Aunt Augusta was originally to have been played by Katherine Hepburn but she was replaced by Smith shortly before production was to begin. Everyone involved had a different story as to why the change was made. Hepburn claimed she hadn't the faintest idea why she'd been replaced but said that when she left Cukor almost went with her. "Don't be impractical. You've worked on the film for two years," Hepburn reportedly told her old friend. For his part Cukor told an interviewer from the New York Daily News that Hepburn still was his first choice for the role, but he couldn't allow some of the changes she demanded in the script. According to the director, Hepburn finally withdrew and the two parted amicably.

p, Robert Fryer, James Cresson; d, George Cukor; w, Jay Presson Allen, Hugh Wheeler (based on the novel by Graham Greene); ph, Douglas Slocombe (Panavision, Metrocolor); m, Tony Hatch; ed, John Bloom; prod d, John Box; art d, Gil Parrondo, Robert W. Laing; set d, Dario Simoni; cos, Anthony Powell, Germinal Rangel; m/l, "Serenade of Love," Jackie Trent, Hatch; makeup, Jose Antonio Sanchez.

Comedy   (PR:C   MPAA:PG)

TRE NOTTI D'AMORE   (SEE: THREE NIGHTS OF LOVE, 1969, Ital.)

TRE NOTTI VIOLENTE   (SEE: WEB OF VIOLENCE, 1966, Ital./Span.)

TRE PASSI NEL DELIRIO   (SEE: SPIRITS OF THE DEAD, 1968, Fr./Ital.)

TREACHERY ON THE HIGH SEAS**   (1939, Brit.) 68m Dela/Film Alliance (GB: NOT WANTED ON VOYAGE)

Bebe Daniels (May Hardy), Ben Lyon (Johnny Hammond), Tom Helmore (Edward Brailstone), Charles Farrell (Logan), Hay Petrie (Brainie), Gordon McLeod (Flemming), James Carew (The Chief).

Boring crime film featuring Lyon as an insurance investigator going undercover as a gangster to get evidence to convict a jewel thief. While part of the gang, he is double-crossed and his passport is stolen by his fellow thugs. Trying to get to the U.S., he takes a disguise again, this time as a member of the ship's crew. After some digging he finds the real jewels have been replaced by fakes. As he investigates, Daniels falls in love with him, even though she is part of the gang of thieves. She changes her allegiance to Lyon, and helps him solve his case. He returns the favor by saving her life at the end. Lyon and Daniels were husband and wife in real life, and appeared in a number of films together.

p, Alexander Dembo de Lasta; d, Emil E. Reinert; w, Charles Lincoln, Harold Simpson (based on the play "Murder in the Stalls" by Maurice Messenger); ph, Roy Fogwell, Jimmy Harvey.

Crime   (PR:A   MPAA:NR)

TREACHERY RIDES THE RANGE½**   (1936) 56m WB bw

Dick Foran (Capt. Red Tyler), Paula Stone (Ruth Drummond), Craig Reynolds (Wade Carter), Monte Blue (Col. Drummond), Carlyle Moore, Jr (Little big Wolf), Monte Montague (Nebraska Bill), Henry Otho (Burley Barton), Don Barclay (Cpl. Bunce), Jim Thorpe (Chief Red Smoke), Frank Bruno (Little Big Fox), Dick Botiller (Antelope Boy), Gene Alsace [Rocky Camron] (Scout Blackbourne), Milt Kibbee, Bud Osborne, Nick Copeland, Tom Wilson, Iron Eyes Cody, William Desmond, Cliff Saum, Frank McCarroll, Frank Ellis, Artie Ortego.

Foran did 12 westerns for Warner Brothers and this is near the top of the dozen. Mistreatment of Indians on the buffalo range is the focus, as a couple of buffalo hunters are trying to stir up some trouble with the Cheyennes. Foran's job as an Army captain is to take Stone through Indian country. But she falls in with the bad hunters, who are breaking the treaty her father had set up. Foran can't help but get tossed in jail while the Indians go on the warpath. He finally gets out, and with help from his special trick horse, catches the crooks and appeases the Indians. He also has time to sing "Ridin' Home" and "Leather and Steel" (M.K. Jerome, Jack Scholl). Famed athlete Jim Thorpe is the leader of the Cheyennes.

p, Bryan Foy; d, Frank McDonald; w, William Jacobs; ph, L. W. O'Connell; ed, Frank McGee; md, Leo F. Forbstein; art d, Ted Smith.

Western   (PR:A   MPAA:NR)

TREAD SOFTLY½**   (1952, Brit.) 70m Albany/Apex bw

Frances Day (Madeleine Peters), Patricia Dainton (Tangye Ward), John Bentley (Keith Gilbert), John Laurie (Angus McDonald), Olaf Olsen (Philip Defoe), Nora Nicholson (Isobel Mayne), Harry Locke (Nutty Potts), Batty Baskcomb (Olivia Winter), Robert Urquhart (Clifford Brett), Michael Ward, Betty Hare, Ronald Leigh-Hunt, Hamilton Keene, Anthony Verner, Colin Croft, Nelly Arno.

A London stage production starring Day is to take place in a reportedly haunted theater. The woman who rents producer Bentley the theater makes only one condition–that the dressing room of her husband, murdered years earlier, remain locked. The owner's son is killed on stage and during the police investigation that follows clues lead to the locked dressing room where Day's corpse is found. A tepid picture which isn't sure if it wants to be a musical or a thriller.

p, Donald Ginsberg, Vivian A. Cox; d, David MacDonald; w, Gerald Verner (based on his radio serial "The Show Must Go On"); ph, Reginald Wyer.

Crime   (PR:A   MPAA:NR)

TREAD SOFTLY STRANGER**   (1959, Brit.) 90m Alderdale/Bentley bw

Diana Dors (Calico), George Baker (Johnny Mansell), Terence Morgan (Dave Mansell), Patrick Allen (Paddy Ryan), Jane Griffiths (Sylvia), Maureen Delany (Mrs. Finnegan), Betty Warren (Flo), Thomas Heathcote (Sgt. Lamb), Russell Napier (Potter), Norman MacOwen (Danny), Wilfrid Lawson (Holroyd), Chris Fay, Terry Baker, Timothy Bateson, John Salew, Joseph Tomelty, Michael Golden, George Merritt, Jack McNaughton, Andrew Keir, Hal Osmond, Norman Pierce, Patrick Crean, Sandra Francis.

Two brothers–embezzler Morgan and gambler Baker–get mixed up in a web of violence when Morgan robs a steel mill in order to keep girl friend Dors in fancy clothes. Morgan kills a night watchman, bringing on an investigation by the dead man's son who finds a witness who happens to be blind. Morgan is fooled into believing that the witness saw him and blurts out a confession. Corny but passable.

p, Denis O'Dell; d, Gordon Parry; w, George Minter, O'Dell (based on the play "Blind Alley" by Jack Popplewell); ph, Douglas Slocombe; m, Tristam Cary; song, "Tread Softly, Stranger," sung by Jim Dale.

Crime (PR:A MPAA:NR)

TREASON, 1937 (SEE: OLD LOUISIANA, 1938)

TREASON, 1950 (SEE: GUILTY OF TREASON, 1950)

TREASURE AT THE MILL½** (1957, Brit.) 60m Wallace-Children's Film Foundation/BL bw

Richard Palmer (*John Adams*), John Ruddock (*Mr. Wilson*), Hilda Fenemore (*Mrs. Adams*), Merrilyn Pettit, Hilary Pettit, Harry Pettit, Jr, Mr. and Mrs. Harry Pettit, Sr (*Themselves*).

Palmer and Ruddock are rivals in a hunt for a treasure hidden in a mill by one of Palmer's ancestors. The mill's new owners, the Pettit family, help Palmer locate the booty that is rightfully his. An exciting children's picture with some surprisingly capable performers.

p, A.V. Curtice; d, Max Anderson; w, Mary Cathcart Borer (based on a story by Malcolm Saville); ph, Jimmy Ewins.

Children's Film (PR:AAA MPAA:NR)

TREASURE HUNT** (1952, Brit.) 79m Romulus/BL-IP bw

Martita Hunt (*Aunt Anna Rose*), Jimmy Edwards (*Hercules Ryall/Sir Roderick*), Naunton Wayne (*Eustace Mills*), Athene Seyler (*Consuelo Howard*), June Clyde (*Mrs. Cleghorn-Thomas*), Miles Malleson (*Mr. Walsh*), Susan Stephen (*Mary O'Leary*), Brian Worth (*Philip*), Mara Lane (*Yvonne*), Maire O'Neill (*Brigid*), Toke Townley (*William Burke*), Bee Duffell, Joseph Tomelty, John McDarby, Tony Quinn, Wilfred Caithness, Hamlyn Benson, Irene Handl, Sheila Carty, Kendrick Owen, Marguerite Brennan, Diana Campbell, John Kelly, Kenneth Kove, Patrick O'Connor, James Page, Roger Maxwell, Nella Occleppo, Michael Ripper, Fred Johnson, Alfie Bass.

A tedious comedy about an Irish mansion owner who invites guests to come and search for hidden treasures that don't actually exist. He is soon unmasked as a phony who doesn't have a penny to his name, but when a fortune in rubies is found his tarnished name shines again.

p, Anatole de Grunwald; d, John Paddy Carstairs; w, de Grunwald (based on a play by M.J. Farrell, John Perry); ph, C. Pennington-Richards.

Comedy (PR:A MPAA:NR)

TREASURE ISLAND*½** (1934) 109m MGM bw

Wallace Beery (*Long John Silver*), Jackie Cooper (*Jim Hawkins*), Lionel Barrymore (*Billy Bones*), Otto Kruger (*Dr. Livesey*), Lewis Stone (*Capt. Alexander Smollett*), Nigel Bruce (*Squire Trelawney*), Charles "Chic" Sale (*Ben Gunn*), William V. Mong (*Pew*), Charles McNaughton (*Black Dog*), Dorothy Peterson (*Mrs. Hawkins*), Douglas Dumbrille ("*Ugly Israel*" *Hands*), Edmund Breese (*Anderson*), Olin Howland (*Dick*), Charles Irwin (*Abraham Gray*), Edward Pawley (*O'Brien*), Richard Powell (*William Post*), James Burke (*George Merry*), John Anderson (*Harry Sykes*), Charles Bennett (*Dandy Dawson*), J.M. Kerrigan (*Tom Morgan*), Westcott Clark (*Allan*), Yorke Sherwood (*Mr. Arrow*), Harry Cording (*Henry*), Tom Mahoney (*Redruth*), Sidney D'Albrook (*Joyce*), Frank Dunn (*Hunter*), Robert Adair (*Tom, Seaman*), Cora Sue Collins (*Child at Inn*), Harold Entwistel (*Ship's Chandler*), Harold Wilson (*Oldster*), Bernice Beatty (*Woman at Inn*), Vernon Downing (*Boy at Inn*), Bobby Bolder (*Mild Man at Inn*), Edith Kingdon (*Wife at Inn*), Wilson Benge (*Friend at Inn*), Shirlee Simpson (*Woman Friend at Inn*), Matt Gillman, Bob Anderson, A.B. Lane, John Kerr, Tom Wilson, James Mason, Edwin J. Brady, Frank Hagney, Bill Booley, Bob Stevenson, Red Burger, Jack Hill, King Mojave (*Pirates*), Kay Deslys, Jane Tallent, Ethel Ransome, Jill Bennett (*Streetwalkers*).

The first sound version of this classic was a winner on several levels. It was previously shot four times in silence (1908, 1912, 1917, 1920). Stevenson's story was his first real hit after having tried his pen at *An Island Voyage* and *The Silverado Squatters* before capturing the imagination of the public with this. Stevenson had married an American woman, Fannie Osbourne, in the U.S. and he wrote this story as a diversion for Osbourne's son, a teenager named Lloyd. With Beery as the famous Long John Silver and Cooper in the role of the doughty lad, the film opens at a rough pub on the sea coast. Cooper meets drunken Barrymore and learns that the old rummy has a secret that is so important men are willing to die to learn it. Cooper finds out that Barrymore has a treasure map of an island in the Caribbean where there is a trove left by a well-known pirate. Barrymore dies and Cooper convinces Bruce and Kurger that they can all become wealthy if they can get to that dot in the sea. The trio book passage on a ship run by Stone. What they don't know, at first, is that practically all of Stone's men are one-time associates of the late pirate and one step from being cutthroats. They all know about the pirate's treasure and want their share of the booty they helped to cull from unsuspecting ships on the bounding main. Beery is the man who leads the brigands and befriends little, blond Cooper. Once they arrive on the island, Beery turns his coat and stages a mutiny against the gentle Stone. To avoid the mutineers, Stone, Bruce, Kruger, Cooper, and the few remaining sailors who stick with Stone build a fortress to stave off any onslaughts by Beery and his men. Beery has the map but can't find the

treasure, thus frustrating him no end. The reason it is unlocatable is that Sale, a hermit who had been stranded on the island, has found the treasure and hidden it elsewhere. Sale had been left on the island by the now dead pirate who owned the treasure and he has a score to settle, so he joins up with Cooper and the others and, knowing every inch of the island that had been his home for so many years, he helps the good guys beat the bad guys. Stone captains the ship as they return to England with the treasure in hand and the mutineers in chains, deep in the ship's hold. But Beery exerts his influence on Cooper and the lad helps the sailor escape before he can face execution. Fleming's direction was superior, though somewhat flagging in spots. He would go on to make THE WIZARD OF OZ, GONE WITH THE WIND, and CAPTAINS COURAGEOUS so the man obviously knew what to do with a good story. Beery, who was known to chew up a set from time to time with his hamminess, was kept in check in this ensemble piece and it was better for the film that he was. Cooper had been a child star and this was the first film in which he began to demonstrate his manhood. A beautiful production, good music by Stothart, and a strong Mahin script all contribute to making this a respectful version of Stevenson's work. The great author loved the South Seas and when he was dying at the young age of 40, he moved to Samoa and passed away there at 44. In his brief life as a writer, starting at the age of 28, he'd written all of the books mentioned previously as well as *Dr. Jekyll and Mr. Hyde*, *The Black Arrow*, *The Master of Ballantrae*, *Kidnapped*, and any number of others. The Samoans revered him and dubbed Stevenson "Tusitala," which, when translated, means "Teller of Tales." How right they were. The excellent sound was by Norma Shearer's brother, Douglas, and a special credit was given to Jack Leggett for his expertise in firearms.

p, Hunt Stromberg; d, Victor Fleming; w, John Lee Mahin, Leonard Praskins, John Howard Lawson (based on the novel by Robert Louis Stevenson); ph, Ray June, Harold Rosson, Clyde DeVinna; m, Herbert Stothart; ed, Blanche Sewell; art d, Cedric Gibbons, Merrill Pye, Edwin B. Willis; cos&tech adv, Dwight Franklin.

Historical Adventure Cas. (PR:A MPAA:NR)

TREASURE ISLAND** (1950, Brit.) 96m Disney/RKO c

Bobby Driscoll (*Jim Hawkins*), Robert Newton (*Long John Silver*), Basil Sydney (*Capt. Smollett*), Walter Fitzgerald (*Squire Trelawney*), Denis O'Dea (*Dr. Livesey*), Ralph Truman (*George Merry*), Finlay Currie (*Capt. Bones*), John Laurie (*Pew*), Francis de Wolff (*Black Dog*), Geoffrey Wilkinson (*Ben Gunn*), David Davies (*Arrow*), Andrew Blackett (*Gray*), Paddy Brannigan (*Hunter*), Ken Buckle (*Joyce*), John Gregson (*Redruth*), Howard Douglas (*Williams*), Geoffrey Keen (*Israel Hand*), William Devlin (*Tom Morgan*), Diarmuid Kelly (*Bolen*), Sam Kydd (*Cady*), Eddie Moran (*Jack Bart*), Harry Locke (*Haggott*), Harold Jamieson (*Scully*), Stephen Jack (*Job Anderson*), Jack Arrow (*Norton*), Jim O'Brady (*Wolfe*), Chris Adcock (*Pike*), Reginald Drummond (*Vane*), Gordon Mulholland (*Durgin*), Patrick Troughton (*Roach*), Leo Phillips (*Spotts*), Fred Clark (*Bray*), Tom Lucas (*Upson*), Bob Head (*Tardy*).

Although technically a U.S. film, this has to be called British because it was made entirely in England with only one actor from the States. There were thousands of pounds "frozen" in Britain that could not be recovered by Disney so the studio elected to spend the money over there by making this, the sixth version of Stevenson's rousing adventure, and, by far, the best. It was shot one more time in the 1970s, but that version, with Orson Welles top-billed, was a disappointment. This was Disney's first totally live-action movie and cost nearly $2 million, a not inconsiderable sum for those days, when one realizes that there were no big stars to attract the patrons. The familiar story begins, as usual, at the inn overlooking the craggy Bristol sea coast. It's the 1700s in England as de Wolff enters the inn and gives a message to Driscoll, the son of the owners, to give to Currie (who appeared in many of Disney's films). When the aged Currie passes away, he hands Driscoll the treasure map to a cache of booty which is stashed on a small island across the sea. Driscoll enlists the aid of O'Dea (a doctor) and Fitzgerald and they get on board the ship helmed by Sydney. Also on the ship is Newton, a one-legged sea cook with nefarious schemes dancing behind his eyes. Newton leads the rebellious faction aboard the ship *Hispaniola*, all of whom want their piece of the treasure buried on the island, mainly because they had served under the late pirate who made the treasure map. Driscoll is not the naive boy he appears to be at first, but he is still taken in by the charm of Newton. The two develop a grudging respect for each other and the film's fulcrum is their relationship. There are battles galore between the pirates loyal to Newton and the honest sailors who follow the lead of their captain, Sydney. As in all the other versions, the treasure has been reburied by the man who was left stranded on the island by the late pirate. This time, he's played by Wilkinson. Alterations have been made in the conclusion of the film, and the major one is that Newton gets a bit of the treasure, jumps in a rowboat, and commands Driscoll to steer him. When Driscoll refuses, having just seen Newton kick Fitzgerald and two crewmen into the water, Newton pulls a gun and says that he'll blast the lad to smithereens. Driscoll shows his pluck by refusing to do as Newton wishes, and Newton responds by not having the black heart to shoot the boy. In the end, Driscoll finally does help Newton to safety and the two friendly enemies wave farewell to each other. Newton is magnificent and anyone who accused him of going overboard with his eye-rolling and his "yo- ho-hos" is not familiar with Stevenson's depiction of the character. Newton was born to play "Long John Silver" and repeated the role in a TV series (shot in Australia) in the late 1950s. Two years after this was released, he did a similar role in BLACKBEARD, THE PIRATE. Director Haskin's teaming with the superb cinematographer Freddie Young gave this a marvelous full-bodied look that never smacked of studio shooting. Newton and Haskin teamed again for LONG JOHN SILVER, but by that time Newton had gone beyond the edge with overplaying. Peter Ellenshaw's matte painting of the backgrounds lent a reality to the proceedings that was breathtaking. By painting the scenes so well, he saved the production millions of dollars that they might have needed to reproduce the many tall ships seen in the port sequence at the start. Driscoll could only work for a few weeks of the production due to the stringent rules governing teenagers and all of his scenes were gang-shot at the start, then he was released. When Disney wanted to re-release the film in the 1970s, the MPAA ratings system was in and, because of some rather graphic violence, the movie was given the dreaded (by Disney) PG rating. The offending scenes had to be snipped to acquire the desired G rating, but that deprived audiences of some excitement. For the record, Driscoll's role had been played by Shirley Mason, a girl, in the 1918 Maurice Tourneur version. Driscoll's career never soared past his work in this. He became a drug addict, moved to New York, and died of a heart attack at age 31. His body was not identified at first and he was buried as a John Doe. One full year later, after an investigation, his fingerprints were identified. He made 19 movies from the age of 6 (LOST ANGEL) to his final film when he was 20, THE PARTY CRASHERS. His life could almost be summed up by the titles of some of his films: WHEN I GROW UP, THE HAPPY TIME, THE BIG BONANZA, FROM THIS DAY FORWARD, and IDENTITY UNKNOWN.

p, Perce Pearce; d, Byron Haskin; w, Lawrence E. Watkin (based on the novel by Robert Louis Stevenson); ph, F.A. Young (Technicolor); m, Clifton Parker; ed, Alan L. Jaggs; prod d, Thomas Morahan; md, Muir Mathieson; makeup, Tony Sforzini; matte artist, Peter Ellenshaw.

Historical Adventure   Cas.   (PR:A-C MPAA:G)

TREASURE ISLAND*   (1972, Brit./Span./Fr./Ger.) 94m
Massfilms-Eguiluz-F.D.L.-CCC/ (LA ISLA DEL TESORO)

Orson Welles (Long John Silver), Kim Burfield (Jim Hawkins), Walter Slezak (Squire Trelawney), Lionel Stander (Billy Bones), Paul Muller (Blind Pew), Maria Rohm (Mrs. Hawkins), Angel Del Pozo (Doctor Livesey), Michel Garland (George, Mary), Rik Battaglia (Capt. Smollett), Jean Lefebvre (Benn Gunn), Aldo Sambrell (Israel Hands), Alibe (Mrs. Silver), Chinchilla (Anderson).

One of many versions of Stevenson's famed story and also one of the most boring. Sets are well-made but the dialog seems wooden. The film is geared strictly for children and the actors and actresses overact accordingly. The ship in this film was also used in the movie THE EMIGRANTS (1971). This was at least the fifth time Treasure Island was put on the screen, including the years 1917, 1920, 1934, and 1950. Many of the voices were badly looped in the English-language dubbing which was necessary for some of the players in this multinational production. Welles' Long John Silver has no such excuse; his playing style is difficult to understand because he chose to mutter and mumble. Young Burfield does well in his second featured role; Mark Lester of OLIVER! (1968) had originally been slated for his part. Director Hough replaced the original helmer, Silvio Narizzano.

p, Harry Alan Towers; d, John Hough; w, Wolf Mankowitz, O.W. Jeeves [Orson Wells] (based on the novel by Robert Louis Stevenson); ph, Cecilio Paniagua, Ginger Gemell (Eastmancolor); m, Natal Massara; ed, Nicholas Wentworth; art d, Frank White; set d, Jose Maria Alarcon.

Adventure   Cas.   (PR:A MPAA:G)

TREASURE OF FEAR   (SEE: SCARED STIFF, 1945)

TREASURE OF JAMAICA REEF, THE zero
          (1976) 96m D&R/Golden-Selected c (AKA: EVIL IN THE DEEP)

Stephen Boyd, Rosey Grier, David Ladd, Cheryl Stoppelmoor [Cheryl Ladd], Chuck Woolery.

Boyd is the scuba-diving seafarer who takes on the big fish in this quick-to-forget adventure thriller inspired by JAWS (1975). He and his crew seek sunken gold, menaced by massive teeth at every turning. Chiefly interesting for the young romantic leads; actress Stoppelmoor married Alan Ladd's son David and changed her surname to his. Woolery scored his first featured film role here; he was better known as a TV game-show host. International star Boyd died a year after the film's release at the age of 49. Football star Grier rounded out the cast.

p, Virginia Stone, J. A. S. McCombie; d, V. Stone; m, Christopher Stone.

Adventure   (PR:C MPAA:PG)

TREASURE OF KALIFA   (SEE: STEEL LADY, THE, 1953)

TREASURE OF LOST CANYON, THE½**   (1952) 82m UNIV c

William Powell (Doc Homer Brown), Julia Adams (Myra Wade), Charles Drake (Jim Anderson), Henry Hull (Lucius Cooke), Rosemary De Camp (Samuella Brown), Tommy Ivo (David), Chubby Johnson (Baltimore Dan), John Doucette (Gyppo), Marvin Press (Paddy), Frank Wilcox (Stranger), Griff Barnett (Judge Wade), Virginia Mullen (Mrs. Crabtree), Paul "Tiny" Newlan (Coach Driver), Jimmy Ogg (Guard), Hugh Prosser (Fire Captain), George Taylor (Clem), Philo McCullough, Ed Hinkle (Miners), Edward Rickard (Bit), Jack Perrin (Sheriff).

It's the battle of the professionals as kindly doctor Powell rescues youngster Ivo from the evil machinations of unscrupulous lawyer Hull, who had placed him in the care of a troupe of traveling medicine show tricksters. The small town physician offers the lad a good home until the two happen upon an old chest filled with valuable treasure. The boy conceals the chest under a waterfall to keep it from the clutches of the larcenous lawyer and from Powell, who suddenly sees his opportunity to return to his former licentious life in the big city. Powell recants, deciding to concentrate on what's best for the boy, and they try to recover the chest from its underwater lair. Powell returned to films after a three-year hiatus to make this one; it hardly seemed worthy of his considerable talents.

p, Leonard Goldstein; d, Ted Tetzlaff; w, Brainerd Dullfied, Emerson Crocker; (based on the story "The Treasure of Franchard" by Robert Louis Stevenson); ph, Russell Metty (Technicolor); ed, Milton Carruth; md, Joseph Gershenson; art d, Bernard Herzbrun, Alexander Golitzen.

Western   (PR:A MPAA:NR)

TREASURE OF MAKUBA, THE**   (1967, U.S./Span.) 84m P.C.
          Memsa-L.M.F.I.S.A./Producers Releasing Organization c (EL TESORO
          DE MAKUBA)

Cameron Mitchell (Coogan), Mara Cruz (Maroa), Jessie Paradise (Mary), Todd Martin (Hank), Al Mulock (Pat), Joseph Luis Lluch (Tony), Pastor Serrador (Duval), Felix Noble (Chief Maola), Walter Zamudio (Ling).

Mitchel, an adventurer, saves native girl Cruz from rape by one of his three pearl-hunting partners on a Polynesian island. The partners, with a murdered friend of Mitchell's, had stolen the pearls, which were then buried in a secret place on the island. The pearls have disappeared, but the grateful Cruz tells Mitchell of their whereabouts: her brother found them and offered them at the ikon of a native god. The would-be rapist, Martin, kills the Polynesian chief, Noble, pins the blame on Mitchell and Cruz, and makes off with the treasure. The romantic pair are saved from a sentence of death by the island's police commissioner, Serrador, and the three pursue the villains. Detained at the dock by their internal squabbling, the latter have not yet sailed away. During a battle, their boat is set afire and two of the wretches are immolated. Mitchell decides that Cruz suffices to make the island paradise enough for him, so he will remain there. Serrador impounds the pearls. A humorless potboiler with little to recommend it.

p, Sidney Pink; d, Joe Lacy; w, Manuel M. Remis, Jose Maria Elorrieta (based on a story by Jose Luis Navarro); ph, Alfonso Nieva, Pablo Ripoll (Eastmancolor); m, Fernando Garcia Morcillo; ed, John Horvath; art d, Wolfgang Burman.

Adventure/Drama   (PR:A MPAA:NR)

TREASURE OF MATECUMBE*½**   (1976) 117m Disney/BV c

Robert Foxworth (Jim), Joan Hackett (Lauriette), Peter Ustinov (Dr. Snodgrass), Vic Morrow (Spangler), Johnny Doran (Davie), Billy Attmore (Thad), Jane Wyatt (Aunt Effie), Robert DoQui (Ben), Mills Watson (Catrell), Val De Vargas (Charlie), Virginia Vincent (Aunt Lou), Don Knight (Skaggs), Dub Taylor (Sheriff Forbes), Dick Van Patten (The Gambler).

A sad effort from the Disney studios focusing on the adventures of two young boys, one black, one white, in search of buried treasure along the Florida coast during the mid-19th Century. Accompanying the kids are three adults, Hackett, Ustinov, and Foxworth, also after the treasure for their own personal reasons. Most of the perils on the trip are a result of continual pursuit by evil Morrow and his gang, but they are not too much of a threat to keep the treasure hunters from pursuing their goal. Very uncustomary for Disney are the slack special effects and process shots, the use of which hurts the continuity of an already lagging story.

p, Bill Anderson; d, Vincent McEveety; w, Don Tait (based on the novel A Journey To Matecumbe by Robert Lewis Taylor); ph, Frank Phillips (Technicolor); m, Buddy Baker; ed, Cotton Warburton; prod d, Robert Clatworthy; art d, John B. Mansbridge; Set d, Frank R. McKelvy; cos, Shelby Anderson; ch, Burch Mann.

Adventure   (PR:AA MPAA:G)

TREASURE OF MONTE CRISTO**   (1949) 76m Lippert/Screen Guild
          bw

Glenn Langan (Edmund Dantes), Adele Jergens (Jean Turner), Steve Brodie (Earl Jackson), Robert Jordan (Tony Torecelli), Michael Whalen (Lt. Perry), George K. Davis (District Attorney), Margia Dean (Nurse), Michael Vallon (Papa Torecelli), Sidney Melton (Tyson), Brian O'Hara (Jailer), Robert Boon

(Boatswain), Jeritza Novak (Miss Jean Turner), Jimmy O'Neil (Pawnbroker), Curtis Jarrett (Deputy Sheriff), Charles Reagan (Bail ey), Larry Barton (Hotel Clerk), Rube Schaeffer (Roberts), Don Junior (Bellboy), Jack Power (Norris), Jamison Shade (Mason), Johnny Casino (Carlo Torecelli), Kem Tang (Chinese Waiter).

A modern tale that takes from the legend of an old one in establishing Langan as a descendant of the Count of Monte Cristo presently working as a mate on a ship that docks in San Francisco. Crooked lawyer Brodie sets up a scheme to get at the treasure of Langan's famed ancestor, and–using the beautiful blond, Jergens,–tries to lure him into a trap. But Langan proves worthy of his heritage, using a gun instead of a sword, and winning both his fortune and Jergens legitimately

p, Leonard S. Picker; d, William Berke; w, Aubrey Wisberg, Jack Pollexfen; ph, Benjamin Kline; m, Albert Glasser; ed, Stanley Frazen; md, Glasser; cos, Sara Simon, Frank & Imback; spec eff, Ray Mercer.

Crime/Drama   **(PR:A   MPAA:NR)**

TREASURE OF MONTE CRISTO, THE
            (SEE: SECRET OF MONTE CRISTO, THE, 1961)

TREASURE OF PANCHO VILLA, THE**
                            (1955) 96m Grainger/RKO c

Rory Calhoun (Tom Bryan), Shelley Winters (Ruth Harris), Gilbert Roland (Juan Castro), Joseph Calleia (Pablo Morales), Carlos Mosquiz (Commandant), Fanny Schiller (Laria Morales), Tony Carvajal (Farolito), Pasquel Pena (Ricardo).

During the Mexican Revolution in 1910, Calhoun and Roland stand off a detachment of Federales in an isolated mountain area of Mexico. In flashback, the events leading to their plight are recounted. Mercenary soldier-of-fortune Calhoun joins Roland and Winters, both supporters of the revolution, in an attempt to transport a gold shipment stolen by Calhoun for the forces of Pancho Villa. The customary sideplay occurs among the acquisitive Calhoun and his idealistic companions as they battle both brigands and troops in their transit. Flashing forward, the matter is resolved after the death of the valiant Roland when Calhoun's dynamite brings a mountain down, burying both troops and treasure. An excessively wordy, banal script is redeemed in part by excellent action sequences.

p, Edmund Grainger; d, George Sherman; w, Niven Busch (based on the story by J. Robert Bren, Gladys Atwater); ph, William Snyder (Superscope, Technicolor); m, Leith Stevens; ed, Harry Marker.

Western   **Cas.**   **(PR:A   MPAA:NR)**

TREASURE OF RUBY HILLS*
                            (1955) 71m AA bw

Zachary Scott (Haney), Carole Mathews (Sherry), Barton MacLane (Reynolds), Dick Foran (Doran), Lola Albright (May), Gordon Jones (Voyle), Raymond Hatton (Scotty), Lee Van Cleef (Emmett), Steve Darrell (Hull), Charles Fredericks (Payne), Stanley Andrews (Garvey), James Alexander (Burt), Rick Vallin (Vernon).

Dreary and overly talky western in which Scott, an outlaw's son, moves to a town to try to set himself up with a nice little homestead. Before this can happen he must contend with two groups of ranchers at each other's necks. He really gets in the middle of things when his water rights are threatened.

p, William F. Broidy; d, Frank McDonald; w, Tom Hubbard, Fred Eggers (based on a story by Louis L'Amour); ph, John Martin; m, Edward J. Kay; ed, Ace Herman; md, Kay.

Western   **(PR:A   MPAA:NR)**

TREASURE OF SAN GENNARO**½
                        (1968, Fr./Ital./Ger.) 102m
Ultra Film-Societe Cinematographique-Lyre-Roxy Film/PAR c (OPERAZIONE SAN GENNARO; OPERATION SAN GENNARO; UNSER BOSS IST EINE DAME)

Nino Manfredi (Dudu), Senta Berger (Maggie), Harry Guardino (Jack), Claudine Auger (Concettina), Toto (Don Vincenzo), Mario Adorf (Sciascillo), Frank Wolff (Frank), Ugo Fangareggi (Agony), Dante Maggio (Captain), Giovanni Bruti (Cardinal), Pinuccio Ardia (Baron), Vittoria Crispo (Assunta), Jean Louis, Ralf Wolter, Solvi Stubing.

Posing as tourists, American swindlers Berger, Guardino, and Wolff journey to Naples with a plan to steal valuables from a church. Wolff, taking full advantage of the citys edible offerings, consumes an excess of pasta and dies before the plan is well under way. Enlisting the aid of petty criminal Manfredi because of his local knowledge, the other two carry out their plan. After the successful robbery, the thieves fall out. Evading Manfredi, Berger murders Guardino, seizes the treasure, and–disguised as a nun–makes tracks for the airport. Manfredi and his friend Adorf hijack the treasure from her before she can board an airplane. Manfredi then makes for the Swiss border with the jewels, in the company of a "fake" cardinal who serves as protective coloration. The cardinal proves to be the genuine article; he returns the treasure to its rightful habitat, the church of the title.

p, Turi Vasile; d, Dino Risi; w, Risi, Adriano Baracco, Ennio De Concini, Nino

Manfredi (based on a story by De Concini, Risi); ph, Aldo Tonti (Eastmancolor); m, Armando Trovajoli; ed, Franco Fraticelli, Lisbeth Neumann; art d, Luigi Scaccianoce; cos, Maurizio Chiari.

Crime/Comedy   **(PR:A   MPAA:NR)**

TREASURE OF SAN TERESA, THE
            (SEE: HOT MONEY GIRL, 1962, Brit./Ger.)

TREASURE OF SILVER LAKE*½
                        (1965, Fr./Ger./Yugo.) 82m
S.N.C.-Rialto-Jadran/COL c (LE TRESOR DU LAC D'ARGENT; DER SCHATZ IM SILBERSEE; BLAGO U SREBRNOM JEZERU)

Lex Barker (Old Shatterhand), Gotz George (Fred Engel), Herbert Lom (Brinkley), Pierre Brice (Winnetou), Karin Dor (Ellen Patterson), Eddi Arent (Duke of Glockenspiel), Marianne Hoppe (Mrs. Butler), Jan Sid (Patterson), Ralf Wolter (Sam Hawkins), Mirko Boman (Gunstick Uncle), Jozo Kovacevic, Slobodan Dimitrijevic, Miliovj Stojanovic, Branko Spoljar, Velimir Hitil, Antun Nalis, Ilija Ivezic.

This European western, one of a popular series made before the the onslaught of spaghetti westerns, sparked little interest when released in the U.S. This is mainly a result of an atrocious dubbing job and the hacking of scenes, an act which really hurt the film's continuity. But in Europe this feature, and others like it, was a tremendous success, helping to establish the mythology of the West across the Atlantic. Barker plays a legendary gunfighter who comes to the assistance of George when the latter's father is murdered over a treasure map. Teaming with Indian Brice, he tracks down the culprit, Lom, at the lake of the title where the other half of the map is waiting for its companion in order to make somebody very rich. If possible, see one of the European versions over the American one.

p, Leif Feilberg; d, Harald Reinl; w, Harald G. Petersson (based on the novel Der Schatz im Silbersee by Karl Friedrich May); ph, Ernst W. Kalinke (CinemaScope, Eastmancolor); m, Martin Bottcher; ed, Hermann Haller; art d, Dusko Jericevic; cos, Irms Pauli; spec eff, Erwin Lange; makeup, Willi Nixdorf, Charlotte Schmidt-Kersten.

Western   **(PR:A   MPAA:NR)**

TREASURE OF THE FOUR CROWNS*   (1983, Span./U.S.) 99m
MTG-Lotus/ Cannon c (IL MISTERO DELLA QUATTRO CORONA

Tony Anthony (J.T. Striker), Ana Obregon (Liz), Gene Quintano (Edmund), Francisco Rabal (Socrates), Jerry Lazarus (Rick), Emiliano Redondo (Brother Jonas), Francisco Villena (Prof. Montgomery), Kate Levan (Possessed Woman), Lewis Gordon (Popo).

Chintzy 3-D adventure picture that throws in so many shots to raise a chill that is destroys that little bit of a plot it has. The plot that does exist, looking much too much like a copy of RAIDERS OF THE LOST ARK, is about Anthony as a daredevil who gets together a specialized group in order to claim an ancient treasure that supposedly holds the secrets to good and evil. On the plus side are decent sets and a score composed by Ennio Morricone.

p, Tony Anthony, Gene Quintano; d, Ferdinando Baldi; w, Lloyd Battista, Jim Bryce, Jerry Lazarus (based on the story by Tony Petito, Quintano); ph, Marcello Masciocchi, Giuseppe Ruzzolini (3-D, Metrocolor); m, Ennio Morricone; ed, Franco Fraticelli; art d, Luciano Spadoni; cos, Eugenia Escriba; spec eff, Freddy Unger, Germano Natali, Carlo De Marchis; stunts, Neno Zamperla.

Adventure   **Cas.**   **(PR:A   MPAA:PG)**

TREASURE OF THE GOLDEN CONDOR***   (1953) 93m FOX c

Cornel Wilde (Jean-Paul), Constance Smith (Clara), Finlay Currie (MacDougal), Walter Hampden (Pierre), Anne Bancroft (Marie), George Macready (Marquis), Fay Wray (Marquise), Leo G. Carroll (Dondel), Konstantin Shayne (Curate), Louis Heminger (Indian Chief), Tudor Owen (Fontaine), Gil Donaldson (Count de Bayoux), Ken Herman (Francois), Bobby Blake (Stable Boy), Jerry Hunter (Jean-Paul, aged 10), Wende Weil (Marie, aged 8 ½), Ray Beltram (Medicine Man), Edna Holland (Fontaine's Wife), Harry Cording (Breton), Crane Whitney (Ruffian), Donald Lawton (Dondel's Clerk), Robert Filmer (Bailiff), Camillo Guercio (Prosecutor), House Peters, Sr (Magistrate), John Parrish (Turnkey), Alphonse Martell (Artist), May Wynn (Maid), Paul Bryar (Guard), Margaret Brayton.

A costume swashbuckler in which Wilde heads to the jungles of Guatemala with Currie in order to search for ancient treasure, the finding of which will allow Wilde to reclaim the estate which his villanous uncle snatched from him. When Wilde returns to France, Currie and his daughter Smith decide to stay in the quiet of Guatemala. After getting his land back and discovering just what type of woman Bancroft, the woman he was set on marrying, is, Wilde decides that the jungle is the best place for him also, and makes the long journey back to it and Smith. The interesting scenery of the Mayan ruins adds interest to a strictly formula venture. A remake of 1942's SON OF FURY.

p, Jules Buck; d&w, Delmer Daves (based on the novel Benjamin Blake by Edison Marshall); ph, Edward Cronjager (Technicolor); m, Sol Kaplan; ed, Robert Simpson; m, Alfred Newman; art d, Lyle Wheeler, Albert Hogsett; cos, Dorothy Jeakins, Charles LeMaire.

Adventure **Cas.** **(PR:A MPAA:NR)**

TREASURE OF THE PIRANHA

(SEE: KILLER FISH, 1979, Ital./Braz.)

TREASURE OF THE SIERRA MADRE, THE***

(1948) 126m WB bw

Humphrey Bogart *(Fred C. Dobbs)*, Walter Huston *(Howard)*, Tim Holt *(Curtin)*, Bruce Bennett *(Cody)*, Barton MacLane *(McCormick)*, Alfonso Bedoya *(Gold Hat)*, A. Soto Rangel *(Presidente)*, Manuel Donde *(El Jefe)*, Jose Torvay *(Pablo)*, Margarito Luna *(Pancho)*, Jacqueline Dalya *(Flashy Girl)*, Bobby Blake *(Mexican Boy)*, Spencer Chan *(Proprietor)*, Julian Rivero *(Barber)*, John Huston *(White Suit)*, Harry Vejar *(Bartender)*, Pat Flaherty *(Customer)*, Clifton Young, Ralph Dunn, Jack Holt *(Flophouse Men)*, Guillermo Calleo *(Mexican Storekeeper)*, Manuel Donde, Ildefonso Vega, Francisco Islas, Alberto Valdespino *(Indians)*, Mario Mancilla *(Youth)*, Ann Sheridan *(Streetwalker)*, Martin Garralaga *(Railroad Conductor)*, Ernesto Escoto *(1st Mexican Bandit)*, Ignacio Villabajo *(2nd Mexican Bandit)*, Roberto Canedo *(Mexican Lieutenant)*.

Huston has produced a number of great films but this tale of greed, fear, and murder in Mexico is undoubtedly his finest, a towering memorable masterpiece with Bogart simply wonderful as the inimitable Fred C. Dobbs. Bogart, within the space of two hours, undergoes an incredible metamorphosis, changing from a rather personable down-and-outer to a carping paranoid prospector to a homicidal maniac willing to kill his closest friends at the drop of a sombrero. On the bum in Tampico, Mexico, gringo Bogart panhandles a peso from a tall man dressed all in white, saying, "Beg pardon, mister but can you stake a fellow American to a meal?" After the man gives him a peso, Bogart goes to a small Mexican diner to eat. While there a Mexican boy, Blake, goes to Bogart and tries to sell him a lottery ticket. He's not interested. The boy is persistent, telling Bogart that "I sell only the winners." Bogart begins to lose his patience with the smiling boy and snaps, "If you don't get away from me I'll throw this glass of water right in your face." Blake won't quit and keeps pitching Bogart who promptly throws the water in his face. Dripping, Blake keeps up his sales pitch and Bogart weakens. "You got all the winners, huh?" he says finally and buys a ticket. On the street, Bogart bums another peso from the same tall man in the white suit. After getting a haircut and a shave which considerably lowers Bogart's hat, he once more approaches the tall man in the white suit with the same pitch about staking "a fellow American to a meal." The man, director Huston himself, glares down at Bogart and says, "Such audacity never came my way," and reminds Bogart that he has put the touch on him twice before in the same day. "Beg pardon, mister," Bogart says, sincerely apologetic, "I never looked at your face, only your shoes." Huston gives him a snort, chomps on his cigar, and slaps another peso into Bogart's outstretched palm, telling him, "From now on you're going to have to make you way through life without my assistance." He gives Bogart one more peso and adds, "And here's another peso so you won't forget!" Bogart goes to the main plaza in Tampico to sit on a park bench and there befriends a clean-cut young American, Holt. Both of them go to work for a shady contractor, MacLane, who takes them to a remote site where they slave away with only food and shelter, their pay held until the job is done. When the work is finished, MacLane tells them at the Tampico dock where the ferry takes them that he must go and pick up the payroll. Bogart and Holt complain that they don't have a cent, even to buy a beer, and he gives them a few dollars. They go to a cantina and drink, then check in at a flophouse, the Oso Negro, where they take bunks next to a colorful, garrulous old man, Walter Huston (the director's father). Huston is regaling other stewbums about prospecting for gold and how he has been at it since the Klondike days, having dug up fortunes and spent them. (One of the tramps listening to Huston is Jack Holt, father of Tim, Bogart's new-found friend.) As Huston spins his tales of gold-seeking, he adds that greed is usually the undoing of all prospectors, ruining them and their associates. Bogart, half drunk, pipes up with a mushy tongue, "It wouldn't happen to me; all I'd want is my fair share." Huston laughs at this, mentioning something about the good intentions of gold-seekers vanishing when the gold is found. Bogart goes to sleep, dreaming of gold. The next day Bogart and Holt look for MacLane but he cannot be found. Another American, Flaherty, tells both men that they have been suckered, that MacLane is a con man who hires gullible workers and then never shows up to pay them. But the duped Bogart and Holt find MacLane on the street with Dalya, obviously playing the role of a Mexican hooker. They push MacLane hard for their money and he sees no escape, sending Dalya on her way, telling her he will see her in a few minutes. He takes Bogart and Holt to a bar, telling them that he hasn't been paid either but Bogart tells him, "We want our money and we want it now!" Holt adds, "We want every cent that's coming to us." MacLane smiles and says he can spare some money. "Let's not stop being friends," he tells them, and orders three drinks. As Bogart lifts his glass, MacLane crashes the bottle on his head and Bogart falls to the floor. In the same movement, MacLane smashes Holt in the face. Bogart gets up and hits MacLane and so does Holt, until they are hitting him from one end of the bar to the other, MacLane finally crashing, a bloody pulp, to the floor. "I'm licked, fellas, I'm licked," he gasps, yanking his wallet out of his pocket and trying to pull money forth. But both his eyes have been closed from the punches he's received and Bogart and Holt take the money due them, leaving what is not theirs with the unconscious con man. They go to the plaza and nurse their wounds. Then Bogart gets an idea, saying to Holt: "You know, Curt, we ain't very smart sticking around Tampico....Maybe that old guy at the Oso Negro was right....Maybe we ought to try our hand at prospecting." They decide to find the old man and when they do, Huston looks up at them with anxious eyes: "Will I go? Sure, I'll go," and he tells them he has a small stake. They tell him that they will put up the money that they have gotten from MacLane but it's not quite enough. Then Blake arrives to tell Bogart the good news that he has won the lottery. Bogart is ecstactic. Things are finally going his way. He gives Blake a handsome tip and, kissing the lottery ticket, says, "That's the kind of sugar Papa likes!" He then offers to put up not only his extra money from the lottery winnings but Holt's, too, telling him that since they're partners it's all the same. They shake hands on it as Huston continues to look at both younger men apprehensively. The trio is now shown on a train heading toward the wild Sierra Mountains but the train is attacked by bandits led by a fierce- looking chieftain, Bedoya. As bullets whine into the passenger cars and plow into the seats and window frames, Bogart, Holt, and Huston join the troops and passengers on the train in battling the bandits, a running fight that does not end until the train snakes safely into a tunnel and beyond the reach of the bandits. Bogart has thoroughly enjoyed the fight, loading his gun and telling his companions: "I think I got three of them! Did you see the one in the gold hat? He must have been their leader." Later, in a small village, the prospectors buy burros and supplies and then head for the hills. In a few days Holt and Bogart are physically exhausted, barely staggering along the dusty trail, gradually climbing, climbing into the high Sierras, but Huston keeps going at a steady clip, outdistancing his younger companions. "He must be part goat," pants Bogart as he looks up to see Huston climbing steadily upward. "Look at him go, will you?" But they cannot go much farther and drop to the ground. Huston turns around with a look of disgust on his face and goes to them. He upbraids them for their lack of strength and then grins widely. "You're so dumb, you don't know the riches you're tredding on." Bogart picks up a rock and threatens to smash Huston's face but Huston is full of elation, telling the pair, as he does a little jig, that they have found a small vein, and they are a "couple of jackasses for not seeing it. But it's not rich enough." He points to the high mountain in front of them. "Up there's where we got to go....Up there....Up there!" They begin climbing with renewed strength, dragging their burros after them. The men find the source of the vein and dig out a mine shaft, working week after week, building a long sluice run and sifting the dirt taken from the shaft, drawing forth the gold. As they begin to accumulate the gold, Huston, in their common tent each night, weighs each day's take and splits it up evenly. Bogart's eyes take on a new and sinister glint as he watches the old man drop the delicate grains of gold onto a scale. Each man hides his share of the gold, which they term "goods" but they become apprehensive about each other, or at least Bogart does. Every little sound in the night causes him to jump up to see if his companions have left the tent. One night he finds Holt gone and asks Huston where he has gone to. The old man tells him he is checking the burros. "I think *I'll* check the burros," Bogart says and grabs his gun and goes out. When Holt returns he notices Bogart missing and asks Huston where he has gone. "He went to check the burros, but if it's all the same to you fellas, I won't take my turn." When Bogart returns, nervously eyeing the others, Huston tells them to go to sleep. While digging in the shaft some days later Bogart strikes a weak wall and part of the roof caves in on him. Holt sees a billow of dust blow out of the shaft and rushes forward, calling Bogart's name. When he gets no answer he pauses, a look on his face saying that if he does not go into the shaft and help Bogart he might profit by his inaction. But the temptation is only brief and Holt rushes forward, dragging Bogart free of debris and outside. When Bogart comes to, Huston tells Bogart that Holt has just saved his life and Bogart says, "Thanks, partner." "It's okay," Holt says guiltily. "You'd have done the same for me." Days pass and Bogart becomes more paranoid about his working companions, mumbling to himself about being asked to go into the village for supplies. Holt tells Huston that "Dobbs is over there talking to himself," and the old man goes to Bogart. Says Huston: "What's the matter, Dobbs? Got something up your nose? Blow it out!" Bogart accuses Huston and Holt of wanting to send him to the village so they can look for his buried gold and nothing Huston can say to him will change his mind. As Huston walks away, Bogart's face scowls in anger and apprehension. "No one's gonna put anything over on Fred C. Dobbs," he promises himself, "No, sir!" Bogart's paranoia reaches epic proportions the next day when he finds Holt trying to turn over a huge rock by prying it upward with a long tree limb. Bogart pulls his gun and tells Holt that he is going to shoot him for trying to steal his gold. Huston comes upon the scene and Holt laughs, telling the old man that he has accidentally found Bogart's hiding place while trying to get at a Gila monster which has just crawled under the rock. Bogart tells Holt that he's lying and that there is no Gila monster under the rock and Holt smirks. "Go on, why don't you, look for yourself." Bogart kneels down and is about to reach beneath the rock when Holt says to Huston, "They never do let go once they bite you, do they Howard?" Bogart's hand pauses at the opening before the rock. He can't bring himself to do it and Holt pries the rock upward so that it rolls away. There, in the shallow pocket of earth is Bogart's cache of little bags containing the gold. Slithering on top of the gold is a Gila monster which Holt shoots and kills. This, however, is no proof that Holt was right, Bogart illogically concludes. Holt goes to the village to get supplies and there runs into another American, Bennett, who asks him questions about who he is and what he is doing in that remote area. Holt tells him that he is a hunter but that game is scarce. "There's no game within a hundred miles of here," Bennett tells him. Holt realizes that Bennett is another prospector and leaves quickly. He tells Bogart and Huston about Bennett when he arrives back at camp and then is surprised when Bennett appears, having followed Holt. Huston, Bogart, and Holt tell Bennett that he's welcome to spend the night at their camp, but they all have a nervous and sleepless night trying to decide what to do about the interloper. In the morning, Bogart finds Bennett drinking some of their water and tells him to stop it. "I didn't think civilized people would begrudge me a little water," Bennett tells him. With that Bogart lets loose a vicious smash to Bennett's face, knocking him down and saying, "Who says we're not civilized?" Bennett then tells Holt, Huston, and Bogart that he wants to be let in on their gold strike but that he won't ask for anything they've dug up so far, only that which he himself is able to mine. He says that they have three choices, to let him stay, drive him off, or kill him. After a short conference the trio decides to shoot the invader, although Huston is reluctant to do so. They approach Bennett who tells them: "So it's number three, is it? Well you'd better look down there first." He tells them that they will need his gun if not his arms to dig for gold and the men look down into the valley to see a stream of riders heading their way. They are bandits. Hurriedly, the four men put their provisions away and take positions to fend off the bandits. Bedoya and his men soon arrive on horseback and discover the camp but as they begin to look for the prospectors, Bedoya spots Bogart who sends a shot in his direction. Bedoya has to be the ugliest bandit ever put on film with his enormous buck teeth, squinty eyes, chinless jaw, and a mustache that appears to be drooping from sheer frustration and exhaustion at having to cling to this gargoyle's face. The bandit tells Bogart that they are lawmen but savvy Bogart, peering over the edge of a mound of dirt as he lies down in a small trench with his pistol aimed at the bandit says, "If you're a lawman let me see your badge." Bedoya's face grows dark with a frown and he steps forward menacingly, spitting out his words, the globs of saliva actually sailing into the air after them. "Badges?" he roars, "We ain't got no badges." He takes another step toward Bogart, raging, "I don't have to show you any stinkin' badges!" He sees Bogart draw down on him and stops in his tracks. Then Bedoya, in a crude, fumbling appeasement attempt, holds up a gold watch, offering this to Bogart in exchange for his gun. "I need my gun," Bogart tells him firmly from his hiding place, his head barely visible from the hole where he is lying. Bedoya goes on telling him about the marvels of the watch until finally Huston has had enough of this primitive ploy on the part of the bandit and fires a single shot that smashes the watch as Bedoya holds it by the chain, sending it spinning in his hand. The bandits scurry into the underbrush, firing on the prospectors and the battle is on. A terrific fusillade is unleashed by the bandits from their hiding places but the prospectors take careful aim and pick off the bandits as they try to flank their positions. Then there is silence, broken by the sound of wood being chopped. Huston tells his friends that "this isn't good....They are building barricades." He explains how they will use these barricades to cover their movements as they close in on them, but before this happens there is the sudden sound of horses riding away at a quick pace. "They've cleared out," Holt says with amazement. The prospectors soon find out why, going to a promontory where they see the bandits riding furiously down the lower ridges and up the valley, scores of federal tropps chasing and firing after them. "Go you federales," Bogart grins, cheering on the federal troops. "I could kiss each and every one of them! Go get 'em! Tear 'em to pieces. Chew 'em up and spit 'em out! " After enjoying the sight, the prospectors look down to see Bennett dead, killed by a bandit bullet. Holt takes his effects, reading a letter Bennett had been writing to his wife, an emotional plea to her to forgive him for his wanderlust and that he promises to return to her once he has struck it rich. The prospectors bury the body and conclude that they have taken enough gold out of the mountain and that the vein has run out. Each has about $35,000 in gold and they are satisfied with their hard-earned take. Before they leave, Huston says they should close up the shaft, that "we have wounded this mountain" and they should repair the damage. Bogart and Holt agree to help him close the shaft before leaving. As they make their way back to civilization, Indians enter their camp one night. They silently move into the camping area and squat about the fire. Huston exchanges cigarettes for the home-grown smoking weeds the Indians offer the prospectors. Bogart squints and says: "I don't get this. We give 'em our smokes, they give us theirs– why don't everyone just smoke their own?" The Indians have come on an important mission and after speaking with them in their native tongue, Huston tells his companions that they have a sick child in their village, one who appears dead, having fallen into a lake, but there are some signs of life. They ask that one of the prospectors go with them to see if they can help the boy. Huston, the most experienced at such matters, agrees to go, and even agrees to allow Holt and Bogart to take his gold into the city for safekeeping, but when the old man leaves with the Indians the next day he glances back furtively at Holt and Bogart going in the other direction with his "goods." From the anxious look on Huston's face, it is clear that his belief in his fellow prospectors, despite their hearty reassurances that they will see him in a few days, is generously mixed with a degree of distrust. Huston goes to the village and there finds a small boy in a comatose state. He begins to work on him, moving his arms methodically up and down. He labors through the day and into the night with the Indians of the village looking down upon him expectantly. (The shots showing the leathery, weather-beaten faces of the Indians are extraordinary, rows of primitive but goodhearted natives peering down on Huston and the boy, black eyes unblinking, almost like a painting by Mexican muralist Diego Rivera.) Huston's intense efforts are rewarded when the little boy suddenly comes to life, crying, his mother running forward, the Indians surrounding a beaming Huston to murmur their gratitude. At the other end of the emotional spectrum are Bogart and Holt. Bogart quickly concludes in his deluded mind that Holt lives for no other purpose that to kill him and take all the gold for himself. He moves through the brush ahead of Holt, trying to waylay him but Holt is going too fast, pulling his own gun and forcing Bogart, now that the cards are on the table, to move ahead and keep in sight of him. That night, Bogart tells Holt as they sit nervously about the campfire that he knows Holt is planning on killing him for the gold. "If you talk like that, Dobbs," says the startled Holt, "there's nothing to do but tie you up at night." Instead Holt tries to stay awake, keeping Bogart's gun and his own trained on Bogart who has now completely gone round the bend. He waits and waits for Holt to fall asleep and when his former friend nods off, Bogart makes a jump for the guns but Holt snaps his eyes open and tells Bogart to get away and sit by the fire where he can watch him. The next day, Holt is groggy from lack of sleep, stumbling down the jungle path, following Bogart and his burros. That night the exhausted Holt falls asleep and Bogart makes his move, jumping him and taking away the guns. He marches Holt into the jungle and there shoots him and goes back to the campfire, talking out loud to himself, justifying his actions. "Maybe he's not dead?" he questions himself, and he races back to where he left the body. It's gone. Bogart then believes that a wild animal probably dragged off Holt's body. "A mountain lion, yeah, sure, that's it." Bogart goes off on his own the next day, driving all the burros ahead of him, but soon he is out of water and stumbles along in a half- conscious state, nearing the village where the burros were purchased. He spots a water hole and drives the burros to the water, then flops down and buries his face in the water. He drinks his fill but then sees the reflection of a Mexican standing behind and over him, one wearing an enormous sombrero. It is the fearfully familiar face of the bandit chieftain, Bedoya. Then two more figures are seen, Bedoya's aides. They are in the same grubby, down-and-out shape as is Bogart and they toy with him. The aides, barefoot, dirty, in rags, hover above Bogart, looking over his wornout shoes, his clothes. They seem to be visualizing Bogart dead and themselves inside of his clothes. He moves away from them warily, pushing the burros from their reach as they begin to pick over the animals. "Get away from my burros," Bogart orders them, but they are like pesky flies around a sugar bowl, moving in on him and the burros, closer and closer. Bedoya asked what Bogart has packed on the burros and he tells them hides, that he is going into the village to sell the hides and burros and he mentions that he has friends who will soon be along. Bedoya looks across the wide stretch of land and sees no one, remarking that Bogart's friend must be a "long way away." Then he says with menace in his voice, "We can sell those burros same as you!" Bogart pulls his pistol and trains it on Bedoya who laughs maniacally. "Who are you kidding?" he spits. "You can't hurt a sick cat with that." The three bandits draw their machetes and move toward Bogart. He squeezes the trigger of his pistol but it only clicks; he is out of bullets, having used them up on shooting Holt. Bedoya and his men jump forward, raising their machetes, hacking and chopping Bogart to pieces and he is no sooner dead than his body is stripped and the burros are hurried off to the village. Holt, who has only been wounded by Bogart, is found and his wounds are tended to by Huston. Both of them pursue Bogart's trail on fast horses. Meanwhile, Bedoya has looked over the burros and, near some ancient ruins, dumped the curious contents from the sacks tied to the animals and kept the hides and the burros, taking these to the village. He begins to barter with the man who sold the burros originally to the three prospectors. A boy notices that the brand on these burros is the same as those bought by Huston, as does the original owner. The boy races off to the office of the federales. Bedoya and his men realize that they are suspected of having stolen the burros and try to back away from the villagers who are now demanding that they tell them where they got the animals. The bandits inch their hands toward their machetes but the villagers press weapons against them and they are soon in custody. (Huston does a marvelous job here by having his actors speak only Spanish during this entire scene; it is clear, from the way he shows the villagers and bandits, exactly what is being said and that English is not necessary to explain the situation, a scene that testifies as to Huston's brilliant perception of visuals to carry understanding.) Mexican justice is swift. For stealing the burros, Bedoya and his men are quickly taken to a wall, and, after being forced to dig their own graves, are lined up in front of a firing squad. The egocentric Bedoya has a final request of the commander in charge of his execution. He wants to wear his enormous sombrero to face the bullets. He is told to put it on. Just as Huston and Holt ride into the outskirts of the village, they hear the volley of shots that kill the bandits. Director Huston shows Bedoya's sombrero on the ground, blown into the grave the bandit now occupies by a gust of wind. The wind begins blowing wildly through the valley as Huston and Holt search the ruins for their gold, finding the empty sacks and realizing in shock that the bandits have dumped it out. By now the wind is blowing fiercely and the gold is carried in tiny grains into the air and along the ground, impossible to recapture. Holt is utterly dejected but Huston begins to laugh loudly, his laughter echoing across the land, carried by the wind along with the precious gold he and Bogart and Holt slaved so hard to get. Huston turns to Holt and between roars of laughter, shouts over the now whistling wind: "Laugh, Curtin, old boy! It's a great joke played on us by the Lord or fate or by nature...whichever you prefer, but whoever or whatever played it, certainly has a sense of humor! The gold has gone back to where we got it! Laugh, my boy, laugh! It's worth 10 months of labor and suffering...this joke is!" He roars with laughter so hard his body quakes and soon Holt grabs onto the crazy sense of it all and begins to laugh, too. Director Huston cuts to the earth they stand on, its dusty soil blowing along with the little grains of gold, and the empty sacks that contained the fortune blowing away into the swirling cloud of dust.

Huston, master of *film noir* (MALTESE FALCON, 1941, THE ASPHALT JUNGLE, 1950), here creates a classic film incisively showing the crime of greed and destruction of morality by gold. He shows the corruption of the human soul in the raw acquisition of riches, his detail grim, his irony overwhelming. The director wrings from his cast amazing performances that for the genre have never been equalled, even by Jean Hersholt and Gibson Gowland in Erich von Stroheim's masterpiece, GREED. And the humor in THE TREASURE OF THE SIERRA MADRE is as black and thorny as the landscape it presents. Inside of every scene there is a sort of grit that infects the speech and mannerisms of the characters, blown through them and later to work its lumpy way out of their pores. Bogart is the epitome of the average man gone wrong for riches, a man whose self-declared "fair share" turns into everyone's share. Nowhere in all the history of film has his performance been matched, an alarming essay of a human being whose mind is clutched and crushed by paranoid fears, agonizing doubts, and irrational murderous solutions to the delusionary devils plaguing him. He is, inside of himself, what the ruthless bandit Bedoya is on the outside, at the end willing to sacrifice friends, dignity, personal honor, or anyone's life except his own to possess wealth. Huston's profile is not a clincal study but a filmic odyssey into the corruption of the human spirit, shown in vivid, day-to-day experiences as healthy ambitions become diseased by cancerous nightmares, where evil overtakes good as subtly and as deadly as a patient, hungry cat inching up on an unsuspecting cheese-nibbling mouse. Huston, as the sanguine, optimistic old man who is painfully aware of the pitfalls awaiting the gold-seekers, is simply marvelous to behold, a perceptive old man whose own experiences and the understanding of them has put caution in his step and wisdom in his eyes. He is a man who sees backward as well as ahead and in his stated fables cryptically predicts the tragic outcome of this tale before it concludes with lightning fatality. The portrayal rendered by Holt is a perfect counterpoint to the aggressive, nonstop Bogart, one of reason, faith, and fairness. Holt has enough strength to survive his tenuous friendship with the lethal Bogart whose real seething subterranean personality is revealed by Holt himself when turning over the rock to find the Gila monster, its scaly tail twitching, squatting on Bogart's bags of hidden gold. The creature beneath the rock and Bogart are one in the same. And the element that saves Holt from being consumed by the same hatred and fears that swallowed Bogart whole is found in Huston's old man. From a magnificent wellspring deep inside of him, Huston produces laughter, the gigantic ability to laugh in the face of a fate that has made of them posturing, groping paupers again through a gush of wind. It is the roaring human laughter at the finish of this film that rises above and drowns out the low moan of evil that has momentarily engulfed the characters, laughter that gives hope, laughter that spreads light so that vision is restored, along with sanity and the prospect of a longer if not richer life. Both director John Huston and his distinguised father, Walter, won Oscars for THE TREASURE OF THE SIERRA MADRE, the only time father and son won the coveted gold statuettes. Son John specifically thought about having his father playing the role of Dobbs when he first read the novel in 1935 and hoped some day to film it, but, as years passed, John saw his father in the role of the old man. Yet he had to argue hard to convince Walter Huston to take on the old prospector part. Walter Huston had been a matinee idol for 20 years and was concerned about his image, although he stated that he would do anything for his son's career. When he first reported to the location site, John asked him to remove his false teeth and gum his way through the role. Walter refused and John and Bogart, according to the plan, literally held him down and pulled the teeth from Walter's mouth. He stood up sputtering, half angry and cursing at being forced to appear so undignified and half laughing at the way he sounded. "That's what I want for this role, " John reportedly said. Throughout the production John Huston and Bogart played pranks on the cast and crew, including the always hungry Bedoya who had had hardly any acting experience and was pulled out of a crowd by Huston to play the heinous bandit chieftain. Bedoya, Bogart and Huston noticed, was always first when the meal bells were rung to call everyone to eat. He gorged himself on the ample meals provided by studio cooks who went on the location shooting, going back two or three times for more helpings. At one point Huston and Bogart affixed strong glue to Bedoya's saddled but stationary stuffed horse and then the director, just before mealtime, insisted that Bedoya pose for some closeup takes. Bedoya jumped on the horse and then the meal bell rang and Huston called a halt to the shooting. As cast and crew went to eat, Bedoya struggled to get off the saddle but was held in place by the glue. He became frantic, sobbing and crying out, terrified of missing a sumptuous meal, becoming so hysterical that Huston couldn't stand Bedoya's caterwauling and ordered the Mexican actor's pants cut away from the saddle so he could run to the chow line. As with most Mexican actors selected from the local population where the film was made, Bedoya's pronunciation of English proved to be atrocious and Huston had a

continuing problem trying to get him to pronounce words correctly. He pronounced "horseback" as "whore's back." With the company on location was a mysterious little man named Hal Croves who claimed to be author B. Traven's representative. The author of THE TREASURE OF THE SIERRA MADRE, Traven, was a mysterious German no one had ever really seen, one who insisted upon total anonymity. When Huston first negotiated for the rights to film the book it was Croves who turned up in his seedy Mexican hotel to arrange things for Traven and who stayed on as an advisor throughout the filming in Mexico. Huston always had a suspicion that Croves was Traven himself. The director managed to obtain a rare photo of Traven and showed it to Bogart and asked him if he knew who it was. "Sure," Bogart replied, "It's that strange little guy, Croves." After finishing the film, Croves vanished forever. THE TREASURE OF THE SIERRA MADRE was the first postwar film produced by a major studio that was shot all on location, except for a few retakes made on the Warner Bros. back lot. After scouting southern Mexico for weeks, Huston selected the rough terrain around Jungapeo, Mexico, as the ideal setting for his story and moved the entire cast and crew to the area. Not since TRADER HORN was made in Africa did a film shot on location cost so much money. The budget soared upward daily as Huston went beyond schedule. Though the rushes shipped back to Jack Warner, head of the studio, impressed the mogul, he nearly went crazy with the weekly expenditures. After viewing one scene of the movie, Warner threw up his hands and shouted to producer Blanke, "Yeah, they're looking for gold all right–mine!" Toward the end of the film, which would cost Warners nearly $3 million, Jack Warner watched Bogart stumbling along, looking frantically for something to drink. Warner jumped up in the middle of the scene and shouted to a bevy of executives, "If that s.o.b. doesn't find water soon I'll go broke!" Warner had some reason to be angry. He had been somewhat misled by Huston and Blanke who told him that the story was simple to make and he concluded–Warner never read scripts so he had no idea what the film was really about–that THE TREASURE OF THE SIERRA MADRE was another western and would be shot at the studio's Calabasas Ranch where Warners made all its westerns. But bit by bit the production slipped south of the border until Warner, too late, realized he had a Mexican colossus on his hands. He didn't like the way Bogart turned mean at the end and thought it was a mistake to have him killed at the finish. His instincts proved initially correct. The public didn't like it, either, but the film was a huge critical success and, in its many re-releases, it more than made back its original investment.

p, Henry Blanke; d&w, John Huston (based on the novel by B. Traven [Berwick Traven Torsvan]); ph, Ted McCord; m, Max Steiner; ed, Owen Marks; md, Leo F. Forbstein; art d, John Hughes; set d, Fred M. MacLean; spec eff, William McGann, H.F. Koenekamp; makeup, Perc Westmore; tech adv, Ernesto A. Romero, Antonio Arriaga.

Adventure/Drama   **Cas.**   **(PR:C   MPAA:NR)**

TREAT EM' ROUGH*½   (1942) 59m UNIV bw

Eddie Albert (*Bill "Panama Kid" Kingsford*), Peggy Moran (*Betty*), William Frawley (*Hotfoot*), Lloyd Corrigan (*Gray Kingsford*), Truman Bradley (*Perkins*), Mantan Moreland (*Snake-Eyes*), Joseph Crehan (*Wetherbee*), Ed Pawley (*Martin*), William Ruhl (*Police Sergeant*), James Flavin (*Trosper*), Peter Leeds (*Davis*), Monte Blue (*Captain*), Dewey Robinson (*Handshaker*), Jack Mulhall (*Waiter*), Mel Ruick (*Police Announcer*).

The old story about the boy who pursues a career against his father's wishes and then comes back to help dad out of a jam, is given no new treatment in this tale in which Albert becomes a boxing champion. His pop is an oil tycoon in dire straits when federal investigators discover over a million barrels of oil unaccounted for. Albert gets into the act and discovers the inner bodies responsible for siphoning off the oil. Not a very good role for Albert.

p, Marshall Grant; d, Ray Taylor; w, Roy Chanslor, Bob Williams; ph, George Robi nson; ed, Maurice Wright.

Drama   **(PR:A   MPAA:NR)**

TREATMENT, THE   (SEE: STOP ME BEFORE I KILL!, 1961, Brit.)

TREE, THE*½   (1969) 92m Robert Guenette bw

Jordan Christopher (*Buck Gagnon*), Eileen Heckart (*Sally Dunning*), George Rose (*Stuey Moran*), James Broderick (*Detective McCarthy*), Ruth Ford (*Mrs. Gagnon*), Fred J. Scollay (*Alex*), Kathy Ryan (*Terry*), Alan Landers (*Jim Wisiewski*), Gale Dixon (*Lorry*), Ed Griffith (*Detective Gorman*), Tom Ahearne (*Joe*), Glenn Scimonelli (*1st Boy on Bicycle*), Alan Zemel (*2nd Boy on Bicycle*), Billy King (*Delivery Boy*), Ben Gerard (*Waiter*).

Highly atmospheric depiction lacking much of a concrete plot, of a half-crazed man who kidnaps his niece while thinking about his cherished sister. We learns that this sister is dead, which sparks memories of their incestual relationship, and inevitably he commits suicide. Performances leave much to be desired, with little personali ty showing through the caricatures.

p,d&w, Robert Guenette; ph. Jesse Paley; m, Kenyon Hopkins; ed, Howard Milkin; prod d, Francis Gudemann.

Drama   **(PR:O   MPAA:NR)**

TREE GROWS IN BROOKLYN, A**   (1945) 128m FOX bw

Dorothy McGuire (*Katie*), Joan Blondell (*Aunt Sissy*), James Dunn (*Johnny Nolan*), Lloyd Nolan (*McShane*), Peggy Ann Garner (*Francie Nolan*), Ted Donaldson (*Neeley Nolan*), James Gleason (*McGarrity*), Ruth Nelson (*Miss McDonough*), John Alexander (*Steve Edwards*), B.S. Pully (*Christmas Tree Vendor*), Ferike Boros (*Grandma Rommely*), Charles Halton (*Mr. Barker*), Patricia McFadden (*Sheila*), Robert Strange (*Doctor*), Robert Tait (*Street Singer*), Teddy Infuhr, Mickey Kuhn (*Boys*), Constance Purdy (*Woman*), J. Farrell MacDonald (*Carney, Junk Man*), Adeline De Walt Reynolds (*Mrs. Waters*), George Melford (*Mr. Spencer*), Mae Marsh, Edna Jackson (*Tynmore Sisters*), Vincent Graeff (*Henny Gaddis*), Susan Lester (*Flossie Gaddis*), Johnnie Berkes (*Mr. Crackenbox*), Lillian Bronson (*Librarian*), Alec Craig (*Werner*), Al Bridge (*Cheap Charlie*), Joseph J. Greene (*Hassler*), Virginia Brissac (*Miss Tilford*), Harry Harvey, Jr. (*Herschel*), Robert Anderson (*Augie*), Art Smith (*Ice Man*), Erskine Sanford (*Undertaker*), Martha Wentworth (*Mother*), Francis Pierlot (*Priest*), Al Eben (*Union Representative*), Harry Seymour (*Floorwalker*), Joyce Tucker (*Girl*), Nick Ray (*Bakery Clerk*), Robert Malcolm (*Doctor*), Norman Field, George Meader (*Principals of Schools*), Peter Cusanelli (*Barber*).

Elia Kazan's first directorial assignment in films proved to be one of the most endearing, honest family dramas of the era and is still timeless enough to be watched and savored decades later. James Dunn won the Best Supporting Actor Oscar, Peggy Ann Garner earned a special Oscar as Best Child Actress, and the script was nominated by the Academy. Set in the Williamsburg area of Brooklyn, in the first years of the 20th Century, it accurately captures the ambiance of the poor people who struggled mightily to eke out an existence against the odds by concentrating on the drama of one Irish family. McGuire is the matriarch of the family, worried about every penny because her husband, Dunn, can't ever seem to earn enough to keep her and their children, Donaldson and Garner, above the hot water they are always immersed in. McGuire is pregnant again and although Dunn means well and truly feels that he is the best singing waiter in all of the borough, he finds success just outside his grasp and takes solace in alcohol. Dunn is not a mean drunk and there's not a scintilla of anger in his body. He is simply one of life's losers and, from the outset, we can sense that. Garner dreams of a better life, a life as a writer, somewhere away from the poverty of Brooklyn and she is the person through whom the story is told. While Donaldson is McGuire's boy, Garner is daddy's little girl. Blondell is the aunt, a woman who takes lovers and husbands with ease and who is quick to offer suggestions to everyone as to how to run their lives, although she can't quite manage her own. In the tenement, there is a small tree that heroically withstands the harsh winter and the humid summer and Garner watches it as it hardily stretches its barren branches and refuses to be bent under the bludgeonings of life. She likens herself to that tree and takes strength from it as the small sapling continues to flourish, despite what is transpiring all around it, not unlike the O. Henry story "The Last Leaf." Dunn dies of pneumonia and Garner fears that her link is gone but McGuire clasps the young girl to her bosom, saying that she is going to ask her to help with the birth of the new baby because "I can't count on Neely– a boy is no use at times like these" (or words to that effect). The movie is a trifle lengthy but never tedious. It's episodic, but life is often episodic and the performances are so real, so richly detailed that one can overlook the segmented way in which the movie is unspooled. Stories about life in the squalor of a big city have often been made. STREET SCENE preceded this as did many other films. It's sentimental although it never descends into treacle. McGuire had only made one movie before, the charming CLAUDIA, and was only about 13 years older than Garner and 13 years younger than Dunn at the time of shooting. Kazan did not fall into the trap so many first-time directors are prey to: i.e. impressing the eye with cinematic tricks. Instead, he wisely concentrated on evoking memorable performances from all concerned, and none was more rewarding than that of Dunn, who had starred in many B movies for years before getting the opportunity to show his stuff here. Dunn, for many years, had been a notorious heavy drinker and when he was first proposed for the role of the Irish singing waiter, Fox executives said no, that he was "unreliable" and "a drunk." But studio boss Zanuck was persuaded that that was exactly what Dunn would be playing and, against all advice, cast the easygoing tippler in the role. Dunn ecstatically met with the press after getting the part and blatantly announced: "They needed a bum so they hired me." Dunn required a tuxedo for his role as the singing waiter but wardrobe had no time to fit him. He found a discarded tuxedo in the studio and wore it for his part. According to the name tag sewn into the tuxedo's lining, the coat had once belonged to Sol M. Wurtzel, king of the B-programmer producers.

p, Louis D. Lighton; d, Elia Kazan; w, Tess Slesinger, Frank Davis (based on the novel by Betty Smith); ph, Leon Shamroy; m, Alfred Newman; ed, Dorothy Spencer; art d, Lyle Wheeler; set d, Thomas Little, Frank E. Hughes; cos, Bonnie Cashin; spec eff, Fred Sersen.

Drama   (PR:C MPAA:NR)

TREE OF LIBERTY   (SEE: HOWARDS OF VIRGINIA, THE, 1940)

TREE OF WOODEN CLOGS, THE*½   (1979, Ital.) 185m G. P. C.
Gruppo/GAU-Sacis-New Yorker c (L' ALBERO DEGLI ZOCCOLI)

Luigi Ornaghi (*Batisti*), Francesca Moriggi (*Batistina*), Omar Brignoli (*Minek*), Antonio Ferrari (*Tuni*), Teresa Brescianini (*Widow Runk*), Giuseppe Brignoli (*Grandpa Anselmo*), Carlo Rota (*Peppino*), Pasqualina Brolis (*Teresina*), Massimo Fratus (*Pierino*), Francesca Villa (*Annetta*), Maria Grazia Caroli (*Bettina*), Battista Trevaini (*Finard*), Giuseppina Sangaletti (*Finarda*), Lorenzo Pedroni (*Grandpa Finar*), Felice Cervi (*Usti*), Pierangelo Bertoli (*Secondo*), Brunella Migliaccio (*Olga*), Giacomo Cavalleri (*Brena*), Lorenza Frigeni (*Brena's Wife*), Lucia Pezzoli (*Maddalena*), Franco Pilenga (*Stefano*), Guglielmo Padoni (*Bridegroom's Father*), Laura Locatelli (*Bridegroom's Mother*), Carmelo Silva (*Don Carlo*), Mario Brignoli (*Master*), Emilio Pedroni (*Bailiff*), Vittorio Capelli (*Friki*), Francesca Bassurini (*Sister Maria*), Lina Ricci (*Sign Woman*).

A naturalistic portrayal of Italian peasants which neither glorifies their lives nor looks down at them--it merely presents them in a truthful and beautiful manner. Director Olmi, who directed, scripted, photographed, and edited the film, concentrates on three peasant families (all acted by nonprofessionals) and their daily existence for the period of about one year. They live on an estate governed by a practically nonexistent landlord and work his land with the greatest of care and devotion. Interestingly, however, the least important facet of THE TREE OF WOODEN CLOGS is its plot. Instead, concentration is placed on the bond between people, as well as their relationship to the land. A memorable picture which takes a sensitive, poetic look at a remarkable group of human beings. Winner of the Golden Palm at the 1978 Cannes Film Festival, making it the second Italian film in a row to take top honors. The 1977 winner was the Taviani Brother's PADRE PADRONE. (In Italian; English subtitles.)

d,w&ph, Ermanno Olmi; m, Johanna Sebastien Bach; ed, Olmi.

Drama   Cas.   (PR:A-C MPAA:NR)

**TREMENDOUSLY RICH MAN, A*½   (1932, Ger.) 73m
Tobis-UNIV/Deutsche-UNIV bw (EIN STEINREICHER MANN)

Curt Bois, Dolly Haas, Adele Sandrock, Liselotte Schaack, Eugen Brosig, Fritz Ley, Paul Horbiger, Willy Schur, Paul Biensfeld, Margarete Kupfer, Friedrich Ettel, Rothauser, Anni Ann.

Poorly directed farce about a young man who accidentally swallows a very expensive jewel, only to put everyone through a lot of fits and exasperating moments to discover that the diamond actually fell into his trouser cuffs. Could have been much better.

d, Stefan Szekely; w, Eugen Szatmary, Ernst Wolff; ph, R. Kuntze; m, Theo Mackeben; m/l, Max Kolpe.

Comedy   (PR:A MPAA:NR)

**TRENCHCOAT*½   (1983) 91m BV c

Margot Kidder (*Mickey Raymond*), Robert Hays (*Terry Leonard*), David Suchet (*Inspector Stagnos*), Gila Von Weitershausen (*Eva Werner*), Daniel Faraldo (*Nino Tenucci*), Ronald Lacey (*Princess Aida*), John Justin (*Marquis DePina*), Pauline Delany (*Lizzy O'Reilly*), Leopoldo Trieste (*Estaban Ortega*), P.G. Stephens (*Sean O'Reilly*), Brizio Montinaro (*Cpl. Lascaris*), Martin Sorrentino (*Afro-Dite*), Luciano Crovato (*Taxi Driver*), Massimo Sarchielli (*Boss Arab*), Jennifer Darling (*Laurie*), Kevork Malikyan (*Arab*), Vic Tablian (*Achmed*), Brian Coburn (*Burly Salt*), Fifi Moyer (*Mother*), Savior Tanti (*Passport Agent*), Nadine Azzopardi (*Stewardess*), Emanuel Abela (*Man at Museum Post*), Nancy Calamatta (*Tour Guide*), Anthony Spiteri (*Bald Man*), Joe Quattromani (*Man in Fez*), Eddie Baldacchino (*Wheelman at Dragonara Casino*), Joe Coppini (*Fishmonger*), Harry Jones (*Man with Duffle Bag*), Michael Kissaun (*Backstage Man*), Charles Darmanin, Joe Abela (*Museum Guards*), Marcello Krakoff, Philip Alexander, Brian Eubanks (*Boys*), Charles Saliba, Benny Farrugia (*Bartenders*), Margaret Von Brockdorff, Ruth Borthwick, Freda Camilleri, Lilly Harding (*Nuns*).

Haphazardly scripted pseudo-farce that just does hold together, stars Kidder as an aspiring mystery novelist taking a few weeks off her office job to churn out a story on the island of Malta. She gets more than she bargained for as she finds herself in the midst of the real thing, giving her plenty of material for her book. It isn't very funny; the attempts to provide the Disney type of charm is nauseating.

p, Jerry Leider; d, Michael Tuchner; w, Jeffrey Price, Peter Seaman; ph, Tonino Delli Colli (Technicolor); m, Charles Fox; ed, Frank J. Urioste; prod d, Rodger Maus; art d, John B. Mansbridge; cos, Gloria Mussetta.

Comedy/Mystery   Cas.   (PR:A MPAA:PG)

TRENT'S LAST CASE   (1953, Brit.) 90m Wilcox-Neagle/BL bw

Margaret Lockwood (*Margaret Manderson*), Michael Wilding (*Philip Trent*), Orson Welles (*Sigsbee Manderson*), John McCallum (*John Marlowe*), Miles Malleson (*Burton Cupples*), Hugh McDermott (*Calvin C. Bunner*), Sam Kydd (*Inspector Murch*), Jack McNaughton (*Martin*).

After international financier Welles turns up dead, a coroner's inquest rules the death a suicide. Investigative reporter Wilding is not convinced and he sets out to prove that it was murder. He uncovers evidence that points to Welles' secretary, McCallum, who has been having an affair with Lockwood, the dead man's widow. He confronts McCallum and Lockwood with what he suspects and that launches a string of flashbacks, the only scenes where Welles is actually on screen. Eventually Wilding concludes that Welles was indeed a suicide, and that he left evidence that would frame McCallum for his own murder. Apart from a good cast, this is mostly a routine murder mystery of the British school. Welles took the part largely because he needed the money, and it marked the beginning of a long string of embarrassing supporting parts with which he was to fill most of his remaining years. His performance here is somewhat overwrought, as indeed most of these later performances were, but he provides whatever reason there is to see this film today. Two versions preceeded; one in 1920 and one in 1929 directed by Howard Hawks.

p&d, Herbert Wilcox; w, Pamela Wilcox Bower (based on the novel by E.C. Bentley); ph, Max Greene [Mutz Greenbaum]; m, Anthony Collins; ed, Bill Lewthwaite; art d, William C. Andrews.

Crime   **(PR:A MPAA:NR)**

TRES NOCHES VIOLENTAS   (SEE: WEB OF VIOLENCE, 1966, Ital./Span.)

TRESPASSER, THE½**   (1929) 91m UA bw

Gloria Swanson (Marion Donnell), Robert Ames (Jack Merrick), Purnell Pratt (Hector Ferguson Lawyer), William Holden (John Merrick, Sr.), Henry B. Walthall (Fuller), Wally Albright ("Jackie" Merrick), Kay Hammond (Catherine "Flip" Merrick), Blanche Frederici (Miss Potter), Marcelle Corday (Blanche), Mary Forbes (Mrs. Ferguson), Bill O'Brien (Butler), Lloyd Whitlock (Member of Board of Directors), Allan Cavan (Doctor), Ed Brady (Moving Man), Henry Armetta (Barber), Stuart Erwin, Dick Cramer, Billy Bevan, Brooks Benedict (Reporters).

The chance for the millions of Swanson fans to actually hear their favorite star talking and singing was an assured success for this early talky venture. Swanson proved to have a pleasant voice, even when it came to singing. Her performance, which as always required her to display an extravagant wardrobe, was good enough to warrant a nomination for an Academy Award. Story is a tearjerker. Swanson as a young mother is dropped by her husband when daddy-in-law exhibits disapproval of his son's wedding and coerces him away with promises of riches. Swanson does okay on her own, getting a job with a lawyer who makes sure that the girl is not wanting, including bequeathing her half a million dollars. Story is constructed well, though concent ration is on bringing out emotion, something audiences went to the theaters in droves to wear.

p, Joseph P. Kennedy; d&w, Edmund Goulding; ph, George Barnes, Gregg Toland; m, Josiah Zoro; ed, Cyril Gardner; m/l, "Love Your Magic Spell is Everywhere," Goulding, Elsie Janis, other songs, Enrico Toselli, Sig Spaeth.

Drama   **(PR:A MPAA:NR)**

TRESPASSER, THE, 1946   (SEE: NIGHT EDITOR, 1946)

TRESPASSER, THE**   (1947) 71m REP bw

Dale Evans (Linda Coleman), Warren Douglas (Danny Butler), Janet Martin (Stevie Carson), Douglas Fowley (Bill Munroe), Adele Mara (Dee Dee), Gregory Gay (Charles), Grant Withers (Kirk), William Bakewell (Bruce Coleman), Vince Barnett (Bartender), Francis Pierlot (Channing Bliss), Joy Barlowe (Mary Lou), Fred Graham (Davis), Dale Van Sickel (Hall), Betty Alexander (Jane), Joseph Crehan (The Doctor).

Highly suspenseful yarn about a rookie newspaper reporter, Martin, who discovers a book-forging racket almost immediately after being assigned to cover the morgue. She tells her findings to the more established Fowley, and the two expose the schemers. Evans is in the plot as romantic interest for Fowley, otherwise she spends her time singing in nightclubs, doing one song for the cameras: "It's Not the First Love" (Eddie Maxwell, Nathan Scott).

p, William J. O'Sullivan; d, George Blair; w, Jerry Gruskin, Darrell McGowan, Stuart E. McGowan (based on the story by Jerry Sackheim, Erwin Gelsey); ph, John Alton; ed, Arthur Roberts; md, Mort Glickman; art d, Frank Hotaling; set d, John McCarthy, Jr., Helen Hansard; cos, Adele Palmer.

Drama/Mystery   **(PR:A MPAA:NR)**

TRESPASSERS, THE**½   (1976, Aus.) 93m Vega/Filmways c

John Derum (Richard), Judy Morris (Dee), Briony Behets (Penny), Hugh Keys-Byrne (Frank), Peter Carmody (Journalist), Max Gilles (Publisher), John Frawley (Politician), Syd Conabere (Harry), John Oresik (Surveyor), Chris Haywood (Sandy), Ross Thompson (Terry), John Bowman (Mark).

A subtly and casually handled depiction of a love triangle that evolves around Derum as the man who lives with Behets but carries on an extra affair with Morris. Behets catches her lover and Morris together, and after getting over a not-too-damaging hurt, develops a close affection for Morris.

Morris and Behets become closer to each other than to Derum, including possibly having a physical relationship, though this is not actually depicted. Atmosphere and attitude are maintained to keep the situations believable. Filmed on location around Melbourne and the Victoria coast.

p,d&w, John Duigan; ph, Vince Monton; m, Bruce Smeaton.

Drama   **(PR:O MPAA:NR)**

TRI   (SEE: THREE, 1967, Yugo.)

TRI SESTRY   (SEE: THREE SISTERS, THE, 1969, USSR)

TRIAL*½   (1955) 105m MGM bw

Glenn Ford (David Blake), Dorothy McGuire (Abbe Nyle), Arthur Kennedy (Barney Castle), John Hodiak (John J. Armstrong), Katy Jurado (Consuela Chavez), Rafael Campos (Angel Chavez), Juano Hernandez (Judge Theodore Motley), Robert Middleton (A. S. "Fats" Sanders), John Hoyt (Ralph Castillo), Paul Guilfoyle (Cap Grant), Elisha Cook, Jr (Finn), Ann Lee (Gail Wiltse), Whit Bissell (Sam Wiltse), Richard Gaines (Dr. Schacter), Barry Kelley (Jim Backett), Frank Cady (Canford), Charles Tannen (Bailiff), David Leonard (County Clerk), John Rosser (Assistant District Attorney), James Todd (Minister), Sheb Wooley (Butteridge), Charlotte Lawrence (Mrs. Webson), Percy Helton (Youval), Dorothy Green (Mrs. Ackerman), Everett Glass (Dean), Grandon Rhodes (Terry Bliss), Charles Evans (Lawyer No. 1), Frank Wilcox (Lawyer No. 2), Wilson Wood (Checker), Robert Bice (Abbott), John Maxwell (Benedict), Michael Dugan (Pine), Vince Townsend (Dr. Abraham Tenfold), Frank Ferguson (Kiley), Robert Forrest, Mort Mills (Reporters), Rodney Bell (Lew Bardman), Richard Tyler (Johnson), Mitchell Lewis (Jury Foreman).

A courtroom drama by its nature alone is hard put to maintain a high level of interest; the bickerings over the case, the enclosed and sterile setting, and the inevitable outcome all seem to follow a format which doesn't allow much versatility. Not so with TRIAL, an unusually good film resulting from extraordinary efforts by everyone involved--a taut script, intriguing performances, the thought and planning that went behind the recording of each shot. Ford plays the lawyer, an inexperienced one, given the job of defending a Mexican youth against a charge of murder. The case very nearly meets its resolution outside the courtroom when an angry mob wishes to impose its own form of justice--a public lynching. For this reason the trial takes on an importance far outside the bounds of court; the lad is undoubtedly innocent but prejudice against his cultural background makes it impossible for him to be judged fairly. In an unusual role for the 1950s, the presiding judge is black, superbly played by Hernandez, conscientiously and subtly showing his desire to see that a fair trial is given the youth. One of the major issues that the film deals with is the Communist use of such a case to help its cause. Unfortunately this creates a strong atmosphere of anti-Communist propaganda, with Kennedy revealed as a man constantly scheming, using Ford as his spokesman, though the lawyer remains naive to this position as he delves into the case wholeheartedly. This line of attack on communism could only hurt the way the picture is viewed outside of the time period in which it was made; mid-1950s Hollywood, a time in which taking pot-shots at Communist ideology was the thing to do. Despite this the picture still remains a highly suspenseful, well performed, and powerful drama.

p, Charles Schnee; d, Mark Robson; w, Don M. Mankiewicz (based on his novel); ph, Robert Surtees; m, Daniele Amfitheatrof; ed, Albert Akst; md, Amfitheatrof; art d, Cedric Gibbons, Randall Duell; set d, Edwin B. Willis, Fred Maclean; spec eff, Warren Newcombe.

Drama   **(PR:A MPAA:NR)**

TRIAL, THE**½   (1948, Aust.) Oesterreichesche Wecheschau & Filmproductions A.G., J.A. Heubler, Kahn & Co. bw (DER PROZESS; IN NAME DER MENSCHLICHKEIT)

Ewald Balser (Dr. Eotvoes), Ernest Deutsch (Scharf), Albert Truby (Moritz), Heinz Moog (Baron Onody), Marcia Ebs (Mrs. Sotymori), Aglaja Schmid (Esther), Ivan Petrovitch (Egnessy), Gustav Diessl (Eoth), Josef Meinrad (Bary), Ladislaus Morgenstern (Salomon Schwarz), Ernest Waldbaum (Wollmer), Frank Pfandler (Peezely), Leopole Rudolf (Reszky), Herman Thimig (Farkas), Otto Schmoele (Prussian), Marinanne Schoenauer (Dr. Eoetvoes' Fiancee), Max Rood (A Jew), Klaramaria Skala (Julca).

After having made two films for the Nazis during World War II, the great G.W. Pabst seemed to be in need of a way to redeem himself in this mediocre, by the standards of what Pabst was capable, condemnation of anti-Semitism. Yarn concerns the trial of several Hungarian Jews for the murder of a young girl who actually committed suicide. Set in the late 19th Century, a famous lawyer takes up the case on the basis of religious freedom for all people, and does a good enough job of proving his points to win a verdict of innocent. Though Pabst was still a very capable filmmaker at this point in his career, he seemed to let sentimentalism get the better part of him in several sequences from this picture. Part of the service in the synagog is sung by famous Hungarian cantor Ladislaus Morgenstern.

p, J.W. Beyer; G.W. Pabst; w, Rudolf Braungraber, Jurt Heuser, Emmerich Robenz; ph, Oskar Schuirch, Helmut Fischer-Ashely; m, Alois Melichar; ed,

Anna Hoeltering; md, Melichar.

Drama   (PR:A MPAA:NR)

TRIAL, THE***   (1963, Fr./Ital./Ger.) 118m Paris
Europa-FI-C-IT-Hisa/Astor bw (LE PROCES; DER PROZESS; IL PRO-
CESSO)

Anthony Perkins *(Josef K)*, Orson Welles *(Hastler, Advocate)*, Jeanne
Moreau *(Miss Burstner)*, Romy Schneider *(Leni)*, Elsa Martinelli *(Hilda)*,
Akim Tamiroff *(Bloch)*, Arnoldo Foa *(Inspector A)*, William Kearns *(1st
Assistant Inspector)*, Jess Hahn *(2nd Assistant Inspector)*, Suzanne Flon
(Miss Pittl), Madelaine Robinson *(Mrs. Grubach)*, Wolfgang Reichmann
(Courtroom Guard), Thomas Holtzmann *(Bert the Law Student)*, Maydra
Shore *(Irmie)*, Max Haufler *(Uncle Max)*, William Chappell *(Titorelli)*,
Fernand Ledoux *(Chief Clerk)*, Maurice Teynac *(Deputy Manager)*, Michael
Lonsdale *(Priest)*, Max Buchsbaum *(Examining Magistrate)*, Jean-Claude
Remoleux *(1st Policeman)*, Raoul Delfosse *(2nd Policeman)*, Karl Studer
(Man in Leather).

Welles applied his bravura directorial style to Kafka's brilliant but
frustrating novel (published in 1925) about an aggressive office clerk
(Perkins) who gets arrested without being told why. The film opens over a
series of pin-screen pictures (a technique using pins, cloth, light, and
shadows created by A. Alexeieff) of a guard in front of a huge door,
preventing a man from entering. For years the man awaits entrance into the
door which leads to the Law, but he never gains admittance. The narrator
(Welles) then explains "It has been said that the logic of this story is the logic
of a dream. Do you feel lost in a labyrinth? Do not look for a way out. You
will not be able to find one... There is no way out." The story of Joseph K
(Perkins) then begins as two men break into the clerk's room and announce
that he is under arrest. Perkins is not told what crime he has committed, nor
is he shackled and dragged away to prison. He is simple told that he is guilty.
Perkins then decides to begin his quest for justice. He is constantly
confronted by bureaucratic obstacles. He works his way to an examining
magistrate but still can get no answers. Through his uncle, Perkins is
introduced to Welles, a powerful defense attorney who has taken on a
number of clients in the same predicament, none of whom, however, has
been acquitted. Perkins becomes overwhelmed by the bureaucratic underworld through which he is dragged in search of the charge against him.
There are mammoth offices with seas of file cabinets and papers, a landscape
of desks and clerks, and the frantic hum of clacking typewriter keys. There
seems to be no end to the red tape–and indeed there isn't. In the process,
Perkins becomes involved with three bizarre women–Moreau, who lives
down the hall; Schneider, who is attracted to condemned men; and
Martinelli, a nymphomaniac who offers her help–none of whom get him any
closer to solving his case. Then one morning, two men accost Perkins in his
room and force him into an abandoned quarry. Hysterical, Perkins refuses
to kill himself with the knife the men supply and is instead dynamited into
oblivion. A visually stunning film, THE TRIAL suffers from a less-than-
subtle adaptation of the novel (Kafka's end has no explosives, only Joseph
K being stabbed in the heart by his captors). While Kafka's novel is surely
one of the finest pieces of 20th-Century European literature, it doesn't
translate well into film. Being far more literary than dramatic, the novel is
dependent on the thoughts and frustrations of Joseph K during his quest.
Instead Welles, has chosen to concentrate on the atmosphere of K's world,
accompanied by the dreamy musical leitmotif of Albinoni's "Adagio." The
sets are typical Welles baroque–massive structures which engulf Perkins in
the same way Xanadu swallowed Charles Foster Kane (it is inevitable that
all Welles' work be compared with CITIZEN KANE). It is for these sets
alone–with their haunting shadows and claustrophobic walls and ceilings–
that THE TRIAL is essential viewing. Welles' enthusiasm for the film is
remarkable; "Say what you like, but THE TRIAL is the best film I ever
made." The film's genesis goes back to Miguel and Alexander Salkind, the
father-and-son producing team, who offered Welles a list of 15 classic novels
which were in public domain. Welles was to choose one which he wanted to
film and, without much enthusiasm (Welles admits he had a "lack of
profound sympathy for Kafka"), he agreed to *The Trial*. Production began
in Zagreb, Yugoslavia, but was soon shut down for lack of funds. Skipping
out on bills owed there, Welles and his entourage returned to Paris to
complete the film at the abandoned Gare d'Orsay train station–an overwhelming structure which seems to have been built with Welles in mind.
Although the film has its admirers, its opening was less than favorable.
Originally scheduled to play the 1962 Venice Film Fest, it did not open until
December 21st of that year in Paris. Not only did Welles have to overcome
financial and scheduling restrictions, but he had problems with the casting.
He had first cast himself as a priest, but when no suitable actor could be
found for "The Advocate," Welles took over the role, scrapping the footage
he had already shot. Much of the controversy surrounding the film's
reception invlved the casting of Perkins in the lead. Although Perkins is
perfect as Joseph K (even if he is a bit more animated than Kafka had
intended), not everyone agreed. In her biography of Welles, Barbara
Lemming quotes Welles as saying, "I think everybody has an idea of K as
some kind of little Woody Allen." Shot in English, the picture was dubbed
in its foreign language releases (which had a variety of running times). Two
players were cut from the U.S. release: Katina Paxinou, whose role was that
of a scientist, and Van Doude, who played an archivist. The chief difference
in Welles' Joseph K and Kafka's is in the question of the character's guilt.

While Kafka stresses ambiguity, Welles is clear in his feelings, "He is a little
bureaucrat. I consider him guilty... He belongs to a guilty society, he
collaborates with it." Welles further points to his differences with Kafka: "I
do not share Kafka's point of view in *The Trial*. I believe that he is a good
writer, but Kafka is not the extraordinary genius that people today see him
as." Unfortunately for Welles, Kafka's story is far more successful as a novel
than as a film.

p, Yves Laplanche, Miguel Salkind, Alexander Salkind; d&w, Orson Welles
(based on the novel by Franz Kafka); ph, Edmond Richard; m, Jean Ledrut,
Tommaso Albinoni; ed, Yvonne Martin; md, Ledrut; art d, Jean Mandaroux;
set d, Jean Charpentier, Francine Coureau; cos, Helen Thibault; makeup,
Louis Dor.

Drama   **Cas.**   (PR:C MPAA:NR)

TRIAL AND ERROR**½   (1962, Brit.) 88m Anatole De
Grunwald/MGM bw (GB: THE DOCK BRIEF)

Peter Sellers *(Morgenhall/Doctor)*, Richard Attenborough *(Fowle/Judge/
Foreman of the Jury/Member of the Public/Character Witness)*, Beryl Reid
(Doris), David Lodge *(Bateson)*, Frank Pettingell *(Tuppy Morgan)*, Eric
Woodburn *(Judge Banter)*, Frank Thornton *(Photographer)*, Tristram Jel-
linek *(Perkins)*, Patrick Newell *(1st Warder)*, Audrey Nicholson *(Morgan-
hall's Girl)*, John Waite *(Clerk of the Court)*, David Drummond *(Policeman)*,
Eric Dodson *(Examiner)*, Ian Curry *(Doctor)*, Henry Kay *(2nd Warder)*.

Sellers and Attenborough set themselves up for humiliation when they try
to thoroughly rehearse their court defense before their day in front of the
judge. The brilliant Sellers plays the cautious attorney defending wife-
murderer Attenborough. Both fall to pieces when the time comes to put their
case to trial. An odd comedy that works well by Hill, a director of many
smart comedies and thrillers.

p, Dimitri De Grunwald; d, James Hill; w, Pierre Rouve (based on the play
by John Mortimer); ph, Edward Scaife; m, Ron Grainer; ed, Ann Chegwidden; md, Grainer; art d, Ray Simm; makeup, Tom Smith.

Comedy   (PR:A MPAA:NR)

TRIAL BY COMBAT   (SEE: DIRTY KNIGHT'S WORK, 1976, Brit.)

TRIAL OF BILLY JACK, THE zero   (1974) 170m Taylor-Laughlin c

Tom Laughlin *(Billy Jack)*, Delores Taylor *(Jean Roberts)*, Victor Izay *(Doc)*,
Teresa Laughlin *(Carol)*, William Wellman, Jr *(National Guardsman)*,
Russell Lane *(Russell)*, Michelle Wilson *(Michelle)*, Geo Anne Sosa *(Joanne)*,
Lynn Baker *(Lynn)*, Riley Hill *(Posner)*, Sparky Watt *(Sheriff Cole)*, Gus
Greymountain *(Blue Elk)*, Sacheen Littlefeather *(Patsy Littlejohn)*, Michael
Bolland *(Danny)*, Jack Stanley *(Grandfather)*, Bong Soo Han *(Master Han)*,
Rolling Thunder *(Thunder Mountain)*, Sandra Ego *(Indian Maiden)*,
Trinidad Hopkins *(Vision Maiden)*, Marianne Hall *(Alicia)*, Jason Clark
(Cowboy No. 1), Johnny West *(Turning Water)*, Buffalo Horse *(Little Bear)*,
Dennis O'Flaherty *(Defense Attorney)*, George Aguilar *(Elk's Shadow)*,
Pepper Rogers *(3rd Trooper)*, Teda Bracci *(Teda)*, Susan Sosa *(Sunshine)*,
Ron Nix *(Cowboy No. 2)*, Michael J. Shigezane *(Karate Expert)*, Ken Tealor
(Ken), Evans Thornton *(Prosecuting Attorney)*, Jack White *(Bugger)*, Hosea
Barnett *(Student)*, David Scott Clark *(Town Boy)*, Jean Newburn *(Militant
Indian Lawyer)*, Debbie Hill *(Debbie)*, Diane Webber *(Belly-Dance Instruc-
tor)*, Oshannah Fastwolf *(Oshannah)*, Kathy Cronkite *(Kristen)*, DeLaura
Henry *(Liz)*, Patricia McCulloch *(Girl)*, Alexandra Nicholson *(Abby)*.

This self-gratifying project by Laughlin is one of the most cliche-ridden,
absurd films ever to force its way onto the screen and down the throats of
millions of people who flocked to theaters to sit through it. Its success
assured yet another sequel, BILLY JACK GOES TO WASHINGTON, about
the peace-loving Indian who is dying to get his chance to kick in the teeth
of the hawkish bourgeoisie who threaten the liberty of his friends at The
Freedom School. He gets his chance when the National Guard encroaches
on school property to quell student attempts to expose political shenanigans
through their TV station. How a small school like this ever got a TV station
is one of the many incongruities placed in this film to help develop the plot.
The whole thing is told in flashback from the point of view of Taylor,
Laughlin's real-life wife and business partner, whose acting ability consists
of crying a lot because people are cruel. When she's not crying, she spouts
out trite philosophy about how the world can become such a wonderful place
to live. Would someone please make THE HANGING OF BILLY JACK.

p, Joe Cramer; d, Frank Laughlin; w, Frank and Teresa Christina Laughlin;
ph, Jack A. Marta (Panavision, Metrocolor); m, Elmer Bernstein; ed, Tom
Rolf, Jules Nayfack, Michael Economou, George Grenville, Michael Karr;
art d, George W. Troast; cos, Moss Mabry.

Drama   **Cas.**   (PR:C MPAA:PG)

TRIAL OF JOAN OF ARC***   (1965, Fr.) 65m Pathe Contemporary
bw (PROCES DE JEANNE D'ARC)

Florence Carrez *(Jeanne D'Arc)*, Jean-Claude Fourneau *(Bishop Cauchon)*,
Marc Jacquier *(Jean Lemaitre, Inquisitor)*, Roger Honorat *(Jean Beaupere)*,
Jean Gillibert *(Jean de Chatillon)*, Andre Regnier *(D'Estivet)*, Michel

Herubel (*Frere Isambart de la Pierre*), Philippe Dreux (*Frere Martin Ladvenu*), Jean Darbaud (*Nicolas de Houppeville*), E.R. Pratt (*Warwick*), Michael Williams (*Englishman*), Harry Sommers (*Bishop of Winchester*), Donald O'Brien (*English Priest*), Gerard Zingg (*Jean-Lohier*), Andre Maurice (*Tiphaine*), Paul-Robert Mimet (*Guillaume Erard*), Yves Leprince (*Pierre Morice*), Arthur Le Bau (*Jean Massieu*).

The most commonly known film rendition of the famous French legend of Joan of Arc is the 1920's version by Dreyer in which Falconetti gave a stunning performance of the girl burned as a witch. From the outset of this newer project, Bresson chose an entirely different angle from that of Dreyer, for he was concerned with creating a more objective rendition, unprejudiced by the filmmaker's camera technique and personal manipulations. His efforts were fairly successful, basing the script solely on the notes from the trial, with Carrez playing Joan in a manner that makes her appear brighter and more scheming than she had usually been pictured. Joan was a French peasant girl brought to trial as an enemy to the government, and after enduring a long court case and torture she was burned as a witch. Unlike the earlier version, Bresson concentrates quite heavily on the psychological and physical torture, showing how Joan broke down during the trial and recanted her faith. The purpose of Bresson was not to destroy the myth of Joan of Arc; what he did was reveal the processes that helped to create a legend.

p, Agnes Delahaie; d&w, Robert Bresson (based on "Proces De Condamnation Et De Rehabilitation De Jeanne D'Arc"); ph, Leonce-Henri Burel; m, Francis Seyrig; ed, Germaine Artus; art d, Pierre Charbonnier; cos, Lucilla Mussini.

Historical Drama   **(PR:C   MPAA:NR)**

TRIAL OF LEE HARVEY OSWALD, THE**   (1964) 100m Falcon
International bw

Arthur Nations (*Prosecuting Attorney*), George Russell (*Defense Attorney*), George Edgley (*Presiding Judge*), George Mazyrack (*Lee Harvey Oswald*), Charles W. Tessmer (*Himself*).

This documentary-style film projects what the trial of Oswald might have been like, had he not himself been assassinated after allegedly killing President John F. Kennedy. An aura of uncertainty is established by not having any verdict announced, leaving the audience to make its own judgment. A television movie was made in 1977 with the same title and the same intent.

p, Harold Hoffman; d&w, Larry Buchanan.

Historical Drama   **(PR:A   MPAA:G)**

TRIAL OF MADAM X, THE*½ (1948, Brit.) 54m Invicta/EPC British
bw

Mara Russell-Tavernan (*Jacqueline*), Paul England (*Perrisard*), Edward Leslie (*Raymond*), Frank Hawkins (*La Roque*), Hamilton Deane (*Noel*), Hamilton Keene (*Louis*), Jean Le Roy (*Madeleine*).

Russell-Tavernan stars in this most obscure version of French playwright Alexandre Bisson's melodramatic tearjerker, filmed many times before and since as MADAME X. It is the story of a married woman whose extramarital affair turns sour and ends in her lover's accidental death. Her marriage dissolves, her life ends up in the gutter, she is blackmailed, she shoots her blackmailer and winds up in court, to be defended by her son (although she doesn't know it is him) and finally she dies. There's enough earth-shattering twists to fill a year's worth of soap operas. For the curious, check out the 1966 version of MADAME X with Lana Turner in the lead.

p, Wyndham T. Vint; d&w, Paul England (based on the play "Madame X" by Alexandre Bisson); ph, Hone Glendinning.

Drama   **(PR:A   MPAA:NR)**

TRIAL OF MARY DUGAN, THE***   (1929) 113m MGM bw

Norma Shearer (*Mary Dugan*), Lewis Stone (*Edward West*), H.B. Warner (*District Attorney Galway*), Raymond Hackett (*Jimmy Dugan*), Lilyan Tashman (*Dagmar Lorne*), Olive Tell (*Mrs. Edgar Rice*), Adrienne D'Ambricourt (*Marie Ducrot*), DeWitt Jennings (*Police Inspector Hunt*), Wilfred North (*Judge Nash*), Landers Stevens (*Dr. Welcome*), Mary Doran (*Pauline Agguerro*), Westcott B. Clarke (*Police Capt. Price*), Charles Moore (*James Madison*), Myra Hampton (*May Harris*), Claude Allister (*Henry Plaisted*).

In her first sound picture, Shearer plays a Broadway show girl accused of killing her boy friend, a rich playboy, by stabbing him with a knife. Stone, a friend of Shearer's, serves as her attorney but decides against cross-examining witnesses. Hackett, Shearer's younger brother and himself a newly appointed member of the bar, is furious with this tactic. Stone mysteriously withdraws from defending Shearer, so Hackett takes over. Eventually it's revealed that Shearer had served as mistress to several wealthy individuals, using the money secured from each man to help finance Hackett's education. Hackett pursues with his defense, finally proving his sister innocent when Stone is uncovered as the real killer. This tense courtroom drama works well thanks to an intelligent script and the skill of the cast. Shearer is fine as the accused woman, showing a range that

improves on the image she built up in silent films. She gives her often emotionally wrought part humanity, without once exaggerating the performance. Stone and Hackett provide good support, with Tashman and D'Armbricourt giving some nice touches in their scenes on the witness stand. The film, like so many early talking pictures, suffers from the limitations of the new sound technology in its pacing and consequently runs a little longer than it should.

d, Bayard Veiller; w, Becky Gardiner, Veiller (based on the play by Veiller); ph, William Daniels; ed, Blanche Sewell; art d, Cedric Gibbons; cos, Adrian.

Crime Drama   **(PR:C   MPAA:NR)**

TRIAL OF MARY DUGAN, THE**   (1941) 90m MGM bw

Laraine Day (*Mary Dugan*), Robert Young (*Jimmy Blake*), Tom Conway (*Edgar Wayne*), Frieda Inescort (*Mrs. Wayne*), Henry O'Neill (*Galway*), John Litel (*Mr. West*), Marsha Hunt (*Agatha Hall*), Sara Haden (*Miss Mathews*), Marjorie Main (*Mrs. Collins*), Alma Kruger (*Dr. Saunders*), Pierre Watkin (*Judge Nash*), Addison Richards (*Capt. Price*), Francis Pierot (*John Masters*), George Watts (*Inspector Hunt*), Ian Wolfe (*Dr. Winston*), Cliff Danielson (*Robert the Chauffeur*), Cliff Clark (*John Dugan*), Milton Kibbee (*Court Clerk*), Nora Perry (*Sally*), Minerva Urecal (*Landlady*), Paul Porcasi (*Ship's Captain*), Larry Wheat (*Court Stenographer*), Walter Lawrence (*Newsboy*), Matt Moore (*Bailiff*), Anna Q. Nilsson (*Juror*), William Tannen (*Driver*), Kay Sutton (*Secretary*), Joe Yule (*Sign Painter*), Joan Barclay, Ernie Alexander, Jessie Arnold, Hal Cooke, William Stelling, Betty Farrington (*Spectators*).

This remake of the 1929 film that starred Norma Shearer in the title role went through numerous revisions in this updated version, resulting in a much less forceful, lifeless drama. It's mainly an attempt to showcase Day, who never regained the popularity she achieved in her role in the DOCTOR KILDARE series. Her role was rewritten to conform with the moral codes of the time. She plays a stenographer on trial for murder, with Young getting the job of defending her. He also happens to be madly in love with her. An adequate cast and decent job of pacing partially make up for the qualities missing from the earlier effort.

p, Edwin H. Knopf; d, Norman Z. McLeod; based on the play by Bayard Veller; ph, George Folsey; ed, George Boemler; art d, Cedric Gibbons, Howard Campbell; set d, Edwin B. Willis; cos, Dolly [Dorothy] Tree.

Drama   **(PR:A   MPAA:NR)**

TRIAL OF PORTIA MERRIMAN, THE
(SEE: PORTIA ON TRIAL, 1937)

TRIAL OF SERGEANT RUTLEDGE, THE
(SEE: SERGEANT RUTLEDGE, 1960)

TRIAL OF THE CATONSVILLE NINE, THE½**
(1972) 85m Melville c

Gwen Arner (*Marjorie Melville*), Ed Flanders (*Father Daniel Berrigan*), Barton Heyman (*John Hogan*), Mary Jackson (*Witness*), Richard Jordan (*George Mische*), Nancy Malone (*Mary Moylan*), Donald Moffatt (*Thomas Melville*), Davis Roberts (*Prosecutor*), Leon Russom (*David Darst*), William Schallert (*Judge*), David Spielberg (*Defense*), Peter Strauss (*Thomas Lewis*), Douglass Watson (*Father Philip Berrigan*).

The motives of young protesters brought to trial for burning their draft cards during the height of the anti-Vietnam War movement are examined in this film based on the play of the same name by one of the real-life participants in the event. The intent is to show that each individual's actions were the result of personal ideals, not mere conformity to the then-fashionable protest of the draft. But attempts to defend this form of individualism don't hold up in court, and a guilty verdict is handed down. The play itself doesn't hold up well on screen, with the actors seeming to do more preaching than acting.

p, Gregory Peck; d, Gordon Davidson; w, Daniel Berrigan, Saul Levitt (based on the play by Berrigan); ph, Haskell Wexler; m, Shelly Manne; ed, Aaron Stell; cos, Albert Wolsky.

Drama   **Cas.**   **(PR:A   MPAA:PG)**

TRIAL OF VIVIENNE WARE, THE**   (1932) 56m FOX bw

Joan Bennett (*Vivienne Ware*), Donald Cook (*John Sutherland*), Richard "Skeets" Gallagher (*Graham McNally*), ZaSu Pitts (*Gladys Fairweather*), Lillian Bond (*Dolores Divine*), Alan Dinehart (*Prosecutor*), Herbert Mundin (*William Boggs*), Howard Phillips (*Joe Garson*), Noel Madison (*Angelo Parone*), J. Maurice Sullivan (*Judge Henderson*), Eddie Dillon (*William Hardy*), Jameson Thomas (*Damon Fenwick*), Christian Rub (*Axel*), Bert Hanlon (*Juror*), Mary Gordon (*Matron*), Clarence Nordstrom (*Cafe Singer*), Edwin Maxwell (*Detective*), John Elliott (*Police Captain*), Bob Perry (*Bailiff*), Ethel Wales, Dale Fuller (*Listeners*), Tom London (*Court Officer*), Ward Bond (*John's Assistant*), Pat Somerset (*Spectator*), Pat O'Malley (*Broadcast Sergeant*), Phil Tead (*Mac the Reporter*), Fred Kelsey (*Cop*), Stanley Blystone (*Cop Who Kills Parone*), Joe King (*Bailiff*), Chuck

Hamilton (Court Officer), Ruth Selwyn (Mercedes Joy), Maude Eburne (Elizabeth Hardy), William Pawley (Gilk), Nora Lane.

This fairly engrossing depiction of a murder trial takes place almost entirely inside the courtroom. As the mystery starts to unravel through the testimony, a woman is about to give the evidence which will point the finger of guilt at the proper party, when she is shot at by a man in the courtroom. He then runs through the courthouse with the police on his tail, going every which way in search of a means of escape. Pitts plays a radio announcer who comments on the drama taking place, adding cohesion to an otherwise sketchy plot.

d, William K. Howard; w, Philip Klein, Barry Conners (based on the novel by Kenneth M. Ellis); ph, Ernest Palmer; ed, Ralph Dietrich; art d, Gordon Wiles, cos, David Cox; m/l, Ralph Freed, James Hanley.

Crime/Drama   (PR:A   MPAA:NR)

TRIAL WITHOUT JURY*½   (1950) 60m REP bw

Robert Rockwell (Bill Peters), Barbra Fuller (Corinne Hollister), Kent Taylor (Jed Kilgore), Audrey Long (Myra Peters), K. Elmo Lowe (John Webb), Stanley Waxman (Arthur Gentry), John Whitney (Riley Wentworth), Barbara Billingsley (Rheta Milford), Ruthelma Stevens (Mrs. Mannings), William Grueneberg (Turner), Christine Larson (Bernice Andrews), James Craven (Producer), William Haade (Kennedy), Bill Baldwin (Ticket Seller), Theodore Von Eltz (Phillip Mannings), Sid Marion (Shuffalong).

This plodding story is about a playwrite who is accused of a murder when his continual snooping arouses suspicion. He was looking for details to help in the mystery he was writing based on the actual events of a murder case. His writing skills would have been put to better use if applied to this awful script.

p, Stephen Auer; d, Philip Ford; w, Albert DeMond, Lawrence Goldman (based on a story by Rose Simon Kohn); ph, John MacBurnie; m, Stanley Wilson; ed, Harold Minter, art d, Frank Hotaling; cos, Adele Palmer.

Mystery   (PR:A   MPAA:NR)

TRIALS OF OSCAR WILDE, THE   (SEE: MAN WITH THE GREEN CARNATION, THE, 1960, Brit.)

TRIBES**   (1970) 90m FOX c

Darren McGavin (Sgt. Drake), Earl Holliman (DePayster), Jan-Michael Vincent (Adrian), John Gruber (Quentin), Danny Goldman (Sidney), Richard Yniguez (Sanchez), Antone Curtis (Marcellus), Peter Hooten (Scrunch), David Buchanan (Armstrong), Rick Weaver (Morton).

Originally made for television and then released theatrically shortly after going over the airwaves, this yarn concerns the induction of a flower child into the Marines. At first the recruiting sergeant, McGavin, shows the prejudice one would expect a hardened Marine to have against a long-haired hippie. But in comparison to the other recruits, Vincent turns out to be better at adapting himself to the strict Marine regulations, his exercises in yoga given the credit for developing his powers of concentration. Respect between the tough sergeant and the hippie recruit starts to emerge, but soon comes up against further obstacles. Despite the obvious cliches, a decent effort is made in trying to make these characters seem human.

p, Marvin Schwartz; d, Joseph Sargent; w, Tracy Keenan Wynn, Schwartz; ph, Russell Metty (DeLuxe Color); m, Al Capps, Marty Cooper; ed, Patrick Kennedy; art d, Jack Martin Smith, Richard Day; set d, Walter M. Scott, Jerry Wunderlich.

Drama   Cas.   (PR:A   MPAA:G)

TRIBUTE***½   (1980, Can.) 123m FOX c

Jack Lemmon (Scottie Templeton), Robby Benson (Jud Templeton), Lee Remick (Maggie Stratton), Kim Cattrall (Sally Haines), Colleen Dewhurst (Gladys Petrelli), John Marley (Lou Daniels), Gale Garnett (Hilary), Teri Keane (Evelyn), Rummy Bishop, John Dee, Bob Windsor (Poker Players).

Hard to believe that the same man who directed PORKY'S did this sensitive adaptation of Bernard Slade's play. Lemmon is guilty of a bit of overacting, but that's understandable here as he'd played the role on the stage in New York and honed his performance for the theater so it wasn't easy to pull back his acting for the screen. When Lemmon quit the show in New York, it promptly closed. He's a smart-mouth Broadway press agent divorced from Remick. His partner is Marley and he spends his time tossing off quips. Then disaster strikes as his doctor, Dewhurst, gives him the bad news that he's a victim of leukemia and he will die unless he submits to the treatment necessary to keep him alive. Benson arrives. He's Lemmon's and Remick's son and the antithesis to Lemmon's rowdy character. Benson is serious, bright, and disdainful of the life Lemmon leads, a life Benson feels is little more than a press pimp because Lemmon devotes himself to getting items

about his clients into the newspapers and will stop at nothing to please his customers. The clash between Benson's sober attitude and Lemmon's seeming not to care about his own life is what makes for the drama and the comedy. On one hand, the situation is dramatic and often heart rendering. On the other hand, Slade's way with witty words (he wrote SAME TIME, NEXT YEAR, and ROMANTIC COMEDY after a very successful TV career) leavens the seriousness just when it approaches maudlin. At the finale, Lemmon agrees to seek treatment, if only to keep him alive long enough to enjoy his new-found relationship with his son. Singer Gale Garnett, who was best-known for the hit "We'll Sing in the Sunshine," does especially well in the showy part of a prostitute who is Lemmon's friend. One funny scene has Lemmon presenting her with a gold watch as she prepares to retire from the World's Oldest Profession. The film was done in Canada and that may have been because writer Slade is Canadian by birth, thereby making the picture eligible for certain Canadian production benefits.

p, Joel B. Michaels, Garth B. Drabinsky; d, Bob Clark; w, Bernard Slade (based on his stage play); ph, Reginald H. Morris (Medallion Film Laboratories Color); m, Kenn Wannberg, Barry Manilow, Jack Feldman, Bruce Sussman, Jack Lemmon, Alan Jay Lerner; ed, Richard Halsey; prod d, Trevor Williams; art d, Reuben Freed.

Comedy/Drama   Cas.   (PR:C   MPAA:PG)

TRIBUTE TO A BADMAN***   (1956) 95m MGM c

James Cagney (Jeremy Rodock), Don Dubbins (Steve Miller), Stephen McNally (McNulty), Irene Papas (Jocasta Constantine), Vic Morrow (Lars Peterson), James Griffith (Barjack), Onslow Stevens (Hearn), James Bell (L.A. Peterson), Jeanette Nolan (Mrs. L.A. Peterson), Chubby Johnson (Baldy), Royal Dano (Abe), Lee Van Cleef (Fat Jones), Peter Chong (Cooky), James McCallion (Shorty), Clint Sharp (Red), Carl Pitti (Tom), Tony Hughes (1st Buyer), Roy Engel (2nd Buyer), Bud Osborne, John Halloran, Tom London, Dennis Moore, Buddy Roosevelt, Billy Dix (Cowboys).

Cagney's third and last western sees him as a tough rancher who ruthlessly guards his vast tracks of Colorado territory in the 1870s. Dubbins, a former grocery clerk from Pennsylvania who has come out West looking for adventure, is ranch by the rancher to work as a hired hand. The naive easterner is shocked by Cagney's swift and terrible actions after the rancher learns that rustlers have taken some of his stock. Accompanied by his men, Cagney catches the thieves and hangs them himself. When some of his horses are stolen, Cagney catches the culprits and forces them to hike barefoot through intense heat over the rocky terrain. Meanwhile, Dubbins finds himself becoming attracted to Cagney's mistress, Papas. Papas, despite the fact that she has seen the warm, gentle, and caring side of Cagney, allows herself to fall for Dubbins, who is much younger than Cagney. Eventually Dubbins and Papas have had enough of Cagney's vicious behavior and decide to leave together. Realizing that his brutality has cost him the woman he loves, Cagney lets Papas go without a fight. Sensing that Cagney's reluctance to seek revenge might mark a turning point in his personality, Papas sees hope for their relationship and returns to the rancher. Grateful for her faith in him, Cagney vows to become a more compassionate man and asks Papas to marry him. Beautifully photographed by Surtees and energetically played by Cagney, TRIBUTE TO A BADMAN boasts little else. The script by Blankfort is bland and uninteresting, with director Wise alternating the pace between breakneck and sluggish. The supporting cast does well, particularly famed Greek actress Papas (in her Hollywood film debut), with Morrow, Dano, and Van Cleef on hand as more menacing rustlers. The production was troubled from the start. Originally titled "Jeremy Rodock," the film was to have starred Spencer Tracy and Grace Kelly. Tracy looked forward to working with Kelly, but the actress hated the role and refused to participate. MGM imported Papas as a replacement. Learning of this, Tracy's enthusiasm waned as well because he disliked the script, was unfamiliar with Papas and director Wise, and wanted to get out of his MGM contract in order to pursue his own projects, especially THE OLD MAN AND THE SEA. Wise had a massive set built high up in the Colorado Rockies and then sat and waited for his star, who showed up six days late without so much as offering a clue to why he was absent. Tracy kept to himself, would disappear from the set when needed, and maintained an attitude of indifference toward the picture. Obviously looking for a way out, Tracy then demanded that the whole set be torn down and moved to a lower elevation because the thin mountain air was bothering his health. Because he was one of MGM's biggest stars, the request was taken seriously. Director Wise had had enough of Mr. Tracy, however, and the matter came to a head when studio vice-president Howard Strickling arrived in Colorado to settle the matter. After much agonizing deliberation between Wise, Tracy, Strickling, and MGM production chief Dore Schary, the decision was made to fire Tracy. Most of MGM was shocked that their star of more than 20 years had been given the ax and the offical reason cited was Tracy's "artistic differences" with director Wise. Cagney was chosen to replace Tracy, but as the actor stated in his autobiography, "I was about as interested in working as I was in flying, which means a considerable level below zero...The result was alright, I guess."

p, Sam Zimbalist; d, Robert Wise; w, Michael Blankfort (based on a short story by Jack Schaefer); ph, Robert Surtees (CinemaScope, Eastmancolor); m, Miklos Rosza; ed, Ralph E. Winters; art d, Cedric Gibbons, Paul Broesse; set d, Edwin B. Willis, Fred MacLean; cos, Walter Plunkett; makeup,

William Tuttle.

Western   **(PR:C   MPAA:NR)**

TRICET JEDNA VE STINU   (SEE: 90 DEGREES IN THE SHADE, 1966, Czech./Brit.)

TRICK BABY*   (1973) 89m UNIV c (AKA: THE DOUBLE CON)

Jan Leighton (*Carlson*), Byron Sanders (*Parkview Clerk*), Dick Boccelli (*Vincent*), Jim Mapp (*Doc*), Bob Brooker (*DuSable Clerk*), Ronald Carter (*Bartender*), Celeste Creech, Deloris Brown-Harper (*Hookers*), Jacqueline Weiss (*Aunt Rose*), Father James Kelly (*Priest*), Charles Weldon (*Tough*), Charles Clarke (*Cab Driver*), Kiel Martin (*White Folks*), Mel Stewart (*Blue Howard*), Dallas Edward Hayes (*Dot Murray*), Beverly Ballard (*Susan*), Vernee Watson (*Cleo Howard*), Donald Symington (*Morrison*), Don Fellows (*Phillips*), Tom Anderson (*Felix the Fixer*), Clebert Ford (*Josephus*), Fuddle Bagley (*Percy*), Ted Lange (*Melvin the Pimp*), Tony Mazzadra (*Nino Parelli*), David Thomas (*Frascatti*), Jim King (*Duke*), Anthony Charnota (*Bobby*), John Aquino (*Frank*).

A number of scenes were thrown together for this black exploitationer mainly for the effect. They do little to provide atmosphere; instead, distract from the development of the already poorly conceived plot. The story deals with two black con men, one of whom can pass for white, who go about pulling a number of amateurish capers. But when they try to pull a fast one off the mob, they get their comeuppance. With performances like these, it is hard to believe that anybody was ever fooled.

p, Marshal Backlar; d, Larry Yust; w, Yust, T. Raewyn, A. Neuberg (based on the novel by Iceberg Slim [Robert Beck]); ph, Isidore Mankofsky (Technicolor); m, James Bond; ed, Peter Parasheles.

Crime   **(PR:O   MPAA:R)**

TRICK FOR TRICK*   (1933) 67m FOX bw

Ralph Morgan (*Azrah*), Victor Jory (*La Tour*), Sally Blane (*Constance Russell*), Tom Dugan (*Albert Young*), Luis Alberni (*Metzger*), Edward Van Sloan (*John Russell*), Willard Robertson (*Dr. Frank Fitzgerald*), Dorothy Appleby (*Susie Henry*), Clifford Jones (*David Adams*), John George (*Magician's Assistant*), Adrian Morris (*Boldy*), Herbert Bunston (*Prof. King*), James Burtis (*Sgt. Lombard*), Boothe Howard, Jimmy Leong.

This confusing and flimsy mishmash is about a bunch of magicians involved in a murder which takes brother tricksters to solve. The only real magic needed is to make this ill-conceived script look presentable, which the director and his crew obviously did not possess.

d, Hamilton MacFadden; w, Howard Green (based on the story by Vivian Crosby, Shirley Warde, Harry Wagstaff Gribble); ph, L.W. O'Connell.

Mystery   **(PR:A   MPAA:NR)**

TRICK OR TREATS*   (1982) 91m Lone Star International Pictures c

Jackelyn Giroux (*Linda*), Peter Jason (*Malcolm*), Chris Graver (*Christopher*), David Carradine (*Richard*), Carrie Snodgress (*Joan*), Jillian Kesner (*Andrea*), Dan Pastorini, Tim Rossovich (*Men in White Shorts*), J.L. Clark (*Bert*), John Blyth Barrymore (*Mad Doctor*), Catherine Coulson (*Nurse Reeves*), Maria Dillon (*Newscaster*), Jason Renard, Paul Bartel (*Winos*), Owen Orr (*Shakespearean Actor*), Allen Wisch (*Bum*), Nike Zachmanoglou (*Connie*).

The title alone lets it be known that this film is another HALLOWEEN ripoff. Again it a case of a person brought to the loonie bin at the beginning of the film who escapes a few years later to seek revenge against those responsible for getting him committed. In this film, Jason is the man who seduces a nurse to gain passage out of the institution, donning the nurse's uniform as a disguise and looking outrageously silly. His object is a confrontation with his former wife Snodgress, only she's not at home, and there's a babysitter watching over her kid. Giroux is the girl who must put up with the antics of Graver, a precocious brat who has her terrorized and therefore ripe for the real events. Though the movie has the usual amount of gore, a modest sense of humor is maintained, making it more enjoyable than most run-of-the-mill slasher films.

p,d,w,ph,ed, Gary Graver (CFI Color); set d, Michael Railsback.

Horror   **Cas.**   **(PR:O   MPAA:R)**

TRICKED   (SEE: BANDITS OF EL DORADO, 1949)

TRIGGER HAPPY   (SEE: DEADLY COMPANIONS, THE, 1961)

TRIGGER FINGERS ½   (1939) 55m Victory bw

Tim McCoy (*Bill Carson*), Ben Corbett (*Magpie*), Jill Martin (*Jessie*), Joyce Bryant (*Margaret*), Carleton Young (*Lee*), Ted Adams (*Jeff*), John Elliott (*Bolton*), Bud McTaggart (*Jerry*), Ralph Peters (*Mort*), Forrest Taylor (*Crane*), Kenne Duncan (*Johnson*), Carl Mathews.

A weak oater has McCoy playing a Mountie going undercover in gypsy garb to round up a gang of rustlers. His ploy is dealing cards to a bunch of cowboys in the hopes of getting their fingerprints. Implausible story line is just the beginning of the film's weaknesses.

p, Sam Katzman; d, Sam Newfield; w, Basil Dickey; ph, Bill Hyer; ed, Holbrook N. Todd.

Western   **(PR:A   MPAA:NR)**

TRIGGER, JR.*   (1950) 68m REP c

Roy Rogers (*Himself*), Dale Evans (*Kay Harkrider*), Pat Brady (*Biffle*), Gordon Jones (*Splinters*), Grant Withers (*Monty Manson*), Peter Miles (*Larry*), George Cleveland (*Col. Harkrider*), Frank Fenton (*Sheriff Pettigrew*), I. Stanford Jolley (*Doc Brown*), Stanley Andrews (*Rancher Wilkins*), Raynor Lehr Circus, Foy Willing and Riders of the Purple Sage, Trigger the Horse.

The stunning footage of wild horses roaming the range is the highlight of this oater which has Rogers and his trusty mount Trigger getting involved in efforts to thwart a crooked official. As the local range patrol officer, Withers has brought in a wild and deadly horse to lay rampage to the other horses in the valley. In this way he manages to collect extra fees, until Rogers figures out who is behind all the shenanigans. The idea of this rampant killer horse stretches credulity but provides for some interesting moments. (See Roy Rogers series, Index.)

p, Edward J. White; d, William Witney; w, Gerald Geraghty; ph, Jack Marta (Trucolor); ed, Tony Martinelli; md, R. Dale Butts; art d, Frank Arrigo; m/l, Peter Tinturin, Foy Willing, Carol Rice.

Western   **Cas.**   **(PR:A   MPAA:NR)**

TRIGGER PALS*   (1939) 60m Cinemart/GN bw

Art Jarrett (*Lucky Morgan*), Lee Powell (*Stormy*), Al St. John (*Fuzzy*), Dorothy Faye (*Doris Allen*), Ted Adams (*Harvey Kent*), Nina Guilbert (*Minnie Archer*), Earl Douglas (*Jake*), Stanley Blystone (*Steve*), Frank LaRue (*Gates*), Ethan Allen (*Sheriff*), Ernie Adams (*Pete*).

One of the worst efforts to impersonate a saddle hero ever is delivered by Jarrett in this rudimentary oater in which he teams up with Powell to bring a gang of rustlers to justice. Jarrett even tries to sing a few tunes, at which he proves no more adept than at gunplay.

p, Phil Krasne; d, Sam Newfield; w, George Plympton (from the story by Plympton and Ted Richmond); ph, Jack Grenhalgh; ed, Roy Luby; m/l, "When a Cowboy Sings," "Lullaby Trail," Lew Porter, Johnnie Lange) sung by Art Jarrett).

Western   **Cas.**   **(PR:A   MPAA:NR)**

TRIGGER SMITH*½   (1939) 59m MON bw

Jack Randall, Joyce Bryant, Frank Yaconelli, Forrest Taylor, Dennis Moore, Dave O'Brien, Sherry Tansey, Ed Cassidy, Jim Corey, Reed Howes, Warner Richmond.

The murder of his brother forces Randall to turn to the gun once again, with his U.S. Marshal father Cassidy lending a hand in rounding up Richmond's gang. This same crew who shot his brother is also doing a pretty good job of making life miserable for everyone else within miles. Strictly routine.

p, Robert Tansey; d, Alan James; w, Robert Emmett; ph, Bert Longnecker; ed, Howard Dillinger.

Western   **(PR:A   MPAA:NR)**

TRIGGER TRAIL*   (1944) 59m UNIV bw

Rod Cameron (*Clint Farrel*), Vivian Austin (*Ann Catlett*), Fuzzy Knight (*Echo*), Eddie Dew (*Bob Reynolds*), Lane Chandler (*Slade*), George Eldredge (*Rance Hudson*), Buzz Henry (*Chip*), Davison Clark (*Silas Farrel*), Michael Vallon (*Bender*), Dick Alexander (*Waco*), Jack Rockwell (*Joe Kincaid*), Budd Buster (*Tug Catlett*), Bud Osborne, Ray Jones, Jack Ingram, Artie Ortego, Ray Whitley and His Bar-6 Cowboys, Ezra Paulette, Lem Giles, Charley Quirt.

A gang of scurrilous businessmen try to trick homesteaders off their land, but Cameron comes along to see that justice catches up with the villains. Routine oater action and fine for fans of the genre.

p, Oliver Drake; d, Lewis D. Collins; w, Ed Earl Repp; ph, William Sickner; ed, Milton Carruth; art d, John B. Goodman, Abraham Grossman.

Western   **(PR:A   MPAA:NR)**

TRIGGER TRICKS*½   (1930) 60m UNIV bw

Hoot Gibson (*Tim Brennan*), Sally Eilers (*Betty Dawley*), Robert E. Homans (*Thomas Kingston*), Jack Richardson (*Joe Dixon*), Monte Montague (*Nick Dalgus*), Neal Hart (*Sheriff*), Max Ascher (*Mike*), Walter Perry (*Ike*), Pete Morrison.

Gibson enters the age old battle between cattle ranchers and sheep farmers when his brother becomes the victim of a ruthless cattleman. He stays at the ranch of Eilers to go about seeking his vengeance, which meets its climax when Hoot tricks the gang of kingpin Homans with a record player. Gibson married Eilers not too long after this production was in the can.

p, Hoot Gibson; d&w, B. Reeves Eason; ph, Harry Neumann; ed, Gilmore Walker.

Western   (PR:A   MPAA:NR)

TRIGGER TRIO, THE*½   (1937) 55m REP bw

Ray Corrigan (*Tucson Smith*), Max Terhune (*Lullaby Joslin*), Ralph Byrd (*Stony Brooke*), Sandra Corday (*Anne*), Robert Warwick (*Evans*), Cornelius Keefe (*Brent*), Sammy McKim (*Mickey*), Hal Taliaferro [Wally Wales] (*Luke*), Willie Fung (*Chong*), Buck the Great Dane.

The Three Mesquiteers are given the job of tracking down a killer and his gang after an inspector from the State Agricultural Service is slain. An outbreak of hoof and mouth disease has this particular culprit in arms at the thought of losing his entire herd. But if his diseased cattle are not killed, the epidemic will continue to spread, and Corrigan, Terhune, and Byrd make sure the latter is not the case. Best performance and scene grabber is the Great Dane Buck who does his best to lend a helping paw. (See: THREE MESQUITEERS series, Index.)

p, Sol C. Siegel; d, William Witney; w, Oliver Drake, Joseph Poland (based on the story by Houston Branch, Poland); ph, Ernest Miller; ed, Tony Martinelli.

Western   **Cas.**   (PR:A   MPAA:NR)

TRILOGY   (SEE: TRUMAN CAPOTE'S TRILOGY, 1969)

TRINITY IS STILL MY NAME**   (1971, Ital.) 121m West/AE c
(CONTINUAVAMO A CHIAMARLO TRINITA)

Terence Hill [Mario Girotti] (*Trinity*), Bud Spencer [Carlo Pedersoli] (*Bambino*), Harry Carey, Jr (*Father*), Jessica Dublin (*Mother*), Yanti Somer (*Pioneer*), Enzo Tarascio (*Sheriff*), Pupo De Luca (*Padre*), Dana Ghia, Emilio Delle Piane, Enzo Fiermonte, Tony Norton, Jean Louis, Franco Ressel, Adriano Mercantoni, Gerald Landry.

This unexciting sequel to THEY CALL ME TRINITY, is another farcical spaghetti western in which brothers Hill and Spencer trade in their badges to try and make a living on the other side of the law. Needless to say they don't accomplish what they set out to do, instead becoming the type of bad men people would love to have rob them. Low on plot, but some of the comic routines make up for this.

p, Italo Zingarelli; d&w, E.B. Clucher [Enzo Barboni]; ph, Aldo Giordani (Widescreen, Technochrome); m, Guido De Angelis, Maurizio De Angelis; ed, Antonio Siciliano; md, Gianfranco Plenizio; art d, Enzo Bulgarelli.

Western/Comedy   (PR:A   MPAA:G)

TRIO*½**   (1950, Brit.) 91m Gainsborough/PAR bw

"The Verger": James Hayter (*Albert Foreman*), Kathleen Harrison (*Emma Foreman*), Felix Aylmer (*Bank Manager*), Lana Morris (*Gladys*), Michael Hordern (*The Vicar*), Glyn Houston (*Ted*), Eliot Makeham (*Sexton*), Henry Edwards (*1st Church Warden*), "Mr. Knowall": Anne Crawford (*Mrs. Ramsay*), Nigel Patrick (*Kelada*), Naunton Wayne (*Mr. Ramsay*), Wilfred Hyde-White (*Grey*), Clive Morton (*Ship's Captain*), Bill Linden Travers (*Fellowes*), Dennis Harkin (*Captain's Steward*), Michael Medwin (*Steward*), "Sanatorium": Jean Simmons (*Evie Bishop*), Michael Rennie (*Maj. Templeton*), Roland Culver (*Mr. Ashenden*), Raymond Huntley (*Mr. Chester*), Betty Ann Davies (*Mrs. Chester*), Andre Morell (*Dr. Lennox*), John Laurie (*Mr. Campbell*), Finlay Currie (*Mr. Macleod*), Mary Merrall (*Miss Atkin*), Marjorie Fielding (*Mrs. Whitbread*), Harry Fowler, Joan Schofield, Michael Ward.

These three stories by Somerset Maugham were brought to the screen after the success of a previous compilation of four Maugham stories called QUARTET. The first piece here, directed by Annakin, deals with Hayter, who is fired from his post as a church verger when the vicar (Hordern) learns that Hayter is illiterate. Hayter decides to go into business for himself, and in a few years is running a successful chain of tobacco stores. As he discusses money with a banking official who is amazed at Hayter's success despite his handicap, the now-wealthy tobacconist explains: "If I could read and write, I'd have been a verger." Annakin's second story, "Mr. Knowall," features Patrick as an obnoxious jeweler taking a holiday aboard a ship. Every passenger tries to avoid the oaf, but eventually, in a roundabout fashion, Patrick is able to prove himself a gentleman. "Sanatorium" is the final story, and the longest of the three. This one was directed by French and chronicles the crossed lives of some patients at a tuberculosis sanatorium. Simmons and Rennie are two younger people who meet there and end up in love. Though doctors warn them marriage could be fatally taxing to their health, the lovers believe that a short-lived happiness is better than a longer, lonely existence. Also residing at this North Scotland sanatorium are two gossipy old ladies and a pair of old men (Laurie and

Currie) who consistently fight with each other. When one of the old men finally dies, the survivor realizes he misses his partner, now having no one to bicker with. Though there is no connecting theme, these varied stories are presented with style and intelligence. The short, humorous pieces are a good counterpoint to the bittersweet feelings of the final story. The casting is uniformly excellent. Hayter is fine as the illiterate, while Patrick has a field day with his rude, odious characterization. A small and highly enjoyable film.

p, Anthony Darnborough; d, Ken Annakin ("The Verger," "Mr. Knowall"), Harold French ("Sanatorium"); w, W. Somerset Maugham, R.C. Sheriff, Noel Langley (based on stories by Maugham); ph, Reginald Wyer, Geoffrey Unsworth; ed, Alfred Roome; m, John Greenwood.

Drama   (PR:A   MPAA:NR)

TRIP, THE*½   (1967) 85m AIP c

Peter Fonda (*Paul Groves*), Susan Strasberg (*Sally Groves*), Bruce Dern (*John, Guru*), Dennis Hopper (*Max*), Salli Sachse (*Glenn*), Katherine Walsh (*Lulu*), Barboura Morris (*Flo*), Caren Bernsen (*Alexandra*), Dick Miller (*Cash*), Luana Anders (*Waitress*), Barbara Renson (*Helena*), Susan Walters, Frankie Smith (*Go-Go Dancers*), Mike Blodget (*Lover*), Tom Signorelli (*Al*), Mitzi Hoag (*Wife*), Judy Lang (*Nadine*), Peter Bogdanovitch, Angelo Rossitto.

In 1967, when LSD tripping was quickly becoming the in thing to do, what better premise than to make a movie exactly on this subject? So here we have this overly long, nonstop bombardment of fantastic visual images supposedly going on in the mind of one embarking on his first trip. Some of the visuals are stunning, but much more fitting for a short subject of 10 to 15 minutes at most. This film is feature length. Fonda plays the television director who decides to clear up problems generated by his complex personal and professional life. Under the guidance of Dern he takes off on a night of images symbolically reflective of his troubled mind, doing such things as dying and being reborn, getting chased after by hooded horsemen, and experiencing sex with a mysterious girl who teaches him to better understand the preceedings. These images more closely resemble a bad dream following an overdose of pepperoni and onion pizza the evening before than the product of ingesting hallucinogenic drugs.

p&d, Roger Corman; w, Jack Nicholson; ph, Arch R. Dalzell (Pathecolor); m, American Music Band, ed, Ronald Sinclair; cos, Richard Bruno,; spec eff, Roger George; makeup, Ted Coodley.

Fantasy   **Cas.**   (PR:O   MPAA:NR)

TRIP, THE   (SEE: CHELSEA GIRLS, THE, 1967)

TRIP, THE   (SEE: VOYAGE, THE, 1974, Ital.)

TRIP TO AMERICA, A   (SEE: VOYAGE TO AMERICA, 1952, Fr.)

TRIP TO ITALY, A   (SEE: STRANGERS, THE, 1955, Ital.)

TRIP TO PARIS, A**   (1938) 63m Fox bw

Jed Prouty (*John Jones*), Shirley Deane (*Bonnie Thompson*), Spring Byington (*Mrs. John Jones*), Russell Gleason (*Herbert Thompson*), Ken Howell (*Jack Jones*), George Ernest (*Roger Jones*), June Carlson (*Lucy Jones*), Florence Roberts (*Granny Jones*), Billy Mahan (*Bobby Jones*), Marvin Stephens (*Tommy McGuire*), Joan Valerie (*Marguerite Varloff*), Harold Huber (*Willie Jones*), Nedda Harrigan (*Countess Varloff*), Armand Kaliz (*Hotel Manager*), Clay Clement (*Duroche*), Leonid Kinskey (*Emile*).

The Jones family celebrates Prouty and Byington's 25th anniversary by taking their first trip abroad, a situation which gives the scripters a chance to capitalize on the family's innocence and boost down-home American values. A good array of laughs are provided though they are easily predicted. (See JONES FAMILY series, Index.)

p, Max Gordon; d, Malcolm St. Clair; w, Robert Ellis, Helen Logan (based on characters created by Katherine Kavanaugh); ph, Edward Snyder; ed, Norman Colbert; md, Samuel Kaylin; cos, Helen A. Myron.

Comedy   (PR:A   MPAA:NR)

TRIP TO TERROR   (SEE: IS THIS TRIP REALLY NECESSARY?
                                                                                                1970)

TRIP WITH ANITA, A   (SEE: LOVERS AND LIARS, 1981, Ital.)

TRIPLE CROSS, THE   (SEE: JOE PALOOKA IN TRIPLE CROSS,
                                                                                                1951)

TRIPLE CROSS*   (1967, Fr./Brit.) 126m Cineurop/WB c

Christopher Plummer (Eddie Chapman/"Fritz Grauman"), Romy Schneider (The Countess), Trevor Howard (Distinguished Civilian), Gert Frobe (Col. Steinhager), Yul Brynner (Baron von Grunen), Claudine Auger (Paulette), Georges Lycan (Leo), Jess Hahn (Comdr. Braid), Harry Meyen (Lt. Keller), Gil Barber (Bergman), Jean-Claude Bercq (Maj. von Leeb), Jean Claudio (Sgt. Thomas), Robert Favart (Gen. Dalrymple), Bernard Fresson (French Resistance Member), Clement Harari (Losch), Howard Vernon (Lisbon Embassy Official), Francis De Wolff (German Colonel-General), Jean-Marc Bory (Resistance Leader), Hubert Noel (von Rundstedt's Staff Officer), Jean Bertrand.

Plummer is a British safecracker whose robbery of a movie theater on one of the Channel Islands lands him in jail for a long term. But while he still has 14 years to serve, WW II breaks out and after the fall of France the islands are abandoned, leaving Plummer in his cell when the Germans come to occupy. He makes a propostion to his new captors: he will spy for them, using his criminal talents, if they let him out and pay a large fee. The Germans are suspicious, but they agree, and Plummer is soon sent to France for training by monocled Brynner, who suspects his student's motives. Finally his training is completed and after he passes a loyalty test Plummer is parachuted into England on a mission of sabotage. He immediately goes to the British intelligence service and offers to be a double agent in return for a full pardon and more cash. The British, like the Germans, are suspicious, but eventually they accept Plummer's offer and help him to fake the sabotage of an aircraft factory. German reconnaissance planes photograph the spurious damage and when Plummer is returned to Occupied Paris, he is awarded the Iron Cross for his deeds. Later the Germans send him back to England, this time to report on the damage caused by the V-1 and V-2 rockets raining down on London. With the help of the British, he feeds the Germans false information that causes them to redirect their missiles into uninhabited countryside. The end of the war finds Plummer drinking in a pub, considering the safe tucked behind the bar. Based on a true story, the film still seems lifeless and contrived. Plummer appears to be thinking of something else the whole time and the others are either cliches from a hundred espionage pictures or automatons like Plummer. Only the opening scenes on the Island of Jersey have any real interest. TRIPLE CROSS was released in Britain in 135- and 140- minute versions but cut to 126 minutes for U.S. distribution.

p, Jacques-Paul Bertrand; d, Terence Young; w, Rene Hardy, William Marchant (based on the book The Eddie Chapman Story by Eddie Chapman as told to Frank Owen); ph, Henri Alekan (Technicolor); m, Georges Garvarentz; ed, Roger Dwyre; prod d, Rene Renoux; art d, Tony Roman; makeup, Marie-Madeleine Paris.

Spy Drama   (PR:C-O   MPAA:NR)

TRIPLE DECEPTION   (1957, Brit.) 85m Rank c (GB: HOUSE OF SECRETS)

Michael Craig (Larry Ellis), Julia Arnall (Diane), Brenda De Banzie (Mme. Ballu), Barbara Bates (Judy), David Kossoff (Van de Heide), Gerard Oury (Pindar), Geoffrey Keen (Burleigh), Anton Diffring (Lauderbach), Eric Pohlmann (Gratz), Eugene Deckers (Vidal), Jacques Brunius (Lessage), Alan Tilvern (Brandelli), Carl Jaffe (Dorffman), Gordon Tanner (Curtice), David Lander (Marseilles Detective), Balbina (Maid), Violet Gould, John Serrett, Jean Driant, Patrick Westwood, Yves Chanteau.

Craig is an innocent British seaman stationed in France who gets involved against his will in a gold smuggling ring. He is mistaken by a gang for their contact, whom he greatly resembles; unbeknownst to the gang, their connection is dead. Before he knows what is going on, Craig is arrested by the authorities and interrogated by a team of international cops. After he manages to convince them of his innocence, they ask him to spy for them. Craig reluctantly agrees, and soon both the crooks and the cops think that he is double-crossing them. This leads to some rather tense moments which see Craig beaten and injured by both sides. Eventually all his hair-raising undercover work pays off, and the cops get their man.

p, Julian Wintle, Vivian A. Cox; d, Guy Green; w, Robert Buckner, Bryan Forbes (based on the novel Storm Over Paris by Sterling Noel); ph, Harry Waxman (VistaVision, Technicolor); m, Herbert Clifford; ed, Sidney Hayers; art d, Alex Vetchinsky.

Crime   (PR:A   MPAA:NR)

TRIPLE ECHO, THE**   (1973, Brit.) 90m Senat/Altura c (AKA: SOLDIERS IN SKIRTS)

Glenda Jackson (Alice), Brian Deacon (Barton), Oliver Reed (Sergeant), Anthony May (Subaltern), Gavin Richards (Stan), Jenny Lee Wright (Christine), Daphne Heard (Shopkeeper).

In this plodding story set during World War II, Jackson is a lonely woman in her country home while her husband is away in a Japanese prisoner of war camp. The drifting Deacon manages to hit a soft spot in the bitter gal, and they soon are lovers. A soldier, he decides not to return to the front, preferring to stay with Jackson. He dons a dress to conceal his identity, but gets over-confident. The gruff Reed, sergeant of a tank unit, passes by and uncovers Deacon's true identity when Deacon allows him to take him out

dancing. Despite the love story and inescapable humor of the situation at the dance, the film's grim realism lasts to its bitter conclusion.

p, Graham Cottle; d, Michael Apted; w, Robin Chapman (based on the novel by H. E. Bates); ph, John Coquillon (Eastmancolor); m, Marc Wilkinson; ed, Barrie Vince.

Drama   (PR:O   MPAA:R)

TRIPLE IRONS*   (1973, Hong Kong) 115m Shaw Bros./NG c (AKA: THE NEW ONE-ARMED SWORDSMAN)

Li Ching (Pa Chiao), David Chiang (Lei Li), Ti Lung (Feng Chun-Chieh), Ku Feng (Lung I-Chih), Chen Hsing (Chen Chen-Nan), Wang Chung (Chin Fen), Cheng Lei (Ho Cheng).

This excessively bloody martial arts picture is about a man who vowed never to return to fighting after having cut off his own arm for losing a championship battle. But as these things go, he returns to battle in order to take vengeance against the men responsible for the murder of a close friend. The only unusual item in this film is the use of a three bladed sword, which somewhat accounts for the amount of blood-letting.

d, Cheng Cheh; w, I. Kuang; ph, Kung Mu-To; ed, Kuo Ting-Hung; md, Chen Yung-Huang; art d, Tsao Chuang-Sheng.

Martial Arts   (PR:O   MPAA:R)

TRIPLE JUSTICE**   (1940) 65m RKO bw

George O'Brien (Brad), Virginia Vale (Lorna), Harry Woods (Reeves, Deputy Sheriff), Peggy Shannon (Mary), Leroy Mason (Gregory), Paul Fix (Cleary), Glenn Strange (Wiley), Malcolm McTaggart (Payson), The Lindeman Sisters, Robert McKenzie, Wilfred Lucas, Herman Nolan, John Judd, Henry Rocquemore, Fern Emmett, Walter Patterson, Paul Everton.

Above average oater that has O'Brien, in his last role as hero for RKO, being mistaken for a bank robber. The friend who could have identified him has been killed. O'Brien, of course, clears his name by tracking down the real robbers. One of the more noteworthy elements about this western was the manner in which horses galloping across the dust were photographed. The camera was placed to the side instead or the customary oater angles.

p, Bert Gilroy; d, David Howard; w, Arthur V. Jones, Morton Grant (based on the story by Arnold Belgard, Jack Roberts); ph, J. Roy Hunt; ed, Frederic Knudtson; m/l, "Lonely Rio," Fred Rose, Ray Whitley.

Western   (PR:A   MPAA:NR)

TRIPLE THREAT**   (1948) 71m COL bw

Richard Crane (Don Whitney), Gloria Henry (Ruth Nolan), Mary Stuart (Marian Rutherford), John Litel (Coach Snyder), Pat Phelan (Joe Nolan), Joseph Crehan (Coach Miller), Regina Wallace (Mrs. Nolan), Syd Saylor (Television Man), Dooley Wilson (Porter), Harry Wismer, Tom Harmon, Bob Kelley (Announcers), Sammy Baugh, Johnny Clement, "Boley" Dancewicz, Paul Christman, Bill Dudley, Paul Governall, "Indian" Jack Jacobs, Sid Luckman, Charles Trippi, Steve Van Buren, Bob Waterfield (Professional Football Players).

Crane plays a conceited college football player who, when he graduates and goes into the professional arena, gets the stuffings knocked out of him. A dull story that plods along to a cliche ending between some lively shots of some gridiron greats in action, but those are newsreel clips and do little to further the action of the story. The football pros in the film are there mostly for introduction sake and do little themselves to make the story sing. TRIPLE THREAT is hardly that to any other B programmer that happens to be around at the time.

p, Sam Katzman; d, Jean Yarbrough; w, Joseph Carole, Don Martin; ph, Vincent Farrar; ed, Jerome Thoms.

Drama   (PR:A   MPAA:NR)

TRIPLE TROUBLE   (SEE: KENTUCKY KERNELS, 1935)

TRIPLE TROUBLE*½   (1950) 66m MON bw

Leo Gorcey (Terrence Aloysius "Slip" Mahoney), Huntz Hall (Horace Debussy "Sach" Jones), Billy Benedict (Whitey), David Gorcey (Chuck), Buddy Gorman (Butch), Gabriel Dell (Gabe Moreno), Bernard Gorcey (Louie Dumbrowski), Richard Benedict (Skeets O'Neil), Pat Collins (Bat Armstrong), Paul Dubov ("Pretty Boy" Gleason), Effie Lairch (Ma Armstrong), Joseph Turkel (Benny the Blood), George Chandler (Squirrely Davis), Eddie Gribbon (Hobo Barton), Lyn Thomas (Shirley O'Brien), Jonathan Hale (Judge), Joseph Crehan (Warden Burnside), Eddie Foster, Frank Marlowe (Ma's Henchmen), Edward Gargan (Murphy), Tom Kennedy (Convict), Lyle Talbot (Guard).

A flatly directed BOWERY series entry has Slip and Sach going to prison to try and uncover the crooks behind a robbery the gang is accused of committing. The mastermind behind the robbery ring is operating from prison via shortwave radio to his cohorts outside. The pair is able to pin down the crook but only after Slip and Sach arouse suspicion and are unable to find any authority willing to listen. An overabundance of illiterate and rough humor that these pictures are noted for, such as Gorcey's attempts to impress through his misuse of big words and the continual harassment of Hall, finally gets excrutiatingly boring. (See BOWERY BOYS series, Index.)

p, Jan Grippo; d, Jean Yarbrough; w, Charles R. Marion, Bert Lawrence; ph, Marcel Le Picard; ed, William Austin; md, Edward Kay; art d, David Milton; set d, Raymond Boltz, Jr.

Comedy   **(PR:A MPAA:NR)**

TRIPOLI½   (1950) 95m PAR c (AKA: FIRST MARINES)

Maureen O'Hara (Countess D'Arneau), John Payne (Lt. O'Bannon), Howard Da Silva (Capt. Demetrios), Philip Reed (Hamet Karamanly), Grant Withers (Sgt. Derek), Lowell Gilmore (Lt. Tripp), Connie Gilchrist (Henriette), Alan Napier (Khalil), Herbert Heyes (Gen. Eaton), Alberto Morin (Il Taiib), Emil Hanna (Interpreter), Grandon Rhodes (Commodore Barron), Frank Fenton (Capt. Adams), Rosa Turich (Seewauk), Ray Hyke (Crawford), Walter Reed (Wade), Paul Livermore (Evans), Gregg Barton (Huggins), Don Summers (Langley), Jack Pennick (Busch), Ewing Mitchell (Elroy).

Silly costume adventure has Payne leading a detachment of U.S. Marines and a company of Greek mercenary cavalry under Da Silva against the marauding Barbary pirates under stylish pasha Reed. O'Hara is the daughter of a French diplomat and Reed's ward, but she disguises herself as a dancing girl and crosses the desert with dashing lieutenant Payne. Pretty but mostly worthless effort from Paramount's resident B movie unit, Pine and Thomas (nicknamed the "Dollar Bills" for their low budget ways), this film takes major liberties with history and actually owes more to World war II movie cliches than the real business of the Marines putting down the Barbary pirates in 1805. Payne is adequate as the handsome hero and O'Hara is lovely to look at (perhaps because her husband directed), but it is Da Silva, playing his mercenary captain for laughs, who steals the picture every time he appears on screen. A few scenes are effective–a march through a sandstorm and the climactic battle especially–but the whole film sinks into the same quagmire of hackneyed action and dialog that has claimed so many other films. The color photography is good, but the lush set designs and ornate costumes seem out of place on the rim of Africa, and anachronisms such as jet contrails streaking the sky and some 1940s slang these 19th Century Marines throw around are not easy to excuse.

p, William H. Pine, William C. Thomas; d, Will Price; w, Winston Miller (based on the story by Price, Miller); ph, James Wong Howe (Technicolor); m, David Chudnow; ed, Howard Smith; art d, Lewis H. Creber; cos, Yvonne Wood; spec eff, Darrell A. Anderson, Alex Weldon.

Historical Drama   **(PR:A MPAA:NR)**

TRISTANA***   (1970, Span./Ital./Fr.) 95m Epoca-Talia-Selenia-Les
                                                          Films Corona/Maron c

Catherine Deneuve (Tristana), Fernando Rey (Don Lope), Franco Nero (Horacio), Lola Gaos (Saturna), Antonio Casas (Don Cosme), Jesus Fernandez (Saturno), Vicente Soler (Don Ambrosio), Jose Calvo (Bellringer), Fernando Cebrian (Dr. Miquis), Candida Losada (Senora Burguesa), Mary Paz Pondal (Girl), Juan Jose Menendez (Don Candido), Sergio Mendizabal (Professor), Antonio Ferrandis, Jose Maria Caffarel, Joaquin Pamplona, Jose Blanch, Alfredo Santa Cruz, Luis Aller, Luis Rico, Saturno Cerra, Jesus Combarro, Vicente Roca, Ximenez Carrillo, Adriano Dominguez, Jose Riesgo, Rosa Gorostegui, Antonio Cintado, Pilar Vela, Lorenzo Rodriguez.

Bunuel's reworking of the novel by Benito Perez Galdos, like all the works of this prolific filmmaker, has much beneath the surface of the tale of a young woman who is seduced by her benefactor and guardian, whom she leaves to pursue a love affair with an artist only to return when stricken with an illness and in need of support. In one respect this woman can be viewed as all of Spain unable to overcome stifling traditional values which keep its people trapped in unfulfilling destinies. In a role that takes advantage of her complacent demeanor and placid beauty, Deneuve is the young woman left in the hands of the aristocratic nobleman Rey, outwardly a devoted protector of the young woman, seeing her as an innocent victim who could not exist without his care. Though preaching against taking advantage of her, Rey does just that, that a perfect example of the hypocritical man. Prior to receiving an inheritance from his sister, Rey is basically impoverished, refusing to work because a man of his social position is above menial labor. Instead, he sells all his belongings. At the same time he sees himself as a leader of the common man, making great speeches to his cronies about improving the lot of the people. Deneuve leaves the protection of Rey's home when she falls in love with Nero, but she is unwilling to make a commitment to him so she returns to Rey, who asks for her hand. She consents after losing a leg because of a tumor, and allows herself to remain in this passionless state despite still being in love with Nero. Perhaps what makes this work most powerfully is the subtle use of key situations to represent much larger ideas, such as the priests, who gather around Rey's death bed in the hope of receiving money from him, greedily stuffing their faces with sweets. In comparison to such masterpieces as VIRIDIANA and LOS OLVIDADOS, TRISTANA can be considered much more tame in terms of cutting remarks against religion and

politics, as well as in visual effects. Yet Bunuel's subtle handling, consisting of very little camera movement and little music, is still effective in establishing a viewpoint that perceives a world that is in desperate need of change.

d, Luis Bunuel; w, Bunuel, Julio Alejandro (based on the novel Tristana by Benito Perez Galdos); ph, Jose F. Aguayo (Eastmancolor); ed, Pedro del Rey; art d, Enrique Alarcon; set d, Luis Arguello; cos, Rosa Garcia; makeup, Julian Ruiz, Vicente Martinez.

Drama   **(PR:C MPAA:GP)**

TRITIY TAYM   (SEE: LAST GAME, THE, 1964, USSR)

TRIUMPH OF SHERLOCK HOLMES, THE***
                                                          (1935, Brit.) 72m REA/Olympic bw

Arthur Wontner (Sherlock Holmes), Ian Fleming (Dr. John H. Watson), Lyn Harding (Prof. Moriarty), Leslie Perrins (John Douglas), Jane Carr (Ettie Douglas), Charles Mortimer (Inspector Lestrade), Minnie Rayner (Mrs. Hudson), Michael Shepley (Cecil Barker), Ben Welden (Ted Baldwin), Roy Emerton (Boss McGinty), Conway Dixon (Ames), Wilfrid Caithness (Col. Sebastian Moran), Edmund D'Alby (Capt. Marvin), Ernest Lynds (Jacob Shafter).

Super-sleuth Sherlock Holmes (Wontner) is called from retirement as a beekeeper in Sussex when an American, who has fled to Europe to avoid union bosses, is murdered. A bit of snooping uncovers that the intended victim had not been killed at all, and in fact is in hiding after killing his would-be assailant. As it turns out the American, Perrins, had to flee from the States from fear of attack by mobsters for his part in the breaking up of a Pennsylvania strike. Harding, as the venomous Dr. Moriarty, was then called upon to see that Perrins was gotten out of the way. Holmes' chief nemesis earlier visited him in retirement to wish him peace and to warn him against returning to his former profession. Adapted from the Doyle novel "The Valley of Fear," this HOLMES entry differs from others in that it is more faithful to the plot structure Doyle laid out. (See SHERLOCK HOLMES series, Index.)

p, Julius Hagen; d, Leslie Hiscott; w, H. Fowler Mear, Cyril Twyford, Arthur Wontner (based on the novel The Valley of Fear by Sir Arthur Conan Doyle); ph, William Luff.

Mystery   **Cas.**   **(PR:A MPAA:NR)**

TRIUMPHS OF A MAN CALLED HORSE*   (1983, US/Mex.) 86m
                                     Redwing-Transpacific Media-Hesperia/Jensen Farley c

Richard Harris (Man Called Horse), Michael Beck (Koda), Ana De Sade (Redwing), Vaughn Armstrong (Capt. Cummings), Anne Seymour (Elk Woman), Buck Taylor (Sgt. Bridges), Simon Andreu (Gance), Lautaro Murua (Perkins), Roger Cudney (Durand), Gerry Gatlin (Winslow), John Davis Chandler (Mason), Miguel Angel Fuentes (Big Bear).

A rip off sequel to A MAN CALLED HORSE (1970) and THE RETURN OF A MAN CALLED HORSE (1976), which merely cashes in on the popularity of its predecessors. Harris briefly appears as an aging Englishman who has headed a Sioux tribe for 30 years, while raising his half-breed son Beck. Father and son try to protect the tribe from an onslaught of gold rush settlers. The Sioux receive aid from Army officer Armstrong, but the battle between settlers and Indians rage. Harris is quickly killed off (before the one-third point of the film), leaving Beck in charge. Bows and arrows successfully fend off bullets and, by the finale, Beck and his Indian sweetheart, De Sade, have driven away the settlers. It's just plain dumb, and anything but a triumph.

p, Derek Gibson; d, John Hough; w, Ken Blackwell, Carlos Aured (based on a story by Jack DeWitt and on a character created by Dorothy M. Johnson); ph, John Alcott, John Cabrera (CFI Color); m, George Garvarentz; ed, Roy Watts; prod d, Alan Roderick-Jones; art d, Marilyn Taylor.

Adventure/Drama   **Cas.**   **(PR:O MPAA:PG)**

TROCADERO**   (1944) 74m REP bw

Rosemary Lane (Judy), Johnny Downs (Johnny), Ralph Morgan (Sim), Dick Purcell (Spike), Sheldon Leonard (Mickey), Marjorie Manners (Marge), Emmett Vogan (Carson), Charles Calvert (Tony), Dewey Robinson (Bullfrog), Ruth Hilliard (Cigarette Girl), Eddie Bartell (M. C.), Cliff Nazarro, Erskine Johnson, Dave Fleischer (Themselves), Ida James, Patricia Kay, Betty Bradley, Jane Ellison, Wingy Mannone, The Stardusters, The Radio Rogues, The Bob Chester, Eddie Le Baron, Matty Malneck, Gus Arnheim Orchestras.

A slight plot of two children inheriting a nightclub from their foster father mainly serves the purpose of providing for some first-rate entertainment during the jazz age. Like the plot, the club doesn't start doing well until the music picks up. Added attractions are comic routines of Nazarro and an appearance by the famous cartoonist Dave Fleischer. Songs include: "Shoo-Shoo Baby" (Phil Moore), "The Music Goes 'Round and Around" (Red Hodgson, Ed Farley, Mike Riley), "Roundabout Way" (Sidney Clare, Lew Porter), "Bullfrog Jump," "How Could You Do That to Me" (Porter), "The

King was Doing the Rhumba" (Jay Chernis, Porter), "Trying to Forget" (Tony Romano), "Can't Take the Place of You" (Walter Colmes, Porter).

p, Walter Colmes; d, William Nigh; w, Allen Gale (based on the story by Charles F. Chaplin, Garret Holmes); ph, Jackson Rose; m, Jay Chernis; ed, Robert Crandall.

Musical   **(PR:A MPAA:NR)**

TROG zero   (1970, Brit.) 91m WB c

Joan Crawford (Dr. Brockton), Michael Gough (Sam Murdock), Bernard Kay (Inspector Greenham), David Griffin (Malcolm Travers), Kim Braden (Ann Brockton), Joe Cornelius (Trog), John Hamill (Cliff), Geoffrey Case (Bill), Thorley Walters (Magistrate), Jack May (Dr. Selbourne), Maurice Good, Rona Newton-John (Reporters), Paul Hansard (Dr. Kurtlimer), Robert Crewdson (Dr. Pierre Duval), Robert Hutton (Dr. Richard Warren), David Warbeck (Alan Davis), Brian Grellis (John Dennis), Simon Lack (Col. Vickers), Chloe Franks (Little Girl), Cleo Sylvestre (Nurse), Golda Casimir (Butcher), Shirley Conklin (Little Girl's Mother), John Baker (Anaesthetist), Bartlett Mullins (Butcher).

Not every star can bow out of the movies with a resoundingly successful film and such was to be the case with Crawford. Sadly, she didn't just leave films on a bad note, but with a bomb that used her status as Pepsi Cola's president in a cheap commercial display as well. When some students are killed by a cave creature, Crawford, an anthropologist, has the beast captured and taken to her laboratory. The troglodyte (nicknamed "Trog") is supposedly the missing link science has been searching for though it looks more like an actor with too much body hair and a bad monkey mask. The creatures loves classical music and hates rock 'n' roll and eventually has his mind tapped to learn its history. His supposed "memory" is just some old footage of THE ANIMAL WORLD, a 1955 Irwin Allen picture, edited into the footage. There's some jealousy by Crawford's colleagues and the inevitable "search and destroy" mission when the misunderstood creature escapes and takes a little girl with him. It could have been great camp fun but the presentation is absolutely wretched. The direction shows no sense of subtlety in the least, slamming home each point with jackhammer force. A real waste of time closes Crawford's superb career.

p, Herman Cohen; d, Freddie Francis; w, Aben Kandel (based on a story by Peter Bryan, John Gilling); ph, Desmond Dickinson (Technicolor); m, Johnny Scott; ed, Oswald Hafenrichter; md, Scott; art d, Geoffrey Tozer; set d, Helen Thomas; spec eff, Willis O'Brien, Ray Harryhausen; makeup, Jimmy Evans.

Science Fiction   **(PR:A MPAA:GP)**

TROIKA*   (1969) 89m Inca/Emerson c

Fredric Hobbs (Himself), Richard Faun (Goodloins), Nate Thurmond (Bug Man), Gloria Rossi, Morgan Upton, Parra O'Siochain, San Francisco Art Center Ensemble.

This three part, avante-garde, surrealistic comedy is hard to put a label on but a treat for those who don't mind standard film forms being blasted like shotgun pellets. Hobbs, who wrote and directed the film in addition to using some of his art work in the backgrounds, plays himself loose by connecting the film's sections. The subject, roughly, is the film business itself as Hobbs carries out conversations with an "Academy Award-winning" director on subjects ranging from art to popcorn, modern pop films, and Variety gross receipts listings. It's told in a wild free form that's enormous fun and quite hysterical. The final sequence features then NBA star Thurmond as a "Bug-man" who serves as leader of a blue-hued civilization. Don't bother trying to figure out what it means, just sit back and enjoy this on its own terms. It's brimming with imagination and creativity and an obvious product of the late 1960s, San Francisco psychedelic culture.

d, Frederic Hobbs, Gordon Mueller; w, Hobbs; ph, William Heick (Eastmancolor); set d, Hobbs.

Comedy   **(PR:O MPAA:R)**

TROIS HOMMES A ABATTRE (SEE: THREE MEN TO DESTROY, 1980, Fr.)

TROIS VERITES (SEE: THREE FACES OF SIN, 1963, Fr./Ital.)

TROJAN BROTHERS, THE*½   (1946) 85m BNF/Anglo-American
                            (AKA: MURDER IN THE FOOTLIGHTS) bw

Patricia Burke (Betty Todd), David Farrar (Sid Nichols), Bobby Howes (Benny Castelli), Barbara Mullen (Margie Castelli), Lesley Brook (Ann Devon), David Hutcheson (Cyril Todd), Finlay Currie (W. H. Maxwell), Wylie Watson (Stage Manager), George Robey (Old Sam), Bransby Williams (Tom Hockaby), Gus McNaughton (Frank), Hugh Dempster (Tommy), H. F. Maltby (Col. Robbins), Joyce Blair (Beryl Johnson), Annette D. Simmonds, Joan Hickson, Carol Lawton, Roma Milne, Grace Arnold, Shirley Renton, Vincent Holman, Vi Kaley, Doorn Van Steyn, Joy Frankau, Patricia Fox, Olive Kirby, Anders Timberg, Dawn Bingham.

Vaudeville partners ply their trade as the front and back ends of a comedy stage horse. Farrar is the northern half and Howes the southern end of the costume. Burke is a cheating society woman involved with Farrar, and Mullen is the dull wife of Howes. This film is completely miscast, creating further problems for an uninspired story. Howes, the stronger personality of the two, is subordinated by his lesser role, and the female leads are similarly miscast as Mullen is a much better comedienne than her counterpart and deserves a meatier role. The direction is all right but often the dialog is terribly inferior.

p, Louis H. Jackson; d, Maclean Rogers; w, Irwin Reiner, Rogers (based on the novel by Pamela Hansford-Johnson); ph, Ernest Palmer, Moray Grant.

Comedy/Drama   **(PR:A MPAA:NR)**

TROJAN HORSE, THE½**   (1962, Fr./Ital.) 105m Europa
Cinematografica-Les Films Modernes-Films Borderie/Colorama-CAP c
(LA GUARRA DI TROIA, LA GUERRE DE TROIE; AKA: THE TRO-
                   JAN WAR, THE MIGHTY WARRIOR)

Steve Reeves (Aeneas), John Drew Barrymore (Ulysses), Juliette Maynie (Creusa), Hedy Vessel (Helen), Lidia Alfonsi (Cassandra), Warner Bentivegna (Paris), Luciana Angelillo (Andromache), Arturo Dominici (Achilles), Mimmo Palmara (Ajax), Nerio Bernardi (Agamemnon), Nando Tamberlani (Menelaus), Carlo Tamberlani (Priam).

Yet another quasi-epic based on Greek mythology for muscleman Reeves. This time he's the leader of some warriors and is opposed for leadership by Bentivegna. Reeves marries Mayniel, who becomes pregnant and is kidnaped during the constant barrage of sword fighting. Under the command of Barrymore, an uplifting cameo that gives the film its needed touch of class, the Greek warriors build the fabled Trojan horse and hide out in its belly. The wooden nag is left outside the city of Troy after word is put out that this is a holy object. The horse is brought into the city and the Greek warriors emerge from it to pillage the town. Reeves finds his wife has been murdered but has given birth to a son. He takes the boy, along with some of his warriors, and together they found the city of Rome. This doesn't exactly stick to all the mythological stories and throws famed characters around like tenpins, but it's good Saturday matinee fare and on that level works with some success.

p, Gianpaolo Bigazzi; d, Giorgio Ferroni; w, Giorgio Stegani, Ugo Liberatore, Federico Zardi; ph, Rino Filippini (Techniscope, Eastmancolor); m, Giovanni Fusco, Mario Ammonini; ed, Antonietta Zita; art d, Pier Vittorio Marchi.

Historical Epic   **(PR:AA MPAA:NR)**

TROJAN WAR, THE (SEE: TROJAN HORSE, THE, 1962, Fr./Ital.)

TROJAN WOMEN, THE**   (1971) 111m Cinerama c

Katharine Hepburn (Hecuba), Genevieve Bujold (Cassandra), Vanessa Redgrave (Andromache), Irene Papas (Helen), Brian Blessed (Tathybius), Patrick Magee (Menelaus), Alberto Sanz (Astyanax).

Outside the ruined walls of Troy four women lament the fate they have suffered since the city fell to the Greeks. The film brings together four top name actresses but this isn't always a guarantee of quality. Previously presented by its director as an off-Broadway play, the film suffers from staginess that works against its cinematic stylizations. The performances, all emphasizing the tragedy of war and its aftermath, range from good to below standard. Hepburn, the featured player as the fallen Queen of Troy who has lost almost her entire family, gives a fine performance but it lacks the depth her character needs. Redgrave and Bujold likewise, missing the spark of passion their characters demand. Pappas is poor Helen of Troy, whose life has caused the war. She plays the role nicely but like the others lacks qualities the role should have. The moody photography creates an air of tragedy in the proceedings, helping the direction and players to a certain extent. It's not the film it could have been but is still worth a look, simply to see four great players working together.

p, Michael Cacoyannis, Anis Nohra; d&w, Cacoyannis (based on Edith Hamilton's English translation of the play by Euripides); ph, Alfio Contini (Eastmancolor); m, Mikis Theodorakis; ed, Cacoyannis; art d, Nicholas Georgiadis; cos, Annalisa Nasalli Rocca; spec eff, Basilio Cortijo; makeup, Francesco Freda.

Drama   **Cas.**   **(PR:C MPAA:GP)**

TROLLENBERG TERROR, THE
                   (SEE: CRAWLING EYE, THE, 1958, Brit.)

TROMBA, THE TIGER MAN*½   (1952, Ger.) 62m Lippert bw
                                              (TROMBA)

Rene Deltgen (Tromba), Angelika Hauff (Ola Orlando), Gustav Knuth (Ernesto Spadoli), Hilde Weissner (Therese Kronbeck), Grethe Weiser (Clare Vets), Gardy Granass (Gardy), Adrian Hoven (Rudolf Weckerle).

Unappealing trash stars Deltgen playing a tiger trainer who uses hypnotism on his beasts as well as the women in his life. He abuses many a lass but eventually his wicked ways catch up with him when Hauff steals the drug that gives him his hypnotic powers. Without this, Deltgen is helpless and eventually is killed by one of his tigers. The story, already hampered by slow direction, suffers from some heavy editing of sex scenes (by 1950s standards) which American censors deemed unacceptable. The players aren't bad but the poor dubbing chops down their performances.

p, Georg Richter; d, Helmut Weiss; w, Weiss, Elisabeth Zimmermann; ph, Werner Krien; m, Adolf Steimel; ed, Luise Dreyer-Sachsenberg.

Drama   (PR:C MPAA:NR)

TRON***   (1982) 96m BV c

Jeff Bridges (Kevin Flynn/Clu), Bruce Boxleitner (Alan Bradley/Tron), David Warner (Ed Dillinger/Sark), Cindy Morgan (Lora/Yori), Barnard Hughes (Dr. Walter Gibbs/Dumont), Dan Shor (Ram), Peter Jurasik (Crom), Tony Stephano (Peter/Sark's Lieutenant), Craig Chudy, Vince Deadrick (Warriors), Sam Schatz (Expert Disc Warrior), Jackson Bostwick (Head Guard), Dave Cass (Factory Guard), Gerald Berns, Bob Neill, Ted White, Mark Stewart, Michael Sax, Tony Brubaker (Guards), Charles Picerni (Tank Commander), Pierre Vuilleumier, Erik Cord (Tank Gunners), Lloyd Catlett, Michael J. Dudikoff II (Conscripts), Richard Bruce Friedman (Video Game Player), Lloyd Catlett (Video Game Cowboy), Rick Feck, John Kenworthy (Boys in Arcade).

Bridges is a computer game designer whose advanced ideas are constantly being stolen by Warner, the perennial villain who plays the computer company head. While trying to obtain information from the main computer's master control program Bridges is scientifically transformed into a component of the computer and must enter the "Tron" dimension. The world inside the computer is a carefully created design that's wonderful to look at. This can't cover the fact that TRON is a simplistic good-versus-bad guys story with plenty of computer-generated animated combat. The film falters, but taken as an adventure story TRON is good fun. Lisberger, an East Coast animator, directed the visuals, combining the actors and computer graphics with amazing results. Disney studio was in a transitory period at the time of the film's release, trying to bridge the market from the near dead "family film" audiences to the more sophisticated viewer. Its first PG production was less than a success, initially doing poorly at the box office. Ironically, when a TRON-inspired video game hit the arcades the film picked up business and eventually found a limited audience.

p, Donald Kushner; d&w, Steven Lisberger (based on a story by Lisberger, Bonnie MacBird); ph, Bruce Logan (Technicolor/Super Panavision 70); m, Wendy Carlos; ed, Jeff Gourson; prod d, Dean Edward Mitzner; art d, John Mansbridge, Al Roelofs; set d, Roger Shook; cos, Elois Jenssen, Rosanna Norton; spec eff, Richard Taylor, Harrison Ellenshaw; m/l, Journey.

Science Fiction   **Cas.**   (PR:A MPAA:PG)

TROOPER, THE   (SEE: FIGHTING TROOPER, THE, 1935)

TROOPER HOOK**½   (1957) 81m UA bw

Joel McCrea (Sgt. Hook), Barbara Stanwyck (Cora Sutliff), Earl Holliman (Jeff Bennett), Edward Andrews (Charlie Travers), John Dehner (Fred Sutliff), Susan Kohner (Consuela), Royal Dano (Trude), Terry Lawrence (Quito), Celia Lovsky (Senora), Rudolfo Acosta (Chief Nanchez), Stanley Adams (Salesman), Pat O'Moore (Col. Weaver), Jeanne Bates (Ann Weaver), Rush Williams (Cpl. Stoner), Dick Shannon (Ryan), D.J. Thompson (Tess), Sheb Wooley (Cooter Brown), Cyril Delevanti (Junius), Paul "Tiny" Newlan, Charles Gray, Mary Gregory, Alfred Linder, Jody McCrea.

After capturing a band of Apaches sergeant McCrea discovers Stanwyck, a kidnaped white woman, in their midst. He is to escort her home to Dehner, her homesteader husband, but problems arise when she refuses to give up Lawrence, the half-breed son she bore in captivity. Acosta, the Apache chief and father of Lawrence, is determined to regain his son. He takes a band of warriors and attacks the stagecoach McCrea, Stanwyck, and Lawrence are aboard. McCrea threatens to kill the boy if Acosta's group attacks, forcing the chief to retreat. Finally the three reach Dehner but he refuses to accept the half-breed boy. Acosta returns and engages Dehner in battle. The two are killed, leaving Stanwyck and McCrea to begin a life together. Initially this was attacked by critics for taking on issues of race and sex. Though the ending is wholly contrived and the script overwritten in parts, TROOPER HOOK is well acted by the leads and raises some interesting issues in an unflinching manner. McCrea and Stanwyck have an interesting chemistry and Acosta gives good support. The title song was sung by series western veteran Tex Ritter.

p, Sol Baer Fielding; d, Charles Marquis Warren; w, Warren, Martin Berkley, David Victor, Herbert Little, Jr. (based on a story by Jack Schaefer); ph, Ellsworth Fredericks; m, Gerald Fried; ed, Fred Berger; md, Fried; art d, Nick Remisoff; cos, Voulee Giokaris; m/l, "Trooper Hook," Fried, Mitzi Cummings (sung by Tex Ritter); makeup, Bill Woods, John Holden.

Western   (PR:C MPAA:NR)

TROOPERS THREE**   (1930) 80m TIF bw

Rex Lease (Eddie Haskins), Dorothy Gulliver (Dorothy Clark), Roscoe Karns (Bugs), Slim Summerville (Sunny), Tom London (Hank Darby), Joseph Girard (Capt. Harris), Walter Perry (Halligan).

When three vaudeville troupers are bounced from the theatrical trade they decide to become troopers of a different nature. Lease, the romantic lead, is aided by the comedy team of Karns and Summerville as they go through various misadventures when they join the army. Gulliver is the romantic opposite for Lease, causing for Lease some jealousy-sparked moments with a superior officer. There are some snappy moments of cornball comedy but this feature is hurt by poor editing toward the finale, apparently done to keep the film at a short program-filler running time.

p, Arthur Guy Empey; d, Norman Taurog, B. Reeves Eason; w, John F. Natteford (based on a story by Empey); ph, Benjamin Kline, Ernest Miller, Jackson Rose; ed, Clarence Kolster; m/l, As Long As You Love Me, (George Waggner, Abner Silver), "The Girl from Oscaloosa," and the last song sung by Rex Lease, "Please Be Good to Me".

Comedy   (PR:AA MPAA:NR)

TROOPSHIP**   (1938, Brit.) 83m UA bw (GB: FAREWELL AGAIN)

Leslie Banks (Col. Harry Blair), Flora Robson (Lucy Blair), Sebastian Shaw (Capt. Gilbert Reed), Patricia Hilliard (Ann Harrison), Robert Cochrane (Carlisle), Anthony Bushell (Roddy Hammond), Rene Ray (Elsie Wainwright), Robert Newton (Jim Carter), Leonora Corbett (Lady Joan), J.H. Roberts (Dr. Pearson), Eliot Makeham (Maj. Swayle), Martita Hunt (Adela Swayle), Edwart Lexy (Sgt. Brough), Maire O'Neill (Mrs. Brough), Wally Patch (Sgt.-Maj. Billings), Margaret Moffatt (Mrs. Billings), Gertrude Musgrove (Lily Toft), Billy Shine (Cpl. Edrich), Alf Goddard (Pvt. Bulger), Edie Martin (Mrs. Bulger), Edmund Willard (Pvt. Withers), Phil Ray (Moore), Janet Burnell (Mrs. Moore), John Laurie (Pvt. McAllister), Jerry Verno (Judd), Vernon Harris (Harry), David Horne (John Carlisle).

After serving five years in the service in India a regiment of British sailors is happy to be returning home. However, their emotions are crushed when it's learned that the homecoming is only temporary, and they only have six hours to reunite with loved ones before returning to sea. Banks, a colonel trapped between loyalty to the services and his sickly wife, Robson; Shaw, a captain involved with the ship's nurse Hilliard, and a romance between a sailor and a dockside shopkeeper comprise the three main story lines. Despite the large cast and several subplots, the film is told with style and depth, rarely pandering to mere manipulation of audience emotions. The ensemble plays well together with standout performances by Banks and Robson. The photography by noted cinematographer Howe is excellent. This was noted director Pommer's second film for Alexander Korda in London, after a brief stay in Hollywood. He is reported to have said that Ufa in Berlin stole the basic plot of the film and used it in A PASS AND A PROMISE with Heinrich George, one of the greatest actors of his time on the German stage and in German films.

p, Erich Pommer; d, Tim Whelan; w, Clemence Dane, Patrick Kirwan (based on a story by Wolfgang Wilhelm); ph, James Wong Howe, Hans Schneeberger; m, Richard Addinsell; ed, Jack Dennis; prod d, Frederick Pusey; md, Muir Mathieson.

Drama   (PR:C MPAA:NR)

TROPIC FURY*   (1939) 62M UNIV bw

Richard Arlen (Dan Burton), Andy Devine ("Tiny" Andrews), Beverly Roberts (Judith Adams), Lou Merrill (Scipio), Lupita Tovar (Maria), Samuel S. Hinds (J.P. Waterford), Charles Trowbridge (Dr. Taylor), Leonard Mudie (Gallon), Adia Kuznetzoff (Soledad), Noble Johnson (Hannibal), Frank Mitchell (Amando), Milburn Stone (Thomas Snell).

When a professor is captured and tortured by jungle natives at an Amazon rubber plantation, it's up to adventurer Arlen and Roberts, the professor's daugther, to rescue him. This is perfunctory from the first frame to the last, involving jungle film stereotypes and cliches. There are no original embellishments in this tepid drama either in front of or behind the camera. The so-called jungle is obviously a cheap studio set. The direction holds no suspense, though there are unintentionally funny moments.

p, Ben Pivar; d, Christy Cabanne; w, Michael L. Simmons (based on a story "Fury of the Tropics" by Maurice Tombragel, Pivar); ph, Jerry Ash; ed, Maurice Wright.

Jungle Adventure   (PR:A MPAA:NR)

TROPIC HOLIDAY**   (1938) 77m PAR bw

Dorothy Lamour (Manuela), Bob Burns (Breck Jones), Ray Milland (Ken Warren), Martha Raye (Midge Miller), Binnie Barnes (Marilyn Joyce), Tito Guizar (Ramon), Elvira Rios (Rosa), Roberto Soto (Roberto), Michael Visaroff (Felipe), Bobby Moya (Pepito), Fortunio Bonanova (Barrera), Pepito (Chico), Matt McHugh (Joe), Ofelia Ascencio, Sara Ascencio, Emmy del Rio (Ascencio del Rio Trio), The San Christobal Marimba Band (Themselves), Chris Pin Martin (Pancho), Frank Puglia (Copilot), Jesus Topete (Pedro), Jesus Castillon, Mario Santos, Jose Mendoza (Ensenada Singers), Carlos

Villarias (*Commandante*), Anna Demetrio (*Shopkeeper*), Blanca Vischer (*French Maid*), Paul Lopez (*Young Man*), Pedro Regas, Charles Stevens (*Peons*), Robert O'Conor (*Enrique the Big Peon*), Victor Romito, Manuel Valencia (*Henchmen*), Duncan Renaldo (*Young Blood*), Eduardo, Castro, Maria and Teresa Olguin (*Bullfighters*), Paula DeCardo, Dolores Casey, Sheila Darcy, Marie Burton, Yvonne Duval, Gwen Kenyon, Ruth Rogers (*Girls*), the Dominquez Brothers (*Themselves*).

On the search for a good movie story, screenwriter Milland heads off to sunny Mexico. There he looks for inspiration amidst the locals while soaking up numerous musical acts, and meets sarong-clad Lamour. A strictly by-the-book musical with Lamour singing a few numbers. Surprisingly, she's overshadowed by Rios, a Mexican who proved to have a much stronger voice. Raye and Burns provide some comic moments with a bullfight, and Burns marvelously parodies Fredric March's death scene in A STAR IS BORN. Music with a Mexican flavor is abundant and the production values are standard for the fare. Songs include: "The Lamp on the Corner," "My First Love" "Tonight We Live," Tropic Night" (Augustin Lara, Ned Washington), "Havin' Myself a Time" (Ralph Rainger, Leo Robin).

p, Arthur Hornblow, Jr.; d, Theodora Reed. w. Don Hartman, Frank Butler, John C. Moffett, Duke Atteberry (story by Hartman, Butler); ph, Ted Tetzlafff ed, Archie Marshek; cos, Edith Head; ch, LeRoy Prinz.

Musical (PR:A MPAA:NR)

TROPIC ZONE*½ (1953) 94m PAR c

Ronald Reagan (*Dan McCloud*), Rhonda Fleming (*Flanders White*), Estelita (*Elena*), Noah Beery, Jr (*Tapachula Sam*), Grant Withers (*Bert Nelson*), John Wengraf (*Lukats*), Argentina Brunetti (*Tia Feliciana*), Rico Alaniz (*Capt. Basilio*), Maurice Jara (*Macario*), Pilar Del Rey (*Victoriana*).

In Central America, Reagan is on the run because of his involvement with an underground political movement. He ends up in a neighboring country working for Wengraf, a banana grower. Reagan becomes his foreman because of his knowledge of banana growing and soon learns his boss wants to monopolize all of the local banana trade. Wengraf appoints Reagan foreman for Fleming's banana plantation in hopes that he'll help overthrow her. However, Reagan falls for Fleming and plots with her and other banana growers to stop Wengraf from carrying out his evil plans. The story is merely western material transplanted to Central America, substituting fruit growing for cattle ranching. There is some good action and Reagan's performance is good, but the film lacks any real feeling. Reagan had recently left Warner Bros. and took up life as an independent actor with this picture. Despite the obvious script flaws he took the assignment, figuring that he owed Paramount a favor for letting him do THE LAST OUTPOST two years previously.

p, William H. Pine, William C. Thomas; d&w, Lewis R. Foster (based on the novel Gentleman of the Jungle by Tom Gill); ph, Lionel Lindon (Technicolor); m, Lucien Cailliet; ed, Howard Smith; art d, Hal Pereira, Earl Hedrick; cos, Edith Head; ch; Jack Baker.

Adventure (PR:A MPAA:NR)

TROPICAL HEAT WAVE*½ (1952) 74n REP bw

Estelita (*Estelita Rodriguez*), Robert Hutton (*Stratford Carver*), Grant Withers (*Norman James*), Kristine Miller (*Sylvia Enwright*), Edwin Max (*Moore*), Lou Lubin (*Frost*), Martin Garralaga (*Ignacio Ortega*), Earl Lee (*Dean Enwright*), Lennie Breman (*Stoner*), Jack Kruschen (*Stickey Langley*).

Estelita arrives from Cuba to become a singer in her uncle's nightclub. Trouble comes in the form of Withers, a gangster who wants to muscle in on the club and threatens Estelita if he can't have his way. Hutton is a professor of criminology who helps the lass by posing as a gangster himself and all ends well. The film is riddled with implausibilities and typical B-movie chases which serve as mere fillers. Estelita gets three numbers including "My Lonely Heart and I" (Sammy Wilson, Arthur T. Horman); "I Want to be Kissed" (Wilson, Nestor Amaral); "What Should Happen to You" (Wilson) but never warbles the famed song which shares this film's title.

p, Sidney Picker; d, R. G. Springsteen; w, Arthur T. Horman; ph, John MacBurnie; m, Stanley Wilson; ed, Harold Minter; set d, John McCarthy, Jr., James Redd; cos, Adele Palmer; m/l, Sammy Wilson, Arthur T. Horman, Nestor Amaral

Musical/Crime (PR:A MPAA:NR)

TROPICAL TROUBLE* (1936, Brit.) 70m City/GFD bw

Douglass Montgomery (*George Masterman*), Betty Ann Davies (*Mary Masterman*), Alfred Drayton (*Sir Montagu Thumpeter*), Natalie Hall (*Louise van der Houten*), Sybil Grove (*Lady Thumpeter*), Victor Stanley (*Albert*), Gerald Barry (*Sir Pomfrey Pogglethwaite*), Morris Harvey (*Chief of the Bungs*), Marie Ault (*Nonnie*), Vernon Harris (*Martindale*), Mabel Mercer, Chela and Doray, Diana Hance, Andrea Malandrinos, Billy Watts.

Drayton is appointed governor of the tropical island of Bunga-Bunga and, along with his aide, Montgomery, soon falls in love with the easy-going life. Unknown to Drayton, Montgomery takes a native wife, though he has one

back home. Wild rumors of the two men's behavior get to England and Drayton's nagging sister and Montgomery's wife come to the island to investigate. The two men are forced to use a series of ruses to fool the women. Decent stage farce loses a lot on the screen.

p, Basil Humphrys w, Harry Hughes; w, Vernon Harris (based on the novel Bunga-Bunga and the play of the same name by Stephen King-Hall).

Comedy (PR:A MPAA:NR)

TROPICANA (SEE: HEAT'S ON, THE, 1943)

TROPICS½** (1969, Ital.) 87m Giannangelo Corte-B.B.G. Cinematografica/New Yorker bw (TROPICI)

Joel Barcelos (*Miguel*), Janira Santiago (*Maria*), Graciele Campos (*Graciele*), Batista Campos (*Batista*), Antonio Pitanga (*Black Man*), Roque Aranjo (*Julio*), Maria Euridice (*Herself*), Giorgio Poppi (*Doctor*).

This film takes a unique approach, telling a fictional story as a setup for a documentary. The first part is the story of a poverty-ridden country family of Brazil. They are forced to leave their home in the country's northeastern section and head for Sao Paulo in hopes of finding work. The journey is hard but eventually Barcelos and Santiago settle their family in a shantytown within Sao Paulo. Barcelos takes a low-paying construction job. The rest of the film gives an explanation of Brazil's feeble economic system (circa 1969) in relation to other countries', especially the prosperous U.S.

p, Gianni Barcelloni; d, Gianni Amico; w, Amico, Francesco Tullio Altan; ph, Giorgio Pelloni; m, Wolfgang Amadeus Mozart; ed, Pelloni.

Drama (PR:O MPAA:NR)

TROTTIE TRUE (SEE: GAY LADY, THE, 1949, Brit.)

TROUBLE* (1933, Brit.) 70m British and Dominions/UA bw

Sydney Howard (*Horace Hollebone*), George Curzon (*Capt. Vansittart*), Dorothy Robinson (*Cora Vansittart*), Hope Davy (*Miss Carruthers*), Muriel Aked (*Miss May*), George Turner (*Nobby Clarke*), Wally Patch (*Chief Steward*), Betty Shale (*Mrs. Orpington*), Abraham Sofaer (*Ali*), Ballard Berkeley, Frank Atherley.

Howard is a steward on a luxury liner. A notorious jewel thief comes aboard and Howard is assigned to watch him. When a valuable diamond is stolen, Howard and his fellow stewards spring to action and bungle their way toward recovering the gem. Not especially good British comedy.

p, Herbert Wilcox; d, Maclean Rogers; w, R.P. Weston, Bert Lee, Jack Marks (based on a story by Dudley Sturrock, Walter Tennyson); ph, F.A. Young.

Comedy (PR:A MPAA:NR)

TROUBLE AHEAD*½ (1936, Brit.) 74 Vogue/Times bw (GB: FALLING IN LOVE)

Charles Farrell (*Howard Elliott*), Mary Lawson (*Ann Brent*), Gregory Ratoff (*Oscar Marks*), H. F. Maltby (*Cummins*), Diana Napier (*Winnie*), Cathleen Nesbitt (*Mother*), Pat Aherne (*Dick Turner*), Margot Grahame (*June Desmond*), Sally Stewart (*Gertie*), Monty Banks (*Film Director*), Marion Harris (*Herself, Cafe Singer*).

When Hollywood movie star Farrell arrives in London to work in his first British picture, he is persecuted by avid admirers. Seeking shelter, he boards a bus and finds himself seated beside sweet young orphan girl Lawson. Delighted with the solace of her company, he arranges for a further meeting. To the dismay of his manager, Ratoff, Farrell evades the duties of a star, avoiding his public and, instead, picnicking and partying with his new-found nonentity. When she learns of her hero's true identity, Lawson tries to disappear from his life. The disgruntled star decides to eschew the production and return to the U.S. This forces manager Ratoff to have a change of heart. Locating the lass, he puts her on a tugboat and pursues the ocean liner carrying Farrell away. The lovers are reunited, production is resumed, and all ends well. Ratoff is superb and the rest of the cast performs well including director Banks, who plays, of all things, a film director.

p, Howard Welsch; d, Monty Banks; w, Fred Thompson, Miles Malleson, John Paddy Carstairs (based on a story by E. Bard, A. Hyman, Lee Loeb); ph, Geoffrey Faithfull; m/l, Carroll Gibbons.

Comedy (PR:A MPAA:NR)

TROUBLE ALONG THE WAY* (1953) 110m WB bw

John Wayne (*Steve Aloysius Williams*), Donna Reed (*Alice Singleton*), Charles Coburn (*Father Burke*), Tom Tully (*Father Malone*), Sherry Jackson (*Carole Williams*), Marie Windsor (*Anne McCormick*), Tom Helmore (*Harold McCormick*), Dabbs Greer (*Father Mahoney*), Leif Erickson (*Father Provincial*), Douglas Spencer (*Procurator*), Lester Matthews (*Cardinal O'Shea*), Chuck Connors (*Stan Schwegler*), Bill Radovich (*Moose McCall*), Richard Garrick (*Judge*), Murray Alper (*Bus Driver*), James Flavin*Buck Holman*, Ned Glass (*Pool Player*), Phil Chanmbers (*Bishop*), Frank Ferguson (*Mike Edwards*), Howard Petrie (*Polo Grounds Manager*), Renata Vanni

(Italian Mother), Tim Graham *(Bill, Team Manager)*, Robert Keys *(Joe, Team Manager)*.

A charming comedy-drama that satrizes big-time college football with a religious undertone that never gets in the way. Wayne top-lines as a former top-notch college football coach who has been fired from his last jobs because he was unable to become part of the academic "system" and rankled under the bureaucracy of his former employers. Coburn is the rector of a New York Catholic college which is in danger of being shuttered unless he can raise nearly $200,000 to take care of operating costs. He has half a year to raise the money or the school will be shut forever. Coburn thinks they would be able to sell tickets to their football games if they had a decent team. But a good team demands a great coach so Coburn approaches Wayne, who refuses the offer because the team was so dreadful the year before that Wayne thinks it would be impossible to whip them into shape quickly. At the same time, Wayne is living with his young daughter, Jackson, while his ex-wife, Windsor, and her new husband, Helmore, are trying to get the youngster back. To that end, Reed, a woman from the Probation Bureau, is sent to look into the life Wayne and Jackson lead. Wayne spots Reed for what she is, a spinster afraid of any romantic entanglements. He soon charms Reed and she gives him time to prove that he is a fit father. Wayne takes the coaching job and moves on the campus with Jackson, if only to flee the threats of Windsor and Helmore. They are given a room in the belfry and have to stop their conversation every half-hour as the bells toll and jangle their ears. Wayne calls for Connors and Radovich, two of his one-time football assistants. He begins a chicanerous recruiting program, getting good players (with poor records in scholastics) into the school; he wheedles his way into securing decent football uniforms; and he even promises his players that they will receive a share of the parking fees and various concessions. It's all underhanded, of course, and the pious Coburn would pop his clerical collar if he knew, but Wayne is a desperate man who wants to prove he can still coach, as well as keep his daughter. Wayne gets the players into shape for the game, which they win, then Coburn finally learns what Wayne has done and cancels the remainder of the games. Wayne begins to tipple a bit and Reed has to withdraw her favorable report about his fitness as a parent. There's a trial which is run by Garrick, as the judge, and it would appear that Jackson will have to be remanded to Windsor and Helmore. Then Coburn shows up and tells the court that he takes full responsibility for what's happened because he made such tough demands on Wayne to win that the coach was forced to take drastic steps. Reed is going to take Jackson away until Coburn offers Wayne his old job back. Coburn decides to step down and Jackson sees that Wayne and Reed are in love and that she wouldn't mind having Reed as her new stepmother. Naturally, it all works out in the end. The synopsis doesn't do justice to the sparkling and witty dialog provided by Shavelson and Rose, two former Bob Hope writers who know their way around a quip. Wayne shows that he can handle comedy as well as he can handle Indians and Nazis and acquits himself well in an unaccustomed role. Director Curtiz moves matters along briskly, and Steiner's music is in keeping with the lighthearted vein of the movie. Excellent family fare.

p, Melville Shavelson; d, Michael Curtiz; w, Shavelson, Jack Rose (based on the story "It Figures" by Douglas Morrow, Robert H. Andrews); ph, Archie Stout; m, Max Steiner; ed, Owen Marks; art d, Leo K. Kuter.

Comedy/Drama   **(PR:O   MPAA:R)**

TROUBLE AT MIDNIGHT*   (1937) 68m UNIV bw

Noah Beery, Jr *(Kirk Cameron)*, Catherine Hughes *(Catherine Benson)*, Larry Blake *(Tony Michaels)*, Bernadene Hayes *(Marion)*, Louis Mason *(Elmer)*, Earl Dwire *(Goff)*, Charles Halton *(Everett Benson)*, Frank Melton *(Frank Gordeen)*, George Humbert *(Nick)*, Edward Hearn *(DeHoff)*, Harlan Briggs *(Sheriff)*, Henry Hunter *(Dick)*, Harry C. Bradley *(Doctor)*, Virginia Sale *(Mrs. Lippencott)*.

It starts off like a war film, turns into a gangster movie, and ends up being a western. This cheap outing from Universal suffers from an obvious thrown-together production, borrowing from each of the three mentioned genres and ultimately creating nothing. Beery plays a dairy farmer who's having trouble when his stock suffers from constant midnight raids. He's also in love with Hughes, a banker's daughter whose pappy (Halton) disapproves of Beery. With the help of Dwire, Beery stops the nefarious activities and ends up with the gal. The production suffers from an unsure story line. The end result fooled no one and the film proved to be a box office bomb.

p, Barney A. Sarecky, Ben Koenig; d, Ford Beebe; w, Beebe, Maurice Geraghty (based on the stories "Night Patrol" by Kimball Herrick and "Midnight Raiders" by Geraghty, Beebe); ph, Jerome Ash; ed, Jack Rawlins.

Western/Crime   **(PR:A   MPAA:NR)**

TROUBLE AT 16   (SEE: PLATINUM HIGH SCHOOL, 1960)

TROUBLE BREWING*   (1939, Brit.) 87m EAL/ABF bw

George Formby *(George Gullip)*, Googie Withers *(Mary Brown)*, Gus McNaughton *(Bill Pike)*, Garry Marsh *(A.G. Brady)*, Joss Ambler *(Lord Redhill)*, Ronald Shiner *(Bridgewater)*, Martita Hunt *(Mme. Berdi)*, C.

Denier Warren *(Maj. Hopkins)*, Beatrix Fielden-Kaye *(Housekeeper)*, Basil Radford *(Guest)*, Esma Cannon *(Maid)*, Tiger Tasker.

Enjoyable Formby vehicle finds him a newspaper printer who wants to be a detective. When he bets on a horse and his winnings turn out to be counterfeit, he sets out to catch the gang of counterfeiters himself. After a series of madcap adventures he tails them to a brewery they're using for a hideout and discovers that his boss is the leader of the gang. Includes the songs "Fanlight Fanny" and "Hitting the Highspots Now."

p, Jack Kitchin; d, Anthony Kimmins; w, Kimmins, Angus McPhail, Michael Hogan; ph, Ronald Neame; ed, Ernest Aldridge; md, Ernest Irving; art d, Wilfred Shingleton.

Comedy   **(PR:A   MPAA:NR)**

TROUBLE CHASER   (SEE: LI'L ABNER, 1940)

TROUBLE-FETE*   (1964, Can.) 95m Cooperatio Prod./France Film
                                                                              bw

Lucien Hamelin, Louise Remy, Percy Rodriguez, Herni Tremblay, Yves Corbeil.

This story of a college kid rebelling against authority is lifted above typical films of this nature, mainly because of its energetic direction and believable performances. Set against the social unrest of 1960s Quebec, the film follows a young man who starts out to fight conformity and ends up causing himself more trouble than intended. The direction throws in some avant-garde style filmmaking that was gaining popularity at the time, thanks to the French New Wave's revolution. Worth a look. (In French.)

p, Jean-Claude Lord; d, Pierre Patry; w, Lord, Patry; ph, Jean Roy; m, Claude Leveilles; ed, Lucien Marleau.

Drama   **(PR:O   MPAA:NR)**

TROUBLE FOR TWO   (1936) 75m MGM bw (GB: SUICIDE CLUB,
                                                                             THE)

Robert Montgomery *(Prince Florizel)*, Rosalind Russell *(Miss Vandeleur [Princess Brenda])*, Frank Morgan *(Col. Geraldine)*, Reginald Owen *(Dr. Franz Noel, President of the Club)*, Louis Hayward *(Young Man with Cream Tarts)*, E. E. Clive *(The King)*, Walter Kingsford *(Malthus)*, Ivan Simpson *(Collins)*, Tom Moore *(Maj. O'Rock)*, Robert Greig *(Fat Man)*, Guy Bates Post *(Ambassador)*, Pedro de Cordoba *(Sergei)*, Leyland Hodgson *(Capt. Rich)*, Pat Flaherty *(Ship Captain)*, Frank Darien *(King's Aide)*, Tom Ricketts *(Excited Club Member)*, Pat O'Malley *(Purser)*, Leonard Carey *(Valet)*, Bill O'Brien *(Club Waiter)*, Paul Porcasi *(Cafe Proprietor)*, Sidney Bracey *(Henchman)*, Frank McGlynn, Jr *(Club Member)*, Larry Steers *(Officer)*, Olaf Hytten *(Butler)*, Edgar Norton *(Herald)*, Fred Graham *(Club Guard)*, David Holt *(Florizel as a Child)*, Virginia Weidler *(Miss Vandeleur as a Child)*.

Three of Stevenson's "Suicide Club" stories were adapted into a single feature with only limited success in this production. Montgomery is a Ruritanian prince who is heir to the throne of Karovia. Before he can take his place as ruler and marry his beloved, Russell, Montgomery must wind his way through a nefarious group of killers who set trap after ingenious trap. Montgomery always manages to stay one step ahead and he is finally united with his princess. The story starts out well, setting an intriguing mood of mystery. All too soon, however, this mood is destroyed by unbelievable coincidences and a lagging pace. The film begins as great fun but is ultimately routine and a by-the-book mystery. Despite some good performances by the cast, TROUBLE FOR TWO is a film of promise that disappointingly never quite delivers.

p, Louis D. Lighton; d, J. Walter Ruben; w, Manuel Seff, Edward E. Paramore, Jr. (based on "The Suicide Club" by Robert Louis Stevenson); ph, Charles Clarke; m, Franz Waxman; ed, Robert J. Kern; art d, Cedric Gibbons.

Mystery   **(PR:A   MPAA:NR)**

TROUBLE IN MOROCCO   (1937) 62m COL bw

Jack Holt *(Paul Cluett)*, Mae Clarke *(Linda Lawrence)*, C. Henry Gordon *(Capt. Nardant)*, Harold Huber *(Palmo)*, Victor Varconi *(Kamaroff)*, Paul Hurst *(Tiger Malone)*, Bradley Page *(Branenok)*, Oscar Apfel *(DeRouget)*.

When a gun-running operation surfaces in Cairo, newspaperman Holt and female journalist Clarke head overseas to investigate. Holt ends up in the foreign legion after taking up with a gangster, then being mistaken for a fellow bad man. He tries to work his way out of the service, but not before engaging in some desert battles with local warriors. The direction keeps the film going at a good, frenzied pace with a natural emphasis on the action. The performances don't fall below the action genre expectations, making for an acceptable film altogether.

p, Larry Darmour; d, Ernest B. Schoedsack; w, Paul Franklin (based on "Sowing Glory" by J. D. Newsom); ph, James S. Brown, Jr.; ed, Dwight Caldwell.

Adventure   (PR:A   MPAA:NR)

TROUBLE IN PANAMA   (SEE: TORCHY BLANE IN PANAMA, 1938)

TROUBLE IN PARADISE**   (1932) 83m PAR bw

Miriam Hopkins (*Lily Vautier*), Kay Francis (*Mariette Colet*), Herbert Marshall (*Gaston Monescu/La Valle*), Charlie Ruggles (*The Major*), Edward Everett Horton (*Francois Filiba*), C. Aubrey Smith (*Adolph Giron*), Robert Greig (*Jacques the Butler*), George Humbert (*Waiter*), Rolfe Sedan (*Purse Salesman*), Luis Alberni (*Annoyed Opera Fan*), Leonid Kinskey (*Radical*), Hooper Atchley (*Insurance Agent*), Nella Walker (*Mme. Bouchet*), Perry Ivins (*Radio Commentator*), Tyler Brooke (*Singer*), Larry Steers (*Guest*).

If you were allowed to see one movie produced and directed by Ernest Lubitsch, it would be difficult to choose between this and the original TO BE OR NOT TO BE. Working from a Hungarian play, scripters Jones and Raphaelson have concocted a Sacher torte that is delicious to watch again and again. Since the movie was made before censor Joe Breen came in to squash double-entendre, it is chock-a-block with sexual overtones, saucy lines, and visual eroticism not seen again until the Code was lifted. Smooth Marshall is a "Raffles" type, a thief with sophistication. His erstwhile partner in crime is Hopkins and their dialog glistens with sharply etched bon mots. Their mark is Francis, a very rich Parisienne widow who owns a successful perfume store which is managed by Smith. Marshall and Hopkins are former crime conspirators and ex-lovers and each sets sights on Francis and manages to inveigle a way into the Francis life style. It's a competition as Marshall finds employment as the widow's secretary and Hopkins signs on as her personal maid. Love blossoms between Marshall and Francis and we wonder if he will eschew his larcenous life for a marriage to the perfumer. At first, it seems that Marshall does love Francis, then we are led to believe that it's a sham he's engaged in, just to wangle his way into her confidence. The picture is filled with surprises as we try to discern what is really happening. Meanwhile, Horton, who is a former dupe of an earlier Marshall scam, keeps furrowing his brow as he tries to recall where it was he first met Marshall. The background is ultra-chic with moments in Venice and Paris and fabulous gowns by Banton, but the true stars are the words given to the actors to speak. At the finale, Marshall and Hopkins are reunited, after a bit of a triangle plot twist, and it is assumed that they will go off and ply their felonious trade again somewhere else. Thin as a cut of boarding house turkey but worth seeing, if only to understand how to take a molehill premise and build it into a mountain of whipped cream. Technically flawless, TROUBLE IN PARADISE was overlooked by the Oscars that year but did manage to be named one of the Ten Best by the National Board of Review. You'll grin from "Paramount Presents" right through "The End." That wonderful character actor Kinskey (sometimes spelled Kinsky) was personally signed by Lubitsch to play the nutty radical after the director saw Kinskey in a Hollywood production of "Wonder Bar", a road show in which he played with Al Jolson.

p&d, Ernst Lubitsch; w, Grover Jones, Samson Raphaelson (based on the play "The Honest Finder" by Laszlo Aladar); ph, Victor Milner; m, W. Frank Harling; art d, Hans Dreier; cos, Travis Banton; m/l, "Trouble in Paradise," "Colet and Company," Harling, Leo Robin.

Comedy   (PR:C   MPAA:NR)

TROUBLE IN STORE½   (1955, Brit.) 85m Rank/REP bw

Norman Wisdom (*Norman*), Margaret Rutherford (*Miss Bacon*), Moira Lister (*Peggy*), Derek Bond (*Gerald*), Lana Morris (*Sally*), Jerry Desmonde (*Freeman*), Megs Jenkins (*Miss Gibson*), Joan Sims (*Edna*), Michael Brennan (*Davis*), Joan Ingram (*Miss Denby*), Eddie Leslie (*Bill*), Michael Ward (*Wilbur*), John Warwick (*Robson*), Perlita Neilson (*Mabel*), Hamlyn Benson, Cyril Chamberlain, Ronan O'Casey, John Warren.

When new clerk Wisdom begins working at a department store, he causes nothing but trouble for boss Desmonde. Soon the bumbling newcomer stumbles onto a plot by some employees who are in cahoots with gangsters. He stops the robbers from carrying out their plans and ends up the hero of the day. This is an amiable comedy and Wisdom shows some real clowning ability in the first of his film farces. The plot is simplistic–a story line right out of any Mack Sennett silent short–with the slapstick to match, but that's all Wisdom needs to create some truly enjoyable moments. Directed with efficiency and featuring a strong supporting cast.

p, Maurice Cowan; d, John Paddy Carstairs; w, Carstairs, Cowan, Ted Willis; ph, Ernest Steward; m, Mischa Spoliansky; ed, Peter Seabourne, Geoffrey Foot; md, Philip Martell; art d, Alex Vetchinsky, John Gow; cos, Yvonne Caffin.

Comedy   (PR:A   MPAA:NR)

TROUBLE IN SUNDOWN½   (1939) 60m RKO bw

George O'Brien (*Bradford*), Rosalind Keith (*Jewell*), Ray Whitley (*Ray*), Brackets Chill Wills (*Whopper*), Ward Bond (*Dusty*), Cyrus W. [Cy] Kendall (*Ross*), Howard Hickman (*Tex*), Monte Montague (*Hartman*), John Dilson (*Cameron*), Otto Yamaoka (*Cook*), Ken Card, Earl Dwire, Robert Burns, The Phelps Brothers.

Fiendish real estate man Kendall robs a bank of all its assets, then makes the banker take the fall. Kendall becomes the institution's receiver and tries to collect on the mortgages for various ranches. Meanwhile, he knows that the funds aren't there and the land will become his. Leave it to good-guy cowpoke O'Brien to stop Kendall's plot, restore banker Hickman to his post, and get Hickman's daughter Keith as well. Some good fight sequences and Wills' typically funny support make this a fairly enjoyable western adventure.

p, Bert Gilroy; d, David Howard; w, Oliver Drake, Dorrell McGowan, Stuart McGowan (based on a story by Charles F. Royal [George F. Royal]); ph, Harry Wild; ed, Frederick Knudtson; m/l, "Prairie Winds," "Home on the Prairie," Ray Whitley.

Western   (PR:A   MPAA:NR)

TROUBLE IN TEXAS½   (1937) 64m GN bw

Tex Ritter (*Tex Masters*), Rita Cansino [Hayworth] (*Carmen*), Earl Dwire (*Barker*), Yakima Canutt (*Squint*), Dick Palmer (*Duke*), Hal Price (*G-Man*), Fred Parker (*Sheriff*), Horace Murphy (*Lucky*), Charles King (*Pinto*), Tom Cooper (*Announcer*), Chick Hannon, Oral Zumalt, Fox O'Callahan, Henry Knight, Bob Crosby, Jack Smith, Shorty Miller, Milburn Morante, George Morrell, Rudy Sooter, Tex Sherman, Glenn Strange, The Texas Tornados, White Flash.

After a series of mysterious rodeo robberies, Ritter–with the assistance of undercover agent Cansino [Hayworth]—gets to the bottom of things. Perennial outlaws Canutt and King are, of course, the bad guys. There's plenty of action (and rodeo stock footage) until the exciting climax, with Ritter and Canutt fighting it out aboard a dynamite-filled runaway buckboard. This is an enjoyable piece crammed full of western action and designed to show off Ritter's riding and singing abilities. Hayworth, in her last film done under the name "Cansino," provides good support as the love interest. Of Ritter's 12 features for Grand National TROUBLE IN TEXAS proved to be the one best publicized by the studio. Songs include: "Down on the Colorado," "Song of the Rodeo," "Cowman's Lament," "Headin' for the Rio Grand," "The Looney Cowboy Band" (sung by Tex Ritter).

p, Ed Finney; d, R.N. Bradbury; w, Robert Emmett [Tansey] (Based on a story by Lindsley Parsons); ph, Gus Peterson; ed, Fred Bain; md, Frank Sanucci; art d, Ralph Burger; cos, Maizie Lewis, Lou Brown.

Western   Cas.   (PR:A   MPAA:NR)

TROUBLE IN THE AIR*   (1948, Brit.) 55m Production Facilities/GFD bw

Jimmy Edwards (*B. Barrington Crockett*), Freddie Frinton (*Fred Somers*), Joyce Golding (*Miss Clinch*), Bill Owen (*1st Spiv*), Sam Costa (*2nd Spiv*), Dennis Vance (*Larry Somers*), Laurence Naismith (*Tom Hunt*), Jon Pertwee (*Truelove*), Malcolm Russell (*Sir Charles Newdigate*), Lionel Murton (*1st Boy*), David Lines (*2nd Boy*), Stella Hamilton (*April Newdigate*), Lisa Lee (*Mrs. Hunt*), Gerald Kent (*Mr. Barnes*), Patsy Drake (*Crockett's Secretary*), Sam Kydd, Harry Fowler.

A team of bellringers is set to broadcast over the BBC, but along with the radio crew and tourists descending on the small village come hoodlums trying to take advantage of the event. A radio announcer broadcasts information on the criminals and foils their scheme. Popular British radio personalities exhibit almost no screen presence.

p, George Black, Alfred Black; d, Charles Saunders; w, Jack Davies, Michael Pertwee, Martin Lane; (based on a story by Black, Black, Davies); ph, Roy Fogwell; m, Arthur Wilkinson; ed, Graeme Hamilton; art d, Donald Russell; md, Muir Mathieson.

Comedy   (PR:A   MPAA:NR)

TROUBLE IN THE GLEN**   (1954, Brit.) 91m REP-Wilcox-Neagle/REP c

Margaret Lockwood (*Marissa Mengues*), Orson Welles (*Sanin Cejadory Mengues*), Forrest Tucker (*Maj. Lance Lansing*), Victor McLaglen (*Parlan*), John McCallum (*Malcolm*), Janet Barrow (*Bishop's Wife*), Eddie Byrne (*Dinny Sullivan*), Albert Chevalier (*Bishop*), George Cormack (*Villager*), Dorothea Dell (*Castillo*), Archie Duncan (*Nolly Dukes*), Ann Gudrun (*Dandy Dinmont*), Grizelda Hervey (*Sheilah*), Alistair Hunter (*Policeman*), William Kelly (*Nurrich*), Moultrie Kelsall (*Luke Carnoch*), Stevenson Lang (*McLaren*), Robin Lloyd (*David*), Margaret McCourt (*Alguin*), Alex McCrindle (*Keegan*), Jack Watling (*Sammy Weller*), Peter Sinclair (*Gillie*), Mary MacKenzie (*Kate Kurnoch*), Duncan McIntyre, Jock McKay, Michael Shepley, Jack Stewart, F.A. Vinyals.

Welles arrives from Brazil to inherit some Scottish land, but he quickly antagonizes the locals by closing a highway that runs through the estate, evicting some tinkers who have long live on the land and upsetting crippled girl McCourt, who asks a visiting U.S. Air Force major, Tucker, to help settle the matter. The displaced tinkers, led by McLaglen and son McCallum, strike back by burning Welles in effigy and stealing his prize cow. Welles escalates the war by importing a gang of Glaswegian thugs. A full-scale battle is avoided, though, when Welles admits he has been wrong and works to get along with the natives. Tucker falls in love with Lockwood, Welles' daughter, and is eventually revealed to be the father of McCourt. Inferior comedy tries to emulate THE QUIET MAN (1952), right down to hiring the same screenwriter, Nugent, to adapt the work of the same author, Walsh, but whatever they brought to this misfired project, it was not enough. No one but Welles seems to take any real interest in what he's doing, and Welles, though he hams it up endearingly, sits under a bouffant hairdo that could make anyone look ridiculous. This was the second film Welles made purely for the money with producer-director Wilcox. One can be generous and assume that the rest of the cast had a similar motive. Some nice color photography of the Scottish landscape starts the picture, but it then moves into horribly artificial-looking studio exteriors for the rest of the story. A film barely worth remembering.

p, Herbert J. Yates, Herbert Wilcox; d, Wilcox; w, Frank S. Nugent (based on a story by Maurice Walsh); ph, Max Greene (Trucolor); m, Victor Young; ed, Reginald Beck.

Comedy   Cas.   (PR:A MPAA:NR)

TROUBLE IN THE SKY**   (1961, Brit.) 76m Bryanston Films-Aubrey Baring Prod./UNIV bw (GB: CONE OF SILENCE)

Michael Craig (*Capt. Hugh Dallas*), Peter Cushing (*Capt. Clive Judd*), Bernard Lee (*Capt. George Gort*), Elizabeth Seal (*Charlotte Gort*), George Sanders (*Sir Arnold Hobbes, Queen's Counsel*), Andre Morell (*Capt. Edward Manningham*), Gordon Jackson (*Capt. Bateson*), Charles Tingwell (*Capt. Braddock*), Noel Willman (*Nigel Pickering*), Delphi Lawrence (*Joyce Mitchell*), Marne Maitland (*Mr. Robinson*), Jack Hedley (*First Officers*), Simon Lack, Hedger Wallace (*Navigators*), Charles Mylne, Howard Pays (*Stewards*), Ballard Berkeley, Charles Lloyd Pack (*Commissioners*), Homi Bode, Anthony Newlands (*Controllers*).

A British airliner crashes in India and its pilot (Lee) is found guilty of a "pilot error." His daughter Seal doesn't believe that Lee is guilty and asks Craig, a crack flying examiner, to look into the case. Soon afterwards, Lee is killed in a similar accident. Craig proves that the plane's designer Willman had been deliberately withholding problems with the plane's design until it could be perfected. Seal takes this new information and finally clears her father of any guilt. An average drama with simplistic characterizations and poorly written dialog.

p, Aubrey Baring; d, Charles Frend; w, Robert Westerby (based on the novel *Cone of Silence* by David Beaty); ph, Arthur Grant; ed, Max Benedict; md, Gerard Schurmann; art d, Wilfred Shingleton; makeup, Freddie Williamson.

Drama   (PR:C MPAA:NR)

TROUBLE MAKERS½**   (1948) 69m MON bw

Leo Gorcey (*Terrence Aloysius "Slip" Mahoney*), Huntz Hall (*Horace Debussy "Sach" Jones*), Billy Benedict (*Whitey*), David Gorcey (*Chuck*), Bennie Bartlett (*Butch*), Gabriel Dell (*Officer Gabe Moreno*), Helen Parrish (*Ann Prescott*), John Ridgely (*Silky Thomas*), Lionel Stander (*Hatchet Moran*), Frankie Darro (*Feathers*), Fritz Feld (*Andre Schmidlapp*), Bernard Gorcey (*Louie Dumbrowski*), Cliff Clark (*Capt. Madison*), William Ruhl (*Jones, a Cop*), David Hoffman (*Morgue Keeper*), John Indrisano (*Lefty*), Charles La Torre (*Needles the Tailor*), Charles Coleman (*Doorman*), Buddy Gorman (*Sandy, the 1st Newsboy*), Kenneth Lundy (*2nd Newsboy*), Pat Moran (*Gimpy the Henchman*), Herman Cantor (*Sam*), Maynard Holmes (*Fat Bellboy*), Carey Loftin (*Hall's Stunt Double*).

A better than usual outing for the Bowery Boys finds the gang caught up in murder. While looking across the street with a telescope, Gorcey and company witness a murder but they don't see the killer's face. After seeing the victim's photo in the paper, Gorcey and Hall go to the morgue to further investigate the crime. There, they meet Parrish, the dead man's daughter who runs the hotel from which the boys witnessed the murder. She hires them as bellboys so they can work undercover. Through mistaken identity, Hall learns more about the killing from gangster Stander. He passes the information on to officer Dell, who is suspended from the force for neglecting his regular duties. The crime is inadvertently solved by the Bowery Boys when they engage the crooks in a wild chase through a laundry chute. TROUBLE MAKERS is a well-handled comedy for the infrequently funny Dead End Kids, making sense with its plot and using the film medium with positive effect. Some solid direction combines the slapstick and suspense elements for a good, brisk pace that gives this a higher quality. (See BOWERY BOYS series, Index.)

p, Jan Grippo; d, Reginald LeBorg; w, Edmond Seward, Tim Ryan, Gerald Schnitzer (based on a story by Schnitzer); ph, Marcel Le Picard; ed, William Austin; md, Edward J. Kay; set d, Raymond Boltz, Jr.

Comedy   (PR:AA MPAA:NR)

TROUBLE MAN*   (1972) 99m FOX c

Robert Hooks (*Mr. "T"*), Paul Winfield (*Chalky Price*), Ralph Waite (*Pete Cockrell*), William Smithers (*Capt. Joe Marks*), Paula Kelly (*Cleo*), Julius W. Harris (*Mr. Big*), Bill Henderson (*Jimmy*), Vince Howard (*Preston*), Larry Cook (*Buddy*), Akili Jones (*Chi*), Rick Ferrell (*Pindar*), Stack Pierce (*Collie*),

Edmund Cambridge (*Sam*), Felton Perry (*Bobby*), Wayne Storm (*Frank*), Virginia Capers (*Macy*), James Earl "Texas Blood" Brown (*Pool Shark*), Jita Hadi (*Leroy*), Tracy Reed (*Policewoman*), John Crawford (*Sgt. Koeppler*), Howie Steindler (*Howie*), Danny Lopez (*Young Boxer*).

An ugly blacksploitation film features Hooks as a smartly dressed, foul-mouthed L.A. private detective with a white Lincoln Mark IV he uses for investigations. Winfield and Waite (soon to become the father in TV's "The Waltons") are a black and white pair of baddies who want Hooks' help when someone starts muscling in on their (already illegal) crap games. Several bullet-ridden corpses later, Hooks has neatly solved the crime, killed a few bad guys, and lifted some guns from right under the police department's nose. Despite some excellent use of Los Angeles locations, TROUBLE MAN is a classic example of what white writers and producers perceive as the black life style. There's plenty of easy sex, fancy duds, and lots of "jive language" and obscenities for so-called street realism. The cast itself has a fine background. Hooks was formerly a member of the noted Negro Ensemble Company of New York and Winfield had given a fine performance in SOUNDER. TROUBLE MAN was simply another example of the racist beliefs that permeated Hollywood through the years, thus reinforcing stereotypes for no other reason than to make a buck. A curious note: Kelly, who played Hooks' girl friend, was a graduate of New York's Juilliard School of Performing Arts and was revealingly photographed for *Playboy Magazine*

p, Joel D. Freeman; d, Ivan Dixon; w, John D. F. Black; ph, Michel Hugo (DeLuxe Color); m, Marvin Gaye; ed, Michael Kahn; art d, Albert Brenner; set d, Morris Hoffman; spec eff, Logan R. Frazee.

Crime   (PR:O MPAA:R)

TROUBLE PREFERRED***   (1949) 63m FOX bw

Peggy Knudsen (*Dale Kent*), Lynne Roberts (*Madge Walker*), Charles Russell (*Lt. Rod Brooks*), Mary Bear (*Sgt. Hazel Craine*), Paul Langton (*Ed Poole*), James Cardwell (*Tuffy Tucker*), June Storey (*Hilary Vincent*), Paul Guilfoyle (*Baby Face Charlie*), Marcia Mae Jones (*Virginia*).

This pre-feminist-era women's picture features Knudsen and Roberts as rookie cops who aren't satisfied with being assigned to desk jobs. The two bend the rules so they can hit the streets and prove themselves when Jones, a distraught would-be suicide, is saved by the pair. Though the film suffers from 1940s sexism, it's still ahead of its time in portraying women's roles. It's acted with good feeling and directed with competence.

p, Sol M. Wurtzel; d, James Tinling; w, Arnold Belgard; ph, Benjamin Kline; m, Lucien Cailliet; ed, Roy Livingston; m, David Chudnow; art d, Eddie Imazu.

Drama   (PR:A MPAA:NR)

TROUBLE WITH ANGELS, THE½**   (1966) 111m COL c

Rosalind Russell (*Mother Superior*), Binnie Barnes (*Sister Celestine*), Camilla Sparv (*Sister Constance*), Mary Wickes (*Sister Clarissa*), Marge Redmond (*Sister Liguori*), Dolores Sutton (*Sister Rose Marie*), Margalo Gillmore (*Sister Barbara*), Portia Nelson (*Sister Elizabeth*), Marjorie Eaton (*Sister Ursula*), Barbara Bell Wright (*Sister Margaret*), Judith Lowry (*Sister Prudence*), Hayley Mills (*Mary Clancy*), June Harding (*Rachel Devery*), Barbara Hunter (*Marvel-Ann*), Bernadette Withers (*Valerie*), Vicky Albright (*Charlotte*), Patty Gerrity (*Sheila*), Vicki Draves (*Kate*), Wendy Winkelman (*Sandy*), Jewel Jaffe (*Ginnie-Lou*), Gail Liddle (*Priscilla*), Michael-Marie (*Ruth*), Betty Jane Royale (*Gladys*), Ronne Troup (*Helen*), Catherine Wyles (*Brigette*), Gypsy Rose Lee (*Mrs. Phipps*), Jim Boles (*Mr. Gottschalk*), Kent Smith (*Uncle George*), Pat McCaffrie (*Mr. Devery*), Harry Harvey, Sr (*Mr. Grissom*), Mary Young (*Mrs. Eldridge*), Jim Hutton (*Mr. Petrie*).

Mills and Harding are a pair of young trouble makers assigned to a convent school run by Russell. Try as she may, Russell is unable to stop the two from wreaking their own brand of havoc on the place. Nuns are surprised by finding bubble bath replacing their dinner table sugar, and one student gets her face covered with quick-drying plaster when the duo tries to make a mask. Despite the antics Russell sees some good in the girls and is determined to win them over. One night she sits up with Harding to make a dress and reveals that she once dreamed of becoming a fashion designer. When one of the convent sisters passes away Mills is deeply moved by the simple, yet devout, funeral service. Finally by graduation Russell's patience has been rewarded, for Mills has completely reformed and wants to become a nun herself. The comedy in the film's first portion suffers from a "one-two-three kick!" pattern run over and over with typically predictable results. Once the film takes the serious turn things improve nicely, helped by some fine performances. Russell and Mills play well off one another and ex-stripper Lee isn't bad as a lay instructor. Overall the large cast works well as an ensemble but the direction is surprisingly perfunctory. This was Lupino's first film since 1953's THE BIGAMIST and the film's structure is little more than connected set pieces. A livelier style would have increased the story's charm. A sequel, WHERE ANGELS GO—TROUBLE FOLLOWS, was made in 1968.

p, William Frye; d, Ida Lupino; w, Blanche Hanalis (based on the book *Life with Mother Superior* by Jane Trahey); ph, Lionel Lindon (Pathe Color); m,

Jerry Goldsmith; ed, Robert C. Jones; art d, John Beckman; set d, Victor Gangelin; cos, Helen Colvig (Nun's habit and Hayley Mills' wardrobe by Sybil Connolly); makeup, Ben Lane.

Comedy   **Cas.**   **(PR:AA MPAA:NR)**

TROUBLE WITH EVE (SEE: IN TROUBLE WITH EVE, 1964, Brit.)

TROUBLE WITH GIRLS (AND HOW TO GET INTO IT), THE*½
(1969) 97m MGM c (AKA: THE CHAUTAUQUA)

Elvis Presley (*Walter Hale*), Marilyn Mason (*Charlene*), Nicole Jaffe (*Betty*), Sheree North (*Nita Bix*), Edward Andrews (*Johnny*), John Carradine (*Mr. Drewcolt*), Anissa Jones (*Carol*), Vincent Price (*Mr. Morality*), Joyce Van Patten (*Maude*), Pepe Brown (*Willy*), Dabney Coleman (*Harrison Wilby*), William Zuckert (*Mayor Gilchrist*), Pitt Herbert (*Mr. Perper*), Anthony Teague (*Clarence*), Med Flory (*Constable*), Robert Nichols (*Smith*), Helene Winston (*Olga Prchlik*), Kevin O'Neal (*Yale*), Frank Welker (*Rutgers*), John Rubinstein (*Princeton*), Chuck Briles (*Amherst*), Patsy Garrett (*Mrs. Gilchrist*), Linda Sue Risk (*Lily-Jeanne*), Charles P. Thompson (*Cabbie*), Leonard Rumery, William M. Paris, Kathleen Rainey (*Farmhands*), Hal James Pederson (*Soda Jerk*), Mike Wagner (*Chowderhead*), Brett Parker (*Iceman*), Duke Snider (*Cranker*), Pacific Palisades High School Madrigals (*Choral Group*).

The former king of rock and roll had taken a mighty deep fall by the time of this release. Presley is woefully miscast as the manager of a traveling chautauqua company circa 1927. He's got a hankering for Mason, a member of the company who's trying to unionize the players. When the company arrives in a small Iowa town, Mason picks local kid Jones (of TV's "Family Affair") to appear with the chautauqua. This upsets local politicos who expected one of their own kids to appear with the company. Coleman, in one of his early roles, plays a sneering pharmacist who employs Jones' mother, North. When he's found dead Teague is blamed but Presley discovers that North is the real murderer. She had done it after Coleman had forced her into an unwanted affair, and Presley convinces the woman to confess. She does and is exonerated of the crime. However, because Presley used the confession as a promotional stunt for the company, Mason is enraged. But Elvis manages to convince her of her integrity in a nice, white-bread ending and all ends happily. Presley has little singing to do in what was his next-to-last film, and merely goes through the acting motions. He sings "Almost" and "Clean Up Your Own Back Yard" by Scott Davis and Billy Strange, and both are all wrong for Presley's style. It's rather sad to see the giant reduced to such piddling material. The story is unbelievable tripe, with bad performances and confusing direction. Surprisingly, period detail is paid close attention, making a handsome but hollow movie. The title is wrong for the story, probably tagged on to try to cash in on Presley's long-gone reputation.

p, Lester Welch; d, Peter Tewksbury; w, Arnold Peyser, Lois Peyser (based on a story by Mauri Grashin and the novel *The Chautauqua* by Day Keene, Dwight Babcock); ph, Jacques Marquette (Panavision, Metrocolor); m, Billy Strange; ed, George W. Brooks; art d, George W. Davis, Edward Carfagno; set d, Henry Grace, Jack Mills; cos, Bill Thomas; ch, Jonathan Lucas; m/l, Strange, Scott Davis; makeup, William Tuttle.

Musical/Drama/Comedy   **(PR:A MPAA:G)**

TROUBLE WITH HARRY, THE***½   (1955) 99m PAR c

Edmund Gwenn (*Capt. Albert Wiles*), John Forsythe (*Sam Marlowe the Painter*), Shirley MacLaine (*Jennifer Rogers, Harry's Wife*), Mildred Natwick (*Miss Graveley*), Mildred Dunnock (*Mrs. Wiggs*), Jerry Mathers (*Arnie Rogers, Harry's Son*), Royal Dano (*Calvin Wiggs*), Parker Fennelly (*Millionaire*), Barry Macollum (*Tramp*), Dwight Marfield (*Dr. Greenbow*), Leslie Woolf (*Art Critic*), Philip Truex (*Harry Worp*), Ernest Curt Bach (*Chauffeur*).

Shirley MacLaine's debut in features was one of the rare Hitchcock box-office losers but as the years pass, and the picture is viewed again, one realizes that it may well have been ahead of its time. The novel was set in England and Hitchcock switched it to rural Vermont, in order to take advantage of the multi-hued backdrop. The colorful scenery was in direct contrast to the black humor and doubtless over the heads of audiences who were flocking to see dramas in 1955 like THE ROSE TATTOO, EAST OF EDEN, PICNIC, INTERRUPTED MELODY, and, of course, MARTY. Harry is a corpse who can't seem to stay dead. Young Mathers is traipsing through the deep woods when he finds a body. Without looking too closely at it, he races home and brings his mother, MacLaine, to the site. She instantly recognizes the corpse as that of her ex-husband. She is certain that Harry died due to her whacking him over the head with a bottle. The body has also been discovered by Gwenn, a retired sea captain, and he thinks that one of his bullets may have done the chap in. Gwenn is given to hunting rabbits and has been known to let some ammo fly without taking too good an aim. Natwick is a dotty old lady who also believes that she is responsible for Harry's passing. The "guilty" parties inter and disinter poor Harry several times until it is finally learned that the deceased died of "natural causes." (Which are, of course, the greatest killers of humans around. Matter of fact, someone should start a telethon to "Help Stamp Out Natural Causes.") Along the way, modern artist Forsythe is enlisted by all of the "culprits" in

aiding them with Harry's movements. Two love stories are interspersed as MacLaine and Forsythe fall for each other and Gwenn and Natwick do the same. For anyone who has ever confused Mildred Natwick with Mildred Dunnock, THE TROUBLE WITH HARRY offers a chance to see them in the same film, thus erasing any doubt as to which is which. Mathers, who went on to be Beaver on "Leave It To..." shows early how well he could steal a scene. In a small role as an eccentric millionaire, note Parker Fennelly, who was, for years, a regular member of Fred Allen's cast on radio when he played Titus Moody on the "Allen's Alley" question-and-answer segment. For lovers of radio trivia, the other members of that panel were Kenny Delmar, who announced and played Senator Claghorn; Alan Reed as Falstaff Openshaw; Minerva Pious as Mrs. Nussbaum; and Peter Donald as Ajax Cassidy. Reed, who was one of the most successful radio voices in history, did not appear often on screen but will be best recalled for his role as Pancho Villa in VIVA ZAPATA. THE TROUBLE WITH HARRY was visually dazzling, mainly because Vermont was so beautiful at that time of year. The company moved to Stowe and used that as the hub of the production, fanning out to Morrisville, East Craftsbury, Craftsbury Common, and Sugarbush. Because of the unpredictability of the weather, much of the photography had to be shot on an indoor set built in a local gymnasium, thus altering Hitchcock's carefully mapped-out production schedule. However, the indoor set was affected by the torrential Vermont storms; its roof was made of tin, causing the sound of the rain to echo throughout. Having fallen behind schedule, Hitchcock and his crew returned to add some finishing touches on the Paramount set, careful to bring with them an ample amount of colorful Vermont leaves. Like the television series "Alfred Hitchcock Presents . . ." (which premiered two days after the premiere of THE TROUBLE WITH HARRY) this film is funny in a chuckling rather than belly-laughing fashion. Much of the humor is derived from the off-handed manner in which the participants talked to the corpse. "Hitchcock," as James B. Allardice (the prolog and epilog writer of "Alfred Hitchcock Presents . . .") described him, "is very objective toward death. Dead bodies are not necessarily sacred to him." Herrmann was scoring his first film for Hitchcock and would do many more until the studio toppers at Universal didn't like Herrmann's music for MARNIE and touted Hitchcock off Herrmann's work. Gwenn and Hitchcock had worked together 24 years prior in THE SKIN GAME and both enjoyed the reunion. It was a satire of murder movies and Hitchcock knew that George Jean Nathan's quote was correct ("Satire is what closes on Saturday night") but he was in such good spirits after his success with TO CATCH A THIEF that he thought he'd take a crack at breaking new ground. While most of his films had some moments of humor in them, Hitchcock seldom went in for full-fledged comedy, with the exception being 1941's MR. AND MRS. SMITH. Aware of the fact that his audience expected something other than black comedy, Hitchcock purposely kept the budget on THE TROUBLE WITH HARRY to a bare minimum. He paid only $11,000 for the rights to Story's novel, hired a talented but relatively unknown cast, and managed to spend only $1 million thereby insuring a profit. MacLaine's rise to fame began when she replaced the injured Carol Haney in "Pajama Game." Associate producer Herbert Coleman saw the redhead, signed her up, made a test, showed it to Hitchcock, and the rest is film history. The advertising log line was "The Unexpected From Hitchcock." What was unexpected was the lack of interest on the part of the public.

p&d, Alfred Hitchcock; w, John Michael Hayes (based on the novel by John Trevor Story); ph, Robert Burks (VistaVision, Technicolor); m, Bernard Herrmann; ed, Alma Macrorie; art d, Hal Pereira, John Goodman; cos, Edith Head; spec eff, John P. Fulton; m/l, "Flaggin' the Train to Tuscaloosa," Mack David, Raymond Scott.

Comedy/Mystery   **Cas.**   **(PR:A-C MPAA:NR)**

TROUBLE WITH WOMEN, THE**   (1947) 90m PAR bw

Ray Milland (*Prof. Gilbert Sedley*), Teresa Wright (*Kate Farrell*), Brian Donlevy (*Joe McBride*), Rose Hobart (*Dean Agnes Meeler*), Charles Smith (*Ulysses S. Jones*), Lewis Russell (*Dr. Wilmer Dawson*), Iris Adrian (*Rita La May*), Frank Faylen (*Geeger*), Rhys Williams (*Judge*), Lloyd Bridges (*Avery Wilson*), Norma Varden (*Mrs. Wilmer Dawson*), James Millican (*Keefe*), Matt McHugh (*Herman*), Jimmie Smith (*Peanuts*), Minor Watson (*Mr. Carver*), Norman Rainey (*Prof. Lovell*), Nestor Paiva (*Tony the Waiter*), Mary Field (*Della*), Will Wright (*Commissioner*), Conrad Binyon (*Newsboy*), Dorothy Adams (*Henry's Mother*), Byron Foulger (*Little Thin Man*), Albert Ruiz (*Glove Man*), Byron Poindexter, Eddie Carnegie, Stan Johnson, Charles Mayon, Jerry James (*Reporters*), William Haade (*Cap*), John Hamilton (*Judge*), Kristine Miller (*Coquette*), Chester Conklin, Eddie Borden (*Comedians*), Esther Howard (*Mrs. Fogarty*), Edward Gargan (*Mr. Fogarty*), George Sorel (*Romain*), Jimmy Conlin, Joseph Crehan, Frank Ferguson.

Absent-minded psychology professor Milland writes a book stating women like to be handled brusquely. This gets a write-up in a local paper and Milland threatens to sue for libel when he's misquoted. The paper sends out reporter Wright, who wrote the damaging piece, to get some dirt on Milland and thus save them from embarrassment. She saves him, but not as originally expected. Instead, in good B-movie fashion, a romance blooms between Wright and Milland. Lively performances help the weak story and routine direction.

p, Harry Tugend; d, Sidney Lanfield; w, Arthur Sheekman (based on a story by Ruth McKenney, Richard Bransten); ph, Lionel Lindon; m, Victor Young, Robert Emmett Dolan; ed, William Shea; art d, Hans Dreier, Earl Hedrick; set d, Sam Comer, George McKinnon; cos, Edith Head; ch, Billy Daniels.

Comedy   **(PR:A MPAA:NR)**

TROUBLED WATERS**½   (1936, Brit.) 70m FOX bw

Virginia Cherrill (*June Elkhardt*), James Mason (*John Merriman*), Alastair Sim (*Mac MacTavish*), Raymond Lovell (*Carter*), Bellenden Powell (*Dr. Garthwaite*), Sam Wilkinson (*Lightning*), Peter Popp (*Timothy Golightly*), William T. Ellwanger (*Ezra Elkhardt*), Sybil Brooke, Ernest Borrow.

A small English town pools its resources to invest in a dying mineral spring water business. When a local man is killed in a car crash a conspiracy is hatched to rule the death as murder. This way the town hopes to gain some publicity that will attract attention to the mineral water business. Mason, a government agent, enters to investigate the death and discovers that it really is a murder. This leads him to a gang of explosives, smugglers whom he exposes. The action is sustained throughout and Mason, as usual, is very good.

p, John Findlay; d, Albert Parker; w, Gerard Fairlie (based on a story by W. P. Lipscomb, Reginald Pound); ph, Roy Kellino.

Mystery   **(PR:A MPAA:NR)**

TROUBLEMAKER, THE***   (1964) 80m Ozymandias-Seneca/Janus bw

Tom Aldredge (*Jack Armstrong*), Joan Darling (*Denver James*), Theodore J. Flicker (*Crime Commissioner*), James Frawley (*Sol/Sal/Judge Kelly*), Buck Henry (*T.R. Kingston*), Charles White (*Building Inspector*), Godfrey Cambridge (*Fire Inspector*), Bernard Reed (*Sanitation Inspector*), Michael Currie (*Electrical Inspector*), Leo Lerman (*Dirty Old Man*), Al Freeman, Jr (*Intern*), Adelaide Klein (*Psychiatrist*), Joy Claussen (*Miss Simmons*), China Lee (*Hooker*), Betty Stanton (*Girl on the Couch*), Robbie Reed (*Kid*), Francis Dux (*Nazi Leader*), Calvin Ander (*Mr. Cohen*), Graziella Narducci (*Sal's Secretary*).

Odd but refreshing comedy stars Aldredge as a former chicken farmer from the Midwest who comes to New York to open a coffeehouse. Gangster Frawley (who plays three roles here) tries to extort money from him, as do a number of city inspectors and officials. He refuses to pay them but his lawyer and old college friend, Henry, is not so scrupulous and he properly greases the way for the place to open. Aldredge persists in his moral indignation at the corruption all around him and Frawley's minions eventually kidnap him and lock him away in a mental institution. He gets out and puts together evidence to put them all away, including the mastermind, Flicker, the city's crime commissioner. Henry joins him and girl friend Darling in cleaning up the crooked mob, but by the end Aldredge has been corrupted and he merely takes over Flicker's position. The film is an offspring of a Greenwich village improvisational comedy troupe known as "The Premise," and it marks the writing and acting debut of Buck Henry, who would go on to write THE GRADUATE (1967), THE MAN WHO FELL TO EARTH (1976), and other interesting works. Also doing his first work for the big screen is director Flicker, who would also direct the terrific satire, THE PRESIDENT'S ANALYST (1968), but who has been too little heard from since. Some of the comedy is terrific, especially scenes like an old woman accidentally walled up, black fire chief Cambridge speaking with an Irish brogue, and Henry's entire performance. The film's failings are the usual failings of improvisational comedy on stage and on screen–vaguely promising ideas are beaten into the ground trying to get a laugh out of them when there's nothing there to laugh at. A lot of the acting is barely more than amateur, and Flicker's direction, despite the occasional flash of inspiration, shows his inexperience. Still, an interesting film of small importance but well worth seeing.

p, Robert Gaffney; d, Theodore J. Flicker; w, Flicker, Buck Henry (based on a story by Henry); ph, Gayne Rescher; m, Cy Coleman; ed, John McManus, William Austin; art d, David Moon; set d, Leif Pedersen.

Comedy   **(PR:O MPAA:NR)**

TROUBLES THROUGH BILLETS   (SEE: BLONDIE FOR VICTORY, 1942)

TROUBLESOME DOUBLE, THE**   (1971, Brit.) 57m
Interfilm/Children's Film Foundation c

Keith Chegwin, Julie Collins, Tracy Collins, Richard Wattis, Josephine Tewson, Larry Martyn.

Okay sequel to EGGHEAD'S ROBOT (1970) has Chegwin the little genius building a robot double for his sister to help her win a swimming contest. Not quite as good as the original, it is still an above-average film for children.

p, Cecil Musk; d, Milo Lewis; w, Leif Saxon; ph, Alfred Hicks.

Children   **(PR:AA MPAA:NR)**

TROUT, THE**   (1982, Fr.) 104m GAU-TFI-SFPC/Triumph c (LA TRUITE)

Isabelle Huppert (*Frederique*), Jean-Pierre Cassel (*Rambert*), Jeanne Moreau (*Lou*), Daniel Olbrychski (*Saint-Genis*), Jacques Speisser (*Galuchat*), Isao Yamagata (*Daigo Hamada*), Lisette Malidor (*Mariline*), Jean-Paul Roussillon (*Pere Perjon*), Roland Bertin (*Count*), Craig Stevens (*Carter, Company President*), Alexis Smith (*Gloria, Rich Widow*), Ruggero Raimundi (*Himself*), Lucas Delvaux (*Young Employee*), Pierre Forget (*Frederique's Father*), Ippo Fujikawa (*Kumitaro*), Yuko Kada (*Akiko*), Anne Francois (*Air Hostess*), Pascal Morand, Frederique Briel (*Frederique's Girl Friends*).

The sexual adventures of a country girl turned business woman are chronicled in this elaborate, often rambling film. Huppert is the title character, a human "trout" who swims upstream against life's troubles. She's an ex-trout farmer herself, now married to a closet homosexual. The marriage has never been consummated and eventually she leaves with her husband's friend Olbrychski for a whirlwind tour of Japan. She returns home after her husband tries to kill himself. The couple is taken in by Moreau's husband who takes a particular liking to Huppert's husband. Moreau discovers what's happening and has it out with her man, who then kills her. Finally Huppert settles down with her now alcoholic husband to run a Japanese trout farm. Losey, an American director who remained in Europe after the 1950s blacklisting period, claimed this was a story he had wanted to do for 20 years. It hardly seemed worth the wait, for despite a lovely mise-en-scene the story is lifeless and more than a little outdated. Issues are only lightly touched on with vagueness substituting for psychology. The performances suffice but the actors, especially Huppert and Moreau, aren't given much to do. (In French; English subtitles.)

p, Yves Rousset-Rouard; d, Joseph Losey; w, Losey, Monique Lange (based on the novel *La Truite* by Roger Vailland); ph, Henri Alekan (Eastmancolor); m, Richard Hartley; ed, Marie Castro Vasquez; prod d, Alexandre Trauner; cos, Annalisa Nasilli-Rocca.

Drama   **Cas.**   **(PR:O MPAA:R)**

TRUANT, THE   (SEE: TERROR IN THE CITY, 1966)

TRUCK BUSTERS**   (1943) 58m WB bw

Richard Travis (*Casey Dorgan*), Virginia Christine (*Eadie Watkins*), Charles Lang (*Jimmy Dorgan*), Ruth Ford (*Pearl*), Richard Fraser (*Limey*), Michael Ames [Tod Andrews] (*Dave Todd*), Frank Wilcox (*Police Capt. Gear*), Don Costello (*Bonetti*), Rex Williams (*Al Wilson*), Bill Crago (*Joe Moore*), Monte Blue (*Scrappy O'Brien*), Bill Kennedy (*Tim Shaughnessy*), William B. Davidson (*Stephen S. Gray*), George Humbert (*Andy Panopolos*), Peggy Diggins (*Babe*), John Harmon (*Maxie*), John Maxwell (*District Attorney Danton*), Glenn Cavender (*Mack*), Frank Ferguson (*George Havelock*), Robert Middlemass (*Landis*), Edward Keane (*Elliott*), Jean Ames (*Waitress*).

It's almost nonstop action as an independent trucking firm led by Travis takes on some big timers who are in cahoots with the mob. Travis' brother Lang is killed in the ensuing fracas and there's a climactic gun battle in this formula programmer. The film moves at a quick pace, giving the actors little to do but go through the prescribed motions.

p, William Jacobs; d, B. Reeves Eason; w, Robert E. Kent, Raymond L. Schrock (based on their story "Night Freight"); ph, Harry Neumann; ed, Clarence Kolster; art d, Hugh Reticker; cos, Milo Anderson; spec eff, Byron Haskin.

Action/Crime   **(PR:A MPAA:NR)**

TRUCK STOP WOMEN**   (1974) 82m LT Films c

Claudia Jennings (*Rose*), Lieux Dressler (*Anna*), John Martino (*Smith*), Dennis Fimple (*Curly*), Dolores Dorn (*Trish*), Gene Drew (*Mac*), Paul Carr (*Seago*), Jennifer Burton (*Tina*).

Good mindless sleaze features Dressler as the proprietor of a robbery and prostitution ring which operates out of a Southwestern truck stop. Martino is a mafioso who wants in on the business and starts a bloody war over it. Surprisingly this isn't as bad as it sounds. Though at points the direction is sloppy, other passages show some real craftsmanship. Dressler gives one of the film's better performances, a good cynical outing that shines above some of the other cartoon-like characters that populate the story. There's plenty of action, as expected with this sort of film, with truck chases and a bloody, climactic gun battle.

p&d, Mark L. Lester; w, Lester, Paul Deason (based on a story by Deason); ph, John A. Morrill (Technicolor); m, Big Mack and the Truckstoppers; ed, Marvin Wallowitz; art d, Tom Hassen; m/l, Red Simpson, Jerry Chestnut, Bob Stanton, Bobby Hart, Jimmy Haskell, Danny Janssen, Guy Hemric (sung by Bobby Hart).

Action   **Cas.**   **(PR:O MPAA:R)**

TRUCK TURNER*½ (1974) 91m Sequoia/AIP c

Isaac Hayes (*Truck Turner*), Yaphet Kotto (*Harvard Blue*), Alan Weeks (*Jerry*), Annazette Chase (*Annie*), Nichelle Nichols (*Dorinda*), Sam Laws (*Nate*), Paul Harris (*Gator*), John Kramer (*Desmond*), Scatman Crothers (*Duke*), Chuck Cypher (*Drunk*), Dick Miller (*Fogarty*), Bob Harris (*Snow*), Jac Emil (*Reno*), Stan Shaw (*Fontana*), Clarence Barnes (*Toro*), Don Watters (*Val*), Eddie Smith (*Druggist*), Esther Sutherland (*Black Mama*), Earl Maynard (*Panama*), Henry Kingi (*Candy Man*), Larry Gabriel (*Travis*), Don Megowan (*Garrity*), Cheryl Samson (*Taffy*), Edna Richardson (*Frenchie*), Bernadette Gladden (*Racquel*), Tara Stronmeier (*Turnpike*), Lisa Farringer (*Annette*), Sharon Madigan (*Nurse*), Mel Novak (*Doctor*), Donnie Williams (*Highway Man*), Randy Gray (*Kid in Hospital*), Annik Borel (*Stalingrad*), Stymie Beard (*Jail Guard*).

Just another quickie blacksploitation feature that's long on violence and short on plot. Hayes, who also provided an unusually unoriginal score, is a bounty hunter who, with partner Weeks, is after Harris, a notorious pimp. They kill him, then must face the wrath of Kotto, a *bad* gangster who's hired to carry out revenge by Harris' girl friend Nichols. It's strictly perfunctory filmmaking, a group of stock characters populating a mindless blood-and-guts action ride. Though the direction shows no flair for action sequences, the cast actually isn't bad. Kotto would later prove himself in such films as BLUE COLLAR and ALIEN. Watch for a brief appearance by Beard, a former "Our Gang" kid now grown up and reduced to this mess.

p, Fred Weintraub, Paul M. Heller; d, Jonathan Kaplan; w, Leigh Chapman, Oscar Williams, Michael Allin (based on a story by Jerry Wilkes); ph, Charles F. Wheeler (Movielab Color); m, Isaac Hayes; ed, Michael Kahn; cos, Ann McCarthy; m/l, (performed by Hayes).

Action **(PR:O MPAA:R)**

TRUE AND THE FALSE, THE*½ (1955, Swed.) 79m Helene Davis bw

Signe Hasso (*Bride-to-Be*), William Langford (*Bridegroom-to-Be*), "La Grande Breteche": Hasso (*Josephine de Merrit*), Langford (*Louis de Merrit*), Michael Road (*Edmond Montez*), Stig Olin (*Goronflot*), Lilli Kjellin (*Gertrude, the Chambermaid*), Naima Wifstrand (*Gertrude, 50 Years Later*), Ragnar Arvedson (*Innkeeper*), Ann Bibby (*Innkeeper's Wife*), "The Old Maid": Hasso (*Agnes Maubert*), Langford (*Andre Morain*), Arvedson (*Agnes' Father*), Ruth Brady (*Helene*), Hjordis Petterson (*Aunt Emilie*), Olin (*Officer*).

Swedish actress Hasso turned producer as well for this film, combining two short stories by Balzac and Maupassant with less than successful results. The stories are connected by an unneeded bridge that has Hasso reading short stories on the night before she is to wed Langford. First is the Balzac story "La Grande Breteche." A couple lives in an abandoned French castle. Hasso is the wife who takes on a lover. One night as she entertains the man, her husband (Langford again) comes home. The lover hides in a closet and the suspicious Langford has his hideaway bricked up, thus sealing the lover to certain death. Next is Maupassant's "The Old Maid." This concerns a young girl who loves a soldier. He feels nothing for her, though, as he only wants a bride with money. Later the girl is horribly frostbitten which permanently disfigures her. Her father passes away leaving her all his money. The girl looks up the soldier who now claims to love her but she only gives him the money and goes to live in seclusion. The two stories are told in a confusing flashback-within-a-flashback style that takes a while to be understood. Once that is cleared the direction still ranks as fairly poor, never really focusing on connecting themes. The cast goes through the motions but without much success. The photography by Ingmar Bergman's photographer Nykvist is only average. (In English.)

p, Signe Hasso; d, Michael Road; w, Bob Condon (based on "La Grande Breteche" by Honore de Balzac and "The Old Maid" by Guy de Maupassant; ph, Sven Nykvist.

Drama **(PR:O MPAA:NR)**

TRUE AS A TURTLE*½ (1957, Brit.) 96m RANK c

John Gregson (*Tony Hudson*), June Thorburn (*Jane Hudson*), Cecil Parker (*Dudley*), Keith Michell (*Harry Bell*), Elvi Hale (*Anne*), Avice Landone (*Valerie*), Jacques Brunius (*Charbonnier*), Gabrielle Brune (*Mary*), Charles Clay (*Sir Harold Brazier*), Betty Stockfield (*Lady Brazier*), Michael Briant (*Paul*), Pauline Drewett (*Susan*), John Harvey (*1st Officer*), Beth Rogan.

Though his new bride Thorburn is against the idea, Gregson talks her into spending their honeymoon aboard the yacht "Turtle." They encounter all sorts of trouble aboard the creaky ship like a flooded engine room and getting caught in fog. For some excitement an insurance man is mistaken by the pair to be a crook. That's all there is to this weak comedy, directed with some heart though there's really not much to work with. Thorburn and Gregson are okay considering what's going on.

p, Peter de Sarigny; d, Wendy Toye; w, John Coates, Jack Davies, Nicholas Phipps (based on a novel by Coates); ph, Reginald Wyer (Eastmancolor); m, Robert Farnon; ed, Manuel del Campo.

Comedy **(PR:A MPAA:NR)**

TRUE CONFESSION*** (1937) 85m PAR bw

Carole Lombard (*Helen Bartlett*), Fred MacMurray (*Kenneth Bartlett*), John Barrymore (*Charley*), Una Merkel (*Daisy McClure*), Porter Hall (*Prosecutor*), Edgar Kennedy (*Darsey*), Lynne Overman (*Bartender*), Fritz Feld (*Krayler's Butler*), Richard Carle (*Judge*), John Murray (*Otto Krayler*), Tom Dugan (*Typewriter Man*), Garry Owen (*Tony Krauch*), Toby Wing (*Suzanne Baggart*), Hattie McDaniel (*Ella*), Bernard Suss (*Pedestrian*), Pat West, Herbert Ashley, Dudley Clements, Walter Soderling, Jim Toney, Gertrude Simpson, Chester Clute, Irving White, George Ovey, Elmer Jerome, Peggy Meon, Jame Loonfboeurrow, George B. French, Anne Cornwall (*Jurors*), Harry Fleischman, Jack Isley (*Policemen*), Bradley Metcalfe, Wesley Giraud, Billy O'Brien, Carmencita Johnson, Rosita Butler, Beaudine Anderson, Seesel Anne Johnson (*Autograph Hunters*), Charlotte Dabney (*Newspaper Sketch Artist*), Wally Maner (*Assistant Prosecutor*), Clarence Sherwood, Marty Faust (*Door Attendants*), Don Roberts (*Court Attendant*), Nick Copeland, Monte Vandergrift (*Guards*).

Carole Lombard's final film for Paramount on her contract was a charming screwball comedy that was entertaining, if lightweight. Lombard is married to MacMurray, an honest attorney (rare!) who won't accept a client unless he knows full well that his charge is innocent. That kind of morality has stood him in bad stead and he's not doing well. To help financial matters, Lombard secures employment as the personal assistant to Murray, a rich and amorous man. Murray finds Lombard attractive and makes a pass, which she responds to by a sharp punch. He fires her and is later found murdered. Since Lombard was the last person to be seen with him and since they had a physical fracas, she is accused of doing him in. The evidence is so strong against her that MacMurray defends her with a justifiable homicide plea on the basis that she was protecting herself against his wolfishness. There's a trial that brings the press flocking to the courtroom, and MacMurray's tactics win the jury over and Lombard is declared innocent. Since the case is so well documented, MacMurray's phone rings off the hook with other clients seeking his counsel. As the picture continues, we soon learn that Lombard is an inveterate liar. Barrymore, a drunken sot, comes to Lombard and says that he knows the truth of Murray's demise and he will tell MacMurray what really happened unless she forks over some cash. MacMurray is outside the door and hears Barrymore's demands and pushes Barrymore into telling the truth. Lombard didn't murder Murray at all (something she implied she had done). Rather, Murray was slain by Barrymore's former brother-in-law, a man who has since perished in an automobile accident. Barrymore leaves when he realizes that there is no reason for anyone to pay him any money because, after all, Lombard was tried and declared not guilty already for a crime she did not commit. But idealistic MacMurray is livid that his own wife lied to him and said she was guilty when she was, in fact, innocent. Since the innocence or guilt of his clients is all that matters to him, MacMurray feels that she has betrayed him and now gets ready to say goodbye to her. To forestall that, Lombard pulls another lie out of her quiver and tells her husband that she is expecting a child. MacMurray wonders if she can tell the truth about anything at all. But love prevails, and even though MacMurray eventually learns that he is not about to become a father, he forgives Lombard and takes her back to his bosom. By making Lombard an unmotivated liar, the underpinning of the story is harmed, but there is so much fun to be found that audiences seemed to overlook that flaw. Edgar Kennedy, who had spent most of his career acting and sometimes directing shorts, gets a good chance to show his wares as a dogged cop. One of the biggest laughs in the movie comes when Hattie McDaniel enters, humming the familiar "Frankie and Johnny," and casually asks MacMurray if he could handle a murder case for her. Although Barrymore was billed third, he doesn't have much to do, but what he does do is hysterical in the role of the tippling criminologist who upsets the domestic apple cart. Usually, a courtroom scene is a culminating section of a movie. Here, it came early and the fireworks between MacMurray and prosecutor Hall are funny and sometimes border on broad. MacMurray and Lombard were appearing together for the fourth time. They would make only seven more films before her tragic death in 1942 in a plane crash. This was remade with Betty Hutton under the title CROSS MY HEART.

p, Albert Lewin; d, Wesley Ruggles; w, Claude Binyon (based on the play "Mon Crime" by Louis Verneuil, Georges Berr); ph, Ted Tetzlaff; m, Frederick Hollander; ed, Paul Weatherwax; md, Boris Morros; art d, Hans Dreier, Robert Usher; set d, A.E. Freudeman; cos, Travis Banton; m/l, "True Confession," Hollander, Sam Coslow.

Comedy **(PR:A MPAA:NR)**

TRUE CONFESSIONS**** (1981) 108m UA c

Robert DeNiro (*Des Spellacy*), Robert Duvall (*Tom Spellacy*), Charles Durning (*Jack Amsterdam*), Ed Flanders (*Dan T. Champion*), Burgess Meredith (*Seamus Fargo*), Rose Gregorio (*Brenda Samuels*), Cyril Cusack (*Cardinal Danaher*), Kenneth McMillan (*Frank Crotty*), Dan Hedeya (*Howard Terkel*), Gwen Van Dam (*Mrs. Fazenda*), Tom Hill (*Mr. Fazenda*), Jeanette Nolan (*Mrs. Spellacy*), Jorge Cervera, Jr. (*Eduardo Duarte*), Susan Myers (*Bride*), Louisa Moritz (*Whore*), Darwyn Carson (*Lorna Keane*), Pat Corley (*Sonny McDonough*), Matthew Faison (*2nd Reporter*), Richard Foronjy (*Ambulance Driver*), Joe Medalis (*Deputy Coroner*), James Hong (*Coroner Wong*), Ron Ryan, Louis Basile, Paul Valentine (*Detectives*), Louise Fitch (*Older Nun*), Margery Nelson (*2nd Nun*), Frederic Cook (*Brenda's*

Trick), Kirk Brennan *(Acolyte)*, Fred Dennis *(Man)*, Shelly Batt *(Girl)*, Mary Munday *(Nun)*, Colin Hamilton *(Headwaiter)*, Amanda Cleveland *(Lois)*, Pierrino Mascarino *(Suspect)*, Michael Callahan *(Sub-Deacon)*, Harry Pavelis *(Cardinal's Attendant)*, Luisa Leschin *(Towel Girl)*, Bob Arthur, Bill Furnell *(Newscasters)*, Sig Frohlich *(Waiter)*, Steve Arvin *(Radio Announcer)*, Steve Powers *(Photographer)*, Joseph H. Choi *(Pathologist)*, Sharon Miller *(Movie Star)*, Kevin Breslin *(Boy)*, Jeff Howard *(2nd Priest)*, Harry Duncan *(Priest at Banquet)*.

Horribly underrated at the time of release, TRUE CONFESSIONS is a fascinating film that exposes the dark underbelly of the Catholic church and fixes it firmly in the seedy, corrupt, and helpless world of *film noir*. The first, and thus far only, on-screen teaming of two of America's greatest actors, DeNiro and Duvall (they appeared in GODFATHER II, but never in the same scene), opens in the year 1960 as a gray-haired Duvall goes out to the desert to visit his brother, DeNiro, a priest at a tiny run-down church. DeNiro informs his brother that he (De Niro) is going to die from a terminal heart disease and the news jars memories for Duvall, taking him back to 1948 when he was a homicide detective for the Los Angeles Police Department. Duvall and his partner McMillan arrive at a sleazy whorehouse to investigate a death. The victim had a heart attack while entertaining himself with a black prostitute. The call is routine except for one thing, the dead man was a prominent Catholic priest. The action then shifts to a wedding ceremony performed by DeNiro, a young monsignor. The bride (who is pregnant) is the daughter of Durning, a former pimp and small-time hood clawing desperately for respectability by making huge donations to the Catholic church. His friend and aide Flanders acts as a go-between with DeNiro and they cut shady deals with Durning's construction company for new churches and schools (DeNiro has even gotten Durning an audience with the Pope). Duvall visits DeNiro at his parish and quietly informs him of the dead priest in the whorehouse. DeNiro thanks his brother for his discretion. Later that day, the remains of a grisly murder are found in an empty lot–the naked body of a young girl who has been cut in two and drained of blood (the case is loosely based on the infamous "Black Dahlia" killing). She is identified as a would-be actress who had drifited into prostitution. While Duvall and McMillan investigate the killing, DeNiro becomes further involved with Durning's, land deals and questionable construction jobs at the urging of cardinal Cusack, who rules his archdiocese with an iron hand and an eye toward the cash box. When an old priest, Meredith, begins to balk at the new, distinctly mercenary turn the church has taken, Cusack hints to DeNiro that the old man's days are numbered. Meanwhile, Duvall tries to warn his brother to steer clear of Durning and he even admits that he was once Durning's bag man during his early days on the force when the fat man was still running whores. McMillan turns up a stag film starring the dismembered girl (a contact at Warner Bros. told him she was an Arab extra in CASABLANCA) and both he and Duvall are surprised to see the black prostitute who was with the priest when he died also in the film. Duvall returns to the whorehouse where the madam, Gregorio, who was also involved with Durning when Duvall was, informs him that she has fired the girl; however, she provides him with the name of the porno producer, "Standard." Upon investigation, the detectives learn that Standard was killed in a car wreck only a few days earlier. Meanwhile, DeNiro, who is beginning to have deep guilt feelings over his dealings with Durning, confesses to Meredith his confusion over the amount of power he has over the church. Fueled by Meredith's affirmation of the fundamentals of faith, DeNiro tells Flanders that the church's association with Durning has ended and that he'll be named "Catholic Layman of the Year" before he is sent off. Cusack agrees with the decision, but also tells DeNiro to fire Meredith who has finally gone too far by telling the cardinal that he is: "less like a priest and more like the employee of a construction company." Meredith is shipped out to a small parish in the desert. DeNiro dislikes the assignment, but is persuaded when Cusack says that he's recommended him for bishop. Meanwhile, Duvall discovers Durning's phone number among the murdered girl's possessions and he sets out to destroy him. Duvall shows up at the height of hypocrisy, Durning's "Catholic Layman of the Year" dinner. "You gotta be a rich pimp to get a sash like that," Duvall comments when Durning is presented with a green sash proclaiming his honor. Duvall confronts Durning in front of many prominent guests and insults him by connecting him sexually with the dead girl. A fight breaks out between the men and both have to be restrained from beating each other. The next day Flanders visits DeNiro in church and reminds the monsignor that they had both met the dead girl a few months before her demise. Flanders insinuates that if Duvall gets too close to Durning, they'll drag him down, too. Eventually Duvall finds the location where the stag film was shot and there is a blood-soaked mattress and bloody footprints leading to the blood-splattered bathtub where the dismemberment was performed. The facts prove that the dead porno filmmaker committed the murder, and Duvall knows it, but the facts do not stop him from trying to implicate Durning in the killing–no matter how unjustified. Feeling the heat from Duvall, Durning has a talk with DeNiro in a confessional and demands that he call his brother off. DeNiro declines, saying that he's just Durning's confessor. Enraged, Durning practically screams: "You're my confessor in here, but you wheel and deal out there! Is that it? Who absolves you? I met the Pope for Christsake! You understand? You hypocrite!" Durning warns DeNiro that if he's ruined by scandal he'll make good on his threat. DeNiro says nothing and Durning leaves. Duvall then enters the confessional and informs his brother that he's about to arrest Durning: "What are you doing giving absolution to that mick pimp? He passed her around like a piece of Christmas candy while you were out playing golf! Catholic Layman of the Year...highest honors bestowed..." DeNiro responds: "Did he do it?" Caught in his obsession, Duvall shouts back, "I don't care! And I don't care whether you go down with him or not!" Filled with guilt and resigned to his fate, DeNiro quietly states, "Either do I." The ensuing scandal becomes a media circus with DeNiro shipped out to the desert parish and Duvall losing respect on the force. Everyone loses. Once again in 1960, Duvall apologizes to his brother for the way their lives have turned out. "No, you were my salvation." TRUE CONFESSIONS paints a distressingly bleak view of society that is truly in the realm of the best *film noir* classics. Adapted by the husband and wife team of Dunne and Didion from Dunne's fine novel, all of the characters in TRUE CONFESSIONS are corrupt to the core and diseased (literally–many of them have terminal physical ailments). While filmgoers are quite used to stories showing corruption in the police department, portrayal of the Catholic church as a cynical, hypocritical, capitalistic, and morally bankrupt entity are almost unheard of in American films. The film takes some big chances in its depiction of the Catholic church and it's a wonder that massive protests weren't staged outside theaters where the film was shown (as happened with Jean- Luc Godard's HAIL MARY in 1985). Cusack, the cardinal, is shown as a man building a private empire with little regard for morality. The ends seem to justify the means in his mind, and as long as the unsavory Durning stears clear of scandal, the church willingly honors him in return for construction favors. Instead of saving souls and comforting the sick, the church has become a upwardly mobile corporation and DeNiro is the fixer. Cusack's Christianity has become so jaded that when he and DeNiro attend a Mexican street festival Cusack says he feels like a fool when wearing the ceremonial sombrero given to him by the parishioners. DeNiro's salvation comes from his brother, the cop. Duvall knows the score and has been living with the contradictions within his profession for years. He has faced the dark side and knows how to handle it, DeNiro has submerged himself in the same seedy milieu, but with the church's arms around him he can't see the forest for the trees until it is too late. While DeNiro is out playing golf, hosting testimonial dinners, and saying mass for Durning–a former pimp–Duvall moves through the run-down brothels, bars, and porno studios that the fat man has left behind him like slime from a snail. The brothers are miles apart emotionally and spiritually but when Duvall decides to damn the consequences and nail Durning, the act finally brings DeNiro out of his pious cocoon. TRUE CONFESSIONS has the look and feel of a *film noir* of the 1940s. The period detail is letter perfect and the cast is as close to a Hollywood studio system stable of superior performers as you can get in the 1980s. Not enough can be said about the acting abilities of DeNiro and Duvall (this was DeNiro's first film since RAGING BULL and nary a trace of the weight he had gained to play Jake LaMotta is evident). The supporting actors are superb, with Meredith, Cusack, Durning, and especially McMillan being standouts. The musical score by Delerue is haunting, evocative, and simply one of the best soundtracks of the decade. TRUE CONFESSIONS is a quiet, thoughtful, sudued, but ultimately deeply disturbing film and its frank, unblinking portrayal of sex, crime, corruption, and murder makes it for adults only.

p, Irwin Winkler, Robert Chartoff; d, Ulu Grosbard; w, John Gregory Dunne, Joan Didion (based on the novel by Dunne); ph, Owen Roisman (Technicolor); m, Georges Delerue; ed, Lynzee Klingman; prod d, Stephen S. Grimes; art d, W. Stewart Campbell; set d, Marvin March; cos, Joe I. Tompkins; ch, Alfonse L. Palermo.

Crime **Cas.** **(PR:O MPAA:R)**

TRUE DIARY OF A WAHINE (SEE: MAEVA, 1961)

TRUE GRIT***** (1969) 128m PAR c

John Wayne *(Reuben J. "Rooster" Cogburn)*, Glen Campbell *(La Boeuf)*, Kim Darby *(Mattie Ross)*, Jeremy Slate *(Emmett Quincy)*, Robert Duvall *(Ned Pepper)*, Dennis Hopper *(Moon)*, Alfred Ryder *(Goudy)*, Strother Martin *(Col. G. Stonehill)*, Jeff Corey *(Tom Chaney)*, Ron Soble *(Capt. Boots Finch)*, John Fiedler *(Lawyer J. Noble Daggett)*, James Westerfield *(Judge Parker)*, John Doucette *(Sheriff)*, Donald Woods *(Barlow)*, Edith Atwater *(Mrs. Floyd)*, Carlos Rivas *(Dirty Bob)*, Isabel Boniface *(Mrs. Bagby)*, H.W. Gim *(Chen Lee)*, John Pickard *(Frank Ross)*, Elizabeth Harrower *(Mrs. Ross)*, Ken Renard *(Yarnell)*, Jay Ripley *(Harold Parmalee)*, Kenneth Becker *(Farrell Parmalee)*, Myron Healey *(A Deputy)*, Hank Worden *(Undertaker)*, Guy Wilkerson *(The Hangman)*, Red Morgan *(Red the Ferryman)*, Robin Morse.

TRUE GRIT is a rollicking western, an enormously entertaining adventure that is as much about the John Wayne image as it is about a girl seeking revenge for her father's murder. Darby is a level-headed 14-year-old girl who goes to Wayne after her father, Pickard, has been killed by his hired man, Corey. Corey has now fled into Indian territory and Darby wants a man of "true grit" to help find the killer and bring him to justice. Wayne, a potbellied U.S. Marshal with a patch over one eye, admires Darby's spunk, and agrees to take on the job. Joining them is Campbell, a Texas Ranger whom Darby despises. He, too, is searching for Corey, hoping to collect a reward the family of a murdered Texas politician has placed on Corey's head. Campbell is reluctant to take Darby into Indian territory. He and Wayne try to evade Darby, but she quickly catches up with them. When the party stops off for a meal, Wayne learns that Corey has joined up with Duvall, an old nemesis of the marshal's. The trio finds Duvall's hideout, then smokes out Slate and Hopper, two gang members holed up in the shack. After handcuffing the men together, Wayne begins questioning them about Duvall's whereabouts. Slate stabs Hopper with a knife, and Wayne responds by shooting him. He then pumps the dying Hopper for information, and learns that Duvall is to return to the hideout in the morning. Wayne, warning Campbell not to fire unless it's absolutely necessary, takes Darby and hides out in the rocky hills above the shack. He and Darby talk awhile, and Wayne reveals some of his unhappy past life to the girl. Later Duvall rides in with some henchmen. Campbell begins shooting from his lookout, forcing Wayne to fire at the group as well. Some of the gang members are killed, but Duvall manages to escape. Wayne, Campbell, and Darby begin trailing the outlaw. Darby goes to a river to wash up, and is surprised there by Corey. Corey is just as surprised to see the girl, and begins taunting her. Taking her father's pistol, Darby shoots Corey, breaking his ribs. Wayne and Campbell hear the shot but before they can get to Darby, Duvall finds the girl. He grabs her, then shouts to Wayne that Darby is a hostage. Wayne and Campbell agree to retreat, and Duvall takes Darby back to his camp. He leaves her there with Corey, then rides off with his gang members. Crossing a meadow, Duvall is shocked to see Wayne sitting tall in the saddle, waiting for the badman. Wayne challenges the four men facing him, telling them they can die now or face the hangman later. "Bold talk for a one-eyed fatman," says Duvall. Wayne, repeating rifle in one hand, six-gun in the other, shouts back, "Fill your hand, you son-of-a-bitch!" then, taking his horse's reins in his teeth, charges across the meadow firing left and right at the badmen. Duvall is the only survivor, though he is badly wounded. Wayne's horse is shot, and the marshal is pinned beneath the animal. Duvall slowly rides in to kill Wayne, but Campbell, who has been watching it all from a hideaway, fires a single shot, killing the outlaw. Wayne and Campbell then go to Duvall's camp to rescue Darby. Campbell arrives first, but he is attacked by Corey. Darby fires her pistol, wounding Corey, but the force of the shot causes her to fall backwards into a pit full of deadly rattlesnakes. She screams for help, and Wayne rides in to save her. He lowers himself into the pit with a rope, then the dying Campbell pulls Wayne and Darby out. Campbell finally collapses but there is no time to help him. Darby's arm is broken and she has been bitten by a snake. Wayne rushes her to a doctor, killing one horse with the furious pace before he steals a wagon to finish the journey. The story jumps to a few months later. Wayne is at Darby's home, standing with the girl by her father's snow-covered grave. She tells Wayne there is a spot for him in the small plot, but Wayne insists he is not ready to die. He jumps his horse over a fence and shouts to Darby, "Come and see an old fat man some time!" As "Rooster" Cogburn, Wayne pokes fun of himself, yet maintains a reverence towards his screen image. The character is fat, drunk, and not entirely honest, but Wayne plays it with an underlying sense of honor, the "true grit" that Darby demands. Though his performances in STAGECOACH and THE SEARCHERS are more complex, TRUE GRIT provides Wayne with some of his most memorable moments. Wayne later said that the sequence where he tells Darby about his past "...is about the best scene I ever did." His two-gun face off with Duvall and his gang is a classic, the quintessential heroic Wayne image. Wayne gave the credit for this unforgettable sequence to his director, Henry Hathaway, saying: "That's Henry at work...it looks almost dreamlike. Henry made it a fantasy and yet he kept it an honest Western." Hathaway's direction is robust, keeping the sprawling action under tight control, with some beautiful shots of the Colorado locations. Roberts adapted the script from Portis' fine novel, using many of its scenes and keeping whole sections of dialog intact. The final scene between Wayne and Darby at the cemetery was Roberts' own creation, a fine piece of work that gives Wayne and Darby one of their best scenes together. Darby was 21 years old when this was made, but she effectively plays a girl seven years younger. Her mature and level-headed demeanor is an excellent counterpart to Wayne's rogue, and the pair make a highly entertaining combination. Campbell, the 1960s pop music star making a much ballyhooed screen debut, is likable as the Texas Ranger, though his performance did not justify the five-film contract producer Wallis gave him. Duvall is an effective villain, memorable in this early role. In a sense, Duvall, along with Hopper, represented the new generation of actors in Hollywood, while Wayne and Hathaway were warhorses from the old studio star system. It made TRUE GRIT a sort of transitional picture in movie history, and the set was not without its problems when the widely different attitudes towards acting and directing met head on. Duvall, who had learned his craft on New York stages, watched one day as Hathaway berated a meek Campbell for some acting indiscretion. Duvall was angered by this, and when Hathaway instructed him on what to do before the camera, the actor responded with an angry tirade. Eventually a compromise was reached, and shooting continued. Portis had written his original novel with Wayne in mind, sending the actor the unpublished galleys in hopes of getting it on the screen. Wayne immediately fell in love with the project, and offered $300,000 for the film rights. Wayne hoped to direct TRUE GRIT as well, but this fell through when Paramount ultimately bought the novel for $500,000. Hathaway came on as director, but Wayne was pacified with a $1 million salary and 35 percent of the gross. TRUE GRIT was an immediate hit, taking in $15 million at the box office and became one of the highest grossing westerns of all time. Wayne won an Oscar for his performance, beating out Dustin Hoffman and Jon Voight for MIDNIGHT COWBOY, Richard Burton for ANNE OF THE THOUSAND DAYS, and Peter O'Toole in GOODBYE, MR. CHIPS. Some arguments were raised that the Duke was being honored more for his career than this specific performance, but Wayne—who later said he hadn't given such heart to a role since STAGE-

COACH—was humbled by the award. After his name was announced as winner, Wayne told the audience: "If I'd a known that, I'd a put on a patch 35 years earlier." Wayne would reprise the role in the 1975 film ROOSTER COGBURN, costarring with Katharine Hepburn, and TRUE GRIT was redone as a made-for-television film in 1978, with Warren Oates in the lead role, but neither project approached this film in either quality or spirit.

p, Hal B. Wallis; d, Henry Hathaway; w, Marguerite Roberts (based on the novel by Charles Portis); ph, Lucien Ballard (Technicolor); m, Elmer Bernstein; ed, Warren Low; prod d, Walter Tyler; set d, Ray Moyer, John Burton; cos, Dorothy Jeakins; spec eff, Dick Johnson; m/l, "True Grit," Bernstein, Don Black, sung by Glen Campbell, "Amazing Grace," John Newton, "Wildwood Flower"; makeup, Jack Wilson, Carol Meikle.

Western   Cas.   (PR:A   MPAA:G)

TRUE STORY OF A WAHINE   (SEE: MAEVA, 1961)

TRUE STORY OF ESKIMO NELL, THE*   (1975, Aus.) 103m
                                                  Quest/Filmways c

Max Gillies (Dead-Eye-Dick), Serge Lazareff (Mexico Pete), Abigail (Esmeralda), Grahame Bond (Bogger), Paddy Madden Victoria Anoux (Eskimo Nell), Elli Maclure (Elly), Kris McQuade, Elke Neidhart, Tony Bazell, Bob Horsfall, Wayne Levy, Paul Jansen, Max Fairchild, Frank Hanilton, Ken Webb, Ernie Bourne, John Bennet, Kurt Beimel, David Byrne, Jerry Thomas, Luigi Villani, Fred Van der Linde.

A wonderful offbeat comedy from Australia features Gillies as a peeping Tom with the moniker "Dead-Eye-Dick." He's looking in on a Mexican woman who's married to a passionately jealous man and ends up rescuing Lazareff, a rogue who has been carrying on with the woman. The two form an odd friendship as Lazareff tries to help the shy Gillies with his lady problems. Gillies Claims he's saving himself for "Eskimo Nell" of Alaska. The pair go off to meet her and run into a few adventures along the way. The picture is great fun thanks to the wonderfully weird chemistry between the two leads. Though the script tends to wander the pair keep it anchored with their surprisingly sensitive and very funny performances. The direction is smooth, showing a good ability to handle off-the-wall material with ease. The photography makes fine use of Australian and Canadian locations.

p, Richard Franklin, Ronald Banneth; d, Franklin; w, Franklin, Alan Hopgood; ph, Vincent Monton; m, Brian May.

Comedy   (PR:O   MPAA:NR)

TRUE STORY OF JESSE JAMES, THE*
                            (1957) 92m FOX c (GB: JAMES BROTHERS, THE)

Robert Wagner (Jesse James), Jeffrey Hunter (Frank James), Hope Lange (Zee), Agnes Moorehead (Mrs. Samuel), Alan Hale, Jr (Cole Younger), Alan Baxter (Remington), John Carradine (Rev. Jethro Bailey), Rachel Stephens (Anne), Barney Phillips (Dr. Samuel), Biff Elliot (Jim Younger), Frank Overton (Maj. Cobb), Chubby Johnson (Askew), Frank Gorshin (Charley), Carl Thayler (Robby), John Doucette (Hillstrom), Robert Adler (Sheriff Trump), Clancy Cooper (Sheriff Yoe), Sumner Williams (Bill Stiles), Tom Greenway (Deputy Leo), Mike Steen (Deputy Ed), Jason Wingreen (Peter), Aaron Saxon (Wiley), Anthony Ray (Bob Younger), Clegg Hoyt (Tucker), Tom Pittman (Hughie), Louis Zito (Clell Miller), Mark Hickman (Sam Wells), Adam Marshal (Dick Liddell), Joseph Di Reda (Bill Ryan), J. Frederik Albeck (Jorgenson), Kellogg Junge, Jr (Archie at age 4), Barry Atwater (Attorney Walker), Marian Seldes (Rowina Cobb).

This remake of the 1939 JESSE JAMES takes a similar story but changes the emphasis and themes, becoming a work that clearly belongs to its director Ray. Wagner is the notorious outlaw who turns to crime with brother Hunter when their post-Civil War South crumbles. First the two are shot at by Union forces despite a white flag of surrender. The brothers are further embittered by how easily their former Confederate neighbors become accustomed to the Union men who settle into their town to rebuild. Because of their steadfast southern sympathies, the James boys are denied work and finally take to robbery just to get money. The two find the criminal life exhilarating and become addicted to the danger and excitement that bank and train robbery brings. Gradually this excitement wears and they feel encumbered as it dawns on them there's no leaving the outlaw life. Wagner meets his doom when a young detective from the Remington Agency kills the outlaw for a $25,000 reward. Ray's pacing builds some good excitement, and as a western alone the film works nicely. But there are deeper things going on, some not entirely successfully worked out, though it's still strong stuff. The feeling of rebellion and impending doom isn't quite as heady as in Ray's classic REBEL WITHOUT A CAUSE but on a lesser intellectual plane these themes are present throughout the story. Some footage from the 1939 film is incorporated into Ray's artistic presentation with good effect.

p, Herbert B. Swope, Jr.; d, Nicholas Ray; w, Walter Newman (based on a screenplay by Nunnally Johnson); ph, Joe MacDonald (CinimaScope, DeLuxe Color); m, Leigh Harline; ed, Robert Simpson; md, Lionel Newman; art d, Lyle R. Wheeler, Addison Hehr; set d, Walter M. Scott, Stuart A. Reiss; cos, Mary Wills.

Western   (PR:A MPAA:NR)

TRUE STORY OF LYNN STUART, THE***   (1958) 78m COL bw

Betsy Palmer (*Phyllis Carter*), Jack Lord (*Willie Down*), Barry Atwater (*Hagan*), Kim Spalding (*Ralph Carter*), Karl Lukas (*Hal Bruck*), Casey Walters (*Eddie Dine*), Harry Jackson (*Husband Officer*), Claudia Bryar (*Nora Efron*), John Anderson ("*Doc*"), Rita Duncan (*Sue*), Lee Farr (*Ben*), Louis Towers (*Jimmy Carter*).

After her nephew is killed in a drug-hazed car crash, Palmer, A Santa Ana housewife, goes to the Orange County police and volunteers to assist in breaking a major drug ring. Atwater, the chief investigator, accepts the offer and soon Palmer infiltrates the dope dealers by becoming Lord's girl friend. She goes with him to Tijuana where they are both arrested and the ring smashed. In an emotional climax, Palmer goes to jail and testifies before a Grand Jury in order to protect her secret identity from mobsters who would kill her if they knew the truth. Based on a series of newspaper articles about a similar case, this is told in a realistic documentary style. Though at points this gets chatty, the story is told with gritty honesty and there are some fine performances. The film hinges on Palmer–had a lesser actress taken the role this would be just another crime story. Her performance here lifts the film and is complemented by sensitive direction that works in tandem with the heroine.

p, Bryan Foy; d, Lewis Seiler; w, John H. Kneubuhl (based on newspaper articles by Pat Michaels); ph, Burnett Guffey: m, Mischa Bakaleinikoff; ed, Saul A. Goodkind; md, Bakaleinikoff; art d, Ross Bellah.

Crime   (PR:A MPAA:NR)

TRUE TO LIFE***½**   (1943) 94m PAR bw

Mary Martin (*Bonnie Porter*), Franchot Tone (*Fletcher Marvin*), Dick Powell (*Link Ferris*), Victor Moore (*Pop Porter*), Mabel Paige (*Mom Porter*), William Demarest (*Jake*), Clarence Kolb (*Mr. Huggins*), Beverly Hudson (*Twips*), Raymond Roe (*Clem*), Ernest Truex (*Oscar Elkins*), Harry Shannon (*Mr. Mason*), Charles Moore (*Gabe the Butler*), Tim Ryan (*Mr. Mammal*), Ken Carpenter (*Announcer*), Nestor Paiva (*Kapopolis*), Betty Farrington (*Mrs. Barkow*), Charles Cane (*Expressman*), J. Farrell MacDonald, Vernon Dent, Fred Santley (*Men*), Grace Hayle, Esther Howard, Ethel Clayton, Gloria Williams (*Women*), Fred A. Kelsey (*Cop*), Stanley Andrews (*Frank*), Foreman of the Bakery, John Hiestand (*Narrator*), Harry Tyler (*Program Director*), Harry Hayden (*Radio Pop*), Ann Doran (*Radio Kitty*), Madora Keene (*Radio Mom*), Shirley Mills (*Radio Sister*), Bill Bletcher (*Radio Heavy*), Bud Jamison (*Radio Jake*), Robert Winkler (*Radio Sonny*), Jack Gardner (*Radio Man*), Christopher King, Maxine Ardell, Yvonne De Carlo, Alice Kirby, Marcella Phillips, Marjorie Deanne, Dorothy Granger (*Girls*), Jack Baxley, Frank Coleman, Edna Bennett (*People on Bus*), Don Kerr (*Guide on Bus*), Dan Borzage (*Beggar*), Matt McHugh (*Taxicab Driver*), Walter Soderling (*Man in Subway*), Constance Purdy (*Woman in Subway*), Edward S. Chandler (*Subway Guard*), Tom Kennedy (*Customer*), Terry Moore (*Little Girl*), Paul Newlan.

A rollicking comedy with a plot that would work today with a bit of a switch. Powell and Tone are scriptwriters of high-priced radio soap operas who have run out of ideas and their show "Kitty Farmer" is in danger of being canceled. Since both men are bachelors, they have no idea what family life is really about and they need to find some new ideas or lose their jobs, which pay each about $50,000 per annum. They encounter waitress Martin and later visit her home, where they are astonished to meet as screwball a family as Hartman and Tugend could have ever dreamed up. Martin's father is eccentric Moore, an inventor of silly items and a part-time air-raid warden who reaches for his helmet every time he hears any kind of siren. Moore's wife is Paige, who is the sanest of the brood but still a few bricks shy of a load. Paige's brother is the indolent Demarest, who has not worked for years and has a running battle of silence with Moore. The scenes cut between the Moore house and the radio show as Tone and Powell take down what's being said in the Moore household, type it up, and put it right on the air where a bevy of radio actors repeat the words. The ratings begin to soar, much to the delight of sponsor Kolb and his two yes-men assistants, Truex and Shannon. Tone is a bit of a roue and would like to get Martin. At the same time, Powell is trying to keep the Moore family away from the radio so they don't hear the popular soap opera and realize that it's their story. Good satire of how they did radio shows in those days and sparkling performances from all concerned. Every role, no matter how small, was well cast and directed by Marshall. Since Powell and Martin were both well-known singers, audiences may have expected a full musical with those stars topping the bill. Instead, they received a comedy with just a few tunes by Johnny Mercer and Hoagy Carmichael. "Mr. Bluebird" was sung by Martin, while Powell did "There She Was" and "The Old Music Master." Also included were "Mister Pollyanna" and "Sudsy Suds Theme Song," sung by Carmichael. In a bit part, note Yvonne De Carlo, age 21, and already in her twelvth movie. If the family of eccentrics feels a bit familiar, they were the staple of many plays and films of the 1930s and 1940s, most notably "You Can't Take It with You" and, perhaps,"The Man Who Came to Dinner." This is one of those pictures that might be a fine remake or even the basis for a musical as the characters are so well drawn and the situations so finely delineated that they could be compressed somewhat and leave plenty of space for a full musical score. Mary Martin, who seldom registered as well

on screen as she did on stage, does one of her best roles in this and handles the comedy with deftness.

p, Paul Jones; d, George Marshall; w, Don Hartman, Harry Tugend (based on a story by Ben Barzman, Bess Taffel, Sol Barzman); ph, Charles Lang; m, Victor Young; ed, LeRoy Stone; md, Young; art d, Hans Dreier, Earl Hedrick; set d, George Sawley.

Comedy   (PR:A MPAA:NR)

TRUE TO THE ARMY***   (1942) 76m PAR bw

Judy Canova (*Daisy Hawkins*), Allan Jones (*Pvt. Bill Chandler*), Ann Miller (*Vicki Marlow*), Jerry Colonna (*Pvt. J. Wethersby "Pinky" Fothergill*), Clarence Kolb (*Col. Marlow*), Edward Pawley (*Junior*), William Wright (*Lt. Danvers*), William Demarest (*Sgt. Butes*), Edwin Miller (*Ice*), Arthur Loft (*Ray*), Gordon Jones (*Pvt. Dugan*), Rod Cameron (*Pvt. O'Toole*), Eddie Acuff (*Sgt. Riggs*), Edgar Dearing (*Target Sergeant*), Mary Treen (*Mae*), Selmer Jackson (*Congressman*), Harry Barris (*Piano Player*), Frank Sully (*Mugg*), Joseph Crehan (*Police Chief*), George Turner (*Military Policeman*), Dorothy Sebastian (*Gloria*), Donald Kerr (*Soldier*), John Miljan (*Drake*), Ralph Dunn (*Officer*), Stanley Blystone (*Police Officer*), Syd Saylor (*Private*).

Canova is a high wire circus performer who wants to be closer to Colonna, her boy friend in the Army. She's being chased by gangsters which is all the excuse she needs to don men's garb and join the armed forces. From there the comedy is entirely predictable with all jokes hinged on when her ruse will be discovered. At the end the camp puts on a show where the gangsters finally catch up with Canova but fortunately the cops arrive and the film ends. Despite the obvious handling of the idea, this is a smooth presentation that generates a few laughs. Despite the weaknesses Canova gives it her best. Songs include: "In the Army," "Need I Speak," "Jitterbug's Lullaby," Spangles onMy Tights," "Wacky for Khaki" (Frank Loesser, Harold Spina), "Swing in Line" (Loesser, Joseph J. Lilley), "Love in Bloom" (Ralph Rainger, Leo Robin), "I Can't Give You Anything But Love" (Dorothy Fields, Jimmy McHugh).

p, Sol C. Siegel; d, Albert S. Rogell; w, Art Arthur, Bradford Ropes, Edmund Hartmann, Val Burton (based on a play by Howard Lindsay and the novel *She Loves Me Not* by Edward Hope), ph, Daniel L. Fapp; ed, Alma Macrorie; md, Victor Young; art d, Hans Dreier, William Flannery.

Comedy   (PR:AAA MPAA:NR)

TRUE TO THE NAVY*½   (1930) 71m PAR bw

Fredric March (*Gunner McCoy*), Clara Bow (*Ruby Nolan*), Harry Green (*Solomon Bimberg*), Rex Bell (*Eddie*), Eddie Fetherston (*Michael*), Eddie Dunn (*Albert*), Ray Cooke (*Peewee*), Harry Sweet (*Artie*), Adele Windsor (*Maizie*), Sam Hardy (*Grogan*), Jed Prouty (*Dancehall Manager*), Charles Sullivan (*Shore Patrol*), Louise Beavers (*The Maid*), Frances Dee (*Girl at Table*), Maurice Black (*Sharpie*).

March is a sailor in port and Bow a soda fountain attendant who flirts with the seamen who pass her way. She meets March and her eyelash-batting days are over as the two fall in love. The romance has the usual pitfalls but ultimately they end up together in a sticky-sweet happy ending. March was woefully miscast in this lighthearted comedy and although he gave a good performance he deserved far better material. Bow, on the other hand, did what she could in a role written specifically for her talents. Thanks to numerous scandals and the advent of sound, her heyday was clearly gone. She was far from her best in this picture. The direction didn't help–an uneven style with no sense of comedy. The jokes are flatly predictable and development is slow. Bow's husband Bell makes an appearance as one of the gobs she flirts with.

d, Frank Tuttle; w, Keene Thompson, Doris Anderson, Herman J. Mankiewicz; ph, Victor Milner; ed, Doris Drought; m/l, L. Wolfe Gilbert, Abel Baer.

Comedy   (PR:A MPAA:NR)

TRUMAN CAPOTE'S TRILOGY***   (1969) 100m AA c

"Miriam": Mildred Natwick (*Miss Miller*), Susan Dunfee (*Miriam*), Carol Gustafson (*Miss Lake*), Robin Ponterio (*Emily*), Beverly Ballard (*Nina*), Jane Connell (*Mrs. Connolly*), Frederick Morton (*Man in Theater*), Richard Hamilton (*Man in Automat*), Phyllis Eldridge (*Woman in Automat*), Tony Ross (*Dwarf*), Brooks Rogers (*Connolly*), Niki Flacks (*Clerk in Shop*), "Among the Paths to Eden": Maureen Stapleton (*Mary O'Meaghan*), Martin Balsam (*Ivor Belli*), "A Christmas Memory": Geraldine Page (*Woman*), Donnie Melvin (*Buddy*), Christine Marler, Lavinia Cassels (*Aunts*), Josip Elic (*Haha*), Lynn Forman (*Woman in Car*), Win Forman (*Storekeeper*), Truman Capote (*Narrator*).

This three-part film adapted by Capote from his stories was originally three different adaptations of his work created for television. However, only one of the stories, "A Christmas Memory," was broadcast; it won both an Emmy and a Peabody Award. The three tales were then re-edited into a theatrical version which saw a limited release before being made available to its intended market of high school and university classrooms. Though each clearly suffers from its shortened length, as a whole this is a strong, sensitive film strengthened by some fine performances. "Miriam" features Natwick as a nanny slowly losing her mind. "The Paths of Eden" is a beautiful story about a spinster (Stapleton) who looks for a husband amidst widowers visiting their wives' graves. Finally there is "A Christmas Memory" which Capote himself narrates. This is a sensitive drama about a young child who slowly watches a loved one lose her memory as years go by. Capote remained in complete control over his material, with fine results. Initially he had been unhappy with the editing of "Miriam" and the entire film was reworked at his insistence.

p&d, Frank Perry; w, Truman Capote, Eleanor Perry (based on the stories "Miriam," "Among the Paths of Eden," "A Christmas Memory" by Capote); ph, Joseph Brun, Harry Sundby, Conrad Hall, Jordon Cronenweth (Eastmancolor); m, Meyer Kupferman; ed, Patricia Jaffe, Ralph Rosenblum, Sheila Bakerman; prod d, Gene Callahan, Peter Dohanos; set d, Leif Pedersen; cos, Anna Hill Johnstone, Frank Thompson.

Drama   (PR:A   MPAA:G)

TRUMPET BLOWS, THE**   (1934) 72m PAR bw

George Raft (Manuel Lopez/Pancho Lopez), Adolphe Menjou (Senor Madrino), Frances Drake (Chulita), Sidney Toler (Pepi Sancho), Edward Ellis (Chato), Nydia Westman (Carmela Ramirez), Douglas Wood (Senor Ramirez), Lillian Elliot (Senora Ramirez), Katherine De Mille (Lupe the Maid), Francis McDonald (Vega), Morgan Wallace (Police Inspector), Gertrude Norman (Grandma Albrentez), Aleth "Speed" Hanson (Singing Beggar), Howard Brooks (Priest), E. Alyn Warren (Station Master), Joyce Compton (Blonde on Train), Charles Stevens (Mojias the Sheriff), Hooper L. Atchley (Detective), Al Bridge (Policeman), Mischa Auer.

Raft is a Mexican who returns home after being educated in the U.S. His older brother, Menjou, is a retired bandit, still sought by the police, who wants Raft to marry the girl he has picked out for him and take a respectable job. Raft, however, falls in love with Menjou's mistress, dancer Drake, and wants to become a bullfighter. He is too much a man of honor to take his brother's woman, but under the tutelage of Ellis does become a matador in Mexico City. There he again meets Drake and soon they are living together. Menjou learns of this domestic arrangement and refuses to speak to his brother again. Menjou's rejection weighing heavy on his mind, Raft drinks heavily and his nerve begins to go. Drake goes to Menjou and asks him to forgive his brother, and he travels to the city although he knows the police are still on the lookout for him. At the arena that afternoon, a bull is about to gore Raft when Menjou jumps into the ring, attracting the attention of the bull and the cops. He pauses briefly to give his blessing to Raft and Drake before making good his escape. One of the worst films Raft ever made, both for the sheer inanity of the plot and the ridiculous miscasting of both Raft and Menjou as Mexicans. A real matador, Jose Ortiz, who was immortalized by Ernest Hemingway, was brought out to Hollywood to coach Raft in the ways of the cape and sword, but to no avail. Raft just looks silly in the matador's "suit of lights" and little hat. Dapper Menjou is even more out of place as a Pancho Villa-type bandit. The two didn't get along well on the set and at one point Menjou punched Raft in the mouth, splitting his lip. This film finally killed Paramount's notion of building Raft into a romantic lead.

d, Stephen Roberts; w, Bartlett Cormack, Wallace Smith (based on a story by Porter Emerson Browne, J. Parker Read, Jr.); ph, Harry Fischbeck; ed, Ellsworth Hoagland.

Drama   (PR:A   MPAA:NR)

TRUNK, THE*½   (1961, Brit.) 72m Donwin/COL bw

Philip Carey (Stephen Dorning), Julia Arnall (Lisa Maitland), Dermot Walsh (Henry Maitland), Vera Day (Diane), Peter Swanwick (Nicholas Steiner), John Atkinson (Matt), Betty Le Beau (Maria), Tony Quinn (Porter), Robert Sansom (Bank Manager), Pippa Stanley (Mrs. Stanhope), Richard Nellor (Sir Hubert), Nicholas Tanner (Country Policeman).

When his ex-girl friend Arnall marries London lawyer Walsh, Carey plots revenge. He fools her into thinking he's killed her husband's former mistress Day. Arnal offers Carey a large sum of money to keep quiet and get rid of the body. However, Carey and Day are seen together by Swanwick, a rejected suitor of Day. When Carey gets his money from Arnall he puts Day into a trunk and drives to a deserted area. There to his horror he discovers that she really is dead, killed by the jealous Swanwick in a manner that will incriminate Carey. The movie is badly produced and too seamy for its own good.

p, Lawrence Huntington; d&w, Donovan Winter (based on a story by Edward Abraham, Valerie Abraham); ph, Norman Warwick; m, John Fox; ed, Reginald Beck; art d, Bill Hutchinson.

Crime   (PR:C   MPAA:NR)

TRUNK CRIME   (SEE: DESIGN FOR MURDER, 1940, Brit.)

TRUNK MYSTERY, THE   (SEE: ONE NEW YORK NIGHT, 1935)

TRUNK TO CAIRO**   (1966, Israel/Ger.) 80m Noah Films-CCC-Filmkunst/AIP c (MIVTZA KAHIR; EINER SPIELT FALSCH)

Audie Murphy (Mike Merrick), George Sanders (Professor Schlieben), Marianne Koch (Helga Schlieben), Hans von Borsody (Hans Klugg), Joseph Yadin (Capt. Gabar), Gila Almagor (Yasmin), Elana Eden (Hadassa), Eytan Priver (Jamil), Zalman (Ephraim), Bomba Zur (Ali), Tikva Mor (Christina), Zeev Berlinski (Benz), Eliezer Young (Dr. Heider), Shlomo Vichinsky (Jacob), Yoel Noyman (Egyptian Colonel), Cesar Suberi (Old Mullah), Shlomo Paz (Joe), Mona Silberstein (Hostess), Anna Shell (Belly Dancer), Suzanna Ratoni (Fraulein Bruckner), Menashe Glazier (Mahmud), Karin (Young German Girl).

In a rare departure from his usual cowboy or war hero characterizations, Murphy plays an agent who's sent to a rendezvous in Cairo with Sanders, a German scientist. He gets involved with the man's daughter Koch and learns her father is working on a nuclear-powered moon rocket that has capabilities as a weapon. Murphy sneaks past Sanders' heavily guarded headquarters and destroys the rocket's blueprints. He encounters a radical Islamic group who want to destroy the rocket themselves but won't trust anyone to do it. To escape a trap set for him Murphy kidnaps Koch as a way of getting Sanders to leave Egypt. After the couple arrives in Rome via submarine they are captured by Egyptian forces. Murphy is put in a trunk and set on a plane for Cairo but when Italian agents capture the Egyptians and try to rescue him, they discover Murphy has replaced himself with one of the guards. The supersleuth has boarded a plane where Koch is held prisoner and takes over after fighting the pilot. He returns Koch to her father and all ends happily for the characters if not for the audience. The story is so muddled it's noteven clear whether Murphy is an Israeli agent or employed by some other country.

p&d, Menahem Golan; w, Marc Behm, Alexander Ramati (story by Behm, Ramati); ph, Itzhak Herbst; m, Dov Seltzer; ed, Dani Schick; art d, Shlomo Zafrir; m/l, "Dangerous Woman," Geula Gil; makeup, Rachel Golan, Daliah Priver.

Action/Thriller   (PR:C   MPAA:NR)

TRUNKS OF MR. O.F., THE****   (1932, Ger.) 80m Tonbild-Syndikat AG/Deutsches Lichtspiel-Syndikat bw (DIE KOFFER DES HERRN O.F.; BAUEN UND HEIRATEN)

Alfred Abel (The Mayor), Peter Lorre (Stix the Reporter), Harald Paulsen (Stark, the Builder), Hedy Kiesler (Helene the Mayor's Daughter), Ludwig Stoessel (Brunn the Hotel Owner), Margo Lion (Viola Volant, Cabaret Star), Ilse Korseck (Mayor's Wife), Liska March (Eve Lune), Aribert Mog (Stark's Assistant), Gaby Karpeles (Assistant in Salon), Hadrian Maria Netto (Jean, a Hairdresser), Hertha Von Walther (Jean's Wife), Franz Weber (Dorn, a Tailor), Maria Karsten (Dorn's Wife), Fred Doderlein (Alexander the Mayor's Son), Bernhard Goetzke (Prof. Smith), Josephine Dora (Jean's Mother-in-Law), Friedrich Ettel (A Druggist), Aenne Gorling (Frau Beck, a Landlady), Meinhardt Maur (The Doctor), Ralf Ostermann (Maitre d'Hotel), Henry Pless (Bank Director), Gertrud Ober (Bank Director's Secretary), Hans Hermann Schaufuss (Peter), R. Hofbauer (A Film Producer), Arthur Mainzer (A Film Director), Eduard Rothauser (Travel Agent).

"Better two steps backward than one step forward" is the motto of the tiny German town of Ostend. The citizens enjoy a peaceful existence, quite separated from modern reality. However, their idyllic lives are interrupted when some expensive trunks, all marked "O.F.," arrive from Cairo, followed by a telegram asking for reservations at the town's only hotel. Since the hotel has only five rooms, the manager evicts its tenants and proceeds to build on five more rooms. Soon the excitement spreads through the citizenry as everyone anticipates the arrival of Mr. O.F. Lorre, wonderful in a rare comic role, is a reporter for the local paper who announces that this O.F. is actually a millionaire. Though no one knows why a millionaire would want to visit their sleepy village the preparations continue. A movie house, casino, opera hall, cabaret and other buildings are built. Ostend slowly grows but still there is no O.F. The town's sudden boom is noticed by all of Europe. Why should little Ostend experience such growth when the rest of the continent is suffering from a depression? An economic summit is held in the town and Lorre at last decides to end it all by announcing that this millionaire (who he made up) has been killed in an auto accident. No one really notices though, for the O.F. momentum has built up the town beyond anyone's wildest dreams and all are anticipating the upcoming Economic Conference. Meanwhile, in a far off office the talent agent for a movie star named Ola Fallon fires his secretary for accidentally sending the actress' trunks to some obscure little town no one has ever heard of. This is a delightful little satire, full of whimsy and marvelous performances. The story is told in an uncomplicated manner, letting the events build to a frenzied pitch and saving a great punchline for the closing moments. Sadly, this fine comedy was a victim of the new Nazi government the next year. Because Jewish performers and writers had contributed their talents to the film it was severely cut to reduce their work. The resulting film was retitled BAUEN UND HEIRATEN (BUILD AND MARRY). Songs include "Hausse-Song," "Cabaretsong," "Barcarole," Die Kleine Ansprache," "Schluss-song" (Erich Kastner).

p, Hans Conradi, Mark Asarow; d, Alexis Granowsky; w, Leo Lania, Granowsky (based on a story by Hans Homberg); ph, Reimar Kuntze, Heinrich Balasch; m, Karol Rathaus; ed, Paul Falkenberg, Curt von Molo; md, Kurt Schroder; art d, Erich Czerwonsky; set d, Czerwonsky; cos, Edward Suhr.

Comedy   **(PR:A   MPAA:NR)**

TRUST THE NAVY**   (1935, Brit.) 71m St. George's/COL bw

Lupino Lane (Nip Briggs), Nacy Burne (Susie), Wallace Lupino (Wally Wopping), Guy Middleton (Lt. Richmond), Miki Hood (Andree Terraine), Ben Welden (Scar), Fred Leslie (Chief Petty Officer), Doris Rogers (Martha), Reginald Long (Serge Chungster), Arthur Rigby (Lambert Terrain), Arthur Stanley, Charles Sewell.

An occasionally funny comedy starring Lane and Lupino as two goofy sailors aboard the HMS *Improbable*. The duo perform the usual comedy bits while combating a gang of smugglers, much to the dismay of their chief petty officer.

p, Ian Sutherland; d, Henry W. George; w, Reginald Long, Arthur Rigby (based on a story by Arthur Rose).

Comedy   **(PR:A   MPAA:NR)**

TRUST YOUR WIFE   (SEE: THE FALL GUY, 1930)

TRUSTED OUTLAW, THE**   (1937) 57m REP bw

Bob Steele (Dan Ward), Lois January (Molly), Joan Barclay (Betty), Earl Dwire (Swain), Charlie King (Bert Gilmore), Dick Cramer (Rogan), Hal Price (Pember), Budd Buster (Adler), Frank Ball (Sheriff), Oscar Gahan, George Morrell, Chick Hannon, Sherry Tansey, Clyde McClary.

Outlaw Steele returns to the family ranch so he can reform. He didn't count on bad men Dwire and King, who want to keep him in the evil fold, but fights temptation and remains on the side of law and order. January is the gal he's coming home to but she loves two-times Steele, nearly getting him killed as well. His heart finally ends up with love interest Barclay. The plot is like most Westerns and the treatment is the same.

p, A. W. Hackel; d, R. N. Bradbury; w, George Plympton, Fred Myton (based on a story by Johnston McCulley); ph, Bert Longenecker; ed, S. Roy Luby.

Western   **(PR:A   MPAA:NR)**

TRUTH, THE**   (1961, Fr./Ital.) 127m Han-Iena-C.E.I.A.P./Kingsley
                      International Pictures bw (LA VERITE; LA VERITA)

Brigitte Bardot (Dominique Marceau), Charles Vanel (Maitre Guerin, Defense Attorney), Paul Meurisse (Eparvier, Prosecuting Attorney), Sami Frey (Gilbert Tellier), Marie-Jose Nat (Annie Marceau), Louis Seigner (President of the Court), Jacqueline Porel (Defense Lawyer), Andre Oumansky (Ludovic), Christian Lude (Colonel), Suzy Willy (Mme. Marceau), Barbara Somers (Daisy), Rene Blancard (Attorney General), Fernand Ledoux (Court Physician), Louis Arbessier (Conservatory Professor), Jacques Perrin, Claude Berri, Jacques Hilling, Colette Castel, M. Cavalier.

Bardot is on trial for murdering her lover. Prosecution says the crime was premeditated and the death penalty should be evoked while the defense says that her crime was one of passion. Bardot's story is told in flashback. She had been living a Bohemian life on the Left Bank. After having an affair with her sister's boyfriend Frey, a young music student, she continues to engage in numerous sexual encounters. But Frey has fallen for her and the two have a terrific fight. She ends up a streetwalker while Frey becomes a celebrated symphony conductor. Bardot learns that Frey has become engaged to her sister (Nat) and comes to realize that Frey is the only man she has ever loved. She goes to his flat and they spend the night together but the next day Frey throws her out, calling Bardot a slut. She decides the only thing to do is kill herself in front of him but he laughs this off with insults. Angered, Bardot shoots Frey and tries to kill herself. The police find her before she dies however and Bardot recovers to be put on trial. When her trial is over Bardot comes to believe that the jury won't take her love for Frey as real because of her past. Distraught, she takes a piece of broken mirror and slashes her wrists.

p, Raoul J. Levy; d, Henri-Georges Clouzot; w, Clouzot, Simone Drieu, Michele Perrein, Jerome Geronimi, Christiane Rochefort, Simone Marescat, Vera Clouzot; ph, Armand Thirard; m, excerpts from Ludwig van Beethoven, "The Firebird" Igor Stravinsky; ed, Albert Jurgenson; art d, Jean Andre.

Drama   **(PR:O   MPAA:NR)**

TRUTH ABOUT MURDER, THE**   (1946) 63m RKO bw (GB: LIE
                                                DETECTOR, THE)

Bonita Granville (Chris Allen, Attorney), Morgan Conway (District Attorney Les Ashton), Rita Corday (Peggy), Don Douglas (Paul Marvin), June Clayworth (Marsha Crane), Gerald Mohr (Johnny Lacka), Michael St. Angel (Hank), Tom Noonan (Jonesy), Edward Norris (Bill Crane).

When a woman photographer is found dead in her studio her husband

Norris is arrested for the crime. He claims innocence but district attorney Conway doesn't believe him. He prosecutes the man for murder but finds this is not helping his love life when his girl friend Granville represents Norris as defense counsel. She's convinced of his innocence and with the help of a lie detector proves it. But her romance with Conway holds up despite the strain. This could have been an interesting programmer but is too slowly paced to hold interest. The novelty of the character relationships alone can't carry the film. The result is a routine and predictable courtroom drama.

p, Herman Schlom; d, Lew Landers; w, Lawrence Kimble, Hilda Gordon, Eric Taylor; ph, Frank Redman; m, Leigh Harline; ed, Edward W. Williams; md, C. Bakaleinikoff; art d, Albert S. D'Agostino, Walter E. Keller.

Drama   **(PR:A   MPAA:NR)**

TRUTH ABOUT SPRING, THE***   (1965, Brit.) 102m UNIV c

Hayley Mills (Spring Tyler), John Mills (Tommy Tyler), James MacArthur (William Ashton), Lionel Jeffries (Cark), Harry Andrews (Sellers), Niall MacGinnis (Cleary), Lionel Murton (Simmons), David Tomlinson (Skelton).

Real life father and daughter John and Hayley Mills play two Americans, a widower and his 18-year-old daughter, living in the Caribbean. The daughter meets MacArthur, the nephew of millionaire Tomlinson. He's bored with his life on his uncle's yacht and stays with the pair on their houseboat. The two young people take an immediate liking to one another but any idyl must be put on hold when MacArthur's former partner Jeffries arrives on the scene. MacArthur has Jeffries invest some money in an expedition that's on the lookout for underwater treasures. MacGinnis is another partner in the venture, which proves to be a waste of money when all that's found in the undersea wrecks are skeletons. MacArthur keeps the money and goes back to his uncle's yacht to hide but realizes he loves Mills. He asks her father for permission to marry her and of course he gets it. Dad leaves the young people on the yacht and takes his houseboat off to new scenery. Though the characters and plot are simplistic, this is played with good feeling. The cast is quite amiable and makes the modest comedy work nicely. Direction is fine for the film, with good light pacing.

p, Alan Brown; d, Richard Thorpe; w, James Lee Barrett (based on the story "Satan: a Romance of the Bahamas" by Henry deVere Stacpoole); ph, Edward Scaife (Technicolor); m, Robert Farnon; ed, Thomas Stanford; art d, Gil Parrondo.

Romance/Comedy/Adventure   **(PR:AA   MPAA:NR)**

TRUTH ABOUT WOMEN, THE**   (1958, Brit.) 98m Beaconsfield/CD
                                                                  c

Laurence Harvey (Sir Humphrey Tavistock), Julie Harris (Helen Cooper), Diane Cilento (Ambrosine Viney), Mai Zetterling (Julie), Eva Gabor (Louise), Michael Denison (Rollo), Derek Farr (Anthony), Elina Labourdette (Comtesse), Roland Culver (Charles Tavistock), Wilfrid Hyde-White (Sir George Tavistock), Catherine Boyle (Diana), Ambrosine Philpotts (Lady Tavistock), Jackie Lane (Saida), Lisa Gastoni (Mary Maguire), Robert Rietty (Sultan), Balbina (Marcelle), Christopher Lee (Francois), Aletha Orr (Mrs. Maguire), Marius Goring (Otto Kerstein), Thorley Walters (Trevor), Ernest Thesiger (Judge), Griffith Jones (Sir Jeremy), Hal Osmond (Baker), John Glyn-Jones (Raven).

Aging baronet Harvey sits in his drawing room with his son-in-law discussing that universal male topic: women. The female gender is inexplicable claims Harvey and through flashbacks he tells of his exploits with the fair sex. At various times in his youthful career as a philanderer Harvey tried his hand at seducing a suffragette, tried kidnaping a young lady from a harem, got involved with a married woman and finally meets Philpotts who becomes the love of his life. This has some funny moments but the going gets repetitive and often tedious. It's not nearly as witty as it thinks it is though Harvey does lend a certain grace to the proceedings. The direction is simply too serious for what should have been a much lighter comedy, so the film falls far short of its intentions. The attention to period detail in the art direction is notable.

p, Sydney Box; d, Muriel Box; w, S. Box, M. Box; ph, Otto Heller (Eastmancolor); m, Bruce Montgomery; ed, Anne V. Coates; md, Muir Mathieson; art d, George Provis; cos, Cecil Beaton.

Comedy   **(PR:A   MPAA:NR)**

TRUTH ABOUT YOUTH, THE**½   (1930) 62m FN bw

Loretta Young (Phyllis Ericson), David Manners (Richard Dane the Imp), Conway Tearle (Richard Carewe), J. Farrell MacDonald (Col. Graham), Harry Stubbs (Horace Palmer), Myrtle Stedman (Mrs. Ericson), Myrna Loy (Kara the Firefly), Yola D'Avril (Babette), Dorothy Mathews (Cherry), Ray Hallor (Hal).

A sort of poor man's version of THE BLUE ANGEL has Loy playing a cabaret singer who goes through men like tissues from a box. Manners is a young naive type who becomes entranced with the haughty woman only to be cast aside for more lucrative middle-aged men. Young is the nice girl who likewise tosses aside the youngster for the older Tearle. Some guys just have no luck at all] This is entertaining material, with some good performances particularly by the utter vamp Loy. In one scene she wears a bikini white sitting astride an elephant. When the beast's trunk swung up between her legs, many a blue nose turned purple] Directed with some style, this is a remake of a 1915 silent feature taken from a Broadway play.

d, William A. Seiter; w, B. Harrison Orkow (based on the play "When We Were Twenty-one" by Henry V. Esmond); ph, Arthur Miller; ed, Frederick Y. Smith.

Drama (PR:A MPAA:NR)

TRUTH IS STRANGER (SEE: WHEN LADIES MEET, 1933)

TRY AND FIND IT (SEE: HI DIDDLE DIDDLE, 1943)

TRY AND GET ME (SEE: SOUND OF FURY, THE, 1950)

TRYGON FACTOR, THE** (1969, Brit.) 87m Rialto-Film Preben Philpsen/WB c

Stewart Granger (Supt. Cooper-Smith), Susan Hampshire (Trudy Emberday), Robert Morley (Hubert Hamlyn), Cathleen Nesbitt (Livia Emberday), Brigitte Horney (Sister General [Mrs. Hamlyn]), Sophie Hardy (Sophie), James Robertson-Justice (Sir John), Eddi Arent (Emil Clossen), Diane Clare (Sister Claire), James Culliford (Luke Emberday), Allan Cuthbertson (Det. Thompson), Colin Gordon (Dice), Yuri Borienko (Nailer), Conrad Monk (Pasco), Russell Waters (Sgt. Chivers), Caroline Blakiston (White Nun), Richardina Jackson (Black Nun), John Barrett (Guide), Jeremy Hawk (Bank Manager), Joseph Cuby (Receptionist), Inigo Jackson (Ballistics Expert), Tom Bowman (Security Guard), Cicely Paget-Bowman (Lady at Hotel), Hilary Wontner (Man at Hotel).

In order to keep their palatial English home Nesbitt and her daughter Hampshire, a photographer, set up a phony convent in an old priory next to the house. Dubbed "The Sisters of Vigilance" the pair, along with the not so bright Culliford, use the so-called convent as a front for a stolen goods operation. A Scotland Yard detective comes round to investigate but quickly disappears, so Granger is then assigned to the case. Meanwhile the "nuns" decide to expand their operation and bring in Arent, a talented safecracker. Granger talks Hardy, a hotel receptionist, into helping him with the case. Some gold is stolen from a local bank with the intention of melting it down so Morley can smuggle it out of the country. Hardy is caught spying on them but Granger arrives just as the gold is being poured into vases. Confusion ensues with Arent getting strangled and Morley drowning in a coffin. Nesbitt shoots Culliford and Hampshire is killed when hit by a molten gold-filled crucible. In the melee Hardy tries to help but ends up knocking out Granger. The ending isn't the only portion where confusion reigns; the story is often muddled by sloppy editing. There are also some gaping holes in the story logic. On the plus side, this film's offbeat black humor works well at times and there are enough cockeyed characters to hold interest throughout.

p, Brian Taylor; d, Cyril Frankel; w, Derry Quinn, Stanley Munro (based on a story by Quinn); ph, Harry Waxman (Technicolor); m, Peter Thomas; ed, Oswald Hafenrichter; art d, Roy Stannard; set d, Hazel Peisei; spec eff, Ted Samuels.

Crime/Comedy (PR:C MPAA:M/PG)

TSAR'S BRIDE, THE*** (1966, USSR) 95m Riga Film Studio/Artkino bw (TSARSKAYA NEVESTA)

Raisa Nedashkovskaya (Marfa), Natalya Rudnaya (Lyubasha), Otar Koberidze (Grigoriy Gryaznoy), G. Shevtsov (Malyuta Skuratov), V. Zeldin (Bomeliy), Nikolay Timofeyev (Sobakin), Viktor Nuzhnyy (Ivan Lykov), M. Maltseva (Dunyasha), T. Loginova (Saburova), Pyotr Glebov (Ivan Groznyy [Ivan the Terrible]), Singing Voices: Galina Oleynichenko (Marfa), Larisa Avdeyeva (Lyubasha), Yevgeniy Kibkalo (Gryaznoy), A. Geleva (Malyuta Skuratov), P. Chekin (Bomeliy), A. Vedernikov (Sobakin), Ye. Raykov (Ivan Lykov), V. Klepatskaya (Dunyasha), T. Tugarinova (Saburova), Bolshoi Theater Chorus.

This Soviet film is an adaptation of the Rimsky-Korsakov opera of 1899 and a play of 1849. Nedashkovskaya is a young Russian aristocrat about to enter into a forced marriage with the cruel Tsar Glebov. However, Glebov's chief bodyguard Koberidze also loves the girl. He persuades a German scientist to make a love potion so that Nedashkovskaya will love him as well. However, Koberidze's mistress Rudnaya learns of this and replaces the love potion with poison. A great feast is held for Glebov to announce his upcoming marriage but before he arrives Nedashkovskaya drinks the poison and goes mad as she dies. Glebov enters and Koberidze admits planting the poison. He is hauled away by guards but suddenly Rudnaya admits her guilt. Koberidze stabs her and is finally taken away by Glebov's men.

d, Vladimir Gorikker; w, A. Donatov, Gorikker (based on the opera "Tsarskaya Nevesta" by Nikolai Andreevich Rimsky-Korsakov and the play "Tsarskaya Nevesta" by Lev Aleksandrovich Mey); ph, Kh. Kukels (Sovscope); m, Rimsky-Korsakov; md, Yevgeniy Svetlanov; art d, G. Balodis.

Opera (PR:C MPAA:NR)

TSARSKAYA NEVESTA (SEE: TSAR'S BRIDE, THE, 1966, USSR)

TSUBAKI SANJURO (SEE: SANJURO, 1962, Jap.)

TU PERDONAS..YO NO (SEE: GOD FORGIVES-I DON'T, 1969, Ital./Span.)

TU SERAS TERRIBLEMENT GENTILLE (SEE: YOU ONLY LOVE ONCE, 1969, Fr.)

TUCSON*½ (1949) 64m FOX bw

Jimmy Lydon (Andy Bryant), Penny Edwards (Laurie Sherman), Deanna Wayne (Jennifer Johnson), Charles Russell (Gregg Johnson), Joe Sawyer (Tod Bryant), Walter Sande (George Reeves), Lyn Wilde (Gertie Peck), Marcia Mae Jones (Polly Johnson), John Ridgely (Ben), Grandon Rhodes (Dean Sherman), Gil Stratton (Jerry Twill), Harry Lauter (George Reeves, Jr.), Cass County Trio.

Lydon, a student at the University of Arizona, prefers training his horse for a college rodeo to doing his homework. His father Sawyer wants him to win so he can show up rival rancher Sande. But Lydon's apathetic attitude in the classroom catches up with him when he nearly blinds a student in chemistry class. This forces him to take a second look at his priorities. He buckles down with the books but manages to win the rodeo in the end. Routine material and a cast that clearly is bored with what they're doing, plus a predictable script and standard direction, doesn't add up to much.

p, Sol M. Wurtzel; d, William Claxton; w, Arnold Belgard; ph, Benjamin Kline; m, Darrell Calker; ed, Frank A. Baldridge; m/l "Nobody's Lost on the Lonesome Trail," "Ringin' the New Year In," I.B. Kornblum, L. Wolfe Gilbert (sung by the Cass County Trio).

Western (PR:A MPAA:NR)

TUCSON RAIDERS**½ (1944) 55m REP bw

"Wild" Bill Elliott (Red Ryder), Robby [Robert] Blake (Little Beaver), George "Gabby" Hayes, Alice Fleming, Ruth Lee, Peggy Stewart, LeRoy Mason, Stanley Andrews, John Whitney, Bud Geary, Karl Hackett, Tom Steele, Tom Chatterton, Edward Cassidy, Edward Howard, Fred Graham, Frank McCarroll, Marshall Reed, Stanley Andrews, Frank Pershing, and the voices of Roy Barcroft, Kenne Duncan, Tom London, Jack Kirk.

After an unsuccessful try at marketing a series western based on Fred Harman's comic strip character Red Ryder in 1940, featuring Don "Red" Barry, Republic Studios shelved the idea until someone noticed "Wild" Bill Elliott's resemblance to Harman's character. In 1944 the studio released TUCSON RAIDERS, the first in a new Red Ryder series of oaters. With little Bobby Blake as his sidekick, Elliott blazed his way out of the pages of a giant Red Ryder book to open the show. The first movie in the series saw Elliott, Blake, and comedy relief king Hayes battling to rid the territory of an evil governor who had stepped on too many toes, including those of Elliott's aunt. The new Red Ryder was a success and Elliott starred in 16 episodes before he retired from the part. Allan "Rocky" Lane took over the Red Ryder role in 1946. (See RED RYDER series, Index.)

p, Eddy White; d, Spencer G. Bennett; w, Anthony Coldeway (based on a story by Jack O'Donnell from the comic strip characters created by Fred Harman); ph, Reggie Lanning; m, Joseph Dubin; ed, Harry Keller; art d, Gano Chittenden.

Western (PR:A MPAA:NR)

TUDOR ROSE (SEE: NINE DAYS A QUEEN, 1936, Brit.)

TUGBOAT ANNIE***½ (1933) 87m MGM bw

Marie Dressler (Annie Brennan), Wallace Beery (Terry Brennan), Robert Young (Alec Brennan), Maureen O'Sullivan (Pat Severn), Willard Robertson (Red Severn), Tammany Young (Shif'less), Frankie Darro (Alec as a Boy), Jack Pennick (Pete), Paul Hurst (Sam), Oscar Apfel (Reynolds), Robert McWade (Mayor of Secoma), Robert Barrat (1st Mate), Vince Barnett (Cabby), Robert E. Homans (Old Salt), Guy Usher (Auctioneer), Willie Fung (Chow the Cook), Hal Price (Mate), Christian Rub (Sailor), Major Sam Harris (Onlooker).

What could have been a sentimental, sappy, and sickly sweet saga turned into a colossal hit for MGM as it reteamed Dressler and Beery (who had starred together in MIN AND BILL) and gave them free rein to strut their stuff. Dressler is the captain of a tugboat and Beery is her drunken husband. Their son is Young, who has aspirations beyond the tugboat and winds up as the captain of an ocean liner. (This is a hole in the story as Young is far too beardless to helm such a large ship.) Young falls in love with O'Sullivan, the daughter of Robertson, a rival to Dressler and Beery, who owns the large liner. Young adores Dressler and would like to get her off the little scow she pilots, but she enjoys her life on the tug and defends Beery when Young makes mention of the fact that his own father is shiftless and a braggart. He tries to get Dressler to leave Beery but her first loyalty is to her husband, and when she refuses to leave him, Young exits, saying that he will not talk to her ever again until she comes to her senses. Beery drunkenly crashes the tugboat and the vessel is damaged, then sold at an auction. It's then repaired and put into service as a garbage ship. Dressler is offered the job of running it and although it breaks her heart to see her ship put to such use, she takes the assignment because she and Beery are out of money. Young is running the liner and one tempestuous night, while Beery and Dressler are far out to sea dumping refuse, they hear an SOS from Young's liner. The small boat is in bad shape and can hardly get up enough steam to effect a rescue, but Beery climbs into the boiler, repairs a leak, and they sail to Young's ship and everyone is saved. Later, Beery receives an award for what he did, the tug is given back to them, and the family is together once again, with Young and O'Sullivan being also united as prospective husband and wife. Dressler and Beery appeared later in DINNER AT EIGHT, but not with each other. The tugboat was later used by Beery (and new costar Marjorie Main) in BARNACLE BILL (1941) after Dressler died in 1934. Marjorie Rambeau and Alan Hale did the roles once more in Warner Bros.' TUGBOAT ANNIE SAILS AGAIN, and Edgar Kennedy and Jane Darwell played the leads in Republic's CAPTAIN TUGBOAT ANNIE (1945). In 1957, Minerva Urecal did the lead for a TV series. The relationship between Beery and Dressler was never again done with as much panache and affection as it was in this, under the direction of young Mervyn LeRoy, who was just 33 at the time. This film and RASPUTIN AND THE EMPRESS were MGM's big hits that year and took the studio out of some difficulty caused by the Depression, which was raging in the U.S. at the time. The success of the movie caused the studio to tear up Beery's term contract and give him a new one. TUGBOAT ANNIE cost $614,000 to make, not an inconsiderable amount in those days, but the box office results more than made up for the production budget.

p, Harry Rapf; d, Mervyn LeRoy; w, Zelda Sears, Eve Green, Norman Reilly Raine (based on the stories by Raine); ph, Gregg Toland; ed, Blanche Sewell; art d, Merrill Pye; set d, Edwin B. Willis.

Comedy/Drama   **(PR:A   MPAA:NR)**

TUGBOAT ANNIE SAILS AGAIN**   (1940) 77m FN-WB bw

Marjorie Rambeau (*Tugboat Annie*), Jane Wyman (*Peggy Armstrong*), Ronald Reagan (*Eddie Kent*), Alan Hale (*Capt. Bullwinkle*), Charles Halton (*Alec Severn*), Clarence Kolb (*J.B. Armstrong*), Paul Hurst (*Pete*), Victor Kilian (*Sam*), Chill Wills (*Shiftless*), Harry Shannon (*Capt. Mahoney*), John Hamilton (*Capt. Broad*), Sidney Bracey (*Limey*), Jack Mower (*Johnson*), Dana Dale (*Rosie*), Josephine Whittell (*Miss Morgan*), Neil Reagan (*Rex Olcott*), George Meader (*Bradley*), Don Turner, Glen Cavander (*Men*), Al Lloyd (*Little Man*), Tom Wilson (*Big Guy*), George Campeau (*Olcott's Announcer*), Lucia Carroll (*Beauty Operator*), Leo White (*Whiter*), Leon Belasco (*Headwaiter*), Creighton Hale (*Chauffeur*).

Released seven years after TUGBOAT ANNIE, this sequel tries awfully hard but never captures the charm of the original. Rambeau plays the title role, this time as a widow. She runs a tugboat in the Northwest in competition with Hale. Her company needs $25,000, which she gets without much trouble. When another skipper takes over the tug for a trip to Alaska, Rambeau goes along for the ride and proves to be more than a passenger when they run into trouble. For romantic interest Reagan and his then off-screen wife Wyman, played the unlikely love team of a sailor and rich socialite. The players give the film a lot of heart, but the script is minor stuff with inadequate direction. This was a surprise considering the studio had invested some otherwise good production values in the film.

p, Edmund Grainger; d, Lewis Seiler, w, Walter De Leon (based on characters created by Norman Reilly Raine); ph, Arthur Edeson; m, Max Steiner; ed, Harold McLernon.

Drama   **(PR:AA   MPAA:NR)**

TULIPS*   (1981, Can), 92m Astral Bellevue Pathe-Bennettfilms/AE c

Gabe Kaplan (*Leland Irving*), Bernadette Peters (*Rutanya Wallace*), Al Waxman (*Bert Irving*), Henry Gibson (*Maurice "Boom Boom" Avocado*), David Boxer (*Dr. Carl Walburn*), Jazzmine Lauzane (*Metermaid*), Malcolm Nelthorpe (*Surgeon*), Sean McCann (*Roger*), Gail Garfinkle (*Nurse*), Jack Creley (*Florist*), Cid Darrows (*Gunshop Owner*).

A strange, Messy, and altogether unfunny comedy has Kaplan as a would-be suicide. He just can't do it right, so he hires a hit man, Gibson, who promises that he'll ignore any last-minute pleadings by Kaplan. Shortly afterwards, Kaplan pulls Peters out of a burning Volkswagon. It seems she was also trying to kill herself to get even with her boy friend, who just happens to be Kaplan's psychiatrist. How's that for a contrived situation? Of course, the two fall in love and Kaplan is faced with how to stop his hired gun. The plot has lots of potential for bizarre comedy, but the production was so riddled with problems that it's amazing this even got as far as the cutting room. Both the credited writer and director are pseudonyms, as the production went through no less than three directors, two of whom worked on the script. Kaplan tried some writing, too, but it was hardly worth the effort. TULIPS is a flat, lifeless comedy that shows no sense of style and only a faint glimpse of the much-needed chemistry between the two leads. Gibson is

unbelievable as the hit man. This mild-mannered boob would no sooner swat a fly than kill a man.

p, Don Carmody; d, Stan Ferris [Mark Warren, Rex Bromfield, Al Waxman]; w, Fred Sappho [Bromfield, Waxman, Henry Olek, Gabe Kaplan]; ph, Francois Protat; m, Eddie Karam; ed, Allan Collins, Yurij Lohovy; art d, Ted Watkins.

Comedy   **Cas.**   **(PR:C   MPAA:PG)**

TULSA**½**   (1949) 90m Wanger/EL c

Susan Hayward (*Cherokee Lansing*), Robert Preston (*Brad Brady*), Pedro Armendariz (*Jim Redbird*), Chill Wills (*Pinky Jimpson*), Harry Shannon (*Nelse Lansing*), Ed Begley (*Johnny Brady*), Jimmy Conlin (*Homer*), Paul E. Burns (*Tooley*), Lloyd Gough (*Bruce Tanner*), Roland Jack (*Steve*), Chief Yowlachie (*Charlie Lightfoot*), Pierre Watkin (*Winters*), Lane Chandler (*Mr. Kelly*), Tom Dugan (*Taxi Driver*), Lola Albright (*Candy Williams*), Iron Eyes Cody (*The Osage Indian*), Dick Wessel (*Joker*), John Dehner, Selmer Jackson (*Oilmen*), Larry Keating (*Governor*), Joseph Crehan (*Judge McKay*), Thomas Browne Henry (*Winslow*), Nolan Leary (*Man with Newspaper*), Fred Graham (*Oil Worker*).

A big, sprawling oil field story served as Hayward's only film for Eagle-Lion and proved to be its most costly and highest- grossing production. Lots of action, romance, a few laughs, and good directorial pace by Heisler. Hayward is the daughter of Shannon. They are cattle folk and when Shannon dies in an oil field explosion which Hayward feels is the fault of Gough, a rich oil man, she is determined to extract revenge for her being left an orphan. Hayward's cousin is Wills and she is going to ask him for some aid in her quest for revenge. She meets Begley and saves him from a beating by a large tough. Begley takes her out for a few drinks, has a few too many, and signs over some of his oil leases to show his appreciation for her having saved him. She realizes that it's the move of a drunken, albeit grateful, man and fully intends giving him the leases the following day, when Begley returns to being sober. That day never dawns as Begley is killed in another battle. Hayward is the legal owner of the oil leases but has no idea of their value until the hated Gough offers her a good deal of money for them. Rather than make a deal with the man she despises, she calls upon Armendariz, an Indian pal who has a few bucks in his jeans. With his money, they start to drill but there doesn't seem to be anything happening under the earth. Preston arrives. He is the young son of the late Begley and a graduate geologist. Since he knows about oil and shale and the like, he says he can help. Hayward suspects his motives at first, but then sees that he is sincere and a man who is dedicated to conserving the oil of the state, rather than raping the land. (This may have been the earliest movie in which anyone ever gives a thought to conservation of natural resources.) Armendariz has no money left and the holes are still dry, so Hayward is forced into making an agreement with Gough. She borrows money from him with the deal being that if she hasn't struck oil by a particular date, Gough will be the recipient of the leases in perpetuity. On the brink of going bankrupt, black gold erupts from the earth and Hayward's fortunes soar as high as the gushers. The landscape is now jagged with one oil rig after another and the land that once was used for cattle grazing is now being ruined. Even Armendariz, who benefits from the oil, feels that there must be a way to compromise between petroleum and cattle. However, there are other Indians, who derive money from the oil in the ground, who pressure Hayward to drill even more wells--as many as Gough has-- so they can increase their percentage of the take. Hayward reluctantly agrees to up production. Preston and Hayward are now in love and although he is totally against her business methods, she convinces him that it will soon be over and they can marry and go away somewhere. To make as much money as she can, Hayward teams up with Gough and they make an agreement to be partners. Then Hayward learns that Gough has committed them for more oil production than they can issue. Preston is disgusted with Hayward's moves and exits, for the time being. To increase the oil output, Gough tells Hayward that they need the land owned by Armendariz, who has long ago told Hayward how much he disagrees with her. Armendariz will not lease his grazing land for oil and Gough attempts to have the Indian declared *non compos mentis* in front of a local magistrate. Seeing how greedy Gough is, Hayward finally puts her little foot down and says "Enough!" This move jeopardizes her entire holdings because they are committed to supply oil. Armendariz returns to his land and when he sees some dead cattle that have perished because they drank polluted water, he tosses a match into the stream and a huge oil fire erupts. A large fire- fight scene ensues with Preston, Gough, Armendariz, and Hayward joining forces to attempt to quell the flames. Armendariz tries to rescue some of his cattle and Hayward follows him, then both are trapped by toppling oil towers and finally saved by Preston, who has commandeered a bulldozer. The fire ends and Hayward and Preston are reunited as they look at the smoking landscape. They vow to start all over again, but this time using some sense and better understanding of how to treat the treasures that the earth has yielded. Preston and Hayward made four films together, this one being the last. The best parts of the movie were the outdoor sequences, especially the fire and the gushers. There have been many attempts at oil field stories, such as OKLAHOMA CRUDE, which was exactly that--crude by comparison.

p, Walter Wanger; d, Stuart Heisler; w, Frank Nugent, Curtis Kenyon (based on a story by Richard Wormser); ph, Winton Hoch (Technicolor); m, Frank

Skinner; ed, Terrell Morse; md, Irving Friedman; art d, Nathan Juran; set d, Armor Marlowe, Al Orenbach; cos, Herschel; spec eff, John Fulton; makeup, Ern Westmore, Del Armstrong; m/l, "Tulsa," Mort Greene, Allie Wrubel.

Drama Cas. (PR:A MPAA:NR)

TULSA KID, THE** (1940) 57m REP bw

Don "Red" Barry (Tom Benton), Noah Beery, Sr (Montana), Luana Walters (Mary), David Durand (Bob Wallace), George Douglas (Dick Saunders), Ethan Laidlaw (Nick), Stanley Blystone (Sam Ellis), John Elliott (Perkins), Jack Kirk (Sheriff), Fred "Snowflake" (Snowball) Toones, Charles Murphy, Joe De LaCruz, Charles Thomas, Art Dillard, Cactus Mack, Jimmy Wakely and his Roughriders.

Beery is Barry's foster father, teaching the young man all his tricks in the gunslinging trade. Later, Barry realizes that the straight and narrow is his true path, and when he defends a cattle ranch, Barry must face his former mentor in a gunfight. Neither can pull the trigger, though, and all ends happily. An average western. Beery does some good work. Sherman helmed 17 of Barry's first 18 films for Republic.

p&d, George Sherman; W, Oliver Drake, Anthony Coldeway; ph, John MacBurnie; ed, William Thompson.

Western Cas. (PR:A MPAA:NR)

TUMBLEDOWN RANCH IN ARIZONA**½ (1941) 60m MON bw

Ray Corrigan (Crash), John King (Dusty), Max Terhune (Alibi), Sheila Darcy (Dorothy), Marian Kerby (Mother Rogers), Quen Ramsey (Gallop), James Craven (Slocum), Jack Holmes (Sheriff Nye), Steve Clark (Shorty), Sam Bernard (Nick), Carl Mathews, Tex Palmer, Tex Cooper, Frank Ellis, Nick Thompson, Frank McCarroll, Chick Hannon, John Elliott, University of Arizona Glee Club.

Good entry in the "Range Busters" series has King a college student. At a rodeo he's flung from his bronc and knocked out. While unconscious he dreams a typical western story. The railroad is going through town, right through Kerby's land. In come the Range Busters to save the day, but King is blamed for a murder. He's proven innocent and Ramsey is found to be the culprit. All is put right and the story ends happily. Some good production values in a film shot on cowboy star Corrigan's ranch. (See RANGE BUSTERS series, Index.)

p, George W. Weeks; d, S. Roy Luby; w, Milton Raison; ph, Robert Cline; ed, Roy Claire; md, Frank Sanucci; songs, "Tumbledown Ranch in Arizona," "All Hail, Arizona," "Wake Up with the Dawn."

Western (PR:A MPAA:NR)

TUMBLEWEED** (1953) 79m UNIV c

Audie Murphy (Jim Harvey), Lori Nelson (Laura), Chill Wills (Sheriff Murchoree), Roy Roberts (Nick Buckley), Russell Johnson (Lam), K. T. Stevens (Louella Buckley), Madge Meredtith (Sarah), Lee Van Cleef (Mary), I. Stanford Jolley (Ted), Ross Elliott (Seth), Ralph Moody (Aguila), Eugene Iglesias (Tigre), Phil Chambers (Trapper Ross), Lyle Talbot (Weber), King Donovan (Wrangler), Harry Harvey (Prospector).

This is a typical western outing for Murphy. He's a guard for a wagon train and wrongly accused of being party to a raid on it. He's saved from hanging by Wills and put in jail. He's sprung from there by a Yaqui Indian he once helped. Wills catches up with him at a waterhole where they battle some Indians. After a fight with the real villain, Johnson (later to play the Professor on TV's "Gilligan's Island"), Murphy proves his innocence. Every Murphy motif is clearly in place and this is no different from most of his other cowboy films. The production values aren't bad, with some good use of color.

p, Ross Hunter; d, Nathan Juran; w, John Meredyth Lucas (based on the novel Three Were Renegades by Kenneth Perkins); ph, Russell Metty (Technicolor); ed, Virgil Vogel; md, Joseph Gershenson; art d, Bernard Herzbrum, Richard H. Riedel.

Western Cas. (PR:A MPAA:NR)

TUMBLEWEED TRAIL** (1946) 57m PRC bw

Eddie Dean (Eddie), Roscoe Ates (Soapy), Shirley Patterson (Robin Ryan), Johnny McGovern (Freckles Ryan), Bob Duncan (Brad Barton), Ted Adams (Alton Small), Jack O'Shea (Gringo), Kermit Maynard (Bill Ryan), Bill Fawcett (Judge Town), The Sunshine Boys: M.H. Richman, J.O. Smith, A.L. Smith, Edward F. Wallace (Ranch Hands), Carl Mathews, Matty Roubert, Lee Roberts, Frank Ellis, Flash the Horse.

Undercover agent Dean heads out after some rustlers with his stuttering sidekick Ates. Patterson is the woman whose father has been murdered. Dean takes a job as a ranch hand with her, and after the usual amounts of gun play and fist-fighting, the bad guy is exposed and the hero gets the girl. Good for what it is, though some of the production values could have been better.

p&d, Robert Emmett Tansey; w, Frances Kavanaugh; ph, Ernest Miller; ed, Hugh Winn; m/l, Eddie Dean, Glenn Strange, Johnny Bond, Ernest Bond, Lou Wayne, Bob Shelton

Western Cas. (PR:A MPAA:NR)

TUMBLING TUMBLEWEEDS*½ (1935) 61m REP bw

Gene Autry (Gene), Smiley Burnette (Smiley), Lucile Browne (Jerry), Norma Taylor (Janet), [Gabby] Hayes (Dr. Parker), Edward Hearn (Craven), Jack Rockwell (McWade), Frankie Marvin (Shorty), George Chesebro (Connors), Eugene Jackson (Eightball), Charles King (Blaze), Charles Whitaker (Higgins), George Burton (Sheriff), Tom London (Sykes), Cornelius Keefe (Harry Brooks), Tommy Coats, Cliff Lyons, Bud Pope, Tracy Layne, Bud McClure, George Morrell, Oscar Gahan, Champion the Horse.

In his first feature for Republic, fledgling cowboy star Autry shows none of the talents that would make him a western movie legend. As a singer and actor, Autry's efforts were so-so and his riding abilities were equally mediocre. He also sported a spare tire around his middle, which later disappeared as his talent grew. Here he's a man returning to his father after a five-year absence. He finds his father has been murdered and Autry's childhood buddy Browne is accused of the crime. With the help of Burnette and Hayes, two friends from Autry's medicine show, the singing cowpoke finds the real murderers and brings them to justice. The film isn't that well made and some sloppy editing makes it look like the heroes are shooting at themselves] The poor production quality could be accounted for by the fact that this was hack-director Kane's first effort for Republic studios, where he was forced to shoot on a six-day schedule with the minuscule budget of only $12,000. Kane would become quite proficient workng under these conditions; he made a total of 17 films starring Autry and 43, (believe it or not) vehicles for Roy Rogers.

p, Nat Levine; d, Joseph Kane; w, Ford Beebe (based on a story by Alan Ludwig); ph, Ernest Miller; songs, "Tumbling Tumbleweeds," "That Silver-Haired Daddy of Mine," "Ridin' Down the Canyon" (sung by Gene Autry).

Western Cas. (PR:AA MPAA:NR)

TUNA CLIPPER**½ (1949) 77m MON bw

Roddy McDowall (Alec), Elena Verdugo (Bianca), Roland Winters (Ransome), Rick Vallin (Silvestre), Dickie Moore (Frankie), Russell Simpson (Fergus), Doris Kemper (Mrs. McLennan), Peter Mamakos (Manuel), Richard Avonde (Peter), Michael Vallon (Papa Pereira).

McDowall is a young man with dreams of becoming an attorney. When a friend gets in trouble with some gamblers, McDowell ships out to try to turn the tide in his pal's favor. He helps the guy make good, but McDowall's proper Scottish family temporarily disowns him. Finally, everything is righted, McDowell returns to his old life, and everyone is happy again. The story is slow at the begining, but once things get going, TUNA CLIPPER becomes a mildly entertaining B film with competent production values. McDowell also served as the film's co-associate producer.

p, Lindsley Parsons; d, William Beaudine; w, W. Scott Darling; ph, William Sickner; m, Edward J. Kay; ed, Leonard W. Herman; art d, Dave Milton; set d, Ray Boltz; md, Kay; makeup, Webb Overlander.

Drama (PR:A MPAA:NR)

TUNDRA* (1936) 78m Dearholt & Stout/Burroughs-Tarzan bw (GB: THE MIGHTY TUNDRA)

Del Cambre (Flying Doctor), William Merrill McCormick, Wally Howe (Trappers), Earl Dwire (Storekeeper), Jack Santos (Half Breed), Fraser Acosta (Eskimo Father), Mrs. Elsie Duran (Eskimo Woman), Bertha Maldanado (Eskimo Girl).

While flying an important vaccine to an Alaskan village that is battling a flu epidemic, Cambre crashes and ends up stranded in the frozen North. He wanders aimlessly, fighting off some unthrilling perils, and befriending two bear cubs. Finally he makes it to the flu-ridden village where, to no one's surprise, all have succumbed to the epidemic. This last portion was wholly unnecessary but provided the only excitement in this poorly made picture. It starts off agreeably enough, but when Cambre begins to wander, so does the story and both go nowhere at all. A poor job by the editor doesn't help things any, though the photography is better than the material needed.

p, George W. Stout; d, Norman Dawn; w, Norton S. Parker, Charles F. Royal (based on a story by Dawn); ph, Dawn, Jacob and Edward Kull; ed, Walter Thompson, Thomas Neff.

Drama (PR:A MPAA:NR)

TUNES OF GLORY***½ (1960, Brit.) 106m HM/Lopert c

Alec Guinness (Lt. Col. Jock Sinclair), John Mills (Lt. Col. Basil Barrow), Dennis Price (Maj. Charlie Scott), Susannah York (Morag Sinclair), John Fraser (Cpl. Piper Fraser), Allan Cuthbertson (Capt. Eric Simpson), Kay Walsh (Mary), John MacKenzie (Pony Major), Gordon Jackson (Capt. Jimmy Cairns), Duncan MacRae (Pipe Maj. MacLean), Keith Faulkner (Piper), Peter McEnery (Lt. David MacKinnon), Paul Whitsun-Jones (Maj. Dusty

Miller), Gerald Harper *(Maj. Hugo MacMillan),* William Marlowe *(Lt. Rory),* Richard Rudd *(Lt. John),* David Webb *(Lt. Alistair),* Andrew Downie *(Cpl. Waiter),* Donald Douglas *(2nd Mess Waiter),* Richard Leech *(Capt. Alec Rattray),* William Young *(Capt. Peter),* Barry Steele, John Barcroft, John Bown, Kay Walsh.

A highly effective and affecting peacetime drama of life in a Scottish regiment. Director Neame and the producers cast against type by offering the suave Guinness the role of the hard-bitten up-from-the-ranks officer who had led his troops to victory at El Alamein and other skirmishes while Mills is given the task of convincing the audience that he is the Etonian and Oxfordian type who is all spit, polish, and protocol. The regiment has been around for 200 years and Mills' grandfather once commanded it. For the moment, Guinness is the interim commander. He's a man of war, he knows how to run the troops ragged while guns are blazing but the theory of peacetime commanding has eluded him and there is a lack of discipline in the ranks, although the men dearly love him. Guinness' daughter is York (in her feature film debut), a nubile lass who lives with him and has eyes for young corporal Fraser. Guinness keeps a loose rein on his men, allows them to bend the rules often, and does things like allow his bagpipers to rehearse in any clothes they want, rather than kilts, because that kind of martinetism doesn't much matter to him. Enter Mills, a veteran of a Japanese prison camp in WW II and a man devoted to restoring the faded glory of the regiment. Mills demands respect from everyone and strides into his new assignment of replacing Guinness like a whirlwind, thus causing the men in the regiment to rankle immediately. The officers who were under Guinness appreciate his personal bravery and his wartime abilities but they hate his boorish ways and some of them flock to Mills in the hopes that he will bring back the days that once were. Mills goes so far as to cause them all to take lessons in dancing one morning. When Guinness finds York in a bar with Fraser, he hits the young man, a major offense. Mills has a choice: he can send this case up higher, which would mean a full court-martial for Guinness, or he can keep it within the regiment. He is hard-pressed to make a decision and his manipulative second in command, Price, pushes Mills to go for the full court-martial. Price, a snob and a prig, has never liked Guinness and feels he isn't one of the old school tie group. Mills is about to turn the case over when Guinness comes to him and makes an impassioned plea that touches Mills, who changes his mind. When that happens, Mills, who is shaky mentally, realizes that he has done wrong and that this indecision is an indication of his inability to command. He does the only thing he thinks he can do and commits suicide. His body is found by McEnery who must tell the news to Guinness. Upon hearing it, Guinness, who was about to retire, goes mad, but his fellow officers, realizing what has caused him to go over the edge, surround and protect him as the film ends. Mills and Guinness are the entire focal points for the movie and it's a tossup as to which one was "better," if that's possible. Mills won the Best Actor Award at the Venice Film Festival but it might have gone either way. Guinness has a superb Scottish accent and wears a reddish wig and mustache, for no apparent reason other than to make him look different from the colonel he'd recently played in THE BRIDGE ON THE RIVER KWAI. Music was by Malcolm Arnold, the British composer who'd done the score for KWAI, ISLAND IN THE SUN, INN OF THE SIXTH HAPPINESS, and BREAKING THE SOUND BARRIER before receiving the assignment for this. Although it was drawn from a novel, Kennaway's Oscar-nominated script might have just as easily been from one of those men-in-service stage plays like THE HASTY HEART or CONDUCT UNBECOMING.

p, Colin Lesslie; d, Ronald Neame; w, James Kennaway (based on his novel); ph, Arthur Ibbetson (Technicolor); m, Malcolm Arnold; ed, Anne V. Coates.

Drama   **(PR:C   MPAA:NR)**

TUNNEL, THE   (SEE: TRANSATLANTIC TUNNEL, 1935, Brit.)

TUNNEL OF LOVE, THE**½   (1958) 98m MGM bw

Doris Day *(Isolde Poole),* Richard Widmark *(Augie Poole),* Gig Young *(Dick Pepper),* Gia Scala *(Estelle Novick),* Elisabeth Fraser *(Alice Pepper),* Elizabeth Wilson *(Miss MacCracken),* Vikki Dougan *(Actress),* Doodles Weaver *(Escort),* Charles Wagenheim *(Day Motel Man),* Robert Williams *(Night Motel Man),* The Esquire Trio *(Themselves).*

Day and Widmark are a young couple who desperately want a child. After being unable to become natural parents, the two decide to adopt. Young and the ever-pregnant Fraser are their next-door neighbors. Scala, a woman from the adoption agency, stops by to pay a visit and surprises Widmark, who is busy chasing mice and wearing only his underwear. She is unimpressed with him and that feeling is reenforced when Young drops by and takes her for a collector for a charity. But Widmark is determined to convince Scala of his worthiness as a potential parent and finds that she is most amiable when away from her job. That evening he takes her out to dinner and both do their share of drinking (Widmark has also been taking tranquilizers). Widmark awakens in a motel room, remembering nothing, but it all comes back to him some months later when Scala informs him that she is pregnant and asks to borrow $1,000. She tells him that she can arrange a child for him to adopt and Widmark sees the writing on the wall. He grows a moustache, hoping it will disguise any resemblance he may have to the soon-to-arrive child. Finally, a boy comes to the home and looks much like his new father. Day threatens divorce, but all is righted when Scala comes

by with a picture of her new baby daughter and proud husband. To top things off, Day admits that she is now pregnant. Overall the film has a certain charm tht has grown over the years. While it was considered to be quite shocking in the 1950s, it seems relatively mild by today's standards. Day and Young are at their best with the comedy, but Widmark, normally a serious actor, was not well-accepted by audiences in this rare foray into humor. The director was Kelly and this was the last film done under his contract with MGM. He was at a point in his career when he wanted to work only behind the camera and he shows a good talent for light comedy with this. Some good glib moments, with a cast that works well together.

p, Joseph Fields, Martin Melcher; d, Gene Kelly; w, Joseph Fields (based on the play by Fields, Peter DeVries and the novel by De Vries); ph, Robert Bronner (CinemaScope); ed, John McSweeney, Jr., art d, William A. Horning, Randall Duell; set d, Henry Grace, Robert Priestly; cos, Helen Rose; m/l, "The Tunnel of Love," Patty Fisher, Bob Roberts (sung by Doris Day), "Runaway, Skidaddle, Skidoo," Ruth Roberts, Bill Katz (sung by Day).

Comedy   **(PR:C   MPAA:NR)**

TUNNEL TO THE SUN**   (1968, Jap.) 198m Mifune-Ishihara/Toho c
(KUROBE NO TAIVO)

Toshiro Mifune *(Kitagawa),* Yujiro Ishihara, Osamu Takizawa, Ryutaro Tatsumi, Jukichi Uno, Eijiro Yanagi, Eiji Okada, Shuji Sano, Mieko Takamine, Fumie Kashiyama, Tomoe Hiiro, Tanie Kitamura.

A dam must be built along a fault line. Mifune, an engineer, is assigned to dig a tunnel so supplies can be brought to the construction site. Because of the danger of the dam's location, Mifune is reluctant to accept the job.

p, Toshiro Mifune, Yujiro Ishihara; d, Kei Kumai; w, Masato Ide, Kumai (based on a story by Sojiro Motoki); ph, Mitsuji Kanu; m, Toshiro Mayuzumi

Drama   **(PR:C   MPAA:NR)**

TUNNEL 28   (SEE: ESCAPE FROM EAST BERLIN, 1962, U.S./Ger.)

TUNNELVISION zero (1976) 75m International Harmony-Woodpecker
Music/Worldwide c

Phil Proctor *(Christian A. Broder),* Rick Hurst *(Father Phaser Gun),* Larraine Newman *(Sonja),* Howard Hesseman *(Sen. McMannus),* Roger Bowen *(Kissinger),* Ernie Anderson *(Quant O'Neil),* Edwina Anderson *(Melanie Edwards),* James Bacon, Chevy Chase, Ron Silver, Roberta Kent, Lorry Goldman, Lynn Marie Stewart, Gerrit Graham, Pamela Toll, Sam Riddle, Betty Thomas, Joe O'Flaherty, Bart Williams, Ron Prince, Nellie Bellflower, Tom Davis, Al Franken, Frank Von Zerneck, Doug Steckley, Wayne Satz, Michael Overly Band, Elizabeth Edwards, Bill Schallert, Frank Alesia, Howard Storm, Julie Mannix, Michael Mislove, Ira Miller, Bill Saluga, Terri Seigel, Neil Israel, Mary McCuster, Jimmy Martinez, Rod Gist, Jose Kent, Michael Popovich, Bo Kaprall, Larry Gelman, Barry Michlin, Danny Dark, Kurt Taylor, Joe Roth, C.D. Taylor, Bob McClurg, Cary Hoffman, Dody Dorn.

An ugly and highly unfunny "satire" of tv in the wasted vein of films like THE GROOVE TUBE. One can only wonder how hungry comedy talents such as Chase, Newman, Franken and Davis, Hesseman, and Proctor were to appear in such tripe as this. Most of the interest lies in watching some fine television performers appear in this early effort. The set pieces include such great yuks as a sit-com about the Manson Family and a game show in which passing gas wins a prize. There are also plenty of obscenities so that you'll know how daring and clever this is. This complete waste of time was shot on videotape and later transferred to film. It looks it, too. Israel went on to direct another distasteful comedy with a similar idea, AMERICATHON.

p, Joe Roth; d, Brad Swirnoff, Neil Israel; w, Israel, Michael Mislove; ph, Don Knight; m, Dennis Lambert, Brian Potter; ed, Roger Parker, Dayle Mustain; art d, C.D. Taylor; makeup, Danielle Gochrach.

Comedy   Cas.   **(PR:O   MPAA:R)**

TURKEY SHOOT   (SEE: ESCAPE 2000, 1983, Aus.)

TURKEY TIME**½   (1933, Brit.) 73m GAU British bw

Tom Walls *(Max Wheeler),* Ralph Lynn *(David Winterton),* Dorothy Hyson *(Rose Adair),* Robertson Hare *(Edwin Stoatt),* Mary Brough *(Mrs. Gather),* Norma Varden *(Ernestine Stoatt),* Veronica Rose *(Louise Stoatt),* D.A. Clarke-Smith *(Westbourne),* Marjorie Corbett *(Florence).*

A durable comedy about two pals, Walls and Lynn, who spend Christmas at the seaside home of Walls fiancee. Walls soon falls for another girl, Hyson, but is saved when Lynn also falls for her. One of an unbroken string of enjoyable comedies from London's Aldwych Theater which featured Walls.

p, Michael Balcon; d, Tom Walls; w, Ben Travers (based on his play); ph, Charles Van Enger.

Comedy   **(PR:A   MPAA:NR)**

TURKISH CUCUMBER, THE* (1963, Ger.) 96m Bavaria-Filmkunst/K. Gordon Murray-Inter-American-Trans-International c/bw (DIE TUR-KISCHEN GURKEN; AKA: WEDDING PRESENT; DADDY'S DELECTABLE DOZEN)

Oskar Sima (*Fruit Merchant*), Susi Nicoletti (*His Wife*), Ruth Stephan (*Their Daughter*), Gunther Philipp, Walter Gross, Hubert von Meyerinck, Ernst Walbrunn, Charly Muller, Ilse Petri, Monika Berger, Angela Monti, Brigitte Wenzel, Angela Hartmann, Edith Peters, Sergio Cosmei, Willy Schultes, Dora Carras, Harry Hertzsch, Lill Babs.

Sima is a man with two happy events to celebrate. He's marking his fiftieth year in the wholesale fruit business and his daughter (Stephan) is getting married. To help him celebrate, his Oriental supplier, a Turkish shiek, gives Sima a harem. This causes the man some trouble as he tries to hide the girls from his daughter and extremely jealous wife.

p, K. Gordon Murray; d, Rolf Olsen; w, Olsen, Peter Loos, Gunther Philipp; ph, Walter Tuch; m, Werner Scharfenberger; art d, Otto Pischinger, Herta Hareiter.

Comedy   (PR:C   MPAA:NR)

TURLIS ABENTEUER   (SEE: PINOCCHIO, 1969, Ger.)

TURN BACK THE CLOCK½**   (1933) 80m MGM bw

Lee Tracy (*Joe Gimlet*), Mae Clarke (*Mary Gimlet*), Otto Kruger (*Ted Wright*), George Barbier (*Pete Evans*), Peggy Shannon (*Elvina Wright*), C. Henry Gordon (*Mr. Holmes*), Clara Blandick (*Mrs. Gimlet*).

Cigar-store owner Tracy has a rich friend come over for dinner. He offers Tracy a business deal but Tracy's wife, Clarke, says nothing doing. Tracy gets drunk and runs out of the house, only to get hit by a car. While knocked out, he dreams of what life might be like were he rich. The comedy is simplistic but amiable and well told. What makes the story work is its good script, co-written by the talented Hecht. Some good, if light, laughs herein and Tracy's not at all bad in the lead.

p, Harry Rapf; d, Edgar Selwyn; w, Selwyn, Ben Hecht; ph, Harold Rosson; Frank Sullivan.

Comedy   (PR:A   MPAA:NR)

TURN OF THE TIDE**   (1935, Brit.) 80m BN/GAU bw

John Garrick (*Marney Lunn*), Geraldine Fitzgerald (*Ruth Fosdyck*), Sam Livesey (*Henry Lunn*), Joan Maude (*Amy*), J. Fisher White (*Isaac Fosdyck*), Wilfrid Lawson (*Luke Fosdyck*), Niall Macginnis (*John Lunn*), Moore Marriott (*Tindal Fosdyck*).

White is the head of a fishing family that has been established in a Yorkshire village for over 400 years. When another family moves in he regards them as foreigners and a feud starts. Leave it to the young people to solve everything when Garrick and Fitzgerald do their version of the "Romeo and Juliet" story. Unlike Shakespeare's classic, this ends happily. The film is well told with some good performances, though it runs much longer than need be.

p, John Corfield; d, Norman Walker; w, L. DuGarde Peach, J.O.C. Orton (based on the novel *Three Fevers* by Leo Walmsley).

Drama   (PR:A   MPAA:NR)

TURN OFF THE MOON**   (1937) 79m Fanchon/PAR bw

Charlie Ruggles (*Elliott Dinwiddy*), Eleanore Whitney (*Caroline Wilson*), Johnny Downs (*Terry Keith*), Kenny Baker (*Himself*), Ben Blue (*Luke*), Marjorie Gateson (*Myrtle Tweep*), Grady Sutton (*Truelove Spencer*), Romo Vincent (*Detective Dugan*), Andrew Tombes (*Dr. Wakefield*), Constance Bergen (*Maizie Jones*), Franklin Pangborn (*Mr. Perkins*), Charles Williams (*Brooks*), Pat West (*Photographer*), The Albee Sisters, The Fanchonettes, Floyd Christy and Hal Gould (*Specialties*), Phil Harris and Orchestra.

Ruggles owns a furniture store and pal Blue serves as night watchman. Gateson is the secretary that Ruggles wants to marry, but he can't make a move unless his astrologer (Tombes) gives him the go-ahead. The film culminates in a big extravaganza celebrating the store's twenty-fifth anniversary. Downs and Whitney are a younger set of lovers equally dependent on Tombes' mumbo jumbo. The tunes are nothing special, but lively direction helps this film along. Some good entertaiment comes from the specialty acts and Vincent does a nice little parody of Charles Laughton in MULTINY ON THE BOUNTY. Dmytryk, who edited this film, went on to gain fame as a director and as a member of the "Hollywood Ten." Songs includes "Turn off the Moon," "Easy on the Eyes," "Jammin', That's Southern Hospitality," and "Little Wooden Soldiers" (Sam Coslow).

p, Fanchon Royer; d, Lewis Seiler; w, Marguerite Roberts, Harlan Ware, Paul Gerard Smith (based on a story by Mildred Harrington); ph, Ted Tetzlaff; ed, Edward Dmytryk; md, Boris Morros; art d, Hans Dreier; ch, LeRoy Prinz.

Musical   (PR:A   MPAA:NR)

TURN ON TO LOVE zero   (1969) 83m Haven International bw

Sharon Kent (*Janice*), Richard Michaels (*Gerard*), Luigi Mastoianni (*Rico*), Jackie Riley (*Randee*).

We all start somewhere. This wretched and downright boring film which is a supposed expose of the underground hippe life is an early directorial effort of Avildsen, who later won the Oscar for his fine job on ROCKY. The paper-thin, quasi-porno plot has Kent playing a young woman dissatisfied with her new husband, Michaels. He's too much of a square, so she heads back to the Village where many of her old hippie friends still hang out. At a "freak out" she meets Mastoianni, an Italian filmmaker, and the pair wind up in the sack. After a couple of love-making sessions and some poorly done slow-motion interludes, Kent realizes that this is no longer the life for her. She returns to Michaels, who miraculously has overcome his "squareness" and is ready to get funky with his wife. The story is ridiculous, using standard cliches about hippie life styles without bothering to explore their nature. The sex scenes are relatively tame but with enough eroticism to have been considered borderline pornography in 1969. (By today's standards this is really nothing at all.) Avildsen's direction shows nothing of what he would be capable later in his career. Here it was often amateurish and provided no insight at all into the subjects. He also did the photography, which was perfunctory at best.

p, L.T. Kurtmann; d, John G. Avildsen; w, Atlas Geodesic, Fred Balachine, (based on a story by Herman Worth); ph, Avildsen; m, Amanda Productions Harmon Thronebury, the Ins and Outs.

Drama   (PR:O   MPAA:NR)

TURN THE KEY SOFTLY**   (1954, Brit.) 81m Chiltern/Astor bw

Yvonne Mitchell (*Monica Marsden*), Terence Morgan (*David*), Joan Collins (*Stella Jarvis*), Kathleen Harrison (*Mrs. Quilliam*), Thora Hird (*Landlady*), Dorothy Alison (*Joan*), Glyn Houston (*Bob*), Geoffrey Keen (*Gregory*), Russell Waters (*Jenkins*), Clive Morton (*Walters*), Richard Massingham (*Bystander*).

A trio of stories are loosely linked by the situations of the characters. Mitchell, Collins, and Harrison are three women who are released from prison on the same morning. Mitchell has served time after helping her boy friend in a burglary and he's quick to have her back at it once she's out. Collins, long before her fame on TV's "Dynasty," is a hooker who wants to reform and be married. She's nearly tempted back to the profession by the excitement of the street, but finally makes it as an honest girl. Last is Harrison, a shoplifter who loves her dog more than anything. Now that she's free, Harrison takes the mutt for a walk, only to see it killed by an auto when it runs into the street. The women all play their roles well and give the film its worth. At times the plot is forcefully contrived and often lacks interest. Essentially, these are three different stories with only a threadbare link between them. The direction is adequate, but doesn't do much with the material other than present it straightforwardly.

p, Maurice Cowan; d, Jack Lee w, Cowan, Lee John Brophy (based on a novel by Brophy); ph, Geoffrey Unsworth; m, Mischa Spoliansky; ed, Lito Carruthers.

Drama   (PR:C   MPAA:NR)

TURNABOUT**   (1940) 83m UA bw

Adolphe Menjou (*Phil Manning*), Carole Landis (*Sally Willows*), John Hubbard (*Tim Willows*), William Gargan (*Joel Clare*), Verree Teasdale (*Laura Bannister*), Mary Astor (*Marion Manning*), Donald Meek (*Henry*), Joyce Compton (*Irene Clare*), Inez Courtney (*Miss Edwards*), Franklin Pangborn (*Mr. Pingboom*), Marjorie Main (*Nora*), Berton Churchill (*Julian Marlowe*), Margaret Roach (*Dixie Gale*), Ray Turner (*Mose*), Norman Budd (*Jimmy*), Polly Ann Young (*Miss Twill*), Eleanor Riley (*Lorraine*), Murray Alper (*Masseur*), Miki Morita (*Ito*), Yolande Mollot (*Marie*), Georges Renavent (*Mr. Ram*).

Hubbard is a partner with Menjou and Gargan in a major advertising agency. He's married to Landis and the pair are always fighting about their respective roles and what the other really should be doing. An ancient Indian god that sits on their mantle hears this arguement just once too often and, presto chango! the two personalities have switched bodies. She discovers what he does at work all day, almost destroying the agency in the process. It's the same at home when an afternoon tea nearly turns into a disaster. Though there are a few chuckles, the presentation is predictable slapstick and takes much longer than need be to get to the main point. The performances aren't bad, though, and the budget allowed for some handsome looking sets. It's based on a novel by the same man who wrote the basis for TOPPER.

p&d, Hal Roach; w, Mickell Novak, Berne Giler, John McClain, Rian James (based on the novel, Thorne Smith); ph, Norbert Brodine; m, Arthur Morton; ed, Bert Jordan; art d, Nicholai Remisoff; spec eff, Roy Seawright.

Comedy   (PR:A   MPAA:NR)

TURNED OUT NICE AGAIN*½　(1941, Brit.) 80m Associated Talking Pictures-EAL/UA bw (AKA: IT'S TURNED OUT NICE AGAIN)

George Formby (*George Pearson*), Peggy Bryan (*Lydia Pearson*), Edward Chapman (*Uncle Arnold*), Elliot Mason (*Mrs. Pearson*), Mackenzie Ward (*Gerald Dawson*), O.B. Clarece (*Mr. Dawson*), Ronald Ward (*Nelson*), John Salew (*Largos*), Wilfrid Hyde-White (*Removal Man*), Hay Petrie (*Drunk*), Michael Rennie (*Diner*), Bill Shine.

Bryan and Formby are newlyweds who can't seem to get on the right track, mainly due to hubby's jealousy. He loses his job as foreman at an underwear factory when he buys a stock of untested material. Bryan leaves for London and displays the see-through underwear she's made of the stuff at a convention, garnering plenty of attention and winning Formby his job back.

p, Basil Dearden; d, Marcel Varnel; w, Austin Melford, John Dighton, Dearden (based on the play "As You Were" by Wells Root, Hugh Mills); ph, Gordon Dines; m, Ernest Irving; ed, Robert Hamer; art d, Wilfred Shingleton, Alberto Cavalcanti.

Comedy　　　　　　　　(PR:A　MPAA:NR)

TURNERS OF PROSPECT ROAD, THE**　(1947, Brit.) 88m GN bw

Wilfrid Lawson (*Will Turner*), Helena Pickard (*Lil Turner*), Maureen Glynne (*Betty Turner*), Amy Veness (*Grandma*), Jeanne de Casalis (*Mrs. Webster*), Shamus Locke (*Terence O'Keefe*), Desmond Tester (*Nicky*), Christopher Steele (*Magistrate*), Giselle Morlaix (*Jacqueline*), Joy Frankau (*Ruby*), Andrew Blackett (*Andrew Carroll*), Gus McNaughton (*Knocker*), Charles Farrell (*Jack*), Leslie Perrins (*Mrs. Webster*), Peter Bull (*J.G. Clarkson*).

A taxi driver finds a greyhound pup in his cab and brings the animal home for his daughter. She raises it and takes the dog to a racing track for some training. There a crooked dog owner who has entered a favored champ in an upcoming race tries to buy this new challenger. He is refused, though, so he sets the cabbie up on a phony drunk-driving charge. It looks rocky for a moment, but all is righted in the end and the cabbie's dog wins the big race. There are some fine moments of humor in this simple film and the playing is good, though not extraordinary. Made on an obviously limited budget, this is a good example of generic filmmaking with an amiable and predictable story populated by cardboard cutouts.

p, Victor Katona; d, Maurice J. Wilson; w, Katona, Patrick Kirwan; ph, Frederick Ford; m, Nicholas Brodszky; ed, Donald Ginsberg, Kenneth Hume; md, Philip Green; art d, George Ward; makeup, Sydney Hill.

Comedy/Drama　　　　　　　(PR:A　MPAA:NR)

TURNING POINT, THE***　　　　(1952) 85m PAR bw

William Holden (*Jerry McKibbon*), Edmond O'Brien (*John Conroy*), Alexis Smith (*Amanda Waycross*), Tom Tully (*Matt Conroy*), Ed Begley (*Eichelberger*), Dan Dayton (*Ackerman*), Adele Longmire (*Carmelina*), Ray Teal (*Clint*), Ted De Corsia (*Harrigan*), Don Porter (*Joe Silbray*), Howard Freeman (*Fogel*), Neville Brand (*Red*), Peter Baldwin (*Boy*), Judith Ames (*Girl*), Mary Murphy (*Secretary*), Leonard George (*Lefty*), Ben Cameron (*Gates*), Russell Johnson (*Herman*), Leonard Bremen (*Doc*), Eugene White (*Pinky*), Buddy Sullivan, Robert Rockwell, Joel Marston, Russell Conway (*Reporters*), George Ford, Charles Sherlock, Lee Phelps, Chalky Williams, George Dempsey (*Policemen*), Charles Campbell (*Cameraman*), Albin Robeling (*Waiter*), Jean Ransome (*Maid*), Gretchen Hale (*Mrs. Conroy*), Grace Hayle (*Mrs. Martin*), Ruth Packard, Hazel Boyne, Carolyn Jones (*Women*), Whit Bissell (*Buck*), Harry Hines (*Maintenance Man*), Franz F. Roehn (*Cashier*), Tony Barr (*Garcia*), Tom Moore (*Drugstore Proprietor*), Jamesson Shade (*Staff Member*), Jerry James (*Man*), John Maxwell (*Ed*), Soledad Jiminez (*Mrs. Manzinates*), Diane Garret (*Woman at Detroit Joint*), Ralph Sanford (*Harry*), Ralph Montgomery (*Driver*), Jay Adler (*Sammy*).

O'Brien is a crusading lawyer appointed to head a commission investigating organized crime. He enlists the help of his friend, investigative reporter Holden, and together they uncover proof that Begley is the head of the local crime syndicate. Holden also discovers that Tully, O'Brien's policeman father, is on the take from Begley. To get the commission off his back, Begley orders Tully killed, but this only serves to strengthen O'Brien's resolve. He and Holden also compete for the affections of Smith, long O'Brien's girl, but rapidly succumbing to Holden's easy charm. The commission subpoenas records from Begley which are kept in a tenement building he owns, and rather than let the incriminating documents fall into the hands of O'Brien's civic crusaders, he has the building burned down, killing dozens of residents. By now the commission has learned of a female witness to a murder committed by one of Begley's henchmen. While O'Brien frantically tries to find her, Holden is lured to a boxing arena where one of Begley's hired guns awaits him. The two play a deadly game of hide-and-seek, but before help in the form of police cars sent by O'Brien can get to him, Holden is shot and dies heroically in Smith's arms. Interesting *film noir* has good performances by the leads and a terrific villain in the person of Begley. When he orders the building containing the records burned down, his cruelty and vicious greed are almost written on his sweaty face. The actual burning of the building– at night, with screams of the victims hanging in the air–is a real shocker. In most other areas, though, the film is flat and flabby. The scenes of O'Brien and Smith are humdrum and it's only the crime scenes that take

on any life under the direction of Dieterle. Holden was almost through with his contract leading- man status. SUNSET BOULEVARD was behind him, STALAG 17 was next, and he was on the verge of superstardom.

p, Irving Asher; d, William Dieterle; w, Warren Duff (based on the unpublished story "Storm in the City" by Horace McCoy); ph, Lionel Lindon; ed, George Tomasini; md, Irving Talbot; art d, Hal Pereira, Joseph McMillan Johnson; set d, Sam Comer, Grace Gregory; cos, Edith Head; spec eff, Gordon Jennings, Farciot Edouart; makeup, Wally Westmore.

Crime　　　　　　　　(PR:C-O　MPAA:NR)

TURNING POINT, THE***　　　　(1977) 119m Hera/FOX c

Anne Bancroft (*Emma Jacklin*), Shirley MacLaine (*Deedee Rodgers*), Mikhail Baryshnikov (*Kopeikine*), Leslie Browne (*Emilia Rodgers*), Tom Skerritt (*Wayne Rodgers*), Martha Scott (*Adelaide*), Antoinette Sibley (*Sevilla*), Alexandra Danilova (*Dahkarova*), Starr Danias (*Carolyn*), Marshall Thompson (*Carter*), James Mitchell (*Michael*), Anthony Zerbe (*Rosie*), Phillip Saunders (*Ethan Rodgers*), Lisa Lucas (*Janina Rodgers*), Scott Douglas (*Freddie Ronoff*), Daniel Levans (*Arnold*), Jurgen Schneider (*Peter*), James Crittenden (*Billy Joe*), David Byrd (*Conductor*), Alexander Minz (*Boys Class Teacher*), Dennis Hahat (*Dennis*), Enrique Martinez (*Ballet Master*), Anne Barlow (*Ballet Mistress*), Saax Bradbury (*Florence*), Hilda Morales (*Sandra*), Donald Petrie (*Barney*), Howard Barr, Martha Johnson (*Pianists*), Lucette Aldous, Fernando Bujones, Richard Cragun, Suzanne Farrell, Marcia Haydee, Peter Martins, Clark Tippet, Marianna Tcherkassky, Martine Van Hamel, Charles Ward (*Ballet Stars*).

A big winner at the box office, recipient of many Oscar nominations (and winner of none), and only the second ballet- based picture (the other was THE RED SHOES) to ever make a dent with popular audiences, THE TURNING POINT is a well-made soap opera with a story that could have been right out of the 1930s backstage musicals except that the dancing here was replete with plies, not bucks and wings. The American Ballet Theatre is touring the U.S. and makes a stop in Oklahoma City. Star of the company is Bancroft, painfully thin, dedicated to dance, and having very little life away from her work. Living in O.C. is her former associate, MacLaine, who opted for love and marriage 20 years before, when both were rivals for the prima ballerina role in the company. MacLaine is married to Skerritt; they have three children and a successful ballet school. MacLaine goes to the performance and is bothered by her choice in life. Had she stayed with the ABT and continued, would that prima ballerina on the stage be her and not Bancroft? MacLaine's daughter is Browne and she is but 19. MacLaine introduces Browne to Bancroft, who recognizes herself and MacLaine in the young, ambitious Browne. Bancroft arranges an audition for Browne and the youngster is accepted. As the new season approaches, Browne bids farewell to MacLaine and Skerritt and goes north to prepare for her work in the ABT. Bancroft has been a star for many years and the time has come for her to hang up her tutu. The leading roles are being given to younger ballerinas and Bancroft realizes that the moment is near when she will begin to teach more than dance. This is depressing for Bancroft and she wonders if MacLaine didn't make the right decision by marrying Skerritt way back then. Browne is comfortably ensconced in New York by now and MacLaine has joined her, apparently as a chaperone. But the truth is that MacLaine wants to see if she did right by leaving the ballet. Browne is the lever between the women as they both coach her in various regimens while keeping an eye on each other. Browne meets Baryshnikov, a Casanova type who dances in between sexual conquests. They have a brief affair, then he breaks her heart by moving on to another dancer. (Both were making their film debuts here.) Bancroft has been having an affair with married Thompson and now that she is going to leave the road and her constant touring, she fully expects Thompson to shed his wife and marry her. However, Thompson has no thoughts of doing that and lets her know, thus depressing her even further. While in New York, MacLaine runs into an old flame she knew before marrying Skerritt. This is Zerbe, and she spends one night in bed with him. The moment Browne learns of that, she leaves the apartment she shares with MacLaine, irate over her mother's cheating. Skerritt comes to New York and he and MacLaine have a scene whereby she reveals that when she married him, it wasn't love as much as it was her needing to prove to the other dancers at ABT that Skerritt was not gay. Since that time, however, she has come to love him deeply. It's the night of Browne's debut in "Swan Lake." Prior to the performance, MacLaine and Bancroft take a walk near the theater for what is the most memorable scene of the film. MacLaine feels that Bancroft manipulated her into marrying Skerritt to get her out of the way and allow Bancroft to assume the prima ballerina position with the company. Bancroft laughs off the accusation and says that MacLaine wouldn't have ever made it in the big-time world of ballet because she is too nice and couldn't have back-stabbed all the people necessary to get to the top. The dialog gets angrier and culminates when the two women assault and maul each other. After enough hair has been pulled, they simultaneously start to laugh as they realize they are fighting over something that happened 20 years before and it is impossible to alter the past. Thus united in friendship again, both women walk into the theater to see Browne as she captivates the crowd with her magnificent technique. Some laughs, lots of maudlin moments, superior dancing from a host of real ballerinas, and a sometimes enlightening script. Browne replaced Gelsey Kirkland, who fell ill, and the odd part of that is Browne's real life paralleled the story in the film and was probably the basis for it. Her family had left

New York to open a ballet school in the hinterlands and did come back to New York, just as it was depicted in the film, and Browne became a topflight dancer. Executive producer Nora Kaye (wife of the director) is herself a former famed ballerina and Ross is a one-time choreographer. Ross showed great intelligence as he managed to shoot scenes of Bancroft "dancing" when, in fact, she didn't dance at all! It was all done with fast cuts and closeups but fooled nobody who really know anything about ballet. To music played by the Los Angeles Philharmonic, the dances included: "Legende" (Henryk Wieniawsky, danced by Richard Cragun, Marcia Haydee, choreographed by John Cranko), "Vortex" (Duke Ellington, danced by Browne, choreographed by Alvin Ailey), "Black Swan Pas de Deux" (from Peter Ilish Tchaikovsky's "Swan Lake," danced by Fernando Bujones, Lucette Aldous, choreographed by Marius Petipa), "Le Corsaire" (Adolphe Charles Adam, danced by Baryshnikov, choreographed by Petipa), "Pas de Deux" (Tchaikovsky, danced by Peter Martins, Suzanne Farrell, choreographed by George Balanchine), "Anna Karenina" (Tchaikovsky, danced by Bancroft, Scott Douglas, choreographed by Dennis Nahat). Other dances were "Chopin Etude" (choreographed by Frederick Ashton, Lev Ivanov, Michel Fokine), "Don Quixote Pas de Deux" (Minkus, choreographed by Petipa), "La Bayadere" (Minkus, choreographed by Alexander Minz, based on choreography by Petipa), "Giselle" (Adam, choreographed by Jules Perrot, Jean Coralli), Czerny's "Etudes" (choreographed by Harald Lander), "Romeo and Juliet" (by Sergei Prokofiev, choreographed by Kenneth MacMillan). Shot in Los Angeles and New York, with interiors at various New York locations.

p, Herbert Ross, Arthur Laurents; d, Ross; w, Laurents; ph, Robert Surtees (Panavision, DeLuxe Color); ed, William Reynolds; prod d, Albert Brenner; md, John Lanchbery; set d, Marvin March; cos, Albert Wolsky; ch, John Cranko, Alvin Ailey, Marius Petipa, George Balanchine, Dennis Nahat, Alexander Minz, Jean Coralli, Jules Perrot, Harald Lander, Kenneth MacMillan, Frederick Ashton, Michel Fokine, Lev Ivanov; makeup, Charles Schram; tech adv, Oliver Smith.

Ballet Drama   **Cas.**   **(PR:C MPAA:PG)**

TUSK*   (1980, Fr.) 119m Yang-Films 21 c

Cyrielle Clair (Elise), Anton Diffring (John Morrison), Serge Merlin (Greyson), Christopher Mitchum (Richard Cairn), Michel Peyrelon (Shakley), Sukumar Anhana (The Maharajah), B. Chandrasherkhra (Deepak), Oriole Henry (Elise at Age 5), Andy Jenny (The Reverend), Krake (The Maharand), Tusk the Elephant.

This confusing, pseudo-art film parallels the life of Clair, a turn-of-the-century English girl in India, with that of Tusk, the elephant of her dreams. The film is utterly incoherent, and culling a story from the mess borders on the impossible. The cast is almost uniformly awful. Clair seems more like she's playing than performing and her supporting cast ranges from tolerable to laughably unfunny. There's plenty of elephant trumpeting on the soundtrack, which is more noisy than anything else. The script went through the hands of several writers, though watching this one might think it went through a meat grinder as well. The director, famous for his EL TORO, publicly acknowledged a love for Luis Bunuel's films and obviously tried to emulate his mentor here. The imitation is pale, lots of pretty pictures wrapped around a wholly empty package. The locations act as the saving grace; they're good to look at and probably the only thing worth watching here.

p, Eric Rochacit; d, Alexandro Jodorowsky; w, Nick Niciphor, Jeffrey O'Kelly, Jodorowsky (based on the novel Poo Lorn of the Elephants by Reginald Campbell); ph, Jean-Jacques Flori (Technicolor); m, Jean-Claude Petit, Guy Skornik; ed, Jean-Philippe Berger; art d, Philip King.

Drama   **(PR: A MPAA:NR)**

TUTTE LE ALTRE RAGAZZE LO FANNO
                         (SEE: ALL THE OTHER GIRLS DO, 1967, Ital.)

TUTTI A CASA   (SEE: EVERYBODY GO HOME! 1962, Fr./Ital.)

TUTTI FRUTTI   (SEE: CATCH AS CATCH CAN, 1968, Fr./Ital.)

TUTTI PAZZI MENO IO   (SEE: KING OF HEARTS, 1967, Fr./Ital.)

TUTTLES OF TAHITI½   (1942) 91m RKO bw

Charles Laughton (Jonas Tuttle), Jon Hall (Chester Tuttle), Peggy Drake (Tamara Taio), Victor Francen (Dr. Blondin), Gene Reynolds (Ru), Florence Bates (Emily Taio), Curt Bois (Jensen), Adeline de Walt Reynolds (Mama Rusu Tuttle), Mala (Nat), Leonard Sues (Fana), Jody Gilbert (Effie), Adams (Paki), Jim Spencer (Tupa), Alma Ross (Hio), Teddy Infuhr (Ala).

Tucked away on a small South Seas island is a clan of life worshipers led by fun-loving Laughton. The family eats, drinks, and makes merry, caring little for anything else, least of all work. As the story unfolds episodically, Laughton and family encounter problems with cock fighting, money, and an always-out-of-gas boat. Bates is the matriarch of a rival family with a totally opposite set of values. This causes some problems when Laughton's son Hall

falls for her daughter Drake. The film's problem is that it's as lackadaisical as Laughton. There's really not enough here to justify an hour and a half though the cast isn't bad. There are some fun moments, but these are stretched out along the film's course with the rest serving as filler. Based on a novel by the authors of Mutiny on the Bounty, this boasted of some lavish special effects during a storm sequence. Nevertheless, this overbudgeted comedy (with a production cast of $847,000) was a poor box office attraction.

p, Sol Lesser; d, Charles Vidor; w, S. Lewis Meltzer, Robert Carson, James Hilton (based on the novel No More Gas by Charles Nordhoff, James Norman Hall); ph, Nicholas Musuraca; ed Frederic Knudtson; spec eff, Vernon L. Walker.

Comedy   **(PR:A MPAA;NR)**

TUXEDO JUNCTION**   (1941) 71 REP bw (GB: THE GANG MADE
                                                          GOOD)

Leon Weaver (Abner), June Weaver (Elviry), Frank Weaver (Cicero), Thurston Hall (Doug Gordon), Frankie Darro (Sock), Sally Payne (Pansy), Clayton Moore (Bill Bennett), Lorna Gray (Joan), Billy Benedict (Piecrust), Kenneth Lundy (Soapy Peters), Howard Hickman (Judge Rivers), Leonard Carey (Jenkins), Betty Blythe (Miss Hornblower), Sam Flint (Judge Lewis), The Little Vagabonds (Themselves).

Those hillbilly Weaver Brothers ride again in this stupid, though pleasant, entry in their series for Republic. The title has nothing to do with the plot, since the boys are trying to put together a float that will outshine everyone else's in the Rose Parade. This one is simple and nice, even if it's not much. Watch for an appearance by a very young Moore, later to become TV's "Lone Ranger." (See WEAVER FAMILY series, Index.)

p, Armand Schaefer; d, Frank McDonald; w, Dorrell McGowan, Stuart McGowan; ph, Ernest Miller; m, Cy Feuer; ed, Charles Craft. cos., Adele Palmer.

Comedy   **(PR:A MPAA:NR)**

TVA LEVANDE OCH EN DOD   (SEE: TWO LIVING, ONE DEAD,
                                                    1964, Brit./Swed.)

TWELFTH NIGHT**½   (1956, USSR) 54m Len film Studio/Artkino c

Katya Luchko (Viola/Sebastian), Anna Larionova (Olivia), Vadim Medvediev (Duke Orsino), M. Yanshin (Sir Toby Belch), G. Vipin (Sir Andrew Aguecheek), Vasili Merkuriev (Malvolio), S. Lukyanov (Antonio), B. Freindlich (Clown), A. Lisyanskaya (Maria), S. Filippov (Fabian), A. Antonov (Sea Captain).

Despite an abbreviated length this Russian adaptation of Shakespeare's great comedy is well done and highly entertaining. Though there are a few minor slow passages, for the most part the story is told with creative flair, using camera and color well. Luchko does a fine job with the dual role of twin brother and sister. The adaptation is faithful to the original play, told with spirit by a good cast and backed with a fine musical score as well.

d&w, Y. Fried (based on the comedy by William Shakespeare); ph, E. Shapiro (Magicolor); m, A. Zhivotov.

Comedy   **(PR:A MPAA:NR)**

12 ANGRY MEN***   (1957) 95m Orion-Nova/UA bw

Henry Fonda (Juror No. 8), Lee J. Cobb (Juror No. 3), Ed Begley (Juror No. 10), E.G. Marshall (Juror No. 4), Jack Warden (Juror No. 7), Martin Balsam (Juror No. 1), John Fiedler (Juror No. 2), Jack Klugman (Juror No. 5), Edward Binns (Juror No. 6), Joseph Sweeney (Juror No. 9), George Voskovek (Juror No. 11), Robert Webber (Juror No. 12), Rudy Bond (Judge), James A. Kelly (Guard), Bill Nelson (Court Clerk), John Savoca (Defendant).

12 ANGRY MEN begins in the final hours of a trial for murder in a hot, muggy New York City courtroom. The tired trial judge gives 12 weary jurors their instructions, exhorting them to adhere to the basic rule that weights the scales of justice: the defendant must be seen to be innocent unless proven guilty beyond a reasonable doubt. The jurors shuffle slowly to their confining chamber of rumination and final judgment, the life of a teen-aged Puerto Rican boy accused of knifing his father to death in their hands. Expecting a rapid verdict in what appears a conclusive case, which will allow the unwilling veniremen to quickly return to their day-to-day lives–as compelling to most as a siren's song–the jury foreman invites an immediate vote on what most believe will be a unanimous guilty verdict. When the ballots are tallied, 11 prove to be for conviction. Fonda is the lone holdout, the one juror who senses that the "reasonable doubt" requirement has not been met. The others breathe a nearly audible collective sigh: there's one in every crowd, their expressions attest. Grudgingly, they agree to re-examine the evidence. Afterwards, another vote is taken; this time, four are for acquittal. Once again, they deliberate among themselves, and the characters of each emerge. Balsam is a man who wants no trouble, a pleasant man who will go with the majority to enhance his popularity among his peers. Fiedler, an unassuming bank clerk, is unaccustomed to framing opinions on his own. Cobb, a bullying entrepreneur who runs a transport

service, insists that his own is the only worthwhile opinion. Businessman Marshall, a calculating rationalist, enjoys deductive reasoning, but seems unable to comprehend that a life is at stake in this "game" of justice. Street-wise Klugman, whose origins are too close to those of the defendant, wants only to forget them. Binns voices the prejudices and sympathies of his own class only. Warden, another small-time entrepreneur, thinks that everything is a Communist plot. Stupid Sweeney is unable to understand the evidence, but becomes the pivotal juror by default. Sour-faced, dyspeptic old Begley believes that authority, as represented by police and prosecution personnel, must by its nature be infallible, as does German-American Voskovec. Advertising executive Webber views the world solely in terms of slogans. Fonda's proves to be the voice of sweet reason as he compels his 11 near-peers into re-evaluating the circumstantial evidence that has nearly convicted the boy. Attitudes are altered in the process, and during the hour-and-a-half (the *real* time taken by the jury's deliberations) of the claustrophobic session, all 12 come to realize that the evidence is insufficient. The unanimous vote is for acquittal. 12 ANGRY MEN, which, at later viewing, appears anachronistic (where are the women, the blacks?) was a landmark film in its day, one which brought a new style to cinema. The teleplay-turned-movie made use of a single static set–an actual New York City jury room–and had a total of 365 separate takes, nearly all of them from different angles. The result was cinema heresy that *worked*. Novice director Lumet, making his film debut (he was an accomplished stage and TV helmer) was teaching lessons to the old-timers. With cameraman Kaufman (the brother of famed Soviet director Dziga Vertov), Lumet carefully plotted and sketched every visual nuance. As had been his habit with theatrical productions, he also rehearsed his cast for a full two weeks before the actual 20-day shoot. The resulting real-time drama made film history. This was Fonda's one experience as a movie producer. He had admired the TV play authored by coproducer Rose and had attempted to get Hollywood's established studios interested in it with little success. He and Rose raised the $340 thousand cost of the production themselves. Released as a conventional booking in large theaters (rather than being distributed only to small art houses, where it might have gained a major following and run for months on the strength of the uniformly favorable reviews it received), the film failed to make a profit, and Fonda never received his deferred salary. The picture *did* continue to be screened for years in schools' and organizations' auditoriums; despite his financial loss, Fonda remembered it fondly as one of his three best efforts (the others were THE GRAPES OF WRATH and THE OX-BOW INCIDENT). Fonda is fine in the picture, and the others in the cast (hand-picked by Fonda) comprised the leading stage and TV actors of Gotham, whose wonderful work was rewarded in many cases by future stardom. The film is an unsettling one in many ways, as much an indictment as an affirmation of America's jury system (one wonders what might have happened had Fonda's voice-of-reason character *not* been present), and the telegraphed conclusion is seldom in doubt, but the picture remains a valuable civics lesson, albeit a disquieting one. Eleanor Roosevelt witnessed a private screening of the movie, and liked it enormously, writing about it in her widely circulated newspaper column, "My Day." Fonda received an Oscar nomination–as a coproducer, not an actor–as did Rose and Lumet. The technique of the film has been repeated since, but this is the one that set the precedent.

p, Henry Fonda, Reginald Rose; d, Sidney Lumet; w, Rose (based on his TV play); ph, Boris Kaufman; m, Kenyon Hopkins; ed, Carl Lerner; art d, Robert Markell.

Drama   Cas.   (PR:A MPAA:NR)

TWELVE CHAIRS, THE*½   (1970) 94m Crossbow-UMC c

Ron Moody (*Ippolit Vorobyaninov*), Frank Langella (*Ostap Bender*), Dom DeLuise (*Father Fyodor*), Mel Brooks (*Tikon*), Bridget Brice (*Young Woman*), Robert Bernal (*Curator*), David Lander (*Engineer Bruns*), Andreas Voutsinas (*Nikolai Sestrin*), Vlada Petric (*Sevitsky*), Diana Coupland (*Mme. Bruns*), Nicholas Smith (*1st Actor*), Elaine Garreau (*Claudia Ivanova*), Will Stampe (*Watchman*), Branka Veselinovic (*Natasha*), Paul Wheeler, Jr. (*Kolya*), Aca Stojkovic (*Capt. Scriabin*), Mavid Popovic (*Makko*), Mladja Veselinovic, Rada Djuricin.

One of Mel Brooks' best films, made before he discovered that nothing succeeds like excess. Based on a Russian novel from the 1920s, which was then translated into English by Doris Mudie and Elizabeth Hill and named *Diamonds to Sit On*, this fast-paced period piece is well-made, funny, and a pleasure to watch from start to completion. Shot on location in Yugoslavia (to resemble Russia), it begins as Moody, a one-time nobleman's son who has now been reduced to working as a clerk for the government, is told by his dying mother that the family fortune was hidden in one of a set of a dozen chairs, 10 years before, to escape the clutches of the Bolsheviks. In an attempt to claim the money, Moody goes back to where the family once lived in splendor and makes the mistake of telling his story to Langella, a beggar with big ideas. Now that Langella knows the secret, he is cut in as a partner when he promises to help Moody. DeLuise is a Russian Orthodox priest who heard the old woman's final confession and is now also searching for the jewels which represent the sum total of Moody's inheritance. DeLuise visits the Department of Housing and Langella masquerades as a clerk there and sends the erstwhile priest on a wild goose chase to Siberia to see Lander, who supposedly has the chairs. Meanwhile, Moody and Langella find a few of the chairs reposited in a museum. They wait until the museum closes,

then attack the chairs, rip them up, and find nothing for their efforts. They next learn that some of the remaining chairs are being used as props by a small theatrical company. Langella and Moody insinuate themselves into the acting company, slash the chairs, and are again stymied when they find zilch. The search continues and they discover that a Russian circus performer is using one of the chairs in a high-wire act. That chair is destroyed and again they come up with nothing. Eleven chairs have been found and there is but one left. They are starving and in need of any roubels they can find. Moody fakes a seizure as Langella passes the hat to sympathetic people on the street and they raise enough cash to take them to their final destination, a railway employees' clubroom where they sadly learn that the final chair was already dismantled by the workers and the jewels were used to provide all of the accouterments and chess games for the retired workers. Their journey has ended sadly and Langella is preparing to jettison Moody when he changes his mind as Moody goes into his epilepsy act and several people stop on the street to toss him some money. Langella and Moody will continue their relationship as long as Moody can quiver and Langella can shout at the passers-by and gather the loose coins in the crowd's pockets. Brooks plays a small role as the one-time valet to Moody's father, who is now acting as the janitor in the house. He does a drunk routine that is a marvel of timing and underplaying (which is rare for Brooks). DeLuise is out of his class against Moody and Langella. Moody's work proves that his brilliance in OLIVER was not a one-time thing. Langella plays it straight, which is perfect in the script by Brooks. DeLuise mugs and frets and seems out of place against the controlled work of the other actors. Good second unit direction by Eric Van Haaren Norman and the production supervisor was a man who was to spend several profitable years working with Woody Allen, Fred Gallo. A charming movie about larceny in Communist Russia, with a few moments of questionable taste that take this out of the G-rated category.

p, Michael Hertzberg; d&w, Mel Brooks (based on the novel by Ilya Arnoldovich Ilf, Yevgeniy Petrov, translated by Elizabeth Hill, Doris Mudie as *Diamonds to Sit On*); ph, Djordje Nikolic (Movielab Color); m, John Morris; ed, Alan Heim; art d, Mile Nokolic; md, Morris, Jonathan Tunick; cos, Ruth Myers; m/l, "Hope for the Best (Expect the Worst)," Brooks.

Comedy   Cas.   (PR:A-C MPAA:GP)

TWELVE CROWDED HOURS½   (1939) 64m RKO bw

Richard Dix (*Nick Green*), Lucille Ball (*Paula Sanders*), Allen Lane (*Dave Sanders*), Donald MacBride (*Inspector Keller*), Cyrus W. Kendall (*Costain*), Granville Bates (*McEwan*), John Arledge (*Red*), Bradley Page (*Tom Miller*), Dorothy Lee (*Thelma*), Addison Richards (*Berquist*), Murray Alper (*Allen*), John Gallaudet (*Jimmy*), Joseph de Stephani (*Rovitch*).

A nice crime film has Dix playing a nosy reporter. When his editor is killed Dix stumbles onto a numbers racket run by the nefarious Kendall. Ball is the love interest for Dix. Lane is her kid brother who's mixed up in the racket, and requiring the usual rescue-from-the-criminal-world by his future brother-in-law. Despite some scripting flaws the cast does its job with vigor. The direction is at a good clip which manages to overcome the unlikely depiction of newspaper life.

p, Robert Sisk; d, Lew Landers; w, John Twist (based on a story by Garrett Fort, Peter Ruric); ph, Nicholas Musuraca; ed, Harry Marker; cos, Renie.

Crime   (PR:A MPAA:NR)

TWELVE GOOD MEN   (1936, Brit.) 64m WB bw

Henry Kendall (*Charles Drew*), Nancy O'Neil (*Ann*), Joyce Kennedy (*Lady Thora*), Percy Parsons (*Hopwood*), Morland Graham (*Victor Day*), Bernard Miles (*Inspector Pine*), Philip Ray (*Higgs*), Frederick Burtwell (*Fortheringay*), Roddy Hughes, Sam Springson, George Hughes, Madge White.

After being convicted and sent to prison, a killer escapes and begins to terrorize the jurors who sent him up by killing two of them. The remaining jurors take refuge in the home of Kendall, an actor who served as a juror in the case. Though the murderer kills a few more people, Kendall stops him from completing his spree. Despite a seemingly unbelievable chain of events the film works nicely, thanks to the skilled writing team of Launder and Gilliat.

p, Irving Asher; d, Ralph Ince; w, Frank Launder, Sidney Gilliat (based on the novel *Murders in Praed Street* by John Rhodes); ph, Basil Emmott.

Crime   (PR:A MPAA:NR)

TWELVE-HANDED MEN OF MARS, THE* (1964, Ital./Span.) 95m Produzione D.S./Epoca Films bw (I MARZIANI HANNO DODICI MANI; SIAMMO QUATTRO MARZIANI; LLEGARON LOS MARCIANOS)

Paolo Panelli (*X1*), Carlo Croccolo (*X2*), Enzo Garinei (*X3*), Alfredo Landa (*X4*), Magali Noel, Cristina Gajonia, Umberto D'Orsi, Margaret Lee, Franco Franchi.

This charming science fiction comedy features Panelli, Croccolo, Garinei, and Landa as four Martians who take human guise for a trip to Earth. They're supposed to be preparing for an invasion by the Red Planet but discover that life on Earth isn't too bad. One gets in the real estate business, another becomes involved in politics, a third falls in love, and the last ends up, of all things, a science fiction author! The comedy is played for big laughs and they come through almost every time. Lots of fun with a good score by Morricone, who wrote the music for A FISTFUL OF DOLLARS and FOR A FEW DOLLARS MORE.

p, Dario Sabatello; d&w, Franco Castellano, G. Pipolo, G. Mocchia, L. Martin; ph, Alfio Contini; m, Ennio Morricone.

Science Fiction/Comedy (PR:A MPAA:NR)

TWELVE HOURS TO KILL* (1960) 83m FOX bw

Nico Minardos (*Martin Fallonis*), Barbara Eden (*Lucy Hall*), Grant Richards (*Lt. Jim Carnevan*), Russ Conway (*Capt. Willie Long*), Art Baker (*Capt. Johns*), Gavin McLeod (*Johnny Carver*), CeCe Whitney (*Clara Carnevan*), Richard Reeves (*Mark Venard*), Byron Foulger (*Shelby Gardner*), Barbara Mansell (*Cynthia Marshall*), Ted Knight (*Denton*), Shep Sanders (*Russo*), Charles Meredith (*Druggist*), Stewart Conway (*Bert, Cop*), Don Collier (*Andy, Cop*), Donald Kerr (*Neighbor*), Ed Sheehan (*Gas Station Attendant*), Bernard Kates (*Desk Editor*), David Thursby (*Cab Dispatcher*), Sid Kane (*George Marshall*), Kitty Kelly (*Woman*).

When Minardos witnesses a murder, the hapless Greek engineer is taken into protective custody by the cops. Unfortunately for him the law is in cahoots with the killers. When he finds this out Minardos goes on the run and so does the film, twisting and turning the plot into total confusion bordering on unintentional self-parody. The actors, some of whom would later be big on TV sitcoms (Eden, Knight, MacLeod), do what they can but eventually are overwhelmed by the shoddy script and confusing, frenetic direction. To the film's credit it looks good and the score isn't bad at all.

p, John Healy; d, Edward L. Cahn; w, Jerry Sohl (based on the *Saturday Evening Post* serial "Set Up for Murder" by Richard Stern); ph, Floyd Crosby (CinemaScope); m, Paul Dunlap; ed, Betty Steinberg; art d, John Mansbridge.

Crime (PR:A MPAA:NR)

TWELVE O'CLOCK HIGH***** (1949) 132m FOX bw

Gregory Peck (*Gen. Frank Savage*), Hugh Marlowe (*Lt. Col. Ben Gately*), Gary Merrill (*Col. Keith Davenport*), Dean Jagger (*Maj. Harvey Stovall*), Millard Mitchell (*Gen. Pritchard*), Robert Arthur (*Sgt. McIllhenny*), Paul Stewart (*Capt. "Doc" Kaiser*), John Kellogg (*Maj. Cobb*), Robert Patten (*Lt. Bishop*), Lee MacGregor (*Lt. Zimmerman*), Sam Edwards (*Birdwell*), Roger Anderson (*Interrogation Officer*), John Zilly (*Sgt. Ernie*), William Short (*Lt. Pettinghill*), Richard Anderson (*Lt. McKessen*), Lawrence Dobkin (*Capt. Twombley*), Kenneth Tobey (*Sentry*), John McKee (*Operations Officer*), Campbell Copelin (*Mr. Britton*), Don Guadagno (*Dwight*), Peter Ortiz (*Weather Observer*), Steve Clark (*Clerk in Antique Shop*), Joyce McKenzie (*Nurse*), Don Hicks (*Lt. Wilson*), Ray Hyke (*Bartender*), Harry Lauter (*Radio Officer*), Leslie Denison (*RAF Officer*), Russ Conway (*Operations Officer*).

Probably the finest drama about the burdens of command ever made, TWELVE O'CLOCK HIGH also includes one of Gregory Peck's finest performances plus magnificent combat footage. The film opens as Jagger walks about London in 1949. He recognizes a small mug in an antique store window and buys it, and later travels out into the countryside to visit an abandoned air base which the mug had reminded him of. His mind wanders back to the war and as he was, a major stationed at a U.S. Air Corps bomber base. The unit is plagued with high casualties and low effectiveness, partly a result of commander Merrill's "overidentification" with the men. Simply put, the men he sends up to possible death every day have become too important to him as individuals and it is impairing his ability to do his job. Peck steps in and assumes command, immediately cutting back on leaves, closing the local bar, and disciplining the men back into line. At first almost every pilot in the unit applies for a transfer, but before long, in the face of declining losses and improved efficiency, they rally to Peck's support. But just as it had Merrill, the strain of the job cracks Peck, and he has to be physically restrained from flying a mission himself. When the men fly off without him, he sits, catatonic and guilty, while the radio brings the battle over Germany into the room. In the end, with most of the planes returning safely, Peck is taken away, the victim of a complete nervous breakdown. One of the first films to look at WW II in the air from a nonheroic standpoint, the story of the commander cracking under the strain of sending lads into battle day after day had previously been seen twice in THE DAWN PATROL and its remake, although the story was actually taken from the true story of Maj. Gen. Frank A. Armstrong, who suffered a nervous breakdown while commanding a bomb group of the Eighth Air Force. During the shooting at Eglin Air Force Base in Florida, the script called for a B-17 to make a wheels-up belly landing. The Air Force refused to let any of its men perform the stunt, though more than 20 volunteered. Word was sent to veteran stunt pilot Paul Mantz, asking him to do the job, but his asking price was too high. Director King, a long-time flyer himself, then sent Mantz a letter saying that unless he did the stunt King was going to do it himself. Mantz, an old friend of King's, immediately cut his price in half and did the stunt. Much of the aerial footage in the film came from German and American archives, and this footage was seamlessly cut into the film. At one point in the researching, a film of a B-17 having its tail sheared off, then

going into a turning dive, around and around toward Berlin below, was found. Researchers later located German footage of the same plane going down and the resulting scene is thoroughly impressive. Peck is superb, his mannerisms slowly betraying the incredible pressure and oncoming breakdown. Even better is Jagger, around whom the story unfolds, and who serves to comment and elucidate what Peck is going through. He received an Oscar for his part here, and never did anything else as good again. The opening scenes, where he flashes back to 1942, are beautiful and powerfully conceived, and the moment when the present gives way to the past is almost unnoticeable. Many films have been made on the subject of the burdens of command since, but none can compare with TWELVE O'CLOCK HIGH.

p, Darryl F. Zanuck; d, Henry King; w, Sy Bartlett, Beirne Lay, Jr. (based on their novel); ph, Leon Shamroy; m, Alfred Newman; ed, Barbara McLean; art d, Lyle R. Wheeler, Maurice Ransford; tech adv, Col. John H. De Russy, Maj. Johnny McKee.

War Drama Cas. (PR:C MPAA:NR)

TWELVE PLUS ONE** (1970, Fr./Ital.) 95m COFCI-CEF c

Sharon Tate (*Pat*), Orson Welles (*Markau*), Vittorio Gassman (*Mike*), Mylene Demongeot (*Judy*), Terry-Thomas (*Albert*), Tim Brooke Taylor (*Jackie*), Vittorio De Sica (*Di Seta*).

Gassman arrives in England where he has inherited a fortune from an eccentric old aunt. He visits her home and finds the place run down so he sells 13 antique chairs to raise money for the fare home. To his horror Gassman later finds a note explaining that the fortune was hidden inside one of the chairs. He goes to Tate who works in the gallery he sold the chairs to and from there it's a mad dash across Europe to find the missing loot. Eventually it's found in a chair that's owned by some nuns raising funds for an orphanage. There are a few good cameos, particularly by Welles and De Sica. On the whole it's still not much. This old Russian fable was done much better by Mel Brooks under the title THE TWELVE CHAIRS. This was Tate's last film for shortly after its completion she and several others were the victims of the brutal bloodbath inflicted by Charles Manson and his "family". Because of the nature of her death the film's original title THIRTEEN was changed to TWELVE PLUS ONE.

p, Claude Giroux; d, Nicolas Gessner; w, Marc Benham, Gessner; ph, Giuseppe Ruzzolini (Eastmancolor); m, Piero Poletto.

Comedy (PR:A MPAA:R)

TWELVE TO THE MOON*½ (1960) 74m COL bw

Ken Clark (*Capt. John Anderson*), Michi Kobi (*Dr. Hideko Murata*), Tom Conway (*Dr. Feodor Orloff*), Anthony Dexter (*Dr. Luis Vargas*), John Wengraf (*Dr. Erik Heinrich*), Anna-Lisa (*Dr. Sigrid Bromark*), Phillip Baird (*Dr. Rochester*), Roger Til (*Dr. Etienne Martel*), Cory Devlin (*Dr. Asmara Makonen*), Tema Bey (*Dr. Selim Hamid*), Robert Montgomery, Jr (*Roddy Murdock*), Richard Weber (*Dr. David Ruskin*), Francis X. Bushman (*Narrator*).

An international crew of 12 goes on a trip to the moon where they have nothing but trouble. First one crew member is killed by some molten silver. Others die from lunar dust. Finally it's revealed that the creatures behind all the deaths are some underground lunar dwellers who ironically are a bunch of peace-seekers. They've been frightened by the Earthmen's intrusions on their planet and threaten to freeze up all of North America unless the survivors tell Earth to stop all wars. Why supposedly timid peace-loving creatures would turn to such rash methods isn't explained but a lot of things are discussed ad infinitum, well past an acceptable level of boredom. The acting is stiff and unnatural and the space flight sequences highly inaccurate to the space-conscious audiences of 1960, let alone today. The camera work isn't bad, though, and some of the special effects almost make up for the problems. The screenplay is by the author of the original CAT PEOPLE and was directed without much excitement by the man who gave us THEY SAVED HITLER'S BRAIN.

p, Fred Gebhardt; d, David Bradley; w, DeWitt Bodeen (based on a story by Gebhardt); ph, John Alton; m, Michael Anderson; ed, Edward Mann; art d, Rudi Feld; set d, John Burton; spec eff, Howard A. Anderson, E. Nicholson.

Science Fiction (PR:A MPAA:NR)

TWENTIETH CENTURY***½ (1934) 91m COL bw

John Barrymore (*Oscar Jaffe*), Carole Lombard (*Mildred Plotka/Lily Garland*), Roscoe Karns (*Owen O'Malley*), Walter Connolly (*Oliver Webb*), Ralph Forbes (*George Smith*), Dale Fuller (*Sadie*), Etienne Girardot (*Matthew J. Clark*), Herman Bing, Lee Kohlmar (*Bearded Men*), James P. Burtis (*Train Conductor*), Billie Seward (*Anita*), Charles Lane (*Max Jacobs*), Mary Jo Mathews (*Emmy Lou*), Ed Gargan (*Sheriff*), Edgar Kennedy (*McGonigle*), Gigi Parrish (*Schultz*), Fred Kelsey (*Detective*), Cliff Thompson (*Lockwood*), Nick Copeland (*Treasurer*), Sherry Hall (*Reporter*), Howard Hickman (*Dr. Johnson*), James Burke (*Chicago Detective*), George Reed (*Uncle Remus*), Clarence Geldert (*Southern Colonel*), Lillian West (*Charwoman*), Fred "Snowflake" Toones (*Porter*), Steve Gaylord Pendleton (*Brother in Play*), King Mojave (*McGonigle's Assistant*), Eddy Chandler (*Cameraman*), Harry Semels (*Artist*), Lynton Brent (*Train Secretary*), Anita

Brown (*Stage Show Girl*), Irene Thompson (*Stage Actress*), George Offerman, Jr. (*Stage Carpenter*), Buddy Williams (*Stage Actor*), Nick Copeland (*Treasurer*).

Even though there are many actors in this, it remains a one-man show for Barrymore as he portrays one of the most preposterous and memorable characters to ever spring from the minds of Hecht and MacArthur (who, it must be admitted, did adapt a play by Milholland). Directed with mile-a-minute speed by Hawks (who did the same thing for MacArthur and Hecht in HIS GIRL FRIDAY), it's the tale of maniacal Broadway director Barrymore who takes a shop girl, Lombard, and transforms her from a talented amateur to a smashing Great White Way success, beloved by the public and the press. Barrymore and Lombard have been together three years and he has been pulling his Svengali routine on her, shaping Lombard's every move, directing her plays, being her lover, and forming her career. They battle like the Hatfields and the McCoys with regularity, then make up with passion. She is a huge star in New York but yearns for some peace away from the manic-excessive Barrymore. One final disagreement does the trick and Lombard departs the concrete jungle of New York for the palm trees of Hollywood and a screen career. Now Barrymore's fortune plummets, with his manager, Connolly, and his press representative, Karns, he boards the Twentieth Century Limited, the cross-country train in Chicago . They are in Chicago with creditors at his heels. They escape the Windy City on their way to New York, and what Barrymore hopes will be a fresh chance at repeating his prior success. As luck would have it, Lombard and her new fiance, football player Forbes, are also on the train. Barrymore despises Forbes and his rugged good looks and doesn't bother to hide his disdain. The train clackety-clacks along the tracks and Barrymore moves in on Lombard, who has become as large a movie star as she was on Broadway. Barrymore plans to produce his version of "The Passion Play" (the same as the one in Europe that runs forever), and he wants Lombard to star in it. The remainder of the picture is a farcical and biting series of verbal exchanges, doors opening and closing, insults hurled, kisses thrown, several weird characters racing through the proceedings, and some of the biggest laughs Barrymore ever received. In the end, as expected, Barrymore has convinced Lombard that Broadway is the place for her, and by the moment they come to a halt at Grand Central Station, she is safely under his influence once more. Barrymore is a wonder, doing imitations of camels, trampling over actors' lines, using foreign phrases to punctuate his dialog and causing everyone else in the movie to appear like little more than stooges for his performance. The picture was not a hit when it first came out, perhaps due to the fact that the theater and the nuts who inhabit it are somewhat outside the ken of the average moviegoer. Years later, it would become a musical by Comden and Green but that presentation was also not nearly the hit which was expected. Although Joe August gets the credit as the cinematographer, some sources also list Joe Walker. The play took place entirely on the train but they wisely held off getting on board until the third reel here. Movies that take place entirely on trains are not easy to sustain and only the mastery of Hitchcock could make it work in THE LADY VANISHES. There is no use analyzing Barrymore's character because it defies parsing, so just sit back and watch hinm take over the screen and make it his. An incredible performance. In small roles as two bearded men who want to be in the religious play, there's some good comic acting by Herman Bing and Lee Kohlmar. This was the basis for the Broadway musical "On The Twentieth Century."

p&d, Howard Hawks; w, Charles MacArthur, Ben Hecht (based on their play, adapted from the play "Napoleon on Broadway" by Charles Bruce Milholland); ph, Joseph August; ed, Gene Havlick.

Comedy   **(PR:A MPAA:NR)**

20TH CENTURY OZ* (1977, Aus.) 100m Count Features/BEF c (OZ)

Joy Dunstan (*Dorothy*), Graham Matters (*The Wizard*), Bruce Spence (*Surfie*), Michael Carmen (*Mechanic*), Gary Waddell (*Bikie*), Robin Ramsay (*The Good Fairy*), Paula Maxwell (*Jane*), Ned Kelly (*Truckie*).

20TH CENTURY OZ is yet another telling of L. Frank Baum's classic story. In this version, Dorothy (Dunstan) is knocked unconscious after her pickup truck crashes when she is out on a date. She wakes up in the new and different world with one idea on her mind: not to return home but to see the farewell performance of the great rock star The Wizard (Matters). Along the trail she meets Spence, a surfer (for the Scarecrow), Carmen, a mechanic (for the Tinman), and Waddell as a biker (for the Lion). The Good Fairy arrives in the form of a boutique christened with the moniker, and the Bad Witch is a 210-pound truck driver who proves to be quite a menace. A charming and often very clever film, it's hampered by the rock score that is often overbearing, particularly the title tune and the unfortunately anticlimactic concert. Dunstan isn't bad, but she could have used a few more acting lessons. The direction is sharp, and a nice job of turning Melbourne side streets into the land of Oz. The film may be a little bawdy for younger viewers, but the teens will get a kick out of it.

p, Chris Lofven, Lyne Helms; d&w, Lofven (based on the book "The Wizard of Oz" by L. Frank Baum); ph, Dan Burstall (Eastmancolor); m, Ross Wilson; ed, Les Luxford.

Fantasy   **(PR:A MPAA:R)**

25TH HOUR, THE** (1967, Fr./Ital./Yugo.) 119m Les Films Concordia-C.C. Champion-Avala Film/MGM c (LA 25E HEURE; LA VENTICINQUESIMA ORA)

Anthony Quinn (*Johann Moritz*), Virna Lisi (*Suzanna Moritz*), Michael Redgrave (*Defense Counsel*), Gregoire Aslan (*Nicolai Dobresco*), Marcel Dalio (*Strul*), Serge Reggiani (*Trajan Koruga*), Drewe Henley (*Capt. Brunner*), Paul Maxwell (*Photographer*), George Roderick (*Goldenberg*), Alexander Knox (*Prosecutor*), Albert Remy (*Joseph Grenier*), Francoise Rosay (*Mme. Nagy*), Jean Desailly (*War Minister's Aide*), Marius Goring (*Col. Muller*), John Le Mesurier (*Magistrate*), Liam Redmond (*Father Koruga*), Kenneth J. Warren (*Varga*), Henia Suchar (*Nora*), Jan Werich (*Sgt. Apostol Constantin*), Harold Goldblatt (*Dr. Nagy*), Meier Tzelniker (*Abramovici*), Jacques Marin (*Fourrier*), Dara Milosevic (*Mrs. Koruga*), Viktor Starcic (*Hurtig*), Stojan Decermic (*Marcou*), Olga Schoberova (*Rosa*), David Sumner (*Ghitza Jon*), Raoul Delfosse (*Usher*).

Quinn is a Rumanian peasant falsely accused of being a Jew by invading German forces. He's sent to a labor camp by Aslan, a local police captain who lusts after Quinn's wife Lisi. Though she loves her husband, Lisi is forced to divorce Quinn so their property won't be confiscated. After a year and a half in the camp, Quinn escapes and flees to Hungary. He tries to get help from some Jewish organizations, but they won't help him because he's Gentile. He's taken by the Germans once more, but this time as an example of the best that Aryan breeding can offer. Unwittingly made an S. S. officer, Quinn is photographed and his face printed on magazine covers circulated throughout occupied Europe. The war ends and Quinn is put on trial. However, a letter arrives from Lisi, who now has a child after being raped by a Russian soldier. This so moves the jury that Quinn is let go and finally reunited with his wife. Despite excellent performances by Quinn and Lisi, the film is a genuine mess. Its episodic structure proved to be overwhelming for the director and writers, veering uncomfortably from comedy to tragedy without any real thought. Quinn is left to carry the weight of the film, a difficult task that he manages to pull off with some degree of success. He gives it his best, but at times it simply isn't enough. MGM didn't even understand the film, which tried hard to be a tragicomedy, and tried a variety of ad campaigns to sell it.

p, Carlo Ponti; d, Henri Verneuil; w, Verneuil, Francoise Boyer, Wolf Mankowitz (based on *La Vingt-Cinquieme Heure* by Constantin Virgil Gheorghiu); ph, Andreas Winding (Franscope, Metrocolor); m, Georges Delerue; ed, Francoise Bonnot; prod d, Robert Clavel; cos, Rosine Delamare; makeup, Monique Archambault.

Drama/Comedy   **(PR:C MPAA:NR)**

24-HOUR LOVER*½ (1970, Ger.) 90m Rob Houwer-Film/AIP c (BENGELCHEN LIEBT KRUEZ UND QUER; BENGELCHEN HAT'S WIRKLICH SCHWER; AKA: CRUNCH)

Harald Leipnitz (*George Weissborn*), Sybille Maar (*Irene*), Herbert Botticher (*Alfred Weissborn*), Brigitte Skay (*Marion*), Monika Lundi (*Lisa*), Renate Roland (*Peggy*), Marianne Wischmann (*Vera*), Claudia Wedekind (*Rosa*), Sylvie Beck (*Monika*), Isolde Brauner (*Mia*), Werner Schwier (*Doctor*), Jana Novakova (*Ulla*), Doris Kiesow (*Lenna*), Herbert Weissbach (*Grandfather*), Inge Langen (*Claudia*), Sammy Drechsel, Henry van Lyck, Nino Korda.

Leipnitz is a roving bachelor wine salesman whose naughty exploits harm the chances of his schoolteacher brother Botticher getting a promotion. When he's hospitalized for exhaustion, the family rejoices as Leipnitz announces he's found true love–his nurse–at last . He talks of an engagement, but the family is more than a little surprised and dismayed when Leipnitz brings home a different fiancee than the one expected. Leipnitz goes through several more fiancees and finally Maar, a distant cousin, is invited to the house in hopes that Leipnitz will fall in love with her. The two eventually marry and Leipnitz's escapades are permanently ended when he injures himself sliding down the bannister at his wedding party.

p, Rob Houwer; d&w, Marran Gosov; ph, Hubs Hagen, Niklas Schilling (Eastmancolor); m, Martin Bottcher; ed, Gisela Haller; art d, Gabriel Bauer.

Comedy   **(PR:O MPAA:R)**

24 HOURS* (1931) 65m PAR bw (LE LIEUTENANT SOURIANT; GB: THE HOURS BETWEEN)

Clive Brook (*Jim Towner*), Kay Francis (*Fanny Towner*), Miriam Hopkins (*Rosie Dugan*), Regis Toomey (*Tony Bruzzi*), George Barbier (*Hector Champion*), Adrienne Ames (*Ruby Wintringham*), Lucille La Verne (*Mrs. Dacklehorse*), Wade Boteler (*Pat Healy*), Charlotte Granville (*Savina Jerrold*), Minor Watson (*David Melbourn*), Thomas E. Jackson (*Police Commissioner*), Robert Kortman (*Dave-the-Slapper*), Malcolm Waite (*Murphy*).

Rich couple Brook and Francis are constantly bickering and close to divorce. Cabaret singer Hopkins is Brook's new interest, but over the course of 24 hours he realizes he loves Francis and returns to her. A well-acted and nicely detailed film. Hopkins is a little disappointing, but Brook handles himself very well.

d, Marion Gering; w, Louis Weitzenkorn (based on the novel by Louis Bromfield and the play by William C. Lengle, Lew Levenson); ph, Ernest

Haller.

Drama   (PR:A   MPAA:NR)

24 HOURS IN A WOMAN'S LIFE****½**   (1968, Fr./Ger.) 86m Ge
Fi-Roxy-Film/c (24 STUNDEN IM LEBEN EINER FRAU; 24 HEURES
DE LA VIE D'UNE FEMME)

Danielle Darrieux (*Alice*), Robert Hoffmann (*Thomas*), Romima Power
(*Mariette*), Lena Skerla (*Mlle. Georges*), Marthe Alycia (*Mme. Di Stefano*).

Darrieux, a widow, returns from a holiday in Italy and relates what
happened as she sits with some friends. After a piano recital, Darrieux is
caught in a rainstorm. She gets on the wrong boat, ending up in Switzerland.
While waiting for the next boat, she kills time in a casino and meets
Hoffmann, a young German who has just lost all his money. She follows him
and the two spend the night together. The next morning, she leaves a note
to arrange a rendezvous with him. Her friends, Skerla and Alycia, avoid her
but teenager Power speaks with her. Hoffmann deliberately comes by late,
but he spends the afternoon walking with Darrieux in the woods. He
explains that he's a deserter from the German army and a compulsive
gambler as well. Darrieux offers to pay his debts and the cost of passage for
him to Zurich, on the condition that Hoffmann will never gamble again. He
agrees and they part. Later, she decides to go with him but misses his train.
She spends the evening wandering about the places the two had been
together and is shocked to find that Hoffmann has returned to the gambling
tables. She confronts him and he shoves money into her hands. Hoffmann
insults his would-be benefactor and sends her off.

p, Louis Emile Galey; d, Dominique Delouche; w, Delouche, Albert Valentin,
Eberhard Keindorff, Johanna Sibelius, Paul Hengge, Marie-France Riviere
(based on the story "Vierundzwanzig Stunden aus dem Leben einer Frau"
by Stefan Zweig); ph, Walter Wottitz (Eastmancolor); m, Jean Podromides
(adapted from Johannes Brahms' themes); ed, Genevieve Winding; art d,
Francois de Lamothe.

Drama   (PR:C   MPAA:NR)

24 HOURS OF A WOMAN'S LIFE
(SEE: AFFAIR IN MONTE CARLO, 1953, Brit.)

24 HOURS OF THE REBEL   (SEE: 9-30-55, 1978)

24 HOURS TO KILL****½**   (1966, Brit.) 94m Grixflag Films/Seven Arts
Pictures c

Lex Barker (*Jamie*), Mickey Rooney (*Norman Jones*), Michael Medwin
(*Tommy*), Wolfgang Lukschy (*Kurt*), Helga Sommerfeld (*Louise*), France
Anglade (*Francoise*), Helga Lehner (*Helga*), Walter Slezak (*Malouf*), Hans
Clarin (*Elias*), Shakib Khouri (*Andronicus*), Maria Rohm (*Claudine*), Nadia
Gamel (*Mimi*).

A plane to Athens develops engine trouble and is forced to land in Beirut.
Rooney, a purser, is hiding out from gold smugglers headed by Slezak.
Rooney gains the confidence of the pilot, ex-Tarzan Barker, as well as the
plane's crew members, who, thought that Rooney was a mobster. The
smugglers try twice to kill Rooney and then they go after stewardess
Sommerfeld, Barker's girl friend. She evades them and Barker learns that
Rooney really is a smuggler on the run, having stolen a large sum of gold
bullion from the gang. Sommerfeld is finally captured by the smugglers who
offer to exchange her for Rooney. She's rescued by the crew after a fight,
however, and Rooney is grabbed by Slezak. He is momentarily saved, but
as the plane takes off Rooney is finally done in by one of Slezak's men. Some
good mild suspense thrills in this feature, filmed on location in Lebanon.

p, Harry Alan Towers; d, Peter Bezencenet; w, Peter Yeldham (based on the
story by Peter Welbeck [Towers]; ph, Ernest Steward (Techniscope, Technicolor); m, Wilfred Josephs; ed, John Trumper; md, Marcus Dods; art d,
Scott MacGregor.

Thriller   (PR:C   MPAA:NR)

20 MILLION MILES TO EARTH**   (1957) 84m Morningside/COL bw

William Hopper (*Calder*), Joan Taylor (*Marisa*), Frank Puglia (*Dr. Leonar-
do*), John Zaremba (*Dr. Judson Uhl*), Thomas B. Henry (*Gen. A.D.
McIntosh*), Tito Vuolo (*Comisario of Police*), Jan Arvan (*Signore Contino*),
Arthur Space (*Sharman*), Bart Bradley (*Pepe*), George Pelling (*Mr. Maples*),
George Khoury (*Verrico*), Don Orlando (*Mondello*), Rollin Moriyama (*Dr.
Koruku*), Ray Harryhausen (*Man Feeding Elephants*), Dale Van Sickel
(*Stuntman*).

The first human expedition to Venus returns to Earth in a crash landing off
the coast of Italy (in an ocean that is part of a set borrowed from MUTINY
ON THE BOUNTY). The only survivor is Hopper and he's frightened that
he may have lost a cannister holding specimens of Venusian life. He has, all
right, and the cannister containing a gelatinous substance is found by a
young boy. The gel hatches and zoologist Puglia puts the tiny creature in a
cage. Imagine his surprise the next morning when the thing is now four feet
long and hungry. It gets loose and begins attacking in the prescribed science
fiction manner, all the while increasing in size. Finally the army is called in

with their bazookas and you know what happens next. The film is unusually
dull and built almost entirely around the special effects of miniature model
animator Harryhausen. In this early effort Harryhausen's effects are only
so-so. They look cheap, reflecting the film's budget, but carry a certain
intrigue about them. A fight between the creature and a miniature elephant
isn't too bad. Fans of the genre will definitely enjoy this more than anyone
else. Watch for a cameo by the special effects man as he feeds elephants at
the zoo.

p, Charles H. Schneer; d, Nathan Juran; w, Bob Williams, Christopher
Knopf (based on a story by Charlott Knight, Ray Harryhausen); ph, Irving
Lippman, Carlos Ventigmilia; m, Mischa Bakaleinikoff; ed, Edwin Bryant;
art d, Cary Odell; spec eff, Harryhausen.

Science Fiction   **Cas.**   (PR:A   MPAA:NR)

TWENTY MILLION SWEETHEARTS***   (1934) 89m FN-WB bw

Pat O'Brien (*Rush Blake*), Dick Powell (*Buddy Clayton*), Ginger Rogers
(*Peggy Cornell*), The Four Mills Brothers, Ted Fiorito and His Band, The
Three Radio Rogues, The Debutantes (*Themselves*), Allen Jenkins (*Pete*),
Grant Mitchell (*Chester A. Sharpe*), Joseph Cawthorne (*Herbert Brockman*),
Joan Wheeler (*Marge*), Henry O'Neill (*Lemuel Tappan*), Johnny Arthur
(*Secretary*), Muzzy Marcellino (*Himself*), Grace Hayle (*Martha Brockman*),
Oscar Apfel (*Manager*), Billy West (*Bellboy*), Gordon 'Bill' Elliott (*1st Man*),
Eddie Kane (*2nd Man*), Larry McGrath (*3rd Man*), Diane Borget (*Girl*), Bob
Perry (*Cafe Manager*), Rosalie Roy (*Girl Operator*), Eddie Foster (*1st
Hillbilly*), Billy Snyder (*2nd Hillbilly*), Matt Brooks (*3rd Hillbilly*), Morris
Goldman (*4th Hillbilly*), Milton Kibbee (*Pete's Announcer*), John Murray
(*2nd Announcer*), Sam Hayes (*Peggy's Announcer*), Dick Winslow (*Page
Boy*), Leo Forbstein (*Brusiloff*), Harry Seymour (*Announcer*), Eddie Shub-
ert, George Chandler, Charles Lane, Dennis O'Keefe (*Reporters*), Sam
McDaniel (*Deacon the Waiter*), William B. Davidson (*Woodcliff Inn Manag-
er*), George Humbert (*Headwaiter*), Charles Halton (*Sound Effects Man*),
Charles Sullivan (*Cabby*), Nora Cecil (*Lady in Bed*).

A pleasant satire on radio with good performances from the stars, especially
O'Brien, who seemed to have been directed by Howard Hawks, rather than
Ray Enright. O'Brien is the catalyst and sails through his scenes with
aplomb. He's an agent who finds singing waiter Powell and plans to make
him the next big radio star. Powell has trouble with "mike fright" though
and that has to be worked out. Meanwhile, Rogers is a radio star who has
just lost her own weekly program and she helps Powell get over his problem.
By the end of the film, Powell and Rogers (who was on loan from RKO) have
become the darlings of the airwaves. Lots of pointed humor about the radio
business that could just as easily be applied today to television. It was
remade with Doris Day in 1949 as MY DREAM IS YOURS. Harry Warren
and Al Dubin wrote several of the songs which included: "Fair and Warmer"
(sung by Ted Fiorito), "What Are Your Intentions?" (The Debutantes), "Out
for No Good" (Ginger Rogers), "I'll String Along with You" (Rogers and
Powell, the biggest hit from the film). Other tunes were "The Man on the
Flying Trapeze" (Walter O'Keefe, sung by Powell), "How'm I Doin'?" (Lem
Fowler, Don Redman, sung by the Mills Brothers), "Oh, I Heard, Yes, I
Heard" (Redman, sung by the Mills Brothers). One piece of special material
(uncredited) was a Yiddish version of "The Last Round-Up" which was sung
by Eddie Foster, Billy Snyder, Morris Goldman, and Matt Brooks. In a small
bit role, note Dennis O'Keefe as a reporter. Long-time musician and
bandleader for Art Linkletter, Muzzy Marcellino, is seen as himself. A very
entertaining picture about radio, and Powell and Rogers made a good team
but O'Brien got all the laughs with his breezy performance.

p, Sam Bischoff; d, Ray Enright; w, Warren Duff, Harry Sauber (based on
the story "Hot Air" by Paul Finder Moss, Jerry Wald); ph, Sid Hickox; ed,
Clarence Kolster; md, Leo F. Forbstein; art d, Esdras Hartley; cos,
Orry-Kelly; makeup, Perc Westmore.

Musical Comedy   (PR:A   MPAA:NR)

TWENTY MULE TEAM***   (1940) 82m MGM bw

Wallace Beery (*Skinner Bill Bragg*), Leo Carrillo (*Piute Pete*), Marjorie
Rambeau (*Josie Johnson*), Anne Baxter (*Jean Johnson*), Douglas Fowley
(*Stag Roper*), Noah Beery, Jr (*Mitch*), Berton Churchill (*Jackass Brown*),
Arthur Hohl (*Salters*), Clem Bevans (*Chuckawalla*), Charles Halton (*A-
dams*), Minor Watson (*Marshal*), Oscar O'Shea (*Conductor*), Lloyd In-
graham (*Stockholder*), Ivan Miller (*Alden*), Eddy Waller (*Horsecollar,
Bartender*), Sam Appel (*Proprietor*), John Beck, Henry Sylvester, Lew Kelly,
Katherine Kenworthy.

This well made, entertaining western features Beery and Carrillo as a mule
skinner and half-breed scout carrying some shipments of borax across the
desert. Some new deposits are found and bad guy Fowley wants to jump
Beery and Carrillo's claim. Baxter (in her film debut) is Rambeau's daughter
and the love interest for the bad guy. There's plenty of action, of course, all
neatly handled within the confines of the slightly unusual western plot. It's
directed with vigor and played nicely by the ensemble. Reviews and box
office for this were both very good and convinced Beery that the western
was the genre for him. He spent most of his remaining career doing films
in that category as a result. Beery had been looking for a female screen
counterpart since the death of Marie Dressler in 1934. This movie was
expected to be the first of a series of films opposite Rambeau. But the actress

was seriously hurt in a car accident after TWENTY MULE TEAM was made, and Marjorie Main became Beery's film partner.

p, J. Walter Ruben; d, Richard Thorpe; w, Cyril Hume, E. E. Paramore, Richard Maibum (based on a story by Robert C. DuSoe, Owen Atkinson); ph, Clyde DeVinna; m, David Snell; ed, Frank Sullivan; cos, Dolly Tree, Gile Steele.

Western   **(PR:A   MPAA:NR)**

29 OCACIA AVENUE   (SEE: FACTS OF LOVE, 1949, Brit.)

TWENTY-ONE DAYS (SEE: TWENTY-ONE DAYS TOGETHER, 1939, Brit.)

TWENTY-ONE DAYS TOGETHER*½   (1940, Brit.) 72m
LFP-Denham/COL bw(GB: TWENTY ONE DAYS; AKA: THE FIRST AND THE LAST)

Vivien Leigh (Wanda), Laurence Olivier (Larry Durrant), Leslie Banks (Keith Durrant), Francis L. Sullivan (Mander), Hay Petrie (John Aloysius Evans), Esme Percy (Henry Walenn), Robert Newton (Tolly), Victor Rietti (Antonio), Morris Harvey (Alexander Macpherson), Meinhart Maur (Carl Grunlich), Lawrence Hanray (Solicitor), David Horne (Beavis), Wallace Lupino (Father), Muriel George (Mother), William Dewhurst (Lord Chief Justice), Frederick Lloyd (Swinton), Elliot Mason (Frau Grunlich), Arthur Young (Asher), Fred Groves (Barnes), Aubrey Mallalieu (Magistrate), John Warwick.

A slow movie that languished two years on the shelves before it was released, mainly on the strength that Leigh and Olivier had, by then, achieved stardom, and the distributing company hoped to cash in on that. Olivier is a bit of a rake and a flake but lovable nevertheless. His brother Banks is a well-known barrister who is on the brink of becoming a judge in the British judicial system and thus fearful of any scandal that might besmirch his name. Olivier meets Leigh, who is estranged from her husband. She is a model and when her husband finds out that she and Olivier are seeing each other, he arrives at Olivier's place and threatens him. Olivier fights back and kills the man in self defense as Leigh watches. A mentally deranged man is taken in for the crime and will be held for 21 days until he comes to trial. Olivier decides to use the three weeks to have some happiness with Leigh before he will give himself up for the murder, rather than allow the innocent man to be tried. Banks, who knows the truth, tells Olivier to keep mum, as he'd rather see the innocent mental case hanged than suffer the slings and arrows of the outraged press. The problem is cleared up when the innocent man dies in jail of heart failure and Olivier and Leigh are now free to take up a happy existence with each other. The picture was reissued in 1944 but fared no better than the first go-around. Producer Alexander Korda directed one sequence of the film which had a working title of "The First and the Last" until the final title was decided on. Although brief at 72 minutes, it seemed like twice the length because everyone appeared to be moving as though they'd just awakened.

p, Alexander Korda; d, Basil Dean; w, Graham Greene, Dean (based on the play "The First and the Last" by John Galsworthy); ph, Jan Stallick; m, John Greenwood; ed, William Hornbeck, Charles Crichton; md, Muir Mathieson; art d, Vincent Korda.

Drama   **(PR:A   MPAA:NR)**

TWENTY PLUS TWO½**   (1961) 102m AA bw

David Janssen (Tom Alder), Jeanne Crain (Linda Foster), Dina Merrill (Nikki Kovacs/Doris Delaney), Agnes Moorehead (Mrs. Delaney), Brad Dexter (Leroy Dane), Robert Strauss (Honsinger), Jacques Aubuchon (Frenchy Pleschette), William Demarest (Slocum), George N. Neise (Walter Collinson), Fredd Wayne (Harris Toomey), Carleton Young (Colonel), Robert H. Harris (Stanley), Billy Varga (Mark), Teri Janssen (Stewardess), Ellie Kent (Blonde), Mort Mills (Harbin), Robert Gruber (Bellboy), Will Wright (Morgue Attendant).

Janssen is a private eye specializing in missing persons cases. When movie star Dexter's secretary is murdered, Janssen links the death to the disappearance of Merrill, a rich woman who had vanished a few years previously. He meets with Dexter and Crain, the dick's former fiancee. He also meets with Merrill, unaware that this is the missing heiress now using an alias. However, Janssen senses something peculiar about her and shortly thereafter is approached by Aubuchon, who asks the detective to look for his missing brother. Janssen runs into Merrill again on an airplane and realizes that he had met her in Japan while he was recuperating from wounds suffered in the Korean conflict. From there Janssen learns that Merrill had gotten mixed up with a guy who had made her pregnant and whom she believed she had killed. To avoid any embarrassment to her family Merrill had fled to Japan. Upon further digging Janssen deduces that Dexter killed both his secretary and the man Merrill thought she had done in. Dexter also proves to be Aubuchon's missing brother and the two siblings square off. Aubuchon kills Dexter, leaving Janssen to renew his romance with Merrill. The film is a little long but plays its hardboiled detective format nicely. Janssen is good as the quintessential private eye. He's given good support by the director and cast. At times the dialog borders on

self-parody, though that's not always a fault. The film is slightly ridiculous as it is and is good pulpy fun at its best moments.

p, Frank Gruber; d, Joseph M. Newmnan; w, Gruber (based on his novel); ph, Carl Guthrie; m, Gerald Fried; ed, George White; art d, David Milton; set d, Joe Kish; spec eff, Milt Olsen; makeup, Harry Maret.

Mystery   **(PR:C-O   MPAA:NR)**

TWENTY QUESTIONS MURDER MYSTERY, THE**
(1950, Brit.) 95m Pax-Pendennis/GN bw (AKA: MURDER ON THE AIR)

Robert Beatty (Bob Beacham), Rona Anderson (Mary Game), Clifford Evans (Tom Harmon), Edward Lexy (Inspector Charlton), Olga Lindo (Olive Tavy), Frederick Leister (Commissioner), Harold Scott (Maurice Emery, King's Counsel), Wally Patch (Tiny White), Meadows White (Frederick Tavy), Kynaston Reeves (Gen. Maitland Webb), Stewart MacPherson, Daphne Padel, Jack Train, Richard Dimbleby, Jeanne de Casalis, Norman Hackforth, Gordon McLeod, Liam Redmond, John Salew, Howard Douglas, Arthur Young, Merle Tottenham, Sonya O'Shea, Homi D. Bode, Philip King.

"Twenty Questions," a popular radio show featuring Train, Dimbleby, Padel, and de Casalis as panelists, becomes embroiled in a game of murder when a killer begins sending clues about his victims to the quartet. It's not long before two reporters catch on to the murderer's identity and then use the panel to trap the man. Even nonmystery buffs will have figured out the pieces of the puzzle presented here long before they are revealed.

p, Steven Pallos, Victor Katona; d, Paul L. Stein; w, Katona, Patrick Kirwan (based on a story by Charles Leeds); ph, Ernest Palmer.

Mystery   **(PR:A   MPAA:NR)**

27A*   (1974, Aus.) 86m Smart St. Films c

Robert McDarra, Bill Hunter, James Kemp, Graham Corry, David Curtis, Haydn Keenan.

An alcoholic voluntarily enters a mental ward in search of a cure. He doesn't get along with one of his male nurses and consequently is declared uncooperative and kept in custody against his will. This is a poorly made and depressing work that shows hardly any sympathy towards its subject. The patients are the film's main focus with all other characters poorly sketched and shunted off to the side. There is little attention paid to simple continuity (characters change clothes from shot to shot with utter abandon) though the camera work isn't too bad, making some use out of the rural Australian scenery.

p, Haydn Keenan; d&w, Esben Storm; ph, Michael Edols; m, Winsome Evans; ed, Storm, Richard Moir.

Drama   **(PR:O   MPAA:NR)**

27TH DAY, THE½**   (1957) 75m Romson/COL bw

Gene Barry (Jonathan Clark), Valerie French (Eve Wingate), George Voskovec (Prof. Klaus Bechner), Arnold Moss (The Alien), Stefan Schnabel (Leader), Ralph Clanton (Mr. Ingram), Frederick Ledebur (Dr. Karl Neuhaus), Paul Birch (Admiral), Azemat Janti (Ivan Godofsky), Mari Tsien (Su Tan), Ed Hinton (Commander), Grandon Rhodes (United Nations Officer), Doreen Woodbury (Woman), Jerry Janger (Officer), Mark Warren (Peter), Don Spark (Harry Bellows), David Bond (Dr. Schmidt), Eric Feldary (Russian Sergeant), Weaver Levy (Chinese Sergeant), Monty Ash (Russian Doctor), Irvin Ashkenszy (2nd Man), Hank Clemin (Hans), Theodore Marcuse (Col. Gregor), Peter Norman (Interrogator), John Bleifer (Spokesman), Mel Welles (Marshall), Sigfrid Tor (Gen. Zamke), John Dodsworth (British Announcer), Jacques Gallo (French Announcer), Charles Bennett (Gorki), Arthur Lovejoy (Brakovich), John Bryant (Federal Agent), John Mooney (M.P. Captain), Paul Power (Army Doctor), Michael Harris (FBI Man), Walda Winchell (Nurse), Tom Daly (Joe the Bartender), Don Rhodes (TV Technician), Emil Sitka (Newsboy), Phil Van Zandt (Taxi Driver), Paul Frees (Newscaster), Ralph Montgomery.

Many science fiction films of the 1950s such as THE INCREDIBLE SHRINKING MAN and INVASION OF THE BODY SNATCHERS served as allegories veiled by their genre to express dangerous viewpoints of those politically charged times. THE 27TH DAY, unlike these two liberal narratives, was clearly an anti-Communist propaganda piece well understood by its post-Sputnik audience. Moss is an alien from a dying planet whose people want to immigrate to Earth. He gives five humans from five different countries special killing capsules. It is against the ethics of Moss' people to kill intelligent life but Earthlings, he observes, seem set on destroying themselves. The capsules he hands out will instantly kill when opened but become useless after 27 days or the death of their bearer. French destroys her batch by tossing them into the ocean and Tsien's are rendered to dust when she commits suicide. Moss broadcasts the name of his five bearers to the world. Barry, Voskovec, and Janti are the only ones left with the capsules and Janti is summoned to the Kremlin by the evil Soviet leader Schnabel. Schnabel wants Janti to destroy the West with these capsules, thus insuring a Soviet-dominated world. Just as Janti is about to give in, he is shot by a KGB guard, and the pills turn to dust. Barry and Voskovec combine forces with French and just before Schnabel declares nuclear war the remaining capsules are released. The entire evil empire of the USSR is wiped out and the aliens come to colonize a new home on Earth where peace and freedom will now reign. In addition, Barry and French wind up together in true romance. As science fiction this isn't too bad an effort, with suspense elements directed nicely. Some footage from EARTH VERSUS THE FLYING SAUCERS was incorporated into the film also with good effect. The acting works well for the simplistic tale but the film's real point of interest is as a barometer of political influences on Hollywood in the late 1950s. The worst of the HUAC blacklisting was slowly drawing to a close in 1957 but problems were still blatant within the studio system. There were still a good number of strongly anti-Communist, anti-Russian cold war stories being churned out to sate the powers that be and THE 27TH DAY is an excellent example. Director Asher went on to direct BEACH PARTY, the first officially recognized "beach" movie.

p, Helen Ainsworth; d, William Asher; w, John Mantley (based on his own novel); ph, Henry Freulich; ed, Jerome Thoms; md, Mischa Bakaleinikoff.

Science Fiction   **(PR:A-C   MPAA:NR)**

20,000 EYES**   (1961) 61m AP/FOX bw

Gene Nelson (*Dan Warren*), Merry Anders (*Karen Walker*), James Brown (*Jerry Manning*), John Banner (*Kurt Novak*), Judith Rawlins (*Girl*), Robert Shayne (*Police Lieutenant*), Paul Maxey (*Ryan*), Rex Holman (*High School Boy*), Ollie O'Toole (*Moore*), Bruno Ve Sota (*Museum Watchman*), Barbara Parkins (*High School Girl*), William O'Connell (*Appraiser*), Rusty Wescoatt (*Policeman*), Vince Monroe Townsend, Jr (*Museum Guard*).

Nelson is an investment counselor who embezzles $100,000 from a client in order to protect his interests in a South American diamond mine. Unfortunately, this client is Banner, a retired gangster. When Banner finds out about the scam he gives Nelson time to raise the money to pay him back on the condition that an insurance policy is taken out on Nelson's life with the gangster as sole beneficiary of its $100,000 payoff. Nelson is informed that unless the cash is raised in five days he'll have an "accident" that will make fund raising unnecessary. In desperation Nelson gets his partner Brown and secretary Anders to help him rob gems from a local museum. This they do, replacing the real gems with clever fakes. Nelson then takes out a $100,000 insurance policy on the diamonds and has Brown steal them so he can collect the money. This appears to be successful until Nelson discovers that the money won't be paid for at least five weeks. He tells Banner this news and the gangster shoots him in the back. Before dying Nelson throws a television at Banner, knocking him into a swimming pool and electrocuting the man. This film was shot in only six days on a budget of just $70,000. Though it suffers from a quick shoot and cheapie production values, it's not such a bad effort. The B-grade plot has some nice elaborations and the direction handles the suspense with adeptness. Characters are somewhat poorly sketched with simplistic motivations but all in all it turned out well, typical of several quick and cheap films Associated Producers was making in conjunction with Twentieth Century Fox at the time.

p&d, Jack Leewood; w, Jack Thomas; ph, Brydon Baker (CinemaScope); m, Albert Glasser; ed, Peter Johnson; art d, John Mansbridge; set d, Harry Reif; makeup, Emile La Vigne.

Crime   **(PR:C   MPAA:NR)**

20,000 LEAGUES UNDER THE SEA****   (1954) 120m Disney/BV c

Kirk Douglas (*Ned Land*), James Mason (*Capt. Nemo*), Paul Lukas (*Prof. Pierre Aronnax*), Peter Lorre (*Conseil, His Assistant*), Robert J. Wilke (*1st Mate of "Nautilus"*), Carleton Young (*John Howard*), Ted De Corsia (*Capt. Farragut*), Percy Helton (*Diver*), Ted Cooper (*Mate of "Abraham Lincoln"*), Edward Marr (*Shipping Agent*), Fred Graham (*Casey Moore*), J.M. Kerrigan (*Billy*), Harry Harvey (*Shipping Clerk*), Herb Vigran (*Reporter*), Esmeralda (*Nemo's Seal*).

The first live-action movie made by Disney at his own studio turned out to be one of the best science-fiction movies ever done. Felton's script hewed closely to Jules Verne's incredible vision (written in 1869) that told of submarines, atomic power, electricity, and several other innovations which were yet to be invented. The time is 1868, and the men of the sea in San Francisco are agog over reports of a "monster" roaming the sea that has taken a toll of any ships that dared venture into its area. Because of the problems, many voyages have been canceled and the government is forced to send a warship out to investigate and clear the sea lanes. That ship is sunk by the heinous "creature" and only three people survive the ordeal: Douglas (a professional harpoonist), Lukas (a professor from the Nautical Museum in Paris), and his aide, Lorre. The men are picked up by the submarine Nautilus which is what they thought was the creature. The sub is captained by Mason, a strange and demented man who is, at once, cultured and fanatical. He's been sinking all these vessels in a misguided attempt to end warfare at sea. Mason knows who Lukas is as his Victorian library aboard the sub is lined with books from all sources, including several by Lukas. Mason is honored to have the famed Lukas on board but shows a passing disdain for Lorre and Douglas. Mason is heading back to his island base on "Vulcania" and takes a route that shows off the undersea to Lukas, Lorre, and Douglas. Mason plays his huge pipe organ and regales his prisoners with bits of Bach in between his rantings. Lukas and Lorre are fascinated by Mason and his incredible ship (it was 200 feet long in Verne's book and

they actually built it to scale for the film) and feel more like guests than prisoners, but Douglas is eager to flee the confines of the craft and cooks up a plan. The sub ports at a lonely island and Douglas gets off the ship, only to be driven back when some local cannibals find him to be a perfect morsel for their dinner. Douglas finds out what the coordinates are for Mason's home island and he puts the latitude and longitude on pieces of paper, slips them into bottles, and sends them bobbing on the ocean in the hope that they will be found. When the sub is hit by shells from a warship, it must go into a power dive and regroup at the bottom of the sea where Mason and his loyal seamen fix the broken shaft that was ruined by a gunshell. Now that they are deeper than any human being has ever been, they see a world of fantastic creatures. Later, they are attacked by a giant squid that almost takes the sub to Davey Jones' locker. In the course of inhuman events, Douglas saves the life of Mason, who responds by telling the trio what his exact plan is. He means to make them ambassadors from his undersea nation who will sue for peace with the rest of the world. When they get to the "Vulcania" harbor, ships are already waiting for them as Douglas' messages have been found and acted upon. Mason manages to get out of the sub and set an atomic bomb in motion which is ready to go off on a delayed reaction. He attempts to return to the sub and is wounded, but orders his men to take the sub straight down to the bottom of the sea. Douglas, Lorre, and Lukas manage to get away from Mason's men and reach safety as they see Vulcania, the sub, and everyone connected with Mason go up in a mushroom cloud. In 1907, Georges Melies made a short, hand-tinted version of the story, then Universal (Stuart Paton) tried a longer version in 1916 which took liberties with Verne's story by adding a girl and explaining that the captain had been an Indian prince before taking to the sea. It was not a large hit and so Universal satirized it the following year with a comedy called THE CROSS-EYED SUBMARINE. Although the interiors were done at Disney's Burbank lot, Disney did not stint on his location work and shot in the Bahama Islands at New Providence as well as in Jamaica at Long Bay. The price of $5 million or so was well worth it as all stops were pulled out to make this the great adventure it turned out to be. Director Fleischer was the son of an early Disney conmpetitor, Max Fleischer, and went on to make many sci-fi films, including SOYLENT GREEN and FANTASTIC VOYAGE. Oscars went to Meehan for his (color) art direction, Kuri for his (color) set direction, and to the entire special effects team for their work. Because this was a fantasy film, Mason was not nominated for his sensational performance as the very complex Captain Nemo, but he should have been. The movie more than doubled its cost on the first release and has proven to be one of Disney's most durable movies over the years and can be found, from time to time, in reissue. There was a documentary shot while they were making the movie and it was shown on Disney's TV show and later won an Emmy. Nemo would appear again in other films (Robert Ryan did him in CAPTAIN NEMO AND THE UNDERWATER CITY), but never done as well as Mason's portrayal. It was the first movie distributed by Buena Vista, the Disney Studios distribution arm. If you've ever wondered where that name came from, be aware that Disney Studios is located on a street called Buena Vista in Burbank. In honor of Verne's amazing ability to look into the future, the U.S. Navy named the first atomic-powered submarine Nautilus when it was commissioned. The fight with the giant squid was shot in a specially built tank in Burbank and didn't work at first because they did it in a calm sea and all the mechanical workings were easily spotted by the camera. It was re-shot in a roiling sea background and looked far better for the alteration. Excellent music by Paul Smith and J.S. Bach, and Douglas sings a tune, "A Whale of a Tale" (Al Hoffman, Norman Gimbel). What is unique about Jules Verne is that he wrote all of his imaginative stories while never leaving his home in Nantes, France. A superb movie helped greatly by the contribution of the man who worked so closely with Disney for so many years, beginning with the creation of "Mickey Mouse," the unsung Ub Iwerks, who handled all the special process shots on the movie. We must be thankful that Disney, Fleischer, and Felton made this movie before Irwin Allen could get his heavy hands on it.

p, Walt Disney; d, Richard Fleischer; w, Earl Felton (based on the novel Vingt Mille Lieues Sous les Mers by Jules Verne); ph, Franz F. Planer, Ralph Hammeras, Till Gabbani (CinemaScope, Technicolor); m, Paul J. Smith, J.S. Bach; ed, Elmo Williams; art d, John Meehan; set d, Emile Kuri; cos, Norman Martien; spec eff, John Hench, Joshua Meador; makeup, Lou Hippe; matte artist, Peter Ellenshaw.

Science Fiction/Fantasy   **Cas.**   **(PR:A   MPAA:NR)**

20,000 MEN A YEAR**   (1939) 83m COS/FOX bw

Randolph Scott (*Brad Reynolds*), Preston Foster (*Jim Howell*), Margaret Lindsay (*Ann Rogers*), Robert Shaw (*Tommy Howell*), Mary Healy (*Joan Marshall*), George Ernest (*Skip Rogers*), Kane Richmond (*Al Williams*), Maxie Rosenbloom (*Walt Dorgan*), Douglas Wood (*Crandall*), Sen Yung (*Harold Chong*), Paul Stanton (*Gerald Grant*), Tom Seidel (*Wally Richards*), Edward Gargan (*Dunk*), Harry Tyler (*Joe Hungerford*), Sidney Miller (*Irving Glassman*), Edwin Stanley (*Chief Pilot Lawson*), Jane Darwell (*Mrs. Allen*).

Scott, in a pre-cowboy role, plays a transport pilot who turns down a mission he deems unsafe. This angers his superiors and he's fired. Scott invests in a rundown airport and starts his own school for pilots. He works with the students but the school almost closes because of money problems. When the government announces a new program for pilot training Scott is given a reprieve. Foster, a government inspector whom had fought with Scott earlier, sends his brother Shaw to the school. He bails out over the Grand Canyon and Scott is nearly killed searching for him. The story is trite, padded out with good footage of planes, particularly in the Grand Canyon sequences. The direction is programmer quality, telling the story without embellishment. The film was tied in with a government program which hoped to recruit "20,000 men a year" for pilot training.

p, Sol M. Wurtzel; d, Alfred E. Green; w, Lou Breslow, Owen Francis (based on a story by Frank Wead); ph, Ernest Palmer; Charles Marshall; ed, Fred Allen; md, Samuel Kaylin.

Drama   **(PR:A MPAA;NR)**

20,000 POUNDS KISS, THE**½   (1964, Brit.) 57m Merton
                                                              Park/Schoenfeld bw

Dawn Addams (Christina Hagen), Michael Goodliffe (Sir Harold Trevitt), Richard Thorp (John Durran), Anthony Newlands (Leo Hagen), Alfred Burke (Inspector Waveney), Mia Karam (Paula Blair), Ellen McIntosh (Ursula Clandon), Paul Whitsun-Jones (Charles Pinder), Noel Hood (Lady Clandon), John Miller (Lord Clandon), Vincent Harding (Detective Sgt. Holt), Susan Denny (Susie), Joyce Hemson (landlady).

In a London apartment, Newlands, a Polish aristocrat, lives with his wife Addams. Their maid (Karam) sees Addams in an embrace with their neighbor Goodliffe, an important member of Parliament. Karam threatens to expose Goodliffe to Newlands unless he pays her off. Goodliffe hires Thorp, a private eye, to check out this young woman but both she and Newlands are found dead. Burke, a Scotland Yard man, comes to investigate the case. He discovers that Goodliffe was the killer and Addams had conspired with her husband and maid to blackmail the politician. Based on a story by the popular mystery writer Wallace.

p, Jack Greenwood; d, John [Llewelyn] Moxey; w, Philip Mackie (based on a story by Edgar Wallace); ph, James Wilson; m, Bernard Ebbinghouse; ed, Gordon Hales, Derek Holding; art d, Peter Mullins; makeup, Michael Morris.

Mystery   **(PR:C MPAA:NR)**

20,000 YEARS IN SING SING****   (1933) 81m FN-WB/WB bw

Spencer Tracy (Tom Connors), Bette Davis (Fay), Lyle Talbot (Bud), Arthur Byron (Warden Long), Grant Mitchell (Dr. Ames), Warren Hymer (Hype), Louis Calhern (Joe Finn), Sheila Terry (Billie), Edward J. McNamara (Chief of Guards), Spencer Charters (Daniels), Nella Walker (Mrs. Long), Harold Huber (Tony), William LeMaire (Black Jack), Arthur Hoyt (Dr. Meeker), Sam Godfrey (2nd Reporter), George Pat Collins (Mike), Rockliffe Fellows, Lucille Collins, Clarence Wilson, Jimmie Donlon.

The praises of a prison, the famous Sing Sing, are sung-sung in this picture authored by its long-term reform warden, Lawes. Cocksure criminal Tracy is sent up the Hudson to the slammer on a felony rap. There he is greeted by the kindly warden, Byron, who offers him the hand of friendship, explaining that good behavior brings the reward of certain privileges. Tough-guy Tracy rejects the proffered offer, believing that his politically connected one-time associates will soon win his release. The troublemaking Tracy establishes his dominance in the prison hierarchy and sets about his invidious mischief. When Tracy starts a near-riot, he is consigned to solitary confinement for a 90-day period. Ruminating in his lonely cell, the convict comes to the conclusion that the only assistance he will get from his former confederates is assistance in dividing the spoils he had amassed, including his sweetheart, Davis. Tracy emerges from his steel-encased vigil an altered man, now believing that escape is his only remaining possibility. When Davis visits him, he laments his ill luck, which appears to the superstitious mobster to be dependent on the day of the week. He points out that he was born on a Tuesday, captured on a Tuesday, sentenced on a Tuesday, and imprisoned on a Tuesday. "And you met me on a Tuesday," responds Davis. Tracy joins some prisoners who are planning an escape attempt, but when he learns that their plan calls for a try at breaching the walls on Tuesday, he drops out. Beaten at last, he determines to win parole through his good behavior. Kindly Byron welcomes the change in the felon's attitude and soon visits on him all the perquisites the prison allows. Meanwhile, moll Davis–attempting to win Tracy's parole for him by other means–seeks the assistance of powerful mob chief Huber. In reward for his beneficence, Huber seeks the use of Davis' beautiful body. While speeding down a street in a car, Davis repels the gangster's groping, and is seriously injured in the resulting automobile crash. When Byron hears of her condition, he offers Tracy–now a trusty–compassionate leave from the prison's walls so that he might visit the bedridden beauty. Tracy takes a solemn oath that he will return to prison that same evening, and then entrains to the big city. Arriving at Grand Central Station, Tracy is recognized by two detectives who, unaware of his pass from prison, follow him to Davis' apartment. There, Tracy finds Calhern, the man responsible for his incarceration. During a furious fight, Tracy knocks Calhern's gun to the floor. Calhern gains the upper hand and Davis, fearing for Tracy's life, crawls from her bed of pain, retrieves the pistol, and shoots him. Hearing the shot, the waiting detectives break down the door as Tracy escapes through a window. With his dying breath, Calhern fingers Tracy as the one who shot him. The latter redeems his promise to warden Byron by returning to Sing Sing, where he

is charged with killing Calhern. At his murder trial, Tracy refuses to testify on his own behalf. Davis tries to tell the prosecutor that she was the one who pulled the trigger, but nobody will believe her. Under sentence of death, Tracy is led from the courtroom to the rising strains of "Happy Days Are Here Again" (Jack Yellen, Milton Ager). The picture ends as it began, with a procession of numerals racing across the screen behind the credits. Tracy's role in the film seems tailored more to James Cagney's cinematic persona than to his own–indeed, Cagney, who made the mold in a number of gangster films, was cinemogul Jack Warner's first choice for the part. Cagney was holding out for a raise in salary; he was asking for $3,000 weekly, rather than the $1,750 specified in his last contract. Tracy handled the characterization beautifully, causing one reviewer to claim that his acting was "... fully on a par with Paul Muni's ..." (Muni played brilliantly that same year in I AM A FUGITIVE FROM A CHAIN GANG). Davis' performance is excessively histrionic; always hard to restrain, not even domineering director Curtiz could always hold the actress back. In comic relief, cellmate Hymer works well with Tracy; the two had teamed together in similar roles in UP THE RIVER (1930) for 20th Century-Fox. This was to be the only time that two-time Oscar winners Davis and Tracy were to work together. The earthy actor and the doughty Davis didn't get along well with each other, but late in their lives both attested that they would like to star again with the other. Author Lawes was, at the time the picture was made, the actual warden of Sing Sing. He cooperated in every possible way for the production; real prisoners played in the mob scenes, and the film crew was permitted to enter the prison to shoot. The film was the first of many to be based on Lawes' accounts of prison life; others include OVER THE WALL (1938), YOU CAN'T GET AWAY WITH MURDER (1939), INVISIBLE STRIPES (1940), and CASTLE ON THE HUDSON (1940), the latter a remake of 20,000 YEARS IN SING SING, which starred John Garfield, Ann Sheridan, and Pat O'Brien. Despite the grimness of its subject matter, the film is laced with wit and humor. Prison life seems not so bad after all in Lawes' benevolent recounting; three square meals a day seemed somewhat tempting to contemporary viewers following the stock market crash of 1929.

p, Robert Lord; d, Michael Curtiz; w, Courtney Terrett, Lord, Wilson Mizner, Brown Holmes (based on the book by Warden Lewis E. Lawes); ph, Barney McGill; m, Bernhard Kaun; ed, George Amy; md, Leo F. Forbstein; art d, Anton Grot; cos, Orry-Kelly.

Prison   **(PR:A MPAA:NR)**

23½ HOURS LEAVE**   (1937) 73m GN bw

James Ellison (Sgt. Gray), Terry Walker (Peggy), Morgan Hill (Tommy), Arthur Lake (Turner), Paul Harvey (General), Wally Maher (Banning), Andy Andrews (Solomon), Murray Alper (Schultz), Pat Gleason (Squibb), John Kelly (Tubbs), Russell Hicks (Barker), Ward Bond (Top Kick).

It's WW I and Ellison is in uniform. While at training camp the wily young soldier bets his buddies that he'll have breakfast with the general (Harvey). It takes a few comic turns to achieve that goal but Ellison gets his breakfast with the big man in the end. Walker is the general's daughter who runs an unlikely (and unbelievable) taxi service for the enlisted men. Lake, later of the BLONDIE series, provides good comedy support, but mostly this is a routine, unfunny affair that was well dated by the time of its release. It was a remake of a 1919 silent comedy with four songs added to liven up matters. They are: "Goodnight, My Lucky Day," "It Must Be Love," "Now You're Talking My Language," "We Happen to Be in the Army" (Sammy Stept, Ted Koehler). MacLean, who starred in the original film, produced this version.

p, Douglas MacLean; d, John G. Blystone; w, Harry Ruskin, Henry McCarty, Samuel J. Warshawsky (based on a story by Mary Roberts Rinehart); ph, Jack Mackenzie; md, Marlin Skiles.

Comedy   **(PR:A MPAA:NR)**

23 PACES TO BAKER STREET***   (1956) 103m FOX c

Van Johnson (Phillip Hannon), Vera Miles (Jean Lennox), Cecil Parker (Bob Matthews, Hannon's Secretary), Patricia Laffan (Miss Alice Mac-Donald), Maurice Denham (Inspector Grovening), Estelle Winwood (Barmaid), Liam Redmond (Mr. Murch/Joe), Isobel Elsom (Lady Syrett), Martin Benson (Pilling), Natalie Norwick (Janet Murch), Terence de Marney (Sgt. Luce), Queenie Leonard (Miss Schuyler), Charles Keane (Policeman), Lucie Lancaster (Miss Marston), A. Cameron Grant (Pin Ball Player), Ashley Cowan (Lift Operator), Les Sketchley (English Cop), Ben Wright (Hotel Porter), Reginald Sheffield (Bespectacled Man), Phyllis Montifiere (Mrs. De Mester), Arthur Gomez (Mr. De Mester), Janice Kane (Invalid Child), Robert Raglan (Police Inspector), Howard Lang (Doorman), Margaret McGrath (Demonstrator), Walter Horsborough (Shop Assistant), Fred Griffith (Taxi Driver), Charles Stanley (Photographer), Robin Alalouf (Bell Boy), Yorke Sherwood (Cabby), Michael Trubshawe.

Van Johnson plays a blind London writer who lives on Baker Street. He overhears a conversation that reveals a kidnaping plot so he rushes to the police. They are polite but refuse to believe him. His friends also prove to be no help, humoring the man with a friendly air. However, Van Johnson knows what he heard is true and engages the help of his fiancee (Miles) and Parker, his secretary, to find the kidnapers. In a darkened room the blind man confronts the kidnaper and is nearly killed in the ensuing struggle. This terrific suspense film takes interesting chances with the genre. Van

Johnson's character is a study in frustration, a portrait of a man investigating something he knows exists but cannot see. The direction builds tension well, and is supported by a fine musical background which heightens the mood. London was subject to what could be termed "creative geography" by the director. Van Johnson's Baker Street home overlooks the Thomas River, which in reality is two miles from the noted London street. The film is full of clever locations like this which add to the confusion felt by the blind man. It's a good way to visually present the problems of a sightless man within a suspense format.

p, Henry Ephron; d, Henry Hathaway; w, Nigel Balchin (based on the novel *A Warrant for X* by Philip MacDonald); ph, Milton Krasner (CinemaScope, DeLuxe Color); m, Leigh Harline; ed, James B. Clark; md, Lionel Newman; art d, Lyle R. Wheeler, Maurice Ransford; set d, Walter M. Scott, Fay Babcock; cos, Charles Le Maire, Travilla; spec eff, Ray Kellogg.

Suspense Cas. (PR:C MPAA:NR)

TWICE A MAN★★ (1964) 55m Gregory J. Markopoulous c

Paul Klib (*Youth*), Albert Torgessen (*Friend*), Olympia Dukakis (*Young Woman/Commentator*), Violet Roditi (*Old Woman*).

This experimental film has good moments that nicely play with the film medium, but unfortunately are overcome by artistic pretensions. The loosely told story involves Klib, a young man loved by both his stepmother and another man. The stepmother is seen as both a young and old woman, which at points is confusing rather than psychologically revealing as intended. The film is a series of well-composed shots wrapped around a confusing tale with Bergmanesque actors who pose rather than perform. It won a top prize at the 1964 Belgian Experimental Film Festival but overall the piece just doesn't quite come together. Shot in 16mm and blown up to 35mm.

p,d, w&ph, Gregory J. Markopolous (Eastmancolor); m, Peter Illich Tschaikovsky; ed, Markopolous.

Experimental (PR:O MPAA:NR)

TWICE BLESSED★½ (1945) 76m MGM bw

Preston Foster (*Jeff Turner*), Gail Patrick (*Mary Hale*), Lee Wilde (*Terry Turner*), Lyn Wilde (*Stephanie Hale*), Richard Gaines (*Sen. John Pringle*), Jean Porter (*Kitty*), Marshall Thompson (*Jimmy*), Jimmy Lydon (*Mickey Pringle*), Gloria Hope (*Alice*), Ethel Smith at her organ.

The Wilde sisters, identical twins, graduated from bit parts in musicals to their own feature with this minor film. They play a pair of sibling opposites, one a regular teenager and the other a whiz kid who has held the nation's top I.Q. five years running. Their parents are divorced, having custody of one girl apiece. The sisters want to get their parents back together so they switch places to facilitate a reconciliation. The script is weak both in dialog and story development, though things happen with appropriate pacing and style. Smith, an organist, plays a Brazilian-flavored number ("Lero, Lero") and had no place in this film other than for padding.

p, Arthur L. Field; d, Harry Beaumont; w, Ethel Hill; ph, Ray June; ed, Douglas Biggs; md, David Snell; art d, Cedric Gibbons, Hans Peters; ch, Arthur Walsh.

Comedy (PR:A MPAA:NR)

TWICE BRANDED★★ (1936, Brit.) 72m GS Enterprises/RKO bw

Robert Rendel (*Charles Hamilton*), Lucille Lisle (*Betty Hamilton*), James Mason (*Henry Hamilton*), Eve Gray (*Sylvia Hamilton*), Mickey Brantford (*Dennis*), Ethel Griffies (*Mrs. Hamilton*), Isobel Scaife (*Mary*), Paul Blake (*Lord Hugo*), Neville Brook, Michael Ripper, Ethel Royale.

After being sentenced to 12 years in prison for his unwitting part in a fraud scheme, Rendel completes his term and returns to his family. The shame of his crime is too much for them to bear, so, rather than tell the truth, Rendel is introduced as "Uncle Charles from South America." When his son, a very young Mason, is framed by the same crook who sent Rendel to prison, "Uncle Charles" takes the fall and goes back behind bars. There he finds happiness in a world where no snobbery or caste system exists. The film is somewhat stagey in presentation and the script is too obvious at times. However, the direction overcomes some of the problems and entertains occasionally. Interesting for Mason fans in particular.

p, A. George Smith; d, Maclean Rogers; w, Kathleen Butler (based on the novel *Trouble in the House* by Anthony Richardson); ph, Geoffrey Faithfull.

Drama (PR:A MPAA:NR)

TWICE AROUND THE DAFFODILS★★★ (1962, Brit.) 89m GWH/Anglo Amalgamated bw

Juliet Mills (*Catty*), Donald Sinden (*Ian Richards*), Donald Houston (*John Rhodes*), Kenneth Williams (*Harry Halfpenny*), Ronald Lewis (*Bob White*), Andrew Ray (*Chris Walker*), Joan Sims (*Harriet Halfpenny*), Jill Ireland (*Janet*), Lance Percival (*George Logg*), Sheila Hancock (*Dora*), Nanette Newman (*Joyce*), Renee Houston (*Matron*), Amanda Reiss (*Dorothy*), Mary

Powell (*Mrs. Rhodes*), Barbara Roscoe (*Mary*).

It's zany, madcap humor in the unlikely setting of a men's tuberculosis sanatorium. The characters are comedy stereotypes, such as the nasty head nurse, and the typical slice-of-life crew of patients includes a chess whiz, a bumpkin, a RAF man with an eye for pretty nurses, and a patient who doesn't seem to be the least bit ill. Episodically told, the predictable situations are given fresh twists with good direction that uses the cast well. Watch for an appearance by Ireland as a nurse in her pre-Charles Bronson's wife-days.

p, Peter Rogers; d, Gerald Thomas; w, Norman Hudis (based on the play "Ring for Catty" by Patrick Cargill, Jack Beale); ph, Alan Hume; m, Bruce Montgomery; ed, John Shirley.

Comedy (PR:A MPAA:NR)

TWICE TOLD TALES★★★ (1963) 119m Admiral/UA c (AKA: NATHANIEL HAWTHORNE'S "TWICE TOLD TALES")

"Dr. Heidegger's Experiment": Vincent Price (*Alex Medbourne*), Sebastian Cabot (*Dr. Carl Heidegger*), Mari Blanchard (*Sylvia Ward*), "Rappaccini's Daughter": Price (*Dr. Rappaccini*), Brett Halsey (*Giovanni Guastconti*), Abraham Sofaer (*Prof. Pietro Baglioni*), Joyce Taylor (*Beatrice Rappaccini*), Edith Evanson (*Lisabetta*), "The House of the Seven Gables": Price (*Gerald Pyncheon*), Beverly Garland (*Alice Pyncheon*), Richard Denning (*Jonathan Maulle*), Jacqueline De Wit (*Hannah*), Floyd Simmons (*Mathew*), Gene Roth (*Cab Driver*).

After Price's success with his Edgar Allan Poe trilogy TALES OF HORROR, another film, this time based on Hawthorne stories, was immediately produced for United Artists. Though the stories take liberties with the source material, this trilogy is an interesting and well-made horror film. The first has Cabot discovering an elixir that keeps Price and him young. It also revives the long-dead corpse of Cabot's fiancee who reveals that Price killed her the night before the wedding in a fit of jealousy. Price completes the job by killing Cabot. The second story, "Rappaccini's Daughter," has Price injecting his daughter with a serum which will cause everyone she touches to die. She falls in love with Halsey, a neighboring student, and Price tries to create an antidote. Halsey's science professor creates one himself but this ends up killing the two lovers. Price is horrified by what he's done and kills himself. Lastly, "The House of the Seven Gables" sends newlywed Price to the ancient family home in search of a fortune. There he confronts the ghost of a man his ancestors had killed for being a warlock. The man had also been the lover of one of Price's wife's ancestors as well. Price kills his sister and dies in a treasure vault he had been in search of. The estate ends up in ruins and Garland, Price's widow, marries Denning, a descendant of the ghost. The story comes full circle in two ways. First is the ancestral love between Garland's ancestor and the ghost rekindled through their descendants. Secondly is Price himself, now playing the older gentleman. In the 1940 version of HOUSE OF THE SEVEN GABLES the much younger Price played the young descendant of the ghost. This well told trilogy is great fun, particularly for fans of the genre. Cinematic flair in the direction gives it the right ambience and Price, as always, is a delight.

p, Robert E. Kent; d, Sidney Salkow; w, Kent (based on "Dr. Heidegger's Experiment," "Rappaccini's Daughter" and *The House of the Seven Gables* by Nathaniel Hawthorne); ph, Ellis W. Carter (Technicolor); m, Richard La Salle; ed, Grant Whytock; art d, Franz Bachelin; set d, Charles Thompson; cos, Marjorie Corso, Tom Welsh; spec eff, Milton Olsen, Pete Faga; makeup, Gene Hibbs.

Horror (PR:C MPAA:NR)

TWICE UPON A TIME★½ (1953, Brit.) 75m LFP/FA bw

Hugh Williams (*James Turner*), Elizabeth Allan (*Carol-Anne Bailey*), Jack Hawkins (*Dr. Matthews*), Yolande Larthe (*Carol Turner*), Charmain Larthe (*Anne Bailey*), Violette Elvin (*Florence la Roche*), Isabel Dean (*Miss Burke*), Michael Gough (*Mr. Lloyd*), Walter Fitzgerald (*Prof. Reynolds*), Eileen Elton, Kenneth Melville (*Ballet Dancers*), Nora Gordon (*Emma*), Isabel George (*Molly*), Cecily Walger (*Mrs. Maybridge*), Molly Terraine (*Miss Wellington*), Martin Miller (*Eipeldauer*), Lily Kann (*Mrs. Eipeldauer*), Jean Stuart (*Mrs. Jamieson*), Margaret Boyd (*Mrs. Kinnaird*), Myrette Morven (*Miss Rupert*), Jack Lambert (*Mr. Buchan*), Archie Duncan (*Doorman*), Colin Wilcox (*Ian*), Pat Baker (*Sonia*), Monica Thomson (*Thelma*), Margaret McCourt (*Wendy*), Alanna Boyce (*Susie*), Ilsa Richardson (*Hilary*).

Twins Yolande and Chamain Larthe separated when their parents divorced but as luck would have it the two now attend the same summer camp. They hatch on to a scheme to take one another's place in an effort to reunite their parents. If the plot sounds familiar, that's because this is almost the same film as the better known THE PARENT TRAP (1961). This version is clearly the lesser of the two, with generally bad acting stretched out over a saccharine story. Both this and the 1961 Disney film are based on DAS DOPPELTE LOTTCHEN, a 1951 German film made from the Erich Kastner book.

p,d&w, Emeric Pressburger (based on the novel *Das Doppelte Lottchen* by Erich Kastner); ph, Christopher Challis; m, Johannes Brahms, Carl Maria von Weber; ed, Reginald Beck; prod d, Arthur Lawson; md, Frederic Lewis.

Comedy (PR:A MPAA:NR)

TWICE UPON A TIME*½ (1983) 75m Ladd-Kortyfilms-Lucasfilm/WB c

The voices of: Lorenzo Music (*Ralph*), Judith Kaham Kampmann (*Fairy Godmother*), Marshall Efron (*Synonamess Botch*), James Cranna (*Rod Rescueman/Scuzzbopper*), Julie Payne (*Flora Fauna*), Hamilton Camp (*Greensleeves*), Paul Frees (*Narrator/Chief of Stage/Judges/Baliff*).

It's good guys versus bad guys in this confusing, plotless animated feature produced in association with the Lucasfilm empire. The world of dreams and nightmares is explored within a cartoon fantasy framework as the characters fight for control of a cosmic clock. Though the animation is first-rate, the emptiness of the storyline is overpowering, proving once again that no matter how good something looks, if there's no story then there's no movie. Director Korty was noted as an independent filmmaker and Music, who provides the voice for the main character, was known as "Carleton, your doorman" on TV's "Rhoda." The film falls somewhere in that great expanse which is too sophisticated for the younger set and too bland for adults. All in all it's a waste of fine animation talent.

p, Bill Couturie; d, John Korty, Charles Swenson; w, Korty, Swenson, Suella Kennedy, Couturie (based on a story by Korty, Couturie, Kennedy); m, Dawn Atkinson, Ken Melville; ed, Jennifer Gallagher; art d, Harley Jessup; spec eff, David Fincher; anim d, Brian Narelle.

Animated Fantasy (PR:A MPAA:PG)

TWILIGHT FOR THE GODS** (1958) 120m UNIV c

Rock Hudson (*Capt. David Bell*), Cyd Charisse (*Charlotte King*), Arthur Kennedy (*First Mate Ramsay*), Leif Erickson (*Harry Hutton*), Charles McGraw (*Yancy*), Ernest Truex (*Reverend Butterfield*), Richard Haydn (*Oliver Wiggins*), Judith Evelyn (*Ethel Peacock*), Wallace Ford (*Old Brown*), Vladimir Sokoloff (*Feodor Morris*), Celia Lovsky (*Ida Morris*), Robert Hoy (*Keim*), Charles Horvath (*Lott*), Maurice Marsac (*Shipping Clerk*), William Challee (*Sweeney*), Morris Ankrum (*Sea Captain*), Arthur Space (*Officer*), William Yip (*Dak Sue*), Kimo Mahi (*Uala*), Virginia Gregg (*Myra Pringle*).

Hudson is an alcoholic court-martialed ship's captain, reduced to running a leaky two-masted schooner between a South Seas island and Honolulu. He takes on the usual slice-of-life group and suffers the usual skullduggery and natural disasters found in films like this. Charisse is a prostitute on the run, Kennedy the untrustworthy first mate, and McGraw is a crew member who wants to mutiny. The performances are adequate for the fare, and occasional excitement is tossed in, but mostly this is a non-suspenseful thriller that quickly becomes as creaky as the ship it takes place on. The film was adapted by Gann from his novel, which was similar to his much better THE HIGH AND THE MIGHTY, essentially the same story aboard a doomed airliner and much better told.

p, Gordon Kay; d, Joseph Pevney; w, Ernest K. Gann (based on his novel); ph, Irving Glassberg (EastmanColor); special ph, Clifford Stine; m, David Raksin; ed, Tony Martinelli; md, Raksin; art d, Alexander Golitzen, Eric Orbom; set d, Russell A. Gausman, Oliver Emert; cos, Bill Thomas; makeup, Bud Westmore.

Drama (PR:A MPAA:NR)

TWILIGHT HOUR*½ (1944, Brit.) 85m BN/Anglo bw

Mervyn Johns (*Maj. John Roberts/"John Smith"*), Basil Radford (*Lord Chetwood*), Marie Lohr (*Lady Chetwood*), A.E. Matthews (*Gen. Fitzhenry*), Lesley Brook (*Virginia Roberts*), Grey Blake (*Michael Chetwood*), Ian Maclean (*Hemingway*), Barbara Waring (*Gladys*), Brefni O'Rorke (*Richard Melville*), Margaret Vyner (*Angela*), Joyce Heron (*Diana*), Christopher Steele, Tonie Edgar Bruce, Roy Russell, Sybil Wise, Ethel Royale, John Howard, Marjorie Caldicott, Rita Varian, Elsa Tee, Gabrielle Day, Victor Wood, Noel Dainton, C. Denier Warren, David Ward, Ruby Miller, Richard Turner, Bertram Wallis, Margaret Emden, Edward Stirling, Violet Gould, Alfred Harris, Marie Ault, Cecil Bevan.

Johns is a gardener suffering from that ever handy movie plot device of amnesia. In actuality he is a wealthy major who had lost his memory after being buried alive in WW I. Now he works for Radford, whose son, Blake, is set to marry actress Brook. Johns is wrongly accused of theft and this charge upsets him to the point that the stress brings back his memory. Since the story thus far has bordered on the unbelievable, it takes the fatal plunge by having Brook turn out to be the gardener *cum* major's daughter as well. Hokey stuff, though Johns does try to give this his best.

p, Louis H. Jackson; d, Paul L. Stein; w, Jack Whittingham (based on the novel by Arthur Valentine); ph, James Wilson.

Drama (PR:A MPAA:NR)

TWILIGHT IN THE SIERRAS**½ (1950) 67m REP c

Roy Rogers (*Roy Rogers*), Dale Evans (*Pat Callahan*), Estelita Rodriguez (*Lola Chavez*), Pat Brady (*Sparrow Biffle*), Russ Vincent (*Ricardo Chavez*), George Meeker (*Matt Brunner*), Fred Kohler, Jr (*Mason*), Edward Keane

(*Judge Wiggins*), House Peters, Jr (*Williams*), Pierce Lyden (*Blake*), Don Frost (*Bartender*), Joseph A. Garro (*Henchman*), William Lester (*Paul Clifford*), Bob Burns, Bob Wilke, Foy Willing and the Riders of the Purple Sage, Trigger.

This combination western-gangster plot finds Rogers a U.S. marshal on the trail of some counterfeiters. The gang kidnaps an ex-outlaw who now follows the straight and narrow so he can help with their scheme. Of course, Rogers saves the day with the usual amount of heroics and music. Some minor suspense moments come in the form of a mountain lion hunt subplot. Rodriguez plays a Latino singer who is a Cuban rather than the usual Mexican. A typical outing for Rogers although the sets don't look so good under the Trucolor process. Songs: "Its One Wonderful Day," "Rootin', Tootin' Cowboy," "Pancho's Rancho."

p, Edward J. White; d, William Witney; w, Sloan Nibley; ph, John MacBurnie (Trucolor); m, Stanley Wilson; ed, Tony Martinelli; Frank Hotaling; m/l, Sid Robin, Foy Willing.

Western **Cas.** (PR:A MPAA:NR)

TWILIGHT OF HONOR**½ (1963) 104m MGM bw (GB: THE CHARGE IS MURDER)

Richard Chamberlain (*David Mitchell*), Joey Heatherton (*Laura Mae Brown*), Nick Adams (*Ben Brown*), Claude Rains (*Art Harper*), Joan Blackman (*Susan Harper*), James Gregory (*Norris Bixby*), Pat Buttram (*Cole Clinton*), Jeanette Nolan (*Amy Clinton*), Edgar Stehli (*Judge James Tucker*), James Bell (*Charles Crispin*), George Mitchell (*Paul Farish*), Donald Barry (*Judson Elliot*), Bert Freed (*Sheriff "Buck" Wheeler*), Robin Raymond (*Therese "Tess" Braden*), June Dayton (*Vera Driscoll*), Vaughn Taylor (*Ballentine*), Linda Evans (*Alice Clinton*), Arch Johnson (*Mr. McWade*), Chubby Johnson (*Jailer*), Bert Mustin (*Court Clerk*), Paul Langton.

In 1963 Chamberlain was instantly recognizable for his "Dr. Kildare" role on television, so it was only natural that MGM would try to parlay his small screen talents into movie success. When Buttram is found murdered in Durango, New Mexico, it's up to Chamberlain, a local attorney, to defend number one suspect Adams. Although at first he believes his client to be guilty, gradually Chamberlain begins to have some doubts. The written confession conflicts with Adams' story and, with the encouragement of retired attorney Rains and daughter Blackman, Chamberlain continues his investigation. At the trial, Gregory, a politically hungry lawyer, refuses to call up several key witnesses, which only confirms Chamberlain's suspicions that his client is being framed. Soon the truth comes out: Adams did indeed kill Buttram but only after he had found the town's leading citizen in bed with his wife (Heatherton.) The prosecution tries to stop this scandal from coming out, but Chamberlain pursues it, resulting in a not guilty verdict from the jury. Chamberlain wins this important case and gets Blackman's love as well. This courtroom drama is a slick piece of entertainment, though somewhat dated by it's language. The writing is well-honed and the direction handles the legal maneuvering with good skill. Chamberlain is good in this character switch and has some nice support from the cast. Audiences did not flock to this as MGM had hoped for it was only a moderate success at the box office.

p, William Perlberg, George Seaton; d, Boris Sagal; w, Henry Denker (based on the novel *Twilight of Honor* by Al Dewlen); ph, Philip Lathrop (Panavision); m, John Green; ed, Hugh S. Fowler; md, Green; art d, George W. Davis, Paul Groesse; set d, Henry Grace, Hugh Hunt; makeup, William Tuttle, Ron Berkeley, Agnes Flanagan.

Drama (PR:C MPAA:NR)

TWILIGHT OF THE DEAD (SEE: GATES OF HELL, THE, 1983, U.S./Ital.)

TWILIGHT ON THE PRAIRIE** (1944) 62m UNIV bw

Johnny Downs, Vivian Austin, Leon Errol, Connie Haines, Eddie Quillan, Milburn Stone, Jimmie Dodd, Olin Howlin, Perc Launders, Dennis Moore, Ralph Peters, Foy Willing and the Riders of the Purple Sage, Jack Teagarden and His Orchestra, The Eight Buckaroos.

A cowboy buckaroo band is given a chance to appear in a Hollywood movie. En route they get stranded in Texas and, deperate for employment, take a job running Austin's ranch. That's all there is to this perfunctory cowboy musical that manages to pack 12 typical cowpoke songs into just over an hour. This routine production was aimed at filling out the bill of 1940s movie houses. Songs include: "Let's Love Again," "Where the Prairie Meets the Sky," "Don't You Ever Be a Cowboy" (Everett Carter, Milton Rosen), "Texas Polka" "Oakley Haldeman, Vic Knight, Lew Porter), "No Letter Today" (Frankie Brown), "I Got Mellow in the Yellow of the Moon" (Jimmie Dodd), "Sip Nip Song" (Don George, Brenda Weisberg), "Salt-Water Cowboy" (Redd Evans), "The Blues" (Jack Teagarden), "Little Brown Jug" (Joseph E. Winner), and "And Then" (Sidney Mitchell, Sammy Stept).

p, Warren Wilson; d, Jean Yarbrough; w, Clyde Bruckman (based on a story by Wilson); ph, Jerome Ash; ed, Fred R. Feitshans, Jr.; art d, John B. Goodman, Abraham Grossman, cos, Vera West.

Western/Musical   (PR:A MPAA:NR)

TWILIGHT ON THE RIO GRANDE*   (1947) 71m REP bw

Gene Autry (Himself), Sterling Holloway (Pokie), Adele Mara (Elena Del
Rio), Bob Steele ("Dusty"), Charles Evans (Henry Blackstone), Martin
Garralaga (Mucho Pesos), Howard J. Negley (Jake Short), George J. Lewis
(Capt. Gonzales), Nacho Galindo (Torres), Tex Terry (Joe), George Magrill,
Bob Burns, Enrique Acosta, Frankie Marvin, Barry Norton, Gil Perkins,
Nina Campana, Kenne Duncan, Tom London, Alberto Morin, Keith Rich-
ards, Anna Camargo, Donna Martell, Jack O'Shea, Steve Soldi, Bud
Osborne, Frank McCarroll, Alex Montoya, Connie Menard, Joaquin
Elizondo, The Cass Country Boys, Champion, Jr, the Horse.

While Autry and Holloway are vacationing just south of the border, they
find that their good pal Steele (in a cameo role) has been murdered. Autry
learns that Steele was probably knifed by some smugglers and the
investigation is on. Mara is a young woman whose father was also knifed
by the same band and, after some urging from the heroes, she agrees to help
find the killers. The badmen turn out to be cantina owner Negley and
crooked attorney Evans and they are soundly defeated in an all-out cowboy
brawl. All is resolved nicely and neatly in this lower quality entry for Autry.
The film freely mixes cowboy motifs of the 1880's with 1947 devices like
telephones and flatbed trucks, using whichever historical period is handy at
the moment. The dialog is weak and somewhat racist towards Mexican-
Americans. The direction is okay considering the film's inherent stupidity.
Songs include: "Twilight on the Rio Grande" (sung by Gene Autry and Cass
County Boys, reprise by Autry, Adele Mara), "The Old Lamplighter," "I
Tipped My Hat and Slowly Rode Away" (sung by Gene Autry), "Pretty
Knife Grinder" (sung by Mara), "01' Grandad" (performed by Cass County
Boys).

p, Armand Schaefer; d, Frank McDonald; w, Dorrell and Stuart E.
McGowan; ph, William Bradford; ed, Harry Keller; md, Morton Scott; art d,
Frank Hotaling; m/l, Charles Tobias, Nat Simon, Smiley Burnette, Larry
Marks, Dick Charles, Jack Elliott.

Western   Cas.   (PR:A MPAA:NR)

TWILIGHT ON THE TRAIL**   (1941) 58m PAR bw

William Boyd (Hopalong Cassidy), Brad King (Johnny Nelson), Andy Clyde
(California), Jack Rockwell (Brent), Wanda McKay (Lucy), Norma Willis
(Kerry), Robert Kent (Drake), Tom London (Gregg), Frank Austin (Steve),
Clem Fuller (Stage Driver), Johnny Powers (Drummer), Frank Ellis, Bud
Osborne, Bob Kortman, Jimmy Wakely Trio: Jimmy Wakely, Johnny Bond,
Dick Rinehart.

By the time this was released, the "Hopalong Cassidy" series was well
entrenched in the minds of movie-going kids everywhere, and this entry is
a good example of how formulized the series had become. Boyd and
sidekicks King and Clyde are on the trail of some rustlers. These outlaws
have been making life difficult for some rancher friends. It seems a crooked
foreman has been helping out the bad guys all along but, thanks to Boyd's
good work and by way of some rootin' tootin' action, all is resolved as usual.
McKay provides the love interest and the production values are the
accepted standard. (See: HOPALONG CASSIDY series, Index.)

p, Harry Sherman; d, Howard Bretherton; w, J. Benton Cheney, Ellen
Corby, Cecile Kramer (based on characters created by Clarence E. Mulford);
ph, Russell Harlan; ed, Fred Feitshans, Jr.

Western   (PR:A MPAA:NR)

TWILIGHT PATH***   (1965, Jap.) 107m Shochiku/Shochiku Films of
America c (DAIKON TO NINJIN; AKA: RADISHES AND CARROTS;
MR. RADISH AND MR. CARROT)

Chishu Ryu (Tokichi Yamaki), Nobuko Otowa (Nobuyo Yamaki), Mariko
Kaga (Keiko Yamaki), Isao Yamagata (Gohei Suzuka), Shima Iwashita (Mie
Kawano), Ryo Ikebe (Kotaki), Mariko Okada (Kyoko), Ineko Arima (Nat-
suko), Yoko Tsukasa (Haruko), Shin-ichiro Mikami (Saburo Suzuka), Kinzo
Shin (Akiyama), Hiroyuki Nagato (Kosuki Yamaki), Daisuke Kato.

Ryu is the manager of an office for a trading company. He lives a good life
with Otowa, his wife, and Kaga, their youngest daughter. The three oldest
girls in the family are married and Kaga is engaged to Mikami, the son of
her father's friend Yamagata. While attending a college reunion, Ryu and
Yamagata fight over whether they should inform Shin, a third friend, that
he is dying of cancer. When Ryu's younger brother, Nagato, informs him
that he (Nagato) has embezzled over a million yen, Ryu is forced to sell
some stocks to raise the money necessary to keep the family name
untainted. But when he has all the money in his briefcase, all caution is
tossed aside, and Ryu impetuously boards a train leaving town. The
daughters all meet with their mother after Ryu's absence and admit their
only concern is the money their parents had saved up. Meanwhile, Ryu has
journeyed to Osaka and checked in to a brothel, thinking it to be a hotel.
There he finds room service to be a most unusual and delightful quality.
After a 10-day stay, he finally decides enough is enough and returns home,
finding some new respect from his family.

d, Minoru Shibuya; w, Yoshio Shirasaka, Shibuya (based on a story by

Yasujiro Ozu); ph, Hiroyuki Nagaoka (Shochiku GrandScope, Eastmancol-
or); m, Toshiro Mayuzumi; art d, Nobutaka Yoshino.

Comedy/Drama   (PR:C MPAA:NR)

TWILIGHT PEOPLE zero   (1972, Phil.) 84m Four
Associates/Dimension c

John Ashley (Matt Farrell), Pat Woodell (Neva Gordon), Jan Merlin
(Steinman), Pam Grier (The Panther Woman), Eddie Garcia (Pereira),
Charles Macaulay (Dr. Gordon), Ken Metcalfe (The Antelope Man), Tony
Gosalvez (The Bat Man), Kim Ramos (The Ape Man), Mona Morena (The
Wolf Woman), Angelo Ventura, Johnny Long, Andres Centenera, Letty
Mirasol, Max Rojo, Cenon Gonzalez, Roger Ocomapo, Vic Unson, Romeo
Mabutol.

This is Romero's second attempt to recreate the ISLAND OF LOST SOULS.
The first time around he acted as the executive producer for TERROR IS
A MAN (1959), but this time he takes both the directing and producing
credits. Former teen heartthrob Ashley is an adventurer who is spirited
away to the mysterious island where a mad scientist creates animal-like
humans. Among the poor creatures who are the results of the scientist's
experiments are an antelope man, a winged bat-man, an apeman, a wolf
woman, and a panther woman (played by TV and blaxploitation veteran
Pam Grier). A Nazi and a tree woman are also on hand for the gory
goings-on. Unfortunately, none of this business is memorable, even on a
camp level. The film is as inept as they come, with some pretty poor makeup
jobs to boot.

p, Eddie Romero, John Ashley; d, Romero; w, Romero, Jerome Small; ph,
(Metrocolor).

Horror   Cas.   (PR:O MPAA:PG)

TWILIGHT STORY, THE**½   (1962, Jap.) 150m Tokyo Eiga/Toho bw
(BOKUTO KIDAN)

Hiroshi Akutagawa (The Teacher), Fujiko Yamamoto (The Prostitute),
Masao Oda (The Uncle), Michiyo Aratama, Eijiro Tono, Nobuko Otowa,
Keiko Awaji, Shikaku Nakamura.

Yamamoto is a small-town girl who becomes a whore in Tokyo in order to
support her sickly mother. She meets Akutagawa, a teacher who tells her
he is unmarried. Yamamoto hopes to marry him, but this dream is dashed
when she learns he is unhappily married to a woman with a child fathered
by another man. He ends up returning to his wife and Yamamoto's life is
further saddened when her uncle (Oda) fritters away the money she has
given him to keep in good faith. Events go from bad to worse; her mother
dies and Yamamoto herself is the victim of illness.

p, Ichiro Sato; d, Shiro Toyoda; w, Toshio Yasumi (based on the book Bokuto
Kidan by Kafu Nagai).

Drama   (PR:O MPAA:NR)

TWILIGHT TIME*½   (1983, U.S./Yugo.) 112m Centaur/MGM-UA c

Karl Malden (Marko), Jodi Thelen (Lena), Damien Nash (Ivan), Mia Roth
(Ana), Pavle Vujisic (Pashko), Dragan Maksimovic (Tony), Stole Arandjelov-
ic (Matan), Petar Bozovic (Rocky), Milan Srdoc (Karlo), Peter Carsten
(Gateman), Bora Todorovic (Nikola), Bozidar Pavicevic (Luka), Davor
Antolic (Driver), Slobodanka Markovic (Kristina), Ethan Stone (Milan),
Bojana Stankovic (Vera), Izabela Gavric (Helena), Predrag Dejanovic
(Vlatko), Nenad Dejanovic (Vladimir), Branislav Ranisavljev (Aldo).

After spending 20 years in the U.S., native Yugoslavian Malden heads back
to the small farming village of his mother country. There he takes charge
of his two grandchildren (Nash and Roth) while their parents work in West
Germany. Thelan is the local schoolteacher who implores Malden to lessen
Nash's chores on the farm so the boy can go to school. By the time of the
aged Malden's death at the end of the film, the children have completely
taken over the farm, rejecting their parents' devil-may-care attitude for
Malden's homebodiness. Malden's performance is touching and sincere in
this unusual production, but unfortunately the rest of the film is mediocre
pap. The supporting cast is far below Malden's quality, with Thelan, so good
in FOUR FRIENDS, being sweet to the point of saccharinity. The dubbing
of Yugoslavian actors with English voices doesn't help. It gives the film an
unnatural rhythm. The direction is trifling at best, never quite sure whether
to take a chance with potentially deeper meanings. The result is a complete
waste of time, save for Malden's fine performance. Critics often complain of
the "family film's" demise and this is a perfect example of the level to which
the genre has sunk.

p, Dan Tana; d, Goran Paskaljevic; w, Paskaljevic, Filip David, Tana,
Rowland Barber; ph, Tomislav Pinter (Frank Color); m, Walter Scharf; ed,
Olga Skrigin; art d, Niko Matul; cos, Marija Danc; ch, Renato Pernic; m/l,
"Twilight Time," Buck Ram, Morty Nevins, Al Nevins.

Drama   (PR:C MPAA:PG)

TWILIGHT WOMEN*** (1953, Brit.) 89m Romulus/Lippert bw (GB: WOMEN OF TWILIGHT)

Freda Jackson *(Helen Alistair)*, Rene Ray *(Vivianne Bruce)*, Lois Maxwell *(Christine Ralston)*, Joan Dowling *(Rosie Gordon)*, Dora Bryan *(Olga Lambert)*, Vida Hope *(Jess Smithson)*, Mary Germaine *(Veronica)*, Ingeborg Wells *(Lilly)*, Dorothy Gordon *(Sally)*, Clare James *(Molly)*, Laurence Harvey *(Jerry Nolan)*, Betty Henderson *(Nurse)*, Ben Williams *(Detective)*, Marguerite Brennan *(Miriam)*, Cyril Smith *(Flinton)*, Katherine Page *(First Landlady)*, Edna Morris *(Second Landlady)*, Bruce Beeby, Dandy Nichols, Michael Corkran, Arnold Bell, Gordon Craig, Cyril Conway, Geoffrey Goodheart, Harry Brunning, Robin Dowell, Liam Gaffney, Roy Russell.

A dark, gripping tale of the black-market baby trade set in a London boarding house. Jackson is the landlady who pretends to be righteous, but really is the wicked cornerstone of the illegal operation. Ray, the pregnant mistress of a condemned killer, checks into the boarding house in an attempt to avoid harmful publicity. She soon receives the usual horrendous treatment by Jackson but fails to make public her abuse. The young mother-to-be is befriended by Maxwell, a boarder who loses her baby when Jackson refuses to phone a doctor. When the landlady's evil ways can no longer be ignored, a fellow worker, Hope, informs the police. Before they arrive, however, Ray is pushed down a flight of stairs by Jackson and left to die. The police finally arrive and Jackson receives her just punishment. An uncharacteristically brutal drama for the time, earning it Britain's first "X" rating.

p, Daniel M. Angel; d, Gordon Parry; w, Anatole de Grunwald (based on the play by Sylvia Rayman); ph, Jack Asher; m, Alan Gray; ed, Ralph Kemplen; art d, William Kellner.

Drama **(PR:C MPAA:NR)**

TWILIGHT ZONE--THE MOVIE** (1983) 102m WB c

Segment 1 and Prolog: Dan Aykroyd *(Passenger)*, Albert Brooks *(Driver)*, Vic Morrow *(Bill)*, Doug McGrath *(Larry)*, Charles Hallahan *(Ray)*, Remus Peets, Kai Wulff *(German Officers)*, Sue Dugan, Debby Porter *(Waitresses)*, Steven Williams *(Bar Patron)*, Annette Claudier *(French Mother)*, Joseph Hieu, Albert Leong *(Vietnamese)*, Stephen Bishop *(Charming GI)*, Norbert Weisser *(Solder No. 1)*, Thomas Byrd, Vincent J. Isaac, William B. Taylor, Domingo Ambriz *(GI's)*, Eddie Donno, Michael Milgram, John Larroquette *(KKK)*, Bill Quinn *(Conroy)*, Martin Garner *(Weinstein)*, Selma Diamond *(Mrs. Weinstein)*, Helen Shaw *(Mrs. Dempsey)*, Murray Matheson *(Agee)*, Peter Brocco *(Mute)*, Priscilla Pointer *(Miss Cox)*, Scott Nemes *(Young Mr. Weinstein)*, Tanya Fenmore *(Young Mrs. Weinstein)*, Evan Richards *(Young Mr. Agee)*, Laura Mooney *(Young Mrs. Dempsey)*, Christopher Eisenmann *(Young Mr. Mute)*, Richard Swingler *(Grey Panther)*, Alan Haufrect *(Conroy's Son)*, Cheryl Socher *(Conroy's Daughter-in-law)*, Elsa Raven *(Nurse)*, Jeremy Licht *(Anthony)*, Kevin McCarthy *(Uncle Walt)*, Patricia Barry *(Mother)*, William Schallert *(Father)*, Nancy Cartwright *(Ethel)*, Dick Miller *(Paisley)*, Cherie Currie *(Sara)*, Bill Mumy *(Tim)*, Jeffrey G. Bannister *(Charlie)*, Abbe Lane *(Senior Stewardess)*, Donna Dixon *(Junior Stewardess)*, John Dennis Johnston *(Co-Pilot)*, Larry Cedar *(Creature)*, Charles Knapp *(Sky Marshall)*, Christina Nigra *(Little Girl)*, Lonna Schwab *(Mother)*, Margaret Wheeler *(Old Woman)*, Eduard Franz *(Old Man)*, Margaret Fitzgerald *(Young Girl)*, Jeffrey Weissman *(Young Man)*, Jeffrey Lambert, Frank Toth *(Mechanics)*, Burgess Meredith *(Narrator)*, Carol Serling *(Passenger)*, Byron McFarland *(Pilot Announcement)*.

Based on television's most popular anthology series, TWILIGHT ZONE - THE MOVIE is a frightfully lopsided ominibus which begins with two wretched episodes–by Landis and Spielberg–and finishes with an engrossing pair–by Dante and Miller–resulting in nothing more than a mediocre film as a whole. The film opens with the familiar voice of Burgess Meredith (in place of the more familiar voice of "TWILIGHT ZONE" creator Rod Serling) and a prolog by Aykroyd and Brooks. As they drive down a deserted highway at night, Aykroyd promises to show Brooks "something really scary." With that we are off into the first episode. The only one not based on an original television episode, Landis' segment stars Morrow as loud-mouthed bigot who shouts his hatred for Jews, blacks, and Vietnamese to his friends while getting drunk in a bar. With the blink of an eye, Morrow finds himself as a Jew in Occupied France during WW II being hunted by Nazis. He falls through time again and is tracked down by the KKK in the racially divided South of th 1960s. He gets another dose of his own medicine when, in Vietnam, he is hunted as the enemy by American soldiers. He is then transported back to the bar where he is carted off to a concentration camp, screaming a plea of help to his friends. The production of this episode brought about more publicity than producers Spielberg and Landis could have ever hoped for–unfortunately for them, however, it was all bad. Morrow, the former star ot TV's "Combat" and the boyhood hero of many, was tragically beheaded in a helicopter accident which also killed two young Vietnamese costars. The scandal not only rocked Hollywood where it made the front page of trade journals, but also found its way onto the evening news all across the country. Criminal charges were brought against Landis, whose defense attempted to shift the responsibility to the helicopter pilot and the pyrotechnics engineer. A fine piece of investigative reporting in *FRolling Stone* magazine charged that the weight of the responsibility rested on Landis' shoulders. The fact that Landis had sole control over his episode– he produced, directed, and worth it–seems to back this up. It was also reported that there were a number of dangers on the set during the Vietnam portion of the episode (in all fairness, there is danger on all movie sets). The shot was to have Morrow being pursued at night through the marshes. From above a helicopter with a searchlight spots Morrow, running with his two small children in his arms. To add to the effect bombs and shotgun blasts were going off around them, sending splashes of water everywhere. One explosion sent a piece of debris flying into the helicopter's tail rotor which sent it spinning out of control and into Morrow. All three actors were killed instantly–a bloody death that was recorded from a number of camera angles. Accusations have been made that Landis ordered the helicopter pilot to fly too low, thereby placing the aircraft in danger from the explosions. Morrow had reportedly expressed fear in completing the scene, but since TWILIGHT ZONE - THE MOVIE was his chance to revitalize his sagging career, he could do little but go along with the program. More controversy floated to the surface when it was charged that the Vietnamese children were being overworked and paid in cash to hid this fact. Unfortunately for Landis, this tragedy would cause him to alter his film. It was originally intended that Morrow be redeemed at the end and see the error in his ways. With Morrow dead, the final scenes could not be shot. Instead footage of Morrow being carted away to a concentration camp was substituted at the end, making the entire episode completely pointless. In light of the tragedy, Landis' episode is justifiably the worst of the lot. As of this writing the case is still pending and Landis is still directing. Spielberg's piece, based on the TV episode "Kick the Can," typifies almost every thing intolerable about the director's work. Crothers, a genial old man, arrives at a retirement home and invites residents to join him in a game of kick the can. The can Crothers provides magically transforms the elderly men and women into youthful incarnations from their days gone by. When the game is over the playersare once again physically old (91 though one man chooses to remain young), but their spirits have been rejuvenated. Crothers departs, taking his magic can to another retirement home. Spielberg's point is as subtle as a lead pipe smashing into a plate glass window. In order for these older people to appreciat e life, they must first reexperience their respective childhoods. Had Spielberg shown any respect for his subject the episode might have held some charm. Instead he bathes the characters in dreamy lighting, backing the image with Goldsmith's heart-tugging music. The result is an indigestible 20 minutes of treacle, with the elderly treated as cute figures rather than fully developed characters. Spielberg's vision is condescending garbage masquerading as a meaning personal statement. The film takes a sharp turn for the better in the third segment, directed by Joe Dante and based on the Twilight Zone episode "It's a Good Life" written by Jerome Bixby. Quinlan, a young woman traveler who has lost her way, stops at a rundown diner and asks for directions. As she leaves, Quinlan accidentally backs her car over a bicycle belonging to Licht, a little boy who has been playing a video game inside the diner. Embarrassed and very sorry, Quinlan offers to load the bicycle in her car and drive the boy home where she will pay his parents for the damage. The boy seems unperturbed about his bicycle and glad to have such a pretty lady as company on the ride home. Things begin to get a bit weird when Quinlan arrives at Licht's house. His family–McCarthy, Barry, Schallert, and Cartwright–seem terrified of the youngster and practically beg to serve his whims. Cartoons are on every channel of the TV and are played at maximum volume. The hallways and rooms of the house are grossly distored, as if they, too, are from a cartoon. On a trip upstairs, Quinlan spots another sister of the boy, Currie, but unbeknownst to her the girl is unable to speak because so has no mouth. Quinlan quickly comes to realize that Licht somehow controls the very fiber of the household and warps it to conform to his whims. Everything in the house has sprung from the imagination of a child. When supper is served it is always the boy's latest favorite meal, consisting of a variety of unnourishing junk-type food, and everyone pretends to enjoy it for fear of making him angry. What the whole family seeks to avoid happens, however, when Licht catches his sister, Cartwright, passing a note to Quinlan begging to be freed from her brother's tyranny. Licht goes wild and sends his sister into cartoonland where the family can see her being chased by hideous cartoon monsters on the TV. He then creates some real-life cartoon creatures that appear in the living room and threaten the family. Seeing that what the boy needs is some firm discipline and understanding, Quinlan risks Licht's wrath by demanding that he stop his tantrum. Miraculously the boy listens and the monsters disappear. She learns that his "family" is not really related to him and that he has trapped them in the house and forced them to play the roles of a typically happy 1950s television family-unit. Quinlan offers to adopt Licht if he will let his prisoners go and use his telekinetic powers for good instead of bad. He agrees and they drive off, with Licht turning the grass into flowers. A wildy imaginative and stunningly directed segment: Dante, set designer Teegarden, and special makeup effects master Bottin turned in some of their best work for this, the most visually stunning of the episodes. Mumy, who played the boy in the original TV version, makes a cameo in the diner scene, as does veteran character actor Dick Mikker who reprises his role as well. Animation fans should note that the cartoon segments were created by Sally Cruikshank, whose independently produced series of cartoons starring an odd character named "Quasi" has developed quite a cult following. The momentum continues with the fourth episode, directed by George Miller of MAD MAX and ROAD WARRIOR fame and penned by Matheson who also wrote the original TV episode, "Nightmare at 20,000 Feet". Lithgow stars as a plane passenger who is deathly afraid of flying. He wrestles with his phobia and manages to keep in control until he sees someone standing out on the wing. No one else sees anything, however–not the passengers, not the stewardess, not the pilot. Lithgow is not crazy; we also see the wingwalker, a crazed demon who is wreaking havoc on the engines. By the time the plane lands, Lithgow has gone completely over the edge. He is carted away in an ambulance (driven by Aykroyd) and Brooks) while plane crews survey damage done to the wing, proving that Lithgow actually *did* see someone on the wing. The story is a basic one and in a lesser director's hands it might have failed miserably. Miller, however, is known for his genius at directing action scenes. MAD MAX and ROAD WARRIOR are two of the fastest, most energetic films ever to grace the screen. In his TWILIGHT ZONE segment Miller is given only one confined location (the inside of the plane) allowing for only a minimum of possible camera angles. Yet he manages to create a film which moves as much as the final car chase in ROAD WARRIOR. Judging from the order of the segments, it seems as if producers Spielberg and Landis were well aware that their episodes were of a lesser caliber. The Dante and Miller half of the film is the reward one gets for living through the Landis and Spielberg drek. The moderate success of TWILIGHT ZONE - THE MOVIE paved the way for a resurgence of the anthology series on television. Spielberg came up with the bright idea for "Amazing Stories," most of which are less than amazing, while "The Twilight Zone" and "Alfred Hitchcock Presents" also were resurrected. Unfortunately, as this film proves, Spielberg and his devoted cronies are too entrenched in television land to breathe much life back into the medium.

p, Steven Spielberg, John Landis; Segment 1 and Prolog: d&w, Landis; ph, Steven Larner (Technicolor); ed, Malcolm Campbell; Segment 2: d, Spielberg; w, George Clayton Johnson, Josh Rogan, Richard Matheson (based on the teleplay "Kick the Can" by Johnson for "The Twilight Zone" created by Rod Serling); ph, Allen Daviau, ed, Michael Kahn; Segment 3: d, Joe Dante; w, Matheson (based on the teleplay "It's a Good Life" by Rod Serling for "The Twilight Zone" from a short story by Jerome Bixby); ph, John Hora; ed, Tina Hirsch; Segment 4: d, George Miller; w, Matheson (based on his teleplay "Nightmare at 20,000 Feet" For "The Twilight Zone"); ph, Daviau; ed, Howard Smith; other credits: m, Jerry Goldsmith; prod d, James D. Bissell; art d, Richard Sawyer, James H. Spencer; set d, William J. Teegarden; cos, Deborah Nadoolman; spec eff, Paul Stewart, Mike Wood; makeup, Rob Bottin, Craig Reardon, Michael McCracken; anim, Sally Cruikshank.

Fantasy **Cas.** **(PR:C-O MPAA:PG)**

TWILIGHT'S LAST GLEAMING*½** (1977, U.S./Ger.) 146m Geria-Lorimar-Bavaria/AA c

Burt Lancaster *(Lawrence Dell)*, Richard Widmark *(Martin MacKenzie)*, Charles Durning *(President Stevens)*, Melvyn Douglas *(Zachariah Guthrie)*, Paul Winfield *(Willis Powell)*, Burt Young *(Augie Garvas)*, Joseph Cotten *(Arthur Renfrew)*, Roscoe Lee Browne *(James Forrest)*, Gerald S. O'Loughlin *(Brig. Gen. Michael O'Rourke)*, Richard Jaeckel *(Capt. Stanford Towne)*, William Marshall *(Attorney Gen. William Klinger)*, Charles Aidman *(Col. Bernstein)*, Leif Erickson *(CIA Director Ralph Whittaker)*, Charles McGraw *(Gen. Peter Crane)*, Morgan Paull *(1st Lt. Louis Cannellis)*, Simon Scott *(Phil Spencer)*, William Smith *(Hoxey)*, Bill Walker *(Willard)*, David Baxt *(Sgt. Willard)*, Glenn Beck *(Lieutenant)*, Ed Bishop *(Maj. Fox)*, Phil Brown *(Rev. Cartwright)*, Gary Cockrell *(Capt. Jackson)*, Don Fellows *(Gen. Stonesifer)*, Werton Gavin *(Lt. Wilson)*, Garrick Hagon *(Driver Alfie)*, Elizabeth Halliday *(Stonesifer's Secretary)*, David Healy *(Maj. Winters)*, Thomasine Heiner *(Nurse Edith)*, Bill Hootkins *(Sgt. Fitzpatrick)*, Ray Jewers *(Sgt. Domino)*, Ron Lee *(Sgt. Rappaport)*, Robert Sherman *(Maj. Le Beau)*, John Ratzenberger *(Sgt. Kopecki)*, Robert MacLeod *(State Trooper Chambers)*, Lionel Murton *(Col. Horne)*, Robert O'Neil *(Briefing Officer)*, Shane Rimmer *(Col. Franklin)*, Pamela Roland *(Sgt. Kelly)*, Mark Russel *(Airman Mendez)*, Rich Steber *(Capt. Kincaid)*, Drew W. Wesche *(Lt. Witkin)*, Kent O. Doering *(Barker)*, Alan Moore, Phil Senini, Rich Demarest *(Sharpshooters)*, Roy E. Glenn *(White House Servant)*.

A flawed, but nonetheless very exciting, political thriller which has some deeply disturbing things to say about the powers that be in America. After the credits sequence–where Billy Preston is heard singing a marvelously soulful and poignant rendition of "My Country 'tis of Thee" over a picturesque view of the Statue of Liberty at sunset, the action begins in the near future of 1981 (the film was released in 1977). The film circles around former U.S. Air Force General Lancaster, a Vietnam veteran who served five years as a POW. Upon his return, Lancaster became a vocal advocate for revealing the truth behind America's involvement in Southeast Asia in the hope that a post-Watergate America would appreciate the gesture, forgive their government, and have renewed faith their leaders. Because of his radicalized attitudes toward the war, the Air Force tried to silence him by making him a one-star general. When this failed, he was sent to prison on trumped up manslaughter charges after a man with whom he had a fight suffered a heart attack and died. Determined to reveal the truth about Vietnam to the American public, Lancaster recruits three inmates, Winfield, Young, and Smith, to escape the prison and take over a nearby SAC base that he helped design. The men move swiftly and skillfully through the maze of procedures, code words, and booby traps until they take over the base. Smith, who has been demonstrating some psychotic tendencies during the takeover (he needlessly kills two men), is coldy executed by Lancaster. The two remaining inmates are shocked, but continue to heed the general's orders. Lancaster holds two Air Force personnel, Jaeckel and Paull, hostage because one of them knows the combination to the safe containing the keys neccessary to launch the nine Titan missiles. Lancaster then contacts his former superior Widmark, the base commander, and informs him that Silo 3 is in hostile hands. Lancaster demands to speak to the president. While confirmation of the takeover is being made by the Air Force, Young and Winfield trick Paull into giving up the combination to the safe. Soon after, Lancaster is on the line with the president, Durning, who has assembled his cabinet and the Joint Chiefs (Cotten, Douglas, Marshall, Erickson, McGraw and O'Laughlin–Durning's personal aide) to listen in. Lancaster demands that $10 million in small bills be given to his men, that they be transported to the country of their choice on Air Force One, that the president himself be offered up as their hostage to ensure safe passage, and that once at their destination, the president reveal to the American people the truth about the Vietnam war by reading the contents of NSC (National Security Council) document Number 9759 on national television. If these demands are not met, Lancaster will send the nine Titan missiles to their targets in the Soviet Union. Durning asks an hour and a half to consider the demands and is given permission to do so. The NSC document in question, which is 20 years old, is copied and distributed among the cabinet members. Durning–a wise politician, but basically a decent, moral man–is shocked by the revelations in the document. The reason America became involved in Vietnam was to prove to the Russians that the United States had the will to senselessly sacrifice thousands of lives in a war they knew they had no hope of winning. This act of madness was designed to impress upon the Soviets that the American government was crazy enough to use nuclear weapons to protect its territory. The whole Vietnam war was designed to lend "credibility" to our foreign policy and defense rhetoric. Durning is outraged by the National Security Council's arrogance and decides that revealing the truth to the American people would be a good idea. He is vetoed by most of the men assembled who think that he cannot, under the circumstances of blackmail and with a gun to his head, reveal the truth. Meanwhile, Widmark has mobilized his forces to execute an operation that will sneak men into Silo 3 by avoiding the security cameras and plant a miniature nuclear device that will kill the terrorists and destroy the silo. Realizing it would be impossible to reveal the truth about Vietnam under the circumstances, Durning gives the go-ahead to Widmark and his men. After some very tense moments when Lancaster uncovers the plot and sends the missiles up out of their silos, the operation proves to be a failure (though Young is killed) and Durning is faced with having to serve as bait to get Lancaster and Winfield out in the open. Not a particularly brave man, Durning at first refuses to sacrifice himself for the sins of a previous administration, knowing there is a good possibility that he will be killed. O'Laughlin, his aide and close friend, tells him that the "buck stops here" and he must do his duty. Durning agrees and makes Douglas, the Secretary of Defense, promise to reveal the NSC document to the public if he is killed. Durning flies to the missile base on Air Force One to escort Lancaster and Winfield out. Three sharpshooters have been positioned to kill the terrorists at the first opportunity. In the silo, Winfield tells Lancaster that they are going to lose. The powers that be will never allow the status quo to be changed and the president is expendable. Lancaster finally admits that Winfield is right and decides to send the missiles to Russia because the government won't honor its word. Winfield stops him. "Nobody honors nothin', but that's no reason to blow up the whole world." The inmate then encourages Lancaster to take the chance–admittedly a slim one–that they can make it out, collect the ransom, and disappear. Lancaster agrees and when the president arrives, he and Winfield arm themselves and come out of the silo. With guns pressed to Durning's head, the three men start the walk to the plane. To avoid being hit by snipers, Lancaster, Winfield and Durning walk in circles, constantly placing Durning in the line of fire. The three snipers protest to Widmark that they do not have a clear line of fire, but are told that under no circumstances should those men make it to Air Force One. The men fire, killing Lancaster and Winfield and fatally wounding Durning. As he lies dying in O'Laughlin's arms, Durning calls for Douglas and asks him if he will keep his word about revealing the NSC document. Douglas says nothing. The president dies, knowing that it was all in vain. TWILIGHT'S LAST GLEAMING is a stunning indictment of the arrogance of America's decision makers and the lengths to which they will go to maintain "business as usual." Our nation's unthinking faith in technology is shown to be so dangerous that it can easily be turned against us if the right person comes along. It comes as a deep shock to the military that their usually reliable machines and detailed procedures seem to have gone haywire on the day of the siege, leaving them powerless to stop Lancaster. Even Widmark's message beeper doesn't work properly and he cannot shut it off. Though the film is a bit slow at the outset and suffers from some occasional lapses of logic, director Aldrich–who shot the film in Germany with no cooperation from the U.S. military–turned in a fascinating, tension-filled film with important things to say about the nature of power. Lancaster turns in a fine performance as the general obsessed with cleaning the nation by revealing the truth to the American people, and Durning is superb as the president who comes to share Lancaster's hopes. Durning's performance is detailed and complex as we see a man struggle with the political realities and moral dilemmas inherent in the job. His president is reminiscent of Jimmy Carter, a man who let his basic decency and morality ultimately outweigh his political sense. Aldrich uses some remarkable spilt-screen techniques in the film which add to the tension and help speed up the complicated exposition passages. Ironically, Vera Miles had a few cameo scenes as Durning's wife that were cut in the final editing, fate which had befallen her before in THE

GREEN BERETS where her scenes as John Wayne's wife had also been cut out completely. Despite some flaws, TWILIGHT'S LAST GLEAMING is a gripping drama that will have you on the edge of your seat until the bitter end.

p, Merv Adelson; d, Robert Aldrich; w, Ronald M. Cohen, Edward Huebsch (based on the novel *Viper Three* by Walter Wager); ph, Robert Hauser (Technicolor); m, Jerry Goldsmith; ed, Michael Luciano, Maury Weintrobe; prod d, Rolf Zehetbauer; art d, Werner Achmann; cos, Tom Dawson; spec eff, Henry Millar, Willy Neuner; m/l, "My Country 'Tis of Thee," sung by Billy Preston.

Drama   **Cas.**   **(PR:O   MPAA:R)**

TWIN BEDS*½   (1929) 70m FN-WB bw

Jack Mulhall (*Danny Brown*), Patsy Ruth Miller (*Elsie Dolan*), Armand Kaliz (*Monty Solari*), Gertrude Astor (*Mrs. Solari*), Knute Erickson (*Pa Dolan*), Edythe Chapman (*Ma Dolan*), Jocelyn Lee (*Mazie Dolan*), Nita Martan (*Bobby Dolan*), ZaSu Pitts (*Tillie, Maid*), Eddie Gribbon (*Red Trapp*), Ben Hendricks, Jr (*Pete Trapp*), Carl Levinus (*Jason Treejohn*), Alice Lake (*Mrs. Treejohn*), Bert Roach (*Edward J. Small*).

Three telephone operators listen in to the their customers, thus learning all there is to know about these out-of-town callers. From there it turns into the old show business story of a girl ditching her boy friend and hooking up with a songwriter to become a Broadway smash. Lots of dumb and unnecessary bits of business are tossed in as well in this confusing, overlong comedy. The film's theme song, "If You Were Mine," gets repeated time after time until the audience knows it almost as well as the cast. The direction lets the slapstick run its course in a simple, unaffected manner. The acting is convincing enough, but the story is too creaky to be effective.

d, Alfred Santell; w, F. McGrew Willis (based on the play by Margaret Mayo and Salisbury Field); ph, Sol Polito; ed, LeRoy Stone.

Musical/Comedy   **(PR:A   MPAA:NR)**

TWIN BEDS**   (1942) 85m UA bw

George Brent (*Mike Abbott*), Joan Bennett (*Julie Abbott*), Mischa Auer (*Nicolai Cherupin*), Una Merkel (*Lydia*), Glenda Farrell (*Sonya Cherupin*), Ernest Truex (*Larky*), Margaret Hamilton (*Norah, Maid*), Charles Coleman (*Butler*), Charles Arnt (*Manager*), Cecil Cunningham (*Secretary*), Thurston Hall.

The third film version of this story (following a 1920 silent and sound treatment done in 1929) has been updated from its 1914 source material with sufficient effectiveness. Brent and Bennett are believable but lack the energy needed for this bedroom farce which relies heavily on slapstick humor. The two are newlyweds living in a lush apartment. Auer, their next door neighbor, is a concert singer and attracted to Bennett. He begins flirting and the jealous Brent leaves town in a huff. That night Auer downs one too many and ends up in Bennett's apartment. Her husband returns the next day and it's a tough job for Bennett as she tries to hide the singer. Adding to her trouble is Farrell, Auer's wife, who shows up to claim her man. This bedroom farce should have been fast and furious, but surprisingly is off the needed pace. The script is over-written, though it picks up in the film's later moments and nearly redeems itself. Auer just about runs away with the film as the comic saving grace.

p, Edward Small; d, Tim Whelan; w, Curtis Kenyon, Kenneth Earl, E. Edwin Moran (based on the play by Margaret Mayo, Salisbury Field); ph, Hal Mohr; m, Dimitri Tiomkin; ed, Francis Lyons; art d, John DuCasse Schulze; cos, Irene, Rene Hubert.

Comedy   **(PR:A   MPAA:NR)**

TWIN FACES*   (1937, Brit.) 67m Premier/PAR bw

Anthony Ireland (*Jimmy the Climber/Michael Strangeways*), Francesca Bahrle (*Judy Strangeways*), Frank Birch (*Ben Zwigi*), Paul Neville (*Comdr. Strangeways*), Victor Hagen (*Inspector Coates*), George Turner (*Maurice*), Ivan Wilmot (*Levenstein*), Frank Tickle (*John Cedar*).

Ireland handles a dual acting chore as both a notorious thief, Jimmy the Climber, and an art dealer's nephew, Michael Strangeways. The nephew is mistakenly identified as the thief and is pursued by Bahrle, the daughter of the police commissioner. She finally is able to prove the nephew's innocence when she gets the twins together in the same place.

p, J. Stevens Edwards; d, Lawrence Huntington; w, Gerald Elliott (based on a story by Douglas Reekie).

Crime   **(PR:A   MPAA:NR)**

TWIN HUSBANDS**   (1934) 68m IN/CHES bw

John Miljan (*Jerry Van Trevor*), Shirley Grey (*Chloe Werrenden*), Monroe Owsley (*Colton Drain*), Hale Hamilton (*Gordon Lewis*), Robert Elliott (*Sgt. Kerrigan*), Wilson Benge (*Butler*), William Franklin (*Chuck*), Maurice Black (*Red*).

Miljan is a conman who is abducted and involved in a plan to bilk some

money by posing as the missing husband of Grey. Owsley is the secretary who hatches the entire scheme, but gradually Miljan begins to see how wrong the life he leads is and tries to go straight. In between there are some mixups with cops, both real and phony, as Miljan's henchmen dress in blue to help their man out. Miljan turns in a fair performance in the lead, but the film is little more than a well-made programmer. The action is confined to four sets, which are used with some flair by the director.

d, Frank Strayer; w, Anthony Coldewey and Robert Ellis (based on a story by Ellis); ph, M.A. "Andy" Anderson; ed, Roland Reed.

Crime   **(PR:A   MPAA:NR)**

TWIN SISTERS OF KYOTO**   (1964, Jap.) 107m Shochiku/Shochiku
                                                           Films of America c(KOTO)

Shima Iwashita (*Chieko/Naeko*), Seiji Miyaguchi (*Takichiro Sada*), Teruo Yoshida (*Ryusuke Mizuki*), Tamotsu Hayakawa (*Shinichi Mizuki*), Hiroyuki Nagato, Michiyo Tamaki.

Iwashita is the daughter of a drygoods merchant in the town of Kyoto. Unbeknownst to her, she is a twin, abandoned along with her sister as an infant because of an old superstition about the bad luck twins bring. To protect her from the humiliation this knowledge would bring, Iwashita's parents tell her that they kidnaped her. She begins to suspect that they are not telling the truth and her suspicions are confirmed when she meets an orphaned villager who is her exact double (Iwashita in a dual role). Both women are engaged in love affairs. Iwashita (the merchant's daughter) is being courted by an educated gentleman, but she begins to think he may be more interested in her sister than in herself.

p, Ryotaro Kuwata; d, Noboru Nakamura; w, Toshihide Gondo (based on the book *Koto* by Yasunari Kawabata); ph, Toichiro Narushima (Shochiku, GrandScope, Eastmancolor); m, Toru Takemitsu; ed, Hishashi Sagara; art d, Jun-ichi Ozumi.

Drama   **(PR:C   MPAA:NR)**

TWINKLE AND SHINE   (SEE: IT HAPPENED TO JANE, 1959)

TWINKLE IN GOD'S EYE, THE***   (1955) 73m Mickey Rooney/REP
                                                                            bw

Mickey Rooney (*Rev. Macklin*), Coleen Gray (*Laura*), Hugh O'Brian (*Marty*), Joey Forman (*Ted*), Don Barry (*Dawson*), Touch [Mike] Connors (*Lou*), Jil Jarmyn (*Millie*), Kem Dibbs (*Johnny*), Tony Garcen (*Babe*), Raymond Hatton (*Yahoo Man*), Ruta Lee (*3rd girl*), Clem Bevans.

After a church in a western town is destroyed by an Indian raid, wide-eyed Rooney, fresh out of the seminary, comes to rebuild it. He raises the church once more and gains a following among the towns-people. Despite some opposition from a gambling-hall owner (O'Brian) and a bad man, Rooney triumphs in the end. The antagonists come to see the truth the new preacher offers and all is resolved. Despite the often hackneyed story line, Rooney gives a surprisingly good performance, projecting an innocent quality that works with good effectiveness. Other than that, this isn't much of a film, as the situations are wholly contrived and direction completely perfunctory. The supporting cast is standard for this fare. Watch for an early appearance by Connors.

p, Herbert Jo Yates; d, George Blair; w, P.J. Wolfson; ph, Bud Thackery; m, Van Alexander; ed, Tony Martinelli; art d, Al Goodman; cos, Adele Palmer; m/l, "Twinkle in God's Eye," Mickey Rooney (sung by Eddie Howard).

Western/Drama   **(PR:A   MPAA:NR)**

TWINKLE, TWINKLE, KILLER KANE
                              (SEE: NINTH CONFIGURATION, THE, 1980)

TWINKY   (SEE: LOLA, 1971, Brit.)

TWINS OF EVIL**   (1971, Brit.) 85m Hammer/UNIV c

Madeleine Collinson (*Frieda Gellhorn*), Mary Collinson (*Maria Gellhorn*), Peter Cushing (*Gustav Weil*), Kathleen Bryon (*Katy Weil*), Dennis Price (*Dietrich*), Damien Thomas (*Count Karnstein*), David Warbeck (*Anton Hoffer*), Isobel Black (*Ingrid Hoffer*), Harvey Hall (*Franz*), Alex Scott (*Hermann*), Katya Wyeth (*Countess Mircalla*), Roy Stewart (*Joachim*), Maggie Wright (*Aleta*), Luan Peters (*Gerta*), Kristen Lindholm (*Young Girl at Stake*), Peter Thompson (*Jailer*), Inigo Jackson (*Woodman*), Judy Matheson (*Woodman's Daughter*), Sheelah Wilcox (*Lady in Coach*).

This run-of-the-mill Hammer Studios vampire film features Madeleine and Mary Collinson, the first twin centerfold girls for *Playboy*, as a pair of orphans who come to visit their spirit-hating, God-fearing uncle Cushing. He lives near the evil Karnstein Castle and, of course, that means evil lurks just around the corner. One of the twins becomes curious about the old castle and takes a look around the place. There she meets Thomas, a handsome young count who also is a member of an elite organization: the undead. He bites her and now the question is: which twin is good and which bad? Unfortunately for the good one, the bad is getting away with murder (literally, with the unusual vampire twist of biting victims on the breast) while the good one takes the blame. Finally, Cushing, after much black magic and a witch burning, catches up with his naughty niece and beheads her. This isn't nearly as bad as it could have been and the Collinsons show some talent. As vampire films go, this has the sufficient amount of blood-letting and cheap thrills to be passable entertainment. It is directed with a balance between the horror and an intentional self-parody. Cushing is his usual sinsister self.

p, Harry Fine, Michael Style; d, John Hough; w, Tudor Gates (based on characters created by J. Sheridan Le Fanu); ph, Dick Bush (Eastmancolor); m, Harry Robinson; ed, Spencer Reeve; art d, Roy Stannard; spec eff, Bert Luxford, Jack Mills; makeup, George Blackler, John Webber.

Horror   Cas.   (PR:O MPAA:R)

TWIST, THE**   (1976, Fr.) 105m Barnabe-Gloria-CCC/ UGC-Parafrance c (FOLIES BOURGEOISES)

Bruce Dern (Writer), Stephane Audran (Wife), Ann-Margret (Charley), Sydne Rome (Nathalie), Jean-Pierre Cassel (Jacques), Curt Jurgens (Jeweller), Maria Schell (Gretel), Charles Azanvour (Doctor).

Infidelity–real and imagined–is at the heiart of this tale which transpires in a decidedly upper-middle class millieu. Dern is an American writer; Audran a French socialite; and Margret "oh so cool". There is suspicion and doubt aplenty, but, despite an excellent cast that boasts some talented American and French performers, this would-be adult comedy never goes anywhere. Chabrol's direction is surprisingly lackluster, showing none of his usual insight into character behavior. The production looks handsome, but that's just not enough to compensate for the lack of laughs, as the comedy misses its intended goals again and again. A real disappointment. This was filmed in both French and English language versions.

d, Claude Chabrol; w, Ennio De Concini, Maria Pafusto, Norman Enfield, Chabrol (based on the book by Licie Faure); ph, Jean Rabier (Eastmancolor); ed, Monique Rossignol.

Comedy   Cas.   (PR:C-O MPAA:NR)

TWIST ALL NIGHT*   (1961) 76m Keelou-Alta Vista/AIP c/bw (AKA: THE CONTINENTAL TWIST; THE YOUNG AND THE COOL)

Prolog–"Twist Craze": Jim Lounsbury, Tobin Mathews and the All Stars, Joe Cavalier, The Parisian Twisters, The Manhattan Twisters, The Windy City Twister, Louis Prima (Louis Evans), June Wilkinson (Jenny), Sam Butera and the Witnesses (Themselves), Gertrude Michael (Miss Letitia Clunker), David Whorf (Riffy), Hal Torry (The Mayor), Ty Perry (Arturo), Fred Sherman (Julius), Dick Winslow (Du Bois), Gil Fry (Cop).

This quickie production was hastily put together in order to beat Chubby Checker and his similarly titled film TWIST AROUND THE CLOCK to the theaters, which it did with a release that preceded the Checker film by 15 days. However, the result was an idiotic mess that smacked of ripoff. The original release was accompanied by an independently produced (Independent Artists) short, "Twist Craze," which served as a prolog. In this nine-minute color piece (which increases the combined running time to 85 minutes when the two are shown together, as they often still are), an energetic emcee introduces his nightclub, some energetic dancers, and that hot new dance, "the Twist." After that the film is bogged down by a story involving Prima as a nightclub owner who is losing money. It seems nothing but freeloading teenagers are coming to his club night after night and not spending a dime. Eventually he discovers that an art gallery owner (Perry) who occupies the space above the club has hired the kids so Prima will be forced out of business. After a fight, Prima learns that his neighbor also engages in art theft and has the man arrested. All ends happily, as one might expect, with a big in-the-street twist party and the club is once again successful. This story, filmed in black-and-white, is utterly without worth, giving its characters the most perfunctory of motivations against the framework of a highly implausible plot line. These films aren't termed exploitation pictured for nothing! Songs include: "When the Saints Go Twistin' In," "Everybody Knows," "The Saints Waltz," "Oh Mama, Twist" (Louis Prima), "Alright, Okay, You Win" (S. Wyche, M. Watts), "Sam's Boogie," "Society Waltz," "International Waltz," "Better Twist Now, Baby," "Twistin' the Blues" (Sam Butera, Prima), "Trombone Staccato" (Prima, Louis Sino), "Chantilly Lace" (J.P. Richardson), "The Continental Twist" (Don Covay, John Berry), "Coolin'" (Sid Kuller, Prima), "Tag That Twistin' Dollie" (Ollie Jones, Lockie Edwards, Jr.), "When You're Smiling" (Mark Fisher, Joe Goodwin, Larry Shay), "Fool Around" (Butera), "I Can't Give You Anything But Love" (Dorothy Fields, Jimmy McHugh), "Mood Indigo" (Duke Ellington, Irving Mills, Albany Bigard), "I Can't Believe That You're in Love With Me" (Clarence Gaskill, McHugh).

"Twist Craze": p&d, Allan David; ph, Warren Lieb; ed, Art Ellis; p, Maurice Duke; d, William J. Hole, Jr.; w, Berni Gould; ph, Gene Polito; ed, John Durant; art d, Gabriel Scognamillo; set d, Armour Goetten; ch, Richard Humphrey; makeup, Tom Miller, Jr.

Comedy   (PR:A MPAA:NR)

TWIST AROUND THE CLOCK**   (1961) 86m Four Leaf/COL bw

Chubby Checker (Himself), Dion (Himself), Vicki Spencer (Herself), The Marcels (Themselves), Clay Cole (Himself), John Cronin (Mitch Mason), Mary Mitchell (Tina Louden), Maura McGiveney (Debbie Marshall), Tol Avery (Joe Marshall), Alvy Moore (Dizzy Bellew), Lenny Kent (Georgie Clark), Tom Middleton (Jimmy Cook), Jeff Parker (Larry), John Bryant (Harry Davis), Ernesto Morelli (Headwaiter), Barbara Morrison (Mrs. Vandeveer), Ezelle Poule (Dowager), Renee Aubry (Girl in Booth), Barry O'Hara (Harvey), Dal McKennon (Proprietor).

With Elvis in the Army, the face of rock'n'roll was slowly undergoing a transformation that would soon be exploded with the British Invasion. As a last gasp from the old era, TWIST AROUND THE CLOCK is a bit of good fun, updating the classic ROCK AROUND THE CLOCK to fit the dance craze that was captivating teenyboppers across the U.S. The simple story line has Cronin playing a rock'n'roll manager who discovers kids dancing the night away to a new fangled dance, the Twist. He books a big Boston society party for his new band, but can't get other gigs because he once spurned the affections of McGiveney, the daughter of a top agent. Several songs and a few simple moments later, Cronin has married Mitchell, one of his dancers, despite a tricky contract designed by McGiveney to prevent just that from happening. The dancers appear on nationwide TV and, of course, are a big smash. Though it's not as good as the original, TWIST AROUND THE CLOCK bears a certain naive charm of a long-gone era, a time when teenagers were more innocent and sophistication meant a milkshake with two straws. This simple story is really just an excuse for plenty of rock tunes including Checker singing something called "Merry Twist-mas" (Mack Wolfson, Wally Hall, Charlie Singleton). The best moments in the film come when great rocker Dion sings two of his classic songs, "Runaround Sue" (E. Meresca, Dion Dimucci), and "The Wanderer" (Meresca). Other songs include: "Twist Around the Clock," "Don't Twist with Anyone Else but Me," (Buddy Kaye, Philip Springer, Clay Cole), "Here, There, Everywhere" (Teddy Vann), "Twistin', U.S.A." (Kal Mann), "Your Lips and Mine," "Twist Along" (Mann, Dave Appell), "The Twist is Here to Stay" (Cole, Fred Karger), "He's So Sweet" (Alonzo Tucker, Gwen Elias, Gordon Evans), "The Majestic" (B.L. Jones, Welton Young).

p, Sam Katzman; d, Oscar Rudolph; w, James B. Gordon; ph, Gordon Avil; ed, Jerome Thoms; art d, George Van Marter; set d, Morris Hoffman; ch, Earl Barton.

Musical   (PR:A MPAA:NR)

TWIST OF FATE   (SEE: BEAUTIFUL STRANGER, THE, 1954, Brit.)

TWIST OF SAND, A**½   (1968, Brit.) 90m Christina/UA c

Richard Johnson (Geoffrey Peace), Honor Blackman (Julie Chambois), Jeremy Kemp (Harry Riker), Peter Vaughan (Johann), Roy Dotrice (David Carland), Guy Doleman (Patrol Boat Commander), James Falkland (Patrol Boat Lieutenant), Jack May (Seekert), Kenneth Cope (Flag Officer), Tony Caunter (Elton), Clifford Evans (Adm. Tringham).

Johnson is a man haunted by his past. During WW II he had captured a Nazi U-boat and under orders killed all surviving crew members. Now he is running a smuggling operation based in Malta with Dotrice, an old shipmate. Kemp, another ex-war buddy approaches the pair with an idea about recovering some diamonds hidden aboard a Spanish galleon. Blackman is the widow of the man who hid the cache of gems and Vaughan is an idiotic German thug who knows the area and its rugged terrain. Though Dotrice and Kemp don't get along, the crew goes after the treasure. While crossing a South African desert, Johnson comes to realize that Vaughan is a survivor of his war crime. Finally, the galleon is found buried in a sand dune and the diamonds uncovered. However, Kemp dislodges a supporting brace on the ship, which causes it to collapse, killing Dotrice and trapping Vaughan. Johnson reveals his past connection to Vaughan and the German recovers, attempting to get at Johnson. Kemp shoots him with a rifle, but, before dying, Vaughan manages to thrust a knife into his killer. Kemp falls and the diamonds are washed out to sea, leaving Johnson and Blackman alone and empty handed. This adventure film is put together with good skill by the director, utilizing all of the genre's tricks with a good payoff. Unfortunately the players overact their roles to some degree, which hampers the overall power of the film. At points the music is also overdone, intruding on the proceedings where it clearly should not. A TWIST OF SAND is not a disappointing film, for the thrills are well-developed. However, it falls just short of being a really good action piece, thus ending up as a well-told run-of-the-mill adventure.

p, Fred Engle; d, Don Chaffey; w, Marvin H. Albert (based on the novel A Twist of Sand by Geoffrey Jenkins); ph, John Wilcox, Stephen Halliday (DeLuxe Color; m, Tristram Carey; ed, Alastair McIntyre; prod d, John Stoll; md, Carey; spec eff, Bill Warrington, Nick Allder.

Adventure   (PR:A MPAA:G)

TWISTED BRAIN (SEE: HORROR HIGH, 1974)

TWISTED LIVES (SEE: LIARS, THE, 1964, Fr.)

TWISTED NERVE** (1969, Brit.) 118m Charter/NG c

Hayley Mills (*Susan Harper*), Hywel Bennett (*Martin Durnley/Georgie Clifford*), Billie Whitelaw (*Joan Harper*), Phyllis Calvert (*Enid Durnley*), Frank Finlay (*Henry Durnley*), Barry Foster (*Gerry Henderson*), Salmaan Peer (*Shashi Kadir*), Thorley Walters (*Sir John Forrester*), Christian Roberts (*Philip Harvey*), Timothy West (*Superintendent Dakin*), Gretchen Franklin (*Mrs. Clarke*), Clifford Cox (*Inspector Goddard*), Robin Parkinson (*Shop Manager*), Richard Davies (*Taffy Evans*), Brian Peck (*Detective Sergeant*), Russell Napier (*Prof. Fuller*), Russell Waters (*Hospital Attendant*), Michael Cadman (*Mac*), Mary Land (*Judy*), Hazel Bainbridge (*Nursing Sister*), Timothy Bateson, Basil Dignam.

Bennett plays a young man who during severe emotional stress assumes the personality of a 6-year-old. When caught stealing a toy duck from a store, Bennett is helped out by Mills, a kindly student who talks the store manager out of pressing charges. Bennett's overprotective mother, Calvert, has to defend the 21-year-old against his stepfather when the schizophrenic young man explains he simply wanted to take the duck to his institutionalized mongoloid brother. Finlay will have none of this and throws his stepson out of the house. Bennett claims he's going to another country but ends up at Mills' home. In his 6-year-old personal, Bennett endears himself to her mother (Whitelaw) and the woman takes him in at her boarding house. A few nights go by and Bennett returns to his old home, brutally murdering his father with a pair of scissors. Bennett's presence at the boarding house causes problems for Mills and her mother. The daughter breaks up with her boy friend and the mother stops an affair with another tenant (Foster). Mills tries to find out more about Bennett. When Whitelaw tries to seduce him, Bennett goes mad and kills her. Mills comes home and seemingly is the next victim. Fortunately, Foster has discovered his former lover's corpse and calls the police, who arrive in the nick of time. This PSYCHO-styled thriller holds some good moments of genuine chills, but the film makes a connection between Bennett and his mongoloid brother that unfortunately permeates the story. Suggesting that mental retardation is hereditarily linked with homicidal tendencies is a cheap exploitative gimmick that overrides much of the film's psychological explanations. It's an ugly theory to put forth and highly irresponsible on the part of the filmmakers. The film was scored by Hitchcock's great composer Herrmann. Interestingly enough, the production and direction team of John and Roy Boulting comprises twin brothers. After completion of this film Roy Boulting and his star Mills were married in spite of a 23-year age difference.

p, John Boulting, George W. George, Frank Granat; d, Roy Boulting; w, R. Boulting, Leo Marks (based on a story by Roger Marshall from an idea by Marshall and Jeremy Scott); ph, Harry Waxman (Technicolor); m, Bernard Herrmann; ed, Martin Charles; md, Herrmann; art d, Albert Witherick.

Thriller (PR:O MPAA:M/PG)

TWISTED ROAD, THE (SEE: THEY LIVE BY NIGHT, 1949)

TWITCH OF THE DEATH NERVE* (1973, Ital.) 82m Hallmark c (ANTEFATTO; AKA: LAST HOUSE ON THE LEFT PART II)

Claudine Auger, Claudio Volonto, Ana Maria Rosati, Laura Betti, Luigi Pistilli, Brigitte Skay.

A typical mad-slasher movie that makes the dubious boast of 13 gory murders. It also carries the equally dubious distinction of influencing FRIDAY THE THIRTEENTH. A re-release of this picture had a few scenes cut and was renamed LAST HOUSE ON THE LEFT PART II, though it had absolutely nothing to do with that cult horror film.

p, Giuseppe Zacciarello; d, Mario Bava; w, Bava, Carlo Reali; ph, Bava; m, Stelvio Copriani.

Horror (PR:O MPAA:R)

TWO½ (1975) 93m Colmar c (AKA: CAPTIVE)

Sarah Venable (*Ellen*), Douglas Travis (*Steven*), Clifford Villeneuve (*Irate Driver*), Ray Houle (*Doctor*), Florence Hadley (*Hardware Customer*), William Green (*Husband*), Thelma Green (*Wife*), Sylvia Harman (*Bank Teller*), Elwyn Miller (*Guard*), Jack Dykeman (*Man in Bank*), Stanley McIntire (*Chief of Police*), Fred Gilbert (*Policeman*), Winston Merrill (*Postal Clerk*).

When Vietnam veteran Travis escapes from an army discharge hospital, he kidnaps Venable and hides away with her in a secluded mountain cabin. Venable manages to calm Travis down and talks him into letting her go if she stays for two days. The two build an unusual rapport over the next 48 hours. Travis goes to town to get some food and robs a bank as well. This robbery upsets the relationship that he's built with the girl and Travis is forced to go back to return the stolen money. Of course, this leads to tragedy and Venable is left alone, a bit wiser and emotionally drained from the ordeal. This independent film, like many of its kind, is a work of mixed artistic result. Venable is a real standout, giving a sensitive performance

with good subtle feeling. Travis, on the other hand, is too stiff in a role that clearly demands some expansion. Both are hampered by a script that, while it gives a good setup, never quite probes as deeply as it should. The direction by the film's author also suffers somewhat from this detached feeling, though the mountain locations are well used, creating a lovely film to look at. For all its problems, there is a certain sincerity to the proceedings, a youthful earnestness that is often found in small, independent features.

p,d&w, Charles Trieschmann; ph, Vilis Lapenieks (Movielab Color); m, Akiva Talmi; ed, David McKenna.

Drama (PR:O MPAA:PG/R)

TWO A PENNY* (1968, Brit.) 98m World Wide c

Cliff Richard (*Jamie Hopkins*), Dora Bryan (*Ruby Hopkins*), Avril Angers (*Mrs. Burry*), Ann Holloway (*Carol Turner*), Geoffrey Bayldon (*Alec Fitch*), Peter Barkworth (*Vicar*), Donald Bisset (*Dr. Berman*), Edward Evans (*Jenkins*), Mona Washbourne (*Mrs. Duckett*), Tina Packer (*Gladys*), Earl Cameron (*Verger*), Noel Davis (*Dennis Lancaster*), Nigel Goodwin (*Hubert*), Charles Lloyd Pack (*Rev. Allison*), Billy Graham (*Himself*), Richard Vanstone (*David*), Warwick Sims (*Bill*), Rudi Patterson (*Sid*), John Watson (*Mr. Baker*), Jo Rowbottom (*Helen*), Daphne Riggs, Barbara Bruce (*Middle-aged Women*), Doreen Keogh (*Mary*), Norman Mitchell (*Attendant*).

Richard, a real-life minor pop star turned religious crusader, plays a young man tempted by easy money into drug dealing. Since his mother works as a receptionist for a doctor, getting the stuff is no problem. Bisset, his mother's employer, also dabbles with psychedelic substances himself. Richard goes with his girl friend, Holloway, to a revival meeting led by the famed evangelist Graham (playing himself in a cameo appearance). She sees the light, but it takes more than one meeting to convince Richard. He's caught stealing from Bisset and tries to double-cross Bayldon, a drug supplier. Gradually, Holloway draws away from Richard and after the expected tribulations he, too, sees the light. This is the sort of film that labels its message on a lead pipe and proceeds to bash the audience over the head with it until they catch on.

p, Frank R. Jacobson; d, James F. Collier; w, Stella Linden; ph, Michael Reed (Eastmancolor); m, Mike Leander; ed, Ann Chegwidden, Eugene Pendleton; art d, Peter Williams; m/l, "Two a Penny," "Love You Forever, Today," "Questions," Cliff Richard, James F. Collier (sung by Richard).

Religious Drama (PR:A MPAA:G)

TWO AGAINST THE WORLD* (1932) 80m WB bw

Constance Bennett (*Dell Hamilton*), Neil Hamilton (*Dave Norton*), Helen Vinson (*Corinne*), Allen Vincent (*Bob*), Gavin Gordon (*Victor Linley*), Oscar Apfel (*District Attorney*), Walter Walker (*Courtnay Hamilton*), Hale Hamilton (*Mr. Mitchell*), Maude Truax (*Dowager*), Clara Blandick (*Aunt Agatha*), Alan Mowbray (*George*), Leila Bennett (*Bootlegger*), Dennis O'Keefe (*Dance Extra*), Roscoe Karns, Eulalie Jensen, Louise Carter, Harold Entwistle, Harold Nelson.

When her no good younger brother commits murder Bennett gallantly takes the blame. However, the socialite finds she's got some problems when the man defending her in court is also the man she loves (Hamilton). The dialog is as contrived as the plot. Motivations in this drama are almost nonexistent and the actors merely go through the motions. Direction is little more than a camera pointing at the action. At least the sets are handsome and so are the women in their fancy costumes.

p, Lucien Hubbard; d, Archie Mayo; w, Sheridan Gibney (based on the play "A Dangerous Set" by Marion Dix, Jerry Horwin); ph, Charles Rosher; ed, Bert Levy.

Drama (PR:A MPAA:NR)

TWO AGAINST THE WORLD** (1936) 64m WB-FN bw (GB: THE CASE OF MRS. PEMBROOK)

Humphrey Bogart (*Sherry Scott*), Beverly Roberts (*Alma Ross*), Linda Perry (*Edith Carstairs*), Carlyle Moore, Jr (*William Sims, Jr.*), Henry O'Neill (*Jim Carstairs*), Helen MacKellar (*Martha Carstairs/Glory Penbrook*), Claire Dodd (*Cora Latimer*), Hobart Cavanaugh (*Tippy Mantus*), Harry Hayden (*Martin Leavenworth, Minister*), Robert Middlemass (*Bertram C. Reynolds*), Clay Clement (*Mr. Banning*), Douglas Wood (*Malcolm Sims*), Virginia Brissac (*Mrs. Marion Sims*), Paula Stone (*Miss Symonds*), Bobby Gordon (*Herman O'Reilly*), Frank Orth (*Tommy*), Howard Hickman (*Dr. Maguire*), Ferdinand Schumann-Heink (*Sound Mixer*).

To gain listeners for his radio station Bogart's boss digs up a murder case of 20 years previous and Bogart is told to broadcast it as a serial. MacKellar is the woman who had been exonerated of the charge originally and gone on to marry. She has never mentioned the case to her daughter (Perry), who is engaged to Moore, the son of a well-to-do manufacturer. Now that her past is being relived for a wide audience, the wedding faces possible cancellation. Unable to live with this, MacKellar and her husband, O'Neill, kill themselves. Bogart, strongly backed by his secretary, Roberts, has been opposed all along to the broadcasts, but Perry, feeling that Middlemass has in effect murdered her parents, goes to the station to kill him. Fortunately Moore follows her and deflects her aim before she fires a pistol. The two renew their love and marry Roberts, who resigns, marries Roberts. This remake of FIVE STAR FINAL (1931) is a boring venture all around. The screenplay is beefed up only when it directly borrows from the original film, otherwise it lacks any real emotion. Bogart is ineffective in this early lead role, heading a cast that is for the most part without much energy. Audiences caught on to the film's many shortcomings and this lackluster piece was a poor box office earner.

p, Bryan Foy; d, William McGann; w, Michel Jacoby (based on the play "Five Star Final" by Louis Weitzenkorn); ph, Sid Hickox; m, Heinz Roemheld; ed, Frank Magee; art d, Esdras Hartley; spec eff, Fred Jackman, Jr., Rex Wimpy.

Drama (PR:A MPAA:NR)

TWO ALONE½ (1934) 75m RKO bw

Jean Parker (Mazie), Tom Brown (Adam), ZaSu Pitts (Esthey), Arthur Byron (Slag), Beulah Bondi (Mrs. Slag), Nydia Westman (Corie), Willard Robertson (Marshall), Charley Grapewin (Sandy), Emerson Treacy (Milt), Paul Nicholson (Sheriff).

Parker is a poor orphan girl stuck on a farm run by Byron, a mean old man who keeps her in slave-like conditions. Along comes Brown, a runaway from reform school, and he, too, ends up a victim of Byron's cruel and evil ways. The two fall in love and are rescued by Robertson, Parker's long lost father, who sees that the young people marry in the end. The film is a struggle for the audience with all the ridiculous and melodramatic twists this story takes. Parker is excellent in one of her early films, but Brown is unbelievable in his role. Pitts, a fine comic actress, is wasted in a part as an applejack swigging neighbor.

p, David Lewis; d, Elliott Nugent; w, Josephine Lovett, Joseph Moncure March (based on the play "Wild Birds" by Dan Totheroh); ph, Lucien Andriot; ed, Arthur Roberts.

Drama (PR:A MPAA:NR)

TWO AND ONE TWO** (1934) 69m FOX bw (DOS MAS UNO DOS)

Rosita Moreno, Valentine Parera, Carmen Rodriguez, Andres de Segurola.

A Spanish language programmer which casts Moreno in dual roles–as a proper young woman of royalty and a carefree modern girl. Parera, a young scientist, falls in love with both before learning that they are one and the same.

p, John Stone; d, John Reinhardt.

Comedy/Romance (PR:A MPAA:NR)

TWO AND TWO MAKE SIX** (1962, Brit.) 89m Prometheus-BL-Bryanston/Union bw (AKA: A CHANGE OF HEART; THE GIRL SWAPPERS)

George Chakiris (Larry Curado), Janette Scott (Irene), Alfred Lynch (Tom), Jackie Lane (Julie), Athene Seyler (Aunt Phoebe), Bernard Braden (Sgt. Sokolow), Malcolm Keen (Harry Stoneham), Ambrosine Phillpotts (Lady Smith-Adams), Jack MacGowran (Night Porter), Robert Ayres (Col. Thompson), Edward Evans (Mack), Harry Locke (Ted), Jeremy Lloyd (Young Man), Marianne Stone (Hotel Receptionist), Nina Parry (Prudence), Ken Wayne (Maj. Calhoun), Gary Cockrell (Leo Kober), Bill Mitchell (Bob Young), Eric Woodburn (Dresser), Bob Kanter, John Gardiner, Billy Edwards, George Sperdakos (Air Policemen), Patricia English (Club Stewardess).

Chakiris is a carefree member of the U.S. Air Force stationed in England. A womanizer, he also loves to play the ponies, and inevitably this brings trouble. He goes AWOL, then knocks out a sergeant who's sent to arrest him. Thinking the man is dead, Chakiris grabs his girl, Lane, and her brother's motorbike, and the two head out to the seaside. At a cafe, they meet Lynch and Scott. Because of the similarity in their boy friends' clothing and motorbikes, the two women end up riding with the wrong men and of course fall for their new partners. Scott convinces Chakiris to give up and return to base. He does so and is given a mild sentence after announcing an impending marriage to Scott. A year goes by and the two women meet again, this time wheeling identical prams. There are some nice moments in this oddball romantic comedy but the film is hampered by a wavering style. It swings between the humorous and the serious without finding a neat middle ground. Scott is a standout, giving her role a fresh and enjoyable appeal.

p, Monja Danischewsky; d, Freddie Francis; w, Danischewsky; ph, Desmond Dickinson, Ron Taylor; m, Norrie Paramor; ed, Peter Taylor; art d, Ted Marshall; m/l, "A Change of Heart," Paramor, Bunny Lewis (sung by Craig Douglas).

Comedy/Drama (PR:C MPAA:NR)

TWO ARE GUILTY** (1964, Fr.) 131m S.N.E.-GAU-Trianon-Ultra/MGM bw (LA GLAIVE ET LA BALANCE; UNO DEI TRE; AKA:THE SWORD AND THE BALANCE)

Anthony Perkins (Johnny), Jean-Claude Brialy (Jean-Philippe), Renato Salvatori (Francois), Pascale Audret (Agnes), Anne Tonietti (Christine),

Marie Dea (Mlle. Winter), Elina Labourdette (Mlle. Darbon), Fernand Ledoux (Prosecutor), Jacques Monod (Pranzani), Michele Mercier (Brigitte), Henri Cremieux (President des Assies), Camille Guerini (Judge), Jean Ozenne (Bernardi), Claude Cerval (Plouzenec), Anne Riviere (Marie), Janine Darcey (Chantal), Gilbert Gil (Inspector Portal), M. Klemens (1st Police Inspector), Lou Bennett, Sonny Criss, Sonny Grey, Kenny Clarke, Mae Mercer (Musical Group), Henri Vilbert, Robert Le Beal, Diana Lepvrier, Helena Manson, Pierre Mirat, Maurice Nasil, Marcel Peres, Robert Rollis, Maurice Chevit, Jean Marchat, Claudine Maugey.

A child is kidnaped and murdered along the French Riviera. Two men are seen fleeing the scene of the crime and are chased by the police. One of the two kills a policeman and the pair then run into a lighthouse. After the police surround the place three men emerge, all dressed in the same garb. Each man claims innocence and states that the other two are the killers. Perkins is an American, a would-be artist involved in a sex scandal back home. Salvatori is a known gigolo with unsavory attitudes towards his women, and Brialy is a real estate man who sometimes uses his sister's sexuality to close deals. They are brought to trial and all are found innocent, but an angry mob of demonstrators kills the trio when they are being transported from court. It is never known who the real killer is in this nifty little thriller from France. For an American actor like Perkins to make an all-French film was a daring career move, but it paid off nicely. His performance is a standout in this clever, well-directed crime picture. Genre fans will love it.

P, Alain Poire; d, Andre Cayatte; w, Cayatte, Henri Jeanson, Charles Spaak; ph, Roger Fellous (Franscope); m, Louiguy; ed, Paul Cayatte; art d, Rino Mondellini.

Crime (PR:C MPAA:NR)

TWO BLACK SHEEP (SEE: TWO SINNERS, 1935)

TWO BLONDES AND A REDHEAD** (1947) 69m COL bw

Jean Porter (Catherine Abbott), Jimmy Lloyd (Tommy Randell), June Preisser (Patti Calhoun), Judy Clark (Vicki Adams), Rick Vallin (Freddie Ainsley), Douglas Wood (Judge Abbott), Charles Smith (Miles Bradbury), Regina Wallace (Mrs. Abbott), John Meredith (Melvin Lounsdale), Diane Fauntelle (Miss Courtley), Joanne Wayne (Jeanette), Tony Pastor and His Orchestra.

Society girl Porter attends an exclusive school. However, her heart really is in show business and she ends up playing hookey to appear as a chorus girl in a musical. When the show closes, she invites chorines Preisser and Clark to join her in a visit home. Some predictable nonsense occurs on their arrival in the form of servant-cum-rich kid Lloyd. The story is given a better-than-average treatment and backed by a fairly good budget but the direction is just standard. The well known Dorothy Fields and Jimmy McHugh tune, "On the Sunny Side of the Street," is featured amoung the musical numbers. Other songs: "It's So Easy," "All I Know is Si Si" (Doris Fisher, Allan Roberts), "Boogie Woogie from Nowhere" (Saul Chaplin).

p, Sam Katzman; d, Arthur Dreifuss; w, Victor McLeod, Jameson Brewer (based on a story by Harry Rebuas); ph, Ira H. Morgan; ed, Jerome Thoms; md, Mischa Bakaleinikoff; art d, Paul Palmentola.

Musical (PR:A MPAA:NR)

TWO BRIGHT BOYS**½ (1939) 70m UNIV bw

Jackie Cooper (Roy O'Donnell), Freddie Bartholomew (David Harrington), Melville Cooper (Hilary Harrington), Dorothy Peterson (Kathleen O'Donnell), Alan Dinehart (Bill Hallet), Willard Robertson (Clayton), J.M. Kerrigan (Mike Casey), Eddie Acuff (Washburn), Hal K. Dawson (Boswell), Harry Worth (Maxwell), Eddy C. Waller (Sheriff).

When the orphaned Cooper inherits some oil rich property in Texas, the unscrupulous Dinehart is more than helpful to the lad. It seems he wants the property for his own but thanks to the ever pure Bartholomew and his pa Melville Cooper all is saved. Despite the routine plotting this is a fairly entertaining piece. The old western style was brought up to date, directed in a fast pace and with just enough comic moments from Cooper to keep it from becoming heavy-handed. This was the second film that year for the Cooper-Bartholomew team following SPIRIT OF CULVER. The studio heads knew a good thing when they saw it for the two boy stars worked well together.

p, Burt Kelly; d, Joseph Santley; w, Val Burton, Edmund L. Hartmann; ph, Elwood Bredell; ed, Phillip Cahn.

Drama (PR:A MPAA:NR)

TWO COLONELS, THE**½ (1963, Ital.) 90m Titanus/Comet Film Distributors bw (I DUE COLONELLI)

Toto (Col. Di Maggio), Walter Pidgeon (Col. Timothy Henderson), Scilla Gabel (Iride), Adriana Facchetti (Penelope), Nino Taranto (Sgt. Quaglia), Francis Lane (Sgt. McIntyre), Toni Ucci (Mazzetta), Roland Bartrop (Maj. Kruger), Gerard Herter (German General), Giorgio Bixio, Nino Terzo.

During World War II Toto is an Italian colonel who leads an invasion of the small town of Montegreco. This Greek-Albanian border town is quite indifferent to Toto and the town's British invader Pidgeon, for between the two Montegreco has been invaded thirty-one times. The townspeople openly fraternize with both sides, caring little which side wins the war. Pidgeon goes to fetch his pipe, forgotten at a local tavern on a previous invasion. The Italians are now occupying the area and hold him prisoner, but he's easily retrieved by his forces. All it takes is two prisoners and two cases of whiskey. Next the British capture Toto but he escapes with Pidgeon's help. When Nazis attack the Greek border, Bartrop orders this little town destroyed. Toto has the German officer arrested but the S.S. captures him and decides he should be executed. Leave it to his friend Pidgeon to save Toto and soon the opposing forces have united to fight a common enemy. The comedy in this war spoof is light and unaffected. Unfortunately the direction and script are not, and rely on stereotypes and obvious humor to make their points. It's the cast that makes this film work, especially the fine leads of Toto and Pidgeon. The two "best of enemies" have a genuine affection that works well, overcoming the production troubles.

p, Gianni Buffardi; d, Steno [Stefano Vanzina]; w, Ruggero Grimaldi, Sergio Corbucci; ph, Tino Santoni.

War/Comedy   **(PR:A MPAA:NR)**

TWO DAUGHTERS*   (1963, India) 114m Satyajit Ray Prod./Janus
                                         Films bw (TEEN KANYA)

"The Postmaster": Anil Chatterjee (*Nandalal*), Chandana Bannerjee (*Ratan*), Nripati Chatterjee (*Bishay*), Kagen Rathak (*Khagen*), Gopal Roy (*Bilas*), "The Conclusion": Aparna Das Gupta (*Mrinmoyee*), Soumitra Chatterjee (*Amulya*), Sita Mukherji (*Jogmaya*), Gita Dey (*Nistarini*), Santosh Dutt (*Kishory*), Mihir Rakhal Chakravarty, Debi Neogy (*Haripada*).

In the first story of this two part film Anil Chatterjee is a city boy who goes to the country for a job as postmaster. In the small village where he works Bannerjee, an orphan girl of 10, serves as his assistant. She had done this for his predecessor, who had treated her cruelly. Now a real friendship develops as the new postmaster treats her kindly. However, rural life doesn't suit Chatterjee, and after a bout with malaria he decides to return to the city. Just before leaving, he comes to realize how close his friendship with the little girl has grown. The second tale has Soumitra Chatterjee playing an unmarried lawyer. He cares nothing for his mother's fix-ups and instead marries Gupta, a carefree tomboy. On their wedding night she tells him that she was forced into the marriage and now resents this loss of freedom. She runs away later in the night but is found and brought back the next day. After Gupta is given the traditional punishment for unwilling brides, Chatterjee sends her home and goes off to Calcutta himself. While he is gone, Gupta realizes that she does love him and finally joins up with her husband. In India this film had a third episode called "Monihara" and the trilogy was known as THREE DAUGHTERS. However only "The Postmaster" and "The Conclusion" were included for the American release.

p,d&w, Satyajit Ray (based on the short stories "The Postmaster" and "The Conclusion" by Rabindranath Tagore); ph, Soumendu Roy; m, Ray; ed, Dulal Dutta; art d, Bansi Chandragupta.

Comedy/Drama   **(PR:A MPAA:NR)**

TWO DOLLAR BETTOR*½   (1951) 72m REA bw (GB: BEGINNER'S
                                                              LUCK)

John Litel (*John Hewitt*), Marie Windsor (*Mary Slate*), Steve Brodie (*Rick Bowers*), Barbara Logan (*Nancy Hewitt*), Robert Sherwood (*Phillip Adams*), Barbara Bestor (*Diane Hewitt*), Walter Kingsford (*Carleton Adams*), Don Shelton (*George Irwin*), Kay La Velle (*Mrs. Irwin*), Carl Switzer (*Chuck Norlinger*), Isabel Randolph (*Mrs. Adams*), Ralph Reed (*Teddy*), Barbara Billingsley (*Miss Pierson*), Ralph Hodges (*Chester*), Madelon Mitchell (*Grace Sheppard*), Phillip Van Zandt (*Ralph Sheppard*).

It's the old story of a good man destroyed by gambling, told in a flat, unoriginal style. Litel is the man who gets into betting at first as a fun little sideline but gradually he becomes an addict. He begins taking funds from the bank he works at in order to pay off his debts. In the end he's killed but his family is saved from disgrace when Litel's employer claims the man was protecting company funds. This contrived ending is appropriate for this unbelievable story. Performances and direction are both perfunctory. Watch for an appearance by Switzer, the "Alfalfa" from OUR GANG comedies, here an adult. Billingsley, later to become the mother of television's "Leave It To Beaver," also has a minor role.

p&d, Edward L. Cahn; w, Howard Emmett Rogers (based on his novel *The Far Turn*); ph, Charles Van Enger; m, Irving Gertz; ed, Sherman Rose; art d, Boris Leven; m/l, "Querido," Jean Logan.

Drama   **(PR:A MPAA:NR)**

TWO ENEMIES   (SEE: BEST OF ENEMIES, THE, 1962)

TWO ENGLISH GIRLS*½   (1972, Fr.) 132m Les Films du
Carosse-Cinetel-Simar/Janus c (LES DEUX ANGLAISES ET LE CONTI-
                                    NENT; GB: ANNE AND MURIEL)

Jean-Pierre Leaud (*Claude Roc*), Kika Markham (*Anne Brown*), Stacey Tendeter (*Muriel Brown*), Sylvia Marriott (*Mrs. Brown*), Marie Mansart (*Madame Roc*), Philippe Leotard (*Diurka*), Irene Tunc (*Ruta*), Mark Petersen (*Mr. Flint*), David Markham (*Palmist*), Georges Delerue (*Claude's Business Agent*), Marcel Berbert (*Art Dealer*), Annie Miller (*Monique de Monferrand*), Christine Pelle (*Claude's Secretary*), Jeanne Lobre (*Jeanne*), Anne Levaslot (*Muriel as a Child*), Sophie Jeanne (*Clarisse*), Rene Gaillard (*Taxi Driver*), Sophie Baker (*Friend in Cafe*), Laura Truffaut, Eva Truffaut, Mathieu Schiffman, Guillaume Schiffman (*Children*), Francois Truffaut (*Narrator*).

TWO ENGLISH GIRLS is a three-sided love story which examines the complications of a romance between one man and two women, along the lines of Truffaut's earlier JULES AND JIM (1961). Leaud stars as a young art critic and aspiring author who charms his way through life at the outset of the 20th Century. In Paris, Leaud meets Markham, a liberated girl, who invites him to spend the summer at the seaside cottage she shares with her sister, Tendeter, and her mother, Marriott. Leaud falls in love with the puritanical Tendeter, but when her mother discovers his desires she orders him to leave. Before he leaves he proposes to Tendeter. He returns to Paris and after six months writes to Tendeter informing her that he wants to break the engagement. Markham pays a visit to Paris and becomes briefly involved with Leaud before running off to Persia with another lover. In an attempt to reunite Leaud and Tendeter, Markham invites her sister to come to Paris. When Tendeter arrives she is shocked to learn that Leaud and her sister had a tryst. Markham returns home only to later die of tuberculosis. After time has passed and Leaud's first book has been published (ironically titled "Jerome and Julien"--an homage to the novel "Jules and Jim") Tendeter, now 30 years old, returns to Paris to visit Leaud. They are immediately attracted to each other and during the night Leaud deflowers virgin Tendeter--a bloody scene which should silence those critics who accuse Truffaut of being "too sweet." When Tendeter awakes the following morning she leaves Leaud, even though she is still very much in love. Many years later Leaud, still obsessed with the thought of Tendeter, sees a young girl in the park who answers to the name "Muriel." Letting his imagination run wild, Leaud thinks that it may be Tendeter's daughter. One of Truffaut's darker films, TWO ENGLISH GIRLS is too quickly compared to its companion pieces JULES AND JIM. Both were based on novels written by Henri Pierre Roche (the only two novels he wrote, both of which were penned while Roche was in his seventies), though the similarities are confined to the surface--a love triangle. In JULES AND JIM it was two friends (Oskar Werner and Henri Serre) in love with a vivacious but dangerous woman (Jeanne Moreau). In TWO ENGLISH GIRLS, however, the aspect of danger is removed while a sibling rivalry (of sorts) is added. Although both pictures can stand independently, it is interesting to see the overlaps in the characters played by Leaud and Moreau. Since Truffaut had access to Roche's personal, unpublished diaries, his information on character in these films was drawn from the author's thoughts--thereby causing Moreau's "Catherine" and Leaud's "Claude" to be unrecognizably intertwined with Roche's own personality. Truffaut's fondness for this film (it owes a great deal to Jean Renoir--Truffaut's greatest influence) is apparent since he was reportedly recutting the picture just shortly before his death. The film was originally released at 132 minutes and included a "picnic on the grass" sequence which is an homage to Renoir's classic short A DAY IN THE COUNTRY (1946) and his PICNIC ON THE GRASS (1959). As in JULES AND JIM and so many other Truffaut pictures, TWO ENGLISH GIRLS is narrated by the director. Executive producer Marcel Berbert and composer Delerue both have small parts in the picture. (In French; English subtitles.)

p, Claude Miler; d, Francois Truffaut; w, Truffaut, Jean Gruault (based on the novel by Henri-Pierre Roche); ph, Nestor Almendros (Eastmancolor); m, Georges Delerue; ed, Yann Dedet; art d, Michel de Broin; cos, Gitt Magrini.

Drama   **Cas.**   **(PR:O MPAA:R)**

TWO EYES, TWELVE HANDS*   (1958, India) 124m Rajkamal
                                              Kalamandir Private Ltd. bw

Shri V. Shantaram, Sandhya.

Six men are jailed for murder, but their jailer feels that no matter what their crime they are basically good and he sets out to prove it. Though at first suspicious, the men gradually come to an understanding with their keeper. They help farm a once barren area and take their produce to market where an unscrupulous dealer tries to wreck all the jailer has worked for. Back on the farm a herd of cattle gets loose, killing the jailer. However the six have come to understand what they are capable of doing and the dead man's dream lives on. This is a well made drama, a bit naive at times, but overall excellent. The cast works well as an ensemble, backed by strong direction that cares about the material. Shantaram, who played the kindly jailer, also served as director.

p&d, Shri V. Shantaram; w, G. D. Madgulkar; ph, G. Balkrishna; m, Vasant Desai.

Drama   **(PR:C MPAA:NR)**

TWO-FACED WOMAN**   (1941) 94m MGM bw

Greta Garbo (*Karin Borg Blake/Katherine Borg*), Melvyn Douglas (*Larry Blake*), Constance Bennett (*Griselda Vaughn*), Roland Young (*O.O. Miller*), Robert Sterling (*Dick Williams*), Ruth Gordon (*Miss Ellis*), George Cleveland (*Sheriff*), George P. Huntley, Jr. (*Mr. Wilson*), James Spencer (*Carl*), William Tannen (*Ski Guide*), Frances Carson (*Miss Dunbar*), John Marston (*Graham*), Olive Blakeney (*Phyllis*), Douglass Newland, Roy Gordon (*Men*), Mary Young (*Wife*), Hilda Plowright, Eula Guy (*Women*), Mark Daniels (*Bellboy*), Vinton Haworth (*Guide*), Connie Gilchrist, Bess Flowers (*Receptionists*), Cliff Danielson, Paul Leyssac (*Clerks*), Walter Anthony Merrill (*Stage Manager*), George Lollier (*Cab Driver*), Arno Frey (*Waiter*), Andre Cheron (*Headwaiter*), Lorin Raker, Tom Herbert, Grace Hayle, Emily Fitzroy (*Rhumba Dancers*), Robert Alton (*Cecil*), Gloria De Haven, Michaele Fallon (*Debutantes*), George Calligas (*Hotel Clerk*).

Because Garbo laughed in 1939's NINOTCHKA, MGM moguls got the mistaken idea in their heads that the great, mysterious Swede should be Americanized and put into a comedy. The result was a new Garbo–her husky voice still in tact, but her hair bobbed, and her enigmatic persona misguided into frivolous dancing, skiing, and swimming (with an awful rubber cap covering her gorgeous hair). The final film is today still a watchable comedy, but it turns Garbo into something she's not. In retaliation, Garbo, still beautiful at age 37, left movies for good. Garbo stars as a ski instructor who gives lessons to gentlemanly playboy Douglas, and, soon after, they marry, despite the fact that he has a girl friend, Bennett, back in New York. Douglas returns to New York and Garbo follows, getting a look at Bennett, a brainy playwright, whom Garbo fears will woo Douglas away again. To keep her man, Garbo devises a scheme in which she poses as her own twin sister, Katherine, hoping that Douglas will fall for her instead of Bennett. Douglas learns of her masquerade, but plays along with Garbo's game without letting on. Garbo then becomes angry that Douglas could fall in love with her own sister, and returns to her ski resort. Douglas manages to win back her love, however, and the pair get together for the final clinch. Seemingly convinced that TWO-FACED WOMAN would fall flat, Garbo agreed to make the film at a reduced salary of $150,000 (down from her 1934 MGM contract which payed $250,000 per film), a figure which represented a healthy portion of the $316,000 budget. Because of the expectation to see "Garbo laugh" once again, she also agreed to put aside her pet project, MADAME CURIE. The lack of enthusiasm for TWO-FACED WOMAN, coupled with the new look MGM was trying to squeeze her into, prompted Garbo to announce a short retirement which would last, she warned them, until the end of WW II. Resisting a number of offers to coax her back onto the screen–MADAME CURIE, a remake of FLESH AND THE DEVIL, a Sarah Bernhardt biography, a Max Ophuls U.S.-Italian coproduction, to name the most interesting–Garbo chose to retire to a semi-reclusive lifestyle. Not surprisingly, the picky Catholic League of Decency pounced on TWO-FACED WOMAN as presenting marriage in an immoral light. The original, objectionable, version had Douglas becoming involved with Garbo's twin without realizing it was actually Garbo, knowingly and wilfully committing adultery with his wife's sister. Scenes were reshot (by Andrew Marton and Charles Dorian), the film was resubmitted, and eventually passed without the League of Decency's black cloud hanging over the marquee.

p, Gottfried Reinhardt; d, George Cukor, (uncredited) Andrew Marton, Charles Dorian; w, S. H. Behrman, Salka Viertel, George Oppenheimer (based on the play by Ludwig Fulda); ph, Joseph Ruttenberg; m, Bronislau Kaper; ed, George Boemler; md, Leo Arnold; art d, Cedric Gibbons, Daniel B. Cathcart; set d, Edwin B. Willis, Cathcart; cos, Adrian; ch, Bob Alton.

Romance   (PR:A   MPAA:NR)

TWO FACES OF DR. JEKYLL   (SEE: HOUSE OF FRIGHT, 1961)

TWO FISTED**   (1935) 60m PAR bw

Lee Tracy (*Hay Hurley*), Roscoe Karns (*Chick Moran*), Grace Bradley (*Marie*), Kent Taylor (*Clint Blackburn*), Gail Patrick (*Sue Parker*), Gordon Westcott (*Parker*), G. P. Huntley, Jr (*Fitz-Stanley*), Billy Lee (*Jimmy*), John Indrisano (*Pinky Duffy*), Samuel S. Hinds, Florence Lake, Sarah Edwards, Lillian Leighton, Ferdinand Munier, Lew Kelly, Akim Tamiroff, Irving Bacon.

Programmer fight picture finds Tracy managing Karns, who clearly is wrong for the part of a pug. The two need some cash so they take jobs as servants-cum-bodyguards to Patrick. She's a socialite who wants to divorce her creepy husband so she can marry another man. Of course this is accomplished but not before Karns engages in a living room bout. Previously made as IS ZAT SO? in the silent era, this minor comedy contains some amiable laughs but that's about it. Patrick shows some good stuff as a scatterbrained lady and Tracy gets in some good lines. The drama and romance aren't that well-developed and direction is nothing out of the norm for such fare.

p, Harold Hurley; d, James Cruze; w, Sam Hellman, Francis Martin, Eddie Moran (based on the screenplay "Is Zat So?" by James Gleason, Richard Taber); ph, Harry Fishbeck; ed, James Smith; cos, Travis Banton.

Comedy   (PR:A   MPAA:NR)

TWO FISTED AGENT   (SEE: BONANZA TOWN, 1951)

TWO-FISTED GENTLEMAN*½   (1936) 63m COL bw

James Dunn (*Mickey*), June Clayworth (*Ginger*), Thurston Hall (*Pop*), George McKay (*Schmidty*), Gene Morgan (*Porky*), Paul Guilfoyle (*Gallagher*), Harry Tyler (*Fieldsie*).

This unbelievable comedy tries to accurately portray the seedy street life of a fighter but the dialog ranges from trite to stupid. The direction is okay and acting fits the stereotyped characters. However, with such a slight story the production team can't do much.

p, Ben Pivar; d, Gordon Wiles; w, Tom Van Dycke; ph, John Stumar; ed, James Sweeney; cos, Lon Anthony.

Comedy   (PR:A   MPAA:NR)

TWO-FISTED JUSTICE*½   (1931) 63m MON bw

Tom Tyler, Barbara Weeks, Bobbie Nelson, Yakima Canutt, John Elliott, G. D. Wood [Gordon DeMain], Kit Guard, William Walling, Pedro Regas, Carl DeLoue, Joe Mills, Si Jenks.

At the start of the Civil War President Lincoln sends Tyler out to Kentucky for service. There he finds the usual assortment of outlaws and Injuns. He rescues a young boy, the sole survivor of an Indian attack on a wagon train. Later Tyler must face off against Walling and his boys when a murder is committed. This is slow to start and despite a few good action sequences never gets off the ground. Some poor photography and too many indoor sequences further detract. Acting is the usual for the genre.

p, Trem Carr; d&w, G. Arthur Durlam.

Western   (PR:A   MPAA:NR)

TWO FISTED JUSTICE*   (1943) 54m MON bw

John King (*Dusty*), David Sharpe (*David*), Max Terhune (*Alibi*), Gwen Gaze (*Joan*), Joel Davis (*Sunny*), John Elliot (*Hodgins*), Charles King (*Trigger*), George Chesebro (*Decker*), Frank Ellis (*Harve*), Cecil Weston (*Miss Adams*), Hal Price (*Sam*), Carl Mathews, Lynton Brent, Kermit Maynard, Dick Cramer, Tex Palmer, John Curtis.

A poor entry in Monogram's "Range Busters" series finds King recruited by the town of Dry Gulch to be the new sheriff. He's got to fight off the usual assortment of outlaws which he does in typical fashion with the help of sidekicks Sharpe and Terhune. Despite the usual amounts of action the film is lackluster, poorly directed and played without spirit. The comedy bits fall completely flat. (See RANGE BUSTERS series, Index.)

p. George W. Weeks; d, Robert Tansey; w, William Nolte; ph, Robert Cline; ed, Roy Claire.

Western   Cas.   (PR:A   MPAA:NR)

TWO-FISTED LAW**   (1932) 64m COL bw

Tim McCoy (*Tim Clark*), Alice Day (*Betty Owen*), Tully Marshall (*Sheriff Malcolm*), Wheeler Oakman (*Bob Russell*), Wallace MacDonald (*Artie*), John Wayne (*Duke*), Richard Alexander (*Zink Yocum*), Walter Brennan (*Depty-Sheriff Bendix*).

McCoy is a rancher who borrows 10 grand from Oakman. It turns out Oakman is a land grabber who lends money and rustles cattle so ranchers can't pay back and lose their land. With the help of a sheriff's posse McCoy captures Oakman, ending his evil reign in the valley. The story is simplistic and not one of McCoy's best outings though it makes up in energy for the meager plot. Wayne (ironically playing a character named "Duke") and Brennan both make early screen appearances in minor roles.

p, Irving Briskin; d, D. Ross Lederman; w, Kurt Kempler (based on a story by William Colt MacDonald); ph, Benjamin Kline; ed, Otto Meyer.

Western   Cas.   (PR:AA   MPAA:NR)

TWO-FISTED RANGERS**   (1940) 62m COL bw

Charles Starrett (*Thad Lawson*), Iris Meredith (*Betty Webster*), Bob Nolan (*Bob*), Kenneth MacDonald (*Jack Rand*), Dick Curtis (*Dick Hogan*), Hal Taliaferro [Wally Wales] (*Sheriff Hanley*), Bill Cody, Jr (*Silver*), Pat Brady (*Pat*), Ethan Laidlaw, James Craig, Bob Woodward, Francis Walker, Sons of the Pioneers.

When Starrett's brother, a sheriff, is murdered, it's up to the cowboy to avenge the death. He heads off after the killer, helped by Meredith whose publisher father was also killed by the outlaws. Though the story and acting are usual western fare the direction is pretty good with some neat little touches in the camera work.

p, Leon Barsha; d, Joseph H. Lewis; w, Fred Myton; ph, George Meehan; ed, Charles Nelson; m/1, Bob Nolan, Tim Spencer.

Western   (PR:A   MPAA:NR)

TWO-FISTED SHERIFF* (1937) 58m COL bw

Charles Starrett (*Dick Houston*), Barbara Weeks (*Molly Herrick*), Bruce Lane (*Bob Pearson*), Edward Peil, Sr (*Judge Webster*), Alan Sears (*Bill Slagg*), Walter Downing (*Doc Pierce*), Ernie Adams (*Sheriff Rankin*), Claire McDowell (*Miss Herrick*), Frank Ellis (*Gargan*), Robert Walker (*Lyons*), George Chesebro (*Prosecutor*), Art Mix, Al Bridge, Dick Botiller, George Morrell, Merrill McCormack, Edmund Cobb, Tex Cooper, Dick Cramer, Dick Alexander, Maston Williams, Ethan Laidlaw, Steve Clark, Wally West, Fred Burns.

This ranks as one of cowboy hero Starrett's best outings. When his pal Lane is wrongly accused of murder Starrett saves him and some other accused killers from a lynch mob. But Lane breaks loose and escapes, which causes Starrett to lose both his job as a lawman and the respect of the townsfolk. To clear both his and Lane's reputation Starrett sets off after the real killer and meets him in a well-handled climactic gun battle. Sears is the murderer, nicely playing his role as one of the western movies' first psychotic badmen. The story is directed with real excitement, backed by solid dialog. Starrett and his supporting cast fill their roles well in this excellent series entry.

p, Harry Decker; d, Leon Barsha; w, Paul Perez (based on a William Colt MacDonald); ph, Allen G. Siegler; ed, William Lyon.

Western (PR:A MPAA:NR)

TWO FLAGS WEST* (1950) 92m FOX bw

Joseph Cotten (*Col. Clay Tucker*), Linda Darnell (*Elena Kenniston*), Jeff Chandler (*Kenniston*), Cornel Wilde (*Capt. Mark Bradford*), Dale Robertson (*Lem*), Jay C. Flippen (*Sgt. Terrance Duffy*), Noah Beery, Jr. (*Cy Davis*), Harry Von Zell (*Ephraim Strong*), John Sands (*Lt. Adams*), Arthur Hunnicut (*Sgt. Pickens*), Jack Lee (*Courier*), Robert Adler (*Hank*), Harry Carter (*Lt. Reynolds*), Ferris Taylor (*Dr. Magowan*), Sally Corner (*Mrs. Magowan*), Everett Glass (*Rev. Simpkins*), Marjorie Bennett (*Mrs. Simpkins*), Roy Gordon (*Capt. Stanley*), Lee MacGregor (*Cal*), Aurora Castillo (*Maria*), Stanley Andrews (*Col. Hoffman*), Don Garner (*Ash Cooper*).

During the Civil War, Cotten is the leader of a band of Confederate prisoners in a Northern camp. Conditions are appalling, but when Wilde, a Union officer wounded out of the war, approaches them with an offer to go West with him to fight Indians, they refuse to help the Union cause in any form. Eventually they change their minds, planning to desert at the first opportunity to head back to the South and the war. They arrive in New Mexico at a fort commanded by Chandler, another wounded Union officer sent West. He is embittered by his inability to fight in the big war and by the death of his brother in an early action. He takes an immediate dislike to the Rebels under his command. Compounding the tension is Darnell, the widow of Chandler's brother, whom Chandler holds an affection for he dares not admit, Wilde falls in love with, and who Cotten shows some interest in. Cotten and his men are about to make their break for freedom when Chandler provokes the local Indians by killing the son of the chief. The full fury of the tribe comes down on the fort and only heroic action by Cotten and his Southerners saves the day. Chandler finally brings an end to the attacks by sacrificing himself to the Indians. Given the stars and the plot, this should have been a better film than it actually turns out to be. Chandler, on whom the whole story pivots, brings almost no depth to his role, and Cotten and Wilde are little more than devices to say important lines. Still, the film does move at a good clip, the Indian attack is exciting, and Wise's direction pushes the right buttons. The cinematography is also quite good, capturing the bleakness of the desert outpost.

p, Casey Robinson; d, Robert Wise; w, Robinson (based on a story by Frank S. Nugent, Curtis Kenyon); ph, Leon Shamroy; m, Hugo Friedhofer; ed, Louis Loeffler; md, Alfred Newman; art d, Lyle Wheeler, Chester Gore.

Western (PR:A MPAA:NR)

TWO FOR DANGER ** (1940, Brit.) 70m WB bw

Barry K. Barnes (*Tony Grigson*), Greta Gynt (*Diana*), Ian Maclean (*Australian*), Gordon McLeod (*German*), Tony Shaw (*American*), David Keir (*Prof. Burns*), Vera Bogetti (*Lady*), Peter Glenville (*Young Latin*), Peter Gawthorne (*Assistant Commissioner Grigson*), George Merritt (*Inspector Canway*), Wilfred Caithness (*Meason*), Cecil Parker (*Sir Richard Frencham*), P. Kynaston Reeves (*Dr. George Frencham*), Henry Oscar (*Claude Frencham*), Gus McNaughton (*Braithwaite*), Leslie Weston (*Welshman*), Jean Capra, Katie Johnson, Leon Lindos, Alec Waugh, Sam Wolsey.

Some valuble art works are being stolen from private collections. Barnes, the lawyer son of a local commissioner, decides to solve the case. He hooks up with Gynt, his fiancee and secretary to an art curator, and it's a merry chase to find the thieves. This is a pleasant light comedy which unfortunately is not given the proper pacing by the direction. Things move just a little too slowly, resulting in a few dead spots. The cast isn't bad though, handing in some fine comic performances. The two leads have a real chemistry and are given the necessary support from the cast.

p, A, M. Salomon; d, George King; w, Brock Williams, Basil Woon, Hugh Gray (based on a story by Williams); ph, Basil Emmott.

Comedy/Crime (PR:A MPAA:NR)

TWO FOR THE ROAD*½ (1967, Brit.) 112m FOX c

Audrey Hepburn (*Joanna Wallace*), Albert Finney (*Mark Wallace*), Eleanor Bron (*Cathy Manchester*), William Daniels (*Howard Manchester*), Claude Dauphin (*Maurice Dalbret*), Nadia Gray (*Francoise Dalbret*), Georges Descrieres (*David*), Gabrielle Middleton (*Ruth Manchester*), Jacqueline Bisset (*Jackie*), Judy Cornwell (*Pat*), Irene Hilda (*Yvonne de Florac*), Dominique Joos (*Sylvia*), Kathy Chelimsky (*Caroline*), Carol Van Dyke (*Michelle*), Karyn Balm (*Simone*), Mario Verdon (*Palamos*), Roger Dann (*Gilbert, "Comte de Florac"*), Libby Morris (*American Lady*), Yves Barsacq (*Police Inspector*), Helene Tossy (*Mme. Solange*), Jean-Francois Lalet (*Boat Officer*), Albert Michel (*Customs' Officer*), Joanna Jones, Sophia Torkeli, Patricia Viterbo, Olga George Picot, Clarissa Hillel (*Joanna's Touring Friends*), Cathy Jones.

TWO FOR THE ROAD is like an inexpensive wine in that it has not aged well. What seemed so chic in 1967 looks like a soap opera with jump-cuts today. Still, one must measure it by the temper of the times and in 1967, it was on the money for audiences and there is still a small cult of aficianados who feel it remains one of the best of the genre. Hepburn and Finney are a married couple taking a trip from England to the French Riviera in their small Mercedes-Benz. He is an architect and they are about to visit the home of Dauphin, the Frenchman who helped the successful Finney get his first break. From the nature of the biting dialog between the two, it's not difficult to discern that this is a marriage in jeopardy. Flash back to a dozen years before when Finney and Hepburn first met. He's a backpacking student looking at European buildings and she's one of a bevy of female music students going to a festival. Finney is attracted to Bisset but winds up with Hepburn as the other women all come down with chicken pox. They travel together to the edge of the sea and decide they are in love and will get married. Flash forward to their next trip on the Continent. They are freshly married and traveling with Daniels and Bron (who is Finney's one-time lover) and their daughter, an incorrigible brat, Middleton. This little girl is enough to sour any woman from having a child but Hepburn manages to overcome her hatred for the little bad seed and they make a pact to never again travel with anyone else. On yet another trip along the same road, Hepburn tells Finney that she is pregnant and they meet Dauphin, who gives Finney his chance to go from minor jobs to major homes in the south of France. The film cuts betweem past, present, and future and we see Finney have a one-night stand with Balm, and Hepburn submit to the amorous advances of Descrieres, a sober intellectual who turns out to be far too dour for Hepburn's lighthearted personality. The two are reunited and realize that, through it all, they love each other and no amount of petty quarreling or even major spats will ever divide them. Finney's character remains essentially the same throughout, a slightly boorish lout. Hepburn changes visibly from a naive waif to a mature wife and mother to a bored matron. Raphael wrote the script directly for the screen and it might be worth the while of a viewer to purchase his published version of the screenplay to see how it was realized in the movie. There were some complaints that Hepburn was too old for Finney, but she is actually just about seven years his senior. However, her career had been twice the length of Finney's and people were just used to seeing her more often. As the years passed, he made more movies than she did, so watching it 20 years later they seem about right for each other. Raphael was nominated for an Oscar and lost that year to William Rose for his original screenplay of GUESS WHO'S COMING TO DINNER? The usually fastidious Hepburn was dressed by Mary Quant, Paco Rabanne, Ken Scott, and others and, wonder of wonders, she even wore blue jeans. Location scenes were done in Paris, Nice, St. Tropez, La Colle sur le Loup, and Beauallon. Good aerial photography by Guy Tabary and an excellent Henry Mancini score. Although Bron played an American, she is actually a British actress who scored in HELP, ALFIE, WOMEN IN LOVE, and has been a foil for the "Monty Python" TV troupe. Donen's direction was a trifle trendy and frantic and the result was sometimes jarring to the eye.

p&d, Stanley Donen; w, Frederic Raphael; ph, Christopher Challis (Panavision, DeLuxe Color); m, Henry Mancini; ed, Richard Marden, Madeleine Gug; art d, Willy Holt, Marc Frederic; set d, Roger Volper; cos, Hardy Amies, Ken Scott, Michele Posier, Paco Rabanne, Mary Quant, Foale and Tuffin; spec eff, Gilbert Manzon; makeup, Alberto De Rossi, Georges Bouban.

Comedy/Drama Cas. (PR:C MPAA:NR)

TWO FOR THE SEESAW ** (1962) 119m Mirisch-Argyle-Talbot-Seven Arts/UA bw

Robert Mitchum (*Jerry Ryan*), Shirley MacLaine (*Gittel Mosca*), Edmon Ryan (*Taubman*), Elisabeth Fraser (*Sophie*), Eddie Firestone (*Oscar*), Billy Gray (*Mr. Jacoby*), Vic Lundin (*Beat Singer*), Shirley Cytron, Cia Dave, Virginia Whitmore, Colin Campbell, Mike Enserro, Moira Turner.

Casting Connecticut-born Mitchum as a Nebraska attorney and Virginia-born MacLaine as a New York Jewish bohemian is tantamount to casting Sidney Poitier and Clifton Webb as The Corsican Brothers. Gibson's play starred Grand Island's Henry Fonda as the Nebraskan and New York's Anne Bancroft as the female lead. The play opened to good reviews in January, 1958, and was later turned into the musical "Seesaw" with Ken Howard and Michele Lee. The original casting for this was Paul Newman and Liz Taylor with Delbert Mann to direct. When that fell apart, Wise was brought in and chose Mitchum and MacLaine. Mitchum is newly arrived in

New York from Omaha. He's lost his position in a law firm and his marriage is on the rocks so he's come to Manhattan to seek some peace and solitude. When an old pal, Firestone, invites Mitchum to a Greenwich Village party, he has nothing better to do so he accepts. He meets a woman quite unlike anyone he's ever met before, a dancer from the Bronx played by MacLaine. They have a sexual, though not necessarily loving, affair, but Mitchum's mind is still in Nebraska, even though his body is in New York. Mitchum gets a good job with a large law firm and sets up MacLaine in a new apartment-studio. She sees that his heart is still in the Midwest and that causes her to feel terribly. Arguments begin and an old ulcer flares up, causing MacLaine to need hospitalization. After recovering, she retuns to the loft where she lives and Mitchum does his best to be doting. Time passes and MacLaine says that she would like to marry Mitchum, just as soon as he is legally free of his entanglement. When she discovers that Mitchum is, in fact, now divorced, she is hurt that he never told her. Both lovers realize that the time has come to call it quits and that Mitchum wants to return to his old life in Nebraska. He calls her up to say goodbye and finally speaks the words she's been yearning to hear, "I Love You," as the picture fades. Locationed in New York, it's a lethargic film that worked better as a play because the large screen magnified the talkiness and lack of emotional fireworks. Why Fonda and Bancroft did not do the film under the direction of the man who staged the show, Arthur Penn, is a mystery. MacLaine is a good actress but could not come close to capturing the ethnic quality of Bancroft, who is Italian. Lenny Bruce put it right, though, when he said: "If you're Italian or Irish or Puerto Rican and you're from New York, you're Jewish. But you could be the president of your synagogue in Kansas City and your're still Gentile." In a small role, note Billy Gray, one of Hollywood's favorite nightclub operators and a sometime actor (SOME LIKE IT HOT, SPECTRE OF THE ROSE).

p, Walter Mirisch; d, Robert Wise; w, Isobel Lennart (based on the play by William Gibson); ph, Ted McCord (Panavision); m, Andre Previn; ed, Stuart Gilmore; prod d, Boris Leven; set d, Edward G. Boyle; cos, Orry-Kelly; makeup, Frank Westmore.

Comedy   (PR:C   MPAA:NR)

TWO FOR TONIGHT*½   (1935) 61m PAR bw

Bing Crosby (Gilbert Gordon), Joan Bennett (Bobbie Lockwood), Mary Boland (Mrs. J.E. Smythe), Lynne Overman (Harry Kling), Thelma Todd (Lilly Bianca), Ernest Cossart (Hompe), James Blakeley (Buster Da Costa), Douglas Fowley (Pooch Donahue), Maurice Cass (Alexander Myers), Charles E. Arnt (Benny the Goof), Leonard Carey (Mr. Myers' Butler), Herbert Evans (Butler), Bert Hanlon (Census Taker), Arthur Housman (Warburton), Harold Minjir (Mr. Myers' Secretary), Lillian West (Nurse), Jack Mulhall (Gordon's Doctor), Charles Levison 'Lane' (Author), Torben Meyer, Jerry Mandy (Waiters), Eddie Kane (Charlie), Hooper Atchley (Manager), Guy Usher (Police Captain), Doris Lloyd (Lady Ralston), Lionel Pape (Lord Ralston), A.S. "Pop" Byron (Jailer), John Gough (Prisoner), Edward Gargan (Taxi Driver), Beulah McDonald (Maid), Suzanne Rhodes, Irene Thompson, Jack Deery, Pat Somerset (Lord Ralston's Guests), Robert Kent, Oscar Rudolph, Jack Chapin, Toby Wing, Dorothy Thompson (College People), Monte Vandegrift, Duke York, Charles Morris, Hal Craig, Clarence L. Sherwood (Cops in Cafe), Alex Melesh (Man for Toupee Gag), Connie Emerald (Woman for Hat Gag), Phillips Smalley (Doctor in Hallway).

Perhaps one of Crosby's weakest films, this one illustrates how several talented people can get wrapped up in a film that goes nowhere. The short length is to its advantage although they attempt to jam several twists and many songs into the proceedings and it winds up splayful rather than playful. Crosby has two half-brothers, Blakeley and Fowley, each by different fathers who were once married to their mother, Boland. Overman is a play producer having trouble with his tempestuous star, Todd. Bennett is Overman's secretary and Crosby, while wooing her, says that he can write a new musical for Todd in a week (seven days). The rest of the film shows the writing of the score and the play within the screenplay. Needless to say, Crosby's show is a hit. He sings all of the songs (Bennett was no chirper) by Harry Revel and Mack Gordon and none of them is memorable. They include "I Wish I Were Aladdin," "From the Top of Your Head to the Tip of Your Toes," "Without a Word of Warning," "Takes Two to Make a Bargain," "You're Beautiful," "Two for Tonight." The script for this looks as though it were written in seven days. Ho-hum.

p, Douglas MacLean; d, Frank Tuttle; w, George Marion, Jr., Jane Storm, Harry Ruskin (based on a play by Max Lief, J.O. Lief); ph, Karl Struss.

Musical Comedy   (PR:A   MPAA:NR)

TWO GALS AND A GUY**   (1951) 70m UA bw

Robert Alda (Deke Oliver), Janis Paige (Della Oliver/Sylvia Latour), James Gleason (Bill Howard), Lionel Stander (Mr. Seymour), Arnold Stang (Bernard), The Three Suns (Three Suns), Rock Rogers (Gabroli), Linda Preston (Maggie), Morris Lieb (Tim), Cecil Clovelly (Herbert), Myrtle Ferguson, Rhea Scott, Ray Morgan, Lupe Garnica, Patti Crowe.

In the early days of television, Alda and his wife Paige are determined to crack this new form of show biz. Paige has a double role, playing both Alda's wife and the TV singing star look-alike who is forced to leave her show. The producers are desperate for someone who looks like her to take over, so who

gets the call? This was intended to be a spoof of TV life but it never takes any real chances. The result is an ordinary backstage musical of limited originality. The players are handicapped by the pedestrian script and the direction doesn't help out much. Songs by David and Nevins include "Laugh and Be Happy," "So Long for Now," and "Sunshowers." At the time of the film's release, Alda was appearing on Broadway in "Guys and Dolls," which may have prompted the similar sounding title.

p, John W. Arents; d, Alfred E. Green; w, Searle Kramer; ph, Gerald Hirschfield; m, Gail Kubik; m/l, Morty Nevins, Hal David.

Comedy   (PR:A   MPAA:NR)

TWO GENTLEMEN SHARING**   (1969, Brit.) 105m PAR/AIP c

Robin Phillips (Roddy), Judy Geeson (Jane), Hal Frederick (Andrew), Esther Anderson (Caroline), Norman Rossington (Phil), Hilary Dwyer (Ethne), Rachel Kempson (Mrs. Ashby-Kydd), Daisy Mae Williams (Amanda), Ram John Holder (Marcus), Earl Cameron (Charles), Shelagh Fraser (Helen), David Markham (Mr. Pater), Avice Landon (Mrs. Pater), Philip Stone (Mr. Burrows), Elspeth March (Mrs. Burrows), Thomas Baptiste (Mutt), Linbert Spencer (Jeff), Willy Payne (Bizerte), Thors Piers (Eugene Valentine), Nathan Dambuza (Chicomo), Robert Burnell (O'Reilly), Hamilton Dyce (Dickson Senior), John Humphrey (Dickson Junior), Harold Lang (Young Man), Lionel Ngakane (Bill), Tommy Ansah (Driver), George Baizley (Caretaker), Harcourt Curacao (Band Leader), Carl Adam (Negro Visitor), Anna Wing (Neighbor), Benny Nightingale (Elevator Operator), Charles Leno (Doorman), Phillamore Davidson, Norman Mitchell, John Chandos, David Edwards, John Snow, Gary Sobers, Les Flambeaux Steele Band.

In London, two young Oxford graduates come to share an apartment. Phillips is a white advertising executive and Frederick, a black Jamaican-born lawyer. The two visit a club with their girl friends one night, but Phillips becomes bored with Dwyer, his rich date. Instead, he is fascinated with Geeson, a young white woman who seems to be charming numerous black men. Later, he takes her home and is surprised to find that she lives in a black-owned home. The next week the roommates plan a trip to Phillips' parents' mansion and Phillips brings Geeson along. His parents are upset when they see the black man and his black girl friend Anderson. The two leave and return to the apartment to make love, only to be interrupted by the racist landlady. She demands that they get out, so Frederick quickly dashes off a note to Phillips before leaving. He and Anderson first move to the ghetto, then plan a return to Jamaica. At a drunken farewell party, Phillips announces he wants to marry Geeson even though it turns out her stepfather is black. She rejects him, seeing Phillips as a weak character. Later at the party, Phillips rejects a homosexual advance by Holder. In the end, the police break up the party and the much-confused Phillips is left all alone. The theme of racial mixing was a daring one for 1969 (Martin Luther King, Jr., had been shot only the year before and there were still many unsettled feelings on racial issues), but unfortunately the treatment here is all too simplistic. At times, the direction seems to go for shock value rather than in-depth character study. Also, emotional feelings are given only passing glances at best. The players are the film's saving grace, making the most they can out of the material with some pretty good performances. Phillips and Frederick work well together, given some fine support from Geeson. However, the film is neither as sophisticated nor as daring as the filmmakers apparently wanted, and the result has not aged well.

p, J. Barry Kulick; d, Ted Kotcheff; w, Evan Jones (based on the novel Two Gentlemen Sharing by David Stuart Leslie); ph, Billy Williams (Movielab Color); m, Stanley Myers; prod d, Ed Harper; art d, Ken Bridgeman; set d, Chris Cook; cos, Gabriella Falk; makeup, Colin Garde.

Drama   (PR:O   MPAA:R)

TWO GIRLS AND A SAILOR***   (1944) 124m MGM bw

Van Johnson (John Dyckman Brown III), June Allyson (Patsy Deyo), Gloria DeHaven (Jean Deyo), Jimmy Durante (Billy Kipp), Tom Drake (Frank Miller), Henry Stephenson (John Dyckman Brown I), Henry O'Neill (John Dyckman Brown II), Ben Blue (Ben), Frank Sully (Pvt. Adams), Donald Meek (Mr. Nizby), Carlos Ramirez (Carlos), Lena Horne, Jose Iturbi, Amparo Novarro, Albert Coates, Virginia O'Brien, The Wilde Twins, Harry James Orchestra with Helen Forrest, Xavier Cugat Orchestra with Lina Romay (Themselves), Lena Horne (Specialty), Gracie Allen (Concerto Number), Frank Jenks (Dick Deyo), Joan Thorsen (Gladys Deyo), Doreen McCann (Patsy, aged two), Eilene Janssen (Patsy, Aged four), Sandra Lee (Jean, Aged one), Ghislaine [Gigi] Perreau (Jean, Aged two and a half), Ava Gardner (Rockette Girl), Billy Lechner, Allen Forienza (Call Boys), William Frambes (Boy Vaudevillian), Don Loper (Small Town Wolf), Charles Hayes (Man in Evening Clothes), Eve Whitney (Bejeweled Woman), Sheldon Jett (Fat Man), Ruth Cherrington (Stout Lady), Hazel Dohlman (Dowager), Lynn Arlen, Patricia Lenn (Debutantes), Florence Wix, Harry Adams, Ed Mortimer (Middle-aged Folk), Diane Mumby, Shelby Payne (Cigarette Girls), Fred Rapport (Captain of Waiters), Leo Mostovoy (Waiter), Eddie Kane (Head-waiter), Lee Bennett (Friend), Arthur Walsh (Lonesome Soldier), Joe Yule (Carpenter), Thomas Louden (Butler), Peggy Maley (Girl), Ralph Gardner, James Carpenter, Mickey Rentschler, Doodles Weaver (Soldiers), Fred G. Beckner (Sailor), Kathleen [Kay] Williams (Girl Flirt), Nolan Leary (Durante's Double), Sol De Garda (Man in Canteen), Buster Keaton

(Durante's Son).

A sheer delight. DeHaven and Allyson play a sister song-and-dance act in a posh New York night club. They do their part for the war effort by bringing soldiers and sailors to their apartment after hours and running their own U.S.O. show in the living room. Being 1944 it's all perfectly innocent of course! One night they bring Drake, a soldier, and Van Johnson, a sailor, and secretly a millionaire to boot. DeHaven is a flirt and charms both men, while the more quiet Allyson is attracted to Van Johnson. The two girls mention that an empty factory next door would be great for a soldiers' canteen so Van Johnson secretly buys the place and develops it for that purpose. Allyson finds out, but believing that he loves her sister, she tries to stay out of Van Johnson's romantic life. Of course DeHaven is ecstatic that she has attracted a millionaire but she comes to realize that he loves her sister more. It's just as well for she really cares for Drake. The romances get together wih the proper partners and it's a happy ending for all. The plot is simple and little more than a redoing of the studio's TWO GIRLS ON BROADWAY from 1940. It doesn't matter though for this is well presented with a charm all it's own. Packing the romantic comedy was a myriad of specialty music numbers of the day ranging from Xavier Cugat's band to Lena Horne and even Gracie Allen (sans George Burns) doing a number. Also on hand was Durante with his famous "Inka Dinka Doo." This was a comeback of sorts for the Great Schnozzola as he had been MGM's great comic hope in the early 1930s before drifting away. Also on hand was Keaton (who had briefly been teamed with Durante in the early sound era). At the time he was working for MGM as a gag man, creating comic bits for such films as AT THE CIRCUS featuring the Marx Brothers. Allyson and DeHaven are wonderful as the two leads, expressing a sense of innocent energy so sadly lacking in the films of today. Van Johnson is at his charming best. The whole picture is bounding with enthusiasm under a steady direction that never makes more out of this musical than need be. Songs included: "Paper Doll" (Johnny Black) in a fine rendition by Horne; a great version of "The Young Man with a Horn" (Ralph Freed, George Stoll) by Allyson backed by the immortal Harry James, a really cute and funny piano piece, "Concerto for Index Finger" performed by the wonderfully daft Gracie Allen, "Take It Easy" (Albert De Bru, Irving Taylor, Vic Mizzy), "Ritual Fire Dance" (De Falla), "Inka Dinka Doo" (Durante, Ben Ryan), "My Mother Told Me" (Freed, Jimmy McHugh), "A Love Like Ours" (Mann Holiner, Alberta Nichols), "In a Moment of Madness" (Freed, McHugh), "Sweet and Lovely" (Gus Arnheim, Jules Lemare, Harry Tobias), "Granada" (Dorothy Dodd, Augustin Lara), "Estrellita" (Manuel Ponce, adapted Frank La Forge), "A-Tisket-A-Tasket" (Al Feldman, Ella Fitzgerald), "Did You Ever Have the Feeling?" "Castles in the Air," "Who Will Be With You When I'm Far Away?" (Durante), "Flash" (James), "Charmaine" (Erno Rapee, Lew Pollack), "Babalu" (Bob Russell, Marguerita Lecuona), "The Thrill of a New Romance" (Harold Adamson, Xavier Cugat), "You Dear" (Freed, Sammy Fain), "Dardanella" (Fred Fisher, Felix Bernard, Johnny S. Black), "My Wonderful One Let's Dance" (Roger Edens, Arthur Freed, Nacio Herb Brown).

p, Joe Pasternak; d, Richard Thorpe; w, Richard Connell, Gladys Lehman; ph, Robert Surtees; ed, George Boemler; md, Georgie Stoll; art d, Cedric Gibbons; cos, Irene, Kay Dean; ch, Sammy Lee.

Musical   **(PR:A   MPAA:NR)**

TWO GIRLS ON BROADWAY½**
(1940) 71m MGM bw (GB: CHOOSE YOUR PARTNERS)

Lana Turner *(Pat Mahoney)*, Joan Blondell *(Molly Mahoney)*, George Murphy *(Eddie Kerns)*, Kent Taylor *("Chat" Chatsworth)*, Richard Lane *(Buddy Bartell)*, Wallace Ford *(Jed Marlowe)*, Otto Hahn *(Ito)*, Chester Clute *(Salesman)*, Lloyd Corrigan *(Judge)*, Don Wilson *(Announcer)*, George Meader *(McChesney)*, May McAvoy, Jessie Arnold *(Secretaries)*, Charles Wagenheim, Cyril Ring *(Assistants)*, Adrienne d'Ambricourt *(Miss Apricots)*, Arthur O'Connell, Lester Dorr, J. Anthony Hughes, Harry Lash *(Reporters)*, Jimmy Conlin *(Poem Vendor)*, Ed Peil, Sr. *(Man)*, George Lollier *(Chauffeur)*, Lee Murray *(Newsboy)*, Maxine Conrad *(Chorus Girl)*, Daisy Bufford *(Maid)*, Jack Gardner *(Messenger Boy)*, Hillary Brooke, Carole Wayne *(Girls)*, Hal K. Dawson *(Clerk)*.

This remake of BROADWAY MELODY (1929) featured Turner and Blondell in the roles played by Anita Page and Bessie Love in the original. Newly married to clarinetist Artie Shaw, Turner was billed above veterans Blondell and Murphy and showed that she could trip the light fantastic without tripping over her own feet. Murphy and Blondell are a dance team and business is bad because vaudeville is bowing out. Murphy is engaged to Blondell and they are planning to be married. Turner is Blondell's younger sister and Murphy falls for her but she holds back, not wanting to hurt Blondell's feelings. Turner is being wooed by wealthy Taylor, who already has a quintet of ex-wives. All of this is witnessed by Ford, a Broadway columnist patterned after Winchell or Ed Sullivan. Taylor tries to get to Turner but she eventually winds up with Murphy, only after Blondell has graciously stepped aside in order to allow her sister to have some happiness with her now ex-fiance. Slim plot but well directed by Simon, who was only 30 but already a veteran behind the camera, and had just finished directing Turner in DANCING CO-EDS and THESE GLAMOUR GIRLS. Nacio Herb Brown, Roger Edens, and Arthur Freed wrote "My Wonderful One, Let's Dance" (performed by Turner and Murphy). Harry Revel and Ted Fetter

contributed "Broadway's Still Broadway." Other tunes were "True Love" and "Ranch Santa Fe" by Walter Donaldson and Gus Kahn, and "Maybe It's the Moon," by Chet Forrest, Bob Wright, and Donaldson. The advertising tag line left no doubt as to why anyone would come to see this movie. The photo was a provocative shot of Turner and the line read: "The Girl They're All Talking About...lovely Lana, America's Blonde Bonfire, in her hottest, most daring role." Now that you know how bland the story was, that should give you an indication of how little reality there is in movie advertising, just in case you didn't know already.

p, Jack Cummings; d, S. Sylvan Simon; w, Joseph Fields, Jerome Chodorov (based on a story by Edmund Goulding); ph, George Folsey; ed, Blanche Sewell; md, Georgie Stoll; art d, Cedric Gibbons, Stan Rogers; set d, Edwin B. Willis; cos, Dolly Tree; ch, Bobby Connolly, Merrill Pye, Eddie Larkin.

Musical Comedy   **(PR:A   MPAA:NR)**

TWO GROOMS FOR A BRIDE*½   (1957) 73m Eros/FOX bw (GB: THE RELUCTANT BRIDE)

John Carroll *(Jeff Longstreet)*, Virginia Bruce *(Laura Weeks)*, Brian Oulton *(Professor Baker)*, Kay Callard *(Lola Sinclair)*, Michael Caridia *(Tony)*, Barbara Brown *(Ra)*, Kit Terrington *(Big)*, Alexander Gauge *(Humbold)*, Donald Stewart *(Cadwell)*, Anita Sharp Bolster *(Mrs. Fogarty)*, Arthur Lowe *(Mr. Fogarty)*, Tim Gill *(MacCarthy)*, Ernest Jay *(Minister)*, Michael Balfour *(Boxer)*, Karen Greer *(Candy Sugar)*, Tucker Maguire *(Claire)*, Ann Doran *(Violet Blue)*.

When a husband and wife team of explorers becomes lost, their four children are left to the man's brother (Carroll) and the woman's sister (Bruce). Whichever marries first will retain full custody. Carroll is a wild American playboy while Bruce is a proper English entomologist. Of course they dislike each other and he's got his eye on a little blonde anyway. But wouldn't you know it? In typical contrived movie plotting the two opposites fall in love and adopt the children together when they marry one another. There's nothing in the least bit surprising in the script or dialog in this thoroughly contrived plot. The ensemble does what it can, though talents are clearly blocked by the material. The direction is straightforward, which helps, but not much.

p, Robert S. Baker, Monty Berman; d, Henry Cass; w, Frederick Stephani; ph, Berman; m, Stanley Black; ed, Maurice Rootes.

Comedy   **(PR:A   MPAA:NR)**

TWO-GUN CUPID   (SEE: BAD MAN, THE, 1941)

TWO-GUN JUSTICE**   (1938) 58m Concord/MON bw

Tim McCoy *(Tim)*, Betty Compson *(Kate)*, Joan Barclay *(Nancy)*, John Morton *(Bart)*, Al Bridges *(Sheriff)*, Tony Patton *(Blinky)*, Alan Craven *(Tex)*, Lane Chandler *(Butch)*, Harry Strange *(Joe)*, Olin Francis *(Blackie)*, Earl Dwire *(Old Timer)*, Enid Parrish *(Secretary)*, Curley Dresden, Jack Ingram.

McCoy shows a little range with his acting ability as a retired lawman who poses as a Mexican bandido. In this guise McCoy infiltrates a gang, led by Morton, which is terrorizing some locals. This soon comes to an end thanks to McCoy's clever planning in this typical western with standard production qualities.

p, Maurice Conn; d, Alan James; w, Fred Myton (based on a story by Myton); ph, Jack Greenhalgh; ed, Richard G. Wray.

Western   **(PR:A   MPAA:NR)**

TWO-GUN LADY**½   (1956) 76m ARC bw

Peggie Castle *(Kate Masters)*, William Talman *(Dan Corbin)*, Marie Windsor *(Bess)*, Earle Lyon *(Ben Ivers)*, Joe Besser *(Doc M'Ginnis)*, Barbara Turner *(Jenny Ivers)*, Robert Lowery *("Big Mike" Dougherty)*, Ian MacDonald *(Jud Ivers)*, Norman Jolley *(Gruber)*.

The all-too-rare western heroine takes charge here as Castle is a gun-toting woman who's looking for her parents' killers. Talman is the U.S. Marshal who lends a hand as she efficiently takes care of a trio of heavies played, oddly enough, by the film's executive producer (Lyon), associate producer (MacDonald), and writer (Jolley). This is well directed with some tense moments, as B Westerns go. Castle plays her role with much believability and the production team makes surprisingly good outlaws.

p&d, Richard H. Bartlett; w, Norman Jolley (based on a story by Jolley, Bartlett); ph, Guy Roe; m, Leon Klatzkin; ed, Carl Pierson.

Western   **(PR:A   MPAA:NR)**

TWO GUN LAW**½   (1937) 58m COL bw

Charles Starrett *(Bob Larson)*, Peggy Stratford *(Mary Hammond)*, Hank Bell *(Cookie)*, Edward J. LeSaint *(Ben Hammond)*, Charles Middleton *(Wolf Larson)*, Alan [Al] Bridge *(Kipp)*, Lee Prather *(Sheriff)*, Dick Curtis *(Edwards)*, Victor Potel *(Cassius)*, George Chesebro, Art Mix, George Morrell, Tex Cooper.

Routine but well made western stars Starrett as the outlaw-gone-straight. He's used and abused by some unscrupulous types, which forces him to reconsider his professional switch. Justice triumphs in the end, of course, after plenty of two-fisted action and gun-fighting. There are also 12 chases to liven things. Good acting and fine workmanlike direction help to make this a better than average programmer.

d, Leon Barsha; w, John B. Rathmell (based on a story by Norman Sheldon); ph, George Meehan; ed, William Lyon.

Western   **(PR:A   MPAA:NR)**

TWO GUN MAN, THE**   (1931) 60m TIF bw

Ken Maynard, Lucille Powers, Lafe McKee, Nita Martin, Charles King, Tom London, Murdock McQuarrie, Walter Perry, Will Stanton, William Jackie, Ethan Allen, Buck Bucko, Roy Bucko, Jim Corey, Jack Ward, Tarzan the Horse.

Well made if routine story starring Maynard who is up against cattle thieves. The film carries its title because just about everyone packs two pistols instead of the usual one. Plenty of hard riding, shooting, and action directed with competence.

p, Phil Goldstone; d, Phil Rosen; w, John F. Natteford, Earle Snell (based on a Natteford).

Western   **(PR:A   MPAA:NR)**

TWO GUN SHERIFF*½   (1941) 56m REP bw

Don "Red" Barry (The Sundown Kid/Bruce McKinnon), Lynn Merrick (Ruth), Jay Novello (Albo), Lupita Tovar (Nita), Milton Kibbee (Jones), Fred Kohler, Jr (Keller), Marin Sais (Mrs. McKinnon), Fred "Snowflake" Toones (Snowflake), Dirk Thane (Duke), Archie Hall (Dunn), Charles Bob Thomas (Tex), Lee Shumway (Sheriff Blake), John Merton, Carleton Young, Curley Dresden, Buck Moulton, Bud McClure, Tex Parker, Herman Nolan, George Plues.

Two is the key word for this film as Barry plays a good and an evil twin. The outlaw kidnaps the good-guy sheriff and takes his identity so he can pull off a robbery. Bad Barry comes to see the evil of his ways with help from his mother (Sais) and goes straight. Barry handles the dual role well but the rest of the cast isn't given much to do in this typically plotted western. Barry's playing a less-than-virtuous hero wasn't popular at the time, but in the course of western film history marked a change in that genre's leading character traits.

p&d, George Sherman; w, Doris Schroeder, Bennett Cohen (based on a story by Cohen); ph, William Nobles; m, Cy Feuer; ed, Tony Martinelli; md, Feuer.

Western   **(PR:A   MPAA:NR)**

TWO-GUN TROUBADOR**   (1939) 58m Spectrum bw (GB: THE LONE TROUBADOR)

Fred Scott (Fred Dean), Claire Rochelle (Helen Bradfield), John Merton (Bill Barton), Harry Harvey (Elmer Potts), Carl Mathews (Kirk Dean), Buddy "Bull Fiddle Bill" Lenhart (Fred, Jr.), Harry Harvey, Jr (Billy Barton as a Boy), Buddy Kelley (Tom Bradfield), Gene Howard (Pedro Yorba), William Woods (Sheriff), Jack Ingram, Bud Osborne, John Ward, Elias Gamboa, Cactus Mack.

A hooded Robin Hood-type western hero rides about seeking revenge on the gang that murdered his father 20 years previously. Though the plot is standard and the dialog weak this story is unlike others of its nature in that the hero's (Scott) identity is kept a secret until the film is nearly over. Other than that it's a routine western with typical direction and acting qualities. Songs include "Cowboy and the Schoolmarm."

p, C. C. Burr; d, Raymond K. Johnson; w, Richard L. Bare, Philip Dunham; ph, Elmer Dyer, Walter Bluemel; m/l, June Hershey, Don Swandler.

Western   **(PR:A   MPAA:NR)**

TWO GUNS AND A BADGE**   (1954) 69m Silvermine/AA bw

Wayne Morris (Jim Blake), Morris Ankrum (Sheriff Jackson), Beverly Garland (Gail Sterling), Roy Barcroft (Bill Sterling), William Phipps (Dick Grant), Damian O'Flynn (Wilson), I. Stanford Jolley (Allen), Robert [Bob] Wilke (Moore), Chuck Courtney (Val Moore), John Pickard (Sharkey), Henry Rowland (Jim Larkin), Gregg Barton.

This is considered by most film historians to be the last series B western ever released by a studio. By this time television had taken over the form completely, producing–week after week–the same format that once ruled the silver screen. Appropriately, the story is routine stuff about ranchers and outlaws, with some romance tossed in as well. Morris is an ex-convict riding into town who is mistaken for a new sheriff, come to clean up the town of bad men. Barcroft is an evil rancher who's causing trouble for everyone in the area and Garland is his daughter, the love interest for Morris. The film is typical of the genre but backed with some good direction and camera work. Morris is a little stiff in the part, but he's supported nicely by the cast.

p, Vincent M. Fennelly; d, Lewis D. Collins; w, Dan Ullman; ph, Joseph M. Novac; m, Raoul Kraushaar; ed, Samuel Fields.

Western   **(PR:A   MPAA:NR)**

TWO WEEKS IN ANOTHER TOWN**   (1962) 107m MGM c

Kirk Douglas (Jack Andrus), Edward G. Robinson (Maurice Kruger), Cyd Charisse (Carlotta), George Hamilton (Davie Drew), Dahlia Lavi (Veronica), Claire Trevor (Clara Kruger), James Gregory (Brad Byrd), Rosanna Schiaffino (Barzelli), Joanna Roos (Janet Bark), George Macready (Lew Jordan), Mino Doro (Tucino), Stefan Schnabel (Zeno), Vito Scotti (Assistant Director), Tom Palmer (Dr. Cold Eyes), Erich Von Stroheim, Jr. (Ravinski), Leslie Uggams (Chanteuse), Janet Lake (Noel O'Neill), Joan Courtenay (Signora Tucino), Margie Liszt (Liz), Franco Corsaro, Edward Comans (Henchman), Edit Angold (German Tourist), Don Orlando (Soundman), Red Perkins (George Jarrett), Albert Carrier (Electrician), James Garde (Sound Engineer), Albert Morin (Cameraman), Beulah Quo (Chinese Sister), Cilly Feindt (Lady Godiva), Lilyan Chauvin, Ann Molinari (Bar Girls), Charles Horvath, John Idrisano (Bouncers), Benito Prezie, Tony Randall, Joe Dante (Ad Libs in Lounge).

This disappointing movie about moviemaking features Douglas as a former Hollywood star who's personal life collapsed as his popularity declined. He has spent three years recuperating in a New England sanatorium, trying to make sense of a life plagued by alcohol, divorce, a nervous breakdown, and a near-fatal car crash. His doctors allow him to go to Rome, where Douglas has been offered a small role in a new film to be directed by the equally has-been Robinson. Together Douglas and Robinson had made some of their greatest pictures, but now these once mighty talents are reduced to making low-budget Italian spectacles. Upon arriving, Douglas learns his minor part has been filled and the picture itself is in deep trouble. Producer Doro is giving Robinson nothing but headaches about budget, and leading lady Schiaffino can barely speak English. Hamilton, the film's other star, is also giving Robinson problems with his disrespectful attitude and constant fights with girl friend Lavi. Robinson implores Douglas to supervise the film's dubbing, hopeful that his friend can save the picture. Douglas reluctantly agrees, and his ego receives a further blow when his ex-wife (Charisse) shows up to see how much power she still wields over him. At an anniversary party, Robinson's shrewish wife Trevor accuses her husband of fooling around with Schiaffino. The two get in a heated argument, which leads to Robinson suffering a heart attack. Douglas replaces him as director, bringing the film in under budget, as well as helping out Hamilton with his personal troubles. Robinson, bitter over his replacement's success, accuses Douglas of trying to ruin his career. Douglas turns to Charisse for comfort and the two embark on a wild night of total abandon. The evening ends with a dangerous car ride, and Douglas realizes he must grab control of his own life. He cuts loose the ties he has made in Rome, then heads alone to Hollywood to begin a new career as a director. Adapted from a trashy Irwin Shaw novel, this film is plagued by poorly written characters, played like cartoon figures rather than flesh and blood human beings. Everyone fits a certain type with no sense of style at all. Only Robinson and Trevor give any real life to their creations, but their efforts are middling at best. At one point Douglas and Robinson reminiscence over former successes, and watch clips from one of their past hits. The clips used are from THE BAD AND THE BEAUTIFUL, the classic film that was also about the movie business. Director Minnelli, Douglas, screenwriter Schnee, and producer Housemann had all worked together on that film, and it is with a sort of perverse irony that this classic motion picture was chosen to represent the successes of the new film's characters. Minnelli admitted that TWO WEEKS IN ANOTHER TOWN was a bad picture, but he put more blame on studio editing of his final cut. In his autobiography I Remember It Well, Minnelli wrote: "What we filmed was a better picture than what was released... The culprit responsible for the hacking of the picture was the head of the studio in New York, who himself would be out of a job in two months. He found the philosophy of the film immoral...and attacked our picture with a meat cleaver. This was the only time in my career such a catastrophe befell me."

p, John Houseman; d, Vincente Minnelli; w, Charles Schnee (based on the novel by Irwin Shaw); ph, Milton Krasner (CinemaScope, Metrocolor); m, David Raksin; ed, Adrienne Fazan, Robert J. Kern, Jr.; art d, George W. Davis, Urie McCleary; set d, Henry Grace, Keogh Gleason; cos, Walter Plunkett, Pierre Balmain; spec eff, Robert R. Hoag; makeup, William Tuttle.

Drama   **(PR:O   MPAA:NR)**

TWO GUYS FROM TEXAS***   (1948) 86m WB c (GB: TWO TEXAS KNIGHTS)

Dennis Morgan (Steve Carroll), Jack Carson (Danny Foster), Dorothy Malone (Joan Winston), Penny Edwards (Maggie Reed), Forrest Tucker ("Tex" Bennett), Fred Clark (Dr. Straeger), Gerald Mohr (Link Jessup), John Alvin (Jim Crocker), Andrew Tombes ("The Texan"), Monte Blue (Pete Nash), Philharmonica Trio (Specialty).

This remake of a COWBOY FROM BROOKLYN (1938) features Carson and Morgan as a low-level song-and-dance team who find themselves stuck on a Texas dude ranch. A variety of hijinks ensues, including jail, rodeos, and romance, the latter coming in the form of Edwards and Malone. There's also some business with Tucker, a nefarious hood who the would-be cowboys end up forcing off the ranch. This spoof of western formulas has some wonderfully witty moments, scripted by Billy Wilder's regular collaborator, Diamond. One enjoyable sequence cuts back and forth between Carson and Morgan, and Edwards and Malone, as the four prepare for bed in gender separated rooms. Also included is a cartoon dream sequence, created by Freleng, one of the best animators at Warners' "Termite Terrace." Carson is amusing in the lead, with Morgan doing a good job as the more romantic member of the duo. Butler's direction, though nothing special, suits the material in a nice, easygoing manner. The songs include: "Every Day I Love You Just a Little Bit More," "Hankerin'," "I Don't Care If It Rains All Night," "There's Music In the Land," and "I Wanna Be a Cowboy In the Movies" (Jule Styne, Sammy Cahn).

p, Alex Gottlieb; d, David Butler; w, I.A.L. Diamond, Allen Boretz (based on the play "Howdy Stranger" by Louis Pelletier, Jr., Robert Sloane); ph, Arthur Edeson, William V. Skall (Technicolor); ed, Irene Morra; md, Leo F. Forbstein; art d, Edward Carrere; ch, Le Roy Prinz; animation, Friz Freleng.

Western Comedy   **(PR:A   MPAA:NR)**

TWO-HEADED SPY, THE*   (1959, Brit.) 93m Sabre/COL bw

Jack Hawkins (*Gen. Alex Schottland*), Gia Scala (*Lili Geyr*), Erik Schumann (*Lt. Reinisch*), Alexander Knox (*Gestapo Leader Mueller*), Felix Aylmer (*Cornaz*), Walter Hudd (*Adm.Canaris*), Edward Underdown (*Kaltenbrunner*), Laurence Naismith (*Gen. Hauser*), Geoffrey Bayldon (*Dietz*), Kenneth Griffith (*Adolf Hitler*), Robert Crewdson (*1st Gestapo Agent*), Michael Caine (*2nd Gestapo Agent*), Harriette Johns (*Karen Corscher*), Martin Benson (*Gen. Wagner*), Victor Woolf (*Pawnbroker*), Richard Grey (*Marshal Wilhelm Keitel*), Ronald Hines (*German Corporal*), Donald Pleasence (*Gen. Hardt*), Martin Boddey (*Gen. Optiz*), Bernard Fox (*Lieutenant*), Deering Wells (*Gen. Merkel*), Nada Beale (*Eva Fischer*), Ian Colin (*Col. Heitz*), Peter Swanwick (*Gen. Toppe*), Desmond Roberts (*Gen. Zeiss*), Victor Fairley (*Gen. Rupert*), Thorp Devereux (*Gen. Kirche*), Peter Welch (*Gestapo Major*), John Dunbar (*Doctor*), John Brooking (*Staff Officer*), Dudley Foster (*Gestapo Man*), Grenville Eves (*Colonel, Field Hospital*), Neil Hallet (*Hitler's Guard*), Bart Allison, Edward Malin (*Orderlies*), John Cabot (*Innkeeper*), Kenneth Earl (*British Soldier*), John McLaren, Martin Sterndale.

After serving as a spy for England during WW I Hawkins is planted in Germany. As the Nazi power grows, Hawkins infiltrates and soon becomes a general in their war machine. While maintaining the facade, the British agent feeds information to his fellow Englishman, Aylmer, who disguises himself as a clock salesman. However, Aylmer is caught and murdered for his actions, leaving Hawkins alone. He is suspected at first, but manages to overcome this and continue his espionage. His next contact is Scala, a beautiful singer he pretends to love so he can feed more information to England. However, he does fall in love and plans to return to England with her. Finally, though, his ruse is discovered and he must flee home as Schumann, his Gestapo aide, murders Scala. Based on truth, this is an interesting and well-told spy picture that nicely builds its levels of tension. Though there is too much use of documentary footage to pad out the historical ends, the cast gives good performances that really make this story work. Hawkins is convincing as the agent, well supported by Scala's relatively minor role. Schumann is appropriately evil as the aide and the rest of the cast fills out the ensemble with some fine work. Watch for an early appearance by Caine as a Nazi. The direction handles the story's inherent trickiness with great skill, always holding the proper balance between seeming safety and fear.

p, Bill Kirby, Hal E. Chester; d, Andre De Toth; w, James O'Donnell (based on a story by J. Alvin Kugelmass); ph, Ted Scaife; m, Gerard Schurmann; ed, Raymond Poulton; md, Muir Mathieson; art d, Ivan King; spec eff, George Blackwell, Jr.; m/l, Peter Hart; tech adv, Col. Alexander Scotland, OBE.

Spy Drama   **(PR:C   MPAA:NR)**

TWO HEADS ON A PILLOW*½   (1934) 68m Liberty bw

Neil Hamilton, Miriam Jordan, Henry Armetta, Lona Andre, Hardie Albright, Dorothy Appleby, Mary Forbes, Edward Martindel, Claude King, Betty Blythe, Edward Kane, Claire McDowell, George Lewis, Emily Fitzroy, Nellie V. Nicholas, Julia Ford, Mary Foy, Jack Kennedy.

Married attorneys Hamilton and Jordan alternate between love and war. Finally they get the marriage annulled. Then the two meet again in the courtroom when they must argue opposite sides in another marriage anullment. The film lacks any real imagination with its contrived plot and some pretty poor dialog. Surprisingly, the cast is able to overcome the material and the majority turn in strong performances. The direction, once it figures out what to do with the weak material, is okay for the fare.

p, M.H. Hoffman; d, William Nigh; w, Albert De Mond (based on "The Eternal Masculine" by Dorothy Canfield); ph, Harry Neumann; m, A.H. Meyer; ed, Mildred Johnston.

Drama   **(PR:A   MPAA:NR)**

TWO HEARTS IN HARMONY**   (1935, Brit.) 70m Time/BIP bw

Bernice Claire (*Micky*), George Curzon (*Lord Sheldon*), Enid Stamp-Taylor (*Sheila*), Paul Hartley (*Bobby*), Nora Williams (*Lil*), Gordon Little (*Joe*), Guy Middleton (*Mario*), Charles Farrell (*Himself*), Chick Endor (*Himself*), Betty Thumling (*Pam*), Sheila Barrett (*Dodo*), Eliot Makeham (*Wagstaff*), Julian Royce (*Carstairs*), Rex Curtis (*Butler*), Victor Rietti (*Calvazzi*), Jack Harris and His Band.

Claire is a cabaret singer who performs along with her friends Endor, Farrell, and Williams. Determined to marry Curzon, a wealthy lord, she becomes governess to his son. Finally she hooks the rich widower and of course lives happily ever after. This simple but pleasant programmer features some amusing acts in the cabaret and good production values. A slow story development doesn't harm the piece; it's charming enough for what it is.

p, John Clein; d, William Beaudine; w, Robert Edmunds, A.R. Rawlinson (based on a story by Samuel Gibson Brown); ph, John Silver; m/l, Eddie Pola, Franz Vienna.

Musical   **(PR:A   MPAA:NR)**

TWO HEARTS IN WALTZ TIME**   (1934, Brit.) 80m
                                                 Nettlefold-Fogwell/GAU bw

Carl Brisson (*Carl Hoffman*), Frances Day (*Helene Barry*), Bert Coote (*Danielli*), Oscar Asche (*Herman Greenbaum*), C. Denier Warren (*Meyer*), Roland Culver (*Freddie*), William Jenkins (*Max*), Peter Gawthorne (*Mr. Joseph*), Valerie Hobson (*Susie*).

A dated musical about a Viennese composer, Brisson, who is commissioned to compose an operetta. While doing so he falls in love with Day, without realizing that she is the star of the opera company. Michael Powell handled the same plot devices with much more finesse in THE RED SHOES (1948).

p, Reginald Fogwell; d, Carmine Gallone, Joe May; w, Fogwell, John McNally (based on a story by Walter Reisch, Franz Schulz).

Musical/Romance   **(PR:A   MPAA:NR)**

TWO HUNDRED MOTELS**   (1971, Brit.) 98m UA c

The Mothers of Invention (*Themselves*), Theodore Bikel (*Rance Muhammitz*), Ringo Starr (*Larry the Dwarf/Frank Zappa*), Keith Moon (*Hot Nun*), Jimmy Carl Black (*Lonesome Cowboy Burt*), Martin Lickert (*Jeff*), Janet Ferguson, Lucy Offerall (*Groupies*), Pamela Miller (*Interviewer*), Don Preston (*Bif Debris*), Dick Barber (*Industrial Vacuum Cleaner*), Jim Pons, Frank Zappa (*Themselves*), Ruth Underwood, Judy Grindley, The Royal Philharmonic Orchestra conducted by John Lowdell.

Always ahead of his time, avant-garde musician Zappa predates the rock video in what can best be described as a visual equivalent to any of his recordings in the late 1960s and early 1970s. TWO HUNDRED MOTELS is a hodgepodge of color and sound linked by ex-Beatle Starr playing Zappa, complete with curly-locked wig and the signature goatee. The film is a marvelous whirl of color and visual effects, with some fine animation and Zappa's delicious wit present throughout the entire production. This was the first color production to be transferred from videotape to film and the technique works well. The special visual effects available at the time were used to create some amazing surreal images and optical illusions. This is certainly not for everyone and sometimes the picture causes eyestrain, but TWO HUNDRED MOTELS is definitely a film to experience. Zappa codirected with Palmer, taking credit for "characterizations." Palmer was said to have directed the visuals and was also responsible for the shooting script from the "story" and screenplay by Zappa. Watch for Moon, the drummer of The Who, in a cameo as a nun]

p, Jerry Good, Herb Cohen; d&w, Frank Zappa, Tony Palmer (based on a story by Zappa); ph, Palmer (Technicolor); m, Zappa; ed, Richard Harrison, Barry Stephens; prod d, Calvin Schenkel; art d, Leo Austin; cos, Sue Yelland; spec eff, Bert Luxford; ch, Gillian Lynne; animation, Mara Kam.

Musical/Fantasy   **Cas.**   **(PR:O   MPAA:R)**

TWO IN A CROWD*   (1936) 82m UNIV bw

Joan Bennett (*Julia Wayne*), Joel McCrea (*Larry Stevens*), Henry Armetta (*Toscani*), Alison Skipworth (*Lillie "The Toad" Eckleberger*), Nat Pendleton (*Flynn*), Reginald Denny (*James Stewart Anthony*), Andy Clyde (*Jonesy*), Elisha Cook, Jr (*Skeeter*), Donald Meek (*Bennett*), Bradley Page (*Tony Bonelli*), Barbara Rogers (*The Lawson Girl*), John Hamilton (*Purdy the FBI Man*), Tyler Brooke (*Charles Brock*), Douglas Wood (*Ralston*), Milburn Stone (*Kennedy the Cashier*), Frank Layton (*Bank Guard*), Robert Murphy (*Bartender*), Matt McHugh (*Taxi Driver*), Ed Gargan (*Policeman*), Jean Rogers (*Blonde at Party*), Paul Porcasi (*Polito the Headwaiter*), Joe Sawyer (*Bonelli's Henchman*), Paul Fix (*Mike, Bonelli's Henchman*), Eddie "Rochester" Anderson (*Swipe*), Eddie Kane (*Bar Manager*), Nena Quartaro (*Celita the Hat Check Girl*), Alan Matthews (*Taxi Driver*), James Quinn (*Ho-Head*), Diana Gibson (*Secretary*), James Morton, Eddy Chandler, Henry Otho, James Flavin (*Policemen*), Evelyn Selbie (*Tenement Woman*), Winter Hall (*Judge*), Jerry Mandy (*Barber*), John George (*Dwarf*), Johnnie Morris (*Balloon Vendor*), Phyllis Crane, Maxine Cantway, Eloise Rozelle (*Molls*),

Carl Andre (*Larry Stevens' Stand-in*), Mary Windsor (*Julia Wayne's Stand-in*), Billy Burrud.

Racing man McCrea is too broke to feed his horse when all appears to be relieved by his finding half of a $1,000 bill. He is able to cash it in but the bill turns out to be loot from a bank robbery. The robbers come in and hold him hostage but all works out and the horse wins the big race as well. This is an overlong comedy which suffers from a bad script as well. The scattered funny moments are tediously stretched out by the slow pace of the direction. The story had potential for some minor laughs but with this treatment it never has a chance. Acting is strictly conventional.

p, Charles R. Rogers; d, Alfred E. Green; w, Lewis R. Foster, Doris Malloy, Earle Snell (based on a story by Foster); ph, Joseph Valentine; ed, Milton Carruth; md, Herman Heller; art d, Albert S. D'Agostino; spec eff, John P. Fulton.

Comedy   (PR:A   MPAA:NR)

TWO IN A MILLION   (SEE: EAST OF FIFTH AVENUE, 1933)

TWO IN A SLEEPING BAG**   (1964, Ger.) 75m
Bavaria-Filmkunst/Holt International, Fouad Said c (KLEINES ZELT UND GROSSE LIEBE)

Susanne Cramer (*The Heiress*), Claus Biederstaedt, Eva Kerbler, Hans Nielsen, Dietmar Schonherr, Heinrich Gretler, Gundel Thormann, Lina Carstens, Ernst Tabe.

Cramer is a poor little rich girl who almost marries a fortune-hunting bachelor. Her father sends the spoiled girl to a strict boarding school but she runs off to rejoin her true love. En route she meets a man who is taking a kayak trip along the Rhine. He offers her a ride and the two spend a few days camping and boating together. Gradually Cramer forgets her old beau as she falls for this new man.

p, Georg Richter; d, Rainer Geis; w, Joachim Wedekind (based on an idea of Arnold Franck); ph, Klaus von Rautenfeld (Agfacolor); m, Franz Grothe; ed, Hilwa von Boro; art d, Hans Berthel.

Comedy   (PR:C   MPAA:NR)

TWO IN A TAXI*½   (1941) 63m COL bw

Anita Louise (*Bonnie*), Russell Hayden (*Jimmy Owens*), Noah Beery, Jr (*Sandy Connors*), Dick Purcell (*Bill Gratton*), Chick Chandler (*Sid*), Fay Helm (*Ethel*), George Cleveland (*Gas Station Proprietor*), Frank Yaconelli (*Tony Vitale*), Ben Taggart (*Sweeny*), Paul Porcasi (*Herman*), Henry Brandon (*Professor*), John Harmon (*Benny*), Ralph Peters (*Zazu*), James Seay (*Cristy Reardon*).

A taxi driver wants to save up enough money so he can buy a gas station and marry his sweetheart. Everything that can go wrong for him does before he finally achieves his goal. Hayden, Hopalong Cassidy's sidekick, plays the hero well and Louise isn't bad as his girl. However, they're hampered by an impossible script, full of unbelievable plot contrivances presented in a most unoriginal fashion. The direction is barely average, showing no creativity, and the camera work is unexciting.

p, Irving Briskin; d, Robert Florey; w, Howard J. Green, Morton Thompson, Malvin Wald; ph, George Meehan; ed, Viola Lawrence; md, M.W. Stoloff; art d, Lionel Banks.

Comedy/Drama   (PR:A   MPAA:NR)

TWO IN REVOLT½**   (1936) 65m RKO bw

John Arledge (*John Woods*), Louise Latimer (*Gloria*), Moroni Olsen (*Cyrus Benton*), Emmett Vogan (*Mason*), Harry Jans (*Crane*), Murray Alper (*Andy*), Max Wagner (*Davis*), Ethan Laidlaw (*Bill*), Lightning the Dog, Warrior the Horse.

Aimed directly at children, this 1930s programmer is the story of a horse and dog born the same day. The two four-legged creatures become fast friends and live together in the wilderness. When a pack of wolves attacks a herd of wild horses both animals fight their instincts and save the herd. Next they return to the civilized world where Arledge trains the horse for a big race. With the encouragement of his canine chum the horse wins despite the interference of Vogan, a nasty gambler. This is the sort of movie that depends on the strengths and believability of its animal performers. Both beasts pass this acid test with high grades. The film is at its best when the two natural performers are allowed to go through their moves. The sequences with the humans, particularly the mushy love story with Arledge and Latimer, detract from this animal tale. But overall it's an entertaining film, enjoyable on its simplistic level. Directed with care for it's animal performers, it makes one wonder just how they got them to do all they did. For that, it's rather remarkable.

p, Robert Sisk; d, Glenn Tryon; w, Frank Howard Clark, Ferdinand Reyher, Jerry Hutchinson (based on the story by Earl Johnson and Thomas Storey); ph, Jack MacKenzie; ed, Frederic Knudtson; md, Alberto Colombo.

Animal Drama   (PR:AAA   MPAA:NR)

TWO IN THE DARK*½   (1936) 72m RKO bw

Walter Abel (*The Man*), Margot Grahame (*Marie Smith*), Wallace Ford (*Hillyer*), Gail Patrick (*Irene Lassiter*), Alan Hale (*Florio*), Leslie Fenton (*Stuart Eldredge*), Eric Blore (*Edmund Fish*), Erin O'Brien-Moore (*Olga Konar*), Erik Rhodes (*Carlo Ghett*), J. Carroll Naish (*Mansfield*), Addison Randall, Russell Hicks, Richard Howard.

After losing his memory from a blow on the head Abel must find out whether he is responsible for a murder. After his landlady locks him out he meets Grahame, who helps him find the truth. Pretty strange thing to do, considering she suspects he may indeed be a killer. From there the film descends into a confusing mess disguised as a mystery. The plot becomes difficult to follow and ends up a disappointment for genre fans. This is a real shame following the very clever opening and considering the solid performances by the leads. The direction makes the film look nice, but the plot twists ultimately bring it down. It was later remade in 1945 as TWO O'CLOCK COURAGE.

p, Zion Myers; d, Benjamin Stoloff; w, Seton I. Miller (based on the novel *Two O'Clock Courage* by Gelett Burgess); ph, Nicholas Musuraca; ed, George Crone; cos, Bernard Newman.

Mystery   (PR:A   MPAA:NR)

TWO IN THE SHADOW½**   (1968, Jap.) 108m Toho c
(MIDARE-GUMO)

Yuzo Kayama (*Shiro Mishima*), Yoko Tsukasa (*Yumiko*), Mitsuko Mori, Mitsuko Kusabue, Daisuke Kato, Nobu Tsuchiya, Yumiko Iida, Naoya Kusakawa.

Kayama is involved in a traffic accident in which a man dies. Though he is proven innocent his company, an import-export operation, transfers him from Tokyo to a branch in Aomori. Kayama prepares to leave but before going the guilt-ridden man offers some money to Tsukasa, the dead man's widow. She refuses at first but finally takes it under pressure from her in-laws. She decides to go to her home town in an effort to get over the past, but the town turns out to be Aomori. Tsukasa and Kayama run into each other often but Tsukasa at first refuses to acknowledge Kayama's efforts to be friends. Kayama tries to transfer to his firm's Pakistani branch but slowly Tsukasa has built up some affection for the man. The two go out and just before he leaves Kayama confesses he's fallen in love with her. She leaves him but on the day he is to go abroad Tsukasa finds that she really wants to go with him. But then the two see a traffic accident similar to the one that made her a widow, leading them both to realize that their love cannot be.

p, Sanezumi Fujimoto, Masakatsu Kaneko; d, Mikio Naruse; w, Nobuo Yamada; ph, Jo Aizawa (Tohoscope); m, Toru Takemitsu; art d, Satoru Nakano.

Drama   (PR:C   MPAA:NR)

TWO IS A HAPPY NUMBER   (SEE: ONE IS A LONELY NUMBER, 1972)

TWO KINDS OF WOMEN*   (1932) 75m PAR bw

Miriam Hopkins (*Emma Krull*), Phillips Holmes (*Joseph Greshan Jr.*), Wynne Gibson (*Phyllis Adrian*), Stuart Erwin (*Hauser*), Irving Pichel (*Sen. Krull*), Stanley Fields (*Glassman*), James Crane (*Joyce*), Vivienne Osborne (*Helen*), Josephine Dunn (*Clarissa Smith*), Robert Emmett O'Connor (*Tim Gohagen*), Larry Steers (*Murchard*), Adrienne Ames (*Jean*), Claire Dodd (*Shiela*), Terrence Ray (*Babe Sevito*), June Nash (*Mrs. Bowen*), Kent Taylor (*Milt Fleisser*), Edwin Maxwell (*Deputy Police Commissioner*), Lindsay McHarrie (*Radio Announcer*).

Hopkins is the daughter of Pichel, a South Dakota senator. He's convinced that New York City is a modern day version of Sodom and/or Gomorrah and heads out East to prove it. While he's arguing with some locals, Hopkins meets Holmes, a high living playboy who's everything her father fears. Of course it's true love for the pair. Holmes is already married to a floozy chorus girl but her convenient suicide makes everything okay. Finally Pichel comes around and all live happily ever after. All this is given the simplest of treatments with character motivation sketchy at best. The dialog lacks the needed bite and any sense of reality is buried beneath the inane plot development. Acting generally is as bad, though Hopkins manages to rise above the senseless material. Holmes is at best ineffective.

d, William C. de Mille; w, Benjamin Glazer (based on the play "This Is New York" by Robert E. Sherwood); ph, Karl Struss.

Drama   (PR:C   MPAA:NR)

TWO KOUNEY LEMELS*   (1966, Israel) 120m Geva/Flying Matchmaker Company c

Mike Bourstein (*Kouney Lemel/Max*), Rafael Klatchkin (*The Matchmaker*), Jermain Unikovsky (*His Daughter*), Shmuel Rodensky (*Reb Pinchas*), Elisheva Michaeli (*His Wife*), Rina Ganor (*His Daughter*), Aharon Meskin (*Kouney Lemel's Father*), Ari Koutay (*Max's Father*).

An illiterate but wealthy man is trying to marry off his daughter. Bourstein is his stuttering son who is also to be married. ("Kouney Lemel" is Yiddish for a sort of hapless, talentless person with a tendency to be pushed around by others.) His intended's family looks down on him but overlooks the fellow's shortcomings because of his father's wealth. Ganor is the girl he loves, but she loves another, the family black sheep who pays little attention to strict Orthodox Jewish customs. This man is also played by Bourstein, and several character switches later, there are two weddings and a very happy village. This is an exuberant, occasionally confusing, but overall enjoyable film. Bourstein is a fine physical comedian who makes the story work. The potential for maudlin drama is always averted thanks to his sensitive and humorous portraits. The direction does well with a light, breezy style. This popular film, the first Israeli musical, inspired several other adventures of the Kouney Lemel character.

p, Mordechai Navon; d, Israel Becker; w, Becker, Alex Maimon (based on a play by Avraham Goldfaden); ph, Romulo Grounni and Adam Grinberg (Technicolor); m, Shaul Perezovsky; md, Shimon Coben; m/l, Moshe Sahar.

Musical   (PR:A MPAA:NR)

TWO-LANE BLACKTOP**   (1971) 102m UNIV c

James Taylor (*The Driver*), Warren Oates (*G.T.O.*), Laurie Bird (*Girl*), Dennis Wilson (*The Mechanic*), David Brake (*Needles Station Attendant*), Richard Ruth (*Needles Station Mechanic*), Rudolph Wurlitzer (*Hot Rod Driver*), Jaclyn Hellman (*Driver's Girl*), Bill Keller (*Texas Hitchhiker*), H.D. [Harry Dean] Stanton (*Oklahoma Hitchhiker*), Don Samuels, Charles Moore (*Texas Policemen*), Tom Green (*Boswell Station Attendant*), W.H. Harrison (*Parts Store Owner*), Alan Vint (*Man in Roadhouse*), Illa Ginnaven (*Waitress*), George Mitchell (*Driver at Accident*), Katherine Squire (*Old Woman*), Melissa Hellman (*Child*), Jay Wheatley, Jim Mitchum (*Men at Race Track*), Kreag Caffey (*Motorcyclist*), Tom Witenbarger (*Pickup Driver*), Glen Rogers (*Soldier*).

Real life rock stars Taylor and Wilson (the latter a member of The Beach Boys) are a pair of car freaks driving down the endless roads of the American Southwest in search of a race. They drive an old 1955 Chevy, using race winnings to keep the souped-up auto in shape. The pair have little to say to each other beyond car talk. At a small Arizona diner they meet Bird, who gets in the car with them, no questions asked. After winning another race, Taylor and Bird make love; the next evening it's Wilson's turn with her. Later the three meet up with Oates, an older drifter who travels across the U.S. in his brand new G.T.O. He challenges them to a cross-country race to Washington, D.C., with the winner taking ownership of the loser's car. Along the way the participants' interest in the race begins to wane. Wilson suggests to Bird that they ride off together. Taylor enters a race in Memphis, and Bird, bored with the younger men, heads off to North Carolina with Oates. Later she takes off with a motorcyclist and Oates continues his aimless driving. Eventually, Wilson and Taylor find another race to run, and the movie ends ominously as they drive away from the camera down a two-lane road and the film burns and melts in the gate, leaving only a bright white light. Certainly not an average car chase movie, TWO-LANE BLACKTOP is perhaps director Monte Hellman's finest film. Known for his small, brooding existential westerns (THE SHOOTING, RIDE IN THE WHIRLWIND, both 1967), Hellman once again brings to life characters desperately searching for meaning in their lives. Oates, a close personal friend of Hellman's and lead player in nearly all is films, is magnificent in TWO-LANE BLACKTOP bringing a perfect blend of comedy, mystery, and pathos to his role. It is a powerful and memorable screen appearance that is somewhat weakened by the amateur support from nonactors Taylor, Wilson, and Bird, whose limited abilities required delicate handling by Hellman. Expectations were high for this somber film, with the studio convinced they had another EASY RIDER on their hands. *Esquire* magazine ran a cover story on the film, reprinted screenwriter Wurlitzer's screenplay in its entirety, and proclaimed it "the movie of the year." The predictions fell far short as the majority of the movie-going public failed to understand the picture and found its portrayal of youthful boredom to be just that: boring. TWO-LANE BLACKTOP is very similar to the work of popular European existential filmmakers, but the fickle American "art house" crowd stayed away in droves, obviously preferring their serious psychological dramas to be imported from abroad.

p, Michael S. Laughlin; d, Monte Hellman; w, Rudolph Wurlitzer, Will Corry (based on a story by Corry); ph, Jackson Deerson (Technicolor); ed, Hellman; cos, Richard Bruno.

Drama   (PR:O MPAA:R)

TWO LATINS FROM MANHATTAN*   (1941) 65m COL bw

Joan Davis (*Joan Daley*), Jinx Falkenburg (*Jinx Terry*), Joan Woodbury (*Lois Morgan*), Fortunio Bonanova (*Armando Rivero*), Don Beddoe (*Don Barlow*), Marquita Madero (*Marianela*), Carmen Morales (*Rosita*), Lloyd Bridges (*Tommy Curtis*), Sig Arno (*Felipe Rudolfo MacIntyre*), Boyd Davis (*Charles Miller*), Antonio Moreno, Rafael Storm (*Latins*), John Dilson (*Jerome Kittleman*), Tim Ryan (*Sergeant*), Don Brodie (*Young Advertisng Man*), Lester Dorr (*Information Attendant*), Bruce Bennett, Ralph Dunn (*Americans*), Stanley Brown (*M.C.*), Eddie Kane (*Manager*), Dick Elliott (*Sylvester Kittleman*), Chuck Morrison, Jack Cheatham (*Cops*), Tyler Brooke (*Hotel Clerk*), Ed Bruce (*Jed*), Ed Fetherston, Tony Merrill (*Stew-*

ards), Ernie Adams (*Stage Doorman*), Mel Ruick (*Radio Announcer*).

Back in the days when there were Latins native to New York City, a pair of Cuban show business sisters are brought to Manhattan by a nightclub owner. When they do not show up for work, Davis, the club's public relations woman, gets her roommates, Woodbury and Falkenburg, to substitute for them. The girls are a big hit but are eventually confronted by the real sisters. This weak B film is unoriginal and often sophomoric, with flat direction and a script that leaves room for nothing more than the bare-bones story. Songs include "Daddy" (Bobby Troup, sung by Davis, Falkenburg), which Sammy Kaye and his orchestra later turned into a hit record.

p, Wallace MacDonald; d, Charles Barton; w, Albert Duffy; ph, John Stumar; ed, Arthur Seid; art d, Lionel Banks; m/l, Sammy Cahn, Saul Chaplin.

Musical/Comedy   (PR:A MPAA:NR)

TWO LEFT FEET*   (1965, Brit.) 93m BL bw

Michael Crawford (*Alan Crabbe*), Nyree Dawn Porter (*Eileen*), Julia Foster (*Beth Crowley*), Michael Craze (*Ronnie*), David Hemmings (*Brian*), Dilys Watling (*Mavis*), David Lodge (*Bill*), Bernard Lee (*Mr. Crabbe*), Cyril Chamberlain (*Miles*), Neil McCarthy (*Ted*), Howard Pays (*Peter*), Douglas Ives (*Joe*), Michael Ripper (*Uncle Reg*), Hazel Coppen (*Mrs. Daly*), Peggy Ann Clifford (*Customer*), Anthony Sheppard (*Policeman*), Bob Wallis and His Storyville Jazzmen.

Porter is a waitress who loves to flirt. She ends up attracting the attention of the much younger Crawford, who tries to seduce her. This proves to be a disaster and Porter heads to a jazz club in search of better catches. The lonely Crawford takes up with Foster, a young shop clerk. At a wedding he sees his old flame and slugs it out with her new beau. Soundly thrashed, he returns to Foster. This minor sex comedy shows an occasional glimpse of wit but it's mostly trite and unfunny. The script is weak, especially in character motivation. The direction tries to make the mess work but does not succeed. Crawford shows a flair for comedy and Foster gives him the needed support.

p, Leslie Gilliat; d, Roy Baker; w, Baker, John Hopkins (based on the novel *In My Solitude* by David Stuart Leslie); ph, Wilkie Cooper, Harry Gillam; m, Phil Green; ed, Michael Hark.

Comedy   (PR:O MPAA:NR)

TWO LETTER ALIBI*½   (1962, Brit.) 60m Playpont/BL bw

Peter Williams (*Charles*), Petra Davies (*Kathy*), Ursula Howells (*Louise*), Ronald Adam (*Sir John Fawcett*), Bernard Archard (*Duke*), Stratford Johns (*Bates*), Peter Howell (*Carlton*).

An off-the-rack crime tale about a TV star whose lover is charged with the murder of his alcoholic wife. Enough clues are unearthed to prove the man's innocence and the real killer is found. Nothing new or interesting here.

p, E.M. Smedley Aston; d, Robert Lynn; w, Roger Marshall (based on the novel *Death and the Sky Above* by Andrew Garve).

Crime   (PR:A MPAA:NR)

TWO LITTLE BEARS, THE½**   (1961) 83m FOX bw

Eddie Albert (*Harry Davis*), Jane Wyatt (*Anne Davis*), Brenda Lee (*Tina Davis*), Soupy Sales (*Officer Pat McGovern*), Butch Patrick (*Billy Davis*), Donnie Carter (*Timmy Davis*), Jimmy Boyd (*Tina's Boy Friend*), Nancy Kulp (*Miss Wilkins*), Milton Parsons (*Psychiatrist*), Ernie Parnell (*School Board Head*), Opal Euard (*Fortuneteller*), Richard Alden (*Tom Provost*), Theo Marcuse (*Janos*), James Maloney (*Jefferson Stander*), Jack Finch (*Psychiatrist*), Jack Lester (*Phil Wade*), Charlene Brooks (*Mary Jergens*).

After receiving instructions from a mysterious gypsy, youngsters Patrick and Carter learn how to turn themselves into bears. This at first confuses their school-principal father Albert, but soon he becomes proud of his boys' unusual ability. His colleagues wonder about him; he is sent to a psychiatrist and recommended for dismissal. Leave it to those two boys to show the town that their father is right, turning into bears right before everyone's eyes. Luckily the football season is approaching and eclipses their interest in metamorphosis. This unusual child fantasy has an odd premise that really works. The direction occasionally panders to the more saccharine elements of the story, but for the most part this minor film has some entertaining moments. The kids will love it and probably get a few ideas as well. Patrick apparently was heavily influenced by the role, for he went on to play Eddie, the wolf-boy son in the TV-sitcom "The Munsters."

p, George W. George; d, Randall Hood; w, George (based on a story by George, Judy George); ph, Floyd Crosby (CinemaScope); m, Henry Vars; ed, Carl Pierson; art d, John Mansbridge; set d, Chester L. Bayhi; cos, Robert Olivas, Paula Giokaris; spec eff, Cinema Research Corp.; ch, Jonathan Lucas; m/l, "Honey Bear," Jay Livingston, Ray Evans, "Speak to Me Pretty," By Dunham, Henry Vars (all sung by Brenda Lee); makeup, Hal Lierley.

Children's Fantasy   (PR:AAA MPAA:NR)

TWO LIVING, ONE DEAD**½   (1964, Brit./Swed.) 92m
Swan-Wera/Emerson bw (TVA LEVANDE OCH EN DOD)

Virginia McKenna (Helen Berger), Bill Travers (Anderson), Patrick McGoohan (Berger), Dorothy Alison (Esther Kester), Alf Kjellin (Rogers), Noel Willman (Inspector Johnson), Pauline Jameson (Miss Larsen), Peter Vaughan (John Kester), Derek Francis (Broms), Michael Crawford (Nils), John Moulder-Brown (Rolf Berger), Isa Quensel, (Mlle. Larousse), Alan Rothwell (Karlson), Peter Bathurst (Engelhardt), Mariane Nielsen (Miss Lind), Mikael Bolin (Peter), Mona Geijer-Kalner (Mrs. Holm), Alan Bair, Georg Skarstedt.

While counting up the day's income one night, three postal workers are surprised by two robbers. Vaughan is killed during the holdup and Travers is badly wounded in the head. McGoohan gives the thieves the money but later is treated as a coward. Travers is given a hero's treatment and rewarded with a promotion that originally had been scheduled for McGoohan. His wife, McKenna, postal authorities, and the police, begin to think McGoohan was in cahoots with the robbers. Later the shamed man learns that Travers was actually in on the plot. He confronts the guilty man with a gun and forces him to admit his part in the robbery, thus regaining the respect he once held. In real life McKenna and Travers are husband and wife. The duo later starred in BORN FREE. Filmed on location in a small Swedish town.

p, Teddy Baird; d, Anthony Asquith; w, Lindsay Galloway (based on the Norwegian novel To Levende Og En Dod by Sigurd Wesley Christiansen); ph, Gunnar Fischer; m, Erik Nordgren; ed, Oscar Rosander; art d, Bibi Lindstrom.

Drama   **(PR:C   MPAA:NR)**

TWO LOST WORLDS*½   (1950) 61m Sterling/EL bw

Laura Elliott (Elaine Jeffries), Jim [James]Arness (Kirk Hamilton), Bill Kennedy (Martin Shannon), Gloria Petroff (Janice Jeffries), Tom Hubbard (John Hartley), Jane Harlan (Nancy Holden), Pierre Watkin (Magistrate Jeffries), Bob Carson (Capt. Allison), Guy Bellis (Governor), James Guilfoyle (Dr. Wakeland), Fred Kohler, Jr (Nat Mercer), Tom Monroe (Capt. Tallman), Tim Grahame (Salty), Richard Bartell (Mr. Davis).

This no-thrills, no-frills thriller has poor lass Elliot being kidnaped by some nasty pirates in Australia. It's up to Arness, in his pre-Matt Dillon ("Gunsmoke") days to rescue her. Later when they all end up shipwrecked, the cast pretends to be frightened by some intercut footage of ONE MILLION B.C. Plenty of gusto with some wonderfully hokey dialog to boot. Kennedy, who plays the head nasty, became a TV movie-show host in the Midwest during the 1950s. It's not known if this was one of that series' more popular attractions.

p, Boris Petroff; d, Norman Dawn; w, Tom Hubbard (based on a story by Hubbard and Phyllis Parker); ph., Harry Neumann; m, Michael Terr; ed, Fred R. Feitshans, Jr.; art d, Denny Hall.

Adventure   **(PR:A   MPAA:NR)**

TWO LOVES*   (1961) 100m MGM c (GB: THE SPINSTER)

Shirley MacLaine (Anna Vorontosov), Laurence Harvey (Paul Lathrope), Jack Hawkins (W.W.J. Abercrombie), Nobu McCarthy (Whareparita), Ronald Long (Headmaster Reardon), Norah Howard (Mrs. Cutter), Juano Hernandez (Rauhuia), Edmund Vargas (Matawhero), Neil Woodward (Mark Cutter), Lisa Sitjar (Hinewaka), Alan Roberts (Seven).

A gigantic bore that suffers from misconception and miscasting, TWO LOVES never should have been made with the script and the actors utilized. The loveliness of Ashton-Warner's novel is all but bypassed in favor of a commercial vehicle that fails to satisfy on many levels. MacLaine is a Pennsylvania native who is now teaching school in a New Zealand community far from any civilization. (How she came to be in New Zealand is never fully explained.) MacLaine is a spinster, a repressed woman who prides herself on being chaste and is shocked by the amorality of the Maoris surrounding her. The children love the way she teaches, as she has brought new methods to an old role. When one student complains that he is sick of writing, MacLaine suggests he practice writing "I am sick of writing." Hawkins is the married man who is the school administrator for the area and makes regular visits to the more remote places in his domain. At first, he is not pleased with her drastic methods but when he sees how the children (all 46 or so of them, of racially mixed backgrounds) respond, he decides to back off and allow her to do as she wishes. As successful as she is at her work, that's how insecure she is in her private life. A virgin, she is frightened of men and stays at arm's length from anyone whose voice is deeper than hers. Harvey is a fellow teacher who yearns to be a singer. He is irresponsible, weak, and neurotic. Harvey tries to break down MacLaine's walls but she keeps rebuffing him. MacLaine's aide at the school is McCarthy, a 15-year-old native. MacLaine learns that McCarthy is pregnant and that no one in the village seems to be concerned that she is unmarried or who the father is. MacLaine can't get over the natural way in which the natives accept this pregnancy and she wonders if her own morality may be out of place in the area and in this film. McCarthy's baby dies at birth and that is followed by Harvey's death in a motorcycle accident, or perhaps it is a suicide. Then MacLaine finds out that McCarthy's dead child had been

sired by Harvey. MacLaine's life is turned around by this and she blames herself for all of it. Had she submitted to Harvey, perhaps he wouldn't have impregnated McCarthy and he might not have killed himself. It is with Hawkins' patient counseling that she is able to come to grips with her imagined guilt. Hawkins offers her affection and love and MacLaine has matured enough to accept it. Southern California doubled for New Zealand but nothing could replace the lack of focus in the film. The only reasons to see this movie are the adorable children and the fine acting by Juano Hernandez as the chief of the Maoris.

p, Julian Blaustein; d, Charles Walters; w, Ben Maddow (based on the novel Spinster by Sylvia Ashton-Warner); ph, Joseph Ruttenberg (CinemaScope, Metrocolor); m, Bronislau Kaper; ed, Fredric Steinkamp; art d, George W. Davis, Urie McCleary; set d, Henry Grace, Hugh Hunt; spec eff, Robert R. Hoag, Lee Le Blanc; makeup, William Tuttle.

Drama   **(PR:C   MPAA:NR)**

TWO-MAN SUBMARINE**   (1944) 62m COL bw

Tom Neal (Jerry Evans), Ann Savage (Pat Benson), J. Carroll Naish (Dr. Augustus Hadley), Robert Williams (Walt Hedges), Abner Biberman (Gabe Fabian), George Lynn (Norman Fosmer), J. Alex Havier (Fuzzytop).

Before penicillin existed, enemy agents from America's opposing forces tried to lay their sneaky hands on a formula created by an American team holed up in South America, according to this WW II-era programmer. The Americans go through the usual trials and tribulations at the hands of the evil-minded Nazis and Japanese (combining forces for this story) until, like the cavalry in a western, a U.S. submarine comes to save the day. The story is an exercise in contrivance.

p, Jack Fier; d, Lew Landers; w, Griffin Jay, Leslie T. White; ph, James Van Trees; ed, Jerome Thoms; md, M.W. Stoloff; art d, Lionel Banks, Cary Odell.

War Drama   **(PR:A   MPAA:NR)**

TWO MEN AND A GIRL   (SEE: HONEYMOON, 1947)

TWO MEN AND A MAID*½   (1929) 73m TIF-Stahl bw

William Collier, Jr (Jim Oxford), Alma Bennett (Rose), Eddie Gribbon (Adjutant), George E. Stone (Shorty), Margaret Quimby (Margaret).

Collier mistakenly believes that his wife has had another lover before him. Filled with shame, he joins the French Foreign Legion and goes to Algeria, where he falls in love with Bennett, the mistress of the cruel adjutant. When their romance is revealed a gun accidentally discharges and Bennett is hit. Before she dies she arranges for Collier's escape. He is finally captured, but the adjutant shows mercy and lets him return to his wife, who waits with her all-forgiving open arms. A typical melodrama which manages to insult modern views of romance and relationships.

d, George Archainbaud; w, Frederic Hatton, Fanny Hatton, Frances Hyland (based on a story by John Francis Natteford); ph, Harry Jackson; m, Hugo Riesenfeld; ed, Desmond O'Brien; m/l, "Love Will Find You," L. Wolfe Gilbert, Abel Baer.

Romance   **(PR:A   MPAA:NR)**

TWO MEN IN TOWN***   (1973, Fr.) 100m Adel-Medusa/Valoria c
(DEUX HOMMES DANS LA VILLE)

Alain Delon (Gino), Jean Gabin (Germaine), Mimsy Farmer (Lucie), Michel Bouquet (Goitreau), Ilaria Occhini (Sophie), Victor Lanoux (Marcel), Christine Fabrega (Genevieve), Bernard Giraudeau (Frederic), Malka Ribovska (Lawyer), Jacques Monod (Prosecutor).

After serving 10 years for bank robbery Delon is let go after some interceding on his behalf by old pal Gabin, a social worker. Delon returns to his wife and respectability despite attempts by his cohorts to have him resume the old life. Later there is a prison riot and Gabin ends up settling in the same town as Delon. The two families become close but Delon's wife is killed in an accident. He remarries but faces scandal when he's hounded by a cop who wants to bring up his gangster past. Delon kills the policeman when the cop mistreats his new wife and goes to trial. He's sentenced to death and executed in one of filmdom's more graphic portrayals of the death penalty put into execution. This is a taut, interesting psychological film that occasionally suffers from preachiness. Delon's performance is very strong and Gabin is equally good in support. This is reminiscent of the old prison pictures from the 1930s and 1940s, given a good updating and strong material.

d&w, Jose Giovanni; ph, Jean-Jacques Tarbes (Eastmancolor); ed, Francoise Javet.

Drama   **(PR:O   MPAA:NR)**

TWO-MINUTE WARNING*   (1976) 115m UNIV c

Charlton Heston (Capt. Peter Holly), John Cassavetes (Sgt. Chris Button), Beau Bridges (Mike Ramsay), Marilyn Hassett (Lucy), David Janssen (Steve), Jack Klugman (Stu Sandman), Gena Rowlands (Janet), Walter

Pidgeon *(Pickpocket)*, Brock Peters *(Paul, McKeever's Assistant)*, David Groh *(Al Spinner, Intern)*, Mitchell Ryan *(Priest)*, Joe Kapp *(Charlie Tyler)*, Pamela Bellwood *(Peggy Ramsay)*, Jon Korkes *(Jeffrey, Lucy's Escort)*, William Bryant *(Lt. Calloway)*, Allan Miller *(Mr. Green)*, Andy Sidaris *(TV Director)*, Ron Sheldon, Stanford Blum *(Assistant TV Directors)*, Warren Miller *(Sniper)*, Vincent Baggetta *(Ted Shelley)*, Stewart Steinberg *(Portman)*, Juli Bridges *(Pickpocket's Accomplice)*, Brooke Mills *(Tyler's Girl Friend)*, Brad Savage, Reed Diamond *(Ramsay Children)*, Lina Raymond *(Sandman's Girl Friend)*, Ross Durfee *(Network Executive)*, Jenny Maybrook *(Girl in TV Truck)*, Gerry Okuneff *(Los Angeles Coach)*, Chuck Tamburro *(Porter)*, Wild Bill Mock *(Gilmore)*, John Armond *(Sutherland)*, Tom Bears *(Baltimore Coach)*, Sandy Johnson *(Button's Wife)*, Edward McNally *(Newsman with Governors)*, Howard Cosell, Frank Gifford, Dick Enberg, Merv Griffin *(Themselves)*, Gary Combs *(Downing)*, Fred Hice *(Innocent Suspect)*, Boris Aplon *(Maitre d')*, Jack Brodsky, Arnold Carr *(Spectators)*, Tom Huff, Patty Elder *(Cyclists)*, Larry Manetti *(Pratt)*, Christine Nelson, Holly Irving *(Old Women at Airport)*, Tom Baker *(Stakowski)*, Trent Dolan *(Fuller)*, Michael Gregory *(Angelo)*, Glen Wilder, David Cass *(Green's Henchmen)*, Buck Young, Jess Nadelman, Allan Eisenman, Richard Feldman, Lisa Lyke, Dick Winslow, Shelley Siverstein, J. A. Preston, James Parkes, Garry Walberg, Kate Archer, Colin Hamilton, Gracia Lee, Robert Ginty, Richard Branda, Forrest Wood, Terry Hinz, Ray Nadeau, John Ramsey, Eugene Daniels, Henry Deas, Sander Peerce, Karl Lukas, Hanna Hetelendy, John West, Sharri Zak.

Another disaster movie that is the embodiment of the term. It's the day of a football playoff game between Los Angeles and Baltimore. The stadium is packed–a disaster is waiting to happen, right? The disaster comes in the form of a sniper who hides out and waits for a victim, supposed to be the president of the U.S. It is up to Heston to save the day with the help of SWAT team leader Cassavetes. After Griffin sings the national anthem (worth the price of admission alone!) we are introduced to the various characters who are going to be in big trouble soon. Klugman is a gambler playing with mob money; Janssen and Rowlands are bickering lovers; Groh, fresh from his divorce on TV's "Rhoda," is a smoothie bachelor; Pidgeon is a pickpocket; and Bridges is a man who's just lost his job and is trying to show his family a good time. Finally it's announced that the President isn't coming and this causes the sniper to start firing away, killing Klugman, Janssen, and Pidgeon. The crowd panics with full force, causing a riot as people try to get out of the stadium. Heston stands up against the sniper fire and kills the man. This mess is no fun until the sniper starts shooting–at least that livens things up a bit. The characters are the same cardboard cutouts seen in any of a dozen disaster movies released in the 1970s. The one fresh aspect is the sniper himself. He's never named or given a phony psychological motivation; he merely exists to kill. For its TV release this was chopped by an hour and replaced with new characters and new subplots. It goes without saying this did nothing to improve the film's quality. Bad!

p, Edward S. Feldman; d, Larry Peerce; w, Edward Hume (based on the novel by George La Fountaine); ph, Gerald Hirschfeld (Technicolor); m, Charles Fox; ed, Eve Newman, Walter Hannemann; art d, Herman A. Blumentahl; set d, John M. Dwyer; stunts, Glen Wilder.

Drama   Cas.   (PR:O MPAA:R)

TWO MINUTES' SILENCE*   (1934, Brit.) 74m PM/UNIV bw

Marie Lorraine, Ethel Gabriel, Frank Leighton, Frank Bradley, Campbell Copelin, Arthur Greenway, Leo Franklyn, Leonard Stephen, Victor Gouriet.

Four people who lost family and friends during WW I reminisce during a nationwide two minutes of silence. An uninteresting tale which borders on documentary.

p&d, Paulette MacDonagh.;

Drama   (PR:A MPAA:NR)

TWO MINUTES TO PLAY*   (1937) 69m Victory bw

Herman Brix [Bruce Bennett] *(Martin Granville)*, Eddie Nugent *(Jack Gaines)*, Jeanne Martel *(Pat Meredith)*, Betty Compson *(Fluff Harding)*, Grady Sutton *(Hank Durkee)*, Duncan Renaldo *(Lew Ashley)*, David Sharpe *(Buzzy Vincent)*, Sammy Cohen *(Abie)*, Forrest Taylor *(Coach Rodney)*, Richard Tucker *(Gaines, Senior)*, Sam Flint *(Granville, Senior)*.

At Franklin University, another mythical movie college, Brix and Nugent are rivals in academics, on the football field, and for the affections of Martel. This is in keeping with an old family tradition, for their fathers (Tucker and Flint) continue a similar rivalry that also began in their own days at good old Franklin U. All is settled on the football field in this strictly by-the-book story backed by some pretty poor production values.

p, Sam Katzman; d, Robert Hill; w, William Buchanan; ph, William Hyer; ed, Charles Henkel.

College Drama   (PR:A MPAA:NR)

TWO MRS. CARROLLS, THE*½**   (1947) 99m WB bw

Humphrey Bogart *(Geoffrey Carroll)*, Barbara Stanwyck *(Sally Morton Carroll)*, Alexis Smith *(Cecily Latham)*, Nigel Bruce *(Dr. Tuttle)*, Isobel Elsom *(Mrs. Latham)*, Pat O'Moore *(Charles Fennington)*, Ann Carter *(Beatrice Carroll)*, Anita Bolster *(Christine)*, Barry Bernard *(Mr. Blagdon, Druggist)*, Colin Campbell *(MacGregor)*, Peter Godfrey, Creighton Hale *(Race Track Touts)*, Leyland Hodgson *(Inspector)*.

A much-underrated Bogart vehicle which casts him in the rather unlikely, and unlikable, role of a psychotic painter with a penchant for killing off his wives. After painting a portrait of his wife as an "Angel of Death," Bogart meets Stanwyck and falls in love with her. To rid himself of the matrimonial bond that keeps him from Stanwyck, Bogart slowly poisons his wife. She first becomes ill and bed-ridden, while Bogart acts the loving husband and brings her a nightly glass of warm milk laced, unknown to her, with increasingly large doses of poison. Bogart sends his daughter, Carter, away to school, during which time the wife dies and he marries Stanwyck. A couple of years later, after having painted Stanwyck as the "Angel of Death," Bogart falls in love with his new neighbor, Smith. He tries his same trick again, slowly poisoning Stanwyck with warm milk. His plan hits a snag, however, when the druggist who supplies the poison, Bernard, hits Bogart with a blackmail demand. Smith also grows anxious and pressures Bogart to run away with her. The demented artist follows his previous footsteps and sends Carter off to school once again. Carter, still emotionally scarred from her mother's death, confides in Stanwyck that the last time she went off to school she returned to find her mother dead. Stanwyck's suspicions are raised, and when she finds the two "Angel of Death" portraits, she turns to former suitor, O'Moore, for help. Receiving a gun from him, Stanwyck begins her fight to stay alive. The next time she is offered a glass of warm milk she pretends to drink it, but actually empties it out the window. Bogart discovers this, however, and is alerted to the fact that she has caught on. When he is unable to get into her locked room, he attempts entry through her bedroom window. Climbing up a tree in a blazing storm, the maniacal Bogart breaks in, dripping with water and seething with hatred. Stanwyck's attempt to draw her gun is thwarted when he wrestles it away from her. At the last second, O'Moore and the police burst into the room and save Stanwyck from becoming the second former Mrs. Carroll. Completed in June, 1945, on the heels of GASLIGHT (which starred Ingrid Bergman who beat out Stanwyck's DOUBLE INDEMNITY performance as Best Actress at the 1944 Academy Awards ceremony), THE TWO MRS. CARROLLS bore too much similarity to that film to please Warner Bros. executives. Instead, they sat on the film for nearly two years, finally releasing it in March, 1947. While unable to boast anything but average showings from its leads (Bogart's often- criticized performance is a laudible attempt to act against type) and saddled with some severely melodramatic excesses, THE TWO MRS. CARROLLS still proves an effective, and sometimes chilling, entertainment.

p, Mark Hellinger; d, Peter Godfrey; w, Thomas Job (based on the play by Martin Vale); ph, Peverell Marley; m, Franz Waxman; ed, Frederick Richards; md, Leo F. Forbstein; art d, Anton Grot; set d, Budd Friend; cos, Edith Head, Milo Anderson; spec eff, Robert Burks; makeup, Perc Westmore.

Crime/Drama   (PR:A-C MPAA:NR)

TWO MULES FOR SISTER SARA*½**   (1970) 114m
                                        UNIV-Malpaso-Sanen/UNIV c

Shirley MacLaine *(Sister Sara)*, Clint Eastwood *(Hogan)*, Manolo Fabregas *(Col. Beltran)*, Alberto Morin *(Gen. LeClaire)*, Armando Silvestre *(1st American)*, John Kelly *(2nd American)*, Enrique Lucero *(3rd American)*, David Estuardo *(Juan)*, Ada Carrasco *(Juan's Mother)*, Pancho Cordova *(Juan's Father)*, Jose Chavez *(Horacio)*, Pedro Galvan, Jose Angel Espinosa, Aurora Munoz, Xavier Marc, Hortensia Santovena, Rosa Furman, Jose Torvay, Margarito Luna, Javier Masse.

This almost makes the grade as high-quality moviemaking, but just never quite gets there. Eastwood is riding through the Mexican desert when he comes upon MacLaine, who has been stripped by three men. They are about to rape her, but the new arrival kills the evil bunch. Though initially attracted to her himself, Eastwood is surprised when he discovers MacLaine, a Juarista sympathizer, is really a nun. He agrees to take her to a revolutionaries' camp site and says if offered enough money, he just might help attack the French garrison at Chihuahua. Along the trail Eastwood gets more surprises from this lady when he sees her smoking a cigar and enjoying a snort of whiskey. As they get closer to their destination Eastwood tries to dynamite a French train loaded with ammunition. He's stopped when a Yaqui Indian hits him square in the shoulder with an arrow. MacLaine gets him drunk and removes the arrow, bandaging his wounded shoulder. She herself sets off the charge by helping him fire a bullet into the explosives. After arriving at the revolutionaries' camp, MacLaine reveals that she is actually a prostitute and has detailed knowledge of the French fort's layout. A plan is devised by the group and Eastwood takes her to the enemy stronghold. He pretends that she is his prisoner, thus gaining the confidence of the French. The gate is opened and the Mexican guerrillas rush in. A brutally violent battle takes place between the two forces. Eastwood and MacLaine grab some loot, make some love, and ride off together. Eastwood gives his usual western performance, that of an expressionless nobody from nowhere, that works time after time. His chemistry with the more lively MacLaine is good. The two make a fine team, building an odd sort of friendship over the course of the film. Eastwood later said that the sequence with her removing the arrow was some of his best work. However, the whole of the film doesn't play as well as the leads. The development is episodic, moving slowly before shifting into the high-action, ugly finish. Some of the final battle's moments contain horrible brutality; one man is hit full-face by a machete. MacLaine and director Siegel didn't get along on set and developed an eggshell working relationship. The Mexican locations proved too much for the fair-skinned redhead; a local was hired to follow MacLaine carrying a protective sun umbrella. Dysentery also infected the cast, except health-food faddist Eastwood. The film was originally scripted by Budd Boetticher, who also was to direct. However, several rewrites later he was dropped. Director Siegel and producer Rackin didn't hit it off. Rackin got final cut, but Siegel shot minimally, editing in the camera to prevent this producer's later interference. Elizabeth Taylor had originally been approached for MacLaine's part. She liked the script, and broached it to Eastwood as a possible venture. When Universal was unwilling to meet Taylor's salary-plus-percentage demands, the studio settled for MacLaine at the reported pittance of only $1 million.

p, Martin Rackin, Carroll Case; d, Don Siegel, w, Albert Maltz (based on a story by Budd Boetticher); ph, Gabriel Figueroa (Panavision, Technicolor); m, Ennio Morricone; ed, Robert F. Shugrue, Juan Jose Marino; art d, Jose Rodriguez Granada; set d, Pablo Galvan; cos, Helen Colvig, Carlos Chavez; spec eff, Frank Brendel, Leon Ortega; makeup, Frank Westmore; stunts, Buddy Van Horn.

Western   **Cas.**   **(PR:C MPAA:M/PG)**

TWO NIGHTS WITH CLEOPATRA*½
(1953, Ital.) 80m
Excelsa-Rosa/Ultra bw (DUE NOTTI CON CLEOPATRA)

Sophia Loren (Cleopatra/Nisca, Cleopatra's Double), Ettore Manni (Marc Antony), Alberto Sordi (Cesarino), Paul Muller, Alberto Talegalli, Rolf Tasna, Gianni Cavalieri, Fernando Bruno, Riccardo Garrone, Carlo Dale.

A silly bedroom romp with Loren starring as an insatiable Queen Cleopatra who must be with her Marc Anthony (Manni) before he goes off to battle. Meantime, a new guard for the queen's chambers, Sordi, has been assigned, replacing the previous guard who was executed one morning after having made love to Loren. Making love to her guards and then having them killed is an obnoxious habit of Loren's, and one of which Sordi is unaware. Loren sneaks out of the palace and, in her place, puts a slave girl as her double (also played by Loren). When Sordi sneaks into the queen's bedroom it is Loren's double that he makes love to. Much to the surprise of his fellow guards, Sordi is seen alive the next day. Before long he has saved Loren from an assassin and managed to rescue the slave girl-queen from the dungeon. Rather than risk his neck by making love to the real queen, he escapes from the palace with the double whom he loves. A ridiculous sex comedy which can only appeal to indiscriminating Italians and die-hard fans of Loren (especially since she practically bears her breasts). In most cases one Sophia Loren in a film is bad enough, but having two of her in TWO NIGHTS WITH CLEOPATRA is insufferable. The picture's coscriptwriter, Scola, in 1984 gained fame in the U.S. as the director of the unique LE BAL.

p, Carlo Ponti, Dino DeLaurentiis; d, Mario Mattoli; w, Nino Maccari 'Ruggero Maccari', Ettore Scola (Ferraniacolor, MoviebLab); ph, Karl Struss, Riccardo Pallottini; m, Armando Trovajoli.

Comedy   **(PR:C MPAA:NR)**

TWO O'CLOCK COURAGE**
(1945) 66m RKO bw

Tom Conway (The Man), Ann Rutherford (Patty), Richard Lane (Haley), Lester Matthews (Mark Evans), Roland Drew (Maitland), Emory Parnell (Brenner), Bettejane [Jane] Greer (Helen), Jean Brooks (Barbara), Edmund Glover (O'Brien), Bryant Washburn (Dilling), Phillip Morris (McCord), Nancy Marlow (Hat-Check Girl), Elaine Riley (Cigarette Girl), Jack Norton (Drunk), Guy Zanett (Headwaiter), Harold de Becker (Judson), Bob Alden (Newsboy), Chester Clute (Mr. Daniels), Almira Sessions (Mrs. Daniels), Eddie Dunn, Bob Robinson (Cops), Charles Wilson (Brant), Sarah Edwards (Mrs. Tuttle), Maxine Seamon (Maid), Chris Drake (Assistant Editor), Carl Kent (Dave Rennick).

After being knocked out, Conway suffers from amnesia. He finds himself in the middle of a murder investigation and all clues point towards him as the probable killer. Rutherford, a lady cab driver, helps him to clear his name. After he's struck by a bullet, Conway's memory miraculously returns and he is proven innocent. This remake of TWO IN THE DARK (1936) is somewhat better than the original, though even that's not saying much. It's presented in an obvious manner with strictly routine situations and dialog. All along the audience knows Conway is innocent, so it's only a matter of time for his name to be cleared. Conway and Rutherford aren't bad as a team, but it's a shame they didn't have better material.

p, Ben Stoloff; d, Anthony Mann; w, Robert E. Kent (based on the novel by Gelett Burgess); ph, Jack Mackenzie; m, Roy Webb; ed, Phillip Martin, Jr.; set d, Darrell Silvera, William Stevens; spec eff, Vernon L. Walker.

Drama   **(PR:C MPAA:NR)**

TWO OF A KIND**
(1951) 75m COL bw

Edmond O'Brien (Lefty Farrell), Lizabeth Scott (Brandy Kirby), Terry Moore (Kathy McIntyre), Alexander Knox (Vincent Mailer), Griff Barnett (William McIntyre), Robert Anderson (Todd), Virginia Brissac (Maida McIntyre), J. M. Kerrigan (Father Lanahan), Claire Carleton (Minnie Mitt), Louis Jean Heydt (Chief Petty Officer).

A wealthy couple will give anything to have their missing son back, so Scott and Knox plan a scheme to get their dough. Knox arranges for O'Brien, a carnival showman, to portray the son who had been lost at age two. Knox is confident that the ruse will fool the couple because they haven't seen their child as a grown man. Driven on by thoughts of money, O'Brien goes as far as smashing his fingers in a car door so they will match the real heir's. He moves in and starts romancing Moore, the couple's slightly daft niece. However, Barnett, the old man, decides not to change his will, meaning O'Brien won't get anything. Knox plans to kill him, but Scott and O'Brien refuse to get involved. Next, Knox tries to kill O'Brien, who in fear explains everything to Barnett. Barnett says he knew all along but kept it quiet because it brought joy to his wife to see their grown "son". Knox is finally disgraced and O'Brien ends up with Scott. This starts off with an interesting premise, but is quickly bogged down to run-of- the-mill suspense action with only a few mild thrills. The dialog is overly talky and the ending wholly unbelievable. The direction paces itself well, however, and the cast isn't bad, giving performances better than the script probably deserved.

p, William Dozier; d, Henry Levin; w, Lawrence Kimble, James Grunn (based on a story by James Edward Grant); ph, Burnett Guffey; m, George Duning; ed, Charles Nelson; md, Morris Stoloff; art d, Walter Holscher.

Suspense/Drama   **(PR:C MPAA:NR)**

TWO OF A KIND zero
(1983) 87m FOX c

John Travolta (Zack), Olivia Newton-John (Debbie), Charles Durning (Charlie), Beatrice Straight (Ruth), Scatman Crothers (Earl), Castulo Guerra (Gonzales), Oliver Reed (Beazley), Richard Bright (Stuart), Vincent Bufano (Oscar), Toni Kalem (Terri), James Stevens (Ron), Jack Kehoe (Chotiner), Ernie Hudson (Detective Staggs), Warren Robertson (Himself), Deborah Dalton (Angie), Tony Crupi (Detective Bruno), Bobby Costanzo (Capt. Cinzari), Kurek Ashley (SoHo Cop), Jill Andre (Gladys), Ann Travolta (Bank Teller), Kathy Bates (Furniture Man's Wife), John Hudkins (Guard), Sheila Frazier (Reporter), Tony Munafo (Furniture Man), Steven Hirsch (Jet Setter), Pam Bowman (Jet Setter's Date), Jacque Foti (Maitre D'), Ted Grossman (Waiter), Joe Cirillo (Cop), Christopher Loomis (Sarge), Dennis McKenzie (Detective), Michael Prince (Judge), Ric DiAngelo (Van Driver), Jerome Michaels (Customer), John Dresden (Bartender), Walter Robles (Bum), Michael Melon, Ellen Whyte, Kitty Muldoon, Michael Aronin (Students), Tammy Brewer, Deborra Hampton, Roxanne Byrd (Loose Ladies), Rochelle Kravit, Dee Griffin, Robin Adler, Phil Romano, Richard C. Adams, Donna Porter, Jeff Lawrence, Gary Woodward (Restaurant Patrons).

God is pretty angry at the human race, but four angels persuade him to give the people another chance. Hopefully, the Lord didn't stick around to watch the rest of this mess; it's pure Hell. Travolta is an inventor-turned-bank robber and Newton-John, a teller who helps pass some money. If the human race must depend on these two then we're all in big trouble. Apparently, some studio head thought the reuniting of the GREASE duo would once more strike box-office lightning. Wrong. Songs include: "Twist of Fate" (Steve Kipner, Peter Beckett), "Living in Desperate Times" (Tom Snow, Barry Alfonso), "Shakin' You" (David W. Foster, Tom Keane, Paul Goedon), "Take a Chance" (Olivia Newton-John, Steven Likather), "The Perfect One" (Boz Scaggs, Foster), "Catch 22[Two Steps Forward, Three Steps Back]- (Kipner, John. L. Parker), "It's Gonna Be Special" (Clif Magness, Glen Ballard, Foster), "Ask the Lonely" (Steve Perry, Jonathan Cain), "Prima Donna" (Peter Cetera, Mark Goldenberg).

p, Roger M. Rothstein, Joe Wizan; d&w, John Herzfeld; ph, Fred Ko-enekamp (Panavision, Deluxe Color); m, Patrick Williams; ed, Jack Hofstra; prod d, Albert Brenner; art d, Spencer Deverell; set d, Kandy Stern, Diane Wager.

Comedy   **Cas.**   **(PR:C MPAA:PG)**

TWO OF US, THE**
(1938, Brit.) 55m Gainsborough-GAU bw

Jack Hulbert (Jack Warrender), Gina Malo (Frances Wilson), J. Robertson Hare (Lionel Fitch), Athole Stewart (Huckle), Felix Aylmer (Benton), H. F. Maltby (Holman), Fewlass Llewellyn (Nicholson), Mary Jerrold (Old Lady), Peggy Simpson (Typist), C. M. Hallard (Henry Kilner), Marcus Barron (Williams), Cecil Parker (Barrington), Ian McLean (Gangster), Bruce Seton, Betty Astell (Dancers), Frederick Piper, Cyril Smith, Netta Westcott, Henry Crocker, Arnold Bell.

After poor schlep Hulbert is hired as a waiter for a fancy party, one of the more inebriated guests thinks him to be one of the wealthy. Hulbert mingles, meets rich girl Malo, and decides to live up to his new reputation. The next day, he goes to the banker (Hare) and blackmails the man into hiring him. From there it's a few career moves up the ladder before he's with the Paris branch. No one knows where he originally came from but never mind–he's one of their own now. Hulbert lives happily and is financially well off with the love of Malo to help him get through his days. There are a few good moments in this mildly entertaining comedy. However, ideas are never developed to their full potential and the whole film has taken on a rushed look. The camera work is definitely below quality standards. Hulbert works hard, however, to make his part believable. He also served as co director.

p, Michael Balcon; d, Jack Hulbert, Robert Stevenson; w, Hulbert, Austin Melford, J.O.C. Orton (based on the play "Youth at the Helm" by Paul Vulpius); ph, Charles Van Enger; m/l, "When There's You There's Me," "Top Your Tootsies."

Comedy (PR:A MPAA:NR)

TWO OF US, THE**** (1968, Fr.) 86m Valoria -P.A.C.-Renn / Cinema V bw (LE VIEIL HOMME ET L'ENFANT; AKA: CLAUDE; THE OLD MAN AND THE BOY)

Michel Simon ("Gramps" , Pepe), Alain Cohen (Claude), Luce Fabiole ("Granny" , Meme), Roger Carel (Victor), Paul Preboist (Maxime), Charles Denner (Claude's Father), Zorica Lozic (Claude's Mother), Jacqueline Rouillard (Teacher), Aline Bertrand (Raymonde), Sylvine Delannoy (Suzanne), Marco Perrin (The Priest), Elisabeth Rey (Dinou), Denise Peronne (Landlady), Didier Perret (Dinou's brother), Kinou the Dog.

The joys and sadnesses of life are given a fine, sensitive treatment in this autobiographical film from the French-Jewish Filmmaker Berri. During the Occupation, Berri was one of many Jewish children sent by his Parisian parents to live safely with a Gentile family in the French countryside. This film, an honest portrait of one such boy, was considered by Francois Truffaut to be one of the best films made about the Occupation. Cohen, in a touching and natural performance, is an 8-year-old boy sent to live with the parents of his father's Catholic friends. The old man (Simon) takes an immediate liking to the boy and tries to teach him about anti-Semitism. He doesn't realize his new friend is a Jew, so the boy plays along. A warm friendship builds up between the two with some genuinely comic moments. One of the film's best scenes has the youngster playing with Simon's prejudices, accusing the old man of being a Jew himself because of his big nose. Still, the two remain the best of friends, bound together by the trials of everyday living, the problems incurred by the war, and Simon's aging dog Kinou. The war finally ends and the boy must return to his parents, leaving the old man and his wife silently waving goodbye. Berri packs his film with a gamut of emotions. A genuine affection for a time and place that could exist only under such unusual circumstances permeates the entire film. This is an enchanting picture, perfect for the entire family.

p, Paul Cadeac; d&w, Claude Berri; w, Berri, Michel Rivelin, Gerard Brach; ph, Jean Penzer; m, Georges Delerue; ed, Sophie Coussein, Denise Charvein; art d, Georges Levy, Maurice Petri.

Drama/Comedy **Cas.** (PR:A MPAA:NR)

TWO ON A DOORSTEP* (1936, Brit.) 71m British and Dominions-PAR British bw

Kay Hammond (Jill Day), Harold French (Jimmy Blair), Anthony Hankey (Peter Day), George Mozart (George), Dorothy Dewhurst (Mrs. Beamish), Frank Tickle (Mr. Beamish), Walter Tobias (Diggle), Ted Sanders.

Mistaken for a bookie with the same last name, Hammond decides to accept some bets in order to clear her brother's debts. She nearly loses everything she owns before winning big at a greyhound track.

p, Anthony Havelock-Allan; d, Lawrence Huntington; w, Gerald Elliott, George Barraud (based on a story by Donovan Pedelty).

Comedy (PR:A MPAA:NR)

TWO ON A GUILLOTINE** (1965) 107m WB bw

Connie Stevens (Melinda Duquesne/Cassie Duquesne), Dean Jones (Val Henderson), Cesar Romero (John "Duke" Duquesne), Parley Baer ("Buzz" Sheridan), Virginia Gregg (Dolly Bast), Connie Gilchrist (Ramona Ryerdon), John Hoyt (Carl Vickers), Russell Thorson (Carmichael).

A standard haunted house thriller about a deranged magician, Romero, who became a widower after lopping his wife's head off during a magic act. His daughter, Stevens, is called to his funeral 20 years later and she learns that in order to claim her father's estate she must spend seven nights in his eerie mansion. Jones is a reporter who volunteers to stay with her (anything for a scoop). By doing so, he saves her from the same fate as her mother–at the hands of Romero, who is alive and ready for blood. Max Steiner penned his final score for this picture after 29 years of adding music to pictures.

p&d, William Conrad; w, Henry Slesar, John Kneubuhl (based on the story by Slesar); ph, Sam Leavitt (Panavision); m, Max Steiner; ed, William Ziegler; art d, Art Loel; set d, William Wallace; makeup, Gordon Bau.

Mystery (PR:C MPAA:NR)

TWO ON THE TILES (SEE: SCHOOL FOR BRIDES, 1952, Brit.)

TWO OR THREE THINGS I KNOW ABOUT HER**
(1970, Fr.) 90m Anouchka-Argos-Films du Carrosse-Parc/New Yorker c (DEUX OU TROIS CHOSES QUE JE SAIS D'ELLE)

Marina Vlady (Juliette Janson), Anny Duperey (Marianne), Roger Montsoret (Robert Janson), Jean Narboni (Roger), Christophe Bourseiller (Christophe), Marie Bourseiller (Solange), Raoul Levy (The American), Joseph Gehrard (Mons. Gerard), Helena Bielicic (Girl in Bath), Robert Chevassu (Meter-Reader), Yves Beneyton (Long Haired Youth), Jean-Pierre Laverne (Writer), Blandine Jeanson (Student), Claude Miler (Bouvard), Jean-Patrick Lebel (Pecuchet), Juliette Berto (Girl Who Talks to Robert), Anna Manga (Woman in Basement), Benjamin Rosette (Man in Basement), Helen Scott (Woman at Pinball Machine), Jean-Luc Godard (Narrator).

Made at the same time as MADE IN U.S.A. (one was shot in the mornings, the other in the evenings), TWO OR THREE THINGS is a document of modern life in Paris (the "HER" of the title), with Vlady starring as a housewife who supplements her husband's income by working as a part-time prostitute. The film is more of a barrage of words, images, and ideas (with whispering narration spoken by Godard and frequently inaudible) than a narrative film. Godard himself qualifies TWO OR THREE THINGS: "I watch myself filming, and you hear me thinking aloud. TWO OR THREE THINGS, in fact, is not a film but an essay at film, presented as such and really forming part of my own personal research. A document rather than a story." Not surprisingly, with those guidelines, TWO OR THREE THINGS (along with MADE IN U.S.A.) was to be Godard's last stab at narrative film until the 1980s, with a long stretch of political and television films in between.

p, Raoul Levy; d&w, Jean-Luc Godard (based on a letter from Catherine Vimenet which appeared in Le Nouvel Observateur); ph, Raoul Coutard (Techniscope, Eastmancolor); m, Ludwig van Beethoven (Quartet No. 16); ed, Francoise Collin, Chantal Delattre; cos, Gitt Marrini; makeup, Jackie Reynal.

Drama (PR:O MPAA:NR)

TWO PEOPLE* (1973) 100m Filmakers Group/UNIV c

Peter Fonda (Evan Bonner), Lindsay Wagner (Deirdre McCluskey), Estelle Parsons (Barbara Newman), Alan Fudge (Fitzgerald, Embassy Official), Philippe March (Gilles), Frances Sternhagen (Mrs. McCluskey), Brian Lima (Marcus McCluskey), Geoffrey Horne (Ron Kesselman).

A talky romance about a Vietnam deserter in Africa, Fonda, and the girl he falls in love with, Wagner, a West Virginia fashion model. They walk around a lot, go to Paris, walk around some more, go to New York, and all the while talk about life in general. They make love and wind up with an illegitimate son, and they eventually return to the U.S., where Fonda turns himself in. Fonda and Wagner (in her film debut) just aren't able to pull it off.

p&d, Robert Wise; w, Richard DeRoy; ph, Henri Decae, Gerald Hirschfeld (Technicolor); m, David Shire; ed, William Reynolds; art d, Henry Michelson; set d, Eric Simon; makeup, Monique Archambault.

Romance (PR:O MPAA:R)

2 + 5 MISSIONE HYDRA (SEE: STAR PILOT, 1977, Ital.)

TWO ROADS (SEE: TEXAS STAGECOACH, 1940)

TWO RODE TOGETHER½** (1961) 108m COL c

James Stewart (Guthrie McCabe), Richard Widmark (Lt. Jim Gary), Shirley Jones (Marty Purcell), Linda Cristal (Elena de la Madriaga), Andy Devine (Sgt. Darius P. Posey), John McIntire (Maj. Frazer), Paul Birch (Edward Purcell), Willis Bouchey (Mr. Harry J. Wringle), Henry Brandon (Chief Quanah Parker), Harry Carey, Jr. (Ortho Clegg), Olive Carey (Abby Frazer), Ken Curtis (Greely Clegg), Chet Douglas (Ward Corbey), Annelle Hayes (Belle Aragon), David Kent (Running Wolf), Anna Lee (Mrs. Malaprop), Jeanette Nolan (Mrs. McCandless), John Qualen (Ole Knudsen), Ford Rainey (Henry Clay), Woody Strode (Stone Calf), O.Z. Whitehead (Lt. Chase), Cliff Lyons (William McCandless), Mae Marsh (Hanna Clay), Frank Baker (Capt. Malaprop), Ruth Clifford (Woman), Ted Knight (Lt. Upton), Major Sam Harris (Post Doctor), Jack Pennick (Sergeant), Chuck Roberson (Comanche), Dan Borzage, Bill Henry, Chuck Hayward, Edward Brophy (Bits), Bob Kenneally, Ed Sweeney (Officers), Big John Hamilton (Settler).

John Ford's attempt at an adult western seems to fall between the cracks as it's too grown-up for the children's audience and much too simplistic to be deemed a psychological film. There are attempts at comedy that barely cause a smile and the picture winds up yawnable, one of Ford's very few to achieve that status. Gorgeous scenery and a fine acting job by Stewart in an unaccustomed semi-villain role don't overcome the lackluster production overseen by TV veteran Shpetner. Stewart is a corrupt sheriff in a small town where he spends most of his time seated on the verandah of the saloon run by Hayes and collecting a 10 percent tithe from any illicit goings-on in the village. Widmark approaches Stewart for some help. Some years before,

Comanche Indians kidnaped a group of whites and Widmark wants to rescue them and bring them back to their anxious families. Stewart reckons he might help but only if Widmark arranges a bounty of $500 to be paid for each hostage recovered. The promise of the fee plus the chance to flee from the matrimonially minded Hayes is enough to get Stewart off his duff and into the plains. They ride into the camp of Indian Brandon and secure the release of Kent, a white boy who has been raised as an Indian, plus Cristal, a Mexican woman who had been the forced squaw of Indian warrior Strode. Strode is not thrilled that they want to take away his woman and he gets into a battle with Stewart, who kills him. Widmark and Stewart bring the duo of Cristal and Kent back to the Army fort and none of the waiting families recognizes Kent. He is finally claimed by Nolan, a woman who is mentally incompetent. She thinks that the wild youth is her son and wants him. She unties Kent and he promptly kills her. Jones is a settler in the area who is in love with Widmark. The settlers capture Kent and string him up before Jones can let them know that the boy is her brother. None of the prissy women at the Army fort will have a thing to do with the tainted Cristal, as any woman who has lived with Indians must be a harlot in their eyes. Cristal is brokenhearted and thinks that the ways of civilization are far too uncivilized. Stewart shrugs and prepares to go back to his old job as sheriff of the small town but he learns that he's lost his position to his deputy, who now occupies the same spot on Hayes' verandah. Stewart takes Cristal's hand, understands that they are both outcasts, and the two of them ride off to find something better over the next hill as the picture goes to black. Filmed in Southwest Texas, it more than resembles Ford's THE SEARCHERS in several ways but came nowhere close to the power of the former. The picture is almost totally devoid of anything to break the despair of a mission unaccomplished. Good supporting work from a host of actors but there is a vague feeling that we've seen it before, and better.

p, Stan Shpetner; d, John Ford; w, Frank Nugent (based on the novel *Comanche Captives* by Will Cook); ph, Charles Lawton, Jr. (Eastmancolor); m, George Duning; ed, Jack Murray; art d, Robert Peterson; set d, James M. Crowe; cos, Frank Beetson; makeup, Ben Lane.

Western   (PR:C MPAA:NR)

TWO SECONDS**   (1932) 68m FN-WB bw

Edward G. Robinson (*John Allen*), Preston Foster (*Bud Clark*), Vivienne Osborne (*Shirley Day*), J. Carrol Naish (*Tony*), Guy Kibbee (*Bookie*), Frederick Burton (*Judge*), Adrienne Dare (*Annie*), Dorothea Wolbert (*Lizzie*), Edward McWade (*Doctor*), Berton Churchill (*Warden*), William Janney (*College Boy*), Lew Brice, Franklin Parker, Frederick Howard (*Reporters*), Helen Phillips (*Mrs. Smith*), June Gittleson (*Fat Girl*), Jill Dennett, Luana Walters (*Tarts*), Otto Hoffman (*Justice of the Peace*), Harry Beresford (*Doctor*), John Kelly, Matt McHugh (*Mashers*), Harry Woods (*Executioner*), Gladys Lloyd (*Woman*).

It only takes two seconds from the moment the executioner pulls the switch until the current charges into the body and kills the recipient. This movie deals with the review of a man's life in the two seconds which elapse between the moment of electrical surge and the moment when he dies. In this way, it owes more than a little to Ambrose Bierce's story "Incident at Owl Creek Bridge," which deals in the second between the instant when the trap is sprung and when the noose snaps the hanged man's neck. The picture begins when the press arrives at a prison like Sing Sing to witness the execution of Robinson, a convicted murderer, who says that he deserves to die, but not for the crime of which he has been convicted. The switch is pulled and we flash back to reveal the circumstances that brought Robinson to the hot seat. Robinson and Foster are best friends, high iron workers. Robinson is a dour man but Foster is an optimist who lives to enjoy. Foster has just won a few dollars at the races and both men had intended to go out on dates but Robinson begs off and later finds himself inside a taxi dance hall where he meets Osborne. They begin dating and one night, when Robinson is in his cups, Osborne tricks him into appearing before a justice of the peace. Foster can't believe Robinson has been sappy enough to marry Osborne, especially after he learns that she has been secretly seeing Naish, the sleazeball who owns the taxi dance hall. Foster tells Robinson the truth and Robinson responds by knocking Foster off their high perch, sending him to his death. The loss of Foster puts Robinson into a terrible depression and he can no longer work on skyscrapers. Osborne tells Robinson that she has had to borrow money from Naish for their food and rent. Robinson saves a few dollars, bets it on the races, and wins almost $400. Later, he finds Osborne with Naish, gives Naish the money they owe him, then shoots Osborne. Flash forward to the electric chair and Robinson again says that he should be dying for Foster's death but not for killing his cheating wife, Osborne. The tragic ending puts a pall on the story and Robinson is guilty of some overacting. Foster had appeared in the Broadway play from whence this sprung. It was his second film after FOLLOW THE LEADER. Slow, laborious, and unsatisfying to Robinson fans who were used to more action from the little guy when he played killers, such as in LITTLE CAESAR. Lots of holes in the story, including the marriage by justice Hoffman which has no witnesses present.

p, Hal Wallis; d, Mervyn LeRoy; w, Harvey Thew (based on the play by Elliot Lester); ph, Sol Polito; ed, Terrill Morse; md, Leo Forbstein; art d, Anton Grot.

Crime Drama   (PR:C MPAA:NR)

TWO SENORITAS   (SEE: TWO SENORITAS FROM CHICAGO, 1943)

TWO SENORITAS FROM CHICAGO*
                            (1943) 68m COL bw (GB: TWO SENORITAS)

Joan Davis (*Daisy Baker*), Jinx Falkenburg (*Gloria*), Ann Savage (*Maria*), Leslie Brooks (*Lena*), Ramsey Ames (*Louise*), Bob Haymes (*Jeff Kenyon*), Emory Parnell (*Rupert Shannon*), Douglas Leavitt (*Sam Grenman*), Muni Saroff (*Gilberto Garcia*), Max Willenz (*Armando Silva*), Stanley Brown (*Mike*), Frank Sully (*Bruiser*), Charles C. Wilson (*Chester T. Allgood*), Romaine Callender (*Miffins*), George McKay (*Gus*), Harry Strang (*Electrician*), Constance Worth (*Sob Sister*), Craig Woods, Johnny Mitchell (*Reporters*), Eddie Laughton (*Western Union Clerk*), Wilbur Mack (*Harry*), Anne Loos (*Designer*), Sam Ash (*Jack*), Harrison Greene (*Sam Gribble*).

A lifeless musical offering about Davis' script-selling scam in which she gets a play produced without even knowing who the real authors are. Falkenburg and Savage hook themselves starring roles, but when the actual authors sell the same play legitimately to another producer, a jail sentence is in order. Haymes, the producer's assistant, saves the day, however, when he comes up with a play he's written and it turns out to be a smash.

p, Frank MacDonald; d, Frank Woodruff; w, Stanley Rubin, Maurice Tombragel (based on a story by Steven Vas); ph, L. W. O'Connell; ed, Jerome Thoms; md, M. W. Stoloff; art d, Lionel Banks; cos, William Travilla; ch, Nick Castle.

Musical/Comedy   (PR:A MPAA:NR)

TWO SINNERS*½   (1935) 72m T/C/REP bw (GB: TWO BLACK
                                                           SHEEP)

Otto Kruger (*Henry Vane*), Martha Sleeper (*Elsie Summerstone*), Minna Gombell (*Mrs. Pym*), Ferdinand Munier (*Monte*), Cora Sue Collins (*Sally Pym*), Harrington Reynolds (*Ritchie*), Olaf Hytten (*French Judge*), Montague Shaw (*Mr. Grylls*), William P. Carlton (*Heggie*), Harold Entwistle (*Pateman*).

Kruger is an ex-convict who gets released after shooting a fellow who made a play for his wife. When he meets Sleeper, his life takes a change for the better, but along with her comes the boisterous little Collins, for whom she is a governess.

p, Trem Carr; d, Arthur Lubin; w, Jefferson Parker (based on the story "Two Black Sheep" by Warwick Deeping); ph, Harry Neumann; ed, Jack Ogilvie.

Drama/Romance   (PR:A MPAA:NR)

TWO SISTERS*   (1938) 79m Graphic Pictures/Foreign Cinema Arts bw

Jennie Goldstein, Muni Seroff [Serebrov], Rebecca Weintraub, Michael Rosenberg, Abraham Teitelbaum, Celia Budkin, Yudel Dubinsky, Joan Carroll, Aneta Hoffman, Sylvia Dell, Jack Wexler, Harvey Kier, Betty Jacobs, Betty Bialis, Anna Levine, Ida Adler.

Geared for Jewish audiences, TWO SISTERS is an exercise in overdramatization with Goldstein as the older sister of Dell, both of whom fall in love with Bronx doctor Seroff. While the girls' mother is on her deathbed, she begs for Goldstein to take care of the younger girl. Goldstein complies by letting her marry the doctor. (In Yiddish; English subtitles.)

d, Ben K. Blake; w, Samuel H. Cohen; ph, George F. Hinners; m, Joseph Rumshinsky; ed, Harry Foster.

Drama   (PR:A MPAA:NR)

TWO SISTERS FROM BOSTON***   (1946) 112m MGM bw

Kathryn Grayson (*Abigail Chandler*), June Allyson (*Martha Canford Chandler*), Lauritz Melchior (*Olstrom*), Jimmy Durante (*"Spike"*), Peter Lawford (*Lawrence Patterson, Jr.*), Ben Blue (*Wrigley*), Isobel Elsom (*Aunt Jennifer*), Harry Hayden (*Uncle Jonathan*), Thurston Hall (*Lawrence Patterson, Sr.*), Nella Walker (*Mrs. Lawrence Patterson, Sr.*), Gino Corrado (*Ossifish*), Jack Roth, Eddie Jackson, Ralph Sanford, Chester Clute, Dewey Robinson, Vince Barnett, Norman Leavitt, Paul "Tiny" Newlan, Byron Foulger, Jimmy Conlin, Grady Sutton, Erville Alderson, Tim Ryan.

Bostonians Grayson and Allyson pack their bags for the Big Apple and find love and music without much effort. Grayson pairs up with piano player-club owner Durante and Allyson does the same with opera sponsor Lawford. Grayson has aspirations to the Metropolitan opera, to the shame and disgruntlement of her back-bay family, including Allyson, who starts out something of a stick. The singing members of the cast deliver the following tunes: "The Fire Chief's Daughter," "There Are Two Sides to Every Girl," "Down by the Ocean," "Nellie Martin," "After the Show," "G'wan Your Mudder's Callin'" (Sammy Fain, Ralph Freed), "Hello, Hello, Hello" (Jimmy Durante), "The Prize Song" (from Wagner's opera "Die Meistersinger").

p, Joe Pasternak; d, Henry Koster; w, Myles Connolly, James O'Hanlon, Harry Crane (operatic sequences, Charles Previn, William Wymetal); ph, Robert Surtees; ed, Douglas Biggs; art d, Cedric Gibbons, Daniel B. Cathcart; ch, Jack Donohue.

Musical/Comedy   (PR:A MPAA:NR)

TWO SMART MEN* (1940, Brit.) 52m Clive/Anglo International bw

Leslie Fuller (*Jimmy*), Wally Patch (*Wally*), Margaret Yarde (*Mrs. Smith*), Pamela Bevan (*Pamela*), George Turner (*Henry Smith*).

A stale comedy which wastes the talents of funnymen Fuller and Patch. They are partners in a casting agency with is failing when they disguise themselves as butler and cook for a high society party. A designer guest at the party makes off with the host's jewels and it's up to Fuller and Patch to save the day. Unfortunately, their antics can't save the movie.

p&d, Widgey R. Newman.;

Comedy   (PR:A   MPAA:NR)

TWO SMART PEOPLE* (1946) 93M MGM bw

Lucille Ball (*Ricki Woodner*), John Hodiak (*Ace Connors*), Lloyd Nolan (*Bob Simms*), Hugo Haas (*Senor Rodriguez*), Lenore Ulric (*Senora Maria Ynez*), Elisha Cook, Jr (*Fly Felleti*), Lloyd Corrigan (*Dwight Chandwick*), Vladimir Sokoloff (*Jacques Dufour*), David Cota (*Jose*), Clarence Muse (*Porter*), George Magrill (*Taxi Driver*), Mary Emory, Maria Dodd, Helen Dickson (*Women*), Bobby Johnson (*Waiter*), Leo Mostovoy (*Headwaiter in French Restaurant*), Shelley Winters (*Princess*), Frank Johnson (*Fat Man*), Lynn Whitney (*Swedish Girl*), Erwin Kalser (*Franz*), Connie Weiler (*Hat Check Girl*), Fred Nurney (*Victoire*), Marek Windheim (*Captain*), William Riley (*Pete the Bellboy*), William Tannen (*Clerk*), Fred "Snowflake" Toones (*Redcap*), Cleo Morgan (*Cleopatra*), Peter Virgo (*Indian Attendant*), Gloria Anderson (*Grecian Girl*), Harold De Garro (*Stilt Walker*), Jimmie Magill (*Reveler*), John Piffl (*Jolly Fat Man*), Tom Quinn (*Sheik*), Gabriel Canzono (*Monkey Man*), Emil Rameau (*Riverboat Waiter*), Paul Kruger (*Cop*), Bess Flowers, Jean Andren (*Policewomen*), Lorenzo Lopez (*Gardener*), Phil Dunham (*Drunk*), Harry Depp (*Spectator*), George Calliga (*Stewart*), Margaret Jackson (*Bystander*).

Hodiak and Ball are swindlers, but Hodiak had the misfortune to be apprehended by lawman Nolan for his transgressions. With five days of freedom left him before he must serve a jail term, Hodiak switches his sins, going from larceny to gluttony. Aware that prison fare will leave much to be desired, he travels the country visiting four-star restaurants and packing away the gourmet provender they provide. He is accompanied in his quest by Ball and Nolan, each of whom is interested in ascertaining the location of the half-million dollars in loot which he has concealed in a place known only to himself. Lust replaces gluttony as Hodiak has his eye on the Ball, and both decide to marry and lead a lawful life after he has paid his debt to society. Fine comic talents are wasted through inane dialog and spotty direction and editing.

p, Ralph Wheelwright; d, Jules Dassin; w, Ethel Hill, Ralph Wheelwright, Leslie Charteris (based on a story by Allen Kenward); ph, Karl Freund; m, George Bassman; ed, Chester W. Schaeffer; art d, Cedric Gibbons, Wade Rubottom; set d, Edwin B. Willis, Keough Gleason; cos, Irene, Valles; m/l, "Dangerous," Bassman, Ralph Blane.

Drama   (PR:A   MPAA:NR)

TWO SOLITUDES* (1978, Can.) 116m Two Solitudes/Compass c

Jean-Pierre Aumont (*Tallard*), Stacy Keach (*McQueen*), Gloria Carlin (*Kathleen*), Christopher Wiggins (*Yardley*), Claude Jutra (*Beaubien*), Raymond Cloutier (*Marius*), Jean-Louis Roux (*Cardinal*).

The conflicts which arose during and after WW I in the French and English-speaking provinces of Canada are brought to the screen as town squire Aumont is finally ruined in his attempts to promote industry in his small town when his own son sides with Keach and exposes his anti-religious sentiments. Since the picture is concerned with the French-versus-English language areas, it is odd that the picture employs only the English language.

d&w, Lionel Chetwynd (based on the book by Hugh McLennan); ph, Rene Verzier; m, Maurice Jarre; ed, Ralph Brunjes.

Drama   (PR:A   MPAA:NR)

TWO SUPER COPS*½ (1978, Ital.) 115m Triton/WB-Col c (DEUX SUPER FLICS)

Terence Hill [Mario Girotti] (*Matt*), Bud Spencer [Carlo Pedersoli] (*Wilbur*), Laura Gemser (*Susy Lee*), Luciano Catenacci (*Fred*).

Hill and Spencer are a couple of struggling crooks who turn into TWO SUPER COPS when they accidentally get themselves on the side of the police. They join the force and succeed in cracking a drug case, but not without some silly spoofing. Nothing super about it, except the title. The spaghetti-western duo with anglicized names, handsome Hill and hulking Spencer, moved to dubbed voices in pictures such as ACE HIGH (1969) before coming to the U.S., where this one was filmed.

p, Salvatore Alabiso; d&w, E. B. Clucher Enzo Barboni; ph, Claudio Cirillo; m, Guido DeAngelis, Maurizio DeAngelis.

Crime/Comedy   (PR:C   MPAA:NR)

TWO TEXAS KNIGHTS (SEE: TWO GUYS FROM TEXAS, 1948)

TWO THOROUGHBREDS** (1939) 62m RKO bw

Jimmy Lydon (*David Carey*), Joan Brodel [Joan Leslie] (*Wendy Conway*), Arthur Hohl (*Thaddeus Carey*), J. M. Kerrigan (*Jack Lenihan*), Marjorie Main (*Hildegarde Carey*), Selmer Jackson (*Bill Conway*), Spencer Charters (*Doc Purdy*), Paul Fix (*Stablemaster*), Al Ferguson (*Rancher*), Bob Perry (*Henchman*), Frank Darien (*Beal, the Mailman*), Crystal Jack (*the Horse*), Rex (*the Dog*).

A pleasant tale about a farm boy, Lydon, who finds a colt wandering around and raises it as his own, much to the consternation of his stern uncle, Hohl. When he learns that it is actually one of his girl friend's father's herd, he needs her help to assure a happy ending with the animal. Joan Brodel later gained fame as Joan Leslie in such pictures as HIGH SIERRA (1941), SERGEANT YORK (1941), and YANKEE DOODLE DANDY (1943).

p, Cliff Reid; d, Jack Hively; w, Joseph A. Fields, Jerry Cady (based on a story by Fields); ph, Frank L. Redman; m, Roy Webb; ed, Theron Warth.

Drama   (PR:A   MPAA:NR)

TWO THOUSAND MANIACS! zero (1964) 88m Box Office Spectaculars c

Connie Mason (*Terry Adams*), Thomas Wood (*Tom White*), Jeffrey Allen (*Mayor Buckman*), Ben Moore (*Lester*), Shelby Livingston (*Bea Miller*), Gary Bakeman (*Rufe*), Jerome Eden (*John Miller*), Michael Korb (*David Wells*), Yvonne Gilbert (*Beverly Wells*), Mark Douglas (*Harper*), Linda Cochran (*Betsy*), Vincent Santo (*Billy*), Andy Wilson (*Policeman*), The Pleasant Valley Boys (*Themselves*).

A pair of vacationing couples are led into a townfull of maniacs (amounting to less than a hundred) thanks to some misplaced detour signs. They soon discover Pleasant Valley isn't too pleasant when they become special guests of honor for the town's centennial. Before long one girl gets hacked apart (in a deranged effort to ease the pain of her thumb), another gets a boulder dropped on her, one man is barbecued, and the last of the four is rolled down a hill in a barrel lined with razor sharp nails. After the four murders, the centennial is complete and we learn that the townsfolk are actually ghosts from the Civil War, expressing their dislike for Northerners. TWO THOUSAND MANIACS is the best of Lewis' gore trash and it still isn't worth any more than a "zero."

p, David F. Friedman; d&w, Herschell Gordon Lewis; ph, Lewis (Eastmancolor); m, Lewis (arranged by Larry Wellington, performed by the Pleasant Valley Boys); ed, Robert Sinise; prod d, Friedman; md, Chuck Scott.

Horror   **Cas.**   (PR:O   MPAA:NR)

2,000 WEEKS½** (1970, Aus.) 85m Eltham-Senior/Boxoffice-COL bw

Mark McManus (*Will Gardiner*), Jeanie Drynan (*Jacky Lewis*), Eileen Chapman (*Sarah Gardiner*), David Turnbull (*Noel Oakshot*), Michael Duffield (*Will's Father*), Stephen Dattner (*Sir George Turnbull*), Bruce Anderson (*Rex Stapleton*), Dominic Ryan (*Will as a Boy*), Nicholas McCallum (*Noel as a Boy*), Anne Charleston (*Will's Mother*).

Australian journalist McManus and his mistress Drynan nearly part ways when their relationship is threatened by a visiting friend, who informs McManus' wife of the goings-on. After some strained emotions between McManus and his pal a fight breaks out, making the journalist realize how much he loves Drynan. Occasionally interesting but it becomes chatty and pretentious.

p, Patrick Ryan, David Bilcock, Sr.; d, Tim Burstall; w, Burstall, Ryan; ph, Robin Copping; m, Don Burrows; ed, David Bilcock, Jr.; art d, Rosemary Ryan; md, Burrows; makeup, Joan Cooly.

Drama   (PR:C   MPAA:NR)

2,000 WOMEN** (1944, Brit.) 97m Gainsborough/GFD bw

Phyllis Calvert (*Freda Thompson*), Flora Robson (*Miss Manningford*), Patricia Roc (*Rosemary Brown*), Renee Houston (*Maud Wright*), Anne Crawford (*Margaret Long*), Jean Kent (*Bridie Johnson*), Reginald Purdell (*Alec Harvey*), James MacKechnie (*Jimmy Moore*), Bob Arden (*Dave Kennedy*), Carl Jaffe (*Sgt. Hentzner*), Muriel Aked (*Miss Meredith*), Kathleen Boutall (*Mrs. Hadfield*), Thora Hird (*Mrs. Burtshaw*), Dulcie Gray (*Nellie Skinner*), John Snagge (*Voice*), Hilda Campbell-Russell, Christina Forbes, Joan Ingram, Christiane de Maurin, Betty Jardine, Paul Sheridan, Dora Sevening, Walter Gotell, Wallace Bosco, William Hatton, Guy le Feuvre, Janette Scott, Anders Timberg, John England, Hazel Bray.

A WW II drama about the goings-on in a one-time spa hotel in France which has been converted by the German occupiers into a detention center for women. When three British airmen are downed on the grounds of the spa, the women prisoners conceal them from the Germans in an attic area, then help them to escape during a camp entertainment. Barring the gender-specific occurrences, a routine prisoner-of-war picture.

p, Edward Black; d, Frank Launder; w, Launder, Sidney Gilliat (based on a story by Launder, Michael Pertwee); ph, Jack Cox.

War (PR:A MPAA:NR)

2000 YEARS LATER*
(1969) 80m WB-Seven Arts c

Terry-Thomas (*Charles Goodwyn*), Edward Everett Horton (*Evermore*), Pat Harrington (*Franchot*), Lisa Seagram (*Cindy*), John Abbott (*Gregorius*), John Myhers (*Air Force General*), Tom Melody (*Senator*), Myrna Ross (*Miss Forever*), Monti Rock III (*Tomorrow's Leader*), Murray Roman (*Superdude*), Michael Christian (*The Piston Kid*), Casey Kasem (*Disc Jockey*), Bert Tenzer (*Mercury's Voice*), Rudi Gernreich (*Himself*), Milton Parsons, Buddy Lewis, Tony Gardner.

A wayward little comedy which attempts to satirize modern civilization and the hedonism it appears to promote. Abbott is a citizen of ancient Rome who is dropped into the Hollywood of the 1960s and learns that it is no place for the uninitiated. He is exploited on a popular television show about culture, turned into an excuse for a Roman marketing fad, and finally seduced by a hip girl from a TV commercial. Casey Kasem, a disk jockey, makes an appearance.

p,d&w, Bert Tenzer; ph, Mario Di Leo (Technicolor); m, Stu Phillips; ed, Donn Cambern; md, Phillips; art d, Michael Haller; set d, Harry Reif; cos, Jerry Alpert, Rudi Gernreich; makeup, Bob Dawn; m/l, Phillips, Chuck Sedacca (performed by Kin Vassy, Jay Paul Kane, The Yellow Crusaders.

Comedy (PR:O MPAA:R)

2001: A SPACE ODYSSEY***½
(1968, U.S./Brit.) 160m
Hawk-MGM/MGM c

Keir Dullea (*David Bowman*), Gary Lockwood (*Frank Poole*), William Sylvester (*Dr. Heywood Floyd*), Daniel Richter (*Moonwatcher*), Leonard Rossiter (*Smyslov*), Margaret Tyzack (*Elena*), Robert Beatty (*Halvorsen*), Sean Sullivan (*Michaels*), Frank Miller (*Mission Controller*), Alan Gifford (*Poole's Father*), Penny Brahms, Edwina Carroll (*Stewardesses*), Vivian Kubrick ("*Squirt, Dr. Floyd's Daughter*"), John Ashley (*Astronaut*), Douglas Rain (*The Voice of HAL*), Glenn Beck, Mike Lovell, Edward Bishop, Bill Weston, Ann Gillis, Heather Downham, David Hines, Jimmy Bell, Tony Jackson, David Charkham, John Jordan, Simon Davis, Scott MacKee, Jonathan Daw, Laurence Marchant, Peter Delmar, Darryl Paes, Terry Duggan, Joe Refalo, David Fleetwood, Andy Wallace, Danny Grover, Bob Wilyman, Brian Hawley, Richard Wood.

A beautiful, confounding picture that had half the audience cheering and the other half snoring. Based on a short story by Arthur C. Clarke. He and Kubrick wrote the screenplay and Kubrick spent the next three years shooting it, beginning his production in December, 1965. The story, such as it is, can be synopsized but can it be understood? For the first half hour or so, we are treated to the dialogless sight and grunts of a tribe of apes, circa 4 million years ago. Kubrick uses actors in ape suits plus a few real animals and they happily cavort as vegetarians in their prehistoric world. Then a large black monolith appears and seems to be calling to the apes. The moment they touch the ebony slab, the peaceful simians become carnivorous, territorial, and begin using the bones of their prey as weapons to keep other apes away from their small domain. A bone is tossed in the air, begins to revolve in slow motion, and the film jumps 4 million years forward to 2001. The rotating bone becomes the rotating space ship known as *Orion*. Sylvester is a scientist aboard the spaceship who is on his way to a lunar station. When he is questioned by Russian colleagues about why they have been banned from the space station, despite having an agreement with the U.S., Sylvester says he has no idea why they are not allowed. Sylvester arrives at the station and talks to several Americans and it turns out he knows full well why the Russians have been kept in the dark but he has been forbidden to speak of it to anyone other than people cleared on the highest classified level. There has been a tremendous discovery and the U.S. government fears that any leak of the "discovery" might cause a panic back on Earth. Sylvester and his compatriots use a lunar buggy to go to the site and come upon the monolith which is, as near as they can determine, 4 million years in age. They approach the edifice and it lets out an ear-piercing screech which seems to be in the direction of Jupiter. Dissolve to a year-and-a-half later as a spaceship is crossing the darkness of the sky on the way to Jupiter. Dullea and Lockwood run the ship with the help of HAL 9000, the most sophisticated computer ever devised. The voice of HAL is that of Douglas Rain, a pleasant tone but with the slightest bit of malevolence under the niceness. (Martin Balsam had originally recorded the voice but was replaced.) There are three other men in a deep freeze and neither Lockwood nor Dullea knows the real mission. HAL does know but he has been programmed not to tell them until they get there. Lockwood and Dullea take care of the minor things aboard the ship, exercise, and try to keep from going nuts as HAL runs the voyage. The computer is not supposed to ever tell a lie or make an error, so they take it as Gospel when HAL says there is a malfunction in the spaceship's antenna. They plan to go outside and do an on-site check. On Earth, the men at Mission Control report that HAL is wrong and that it is impossible for such a thing to have happened. Lockwood and Dullea wonder now about the efficacy of their on-board computer. Lockwood goes outside the spaceship and HAL arranges to have the life line cut. Lockwood is floating in space and Dullea attempts to rescue him but fails. At the same time, HAL shuts off the units that are keeping

the deep-frozen astronauts alive. Dullea tries to get back on board but is being stopped by the machinations of HAL and he finally gets back on the ship by manually overriding the computer. Once on board, Dullea cuts off the electrical system that keeps HAL going and now learns about the slab found on the moon. The ship approaches Jupiter and Dullea sees a slab go past his ship. The next sequence has Dullea in a light show as he is in a vast array of many-colored oceans and seas and skies and explosions, none of which he can fathom and all of which were sheer delight to the drug-laden viewers who thought this movie was a message from Heaven. Next thing he knows, he is in a bedroom circa 1700 and he discovers an old man, himself at 100 years old. Dullea is both characters and they have an enigmatic conversation, then a monolith appears in the room and moves toward the bed. Finally, an embryo that looks vaguely like Dullea is seen floating toward Earth as the film concludes. Kubrick was delighted by the confusion the movie caused and maintained that he deliberately kept questions unanswered because he wanted to pique the curiosity of audiences. Made at a cost of only $10.5 million, it began to build slowly but eventually took in almost $15 million in North America, then about half that upon re-release in the slightly shorter version (141 minutes) in 1972. Clarke's short story was first made into a novel, then into the screenplay that MGM financed for $6 million. The budget kept rising and the studio toppers feared a disaster. They didn't reckon with Kubrick's vision. The rebirth of Dullea at the film's end has been thought to signify the next leap forward of humankind but that is still open for discussion. Understandably, the movie won the Oscar for Best Special Effects in 1968. It also took the BFA Awards for Best Cinematography, Best Sound, and Best Art Direction. Made at Boreham Wood's British Studios in England, it featured many classical tunes as the background score. They include Aram Khatchaturian's "Gayane Ballet Suite" (played by the Leningrad Symphony Orchestra, conducted by Gennadi Rozhdestvensky), Richard Strauss' "Thus Spake Zarathustra" (played by the Berlin Symphony Orchestra, conducted by Karl Boehm), Johann Strauss' "Blue Danube Waltz" (played by the Berlin Symphony, conducted by Herbert von Karajan), Gyorgy Ligeti's "Atmospheres"(played by the Southwest German Radio Orchestra, conducted Ernst Baur), Ligeti's "Lux Aeterna" (played by the Stuttgardt State Orchestra, conducted by Clytus Gottwald), and Ligeti's "Requiem for Soprano, Mezzo-Soprano, Two Mixed Choirs and Orchestra" (played by the Bavarian Radio Orchestra, conducted by Francis Travis). Lots of jokes in the movie that include Woody Allen-like jibes at Howard Johnson's, Hilton Hotels, and others. It continues to annoy and delight audiences, years later, and the real meaning of the picture cannot be explained to anyone's liking. Kubrick has only given the merest inklings of what he intended in his interviews and prefers allowing viewers to read whatever they like into the movie. For sheer spectacle, it may be unsurpassed. As an example of storytelling, it stays as dark and deep as the monolith which is the focal point for the story. The casting of Lockwood, Dullea, and Sylvester, three undynamic actors (in these roles), must have been deliberate, as Kubrick didn't want anything in the way of his vision, whatever that was. Some have said that it broke new ground by creating a new film language. We think that a bit more story would have helped, or at least a translation of this new language that Kubrick invented. Followed by a sequel in 1984, 2010.

p&d, Stanley Kubrick; w, Kubrick, Arthur C. Clarke (based on the short story "The Sentinel" by Clarke); ph, Geoffrey Unsworth, John Alcott (Super Panavision, Cinerama, Technicolor, Metrocolor); ed, Ray Lovejoy; prod d, Tony Masters, Harry Lange, Ernest Archer; art d, John Hoesli; cos, Hardy Amies; spec eff, Kubrick, Wally Veevers, Douglas Trumbull, Con Pederson, Tom Howard, Colin J. Cantwell, Bryan Loftus, Frederick Martin, Bruce Logan, David Osborne, John Jack Malick; makeup, Stuart Freeborn; scientific consultant, Frederick I. Ordway III.

Science Fiction Cas. (PR:A MPAA:NR)

TWO TICKETS TO BROADWAY***
(1951) 106m RKO c

Tony Martin (*Dan Carter*), Janet Leigh (*Nancy Peterson*), Gloria De Haven (*Hannah Holbrook*), Eddie Bracken (*Lew Conway*), Ann Miller (*Joyce Campbell*), Barbara Lawrence (*S.F. "Foxy" Rogers*), Bob Crosby (*Himself*), The Charlivels (*Acrobatic Specialty*), Joe Smith (*Harry*), Charles Dale (*Leo*), Taylor Holmes (*Willard Glendon*), Buddy Baer (*Sailor*), Frieda Stoll (*Wardrobe Woman*), Fred L. Gillett (*Bus Driver*), Norval Mitchell (*Mr. Peterson*), Helen Spring (*Mrs. Peterson*), John Gallaudet (*McGiven*), Isabel Randolph (*Housekeeper*), Donald MacBride (*Bus Terminal Guard*), John Sheehan (*Desk Clerk*), Don Blackman (*Porter*), Vera Miles, Jean Corbett, Helen Hayden Claudette Thornton, Hazel Shaw, Barbara Logan, Charlotte Alpert, Victoria Lynn, Jeane Dyer, Pat Hall, Maura Donatt (*Chorus Girls*), Joi Lansing (*Redhead*), Mara Corday, Joan Evans, June McCall, Joan Olander, Noreen Mortensen, Joel Robinson, Georgia Clancy, Elizabeth Burgess, Barbara Thatcher, Carol Brewster, Shirley Buchanan, Mildred Carroll, Carmelita Eskew, Joanne Frank, Mary Ellen Gleason, Joan Jordan, Lola Kendrick, Shirley Kimball, Evelyn Lovequist, Kathleen O'Malley, June Paul, Marylin Symons, Beverly Thomas, Joan Whitney, Barbara Worthington (*Showgirls*), George Nader, Lester Dorr, Garry Owen (*Men*), Linda Williams (*Brunette*), Ann Zika (*Blonde*), Libby Taylor (*Maid*), Herman Cantor, Jimmy Dundee (*Doormen*), Millicent Deming (*Receptionist*), Jerry Hausner (*Agent*), Jack Gargan (*Dispatcher*), Jane Easton, Shirley Tegge, Martha O'Brian, Lucy Knoch, Rosalee Calvert, Joan Shawlee, Joan Barton, Shirley Whitney, Marilyn Johnson, Gwen Caldwell, Barbara

Freking, Mona Knox, Rosemary Knighton, Kathy Case, Eileen Coghlan, Marie Thomas *(Girls)*, Billy Curtis *(Midget)*, Mike Lally, Bennett Green *(Men with Tuxes)*, Larry Barton *(Waiter)*, Gene Banks *(Usher)*, Vincent Graeff *(Cheerleader)*, Maxine Willis, Joann Arnold *(Secretaries)*, Ann Melton, Ann Kramer *(Women in Evening Gowns)*, Marg Pemberton *(Woman Hotel Guest)*, Ann Kimball *(Western Union Girl)*, Anne O'Neal, Charlete Hardy *(Women)*, Lillian West *(Old Lady)*, Sid Tomack *(Bus Driver)*, Tony Felice, Marty Rhiel, Buris De Jong, Gene Marshall *(Ad-lib Men)*, Marie Allison *(Ad-lib Woman)*, Miles Shepard, Bob Thom *(Cops)*, Ralph Hodges, Michael Pierce *(Hot Rod Passengers)*, Suzanne Ames *(Beautiful Girl)*.

Old-fashioned but fun vehicle with loads of songs, a bit of comedy, and a story that was hirsute when Aristophanes was a youth. Leigh is a small-town girl who is leaving her family and friends to make it in New York. She climbs on a bus, waves farewell, and immediately meets Lawrence, De Haven, and Miller, a femme trio on its way to New York after having bombed with their act on a showboat. Martin is a singer on the bus and Bracken is the trio's flip agent, a man who is as incompetent as the average congressman and twice as dishonest. Martin is disgusted with show business and wants to find some honest profession. His luggage is inadvertently confused with Leigh's and when he returns it to Leigh, they fall in love, as only movie leads can. Bracken has told the trio that he has a spot for them on the TV show hosted by Crosby. But if they are going to appear on national TV, they have to get new clothes and Bracken hustles Smith and Dale, the men who own the local deli, into laying out a few bucks. Bracken is lying and not only can't get the girls on the show, he can't even get past the security guards at the studio. Leigh has joined the other three and they are deep into rehearsal. Since they believe the nonsense that Bracken has been telling them, Leigh notifies her hometown paper that she will soon be lighting up their cathode tubes. Bracken is stuck for an idea so he hires Holmes, a failed actor, to play the role of Crosby's manager. There's a benefit coming up and Bracken hopes that the girls' act will be such a success there that Crosby will hear about it and give them their big chance. When the plot is uncovered, Leigh is disgusted and, thinking that Martin has been part of the plan, she decides to give up her dreams of a show business career and go home to the burg from whence she came. Martin adores Leigh and doesn't want her to leave, so he manages to get past all of Crosby's minions and convinces the bandleader to see the girls. Crosby takes Martin's word for the talent of the quartet but Leigh has already left. The show will be going on "live" and Martin has to race after Leigh's bus, get it to stop, and turn around and bring her back to the studio where the other three are waiting. Baer, a huge sailor, helps Martin achieve that and Leigh gets to the studio just as the show is about to go on. The picture ends with everyone performing and delighting the studio audience. Famed vaudevillians Smith and Dale (who were the inspiration for THE SUNSHINE BOYS) do well in their small roles and viewers with sharp eyes will note bit parts being played by Vera Miles, George Nader, Joan Shawlee, and Joi Lansing, among others. An expensive movie that lost more than $1 million, it had inventive choreography by Busby Berkeley and a host of tunes from various writers which included: "Let the Worry Bird Worry for You" (Jule Styne, Leo Robin, performed by Lawrence, DeHaven, Miller), "Pagliacci" (Leoncavallo, sung by Tony Martin), "There's No Tomorrow" (Leon Carr, Al Hoffman, Leo Corday, sung by Martin), "Manhattan" (Richard Rodgers, Lorenz Hart, sung by Martin), "Big Chief Hole in the Ground" (Styne, Robin, performed by Miller, Lawrence, De Haven). Other tunes by Styne and Robin were "The Closer You Are," "Baby, You'll Never Be Sorry," "Pelican Falls High," "It Began in Yucatan," and "Are You a Beautiful Dream?" Sammy Cahn and Bob Crosby wrote "Let's Make Comparisons" (sung by Crosby and his BobCats), Howard Hughes was thought to be the producer but he was really the presenter as Jerry Wald and Norman Krasna did most of the work. An example of Hughes' excesses is that he was located at Goldwyn on Santa Monica Boulevard and Formosa while the film was being shot on Melrose Avenue at Gower, a distance of a few miles. Rather than drive, Hughes had the sets dismantled at RKO and rebuilt at Goldwyn where he could look at and approve them. Once that was done, he ordered the sets brought back to the Melrose lot. Good fun in the Kanter-Silvers script although the film was an idea that had come and gone and Hughes must thought it was coming back again. Lively but, in the final analysis, empty. Sound recordist John O. Aalberg was Oscar-nominated.

p, Howard Hughes, (uncredited) Jerry Wald, Norman Krasna; d, James V. Kern; w, Sid Silvers, Hal Kanter (based on a story by Sammy Cahn); ph, Edward Cronjager, Harry J. Wild (Technicolor); m, Walter Scharf; ed, Harry Marker; art d, Albert S. D'Agostino, Carroll Clark; set d, Darrell Silvera, Harley Miller; cos, Michael Woulfe; ch, Busby Berkeley; makeup, Mel Berns.

Musical Comedy   **(PR:A   MPAA:NR)**

TWO TICKETS TO LONDON**   (1943) 77m UNIV bw

Michele Morgan *(Jeanne)*, Alan Curtis *(Dan Driscoll)*, C. Aubrey Smith *(Fairchild)*, Barry Fitzgerald *(Capt. MacCardle)*, Tarquin Olivier *(Roddy)*, Mary Gordon *(Mrs. Tinkle)*, Robert Warwick *(Ormsby)*, Matthew Boulton *(Brighton)*, Oscar O'Shea *(Mr. Tinkle)*, Doris Lloyd *(Emmie)*, Holmes Herbert *(Kilgallen)*, Stanley Logan *(Nettleton)*, Lester Matthews *(Treathcote)*, Harold de Becker *(Benson)*, John Burton *(Royce)*, Mary Forbes *(Dame Dunne Hartley)*, Dooley Wilson *(Accordionist)*, Shirley Collier *(Little Girl)*, Colin Kenny *(Gordon)*.

A standard programmer which has had its story told hundreds of times. It is about a Navy man charged with treason after he reportedly had signaled to a German submarine while in convoy. He is innocent of all charges and sets off for London to convince the authorities of the truth. He takes beautiful Morgan, a showgirl, along and they fall in love while being pursued. He is captured, put to trial, and exonerated for the final clinch with Morgan.

p&d, Edwin L. Marin; w, Tom Reed (based on a story by Roy William Neill); ph, Milton Krasner; ed, Milton Carruth; cos, Vera West; m/l, "You Are My Sunshine," Jimmie Davis, Charles Mitchell (sung by Dooley Wilson), "Lead, Kindly Light" (sung by Wilson).

Drama   **(PR:A   MPAA:NR)**

TWO TICKETS TO PARIS*   (1962) 90m COL bw

Joey Dee *(Joey)*, Gary Crosby *(Gary)*, Kay Medford *(Aggie)*, Jeri Lynne Fraser *(Piper)*, Lisa James *(Coco)*, Charles Nelson Reilly *(Claypoole)*, Richard Dickens *(Tony)*, Nina Paige *(Dumb Blonde)*, Sal Lombardo *(Marmaduke)*, Jeri Archer *(Mrs. Patten)*, Michele Moinet *(Le Claire)*, Jay Burton *(Charles)*, The Starliters.

Inept movie with a fun bunch of musical acts, TWO TICKETS TO PARIS served mainly as a vehicle for Joey Dee and the Starliters, who had become the twistingest group of musicians since Chubby Checker. The scant story line has Dee and Fraser on board the *SS France* en route to Paris, but both end up with other mates. Film was shot in New York City and on the docked *SS France*. Dee and his group perform: "C'est Si Bon" (Jerry Sielen, Henry Betti), "Willy Willy," "This Boat," "Twistin' on a Liner," "Everytime" (Henry Glover, Joey Dee, Morris Levy), "Open Sea," "Left Bank Blues" (Glover, Dee, Levy). Other tunes include: "Instant Man" (Hal Hackady, Don Gohman), "Teenage Vamp" (Albert Seigal), "Baby Won't You Please Come Home" (Charles Warfield, Clarence Williams), "The Lady Wants to Twist" (Jerry Leiber, Mike Stoller), "C'est La Vie" (Edward R. White, Mack Wolfson), "Swingin' Shepherd Blues" (Rhoda Roberts, Kenny Jacobson, Moe Koffman), "What Kind of Love Is This?" (Johnny Nash).

p, Harry Romm; d, Greg Garrison; w, Hal Hackady; ph, William O. Steiner, Sr.; m, Henry Glover; ed, Ralph Rosenblum; art d, Albert Brenner; cos, Natalie Walker; makeup, Robert Jiras.

Musical   **(PR:A   MPAA:NR)**

TWO TIMES TWO (SEE: START THE REVOLUTION WITHOUT ME, 1970)

TWO VOICES*½   (1966) 80m Film-Makers Cooperative bw (DEUX VOIX)

Elektrah Lobel *(Her)*, John Heuer *(Him)*, Finnegan *(A Cat)*.

A pretentious New York independent picture about a woman who spends a considerable amount of time in her apartment alone, except for her cat. She makes a visit to a nearby playground one day and meets a man. After a number of rendezvous at her apartment the woman decides that she prefers the company of the cat. In order to assure the film's "artsiness" the filmmaker gave the picture a French-language title.

p&d, Rosalind A. Stevenson; m, Steve McCord.

Drama   **(PR:C   MPAA:NR)**

TWO-WAY STRETCH***½   (1961, Brit.) 87m Shepperton-Vale-John Harvel- BL/International-Show Corporation of America bw

Peter Sellers *(Dodger Lane)*, Wilfrid Hyde-White *(Rev. Basil "Soapy" Fowler)*, David Lodge *(Jelly Knight)*, Bernard Cribbins *(Lennie Price)*, Maurice Denham *(Comdr. Horatio Bennet, Prison Governor)*, Lionel Jeffries *(Sidney Crout)*, Irene Handl *(Mrs. Price)*, Liz Fraser *(Ethel)*, George Woodbridge *(Warder Jenkins)*, Cyril Chamberlain *(Warder George)*, Edwin Brown *(Warder Charlie)*, John Glyn-Jones *(The Lawyer)*, Beryl Reid *(Miss Pringle)*, Noel Hood *(Miss Meakin)*, Myrette Morven *(Miss Prescott)*, Thorley Walters *(Col. Arkwright)*, Walter Hudd *(Rev. Butterworth)*, Olga Dickie *(Woman in Pub)*, Joe Gibbons *(Dustman)*, John Wood *(Captain)*, Robert James *(Police Superintendent)*, Warren Mitchell *(Tailor)*, Ian Wilson *(Milkman)*, Eynon Evans *(Solicitor)*, Wallas Eaton *(Night Warder)*, Larry Taylor *(Warder at Rockhampton)*, Andrew Downie *(Warder in Prison Garden)*, William Abney *(Visiting Room Warder)*, John Vivyan *(Little Prisoner)*, Mario Fabrizi *(Jones)*, John Harvey.

A very funny British prison comedy that owes a bit to the 1938 film CONVICT 99 which also dealt with a lax jail. Sellers, Lodge, and Cribbins are inmates at what must be the happiest prison in all of England. Denham is the jail's warden and treats the men as though they were guests. The cells are like Holiday Inn rooms, newspapers are delivered daily with fresh milk, and the men are treated to a multitude of classes to improve their lives once they are released. Hyde-White fakes his way into the jail by masquerading as a vicar visiting inmates. He proposes a plan for the trio: a daring robbery that they can pull off quickly and be back in jail, with a perfect alibi, before anyone is the wiser. The crime involves a visiting Eastern potentate who is weighed against a bucketful of jewels (the Aga Khan actually did this regularly) on his birthday. The robbery is meticulously planned and the crooks have a way to leave, do the job, and get back. Just as they are to break out, Denham is replaced by Jeffries, a man who has other thoughts about criminals and who thinks all of them should be clapped in irons and flogged regularly. Now that the clamp is down, leaving the jail is more difficult but Hyde-White manages to get them out of jail in a police vehicle. With Fraser, Sellers' girl friend, and Handl, Cribbins' mother, to help, they successfully steal the jewels. Now the question is where to keep such a fortune? The best place is in the safe of the warden so they bring the diamonds into jail and hide them there. On the following day, Sellers, Cribbins, and Lodge receive their walking papers from jail, nab the diamonds, and stroll out. Through the usual stroke of fate, Sellers makes a mistake on the train bringing them back to town and the diamonds are discovered. Hyde-White is spotted by the vigilant Jeffries who sees through his clerical collar and Church of England ways and sees that he is arrested. Later, Sellers, Cribbins, and Lodge are seen at the weighing in ceremony for the potentate and eye the recovered jewels and we can see that their nefarious plans for untold riches are still in order. Lots of slapstick, some adult dialog, and fast-moving direction by Day make this a most entertaining film which doesn't slow up for an instant. Director Day's career has been up and down. Some of his "ups" include THE GREEN MAN, and CALL ME GENIUS. His "downs" are several ordinary "Tarzan" movies. He is married to actress Dorothy Provine (THE GREAT RACE, THAT DARN CAT, WHO'S MINDING THE MINI? etc). TWO-WAY STRETCH was filmed in London, at Aldershot, Maidstone, Windsor, and Pirbright and was tentatively titled "Nothing Barred" until they came up with the final name. It may have been the inspiration for a British TV series about prison called "Porridge," which was later unsuccessfully adapted to U.S. TV for a short run as "On the Rocks."

p, E.M. Smedley-Aston; d, Robert Day; w, John Warren, Len Heath, Alan Hackney (based on a story by Warren, Heath); ph, Geoffrey Faithfull; m, Ken Jones; ed, Bert Rule; md, Jones; art d, John Bos; set d, Roy Rossotti; makeup, Jimmy Evans.

Comedy   Cas.   (PR:A-C MPAA:NR)

TWO WEEKS IN SEPTEMBER*½   (1967, Fr./Brit.) 95m Francos-Les Films du Quadrangle-Films Pomereu-Kenwood/PAR c (A COEUR JOIE)

Brigitte Bardot (Cecile), Laurent Terzieff (Vincent), Jean Rochefort (Philippe), James Robertson Justice (McClintock), Michael Sarne (Dickinson), Georgina Ward (Patricia), Carole Lebel (Monique), Annie Nicholas (Chantal), Murray Head (Dickinson's Assistant).

A hopeless Bardot vehicle which appropriately has its star cast as a fashion model. She takes a trip to London, leaving her lover behind in Paris. Just about every man who sees her falls for her, but it's Terzieff, a persistent geologist, who charms her off her feet. They go to Scotland and make love in a castle, deciding to part by the story's finale. The film's failure is no one's fault but Bardot's, who personally chose the story and the director, neither of which were worth much. As usual, murmurs of romance surrounded the set with Bardot jilting one lover for a new husband just weeks before the shoot and reportedly carrying on with Sarne, who is cast as a cliched photograph er.

p, Francis Cosne, Kenneth Harper; d, Serge Bourguignon; w, Vahe Katcha, Pascal Jardin, Bourguignon; ph, Edmond Sechan (Franscope, Eastmancolor); m, Michael Magne; ed, Jean Ravel; art d, Rino Mondellini; cos, Tanine Autre; makeup, Odette Berroyer; English adaptation, Sean Graham.

Romance   (PR:O MPAA:NR)

TWO WEEKS OFF*   (1929) 88m FN bw

Dorothy Mackaill (Kitty Weaver), Jack Mulhall (Dave Pickett), Gertrude Astor (Agnes), Jimmie Finlayson (Pa Weaver), Jed Prouty (Harry), Eddie Gribbon (Sid Winters), Dixie Gay (Maizie Loomis), Gertrude Messinger (Tessie McCann).

A talky talkie which only has dialog for about 20 of its 88 minutes. It's basically the story of a home town plumber who poses as a film star and meets Mackaill while on a two-week vacation. She falls for his scam until a lifeguard, also interested in her, blows the plumber's cover.

d, William Beaudine; w, F. McGrew Willis, Joseph Poland; Richard Well (based on a story by Kenyon Nicholson, Thomas Barrows); ph, Sid Hickox; ed, Ralph Holt; m/l, "Love Thrills," Al Bryan, George W. Meyer.

Comedy   (PR:A MPAA:NR)

TWO WEEKS TO LIVE*   (1943) 76m RKO bw

Chester Lauck (Lum), Norris Goff (Abner), Franklin Pangborn (Mr. Pinkney), Kay Linaker (Mrs. Carmen), Irving Bacon (Gimpel), Herbert Rawlinson (Stark, Sr.), Ivan Simpson (Prof. Frisby), Rosemary LaPlanche (Nurse), Danny Duncan (Postman), Evalyn Knapp (Secretary), Charles Middleton (Kelton), Luis Alberni (Van Dyke), Jack Rice (Hotel Clerk), Tim Ryan (Higgens), Oscar O'Shea (Squire Skimp), Edward Earle (Doctor).

Lauck and Goff continue as Lum and Abner in TWO WEEKS TO LIVE, which sends the homey boys to Chicago to claim a railroad they've been

willed. They have to come up with a hefty sum of cash before it's theirs, however, sending Goff off on a number of zany expeditions to raise the bills. He learns that he's terminally ill (hence the title) and agrees to be sent to Mars in a rocket. (See LUM AND ABNER series, Index.)

p, Ben Hersh; d, Malcolm St. Clair; w, Michael L. Simmons, Roswell Rogers; ph, Jack MacKenzie; ed, Duncan Mansfield; md, Lud Gluskin; art d, F. Paul Sylos.

Comedy   Cas.   (PR:A MPAA:NR)

TWO WEEKS WITH LOVE½**   (1950) 92m Metro c

Jane Powell (Patti Robinson), Ricardo Montalban (Demi Armendez), Louis Calhern (Horatio Robinson), Ann Harding (Katherine Robinson), Phyllis Kirk (Valerie Stresemann), Carleton Carpenter (Billy Finley), Debbie Reynolds (Melba Robinson), Clinton Sundberg (Mr. Finlay), Gary Gray (McCormick Robinson), Tommy Rettig (Ricky Robinson), Charles Smith (Eddie Gavin).

Though not yet a major star, Debbie Reynolds stole the show in this entertaining comedy about a family that heads for the Catskills on a two-week vacation. Reynolds and older sis Powell fall for a couple of fellows, but find themselves falling somewhere between girlhood and womanhood. Powell goes for Montalban and even has a bizarre dream about home which equates her desires to wear a corset with her love for her man. Reynolds is a charmer as she makes a play for Carpenter. Two years previous to this picture, Reynolds was being crowned "Miss Burbank"; in two more years she would be dancing and SINGING IN THE RAIN. Songs: "Aba Daba Honeymoon" (Arthur Fields, Walter Donovan), "The Oceana Roll" (Roger Lewis, Lucien Denni), "A Heart That's Free" (Thomas T. Railey, Alfred G. Robyn), "By the Light of the Silvery Moon" (Gus Edwards, Edward Madden), "My Hero" (Stanislau Stange, Oscar Straus), "Row Row Row" (William Jerome, James V. Monaco), "That's How I Need You" (Joe McCarthy, Joe Goodwin), "Beautiful Lady (Ivan Caryll, C.H.S. McClellan).

p, Jack Cummings; d, Roy Rowland; w, John Larkin, Dorothy Kingsley (based on a story by Larkin); ph, Alfred Gilks; ed, Irvine Warburton; md, Georgie Stoll; art d, Cedric Gibbons, Preston Ames; set d, Edwin B. Willis, Richard A. Pefferle; cos, Helen Rose, Walter Plunkett; spec eff, Warren Newcombe; ch, Busby Berkeley; makeup, William Tuttle.

Musical   (PR:A MPAA:NR)

TWO WHITE ARMS   (SEE: WIVES BEWARE, 1933, Brit.)

TWO WHO DARED**   (1937, Brit.) 78m GN bw (GB: A WOMAN ALONE)

Anna Sten (Maria), Henry Wilcoxon (Capt. Nicolai Ilyinski), Viola Keats (Olga Ilyinski), John Garrick (Yakov Sharialev), Romilly Lunge (Lt. Tuzenbach), Esme Percy (General), Francis L. Sullivan (Prosecutor), Guy Middleton (Alioshka), Peter Gawthorne (President Of Court Martial), Frank Atkinson (Porter), Minnie Rayner (Lousha), Pat Noonan (Sergeant), Ballets de Leon Woizikovski.

The closeups of Anna Sten are the best thing about this average tale set in Russia at the turn of the century. She plays a peasant girl who loses her officer beau to the socially prominent Keats, and ends up with a private, Garrick. Eventually, however, the triangle flares and strained emotions turn bitter. Sten was married to Frenke, this picture's director.

p, Robert Garrett, Otto Klement; d, Eugene Frenke; w, Leo Lania, Warren Chetham Strode (based on the story "Woman Alone" by Fedor Oztep); ph, Jack Cox; ed, Winifred Cooper.

Romance   (PR:A MPAA:NR)

TWO WISE MAIDS**   (1937) 70m REP bw

Alison Skipworth (Agatha Stanton), Polly Moran (Prudence Matthews), Hope Manning (Ellen), Donald Cook (Bruce), Jackie Searl (Elliott), Lila Lee (Ethel Harriman), Luis Alberni (Guili), Maxie Rosenbloom (Champ), Marcia Mae Jones (Jerry), Harry Burns (Zackorackus), Clarence Wilson (Twitchell), Selmer Jackson (MacIntyre), John Hamilton (Wentworth), Teresa Conover (Mrs. Braxton), Raymond Brown (Pierpont), James C. Morton (Sgt. Abbot), Stanley Blystone (Butch).

An adequate programmer which drives home the importance of reading, writing, and arithmetic, with Skipworth and Moran cast as a tough old pair of schoolteachers. A little romance is tossed into the school halls when young principal Cook falls for substitute teacher Manning. A pleasant little slice of Americana.

p, Nat Levine; d, Phil Rosen; w, Sam Ornitz (based on the story by Endre Bohem); ph, Ernest Miller; ed, Ernest Nims; cos, Eloise.

Drama   (PR:A MPAA:NR)

TWO WIVES AT ONE WEDDING** (1961, Brit.) 66m Danziger/PAR bw

Gordon Jackson (*Tom*), Christina Gregg (*Janet*), Lisa Daniely (*Annette*), Andre Maranne (*Paul*), Humphrey Lestocq (*Mark*), Viola Keats (*Mrs. Ervine*), Douglas Ives (*Jessop*), John Serret (*Larouche*).

Jackson is a respected doctor who marries socialite Gregg, but soon receives blackmail threats from Daniely, a French girl who claims she married him years earlier. His past in the underground movement surfaces and nearly ruins his life. An intriguing premise which suffers from some unbelievable plot twists and turns.

p, Brian Taylor; d, Montgomery Tully; w, Brian Clemens, Eldon Howard.

Crime (PR:A MPAA:NR)

TWO WOMEN**½ (1940, Fr.) 97m Paragon bw (L'EMPREINTE DU DIEU)

Pierre Blanchar (*Van Bergen*), Annie Ducaux (*Wilfrida*), Blanchette Brunoy (*Karelina*), Jacques Dumesnil (*Gomar*), Pierre Larquey (*Mosselmann*), Ginette Leclerc (*Fanny*).

The two women of the title are Ducaux, the wife of Blanchar, and Brunoy, the wife of the wicked Dumesnil. Brunoy flees to Ducaux's home after a battle with her husband, only to have it revealed that she had a child by Blanchar. This news sends Dumesnil into a rage which results in the death of his wife's former lover. Able direction, fine performances, and beautiful location photography are all pluses. (In French; English subtitles.)

p, E. Zama; d, Leonid Moguy; w, Charles Spaak (based on the novel *L'Empreinte Du Dieu* by Maxence van der Meersch); ph, Otto Heller; English titles, Julian Leigh.

Drama (PR:A MPAA:NR)

TWO WOMEN**** (1961, Ital./Fr.) 105m C.C. Champion-Les Films Marceau- Cocinor-S.G.C./EM bw (LA CIOCIARA)

Sophia Loren (*Cesira*), Jean-Paul Belmondo (*Michele*), Eleonor Brown (*Rosetta*), Raf Vallone (*Giovanni*), Renato Salvatori (*Florindo*), Carlo Ninchi (*Michele's Father*), Andrea Checchi (*Fascist*), Pupella Maggio, Emma Baron, Bruna Cealti, Mario Frera, Luciana Coltellesi, Toni Calio, Elsa Mancini, Luigi Terribile, Antonio Gastaldi, Antonella De La Porta, Franco Balducci, Curt Lowens, Remo Galavotti, Giuseppina Ruggeri, Luciano Igozzi, Carolina Carbonare.

Sophia Loren's finest hour was in this Italian picture which brought her an Oscar. It was the first time an Oscar had been awarded to an actress who spoke anything other than English in a film. The screenplay by De Sica and Zavattini was a marvel of neorealism that felt more like a documentary than a scripted feature. It's 1943 in Italy and Loren is a recent widow. She's living in the town of San Lorenzo and the Allies are bombing the area so she leaves her tiny grocery store in the hands of her occasional boy friend, Vallone, and departs the suburb of Rome in order to return to her home village, which is a distance away. Traveling with her teenage daughter, Brown, they walk, train, and ride mules as the skies are filled with fighters and bombers that pock the landscape with their deadly loads. Finally arriving at her tiny town, the mother and daughter move into an unmarked house that serves as a meeting place for the citizenry. There they meet Belmondo, an intellectual whose father is a farmer in the area. Brown's young heart flutters at the sight of Belmondo but he finds himself falling for Loren. The town is barraged by the Allies and food and shelter are becoming but memories for many of the people. Some Germans who had occupied the town are about to leave and force Belmondo to guide them through the woods to safety in Austria. Loren and Brown depart the cottage and seek shelter in a bombed-out church. Some invading Morroccan soldiers, part of the Allied forces, jump on the mother and daughter and both are brutally raped. Brown is numbed into shock. Loren takes her daughter into her arms and tries to bring the youngster back to reality. They leave the area to return to Rome and are given a lift by a sympathetic truck driver, Salvatori, who has them bed down at his home to rest and restore their sanity. When Loren gets up from sleep, she is stunned to see that Brown is missing. Later, Brown returns home after a night of carousing with Salvatori during which she has given herself to him for the price of a pair of nylon stockings. The little girl is no longer a girl, she is now a woman. Loren is hurt terribly and feels that her relationship with Brown is no longer. Then Loren tells Brown that the man they both loved, Belmondo, has been killed and the two women are united in their grief and fall into each others' arms, seeking solace in the mother-daughter bond. The rape scene is brutal and unforgettable and the close-up of Brown's face as the men attack her is frozen in the memory of anyone who has ever seen it. Loren also won the Best Actress Award at Cannes; at Cork, Ireland; and at the British Film Academy. Formerly known as a sexpot and little more, Loren proved with this film that she was a mature actress who could hold an audience with her talent. Originally conceived as a vehicle for Anna Magnani (with Loren as the daughter), Magnani rebelled against the thought of playing Loren's mother and backed off, even though George Cukor had been spoken of to direct. As good as Magnani can be, it's hard to imagine that any actress might have given a finer performance than Loren in this role. The movie was later re-issued in a dubbed-into-English version and captivated millions more. Loren's final

scene, as she tries to get through to Brown, is a treasure and should be included in any reel of great performances by actresses. This was another of Joe Levine's terrific acquisitions for a pittance that he turned into gold at the box office when he presented it stateside. (In Italian; English subtitles.)

p, Carlo Ponti; d, Vittorio De Sica; w, Cesare Zavattini, De Sica (based on the novel by Alberto Moravia); ph, Gabor Pogany, Mario Capriotti (Cinema-Scope); m, Armando Trovajoli; ed, Adriana Novelli; art d, Gastone Medin; set d, Elio Costanzi; cos, Costanzi; makeup, Giuseppe Annunziata.

Drama (PR:C-O MPAA:NR)

TWO WORLD** (1930, Brit.) 74m Wardour/BIP bw (ZWEI WELTEN)

Norah Baring (*Esther Goldscheider*), John Longden (*Lt. Stanistaus von Zaminsky*), Donald Calthrop (*Mendel*), Randle Ayrton (*Simon Goldscheider*), Constance Carpenter (*Mizzi*), C.M. Hallard (*Col. von Zaminsky*), Jack Trevor (*Capt. Stanislaus*), Andrews Englemann (*Lieutenant*), Gus Sharland (*Major*), Boris Ranevsky (*Ensign*), Georges Marakoff (*Colonel*), John Harlow (*Corporal*), Teddy Hill, Meinhard Juenger, Mirjam Elias, John McMahon, John St. John.

Another visually arresting but slow-moving drama from E.A. Dupont, the director of the classic silent VARIETY. An Austrian officer is wounded when his troops pull out of an occupied town. A young woman, the daughter of a Jewish clockmaker, finds the officer and brings him back to the house, ignoring the protests of her father. The Austrian is not welcome because he is responsible for the death of the clockmaker's son, as well as the imprisonment of the old man. The clockmaker attempts to notify the Russian troops of where the Austrian is hiding, but the message gets intercepted by the officer's father, who forbids the boy to remain in the house. The romance which had begun to bud between the two youngsters is nipped and each are returned to their own worlds.

p&d, E.A. Dupont; w, Miles Malleson, Norbert Falk, Franz Schulz (based on the story by Dupont, Thekla von Bodo); ph, Charles Rosher, Mutz Greenbaum; ed, Emile de Rulle; art d, Alfred Junge.

War Drama (PR:A MPAA:NR)

TWO WORLDS OF CHARLY GORDON, THE (SEE: CHARLY, 1968)

TWO YANKS IN TRINIDAD** (1942) 84m COL bw

Pat O'Brien (*Tim Reardon*), Brian Donlevy (*Vince Barrows*), Janet Blair (*Patricia Dare*), Roger Clark (*James W. Buckingham III*), Donald MacBride (*Sgt. Valentine*), John Emery (*Chicago Hagen*), Frank Jenks (*Joe Scavenger*), Frank Sully (*Mike Paradise*), Veda Ann Borg (*Bubbles*), Clyde Fillmore (*Col. Powers*), Dick Curtis (*Sea Captain*), Sig Arno (*Maitre d'*), Dewey Robinson (*Tony*), George Allen, John Daheim, Dave Harper, Duke Taylor, Earl Bunn, William "Bing" Conley (*Seamen*), Al Hill, Bud Geary (*Bartenders*), Ralph Peters (*Sentry*), William "Billy" Newell (*Taxi Driver*), Julius Tannen (*Doctor*).

A fine cast makes this standard wartime programmer watchable as O'Brien and Donlevy play a couple of hoods who have a falling out. Donlevy joins the Army to escape O'Brien's hoods, only to be followed all the way to Trinidad by O'Brien. The friendship is reaffirmed, however, when they bring in a Nazi spy. Rollicking fun in several parts, as hood Donlevy continually disregards Army discipline.

p, Samuel Bischoff; d, Gregory Ratoff; w, Sy Bartlett, Richard Carroll, Harry Segall, Jack Henley (based on the story by Bartlett); ph, Phillip Tannura; ed, Viola Lawrence; cos, William Travilla; m/1, "Trinidad," Sammy Cahn, Saul Chaplin.

War/Comedy (PR:A MPAA:NR)

TWO YEARS BEFORE THE MAST***½ (1946) 98m PAR bw

Alan Ladd (*Charles Stewart*), Brian Donlevy (*Richard Henry Dana*), William Bendix (*Amazeen*), Barry Fitzgerald (*Dooley*), Howard da Silva (*Capt. Francis Thompson*), Esther Fernandez (*Maria Dominguez*), Albert Dekker (*Brown*), Luis Van Rooten (*Foster*), Darryl Hickman (*Sam Hooper*), Roman Bohnen (*Macklin*), Ray Collins (*Mr. Gordon Stewart*), Theodore Newton (*Hayes*), Tom Powers (*Bellamer*), James Burke (*Carrick*), Frank Faylen (*Hansen*), Duncan Renaldo (*Mexican Captain*), Kathleen Lockhart (*Mrs. Gordon Stewart*), Rosa Rey (*Mercedes, Maria's Maid*), Pedro deCordoba (*Don Sebastian*), Ethan Laidlaw (*Clark, Sailor*), Robert F. Kortman (*Bobson, Sailor*), John Roy, Bink Hedberg, George Bruggeman, Clint Dorrington, Carl Voss, John "Blackie" Whiteford, Mike Lally, Joe Palma, Dave Kashner (*Sailors*), Rex Lease (*Rider*), Barry Macollum (*Chief Clerk*), Edwin Stanley (*Blake*), Crane Whitley (*Broker*), George M. Carleton (*Hallet*), Arthur Loft (*Crabtree*), Pierre Watkin (*Staunton*), James Flavin (*Crimp with Amazeen*), David Clyde (*Butler*), Stanley Andrews (*Policeman*).

Ladd is the spoiled son of a shipowner who, while drinking in a waterfront dive in Boston one evening, finds himself the victim of Bendix and his gang and wakes up shanghaied, on board the *Pilgrim* bound for the California coast and back. Conditions on the ship are appalling, and the captain, da Silva, drives the men ruthlessly in quest of a record time on his voyage. Da

Silva had earlier been drummed out of the Navy for cruelty to his men and his manners have improved none since. Men are flogged for the slightest offense, with first mate Bendix working as the captain's enforcer. Ladd develops an ally in the person of Donlevy, whose brother died on one of da Silva's voyages and who is gathering material to write a book on the horrid conditions seamen are forced to endure. They reach California and pick up a passenger, the beautiul Fernandez. The men want to go ashore to gather fresh fruit and water, but da Silva wants to get back underway immediately. On the return voyage, scurvy breaks out among the crew and mutinous thoughts spread. Pushed beyond all endurance, Ladd steals two guns and tries to take over the ship, but he is quickly subdued by Bendix and put in irons. Eventually, da Silva goes too far and even Bendix turns against him. Without hesitation, da Silva kills his first mate. Now the crew rises up en masse and kills the tormentor. They argue for taking the ship to China, but Ladd and Donlevy persuade them to sail back to Boston to face the charges. The trial causes a sensation, and the controversy eventually comes up before Congress, which, thanks also to the book Donlevy has written, passes legislation guaranteeing the rights of men on the high seas. A depressing and dark film that conveys effectively the oppressive conditions endured by sailors of the period. Ladd is better than usual as the spoiled young man who grows in character as he suffers under the lash. Donlevy is intelligent and concerned and more believable than such a character should be. Fitzgerald is effective as the cook with a sinister streak, but it is da Silva, as the tyrannical Captain Thompson, who steals the picture. His bearing of formality and discipline masks a sadist. Though the filming went smoothly, the same cannot be said of the cast's stomachs. The ship set was built in four pieces, all of them on hydraulic lifts that could recreate the rolling motion of a ship on the ocean. Da Silva recalled later that most of the cast came down with seasickness even though they were inside a Hollywood sound stage. Shot in 1944, the film was held up for two years for an assortment of reasons before finally emerging in 1946, to excellent reviews and a healthy return at the box office.

p, Seton I. Miller; d, John Farrow; w, Miller, George Bruce (based on the novel by Richard Henry Dana, Jr.); ph, Ernest Laszlo; m, Victor Young; ed, Eda Warren; art d, Hans Dreier, Franz Bachelin; spec eff, Gordon Jennings, J.D. Jennings.

Drama						**(PR:C MPAA:NR)**

TWO YEARS HOLIDAY	(SEE: STOLEN DIRIGIBLE, THE, 1966, CZCH.)

TWONKY, THE*						(1953) 72m UA bw

Hans Conried (*Kerry*), Billy Lynn (*Coach Trout*), Gloria Blondell (*Eloise*), Janet Warren (*Caroline*), Ed Max (*Ed*), Al Jarvis (*Mailman*), Norman Field (*Doctor*), Trilby Conried (*Baby*), William Phipps (*Student*), Steve Roberts (*Government Agent*), Florence Ravenel (*Nurse*).

An anti-television picture produced, directed, and written by a radio producer, Oboler, whose dislike for the medium is clearly presented. The execution, however, verges toward silliness as philosophy professor Conried's TV set begins to live. It walks around, tells Conried what he should and shouldn't eat, hypnotizes anyone who tries to stop it, and does the housework. In short, the tube takes over his life. But before long Conried fights back and destroys the set. As capricious as it sounds, Oboler deadens if with seriousness, resulting in nothing more than a drawn-out sermon.

p,d&w, Arch Oboler; w, (based on the story written by Lewis Padget [Henry Kuttner]; ph, Joseph Biroc; m, Jack Meskin; ed, Betty Steinberg.

Science-Fiction						**(PR:A MPAA:NR)**

TWO'S COMPANY**	(1939, Brit.) 64m British and Dominions/Times bw

Ned Sparks (*Al*), Henry Holman (*B.G. Madison*), Olive Blakeney (*Mrs. Madison*), Mary Brian (*Julia Madison*), Gibb McLaughlin (*Toombs*), Morton Selten (*Earl of Warke*), Patric Knowles (*Lord Jerry Wendover*), Gordon Harker (*Muggridge*), Syd Crossley (*Ives*), H.F. Maltby (*Otto Stump*), Robb Wilton (*Mr. Muddlecombe, J.P.*), Robert Nainby (*Assistant J.P.*).

The gap between the British and Americans is closed in this entertaining but familiar comedy which has the daughter (Brian) of a millionaire American businessman (Holman) falling in love with the son (Knowles) of a stodgy earl (Selten). Of course the fathers oppose the relationship but by the finale everything is cleared up and Sparks walks away with honors as the irascible lawyer of Holman who shoots barbs of dark wit at all and sundry.

p, Paul Soskin; d, Tim Whelan; w, Tom Geraghty, Roland Pertwee, J.B. Morton, Tim Whelan, John Paddy Carstairs (based on the novel *Romeo and Julia* by Sidney Horler); ph, F.A. Young.

Comedy/Romance						**(PR:A MPAA:NR)**

TYCOON**						(1947) 128m RKO bw

John Wayne (*Johnny Munroe*), Laraine Day (*Maura Alexander*), Sir Cedric Hardwicke (*Frederick Alexander*), Judith Anderson (*Miss Braithwaite*), James Gleason (*Pop Mathews*), Anthony Quinn (*Enrique "Ricky" Vargas*),

Grant Withers (*Fog Harris*), Paul Fix (*Joe*), Fernando Alvarado (*Chico*), Michael Harvey (*Curly Messenger*), Harry Woods (*Holden*), Charles Trowbridge (*Senor Tobar*), Martin Garralaga (*Chavez*), Sam Lufkin, Wayne McCoy, Frank Leyva, Joe Dominguez, Tom Coffey, John Eberts, Sheila Raven, Diane Stewart, Clarise Murphy, Fred Aldrich, Brick Sullivan, Jane Adrian, Rudolph Medina, Al Murphy, Trevor Bardette, Argentina Brunetti, Max Wagner, Lucio Villegas, Blanca Vischer, Nacho Galindo, Eduardo Noriega.

Overlong and boring, TYCOON features Wayne as an engineer hired to build a railroad in the Andes Mountains for Hardwicke, a wealthy American with mining interests in the area. At one point there is a river where Wayne wants to build a bridge. Hardwicke wants Wayne to tunnel through a mountain, a shorter but more dangerous way to complete the railroad. Wayne finally gives in, causing friction between the two. After a night of heavy drinking Wayne spies Day and follows her to church. Despite a severe hangover he continues eyeing her, which intrigues the cloistered Day. Wayne hires some musicians to serenade Day and can no longer resist his attentions. She invites him home where Wayne unhappily learns Day is Hardwicke's daughter. His employer orders Wayne never to see her again. The two meet in secret with the help of Anderson, Day's duenna, and Day's cousin Quinn. Wayne and Day go for a ride in his Jjeep but end up getting lost and running out of gas in some ancient Inca ruins. After spending the night there, Wayne decides to try a little romance. He starts to kiss Day but is thwarted by the unexpected intrusion of Hardwicke, who has been searching for his missing daughter. The lovers marry despite Hardwicke's disapproval and Day moves in with Wayne at the construction camp. Wayne has little time for his bride, becoming more involved with the problems of constructing the tunnel. Hardwicke adds to the trouble by deliberately withholding much-needed materials. After the tunnel collapses on a worker friend, Wayne, angered at himself for compromising with Hardwicke, blows up what's left of the tunnel and proceeds to finish with his original plans. Promising to complete the line on schedule within the original budget, Wayne cuts back on safety measures. This causes most of the crew to leave. Day leaves as well, going back to her father. A new crew is hired but a torrential rain threatens them. After the new men leave Wayne tries to finish the work by himself despite the danger. The old crew returns to help Wayne in completing the job. After testing the bridge, Wayne and Hardwicke realize that their personal differences can be overcome. Hardwicke finally approves of Day's marriage and finds romance himself as he marries Anderson. Though Wayne gives a valiant try, he simply can't rise above the weaknesses within the film. The story is unbelievable, padded with superficial characters and ridiculous plot twists. The ending requires the suspension of disbelief normally required for films such as THE WIZARD OF OZ. Day is barely competent as the love interest, slogging through her part without giving it much life. The writer and director tried, to inject an epic feel but the film plays for what it is: an overblown melodrama. The studio sank $3,209,000 into this turkey and ended up losing $1,035,000. Quinn, sick of playing Latin characters in film after film, went directly to the Broadway stage after finishing his minor role here. At the time, Day was married to baseball personality Leo Durocher, a man known for his explosive temper. Durocher grew jealous whenever Wayne played a love scene opposite Day. He became a regular fixture around the set, firing angry stares in the Duke's direction. This, along with the ballplayer's nasty remarks, forced Wayne to take some severeaction. He demanded a closed set, the only time in his career Wayne made such a request. This unusual move by the normally genial Wayne was approved and the love scenes were filmed without further interruption by the jealous shortstop.

p, Stephen Ames; d, Richard Wallace; w, Borden Chase, John Twist (based on the novel by C. E. Scoggins); ph, Harry J. Wild, W. Howard Greene (Technicolor); m, Leigh Harline; ed, Frank Doyle; md, C. Bakaleinikoff; art d, Albert S. D'Agostino, Carroll Clark; spec eff, Vernon L. Walker.

Drama			**Cas.**			**(PR:A MPAA:NR)**

TYPHOON**½						(1940) 70m PAR c

Dorothy Lamour (*Dea*), Robert Preston (*Johnny Porter*), Lynne Overman (*Skipper Joe*), J. Carroll Naish (*Mekaike*), Chief Thundercloud (*Kehi*), Frank Reicher (*Doctor*), John Rogers (*Barkeep*), Paul Harvey (*Dea's Father*), Norma Nelson (*Dea as a Child*), Jack Carson (*Mate*), Al Kikume (*Cook*), Angelo Cruz, Paul Singh (*Kehi's Bodyguards*).

Sarong girl Lamour is seen in living color in this adventure as the lone inhabitant of a remote island in the tropics. Preston is a hard-drinking ex-Navy man who gets hooked up as a submarine navigator for pearl diver Overman. When natives attack their sub, Preston is rescued by Lamour and brought back to her tree-top island hut (every man's dream come true). Overman finds himself under pressure from an island official and tries to escape by setting a fire. A roaring typhoon, however, comes along and dampens his plans, bringing Lamour and Preston even closer together. The quality is raised somewhat by the frolicking of an intelligent chimp and some admirable usage of miniatures.

p, Anthony Veiller; d, Louis King; w, Allen Rivkin (based on the story by Steve Fisher); ph, William C. Mellor (Technicolor); m, Frederick Hollander; ed, Alma Macrorie; art d, Hans Dreier, John Goodman; spec eff, Gordon Jennings; m/l, "Palms of Paradise," Frederick Hollander, Frank Loesser (sung by Dorothy Lamour).

Adventure/Romance   (PR:A   MPAA:NR)

TYPHOON TREASURE*   (1939, Brit.) 68m COM/Ace bw

Campbell Copelin (Alan Richards), Gwen Munro (Jean Roberts), Joe Valli (Scotty McLeod), Douglas Herald (Buck Thompson), Kenneth Brampton (Alfred Webb), Norman French (Patrol Officer), Utah (The Native).

A technically shabby adventure with a jungle backdrop that has a couple of good guys trying to beat a couple of bad guys to a lost treasure. Hampering their efforts are a typhoon, natives, and a crocodile. It's all formula footage, with some underwater photography the only things of interest.

p, R.L. Wilkinson; d, Noel Monkman; w, John P. McLeod (based on the story by Monkman); ph, George Malcolm, Harry Malcolm, A.B. Cummings.

Adventure   (PR:A   MPAA:NR)

TYRANT OF SYRACUSE, THE

(SEE: DAMON AND PYTHIAS, 1962)

TYRANT OF THE SEA**   (1950) 70M COL bw

Rhys Williams (Capt. William Blake), Ron Randell (Eric Hawkins), Valentine Perkins (Betsy Blake), Doris Lloyd (Elizabeth Blake), Lester Matthews (Lord Horatio Nelson), Harry Cording (Sampson Edwards), Terry Kilburn (Dick Savage), Maurice Marsac (Phillipe Domer), William Fawcett (Shawn O'Donnell), Ross Elliott (Howard Palmer), Don Harvey (John Moriarity), James Fairfax (Oliver Sibley).

Williams is a rough 'n' ready sea captain who runs his ship with dictatorial authority and is the only person who can stop Napoleon's forces from invading England. He does so buy steering his men into a battle with a French vessel and engaging in some swift-handed swordplay.

p, Sam Katzman; d, Lew Landers; w, Robert Libott, Frank Burt; ph, Ira H. Morgan; ed, Edwin Bryant; md, Mischa Bakaleinikoff; art d, Paul Palmentola.

War/Adventure   (PR:A   MPAA:NR)

TYSTNADEN   (SEE: SILENCE, THE, 1964, Swed.)

U

U KRUTOGO YARA   (SEE: SHE-WOLF, THE, 1963, USSR)

U.S.S. TEAKETTLE   (SEE: YOU'RE IN THE NAVY NOW, 1951)

U-BOAT PRISONER*   (1944) 65m COL bw

Bruce Bennett (*Archie Gibbs*), Erik Rolf (*Kapitan Ganz*), John Abbott (*Alfonse Lamont*), John Wengraf (*Rudehoff*), Robert Williams (*Comdr. Bristol*), Kenneth MacDonald (*Clyde Hamilton*), Erwin Kalser (*Biencawicz*), Egon Brecher (*Sigo van Der Brek*), Frederick Gierman (*First Officer Kerck*), Arno Frey (*Hagemann*), Sven-Hugo Borg (*Dorner*), Nelson Leigh (*Lt. Hagen*), Fred Graff (*Lt. Blake*), Trevor Bardette (*Comdr. Prentiss*), Paul Conrad (*Lt. Nolan*), Eric Feldary (*Braustig*).

Based on the story of a former merchant seaman, this wartime tale is awfully tough to swallow. Bennett is cast as a Yankee seaman who single-handedly knocks out a German sub by posing as a Nazi. He gets on board during a rescue operation completely undetected, renders everyone helpess with some flying fists, and then allows a U.S. destroyer to sink the sub. He shows a touch of humanity, however, by rescuing the crew from certain death. The only people who would believe this story are the same ones who think the Third Reich never fell.

p, Wallace MacDonald; d, Lew Landers; w, Aubrey Wisberg (based on a story by Archie Gibbs); ph, Burnett Guffey; ed, Paul Borofsky; art d, Lionel Banks, Perry Smith.

War   (PR:A   MPAA:NR)

U-BOAT 29*   (1939, Brit.) 77m Harefield/COL bw (GB: THE SPY IN BLACK)

Conrad Veidt (*Capt. Hardt*), Valerie Hobson (*Joan the Schoolmistress*), Sebastian Shaw (*Comdr. Davis Blacklock*), Marius Goring (*Lt. Schuster*), June Duprez (*Anne Burnett*), Athole Stewart (*Rev. Hector Matthews*), Agnes Lauchlan (*Mrs. Matthews*), Helen Haye (*Mrs. Sedley*), Cyril Raymond (*Rev. John Harris*), Hay Petrie (*Chief Engineer*), Grant Sutherland (*Bob Bratt*), Robert Rendel (*Admiral*), Mary Morris (*Chauffeuse*), George Summers (*Capt. Ratter*), Margaret Moffatt (*Kate*), Kenneth Warrington (*Comdr. Dennis*), Torin Thatcher (*Submarine Officer*), Bernard Miles (*Hans, Hotel Clerk*), Esma Cannon, Skelton Knaggs.

A good spy picture with a couple of fine performances and some unexpected twists. Veidt is a German submarine commander during WW I. He is cruising off England when he gets word that he is to proceed forthwith to the northern Orkney Islands (which are part of Scotland), where he is to meet a woman who will give him further instructions. The bleak Orkneys (where author George Orwell lived for years until his death) never looked starker as Veidt arrives and meets Hobson, a schoolteacher in the employ of the Kaiser. She is with a traitorous British naval officer, Shaw, and the two of them tell Veidt that there are 15 ships in and around the area that Veidt is to sink. Veidt is not so sure these people are legitimate and when he learns that they are triple agents (British agents pretending to be German agents pretending to be British patriots), he must now make his getaway aboard a channel ship which is transporting some German prisoners. Veidt releases them and takes command of the craft, piloting it to the location of his U-boat, hoping to keep it from carrying out its misguided mission. The U-boat crew, thinking themselves under attack, fire on the vessel, sinking it; the German submersible is itself then sunk by British torpedoes. Veidt is sensational in one of the many German roles he played (most notably in CASABLANCA). He often essayed Nazis and the oddity there was that he was forced to leave his native Germany because he was happily married to a Jewish wife. Veidt had great success in England and became a citizen there in 1939, then came to the U.S. in 1940 to make eight films before his death at the age of only 50 in 1943. The other two men who will be most recalled for their gauleiter roles are Otto Preminger and Erich von Stroheim, both of whom were Jewish. Powell and Pressburger went on to applause in later years with THE RED SHOES, STAIRWAY TO HEAVEN, BLACK NARCISSUS, and many others. They must have liked Goring's work as they gave him the role of the male lead opposite Moira Shearer in THE RED SHOES.

p, Irving Asher; d, Michael Powell; w, Emeric Pressburger, Roland Pertwee (based on the novel *The Spy In Black* by J. Storer Clouston); ph, Bernard Browne; m, Miklos Rozsa; ed, William Hornbeck, Hugh Stewart; prod d, Vincent Korda; md, Muir Mathieson; art d, Frederick Pusey.

War/Spy Drama   (PR:A   MPAA:NR)

UCCELLACCI E UCCELLINI
          (SEE: HAWKS AND THE SPARROWS, THE, 1967, Ital.)

UCCIDERO UN UOMO (SEE: THIS MAN MUST DIE, 1970, Ital./Fr.)

UCHUJIN TOKYO NI ARAWARU
          (SEE: MYSTERIOUS SATELLITE, THE, 1956, Jap.)

UFO   (SEE: UNIDENTIFIED FLYING ODDBALL, 1979, Brit.)

UFO: TARGET EARTH*   (1974) 80m Centrum International c

Nick Plakias, Cynthia Cline, Phil Erickson.

Horrible science fiction story about an alien flying saucer at the bottom of a lake and the attempts of a scientist to recover it. Unintended laughs abound in the tiny budget feature.

p&d, Michael A. de Gaetano.

Science Fiction   (PR:A   MPAA:G)

U-47 LT. COMMANDER PRIEN*½   (1967, Ger.) 91m Arca/United
          Film Enterprises bw (U-47–KAPITANLEUTNANT PRIEN)

Dieter Eppler (*Gunther Prien*), Sabina Sesselmann (*His Wife*), Joachim Fuchsberger (*1st Lieutenant*), Dieter Borsche (*Preacher*), Joachim Mock (*Kaleu Schopf*), Richard Haussler (*German U-Boat Fleet Commander*), Harald Juhnke, Ute Hallant, Olga Tschechowa, Ernst Reinhold, Raidar Muller, Mathias Fuchs, Rolf Mobius, Michael Cramer, Peter Carsten, Heinz Engelmann, Rolf Weih.

The WW II experiences of a German U-boat commander, Gunther Prien (Eppler), are brought to the screen as he becomes a hero for an attack on a Scottish bay which resulted in the destruction of a battleship and the safe retreat of his submarine. The British soon retaliate, however, and his U-boat is eventually sunk. He is taken prisoner on a ship by the English but is again sunk, this time by another German submarine, which, in turn, is sunk by a British airplane. Far more sinkings than dramatic moments. First released in Germany in 1958.

d, Harald Reinl; w, Joachim Bartsch (based on a story by Udo Wolter about the war experiences of Gunther Prien); ph, Ernst W. Kalinke; m, Norbert Schultze; art d, Erich Kettelhut, Hans Auffenberg; makeup, Ludwig Ziegler.

War   (PR:A   MPAA:NR)

UGETSU***   (1954, Jap.) 96m Daiei/Edward Harrison bw (AKA:
          UGETSU MONOGATARI)

Machiko Kyo (*Lady Wakasa*), Masayuki Mori (*Genjuro, Pottery Maker*), Kinuyo Tanaka (*Miyagi, Genjuro's Wife*), Sakae Ozawa (*Tobei, Genjuro's Brother-in-Law*), Mitsuko Mito (*Ohama, Tobei's Wife*), Sugisaku Aoyama (*Old Priest*), Ryosuke Kagawa (*Village Chief*), Kichijiro Tsuchida (*Silk Merchant*), Mitsusaburo Ramon (*Captain of Tamba Soldiers*), Ichisaburo Sawamura (*Genichi*), Kikue Mori (*Ukan*), Syozo Nanbu (*Shinto Priest*).

This lyrical and enchanting tale is considered by many to be one of the greatest Japanese masterpieces. The setting is 16th-century Japan, during a period of intense warfare that spreads throughout the land. Mori and Ozawa are two brothers, peasant potters who dream of success and glory, Mori as a rich man and his brother a samurai. After an initial taste of the money that is to be made through the sale of pottery, the two devote themselves day and night to producing pottery to sell at market, almost killing themselves in the process. Setting out with both their wives they head for the big city in the hope of reaching their goals. Because the fighting seems too dangerous, Mori leaves his wife and child behind while the others go on ahead. Man and wife are never to meet again, for the woman is killed by rampaging soldiers. Mori is taken in by a beautiful woman of noble birth, who in reality is a ghost able to supply the potter with any material desire, keeping him inside a beautiful estate far from the sorrows caused by war. With the first sign of money, the other brother runs off to buy a sword and a samurai outfit in order to become part of the army. Though at first treated as a buffoon by the soldiers, he witnesses the slaying of a great fighter and claims to have been the one responsible for the death. This gives him the chance to become a soldier. His wife, abandoned and left to fend for herself, is raped by soldiers and forced to seek a living as a prostitute. Mito comes upon her while vainly bragging about his exploits in a brothel, unaware that his wife is one of the employees. After their experiences, both brothers head back home to continue with the meager, but fulfilling forms of labor they had before their journey. Mori managed to escape the spell of the ghost through the aid of a priest, his own wife now a ghost, looking over him and his child as they toil away at the potter's wheel. The combination of fantastic elements and realistic ones make UGETSU a complicated story for Western audiences. This is especially true because ghosts and legends are dealt with in a manner that does not break up the normal endeavors of the peasants. Though many sub-themes can be found beneath this simple tale, ones that strongly parallel the plight of Japan after World War II, the real beauty of this film lies in the magnificent, almost painterly images, and the subtle combination of sound and picture. The soundtrack is filled with background noises that produce a particularly eerie atmosphere, which lends itself to Mizoguchi's flair for allowing the environment to dominate his film and take control of the story.

p, Masaichi Nagata; d, Kenji Mizoguchi; w, Matsutaro Kawaguchi, Yoshikata Yoda (based on two classic tales by Akinari Ueda); ph, Kazuo Miyagawa; m, Fumio Hayasaka, Ichiro Saito; ed, Mitsuji Miyata; art d, Kisaku Ito; cos, Kusune Kainosho; ch, Kinshichi Kodera.

Drama/Fantasy   **Cas.**   **(PR:A MPAA:NR)**

UGLY AMERICAN, THE**½   (1963) 120m UNIV c

Marlon Brando *(Harrison Carter MacWhite)*, Eiji Okada *(Deong)*, Sandra Church *(Marion MacWhite)*, Pat Hingle *(Homer Atkins)*, Arthur Hill *(Grainger)*, Jocelyn Brando *(Emma Atkins)*, Kukrit Pramoj *(Prime Minister Kwen Sai)*, Judson Pratt *(Joe Bing)*, Reiko Sato *(Rachani)*, George Shibata *(Munsang)*, Judson Laire *(Sen. Brenner)*, Philip Ober *(Sears)*, Yee Tak Yip *(Sawad)*, Stefan Schnabel *(Andrei Krupitzyn)*, Pock Rock Ann *(Col. Chee)*, Carl Benton Reid, Simon Scott, Frances Helm, James Yagi, John Day, Leon Lontoc, Bill Stout.

An admirable attempt at illuminating the public about the Vietnam situation through a movie. It was too talky and so sincere that audiences minded being lectured and would rather have been entertained. Heavy going despite Marlon Brando's complex performance. The mythical country of Sarkhan resembles Vietnam by more than a passing glance. Brando is the new ambassador from the U.S. He's received the appointment above the disgruntlement of many senators. A newspaperman by trade, Brando has enjoyed a long relationship with Okada, who is a revolutionary in Sarkhan, and the U.S. is hoping that their friendship will help ameliorate the troubles in the small land. When Brando arrives with wife Church and assistant Hill, the ceremonial welcome soon becomes a riot by the people who protest the U.S. involvement. Okada is busily courting the Red leaders in the country in an attempt to bind the wounds that separate them. Brando visits Okada and his wife Sato and their affection for each other is soon shattered when Okada lets it be known that he opposes Brando's idea for a project which he sincerely feels will aid the Sarkhanese. It's a highway to be called "The Freedom Road," but Okada thinks Brando is being used by his government in his passion for the road and that it is little more than something which will only benefit the puppet dictatorship overseen by Pramoj, the leader of the small country. Brando will not be deterred and the road is now in the first stages of construction. He goes to see the chief engineer, Hingle, and his wife, Jocelyn Brando (Marlon's sister). The couple are running a clinic-home for Sarkhanese orphans and Brando thinks that's a good step in impressing the natives of the sincerity of the U.S. At the same time, he voices objections to Hingle anent the route of the road and feels that it should go straight into the area run by the Communists. Pramoj thinks they may run into trouble from the countries that support the Communist faction if that is done but Brando says the project will be backed all the way by the U.S. When Okada learns of this decision, he decides that he can no longer tolerate U.S. intervention in Sarkhan and joins with the Communists and plans an insurrection. The anniversary of the land's independence is to be celebrated and the revolutionaries use the state occasion to wreak havoc. They detonate bombs at the road's construction headquarters, blow up the oil storage tanks, and destroy the clinic. Pramoj proves to Brando that it was all a plot by the Reds and that the Communists have a further plot–they mean to kill Okada, blame it on the loyalist forces, and use the death to justify any further outbreaks against the government. Brando manages to get to Okada and tells him what his Communist allies have in mind. At first, Okada thinks it's more American chicanery, but he finally realizes that Brando is speaking the truth and agrees to withdraw his support of the Reds and ally with Pramoj and the elected government. Okada is about to put his plan into place when he is shot by Yip, a Communist who is part of the cabal. Okada dies, but not before he reveals the extent of the treachery of the Reds and assures the Sarkhanese that Brando is a good man who wants only the best for them. Brando sees that he is no match for the machinations of the Southeast Asians and resigns his post, understanding that his road, while being paved with good intentions, is also filled with potholes. Brando is interviewed on TV and makes an impassioned plea that is seen all over the U.S. He waxes on about the indifference of the American people and how it is important to know exactly why there is a cold war going on in that part of the world. As he is speaking, an unidentified man is watching Brando on TV and switches him off to find something more entertaining on another channel. Pramoj had been the Thai finance minister in real life and was hired as technical advisor. Brando and the others were impressed by his powerful charisma and gave him the role of the premier. They were quite right as he delivered the goods in the part. The company shot for nearly three months in Thailand, then built an Asian village on several acres in the San Fernando Valley, as well as a number of interiors. It's impossible to truly detail the woes of the area in two hours, and the result was a somewhat naive synthesis that only dusted the surface.

p&d, George Englund; w, Stewart Stern (based on the novel by William J. Lederer, Eugene Burdick); ph, Clifford Stine (Eastmancolor); m, Frank Skinner; ed, Ted J. Kent; art d, Alexander Golitzen, Alfred Sweeney; set d, Oliver Emert; cos, Rosemary Odell; makeup, Bud Westmore; tech adv,

Kukrit Pramoj, Sasidhorn Bunnag.

Drama   **(PR:A-C MPAA:NR)**

UGLY DACHSHUND, THE**   (1966) 93m Disney/BV c

Dean Jones *(Mark Garrison)*, Suzanne Pleshette *(Fran Garrison)*, Charlie Ruggles *(Dr. Pruitt, Veterinarian)*, Kelly Thordsen *(Officer Carmody)*, Parley Baer *(Mel Chadwick)*, Robert Kino *(Mr. Toyama)*, Mako *(Kenji)*, Charles Lane *(Judge)*, Gil Lamb *(Milkman)*, Dick Wessel *(Garbageman)*, Hal Smith.

Happily wed Jones and Pleshette bring a Great Dane pup home from the veterinarian along with a litter of Dachshunds. Since all the pups are raised together the Great Dane grows up thinking it is a Dachshund, leading to numerous outrageous moments. Each has a favorite breed; Jones enters the Great Dane in a dog show to compete against Pleshette's Dachshund. Jones' animal nearly loses the show by acting like a Dachshund but in the end takes the Blue Ribbon. One of the more mindless and predictable of the Disney family entries which probably explains why it was the 11th-largest-grossing picture of the year, raking in $6 million.

p, Walt Disney, Winston Hibler; d, Norman Tokar; w, Albert Aley (based on the book *Dogs in an Omnibus* by Gladys Bronwyn Stern); ph, Edward Colman (Technicolor); m, George Bruns; ed, Robert Stafford; art d, Carroll Clark, Marvin Aubrey Davis; set d, Emile Kuri, Frank R. McKelvy; cos, Chuck Keehne, Gertrude Casey; spec eff, Eustace Lycett; makeup, Pat McNalley; dog trainers, William R. Koehler, Glenn Randall, Jr.

Comedy   **(PR:AAA MPAA:NR)**

UGLY DUCKLING, THE**   (1959, Brit.) 84m Hammer/COL bw

Bernard Bresslaw *(Henry Jekyll/Teddy Hyde)*, Reginald Beckwith *(Reginald)*, Jon Pertwee *(Victor Jekyll)*, Maudie Edwards *(Henrietta Jekyll)*, Jean Muir *(Snout)*, Richard Wattis *(Barclay)*, Elwyn Brook-Jones *(Dandy)*, Michael Ripper *(Benny)*, David Lodge *(Peewee)*, Harold Goodwin, Norma Marla, Keith Smith, Michael Ward, John Harvey, Jess Conrad, Mary Wilson, Geremy Philips, Vicky Marshall, Jill Carson, Cyril Chamberlain, Alan Coleshill, Jean Driant, Nicholas Tanner, Shelagh Dey, Ian Wilson, Verne Morgan, Sheila Hammond, Ian Ainsley, Reginald Marsh, Roger Avon, Richard Statman, Robert Desmond, Alexander Dore.

In a chemist's laboratory young Bresslaw, a descendant of the notorious Dr. Jekyll, mixes up a potion which brings out a suave, Raffles-like Mr. Hyde personality in him. He commits a jewel robbery as Hyde, is later transformed into Jekyll again, and successfully rounds up a gang of thieves. An attempt at comedy which never really pays off.

p, Tommy Lyndon-Hayes; d, Lance Comfort; w, Sid Colin, Jack Davies (based on characters created by Robert Louis Stevenson); ph, Michael Reed; m, Douglas Gamley; ed, James Needs, John Dunsford; art d, Bernard Robinson.

Comedy   **(PR:A MPAA:NR)**

UGLY ONES, THE*½   (1968, Ital./Span.) 96m Tecisa-Discobolo/UA c
          (EL PRECIO DE UN HOMBRE; AKA: THE BOUNTY KILLERS)

Richard Wyler *(Luke Chilson)*, Tomas Milian *(Jose Gomez)*, Ella Karin *(Eden)*, Mario Brega, Hugo Blanco, Glenn Foster, Ricardo Canales, Lola Gaos, Saturno Cerra, Manuel Zarzo, Tito Garcia, Antonio Iranzo, Fernando Sanchez Polack, Chiro Bermejo, Antonio Cintado, Ricardo Palacios, Gonzalo Esquiroz, Enrique Navarro, Rafael Vaquero.

An average spaghetti western about a bounty hunter, Wyler, determined to bring in Mexican bandit Milian. With the help of Karin, Milian escapes the law, returns to his home town, and rallies the support of the locals as well as re-forming his old gang. When Wyler shows up on the scene, he is promptly captured, tied up, and tortured by Milian, who then proceeds to rob and kill some of the townspeople. Karin sees the error of her ways and lets Wyler go free. After a shootout, Milian and all of his gang members are dead, and Wyler is wealthier by the amount of the bounties on their heads.

p, Giuliano Simonetti; d, Eugenio Martin; w, Martin, Don Prindle, Jose G. Maesso, Biancini (based on the novel *The Bounty Killer* by Marvin H. Albert); ph, Enzo Barboni, Jose Herrero (DeLuxe Color); m, Stelvio Cipriani; ed, Jose Rocco, Gisa Levi Radicchi; art d, Francisco Canet.

Western   **(PR:O MPAA:R)**

UKIGUSA   (SEE: FLOATING WEEDS, 1970, Jap.)

ULTIMATE CHASE, THE   (SEE: ULTIMATE THRILL, THE, 1974)

ULTIMATE THRILL, THE*½   (1974) 80m Centaur/General Cinema c
                              (AKA: THE ULTIMATE CHASE)

Barry Brown *(Joe)*, Britt Ekland *(Michele)*, Eric Braeden *(Roland)*, Michael Blodgett *(Tom)*, John Davis Chandler *(Evans)*, Ed Baierlein *(Webster)*, Paul Felix *(Fielder)*, Gary Tessler *(Night Clerk)*, Ron Schwary *(Danny)*, Mary Hampton *(Woman at Deli)*, Carol Adams *(Secretary)*, June Goodman

(Pretzel), David Kahn *(Denver Clerk)*, Hallie McCollum *(Day Clerk)*, Sam Darling *(Bartender)*.

Brown is an executive married to unfaithful Ekland. He grows paranoid over her indiscretions and follows her to Colorado, stalking her lovers. Brown gives it a try with an underplayed performance, but the film is dragged down by a bad script and too many (albeit well handled) skiing sequences.

p, Peter S. Traynor, William D. Sklar; d, Robert Butler; w, John W. Zodrow (based on a story by Jim McGinn); ph, Isidore Mankofsky (Eastmancolor); m, Ed Townsend; ed, Peter Parasheles; cos, Ray Summers.

Crime   **Cas.**   (PR:A-C MPAA:PG)

ULTIMATE WARRIOR, THE**½   (1975) 94m WB c

Yul Brynner *(Carson)*, Max von Sydow *(The Baron)*, Joanna Miles *(Melinda)*, William Smith *(Carrot)*, Richard Kelton *(Cal)*, Stephen McHattie *(Robert)*, Darrell Zwerling *(Silas)*, Nate Esformes *(Garon)*, Lane Bradbury *(Barrie)*, Mel Novak *(Lippert)*, Mickey Caruso *(B. Harkness)*, Gray Johnson *(L. Harkness)*, Susan Keener *(Angry Woman)*, Stevie Myers *(Ice House Woman)*, Fred Slyter *(Store Room Clerk)*, Reggie Parton, Larry Bischof *(Baron's Guards)*, Pat Johnson, Henry Kingi *(Carrot's Men)*, Alex Colon.

A two-fisted, action-packed, futuristic comic-book thriller set in New York after plague has taken its effect. Von Sydow is the community leader who hoards anything of value, while Brynner is the ultimate stranger who passes through and lends his aid to scientist Kelton and his pregnant wife Miles. Brynner carries his WESTWORLD (1973) persona a step further (and appears as somewhat of a precursor to Kurt Russell's character in ESCAPE FROM NEW YORK, 1981) as he leads the young woman to safety while defeating the enemy in mythic proportions. He then shows a gentle strain by delivering Miles' baby at the finale.

p, Fred Weintraub, Paul Heller; d&w, Robert Clouse; ph, Gerald Hirschfeld (Technicolor); m, Gil Melle; ed, Michael Kahn; art d, Walter Simonds; set d, Bill Calvert; cos, Ann McCarthy; spec eff, Gene Griggs; makeup, Marvin Westmore; stunts, Pat Johnson, Reggie Parton.

Science Fiction/Adventure   (PR:O MPAA:R)

ULTIMATUM**   (1940, Fr.) 88m Forrester-Parant/Hoffberg bw

Erich von Stroheim *(Gen. Simovic)*, Dita Parlo *(Anna Salic)*, Abel Jacquin *(Capt. Karl Burgstaller)*, Bernard Lancret *(Comdr. Stanko Salic)*, Georges Rollin *(Lt. Ristic)*, Marcel Andre *(Legrain)*, Aimos *(Usir)*.

In the war-threatened Balkans just prior to the outbreak of WW II, nationalism rears its ugly head as Serbian soldier Lancret's marriage to Austrian Parlo is complicated by the presence of her countryman Jacquin. Stock footage from other war films is used for the few battle scenes; the bulk of the film comprises on-set dalliances among the overemoting characters. Von Stroheim does his customary Prussian strutting as a Serbian general. This was the final film of producer/director Wiene, who made his major mark with the silent classic THE CABINET OF DR. CALIGARI (1919). Wiene died in 1938 four months before the Paris premiere of ULTIMATUM. Robert Siodmak reportedly had taken over the helm from the ailing Wiene, but Siodmak remained uncredited.

p&d, Robert Wiene; w, Leo Lania, Alexandre Arnoux; ph, Ted Pahle, Mercanton; m, Adolphe Borchard.

Drama   (PR:A MPAA:NR)

ULYSSES***   (1955, Ital.) 104m Lux/PAR c (AKA: ULISSE)

Kirk Douglas *(Ulysses)*, Silvana Mangano *(Penelope/Circe)*, Anthony Quinn *(Antinous)*, Rossana Podesta *(Nausicaa)*, Sylvie *(Euriclea)*, Daniel Ivernel *(Euriloco)*, Jacques Dumesnil *(Alicinous)*, Franco Interlenghi *(Telemachus)*, Elena Zareschi *(Cassandra)*, Evi Maltagliati, Ludmilla Dudarova, Tania Weber, Piero Lulli, Ferruccio Stagni, Alessandro Ferson, Oscar Andriani, Umberto Silvestri, Gualtiero Tumiati, Teresa Pellati, Mario Feliciani, Michele Riccardini.

This adequate and fairly entertaining version of Homer's epic poem has Douglas the bearded hero taking the slow route home from the Trojan War. The film opens with Quinn and other suitors trying to convince Douglas's wife, Mangano, that her long-missing husband is dead and that she must pick one of them as a replacement. Meanwhile the amnesiac Douglas washes up on a beach on the island of Phaeacia. He is nursed back to health by a princess, Podesta, who falls in love with him, but Douglas spends most of his time staring out at the sea, trying to remember. In flashbacks he remembers killing the cyclops, lashing himself to the mast of his ship to hear the call of the sirens, and the sorceress Circe (also Mangano) turning his entire crew into pigs. Soon his memory is completely restored and after saying goodbye to Podesta he sails back home to Ithaca. When he arrives he disguises himself as a beggar to check out the situation. The obnoxious suitors are still there and they insult and harass the beggar. Mangano sets a task to determine her new husband. Whoever can bend the heavy bow of Ulysses will have her hand. One after another the suitors try and fail. Finally Douglas comes forth and–while the others jeer him–he bends the bow and sends its arrow through Quinn and then makes short work of the others. A

decent attempt to film the original epic fails as it inevitably must, the result of too much condensation and the reduction of high drama into low soap opera. But these failings aside, the film is a tasteful and surprisingly literate work. Douglas gives a restrained and thoughtful performance and the production values are way above the run of Italian sword-and-sandal epics. Excellent camera work by Hollywood veteran Rosson and a number of small but well-played supporting parts add greatly to the quality, and the film is probably as good a job as one can do with the subject.

p, Dino De Laurentiis, Carlo Ponti, William W. Schorr; d, Mario Camerini; w, Franco Brusati, Camerini, Ennio de Concini, Hugh Gray, Ben Hecht, Ivo Perilli, Irwin Shaw (based on Homer's *The Odyssey*); ph, Harold Rosson (Technicolor); m, Alessandro Cicognini; ed, Leo Cattozzo; md, Franco Ferrara; art d, Flavio Mogherini; set d, Andrea Tommasi; cos, Giulio Coltellacci, Mme. Gres; makeup, Eugene Schuftan.

Adventure   **Cas.**   (PR:C MPAA:NR)

ULYSSES***   (1967, U.S./Brit.) 140m Ulysses/CD bw

Barbara Jefford *(Molly Bloom)*, Milo O'Shea *(Leopold Bloom)*, Maurice Roeves *(Stephen Dedalus)*, T. P. McKenna *(Buck Mulligan)*, Martin Dempsey *(Simon Dedalus)*, Sheila O'Sullivan *(May Goulding Dedalus)*, Graham Lines *(Haines)*, Peter Mayock *(Jack Power)*, Fionnuala Flanagan *(Gerty MacDowell)*, Anna Manahan *(Bella Cohen)*, Maureen Toal *(Zoe Higgins)*, Maureen Potter *(Josie Breen)*, Chris Curran *(Myles Crawford)*, Maire Hastings *(Mary Driscoll)*, Eddie Golden *(Martin Cunningham)*, Joe Lynch *(Blazes Boylan)*, Ruadhan Neeson *(Cyril Sargent)*, Biddie White-Lennon *(Cissy Caffrey)*, Meryl Gourley *(Mrs. Mervyn Talboys)*, Ann Rowan *(Mrs. Bellingham)*, Rosaleen Linehan *(Nurse Callan)*, Robert Carlisle, Jr *(Dr. Dixon)*, O. Z. Whitehead *(Alexander J. Dowie)*, Cecil Sheridan *(John Henry Manton)*, Tony Doyle *(Lt. Gardner)*, James Bartley *(Pvt. Carr)*, Colin Bird *(Pvt. Compton)*, Jack Plant *(Denis Breen)*, Dave Kelly *(Garrett Deasy)*, Des Keogh *(Joe Hynes)*, Leon Collins *(Lynch)*, Robert Somerset *(Lenehan)*, May Cluskey *(Mrs. Yelverton Barry)*, Desmond Perry *(Bantam Lyons)*, John Molloy *(Corny Kelleher)*, Clare Mullen *(Florry)*, Pamela Mant *(Kitty)*, Paddy Roche *(Madden)*, Brendan Cauldwell *(Bob Doran)*, Eugene Lambert *(Costello)*, Danny Cummins *(The Drinker)*, Geoffrey Golden *(The Citizen)*, Frank Bailey, Brenda Doyle, Barry Cassin, Don Irwin, Thomas MacAnna, Pauline Melville, Maire Ni Ghrainne, Derry Power, Lillian Rapple, Charlie Roberts, Cecil Sheehan, Ritchie Stewart.

James Joyce's unfilmable novel is brought to the screen in this interesting but flawed movie. O'Shea is Joyce's Jewish protagonist. Wandering the Dublin streets, he thinks about his dead son, his cuckolding wife, and his own impotence. During his travels he meets a one-eyed man who taunts him with anti-Semitic remarks. Later he meets young student and poet Roeves and the pair go to a brothel where O'Shea is beset by frightening fantasies. Afterwards the two men sit up all night talking at O'Shea's house and after Roeves leaves, Jefford, O'Shea's wife, lies awake in bed thinking about her present and past loves and the notion of an affair with Roeves. There was no way Joyce's dense stream-of-consciousness prose could be translated into filmic terms, so the producers settled for a superficial record of O'Shea's peregrinations and only went into depth for two scenes–the brothel fantasies, where O'Shea sees himself as an oriental emperor, the mayor of Dublin, and the victim of an anti-Semitic judge, and Jefford's soliloquy as she muses on love, sex, and the impotent husband in bed beside her. The best thing here is that large chunks of Joycean prose make the soundtrack intact as voiceovers from the characters, and a lot of that voiceover is the same material that got the book banned in America for more than thirty years, especially Jefford's monolog. The cast is almost entirely Irish and the film is shot in the same locations mentioned in the book. Technically everything is very good, particularly the crisp black-and-white photography. There is no way any film can do justice to this classic modern novel, but this film comes as close as is ever likely.

p&d, Joseph Strick; w, Strick, Fred Haines (based on the novel by James Joyce); ph, Wolfgang Suschitzky (Panavision); m, Stanley Myers; ed, Reginald Mills; Md, Myers; art d, Graham Probst.

Drama/Fantasy   (PR:C MPAA:NR)

ULZANA'S RAID***   (1972) 103m UNIV c

Burt Lancaster *(McIntosh)*, Bruce Davison *(Lt. Garnett DeBuin)*, Jorge Luke *(Ke-Ni-Tay)*, Richard Jaeckel *(Sergeant)*, Joaquin Martinez *(Ulzana)*, Lloyd Bochner *(Capt. Gates)*, Karl Swenson *(Rukeyser)*, Douglass Watson *(Maj. Cartwright)*, Dran Hamilton *(Mrs. Riordan)*, John Pearce *(Corporal)*, Gladys Holland *(Mrs. Rukeyser)*, Margaret Fairchild *(Mrs. Ginsford)*, Aimee Eccles *(McIntosh's Indian Woman)*, Richard Bull *(Ginsford)*, Otto Reichow *(Steegmeyer)*, Dean Smith *(Horowitz)*, Larry Randles *(Mulkearn)*, Hal Maguire, Ted Markland, R. L. Armstrong, John McKee, Tony Epper, Nick Cravat, Richard Farnsworth, Walter Scott, Jerry Gatlin, Fred Brookfield, Bill Burton, Henry Camargo, Gil Escandon, Frank Gonzales, Larry Colelay, George Aguilar, Marvin Fragua, Benny Thompson, Wallace Sinyella.

Lancaster is cast as a hard-riding, weather-worn scout who rides with Davison, a young idealist who hasn't lived at all in comparison. Together they chase down a group of renegade Apaches led by Martinez who rape the women and kill the men who cross their path. A conflict brews between the two riders on how best to deal with Ulzana Martinez and his men. Values are explored and campfires shed light on their differing ideologies until, at the finale, Davison sheds his naive idealism as Lancaster is left behind to die. Viewed by some as an allegorical indictment of the Vietnam war, ULZANA'S RAID avoids the preachy soapbox stance of similar westerns (SOLDIER BLUE, 1970, for example) by working from a well-developed script by Sharp (NIGHT MOVES, 1975) that is given a stark, violent treatment by Aldrich in this bloody picture (which was rated "unacceptable" by the American Humane Association because of the use of trip wires to fell the horses). Depending on where you've seen this film, the U.S. or Europe, you'll have seen different takes and slightly different scene construction (notably at the opening), though most versions are equally penetrating. This was the third time the now-crusty Lancaster and director Aldrich had worked together after a lapse of 18 years (the previous films were APACHE and VERA CRUZ, both in 1954).

p, Carter De Haven; d, Robert Aldrich; w, Alan Sharp; ph, Joseph Biroc (Technicolor); m, Frank DeVol; ed, Michael Luciano; art d, James Vance; set d, John McCarthy.

Western   **Cas.**   **(PR:O   MPAA:R)**

UMBERTO D***** (1955, Ital.) 89m Amato-Rizzoli/Harrison-Davidson bw

Carlo Battisti (*Umberto Domenico Ferrari*), Maria Pia Casilio (*Maria*), Lina Gennari (*Landlady*), Alberto Albani Barbieri (*Fiance*), Elena Rea (*Sister*), Ileana Simova (*Surprised Woman*), Memo Carotenuto (*Voice of Light*).

A powerful, shattering portrait of an old man that is simple on the surface but multi-layered beneath and serves as an indictment of postwar Italy and the manner in which they treated the aged. De Sica and his longtime associate, screenwriter Zavattini, have written a grim script that was a resounding dud at the box office because films about old people have been poison since before the silents gave way to sound. The title character is played by non-pro Battisti (a university professor in real life). He's a retired civil servant with no friends, no family, and no prospects. His only pal is his dog, Flike. At the present time, he is far behind in his rent and his meager pension does not provide him with enough to both eat and have shelter. He's been living in the same room for three decades and when he used to work during the day, his landlady, Gennari, would rent his room out to lovers who needed a place for a few hours to tryst. Gennari is planning to evict him now that his presence is cutting into her income. Battisti is one of a series of elderly who voice their opposition to the way the government is treating the pensionsers and he is depressed by the lack of response. Gennari is to marry Barbieri and wants the room but Battisti thinks he can stay if he can only raise the money to pay the back rent. He tries several times to make the cash but cannot and so he determines there is no way out but suicide. Those thoughts are put aside when he realizes that if he did that, his dog would be at the mercy of the streets and probably be slain and eaten. From time to time, Battisti talks with the servant, Casilio, but that hardly satisfies his need for human companionship. He hits upon a plan to kill himself and his dog and fails at that. He is now hopelessly alive and there doesn't seem to be a glimmer of happiness on the horizon to alter his despair. Battisti shrugs and decides he'd better just go along and see what further pitfalls life has to offer. There is no sentimentality, not even any elicitation of sympathy on the part of the director. Rather, the story is presented in as straightforward a fashion as Lynn Littman's Oscar-winning documentary NUMBER OUR DAYS which told of the plight of the aged Jews in the Venice Beach area of Los Angeles. The movie was made in 1952 and did not secure a release in the U.S. for 3 years, probably because everyone in the distribution business recognized that this was hardly MARY POPPINS. De Sica made many movies about ordinary people such as SHOE SHINE and BICYCLE THIEF and in those, and other films, he preferred amateurs in the leading roles because he felt, like Charles Chaplin often said, that using a non-professional meant there was nothing for the actors to "unlearn" and he could mold them more easily. The attention to detail is what makes this such a moving experience. Battisti, a proud but impoverished man, is forced to beg on the Roman streets; his thoughts about suicide are felt rather than spoken as the camera zooms from in back of him to the street below and we know that he is considering a jump from the high floor. De Sica's father's name was Umberto and it is to his memory that the movie is dedicated. It is a bleak film, non-sparing of emotions in the presentation, heart-rending without ever appearing manipulative, and the result was that the movie got trounced by the Italian government for being what they felt was a poor description of life in the Boot. After the movie was released, there was a move afoot to keep any Italian films which were "detrimental to the image of Italy" from being seen outside the country's confines. Zavattini was nominated for an Oscar for his original story, and the picture won the New York Film Critics Award for Best Foreign Film (which it shared with DIABOLIQUE).

p&d, Vittorio De Sica; w, Cesare Zavattini, De Sica (based on a story by Zavattini); ph, Aldo Graziati 'G.R. Aldo'; m, Alessandro Cigognini; ed, Eraldo di Roma; prod d, Virgilio Marchi.

Drama   **Cas.**   **(PR:C   MPAA:NR)**

UMBRELLA, THE**   (1933, Brit.) 56m Real Art/RKO bw

Kay Hammond (*Mabel*), Harold French (*Freddie Wallace*), S. Victor Stanley (*Victor Garnett*), Dick Francis (*Michael Frankenstein*), Barbara Everest (*Mrs. Wynne*), Kathleen Tremaine (*Mary Wynne*), John Turnbull (*Governor*), Syd Crossley (*Police Constable*), Ernest Mainwaring.

A couple of crooks are released from prison and their valuables are returned to them. One of these possessions is an umbrella which has some stolen jewels hidden in the handle. It mistakenly ends up in the wrong hands and eventually winds up with Hammond after French lends it to her. By the finale French has informed the police and the crooks are rounded up at a masked ball.

p, Julius Hagen; d, Redd Davis; w, H. Fowler Mear (based on a story by Lawrence Meynell); ph, Ernest Palmer.

Comedy   **(PR:A   MPAA:NR)**

UMBRELLAS OF CHERBOURG, THE**½**   (1964, Fr./Ger.) 90m Madeleine-Parc-Beta/Laundau c (LES PARAPLUIES DE CHERBOURG; DIE REGENSCHIRME VON CHERBOURG)

Catherine Deneuve (*Genevieve Emery*), Nino Castelnuovo (*Guy*), Anne Vernon (*Mme. Emery*), Ellen Farner (*Madeleine*), Marc Michel (*Roland Cassard*), Mireille Perrey (*Aunt Elise*), Jean Champion (*Aubin*), Harald Wolff (*Dubourg*), Dorothee Blank (*Girl in Cafe*).

A charming cinematic operetta without a word of spoken dialog. Instead, everything is sung and the music of Legrand and the lyrics of screenwriter-director Demy have become part of the fabric of popular music. The English lyrics for the songs were written by Norman Gimbel and it is those that are recalled in the U.S. Set, of course, in Cherbourg, the story takes place over a six-year period and begins in the winter of 1957. Deneuve is the teenaged daughter of Vernon, a widow who owns an umbrella shop. Castelnuovo is Deneuve's boy friend, a gas station attendant who lives with his aunt, Perrey, a crippled woman. The two youngsters would love to get married but are stopped by Vernon who thinks that Deneuve should wait a bit, at least until she is out of her teens, before taking such an important step. The store is not making money so Vernon goes to the local jewelry shop to sell her treasured pearl strand. While there, Michel, a rich man who deals in gems, sees Deneuve, and is instantly fascinated by her. In order to ingratiate himself with Deneuve's mother, he buys the pearls. Deneuve is still a virgin, but when Castelnuovo is drafted to fight for France in Algeria and there will be a separation of two years, she finally decides that she will sleep with him as a going-away present and to seal their love. A couple of months later Deneuve is pregnant and has not had one word in the mail from the father-to-be. Vernon invites Michel to dinner and he continues to be smitten by Deneuve and offers to make her his wife. A few weeks later, Deneuve receives word from Castelnuovo; he's alive and thrilled that they are going to be parents but the war rages on and he can only hope that he will live long enough to see the child. It's the days before Lent and Vernon says Deneuve would be a fool to wait for Castelnuovo. She will already have a child more than a year old if and when he comes home and she tells Deneuve that Michel would make her a fine husband. Michel is traveling and returns to Cherbourg to assure Deneuve that he will raise her child as though he were the father. With that assurance, Deneuve and Michel are married in June. Many months pass and a slightly wounded Castelnuovo returns home to Cherbourg and is shocked to learn that Deneuve and Michel are wed and now living in Paris. His aunt is being cared for by Farner, a young woman who has always loved Castelnuovo but never made her love known to him because he was so mad for Deneuve. Castelnuovo is a changed man now. Gone is the youth and the snap in his step. The man who has returned from the war is a hardened veteran and unable to deal with civilian life. When Perrey dies, Farner's custodial job is done but Castelnuovo, who is now alone in the world, asks her to remain in the house. After Perrey's will is read, there's enough money for Castelnuovo to buy his own service station. He is somewhat happier now and feels that it is Farner who has made him a better man so he asks for her hand. She's not sure if he still doesn't love Deneuve but he assures her that he's in love with her and will make her a good husband. Almost four years have gone by when, one Christmas Eve, the snow is drifting down and all seems right with the world. Castelnuovo is working late, bids *au revoir* to Farner and their young son as the two are going out to buy the lad a few toys. A moment later, Deneuve pulls into the gas station in a sleek car. Inside the car is their daughter and the moment between them is shattering as both strive to suppress the swell of emotion at seeing the other. Deneuve wonders if he would enjoy seeing their daughter but he shakes his head and suggests that they both might be better off if she left right now. It is not spoken with rancor, just matter-of-fact, and both of them understand why it has to be said. The car quietly pulls into the street and Farner, having seen it all, races to Castelnuovo and clasps him, now secure in the knowledge that he is hers forever. A sweet love story with a number of hit songs such as, "I Will Wait for You" and "Watch What Happens." Grand Prize winner at Cannes in 1964 and nominated as Best Foreign Language Film by the Academy in 1964 (losing to YESTERDAY, TODAY AND TOMORROW). In 1965, it was Oscar-nominated for Best Story and Screenplay (Demy) as well as for "I Will Wait for You" as Best Song and two further nominations to Legrand for his composition and his scoring. In 1979, it was attempted as a stage musical in an Off-Broadway house and subsequently had many other stagings. Gorgeous colors and fine dubbed voices (most of the actors couldn't sing a note) make this a pleasure for the eyes and ears and emotions. (In French; English subtitles.) Sequel: THE YOUNG GIRLS OF ROCHEFORT.

p, Mag Bodard; d&w, Jacques Demy; ph, Jean Rabier (Eastmancolor); m, Michel Legrand; ed, Anne-Marie Cotret; md, Legrand; art d, Bernard Evein; cos, Real, Jacqueline Moreau; m/l, Legrand, Demy (English lyrics, Norman Gimbel).

Musical   **Cas.**   **(PR:A-C MPAA:NR)**

UN AMOUR DE POCHE   (SEE: NUDE IN HIS POCKET, 1962, Fr.)

UN CARNET DE BAL½   (1938, Fr.) 109m Sigma bw (AKA: LIFE DANCES ON, CHRISTINE)

Marie Bell (Christine Sugere), Francoise Rosay (Madame Audie), Louis Jouvet (Jo [Pierre Verdier]), Harry Baur (Pere Alain Regnault), Pierre-Richard Willm (Eric Irvin), Raimu (Francois Patusset), Pierre Blanchar (Dr. Thierry), Fernandel (Fabien Coutissol), Robert Lynen (Jacques Dambreval), Roger Legris (Jo's Accomplice), Sylvie.

The widowed Bell discovers a 20-year-old dance program from a ball and decides to seek out the men she danced with. The story is told in episodic fashion as she becomes disillusioned with what she finds–Blanchar is an abortionist, Jouvet is a sleazy lawyer, Fernandel has become a hairdresser, and Baur has found God. She finds that the only one she really loved has killed himself, leaving behind a son whom Bell adopts. An uneven and often overwrought script hampers what in the 1930s was a vastly popular picture, taking a top prize at the Venice Film Festival. It was one of the first films of an episodic nature in France, paving the way for a number of such pictures. Today, however, it is of little interest except for devotees of Duvivier. Duvivier trod the same path again in his Hollywood period with LYDIA (1941).

d, Julien Duvivier; w, Duvivier, Jean Sarment, Pierre Wolff, Yves Mirande, Henri Jeanson, Bernard Zimmer (based on a story by Duvivier); ph, Michel Kelber, Philippe Agostini, Pierre Levent; m, Maurice Jaubert; ed, Andre Versein;

Drama   **(PR:A MPAA:NR)**

UN, DEUX, TROIS, QUATRE!   (SEE: BLACK TIGHTS, 1962, Fr.)

UNE FEMME DEUCE   (SEE: GENTLE CREATURE, A, 1971, Fr.)

UN FILE   (SEE: COP, A, 1973, Fr.)

UN HOMME ET UNE FEMME   (SEE: MAN AND A WOMAN, A, 1966, Fr.)

UNE MERE, UNE FILLE   (SEE: ANNA, 1981, Fr./Hung.)

UN SEUL AMOUR   (SEE: MAGNIFICENT SINNER, 1963, Fr.)

UN TAXI MAUVE   (SEE: PURPLE TAXI, THE, 1977, Fr./Ital./Ire.)

UN UOMO, UN CAVALLO, UNA PISTOLA
        (SEE: STRANGER RETURNS, THE, 1968, U.S./Ital./Ger.)

UNA MOGLIE AMERICANA   (SEE: RUN FOR YOUR WIFE, 1966, Fr./Ital.)

UNA SIGNORA DELL'OVEST½   (1942, Ital). 88m Scalera bw

Michel Simon, Isa Pola, Rossano Brazzi, Valentina Cortese, Renzo Merusi, Carlo Duse.

Cortese is a dance-hall girl whose husband is killed by Simon, who then gets her again by framing her new lover. Simon consoles her until she discovers what really happened, returning to her lover only to find him with a wife that she didn't know he had. This is Italy's first Western...and it looks like it. Cortese is seen in an early role, much later appearing in Truffaut's DAY FOR NIGHT as the aging Italian actress.

p, Franco Magli; d, Carlo Koch; w, Koch, Lotte Reiniger (based on the opera by Puccini and the play by David Belasco entitled "The Girl Of The Golden West"); ph, Ubaldo Arata.

Western   **(PR:A MPAA:NR)**

UNAKRSNA VATRA   (SEE: OPERATION CROSS EAGLES, 1969, U.S./YUGO)

UNASHAMED½   (1932) 75m MGM bw

Helen Twelvetrees (Joan Ogden), Robert Young (Dick Ogden), Lewis Stone (Henry Trask), Jean Hersholt (Mr. Schmidt), John Miljan (District Attorney Harris), Monroe Owsley (Harry Swift), Robert Warwick (Mr. Ogden), Gertrude Michael (Marjorie), Wilfred North (Judge Ambrose), Tommy [Thomas] Jackson (Capt. Riordan), Louise Beavers (Amanda).

A weak courtroom drama about murder, marriage, and family honor which casts Twelvetrees as the rebellious daughter of Warwick and sister of Young. She's in love with a scoundrel who wants nothing but her money and her body, and tries to talk her father into permitting her marriage. When her father refuses, the lovers run off together, but Young follows and kills the caddish suitor. A trial follows, with Twelvetrees only contributing to her brother's probable guilty verdict. At the last moment she turns on an act which keeps Young from being sent to the chair.

d, Harry Beaumont; w, Bayard Veiller; ph, Norbert Brodine; ed, William S. Gray.

Drama   **(PR:A MPAA:NR)**

UNASHAMED zero   (1938) 65m Cine-Grand bw

Rae Kidd (Rae Lane), Robert Stanley (Robert Lawton), Lucille Shearer (Barbara Pound), Emily Todd (Emma), Joseph W. Girard (Dr. Malvin), Frances Grey (Maizie), Joan Charles (Rose), Woody McGillicuddy (Himself), Ross Lynn (Dad McGillicuddy).

A secretary, Kidd, persuades her chronically ill boss, Stanley, that the cure for his malaise is to get back to nature. She gets doctor Girard to prescribe a curative trip to an appropriate camp. When he shows up, he discovers the campers–including his love-smitten secretary–in the buff. Surprise, surprise: it's a nudist camp. Adjusting to the situation, he discovers that Kidd isn't a bad looking girl when she takes off her glasses (and the rest of her things, as well), and romance blossoms. But, lo! A snake appears in this Eden in the person of a glamorous heiress, who preceeds to win Stanley's affections. During an evening storm, the two tryst in the trees, watched by the dolorous Kidd. Disaffected and rejected, the naked naiad climbs to a cliff and leaps to her death. Except for the climb to the cliff, the photography remains above the pelvis in frontal shots, which got the film past the National Board of Review. An exception to this rule was Woody McGillicuddy, a ventriloquist's dummy who provided–with the help of Lynn–much of the comic relief. One of the best of the nudism-promulgating films which came out in profusion in pre-Hays Office times,–when censorship was up to individual states,–this one has a real story line. One song: "Back to Nature" (Richard B. Gump, Howard Sprague).

d, Allen Stuart; w, William Lively (based on a story by Captain C. P. Prescott-Richardson); ph, George Sergeant; m, Frederic Chapin; ed, Holbrook N. Todd.

Drama/Nudist   **(PR:O MPAA:NR)**

UNCANNY, THE**   (1977, Brit./Can.) 85m Cinevideo-Tor-Subotsky and Heroux/RANK c

Peter Cushing (Wilbur), Ray Milland (Frank), "Malkin Story": Susan Penhaligon (Janet), Joan Greenwood (Miss Malkin), Roland Culver (Wallace), Simon Williams (Michael), "Black Magic Story": Alexandra Stewart (Mrs. Blake), Donald Pilon (Mr. Blake), Chloe Franks (Angela), Renee Giraud (Mrs. Maitland), Katrina Holden (Lucy), "Film Studio Story": Donald Pleasence (Valentine De'Ath), Samantha Eggar (Edina), John Vernon (Pomeroy), John LeClerc (Barrington), Sean McCann (Inspector), Catharine Begin (Madeline).

Mediocre horror anthology has framing story of Cushing, an author, trying to sell a book charging that cats are plotting to take over the world to skeptical Milland. He tells three stories involving felines. In the first, Greenwood is an old woman eaten by her pet kitties: in the second, a girl shrinks to tiny size and is terrorized by her now giant cat (a story stolen from one scene in THE INCREDIBLE SHRINKING MAN). The final episode has Pleasence building a pit-and-pendulum type gadget to rid himself of a bothersome wife, but her cat avenges her mistress's death. Never released theatrically in the U.S.

p, Claude Heroux, Rene Dupont; d, Denis Heroux; w, Michael Parry; ph, Harry Waxman, James Bawden; m, Wilfred Josephs; prod d, Wolf Kroeger, Harry Pottle; spec eff, Michael Albrechtsen.

Horror   **Cas.**   **(PR:C MPAA:NR)**

UNCENSORED½   (1944, Brit.) 83m Gainsborough/FOX bw

Eric Portman (Andre Delange), Phyllis Calvert (Julie Lanvin), Griffith Jones (Father de Gruyte), Raymond Lovell (Von Koerner), Peter Glenville (Charles Neels), Frederick Culley (Victor Lanvin), Irene Handl (Frau von Koerner), Carl Jaffe (Kohlmeier), Felix Aylmer (Col. Von Hohenstein), Eliot Makeham (Abbe De Moor), Walter Hudd (Van Heemskirk), Stuart Lindsell (Press Officer), J. H. Roberts (Father Corot), John Slater (Theophile), Lloyd Pearson (Cabaret Manager), Philip Godfrey (Lou), Arthur Goullet (Gaston), Ben Williams (Arthur Backer), Aubrey Mallalieu (Louis Backer), Kathleen Boutall, Phyllis Monkman (The Pony Act), Allan Jeayes, Clifford Cobbe,

Johnnie Schofield, John Snowden, Ian Kenyon, Antony Holles, Corey Ellison, Everley Gregg, Charles Paton, Charlton Morton, Charles Doe, Norman Pierce, Lawrence O'Madden, Arthur Denton, Peter Cozens, James Carson, Josephine Wilson.

In Nazi-occupied Belgium, a group of underground fighters revive an anti-Nazi publication, much to the chagrin of the occupying forces. Cabaret entertainer Portman is the publisher and Calvert his assistant, but their plans are short-circuited by Glenville, Portman's jealous cabaret partner, who informs on them. Portman and Calvert escape a Nazi raid, but the rest of the staff is arrested. The two are able to get out another edition, forcing the befuddled Nazis to release their prisoners. An appealing concept which doesn't deliver what it promises.

p, Edward Black; d, Anthony Asquith; w, Wolfgang Wilhelm, Terence Rattigan, Rodney Ackland (based on the novel by Oscar E. Millard); ph, Arthur Crabtree; ed, R. E. Dearing; md, Louis Levy; art d, Alex Vetchinsky.

War Drama   **(PR:A   MPAA:NR)**

UNCERTAIN GLORY***   (1944) 102m WB bw

Errol Flynn (Jean Picard), Paul Lukas (Marcel Bonet), Jean Sullivan (Marianne), Lucile Watson (Mme. Maret), Faye Emerson (Louise), James Flavin (Captain, Mobile Guard), Douglas Dumbrille (Police Commissioner), Dennis Hoey (Father Le Clerc), Sheldon Leonard (Henri Duval), Odette Myrtil (Mme. Bonet), Francis Pierlot (Prison Priest), Wallis Clark (Razeau), Victor Kilian (Latour), Ivan Triesault (Saboteur), Albert van Antwerp (Vitrac), Art Smith (Warden), Carl Harbaugh (Innkeeper), Mary Servoss (Drover's Wife), Charles La Torre (Restaurant Keeper), Pedro De Cordoba (Executioner), Bobby Walberg (Pierre Bonet), Erskine Sanford (Drover), Felix Basch (German Officer), Joel Friedkin (Veterinary), Creighton Hale (Prison Secretary), Joyce Tucker (Michele Bonet), Paul Panzer (Train Guard), Hans Schumm (Gestapo Agent), Zina Torchina (Peasant Girl), Sarah Padden (Peasant Woman on Bus), Trevor Bardette, Michael Mark (Passengers on Train).

In Occupied Paris during WW II, Flynn is a thief and murderer about to be guillotined. He rejects the priest saying prayers for his soul and refuses to let the prison barber shave his neck. He is about to lose his head when British planes raid Paris, and the falling bombs hit the prison and give Flynn a chance to escape. He flees toward Spain, with his old nemesis, Surete inspector Lukas, in hot pursuit. Eventually Lukas recaptures Flynn and the two are on a train returning to Paris when saboteurs blow up the bridge ahead of them. The two are forced to spend some time in a small village where Flynn charms local girl Sullivan. The Nazis, searching for the saboteurs, take 100 hostages and threaten to kill them if the culprits do not step forth. Flynn makes a proposition to Lukas. Since he is going to die one way or another, he will confess to the sabotage and die in front of a German firing squad rather than have his head chopped off, a fate of which he has a mortal fear. Flynn is actually simply stalling while he figures a way to escape again, but when he learns that Sullivan is among the hostages he goes through with his self-sacrifice. Although far from being one of Flynn's best films, the first half of this film is fascinating as it develops his character, much of it at Flynn's own suggestion. As originally written, the script called for Flynn to go to the guillotine sullen and resigned, but Flynn turned his character angry and resentful, and Lukas, as the man determined to see justice done, is equally intriguing. But whatever power the first half of the film has is dissipated in the second half, as this cynical criminal suddenly turns noble and sacrifices himself for a young girl. Director Walsh showed little more than cursory interest in the film and in his autobiography writes it off along with two others he made that year as "quickies."

p, Robert Buckner; d, Raoul Walsh; w, Laszlo Vadnay, Max Brand (based on a story by Joe May, Vadnay); ph, Sid Hickox; m, Adolph Deutsch; ed, George Amy; md, Leo F. Forbstein; art d, Robert Haas; set d, Walter F. Tilford; spec eff, E. Roy Davidson; makeup, Perc Westmore; tech adv, Paul Coze.

War Drama   **(PR:A   MPAA:NR)**

UNCERTAIN LADY*   (1934) 65m UNIV bw

Edward Everett Horton (Elliot), Genevieve Tobin (Doris), Renee Gadd (Myra), Paul Cavanagh (Bruce), Mary Nash (Edith), George Meeker (Garrison), Dorothy Peterson (Cicily), Donald Reed (Garcia), Herbert Corthell (Butler), Arthur Hoyt (Superintendent), Gay Seabrook (Secretary), Dick Winslow (Boy), James Durkin.

Woman executive Tobin, busy with business, has lost her spouse (Horton) to another woman. Not one to accept defeat easily, she plans to win him back. She enlists the assistance of an attractive male to evoke jealousy in husband Horton during a lavish dinner party. Her strategy doesn't work out as planned, however; she finds that she is falling for the decoy love interest. Typical drawing-room comedy of its period with Horton playing his stereotyped role.

p, Dale Van Every; d, Karl Freund; w, George O'Neill, Doris Anderson, Daniel Evans, Don Ryan (based on the play "The Behavior Of Mrs. Crane" by Harry Segall); ph, Charles Stumar; ed, Edward Curtiss.

Comedy   **(PR:A   MPAA:NR)**

UNCHAINED**   (1955) 75m WB bw

Elroy Hirsch (Steve Davitt), Barbara Hale (Mary Davitt), Chester Morris (Kenyon J. Scudder), Todd Duncan (Bill Howard), Johnny Johnston (Eddie Garrity), Peggy Knudsen (Elaine), Jerry Paris (Joe Ravens), John Qualen (Leonard Haskins), Bill Kennedy (Sanders), Henry Nakamura (Jerry Hakara), Kathryn Grant (Sally Haskins), Bob Patten (Swanson), Don Kennedy (Gladstone), Mack Williams (Mr. Johnson), Saul Gorss (Police Captain), Tim Considine (Win Davitt).

A prison drama in which the facts that the film is based on are more interesting then the fiction. UNCHAINED tells the story of a group of prisoners in the unwalled, 2,600 acre prison farm at Chino, California, where the men are treated like humans instead of numbers. There are no armed guards, no lockups, and no uniforms. The idea is that the criminals will lose their will to escape and accept the fact that they must do their time. Hirsch is imprisoned at Chino and, as expected, soon becomes used to the idea. Morris turns in a controlled performance as the kindly warden, more interested in the honor system than in violence. Includes the tune "Unchained Melody" by Alex North and Hy Zaret. The film premiered at a preview attended by press, prisoners, and guests in the mess hall of its subject area, the California Institution for Men at Chino, California. The 31-year-old producer/director/writer/social reformer, Bartlett, had previously made two films, one of them–CRAZYLEGS (1953)–a filmed biography of his leading actor here, former football great Elroy "Crazylegs" Hirsch.

p,d&w, Hall Bartlett (based on the book Prisoners Are People by Kenyon J. Scudder); ph, Virgil E. Miller; m, Alex North; ed, Cotton Warburton.

Prison Drama   **(PR:A   MPAA:NR)**

UNCHAINED   (SEE: ANGEL UNCHAINED, 1970)

UNCIVILISED**   (1937, Aus.) 82m Expeditional/Box Office
                                                          Attractions bw

Dennis Hoey (Mara), Margot Rhys (Beatrice Lynn), Marcelle Marnay (Sondra), Ashton Jarry (Akbar Jhan), Kenneth Brampton, Victor Fitzherbert, E. G. Howell, Edward Silveni, P. Dwyer, Rita Aslim, John Fernside, Jessica Malone, Richard Mazar, Z. Gee, D. McNiven, P. Rutledge, C. Francis.

Australia serves as the star of this passable adventure which casts Rhys as a reporter sent to an uncivilised region in order to locate Hoey. The Tarzan-like white man she's looking for heads an aborigine tribe and could be valuable in providing information for a book she is authoring. Of course romance plays a part, as do the natives of the aboriginal tribes. Directed by Charles Chauvel whose IN THE WAKE OF THE BOUNTY in 1933 first brought Hollywood's attention to Errol Flynn.

d&w, Charles Chauvel (based on a story by E. Timms); ph, Tasman Higgins; m, Lindley Evans.

Drama/Adventure   **(PR:A   MPAA:NR)**

UNCLE, THE***   (1966, Brit.) 87m Play-Pix-BL/Lenart bw

Rupert Davies (David), Brenda Bruce (Addie), Robert Duncan (Gus), William Marlowe (Wayne), Ann Lynn (Sally), Christopher Ariss (Tom), Maurice Denham (Mr. Ream), Helen Fraser (Mary Ream), Barbara Leake (Emma), John Moulder-Brown (Jamie), Jane Ratcliffe (Susie).

A refreshing story about a 7-year-old boy who is the uncle of a boy the same age as he. This fact disturbs him and upsets his method of dealing with children his own age–at times feeling like a child, while occasionally feeling the awesome responsibility of being an uncle. He removes himself from his friends and family, but eventually grows to care for his nephew and his father more than ever before. A fine treatment of an unusual situation. Some controversy surrounded the film when director Desmond Davis and executive producer Leonard Davis (no relation) found themselves in a tangle of disagreement over some allegedly unauthorized re-editing on the producer's part.

p, Robert Goldston; d, Desmond Davis; w, Davis, Margaret Abrams (based on the novel by Abrams); ph, Manny Wynn; ed, Brian Smedley-Aston; art d, Edward Marshall; makeup, Michael Morris.

Drama   **(PR:A   MPAA:NR)**

UNCLE HARRY***½   (1945) 80m UNIV bw (AKA: THE STRANGE
                                                    AFFAIR OF UNCLE HARRY)

George Sanders (John Quincy), Geraldine Fitzgerald (Lettie Quincy), Ella Raines (Deborah Brown), Sara Allgood (Nona), Moyna MacGill (Hester), Samuel S. Hinds (Dr. Adams), Harry Von Zell (Ben), Ethel Griffies (Mrs. Nelson), Judy Clark (Helen), Craig Reynolds (John Warren), Will Wright (Mr. Nelson), Arthur Loft (Mr. Follinsbee), Irene Tedrow (Mrs. Follinsbee), Coulter Irwin (Biff Wagner), Dawn Bender (Joan Warren), Ruth Cherrington (Matron), Rodney Bell (Joe the Greek), Harry Hayden (Slavin), Holmes Herbert (Warden), William Hall, Matt McHugh (Moving Men), Harlan Briggs (Hangman), Barbara Pepper (Annie), Robert Malcolm (Connors), Robert Dudley (Stationmaster), Sara Selby (Alice), Walter Soderling (Jed Jessup), Rev. Neal Dodd (Minister), Fred Santley (Waiter), Bob McKenzie

(Manager), Wally Scott *(Barman)*, Frank Jaquet *(Salesman)*, Robert Anderson, Gregory Muradian, Billy Gray, Mike Clifton *(Children)*, Bill Henderson *(Johnny)*, Norman Nielson, Clarence Badger, Alan Watson, Jan Williams *(Quartet)*.

Unsatisfying adaptation of a successful drama that played Broadway for a season, starring Joseph Schildkraut and Eva Le Gallienne. In the play, the story unfolded in a series of flashbacks. The screenplay by Longstreet opted to tell the tale in a more traditional narrative form with a cop-out ending that had to be tacked on to appease the Hays Office. Sanders is a fabric designer who lives a life of quiet desperation with his old maid sisters, MacGill and Fitzgerald, in their New Hampshire mansion. While visiting the mill in Quincy, Sanders meets and falls for Raines, a fashion mavin who has come up from New York. She is charming, bubbly, and the antithesis of the dour spinsters. Love blossoms quickly and Sanders soon asks for Raines' hand in marriage. Raines meets the sisters and MacGill is delighted that their brother has someone to love, but Fitzgerald, who harbors an almost incestuous jealousy for Sanders, can barely stand the thought and feigns a heart seizure upon hearing of the troth. Sanders is angered enough by Fitzgerald's behavior to want to do away with her so he poisons her nightly cup of cocoa to get her out of the way of his happiness. By mistake, MacGill drinks the lethal brew and expires. The evidence points to Fitzgerald as the killer and she is arrested, tried, and convicted of a crime she did not commit. Fitzgerald can get herself off the hook by telling of Sanders' desire to see her dead and that he is the probable killer, but she keeps mum as she knows that Raines will probably leave Sanders and he will never have a moment's peace. At the conclusion, Sanders wakes up to find that it's all been (ugh) a dream. Producer Harrison (long-time Alfred Hitchcock associate) was so incensed at the ending that she strolled from Universal. Director Siodmak must have enjoyed the good sister-bad sister plot because he is also the man who helmed THE DARK MIRROR, about a pair of good-bad twins, played by Olivia de Havilland. The incest is subtly depicted, but any child over the age of six will recognize the implications.

p, Joan Harrison; d, Robert Siodmak; w, Stephen Longstreet, Keith Winter (based on the play by Thomas Job); ph, Paul Ivano; ed, Arthur Hilton; md, Hans J. Salter; art d, John Goodman, Eugene Lourie; set d, Russell A. Gausman; cos, Travis Banton; spec eff, John P. Fulton.

Mystery (PR:C MPAA:NR)

UNCLE JOE SHANNON* (1978) 108m UA c

Burt Young *(Joe Shannon)*, Doug McKeon *(Robbie)*, Madge Sinclair *(Margaret)*, Jason Bernard *(Goose)*, Bert Remsen *(Braddock)*, Allan Rich *(Dr. Clark)*.

The word "maudlin" is given new scope in this babbling piece of sentimentality written by and starring Burt Young as a trumpet player who's hit rock bottom in a big way. When his wife and child are killed in a fire, Young approaches suicide, but his life is brightened by crippled youngster McKeon. The stereotypical character development has both Young and McKeon battling their obstacles through each other's encouragement. McKeon handles his role with an excess of hamminess, though admittedly most of the problems stem from the script. Maynard Ferguson handled the trumpet-blowing solos, and it becomes obvious when you catch Young failing to even move his fingers as he plays.

p, Robert Chartoff, Irwin Winkler; d, Joseph C. Hanwright; w, Burt Young; ph, Bill Butler; m, Bill Conti; ed, Don Zimmerman; prod d, Bill Kenney; cos, Bobbie Mannix.

Drama (PR:C MPAA:PG)

UNCLE SCAM zero (1981) 105m New World Pictures of Philadelphia c

Tom McCarthy *(Tom Ryan)*, Maxine Greene *(Ginger)*, John Russell *(Art)*, James E. Myers *(Steve Vitali)*, Sharon Victoria *(Linda)*, David Cassling *(Herbie)*, Matt Myers *(Governor Jones)*, Pat Cooper *(Agency Chief)*, Joan Rivers *(Herself)*, Alan Jay *(Harry)*, Shari Thomas *(Secretary)*, Diane Moore *(Congresswoman Starr)*, Pat Canuso *(Donna)*, Elaine Filoon *(Selma)*, Marvin Stafford *(Sidney)*, Joe Pileggi *(Sal)*.

The biggest scam most audience members will recognize in this picture is shelling out cash to see it. It's a treacherously lame comedy about a group of federal agents trying to catch some bribes on film a la the Abscam scandal. The perpetrators are caught, but do manage to turn the camera on the feds and film some extramarital activities. Co-producers, directors, and writers Pileggi and Levanios, Jr. don't have much of a track record–Pileggi is a Philadelphia real estate developer who helped fund Joan Rivers' RABBIT TEST (1978), and Levanios is an industrial filmmaker–so it's not surprising that the film's quality is poor. Rivers turns up in the form of a nightclub appearance–it's brief, but more than most people can handle. Also cast is James E. Myers, who helped pen "Rock Around The Clock." Pileggi, having assembled his nepotism-packed production team, reportedly purchased a large area of Bucks County, Pennsylvania, planning to build a studio for the production of still more such cream-cheese pictures. One is reminded of W. C. Fields' self-penned epitaph: "On the whole, I'd rather be in Philadelphia."

p&d, Tom Pileggi, Michael Levanios, Jr.; w, Pileggi, Levanios, Jr., Tom Pilong, Joe Ryan; ph, John Burke; m, Michael Levanios III; ed, Levanios, Jr.

Comedy (PR:O MPAA:R)

UNCLE SILAS (SEE: INHERITANCE, THE, 1951, Brit.)

UNCLE TOM'S CABIN*½ (1969, Fr./Ital./Ger./Yugo.) 118m Melodie-CCC-Filmkunst-A vala-S.I.P.R.O.-Debora/Kroger Babb c (ONKEL TOMS HUTTE; LA CASE DE L'ONCLE TOM ; CENTO DOLLARI D'O-DIO; CICA TOMINA KOLIBA)

John Kitzmiller *(Uncle Tom)*, O. W. Fischer *(Saint-Claire)*, Herbert Lom *(Simon Legree)*, Eleanora Rossi-Drago *(Mrs. Saint-Claire)*, Gertraud Mittermayr *(Little Eva Saint-Claire)*, Mylene Demongeot *(Harriet)*, Juliette Greco *(Dinah)*, Olive Moorefield *(Cassy)*, Catana Cayetano *(Eliza)*, Rhet Kirby *(Topsy)*, Eartha Kitt *(Singer)*, Charles Fawcett *(Mr. Shelby)*, Thomas Fritsch *(George Shelby)*, Bibi Jelinek *(Virginia)*, Aziz Saad *(Napoleon)*, Harry Tamekloe *(Andy)*, George Goodman *(Sambo)*, Harold Bradley *(Harris)*, Erika von Thellmann *(Aunt Ophelia)*, Dorothee Ellison *(Uncle Tom's Mama)*, Felix White *(Dolph)*, Vilma Degischer *(Mrs. Shelby)*, Claudio Gora, the Voice of Ella Fitzgerald.

The classic tale of slavery and southern plantations is brought to the screen by veteran Hungarian director Radvanyi, who chose to film in Yogoslavia. It doesn't take a geography major to notice that Yugoslavia doesn't pass for Kentucky, and that Serbians don't look like black slaves. This tale of life among the lowly, while keenly acted, suffers from endless historical inaccuracies and a tendency to wander too far from the original material. Author Stowe's powerful but provincial tale here has turned epic, with such additions as the assassination of Abraham Lincoln being depicted to reinforce the political ferment of the period. The music is an odd mix, with Jerome Kern's "Old Man River" blending badly with Aram Khatchaturian's "Sword Dance." Oddly, this is the only sound version, though 8 silents were filmed.

p, Aldo von Pinelli (U.S. version supervised by Kroger Babb); d, Geza von Radvanyi; w, Radvanyi, Fred Denger (based on the novel by Harriet Beecher Stowe); ph, Heinz Holscher (70mm Superpanorama, Eastmancolor); m, Peter Thomas; ed, Victor Palfi (U.S. version ed, Will Williams); art d, Willi Schatz; cos, Herbert Ploberger.

Historical Drama (PR:C MPAA:G)

UNCLE VANYA* (1958) 98m Uncle Vanya/CD bw

Mary Perry *(Marina)*, Franchot Tone *(Dr. Mikhail Lvovich Astroff)*, George Voskovec *(Ivan Petrovich "Uncle Vanya" Voinitsky)*, Clarence Derwent *(Prof. Alexander Vladimirovich Serebriakoff)*, Peggy McCay *(Sofia Alexandrovna)*, Dolores Dorn-Heft *(Dorn)* *(Elena Andreevna Serebriakoff)*, Gerald Hiken *(Ilya Ilyich Telegin)*, Shirley Gale *(Maria Vasilievna Voinitskaya)*.

A reproduction of the Chekhov play which ran off Broadway which here, unfortunately, makes minimum use of the film medium. As faithful as it is to the original, it is overly talky in its telling of a country doctor (Tone) who devotes his attentions to his work, but still falls in love with an unattainable beauty. Voskovec is cast in the title role, a frustrated old man who realizes that he hasn't lived his life to the fullest. The same cast as the stage production four years earlier with the exception of Dorn-Heft, who replaced Signe Hasso.

p, Marion Parsonnet, Franchot Tone; d, John Goetz, Tone; w, Stark Young (based on his translation of Anton Chekhov's play); m, Werner Jannssen; art d, Kim E. Swados

Drama (PR:A MPAA:NR)

UNCLE VANYA½ (1972, USSR) 110m Mosfilm/Artkino bw/c (DIADIA VANYA)

Innokenty Smoktunovsky *(Ivan "Uncle Vanya" Voynitsky)*, Sergei Bondarchuk *(Dr. Astrov)*, Vladimir Zeldin *(Alexander Serebryskov)*, Irina Kupchenko *(Sonya Serebryskov)*, Irina Miroshnichenko *(Yelena Serebryskov)*, Irina Anisimova-Wolf *(Mother)*, Nikolai Pastukov *(Telyegin)*.

A slow but insightful version of Chekhov's stage play about hopelessness and the relationships between a pathetic old uncle (Smoktunovsky), a devoted doctor (Bondarchuk), and a visiting professor who arrives with his lovely new wife. Wordy and somewhat claustrophobic in its near-exclusive use of indoor locations. Bondarchuk is not only one of the top post-WW II Russian actors but also a respected director, who directed the 8 ½-hour, $40 million epic version of Tolstyo's WAR AND PEACE. (Russian; English subtitles.)

d&w, Andrei Mikhalkov-Konchalovsky (based on the play by Anton Chekhov); ph, Georgy Rerberg, Yevgeny Guslinsky (Partial Sovcolor); m, A. Shnitke; art d, N. Dvigubsky.

Drama (PR:A MPAA:G)

UNCLE VANYA* (1977, Brit.) 120m British Home Entertainment/Arthur Cantor bw

Sybil Thorndike *(Nurse)*, Laurence Olivier *(Dr. Astrov)*, Michael Redgrave *(Uncle Vanya)*, Lewis Casson *(Telyegin)*, Joan Plowright *(Sonya)*, Rosemary

Harris (*Yelena*), Fay Compton (*Mother*), Robert Lang (*Yefim*), Max Adrian (*Professor*).

The 1963 Chichester Festival production of the classic Chekhov play is recorded in this oddly uninteresting film. The direction keeps most of the action confined to closeups and two-shots, and the audience loses any sense of where the characters are in relation to each other and the larger space of the stage. What does show through of the original production with its amazing cast is still worth watching for theater fans.

d, Stuart Burge (based on the stage play directed by Laurence Olivier); w, Anton Chekhov (translation by Constance Garnett).

Drama   **(PR:A MPAA:NR)**

UNCOMMON THIEF, AN**   (1967, USSR) 93m Mosfilm/Artkino bw
                                            (BEREGIS AVTOMOBILYA!)

Innokenty Smoktunovsky (*Detochkin*), Oleg Yefremov (*Maksim Podberyozovikov*), Anatoliy Papanov (*Sokol-Kruzhkin*), Lyubov Dobrzhanskaya, Olga Aroseva, Andrey Mironov, Tatyana Gavrilova, Georgiy Zhzhyonov, Yevgeniy Yevstigneyev, Sergey Kulagin, Viktoria Radunskaya, G. Roninson, B. Runge, Ya. Lents, V. Nevinnyy, D. Banionis, G. Volchek, L. Sokolava, A. Maksimova.

Smoktunovsky is the amateur thief with an uncommon habit of stealing the cars of criminals who have not justly been dealt with by the law. He then sells the cars and donates the cash to an orphanage. He is eventually caught when he tell his actions to a police investigator assigned to the case who happens to be acting with the crook in a stage production of Hamlet. The investigator sides with the thief, however, and when the trial comes along Smoktunovsky is freed.

d, Eldar Ryazanov; w, Emil Veniaminovich Braginskiy, Ryazanov; ph, Anatoliy Mukasey, Vladimir Nakhabtsev; m, Andrey Petrov; art d, Boris Nemechek, Lev Semyonov.

Comedy/Drama   **(PR:A MPAA:NR)**

UNCOMMON VALOR**   (1983) 105m PAR c

Gene Hackman (*Col. Rhodes*), Robert Stack (*MacGregor*), Fred Ward (*Wilkes*), Reb Brown (*Blaster*), Randall "Tex" Cobb (*Sailor*), Patrick Swayze (*Scott*), Harold Sylvester (*Johnson*), Tim Thomerson (*Charts*), Alice Lau [Lau Nga Lai] (*Lai Fun*), Kwan Hi Lim (*Jiang*), Gail Strickland (*Mrs. Helen Rhodes*), Kelly Yunkermann (*Paul MacGregor*), Todd Allen (*Frank Rhodes*), Jeremy Kemp (*Ferryman*), Jane Kaczmarek (*Mrs. Wilkes*), Gloria Stroock (*Mrs. MacGregor*), Constance Forslund (*Mrs. Charts*), Charles Aidman (*Sen. Hastings*), Debi Parker (*Mai Ling*), Jan Triska (*Gericault*), James Edgcomb (*CIA Agent*), Ken Farmer (*Jail Guard*), Tad Horino (*Mr. Ky*), Michael Dudikoff (*Blaster's Assistant*), Bruce Paul Barbour (*Helicopter Pilot*), Jerry Supiran (*Frank at Age 9*), Juan Fernandez (*Orderly*), Darwyn Carson (*Secretary*), Emmett Dennis III (*Medic*), Charles Faust, David Austin (*GIs*), Le Tuan (*Guard*), Steven Solberg, Laurence Neber, Don Mantooth (*POWs*), Brett Johnson, Barret Oliver, Marcello Krakoff, Justin Bayly, Kevin Brando, Angela Lee (*Kids*), Nancy Linari, David Dangler (*Reporters*), William S. Hamilton, Napoleon Hendrix, Chip Lally, Michael P. May, Tom Randa, Larry Charles White (*Soldiers*).

One of a string of "Let's go back and rescue our boys" pictures which has an angry hero trying to win in Vietnam "this time." Hackman stars and contributes a different persona to the role than Chuck Norris in his MISSING IN ACTION pictures, or Stallone in the baffling, stupid RAMBO. He gathers together a group of veterans and leads them back into the jungles in the hopes of finding his missing-in-action son. Hackman makes it watchable, but the politics and emotions that accompany these types of films are disturbing. Coproducer Milius carries this right-wing propaganda even further in his anti-Red, pro-survivalist RED DAWN (1984). Beautifully photographed by the consistent Burum, who also shot the visually poetic RUMBLE FISH (1983).

p, John Milius, Buzz Feitshans; d, Ted Kotcheff; w, Joe Gayton; ph, Stephen H. Burum, Ric Waite (Movielab Color); m, James Horner; ed, Mark Melnick; prod d, James L. Schoppe; art d, Jack G. Taylor, Jr; set d, John H. Anderson, George Gaines.

Adventure   **Cas.**   **(PR:O MPAA:R)**

UNCONQUERED***½   (1947) 146m PAR c

Gary Cooper (*Capt. Christopher Holden*), Paulette Goddard (*Abigail Martha "Abby" Hale*), Howard da Silva (*Martin Garth*), Boris Karloff (*Guyasuta, Chief of the Senecas*), Cecil Kellaway (*Jeremy Love*), Ward Bond (*John Fraser*), Katherine DeMille (*Hannah*), Henry Wilcoxon (*Capt. Steele*), C. Aubrey Smith (*Lord Chief Justice*), Victor Varconi (*Capt. Simson Ecuyer*), Virginia Grey (*Diana*), Porter Hall (*Leach*), Mike Mazurki (*Dave Bone*), Richard Gaines (*Col. George Washington*), Virginia Campbell (*Mrs. John Fraser*), Gavin Muir (*Lt. Fergus McKenzie*), Alan Napier (*Sir William Johnson*), Nan Sutherland (*Mrs. Pruitt*), Marc Lawrence (*Sioto, Medicine Man*), Jane Nigh (*Evelyn*), Robert Warwick (*Pontiac, Chief of the Ottawas*), Lloyd Bridges (*Lt. Hutchins*), Oliver Thorndike (*Lt. Billie*), Rus Conklin (*Wamaultee*), John Mylong (*Col. Henry Bouquet*), Raymond Hatton (*Venan-*

go *Scout*), Julia Faye (*Widow Swivens*), Paul E. Burns (*Dan McCoy*), Clarence Muse (*Jason*), Jeff York (*Wide-Shouldered Youth*), Dick Alexander (*Slave*), Syd Saylor (*Spieler for Dr. Diablo*), Si Jenks (*Farmer*), Bob Kortman (*Frontiersman*), Edgar Dearing, Hugh Prosser, Ray Teal (*Soldiers-Gilded Beaver*), Chief Thundercloud (*Chief Killbuck*), Noble Johnson (*Big Ottawa Indian*), John Merton (*Corporal*), Buddy Roosevelt (*Guard*), John Miljan (*Prosecutor*), Jay Silverheels (*Indian*), Lex Barker (*Royal American Officer*), Jack Pennick (*Joe Lovat*), Byron Foulger (*Townsman*), Denver Dixon (*Citizen*), Fred Kohler, Jr. (*Sergeant*), Tiny Jones (*Bondswoman*), Charles B. Middleton (*Mulligan*), Dorothy Adams (*Mrs. Bront*), Davison Clark (*Mr. Carroll*), Griff Barnett (*Brother Andrews*), Francis Ford, Gertrude Valerie, Christopher Clark, Bill Murphy, Greta Granstedt, Ottola Nesmith, Al Ferguson, Constance Purdy, Rose Higgins, Inez Palange, Mimi Aguglia, Clare DuBrey, Fernanda Eliscu, Belle Mitchell, Charmienne Harker, Isabel Chabing Cooper, Anna Lehr, Lane Chandler, Mike Killian, Erville Alderson, Jeff Corey, William Haade, Iron Eyes Cody, Olaf Hytten, Eric Alden, Frank Hagney, Sally Rawlinson, Chuck Hamilton, Ethel Wales, Francis McDonald, June Harris.

Another of Cecil B. DeMille's bloated epics about the shaping of America. Goddard is an indentured servant sentenced to 14 years of servitude in the American colonies. On the voyage across from England, she meets Cooper, a Virginia militia captain who takes an immediate liking to her, despite the fact that he is already engaged to be married. She also attracts the eye of da Silva, a scurrilous trader. When his attentions grow too lewd, she slaps him hard, which makes him want to buy her contract and make her his own. He is foiled on the docks, though, when Cooper bids a higher price. Cooper immediately gives Goddard her freedom. Da Silva has too many other nefarious schemes in the works to be bothered by a little setback like this. He marries the daughter of Seneca chief Karloff and agitates the Indians to unite to drive the white men back into the sea, using muskets he sells them. At Fort Pitt, Cooper's fiancee arrives to tell him that she has fallen in love with another man, a development that doesn't bother him too much. Goddard, however, falls into da Silva's hands again when he manages to get hold of her contract and convince her that Cooper's purchase had been fraudulent. He puts her to work in a saloon he owns managed by crude Mazurki. She scrubs the floor while the men make rude comments, but Cooper isn't long in rescuing her at knifepoint. Da Silva's Indian wife is jealous of her husband's attentions toward Goddard, so she arranges with the tribe to have her kidnaped. Goddard is tied to a stake and is about to be tortured when Cooper comes on the scene to rescue her yet again. They arrive back at the fort just as the Indians attack with flaming arrows. Cooper helps the settlers fight off the Indians, then manages to kill da Silva and Mazurki in a shootout in a stable afterward. As the film ends he and Goddard are about to be married. A huge and expensive production that just didn't come off. Over $5 million and 102 days were spent on the production, but it was savaged by the critics when it came out and the public stayed away. Goddard gave the director trouble when she refused to climb the ramparts of the fort during the attack sequence for fear of the flaming arrows that had already sent 30 extras to the hospital with burns. To teach her a lesson DeMille picked one lowly extra for an important part in the scene, succoring the wounded on the ramparts. Goddard was vindicated, though, when the extra joined the others at the hospital. Karloff wasn't very good as the Indian chief, though his dedication to the part was impressive. He had originally intended to speak the role in gibberish, but DeMille insisted that he learn Seneca, which he did. In addition, the actor had recently undergone back surgery and under his bonnet and furs and loincloth was a massive brace. The expert in Indian regalia who dressed Karloff (deaf-mute Joe De Yong) sent a note to DeMille saying of Karloff, "This man is as patient as a horse." Cooper is good, but beginning to look a little old to be gallivanting about the frontier, and Goddard tries too hard to be glamorous, destroying her character. Da Silva is a worthy villain and the rest of the cast is more than adequate, but the whole thing sinks under its own grand weight. DeMille simply tries too hard to get in everything, even one of his patented bathtub scenes, played here in a barrel by Goddard. The film lost of fortune at the box office.

p&d, Cecil B. DeMille; w, Charles Bennett, Frederic M. Frank, Jesse Lasky, Jr. (based on the novel *The Judas Tree* by Neil H. Swanson); ph, Ray Rennahan (Technicolor); m, Victor Young; ed, Anne Bauchens; art d, Hans Dreier, Walter Tyler; set d, Sam Comer, Stanley Jay Sawley; cos, Gwen Wakeling, Mme. Barbara Karinska; spec eff, Gordon Jennings, Farciot Edouart, W. Wallace Kelley, Paul Lerpae, Devereux Jennings; ch, Jack Crosby; makeup, Wally Westmore; m/l, "Whippoorwills-a-Singing," Ray Evans, Jay Livingston; tech adv, Iron Eyes Cody, Capt. Fred F. Ellis, BMM (ret.).

Historical Adventure   **Cas.**   **(PR:A MPAA:NR)**

UND IMMER RUFT DAS HERZ   (SEE: MOONWOLF, 1966, Ger.)

...UND MORGEN FAHRT IHR ZUR HOLIE
                              (SEE: DIRTY HEROES, 1969, Fr./Ital./Ger.)

UNDEAD, THE**   (1957) 71m AIP bw

Pamela Duncan (*Helene/Diana Love*), Richard Garland (*Pendragon*), Allison Hayes (*Livia*), Val DuFour (*Quintus*), Mel Welles (*Smolkin*), Dorothy Neuman (*Meg Maud*), Billy Barty (*The Imp*), Bruno Ve Soto (*Scroop, Innkeeper*), Aaron Saxon (*Gobbo*), Richard Devon (*Satan*), Dick Miller.

A Roger Corman cheapie about a prostitute who gets sent back into the Middle Ages as a result of an experiment. She finds herself as a witch condemned to die and tries to fight off fate. Eventually she accepts her scheduled beheading in order to let her future lives exist. Another piece of guesswork revolving around reincarnation–a popular subject of the time. Plenty of blood and bosoms.

p&d, Roger Corman; w, Charles Griffith, Mark Hanna; ph, William Sickner; m, Ronald Stein; ed, Frank Sullivan.

Horror   **(PR:A   MPAA:NR)**

UNDEFEATED, THE**   (1969) 119m FOX c

John Wayne (*Col. John Henry Thomas*), Rock Hudson (*Col. James Langdon*), Tony Aguilar (*Gen. Rojas*), Roman Gabriel (*Blue Boy*), Marian McCargo (*Ann Langdon*), Lee Meriwether (*Margaret Langdon*), Merlin Olsen (*Big George*), Melissa Newman (*Charlotte Langdon*), Bruce Cabot (*Jeff Newby*), [Jan-Michael] Michael Vincent (*Bubba Wilkes*), Ben Johnson (*Short Grub*), Edward Faulkner (*Anderson*), Harry Carey, Jr (*Webster*), Royal Dano (*Major Sanders*), Richard Mulligan (*Dan Morse*), Paul Fix (*Gen. Joe Masters*), arlos Rivas (*Diaz*), John Agar (*Christian*), Guy Raymond (*Giles*), Don Collier (*Goodyear*), Big John Hamilton (*Mudlow*), Dub Taylor (*McCartney*), Cook, Henry Beckman (*Thad Benedict*), Victor Junco (*Maj. Tapia*), Robert Donner (*Judd Mailer*), Pedro Armendariz, Jr (*Escalante*), James Dobson (*Jamison*), Rudy Diaz (*Sanchez*), Richard Angarola (*Petain*), James McEachin (*Jimmy Collins*), Gregg Palmer (*Parker*), Juan Garcia (*Col. Gomez*), Kiel Martin (*Union Runner*), Bob Gravage (*Joe Hicks*), Chuck Roberson (*Yankee Officer*).

An average western which looks even more mediocre following the performance John Wayne gives in the same year's TRUE GRIT. Here he plays a Union colonel who is leading a herd of 3,000 horses into Mexico with Gabriel, his adopted Indian son, by his side. Also en route to Mexico is Confederate colonel Hudson who is leading an exodus of fellow Southerners to a place where they won't have to see their land devoured by carpetbaggers. The two colonels meet and unite in a fight against Mexican bandits. Wayne eventually has to come to Hudson's aid when the Southerners are captured by Aguilar, a supporter of Benito Juarez, who plans to kill his prisoners unless Wayne turns over his herd. Complications arise involving the French cavalry, which plans to take the horses and deliver them themselves. Wayne, however, delivers the horses to Aguilar and secures Hudson's freedom. A poor attempt at paying tribute to John Ford is clearly present in McLaglen's direction, especially in a 4th of July party which has both Hudson's Southerners and Wayne's Northerners whacking away at each other. THE UNDEFEATED adds up to nothing more than a weak imitation–paying little or no heed to originality. A pair of Los Angeles Rams football players make an appearance–Gabriel, as Wayne's Indian aide, and Merlin Olsen, as a kindly blacksmith.

p, Robert L. Jacks; d, Andrew V. McLaglen; w, James Lee Barrett (based on a story by Stanley L. Hough); ph, William Clothier (Panavision, DeLuxe Color); m, Hugo Montenegro; ed, Robert Simpson; md, Montenegro; art d, Carl Anderson; set d, Walter M. Scott, Chester L. Bayhi; cos, Bill Thomas; spec eff, L. B. Abbott, Art Cruikshank; makeup, Dan Striepeke; stunts, Hal Needham.

Western   **Cas.**   **(PR:A   MPAA:G)**

UNDER A CLOUD*   (1937, Brit.) 67m Triangle/PAR bw

Edward Rigby (*Jimmy Forbes*), Betty Ann Davies (*Diana Forbes*), Bernard Clifton (*George Forbes*), Renee Gadd (*Judy St. John*), Hilda Bayley (*Mrs. Forbes*), Moira Reed (*Mary Jessyl*), Brian Buchel (*Arnold Gill*), Peter Gawthorne (*Sir Edmund Jessyl*), Jack Vyvyan (*Inspector Bryan*), Billy Watts.

Rigby flees England for Australia with the police after him, but returns 20 years later when the heat is off. He sets about fixing his family's troubles, including getting his daughter away from a gigolo and clearing his son, accused of murdering a blackmailer. He also offers his wife a divorce, but in the end she hops a boat and and goes back with him to Australia.

p&d, George King; w, M.B. Parsons (based on a story by Gordon Francis); ph, Hone Glendinning.

Crime   **(PR:A   MPAA:NR)**

UNDER A TEXAS MOON**   (1930) 82m WB c

Frank Fay (*Don Carlos*), Raquel Torres (*Raquella*), Myrna Loy (*Lolita Romero*), Armida (*Dolores*), Noah Beery, Sr (*Jed Parker*), Georgie [George E.] Stone (*Pedro*), George Cooper (*Philipe*), Fred Kohler (*Bad Man*), Betty Boyd (*Girl*), Charles Sellon (*Jose Romero*), Jack Curtis (*Buck Johnson*), Sam Appel (*Pancho Gonzalez*), Tully Marshall (*Gus Aldrich*), Mona Maris (*Lolita Roberto*), Francisco Maran (*Antonio*), Tom Dix (*Tom*), Jerry Barrett (*Jerry*),

Inez Gomez (*Mother*), Edythe Kramera (*Moza*), Bruce Covington (*Don Roberto*).

Fay is cast as the womanizing Don Carlos who agrees to bring in a cattle rustler within 10 days, but instead makes a play for every senorita in sight. Fay, better known for his stage and radio appearances than for his cinema work, is an odd choice as the amorous *bandido*. His freckled Irish face notwithstanding, he does a fine comic job. Reportedly, a clash of enlarged egos occurred during filming, with director Curtiz and Fay getting surprisingly good results from their collaboration considering that they were not on speaking terms. Armida's staccato speech is outstanding as she vocally emulates a machine gun. Curtiz apparently was entranced by Loy, who got a lot of footage in one of her early stock ethnic roles as a languorous Latin lovely, one of the many romanced by the satyriasis-suffering Fay. An enjoyable, aptly-directed comic western, which is the first of the genre to be shot in color, making bold use of it in the Mexican settings. Includes the song "Under a Texas Moon" (Ray Perkins).

d, Michael Curtiz; w, Gordon Rigby (based on the story "Two-Gun Man" by Stewart Edward White); ph, Bill Rees (Two-color Technicolor); m, Ray Perkins; ed, Ralph Dawson.

Western/Comedy   **(PR:A   MPAA:NR)**

UNDER AGE*½   (1941) 60m COL bw

Nan Grey (*Jane Baird*), Tom Neal (*"Rocky" Stone*), Mary Anderson (*Edie Baird*), Alan Baxter (*Tap Manson*), Leona Maricle (*Mme. Burke*), Don Beddoe (*Albert Ward*), Yolande Mollot (*Lily Fletcher*), Richard Terry (*Grant*), Wilma Francis (*Rhoda*), Patti McCarty (*Minnie*), Billie Roy (*Boots*), Gwen Kenyon (*Gladys*), Barbara Kent (*Jackie*), Nancy Worth (*Nell*).

Grey leads a cast of young women who are forced into working for mobsters after their release from detention centers. They are hired to lure wealthy men into bogus tourist resorts where they are then relieved of all their earnings by gambling racketeers. When Neal gets most of his jewel firm's gems stolen, the police intervene and the gang is cracked. Plenty of sweatered starlets for the prurient in this B offering.

p, Ralph Cohn; d, Edward Dmytryk; w, Robert D. Andrews (based on a story by Stanley Roberts); ph, John Stumar; ed, Richard Fantl; art d, Lionel Banks.

Crime   **(PR:A-C   MPAA:NR)**

UNDER AGE*   (1964) 90m Falcon/AIP bw

Anne MacAdams (*Ruby Jenkins*), Judy Adler (*Linda Jenkins*), Roland Royter (*George Gomez*), George Russell (*Defense Atty. Tyler*), John Hicks (*Prosecuting Atty. Adkins*), George Edgley (*The Judge*), Tommie Russell (*Mrs. Sybel Riley*), Regina Cassidy (*Dr. Vivian Scott*), Joseph Patrick Cranshaw (*W. J. Earnhardt, Justice of the Peace*), Raymond Bradford (*Wilbur Neal*), Jonathan Ledford (*Barney Jenkins*), Howard Ware (*Bailiff*), Joretta Cherry (*Court Reporter*), Robert Alcott (*Assistant District Attorney*), William Peck (*News Photographer*), Barnett Shaw (*News Reporter*).

A divorced mother is brought to trial and charged with rape under a Texas law which stipulates that if a person encourages an illegal act that person too can be tried for the crime. The court must decide whether or not MacAdams is responsible for the sexual contact that occurred between her 14-year-old daughter Adler and the girl's Mexican boy friend Royter. It turns out that the audience members must judge for themselves since the film ends with the jury in deliberation. The suspense is just killing us. Songs: "Boil Them Cabbage Down" (The Alpine Trio), "Turtledove Song" (The Lost River Trio), and the title song (Harold Hoffman, Larry Buchanan).

p, Harold Hoffman; d, Larry Buchanan; w, Hoffman, Buchanan; ph, Henry Kokojan; ed, Buchanan.

Courtroom Drama   **(PR:O   MPAA:NR)**

UNDER ARIZONA SKIES**   (1946) 59m MON bw

Johnny Mack Brown, Raymond Hatton, Reno Blair [Browne], Riley Hill, Tristam Coffin, Reed Howes, Ted Adams, Ray Bennett, Frank LaRue, Steve Clark, Jack Rockwell, Bud Geary, Ted Mapes, Kermit Maynard, Ray Jones, Smith Ballew and the Sons of the Sage, Reno the Horse.

Yet another Johnny Mack Brown oater, this time with the stern-faced hero fighting cattle rustlers. Indistinguishable from scores of other films the big money-making cowboy starred in.

p, Scott R. Dunlap; d, Lambert Hillyer; w, J. Benton Cheney (based on a story by John McCarthy); ph, Harry Neumann; ed, Fred Maguire; md, Edward J. Kay.

Western   **(PR:A   MPAA:NR)**

UNDER CALIFORNIA SKIES   (SEE: UNDER CALIFORNIA STARS, 1948)

UNDER CALIFORNIA STARS*½   (1948) 70m REP/(AKA: UNDER CALIFORNIA SKIES)

Roy Rogers (Himself), Jane Frazee (Caroline Maynard), Andy Devine (Cookie Bullfincher), George H. Lloyd (Jonas "Pop" Jordan), Wade Crosby (Lye McFarland), Michael Chapin (Ted Conover), House Peters, Jr (Ed), Steve Clark (Sheriff), Joseph Garro (Joe), Paul Power (Director), John Wald (Announcer), Bob Nolan and The Sons of the Pioneers, Trigger the Horse.

Trigger is the center of this oater's plot when he is kidnaped and held for a $100,000 ransom. Rogers and his ranch hands get tough and are able to retrieve the animal as well as bring the culprits to justice. Marred by some noticeably cheap effects such as a dummy stand-in which receives a kick from Trigger, and a stunt double for the star who bears him no resemblance.

p, Edward J. White; d, William Witney; w, Sloan Nibley, Paul Gangelin (based on a story by Gangelin); ph, Jack Marta (Trucolor); m, Morton Scott; ed, Tony Martinelli; art d, Frank Hotaling; set d, John McCarthy, Jr., George Milo; spec eff, Howard Lydecker, Theodore Lydecker; makeup, Bob Mark.

Western   **Cas.**   **(PR:A MPAA:NR)**

UNDER CAPRICORN**   (1949) 117m TRA/WB c

Ingrid Bergman (Lady Henrietta Flusky), Joseph Cotten (Sam Flusky), Michael Wilding (Hon. Charles Adare), Margaret Leighton (Milly), Cecil Parker (Governor), Dennis O'Dea (Corrigan), Jack Watling (Winter), Harcourt Williams (Coachman), John Ruddock (Mr. Potter), Ronald Adam (Mr. Riggs), Francis de Wolff (Commissioner), G. H. Mulcaster (Dr. McAllister), Olive Sloane (Sal), Maureen Delany (Flo), Bill Shine (Mr. Banks), Julia Lang (Susan), Betty McDermott (Martha), Roderick Lovell, Victor Lucas.

An ill-conceived and muddled costume epic that cost (and lost) a fortune. Casting Bergman as an Irish girl and Leighton as an evil housemaid are just two of the many flaws in this heavy production that came in at nearly $2.5 million and failed to recover from the yawning reception given by critics and public. Set in 1831 Australia, it picks up in mid-story and we learn, through exposition, that Cotten, an Irish horse groom, had run off with Bergman, the daughter of a titled Irish aristocrat. When her brother attempted to stop the couple, he was killed and Cotten was tried and convicted of the slaying and sent to Australia. Tossed aside by her family and now with no funds, Bergman tailed her husband to the Island Continent. The law, at that time, stated that anyone who had served a term would be allowed to begin again and since Australia had so many former felons, Cotten was in his element and waxed wealthy as a real estate entrepreneur. Despite his wealth, Cotten is not accepted by the doyennes of Australia who raise their collective noses at this nouveau riche couple. This treatment forces Bergman to head straight for the bottle which causes her mind to become addled and creates a problem as to who is the mistress of the estate, she or Leighton. The latter is a strong-willed woman who sees an opportunity to ease the besotted Bergman out of the way so she can move in on Cotten. Bergman becomes increasingly unable to take care of the house or herself and Leighton continues to embarrass Bergman whenever she can. Wilding is Bergman's cousin. He's a smiling and amiable young man who has come to Australia to find his own way in life and he gets in touch with Bergman. He is shocked by the manner in which matters are conducted at the Cotten-Bergman home and wants to do what he can to bring back her old bloom. Cotten thinks that's a good idea as Bergman has no real friends and it just might be beneficial if she and Wilding pal around together for a while, talk about the fun they had as children, and so forth. Leighton watches this closely and subtly hints to Cotten that Bergman and Wilding may have a bit more than a familial relationship. It's the truth, at least on Wilding's part, as he soon finds himself enamored of Bergman. Things aren't moving fast enough for Leighton so she tries to eliminate Bergman with poison. Before the deed is done, Cotten discovers what Leighton is up to and banishes her from the estate, but not before she hurls accusations that Wilding and Bergman have been romantic lovers. Cotten is beginning to doubt his wife's fidelity. They are invited to a society party and Cotten verbally lashes Bergman, perhaps due to what Leighton has said or it could be because the hoity-toity ways of the people at the function have made him feel out of place. Wilding springs to Bergman's defense and the two men tussle, with Wilding coming out on the short end. Wilding is ready to press charges and the government, knowing that Cotten is already a convicted killer, already thinks the worst of him. Now Bergman drops a bombshell as she reveals that she was the person who killed her brother long ago and that Cotten took the rap for it. Further, it was that long-ago crime which caused her to seek solace in booze. Wilding's gunshot wound is a minor one and he elects to drop the charge against Cotten and tells the authorities that it was an accident. Now, there is still a charge against Bergman for killing her brother but Cotten will not verify that (since he has already done the time for the murder and since he loves her so much, it's the only gentlemanly thing to do), so both are released. Wilding sees that he is a fifth wheel and returns to Ireland, thus allowing Bergman and Cotten to reawaken their love for each other and face the remainder of their lives as a couple. Talky, with little of the Hitchcock suspense. One grisly sequence as a shrunken mummified head is seen but that's about it. Hitchcock's metier was not in the costume drama (although he did do JAMAICA INN 10 years before) and he wisely decided to stay out of the genre after this. Long sequences with no cuts added up to a very wordy picture. Hitchcock had just finished ROPE, which featured 10-minute takes and he liked the freedom, but the actors, mainly Bergman,

rebelled and there was more friction on the set than on the screen. Made by Hitchcock's own Transatlantic Pictures, it was eventually taken back by the bank which put up the money and marked the end of the director's company.

p, Sidney Bernstein, Alfred Hitchcock; d, Hitchcock; w, James Bridie, Hume Cronyn (based on the play by John Colton, Margaret Linden, and the novel by Helen Simpson); ph, Jack Cardiff, Paul Beeson, Ian Craig, David McNeilly, Jack Haste (Technicolor); m, Richard Addinsell; ed, A.S. Bates; md, Louis Levy; art d, Tom Morahan; cos, Roger Furse.

Historical Drama   **Cas.**   **(PR:C MPAA:NR)**

UNDER COLORADO SKIES**½   (1947) 65m REP c

Monte Hale (Himself), Adrian Booth (Julia), Paul Hurst ("Lucky" John Hawkins), William Haade (Marlowe), John Alvin (Jeff), LeRoy Mason (Faro), Tom London (Sheriff Blanchard), Steve Darrell (Clip), Gene Evans (Red), Ted Adams (Doc Thornhill), Steve Raines (Pony), Hank Patterson (Slim), Foy Willing and The Riders of the Purple Sage.

Hale is a medical student and part-time bank employee accused of working with Haade's bank-robbing gang. It turns out that Hale is only trying to protect his fiancee's brother, but by the finale the truth comes out and Hale is cleared. Includes the song "San Antonio Rose" performed by The Riders of the Purple Sage.

p, Melville Tucker; d, R. G. Springsteen; w, Louise Rousseau; ph, Alfred S. Keller (Trucolor); ed, Arthur Roberts; md, Mort Glickman; art d, Frank Hotaling; set d, John McCarthy, Jr., Helen Hansard; spec eff, Howard Lydecker, Theodore Lydecker; m/l, Bob Wills, Foy Willing, Sid Robin.

Western   **(PR:A MPAA:NR)**

UNDER COVER OF NIGHT**   (1937) 70m MGM bw

Edmund Lowe (Christopher Cross), Florence Rice (Deb), Nat Pendleton (Sgt. Lucks), Henry Daniell (Prof. Marvin Griswald), Sara Haden (Janet Griswald), Dean Jagger (Alan), Frank Reicher (Rudolph Brehmer), Zeffie Tilbury (Mrs. Nash), Henry Kolker (District Atty. Prichard), Marla Shelton (Tonya Van Horne), Theodore von Eltz (John Lamont), Dorothy Peterson (Susan), Harry Davenport (Dr. Reed).

A stock murder mystery which isn't all that mysterious. Lowe is the detective on the trail of professor Daniell, who has been taking all the credit for his wife's research. When she threatens to leave him, he kills her. He soon realizes that she confided in other members of the college, forcing him to bump off a couple more. Rice was lucky enough to be saved from Daniell's murderous clutch by Lowe, who proved his competence as a gumshoe.

p, Lucien Hubbard, Ned Marin; d, George B. Seitz; w, Bertram Milhauser; ph, Charles Clarke; ed, Ben Lewis.

Crime/Mystery   **(PR:A MPAA:NR)**

UNDER COVER ROGUE   (SEE: WHITE VOICES, 1964, Fr./Ital.)

UNDER EIGHTEEN*½   (1932) 80m WB bw

Marian Marsh (Marge Evans), Regis Toomey (Jimmie, Grocery Clerk), Warren William (Howard Raymond), Anita Page (Sophie), Emma Dunn (Mrs. Evans), Joyce Compton (Sybil), J. Farrell MacDonald (Pop Evans), Norman Foster (Alf), Dorothy Appleby (Elsie), Maude Eburne (Mrs. Ged), Claire Dodd (Babsy), Paul Porcasi (Francois), Mary Doran (Lucille), Murray Kinnell (Walters), Walter McGrail (Gregg), Judith Vosselli (Miss Gray).

Marsh is a young girl in dire financial straits who gets herself mixed up with a lecherous theatrical producer who resides in a luxurious penthouse. She is saved from this den of dancing, drink, and god-only-knows-what by Toomey, the kind-hearted, two-fisted grocery boy who can give her love but not money.

d, Archie Mayo; w, Charles Kenyon, Maude Fulton (based on the story "Sky Life" by Frank M. Dazey); ph, Sid Hickox; ed, George Marks.

Romance   **(PR:A MPAA:NR)**

UNDER FIESTA STARS**   (1941) 64m REP bw

Gene Autry, Smiley Burnette, Carol Hughes, Frank Darien, Joe Straugh, Jr, Pauline Drake, Ivan Miller, Sam Flint, Elias Gamboa, John Merton, Jack Kirk, Inez Palange, Curley Dresden, Hal Taliaferro, Frankie Marvin, Pascale Perry, Champion the Horse.

Autry inherits a gold mine, and finds more trouble than ore when he goes to claim it. Routine stuff, just about like all the other Autry movies.

p, Harry Grey; d, Frank McDonald; w, Karl Brown, Eliot Gibbons (based on a story by Brown); ph, Harry Neumann; ed, Tony Martinelli.

Western   **(PR:A MPAA:NR)**

UNDER FIRE** (1957) 78m FOX bw

Rex Reason (*Lt. Rogerson*), Henry [Harry] Morgan (*Sgt. Dusak*), Steve Brodie (*Capt. Linn*), Peter Walker (*Lt. Sarris*), Robert Levin (*Pvt. Pope*), Jon Locke (*Cpl. Crocker*), Gregory LaFayette (*Cpl. Quinn*), Karl Lukas (*Sgt. Hutchins*), Frank Gerstle (*Col. Dundee*), Tom McKee (*Capt. O'Mar*), John Murphy (*M.P. Sergeant*), Edmund Penney (*Capt. Linn's Assistant*), Seymour Green, Dave Tomack, Walter Maslow, David Carlisle (*Court Officers*), William Allyn (*Lt. Stagg*), Rita Paul (*Singer*), Kay Kuter (*Pvt. Swanson*), Keith Byron (*Capt. Tanner*), Neyle Morrow (*Lt. Conroy*), K. L. Smith (*Pvt. Finley*), Robert Hinkle (*Pvt. Barton*), Robert Colbert (*M.P. Sentry*), Al Shelley (*M.P. Lieutenant*), Troy Patterson (*Lieutenant*), Dehl Berti (*Col. Jason*), Ronald Foster (*Lieutenant D.S.C.*), Sid Melton (*1st GI*), George Chakiris (*Pvt. Steiner*), Ed Hinton (*Colonel D.S.C.*), Nico Minardos (*Pvt. Tartolia*), Calvin Booth (*2nd GI*), Lorraine Martin (*Nurse*), Mary Townsend (*Waitress*).

Four American soldiers–Morgan, Locke, LaFayette, and Levin–are court-martialed after being accused of deserting and killing a fellow soldier. Reason, the defense attorney, proves that four Germans disguised as Americans did the actual killing, clearing the names of his clients. This was the directorial debut for veteran 20th Century Fox editor Clark, and his pacing (intercutting action scenes with courtroom questioning) results from his past experience. Producer Skouras proves that there's sometimes merit in nepotism in this, his second production for his dad, studio chief Spyros Skouras. On July 4th, over two months before the picture's release, LaFayette and his wife, actress Judy Tyler (who had just finished JAIL-HOUSE ROCK) were both killed in a car wreck.

p, Plato Skouras; d, James B. Clark; w, James Landis; ph, John M. Nickolaus, Jr. (Regalscope); m, Paul Dunlap; ed, Jodie Copelan; art d, Rudi Feld.

War/Courtroom Drama (PR:A MPAA:NR)

UNDER FIRE*** (1983) 127M Lion's Gate/Orion c

Nick Nolte (*Russell Price*), Ed Harris (*Oates*), Gene Hackman (*Alex Grazier*), Joanna Cassidy (*Claire*), Alma Martinez (*Isela*), Holly Palance (*Journalist*), Ella Laboriel (*Nightclub Singer*), Samuel Zarzosa, Jonathan Zarzosa, Raul Picasso (*Jazz Combo*), Oswaldo Doria (*Boy Photographer*), Fernando Elizondo (*Businessman*), Hamilton Camp (*Regis Seydor*), Jean-Louis Trintignant (*Jazy*), Richard Masur (*Hub Kittle*), Jorge Santoyo (*Guerrilla Leader*), Lucina Rojas (*Guerrilla Woman*), Raul Garcia (*Waiter*), Victor Alcocer (*Capture Businessman*), Eric Valdez (*Time Stringer*), Andaluz Russel (*Young Journalist*), E. Villavicencio (*Arresting Officer*), Enrique Lucero (*Prison Priest*), Enrique Beraza (*Interrogating Officer*), Jenny Gago (*Miss Panama*), Elpidia Carrillo, Martin Palmares, Gerardo Morena (*Sandinistas*), Eloy Phil Casados (*Pedro*), Carlos Romano (*Priest*), Rene Enriquez (*Somoza*), Jose Campos, Jr (*Soldier*), Halim Camp, Antonio Mata, Jr (*TV Camera Crew*), Julio Cesar Vazquez (*Small Boy*), Martin LaSalle (*Commandante Cinco*), Filipe Ytuarte (*Commandante*), Jorge Zepeda (*Rafael*), Alfredo Gutierrez, Jose Marin, J. A. Ferral, E. Baramona, Octaio Cruz (*Soldiers*), Leonor Llausas (*Woman*), Juan Carlos Meizveiro (*Boy Soldier*), Humberto Vilches (*Squadron Commander*), Roberto Dumant (*Hotel Clerk*), Ahui Camacho, Arturo R. Doring, Bruno Bichir (*Muchachos*), Ricardo Ramirez, Jose Carlos Rodriguez (*Sandinistas with Radio*), Enrique Hernandez (*Boy on Bike*), Monica Miguel (*Doctor*), Luisa Sanchez M (*Woman, Refugee Camp*), Carlos Lenin Vazuez (*Boy*), "Los Folkloristas" (*Singing Group*), Clay Wright (*Helicopter Pilot*), Michael Crowley, Eugene Vagnone (*Helicopter Gunners*), Gilbert Combs, Gene Walker, Benny Moore, Harold Jones, Tanya Russell, Mike Vendrell, Kerrie Cullen, George Fisher, Bruce Barbour, David Zelletti, Lamont Cox, Eddie Smith, Tony Brubaker, Alex Brown, John Ashby (*Stunt People*).

A somewhat naive but nonetheless interesting look at the revolution in Nicaragua as seen through the eyes of Nolte, an American press photographer who chooses to distance himself from reality with the lens of his camera ("I take pictures. I don't take sides."). The film begins in Chad as Nolte and his reporter friends Cassidy and Hackman (who are lovers) cover the revolution. Nolte takes some superb pictures of the fighting, and one of them is chosen for the cover of Time magazine. As the revolution draws to a close, so does Hackman and Cassidy's romance. Hackman decides to accept an anchorman job in New York, while Cassidy chooses to cover the fighting in Nicaragua. Nolte, too, is going to Central America, and he sees this as his chance to start a love relationship with Cassidy. Before leaving Chad, Nolte runs into an American mercenary, Harris, a totally amoral man who also decides to see which side might pay more for his services in Nicaragua. In Managua, Nolte finds his noncommital attitude being put to the test. The contrast between how the supporters of President Somoza (Enriquez) live and the lifestyle of the Sandinistas is startling. Nolte begins to notice that his shelter in the plush Hotel Continental, home of the press corps, is an obscene form of imperialism, further distancing the reporters from the people about whom they are reporting. These beliefs have long been held by Cassidy, and it is Nolte's contact with her that begins to change his perspective. Cassidy and Nolte soon find themselves traveling with the Sandinista rebels who are led by the charismatic and mysterious Zepeda. In a battle against troops (where Nolte again runs into Harris, who's fighting for Somoza), Zepeda is killed, and the Sandinista leaders try to persuade Nolte to fake a photograph of the dead man that would make him appear

alive and very much in command so that their troops will not lose morale. Nolte takes the ultimate step into personal involvement and makes the picture. News of Zepeda's resurrection sweeps the world and Hackman leaves New York to personally cover the story for the network. While out driving with Nolte, Hackman loses his way and goes to ask government troops directions. In an irrational spasm of violence, a trooper shoots and kills Hackman (based on the horrifying true-life murder of ABC correspondent Bill Stewart, who was killed by Somoza's troops in 1979–an event which was captured on videotape and shown to a shocked world). Nolte, who is a safe distance away, captures the whole incident on film. Nolte's pictures create worldwide outrage and help sound the death knell for Enriquez's government. Enriquez and his cronies flee the country and the Sandinistas roll into Managua victorious. During the joyous street celebration Nolte is surprised to find Harris who ominously intones that some day the people will probably be fed up with the Sandinistas and he'll be back. In the meantime, there are plenty of wars to fight and he'll go to the highest bidder. With that, the mercenary once again disappears. Forever changed by the experience, Nolte watches the parade and wonders where he'll end up next. UNDER FIRE is an insightful look at the world of journalism on a global scale. Nolte gives one of his best performances as the photographer who suddenly finds himself looking past what he sees through the viewfinder. Cassidy, in one of the best female roles of recent years (that thankfully wasn't given to Jane Fonda), proves herself to be a major talent who deserves to escape the television limbo in which her career seemed stuck. Hackman, always a superior actor, manages to vividly convey a complex and fascinating character in the brief amount of screen time given him. Harris, also in a brief supporting role, creates a wholly believable rogue who presents a different and valuable perspective on the action at hand. A real surprise is Enriquez (best known at the time as Lt. Callento on TV's "Hill Street Blues") as Anastazio Somoza. A native Nicaraguan who was related to murdered newspaper editor Joaquin Chamorro (a killing that he claims accelerated the revolution), Enriquez uses his personal knowledge of the dictator to full advantage. Also notable is Trintignant as a French CIA agent who is shrouded in mystery. Director Spottiswoode, who had edited Sam Peckinpah's STRAW DOGS, THE GETWAY, PAT GARRETT, AND BILLY THE KID, Walter Hill's HARD TIMES, Karl Reisz' WHO'LL STOP THE RAIN, and directed TERROR TRAIN and THE PURSUIT OF D. B. COOPER, succeeds in creating the chaotic last days of Somoza's government and spinning a tale of personal revelation and romance around it. Where the film fails is in its simplistic view of Somoza and the Sandinistas. Shown to be the white knights riding to the rescue of the oppressed masses, the Sandinistas are given embarrassingly reverent treatment with no hint of the vicious purges, ideological divisions, confusion, and suffering that would follow their takeover. In the end, Harris' mercenary seems to be the only character aware of the harsh reality of the situation. In fact, Zepeda's Sandinista leader–a wholly fictitious character created by the filmmakers–works against them and actually cheapens the commitment of the other revolutionaries by suggesting that they couldn't go on without him. Politically, this is a confused film that doesn't seem to be particularly well thought out in its treatment of a highly complex situation. On both sides, party in power and revolutionary, there are shades of gray that are simply not considered here. As a story of one man's personal awakening, UNDER FIRE succeeds. As a relevant, insightful political statement, it falls flat on its face.

p, Jonathan Taplin; d, Roger Spottiswoode; w, Ron Shelton, Clayton Frohman (based on a story by Frohman); ph, John Alcott (Technicolor); m, Jerry Goldsmith; ed, John Bloom; art d, Agustin Ytuarte, Toby Rafelson; set d, Enrique Estevez; Cos, Cynthia Bales; spec eff, Laurencio Cordero, Jesus Duran; m/l, "Our Love May Never See Tomorrow," Peggy Turner, "Dear John," Pat Metheny (sung by Metheny); makeup, Ed Henriques; stunts, Gary Combs.

Drama Cas. (PR:O MPAA:R)

UNDER MEXICALI SKIES (SEE: UNDER MEXICALI STARS, 1950)

UNDER MEXICALI STARS**½ (1950) 67m REP bw (AKA: UNDER MEXICALI SKIES)

Rex Allen (*Himself*), Dorothy Patrick (*Madeline Wellington*), Roy Barcroft (*Hays Lawson*), Buddy Ebsen (*Homer Oglethorpe*), Percy Helton (*Nap Wellington*), Walter Coy (*Giles Starkey*), Steve Darrell (*Sheriff Meadows*), Alberto Morin (*Capt. Gomez*), Ray Walker (*Handley*), Frank Ferguson (*Goldie*), Stanley Andrews (*Announcer*), Robert Bice (*Deputy*), Koko the Horse.

A gang of smugglers is sneaking gold across the border into Mexico via a helicopter and then having it turned into counterfeit coins. This raises an eyebrow or two at the U.S. Treasury Department and Allen is sent out with sidekick Ebsen (replacing Fuzzy Knight in Allen's series) to put an end to the gang's activities. They succeed and along the way Allen delivers the following tunes: "Old Black Mountain Trail," "Born in the Saddle," and "The Railroad Corral."

p, Melville Tucker; d, George Blair; w, Bob Williams; ph, John MacBurnie; ed, Harold Minter; md, Stanley Wilson; art d, Frank Arrigo.

Western (PR:A MPAA:NR)

UNDER MILK WOOD*** (1973, Brit.) 90m Timon/Altura Films International c

Richard Burton (1st Voice), Elizabeth Taylor (Rosie Probert), Peter O'Toole (Capt. Cat), Glynis Johns (Myfanwy Price), Vivien Merchant (Mrs. Pugh), Sian Phillips (Mrs. Ogmore-Pritchard), Victor Spinetti (Mog Edwards), Ryan Davies (2nd Voice), Angharad Rees (Gossamer Beynon), Ray Smith (Mr. Waldo), Michael Forrest (Sinbad Sailors), Ann Beach (Polly Garter), Glynn Edwards (Mr. Cherry Owen), Bridget Turner (Mrs. Cherry Owen), Talfryn Thomas (Mr. Pugh), Wim Wylton (Mr. Willy Nilly), Bronwen Williams (Mrs. Willy Nilly), Meg Wynn Owen (Lily Smalls), Hubert Rees (Butcher Beynon), Mary Jones (Mrs. Beynon), Aubrey Richards (Rev. Eli Jenkins), Mark Jones (Evans the Death), Dillwyn Owen (Mr. Ogmore), Richard Davies (Mr. Pritchard), David Jason (Nogood Boyo), Davydd Havard (Lord Cut Glass), David Davies (Utah Watkins), Maudie Edwards (Mrs. Utah Watkins), Griffith Davies (Ocky Milkman), Peggyann CliffordBessie Bighead, Dudley Jones (Dai Bread), Dorothea Phillips (Mrs. Dai Bread One), Ruth Madoc (Mrs. Dai Bread Two), David Harries (Police Constable Attila Rees), Rachael Thomas (Mary Ann Sailors), Andree Gaydon (Waldo Wife One), Eira Griffiths (2nd Woman/Waldo Wife Two), Margaret Courtenay (1st Neighbor/Waldo Wife Three), Rhoda Lewis (1st Woman/Waldo Wife Four), Pamela Miles (Waldo Wife Five), John Rees (Jack Black), Jill Britton (Mrs. Rose Cottage), Susan Penhaligon (Mae Rose Cottage), Edmond Thomas (Inspector), Richard Parry (Organ Morgan), Dilys Price (Mrs. Organ Morgan), Olwen Rees (Gwennie), Iris Jones (Mother), Gordon Styles, Brian Osbourne (Fishermen), Shane Shelton, Paul Grist, Bryn Jones, John Rainer, Bryn William (Drowned Sailors), Aldwyn Francis, Ifor Owen, Dudley Owen, Gladys Wykeham-Edwards (Villagers in "Sailors Arms"), Ieuan Rhys Williams (Gomer Owen), T.H. Evans (Old Man), Gwyneth Owen, Lucy Griffiths, Angela Brinkworth (Neighbors).

All things considered, this is a fairly good adaptation of an impossible play to adapt. Dylan Thomas wrote it as a "play for voices" for the BBC. It was later done on the stage and this film was made mainly because Burton, Taylor, and O'Toole (a former classmate of the screenwriter-director) agreed to work for little money and large points in the profits, of which there were none. Burton is a voice-over and occasional on-screen persona as he keeps matters moving in the episodic tale of a day or so in the lives of the people in the town of Llareggub, a Welsh village by the sea. It's night and blind O'Toole (with the help of heavy makeup and trick contact lenses) is telling Burton about his life. O'Toole is a retired sea captain and he fondly recalls those old pals who went down to the bottom as well as his memories of Taylor, a whore who was O'Toole's one and only love. Cut to Johns and Spinetti, two of the local store owners, as they snooze and dream of each other and the sex that has never happened between them. Cut to Phillips, a twice-widowed woman who orders her two late husbands, Owen and Davies, to do the housework. The evening slides by and dawn is on the horizon. While the local reverend, Richards, offers his morning prayer to the Lord, the baker, Dudley Jones, runs to his shop to sell his wares, and the postman, Wylton, begins his daily stroll. The day wears on and mild-mannered Thomas happily contemplates slipping some poison to still the tongue of his shrewish wife, Merchant; the meat vendor, Hubert Rees, teases his spouse, and more and more. O'Toole is blind as a bat but he senses what's happening around him and continues his talk with Burton while Forrest chases after Rees' daughter Olwen Rees. Smith begins drinking to forget his late wife and the reverend works on his nightly song of praise. Phillips begins to dream about her late husbands as the night comes, and Smith sleeps with Beach as she mourns her late lover. Burton's sonorous voice permeates the screen and brings the Dylan Thomas words to rich, rewarding life. Nobody went to see the movie and it remains a curiosity piece that was made almost as a "vanity" movie by the stars and the hordes of nonprofessionals recruited from the Gwaun Valley of Wales. It's doubtful that anyone thought it would be a large commercial hit but someone wanted to commit the Thomas play to the screen and for that we must be thankful. Burton also recorded the play on a Westminster Records album. Since it's almost impossible to see this film on TV, perhaps the purchase of the record will suffice.

p, Hugh French, Jules Buck; d&w, Andrew Sinclair (based on the radio play by Dylan Thomas); ph, Bob Huke (Technicolor); m, Brian Gascoigne; ed, Willy Kemplen; art d, Geoffrey Tozer.

Drama (PR:C MPAA:PG)

UNDER MONTANA SKIES*½ (1930) 58m TIF bw

Kenneth Harlan (Clay Conning), Dorothy Gulliver (Mary), Slim Summerville (Sunshine), Nita Martan (Blondie), Harry Todd (Abner Jenkins), Ethel Wales (Martha Jenkins), Lafe McKee (Pinky), Christian J. Frank (Frank Blake).

Harlan keeps himself busy in this oater by belting out a few tunes, while befriending Gulliver and helping a traveling stage show fend off the bad guys. More concentration on dancing and singing ladies than on drawing guns and clenching fists.

d, Richard Thorpe; w, James A. Aubrey, Bennett Cohen; ph, Harry Zech; ed, Carl Himm; set d, Ralph De Lacy.

Western/Comedy (PR:A MPAA:NR)

UNDER MY SKIN*** (1950) 86m FOX bw

John Garfield (Dan Butler), Micheline Prelle 'Presle' (Paule Manet), Luther Adler (Louis Bork), Orley Lindgren (Joe), Noel Drayton (George Gardner), A.A. Merola (Maurice), Ott George (Rico), Paul Bryar (Max), Ann Codee (Henriette), Steve Geray (Bartender), Joseph Warfield (Rigoli), Eugene Borden (Doctor), Loulette Sablon (Nurse), Alphonse Martell (Detective), Ernesto Morelli (Hotel Clerk), Jean Del Val (Express Man), Hans Herbert (Attendant), Esther Zeitlin (Flower Woman), Maurice Brierre (Doorman), Gordon Clark (Barman), Frank Arnold (Official), Elizabeth Flournoy (American Mother), Mario Siletti (Italian Officer), Guy Zanette (Porter), Andre Charise (Gendarme), Harry Martin (Drake).

Ernest Hemingway's sparse, somewhat grim short story "My Old Man" was turned into something resembling THE CHAMP on horseback instead of in a boxing ring. Though Hemingway's story was considerably altered and expanded to fit a feature length film, the resulting picture retains much of the basic flavor of the author's work. Garfield stars as a crooked jockey who has been barred from working in the U.S. The film opens in Italy where Garfield has just run out of luck with the local gangsters. Garfield and his young son Lindgren quickly pack their bags to leave the country, but the gangsters catch up with them in their hotel. While Garfield tries to talk his way out of the situation, Lindgren heads for the roof and escapes. The mobsters aren't interested in what Garfield has to say, however, and police arrive in time to stop the jockey from being beaten to death. Recovering from his wounds, Garfield decides to give the ponies in France a try. In Paris, Garfield and his son run into Prelle, a beautiful woman who owns her own nightclub on the Left Bank. Prelle and Garfield had met years before and Prelle was interested in the jockey, but Garfield never took advantage of the situation. On the rebound, Prelle became involved with a friend of Garfield's, but the man was killed by gamblers with whom he and Garfield had become involved. Since then, Prelle had always blamed Garfield for her lover's death, but now, seeing his devotion to the child, she rekindles her attraction to the jockey. Lindgren takes an immediate liking to Prelle and she becomes a mother figure for the boy. Garfield, however, is a bit wary of relationships with women and sees Prelle only because of his son. Meanwhile, Garfield finds work at the Paris racetracks and soon becomes involved with big-time gambler Adler, who uses the crooked jockey to make some money. Lindgren finally learns that the father he idolizes is a crook, and the news is devastating. At the same time, Garfield's relationship with Prelle becomes seriously romantic and he makes the decision to go straight, get married, return to the States, and give his son a real family life. To finance the dream, Garfield tricks Adler and makes off with a big sum of money. Adler catches up with him and demands that he throw the next big race as repayment for the money he filched. Garfield pretends to agree, but he knows he is riding a horse capable of winning the race and decides to do so. Adler suspects the double cross, so he arranges for another jockey to knock Garfield off his horse if it appears he might win the race. During the intense race Garfield pulls ahead and Adler's jockey catches up with him at the last hurdle. The rival jockey crashes his horse into Garfield's in an effort to dump the rider, but Adler's jockey falls instead and is killed. Garfield makes it across the finish line and wins the race, but the dead jockey's riderless horse crashes into Garfield's horse and he is thrown. Badly injured, Garfield is brought to the emergency room where he dies. Lindgren is with his father at the final moment, and is comforted by Drayton, a friend of Garfield's who assures the boy that his father was a great jockey and a decent man. Lindgren leaves the track with Prelle who tells the boy that they should fulfill Garfield's wish and start a new life in America with the prize money. Though the Hemingway story ends on a much more bitter note–the Garfield character is killed and only then does the boy learn that his father was a crook–UNDER MY SKIN offers a a ray of hope for the boy through the character played by Prelle (who doesn't appear in the story). It should be noted that screenwriter Robinson, director Negulesco, and, for that matter, the studio, allowed the Garfield character to die rather than go for the usual Hollywood ending that sees the near-tragic figure miraculously survive his ordeal (as in the film version of Hemingway's THE SNOWS OF KILIMANJARO). Garfield had great enthusiasm for this film, and rumor had it that the reason was French actress Prelle. Garfield met Prelle when she came to America to sign a contract with 20th Century-Fox in 1947. The studio was anxious to capitalize on the actress, who had created a sensation with her performance in THE DEVIL IN THE FLESH. Garfield was infatuated with the cultured Frenchwoman and may have pushed to have her star opposite him in UNDER MY SKIN. Unfortunately for Garfield, Prelle was involved in a serious romantic relationship with Hollywood producer Bill Marshall and they were married during the production. Garfield's health began to plague him as well, and he collapsed after playing tennis one day. A myocardial condition (heart muscle strain) was diagnosed and he was ordered to avoid physical exertion (advice he ignored). Shooting was held up for a month. UNDER MY SKIN was coolly received by critics and the public. Though Garfield's strong performance was noted, Miss Prelle failed to make much of an impression and she soon found herself back in France.

p, Casey Robinson; d, Jean Negulesco; w, Robinson (based on the story "My Old Man" by Ernest Hemingway); ph, Joseph LaShelle; m, Daniele Amfitheatrof; ed, Dorothy Spencer; art d, Lyle Wheeler, Maurice Ransford; set d, Thomas Little, Walter M. Scott; spec eff, Fred Sersen; m/l, Alfred Newman, Mack Gordon, Jacques Surmagne.

Drama   (PR:A   MPAA:NR)

UNDER NEVADA SKIES**½   (1946) 69m REP bw

Roy Rogers (Himself), George ["Gabby"] Hayes (Gabby Whittaker), Dale
Evans (Helen Williams), Douglas Dumbrille (Arthur Courtney), Leyland
Hodgson (Tom Craig), Tristram Coffin (Dan Adams), Rudolph Anders
(Alberti), LeRoy Mason (Marty Fields), George Lynn (LeBlane), George J.
Lewis (Flying Eagle), Tom Quinn (Hoffman), Iron Eyes Cody, Bob Nolan and
The Sons of the Pioneers, Trigger.

An energetic Rogers entry with Evans and sidekick Hayes helping to
recover a secret map which indicates the location of pitchblende deposits.
When a gang of outlaws gets its hands on the map, Rogers leads a posse of
Indians against the bandits. This was the last in a long series of Rogers'
westerns to be directed by MacDonald; he was replaced at the helm by
William Witney. Songs include: "Under Nevada Skies," "Anytime That I'm
With You," "Ne-hah-nee," "I Want to Go West," and "Sea-Goin' Cowboy."

p, Edward J. White; d, Frank McDonald; w, Paul Gangelin, J. Benton
Cheney (based on a story by M. Coates Webster); ph, William Bradford; ed,
Edward Mann; md, Dale Butts; art d, Paul Youngblood; set d, John
McCarthy, Jr., Otto Siegel.

Western   Cas.   (PR:A   MPAA:NR)

UNDER NEW MANAGEMENT   (SEE: HONEYMOON HOTEL, 1946,
                                                              Brit.)

UNDER PRESSURE**½   (1935) 72m FOX bw

Edmund Lowe (Shocker), Victor McLaglen (Jumbo), Florence Rice (Pat),
Marjorie Rambeau (Amy), Charles Bickford (Nipper Moran), Siegfried
Rumann (Doctor), Roger Imhof (George Breck), George Walsh (Tug), Warner
Richmond (Weasel), Jack Wallace (The Kid), James Donlan (Corky).

A programmer about two rival tunnel-digging crews, one led by McLaglen,
the other by Bickford. Infighting occurs in McLaglen's crew when he and his
partner Lowe both fall for journalist Rice. They patch things up, however,
when McLaglen saves Lowe's life. Because of an injury to McLaglen, Lowe
takes control of the crew, but the leader proves his worth by defeating
Bickford and guiding his crew past his rival's. Expertly photographed by
Hal Mohr, who the same year shot CAPTAIN BLOOD and won an Academy
Award for A MIDSUMMER NIGHT'S DREAM.

p, Robert T. Kane; d, Raoul Walsh; w, Borden Chase, Noel Pierce. Lester
Cole, Edward J. Doherty (based on the novel East River by Chase); ph, Hal
Mohr, L. W. O'Connell; m, Louis De Francesco; Cos, William Lamberto.

Drama   (PR:A   MPAA:NR)

UNDER PROOF*   (1936, Brit.) 50m FOX British bw

Betty Stockfield (Vivian), Tyrell Davis (Dudley), Judy Kelly (Corone), Guy
Middleton (Bruce), Charles Farrell (Spike), Viola Compton (Mrs. Richards),
David Horne (Dr. Walton), Edward Ashley (Ward Delaney), Henry Long-
hurst (Inspector Holt), Harry Watson, Andrea Malandrinos, Peter Popp,
Tuff de Lyle the Dog.

Travelers caught in a storm seek shelter at a remote house of a vacationing
friend. When they arrive, cowardly Davis accidentally says a password that
bootleggers, hiding out in the house, are waiting for and they take him for
their leader. A swallow of bootleg brandy gives him the courage to maintain
the ruse until the police arrive to arrest the lot. Spectacularly unfunny
comedy, one to avoid.

p, John Findlay; d, Roland Gillett; w, Tod Waller (based on his play "Dudley
Does It"); ph, Stanley Grant.

Comedy   (PR:A   MPAA:NR)

UNDER SECRET ORDERS*½   (1933) 60m Monarch/Syndicated
                                        Exchanges-Progressive bw

Donald Dillaway (Henry Ames), J. Farrell MacDonald (John Burke), Nena
Quartero (Carmencita Alverez), Phyllis Barrington (Jane Lawrence), Don
Alvarado (Don Federico), Lafe McKee (Franklyn Lawrence), Matthew Betz
(Senor Cevallos), Paul Ellis, Leon Holmes.

Dillaway is a naive fellow who gets an assignment to deliver some secret
papers but has one drink too many and loses them. Actually, MacDonald has
grabbed them and kept them for safety. In the meantime Dillaway has fallen
in love with the daughter of the man for whom the papers are intended. It
turns out that the recipient is dead and the papers are a will which makes
the daughter the heir. The finale has Dillaway marrying the girl. How cute.

d, Sam Newfield; w, Eustace L. Adams; ph, Jules Cronjager; ed, Walter
Thompson.

Drama/Romance   (PR:A   MPAA:NR)

UNDER SECRET ORDERS   (1943, Brit.) 66m
                                       Grafton-Trafalgar/Guaranteed bw

Dita Parlo (Dr. Anne-Marie Lesser), John Loder (Lt. Peter Carr), Erich von
Stroheim (Col. Mathesius/"Simonie"), Claire Luce (Gaby), Gyles Isham (Lt.
Hans Hoffman), Clifford Evans (Condoyan), John Abbott (Armand), Antony
Holles (Mario), Edward Lexy (Carr's Orderly), Robert Nainby (French
General), Brian Powley (Col. Burgoyne), Molly Hamley Clifford (Proprietor
of "The Blue Peacock"), Raymond Lovell (Col. von Steinberg), Frederick
Lloyd (Col. Marchand), Claud Horton (Capt. Fitzmaurice), Stewart Granger.

In the midst of WW I Parlo is a German doctor who gains some notoriety
for her espionage activities. She infiltrates the British side to find the man
who killed her lover. Once ingratiated with the enemy, Parlo meets and falls
in love with Loder, only to discover he's the very man she has been looking
for. Parlo steals some plans for an air raid, and Loder is killed in the
subsequent attack. This heavy-handed remake of a French film was itself
remade some 30 years later under the title FRAULEIN DOKTOR. This was
one of many minor films von Stroheim (the man you love to hate) appeared
in after his directing career fell apart.

p, Max Schach; d, Edmond T. Greville; w, Jacques Natanson, Marcel
Archard, Ernest Betts (based on a story by Georges Hereaux, Irma Von
Cube); ph, Otto Heller.

Drama   Cas.   (PR:A-C   MPAA:NR)

UNDER STRANGE FLAGS**   (1937) 61m Crescent/States Rights bw

Tom Keene (Tom Kenyon), Luana Walters (Dolores de Vargas), Budd Buster
(Tequilla), Maurice Black (Pancho Villa), Roy D'Arcy (Morales), Paul
Sutton (Geor. Barranca), Paul Barrett (Denny), Donald Reed (Garcia), Jane
Wolfe (Mrs. Kenyon).

Pancho Villa (Black) lends a hand to Keene when Walters' silver mine is
nearly taken over by mendacious Federales assisted by Black's treacherous
aide D'Arcy during a period of revolution. Keene and Black uncover the
marauder's deceit and save Walters' fortune.

p, E.B. Derr; d, I.V. Willat; w, Mary Ireland (based on a story by John Auer);
ph, Arthur Martinelli.

Western   (PR:A   MPAA:NR)

UNDER SUSPICION*   (1931) 66m Fox bw

Lois Moran (Alice Freil), J. Harold Murray (John Smith), J. M. Kerrigan
(Doyle), Erwin Connelly (Darby), Lumsden Hare (Freil), George Brent
(Inspector Turner), Marie Saxon (Suzanne), Rhoda Cross (Marie), Herbert
Bunston (Maj. Manners), Vera Gerald (Ellen).

Set in the Canadian wilderness, this Canadian Mounted Police picture has
Moran out in the woods with singing Mountie Murray, trying to survive
blazing fires and his wretched voice. A lame entry on all accounts which
devotes more time to scenery than to action.

d, A. F. Erickson; w, Tom Barry; ph, George Schneiderman; ed. J. Edwin
Robbins; m/l, James F. Hanley, Joseph McCarthy.

Adventure   (PR:A   MPAA:NR)

UNDER SUSPICION**   (1937) 61m COL bw

Jack Holt (Robert Bailey), Katherine De Mille (Mary Brookhart), Luis
Alberni (Luigi), Rosalind Keith (Doris), Purnell Pratt (Rogers), Granville
Bates (K.Y. Mitchell), Maurice Murphy (Ralph), Morgan Wallace (MacGre-
gor), Craig Reynolds (Nelson Dudley), Robert Emmett Keane (Mr. Walters),
Margaret Irving (Mrs. Walters), Clyde Dilson (Eddie), George Anderson
(Bill), Esther Muir (Frances), Guy D'Ennery, Lee Phelps, Dorothy Brad-
shaw, Robert Noble, Harry Hervey, Otto Fries.

A standard murder mystery which casts Holt as an automobile manufacturer who no longer wants to be involved with his company. When he
announces plans to give his stock to his employees and turn his energies to
his hunting hobby, a few people get upset and try to prevent him from doing
so. The guilty party is his attorney, who is Holt's executor in case anything
should happen to him, and who covets the prospective fees. Well-crafted but
offering nothing new.

p, Larry Darmour; d, Lewis D. Collins; w, Joseph Hoffman, Jefferson
Parker, (based on a story by Philip Wylie); ph, James S. Brown, Jr.; ed,
Dwigt Caldwell.

Crime Drama   (PR:A   MPAA:NR)

UNDER TEN FLAGS***½   (1960, U.S./Ital.) 92m DD/PAR bw

Van Heflin (Reger), Charles Laughton (Adm. Russell), Mylene Demongeot
(Zizi), John Ericson (Krueger), Liam Redmond (Windsor), Alex Nicol
(Knoche), Gregoire Aslan (Master of Abdullah), Cecil Parker (Col. Howard),
Eleonora Rossi-Drago (Sara), Gian Maria Volonte (Braun), Philo Hauser
(Clown), Dieter Eppler (Dr. Hartmann), Ralph Truman (Adm. Benson),
Peter Carsten (Lt. Mohr), Folco Lulli (Paco).

Heflin is the commander of a German merchant raider during WW II who adopts a bewildering array of disguises–repainting the ship, flying neutral flags, erecting false smokestacks, and even having crewmen dress as women passengers promenading up and down the deck–to lure Allied ships near enough to drop the disguise, hoist high the Nazi ensign, and blow the ship out of the water with his concealed guns. Despite this trickery, Heflin is a compassionate man who picks up survivors out of the water, to the dismay of fanatical Nazi lieutenant Ericson, who thinks they should be left to drown. Meanwhile, at the British Admiralty offices, admiral Laughton is assigned to discover the cause of the mysterious sinkings, and although the two men never meet, the film concerns the battle of wits between them. Laughton finally gets his big break when Nicol, an American agent in Paris who bears a striking resemblance to a certain German naval officer, boldly walks into the German headquarters in broad daylight and walks out again with pictures of the German coded sea chart in his miniature camera. From then on the fate of Heflin's ship is sealed. The British dispatch a number of ships to the area where they know the ship to be working and destroy it, although Heflin survives. The scenes that deal directly with the conflict are the best, and Nicol's theft of the Nazi codes is quite suspenseful, but the film is bogged down in subplots, including Ericson's attraction to a busty French prisoner aboard, Demongeot, who rejects him when she discovers the depth of his Nazi sentiments, and Heflin's philosophic discussions with another of his prisoners. Laughton is simply outrageous as he mugs his way through one of his last roles, but Heflin is excellent as the intelligent, humanitarian German commander. Based on the true story of the German raider *Atlantis* as written by her commander after the war.

p, Dino De Laurentiis; d, Duilio Coletti; w, Vittoriano Petrilli, Coletti, Ulrich Moh, William Douglas-Home (based on original diaries by Bernhard Rogge); ph, Aldo Tonti; m, Nino Rota; ed, Jerry Webb; art d, Mario Garbuglia; cos, Piero Cherardi.

War   **(PR:C   MPAA:NR)**

UNDER TEXAS SKIES**   (1931) 57m SYN bw

Bob Custer, Natalie Kingston, Tom London, Bill Cody, Lane Chandler, William McCall, J. S. Marba, Bob Roper.

Kingston is an orphaned girl whose father left her a herd of horses which Army officer Cody plans to buy for the cavalry. He is captured, however, by a bandit gang led by Chandler. Chandler then poses as the officer and tries to gain the girl's confidence. In the meantime, a mysterious cowboy, Custer, has arrived and also tries to befriend the girl. She has trouble deciding which of the two men is legitimate and finally realizes that Chandler is part of the horse-rustling gang. An interesting low-budget western. Producer Johnston's Syndicate Pictures was one of the two major sources of westerns during this period. The same featured male players worked in many of Syndicate's films, but the leading-man roles changed around. It was Custer's turn to be the hero in this one.

p, W. Ray Johnston; d, J. P. McGowan; w, G. A. Durlam; ph, Otto Himm; ed, Alfred Brook.

Western   **(PR:A   MPAA:NR)**

UNDER TEXAS SKIES*   (1940) 57m REP bw

Robert Livingston (*"Stony" Brooke*), Bob Steele (*"Tucson" Smith*), Rufe Davis (*"Lullaby" Joslin*), Lois Ranson (*Helen*), Henry Brandon (*Blackton*), Wade Boteler (*Sheriff Brooke*), Rex Lease (*Marsden*), Walter Tetley (*Theodore*), Yakima Canutt (*Talbot*), Earle Hodgins (*Smithers*), Curley Dresden (*Jackson*), Jack Ingram (*Finley*), Jack Kirk, Ted Mapes, Vester Pegg.

A much-shuffled lineup left this THREE MESQUITEERS entry with only one original cast member–Livingston–with Raymond Hatton being replaced by Davis, and Duncan Renaldo stepping aside for Steele. The story, however, is far from new with Livingston returning home after a long absence to find that his father has been killed. When he hears that Steele has been accused he knows that something is up and finally uncovers a plot by new sheriff Brandon to frame the Mesquiteer. Proof that change doesn't always bring progress with it. Love-interest Ranson seems uncomfortable with this fare; she was more at home in musical comedies (the studio was grooming her for proposed major singing-dancing roles). (See THREE MESQUITEERS series, Index.)

p, Harry Grey; d, George Sherman; w, Anthony Coldeway, Betty Burbridge (based on characters created by William Colt MacDonald); ph, William Nobles; m, Cy Feuer; ed, Tony Martinelli.

Western   **(PR:A   MPAA:NR)**

UNDER THE BANNER OF SAMURAI**½
(1969, Jap.) 166m Mifune/Toho c (FURIN KAZAN; AKA: SAMURAI BANNERS)

Toshiro Mifune (*Kansuke Yamamoto*), Kinnosuke Nakamura (*Shingen Takeda*), Yoshiko Sakuma (*Princess Yufu*), Kankuro Nakamura (*Katsuyori Takeda*), Mayumi Ozora (*Princess Okoto*), Ganemon Nakamura (*Mobukata Itagaki*), Katsuo Nakamura (*Nobusato Itagaki*), Masakazu Tamura (*Nobushige Takeda*), Yujiro Ishihara (*Kenshin Uesugi*), Ken Ogata.

A fine samurai film produced by Tishiro Mifune's production company and starring the veteran samurai actor who has starred in such greats as THE SEVEN SAMURAI (1954) and THRONE OF BLOOD (1957). As expected, he plays a veteran samurai hired for advice by a great warlord. The warlord at first fails to pay heed to Mifune's advice, which eventually leads to Mifune's carrying out a vengeful deed without the approval of the warlord. Romance then plays a part in the relationship between the warlord and his samurai as both fall in love with a princess, the daughter of the man Mifune killed. She hates Mifune for what he did, and chooses to marry the warlord. After a number of years Mifune is killed in a major battle, fighting beside the warlord. Running nearly three hours, the picture is long, but filled with Mifune's excellent characterization and an entrancing 16th-Century atmosphere.

d, Hiroshi Inagaki; w, Shinobu Hashimoto (based on the novel *Furin Kazah* by Yasushi Inoue); ph, Kazuo Yamada (Tohoscope, Eastmancolor); m, Masaru Sato; art d, Hiroshi Ueda

Action/Drama   **(PR:C   MPAA:NR)**

UNDER THE BIG TOP*½   (1938) 63m MON bw

Anne Nagel (*Penny*), Marjorie Main (*Sara*), Jack LaRue (*Ricardo*), Grant Richards (*Pablo*), George Cleveland (*Joe*), Herbert Rawlinson (*Herman*), Rolfe Sedan (*Pierre*), Betty Compson (*Marie*), Snowflake [Fred Toones] (*Juba*), Harry Harvey (*McCarthy*), Charlene Wyatt (*Penny as a Child*), Speed Hansen (*Marty*).

Romance takes the form of a triangle when a circus owner introduces her niece, Nagel, into an aerial act. The girl soon becomes the greatest aerialist in the world and the "Three Flying Pennies," as the act is called, soar to the top. Her two male counterparts have both fallen for Nagel, but she choses Richards over his brother, LaRue. Tensions flare, the act dissolves, but finally is reformed at the circus owner's request.

p, Charles J. Bigelow; d, Karl Brown; w, Marion Orth (based on a story by Llewellyn Hughes); ph, Gilbert Warrenton; ed, Russell Schoengarth.

Drama   **(PR:A   MPAA:NR)**

UNDER THE CLOCK   (SEE: CLOCK, THE, 1945)

UNDER THE GREENWOOD TREE**   (1930, Brit.) 84m BIP bw

Marguerite Allan (*Fancy Day*), Peggie Robb-Smith (*Voice of Allan*), John Batten (*Dick Dewey*), Nigel Barrie (*Shinar*), Maud Gill (*Old Maid*), Wilfred Shine (*Parson Maybold*), Robert Abel (*Penny*), Antonia Brough (*Maid*), Tom Coventry (*Tranter Dewey*), Robison Page (*Grandfather Dewey*), Tubby Phillips (*Tubby*), Billy Shine (*Leaf*), Sid Ellery, Harry Stafford, Queenie Leighton, The Gotham Singers.

A charming but poorly cast drama set in the English countryside which has the town squire replacing the church choir with an organ, thereby dispossessing a hundred or more years of tradition. His plan is to get close to a young lovely new to town who plays the organ. She catches on to the scheme and soon things are returned to normal. Based on a novel by Thomas Hardy.

d, Harry Lachman; w, Lachman, Rex Taylor, Frank Launder, Monkton Hoffe (based on the novel by Thomas Hardy); ph, Claude Friese-Greene; ed, Emile De Ruelle.

Drama   **(PR:A   MPAA:NR)**

UNDER THE GUN**½   (1951) 84m UNIV bw

Richard Conte (*Bert Galvin*), Audrey Totter (*Ruth Williams*), John McIntire (*Langley*), Sam Jaffe (*Gower*), Shepperd Strudwick (*Milo Bragg*), Gregg Martell (*Nero*), Phillip Pine (*Gandy*), Don Randolph (*Sherbourne*), Royal Dano (*Nugent*), Richard Taber (*Five Shot*).

An intriguing prison drama about a New York gambler, Conte, who gets sent up the river for murder for 20 years. In a Florida prison he soon learns of a "trusty" system by which certain inmates guard others. He works his way into this position and devises a plan by which he tricks prison philosopher Jaffe into escaping. During the escape attempt he kills Jaffe and is rewarded with a parole. His plan backfires, however, when Jaffe's diary is read, revealing the planned escape with Conte as his partner. Conte is chased down by sheriff McIntire and eventually shot down. Includes the song "I Cried for You" (Arthur Freed, Gus Arnheim, Abe Lyman).

p, Ralph Dietrich; d, Ted Tetzlaff; w, George Zuckerman (based on a story by Daniel B. Ullman); ph, Henry Freulich; m, Joseph Gershenson; ed, Virgil Vogel; art d, Bernard Herzbrun, Edward L. Ilou; cos, Orry-Kelly.

Prison Drama   **(PR:A   MPAA:NR)**

UNDER THE PAMPAS MOON**½   (1935) 78m FOX bw

Warner Baxter (*Cesar Campo*), Ketti Gallian (*Yvonne LaMarr*), J. Carrol Naish (*Tito*), John Miljan (*Graham Scott*), Armida (*Rosa*), Ann Codee (*Mme. LaMarr*), Jack LaRue (*Bazan*), George Irving (*Don Bennett*), Rita Cansino [Hayworth] (*Carmen*), Veloz and Yolanda (*Dancers in Cafe*), Tito Guizar

(Cafe Singer), Chris-Pin Martin *(Pietro)*, Max Wagner *(Big Jose)*, Philip Cooper *(Little Jose)*, Sam Appel *(Bartender)*, Arthur Stone *(Rosa's Father)*, George Lewis *(Aviator)*, Paul Porcasi *(Headwaiter)*, Lona Andre *(Girl)*, Blanca Vischer *(Elena)*, Lucio Villegas *(Magistrate)*, Martin Garralaga *(Court Clerk)*, Frank Amerise, Tommy Coates, John Eberts, Enrique Lacey, Charles Ramos, Vinegar Roan, Antonio Samaniego, Manuel Valencia, Mariano Valenzuala *(Cesar's Gauchos)*, Mariano Betancourt, Frank Cordell, Antonio Manifredi, Joseph Rickson, Paul Perodi *(Bazan's Gauchos)*, Jean De Briac *(Stenographer)*, Jacques Vanaire *(Hairdresser)*, Catherine Cotter *(Maid)*, Charles Stevens *(Groom)*, Bobby Rose, Pedro Regas *(Jockeys)*, Fred Malatesta, Francesco Maran *(Doormen)*, Rafael Storm *(Barber)*, Ambrose Barker *(Valet)*, Juan Ortiz *(Police Sergeant)*, Joe Dominguez *(Newsboy)*, Nick Thompson, Manuel Perez *(Waiters)*, Soledad Jiminez *(Senora Campo)*, Princess Mural Sharado.

Baxter returns in the Cisco Kid-type role that won him an Oscar for IN OLD ARIZONA (1929), this time chasing after a horse in Buenos Aires which has been stolen from him. While down there he also chases after Gallian, a singer who is managed by the man suspected of nabbing the horse. By the finale he gets both the horse and the girl. Annoyingly disparate, obviously fake Hispanic accents are used throughout the film. Some funny moments, mostly centering about Jiminez, who plays Baxter's mother. Making an early appearance is Rita Hayworth, here billed as Rita Cansino, which was short for Margarita Cansino. The name Hayworth came from her mother's maiden name, Haworth, which was amended with an extra "y" by producer Harry Cohn. She plays a dance hall girl-waitress who dances a tune called "Zamba" (Arthur Wynter-Smith). Other songs include: "The Gaucho" (Buddy De Sylva, Walter Samuels), "Querida Mia (Paul Francis Webster, Lew Pollack), "Love Song of the Pampas," "Veredita," "Je t'Adore" (Miguel de Zarraga, Cyril J. Mockridge).

p, B. G. ["Buddy"] De Sylva; d, James Tinling; w, Ernest Pascal, Bradley King, Henry Jackson (based on the story by Gordon Morris); ph, Chester Lyons; ed, Alfred DeGaetano; md, Arthur Lange; ch, Jack Donahue; cos, Rene Hubert; makeup, Ernest [Ern] Westmore.

Western/Musical   **(PR:A   MPAA:NR)**

UNDER THE RAINBOW zero   (1981) Orion-WB c

Chevy Chase *(Bruce Thorpe)*, Carrie Fisher *(Annie Clark)*, Billy Barty *(Otto Kriegling)*, Eve Arden *(Duchess)*, Joseph Maher *(Duke)*, Robert Donner *(Assassin)*, Mako *(Nakamuri)*, Cork Hubbert *(Rollo Sweet)*, Pat McCormick *(Tiny)*, Adam Arkin *(Henry Hudson)*, Richard Stahl *(Lester)*, Freeman King *(Otis)*, Peter Isacksen *(Homer)*, Jack Kruschen *(Louie)*, Bennett Ohta *(Akido)*, Gary Friedkin *(Wedgie)*, Michael Lee Gogin *(Fitzgerald)*, Pam Vance *(Lana)*, Louise Moritz *(Operator)*, Anthony Gordon *(Inspector)*, John Pyle *(Steward)*, Bill Lytle *(Clerk)*, Ted Lehmann *(Adolf Hitler)*, Patty Maloney *(Rosie)*, Zelda Rubinstein *(Iris)*, Bobby Porter *(Ventriloquist)*, Charlie Messenger *(Hitler's Aide)*, Robert Murvin *(Lefty)*, David Haney *(Dispatcher)*, Leonard Barr *(Pops)*, Geraldine Papel *(Waitress)*.

A pathetic little nothing of a film which resorts to tasteless humor at the expense of its largely midget cast. It is set in 1938-the same time as the lensing of MGM's THE WIZARD OF OZ-and supposedly follows the escapades of the hundreds of midget actors needed for that picture. Perhaps that story of the life led during OZ's production is interesting, but it doesn't appear that way in UNDER THE RAINBOW. Instead we have Chase trying to be romantically cute with Fisher, who spends most of her time in munchkinland. Then there's a plot about Nazi agents led by Billy Barty who are involved in an attempted overthrow of the U.S. government. Whose idea was this anyway? UNDER THE RAINBOW is the type of picture that makes an audience long for a revival of THE TERROR OF TINY TOWN (1938).

p, Fred Bauer; d, Steve Rash; w, Pat McCormick, Harry Hurwitz, Martin Smith, Pat Bradley, Bauer (based on a story by Bradley, Bauer); ph, Frank Stanley (DeLuxe Color); m, Joe Renzetti; ed, David Blewitt; prod d, Peter Wooley; cos, Mike Butler.

Comedy   **Cas.**   **(PR:C MPAA:PG)**

UNDER THE RED ROBE*****½**   (1937, Brit.) 80m New World/FOX bw

Conrad Veidt *(Gil de Berault)*, Annabella *(Lady Marguerite)*, Raymond Massey *(Cardinal Richelieu)*, Romney Brent *(Marius)*, Sophie Stewart *(Elise, Duchess of Foix)*, F. Wyndham Goldie *(Edmond, Duke of Foix)*, Lawrence Grant *(Father Joseph)*, Baliol Holloway *(Clon)*, Haddon Mason *(Count Rossignac)*, J. Fisher White *(Baron Breteuil)*, Ben Soutten *(Leval)*, Anthony Eustrel *(Lt. Brissac)*, Shayle Gardner *(Louis)*, Desmond Roberts *(Capt. Rivarolle)*, Frank Damer *(Pierre)*, James Regan *(Jean)*, Edie Martin *(Maria)*, Eric Hales *(Lieutenant at Castle)*, Ralph Truman *(Captain at Castle)*.

Famed Swedish director Victor Seastrom (Sjostrom in Sweden) interrupted his semiretirement and ventured to England to direct what was to be his last film. Handsomely mounted and boasting a strong cast, UNDER THE RED ROBE is a costume drama set in France during the reign of Louis XIII. Veidt, a notorious gambler and duelist, finds himself facing the gallows. At the last moment he is offered a reprieve by Cardinal Richelieu (Massey) if he will seek out and kill a duke suspected of being the leader of the

Huguenots, an antimonarchy group that worries Massey and the king. Veidt agrees and finds himself accompanied by Brent, Massey's trusted assassin who is dispatched to insure that the job is done. Veidt traces the rebel leader to a castle and infiltrates his stronghold, only to fall in love with the rebel's beautiful sister, Annabella. Veidt captures the duke, but rather than kill him or bring him back to Massey for execution, he lets the rebel escape to England. When Veidt returns to Massey and King Louis and explains his actions, the king praises him for the clever way he removed the threat to the crown. Angered, but forced to concur, Massey also congratulates Veidt. His neck out of the noose, Veidt returns to Annabella to renew their romance. While certainly not among director Seastrom's masterworks, UNDER THE RED ROBE is a fine costume adventure. Massey attacks his menacing role with relish, while Veidt, who was a bit too old for his role, rises to the occasion and pulls off the action scenes as well as the romance. French actress Annabella, who was treated as a national treasure by her countrymen following her performances in Rene Clair's LE MILLION (1931) and JULY 14TH (1933), left France for England to make this picture and two others. She then went to Hollywood where she failed to distinguish herself. Seastrom never made another film, but concentrated on acting and appeared in several films, including a superb performance in Ingmar Bergman's WILD STRAWBERRIES (1957).

p, Robert T. Kane; d, Victor Seastrom 'Sjostrom'; w, Lajos Biro, Philip Lindsay, J.L. Hodson, Arthur Wimperis (based on the play by Edward Rose and the novel by Stanley J. Weyman); ph, Georges Perinal, James Wong Howe; m, Arthur Benjamin; ed, James Clark; md, Muir Mathieson; cos, Rene Hubert.

Drama   **(PR:A   MPAA:NR)**

UNDER THE ROOFS OF PARIS********   (1930, Fr.) 96m Tobis/Images bw (SOUS LES TOITS DE PARIS)

Albert Prejean *(Albert)*, Pola Illery *(Pola)*, Edmond Greville *(Louis)*, Gaston Modot *(Fred)*, Paul Olivier *(Drunkard)*, Bill Bocket *(Bill)*, Jane Pierson *(Neighborhood Woman)*, Raymond Aimos *(Thief)*, Thomy Bourdelle *(Francois)*.

Billed upon its release as "The most beautiful film in the world," UNDER THE ROOFS OF PARIS may well have fit that description, at least at that time. In the first "100 percent French talking and singing film," Rene Clair was determined to make a picture that successfully used sound as an equal to the picture. Instead of simply employing synchronous sound techniques he chose to use sound only when needed- not content with tossing in dialog just for the sake of doing so. Clair expressed the film's meaning "essentially in images with words used only when helpful and to avoid lengthy visual explanations." The story itself is a simple one (which without much effort could, in fact, be told silently). Street singer Prejean and Illery are lovers, though she enjoys flirting with his best friend, Greville. Prejean finds himself in prison for a crime he didn't commit, and while serving his sentence leaves the doors open for Illery and Greville to become lovers. He is angered when he gets out of jail, but soon sees how happy the two are together. The three then carry on as the best of friends. With practically the same set of technicians, Clair went on to make what many consider his masterpiece, A NOUS LA LIBERTE, the following year. Marcel Carne, himself one of the great figures of French cinema, worked as an assistant director on this picture.

d&w, Rene Clair; ph, Georges Perinal, Georges Raulet; ed, Rene Le Henaff; md, Armand Bernard; art d, Lazare Meerson; m/l Raoul Moretti, Rene Nazelle.

Drama   **Cas.**   **(PR:A MPAA:NR)**

UNDER THE SUN OF ROME*******   (1949, Ital.) 100m UA bw (SOTTO IL SOLE DI ROMA)

Oscar Blando *(Ciro)*, Liliana Mancini *(Iris)*, Francesco Golisano *(Geppa)*, Enno Fabeni *(Bruno)*, Alfredo Locatelli *(Nerone)*, Gaetano Chiurazzi *(Bellicapelli ["Curly"])*, Anselmo di Biagio *(Dottorino)*, Ferruccio Tozzi *(Ciro's Father)*, Maria Tozzi *(Ciro's Mother)*, Giuseppina Fava *(Janitor)*, Raffaele Caporilli *('Mbriachella)*, Ilario Malaschini *(Pirate)*, Omero Paoloni *(Coccolone)*, Gisella Monaldi *(Tosca)*, Alberto Sordi, Lorenzo di Marco.

Often called the "director of youth" in the Italian cinema, Castellani made himself an overnight success with this spirited but flawed portrayal of a post-WW II group of adolescents, concentrating on a few years in the life of Blando. His life (as is the case with all the characters) is seen in an episodic, chronicled manner detailing various incidents including the death of his parents due to his irresponsibility. Mixed in with the surprisingly humorous neo-realist nature of the film is an overwrought and melodramatic romance which is perhaps its greatest drawback. Castellani followed this picture with two more in the same optimistic vein. (In Italian; English subtitles.)

p, Sandro Ghenzi; d, Renato Castellani; w; Castellani, Fausto Tozzi, Sergio Amidei, Emilio Cecchi, Ettore Margadonna; ph, Domenico Scala; m, Nino Rota; ed, Giuliano Betti.

Drama   **(PR:A   MPAA:NR)**

UNDER THE TONTO RIM*½   (1933) 63m PAR bw

Stuart Erwin (*Tonto Duley*), Fred Kohler, Sr (*Murther*), Fuzzy Knight (*Porky*), Verna Hillie (*Nina Weston*), John Lodge (*Joe Gilbert*), George Barbier, Patricia Farley, Edwin J. Brady, Marion Burdell, Allan Garcia, Raymond Hatton, Kent Taylor.

One of eight Zane Grey adaptations helmed by Hathaway within a two-year period, UNDER THE TONTO RIM lacks one major contribution that his other Grey pictures had–Randolph Scott. Erwin turns in a barely average performance as a not-too-bright cowpoke who proves his worth and wins over his boss' daughter by doing so. A remake of a 1928 silent, which bears almost no similarities to this picture. The story again made it to the screen in 1947, and again had nothing in common with either of the others but the title.

p, Adolph Zukor; d, Henry Hathaway; w, Jack Cunningham, Gerald Geraghty (based on the novel by Zane Grey); ph, Archie Stout; art d, Earl Hedrick.

Western   **(PR:A   MPAA:NR)**

UNDER THE TONTO RIM½**   (1947) 61m RKO bw

Tim Holt (*Brad*), Nan Leslie (*Lucy*), Richard Martin (*Chito*), Richard Powers [Tom Keene] (*Dennison*), Carol Forman (*Juanita*), Tony Barrett (*Patton*), Harry Harvey (*Sheriff*), Jason Robards [Sr.] (*Capt. McLean*), Robert Clarke (*Hooker*), Jay Norris (*Andy*), Lex Barker (*Deputy Joe*), Steve Savage (*Curly*), Herman Hack.

Holt is a stagecoach operator whose stage gets held up; one of his drivers is killed. He is determined to get revenge and goes under cover, befriending one of the gang members in prison. They escape; he is then led to the bandits' hideout where he busts the gang wide open. In the meantime he falls in love with Leslie, the sister of gang leader Powers. Saved by Landers' snappy direction and top-notch camerawork.

p, Herman Schlom; d, Lew Landers; w, Norman Houston (based on the novel by Zane Grey); ph, J. Roy Hunt; m, Paul Sawtell; ed, Lyle Boyer; md, Constantin Bakaleinikoff; art d, Albert S. D'Agostino, Charles F. Pyke; set d, Darrell Silvera, John Sturtevant.

Western   **(PR:A   MPAA:NR)**

UNDER THE YUM-YUM TREE½**   (1963) 110m Sonnis-Swift/COL c

Jack Lemmon (*Hogan*), Carol Lynley (*Robin*), Dean Jones (*David*), Edie Adams (*Irene*), Imogene Coca (*Dorkus*), Paul Lynde (*Murphy*), Robert Lansing (*Charles*), James Millhollin (*Thin Man*), Pamela Curran (*Dolores*), Asa Maynor (*Cheryl*), Jane Wald (*Liz*), Bill Bixby (*Boy, Track Team*), Vera Stough (*Girl in Class*), Bill Erwin (*Teacher*), Maryesther Denver (*Woman in Bus*), Erskine Johnson, Army Archerd (*Writers*), Lyn Edgington (*Peggy*), Patty Joy Harmon (*Ardice*), Phil Arnold (*Deliveryman*), Almira Sessions (*Woman*), Gary Waynesmith (*Josh*), Irene Tsu (*Suzy*), Gloria Calomee (*Sandy*), Cliff Carnell (*Athletic Instructor*), Matty Jordan (*Maitre d'*), John Indrisano (*Boxing Instructor*), Laurie Sibbald (*Eve*), Jerry Antes (*Adam*).

An indulgent movie that was slightly too late to catch the "sex comedy" trend begun by the Doris Day-Rock Hudson pictures. Lemmon's career was somewhat tarnished by this film and he went into the doghouse of the critics for a couple of years. He didn't much like the movie either and was quoted as saying it was "a real crock." Be that as it may, looking at it today reveals that it's all quite innocent. Lemmon runs an apartment building and will only rent flats to single, attractive women, with all of whom he engages in hanky-panky. Adams moves out of her place and sublets it to Lynley, her niece. Adams has left the apartment to take up with her new lover, Lansing, and Lemmon looks delightedly at Lynley, thinking he has a new conquest. Lansing is a professor and Adams is a marriage counselor who has advised Lynley and her boy friend, Jones, that they should move in together, on a platonic level, and see if they are totally compatible in every way but sexually before they decide to get married. Adams doesn't know that Lemmon is intending to use his wiles to seduce Lynley, and Lemmon doesn't know about the agreement between Jones and Lynley. When he does learn about it, he spends several days trying to devise a way to get Jones out of the way. Lemmon's building is the ultimate bachelor's dream. It's chock full of gorgeous women, all of whom have fallen prey to Lemmon's lust. His own apartment is a riot of devices, all of which have been put there to satisfy any woman's desire, no matter how outre. Lemmon does such a good job of establishing himself as a cad, a rake, and roue that any sympathy for his character goes right out the window. When Lemmon begins to move in on Lynley (who steals the movie away from everyone), Adams sees his plan and takes steps to undermine it. She knows exactly what he is up to because she went through the same experience herself when she first moved into the building. Jones has finally caught on and is furious at Lemmon's attempts to deflower Lynley. Jones decides to take direct action and change his platonic relationship with Lynley in favor of a more amorous liaison. He goes to great lengths to plan the perfect romantic evening and seduce her, but before he can go all the way (which would end their relationship), Jones is overcome by guilt and exits. Jones does return (as we knew he would), and he and Lynley elope to live happily ever after. Adams and Lansing are now totally in love and Lemmon has an empty apartment, which he promptly rents to a new young thing as he rubs his hands and licks his lips in

anticipation of his latest amour. Roman's stage play had been a big hit, but too much time had elapsed between the stage presentation and the film and Swift and Roman wrote a script that was a trifle blatant for the times without much subtlety. Coca and Lynde score with some laugh scenes and, in small roles, note Bill Bixby and Jerry Antes, who had a brief career as a singer. Gary Waynesmith spent half his time acting and the other half as an executive at *TV Guide* when he wasn't before the cameras. Whereas the Hudson-Day comedies showed some restraint, this one snickered, smarmed, and went too far for most audiences.

p, Frederick Brisson; d, David Swift; w, Lawrence Roman, Swift (based on the play by Roman); ph, Joseph Biroc (Eastmancolor); m, Frank DeVol; ed, Charles Nelson; prod d, Dale Hennesy; set d, William Kiernan; cos, Don Feld; ch, Robert Tucker; m/l, "Under the Yum-Yum Tree," Sammy Cahn, James Van Heusen (sung by James Darren); makeup, Harry Ray.

Comedy   **(PR:C-O   MPAA:NR)**

UNDER TWO FLAGS*½**   (1936) 105m FOX bw

Ronald Colman (*Cpl. Victor*), Claudette Colbert (*Cigarette*), Victor McLaglen (*Maj. Doyle*), Rosalind Russell (*Lady Venetia*), J. Edward Bromberg (*Col.-Ferol*), Nigel Bruce (*Capt. Menzies*), Herbert Mundin (*Rake*), Gregory Ratoff (*Ivan*), C. Henry Gordon (*Lt. Petaine*), John Carradine (*Cafard*), William Ricciardi (*Cigarette's Father*), Lumsden Hare (*Lord Seraph*), Fritz Leiber (*French Governor*), Onslow Stevens (*Sidi Ben Youssiff*), Louis Mercier (*Barron*), Francis McDonald (*Husson*), Thomas Beck (*Pierre*), Harry Semels (*Sgt. Malines*), Frank Lackteen (*Ben Hamidon*), Jamiel Hasson (*Arab Liaison Officer*), Frank Reicher (*French General*), Gwendolyn Logan (*Lady Cairn*), Hans von Morhart (*Hans*), Tor Johnson (*Bidou*), Marc Lawrence (*Grivon*), George Regas (*Keskerdit*), Douglas Gerrard (*Col. Farley*), Ronald J. Pennick (*Cpl. Veux*), Rolfe Sedan (*Mouche*), Eugene Borden (*Villon*), Harry Worth (*Dinant*), Tony Merl (*Catouche*), Alex Palasthy (*Hotel Manager*), Gaston Glass (*Adjutant*), Nicholas Soussanin (*Levine*), Rosita Earlan (*Ivan's Girl*), Fred Malatesta (*Chasseur Lieutenant*), Hector Sarno (*Arab Merchant*), George Ducount (*Soldier*), George Jackson (*Sentry*).

A rousing adaptation of the novel by Ouida that had already been a successful stage play and filmed twice before without sound. Zanuck is listed as the producer but his associate, Raymond Griffith, was the "on-line" man and is to be credited with the excellent result. Colman is a member of the French Foreign Legion, where no one ever asks why you're there or where you came from. Mundin had been his valet in England and follows him into the service when Colman is accused of having committed a crime (actually Colman is covering up for the real culprit, his kid brother). While in the service, Colman meets Colbert, a camp follower who adores men in uniform and will stop at nothing to prove it. McLaglen is the Legion's commander and jealous of the way Colbert tosses herself at Colman so he deliberately makes the hard life even harder for Colman. Russell, an English lady, arrives in the area and Colman immediately goes for her, thus throwing in the added twist of a romantic triangle with a man at the fulcrum. When Colman eventually says farewell to Colbert, as he prefers Russell, she is terribly hurt. McLaglen sends Colman off on an impossible mission and hopes he won't come back. Colman is captured by Stevens, an Arab chieftain who just happened to attend the same college (Oxford) as Colman. But the old school tie doesn't work out in the parched desert and it looks as though Colman might get his. Colbert knows where Colman is being hidden and she can lead the Legionnaires there, if she so chooses. She is torn between letting him die like a dog (after all, Hell hath no fury like a woman scorned), or she can do the good thing and save his life. Need we tell you which course she chooses? Colbert leads the soldiers to the den of Stevens and, in doing so, is mortally wounded and dies with her arms around the man whose life she has just saved, Colman. The picture ends as the tart is given a military burial while the Legionnaires watch with tears in their eyes at the memory of Colbert. Colman leaves for England with Russell and the French Foreign Legion goes back to work. Lots of action, some of which was reminiscent of BEAU GESTE. If the men look as though they are tired and terribly hot, they are not acting. It was shot in the dry, dusty Arizona desert under worse conditions than the Legion faced in the Sahara. A few laughs to punctuate the battles, mostly by Ratoff. The play was first staged in 1870, and Theda Bara starred as "Cigarette" in one of the silent versions. This was Colman's final film with Fox Studios. Later, he went onto the free-lance market and upped his price considerably to a quarter of a million per movie. Hungarian-born J. Edward Bromberg made his debut here at the age of 33. During the next 15 years before his death in 1951, this very busy actor would appear in more than 30 films, including SEVENTH HEAVEN, SUEZ, SALOME, as well as some other movies which did *not* begin with the letter "S." He may have been the only actor to have ever made three films about the James brothers, having appeared in JESSE JAMES, I SHOT JESSE JAMES, and THE RETURN OF FRANK JAMES.

p, Darryl F. Zanuck; d, Frank Lloyd, (battle sequences Otto Brower); w, W.P. Lipscomb, Walter Ferris (based on the novel by Ouida); ph, Ernest Palmer, Sidney Wagner; m, Louis Silvers; ed, Ralph Dietrich; md, Silvers.

Action/Adventure   **Cas.**   **(PR:A-C   MPAA:NR)**

UNDER WESTERN SKIES*½ (1945) 57m UNIV bw

Martha O'Driscoll (Katie), Noah Beery, Jr (Tod), Leo Carrillo (King Randall), Leon Errol (Willie), Irving Bacon (Sheriff), Ian Keith (Prof. Moffett), Jennifer Holt (Charity), Edna May Wonacott (Faith), Earle Hodgins (Mayfield), Shaw and Lee (The Barton Brothers), Dorothy Granger (Maybelle), Jack Rice (Neil Matthews), Gladys Blake (Lulu), George Lloyd (Proprietor), Claire Whitney (Mrs. Simms), Frank Lackteen (Dan Boone), Jack Ingram (Red Hutchins), Patsy O'Byrne (Mrs. Bassett), Nan Leslie (Prudence), Eddy Waller (Preacher), Perc Launders (Hank), Donald Kerr (Stable Owner), Warren Jackson, Charles Sherlock (Young Bucks).

A traveling vaudeville troupe makes a stop in a little Arizona town which is less than hospitable. They are befriended by Beery, who not only gets rid of a pesty bandit, but falls in love with the show's star, O'Driscoll. Includes a handful of easily forgettable ditties: "Under Western Skies," "Don't Go Making Speeches," "An Old Fashioned Girl," "All You Kids" (Everett Carter, Milton Rosen).

p, Warren Wilson; d, Jean Yarbrough; w, Stanley Roberts, Clyde Bruckman (based on a story by Roberts); ph, Charles Van Enger; ed, Arthur Hilton; md, Frank Skinner; art d, John B. Goodman.

Western/Musical (PR:A MPAA:NR)

UNDER WESTERN STARS**½ (1938) 67m REP bw

Roy Rogers (Himself), Smiley Burnette (Frog), Carol Hughes (Eleanor), Maple City Four (Themselves), Guy Usher (Fairbanks), Tom Chatterton (Marlowe), Kenneth Harlan (Richards), Alden Chase (Andrews), Brandon Beach (Sen. Wilson), Earle Dwire (Mayor Biggs), Jean Fowler (Mrs. Wilson), Dora Clement (Mrs. Marlowe), Dick Elliott (Scully), Burr Caruth (Larkin), Charles Whitaker (Tremaine), Jack Rockwell (Sheriff), Frankie Marvin (Deputy Pete), Jack Kirk, Fred Burns, Curley Dresden, Bill Wolfe, Trigger the Horse, Jack Ingram, Tex Cooper.

Rogers is a singing, hard-riding congressman from a dust-bowl state who journeys to Washington, D. C., after being elected by fellow ranchers and cowpokes. His platform? That which in another time might have been called socialism: he advocates public ownership of utilities (remember, this was the time of the New Deal; the Tennessee Valley Authority was beginning to deliver electric power to farmers under the aegis of the federal government). Specifically, he wants free water supplies for his drought-ridden constituents. With the help of sidekick Burnette and others, his platform wins out. He gains support by showing influential Washingtonians a documentary film dealing with the ravages of the dust bowl, demonstrating once again the power of cinema. This was the first starring film for "The King of the Cowboys," and it made Rogers an instant success. Studio head Herbert J. Yates had groomed Rogers for stardom as a tactic in his continuing battle with his most profitable star, the mettlesome but extremely popular Gene Autry. The result exceeded all expectations. The old king was dead; long live the king! Not one to tamper with success, Yates extended the victory by having director Kane at the helm of 41 more of Rogers' starring vehicles.

p, Sol C. Siegel; d, Joseph Kane, w, Dorrell McGowan, Stuart McGowan, Betty Burbridge (based on the story by Dorrell McGowan, Stuart McGowan); ph, Jack Marta; ed, Lester Orlebeck; md, Albert Colombo; m/l, Jack Lawrence, Peter Tinturin, Chalres Rosoff, Johnny Marvin, Eddie Cherkose.

Western (PR:A MPAA:NR)

UNDER YOUR HAT** (1940, Brit.) 79m BL/REP bw

Jack Hulbert (Jack Millett), Cicely Courtneidge (Kay Millett), Austin Trevor (Boris Vladimir), Leonora Corbett (Carole Markoff), Cecil Parker (Sir Geoffrey Arlington), Tony Hayes (George), Charles Oliver (Carl), H. F. Maltby (Col. Sheepshanks), Mary burton (Mrs. Sheepshanks), Glynis Johns (Winnie), Myrette Morven (Miss Stevens), The Rhythm Brothers.

Hulbert and his wife Courtneidge are a popular song-and-dance pair. Husband Hulbert doubles as a secret agent for his government. Between pictures, Hulbert is assigned the secret mission of keeping tabs on glamorous foreign spy Corbett. True to his trade, he keeps the real reason for his involvement with the ardent agent a secret from his wife. Piqued no end by his apparent amorous entanglement, Courtneidge dons a disguise and gets a job as maid to the sexy spy. Noting that his wife's skill at surveillance exceeds even his own, Hulbert relents and solicits her assistance. Together–with the help of their show-business acumen– the two uncover master-spy Trevor, who has fitted a prototype of a new design of carburetor to his own airplane, planning to take it aboard. Posing as mechanics, the husband-and-wife team stow away aboard the aircraft. Forcing the pilot to bail out, they fly back to Blighty with the valuable prototype. Redolent of the THIN MAN series, with the added fillip of the musical-stage talent, but lacking the charisma of the stars of that series. Musical numbers include "Can't Find That Tiger," sung by The Rhythm Brothers.

p, Jack Hulbert; d, Maurice Elvey; w, Rodney Ackland, Anthony Kimmins, L. Green (based on the play by Hulbert, Archie Menzies, Geoffrey Kerr, Arthur Macrae); ph, Mutz Greenbaum; m, Lew Stone; cos, Joe Strassner.

Spy Drama/Comedy (PR:A MPAA:NR)

UNDER YOUR SPELL*½ (1936) 62m FOX bw

Lawrence Tibbett (Anthony Allen), Wendy Barrie (Cynthia Drexel), Gregory Ratoff (Petroff, Manager), Arthur Treacher (Botts, Butler), Gregory Gaye (Count Raul Du Rienne), Berton Churchill (Judge), Jed Prouty (Mr. Twerp), Claudia Coleman (Mrs. Twerp), Charles Richman (Uncle Bob), Madge Bellamy (Miss Stafford), Nora Cecil (School Teacher), Bobby Samarzich (Pupil), Joyce Compton, June Gittelson (Secretaries), Clyde Dilson, Boyd Irwin, John Dilson, Lloyd Whitlock, Frank Sheridan, Edward Mortimer, Sam Blum, Jay Eaton, Scott Mattraw, Harry Stafford (Sponsors), Edward Gargan, Frank Fanning (Detectives), Cedric Stevens (Steward), Creighton Hale, Harry Harvey, Charles Sherlock (Photographers), Edward Cooper (Butler), Lee Phelps, Bruce Mitchell (Bailiffs), Pierre Watkin (Allen's Lawyer), Theodore Von Eltz (Cynthia's Lawyer), Sherry Hall, Jack Mulhall (Court Clerks), Dink Trout (Small Man), Kate Murray, Mariska Aldrich (Tall Women), Frank Arthur Swales (Man with Glasses), Troy Brown (Porter), Florence Wix (Dowager), George Magrill (Angry Man), Josef Swickard (Amigo), Ann Gillis (Gwendolyn), Robert Dalton (Announcer), Muriel Evans (Governess), Alan Davis (Pilot).

A weak Tibbett vehicle which casts him as a singer tired of fame and publicity who runs away in search of relaxation and ends up on a ranch in Mexico. His manager, Ratoff, isn't too fond of the idea and sends Barrie to fetch him. He puts up with the pretty young socialite's pestering for a while and then finally marries her. A less-than-inspired showing from Preminger in his Hollywood directorial debut. Songs include: "Amigo," "My Little Mule Wagon," "Under Your Spell" (Arthur Schwartz, Howard Dietz), and operatic arias from Mozart's "The Marriage of Figaro" and Gounod's "Faust."

p, John Stone; d, Otto Preminger; w, Frances Hyland, Saul Elkins (based on a story by Bernice Mason, Sy Bartlett); ph, Sidney Wagner; ed, Fred Allen; md, Arthur Lange; cos, Herschel; ch, Sammy Lee.

Musical (PR:A MPAA:NR)

UNDERCOVER (SEE: UNDERGROUND GUERRILLAS, 1944, Brit.)

UNDERCOVER AGENT** (1939) 65m MON bw (GB: SWEEPSTAKE RACKETEERS)

Russell Gleason (Bill Trent), Shirley Deane (Betty Madison), J. M. Kerrigan (Tom Madison [Pop]), Maude Eburne (Mrs. Minnow), Oscar O'Shea (Pat Murphy), Selmer Jackson (Graham), Ralf Harolde (Bartel), Ray Bennett (Pussyfoot), Ralph Sanford (Joe Blake).

Gleason has aspirations of becoming a postal inspector but gets himself in trouble when he carries a gun around while off duty. He earns the government's respect when he cracks open a case involving the counterfeiting of sweepstakes tickets. Deane (who costarred with Gleason in Republic's JONES FAMILY series) takes the role of the female lead, with Kerrigan her drunken Shakespearean actor father who kicks the bottle by the finale.

p, E. B. Derr; d, Howard Bretherton; w, Milton Raison (based on a story by Martin Mooney); ph, Arthur Martinelli; ed, Russell Schoengarth.

Crime (PR:A MPAA:NR)

UNDERCOVER AGENT** (1935, Brit.) 68m Merton Park/Lippert bw (GB: COUNTERSPY)

Dermot Walsh (Manning), Hazel Court (Clare), Hermione Baddeley (Del Mar), James Vivian (Larry), Archie Duncan (Jim), Alexander Gauge (Smith), Frederick Schrecker (Plattnauer), Hugh Latimer (Barlow), Bill Travers (Rex), John Penrose (Paulson), Gwen Bacon (Matron), Maxwell Foster (Dr. Stevenson), Howard Lang (Policeman), Beryl Baxter (Girl), Monti de Lyle, Stuart Saunders, Ann Wrigg, Fred Buckland.

A routine spy picture which has mild-mannered chartered accountant Walsh receiving a secret package that contains valuable plans. Of course, there's a spy ring that wants the plans and the spies kidnap Walsh and wife Court in order to get them. He is saved, however, when the police discover his location and bring the criminals to justice.

p, W. H. Williams; d, Vernon Sewell; w, Guy Elmes, Michael Le Fevre (based on the novel Criss Cross Code by Julian Symons); ph, A.T. Dinsdale; m, Eric Spear; ed, G. Muller.

Spy Drama (PR:A MPAA:NR)

UNDERCOVER DOCTOR** (1939) 67m Harold Hurley/PAR bw

Lloyd Nolan (Robert Anders), Janice Logan (Margaret Hopkins), J. Carroll Naish (Dr. Bartley Morgan), Heather Angel (Cynthia Weld), Broderick Crawford (Eddie Krator), Robert Wilcox (Tom Logan), Richard Carle (Elmer Porter), Stanley Price (Johnny Franklin), John Eldredge (Gordon Kingsley), George Meeker (Dapper Dan Barr), Raymond Hatton (Dizzy Warner), Philip Warren (Spats Edwards), Paul Fix (Monk Jackson).

The FBI is made to look like a picture of glory in this standard programmer about, as the title implies, a doctor who serves the underworld. He lives a life of luxury until G-man Nolan catches on to the nature of his patients. The finale drives home the familiar philosophy that criminals must be punished by killing off all of them at the hands of the feds. One-time FBI head J. Edgar Hoover (who penned the story!) had the final cut on this picture, as well as control over the ad campaign, so be prepared for some hard-core propaganda in favor of the bureau. This was the second in a series of G-men glorification pictures made by executive producer Harold Hurley under his deal with the publicity-hungry Hoover; the first was PERSONS IN HIDING (1939). The film is very loosely based on the life and times of Joseph P. "Doc" Moran, a practicing physician with mob connections who specialized in laundering mob money and performing plastic surgery to alter the appearance of wanted criminals. Author Hoover's FBI had nothing to do with the death of the hard-drinking doctor; he was murdered by two disgruntled ex-patients whose plastic surgery had been painfully unsuccessful. The two were wanted criminals Freddie Barker and Alvin Karpis, whom Hoover's agency had been unsuccessfully seeking at the time.

p, Edward T. Lowe; d, Louis King; w, Horace McCoy, William R. Lipman (based on a story by J. Edgar Hoover); ph, William C. Mellor; ed, Arthur Schmidt.

Crime   (PR:A   MPAA:NR)

UNDERCOVER GIRL   (SEE: UNDERCOVER MAISIE, 1947)

UNDERCOVER GIRL**   (1950) 83m UNIV bw

Alexis Smith (Christine Miller/"Sal Willis"), Scott Brady (Lt. Mike Trent), Richard Egan (Jess Taylor), Gladys George (Liz Crow), Edmon Ryan (Doc Holmes), Gerald Mohr (Reed Menig), Royal Dano (Moocher), Harry Landers (Tully), Connie Gilchrist (Capt. Parker), Angela Clarke (Babe Snell), Regis Toomey (Hank "Butt" Miller), Lynn Ainley (Pat Gibson), Tristram Coffin (Robbie), Lawrence Cregar (Murph), Harold Gary (Wally), Ed Rand (Lew), Mel Archer (Collar), Betty Lou Gerson (Pat the Nurse).

Smith plays a policewoman trainee involved in a narcotics case with cop Brady. She nearly gets herself killed but by the finale, after a search through a deserted house, she smashes the drug ring. At the time this may have been a novel idea, but later you could turn on the TV seven days a week, 52 weeks a year, and see the same exact plot.

p, Aubrey Schenck; d, Joseph Pevney; w, Harry Essex (based on a story by Robert Hardy Andrews, Francis Rosenwald); ph, Carl Guthrie; ed, Russell Schoengarth; md, Joseph Gershenson; art d, Bernard Herzbrun, Emerich Nicholson; cos, Bill Thomas.

Crime   (PR:A   MPAA:NR)

UNDERCOVER GIRL*   (1957, Brit.) 68m But bw

Paul Carpenter (Johnny Carter), Kay Callard (Joan Foster), Monica Grey (Evelyn King), Bruce Seton (Ted Austin), Jackie Collins (Peggy Foster), Maya Koumani (Miss Brazil), Kim Parker (Maid), Tony Quinn (Mike O'Sullivan), John Boxer, Alexander Field, Paddy Ryan, Milton Reid, Eleanor Leigh, Robert Raglan, George Roderick, Michael Moore, Totti Truman Taylor, Mark Hashfield, Gerry Collins.

A lame crime programmer from across the Atlantic which stars Carpenter as the brother of a murdered journalist who came too close to busting open a drug ring. With the help of Callard, a nightclub employee, Carpenter is able to track down the murderer, as well as extinguish the narcotics sales.

p, Kay Luckwell, Derek Winn; d, Francis Searle; w, Bernard Lewis, Bill Luckwell (based on a story by Lewis); ph, Jimmy Harvey.

Crime   (PR:A   MPAA:NR)

UNDERCOVER MAISIE**   (1947) 90m MGM bw (GB: UNDERCOVER GIRL)

Ann Sothern (Maisie Ravier), Barry Nelson (Lt. Paul Scott), Mark Daniels (Chip Dolan), Leon Ames [Willis Farnes]), Clinton Sundberg (Guy Canford), Dick Simmons (Gilfred I. Rogers), Charles D. Brown (Capt. Mead), Gloria Holden (Mrs. Guy Canford), Douglas Fowley (Daniels), Nella Walker (Mrs. Andrew Lorrison), Gene Roberts (Viola Trengham), Celia Travers (Isabelle), Morris Ankrum (Parker).

Ann Sothern's MAISIE series drew to a close after eight years with this 10th entry as the flippant blonde goes under cover with the Los Angeles police in order to finger a gang of confidence men. She's nearly suspected of being a real gangster before she manages to bring in the culprits. (See MAISIE series, Index.)

p, George Haight; d, Harry Beaumont; w. Thelma Robinson; ph, Charles Salerno; m, David Snell; ed, Ben Lewis; art d, Cedric Gibbons, Gabriel Scognamillo; cos, Irene.

Crime   (PR:A   MPAA:NR)

UNDER-COVER MAN**   (1932) 74m PAR bw

George Raft (Nick Darrow), Nancy Carroll (Lora Madigan), Lew Cody (Kenneth Mason), Roscoe Karns (Dannie), Noel Francis (Connie), Gregory Ratoff (Martoff), David Landau (Inspector Conklin), Paul Porcasi (Sam Dorse), Leyland Hodgson (Gillespie), William Janney (Jimmy Madigan),

George Davis (Bernie), Robert E. Homans (Flannagan), Hal Price (Detective).

Raft agrees to work with the police after his father is killed by Wall Street bond thieves, going under cover to do so. He hooks up with Carroll, whose bond messenger brother was also killed, and together they infiltrate the underworld. While she makes a play for gang boss Cody, he snoops around and becomes pals with gang members Ratoff. They soon have enough information to make the gang crumble and turn master-criminal Cody over to the police. Raft and Carroll then let romance carry them away. This was one-time hoofer Raft's first starring role, one that helped him establish the gangster persona that he tried to carry over into real life. Aging ingenue Carroll, in a distinctly secondary part, had been in a career slump. Her miscasting here didn't help her.

d, James Flood; w, Garrett Fort, Francis Faragoh, Thomson Burtis (based on a story by John Wilstach); ph, Victor Milner.

Crime   (PR:A   MPAA:NR)

UNDERCOVER MAN**   (1936) 57m REP bw

Johnny Mack Brown, Suzanne Karen, Ted Adams, Lloyd Ingraham, Horace Murphy, Edward Cassidy, Frank Ball, Margaret Mann, Frank Darien, Dick Morehead, George Morrell.

Brown is a Wells Fargo agent who goes under cover to catch a criminal sheriff and his accomplice deputies. Not bad for a B western, but only fans of the genre will be entertained.

p, A.W. Hackel; d, Albert Ray; w, Andrew Bennison.

Western   Cas.   (PR:A   MPAA:NR)

UNDERCOVER MAN*½   (1942) 68m UA bw

William Boyd (Hopalong Cassidy), Andy Clyde (California), Jay Kirby (Breezy Travers), Antonio Moreno (Tomas Gonzales), Chris-Pin Martin (Miguel), Nora Lane (Louise Saunders), Esther Estrella (Dolores Gonzales), Alan Baldwin (Bob Saunders), Eva Puig (Rosita Lopez), Jack Rockwell (Capt. John Hawkins), John Vosper (Ed Carson), Tony Roux (Chavez), Pierce Lyden (Bert), Ted Wells (Jim, a Rancher), Martin Garralaga (Cortez), Joe Dominguez (Caballero), Earle Hodgins (Sheriff Blackton), Frank Ellis, Bennett George.

A tired oater in the HOPALONG CASSIDY series which trudges through a weak script about a bandit who empties the pockets of Americans and Mexicans alike. His lack of discrimination causes some ill feelings as each side of the border places blame on the other. Boyd gets involved and before a major dispute starts the Rio Grande is squeaky clean. Originally slated for release by Paramount, but United Artists took over a handful of the pictures for release; this was the first of that handful. (See HOPALONG CASSIDY series, Index.)

p, Harry Sherman; d, Lesley Selander; w, J. Benton Cheney (based on characters created by Clarence E. Mulford); ph, Russell Harlan; ed, Carrol-Lewis; md, Irvin-Talbot; art d, Ralph Berger.

Western   (PR:A   MPAA:NR)

UNDERCOVER MAN, THE½**   (1949) 85m COL bw

Glenn Ford (Frank Warren), Nina Foch (Judith Warren), James Whitmore (George Pappas), Barry Kelley (Edward O'Rourke), David Wolfe (Stanley Weinburg), Frank Tweddell (Inspector Herzog), Howard St. John (Joseph S. Horan), John F. Hamilton (Sgt. Shannon), Leo Penn (Sidney Gordon), Joan Lazer (Rosa Rocco), Esther Minciotti (Maria Rocco), Angela Clarke (Theresa Rocco), Anthony Caruso (Salvatore Rocco), Robert Osterlohk (Manny Zanger), Kay Medford (Gladys LaVerne), Patricia White (Muriel Gordon), Peter Brocco (Johnny), Everett Glass (Judge Parker), Joe Mantell (Newsboy), Michael Cisney (Fred Ferguson), Marcella Cisney (Alice Ferguson), Sidney Dubin (Harris), William Vedder (Druggist), James Drum, Pat Lane, Allen Mathews, Robert Malcolm, Brian O'Hara, Joe Palma (Policemen), Esther Zeitlin, Irene Martin, Virginia Farmer, Rose Plumer, Stella LeSaint (Women), Harlan Warde, Cy Malis, Jack Gordon, Paul Marion, Ted Jordan, Glen Thompson, Roy Darmour, Wally Rose, Saul Gorss (Hoodlums), Tom Coffey, William Rhinehart (Gunmen), Ralph Volkie (Big Fellow/Man in White), Ken Harvey (Big Fellow), Al Murphy, Daniel Meyers, Franklin Parker, Robert Haines, Sam LaMarr, Bernard Sell, Edwin Randolph (Men), Silvio Minciotti (Vendor), John Butler (Grocer), Richard Bartell (Court Attendant), Ben Erway (Court Clerk), Franklin Farnum (Federal Judge), Frank Mayo (Jury Foreman), Wheaton Chambers (Secretary), George Douglas (District Attorney), Helen Wallace (Mrs. O'Rourke), Peter Virgo (Cigar Store Owner), Edwin Max (Manager), Billy Nelson (Bouncer), Billy Stubbs (Crap Dealer), Tom Hanlon (Newsreel Announcer).

Although Treasury Department detectives wouldn't seem to live a life of danger, Ford does in this picture as he tries to prove an underworld crime boss, known only as the "Big Fellow," guilty of tax evasion. The hood owes $3 million in back taxes so Ford and partner Whitmore head to Chicago to crack the case. They begin asking a lot of questions–too many for the Big Fellow and his corrupt Italian "family." When they try to get some answers from the mob's bookkeeper, the man is silenced with a gunshot. One by one the contacts are bumped off. When Ford's wife's safety is placed in jeopardy, Ford seriously debates giving up the Treasury Department for a quiet life with his family. He is put back on track, however, by a stirring patriotic speech delivered by the old Italian mother of one of the dead contacts. The dead man's daughter then supplies Ford with the necessary figures and records, which gives him solid evidence. With assistance from the Big Fellow's disloyal lawyer, Ford and the feds topple the Big Fellow. Clearly based on the methods the government used to convict Al Capone of tax evasion, THE UNDERCOVER MAN is based on an article written by Frank J. Wilson, who reportedly was the man behind the bust of Capone.

p, Robert Rossen; d, Joseph H. Lewis; w, Sydney Boehm, Malvin Wald, Jerry Rubin (based on article "Undercover Man: He Trapped Capone" by Frank J. Wilson); ph, Burnett Guffey; m, George Duning; ed, Al Clark; md, M.W. Stoloff; art d, Walter Holscher; set d, William Kiernan; cos, Jean Louis.

Crime   (PR:C   MPAA:NR)

UNDERCOVER WOMAN, THE**   (1946) 56m REP bw

Stephanie Bachelor *(Marcia Conroy)*, Robert Livingston *(Sheriff Don Long)*, Richard Fraser *(Gregory Vixon)*, Isabel Withers *(Penny Davis)*, Helene Heigh *(Laura Vixon)*, Edythe Elliott *(Mrs. Grey)*, John Dehner *(Walter Hughes)*, Elaine Lange *(Juanita Gillette)*, Betty Blythe *(Cissy Van Horn)*, Tom London *(Lem Stone)*, Larry Blake *(Simon Gillette)*.

An entertaining combination of mystery and comedy brightens up the dude-ranch locale of this programmer. Bachelor is a private eye hired to shadow an adulterous husband, but when the fellow gets killed the case takes on a larger meaning. Bachelor enlists the aid of sheriff Livingston and together they discover the identity of the culprit. Not a western though set in the West and costarring one of the best-known B western actors, Livingston, who had played the character "Stoney Brooke" in the THREE MESQUITEERS series 29 times, and then went on to become the protagonist in the LONE RIDER series.

p, Rudolph E. Abel; d, Thomas Carr; w, Jerry Sackheim, Sherman L. Lowe, Robert Metzler (based on a story by Sylvia G. L. Dannet); ph, Bud Thackery; ed, Fred Allen; md, Richard Cherwin; art d, Hilyard Brown; cos, Adele Palmer; spec eff, Howard Lydecker, Theodore Lydecker.

Mystery/Comedy   (PR:A   MPAA:NR)

UNDERCOVERS HERO* (1975, Brit.) 95m Charter/UA c (GB: SOFT BEDS AND HARD BATTLES)

Peter Sellers *(Gen. Latour/Maj. Robinson/Schroder/Adolf Hitler/Prince Kyoto/President of France)*, Lila Kedrova *(Mme. Grenier)*, Curt Jurgens *(Gen. Von Grotjahn)*, Beatrice Romand *(Marie-Claude)*, Rex Stallings *(Alan Cassidy)*, Jenny Hanley, Francoise Pascal, Gabriella Licudi, Rula Lenska, Daphne Lawson, Carolle Rousseau, Hylette Adolphe *(Grenier's Girls)*, Nicholas Loukes *(Schroeder's Aide)*, Vernon Dobtcheff *(Priest)*, Patricia Burke *(Mother Superior)*.

A feeble attempt at comedy which tries to depend on Sellers handling a half-dozen different roles, each one of them unfunny as the next. The premise is that a brothel full of ladies helps the anti-Nazi cause by ridding the world of the enemy in the bedroom. More offensive than the premise is the fact that it could have been quite funny if scripted with any life.

p, John Boulting; d, Roy Boulting; w, Leo Marks, Roy Boulting; ph, Gil Taylor (Eastmancolor); m, Neil Rhoden, Roy Boulting ed, Martin Charles; art d, John Howell; set d, Patrick McLoughlin.

Comedy   (PR:O   MPAA:R)

UNDERCURRENT**½   (1946) 116m MGM bw

Katharine Hepburn *(Ann Hamilton)*, Robert Taylor *(Alan Garroway)*, Robert Mitchum *(Michael Garroway)*, Edmund Gwenn *(Prof. Dink Hamilton)*, Marjorie Main *(Lucy)*, Jayne Cotter *(Sylvia Burton)*, Clinton Sundberg *(Mr. Warmsley)*, Dan Tobin *(Prof. Herbert Bangs)*, Kathryn Card *(Mrs. Foster)*, Leigh Whipper *(George)*, Charles Trowbridge *(Justice Putnam)*, James Westerfield *(Henry Gilson)*, Billy McLain *(Uncle Ben)*, Milton Kibbee *(Minister)*, Jean Andren *(Mrs. Davenport)*, Forbes Murray *(Sen. Edwards)*, Bert Moorehouse *(1st Man)*, David Cavendish, Ernest Hilliard, Clive Morgan, Reginald Simpson, Oliver Cross, Harold Miller, Frank Leigh, Dick Earle, James Carlisle, Ann Lawrence, Florence Fair, Laura Treadwell, Ella Ethridge, Hazel Keener, Maxine Hudson, Bess Flowers, Hilda Rhoades, Joan Thorsen, Barbara Billingsley *(Guests)*, Sarah Edwards *(Manager)*, Ellen Ross *(Gwen)*, Betty Blythe, Moyna Andre *(Saleswomen)*, Helyn Eby-Rock *(Fitter)*, Sylvia Andrew *(Nora)*, Eula Guy *(Housekeeper)*, Wheaton Chambers *(Proprietor)*, James Westerfield *(Henry Gilson)*, Gordon Richards *(Headwaiter)*, Frank Dae *(2nd Man)*, Nina Ross, Dorothy Christy, Jane Green *(Women)*, Dan Kerry *(Elevator Man)*, Sydney Logan *(Model)*, Hank Worden *(Attendant)*, Robert Emmett O'Connor *(Stationmaster)*, Rudy Rama *(Headwaiter)*, William Eddritt *(Butler)*, Phil Dunham *(Elevator Man)*, Jack Murphy, William Cartledge *(Messengers)*.

Taylor's first film after coming back from WW II service had him in the unaccustomed role of a villain in director Minnelli's only *film noir* assignment. Hepburn is a dowdy spinster who lives a very quiet existence

with her professor father, Gwenn. (Hepburn had been Gwenn's daughter once before in SYLVIA SCARLETT, 1936.) There is no love on the horizon for Hepburn so she is more than eager when she meets Taylor, a well-to-do manufacturer of airplanes. Their courtship and marriage are seen in scant minutes and the couple are united. No sooner is the ring slipped on the finger than Hepburn sees Taylor is not nearly the solid citizen he appeared to be on the surface. His face grows dark when he speaks of his long-lost brother, Mitchum, and he maintains that Mitchum cheated him on a business deal. Hepburn can't believe that her normally gentle husband could muster so much rancor so she begins to investigate and learns that Taylor has been lying. Mitchum is anything but a snake and Taylor may be the person responsible for Mitchum's disappearance he may have murdered him. Further information she gleans leads her to believe that Taylor may have framed Mitchum on a robbery charge and he also may have killed a scientist and stolen his invention. It was that asset that put Taylor's company on the map and gave him such riches. (If we are to believe Honore de Balzac, then it's true that "behind every great fortune there is a great crime.") Hepburn takes it upon herself to go out to Mitchum's small ranch. While there, she meets a man she thinks is the caretaker. It takes a while, but she finally learns that the man is Mitchum. She is taken by her naivete and worries that Taylor's chicanery might ruin her innocent life. Mitchum goes to see Taylor and we discover the truth about why he left the family company. Mitchum had always thought Taylor killed the scientist and he couldn't bear living with that guilt. Taylor tells Mitchum that he loves Hepburn and would never dream of involving her in any criminal schemes. Mitchum is placated enough to cease his harangue of Taylor. Hepburn has been acting standoffish towards Taylor and he can tell that the love has disappeared from their marriage. (Brahms' Third Symphony is used effectively here.) With that gone, she has become an albatross around his neck so he seeks to remove her by murder. Instead, he is himself killed when Mitchum's horse stomps him to death. In the end, Hepburn and Mitchum will get together as she feels that he is a man with whom she can have a meaningful relationship. Good musical score by Stothart highlights the suspense, but the movie fails to engender enough thrills to make it effective. Mitchum had been loaned out by David Selznick, with whom he had a personal contract, and was working on three–that's right, three movies–at the same time. He shot DESIRE ME for MGM in the afternoon, this film in the morning, and THE LOCKET for RKO at night. Since he was not yet 30 years of age, it is assumed that he had a great deal of stamina, but it must have taken a toll because he seemed to go into a permanent sleepwalk mode for the remainder of his career. Taylor was 35 and no longer the pretty boy of CAMILLE and his other films before the war. This was one of his most difficult acting jobs because it wasn't one-note, it was a huge range of tones and he was equal to the task. It was also Clinton Sundberg's film debut after Hepburn discovered him on the stage. Minnelli's distinguished career ended when he turned down assignment after assignment in the 1970s and 1980s because he felt that the movie industry was paying too much attention to sex and violence and had lost the charm it once embraced. He died in late July, 1986, leaving a legacy of many memorable films.

p, Pandro S. Berman; d, Vincente Minnelli; w, Edward Chodorov, Marguerite Roberts, George Oppenheimer (based on *You Were There* by Thelma Strabel); ph, Karl Freund; m, Herbert Stothart; ed, Ferris Webster; md, Stothart; art d, Cedric Gibbons, Randall Duell; set d, Edwin B. Willis, Jack D. Moore; cos, Irene; makeup, Jack Dawn.

Spy Drama   (PR:A-C   MPAA:NR)

UNDERDOG, THE**   (1943) 65m PRC bw

Barton MacLane *(John Tate)*, Bobby Larson *(Henry Tate)*, Jan Wiley *(Amy Tate)*, Charlotte Wynters *(Mrs. Bailey)*, Conrad Binyon *(Spike)*, Elizabeth Valentine *(Mrs. Connors)*, Kenneth Harlan *(Eddie Mohr)*, George Anderson *(Kraeger)*, Jack Kennedy *(Officer O'Toole)*, Hobo the Dog.

The conflict between the simple down-home verities of the farm country and the self-serving survivalist way of life in the big city forms the basis for this "family" picture. MacLane–in a switch from his usual casting–is a dispossessed farmer, a victim of drought, on whose farm a bank has foreclosed. He, wife Wiley, and son Larson have emigrated to an urban area in the hope of making a more certain living. Young Larson, in particular, has difficulty in adjusting to his new environs because of the local gang of young toughs. His dog Hobo, though rejected by the armed forces for service in WW II, proves to be heroic on the home front. With his young master, Hobo rounds up a gang of saboteurs and saves former farmer MacLane from a fiery death, activities which appear to portend a reasonable adjustment to urbanity. Its many sure-winner story elements make this one a classic in the "I Made Love to a Bear for the FBI and Found God" sweepstakes.

p, Max Alexander; d. William Nigh; w, Ben Lithman (based on a story by Lawrence E. Taylor, Malvin Wald); ph, Robert Cline; ed, Charles Henkel, Jr.; md, Lee Zahler.

Drama   (PR:A   MPAA:NR)

UNDERGROUND**½   (1941) 95m WB bw

Jeffrey Lynn *(Kurt Franken)*, Philip Dorn *(Eric Franken)*, Kaaren Verne *(Sylvia Helmuth)*, Mona Maris *(Fraulein Gessner)*, Peter Whitney *(Alex)*, Martin Kosleck *(Heller)*, Erwin Kalser *(Dr. Franken)*, Ilka Gruning *(Frau*

Franken), Frank Reicher *(Prof. Baumer),* Egon Brecher *(Herr Director),* Ludwig Stossel *(Herr Muller),* Hans Schumm *(Heller's Aide),* Wolfgang Zilzer *(Hoffman),* Roland Varno *(Ernst Demmler),* Henry Brandon *(Rolf),* Lotte Palfi *(Greta Rolf),* Lisa Golm *(Ella, Maid),* Louis Arco *(Otto),* Roland Drew *(Gestapo),* Lionel Royce *(Captain),* Robert O. Davis, Carl Ottmar *(Officials),* Ernest Hausman *(Rudd),* Paul Panzer *(Janitor),* Willy Kaufman *(Customer),* Ludwig Hardt *(Clerk),* Hans Wollenberger *(News Vendor),* Lester Alden *(Herr Krantz),* Henry Rowland *(Paul),* John Piffl *(Herr Mazel),* Erno Verebes *(Head Waiter),* Hans Conried *(Herman),* David Hoffman *(Willi),* Edith Angold *(Cashier),* William von Brincken *(Capt. Bornsdorff),* Norbert Schiller *(Blind Man),* Glen Cavender *(Man),* Louis Alden *(Attendant),* Gretl Sherk *(Landlady),* Arno Frey *(Guard),* Walter Bonn *(Lieutenant),* Fred Giermann, Rolf Landau *(Radio Men),* Crane Whitley, Henry Victor, Hans von Morhart, Otto Reichow, Bob Stevenson *(Gestapo Men).*

For its time, UNDERGROUND was a hard-hitting wartime drama which exposed the dark underbelly of Nazism and the Third Reich. The conflict is between two brothers in the Nazi regime, one of whom exposes the evils of the system to the other and finally convinces him of the immoral stance that marches under the symbol of the swastika. Warner Bros. tried to make the picture as timely as it could by including references to the flight of Nazi leader Rudolf Hess and to the sinking of the German pocket battleship Bismarck.

p, Jack L. Warner, Hal B. Wallis; d, Vincent Sherman; w, Charles Grayson (based on a story by Oliver H. P. Garrett, Edwin Justus Mayer); ph, Sid Hickox; m, Adolph Deutsch; ed, Thomas Pratt; md, Leo F. Forbstein; art d, Charles Novi.

War Drama   **(PR:A   MPAA:NR)**

UNDERGROUND*½   (1970, Brit.) 100m Brighton/UA c

Robert Goulet *(Maj. Joe Dawson),* Daniele Gaubert *(Yvonne),* Lawrence Dobkin *(Boule),* Carl Duering *(Gen. Stryker),* Joachim Hansen *(Hessler),* Roger Delgado *(Xavier),* Alexander Peleg *(Moravin),* George Pravda *(Menke),* Leon Lissek *(Sergeant in Bistro),* Harry Brooks, Jr *(Panzer Sergeant),* Sebastian Breaks *(Condon),* Nicole Croisille *(Bistro Singer),* Derry Power *(Pommard),* Paul Murphy *(Jean),* Gerry Sullivan *(Fosse),* Eamonn Keane *(Emile),* Andre Charise *(Gerrard),* Martin Crosbie *(RAF Sergeant),* Andreas Malandrinos *(Jacquard),* Liam O'Callaghan *(Imhoff),* David Leland *(Paul),* Vincent Smith *(Sentry),* James Bartley *(1st Maquis),* Gerry Alexander *(2nd Maquis),* Chris O'Neill *(Aid Man),* Bill Golding *(German Staff Sergeant),* Stephen Follett *(Boy in Church),* Maura Keeley *(Mother),* Frank Hayden *(Motorcycle Lieutenant),* Robert Carlisle, Jr *(Corporal),* Conor Evans *(German Officer in Church),* Brendan Mathews *(German Officer),* Joe Pilkington, Fred Meany *(Enlisted Men),* Barry Cowan *(1st Radarman),* Jeremy Jones *(2nd Radarman).*

An actioner against a WW II backdrop with Goulet as a determined U.S. intelligence agent attempting to kidnap a top Nazi general. French Resistance fighters Dobkin and Gaubert unwillingly lend their help to Goulet, whom they believe to be unduly cold-blooded. They soon discover, however, that Goulet's previous attempt to capture the general led to the torture and death of the agent's wife. Gaubert sympathizes with Goulet's cause and inevitably falls in love with him, while the general is successfully abducted. If you can buy Goulet, in his least expressive manner, as a Nazi fighter then you'll believe anything. A touch of late-1960s modernism comes into the picture in the form of some innuendo which might have been a bit too suggestive to be in a film made during the period of this one's setting. The German general's relationship with his young male aide appears to be more than casual. Also, while Goulet and Gaubert are posing as a French baker and his wife, respectively, a German sergeant who stops them gets a crush, not on the beauteous Gaubert, but rather on the bearded Goulet. Were they really messing around with each other in those Panzer tanks during the blitzkriegs? No wonder those decadents lost the war. Filmed in Ireland–probably for financial reasons, since the producers are from the U.S.

p, Jules Levy, Arthur Gardner, Arnold Laven; d, Arthur H. Nadel; w, Ron Bishop, Andy Lewis (based on a story by Marc L. Roberts, Bishop); ph, Kenneth Talbot (DeLuxe Color); m, Stanley Myers; ed, Tom Rolf; art d, Frank White; spec eff, Thomas "Knobby" Clark.

War Drama   **(PR:C   MPAA:GP)**

UNDERGROUND AGENT*½   (1942) 70m COL bw

Bruce Bennett [Herman Brix] *(Lee Graham),* Leslie Brooks *(Ann Carter),* Frank Albertson *(Johnny Davis),* Julian Rivero *(Miguel Gonzales),* George McKay *(Pete Dugan),* Rhys Williams *(Henry Miller),* Henry Victor *(Johan Schrode),* Addison Richards *(George Martin),* Rosina Galli *(Maris Gonzales),* Warren Ashe *(John Ward),* Russel Gaige *(Dr. Fenwick),* Crane Whitley *(Guiseppe Ormanti),* Leonard Strong *(Count Akiri),* Hans Conried *(Hugo),* Hans Schumm *(Hans),* Sonny Schulman *(Jose),* Jovanhy Blake *(Elena),* Ben Taggart *(Police Chief),* Kenneth MacDonald *(Clyde),* Jayne Hazard *(Secretary),* Lynton Brent *(Engineer),* Lloyd Bridges *(Chemist),* Oscar "Dutch" Hendrian, George Magrill *(Men),* Jack Shay *(Hank),* Bud Geary *(Fred),* William Caldwell, Sandy Sanford, William Stahl *(Telephone Men),* Ralph Sanford *(Big Guy),* Johnny Tyrrell *(Assistant).*

A standard espionage film with one-time Tazan Bennett as a government agent hired to stop the enemy from eavesdropping at a defense plant. He invents a word scrambler which makes things tough for Axis ears and eventually rounds up the perpetrators. Brooks is the female lead whom Bennett hires as a member of his anti-espionage team after he inadvertently gets her fired from her plant job. This was one of two similar films starring Bennett released by Columbia during the same year; the other was SABOTAGE SQUAD. Each film featured a roster of unusual sidekicks played by fine character actors such as Albertson, who manage to inject some good moments into these B features.

p, Sam White; d, Michael Gordon; w, J. Robert Bren, Gladys Atwater; ph, L. W. O'Connell; ed, Arthur Seid; art d, Lionel Banks, Jerome Pycha, Jr.; set d, George Montgomery.

Spy Drama   **(PR:A   MPAA:NR)**

UNDERGROUND GUERRILLAS**   (1944, Brit.) 82m Ealing Studios/COL bw (GB: UNDERCOVER; AKA: CHETNIK)

John Clements *(Milosh Petrovitch),* Tom Walls *(Kossan Petrovitch),* Mary Morris *(Anna Petrovitch),* Godfrey Tearle *(Gen. Von Staengel),* Michael Wilding *(Constantine),* Niall MacGinnis *(Dr. Jordan),* Robert Harris *(Col. Von Brock),* Rachel Thomas *(Maria Petrovitch),* Stephen Murray *(Dr. Stevan Petrovitch),* Charles Victor *(Sergeant),* Ben Williams *(Dragutin),* George Merritt *(Yugoslav General),* Ivor Barnard *(Station Master),* Stanley Baker *(Peter),* Terwyn Jones *(Danilo),* Eynon Evans *(Lt. Ranse),* Norman Pierce *(Lt. Franke),* Eric Micklewood *(Lt. Von Klotz),* Finlay Currie *(Father),* John Slater, Brynmore Thomas.

Set in Yugoslavia during WW II, UNDERGROUND GUERRILLAS tells the story of the Petrovitch clan which fights against the invading Nazi troops in its small village. Peasant resistance to the Germans is seen in Clements' underground tactics which survive through information he receives from his doctor brother Murray, who pretends to be a collaborator. The family's attacks on Nazi soldiers and their posts is finally ended, however, when the Petrovitch clan is attacked by the enemy. Released in Britain in 1943, the film was made at a time when the Chetnik fighters under the command of Draja Mihailovitch were still being touted as resistance heroes (they actually collaborated with the Nazis against Tito's partisan force), and was originally titled CHETNIK. However, a conflict arose when 20th Century-Fox released its CHETNIKS in the same year (starring Philip Dorn as Mihailovitch), and the name was changed.

p, Michael Balcon; d, Sergei Nolbandov; w, John Dighton, Monja Danischewsky, Nolbandov, Milosh Sokulich (based on a story by George Slocombe); ph, Wilkie Cooper; m, Frederick Austin; ed, Sidney Cole, Eily Boland; art d, Duncan Sutherland; spec eff, Roy Kellino.

War Drama   **(PR:A   MPAA:NR)**

UNDERGROUND RUSTLERS**   (1941) 56m MON bw

Ray Corrigan *(Crash),* John King *(Dusty),* Max Terhune *(Alibi),* Gwen Gaze *(Irene),* Robert Blair *(Ford),* Forrest Taylor *(Bently),* Tom London *(Tom),* Steve Clark *(Jake),* Bud Osborne *(Sheriff),* Dick Cramer, John Elliott, Tex Palmer, Edward Piel, Sr, Carl Mathews, Tex Cooper, Frank McCarroll.

Former Mesquiteers Corrigan and Terhune team with King in this RANGE BUSTERS entry which uses the gold-hungry days in California as its backdrop. It's a familiar oater outing with the same old fights, same old situations, same old romances (Corrigan and King falling for Gaze), and much the same old tunes. The singing King–formerly with Ben Bernie's orchestra–delivers "Following the Trail" and "Sweetheart of the Range." (See RANGE BUSTERS series, Index.)

p, George W. Weeks; d, S. Roy Luby; w, Bud Tuttle, Elizabeth Beecher, John Vlahos (based on a story by John Rathmell); ph, Robert Cline; ed, Roy Claire; m/l, Jean George, Harry Tobias, Roy Ingraham, Mickey Ford.

Western   **Cas.**   **(PR:A   MPAA:NR)**

UNDERGROUND U.S.A.**   (1980) 85m New Cinema c

Patti Astor *(Vickie),* Eric Mitchell *(Hustler),* Rene Ricard *(Kenneth),* Tom Wright *(Frank),* Jackie Curtis *(Roommate),* Cookie Mueller, Taylor Mead, Duncan Smith, Steve Mass, Terry Toye, John Lurie.

An independent 16mm production from New York which tries to elevate its underground "scene" to some level of relevance simply by devoting screen time to it. Producer, director, writer Mitchell also takes the starring role as a hustler who becomes involved with fizzling screen star Astor, who follows a path to suicide. If you want to get a peek at the art crowd, this is it. At least you'll hear a decent soundtrack which, as in most pictures of this kind, is the best thing about the film. The sound man on UNDERGROUND U.S.A. was Jim Jarmusch, who received great acclaim for his picture STRANGER THAN PARADISE which starred John Lurie, who also appeared here and was a member of The Lounge Lizards.

p, Eric Mitchell, Erdner Rauschalle; d&w, Mitchell; ph, Tom DiCillo; m, James White and the Blacks, The Lounge Lizards, Walter Stedding; ed, J. P. Roland-Levy

Drama   (PR:O MPAA:NR)

UNDERNEATH THE ARCHES**   (1937, Brit.) 71m
Twickenham/Wardour bw

Bud Flanagan *(Bud)*, Chesney Allen *(Ches)*, Stella Moya *(Anna)*, Lyn Harding *(Pedro)*, Enid Stamp-Taylor *(Dolores)*, Edmund Willard *(Chief Steward)*, Edward Ashley *(Carlos)*, Aubrey Mather *(Professor)*.

Flanagan and Allen find themselves inadvertently stowed away on a South America-bound ship where they get mixed up with a band of revolutionaries. The rebels try to steal a special "peace" gas but are stopped by Flanagan and Allen. The film's title is borrowed from a popular English music-hall song, and bespeaks the nominal evening resting place of its two wayfaring leading men: under one of the bridges of the River Thames. This film sparked a number of others featuring members of the famed "Crazy Gang." An entertaining comedy.

p, Julius Hagen; d, Redd Davis; w, H. Fowler Mear (based on a story by Alison Booth); ph, Sydney Blythe.

Comedy   (PR:A MPAA:NR)

UNDER-PUP, THE**½   (1939) 88m UNIV bw

Gloria Jean *(Pip-Emma)*, Robert Cummings *(Dennis King)*, Nan Grey *(Priscilla Adams)*, C. Aubrey Smith *(Grandpa)*, Beulah Bondi *(Miss Thornton)*, Virginia Weidler *(Janet Cooper)*, Margaret Lindsay *(Mrs. Cooper)*, Raymond Walburn *(Mr. Layton)*, Ann Gillis *(Letty Lou)*, Paul Cavanagh *(Mr. Cooper)*, Billy Gilbert *(Tolio)*, Kenneth Brown, Bill Lenhart *(Tolio's Sons)*, Frank Jenks *(Uncle Dan)*, Shirley Mills *(Cecilia Layton)*, Samuel S. Hinds *(Dr. McKay)*, Ernest Truex *(Mr. Binns)*, Doris Lloyd *(Mrs. Binns)*, Dickie Moore *(Jerry Binns)*, Spencer Charters *(Man)*.

After making a name of Deanna Durbin in THREE SMART GIRLS, producer Joe Pasternak hit the jackpot again with the pre-teen Gloria Jean who made her debut in this picture. She is a youngster in rags who gets to hang around with the rich kids when she gets a chance to spend a holiday in an exclusive camp. After initial ostracism, she soon is giving away advice to all the snobbish girls, who seem impressed with Gloria Jean's common sense. Weidler benefits most from the advice, learning how to cope with her parents' prospective divorce. Producer Pasternak was noted for his discoveries of kiddie talent. After production started on this film, he came up with two more winners, Brown and Lenhart, 7 and 8 years old respectively. The pair had been performing at Los Angeles benefits doing a comedy act with bass violin and accordion. Pasternak had a little rewriting done on the picture to fit the comical kids in as the children of camp caretaker Gilbert, with excellent results. Musical numbers: "March of the Penguins (High School Cadet's March)" (John Philip Sousa), "Annie Laurie" (Lady John Douglas Scott), "Lo! Hear the Gentle Lark" (Henry Bishop, from Shakespeare's "Venus and Adonis"), "Choir Song" (Reinke), "Shepherd's Lullaby" (Mozart), "I'm Like a Bird".

p, Joe Pasternak; d, Richard Wallace; w, Grover Jones (based on a story by I. A. R. Wylie); ph, Hal Mohr; m, Ralph Freed, Harold Adamson; ed, Frank Gross; md, Charles Previn.

Musical   (PR:A MPAA:NR)

UNDERSEA GIRL zero   (1957) 74 m Nacirema/AA bw

Mara Corday *(Val Hudson)*, Pat Conway *(Brad Chase)*, Florence Marly *(Leila Graham)*, Dan Seymour *(Mike Travis)*, Ralph Clanton *(Sam Marvin)*, Myron Healey *(Swede Nelson)*, Lewis Charles *(Phil Barry)*, Jerry Eskow *(Dwyer)*, Dehl Berti *(Joe)*, Sue George *(Susie)*, Mickey Simpson *(Larkin)*, Mike Mason *(Don Carson)*, Brick Sullivan, Don Warren, Jess Kirkpatrick, Russ Thorsen, Corrine Laine, William Kendis, Mack Chandler.

A water-logged script and some equally soggy performances can't help this actioner about $2 million in missing Navy money. An answer to the mystery is stumbled upon by newsgirl skindiver Corday, who finds the corpse of a tuna fisherman with $1,800 of the missing money. Corday realizes that something smells fishy and it's not just the dead man's body. She informs her Navy lieutenant boy friend, Conway, and together they get to the bottom of the shady dealings. It turns out that Clanton is behind everything and all the cash is recovered and returned. Includes the completely forgettable tune "Daydreams" (Alexander Courage, Hal Levy).

p, Norman T. Herman; d, John Peyser; w, Arthur V. Jones; ph, Hal McAlpin, Edwin Gillette; m, Alexander Courage; ed, Richard C. Meyer; md, Courage; art d, Nicolai Remisoff.

Action/Adventure   (PR:A MPAA:NR)

UNDERSEA ODYSSEY, AN   (SEE: NEPTUNE FACTOR, THE, 1973, Can.)

UNDERTAKER AND HIS PALS, THE zero
(1966) 60m Eola/Geneni-Howco c

Ray Dannis *(The Undertaker)*, Warrene Ott, Rad Fulton, Robert Lowery, Marty Friedman, Sally Frei, Rick Cooper, Ryck Rydon, Charles Fox, Karen

Ciral.

A gore exploitationer with a sense of humor (well, sort of) that has some fun with the genre, but still is pretty despicable. Dannis is an undertaker whose funeral home gives great deals (and trading stamps!) to the families of people he and his pals have killed. The best joke in the film has a woman getting her leg cut off and later having it show up as part of a dinner–the punch line is the woman's name–Miss Lamb. Get it? Leg of Lamb.

p&d, David C. Graham; w, T. L. P. Swicegood; ph, Andrew Janczak (Eastmancolor); m, Johnny White; art d, Mike McCloskey.

Horror   (PR:O MPAA:NR)

UNDERTOW*   (1930) 56m UNIV bw

Mary Nolan *(Sally Blake)*, Johnny Mack Brown *(Paul Whalen)*, Robert Ellis *(Jim Paine)*, Churchill Ross *(Lindy)*, Audrey Ferris *(Kitty)*.

A humorless drama which casts Brown as a lighthouse keeper who marries Nolan and soon afterward goes blind. A Coast Guardsman then comes along and steals away the wife, but Brown regains his sight, and shortly afterwards his wife.

d, Harry A. Pollard; w, Winifred Reeve, Edward T. Lowe, Jr. (based on the story "Ropes" by Wilbur Daniel Steele); ph, Jerome Ash; ed, Daniel Mandel.

Drama   (PR:A MPAA:NR)

UNDERTOW**½   (1949) 71m UNIV bw

Scott Brady *(Tony Reagan)*, John Russell *(Danny Morgan)*, Dorothy Hart *(Sally Lee)*, Peggy Dow *(Ann McKnight)*, Charles Sherlock *(Cooper)*, Robert Easton *(Fisher)*, Bruce Bennett [Herman Brix] *(Reckling)*, Gregg Martell *(Frost)*, Robert Anderson *(Stoner)*, Daniel Ferniel *(Gene)*, Roc [Rock] Hudson *(Detective)*, Ann Pearce *(Clerk)*, Marjorie Bennett *(Woman in Las Vegas)*.

Brady becomes the victim of a plot by his fiancee Hart and his best friend Russell who attempt to frame the innocent fellow on a murder charge. With the help of Dow, whom he casually met on an airplane flight, Brady is able to clear his name while hiding out in her apartment. Filmed in Chicago, UNDERTOW marked an early screen appearance–his second–for Rock Hudson in the role of a detective.

p, Ralph Dietrich; d, William Castle; w, Lee Loeb, Arthur T. Horman (based on the story "The Big Frame" by Horman); ph, Irving Glassberg; ed, Ralph Dawson; md, Milton Schwarzwald; art d, Bernard Herzbrun, Nathan Juran; set d, Russell A. Gausman, A. Roland Fields; cos, Orry-Kelly; spec eff, David S. Horsley; makeup, Bud Westmore, Joe Stington.

Crime Drama   (PR:A MPAA:NR)

UNDERWATER!**   (1955) 99m Howard Hughes/RKO c

Jane Russell *(Theresa)*, Gilbert Roland *(Dominic)*, Richard Egan *(Johnny)*, Lori Nelson *(Gloria)*, Robert Keith *(Father Cannon)*, Joseph Calleia *(Rico)*, Eugene Iglesias *(Miguel)*, Ric Roman *(Jesus)*, Max Wagner *(Bartender)*, Robert Polo *(Deck Hand)*, Dan Bernaducci *(Waiter)*, Jamie Russell *(Cab Driver)*.

An absurd and outlandish picture which is actually better known for the excessive hype which surrounded it than for the film itself. Russell and Egan are a husband-and-wife diving team who discover a sunken Spanish galleon deep beneath the Caribbean. They enlist the help of adventurer Roland and together scout the ocean floor for the galleon's treasure. Also along for the ride are Keith, a priest who advises Russell and Egan on their treasure, and Nelson, a scantily clad beauty. What little suspense the film holds is in the divers' attempts to salvage the treasure before the galleon teeters off the underwater ridge it rests on and sinks to an unreachable depth. Rather than tell a story, billionaire Howard Hughes (the "mastermind" behind the film) set his sights on two things—exploiting Russell's figure once again (his first of many attempts was in 1943's THE OUTLAW), and showing off scuba gear, a relatively new invention. This would be the final film that Russell and Hughes completed together, though he did sign her to another contract, unlike any before in Hollywood. He paid her a million dollars to make six pictures on loan-out (meaning Hughes would not make the films but loan her to other studios for filming). Russell in return received complete control over her career, the freedom to enter any other professional deals, and the choice of a project's director.

p, Harry Tatelman; d, John Sturges; w, Walter Newman (based on the story "The Big Rainbow" by Hugh King, Robert B. Bailey); ph, Harry J. Wild (SuperScope, Technicolor); m, Roy Webb; ed, Stuart Gilmore; md, Constantin Bakaleinikoff; cos, Michael Woulfe; underwater ph, Lamar Boren

Adventure   **Cas.**   (PR:C-O MPAA:NR)

UNDERWATER CITY, THE zero   (1962) 78m Neptune/COL bw

William Lundigan *(Bob Gage)*, Julie Adams *(Dr. Monica Powers)*, Roy Roberts *(Tim Graham)*, Carl Benton Reid *(Dr. Halstead)*, Chet Douglas *(Chuck "Cowboy" Marlow)*, Paul Dubov *(George Burnett)*, Karen Norris *(Phyllis Gatewood)*, Kathie Browne *(Dotty)*, Edward Mallory *(Lt. Wally*

Steele), George De Normand (*Dr. Carl Wendt*), Edmund Cobb (*Meade*), Roy Damron (*Winchell*), Paul Power (*Civilian*).

Interesting perhaps only to those with a grave interest in architecture and interior design, THE UNDERWATER CITY is about as exciting as watching seaweed grow. This below-sea-level nonsense has people inhabiting the sea floor in a domed city which eventually collapses and leaves only the two starfishy-eyed lovers–Lundigan and Adams–alive, prepared to build again. Filmed in Eastmancolor, Columbia decided to release this picture in black-and-white for some unknown reason. Badly directed and unconvincingly acted, this one could never qualify as the rapture of the deep.

p. Alex Gordon; d, Frank McDonald; w, Owen Harris (based on an idea by Gordon, Ruth Alexander); ph, Gordon Avil (FantaScope); m, Ronald Stein; ed, Al Clark, Don Starling; art d, Don Ament; spec eff, Howard Lydecker; makeup, Ben Lane.

Science Fiction/Adventure   (PR:A MPAA:NR)

UNDERWATER ODYSSEY, AN   (SEE: NEPTURE FACTOR, THE, 1973, Can.)

UNDERWATER WARRIOR**   (1958) 90m MGM bw

Dan Dailey (*Comdr. David Forest*), Claire Kelly (*Anne Whitmore*), James Gregory (*Comdr. William Arnold*), Ross Martin (*Joe O'Brien*), Raymond Bailey (*Adm. Ashton*), Alex Gerry (*Captian of Battleship*), Genie Coree (*Marie*), Charles Keane (*Captain*), Jon Lindbergh (*Boat Officer*), Zale Parry (*Girl Swimmer*), Alex Fane (*Davey, Jr.*).

Dailey stars as a frogman in this episodic tale which stretches from pre-WW II times to the "police action" in Korea. A great deal of unusual underwater footage, including swimming among sharks and a 300-foot dive, adds excitement to Dailey's adventures, but the picture loses steam when it takes to land. Besides battling the enemy, Dailey also has to deal with a wife who has trouble understanding why his job is so important to him. Based on the real-life adventures of a naval commander named Francis D. Fane. Charles A. Lindbergh's son Jon plays the part of one of the officers on the divers' boat. Another undersea epic from subsurface solon Tors, Hollywood's answer to Jacques-Yves Cousteau.

p, Ivan Tors; d, Andrew Marton; w, Gene Levitt; ph, Joseph Biroc, Lamar Boren (CinemaScope); m, Harry Sukman; ed, Charles Craft; md, Sukman.

Adventure   (PR:A MPAA:NR)

UNDERWORLD**   (1937) 69m Micheaux bw

Sol Johnson (*Paul*), Bee Freeman (*Dinah*), Oscar Polk, Alfred "Slick" Chester, Ethel Moses, Larry Seymore.

Johnson is a black man who has graduated from a southern college and heads to Chicago for a shot at success. He boards at a hotel which he soon discovers is a cover for a brothel. Freeman takes a liking to him and drags him into the criminal activities of the underworld. Johnson is backed into a corner when Freeman frames him for the murder of her lover. Freeman then goes out on a drinking spree and is hit by a train, thereby destroying Johnson's only alibi. He is saved from certain prosecution by a last-minute witness who testifies on Johnson's behalf. A bleak look at city life which differs from other crime stories only in its all-black cast. Features Oscar Polk who later played "Pork" in GONE WITH THE WIND.

d, Oscar Micheaux.

Crime   (PR:A-C MPAA:NR)

UNDERWORLD AFTER DARK   (SEE: BIG TOWN AFTER DARK, 1947)

UNDERWORLD INFORMERS**   (1965, Brit.) 105m RANK/CD bw
                                            (GB: THE INFORMERS; THE SNOUT)

Nigel Patrick (*Chief Inspector Johnnoe*), Margaret Whiting (*Maisie*), Colin Blakely (*Charlie Ruskin*), Derren Nesbitt (*Bertie Hoyle*), Frank Finlay (*Leon Sale*), Catherine Woodville (*Mary Johnnoe*), Harry Andrews (*Superintendent Bestwick*), John Cowley (*Jim Ruskin*), Michael Coles (*Ben*), Allan Cuthbertson (*Smythe*), Roy Kinnear (*Shorty*), Ronald Hines (*Lewis*), Peter Prowse (*Lonergan*), George Sewell (*Hill*), Kenneth J. Warren (*Lou Waites*), Brian Wilde (*Lipson*).

Patrick gets himself into hot water with his Scotland Yard superiors when he refuses to inform on his sources, who have underworld ties. The Yard doesn't like its inspectors getting information from criminal sources, but Patrick pays little attention to their warnings until one of his informants gets murdered. He sets out to uncover the identity of the culprit and winds up as a victim of a frame-up by prostitute Whiting before delivering the killer to the authorities with the help of the murder victim's mobster brother Blakely and his gang.

p, William MacQuitty; d, Ken Annakin; w, Alun Falconer, Paul Durst (based on the novel Death of a Snout by Douglas Warner); ph, Reginald Wyer; m, Clifton Parker; ed, Alfred Roome; md, Muir Mathieson; art d, Alex Vetchinsky.

Crime   (PR:A MPAA:NR)

UNDERWORLD STORY, THE   (SEE: WHIPPED, THE, 1950)

UNDERWORLD U.S.A.***½   (1961) 98m Globe/COL bw

Cliff Robertson (*Tolly Devlin*), Dolores Dorn (*Cuddles*), Beatrice Kay (*Sandy*), Paul Dubov (*Gela*), Robert Emhardt (*Conners*), Larry Gates (*Driscoll*), Richard Rust (*Gus*), Gerald Milton (*Gunther*), Allan Gruener (*Smith*), David Kent (*Tolly at 12*), Tina Rome (*Woman*), Sally Mills (*Connie*), Robert P. Lieb (*Officer*), Neyle Morrow (*Barney*), Henry Norell (*Prison Doctor*), David Fresco (*Convict*), Peter Brocco (*Vic Farrar*), Joni Beth Morris (*Jenny*), Alan Aaronson, Donald Gamble (*Boys*), Rickie Sorenson (*Harry*), Audrey Swanson (*Mother*), Tom London, Bob Hopkins (*Drunks*), Charles Sterrett, Bernie Hamilton (*Investigators*), Jerry Mann (*Cashier*), Don Douglas (*Man*), James R. Bacon (*Newspaperman*).

A gritty tale of vengeance in which Robertson feigns loyalty to both the government (a federal crime commission) and organized crime in order to kill the men who murdered his father. As a boy, Robertson was orphaned when his father was beaten to death in an alley by four men. Having witnessed the beating, Robertson vowed to find the men. Kay, a friend of the boy's father, does her best to mother the boy, but he soons winds up in prison. While behind bars Robertson learns that one of the four men, Brocco, is on his deathbed in the hospital infirmary. Persistence pays off and Robertson learns the names of the remaining three–Dubov, Milton, and Gruener–who have by now become big shots in an underworld organization known as National Projects. When Robertson is released from prison he calls on Kay, only to find that her bar is being run by Dubov. Dubov knows Robertson is the dead man's son, but admires his loyalty and makes a place for him in the organization. in the meantime, Robertson meets and falls in love with gang moll Dorn. A federal agent, Gates, who is investigating the underworld, meets with Robertson and persuades him to help the government with its case. By pitting the underworld against the law, Robertson raises the suspicions of mob boss Emhardt, who can no longer be sure of the loyalty of his men. To further disrupt the mob, Robertson arranges with Gates to doctor some files on the supposedly loyal criminals. Emhardt then orders the men killed by Rust, his top assassin. Having avenged his father's death, Robertson bids farewell to Gates. Gates, however, still wants to pin Emhardt and thereby completely topple the mob. Robertson, who has finally agreed to marry Dorn, holds no loyalty to Gates and isn't easily convinced. When Emhardt orders Robertson to kill Dorn a different sort of loyalty forms in his head–one based on a man's love for a woman. Rather than kill Dorn, Robertson drowns Emhardt in his penthouse pool. Robertson cannot escape his fate, however, and is gunned down by Rust. He dies in Dorn's arms in the same alley where his father was killed.

p,d&w, Samuel Fuller (based on Saturday Evening Post articles by Joseph F. Dinneen); ph, Hal Mohr; m, Harry Sukman; ed, Jerome Thoms; art d, Robert Peterson; set d, William Calvert; cos, Beatrice Pontrelli; makeup, Ben Lane.

Crime   (PR:C MPAA:NR)

UNDYING MONSTER, THE**   (1942) 63m FOX bw (GB: THE HAMMOND MYSTERY)

James Ellison (*Bob Curtis*), Heather Angel (*Helga Hammond*), John Howard (*Oliver Hammond*), Bramwell Fletcher (*Dr. Geoffrey Covert*), Heather Thatcher (*Christy*), Aubrey Mather (*Inspector Craig*), Halliwell Hobbes (*Walton*), Eily Malyon (*Mrs. Walton*), Heather Wilde (*Millie*), Charles McGraw (*Stredwick*), Alec Craig (*Will*), Holmes Herbert (*Constable*), Clive Morgan (*Foster*), Dave Thursby (*Miles McGregor*), Donald Stuart (*Charles Clagpool*), John Rogers (*Tom Clagpool*), Matthew Boulton (*Coroner*).

Howard is the male heir to a wealthy British estate but is soon discovered to be a werewolf. The heir's sister, Angel, enlists the assistance of Scotland Yard investigator Ellison, who helps her locate the corpses of murdered family members. Some eerie atmosphere with a foggy English moorland location. Studio moguls were apparently attentive to the box-office draw of Universal's film THE WOLF MAN a year previously; unfortunately, this one didn't do as well. Considering the female leads, it's a wonder that the victims weren't Heathered to death.

p, Bryan Foy; d, John Brahm; w, Lillie Hayward, Michael Jacoby (based on, novel by Jessie Douglas Kerruish); ph, Lucien Ballard; m, Emil Newman, David Raskin; ed, Harry Reynolds; art d, Richard Day, Lewis Creber.

Horror   Cas.   (PR:A MPAA:NR)

UNE FEMME EST UNE FEMME   (SEE: WOMAN IS A WOMAN, A, 1961, Fr.)

UNE HISTOIRE IMMORTELLE   (SEE: IMMORTAL STORY, THE, 1968, Fr.)

UNE JEUNE FILLE   (SEE: MAGNIFICENT SINNER, 1963, Fr.)

UNE PARISIENNE   (SEE: LA PARISIENNE, 1958, Fr./Ital.)

UNEARTHLY, THE*   (1957) 73m American Broadcast-Paramount
                                                 Theatres/REP bw

John Carradine (*Prof. Charles Conway*), Allison Hayes (*Grace Thomas*),
Myron Healey (*Mark Houston*), Sally Todd (*Natalie*), Marilyn Buferd (*Dr.
Gilchrist*), Arthur Batanides (*Danny Green*), Tor Johnson (*Lobo*), Harry
Fleer (*Jedrow*), Roy Gordon (*Dr. Loren Wright*), Guy Prescott (*Capt. Rogers*),
Paul MacWilliams (*Police Officer*).

A dull and slow-moving mad-scientist-operates-on-humans picture which
casts Carradine in the role of experimenter. As usual he is trying to achieve
immortality and (again as usual) is helped in his operations by a mutant
assistant named Lobo (played by Johnson, who's probably best known for his
role in PLAN 9 FROM OUTER SPACE.) Hayes and Healey wind up in
Carradine's clutches and fall in love while fearing for their lives. Johnson
finally comes to their aid and helps them with their escape in a final
redemption for his master's evil ways. Keeping to tradition, all the evil folks
are killed off by the finish. When the police finally arrive to search the
premises, they find the killers in the cellar; horribly mutilated subhuman
creatures, Carradine's failed experiments. The film closes on one policeman's query: "What if they *do* live forever?"

p&d, Brooke L. Peters; w, Geoffrey Dennis, Jane Mann (based on a story by
Mann); ph, Merle Connell; ed, Richard Currier; md, Henry Vars, Michael
Terr; art d, Dan Hall.

Science Fiction   Cas.   (PR:O MPAA:NR)

UNEARTHLY STRANGER, THE*   (1964, Brit.) 75m Independent
                                          Artists/AIP bw (GB: UNEARTHLY STRANGER)

John Neville (*Dr. Mark Davidson*), Gabriella Licudi (*Julie Davidson*), Philip
Stone (*Prof. John Lancaster*), Patrick Newell (*Maj. Clarke*), Jean Marsh
(*Miss Ballard*), Warren Mitchell (*Dr. Munro*).

A gripping science-fiction picture which is surprisingly sharp in its approach. Instead of getting lost in the usual science-fiction traps of space and
time chatter, THE UNEARTHLY STRANGER concentrates on a rather
touching love story. The romance between the leads–earthling Neville and
alien Licudi–is an impossible love but leads to marriage before husband
Neville discovers that his wife has unusual traits. When he notices that she
sleeps with her eyes open, has no pulse, and doesn't react to heat, he begins
to put two and two together. This, coupled with the fact that practically his
entire team of scientists has mysteriously died, leads Neville to the
conclusion that his wife's a bit odd. She admits that she's part of an alien
project but insists that she loves Neville. Her alien mind controllers have her
dying in his arms with her face being disintegrated by tears. When Neville,
distraught, goes to his workplace, secretary Marsh–another alien, one who
does not love him–tries to kill him. He is saved by fellow scientist Stone;
Marsh falls from a window and disintegrates, but not before proclaiming,
"There are too many of us, and few as weak as [Licudi]." As the two
surviving scientists leave the laboratory, they find themselves among a
group of women, none of whom appears to be able to blink. The film is a little
too earnest in its intent, but a cast of fine actors and an appealing premise
overcome many of its limitations.

p, Albert Fennell; d, John Krish; w, Rex Carlton; ph, Reg Wyer; m, Edward
Williams; ed, Tom Priestley; md, Marcus Dods; art d, Harry Pottle; makeup,
Trevor Crole Rees.

Science Fiction/Romance   (PR:A MPAA:NR)

UNEASY TERMS*   (1948, Brit.) 91m BN/Pathe bw

Michael Rennie (*Slim Callaghan*), Moira Lister (*Corinne Alardyse*), Faith
Brook (*Viola Alardyse*), Joy Shelton (*Effie*), Patricia Goddard (*Patricia
Alardyse*), Barry Jones (*Inspector Gringall*), Marie Ney (*Honoria Wymer-
ing*), Paul Carpenter (*Windy Nicholls*), Nigel Patrick (*Lucien Donnelly*),
Sydney Tafler (*Maysin*), J. H. Roberts (*Sallins*), Joan Carol (*Matron*), Mary
Horn (*La Valliere*), John Robinson (*Brighton Detective Inspector*), Tony
Quinn (*Patrick*), George Street (*Brighton Police Inspector*), John England
(*Wilkie*), Etienne Bonichon (*1st Croupier*), Harry Brooks (*Rosy*), Chick Rolfe
(*George*), Roy Russell (*Col. Stenhurst*), Lionel Newbold (*Country Doctor*),
Mark Stone (*Profiteer*), Julien Henry ("*Two Friars*" *Waiter*), Gordon
Plunkett (*2nd Croupier*), Kathleen Heath (*Maid at "Two Friars"*), George
Rigby (*Mardene Club Waiter*), Raphael Norman (*Dark Spinney Police
Sergeant*), William Forbes (*Receptionist at Mardene Club*), Robert Moore
(*Porter at Mardene Club*), Clifford Buckton (*Brighton Police Sergeant*),
William Bridger (*Brighton Police Constable*), Delia Digby (*Corinne's Maid*),
Margaret Allworthy (*Profiteer's Girl Friend*), Alec Bernard (*Bar Attendant
at Mardene Club*), Doreen English.

A flat thriller which has Rennie cast as a private eye whose client turns up
dead leaving behind a trail of suspects. It clearly seems that Brook, the
eldest of the victim's three stepdaughters, is the guilty one but after
trudging through clues and romance, Rennie points the finger at the real
culprit. Based on author Cheyney's best-selling mystery novel. The screen
credits fail to mention a script writer, but all the evidence clearly points to
Cheyney himself, a capable novelist but a novice at screen transpositions.

p, Lois H. Jackson; d, Vernon Sewell; w, Peter Cheyney (based on his novel);
ph, Ernest Palmer; m, Hans May; ed, Monica Kimick; md, May; art d, R.
Holmes Paul; cos, Rahvis; makeup, Henry Hayward.

UNEASY VIRTUE*   (1931, Brit.) 83m BIP/Wardour bw (AKA:
                                                   FLIRTING WIVES)

Fay Compton (*Dorothy Rendell*), Edmond Breon (*Harvey Townsend*),
Francis Lister (*Bill Rendell*), Margot Grahame (*Stella Tolhurst*), Donald
Calthrop (*Burglar*), Garry Marsh (*Arthur Tolhurst*), Dodo Watts (*Sylvia
Fullerton*), Adele Dixon (*Consuelo Pratt*), Hubert Harben (*Frank K. Pratt*),
Gerard Lyley (*Sosso Stephens*), Margaret Yarde (*Mrs. Robinson*), Molly
Lamont (*Ada*).

Compton is determined to get her husband jealous and when a few other
couples visit for a game of bridge she gets her chance. A burglar makes his
way in and is hidden in a bedroom with one of the wives, though none of
the husbands is sure which one. Compton goes to great lengths to make it
seem as if she's been cheating but laughter and reconciliation finally occur.
This latter-day restoration comedy was never released across the water; U.S.
reception to British farces had been lukewarm at best, so British International decided not to bother.

d&w, Norman Walker (based on the play "The Happy Husband" by
Harrison Owens); ph, Claude Friese-Greene.

Comedy   (PR:A MPAA:NR)

UNEXPECTED FATHER*½   (1932) 71m UNIV bw (AKA: THE
                                                      UNEXPECTED FATHER)

Slim Summerville (*Jasper Jones*), ZaSu Pitts (*Polly Perkins*), Cora Sue
Collins (*Judge*), Alison Skipworth (*Mrs. Hawkins*), Dorothy Christy (*Evelyn
Smythe*), Grace Hampton (*Mrs. Smythe*), Claude Allister (*Claude*), Tyrell
Davis (*Reggie*), Tom O'Brien, Richard Cramer (*Policemen*).

Summerville is saved from a marriage to a gold-digger when the young
Collins shows up in Summerville's car one day. The fiancee is far from
pleased at the moppet's arrival, especially when nursemaid Pitts is hired
and falls for Summerville. Collins then plays matchmaker by pairing her
adopted dad with nursemaid Pitts, leaving the bride-to-be without a groom.

p, Stanley Bergerman; d, Thornton Freeland; w, Robert Keith, Max Lief,
Dale Van Every (based on a story by Van Every); ph, Jerome Ash.

Comedy   (PR:A MPAA:NR)

UNEXPECTED FATHER**   (1939) 73m UNIV bw (GB: SANDY
                                                        TAKES A BOW)

Baby Sandy [Sandra Lee Henville] (*Sandy*), Shirley Ross (*Diana Donovan*),
Dennis O'Keefe (*Jimmy Hanley*), Mischa Auer (*Boris Bebenko*), Joy Hodges
(*Peg*), Dorothy Arnold (*Sally*), Anne Gwynne (*Kitty*), Donald Briggs (*Allen
Rand*), Richard Lane (*Leo Murphy*), Paul Guilfoyle (*Ed Stone*), Mayo Methot
(*Mrs. Stone*), Jane Darwell (*Mrs. Callahan*), Spencer Charters (*Magistrate*),
Anne Nagel (*Beulah*), Dorothy Vaughn (*Nurse*), Ed Stanley (*Dr. Evans*),
Frank Reicher (*Referee*), Ygor and Tanya (*Dance Specialty*).

O'Keefe finds himself playing dad when he takes custody of an orphaned
baby, which leads him into the courts in order to keep it from an orphanage.
He avoids a legal battle by marrying Ross, who also wants custody of the
youngster. Similar to a previous Baby Sandy (as she was known in the
credits) picture entitled EAST SIDE OF HEAVEN which had Bing Crosby
in the starring spot.

p, Ken Goldsmith; d, Charles Lamont; w, Leonard Spigelgass, Charles
Grayson (based on a story by Spigelgass); ph, George Robinson; ed, Ted
Kent; md, Charles Previn; art d, Jack Otterson.

Drama/Comedy   (PR:A MPAA:NR)

UNEXPECTED GUEST½**   (1946) 61m UA bw

William Boyd (*Hopalong Cassidy*), Andy Clyde (*California Carlson*), Rand
Brooks (*Lucky Jenkins*), Una O'Connor (*Miss Hackett, Housekeeper*), John
Parrish (*David Potter, Attorney*), Earle Hodgins (*Joshua Coulter*), Robert B.
Williams (*Ogden*), Patricia Tate (*Ruth Baxter*), Ned Young (*Ralph Baxter*),
Joel Friedkin (*Phineas Phipps*), Ian Wolfe.

An entertaining Hopalong oater which has Clyde inheriting a ranch along
with five other relatives. The will, however, includes a stipulation that if one
member dies, the others share in his portion. Sure enough, people start
dying, but Clyde's buddy Boyd fingers the culprit after only a couple of
casualties. Full of suspense and a playful ranch setting which comes
complete with hidden passages and sliding panels. (See HOPALONG
CASSIDY series, Index.)

p, Lewis J. Rachmil; d, George Archainbaud; w, Ande Lamb; ph, Mack
Stengler; m, David Chudnow; ed, Fred W. Berger; art d, Harvey T. Gillett;
set d, George Mitchell.

Western/Mystery   (PR:A MPAA:NR)

UNEXPECTED UNCLE*   (1941) 67m RKO bw

Anne Shirley (*Kathleen Brown*), James Craig (*Johnny Kerrigan*), Charles
Coburn (*Seton Manley*), Ernest Truex (*Wilkins, Butler*), Renee Haal
[Godfrey] (*Carol West*), Russell Gleason (*Tommy Turner*), Astrid Allwyn

(Sara Cochran), Jed Prouty (Sanderson), Thurston Hall (Jerry Carter), Virginia Engels (Mrs. Carter), Hans Conried (Clayton, Store Manager), Arthur Aylesworth (Quenton), Matt Moore (Detective), Jack Mulhall (Policeman), Russell Hicks (Tony, Cafe Manager), Eleanor Counts (Cigarette Girl), Pat Flaherty (Mounted Cop), George Dolenz (Headwaiter), Joey Ray (Club Singer), Mary Gordon (Landlady), Edith Conrad (Flower Woman), Tom Dugan (Bus Driver), Jimmy Conlon (Landlord), Robert E. Homans (Cop), Wade Boteler (Joe the Doorman).

Shirley is a lingerie salesgirl who gets involved with wealthy manufacturer Craig while receiving advice from her "uncle," Coburn. Coburn himself is a former tycoon who decided to give up luxury in order to live a happy and honest life. Frank Capra's type of film, but without any of his talent. Actress Haal comes off best, probably because director Godfrey's attention was focused on her (she was his wife, who later used his surname in films).

p, Tay Garnett; d, Peter Godfrey; w, Delmer Daves, Noel Langley (based on a novel by Eric Hatch); ph, Robert de Grasse; m, Anthony Collins; ed, William Hamilton; art d, Albert S. D'Agostino.

Drama (PR:A MPAA:NR)

UNFAITHFUL**½ (1931) 70m PAR bw

Ruth Chatterton (Fay), Viscountess Kilkerry, Paul Lukas (Colin Graham), Paul Cavanagh (Ronald, Viscount Kilkerry), Juliette Compton (Gemma Houston), Donald Cook (Terry Houston), Emily Fitzroy (Auntie Janie), Leslie Palmer (Claire), Syd Saylor (Buck), Bruce Warren (Steve), Arnold Lucy (Bishop), Dennis D'Auburn (Gerald), Ambrose Barker (Tinkler), Stella More (Iris), Capt. George Jackson (Count Carini), Eric Kalkhurst (Frank), Douglas Gilmore (Drunk), Jack Richardson (Armstrong), Donald MacKenzie (Inspector).

Chatterton finds herself wedged between a marriage to the adulterous Cavanagh and responsibility to her social class. She is expected to ignore her husband's activities, as a divorce would cause a scandal, especially since he is carrying on with the wife of Chatterton's brother, Cook. She decides to indulge herself and takes off to Switzerland, where she gets involved with Lukas. The finale has Cavanagh and his mistress (Compton) involved in a car crash which kills the adulterous husband. Chatterton destroys her own reputation by explaining that Cavanagh and Compton were together only in an attempt to prevent a rendezvous with her and Lukas. Since she has broken the rules of the upper class' game, Chatterton is now free to marry Lukas, whom she has loved all along.

d, John Cromwell; w, Eve Unsell, John Van Druten (based on a story by Van Druten); ph, Charles Lang.

Drama (PR:A MPAA:NR)

UNFAITHFUL, THE**½ (1947) 109m WB bw

Ann Sheridan (Chris Hunter), Lew Ayres (Larry Hannaford), Zachary Scott (Bob Hunter), Eve Arden (Paula), Jerome Cowan (Prosecuting Attorney), Steven Geray (Martin Barrow), John Hoyt (Detective-Lt. Reynolds), Peggy Knudsen (Claire), Marta Mitrovich (Mrs. Tanner), Douglas Kennedy (Roger), Claire Meade (Martha), Frances Morris (Agnes), Jane Harker (Joan), Joan Winfield (Girl), Maude Fealy (Old Maid), Cary Harrison (Seedy Man), Dick Walsh, Betty Hill, Charles Marsh, Bob Lowell (Reporters), John Elliott (Judge), George Hickman, Bob Alden (Newsboys), Paul Bradley (Mr. Tanner), Ray Montgomery (Secretary), Mary Field (Receptionist), Monte Blue (Businessman), Jack Mower (Plainclothesman), Jean De Briac (Maitre D'), Lois Austin (Middle-Aged Woman), Ross Ford (Young Man), Eve Whitney (Young Woman), Dorothy Christy (Mrs. Freedley), Paul Bradley (Mr. Tanner), Charles Jordan (Attendant).

A satisfying remake of THE LETTER which makes a comment on the social aspects of divorce and adultery. Sheridan is stricken with guilt over an affair she had while her husband was in the service. The relationship survives until Sheridan kills an attacker outside of her home who is identified as her lover. The marriage breaks apart, which only allows for a reconciliation at the finale. Coscripted by pulp writer David Goodis, whose work became the inspiration for a handful of French New Wave Films.

p, Jerry Wald; d, Vincent Sherman; w, David Goodis, James Gunn (based, uncredited, on the play by W. Somerset Maugham); ph, Ernest Haller; m, Max Steiner; ed, Alan Crosland, Jr.; md, Leo F. Forbstein; art d, Leo Kuter; set d, William Wallace; spec eff, William McGann, Robert Burks.

Drama (PR:A MPAA:NR)

UNFAITHFUL WIFE, THE (SEE: LA FEMME INFIDELE, 1969, Fr./Ital.)

UNFAITHFULLY YOURS***** (1948) 105m FOX bw

Rex Harrison (Sir Alfred de Carter), Linda Darnell (Daphne de Carter), Barbara Lawrence (Barbara Henshler), Rudy Vallee (August Henshler), Kurt Kreuger (Anthony), Lionel Stander (Hugo Standoff), Edgar Kennedy (Detective Sweeney), Alan Bridge (House Detective), Julius Tannen (Tailor), Torben Meyer (Dr. Schultz), Robert Greig (Jules), Evelyn Beresford (Mme. Pompadour), Georgia Caine (Dowager), Harry Seymour (Musician), Isabel

Jewell, Marion Marshall (Telephone Operators), Maj. Sam Harris, Douglas Gerrard (Bit Men), Dave Morris, Franz Roehn, George Matthews (Musicians), Charles Tannen (Information Man), Harry Carter (Reporter), Pati Behrs (Bit Girl), J. Farrell MacDonald (Doorman), George Melford (Elderly Man in Audience), Billy Cartledge (Page Boy), George Beranger (Maitre d'), Tamara Schee (Mme. La Lotte), Ruth Clifford (Saleslady), Frank Moran (Fire Chief), Laurette Luez (Hatcheck Girl).

This farce of misconceptions, infidelities, and murder is a stylish work, a brilliant concoction from Sturges that imaginatively squeezes every use it can from the film medium. Harrison, in a marvelous performance, is a famous British concert conductor married to Darnell. The two are much in love, but when Harrison returns from Europe a seed of jealously is planted in his mind by his brother-in-law, Vallee. While Harrison has been away, Vallee took the liberty of having a private detective, Kennedy, follow Darnell through her daily activities. Kennedy's report, which Harrison refuses to look at, suggests that perhaps Darnell indulged in some extracurricular activities with Harrison's private secretary, Kreuger, when the conductor was abroad. Harrison tears up the report and throws it out of his hotel room. Eventually the report is put back together and winds up back in Harrison's hands. This time Harrison burns the document, nearly setting his entire dressing room ablaze. However, Harrison slowly begins to think there just might be something to the report and he goes to Kennedy's office. Kennedy, it turns out, is a big fan of Harrison's (he loves how the conductor "handles Handel") and dredges up the original report from his files. Now Harrison's jealous imagination goes wild. That night, as he begins conducting Rossini's "Semiramide" overture at a concert, the camera zeros in on Harrison's eye. The story flashes to Harrison and Darnell as they return to their hotel room. As part of an elaborate plan, Harrison arranges for Darnell to spend a night on the town with Kreuger. Using his straight razor, Harrison gleefully murders his wife, then sets up the room so Kreuger will appear to be the culprit. Harrison's plan works to perfection, and the conductor laughs maniacally when Kreuger is found guilty of the crime. The music comes to a conclusion, and the camera pulls away from Harrison's eye, back to the concert. The entire scenario has all taken place in his mind, as do the next two sequences. To the accompaniment of Wagner's "Tannhauser" overture, Harrison imagines writing a fat check for Darnell, enabling her to run off with her young lover. Finally, with Tchaikovsky's "Francesca da Rimini" wafting in the background, Harrison challenges Darnell and Kreuger to a game of Russian roulette. He ends up with a bullet in his temple, and, back in reality, the concert comes to an end. Harrison, now convinced that Darnell and Kreuger are dallying behind his back, returns to his hotel room and tries to set up the murderous plan he had imagined during the concert. His real-life plans are a disaster, and Harrison finally realizes that Kennedy's report was the result of too many misconceptions. UNFAITHFULLY YOURS is a near perfect combination of sound and image. Sturges orchestrates the fantasy sequences with care and precision, using editing and performance rhythms that are in perfect synch with the underscoring music. Harrison is sheer delight, turning in a devilish performance brimming with wit and style. Darnell, Kreuger, Vallee, and Lawrence fill out lead roles just as nicely, bringing this comedy the needed elegance, while Kennedy, one of the best character actors ever to grace film comedy, adds a nice touch of buffoonery. Sturges had gotten the idea of music affecting the conductor's thoughts while writing the screenplay for his film THE POWER AND THE GLORY. "I had a scene all written and had only to put it down on paper. To my surprise, it came out quite unlike what I had planned," Sturges said later. "I sat back wondering what the hell had happened, then noticed that someone had left the radio on in the next room and realized that I had been listening to a symphony broadcast from New York and that this, added to my thoughts, had changed the total." (Quoted from Between Flops by James Curtis) Sturges wore a bright red fez all through the filming so there would never be any problem finding him on the set. Harrison later recalled that Sturges had a marvelous time during production, saying: "The whole thing was like a party....He would have a Doberman pinscher on set with him. Before he would start, he would stuff a handkerchief in his mouth to stop from laughing." One of Lawrence's dresses in the film was made from a highly flammable material that could burst into flame if it so much as brushed against an electrical outlet. Consequently she was watched during the production by her own personal fireman. Though Sturges took a good deal of time in cutting this film, studio chief Darryl F. Zanuck felt the original running time of 126 minutes was much too long. Zanuck personally supervised UNFAITHFULLY YOURS' trimming, excising some 21 minutes from the final cut. Expectations for the film were high but its release was held back due to unexpected circumstances. On July 6, 1948, Hollywood was rocked by the suicide of Carole Landis. She had been romantically linked with Harrison, who was married to Lily Palmer at the time. The release of UNFAITHFULLY YOURS was held back from summer until Christmas, but the film proved to be a box-office bomb. Despite some fine critical plaudits, UNFAITHFULLY YOURS never caught on with the public and Zanuck observed: "...we are certainly in for one of the biggest beatings in our history." It was an undeserved fate for a film of such brilliance. In 1984 this was remade with Dudley Moore in the Harrison role.

p,d,&w, Preston Sturges; ph, Victor Milner; m, Gioacchino Rossini, Richard Wagner, Peter Ilich Tchaikovsky; ed, Robert Fritch; md, Alfred Newman; art d, Lyle Wheeler, Joseph C. Wright; set d, Thomas Little, Paul S. Fox; cos, Bonnie Cashin; spec eff, Fred Sersen; makeup, Ben Nye.

Comedy **Cas.** **(PR:A-C MPAA:NR)**

UNFAITHFULS, THE** (1960, Ital.) 89m Ponti-DeLaurentiis/AA bw
(LE INFEDELI)

Gina Lollobrigida (*Lulla Possenti*), May Britt (*Liliana*), Anna Maria Ferrero (*Cesarina*), Pierre Cressoy (*Osvaldo*), Marina Vlady (*Marisa*), Irene Papas (*Mrs. Azzali*), Carlo Romano (*Mr. Azzali*), Tina Lattanzi (*Carla Bellaria*), Charles Fawcett (*Henry Rogers*), Paolo Ferrera (*Police Inspector*), Giulio Cali (*Agency Head*), Margherita Bagni (*Marisa's Mother*), Tania Weber (*Lulla's Friend*), Carlo Lamas (*L'Autista*), Bernardo Tafuri (*Guilio Possenti*), Franco Rossi (*Guido Luicidi*).

A blackmailer disrupts the lives of married adulterous couples by bringing their relationships into the open. When a servant girl is falsely accused of having a lover she commits suicide which eventually leads to the murder of the blackmailer. One of eight comedies that Steno and Monicelli directed together. Dubbed in English for this version, it was released in Italy in 1953.

p, Dino DeLaurentiis, Carlo Ponti; d, Mario Monicelli, Stefano Steno; w, Ivo Perilli, Franco Brusati, Monicelli, Steno (based on the story by Perilli); ph, Aldo Tonti; m, Trovajoli.

Comedy **(PR:A MPAA:NR)**

UNFINISHED BUSINESS** (1941) 96m UNIV bw

Irene Dunne (*Nancy Andrews*), Robert Montgomery (*Tommy Duncan*), Preston Foster (*Steve Duncan*), Eugene Pallette (*Elmer the Butler*), Dick Foran (*Frank*), ESther Dale (*Aunt Mathilda*), Walter Catlett (*Billy Ross*), Richard Davies (*Jimmy*), Kathryn Adams (*Katy*), Samuel S. Hinds (*Uncle*), June Clyde (*Clarisse*), Phyllis Barry (*Sheila Duncan*), Thomas W. Ross (*Lawyer*), Chester Clute, Paul Everton, John Sheehan, Matt McHugh, William Haade, Larry Kent, Fred Santley, Reed Hadley, Boyd Irwin, Quen Ramsey (*Men*), Pierre Watkin (*Lawyer*), Helen Lynd, Phyllis Kennedy, Norma Drury, Carol Tevis, Margaret Armstrong, Grace Hayle, Dorothy Vaughan, Grace Stafford, Dorothy Granger, Dora Clement, Hillary Brooke, Sheila Darcy, Flo Wix, Virginia Engels, Gwen Seager, Isabelle LaMal, Dorothy Haas, Ruth Dwyer (*Women*), Paul Fix, Monte Collins, Jack Voglin, Eddie Fetherstone (*Reporters*), Renie Riano (*Secretary*), Virginia Brissac (*Aunt*), Josephine Whittell (*Wardrobe Woman*), Mary Gordon (*Charwoman*), George Davis, Bob Perry (*Waiters*), Harry Rosenthal (*Pianist*), Helen Millard (*Helen*), Fortunio Bonanova (*Impresario*), Rev. Neal Dodd (*Minister*), Hope Landin (*Groom's Mother*), Frank Coghlan, Jr (*Page Boy*), Jacques Vanaire (*Headwaiter*), Yolande Mellot (*Manicurist*), Frank Shannon (*Groom's Father*), Hugh Beaumont (*Groom*), Eugene Jackson (*Bootblack*), Lester Dorr (*Yes Man*), Mary Jo Ellis (*Bridesmaid*), Amanda McFarland (*Baby*).

A romantic comedy which has Dunne first falling for Foster but then marrying his brother Montgomery. The newlyweds hop from nightclub to nightclub and eventually settle down. The marriage quickly hits the rocks, sending Montgomery into the army and Dunne off to an opera company. Foster gets in the middle of their attempts at reconciliation which doesn't come for a full year, and Montgomery finds he is the father of Dunne's child. Includes a tune sung by Dunne, "When You and I Were Young Maggie Blues" (Jimmy McHugh, Jack Frost).

p&d, Gregory La Cava; w, Eugene Thackery; ph, Joseph Valentine; m, Franz Waxman; ed, Russell Schoengarth; md, Charles Previn; art d, Jack Otterson.

Romance/Comedy **(PR:A MPAA:NR)**

UNFINISHED DANCE, THE** (1947) 101m MGM c

Margaret O'Brian ("*Meg*" *Merlin*), Cyd Charisse (*Mlle. Ariane Bouchet*), Karin Booth (*La Darina*), Danny Thomas (*Mr. Paneros*), Esther Dale (*Olga*), Thurston Hall (*Mr. Ronsell*), Harry Hayden (*Murphy*), Mary Eleanor Donahue (*Josie*), Connie Cornell (*Phyllis*), Ruth Brady (*Miss Merlin*), Charles Gradstreet (*Fred Carleton*), Ann Codee (*Mme. Borodin*), Gregory Gaye (*Jacques Lacoste*).

Movies about ballet have always been a precarious risk. Only a few have ever earned back their negative cost. This was one that didn't quite make it. Danny Thomas makes his film debut and showed immediately that he could act as well as toss off quips. O'Brien wants to be a ballerina an begins shadowing star Charisse. When O'Brian thinks that Charisse may be replaced in the ballet company by new ballerina Booth, the little O'Brian arranges an accident which incapacitates Booth to the point where she can no longer dance. In the end, O'Brian makes friends with Booth and there is a happy conclusion to a lachrymose plot. It's a remake of the French BALLERINA, a 1938 film based upon Paul Morand's story "La Mort du Cygne." The musical highlight of the movie is a ballet by Lichine to the strains of David Rose's "Holiday for Strings." Other musical numbers include: "I went Merrily on My Way: (Irving Kahal, Sammy Fain), Kreisler's "Liebesfreud," Beethoven's "Symphony No. Two," Tchaikovsky's "Swan Lake," and bits and pieces from Smetana's "The Bartered Bride," A gaping hole in the story is that the injured Booth never seems to be injured, not even with a limp, so it's hard to believe that her dancing years are over. The film was pretty to look at and the actors struggled to lend believability to it, but the script by Connolly and the direction by veteran Koster were second-rate.

p, Joe Pasternack; d, Henry Koster; w, Myles Connolly; (based on the story "La Mort du Cygne" by Paul Morand); ph, Robert Surgees (Technicolor); m, Herbert Stothard; ed, Douglas Briggs; art d, Cedric Gibbons, Daniel B. Cathcart; ch, David Lichine.

Musical/Ballet **(PR:A MPAA:NR)**

UNFINISHED SYMPHONY, THE*** (1953, Aust./Brit.) 84m
Cine-Allianz-GAU/FOX bw

Martha Eggerth (*Caroline Esterhazy*), Hans Yaray (*Franz Schubert*), Helen Chandler (*Emmie Passenter*), Ronald Squire (*Count Esterhazy*), Paul Wagner (*Lt. Folliot*), Esme Percy (*Huettenbrenner*), Hermine Sperler (*Princess Kinsky*), Eliot Makeham (*Joseph Passenter*), Cecil Humphreys (*Salieri*), Beryl Laverick (*Mary Esterhazy*), Brember Wills (*Secretary*), Frieda Richard (*Schubert's Landlady*), Vienna Philharmonic Orchestra, Vienna Opera Choir, Vienna Boy's Choir, Gypsy Band Gyula Howath.

The life of Franz Schubert is trivialized in this English-language version of an Austrian film. Yaray is the great composer, impoverished, unknown, and unable to finish the symphony he has been working on. A friend lands him a performance for a princess, Sperler, but while the composer is passionately pouring his heart into the performance, aristocratic Eggerth laughs out loud at some private joke. His concentration ruined, Yaray angrily stomps out. Eggerth takes a fancy to this hotheaded musician and she convinces her father to hire him as her music teacher. They fall in love over the keyboard and, inspired, he finishes his symphony. They are forbidden to marry, though, because of the class difference. After she marries a suitably titled young man, Yaray tears up the final pages of the symphony, leaving it, like his love, incomplete. Film biographies of great composers are, almost as a rule, sentimental glossy romances with great hunks of watered-down classical music underscoring every scene. This film falls into a lot of the same traps, but it is still above average for this sort of thing. Asquith was happy to take on this project as Schubert was his favorite composer, but the story was maudlin soap opera and he didn't have much room to change it as he had to follow the Austrian film fairly closely. Good quality filmmaking that was quite successful with the public.

p, Willy Forst; d, Forst, Anthony Asquith; w, Benn Levy, Walter Reisch; ph, Franz Planer; m, Franz Schubert.

Biography **(PR:A MPAA:NR)**

UNFORGIVEN, THE*** (1960) 125m Hecht-Hill-Lancaster/UA c

Burt Lancaster (*Ben Zachary*), Audrey Hepburn (*Rachel Zachary*), Audie Murphy (*Cash Zachary*), John Saxon (*Johnny Portugal*), Charles Bickford (*Zeb Rawlins*), Lillian Gish (*Mattilda Zachary*), Albert Salmi (*Charlie Rawlins*), Joseph Wiseman (*Abe Kelsey*), June Walker (*Hagar Rawlins*), Kipp Hamilton (*Georgia Rawlins*), Arnold Merritt (*Jude Rawlins*), Carlos Rivas (*Lost Bird*), Doug McClure (*Andy Zachary*).

In 1850s Texas, the Zachary family, led by matriarch Gish and eldest son Lancaster, raises cattle and sporadically battles the Kiowa Indians. One day a ragged stranger, Wiseman, rides through and starts spreading stories about Hepburn, the adopted daughter of Gish, telling neighbors that she actually was a Kiowa baby. He rides off again and before long a party of Kiowa braves shows up, offering to buy back Hepburn. Rebuffed, they content themselves with killing one of her suitors as he rides home one night. Lancaster and brothers Murphy and McClure ride out to bring Wiseman back, planning to force him to admit he lied. But even with a noose around his neck, he persists in his accusations until Gish shuts him up by hitting his horse with a branding iron and leaving him swinging. Gish finally admits that Hepburn really was a Kiowa baby, and when racist Murphy wants to give her back, Lancaster forbids it, and Murphy storms out. The Kiowas return to take Hepburn by force and the besieged family makes a fight of it, repulsing several assaults. Gish is killed and it looks grim for the rest as the ammunition runs out, but in the nick of time Murphy returns and the Indians are put to rout. Lancaster and Hepburn, upon learning they're not blood kin, make plans to wed. An interesting western that director Huston now disavows as the only one of his films he actively dislikes. He fought continuously with the producers over the direction the film was to take. Huston wanted to make a story about racism on the frontier, close in spirit to the original novel by Alan LeMay, who also wrote the novel that became the definitive film about captive children and Indian haters, THE SEARCHERS (1956). The producers, Hecht-Hill-Lancaster, were more interested in an action western that would make big profits for their failing concern. On location the production was hampered by several disasters. Hepburn, who hadn't told any of the producers that she was pregnant, fell off a horse, broke her back, and suffered a miscarriage. Murphy was out duck hunting one day when his boat overturned. Because of a war injury to his hip he couldn't swim and the men he was with wouldn't leave him so they clung to the side of the boat. Still photographer Inge Morath, a former swimming champ, spotted the men through her telephoto lens and stripped down to bra and panties and dove in for the rescue. Newspapers regarded it as a publicity stunt. Later, three technicians died when their plane crashed. Despite all of these problems and other–notably the utter miscasting of Hepburn as an Indian–the film does have some memorable moments, like Gish cutting Wiseman off in midsentence by driving his horse off and leaving him to hang, and a surreal scene during the siege in which

Lancaster, responding to the Kiowasg war flutes playing in the darkness, pushes the family piano outside and has Gish play some classics for the Indians. Later the frenzied Indians are seen chopping at the instrument with tomahawks. By no means as bad a film as the director claims, the movie garnered mixed reviews and failed at the box office, putting an end to Hecht-Hill-Lancaster productions.

p, James Hill; d, John Huston; w, Ben Maddow (based on a novel by Alan LeMay); ph, Franz Planer (Panavision, Technicolor); m, Dimitri Tiomkin; ed, Hugh Russell Lloyd; md, Tiomkin; art d, Stephen Grimes; makeup, Frank McCoy.

Western   **(PR:C   MPAA:NR)**

UNGUARDED HOUR, THE½**   (1936) 90m MGM bw

Loretta Young (*Lady Helen Dearden*), Franchot Tone (*Sir Alan Dearden*), Roland Young (*Bunny Jeffers*), Lewis Stone (*Gen. Lawrence*), Dudley Digges (*Metford*), Henry Daniell (*Hugh Lewis*), Jessie Ralph (*Lady Hathaway*), Robert Greig (*Henderson*), E.E. Clive (*Lord Hathaway*), Wallis Clark (*Grainger*), John Buckler (*Defense Counsel*), Aileen Pringle (*Diana Roggers*), Yola D'Avril (*French Maid*), Leonard Carey (*Alan's Assistant*), Montague Shaw (*Registrar*).

Tone is a prosecuting attorney at a trial involving a man who supposedly pushed his wife off a cliff. There is only one witness and it happens to be a former mistress of Tone's. Unknown to Tone, however, is the fact that his wife, Loretta Young, has been paying blackmailer Daniell to keep harmful letters Tone wrote to his mistress out of the public eye, thereby damaging his chance to become attorney general. Before long the prosecuting attorney is forced to reveal his past, realizing that his case parallels the one he is trying. Heavily melodramatic but helped along by an interesting, if not complex, plot.

p, Lawrence Weingarten; d, Sam Wood; w, Howard Emmett Rogers, Leon Gordon (based on the play by Ladislaus Fodor); ph, James Van Trees; m, Dr. William Axt; ed, Frank E. Hull; art d, Cedric Gibbons.

Drama   **(PR:A   MPAA:NR)**

UNGUARDED MOMENT, THE½**   (1956) 95m UNIV c

Esther Williams (*Lois Conway*), George Nader (*Harry Graham*), John Saxon (*Leonard Bennett*), Edward Andrews (*Mr. Bennett*), Les Tremayne (*Mr. Pendleton*), Jack Albertson (*Professor*), Dani Crayne (*Josie Warren*), John Wilder (*Sandy*), Edward C. Platt (*Attorney Briggs*), Eleanor Audley (*Pendleton's Secretary*), Robert B. Williams (*Detective*).

Williams (in her first nonswimming role) is cast as a high school instructor who receives obscene notes from an unidentified student, while becoming friends with student Saxon (Universal's attempt at finding a new James Dean). It turns out that Saxon is really a deranged goon and is responsible for sending the notes. His problem is blamed on an equally demented father who lost control when his wife left him. Police lieutenant Nader helps Williams out of her dangerous predicament and in the meantime falls in love with her.

p, Gordon Kay; d, Harry Keller; w, Herb Meadow, Larry Marcus (based on the story "The Gentle Web," by Marcus, Rosalind Russell); ph, William Daniels (Technicolor); m, Herman Stein; ed, Edward Curtiss; md, Joseph Gershenson; art d, Alexander Golitzen, Alfred Sweeney; cos, Jay Morley, Jr.

Drama   **(PR:A   MPAA:NR)**

UNHINGED zero   (1982) 79m Anavisio c

J. E. Penner (*Marion*), Laurel Munson, Sara Ansley, Virginia Settle.

In an aging house somewhere in Oregon things are somewhat amiss. The terror comes in various forms, including bludgeonings and hackings via scythe and machete. If you've seen one "mad slasher on the loose" film....

p&d, Don Gronquist; w, Gronquist, Reagan Ramsey; ph, Richard Blakeslee; m, Jonathan Newton; prod d, Sol Leibowitz; makeup, Janet Scoutten.

Horror   **(PR:O   MPAA:NR)**

UNHOLY DESIRE½**   (1964, Jap.) 150m Nikkatsu/Toho bw (AKAI
                                                                    SATSUI)

Masumi Harukawa (*Sadako Takahashi*), Akira Nishimura (*Koichi Takahashi*), Shigeru Tsuyuguchi (*Hiraoko*), Yuko Kusonoki (*Yoshiko Masuda*), Haruo Itoga (*Yasuo Tamura*).

An interesting picture about sexual violence turning to romance as Harukawa, a bored housewife, is raped one evening while her husband is away. The following morning she finds herself unable to tell her husband of the attack, and instead looks ahead to the night when her rapist will return. Without much struggle, she gives in and becomes obsessed with her attacker-lover, finding it difficult to rid herself of him. She decides to poison him, but before she can he dies of a heart problem which had been ailing him. She returns to her uneventful existence as a housewife.

d, Shohei Imamura; w, Keiji Hasebe, Imamura (based on a story by Shinji

Fujiwara); ph, Masahisa Himeda (Nikkatsu Scope); m, Toshiro Mayuzumi.

Drama   **(PR:O   MPAA:NR)**

UNHOLY FOUR, THE**   (1954, Brit.) 78m Hammer/Lippert bw (GB:
                                                                    THE STRANGER CAME HOME)

Paulette Goddard (*Angie Vickers*), William Sylvester (*Philip Vickers*), Patrick Holt (*Job Crandall*), Paul Carpenter (*Bill Saul*), Alvys Maben (*Joan Merrill*), Russell Napier (*Inspector Treherne*), David King-Wood (*Sessions*), Pat Owens (*Blonde*), Kay Callard (*Jenny*), Jeremy Hawk (*Sgt. Johnson*), Jack Taylor (*Brownie*), Kim Mills (*Roddy*), Owen Evans, Philip Lennard.

Amnesiac Sylvester returns home from a fishing trip in Portugal which he took three years previously with three friends, all of whom are now interested in his "widow." He tries to find out who bopped him on the head and is understandably less than friendly upon his return. Coinciding with his arrival, however, is a murder which he, of course, is blamed for. With the help of Goddard, he clears his name and reconciles his relationship with her. Goddard wasn't to be seen on the screen again until 1964, in TIME OF INDIFFERENCE.

p, Michael Carreras; d, Terence Fisher; w, Carreras (based on the novel *Stranger At Home* by George Sanders); ph, James Harvey; m, Ivor Slaney; ed, Bill Lenney; art d, Jim Elder Wills.

Crime/Mystery   **(PR:A   MPAA:NR)**

UNHOLY FOUR, THE*   (1969, Ital.) 96m BRC/Atlas c (CIAK MULL,
                                                                    L'UOMO DELLA VENDETTA)

Leonard Mann, Woody Strode, Helmut Schneider, Evelyn Stewart, Luca Montefiore, Andrew Ray.

A posse of half-crazed gunmen tracks down an evil gang led by Montefiore. A typical spaghetti western which benefits mainly from some competent performances, especially Strode's.

p, Manolo Bolognini; d, E.B. Clucher [Enzo Barboni]; w, Franco Rossetti, Mario di Nardo; ph, Mario Mantuori.

Western   **(PR:C   MPAA:NR)**

UNHOLY GARDEN, THE*   (1931) 85m Goldwyn/UA bw

Ronald Colman (*Barrington Hunt*), Fay Wray (*Camille de Jonghe*), Estelle Taylor (*Eliza Mowbray*), Tully Marshall (*Baron de Jonghe*), Ulrich Haupt (*Col. Von Axt*), Henry Armetta (*Nick the Goose*), Lawrence Grant (*Dr. Shayne*), Warren Hymer (*Smiley Corbin*), Mischa Auer (*Prince Nicolai Poliakoff*), Morgan Wallace (*Capt. Krugor*), Kit Guard (*Kid Twist*), Lucille LaVerne (*Lucie Villars*), Arnold Korff (*Lautrac*), Charles Hill Mailes (*Alfred de Jonghe*), Nadja (*Native Dancer*), Henry Kolker, William von Brincken.

This silly bit of business was Colman's worst movie. He's a Raffles-type thief who has had to seek refuge in Algeria where he's taken up with a corps of crooks at an oasis. Wray is the granddaughter of Marshall, an ancient embezzler in a wheelchair. He's secreted some of his ill-gotten gains and she means to protect them. Colman and his pal, Hymer, are at a hotel in the Sahara which has hot and cold running felons in every room. When the local cops learn that Colman is in the area, they send in Taylor, a plainclothes-woman, to get him away from the sanctuary so he can be arrested. By that time, Colman is making eyes at Wray. The members of the gang at the hotel would like to get their hands on Marshall's cache of francs. Guard and Haupt lead that group and they think Colman is making a mistake by getting too close to Wray, who is, after all, related by blood to Marshall. Colman is taking his time in trying to uncover the loot but Auer, one of the gang, thinks it's taking too long so he plans to shoot Marshall. Taylor arrives and tries to vamp Colman. The two go out for a spin in her car and he realizes that something is definitely not kosher when he learns that the car in which they are riding is the property of Korff, the local police chief. Colman tries a double double-cross and tells Taylor that he is going to pull out the rug from beneath his gang's feet. What he really means to do is protect the money and give it to Wray. Taylor is jealous of the manner in which Colman goes for Wray and she blows the whistle on him to the other members of the gang after they get her drunk. When Haupt learns this, he and the others, Auer, Guard, and Armetta, attempt to stem Colman's plan. With Hymer in his corner, Colman gets the money, gives it to Wray, and tells her to get out of there with it, and with Marshall, before the old man is done in. Wray wants to stick with him, but Colman tells her that a life with him would be a life on the run and she'd be better off to leave right away. Colman and Hymer are about to leave when Hymer asks where the money is. Colman shrugs and says that he "just met a dame" and gave it to her. Hymer shakes his head and the two men drive off in Korff's car. A dumb movie that falls between comedy and drama and is neither, THE UNHOLY GARDEN (an unfortunate title) marked the final collaboration between Colman and director Fitzmaurice after eight films together. There is hardly anything as rare as a mediocre script by Hecht and MacArthur but this was, although there is some speculation that they didn't write the script at all. They had told Goldwyn the story and he paid them for a script. Suddenly, a more attractive job (SCARFACE) came along and since they couldn't give attention to two movies at once, legend has it that two nameless writers pounded this one out. Goldwyn hated the final script but the picture was scheduled to shoot immediately and so it went before the cameras in the condition it was in, thus proving the old adage that "if it ain't on the page, it ain't on the stage." Goldwyn's customary lavish sets and costumes could not save the innate stupidity of the badly written script. Goldwyn and Colman were feuding at the time and Fitzmaurice and Goldwyn's aide, Arthur Hornblow, spent most of their time keeping the two men away from each other. The result was a sleepwalking performance from Colman and an increased desire on his part to get away from any long-term contracts in the future. That dream was realized about two years later when he went freelance and made a great deal more money with that decision. Whatever comedy is in the film comes from Hymer. Had Hecht and MacArthur really written the script, you may be certain it would have been funnier, almost a parody of RAFFLES and the other similar films of the era.

p, Samuel Goldwyn; d, George Fitzmaurice; w, Ben Hecht, Charles MacArthur; ph, Gregg Toland, George Barnes; m, Alfred Newman; ed, Grant Whytock; art d, Richard Day, Willy Pogany.

Crime Drama (PR:A MPAA:NR)

UNHOLY LOVE* (1932) 77m Hollywood bw

H.B. Warner (Dr. Gregory), Lila Lee (Jane Bradford), Beryl Mercer (Mrs. Cawley), Joyce Compton (Sheila Bailey), Lyle Talbot (Jerry Gregory), Ivan Lebedeff (Alex Stockmar), Jason Robards (Simmington), Kathlyn Williams (Mrs. Bradford), Frances Rich (Gail Abbot), Richard Carlyle (Mr. Bailey).

Warner and Lee head a cast of overdramatic actors in this updating of Flaubert's classic *Madame Bovary*, which is thankfully disguised by a new title. The story has been filmed with little concern for the original, casting Warner as forgiving father and Lee as forgiving fiancee who continually sacrifice for dopey youth Talbot. Luckily Flaubert was long dead before this flop hit the theaters.

p, M.H. Hoffman; d, Albert Ray; w, Frances Hyland (based on Gustave Flaubert's novel *Madame Bovary*); ph, Harry Neumann, Tom Galligan; ed, Mildred Johnston.

Drama (PR:A MPAA:NR)

UNHOLY NIGHT, THE** (1929) 92m MGM bw

Ernest Torrence (Dr. Ballou), Roland Young (Lord Montague), Dorothy Sebastian (Lady Efra), Natalie Moorhead (Lady Vi), Claude Fleming (Sir James Ramsey), John Miljan (Maj. Mallory), Richard Tucker (Col. Davidson), John Loder (Capt. Dorchester), Philip Strange (Lt. Williams), Polly Moran (Maid), Sojin (Mystic), Boris Karloff (Abdoul), Sidney Jarvis (Butler), Clarence Geldert (Inspector Lewis), John Roche (Lt. Savor), Lionel Belmore (Maj. Endicott), Gerald Barry (Capt. Bradley), Richard Travers (Maj. McDougal), George Cooper (Orderly).

When a number of company officers are found strangled in the thick-fogged London streets, Young gathers the survivors at his home for dinner. A will is read which announces that half of a dead officer's fortune will go to his fellows, and as usual, if any of them should die the survivors would split his share. No one is allowed to leave Young's house until the murderer confesses, which he (or she) eventually does. The second film credit for Ben Hecht (after UNDERWORLD and the uncredited THE BIG NOISE) of which a silent version also exists. THE UNHOLY NIGHT also marks an early appearance for Boris Karloff, who always referred to the film as THE GREEN GHOST, its working title and French release title.

d, Lionel Barrymore; w, Edwin Justus Mayer, Dorothy Farnum, Joe Farnham (based on a story by Ben Hecht); ph, Ira Morgan; ed, Grant Whytock; art d, Cedric Gibbons; cos, Adrian.

Mystery (PR:A MPAA:NR)

UNHOLY PARTNERS½** (1941) 94m MGM bw

Edward G. Robinson (Bruce Corey), Laraine Day (Miss Cronin), Edward Arnold (Merrill Lambert), Marsha Hunt (Gail Fenton), William T. Orr (Tommy Jarvis), Don Beddoe (Mike Reynolds), Charles Dingle (Clyde Fenton), Charles Cane (Inspector Brody), Walter Kingsford (Managing Editor), Charles Halton (Kaper), Clyde Fillmore (Jason Grant), Marcel Dalio (Molyneaux), Frank Faylen (Roger Ordway), Joseph Downing (Jerry), William Benedict (Boy), Charles B. Smith (Copy Boy), Frank Dawson (Old Man), Tom Seidel (Reporter), Tom O'Rourke (Young Man), George Ovey (Old Timer), Emory Parnell (Col. Mason), Al Hill (Rector), Jay Novello (Stick Man), John Dilson (Circulation Man), Billy Mann (Barber), Ann Morrison (Hazel), Lester Scharff (Tony), June MacCloy (Glamor Girl), Don Costello (Pelotti), Larraine Krueger, Natalie Thompson (Girls at Party), Florine McKinney (Mary), Charles Jordan (Gorilla), Ann Pennington (Operator), Lee Phelps (Mechanic), Lester Dorr (Circulation Manager), Gertrude Bennett, Estelle Etterre (Newspaper Women), Milton Kibbee (Drunk).

An entertaining but not very substantial drama which stars Robinson as a WW I veteran who returns from France, where he covered the war, to his former job as a domestic newspaperman. His paper, however, is too conservative, so, with the financial help of gangster Arnold, Robinson starts his own hard-hitting, sensational tabloid. The control of the paper is split 50-50 between Robinson and Arnold, but before long the partners are at

odds. Arnold disapproves of Robinson's tactics and begins an attempt to wrestle away control. In the meantime, Robinson's closest aide, Orr, is becoming involved with a pretty singer, Hunt, who spends an inordinate amount of time with Arnold. Orr grows increasingly jealous of Hunt's closeness to the gangster and begins snooping for clues. He discovers that Hunt's father has run up a large debt to Arnold and has been forced into buying an inflated insurance policy from him in return. When Robinson threatens to expose Arnold's scam, the tensions between the two partners flare. Arnold kidnaps Orr and holds him for a pricey ransom-the remaining control of the newspaper. After a quarrel, Robinson is forced to shoot Arnold in self-defense. Knowing that his time is up, Robinson dictates a confession to secretary Day and then sets off on a suicidal transatlantic flight as part of a publicity campaign. The plane goes down and Robinson is killed, but rather than release the confession, Day burns it. Although Robinson's life has ended, the newspaper continues under the managerial hand of Orr and his new wife, Hunt. Essentially, UNHOLY PARTNERS is a nostalgic throwback to the films and people of an earlier era, specifically the post-WW I ground which had already been trod in FIVE STAR FINAL, also directed by LeRoy. In his autobiography, Robinson writes that UNHOLY PARTNERS is "I think, best forgotten." Not necessarily so; it simply seems to have gotten lost in a Hollywood that was swamped with WW II pictures and had no place for a post-WW I movie, especially one dealing with the 1930s themes of newspapermen and gangsters. Robinson and Arnold both turn in fine performances and LeRoy's direction is solid, but the film itself never rises above the ranks of B movie status. Hunt delivers one tune, "After You've Gone," penned by Henry Creamer and Turner Layton.

p, Samuel Marx; d, Mervyn LeRoy; w, Earl Baldwin, Bartlett Cormack, Lesser Samuels; ph, George Barnes; m, David Snell; ed, Harold F. Kress; art d, Cedric Gibbons.

Crime Drama (PR:A MPAA:NR)

UNHOLY QUEST, THE½** (1934, Brit.) 57 Equity British bw

Claude Bailey (Prof. Sorotoff), Terence de Marney (Frank Davis), Christine Adrien (Vera), John Milton (Hawkins), Harry Terry (Soapy), Ian Wilson (Wilky).

A mad professor works in his laboratory trying to bring corpses back to life. There is a mysterious prowler around the house at night, and the ex-convict butler kills a blackmailer, whose corpse the professor can then use. He runs into technical difficulties and ends up killing himself during his big experiment.

p, Widgey R. Newman, Reginald Wyer, Bert Hopkins; d, R.W. Lotinga; w, Newman.

Horror (PR:A MPAA:NR)

UNHOLY ROLLERS** (1972) 88m Roger Corman/AIP c (AKA: LEADER OF THE PACK)

Claudia Jennings (Karen), Louis Quinn (Stern), Betty Anne Rees (Mickey), Roberta Collins (Jennifer), Alan Vint (Greg), Candice Roman (Donna), Jay Varela (Nick), Charlene Jones (Beverly), Joe E. Tata (Marshall), Maxine Gates (Angie Striker), Kathleen Freeman (Karen's Mother), John Harmon (Doctor), John Mitchell (Horace McKay), Dennis Redfield (Duane), Carl Rizzo, Mike Miller (Referees), John Steadman (Guard), Roxanna Bonilla (Consuelo), Louie and the Rockets (Band in Bar), Dan Seymour, Eve Bruce, Alvin Hammer, Vic Argo, Jack Griffin, Ray Galvin, Louis Pampino, Matt Bennett, Hunter Von Leer, Rick Hurst, Terry Wolfe, Ray O'Keefe, Perry Cook, Abbi Henderson, Kres Mersky, Cecil Reddick, Kathleen Pagel, Margaret Smith, Betty Mauk, Judy Rapp, Mia Abbott, Gloria Clerk, Lynette Sanchez, Jerry Petty, Sparky Blaine, Richard Rapp, William Mauk, James Tanioka, Daniel Rainor, John Taylor, James Barbarino, "Baby" Roacho, Ginger Barbarino, Gail Franklin, Jean David, Joan Spangehl, Joe Aragon, Eddie Smith, Rudy Calvo, Danny Fuentes, Ronald Jones, Luis Sanchez, Joe Madrid.

A fast-paced look at the roller-derby circuit with Jennings taking the starring role as a factory worker who turns to skating. She becomes the top in her field when she decides to ignore the staged brawls and violence and go in for the real thing. Her fellow players hate her, but she leaves the audience always wanting more. Heavy on violence and four-letter words, while short on character, but that seems to make the picture true to form. The producers had hoped to get it into the theaters before KANSAS CITY BOMBER (1972), another roller-derby picture with a larger budget, but the Raquel Welch starrer beat them to the punch.

p, John Prizer, Jack Bohrer; d, Vernon Zimmerman; w, Howard R. Cohen (based on a story by Zimmerman, Cohen); ph, Mike Shea (DeLuxe Color); m, Bobby Hart; ed, George Trirogoff, Yeu-Bun Yee; art d, Spencer Quinn; m/l, "Stay Away From Karen," Hart, Danny Janssen (performed by Louie And The Rockets); tech adv, Sparky Blaine.

Action/Sports (PR:O MPAA:R)

UNHOLY THREE, THE***   (1930) 75m MGM bw

Lon Chaney (Prof. Echo), Lila Lee (Rosie O'Grady), Elliott Nugent (Hector McDonald), Harry Earles (Midget), John Miljan (Prosecuting Attorney), Ivan Linow (Hercules), Clarence Burton (Regan), Crauford Kent (Defense Attorney).

For his first and only talking picture, Lon Chaney decided to return to the safety of one of his biggest grossing pictures, the 1925 Todd Browning-directed silent film THE UNHOLY THREE. The 1930 version tells essentially the same story. Chaney plays a carnival ventriloquist who shares the stage with strongman Linow and midget Earles, while the vampish Lee picks the pockets of the audience members. Eventually they are exposed and have to close down the carnival. Chaney, however, comes up with a new idea. Disguised as a little old lady named Mrs. O'Grady, he opens a pet shop, with Linow as "her" son-in-law, Lee as the daughter, and Earles as their baby boy. Chaney scams his wealthy clientele by selling them parrots which can supposedly talk, though he is actually mimicking bird sounds and throwing his voice. When a customer later complains that the parrot cannot talk, Chaney visits the house, checks out the valuables, and then eventually robs it. Their system gets fouled up when Nugent, a pet shop clerk, falls in love with Lee. Since he fails to suspect his coworkers of any wrongdoing, they decide to leave the stolen goods in his room. When Linow and Earles commit a murder, the police come snooping around and, finding Nugent's room full of valuables, arrest the unsuspecting clerk. He is put on trial and faces the death penalty when Chaney, dressed as a little old lady, takes the stand in the clerk's defense. The jury is nearly convinced when "her" voice accidentally lowers. Chaney's disguise is revealed and Nugent is cleared. In the meantime, Linow has killed Earles and has himself been killed by a rather menacing gorilla which has been kept in the pet shop. In light of the circumstances, the jury goes easy on Chaney and sentences him to a short five year prison term. After three years of refusing to appear in a talkie ("I have a thousand faces, but only one voice"), Chaney finally gave in to audience and studio pressure. The master of disguises would not be satisfied with talking only in his own voice and, to quiet his critics (who had begun rumors that Chaney was mute), spoke in five different voices–his own, the old woman's, a parrot's, a child's, and a ventriloquist's dummy's. It was also rumored that his transition to talkies was quickened by a new MGM contract which would pay a handsome $5,000 weekly. Anticipating a critical backlash, Chaney prepared an affidavit which guaranteed that "in no place in said photoplay was a 'double' or substitute used for my voice." This all-out effort by Chaney was typical of what people had come to expect from him, and he had no thoughts of letting them down. "I'll tell you frankly that my first talking picture is going to make me or break me. Inside, I mean...," Chaney is quoted as saying. "I hope they like my first talkie. I'm going to try my darndest to make them like it." His careful study of sound technique and recording, the recording of voice tests (which he vehemently denied), and his perfection of the five voices, all paid off for Chaney as THE UNHOLY THREE was a popular box office hit. Although not as critically admired as the original (mainly because director Tod Browning had a visual style that far surpassed that of Jack Conway), it guaranteed Chaney a future in sound films. MGM quickly lined him up for DRACULA, THE SEA BAT, THE BUGLE SOUNDS, and CHERI BIBI. Fate, however, interfered and, seven weeks after the opening of THE UNHOLY THREE, Chaney succumbed, in perverse irony, to throat cancer. Based on the story "The Terrible Three," which was also published under the titles "The Unholy Three" and "The Three Freaks."

d, Jack Conway; w, J.C. Nugent, Elliott Nugent (based on the story "The Terrible Three" by 'Tod' Clarence Aaron Robbins); ph, Percy Hilburn; ed, Frank Sullivan; art d, Cedric Gibbons; cos, David Cox.

Crime Drama   (PR:C MPAA:NR)

UNHOLY WIFE, THE**½   (1957) 94m RKO-Treasure/UNIV c

Diana Dors (Phyllis Hochen), Rod Steiger (Paul Hochen), Tom Tryon (San), Beulah Bondi (Emma Hochen), Marie Windsor (Gwen), Arthur Franz (Rev. Stephen Hochen), Luis Van Rooten (Ezra Benton), Argentina Brunetti (Theresa), Tol Avery (Carl Kramer), James Burke (Sheriff Wattling), Steve Pendleton (Deputy Watkins), Gary Hunley (Michael), Douglas Spencer (Judge), Joe De Santis (Gino Verdugo).

A provocative crime thriller which has Dors (in the British actress' first U.S. picture) marrying wealthy wine seller Steiger and then falling in love with rodeo star Tryon. She concocts a plan to kill Steiger and use as her alibi a prowler that her mother-in-law has reported outside their home. In actuality, the prowler is Tryon who secretly visits Dors whenever Steiger isn't around. Her plan backfires when she kills a friend of Steiger's instead, though she is able to con her husband into taking the blame. Sure that he will be acquitted, Steiger agrees but then winds up in the slammer after Dors' false testimony. She then is convicted of poisoning her mother-in-law–a crime she did not commit. All in all, an example of justice working in mysterious ways. As good as the film is, it in no way lived up to its ad campaign–"Half Angel, Half Devil, She Made Him Half A Man." THE UNHOLY WIFE is a remake of THEY KNEW WHAT THEY WANTED (1940), though the similarities between that film and this one are limited.

p&d, John Farrow; w, Jonathan Latimer (based on a story by William Durkee); ph, Lucien Ballard (Technicolor); m, Daniele Amfitheatrof; ed, Eda

Warren; md, Amfitheatrof; art d, Albert D'Agostino, Franz Bachelin; cos, Howard Shoup.

Drama/Crime   **Cas.**   (PR:A MPAA:NR)

UNIDENTIFIED FLYING ODDBALL, THE**½
(1979, Brit.) 93m Disney/BV c (GB: THE SPACEMAN AND KING ARTHUR; AKA: UFO)

Dennis Dugan (Tom Trimble), Jim Dale (Sir Mordred), Ron Moody (Merlin), Kenneth More (King Arthur), John Le Mesurier (Sir Gawain), Rodney Bewes (Clarence), Sheila White (Alisande), Robert Beatty (Sen. Milburn), Cyril Shaps (Dr. Zimmerman), Kevin Brennan (Winston), Ewen Solon (Watkins), Pat Roach (Oaf), Reg Lye (Prisoner).

Dugan is a NASA brain who, along with his robot double, gets sent into the past, landing in medieval England. He soon finds himself at the mercy of Merlin the Magician (Moody) a la Twain's classic A Connecticut Yankee in King Arthur's Court. However, Dugan is saved by the charm he lays on the Englishmen. Pleasantly humorous, though the jokes are aimed at those interested in history. The Twain novel was first filmed in 1921 and subsequently made as A CONNECTICUT YANKEE (1931) and as A CONNECTICUT YANKEE IN KING ARTHUR'S COURT (1949).

p, Ron Miller; d, Russ Mayberry; w, Don Tait (based on the novel A Connecticut Yankee in King Arthur's Court by Mark Twain); ph, Paul Beeson (Technicolor); m, Ron Goodwin; ed, Peter Boita; art d, Albert Witherick; cos, Phyllis Dalton; spec eff, Cliff Culley, Ron Ballanger, Michael Collins.

Comedy   (PR:A MPAA:G)

UNIFORM LOVERS   (SEE: HOLD 'EM YALE, 1935)

UNINHIBITED, THE*½   (1968, Fr./Ital./Span.) 95m
CICC-Borderie-Francos-Standard-Tera Explorer-Cesaro Gonzales-Precitel/ Peppercorn-Wormser c (LES PIANOS MECANIQUES; AMORI DI UNA CALDA ESTATE; LOS PIANOS MECANICOS)

Melina Mercouri (Jenny), James Mason (Pascal Regnier), Hardy Kruger (Vincent), Didier Haudepin (Daniel Regnier), Renaud Verley (Serge), Martine Ziguel [Sophie Dares] (Nadine), Keiko Kishi (Nora), Maurice Teynac (Reginald), Karin Mossberg (Orange the Mistress), Jose Maria Mompin (Tom), Luis Inouni (Bryant), Rafael Luis Calvo, Maria Albaicin.

Lacking any clear direction, this melodrama just stumbles along for 95 of its 95 minutes as Kruger pays a visit to a Spanish town after suffering a nervous breakdown. He has an affair with Mercouri, the local nightclub owner, but their romance ends when she becomes attracted to Mason, the proverbial alcoholic writer who lacks inspiration. Kruger eventually returns to his home town, while Mason stays on with Mercouri and picks up his pen again. Sources conflict on the credit for the role of Nadine.

d, Juan Antonio Bardem; w, Bardem, Henri-Francois Rey (based on the novel Les Pianos Mecaniques by Rey); ph, Gabor Pogany (Eastmancolor); m, Georges Delerue; ed, Bardem; art d, Enrique Alarcon.

Drama   (PR:C MPAA:NR)

UNINVITED, THE****   (1944) 98m PAR bw

Ray Milland (Roderick Fitzgerald), Ruth Hussey (Pamela Fitzgerald), Donald Crisp (Comdr. Bench), Cornelia Otis Skinner (Miss Holloway), Dorothy Stickney (Miss Hird), Barbara Everest (Lizzie Flynn), Alan Napier (Dr. Scott), Gail Russell (Stella Meredith), Jessica Newcombe (Miss Ellis), John Kiernan (Foreword Narrator), Rita Page (Annie, Maid), David Clyde (Boot Owner), Norman Ainsley (Chauffeur), Evan Thomas (Col. Carlton), Ottola Nesmith (Mrs. Carlton), Evan P. Simpson (Will Hardy, Tobacconist), Moyna Macgill (Mrs. Coatsworthy), Queenie Leonard (Mrs. Taylor), Betty Farrington (Voice of Mary Meredith), Leyland Hodgson (Taxi Driver), Holmes Herbert (Charlie Jessup), Helena Grant (Servant), George Kirby (Gas Station Attendant), Elizabeth Russell (Portrait of Mary Meredith), Lynda Grey (Ghost of Mary Meredith/Body for Portrait).

An unusual and fascinating item, a ghost story that takes itself seriously. Milland and his sister buy a house on the Cornish cliffs, but soon various inexplicable phenomena occur, such as cold spots in rooms, the smell of mimosas permeating the air, and the dog refusing to even go upstairs. They frequently receive a visitor, local girl Russell, whose grandfather, Crisp, forbids her to go into the house. The ghost is suspected to be Russell's mother, who fell off the cliffs to her death. More strange things happen, like flowers wilting immediately in a room, and eventually the phantom itself is seen, ectoplasmic at the top of the stairs (probably the most convincing and scary ghost to appear on the screen). Russell is confined by her grandfather to an asylum, but Milland and Hussey figure out that it is not one but two ghosts that haunt their home, carrying their rivalry from life beyond the grave. They expose the facts concerning Russell's mother's death, and with that out, the ghosts fade away and leave the house in peace. Greatly influenced by Val Lewton's productions for RKO in which the horror is only suggested, and almost never shown–for the monster in one's mind is much more frightening than the one on the screen. Some of the film doesn't work so well; it drags in spots and much of it seems a direct cop from REBECCA (house on the cliffs, scary folks coming in and out talking about the dead woman who lived there before, etc., and the advertising for the film went out of its way to compare itself to the Hitchcock film). Milland is as good as ever, and the rest of the cast does an admirable job, particularly Crisp and Skinner. Although the film garnered favorable reviews and decent returns at the box office, it would be many years before Hollywood would get serious about the spirit world again (THE HAUNTING, 1963).

p, Charles Brackett; d, Lewis Allen; w, Dodie Smith, Frank Partos (based on the novel by Dorothy Macardle); ph, Charles Lang; m, Victor Young; ed, Doane Harrison; art d, Hans Dreier, Ernst Fegte; set d, Stephen Seymour; spec eff, Farciot Edouart.

Horror   **(PR:C   MPAA:NR)**

UNION CITY**   (1980) 87m Kinesis c

Dennis Lipscomb (Harlan), Deborah Harry (Lillian), Irina Maleeva (Contessa), Everett McGill (Larry Longacre), Sam McMurray (Young Vagrant), Terina Lewis (Evelyn, Secretary), Pat Benatar (Jeanette), Tony Azito (Alphonse), Paul Andor (Ludendorf), Taylor Mead (Man in Taxi), Cynthia Crisp (Woman in Taxi), Charles Rydell (Cabbie).

A black-comedy feel mixed with a *film noir* look helps this otherwise disappointing independent which is best known for being the dramatic debut of then-popular singer Debbie Harry of the group Blondie (she had previously appeared in ROADIE). She is brunette this time out, cast as a New Jersey housewife in 1953 who is married to the increasingly neurotic Lipscomb. Her husband is obsessed with wreaking vengeance on McMurray, a war vet who insists on taking a drink every morning from Lipscomb's delivered bottle of milk. One day, Lipscomb flips and smashes the vagrant's head into the floor when McMurray accuses him of impotence. He then hides the body in the neighboring apartment and is tormented to the point of suicide when a family moves in. Rock singer Pat Benatar also appears in a minor role. Exquisitely photographed by Lachman, whose work with such directors as Jean-Luc Godard, Wim Wenders, Werner Herzog, and Ingmar Bergman cameraman Sven Nykvist is proof of his talent. Chris Stein, fellow Blondie member and husband of Harry, provided the picture's musical track.

p, Graham Belin; d&w, Mark Reichert (based on the short story "The Corpse Next Door" by Cornell Woolrich); ph, Edward Lachman; m, Chris Stein; ed, Eric Albertson, Lana Tokel, J. Michaels; art d, George Stavrinos.

Drama   **Cas.**   **(PR:A   MPAA:PG)**

UNION DEPOT***½   (1932) 75m FN-WB bw (GB: GENTLEMAN FOR
                                              A DAY)

Douglas Fairbanks, Jr. (Chic Miller), Joan Blondell (Ruth), Guy Kibbee (Scrap Iron), Alan Hale (The Baron), George Rosener (Bernardi), Dickie Moore (Little Boy), Ruth Hall (Welfare Worker), Mae Madison (Waitress), Polly Walters (Mabel), David Landau (Kendall), Lillian Bond (Actress on Train), Frank McHugh (The Drunk), Junior Coghlan 'Frank Coghlan, Jr.' (Ragged Urchin), Dorothy Christy (Society Woman), Adrienne Dore (Sadie), Eulalie Jensen (Cafe Proprietress), Virginia Sale (Woman on Platform), George McFarlane (Train Caller), Earle Foxe (Parker), Mary Doran (Daisy), Walter McGrail, Ed Brody.

Yet another variation on the GRAND HOTEL style, UNION DEPOT actually beat the MGM blockbuster into the theaters by a few months. Critics of the day were quick to notice the similarity between this picture (and two others which predated GRAND HOTEL– HOTEL CONTINENTAL and DEVIL'S LOTTERY) and the Vicki Baum play and novel which served as a basis for GRAND HOTEL. This time the location was a bustling train station, alive with scurrying passengers, vacationing couples, new immigrants, and low-life vagabonds. Fairbanks stars as a disheveled young tramp who wanders the roads and rails with his good friend, Kibbee. While in the station's washroom, Fairbanks finds a forgotten bag full of cash and a new suit of clothes and transforms himself into a respectable citizen. Another character in the terminal is Hale, a bogus baron who carries around a violin case, which he eventually deposits in the checkroom. Rounding out the rest of the nearly two dozen other characters are McHugh, an amicable drunk; Rosener, a fast-moving lecher; Landau, an undercover man hunting for a counterfeiter; and Blondell, a comely chorus girl who needs $64 to get a train to Salt Lake City. Amongst all the activity, Hale gets his billfold snatched. Luckily for Kibbee he finds it, pockets the wad of cash hidden inside, and finds the claim ticket for the violin case. Kibbee and Fairbanks, both of whom are reveling in their recently acquired riches, claim the violin and bring it to a pawnbroker. When they look inside the case, however, they find it stuffed with bills, and quickly leave the shop. By now Fairbanks has met Blondell, but assumes that her hard-luck story is just an attempt to separate him from some of his cash. Fairbanks is finally convinced of Blondell's sincerity and gets her safely on her way to Salt Lake City. While UNION DEPOT pales in comparison to the masterful GRAND HOTEL (which was blessed with a far superior cast), it is still wonderfully smart in that 1930s tradition–rapid dialog, tight editing, sweeping camerawork, and a snappy pace. Unfortunately, this fine film was overshadowed by the great success that GRAND HOTEL garnered when it opened three months later.

d, Alfred E. Green; w, Kenyon Nicholson, Walter De Leon, John Bright, Kubec Glasmon (based on the play by Gene Fowler, Douglas Durkin, Joe Laurie); ph, Sol Polito; ed, Jack Killifer.

Drama/Comedy   **(PR:A   MPAA:NR)**

UNION PACIFIC****   (1939) 135m PAR bw

Barbara Stanwyck (Mollie Monahan), Joel McCrea (Jeff Butler), Akim Tamiroff (Fiesta), Robert Preston (Dick Allen), Lynne Overman (Leach Overmile), Brian Donlevy (Sid Campeau), Robert Barrat (Duke Ring), Anthony Quinn (Jack Cordray), Stanley Ridges (Gen. Casement), Henry Kolker (Asa M. Barrows), Francis McDonald (Gen. Grenville M. Dodge), Willard Robertson (Oakes Ames), Harold Goodwin (E.E. Calvin), Evelyn Keyes (Mrs. Calvin), Richard Lane (Sam Reed), William Haade (Dusky Clayton), Regis Toomey (Paddy O'Rourke), J.M. Kerrigan (Monahan), Fuzzy Knight (Cookie), Harry Woods (Al Brett), Lon Chaney, Jr. (Dollarhide), Joseph Crehan (Gen. U.S. Grant), Julia Faye (Mame), Shelia Darcy (Rose), Joe Sawyer (Shamus), Byron Foulger (Andrew Whipple), Jack Pennick (Harmonica Player), Dick Alexander, Max Davidson, Oscar G. Hendrian, Jim Pierce (Card Players), Walter Long (Irishman), Monte Blue (Indian), John Merton (Laborer), Jim Farley (Paddy), Buddy Roosevelt (Fireman), Richard Denning, David Newell (Reporters), Chief Thundercloud, Mala 'Ray Mala', Iron Eyes Cody, Sonny Chorre, Gregg Whitespear, Richard Robles, Tony Urchel (Indian Braves), Earl Askam (Bluett), John Marston (Dr. Durant), Selmer Jackson (Jerome), Morgan Wallace (Sen. Smith), Russell Hicks (Sergeant), May Beatty (Mrs. Morgan), Stanley Andrews (Dr. Harkness), Ernie Adams (Gen. Sheridan), William J. Worthington (Oliver Ames), Guy Usher (Leland Stanford), James McNamara (Mr. Mills), Gus Glassmire (Gov. Stafford), Paul Everton (Rev. Dr. Tadd), Frank Yaconelli (Accordion Player), Elmo Lincoln (Card Player), Syd Saylor (Barker), Lane Chandler (Conductor), James Flavin (Paddy), Nestor Paiva (C.P. Conductor), Jack Richardson, Mary MacLaren, Jane Keckley, Frank Shannon, Maude Fealy, Stanhope Wheatcroft, Ida May, Nora Cecil, Noble Johnson, Florence Lake, Si Jenks, Louis Natheaux, Wilbur Mack, Emory Parnell, Patrick Moriarity, Walter Long, Robert Homans, Ed Le Saint, Sam McDaniel, Byron Stevens, William Pawley.

After finishing his pirate epic THE BUCCANEER, DeMille was caught in a quandary regarding his next picture. Should it concern flying, ships, or trains? He finally decided on trains but then faced the dilemma of which story to tell: the Union Pacific or the Sante Fe? The producer-director of spectacles reportedly flipped a coin, called tails, and UNION PACIFIC landed face up. McCrea stars in this lavishly produced western as the overseer of the construction of the Union Pacific Railroad. While on the job McCrea meets Stanwyck, the daughter of a railroad engineer who mixes her femininity with an assured toughness that signals that she can handle herself in any situation. Stanwyck works as the Union Pacific's postmistress and McCrea falls for her. Meanwhile, a seedy politician with a financial interest in the Central Pacific (the Union Pacific's rival), Kolker, hires a crooked gambler, Donlevy, to work out a variety of schemes to delay construction of the line. Aided by Preston, a Civil War comrade of McCrea's, Donlevy sets up a gambling den and begins distracting the workers of the Union Pacific by offering games of chance, strong drink, and fast women. The lure of a good time causes havoc at the railroad, as does the robbery of the payroll, performed by Preston. Stanwyck, who has been seeing Preston as well as McCrea, learns that Preston is responsible for the theft and talks him into returning the money. Soon after, the train is attacked by Indians and Stanwyck holds her ground and fights alongside McCrea and Foster. Just as it looks as though they will be slaughtered, the U.S. Cavalry arrives and saves them, but not before the now-reformed Preston is murdered by his former boss Donlevy, who in turn pays for his crimes. With the villains dispatched, the Union Pacific is finally completed and the film ends in a massive celebration as the golden spike is driven into the last rail at Promontory Point. UNION PACIFIC is a big, sprawling western epic produced with the usual DeMille extravagance and eye for detail. DeMille gained the cooperation of the Union Pacific Railroad which made available tons of old records and papers pertaining to the line's construction. In addition to the research assistance, the Union Pacific supplied DeMille with vintage trains and experienced crews to run them. The film was shot on locations in Utah, Oklahoma, and at the Canoga Park lot in Hollywood where the reenactment of the "golden spike" ceremony was staged. The actual golden spike (which was driven on May 10, 1869) used at the ceremony was loaned to the production by Stanford University and brought to Hollywood under great secrecy. DeMille assembled his usual cast-of-thousands for the production and was delighted by Stanwyck's professional enthusiasm as she toughed it through the physical scenes with the men. The director was stricken with a prostate problem during the production and had to be operated on. He was absent for several weeks and much of the location shooting was directed by Arthur Rosson and James Hogan. When DeMille returned to the set he directed from a stretcher and was carried from set to set by crew members. The premiere of UNION PACIFIC was a spectacle in itself. DeMille arranged for a special Union Pacific train carrying the cast on a five-day trip from Los Angeles to Omaha, Nebraska, where the film was being premiered (Omaha was where the railway line started). There were stops along the way, of course, and special events were planned at each. In Omaha a three-day celebration with the citizenry in period costume was held, and the cast of the film–in costumes–joined in. The film was a big hit at the box office and DeMille was finally given *carte blanche* by Paramount Studios on future productions.

p&d, Cecil B. DeMille; w, Walter DeLeon, C. Gardner Sullivan, Jesse Lasky, Jr., Jack Cunningham (based on the novel *Trouble Shooters* by Ernest Haycox); ph, Victor Milner, Dewey Wrigley; m, George Antheil, Sigmund Krumgold, John Leipold; ed, Anne Bauchens; md, Irvin Talbot; art d, Hans Dreier, Roland Anderson; set d, A.E. Freudeman; cos, Natalie Visart; spec eff, Gordon Jennings, Loren L. Ryder, Farciot Edouart.

Western   **Cas.**   **(PR:A   MPAA:NR)**

UNION STATION*½   (1950) 80m PAR bw

William Holden (*Lt. William Calhoun*), Nancy Olson (*Joyce Willecombe*), Barry Fitzgerald (*Inspector Donnelly*), Lyle Bettger (*Joe Beacom*), Jan Sterling (*Marge Wrighter*), Allene Roberts (*Lorna Murcall*), Herbert Heyes (*Henry Murcall*), Don Dunning (*Gus Hadder*), Fred Graff (*Vince Marley*), James Seay (*Detective Shattuck*), Parley E. Baer (*Detective Gottschalk*), Ralph Sanford (*Detective Fay*), Richard Karlan (*Detective George Stein*), Bigelow Sayre (*Detective Ross*), Charles Dayton (*Howard Kettner*), Jean Ruth (*Pretty Girl*), Paul Lees (*Young Man Masher*), Harry Hayden (*Conductor Skelly*), Ralph Byrd (*Priest*), Edith Evanson (*Mrs. Willecombe*), Queenie Smith (*Landlady*), George M. Lynn (*Moreno*), Richard Barron (*Halloran*), Joe Warfield (*Manny*), Trevor Bardette, Robert Wood, Mike Mahoney (*Patrolmen*), Robert R. Cornthwaite (*Orderly*), Clifton Young, Freddie Zendar (*Ambulance Drivers*), Howard J. Negley (*Conductor*), Dick Elliott (*Employee*), Douglas Spencer (*Stationmaster*), Byron Foulger (*Horace*), Edgar Dearing, Thomas E. Jackson, Al Ferguson, Howard Mitchell (*Detectives*), Sumner Getchell (*Police Car Driver*), Bob Easton (*Cowboy*), Bob Hoffman (*Messenger*), Ralph Montgomery, Jerry James (*City Slickers*), Bernard Szold (*Counterman*), Joe Recht (*Messenger*), John Crawford (*Hackett, Clerk*), Gil Warren, Eric Alden, Charles Sherlock (*Doctors*), Jack Gargan (*Police Stenographer*), Bill Meader (*Projectionist*), Hans Moebus (*Charles, Chauffeur*), Jack Roberts (*Freddie*), Mike P. Donovan (*Watchman*), Laura Elliot, Barbara Knudson, Gerry Ganzer, Charmienne Harker, Freddie Zendar, Isabel Cushin (*Clerks*), June Earle (*Nurse*), Betty Corner (*Woman*).

Holden's first film after SUNSET BOULEVARD was a big comedown back to the routine pictures in which he had long been appearing. Here he is the chief of the railway police at Chicago's Union Station when Olson approaches him to report on the suspicious activities of two gun-toting thugs. This leads to the conclusion that the blind daughter (Roberts) of Olson's wealthy employer (Heyes) has been kidnaped and that the culprits have decided on Holden's station as the pickup point for the ransom. When the time comes, Holden has the place completely secured. Despite the diversions afforded by the crowded terminus, the kidnapers are observed picking up the loot. The gang leader, Bettger, gets away with the money, but his two accomplices are less lucky. The first is chased into Chicago's historic stockyards, where a gun battle panics cattle which stampede, leaving the kidnaper trampled in their dust. The second accomplice is caught, and police threaten to throw him into the path of a train unless he tells them the whereabouts of the girl and Bettger, the ringleader of the gang. He tells them and they go there, but the villain has fled with the girl. They learn from his mistress, Sterling, that he intends to kill the girl after he gets the money. Bettger murders Sterling for her stooling, but Holden picks up the trail and the final chase occurs in a service tunnel under the station where the heavy is shot down. The suitcase breaks open and the ransom money falls all over the tunnel. Stylish direction under the hand of cameraman-turned-director Mate. Less episodic than many of the multitude of GRAND HOTEL-style pictures, all of which used a public-access place to integrate a complex variety of stories, UNION STATION still has many minor tales interwoven into its major theme. These lesser stories, deliberately diverting–as they are to the security forces pursuing the kidnapers–are relevant in the context of the chase in this unusual *film noir*. Capable performances from Holden and Olson, paired romantically here, as in SUNSET BOULEVARD that same year, and with a strong cast of reliable character actors (Fitzgerald performing exceptionally well in an unusual piece of casting as a high police official), the film did well at the box office.

p, Jules Schermer; d, Rudolph Mate; w, Sydney Boehm (based on the story "Nightmare in Manhattan" by Thomas Walsh); ph, Daniel L. Fapp; ed, Ellsworth Hoagland; md, Irvin Talbot; art d, Hans Dreier, Earl Hedrick; set d, Sam Comer, Ray Moyer; cos, Mary Kay Dodson; makeup, Wally Westmore.

Crime   **(PR:C   MPAA:NR)**

UNIVERSAL SOLDIER*½   (1971, Brit.) 96m Appaloosa/Ionian c

George Lazenby, Edward Judd, Benito Carruthers, Germaine Greer, Rudolph Walker.

Upon returning home to London a soldier of fortune finds his past life to be a continual haunt. Fairly intelligent, if overly grave, drama. Lazenby does well in this low-budget job, one of only a few the one-time male model from Australia had following his role as "James Bond"–his first starring part–in ON HER MAJESTY'S SECRET SERVICE (1969).

p, Frank J. Schwarz, Donald L. Factor; d&w, Cy Endfield; ph, Tony Imi; m,

Philip Goodhand-Tait.

Drama   **(PR:C   MPAA:NR)**

UNIVERSITY OF LIFE**   (1941, USSR) 90m Soyuzdetfilm/Artkino
                                        bw (MOI UNIVERSITETI; AKA: MY UNIVERSITY)

N. Valbert (*Gorky*), S. Kayukov (*Semyonov, Baker*), N. Dorokhin (*Ossip*), N. Plotnikov (*Nikiforitch*), D. Segal (*Guri Pletnev*), I. Fyedotova (*Masha*), L. Sverdlin (*Old Tatar*), V. Maruta (*Romas*), Pavlik Dojdev (*Yashka*).

The third part in Donskoy's trilogy based on the life of Russian writer Maxim Gorky follows THE CHILDHOOD OF MAXIM GORKY and ON HIS OWN. As a young man Gorky travels to the shipyards and meets the workers where they drink an abundance of vodka and talk philosophy and politics. One of the most picturesque films to come out of Russia in the 1930s and 1940s, the movie brutally portrays the country's streets filled with derelicts and vagabonds and secures Donskoy's place in the history of Russian film.

d, Mark Donskoy; w, Donskoy, I. Gruzdev (based on the memoirs of Maxim Gorky); ph, Pyotr Yermolov; m, Lev Schwartz; art d, I. Stepnaov.

Biography   **(PR:C   MPAA:NR)**

UNKILLABLES, THE   (SEE: DARING GAME, 1968)

UNKISSED BRIDE, THE   (SEE: MOTHER GOOSE A GO-GO, 1966)

UNKNOWN, THE**   (1946) 70m COL bw

Karen Morley (*Rachel Martin*), Jim Bannon (*Jack Packard*), Jeff Donnell (*Nina Arnold*), Robert Scott (*Reed Cawthorne*), Robert Wilcox (*Richard Arnold*), Barton Yarborough (*Doc Long*), James Bell (*Edward Martin*), Wilton Graff (*Ralph Martin*), Helen Freeman (*Phoebe Martin*), J. Louis Johnson (*Joshua*), Boyd Davis (*Capt. Selby Martin*).

Based on the "I Love a Mystery" radio series, THE UNKNOWN brings to the screen a collection of demented heirs who all arrive at a creepy mansion for the reading of a will. Morley, the only sane one in the bunch, arrives to receive her share, but ends up as the victim of a murder plot. The story is filled with all the things that are guaranteed to make audiences jump out of their seats, such as hidden passageways, a hooded grave robber, eerie shadows, and mysterious killings.

p, Wallace MacDonald; d, Henry Levin; w, Malcolm Stuart Boylan, Julian Harmon (based on the novel by Carleton E. Morse, adapted by Charles O'Neal, Dwight Babcock); ph, Henry Freulich; ed, Arthur Seid; md, Mischa Bakaleinikoff; art d, George Brooks.

Mystery   **(PR:A   MPAA:NR)**

UNKNOWN BATTLE, THE   (SEE: HEROES OF TELEMARK, 1965, Brit.)

UNKNOWN BLONDE*   (1934) 65m Majestic bw (GB: THE MAN
                                        WHO PAWNED HIS SOUL)

Edward Arnold, Barbara Barondess, Barry Norton, John Miljan, Dorothy Revier, Leila Bennett, Walter Catlett, Helen Jerome Eddy, Claude Gillingwater, Arletta Duncan, Maidel Turner, Franklin Pangborn, Esther Muir, Clarence Wilson, Arthur Hoyt.

Arnold is a lawyer who resorts to illegal means in order to pay off his wife's stock debts and then gets dropped by her in favor of another fellow. He is determined to prove that she made a mistake with her new hubby, trying to convince her that she's better off with him. The movie is technically shaky, with a script that's not much better.

d, Hobart Henley; w, Leonard Fields, Davis Silverstein (based on the novel *Collusion* by Theodore D. Irwin); ph, Ira Morgan; ed, Otis Garrett.

Drama   **(PR:A   MPAA:NR)**

UNKNOWN GUEST, THE**   (1943) 61m MON bw

Victor Jory (*Chuck Williams*), Pamela Blake (*Julie*), Harry Hayden (*Nadroy*), Veda Ann Borg (*Helen*), Nora Cecil (*Martha Williams*), Lee White (*Joe Williams*), Paul Fix (*Fats*), Emory Parnell (*Sheriff*), Ray Walker (*Swarthy*), Edwin Mills (*Sidney*).

Jory is suspected of murder by his sweetheart, Blake, when he takes over his aunt and uncle's inn while they take off on holiday. She thinks that he buried his relatives in the basement and suspense builds as she must decide whether or not to inform on him. When the relatives return home, Jory and Blake's romance resumes hotter than ever.

p, Maurice King; d, Kurt Neumann; w, Philip Jordan (based on a story by Maurice Franklin); ph, Jackson Rose; m, Dimitri Tiomkin; ed, Martin G. Cohen; md, David Chudnow; art d, Neil McGuire, Dave Milton.

Mystery   **(PR:A   MPAA:NR)**

UNKNOWN ISLAND*   (1948) 76m Film Classics c

Virginia Grey (*Carole Lane*), Philip Reed (*Ted Osborne*), Richard Denning (*John Fairbanks*), Barton MacLane (*Capt. Tarnowski*), Richard [Dick] Wessel (*Sanderson*), Daniel White (*Edwards*), Philip Nazir (*Golab*).

An exhibition travels to the title island located somewhere in the Pacific in the hopes of photographing dinosaurs which supposedly still roam the forests. Reed brings fiancee Grey along but loses her to the more attentive Denning after failing to put down his camera long enough to please the gal. The dinosaurs are absurdly fake and the script has no surprises, only cliches.

p, Albert Jay Cohen; d, Jack Bernhard; w, Robert T. Shannon, Jack Harvey (based on a story by Shannon); ph, Fred Jackman, Jr. (Cinecolor); ed, Harry Gerstad; spec eff, Howard A. Anderson, Ellis Burman.

Adventure   (PR:A MPAA:NR)

UNKNOWN MAN, THE*½   (1951) 86m MGM bw

Walter Pidgeon (*Dwight Bradley Mason*), Ann Harding (*Stella Mason*), Barry Sullivan (*Joe Buckner*), Keefe Brasselle (*Rudi Wallchek*), Lewis Stone (*Judge Hulbrook*), Eduard Franz (*Andrew Jason Layford*), Richard Anderson (*Bob Mason*), Dawn Addams (*Ellie Fansworth*), Phil Ober (*Wayne Kellwin*), Mari Blanchard (*Sally Tever*), Konstantin Shayne (*Peter Hulderman*), Don Beddoe (*Fingerprint Man*), Holmes Herbert (*Rev. Michael*), Jean Andren (*Secretary*), Richard Hale (*Eddie Caraway*), Jeff York (*Guard*), John Maxwell (*Dr. Palmer*), John Butler, Harry Hines, Ronald Brogan, Robert Scott, Robert Griffin, Frank Gerstle, Jimmy Dodd, Larry Carr, Eric Sinclair (*Reporters*), King Donovan, Frank Scannell (*Photographers*), Katherine Meskill (*Telephone Operator*), Phil Tead (*Attendant*), Dabbs Greer (*Driver*), Mira McKinney, Rhea Mitchell (*Maids*), Wheaton Chambers (*Bailiff*), Richard Karlan (*Lieutenant*), Bradford Hatton (*Plainclothesman*), Robert Fould (*Sergeant*), Emmett Vogan (*Court Clerk*), Paul Kruger (*Prison Guard*), Jack Gargan (*Male Secretary*), Fred Rapport (*Butler*), Monya Andre, Anna Q. Nilsson, Bess Flowers (*Guests*), Mae Clarke Langdon (*Stella's Friend*), Estelle Etterre (*Saleswoman*), Fred Aldrich (*Bailiff*), Harte Wayne (*Court Clerk*), Tay Dunne (*Court Reporter*), Harry Cody (*Detective*), Frank Pershing (*Foreman of Jury*), John Alvin (*Photographer*), Jack Shea (*Sash*).

Heavily plotted and plodding contrivance that features long courtroom sequences which are better than sleeping pills for insomniacs. Sullivan is a district attorney who is giving a speech to a group of law students about to graduate. Instead of telling them the usual stuff, he decides to relate a story about his good friend, the late Pidgeon. While Pidgeon's son (Anderson) is seated in the graduating class audience, Sullivan sends the movie into flashback as he tells the tale. Brasselle is a young man accused of murder and Pidgeon takes the case and wins the boy his freedom, but he has the nagging feeling that Brasselle may have been guilty. His worst fears are proven true when he finds the missing murder weapon, a knife that is part of a cane owned by Brasselle. Now that Brasselle has already been tried and acquitted, he cannot be tried again and Pidgeon is at a loss as to what to do. He seeks the counsel of Franz, a powerful local man who heads the crime commission. What he doesn't know is that Franz is the man behind the crime, having sent Brasselle on the job to commit the murder because the dead man was about to blow the whistle on a large crime ring. Pidgeon is incensed when he uncovers the truth and kills Franz. However, Pidgeon is smart enough to make it look as though Brasselle is the killer and when the young man is caught and accused of the murder, he naturally turns to the lawyer who got him off on the first charge. Brasselle feels confident in choosing Pidgeon because the lawyer had him cleared for a crime he committed. Now that he's in for a crime of which he is innocent, it should be a piece of cake. But Pidgeon arranges his defense to make certain that Brasselle is tried and convicted for Franz's death and is now facing execution. However, Pidgeon is overcome by guilt and goes to D.A. Sullivan to tell him what happened. Sullivan suggests Pidgeon keep mum. Brasselle will die for the wrong death but he is, in fact, a killer, so what's the difference? And Franz, as part of the original cabal, was just as guilty of murder as the man who used the knife. Now that Franz has been killed, he has paid for his crime. Pidgeon doesn't see it that way, though, and goes to visit Brasselle in the jail cell which will be the man's final residence. Pidgeon tells Brasselle what he's done and deliberately leaves a knife near Brasselle so the young man can kill him, which, of course, he does, thus completing the circular movement of the story. Pidgeon has, in effect, committed suicide by allowing himself to be killed by Brasselle, who now has a legit reason to be put to death. Had enough? There are huge holes in the story, such as how did Pidgeon sneak a knife into a maximum security area in a prison? And how did Sullivan keep his job after encouraging the suppression of justice? Harding plays Pidgeon's wife and doesn't have much to do, while Lewis Stone is seen in his familiar role as a judge. In small roles, look for Dabbs Greer, who later enjoyed a large career in TV, and Jimmy Dodd, who will be best recalled as the leader of "The Mickey Mouse Club."

p, Robert Thomsen; d, Richard Thorpe; w, Ronald Millar, George Froeschel; ph, William Mellor; m, Conrad Salinger; ed, Ben Lewis; art d, Cedric Gibbons, Randall Duell; set d, Edwin B. Willis, Jacques Mapes; cos, Helen Rose.

Crime Drama   (PR:C MPAA:NR)

UNKNOWN MAN OF SHANDIGOR, THE*½
                (1967, Switz.) 90m Frajea bw (L'INCONNU DE SHANDIGOR)

Marie-France Boyer (*Sylvaina*), Ben Carruthers (*Manual*), Daniel Emilfork (*Von Krantz*), Howard Vernon (*Yank*), Jacques Dufilho (*Russian*), Serge Gainsbourg.

A James Bond copy has Carruthers coming to the aid of some secret agents while helping Boyer, the daughter of mad scientist Emilfork, out of a predicament. Emilfork is wanted by the U.S. and Russia after he develops a weapon which renders nuclear arms inactive. Luckily the film doesn't take itself too seriously; the villain gets eaten by a sea monster, and the movie is saved from the pomposity of most Bond imitations.

p, Gabriel Arout; d, Jean-Louis Roy; w, Roy, Arout; ph, Roger Bimpage.

Action/Spy Drama   (PR:A MPAA:NR)

UNKNOWN RANGER, THE**   (1936) 57m COL bw

Bob Allen (*Bob*), Martha Tibbetts (*Ann*), Harry Woods (*Van*), Hal Taliaferro [Wally Wales] (*Chuckler*), Robert "Buzz" Henry (*Buzzy*), Edward Hearn.

This average oater marked the entry of Bob Allen into the cowboy role, here working to defeat a gang of rustlers. He joins up with Tibbetts' ranch, helping to foil the plans of the villainous Woods. Much screen time is devoted to the horses Woods tries to take as his own, with a fight between his animal and a wild stallion being the high point.

p, Larry Darmour; d, Spencer Gordon Bennett; w, Nate Gatzert; ph, James S. Brown, Jr.; ed, Dwight Caldwell.

Western   (PR:A MPAA:NR)

UNKNOWN SATELLITE OVER TOKYO
            (SEE: MYSTERIOUS SATELLITE, THE, 1956, Jap.)

UNKNOWN TERROR, THE*   (1957) 76m Regal/FOX bw

John Howard (*Dan Mathews*), Mala Powers (*Gina Mathews*), Paul Richards (*Pete Morgan*), May Wynn (*Concha*), Gerald Milton (*Dr. Ramsey*), Duane Gray (*Lino*), Charles Gray (*Jim Wheatly*), Charles Postal (*Butler*), Patrick O'Moore (*Dr. Willoughby*), William Hamel (*Trainer*), Richard Gilden (*Raul Kom*), Martin Garralaga (*Old Indian*), Sir Lancelot (*Himself*).

Powers and her husband Howard set out on a journey to the South American Cave of Death (or, for the bilinguals, Cava Muerta) in order to locate her missing brother. They find him, but he has lost his mind and now conducts experiments which turn humans into fungus-men (who look more like they've been dipped in soap suds, however). It's not art, but its camp value sort of grows on you–like a fungus.

p, Robert Stabler; d, Charles Marquis Warren; w, Kenneth Higgins; ph, Joseph Biroc (RegalScope); m, Raoul Kraushaar; ed, Fred W. Berger; md, Kraushaar; art d, James M. Sullivan.

Science Fiction   **Cas.**   (PR:A MPAA:NR)

UNKNOWN VALLEY**   (1933) 64m COL bw

Charles "Buck" Jones (*Joe Gordon*), Cecelia Parker (*Sheila*), Carlotta Warwick (*Mary James*), Arthur Wanzer (*Tim*), Wade Botelor (*Elder Crossett*), Frank McGlynn (*Debbs*), Charles Thurston (*Younger*), Ward Bond (*Snead*), Gaylord [Steve] Pendleton (*Bennson*), Bret Black, Alf James, Silver the Horse.

Not the usual western, UNKNOWN VALLEY casts oater star Buck Jones as part of an an isolated community living in a desolate section of the desert. Jones is determined to find his father and in the meantime helps Parker stay out of a marriage she doesn't want.

d&w, Lambert Hillyer (based on a story by Donald W. Lee); ph, Al Siegler; ed, Clarence Kolster.

Drama/Western   (PR:A MPAA:NR)

UNKNOWN WOMAN**   (1935) 66m COL bw

Richard Cromwell (*Larry Condon*), Marian Marsh (*Helen Griffith*), Douglas Dumbrille (*Phil Gardner*), Henry Armetta (*Joe Scalise*), Arthur Hohl (*Lansing*), George McKay (*Gus*), Robert Middlemass (*Hammacher*), Nana Bryant (*Aunt Mary*), Arthur Vinton (*Whitey*), Jerry Mandy (*Tony*), Ben Taggart (*Shanley*), Nellie V. Nichols (*Rosa*), Bob Wilbur (*Mitch*), Eddie Chandler (*Hank*).

Familiar territory is covered in this routine crime drama about young attorney Cromwell who falls in love with a girl who turns out to be a federal agent. Cromwell is on a case involving Dumbrille and some stolen bonds, which leads to a fishing boat fight in which he is helped out by fisherman Armetta. Romance blooms by the finale and, to make for a storybook finish, Cromwell is made a deputy U.S. attorney.

d, Albert Rogell; w, Albert DeMond, Fred Niblo, Jr (based on the story by W. Scott Darling); ph, Henry Freulich; ed, Gene Havlick.

Crime Drama   (PR:A   MPAA:NR)

UNKNOWN WORLD*½   (1951) 73m Lippert bw

Victor Kilian (*Dr. Jeremiah Morley*), Bruce Kellogg (*Wright Thompson*), Otto Waldis (*Dr. Max A. Bauer*), Jim Bannon (*Andy Ostengaard*), Tom Handley (*Dr. James Paxton*), Dick Cogan (*George Coleman*), Marilyn Nash (*Joan Lindsey*), George Baxter (*Presiding officer*).

This interesting picture lacks the finesse a better director might have given it. The story concerns a group of citizens led by scientist Kilian who try to drill to the center of the Earth to find the ideal fallout shelter. Their vehicle–a cyclotram–forces its way to the core, but is pushed back to the surface by an erupting volcano. All this activity was filmed in New Mexico's Carlsbad Caverns.

p, Jack A Rabin, Irwin A. Block; d, Terrell O. Morse; w, Millard Kaufman; ph, Allen G. Siegler, Henry Freulich; m, Ernest Gold; ed, Morse; spec eff, Rabin, Block.

Science Fiction   **Cas.**   (PR:A   MPAA:NR)

UNMAN, WITTERING AND ZIGO½**   (1971, Brit.) 100m
                                                 Mediarts/PAR c

David Hemmings (*John Ebony*), Douglas Wilmer (*Headmaster*), Anthony Haygarth (*Cary Farthingale*), Carolyn Seymour (*Silvia Ebony*), Hamilton Dyce (*Mr. Winstanley*), Barbara Lott (*Mrs. Winstanley*), Donald Gee (*Stretton*), David Jackson (*Clackworthy*), Hubert Rees (*Blisterine*), Lower Five B: David Auker (*Aggeridge*), Tom Morris (*Ankerton*), Richard Gill (*Borby*), Michael Kitchen (*Bungabine*), Nicholas Hoye (*Cloistermouth*), Tom Owen (*Cuthbin*), Toby Simpson (*Hogg*), James Wardroper (*Lipstrob*), Clive Gray (*Muffett*), Rodney Paulden (*Munn Major*), Keith Janess (*Orris*), Christopher Moran (*Root*), Michael Cashman (*Terhew*), Paul Aston (*Trimble*), Michael Howe (*Unman*), Colin Barrie (*Wittering*).

This psychological murder drama set in an English boys' school makes the youngsters in LORD OF THE FLIES look tame. Hemmings quits his advertising job and becomes a teacher, filling a vacancy left by a previous instructor who fell to his death from a nearby cliff. Hemmings is soon shocked to learn that his students claim responsibility for the murder, insisting they killed the teacher after he refused to follow their orders. The students threaten to deal Hemmings the same fate if he doesn't give them all passing grades and place their bets at the racetrack. The headmaster and other adults insist that it is just a schoolboy prank, but Hemmings is proven correct when his wife is nearly gang raped. From this point, however, the film takes a leap into obscurity as the boys plead for Hemmings' help in finding the missing Wittering (Barrie). He turns out to have committed suicide and left a note confessing to the murder of the previous teacher in an attempt to gain his peers' respect. For some reason the third member of the title Zigo is nowhere to be found in the film or credits, seeming to represent a mysterious perpetrator (always absent from class during roll call) of the students' rebellion. The film was produced in association with Hemmings from a 1957 radio play, preceding the British-boys'-school-revolt picture IF... by a number of years.

p, Gareth Wigan; d, John Mackenzie; w, Simon Raven (based on a television and radio play by Giles Cooper); ph, Geoffrey Unsworth (Eastmancolor); m, Michael J. Lewis; ed, Fergus McDonell; art d, William MacCrow; cos, Judy Moorcroft; makeup, Neville Smallwood.

Drama/Mystery   (PR:C   MPAA:GP)

UNMARRIED**   (1939) 63m PAR bw (GB: NIGHT CLUB HOSTESS)

Helen Twelvetrees (*Pat Rogers*), Buck Jones (*Slag Bailey*), Donald O'Connor (*Ted Streaver at Age 12*), John Hartley (*Ted Streaver*), Robert Armstrong (*Pins Streaver*), Sidney Blackmer (*Cash Enright*), Larry ["Buster"] Crabbe (*Buzz Kenton*), Edward Pawley (*Swade*), William Haade (*Waiter*), Philip Warren (*Joe*), Dorothy Howe (*Petty Reed*), Lucien Littlefield (*School Principal*).

Sentimentality seeps through the screen in this harmless melodrama about a has-been fighter, Jones (in his first non-western role for some time), and a prohibition-affected nightclub owner, Twelvetrees, who find themselves with little left in life. They head for the home of Jones' recently killed former manager and live there. When the dead man's young son arrives home from school they vow to take care of him, sending him through high school and college, gearing him up for a career in the ring...just like dad. The youngster, Donald O'Connor, in real life grew up to gain fame singing and dancing.

d, Kurt Neumann; w, Lillie Hayward, Brian Marlow (based on a story by Grover Jones, William Slavens McNutt); ph, Harry Fischbeck; ed, Stuart Gilmore; md, Boris Morros; art d, Hans Dreier, Robert Odell.

Drama   (PR:A   MPAA:NR)

UNMARRIED WOMAN, AN**   (1978) 124m FOX c

Jill Clayburgh (*Erica*), Alan Bates (*Saul*), Michael Murphy (*Martin*), Cliff Gorman (*Charlie*), Pat Quinn (*Sue*), Kelly Bishop (*Elaine*), Lisa Lucas (*Patti*), Linda Miller (*Jeannette*), Andrew Duncan (*Bob*), Daniel Seltzer (*Dr.*

Jacobs*), Matthew Arkin (*Phil*), Penelope Russianoff (*Tanya*), Novella Nelson (*Jean*), Raymond J. Barry (*Edward*), Ivan Karp (*Herb Rowan*), Jill Eikenberry (*Claire*), Michael Tucker (*Fred*), Chico Martinez (*Cabbie*), Clint Chin (*Chinese Waiter*), Ken Chapin (*Man at Bar*), Tom Elios (*Ice Vendor*), Karen Ford (*Executive Secretary*), Alice J. Kane (*Waitress*), Paul Mazursky (*Hal*), Pamela Meunier (*Hat Check Girl*), Donna Perich (*Sophie*), Vincent Schiavelli (*Man at Party*), John Stravinsky (*Bartender*), Ultra Violet (*Lady MacBeth*).

This was one of the key "women's films" of the 1970s but in retrospect it becomes a trifle cliched, though it was–for it's time–a breakthrough and so must be given credit for the bold stroke. Several movies of this genre, such as ALICE DOESN'T LIVE HERE ANYMORE and DIARY OF A MAD HOUSEWIFE, preceded this, but none went as deeply. Eventually, as any stereotypes were developed in successive films as AN UNMARRIED WOMAN attempted to erase. Clayburgh works in a Manhattan art gallery and has been happily married to Murphy (or so she thinks) for the last 15 years. Everything seems to be going well enough when, one day, the two take a walk in SoHo (that area South Of Houston Street in New York and thus named SoHo) and Murphy, in tears, tells her that he's leaving her to run off with a chippie he met in Bloomingdale's. Clayburgh is shocked, enraged, storms away, throws up, begins to sob, and is now a woman alone. Murphy exits their fashionable East Side high-rise apartment and Clayburgh submerges herself in self-doubt for several weeks. She finally decides to consult a therapist, Russianoff (who is, we are told, a real therapist), and the woman pushes Clayburgh into an attempt to forget the past and return to the mainstream of life in the Big City. It's not as easy as that, but Clayburgh makes the attempt, goes to a bar, and meets fast-talking, aggressive Gorman, a slick hotshot artist who has been after Clayburgh's body since he first met her. In the past, Clayburgh fended him off, as she was a lawfully wedded wife. Now that she is free to do as she wishes, Clayburgh decides to test the waters and see what it would be like to be with another man. They have an evening together that is okay, but bells don't ring and the earth doesn't move under Clayburgh's feet. Gorman likes her very much and might like to engage upon that most fearful of all voyages for a bachelor; a "relationship." This time the high-heeled pump has been switched to a different limb and Clayburgh tosses Gorman aside, preferring to continue her quest for independence and the ability to function without a regular man. Clayburgh goes to an exhibition of works by Bates, a British artist of some repute. She is accustomed to arrogants like Gorman so Bates, a decent and gentle man, comes as a great and pleasant surprise to her. They begin seeing each other and, once the heat of passion is out of the way, they discover that there is much to like and savor between the two. The one insect in the salve is Clayburgh's teenaged daughter, Lucas, who doesn't much cotton to Bates, or any other man for that matter. Lucas is resentful of Murphy's leaving and wonders if her mother may have driven her father away. She doesn't like the fact that Clayburgh seems so close to Bates and so soon. Bates is so swell, though, that he soon wins her over. (This is a hole in the story in that Bates' character is too good to be true, so he must be false, although women in the audience loved him and arguments erupted between husbands and wives and boy friends and girl friends as couples walked out of the theater after the movie with the women, almost universally, saying, "Why can't *you* be more like that?" Everything is hunky and/or dory between them and now Bates, who has been on his own for some time, presses Clayburgh for more of a commitment. In a reverse of what is usually the case, Clayburgh maintains that this time, love will be on *her* terms and she insists that she keep her independence. Murphy's younger mistress has dumped him, and he comes back to Clayburgh and wants to rekindle their marriage. Clayburgh douses those dreams and says that she likes her life just the way it is and that doesn't include him. Clayburgh gets a better job and a new apartment, takes an idyllic holiday in New England with Bates and, in the end, steadfastly stands alone, insisting that she keep her freedom and still continue their relationship. The decision is left to Bates, and he agrees with Clayburgh's terms as the movie comes to a sentimental conclusion. The audience is left with no doubt that as soon as Clayburgh comes to her senses and realizes that Bates is a jewel, she will marry him. Now, if that synopsis sounds slushy, be on notice that it is also immensely funny and that writer-director Mazursky spares nobody and nothing with his comic darts. Clayburgh and three pals (Quinn, Bishop, and Miller) have regular luncheons that are hysterically funny as the women let their hair down and talk about their sex lives with a frankness seldom heard in anything short of a John Holmes movie. There's a telling moment as Clayburgh is fixed up with a blind date, Duncan, a man who is one of life's losers and is about as suave as Dom De Luise might be at the Queen's tea party. For almost three-fourths of this movie, there's hardly a false note, except for the fact that Bates is the handsome prince to Clayburgh's "Snow White." As the movie rushes to the conclusion, Conti's bouncy, jazzy score begins to get so syrupy (in keeping with what's on screen) it could give anyone a high blood sugar count. Good set pieces all the way through the film and an insightful screenplay filled with sharp dialog. The movie made a ton of money and proved there was a market for feature films about adults. After all, here was a woman at 40 or so and precious little was presented to appeal to the teeny-bopper crowd. Oscar nominations were handed out to the movie, to Clayburgh as Best Actress and to Mazursky for his screenplay, which also won the New York Film Critics' Award. Honesty was the best policy, and Mazursky elected to go for it on all levels (except for Bates), and the result was a movie that combined wit, intelligence, and drama, and conveyed the vulnerability of a woman beginning her second stage and proving that there is life after divorce. Mazursky plays a small role, as he usually does, and shows that he knows his stuff in front of the camera as well as he does behind it. Gorman's part is small, but effective. After his success on the Broadway stage in "Lenny" (which he lost to Dustin Hoffman in the film) and a few other notable cameos in films (THE BOYS IN THE BAND, ALL THAT JAZZ, etc.), great things were predicted for his career, but that had not, as of 1986, come to fruition yet. The language and the frank sexual scenes make this a poor choice for younger viewers.

p, Paul Mazursky, Tony Ray; d&w, Mazursky; ph, Arthur Ornitz (Movielab Color); m, Bill Conti; ed, Stuart H. Pappe; prod d, Pato Guzman; set d, Edward Stewart; cos, Albert Wolsky; makeup, Mike Maggi.

Drama/Comedy   **Cas.**   **(PR:C-O MPAA:R)**

UNMASKED**   (1929) 62m Weiss Brothers Artclass bw

Robert Warwick (*Craig Kennedy*), Milton Krims (*Prince Hamid*), Sam Ash (*Billy Mathews*), Charles Slattery (*Inspector Collins*), Susan Conroy (*Mary Wayne*), Lyons Wickland (*Larry Jamieson*), William Corbett (*Franklin Ward*), Roy Byron (*Cafferty*), Marie Burke (*Mrs. Brookfield*), Kate Roemer (*Madam Ramon*), Helen Mitchell (*Mrs. Ward*), Waldo Edwards (*Gordon Hayes*), Clyde Dilson (*Imposter*).

A group of people gather at the home of Burke to listen as Warwick, a detective, relates a story involving one of his unsolved cases. In flashback, Conroy, who later will become Warwick's fiancee, is suspected in the poisoning death of Mitchell. It seems that she committed the crime while under the hypnotic influence of Krims, a mystic who has tried to bilk Mitchell's husband, Corbett, as well. It turns out that Warwick's story is all part of a plan to expose Krims (who is attending the gathering under the guise of a count) and bring him to justice. Average for its time.

d, Edgar Lewis; w, Albert Cowles, Bert Ennis, Edward Clark (based on a story by Arthur B. Reeve); ph, Thomas Malloy, Buddy Harris, Irving Browning; ed, Martin G. Cohn.

Mystery/Crime   **(PR:A MPAA:NR)**

UNMASKED**   (1950) 60m REP bw

Robert Rockwell (*James Webster*), Barbara Fuller (*Linda Jackson*), Raymond Burr (*Roger Lewis*), Hillary Brooke (*Doris King*), Paul Harvey (*Harry Jackson*), Norman Budd (*Biggie Wolfe*), John Eldredge (*Rocco*), Emory Parnell (*Pop Swenson*), Russell Hicks (*George Richards*), Grace Gillern (*Mona*), Lester Sharpe (*Mr. Schmidt*), Charles Quigley (*Newcombe*), Barbara Pepper (*Mrs. Schmidt*), Charles Trowbridge (*Dr. Lowell*), Harry Harvey (*Saunders*).

Burr turns in an enjoyably evil performance as a scandal sheet editor who kills a lady he's been blackmailing and then finds himself in the clear when her spineless husband, framed for the crime, kills himself. But Burr's plan soon is weakened when some stolen jewelry implicates him, necessitating another murder. The efforts of the dead man's daughter, Fuller, and a hard-hitting cop, Rockwell, lead to exposure of Burr's ways.

p, Stephen Auer; d, George Blair; w, Albert DeMond, Norman S. Hall (based on a story by Manuel Seff, Paul Yawitz); ph, Ellis W. Carter; m, Stanley Wilson; ed, Robert M. Leeds; art d, Frank Hotaling; cos, Adele Palmer.

Crime Drama   **(PR:A MPAA:NR)**

UNO DEI TRE   (SEE: TWO ARE GUILTY, 1964, Fr./Ital.)

UNPUBLISHED STORY**   (1942, Brit.) 91m TC/COL bw

Richard Greene (*Bob Randall*), Valerie Hobson (*Carol Bennett*), Basil Radford (*Lamb*), Roland Culver (*Stannard*), Brefni O'Rorke (*Denton*), Miles Malleson (*Farmfield*), Andre Morell (*Marchand*), Frederick Cooper (*Trapes*), Renee Gadd (*Miss Hartley*), Henry Jorell (*Wigmore*), George Carney (*Landlord*), Muriel George (*Landlady*), Aubrey Mallalieu (*Warden*), George Thorpe (*Maj. Edwards*), Henry Morrell, Claude Bailey, Ronald Shiner, Wally Patch, D.J. Williams, Anthony Shaw, John Longden, Peter Cozens, Townsend Whitling, Tony Quinn, Edie Martin, John Ojerholm.

Greene is a war correspondent who digs up information on a Nazi group cloaked as a peace organization. He and his reporter girl friend, Hobson, nearly get killed, and he gets kidnaped, while trying to break the story. Their publisher, even after the Nazis are dealth with, refuses to publish the story.

p, Anthony Havelock-Allan; d, Harold French; w, Anatole de Grunwald, Lesley Storm, Patrick Kirwan, Sidney Gilliat (uncredited) (based on the story by Havelock-Allan, Allan Mackinnon); ph, Bernard Knowles, Cyril Knowles.

War Drama   **(PR:A MPAA:NR)**

UNRECONCILED   (SEE: NOT RECONCILED, OR "ONLY VIOLENCE HELPS WHERE IT RULES," 1969, Ger.)

UNRUHIGE NACHT   (SEE: RESTLESS NIGHT, THE, 1964, Ger.)

UNSATISFIED, THE½   (1964, Span.) 89m I.F.I.
Espana-Bellucci/Cambist bw (JUVENTUD A LA INTEMPERIE)

Rita Cadillac (*Wilma*), Colette Descombes (*Suzanne*), Maria del Sol, Angela Tamayo, Fernando Leon, Julian Mateos, Adriano Rimoldi, Luis Induni, Juan Capri, Manolo Gil, Jose Thelman.

An uneventful melodrama about a police commissioner's son who falls in love with a girl involved in a gambling scheme. While luring men into card games with a skillful cheat, she falls for a handsome playboy and informs him that her boss is a cheat, which leads to her death. Naturally, the commissioner's son is blamed, but an investigation clears his name and breaks up the ring. Opened in Spain in 1961.

p&d, Ignacio F. Iquino; w, Federico de Urrutia; ph, Ricardo Albinana; m, Enrique Escobar; ed, Juan Louis Oliver (U.S. version, Jack Curtis); art d, Manuel Infiesta.

Drama   **(PR:A MPAA:NR)**

UNSEEN, THE**½   (1945) 81m PAR bw

Joel McCrea (*David Fielding*), Gail Russell (*Elizabeth Howard*), Herbert Marshall (*Dr. Charles Evans*), Phyllis Brooks (*Maxine*), Isobel Elsom (*Marian Tygarth*), Norman Lloyd (*Jasper Goodwin*), Mikhail Rasumny (*Chester*), Elisabeth Risdon (*Mrs. Norris, Housekeeper*), Tom Tully (*Sullivan*), Nona Griffith (*Ellen Fielding*), Richard Lyon (*Barnaby Fielding*), Victoria Horne (*Lily*), Mary Field (*Miss Budge*).

A chilling murder mystery which has widower McCrea living with his two children after the mysterious death of his wife, for which he was blamed. Next door to their house is a vacant, boarded-up house which is filled with odd goings-on. When one of McCrea's maids is found murdered, his new governess begins to think that he may be a killer after all. The mystery is solved, however, and, as we all expected, McCrea is squeaky clean. Co-scripted by Raymond Chandler, THE UNSEEN is a slightly better-than-average follow-up to the superior THE UNINVITED.

p, John Houseman; d, Lewis Allen; w, Raymond Chandler, Hagar Wilde, Ken Englund (based on the novel *Her Heart in Her Throat* by Ethel Lina White); ph, John F. Seitz; m, Ernst Toch; ed, Doane Harrison; art d, Hans Dreier, Earl Hedrick; set d, George Sawley.

Mystery   **(PR:A MPAA:NR)**

UNSEEN, THE*   (1981) 89m Triune/World Northal c

Barbara Bach (*Jennifer*), Sydney Lassick (*Ernest Keller*), Stephen Furst (*Junior*), Lelia Goldoni (*Virginia Keller*), Karen Lamm (*Karen*), Doug Barr (*Tony*), Lois Young (*Vicki*).

A vile and perverse horror film which is of minor interest because of its treatment of the taboo subject of incest. Bach is a news reporter who, with her two female companions, gets stuck staying overnight in an eerie mansion owned by Lassick. Bach's part, as poor as it is (as usual, she must have been hired for her exotic looks), is negligible, included just to have a screaming woman that the audience is supposed to identify with. The film takes a tasteless (but disturbingly compelling) turn as it concentrates on the maliciousness of Lassick, who beats the moronic, oversized child he hides in the basement–a mutant offspring from an incestuous act with his sister. The son kills off Bach's companions in grisly fashion, but still remains sympathetic in relation to his even more disgusting father. One wonders, however, if any of this was intentional. Stephen Furst (of NATIONAL LAMPOON'S ANIMAL HOUSE) dons a fine makeup job in his role as "Junior." For the most part, this picture, as the title implies, should remain unseen by all but the most ardent horror fans.

p, Anthony Unger, Don P. Behrns; d, Peter Foleg; w, Michael L. Grace; ph, Roberto Quezada, Irv Goodnoff, James Carter (Metrocolor); m, Michael J. Lewis; ed, Jonathan Braun; art d, Dena Roth; spec eff, Harry Woolman; makeup, Craig Reardon; stunts, Sonny Shields.

Horror   **(PR:O MPAA:R)**

UNSEEN ENEMY*½   (1942) 61m UNIV bw

Leo Carrillo (*Nick*), Andy Devine (*Sam*), Irene Hervey (*Gen*), Don Terry (*Bill*), Lionel Royce (*Roering*), Turhan Bey (*Ito*), Frederick Gierman (*Muller*), William Ruhl (*Callahan*), Clancy Cooper (*Davies*), Eddie Fetherston (*Badger*).

U.S. agent Devine and Canadian intelligence operative Terry are on the trail of Carrillo, who has hooked up with Axis provacateurs. These "enemies of democracy" try to come up with a crew for a Japanese ship that is docked in San Francisco. Their plan is to make a getaway from the harbor and wreak havoc on West Coast shipping. Terry helps break up this operation and also falls for Hervey, a cafe singer and the stepdaughter of Carrillo.

p, Marshall Grant; d, John Rawlins; w, Roy Chanslor, Stanley Rubin (based on an idea by George Wallace Sayre); ph, John Boyle; ed, Edward Curtiss; m/l, "Lydia" (sung by Irene Hervey).

War Drama   (PR:A MPAA:NR)

UNSEEN HEROES   (SEE: MISSILE FROM HELL, 1960, Brit.)

UNSENT LETTER, THE   (SEE: LETTER THAT WAS NEVER SENT,
                                              THE, 1962, USSR)

UNSER BOSS IST EINE DAME
        (SEE: TREASURE OF SAN GENNARO, 1968, Fr./Ital./Ger.)

UNSINKABLE MOLLY BROWN, THE***
                            (1964) 128m Marten/MGM c

Debbie Reynolds (*Molly Brown*), Harve Presnell (*Johnny Brown*), Ed Begley (*Shamus Tobin*), Jack Kruschen (*Christmas Morgan*), Hermione Baddeley (*Mrs. Grogan*), Vassili Lambrinos (*Prince Louis de Laniere*), Fred Essler (*Baron Karl Ludwig von Ettenburg*), Harvey Lembeck (*Polak*), Lauren Gilbert (*Mr. Fitzgerald*), Kathryn Card (*Mrs. Wadlington*), Hayden Rorke (*Broderick*), Harry Holcombe (*Mr. Wadlington*), Amy Douglass (*Mrs. Fitzgerald*), George Mitchell (*Monsignor Ryan*), Martita Hunt (*Grand Duchess Elise Lupovinova*), Vaughn Taylor (*Mr. Cartwright*), Anthony Eustrel (*Roberts*), Audrey Christie (*Mrs. McGraw*), Grover Dale (*Jam*), Brendan Dillon (*Murphy*), Maria Karnilova (*Daphne*), Gus Trikonis (*Joe*), Mary Ann Niles (*Dancehall Girl*), Anna Lee (*Passenger*), George Nicholson (*Hotchkiss*), C. Ramsay Hill (*Lord Simon Primdale*), Moyna MacGill (*Lady Primdale*), Pat Benedetto (*Count Feranti*), Mary Andre (*Countess Feranti*), Pat Moran (*Vicar*), Herb Vigran (*Spieler*), Eleanor Audley (*Mrs. Cartwright*).

A rambunctious and spirited effort from Reynolds as the rags-to-riches title character who saves this otherwise weakly scripted, familiar musical from the long list of forgotten pictures. Cast as a penniless tomboy orphan, Reynolds makes her move into Denver's elite by marrying Presnell (recreating his Broadway role), who shortly thereafter strikes it rich. In order to insure her acceptance in high society, Reynolds heads for Europe and makes friends with royalty, bringing them home to meet the Denverites. The admiration of a prince nearly causes her to lose Presnell so, after another trip to Europe, she returns home to her loving husband. The ship she chooses, however, is the unsinkable *Titanic*. She gains her "unsinkable" tag by surviving the iceberg smash and rescuing countless souls from the icy waters. Based on a real-life character, Reynolds' performance won her an Academy Award nomination and fervent critical acclaim. Also taking home an Oscar nomination was Daniel L. Fapp for his awesome, sometimes gaudy, cinematography. THE UNSINKABLE MOLLY BROWN, despite some negative press, became the third largest grossing picture of 1964, raking in $7.5 million. Meredith Wilson songs include: "Colorado Is My Home," "Leadville Johnny Brown (Soliloquy)" (sung by Harve Presnell), "I Ain't Down Yet," "Belly Up to the Bar Boys," "I'll Never Say No" (sung by Debbie Reynolds), "He's My Friend" (sung by Reynolds, chorus), "I've Already Started," "The Beautiful People of Denver," "I May Never Fall in Love with You," "Up Where the People Are," "Dolce Far Niente".

p, Lawrence Weingarten; d, Charles Walters; w, Helen Deutsch (based on the stage musical by Meredith Willson, Richard Morris); ph, Daniel L. Fapp (Panavision, Metrocolor); m, Willson; ed, Fredric Steinkamp; md, Robert Armbruster; art d, George W. Davis, Preston Ames; set d, Henry Grace, Hugh Hunt; cos, Morton Haack; spec eff, A. Arnold Gillespie, Robert R. Hoag, J. McMillan Johnson; ch, Peter Gennaro; makeup, William Tuttle.

Musical   **Cas.**   (PR:A MPAA:NR)

UNSTOPPABLE MAN, THE*½   (1961, Brit.) 68m Argo/Sutton bw

Cameron Mitchell (*James Kennedy*), Marius Goring (*Inspector Hazelrigg*), Harry H. Corbett (*Feist*), Lois Maxwell (*Helen Kennedy*), Denis Gilmore (*Jimmy Kennedy*), Humphrey Lestocq (*Sgt. Plummer*), Ann Sears (*Pat Delaney*), Timothy Bateson (*Rocky*), Kenneth Cope (*Benny*), Brian Rawlinson (*Moonlight Jackson*), Tony Quinn (*Casey*), Tony Doonan (*Alan*), Susan Denny (*Milly*), Jean Marlow (*May*), Edward Harvey (*Lewis*), Emrys Leyshon (*Lab Assistant*), Tony Hawes (*TV Interviewer*), Alan Edwards (*Station Constable*), John Baker (*reporter*), Liza Page (*Club Girl*), Donald Auld (*Doorman*), Graham Stewart (*Taxi Driver*).

Mitchell is a tough American businessman living in England who decides to handle his son's kidnaping without the aid of Scotland Yard. He sends the culprits twice the ransom requested, which, as Mitchell hoped, causes in-fighting among the gang members. One is killed, leaving clues to where the boy is being held. Equipped with a flame thrower (what ever happened to good old American handguns?), Mitchell storms the hideout and saves his son, while Scotland Yard captures the kidnapers.

p, John Pellatt; d, Terry Bishop; w, Bishop, Alun Falconer, Paddy Manning O'Brien (based on the novel *Amateur in Violence* by Michael Francis Gilbert); ph, Arthur Grant; m, Bill McGuffie; ed, Anthony Gibbs; art d, Tony Masters.

Crime Drama   (PR:A MPAA:NR)

UNSTRAP ME*   (1968) 78m Hawk Serpent c

Walter Gutman (*Uncle Bojo Wurlitzer*), George Segal (*Himself*), Janine Soderhjelm, Donna Kerness, Lucinda Love, Frank Meyer, Dorian West, Hanne Weaver, Corky Cristians, Floraine Connors, Doris Zeitlen, Iris Holtzman, Francis Leibowitz, Helen Segal, Hope Morris, Lucien Boujema, Lea Bobey, Inga Nyrod.

Underground filmmaker George Kuchar delivers this weakly structured and ponderous look at a 65-year-old man who decides to start living. He leaves the Big Apple behind and has affairs with some younger women while traveling around the country. He even manages to stop in on sculptor George Segal as well as to pay a visit to Ringling Brothers, deserted circus headquarters. Filled with optical effects, the 16mm UNSTRAP ME, like many of Kuchar's films, is of interest mainly to film students taking optical printing classes.

p, Hawk Serpent; d&w, George Kuchar (based on the story "The Trip to Chicago" by Walter Gutman); m, Michael Snow, Bob Cowan cos, Hope Morris; m/l, "The End of the World," Dorian West.

Drama   (PR:O MPAA:NR)

UNSUITABLE JOB FOR A WOMAN, AN***   (1982, Brit.) 94m
                                              Boyd's/Goldcrest c

Billie Whitelaw, Paul Freeman, Pippa Guard, Dominic Guard, Elizabeth Spriggs, David Horovitch, Dawn Archibald, Bernadette Short, James Gilbey, Kelda Holmes, Margaret Wade, Alex Guard.

A gripping murder mystery about the suicide of a tycoon's son who is found hanging in a well. The female private investigator–hence the title–becomes increasingly engrossed in the case, living in the dead boy's quarters, nearly hanging herself while examining the well, and even making love to the boy's father. Her snooping points to the fact that the boy was actually killed, implicating the least suspect of the characters. Aptly directed by Petit, whose camera never seems to be in a rush to photograph a scene–always lingering on the subject a little longer than necessary, which adds an offbeat atmosphere to the film. It includes a fine score by British pop musician Chas Jankel.

p, Michael Relph, Peter McKay; d, Christopher Petit; w, Elizabeth McKay, Brian Scobie, Petit (based on the novel by P.D. James); ph, Martin Schafer (Gevacolor); m, Chas Jankel; ed, Mick Audsley; prod d, Anton Furst; art d, John Beard.

Mystery   **Cas.**   (PR:CO MPAA:NR)

UNSUSPECTED, THE**½   (1947) 103m Michael Curtiz/WB bw

Joan Caulfield (*Matilda Frazier*), Claude Rains (*Alexander Grandison*), Audrey Totter (*Althea Keane*), Constance Bennett (*Jane Moynihan*), Hurd Hatfield (*Oliver Keane*), Michael North (*Steven Francis Howard*), Fred Clark (*Richard Donovan*), Harry Lewis (*Max*), Jack Lambert (*Mr. Press*), Ray Walker (*Donovan's Assistant*), Nana Bryant (*Mrs. White*), Walter Baldwin (*Justice of the Peace*), Barbara Woodell (*Roslyn*), Douglas Kennedy (*Bill*), Ross Ford (*Irving*), Art Gilmore (*Announcer*), Lucile Vance (*Frizzy Haired Woman*), David Leonard (*Dr. Edelman*), Cecil Stewart (*At the Piano Player*), Faith Kruger, Bunty Cutler (*Women*), George Meader (*Fritz*), Bob Alden (*Messenger*), Dick Walsh, Ross Ford, Ray Montgomery (*Reporters*), Ed Parks (*Waiter*), Eleanor Counts (*Bride*), Alan Ray (*Groom*), Jean Andren (*Mother of the Bride*), Hal Craig, Jack Cheatham (*Policemen*), Joleen King (*Maid*), Harriet Matthews (*Mannish Woman*), Martha Crawford, Wendy Lee (*Guests*), George Eldredge, Rory Mallison.

Rains turns in a compelling performance as a deranged radio personality who hosts a murder mystery show in which he recreates the crimes with startling reality. It's not surprising that his show is so successful once we learn that he actually is a murderer. Rains kills one of his female employees, but this "perfect murder" is endangered by the presence of North, who wants to avenge his fiancee's death. He pulls Rains' niece Caulfield into the picture by attempting to convince her that he is her long-lost husband. Rains tries to poison Caulfield, but is exposed as the killer that he is and receives just punishment. The stylish *film noir* atmosphere created by director Curtiz owed much to Bredell's stunning camerawork. Jack Meredyth Lucas also made an important contribution as the dialog director.

p, Charles Hoffman; d, Michael Curtiz; w, Ranald MacDougall, Bess Meredyth (based on novel by Charlotte Armstrong); ph, Woody Bredell; m, Franz Waxman; ed, Frederick Richards; md, Leo F. Forbstein; art d, Anton Grot; set d, Howard Winterbottom; cos, Milo Anderson; spec eff, David C. Kertesz, Harry Barndollar, Robert Burks; makeup, Perc Westmore.

Crime Drama   (PR:A MPAA:NR)

UNTAMED**½   (1955) 111m FOX c

Tyrone Power (*Paul Van Riebeck*), Susan Hayward (*Katie O'Neill*), Richard Egan (*Kurt Hout*), John Justin (*Shawn Kildare*), Agnes Moorehead (*Aggie*), Rita Moreno (*Julia*), Hope Emerson (*Maria De Groot*), Brad Dexter (*Christian*), Henry O'Neill (*Squire O'Neill*), Paul Thompson (*Tschaka*), Alexander D. Havemann (*Jan*), Louis Mercier (*Joubert*), Emmett Smith (*Jantsie*), Jack Macy (*Simon*), Trude Wyler (*Mme. Joubert*), Louis Polliman

Brown (Bani), Edward Mundy (Grandfather Joubert), Catherine Pasques (Miss Joubert), Christian Pasques (Young Joubert), John Dodsworth (Capt. Richard Eaton), Robert Adler (York), Alberto Morin (Driver--Bree Street), Philip Van Zandt (Schuman), Kevin Corcoran (Young Paul), Eleanor Audley (Lady Vernon), John Carlyle (Cornelius), Cecil Weston, Anne Cornwall, Myra Cunard (Women), Forest Burns (Commando), Leonard Casey (Hansen), Alan Maraton (English Sailor), Nya Van Horn, Robin Hughes (Couple at Irish Ball), Linda Lowell, Tina Thompson, Gary Diamond, Bobby Diamond, Brian Corcoran (Maria's Children), Kim Dibbs, Michael Ross (Outlaws), Charles Evans (Sir George Gray).

Dubbed by many as an African version of GONE WITH THE WIND, this epic adventure-romance opens in the Irish countryside. Power is a South African Boer leader who has come to County Limerick to buy some horses. There he meets Hayward, but any romantic hopes between the two are short-lived as Power must return to South Africa to help fight in the Dutch Free State movement. Hayward eventually marries Justin, though she continues to harbor feelings for Power. When the potato famine sweeps Ireland, the now pregnant Hayward insists the couple emigrate to South Africa. They take along Moorehead, a servant, and Hayward ends up having her baby on board the ship. Arriving in Capetown, the small party is greeted by Emerson, who happily goes out of her way to help them. They join up with a wagon train heading into the African interior, and Hayward captures the attentions of Egan, leader of the outriders. Egan's mistress Moreno grows jealous, and begins harboring ill feelings towards Hayward. Without warning, Zulu natives stage a raid on the wagon train but this is stopped when Power and his men unexpectedly come to the rescue. Justin is killed in the fighting, and Power's interest in Hayward is renewed. Egan, who turns out to be a long-time friend of Power's, makes his own intentions perfectly clear. The homesteaders finally reach the Hoffen Valley under Power's watchful eye, and there they celebrate the end of the journey. Hayward makes a pass at Power, which incurs Egan's wrath. He attacks Power with his bullwhip, but Power is able to defend himself in the vicious brawl that follows. After beating Egan, Power settles in with Hayward, though this soon comes to an end. He cannot turn his back on the Dutch cause and finally leaves, unaware that Hayward is pregnant with his child. Hayward is angered by this, and has Power's old friend and rival become the foreman for her homestead. Egan continues to pursue Hayward, though she resists his advances. A violent storm destroys her home and Egan is badly injured. Hayward gives birth a second time, then cons local natives out of gold and raw diamonds. She returns to Capetown with these valuable minerals, and there achieves financial independence. Once more she runs into Power, and the romance continues. Power learns about the baby, and demands to know why he was never told about the birth. This leads to a bitter argument between the two, and again Power leaves. Hayward runs into some money problems, so she goes to the diamond fields in hopes of gaining more capital. There she is captured by bandits led by Egan, who have taken over the area. Power rides in with his men and kills his rival in an ambush. After bringing the Zulus under control, Power's dream of a Dutch Free State has finally come to fruition. Now he is ready to settle down with Hayward, and they return to the Hoffen Valley to begin their life together. The studio advertised this as being "Africolossal," though it's really not much more than an entertaining romance blown up with CinemaScope. Power and Hayward, as the South African Rhett and Scarlett, play well off one another, though clearly their talents deserved better material. The script is packed with contrivances and unbelievable coincidences that could only be swallowed with a healthy suspension of disbelief. On the other hand, the Zulu action sequences have some real excitement, and the scenery is lusciously photographed with effective use of the CinemaScope process. Rather than film on location, a 40- member crew was sent to Africa to shoot footage later used in Hollywood studios on a rear-screen projector. Locations were also re-created on set, and the results were indistinguishable from real life. At one point, some 3,000 Zulu natives were needed on an African location in the Natal province. Using both planes and oxcarts, the needed extras were shipped in and the production team had a small town constructed for them. This hamlet was dubbed "Zanuck-ville" in honor of famed producer Darryl F. Zanuck. Reportedly, King cared little for the novel the film was based on, and considered the first version of the script to be just as bad as the source material. Casting of the leads was incomplete when the production began, and King toyed with the idea of having Robert Mitchum play Paul Van Riebeck. He did some shooting using a Mitchum double silhouetted against the sun, but Zanuck, upon seeing this footage, wired King: "Don't get too close on your double. I haven't signed the contract yet." Eventually Power was cast, fulfilling the last required picture in his 19-year contract with the studio. Victor Mature was intended as his rival, though the role eventually went to Egan. As is usually the case, Hayward also beat out a number of contenders for her part, including Eleanor Parker, Joan Crawford, Lana Turner, and Jane Wyman. This was the fourth time she was to work with King, and the second film in which she costarred with Power. For some inexplicable reason, the studio held UNTAMED's world premiere in Miami, Florida. Hayward was presented with a key to the city, and the festivities were faithfully recorded by the newsreel cameras of Fox-Movietone News.

p, Bert E. Friedlob; d, Henry King; w, Talbot Jennings, Frank Fenton, Bacher, Michael Blankfort (based on the novel by Helga Moray); ph, Leo Tover (CinemaScope, DeLuxe Color); m, Franz Waxman; ed, Barbara McLean; art d, Lyle Wheeler, Addison Hehr; set d, Walter M. Scott,

Chet Bayhi; cos, Renie; spec eff, Ray Kellogg; ch, Stephen Papich; makeup, Ben Nye.

Drama/Romantic Epic   **(PR:C-O   MPAA:NR)**

UNTAMED½**   (1940) 83m PAR c

Ray Milland (Dr. William Crawford), Patricia Morison (Alverna Easter), Akim Tamiroff (Joe Easter), William Frawley (Les Woodbury), Jane Darwell (Mrs. Maggie Moriarty), Esther Dale (Mrs. Smith), J.M. Kerrigan (Angus McGavity), Eily Malyon (Mrs. Sarah McGavity), Fay Helm (Miss Olcott), Clem Bevans (Smokey Moseby), Sibyl Harris (Mrs. Dillon), Roscoe Ates (Bert Dillon), J. Farrell MacDonald (Dr. Billar), Gertrude W. Hoffman (Miss Rhine), Charles Waldron (Dr. Hughes), Darryl Hickman (Mickey Moriarty), Charlene Wyatt (Milly Dee), Babe Denetdeel (Skoodum), Donna Jean Lester (Judy), Byron Foulger (Nels), Helen Brown (Mrs. Jarvis), Guy Wilkerson (Sim Jarvis), Susan Paley, Marion Martin (Girls), Charles Stevens (Indian Trapper), Brenda Fowler (Chief Nurse), Hazel Keener (Nurse in Apartment), Ann Doran, Pauline Haddon, Dorothy Adams (Nurses), Betty Ross Clarke (Mother), Wilfred Roberts (Intern).

Standard love-triangle cliches abound in this picture set in Canada. Milland stars as a visiting doctor who steals Morison away from her husband, Tamiroff. An epidemic strikes the snow-assaulted country and Milland takes Morison with him on a treacherous mission to obtain some much-needed medicine. They become stranded and Tamiroff comes by dogsled to rescue them. When Tamiroff freezes to death later in the picture, Milland and Morison are free to carry on their romance.

p, Paul Jones; d, George Archainbaud; w, Frederick Hazlitt Brennan, Frank Butler (based on the novel Mantrap by Sinclair Lewis); ph, Leo Tover, W. Howard Greene (Technicolor); M. Victor Young; ed, Stuart Gilmore; art d, Hans Dreier, William Flannery.

Adventure/Romance   **(PR:A   MPAA:NR)**

UNTAMED**   (1929) 88m MGM bw

Joan Crawford (Bingo), Robert Montgomery (Andy), Ernest Torrence (Ben Murchison), Holmes Herbert (Howard Presley), John Miljan (Bennock), Gwen Lee (Marjory), Edward Nugent (Paul), Don Terry (Gregg), Gertrude Astor (Mrs. Mason), Milton Fahrney (Jollop), Lloyd Ingraham (Dowling), Grace Cunard (Billie), Wilson Benge (Bilcombe).

Crawford made the change from silents to sound with this movie and she was the best thing about it, which is not saying much. Crawford plays an oil heiress to millions. She's been living in the interior since she was a little child and has no idea of what life is like in the big city. The money has been left to her but will be overseen by her late father's associates, Torrence and Herbert, a pair of tough old birds. They think that their charge is a diamond who needs buffing so they take her north to New York where she can acquire the sophistication that she'll need to go along with her new wealth. They are taking a liner and Crawford meets and falls for Montgomery, a handsome young man who has everything to recommend him as a prospective husband for Crawford, with the possible exception of the fact that he'd have to borrow money from a churchmouse to make ends meet. The two are madly in love but Montgomery is a proud man and the moment he finds out that Crawford is rich, he backs away because he does not want to live on her money. That's just fine with Torrence and Herbert as they are not thrilled with Montgomery and have been trying to break up the duo anyhow. In New York, the untamed Crawford is a fish out of water. She won't tolerate any nonsense and uses her fists to make the point. This kind of untrammeled behavior raises eyebrows in polite society, but the fact that she is so rich mitigates any disapproval. Crawford makes no bones about her love for Montgomery but he tries to fend her off, hoping that he will eventually make it on his own so he can ask for her hand. When that doesn't seem to be happening, he thinks he has to jettison Crawford entirely and this he does by running off with Lee. The moment Crawford finds out about this, she is suddenly a primal creature again and retaliates by shooting Montgomery. It's just a flesh wound in the arm but it proves to Montgomery how much Crawford loves him and to what lengths she will go. Herbert and Torrence cease attempting to break up the couple and Montgomery is offered a position with the oil company and tosses aside the pride that wenteth before his fall and he and Crawford will be married. Crawford sings "Chant of the Jungle"(Nacio Herb Brown, Arthur Freed) and the film also includes the number "That Wonderful Something Is Love" (Joe Goodwin, Louis Alter).

d, Jack Conway; w, Willard Mack, Sylvia Thalberg, Frank Butler (based on a story by Charles E. Scoggins); ph, Oliver Marsh; ed, William Gray, Charles Hockberg; art d, Cedric Gibbons, Van Nest Polglase; cos, Adrian; titles, Lucile Newmark.

Musical/Romance   **(PR:A-C   MPAA:NR)**

UNTAMED BREED, THE*½   (1948) 79m COL c

Sonny Tufts (Tom Kilpatrick), Barbara Britton (Cherry Lucas), George "Gabby" Hayes (Windy Lucas), Edgar Buchanan (John Rambeau), William Bishop (Larch Keegan), George E. Stone (Pablo), Joe Sawyer (Hoy Keegan), Gordon Jones (Happy Keegan), James Kirkwood (Sheriff), Harry Tyler

(*Elisha Jones*), Virginia Brissac (*Mrs. Jones*), Reed Howes (*Oklahoma*).

Tufts is awkwardly miscast in this ineffective western as a rancher who comes up with the bright idea of having his Brahma bull breed with Texas cattle in the hope of improving the strain. No such luck, however, as the bull goes on a rampage and destroys some neighboring ranches. Despite this scenario, there is little excitement to be found in this one.

p, Harry Joe Brown; d, Charles Lamont; w, Tom Reed (based on a story by Eli Colter); ph, Charles Lawton, Jr. (Cinecolor); ed, Jerome Thoms; md, M.W. Stoloff; art d, George Brooks.

Western   **(PR:A MPAA:NR)**

UNTAMED FRONTIER*½   (1952) 75m UNIV c

Joseph Cotten (*Kirk Denbow*), Shelley Winters (*Jane Stevens*), Scott Brady (*Glenn Denbow*), Suzan Ball (*Lottie*), Minor Watson (*Matt Denbow*), Katherine Emery (*Camilla Denbow*), Antonio Moreno (*Bandera*), Douglas Spencer (*Clayton Vance*), John Alexander (*Max Wickersham*), Lee Van Cleef (*Dave Chittun*), Richard Garland (*Charlie Fentress*), Robert Anderson (*Ezra McCloud*), Fess Parker (*Clem McCloud*), Ray Bennett (*Sheriff Brogan*).

A below-average, conventional western starring Cotten as the nephew of crippled cattle-tycoon Watson. When Watson refuses to let settlers travel across his property, tensions flare and Cotten finds himself in the middle of the conflict. He also finds himself in love with Winters, who has been tricked into marrying Watson's son, Brady, after witnessing him kill a man. Since she is his wife, she cannot take the stand against him. She is soon his widow, however, when he is killed rustling cattle. Next, Winters is without a father-in-law as Watson gets offed by angry homesteaders who take the law into their own hands. A decent cast with a thoroughly uninteresting script. Sources conflict on the role of Bandera: some credit Moreno; others credit Jose Torvay.

p, Leonard Goldstein; d, Hugo Fregonese; w, Gerald Drayson Adams, John Bagni, Gwen Bagni, Polly James (based on a story by Houston Branch, Eugenia Night); ph, Charles P. Boyle (Technicolor); m, Hans J. Salter; ed, Virgil Vogel; art d, Bernard Herzbrun, Nathan Juran; set d, Russell A. Gausman, Ruby R. Levitt; cos, Bill Thomas.

Western   **(PR:A MPAA:NR)**

UNTAMED FURY**   (1947) 65m Danches Bros./PRC bw

Gaylord [Steve] Pendleton (*Jeff Owen*), Mikel Conrad (*Gator-Bait Kirk*), Leigh Whipper (*Uncle Gabe*), Mary Conwell (*Judie Kirk*), Althea Murphy (*Patricia Wayburn*), Jack Rutherford (*Sam Kirk*), Charles Keane (*Crane Owen*), Rodman Bruce (*Lige*), Paul Savage (*Swamper*), E. G. Marshall (*Pompano*), Norman MacKay (*John Bradbury*).

Against the background of the Okefenokee swamp, UNTAMED FURY centers on the relationship between two childhood friends–Pendleton and Conrad–who've grown up to become two very different people. While Conrad stays in the swamp, Pendleton goes on to college and graduates as an engineer. Pendleton returns to his hometown in the hope of modernizing the area, against the protests of Conrad, who strongly resists any change. By the finale, however, Conrad accepts Pendleton's new ideas. Colored with some nice locations and tense underwater alligator sequences.

p&d, Ewing Scott; w, Taylor Caven, Paul Gerard Smith (based on the story "Gator Bait" by Scott); ph, Ernest Miller; m, Alexander Laszlo; ed, Robert Crandall; md, Laszlo.

Drama   **(PR:A MPAA:NR)**

UNTAMED HEIRESS*   (1954) 70m REP bw

Judy Canova (*Judy*), Donald Barry (*Spider Mike*), George Cleveland (*Andrew "Cactus" Clayton*), Taylor Holmes (*Walter Martin*), Chick Chandler (*Eddie Taylor*), Jack Kruschen (*Louie*), Hugh Sanders (*Williams*), Douglas Fowley (*Pal*), William Haade (*Friend*), Ellen Corby (*Mrs. Flanny*), Richard [Dick] Wessel (*Cruncher*), James Flavin (*Cop*), Tweeny Canova (*Tweeny*).

Chiefly a vehicle for J. Canova's singing, UNTAMED HEIRESS tells a muddled tale about a gold prospector, Cleveland, who once loved Canova's opera star mother. He hires a couple of private eyes to find his former sweetheart, who unknown to him has passed away, but all they can come up with is Canova. In the meantime, Canova gets mixed up with some gangsters who help her get Cleveland out of the clutches of the malicious Sanders. All this in only 70 minutes–plus the following songs: "A Dream for Sale" (Jack Elliott, Donald Kahn), "Sugar Daddy" (Elliott), "Welcome" (all sung by Judy Canova).

p, Sidney Picker, Herbert J. Yates; d, Charles Lamont; w, Barry Shipman (based on a story by Jack Townley); ph, Reggie Lanning; m, Stanley Wilson; ed, Arthur Roberts; art d, Frank Arrigo; cos, Adele Palmer; spec eff, Howard Lydecker, Theodore Lydecker.

Musical/Comedy   **(PR:A MPAA:NR)**

UNTAMED MISTRESS zero   (1960) 78m Brenner bw

Allan Nixon, Jacqueline Fontaine.

A *menage-a-trois* of sorts composes the story of this strange and wholly forgettable nonsense. Fontaine must choose between two would-be beaus: the handsome Nixon or an ape. Some girls have all the luck! The advertising campaign warned audiences the film would "shock Dr. Kinsey!" but the only shock the good doctor might get from this would be if he had trouble plugging in the projector.

p,d&w, Ron Ormand.

Horror   **(PR:O MPAA:NR)**

UNTAMED WEST, THE   (SEE: FAR HORIZONS, THE, 1955)

UNTAMED WOMEN zero   (1952) 70m Jewell Enterprise/UA bw

Mikel Conrad (*Steve*), Doris Merrick (*Sandra*), Richard Monahan (*Benny*), Mark Lowell (*Ed*), Morgan Jones (*Andy*), Midge Ware (*Myra*), Judy Brubaker (*Valdra*), Carol Brewster (*Tannus*), Autumn Rice (*Cleo*), Lyle Talbot (*Col. Loring*), Montgomery Pittman (*Prof. Warren*), Miriam Kaylor (*Nurse Edmunds*).

On an invisible budget and with less than a week's worth of production, UNTAMED WOMEN looks just like what you would expect. Conrad is shipwrecked on an uncharted island (one would think that someone would have gone out and charted these islands by now) which is inhabited by barely dressed women, refugee dinosaurs from ONE MILLION B.C. (compliments of the film library), and "hairmen." It's all told in flashback by the rescued Conrad from his hospital bed.

p, Richard Kay; d, W. Merle Connell; w, George W. Sayre; ph, Glen Gano; m, Raoul Kraushaar; ed, William O'Connell; art d, Paul Sprunck; set d, James R. Connell; spec eff, Sprunk, Alfred Schmid.

Science Fiction   **Cas.**   **(PR:A MPAA:NR)**

UNTAMED YOUTH*   (1957) 80m Devonshire/WB bw

Mamie Van Doren (*Penny*), Lori Nelson (*Janey*), John Russell (*Tropp*), Don Burnett (*Bob*), Eddie Cochran (*Bong*), Lurene Tuttle (*Mrs. Steele*), Yvonne Lime (*Baby*), Jeanne Carmen (*Lillibet*), Robert Foulk (*Mitch*), Wayne Taylor (*Duke*), Jerry Barclay (*Ralph*), Keith Richards (*Angelo*), Valerie Reynolds (*Arkie*), Lucita (*Margarita*), Glenn Dixon (*Landis*), Wally Brown (*Pinky*), The Hollywood Rock and Rollers.

A rock 'n' roll prison farm where all the inmates dance to the 1950s teen beat. Van Doren and Nelson are a shapely pair who get tossed in the slammer for 30 days after being caught hitchhiking (they probably should have gotten the chair, the lousy vagrants). It turns out that the prison farm is a front for Russell's cotton-picking operation. When one girl is over-worked, has a miscarriage, and dies, trouble comes along and dances the twist on Russell's illegitimate scheme. Why does Eddie Cochran, one of the 1950s' top rockers, only get to sing one song? He delivers "Cottonpicker" (Les Baxter), while Van Doren (not one of the 1950s' top rockers) belts out "Salamander," "Go, Go, Calypso" (Baxter), "Rolling Stone" (Baxter, Lenny Adelson), and "Oobala Baby" (Baxter, Adelson, Eddie Cochran, Jerry Capehart).

p, Aubrey Schenck; d, Howard W. Koch; w, John C. Higgins (based on a story by Stephen Longstreet); ph, Carl Guthrie; m, Les Baxter; ed, John F. Schreyer; art d, Art Loel.

Musical Drama   **(PR:A MPAA:NR)**

UNTER GEIER   (SEE: FRONTIER HELLCAT, 1966, Fr./Ital./Ger./Yugo.)

UNTIL THEY SAIL**½   (1957) 95m MGM bw

Jean Simmons (*Barbara Leslie Forbes*), Joan Fontaine (*Anne Leslie*), Paul Newman (*Capt. Jack Harding*), Piper Laurie (*Delia Leslie*), Charles Drake (*Capt. Richard Bates*), Sandra Dee (*Evelyn Leslie*), Wally Cassell (*"Shiner" Phil Friskett*), Alan Napier (*Prosecution*), Ralph Votrian (*Max Murphy*), John Wilder (*Tommy*), Adam Kennedy (*Lt. Andy*), Patrick MacNee (*Pvt. Duff*), Ben Wright (*Defense*), Kendrick Huxham (*Justice*), James Todd (*Consul*), David Thursby (*Trainman*), Hilda Plowright (*Woman*), Dean Jones (*Marine Lieutenant*), Robert Keys (*Maj. Campbell*), Ann Wakefield (*Mrs. Campbell*), Vesey O'Davoren (*Minister*), Pat O'Hara (*Police Inspector*), Stanley Fraser (*Court Crier*), James Douglas (*Marine with Girl*), Tige Andrews, Mickey Shaughnessy, Nicky Blair, Morgan Jones, Pat Waltz, William Boyett, Jimmy Hayes, Pat Colby, Dan Eitner, Tom Mayton, Roger McGee, John Rosser, Jim Cox (*Marines*), Alma Lauton, Dee Humphrey, Dorris Riter, Pamela Light, Phyllis Douglas (*New Zealand Girls*).

A four-way love story based on a Michener book serves as the plot for this soap opera set in New Zealand during WW II. There is a quartet of New Zealand sisters, each with her own problem. Most of the local men have gone off to war so when a horde of fun- loving American soldiers descend on the city of Christchurch, it throws the local female citizenry for a loop. Fontaine is the spinster sister, a woman who hides her emotions and keeps men at arm's length until she meets Drake, a captain, and falls hard and fast for him. He is slain in action and she is left with a living memory inside her, a child he has fathered during their brief but ecstatic romance. Laurie is just as fun-loving as the Americans and perhaps even more passionate. With no parents to guide her (they've died and her sole brother was killed in service), she gives vent to her emotions and marries sleazeball Cassell, who then goes off to fight. The youngest sister is Dee, who watches the problems of her older sisters and waits patiently for her love to come home from the service. Simmons is the main story. She's a widow with a good head on her shoulders and a happy memory of the life she shared with her husband, who was also a victim of the Japanese. Newman's job as Marine captain is to check on the soldiers' requests to marry the local women. He is divorced, stiff, and somewhat of a drinker until he meets and falls for Simmons. While Cassell is gone, Laurie becomes an insatiable nymphomaniac. Cassell returns, sees what's gone on, and kills her, while Dee's childhood sweetheart returns unscathed. Good love scenes between Newman and Simmons contributed strongly to his becoming a matinee idol when this picture was released. While all the women were good in their roles, it's doubtful that the real New Zealand women would have enjoyed being portrayed as so love-starved that they fell easy prey to the dashing Americans. It was Newman's fifth film and his second with director Wise, who had also helmed the excellent SOMEBODY UP THERE LIKES ME.

p, Charles Schnee; d, Robert Wise; w, Robert Anderson (based on a story by James A. Michener); ph, Joseph Ruttenberg (CinemaScope); m, David Raksin; ed, Harold F. Kress; art d, William A. Horning, Paul Groesse; m/l, "Until They Sail," Raksin, Sammy Cahn (sung by Eydie Gorme).

War Drama   (PR:C   MPAA:NR)

UNTITLED   (SEE: HEAD, 1968)

UNTOUCHABLES, THE   (SEE: SCARFACE MOB, THE, 1962)

UNTOUCHED*½   (1956) 85m Excelsior bw

Ricardo Montalban, Ariadna Welter, Victor Parra.

Tepid action-adventure drama dubbed into English follows Montalban and company into the dense jungles of Vera Cruz as they search for the wonder drug cortisone. Unfortunately, this exploration into a cure for rheumatoid arthritis and gout is less than engrossing.

p, Walter Bibo; w, Roberto Gavaldon, Luis Alcoriza (based on the novel *Green Shadow* by Ramiro Torres Septien).

Drama   (PR:A   MPAA:NR)

UNVANQUISHED, THE   (SEE: APARAJITO, 1959, India)

UNWED MOTHER*   (1958) 74m AA bw

Norma Moore (Betty Miller), Robert Vaughn (Don Bigelow), Diana Darrin (Mousie), Billie Bird (Gertie), Jeanne Cooper (Mrs. Horton), Ron Hargrave (Ben), Kathleen Hughes (Linda), Sam Buffington (Mr. Paully), Claire Carleton (Mrs. Miller), Collette Jackson (Louella), Ken Lynch (Ray Curtis), Dorothy Adams (Mrs. Paully), Ralph Gamble (Minister), Timothy Carey (Doctor).

A thoroughly unbelievable mega-melodrama about, you guessed it, an unwed mother. Moore is a country gal recently arrived in Los Angeles who finds herself in a family way thanks to the scoundrel Vaughn. He promises to marry her but doesn't follow through. Moore decides to give her baby up for adoption but after giving birth, tries to get the kid back, chasing down the foster parents in her car. Not surprisingly UNWED MOTHER is a product of the director of TV's "Peyton Place," Doniger.

p, Joseph Justman; d, Walter A. Doniger; w, Anson Bond, Alden Nash (based on a story by Bond); ph, Lothrop Worth; m, Emil Newman; ed, Lou Moss, Neil Brunnenkant; art d, David Milton; m/l, "Unwed Mother," Ron Hargrave, Hal Brandle (sung by Hargrave).

Drama   (PR:C-O   MPAA:NR)

UNWELCOME STRANGER*   (1935) 64m COL bw

Jack Holt (Howard Chamberlain), Mona Barrie (Madeline Chamberlain), Jackie Searl (Gimpy), Ralph Morgan (Mike), Bradley Page (Lucky Palmer), Frankie Darro (Charlie Anderson), Sam McDaniel (Pot Roast), Frank Orth (Jackson).

A harmless racetrack picture which casts Holt as a horse owner suspicious of orphans--ponies and people alike--since he himself was raised in an orphanage. The young Searl approaches Holt with the hope of getting involved in racing. Holt takes him in and grows quite fond of him . . . then he discovers that the boy is an orphan. He's too attached to the boy, however, to turn him away and gives in to Searl's desire to jockey a horse. Searl takes first place and Holt's superstition is broken.

d, Phil Rosen; w, Crane Wilbur (based on a story by William Jacobs); ph, John Stumar; ed, Arthur Hilton.

Drama   (PR:A   MPAA:NR)

UNWELCOME VISITORS   (SEE: LONE STAR PIONEERS, 1939)

UNWILLING AGENT*   (1968, Ger.) 95m

Filmaufbau-I.F.C.-Bavaria-Filmkunst/United Film Enterprises bw
(MENSCHEN IM NETZ)

Hansjorg Felmy (Klaus Martens), Johanna von Koczian (Gitta Martens), Hannes Messemer (Braun), Ingeborg Schoner, Rosl Schafer, Olga von Togni, Max Mairich, Hanns Lothar, Peter Luhr, Alexander Hunzinger, Paul Verhoeven, Helmut Brasch, Ettore Cella, Gernot Duda, Klaus Havenstein, Gerhard Just, Rolf Kralowitz, Franziska Liebing, Anton Reimer, Willy Semmelrogge.

Originally released in West Germany in 1959, this espionage thriller has a West German prisoner released from prison after serving only a portion of his sentence. He learns that his wife collaborated with an East German spy ring in order to secure his release. She is later killed by the spies, causing her husband to take matters into his own hands. He is aided by a police commissioner who succeeds in smashing the ring.

d, Franz Peter Wirth; w, Herbert Reinecker (based on newspaper reports by Will Tremper and the book by Erich Kern), ph, Gunter Senftleben; m, Hans-Martin Majewski; ed, Claus von Boro; art d, Franz Bi, Max Seefelder; cos, Ilse Dubois; makeup, Max Rauffer, Gertrud Weinz-Werner.

Spy Drama   (PR:A   MPAA:NR)

UNWRITTEN CODE, THE*   (1944) 61m COL bw

Ann Savage (Mary Lee Norris), Tom Neal (Sgt. Terry Hunter), Roland Varno (Cpl. Karl Richter), Howard Freeman (Mr. Norris), Mary Currier (Mrs. Norris), Bobby Larson (Willie Norris), Teddy Infuhr (Dutchy Schultz), Otto Reichow (Heinrich Krause), Fred Essler (Schultz), Frederick Giermann (Luedtke), Tom Holland (Kunze), Phil Van Zandt (Ulrich), Carl Ekberg (Schroeder), Alan [Al] Bridge (Sheriff).

Varno is a Nazi who manages to sneak into the States by assuming the identity of a murdered British soldier. He then prepares to set free a number of Nazi prisoners but gets shot down before he can carry out his scheme. An unwritten script seems to be the problem with this ill-conceived tale.

p, Sam White; d, Herman Rotsten; w, Leslie T. White, Charles Kenyon (based on a story by Kenyon, Robert Wilmot); ph, Burnett Guffey; ed, Gene Havlick; md, Mischa Bakaleinikoff; art d, Perry Smith.

Drama   (PR:A   MPAA:NR)

UNWRITTEN LAW, THE*½   (1932) 66m Majestic bw

Greta Nissen (Fifi La Rue), Skeets Gallagher (Pete Brown), Mary Brian (Ruth Evans), Louise Fazenda (Lulu Potts), Lew Cody (Roger Morgan), Hedda Hopper (Jean), Purnell Pratt (Stephen McBain), Theodore Von Eltz (Val Lewis), Mischa Auer (Abu Eyd), Arthur Rankin (Frank Woods), Wilfred Lucas (Capt. Kane), Ernie Adams (Ed Riley), Howard Foshay (Steward), Betty Tyree (Script Girl).

A sub-standard murder mystery that has a movie producer getting offed and everyone being seen as suspects. The likely culprits include: Brian, the girl the filmmaker loves; a detective-story writer left for dead on an African location; a resentful crew member who has nearly killed him once already; and Brian's mother, who also happens to be married to the writer. On board a ship bound for the new location, the murder occurs, suspects are rounded up, an inquiry is held, and a confession is finally received. Unfortunately THE UNWRITTEN LAW follows the mystery blueprint to the letter, never offering any deviation.

d, Christy Cabanne; w, Edward T. Lowe (based on a story by John Krafft); ph, Ira Morgan; ed, Otis Garrett.

Mystery   (PR:A   MPAA:NR)

UP FOR MURDER*   (1931) 75m UNIV bw (AKA: FIRES OF YOUTH)

Lew Ayres (Robert Marshall), Genevieve Tobin (Myra Deane), Purnell B. Pratt (William Winter), Richard Tucker (Herk), Frank McHugh (Collins), Louise Beavers (Maid), Frederick Burt (City Editor), Dorothy Peterson (Mrs. Marshall), Kenneth Thompson, Betty Jane Graham, Aileen Manning.

An all-too-familiar melodrama about a young newspaper reporter, Ayres, who falls in love with society editor Tobin. She, however, is the publisher's mistress. The obligatory struggle ensues between the two men, followed by the obligatory accidental death of the publisher. Surrender, trial, and preparation for a hanging follow suit until, at the last obligatory moment, Tobin tells all and saves Ayres' life. If you can't guess how this one ends, you shouldn't be looking in this book. A remake of the 1927 silent MAN, WOMAN AND SIN.

d, Monta Bell; w, James Whitaker (based on a story by Bell); ph, Karl Freund; ed, Ted Kent.

Drama (PR:A MPAA:NR)

UP FOR THE CUP** (1931, Brit.) 76m British and Dominions/Wolfe and Freedman bw

Sydney Howard (*John Willie Entwhistle*), Joan Wyndham (*Mary Murgatroyd*), Stanley Kirk (*Cyril Hardcastle*), Sam Livesey (*John Cartwright*), Marie Wright (*Mrs. Entwhistle*), Moore Marriott (*James Hardcastle*), Hal Gordon (*Proprietor*), Herbert Woodward (*Tom*), Jack Raymond (*Railway Clerk*).

A pleasant comedy about the problematic adventures of Howard, a loom inventor who journeys to London for the FA Cup Final. Once there, he loses his wallet to thieves; then his girl friend, Wyndham, fails to turn up. By the time the final credits roll up, Howard not only has his girl, but also a contract for his invention and a large sum of cash to accompany it. Remade in 1950.

p, Herbert Wilcox; d, Jack Raymond; w, Con West, R.P. Weston, Bert Lee; ph, F.A. Young.

Comedy (PR:A MPAA:NR)

UP FOR THE CUP**½ (1950, Brit.) 76m Citadel-Byron/ABF bw

Albert Modley (*Albert Entwhistle*), Mai Bacon (*Maggie Entwhistle*), Helen Christie (*Jane*), Harold Berens (*Auctioneer*), Wallas Eaton, Jack Melford (*Barrowboys*), Charmian Innes (*Clippie*), Fred Groves (*Hardcastle*), John Warren (*Cartwright*), Arthur Gomez, Lilli Molnar.

Modley stars in this remake of the 1931 picture about a loom inventor whose wife and wallet both disappear enroute to London's Cup Final soccer match. All ends well for the likable sap before the picture concludes. Directed by Raymond, who also directed the original.

p, Henry Halstead; d, Jack Raymond; w, Con West, Jack Marks (based on a story by R.P. Weston, Bert Lee); ph, Henry Harris.

Comedy (PR:A MPAA:NR)

UP FOR THE DERBY** (1933, Brit.) 70m British & Dominions/GAU bw

Sydney Howard (*Joe Burton*), Dorothy Bartlam (*Dorothy Gordon*), Mark Daly (*Jerry Higgs*), Tom Helmore (*Ronnie Gordon*), Frederick Lloyd (*Maj. Edwards*), Frank Harvey (*George Moberley*), Franklyn Bellamy (*Palmer*).

Funny man Howard is up for more laughs in this comedy about a stable boy who buys a horse from his bankrupt boss and ends up winning the Derby with it. However, this isn't a winner-take-all situation, as the chubby comedian discovers that the girl he loves is already spoken for. It's all rather predictable, but pleasing all the same.

p, Herbert Wilcox; d, Maclean Rogers; w, R.P. Weston, Bert Lee, Jack Marks; ph, F.A. Young.

Comedy (PR:A MPAA:NR)

UP FROM THE BEACH**½ (1965) 98m Panoramic/FOX bw

Cliff Robertson (*Sgt. Edward Baxter*), Red Buttons (*Pfc. Harry Devine*), Irina Demick (*Lili Rolland*), Marius Goring (*German Commandant*), Slim Pickens (*Artillery Colonel*), James Robertson Justice (*British Beachmaster*), Broderick Crawford (*U.S. MP Major*), Georges Chamarat (*Mayor*), Francoise Rosay (*Lili's Grandmother*), Raymond Bussieres (*Dupre*), Fernand Ledoux (*Barrelmaker*), Louise Chevalier (*Marie*), Germaine Delbat (*Seamstress*), Paula Dehelly (*Widow Clarisse*), Gabriel Gobin (*Trombonist*), Charles Bouillaud (*French Horn Player*), Georges Adet (*Drummer*), Pierre Moncorbier (*Field-Keeper*), Nicole Chollet (*Post Office Clerk*), Raoul Marco (*Cobbler*), Charlotte Eizlini (*Cobbler's Wife*), Pierval (*Grocer*), Renee Gardes (*Grocer's Wife*), Paul Maxwell (*U.S. Cpl. Evans*), Ken Wayne (*U.S. Pfc. Solly*), Brian Davies (*U.S. Pfc. Dinbo*), Robert Hoffmann (*SS Captain*), Michael Munzer (*SS Sergeant*), Henri Kuhn (*SS Corporal*), Jean-Claude Berva (*Resistance Fighter*), Bibi Morat (*Picot*), Frawley Becker (*Grocer's Assistant*), Roy Stephens (*Colonel's Driver*), Jo Warfield (*Medic Driver*), Rod Calvert (*Other Medic*), Alexandre Grecq (*German Pilot*), Tracy Wynn (*Soldier in Truck*), Billy Kearns (*Colonel in Bunker*), Thomas Farnsworth (*Major in Bunker*).

On June 7, 1944, the day after the Allied invasion of Normandy, a squad of American soldiers under Robertson liberates a number of French civilians who were held hostage by the retreating Germans and captures the German commander, Goring. The soldiers receive orders to accompany the civilians to the beach, where they are to be evacuated from the battle zone to England. At the beach, however, beachmaster Justice knows nothing about any evacuation and, although sympathetic, he sends the group back to the village. Later they make the walk to the beach two more times, but each time confusion and lack of communication make their trips futile. Hungry, they are allowed to steal some army provisons while MP major Crawford generously looks the other way. The Germans begin shelling the village and the captured German, Goring, who is not a bad sort, suggests they take shelter in the vault under the church. Goring leads the way and is killed by a booby trap left behind by his own retreating troops. Eventually the bombardment lifts and Robertson and the squad join the advancing army,

the French civilians singing "The Marseillaise" to them as they march through the streets of the town. This interesting war drama concentrates not on the battles, but on the problems of civilians who awaken one day to find the war outside their doors. Good performances, especially memorable supporting turns by Justice and Crawford, and an intelligent script that rarely sinks to the obvious put this film a notch above the run of war films.

p, Christian Ferry; d, Robert Parrish; w, Stanley Mann, Claude Brule, Howard Clewes (based on the novel *Epitaph for an Enemy* by George Barr); ph, Walter Wottitz (CinemaScope); m, Edgar Cosma; ed, Samuel E. Beetley; md, Cosma; prod d, Albert Rajau; art d, Willy Holt; spec eff, Georges Iaconelli; Karl Baumgartner, Daniel Braunschweig.

War Drama (PR:A MPAA:NR)

UP FROM THE DEPTHS zero (1979, Phil.) 75m New World c

Sam Bottoms (*Greg Oliver*), Susanne Reed (*Rachel McNamara*), Virgil Frye (*Earl Sheridan*), Kedric Wolfe (*Oscar Forbes*), Charles Howerton (*David Whiting*), Denise Hayes (*Iris Lee*), Charles Doherty (*Ed*), Helen McNelly (*Louellen*).

A satire of the JAWS-type scary-creature-in-the-water picture that is dubbed in the worst possible way. Directed by former Roger Corman associate Griffith, UP FROM THE DEPTHS is occasionally funny but, more often than not, just plain bad. An underwater fish is terrorizing a seaside resort and the inhabitants take part in a contest in which they try to kill the finned pest.

p, Cirio H. Santiago; d, Charles B. Griffith; w, Alfred Sweeney; ph, Rick Remington (Metrocolor); m, Russell O'Malley; ed, G.V. Bass.

Comedy/Horror Cas. (PR:O MPAA:R)

UP FRONT*** (1951) 92m UNIV bw

David Wayne (*Joe*), Tom Ewell (*Willie*), Marina Berti (*Emi*), Jeffrey Lynn (*Capt. Ralph Johnson*), Richard Egan (*Capa*), Maurice Cavell (*Vuaglio*), Vaughn Taylor (*Maj. Lester*), Silvio Minciotti (*Peppa Rosso*), Paul Harvey (*Col. Akeley*), Roger De Koven (*Sabatelli*), Grazia Narciso (*Signora Carvadossi*), Tito Vuolo (*Tarantino*), Mickey Knox (*Driver*).

Fairly amusing WW II comedy starring Ewell and Wayne as Willie and Joe, characters created by cartoonist Bill Mauldin during the war. The film follows the pair of U.S. "dogfaces" while they battle their way through Italy. Stuck in a hopelessly undermanned infantry unit on the front, Ewell and Wayne bravely make the best of the situation until Wayne is wounded and sent to Naples to recuperate. Never missing a trick, Ewell manages to get a three-day pass and goes to the hospital to visit his buddy. His trip is hampered somewhat by noncombat MP's, who chase Ewell around Naples because he's out of uniform. Eventually, Ewell gets to the hospital to visit Wayne, and the pair soon leave to return to the front. Before they have a chance to leave Naples, however, the soldiers become involved with a beautiful Italian girl, Berti, and her father, Minciotti, who is a black marketeer. Of course, the MP's are soon after them again, and the climax sees Ewell and Wayne driving a truckload of black market goods to their buddies at the front, while a small army of MP's give chase. Silly stuff, but a lot of fun, with Ewell and Wayne turning in surprisingly good performances. A sequel, BACK AT THE FRONT, followed in 1952.

p, Leonard Goldstein; d, Alexander Hall; w, Stanley Roberts (based on the book *Up Front* by Bill Mauldin); ph, Russell Metty; m, Joseph Gershenson; ed, Milton Carruth; art d, Bernard Herzbrun, Alexander Golitzen.

War/Comedy (PR:A MPAA:NR)

UP GOES MAISIE** (1946) 89m MGM bw (GB: UP SHE GOES)

Ann Sothern (*Maisie Ravier*), George Murphy (*Joseph Morton*), Hillary Brooke (*Barbara Nuboult*), Horace [Stephen] McNally (*Tim Kingby*), Ray Collins (*Mr. Henderickson*), Jeff York (*Elmer Saunders*), Paul Harvey (*Mr. J.G. Nuboult*), Murry Alper ("*Mitch*"), Lewis Howard (*Bill Stuart*), Jack Davis (*Jonathan Marbey*), Gloria Grafton (*Miss Wolfe*), John Eldredge (*Benson*), Lee Phelps (*1st Cop*), Glenn Strange (*2nd Cop*), James Davis (*Businessman*).

Ann Sothern's series of "Maisie" films was just about out of gas in 1946, and UP GOES MAISIE opens as she retires from doing war-related work and plunges into a new and exciting career in peacetime technology. Sothern soon finds herself assisting brilliant young inventor Murphy, who is developing an important new helicopter that has an automatic pilot capability. Of course, there's a rival aircraft company out to sabotage Murphy's machine, but through Sothern's clever efforts (she rescues the helicopter from the villain's evil clutches and fies the machine to safety herself), the inventor is able to reap the rewards from his labors. Standard stuff. (See MAISIE series, Index.)

p, George Haight; d, Harry Beaumont; w, Thelma Robinson (based on the character created by Wilson Collison); ph, Robert Planck; m, David Snell; ed, Irvine Warburton; art d, Cedric Gibbons, Richard Luce; cos, Irene; spec eff, A. Arnold Gillespie.

Comedy (PR:A MPAA:NR)

UP IN ARMS**** (1944) 106m Goldwyn/RKO c

Danny Kaye (*Danny Weems*), Constance Dowling (*Mary Morgan*), Dinah Shore (*Virginia Merrill*), Dana Andrews (*Joe Nelson*), Louis Calhern (*Col. Ashley*), George Mathews (*Blackie*), Benny Baker (*Butterball*), Elisha Cook, Jr. (*Info Jones*), Lyle Talbot (*Sgt. Gelsey*), Walter Catlett (*Maj. Brock*), George Meeker (*Ashley's Aide*), Richard Powers 'Tom Keene' (*Captain, Ashley's Aide*), Margaret Dumont (*Mrs. Willoughby*), Edward Earle (*Sherwood*), Harry Hayden (*Dr. Weavermacher*), Sig Arno (*Waiter*), Oliver Blake, Larry Steers (*Board Members*), Stanley Gilbert (*Man in Lobby*), Isabel Withers, John Hamilton (*Couple*), Eddie Kane (*Wedding Guest in Dream*), Terrance Ray, Matt Willis (*Sentries in Hold*), Frosty Royce (*Bakery Man*), Al Benault (*Cop*), Donald Dickson (*Singer at Dock*), Charles Arnt (*Mr. Higginbotham*), Charles Halton (*Dr. Freyheisen*), Charles D. Brown (*Dr. Campbell*), Maurice Cass (*Dr. Jones*), Tom Dugan (*Master of Ceremonies*), Fred Essler (*Head Waiter*), Leonard Strong (*Interrogator*), Rudolph Friml, Jr. (*Bandmaster*), Betty Alexander, Gale Amber, Gloria Anderson, Jan Bryant, Alma Carroll, Joan Chaffee, Linda Christian, Virginia Cruzon, Helen Darling, Myrna Dell, Dorothy Gardner, Inna Gest, Renee Godfrey, Ellen Hall, June Harris, Eloise Hart, Mary Ann Hyde, June Lang, Rosalyn Lee, Florence Lundeen, Mickey Maloy, Virginia Mayo, Dorothy Merritt, Lorraine Miller, Mary Moore, Kay Morley, Diana Mumby, Lee Nugent, Dorothy Patrick, Shelby Payne, Helen Talbot, Ruth Valmy, Ricki Van Dusen, Alice Wallace, Virginia Wicks, Audrey Young (*The Goldwyn Girls*), William Davidson, Larry Steers, Eddie Waller, Oliver Prickett 'Blake', Maxine Armour, Bonnie Barlowe, Karen Knight, Audrey Korn, Helen McAllister, Marjorie Raymond, Joet Robinson, Eleanor Shaw, June Wayne, Barbara Williams (*Dancers*), Matt McHugh, Pete Cusanelli, Maryon Adair, Herbert Evans, Stanley Gilbert, John Hamilton, Isabel Withers, Hans Schumm, Eddie Kane, Frank O'Connor, Anne O'Neal, Virginia Farmer, Bill Hunter, George McKay, George Magrill, James Harrison, Lillian Randolph, Peter Chong, Bruce Wong, Benson Fong, George T. Lee, Knox Manning.

Samuel Goldwyn, the man who put the "G" in MGM, produced this lavish musical comedy which introduced 31-year-old vaudeville and stage star Danny Kaye to a panting movie audience. Goldwyn's faith in Kaye was justified as the blond (whose hair was originally red but was dyed for the movies) burst onto the screen and immediately became a household name. Kaye plays a confirmed hypochondriac who is so frightened of maladies that he has secured employment in a medical building as an elevator operator so that when a disease strikes, help is no more than a scream away. Kaye and his best pal, Andrews, are drafted by the Army and Kaye must reluctantly tell the woman he loves, Dowling, that the two men are going off to war. Dowling really likes Andrews and when she learns that the two guys are being inducted, she joins the WACS and her friend, Shore, joins the service as a nurse. At the moment, Shore is ga-ga about Kaye but he only has eyes for Dowling. After basic training, Kaye and Andrews are shipped off to the Far East aboard a ship. Through the intervention of fate (and the screenwriters' imaginations), Shore and Dowling, who had sneaked away from their jobs to bid the boys goodbye, are trapped on the departing ship. Shore's job as a nurse allows her to be aboard but Dowling has to be kept a stowaway because if she were to be found there would be a court-martial on several charges. Calhern is the ship's captain and Dowling is shunted from place to place on the ship to be hidden from his eagle eye. He is a martinet and keeps the soldiers on their toes and in fear of his rigid ways. After the usual switches and such, Calhern finally discovers Dowling and things look bleak. Kaye then tells the captain that he must take all the responsibility for Dowling being aboard and will accept the punishment. The boat docks and Kaye is taken to a cell on the rim of the Army base. No sooner does that happen than the Japanese attack the base and take prisoners, Kaye among them. Then, through a series of wonderfully funny escapades, Kaye manages to escape his captors and even manages to nab some of the Japanese, thereby taking the movie out of the realm of believability and into the world of fantasy. All the steam goes out of the movie at this contrived ending and they rightly conclude the picture shortly thereafter. Kaye's superb comic timing, which he perfected in the Catskill Mountains resorts and on various nightclub stages, stands him in great stead as he totally dominates the movie in every scene. Excellent choreography, superb sets, fine costumes, and a host of songs, including several by Harold Arlen and Ted Koehler: "Now I Know" (sung by Shore), "All Out for Freedom," (sung by Donald Dickson, The Goldwyn Girls, Men's Chorus), "Tess' Torch Song" (sung by Shore), "Jive Number" (sung by Kaye, Shore, The Goldwyn Girls). Kaye's wife-to-be, Sylvia Fine, and the man who produced Kaye's show on Broadway ("The Straw Hat Revue" in 1939), Max Liebman, wrote "Manic-Depressive Pictures Presents" (also known as "The Lobby Number") and "Melody in 4-F," a tune they'd originally done for Cole Porter's musical "Let's Face It" in 1941. Porter gave them permission to use it again in this film and Kaye did it brilliantly. This was Shore's second film and the ageless singer seems to have mellowed with time and looked better in 1986 (at the age of 69) than she did in 1944. Kaye had done a few short films in 1937 and 1938 with such tyros as June Allyson and Imogene Coca, then he went to Broadway in "The Straw Hat Revue," "Lady in the Dark," and "Let's Face It." After a phenomenal success at Billy Rose's Diamond Horseshoe nightclub in New York in 1943, Kaye was signed by Goldwyn for five pictures at $150,000 per movie. UP IN ARMS opened at the Radio City Music Hall and Kaye became an instant star. In later years, he would devote himself to charitable causes and represent UNICEF. Heindorf, Forbes, and the song "Now I Know" were nominated for Oscars.

p, Samuel Goldwyn; d, Elliott Nugent; w, Don Hartman, Allen Boretz, Robert Pirosh (based on the play "The Nervous Wreck" by Owen Davis); ph, Ray Rennahan (Technicolor); m, Ray Heindorf; ed, Daniel Mandell, James Newcom; md, Louis Forbes; art d, Perry Ferguson, Stewart Chaney, McClure Capps; set d, Howard Bristol; spec eff, Clarence Slifer, R.O. Binger; ch, Danny Dare; tech adv, Lt. Richard Day, Lt. Eunice C. Hatchitt.

Musical/Comedy (PR:AA MPAA:NR)

UP IN CENTRAL PARK** (1948) 88m UNIV bw

Deanna Durbin (*Rosie Moore*), Dick Haymes (*John Matthews*), Vincent Price (*Boss Tweed*), Albert Sharpe (*Timothy Moore*), Tom Powers (*Regan*), Hobart Cavanaugh (*Mayor Oakley*), Thurston Hall (*Gov. Motley*), Howard Freeman (*Myron Schultz*), Mary Field (*Miss Murch*), Tom Pedi (*O'Toole*), Moroni Olsen (*Big Jim Pitts*), William Skipper, Nelle Fisher (*Dancers*), Patricia Alphin, Nina Lunn, Bunny Waters (*Guests*), Wayne Tredway, Frank McFarland, Harry Denny, Hal Taggart, Ed Peil, Sr. (*Politicians*), G. Pat Collins (*Ward Heeler*), Curt Bois (*Maitre d'*), George Spaulding (*Barton*), Billy Newell (*Stage Manager*), Martin Garralaga (*Bertolli*), Thomas Jackson, Tom P. Dillon (*Officials*), Richard Kipling (*Waiter with Trick Tray*), Alice Backes (*Swedish Immigrant Girl*), Charles Miller (*Jones*), Tudor Owen (*Footman*), Bert Moorhouse (*Democrat*), Carol Dawn Pierson (*Little Girl Dancing*), Eve Pearson (*Ticket Seller*), Carl Sepulveda (*Carriage Driver*), Charles Weskin (*Alderman*), Stuart Holmes, Art Thompson (*Judges*), Rod de Medici (*Immigrant*), Boyd Ackerman, Leslie Sketchley (*Policemen*).

An amiable adaptation of the successful Broadway musical of the same name which had been ballyhooed into a hit by producer Mike Todd. After a run of 504 performances, the studio wouldn't leave well enough alone and removed much of the tuneful Romberg score in favor of an attempt at a story. Big mistake. The paper-thin plot had Haymes, a *New York Times* reporter, teaming up with Durbin, a beauteous Irish immigrant (who was oddly devoid of any Irish accent), to expose the infamous Boss Tweed (Price) for the political scalliwag he was. Durbin, as the lively but naive daughter of park superintendent Sharpe, did what she could to buoy matters in this, her penultimate movie. Nothing much helped and this turn-of-the-century story fell flat. The only two songs from the original play score were "When She Walks in the Room" (Sigmund Romberg, Dorothy Fields, sung by Haymes) and "Carousel in the Park" (Romberg, Fields, sung by Durbin and Haymes). Romberg and Fields wrote a new song, "Oh Say Do You See What I See?" (sung by Durbin), but their hit "Close as Pages in a Book" is only used in the background. Durbin also gets the chance to sing "Pace, Pace, Mio Dio" from Verdi's "La Forza Del Destino." It might have looked better in color, especially the skating ballet, which was designed to look like a print from Currier and Ives and was a direct lift from the stage show, which starred Noah Beery, Betty Bruce, Wilbur Evans, and Maureen Cannon, and had some wonderful tunes, including the aforementioned and "It Doesn't Cost You Anything to Dream," as well as "The Big Back Yard." Removing the songs was a mistake on the part of the producers because the plot was hardly enough to carry the picture without them. Durbin was gaining weight by this time and would make only FOR THE LOVE OF MARY later in 1948 before hanging up her arias at the age of 27 and retiring to France with her wealthy third husband, Charles David.

p, Karl Tunberg; d, William A. Seiter; w, Tunberg (based on the play by Dorothy Fields, Herbert Fields, Sigmund Romberg); ph, Milton Krasner; m, Romberg; ed, Otto Ludwig; prod d, Howard Bay; md, Johnny Green; prod d, Howard Bay; set d, Russell A. Gausman, Ted Offenbecker; cos, Mary Grant; spec eff, David S. Horsley; ch, Helen Tamiris; makeup, Bud Westmore.

Musical/Comedy (PR:A MPAA:NR)

UP IN MABEL'S ROOM**½ (1944) 76m UA bw

Marjorie Reynolds (*Geraldine Ainsworth*), Dennis O'Keefe (*Gary Ainsworth*), Gail Patrick (*Mabel Essington*), Mischa Auer (*Boris*), Charlotte Greenwood (*Martha*), Lee Bowman (*Arthur Weldon*), John Hubbard (*Jimmy Larchmont*), Binnie Barnes (*Alicia Larchmont*), Janet Lambert (*Priscilla*), Fred Kohler, Jr (*Johnny*), Harry Hayden (*Justice of the Peace*).

Pleasant enough bedroom farce based on a popular 1926 stage play. The film stars O'Keefe as a wimpy newlywed who becomes innocently involved with young looker Patrick, who is engaged to marry O'Keefe's business partner, Bowman. Needless to say, Bowman and O'Keefe's wife, Reynolds, misunderstand the nature of the relationship and the usual goofy comedy situations arise. A silent film, also in 1926, preceded this version of the story.

p, Edward Small; d, Allan Dwan; w, Tom Reed, Isobel Dawn (based on the play by Otto Harbach, Wilson Collison); ph, Charles Lawton, Jr.; ed, Grant Whytock; md, Edward Paul; art d, Joseph Sternad; cos, Kay Nelson; spec eff, George Emick.

Comedy (PR:A MPAA:NR)

UP IN SMOKE* (1957) 64m AA bw

Huntz Hall (*Horace Debussy "Sach" Jones*), Stanley Clements (*Stanislaus "Duke" Coveleske*), Judy Bamber (*Mabel*), Eddie LeRoy (*Blinky*), David Gorcey (*Chuck*), Ric Roman (*Tony*), Byron Foulger (*Mr. Bub, the Devil*), Dick

Elliott *(Mike Clancy)*, Ralph Sanford *(Sam)*, Joe Devlin *(Al)*, James Flavin *(Policeman)*, Earle Hodgins *(Friendly Frank, Used Car Dealer)*, John Mitchum *(Desk Sergeant)*, Jack Mulhall *(Police Clerk)*, Fritz Feld *(Dr. Bluzak)*, Wilbur Mack *(Druggist)*, Benny Rubin *(Bernie)*.

The next-to-last Bowery Boys movie sees Hall sell his soul to the Devil, Foulger, so that he can replace the charity money he lost by winning big at the race track. When the mob learns that Hall has a special foresight into the names of the winning horses, they go after the hapless Bowery Boy in an effort to make him work for them. Hall refuses and winds up as the jockey of one of the winning horses. He tries to force the horse to slow down and lose, but the horse wins the race in spite of Hall's efforts. Luckily, since Hall illegally rode the horse, it is disqualified from the race. Since the Devil's prediction didn't come true, his pact with Hall is broken and Satan is forced to do penance by working in Elliott's diner. This entry in the series is pretty lame, even for the Bowery Boys, and the only reason this and the final entry in the series were made was that the studio decided to run out Huntz Hall's contract by making a pair of quickies rather than just pay him off to do nothing. (See BOWERY BOYS Series, Index.)

p, Richard Heermance; d, William Beaudine; w, Jack Townley (based on a story by Elwood Ullman, Bert Lawrence); ph, Harry Neumann; ed, William Austin; md, Marlin Skiles; art d, David Milton; set d, Joseph Kish.

Comedy   **(PR:A   MPAA:NR)**

UP IN SMOKE zero   (1978) 86m PAR c

Cheech Marin *(Pedro De Pacas)*, Tommy Chong *(Man Stoner)*, Stacy Keach *(Sgt. Stedenko)*, Tom Skerritt *(Strawberry)*, Edie Adams *(Tempest Stoner)*, Strother Martin *(Mr. Stoner)*, Louisa Moritz *(Officer Gloria)*, Zane Buzby *(Jade East)*, Anne Wharton *(Debbie)*, Mills Watson *(Harry)*, Karl Johnson *(Clyde)*, Rick Beckner *(Murphy)*, Harold Fong *(Chauffeur)*, Richard Novo *(Richard)*, Jane Moder, Pam Bille *(Jail Baits)*, Arthur Roberts *(Arresting Officer)*, Marian Beeler *(Judge Gladys Dykes)*, Donald Hotton *(Bailiff)*, Jon Ian Jacobs *(Prosecuting Attorney)*, Christopher Joy *(Curtis)*, Ray Vitte *(James, Bass Player)*, Michael Caldwell *(Duane, Guitarist)*, Jose Pulido *(Juan, 1st Trumpeter)*, Ruben Guevara *(Tom, 2nd Trumpeter)*, Miguel Murillo *(Ollie, 3rd Trumpeter)*, June Fairchild *(Ajax Lady)*, Rainbeaux Smith *(Laughing Lady)*, Gary Mule Deer *(Freak with Basketball)*, Angelina Estrada *(Aunt Bolita)*, Ernie Fuentes *(Upholstery Shop Foreman)*, Val Avery *(Factory Boss)*, Ben Marino *(Bennie)*, Akemi Kikumura *(Toyota Kawasaki)*, Joe Creaghe, Roy Stocking *(Border Guards)*, Marcia Wolf *(Sister Mary Vogue)*, Andi Nachman *(Sister Mary Secretary)*, Betty McGuire *(Sister Mary Quacker)*, Cheryl Jeffrey *(Sister Mary Arabian)*, Gayna Shernen *(Sister Mary Mary)*, June Creaghe *(Sister Mary Yuma)*, Patty Proudfoot *(Sister Mary Indian)*, Otto Felix *(Motorcycle Cop)*, Rodney Bingenheimer *(Himself)*, Curt Kaufman, David Nelson *(Roxy Doormen)*, Hal Goplerud *(Punk on Stairs)*, Wayne Hazelhurst *(Tow Truck Driver)*, Berlin Brats, The Dills, The Whores *(The Groups)*.

Cheech and Chong, the witless comedy duo with an enormous cult following, made their film debut in this homage of sorts to the Los Angeles dope scene. The bare-bones plot has Marin picking up Chong hitchhiking along the road after Chong's cruel parents have booted their flea-bitten son from the family nest. Marin invites Chong to join his rock band, then the two ingest a variety of chemicals. After some run-ins with the law, both head down to Tijuana. They end up driving back a van made out of something called "Fibreweed," which is actually pure marijuana. After a border skirmish, Marin and Chong go back to L.A. to enter their group in a "battle of the bands" competition. Lots of marijuana smoke later, Marin and Chong are a success, the law is foiled, and the two dopesters swerve their car off into the sunset. Every joke in this moronic mess depends on drugs, bodily functions, or humiliation to dredge up a laugh. The production qualities are barely tolerable, and the whole thing appears to have been made up as the comedians went along. Producer-director Adler owned the Roxy nightclub where the band contest is held, thus giving himself a nice little plug (this sequence was based on a real-life incident where the comedy team stole the show at a Vancouver "Battle of the Bands" competition). UP IN SMOKE, made on a bargain-basement budget, grossed an amazing $28 million dollars at the box office. Yet big bucks don't necessarily mean intelligent comedy, as this sludge proves. Why do you think they call it dope?

p, Lou Adler, Lou Lombardo; d, Adler; w, Tommy Chong, 'Richard' Cheech Marin; ph, Gene Polito, Jack Willoughby (Panavision, Metrocolor); ed, Lombardo; art d, Leon Ericksen; spec eff, Knott Limited; m/l, title song, Marin, Chong, other songs, Danny "Kootch" Korchmar, Waddy Wachtel; makeup, Wes Dawn.

Comedy   **Cas.**   **(PR:O   MPAA:R)**

UP IN THE AIR**   (1940) 62m MON bw

Frankie Darro *(Frankie)*, Marjorie Reynolds *(Anne)*, Mantan Moreland *(Jeff)*, Gordon Jones *(Tex)*, Lorna Grey *(Rita Wilson)*, Tristram Coffin *(Farell)*, Clyde Dilson *(Marty)*, Dick Elliott *(Hastings)*, John Holland *(Quigley)*, Carleton Young *(Stevens)*.

Lively little whodunit starring Darro as an ambitious young page boy at a local radio station who pushes to get a comedy program aired featuring himself and his buddy, black porter Moreland. Their friend, Reynolds, an

aspiring singer and station receptionist, fully supports them in their efforts and hopes to make her singing debut on their show if it ever gets off the ground. Soon it looks as though Darro and company may get their big break when several of the station's top acts are shot dead while on the air. Darro and his friends solve the murders for the police and Reynolds makes her musical debut by filling in for the station's murdered songstress.

p, Lindsley Parsons; d, Howard Bretherton; w, Ed Kelso; ph, Fred Jackman, Jr.; ed, Jack Ogilvie; m/l, "By the Looks of Things," "Something or Other," Edward J. Kay, Harry Tobias (sung by Marjorie Reynolds), "Doin' the Conga," Lew Porter, Johnny Lange (sung by Lorna Grey).

Comedy/Mystery   **(PR:A   MPAA:NR)**

UP IN THE AIR**½**   (1969, Brit.) 55m Fanfare/Children's Film Foundation c

Gary Smith *(Freddie)*, Jon Pertwee *(Figworthy)*, Felix Felton *(Sir Humphrey)*, Mark Colleano *(Moriarty)*, Susan Payne *(Mary)*, Gary Warren *(Hubert)*, Julian Close *(Ben)*, Earl Younger *(Rollo Sadby)*, Brenda Cowling *(Lady Pennyweight)*, Leslie Dwyer *(Driver)*.

An entertaining children's film set in victorian England which chronicles the efforts of a group of school children trying to escape their depressing boarding school. The kids devise a way to build a hot air balloon and plan to float away from their nasty teacher. Charming moments throughout.

p, George H. Brown; d, Jan Darnley Smith; w, Wally Bosco, Smith (based on a story by Bosco).

Children's   **(PR:AA   MPAA:NR)**

UP IN THE CELLAR**½**   (1970) 92m AIP c (AKA: THREE IN THE CELLAR)

Wes Stern *(Colin Slade)*, Joan Collins *(Pat Camber)*, Larry Hagman *(Maurice Camber)*, Nira Barab *(Tracy Camber)*, Judy Pace *(Harlene Jones)*, David Arkin *(Hugo Cain)*, Joan Darling *(Mme. Krigo)*, Bill Svanoe *(Campus Policeman)*, Charles Pinney, David Cargo.

Stern stars as a failing college student out to get revenge on Hagman, a politically ambitious college president who sees to it that Stern's academic problems are dealt with as harshly as possible in this AIP comedy. Seeking an avenue to vent his anger, Stern falls in with Arkin, the leader of an underground group of Young-Republican types who are awaiting the "Ultimate Revolution" by letting all the radicals wipe each other out, leaving the New Right to take over. Arkin suggests that Stern kill himself in public while Hagman makes his Senate campaign announcement. Stern agrees and is about to jump off a nearby radio tower when he is rescued by Hagman. Disgusted that his stupidity has turned his hated rival into a hero in the public eye, Stern decides to scandalize Hagman by seducing his wife, Collins, his daughter, Barab, and his girl friend, Pace. He succeeds in bedding all three women and even goes so far as to film Hagman's daughter in the nude. Stern administers the *coup de grace* to Hagman by substituting his homemade nudie film for THE SOUND OF MUSIC in the program of a Decency rally held by the Senate hopeful. Unfortunately, these public embarrassments only strengthen Hagman's campaign because the voters begin to feel sorry for him. In the end, Hagman divorces his wife and takes up with Pace, leaving Collins and Barab to Stern.

p, James H. Nicholson, Samuel Z. Arkoff; d&w, Theodore J. Flicker (based on the novel *The Late Wonder Boy* by Angus Hall); ph, Earl Rath (Movielab Color); m, Don Randi; ed, Richard Halsey; m/l, "Didn't I Turn Out Nice," Dory Previn (performed by Hamilton Camp), "Ted's Tune," Randi, "Three Loves," Randi, Bob Silver; makeup, Beau Wilson.

Comedy   **(PR:C   MPAA:R)**

UP IN THE WORLD**   (1957, Brit.) 90m RANK bw

Norman Wisdom *(Norman)*, Maureen Swanson *(Jeannie Andrews)*, Jerry Desmonde *(Maj. Willoughby)*, Ambrosine Phillpotts *(Lady Banderville)*, Colin Gordon *(Fletcher Hethrington)*, Michael Caridia *(Sir Reginald Banderville)*, Michael Ward *(Maurice)*, Jill Dixon *(Sylvia)*, Cyril Chamberlain *(Harper)*, William Lucas *(Mick Bellman)*, Eddie Leslie *(Max)*, Hy Hazell *(Yvonne)*, Edwin Styles *(Conjuror)*, Lionel Jeffries *(Wilson)*, Bernard Bresslaw *(Williams)*, Ian Wilson.

Routine British comedy starring Wisdom as a hapless window washer who loses his job in London and is forced to move to the country, where he lands a job cleaning the windows of a monstrous mansion that has more windows than any other building in England. If that isn't bad enough, the young, spoiled heir of the manor, Caridia, makes Wisdom take him to a nightclub. Some crooks see this as a good opportunity to kidnap the rich heir and they make an attempt in the club, but Wisdom successfully fights them off. Unfortunately, Caridia hits his head during the struggle and develops amnesia. Wisdom is accused of kidnaping and is sentenced to 25 years. Not one to take injustice lying down, Wisdom escapes prison and takes it on the lam. Luckily, Caridia hits his head again, remembers the true facts regarding the kidnap attempt, and clears the window washer's name.

p, Hugh Stewart; d, John Paddy Carstairs; w, Jack Davies, Henry E. Blyth, Peter Blackmore; ph, Jack Cox; m, Philip Green; ed, John Shirley.

Comedy   (PR:A MPAA:NR)

UP JUMPED A SWAGMAN** (1965, Brit.) 87m Ivy/Elstree-WB-Pathe
c

Frank Ifield (*Dave Kelly*), Annette Andre (*Patsy*), Ronald Radd (*Harry King*), Suzy Kendall (*Melissa Smythe-Fury*), Richard Wattis (*Lever, Music Publisher*), Donal Donnelly (*Bockeye*), Bryan Mosley (*Jo-Jo*), Martin Miller (*Herman*), Harvey Spencer (*Luigi*), Carl Jaffe (*Analyst*), Cyril Shaps (*Phil Myers*), Frank Cox (*Wilkinson*), Fred Cox (*Docherty*), Joan Geary (*Mrs. Hawkes Fenhoulet*), William Mervyn (*Mr. Hawkes Fenhoulet*), Ian Peterson (*Policeman*), Paddy Joyce (*Pat*).

Pretty silly film starring Australian singer Ifield as, surprisingly, an Australian singer who comes to London to make it big on the pop charts. Ifield lives in a foggy world where the lines between reality and fantasy are constantly blurred (leaving the audience to wonder just what is supposed to be real). Once in London, Ifield begins romancing a homey, unpretentious girl, Andre, and a flighty debutante, Kendall (in her movie debut). While juggling his women, Ifield becomes embroiled with a robber, Radd, and his gang of thieves, who use the singer's home as a base from which to rob jewelry. Eventually, all the loose ends are tied up, allowing Ifield to warble a number of tunes including "Waltzing Matilda" (Marie Cowan, A.B. Paterson) and "I Remember You."

p, Andrew Mitchell; d, Christopher Miles; w, Lewis Greifer; ph, Ken Higgins (CinemaScope, Technicolor); m, Norrie Paramor; ed, Jack Slade; ch, Pam Devis.

Comedy/Musical   (PR:A MPAA:NR)

UP PERISCOPE**½   (1959) 111m Lakeside/WB c

James Garner (*Ken*), Edmond O'Brien (*Stevenson*), Andra Martin (*Sally*), Alan Hale, Jr (*Malone*), Carleton Carpenter (*Carney*), Frank Gifford (*Mount*), William Leslie (*Doherty*), Richard Bakalyan (*Peck*), Edward [Edd] Byrnes (*Ash*), Sean Garrison (*Floyd*), Henry Kulky (*York*), George Crise (*Murphy*), Warren Oates.

Fairly interesting WW II submarine film starring Garner as a rebellious demolition specialist assigned to serve on a sub commanded by O'Brien, a nasty captain who does everything by the book. Garner's mission is to venture to a tiny Japanese-held island and obtain a secret code. Once the sub reaches the island, Garner must sneak into the Japs' compound, locate the top-secret code book, and bring it back to the sub for deciphering. En route to the island, Garner and O'Brien bicker back and forth on how to run the ship, and there is a distinct possibility that O'Brien will not wait too long for Garner to complete his mission before taking the sub back underwater. Pretty routine stuff, but well-played. Look for a young Warren Oates as a sailor who is always eating in the mess hall.

p, Aubrey Schenck; d, Gordon Douglas; w, Richard Landau (based on the novel by Robb White); ph, Carl Guthrie (WarnerScope, Technicolor); m, Ray Heindorf; ed, John F. Schreyer; art d, Jack T. Collis.

War   **Cas.**   (PR:A MPAA:NR)

UP POMPEII**   (1971, Brit.) 90m Associated London/MGM-EMI c

Frankie Howerd (*Lurcio*), Patrick Cargill (*Nero*), Michael Hordern (*Ludicrus*), Barbara Murray (*Ammonia*), Lance Percival (*Bilius*), Bill Fraser (*Prosperus*), Adrienne Posta (*Scrubba*), Julie Ege (*Voluptua*), Bernard Bresslaw (*Gorgo*), Royce Mills (*Nausius*), Madeline Smith (*Erotica*), Rita Webb (*Cassandra*), Ian Trigger (*Odius*), Aubrey Woods (*Villanus*), Hugh Paddick (*Priest*), Laraine Humphreys (*Flavia*), Roy Hudd (*M.C.*), George Woodridge (*Fat Bather*), Andrea Lloyd (*Dolly Bird*), Derek Griffiths (*Steam Slave*).

Inspired by the success of Britain's long-running "Carry On" series of comedies, the makers of UP POMPEII attempted to inject some of the same wackiness into this effort. The result is a sporadically funny send-up of the Roman Empire that suffers from the same infantile sense of humor that characterized the "Carry On" films. Howerd stars as an incompetent slave owned by Nero. When it is learned that a plot against Nero is in the works and that a scroll containing the names of the conspirators is in Howerd's unwitting possession, a free-for-all ensues which sees both Nero's men and the assassins after the slave for the scroll. The rest is predictable, with scads of sexual double entendres that may amuse dirty-minded 10-year-olds. Howerd had been in a similar British series that was shown on American public television.

p, Ned Sherrin; d, Bob Kellett; w, Sid Colin (based on an idea by Talbot Rothwell); ph, Ian Wilson (Eastmancolor); ed, Al Geil; art d, Sean Flannery; cos, Penny Lowe; m/l, "Up Pompeii," Ken Howard, Alan Blaikley.

Comedy   **Cas.**   (PR:O MPAA:R)

UP POPS THE DEVIL**   (1931) 85m PAR bw

Skeets [Richard] Gallagher (*Biney Hatfield*), Stuart Erwin (*Stranger*), Carole Lombard (*Anne Merrick*), Lilyan Tashman (*Polly Griscom*), Norman Foster (*Steve Merrick*), Edward J. Nugent (*George Kent*), Theodore Von Eltz

(*Gilbert Morrell*), Joyce Compton (*Luella May Carroll*), Eulalie Jensen (*Mrs. Kent*), Harry Beresford (*Mr. Platt*), Effie Ellsler (*Mrs. Platt*), Sleep N. Eat [Willie Best] (*Laundryman*), Guy Oliver (*Waldo*), Pat Moriarity (*Kelly*), Matty Roubert (*Subscription Boy*).

Foster, a struggling writer married to Lombard, meets wealthy publisher Von Eltz who agrees to give him an advance on the first two chapters of his novel. To help the household financially, Lombard gets a job as a dancer in a nightclub revue. Unfortunately, with no one to run interference for him, Foster is left at home to deal with a steady stream of household problems and unexpected visitors which hamper his writing. One of the visitors, a southern belle played by Compton, threatens to distract Foster not only from his novel, but from his marriage as well. Meanwhile, publisher Von Eltz has taken a fancy to Lombard and tries to woo her with money. She innocently assumes that the cash is meant as an additional advance on her husband's book. Eventually both parties become suspicious of the other's fidelity and they separate. Once Foster becomes a successful author, he realizes that it is Lombard he truly loves and the couple is reunited.

d, A. Edward Sutherland; w, Arthur Kober, Eve Unsell (based on the play by Albert Hackett, Francis Goodrich); ph, Karl Struss.

Drama   (PR:A MPAA:NR)

UP SHE GOES   (SEE: UP GOES MAISIE, 1945)

UP THE ACADEMY*   (1980) 96m WB c (AKA: MAD MAGAZINE'S UP THE ACADEMY; THE BRAVE YOUNG MEN OF WEINBERG)

Ron Liebman (*Major*), Wendell Brown (*Ike*), Tom Citera (*Hash*), J. Hutchinson (*Oliver*), Ralph Macchio (*Chooch*), Harry Teinowitz (*Ververgaert*), Tom Poston (*Sisson*), Ian Wolfe (*Commandant Caseway*), Stacy Nelkin (*Candy*), Barbara Bach (*Bliss*), Leonard Frey (*Keck*), Antonio Fargas (*Coach*), Luke Andreas (*Vitto*), Candy Ann Brown, King Coleman, Rosalie Citera, Yvonne Francis, James G. Robertson, Rosemary Eliot, Louis Zorich, Robert Lynn Mock, Tyrees Allen, Eric Hanson, Ken White, Patrick McKenna, Robert Scopa.

Notable only because its star, Ron Liebman, sued the studio to have his name removed from the credits and advertising (as if his name meant big box office!), UP THE ACADEMY is just another in the seemingly endless parade of obnoxious, infantile, and offensive teenage comedies that have flooded the market since the late 1970s. This one was produced by the *Mad* magazine people in response to their more mature (the term is relative) competitor in the comedy magazine field, *National Lampoon*, who created the raunchy teenage film genre with the vastly superior ANIMAL HOUSE. UP THE ACADEMY, however, is composed exclusively of the, all-too-familiar stream of tasteless gags that manage to insult every adult sensibility. Racist, sexist, bigoted, and gross, the film's plot revolves around a group of teenagers struggling under the tyrannical rule of Liebman, who runs the local military academy wherein our heroes are enrolled. This is trash, but it's not as bad as much of the genre (the PORKY'S saga comes immediately to mind), which isn't saying much.

p, Marvin Worth, Danton Rissner; d, Robert Downey; w, Tom Patchett, Jay Tarses; ph, Harry Stradling (Panavision, Technicolor); m, Jody Taylor Worth; ed, Bud Molin; prod d, Peter Wooley; set d, Mary Swanson.

Comedy   **Cas.**   (PR:O MPAA:R)

UP THE CHASTITY BELT*½   (1971, Brit.) 94m EMI/Associated London-International Co-Productions c

Frankie Howerd, Graham Crowden, Bill Fraser, Roy Hudd, Hugh Paddick, Anna Quayle, Eartha Kitt, Dave King, Fred Emney.

A silly and often crude comedy, this film tells the medieval adventures of a knight and his serf. The humor is of the ribald slapstick school that's often popular with British comedy (witness Monty Python) but this never approaches the level of daring it pretends to, resulting in rather juvenile antics.

p, Ned Sherrin; d, Bob Kellett; w, Sid Colin, Ray Galton, Alan Simpson; ph, Ian Wilson (Technicolor); m, Carl Davis.

Comedy   (PR:O MPAA:PG)

UP THE CREEK***   (1958, Brit.) 83m Byron/Dominant bw

David Tomlinson (*Lt. Humphrey Fairweather*), Peter Sellers (*Bosun Docherty*), Wilfrid Hyde-White (*Adm. Foley*), Vera Day (*Lily*), Liliane Sottane (*Susanne*), Tom Gill (*Flag Lieutenant*), Michael Goodliffe (*Nelson*), Reginald Beckwith (*Publican*), Lionel Murton (*Perkins*), John Warren (*Cooky*), Lionel Jeffries (*Steady Barker*), Sam Kydd (*Bates*), Frank Pettingell (*Stationmaster*), Donald Bisset (*Farm Laborer*), Leonard Fenton (*Policeman*), Basil Dignam (*Coombes*), Peter Coke (*Comdr. Price*), Jack McNaughton (*Regulating Petty Officer*), Larry Noble (*Chief Petty Officer*), Patrick Cargill (*Commander*), Michael Ripper (*Decorator*), Howard Williams (*Bunts*), Peter Collingwood (*Chippie*), Barry Lowe (*Webster*), Edwin Richfield (*Bennett*), David Lodge (*Scouse*), Max Butterfield (*Lofty*), Malcolm Ransom (*Small Boy*).

A lively remake of the 1937 British comedy OH MR. PORTER, which was itself a remake of the 1931 film THE GHOST TRAIN, which had originally been filmed as a silent in 1927. Seeing how many different versions of this material have flickered across the screen, it is a surprise that UP THE CREEK is as fresh and amusing as it is. Tomlinson stars as an overly eager naval officer who dabbles in the art of rocket-making. Unfortunately, his hobby has frequently gotten out of hand and he has destroyed untold pounds worth of naval property with his experiments. Seeking to put the innocently dangerous officer somewhere where he can do little harm, the naval brass assign Tomlinson to command a decrepit destroyer that is stationed in the middle of nowhere on the British coast. The ship hasn't had a commander in over two years and the men have gotten pretty used to listening to the bosun, Sellers. On his arrival Tomlinson soon learns that his men, led by Sellers, have been operating a very lucrative black market out of the vessel, using naval services and supplies and selling them to the local townsfolk. Before Tomlinson can raise a hand to stop the illegal activities, he finds himself embroiled in them. Trouble looms when a doddering old admiral (played with relish by Hyde-White) arrives for inspection. It looks as if the jig is up until Hyde-White accidentally sets off one of Tomlinson's rockets and sinks the old destroyer, wiping out all the evidence. Sellers, in one of his earliest roles, steals the show. A sequel entitled FURTHER UP THE RIVER was made, sans Sellers.

p, Henry Halstead; d, Val Guest; w, Guest, Len Heath, John Warren; ph, Arthur Grant, Moray Grant (Hammerscope); m, Tony Fones, Tony Lowry.

Comedy   **(PR:A   MPAA:NR)**

UP THE DOWN STAIRCASE**½   (1967) 120m Park Place/WB c

Sandy Dennis (*Sylvia Barrett*), Patrick Bedford (*Paul Barringer*), Eileen Heckart (*Henrietta Pastorfield*), Ruth White (*Beatrice Schracter*), Jean Stapleton (*Sadie Finch*), Sorrell Booke (*Dr. Bester*), Roy Poole (*Mr. McHabe*), Florence Stanley (*Ella Friedenberg*), Vinette Carroll (*Mother*), Salvatore Rasa (*Harry A. Kagan*), John Fantauzzi (*Ed Williams*), Maria Landa (*Carole Blanca*), Lewis Wallach (*Lou Martin*), Jose Rodriguez (*Himself*), Ellen O'Mara (*Alice Blake*), Jeff Howard (*Joe Ferone*), Loretta Leversee (*Social Studies Teacher*), Robert Levine (*Mr. Osborne*), Elena Karam (*Nurse Eagen*), Frances Sternhagen (*Charlotte Wolf*), Candace Culkin (*Linda Rosen*), Janice Mars (*Miss Gordon*).

This film seemed to be the inspiration for TV's "Welcome Back, Kotter" along with several other movies that used the same backdrop, beginning with THE BLACKBOARD JUNGLE. It deals with a naive teacher in an integrated school and was based on an article in the *Saturday Review* that later became Bel Kaufman's best-selling novel. Dennis is a newly graduated teacher who is bound and determined to introduce the finer points of English literature to her motley charges. The other teachers and administrators are darn near as motley and so she faces problems galore. The chief administrator is Poole, who wants to run his school the way Patton ran his army, with heavy discipline and total obedience. Booke is the principal and your basic softie so he is ever harassed. Bedford is an unpublished author who will probably never finish his Great American Novel but he does find enough time to chase after Dennis. Heckart is a shrill and emotional teacher on the brink of a nervous breakdown at all times, Karam is a dingbat who is not fit to instruct kindergarten students, and Stanley is a pompous pedant who is full of herself. The students are far better drawn although also cliched. Howard is a youngster in whom Dennis takes a teacherly interest and the result is that the boy mistakes her attitude and comes close to violating her. Fantauzzi is a bitter young black boy who feels that nobody ever gives a dark-hued person an even chance at making it. O'Mara is a lovesick and unattractive girl who finally screws up courage and hands a love letter to Bedford, then almost kills herself after Bedford reads the letter and gives it back with the grammatical and spelling errors corrected. One excellent scene finds the students and teachers mixing at a school dance without any academic talk, but most of the movie is too episodic. The best subplot (after the O'Mara-Bedford tale) is Dennis' relationship with shy, retiring Rodriguez (who used his real name in the movie). Dennis is ready to give up, resign and find some other employment, but she is inspired by the transformation of Rodriguez when he is assigned the task of being a classroom judge and suddenly gains leadership and confidence, which convinces Dennis that her work has not been in vain. The major problem with the movie is that it has a tendency to be white bread when pumpernickel was called for. Dennis stays at Calvin Coolidge High School, which was to be expected, and the movie ends on an uplifting note as she is ready to tackle her next class. Although Dennis won the Best Actress award at the Moscow Film Festival, she remains the most mannered actress in films and even under Mulligan's sensitive direction, her fluttery, stop-and-go way of performing can become grating. The teachers get the blame for the educational system in this movie and the students are shown to be the better people. Whether or not that's true is a bone of contention. The Moscow award was the result of the movie having been submitted by the U.S. State Department to show that there was racial integration in schools. Filmed in New York City, it avoided many subjects which might have made it a far more important picture. In a small role, note Jean Stapleton in her fourth movie.

p, Alan J. Pakula; d, Robert Mulligan; w, Tad Mosel (based on the novel by Bel Kaufman); ph, Joseph Coffey (Technicolor); m, Fred Karlin; ed, Folmar

Blangsted; art d, George Jenkins; cos, Ann Roth; makeup, Irving Buchman.

Drama   **Cas.**   **(PR:A-C   MPAA:NR)**

UP THE FRONT*   (1972, Brit.) 89m EMI/Associated London c

Frankie Howerd, Bill Fraser, Zsa Zsa Gabor, Stanley Holloway, Hermione Baddeley, Robert Coote, Lance Percival, Dora Bryan.

A British house servant undergoes hypnosis and ends up joining the army during WW I. Complications arise when some plans supposedly belonging to the enemy end up as a tattoo on his derriere. Inane nonsense.

p, Ned Sherrin; d, Bob Kellett; w, Sid Colin, Eddie Braben; ph, Tony Spratling (Technicolor); m, Patrick Greenwell; art d, Seamus Flannery.

Comedy   **(PR:C   MPAA:NR)**

UP THE JUNCTION**   (1968, Brit.) 119m British Home
                                          Entertainment-Collinson-Crest o/PAR c

Suzy Kendall (*Polly*), Dennis Waterman (*Peter*), Adrienne Posta (*Rube*), Maureen Lipman (*Sylvie*), Michael Gothard (*Terry*), Liz Fraser (*Mrs. McCarthy*), Hylda Baker (*Winny*), Alfie Bass (*Charlie*), Linda Cole (*Pauline*), Doreen Harrington (*Rita*), Jessie Robins (*Lil*), Barbara Archer (*May*), Ruby Head (*Edith*), Susan George (*Joyce*), Sandra Williams (*Sheilah*), Michael Robbins (*Figgins*), Aubrey Morris (*Creely*), Billy Murray (*Ray*), Michael Standing (*John*), Stephen Wittaker (*Alf*), Shaun Curry (*Ted*), Leslie Meadows (*Ron*), Anthony Sharman (*Tom*), Peter Attard (*Bert*), Douglas Sheldon (*Villain*), Queenie Watts (*Mrs. Hardy*), Olwen Griffith (*Fat Lil*), Lockwood West (*Magistrate*), Michael Barrington (*Barrister*), Mark Ross (*Policeman*), Yvonne Manners (*Hotel Receptionist*), Harry Hutchinson (*Hotel Porter*), Larry Martyn (*Barrow Boy*), Ronald Clarke (*Mate*), Michael Martin (*Police Inspector*), Jack Phillips (*Old Man*), Gladys Dawson (*Woman*), Derek Ware (*Ted's Friend*), The Delacardos (*Pop Group*).

Despite the fact that UP THE JUNCTION is based on a successful 1963 book by Nell Dunn that was turned into a television movie in 1965 and eventually adapted for the screen in 1968 (becoming that year's top British moneymaker), it just so happens that the film itself (and the material) isn't all that good. Kendall stars as a young, rich, bored upper-class girl from Chelsea, who for reasons only known to herself and never explained to the audience, decides to abandon her lush life style and move to Battersea, a depressed area of London. There she gets a job working in a candy factory (if jobs are so hard to get, how can a rich girl from Chelsea land one so easily?) and becomes fast friends with sisters Posta and Lipman. Soon Kendall begins dating poor boy Waterman, who hates his existence and wants nothing better than to leave Battersea forever. When it becomes obvious that Waterman wants what Kendall had when she was wealthy, the content-to-be-poor girl realizes that they will never be compatible. In a sub-plot Posta becomes pregnant by her boy friend and is left to visit a sleazy abortionist accompanied by Kendall. After this ordeal, Posta's boy friend agrees to marry her, but he is killed in a motorcycle wreck before the wedding. Kendall and Waterman break up, and he is soon arrested for stealing an expensive car. While the effort to show what life is like in this poverty-stricken area of London is admirable (examining both its tragedy and triumph), the film is deceptive, contrived, and manipulative. Because the main character is a rich girl "slumming" in Battersea, we are given a person from another class to identify with. This in itself is bad enough (as if the characters from Battersea are not sympathetic, vital, or intelligent enough on their own to carry a film), but Kendall's character is given scant motivation for what she does, providing little insight into her character.

p, Anthony Havelock-Allan, John Brabourne; d, Peter Collinson; w, Roger Smith (based on the book by Nell Dunn); ph, Arthur Lavis (Techniscope, Technicolor); m, Mike Hugg, Manfred Mann; ed, John Trumper; art d, Ken Jones; makeup, Dore Hamilton.

Drama   **(PR:O   MPAA:R)**

UP THE MACGREGORS**   (1967, Ital./Span.) 93m Produzione
                    D.S.-Jolly-Talia/COL c (SETTE DONNE PER I MCGREGOR; SIETE
                                              MUJERES PARA LOS MACGREGOR)

David Bailey (*Gregor MacGregor*), Agatha Flory [Agata Flori] (*Rosita Carson*), Leo Anchoriz (*Maldonado*), Robert Camardiel [Roberto Camardiel] (*Donovan*), Cole Kitosh [Alberto Dell'Acqua] (*Dick MacGregor*), Nick Anderson [Nazareno Zamperla] (*Peter MacGregor*), Paul Carter (*Paolo Magalotti*) (*Kenneth MacGregor*), Julio Perez Tabernero (*Mark MacGregor*), Hugo Blanco (*David MacGregor*), Saturnino Cerra (*Johnny MacGregor*), George Rigaud (*Alastair MacGregor*), Roy Bossier (*Apache*), Victor Israel (*Trevor the Dentist*), Ann Casares (*Dolly*), Francesco Tensi (*Harold*), Jesus Guzman (*The Priest*), King Black (*Tom*), Antonio Vico (*Frank James*), Elena Montoya (*The Child from San Raphael*), Tito Garcia (*Miguelito*), Anne Marie Noe [Ana Maria Noe] (*Mamie*), Margaret Horowitz [Margherita Orowitz] (*Annie*), Margaret Merritt (*Dublin*), Kathleen Parker (*Belfast*), Ana Maria Mendoza (*Kilkenny*), Julie Fair (*Galway*), Fern Water (*Tralee*), Judith Shepard (*Dundalks*), Joe Hamlin (*Tipperary*), Catherine Hamlin (*Kilarney*), Nino Scarciofolo, Riccardo Pizzuti, Rinaldo Zamperia, Alberto Cevenini (*Bandits*), Harry Cotton.

Believe it or not, this is a rather tame, *family oriented* spaghetti western that is fun, intelligent, and well-produced. It is also a sequel to SEVEN GUNS FOR THE MACGREGORS, which was released in the U.S. *after* UP THE MACGREGORS. The film involves two families of British immigrants who have settled in Texas during the 1880s, the MacGregors from Scotland and the Donovans from Ireland. A friendly rivalry exists between the clans but the relationship is warm because the six MacGregor boys are engaged to marry the six Donovan girls. During the celebration of Bailey's engagement to Flory, a gang of bandits led by Anchoriz invades the homestead and rides off with the trunk that holds all of the MacGregors' wealth. The MacGregor boys go off after the bandits and eventually track them down at their hideout. Fearing that Bailey will be seduced by the bandits' vixen women, Flory goes off after him and is captured by the crooks. Bailey comes to her rescue, but he, too, is captured, forcing his brothers, the Donovans, and some friendly Indians to attack the bandits and drive them off. Good humor, little violence, lots of fun, and boasting a typically fine score from Morricone.

p, Dario Sabatello; d, Frank Grafield [Franco Giraldi]; w, Fernand Lion [Fernando Di Leo], Vincent Eagle [Enzo Dell'Aquila], Paul Levy [Paolo Levi], Jose Maria Rodriguez, Franco Giraldi (based on a story by Di Leo, Dell'Aquila); ph, Alexander Ulloa [Alejandro Ulloa] (Techniscope, Technicolor); m, Ennio Morricone; ed, Nino Baragli; art d, Adolfo Cofino, Ottavio Scotti, Augusto Lega.

Western/Comedy **(PR:A MPAA:NR)**

UP THE RIVER*** (1930) 92m FOX bw

Spencer Tracy *(St. Louis)*, Warren Hymer *(Dannemora Dan)*, Humphrey Bogart *(Steve)*, Claire Luce *(Judy)*, Joan Lawes *(Jean)*, Sharon Lynn *(Edith La Verne)*, George MacFarlane *(Jessup)*, Gaylord 'Steve' Pendleton *(Morris)*, Morgan Wallace *(Frosby)*, William Collier, Sr. *(Pop)*, Robert Emmett O'Connor *(Guard)*, Louise MacIntosh *(Mrs. Massey)*, Edythe Chapman *(Mrs. Jordan)*, Johnny Walker *(Happy)*, Noel Francis *(Sophie)*, Mildred Vincent *(Annie)*, Mack Clark *(Whitelay)*, Goodee Montgomery *(Kit)*, Althea Henley *(Cynthia)*, Carol Wines *(Daisy Elmore)*, Adele Windsor *(Minnie)*, Richard Keene *(Dick)*, Elizabeth Keating, Helen Keating *(May and June)*, Robert Burns *(Slim)*, John Swor *(Clem)*, Pat Somerset *(Beauchamp)*, Joe Brown *(Deputy Warden)*, Harvey Clark *(Nash)*, Black and Blue *(Slim and Klem)*, Robert Parrish.

Spencer Tracy made his film debut in this prison comedy all but lost today. The film opens with Tracy and his slow-witted sidekick, Hymer, breaking out of jail. They go their separate ways but meet up years later when Tracy sees Hymer preaching in front of a Salvation Army band. Tracy taunts him with shouts of "Crime doesn't pay!" until the fugitive can take no more and swings at Tracy. They brawl and are thrown into prison again, only this time in a medium security lockup that the two have no desire to break out of. Here they have more comforts than home, including dramatics, a baseball league, and women just on the other side of a dividing wall. Messages are smuggled from one side to the other in the hems of lady reformers who come to the prison. Tracy and Hymer share their cell with Bogart (in his second film appearance), convicted of accidental manslaughter. Bogart's wealthy New England family does not know of his incarceration, thinking their son is in China, and Bogart wants to keep it that way. He falls in love with Luce, a female convict framed by crooked broker Wallace. When Bogart is released he tries to go straight and wait for Luce to get out, but Wallace threatens to reveal his past to his parents if he doesn't help him in a corrupt scheme. Bogart doesn't know what to do and asks his friends Tracy and Hymer to help. The two bust out of jail during the talent show, dressed in women's clothes, and make their way to Bogart. After checking out the situation, they manage to work Wallace's own associates against him, resulting in the crook's death. After receiving the thanks of Bogart, the two men break back into jail just in time for the big baseball game against Sing-Sing. Tracy was appearing on Broadway in "The Last Mile" at the time and John Ford, who saw the performance, persuaded the actor to take a six-week leave from the production to make a film based on the riots a year earlier at Auburn Prison. Tracy went west, but before the film could get underway, MGM came out with THE BIG HOUSE, their film based on the Auburn riots. Ford worked quickly then, changing the whole story and reworking it into a comedy. The film was shot in two weeks so that Tracy could get back to New York in time to resume his role. None of the performances is especially memorable, despite the cast of soon-to-be stars, but the film is still quite entertaining. The usual Ford touches are in evidence, dealing with one of his usual subjects, the society of men cut off from the world. Tracy later recalled this as the most pleasant film he ever worked on, although Hymer's memories were not so pleasant. For one scene, the actor had to stand against a board while a knife thrower threw knives at him. Hymer was terrified and Ford walked up and asked him, "If I do it, will you?" Embarrassed, Hymer nodded weakly. Ford then took his place and the thrower did his business. One of the blades caught the director's fingertip, though. Sucking the blood from his finger, Ford asked Hymer if he was ready. Although his knees were shaking, the actor managed to pull off the scene. The film was remade in 1938.

p, William Fox; d, John Ford; w, Maurine Watkins, (uncredited) Ford, William Collier, Sr.; ph, Joseph H. August; ed, Frank E. Hull; set d, Duncan Cramer; m/l, Joseph McCarthy, James F. Hanley.

Comedy **(PR:A MPAA:NR)**

UP THE RIVER½** (1938) 75m FOX bw

Preston Foster *(Chipper Morgan)*, Tony Martin *(Tommy Grant)*, Phyllis Brooks *(Helen)*, Slim Summerville *(Slim Nelson)*, Arthur Treacher *(Darby Randall)*, Alan Dinehart *(Warden Willis)*, Eddie Collins *(Fisheye Conroy)*, Jane Darwell *(Mrs. Graham)*, Sidney Toler *(Jeffrey Mitchell)*, Bill Robinson *(Memphis Jones)*, Edward Gargan *(Tiny)*, Robert Allen *(Ray Douglas)*, Dorothy Dearing *(Martha Graham)*, Charles D. Brown *(Warden Harris)*.

Decent remake of John Ford's 1930 Spencer Tracy-Humphrey Bogart prison comedy, this time starring Foster and Treacher as two con men who find themselves as the stars of the prison football team (the sport was baseball in 1930). When one of their prison buddies, Martin, learns that his mother is being conned by some unscrupulous crooks led by Toler, the experienced con men-football stars decide to help by breaking out (they dress up as women) and taking care of the villains. When their escape is discovered, prison warden Dinehart goes into a frenzy–not because they have escaped justice, but because he has bet a fortune on the upcoming football game and the team can't win without them. After setting things straight with Toler, Foster and Treacher calmly return to prison where they are hustled onto the football field to win the game in the ever-popular *final moments*.

p, Sol M. Wurtzel; d, Alfred Werker; w, Lou Breslow, John Patrick (based on a story by Maurine Watkins); ph, Peverell Marley; ed, Nick DeMaggio; md, Samuel Kaylin; art d, Bernard Herzbrun, Chester Gore; cos, Sophie Wachner; ch, Nicholas Castle, Geneva Sawyer; m/l, "It's the Strangest Thing," Sidney Clara, Harry Akst (sung by Tony Martin).

Comedy **(PR:A MPAA:NR)**

UP THE SANDBOX** (1972) 97m First Artists/NG c

Barbra Streisand *(Margaret Reynolds)*, David Selby *(Paul Reynolds)*, Ariane Heller *(Elizabeth)*, Terry/Gary Smith *(Peter)*, Jane Hoffman *(Mrs. Yussim)*, John C. Becher *(Mr. Yussim)*, Jacobo Morales *(Fidel Castro)*, Paul Benedict *(Dr. Beineke)*, George Irving *(Dr. Keglin)*, Jane House *(Mrs. Keglin)*, Pitt Herbert *(Uncle Dave)*, Janet Brandt *(Aunt Ida)*, Pearl Shear *(Aunt Till)*, Carl Gottlieb *(Vinnie)*, Joseph Bova *(John)*, Mary Louise Wilson *(Betty)*, Marilyn Curtis *(Judy)*, Iris Brooks *(Vicki)*, Tammy Lee *(Bibs)*, Randy Ginns *(Becky)*, Stanley Appleman *(Tommy)*, Moosie Drier *(Billy)*, Jessamine Milner *(Nanny)*, Cynthia Harris *(Stella)*, Mark Vahanian *(David)*, Vassili Lambrinos *(Jack Lawford)*, Marina Durell *(Dr. Lopez)*, Barbara Rhodes *(Dr. Boden)*, Isabel Sanford *(Maria)*, Carol White *(Miss Spittlemeister)*, Danny Black *(Leon)*, David Downing *(John, Black Militant)*, Ji-Tu Cumbuka *(Black Captain)*, Juan DeCarlos *(Blackman)*, Paul Dooley *(Statue of Liberty Guard)*, Conrad Bain *(Dr. Gordon)*, Jane Betts *(Woman Doctor)*, Anne Ramsey *(Battleaxe)*, Margo Winkler *(Hospital Clerk)*, Cryn Matchinga *(Woman Patient)*, John Dennis *(Officer)*, Norman Field *(Reporter)*, Efrain Lopez Neris *(Castro's Aide)*, Lois Smith *(Elinore)*, Steven Britt *(Elinore's Boy)*, Renee Lippin *(Connie)*, Terry O'Mara *(Cathie)*, Jennifer Darling *(Joanne)*, Stockard Channing *(Judy Stanley)*, Rita Karin *(Mrs. Grossbard)*, Marilyn Coleman *(Rose White)*, Dee Timberlake *(Black Girl)*, Juan Canos *(Anti-Cuban)*, Alicia Castro-Leal *(Pro-Cuban)*, Conrad Roberts *(Clay)*, Kevin Bersell *(Kid on Bike)*, Sully Boyer *(Fat Man)*, Lee Chamberlin *(Jan)*, Miriam W'Abdullah *(Chieftess)*, Beth Luzuka *(Gupa)*, National Senegalese Dance Company *(Dancers)*, Somburu Tribe of Kenya *(Tribal Population)*.

UP THE SANDBOX was a controversial picture in that almost everyone had a different opinion of how to interpret this "Women's Liberation" film. Some loved it, more hated it, and we stand somewhere firmly planted with our feet in midair on the subject. Streisand is a married mother of two and in the process of having a third child. She is married to Selby, a professor, and she possesses one of the world's great imaginations. The film consists of a series of vignettes into which Streisand insinuates herself, and the message received is that she is not quite certain of her own sexual identity. Richardson Roiphe's book, upon which the film is based, offers three separate points of view. The first is that Streisand's character is not at all a contemporary woman because it appears that she enjoys being kept "barefoot and pregnant" and safe in that role. Secondly, she can be interpreted as a person who enjoys the job of wife and mother but does have a yearning for some semblance of freedom away from the diapers and Pablum. The third way to look at it is that she hates the life she leads and wants to abandon her family in order to do all the things she feels she must do to fulfill herself as a liberated woman. As the movie unspools, it's not easy to know which of the vignettes are real and which are imagined. Selby doesn't know that Streisand is expecting again and when she visits the college where he is employed and finds him deep in "conference" with Rhodes, a luscious associate, she walks away without giving him the news and her trips to Fantasy Land commence. She thinks that Selby is having an affair, then she goes off in a nether world and dreams of Castro (Morales). When the bearded Cuban leader tries to seduce Streisand in her dream, he suddenly reveals himself to be a woman! She next squires her kids to the local playground and recalls a street fight that sends her off into dreams again as she leads a group of revolutionaries in a plot to dynamite the Statue of Liberty. In real life, she and Selby attend her parents' 33rd wedding anniversary party and she imagines herself pushing her mother (Hoffman) into the large cake and then having a battle with the woman as they roll on the floor and pull out fistfuls of each other's hair. Next, they go to a college cocktail party tossed in honor of a famed anthropologist, Benedict, and she is miffed when Selby shows some interest in Brooks, a comely student. That sets her off on another dream sequence in which she and Benedict travel to Kenya and meet a group of natives who are fat as cows but have discovered an amazing way in which they can give birth with no pain. Streisand now thinks it may be better if she has an abortion and tells Selby to take their kids to a park for the afternoon. A dream takes her to an abortion clinic where Selby arrives just in time to stop her from destroying her unborn child. She returns to reality and goes to the park to tell Selby that she is expecting (while dreaming that she is racing through the park on a hospital gurney that is somehow propelled by unseen power). When she breaks the news about the new baby to Selby, he turns out to be thrilled and not nearly the ogre she'd expected. Selby agrees with Streisand when she informs him that she needs some time off from the torture of being a mother and he shows his understanding by acquiescing. The acting was good, if one can stand Streisand's shrill ways, but acting alone cannot make a movie. It's far too diffuse, the script is vague, and the direction is often haphazard. The combination of the reality of her life and the bizarre quality of her fantasies is jarring. UP THE SANDBOX was filmed in New York, Kenya, and Hollywood. Streisand's long-time manager, Marty Erlichman, is listed as the associate producer. Producer Winkler has used various of his relations in other movies and does so again here as Margo Winkler plays the clerk in the hospital.

p, Robert Chartoff, Irwin Winkler; d, Irvin Kershner; w, Paul Zindel (based on the novel by Anne Richardson Roiphe); ph, Gordon Willis (Technicolor); m, Billy Goldenberg; ed, Robert Lawrence; prod d, Harry Horner; set d, David M. Haber, Rodger Maus, Robert De Vestel; cos, Albert Wolsky; spec eff, Richard F. Albain; makeup, Lee C. Harman.

Comedy   Cas.   (PR:C-O MPAA:R)

UP TIGHT   (SEE: UPTIGHT, 1968)

UP TO HIS EARS***   (1966, Fr./Ital.) 94m Ariane-Les Productions Artistes Associes-Vides/Lopert c (LES TRIBULATIONS D'UN CHINOIS EN CHINE; L'UOMO DI HONG KONG)

Jean-Paul Belmondo (*Arthur Lempereur*), Ursula Andress (*Alexandrine Pinardel*), Maria Pacome (*Suzy*), Valerie Lagrange (*Alice Ponchabert*), Jess Hahn (*Cornelius*), Valery Inkijinoff (*Mr. Goh*), Jean Rochefort (*Leon*), Darry Cowl (*Biscoton*), Paul Preboist (*Cornac*), Mario David (*Roquentin*), Boris Lenissevitch (*Russian Professor*), Joe Said (*Charlie Fallinster*).

Goofy black comedy starring Belmondo as a depressed young heir who is so bored that death seems an exciting alternative to his current life style. After trying and failing nine times to kill himself, Belmondo learns that his fortune has been lost in a stock market crash. This greatly upsets his fiancee, Lagrange, and her mother, Pacome, but he sees it as another good excuse to kill himself. His business manager, Inkijinoff, has a better idea. Instead of killing himself and leaving his loved ones nothing, Inkijinoff suggests that Belmondo take out a life insurance policy for $2 million and then hire someone to assassinate him. Belmondo agrees and the plan is set into motion. Unfortunately he meets an attractive stripper, Andress (she studies archaeology on her days off), and falls in love. Having changed his mind about dying, but unable to stop the plot, he is soon running throughout the Far East being chased by killers. Eventually he makes his way to safety and learns that the "killers" were actually insurance agents and that his fortune has doubled on the stock market. A contrived ending weakens this otherwise funny film.

p, Alexandre Mnouchkine, Georges Dancigers; d, Philippe de Broca; w, Daniel Boulanger, de Broca (based on a novel by Jules Verne); ph, Edmond Sechan (Eastmancolor); m, Georges Delerue; ed, Francoise Javet; art d, Francois de Lamothe; cos, Jacqueline Moreau; spec eff, Gil Delamare, Georges Lagonelli; stunts, Delamare.

Comedy   (PR:C MPAA:NR)

UP TO HIS NECK**   (1954, Brit.) 90m GFD bw

Ronald Shiner (*Jack Carter*), Laya Raki (*Lao Win Tan*), Harry Fowler (*Smudge*), Brian Rix (*Wiggy*), Michael Brennan (*CPO Brazier*), Gerald Campion (*Skinny*), Anthony Newley (*Tommy*), Bryan Forbes (*Subby*), Colin Gordon (*Lt. Comdr. Sterning*), John Warwick (*Lt. Truman*), Martin Boddey (*Chang*), Alec Mango (*Badit General*), Hattie Jacques (*Rakiki*), Roland Curram, Jan Miller, Norman Mitchell, Kim Parker, Shirley Burniston, Ruth Sheal, Eileen Sands, Harold Kasket.

Tepid remake of JACK AHOY! (1934) starring Shiner as a British navy seaman left alone on a South Sea island to guard supplies. Ten years later everyone has forgotten him and he has been made king of the island by the natives. Eventually the navy realizes that he's been left there and a ship is sent to the island to save him. Shiner doesn't want to be saved, however, but he is ordered to train some navy jungle commandos who have been assigned to recapture a submarine that was stolen by bandits. Shiner is soon captured by the baddies, but his native girl friend, Raki, comes to his rescue and the sub is recovered.

p, Hugh Stewart; d, John Paddy Carstairs; w, Carstairs, Patrick Kirwan, Ted Willis, Maurice Cowan (based on the novel *Jack Ahoy* by Sidney Gilliat, John Orton); ph, Ernest Steward; cos, Joan Ellacott.

Comedy   (PR:A MPAA:NR)

UP TO THE NECK½**   (1933, Brit.) 73m British and Dominions/UA bw

Ralph Lynn (*Norman B. Good*), Winifred Shotter (*April Dawne*), Francis Lister (*Eric Warwick*), Reginald Purdell (*Jimmy Catlin*), Mary Brough (*Landlady*), Marjorie Hume (*Vera Dane*), Grizelda Hervey (*Miss Fish*).

Lynn stars as a humble bank clerk who inherits a fortune and decides to fulfill his ambition to be a theater mogul. After falling in love with chorus girl Shotter, he sinks most of his fortune into an expensive production guaranteed to make her a star. The show flops. When Lynn mounts the stage in a desperate move to improve the deadly serious piece by playing the lead, his monocle and toothy grin win him raves as a comic genius, despite the fact that he tried to play the role straight, and the show becomes a comedy hit.

p, Herbert Wilcox; d, Jack Raymond; w, Ben Travers; ph, Cyril Bristow.

Comedy   (PR:A MPAA:NR)

UP WITH THE LARK*   (1943, Brit.) 83m New Realm bw

Ethel Revnell (*Ethel*), Gracie West (*Gracie*), Antony Holles (*Martel*), Anthony Hulme (*Mr. Britt*), Johnnie Schofield (*Mr. Tanner*), Lesley Osmond (*Mabel*), Alan Kane (*Fred Tompkins*), Ian Fleming (*Rev. Swallow*), Alma and Bobby, Van Straten's Piccadilly Dance Band.

Wartime comedy starring BBC radio comediennes Revnell and West as two bumbling female detectives who pose as Land Army girls in order to reveal a local hotel owner as a black marketeer. After a series of boring and predictable slapstick adventures the villains are captured more or less in spite of the women's efforts. Painfully stupid.

p, E.J. Fancey; d, Phil Brandon; w, James Seymour (based on an original story by Val Valentine); ph, Stephen Dade.

Comedy   (PR:A MPAA:NR)

UP YOUR TEDDY BEAR zero   (1970) 89m Joslyn/Geneni-Richard c (AKA: THE TOY GRABBERS; MOTHER)

Wally Cox (*Clyde*), Julie Newmar (*Toy Company Director*), Victor Buono (*Skippy*), Claire Kelly, Angelique Pettyjohn, Thordis Brandt, Valora Noland, Amy Thomson, Vicki Ellison.

Cox, a shy salesman for the Mother Knows Best Toy Company, creates his own wooden dolls as a hobby. Newmar (best remembered for the sexual tension she brought to television's "Batman" series as the Catwoman), the company's director, wants Cox's dolls for the company but he won't part with them. Since Cox's other hobby involves fantasizing about beautiful women, Newmar's son Buono gets a prostitute to try to seduce the dolls away from Cox. This plan fails, however, because Cox has a sort of Oedipus complex on Newmar, who reminds him of his own mother. That good woman instilled a "sex is dirty" ethic in her boy which now works to Newmar's disadvantage. Only Freudians in desperate need of a laugh might find anything remotely funny here.

p,d&w, Don Joslyn; ph, Robert Maxwell; m, Quincy Jones, The Eyes of Blue; ed, John Joyce, John Levine; art d, Bud Costello.

Comedy   (PR:O MPAA:R)

UPPER HAND, THE**   (1967, Fr./Ital./Ger.) 86m Copernic-Fida-Gloria/PAR c (DU RIFIFI A PANAME; RIFIFI INTERNAZIONALE; RIFIFI IN PARIS)

Jean Gabin (*Paulo Berger*), George Raft (*Charles Binaggio*), Gert Frobe (*Walter*), Nadja Tiller (*Irene*), Mireille Darc ("*Lili Princesse*"), Claudio Brook (*Mike Coppolano*), Claude Brasseur (*Giulio*), Daniel Ceccaldi (*Commissioner Noel*), Claude Cerval (*Rene*), Dany Dauberson (*Lea*), Marcel Bozzufi (*Marque Mal*), Jean-Claude Bercq (*Jo le Pale*), Carlo Nell (*Sergio*), Christa Lang (*Girl*), Yves Barsacq, Philippe Clair, Mino Doro, Maurice Jacquin, Jr, Franco Ressel, Tommaso Alvieri.

Decent cast has trouble rescuing this stale hoodlum drama starring Gabin and Frobe as aging gangsters who run an international gold smuggling organization. Seeking fresh, unknown faces to transport their booty throughout Europe, the gangsters hire unemployed journalist Brook, who is in reality a U.S. government agent out to smash Gabin and Frobe's operation because the two are suspected of having connections with American mobster Raft, who is selling guns to the Cubans. After some digging it is obvious to Brook that Gabin has never allowed himself to be taken in by the Mafia, but after Raft and his men cripple Gabin's operation, the gold runner is forced to capitulate. Meeting with Raft, Gabin pretends to be under his thumb, but plants a bomb and flees before the explosion kills everyone. Brook reveals his true identity to Gabin, stating that he admires the old gangster's courage, but Gabin spurns any compliments from the law.

p, Maurice Jacquin; d, Denys de La Patelliere; w, de la Patelliere, Alphonse Boudard; ph, Walter Wottitz (Eastmancolor); m, Georges Garvarentz; ed, Claude Durand; art d, Robert Clavel; cos, Jacques Fonteray.

Crime   (PR:C   MPAA:NR)

UPPER UNDERWORLD   (SEE: RULING VOICE, THE, 1931)

UPPER WORLD**½   (1934) 72m WB bw (AKA: UPPERWORLD)

Warren William (*Alexander Stream*), Mary Astor (*Mrs. Hettie Stream*), Ginger Rogers (*Lilly Linder*), Theodore Newton (*Rocklen*), Andy Devine (*Oscar the Chauffeur*), Dickie Moore (*Tommy Stream*), J. Carroll Naish (*Lou Colima*), Robert Barrat (*Commissioner Clark*), Robert Greig (*Caldwell the Butler*), Ferdinand Gottschalk (*Marcus*), Willard Robertson (*Capt. Reynolds*), Mickey Rooney (*Jerry*), John M. Qualen (*Chris the Janitor*), Henry O'Neill (*Banker*), Sidney Toler (*Officer Moran*), Frank Sheridan (*Inspector Kellogg*), Nora Cecil (*Housekeeper*), Lester Dorr (*Steward*), Wilfred Lucas (*Captain*), Cliff Saum (*Sailor*), William Jeffrey (*Bradley*), Edward Le Saint (*Henshaw*), John Elliott (*Crandall*), Armand Kaliz (*Maurice*), Milton Kibbee (*Pilot*), Marie Astaire, Joyce Owen, Lucille Collins (*Chorus Girls*), Jay Eaton (*Salesman*), James P. Burtis, Henry Otho (*Cops*), Douglas Cosgrove (*Johnson*), Guy Usher (*Carter*), Clay Clement (*Medical Examiner*), James Durkin, Monte Vandergrift, Jack Cheatham (*Detectives*), William B. Davidson (*City Editor*), Edwin Stanley (*Fingerprint Expert*), Howard Hickman (*Judge*), Frank Conroy (*Attorney*), Tom McGuire (*Bailiff*), Bert Moorhouse (*Court Clerk*), Sidney De Grey (*Foreman*), Harry Seymour (*Passerby*).

William is a wealthy businessman whose socialite wife, Astor, has little time for him. He takes up with burlesque queen Rogers, setting her up in an apartment. Her employer, Naish, wants to use this cozy arrangement to blackmail William, and one night as the proposed victim visits Rogers, Naish pulls a gun on him. Rogers sacrifices her life by stepping in front of the bullet, and William quickly guns down Naish in self-defense and flees. Detective Toler, vindictive since William had him transferred to the Bronx for giving him a speeding ticket, finds a fingerprint and prepares to arrest William during a swank party the businessman is giving at his home. Astor stands beside him in court and he is acquitted. Good, literate script by Ben Hecht puts this production a notch above the usual run of romantic triangles-turned-murder dramas that were very popular in 1934. Nothing unique here, apart from Rogers' death—the only time she was ever to die on screen. Another curious aspect is the effect of the newly established Motion Picture Code that forced the screenwriters to go to great lengths to show that the relationship between Rogers and William is completely innocent despite the apartment he furnishes her with and the fact that he is going to be blackmailed for his involvement with the showgirl. Thanks to the script and good performances by all the leads, this film holds up surprisingly well today.

p, Robert Lord; d, Roy Del Ruth; w, Ben Markson (based on a story by Ben Hecht); ph, Tony Gaudio; ed, Owen Marks; md, Leo F. Forbstein; art d, Anton Grot; cos, Orry-Kelly; makeup, Perc Westmore.

Crime   (PR:A   MPAA:NR)

UPSTAIRS AND DOWNSTAIRS**   (1961, Brit.) 101m RANK/FOX c

Michael Craig (*Richard Barry*), Anne Heywood (*Kate Barry*), Mylene Demongeot (*Ingrid Gunnar*), James Robertson Justice (*Mansfield*), Claudia Cardinale (*Maria*), Sidney James (*Police Constable Edwards*), Joan Hickson (*Rosemary*), Joan Sims (*Blodwen*), Joseph Tomelty (*Arthur Farringdon*), Nora Nicholson (*Mrs. Edith Farringdon*), Daniel Massey (*Wesley Cotes*), Austin Willis (*McGuffey*), Margalo Gillmore (*Mrs. McGuffey*), Reginald Beckwith (*Parson*), Cyril Chamberlain (*Guard*), Dilys Laye (*Agency Girl*), Irene Handl (*Large Woman*), William Mervyn (*Kingsley*), Eric Pohlmann (*Mario*), Jean Cadell (*1st Old Lady*), Barbara Everest (*2nd Old Lady*), Stephen Gregson (*Paul*), Nicholas Phipps (*Harry*), Jeremy Burnham (*Frank*), Nicholas Parsons (*Brian*), Madge Ryan (*Sgt. Tuck*), Betty Henderson (*Bridget*), Barbara Steele (*Mary*), Gaylord Cavallero, Bill Edwards, David Cargill, Shirley Lawrence, Shirley Ann Field, Susan Hampshire.

Dim-witted British comedy about the difficulty in hiring domestic help in England stars Craig as an ambitious executive who marries the boss' daughter, Heywood, and inherits the task of entertaining important clients at his home. Craig and Heywood set out to hire some competent domestic help and wind up with a revolving door of loony maids, each one worse than the last. The first, an Italian girl played by Cardinale, turns out to be a rabid nympho with a penchant for sailors. The next, Hickson, is a raving alcoholic whose best friend is a large sheepdog. The third, Sims, is a shy, clumsy girl who has just left her remote Welsh home for the first time. The fourth is an elderly couple who only pose as domestics but who in reality are bank robbers using the house as a front for their crimes. The last, Demongeot, is Swedish and very good, but she takes a liking to Craig and soon more trouble arises from her flirtations and other boy friends and she eventually quits. The distraught couple settles on an ex-policeman who makes an ideal servant. Some clever moments, but mostly predictable.

p, Betty E. Box; d, Ralph Thomas; w, Frank Harvey (based on the novel by Ronald Scott Thorne); ph, Ernest Steward (DeLuxe Color); m, Phil Green; ed, Alfred Roome; cos, Joan Ellacott.

Comedy   (PR:A   MPAA:NR)

UPSTATE MURDERS, THE   (SEE: SAVAGE WEEKEND, 1983)

UPTIGHT**   (1968) 104m Marlukin/PAR c

Raymond St. Jacques (*B.G.*), Ruby Dee (*Laurie*), Roscoe Lee Browne (*Clarence*), Julian Mayfield (*Tank*), Janet MacLachlan (*Jeannie*), Max Julien (*Johnny*), Juanita Moore (*His Mother*), Richard Anthony Williams (*Corbin*), Michael Baseleon (*Teddy*), Ji-Tu Cumbuka (*Rick*), John Wesley Rodgers (*Larry*), Ketty Lester (*Alma*), Robert DoQui (*Street Speaker*), Leon Bibb (*Mr. Oakley*), Jim McEachin (*Mello*), Vernett Allen (*Ralph*), Errol Jaye (*Mr. Oakley*), Isabelle Cooley, Alice Childress, David Moody, Kirk Kirksey, Van Kirksey, Mello Alexandria.

Ill-conceived updating of John Ford's 1935 classic THE INFORMER, featuring a strong cast of black actors. Mayfield stars as a weak-willed black who sells his militant friend Julien (who killed a guard while robbing an armory) down the river for a measly $1,000 with which to help his girl-turned-hooker feed her children. Julien is killed by the cops after a vicious gun battle when he is cornered at his mother's flat, and Mayfield's subsequent erratic and suspicious behavior sets militant leader St. Jacques wondering if he was the one who informed on Julien. Soon Mayfield is hauled before a militant "court" and found guilty. He escapes his captors, but is killed by the blacks after visiting Dee for the last time. While UPTIGHT follows the structure of THE INFORMER very closely, the filmmakers are trying to stuff a square peg into a round hole by making the assumption that the black militant (i.e. violent) cause in America is as tragic, frustrating, and noble as the IRA's was against England in the early 1920s when the book was written.

p&d, Jules Dassin; w, Dassin, Ruby Dee, Julian Mayfield (based on the novel *The Informer* by Liam O'Flaherty); ph, Boris Kaufman (Technicolor); m, Booker T. Jones; ed, Robert Lawrence; prod d, Alexandre Trauner; art d, Phillip Bennett; set d, Ray Moyer; cos, Theoni V. Aldredge; m/l, Jones (performed by Booker T. and the MGs, Judy Clay); makeup, Bob Sidel, Bob Morley.

Drama   (PR:O   MPAA:PG)

UPTOWN NEW YORK**   (1932) 80m KBS/World Wide bw

Jack Oakie (*Eddie Doyle*), Shirley Grey (*Patricia Smith*), Leon Waycoff [Ames] (*Max Silvers*), George Cooper (*Al*), Lee Moran (*Hotel Clerk*), Alexander Carr (*Papa Silver*), Raymond Hatton (*Slot Machine King*), Henry Armetta (*Restaurant Keeper*).

Routine tragic romance starring Waycoff [Ames] as a young Jew pressured by his upward-thinking family to marry a rich girl rather than the poor Miss Grey, whom he really loves. Shocked, hurt, and confused, Grey meets and marries Irishman Oakie as revenge. Eventually Oakie learns that their marriage is loveless and offers to divorce Grey, but she decides to remain with him despite the fact that she still loves Waycoff.

d, Victor Schertzinger; w, Warren B. Duff (based on the story "Uptown Woman" by Vina Delmar); ph, Norbert Brodine; ed, Rose Loewinger.

Drama   (PR:A   MPAA:NR)

UPTOWN SATURDAY NIGHT***   (1974) 104m First Artists/WB c

Sidney Poitier (*Steve Jackson*), Bill Cosby (*Wardell Franklin*), Harry Belafonte (*Geechie Dan Beauford*), Flip Wilson (*The Reverend*), Richard Pryor (*Sharp Eye Washington*), Rosalind Cash (*Sarah Jackson*), Roscoe Lee Browne (*Congressman Lincoln*), Paula Kelly (*Leggy Peggy*), Lee Chamberlin (*Mme. Zenobia*), Johnny Sekka (*Geechie's Henchman*), Calvin Lockhart (*Silky Slim*), Lincoln Kilpartick (*Slim's Henchman No. 1*), Ketty Lester (*Irma Franklin*), Don Marshall (*Slim's Henchman No. 2*), Harold Nicholas (*Little Seymour*).

A fine comedy starring and directed by Sidney Poitier, who plays a bored factory worker. He, along with his taxi-driving friend Cosby, decides to live it up one night and venture into a seedy, illegal, underground gambling den for some fun. While they are at the club, gangsters hold up the guests, making off with jewelry, cash, and wallets. When Poitier and Cosby learn that the lottery ticket in Poitier's stolen wallet happens to be worth $50,000, the desperate friends plunge head first into the criminal underworld to retrieve it. Pryor turns up as an incompetent private eye, Wilson is a preacher, Browne plays a shady black congressman, and Belafonte steals the movie with a hilarious parody of Marlon Brando's "Godfather" as the mobster who owns the town. The film spawned two sequels: LET'S DO IT AGAIN (1975) and A PIECE OF THE ACTION (1977).

p, Melville Tucker; d, Sidney Poitier; w, Richard Wesley; ph, Fred J. Koenekamp (Technicolor); m, Tom Scott; ed, Pembroke J. Herring; prod d, Alfred Sweeney; set d, Robert de Vestel; spec eff, Charles Spurgeon; makeup, Monty Westmore; m/l, title song, Tom Scott, Morgan Ames (sung by Dobie Gray).

Comedy   Cas.   (PR:C   MPAA:PG)

UPTURNED GLASS, THE**   (1947, Brit.) 87m Triton/UNIV bw

James Mason (Michael Joyce), Rosamund John (Emma Wright), Pamela Kellino (Kate Howard), Ann Stephens (Ann Wright), Morland Graham (Clay), Brefni O'Rourke (Dr. Farrell), Peter Cotes (Questioner), Henry Oscar (Coroner), Jane Hylton (Miss Marsh), Sheila Huntington, Susan Shaw (Students), Howard Douglas (Lorry Driver), Richard Afton (Lorry Driver's Mate), Cyril Chamberlain (Junior Doctor), John Stone (Male Student), Nuna Davey (Mrs. Deva), Jno P. Monoghan (U.S. Driver), Maurice Denham (Mobile Policeman), Janet Burnell (Sylvia), Margaret Withers (Party Guest), Beatrice Varley (Injured Girl's Mother), Helene Burls (Farm Laborer's Wife), Lyn Evans (County Policeman), George Merritt, Glyn Rowland (Policemen).

A bad title didn't help the screenplay for this heavy drama which was cowritten by Mason's wife, who used her maiden name of Kellino in both the writing credit and her screen acting credit. Mason is a successful brain surgeon who falls madly in love with John, a married woman. He has saved John's daughter, Stephens, from blindness with his brilliant surgery. John's husband is conveniently traveling on the Continent while Mason is looked after by his sister-in-law, Kellino, a widow who is jealous of his attentions to John. Mason and John realize they can't keep their love together and elect to part so John can raise her daughter with no fear of impropriety being attached to her life. Then John dies mysteriously, having fallen from a window. Mason suspects that she may have been killed by Kellino and he sets out to prove his intuition by wooing Kellino and gaining her confidence. Once that's done, Mason takes Kellino to the same room in the same house from which John fell. Then he tosses Kellino out the window to her death. He thinks he's committed the perfect crime as nobody has seen the two together. Mason stuffs Kellino's body in his car and is on his way to get rid of it when he runs into a fog bank and is stopped by another doctor, O'Rourke, who asks him to help take care of a child who has been hurt in a car accident caused by the thick weather. Mason can't decide what to do. If he leaves the area, the child may die. If he stays, Kellino's body may be discovered. The oath of Hippocrates wins out and he remains to save the life of the little girl. O'Rourke (who died right after finishing this film) sees the body and accuses Mason of being insane. Mason, who more or less agrees, races off and kills himself by leaping off a cliff. The first part of the story is told in flashback by Mason who boldly outlines the coming crime while relating the story of a nameless surgeon to his class of students. Everyone underplays to the point of somnambulism, with the exception of Kellino, who emotes so loudly that she seems to be in a different movie. Mason coproduced with the brother-sister team of Sydney Box and Betty Box (credited as associate producer). Sidney Box had also made THE SEVENTH VEIL and the two would go on to oversee many films between them and apart, including DOCTOR IN THE HOUSE, THE BROTHERS, QUARTET, THE PRISONER, and many more. Sydney Box's wife, Muriel, wrote THE SEVENTH VEIL and later became a director with credits that included THE HAPPY FAMILY and RATTLE OF A SIMPLE MAN.

p, Sydney Box, James Mason; d, Lawrence Huntington; w, John P. Monoghan, Pamela Kellino (based on a story by Monoghan); ph, Reginald Wyer; m, Bernard Stevens; ed, Alan Osbiston; md, Muir Mathieson; art d, Andrew Mazzei; makeup, Nell Taylor.

Crime   (PR:A-C   MPAA)

URANIUM BOOM*½   (1956) 66m COL bw

Dennis Morgan (Brad Collins), Patricia Medina (Jean Williams), William Talman (Grady Mathews), Tina Carver (Gail Windsor), Philip Van Zandt (Navajo Charlie), Bill Henry (Joe McGinns), Mel Curtis (Phil McGinns), Henry Rowland (Harry), S. John Launer (Mac), Michael Bryant (Peterson), Frank Wilcox (Floyd Gorman), Ralph Sanford (Old Timer), Carlyle Mitchell (Mr. Aldrich), Nick Tell (Reporter).

Talman and Morgan play prospecting partners scouring the Colorado Territory for uranium. Things go great for the intrepid fortune-hunters until trouble arises in the form of sexy Miss Medina, over whom the friends have a vicious falling out. Under Medina's influence, Talman works against Morgan and nearly forces him out of the partnership, but honor and reason prevail and the two buddies dump the woman and make up.

p, Sam Katzman; d, William Castle; w, George F. Slavin, George W. George, Norman Retchin (based on a story by Slavin, George); ph, Fred Jackman, Jr.; m, Mischa Bakaleinikoff; ed, Edwin Bryant; art d, Paul Palmentola.

Drama   (PR:A   MPAA:NR)

URBAN COWBOY**   (1980) 135m PAR c

John Travolta (Bud), Debra Winger (Sissy), Scott Glenn (Wes), Madolyn Smith (Pam), Barry Corbin (Uncle Bob), Brooke Alderson (Aunt Corene), Cooper Huckabee (Marshall), James Gammon (Steve Strange), Betty Murphy (Bud's Mom), Ed Geldart (Bud's Dad), Leah Geldart (Bud's Sister), Keith Clemons, Howard Norman (Bud's Brothers), Sheryl Briedel, Sean Lawler (Bud's Cousins), Gator Conley (Gator), David Ogle (Killer), Bettye Fitzpatrick (Sissy's Mom), Jim Gough (Sissy's Dad), Christopher Saylors (Bubba), Mickey Gilley, Johnny Lee, Bonnie Raitt, The Charlie Daniels Band, Minnie Elerick, Bret Williams, Tamara Matusian, Becky Conway, Sherwood Cryer, Jerry Hall, Cyndy Hall, Lucky Mosley, Zetta Raney, Ellen

March, Gina Alexander, Steve Chambers, Ann Travolta, Anson Downs, W.P. Wright III, Steve Strange, Norman Tucker, Debie Tucker, Jesse LaRive, Connie Hanson, Glenn Holtzman, Daniel Heintschel, Jr, Ben F. Brannon III, Robert Herridge, Robert Bush, James N. Harrell, Julie Bailey, Gene McLaughlin.

If one can accept Travolta as a Texan one has gotten only halfway through the problems with URBAN COWBOY. Travolta stars as a young farm-raised Texan who ventures to the big city to work at an oil refinery. Soon he is ushered into the local nightlife which revolves entirely around Gilley's, a cavernous honky-tonk populated with seemingly hundreds of good 'ol boys and good 'ol gals looking for some action. Gilley's (and the film's) main attraction is a nasty mechanical bull which the bravest (and most drunken) male patrons test their bravery upon. In this redneck den of iniquity Travolta meets the sexy and spunky Winger (one of the few performances that makes this plodding cow of a film tolerable-at least she's got her accent down) and after a brief, intense courtship (Winger responds to every suggestion Travolta makes with a complacent "'kay") the two are married. Almost as fast as the marriage is the speed with which it disintegrates. Travolta is soon wooed away from Winger by Smith, a mindless blonde hussy, and Winger takes up with sleazy bad -guy Glenn (the only other reason to sit through this film). After a number of dirty looks, quick fistfights and more drinking and carousing the film lumbers fitfully to its end. Aside from Winger's acclaimed steamy mechanical bull ride, there is not much else of interest. Director Bridges' fatal flaw in dramatizing the dull, vapid lives of these southern singles is that the film itself is dull, vapid, and long, despite interesting performances from Winger and Glenn.

p, Robert Evans, Irving Azoff; d, James Bridges; w, Bridges, Aaron Latham (based on a story by Latham); ph, Ray Villalobos (Panavision, Movielab Color); m, Ralph Burns; ed, Dave Rawlins; prod d, Stephen Grimes; art d, Stewart Campbell; set d, Geore R. Nelson; ch, Patsy Swayze.

Drama   **Cas.**   (PR:C   MPAA:PG)

URGENT CALL   (SEE: AGAINST THE LAW, 1934)

URGE TO KILL**   (1960, Brit.) 58m Merton Park/AA bw

Patrick Barr (Supt. Allen), Howard Pays (Charles Ramskill), Ruth Dunning (Auntie B), Terence Knapp (Hughie), Anna Turner (Lily Willis), Christopher Trace (Sgt. Grey), Margaret St. Barbe West (Mrs. Willis), Yvonne Buckingham (Gwen).

When a local barkeep's daughter is found dead on a nearby dock, her body naked and mutilated, all the evidence points to a young retarded boy as the culprit. The police superintendent isn't convinced of the boy's guilt, however, and when another girl turns up murdered, he is able to locate the real killer.

p, Jack Greenwood; d, Vernon Sewell; w, James Eastwood (based on the story "Hand in Glove" by Gerald Savory, Charles Freeman).

Crime   (PR:C   MPAA:NR)

URSUS   (SEE: MIGHTY URSUS, 1962, Ital./Span.)

URSUS, IL GLADIATORE RIBELLE
          (SEE: REBEL GLADIATORS, THE, 1963, Ital.)

USED CARS***½   (1980) 113m COL c

Kurt Russell (Rudy Russo), Jack Warden (Roy L. Fuchs/Luke Fuchs), Gerrit Graham (Jeff), Frank McRae (Jim the Mechanic), Deborah Harmon (Barbara Fuchs), Joseph P. Flaherty (Sam Slaton), David L. Lander (Freddie Paris), Michael McKean (Eddie Winslow), Michael Talbott (Mickey), Harry Northup (Carmine), Alfonso Arau (Manuel), Al Lewis (Judge Harrison), Woodrow Parfrey (Mr. Chertner), Andrew Duncan (Charlie), Dub Taylor (Tucker), Claude Earl Jones (Al), Dan Barrows (Stanley Dewoski), Cheryl Rixon (Margaret), Marc McClure, Susan Donovan, Don Ruskin, Jan Sandwich, Tracy Lee Rowe, Kurtis Sanders, Clint Lilley, Patrick McMorrow, Joseph Barnaba, Diane Hill, Dick Miller, Rita Taggart, Dave Herrera, Walter Jackson, Gene Blakely, Betty Thomas.

Before director-writer Bob Zemeckis found huge box-office, Spielberg-cloned (Steven Spielberg is personally responsible for Zemecki's career) success with such hits as ROMANCING THE STONE and BACK TO THE FUTURE, he directed this raunchy, hysterically funny comedy which is about as far from his mentor's "innocence of childhood" dramas as one can get. Russell turns in a bravura performance as the unscrupulous-but-likable head salesman of a dying used car lot owned by Warden, who is competing with his hated wealthier brother (also played by Warden) who runs a lucrative though shady used car lot across the street and is trying to snatch up his sibling's property. Russell and his partner, Graham, will try anything to sell a car, including pushing a rock under the rear tire of a decrepit station wagon (so that when it moves forward the driver will think he ran over something) and using their dog, who plays dead upon command, to guilt-trip a customer into buying the vehicle by pitifully screaming, "Mister, you killed my dog!" Another trick the salesmen employ is jamming the airwaves during a nationally televised presidential address with bizarre, R-rated commercials populated with naked women to entice customers to the lot. The loose plot sees Russell and Graham trying to keep their small lot open despite the untimely death of Warden (a morbidly hilarious scene) which they try to keep a secret from both his evil brother (who was responsible for the death) and Warden's daughter, Harmon. The plot twists in this wacky film are nearly impossible to describe. Suffice it to say that the "good" (less sleazy) guys and true love win in the end. Fans of television's "Hill Street Blues" may want to look for Betty Thomas as one of the topless dancers bumping and grinding in one of Russell's more racy used car TV ads (no doubt a role she'd rather forget).

p, Bob Gale; d, Robert Zemeckis; w, Zemeckis, Gale; ph, Donald M. Morgan (Metrocolor); m, Patrick Williams; ed, Michael Kahn; prod d, Peter M. Jamison; set d, Linda Spheeris; m/l, Williams, Norman Gimbel; stunts, Terry J. Leonard.

Comedy   **Cas.**   **(PR:O   MPAA:R)**

USCHI DAI SENSO   (SEE: BATTLE IN OUTER SPACE, 1960, Jap.)

UTAH**½   (1945) 78m REP bw

Roy Rogers (*Himself*), George "Gabby" Hayes" (*Gabby*), Dale Evans (*Dorothy Bryant*), Peggy Stewart (*Jackie*), Beverly Loyd (*Wanda*), Grant Withers (*Ben Bowman*), Jill Browning (*Babe*), Vivien Oakland (*Stella Mason*), Hal Taliaferro (*Steve Lacey*), Jack Rutherford (*Sheriff*), Emmett Vogan (*District Attorney*), Edward Cassidy, Ralph Colby, Bob Nolan and Sons of the Pioneers, Trigger the Horse.

Sidekick Gabby Hayes returned to the Roy Rogers series with this film which sees Roy desperately trying to convince greenhorn musical comedy star Evans not to sell her inherited, unseen ranch to finance her show in Chicago. Rogers, who is the foreman on her ranch, persuades Evans to travel to Utah and see her inheritance in the hope that she will fall in love with it and not sell. Eventually she sees the light and everyone sings for the fade.

p, Donald H. Brown; d, John English; w, Jack Townley, John K. Butler (based on an original story by Gilbert Wright, Betty Burbridge); ph, William Bradford; ed, Harry Keller; m, Morton Scott; art d, Gano Chittenden; cos, Adele Palmer; ch, Larry Ceballos; m/l, Charles Henderson, Dave Franklin, Bob Palmer, Glen Spencer, Tim Spencer, Bob Nolan, Ken Carson.

Western   **Cas.**   **(PR:A   MPAA:NR)**

UTAH BLAINE**   (1957) 75m COL bw

Rory Calhoun (*Utah Blaine*), Susan Cummings (*Angie Kinyon*), Angela Stevens (*Mary Blake*), Max Baer (*Gus Ortmann*), Paul Langton (*Rip Coker*), George Keymas (*Rink Witter*), Ray Teal (*Russ Nevers*), Gene Roth (*Tom Corey*), Norman Fredric (*Davis*), Ken Christy (*Joe Neal*), Steve Darrell (*Lud Fuller*), Terry Frost (*Gavin*), Dennis Moore (*Ferguson*), Jack Ingram (*Clel Miller*).

Routine oater starring Calhoun as a noble saddlebum who rescues an unfortunate ranch owner who has been hanged and left for dead by the villainous Teal and his men who want the rancher's land. Calhoun saves the man's life and earns enough gratitude to inherit half the ranch (the other half going to love interest Cummings) after Teal and his hoods find the reprieved rancher and this time gun him down. Aided by Baer, Langton, and lots of firearms, Calhoun eventually runs the villains off.

p, Sam Katzman; d, Fred F. Sears; w, Robert E. Kent, James B. Gordon (based on the novel by Louis L'Amour); ph, Benjamin H. Kline; m, Ross Di Maggio; ed, Charles Nelson; art d, Paul Palmentola.

Western   **(PR:A   MPAA:NR)**

UTAH KID, THE**   (1930) 57m TIF bw

Rex Lease (*Cal Reynolds*), Dorothy Sebastian (*Jenny Lee*), Tom Santschi (*Butch*), Mary Carr (*Aunt Ada*), Walter Miller (*Sheriff Bentley*), Lafe McKee (*Parson Joe*), Boris Karloff (*Baxter*), Bud Osborne (*Deputy*).

Sebastian stars as a wholesome schoolteacher who stumbles into the hideout of a ruthless gang of robbers. One of the crooks, Lease, marries the girl so that his fellow outlaws will leave her alone. Miller, the local sheriff, is in love with Sebastian and is determined to smash the gang and rescue her, which he does, but when he sees that she really loves Lease he lets the young outlaw go and gives him a chance to straighten out. Notable only because Boris Karloff played his last bit part, a bandit in an oater.

d, Richard Thorpe; w, Frank Howard Clark; ph, Arthur Reed; ed, Billy Bolen.

Western   **(PR:A   MPAA:NR)**

UTAH TRAIL**   (1938) 60m GN bw

Tex Ritter (*Tex Lawrence*), Horace Murphy (*Ananias*), Snub Pollard (*Pee Wee*), Adele Pearce (*Sally Jeffers*), Karl Hackett (*Slaughter*), Charles King (*Badger*), Edward Cassidy (*Sheriff*), David [Dave] O'Brien (*Mason*), Bud Osborne (*Hank*), Lynton Brent (*Cheyenne*), Rudy Sooter (*Orchestra Leader*).

Strange Ritter oater (His last for Grand National, which soon after went bankrupt) based on his original idea–not that the idea was all that original. Ritter plays a lawman hired to stop the cattle-rustling activities of a gang of crooks who use their secret railroad to shuttle trainloads of beef into a valley where no one can find them. Except Ritter, that is. Super-cheap production hampers what could have been a fairly interesting story.

p, Edward Finney; d, Al Herman; w, Edmund Kelso (based on a story by Lindsley Parsons, Kelso); m/l, Bob Palmer, Frank Harford, Rudy Sooter.

Western   **Cas.**   **(PR:A   MPAA:NR)**

UTAH WAGON TRAIN**   (1951) 67m REP bw

Rex Allen (*Himself*), Penny Edwards (*Nancy Bonner*), Buddy Ebsen (*Snooper Trent*), Roy Barcroft (*Driscoll*), Sarah Padden (*Sarah Wenover*), Grant Withers (*Bancroft*), Arthur Space (*Hatfield*), Edwin Band (*Sutton*), Robert Karnes (*Scully*), William Holmes (*Millan*), Stanley Andrews (*Sheriff*), Frank Jenks (*Hap*), Koko the Horse.

A western whodunit sees Allen guide a group of settlers along an ancient wagon train trail after his father, who was supposed to play guide, is murdered. Figuring he can solve the crime on the trail, Allen casts a suspicious eye on all the pioneers until it is finally revealed that a phony preacher, Space, is the villain intent on uncovering a $500,000 fortune in gold hidden by settlers nearly 100 years ago.

p, Melville Tucker; d, Philip Ford; w, John K. Butler; ph, John MacBurnie; m, Stanley Wilson; ed, Edward H. Schroeder; m/l, "Toolie Rollum," "The Colorado Trail," Rex Allen.

Western   **Cas.**   **(PR:A   MPAA:NR)**

UTILITIES**   (1983, Can.) 91m New World c (AKA: GETTING EVEN)

Robert Hays (*Bob*), Brooke Adams (*Marion*), John Marley (*Roy*), James Blendick (*Kenneth*), Ben Gordon (*Eddie*), Jane Mallet (*Dr. Rogers*), Toby Tarnow (*Gilda*), Helen Burns (*Ruby*), Lee Broker (*Jack*).

Hays is a social worker who decides to take on the local utility companies in a seemingly futile battle. Is he doing this out of a genuine concern for the environment? Maybe, but winning the affections of Adams, a local policewoman, also plays a decisive hand in his dealings. There are some attempts at satire but these fall flat, making it a highly forgettable comedy.

p, Robert Cooper; d, Harvey Hart; w, David Greenwalt, M. James Kouf, Jr.; ph, Richard Leiterman; m, John Erbe, Mickey Solomon; ed, John Kelly; prod d, Bill Boeton.

Comedy/Romance   **Cas.**   **(PR:C-O   MPAA:R)**

UTOPIA**½   (1952, Fr./Ital.) 80m Les Films Sirius-Franco-London-Fortezza/Exploitation bw (GB: ESCAPADE; AKA: ATOLL K; ROBINSON CRUSOE-LAND)

Stan Laurel (*Himself*), Oliver Hardy (*Himself*), Suzy Delair (*Cherie Lamour*), Max Elloy (*Kokken Antoine*), Suzet Mais (*Mrs. Dolan*), Felix Oudart (*Mayor*), Robert Murzeau (*Capt. Dolan*), Luigi Tosi (*Lt. Jack Frazer*), Michael Dalmatoff (*Alecto*), Adriano Rimoldi (*Giovanni Copini*), Charles Lemontier, Simone Voisin, Olivia Hussenot, Lucien Callamand, Robert Vattier, Gilbert Morfau, Jean Verner, Andre Randall, C. May, R. Legris (*Fortune Hunters and Subversives*), Paul Frees (*English Narrator*).

The final film of Laurel and Hardy as a team was a disappointment for the members of the "Sons of the Desert" (which is the name of the L&H fan club). Although Joannon and Berry are listed as the directors, there were three other names indicated in that department. Isabelle Kloukowski and Jean-Claude Eger were named for "directorial assistance" and Al Goulding had his name attached for "special directorial assistance." Too many cooks spoiled whatever broth remained in the duo. The boys inherit a ship and an island somewhere in the South Pacific and they set out for their island. Much of their money has been taken by taxes and they are looking forward to cashing in on what's left. Rimoldi is a stowaway and Elloy is a stateless Frenchman who offers to be their cook if they will let him stay on their island. As they approach the shore of the tropical paradise, the ship begins to go down in a storm. Suddenly, an atoll emerges from the rolling sea and juts up to form an island where they can stay. They begin life as a quartet of Robinson Crusoes, then Delair lands on their atoll. She's running from a jealous lover (Tosi) and seeks refuge with them. They begin their own government and declare the island a republic. Soon, they discover that their island is a huge repository of one of the world's most important minerals–uranium. Once that word gets out, they are besieged by all of the governments of the world and their Eden is overrun as a horde of people descend on them. It gets so dicey that the group is about to be executed (in an unbelievable series of twists and turns) when fate takes a hand and sinks the atoll. They are rescued by a ship, Delair goes back to her boy friend, and L&H finally make it to their island to learn that they can never afford to pay all the inheritance taxes which still remain and they will never live the Life of Riley that they'd hoped for. It was made in 1950 and 1951 and the lag in shooting was due to Laurel's prostate illness that called for an operation in Paris. He was in pain before and after the surgery and that's indicated by the grimaces on his face. The movie was known as ESCAPADE in Britain and briefly released as ROBINSON CRUSOE-LAND in the U.S. with an English-language narration added by Paul Frees, the same man who does so much of the narration at Disneyland in California. The entire affair was marred by a limited budget and the problems of having to deal with a crew that came from several countries. It was not distributed in the U.S. until 1955, perhaps due to the fact that the film's co-director, Berry, was alleged to be one of the many film people who were deemed "unfriendly" by the Communist witch-hunters. The dubbing was awful and many of the gags lacked the old zing. Laurel was 60 years of age when the movie was made and Hardy was 58 and time was taking a toll on their maneuverability, so a lot of their old slapstick had to be substituted by verbal wit. Despite not being up to the quality of much of their other work, it is still funny in spots and has a few wonderful bits. Fans of the duo will know that the moment they teamed up, Laurel never worked alone. Hardy, however, did three movies without Laurel. He appeared in ZENOBIA in 1939 for their boss Hal Roach, then did a neat cameo with John Wayne in THE FIGHTING KENTUCKIAN, and completed his solo work in RIDING HIGH for Frank Capra in 1950. One of the highlights of their lives was the "This is Your Life" segment done just before Hardy's death. The rights to the Laurel and Hardy characterizations have been held for some years by Larry Harmon, who is the man behind the makeup of "Bozo the Clown." Harmon likes to do Laurel in the various commercials but he is woefully inadequate when seen next to veteran impressionist Jim McGeorge, who works with Chuck McCann (as Hardy) on many TV spots. Both were seen on the Oscar Awards in 1986.

McGeorge played Laurel in the musical play "Chaplin" and was so good at it that an audience member was heard to exclaim at McGeorge's entrance, "That's Stan Laurel. I thought he was dead. I guess I was wrong."

p, R. Eger; d, John Berry, Leo Joannon; w, Rene Wheeler, P. Tellini (based on an idea by Joannon); ph, Armand Thirard, Louis Nee; ed, Raymond Isnardon; md, Paul Misraki.

Comedy   **Cas.**   **(PR:A   MPAA:NR)**

U-TURN*½   (1973, Can.) 97m Cinepix c

David Selby (Scott), Maud Adams (Paula/Tracy), Gay Rowan (Bonnie), William Osler (Prof. Bamberger), Diane Dewey (Holly).

Lovestruck lawyer Selby spends two years seeking Adams, the beauty he briefly met and instantly adored, despite his long-time liaison with his live-in girl friend. When at last he chances upon his lost love, he discovers that she, too, was smitten and sought him as well, even though she is married and multiparous. After a brief, touching, romantic meeting, they separate forever. Selby returns to comfortable unfulfillment and continued fantasy.

p&d, George Kaczender; w, Douglas Bowie; ph, Miklos Lente (Eastmancolor); m, Neil Chotem; ed, Kaczender.

Drama/Romance   **(PR:C   MPAA:NR)**

V.D. zero   (1961) 91m Donna-Big Ten/MY c (AKA: DAMAGED GOODS)

Charlotte Stewart (*Judy Jackson*), Mory Schoolhouse (*Jim Radman*), Dolores Faith (*Kathy Durham*), Michael Bell (*Monk Monahan*), Joan Yarborough (*Mary Jackson*), Terry Reagan (*Fred Jackson*), George Martin (*Singer*).

The horrors of venereal disease are dramatized in this feature-length public service announcement which follows the sexual escapades of a group of high-school students. Stewart and Schoolhouse play young lovers planning to get married someday. When Schoolhouse's wild friend Bell introduces vixenish girl Faith into the group, there's some tension between the young couple when it is obvious she is attracted to Schoolhouse. When Stewart's parents learn that their daughter is harboring thoughts of matrimony, they take her away for a weekend in the mountains to dissuade her. This leaves Schoolhouse bored and alone, so he runs off to a nearby seaside town with his buddies. The boys get drunk, pick up some local prostitutes, and you guessed it, they contract venereal disease. When Stewart learns of this horror she dumps Schoolhouse like a hot potato, forcing her former beau into the waiting arms of Faith. Soon Faith is infected with the dread disease which spreads like wildfire among the tightly knit (and apparently quite friendly) group of teenagers. Eventually all the gang troops down to the local doctor who shows them a five-minute V.D. film and cleans up their problems with a little penicillin. Now that Schoolhouse's plumbing is once again bug-free, Stewart relents and agrees to resume their engagement. What more can one say?

p, Sid Davis; d&w, Haile Chace; ph, Vilis Lapenieks; ed, Warren Brown.

Drama   (PR:O   MPAA:NR)

V.I.P.s, THE*½   (1963, Brit.) 119m MGM-Taylor/MGM c

Elizabeth Taylor (*Frances Andros*), Richard Burton (*Paul Andros*), Louis Jourdan (*Marc Champselle*), Elsa Martinelli (*Gloria Gritti*), Margaret Rutherford (*Duchess of Brighton*), Maggie Smith (*Miss Mead*), Rod Taylor (*Les Mangam*), Orson Welles (*Max Buda*), Linda Christian (*Miriam Marshall*), Dennis Price (*Comdr. Millbank*), Richard Wattis (*Sanders*), Ronald Fraser (*Joslin*), David Frost (*Reporter*), Robert Coote (*John Coburn*), Joan Benham (*Miss Potter*), Michael Hordern (*Airport Director*), Lance Percival (*BOAC Official*), Martin Miller (*Dr. Schwutzbacher*), Peter Sallis (*Doctor*), Stringer Davis (*Hotel Waiter*), Clifton Jones (*Jamaican Passenger*), Moyra Fraser, Jill Carson (*Air Hostesses*), Joyce Carey (*Mrs. Damer*), Peter Illing (*Mr. Damer*), Griffiths Davis (*Porter*), Maggie McGrath (*Waitress*), Frank Williams (*Assistant to Airport Director*), Rosemary Dorken, Pamela Buckley (*Airport Announcers*), Ray Austin (*Rolls Chauffeur*), Angus Lennie (*Meteorological Man*), Duncan Lewis (*Hotel Receptionist*), Richard Briers (*Meteorological Official*), Terence Alexander (*Captain*), Richard Caldicot (*Hotel Representative*), Ann Castle (*Lady Reporter*), Clifford Mollison (*Mr. River the Hotel Manager*), Gordon Sterne (*Official*), Reginald Beckwith (*Head Waiter*), John Blythe (*Barman*), Virginia Bedard, Cal McCord (*Visitors*).

A slick, glossy multi-character soap opera set in London's airport. Next to CLEOPATRA, Burton and Elizabeth Taylor shine in this film, which was shot after CLEOPATRA was made but released to a panting public before the aforementioned epic left the "Road Show" theaters. Burton signed on to do the movie and Taylor kiddingly suggested that it's hard to be in it as well and was offered the role on the spot. As fog rolls in over London, the regular flight to the U.S. has been temporarily grounded by the pea soup. Several people are desperate to get off the ground that night for various reasons. They are all strangers but in the time they must spend in the airport's waiting lounge they get to know each other fast. Taylor is a fleeing wife who has left her immensely wealthy husband, Burton, to seek a new life in the U.S. with Jourdan, her lover. She is convinced that Burton no longer cares for her and she will not play second fiddle to anyone. She'd left him a "Dear Paul" letter and after reading it, Burton makes a beeline to the airport in the hopes of winning his spouse back. She thought that he wouldn't read the note until she was safe in the sky. The implausible part of this is that playboy Jourdan and Burton are perceived as such opposites that it's hard to reckon two more unalike men in love with the same woman. In this, the first of the stories, Burton and Taylor eventually do reconcile, but not before Burton has some agonizing moments as he contemplates how lonely his life would be without her. He comes out of his macho shell, tells her straightaway how much he adores her, and that problem is solved. But there are other woeful people seated in that lounge. Welles (doing a fine impersonation of Welles as a mittel-European film director) is in the lounge with his accountant, Miller, and his latest "discovery," Martinelli. He is a rich director who spends his time in various countries to avoid paying income taxes anywhere. If he's not out of England by midnight, all of his money will be erased by the high taxes. Miller, a conniving accountant with Byzantine ideas, comes up with the answer. If Welles marries Martinelli, he can legally transfer his wealth to her, thus avoiding the Inland Revenue scythe. Rod Taylor is an Australian entrepreneur who must get to New York by the following day

to secure financing in order to hold off a hostile takeover of his tractor manufacturing company. Smith is Taylor's devoted secretary and secretly in love with him. She prevails on the rich Burton to lend Taylor the money to tide him over. The final, and most delightful of all the plots, concerns Rutherford as a dotty duchess. She is in danger of losing her estate because she can't afford to keep it up. Thus she has secured a job in Florida as a social hostess so she can raise the cash. Rutherford is losing her marbles and has to take pills to relieve her fear of flying. She is rescued from having to fly by Welles' deciding to shoot his next film on her estate and paying her in advance for the rental. Lots of humor, especially from Rutherford in a role that won her the Best Supporting Actress Award. TV's David Frost made his film debut here as a reporter and all of the other actors were splendid. This kind of movie, a GRAND HOTEL in a smaller space, could have been a crashing bore, but Asquith's snappy direction and some bright lines from Rattigan's script saved the day. Filmed in England for a reasonable figure, it made scads of money wherever it was shown. While shooting, the title was tentatively "International Hotel." Smith was excellent and it was a tossup as to which actress would be nominated for the Oscar. Rozsa's score sounded a little too much like his music for BEN-HUR.

p, Anatole de Grunwald; d, Anthony Asquith; w, Terence Rattigan; ph, Jack Hildyard (Panavision, Metrocolor); m, Miklos Rozsa; ed, Frank Clarke; art d, William Kellner; set d, Pamela Cornell; cos, Hubert de Givenchy, Pierre Cardin; spec eff, Tom Howard; makeup, Dave Aylott, Tom Smith, Eric Allwright.

Drama/Comedy   (PR:A   MPAA:NR)

V1   (SEE: MISSILE FROM HELL, 1960, Brit.)

VACATION, THE zero   (1971, Ital.) 101m Lion c (LA VACANZA)

Vanessa Redgrave (*Immacolata*), Franco Nero (*The Poacher*), Leopoldo Trieste (*Judge*), Corin Redgrave (*Gigi*), Osiride Pevarello (*Olindo*), Countessa Veronica (*Iside*), Germana Monteverdi (*Mercedes*), Margherita Lozano (*Ra*), Fany Sakantany (*Alpi*).

A dreadful, self-indulgent piece of claptrap directed by the man who gave the world CALIGULA, Tinto Brass. Redgrave is a supposed mental case who gets a brief leave from the asylum where she has been residing. There is a theory that if she can make it in the outside world for a short while, then she is on the road to recovery. She goes home to her family who turn a blind eye and a deaf ear to her and she is sold to one of the family's creditors. She escapes that fate and marches into the woods where she meets Nero, a professional poacher who makes his living killing animals that don't belong to him. She tells Nero how and why she came to be in this predicament and we flash back to see that she had been having an affair with a local nobleman and he is the person who had her tossed into the asylum to get her out of his hair. Nero and Redgrave go off on various adventures that bring them into contact with a band of gypsies, a British panty salesman (played by Redgrave's brother, Corin), and a few other oddballs. In the end, the cops kill Nero and Redgrave is thrown back into the asylum. There appears to be a great deal of improvisation in the movie, a typical reaction of egocentric actors who think they can make up better dialog and action than the writers who are expert at it. The best part of the movie is the beautiful landscape of the area surrounding Venice. A number of local folk tunes also help define the locale but Redgrave and Nero do nothing to help matters. It was in 1967 that Redgrave met Nero on the set of CAMELOT when he played "Lancelot" to her "Guinevere." They appeared to be having a marvelous time making this movie. Wish we could say the same watching it.

p, Tinto Brass; w, Vincenzo M. Siniscalchi, Brass, Roberto Lerici; ph, Silvano Ippoliti (Technichrome); m, Florenzo Carpi; ed, Brass; art d, Carla Cipriani

Drama   (PR:C   MPAA:NR)

VACATION DAYS*   (1947) 68m MON bw

Freddie Stewart, June Preisser, Frankie Darro, Warren Mills, Noel Neill, Milt Kibbee, Belle Mitchell, John Hart, Hugh Prosser, Terry Frost, Edythe Elliott, Claire James, Spade Cooley, Jerry Wald.

High school-age romance grows between Stewart and Preisser during summer vacation. Lightweight drama with Cooley contributing some western swing tunes.

p, Sam Katzman; d, Arthur Dreifuss, w, Hal Collins; ph, Ira Morgan; ed, Ace Herman; md, Edward J. Kay; art d, Dave Milton.

Romance   (PR:A   MPAA:NR)

VACATION FROM LOVE**   (1938) 66m MGM bw

Dennis O'Keefe (*Bill Blair*), Florence Rice (*Patricia Lawson*), Reginald Owen (*John Hodge Lawson*), June Knight (*Flo Heath*), Edward S. Brophy (*Barney Keenan*), Truman Bradley (*Mark Shelby*), Tom Rutherford (*T. Ames*

Piermont III), Andrew Tombes *(Judge Brandon)*, Herman Bing *(Oscar Wittlesbach)*, George Zucco *(Dr. Waxton)*, Paul Porcasi *(French Judge)*, J. M. Kerrigan *(Danny Dolan)*, Armand Kaliz *(M. Fumagally)*.

Dull drama starring O'Keefe as a saxophone player who meets, romances, and marries rich debutante Rice. Their union is blissful until O'Keefe succumbs to family pressures and enters his father-in-law's business, which keeps him away from home frequently. Eventually these long absences lead to marital problems and a separation of the couple which seems certain to end in divorce. Luckily the two have a last minute change of heart and they patch things up in time for the end credits.

p, Orville O. Dull; d, George Fitzmaurice; w, Patterson McNutt, Harlan Ware; ph, Ray June; ed, Ben Lewis; m/1, Edward Ward, Bob Wright, Chet Forrest.

Drama   (PR:A   MPAA:NR)

VACATION FROM MARRIAGE***   (1945, Brit.) 111m MGM-LFP
                                                  bw(GB: PERFECT STRANGERS)

Robert Donat *(Robert Wilson)*, Deborah Kerr *(Catherine Wilson)*, Glynis Johns *(Dizzy Clayton)*, Ann Todd *(Elena)*, Roland Culver *(Richard)*, Elliot Mason *(Mrs. Hemmings)*, Eliot Makeham *(Mr. Staines)*, Brefni O'Rorke *(Mr. Hargrove)*, Edward Rigby *(Charlie)*, Muriel George *(Minnie)*, Allan Jeayes *(Commander)*, Ivor Barnard *(Chemist)*, Henry B. Longhurst *(Petty Officer)*, Bill Shine *(Webster)*, Billy Thatcher *(Essex)*, Brian Weske *(Gordon)*, Rosamund Taylor *(Irene)*, Harry Ross *(Bill)*, Vincent Holman *(ARP Warden)*, Leslie Dwyer *(Strupey)*, Caven Watson *(Scotty)*, Jeanine Carre *(Jeannie)*, Molly Munks *(Meg)*, Roger Moore, Bill Rowbotham.

Excellent wartime drama has Donat and Kerr, an unhappily married couple barely tolerating each other, suddenly separated by the war. Donat joins the Royal Navy and the service life loosens him up considerably. He even has an affair with widowed nurse Todd. Kerr joins the Wrens and becomes friends with daffy Johns, who teaches her to smoke, wear lipstick, and have a fling with Culver. When the war is over each dreads their marital reunion but when they see how the other has changed, they fall in love again. Excellent performances by Kerr and Donat and good production values, despite the fact that London was suffering through the height of the flying bomb attacks during production. Two years before the film opened, Korda's London Films signed a coproduction deal with MGM and announced a number of prestigious projects, including a production of WAR AND PEACE to be directed by and starring Orson Welles with Merle Oberon. VACATION FROM MARRIAGE was the only film to be completed. An Oscar went to Dane for Best Original Story.

p&d, Alexander Korda; w, Clemence Dane, Anthony Pelissier (based on a story by Dane); ph, Georges Perinal; m, Clifton Parker; ed, E.B. Jarvis; prod d, Vincent Korda; md, Muir Mathieson; spec eff, Percy Day.

Drama   (PR:A   MPAA:NR)

VACATION IN RENO**   (1946) 60m RKO bw

Jack Haley *(Jack Carroll)*, Anne Jeffreys *(Eleanor)*, Wally Brown *(Eddie Roberts)*, Iris Adrian *(Bunny Wells)*, Morgan Conway *(Joe)*, Alan Carney *(Angel)*, Myrna Dell *(Mrs. Dumont)*, Matt McHugh *(Dumont)*, Claire Carleton *(Sally Beaver)*, Jason Robards, Sr *(Sheriff)*, Matt Willis *(Hank)*.

Silly marital farce starring Haley and Jeffreys as a young married couple whose first big spat causes untold troubles. After the fight, Haley takes off to Reno on a two-week vacation in search of buried gold. Jeffreys doesn't buy his prospecting tale and becomes convinced he's gone there for a quick divorce. She follows. When she arrives in the desert she finds Haley entangled in a scheme by some goofy bank robbers, Conway, Carney, and Adrian, to pull a heist. After some tired slapstick Haley turns out a hero when he puts the robbery gang in jail and the married couple make up.

p&d, Leslie Goodwins, w, Charles E. Roberts, Arthur Ross (based on a story by Charles Kerr); ph, George E. Diskant; m, Paul Sawtell; ed, Les Millbrook; spec eff, Russell A. Cully.

Comedy   (PR:A   MPAA:NR)

VADO...L'AMMAZZO E TORNO (SEE: ANY GUN CAN PLAY, 1968,
                                                                            Ital.)

VAGABOND KING, THE***   (1930) 104m PAR c

Dennis King *(Francois Villon)*, Jeanette MacDonald *(Katherine de Vaucelles)*, O.P. Heggie *(King Louis XI)*, Lillian Roth *(Huguette)*, Warner Oland *(Thibault)*, Arthur Stone *(Oliver the Barber)*, Thomas Ricketts *(The Astrologer)*, Lawford Davidson *(Tristan)*, Christian J. Frank *(Executioner)*, Elda Voelkel *(Girl)*, Dorothy Davis, Thora Waverly, Cecile Cameron *(Brunettes)*, Jean Douglas, Eugenia Woodbury, Rae Murray, Blanche Saunders, Francis Waverly *(Blondes)*, Gloria Faith, Theresa Allen, Sue Patterson *(Pages)*.

One of the most often filmed stories in history is done well here as Paramount's first talkie in full color. King, reprising his successful stage run, goes over the top in his portrayal, paying no attention to the limitations

of the camera and preferring to shout and strut and fret as though he were acting in the Hollywood Bowl without a microphone. Heggie is the weak-willed Louis XI and can't make up his mind about how to combat the forces of the Duke of Burgundy, who wants to come in and take over. Heggie's own grand marshal is Oland and he is dealing treacherously with the Duke in an attempt to dethrone Heggie. Meanwhile, the poor people of Paris have flocked behind King, a poet-adventurer, and his sweetheart, Roth. The duo have been spending their time singing insulting ditties about Heggie. When the boisterous crowd kidnaps MacDonald, Heggie's niece, King manages to save her from death and they soon fall in love, much to the dismay of Roth. There is a huge party for Heggie and Oland plans to kill the man but is thwarted by King. Roth gives up her life to save King when he is in danger and King then rallies the people to help him fight the Burgundians and keep the monarchy. No matter how atrocious Heggie is, he is still better than the men who mean to assassinate him. Lots of huge production numbers and a good bit of acting by Roth, who was still a teenager at the time and in her fourth film. It began as a novel by R.H. Russell, then went to the stage in 1901 as "If I Were King." In 1920, it was filmed with that title by Fox, starring William Farnum. In 1938, Ronald Colman starred in the remake with Frances Dee. The musical version played New York from September, 1925, went to London in 1927, and was made as this picture. John Barrymore starred in THE BELOVED ROGUE, another version of the Villon story in 1926, and the musical was again made in 1956 as THE VAGABOND KING, starring Kathryn Grayson. If the lyricist's name seems familiar, that's because Brian Hooker was responsible for what is acknowledged to be the best translation of Rostand's "Cyrano de Bergerac," the one that served as the basis for the Jose Ferrer film. This film was dubbed and had to be sent out as a silent film with titles overseas. One of the major problems is that it seems more like a filmed version of a stage play rather than a movie and the fault has to be laid at the feet of Berger, a German director who was making his first sound feature and must have been somewhat in awe of King. The songs by composer Friml and wordsmith Hooker were: "Song of the Vagabonds" (sung by the male chorus), "Some Day" (sung by MacDonald), "Only a Rose" (MacDonald, King), "Huguette's Waltz" (sung by Roth), "Love Me Tonight" (MacDonald, King), "Nocturne" (chorus), with several reprises. Other songs were "King Louie" (Sam Coslow, Leo Robin, Newell Chase, sung by King), "Mary, Queen of Heaven" (Coslow, Robin, Chase, sung by the chorus), "If I Were King" (Coslow, Robin, Chase, sung by King), "What France Needs" (Chase, Robin, sung by King, chorus), and "Death March" (Robin, Chase). Other versions of the story included a one reeler in 1911, a radio presentation starring MacDonald in 1934, another radio version (both on "Lux Radio Theatre") in 1936 starring John Boles and Evelyn Venable, and still another "Lux" show in 1944 which starred Kathryn Grayson and Dennis Morgan. The screenwriter for this one was the same man who collaborated with Orson Welles on CITIZEN KANE.

p, Adolph Zukor; d, Ludwig Berger; w, Herman Mankiewicz (based on a novel by R.H. Russell, the play "If I Were King" by Justin Huntly McCarthy and the operetta "The Vagabond King" by William H. Post, Rudolf Friml, Brian Hooker); ph, Henry Gerrard, Ray Rennahan; m, Friml; ed, Merrill White; art d, Hans Dreier; cos, Travis Banton.

Musical   (PR:A   MPAA:NR)

VAGABOND KING, THE***   (1956) 88m PAR c

Kathryn Grayson *(Catherine De Vaucelles)*, Oreste 'Kirkop' *(Francois Villon)*, Rita Moreno *(Huguette)*, Sir Cedric Hardwicke *(Tristan)*, Walter Hampden *(King Louis XI)*, Leslie Nielsen *(Thibault)*, William Prince *(Rene)*, Jack Lord *(Ferrebone)*, Billy Vine *(Jacques)*, Harry McNaughton *(Colin)*, Florence Sundstrom *(Laughing Margot)*, Lucie Lancaster *(Margaret)*, Raymond Bramley *(The Scar)*, Gregory Morton *(Gen. Antoine De Chabannes)*, Richard Tone *(Quicksilver)*, Ralph Sumpter *(Bishop of Paris and Turin)*, G. Thomas Duggan *(Burgundy)*, Gavin Gordon *(Major-domo)*, Joel Ashley *(Duke of Normandy)*, Ralph Clanton *(Duke of Anjou)*, Gordon Mills *(Duke of Bourbon)*, Vincent Price *(Narrator)*, Sam Schwartz *(One Eye)*, Phyllis Newman *(Lulu)*, Slim Gaut *(Jehan "The Wolf")*, Albie Gaye *(Jeannie)*, Laura Raynair, Frances Lansing, Jeanette Miller *(Ladies in Waiting)*, Richard Shannon *(Sergeant)*, Larry Pennell *(1st Soldier)*, Nancy Bajer *(Blanche)*, Rita Marie Tanno *(Belle)*, Dolores Starr, David Nillo *(Specialty Dancers)*.

By far the most lavish of all the versions of this story but the money spent was not returned. Perhaps it was made at the wrong time or it might have been that Oreste, the Maltese tenor whom Paramount hoped would be their answer to Mario Lanza, just didn't have the fire to bring off the flashy role of Francois Villon, the rogue-poet who saved the monarchy of King Louis XI. The plot remains essentially the same: the weak king (Hampden) is being threatened by the forces of the Duke of Burgundy, Duggan. There are traitors in Hampden's midst, led by Neilsen and Morton. On the streets of Paris, satirical songs about Hampden are being sung by Oreste and his girl friend, Moreno. Oreste is asked by the enemy to be part of their forces and, at first, agrees. Then, when he learns that Hampden really does care about his people, Oreste switches his allegiance after taking up with Grayson, the niece of Hampden. In the ensuing battle, Moreno is killed, Oreste's bests the bad guys with the help of the Parisians, and he winds up with Grayson, who had earlier offered herself in Oreste's place when the poet was under sentence for previous crimes. Not that many of the tunes from the original Rudolf Friml, Brian Hooker, William H. Post show are in evidence. The only ones remaining were "Some Day" (sung by Grayson), "Huguette's Waltz" (Moreno), "Song of the Vagabonds" (chorus), and "Love Me Tonight." Friml was in his nineties when he wrote some new music which had special lyrics by Johnny Burke. The fresh airs included "Vive Le You" (sung by Moreno), "Watch Out for the Devil," "This Same Heart," "Bon Jour," "Comparisons," and something called "Lord, I'm Glad I Know Thee," which was supposedly written by two people named V. Giovane and K.C. Rogan, but Burke has been known to use the Rogan name as a *nom de lyric* so we can only assume that Friml used the other name. Jack Lord was still in his twenties when he made his appearance in this film, his third after CRY MURDER and THE COURT MARTIAL OF BILLY MITCHELL. Vincent Price lends his dulcet tones as the narrator, as though the action weren't enough to carry the movie. The male lead's full name was Oreste Kirkop and, as far as we can determine, he sank into the Maltese sunset right after this. Grayson's career was also on the wane at age 34, and she left the screen to work on stage and in nightclubs following her work here. Lots of good music, terrific sets and costumes but the fun of the prior versions seemed to have been gone in a flurry of color and a very studied sense of direction by Curtiz. Still, if you like your musicals old-fashioned, you'll enjoy THE VAGABOND KING in its latest incarnation, which is, hopefully, the last time around for this war horse. In a very small role, look hard for Phyllis Newman, who later married Adolph Green (of Comden and) and went on to have a satisfying New York stage career. Remake of THE BELOVED ROGUE, 1928, and IF I WERE KING, 1938.

p, Pat Duggan; d, Michael Curtiz; w, Ken Englund, Noel Langley (based on a novel by R.H. Russell, the play "If I Were King" by Justin Huntly McCarthy, and the musical "The Vagabond King" by Rudolph Friml, Brian Hooker, William H. Post); ph, Robert Burke (VistaVision, Technicolor); m, Victor Young; ed, Arthur Schmidt; art d, Hal Pereira, Henry Bumstead; cos, Mary Grant; ch, Hanya Holm; spec eff, John P. Fulton.

Musical   (PR:A   MPAA:NR)

VAGABOND LADY*½   (1935) 75m MGM bw

Robert Young (*Tony Spear*), Evelyn Venable (*Josephine Spiggins*), Berton Churchill (*R. D. Spear*), Reginald Denny (*John Spear*), Frank Craven (*"Spiggs" Spiggins*), Forester Harvey (*Corky Nye*), Dan Crimmins (*Willie*), Ferdinand Gottschalk (*Mr. Higginbotham*), Fuzzy Knight (*Swan*), Herbert [Herb] Vigran (*Edgar*), Harry Todd (*Crabby Clerk*), Herman Bing, Arthur Hoyt, Ferdinand Munier (*Department Heads*), "Shep" Shepard (*Stand-In for Robert Young*), Pat Scott (*Stand-In for Evelyn Venable*), George Becker (*Stand-In for Reginald Denny*), Rose Plummer, Elizabeth Rhoades (*Old Women*), John Elliott (*Master of Ceremonies*).

Slow-moving romantic comedy starring Venable as the young daughter of a janitor who finds herself being courted by her boss' two sons, Young being rowdy and carefree, Denny stuffy and polite. Her sense of reason tells her to marry Denny, but in the end she allows herself to be swept away by the looney Young as she's about to say "I do" to his brother. Hal Roach was executive producer; the film was made at his studio, one of the few made there in this period which did *not* star Stan Laurel and Oliver Hardy.

p&d, Sam Taylor; w, Frank Butler; ph, Jack MacKenzie; ed, Bernard Burton.

Comedy/Romance   (PR:A   MPAA:NR)

VAGABOND LOVER*   (1929) 65m RKO bw

Rudy Vallee (*Rudy Bronson*), Sally Blane (*Jean*), Marie Dressler (*Mrs. Whitehall*), Charles Sellon (*Officer Tuttle*), Eddie Nugent (*Sport*), Nella Walker (*Mrs. Todd Hunter*), Malcolm Waite (*Ted Grant*), Alan Roscoe (*Manager*), The Connecticut Yankees.

Rudy Vallee made his movie debut in this dull but inexplicably successful little talkie, which cast him as a rube from small town America who learns to play the saxophone from a correspondence course offered by Waite, the East Coast "Saxophone King." Infused with enthusiasm (though you couldn't tell from Vallee's wooden performance), Vallee ventures out to Long Island to meet his mentor. Much to his surprise, Waite brushes Vallee off and refuses to give the adoring fan an audience. There is nothing like the wrath of a rabid fan scorned, however, and Vallee gets revenge by posing as Waite himself. This deception is mildly successful and Vallee gets some hot notices until it is revealed he is an imposter. Luckily, all is forgiven, and Waite hires Vallee to work for him. Dressler steals the show (so what else is new?) as a high-society dowager who puts her snobby, upper-crust contemporaries in their place. Songs include: "If You Were the Only Girl in the World" (Clifford Grey, Nat D. Ayer), "A Little Kiss Each Morning," "Heigh Ho Everybody" (Harry M. Woods), "Piccolo Pete" (Phil Baxter), "I Love You" (Ruby Cowan, Philip Bartholomae, Phil Boutelje), "I'll Be Reminded of You" (Ken Smith, Edward Heyman), and "I'm Just a Vagabond Lover" (Leon Zimmerman, Rudy Vallee).

p, James Ashmore Creelman, Louis Sarecky; d, Marshall Neilan; w, Creelman; ph, Leo Tover; md, Victor Barravalle; art d, Max Ree.

Musical   **Cas.**   (PR:A   MPAA:NR)

VAGABOND QUEEN, THE*   (1931, Brit.) 62m BIP/Wardour bw

Betty Balfour (*Sally/Princess Xonia*), Glen Byam Shaw (*Jimmie*), Ernest Thesiger (*Katoff*), Harry Terry (*Winkleburg*), Charles Dormer (*Prince Adolphe*), Dino Galvani (*Ilmar*), Ralph Leslie.

Balfour plays a double role, as a London girl and the Ruritanian princess whose double she is. The commoner takes the place of the princess to help foil an assassination plot. Filmed as a silent in Germany, the movie had sound added in 1930.

d, Geza von Bolvary; w, Rex Taylor, Val Valentine (based on a story by Douglas Furber); ph, Charles Rosher.

Comedy   (PR:A   MPAA:NR)

VAGABOND VIOLINIST   (SEE: BROKEN MELODY, THE, 1934, Brit.)

VAGHE STELLE DELL'ORSA   (SEE: SANDRA, 1966, Ital.)

VALACHI PAPERS, THE*   (1972, Ital./Fr.) 125m DD-Euro-France/COL c (JOE VALACHI: I SEGRETTI DI COSA NOS-TRA)

Charles Bronson (*Joseph Valachi*), Lino Ventura (*Vito Genovese*), Joseph Wiseman (*Salvatore Maranzano*), Jill Ireland (*Maria Valachi*), Walter Chiari (*Dominick "The Gap" Petrilli*), Gerald S. O'Loughlin (*FBI Agent Ryan*), Amedeo Nazzari (*Gaetano Reina*), Guido Leontini (*Tony Bender*), Allesandro Sperli (*Giuseppe Masseria*), Maria Baxa (*Donna Petrillo*), Pupella Maggio (*Rosanna Reina*), Fausto Tozzi (*Albert Anastasia*), Mario Pilar (*Salerto*), Franco Borelli (*Buster from Chicago*), Angelo Infante (*Charles "Lucky" Luciano*), Fred Valleca (*Johnny Beck*), John Alarimo (*Steven Ferrigno*), Arny Freeman (*Penitentiary Warden*), Giancomino De Michelis (*Little Augie*), Sylvester Lamont (*Commander of Fort Monmouth*), Sabine Sun (*Jane*), Isabelle Marchal (*Mary Lou*), Imelde Marani (*Donna's Girl Friend*), Jason McCallum (*Donald Valachi*), Saro Urzi (*Masseria*), Frank Gio (*Frank*), Steve Belouise (*Vinnie*), Anthony Dawson 'Antonio Margheriti' (*Federal Investigator*), Don Koll (*State Trooper*).

An episodic quasi-documentary covering 32 years–mainly through flash-back–unfolding that ever-fascinating subculture, the Outfit. Real names are used in a part-factual, part-fictional recounting of the development and growth of the organized Italian-American crime syndicate known as the Cosa Nostra, seen from the perspective of a minor "soldier" in the ranks, played by Bronson. Serving a 15-year sentence at the Atlanta Federal Penitentiary on a narcotics charge, Bronson learns that his ex-boss Ventura–a powerful *capo* in the hierarchy–has put out a "contract" on his life, believing Bronson to be responsible for his own incarceration. Frightened for his safety, Bronson alerts prison authorities that he is willing to talk about his past activities in return for extra security in a different prison. FBI agent O'Loughlin responds to Bronson's request. Bronson begins his long monolog, recounting details of his past as the visuals flash back to the year 1929, when he began his criminal career. The 30-year-old Bronson gets a job as driver for Mafia chieftain Nazzari who, in a dispute over territory, is killed by Ventura and Infanti. Bronson–seen by the killers to be ruthless, ambitious, and efficient, and thus grist for their own gangland mill–goes to work for them, along with his good friend and compatriot Chiari. Boss of bosses Wiseman, to avoid further internecine disputes, organizes the Outfit into "families," each with its own turf, and the rising young mafioso marries Ireland, the daughter of his murdered ex-employer, in a massive marriage ceremony, his peers bringing costly gifts to the grandiose hotel ballroom setting. Later, in 1963, Infanti is convicted of a felony and Ventura flees temporarily to Italy for sanctuary, appointing Chiari as bodyguard for his mistress Baxa during his absence. Upon his return, Ventura discovers that Chiari and Baxa have formed a romantic attachment, and orders that Chiari be castrated in as graphic a demonstration of punishment-fitting-crime as ever rendered on screen. Finding his friend so mutilated, Bronson puts the man out of his misery. The panoply of crime continues to unroll as the stolid monster brings his avid FBI listener up through the year 1957, when a secretly bugged meeting of major mobsters is convened in Appalachia in a country estate. The conference is raided by federal agents, who place both Ventura and Bronson under arrest. The string of flashbcks ends back in Bronson's cell. O'Loughlin persuades Bronson to testify before a U.S. Senate subcommittee on crime in 1963, whereupon Ventura increases the reward for his head to $100,000. Remorseful at having broken *omerta*–the Mafia code of silence–Bronson tries unsuccessfully to hang himself in his cell, using as a noose the cord of the TV set on which he viewed himself testifying before the subcommittee. Ultimately, Bronson dies of a heart attack–ironically six months after the death of his incarcerated enemy, Ventura. Author Maas' book– enormously popular with a reading public fascinated by details of the inner workings of a much-feared secret society of hoodlums and killers–was based partly on minor mobster Valachi's Senate subcommittee testimony and partly on follow-up interviews with the imprisoned hoodlum, whose revelations broke the chain of secrecy surrounding the highly structured Cosa Nostra ("Our Thing," literally). Director Francis Ford Coppola's enormously successful movie version of Mario Puzo's *The Godfather* had preceded THE VALACHI PAPERS to the marketplace, and audiences thought this film–which seems somewhat hastily constructed–

had been quickly put together to exploit the earlier blockbuster's popularity. In reality, Maas' book had been published *before* Puzo's, and film rights had been sold before the release of THE GODFATHER. Production difficulties slowed the shooting in the U.S. when New York-based Mafia mobsters arranged a series of "accidents" hoping to prevent the picture from being made. (Even after the film's completion, the producers were plagued with such events; a bomb threat emptied a preview screening room of critics in Manhattan.) Ultimately, producer De Laurentiis had to do most of the filming at his own studios in Rome. The book was bowdlerized somewhat in the movie; Chiari's castration appears to have been invented for visual effect—in fact, Chiari himself plays an amalgam of two different characters in the book. On initial release, the picture was pilloried by the critics, many of whom thought it—despite its litany of gore– ultimately boring. Despite its negative reviews, it did well at the box office, bringing in $9.4 million in the first eight months of release. Much of this take may have resulted from the popularity of superstar Bronson, then thought to be the world's biggest movie draw. Initially loath to play his part in the picture, Bronson was finally persuaded by a lucrative three-film contract which gave him a million dollars for each picture, as well as a percentage of the gross profits, making him one of the highest paid actors in history. Bronson's wife Ireland plays his screen wife here–an additional inducement to the actor, who wanted to keep his family together during his filmic excursions abroad. Paramount had planned to release the film, but the studio planners quarreled with De Laurentiis over the details of distribution, and so lost the lucrative rights. Director Young does well with many of the violent action scenes–his forte, since he directed three of the best of another type of crime caper in the James Bond series (see Index), including one with Capo Mafioso-player Wiseman, DR. NO (1963). He does less well with his international cast of players, whose comic-opera dialects are sometimes downright laughable. Young had directed Bronson before (COLD SWEAT, 1971, and RED SUN, 1972), and got an appropriately wooden response from the actor.

p, Dino De Laurentiis; d, Terence Young; w, Stephen Geller (based on the book by Peter Maas); ph, Aldo Tonti (Technicolor); m, Riz Ortolani; ed, John Dwyre; art d, Mario Carbuglia; set d, John Godfrey, Ferdinando Ruffo; cos, Ann Roth, Giorgio Desideri; spec eff, Eros Baciucchi; makeup, Gianetto De Rossi, Mirella Sforza.

Crime   (PR:O   MPAA:R)

VALDEZ IS COMING½   (1971) 90m Norlan-Ira Steiner/UA c

Burt Lancaster *(Bob Valdez)*, Susan Clark *(Gay Erin)*, Jon Cypher *(Frank Tanner)*, Barton Heyman *(El Segundo)*, Richard Jordan *(R.L. Davis)*, Frank Silvera *(Diego)*, Hector Elizondo *(Mexican Rider)*, Phil Brown *(Malson)*, Ralph Brown *(Beaudry)*, Juanita Penaloza *(Apache Woman)*, Lex Monson *(Rincon)*, Roberta Haynes *(Polly)*, Maria Montez *(Anita)*, Marta Tuck *(Rosa)*, Jose Garcia *(Carlos)*, James Lemp *(Bony Man)*, Sylvia Poggioli *(Segundo's Girl)*, Werner Hasselman *(Sheriff)*, Concha Hombria *(Inez)*, Per Barclay *(Bartender)*, Vic Albert *(Rancher)*, Allan Russell *(Rancher)*, Michael Hinn *(Merchant)*, Rudy Ugland, Joaquin Parra, Losada *(Trackers)*, Santiago Santos, Losardo Iglesias *(Riders)*, Juan Fernandez *(Mexican Buyer)*, Tony Eppers *(Bodyguard)*, Mario Barros, Raul Castro, Nick Cravat, Santiago Garcia, Jeff Kibbee, Linc Kibbee, Ian Maclean, Tom McFadden, Jose Morales, Mario Sanz, Lee Thaxton, Robin Thaxton, Julian Vidrie, Manolin Vidrie *(Gang Members)*.

Lancaster is a Mexican-American peace officer who runs across a party of men blasting guns at a shack. He learns the men are trying to bring out Monson, a black man accused of murdering a local trader. After Lancaster calms the group, Monson comes out, only to be shot at by a still angry vigilante. Monson fires back and Lancaster is forced to kill him. Cypher, a wealthy rancher heading the party, looks at the corpse and realizes they killed the wrong man. Lancaster tries to raise $200 to give Monson's widow. Locals agree to provide half the money with the understanding that Cypher will put up the rest. When Lancaster confronts the man he is rebuffed, then tied to a cross and left to wander in the desert. Lancaster vows revenge and sends Cypher a message: "Valdez is coming." He kidnaps Clark, Cypher's mistress and the murdered trader's widow. She admits to killing her husband and ends up in a love affair with Lancaster. A posse hired by Cypher goes out after Lancaster but he takes them on handily. Eventually they capture the wily man but Lancaster's life is spared. The men have grown to admire Lancaster and leave him to have it out with Cypher. The rich man, broken by Lancaster's spirit, pays off the $100 his adversary has been demanding. The film tries to make a statement about race relations but unfortunately gets bogged down under obvious characterizations and a good deal of gratuitous violence. Shot in Spain, this marked the directoral debut for Sherin who was highly praised for his production of "The Great White Hope" on Broadway. He shows little sense for film, though, creating a movie that differs little from any other minor western effort of the early 1970s. One scene has Lancaster and Clark colliding while on horseback, which prompted a condemnation of the film by the American Humane Association. Though the film is unsatisfying, Lancaster does give it his best. In order to create a realistic character he went to a language coach with questions about speech patterns of Mexicans living in the 1890s American Southwest. He also consulted students of Mexican-Chicano programs at a Los Angeles college and took advice from a Mexican script boy to add further perspective to his interpretation.

p, Ira Steiner; d, Edwin Sherin; w, Roland Kibbee, David Rayfiel (based on the novel by Elmore Leonard); ph, Gabor Pogany (DeLuxe Color); m, Charles Gross; ed, James T. Heckert; art d, Jose Maria Tapiador, Jose Maria Alarcon; set d, Rafael Salazar; cos, Louis Brown; spec eff, Chuck Gaspar, Linc Kibbee; stunts, Al Wyatt; makeup, Mariano Garcia Rey, Alberto Comenar.

Western   **Cas.**   (PR:O   MPAA:GP)

VALENTINO**   (1951) 102m COL c

Eleanor Parker *(Joan Carlisle)*, Richard Carlson *(William King)*, Patricia Medina *(Lila Reyes)*, Joseph Calleia *(Luigi Verducci)*, Dona Drake *(Maria Torres)*, Lloyd Gough *(Eddie Morgan)*, Anthony Dexter *(Rudolph Valentino)*, Otto Kruger *(Mark Towers)*, Marietta Canty *(Tilly)*, Paul Bruar *(Photographer)*, Eric Wilton *(Butler)*.

The life of Hollywood's Latin Lover, Rudolph Valentino, is reduced to a collection of cinematic cliches in this ridiculous, highly fictionalized screen biography. Dexter plays the star, who arrives in the U.S. as a member of an Italian dance troupe. On board ship he meets Parker, whom he begins to pursue, not realizing she is an important film star traveling under an assumed identity. Moreno, the dance troupe's supervisor, grows jealous with all the attention Dexter is giving Parker, but Dexter solves this by leaving the company. Forced to find employment in New York, Dexter takes a job washing dishes, though this comes to an abrupt end when he punches another employee who calls him a greaseball. Fortunately, Dexter's skills as a dancer soon get him another job, working as a gigolo at a fancy dance hall. As he guides thrilled women around the floor, Dexter once again runs into Parker, who is accompanied by film director Carlson. Though Carlson insists his star is tired, Dexter sweeps Parker off her feet and together they dance the tango. Parker claims she feels nothing for Dexter, who replies, "Then why is your heart pounding as it did that night on the boat?" Carlson watches the two and sees a certain charisma in Dexter. He has Dexter appear as an Apache dancer in a film, and realizes he is on to something. Medina, another actress, is attracted to Dexter but he is only interested in a romance with Parker. He realizes his future lies in Hollywood, so, after borrowing money from a friend, he heads west. Once in California, Dexter finds the studios uninterested in his talents. Medina, who is driving by, sees Dexter on the street and offers him a ride while she picks up a script. When she leaves him in the car, Dexter spots a sign advertising a new film: THE FOUR HORSEMEN OF THE APOCALYPSE. The sign tantalizes Dexter, as it implies that the search is still on for an actor to play the role of Julio. Dexter gets hold of the script but cannot get an interview with Kruger, the film's producer. He crashes Kruger's birthday party, then tells the shocked man he will perform a dance number that could serve as the film's prolog. Kruger likes what he sees and the part is Dexter's. After the film's release Dexter becomes an overnight sensation. He continues to have professional success after success, but remains unsatisfied as Parker still spurns his attentions. This changes quickly when Kruger buys a property called THE SHEIK, in which he plans to cast the two as lovers. Dexter feels uncomfortable with the part, for Carlson (now Parker's husband) is assigned to direct the film. Kruger is disturbed that the "Latin Lover" is so unusually restrained in his love scenes. Finally the two costars play with more passion, and Dexter later tells Parker that perhaps they should not have done this film. Both balk at doing a sequel, which angers their producer. Dexter, while out driving, experiences sharp pains in his stomach that force him to stop the car. He goes to bed for rest, but is disturbed by a call from Parker, who begs to see him. She goes to Dexter's home, not realizing that a gossip columnist and photographer are trailing her. When Dexter and Parker leave the house, the photographer surprises them with his flash camera. Dexter angrily smashes the camera, then goes after the two men. He takes several blows in his already pained middle, and the reporter promises to smear both of them in the newspapers. To save face and Parker's honor, Dexter goes back to New York, where he calls the reporter. Dexter tells the man he is about to elope with Medina, though this is hardly the truth. Dexter's stomach pains force him to go into the hospital. As he lies in his sickbed, he has a friend pull up the shades to let sunshine into the room. As the beams grace his face, Dexter quietly passes away. His death causes riots among fans, who come in droves to his funeral. Carlson comforts his wife, while telling reporters he knew what went on between Parker and the late screen idol. Twenty-five years go by, and, as a narrator informs the audience, a mysterious "Lady in Black" continues to lay a wreath at Dexter's tomb each year on the anniversary of his death. The Valentino story, as presented here, is a lifeless soap opera brimming with fanciful situations that blatantly ignore the truth behind the legend. Dexter never conveys the electricity that Valentino radiated on-screen, though he brings enthusiasm (if not much talent) to the role. Dexter is further hampered by the cliche-ridden script and the often ridiculous lines he must recite. Allen's direction is lackluster, simply delivering an assignment without giving the story any of its much needed spice. Columbia interviewed nearly 2,000 actors to find the perfect Valentino before finally deciding on Dexter, a relatively unknown stage actor. He spent three years working on the part, and at the time of VALENTINO's production was already a year older than the Latin Lover was when he died at age 31. Though the majority of the film is fiction, Valentino's brother Alberto and his sister, Maria Strada, sued Columbia for $700,000. The two claimed they had never been consulted about their brother's life, which made this an unauthorized biography, humiliating the family. Alice Terry, the widow of Rex Ingram (Valentino's costar in THE FOUR HORSEMEN OF THE APOCALYPSE), also filed suit. Eventually these legal troubles were settled out of court. The legend of Valentino is one that has always intrigued Hollywood. At one point Tyrone Power was considered for the part of filmdom's greatest lover, and 26 years after this film Ken Russell made his own version of the Valentino myth, featuring ballet star Rudolph Nureyev in the title role.

p, Edward Small; d, Lewis Allen; w, George Bruce; ph, Harry Stradling (Technicolor); m, David Chudnow; ed, Daniel Mandell; art d, William Flannery.

Biography (PR:C MPAA:NR)

VALENTINO½** (1977, Brit.) 132m UA c

Rudolf Nureyev (*Rudolph Valentino*), Leslie Caron (*Nazimova*), Michelle Phillips (*Natasha Rambova*), Carol Kane (*"Fatty's" Girl*), Felicity Kendal (*June Mathis*), Seymour Cassel (*George Ullman*), Peter Vaughan (*Rory O'Neil*), Huntz Hall (*Jesse Lasky*), David De Keyser (*Joseph Schenck*), Alfred Marks (*Richard Rowland*), Anton Diffring (*Baron Long*), Jennie Lindon (*Agnes Ayres*), William Hootkins (*"Fatty"*), Bill McKinney (*Jail Cop*), Don Fellows (*George Melford*), John Justin (*Sidney Olcott*), Linda Thorson (*Billie Streeter*), June Bolton (*Bianca De Saulles*), Penny Milford (*Lorna Sinclair*), Dudley Sutton (*Willie*), Robin Brent Clarke (*Jack De Saulles*), Anthony Dowell (*Vaslav Nijinsky*), James Berwick, Marcella Markham, Leland Palner, John Alderson, Hal Galili, Percy Herbert, Nicolette Marvin, Mark Baker, Mildred Shay, Lindsay Kemp, John Tarzenberger, Norman Chancer, Robert O'Neil, Christine Carlson.

A typical Ken Russell movie that is high on visual content and low on humanity. VALENTINO is the bizarre, fascinating biography of the famed silent screen actor. As in his other biographies, Russell doesn't appear to be too intrigued by the details of his lead's life so he takes various elements of episodes and stages them surrealistically, with a fury that hardly befits the nature of some of the scenes. Russell seems more concerned with the reasons for the star's success as a sex symbol than with his relationships. Nureyev looks nothing like Valentino and is not a very good actor but his screen charisma almost makes up for his lack of thespian ability. The movie commences as Nureyev is about to be buried at the mob scene in New York which marked his final moments above ground. People riot and press in to break the windows of the funeral parlor and then Russell goes into a CITIZEN KANE flashback as the press questions various people in the actor's life. We see Nureyev as a ballroom dancing instructor, including one funny bit where Nureyev teaches Dowell (as the famous Nijinsky) how to do the tango. Next, Nureyev falls hard for the girl friend of a mobster and has to leave New York in a hurry, winding up doing a dance act in Hollywood with a drunken partner. While Hootkins (as Fatty Arbuckle) gives him a hard time, Nureyev manages to keep his cool. He meets and marries actress Kane and gets into films when he is discovered by Kendal (playing June Mathis, the head film cutter at MGM), who pulls him out of low-class comedies and recommends him for the role in THE FOUR HORSEMEN OF THE APOCALYPSE which makes him a national sensation. Nureyev soon divorces Kane and meets the Russian Caron (playing Alla Nazimova) and Phillips, who plays Rambova. Nureyev marries Phillips but is soon charged with bigamy as his Mexican divorce from Kane is not recognized by California's courts. He's tossed into a tough clink where the criminals resent his fame and make it hard for him. These scenes are particularly distasteful and feature orgy-like moments which are out of place. There is some question as to the actor's masculinity so he agrees to battle a man who has challenged him and is whacked about when that man is replaced by a huge thug. It takes place in a nightclub and may be a figment of Russell's imagination, at least as far as we can tell. Nureyev wins the fight but the pounding he takes eventually leads to his becoming ill when he begins drinking heavily. The movie ends where it began, with the actor on his bier about to be interred. Nureyev's first movie showed that he had something but what it was is yet to be determined. As was the case with Russell's other film bios, audiences were alternately outraged or charmed by his work but even the most severe detractors had to admit that it was different. The story of Valentino's life had been badly made in 1951 with Tony Dexter in the lead. An odd bit of offbeat casting was the selection of "Bowery Boy" Huntz Hall to play the role of movie czar Jesse Lasky. There are special effects galore and Russell's well-known penchant for *outre* camera angles is seen again and again. In a small role, see if you can spot Linda Thorson, who replaced Diana Rigg as "Emma Peel" on the TV show "The Avengers." Coproducer Winkler, who usually casts a member of his family in some small role, did not do that here, which may have been due to Russell's insistence that he hand-pick everyone in the cast.

p, Irwin Winkler, Robert Chartoff; d, Ken Russell; w, Russell, Mardik Martin (based on the nonfiction story "Valentino, an Intimate Expose of the Sheik" by Brad Steiger, Chaw Mank); ph, Peter Suschitzky; m, Ferde Grofe, Stanley Black; ed, Stuart Baird; art d, Philip Harrison, Malcolm Middleton; set d, Ian Whittaker; cos, Shirley Russell; ch, Gillian Gregory; m/l, "Words of Parody," Russell.

Biography (PR:C-O MPAA:R)

VALERIE** (1957) 84m UA bw

Sterling Hayden (*John Garth*), Anita Ekberg (*Valerie*), Anthony Steel (*Rev. Blake*), Peter Walker (*Herb Garth*), John Wengraf (*Louis Horvat*), Iphigenie Castinglioni (*Mrs. Horvat*), Jerry Barclay (*Mingo*), Robert Adler (*Lundy*), Tom McKee (*Dave Carlin*), Gage Clarke (*Lawyer Griggs*), Sidney Smith (*Judge Frisbee*), Juney Ellis (*Nurse Linsey*), Stanley Adams (*Dr. Jackson*), Brian O'Hara, John Dierkes.

A pretty contrived oater that takes the delicate structure of Akira Kurosawa's masterpiece RASHOMON (1951) and drives it right into the ground. The film opens at the trial of upstanding Civil War vet Hayden who is being tried for the murder of his wife's parents and the attempted murder of Ekberg, his wife. As the evidence unfolds, the jury (and audience) are treated to three separate accounts of the events on that violent day. According to Ekberg's supposed lover, preacher Steel, Hayden had driven his poor wife away with months of abuse and cruelty. When she sought solace with the Lord, Steel took pity on her and brought her to her parents' home. Soon after, Hayden and his men arrived and slaughtered them. Hayden, however, testifies that his wife was a loose and wandering woman from the day they married, one who only married him for his money. He became enraged when he learned she had seduced his younger brother, Walker. In the end, it is the raspy testimony of Ekberg herself, who struggled out of her death bed to relate the sad tale, that the jury believes. She states that Hayden had married her in order to get at her lucrative dowry. She contends that he had invented her affair with Walker as an excuse to kill them both and walk off with the inheritance. When that plan failed Hayden tried to wipe her and her family out. At this moment one of Hayden's hoodlums pulls a gun in the courtroom and rescues his boss, but in the end Hayden is killed by his brother in a showdown.

p, Hal R. Makelim; d, Gerd Oswald; w, Leonard Heideman, Emmett Murphy; ph, Ernest Laszlo; m, Albert Glasser; ed, David Bretherton; art d, Frank Smith.

Western (PR:C MPAA:NR)

VALIANT, THE* (1929) 66m FOX bw

Paul Muni (*James Dyke*), Marguerite Churchill (*Mary Douglas*), DeWitt Jennings (*Warden*), Henry Kolker (*Judge*), Edith Yorke (*Mrs. Douglas*), Richard Carlyle (*Chaplain*), John Mack Brown (*Robert Ward*), Clifford Dempsey (*Police Lieutenant*), George Pearce (*Dr. Edmondson*), Don Terry (*Policeman*).

Muni makes his film debut playing a drifter who murders a man. After being sentenced to die in the electric chair, Muni denies who he really is so that his mother and sister (Yorke and Churchill) won't have to live under the burden of his shame. Muni had developed into an actor of considerable talents on the stages of the American Yiddish theater (performing under his given name of Muni Weisenfreund). The drama here is grim, but strong for its time with an unflinching attitude toward the subject. The cast gives this realism, lead by Muni's strong performance. After establishing himself on Broadway, Muni was signed by Fox and production on THE VALIANT was begun. Studio head William Fox, upon seeing the film's rushes, decided Muni had no sex appeal whatsoever. He ordered production halted, but because the film was well along the way to completion, Winfield Sheehan, the studio's production chief, implored that it would wind up costing more to kill the project than it would to finish it. Fox finally agreed, but had the budget considerably slashed. Muni's talents survived this stupidity, and he was nominated for his first Oscar for Best Actor. Although critical praise for Muni was high, the film died at the box office. Supporting cast member Brown later garnered considerable fame as the hero of numerous B westerns.

d, William K. Howard; w, Tom Barry, James Hunter Booth (based on the play by Robert Middlemass, Holworthy Hall); ph, Lucien Andriot, Glen MacWilliams; ed, Jack Dennis.

Crime Drama (PR:A-C MPAA:NR)

VALIANT, THE½** (1962, Brit./Ital.) 100m B.H.P.-Euro International/UA bw (L'AFFONDAMENTO DELLA VALIANT)

John Mills (*Capt. Morgan*), Ettore Manni (*Luigi Durand de La Penne*), Roberto Risso (*Emilio Bianchi*), Robert Shaw (*Lt. Field*), Liam Redmond (*Surgeon Comdr. Reilly*), Ralph Michael (*Comdr. Clark*), Colin Douglas (*Chief Gunners Mate*), Dinsdale Landen (*Norris*), John Meillon (*Bedford*), Patrick Barr (*Rev. Ellis*), Moray Watson (*Turnbull*), Charles Houston (*Medical Orderly*), Gordon Rollings (*Payne*), Laurence Naismith (*Admiral*), Leonardo Cortese.

Slow-moving WW II naval suspense thriller starring Mills as the tough captain of a British battleship stationed in Alexandria Harbor in 1941. When two Italian frogmen are captured while attempting to mine the vessel, Mills tries to force them to reveal if they had indeed planted any mines, and, if so, when they are set to explode. The Italians refuse to talk, and–pressed to come up with the information–Mills lets them sit (one is wounded) with the crew awaiting the explosions. The tension begins to get to the British sailors, who question their commander's wisdom and ethics. Eventually the Italians reveal that there is a mine, but they refuse to tell the location or time of the explosion. Mills evacuates the ship, leaving the prisoners behind, but he remains and overhears them discussing where they have put the mine after they think the ship is empty. Having gained the information Mills tries to have the mine removed. Before he can mobilize his men, the mine explodes, crippling the ship. Knowing that Italian reconnaissance planes will be arriving to report whatever damage the ship sustained, Mills fakes them out by having some of his men go on the deck and act as if all is well, while the rest of the sailors go below and try to repair the ship. In the end it appears that both the British and the Italians have won the battle of nerves.

p, Jon Penington; d, Roy [Ward] Baker, Giorgio Capitani; w, Willis Hall, Keith Waterhouse, Capitani (based on the play "L'Equipage au Complet" by Robert Mallet); ph, Wilkie Cooper (CinemaScope); ed, John Pomeroy; md, Christopher Whelen; art d, Arthur Lawson; spec eff, Wally Veevers.

War   **(PR:A   MPAA:NR)**

VALLIANT HOMBRE, THE**   (1948) 60M UA bw

Duncan Renaldo (Cisco), Leo Carrillo (Pancho), John Litel (Lon Lansdell), Stanley Andrews (Sheriff Dodge), John James (Paul Mason), Barbara Billingsley (Linda Mason), [Lee] "Lasses" White (Old Prospector), Frank Ellis, Herman Hack, Ralph Peters, Daisy the Wonder Dog.

The Cisco Kid rides again in another routine adventure. This time out Renaldo and his silly sidekick Carrillo hit the trail to investigate the disappearance of James, the owner of a cute little doggie who comes to Cisco and Pancho looking for help in locating her vanished master. When our heroes discover Billingsley, James' sister, they learn that her brother had just struck it rich on a gold mine and disappeared soon after. Eventually the hombres uncover saloonkeeper Litel as the villain, recover James, and justice is done. (See CISCO KID series, Index.)

p, Philip N. Krasne; d, Wallace Fox; w, Adele Buffington (based on a character created by O. Henry); ph, Ernest Miller; m, Albert Glasser; ed, Martin G. Cohn.

Western   **(PR:A   MPAA:NR)**

VALIANT IS THE WORD FOR CARRIE**   (1936) 110m PAR bw

Gladys George (Carrie Snyder), Arline Judge (Lady), John Howard (Paul Darnley), Dudley Digges (Dennis Ringrose), Harry Carey (Phil Yonne), Isabel Jewell (Lilli Eipper), Hattie McDaniel (Ellen Hale), William Collier, Sr (Ed Moresby), John Wray (George Darnley), Jackie Moran (Paul Darnley as a Child), Charlene Wyatt (Lady as a Child), Maude Eburne (Maggie Devlin), Lew Payton (Lon Olds), Grady Sutton (Mat Burdon), Janet Young, Adrienne D'Ambricourt, Helen Lowell, George F. ["Gabby"] Hayes, Irving Bacon, Olive Hatch, Nick Lukats.

Another overwrought melodrama about a fallen woman who must sacrifice all for her young wards. George makes her film debut in this tearjerker playing a Louisiana harlot who, though wealthy from all the money she has made as a lady of the night, is pressured to give up the children (played by Moran and Wyatt as children and then Howard and Judge as teenagers) whom she has successfully sheltered from the realties of her business. Years later, when the kids are nearly grown and George faces charges that could send her to prison, she opts for jail rather than a jury trial that will reveal her secrets and spoil her children's chances in life. This was the first screen role for George, a fine comic actress who was inappropriately cast as a tragedienne by the studio which recruited her because of her work in the stage play "Personal Appearance." When the latter was filmed as GO WEST, YOUNG MAN (1936), George's part went to Mae West, who also got the screenwriting credit.

p&d, Wesley Ruggles; w, Claude Binyon (based on the novel by Barry Benefield); ph, Leo Tover; ed, Otho Lovering.

Drama   **(PR:A-C   MPAA:NR)**

VALLEY GIRL***½   (1983) 95m Atlantic c

Nicholas Cage (Randy), Deborah Foreman (Julie Richman), Elizabeth Daily (Loryn), Michael Bowen (Tommy), Cameron Dye (Fred), Heidi Holicker (Stacey), Michelle Meyrink (Suzie), Tina Theberge (Samantha), Lee Purcell (Beth Brent), Colleen Camp (Sarah Richman), Frederick Forrest (Steve Richman), Richard Sanders (Driving Education Teacher), David Ensor, Joanne Baron, Tony Plana, Tony Markes, Christopher Murphy, Robby Romero, Camille Calvert, Lisa Antille, Theresa Hayes, Andrew Winner, Betsy Bond, Laura Jacoby, Karl Johnson, Joyce Heiser, Michael Wyle, Stephen Sayre, Wayne Crawford.

After the American public was tortured with years of endless, mindless, and heartless teenage sex comedies, director Martha Coolidge's charming VALLEY GIRL hit the screen like a breath of fresh air. Insightful, genuine, warm, and downright romantic, VALLEY GIRL tells the unlikely tale of a deb from the Vally, Foreman, and a punker from Hollywood, Cage, falling hopelessly in love like Romeo and Juliet. After meeting at a dull party which Cage and his friend Dye crashed, Foreman and the punker stay out all night and engage in some innocent fun. Cage worries needlessly that Foreman's parents, Forrest and Camp, will react badly to her staying out all night because he doesn't know that they are laid-back children of the 1960s who are actually more liberal than their daughter. While the two are deeply in

love, Foreman begins to crack under the pressure from her friends to come back to the fold and stop dating that "creep" from "Hollyweird." With prom time coming up, Foreman relents and dumps Cage for her old boy friend Bowen, a mindless jock. Cage sinks into a bit of self-pity until his buddy talks him into wooing his girl back. After donning a number of disguises to get her to notice him (fast-food worker, usher at a movie theater, etc.), none of which make her return to him (though it is obvious she wants to), Cage reluctantly decides to go to the prom and force a confrontation. Just as the suburban couple is about to be announced as prom king and queen, Cage steals Foreman back and marches (actually he runs) down the aisle with the delighted girl on his arm (he barely escapes the small army of jock-types out to kill him). Though the plot is a simple Romeo and Juliet tale, it is written and performed with such heart and care that it is impossible to dislike. The cast is wonderful, headed by Cage and Foreman who make one of the most charming and engaging screen couples in recent memory. Coolidge proves that one doesn't have to wallow in nudity or sex to create a lively, interesting, witty film about teenagers that stresses wholesome, honest values. The basic messages of strength, friendship, and love are well-stated and refreshing (as opposed to the Peeping-Tom, get-it-while-you-can gross-ness of most other teenage films). Not only that, but VALLEY GIRL also boasts the best musical score of any teenage film in recent memory with songs by Modern English, Josie Cotton, Men at Work, The Plimsouls, Sparks, Psychedelic Furs, and Eddie Grant, among others.

p, Wayne Crawford, Andrew Lane; d, Martha Coolidge; w, Crawford, Lane; ph, Frederick Elmes; m, Scott Wilk, Marc Levinthal; ed, Eva Gordos; prod d, Mary Delia Javier; set d, Carl Aldana.

Romance   **Cas.**   **(PR:C   MPAA:R)**

VALLEY OF DEATH, THE   (SEE: TANK BATTALION, 1958)

VALLEY OF DECISION, THE***   (1945) 111m MGM bw

Gregory Peck (Paul Scott), Greer Garson (Mary Rafferty), Donald Crisp (William Scott), Lionel Barrymore (Pat Rafferty), Preston Foster (Jim Brennan), Gladys Cooper (Clarissa Scott), Marsha Hunt (Constance Scott), Reginald Owen (McCready), Dan Duryea (William Scott, Jr.), Jessica Tandy (Louise Kane), Barbara Everest (Delia), Marshall Thompson (Ted Scott), Mary Lord (Julia Gaylord), John Warburton (Giles, Earl of Moulton), Mary Currier (Mrs. Gaylord), Arthur Shields (Callahan), Russell Hicks (Mr. Gaylord), Geraldine Wall (Kate Shannon), Norman Ollstead (Callahan's Son), Evelyn Dockson (Mrs. Callahan), Connie Gilchrist (The Cook), Willa Pearl Curtis (Maid), William O'Leary (O'Brien), Richard Abbott (Minister), Dean Stockwell (Paulie), Joy Harrington (Stella), Lumsden Hare (Dr. McClintock), Anna Q. Nillson (Nurse), Sherlee Collier (Clarrie), Mike Ryan (Timmie).

A huge, sprawling poor-girl-meets-rich-boy story set against the steel industry in Pittsburgh in 1880. Garson, the Queen of MGM, is an Irish lass who takes a job as a maid in the huge home of Crisp, a steel magnate. Garson's father, Barrymore, is totally against her doing that because Crisp is the enemy, as Barrymore, a one-time steel worker, had been permanently crippled in an accident at the mill owned by Crisp, an accident Barrymore feels might have been prevented had the needed safety precautions been in place. Once inside the estate, Garson soon becomes invaluable to Crisp's wife, Cooper, and is beloved by all four of their children, Peck, Thompson, Hunt, and even Duryea, who is a sneaky type. Garson helps Hunt through her various trials and is elevated to far more than a servant, she is a confidante and friend. Peck and Garson fall in love but she believes that there is no way a marriage could take place, due to the difference in their castes. Crisp adores Garson and reckons she would make a fine wife for Peck but the couple's happiness is short-lived as a strike takes place against the mill and that action is backed by Garson's father, thereby sending any thoughts of immediate marriage onto the slag heap. Crisp calls for some professional strikebreakers but Garson tries to pour oil on the waters and arranges a face-to-face meeting between Barrymore and Crisp. The strikers arrive, led by Barrymore, but then the goons arrive as well and Barrymore is incensed and rallies his men behind him. The result is a free-for-all with heads being broken and noses smashed. In the turmoil, Barrymore and Crisp are both killed and Garson feels responsible. She quickly leaves her employment and the love of Peck and spends the next decade a lonely woman. Meanwhile, Peck has married Tandy, a shrew who is a world-class expert at carping. He is not happy with this marriage but has nowhere else to go. Cooper suffers a heart attack and asks for Garson to come to her side, which riles Tandy because she thinks that if Garson comes back into Peck's life, he may leave her. Cooper passes away and now the steel company is owned by the four children and Garson. Cooper's will had asked that her share of the mill be ceded to Garson as she knew in her heart that the young woman would not do anything to harm the family's interests. Duryea, Hunt, and Thompson would like to sell out but Peck insists that they keep the mill. Garson sides with Peck, then persuades Hunt to do the same. Tandy, by this time, hates Garson and verbally abuses her, causing Peck to become angry. The picture ends and we are not quite certain whether Peck will leave Tandy for Garson but there appears to be a glimmer of hope in that direction. Peck had established himself in DAYS OF GLORY and KEYS OF THE KING-DOM and was being wooed by a few studios (RKO and FOX among them) but he wanted to maintain his independence. Mayer appealed to him in one famous meeting where the little mogul actually began to cry in order to get

Peck to sign an exclusive contract. Peck suspected that Mayer did that regularly and held out for a nonexclusive deal, which he eventually received. THE VALLEY OF DECISION was filmed entirely on MGM's huge back lot and the reality of the sets is a tribute to the art directors and set decorators. Stothart's music was nominated for an Oscar and Garson received her fifth Best Actress nomination in a row for her work, with the prior accolades being given for BLOSSOMS IN THE DUST, MRS. MINI-VER (winner), MADAME CURIE, and MRS. PARKINGTON. This marked Thompson's first picture and he replaced Hume Cronyn when it was obvious that the diminutive Cronyn and the lanky Peck could never be perceived as brothers. This movie was a huge success, earning nearly $6 million on the initial release. It also won the *Photoplay* Gold Medal and was high on the "Ten Best" list of *Film Daily*. It was right after this that Garson decided to alter the image that Mayer had given her. Over his vociferous objections, she chose to play a tart in ADVENTURE and made several more films which tarnished the carefully conceived legend Mayer had built. Mayer, for all his chicanery and phony theatrics, was an old-line producer who could judge things instinctively and his feelings about Garson and the aura she projected were quite right. Her career never went as high as it did when he was choosing the movies.

p, Edwin H. Knopf; d, Tay Garnett; w, John Meehan, Sonya Levien (based on the novel by Marcia Davenport); ph, Joseph Ruttenberg; m, Herbert Stothart; ed, Blanche Sewell; art d, Cedric Gibbons, Paul Groesse; set d, Edwin B. Willis; Mildred Griffiths; spec eff, A. Arnold Gillespie, Warren Newcombe.

Drama   **(PR:A MPAA:NR)**

VALLEY OF EAGLES*½   (1952, Brit.) 86m Independent Sovereign/Lippert bw

Jack Warner (*Inspector Petersen*), Nadia Gray (*Kara Niemann*), John McCallum (*Dr. Nils Ahlen*), Anthony Dawson (*Sven Nystrom*), Mary Laura Wood (*Helga Ahlen*), Norman Mac Owan (*McTavish*), Alfred Maurstad (*Trerik*), Martin Boddey (*Headman*), Christopher Lee (*1st Detective*), Ewen Solon (*2nd Detective*), Niama Wiwstrand (*Baroness Erland*), Peter Blitz (*Anders*), Sarah Crawford (*Noma*), Molly Warner (*Frau Lund*), Trillot Billquist (*Col. Strand*), Gosta Cederlund (*Prof. Lind*), Sten Lindgren (*Director General*), George Willoughby (*Bertil*), Kurt Sundstrom, Holger Kax.

McCallum plays a Swedish scientist who enlists the aid of police inspector Warner in tracking down his unfaithful wife, Wood, and disloyal assistant, Dawson, who have fled with some of his valuable scientific equipment which can produce energy from sound waves. The chase takes them to Lapland, where the scientist and the inspector are attacked by wolves. Local hunters with their trained eagles rescue them and eventually the villainous lovers are killed in an avalanche. The lively sequence where the Lapps hunt wolves with eagles was filmed by the National Geographic Society and used in the picture. Lee, who always had boasted about his love affair with Sweden, later said that making this film was the beginning of his affection for that cold country. He was quoted as saying that he learned a lot there at the time, and it was where he had his first contact with singing in opera.

p, Nat A. Bronsten, George Willoughby; d&w, Terence Young (based on a story by Paul Tabori, Bronsten); ph, Harry Waxman; m, Nino Rota; ed, Lito Carruthers; md, Muir Mathieson; art d, J. Elder Wills.

Adventure/Crime   **(PR:A MPAA:NR)**

VALLEY OF FEAR   (SEE: SHERLOCK HOLMES AND THE DEADLY NECKLACE, 1962, Ger.)

VALLEY OF FIRE**   (1951) 70m COL bw

Gene Autry (*Himself*), Pat Buttram (*Breezie Larrabee*), Gail Davis (*Laurie*), Russell Hayden (*Steve Guilford*), Christine Larson (*Bee Laverne*), Harry Lauter (*Tod Rawlings*), Terry Frost (*Grady McKean*), Barbara Stanley (*Gail*), Teddy Infuhr (*Virgil*), Marjorie Liszt (*Widow Blanche*), Riley Hill (*Colorado*), Victor Sen Young (*Ching Moon*), Gregg Barton (*Blackie*), Sandy Sanders (*Banjo*), Bud Osborne (*Beardsley*), Fred Sherman (*"Panhandle" Jones*), James Magill (*Bartender*), Duke York (*Piano*), Frankie Marvin, Pat O'Malley, Wade Crosby, William Fawcett, Syd Saylor, John Miller, Champion, Jr. the Horse.

Autry is the mayor of a booming frontier town that is faced with a monumental crisis–there just aren't any women around. To quell the passion-turned-to-rowdiness of the men in his town, Autry sends out for a wagon train of women willing to settle in the area. Too bad for Gene that villains Lauter and Hayden learn of the ladies' arrival and try to hijack the shipment in order to sell the women to a group of love-starved miners. Of course Autry and his town come to the rescue and bring the women home to their valley. A bit sexist, but it was 1951.

p, Armand Schaefer; d, John English; w, Gerald Geraghty (based on a story by Earle Snell); ph, William Bradford; ed, James Sweeney; md, Mischa Bakaleinikoff; art d, Charles Clague.

Western   **Cas.**   **(PR:A MPAA:NR)**

VALLEY OF FURY   (SEE: CHIEF CRAZY HORSE, 1955)

VALLEY OF GWANGI, THE***½   (1969) 95m Morningside/WB c

James Franciscus (*Tuck Kirby*), Gila Golan (*T.J. Breckenridge*), Richard Carlson (*Champ Connors*), Laurence Naismith (*Prof. Horace Bromley*), Freda Jackson (*Tia Zorina*), Gustavo Rojo (*Carlos dos Orsos*), Dennis Kilbane (*Rowdy*), Mario de Barros (*Bean*), Curtis Arden (*Lope*), Jose Burgos (*Dwarf*).

Special effects animator Ray Harryhausen dusted off an old script written by his mentor, Willis O'Brien (KING KONG, 1933), entitled "The Valley of the Mist" and decided to make it his next project. Two years later the retitled film, now THE VALLEY OF GWANGI, opened to mediocre reviews and a disinterested public. Had anyone bothered to notice, Harryhausen's movie contains some of the most breathtaking stop-motion effects sequences ever put on film. Set in a small Mexican town in the year 1912, the film follows circus promote Franciscus into a strange valley where time has stopped and prehistoric creatures still live, which he and his men stumble across while trying to capture a tiny horse (believed extinct 50 million years ago) that turned up in the village. What the little animal leads them to is a giant, ferocious allosaur which the cowboys try to lasso (this scene stands among Harryhausen's finest moments). After several run-ins with the beast (and other prehistoric creatures, including a pteranodon and a styracosaur), Franciscus and his men eventually subdue the dinosaur and take him back to the circus to be put on display. Of course the monster escapes (shades of KONG) and wreaks havoc on the Mexican town before meeting his doom in a burning cathedral. While the human action in the film is a bit stiff (once again), the special effects are exhilarating. Harryhausen was able to achieve an incredible fluidity to his creatures' movements and the matte work is nearly perfect. Well worth a look, it is a real shame that THE VALLEY OF GWANGI never really found an audience outside the circle of Harryhausen cultists.

p, Charles H. Schneer; d, James O'Connolly; w, William E. Bast, Julian More (based on the story "Gwangi" by Bast); ph, Erwin Hillier (Dynamation, Technicolor); m, Jerome Moross; ed, Henry Richardson; art d, Gil Parrondo; cos, John Furness; spec eff, Ray Harryhausen.

Fantasy/Western   **(PR:A MPAA:G)**

VALLEY OF HUNTED MEN**½   (1942) 60m REP bw

Bob Steele (*Tucson Smith*), Tom Tyler (*Stony Brooke*), Jimmie Dodd (*Lullaby Joslin*), Anna Marie Stewart (*Laura*), Edward Van Sloan (*Dr. Henry Steiner*), Roland Varno (*Carl Baum*), Edythe Elliott (*Mrs. Schiller*), Arno Frey (*Von Breckner*), Richard French (*Toller*), Robert Stevenson (*Kruger*), George Neiss (*Schiller*), Duke Aldon, Budd Buster, Hal Price, Billy Benedict, Charles Flynn, Rand Brooks, Kenne Duncan, Jack Kirk.

Bizarre THREE MESQUITEERS oater sees a Nazi on the run assume the identity of the nephew of a trusted German refugee who has developed a system to obtain valuable rubber from culebra plants. Steele, Tyler, and Dodd become a bit suspicious of this German (after all, it was wartime) and they bring the real nephew's mother in to identify her son. She blows the whistle on the Nazi imposter and the cowboys round him up in short order. (See THREE MESQUITEERS series, Index.)

p, Louis Gray; d, John English; w, Albert DeMond, Morton Grant (based on an idea by Charles Tetford and on characters created by William Colt MacDonald); ph, Bud Thackery; m, Mort Glickman; ed, William Thompson; art d, Russell Kimball.

Western   **(PR:A MPAA:NR)**

VALLEY OF MYSTERY**   (1967) 94m UNIV c

Richard Egan (*Wade Cochran, the Pilot*), Peter Graves (*Ben Barstow, the Author*), Joby Baker (*Pete Patton*), Lois Nettleton (*Rita Brown, the Girl*), Harry Guardino (*Danny O'Neill*), Julie Adams (*Joan Simon*), Fernando Lamas (*Francisco Rivera, the Killer*), Alfred Ryder (*Dr. Weatherly*), Karen Sharpe (*Connie Lane*), Barbara Werle (*Ann Dickson*), Lee Patterson (*Dino Doretti*), Rodolfo Acosta (*Manuel Sanchez*), Douglas Kennedy (*Charles Kiley*), Don Stewart (*Jim Walker*), Leonard Nimoy (*Spence Atherton*), Tony Patino (*Juan Hidalgo*), Otis Young (*Dr. John Quincy*), Lisa Gaye (*Margalo York*), George Tyne (*Forest Hart*), Larry Domasin (*Indian Boy*), Eddie Little Sky (*M'Tu*), William Phipps (*Immigration Inspector*).

Lame plane disaster movie that was originally intended as a television series pilot but later expanded to feature length and released in theaters. Egan stars as the brave pilot of a jumbo jet that is blown off course and forced to crash-land in the dense jungles of South America. All the passengers survive save one, a lawman escorting dangerous killer Lamas to the executioner (Lamas killed him in the excitement). While the plane was carrying over a hundred passengers, only a handful are seen on screen and they are the standard set of stereotypical disaster-film characters. Baker is a famous singer, Guardino a has-been comedian, Adams a disturbed schoolteacher, and Graves a novelist searching for his sister who is married to a missionary stationed in the area. It is Graves' quest that serves as the basis for the rest of the action as the plane has crashed not too far from where he was to begin his search. Graves soon finds some answers and is shocked to learn that his sister is dead and her missionary husband, Ryder, has gone completely insane and set himself up as the ruler of the local tribe of natives. The goofy zealot is about to offer up Graves and some passengers as human sacrifices when they are rescued by a rival, more friendly, tribe of natives who take them back to the wreckage in time to be saved by navy helicopters.

p, Harry Tatelman; d, Josef Leytes; w, Richard Neal, Lowell Barrington (based on the story by Neal, Lawrence B. Marcus); ph, Walter Strenge (Technicolor); m, Jack Elliott; ed, Gene Milford; art d, Russell Kimball, Howard E. Johnson; set d, John McCarthy, John M. Dwyer; cos, Burton Miller; makeup, Bud Westmore.

Adventure   **(PR:A   MPAA:NR)**

VALLEY OF SONG   (SEE: MEN ARE CHILDREN TWICE, 1953, Brit.)

VALLEY OF THE DOLLS zero   (1967) 123m Red Lion/FOX c

Barbara Parkins (*Anne Welles*), Patty Duke (*Neely O'Hara*), Paul Burke (*Lyon Burke*), Sharon Tate (*Jennifer North*), Tony Scotti (*Tony Polar*), Martin Milner (*Mel Anderson*), Charles Drake (*Kevin Gilmore*), Alexander Davion (*Ted Casablanca*), Lee Grant (*Miriam*), Naomi Stevens (*Miss Steinberg*), Robert H. Harris (*Henry Bellamy*), Jacqueline Susann (*Reporter*), Robert Viharo (*Director*), Mikel Angel (*Man in Hotel Room*), Barry Cahill (*Man in Bar*), Richard Angarola (*Claude Chardot*), Joey Bishop (*MC at Telethon*), George Jessel (*MC at Grammy Awards*), Susan Hayward (*Helen Lawson*), Judith Lowry (*Aunt Amy*), Jeanne Gerson (*Neely's Maid*), Linda Peck, Pat Becker, Corinna Tsopei (*Telephone Girls*), Robert Street (*Choreographer*), Robert Gibbons (*Desk Clerk at Lawrenceville Hotel*), Leona Powers (*Woman at Martha Washington Hotel*), Barry O'Hara (*Assistant Stage Manager*), Norman Burton (*Neely's Hollywood Director*), Margot Stevenson (*Anne's Mother*), Jonathan Hawke (*Sanitarium Doctor*), Marvin Hamlisch (*Pianist*), Billy Beck (*Man Sleeping in Movie House*), Dorothy Neumann, Charlotte Knight (*Neely's Maids*), Robert McCord (*Bartender at New York Theater*), Peggy Rea (*Neely's Voice Coach*), Gertrude Flynn (*Ladies' Room Attendant*).

Pure trash, based on a trashy book, filled to the brim with trashy performances, now becomes a trashy cult film. Based on Jacqueline Susann's novel detailing the horrors of stardom (the author also has a bit part as a journalist–which she has trouble pulling off), the film stars Tate, Parkins, and Duke as three aspiring actresses who each attain a degree of success followed by a dependence on pills (nicknamed "dolls"). Tate, who is told by everyone she meets that she has no talent but a great body, meets and marries a young singer, Scotti, who soon is stricken with a fatal illness requiring expensive hospitalization. To pay the bills, Tate appears in European porno films and becomes quite a sensation. Unfortunately, she soon discovers she has breast cancer and needs to have her "talent" removed. Realizing there is no future in porno after such surgery, Tate kills herself by taking an overdose of sleeping pills. Duke (who turns in the worst performance of the three–only because she is capable of so much more) plays a young actress who lands a minor part in a new Broadway show opposite aging superstar Hayward (who replaced the originally cast Judy Garland, a dropout despite the perquisites proffered by the studio, including the dressing-room pool table she had demanded). The ambitious newcomer makes herself such a nuisance that she soon finds herself out of a job. As luck would have it, Duke winds up doing a quick singing spot on a national television fund-raiser and becomes a superstar overnight (oh, sure). Of course her sudden success leads to a horrible drug addiction which eventually turns her into a pathetic, whining has-been who *should* commit suicide to end the audience's suffering. Unfortunately, she doesn't. Not all success stories are grim, however, as we follow the likable Parkins from her small East Coast town to New York where she hits it big as a model. This, once again, leads to a bout with the ever-present pills and an unstable love life, but Parkins eventually finds the inner strength to abandon her success and hightail it back to her home town before she winds up as just another tragic statistic. Banal, ignorant, and just plain lousy, this wretched film went on to gross over $20 million, becoming one of 20th Century-Fox's biggest hits ever and reaffirming the belief that the public deserves what it gets. A sequel of sorts followed (although Fox sued and won a settlement over it) entitled BEYOND THE VALLEY OF THE DOLLS that was another entry in the Russ Meyer soft-core porno parade (hey, it's better than VALLEY OF THE DOLLS) which was authored by none other than the Pulitzer Prize-winning film critic for the Chicago Sun-Times, Roger Ebert, who also wrote Meyer's BENEATH THE VALLEY OF THE ULTRA VIXENS (he used a pseudonym this time). In 1981 a made-for-TV remake appeared, entitled JACQUELINE SUSANN'S VALLEY OF THE DOLLS.

p, David Weisbart; d, Mark Robson; w, Helen Deutch, Dorothy Kingsley (based on the novel by Jacqueline Susann); ph, William H. Daniels (Panavision, DeLuxe Color); m, Johnny Williams; ed, Dorothy Spencer; md, Williams; art d, Jack Martin Smith, Richard Day; set d, Walter M. Scott, Raphael Bretton; cos, Travilla; spec eff, L.B. Abbott, Art Cruickshank, Emil Kosa, Jr.; ch, Robert Sidney; m/l, Andre Previn, Dory Previn; makeup, Ben Nye.

Drama   **Cas.**   **(PR:O   MPAA:GP)**

VALLEY OF THE DRAGONS*½   (1961) 79m ZRB/COL bw

Cesare Danova (*Hector Servadac*), Sean McClory (*Denning*), Joan Staley (*Deena*), Danielle De Metz (*Nateeta*), Gregg Martell (*Od-Loo*), Gil Perkins (*Tarn/Doctor*), I. Stanford Jolley (*Patoo*), Michael Lane (*Anoka*), Roger Til (*Vidal*), Mark Dempsey (*Andrews*), Jerry Sunshine (*LeClerc*), Dolly Gray (*Mara*).

Silly adaptation of a Jules Verne story starring Danova and McClory as two 19th-Century duelists who are suddenly swept onto a passing comet by a violent windstorm. On the comet the bewildered travelers discover another world populated by dinosaurs and cave men. Circumstances force Danova and McClory to split up and soon each finds himself allied with opposing tribes in a cave-man war. The men fall in love with rival cave women and teach the tribes to live in peace.

p, Byron Roberts; d&w, Edward Bernds (based on a story by Donald Zimbalist, and the novel *Career of a Comet* by Jules Verne); ph, Brydon Baker (Monstascope); m, Ruby Raksin; ed, Edwin Bryant; art d, Don Ament; spec eff, Richard Albain; makeup, Ben Lane.

Science Fiction   **(PR:A   MPAA:NR)**

VALLEY OF THE GIANTS   (1938) 79m WB c

Wayne Morris (*Bill Cardigan*), Claire Trevor (*Lee Roberts*), Frank McHugh ("*Fingers*" *McCarthy*), Alan Hale ("*Ox*" *Smith*), Donald Crisp (*Andy Stone*), Charles Bickford (*Howard Fallon*), Jack LaRue (*Ed Morrell*), John Litel (*Hendricks*), Dick Purcell (*Creel*), El Brendel (*Fats*), Russell Simpson (*McKenzie*), Cy Kendall (*Sheriff Graber*), Harry Cording (*Greer*), Wade Boteler (*Joe Lorimer*), Helen MacKellar (*Mrs. Lorimer*), Addison Richards (*Hewitt*), Jerry Colonna.

Another technicolor tale of rugged lumberjacks blazing a path through the redwoods. Morris plays the lead, a tough lumberman out to stop thieving wood-rustlers. Trevor is the equally tough girl whom he woos. Routine in all respects. A second remake of a silent made by Paramount in 1919. Some footage later appeared in THE BIG TREES (1952).

p, Lou Edelman; d, William Keighley; w, Seton I. Miller, Michael Fessier (based on a story by Peter B. Kyne); ph, Allen M. Davey (Technicolor); ed, Jack Killifer; md, Leo F. Forbstein; art d, Ted Smith.

Adventure   **(PR:A   MPAA:NR)**

VALLEY OF THE HEADHUNTERS*½   (1953) 67m COL bw

Johnny Weissmuller (*Jungle Jim*), Christine Larson (*Ellen Shaw*), Robert C. Foulk (*Arco*), Steven Ritch (*Lt. Barry*), Nelson Leigh (*Mr. Bradley*), Joseph Allen, Jr (*Pico Church*), George Eldredge (*Commissioner Kingston*), Neyle Morrow (*Cpl. Bono*), Vince M. Townsend, Jr (*M'Gono*), Don Blackman (*Chief Bagava*), Paul Thompson (*Chief Gitzhak*), Tamba the Chimpanzee.

Weissmuller stars once again as Jungle Jim, who this time is assigned by the government to gain valuable mineral rights from a group of agreeable natives. Agreeable, that is, until nasty villains Foulk and Allen, Jr. get the natives so upset that they go on the warpath in search of white men's heads. Luckily Weissmuller is able to calm everybody down and get the villains *and* the mineral rights. (See JUNGLE JIM series, Index.)

p, Sam Katzman; d, William Berke; w, Samuel Newman (based on the newspaper feature "Jungle Jim" by Alex Raymond); ph, William Whitley; ed, Gene Havlick; md, Mischa Bakaleinikoff; art d, Paul Palmentola.

Adventure   **(PR:A   MPAA:NR)**

VALLEY OF THE KINGS   (1954) 86m MGM c

Robert Taylor (*Mark Brandon*), Eleanor Parker (*Ann Mercedes*), Carlos Thompson (*Philip Mercedes*), Kurt Kasznar (*Hamed Bachkour*), Victor Jory (*Taureg Chief*), Leon Askin (*Valentine Arko*), Aldo Silvani (*Father Anthimos*), Samia Gamal (*Dancer*).

The romance in this movie was given an added dimension by the realism of the stars' affection for each other. Taylor and Parker were allegedly lovers off screen as well as on and publicity about the duo helped improve the picture's box-office share, perhaps beyond what it deserved. The unoriginal story was somewhat enhanced by the superb photography of Egyptian scenery, such as the Nile, the Pyramids, the Sphinx, the Suez Canal, Mount Sinai, the Red Sea, and various streets in Cairo. It's 1900 in Egypt and Taylor is an archeologist on a dig to uncover the hidden treasures and secrets of the Pharoah Ra-Hotep, an 18th Dynasty ruler of Egypt. One of the aides is Thompson and he is married to Parker but it's not long before Parker and Taylor are making eyes at each other. A subplot has Parker attempting to prove a theory her late father came up with based on the Bible story that tells us there were seven years of abundance followed by an equal period of famine. Parker thinks they might be able to find some records on their expedition as well as proof that Joseph (of the multicolored coat) existed and did make the trip to Egypt as read in the Bible (and seen on the stage in the Tim Rice-Andrew Lloyd Webber musical). The intellectual side of the movie managed to bore audiences and seemed to cause ennui in Taylor as well. There is some heat in the presence of Thompson as a man who is watching his wife being magnetized by a man before his eyes.

Further, it turns out he's a rotter because he's part of a ring of thieves who have already ransacked the tomb and sold the treasures to the highest bidders on the black market. Thompson's partner in the crime is Kasznar, and Askin is seen as a swarthy antique dealer who keeps his feet on both sides as he tries to make a score. At one point, Taylor unbuckles his swash and engages in an excellent bit of swordplay against Jory. Later, Taylor and Thompson do battle on a statue and you have one guess as to who comes out the victor in that skirmish. As noted, the cinematography is excellent and probably should have nabbed at least an Oscar nomination for Surtees. Thompson had a brief acting career that began in Argentina, where he was born, then segued to the U.S. for a few films, then off to Europe where he worked in French, German, and Austrian movies. He eventually married actress Lilli Palmer and settled in Switzerland. VALLEY OF THE KINGS finally wraps up proceedings with an anticlimactic denouement of the subplot, but by that time most people were aching to go back to the refreshment stand for a popcorn refill. It might have worked better if they dealt with the subplot earlier and concluded with the big fight, which was exciting. According to the credits, the film was suggested by material out of C.W. Ceram's book *Gods, Graves and Scholars*. For anyone intrigued by archaeology, we must recommend that tome. It is a thumbnail guide to the great finds, including the discovery of Troy, the uncovering of Pompeii, and several more. Although essentially a classroom text, the book is so well written and so exciting in theory that it's one of those works you will treasure and it is also infinitely more informative and uplifting than this movie. As you will note, there is no credit given for the producer. Whoever it was who oversaw this film saw fit to ask that his (or her) name be deleted from the final release print. The picture wasn't great, but it also wasn't that bad, although the uncomfortable feeling that we'd seen it all before was consistent.

d, Robert Pirosh; w, Pirosh, Karl Tunberg (based on historical data in the book *Gods, Graves and Scholars* by C.W. Ceram); ph, Robert Surtees (Eastmancolor); m, Miklos Rozsa; ed, Harold F. Kress; cos, Walter Plunkett.

Mystery   (PR:A-C MPAA:NR)

VALLEY OF THE LAWLESS**   (1936) 56m Supreme/William Steiner
bw

Johnny Mack Brown, Joyce Compton, George Hayes, Dennis Meadows [Moore], Bobby Nelson, Frank Hagney, Charles King, Jack Rockwell, Frank Ball, Horace Murphy, Steve Clark, Edward Cassidy, Robert McKenzie, Forrest Taylor, George Morell, Jack Evans.

Brown goes searching for a lost treasure and finds trouble. Routine Brown oater that fans of the genre should find acceptable.

p, R.W. Hackel; d&w, Robert N. Bradbury.

Western   (PR:A MPAA:NR)

VALLEY OF THE REDWOODS**   (1960) 62m FOX bw

John Hudson (*Wayne Randall*), Lynn Bernay (*Jan Spencer*), Ed Nelson (*Dino Michaelis*), Michael Forest (*Dave Harris*), Robert Shayne (*Capt. Sid Walker*), John Brinkley (*Willie Chadwick*), Bruno Ve Sota (*Joe Wolcheck*), Hal Torey (*Philip Blair*), Chris Miller (*Charlotte Walker*).

Low-budget caper film starring Hudson, Bernay, and Nelson as thieves out to pull a daring payroll job. The well-planned robbery goes afoul, resulting in the wounding and capture of Hudson and the escape of Bernay and Nelson with the loot. While on the lam through picturesque pine country in northern California, Bernay kills Nelson when he tries to ditch her with the dough in tow. Eventually she too meets with a sticky end. Pretty basic stuff, but it has some redeeming moments. Produced by Roger Corman's brother Gene, with a fine performance by splatter-film regular Ve Sota.

p, Gene Corman; d, William Witney; w, Leo Gordon, Daniel Madison (based on a story by Corman); ph, Kay Norton (CinemaScope); m, Buddy Bregman; ed, Marshall Neilan, Jr.; art d, Daniel Haller.

Crime   (PR:A MPAA:NR)

VALLEY OF THE SUN**   (1942) 84m RKO bw

Lucille Ball (*Christine Larson*), James Craig (*Jonathan Ware*), Sir Cedric Hardwicke (*Warrick*), Dean Jagger (*Jim Sawyer*), Peter Whitney (*Willie, Idiot*), Billy Gilbert (*Justice of the Peace*), Tom Tyler (*Geronimo*), Antonio Moreno (*Chief Cochise*), George Cleveland (*Bill Yard*), Hank Bell (*Shotgun*), Richard Fiske, Don Terry (*Lieutenants*), Chris Willow Bird (*Apache Indian*), Fern Emmett (*Spinster*), Carleton Young (*Nolte*), Carl Sepulveda (*Pickett*), George Melford (*Dr. Thomas*), Pat Moriarty (*Mickey Maguire*), Stanley Andrews (*Major*), Chester Clute (*Secretary*), Al St. John, Harry Lamont, Al Ferguson, Chester Conklin, Ed Brady, Lloyd Ingraham, Frank Coleman (*Men on Street*), Ethan Laidlaw (*Johnson*), Steve Clemente (*Knife Thrower*), George Lloyd (*Sergeant*), Bud Osborne (*Rose*), Tom London (*Parker, Trooper*), Francis McDonald (*Interpreter*), Harry Hayden (*Governor*), Jay Silverheels, Iron Eyes Cody (*Indians*).

Dull western ballyhooed as a massive outdoor epic on par with 1930's CIMARRON upon its release. The result is something of a dud. Jagger stars as an evil Indian agent stationed in the Arizona Territory who bilks the redskins for all they're worth. Craig plays the government agent sent to clean house by posing as a renegade Indian scout to get the goods on Jagger. While playing cat-and-mouse, both men romance restaurant owner Ball. Needless to say Craig gets his man, and his woman. Decent cameo performances by Gilbert as a justice of the peace and Tyler as Geronimo make this one fairly interesting.

p, Graham Baker; d, George Marshall; w, Horace McCoy (based on a story by Clarence Budington Kelland); ph, Harry Wild; m, Paul Sawtell; ed, Desmond Marquette; spec eff, Vernon L. Walker.

Western   (PR:A MPAA:NR)

VALLEY OF THE SWORDS   (SEE: CASTILIAN, THE, 1963,
U.S./Span.)

VALLEY OF THE WHITE WOLVES
(SEE: MARA OF THE WILDERNESS, 1966)

VALLEY OF THE ZOMBIES*½   (1946) 56m REP bw

Robert Livingston (*Dr. Terry Evans*), Adrian Booth (*Susan Drake*), Ian Keith (*Ormand Murks*), Thomas Jackson (*Blair*), Charles Trowbridge (*Dr. Rufus Maynard*), Earle Hodgins (*Fred Mays*), LeRoy Mason (*Hendricks*), William Haade (*Tiny*), Wilton Graff (*Dr. Garland*), Charles Cane (*Inspector Ryan*), Russ Clark (*Lacy*), Charles Hamilton (*The Driver*).

Once again Republic tried to make a horror film, and once again the results weren't too impressive. Keith stars as a mad undertaker who returns from the dead seeking revenge on those who had him committed to an insane asylum (he was alive at the time) by draining them of their blood. In the end Keith falls off a building and dies for a second time. Yes, you're right, the title doesn't really make much sense. Republic should have stuck to oaters.

p&w, Dorrell and Stuart McGowan (based on an original by Royal K. Cole, Sherman L. Lowe); d, Philip Ford; ph, Reggie Lanning; ed, William P. Thompson; md, Richard Cherwin; art d, Hilyard Brown; spec eff, Howard and Theodore Lydecker.

Horror   **Cas.**   (PR:C MPAA:NR)

VALLEY OF VENGEANCE*½   (1944) 56m PRC bw (GB:
VENGEANCE)

Buster Crabbe (*Billy Carson*), Al "Fuzzy" St. John (*Fuzzy Jones*), Evelyn Finley (*Helen*), Donald Mayo (*Young Billy*), David Polonsky (*Young Fuzzy*), Glenn Strange (*Marshal Baker*), Charles King (*Burke*), John Merton (*Kurt*), Lynton Brent (*Carr*), Jack Ingram (*Brett*), Bud Osborne (*Dad Carson*), Nora Bush (*Ma Carson*), Steve Clark (*Happy*), Budd Buster, Edward Cassidy.

Crabbe sets out to revenge the murders of his and a friend's family by a bloodthirsty gang of outlaws who had slaughtered the innocent folk 20 years before. Eventually he catches up with the crooks and calls them out on their own turf-a town they own lock, stock, and barrel. Of course he wins. (See BILLY CARSON series, Index.)

p, Sigmund Neufeld; d, Sam Newfield; w, Joe O'Donnell; ph, Jack Greenhalgh; ed, Holbrook N. Todd.

Western   (PR:A MPAA:NR)

VALUE FOR MONEY**½   (1957, Brit.) 89m RANK c

John Gregson (*Chayley Broadbent*), Diana Dors (*Ruthine West*), Susan Stephen (*Ethel*), Derek Farr (*Duke Popplewell*), Frank Pettingell (*Higgins*), Jill Adams (*Joy*), Charles Victor (*Lumm*), James Gregson (*Oldroyd*), Ernest Thesiger (*Lord Dewsbury*), Donald Pleasence (*Limpy*), Joan Hickson (*Mrs. Perkins*), Hal Osmond (*Mr. Hall*), Sheila Raynor (*Mrs. Hall*), Charles Lloyd Pack (*Mr. Gidbrook*), Ferdy Mayne (*Waiter*), John Glyn Jones (*Arkwright*), Leslie Phillips (*Robjohns*), Molly Weir (*Mrs. Matthews*), Paddy Stone, Irving Davies (*Dancers*), Gillian Lutyens, George Benson, Ronnie Stevens, Cyril Smith, Vic Wise, Ronald Chesney, Diana Munks, Eleanor Fazan, Sheila O'Neil, Aleta Morrison, Pamela Davis, Francis Pidgeon, Hermione Harvey, Jane Dore, Mavis Traill, Diana Satow, Julia Arnall, Patricia Webb, Carol Day, Mavis Greenaway, Ruth Sheil, Hanwell Silver Band.

Typical British comedy featuring Gregson as a wealthy Yorkshire rag magnate who takes off to London after a fight with his girl friend, Stephen, and soon begins romancing the ever-voluptuous Dors, who is a showgirl. While Dors likes Gregson, she figures he's a pauper and turns down his marriage proposal. When she eventually finds out that Gregson's a millionaire, she rushes into his arms and agrees to marriage. Gregson, however, has had second thoughts, and after Dors confirms his suspicions by quickly spending a fortune, he returns to his old girl friend. After having a taste of wealth, Dors doesn't give up, and winds up finding another rich Yorkshireman to marry.

p, Sergei Nolbandov; d, Ken Annakin; w, R. F. Delderfield, William Fairfield (based on the novel by Derrick Boothroyd); ph, Geoffrey Unsworth (Vistavision, Technicolor); m, Malcolm Arnold; ed, Geoffrey Foot; md, Muir Mathieson; art d, Alex Vetchinsky; ch, Paddy Stone, Irving Davies; m/l, John Pritchett, Peter Myers, Alec Grahame.

Comedy   (PR:A MPAA:NR)

VAMPIRA   (SEE: OLD DRACULA, 1975, Brit.)

VAMPIRE, THE   (SEE: VAMPYR, 1932, Fr./Ger.)

VAMPIRE, THE*   (1957) 74m UA bw (AKA: MARK OF THE
                                                             VAMPIRE)

John Beal (*Dr. Paul Beecher*), Coleen Gray (*Carol Butler*), Kenneth Tobey
(*Buck Donnelly*), Lydia Reed (*Betsy Beecher*), Dabbs Greer (*Dr. Will
Beaumont*), Herb Vigran (*George Ryan*), Ann Staunton (*Marion Wilkins*),
James Griffith (*Henry Winston*), Paul Brinegar (*Willie*), Natalie Masters,
Raymond Greenleaf, Mauritz Hugo, Louise Lewis, Wood Romoff, Brad
Morrow, Hallene Hill, Anne O'Neal, George Selk, Walter A. Merrill,
Christine Rees, Arthur Gardner.

Offensive horror movie without a single shudder to be found. Beal is a
scientist who comes across some strange pills made by a recently deceased
colleague. He takes some, of course, and turns into a scaly looking
bloodsucker. A late-night television staple.

p, Arthur Gardner, Jules Levy, Arnold Laven; d, Paul Landres; w, Pat
Fielder; ph, Jack McKenzie; m, Gerald Fried; ed, Johnny Faure; art d, James
Vance; makeup, Don Robertson.

Horror   (PR:C MPAA:GP)

VAMPIRE, THE½**   (1968, Mex.) 84m
            Cinematografica/Trans-International A.B.S.A. bw (EL VAMPIRO)

Abel Salazar (*Henry*), the Doctor, Ariadne Welter (*Marta*), German Robles
(*Count Duval/Lavud*), Carmen Montejo, Jose Luis Jimenez, Alicia Mon-
toya, Mercedes Soler, Margarito Luna, Julio Daneri, Jose Chavez, Amando
Zumaya, Dick Barker, Edward Tucker, Lydia Mellon.

Mexican horror film sees Robles as a vampire terrorizing modern-day
Mexico while trying to weasel the family fortune out of the lovely Welter.
Robles succeeds in wooing his way into the good graces of the young girl's
aunt and even goes so far as to bury Welter alive, but the heroine is
eventually rescued from her terrible fate and the vampire is dispatched with
the proverbial stake-through-the-heart. El stinko. Released in Mexico in
1957.

p, Abel Salazar; d, Fernando Mendez (English version, Paul Nagle); w,
Henrich Rodriguez, Ramon Obon (based on a story by Obon); ph, Rosalio
Solano; m, Gustavo Cesar Carrion; ed, Jose Bustos; art d, Gunther Gerszo.

Horror   (PR:C MPAA:NR)

VAMPIRE AND THE BALLERINA, THE zero
            (1962, Ital.) 86m Consorzio Italiano/UA bw (L'AMANTE DEL VAM-
                                                             PIRO)

Helene Remy (*Luisa*), Maria Lusia Rolando (*The Contessa*), Tina Gloriani
(*Francesca*), Walter Brandi (*Luca*), Isarco Ravaioli (*Servant*), John Turner,
Pierugo Gragnani, Stefania Sabatini, Ugo Gragnani.

Large-breasted ballerinas find themselves stranded in a castle owned by
beautiful vampire Rolando who is assisted in her nocturnal escapades by her
dwarfish assistant Ravaioli. One of the quick-thinking dancers whips out a
gold crucifix after figuring out the truth behind the mysterious goings-on
and manages to hold off Rolando until sunlight turns her to dust.

p, Bruno Bolognesi; d, Renato Polselli; w, Polselli, Ernesto Gastaldi,
Giuseppe Pellegrini; ph, Angelo Baistrocchi; m, Aldo Piga; art d, Amedeo
Mellone; ch, Marissa Ciampaglia.

Horror   (PR:C MPAA:NR)

VAMPIRE AND THE ROBOT, THE
                  (SEE: MY SON, THE VAMPIRE, 1963, Brit.)

VAMPIRE BAT, THE**   (1933) 63m Majestic bw

Lionel Atwill (*Dr. Otto von Niemann*), Fay Wray (*Ruth Bertin*), Melvyn
Douglas (*Karl Brettschneider*), Maude Eburne (*Gussie Schnappmann*),
George E. Stone (*Kringen*), Dwight Frye (*Herman Gleib*), Robert Frazer
(*Emil Borst*), Rita Carlisle (*Martha Mueller*), Lionel Belmore (*Burgermeist-
er Gustave Schoen*), William V. Mong (*Sauer*), Stella Adams (*Georgiana*),
Paul Weigel (*Holdstadt*), Harrison Greene (*Weingarten*), William Hum-
phrey (*Dr. Haupt*), Fern Emmett (*Gertrude*), Carl Stockdale (*Schmidt the
Morgue Keeper*).

Small independent Majestic Studios tried to capitalize on the horror boom
of the earlier 1930s by creating this unusual hybrid made up of borrowed
sets, props, and performers from Universal and Warner Bros. Atwill and
Wray make their third and last horror appearance together (DR. X and THE
MYSTERY OF THE WAX MUSEUM were the first two) with the former
playing yet another mad scientist and the latter yet another terrified victim.
The film opens with the small European village of Kleinschloss gripped in
an epidemic of murder. Several villagers have been found dead in their beds,

drained of all blood. Despite police inspector Douglas' conviction that the
killer is a common criminal, the villagers all believe the murders to be the
work of a vampire. Their suspicions seem confirmed by the huge swarm of
bats which has infested the village. In fact, the citizens suspect the village
idiot, Frye, of being the culprit because of his unusual affection for bats.
When Atwill, a local doctor, pronounces another woman dead and then
states that it was definitely the work of a vampire, the villagers chase Frye
to his death. To ensure that he does not return, the villagers drive a stake
through his heart. Meanwhile, it is revealed that Atwill has been conducting
some strange experiments without the knowledge of his assistants, Wray
and Frazer. Atwill has been using the blood of the locals to feed a living blob
of flesh he has created. The mad doctor hypnotizes Frazer and has him
strangle Adams, his servant. Frazer later awakes in his bed, completely
unaware of his role in the murder. When Adams' body is found, the police
suspect Frye, but when they learn that Frye has been murdered as well,
police inspector Douglas launches a full-scale investigation. Worried that
Douglas will discover the truth, Atwill again hypnotizes Frazer and sends
him off to kill the police inspector. This time, however, Wray stumbles
across the plan and tries to stop it. Atwill subdues the woman and ties her
up. While the hypnotized Frazer goes off to do his murderous work, Atwill
babbles to Wray about the brilliance of his fleshy artificial creation.
Meanwhile, Douglas manages to defend himself against Frazer and snap
him out of his hypnosis. The two men return to the castle, and when Frazer
realizes that he has murdered under Atwill's control, he attacks the
scientist. During the struggle the blood-sucking lifeform is destroyed and
both creator and assistant are killed. Majestic Studios filmed THE VAM-
PIRE BAT on Universal Studio's back lot. Using the village set from
FRANKENSTEIN, the house from THE OLD DARK HOUSE, and furnish-
ings from the silent version of THE CAT AND THE CANARY, the film has
a familiar look to it. This, combined with the casting of Frye in a role almost
identical to his "Renfield" in DRACULA and Belmore re-doing his burgermeister role from FRANKENSTEIN, the film looks and sounds like a
Universal production. Warner Bros'. popular terror duo Atwill and Wray
were added to the brew, giving VAMPIRE BAT a very strange feel. It is as
if two studios had collided and their productions had gotten intertwined.
Atwill is quite good here, having had much practice at the mad scientist
game, and Wray is her usual screamingly attractive self. While the
production was a bit too cheap to have the power of DRACULA, FRANKEN-
STEIN, or THE MYSTERY OF THE WAX MUSEUM, THE VAMPIRE BAT
is a solid effort that should please fans of early 1930s horror.

p, Phil Goldstone; d, Frank R. Strayer; w, Edward T. Lowe; ph, Ira Morgan;
ed, Otis Garrett; art d, Daniel Hall.

Horror   Cas.   (PR:C MPAA:NR)

VAMPIRE BEAST CRAVES BLOOD, THE
                  (SEE: BLOOD BEAST TERROR, 1969, Brit.)

VAMPIRE CIRCUS**½**   (1972, Brit.) 84m Hammer/FOX c

Adrienne Corri (*Gypsy Woman*), Laurence Payne (*Prof. Mueller*), Thorley
Walters (*Burgermeister*), John Moulder-Brown (*Anton Kersh*), Lynne Frede-
rick (*Dora Mueller*), Elizabeth Seal (*Gerta Hauser*), Anthony Corlan (*Emil*),
Richard Owens (*Dr. Kersh*), Domini Blythe (*Anna Mueller*), Robin Hunter
(*Hauser*), Robert Tayman (*Count Mitterhouse*), Mary Wimbush (*Elvira*),
Lalla Ward (*Helga*), Robin Sachs (*Heinrich*), Roderick Shaw (*Jon Hauser*),
Barnaby Shaw (*Gustav Hauser*), Christina Paul (*Rosa*), Dave Prowse
(*Strongman*), Jane Darby (*Jenny*), Skip Martin (*Michael*), Milovan and
Serena (*The Webbers*), John Brown (*Schilt*), Sibylla Kay (*Mrs. Schilt*),
Dorothy Frere (*Grandma Schilt*), Jason James (*Foreman*), Arnold Locke
(*Old Villager*), Bradford and Amoro (*Helga and Heinrich's Doubles*).

Stylish Hammer horror film about a strange circus that arrives in a small
Serbian village to enact an elaborate and horrible revenge on the townsfolk
that murdered their relative, an evil vampire-count, 100 years before. Soon
after the circus' arrival, a mysterious plague forces the village to be
separated from the outside world, leaving the townsfolk at the mercy of the
macabre performers. Soon many of the burg's leading citizens are horribly
murdered by the vampire circus whose members are able to transform
themselves into animals at will. Eventually a full-scale battle between the
remaining townsfolk and the vampires ensues, resulting in the bloody
staking and decapitation of the undead leader of the fiends. The plot is
somewhat overly complicated, but the production values are high and there
are some truly chilling moments.

p, Wilbur Stark; d, Robert Young; w, Judson Kinberg (based on a story by
George Baxt, Stark); ph, Moray Grant (DeLuxe Color); m, David Whittaker;
ed, Peter Musgrave; md, Philip Martell; art d, Scott MacGregor; spec eff, Les
Bowie.

Horror   (PR:C-0 MPAA:R/PG)

VAMPIRE GIRLS, THE   (SEE: THE VAMPIRES, 1969, Mex.)

VAMPIRE HOOKERS, THE zero (1979, Phil.) 88m Capricorn Three c
(AKA: SENSUOUS VAMPIRES; CEMETERY GIRLS)

John Carradine, Bruce Fairbairn, Trey Wilson, Karen Stride, Lenka Novak, Katie Dolan, Lex Winter.

The ads exclaimed, "Warm Blood Isn't All They Suck!" With that bit of enticement, the intrepid horror fan is about to subject himself to the torture of watching the 73-year-old John Carradine as a vampire count send his voluptous minions out to seduce hapless young studs back to his castle for a bloody feast. Truly wretched, even if it's *supposed* to be funny.

p, Robert E. Waters; d, Cirio H. Santiago; w, Howard Cohen; m, Jaime Mendoza-Nava.

Horror   (PR:O MPAA:R)

VAMPIRE LOVERS, THE½** (1970, Brit.) 91m Hammer/AIP c

Ingrid Pitt (*Carmilla/Mircalla/Marcilla Karnstein*), Pippa Steele (*Laura Spielsdorf*), Madeleine Smith (*Emma Morton*), Peter Cushing (*Gen. Spielsdorf*), George Cole (*Roger Morton*), Dawn Addams (*The Countess*), Kate O'Mara (*Mme. Perrodot*), Douglas Wilmer (*Baron Hartog*), Jon Finch (*Carl Ebbhardt*), Kirsten Betts (*1st Vampire*), Harvey Hall (*Renton, Butler*), Janet Key (*Gretchen*), Charles Farrell (*Landlord*), Ferdy Mayne (*Doctor*), John Forbes Robertson (*Man in Black*), Shelagh Wilcox (*Housekeeper*), Graham James, Tom Browne (*Young Men*), Joanna Shelley (*Woodman's Daughter*), Olga James (*Village Girl*).

Hammer's first nudie-lesbian vampire movie and, believe it or not, it's not half bad. The lovely Ingrid Pitt stars as a sexy vampire who arrives at a remote eastern European town to exact revenge upon the townsfolk who killed off her fellow vampires several years before. Pitt seduces her way into the household of the respectable general, Cushing, and his beautiful daughter, Steele. Soon after her arrival Pitt manages to bed Steele and slowly drain her blood after numerous lesbian encounters. Having killed off the daughter of one upstanding villager, Pitt moves on to seduce Smith, the young best friend off the now-deceased Steele and daughter of Cole. Once again Pitt begins to slowly suck the life out of another young woman during sex and after Pitt kills the girl's doctor, Cole hires Wilmer, a famed vampire killer, to investigate. After concluding that Pitt is indeed a vampire, Wilmer and Cole manage to wrest Smith from her lover's grasp and force a confrontation which ends with Pitt's decapitation. Directed with considerable flair, the material is handled as tastefully as possible, adding a new variation on an old horror theme. Roger Vadim had handled the same theme–adapted from the same story– in his BLOOD AND ROSES, released in the U.S. in 1961, lessening the shock power of this adaptation.

p, Harry Fine, Michael Style; d, Roy Ward Baker; w, Tudor Gates, Fine, Style (based on the story "Carmilla" by J. Sheridan Le Fanu); ph, Moray Grant (Technicolor); m, Harry Robinson; ed, James Needs; art d, Scott MacGregor; cos, Brian Box; makeup, Tom Smith.

Horror   (PR:O MPAA:R)

VAMPIRE MEN OF THE LOST PLANET
(SEE: HORROR OF THE BLOOD MONSTERS, 1970, US (Phil.)

VAMPIRE OVER LONDON (SEE: MY SON, THE VAMPIRE, 1963, Brit.)

VAMPIRE PEOPLE, THE (SEE: BLOOD DRINKERS, THE, 1966, US/(Phil.)

VAMPIRES (SEE: DEVIL'S COMMANDMENT, THE, 1957, Ital.)

VAMPIRES, THE* (1969, Mex.) 91m Vergara/COL c (AKA: LAS VAMPIRAS; THE VAMPIRE GIRLS)

John Carradine, Pedro Armendariz, Jr, Mil Mascaras, Maria Duval, Maura Monti, Martha Romero, Elsa Maria, Dagoberto Rodriguez, Jessica Munguia, Vianey Larriaga, Manuel Garay, Rossi Ceballos, Sara Bentz.

Carradine made four cheap vampire movies in Mexico and thankfully this is the last of them. In this one he's the leader of an all-female clan of bloodsuckers, who are costumed in winged body stockings. Duval is one of his followers who takes over and tosses her leader in a cage. Mascaras, a wrestler, comes to save the day. Cheap and worthless.

p, Luis Enrique Vergara; d, Federico Curiel; w, Adolfo Torres Protillo, Curiel (based on a character created by Bram Stoker); ph, Alfredo Uriba; m, Gustavo Cesar Carreon; ed, Juan Jose Munguia; art d, Octavio Ocampo, Jose Mendez; makeup, Maria Eugenia Luca.

Horror   (PR:O MPAA:NR)

VAMPIRE'S COFFIN, THE½** (1958, Mex.) 86m Cinematografica/K. Gordon Murray bw (EL ATAUD DEL VAMPIRO; EL ATAUD DEL COFFIN)

Abel Salazar (*Henry*), Ariadne Welter (*Marta*), German Robles (*Count*

Lavud), Alicia Rodriguez, Yerye Beirute, Guillermo Orea, Antonio Raxell, Carlos Ancira.

A sequel to THE VAMPIRE once again starring Robles as the count who is revived in his coffin by a servant who pulls the stake out of his heart. Armed with a change of identity (he spelled his name backwards, making Duval into Lavud) the vampire changes into a bat and begins terrorizing the Mexicans once again. This time old Lavud-Duval is killed by being speared while still in his bat configuration.

p, Abel Salazar (U.S. version, K. Gordon Murray), d, Fernando Mendez (U.S. version, Paul Nagle); w, Ramon Obon (based on a story by Raul Zenteno); ph, Victor Herrera; m, Gustavo Cesar Carrion; ed, Alfredo Rosas Priego; art d, William Hayden, Gunther Gerszo.

Horror   Cas.   (PR:O MPAA:NR)

VAMPIRE'S GHOST, THE*½ (1945) 59m REP bw

John Abbott (*Webb Fallon*), Charles Gordon (*Roy Hendrick*), Peggy Stewart (*Julie Vance*), Grant Withers (*Father Gilchrist*), Adele Mara (*Lisa*), Emmett Vogan (*Thomas Vance*), Roy Barcroft (*Jim Barrat*), Martin Wilkins (*Simon Peter*), Frank Jaquet (*The Doctor*), Jimmy Aubrey (*The Bum*), Zach Williams, Floyd Shadelford, George Carlton, Fred Howard.

Republic studios took another chance on horror and failed again. Abbott stars as a 400-year-old zombie-vampire who runs the underworld on the west coast of Africa. He has been condemned to wander the Earth forever due to an ancient curse laid on his head back in 1588 and he can't be killed. Well, at least until he finally crumbles under the onslaught of silver-tipped spears, fire, and a falling idol in a voodoo temple. The highlight sees Abbott able to continue his undead wanderings in the daytime by wearing sunglasses]

p, Rudolph E. Abel; d, Lesley Selander; w, Leigh Brackett, John K. Butler (based on an original story by Brackett suggested by Polidori's story "The Vampyre"); ph, Ellis Thackerey, Robert Pittack; ed, Tony Martinelli; md, Richard Cherwin; art d, Russell Kimball; ch, Jerry Jarrette.

Horror   (PR:C MPAA:NR)

VAMPIRE'S NIGHT ORGY, THE*½ (1973, Span./Ital.) 86m International Amusement c (LA ORGIA NOCTURNA DE LOS VAMPIROS)

Jack Taylor, Charo Soriano, Dianik Zurakowska, John Richard.

Taylor stars as one of a group of unfortunate tourists who venture into a mysterious European town that happens to be populated by vampires.

p, Jose Frade; d, Leon Klimovsky; w, Gabriel Burgos, Antonio Fos.

Horror   (PR:O MPAA:R)

VAMPYR***** (1932, Fr./Ger.) 83m Dreyer-Tobis-Klangfilm bw (VAMPYR, OU L'ETRANG E AVENTURE DE DAVID GRAY; VAMPYR, DER TRAUM DES DAVID GRAY; AKA: NOT AGAINST THE FLESH; CASTLE OF DOOM; THE STRANGE ADVENTURE OF DAVID GRAY; THE VAMPIRE)

Julian West [Baron Nicolas de Gunzburg] (*David Gray*), Henriette Gerard (*Marguerite Chopin*), Jan Hieronimko (*Doctor*), Maurice Schutz (*Lord of the Manor*), Rena Mandel (*His Daughter Gisele*), Sibylle Schmitz (*His Daughter Leone*), Albert Bras (*Servant*), N. Babanini (*The Girl*), Jane Mora (*The Religious Woman*).

Much to the dismay of his admirers, Danish director Carl Theodor Dreyer followed his silent masterpiece THE PASSION OF JOAN OF ARC (1927) with a horror film that was to be his first foray into sound. The resulting film is a masterpiece of subtle terror which is the stuff of true nightmares. Loosely based on *In a Glass Darkly*, a collection of horror stories by Joseph Sheridan Le Fanu, the film begins as a young man, West, arrives in a dark, mysterious European village and finds that a room has been booked for him at the inn. West takes the room and that night he is visited by a strange old man, Schutz, who gives West a package and tells him that it should be opened upon his death. The old man then disappears, leaving a confused West wondering whether the encounter was a dream. Unable to sleep, West wanders the village and begins following a disembodied shadow of a one-legged man. The shadow leads West to a house where more shadows dance insanely to odd music. An old woman, Gerard, enters the room and orders the music and dancing to stop. The village doctor, Hieronimko, meets with the old woman. Hieronimko gives Gerard a bottle of poison. Meanwhile, the one-legged shadow reunites with its body, that of a gamekeeper, and the man goes about building coffins. Once again, the shadow leaves its body and West follows it to a mansion. There he meets Schutz, the mysterious old man who had given him the package, and learns that he is the owner of the house. There is the sound of a gunshot and Schutz dies in the arms of his daughter, Mandel. West learns that Mandel's sister, Schmitz, is suffering from a strange malaise. Remembering the package Schutz gave him, West opens it and finds a book entitled *Strange Tales of Vampires*. Later, Schmitz is found to have wandered the mansion grounds in her sleep. The old woman, Gerard, is spotted hovering over the girl's prostrate body, but she quickly disappears. Schmitz has lost a dangerous amount of blood, and West volunteers his blood for a transfusion. During the procedure, West dreams he is being buried alive. The coffin has a window and he sees Gerard peering in at him. Staring out, West sees the tops of buildings and trees as a cart takes his coffin to the cemetery. It is then that he realizes that Gerard is a vampire and the doctor is her assistant. West awakens from his hallucination to find that he has wandered into the cemetery. There he is met by Bras, Schutz's servant, and together they find the grave of Gerard. Taking an iron pole from West, Bras plunges it through the heart of the vampire. The flesh fades from her body and she turns to dust. At the mansion, Schmitz is freed from her spell. Now that the vampire is dead, the spirits of her victims rise from their graves and enact revenge upon the gamekeeper and the doctor. The gamekeeper is thrown down a flight of stairs to his death, while the doctor is trapped in a mill and buried alive in flour. The evil gone, West and Mandel face the dawn. In VAMPYR Dreyer conveys a deep sense of terror by suggesting the evil, not showing it. Nothing is seen that shocks or repulses in this nightmarish vision, but we are left with a sense of unease and dread. The vampire's power is never overtly shown, only felt. Dreyer shot a scene where the vampire summons a pack of wolves to do her bidding, but upon reflection the director decided that the scene was too overt a demonstration of the vampire's power and left it out. In his search for freshness and natural faces, Dreyer had his crew search for actors in every place from flophouses to bridge viaducts. The actors in the film, with the exception of Schmitz and Schutz, are nonprofessionals. West, whose real name was Baron Nicolas de Gunzburg, financed the film. Hieronimko, the doctor, was a Polish journalist, and Gerard was the mother of an actress. The hazy look of the film was discovered quite accidentally. The director was dissatisfied with the crispness of the cinematography but became excited when one reel that had been shot came out gray and foggy. An unwanted light leak had affected the film, and it was the perfect look Dreyer wanted for the film. From then on, cinematographer Mate purposely fogged the image for the desired effect. VAMPYR moves slowly through its bizarre world, and from the point West leaves his room at the inn, we are led through a strange, eerie world where shadows leave their masters and things are not as they seem. The village is caught in a haze of evil and we follow West through it as if in a dream. The scene where West is buried alive (shot mostly from his point of view) is a classic moment of horror, as is the scene where Schmitz looks hungrily at her sister, craving blood. Without much trickery or fanfare, Dreyer slowly brings us into this misty netherworld and holds us there until the end. The director's use of sound is brilliant. Phrases are purposely muffled and half-heard from off screen, giving West (and us) the impression that something is going on that we can't quite comprehend. The sounds of unseen dogs barking and babies crying add to the tension and confusion. As in all of Dreyer's works, viewers must decelerate their normal narrative expectations and allow the film to wash over them. VAMPYR is a sensual film of mood and emotion, not of plot and thrills. Because of this, the film did poorly at the box office worldwide. U.S. distributors tried to cut footage from the film to pick up the pace, but as William K. Everson states in his book *Classics of the Horror Film*, "...you can only shorten a Dreyer film, you cannot speed it up." VAMPYR was retitled CASTLE OF DOOM and set before audiences accustomed to the more visceral thrills of Universal's DRACULA and FRANKENSTEIN. It failed miserably. Financial failure notwithstanding, VAMPYR is one of the true classics of the horror film genre because of its unparalleled subtle evocation of terror that chills down to the bone. No filmmaker has come near this brand of horror, most preferring a more tangible approach, with the exception of producer Val Lewton whose chillers of the 1940s once again evoked the unseen, not the graphic. To attempt to describe VAMPYR in mere words is impossible; this is a film to be seen and savored as an example of filmmaking at its most evocative.

p, Baron Nicolas de Gunzberg, Carl Theodor Dreyer; d, Dreyer; w, Dreyer, Christen Jul (based on stories from *In a Glass Darkly* by Joseph Sheridan Le Fanu); ph, Rudolph Mate, Louis Nee; m, Wolfgang Zeller; art d, Hermann Warm, Hans Bittmann, Cesare Silvagni.

Horror   **Cas.**   **(PR:O   MPAA:NR)**

VAMPYRES, DAUGHTERS OF DRACULA**½
                              (1977, Brit.) 87m Cambist c (AKA: VAMPYRES)

Marianne Morris *(Fran)*, Anulka *(Miriam)*, Murray Brown *(Ted)*, Brian Deacon *(John)*, Sally Faulkner *(Harriett)*, Michael Byrne *(Playboy)*, Karl Lanchbury *(Rupert)*, Bessie Love, Elliott Sullivan *(Elderly Couple)*.

Interesting vampire movie has Morris and Anulka *(Playboy's* May 1973 centerfold) a pair of undead lovers who pass the day in a double coffin, and spend the night preying on the men and women who drop by to camp on the grounds of their castle. Although the script is never completely coherent, the film still generates a great deal of erotic energy and spills a goodly amount of blood, too.

p, Brian Smedley-Aston; d, Joseph Jose Larraz; w, D. Daubeney; ph, Harry Waxman; m, James Clark; ed, Geoff R. Brown; art d, Ken Bridgeman.

Horror   **(PR:O   MPAA:R)**

VAN, THE*½   (1977) 90m Crown c

Stuart Getz *(Bobby Hampton)*, Deborah White *(Tina)*, Harry Moses *(Jack Crandall)*, Marcie Barkin *(Sue)*, Bill Adler *(Steve)*, Stephen Oliver *(Dugan Hicks)*, Connie Lisa Marie *(Sally Johnson)*, Danny DeVito *(Andy)*, Jim

Kester *(Tom)*, Michael Gitomer *(Jim)*, Chuck Hastings *(Fat Policeman)*, Steven Stinebaugh *(Thin Policeman)*, David Ellenstein *(Basketball Player)*, Howard Dayton *(Friendly)*, Donald Elson *(Mr. Hump)*, Jean Howell *(Nora Hampton)*, Richard Karie *(Jaguar Owner)*, Walter Maslow *(Henry Hampton)*, Lilyan McBride *(Bertha)*, Duncan McLeod *(Man in Driveway)*, Michael G. Meday *(Drag Racer)*, Janie Mudrick *(Pinball Girl)*, James Oliver *(Van Customizer)*, Rock Riddle *(Beach Boy)*, Elizabeth Rogers *(Mrs. Eastman)*, Adina Ross *(Blonde)*, Cherise Wilson *(Mexican Girl)*, Jacqueline Jacobs *(Graduation Guest)*.

On his graduation from high school, eager-eyed Getz uses his graduation money as down payment for a gaudy van that would make any others his age green with jealousy. Rather than go to college, he disappoints his folks by deciding to spend the rest of his life trying to lure girls into the water-bed-equipped vehicle. A pal fixes him up with nice girl White. They like each other but Getz's sexual drives cause an inevitable rift. Later Getz meets up with his old boss DeVito (in a role prior to his great success as the curmudgeon Louie on the sit-com "Taxi"), who desperately needs $200 to pay off a gambling debt. Getz gives him the cash, though this was to be a payment on his beloved van. Later Getz makes a pass at Marie, but this is interrupted by her boy friend, Oliver. Getz runs into White and impulsively tells her she's the girl for him. Next thing you know, it's lovemaking time in the back of the van. But wait! Getz still needs some money for his down payment. He meets Oliver in a van drag race, which he naturally wins along with the everlasting love of White. There are some moments in THE VAN where the filmmakers try to rise above the teenage make-out movie genre by injecting a little humanity into the characters. However, one can't enter a pigpen without coming up muddy. The miniscule good moments are overshadowed by the macho attitudes and general stupidity of the characterizations. In the end, this is indistinguishable from any other "California kid and his car" movie.

p, Paul Lewis; d, Sam Grossman; w, Robert Rosenthal, Celia Susan Cotelo; ph, Irvin Goodnoff (DeLuxe Color); ed, Fabien Tordjman, Pierre Jalbert; md, Michael Lloyd; art d, Russell Schwartz; m/l, Sammy Johns (performed by Johns); makeup, Nancy Frechtling; stunts, Eddy Donno.

Teenage Drama   **Cas.**   **(PR:O   MPAA:R)**

VAN NUYS BLVD.**   (1979) 93m Marimark Crown International c

Bill Adler *(Bobby)*, Cynthia Wood *(Moon)*, Dennis Bowen *(Greg)*, Melissa Prophet *(Cameille)*, David Hayward *(Chooch)*, Tara Strohmeier *(Wanda)*, Dana Gladstone *(Al Zass)*, Di Ann Monaco *(Motorcycle Girl)*, Don Sawyer *(Jason)*, Jim Kester *(Frankie)*, Minnie E. Lindsey *(Nurse Bradley)*, Susanne Severeid *(Jo)*, Doug Bailey, Stephen Morrell, Bella Bruck, Mary Ellen O'Neill, Mario Bellini, Rena Harmon, Matthew Tobin, Michael Castle, Cecil Reddick, Diana Daniels, Nancy McCauley, Brando Caffey, Debbie Chenoweth, Louis Rivera, Jacqueline Jacobs.

Fairly engaging teenage drag race film starring Adler as a bored country boy who ventures to the San Fernando Valley for 90 minutes of hanging out, picking up girls, going dancing, and, of course, racing cars. Eventually he gives up these childish pursuits when he falls in love with fellow dragster and former *Playboy* Playmate Wood (she also appeared in APOCALYPSE NOW as the Playmate of the Year outfitted in a skimpy cowboy suit).

p, Marilyn J. Tenser; d&w, William Sachs; ph, Joseph Mangine (DeLuxe Color); m, Ron Wright, Ken Mansfield; ed, George Bowers; art d, Kenneth H. Hergenroeder; cos, Diana Daniels; ch, Sandy Hendrick Adler.

Romance   **Cas.**   **(PR:O   MPAA:R)**

VANDERGILT DIAMOND MYSTERY, THE*   (1936) 60m RKO bw

Elizabeth [Betty] Astell *(Mary)*, Bruce Seton *(Hardcastle)*, Hilary Pritchard *(Briggs)*, Charles Paton *(Mr. Throstle)*, Ethel Royale *(Mrs. Throstle)*, Ben Graham Soutten *(The Boss)*, William Holland *(Carponi)*, Henry B. Longhurst *(Inspector Greig)*, Brian Herbert, John Miller.

Dimwitted British comedy about the search for a diamond necklace that was stolen from a rich woman and then accidentally dropped into the golf bag of an unsuspecting young man. Astell plays the honorable girl out to retrieve the jewels before the gang of thieves can locate the man and get the necklace back. Eventually the crooks are trapped by the man's neighbors.

p&d, Randall Faye; w, Margaret Houghton (based on a story by Michael Crombie).

Comedy   **(PR:A   MPAA:NR)**

VANESSA, HER LOVE STORY**   (1935) 74m MGM bw (GB: VANESSA)

Helen Hayes *(Vanessa)*, Robert Montgomery *(Benjie)*, Otto Kruger *(Ellis)*, May Robson *(Judith)*, Lewis Stone *(Adam)*, Henry Stephenson *(Barney)*, Violet Kemble-Cooper *(Lady Herries)*, Donald Crisp *(George)*, Jessie Ralph *(Lady Mullion)*, Agnes Anderson *(Marion)*, Lionel Belmore *(Leathwaite)*, Lawrence Grant *(Amery)*, Howard Leeds *(Jamie)*, Ethel Griffies *(Winifred Trent)*, Elspeth Dudgeon *(Vera Trent)*, Mary Gordon *(Mrs. Leathwaite)*, George K. Arthur *(Porter)*, Crauford Kent *(Timothy)*.

Overly sentimental and contrived soap opera which sees Hayes married to the increasingly erratic Kruger who is suffering from genetically inherited insanity. Unhappy in her marriage (Hayes doesn't realize that her husband is suffering from a family disease), she takes on a lover, Montgomery, who is soon shipped off to Egypt with the British army. Montgomery gets his arm blown off in battle, Kruger eventually dies, and the illicit couple marry. After VANESSA, HER LOVE STORY, Hayes would all but disappear from the screen until 1951 when she starred in MY SON JOHN. Famed novelist Walpole, who collaborated on the screenplay made from this fourth and last of his "Herries Chronicle" novels, had been brought to Hollywood by producer Selznick primarily to work on the studio's screenplay for DAVID COPPERFIELD (1935). Like Hayes, he didn't remain long in Babylon after this bomb.

p. David O. Selznick; d, William K. Howard; w, Lenore Coffee, Hugh Walpole (based on a novel by Walpole); ph, Ray June; ed, Frank Hull; cos, Dolly Tree.

Drama   **(PR:A MPAA:NR)**

VANISHING AMERICAN, THE**   (1955) 90m REP bw

Scott Brady (Blandy), Audrey Totter (Marian Warner), Forrest Tucker (Morgan), Gene Lockhart (Blucher), Jim Davis (Glendon), John Dierkes (Friel), Gloria Castillo (Yashi), Julian Rivero (Etenia), Lee Van Cleef (Jay Lord), George Keymas (Coshonta), Charles Stevens (Quah-Tain), Jay Silverheels (Beeteia), James Millican (Walker), Glenn Strange (Beleanth).

Routine western starring Brady as a young Navajo brave who stands up to the evil whites and turncoat Apaches who are trying to drive his people off their land. Tucker plays the slimy white trader and Lockhart the dishonest Indian agent who attempt to monopolize all the waterholes in the territory. Totter plays the brave lady rancher who teams up with Brady in order to save her land which has been marked by the baddies for takeover as well. Stevens, who has a small part as an Indian, was in reality Geronimo's grandson. This remake of the remarkable silent picture (1926) which gave Richard Dix his finest screen role differs in important respects from its precursor. The times had changed; implications of miscegenation were no longer against the code of the screen. In this one, Indian Brady appears to actually walk away with Caucasian Totter.

p, Herbert J. Yates; d, Joseph Kane; w, Alan LeMay (based on the novel by Zane Grey); ph, John L. Russell, Jr.; m, R. Dale Butts; ed, Richard L. Van Enger; art d, Walter Keller; cos, Adele Palmer.

Western   **(PR:A MPAA:NR)**

VANISHING FRONTIER, THE**   (1932) 65m Larry Darmour/PAR bw

Johnny Mack Brown (Kirby Tornell), Evalyn Knapp (Carol Winfield), ZaSu Pitts (Aunt Sylvia), Raymond Hatton (Waco), J. Farrell MacDonald (Hornet), Wallace MacDonald (Capt. Kearney), Ben alexander (Lucien Winfield), George Irving (Gen. Winfield), Joyselle (Dolores).

Silly-but-fun oater which sees Brown playing a Latin Robin Hood character who sings and plays the piano between bouts with the Army. As a final irony, Brown rides off into the sunset with Knapp, who happens to be the general's daughter. One of the second-string features contract player Brown appeared in immediately following the studio's decision to concentrate on the career of his competitor, Clark Gable, rather than on that of the talented ex-football hero. Producer Jaffe is not the well-known character actor with the same name.

p, Sam Jaffe; d, Phil Rosen; w, Stuart Anthony; ph, James S. Brown.

Western   **(PR:A MPAA:NR)**

VANISHING FRONTIER, 1962   (SEE: BROKEN LAND, THE, 1962)

VANISHING OUTPOST, THE**   (1951) 58m REA bw

Lash La Rue (U.S. Marshal), Al St. John (Fuzzy Q. Jones), Riley Hill (Walker), Clarke Stevens (Denton), Bud Osborne (Outlaw Chief), Lee Morgan (Outlaw Guard), Ted Adams (Detective), Ray Broome (His Assistant), Cliff Taylor (Bartender), Archie Twitchell (Matt), Sharon Hall (Nancy Walker), Sue Hussey (Sue), Johnny Paul (Rider).

La Rue plays a whip-cracking U.S. marshal who teams up with the Pinkerton Detective Agency in order to smash a gang of sophisticated crooks who use a primitive telegraph to set up their robberies. One of the terrible films directed by Ormond–who had only produced the series previously; he began directing under the aegis of independent financiers J. Frances white and Joy Houck–this was, except for an X-rated film made during the late 1960s, La Rue's last starring film as "Lash" (although some others were released later).

p&d, Ron Ormond; w, Alexander White; ph, Ernest Miller; m, Walter Greene; ed, Hugh Winn; art d, Fred Preble; set d, Fred Offenbecker; makeup, Paul Stanhope.

Western   **(PR:A MPAA:NR)**

VANISHING POINT**½   (1971) 99m Cupid/FOX c

Barry Newman (Kowalski), Cleavon Little (Super Soul), Dean Jagger (Prospector), Victoria Medlin (Vera), Paul Koslo (Young Cop), Bob Donner (Older Cop), Timothy Scott (Angel), Gilda Texter (Nude Rider), Anthony James (1st Male Hitch-Hiker), Arthur Malet (2nd Male Hitch-Hiker), Karl Swenson (Clerk at Delivery Agency), Severn Darden (J. Hovah's Agency), Delaney & Bonnie & Friends [including Rita Coolidge] (J Hovah's Singers), Lee Weaver (Jake), Cherie Foster (1st Girl), Valerie Kairys (2nd Girl), Tom Reese (Sheriff), Owen Bush (Communications Officer).

A fairly interesting, but somewhat muddled and pretentious road movie starring Newman as an ex-cop who now drives cars from Denver to San Francisco for a living. Once in Denver, he bets a friend that he can drive a new Dodge Charger to San Francisco in 15 hours. Knowing that the feat is impossible, the bet is on and Newman loads up with amphetamines and takes off ignoring all speed laws. Soon word of Newman's folly leaks out and a blind, black radio station disc jockey, Little, begins hailing him as an American hero, "the last free man on Earth." By this time the cops in several states have become aware of Newman's race and have banded together to stop him. Along the way Newman picks up a variety of strange characters including an old desert rat, Jagger, who catches snakes and sells them to a cult for a living; two psychotic homosexuals who try to hijack him; a lone outlaw biker and his girl friend who provide him with pep pills and smokes, etc. Somehow Little and Newman form a psychic bond enabling the DJ to sense what the police have in store for the driver and warn him over the air of what to anticipate. Eventually the police send a pair of plainclothesmen to stop Little's broadcast. The lawmen beat the blind DJ up and force him to direct Newman into a trap. Newman senses that Little is being forced to broadcast harmful information and takes another route. Unfortunately, the route he takes has also been blocked, this time with heavy bulldozers, and instead of giving up, Newman roars right into them, committing suicide. Despite some weak flashbacks purporting to show what possesses Newman to pull such a self-destructive stunt, VANISHING POINT provides very little in the way of character motivation or development. While there is really nothing wrong with ambiguity (TWO-LANE BLACKTOP succeeds brilliantly), this film tries to be both an exciting crash-and-burn car chase and a heavy, message laden preachment accompanied by a fairly irritating musical score which really hammers confusing messages of Christian morality into the viewer's head. Director Sarafian has stated that his film was cut extensively by the studio and the ending changed (Newman's death should be perceived as some sort of uplifting transcendental experience) so that the movie was less "esoteric". Among the cuts is a scene that still exists in the British print between Charlotte Rampling (who represents Death) and Newman where they meet and make love. Perhaps the U.S. audiences were lucky that they weren't subjected to another grim and obvious metaphor. Songs and musical numbers include: "You Got to Believe" (Delaney Bramlett, sung by Delaney and Bonnie and Friends); "I Can't Believe It" (Longbranch/Pennywhistle, sung by them); "Super-Soul Theme," "Freedom of Ex-Pression" (The J. B. Pickers, sung by them); "Got It Together" (Mike Settle, sung by Bobby Doyle); "Where Do We Go from Here" (Settle, sung by Jimmy Walker); "Runaway Country" (The Doug Dillard Expedition, sung by them); "So Tired" (Eve, sung by her); "Dear Jesus God," "Over Me" (Segarini/Bishop, sung by them); "Welcome to Nevada" (Don Lanier, Joe Bob Barnhill, played by Jerry Reed); "Mississippi Queen" (West, Lang, Pappalardi, and Rea, sung by Mountain); "Sweet Jesus" (Red Steagal, sung by him); "Love Theme" (Jimmy Bowen, Pete Carpenter, played by Bowen); "Sing Out for Jesus" (Kim Carnes, sung by Big Mama Thornton); "Nobody Knows" (Settle, sung by Carnes).

p, Norman Spencer; d, Richard C. Sarafian; w, Guillermo Cain (based on a story outline by Malcolm Hart); ph, John A. Alonzo (DeLuxe Color); m, Jimmy Bowen, Pete Carpenter, Tom Thacker; ed, Stefan Arnsten; set d, Glen Daniels, Jerry Wunderlich; stunts, Cary Loftin, Louis Elias; make up, Del Acevedo.

Drama   **Cas.**   **(PR:C MPAA:GP)**

VANISHING VIRGINIAN, THE**   (1941) 97m MGM bw

Frank Morgan (Robert Yancey), Kathryn Grayson (Rebecca Yancey), Spring Byington (Rosa Yancey), Natalie Thompson (Margaret Yancey), Douglass Newland (Jim Shirley), Mark Daniels (Jack Holden), Elizabeth Patterson (Grandma), Juanita Quigley (Caroline Yancey), Scotty Beckett (Joel Yancey), Dickie Jones (Robert Yancey, Jr.), Leigh Whipper (Uncle Josh), Louise Beavers (Aunt Emmeline), J. M. Kerrigan (John Phelps), Harlan Briggs (Mr. Rogard), Katharine Alexander (Marcia Marshall).

Routine family saga starring Morgan as the patriarch of a Virginia clan consisting of his wife, Byington, and his five children. Basically a slice of life in the South from 1918 to 1929, the story follows Morgan during his tenure as a hardworking, honest, no-nonsense public prosecutor. Of course Morgan relies on the love and stability of his family life to see him through. Not bad, but nothing special. Grayson's second feature film (she went on to better things) allows her to exercise her vocal talents on "The World Was Made for You" (music by Johann Strauss), and the traditional "Evening by the Moonlight" and "Bill Bailey."

p, Edwin Knopf; d, Frank Borzage; w, Jan Fortune (based on a novel by Rebecca Yancey Williams); ph, Charles Lawton; m, David Snell, Lennie

Hayton; ed, James E. Newcom; art d, Cedric Gibbons; cos, Robert Kalloch, Gile Steele.

Drama (PR:A MPAA:NR)

VANISHING WESTERNER, THE½** (1950) 60m REP bw

Monte Hale (*Chris Adams*), Paul Hurst (*Waldorf Worthington*), Aline Towne (*Barbara*), Roy Barcroft (*"Sand" Sanderson*), Arthur Space (*John Fast*), Richard Anderson (*Jeff Jackson*), William Phipps (*Bud*), Don Haggerty (*Art*), Dick Curtis (*Bartender*), Rand Brooks (*Tim*), Edmund Cobb (*Morton*), Harold Goodwin (*Glumm the Undertaker*).

Unusual series oater starring Hale as a cowboy falsely accused of murdering a sheriff played by Space. Space–who isn't really dead–disappears, only to return in the guise of his twin brother from England, a titled nobleman. The Britisher arrives in town and whips up the locals into a frenzy which sends a lynch mob after the innocent Hale. While trying to extricate himself from this mess, Hale, with the help of sidekick Hurst, discovers that Space and his *compadre*, Barcroft, have staged the whole thing to cover a series of robberies. In the end, justice triumphs.

p, Melville Tucker; d, Philip Ford; w, Bob Williams; ph, Ellis W. Carter; m, Stanley Wilson; ed, Richard L. Van Enger.

Western **Cas.** (PR:A MPAA:NR)

VANITY** (1935) 76m GS Enterprises/COL bw

Jane Cain (*Vanity Faire*), Percy Marmont (*Jefferson Brown*), John Counsell (*Dick Broderick*), H. F. Maltby (*Lord Cazalet*), Moira Lynd, Nita Harvey.

Cain plays an unbelievably egotistical actress who stages her own "death" in order to bask in the sorrow of her adoring fans. Pretty contrived material, but interesting nonetheless.

p, A. George Smith; d&w, Adrian Brunel (based on the play by Ernest Denny); ph, Geoffrey Faithfull.

Drama (PR:A MPAA:NR)

VANITY FAIR* (1932) 67m Allied/Hollywood Exchange bw

Myrna Loy (*Becky Sharp*), Conway Tearle (*Rawdon Crawley*), Barbara Kent (*Amelia Sedley*), Walter Byron (*George Osborne*), Anthony Bushell (*Dobbin*), Billy Bevan (*Joseph Sedley*), Montagu Love (*The Marquis of Steyne*), Herbert Bunston (*Mr. Sedley*), Mary Forbes (*Mrs. Sedley*), Lionel Belmore (*Sir Pitt Crawley*), Lilyan Irene (*Polly*).

For reasons that have never been fully explained, MGM lent one of its stars to a small independent company to make this modern-dress version of Thackeray's well-known drama. The original story caused a great brouhaha in England because it raked the doyennes of London's society over the coals but Loy, no matter how good she was, couldn't personally save this movie, which was ill-conceived from the start, almost as though someone decided to take a classic like A TALE OF TWO CITIES and cast Sylvester Stallone in the role of the two men, then place it in Cleveland and Cincinnati. Loy plays the role of the nimble woman who uses her wiles and native wit and tramples her way through several hearts until she winds up in a marriage that she thinks will be the answer to all of her cunning prayers. It isn't, of course, and she receives her comeuppance in the conclusion. Loy, born Myrna Williams in Montana, was only 27 at this time and already appearing in her 58th film! The direction for this was slack, the dialog trite, and the cinematography ordinary although none of the actors can be faulted. Note veteran comedian Bill Bevan, an Australian who appeared in many Mack Sennett shorts, in a dramatic role. Odd that such a misfire could come from the typewriter of the usually excellent F. Hugh Herbert, who began writing in 1927 for the screen and would later be responsible for the scripts for SITTING PRETTY, SCUDDA HOO, SCUDDA HAY, KISS AND TELL, and THE MOON IS BLUE, among many others. Director Franklin, brother of Sidney Franklin, never quite caught the nuances of the story and was a poor choice for the task. It was remade three years later with Miriam Hopkins as BECKY SHARP in a color production. The first attempt at this story was a 1923 silent. None of the three did justice to it.

p, M.H. Hoffman; d, Chester M. Franklin; w, F. Hugh Herbert (based on the novel by William Makepeace Thackeray); ph, Harry Neumann, Tom Galligan; art d, Jean Hornbustal.

Drama **Cas.** (PR:C MPAA:NR)

VANITY STREET*½ (1932) 68m COL bw

Charles Bickford (*Brian*), Helen Chandler (*Jeanie*), Mayo Methot (*Fern*), George Meeker (*Val*), Arthur Hoyt (*Mr. Kerr*), Raymond Hatton (*Shorty*), Ruth Channing (*Rose Marie*), Dolores Ray (*Susan*), Claudia Morgan (*Lou*), Ann Fay (*Mary Ann*), Kathrin Claire Ward (*Mary Ann's Mother*), May Beaty (*Mrs. Dantry*), Dutch Hendrian (*Grogan*), Eddie Boland (*Joe*).

Melodrama starring Chandler as a starving waif who decides to break a store window so that she'll get thrown into jail and be able to eat. Things don't quite work out as she planned when sympathetic cop Bickford gives her a free meal and sets her up with a job as a dancer in the Follies. Though

Bickford's interest in Chandler seems purely professional, she falls deeply in love with her savior and grows angry and frustrated when her attentions are not reciprocated. To get attention, Chandler dates sleazy gigolo Meeker, who tries to bed her in his apartment. She scrambles just before the point of no return and leaves. Soon after, Meeker is found murdered (another of his lovers, Methot, did the deed) and all the evidence points to Chandler. Bickford, of course, has to arrest his protege, but he eventually clears her name and soon they are married.

d, Nicholas Grinde; w, Gertrude Purcell (based on a story by Frank Cavett, Edward Roberts); ph, Joseph August.

Drama (PR:A MPAA:NR)

VANQUISHED, THE*½ (1953) 84m PAR c

John Payne (*Rock Grayson*), Coleen Gray (*Jane Colfax*), Jan Sterling (*Rose Slater*), Lyle Bettger (*Roger Hale*), Willard Parker (*Capt. Kirby*), Roy Gordon (*Dr. Colfax*), Russell Gaige (*Rev. Babcock*), Leslie Kimmel (*Col. Ellansby*), Voltaire Perkins (*Harvey Giddens*), Sam Flint (*Connors*), Freeman Morse (*Randy Williams*), Charles Evans (*Gen. Hildebrandt*), Richard Shannon (*Lt. Adams*), John Dierkes (*Gen. Morris*), Karen Sharpe (*Lucy Colfax*), Ernestine Barrier (*Mrs. Colfax*), Ellen Corby (*Mrs. Barbour*), Louis Jean Heydt (*Luke Taylor*), Howard Joslin, Llewellyn Johnson, John Halloran, Harry Cody, William Beery, Sam Harris, Jack Hill, Richard Beedle, Richard Bartell, Brad Mora.

Dull oater starring Payne as a Confederate soldier who was held as a prisoner by the Union and, now that the war is over, must return home. Upon his arrival he is shocked to learn that his town is now run by a dishonest, paranoid man, Bettger, who is ruling the area as if he were a king. When the townsfolk see that Payne has returned, they attempt to get him to lead a revolt against Bettger, but Payne refuses and appears to turn against them by getting a job as the tax collector. Little do the villagers know that Payne is only pretending to be on Bettger's side in order to gather enough evidence to legally throw the bum out of office. Bettger proves to be no dummy, however, and soon learns of Payne's scheme. To combat this, the evildoer frames Payne on a murder charge, which forces the hero to take it on the lam. In the end Payne manages to clear his name and run Bettger and his cronies out of town.

p, William H. Pine, William C. Thomas; d, Edward Ludwig; w, Winston Miller, Frank L. Moss, Lewis R. Foster (based on the novel by Karl Brown); ph, Lionel Lindon (Technicolor); m, Lucien Caillet; ed, Frank Bracht; art d, Hal Pereira, Earl Hedrick; cos, Edith Head.

Western (PR:A MPAA:NR)

VARAN THE UNBELIEVABLE*½ (1962, U.S./Jap.) 70m
Toho-Dallas-Cory/Crown Interna tional bw (DAIKAIJU BARAN; AKA: THE MONSTER BARAN)

Myron Healey (*Comdr. James Bradley*), Tsuruko Kobayashi (*Anna*), Clifford Kawada (*Capt. Kishi*), Derick Shimatsu (*Matsu*), Kozo Nomura, Ayumi Sonoda, Koreya Senda, Akihiko Hirata, Hideo Imamura, George Sasaki, Hiroshi Hisamune, Yoneo Iguchi, Michael Sung, Roy Ogata.

Dumb American scientist Healey accidentally revives GODZILLA lookalike Varan after performing some salt-water experiments in a remote lagoon, despite the warnings of the local Japanese. Now unleashed, Varan wanders toward Tokyo destroying everything in his path (so what else is new?) and frustrating the army's attempts to stop him. Eventually Healey invents a serum that will nullify the monster and has it shot into Varan's soft underbelly, ending the terror. Pretty laughable. The Japanese original was severely cut, and many scenes were added for U.S. consumption (including all of those featuring Healey, who did not appear in the original 1958 Japanese version). It seems safe to state that most of the monster special effects are the work of the oriental craftsmen.

Japanese version: d, Inoshiro Honda; w, Shinichi Sekizawa (based on an idea by T. Kuronuma, story by Hajime Koizumi); ph, Koizumi; m, Akira Ifukube; art d, K. Shimizu; spec eff, Eiji Tsuburaya. U.S. version: p&d, Jerry A. Baerwitz; w, Sid Harris; ph, Jack Marquette; ed, Jack Ruggiero, Ralph Cushman; md, Peter Zinner; cos, Robert O'Dell; spec eff, Howard Anderson; makeup, Robert Cowan.

Science Fiction **Cas.** (PR:A MPAA:NR)

VARELSERNA (SEE: LES CREATURES, 1969, Fr./Swed.)

VARIETY*½ (1935, Brit.) 86m Argyle/But bw

Sam Livesey (*Charlie Boyd*), Cassie Livesey (*Maggie Boyd*), Jack Livesey (*Matt Boyd*), Barry Livesey (*Victor Boyd*), April Vivian (*Joan*), George Carney, W. G. Saunders, Bertha Wilmott, Tessa Deane, Nellie Wallace, The Houston Sisters, Harry Brunning, Phyllis Robins, Olsen's Sea Lions, Denis O'Neil, Sam Barton, John Rorke, Bobbie "Uke" Henshaw, The Sherman Fisher Girls, Billy Cotton and His Band, Horace Sheldon and His Orchestra, Bobby Slater, Sybil Wise, W. Dolphin, Ted Sanders, William Daunt, Lily Morris, Van Dock, Johnnie Schofield, Rita Cave, Roy Sharpe, John Clay, The Can Can Dancers.

The trials and tribulations of running a music hall are detailed in VARIETY which stars the Livesey family (who were a real-life show business clan) as the Boyd family, the people who own the music hall. Basically an excuse to film some popular stage acts of the day with a mildly interesting plot tacked on. Oddly absent from this family epic is well-known screen actor Roger Livesey, brother of Jack and Barry and son of Sam.

p, John Argyle; d, Adrian Brunel; w, Oswald Mitchell, Brunel (based on a story by Mitchell); ph, Desmond Dickinson.

Musical   **(PR:A MPAA:NR)**

VARIETY GIRL***   (1947) 83m PAR bw-c

Mary Hatcher (*Catherine Brown*), Olga San Juan (*Amber La Vonne*), De Forrest Kelley (*Bob Kirby*), Bing Crosby, Bob Hope, Gary Cooper, Ray Milland, Alan Ladd, Barbara Stanwyck, Paulette Goddard, Dorothy Lamour, Veronica Lake, Sonny Tufts, Joan Caulfield, William Holden, Lizabeth Scott, Burt Lancaster, Gail Russell, Diana Lynn, Sterling Hayden, Robert Preston, John Lund, William Bendix, Barry Fitzgerald, Cass Daley, Howard da Silva, Billy De Wolfe, Macdonald Carey, Arleen Whelan, Patric Knowles, Mona Freeman, Virginia Field, Richard Webb, Cecil Kellaway, Johnny Coy, Stanley Clements, Cecil B. DeMille, Mitchell Leisen, Frank Butler, George Marshall, Jim Mulcay, Mildred Mulcay, Spike Jones and His City Slickers, Mikhail Rasumny, Sally Rawlinson, Barney Dean, Mary Edwards, Virginia Welles, George Reeves, Patricia White 'Barry', Wanda Hendrix, Nanette Parks, Rae Patterson, Andra Verne (*Themselves*), William Demarest (*Barker*), Frank Faylen (*Stage Manager*), Frank Ferguson (*J.R. O'Connell*), Roger Dann (*French Number*), Pearl Bailey (*Specialty*), Glenn Tryon (*Bill Farris*), Jack Norton (*Busboy at Brown Derby*), Torben Meyer (*Andre the Headwaiter at Brown Derby*), Nella Walker (*Mrs. Webster*), Elaine Riley (*Cashier*), Charles Victor (*Assistant to Mr. O'Connell*), Gus Taute (*Assistant to Assistant*), Harry Hayden (*Stage Manager at Grauman's Chinese Theater*), Janet Thomas, Roberta Jonay (*Girls*), Wallace Earl (*Girl with Sheep Dog*), Dick Keene (*Dog Trainer*), Ann Doran (*Hairdresser*), Jerry James (*Assistant Director*), Eric Alden (*Makeup Man*), Frank Mayo (*Director*), Lucille Barkley, Carolyn Butler (*Secretaries*), Pinto Colvig (*Special Voice Impersonation*), Edgar Dearing (*Cop*), Russell Hicks, Crane Whitley, Charles Coleman, Hal K. Dawson, Eddie Fetherston, Len Hendry, Lorin L. Raker (*Men at Steam Bath*), Sammy Stein (*Masseur*), Douglas Regan, Warren Joslin (*Boys*), John Stanley, Joel Friend, Al Ruiz (*Specialty Dancers*), Pat Templeton, Larry Badagliacca (*Boys at Grauman's Theater*), Bob Alden (*Autograph Seeker*), Pat Moran (*Drunken Tumbling Act*), Willa Pearl Curtis (*Sister Jenkins*), Mildred Boyd (*Sister Jenkins' Daughter*), Lee Emery, Marilyn Gray, Renee Randall (*Usherettes*), Audrey Saunders, Ray Saunders, Russ Saunders, Ted DeWayne, William Snyder, Fay Alexander (*Six DeWaynes*), Raymond Largay (*Director of Variety Club*), Alma Macrorie (*Proprietress*), Duke Johnson (*Juggler*), Catherine Craig, Mavis Murray, Lucille Barkley, Pat White.

Star-packed musical extravaganza featuring just about everyone who was under contract at Paramount, with the exception of Betty Hutton, who was pregnant at the time, and Eddie Bracken. Made in cooperation with the Variety Club organization, it's the thin tale of two young Hollywood hopefuls who come to Paramount Studios and meet the entire work force. The Variety Clubs began when a child was discovered in the theater owned by John Harris in Pittsburgh. She was named Catherine Variety Sheridan (the name of the variety house was The Sheridan") and that's what began the Variety Clubs. Harris was also the man behind "Ice Capades" and a few other shows. In the movie, Mary Hatcher (in her film debut) comes to Hollywood, after a brief flashback to establish her heritage of being almost born in a trunk. She meets San Juan and the two youngsters manage to get on the studio's Melrose Avenue lot where they meet all of the stars mentioned above. There's a small plot twist in which San Juan is mistaken for Hatcher as the "Variety Girl" but eventually Hatcher convinces everyone that she's the right person and there's a huge show benefitting the Variety Clubs at the conclusion of the picture. Hatcher was working as the lead in "Oklahoma" on Broadway and great plans were made for her career which never really materialized. The movie is a "Who's Who" as well as a "Where's Where" of Hollywood, as it goes to the now- destroyed Brown Derby restaurant, various apartment buildings, and covers nearly every inch of the Paramount lot. Frank Loesser wrote many of the songs for the film which include: "Tallahassee" (sung by Dorothy Lamour–as a stewardess–and Alan Ladd–as the pilot on an airliner), "He Can Waltz," "The French," "Your Heart Calling Mine," "Impossible Things," "I Want My Money Back," "I Must Have Been Madly in Love." Johnny Burke and Jimmy Van Heusen wrote the duet "Harmony" for Hope and Crosby, who did a very funny golf sequence. Pearl Bailey sang "Tired" (Allan Roberts, Doris Fisher), and Edward Plumb's "Romeow and Julicat" was seen as part of a George Pal "Puppetoon" sequence. "Mildred's Boogie" was written by Mildred and James Mulcay, while Jelly Roll Morton's "Tiger Rag" was performed by the Original Dixieland Jazz Band. Several famous directors (De Mille, Leisen, Butler, and Marshall) appeared as themselves and even Bill Holden sang and danced in a quartet with dashing Ray Milland, Cass Daley, and Joan Caulfield. No question that the picture was a potpourri with, perhaps, too many things happening at once but the entertainment comes at the eye so briskly and with such good humor under Marshall's capable direction that one can overlook any shortcomings in the Swiss cheese story. For anyone who didn't realize that Ladd had a pleasant

baritone, he did some musical shorts in his early years and more than held his own with Lamour. Lake was pregnant at the time of production and only appeared for an instant in the finale. Many of the stars listed were only on screen for the batting of an eye, such as when Gary Cooper is seen aboard a carousel's wooden horse. A lot of the dialog was missed in the theater, as people shouted out the names of their favorites as they paraded by on screen.

p, Daniel Dare; d, George Marshall; w, Edmund Hartmann, Frank Tashlin, Robert Welch, Monte Brice; ph, Lionel Lindon, Stuart Thompson; ed, LeRoy Stone; md, Joseph J. Lilley; art d, Hans Dreier, Robert Clatworthy; set d, Sam Comer, Ross Dowd; cos, Edith Head; ch, Billy Daniels, Bernard Pearce; spec eff, Gordon Jennings, Farciot Edouart; makeup, Wally Westmore; Puppetoon sequence (in Technicolor), George Pal, Thornton Hee, William Cottrell.

Musical   **(PR:AA MPAA:NR)**

VARIETY HOUR*½   (1937, Brit.) 66m FOX bw

Clapham and Dwyer, The Weir Brothers, Jack Donohue, Helen Howard, Raymond Newell, Carson Robinson and His Pioneers, Brian Lawrence and His Lansdowne Band, Kay, Katya and Kay, Norwich Trio, The Music Hall Boys.

Comedians Clapham and Dwyer try to make it in the big time by posing as American radio commentators. Just another excuse to show off some then-popular radio and music hall personalities on the silver screen. Sparse amusement.

p, Herbert Smith; d, Redd Davis.

Comedy   **(PR:A MPAA:NR)**

VARIETY JUBILEE**   (1945, Brit.) 92m But bw

Reginald Purdell (*Joe Swan*), Ellis Irving (*Kit Burns*), Lesley Brook (*Evelyn Vincent*), Marie Lloyd, Jr (*Marie Lloyd*), Tom E. Finglass (*Eugene Stratton*), John Rorke (*Gus Elen*), Betty Warren (*Florrie Forde*), George Robey, Charles Coburn, Ella Retford, Charles Shadwell, Joan Winters, Nat D. Ayer, Slim Rhyder, Tessa Deane, Ganjou Bros. and Juanita, Wilson Keppel and Betty, Band of HM Coldstream Guards, George Merritt, Arthur Hambling, Pat McGrath, Louis Bradfield, Six Can Can Dancers, Jubilee Girls, Plantation Girls.

A family melodrama that spans three generations sees Irving and Purdell as two stage stars at the turn of the century who decide to become business partners and open up a music hall. The place is a success, but WW I arrives and Irving's son is killed in an aerial dogfight. After the war the popularity of the music hall dwindles and things look grim until Irving's grandson decides to resurrect the music hall and join the RAF when WW II breaks out. Sentimental treatment of a family dynasty padded with many popular stage acts of the day.

p, F. W. Baker; d, Maclean Rogers; w, Kathleen Butler (based on a story by Mabel Constanduros); ph, Geoffrey Faithfull.

Musical   **(PR:A MPAA:NR)**

VARIETY LIGHTS**½   (1965, Ital.) 93m Capitolium/Pathe bw (LUCI DEL VARIETA; GB: LIGHTS OF VARIETY)

Peppino De Filippo (*Checco Dal Monte*), Carla Del Poggio (*Liliana "Lily" Antonelli*), Giulietta Masina (*Melina Amour*), Folco Lulli (*Adelmo Conti*), Lover, Trumpet Player, Dante Maggio (*Remo, Comedian*), Carlo Romano (*Enzo La Rosa*), Gina Mascetti (*Valeria del Sole*), Checco Durante (*Theater Owner*), Joe Falletta (*Bill*), Enrico Piergentili (*Melina's Father*), Mario De Angelis (*Maestro*), Fanny Marchio (*Soubrette*), Giacomo Furia (*Duke*), Silvio Bagolini (*Bruno Antonini, Journalist*), Vanja Orico (*Gypsy Singer*), Franca Valeri (*Hungarian Designer*), Giulio Cali (*Edison Will, Swami*), Vittorio Caprioli, Alberto Bonucci (*Duet*), Renato Malavasi (*Hotelkeeper*), Marco Tulli (*Spectator*), Alberto Lattuada (*Theater Attendant*).

After years of writing (and a bit of acting) for other directors, Federico Fellini was finally given the opportunity to direct his own film (under the watchful eye of established veteran Alberto Lattuada). Even in this early effort the whimsical, odd world of Fellini comes dancing forth. The story follows a troupe of traveling entertainers who wander about the countryside trying to make a buck. Del Poggio plays a young local girl who falls in love with the band of traveling performers and runs away to join them on the road. After winning over the troupe and manager De Filippo with her vibrant dancing, Del Poggio soon becomes the star attraction. Eventually she becomes famous and soon she leaves De Filippo and the troupe to perform in high-class productions. Many of the standard Fellini elements are here including a look at backstage intrigue and a fascination for the bizarre. Lattuada's wife Del Poggio plays the star a-borning; Fellini's wife Masina plays De Filippo's long-suffering mistress. Released in Italy in 1951.

p&d, Alberto Lattuada, Federico Fellini; w, Fellini, Lattuada, Tullio Pinelli, Ennio Flaiano (based on a story by Fellini); ph, Otello Martelli; m, Felice Lattuada; ed, Mario Bonotti; art d, Aldo Buzzi; cos, Buzzi.

Drama   **(PR:A MPAA:NR)**

VARIETY PARADE**   (1936, Brit.) 83m Malcolm/But bw

Mrs. Jack Hylton and Her Boys, Sam Browne, Teddy Brown, G. S. Melvin, Archie Glen, Ernest Shannon, Corona Kids, Harry Tate, Dave and Joe O'Gorman, Nini and Partner, Radio Three, Ivor Vintnor and Ann Gordon, Sherman Fisher Girls, Ronald Tate, Harry Beasley, The Three Nagels.

Musical comedy revue starring comedian Harry Tate as the owner of a hotel who hires a number of variety acts to perform in his establishment. Standard all-star vehicle that is unfortunately hampered by sporting a cast of fairly mediocre stars.

p, Ian Sutherland, Reginald Long; d, Oswald Mitchell; w, Con West.

Musical   (PR:A   MPAA:NR)

VARSITY*½   (1928) 67m PAR bw

Charles ["Buddy"] Rogers (Jimmy Duffy), Mary Brian (Fay), Chester Conklin ("Pop" Conlan, Janitor), Phillips R. Holmes (Middlebrook), Robert Ellis (Rod Luke), John Westwood (The Senior).

A very early talkie (only 13 minutes of dialog, mostly in the last 10 minutes of the film) starring Rogers as a young Princeton student who believes he is an orphan. Little does he know that his father, Conklin, is actually the janitor in his dormitory. Conklin had dropped out of sight early in Rogers' youth due to a severe drinking problem, and now the old man is keeping a close eye on his son to ensure that he doesn't reach for the bottle as well. Dull romantic subplot sees Rogers falling in love with Brian, a carnival girl he met in Trenton. When he graduates they marry and settle down until a pair of evil carnival men frame Rogers for the theft of some money donated to Princeton by the sophomore class. This, of course, requires a bit of emotional upheaval until Rogers can clear his name. The experienced Conklin is the only actor to shine in this film, the first to star Rogers, who went on to marry "America's Sweetheart," Mary Pickford. Author Root, a Yale alumnus, had set his story at that university's New Haven campus, but the school wisely refused to lend itself to such sophomorism. The story was shifted to Princeton, whose regents appeared to know no better. All the dialog was recorded on the campus after the major scenes were shot at Paramount's West Coast studios; only the three principal actors went East to act their lines.

d, Frank Tuttle; w, Howard Estabrook (based on a story by Wells Root); ph, A. J. Stout; ed, Verna Willis; m/l, "My Varsity Girl, I'll Cling to You" Al Bryan, W. Franke Harling.

Drama   (PR:A   MPAA:NR)

VARSITY SHOW**½   (1937) 120m WB bw

Dick Powell (Charles "Chuck" Daly), Fred Waring (Ernie Mason), Priscilla Lane (Betty Bradley), Walter Catlett (Prof. Sylvester Biddle), Ted Healy (William Williams), Rosemary Lane (Barbara "Babs" Steward), Johnny Davis (Buzz Bolton), Lee Dixon (Johnny "Rubberlegs" Stevens), Mabel Todd (Cuddles), George MacFarland (Hap), Halliwell Hobbes (Dean Meredith), Ed Brophy (Mike Barclay), Emma Dunn (Mrs. Smith), Buck and Bubbles (Themselves), Sterling Holloway (Trout), Scotty Bates (Scotty), Poley McClintock (Poley), Roy Atwell (Prof. Washburn), Ben Welden (Hammer), Fred Waring's Pennsylvanians.

Overlong campus musical (some TV prints have as much as 40 minutes cut out) starring Powell as a Winfield College alumnus–now a successful Broadway producer–who heeds the call of his alma mater when the students can't afford to stage their annual show, nor have they anyone to produce it. Powell volunteers to produce the show to the delight of coed Lane and her buddies. Unfortunately, their faculty advisor, Catlett, voices opposition to Powell's "trashy" Broadway ideas and would prefer the students to stage something a little more conservative. Not wanting to get the students in hot water, Powell bows out of the production and returns to New York City. The students will not be moved however, and on spring break Priscilla Lane (who is in love with Powell) and her cohorts travel to New York, find their producer, occupy an empty theater, and put on Powell's show. Of course it's a big hit and the finale–staged by Busby Berkeley–is a stunning tribute to colleges throughout the nation. The two singing Lanes–sister Lola was missing from this one– had been on tour with Waring and his band. This was the film debut of Waring and of the sisters. Songs include: "Love Is on the Air Tonight," "Moonlight on the Campus," "Old King Cole," "Have You Got Any Castles, Baby?" "We're Working Our Way Through College," "On with the Dance," "You've Got Something There," and "When Your College Days Are Gone" (Johnny Mercer, Richard A. Whiting).

p, Lou Edelman; d, William Keighley; w, Jerry Wald, Richard Macaulay, Sig Herzig, Warren Duff (based on an original story by Duff, Herzig); ph, Sol Polito, George Barnes; ed, George Amy; ch, Busby Berkeley.

Musical   (PR:A   MPAA:NR)

VAULT OF HORROR, THE**½   (1973, Brit.)
Metromedia-Amicus/Cinerama c (AKA: TALES FROM THE CRYPT II)

"Midnight Mess:" Daniel Massey (Rogers), Anna Massey (Donna), Mike Pratt (Clive), Erik Chitty (Old Waiter), Frank Forsyth, Jerold Wells (Waiters), "Bargain in Death:" Michael Craig (Maitland), Edward Judd

(Alex), Robin Nedwell (Tom), Geoffrey Davies (Jerry), Arthur Mullard (Gravedigger), "This Trick'll Kill You:" Curt Jergens (Sebastian), Dawn Addams (Inez), Jasmina Hilton (Indian Girl), Ishaq Bux (Fakir), "The Neat Job:" Terry-Thomas (Critchit), Glynis Johns (Eleanor), Marianne Stone (Jane), John Forbes-Robertson (Wilson), "Drawn and Quartered:" Tom Baker (Moore), Denholm Elliott (Diltant), Terence Alexander (Breedley), John Witty (Gaskill).

Another weak film adaptation of the marvelous E.C. horror comics from the 1950s in which five tales (none of them taken from "The Vault of Horror" comics, but from its sister publication "Tales from the Crypt") of the macabre are presented. The first stars Daniel Massey (son of Raymond) as a man who goes to visit his sister in a spooky small town. His sister, Anna Massey (his real-life sister as well), turns out to be a vampire and soon Daniel finds himself strung up by his heels with a tap on his neck while vampires fill their wine glasses with his blood. Another story stars Terry-Thomas as a compulsively neat man who drives his wife, Johns, insane with his obsession. She eventually kills him with an ax and neatly stores all his dismembered body parts in little jars. A third tale sees Jurgens steal a rope trick from India which eventually spells doom. A fourth story (which contains several "in" jokes regarding E.C. comics) sees Judd double-cross Craig and the last segement stars the most popular "Dr. Who", of TV, Tom Baker, as an insane artist who mutilates part of a portrait, whereupon the person in the portrait becomes mutilated. Though better than its predecessor, TALES FROM THE CRYPT (1972), THE VAULT OF HORROR is still no substitute for the comics themselves, which were filled with a lively sense of the macabre, heavy doses of black humor, and impressive illustrations.

p, Max J. Rosenberg, Milton Subotsky; d, Roy Ward Baker; w, Subotsky (based on episodes from William Gaines' E. C. Comics by Al Feldstein, Gaines); ph, Denys Coop (Eastmancolor); m, Douglas Gamley; ed, Oswald Hafenrichter; art d, Tony Curtis; makeup, Roy Ashton.

Horror   Cas.   (PR:C-O   MPAA:PG)

VAXDOCKAN   (SEE: DOLL, THE, 1964, Swed.)

VECHERA NA KHUTORE BLIZ DIKANKI
                          (SEE: NIGHT BEFORE CHRISTMAS, 1963, USSR)

VEIL, THE   (SEE: HAUNTS, 1977)

VEILED WOMAN, THE**   (1929) 58m FOX bw

Lia Tora (Nanon), Paul Vincenti (Pierre), Walter McGrail (Diplomatic Attache), Josef Swickard (Col. De Selincourt), Kenneth Thomson (Dr. Donald Ross), Andre Cheron (Count De Bracchi), Ivan Lebedeff (Capt. Paul Fevier), Maude George (Countess De Bracchi), Lupita Tovar (Young Girl).

Tora relates her life story to a young girl she has saved from a seducer. She tells how she was befriended by Vincenti, the owner of a gambling den, who gave her a job at the roulette wheel. Later, she killed a man and left town, leaving Vincenti behind. She then met another man whom she married, but who later divorced her upon hearing of her past. When the flashbacks end Tora is seen trying to get the girl a taxi. The driver turns out to be Vincenti, who gave up his former life when Tora left him. She agrees to go off with him and start life anew. Director Flynn had a busy career during the silent days but gave it up when sound took over. THE VEILED WOMAN is one of his ventures into sound before throwing in the towel for good.

d, Emmett Flynn; w, Douglas Z. Doty (based on a story by Julio De Moraes, Lia Tora); ph, Charles Clarke.

Drama   (PR: MPAA:NR)

VEILS OF BAGDAD, THE**   (1953) 82m UNIV c

Victor Mature (Antar), Mari Blanchard (Selena), Virginia Field (Rosanna), Guy Rolfe (Kasseim), James Arness (Targut), Palmer Lee [Gregg Palmer] (Oaman), Nick Cravat (Ahmed), Ludwig Donath (Kaffar), Dave Sharpe (Ben Ali), Jackie Loughery (Handmaiden), Leon Askin (Pascha Hamman), Howard Petrie (Karsh), Charles Arnt (Zapolya), Glenn Strange (Mik-Kel), Sammy Stein (Abdullah), Bobby [Robert] Blake (Beggar Boy), Charles Wagenheim (Bedouin Spy), Bob St. Angelo (Soldier Guard), Stuart Whitman (Sergeant), Ben Welden (Stout Wrestler), George J. Lewis (Captain), Dale Van Sickel (Messenger), Thomas Browne Henry (Mustapha), Chester Hayes, Hans Schnabel, Tom Renesto, Vic Holbrook (Wrestlers), Russ Saunders Troupe (Acrobatic Act).

Uninspired sword-and-sandal epic which sees weak-willed ruler Askin and evil vizier Rolfe grabbing Bagdad by the throat and squeezing all the tax money they can out of the innocent citizens in order to finance an insane war against the Ottoman empire. Noble commoner Mature arrives on the scene; with the aid of a small army of wrestlers he topples the evildoers and is crowned the new prince of Bagdad by the grateful locals.

p, Albert J. Cohen; d, George Sherman; w, William R. Cox; ph, Russell Metty (Technicolor); ed, Paul Weatherwax; md, Joseph Gershenson; art d, Alexander Golitzen, Emrich Nicholson; cos, Rosemary Odell; ch, Eugene Loring.

Adventure (PR:A MPAA:NR)

VELVET HOUSE (SEE: CRUCIBLE OF HORROR, 1971, Brit.)

VELVET TOUCH, THE*** (1948) 97m Independent Artists/RKO bw

Rosalind Russell (*Valerie Stanton*), Leo Genn (*Michael Morrell*), Claire Trevor (*Marian Webster*), Sydney Greenstreet (*Capt. Danbury*), Leon Ames (*Gordon Dunning, Producer*), Frank McHugh (*Ernie Boyle*), Walter Kingsford (*Peter Gunther*), Dan Tobin (*Jeff Trent, Columnist*), Lex Barker (*Paul Banton*), Nydia Westman (*Susan Crane*), Theresa Harris (*Nancy, Maid*), Irving Bacon (*Albert*), Esther Howard (*Pansy Dupont*), Harry Hayden (*Mr. Crouch*), William Erwin (*Howard Forman*), Martha Hyer (*Helen Adams*), Steven Flagg [Michael St. Angel] (*Jimmy*), Louis Mason (*Terry*), James Flavin (*Sgt. Oliphant*), Charles McAvoy (*Mr. Soper*), Dan Foster (*Eddie Brown*), Bess Flowers (*Woman at Party*), Jim Drum, Allen Ray, Gill Wallace (*Reporters*), Cast of "Hedda Gabler": Rosalind Russell (*Hedda Gabler*), Russell Hicks (*Judge Brack*), James Todd (*George Tesman*), Joyce Arling (*Mrs. Elvested*), Ida Schumaker (*Juliana Tesman*), Phillip Barnes (*Ejlert Lovborg*), Besse Wade (*Bertha*).

Russell is fine as a frustrated stage star who kills her producer, Ames, with a statuette after he tries to stop her production of Ibsen's play "Hedda Gabler" and also to prevent her upcoming marriage to another man. Circumstances provide Russell with an airtight alibi and she seems to get away with murder. When the police, led by theater-loving detective Greenstreet, surmise that Ames' former lover, Trevor, did the dirty deed, they arrest her and she is convicted of murder. This sends Russell into a deep moral dilemma, but she chooses to keep her mouth shut. Trevor eventually commits suicide rather than face prison, and Russell is finally driven to confess her crime, despite the fact that the cops don't have a shred of evidence against her. A bit overwrought, but entertaining nonetheless. The denouement occurs as a result of Russell's involvement with her character in the play-within-a-movie performance of "Hedda Gabler." This was the first independent production for the husband-and-wife team of Russell and producer Brisson.

p, Frederick Brisson; d, John Gage; w, Leo Rosten, Walter Reilly (based on a story by William Mercer, Annabel Ross); ph, Joseph Walker; m, Leigh Harline; ed, Chandler House; md, C. Bakaleinikoff; prod d, William Flannery; set d, Darrell Silvera, Maurice Yates; cos, Travis banton; spec eff, Russell A. Cully; m/l, "The Velvet Touch," Harline, Mort Greene; makeup, Fred Phillips.

Drama/Crime (PR:A MPAA:NR)

VELVET TRAP, THE zero (1966) 80m Gillman bw

Jamie Karson (*Julie*), Alan Jeffory (*Brad Collins*), James F. Hurley, Bret Steel, Mike Harvey, Robert Terry, Bob Pollard, Dick Hamilton, Stirling Welker, Betty Coryell, Irene Graham, John Scovern, Royce Weyers, Lorie Stark, Jerome Parentae, Ray Vegas, June Harlow.

Total garbage about an innocent young girl, Karson, who runs away from home after being raped by her boss. She soon finds herself in Las Vegas where she becomes an unwilling prostitute. Her first customer dies of a heart attack and the frightened girl runs from the whorehouse and is killed by a speeding truck. Wretched exploitation film.

p, Daniel P. Foley; d&w, Ken Kennedy; ph, Sherwood Strickler, Don McIntosh, Elmer Hohnber.

Drama (PR:O MPAA:NR)

VELVET VAMPIRE, THE*½ (1971) 82m New World c (AKA: THROUGH THE LOOKING GLASS; CEMETERY GIRLS)

Michael Blodgett (*Lee Ritter*), Sherry Miles (*Susan Ritter*), Celeste Yarnall (*Diane*), Jerry Daniels (*Juan, Servant*), Gene Shane (*Carl, Gallery Owner*), Paul Prokop (*Cliff, Mechanic*), Sandy Ward (*Amos, Gas Station Owner*), Chris Woodley (*Mechanic's Girl*), Bob Thessier (*Motorcycle Rapist*).

Disappointing horror film from femme director Stephanie Rothman, whose film TERMINAL ISLAND (1973) is one of the more interesting exploitation items from the 1970s. In THE VELVET VAMPIRE newlyweds Blodgett and Miles meet mysterious and sexy woman Yarnall at an art gallery and accompany her to her expensive desert home. Soon it becomes apparent that their hostess is a vampire and she wastes no time in seducing Blodgett. Later, when Blodgett discovers a corpse drained of its blood on the grounds, he decides to take his wife and leave, but Miles, too, has developed a sexual attraction to Yarnall and refuses to depart. Miles soon snaps back to reality, however, when she stumbles across the bloodless corpse of her husband. Attempting to flee, Miles is followed by Yarnall who is able to survive in sunlight because of her wide-brimmed hat and sunglasses (this gets a bit laughable). Trapped in a crowd, Miles cleverly hands out crosses from a vendor's stand to the people on the streets and together they kill Yarnall who withers away and dies. While the film has its moments, there is plenty of gratuitous nudity and blood coupled with some truly awful performances.

p, Charles S. Swartz; d, Stephanie Rothman; w, Maurice Jules, Swartz, Rothman; ph, Daniel Lacambre (Metrocolor); m, Clancy B. Grass III, Roger

Dollarhide; ed, Stephen Judson; art d, Teddi Petersen; m/l, Johnny Shines.

Horror Cas. (PR:O MPAA:R)

VENDETTA* (1950) 84M RKO bw

Faith Domergue (*Columba Della Rabbia*), George Dolenz (*Orso Della Rabbia*), Hillary Brooke (*Lydia Nevil*), Nigel Bruce (*Sir Thomas Nevil*), Joseph Calleia (*Mayor Barracini*), Hugo Haas (*Brando*), Robert Warwick (*Prefect*), Donald Buka (*Pardino*).

Rotten Howard Hughes epic in which the nutty millionaire sunk untold dollars and several years into a starring vehicle for his latest sexual obsession, Faith Domergue (best remembered for her supporting roles [i.e., screaming a lot! in THIS ISLAND EARTH–1954–and IT CAME FROM BENEATH THE SEA–1955), who couldn't act to save her life. The story sees Domergue as a tough Corsican girl out to avenge the murder of her father despite the fact that her brother, Dolenz, thinks she's gone goofy. Eventually she motivates him to join her and together they battle the rival Corsican clan that had murdered their father. In the end her brother is ambushed and she is killed in a duel. This slow-moving, silly effort was begun by writer-director Preston Sturges who had a falling out with Hughes and left. Max Ophuls was then hired to direct and he too was replaced by Hughes himself. Then Hughes lost interest in the project (and presumably in Miss Domergue), leaving RKO to deal with his mess. The hapless Mel Ferrer was drafted to clean up (his fourth directorial effort) after Hughes, but it was a losing battle. The studio, saddled with a turkey, dumped the film on a handful of theaters with virtually no advertising and took its lumps.

p, Howard Hughes [Preston Sturges uncredited]; d, Mel Ferrer [Max Ophuls, Sturges, Stuart Heisler, Hughes uncredited]; w, W. R. Burnett, Peter O'Crotty [Sturges uncredited] (based on the novel *Columba* by Prosper Merimee); ph, Frank [Franz F.] Planer, Al Gilks; m, Roy Webb; ed, Stuart Gilmore; md, C. Bakaleinikoff; art d, Robert Usher; makeup, Norbert Miles.

Drama (PR:A MPAA:NR)

VENDETTA, 1965 (SEE: MURIETA, 1965, Span.)

VENDETTA DELLA MASCHERA DI FERRO (SEE: PRISONER OF THE IRON MASK, 1962, Fr./Ital.)

VENDREDI 13 HEURES (SEE: WORLD IN MY POCKET, THE, 1962, Fr./Ital./Ger.)

VENETIAN AFFAIR, THE** (1967) 92m MGM c

Robert Vaughn (*Bill Fenner*), Elke Sommer (*Sandra Fane*), Felicia Farr (*Claire Connor*), Karl Boehm (*Robert Wahl*), Boris Karloff (*Dr. Pierre Vaugiroud*), Roger C. Carmel (*Mike Ballard*), Edward Asner (*Frank Rosenfeld*), Joe De Santis (*Jan Aarvan*), Fabrizio Mioni (*Russo*), Wesley Lau (*Neill Carlson*), Luciana Paluzzi (*Giulia Almeranti*), Bill Weiss (*Goldsmith*).

Ponderous espionage thriller apparently cranked out by MGM to capitalize on the success of star Robert Vaughn in TV's "The Man From U.N.C.L.E." After an American diplomat inexplicably explodes a bomb during an international peace conference in Venice, killing himself and everyone in the room, CIA boss Asner calls ex-agent Vaughn in on the case (Asner had previously fired Vaughn when it was discovered that the agent's wife, Sommer, was a Communist). Informing Vaughn that his wife was known to be associating with enemy agents who may have had something to do with the bombing, Asner sends the agent off to find his wife and obtain a secret report written by political scientist Karloff, who purports to know the answers behind the plot. Eventually Vaughn finds Sommer, who is in hiding from Boehm, the man behind the bombing. Vaughn contacts Boehm and pretends to want a ransom for Sommer's return. When Boehm sends the cash, Vaughn double-crosses him, disguises Sommer as a nun, and puts her on a train to safety. He then steals Karloff's report and goes to join her, but when he arrives he is trapped by Boehm. Boehm kills Sommer and then drugs Vaughn and Karloff (who had been kidnaped). The drug moves Karloff to become a zombie and agree to bomb the second international conference, but luckily Vaughn overcomes the drug's effects, kills Boehm, and stops Karloff in the nick of time.

p, Jerry Thorpe, E. Jack Neuman; d, Thorpe; w, Neuman (based on the novel by Helen MacInnes); ph, Milton Krasner, Enzo Serafin (Panavision, Metrocolor); m, Lalo Schifrin; ed, Henry Berman; art d, George W. Davis, Leroy Coleman; set d, Henry Grace, Hugh Hunt; spec eff, Carroll L. Shepphird; m/l, Schifrin, Hall Winn; makeup, William Tuttle.

Spy Drama (PR:C MPAA:NR)

VENETIAN BIRD (SEE: ASSASSIN, 1953, Brit.)

VENETIAN NIGHTS   (SEE: CARNIVAL, 1931, Brit.)

VENGEANCE*½   (1930) 66m COL bw

Jack Holt (*John Meadham*), Dorothy Revier (*Margaret Summers*), Philip Strange (*Charles Summers*), George Pearce (*Doctor*), Hayden Stevenson (*Ambassador*), Irma A. Harrison (*Nidia*), Onest A. Conly.

Holt plays a man whiling away his time under the African sun when a crude Englishman, Strange, comes to relieve him of his job. The hero responds by relieving Strange of his wife. Mild adventure given some spunk through the tension of the relationship between Strange and Holt.

p, Harry Cohn; d, Archie Mayo; w, F. Hugh Herbert (based on a story by Ralph Graves); ph, Ben Reynolds; ed, Gene Milford; art d, Harrison Wiley.

Adventure/Drama   (PR:A   MPAA:NR)

VENGEANCE, 1944   (SEE: VALLEY OF VENGEANCE, 1944)

VENGEANCE, 1945   (SEE: TRAIL TO VENGEANCE, 1945)

VENGEANCE*½   (1964) 79m BadAxe/Crown International bw

William Thourlby (*Capt. Lafe Todd*), Melora Conway (*Jean Harmon*), Owen Pavitt (*Slade*), Ed Cook (*Clay*), Byrd Holland (*Sheriff*), John Bliss (*Deputy Sam*), Larry Gerst (*Will Harmon*), Gordon Wynn (*Col. Carl Dorsett*), Donald Cook (*Billy Todd*), James Cavanaugh (*Uncle Ben*), Tiger Joe Marsh, The Great John L (*Bullies*).

Former Confederate Thourlby is out to seek vengeance against the Yankee responsible for his brother's death. The ensuing chase sees several other people becoming involved, including the man actually responsible for the murder. Routine oater for the 1960s.

p, William Thourlby; d, Dene Hilyard; w, Alex Sharp, Ed Erwin; ph, Richard Kendall; ed, Ewing Brown.

Western   (PR:A   MPAA:NR)

VENGEANCE, 1965   (SEE: BRAIN, THE, 1965, Brit./Ger.)

VENGEANCE**   (1968, Ital./Ger.) 81m Super International/Top Film c (JOKO, INVOCO DIO...E MOURI)

Richard Harrison, Claudio Camaso, Werner Pochat, Paolo Gozlino, Sheyla Rosia, Freddy Unger.

Spaghetti western that puts more importance in the image provided than the plot, has Harrison (in the tradition of "the man with no name") seeking the men responsible for the gruesome murder of his buddy. Harrison's rendition is a bit hard to take but at least-he fits in nicely with the backgrounds.

p, Renato Savino; d, Anthony Dawson [Antonio Margheriti]; w, Savino, Dawson; ph, Riccardo Pallottini.

Western   (PR:C   MPAA:NR)

VENGEANCE IS MINE*½   (1948, Brit.) 59m Eros bw

Valentine Dyall (*Charles Heywood*), Anne Firth (*Linda Farrell*), Richard Goolden (*Sammy Parsons*), Sam Kydd (*Stacey*), Arthur Brander (*Richard Kemp*), Alex Wright (*Doctor*), Ethel Coleridge (*Caretaker*), Bob Connor, Jack Hart, Alex Graham, Michael Darbyshire, Bart Allison, Betty Taylor, Manville Tarrant, Pat Drake, Russell Westwood.

After being told he has only six months to live, Dyall decides to settle an old account. He hires a man to kill him and make the murder look like the work of Brander, who had wrongly sent Dyall to prison. However, the reports of Dyall's terminal illness prove to be false and, what's more, his hit man has died. Brander still puts the muscle on Dyall, though, who is forced to shoot his former nemesis in self-defense. Dyall's life is now free of burdens and so is the viewer's after having to waste 59 minutes sitting through this. There's not a gram of believability in the plot and the cast just goes through the motions.

p, Ben Arbeid; d&w, Alan Cullimore; ph, Bill Oxley.

Crime   (PR:A   MPAA:NR)

VENGEANCE IS MINE*   (1969, Ital./Span.) 94m Leone-Daiano/Atlantida c (QUEI DISPE RATI CHE PUZZANO DI SUDORE ET DI MORTE)

George Hilton, Ernest Borgnine, Alberto de Mendoza, Leo Anchoriz, Annabella Incontrera, Manuel Miranada.

Dreary spaghetti western with Hilton out to get the man who let his family die of cholera while he was away fighting in the Civil War. This culprit is Borgnine, whose talents were put to waste in a heavy role in which he should have been brilliant.

p, Elio Scardamaglia, Ugo Guerra; d, Julio Buchs; w, Buchs, Guerra, Jose

Luis Martinez Mollo, Frederico de Urnutia; ph, Francisco Sempere.

Western   (PR:A   MPAA:NR)

VENGEANCE IS MINE***   (1980, Jap.) 128m Shochiku c (FUKUSHU SURUWA WARE NI ARI)

Ken Ogata (*Iwao Enokizue*), Rentaro Mikuni (*Shizuo Enokizu*), Chocho Mikayo (*Kayo Enokizu*), Mitsuko Baisho (*Kazuko Enokizu*), Mayumi Ogawa (*Haru Asano*), Nijiko Kiyokawa (*Hisano Asano*).

Based on a novel spawned from a true incident, VENGEANCE IS MINE immediately calls upon comparison to IN COLD BLOOD. Like the earlier American film, this one is a methodical retelling of very violent actions. The narrative leaps about in flashback form as it details the events that have shaped the life of brutish Ogata. Events from his deprived childhood, a stay in prison, and a mistrusting marriage are depicted as being the possible causes which have led him to brutally murder two men in an act of anger and rebellion against a society from which Ogata feels estranged. Imamura effectively portrays some of the more negative aspects of the forces that have shaped modern Japanese people. In this manner the picture resembles his chilling films of teenage wanderlust made in the 1950s. (In Japanese; English subtitles).

p, Kazuo Inoue; d, Shohei Imamura; w, Masaru Baba (based on the book by Ryuzo Saki); ph, Shinsaku Himeda; m, Shinichiro Ikebe; ed, Keiichi Uraoka.

Crime   (PR:O   MPAA:NR)

VENGEANCE OF FU MANCHU, THE*½   (1968, Brit./Ger./Hong Kong/Ireland) 91m Babasd ave/WB bw-c (DIE RACHE DAS FU MAN CHU)

Christopher Lee (*Fu Manchu*), Tony Ferrer (*Inspector Ramos*), Tsai Chin (*Lin Tang*), Douglas Wilmer (*Nayland Smith*), Wolfgang Kieling (*Dr. Lieberson*), Suzanne Roquette (*Maria Lieberson*), Howard Marion Crawford (*Dr. Petrie*), Noel Trevarthen (*Mark Weston, FBI Agent*), Horst Frank (*Rudy Moss*), Peter Carsten (*Kurt*), Maria Rohm (*Ingrid*), Mona Chong (*Jasmin Fu Shen*), Eddie Byrne (*Ship's Captain*), Bert Kwouk.

The third of writer-producer Towers' series based on the turn-of-the-century oriental archcriminal and his English nemesis, this is one of the worst (see FU MANCHU series, Index). Fiend Lee and his daughter Tsai, both thought to be dead, return to Lee's Mongolian habitat to plot vengeance against their enemy, Scotland Yard commissioner Wilmer. Kidnaping famed physician Kieling and his daughter Roquette, Lee forces Kieling to transform the face of one of his other prisoners into that of his arch-enemey Wilmer. The latter, who has been attempting to establish an international police organization which will combat just such over-the-border crimes, is also abducted by the sinister Lee. Substituting the surgically transformed doppelganger for the real Wilmer, Lee sends the former to London where–under hypnotic control–he commits a murder. Lee plans to execute the real Wilmer at the very moment that his double hangs for the crime. In the interim, the master criminal has been occupied with other plans for conquest (he's been far too busy to trim his foot-long fingernails). Hong Kong gangster Frank has joined with Lee to form an international syndicate of crime, the alter ego of the organization that Wilmer had planned. Fortunately, Frank has been under surveillance by police inspector Ferrer who, with the help of FBI agent Trevarthen, storms Lee's headquarters and rescues the prisoners. As the villain's headquarters explode, his voice is heard, saying: "You will hear from me again." And so we will, two more times in the series. Shot in color, the picture was mysteriously released in the U.S. in black-and-white. Could it have been a plot by the sinister Dr. Fu Manchu? Lee said of the location shots (the picture was the first European film to be shot mostly in Hong Kong) that the actors and crew suffered from the 100-degree temperatures. The Chinese extras, he stated, were by no stretch of the imagination inscrutable; one pushy extra, who tried to be in every scene, was actually killed by his colleagues for his rudeness. Hollywood, take note.

p, Harry Alan Towers; d, Jeremy Summers; w, Peter Welbeck [Towers] (based on the characters created by Sax Rohmer); ph, John Von Kotze (Eastmancolor, also released in black-and-white); m, Malcolm Lockyer; ed, Allan Morrison; md, Lockyer; art d, Scott MacGregor, Peggy Gick.

Crime   (PR:A   MPAA:NR)

VENGEANCE OF GREGORY   (SEE: FEUD OF THE WEST, 1936)

VENGEANCE OF SHE, THE*   (1968, Brit.) 101m Hammer-Seven Arts/FOX c (AKA: THE RET URN OF SHE)

John Richardson (*King Killikrates*), Olinka Berova (*Carol*), Edward Judd (*Philip Smith, Psychiatrist*), Colin Blakely (*George Carter*), Jill Melford (*Sheila Carter*), George Sewell (*Harry Walker*), Andre Morell (*Kassim*), Noel Willman (*Za-Tor, High Priest*), Derek Godfrey (*Men-Hari*), Daniele Noel (*Sharna*), Gerald Lawson (*Seer*), Derrick Sherwin (*No. 1*), William Lyon Brown (*Magus*), Charles O'Rourke (*Servant*), Zohra Segal (*Putri*), Christine Pocket (*Dancer*), Dervis Ward (*Lorry Driver*).

There was absolutely no reason to try to create a sequel to SHE, the film in which Ursula Andress played an immortal beauty, but that didn't stop the makers of this flat effort. The king of the lost city of Kuma (Richardson) longs to be reunited with his queen, so the high priest (Willman) puts a spell on Berova that draws the dead ringer for the queen from that south of France to Kuma. But Berova's doctor boy friend (Judd) follows her and m anages to convince the king that he has been deceived by his high priest. Nothing much of interest takes place, and although Berova is quite stunning to look at, her talents don't appear to reach very deep, at least as revealed with this material.

p, Aida Young; d, Cliff Owen; w, Peter O'Donnell (based on characters created by H. Rider Haggard); ph, Wolf Suschitzky (DeLuxe Color); m, Mario Nascimbene; ed, James Needs, Raymond Poulton; prod d, Lionel Couch; cos, Carl Toms; spec eff, Bob Cuff; makeup, Michael Morris.

Fantasy   **(PR:A MPAA:G)**

VENGEANCE OF THE DEEP*   (1940, Aus.) 70m Astor bw

Lloyd Hughes (*Daubeney Carshott*), Shirley Ann Richards [Ann Richards] (*Lorna*), James Raglan (*Craig*), Elaine Hamill (*Stella Raff*), Campbell Copelin (*Archie*), Sydney Wheeler (*Capt. Quid*), Frank Harvey (*Manager*), Ronald Whelan (*Mendoza*), Alec Kellaway (*McTavish*), Charlie Chan (*Kishimuni*), Marcelle Marney, Leslie Victor.

An unexciting early Australian feature taking place on the Thursday Islands has two divers competing for a valuable pearl as well as a pretty girl. The prize for finding the gem is the hand of the lady, showing just what type of stuff she is made of. This picture's most valuable asset, the beauty of the South Seas locale, does not even make much of an impression because of the obviously untrained eye behind the camera.

p&d, Ken G. Hall; w, Frank Harvey; ph, George Heath; ed, William Shepherd.

Adventure/Drama   **(PR:A MPAA:NR)**

VENGEANCE OF THE VAMPIRE WOMEN, THE zero
(1969, Mex.) 90m Cinematografica Flama /Peliculas Latinoamericanas) c (SANTO EN LA VENGANZA DE LAS MUJERES VAMPIRO; L A VENGANZA DE LAS MUJERES VAMPIRO)

Gina Romand (*Mayra*), Victor Junco (*Dr. Brancor*), Patricia Ferrer, Carlos Suarez, Alfonso Munguia, Yolanda Ponce, Fernando Oses, Aldo Monti, Norma Lazareno.

Another in the long list of Mexican wrestler pictures in which Santo the powerful masked grappler (actually a fat and grotesque slob) battles supernatural villains. In this one he faces a bunch of blood-hungry vampires led by Romand. She is particularly anxious to get her teeth into him because he is a descendant of the man responsible for the killing of her ghoulish ancestors. These films made a lot of money, and when the sex angle was incorporated, they became even more popular. Although uncredited, speculation has it that Santo was played by Eric del Castillo.

p, Jose Garcia Besne; d, Federico Curiel; w, Besne, Fernando Oses; ph, Jose Ortiz Ramos.

Fantasy   **(PR:O MPAA:NR)**

VENGEANCE VALLEY**   (1951) 83m MGM c

Burt Lancaster (*Owen Daybright*), Robert Walker (*Lee Strobie*), Joanne Dru (*Jen Strobie*), Sally Forrest (*Lily Fasken*), John Ireland (*Hub Fasken*), Carleton Carpenter (*Hewie*), Ray Collins (*Arch Strobie*), Ted de Corsia (*Herb Backett*), Hugh O'Brian (*Dick Fasken*), Will Wright (*Mr. Willoughby*), Grace Mills (*Mrs. Burke*), James Hayward (*Sheriff Con Alvis*), James Harrison (*Orv Esterly*), Stanley Andrews (*Mead Calhoun*), Glenn Strange (*Dave Allard*), Paul E. Burns (*Dr. Irwin*), John R. McKee (*Player*), Tom Fadden (*Obie Rune*), Margaret Bert (*Mrs. Calhoun*), Harvey Dunn (*Dealer*), Robert E. Griffin (*Cal*), Monte Montague, Al Ferguson, Roy Butler (*Men*), Norman Leavitt, Dan White, Bob [Robert] Wilke, Louis Nicoletti (*Cowhands*).

A decent western that places more emphasis on character development than the usual oater, this film has Lancaster and Walker as foster-brothers. Walker, a real louse, has always depended on Lancaster to get him out of sticky situations, but he goes too far when he sees to it that Lancaster is falsely blamed for fathering an illegitimate baby, an accusation that causes the mother's brothers to pursue Lancaster with the intent of making him pay for his cowardly deed. Walker even joins in with the brothers, hoping to secure Lancaster's portion of the ranch. Solid performances and a penetrating script are hampered by an uneven direction, which was obviously more at ease with the action than with the interpersonal segments.

p, Nicholas Nayfack; d, Richard Thorpe; w, Irving Ravetch (based on the novel by Luke Short); ph, George J. Folsey (Technicolor); m, Rudolph G. Kopp; ed, Conrad A. Nervig; art d, Cedric Gibbons, Malcolm Brown; cos, Walter Plunkett.

Western   **Cas.**   **(PR:A MPAA:NR)**

VENOM*   (1968, Den.) 96m ASA-Nordisk/Peppercorn-Wormser-Times bw (AKA: GIFT)

Soren Stromberg (*Per*), Sisse Reingaard (*Susanne*), Poul Reichhardt (*Henrike Steen*), Astrid Villaume (*Mrs. Steen*), Judy Gringer (*Sonja*), Grethe Morgensen (*Frau Jacobsen, the Secretary*), Karl Stegger (*Caretaker*), Vic Salomonsen, Tine Schmedes, PEr Goldschmidt, Jess Kolpin (*Teenagers*).

A sordid attempt at exposing problems within a family plagued by conflicting moral values, especially in the area of sex. Reichhardt plays a man who conducts a hushed affair with his secretary, while his daughter brings a hardy youth into their home who has no qualms at all about open sex, going so far as to proposition the mother and make porno film with the daughter. Pretty pointless.

p, Knud Leif Thompson; Henning Karmack; d&w, Thomsen; ph, Claus Loof, Arne Abrahamsen; m, Niels Viggo Bentzon, The Matadors; ed, Birger Lind.

Drama   **(PR:O MPAA:NR)**

VENOM, 1976 (SEE: LEGEND OF SPIDER FOREST, THE, 1976, Brit.)

VENOM*   (1982, Brit.) 93m Venom-Handmade/PAR c

Klaus Kinski (*Jacmel*), Oliver Reed (*Dave*), Nicol Williamson (*Comd. William Bulloch*), Sarah Miles (*Dr. Marion Stowe, Toxicologist*), Sterling Hayden (*Howard Anderson*), Cornelia Sharpe (*Ruth Hopkins*), Mike Gwilym (*Detective Constable Dan Spencer*), Lance Holcomb (*Philip Hopkins*), Susan George (*Louise*), Paul Williamson (*Detective Sgt. Glazer*), Michael Gough (*David Ball, Snake Handler*), Hugh Lloyd (*Taxi Driver*), Rita Webb (*Mrs. Lowenthal*), Edward Hardwicke (*Lord Dunning*), John Forbes-Robertson (*Sgt. Nash*), Ian Brimble (*Constable in Police Station*), Peter Porteous (*Hodges*), Maurice Colbourne (*Sampson*), Nicholas Donnelly (*Police Superintendent*), Cyril Conway (*Man in 17*), Sally Lahee (*Woman in 17*), David Sterne (*Driver*), Charles Cork (*Driver's Mate*), Howard Bell (*Constable*), Alan Ford (*Peters*), Norman Mann (*Williams*), Tony Meyer (*Martin*), Michael Watkins (*Rogers*), Gerald Ryder (*Smith*), Moti Makan (*Murkerjee*), Katherine Wilkinson (*Susan Stowe*), Eric Richard (*Airline Clerk*), Arnold Diamond (*Headwaiter*).

A deadly snake gets out of its cage and goes about terrorizing London, especially the people responsible for the kidnaping of the boy who had come into possession of the black mamba. Kinski, Reed, and George are the only people the snake bites, as it leaves all the well-meaning people alone, though sending plenty of chills up their spines. Shots from the snake's point of view are thrown in for obvious effect and look silly. But that is about par for this thriller, which boasts one of the best casts to accompany a British film in quite a long time. But surely they could have been used for something a bit more...let's say sophisticated and leave it at that. Without the snake, this could have been an intriguing picture resting on strong performances and a taut script. Sadly, that is not the case.

p, Martin Bregman; d, Piers Haggard; w, Robert Carrington (based on the novel by Alan Scholefield); ph, Gilbert Taylor, Denys Coop (Technicolor); m, Michael Kamen; ed, Michael Bradsell; art d, Tony Curtis; spec eff, Alan Whibley, Richard Dean; makeup, Basil Newall; stunts, Roy Scammell.

Thriller/Crime   **Cas.**   **(PR:O MPAA:R)**

VENTO DELL'EST   (SEE: WIND FROM THE EAST, 1970, Fr./Ital./Ger.)

VENUS DER PIRATEN   (SEE: QUEEN OF THE PIRATES, 1961, Ital./Ger.)

VENUS IN FURS*½   (1970, Ital./Brit./Ger.) 86m Cineproduzioni Associate-Terra Filmkunst-Towers of London/AIP c (PAROXISMUS; PUO UNA MORTA RIVIVERE PER AMORE?; VENUS IN PELTZ)

James Darren (*Jimmy Logan*), Barbara McNair (*Rita*), Maria Rohm (*Wanda Reed/Venus*), Adolfo Lastretti (*Inspector*), Paul Muller (*Nightclub Owner*), Klaus Kinski (*Ahmed*), Margaret Lee (*Olga*), Dennis Price (*Kapp*), Mirella Pamphili.

A novelette by Leopold von Sacher-Masoch (from whose name the word "masochism" was derived) provided the impetus for this weird tale that makes a stab at filming mystical occurrences as they transpire in the mind of musician Darren. After witnessing the brutal murder of a beautiful woman by three sexual deviants--Kinski, a sadist, Lee, a lesbian, and Price, a homosexual--Darren encounters the same woman in a nightclub many, many miles away. The three killers also popup again, but this time are the victims, as they indulge in sexual encounters with the girl that leave them dead. Darren walks away with the pretty thing, though perhaps his mind runs away with him. Several interpretations could be given to explain the strange narrative, one such being Darren's own sexual confusion, but this is not fully developed. A proper atmosphere is maintained through the structure and mood, but the dialog and narration are something else. (Dubbed in English.)

p, Harry Alan Towers; d, Jess Franco; w, Malvin Wald, Franco, Bruno Leder, Carlo Fadda, Milo G. Cuccia (based on a story by Franco, from the book

Venus Im Pelz by Leopold von Sacher-Masoch); ph, Angelo Lotti (Movielab Color); m, Manfred Mann, Mike Hugg; ed, Henry Batista, Mike Pozen, Nicholas Wentworth; spec eff, Howard A. Anderson; m/l, "Let's Get Together," Robert B. Sherman, Richard M. Sherman (sung by Barbara McNair), "Venus in Furs" (sung by McNair).

Drama   **Cas.**   **(PR:O MPAA:R)**

VENUS MAKES TROUBLE*   (1937) 58m COL bw

James Dunn *(Buzz Martin)*, Patricia Ellis *(Kay Horner)*, Gene Morgan *("Happy" Hinkle)*, Thurston Hall *(Harlan Darrow, Banker)*, Beatrice Curtis *(Ruth Milner)*, Donald Kirk *(Lon Stanton)*, Astrid Allwyn *(Iris Randall)*, Thomas Chatterton *(Kenneth Rowland)*, Spencer Charters *(Joel Willard)*, Howard Hickman *(Howard Clark)*, Charles Lane *(District Attorney)*.

Dunn, a young man with a miraculous gift for gab, uses his special talent to pull off big promotions for a bank and theater in a small Pennsylvania town. As if these accomplishments aren't amazing enough, in the wink of an eye he finds himself in a big job in the Big Apple. Not to be believed for a second, this film was basically a vehicle for Dunn, who was trying to establish himself as a leading man of the "good Joe" variety.

p, Wallace McDonald; d, Gordon Wiles; w, Michael Simmons; ph, Lucien Ballard; ed, James Sweeney; cos, Robert Kalloch.

Drama   **(PR:A MPAA:NR)**

VENUSIAN, THE   (SEE: STRANGER FROM VENUS, THE, 1954, Brit.)

VERA CRUZ***   (1954) 94m Hecht-Hill-Lancaster/UA c

Gary Cooper *(Benjamin Trane)*, Burt Lancaster *(Joe Erin)*, Denise Darcel *(CountessMarie Duvarre)*, Cesar Romero *(Marquis de Labordere)*, Sarita Montiel *(Nina)*, George Macready *(Emperor Maximilian)*, Ernest Borgnine *(Donnegan)*, Morris Ankrum *(Gen. Aguilar)*, Henry Brandon *(Danette)*, Charles Buchinsky [Bronson] *(Pittsburgh)*, Jack Lambert *(Charlie)*, Jack Elam *(Tex)*, James McCallion *(Little Bit)*, James Seay *(Abilene)*, Archie Savage *(Ballard)*, Charles Horvath *(Reno)*, Juan Garcia *(Pedro)*.

A broadly played, action-packed western which teams Cooper and Lancaster as two American soldiers-of-fortune on a foray into Mexico during the revolution of 1866. Cooper, a former Confederate major and Lancaster, a constantly grinning outlaw, leave the U.S. in search of mercenary work. It doesn't matter to them which side they fight for, as long as one pays better than the other. In Mexico they meet a beautiful young girl, Montiel, who falls for Cooper and begs him and his partner to fight for Juarez and the revolutionaries. The American gunslingers are tugged in the opposite direction by Romero, a supporter of Maximilian, who offers them huge sums of cash. While mulling the offers over, Cooper and Lancaster encounter Darcel, a seductive and extremely rich countess who asks them to escort her while she transports a gold shipment from Mexico City to Maximilian's forces in Vera Cruz. The men agree and quickly assemble a motley crew of gunfighters and government regulars to accompany them through the rough territory. On the trail, the wily Darcel suggests that they steal the gold and split it three ways. The Americans agree to the plan, with each suspecting the other of planning double crosses. Maximilian loyalist Romero discovers the plot and takes off with the gold to make sure it gets delivered. The Americans chase Romero to the fort in Vera Cruz, and after a bloody battle, Lancaster manages to get his hands on the gold. Cooper, however, has had a change of heart due to Montiel's revolutionary fervor, and demands Lancaster hand over the gold to Juarez's forces. Lancaster doesn't buy Cooper's commitment to the revolution and refuses to release the gold. Cooper is forced to kill Lancaster in a showdown and then gives the gold to Montiel. Directed with emphasis on action by Aldrich (who had just guided Lancaster through APACHE the year before), most of the actors in VERA CRUZ are allowed to ham it up quite a bit. For contrast there is Cooper, forever the tight-lipped and serious professional man wary of those around him, especially Lancaster's grinning gunman. The film was produced by Lancaster's own company on a budget of $1.7 million and became quite a hit, grossing more than $11 million worldwide, though critical opinion at the time was extremely negative. Lancaster gladly gave top billing to Cooper, well aware of the older actor's box-office pull. As is typical with director Aldrich's work, the violence is well staged and frequent, going a bit overboard at times specifically with regard to Darcel, who is shown being slapped and knocked about by Lancaster more than once. Aldrich and Lancaster would collaborate again in the 1970s with ULZANA's RAID (1972) and TWILIGHT'S LAST GLEAMING (1977).

p, James Hill; d, Robert Aldrich; w, Roland Kibbee, James R. Webb (based on the story by Borden Chase); ph, Ernest Laszlo (SuperScope, Technicolor); m, Hugo Friedhofer; ed, Alan Crosland, Jr.; md, Raul Lavista; m/l, title song, Friedhofer, Sammy Cahn.

Western   **Cas.**   **(PR:C-O MPAA:NR)**

VERBOTEN!***   (1959) 93m Globe-RKO/COL bw

James Best *(Sgt. David Brent)*, Susan Cummings *(Helga Schiller)*, Tom Pittman *(Bruno Eck art)*, Paul Dubov *(Capt. Harvey)*, Harold Daye *(Franz Schiller)*, Dick Kallman *(Helmuth)*, Stuart Randall *(Colonel)*, Steven Geray *(Burgermeister)*, Anna Hope *(Frau Schiller)*, Robert Boon *(SS Officer)*, Sasha Harden *(Erich)*, Paul Busch *(Guenther)*, Neyle Morrow *(Sgt. Kellogg)*, Joseph Turkel *(Infantryman)*, Charles Horvath *(Man with Bald Woman)*.

This hard-hitting expose of postwar Germany from the maker of PICK-UP ON SOUTH STREET provided a perfect vehicle for Fuller to expostulate on human cruelty and misunderstanding. Though at times appearing a bit too preachy, with actual footage from the concentration camps, he effectively weaves two separate stories into one centering on Best as an American soldier assigned to the peacekeeping force. Because of his love for the German girl Cummings, the woman who saved him from falling into the grip of the Gestapo during the last days of the war, he quits his post to marry her–there being a regulation which doesn't allow soldiers to have relations with German women. Although Cummings does not at first love Best, marrying him mainly as a meal ticket, her affection for her husband continues to grow. She also has a 15-year-old brother, Daye, who is a member of the neo-Nazi group known as the Werewolves, an organization which continues to follow the pronouncements of Adolf Hitler. These young punks are the main concern of the peacekeeping force, and it is through Daye's cooperation that their activities are brought to a halt. Cummings takes her brother to the trials at Nuremberg, where he finally is made aware of the atrocities his beloved Fuhrer was guilty of and the youth quickly repents. Although films depicting Nazis and their world have been made ad nauseam since this one, the appearance of Fuller's work was a timely reminder of occurrences that people wanted to forget, but should never be allowed to. Somehow an awful and misused song sung by Paul Anka made it into the soundtrack.

p,d&w, Samuel Fuller; ph, Joseph Biroc; m, Harry Sukman, Ludwig von Beethoven, Richard Wagner; ed, Philip Cahn; art d, John Mansbridge; set d, Glen L. Daniels; cos, Bernice Pontrelli, Harry West; spec eff, Norman Breedlove; m/l, "Verboten," Mack David, Sukman (sung by Paul Anka).

Drama   **(PR:C MPAA:NR)**

VERBRECHEN NACH SCHULSCHLUSS
                    (SEE: YOUNG GO WILD, THE, 1962, Ger.)

VERDICT, THE***½   (1946) 86m WB bw

Sydney Greenstreet *(George Edward Grodman)*, Peter Lorre *(Victor Emmric)*, Joan Lorring *(Lottie)*, George Coulouris *(Supt. Buckley)*, Rosalind Ivan *(Mrs. Benson)*, Paul Cavanagh *(Clive Russell)*, Arthur Shields *(Rev. Holbrook)*, Morton Lowry *(Arthur Kendall)*, Holmes Herbert *(Sir William Dawson)*, Art Foster *(P.C. Warren)*, Clyde Cook *(Barney Cole)*, Janet Murdock *(Sister Brown)*, Ian Wolfe *(Jury Foreman)*.

Don Siegel, who had worked at Warner Bros. for years as everything from film librarian to respected second-unit director and montage specialist, was finally given the chance to direct his first feature film–ironically, it was the last film that the popular duo of Greenstreet and Lorre would ever appear in together. Set in the fog-shrouded London of 1890, Greenstreet plays the aging superintendent of Scotland Yard who is finally forced out when a man he had caught and helped convict of murder is found innocent–after his execution. Greenstreet is replaced by a pompous inspector, Coulouris, who ridicules the outgoing superintendent's methods and boasts about his own crime solving abilities. Soon after, the landlady at the boarding house across the street from where Greenstreet lives arrives in a panic claiming something bad may have happened to Lowry, one of her tenants who is locked in his room. Greenstreet accompanies the worried woman back to the house and when there is no response, he breaks down the door. Lowry is seen lying prone and the woman immediately goes to call police. When the men from Scotland Yard arrive, they discover that Lowry has been stabbed to death. Greenstreet watches Coulouris' handling of the case with interest. Also interested in the case is Lorre, an artist and good friend of Greenstreet's who is known for his ghastly illustrations and is working on the pictures to accompany the book on crime detection Greenstreet is now writing. The murder is a puzzler because the victim was found murdered in a room that was locked from the inside. Anxious to prove to Greenstreet that he is a better superintendent, Coulouris makes some quick conclusions and arrests Cavanagh, another friend of Greenstreet's, and charges him with murder. Armed with circumstantial evidence, Coulouris railroads the case through the courts and helps convict Cavanagh. The execution date is set. Greenstreet knows his friend is innocent and learns from Lorring, a cabaret singer, that a woman who could provide Cavanagh with an alibi has fled to the continent. Greenstreet tracks the woman down, but finds that she has died. Because he cannot provide an alibi for his innocent friend, Greenstreet is forced to confess that he is the murderer. Greenstreet explains that the victim was the true culprit of the murder that the innocent man was hanged for. In order to enact crude justice and prove to Coulouris that his arrogant boasting could get him into the same type of trouble that Greenstreet found himself in, the former superintendent concocted the "perfect" crime. Greenstreet had previously drugged his victim so that he would return home, lock himself in and pass out. When the landlady's pounding failed to arouse Lowry, she immediately went to Greenstreet, who feigned concern and broke down the door. What the landlady saw was the prone, but very much alive, body of Lowry. When she went to call the police, Greenstreet stabbed the unconscious man to death. From the landlady's testimony, the room was locked and Lowry was dead when Greenstreet broke down the door. Though Greenstreet has graphically proved his point, he now faces the gallows. Siegel, who would soon prove himself to be a skillful and versatile craftsman with such films as RIOT IN CELL BLOCK 11, THE INVASION OF THE BODY SNATCHERS, FLAMING STAR, HELL IS FOR HEROES, MADIGAN, COOGAN'S BLUFF, DIRTY HARRY, THE SHOOTIST, and ESCAPE FROM ALCATRAZ, demonstrated a keen understanding of mood, lighting, and composition in THE VERDICT. The film was shot on the Warner backlot on 25 outdoor and indoor sets. There was a strike during production, however, and it became necessary to shoot the film quickly with whatever personnel available–which must have frazzled the already jittery nerves of the rookie director. Luckily his stars, Greenstreet and Lorre, liked each other and worked well together. The director and his stars shared the same sense of dry humor and the film is filled with subtle jokes that may be missed by most viewers–Lorre morbidly stating that the exhuming of a grave is "exciting," and the corpulent Greenstreet stating that Coulouris is, "...getting too big for his breeches, but not big enough for mine!," being two of the standouts. This was the third filming of Zangwill's novel, one of the earliest of many locked-room mysteries to come. F.B.O. had filmed it in 1928, with the title THE PERFECT CRIME, as a quasi- comedy. The studio had not yet entirely mastered the new technique of synchronous-sound recording, and the picture is a jumble, mingling dialog with subtitles. The studio was later acquired by RKO, and the story was once again given a film treatment as THE CRIME DOCTOR (1934). Warner Bros. purchased the rights to the story from RKO in 1944 for a reported price of $13,500 to use as a vehicle for their famous scary pair, Lorre and Greenstreet.

p, William Jacobs; d, Don Siegel; w, Peter Milne (based on the novel *The Big Bow Mystery* by Israel Zangwill); ph, Ernest Haller; m, Frederick Hollander; ed, Thomas Reilly; art d, Ted Smith.

Crime   Cas.   (PR:C   MPAA:NR)

VERDICT, THE**   (1964, Brit.) 55m Merton Park/AA bw

Cec Linder (*Joe Armstrong*), Zena Marshall (*Carola*), Nigel Davenport (*Larry Mason*), Paul Stassino (*Danny Thorne*), Derek Francis (*Supt. Brett*), John Bryan (*Prendergast*), Derek Partridge (*Peter*), Glyn Jones (*Harry*), Dorinda Stevens (*Molly*).

An American in England is arrested for murder. He attempts to have his partner rig the jury in his favor, but instead is the victim of blackmail and a double cross. Average.

p, Jack Greenwood; d, David Eady; w, Arthur La Bern (based on the story "The Big Four" by Edgar Wallace).

Crime   (PR:A   MPAA:NR)

VERDICT**   (1975, Fr./Ital.) 95m PECF-Concordia-Compagnia/AE (LE TESTAMENT; AKA: JURY OF ONE) c

Sophia Loren (*Teresa Leoni*), Jean Gabin (*President Leguen*), Henri Garcin (*Maitre Lannelongue*), Julien Bertheau (*Advocate Gen. Verlac*), Michel Albertini (*Andre Leoni*), Gisele Casadessus (*Nicole Leguen*), Muriel Catala (*Annie Chartier*), Jean-Francois Remi (*Antoine Bertolucci*), Mario Pilar (*Joseph Sauveur*), Daniel Lecourtois (*Public Attorney*), Francois Vibert (*Guichard*), Michel Robin (*Vericel, a Witness*), Maurice Nasil (*Cacharel, a Neighbor*).

A judicial melodrama which stars Loren as the mother of Albertini, a young man on trial for the murder of Catala. Because of Albertini's father's reputation as a gangster, the outlook seems dim for the young man. Hoping to free her son, Loren calls on Gabin, an influential French judge in Lyon. She secures her son's acquittal by kidnaping the diabetic wife of Gabin, forcing Gabin to be lenient. Eventually, Albertini is freed, though he later admits to his mother that he did indeed murder the girl. Gabin then learns he defied justice for nothing, finding his wife dead after refusing to take her insulin shots. Distraught, Loren crashes her car into a brick wall, taking her own life in a manner of high tragedy. While not especially interesting, VERDICT is worth watching if only for the magnificence and charm Gabin exudes. Unfortunately, however, this is Loren's film and she receives the most attention, relegating Gabin to a supporting role. This would be his second-to-last film role; he appeared in just one more before his death in 1976.

p, Carlo Ponti; d, Andre Cayatte; w, Andre Cayatte, Henri Coupon, Pierre Dumayet, Paul Andreota; ph, Jean Badal (Eastmancolor); m, Louiguy; ed, Paul Cayatte; art d, Robert Clavel.

Drama   (PR:C   MPAA:NR)

VERDICT, THE****   (1982) 129m FOX c

Paul Newman (*Frank Galvin*), Charlotte Rampling (*Laura Fischer*), Jack Warden (*Mickey Morrissey*), James Mason (*Ed Concannon*), Milo O'Shea (*Judge Hoyle*), Lindsay Crouse (*Kaitlin Costello Price*), Edward Binns (*Bishop Brophy*), Julie Bovasso (*Maureen Rooney*), Roxanne Hart (*Sally Doneghy*), James Handy (*Kevin Doneghy*), Wesley Addy (*Dr. Towler*), Joe

Seneca (*Dr. Thompson*), Lewis Stadlen (*Dr. Gruber*), Kent Broadhurst (*Joseph Alito*), Colin Stinton (*Billy*), Burtt Harris (*Jimmy the Bartender*), Scott Rhyne (*Young Priest*), Susan Benenson (*Deborah Ann Kaye*), Evelyn Moore (*Dr. Gruber's Nurse*), Juanita Fleming (*Dr. Gruber's Maid*), Jack Collard (*Bailiff*), Ralph Douglas (*Clerk*), Gregor Roy (*Jury Foreman*), John Blood (*Funeral Director*), Dick McGoldrick (*Manager, 2nd Funeral Parlor*), Edward Mason (*Widow's Son*), Patty O'Brien, Maggie Task (*Irish Nurses*), Joseph Bergman (*Friedman*), Herbert Rubens (*Abrams*), J.P. Foley (*John, Cigar Stand*), Leib Lensky (*Wheelchair Patient*), Clay Dear (*Courthouse Lawyer*), J.J. Clark (*Courthouse Guard*), Greg Doucette (*Waiter, Sheraton Bar*), Tony LaFortezza (*Sheraton Bartender*), Marvin Beck, Herb Peterson (*Sheridan Patrons*).

This examination of one man's fight to regain his dignity is a powerful study, marked by Newman's excellent performance as a failed attorney. Having lost a once brilliant career, as well as his marriage, in the wake of a legal scandal, Newman is now reduced to hearse chasing, going from funeral to funeral in hopes of picking up clients. Another attorney, Warden, offers to help out Newman by giving his friend a seemingly open-and-shut case of malpractice. Newman agrees to take the case, in which a woman lapsed into a coma while having a baby, the apparent victim of a mistake by an anesthesiologist at a prominent Boston Catholic hospital. At first Newman is willing to take a settlement for the victim's family, of which he will pocket one- third. However, after visiting the comatose woman, Newman realizes that he cannot simply let this case go. Fighting the church and its powerful lawyer, Mason, Newman works to build a case, and, with it, renewed self-respect. Newman must also fight his dependence on alcohol, another reason behind his downfall. Though Newman has a powerful witness in a doctor eager to see justice done, his case nearly collapses when he learns the doctor has suddenly gone on vacation. Newman appeals to O'Shea, the presiding judge, but O'Shea refuses to help, clearly siding with Mason. Newman's problems increase further when he learns that his girl friend, Rampling, is being paid off by Mason to provide the powerful attorney with information. Fighting all odds, Newman manages to bring in a surprise witness, a former admitting nurse (Crouse) who has proof that there was negligence on the part of the hospital. However, Mason, though momentarily stunned by this unexpected tactic, is able to cite some obscure rulings that effectively dismiss Crouse's damning testimony from the court record. Newman's case appears to be lost, but the jury votes in favor of his client, asking if they can award more than the desired sum in damages. Newman's joy is poisoned, though, by the knowledge that Rampling had been using him. In a bitter conclusion, Newman sits alone in his office with a drink in hand. His phone continues to ring but he refuses to pick it up, knowing Rampling is on the other end. Newman portrays his character in a sympathetic and totally candid performance. Every wart shows, from his alcoholism to the ill-prepared opening statement he delivers in a nervous stammer to the packed courtroom. Newman makes his small moments into something special, and the actor received a well-deserved Oscar nomination for his performance. Lumet directs effectively, keeping the tension strong, and unfolding Mamet's intelligent screenplay slowly but with maximum impact. At one point, Robert Redford was considered for Newman's role, though Redford turned it down, disagreeing with the filmmakers on how the character should be interpreted.

p, Richard D. Zanuck, David Brown; d, Sidney Lumet; w, David Mamet (based on the novel by Barry Reed); ph, Andrzej Bartkowiak (Panavision, DeLuxe Color); m, Johnny Mandel; ed, Peter Frank; prod d, Edward Pisoni; art d, John Kasarda; cos, Anna Hill Johnstone.

Drama   Cas.   (PR:C-O   MPAA:R)

VERDICT OF THE SEA*½   (1932, Brit.) 65m Regina/Pathe bw

John Stuart (*Gentleman Burton*), Moira Lynd (*Paddy*), Cyril McLaglen (*Fenn*), David Miller (*Captain*), Hal Walters (*Shorty*), H. Saxon-Snell (*Myers*), Billy Shine (*Slim*), Fred Rains (*Martin*).

While a ship's captain plans on delivering some gems to their rightful owner, a gang of malcontents plots to grab the diamonds for themselves. Thanks to the help of a former doctor the plot is foiled. Pronounce this one toofeeble to stand up.

p, Clayton Hutton; d, Frank Miller, Sydney Northcote; w, Miller.

Crime/Adventure   (PR:A   MPAA:NR)

VERFUHRUNG AM MEER   (SEE: SEDUCTION BY THE SEA, 1967, Ger./Yugo.)

VERGELTUNG IN CATANO   (SEE: SUNSCORCHED, 1966, Span./Ital.)

VERGINITA**   (1953, Ital.) 94m Romana /I.F.E. bw

Irene Genna (*Gina*), Eleonora Rossi-Drago (*Mara*), Leonardo Cortese (*Franco*), Otello Toso (*Giancarlo*), Franca Marzi (*Landlady*), Arnaldo Foa (*Rene*), Tamara Lees (*M. Finzi*).

Genna plays a young girl who comes to the big city for a beauty contest and quickly becomes a procurement for the white-slave industry when she applies for work at a model agency. Cortese is the candy salesman-cum-hero who sees to it that Genna escapes this wretched fate. The script is uneven and is a bit hazy in establishing motivation. (In Italian; English subtitles.)

d, Leonardo De Mitri; w, De Mitri, G. Prosperi, Diego Fabbri, Turi Vasile (based on a story by De Mitri, Prosperi); ph, Giuseppe La Torre.

Drama   (PR:A-C MPAA:NR)

VERKLUGENE MELODIE   (SEE: DEAD MELODY, 1938, Ger.)

VERMILION DOOR**   (1969, Hong Kong) 120m Shaw Bros. c

Li Li-hua (Lo Hsiang-chi), Ivy Ling Po (Mei Pao), Kwan Shan (Chiu Hai-tang), Hsia Yi-chiu (The Deaf Maid), Yang Chi-ching (Chi Shao-shiung), Ching Miao (Yuan Pao-fan), Tien Feng (Shang Lao-er), Ho Fan (Lo Shao-hua), Woo Wei (Mrs. Meng), Chao Ming (Han Shao-wen), Li Kuan (Shiao K'ao-tse), Ruey Ming (Old Man Han), Chiang Kuang-chao (Chao Eu-K'un).

The tragic tale of a love affair set in the days when the Republic of China was initially establishing itself. Li and Po are the two lovers who can only meet in secret. Mishaps mar even these stolen moments; then the pair must endure total separation for a period of 17 years. Only at the very end of their lives are they able to be together for a fleeting moment.

p, Run Run Shaw; d, Lo Chen; w, Chin Ko; ph, Liu Chi (Shawscope, Eastmancolor); m, Wang Ju-jen; ed, Ching Hsing-lung.

Drama   (PR:A MPAA:NR)

VERONA TRIAL, THE**½   (1963, Ital.) 120m Duilio
Cinematografica/DD bw (IL PROC ESSO DI VERONA)

Silvana Mangano (Edda Ciano), Frank Wolf (Count Galeazzo Ciano), Vivi Giol (Donna Rachele), Francoise Prevost (Frau Betz), Salvo Randone (Judge), Giorgio DeLullo (Pavolini), Ivo Garrani (Farinacci), Andrea Checchi (Dino Grandi), Henri Serre (Pucci), Claudio Gora (Cerosimo).

An intriguing look into the desperate final days of Count Galeazzo Ciano (Wolf), the son-in-law of Mussolini, who was convicted of treason against the Fascist government of Italy. Wolf and his wife (Mangano) seek clemency from Il Duce, but when their pleas prove fruitless, they turn to the Nazis in the hope of striking a deal that will save Wolf's life. The picture effectively depicts the atmosphere in Italy during the final days of Mussolini's reign, though Ciano's widow found enough fault with this telling of her husband's story to take the filmmakers to court. Aimed primarily at Italian audiences, some of the film will be lost on those not familiar with the nuances of the historical moment. Longtime Italian leading lady Mangano turns in an arresting performance.

d, Carlo Lizzani; w, Ugo Pirro; ph, Leonida Barboni; m, Mario Nascimbene; ed, Franco Fraticelli.

Historical Drama   (PR:A MPAA:NR)

VERONIKA VOSS**½   (1982, Ger.) 105m
Rialto-Maran-Larua-Tango/UA bw (DIE SEHNS UCHT DER VERONI-KA VOSS)

Rosel Zech (Veronika Voss), Hilmar Thate (Robert Krohn), Cornelia Froboess (Henriette), Annemarie Duringer (Dr. Katz), Doris Schade (Josefa), Erik Schumann (Dr. Edel), Peter Berling (Fat Film Producer), Gunther Kaufmann (G.I. Dealer), Sonja Neudorfer (Saleswoman), Lilo Pempeit (Her Boss), Volker Spengler, Peter Zadek (Directors), Herbert Steinmetz (Gardener), Elisabeth Volkmann (Grete), Hans Wyprachtiger (Head Editor), Tamara Kafka (Arztin), Juliane Lorenz (Secretary), Dieter Schidor (Kripobeamter), Johanna Hofer, Rudolf Platte (Old Couple), Armin Mueller-Stahl, Peter Luhr, Brigitte Horney, Karl-Heinz von Hassel, Thomas Schuhly, Harry Baer, Georg Lehn, Rainer Werner Fassbinder.

A visually remarkable picture about German corruption, the UFA star system, and the loneliness of a once-famous screen star played by Zech. The fading star is drawn into an affair with sportswriter Thate, who soon discovers the actress' dependency on drugs. It is her doctor, Duringer, who fuels her addiction, forcing Zech to turn over all of her personal property in exchange for more morphine. Thate and his girl friend bring the doctor to the attention of the authorities, unaware, however, that they too are involved in the doctor's scheme. On Easter Sunday, Zech is locked in her room by the doctor. Suffering from withdrawal symptoms after being refused morphine, she is given enough sleeping pills to kill herself, which she eventually does. Thate is unsuccessful in his crusade, while his girl friend is run over "mysteriously" after learning some incriminating information. One of the most stylish of Fassbinder's many films, VERONI-KA VOSS features dizzying camerawork and black-and-white photography which is blaringly clinical in its use of overexposed whites. Based loosely on the life of Sybille Schmitz, a German film star who committed suicide in the mid-1950s, unable to cope with her fall from the public eye.

p, Thomas Schuhly; d, Rainer Werner Fassbinder; w, Peter Marthesheimer, Pea Frolich, Fassbinder; ph, Xaver Schwarzenberger; m, Peer Raben; ed, Juliane Lorenz; prod d, Rolf Zehetbauer.

Drama   Cas.   (PR:O MPAA:R)

VERSPATUNG IN MARIENBORN   (SEE: STOP TRAIN 349, 1964, Fr./Ital./Ger.)

VERTIGO***   (1958) 127m PAR c

James Stewart (John "Scottie" Ferguson), Kim Novak (Madeleine Elster/Judy Barton), Barbara Bel Geddes (Midge), Tom Helmore (Gavin Elster), Henry Jones (Coroner), Raymond Bailey (Doctor), Ellen Corby (Manageress), Konstantin Shayne (Pop Leibel), Lee Patrick (Older Mistaken Identity), Paul Bryar (Capt. Hansen), Margaret Brayton (Saleswoman), William Remick (Jury Foreman), Julian Petruzzi (Flower Vendor), Sara Taft (Nun), Fred Graham (Policeman), Mollie Dodd (Beauty Operator), Buck Harrington (Gateman), John Benson, Don Giovanni (Salesmen), Nina Shipman (Young Mistaken Identity), Dori Simmons (Middle-Aged Mistaken Identity), Roxann Delmar (Model), Bruno Santina (Waiter), Ed Stevlingson (Attorney), Roland Gotti (Maitre d'), Carlo Dotto (Bartender), Jack Richardson (Man Escort), June Jocelyn, (Miss Woods), Miliza Milo (Saleswoman), Jack Ano (Extra), Joanne Genthon (Girl in Portrait).

Hitchcock's most intensely personal and frighteningly self-revealing picture, VERTIGO is the story of a man possessed by the image of a former love, becoming increasingly demonic in his desire to re-create her in another woman. Stewart is that man, appearing at first as gentle, likable, and average. A San Francisco police officer, Stewart leaves the force after causing the death of a fellow officer. During a rooftop chase, Stewart loses his footing and slides down the incline of the roof, until he hangs suspended over the street below only by a sagging rain gutter. As Stewart looks below, he experiences a sense of vertigo, a dizzying sensation brought on by his acrophobia, or fear of heights. His fellow officer tries to pull him to safety but in doing so loses his grip and falls to his death. Having given up policework, Stewart spends time with his friend and former fiancee, Bel Geddes, a prim, business-minded, bespectacled woman who designs brassieres for a living. When Stewart gets a call from a former classmate, shipping magnate Helmore, he pays the man a visit. Helmore, knowing of Stewart's police experience, asks Stewart to play detective and shadow his wife, Novak, who Helmore fears is going to wind up dead. Helmore ominously asks Stewart, "Do you believe that someone dead, someone out of the past, can take possession of a living being?" Stewart doesn't believe it, but is persuaded to take the job. He begins by following the icy, alluring, gray-suited blonde to a flower shop, voyeuristically peeking through a barely open door as she purchases a small bouquet. He follows her to a cemetery, where she lays the flowers at the grave of a Carlotta Valdes. He then tracks her to a museum where she sits entranced in front of a portrait of Carlotta Valdes. Stewart notices that she and Carlotta have the same hairstyle–the hair pulled tightly to the back of the head and pinned into a bun. Novak then leads him to a hotel, where Stewart learns from the proprietor, Corby, that Miss Valdes, Novak, comes there every couple of weeks. From Helmore, Stewart learns more. Novak is possessed by thoughts of a dead relative, Valdes, though this possession is entirely subconscious. The hotel is where Valdes grew up, Novak being drawn there by her ancestor's presence. Stewart, searching for more answers, has Bel Geddes take him to a bookshop run by Shayne, an authority on obscure San Francisco history. He learns more–that Carlotta went mad after her husband left her, wandering the streets in a daze searching for her child, then finally killing herself at age 26, the same age as Novak. Later, while intensely following Novak, by whom he is becoming increasingly fascinated, Stewart watches her as she walks near the edge of San Francisco Bay, the Golden Gate Bridge overwhelmingly large in the background. She jumps into the choppy waters, trying, like Carlotta, to kill herself. Stewart fishes her out and takes the entranced Novak back to his apartment. The following morning, she awakes from her unconscious state, naked under the bedsheets, her clothes and stockings hanging to dry. The implications of the night before fill the air, but Novak seems to be too dazed to remember any of it. She leaves, but later comes back to leave Stewart a thank you note for saving her. They go together for a ride to a rocky beachfront, where they kiss as the waves batter the rocks and splash violently behind the lovers. When Stewart returns he is greeted by Bel Geddes who has a surprise to show him–a painting that she has just finished of herself, with her glasses, as Carlotta. Stewart fails to find the humor in the painting, feeling as if he is being ridiculed by his friend, and also realizing that Bel Geddes is not the type of woman that he desires. Realizing her mistake, Bel Geddes destroys the painting. That evening, Novak arrives at Stewart's apartment and begins describing a dream she had. Stewart recognizes the place she describes as a Mexican mission town called San Juan Batista, which has been restored to its original state. Another romantic kiss brings the two together in a barn at San Juan Batista. Novak, however, runs out of the barn towards a church bell tower, telling him that she must climb to the top. Stewart, trying to help her overcome her possession by Carlotta, tells her, "No one possesses you...you're safe with me." "It's too late, there's something I must do," cries Novak. "It shouldn't have happened this way." She pulls free from Stewart's grasp and runs into the church and up the stairs. Stewart tries to follow but cannot because of his vertigo. He struggles with his fear of heights, but whenever he looks down the walls distort and the floor seems to get closer. Before he can move any farther, he hears a scream and sees Novak's body falling past the window, landing with a hard thud below. Unable to accept Novak's death or his own weakness, Stewart runs away. An informal trial follows, which lays to rest any claims of foul play that might be leveled against Stewart, and clearly proves that the emotionally confused Novak, thinking she was one of her suicidal ancestors, killed herself. Helmore expresses his grief to Stewart, and accepts the death with dignity. Stewart, however, falls apart and is committed to an asylum where his treatment consists mainly of listening to the calming strains of Mozart. Furious with his treatment, Bel Geddes verbally attacks Stewart's doctor and leaves (this is the last time we see Bel Geddes in the film). After many months of treatment, Stewart re-enters society, returning to the places where he used to see Novak–her house, the museum, a restaurant–occasionally spotting blonde, gray- suited women who resembles his dead love. While roaming the hilly, San Francisco streets, he spots a rather plain brunette who bears a striking resemblance to Novak (indeed, she is played by Novak). Although she initially resists, Novak agrees to talk with Stewart and have dinner with him. Stewart stares demonically at this reincarnation of his former love, the dead woman's image completely possessing Stewart. He begins to fall in love with the new Novak, not with the person but with the image. He boldly tries to re-create the icy blonde. He buys her an identical gray suit, over the new Novak's objections, and buys her an identical pair of shoes. Novak is in love with Stewart, but cannot deal with her past. She prepares to run out on him, penning a letter which admits that she was Helmore's lover, and was involved in the murder of Helmore's wife. She agreed to let Helmore dress her and make her up as his wife, and then push the already dead woman out of the bell tower. What she didn't plan, however, was that she would fall in love with Stewart, who was just supposed to be a pawn in the game–Helmore's witness to his wife's suicidal emotional state. Novak destroys the letter, however, since she loves Stewart too much to leave him. Novak's partial makeover still isn't enough for Stewart. "Let me take care of you," he demands, seeing Novak in silhouette, looking exactly like he remembers. Stewart grows increasingly intent on redressing Novak, psychologically stripping off her real self and turning her into his past love. "Couldn't you like me the way I am?" she begs. When it seems as if Stewart may finally come to his senses, he makes another demand: "The color of your hair...it can't matter to you." She agrees to dye her hair blonde, returning from the hairdresser with her hair at shoulder length, as if making one last attempt to hold on to part of her real self. Stewart forces her to put it in a bun. Novak agrees, not caring anymore what she looks like and willing to do anything just to keep Stewart. She comes out of the bathroom looking exactly as Stewart remembered, but walking through a hazy fog and appearing as if she's an aberration. Novak and Stewart kiss. As the camera revolves around them we see the hotel room blend into the barn at San Juan Batista and then back into the room. Later, as Novak is getting ready for dinner, having seemingly accepted her fate as the living memory of Stewart's past love, she puts on a necklace which Stewart recognizes as being an heirloom of Carlotta's. He then realizes that his two Novaks are indeed one and the same. He takes her to San Juan Batista to relive her "death," dragging her into the bell tower, forcing her to admit that it was all a plot. Stewart maniacally interrogates her about Helmore: "He made you over just like I made you over–only better. Not only the clothes and the hair, but the looks and the manner and the words. And those beautiful phony trances. And then what did he do? Did he train you? Did he rehearse you? Did he tell you exactly what to do and what to say? You were a very apt pupil, weren't you? You were a very apt pupil!" By now Stewart has overcome his vertigo and he has made it to the top of the tower. He discovers that he does love her after all, even knowing that her hair and clothes and words are phony. The commotion arouses the attention of a church nun whose looming shadow frightens the unstable Novak. As Novak lurches back, she falls off the edge of the tower to her death. A shocked, destroyed Stewart, who has again lost Novak off the bell tower, stands perched at the edge looking down at her dead body. Based on a novel by Pierre Boileau and Thomas Narcejac, who previously supplied the source material for DIABOLIQUE, VERTIGO appealed to Hitchcock for reasons which become more clear the more one knows about the director. It is well known that Hitchcock had very obsessive fascinations with the women he starred in his films–usually cold, icy women (Novak, Grace Kelly, Vera Miles, Joan Fontaine, Ingrid Bergman) whose sexuality was repressed by their sophistication–and carefully molded their appearances and actions to comply with his rigid rules of beauty. Originally cast for the lead in VERTIGO was Vera Miles, who, having just finished THE WRONG MAN, married and became pregnant. Previous to that, however, Hitchcock had carefully groomed Miles for superstardom according to his standards of beauty and sexuality. He had a wardrobe, hairstyle, and makeup specially created for her which she was to wear not only during the shooting but off the set as well. In his published interview with Francois Truffaut, Hitchcock said that Miles "became pregnant just before the part that was going to turn her into a star. After that I lost interest..." He then cast Novak. "I went to Kim Novak's dressing room and told her about the dresses and hairdos that I had been planning for several months." VERTIGO is, in fact, nothing less than Hitchcock revealing himself to his audience–the director's obsessions and desire to make over women are embodied in Stewart, while the perfect Hitchcock woman is embodied in Novak. Hitchcock makes this even more complex (and revealing) by casting Novak as an actress, of sorts–a woman who plays a role in order to help one man (Helmore) and entrap another (Stewart). At both Helmore's and Stewart's request, Novak dresses up and plays a part, just to please them. Although Stewart's role is the central one in VERTIGO, Novak's is equally intriguing, and frightening. She is a woman who is compelled to change herself and allow herself to be physically degraded just to please a man. Stewart, the seemingly "normal" hero who becomes warped in his desire for Novak, finally comes to realize by the film's end what he has done. Pulling her up the bell tower he screams at her, "Did he train you? Did he rehearse you? Did he tell you exactly what to do and what to say?"–lines that could easily refer to Hitchcock himself, the master who obsessively trains his pupil-actress. What Stewart and Hitchcock are both trying to find in their perfect woman is the erotic, carnal female that hides beneath the gray suit and the pinned-up hair. For Stewart (and Hitchcock), the attraction to Novak is something he doesn't feel towards Bel Geddes. Rather than repress her sexual freedom and hide her nudity, Bel Geddes is out in the open, clearly displaying a brassiere to Stewart, and going so far as to discuss its mechanics in comparison to a cantilever bridge. Novak, on the other hand, never reveals herself openly, but does still manage to excite. Hitchcock has said of Novak in the film, "She doesn't wear a brassiere. As a matter of fact, she's particularly proud of that." VERTIGO'S most telling, and disturbing, scene occurs after Stewart pulls Novak from the water. The following morning in his apartment, Novak wakes up nude, her clothes hanging up to dry. Since she was in a trance, Stewart obviously undressed her, and most likely made love to her unconscious body (a reference to the "form of necrophilia," as Hitchcock says, that Stewart indulges in). In reality, however, Novak's drowning was all part of the scheme to hook Stewart (we learn later that she is an excellent swimmer), which means that her trance was an act too, and that she was merely pretending to be unconscious when Stewart undressed and made love to her. When Stewart loses Novak to "suicide," he can no longer function (Hitchcock, when losing Miles to marriage and pregnancy, said about filming VERTIGO, "I lost interest, I couldn't get the rhythm going with her again."), and must recreate her image in the new Novak. The person under the disguise doesn't matter to Stewart, however, as long as she looks and acts like that "ideal woman." Because Stewart is more concerned with loving an image than with loving a person, he has this image taken away from him at the very end. It is most probable that Stewart, had the film gone on, would have spent more time in an asylum, and then found yet another woman to dress up in Novak's image. VERTIGO was less than a box-office smash, though it did find its usual Hitchcock audience, but it has, over the years, become a classic Hitchcock picture, at least in terms of studying the director himself. With the *politique des auteurs*, or "the auteur theory," and the film school interest in directors' lives and careers (as well as a number of books which delve in the "dark side" of the director), VERTIGO has become an important, self-revealing piece of art which, more than any other Hitchcock film, gives the audience a sense of who the director really is. VERTIGO is also a masterpiece of filmmaking skills, including one of the most important technical discoveries since the dawn of cinema--the dolly-out, zoom-in, shot, which visually represents the sensation of vertigo that Stewart feels. As Hitchcock describes to Truffaut, "I always remember one night at the Chelsea Arts Ball at Albert Hall in London when I got terribly drunk and I had the sensation that everything was going far away from me." First attempting to visualize this sensation in REBECCA, Hitchcock was unsatisfied with the effect, thinking about the problem for 15 years. For the vertigo effect in the bell tower (which is used a couple of other times throughout the film), he finally hit upon the idea of dollying the camera away from the stairs (which meant physically pulling the camera away) while, simultaneously, zooming the lens in on them. When presenting the idea to his crew Hitchcock was told it would cost $50,000: "When I asked why, they said, 'Because to put the camera at the top of the stairs we have to have a big apparatus to lift it, an hold it up in space.'" Hitchcock argued that since no characters were in the shot, "Why can't we make a miniature of the stairway and lay it on its side, then take our shot by pulling away from it?" The result, which cost $19,000 to produce, is up on the screen and is a shot unique to Hitchcock, unlike any other before in film.

p&d, Alfred Hitchcock; w, Alex Coppel, Samuel Taylor (based on the novel *D'Entre Les Morts* by Pierre Boileau, Thomas Narcejac); ph, Robert Burks (VistaVision, Technicolor); m, Bernard Herrmann; ed, George Tomasini; art d, Hal Pereira, Henry Bumstead; set d, Sam Comer, Frank McKelvey; cos, Edith Head; spec eff, John Fulton; spec ph eff, Farciot Edouart, Wallace Kelly; special sequence designer, John Ferren; makeup, Wally Westmore.

Drama						Cas.						**(PR:C MPAA:NR)**

VERY BIG WITHDRAWAL, A			(SEE: MAN, A WOMAN, AND A BANK, A, 1979, Can.)

VERY CURIOUS GIRL, A**   (1970, Fr.) 107m Cythere /REG-UNIV C (LA FIANCEE DU PIRATE; AKA: DIRTY MARY; PIRATE'S FIAN-CEE)

Bernadette Lafont (*Marie*), Georges Geret (*Gaston Duvalier*), Michel Constantin (*Andre*), Julien Guiomar (*Le Duc*), Jean Paredes (*Mons. Paul*), Francis Lax (*Emile*), Claire Maurier (*Irene*), Henry Czarniak (*Julien*), Jacques Marin (*Felix Lechat*), Pascal Mazzotti (*Father Dard*), Marcel Peres (*Pepe*), Micha Bayard (*Melanie Lechat*), Fernand Berset (*Jeanjean*), Gilberte Geniat (*Rose*), Jacques Masson (*Hippolyte*), Renee Duncan (*Delphine*), Claire Oliver (*Mother*), Louis Malle (*Jesus*), Claude Makovski (*Victor*).

Lafont plays a young country girl who learns how to use her sexuality to her best advantage. Eventually she turns her skills to blackmail when the hypocritical villagers speak out agaist her antics and go so far as to kill her beloved goat. In a great vengeance scene, she visits a Sunday mass and leaves behind a blaring tape recording that reveals the true personalities of the town's most prominent men.

p, Claude Makovski; d, Nelly Kaplan; w, Kaplan, Makovski, Jacques Berguine, Michel Fabre; ph, Jean Badal (Technicolor); m, Georges Moustaki; ed, Kaplan, Gerard Pollicand, Noelle Boisson, Suzanne Lang-Willar; art d, Michel Landi, Patrick Lafarge, Jean-Claude Landi; m/l, "Moi, Je Me Balance" (sung by Barbara).

Drama   (PR:O MPAA:R)

VERY EDGE, THE**   (1963, Brit.) 82m BL-Garrick bw

Anne Heywood (*Tracey Lawrence*), Richard Todd (*Geoffrey Lawrence*), Jack Hedley (*McInnes*), Nicole Maurey (*Helen*), Jeremy Brett (*Mullen*), Barbara Mullen (*Dr. Shaw*), Maurice Denham (*Crawford*), William Lucas (*Inspector Davies*), Gwen Watford (*Sister Holden*), Patrick Magee (*Simmonds*), Verina Greenlaw (*Selina*).

An effectively handled psychodrama in which Heywood and Todd are a content couple indulging in the idea of becoming parents. Their dreams are destroyed when Heywood, a former model, is brutally attacked by a man who breaks into their house. She suffers a miscarriage and is repulsed by the thought of physical contact with men, including her husband. This situation continues, putting severe strain on their marriage, until the attacker is brought to justice once and for all.

p, Raymond Stross; d, Cyril Frankel; w, Elizabeth Jane Howard (based on a story by Vivian Cox, Leslie Bricusse, Stross); ph, Bob Huke; m, David Lee; ed, Max Benedica.

Drama   (PR:C MPAA:NR)

VERY HANDY MAN, A**   (1966, Fr./Ital.) 95 m Napoleon-Franco London-Federiz-Francinex-Cinecitta/Rizzoli bw (LIOLA)

Ugo Tognazzi (*Liola*), Giovanna Ralli (*Tuzza Azzara*), Pierre Brasseur (*Simone Palumbo*), Anouk Aimee (*Mita*), Elisa Cegani (*Aunt Geas*), Dolores Palumbo, Umberto Spadaro, Rocco D'Assunta, Carlo Piscane, Claudio Micheli, Antonio Piretti, Stefano Maggi, Carlo Angeletti, Massimo Giuliani, Mariettino, Giulio Tomasini, Angela Lavagna, Miranda Poggi, Vera Drudi, Gian Gabella, Giuseppe Stagnitti, Solveig D'Assunta, Nino Musco, Graziella Granata, Renato Terra, Vanda Tibursi, Erina Torelli.

The makeshift plot of this sex farce revolves around the amorous adventures of Tognazzi, a lowly village laborer who has fathered a number of illegitimate children by various women while maintaining the life of a carefree bachelor. Matters become more complicated for him when he becomes embroiled in a village feud over water rights. But despite the efforts of the more scheming villagers, Tognazzi comes out smelling like a rose, siring two more children, his improbable contribution to the resolution of the squabble. All of which allows for some hardy chuckles at the expense of the knaving and less likable members of the cast, but which doesn't help to overcome the silliness of the plot's basically one-joke premise.

p, Nino Krisman; d, Alessandro Blasetti; w, Sergio Amidei, Elio Bartolini, Carlo Romano, Adriano Bolzoni, Blasetti (based on the play "Liola" by Luigi Pirandello); ph, Leonida Barboni, Tonino Delli Colli, Carlo Di Palma; m, Carlo Savina.

Comedy   (PR:C MPAA:NR)

VERY HAPPY ALEXANDER***   (1969, Fr.) 94m Productions de la Gueville-Madeleine Films de la Colombe/Cinema V c (ALEXANDRE LE BIENHEUREUX; AKA: HAPPY ALEXANDER; ALEXANDER)

Philippe Noiret (*Alexander*), Francoise Brion (*La Grande*), Marlene Jobert (*Agathe*), Antoinette Moya (*Angele Sanguin*), Paul Le Person (*Sanguin*), Pierre Richard (*Colibert*), Jean Carmet (*La Fringale*), Tsilla Chelton, Leonce Corne, Jean Saudray, Kaly, Pierre Barnley, Marcel Bernier, Bernard Charlan, Madeleine Damien, Pierre Maguelon, Marie Marc, Francois Vibert.

A delightfully funny and pleasant comedy from the director of THE TALL BLOND MAN WITH the ONE BLACK SHOE, in which Noiret plays an incredibly lazy farmer who doesn't see much of a reason for putting forth an effort in anything. His ideal is to just lie in bed all day, pursuing the smallest amount of labor possible, a life he finally gets to lead when his pushy wife dies. Noiret does exactly what he dreamed, having his dog take care of chores such as going to the market. He eventually meets a young girl who seems to agree with his life style, but when the wedding comes, she shows the same characteristics as Noiret's first wife. So Noiret runs from the altar to the carefree life with his dog. Although in French, this is the type of film that could easily be understood and enjoyed without understanding the dialog. The story is simple, gracefully handled by Robert, with a theme that is universally appreciated. (In French; English subtitles.)

p, Daniele Delorme, Yves Robert; d, Robert; w, Robert, Pierre Levy-Corti (based on a story by Robert); ph, Rene Mathelin (Eastmancolor); m, Vladimar Cosma; ed, Andree Werlin; md, Cosma; art d&set d, Jacques d'Orvidio; English subtitles, Noelle Gillmor.

Comedy   (PR:A MPAA:G)

VERY HONORABLE GUY, A**   (1934) 62m WB-FN bw

Joe E. Brown (*Feet Samuels*), Alice White (*Hortense*), Robert Barrat (*Dr. Snitzer*), Alan Dinehart (*The Brain*), Irene Franklin (*Toodles*), Hobart Cavanaugh (*Benny*), Arthur Vinton (*Moon O'Hara*), George Pat Collins (*Red*), Harold Huber (*Joe*), James Donlan (*O'Toole*), Harry Warren (*Harry*), Al Dubin (*Al*), Joe Cawthorne.

Silly Brown vehicle in which he plays a man who has gambling debts he is unable to pay. Not wanting to be shod in concrete at the bottom of a river, Brown sells his body to a scientist, pays back the hood and basks in his new-found wealth. But he still has agreed to give up his most valued item, himself, to the mad scientist. Except for a moment or two, it isn't all that funny.

p, Robert Lord; d, Lloyd Bacon; w, Earl Baldwin (based on the story by Damon Runyon); ph, Ira Morgan; ed, William Holmes; art d, Jack Okey; cos, Orry-Kelly.

Comedy   (PR:A MPAA:NR)

VERY IDEA, THE*½   (1929) 65m RKO bw

Frank Craven (*Alan Camp, Eugenics Author*), Theodore Von Eltz (*George Green*), Doris Eaton (*Edith Goodhue, Alan's Sister*), Allen Kearns (*Gilbert Goodhue, Alan's Brother-in-Law*), Hugh Trevor (*Joe Garvin, Chauffeur*), Sally Blane (*Nora, Maid*), Jeanne De Bard (*Dorothy Green*), Olive Tell (*Marion Green*), Adele Watson (*Miss Duncan*).

Poorly produced and conceived comedy that centers around the inability of a wealthy couple to produce an offspring. The wife's brother comes up with the seemingly brilliant idea of having others make the baby for them, the chosen being the couple's maid and chauffeur. When the baby finally arrives this pair doesn't want to part with the tot. But that's okay as the childless couple are expecting their own child anyway. Not a very tasteful subject for lighthearted comedy.

p, Myles Connolly; d, Richard Rosson, William Le Baron; w, Le Baron (based on his play); ph, Leo Tover; ed, Ann McKnight, George Marsh; art d, Max Ree.

Comedy   (PR:A MPAA:NR)

VERY IMPORTANT PERSON, A   (SEE: COMING-OUT PARTY, A, 1962, Brit.)

VERY NATURAL THING, A½**   (1974) 80m Montage/New Line c

Robert Joel (*David*), Curt Gareth (*Mark*), Bo White (*Jason*), Jay Pierce (*Alan*), Barnaby Rudge (*Hughey*), Marilyn Meyers (*Valerie*), A. Bailey Chapin (*Minister*), Robert Grillo (*Edgar*), Kurt Brandt (*Charles*), George Diaz (*Miguel*), Deborah Trowbridge (*Jason's Ex-Wife*), Jesse Trowbridge (*Jason's Child*), Michael Kell, Sheila Rock, Linda Weita (*Boating Family*).

A man falls in love, his lover grows disillusioned, and he must find another. What makes this story different is that the principals are all male. A VERY NATURAL THING takes an honest look at the subject of homosexuality. Instead of focusing on the sexual aspects of the story, however, director Larkin deals with the mixed emotions his protagonist feels. Joel is a high school teacher who understands his sexual predelictions but fears for his job should his secret become public. Joel's feelings and situations are dealt with in an open manner but presented in a standard form. The film has nothing new to say about the gay life style other than its being an honest portrait of one man's experiences within the culture. This easily could be a film about a man who has left his wife for another woman rather than for a man. The characterizations are believable, never turning into the commonplace types associated with movie homosexuals. An almost, but not quite, important film on an often unsettling issue.

p&d, Christopher Larkin; w, Larkin, Joseph Coencas; ph, C. H. Douglass (Technicolor); m, Bert Lucarelli, Gordon Gottlieb, The Musemorphoses; ed, Terry Manning.

Drama   (PR:O MPAA:R)

VERY PRIVATE AFFAIR, A**   (1962, Fr./Ital.) 95m Pro Ge Fi-CIPRA-Jacques Bar-C.C.M./MGM c (LA VIE PRIVEE; VITA PRIVA-TA)

Brigitte Bardot (*Jill*), Marcello Mastroianni (*Fabio*), Gregor von Rezzori (*Gricha*), Eleonore Hirt (*Cecile*), Ursula Kubler (*Carla*), Dirk Sanders (*Dick*), Paul Soreze (*Maxime*), Jacqueline Doyen (*Juliette*), Antoine Roblot (*Alain*), Nicolas Bataille (*Edmond*), Marco Naldi (*Italian Grocer*), Francois Marie (*Francois*), Elie Presman (*Olivier*), Gilles Queant (*Trovar*), Christian de Tillere (*Albert*), Stan Kroll (*Maxine's Chauffeur*), Jeanne Allard (*Charwoman*), Gloria France (*Anna*), Louis Malle (*Journalist*), Fred Surin (*Director*), Paul Apoteker (*Cameraman*), Claude Day (*Publicist*), Isarco Ravaioli, Simonetta Simeoni, Jacques Gheusi.

Released just after Marilyn Monroe's death, this picture may have made more money than it deserved because it was a so-called "inside look" at what it meant to be a movie star and was supposedly patterned after Bardot's real life. It begins as Bardot is 18 and living with her mother in a huge estate overlooking Lake Geneva in Switzerland. She is infatuated with Mastroianni, a magazine publisher and theatrical director from Italy who is married to Kubler, a good friend of hers. He pays little attention to her teenaged moon-eyes and she decides to leave Switzerland and the easy life she leads to settle in Paris, where she plans to become a ballerina. But that regimen usually begins for a young girl while she is little more than an infant and Bardot soon tosses that dream out the window to try her luck at modeling. Her saucy looks are the talk of the town and a film producer spots her and decides that she will be the recipient of his mighty publicity machine. In no time at all, Bardot is known across the world after a mere three years of making movies. But she can't take success and the accomodations she must make to the bitch goddess. When she is nearly trampled by a horde of adoring fans, she decides to leave the screen and seek a quieter life. Disguised in a black hairpiece to cover her normally reddish-blonde hues, she returns to Geneva and finds Mastroianni once more. Since their first meeting, he has shed his wife, thus paving the way for Bardot and him to consummate their relationship. Mastroianni is on his way to Spoleto where he is directing the action and designing the sets for Kleist's "Katchen von Heilbronn" for the annual festival. The two share a happy tryst together until the press spots her and moves in along with waves of sycophants and star-lovers. Mastroianni is busy with his work and she is too frightened to go out alone because she will be mobbed. Thus, she has to stay in their hotel room and she begins to pout at Mastroianni's lack of attention to her. This causes any number of quarrels between them and she becomes increasingly depressed. On the opening night of the festival, Bardot steps out on the hotel room's high balcony to see the activity and is momentarily blinded by a flash bulb shot by a photographer who has been waiting for the moment. The flash causes her to lose her balance and she falls to her death, killed by the same item that started her on her brief, tragic career. The idea of the poor little star who can't find anyone to understand her had been already done to death by the time this was released. Paddy Chayefsky covered it with his screenplay for THE GODDESS and Frances Farmer's life had already been well-documented. Bardot, who worked on the screenplay without credit, said she didn't think she wanted to make any films after this but she was not true to her word and filmed at least 10 more. Director Malle was the wrong choice for the film, as he was too studied and devoted more time to the technical side than to extracting performances from those involved. Many of the incidents were said to be directly taken from Bardot's life, including one particularly brutal confrontation with a maid who berates her as a slut. It was shot in Lake Geneva, Paris, and Spoleto and was later released in a English-dubbed version. (In French; English subtitles.)

p, Christine Gouse-Renal; d, Louis Malle; w, Malle, Jean-Paul Rappeneau, Jean Ferry; ph, Henri Decae (Eastmancolor); m, Fiorenzo Carpi; ed, Kenout Peltier; art d, Bernard Evein; cos, Les Maisons Marie-Martine and Real; makeup, Maud Begon; m/l, "Sidonie," Jean Max Riviere, Jean Spanos, Charles Cros (sung by Brigitte Bardot).

Drama   **Cas.**   **(PR:C   MPAA:NR)**

VERY SPECIAL FAVOR, A**   (1965) 105m Lan Kershim/UNIV c

Rock Hudson (*Paul Chadwick*), Leslie Caron (*Lauren Boullard*), Charles Boyer (*Michel Boullard*), Walter Slezak (*Etienne, Proprietor*), Dick Shawn (*Arnold Plum*), Larry Storch (*Harry, Taxi Driver*), Nita Talbot (*Mickey, Switchboard Operator*), Norma Varden (*Mother Plum*), George Furth (*Pete*), Marcel Hillaire (*Claude*), Jay Novello (*Rene*), Stafford Repp (*Bartender*), Alvy Moore (*Ralph*), Jesslyn Fax (*Miss Feeny*), Frank DeVol (*Desk Clerk*), Don Beddoe (*Mr. Ruthledge*), Allen Joseph (*Man at Group Therapy*), Sheila Rogers (*Dorothy*), Irene Martin (*Sandra*), Helen Brown (*Mrs. Ruthledge*), Frank Kreig (*Man with Cigar*), Jimmy Hayes (*Ambulance Attendant*), Patricia Winters (*Seducing Woman*), Barry O'Hara (*Man at Airport*), Danica D'Hondt (*Jacqueline*), John Harding (*Dr. Lambert*).

Hudson is up to his usual antics as the irresisstible bachelor with whom women can't help but fall in love with. In the Doris Day spot is Caron, and the matchmaker is played by the charming Boyer as Caron's father whom she's seeing for the first time in 25 years. Starting out in Paris, Texas oilman Hudson beats Boyer in a court case by resorting to the typical French maneuver (at least in Hudson's eyes) of seducing the lady judge. To make up the damage to Boyer's pride, Hudson offers to do a favor for the elderly man. This comes when Boyer meets Caron and finds his daughter fast becoming a spinster, even though she is engaged to be married to Shawn, a wimp. Boyer's request of Hudson is that he provide her with the romantic experience necessary for Caron to fulfill her womanly role. Rock agrees, and after the nominal amount of game playing on behalf of both parties, true love develops with the next stop the altar. A glossy directorial and scripting effort that makes no pretensions at seriousness. The most impressive performances come from Storch as an uppity cab driver and Talbot as the switchboard operator who nearly faints each time the Rock passes. It has as much impact as the popcorn sold in the theater.

p, Stanley Shapiro; d, Michael Gordon; w, Shapiro, Nate Monaster; ph, Leo Tover (Technicolor); m, Vic Mizzy; ed, Russell F. Schoengarth; art d, Alexander Golitzen, Walter Simonds; set d, John McCarthy, John Austin; cos, Yves Saint Laurent; ch, David Robel; makeup, Bud Westmore.

Comedy   **(PR:A   MPAA:NR)**

VERY THOUGHT OF YOU, THE*   (1944) 99m WB bw

Dennis Morgan (*Sgt. Dave Stewart*), Eleanor Parker (*Janet Wheeler*), Dane Clark (*"Fixit"*), Faye Emerson (*Cora*), Beulah Bondi (*Mrs. Wheeler*), Henry Travers (*Pop Wheeler*), William Prince (*Fred*), Andrea King (*Molly Wheeler*), John Alvin (*Cal Wheeler*), Marianne O'Brien (*Bernice, His Wife*), Georgia Lee Settle (*Ellie*), Dick [Richard], Erdman (*Soda Jerk*), Francis Pierlot (*Minister*).

Dreary depiction of a wartime romance between soldier Morgan and Parker, the girl he falls in love with while on leave in Southern California. They're quick to get married and have a baby, but the film takes far too much time detailing these events without adding much.

p, Jerry Wald; d, Delmer Daves; w, Alvah Bessie, Daves (based on the story by Lionel Wiggam); ph, Bert Glennon; m, Franz Waxman; ed, Alan Crosland, Jr.; md, Leo F. Forbstein; art d, Leo Kuter; cos, Milo Anderson; spec eff, Warren Lynch.

Drama   **(PR:A   MPAA:NR)**

VERY YOUNG LADY, A**   (1941) 75m FOX bw

Jane Withers (*Kitty Russell*), Nancy Kelly (*Alice Carter*), John Sutton (*Dr. Meredith*), Janet Beecher (*Miss Steele*), Richard Clayton (*Tom Brighton*), June Carlson (*Madge*), Charles Halton (*Brixton*), Cecil Kellaway (*Prof. Starkweather*), Marilyn Kinsley (*Susie*), JoAnn Ransom (*Linda*), Catherine Henderson (*Jean*), Lucita Ham (*Sarah*), June Horne (*Beth*).

Basically a vehicle to preen Withers for more adult roles, which never took, her most successful role in adult life being as TV's Josephine the Plumber. Here she's sent off to a fashionable finishing school to curb some of her boyish mannerisms, something she isn't too fond of until she develops a walloping crush on headmaster Sutton. This takes the form of her writing imaginary letters, which she never sends but are made public when an elderly teacher stumbles onto them. The play upon which the film was based had been made into a film called GIRL'S DORMITORY a few years earlier.

p, Robert T. Kane; d, Harold Schuster; w, Ladislas Fodor, Elaine Ryan (based on the play by Fodor); ph, Edward Cronjager; ed, James B. Clark; md, Cyril J. Mockbidge; art d, Richard Day, Joseph G. Wright.

Drama   **(PR:A   MPAA:NR)**

VESSEL OF WRATH   (SEE: BEACHCOMBER, THE, 1938, Brit.)

VET IN THE DOGHOUSE   (SEE: IN THE DOGHOUSE, 1964, Brit.)

VETERAN, THE   (SEE: DEATHDREAM, 1972, Can.)

VIA MARGUTTA   (SEE: RUN WITH THE DEVIL, 1963, Fr./Ital.)

VIA PONY EXPRESS*   (1933) 60m Majestic bw

Jack Hoxie, Marceline Day, Lane Chandler, Julian Rivero, Doris Hill, Mathew Betz, Joseph Girard, Charles K. French, Bill Quinlan, Yakima Canutt.

A mishmash of ideas went in to try to hide the fact that this was just another routine western starring Hoxie as the pony express rider who must put up with thieves who hang him from trees, among various things that get in his path. But as the saying goes: "The mail must go through."

p, Larry Darmour; d, Lew Collins; w, Collins, Oliver Drake (based on a story by Drake).

Western   **(PR:A   MPAA:NR)**

VIAGGIO IN ITALIA   (SEE: STRANGERS, THE, 1955, Ital.)

VIBRATION*½   (1969, Swed.) 85m Nordisk Tonefilm/Audubon bw (LEJONSOMMAR)

Essy Persson (*Eliza*), Margareta Sjodin (*Barbro*), Sven-Bertil Taube (*Mauritz*), Ulf Brunnberg (*Jonas*), Ardy Struwer (*Kono Tahiri [Jurgen]*), Lars Aberg (*Gunnar*), Yvonne Persson (*Annika*), Ann-Christine Magnussen (*Mari [Britta]*), Annmari Engwall (*Louise*), Hasse Wallbom, Thyra Pettersson, William Pettersson, Inez Graaf.

Lackluster story about vacationing writer Taube who tries to bed as many women as possible without becoming attached to any of them. The writer's handicraft is a far cry from his earlier intellectual intensity, so his unwillingness to fall in love can be attributed to his inability to make a commitment to his work. Thus he comes out a very shallow individual.

p&d, Torbjorn Axelman; w, Axelman, Bengt V. Vall, Sandro Key-Aberg, Ardy Struwer, Lars Aberg; ph, Hans Dittmer; m, Sven-Bertil Taube; ed, Margit Nordqvist.

Drama   **(PR:O   MPAA:NR)**

VICAR OF BRAY, THE   (1937, Brit.) 66m JH Productions/ABF bw

Stanley Holloway (The Vicar of Bray), Hugh Miller (King Charles I), K. Hamilton Price (Prince Charles Stuart), Felix Aylmer (Earl of Brendon), Margaret Vines (Lady Norah Brendon), Garry Marsh (Sir Richard Melross), Esmond Knight (Dennis Melross), Martin Walker (Sir Patrick Condon), Eve Gray (Meg Clancy), Kitty Kirwan (Molly), Fred O'Donovan (Tim Connor), George Merritt (Oliver Cromwell).

Holloway plays an Irish priest during the days of Charles I given the privileged job of tutor to the future king's. Years later Holloway is allowed to make a request of the king, which the latter promised to grant as a result of the priest's role as teacher. The request is to let a member of the priest's parish free--even though the man is a political prisoner, the wish is granted. An entertaining role for Holloway, but the accompanying musical numbers are pretty sour.

p, Julius Hagen; d, Henry Edwards; w, H. Fowler Mear (based on the story by Anson Dyer); ph, William Luff.

Historical Drama   (PR:A   MPAA:NR)

VICE AND VIRTUE½   (1965, Fr./Ital.) 108m SNE Gaumont-Trianon-Ultra/MGM bw (LE VICE ET LA VERTU; IL VIZIO E LA VIRTU)

Annie Girardot (Juliette), Catherine Deneuve (Justine), Robert Hossein (SS Col. Schorndorf), Otto Edward [O.E.] Hasse (Gen. von Bamberg), Philippe Lemaaire (Hans), Serge Marquand (Ivan), Luciana Paluzzi (Helena), Valeria Ciangottini (Manuela), Georges Poujouly (Hoech), Michel de Re (Astrologer), Paul Geauff (SS Doctor), Jean-Pierre Honore (Jean), Howard Vernon (SS Man), Lena von Martens, Henri Virlogeux, Jean-Daniel Simon, Pierre Gualdi, Jean Levitte, Dorothee Blank, Lucien Guervil, Marianne Hardy, Juliette Hervieu, Michel Jourdan, Rudy Lenoir, Anne Libert, Monique Messine, Jose Quaglio, Jean-Michel Rouziere, Jacques Seiler, Henri Attal, Dominique Zardi.

Roger Vadim attempted to bring the Marquis de Sade up to date, and what better place to present his ideas than in the Nazi court of Paris during WW II. However, lacking the firm political commitment of his influence, Vadim's efforts look like another of his attempts to delve into sexual exploitation. Girardot and Deneuve play two sisters captured by the Nazis and forced to become sexual playthings for the commanding officers. Somehow Deneuve manages to repel the advances of the soldiers, thus earning the virtue part of the title, but her sister isn't so dedicated and becomes mistress to an SS officer. Part was filmed at the chateau of Fenelon and Treyne.

p&d, Roger Vadim; w, Vadim, Roger Vailland, Claude Choublier (based on the writings Justine and La Nouvelle Justine of Donatien Alphonse Francois [Marquis de] Sade); ph, Marcel Grignon (Franscope); m, Michel Magne; ed, Victoria Mercanton; md, Jean Gitton; set d, Jean Andre; cos, Marc Doelnitz; spec eff, Pierre Durin; makeup, Odette Berroyer.

Drama   (PR:O   MPAA:NR)

VICE DOLLS½   (1961, Fr.) 92m Vascos/William Mishkin bw (LES CLANDESTINES)

Philippe Lemaire (Pierre), Nicole Courcel (Veronique), Maria Mauban, Dominique Wilms, Andre Roanne, Alex D'Arcy, Michele Philippe, Paul Demange, Simone Berthier, Robert Chandeau, Yoko.

Lemaire plays a young man who attempts to get even with a bunch of crooks for causing his grandfather to commit suicide. Not knowing the elements he's up against, Lemaire is kept from the same fate as his grandfather only with the assistance of an innocent prostitute who takes a liking to the youth. Originally opened in Paris in 1954.

p, Raymond Logeart; d, Raoul Andre; w, Raymond Caillava; ph, Roger Fellous; ed, Gabriel Rongier; art d, Louis Le Barbenchon; cos, Henriette Ridard, Renee Rouzot; makeup, Louis Dor.

Crime/Drama   (PR:C   MPAA:NR)

VICE GIRLS, LTD.   (1964) 79m Artscope/Sam Lake bw

Linda Bennet (Christine), Brooks Clift (Nolan), Joann Brier (Jackie Miller), Richard DeHavilland (Merlin), F. Kende Hart (Mr. Lyle), Milton Carlyle (Ivanoff), Anna Stanovich (Gina), Norman Glind (Robert Havershire), Tony Wade (Tommy), Rick Fields (Billy), Don Craig (Thompson).

Dreary account of high-class call girls being preened by a tyrannical pimp whose goal is to get incriminating evidence against men in high places.

p, Jerry Gross, Amin Chaudhri; d, Chaudhri; w, Gross; ph&ed, Chaudri.

Crime   (PR:O   MPAA:NR)

VICE RACKET   (1937) 70m Al Dezel/State Rights bw

Martha Chapin (Mrs. Miller), Wheeler Oakman (Lucky Wilder), Bryant Washburn (Taylor), Jay Sheridan (Phillips), Vera Stedman (Molly), ed Keane (Attorney), Robert Frazer (Dr. Miller), Gaston Glass (Officer), Florence Dudley (Jean), Eddie Laughton (Nick).

This is one of those pictures that's so bad its almost funny, though that isn't its intention, as it makes a claim of showing the elements which lead a perfectly normal woman astray. The performances are forced, the dialog ridiculous, and the direction...well, the direction is missing.

p, Al Dezel;

Crime/Drama   (PR:A   MPAA:NR)

VICE RAID   (1959) 71m Imperial/UA bw

Mamie Van Doren (Carol Hudsone), Richard Coogan (Sgt. Whitey Brandon), Brad Dexter (Vince Malone), Frank Gerstle (Lt. Brennan), Barry Atwater (Phil Evans), Carol Nugent (Louise Hudson), Joseph Sullivan (Ben Dunton), Chris Alcaide (Eddie), Jeanne Bates (Marilyn), Julie Redings (Gertie), Shep Sanders (Mugsie), George Cisar (Marty Heffner), Nestor Paiva (Frank Burke), Jack Kenney (Leo Dempsey), Russ Bender (Lawyer Drucker), Tom McKee (Doctor), George Eldredge (Police Advocate), John Zaremba (City Prosecutor Marsh), Alex Goda (Officer Hennessy), John Hart (Tom), Lester Dorr (Man at Desk), Evans Davis (Policeman).

Another uneventful outing for Van Doren, this time as a prostitute called to New York from Detroit to help frame a cop, Coogan, whose good work has ben giving the mob a tough time. Coogan gets kicked off the force, but when Van Doren realizes the type of scum she's working for (one of them takes undue advantage of her young sister) she aids the ex-cop in pinning the goods on the mob. Van Doren showed more talent in this picture than usual, giving a fairly convincing portrayal of a call girl.

p, Robert E. Kent; d, Edward L. Cahn; w, Charles Ellis; ph, Stanley cortez; m, Paul Sawtell, Bert Shefter; ed, Grant Whytock; art d, Bill Glasgow.

Crime   (PR:C   MPAA:NR)

VICE SQUAD, THE½   (1931) 80m PAR bw

Paul Lukas (Stephen Lucarno), Kay Francis (Alice Morrison), Helen Johnson [Judith Wood] (Madeleine Hunt), William B. Davidson (Magistrate Morrison), Rockliffe Fellowes (Detective Sgt. Mather), Esther Howard (Josie), Monte Carter (Max Miller), G. Pat Collins (Pete), Phil Tead (Tony), Davison Clark (Doctor), Tom Wilson (Court Attendant), James Durkin (Another Magistrate), William Arnold (Prosecutor), Lynton Brent (Court Clerk).

An interesting twist is given to this copper picture, in that Lukas plays a man forced into turning informer for the police in order to save his neck and a woman's. This almost totally ruins the man, who had a standing of some prominence. Just when Lukas is about to get back on his feet, the cops have the gall to pound on his door again for evidence. He gives it in order to save the girl he has fallen in love with. The intent of this picture was to throw light on a police custom that was not totally legitimate and incriminating to innocent people, such as the Lukas character. Lukas eventually gets his chance to get even wih the cops who have taken to harassing him when called before an investigating court on the nature of the use of stool pigeons.

d, John Cromwell; w, Oliver H.P. Garrett; ph, Charles Lang.

Crime   (PR:A   MPAA:NR)

VICE SQUAD   (1953) 88m UA bw (GB: THE GIRL IN ROOM 17)

Edward G. Robinson (Capt. Barnaby), Paulette Goddard (Mona), K.T. Stevens (Ginny), Porter Hall (Jack Hartrampf, Undertaker), Adam Williams (Marty Kusalich), Edward Binns (Al Barkis), Jay Adler (Frankie Pierce), Joan Vohs (Vickie Webb), Lee Van Cleef (Pete Monte), Dan Riss (Lt. Imlay), Mary Ellen Kay (Carol Lawson), Barry Kelley (Hartrampf's Lawyer).

Robinson plays a tough Los Angeles cop investigating the murder of a fellow cop. The witness to the crime, Hall, refuses to talk for fear of problems which may arise in his personal life. So using the usual possibilities for leads, and keeping Hall around just in case, Robinson gets a tip on a bank robbery in the planning for that day. He sends a detachment to cover the bank, and when the robbery takes place, the two men responsible for the murder turn up, but they get away by taking a clerk hostage. Continued pursuit pins the two culprits in their hideout, and Robinson finally captures the killers he set out to grab earlier that morning. An attempt is made to give a realistic depiction of police life by having Robinson go through his job as if it were all in a day's work. Robinson is quite convincing at pulling this off, his performance being what takes this picture above the routine.

p, Jules V. Levy, Arthur Gardner; d, Arnold Laven; w, Lawrence Roman (based on the novel Harness Bull by Leslie T. White); ph, Joseph C. Biroc; m, Herschel Burke Gilbert; ed, Arthur H. Nadel; md, Gilbert; art d, Carroll Clark.

Crime   (PR:A   MPAA:NR)

VICE SQUAD½   (1982) 97m AE-Hemdale-Brent Walker c

Season Hubley (Princess), Gary Swanson (Tom Walsh), Joseph DiGiroloma (Kowalski), Wings Hauser (Ramrod), Pepe Serna (Pete Mendez), Beverly Todd (Louise Williams), Maurice Emmanuel (Edwards), Wayne Hackett (Christian Sorenson), Nina Blackwood (Ginger), Sudana Bobatoon (Dixie),

Lydia Lei *(Coco)*, Kelly Piper *(Blue Chip)*, Kristoffer Anders *(Sgt. Brooks)*, Joseph Baroncini *(Ted)*, Fred A. Berry *(Dorsey)*, Tom Brent *(Happy)*, Grand Bush *(Black Pimp)*, Marilyn Coleman *(Beatrice)*, Michael Ensign *(Chauffeur)*, Nate Esformes *(The John)*, Stacy Everly *(Junkie)*, clifford Frazier *(Mace)*, Lyla Graham *(Mrs. Cruikshank)*, Peter Harrell *(Dude)*, Jonathan Haze *(Dapper Man)*, Vincent J. Isaac *(Silky)*, Cyndi James-Reese *(Black Whore)*, Ben Kronen *(Elderly Man)*, Bob Laird, Doug Laird *(Motorcycle Officers)*, Robert Miano *(Sergeant)*, Richard Milholland *(Driver)*, Vahan Moosekian *(Doctor)*, Mark Ness *(Cab Driver)*, Stack Pierce *(Rosco)*, Barbara Pilavin *(Derelict)*, Donald Rawley *(Gregory)*, David Ross *(Officer)*, Stan Ross *(Drunk)*, Cheryl Smith *(White Whore)*, Hugo Stanger *(Old Man at Mansion)*, Arnold Turner *(Bass Player)*, Nicole Volkoff *(Lisa)*, Richard Wetzel *(Fast Eddie)*, Ark Wong *(Mr. Wong)*.

Stereotyped revamping of every cop-psycho picture ever made stars Hubley as the honest girl turned hooker in order to support her kid. She is forced into going under cover to help detective Swanson pin a murder on pimp Hauser. The pimp is convicted, but escapes, with Hubley as his next target. It's up to Swanson to make sure that Hubley does not meet with the same fate as her hooker friend. Filmed on the streets of Hollywood, the appropriate atmosphere is maintained, but it's one of dark alleys and seedy streets and only heightens the expected. Performances are little more than attempts to fulfill the caricatures provided, which they do convincingly, considering that such images have already been thrust down people's throats in numerable times.

p, Brian Frankish; d, Gary A. Sherman; w, Sandy Howard, Kenneth Peters, Robert Vincent O'Neil; ph, John Alcott (CFI Color); m, Keith Rubinstein; ed, Roy Watts; prod d, Lee Fischer; cos, Bernadette O'Brien.

Crime   **Cas.**   **(PR:O MPAA:R)**

VICE VERSA**½   (1948, Brit.) 111m TC/GFD bw

Roger Livesey *(Paul Bultitude)*, Kay Walsh *(Mrs. Verlayne)*, David Hutcheson *(Marmaduke Paradine)*, Anthony Newley *(Dick Bultitude)*, James Robertson Justice *(Dr. Grimstone)*, Petula Clark *(Dulcie Grimstone)*, Patricia Raine *(Alice, Maid)*, Joan Young *(Mrs. Grimstone)*, Vida Hope *(1st Nanny)*, Vi Kaley *(2nd Nanny)*, Ernest Jay *(Boaler, Butler)*, Kynaston Reeves *(Dr. Chawner)*, Harcourt Williams *(Judge)*, [William] Bill Shine *(Lord Gosport)*, Andrew Blackett *(Duke of Margate)*, John Willoughby *(Lord Sevenoaks)*, Stanley Van Beers *(Earl of Broadstairs)*, Robert Eddison *(Mr. Blinkhorn)*, James Hayter *(Bandmaster)*, Alfred [Alfie] Bass *(1st Urchin)*, Hugh Dempster *(Col. Ambrose)*, Peter Jones *(Chawner, Jr.)*, John Glyn-Jones *(Bindabun Doss)*, Frank Tickle *(Clegg)*, Schoolboys: James Kenney *(Coggs)*, Michael McKeag *(Jolland)*, Timothy [Tim] Bateson *(Coker)*, Malcolm Summers *(Kiffen)*.

This whimsical farce was Ustinov's second effort at the helm, in which a far-fetched ploy is used in order to create an identity switch. In this case father and son, Livesey and Newley respectively, pull the old switch-a-roo when a magic stone is placed in front of the father and he wishes he could be a boy again. This comes immediately after Livesey had been berating the lad for his poor showing at school. The two live in their new roles retaining the perceptions of their original selves. This makes for some interesting moments and gives Ustinov a chance to make a number of witty jabs, the English school system being the end of most of these. Despite its cleverness, and the moralistic statement about differing perceptions, the story slackens and seems a bit pointless after a while.

p, Peter Ustinov, George H. Brown; d&w, Ustinov (based on the novel by F. Anstey); ph, Jack Hildyard; m, Anthony Hopkins; ed, John D. Guthridge; md, Muir Mathieson; art d, Carmen Dillon; cos, Nadia Benois; spec eff, Henry Harris; makeup, Geoffrey Rodway.

Comedy   **(PR:A MPAA:NR)**

VICIOUS CIRCLE, THE*   (1948) 77m bw (GB: WOMAN IN BROWN; AKA: THE CIRCLE)

Conrad Nagel *(Karl Nemesch)*, Fritz UA Kortner *(Joseph Schwartz)*, Reinhold Schnuzel *(Baron Arady)*, Philip Van Zandt *(Balog)*, Lyle Talbot *(Miller)*, Eddie Leroy *(Samuel Schwartz)*, Edwin Maxwell *(Presiding Judge)*, Frank Ferguson *(Stark)*, David Alexander *(Fisher)*, Robert Cherry *(Marten)*, Nina Hansen *(Mrs. Schwartz)*, Sam Bernard *(Herman)*, Rita Gould *(Ethel Mihaly)*, Rudolph Cameron *(Dr. Darosch)*, Peter Brocco *(Dr. Sarwasch)*, Belle Mitchell *(Mrs. Horney)*, Ben Welden *(Constable)*, Michael Mark *(Mr. Horney)*, Nan Boardman, Christina Vale, Lester Dorr, Donald Harvey, Fred Fox, Peggy Wynne, Manfred Furst, Reuben Wendorf, Herman Waldman, Paul Baratoff.

Lifeless courtroom drama set in Hungary during 1882, centering on the trail of five Jews accused of murdering a man who, in actuality, committed suicide. In a stilted performance, Nagel plays the attorney who believes in the Jews' innocence despite the rampant prejudice being shown against the defendants. Prime among the bigots is the greedy landowner who accuses the men of the murder out of pure hatred and the desire to get them out of the way.

p&d, W. Lee Wilder; w, Heinz Herald, Guy Endore (based on the play "The Burning Bush" by Herald and Geza Herczeg); ph, George Robinson; ed, John F. Link; md, Paul Dessau; art d, Rudi Feld.

Drama   **(PR:A MPAA:NR)**

VICIOUS CIRCLE, THE, 1959   (SEE: CIRCLE, THE, 1959, Brit.)

VICIOUS YEARS, THE**   (1950) 81m Emerald/FC bw

Tommy Cook *(Mario)*, Sybil Merritt *(Dina)*, Eduard Franz *(Emilio)*, Gar Moore *(Luca)*, Anthony Ross *(Spezia)*, Marjorie Eaton *(Zia Lola)*, Rusty [Russ] Tamblyn *(Tino)*, Eve Miller *(Giulia)*, Lester Sharpe *(Matteo)*, John Doucette *(Giorgio)*, Crane Whitley *(Leopoldi)*, Paul Gardini *(Waiter)*, Carlo Tricoli *(Doctor)*, James Lombardo *(Schoolboy)*, Ida Smeraldo *(Innkeeper)*, Nick Thompson *(Fisherman)*, Myron Welton, Fred Gavlin.

Set in Italy shortly after the war had torn the normal structures of that country apart, Cook plays a young street urchin who uses his witnessing of a murder to gain entrance to the home of a once wealthy family. His manners and attitudes change as he feels the sense of warmth and belonging that comes from staying with the family. His way of getting there continues to lurk in the closet, as the son of the family, Moore, the person Cook saw commit the murder, still harbors schemes against the youth. Heavy on atmosphere which partially makes up for the tension lacking in the script.

p, Anson Bond; d, Robert Florey; w, N. Richard Nash; ph, Henry Freulich; m, Arthur Lange; ed, Fred Allen.

Crime/Drama   **(PR:A MPAA:NR)**

VICKI**½   (1953) 85m FOX bw

Jeanne Crain *(Jill)*, Jean Peters *(Vicki Lynn)*, Elliot Reid *(Steve Christopher)*, Richard Boone *(Lt. Ed Cornell)*, Casey Adams [Max Showalteh] *(Larry Evans, Columnist)*, Alex D'Arcy *(Robin Ray)*, Carl Betz *(McDonald)*, Aaron Spelling *(Harry Williams, Hotel Night Clerk)*, Billy Nelson *(Wino)*, John Dehner *(Chief)*, Richard Garland *(Reporter)*, Ramsay Ames *(Cafe Photographer)*, Frank Fenton *(Eric)*, Izetta Jewel *(Mrs. McVale)*, Helene Hayden *(Connie)*, Harry Seymour *(Bartender)*, Irene Seidner *(Cleaning Woman)*, Richard West *(Delivery Man)*, Chet Brandenburg *(Milkman)*, Bonnie Paul *(Girl)*, Ron Hargrave *(Boy)*, Kathryn Sheldon *(Hotel Clerk)*, Burt Mustin *(Bellboy)*, June Glory, Ethel Bryant *(Women)*, Charles Wagenheim *(Seedy Man)*, Al Hill *(Bum)*, Kenneth Gibson, Hershel Graham, R. C. McCracken, Brandon Beach, Heinie Conklin *(Men)*, Robert Adler, Harry Carter, Paul Kruger *(Policemen)*, Roy Engel, Frank Gerstle, Stuart Randall, Russ Conway, Parley Baer, Jack Gargan, Norman Stevens, Jack Mather, Jerome Sheldon, Mike Stark *(Detectives)*.

A tale of obsession and jealousy set around the investigation of model Peters' murder. Boone plays a detective who cancels his vacation in order to turn his energies to Peters' case, having been in love with the girl before she started to attract the attention of more influential men, particularly Reid, who acted as her agent. As it turns out Boone never got over the girl, his admiration growing into a strange obsession, evidenced in the film's final sequence where his apartment reveals an idolatry of photographs of the dead Peters. He could never keep from blaming the success of Peters on Reid, and therefore unduly harasses the press agent into admitting to the murder. This allows the real murderer, of whom Boone is aware, to go free, but permits Boone to attempt his vengeance. A stark, alienating world is created, with none of the characters allowing normal viewer identification, each being motivated by his or her selfish desire. A highly suspenseful effort that adds confusion to its unfolding via the use of flashback. A 1942 feature, I WAKE UP SCREAMING, was made from the same novel as VICKI.

p, Leonard Goldstein; d, Harry Horner; w, Dwight Taylor, Harold Greene, Leo Townsend (based on the novel *I Wake Up Screaming* by Steve Fisher); ph, Milton Krasner; m, Leigh Harline; ed, Dorothy Spencer; md, Lionel Newman; art d, Lyle Wheeler, Richard Irvine; set d, Claude Carpenter; cos, Charles LeMaire, Renie; spec eff, Ray Kellogg; m/l, "Vicki," Ken Darby, Max Showalter [Casey Adams]; makeup, Ben Nye.

Crime/Drama   **(PR:C MPAA:NR)**

VICTIM***   (1961, Brit.) 100m Parkway-Allied/Pathe bw

Dirk Bogarde *(Melville Farr)*, Sylvia Syms *(Laura Farr)*, Dennis Price *(Calloway)*, Anthony Nicholls *(Lord Fullbrook)*, Peter Copley *(Paul Mandrake)*, Norman Bird *(Harold Doe)*, Peter McEnery *(Jack Barrett)*, Donald Churchill *(Eddy Stone)*, Derren Nesbitt *(Sandy Youth)*, John Barrie *(Detective Inspector Harris)*, John Cairney *(Bridie)*, Alan MacNaughtan *(Scott Hankin)*, Nigel Stock *(Phip)*, Frank Pettitt *(Barman)*, Mavis Villiers *(Madge)*, Charles Lloyd Pack *(Henry)*, Hilton Edwards *(P.H.)*, David Evans *(Mickey)*, Margaret Diamond *(Miss Benham)*, Alan Howard *(Frank)*, Noel Howlett *(William Patterson)*, Dawn Beret *(Sylvie)*.

A powerful film that deals with homosexuality in England and the fact that most of the blackmail cases in that country were aimed against men who were trying to stay in the closet. In 1961, any homosexual acts were illegal and, while this is hardly an overt plea to change the laws, it did have some impact and a few years later homosexuality was no longer punishable by time in jail. Bogarde, in his best role after several terrible movies, is a lawyer with homosexual tendencies and skeletons in his closet. He is married now to Syms, who knows about his past dalliances, but accepts him nonetheless. Some years before, Bogarde had an affair with construction worker

McEnery but denies it. McEnery is now a wanted man, having stolen money from his building company. When he's caught by policeman Barrie, the truth emerges that McEnery doesn't have a brass farthing to his name. Since a great deal of money had been purloined, this sets Barrie wondering where it all went. McEnery needs a lawyer and tries to get Bogarde but the eminent queen's counsel avoids him and officer Barrie can't imagine the reason. McEnery hangs himself rather than answer any police questions and Bogarde realizes that the reason for the suicide was to protect his good name. Someone had been blackmailing McEnery and he paid him with his stolen money. Once he ran out of cash, he did himself in rather than involve Bogarde, whom he still loved. The blackmailers are extracting money from several people, none of whom falls into the stereotypical homosexual mold. They include Price, Pack, Stock, Bird, and Nicholls and their jobs are right out of the yellow pages as they are seen to be employed in various positions such as a barber, an actor, a salesman of used cars, a photographer, and from about every walk of life. Bogarde makes a vow to track down the bloodsuckers but the best way to get rid of blackmail is to get rid of the law that causes it. The villains are caught and Bogarde wants to prosecute them himself. (In England, there is a different type of legal system. One day, a barrister can be representing a defendant and the following day he can be speaking on behalf of the crown.) When Bogarde must reveal his own background, it's a shock to some but applauded by others. Syms will stick by his side with a stiff upper lip. This was a socially important film in that it depicted homosexuals in a light that had never been seen on a screen. For that alone, it was ranked controversial and refused the Seal from the MPAA. The acting was superb, the writing cogent, and the direction was on the money. Every role, no matter how small, had been intelligently cast. Whether a person agrees or disagrees with the concept that sex between people of the same gender is illegal, immoral, or against Biblical beliefs has nothing to do with the fine movie they made about it. The blackmailers were even well drawn, with one being a hoodlum tough, Nesbitt (to be expected), but the other seen as a prissy, frustrated old maid, Diamond. Dennis Price, as the homosexual actor being blackmailed, is a standout in his role. The team behind the film had all worked on the excllent SAPPHIRE. Dearden was the director, Relph the producer, and the script was by Green and McCormick. It is not a film for children and will enrage homophobes.

p, Michael Relph; d, Basil Dearden; w, Janet Green, John McCormick; ph, Otto Heller; m, Philip Green; ed, John Guthridge; art d, Alex Vetchinsky.

Crime Drama   **(PR:C-O   MPAA:NR)**

VICTIM FIVE   (SEE: CODE 7, VICTIM 4! 1964, Brit.)

VICTIMS OF PERSECUTION*½   (1933) 62m Bud Pollard bw

Mitchell Harris (*Judge Aaron Margolies*), Betty Hamilton (*Ruth Margolies*), Juda Bleich (*Judah Rosenbach*), Shirling Oliver (*Frederick Morgenstern*), John Willard (*John McLean Carter*), Bud Pollard (*George Carter*), Ann Lowenworth (*Sarah*), Dan Michaels (*Henry*), Charles Adler (*Doctor*), David Leonard (*Herschel*).

After being unfairly sentenced to death, a black man takes his case to a higher court presided over by Harris. This Jewish judge ignores all prejudices that have been stirred up against the case and gives the man a fair trial. Despite threats against him and his family (including a bombing) Harris listens only to his conscience and finds the man innocent. In the end his career is ruined but Harris knows he has done the right thing. What could have been an interesting drama dealing with some hard issues is unfortunately reduced to a naive melodrama thanks to unimaginative filmmaking. By 1933 the camera had achieved mobility but this looks like a filmed play, with actors remaining firmly in place most of the time. The cast is sincere, but sincerity doesn't always assure quality. This was an independent production and the first in a proposed series dealing with the problems of Jewish Americans.

p, William Goldberg; d, Bud Pollard; w, David Leonard; ph, Don Malkames.

Drama   **(PR:A MPAA:NR)**

VICTIMS OF THE BEYOND   (SEE: SUCKER MONEY, 1933)

VICTOR FRANKENSTEIN½**   (1975, Swed./Ireland) 92m
Aspect/Films Around The World c (AKA: TERROR OF FRANKEN-
STEIN)

Leon Vitali (*Victor Frankenstein*), Per Oscarsson (*The Monster*), Nicholas Clay (*Henry*), Stacey Dorning (*Elisabeth*), Jan Ohlsson (*William*), Henricsson (*Capt. Waldon*), Archie O'Sullivan (*Prof. Waldhem*), Olof Bergstrom (*Father*), Harry Brogan (*Blind Man*).

A faithful adaptation of Mary Shelley's novel which tells the familiar tale of the scientific genius, Vitali, who becomes obsessed with the thought of bringing the dead back to life. The hours of work are exhausting and take a physical toll on his body but Vitali finally makes his monster. Oscarsson (a superb Swedish actor who is best known for his role in HUNGER, 1968) doesn't look like the Karloff monster. He instead looks like a lifeless man who has recently been brought back from the dead. The monster desiring a bride of his own, tries to take Vitali's, but instead kills her. A chase then

begins with the monster leading Vitali through the bitter snows of the Arctic. On par with the made-for-TV film FRANKENSTEIN: THE TRUE STORY (1973), VICTOR FRANKENSTEIN successfully retells Shelley's story without gore or sensationalism, relying instead on characterizations and an authentic period atmosphere. (See FRANKENSTEIN series, Index.)

p&d, Calvin Floyd; w, Calvin Floyd, Yvonne Floyd (based on the novel by Mary Shelley); ph, Tony Forsberg, John Wilcox (Eastmancolor); m, Gerard Victory; ed, Susanna Linnman; cos, Kersti Gustafsson; makeup, Kerstin Elg.

Horror   **(PR:C   MPAA:NR)**

VICTOR/VICTORIA*   (1982) 133m MGM/UA c

Julie Andrews (*Victor/Victoria*), James Garner (*King*), Robert Preston (*Toddy*), Lesley Ann Warren (*Norma*), Alex Karras (*Squash*), John Rhys-Davies (*Cassell*), Graham Stark (*Waiter*), Peter Arne (*Labisse*), Sherloque Tanney (*Bovin*), Michael Robbins (*Hotel Manager*), Norman Chancer (*Sal*), David Gant (*Restaurant Manager*), Maria Charles (*Madame President*), Malcolm Jamieson (*Richard*), John Cassady (*Juke*), Mike Tezcan (*Clam*), Christopher Good (*Stage Manager*), Matyelock Gibbs (*Cassell's Receptionist*), Jay Benedict (*Guy Langois*), Olivier Pierre (*Langois' Companion*), Martin Rayner (*Concierge*), George Silver (*Fat Man with Eclair*), Joanna Dickens (*Large Lady in Restaurant*), Terence Skelton (*Deviant Husband*), Ina Skriver (*Simone Kallisto*), Stuart Turton (*Boy Friend to Actress*), Geoffrey Beevers (*Police Inspector*), Sam Williams, Simon Chandler (*Chorus Boys*), Neil Cunningham (*Nightclub Master of Ceremonies*), Vivienne Chandler (*Chambermaid*), Bill Monks (*LeClou*), Perry Davey (*Balancing Man*), Elizabeth Vaughan (*Opera Singer*), Paddy Ward (*Photographer*), Tim Stern (*Desk Clerk*).

Blake Edwards returned to top form with this sex farce-musical that doubled as a romantic comedy and was done in such a good nature that it only came in with a "PG" rating from the MPAA, a tribute to Edwards' taste. Andrews and Preston are a pair of down and out performers stranded in Paris with no prospects and hardly a *sou* in their purses. They are both hungry and, in an hysterical scene, manage to eat well in a Paris cafe, then pull the old "Waiter, there's a fly in my soup" routine by slipping a large roach in the food and having the restaurant pick up the tab. Preston is an aging homosexual performer who has fallen on hard times and Andrews is a British singer who can't find employment until Preston devises a bold plan. He models Andrews as a singer-dancer who is supposed to be a man dressing up as a woman. She is an immediate hit at one of the gay clubs. Enter Garner, a gangster from Chicago traveling with his blowsy girl friend, Warren, and his bodyguard, Karras. Garner finds himself attracted to Andrews when he sees her perform and this causes sexual confusion on his part. Garner can't understand his feelings but he thinks he'd better get ditsy Warren out of the way so he sends her back to Illinois. (Warren is sensational and gives new meaning to the stereotypical "dumb blonde" role.) Karras stays close to Garner and watches amazedly as his *macho* boss seems to be altering his yen for beautiful women and turning toward men. This pays off hysterically when Karras is suddenly revealed at the end to be a homosexual who has been masquerading in heterosexual clothing. Karras keeps bailing out Garner as his boss gets into one scrape after another. Preston has a affair with a young man but manages to keep that side of his life under wraps as he continues to advise Andrews in her act. Eventually, Garner learns that Andrews is a woman (phew!) and that his desires were, after all, normal. The two of them have a romance but it has to be kept well hidden or her entire career will be shattered by the revelation that the *he* masquerading as a *she* is really a *she* after all. At the conclusion, Garner and Andrews do wind up together (no surprise to anyone) but the journey has been a hundred laughs. Although a complex story, Edwards makes it easy to watch and simple to understand. It was shot in England and 1934 Paris was totally recreated on a set designed by Rodger Maus. The illusion is pulled off quite well and other than some anachronistic dialog that sounds as though it's strictly from the 1980s, the feeling of the period is firmly entrenched. Andrews gave her best performance since THE SOUND OF MUSIC under her husband's direction. Although some of the gags fall slightly flat, there is enough in this movie to make the grimmest face smile and it made nothing but money at the box office. VICTOR/VICTORIA and GREASE proved that a quality musical can still make it in and transcend the age barrier that had kids going to see teenage movies and adults marching in droves to view KRAMER VS. KRAMER. The score, by Henry Mancini and Leslie Bricusse, was successfully interpolated because most of the numbers were tunes sung either by Andrews or Preston. They include "Crazy World," "The Shady Dame from Seville," "Le Jazz Hot" (sung by Andrews), "You and Me" (Andrews, Preston), "Gay Paree" (Preston), "Chicago, Illinois" (Warren), "Alone in Paris," "Kings Can," "Cat and Mouse."

p, Blake Edwards, Tony Adams; d&w, Edwards (based on the film VICTOR UND VIKTORIA by Rheinhold Schuenzel, Hans Hoemburg); ph, Dick Bush (Panavision, Metrocolor); m, Henry Mancini; ed, Ralph E. Winters; prod d, Rodger Maus; art d, Tim Hutchinson, William Craig Smith; set d, Harry Cordwell; cos, Patricia Norris; ch, Paddy Stone; m/l, Mancini, Leslie Bricusse.

Comedy   **Cas.**   **(PR:O   MPAA:PG)**

VICTORIA THE GREAT** (1937, Brit.) 110m Imperator/RKO bw-c

Anna Neagle (Queen Victoria), Anton Walbrook (Prince Albert), Walter Rilla (Prince Ernest), Mary Morris (Duchess of Kent), H.B. Warner (Lord Melbourne), Grete Wegener (Baroness Lehzen), C.V. France (Archbishop of Canterbury), James Dale (Duke of Wellington), Charles Carson (Sir Robert Peel), Hubert Harben (Lord Conyngham), Felix Aylmer (Lord Palmerston), Arthur Young (Mr. Gladstone), Derrick de Marnek (Young Disraeli), Hugh Miller (Old Disraeli), Percy Parsons (Abraham Lincoln), Lewis Casson (Archbishop of Canterbury, Jubilee), Henry Hallatt (Joseph Chamberlain), Gordon McLeod (John Brown), Wyndham Goldie (Cecil Rhodes), Tom Hesslewood (Sir Francis Grant), Miles Malleson (Physician), Paul Leyssac (Baron Stockmar), Joan Young (Miss Pitt), Frank Birch (Sir Charles Dilke), William Dewhurst (John Bright), Ivor Barnard (Assassin), Moore Marriott, Paul von Henreid 'Paul Henreid', Albert Lieven.

This beautiful and elaborate film gives a humanistic portrait of England's long-reigning monarch, concentrating initially on the first years of her reign, and finishing with the Diamond Jubilee celebration of Victoria's rule. Neagle, in an excellent performance, assumes the throne at the tender age of 18. The film explores Victoria's early days, as she is courted by and then married to Prince Albert (Walbrook). An attempt is made on Neagle's life, but Walbrook risks his own life by placing himself between the would-be assassin and Neagle. The story then concentrates on Neagle and Walbrook's domestic life, with such famous names as Disraeli, Wellington, and Lincoln making peripheral appearances. VICTORIA THE GREAT closes with the Diamond Jubilee, switching, for this sequence, from black and white to a brilliant Technicolor. Fictionalizing the lives of the royal family has long been a touchy issue in England, but producer-director Wilcox treats his subject with respect, never dipping into treacly sentiment. Neagle (who would later marry Wilcox) takes her character from young girl to octogenarian with total believability. Her performance is a marvel to watch: an actress transcends her craft and becomes the character. This film, released 100 years after Victoria began her reign, was enormously popular in England and prompted Wilcox, Neagle, and Walbrook to make a sequel, SIXTY GLORIOUS YEARS (1938), an all-color production that concentrated more on the political elements missing in VICTORIA THE GREAT. In 1942, Wilcox cut the first portion of this film into the latter half of SIXTY GLORIOUS YEARS to create a single feature, simply titled QUEEN VICTORIA. Wilcox began production on VICTORIA THE GREAT after King Edward VIII (who later abdicated to marry American divorcee Wallis Warfield Simpson) personally requested that the filmmaker produce a feature about his famed relation. It took an amazingly short five weeks to film, and attention to period detail was immaculate. Neagle's costumes were copied from Victoria's actual dresses kept at the British Museum. Released in America through RKO, VICTORIA THE GREAT was popular in its initial run at Radio City Music Hall, where it turned a handsome profit, but did not fare as well in smaller cities. Both Neagle and Wilcox made a tour of the U.S. to promote the film, though this was not as successful as hoped. However, Wilcox's association with RKO did result in a lucrative agreement with RKO under which the independent producer was to turn out a number of feature pictures under the American company's banner, an arrangement which helped reduce the burden of the United Kingdom's restrictive quotas on domestic screenings of imported films. In a small role, note Paul Henreid in his first British film, using his real name.

p&d, Herbert Wilcox; w, Miles Malleson, Charles de Grandcourt (based on the play "Victoria Regina" by Laurence Housman); ph, Frederick A. Young (part Technicolor); m, Anthony Collins.

Historical Drama   (PR:A MPAA:NR)

VICTORS, THE*½** (1963) 175m Highroad-Open Road/COL bw

Vincent Edwards (Baker), Albert Finney (Russian Soldier), George Hamilton (Cpl. Trower), Melina Mercouri (Magda), Jeanne Moreau (Frenchwoman), George Peppard (Cpl. Chase), Maurice Ronet (French Lt. Cohn), Rosanna Schiaffino (Maria), Romy Schneider (Regine), Elke Sommer (Helga), Eli Wallach (Sgt. Craig), Michael Callan (Eldridge), Peter Fonda (Weaver), Jim Mitchum (Grogan), Senta Berger (Trudi), Joel Flateau (Jean-Pierre), Albert Lieven (Herr Metzger), Mervyn Johns (Dennis), Tutte Lemkow (Sikh Soldier), Peter Vaughan (Policeman), George Roubicek, George Mikell (Russian Sentries), Alf Kjellin (Priest), Alan Barnes (Tom), John Rogers (Young British Soldier), Marianne Deeming (Frau Metzger), Patrick Jordan (Tank Sergeant), Elizabeth Ercy (Young French Girl), Milo Nappi (Concentration Camp Prisoner), Malya Nappi (Barmaid), Vanda Godsell (Nurse), Bee Duffell (Joan), James Chase (Condemned Soldier), Riggs O'Hara, Larry Caringi, Ian Hughes, Charles De Temple, Al Waxman, Tom Busby, Robert Nichols, Graydon Gould, Anthony McBride (The Squad), Colin Maitland, Tony Wallace, John Crawford, Russ Titus, Sean Kelly, Mickey Knox, Peter Arne, Veite Bethke.

Carl Foreman may have set out to make the antiwar film to end all antiwar films, but with a disjointed script, awful performances by most of the cast, and squabbles over the cutting between the director and the producers, what emerged was a sprawling, ugly mess that occasionally succeeded in packing a punch. The film follows the exploits of one infantry squad from Sicily through the invasion of France and into Germany and on to the occupation at WW II's end. Each scene stands alone, focusing on a different character and incident, while other characters take on lesser importance or perhaps disappear altogether, never to be explained. Between each vignette is a scene of home front silliness culled from newsreels. One man sleeps with an Italian woman whose soldier husband is missing. Peppard falls in love with a beautiful woman who tries to get him to desert to help in her black market operations. Hamilton falls in love with a woman whom he later discovers is a prostitute. A race riot breaks out between white and black troops. A soldier adopts a dog that other soldiers shoot for target practice when it tries to follow their truck when the men ship out. Sergeant Wallach is wounded and sent to the hospital and when Peppard comes to visit him he finds most of his face has been blown off. The men are sent to witness an execution on a snowy night (closely based on the Eddie Slovik execution) while the soundtrack has Frank Sinatra crooning "Have Yourself a Merry Little Christmas." At film's end Hamilton is living in Berlin with a young woman whose sister has become the mistress of a Russian officer. When his girl friend leaves him to take up with a Russian, Hamilton stumbles home drunk. He encounters a similarly drunken Russian (Finney) and the two begin shouting. Each unable to understand the other, they pull knives and kill each other. The film tries to re-create the actual feel of the war, in which one never is sure what has happened to a lot of the guys around him. Men come and go, are wounded, killed, captured, vanish. The first 20 minutes of the film center on Edwards. But when the film returns after a newsreel segue, he is gone and is never mentioned again. The film as cut by Foreman failed to find its audience quickly and the producers immediately pulled it out of circulation and recut to emphasize the action elements. But this isn't the only flaw. The cast is as untalented a collection of actors as ever were assembled for a "serious" movie. Peppard and Hamilton have never given a decent performance. The international starlets who perform the women's roles are too glamorous to be the battle-scarred trollops they're mostly portrayed as. Only Wallach comes out of this film favorably, and the scene where Peppard, not knowing the magnitude of the old sarge's wounds, goes to visit him with a bottle of whiskey, only to find a grotesque remainder of a face shouting at him to get the hell out, is unforgettable. Other scenes, though, come off without impact and leave one appalled at the filmmakers for showing them to us: Mitchum shooting the dog as it follows the truck...a small French boy who propositions the men for homosexual relations, telling them, "The Germans were brave, and they liked me"...the sheer bad taste of playing Christmas carols over a firing squad sequence. All of it becomes numbing over the film's nearly three-hour running time. Still, it is memorable but the memories, like memories of war, aren't pleasant. Songs include: "March of the Victors," "Sweet Talk," "No Other Man" (Sol Kaplan, Freddy Douglass), "Theme from the Victors (My Special Dream)" (Kaplan, Douglass, Howard Greenfield), "Does Goodnight Have to Mean Goodbye?" (Jack Keller, Gerry Goffin, Greenfield), "Have Yourself a Merry Little Christmas" (Ralph Blanc, Hugh Martin, sung by Frank Sinatra).

p,d&w, Carl Foreman (based on the book The Human Kind by Alexander Baron); ph, Christopher Challis (Panavision); m, Sol Kaplan; ed, Alan Osbiston; prod d, Geoffrey Drake; art d, Maurice Fowler; cos, Olga Lehmann; spec eff, Cliff Richardson, Wally Veevers; makeup, Ernest Gasser; tech adv, Capt. Nils Runelundquist

War   (PR:O MPAA:NR)

VICTORY** (1940) 78m PAR bw

Fredric March (Hendrik Heyst), Betty Field (Alma), Cedric Hardwicke (Mr. Jones, Narrator), Jerome Cowan (Ricardo), Sig Rumann (Mr. Schomberg), Margaret Wycherly (Mrs. Schomberg), Fritz Feld (Makanoff), Lionel Royce (Pedro), Rafaela Ottiano (Mme. Makanoff), Chester Gan (Wang).

Translating the dark, moody prose of Joseph Conrad to the screen has never been easy. In this case, it was almost impossible. In 1919, Maurice Tourneur tried Conrad's story as a silent, then William Wellman attempted it again in 1932 as DANGEROUS PARADISE but it remains too elusive. March is a hermit-type who has taken refuge on a small island in the Dutch East Indies. His father had always told him that his fellow man could not be trusted and March has discovered that Father Knew Best so he's entrenched himself far from anywhere. March visits a neighboring island and meets Field, a musician who is marooned. She is fending off the advances of the hotel keeper and March takes her with him to his island, where, legend has it, he has buried a fortune in money. It isn't long before March falls in love with Field but he will not allow himself to go too far so he intends sending her back to civilization on the next boat out. Meanwhile, Hardwicke, his wolfish aide, Cowan, and near-idiot Royce mean to steal March's money. The hotel man has given them some malarkey about a fortune and wants to wreak revenge for March having stolen Field from him. So the murderous trio goes to March's island with every intention of slitting his throat and taking the cache. The remainder of the picture is a cat-and-mice game as March manages to fend them off and protect himself and Field. In the end, March finally realizes that he has to stop being a recluse and come out into the world again. The philosophical point made is that if one is to grow and mature, one must accept that there is evil in the world, combat it, and then take advantage of the good that is also there (e.g. Field). March has been an avowed coward who has avoided any sort of physical confrontation, but when he is forced to take steps he understands that his fear was self-induced. Hardwicke's performance as the tough, mean leader of the pack was a standout and Cowan showed that he could play roles other than harassed lawyers or ineffective police officers. In an early cut of the movie, Alan Ladd was alleged to have played March as a teenager but it's never been seen. VICTORY gets tedious at times and no amount of cinematic technique can conjure up the steamy tropics Conrad wrote about. The story was changed to fit the supposed tastes of the public and Conradicals will not be pleased with the alterations. Many of the Polish-Ukrainian author's works have been made into movies, including LORD JIM (1926, 1965), SABOTAGE (1937), AN OUTCAST OF THE ISLANDS (1952), LAUGHING ANNE (1953), and even APOCALYPSE NOW owes a debt to his *Heart of Darkness.*

p, Anthony Veiller; d, John Cromwell; w, John L. Balderston (based on the novel by Joseph Conrad); ph, Leo Tover; m, Frederick Hollander; ed, William Shea; art d, Hans Dreier, Robert Usher.

Adventure/Drama   **(PR:A-C   MPAA:NR)**

VICTORY   (1981) 117m Victory-Lorimar/PAR c (GB: ESCAPE TO VICTORY)

Sylvester Stallone *(Robert Hatch),* Michael Caine *(John Colby),* Pele *(Luis Fernandez),* Bobby Moore *(Terry Brady),* Osvaldo Ardiles *(Carlos Rey),* Paul Van Himst *(Michel Fileu),* Kazimierz Deyna *(Paul Wolchek),* Hallvar Thorensen *(Gunnar Hilsson),* Mike Summerbee *(Sid Harmor),* Co Prins *(Pieter Van Beck),* Russell Osman *(Doug Clure),* John Wark *(Arthur Hayes),* Soren Linsted *(Erik Borge),* Kevin O'Calloghan *(Tony Lewis),* Max Von Sydow *(Maj. Karl Von Steiner),* Gary Waldhorn *(Coach Mueller),* George Mikell *(Kommandant),* Laurie Sivell *(Goalie),* Arthur Brauss *(Lutz),* Robin Turner *(Player),* Michael Wolf *(Lang),* Jurgen Andersen *(Propaganda Civilian),* David Shawyer *(Strauss),* Werner Roth *(Team Captain Baumann),* Amidou *(Andre),* Benoit Ferreux *(Jean Paul),* Jean Francois Stevenin *(Claude),* Jack Lenoir *(Georges),* Folton Gera *(Viktor),* Carole Laure *(Renee),* Tim Pigott-Smith *(Rose),* Julian Curry *(Shurlock),* Clive Merrison *(The Forger),* Maurice Roeves *(Pyrie),* Michael Cochrane *(Farrell),* Jack Kendrick *(Williams),* Daniel Massey *(Col. Waldron),* Anton Diffring *(Chief Commentator),* Gunter Wolbert *(German),* Capacci Eolo *(Italian),* Michel Drhey *(French).*

An ordinary "prisoner-of-war" film with a sports angle that was mainly notable for some of the amazing soccer plays featuring legend Pele and other international players. Soccer still had not caught on in the U.S. with the same kind of fervor as elsewhere so the film did far better in Europe and South America than it did in the 50 states. During WW II, Von Sydow runs a POW camp. He is a former player for Germany and arranges a game between the prisoners and his troops to build morale. (The same thing was seen in THE LONGEST YARD about crooks and guards playing football in a jail). The prisoners under Von Sydow's Teutonic thumb include Stallone, Pele, and Caine, as a British army officer who had once been a professional for West Ham and in international matches for England. When Von Sydow's chiefs hear about the proposed game, they decide to expand matters and take advantage of worldwide publicity by staging an "All-Star" match between the German national team and captured soccer stars from all over the world. The venue is changed to Paris where the huge stadium in the occupied city will be filled with supporters of the Nazis. In a twist that was later used in STIR CRAZY, the Allied High Command thinks that this might be the perfect place to break the prisoners out of their captivity. With the aid of the French Resistance, a plan is calculated and all of the players are aware. The day of the game dawns and the plan is to be put into action. However, since the game is being broadcast all around the world, winning the game means more to the players than getting away so they delay their escape until after they have trounced the Germans in the match. Lots of contrivances mar the plot. In one, Stallone, who has fled the prison to get in touch with the French Resistance, allows himself to be taken back to jail just so he can lead his team. The second is, of course, the willingness of the entire team to play the game out before they even think about fleeing. Stallone is obviously not a runner so he is given the job of goalie but many of the other parts are played by revered soccer men, such as Bobby Moore (England), Osvaldo Ardiles (Argentina), and Paul Van Himst (Belgium). The entire movie was shot in Hungary, where it was more of a hit than it was in the U.S., and in other countries where soccer doesn't rank high on the sports list. Conti's music is stirring enough, just as he helped Stallone's ROCKY with his theme, but music can't overcome the general lack of interest. Produced in association with Tom Stern, Andy Vajna and Mario Kassar, it was not one of director Huston's finest hours. Hard-core Stallone fans seem to only like him when he is bare-chested in the jungle or the ring and with either boxing gloves on his fists or an automatic rifle in his hands.

p, Freddie Fields; d, John Huston; w, Evan Jones, Yabo Yablonsky (based on a story by Yablonsky, Djordje Milicevic, Jeff Maguire); ph, Gerry Fisher (Panavision, Metrocolor); m, Bill Conti; ed, Roberto Silvi; prod d, J. Dennis Washington; cos, Tom Bronson; soccer plays, Pele.

War/Sports Drama   **Cas.**   **(PR:A-C   MPAA:PG)**

VIDEO MADNESS   (SEE: JOYSTICKS, 1983)

VIDEODROME   (1983, Can.) 88m Filmplan International/UNIV c

James Woods *(Max Renn),* Sonja Smits *(Bianca O'Blivion),* Deborah Harry *(Nicki Brand),* Peter Dvorsky *(Harlan),* Les Carlson *(Barry Convex),* Jack Creley *(Prof. Brian O'Blivion),* Lynne Gorman *(Masha),* Julie Khaner *(Briley),* Reiner Schwarz *(Moses),* David Bolt *(Rafe),* Lally Cadeau *(Rena*

King), Sam Malkin *(Bum),* Bob Church *(Newscaster),* Jayne Eastwood *(Caller),* Franciszka Hedland *(Bellydancer),* Harvey Chao, David Tsubouchi *(Salesmen),* Henry Gomez *(Brolley),* Kay Hawtrey *(Matron).*

Woods stars as an ambitious cable TV programmer who, in his off hours, is a closet voyeur of sex and violence. Looking for something new, something "sensational" for his cable station, Woods stumbles across a show called "Videodrome" while pirating signals from satellite dishes. The show seems to depict the actual torture and murder of a different victim every night. Fascinated (and excited) by the program, Woods tries to find out where the show comes from and during the investigation he becomes deeply embroiled in a bizarre, utterly confusing and nonsensical fusion of television, politics, and mind-control which seems to herald some sort of "New Order" for society. Once again Canadian director Cronenberg comes up with a fairly interesting concept for a horror film and then drives it headlong into the ground with his penchant for impenetrable plot lines and ludicrous sequences that look as if they belong in some other movie. VIDEODROME very well may be the most incomprehensible mainstream film ever made. A small army of critics champions this film as a progressive, unique, compulsively engrossing minor masterpiece, but they must perform analytical gymnastics to justify this position. While some of the ideas fitfully presented are potentially interesting and important, Cronenberg suddenly lets his taste for bizarre visual images take over and we are bombarded with such delights as open stomach cavities that people stick their hands into, throbbing television sets, and humans who crack open and spew forth all manner of flesh, blood, and multi-colored goo. While some of these images are undeniably powerful (the throbbing, *living* TV set is amazing), the film wallows in disconnected episodes of special effects trickery and never really gets to the point of all this. Therefore, VIDEODROME winds up as just another cold, empty, gross, and frustrating exercise in concept and style from Cronenberg.

p, Claude Heroux; d&w, David Cronenberg; ph, Mark Irwin; m, Howard Shore; ed, Ronald Sanders; prod d, Carol Spier; art d, Nick Kosonic; cos, Delphine White; spec eff, Frank Carere, Michael Lennick; ch, Kirsteen Etherington; makeup Rick Baker.

Horror   **Cas.**   **(PR:O   MPAA:R)**

VIENNA, CITY OF SONGS   (1931, Ger.) 82m Atlas bw (WIEN, DU STADT DER LIEDER; CITY OF SONGS)

Charlotte Ander *(Steffi),* Sigi Hofer *(Steffi's Father),* Paul Morgan *(Tailor),* Igo Sym *(Pepi),* Max Ehrlich *(Old Printer),* Dora Hrach, Max Hamsen, Irene Ambrus, Grete Natzler, Sigefried [Sig] Arno, Gusti Stark-Gstettenbauer, Paul Graetz.

There's an old joke about the world's thinnest books. One of them is supposed to be "One Thousand Years Of German Humor!" Never was that better illustrated than in this film. Director Richard Oswald has a hand like a foot as he attempts to place six comedians in search of a story. This is one of Germany's earliest sound films and the inexperience is evident as the recording ranges from shrill to mushy. It is especially poor in the singing sequences of Max Hamsen. The plot, even if you understand the Berlin dialect of German, is thin at best, and the overplaying of all the actors, except for Ehrlich, is strictly from coernsville.

p&d, Richard Oswald; w, Ernst Neubeck; m, Hans May.

Comedy   **(PR:A   MPAA:NR)**

VIENNA WALTZES   (1961, Aust.) 90m Vindobona Filmgesellschaft-Cordial Film/H offberg Productions bw (WIEN TANZT)

Anton Walbrook *(Johann Strauss),* Marthe Harell *(Millie Trampusch),* Lilly Stepanek *(Anna Strauss),* Fritz Imhoff *(Oberstrasser),* Eva Leiter *(Frau Reisner),* Lotte Lang, Eric Frey, P. Czeike, Fritz Berger, H. Meixner, A. Truby, Karl Ehmann, F. Czepa.

The life and times of Johann Strauss the elder and his final deference to his son, Johann, Jr. English actor Walbrook returned to his native Vienna to play the famed waltz king who, while leading a band in a restaurant, develops a new beat. With the help of his milliner mistress Harell, who invents some dance steps to go with his compositions, Walbrook becomes the toast of Vienna. Newly wealthy, he deserts wife Stepanek and his three children and tours Europe with Harell. On his return years later, he discovers that his now-grown son, Johann, Jr., has achieved prominence as a composer, which irritates the irascible old man. A deathbed reconciliation is effected after Walbrook hears his boy's music. Punctuated with musical compositions of the two Strausses. Released in Europe in 1951.

p, Karl Ehrlich; d, Emile Edwin Reinert; w, Benno Vigny, Jacques Companeez (based on a story by Hans Gustl Kernamyr); ph, Gunther Anders; set d, Otto Niedermoser.

Biography/Drama   **(PR:A   MPAA:NR)**

VIENNESE NIGHTS   (1930) 107m WB c

Alexander Gray *(Otto),* Vivienne Segal *(Elsa),* Jean Hersholt *(Hochter),* Walter Pidgeon *(Franz),* Louise Fazenda *(Gretl),* Alice Day *(Barbara),* Bert Roach *(Gus),* June Purcell *(Mary),* Milton Douglas *(Bill Jones),* Lothar

Mayring (Baron), Bela Lugosi (Ambassador).

The color photography and a fine score composed by Hammerstein and Romberg were among the highlights of this early musical. Yarn concerns the thwarted love affair between a young composer, Gray, and Segal, the woman he is destined to marry, but doesn't because of a jealous misunderstanding. She goes on to marry the wealthy Pidgeon, while he gets involved in his own unhappy marriage to a woman who doesn't understand his passion for music. After a period of 40 years, when Gray is long dead and Segal is listening to the symphony her former lover composed, their grandchildren do eventually marry. Story is a bit heavy on the sentiment, but stacks up for some decent entertainment. Worthwhile if only for the chance to listen to one-time crooner Pidgeon's reedy, nasal baritone singing voice, a remarkable revelation. Unlike most other Romberg and Hammerstein works, this one was especially written for the screen, rather than being a stage adaptation. Songs include: "I Bring a Love Song," "I'm Lonely," "You Will Remember Vienna," "Here We Are," "Regimental March," "Yes, Yes, Yes," "Goodbye My Love," and "Viennese Nights."

d, Alan Crosland; w, Oscar Hammerstein II, Sigmund Romberg; ph, James Van Trees (Two-color Technicolor); m, Romberg; ed, Hal McLaren; md, Louis Silvers; ch, Jack Haskell; m/l, Romberg, Hammerstein.

Muscial   **(PR:A MPAA:NR)**

VIEW FROM POMPEY'S HEAD, THE½**
(1955) 97m FOX c (GB: SECRET INTERLUDE)

Richard Egan (Anson Page), Dana Wynter (Dinah Higgins), Cameron Mitchell (Mickey Higgins), Sidney Blackmer (Garvin Wales), Marjorie Rambeau (Lucy Wales), Dorothy Patrick Davis (Meg), Rosemarie Bowe (Kit), Jerry Paris (Ian Garrick), Ruby Goodwin (Esther), Pamela Stufflebeam (Julia), Evelyn Rudie (Cecily), Howard Wendell (Duncan), Dayton Lummis (Barlowe), Bess Flowers (Miss Mabry), Cheryl Calloway (Debbie), Charles Herbert (Pat), Florence Mitchell (Garrick's Secretary), De Forest Kelley (Hotel Clerk), Robert Johnson (Bellhop), Anna Mabry (Maid), Wilma Jacobs (Betty Jo-Ann), Bill Walker (Pullman Porter), Frances Driver (Servant), Jack Mather (Policeman), Charles Watts (Police Sergeant), Wade Duman (Groom), Tom Wilson (Trainman).

Egan, is a New York lawyer who returns to his southern hometown of Pompey's Head when Rambeau requests his services to investigate her husband, Blackmer, an aging author who has gone blind. Some of his royalty checks are missing and Rambeau suspects Blackmer of cashing them without his knowledge. Egan's trip turns nostalgic when he sees Wynter, his childhood sweetheart. Though she is now married to Mitchell, a man rich and gross, a slob, Wynter feels the old attraction heat up. Eventually, Egan discovers what Blackmer has been doing with the money. His mother was a black woman, the mistress of Blackmer's father. Rather than risk scandal, Blackmer has been quietly paying her off in return for her silence. Egan finally cools the romance with Wynter, knowing the affair will only lead to trouble. Though a potentially shocking drama, this is an unusually subdued film. The plot unfolds quietly, lacking the inherent passion that constantly lurks behind events. The racial climate of the American South was tense during the 1950s and undoubtedly this held some influence over the black-white controversy in the story. There's also a missing spark between Egan and Wynter within their romance. The two actors play well off of one another, their accents and mannerisms accurate, showing the characteristics of southerners with a realistic feeling. Dunne's direction, though never probing enough, handles the job adequately. The drama is presented with intelligence and style, capturing the color of the South with an effective use of CinemaScope. There have been several dramas portraying the people and passion of the American South (most notably in the work of Tennessee Williams) and this only gives a glimpse at something which runs much deeper.

p,d&w, Phillip Dunne (based on a novel by Hamilton Basso); ph, Joe MacDonald (CinemaScope, DeLuxe Color); m, Elmer Bernstein; ed, Robert Simpson; md, Lionel Newman; art d, Lyle Wheeler, Leland Fuller; set d, Walter M. Scott, Paul S. Fox.

Drama   **(PR:C-O MPAA:NR)**

VIEW FROM THE BRIDGE, A½   (1962, Fr./Ital.) 110m
Transcontinental-Produzione Intercontinentali/CD bw

Raf Vallone (Eddie Carbone), Jean Sorel (Rodolpho), Maureen Stapleton (Beatrice Carbone), Carol Lawrence (Catherine), Raymond Pellegrin (Marco), Morris Carnovsky (Mr. Alfieri), Harvey Lembeck (Mike), Mickey Knox (Louis), Vincent Gardenia (Lipari), Frank Campanella (Longshoreman).

Arthur Miller's powerful drama gets a somewhat shabby production here by a consortium of Italian and French filmmakers. Although written about Brooklyn (location shots were done there), the interiors were all shot in Paris with a cast of French, Italian, and U.S. actors. Vallone, who played the role in the Parisian version of the play, is an Italian-American longshoreman who has come from Sicily to earn his living. Vallone is married to Stapleton (why she doesn't have the same thick Italian accent is never explained) and the two of them have raised Lawrence, their niece, since she was a baby. There has been a great deal of talk about "submarines" (which is the term for the illegal immigrants), and when two of them arrive at the Red Hook

home of Vallone and Stapleton, problems begin. Pellegrin and Sorel are the "subs" and Vallone resents the obvious attraction Lawrence and Sorel have for each other. He questions Sorel's intentions and wonders if the man is talking about marriage to Lawrence out of real love or because a union with her will guarantee his U.S. citizenship. All of this is to hide his own attraction for Lawrence which borders on incestuous. Lawrence refuses to be put off by Vallone's entreaties and so Vallone does a desperate thing by saying that Sorel is a homosexual. To prove his point, he kisses Sorel on the lips (and now we begin to wonder whether or not Vallone is bisexual as well as incestuous). Instead of turning Lawrence away from Sorel, she moves even closer to the young man and they start talking seriously about marriage. Vallone can't bear the thought of losing Lawrence so he informs on Sorel and Pellegrin to the immigration office and the young men are arrested and taken away, but not before Pellegrin spits in Vallone's face and brands him as a fink. It all seems bleak until a local attorney springs Sorel out of jail because he is about to marry Lawrence. Pellegrin has no such luck and is scheduled to be shipped back to Italy. Pellegrin is released on bail and goes immediately to the home of Vallone where the most dramatic scene of the film takes place. The angry deportee forces Vallone to his knees and, while friends and family watch, makes the man recant all he's done. Not satisfied with that, Pellegrin slays Vallone by putting a huge longshoreman's hook into the man's chest. Although ostensibly an Italian story, it could have been any ethnic background which provided the stage for the drama. The lack of money spent on the film resulted in some very long and stagy takes. Vallone, Sorel, and Pellegrin are superb but the rest of the cast appears to be from another play. Stapleton is, at best, bland, with none of the fire that an Anna Magnani might have brought to the role. Pellegrin's character is, perhaps, the most interesting in that he is seen as a married man who has left his wife and family and risked imprisonment in order to make enough money to bring his flock to the U.S., so his anger and his ultimate murder of Vallone are justified. In small roles, note Harvey Lembeck and Vince Gardenia, who went on to do memorable work in many films and TV series. This was Lumet's fifth feature assignment after a successful career in TV but it did not measure up to some of his earlier work (THE FUGITIVE KIND, 12 ANGRY MEN) or much of his later work (DOG DAY AFTERNOON, SERPICO, and NETWORK).

p, Paul Graetz; d, Sidney Lumet; w, Norman Rosten (based on the play by Arthur Miller); ph, Michel Kelber; m, Maurice Le Roux; ed, Francoise Javet; art d, Jacques Saulnier.

Drama   **(PR:C MPAA:NR)**

VIGIL IN THE NIGHT**   (1940) 96m RKO bw

Carole Lombard (Anne Lee), Brian Aherne (Dr. Prescott), Anne Shirley (Lucy Lee), Julien Mitchell (Matthew Bowley), Robert Coote (Dr. Caley), Brenda Forbes (Nora), Rita Page (Glennie), Peter Cushing (Joe Shand), Ethel Griffies (Matron East), Doris Lloyd (Mrs. Bowley), Emily Fitzroy (Sister Gilson).

Medical doctor and novelist A.J. Cronin supplied the story for this movie, a heavy drama that had no leavening humor and lost just as heavily at the box office. Pandro Berman (who was "in charge of production" on this one) and Stevens left the studio after having a contretemps with the president of RKO and this film was hardly fitting as their final legacy. Set in Manchester, England, it's the story of two sisters, Lombard and Shirley, who work as nurses. Shirley is a student nurse who errs in her judgment at the hospital which leads to a child's death. Lombard, who is far more dedicated, assumes the guilt for the mishap and claims that she was responsible, thus getting Shirley off the hook and allowing her to finish her training. Lombard gets a job at another hospital where she meets Aherne. The hospital is large, badly equipped, and understaffed. The head of the facility is Mitchell and he puts an amorous move on Lombard which she repels because she is becoming enamored of Aherne. Mitchell can't handle the rebuff and he arranges to have her fired. Soon, a huge epidemic breaks out and Lombard and Shirley volunteer their Nightingale services to the hospital. When Mitchell's young son is infected by the disease and appears to be dying, Shirley bends down to give the youngster mouth-to-mouth resuscitation and, in doing so, catches the unnamed disease and expires shortly thereafter. By this time, the members of the hospital's board of directors have seen the kind of selfless person Lombard is and so she gets her old job back. Further, Aherne's efforts pay off when the board votes enough money for the hospital to have a new unit they so desperately need. Aherne and Lombard wind up together but there is no passion in their scenes, only devotion to the medical world. The movie is grim, very realistic, and unremitting in its powerful indictment of certain factions in the hospital world. Lombard, who was so good at light roles, shows none of her comedic touch and the result is that the movie is tough to watch and even more dour than it had to be. This was Peter Cushing's third U.S. film, after THE MAN IN THE IRON MASK and A CHUMP AT OXFORD. It's somewhat too realistic for young eyes and might turn children off the idea of ever seeing a doctor again.

p&d, George Stevens; w, Fred Guiol, P.J. Wolfson, Rowland Leigh (based on the novel by A.J. Cronin); ph, Robert de Grasse; m, Alfred Newman; ed, Henry Berman; art d, Van Nest Polglase; set d, Darrell Silvera; cos, Walter Plunkett.

Drama   **(PR:C MPAA:NR)**

VIGILANTE*½   (1983) 90m Magnum-Artists Releasing/Film Ventures
c (AKA: STREET GANG)

Robert Forster (*Eddie*), Fred Williamson (*Nick*), Richard Bright (*Burke*),
Rutanya Alda (*Vickie*), Don Blakely (*Prago*), Joseph Carberry (*Ramon*),
Willie Colon (*Rico*), Joe Spinell (*Eisenberg*), Carol Lynley (*District Attorney
Fletcher*), Woody Strode (*Rake*), Vincent Beck (*Judge Sinclair*), Bo Rucker
(*Horace*), Peter Savage (*Mr. "T"*).

This is the type of film aimed at making city dwellers who feel harassed by
gangs stand up and cheer. Forster plays a factory worker who refuses to
become part of the vigilante group formed by Williamson and his other
coworkers, that is until his own family becomes victimized by a Puerto Rican
gang, leaving his son dead. The leader of the gang goes free because of the
corrupt judicial system, while Forster is placed in jail for blowing his lid. He
comes out of prison ready and willing to join Williamson's gang in their
bloodletting sprees. Idea is totally far-fetched, but worth seeing just for a
chance to catch Woody Strode as a soft-spoken prisoner who packs a mean
wallop. One more in the litany of vengeance films in the wake of DEATH
WISH (1974), this film follows the splatter film MANIAC (1980) from the
same production team.

p, Andrew Garroni, William Lustig; d, Lustig; w, Richard Vetere; ph, James
Lemmo (TVC Color); m, Jay Chattaway; ed, Lorenzo Marinelli; prod d,
Mischa Petrow; spec eff, Gary Zeller; makeup, Cecilia Verandi.

Crime/Drama   **Cas.**   **(PR:O MPAA:R)**

VIGILANTE FORCE**   (1976) 89m UA c

Kris Kirstofferson (*Aaron Arnold*), Jan-Michael Vincent (*Ben Arnold*),
Victoria Principal (*Linda*), Bernadette Peters (*Dee*), Brad Dexter (*Mayor*),
Judson Pratt (*Harry, Police Chief*), David Doyle (*Homer Arno*), Antony
Carbone (*Freddie Howe*), Andrew Stevens (*Paul Sinton*), Shelly Novack
(*Viner*), Paul X. Gleason (*Michael Loonius*), John Steadman (*Shakey
Malone*), Lilyan McBride (*Boots, Landlady*), James Lydon (*Tom Cousy*),
Peter Coe (*Lu*), Debbie Lytton (*Molly*), Charles Cybbers (*Perry*), Carmen
Argenziano (*Brian*), Don Pulford (*David*), Suzanne Horton (*Sally*).

When growing numbers of incoming oil workers become more than the local
police force of a backwoods California town can manage, Kristofferson is
called in to try to maintain order. A Vietnam veteran, he brings in some of
his buddies, and soon gets the town under control. Their newfound power
goes to their heads and they virtually take over the small town. So
Kristofferson's brother, Vincent, arranges his own group to put the law
officers out of business. Performances are totally stereotyped, and the script
undeveloped, depending upon sheer action for impact.

p, Gene Corman; d&w, George Armitage; ph, William Cronjager (DeLuxe
Color); m, Gerald Fried; ed, Morton Tubor; art d, Jack Fisk; spec eff, Roger
George; stunts, Joe Buddy Hooker

Adventure/Drama   **(PR:C MPAA:PG)**

VIGILANTE HIDEOUT**   (1950) 60m REP bw

Allan "Rocky" Lane (*Himself*), Eddy Waller (*Nugget Clark*), Roy Barcroft
(*Muley Price*), Virginia Herrick (*Marigae Sanders*), Cliff Clark (*Howard
Sanders*), Don Haggerty (*Jim Benson*), Paul Campbell (*Ralph Barrows*),
Guy Teague (*Blackie*), Art Dillard (*Pete*), Chick Hannon, Bob Woodward,
Black Jack the Horse.

Lane and his trusty black stallion are on hand to help old-timer Waller in
his efforts to find water for a town which is threatening to fold up unless
something can be done about the water situation. Some crooked townsfolk
don't want the water to be found, thereby collecting on the $25,000 being
stashed away for an aqueduct. Lane's job is to make sure these people don't
pose too much of a problem, while Waller goes about finding the water. The
characterization of Waller as a crazed inventor of gadgets is an added
attraction to this oater with a realistic bent.

p, Gordon Kay; d, Fred C. Brannon; w, Richard Wormser; ph, John
MacBurnie; m, Stanley Wilson; ed, Robert M. Leeds.

Western   **(PR:A MPAA:NR)**

VIGILANTE TERROR**   (1953) 70m Westwood/AA bw

"Wild Bill" Elliott, Mary Ellen Kay, Myron Healey, Fuzzy Knight, I.
Stanford Jolley, Henry Rowland, George Wallace, Zon Murray, Richard
Avonde, Michael Colgan, Denver Pyle, Robert Bray, Al Haskell, John
James.

All is going well in the life of a western storekeeper until a gang of masked
vigilantes enter the picture. The man is accused of a robbery committed by
the group but Elliott proves the storekeeper's innocence.

p, Vincent M, Fennelly; d, Lewis Collins; w, Sid Theil; ph, Ernest Miller; m,
Raoul Kraushaar; ed, Sam Fields.

Western   **(PR:A MPAA:NR)**

VIGILANTES OF BOOMTOWN**   (1947) 56m REP bw

Allan Lane (*Red Ryder*), Bobby [Robert] Blake (*Little Beaver*), Martha
Wentworth (*The Duchess*), Roscoe Karns (*Delaney*), Roy Barcroft (*McKean*),
Peggy Stewart (*Molly McVey*), George Turner (*James J. Corbett*), Eddie Lou
Simms (*1st Sparring Partner*), George Chesebro (*Dink*), Bobby Barber (*2nd
Sparring Partner*), George Lloyd (*Thug*), Ted Adams (*Sheriff*), John Dehner
(*Bob Fitzsimmons*), Earle Hodgins (*Governor*), Harlan Briggs (*Judge*), Budd
Buster (*Goff*), Jack O'Shea (*Referee*), Tom Steele.

Decent entry from the RED RYDER series in which Lane is on hand in
Carson City to try to ensure that the local bank is not robbed during a
championship "prize" fighting bout between Dehner and Turner. Complications arise when Stewart gets in the way; she does everything possible to see
that the fight does not take place. This includes the proposed kidnaping of
Turner just before the start of the fight. Lane is grabbed by mistake and
must make it back to town before the hold-up takes place. Plenty of
well-paced action. The picture is loosely based on an actual heavyweight
championship match that took place between champion James J, Corbett
and challenger Bob Fitzsimmons in Carson City, Nevada, in 1897. Corbett,
played by Turner, might well have wished that he *had* been kidnaped; he
was the loser. (See RED RYDER series, Index.)

p, Sidney Picker; d, R. G. Springsteen; w, Earle Snell (based on the
characters from Fred Harman's comic strip); ph, Alfred Keller; ed, William
P. Thompson; md, Mort Glickman; art d, Fred A. Ritter.

Western   **Cas.**   **(PR:A MPAA:NR)**

VIGILANTES OF DODGE CITY**   (1944) 54m REP bw

"Wild Bill" Elliott (*Red Ryder*), Bobby [Robert] Blake (*Little Beaver*), Alice
Fleming, Linda Stirling, LeRoy Mason, Hal Taliaferro, Tom London, Stephen
Barclay, Bud Geary, Kenne Duncan, Bob Wilke, Horace B. Carpenter, Stan-
ley Andrews.

Problems arise for a woman when a gang of thieves move in on her freight
company. Enter Elliott and his ever-present sidekick Blake to right all
wrongs. (See RED RYDER series, Index)

p, Stephen Auer; d, Wallace Grissell; w, Norman S. Hall, Anthony Coldeway
(based on a story by Hall); ph, William Bradford; m, Joseph Dubin; ed, Charles
Craft; art d, Fred A. Ritter.

Western   **(PR:AA MPAA:NR)**

VIGILANTES RETURN, THE**   (1947) 67m UNIV c (GB: THE
RETURN OF THE VIGILANTES)

Jon Hall (*Johnnie Taggart*), Margaret Lindsay (*Kitty*), Paula Drew (*Louise
Holden*), Andy Devine (*Andy*), Robert Wilcox (*Clay Curtwright*), Jonathan
Hale (*Judge Holden*), Arthur Hohl (*Sheriff*), Wallace Scott (*Bartender*), Joan
Fulton [Shawlee] (*Ben's Girl*), Lane Chandler (*Messenger*), Jack Lambert
(*Ben*), John Hart, Monte Montague, Bob [Robert J.] Wilke (*Henchmen*),
George Chandler.

Hall plays a U.S. Marshal who goes undercover in order to pin down the
cause of extensive violence and crimes in ranching area. He hooks up with
the gang led by Wilcox, owner of a saloon and gambling house, where Hall's
old gal is employed. His cover blown, the gang pins a murder on Hall, but
he escapes from jail in time to round up a group of vigilantes to oust the gang
for good.

p, Howard Welsch; d, Ray Taylor; w, Roy Chanslor; ph, Virgil Miller
(Cinecolor); ed, Paul Landres; md, Paul Sawtell; art d, Jack Otterson, Frank
A. Richards; set d, Russell A. Gausman, Don Webb; m/l, "One Man Woman,"
Jack Brooks, Milton Schwarzwald.

Western   **(PR:A MPAA:NR)**

VIGOUR OF YOUTH   (SEE: SPIRIT OF NOTRE DAME, 1931)

VIKING, THE*½   (1931) 70m J. D. Williams bw

Louise Huntington (*Mary Joe*), Charles Starrett (*Luke*), Capt. Bob Bartlett
(*Capt. Barker*), Arthur Vinton (*Jed*), Sir Wilfred Grenfell (*Prolog Voice*).

Starrett, believed by his fellow Newfoundlanders to be a jinx, is shamed by
Vinton into joining him on a seal-hunting expedition in the icy waters of the
arctic; the real reason for Vinton's taunting is that he doesn't want to leave
Starrett behind in close proximity to the girl they both desire, Huntington.
The two get stranded on ice floes after a hunting party leaves the sealing
ship *The Viking*, commanded by Bartlett. The perfidious Vinton attempts
unsuccessfully to shoot his hated rival, but, snowblind, he misses. Starrett
heroically helps the blinded bully back to the vessel, braving many arctic
terrors in the process. Recovered, the chastened Vinton avers to all that he'll
beat the tar out of any man who says that Starrett is a jinx or a coward.
Made well before Starrett starred in series westerns, the picture was
plagued with tragedy. Producer Frissell and about 20 others died when the
title ship exploded and sank while on a voyage intended to get filler footage
of an iceberg turning over. Famed explorer Grenfell did a prolog eulogy
recounting the unfortunate event. The photography is superb and the

sound–considering that it was shot on location in the polar area–is excellent, more than making up for the hackneyed story.

p, Varick Frissell; d, George Melford; w, Garnett Weston, T. Bell Sweeney, Jr. (based on a story by Frissell); ph, Maurice Kellerman, Alfred Gandolfi, E. A. Penrod; ed, R. P. Carver.

Adventure   Cas.   (PR:A MPAA:NR)

VIKING QUEEN, THE** (1967, Brit.) 91m Seven Arts-Hammer/FOX c

Don Murray (Justinian), Carita (Salina), Donald Houston (Maelgan), Andrew Keir (Octavian), Adrienne Corri (Beatrice), Niall MacGinnis (Tiberion), Wilfrid Lawson (King Priam), Nicola Pagett (Talia), Percy Herbert (Catus), Patrick Troughton (Tristram), Sean Caffrey (Fergus), Denis Shaw (Osiris), Philip O'Flynn (Merchant), Brendan Mathews (Nigel), Gerry Alexander (Fabian), Bryan Marshall (Dominic), Jack Rodney (Boniface), Patrick Gardiner (Benedict), Paul Murphy (Dalan, Maelgan's Son), Arthur O'Sullivan (Old Man at Tax Enquiry), Cecil Sheridan (Shopkeeper at Protest Gathering), Anna Manahan (Shopkeeper's Wife), Nita Lorraine (Nubian Girl-Slave).

Sex and swordplay fill the screen as the mantle of the ancient British Iceni tribe falls to the glamorous, lightly clad Carita during the long Roman occupation of that land. On his deathbed Lawson, her father, has urged the new queen–whose mother was a Viking–to maintain peace among the warlike British tribes and their foreign conquerors. Carita joins with Murray, the Roman military governor, in this endeavor; their association blossoms into romance. Murray's second-in-command, Keir–who, like Caesar, seems ambitious–subverts these peaceful intentions by fomenting a rebellion, forcing Murray to lead his legions away to the other side of Hadrian's wall. His leader gone, Keir seizes the opportunity to arrest and flog Carita, rape her younger sister, and start an open war between the Romans and the combined forces of the Iceni and the Druids. Murray returns, but too late: Carita, escaping imprisonment, has been forced to join the fray, charging the Roman legions with her knife-hubbed chariot. Wounded in the battle, she dies in Murray's arms. An interesting attempt to spectacularize the land of the blue-painted troglodytes during a time when few records were kept. Well photographed, and the costumes reveal more flesh than might have been wise in the cold, damp climate of the Irish mountains where location scenes were shot. Murray, the lone U.S. national in the cast, is also the only well-known name. Carita, one of a limited number of non-Latin no-surname stars, is not Hispanic as one might expect, but Finnish. This was her screen debut, from which she faded back into obscurity.

p, John Temple-Smith; d, Don Chaffey; w, Clarke Reynolds (based on a story by Temple-Smith); ph, Stephen Dade (DeLuxe Color); m, Gary Hughes; ed, Peter Boita; prod d, George Provis; cos, John Furness; spec eff, Allan Bryce; makeup, Charles Parker.

Adventure   (PR:A MPAA:NR)

VIKING WOMEN AND THE SEA SERPENT
(SEE: SAGA OF THE VIKING WOMEN AND THEIR VOYAGE TO THE WATERS OF THE GREAT SEA SERPENT, 1957)

VIKINGS, THE***   (1958) 114m Bryna/UA c

Kirk Douglas (Einar), Tony Curtis (Eric), Ernest Borgnine (King Ragnar), Janet Leigh (Princess Morgana), James Donald (Lord Egbert), Alexander Knox (Father Godwin), Frank Thring (King Aella), Maxine Audley (Enid), Eileen Way (Kitala), Edric Connor (Sandpiper), Dandy Nichols (Bridget), Per Buckhoj (Bjorm), Almut Berg (Pigtails).

At the height of the Dark Ages, Viking warriors led by Borgnine raid the English coast, raping and plundering. In one small kingdom he kills the king and rapes the queen, who later bears a child from that assault. That child grows up to be Curtis, a Viking slave who knows nothing of his parentage. He and Douglas, Borgnine's legitimate son, take a disliking to each other and fight a duel, during which Curtis' pet falcon claws out one of Douglas' eyes. Enraged, the monocular Norseman orders the slave tossed into a pit of giant crabs kept for such occasions. Curtis is saved when Donald, who was banished from England and is planning his return with Viking help, recognizes an amulet Curtis wears and the slave's true identity. On another raid, the Norsemen carry off princess Leigh, and Douglas decides he wants her, although she has fallen in love with Curtis. Leigh and Curtis escape one night, and when Douglas and Borgnine chase them, the pursuing boat crashes on the rocks in the fjord and sinks. Borgnine is pulled aboard by Curtis and taken to England as a gift for evil king Thring. Thring orders the old Viking chieftain thrown to meet their more civilized variation of the giant crab pit–the ravenous wolf pit. Thring laughs when Borgnine asks to die like a Viking, with a sword in his hand, but Curtis takes pity and cuts his hands free and gives him his own sword. Borgnine almost gleefully jumps into the pit with a shout and manages to take a few wolves to Valhalla with him before the others kill him. Thring is outraged, mostly at the loss of his precious wolves, and orders that Curtis' hand be chopped off and he be set adrift in the North Sea. The boat, of course, drifts straight back to Norway where Curtis tells Douglas the fate of his father, and the two decide to put aside their mutual hatred to seek vengeance on Thring. Their Viking army sails to England and attacks the castle. Douglas then frees Leigh and

proposes marriage. She tells him she loves Curtis and when Douglas vows to kill him, she reveals that they are half-brothers. Curtis shows up and the two fight a pitched duel on the battlements of the castle. Douglas gets the upper hand and is about to kill Curtis when he hesitates, apparently reluctant to kill his own kin. Curtis, however, knows nothing about any blood ties and uses Douglas' moment of indecision to drive his own blade into his foe. The film concludes as Douglas is given a Viking funeral, set adrift on a burning longship. A rousing adventure, despite a great deal of out-and-out silliness, this film was a major ordeal to make. The projected $2.5 million budget doubled as they leased the rights to an entire fjord, constructed a Viking village on a rock in the middle of it, and built a fleet of longships copied from reproductions in museums. The cast and crew were housed on two ships moored in the fjord and were shuttled back and forth by a fleet of 17 old PT boats. Weather, too, proved a problem, and of the 60 shooting days in Norway, 49 were rainy and dark, driving Bresler, the exasperated producer, to ask one young Norwegian extra, "Does it always rain here?" The answer came back, "I don't know, I'm only eighteen." Finally the camera crew improvised a way to protect the camera from the elements and some haunting shots of Viking longships gliding through the rain and fog were captured. Douglas and Borgnine give memorably bombastic performances–Douglas leering with his milked-over eye and Borgnine shouting war cries through his bushy beard as he happily meets his death like a Viking in the wolf pit. Curtis is less memorable and seems as out of place as he always does in these swashbucklers. The production values are all top drawer and thanks to a publicity campaign that included sending Viking dagger letter openers to reviewers, having seven Norwegians sail a longship from Oslo to New York, and lifting another longship onto the marquee of the New York theater where it debuted, the film was a big moneymaker.

p, Jerry Bresler; d, Richard Fleischer; w, Dale Wasserman, Calder Willingham (based on the novel The Viking by Edison Marshall); ph, Jack Cardiff (Technirama, Technicolor); m, Mario Nascimbene; ed, Elmo Williams; prod d, Harper Goff; md, Franco Ferrara; makeup, John O'Gorman, Neville Smallwood.

Adventure   Cas.   (PR:C MPAA:NR)

VILLA!**   (1958) 72m FOX c

Brian Keith (Bill Harmon), Cesar Romero (Fierro Lopez), Margia Dean (Julie North), Rodolfo Hoyos (Pancho Villa), Rosenda Monteros (Mariana), Carlos Muzquiz (Cabo), Elisa Loti (Manuela), Enrique Lucero (Tenorio), Jorge Trevino (Capt. Castillo), Rafael Alcayde (Don Alfonso), Mario Navarro (Pajarito), Jose Espinoza (Posado), Lee Morgan (Rancher), Felix Gonzalez (Don Octavio), Gisela Martinez (Bailarina Flamenca), Jose Trowe (Col. Martinez), Raphael Sevilla, Jr (Carlos), Lamberto Gayou (Perez), Jose Lopez (Abraham Gonzales), Angelina Regis (Mujer Elegante Tren), Carlos Guarneros (Ballarin), Jorge Russek (Teniente Rurale), Eduardo Pliego (Alcaide), Ben Wright (Francisco Madero), Alberto Gutierrez (Maj. Dono), Guillermo Bianchi (Car Driver), Alberto Pedret (Detective).

No history lesson, this film depicts the famed bandido patriot as a peasant playboy who robs and romances widely until his conversion to the cause of the Mexican revolution. Saloon singer Dean is the object of Hoyos' attentions, as well as those of gringo gun-runner Keith. The latter is a peso-hungry rascal until, like Hoyos, he too is evangelized to the peasant cause through witnessing their suffering at the hands and whips of the greedy landowners. Hoyos, as Villa, finally sends Keith and Dean back over the border when he joins the forces of Francisco Madero (played by Wright) in an attack on the Mexican capitol. A good action yarn, well photographed in Mexico.

p, Plato A. Skouras; d, James B. Clark; w, Louis Vittes; ph, Alex Phillips (CinemaScope, DeLuxe Color); m, Paul Sawtell, Bert Shefter; ed, Benjamin Laird; art d, John Mansbridge; m/l, Lionel Newman, Ken Darby, Tom Walton, Walter Kent, Margia Dean.

Western   (PR:A MPAA:NR)

VILLA RIDES**   (1968) 125M PAR c

Yul Brynner (Pancho Villa), Robert Mitchum (Lee Arnold), [Maria] Grazia Buccella (Fina Gonzalez), Charles Bronson (Fierro), Robert Viharo (Urbina), Frank Wolff (Capt. Francisco Ramirez), Herbert Lom (Gen. Huerta), Alexander Knox (President Francisco Madero), Diana Lorys (Emilita), Robert Carricart (Don Luis Gonzalez), Fernando Rey (Col. Fuentes), Regina de Julian (Lupita Gonzalez), Andres Monreal (Capt. Herrera), Antonio Padilla Ruiz (Juan Gonzalez), John Ireland (Dave, Man in Barber Shop), Jill Ireland (Girl in Restaurant), Jose Maria Prada.

Considering the writing and perfoming talents involved here, this should have been a fascinating action-adventure film. Unfortunately what sprang from Kulik's inept direction is a confused, overlong, watered-down mess that most of the creative participants disowned. In Mexico in 1912, American pilot Mitchum smuggles guns from Texas to counterrevolutionary captain Wolff, who is battling General Huerta (Lom) and his underling Pancho Villa (Brynner). Mitchum's plane sustains some damage on one trip and he waits in a Mexican village for it to be repaired. During his wait, Mitchum witnesses a vicious attack by Wolff and his men on the village, which is suspected to be sympathetic to Brynner and the revolution. Wolff's troops are defeated by Brynner's loyal and sadistic aide, Bronson, who saves ammunition by lining up three prisoners, one behind the other, and shooting them all through the heart with only one bullet. When the loyalists learn that Mitchum has been running guns for the opposition, he is arrested and sentenced to be executed. Before facing a firing squad, however, the American pilot is given a chance to save himself if he agrees to fly for the revolution. He does and his first assignment is to bomb government troops with home-made hand grenades while Brynner and his men attack a train and a nearby town. Meanwhile, Lom is embroiled in a power struggle with Brynner. The evil, alcoholic commander sends Brynner on an impossible mission which should ensure his death. Much to Lom's anger and surprise, Brynner succeeds brilliantly with aerial support from Mitchum who goes so far as to crash his airplane into the barbed wire that blocks Brynner's men. Still desperate to be rid of Brynner, Lom has him arrested for disobeying his orders. Mitchum manages to escape and make his way back to Texas. When Brynner learns that Lom has assassinated the president, Knox, and set himself up as dictator, he also escapes and traces Mitchum to Texas where he convinces the American to rejoin the revolution. Originally written by Sam Packinpah in 1959, the writer-director had long hoped to make VILLA RIDES himself, but was forced to sell the property outright during his unofficial blacklisting in Hollywood after causing trouble with producers over MAJOR DUNDEE and being fired from directing THE CINCINNATI KID. The star, Yul Brynner, decided Peckinpah didn't know anything about Mexico and demanded the script be rewritten. This request seemed ridiculous to Peckinpah, who, in an interview in Take One magazine in 1969, explained, "I've spent a great many years in Mexico, I married a Mexican girl, and I know Mexican history." Brynner's judgment seems equally absurd when one considers the vivid, detailed portrayals of Mexico and its variety of people in Peckinpah's MAJOR DUNDEE, THE WILD BUNCH, and BRING ME THE HEAD OF ALFREDO GARCIA. The rewrite job was given to Robert Towne, future writer of THE LAST DETAIL, CHINA-TOWN, and SHAMPOO, who later denounced the film and said it was "a textbook on How Not to Make a Movie," in an interview with John Brady in the book The Craft of the Screenwriter. Peckinpah concurred with Towne's summation of the film and called it "terrible. Bloody awful," in the Take One interview. Peckinpah was outraged at the historical inaccuracies and thought Brynner hopelessly miscast as Pancho Villa. He was right. The actor demonstrates none of the passion, volatility, or charisma necessary for a truly interesting portrayal. Brynner's Villa is boring and it falls on Bronson, who turns in a surprisingly good performance, to inject some life into the goings on. Mitchum is Mitchum and he does fine doing what he does best, exuding a "what the hell" nonchalance throughout the proceedings. Kulik's disinterested direction never gets a grasp on the plot, the milieu, or the characters and only seems to concentrate on the violence. Another sad case of what could have been if the cards had come up differently.

p, Ted Richmond; d, Buzz Kulik; w, Robert Towne, Sam Peckinpah (based on the book Pancho Villa by William Douglas Lansford); ph, Jack Hildyard (Panavision, Eastmancolor); m, Maurice Jarre; ed, David Bretherton; md, Jarre; prod d, Ted Haworth; art d, Jose Alguero; set d, Roman Calatayud; cos, Eric Seelig; spec eff, Milt Rice; makeup, Richard Mills.

Western   Cas.   (PR:O   MPAA:R)

VILLAGE, THE**   (1953, Brit./Switz.) 98m UA bw

John Justin (Alan Manning), Eva Dahlbeck (Wanda Piwonska), Sigfrit Steiner (Heinrich Meili), Mary Hinton (Miss Worthington), Guido Lorraine (Mr. Karginski), W. Woytecki (Dr. Stefan Zielinski), Maurice Regamey (Mr. Faure), Helen Horton (Miss Sullivan), Rolando Catalano (Signore Belatti), Krystina Bragiel (Anja), Voytek Dolinsky (Andrzej), Trevor Hill (Michael), Teachers and Children of the Pestalozzi Village, Switzerland.

Uneven story that centers around a Swiss school designed to provide homes for the war orphans of WW II. The handling of the children is done in a realistic and efficient manner, depicting their various frustrations, desires, and longings. However, the love affair between two teachers from the school, Justin and Dahlbeck, softens the impact of the children's tribulations, without being all that interesting itself.

p, Lazar Wechsler, Kenneth L. Maidment; d, Leopold Lindtberg; w, David Wechsler, Lindtberg, Elizabeth Montagu (based on a story by David Wechsler and Kurt Fruh); ph, Emil Berna; m, Robert Blum; ed, Gordon Hales; md, Muir Mathieson; art d, Ivan King.

Drama   (PR:A   MPAA:NR)

VILLAGE BARN DANCE**   (1940) 74m REP bw

Richard Cromwell (Dan), Doris Day (Betty), George Barbier (Uncle Si), Esther Dale (Minerva Withers), Robert Baldwin (James Rutherford), Andrew Tombes (Rutherford), Lulubelle and Scotty, Barbara Jo Allen ["Vera Vague"], Don Wilson, The Kidoodlers, Texas Wanderers, Helen Troy, Frank Cook.

The town merchants are going broke, so Day decides to save her community by marrying rich industrialist Baldwin, who has promised to bring jobs to the area if she will do so. Itinerant engineer Cromwell, who has fallen hard for Day, is devastated by the news of the impending nuptials. With the townsfolk, he's been working up a radio program. On the eve of the wedding, the news arrives that a large commercial sponsor has agreed to subsidize the broadcasting. Day deserts her intended at the altar and rejoins her true love Cromwell. This Day is not the eternal virgin who played in so many frothy

farces with actor Rock Hudson; that one made her first film in 1948 after a successful career as a big-band singer. The Day in this film had a very limited career, hindered as she was by a poor appearance in profile (nose jobs had yet to become popular, and Barbra Streisand hadn't been born). Many of the cast members were popular radio performers of the time; like other small studios, Republic tried to take advantage of their wide airwave exposure to boost the box office. Songs and musical numbers include "What are Little Girls Made Of?" "When I Yoo Hoo in the Valley" (Scotty Wiseman, John Lair, sung by Lulubelle and Scotty); "Howdy Neighbor" (Eddie Cherkose); "Hail to Lyndale" (Cherkose, Raoul Kraushaar); and "When the Circus Comes to Town," played –among other numbers–on toy instruments by The Kidoodlers.

p, Armand Schaefer; d, Frank McDonald; w, Dorrell and Stuart McGowan; ph, Ernest Miller; ed, Murray Seldeen; md, Cy Feuer; art d, John Victor Mackay; cos, Adele Palmer.

Musical/Drama   (PR:A   MPAA:NR)

VILLAGE OF DAUGHTERS*½   (1962, Brit.) 86m MGM bw

Eric Sykes (Herbert Harris), Scilla Gabel (Angelina Vimercati), Gregoire Aslan (Gastoni), John Le Mesurier (Don Calogero), Eric Pohlmann (Marcio), Warren Mitchell (Puccelli), Peter Illing (Alfredo Predati), Graham Stark (Postman), Monty Landis (Faccino), Harold Kasket (Bus Driver), Martin Benson (1st Pickpocket), George Pastell (2nd Pickpocket), Yvonne Romaine (Annunziata Gastoni), Jill Carson (Lucia Puccelli), Talitha Pol (Gioia Spartaco), Bettine Le Beau (Aliza), Dalia Penn (Sophia), Carol White (Natasha), Ina De La Haye (Maria Gastoni), Golda Casimir (Carlotta Passati), Eileen Way (Gloria Balbino), Mario Fabrizi (Antonio Durigo).

Traveling salesman Sykes arrives in an Italian village which, hard-hit by local economic depression, has lost all its young men to emigration to busier communities. One of the emigrants, having struck it rich, writes the town's mayor to ask his help in selecting a suitable village maiden as a potential bride. All the local beauties vie for the honor, urged on by their parents, to the ultimate consternation of the village elders. The latter decide that the first outsider to visit their community will be the one to make the choice; the outsider proves to be salesman Sykes. The resulting contest, with its pageant of local lovelies, proves to be an entertaining farce, thanks largely to the talent of popular British TV comedian Sykes. One of the first of a series of films made by MGM British in an expansion program, the picture was never released in the U.S.

p, George H. Brown; d, George Pollock; w, David Pursall, Jack Seddon; ph, Geoffrey Faithfull; m, Ron Goodwin; ed, Tristam Cones; cos, Elizabeth Haffenden; m/l, title song, Norman Newell, Ron Goodwin.

Comedy   (PR:A   MPAA:NR)

VILLAGE OF THE DAMNED***   (1960, Brit.) 77m MGM bw (AKA: THE VILLAGE OF THE DAMNED)

George Sanders (Gordon Zellaby), Barbara Shelley (Anthea Zellaby), Michael Gwynne (Maj. Alan Bernard), Laurence Naismith (Dr. Willers), John Phillips (Gen. Leighton), Richard Vernon (Sir Edgar Hargraves), Jenny Laird (Mrs. Harrington), Richard Warner (Mr. Harrington), Thomas Heathcote (James Pawle), Alexander Archdale (Coroner), Martin Stephens (David Zellaby), Charlotte Mitchell (Janet Pawle), Rosamund Greenwood (Miss Ogle), Bernard Archard (Vicar), Susan Richards (Mrs. Plumpton), Pamela Buck (Milly), John Stuart (Mr. Smith), Sarah Long (Evelyn Harrington), Peter Vaughan (Police Constable Gobbey), Robert Marks (Paul Norman), Billy Lawrence (John Bush).

An incredibly frightening adaptation of the John Wyndham novel about a small English village which becomes the victim of a visit from unfriendly aliens. During a 24-hour period all the inhabitants of Midwich are put to sleep, waking to find a dozen of the women pregnant. They have the children, care for them, and love them as if they were their own. The children all look the same, with bright blond hair, and are possessed of superior intelligence and telekinetic powers. Sanders, a physicist and husband of Shelley, who has given birth to the leader of the children, undertakes the job of educating these youngsters and soon discovers that their mission is not a friendly one, but a plan to take control of the entire planet. He then sees that the children are destroyed, killing himself in the process. Sanders was not given a very suitable role; it required more emotional attachment than he had in his repertoire, but this is easily overlooked in the atmosphere provided by the children, with their blond hair and hypnotic gazes symbolizing a greater threat. Made in England for less than $300,000, the picture grossed more than $1.5 million in initial release in the U.S. and Canada alone. It spawned a host of possessed-children-as-villains films, including THE OMEN (1976) and THE BOYS FROM BRAZIL (1978) with its young Hitler clones. This intriguing story warranted a followup with 1963's CHILDREN OF THE DAMNED, which proved every bit as good as the original.

p, Ronald Kinnoch; d, Wolf Rilla; w, Rilla, Sterling Silliphant, George Barclay (based on the novel The Midwich Cuckoos by John Wyndham); ph, Geoffrey Faithfull (Metroscope); m, Ron Goodwin; ed, Gordon Hales; art d, Ivan King; spec eff, Tom Howard; makeup, Eric Aylott.

Fantasy/Horror   Cas.   (PR:C   MPAA:NR)

VILLAGE OF THE GIANTS½ (1965) 81m Berkeley EM/EM c

Tommy Kirk (*Mike*), Johnny Crawford (*Horsey*), Beau Bridges (*Fred*), Ronny Howard (*Genius*), Joy Harmon (*Merrie*), Bob Random (*Rick*), Tisha Sterling (*Jean*), Charla Doherty (*Nancy*), Tim Rooney (*Pete*), Kevin O'Neal (*Harry*), Gail Gilmore (*Elsa*), Toni Basil (*Red*), Hank Jones (*Chuck*), Jim Begg (*Fatso*), Vicki London (*Georgette*), Joseph Turkel (*Sheriff*), The Beau Brummels, Freddy Cannon, Mike Clifford (*Singers*).

Attributed to an H. G. Wells novel, but bearing it no discernible resemblance, is this teenage musical fantasy dealing with the remarkable odyssey of a youthful octet who, stranded by an avalanche that destroys their auto, steal some food and grow to massive proportions. Young Howard–later a talented director–plays "Genius", the brat who has invented the monstrous manna. The eight delinquents, averaging 30 feet in height, terrorize the town's ordinary folks, to the dismay of young lovers Kirk and Doherty, the latter Howard's sister. Ultimately, Howard comes up with a vaporous antidote (a smoking-stunts-the-growth allegory, perhaps) which reduces the juvenile offenders to manageable proportions. Producer Gordon made a later movie, not intentionally funny, from the nominal source of this one, THE FOOD OF THE GODS (1976). Unlike the latter, this one has some entertaining moments, including a rain-and-mud ballet and camera concentration on massive mammaries and, especially, big buttocks. This was to have been the first of a series of 13 low-budget fantasies made by producer Gordon in an equal-partnership deal with Joseph E. Levine. Songs and musical numbers include "Woman," "When it Comes to Your Love" (Ron Elliott, sung by The Beau Brummels), "Little Bitty Corrine" (Frank C. Slay, Frederick A. Picariello, sung by Freddy Cannon); "Marianne," "Nothing Can Stand in My Way" (Jack Nitzsche, Russ Titelman, sung by Mike Clifford).

p&d, Bert I. Gordon; w, Alan Caillou (loosely based on H. G. Wells' novel *The Food of the Gods*; ph, Paul C. Vogell; ("Perceptovision," Pathe Color); m, Jack Nitzsche; ed, John Bushelman; md, Nitzsche; art d, Franz Bachelin; set d, Robert R. Benton; spec eff, Bert I. Gordon, Flora Gordon; cos, Leah Rhodes, Frank Richardson; ch, Toni Basil; makeup, Wally Westmore.

Fantasy Cas. (PR:A MPAA:NR)

VILLAGE SQUIRE, THE* (1935, Brit.) 66m British and Dominions/PAR British bw

David Horne (*Squire Hollis*), Leslie Perrins (*Richard Venables*), Moira Lynd (*Mary Hollis*), Vivien Leigh (*Rose Venables*), Margaret Watson (*Aunt Caroline*), Haddon Mason (*Dr. Blake*), Ivor Barnard (*Mr. Worsfold*), David Nichol.

Perrins is an actor on vacation who wanders into a village which is preparing a stage production of "Macbeth." He saves the village squire, Horne, from turning out an embarrassing stage show and winds up falling in love with his comely daughter, Lynd. THE VILLAGE SQUIRE marked Leigh's first billed performance. She had previously had a small part as a schoolgirl in THINGS ARE LOOKING UP (1935).

p, Anthony Havelock-Allan; d, Reginald Denham; w, Sherard Powell (based on a play by Arthur Jarvis Black).

Comedy (PR:A MPAA:NR)

VILLAGE TALE*½ (1935) 80m RKO bw

Randolph Scott (*Slaughter Somerville*), Kay Johnson (*Janet Stevenson*), Arthur Hohl (*Elmer Stevenson*), Robert Barrat (*Drury Stevenson*), Janet Beecher (*Amy Somerville*), Edward Ellis (*Old Ike*), Dorothy Burgess (*Lulu Stevenson*), Donald Meek (*Charlie*), Andy Clyde (*Storekeeper*), Ray Mayer (*Gabby*), Guinn "Big Boy" Williams (*Ben Roberts*), T. Roy Barnes (*Goggy Smith*), DeWitt Jennings (*Sheriff*).

Starkly redolent of Sinclair Lewis' 1920 novel *Main Street*, this picture relates with unrelenting severity the dark side of small town life. Gossipmongers, bigots, Babbitts, and hypocrites gather around the cracker barrel to destroy the lives of the innocent. The peaceful Scott–Inaptly named "Slaughter"–is victimized as a result of his unfulfilled love for Hohl's wife, Johnson. Through innuendo and deceit, the yokels drive Hohl to make an unsuccesful attempt on Scott's life in the belief that the latter has cuckolded him. During brief intervals of boredom, they also conspire to drive another townsman to suicide. Unrelieved by any touch of humor, this film was seen as one of the worst in the career of a fine director.

p, David Hempstead; d, John Cromwell; w, Allen Scott (based on the novel by Phil Stong); ph, Nick Musuraca; m, Al Colombo; ed, William Morgan; art d, Van Nest Polglase, Carroll Clark.

Drama (PR:A MPAA:NR)

VILLAIN zero (1971, Brit.) 97m Anglo-EMI MGM c

Richard Burton (*Vic Dakin*), Ian McShane (*Wolfe Lissner*), Nigel Davenport (*Bob Matthews*), Donald Sinden (*Gerald Draycott*), Fiona Lewis (*Venetia*), T.P. McKenna (*Frank Fletcher*), Joss Ackland (*Edgar Lowis*), Cathleen Nesbitt (*Mrs. Dakin*), Elizabeth Knight (*Patti*), Colin Welland (*Tom Binney*), Tony Selby (*Duncan*), John Hallam (*Terry*), Del Henney (*Webb*), Ben Howard (*Henry*), James Cossins (*Brown*), Anthony Sagar (*Danny*), Clive Francis (*Vivian*), Stephen Sheppard (*Benny Thompson*), Brook Williams

(*Kenneth*), Wendy Hutchinson (*Mrs. Lewis*), Michael Robbins (*Barzun*), Sheila White (*Veronica*), Cheryl Hall (*Judy*), Shirley Cain (*Mrs. Matthews*), Lindy Miller (*Gilly*), Godfrey James (*Car Lot Manager*), Bonita Thomas (*Strip Dancer*), Leslie Schofield (*Detective Constable*).

A sleazy slumgullion of a film with unquenched violence and no redeeming values. Adapted by actor Al Lettieri from Barlow's novel, the script was by two veteran writers who should have known better, Clement and La Frenais. If every four letter word were taken out of the script, it might have run a full hour shorter and if all the gratuitous violence were deleted, it would go by in an instant. Burton is the homosexual leader of a brutal gang of London thugs and the cops would like to get their hands on him but he has friends all over the place and every time there's a crime he has an alibi prepared. Burton viciously slashes an informer to death with a razor right at the start, then goes home to tend his aged "mum," Nesbitt, who played the same role when she was homosexual Burton's mother in STAIRCASE. Burton dearly loves Nesbitt and we are supposed to allow that to mitigate the blood he has just shed. Burton's current amour is McShane, a blackmailing pimp who makes his money by supplying women for the likes of Sinden, a member of Parliament who enjoys orgies. Burton is about to make love to McShane but his idea of foreplay is to beat his boy friend to a pulp before they consummate their love for each other. Burton's aides-de-camp are Ackland (who suffers from a mean ulcer) and McKenna. The trio unites to pull off a payroll robbery of a chemical company but they are so inept that Ackland's fingerprints are found. Ackland's job was to stash the money and when he is caught by the cops, he is tight-lipped. McShane gets Sinden to provide an alibi for Burton by threatening to expose his sexual proclivities and Burton appears to be safe. Still, the cop in charge, Davenport, has vowed to nail Burton and will stop at nothing in his quest. He has devised a plan to entrap Burton. Ulcer- sufferer Ackland is taken to a civilian hospital from which it will be easy to spring a prisoner. It's a deliberate ploy by Davenport, as he hopes Burton will try to kidnap his associate before the beans are spilled, the cops will follow them, and the payroll money will be found. Nesbitt dies and Burton is inconsolable. He travels to McShane's apartment for sympathy and is stunned to find that his lover swings both ways and is in the sack with a *woman*, of all things. It's pretty Lewis and Burton explodes and tosses the femme out, beats up McShane again (it's getting to be a habit), then jumps into bed with him. Afterward, he gets McShane to promise to nab Ackland. McShane pulls off the coup and brings Ackland to Burton. The three men then travel to a rough area under a railway bridge that is no longer in use. Ackland has hidden the money there but the cops are right on their tails. When Burton sees the police closing in, he thinks that Ackland has done this so he shoots his associate, then tries to get away. McShane wisely gives himself up rather than face a hail of bullets and Burton realizes that he can stay with his lover in jail so he capitulates. This was Tuchner's first feature credit and should have been his last. But he did go on to make FEAR IS THE KEY, the dreadful MR. QUILP, and THE LIKELY LADS. How an intelligent man like Burton could have gotten mixed up with such trash is beyond reason. McShane's performance is the only one that showed any merit. A slimy piece of business and the real villains are the people behind it. It sank quickly out of sight, which is a tribute to the taste of the viewing public, something that was not in the kit bag of the men who made this. If there were a rating that was less than "zero," this movie would have earned it. Hard to believe that Alan Ladd, Jr. (who went on to make many fine pictures) and Jay Kanter, who became an executive at MGM after years in Universal's London office, could have been associated with VILLAIN.

p, Alan Ladd, Jr., Jay Kanter; d, Michael Tuchner; w, Dick Clement, Ian La Frenais, Al Lettieri (based on the novel *The Burden of Proof* by James Barlow); ph, Christopher Challis (Panavision, Technicolor); m, Jonathan Hodge; ed, Ralph Sheldon; art d, Maurice Carter; set d, Andrew Campbell; makeup, Alec Garfath.

Crime Drama (PR:O MPAA:R)

VILLAIN, THE* (1979) 93m Rastar/COL c (AKA: CACTUS JACK)

Kirk Douglas (*Cactus Jack*), Ann-Margaret (*Charming Jones*), Arnold Schwarzenegger (*Handsome Stranger*), Paul Lynde (*Nervous Elk*), Foster Brooks (*Bank Clerk*), Ruth Buzzi (*Damsel in Distress*), Jack Elam (*Avery Simpson*), Strother Martin (*Parody Jones*), Robert Tessier (*Mashing Finger*), Mel Tillis (*Telegrapher*), Laura Lizer Sommers (*Working Girl*), Ray Bickel (*Man*), Jan Eddy (*Sheriff*), Mel Todd (*Conductor*), Jim Anderson (*Bartender*), Ed Little, Dick Dickinson, Richard Brewer, Charles Haigh, Ron Duffy, Earl W. Smith, Mike Cerre, Lee Davis, Dick Armstrong, Sheldon Rosner, Budd Stout.

This spoof of B western stereotypes fails to work despite the talents of a number of fine performers. Douglas is the classical villain who continually attempts to abduct fair damsel Ann-Margaret and is as continually thwarted by handsome, taciturn hero Schwarzenegger. Douglas' involved plots are routinely run over and foiled in a complex of cameos in this cartoon-like feature which was widely viewed as no more than a ROADRUNNER episode using live actors. The denouement has the fair damsel electing to go with the incompetent Douglas, his lustfulness seeming superior to Schwartzenegger's sterile valor. Another broad-brush, unfunny feature from one-time stunt director Needham.

p, Mort Engelberg; d, Hal Needham; w, Robert G. Kane; ph, Bobby Byrne

(Metrocolor); m, Bill Justis; ed, Walter Hannemann; art d, Carl Anderson; stunts, Gary Combs.

Western/Comedy   **Cas.**   **(PR:A MPAA;PG)**

VILLAIN STILL PURSUED HER, THE*
(1940) 65m Franklin-Blank/RKO bw

Hugh Herbert (Healy, a Philanthropist-Reformer), Anita Louise (Mary, a Long-Suffering Heroine), Alan Mowbray (Cribbs the Villain), Buster Keaton (William, a Staunch Friend to the Last), Joyce Compton (Hazel the Half-Wit Sister), Richard Cromwell (Edward the Hero, Woe to Him--a Drinking Man), Billy Gilbert (Announcer, the Master of Ceremonies), Margaret Hamilton (Mrs. Wilson the Heroine's Loving Mother), William Farnum (Vagabond, Another Victim of Demon Rum), Franklin Pangborn (Bartender, an Instrument of the Devil), Diane Fisher (Julia, Angel Daughter of Mary and Edward).

Producer Franklin, one-time head of RKO's theater chain, came up with the idea of transposing a traditional temperance melodrama of the stage to the silver screen. In a prolog, audiences were urged to hiss and boo the villain and cheer the hero. Cromwell, the hero, is suborned by villain Mowbray into consuming a glass of strong spirits, which immediately plunges him into the gutter, at the expense of wife Louise and angel daughter Fisher. The lecherous Mowbray's evil intent is to win for himself the affections of the pure and comely Louise. With the aid of philanthropist Herbert and true friend Keaton, Cromwell painfully wrests himself up from the trough and wins through. Overlong, the joke wears thin quickly. W. C. Fields did it much better in his short THE FATAL GLASS OF BEER.

p, Harold B. Franklin; d, Edward F. Cline; w, Elbert Franklin (based on the traditional melodrama "The Fallen Saved"); ph, Lucien Ballard; ed, Arthur-Hilton; md, Frank Tours; art d, Lewis Rachmil.

Comedy   **Cas.**   **(PR:A MPAA:NR)**

VILLE SANS PITTE   (SEE: TOWN WITHOUT PITY, 1961, U.S./Switz./Ger.)

VILLIERS DIAMOND, THE* (1938, Brit.) 50m FOX British bw

Edward Ashley (Capt. Dawson), Evelyn Ankers (Joan Dawson), Frank Birch (Silas Wade), Liam Gaffney (Alan O'Connel), Leslie Harcourt (Barker), Julie Suedo (Mrs. Forbes), Sybil Brooke (Miss Waring), Billy Shine (Joe), Margaret Davidge.

A vapid crime story about a former criminal, Ashley, who gets his hands on the sought-after Villiers diamond. Harcourt, the man who acquired the diamond, wants Ashley to cough up some money. Daughter Ankers also wants some cash, returning to England penniless after having been kicked out of her finishing school in Switzerland. Ashley stages a fake robbery but his scheme misfires and he is put behind bars, as is Harcourt, while Ankers is left broke and alone. Thankfully it's only 50 minutes long.

p, John Findlay; d, Bernard Mainwaring; w, David Evans (based on a story by F. Wyndham-Mallock); ph, Stanley Grant.

Crime   **(PR:A MPAA:NR)**

VILNA LEGEND, A* (1949, U.S./Pol.) 81m Jewish Films bw

American cast: Joseph Buloff (The Storyteller), Jacob Mestel (1st Traveler), Louis Kadison (2nd Traveler), Bosenko (3rd Traveler), Benjamin Fishbein (Tavernkeeper), Russian-Jewish cast: Lev Mogliov (The Boy), Eda Kaminsky (The Girl), Zigmund Turcoff (The Prophet Elijah), Simchah Balanoff (The Playboy).

A VILNA LEGEND is actually a 1924 silent film shot in Poland with a Russian and Jewish cast. In 1949 new scenes were shot to provide a framing story, with Buloff entertaining some travelers with his tale. The story, an incredibly dated one, is about two students who decide that when they have children, those offspring shall marry each other. Years later, however, that proves to be a difficult task. Helping them keep their pledge is the prophet Elijah, who manages to get the pair to marry. The 1924 portion is livened up with some Yiddish-language narration. (In Yiddish).

d, George Rolland; w, Jacob Mestel.

Drama/Romance   **(PR:A MPAA:NR)**

VINETU   (SEE: APACHE GOLD, 1965, Fr./Ital./Ger./Yugo.)

VINETU II   (SEE: LAST OF THE RENEGADES, 1966, Fr./Ital./Ger./Yugo.)

VINETU III   (SEE: DESPERADO TRAIL, THE, 1967, GER/Yugo.)

VINTAGE, THE*½   (1957) 92m MGM c

Pier Angeli (Lucienne), Mel Ferrer (Giancarlo Barandero), John Kerr (Ernesto Barandero), Michele Morgan (Leonne Morel), Theodore Bikel (Eduardo Uriburri), Leif Erickson (Louis Morel), Jack Mullaney (Etienne Morel), Joe Verdi (Uncle Ton Ton).

Boring romantic drama, which has Ferrer and Kerr taking refuge in the French vineyards of Erickson after fleeing Italy for Kerr's part in a murder.

The two criminals soon ignite the passions of Erickson's wife, Morgan, and her sister, Angeli, who have been bored out of their skulls there amidst the grapes. The police eventually come and conveniently put a stop to the behind-the-scenes romance by killing Kerr, relieving everyone from the tedium. Filmed in France with an international cast and an odd admixture of accents.

p. Edwin H. Knopf; d, Jeffrey Hayden; w, Michael Blankfort (based on the novel by Ursula Keir); ph, Joseph Ruttenberg) (CinemaScope, Metrocolor); m, David Raksin; ed, Ben Lewis; art d, Jean Donarinou.

Drama   **(PR:A MPAA:NR)**

VINTAGE WINE**   (1935, Brit.) 81m Real ARt/GAU bw

Seymour Hicks (Charles Popinot), Claire Luce (Nina Popinot), Eva Moore (Josephine Popinot), Judy Gunn (Blanche Popinot), Miles Malleson (Henri Popinot), P. Kynaston Reeves (Benedict Popinot), Michael Shepley (Richard Emsley), A. Bromley Davenport (Pierre), Amy Brandon Thomas, Meriel Forbes, Brian Buchel. Kathleen Weston, Andrea Malandrinos, [Mary] Hayley Bell, Stella Mantovani, Sonia Somers, Tony de Lungo, Enrico Muzio.

The marriage between an elderly vintner, Hicks, and the young Luce, ignites severe disapproval from his strait-laced sons, who pop their noses into the picture and try to destroy the relationship. Their appearance also enlightens Luce to the true age of her husband; she thought he was 45 when he's really 62. She walks off in a pique for being deceived, but his granddaughter Gunn plays matchmaker. A bit too stagey, but an otherwise pleasant farce.

p, Julius Hagen; d, Henry Edwards w, Seymour Hicks, Ashley Dukes, H. Fowler Mear) based on the play "Der Ewige Jungeling" by Alexander Engel); ph, Sydney Blythe, cos, Louis Brooks.

Comedy   **(PR:A MPAA:NR)**

VIOLATED* (1953) 78m Panther/Palace bw

Wim Holland (Jan C. Verbig), Lili Dawn (Lili DeMar), Mitchell Kowal (Lt. MacCarthy), Vicki Carlson (Sue Grant), William Martel (Detective Dana), Jason Niles (Dr. Jason), Michael Keene (Gardner), Fred Lambert (George Mastro), William Paul Mishkin (Louis Quinto), Sally Peters (Ellen Tinker), Mary Noble (Mrs. Grant), Charles Uday (Joe Summers), Juana (Mary Barrow), Pete Caudreaux (Janitor), Wambly Bald (District Attorney), .

A sad looking production about the attempts of New York police to track down a sex-maniac murderer. They do so in such a contrived manner it's hard to believe they could capture a 10 year old stealing candy. A bad picture with pretensions of showing the seedier side of life.

p, William Holand; d, Walter Strate; w, William Paul Mishkin; ph, Pat Rich; M, Tony Mottola.

Crime   **(PR:C MPAA:NR)**

VIOLATED LOVE**   (1966, Arg.) 72m Productores Argentinos Asociados/CIP Ltd. bw (TESTIGO PARA UN CRIMEN)

Libertad Leblanc (Blondie), Jose Maria Langlais (Martin Pena), Alfonso de Grazia (Raul Pena), Amadeo Novoa (Ricci), Charles Carell (Otero), Marion Bauza (Loco), Eduardo Munoz (Inspector Santoni), Julea DeGrace (Romero), Dora Baret (Marguerite).

A wealthy man sets about to avenge the murder of his brother, getting involved in a number of seedy gangland activities thinking this will lead him to the real murderer. After a number of double crosses, he proves to be a one-man hit squad in wiping out an entire gang. However, it turns out that the murderer was totally unrelated to the people he had been pursuing.

p, Orestes Trucco; d, Emilio Vieyra; w, Abel Santa Cruz, Vito De Martini; ph, Anibal Gonzalez Paz; m, Victor Buchino; ed, Oscar Esparza, Ralph Dell, Delia Manuel; cos, Libertad de Baiza; makeup, Orlando Vilone, George Bruno.

Crime   **(PR:C MPAA:NR)**

VIOLATED PARADISE*½ (1963, Ital./Jap.) 68m Victoria-Times Film c (AKA: DIVING GIRLS OF JAPAN; THE DIVING GIRL'S ISLAND; SCINTILLATING SIN; SEA NYMPHS)

Kazuko Mine (Tomako), Paulette Girard (Narrator).

Uneventful tale of a girl from a small Japanese village who goes to the big city in hopes of discovering the adventures she had romanticized. Instead she finds that city life isn't what it's cracked up to be, and that her heart belongs in a small pearl-fishing village. Luckily she gets her chance to return when she re-meets and marries a fisherman.

p&d, Marion Gering; w, Tom Rowe (based on the novels L'Isola Delle Pescatrici and Ore Giapponesi by Fosco Maraini; ph, Maraini, Roy M. Yaginuma (Eastmancolor); m, Marcello Abbado, Sergo Pagnio

Drama   **(PR:O MPAA:NR)**

VIOLATORS, THE* (1957) 76M RKO-Galahad/UNIV bw

Arthur O'Connell (Solomon Baumgarden), Nancy Malone (Debbie Baumgarden), Fred Beir (Jimmy Coogan), Clarice Blackburn (Eva Baumgarden),

Henry Sharp (*David Baumgarden*), Mary Michael (*Mrs. Riley*), Joe Julian (*Mr. Riley*), Bill Darrid (*Anthony Calini*), Sheila Copelan (*Sheron Riley*), Bernie Lenrow (*Judge McKenna*), Martin Freed (*Barnie*), Mercer McLeod (*Judge Blatz*), Eva Stern (*Jean*), Norman Rose (*Stephen*), Maxine Stewart (*Salesgirl*), Margaret Draper (*Mollie*), Frank Maxwell (*Sam*), John McGovern (*Mr. Coogan*), Norman Feld (*Ray*), Tom Middleton (*Ralph*).

O'Connell is a colorless, hard-working probation officer supporting his motherless daughter Malone and his spinster sister Blackburn. He is forced to closely examine his rote dealings with criminals when Malone's fiance Beir, strapped for cash, commits a felony, Made in New York by radio serial producer Brown as part of a four-picture deal for RKO. The radio roots of the producer are close to the surface in this relatively action-free film.

p, Himan Brown; d, John Newland; w, Ernest Pendrell (based on a novel by Israel Beckhardt, Wenzell Brown); ph, Morris Hartzband; m, Elliot Lawrence; ed, David Cooper; md, Lawrence.

Drama   **(PR:A MPAA:NR)**

VIOLENCE**   (1947) 72m MON bw

Nancy Coleman (*Ann Mason*), Michael O'Shea (*Steve Fuller*), Sheldon Leonard (*Fred Stalk*), Peter Whitney (*Joker Robinson*), Emory Parnell (*True Dawson*), Frank Reicher (*Pop*), Pierre Watkin (*Ralph Borden*), Gay Forester (*Mrs. Donahue*), John Hamilton (*Dr. Chambers*), Richard Irving (*Latimer*), Carol Donne (*Bess Taffel*), Jimmy Clark (*Joe Donahue*), William Gould (*Mr. X*), Mary Donovan, Helen Servis, Harry Deep, Frank Cady, Dick Rich, William Ruhl, Drew Demerest, Billy Green.

Tautly conceived script that has Coleman and O'Shea going undercover to expose a group that recruits WW II veterans and uses the guise of American patriotism to cover up a variety of violent, underhanded activities. Direction is slack, but other facets of production, including performances, are more than adequate.

p, Jack Bernhard, Bernard Brandt; d, Bernhard; w, Stanley Rubin, Lewis Lantz; ph, Henry Sharp; m, Edward J. Kay; ed, Jason Bernie, md, Kay; art d, Oscar Yerg; Cos, Lorraine Maclean.

Crime   **(PR:A MPAA:NR)**

VIOLENT AND THE DAMNED, THE**   (1962, Braz.) 60m Artistas Associadas-Maristola/A . .D.P. Productions bw MAOS SANGRENTAS; ASSASSINOS)

Arturo de Cordova (*Adriano/Rick Marson*), Tonia Carrero (*Sangerin*), Carlos Cotrim (*"Tiger"*), Jackson de Souza (*Carioca*), Sadi Cabral (*Professor*), Oswaldo Louzada (*"Rat"*), Ramiro Magalhaes (*Bacana*).

Intense crime drama set in the jungles of South America has de Cordova making a break from a Panamanian jail amidst an excessive amount of bloodshed during a prison riot. De Cordova attempts to escape pursuing officers by hiding out in the jungle, but is unable to sustain his existence for very long, coming out to the hands of the waiting law.

p, Gregory Wallerstein, Robert Acacio; d, Carlos Hugo Christensen; w, Christensen, Pedro Juan Vignalle; ph, Mario Pages; m, Ruy Alvez, Alexandre Guatalli.

Drama   **(PR:C MPAA:NR)**

VIOLENT ANGELS, THE   (SEE: ANGELS DIE HARD!, 1970)

VIOLENT CITY   (SEE: FAMILY, THE, 1974, Fr./Ital.)

VIOLENT ENEMY, THE*½   (1969, Brit.) 94m Trio-Group W/Monarch c

Tom Bell (*Sean Rogan*), Susan Hampshire (*Hannah Costello*), Ed Begley (*Colum O'More*), Jon Laurimore (*Austin*), Michael Standing (*Fletcher*), Noel Purcell (*John Michael Leary*), Philip O'Flynn (*Inspector Sullivan*).

Ireland is the backdrop for yet another IRA tale about a plan to blow up a British power station. An escaped Republican prisoner learns of the plan and uses his resources to stop the destruction.

p, William Gell, Wilfred Eades; d, Don Sharp; w, Edmund Ward (based on the novel *A Candle for the Dead* by Hugh Marlowe).

Crime   **(PR:A MPAA:NR)**

VIOLENT FOUR, THE**   (1968, Ital.) 98m DD/PAR c (BANDITI A MILANO)

Gian Maria Volonte (*Cavallero*), Tomas Milian (*Inspector Basevi*), Margaret Lee (*Prostitute*), Carla Gravina (*Telephone Victim*), Don Backy (*Notarnicola*), Ezio Sancrotti (*Rovoletto*), Raymond Lovelock (*Lopez*), Piero Mazzarella (*Piva*), Peter Martell (*"Protector"*), Carlo Lizzani, Nino Krisman (*Police Officials*), Laura Solari, Enzo Fisichella, Gianni Bortolotti, Maria Rosa Schlauzero, Ida Meda, Emy Rossi Scotti, Aldo Vigorelli, Umberto Di Grazia, Enzo Consoli, Giorgio Osfuri.

A gang of robbers responsible for a large number of bank robberies in the city of Milan make an accidental mistake during a highly planned job. This blows their cover as legitimate law abiding citizens, and releases a widespread police search to track the robbers down. As the man behind all the scheming, Volonte discovers the romantic image he has of himself is not in accordance with the sentiments of the rest of Milan's citizens.

p, Dino De Laurentiis; d, Carlo Lizzani; w, Lizzani, Dino Maiuri, Massimo De Rita; ph, Otello Spila, Giuseppe Ruzzolini (Techniscope, Technicolor); m, Riz Ortolani; ed, Franco Fraticelli; prod D, Mimmo Scavia; cos, Sebastiano Soldati; spec eff, Eros Bacciucchi.

Crime   **(PR:A MPAA:M)**

VIOLENT HOUR, THE   (SEE: DIAL 1119, 1950)

VIOLENT JOURNEY   (SEE: FOOL KILLER, THE, 1966)

VIOLENT LOVE   (SEE: TAKE HER BY SURPRISE, 1967, Can.)

VIOLENT MEN, THE***   (1955) 96m COL c (GB: ROUGH COMPANY)

Glenn Ford (*John Parrish*), Barbara Stanwyck (*Martha Wilkison*), Edward G. Robinson (*Lew Wilkison*), Dianne Foster (*Judith Wilkison*), Brian Keith (*Cole Wilkison*), May Wynn (*Caroline Vail*), Warner Anderson (*Jim McCloud*), Basil Ruysdael (*Tex Hinkleman*), Lita Milan (*Elena*), Richard Jaeckel (*Wade Matlock*), James Westerfield (*Magruder*), Jack Kelly (*DeRosa*), Willis Bouchey (*Sheriff Martin Kenner*), Harry Shannon (*Purdue*), Peter Hanson (*George Menefee*), Don C. Harvey (*Jackson*), Robo Bechi (*Tony*), Carl Andre (*Dryer*), James Anderson (*Hank Purdue*), Katharine Warren (*Mrs. Vail*), Tom Browne Henry (*Mr. Vail*), Bill Phipps (*Bud Hinkleman*), Edmund Cobb (*Anchor Rider*), Frank Ferguson (*Mahoney*), Raymond Greenleaf (*Dr. Henry Crowell*), Ethan Laidlaw (*Barfly*), Kenneth Patterson (*1st Farmer*), John Halloran (*2nd Farmer*), Walter Beaver (*Hinkleman's Son*), Robert Bice.

Ford is a small rancher who comes up against crippled land baron Robinson, who is pushing out the small ranchers and farmers of the area spurred on by his grasping wife (Stanwyck) and evil brother (Keith). Robinson little suspects that the two are carrying on an affair behind his back. Ford is a pacifist since his horrific experiences in the Civil War, and his refusal to fight eventually causes his fiancee, Wynn, to leave him. When one of Robinson's hired guns, Jaeckel, kills one of Ford's hired hands, Ford is finally pushed over the edge and he tracks Jaeckel down and shoots him dead. Now Ford begins a guerrilla campaign against Robinson that includes setting brush fires and stampeding horses. Keith and Stanwyck are killed in an ambush and Robinson, his home and family destroyed, finally gives up his dream of empire. Ford, meanwhile, manages to win the hand of Robinson's daughter, Foster, who had long been appalled by the behavior of her mother and uncle. A not terribly interesting film that Robinson, in his autobiography, calls one of the B movies that marked the beginning of his decline from stardom. Director Mate was a former cinematographer (he had shot Stanwyck in one of her best films, STELLA DALLAS, 1937), and he shows a good pictorial sense, filling the wide-screen frame with Technicolor action. His ability to direct actors, though, is a different matter entirely; the film drags in many spots and never develops any real power.

p, Lewis J. Rachmil; d, Rudolph Mate; w, Harry Kleiner (based on the novel *Rough Company* by Donald Hamilton); ph, Burnett Guffey, W. Howard Greene (CinemaScope, Technicolor); m, Max Steiner; ed, Jerome Thoms; md, Morris Stoloff; art d, Carl Anderson, Ross Bellah; set d, Louis Diage; cos, Jean Louis.

Western   **(PR:A MPAA:NR)**

VIOLENT MIDNIGHT   (SEE: PSYCHOMANIA, 1964)

VIOLENT MOMENT*½   (1966, Brit.) 61m Independent Artists/Schoenfeld bw

Lyndon Brook (*Douglas Baines*), Jane Hylton (*Daisy Hacker*), Jilly Browne (*Janet Greenway*), John Paul (*Sgt. Ranson*), Rupert Davies (*Bert Glennon*), Moira Redmond (*Kate Glennon*), Bruce Seton (*Inspector Davis*), Martin Miller (*Hendricks*), Gerald Anderson, Leonard White, Frederick Piper, Martin Boddey.

Shakily conceived drama in which Brook plays a man obsessed with the doll that belonged to his son, the illegitimate child of his union with Hylton, a woman he murdered after she sold their son for adoption. His attempts to retrieve the doll when it temporarily leaves his possession lead to his admission of the earlier murder, proving that grown men should not play with dolls.

p, Bernard Coote; d, Sidney Hayers; w, Peter Barnes; ph, Phil Grindrod; m, Stanley Black; ed, Hayers; art d, Eric Saw.

Drama   **(PR:C MPAA:NR)**

VIOLENT ONES, THE*½   (1967) 84m Madison-Harold
                                    Goldman)/Feature Film c

Fernando Lamas *(Manuel Vega)*, Aldo Bay *(Joe Vorzyck)*, Tommy Sands
(Mike Marain), David Carradine *(Lucas Barnes)*, Lisa Gaye *(Dolores)*,
Melinda Marx *(Juanita)*.

A plot with an underlying theme that speaks out against prejudice in a less
than original and inventive style. Lamas, who also directed, stars as the
sheriff in a small Mexican village where a girl is brutally raped and later
dies. The only evidence is that the assailant was a gringo, so Lamas rounds
up the three in the vicinity and tries to ward off an angry mob of villagers,
stirred up by the victim's father. The son of a famous father (John),
Carradine, proves to be the rape-murderer of the daughter of a famous
father (Groucho), Marx. All the gringos hate the Mexicans, and vice-versa,
making the characters seem shallow and the story callous. The actors
seemed to realize this, which their performances make evident.

p, Robert W. Stabler; d, Fernando Lamas; w, Doug Wilson, Charles Davis
(based on a story by Fred Freiberger, Herman Miller); ph, Fleet Southcott
(Eastmancolor); m, Marlin Skiles; ed, Fred W. Berger; art d, Paul Sylos, Jr.

Drama   **(PR:C   MPAA:NR)**

VIOLENT PLAYGROUND**½   (1958, Brit.) 108m Rank bw

Stanley Baker *(Sgt. Truman)*, Anne Heywood *(Cathie Murphy)*, David
McCallum *(Johnny Murphy)*, Peter Cushing *(Priest)*, John Slater *(Sgt.
Walker)*, Clifford Evans *(Heaven Evans)*, Moultrie Kelsall *(Superintendent)*,
George A. Cooper *(Chief Inspector)*, Brona Boland *(Mary Murphy)*, Fergal
Boland *(Patrick Murphy)*, Michael Chow *(Alexander)*, Tsai Chin *(Primrose)*,
Sean Lynch *(Slick)*, Oonagh Quinn, Irene Arnold, Christopher Cooke, Sheila
Raynor, Fred Fowell, Benice Swanson, Gerrard Gibson.

Baker plays a Liverpool cop pulled off his sleuthing of a series of arson fires
and given the job of Juvenile Liaison Officer. One of the families assigned
to his jurisdiction, comprising, McCallum, Heywood, and two young children
finds a particular place in his heart as he falls for the elder sister. McCallum
proves to be responsible for the fires Baker had been investigating. When
the youth is caught red-handed, he gets hold of a gun and holds out in a
classroom using his young siblings as hostages. A tautly scripted effort given
a realistic bent through the atmospheric photography and the subtle
handling of the children.

p, Michael Relph; d, Basil Dearden; w, James Kennaway (based on his
novel); ph, Reginald Wyer; ed, Arthur Stevens.

Crime/Drama   **(PR:A   MPAA:NR)**

VIOLENT ROAD**   (1958) 86m WB bw (AKA: HELL'S HIGHWAY)

Brian Keith *(Mitch)*, Dick Foran *(Sarge)*, Efrem Zimbalist, Jr *(George
Lawrence)*, Merry Anders *(Carrie)*, Sean Garrison *(Ken Farley)*, Joanna
Barnes *(Peg Lawrence)*, Perry Lopez *(Manuelo)*, Arthur Batanides *(Ben)*, Ed
Prentiss *(Nelson)*, Ann Doran *(Edith)*, John Dennis *(Pat Farley)*, Venetia
Stevenson, Bob Alderette.

With a plot closely resembling Henri-Georges Clouzot's THE WAGES OF
FEAR (1955), this flashback-filled film details the story of six risk-takers
who drive truckloads of volatile rocket fuel through dangerous terrain, with
rockfalls threatening them at almost every turn. Each, in his own episodic
vignette, proves to have a reason for making the trip. Most need the $5,000
each has been promised, but only Zimbalist has a deeper reason: he is the
developer of the highly explosive fuel which, in a freak mishap, contributed
to the deaths of his wife and children. With the exception of Foran, all the
adventurers make it to safety.

p, Aubrey Schenck; d, Howard W. Koch; w, Richard Landau (based on the
story "Hell's Highway" by Don Martin); ph, Carl Guthrie; m, Leith Stevens;
ed, John F. Schreyer; art d, Jack Collis.

Drama   **(PR:A   MPAA:NR)**

VIOLENT SATURDAY***½   (1955) 91m FOX c

Victor Mature *(Shelley Martin)*, Richard Egan *(Boyd Fairchild)*, Stephen
McNally *(Harper)*, Virginia Leith *(Linda)*, Tommy Noonan *(Harry Reeves)*,
Lee Marvin *(Dill)*, Margaret Hayes *(Emily)*, J. Carrol Naish *(Chapman)*,
Sylvia Sidney *(Elsie)*, Ernest Borgnine *(Stadt)*, Dorothy Patrick *(Helen)*,
Billy Chapin *(Steve Martin)*, Brad Dexter *(Gil Clayton)*, Donald Gamble
(Bobby), Raymond Greenleaf *(Mr. Fairchild)*, Richey Murray *(Georgie)*,
Robert Adler *(Stan)*, Ann Morrison *(Mrs. Stadt)*, Donna Corcoran *(Anna
Stadt)*, Kevin Corcoran *(David Stadt)*, Noreen Corcoran *(Mary Stadt)*, Boyd
"Red" Morgan *(Slick)*, Harry Seymour *(Conductor)*, Jeri Weil, Pat Weil,
Sammy Ogg *(Amish Children)*, John Alderson *(Amish Farmer)*, Esther
Somers *(Amish Woman on Train)*, Harry Carter *(Bart)*, Florence Ravenel
(Miss Shirley), Dorothy Phillips *(Bank Customer)*, Virginia Carroll *(Marion,
Secretary)*, Ralph Dumke *(Sidney)*, Robert Osterloh *(Roy, Bartender)*, Helen
Mayon *(Mrs. Pilkas)*, Fred Shellac *(Signalman)*, Ellen Bowers *(Bank Teller)*,
Joyce Newhard *(Dorothy)*, Mack Williams *(Drug Clerk)*, Richard Garrick.

This interesting study of small-town America in the mid-1950s opens as
three men, Naish, McNally, and benzedrine-sniffing Marvin, plot a robbery.

Their target is the local bank in a small Arizona mining town. They check
into a nearby hotel, and there plan the caper down to the last detail. The
town, like any other rural community, is beset by its own troubles. Egan
owns the mine the municipality revolves around, but he spends more time
working than paying attention to his wife, Hayes. Hayes resents the dull life
style her husband's business has imposed on her, so she busies herself with
golf and numerous affairs. Her extracurricular activities are no secret, and
Egan is driven to the bottle to escape his pain. Mature is an engineer who
works under Egan. Though his own marriage seems to be in control, Egan's
son is ashamed that his father is the only local man who did not fight in the
war. At the library, head librarian Sidney is facing a bank foreclosure on her
home. When a wealthy woman accidentally leaves her purse at the library,
Sidney quietly helps herself to the money inside. Later she's seen by
Noonan, a mild mannered bank teller, as Sidney tries to dispose of the
evidence. Sidney holds a secret over Noonan's head, though, as she discovers
the meek individual is a voyeur. She catches him looking in on Leith, a
nurse, as she undresses, and threatens to expose Noonan if he turns her in.
Friday night comes, and the three robbers decide to have a drink. They go
to a local bar, where Egan is trying to seduce Leith. Leith doesn't want to
go to bed with him and takes Egan back to his house. As she puts him into
bed, Hayes returns from a dalliance. Leith tells Hayes that she just might
lose her husband, then beats a hasty retreat. The couple argue but in the
morning agree to give the marriage another try. They decide to take a
vacation, and to this end Hayes goes to the bank to fetch some traveler's
checks. Sidney is also there, reading her stolen funds for the mortgage
payment. Marvin, Naish, and McNally arrive on schedule for the holdup.
Sidney becomes frantic when her money is taken, while Noonan reaches for
a gun in a heroic effort to stop the crime. There is some shooting, and Hayes
is struck by a bullet. She is killed, and the trio of robbers make their escape.
They hijack Mature and his car, driving out to an isolated area where
Borgnine, an Amish farmer, lives with his family. They tie up the family,
along with Mature, but the Amish manage to break their bonds. Mature kills
one of the robbers, takes his gun, and tries to get at the other two. Borgnine,
whose religious beliefs won't allow him to commit a violent act, refuses to
help until one of his children is accidentally gunned down. To protect his
family, Borgnine grabs a pitchfork and helps Mature kill the other two
robbers. In the aftermath of this violent day, Mature's son accepts his
father's heroic actions as a substitute for war combat experience, while
Borgnine must come to terms with his religion's strict codes and the
encroaching modern society he can no longer ignore. Egan is shattered by
the death of his wife, though Leith offers him comfort and a possibility of
future romance. As a cinematic study of small-town life, this is a fascinating
portrait. The residents carry their problems under their cloaks as neurotic
baggage, hoping to keep everything covered, and terrified at the slightest
hint of their problems surfacing. No one is safe from this specter, not even
Borgnine, as he is forced to meet his worst fears head-on. The trio of
hoodlums is a symbolic blasting cap, ripping open hidden feelings with their
sudden, unexpected violence. Fleischer carefully balances the caper's
development with the town life, drawing a taut line between the two as he
builds towards the explosive climax. The performances here are strong,
particularly Marvin's sadistic gangster, and Borgnine's pacifist farmer.

p, Buddy Adler; d, Richard Fleischer; w, Sydney Boehm (based on the novel
by William L. Heath); ph, Charles G. Clarke (CinemaScope, DeLuxe Color);
m, Hugo Friedhofer; ed, Louis Loeffler; md, Lionel Newman; art d, Lyle
Wheeler, George W. Davis; cos, Kay Nelson.

Crime Drama   **(PR:O   MPAA:NR)**

VIOLENT STRANGER*½   (1957, Brit.) 83m Merton Park-Anglo
  Amalgamated/Anglo Amal gamated bw (GB: MAN IN THE SHADOW)

Zachary Scott *(John Sullivan)*, Faith Domergue *(Barbara Peters)*, Peter
Illing *(Carl Raffone)*, Faith Brook *(Joan Lennox)*, Kay Callard *(Pamela
Norris)*, Gordon Jackson *(Jimmy Norris)*, John Welsh *(Inspector Hunt)*,
John Horsley *(Alan Peters)*, Julian Strange *(Detective Sergeant)*, Fabia
Drake *(Sister Veronica)*, Derek Sydney *(Consini)*, Catharina Ferraz *(Sister
Cristina)*, Harold Siddons *(Colin Wells)*, George Bishop *(Wells, Sr.)*, Alec
Finter *(Mr. Holman)*, Charlie Bird *(1st Warder)*, George Barker *(2nd
Warder)*, Frank Hawkins, Michael Nightingale, Anthony Pendrell *(British
European Airlines Officials)*, Lance Maraschal *(Consul)*, Charles Hill, David
Saire *(Reception Clerks)*, Roger Delgado *(Alberto)*, Bruno Barnabe *(Italian
Barber)*, Malou Pantera *(Girl Cashier)*, Douglas Hays *(Porter)*, Richard
Golding *(Interpreter)*, Tom Symonds *(Italian Policeman)*, Philip Leaver
(Passport Official), Douglas Ives *(Left Luggage Attendant)*, Martin Boddey
(Doctor), Katherine Page *(Landlady)*, Peter Hobbes *(Doctor at Newhaven)*,
Stella Bonheur *(Sister at Newhaven)*, Barry Raymond *(Policeman)*, Marga-
ret Homes *(Nurse)*, Philip Baird *(Detective)*, Basil Dignam.

In the twilight of his career, Scott went to England to make this confusing
picture, which cast him in his usual role of the suave no-gooder. Here he is
the object of vengeance for Domergue, whose husband Horsley had been
convicted and sentenced to death for a murder that Scott actually committed. The inclusion of a number of subplots only serves to take away from the
film's pacing and movement.

p, Alec Snowden; d, Montgomery Tully; w, Stratford Davis; ph, Philip
Grindrod.

Crime   **(PR:A   MPAA:NR)**

VIOLENT STREETS   (SEE: THIEF, 1981)

VIOLENT SUMMER½   (1961, Fr./Ital.) 95m Titanus-S.G.C./Around
The World-Don K ay bw (ESTATE VIOLENTA; ETE VIOLENT; AKA:
                                                      THE WIDOW IS WILLING)

Eleonora Rossi Drago *(Roberta Parmesa)*, Jean-Louis Trintignant *(Carlo
Romanazzi)*, Jacqueline Sassard *(Rossanna)*, Lilla Brignone *(Signorina
Raluisa)*, Federica Ranchi *(Maddalena)*, Raf Mattioli *(Guilio)*, Enrico Maria
Salerno *(Carlo's Father)*, Cathia Caro *(Gemma)*, Bruno Carotenuto, Giam-
piero Littera, Xenia Valderi, Tina Gloriani, Nadia Gray.

The summer romance between the son of a prominent fascist, Trintignant,
and the lovely widow, Rosssi Drago, is violently distrupted when the Allied
forces land near the seaside resort where the two have had no contact with
the outside conflict. Fleeing southward, their train is bombed. For the first
time, Trintignant is forced to witness the war, something he was able to
avoid because of his fascist father's officialposition while other men his age
were sent to die in battle. Overcome with guilt, he ends his ideal affair and
does what he can to help the wounded. A lot of footage is spent on the pair's
love-making and there is also one completely unnecessary nude scene of
Rossi-Drago.

p. Silvio Clementelli; d, Valerio Zurlini; w, Zurlini, Suso Cecchi D'Amico,
Giorgio Prosperi; ph, Tino Santoni; m, Mario Nascimbene; ed, Mario
Serandrei; set d, Dario Cecchi, Massimiliano Capriccioli.

Drama/War   (PR:C MPAA:NR)

VIOLENT WOMEN**   (1960) 63m Brenner

Jennifer Statler *(Jo)*, Jo Ann Kelly *(Billy)*, Sandy Lyn *(Beverly)*, Eleanor
Blair *(Thelma)*, Pati Magee *(Brenda)*, Paula Scott *(Ginger)*.

Five woman convicts attempt a prison break by tunneling to a nearby sewer.
Despite their penetrating efforts and determination, the ending has all five
convicts meeting with death. An unusual depiction of women in American
films, showing them involved in antics that would make the hardest
criminal cringe.

p&d, Barry Mahon.;

Crime/Drama   (PR:O MPAA:NR)

VIOLENT YEARS, THE zero   (1956) 85m Headliner Productions bw
                                                            (AKA: FEMALE)

Jean Moorehead, Barbara Weeks, Glenn Corbett, Gloria Parr, Lee Constant,
Art Millan, I. Stanford Jolley.

Terrifically corrupt exploitation film has the mild-looking daughter of a
newspaper man forming a gang of vicious girls who roam the highways and
streets, robbing gas stations, assaulting men, and throwing wild pajama
parties. When they kill a cop they go to jail, where Moorehead dies giving
birth to an illegitimate child, to which all the other sad girls in this poor
misguided troupe say, "So what?" Screenwriter Wood directed the unforget-
tably awful PLAN 9 FROM OUTER SPACE (1959).

p, O'Camp, A.O. Bayer; d, Franz Eichorn; w, Edward D. Wood, Jr.

Crime   **Cas.**   (PR:C-O MPAA:NR)

VIOLENZA PER UNA MONACA
                     (SEE: NUN AT THE CROSSROADS, A, 1970, Ital./Span.)

VIOLETTE***   (1978, Fr.) 123m GAU/New Yorker c (AKA: VIOLETTE
                                                                 NOZIERE)

Isabelle Huppert *(Violette Noziere)*, Stephane Audran *(Germaine Noziere)*,
Jean Carmet *(Baptiste Noziere)*, Jean-Francois Garreaud *(Jean Dabin)*, Lisa
Langlois *(Maddy)*, Guy Hoffman *(the Judge)*, Bernard Lajarrige *(Andre De
Pinguet)*, Bernadette Lafont *(Violette's Cellmate)*, Jean Dalmain *(Mr.
Emile)*, Jean-Pierre Coffe *(Dr. Deron)*, Zoe Chaveau *(Zoe the Maid)*, Francois
Maistre *(Mayeul)*, Francois-Eric Gendron *(1st Student)*, Gregory Germain
(Black Musician), Dominique Zardi *(Boy in Cafe)*, Jean-Francois Dupas
(Inspector Champs-de-Mars), Henri-Jacques Huet *(Commissioner Guil-
leaume)*, Maurice Vaudaux *(Willy)*, Fabrice Luchini *(Camus)*.

In the 1930s Paris was both shocked and titillated by the sensational
patricide committed by 19-year old Violette Noziere. She was sentenced to
death for the poisoning death of her father and an attempt on her mother's
life as well; the sentence was commuted to life imprisonment. The case held
great fascination for many artists of the era. Claude Chabrol filmed his
version some 45 years later and though not entirely successful it still makes
for interesting viewing. Huppert, in a stunning performance, plays the
young woman who is bored with life and seeks excitement in seedy Parisian
cafes, where she meets her lover. In order to inherit money from her parents
to give to this lover, Huppert attempts to poison the unsuspecting Audran
and Carmet. Carmet dies but Audran survives and sends her daughter to
prison. Only in prison does Huppert at last find a perverse sort of happiness,
freed from the madness of the outside world. Chabrol's strengths are in the
set design and his camera work. This is a very beautiful film to look at

despite the repulsive nature of its story. Huppert is sensational, creating
some genuine sympathy for a woman who blames her parents when she gets
syphilis, then proceeds to poison them. Chabrol falters though within his
story construction. There are moments that could be better connected and
developed. This aside, VIOLETTE is still a fascinating portrait that should
not be missed. (In French; English subtitles.)

p, Roger Morand; d, Claude Chabrol; w, Odile Barski, Herve Bromberger,
Frederic Grendel (based on the book by Jean-Marie Fitere); ph, Jean Rabier;
m, Pierre Jansen; artd, Jacques Brizzio); cos, Pierre Nourry.

Crime/Drama   **Cas.**   (PR:O MPAA:R)

VIOLIN AND ROLLER½   (1962, USSR) 55m Mosfilm/Artkino c
(KATOK I SKRIPKA; AKA : THE SKATING-RINK AND THE VIOLIN;
                                                 THE VIOLIN AND THE ROLLER)

Igor Fomchenko *(Sasha)*, V. Zamanskiy *(Sergey)*, Nina Arkhangelskaya
(The Girl), Marina Adzhubey, Yura Brusser, Slava Borisov, Sasha Vitoslav-
skiy, Sasha Ilin, Kolya Kozarev, Gena Klyachkovskiy, Igor Korovikov,
Zhenya Fedchenko, Tanya Prokhorova, A. Maksimova, L. Semyonova, G.
Zhdanova, M. Figner.

Made as a student project during his training at The All-Union State
Institute of Cinematography (VGIK) in Moscow by Tarkovskiy in collaboration with his friends and fellow students Konchalovskiy (who is credited by
some as co-director) and cinematographer Yusov, this film is the touching
story of a day in the life of two unlikely friends. Zamanskiy is a
tractor-driving road worker who defends young violin student Fomchenko
from a group of teasing hooligans. The seven-year-old artist then shares the
proletarian's lunch with him as they converse. The boy takes a ride on the
road-rolling vehicle, and in return plays his violin for the driver. The
experience is revelatory for them both. A perspective of the world as
revealed through the observations of the very young is a familiar theme in
Soviet cinema, and the creators of this picture have handled it beautifully
here. Their sensitivity with sound, and the nuances of Ovchinnikov's score,
work wonderfully with the visuals. Due to difficulties with the Cyrillic
alphabet, the names of the cast and crew members are often spelled in
different ways when translated into English; one source credits direction to
Alexi Tartovsky. However the name is spelled, the talented director went
on after graduation to become one of the Soviet Union's most respected
helmers, as did his coscripter Konchalovskiy.

d, Andrey Tarkovskiy; w, Tarkovskii, Andrei Konchalovskiy (based on a
story by S. Bakhmetyeva); ph, Vadim Yusov (Sovcolor); m, Vyacheslav
Ovchinnikov; ed, L. Butuzova; md, E. Khachaturyan; art d, S. Agoyan; cos,
A. Martinson; spec eff,B. Pluzhnikov, V. Sevostyanov, A. Rudachenko;
makeup, A. Makasheva.

Drama   (PR:A MPAA:NR)

VIPER, THE*½   (1938, Brit.) 75m WB/FN bw

Claude Hulbert *(Cedric Gull)*, Betty Lynne *(Gaby Toulong)*, Hal Walters
(Stiffy Mason), Lesley Brook *(Jenny)*, Fred Groves *(Inspector Bradawl)*, Dino
Galvani *(The Viper)*, Boris Ranevsky *(Carlos)*, Harvey Braban *(Jagger)*,
Reginald Purdell *(Announcer)*, Julian Henry, John F. Traynor.

Detective Hulbert and his right-hand man Walters investigate the story
behind Brook being accused of stealing. She's the detective's niece and
something seems amiss. Lynne, a dancer, also has some troubles as she's
being chased by Galvani, an escapee from Devil's Island. It's discovered that
a diamond is hidden in Lynne's shoe and all comes to a satisfactory
conclusion. Pretty nonsensical stuff with too many costume changes by the
plucky detective, none of which adds to the comedy.

p, Irving Asher; d, Roy William Neill; w, Reginald Purdell, John Dighton,
J.O.C. Orton; ph, Basil Emmott.

Comedy/Crime   (PR:A MPAA:NR)

VIRGIN AND THE GYPSY, THE*½   (1970, Brit.) 92m
                                       Kenwood-London Screenplays/Chevron c

Joanna Shimkus *(Yvette)*, Franco Nero *(Gypsy)*, Honor Blackman *(Mrs.
Fawcett)*, Mark Burns *(Maj. Eastwood)*, Maurice Denham *(The Rector)*, Fay
Compton *(Grandma)*, Kay Walsh *(Aunt Cissie)*, Harriet Harper *(Lucille)*,
Norman Bird *(Uncle Fred)*, Imogen Hassall *(Gypsy's Wife)*, Jeremy Bulloch
(Leo), Roy Holder *(Bob)*, Margo Andrew *(Ella)*, Janet Chappell *(Mary)*,
Helen Booth *(Cook)*, Laurie Dale *(Thomas)*, Lulu Davies *(Gypsy Grandmoth-
er)*.

This adaptation of the posthumously published novella by D.H. Lawrence,
does a better job of capturing the themes of sexual repression in strait-laced
society and the hypocrisy of those who uphold it than most film renditions.
Unlike Ken Russell's WOMEN IN LOVE, which focused on lush atmosphere
as an allegory representing the inner awakenings of its characters, THE
VIRGIN AND THE GYPSY opts for an almost literal translation of the
master's work. This has both its good points and bad; the latter because of
the literary conventions of Lawrence's era which seem hackneyed when
brought to the modern cinema. But for capturing the inhibitions and sense
of entrapment felt by a young woman in 1920s England, director Miles

(brother of actress Sarah) has done a fine job in his feature directorial debut. Shimkus plays a young graduate of a provincial French school who returns home to Northern England, along with her sister Harper, to the house lorded over by her strict father Denham and spinster aunt Walsh. This inhibiting home environment is contrasted to the looseness of a gypsy camp, where Shimkus encounters Nero, resulting in meetings which evoke deep sexual feelings she is later to discuss with Blackman and Burns, an unmarried couple, the object of the town's derision because of their "immoral ways. "The breaking of a dam causes a flood which kills Shimkus' grandmother, but the young woman is saved through the efforts of gypsy Nero, who takes Shimkus upstairs for her first sexual encounter. The rising-water metaphor could have been handled in a more sophisticated manner, but Miles' insistence on remaining true to his source didn't allow him to see where changes might have helped the development of the film. The picture is extremely well cast. Actress Margaret Rutherford was originally signed to play Compton's role as the feisty old grandmother, but her increasing senility prevented her from learning her lines. Songs include "Keep Your Hand on Your Halfpenny" (Alex Glasgow); "My Latest (Millionaire" (Ronald Cass); "The Charleston Hop" (Peter Myers).

p, Kenneth Harper; d, Christopher Miles; w, Alan Plater (based on the novella by D. H. Lawrence); ph, Bob Huke (Movielab Color); m, Patrick Gowers; ed, Paul Davies; prod d, Terence Knight; md, Gowers; art d, David Brockhurst, cos, Deirdre Clancy.

Drama (PR:O MPAA:R)

VIRGIN AQUA SEX, THE (SEE: MERMAIDS OF TIBURON, 1962)

VIRGIN COCOTTE, THE (SEE; COQUETTE, 1929)

VIRGIN FOR THE PRINCE, A (SEE: MAIDEN FOR A PRINCE, A, 1967, Ital.)

VIRGIN ISLAND** (1960, Brit.) 84m
Countryman/Films-Around-The-World c (AKA: OUR VIRGIN ISLAND)

John Cassavetes (Evan, Archaeologist), Virginia Maskell (Tina Lomax), Sidney Poitier (Marcus), Isabel Dean (Mrs. Lomax), Colin Gordon (The Commander), Howard Marion Crawford (Prescott), Edric Connor (Capt. Jason), Ruby Dee (Ruth), Gladys Boot (Mrs. Carruthers), Julian Mayfield (Band Leader), Reginald Hearne (Doctor), Arnold Bell (Heath), Alonzo Bozan (Grant).

A unpretentious effort designed to do nothing more than conjure up pleasant thoughts or memories during its hour and a half duration. Cassavetes is the young intellectual who has an idea about living a life away from the rat race; his meeting with Maskell gives him the perfect mate to while away his time with on a tropical island. The newlywed couple buys a small island for $85, set up their love nest with the assistance of local Poitier, and live the dream many people have some place in the back of their minds. A baby pops into the picture, providing the highest dramatic point when his arrival time coincides with Cassavetes and Maskall being stranded in a boat. Notwithstanding the absence of plot and technical problems, the picture manages to hold up through the performaces of Cassavetes and Poitier, their energy coming through even when the script doesn't call for it.

p, Leon Clore, Grahame Tharp; d, Pat Jackson; w, Jackson, Philip Rush (based on the novel Our Virgin Island by Robb White); ph, Freddie Francis; m, Clifton Parker; ed, Gordon Pilkington.

Drama (PR:C MPAA:NR)

VIRGIN OF NUREMBURG, THE (SEE: HORROR CASTLE, 1963, Ital.)

VIRGIN PRESIDENT, THE* (1968) 71m New Line cinema bw

Severn Darden (Henry F. Millmore/Fillard Millmore/The Narrator/Millmore's Ghost), Richard Neuweiler (Secretary of State Schuyler Colfax), Andrew Duncan (Secretary of Defense William Salvo), Louis Walden (CIA Chief Jock Steel), Richard Schaal (Hugh Mugababy), Paul Benedict (Rutherford Melon), Sudie Bond (Mom Millmore), Anthony Holland (Machiavelli von Clausewitz), Conrad Yama (The Chinese Prime Minister), L'nelle Hamanaka (Prime Minister's Daughter), Sabrini Scharf (President's Girl Friend), Peter Boyle (Gen. Heath), Charlotte Baumgartner (White House Courtesan).

Silly concoction about a future president of the U.S. who is being used by his cabinet members to create programs which they see as beneficial. One such plan is the dropping of a bomb on New York to try and boost the stock market. Darden and Ferguson came up with the story outline for this, but the film's dialog was improvised.

p, Severn Darden, Graeme Ferguson, Jim Hubbard; d, Ferguson; w, Darden, Ferguson; ph, Ferguson; m, Teiji Ito; ed, Mark Rappaport, Burt Rashby, Thelma Schoonmaker.

Satire (PR:A MPAA:NR)

VIRGIN QUEEN, THE*** (1955) 92m FOX c

Bette Davis (Queen Elizabeth), Richard Todd (Sir Walter Raleigh), Joan Collins (Beth Throgmorton), Jay Robinson (Chadwick), Herbert Marshall (Lord Leicester), Dan O'Herlihy (Lord Derry), Robert Douglas (Sir Christopher Hatton), Romney Brent (French Ambassador), Marjorie Hellen 'Leslie Parrish' (Anne), Lisa Daniels (Mary), Lisa Davis (Jane), Barry Bernard (Patch Eye), Robert Adler (Postillion Rider), Noel Drayton (Tailor), Ian Murray (Gentleman of the Bedchamber), Margery Weston (Dame Bragg), Rod Taylor (Cpl. Gwilym), David Thursby (Landlord), Arthur Gould-Porter (Randall the Ship Builder), John Costello (Town Crier), Nelson Leigh, Frank Baker (Physicians), Ashley Cowan (Sailor).

Davis is the glue that holds this movie together. Without her reprise as Queen Elizabeth (she's done it before in 1939 with Errol Flynn in ELIZABETH AND ESSEX), it would have been an ordinary costumer starring Richard Todd and Joan Collins. Todd is the man who lent his name to the pipe tobacco and returns to 1581 England after having been honored for his work in the war against the Irish. His swashbuckling feats have impressed Marshall, who is, as they say, "close to the queen." Marshall likes Todd and arranges to have the young man presented at court. In order to make a good impression on Davis, Todd has a new cloak made, one he can ill afford. He wants to convince Davis to finance a projected trip to the Americas where he believes he will find much treasure. There's a mud puddle in the courtyard and Todd gallantly lays his expensive garment down so Davis can cross without getting her tiny feet soiled. This chivalrous move wins her over, but perhaps it's too far over because the aged monarch begins acting like a silly schoolgirl whenever Todd strides into view. It's the talk of the castle and environs and Davis twitters and bats her eyelashes until it almost becomes ludicrous. Robinson is another confidante of Davis and he takes an immediate dislike to Todd, who he suspects is an opportunist. When Davis names Todd as captain of the guard, Robinson seethes because he had recommended against it. Now that Todd is living at the castle and near the seat of power, he begins casting his roving eye around the area and soon spots Collins, a lady-in- waiting. Collins is just as attracted to Todd but wonders how in the world she can get to him when her rival for his affections is her very own queen. Todd now directly asks if Davis will put up the pounds for his expedition that requires three ships. Davis cuts him down to one ship only and says she'll think about it. Meanwhile, the love between Todd and Collins has burgeoned and they can contain themselves no longer so they are surreptitiously wed. Davis decides that Todd can have his boat and takes him to her bedchamber where she dubs him "sir." Her joy at having made him a peer is soon shattered when she discovers that Todd and Collins have tied the knot. Enraged by this turn of events (who would dare to spurn a queen?), she has the blighter arrested and dragged to the Tower of London, the traditional jumping-off place for peers and ladies who are to be separated from their heads. The night before Todd is to be executed, Davis makes a trip to his cell and recalls it as the same cell where her own mother spent her last night before being dispatched. Her heart is softened somewhat by the surroundings and she comes to the realization that Todd was not really toying with her affections but he was only trying to butter her up to get the money for his voyage. Davis relents and frees Todd so he and Collins can go across the seas and seek the fortunes which he will bring back for England. In real life, James I released Sir Walter to go explore the Orinoco River's gold area but with strict orders that he would not attempt to take gold from any Spanish possession. Raleigh and his son arrived at the mouth of the Orinoco on December 31, 1617. He sent his ships up the river with his son and nephew while he stayed in Trinidad suffering from fever. A battle between the British and Spanish took place in which Raleigh's son was killed and when Raleigh returned to England, he was executed at the age of 66 in order to fulfill James' promise to Spain that if Raleigh engaged in any piracy, he would be executed. And so he was. But we digress. The acting in the movie was all good, with Davis taking most of the honors. The movie originally figured to be a Todd-Collins starrer but when Davis joined the cast, the script was rewritten to accommodate her wishes and increase her role. She shot all of her scenes in less than 12 days but her presence is so dominating one gets the feeling that she is all through the movie. It was 16 years since she had played Elizabeth the first time and she showed great insight as she became suspicious, greedy, lonesome, and sometimes evil. The sets were not up to Fox's usual style and appeared as though they were just a trifle low-budget.

p, Charles Brackett; d, Henry Koster; w, Harry Brown, Mindret Lord; ph, Charles G. Clarke (CinemaScope, DeLuxe Color); m, Franz Waxman; ed, Robert Simpson; art d, Lyle Wheeler, Leland Fuller; cos, Mary Wills.

Historical Drama **Cas.** (PR:A-C MPAA:NR)

VIRGIN SACRIFICE*½ (1959) 63m Pan American/Releasing Corp. of Independent Pro ducers-States Rights c

David DaLie (Samson), Antonio Gutierrez (Tumic), Angelica Morales (Morena), Fernando Wagner (Fernando), Linda Cordova, Philip Pearl, Hamdy Sayed, Vicuni Indian Tribe Dancers: Clarence Landry, Nina Peron, Bob Larca, Lydia Goya, Joe Lanza.

DaLie, in a role based upon his own exploits as a big-game hunter, plays a man looking for jaguars in the jungles of Guatemala. When the body one of the members of his camp is found badly mutilated, suspicion is placed on the neighboring Vicuni Indians, a primitive people who have been known to sacrifice humans to their jungle gods. This was one of the first pictures to use the jungles of Guatemala, which are effectively captured in the color photography.

p, John F. Horn; d, Fernando Wagner; w, V. and J. Rhems (based on an idea by David DaLie); ph, Walter Reuter (Tropicolor).

Adventure   **(PR:C MPAA:NR)**

VIRGIN SOLDIERS, THE**½   (1970, Brit.) 96m Open Road-Highroad/COL c

Lynn Redgrave (*Phillipa Raskin*), Hywel Bennett (*Pvt. Brigg*), Nigel Davenport (*St. Driscoll*), Nigel Patrick (*Regimental Sergeant Major Raskin*), Rachel Kempson (*Mrs. Raskin*), Jack Shepherd (*Sgt. Wellbeloved*), Michael Gwynn (*Lt. Col. Bromley-Pickering*), Tsai Chin (*Juicy Lucy*), Christopher Timothy (*Cpl. Brook*), Don Hawkins (*Tasker*), Geoffrey Hughes (*Lantry*), Roy Holder (*Fenwick*), Riggs O'Hara (*Sinclair*), Gregory Phillips (*Foster*), Wayne Sleep (*Villiers*), Peter Kelly (*Sandy Jacobs*), Mark Nicholls (*Cutler*), Alan Shatsman (*Longley*), Jonty Miller (*Forsyth*), Jolyon Jackley (*Lance Cpl. Browning*), Robert Bridges (*Sgt. Fred Organ*), James Cosmo (*Waller*), Graham Crowden (*Medical Officer*), Dudley Jones (*Doctor*), Mathew Guinness (*Maj. Cusper*), Naranjan Singh (*Sikh*), F. Yew (*"Hallelujah"*), Brenda Bruce (*Nursing Sister*), Barbara Keogh (*W.R.A.C.*).

An amusing and, to some extent, insightful look into the lives of young British soldiers serving in Malaya. Their major concern, outweighing the threat of rebel revolt, is the pursuit of sexual conquests. With most of the young men naive about romance as well as war, the film concentrates on the exploits of Bennett as a clerk with a fancy for Redgrave, a local school teacher and daughter of Regimental Sergeant major Patrick. Both have had no experience in the subtler aspects of romance, so their attempts result in rather embarrassing spectacles. Eventually, they do hit it off, the opportune moment coming during a raid, and only after they both have had sexual experiences elsewhere. Though there are many performances which could easily take on stereotypical characteristics, director Dexter avoids this trap and the result is genuine, heartfelt humor. STAND UP VIRGIN SOLDIERS (1977) was the sequel to this.

p, Leslie Gilliat, Ned Sherrin; d, Johm Dexter; w, John Hopkins, John McGrath, Ian La Fresnais (based on the novel by Leslie Thomas); ph, Ken higgins (Technicolor); m, Peter Greenwell, "The Virgin Soldiers March," Raymond Douglas Davies; ed, Thelma Connell; md, Greenwell; art d, Frank White; makeup, Philip Leakey.

Comedy/Drama   **(PR:O MPAA:R)**

VIRGIN SPRING, THE***   (1960, Swed.) 88m Svensk Filmindustri/JANUS bw (JUNGFRUKALLAN)

Max von Sydow (*Herr Tore*), Birgitta Pettersson (*Karin Tore*), Birgitta Valberg (*Mareta Tore*), Gunnel Lindblom (*Ingeri*), Axel Duberg (*Thin Herdsman*), Tor Isedal (*Mute Herdsman*), Ove Porath (*Boy*), Allan Edwall (*Beggar*), Gudrun Brost (*Frida*), Oscar Ljung (*Simon*), Axel Slangus (*Old Man at River Ford*), Tor Borong, Leif Forstenberg (*Farmhands*).

Despite the fact that this movie won Bergman his first Oscar (Best Foreign Film) and is regarded by Bergmaniacs as a "classic," we found it heavy going. Based on a medieval ballad, "The Daughter of Tore of Vange," it takes place in 14th-Century Sweden where Christianity and various heathen faiths were vying for the people's attentions. Pettersson is a 15-year-old virgin who is spoiled by her parents and has her mother, Valberg, in the palm of her hand. Pettersson is to go to church to light candles to the Virgin Mary and asks Valberg if she can be allowed to wear a special gown that has been handmade by 15 virgins. Her father is von Sydow and she begs him to allow her foster sister, Lindblom, to come along. Lindblom is carrying an illegitimate child and harbors a great jealousy for the more attractive Pettersson. Both girls ride to the rim of the woods and meet Slangus, the keeper of the bridge, who invites them to rest at his house. Lindblom stays there and Pettersson moves on alone. Deep in the forest, Pettersson meets three sheepherders– two older men and a young boy. They appear hungry and she climbs off her expensive horse (von Sydow is a wealthy land owner who can afford the best of everything) to share her food with them. After they finish eating, the two older men rape Pettersson while the young boy, Porath, watches. Also watching is Lindblom, who has left the home of Slangus. She is powerless to help and one feels she may actually be enjoying the plight of Pettersson. Once the rape is done, Pettersson is crying bitterly and the men realize they can't allow her to live so they beat her to death with a thick stick, then take her gown which they hope to sell. A few hours later, the trio come out of the woods and find themselves at the home of von Sydow and Valberg. They ask for and are granted a place to sleep and some victuals. In the middle of the night, Porath lets out a yelp and Valberg is roused. She comes to see the boy and he shows her the gown made by 15 virgins and says that it belonged to his sister. Valberg's face turns white but she doesn't betray the fact that she recognizes the bloody garment. Valberg locks the door on the shed where the men are staying and wakes von Sydow, telling him what she's learned. When Lindblom returns and tells him what she saw, von Sydow takes a huge sheep-killing knife and hacks the trio to death as they sleep. Valberg and von Sydow go into the woods and find the lifeless and violated body of Pettersson and von Sydow begins to question the existence of the God he always believed looked after him. He wonders

how this all could have happened, how Pettersson could have been raped and killed, and even how he came to kill the three men who perpetrated the deed. He leans down and lifts the frail corpse and a fresh spring of water erupts where Pettersson had been, a moment after von Sydow had sworn that he would build a church on the spot in her honor. The European print had more of the rape scene in it than the U.S. version and the brutality and naturalism of that sequence is what may have sold the movie on the continent. The acting is excellent and even though it's all in Swedish, there is no mistaking the emotions of the people as they speak. Many of those who have seen this and other Bergman films have been quick to read all sorts of mystical meanings in the narrative. It appears to be about guilt, about revenge, about religion, about violence, about evil, and about 10 minutes too long. (In Swedish; English subtitles.)

p, Ingmar Bergman, Allan Ekelund; d, Bergman; w, Ulla Isaksson (based on the 14th-Century ballad "Tores Dotter I Vange"); ph, Sven Nykvist, Rolf Halmquist; m, Erik Nordgren; ed, Oscar Rosander; art d, P.A. Lundgren; cos, Marik Vos.

Historical   **(PR:C MPAA:NR)**

VIRGIN WITCH, THE*   (1973, Brit.) 87m Univista/Joseph Brenner c (AKA: LESBIAN TWINS)

Anne Michelle (*Christine*), Patricia Haines (*Sybil Waite*), Vicki Michelle (*Betty*), Keith Buckley (*John*), James Chase (*Peter*), Neal Hallett (*Gerald Amberley*), Helen Downing (*Abby Drake*), Paula Wright (*Mrs. Wendell*).

A very bad picture that takes a couple of provincial girls, Michelle and Haines, to London where they hope to enter the world of high fashion as models. Instead they become prey for a lesbian who supplies a coven of "good" witches and warlocks with prospective members. Made in Britain in 1970, this combination of soft-core sex and witchcraft was dredged up for U.S. release a couple of times by Joseph Brenner, the first time in 1973, then again in 1978.

p, Ralph Solomons, Dennis Durack, Edward Brady; d, Ray Austin; w, Klaus Vogel (based on the novel by Vogel); ph, Gerald Moss (Eastmancolor); m, Ted Dicks; ed, Philip Barknel.

Horror   **Cas.**   **(PR:O MPAA:R)**

VIRGINIA*½   (1941) 110m PAR c

Madeleine Carroll (*Charlotte Dunterry*), Fred MacMurray (*Stonewall Elliott*), Sterling Hayden (*Norman Williams*), Helen Broderick (*Theo Clairmont*), Carolyn Lee (*Pretty Elliott*), Marie Wilson (*Connie Potter*), Paul Hurst (*Thomas*), Tom Rutherford (*Carter Francis*), Leigh Whipper (*Ezechial*), Louise Beavers (*Ophelia*), Darby Jones (*Joseph*), Edward Van Sloan, John Hyams (*Ministers*), William Russell (*Loafer*), Thomas Louden, Wilson Benge (*Butlers*), Wanda McKay (*Girl*), Sam McDaniel, Charles R. Moore (*Servants*), George Mitchell, Jan Buckingham (*Guests*).

Scenic Virginia backgrounds and a decent cast could do little to save this dreary story about the New York showgirl who goes back home to the southern state to make claim on an inheritance. As the girl who could only think sell, Carroll soon finds herself involved in a love triangle with MacMurray and Hayden, the latter mainly because of the affluence and financial security he can offer. This was Hayden's first screen appearance, and like the others in the cast, he was handcuffed by the material. A year prior to the release of VIRGINIA, MacMurray, Carroll, Griffith, and Van Upp collaborated on the successful CAFE SOCIETY and HONEYMOON IN BALI, and they had every reason to believe that this film would do equally well. They were mistaken.

p&d, Edward H. Griffith; w, Virginia Van Upp (based on a story by Griffith, Van Upp); ph, Bert Glennon, William V. Skall (Technicolor); ed, Eda Warren; art d, Hans Dreier, Ernst Fegte.

Drama   **(PR:A MPAA:NR)**

VIRGINIA CITY***½   (1940) 121m WB bw

Errol Flynn (*Kerry Bradford*), Miriam Hopkins (*Julia Hayne*), Randolph Scott (*Vance Irby*), Humphrey Bogart (*John Murrell*), Frank McHugh (*Mr. Upjohn*), Alan Hale (*Olaf "Moose" Swenson*), Guinn "Big Boy" Williams (*"Marblehead"*), John Litel (*Marshal*), Moroni Olsen (*Dr. Cameron*), Russell Hicks (*Armistead*), Douglass Dumbrille (*Maj. Drewery*), Dickie Jones (*Cobby*), Monte Montague, Bud Osborne (*Stage Drivers*), Lane Chandler (*Soldier Clerk*), Trevor Bardette (*Fanatic*), Frank Wilcox, Ed Keane (*Officers*), George Regas (*Half-Breed*), Russell Simpson (*Gaylord*), Thurston Hall (*Gen. Meade*), Charles Middleton (*Jefferson Davis*), Victor Kilian (*Abraham Lincoln*), Charles Trowbridge (*Seddon*), Howard Hickman (*Gen. Page*), Charles Halton (*Ralston*), Roy Gordon (*Maj. Gen. Taylor*), Ward Bond (*Sgt. Sam McDaniel*), Spencer Charters, George Guhl (*Bartenders*), Ed Parker, DeWolfe Hopper (*Lieutenants*), Paul Rix (*Murrell's Henchman*), Walter Miller, Reed Howes (*Sergeants*), George Reeves (*Telegrapher*), Wilfred Lucas (*Southerner*), Brandon Tynan (*Trenholm*), Tom Dugan (*Spieler*), Harry Cording (*Scarecrow*).

A followup to 1939's DODGE CITY (though by no means a sequel) features Flynn as a Union officer who manages to escape from the Confederate prison where he has been held captive. Flynn wants to stop a $5 million gold shipment, sent from the North by Southern sympathizers who want to help the Confederacy's battered economy. Scott takes a westbound stagecoach, where he meets Hopkins. The coach is held up by Bogart, a half-breed outlaw with a pencil mustache (something rarely seen in the movies on Bogie's famous top lip). Arriving in Virgina City, Nevada, Flynn learns that Scott, who formerly ran the prison he escaped from, is going to send the gold by wagon train to Richmond, Virginia. Flynn falls for Hopkins, not realizing that she is really a Southern spy. With her help, Scott manages to recapture Flynn. Scott then meets with Bogart, and arranges for the outlaw and his band to attack Union troops so the wagon train can leave town unnoticed. The plan is a success, but later the caravan is inspected by some Union troops located in the desert. The Confederates fire at the bluecoats, and Flynn manages to escape. He then gets to Dumbrille, telling the general about the attack. Dumbrille and his cavalry men ride in, but end up taking the wrong route, victims of a trick. When Flynn is able to catch up to the wagon train, he sees Bogart and his men trying to get their hands on the gold. Flynn helps fight off the bandit, but his nemesis Scott is killed. Flynn then buries the loot, and Dumbrille finally rides in with his men, fending off the outlaws and killing Bogart. Because Flynn refuses to reveal where he has buried the gold, he is court-martialed by his superiors and sentenced to die. Hopkins, who has fallen in love with Flynn, goes to Washington D.C. and begs President Lincoln (Kilian, who is seen only in shadow) to spare Flynn's life. The film, based partially on a true Civil War incident, is not a particularly memorable film, though Flynn and Scott do give it some fine moments. The action sequences have some real flash to them, and once again, Yakima Canutt proves why he was considered the best stuntman in the movie business. At one point, just as in STAGECOACH, Canutt jumps between horses on a fast-moving wagon, coming within inches of the powerful hooves and wagon wheels before pulling himself back up. It's an amazing feat and well worth the price of admission. That the film actually was completed was something of a miracle in itself. Flynn cared little for Curtiz as a director and tried to get him removed from the film. Curtiz felt the same way about Flynn, and cared little for Hopkins as well. To add fuel to this personality fire, Bogart reportedly did get on well with Scott or Flynn. The film began without a finished script, which had angered Flynn. Curtiz then accused Flynn of bearing the subtlety of a Nazi stormtrooper on the set. After sending a telegram to Hal B. Wallis, expressing his anger with the partial script, Flynn received a reply which read: "Dear Heinrich Himmler Flynn: Will show you copy just as soon as ready. Thanks old fellow, keep up the good work. Regards. Hal." Flynn's misery was compounded by the constant rains that besieged the Flagstaff, Arizona locations. The rain caused the actor to suffer from painful headaches, sending him to bed in an unfitful sleep. Despite the troubles, VIRGINIA CITY turned out to be an entertaining picture. It was later put on a double bill with DODGE CITY in some markets. Although Tony Martin sang the title theme, it was deleted from the picture just before its national release. It was issued, however, on RCA Victor records.

p, Robert Fellows; d, Michael Curtiz; w, Robert Buckner, (uncredited) Norman Reilly Raine, Howard Koch); ph, Sol Polito; m, Max Steiner; ed, George Amy; art d, Ted Smith; spec eff, Byron Haskin, H.F. Koenekamp; makeup, Perc Westmore

Western   **(PR:A   MPAA:NR)**

VIRGINIA JUDGE, THE**   (1935) 62m PAR bw

Walter C. Kelly *(Judge Davis)*, Marsha Hunt *(Mary Lee Calvert)*, Stepin Fetchit *(Spasm Johnson)*, Johnny Downs *(Bob Stuart)*, Robert Cummings *(Jim Preston)*, Virginia Hammond *(Martha Davis)*, Dudley Dickerson, Willard Roberton, Davison Clark, Charles Aylesworth, Bernard Carr, LeRoy Broomfield, Spencer Williams, Billy McClain, Etta McDaniel, J.H. Allen, Darby Jones, James Pierce, Irving Bacon, Al Hill, Anna Lee Johnson, John Hyams, Mme. Bonita.

Routine fare about a kindly southern judge with a stepson who can't keep his head above water. Cummings is the young lad who shoots a man in a jealous pique, while Kelly sits behind the desk of the law conceiving a way to set the youngster on the right track. Former vaudevillian Kelly does a decent job in portraying the judge, though his performance is little more than a caricature. The direction helps move the picture along with a few deft touches of comedy at the expense of Stepin Fetchit.

p, Charles R. Rogers; d, Edward Sedgwick; w, Henry Johnson, Frank Adams, Inez Lopez (based on a story by Octavus Roy Cohen, Walter C. Kelly); ph, Milton Krasner; ed, Richard Currier.

Drama   **(PR:A   MPAA:NR)**

VIRGINIAN, THE***½   (1929) 92m FP-PAR bw

Gary Cooper *(The Virginian)*, Walter Huston *(Trampas)*, Mary Brian *(Molly Stark Wood)*, Richard Arlen *(Steve)*, Helen Ware *("Ma" Taylor)*, Chester Conklin *(Uncle Hughey)*, Eugene Pallette *("Honey" Wiggin)*, Victor Potel *(Nebraskey)*, E.H. Calvert *(Judge Henry)*, Tex Young *(Shorty)*, Charles Stevens *(Pedro)*, Jack Pennick *(Slim)*, George Chandler *(Ranch Hand)*, Willie Fung *(Hong the Cook)*, George Morrell *(Rev. Dr. McBride)*, Ernie S. Adams *(Saloon Singer)*, Ethan Laidlaw *(Posse Man)*, Ed Brady *(Greasy)*, Bob Kortman *(Henchman)*, James Mason *(Jim)*, Fred Burns *(Ranch Hand)*,

Nena Quartero *(Girl in Bar)*, Randolph Scott *(Rider)*.

Cooper made his first all-talker and a permanent mark on popular culture with this film adaptation of Owen Wister's popular novel. As the title character, Cooper is foreman of a Wyoming ranch. He gives a job to an old friend, Arlen, and they vie for the affections of schoolmarm Brian. Cooper wins out and Arlen goes bad, taking up with local villain Huston to rustle cattle from Cooper's herd. Cooper catches his friend changing brands and warns him, and when Arlen is later caught along with two other rustlers stealing more cattle, Cooper oversees the lynching of all three. Plagued by guilt, Cooper swears to get Huston, whom he knows to be the leader of the gang. When Brian finds out what Cooper has done, she rejects him. Later, though, in a skirmish with Huston, Cooper is wounded and Brian takes care of him, eventually agreeing to marry him. On the wedding day Huston brings matters to a head and the two men square off in the street for a showdown. Cooper is faster on the draw and Huston dies in the dust. This was the third film of the novel, previously done in 1921 starring Dustin Farnum and in 1923 starring Kenneth Harlan. Cooper played his role well, and it helped him escape the "It Boy" tag he had been saddled with. Now he could play rugged male leads instead of juvenile lovers. Huston is better, his Trampas the essence of western villainy and the standard to be imitated for years to come. Cooper was coached in the Virginia accent he would use by a real Virginian, and a bit actor in the film, Randolph Scott. The bit for which this film is most remembered, is Cooper's line when Huston, while playing cards, calls him a name. Cooper pulls his gun out, lays it on the table and says, "If you want to call me that, smile." (Somehow, this phrase has been perpetuated as "When you call me that, smile"– the line from the book.) The phrase caught on immediately and was used extensively in advertising for the film. It was a major box office success and was remade in 1946 with Joel McCrea, and became a TV series in 1962.

p, Louis D. Lighton; d, Victor Fleming; w, Howard Estabrook, Edward E. Paramore, Jr., Grover Jones, Keene Thompson (based on the play by Owen Wister, Kirk La Shelle, and the novel by Wister); ph, J. Roy Hunt, Edward Cronjager; ed, William Shea; titles, Joseph L. Mankiewicz.

Western   **(PR:A   MPAA:NR)**

VIRGINIAN, THE**½   (1946) 90m PAR c

Joel McCrea *(The Virginian)*, Brian Donlevy *(Trampas)*, Sonny Tufts *(Steve)*, Barbara Britton *(Molly Wood)*, Fay Bainter *(Mrs. Taylor)*, Henry O'Neill *(Mr. Taylor)*, William Frawley *(Honey Wiggen)*, Bill Edwards *(Sam Bennett)*, Minor Watson *(Judge Henry)*, Tom Tully *(Nebraska)*, Vince Barnett *(Baldy)*, Martin Garralaga *(Spanish Ed)*, Paul Guilfoyle *(Shorty)*, Marc Lawrence *(Pete)*, James Burke *(Andy Jones)*, Al Bridge *(Sheriff)*, Nana Bryant *(Mrs. Wood)*.

Uninspired remake of the oft-filmed Owen Wister story has little going for it except a few good performances. McCrea is the title character this time, following in the steps of Dustin Farnum, Kenneth Harlan, and Gary Cooper. When a friend, Tufts, takes up with rustler Donlevy, McCrea first tries to warn him off, and later stands by while a posse hangs Tufts after his depredations continue. Britton rejects him after this episode but they are later reconciled when McCrea takes a bullet from Donlevy. On the day McCrea and Britton are to be married, there is a final showdown with Donlevy, and McCrea comes out on top. Paramount tried to revamp the familiar story with the addition of Technicolor and a more adult approach to the plot, but to no avail. Although McCrea is probably better in his role than Cooper, and Donlevy is always a terrific heavy, the public had little interest in the film and it passed virtually unnoticed. This version did, however, have the correct reading of the line for which everyone remembers this story: "When you call me that, smile."

p, Paul Jones; d, Stuart Gilmore; w, Frances Goodrich, Albert Hackett, Edward E. Paramore, Jr., Howard Estabrook (based on the play by Owen Wister, Kirk La Shelle and the novel by Wister); ph, Harry Hallenberger; m, Daniele Amfitheatrof; ed, Everett Douglas; art d, Hans Dreier, John Meehan; set d, John McNeil; spec eff, Gordon Jennings.

Western   **(PR:A-C   MPAA:NR)**

VIRGINIA'S HUSBAND**   (1934, Brit.) 71m FOX bw

Dorothy Boyd *(Virginia Trevor)*, Reginald Gardiner *(John Craddock)*, Enid Stamp-Taylor *(June Haslett)*, Ena Grossmith *(Elizabeth)*, Annie Esmond *(Mrs. Elkins)*, Sebastian Smith *(Mr. Ritchie)*, Wally Patch *(Police Sergeant)*, Tom Helmore *(Barney Hammond)*, Andrea Malandrinos *(Headwaiter)*, Hal Walters *(Mechanic)*, Vi Kaley, May Hallatt.

Boyd plays a feminist (long before the word was common coin) with an avowed passion against men. However, she is quickly forced to change her ways when her aunt, Esmond, who has been supporting her, arrives unexpectedly in London. Esmond thinks her niece is married, forcing Boyd to take on Gardiner as a husband cover. Some amusing moments but not enough to sustain the comedy throughout. A remake of a 1928 silent film.

p, George Smith; d, Maclean Rogers; w, H. Fowler Mear (based on the play by Florence Kilpatrick).

Comedy   **(PR:AAA   MPAA:NR)**

VIRIDIANA***** (1962, Mex./Span.) 90m Uninci S.A.-Films 59-Gustavo Alatriste/Kingsley International bw

Silvia Pinal *(Viridiana)*, Francisco Rabal *(Jorge)*, Fernando Rey *(Don Jaime)*, Margarita Lozano *(Ramona)*, Victoria Zinny *(Lucia)*, Teresa Rabal *(Rita)*, Jose Calvo, Joaquin Roa, Luis Heredia, Jose Manuel Martin, Lola Gaos, Juan Garcia Tienda, Maruda Isbert, Joaquin Mayol, Sergio Mendizabal, Palmira Guerra, Milagros Tomas, Alicia Jorge Barriga *(The Beggars)*.

Away from his native land for over 25 years, Bunuel was invited by the Franco government to produce a film in Spain as an effort to welcome home that country's greatest filmmaker. Bunuel, admittedly a bit anxious to return to the land of his youth, graciously accepted the offer and was allowed to choose any subject he desired, as long as the censors approved it. The result was what many critics consider to be his greatest film. Ironically, VIRIDIANA was never shown theatrically in Spain, having been banned by the government immediately after its opening at the Cannes Film Festival, where it won the Golden Palm. Bunuel was as capable of creating a stir at 60 as he was at 30 when his L'AGE D'OR had patrons tearing apart the Parisian theater where it premiered. VIRIDIANA follows the sojourn of a young religious novitiate, Pinal, as she is about to take the vows which will sever her contacts with the outside world forever. Before she undertakes this giant step, the mother superior begs Pinal to visit Rey, her wealthy uncle and last remaining relative, who has selflessly supported her. At first Pinal insists she be allowed to remain at the convent and immediately take her vows so that she can start doing the "good work"; she also has a preconception of Rey as a shiftless ogre. Espousing her idealistic values, Pinal eventually visits her uncle, firmly intent on denying the luxuries that surround her at his estate. To her surprise she finds Rey to be a most gracious host; always kind and polite, he treats Pinal with complete tenderness. However, beneath Rey's calm demeanor he has been harboring plans for the young woman. He is obsessed with Pinal's resemblance to his late wife, who died 30 years earlier on their wedding night. The intense love he felt for her has never subsided, but instead increased to the point of a sick indulgence. At one point Rey even puts on her wedding dress and parades around the bedroom. As Pinal plans her return to the convent, Rey makes one final request–that she put on his wife's wedding gown. Because Rey has been so kind, she agrees to comply with the strange request. The devious Rey has his maid, Lozano, drug Pinal's tea to allow him complete control over her. Carrying Pinal to the bridal suite, he lays her on the bed with the intent of possessing her, but at the last minute he is unable to follow through with his plan. The next morning, as Pinal is preparing to return to the convent, Rey tells her that she can no longer become a nun because she has lost her purity. Rey intends to persuade Pinal not to return to the convent and to remain with him. Instead, she immediately rushes from the house, leading Rey to such deep remorse and guilt that he commits suicide, hanging himself with the jump rope Lozano's daughter had earlier been playing with. Before Pinal boards the bus that will take her away, she is informed of Rey's death. She returns to the estate, which she, along with Rey's illegitimate son Rabal, now owns. Forsaking the convent, Pinal decides to remain at the estate, determined to do her good works for those most desperately in need of assistance. She gathers a number of beggars and other outcasts on the estate and agrees to provide them with food and shelter as long as they pitch in and perform some chores. The beggars do as little work as possible, openly deceive and take advantage of Pinal, and continuously fight among themselves. In contrast, Rabal devotes himself to the rehabilitation not of people but of the dilapidated villa and farmland, which his father had allowed to decay. Rabal is a hard-working, practical sort who has no qualms about indulging in the good life. Originally appearing at the estate with a mistress, he quickly sends her on her way and enters into a casual liaison with Lozano. He looks upon Pinal's efforts as pure hogwash, not wishing to have anything to do with worthless vagabonds who fill her estate, but allowing them to remain to please Pinal. But Rabal is not a completey cold-hearted person; when he sees a dog tied to a passing wagon forced to keep up with the wagon's fast pace, he is so upset that he buys the dog. Ironically, another cart passes in the background, pulling another helpless dog. When Rabal, Pinal, and their servants go to the village to attend to some business, the beggars break into the house and treat themselves to a lively feast at the owners' expense. In one of Bunuel's most cutting jabs at the Catholic Church, he has the beggars line up at the long banquet table in a manner that replicates Da Vinci's "Last Supper." A blind beggar, the most devious of the bunch (Bunuel has admitted a certain disgust for blind people), takes the position held by Christ in the painting, while a woman lifts up her skirt and pretends to take a snapshot. While all this is occurring, the "Halleluah Chorus" from Handel's "Messiah" is blaring out over a record player. Suddenly one of the beggars informs the blind man that one of their bunch has sneaked off with his girl. The blind man lashes out with his cane, destroying expensive china and other contents of the room. As Rabal and Pinal return, most of the beggars sneak away, leaving behind a couple of stragglers who attack Rabal and attempt to rape Pinal. Only Rabal's quick response saves her. (He pays one of the mendicants to murder the would-be rapist.) Later, Lozano and Rabal are in the sitting room playing cards when Pinal walks into the room to indicate that she is willing to become part of their family. Lozano gets up as if to leave, but Rabal insists that she remain so that all three of them can play together. As in all of Bunuel's films, VIRIDIANA is filled with allegories concerning the general state of the world and Spain in particular. The religious idealism that had kept Spain locked in the Middle Ages was greatly

in need of change if that country was to avoid becoming a decaying, unfertile mess like Rey's estate. VIRIDIANA is not without a strong positive message, which appears in the form of Rabal, who pursues the needed changes through pragmatism, not via some obtuse idealism that accomplishes nothing in the real world. The changes he attempts to realize, such as buying the suffering dog to relieve it from its misery, will not cure all the pain, poverty, and misery in the world, but at least some good comes of his efforts. Bunuel's idea for VIRIDIANA came as he was traveling from Mexico to Spain by boat. Viridiana was a minor saint Bunuel had come upon as a child; her story became the basis for his new screenplay. In his autobiography, *My Last Sigh*, he further indicates: "As I worked I remembered my old erotic fantasy about making love to the Queen of Spain when she was drugged, and decided somehow to combine the two." The final script of VIRIDIANA had to meet the approval of the Spanish censors, who passed it with only one minor change regarding the ending. Originally Pinal was to come knocking at Rabal's bedroom door, but the censors found this much too suggestive and insisted upon the card-playing scene. Actually Bunuel was much more pleased with this new ending, finding it more subtle in its implications. Immediately after the film was shot, it was shipped over the border to Paris where it was quickly edited in time for Cannes. None of the Spanish authorities had seen the final print before the showing at the festival and were shocked when it won the Golden Palm. Further scandal followed VIRIDIANA to Italy where its showing in Milan had the public prosecutor threatening Bunuel with a prison sentence if he entered the country. Despite all this controversy, VIRIDIANA has a simple quality stemming from the poetic formality with which Bunuel allows the picture to unfold. He steered away from complex and confusing images and camera movement, and the result is perhaps the greatest film from a filmography that includes a number of great films. (In Spanish; English subtitles.)

p, Ricardo Munoz Suay; d, Luis Bunuel; w, Bunuel, Julio Alejandro (based on a story by Bunuel); ed, Pedro del Rey; md, Gustavo Pitaluga; art d, Francisco Canet; m/l, "The Messiah," George Frederick Handel, "Requiem," Wolfgang Amadeus Mozart.

Drama   **Cas.**   **(PR:C-O   MPAA:NR)**

VIRTUE* (1932) 87m COL bw

Carole Lombard *(Mae)*, Pat O'Brien *(Jimmy)*, Ward Bond *(Frank)*, Willard Robertson *(MacKenzie)*, Shirley Grey *(Gert)*, Ed Le Saint *(Magistrate)*, Jack LaRue *(Toots)*, Mayo Methot *(Lil)*.

Lombard is a hooker who promises to leave town in exchange for a suspended jail term. Having no intention of honoring her pledge, she disentrains uptown and she taxis back to the center of the city, intending to bilk driver O'Brien of his fare. O'Brien spouts jokes and philosophy about women. Lombard takes a liking to him and romance blooms. She gives up the street life and marries O'Brien. On their wedding night the police come to arrest Lombard but O'Brien sticks up for her. Lombard later goes to a hotel intending to collect $200 loaned earlier to a girl friend. O'Brien hears about this and assumes the worst. When someone is murdered at the hotel, evidence points to Lombard as the culprit. She claims innocence and O'Brien agrees, helping to clear his wife of all charges. Future stars Lombard and O'Brien were only minor contract players in 1932, and consequently they were cast in this low-budget programmer. Their combined talents make this one better than most, creating flesh-and-blood characterizations within cliched situations. Buzzell's direction has good pacing, balancing elements of drama and comedy with a fine sense of realism. VIRTUE is historically interesting as a showcase for Lombard's and O'Brien's pre-superstardom work.

d, Edward Buzzell; w, Robert Riskin (based on the story by Ethel Hill); ph, Joseph Walker.

Drama   **(PR:C   MPAA:NR)**

VIRTUOUS HUSBAND (1931) 75m UNIV bw (GB: WHAT WIVES DON'T WANT)

Elliott Nugent *(Daniel Curtis)*, Jean Arthur *(Barbara Olwell)*, Betty Compson *(Inez Wakefield)*, J.C. Nugent *(Mr. Olwell)*, Allison Skipworth *(Mrs. Olwell)*, Tully Marshall *(Ezra Hunniwell, Lawyer)*, Eva McKenzie *(Hester)*.

A clever stage farce whose adaptation to the screen was mishandled, both in terms of direction and technical assets. Nugent plays a young man about to marry Arthur, but a considerable strain is put on their relationship when he insists on committing himself to the instructions left by his dead mother on how he should lead his life. Arthur doesn't exactly see things in the same light and quickly lets this be known. Paramount lent her to Universal for this one; Compson appeared courtesy of Radio, and Anthony Brown helped Moore take them through their paces as the dialog director.

d, Vin Moore; w, Dale Van Every, C. Jerome Horwn, Edward Luddy, Fred Niblo, Jr. (based on the play "Apron Srtings" by Dorrance Davis); ph, Jerome Ash; ad, Arthur Hilton

Comedy   **(PR:A   MPAA:NR)**

VIRTUOUS SIN, THE   (1930) 80m PAR bw

Walter Huston (*Gen. Gregori Platoff*), Kay Francis (*Marya Ivanovna*), Kenneth MacKenna (*Lt. Victor Sablin*), Jobyna Howland (*Alexandra Stroganov*), Paul Cavanagh (*Capt. Orloff*), Eric Kalhurst (*Lt. Glinka*), Oscar Apfel (*Maj. Ivanoff*), George McLeod (*Col. Nikitin*), Youcca Troubetzkoy (*Capt. Sobakin*), Victor Potel (*Sentry*).

Set in the Russia of 1917, Francis plays a woman married to medical officer MacKenna, a man destined for trouble because of his inability to adapt to war. His wife goes about seducing Huston, the general who holds the fate of MacKenna in his hands. The twist to the yarn is that Francis actually falls in love with the man she is trying to sway. The performances are satisfactory, but much of the plot is not developed effectively. This was Cukor's second take at the helm; he shared the duties with Louise Gasnier, neither of whom took very well to the story they were trying to tell.

d, George Cukor, Louis Gasnier; w, Martin Brown, Louise Long (based on the play "The General" by Lajos Zilahy); ph, David Abel; ed, Otho Lovering.

Drama   (PR:A MPAA:NR)

VIRTUOUS TRAMPS, THE   (SEE: DEVIL'S BROTHER, THE, 1933)

VIRTUOUS WIFE, THE   (SEE: MEN ARE LIKE THAT, 1931)

VIRUS**½   (1980, Jap.) 155m Toho/Media c (FUKKATSU NO HI)

Sonny Chiba (*Dr. Yamauchi*), Chuck Connors (*Capt. MacCloud, British Sub Commander*), Stephanie Faulkner (*Sarah Baker*), Glenn Ford (*Richardson, American President*), Stuart Gillard (*Dr. Mayer*), Olivia Hussey (*Marit*), George Kennedy (*Adm. Conway*), Masao Kusakari (*Yoshizumi, Scientist*), Cecil [Cec] Linder (*Dr. Latour*), Isao Natsuki (*Dr. Nakanishi*), Ken Ogata (*Prof. Tsuchiya*), Edward J. Olmos (*Capt. Lopez*), Henry Silva (*Garland, American Chief of Staff*), Bo Svenson (*Maj. Carter*), Yumi Takigawa (*Noriko, Nurse*), Robert Vaughn (*Senator Barkley*).

An all-star international cast and location shooting done all over the globe contributed to the $17 million price tag for this, one of the most expensive films ever to come out of Japan. The yarn concerns the near destruction of the world, brought about by the accidental release of germs developed for chemical warfare and fueled by the U.S. nuclear response to this "communist plot." The few hundred people who survive these apocalyptic events do so because they are living in Antarctica, a place immune to the germs because of the immense cold. These people are given the task of rebuilding the world, and since there are only eight women among their number, one-to-one relationships between the survivors will be unthinkably detrimental. Though some intriguing ideas are introduced, many of the sequences are just cliched leftovers from sci-fi predecessors. The exception here is that fear of death and mass destruction is effectively conveyed by a number of the characters. But this was not enough to win back even a fraction of the money sunk into this ill-fated project which was never released theatrically in the U.S., but was instead sold directly to cable TV. En route to a location in the Antarctic, the ship carrying the film's crew and company even had the misfortune of striking a reef, perilously stranding them for several days and further plaguing the production.

p, Haruki Kadokawa; d, Kinji Fukasaku; w, Fukasaku, Koji Takada, Gregory Knapp; (based on the novel by Sakyo Komatsu); ph, Daisaku Kimura; m, Teo Macero.

Fantasy/Disaster   Cas.   (PR:C MPAA:NR)

VISA TO CANTON   (SEE: PASSPORT TO CHINA, 1961, Brit.)

VISCOUNT, THE**½   (1967, Fr./Span./Ital./Ger.) 98m Waterview-Criterion-Producci ones Cinematografica D.I.A-Franca-C.C.M.-Senior Cinematografica-Omnia Deutsche/WB c (LE VICOMTE REGLE SES COMPTES; LES AVENTURES DU VICOMTE; ATRACO AL HAMPA; LAS AVENTURAS DEL VIZCONDE; THE VISCOUNT, FURTO ALLA BANCA MONDIALE)

Kerwin Mathews (*Clint de la Roche, the Viscount*), Edmond O'Brien (*Ricco Barone*), Jane Fleming [Silvia Sorente] (*Lili Dumond*), Yvette Lebon (*Claudia*), Jean Yanne (*Billette*), Fernando Rey (*Marco Demoigne*), Maria Latour (*Tania*), Jose Manuel Martin (*Manuel*), Alain Saury (*Vincento*), Luis Davila (*Steve Heller*), Franco Fabrizi (*Ramon*), Pierre Massimi (*Louis*), Christian Ferville (*Paul*), Alvaro de Luna (*Jean*), Emilio Rodriguez (*Bank Director*), Armand Mestral (*Claude Peroux*).

A tacky and far-fetched picture in which Mathews plays a suave insurance investigator, who uses his supreme skill, not to be believed for a second, to bring about the demise of two notorious gangs involved in a drug war. And his original goal was just to figure out why a bank was robbed. Stylishly nauseating. French- and Spanish-language versions of the film were also produced.

exec p, Nat Wachsberger; d, Maurice Cloche; w, Clark Reynolds (based on the novel by *Bonne Mesure* by Jean Bruce); ph, Henri Raichi (Techniscope, Technicolor); m, Georges Garvarentz; ed, Ray Leboursier; art d, Jean Douarinou; cos, Antonio Cortes; m/l, "The Investigator," Garvarentz, Bill

Martin, Philips Coulper (sung by Tony Allen).

Crime/Drama   (PR:C MPAA:NR)

VISIT, THE**½   (1964, Ger./Fr./Ital./U.S.) 100m Deutschefox-Les Films du Siecle-P.E.C.F.-Dear/FOX bw (DER BESUCH; LA RANCUNE; LA VENDETTA DELLA SIGNORA)

Ingrid Bergman (*Karla Zachanassian*), Anthony Quinn (*Serge Miller*), Paolo Stoppa (*Doctor*), Romolo Valli (*Town Painter*), Claude Dauphin (*Bardick*), Jacques Dufilho (*Fisch*), Hans-Christian Blech (*Capt. Dobrik*), Richard Munch (*Teacher*), Ernst Schroder (*Mayor*), Leonard Steckel (*Priest*), Valentina Cortese (*Mathilda Miller*), Irina Demick (*Anya*), Eduardo Ciannelli (*Innkeeper*), Marco Guglielmi (*Chesco*), Lelio Luttazzi (*1st Idler*), Dante Maggio (*Cadek*), Renzo Palmer (*Conductor*), Fausto Tozzi (*Darvis*).

A weird premise wavers the believability of this international film that had assistance from four different countries. Bergman is the richest woman in the world, the widow of the richest man in the world. She comes back to the small European town where she was born and chastised and she is determined to wreak revenge. The little town is on the skids financially and the news that she is returning sends their hopes soaring as they sincerely believe she might beqeath a few bob on them and take the town out of the doldrums. She has something else in mind. Bergman comes to town in a classic Rolls-Royce with an entourage and a pet leopard. The town honors her with a large dinner for the local girl who made good and make them an offer that she thinks they will be unable to refuse. Quinn, a big man in town who married well after having been Bergman's lover when she was a teenager, is the target of her wrath. She offers a price of $2 million if the town will murder Quinn! Years before, Quinn had impregnated her and then he arranged to have some of his pals disburse the word that she was a harlot. The result was that she was forced to leave the small town and her child died. Later, she took up harlotry for a living in Trieste and met the old, fabulously rich man who became her husband. The people of the town listen and gape and some even consider the offer but they ultimately refuse. Soon, a series of trucks begins arriving with loads of goods for the people. At first, they are suspicious of her intentions but when she begins to distribute the merchandise and asks for nothing in return, the town begins to shift its thinking. Her pet leopard gets away and the locals get their guns and go after the missing feline. Now, if Quinn should *happen* to be hit by a bullet gone astray, that's the breaks, isn't it? Quinn realizes that's exactly what could happen so he goes into hiding until the big cat is nabbed. Quinn approaches Bergman directly and begs her to call off her plan but she reminds him that he married another woman who had a larger dowry and forced her into a life of prostitution. The fact that she made out well in the end doesn't matter to her, she just wants her pound of flesh as vengeance. Quinn makes an attempt to flee but is thwarted. The local people plead with her to stop her plan and spend some money in the town, then she informs them that she already owns the entire town and everything around it. Quinn is put on trial and the people find him guilty of a trumped-up charge and sentence him to death. Bergman meets a young servant, Demick, who is carrying on with a local married policeman and she recognizes herself two decades ago. She gives Demick money and tells her to get away from this town as soon as she can. Quinn's wife is Cortese and she sticks by him, barely. The sentence is passed and Bergman tells the packed courtroom that she will allow him to be set free if anyone speaks up and says that this has been a kangaroo court. Not one person says a word. Then Bergman lifts the death sentence and declares that Quinn must now spend the rest of his miserable life among the people who would have let him die for money. Bergman takes Demick by the hand, tells everyone that her visit is now over, and the two women depart. The Durrenmatt play (and the translation by Valency that was a hit in New York) had both parties a great deal older than Quinn and Bergman. Alfred Lunt and wife Lynn Fontanne played it in New York in May 1958. It might have made more sense with older stars in order to emphasize the festering hatred. Bergman was cast against type and Quinn was little more than a human dart board for her anger. Made at Cinecitta Studios in Rome with locations in Italy, THE VISIT featured some good acting from the smaller roles, including the mayor (Schroder) and the police chief (Blech) among others. Trying Quinn on the 20-year-old charge of seducing Bergman and then paying his pals to say she was a whore is hardly enough to merit a death penalty. The same theme that "people will do anything for money" was seen in the comedy THE MAGIC CHRISTIAN.

p, Julien Derode, Anthony Quinn; d, Bernhard Wicki; w, Ben Barzman (based on the play by Friedrich Durrenmatt, translated into English by Maurice Valency); ph, Armando Nannuzzi (CinemaScope); m, Hans-Martin Majewski, Richard Arnell; ed, Samuel E. Beetley, Francoise Diot; md, Majewski, Arnell; art d, Leon Barsacq; set d, Robert Christides; cos, Rene Hubert; makeup, John O'Gorman.

Drama   Cas.   (PR:C MPAA:NR)

VISIT TO A CHIEF'S SON**½   (1974) 92m Entertainment from Transamerica/UA c

Richard Mulligan (*Robert, Anthropologist*), Johnny Sekka (*Nemolok, Tribal Leader*), John Philip Hodgdon (*Kevin, Anthropologist's Son*), Jesse Kinaru (*Kondonyo, Tribal Chief's Son*), Chief Lomoiro (*Tribal Chief*), Jock Anderson (*Jock, Safari Leader*), People of the Masai Tribe in Kenya, East Africa.

The favorite Shakespearan theme of nature restoring harmony to a person's life was adroitly handled in this simple tale about an anthropologist and his son's trip to the wilds of Africa. As the anthropologist, Mulligan uses the ploy of photographing an eclipse to witness sacred rituals of the Masai tribe, and in the process discovers the warm companionship of the tribal leader Sekka. Likewise, his son Hodgdon temporarily avoids the problems of a youth growing up in Western culture through his association with the chief's son.

p, Robert Halmi; d, Lamont Johnson; w, Albert Ruben (based on the novel by Halmi); ph, Ernest Day, James Wells (DeLuxe Color); m, Francis Lai; ed, Tom Rolf.

Drama   **(PR:AA MPAA:G)**

VISIT TO A SMALL PLANET**   (1960) 85m Wallis-Hazen/PAR bw

Jerry Lewis (Kreton), Joan Blackman (Ellen Spelding), Earl Holliman (Conrad), Fred Clark (Maj. Roger Putnam Spelding, TV Commentator), Lee Patrick (Rheba Spelding), Gale Gordon (Bob Mayberry), Civil Defense Watcher, Jerome Cowan (George Abercrombie), John Williams (Delton, Alien Chief), Barbara Lawson (Desdemona, Beatnik Dancer), Ellen Corby (Mrs. Mayberry), Frank Socolow, Don Bagley, Jack Costanzo.

An unexciting Jerry Lewis vehicle which has him as an extraterrestrial who is extremely interested in the ways of Earth and finally gets a chance to visit it when he goes against the rules of his planet and takes a spaceship there. He manages to befriend the family of news commentator Clark, a man who just happens to have presented a program in which he debunked the craze for searching for flying saucers. Lewis wins the family's confidence by using his supernatural skills to help them; they return the favor by taking the alien under their wings and teaching him about the behavior of an average Earthling family. The bulk of this teaching process falls on the shoulders of daughter Blackman, who takes Lewis to clubs and coaches him in some of the more intimate habits of humans. It is not too long before Lewis falls in love with Blackman, wishing to stay on Earth and marry the girl. But that doesn't sit too well with her beau Holliman, who rushes her off to elope. Watching all of the proceedings from the home planet is Williams, who, upon hearing Lewis' request to become just like a human, takes away some of his supernatural powers. Lewis now has the chance to feel some of the less admirable human qualities, such as pain when being struck, jealously at having a rival in love, and just plain fear. It doesn't take long before Lewis is hopping in his spaceship and gliding back to his peaceful planet, having learned his lesson and being willing to serve out his time at home. Adapted from the play by Gore Vidal, the power and effectiveness of his themes were extremely watered down to allow for the slapstick routines by Lewis, none of which was nearly as funny as it could have been. What remains is a very forcibly acted, glossy production, lacking any of the subtleties that create good satire. However, there is one really fine sequence that makes light of the beat generation: Blackman takes Lewis to a "way out" nightclub where the spaceman grooves with the beatniks and spouts lingo that baffles the hep cats. Dressed in his silver spacesuit, he performs a dance routine with Lawson that even the denizens of the club can't handle–literally "out of this world."

p, Hal B. Wallis; d, Norman Taurog; w, Edmund Beloin, Henry Garson (based on the play by Gore Vidal); ph, Loyal Griggs; m, Leigh Harline; ed, Frank Bracht, Warren Low; art d, Hal Pereira, Walter Tyler; set d, Sam Comer, Arthur Krams; cos, Edith Head; spec eff, John P. Fulton, Farciot Edouart; ch, Miriam Nelson.

Fantasy/Comedy   **Cas.**   **(PR:A MPAA:NR)**

VISITING HOURS*   (1982, Can.) 105m Filmplan International/FOX c
(AKA: THE FRIGHT; GET WELL SOON)

Michael Ironside (Colt Hawker), Lee Grant (Deborah Ballin), Linda Purl (Sheila Munroe), William Shatner (Gary Baylor), Lenore Zann (Lisa), Harvey Atkin (Vinnie Bradshaw), Helen Hughes (Louise Shepherd), Michael J. Reynolds (Porter Halstrom), Kirsten Bishopric (Denise), Debra Kirschenbaum (Connie Wexler), Elizabeth Leigh Milne (Patricia Ellis), Maureen McRae (Elizabeth Hawker), Dustin Waln (Hawker), Neil Affleck (Officer), Damir Andrei (Paramedic), Dorothy Barker (Sally), Steve Bettcher (Anesthetist), Walker Boone, Richard Briere (Police), Terrance P. Coady (Security Officer), Dora Dainton (Mrs. Corrigan), Sylvie Desbois (Desk Nurse), Tali Fischer (Bridget), Kathleen Fee, Sarita Elman, Yvan Ducharme, Richard Comar.

Another slasher picture that pays homage to those early ventures which molded this most prolific genre, borrowing from the likes of PEEPING TOM, HALLOWEEN, and PSYCHO to turn out a totally predictable and disgusting venture. Ironside is the slasher who attacks his innocent femmes and photographs his handiwork. He assaults Grant, a crusading journalist, and then looses his fury on the hospital where she is taken to recover. But by the picture's end the attacker has become the attacked.

p, Claude Heroux; d, Jean Claude Lord; w, Brian Taggert; ph, Rene Verzier; m, Jonathan Goldsmith; ed, Lord, Lise Thouin; art d, Michel Proulx; cos, Delphine White; spec eff, Gary Zeller, Don Berry, Renee Rousseau; makeup, Stephen Dupuis.

Horror/Thriller   **Cas.**   **(PR:O MPAA:R)**

VISITOR, THE**½   (1973, Can.) 93m Highwood c

Pia Shandel (Becca), Eric Peterson (Michael), Hetty Clews, Alan Robertson, Scott Hylands, Joyce Doolittle, John Heywood, Joseph Gollard, Georgie Collins, V.F. Mitchell, Amy Doolittle, Patricia Vickers.

An unusual independent production involves Shandel as a student who rents a house for three weeks to do research, but soon discovers that the house has an occupant. Peterson, a ghost from another era, is also a resident and Shandel's studies take some unusual bends. The two fall in love and teach one another about their respective cultures until at last Shandel can no longer take an ethereal lover. Her sanity becomes questionable and she flees from the house. This quirky, low-budgeted production could have been unintentionally campy, but the unusual premise works thanks to the skill of the two leads. The anachronistic love affair is honest and believable through Shandel and Peterson's fine chemistry. Direction takes care with the subject, giving a few Ingmar Bergman-inspired touches within the telling that greatly enhance the story's atmosphere.

p. Margaret Dallin; d&w, John Wright; ph, Doug McKay (Kodak Color); m, Luigi Zaninelli; ed, Homer Powell.

Drama   **(PR:C-O MPAA:NR)**

VISITOR, THE*   (1980, Ital./U.S.) 90m International Picture
Show-Marvin c (IL VISITATORE)

Mel Ferrer (Dr. Walker), Glenn Ford (Detective), Lance Henriksen (Raymond), John Huston (Jersey Colsowitz, the Visitor), Paige Conner (Katie Collins), Joanne Nail (Barbara Collins), Shelley Winters (Jane Phillips), Sam Peckinpah (Sam), J. Townsend, Jack Dorsey, Johnny Popwell, Steve Somers, Wallace Williamson, Lew Walker, Walter Gordon, Sr, Calvin Fenbry, Betty Turner, Steve Cunningham, Neal Bortz, Bill Ash, Charley Hardnett, Jack H. Gordon, Steve Belzer, Hsio Ho Chao.

Ferrer plays a wealthy member of an occult group; his wife is full of genetic evil, and under the influence of his nefarious cohorts, he seeks to sire a demonic child. There is plenty of mysterious hanky-panky here, but it amounts to nothing more than an overabundance of gore. Ford and Winters should have known better. Set in Atlanta and partially shot there.

p, Ovidio Assonitis; d, Michael J. Paradise [Giulio Paradisi]; w, Lou Comici, Robert Mundi (based on a story by Paradisi, Assonitis); ph, Ennio Guarnieri; m, Franco Mikalizzi; ed, Robert Curi; md, Mikalizzi; art d, Frank Venorio.

Horror   **Cas.**   **(PR:O MPAA:R)**

VISITORS, THE**   (1972) 88m Home Free/UA c

Patrick McVey (Harry Wayne), Patricia Joyce (Martha Wayne), James Woods (Bill Schmidt), Chico Martinez (Tony Rodriguez), Steve Railsback (Mike Nickerson).

The maker of such commercially successful films as ON THE WATERFRONT, Elia Kazan, decided to opt out of the traditional system to try his hand at more personal and meaningful films. THE VISITORS proves that this was perhaps not the wisest move. What is irksome is to see a man of such ability wasting his talent on concepts that are not really worth the cost of the film. Woods plays a Vietnam veteran living a peaceful existence on a Connecticut farm with his girl friend (Joyce) and their infant son. Also living in the area is Joyce's father, McVey, a macho alcoholic writer who is not very fond of Woods' liberal attitude and passive nature. Coming to disturb this serene little picture (though some really big problems are lurking beneath this veil) are two former army acquaintances of Woods', men fresh out of jail, having been imprisoned for the rape and murder of a Vietnamese woman. Woods is the man who gave the testimony which allowed these two rednecks to be convicted, so the minute they pop up a lot of tension is brought to the surface which is just waiting for relief. This is exactly what happens in the end as McVey fills the young men with beer and brings them back to Woods' house to be entertained by the ungracious host and hostess. It isn't too long before Joyce is dancing with one of them, with Wood going into a huff as the man is allowed to go a bit too far. When Woods overcomes his passivity for just a bit he is beaten to a pulp and his wife brutally raped. This was supposedly a sort of treatise on the problems of Vietnam soldiers returning home with the same values that allowed them to be mass murderers. Thrown into the thematic message is a bit of the phoniness lurking behind the ideals of those trying to continue with a "hippie" type existence. Neither of these themes is treated very fairly; both are based on shallowly developed conceptions that take a second seat to the anxiety inherent in the situation. Kazan's son Chris wrote the script and is probably to blame for most of the inadequacies. Shot in 16mm and blown up for release, the film was made at a cost of only $150,000 (the non-union actors received a total of $1,200 for their salaries; director Kazan took 10 percent of the profits, if any). The picture was made entirely on the Kazans' home turf in Newton, Connecticut. Oddly enough, another home-movie-style feature release in the previous year was, thematically and in other ways, a nearly identical twin to this one: GLORY BOY. Director Kazan was accused of union-busting for this low-budget effort; the film was put on the "unfair" list of the Screen Actors Guild.

p, Chris Kazan, Nick Proferes; d, Elia Kazan; w, Chris Kazan; ph, Proferes. m, "Lute Suite No. 1," Johann Sebastian Bach; ed, Proferes.

Drama   (PR:O MPAA:R)

VISITORS FROM THE GALAXY**½   (1981, Yugo.) 90m Zagreb
/Jadran c (GOSTI IZ GALA KSIJE)

Zarko Potocnjak, Ljubisa Samardzic, Lucie Zulova.

The maker of the Academy Award-winning ERSATZ created this likable
feature in which a boy has the characters he's created in his stories, mostly
science fiction, actually coming to life and causing massive disequilibrium
in the small community. Director Vukotic, the first of Yugoslavia's talented
catoon specialists to break away from the "Walt Disney style," was a
cofounder of the famed Duga Film studio in Yugoslavia in 1951. Most
recently–as here–he specialized in mixing live action with animation.

d, Dusan Vukotic; w, Milos Macourek, Vukotic; ph, Jiri Macak.

Fantasy   (PR:AA MPAA:NR)

VISKINGAR OCH ROP (SEE: CRIES AND WHISPERS, 1972, Swed.)

VITA PRIVATA (SEE: VERY PRIVATE AFFAIR, A, 1962, Fr./Ital.)

VITE PERDUTE (SEE: LOST SOULS, 1961, Ital.)

VITELLONI**** (1956, Ital./Fr.) 103m Peg-Cite/AFI-Janus bw (AKA:
THE YOUNG AND THE PASSIONATE; I VITELLONI; SPIVS)

Franco Interlenghi (*Moraldo*), Franco Fabrizi (*Fausto*), Alberto Sordi
(*Alberto*), Leopoldo Trieste (*Leopoldo*), Riccardo Fellini (*Riccardo*), Leonora
Ruffo (*Sandra*), Lida Baarowa (*Guilia, Wife of Michele*), Arlette Sauvage
(*Woman in the Cinema*), Maja Nipora (*Actress*), Jean Brochard (*Father of
Fausto*), Claude Farere (*Sister of Alberto*), Carlo Romano (*Michele, Anti-
quary*), Enrico Viarisio (*Sandra's Father*), Paola Borboni (*Sandra's Mother*),
Achille Majerone (*Natale, the Homosexual Actor*), Silvio Bagolini (*Giudizio,
the Simpleton*), Vira Silenti (*Leopoldo's "Chinese" Date*), Franco Gandolfi,
Gondrano Trucchi, Guido Marturi, Milvia Chianelli.

This somewhat autobiographical work by Federico Fellini was really the
first film to bring him world attention, as well as a step away from the
Neorealist movement which seemed to engulf Italian filmmaking during the
first half of the 1950s. As in AMARCORD (Fellini's film of nearly two
decades later) the setting is the seaside town of Rimini, the birthplace of
Fellini and the wellspring of the experiences which were to color this and
other films. The plot follows the adventures of five youths who refuse to
grow up and accept responsibility. Only one of the gang (Interlenghi, the
young boy from SHOESHINE, 1946) comes to understand that life in the
small town is a relatively empty existence. By the end of the film he is ready
to pack off to someplace where he can grow, leaving his friends to continue
with their meaningless games, something that gives them momentary
security but ultimately makes them puppets to forces beyond their control.
Of the gang, Fabrizi's plight is concentrated upon most heavily. Considered
the Don Juan of the group because of his successes with women, the others
look up to him with admiration. But he eventually gets one woman
pregnant, and is forced into a marriage which will undoubtedly prove tragic.
Fabrizi continues with his amorous adventures even after marriage,
frustrating his wife to the point where she leaves him and he is forced to
return to his father. Here he is treated just like the child he is and will
always be, given a ferocious beating by his father, the only language that
he understands. Sordi, the most effeminate of the group, is basically a lazy
oaf, dependent upon his sister for support. In a fascinatingly filmed festival
scene, Sordi's plight is made known. In a drunken stupor and dressed like
a woman, he swaggers about the floor dancing with a papier-mache doll, the
camera twirling in a fashion that corresponds to Sordi's own movements.
These are just a few of the experiences Interlenghi takes in that help give
him the impression that there must be something more to life than Rimini,
where he may be able to have fun for a short period, but at the expense of
never reaching any form of advancement or enrichment. Filled with many
of the cinematic excesses that were to clutter Fellini's later films, which here
seem much more insightful in describing the tribulations which bring a
youth from boyhood into the adult world.

p, Mario de Vecchi; d, Federico Fellini; w, Fellini, Ennio Flaiano (based on
the story by Fellini, Flaiano, Tullio Pinelli); ph, Otello Martelli, Luciano
Trasatti, Carlo Carlini; m, Nino Rota; ed, Rolando Benedetti; art d, Mario
Chiari.

Drama   (PR:C MPAA:NR)

VIVA CISCO KID*   (1940) 70m FOX bw

Cesar Romero (*Cisco Kid*), Jean Rogers (*Joan Allen*), Chris-Pin Martin
(*Gordito*), Minor Watson (*Jesse Allen*), Stanley Fields (*Ross*), Nigel De
Brulier (*Moses*), Harold Goodwin (*Gunther*), Francis Ford (*Proprietor*),
Charles Judels (*Pancho*).

In one of his frequent stints as the legendary Mexican hero, Romero teams
up with sidekick Martin to stop the plans of Fields to kill Watson and take
total control of his business. Braving such adversities as being sealed in a
mine shaft with the beauteous Rogers, Romero sees to it that no such

scheme is carried out. Romero, the second Cisco of the movies (Warner
Baxter was the first), here enacts the role for the second time. He had
appeared in some of the Baxter-starring Cisco pictures as a secondary
sidekick along with Martin. (See CISCO KID series, Index.)

p, Sol M. Wurtzel; d, Norman Foster; w, Samuel G. Engel, Hal Long (based
on characters created by O. Henry); ph, Charles Clarke; ed, Norman Colbert;
md, Samuel Kaylin.

Western   (PR:A MPAA:NR)

VIVA ITALIA*½   (1978, Ital.) 90m Dean/Cinema 5 c (I NUOVI
MOSTRI; AKA: THE NEW MONSTERS)

"The Canary of Padana Valley": Ugo Tognazzi, Orietta Berti, "Tantum
Ergo": Vittorio Gassman, Luigi Diberti, "Abduction of a Loved One":
Gassman, "First Aid": Alberto Sordi, "Pornodiva": Eros Pagni, Fiona
Florence, "Like A Queen": Sordi, Emilia Fabi, "The Inn": Gassman, Ugo
Tognazzi, "Funeral Elegy": Sordi.

These nine short vignettes are all basically one-joke sketches with a very
dark sense of humor. The common theme is that men are a pretty rotten and
selfish lot, with only the comic energies of Sordi, Gassman, and Tognazzi
giving the sketches life.

p, Pio Angeletti, Adriano De Micheli; d, Mario Monicelli, Dino Risi, Ettore
Scola; w, Age, Scarpelli, Ruggero Maccari, Bernardino Zapponi; ph, Tonino
Delli Colli (Technispes Color); m, Armando Trovajoli: ed, Alberto Gallitti;
prod d, Luciano Ricceri; set d, Ricceri.

Comedy   (PR:O MPAA:R)

VIVA KNIEVEL!*   (1977) 104m Metropolitan/WB c (AKA: SECONDS
TO LIVE)

Evel Knievel (*Himself*), Gene Kelly (*Will Atkins, Mechanic*), Lauren Hutton
(*Kate Morgan*), Red Buttons (*Ben Andrews*), Leslie Nielson (*Stanley
Millard*), Frank Gifford (*Himself*), Sheila Allen (*Sister Charity*), Cameron
Mitchell (*Barton*), Eric Olson (*Tommy Atkins*), Albert Salmi (*Cortland*),
Dabney Coleman (*Ralph Thompson*), Ernie Orsatti (*Norman Clark*), Sidney
Clute (*Andy*), Robert Tafur (*Governor Garcia*), Marjoe Gortner (*Jessie
Hammond*).

Evel Knievel stars as Evel Knievel in a film about Evel Knievel. Nothing
more need be said as he shows that he should definitely stick to motorcycles,
and not give up one successful career to make an embarrassment of himself
in pictures. An inane plot has this American hero of the absurd the center
of a scheme by Nielson to use Knievel's trip to Mexico as a way to smuggle
cocaine into the United States. Neilson's plans require that Knievel turn up
dead, which of course he doesn't because the scriptwriter designed a
contrived situation where Gortner takes his place and is killed instead. An
aura of sadness covers this entire production as we witness the level to
which a great actor and entertainer like Gene Kelly stooped in order to get
work. This was the second film about the bucking biker; the first, EVEL
KNIEVEL (1972), featured George Hamilton as Knievel. Hamilton was
better.

p, Stan Hough; d, Gordon Douglas; w, Norman Katkov, Antonio Santillan
(based on a story by Santillan); ph, Fred Jackman (Panavision, Technicolor);
m, Charles Bernstein; ed, Harold F. Kress; prod d, Ward Preston; set d,
Stuart Reiss; cos, Paul Zaputnevich; spec eff, L. B. Abbott, Van Der
Veer Photo Effects; makeup, Fred Phillips; stunts, Gary Davis.

Drama/Crime   **Cas.**   (PR:A MPAA:PG)

VIVA LAS VEGAS   (SEE: MEET ME IN LAS VEGAS, 1956)

VIVA LAS VEGAS**   (1964) 85m MGM c (GB: LOVE IN LAS
VEGAS)

Elvis Presley (*Lucky Jackson*), Ann-Margret (*Rusty Martin*), Cesare Danova
(*Count Elmo Mancini*), William Demarest (*Mr. Martin*), Nicky Blair (*Shorty
Farnsworth*), Jack Carter (*Himself*), Robert B. Williams (*Swanson*), Bob
Nash (*Big Gus Olson*), Roy Engel (*Baker*), Barnaby Hale (*Mechanic*), Ford
Dunhill (*Driver*), Eddie Quillan (*M. C.*), George Cisar (*Manager*), Ivan
Triesault (*Head Captain*), Francis Raval (*Francois*), Mike Ragan [Holly
Bane] (*Man*).

Like any Elvis picture, this offering can never be taken seriously, and is just
an excuse to show off "The King," get him to sing a few tunes, and send chills
through teeny-boppers, spines when some girl manages to snatch him.
However, in this case the girl is Ann-Margret, endowed with more talent
than any of the other femmes to share center stage with Elvis. The
combination couldn't help but be a smash, and if the triteness of the story
is overlooked, it provides plenty of fun. Presley is a race car driver who
wanders into Las Vegas to compete in the upcoming Grand Prix, which will
require running against his arch-rival Danova. Because Elvis' car needs a
new engine, he gets a job as a waiter at a casino, spending his spare time
waiting for the race by romancing Ann-Margret. Of course Presley manages
to get his car together just in time for the big race and win. Songs include:
"The Lady Loves Me" (Sid Tepper, Roy C. Bennett), " Viva Las Vegas" (Doc
Pomus), "What'd I Say" (Ray Charles), "I Need Somebody to Lean On"

(Pomus), "Come On, Everybody" (Stanley Chianese), "Today, Tomorrow and Forever" (Bill Giant, Bernie Baum, Florence Kaye), "If You Think I Don't Need You" (Bob "Red" West), "Appreciation," "My Rival" (Marvin More, Bernie Wayne), "The Climb," "The Yellow Rose of Texas" (Don George), and "The Eyes of Texas Are Upon You."

p, Jack Cummings, George Sidney; d, Sidney; w, Sally Benson; ph, Joseph Biroc (Panavision, Metrocolor); m, George Stoll; ed, John McSweeney, Jr.; art d, George W. Davis, Edward Carfagno; set d, Henry Grace, George R. Nelson; cos, Don Feld; ch, David Winters; makeup, William Tuttle.

Mucsial/Drama   Cas.   (PR:A MPAA:NR)

VIVA MARIA½** (1965, Fr./Ital.) 120m NEF-Artistes Associes-Vides Film/UA c

Jeanne Moreau (Maria I), Brigitte Bardot (Maria Fitzgerald O'Malley/ Maria II), George Hamilton (Flores), Paulette Dubost (Madame Diogene), Gregor von Rezzori (Diogene), Poldo Bendandi (Wether), Claudio Brook (Rodolfo), Carlos Lopez Moctezuma (Don Rodriguez), Jonathan Eden (Juanito), Francisco Reiguera (Father Superior), Adriana Roel (Janine), Jose Baviera (Don Alvaro), Jose Angel Espinosa [Ferresquilla] (El Presidente), Fernando Wagner (Father of Maria II), Jose Luis Campa, Roberto Campa, Eduardo Murillo, Jose Esqueda (The "Turcos"), Luis Rizo (Strongman).

A lively and zesty film that brought two of France's sexiest and most talented actresses together, Bardot and Moreau. Bardot is the daughter of an Irish anarchist who is killed during an upheaval in Central America, leaving the girl to take up where daddy left off. She meets the circus troupe of which Moreau is a part, and the two become partners in a song-and-dance routine. During one such performance, Bardot accidentally loses her skirt, something the audience likes so much they incorporate the stunt into their act. As the company travels across impoverished Latin America the two become more and more touched by the shameful treatment of the peasants, until they eventually turn revolutionaries themselves. This occurs after a love affair between Hamilton and Moreau, the former a revolutionary leader who is later killed, leaving his lover and friend to continue with his work. The teaming of Moreau and Bardot was a stroke of genius, one quiet and subdued, the other ravishing and bursting with energy, but each filling the screen with a unique style.

p, Louis Malle, Oscar Dancigers; d, Malle; w, Malle, Jean-Claude Carriere; ph, Henri Decae (Panavision, Eastmancolor); m, Georges Delerue; ed, Kanout Peltier, Suzanne Baron; art d, Bernard Evein; cos, Ghislain Uhry; spec eff, Lee Zavitz; m/l, Delerue, Malle, Carriere; makeup, Odette Berroyer, Simone Knapp.

Comedy/Adventure   (PR:C MPAA:NR)

VIVA MAX!½** (1969) 93m Commonwealth United c

Peter Ustinov (Gen. Maximilian Rodrigues de Santos), Pamela Tiffin (Paula Whitland), Jonathan Winters (Gen. Billy Joe Hallson), John Astin (Sgt. Valdez), Harry Morgan (Police Chief George Sylvester), Keenan Wynn (Gen. Barney LaComber), Alice Ghostley (Hattie Longstreet Daniel), Kenneth Mars (Dr. Sam Gillison), Ann Morgan Guilbert (Edna Miller), Bill McCutcheon (Desmond Miller), Gino Conforti (Contreras), Chris Ross (Gomez), Larry Hankin (Romero), Paul Sand (Moreno), Don Diamond (Hernandez), Jack Colvin (Garcia), Jessica Myerson (Mrs. Dodd), Ted Gehring (Customs Guard Collins), Jim B. Smith (Customs Guard Michaels), Eldon Quick (Quincy), Jack Wakefield (Policeman Milton), Glenn Tucker (Capt. Harris), Lee Brandt (Sentry Bus Driver), King Cotton the Horse.

A silly farce which has a balanced number of laughs and dull moments as Ustinov, a blundering Mexican general, organizes an army and invades the Alamo. This is not, however, 1836 but 1969 and for most Texans the Alamo has become sacred ground. Under the pretense of marching in a George Washington's Day parade, Ustinov's unarmed troops "storm" the fortress. Not surprisingly they find little opposition. Ustinov is proud of himself, having finally proven his worth as a soldier (like his father and grandfather) and as a man. He hopes that this will be enough to win back his fiancee. When confronted by authorities, Ustinov refuses to give up his stronghold. The head of the National Guard is called in, the dunderheaded Winters, who earns a living as a used furniture salesman and complains that he saw no action in WW II because he was too busy changing fluorescent lights in a camp. Meanwhile, inside the Alamo's walls, Ustinov takes a couple of prisoners, Tiffin, a tour guide, and Ghostley, a raving anti-Communist. Tiffin grows sympathetic to Ustinov, but Ghostley has ideas of her own. She contacts her nephew, Mars, who heads a paramilitary neofascist group called The Sentries. Outside the walls of the Alamo confusion reigns as everyone tries to implement his own plan of attack, Morgan, Wynn, Winters, and The Sentries. A mere 24 hours after raising the Mexican flag over the Alamo, Ustinov leads his troops quietly back to their own country. Since Texans hold an undying reverence for the Alamo it should come as no shocker that many extremists opposed even a fictional takeover. During filming, one crazed defender of the Lone Star state was hauled away by police after waving a rifle and promising to shoot anyone who raised the Mexican flag over the Alamo. Another group of patriots felt that by slashing the film crew's power cables they were performing a national service. The production survived those who conspired against its completion and still

managed to convey a lighthearted humor directed against both Texans and Mexicans. Mexico proceeded to ban the film, proving that the people of Texas were better at taking a joke.

p, Mark Carliner; d, Jerry Paris; w, Elliot Baker (based on the novel by James Lehrer); ph, Henri Persin (Eastmancolor); m, Hugo Montenegro, Ralph Dino, John Sembello; ed, Bud Molin, David Berlatsky; md, Charles Koppleman; prod d, James Hulsey; art d, Carl Braugner; cos, Annalisa Nasalli-Rocca; makeup, Monique Archambault; stunts, Frank Orsatti.

Comedy   Cas.   (PR:A MPAA:G)

VIVA VILLA!** (1934) 115m MGM bw

Wallace Beery (Pancho Villa), Fay Wray (Teresa), Stuart Erwin (Johnny Sykes), Leo Carillo (Sierra), Donald Cook (Don Felipe), George E. Stone (Chavito), Joseph Schildkraut (Gen. Pascal), Henry B. Walthall (Madero), Katherine De Mille (Rosita), David Durand (Bugle Boy), Phillip Cooper (Villa as a Boy), Frank Puglia (Villa's Father), John Merkel (Pascal's Aide), Charles Stevens, Steve Clemento, Pedro Regas (Staff), Carlos De Valdez (Old Man), Harry Cording (Major domo), Sam Godfrey (Prosecuting Attorney), Nigel De Brulier (Judge), Charles Requa, Tom Ricketts (Grandees), Clarence H. Wilson (Jail Official), James Martin (Mexican Officer), Anita Gordiana (Dancer), Francis McDonald (Villa's Man), Harry Semels (Soldier), Julian Rivero (Telegraph Operator), Bob McKenzie (Bartender), Dan Dix (Drunk), Paul Stanton (Newspaperman), Mischa Auer (Military Attache), Belle Mitchell (Wife), John Davidson, Brandon Hurst, Leonard Mudie (Statesmen), Herbert Prior, Emile Chautard (Generals), Henry Armetta, Adrian Rosley, Hector V. Sarno (Mendoza Brothers), Ralph Bushman 'Francis X. Bushman, Jr.' (Calloway), Arthur Treacher (English Reporter), William Von Brincken (German Reporter), Andre Cheron (French Reporter), Michael Visaroff (Russian Reporter), Shirley Chambers (Wrong Girl), Arthur Thalasso (Butcher), Chris-Pin Martin, Nick De Ruiz (Peons), George Regas (Don Rodrigo), Leon White (Man), H.B. Warner (Bit).

The life of the famous Mexican bandit and revolutionary is told in this exciting action drama. The film opens as young Villa (Cooper) watches a soldier whips his father to death for some minor offense. Soon afterward, the boy murders the soldier and takes to the hills where he grows into Beery and gathers a band of followers who join him in swooping out of the mountains on isolated haciendas and pillaging the homes of the rich, giving part of the proceeds to the poor in classic Robin Hood style. On one of these raids he meets American reporter Erwin, and the two become close friends. Later he meets wealthy landowner Cook and his sister, Wray, who are sympathetic to Berry and his goals. They introduce him to Walthall, the intellectual figurehead of the peon revolt starting to gather strength. Walthall persuades Beery to add his forces to the peasant army as its fighting core. Soon a renegade army general, Schildkraut, joins the rebels with his forces, and they soon sweep through Mexico to victory. The president resigns and Walthall is named in his place. Berry's army is disbanded and he is sent home to his ranch. Beery is not terribly bright, and he thinks banks exist only to give out money. When a bank teller refuses to do this, Berry blackjacks him, killing the man. Schildkraut takes the opportunity to eliminate his closest rival and orders Berry executed for murder. Walthall steps in and pardons Beery on the condition that he leave the country. He does and Schildkraut quickly murders Walthall and seizes power for himself. Beery returns and reorganizes his army to fight Schildkraut, but without Walthall as a guiding intelligence behind him, Beery and his men run wild, robbing and killing almost at random. Cook and Wray refuse to support him this time, and he attacks Wray, who shoots him in the arm. She turns against him and he orders her flogged. Later a stray bullet fired by one of Beery's men kills her. Beery's forces triumph over Schildkraut's and when the general is captured Beery has him covered in honey and left out for the ants to eat. "Put it on his ears, his eyes, his nose, his mouth," Beery rants, "put it every place on him–every place!" Schildkraut dies screaming. Beery takes over as president, but his limited education makes the job too much for him. He retires again to his ranch. Some time later he comes to Mexico City for a visit and runs again into his old friend Erwin. As they talk, they are spotted by Cook, who blames Beery for his sister's death. He seizes a rifle and shoots Beery down. He lies in a butcher shop, mortally wounded, with Erwin cradling his head. Beery tells his journalist friend, "I hear about big men what they say when they die. You write something very big about me." Erwin tells him, "I'll write about how Pancho Villa died with a medal that had once been given him for the rescue of Mexico still around his neck." "What else, Johnny?" Beery asks. "The peons. From north and south, the peons who had loved him came to see him." Erwin says. "That's fine, Johnny, you tell me more." Erwin goes on, "Pancho Villa spoke for the last time. He said, he said...." "Hurry, Johnny. Johnny. What were my last words?" "'Goodbye, my Mexico' said Pancho Villa. 'Forgive me for my crimes. Remember, if I sinned against you, it was because I loved you too much.'" Confused, Beery looks at his friend and asks "Forgive me? Johnny, what I done wrong?" Berry's performance as Villa is one of the highlights of his long and diverse career, and his portrayal of the man as equal parts child, crusader, peasant, and murderous bandito is near perfect. The production was greatly troubled, mostly as a result of an episode involving Lee Tracy, who was originally cast as Johnny Sykes. Tracy was a notorious drunk, and while the crew was in Mexico filming location scenes under the direction of Howard Hawks, he stumbled, naked onto the balcony of his hotel room and urinated on a passing parade of Mexican soldiers. Tracy was arrested for a time, and then called back to MGM in Hollywood, where he was fired. Hawks was called on to testify against Tracy and refused, so he was fired as well, and Conway given the job of finishing the film. Later, a plane carrying a couple of weeks worth of exposed film crashed and burned, putting the schedule back while the scenes were reshot. The swarms of Mexican extras also gave the production trouble. Between 500 and 6,000 were used in various scenes, but they received only half of their $1-a-day rate. When finally completed, the film proved a huge success, earning stacks of money for MGM. It was nominated for an Academy Award as best picture, but lost out to IT HAPPENED ONE NIGHT.

p, David O. Selznick; d, Jack Conway (uncredited, Howard Hawks); w, Ben Hecht (based on the book by Edgcumb Pinchon, O.B. Stade); ph, James Wong Howe; m, Herbert Stothart; ed, Robert J. Kern; art d, Harry Oliver; set d, Edwin B. Willis; cos, Dolly Tree.

Historical Drama **(PR:A-C MPAA:NR)**

VIVA ZAPATA!***** (1952) 113m FOX bw

Marlon Brando *(Emiliano Zapata)*, Jean Peters *(Josefa Espejo)*, Anthony Quinn *(Eufemio Zapata)*, Joseph Wiseman *(Fernando Aguirre)*, Arnold Moss *(Don Nacio)*, Alan Reed *(Pancho Villa)*, Margo *(La Soldadera)*, Harold Gordon *(Don Francisco Madero)*, Lou Gilbert *(Pablo)*, Mildred Dunnock *(Senora Espejo)*, Frank Silvera *(Huerta)*, Nina Varela *(Aunt)*, Florenz Ames *(Senor Espejo)*, Bernie Gozier *(Zapatista)*, Frank De Kova *(Col. Guajarado)*, Joseph Granby *(Gen. Fuentes)*, Pedro Regas *(Innocente)*, Fay Roope *(Diaz)*, Will Kuluva *(Lazaro)*, Richard Garrick *(Old General)*, Harry Kingston *(Don Garcia)*, Ross Bagdasarian *(Officer)*, Leonard George *(Husband)*, Fernanda Eliscu *(Fuentes' Wife)*, Abner Biberman *(Captain)*, Phil Van Zandt *(Commanding Officer)*, Lisa Fusaro *(Garcia's Wife)*, Belle Mitchell *(Nacio's Wife)*, Ric Roman *(Overseer)*, Henry Silva *(Hernandez)*, Guy Thomajan *(Eduardo)*, George J. Lewis *(Rurale)*, Henry Corden *(Senior Officer)*, Nestor Paiva *(New General)*, Robert Filmer *(Captain)*, Salvador Baquez, Peter Mamakos *(Soldiers)*, Julia Montoya *(Wife)*.

Brando and Kazan united to make a stirring and powerful biography of the legendary Mexican revolutionary, Zapata, one that remains vivid and meaningful to this day. The film opens in the grand presidential palace of tyrant Diaz in Mexico City. Roope, playing a patronizing Diaz, allows a group of peons from the state of Moreles to petition for grievances. The peons, poor farmers in cheap white cotton shirts and pants, wearing sandals and nervously clutching their straw sombreros, quietly tell Roope that their lands have once more been taken away from them by the rich landowners of their district. When Roope tells his peasants to be patient, to check their boundary lines, a tall, slender man steps forth from their midst, telling Roope that the corn must be planted in order for the people to eat. Roope repeats his statement about the boundary lines and ancient grants and the man, Brando, nods quietly, saying, "We shall do as you suggest, my President." Roope realizes that Brando is no simple-minded peon and when the delegation files out, he takes the list of names of the group and circles the name of Emiliano Zapata, a man to be watched. Brando and his brother, Quinn, later lead a group of peasants into a huge cornfield, checking the boundary markers. Suddenly, mounted police begin to ride down the helpless peons and a police machine gun opens up, cutting the peaceful farmers down. Brando, mounted on a beautiful white horse, charges the machine gun, lassos it, and knocks its gunners down. This act causes Brando and Quinn to be branded outlaws and they hide out on a remote mountaintop. Gilbert, one of Brando's men, urges Brando to establish ties with Francisco Madero (Gordon) a respected Mexican intellectual who is leading the fight against Diaz's despotic regime. Brando asks that, if Gordon is such a fine opponent to Roope, why is he leading the fight against the despot from across the border in the United States? Reinforcing Gilbert's belief in Gordon is an eccentric newsman, Wiseman, who brings a personal appeal from Gordon, asking for Brando's support. Brando sends Gilbert to "look into Madero's eyes and tell me what you see," and then departs with Quinn and camp follower Margo, leaving Wiseman to watch them go with a quizzical look on his face and uttering the words: "This is all very disorganized." But Brando is a man pulled in two directions. Part of him wants to help his downtrodden people, the other part wants to marry beautiful Peters, daughter of a successful merchant. He meets with her in a church and promises that he will reform and make of himself a man of property. Going to horse breeder Moss, Brando is given an important job rearing thoroughbreds but he sees a boy taking some food from the horses and being whipped for it. Brando jumps on the man wielding the whip and smashes him unconscious. Moss leaps forward, restraining Brando, telling him he cannot act like that and work for him. "But the boy was hungry!" yells Brando. "You cannot be the conscience of the world!" Moss tells him. Brando calms down and even apologizes to the whip-wielder. Gilbert shows up and tells Brando that revolutionary leader Gordon is a man to be trusted, but Brando seems no longer to care about freeing Mexico from a tyrant. "I can't be the conscience of the whole world," he says, repeating Moss' line. But along the road, riding with Quinn, Brando encounters two mounted policemen dragging a peon behind them, a peasant with a rope around his neck. Brando rides abreast of one of the policemen and asks what the peon's offense has been. "Who knows?" shrugs the indifferent policeman, tightening the rope so that the peon must move faster to keep up with the horses. "What did he do?" Brando demands. "They are always doing something," replies the policeman, and this time he yanks so hard on the rope that the man stumbles in the dust. Brando rests his hand on his pistol as he rides along, then says to the policeman, "I think you'd better let him go." With that, the policeman tries to strike Brando, who fights with him. The horses of the policemen bolt forward, dragging the peon by the neck. Brando races after them, riding alongside the man on the ground, swinging his machete so that the rope is cut and the man rolls into a corn field while the police flee, Quinn after them. Brando dismounts and holds the peon in his arms. He is dead. Other farmers flock around Brando, telling him he will now be a hunted man. One offers shelter to him, another offers him his house. He is the reluctant hero the people have been waiting for, patiently waiting for him to lead them out of their misery. Quinn returns to tell Brando that he could not catch the policeman and then sees the peon dead, telling Brando, "You should have cut the rope sooner." Brando next courts Peters in her home, exchanging parables with her mother and aunts in a stuffy parlor. Then Brando emerges from the parlor and enters the dry goods store owned by the father, Ames. The father tells Brando that he is not suited to be his son-in-law and Brando asks, "What is wrong with me?" Spits back Ames: "A fighter, a brawler, these things you are, but a man of substance, no." Brando leans close to Ames and says, "Find her a mousy, moth-eaten man like yourself." He marches from the store but the moment he steps outside, he is jumped by policemen and dragged away. This time he has a rope around his own neck as he is led from the village square by two policemen on horseback. Quinn and Gilbert, seeing this, follow Brando and his captors. More peons begin to follow and, as Brando is led along a back road, dozens, then hundreds, then thousands of peasant farmers and their families throng onto the road, pouring out of the forests and fields, a mighty mass of people who so thickly wedge their bodies next to the nervous policemen that they cannot move. One of the farmers approaches a policeman, now sweating and looking about anxiously at the throng surrounding him, all holding machetes. "What are you doing?" the policeman asks and the peasant farmer replies, "Protecting the prisoner, because if he escaped you would be forced to shoot him in the back." The policeman, realizing that the situation is hopeless, dismounts and goes to a smiling Brando, removing the rope from his neck and cutting the rope that holds his hands behind his back. Quinn, Gibert, and Wiseman race up on horseback and before Brando leaves, Wiseman screams (he never talks when shouting will do in this film), "Cut the wire! He'll use it!" Wiseman points upward to a telegraph pole and the wire running from it, meaning that the policeman will use the wire to contact headquarters. Brando nods and Quinn races forward to pull out his machete. "Stop," yells the policeman in charge. "Cut that wire and you'll be committing sedition!" Brando thinks only for a moment and then orders Quinn: "Cut the wire!" Quinn hacks away at the wire and the next scene shows Brando, selected by his people to lead them, inspecting a troop train his men have just blown up and are looting of military supplies, mostly gunpowder. Brando says that the captured gunpowder will have to be sufficient for their needs, which are made evident in the next scene. The small fortress in the town is occupied by federal troops under the command of Biberman. The place is full of casualites and is smoking from siege. Biberman looks over a rampart to see if the revolutionaries are going to attack again but only the village women with flower baskets are seen. "That's a good sign, don't you think, captain?" asks a hopeful aide of Biberman's. Then, suddenly, the women–Margo in the lead–race toward the fortress and stack their flower baskets, all packed with gunpowder, before the gates, a long trail of powder running from the baskets. Biberman sees the plot unfolding and orders his men to shoot down a woman running toward the trail of black powder with a burning torch in her hand. She is shot down but crawls the distance to the powder line and ignites it with the torch. The flame runs to the basket and a terrific explosion blows open the gates and then Brando's men come dashing forward on horseback to take the fortress. Following the battle, Brando bestows gifts upon his valiant citizen-soldiers–pigs, chickens, and other simple spoils of war. One boy, who has lost two brothers and has killed several federales, requests Brando's horse. The great white steed stands nearby and Brando looks at him lovingly, saying, "That's a good horse." "That's why he wants him," answers an aide. Brando tells the boy to take the horse, a gesture that endears him even more in the hearts of his already adoring followers. Now the stuffy merchant, Ames, is all too happy to have Brando as a son-in-law, now that he is winning the revolution in the south. Peters and Brando are married, but on his wedding night, Brando is restless and cannot sleep. He tells Peters that he is disturbed because he cannot read. She promises to teach him and he gets a book and tells her to start, that night, their wedding night. She does. Outside, Quinn and others get drunk and serenade Brando, but Wiseman does not drink nor celebrate, reminding Quinn that there will be more battles. Quinn says he knows it, but he and the others need some enjoyment. Then, almost as suddenly as it began, the revolution ends as Roope flees Mexico and Gordon is made the new president. Brando and some of his men ride into Mexico City to meet the new president, who tells Brando he is going to give him a huge ranch for his services. "I didn't fight for a ranch!" roars Brando, and insists that the land be given back to the peons. Gordon promises that he will do all in his power to return the land to the farmers but tells Brando that it will take time. He then asks that Brando order his army to lay down its arms so that civilian authority can resume control of the government. Brando tells Gordon that if his men disarm they will stand no chance of ever getting their lands back. He graphically demonstrates his point by aiming his rifle at Gordon's head, demanding his watch. The timorous president hands over his gold watch with quaking hands, Brando then takes his rifle and thrusts it butt first under Gordon's arm and says, now that the gun is pointing at *him*, Brando, "*Now* you can have your watch back." Gordon gets the point and promises to act fast. Brando tells him that he will take his men back to Moreles and wait, but that he will not wait too long. After Brando departs, Silvera, playing the scheming, ruthless General Huerta, comes in from a side office with his military staff, telling Gordon to "shoot that Zapata now!" Gordon tells him that Brando is a good man and that everyone has their good points, even Silvera. Gordon exits and Silvera tells his aides that he cannot abide either Gordon or Brando and both must go. "Oh, the odor of goodness," he sneers when thinking about both men. When Brando's men do not disarm, Gordon travels to the state of Moreles and persuades the revolutionary leader to have his men stack their arms. News arrives that Silvera's troops are invading the state and Gordon tells Brando that it must be a mistake, that Silvera had no such instructions from him. Gordon returns to Mexico City and is summarily assassinated by Silvera's men as Silvera looks on stoically. Brando battles Silvera and defeats him but the price is high, hundreds of his men being killed. Gilbert, who had tried to effect a truce, is considered a traitor for meeting with the enemy, and Brando himself, at Gilbert's request, executes him, but not before Gilbert asks him pointedly, "Can good come from a bad thing?" After Silvera's evil regime falls, Brando goes to Mexico City once more to meet with Pancho Villa who, with Brando, has helped to beat the tyrant. The two men—Reed playing Villa, and Brando—have photos taken sitting in the throne chairs of the national palace and then take a siesta on a little island to decide who should be president of Mexico. Reed looks at Brando and asks him if he can read. When Brando nods, Reed says, "It's settled then, you're the president." But Brando bristles at having to administrate a corrupt system and when a delegation from his own state arrives he finds himself trying to placate the farmers as he and others were once mollified by Roope years earlier. He even circles the name of a defiant peon (Silva), and remembers back to the time when his own name was encircled by Roope. He sees himself becoming the very thing he hates and has fought against. He tells the farmers to wait for him, that he is returning to Moreles with them to get their land back for them. When he walks into the side office to retrieve his rifle and ammunition, Wiseman stops him, telling him he's making a mistake, pointing to a chair and saying that if he leaves his enemies will be sitting in that chair the next day. Brando gives Wiseman a long look and says meaningfully: "I know you now—no friends, no woman. And now do you know what you will do? You will go to Carranzo or Obregon 'Brando's enemies'...and you will never change!" He marches out of the room while Wiseman screams for him to stay. Once back in Moreles, Brando goes to a great but dilapidated hacienda where he finds his own brother, Quinn, who has taken the land from the peasants and also stolen the wife of one farmer. He finds Quinn drunk and saying to him, "Be careful what you say to me, brother." Brando reaches forth and grabs Quinn by the hair, yanking his head upward, shouting, "You drunken pig!" Quinn admits that he took the land and the woman, then stands up, shouting: "We beat Diaz—he's living in a palace in Spain! We beat Huerta—he's a rich man living in the United States! Look at me—I'm a general!" He turns an empty pocket inside out. "Here's my pay– a hunk of dust!" Quinn moves out of the room with the farmer's wife and Brando sits down disgustedly as the peons come close to him for counsel. He tells them that "there are no strong men...they die, they desert." He motions to his brother, an alcoholic hulk, walking away, "they change." He tells them that they must look to themselves and that the only strong country is one led by "a strong people." Quinn is lurching down a hallway, taking the wife of one of the farmers present with him, staggering to a bedroom, slovenly drinking as he goes, sending the woman into a bedroom. The farmer, beside himself with rage, runs down the hallway, shooting Quinn who shoots the farmer. Quinn cries out for Brando who dashes down the hallway to cradle his dying brother in his arms. The peons, out of respect for Brando, offer to bury Quinn as a general with full military honors, but, as he weeps, pressing Quinn's head to his, he says, "No, he did not die in battle." Brando's fortunes dip, his troops die and desert as his enemies in Mexico City grow stronger. He has taken to the mountains with a few men, where he lives with Peters in a small hut. Silva comes to him to tell him that a federal colonel is ready to come over to him, turning over his fortress and well-stocked arsenal. Though Peters protests his going, Brando rides off to meet with the colonel, De Kova, a cross-eyed, lean-faced, bowlegged, pigeon-toed officer greeting him inside a walled hacienda in Chinemeca. Brando inspects his guns and ammunition and then spots his old horse, the great white steed on which he rode to glory years earlier. "A federal officer had him," De Kova tells him. Brando goes to the horse and affectionately strokes it, saying: "You've changed...gotten old." At that moment the horse breaks away and hundreds of federal troops suddenly rear themselves up from behind the walls of the hacienda, unleashing a fierce fusillade of bullets that riddle Brando, who curls up in a ball and dies. The white horse races out of the hacienda and Wiseman, who had developed the insidious assassination plan, runs from cover screaming for the troopers to "Shoot the horse! Shoot the horse!" The hundreds of soldiers turn their guns on the horse and fire, kicking up dust behind the animal's hooves, but none hits the fast-disappearing animal. When a federal general steps forth to look at Wiseman suspiciously for ordering the horse killed, the eternal revolutionary mumbles: "These people are superstitious. If you shoot the man you must shoot his horse." Brando's body is taken to the main square of his home village and dumped on the fountain. Women come running and cover his mutilated body with flowers. Then peasants arrive and one says, "He could be anybody, shot up that way." The legend of Zapata begins at that moment as the peasants refuse to believe that the great populist leader is dead. "Whenever we need him, he will come. He's in the mountains." "Yes," says another peasant, looking toward the mountains in the distance, "he is in the mountains." Brando's white horse is shown high in the mountains, overlooking the spreading valley beneath, rearing up magnificently as the film ends. Kazan directs this exciting biography with great flair for authenticity and period, injecting vitality in almost every frame, working his cameras as hard as the Zapatistas rode their horses, graphically capturing a bloody, bygone era of the Mexican past and profiling, through an electrifying performance from Brando, one of that country's most controversial heroes. The real Emiliano Zapata was a small man with large, dark almond eyes and delicate hands, a tenant-farmer who finally rose up against the tyrannical ways of Porfirio Diaz, as did Pancho Villa in the north, and lead an army to victory over Diaz. He waged his civil wars, 1911-1919, not to conquer Mexico but to free the land for the peasants of Moreles and other southern provinces. Although Brando presents an idealized version of the great leader, he was in reality more barbaric, and did not hesitate to execute his enemies en masse. Though this film has been criticized for showing Zapata's life in uneven episodes, such criticism is invalid; there is no other way in which this film could have presented an intelligent portrait of the revolutionary leader over a long period of time. Brando is superb in this role, understating the character and, while the world is in chaos, speaking softly, even when firing his rifle. Brando respected the image of Zapata and his essaying of the man is one of respect. He made Zapata come mightily alive, a giant stepping forth from the masses to fight for the common man and win for him again and again until battle was without purpose and death the only symbol of Zapata's leadership, especially his own death. Quinn, who won an Oscar for Best Supporting Actor, is marvelous as the hard-riding, hard-drinking brother willing to die for a cause of a cuckolding woman. Silvera as Huerta, Roope as Diaz, and Wiseman as the intense warmongering journalist, are startling villains not far from their real-life counterparts in posture and character. Gilbert, who acts as Brando's intellectual conscience, is a bit too dramatic and unbelievable in certain scenes. Margo hardly has a word in the film. Gordon as Madero gives a realistic profile and Peters is good, if ancillary, as the sultry wife. Though he is on camera for only a few scenes, Reed, playing Pancho Villa, captures the bigness of the revolutionary leader. Kazan had long wanted to do a film about Zapata and went to Zanuck, convincing him that the project was vital. The producer endorsed the idea and Steinbeck wrote a moving, literate, original screenplay, carefully profiling Zapata as the simple man he truly was. The Mexican government, however, refused to cooperate with Zanuck in the production, remembering what had been done to the life of Pancho Villa in VIVA VILLA, where Wallace Beery played Villa as a bumbling enchilada-gulper. Undaunted, Zanuck personally scouted sites in southwest Texas and found the area where the Rio Grande and Pecos Rivers meet to be identical to the state of Moreles as depicted in the script, remodeling small Texas communities to conform to the look of turn-of-the-century Mexico, using a host of Mexican advisors on the film. Kazan and Zanuck studied endless photos of the principals portrayed in the film and matched them physically. Brando himself went to Mexico and studied Zapata in Sonora and then designed his own makeup, taping his eyelids to round them, wearing brown contact lenses, and flaring his nostrils with metal rings. While filming in Roma, Texas, he would take out his contact lenses and put them in his mouth, but he accidentally swallowed them one day and they had to be replaced. Critics wrongly accused Brando of making himself look Oriental, but any student of the part-Indian Zapata who has looked at the Diego Rivera painting of the great leader and studied the famous Casasola photograph collection showing Zapata can easily realize that Brando duplicated the appearance of the Mexican leader perfectly. It was thought that Brando and Quinn would be antagonistic toward one another, both having starred in "A Streetcar Named Desire" in various theatrical productions, although it was Brando who made the part of Stanley Kowalski his own. Quinn was reportedly upset at newcomer Brando getting the lead role. "I thought I'd play Zapata," Quinn was later quoted as saying, "and was really angry when I found out that the part had gone to Brando." Reportedly the two became friends after urinating in the Rio Grande together when on location, having a crude contest as to which could project his emission farther. The river also provided headaches for Kazan. From the Mexican side of the river almost every day swam hordes of Mexican men, stripping naked and swimming over to the U.S. side to try get on camera in the altogether. Kazan, who had been told by Mexican authorities that they did not appreciate his presumptuously making a film of one of their greatest heroes, thought it was all a plot by the Mexican government to ruin his film. It is clear that Kazan was much influenced by Sergei Eisenstein's QUE VIVA MEXICO here, but the film still bears his indelible stamp of creativity. One of the bit players appearing in the film was Maria Luisa Castenada, who—under the name of Movita at age 17–had played Clark Gable's sultry Polynesian mistress in MUTINY ON THE BOUNTY (1936). Brando, always attracted to dark-complexioned women, soon became involved with the older actress who had fallen on hard times. They would begin their life together during the production of VIVA ZAPATA, an 11-year affair which culminated in marriage and divorce.

p, Darryl F. Zanuck; d, Elia Kazan; w, John Steinbeck (based on the novel *Zapata the Unconquered* by Edgcumb Pichon); ph, Joe MacDonald; m, Alex North; ed, Barbara McLean; md, Alfred Newman; art d, Lyle Wheeler, Leland Fuller.

Biography   **Cas.**   **(PR:C MPAA:NR)**

VIVACIOUS LADY*½**   (1938) 90m RKO bw

Ginger Rogers *(Frances Brent)*, James Stewart *(Peter Morgan)*, James Ellison *(Keith Beston)*, Charles Coburn *(Dr. Morgan)*, Beulah Bondi *(Mrs. Morgan)*, Frances Mercer *(Helen)*, Phyllis Kennedy *(Jenny)*, Alec Craig *(Joseph the Chauffeur)*, Franklin Pangborn *(Apartment Manager)*, Grady Sutton *(Culpepper)*, Hattie McDaniel *(Maid)*, Jack Carson *(Waiter Captain)*, Willie Best, Floyd Shackelford *(Porters)*, Dorothy Moore *(Hat Check Girl)*, Maurice Black *(Headwaiter)*, Frank M. Thomas *(Train Conductor)*, Spencer Charters, Maude Eburne *(Husband and Wife on Train)*, Jane Eberling *(Girl on Bus)*, Ray Mayer, George Chandler *(Men on Train)*, Bobby Barber *(Italian)*, June Johnson *(Miss Barton)*, Marvin Jones *(Young Man on Bus)*, Jack Arnold *(Druggist)*, Ed Mortimer *(Publisher)*, Lloyd Ingraham *(Noble the Professor)*, Lee Bennett *(Student)*, Tom Quinn *(Maitre d')*, Harry Campbell, Kay Sutton, Phyllis Fraser, Bud Flanagan 'Dennis O'Keefe', Edgar Dearing, Helena Grant, Vivian Reid, William Brisbane, Vernon Dent, Katharine Ellis, June Horne, Dorothy Johnson, Phoebe Terbell, Robert Wilson, Stanley Blystone, Barbara Pepper.

A charming, fast-moving comedy that shows Rogers didn't have to chirp and tap in order to be a star. Stewart is a mild-mannered botany professor who lives in a college town and works in the university headed by his pedantic father, Coburn, who dominates his son and everyone else around him. Stewart's cousin is Ellison (a longtime western star who was being seen in a rare movie without chaps, guns, and a Stetson) and he has been haunting the nightspots in New York. Stewart is sent to the Big Apple to bring Ellison back. While there, Stewart meets and falls for Rogers, a bouncy, sprightly nightclub performer who is totally unlike any women he knows back home. In the brief span of one night, the two fall in love and are married. Stewart brings Rogers back to his small town and now has to figure some way to break the news of his marriage to his former fiancee (Mercer), his father, and his mother (Bondi), who has regular "heart seizures" whenever anything happens that she doesn't like. Bondi's heart condition is strictly phony but it does frighten Stewart enough that he feels he has to soft-pedal the news. Stewart resolves to tell them all but when push comes to shove, he finds that he is too frightened to do it. It's basically a one-joke premise but there are so many twists that they manage to extend the one joke for an entire movie until Stewart finally comes clean and the traditional and hidebound family members do accept Rogers. Before that happens, there is a hysterical hair-pulling fight between Rogers and Mercer that is a comedic highlight and it's a wonder that both women didn't come out of the fracas bald. Stewart has many emotions he must deal with and successfully handles all of them. He is a remarkable actor in that he was able to be quite different under the guidance of Alfred Hitchcock, Frank Capra, various western directors, and so many comedy directors and still not lose his basic likable innocence which always shone through. Rogers sings "You'll Be Reminded of Me" (Ted Shapiro, Ted Meskill, George Jessel), then dances "The Big Apple" with Bondi, Ellison, and Coburn. This was the second successful collaboration for Stevens and Rogers, as he had directed her and Astaire in SWING TIME. An Oscar nomination was given to de Grasse for his cinematography and the sound department of RKO also received a nomination. Stewart was signed to MGM at this time and was loaned out by the studio for the movie. In another day, this would have made a fine full musical because the story and screenplay were filled with delightful moments and rich characterizations. Some of the best comedy second bananas appear to great advantage, including Jack Carson, prissy Grady Sutton and prissier Franklin Pangborn.

p&d, George Stevens; w, P.J. Wolfson, Ernest Pagano (based on a story by I.A.R. Wylie); ph, Robert de Grasse; m, Roy Webb; ed, Henry Berman; art d, Van Nest Polglase, Carroll Clark; set d, Darrell Silvera; cos, Irene and Bernard Newman; makeup, Mel Burns.

Comedy   **Cas.**   **(PR:A MPAA:NR)**

VIVEMENT DIMANCHE! (SEE: CONFIDENTIALLY YOURS, 1983, Fr.)

VIVERE PER VIVERE   (SEE: LIVE FOR LIFE, 1967, Fr./Ital.)

VIVIAMO OGGI (SEE: DAY AND THE HOUR, THE, 1963, Fr./Ital.)

VIVIR DESVIVIENDOSE   (SEE: MOMENT OF TRUTH, 1965, Ital./Span.)

VIVO PER LA TUA MORTE   (SEE: LONG RIDE FROM HELL, A, 1970, Ital.)

VIVRE POUR VIVRE   (SEE: LIVE FOR LIFE, 1967, Fr./Ital.)

VIVRE SA VIE   (SEE: MY LIFE TO LIVE, 1963, Fr.)

VIXEN**   (1970, Jap.) 95m Daiei c (JOTAI)

Ruriko Asaoka *(Michi)*, Eiji Okada *(Nobuyuki Ishido)*, Kyoko Kishida *(Akie)*, Eiko Azusa *(Ishido's Sister)*, Takao Ito *(Akizuki)*, Yusuke Kawazu *(Goro)*, Eitaro Ozawa.

Asaoka plays a young woman who uses blackmail to get 2 million yen out of the older Okada but isn't satisfied until she completely draws him away from his wife and is supporting her. He even buys her a bar, but she continues seeking her own forms of obsessive satisfaction despite the harm that comes to just about all who cross her path. A dark depiction of the decay of traditional values among modern Japanese youth.

d, Yasuzo Masumura; w, Masumura, Ichiro Ikeda; ph, Setsuo Kobayashi (Daiei Scope, Fujicolor,); m, Hikaru Hayashi; art d, Takesaburo Watanabe.

Drama   **(PR:O MPAA:NR)**

VIXENS, THE*   (1969) 82m Trio-International Film Artists/International Film Arti sts-Stratford bw (AKA: FRIENDS AND LOVERS; THE WOMEN)

Anne Linden *(Betty)*, Mary Kahn *(Ann)*, Peter Burns *(Bob)*, Steven Harrison *(Alan)*, Claudia Bach *(Judy)*, Robert Raymond *(Harold)*, Hector Elizondo *(Inspector)*.

Trying tale set in the late 1960s about two women involved in dead-end marriages who become close to each other due to their common revulsion to their husbands and their swinging neighborhood. The whole sordid story is being told to a police inspector after one of the husbands is killed. It's easy to understand how these characters would elicit revulsion.

p, Sande N. Johnsen; d, Harvey Cort; w, Cort, Al Rosati; ph, Harry Petricek; ed, Pat Follmer.

Drama   **(PR:O MPAA:NR)**

VOGUES   (SEE: VOGUES OF 1938, 1937)

VOGUES OF 1938**½**   (1937) 105m UA c (AKA: ALL THIS AND GLAMOUR TOO; VOGUES)

Warner Baxter *(George Curson)*, Joan Bennett *(Wendy Van Klettering)*, Helen Vinson *(Mary Curson)*, Mischa Auer *(Prince Muratorv)*, Alan Mowbray *(Henry Morgan)*, Jerome Cowan *(Mr. Brockton)*, Alma Kruger *(Sophie Miller)*, Marjorie Gateson *(Mrs. Lemke)*, Dorothy McNulty [Penny Singleton] *(Miss Sims)*, Polly Rowles *(Betty Mason)*, Marla Shelton *(Violet)*, Hedda Hopper *(Mrs. Van Klettering)*, Roman Bohnen *(Lawyer)*, Georgie Tapps, Virginia Verrill, Fred Lawrence, Gloria Gilbert, The Olympic Trio, The Wiere Brothers, The Four Hot Shots *(Specialties)*, Rocco and Saulters *(Cotton Club Dancers)*, Victor Young and His Orchestra *(Themselves)*, Frank McGrath *(Warner Baxter's Stand-In)*, Dick Wessel *(Boxer)*, Jean Acker *(Extra)*, Rosemary Theby, Harry Myers *(Dress Extras)*, Peggy Calvin, Betty Wyman, Martha Heveran, Phyllis Gilman, Elizabeth "Libby" Harben, Ida Vollmar, Dorothy Day, Mary Oakes, Kay Aldridge, Olive Cawley, Frances Joyce, Noreen Carr, Ruth Martin, Betty Douglas *(Walter Wanger Models)*, Irving Bacon, Dick Elliott, Hal K. Dawson, Rex Evans, Charles Williams.

The title says everything for this display of the then prominent styles marching across the stage in beautiful Technicolor. Baxter is the owner of a chic boutique who must contend with innumerable obstacles in order to sell the latest fashions, including a nagging wife, demanding customers, and an astute rival just waiting for him to make a mistake. But he fares all right, and in fact seems to enjoy all the excitement. Though its obvious selling line was the sparkling fashions presented in terrific hues by top models of the day (Miss Lucky Strike and Miss Lux Soap among others), VOGUES was a neatly conceived and tightly directed effort, with some lively well placed tunes. Songs include: "That Old Feeling" (Lew Brown, Sammy Fain, Sung by Virginia Verrill), "Lovely one" (Frank Loesser, Manning Sherwin), "Turn On The Red Hot Heat (Burn The Blues Away)" (Paul Francis Webster, Louis Alter), "King Of Jam" (Alter).

p, Walter Wanger; d, Irving Cummings; w, Bella and Samuel Spewack; ph, Ray Renahan (Technicolor); ed, Otho Lovering, Dorothy Spencer; md, Boris Morros; art d, Alexander Toluboff; cos, Helen Taylor; ch, Seymour Felix.

Musical/Comedy   **(PR:A MPAA:NR)**

VOICE IN THE MIRROR**½**   (1958) 105m UNIV bw

Richard Egan *(Jim Burton)*, Julie London *(Ellen Burton)*, Arthur O'Connell *(William Tobin)*, Walter Matthau *(Dr. Leon Karnes)*, Troy Donahue *(Paul Cunningham)*, Harry Bartell *(Harry Graham)*, Peggy Converse *(Paul's Mother)*, Ann Doran *(Mrs. Devlin)*, Mae Clarke *(Mrs. Robbins)*, Casey Adams [Max Showalter] *(Don Martin)*, Hugh Sanders *(Mr. Hornsby)*, Ken Lynch *(Frank)*, Doris Singleton *(Liz)*, Dave Barry *(Pianist)*, Alan Dexter *(Bartender)*, Richard Hale *(Gaunt Man)*, Bart Bradley *(Gene Devlin)*, Phil Harvey *(Phil Perkins)*.

Poignant drama in which successful commerical artist Egan takes to drink after the death of his small daughter. His drinking gets worse and worse, and though he wants to stop he can't, not even given the support of devoted wife, London, and advice of doc Mattau. His recovery only comes after meeting a man in a similar position and they give each other the support and understanding needed to kick the habit. Egan goes on to create an organization (presumably Alcoholics Anonymous) operating under the premise that "only a drunk can help a drunk." The film helps ensure realism by using downtown Los Angeles as a backdrop. Egan convincingly portrays the problems of a drunk without rather obvious stereotypes.

p, Gordon Kay; d, Harry Keller; w, Larry Marcus; ph, William Daniels; (CinemaScope) m, Henry Mancini; ed, George Gittens; md, Joseph Gershenson; art d, Alexander Golitzen, Richard H. Riedel; cos, Bill Thomas; m/l, title song, Bobby Troup, Julie London (sung by London).

Drama   (PR:A   MPAA:NR)

VOICE IN THE NIGHT*   (1934) 60m COL bw

Tim McCoy (*Tim Dale*), Billie Seward (*Barbara*), Joseph Crehan (*Robinson*), Ward Bond (*Bob*), Kane Richmond (*Jack*), Frank Layton (*Matthews*), Guy Usher (*Benton*), Francis McDonald (*Jackson*), Alphonse Ethier (*W.T. Dale*).

Off his horse for a change, McCoy is working for a telephone company, putting up lines across the desert and landing smack dab in the middle of wars between companies. This gives him ample opportunity to bust the jaws of as many villains as are thrown at him, as well as to perform daring stunts atop telephone poles.

d, Charles C. Coleman; w, Harold Shumate; ph, John Stumar; ed, John Rawlins.

Action/Drama   (PR:A   MPAA:NR)

VOICE IN THE NIGHT, A**   (1941, Brit.) 83m TC/COL bw (GB: FREEDOM RADIO)

Clive Brook (*Dr. Karl Roder*), Diana Wynyard (*Irena Roder*), Raymond Huntley (*Rabenau*), Derek Farr (*Hans Glaser*), Joyce Howard (*Elly*), Howard Marion-Crawford (*Kummer*), John Penrose (*Otto*), Morland Graham (*Father Landbach*), Ronald Squire (*Spiedler*), Reginald Beckwith (*Fenner*), Clifford Evans (*Dressler*), Bernard Miles (*Muller*), Gibb McLaughlin (*Dr. Weiner*), Muriel George (*Hanna*), Martita Hunt (*Concierge*), Hay Petrie (*Sebastian*), Katie Johnson (*Grannie Schmidt*), George Hayes (*Policeman*), Manning Whiley (*S.S. Trooper*), Abraham Sofaer (*Heini Meyer*).

Typical wartime propaganda sees Viennese doctor Brook, who is held in high regard by the Nazis, becoming increasingly disillusioned with the repressive regime as he watches his friends persecuted and his wife's slow seduction by it. With the help of engineer Farr, Brook sets up an underground radio station and in his broadcasts condemns Hitler and holds out the promise that one day a "better" Germany will emerge from the rubble.

p, Mario Zampi; d, Anthony Asquith; w, Anatole de Grunwald, Basil Woon, Jeffrey Dell, Louis Golding, Gordon Wellesley, Bridget Boland, Roland Pertwee (based on the story "Freedom Radio" by Wolfgang Wilhelm, George Campbell); ph, Bernard Knowles; m, Nicholas Brodszky; ed, Reginald Beck; art d, Paul Sheriff.

Drama/War   (PR:A   MPAA:NR)

VOICE IN THE NIGHT (SEE: WANTED FOR MURDER, 1946, Brit.)

VOICE IN THE WIND*   (1944) 85m UA bw

Francis Lederer (*Jan Volny/El Hombre*), Sigrid Gurie (*Marya*), J. Edward Bromberg (*Dr. Hoffman*), J. Carrol Naish (*Luigi*), Alexander Granach (*Angelo*), David Cota (*Marco*), Olga Fabian (*Anna*), Howard Johnson (*Capt. von Neubach*), Hans Schumm (*Piesecke*), Luis Alberni (*Bartender*), George Sorel (*Detective*), Martin Garralaga (*Policeman*), Jacqueline Dalya (*Portuguese Girl*), Rudolph Myzet (*Novak*), Fred Nurney (*Vasek*), Bob Stevenson, Otto Reichow (*Guards*), Martin Berliner (*Refugee*).

An attempt to create a dark thriller set in the oppressive era of Nazidom, this picture was doomed from the start when given an incredibly small budget and an absurd 12-day shooting schedule. A young Czech pianist gets himself into a lot of trouble with the Nazis by playing a song that has been outlawed. The song was good, in fact, the best part of this movie, but not worth getting killed over. A weak script is accompanied by horrible photography and the absence of any form of acting.

p, Rudolph Monter, Arthur Ripley; d, Ripley; w, Frederick Torberg (based on a story by Ripley); ph, Dick Fryer; m, Michael Michelet, "Moldau," Bedrich Smetana; ed, Holbrook N. Todd; md, Yascha Paii; art d, Rudy Feld.

Drama/War   (PR:A   MPAA:NR)

VOICE IN YOUR HEART, A*½   (1952, Ital.) 98m Scalera/Lupa bw (UNA VOCE NEL TUO CUORE)

Vittorio Gassman (*Paul*), Florella C. Forti (*Helen*), Gino Bechi (*Bechi*), Beniamino Gigli (*Gigli*), Constance Dowling (*Dolly*), Nino Pavese (*David*),

Michele Riccardini (*Enrico*), Iolanda Del Fabro (*Anna*), Riccardo Billi (*Ciccillo*), Olimpio Holt (*Maestro*).

War correspondent Gassman falls for the singer Forti, talking her out of the nightclubs and into the opera house. When he turns up wounded during an Arab-Israeli conflict, she thinks he's forgotten about her. Old girl friend Dowling sees to it that Gassman's letters don't get through to Forti. Decent performances can't overcome plot's structural weakness or the uneveness of the script. Nonetheless, the opera sequences are of particular interest, featuring the legendary Italian tenor Beniamino Gigli. (In Italian; English subtitles.)

d, Alberto D'Aversa; w, Rodolfo Lombardi, Pietro Nardi, D'Aversa (based on a story by D'Aversa); ph, G. Lombardi; m, Wolfgang Amadeus Mozart, Vincenzo Bellini, Gaetano Donizetti; English subtitles, Guido Beverini.

Drama   (PR:C   MPAA:NR)

VOICE OF BUGLE ANN**   (1936) 70m MGM bw

Lionel Barrymore (*Springfield Davis*), Maureen O'Sullivan (*Camden Terry*), Eric Linden (*Benjy Davis*), Dudley Digges (*Jacob Terry*), Spring Byington (*Ma Davis*), Charley Grapewin (*Cal Royster*), Henry Wadsworth (*Bake Royster*), William "Billy" Newell (*Mr. Tanner*), James Macklin (*Del Royster*), Jonathan Hale (*District Attorney*), Frederick Burton (*The Warden*).

Barrymore plays a backwoods farmer with a deep love for his hunting dogs, especially one that is killed by mean-spirited Digges. In retaliation Barrymore kills Digges, which doesn't help the love affair between Barrymore's son and Digges' daughter, but things manage to work themselves out, with the dog being missed more than Digges. Interesting footage of the Missourians during a hunt is melded into the unfolding of the weak plot. The dog gave her name to the film barked so incessantly during the shooting that Barrymore took her home with him at one point, hoping that familiarity would result in less contempt in this breed.

p, John W. Considine, Jr.; d, Richard Thorpe; w, Harvey Gates, Samuel Hoffenstein (based on the novel by Mackinlay Kantor); ph, Ernest Haller; m, Rudolph Kopp; ed, George Boemler; cos, Dolly Tree.

Drama   (PR:A   MPAA:NR)

VOICE OF MERRILL, THE   (SEE: MURDER WILL OUT, 1953, Brit.)

VOICE OF TERROR   (SEE: SHERLOCK HOLMES AND THE VOICE OF TERROR, 1942)

VOICE OF THE CITY**   (1929) 81m MGM bw

Robert Ames (*Bobby Doyle*), Willard Mack (*Biff Myers*), Sylvia Field (*Beebe*), James Farley (*Wilmot*), John Miljan (*Wilkes*), Clark Marshall (*"Johnny The Hop"*), Duane Thompson (*Mary*), Tom McGuire (*Kelly*), Alice Moe (*Martha*), Beatrice Banyard (*Betsy*).

Ames stars in this crime melodrama as a man framed for the murder of a policeman. He is sent to prison for a 20-year stretch but escapes and takes refuge in the home of a friend, Marshall. Miljan, who is out to put Ames away permanently, is determined to make him emerge from his hideout. Miljan puts the moves on Ames' girl, Field, leading to a confrontation between the two men. Police detective Mack arrives on the scene and guns down Miljan. Ames is cleared and returns to a happy life with his sweetheart. A standard story with the usual excess of sentimentality and unbelievability. Also released in a silent version.

d&w, Willard Mack; ph, Maximilian Fabian; ed, William S. Gray, Basil Wrangell; art d, Cedric Gibbons.

Drama/Crime   (PR:A   MPAA:NR)

VOICE OF THE HURRICANE**½   (1964) 80m RAM-Moral Re-Armament/Selected Pictures c

Muriel Smith (*Mary, "Mbali"*), Phyllis Konstam (*Janet Lord*), Reginald Owen (*Nigel Charter, District Officer*), William Close (*Mark Pearce*), Jane Wax (*Dolly Charter*), David Cole (*Richard Lord*), William Pawley, Jr (*Humphrey Lord*).

The attempts to make moral messages via film usually result in preachy, overly talky comments about man's need to be nicer to man. This is a consequence of trying to approach the moral problem directly, instead of in the more subtle contexts of character and plot development. VOICE OF THE HURRICANE differs not a speck from earlier efforts, with British East Africa being the setting for young white liberals in the middle of a battle between bigoted colonial rulers and angry black revolutionaries. The characters come out looking like grotesque sterotypes, with words instead of actions explaining motivation. The Moral Re-Armament movement was responsible for this particular bit of cinematic moral posturing. Founded at Oxford University in the 1920s by Frank Nathan Daniel Buchman, a German-American evangelist, the group eventually gained a foothold in the U.S. and produced an earlier message film, THE CROWNING EXPERIENCE, in 1960.

p, Scoville Wishard; d, George Fraser; w, Alan Thornhill (Based on the play "The Hurricane" by Thornhill, Peter Howard); ph, Rickard Tegstrom (Technicolor); m, Ian Freebairn-Smith; ed, Harry Marker; md, Freebairn-Smith; art d, W. Cameron Johnson; cos, Athena; spec eff, Thol O. Simonson.

Drama   **(PR:A MPAA:NR)**

VOICE OF THE TURTLE, THE* **   (1947) 103m WB bw (AKA: ONE FOR THE BOOK)

Ronald Reagan (*Sgt. Bill Page*), Eleanor Parker (*Sally Middleton*), Eve Arden (*Olive Lashbrooke*), Wayne Morris (*Comdr. Ned Burling*), Kent Smith (*Kenneth Bartlett*), John Emery (*George Harrington*), Erskine Sanford (*Storekeeper*), John Holland (*Henry Atherton*), Nino Pepitone (*Headwaiter*), Helen Wallace, Sarah Edwards (*Women*), William Gould (*Man*), Frank Wilcox (*Stanley Blake*), Ross Ford (*Soda Clerk*), Bunty Cutler (*Girl at Telephone*), Dick Bartell (*Ticket Agent*), Jack Lee (*Director*), Doris Kemper (*Woman in Delicatessen*), Nicodemus Stewart (*Elevator Boy*), Janet Warren, Tristram Coffin, Lois Austin (*Theater Party*), Philip Morris (*Doorman*), Alan Foster (*Vendor*), Brian O'Hara (*Box-Office Clerk*), Joan Lawrence (*Bill's Ex-Girl Friend*), Ernest Anderson (*Elevator Man*), Peter Camlin, Suzanne Dulier (*French-Speaking Couple*), Bernard DeRoux (*French-Speaking Waiter*), Noel Delorme (*French Hat Check Girl*), Douglas Kennedy (*Naval Officer*), Robert Spencer (*Boy*).

A three-character play that was widened by the original author to fit the screen proved to be a winner in Reagan's career, even though he tried every which way to get out of doing the picture. Parker is an actress who loves being in love but the pickings are poor in the male department during the war and she has not found the man of her dreams. At present, Parker is dating Smith, her producer, but when he gives her the air, her mood becomes blacker than the inside of a cow. Parker meets Reagan, an Army sergeant who is in New York to meet Arden, another actress who is given to promiscuous behavior and sharp wisecracks. By this time, Arden has totally forgotten her date with Reagan and is out with Morris, a Navy commander. When Reagan wonders who Morris is, Arden tells him that it's her husband. Reagan is stuck for a place to rest his wavy head and Parker offers to put him up in her flat, but strictly on a platonic basis. Well, *you* know what happens. The two of them get closer and closer after Parker lets down her hair. Meanwhile, Arden has discovered that she likes Reagan as well and can't bear losing him to Parker so she tries several ploys to break up the duo, including countless telephone calls and staying as close to the two as she can. It's all for naught and Parker and Reagan wind up together. "The Great Communicator" actually lost a battle here but won the war, which must have been good practice for the second career he chose after playing the vicious gangster in THE KILLERS remake. Reagan was under contract to Warners and Jack Warner insisted that he take this role over Reagan's many objections. John Huston had offered Reagan the Bruce Bennett role in THE TREASURE OF THE SIERRA MADRE, a film Reagan preferred to this, but Warner believed Reagan's career would be better aided by a starring assignment in this hit play (which had already been on stage about four years and was still on Broadway when the film was released). Reagan asked for June Allyson as his costar because he really didn't know Parker and wasn't sure if they could play off each other. That was denied and production began with Parker, wearing a Margaret Sullavan hairdo (she had starred in the play and was bypassed for the movie) and doing what amounted to a Margaret Sullavan impression. Bets were made that this very chic play about manners and morals during wartime could not be translated to the big screen but getting Van Druten to adapt his own play was a great help and the result was a delightful movie. Good character performances by all concerned and slick direction by Rapper for producer Charles Hoffman, who later moved into TV for years.

p, Charles Hoffman; d, Irving Rapper; w, John Van Druten, Hoffman (based on the play by Van Druten); m, Max Steiner; ed, Rudi Fehr; md, Leo F. Forbstein; art d, Robert Haas; set d, William Kuehl; cos, Leah Rhodes; spec eff, Harry Barndollar, Edwin DuPar.

Comedy   **(PR:A MPAA:NR)**

VOICE OF THE WHISTLER**½   (1945) 60m COL bw

Richard Dix (*John Sinclair*), Lynn Merrick (*Jean Martin*), Rhys Williams (*Ernie Spartow*), James Cardwell (*Fred Graham*), Tom Kennedy (*Ferdinand*), Donald Woods (*Paul Kitridge*), Egon Brecher (*Dr. Rose*), Gigi Perreau (*Bobbie*).

Thinking that he has only six months to live, Dix marries Merrick, promising her vast wealth on his death. She takes the offer, moving with him to an isolated lighthouse, with thoughts of supplying her intern fiance with a hefty sum in a half year. But things don't go quite as planned: Dix regains his health, and he and Merrick fall in love in the process. The jealous fiance shows up planning to murder Dix, only to get himself killed. Finaly, Dix is taken to the chair, leaving Merrick to pass her days alone in the lighthouse. Despite a good idea and the proper atmosphere, the story is not brought to the screen effectively, making for tough going as the plot drags itself out. (See: WHISTLER series Index.)

p, Rudolph C. Flothow; d, William Castle; w, Castle, Wilfred H. Pettit Based on a story by Allan Rader from the radio program "The Whistler"); ph, George Meehan; ed, Dwight Caldwell; md, Mischa Bakaleinikoff.

Drama   **(PR:C MPAA:NR)**

**VOICE WITHIN, THE*½   (1945, Brit.) 74m GN bw

Barbara White (*Kathleen*), Keiron O'Hanrahan [Moore] (*Denis O'Shea*), Shaun Noble (*Roy O'Shea*), Violet Farebrother (*Grandma*), Olive Sloane (*Fair Owner's Wife*), Brefni O'Rorke (*Sgt. Sullivan*), George Merritt (*McDonnell*), Paul Merton (*Patrick O'Day*), Hay Petrie (*Fair Owner*), Johnnie Schofield.

A weak tale about two brothers–O'Hanrahan and Noble–both of whom are in the IRA and in love with the same woman, their adopted sister White. Noble needs to leave the country, so O'Hanrahan offers to help him in order to get White to himself. O'Hanrahan inadvertanly kills a constable while smuggling and tries to frame his brother. By the finale, he is caught and blurts out a confession.

p, Isadore Goldsmith; d, Maurice J. Wilson; w, Stafford Dickens, Herbert Victor, B. Charles-Deane (based on a story by Michael Goldsmith); ph, R. Francke, Jan Sikorski.

Crime   **(PR:A MPAA:NR)**

VOICES**½   (1973, Brit.) 91m Warden/Hemdale c

David Hemmings, Gayle Hunnicutt, Lynn Fairleigh, Russell Lewis, Adam Bridge, Eva Griffiths, Peggy Ann Clifford.

A young married couple living in an old house in the country try to get over the death of their son. This proves to be impossible when the dead boy's voice is heard throughout the home. This isn't an original idea but the treatment has a few interesting quirks. The film's main problem is not having much to say and taking to long too say it.

p, Robert Enders; d, Kevin Billington; w, George Kirgo, Enders (based on the play by Richard Lortz); ph, Geoffrey Unsworth (Technicolor); m, Richard Rodney Bennett.

Horror   **Cas.**   **(PR:O MPAA:NR)**

VOICES   (1979) 106m MGM/UA c

Michael Ontkean (*Drew Rothman*), Amy Irving (*Rosemarie Lemon*), Alex Rocco (*Frank Rothman*), Barry Miller (*Raymond Rothman*), Herbert Berghof (*Nathan Rothman*), Viveca Lindfors (*Mrs. Lemon*), Allan Rich (*Montrose Meier*), Joseph Cali (*Pinky*), Jean Ehrlich (*Snowflake*), Rik Colitti (*String*), Thurman Scott (*Patterson*), Melonie Mazman (*Debbie*), Arva Holt (*Helen*), Richard Kendall (*Scott Gunther*), Mary Serrano (*Ceryl*), Thom Christopher (*Paul Janssen*), Hubert Kelly (*Drummer*), Rory Anthony (*Bass*), Frank Lombardi (*Organist*), Dale Stroever (*Guitarist*), Peter Lawrence Cherone (*Saxophonist*), Jerry MacLauchlin (*Choreographer*), Tom Quinn (*Fat*), Tony Munafo (*Ned*), Pedro O'Campo (*Bus Driver*), Nelson Hailparn (*Johnny*), Franc Luz (*Bobby*), Heidi Bohay (*Girl Friend*), Jean Busada, Peggy Waller (*Dancers*), Bill Baldwin (*Announcer*), Ray Serra (*Track Regular*), Jose Rabelo (*Cuban Customer*), Thelma Lee (*Secretary*), Ida Beecher (*Cashier*), Rob DeRosa (*Demetrius*), Ray Suideau (*Bartender*).

A tearjerker in which truck driver Ontkean romances the deaf Irving. Incorporated into the goings on are his desire to become a singer and her dream of dancing. This and the fact that neither of them are totally at ease with their families are the binding forces in their relationship. The film could have been a lot sappier than it is, with high points coming from the characterizations of the misanthropic members of Ontkean's family. Director Markowitz also makes interesting use of the soundtrack, emphasizing Irving's deafness by contrasting soundless moments with a rock 'n' roll soundtrack. Songs include; "Champagne Jam" (performed by the Atlanta Rhythm Section), "Voices," "On a Stage," "Drunk As a Punk" (performed by Burton Cummings), "Anything That's Rock and Roll" (performed by Tom Petty and the Heartbreakers), and "Bubbles in My Beer" (performed by Willie Nelson).

p, Joe Wizan; d, Robert Markowitz; w, John Herzfeld; ph, Alan Metzger (Panavision, Metrocolor); m, Jimmy Webb; ed, Danford B. Green; art d, Richard Bianchi; cos, John Boxer; ch, Stuart Hodes.

Drama   **(PR:C MPAA:PG)**

VOLCANO**½   (1953, Ital.) 106m Panaria/A UA bw (AKA: VULCANO)

Anna Magnani (*Maddalena Natoli*), Rossano Brazzi (*Donato*), Geraldine Brooks (*Maria*), Edward Cianelli [Eduardo Ciannelli] (*Giulio*), Enzo Staiola (*Nino*), Rinaldo Ambrogi (*Don Antonio*), Lucia Belfadel (*Carmela*), Rosina Galli (*A Worker*), Giulio Cesare Giuffre (*Alvero*), Francesco Cupano (*Merchant*), Ignazio Consiglio (*Boat Captain*).

Set on a small Italian island, this tale begins with Magnani's return to her home village after being kicked out of Naples for being a prostitute. She encounters Staiola, the brother she has never seen, and Brooks, the sister she last saw as a baby, who is now a beautiful young woman. She also meets with indignation from the rest of the villagers, who go so far as to refuse Magnani entrance into the church. In a touching scene of defiance and faith, she prays on the ground in front of the spurning women. Brazzi is a young diver with a disreputable past, who entices the young Brooks to fall in love with him. As the knowing sister wishing to keep Brooks from a troubled future, Magnani drowns Brazzi, leaving her with a guilt that prevents her from saving herself when the active volcano on the island explodes. Director Dieterle brought an entire crew to a small island that had nothing to offer the visitors in terms of modern conveniences. Under such circumstances Dieterle did a very creditable job, always under the threat of a possible eruption from the active volcano. The sequences with the bubbling volcano, as well as other odd features of life on the island, are the worthy results of his efforts.

p&d, William Dieterle; w, Piero Tellini, Victor Stoloff, Erskine Caldwell (based on a story by Renzo Avanzo); ph, Arturo Gallea; m, Enzo Masetti; ed, Gian Carlo Cappelli.

Drama   **(PR:A MPAA:NR)**

VOLCANO, 1969   (SEE: KRAKATOA, EAST OF JAVA, 1969)

VOLPONE**½   (1947, Fr.) 98m Ile de France/Siritzky International bw

Harry Baur (Volpone), Louis Jouvet (Mosca, Steward), Fernand Ledoux (Corvino, Silk Merchant), Marion Dorian (Canina), Jean Temerson (Voltore), Alexandre Rignault (Leone), Charles Dullin (Corbaccio), Jacqueline Delubac (Columba).

Filmization of the classic play by the English man-of-letters Ben Jonson takes a satirical look at a greedy merchant who feigns illness in order to gain the attention (and money) of three would-be inheritors. These three are equally as greedy as Volpone and will do anything to be named his heir, one going so far as to put his wife at the gentleman's disposal. Though originally made in 1939, the film didn't make it to the States until after WW II, by which time several of the people involved in the production had died. Foremost among the missing was the lead player Baur, who was superb in an uncharacteristic comic role. He died mysteriously in 1943, shortly after release from a period of incarceration in a Nazi prison. (In French; English subtitles.)

d, Maurice Tourneur; w, Jules Romains, Stefan Zweig (based on the play by Ben Jonson); m, Marcel Delannoy; set d, A. Baracq.

Comedy   **(PR:A MPAA:NR)**

VOLTAIRE**   (1933) 72m WB bw

George Arliss (Francois Marie Arouet Voltaire), Doris Kenyon (Mme. de Pompadour), Margaret Lindsay (Nanette Calas), Theodore Newton (Francois), Reginald Owen (King Louis XV), Alan Mowbray (Count de Sarnac, Minister of Finance), David Torrence (Dr. Tronchin), Murray Kinnell (Emile), Doris Lloyd (Mme. Clairon), Leonard Mudie (Morteau), Helena Phillips (Mme. Denis), Douglas Dumbrille (Oriental King), Ivan Simpson (Lekain), Gordon Westcott (The Captain).

A romanticized account of a period in the life of the famed French writer and philosopher, with Arliss, in the title role, taking under his protection the harassed Lindsay, producing a play for the king which almost lands the thinker in jail, and, finally, using his superior wit to see that the real villain, Mowbray, receives his just reward. The attempts to add the political flavor of the times hurt the overall flow of the plot, but otherwise this is an intriguing biography. Arliss had seemed like a natural choice to play the famous Frenchman after having scored in the lead role in DISRAELI (1929), an earlier larger-than-life Warner Bros. biography.

p, Ray Griffith; d, John G. Adolfi; W, Paul Green, Maude T. Howell (based on the novel by George Gibbs, E. Lawrence Dudley); ph, Tony Gaudio; ed, Owen Marks; cos, Orry-Kelly.

Historical Drama   **(PR:A MPAA:NR)**

VON RICHTHOFEN AND BROWN**
                        (1970) 97m UA c (AKA: THE RED BARON)

John Philip Law (Baron Manfred von Richthofen), Don Stroud (Roy Brown), Barry Primus (Hermann Goering), Peter Masterson (Maj. Oswald Boelcke), Robert Latourneaux (Ernst Udet), George Armitage (Wolff), Steve McHattie (Voss), Brian Foley (Lothar von Richthofen), David Osterhout (Holzapfel), Clint Kimbrough (Maj. Von Hoeppner), Gordon Phillips (Cargonico), Peadar Lamb (German Staff Major), Seamus Forde (Kaiser), Karen Huston (Ilse), Ferdy Mayne (Father Richthofen), Maureen Cusack (Mother Richthofen), Fred Johnson (Jeweler), Hurd Hatfield (Anthony Fokker), Vernon Hayden (Trackl), Michael Fahey (Richthofen at Age 3), Corin Redgrave (Maj. Lanoe Hawker), Tom Adams (Owen), David Weston (Murphy), Brian Sturdivant (May), Des Nealon (British Intelligence Officer), John Flanagan (Thompson), Lorraine Rainier (Girl in Woods), Robert Walsh (Richthofen at Age 13).

Produced and directed by the brother team of Gene and Roger Corman, this was an ambitious attempt at the telling of the famous "Red Baron" story that was exciting when it was in the air but came to a screeching halt whenever the actors stopped shooting at each other and stopped to speak. Law is von Richthofen, a 23-year-old who joins the unit headed by fighter pilot Masterson. WW I is raging and good men are needed to battle the

Allies. Law is a snob and a bit of a blowhard but he has the flying skills to back that up and immediately becomes the target of the ire of Primus (as Hermann Goering), himself a pilot and a man with big ideas about where he belongs in the scheme of things and an appetite to match his ego. Meanwhile, on the other side of the fracas, Canadian Stroud (as Brown) arrives and resents the way his British compatriots treat the war. They seem to look at it as sort of a sporting event not unlike cricket. Brown is angry when they raise their glasses to Law because he is the No.1 ace on the German side. Instead, Stroud toasts the memory of a pilot who went down on his side and publicly states that he intends to get Law and bring him down to earth. German squadron leader Masterson is killed and Law takes over the duties as boss. He immediately has all of the German planes done in bright colors and his plane is painted blood red, thereby earning the squadron the designation "The Flying Circus," with Law being monikered "The Red Baron." The British are using the same kind of gentlemanly tactics that lost them the Revolutionary War and Stroud presses them to abandon those lifted-pinky ideals and go right for the enemy's throat. Stroud leads the British on a surprise attack that successfully ruins several parked German planes, destroys their hospital, and levels almost everything that was standing. Flushed with success, they fly back toward their base but Law and Primus have raced ahead in some powerful new Fokker triplanes that almost double the speed of their former ships. They get to the British base and wreak terrible havoc on it, with Primus machine-gunning unarmed female nurses like ducks on a pond. Time passes and the Germans see that there is no way they can triumph so Law is asked by his superiors to give up active service. He is such a hero to the people that they want to enlist his political clout to help them run the government that will be formed after the war. Law can't handle the thought that all of his bravery will have been for nothing so he returns to the action and keeps shooting down Allied planes. Law has about 80 "kills" to his credit when he finally meets his match in Stroud. They have a lengthy dogfight which ends when Law is killed in midair but his red Fokker makes a miraculous landing by itself (it really did happen, according to air lore). The picture cost almost a million, which was a great deal for Corman, although there are many stars who get that as their fees these days. Real WW I planes were used but there were a couple of crashes during filming which resulted in one death (stunt pilot Charles Bodington) and a few injuries, most notably to Stroud. A nude love scene between Law and Huston was so ludicrous that West Coast preview audiences laughed hard and it was deleted from the final print. A bad soundtrack and horrendous dubbing didn't help matters but the hardest thing to figure out was who was shooting at whom in the air sequences. Filmed in Ireland, which looks exquisite. In a small role, note Hurd Hatfield, who will always be remembered as "Dorian Gray" in you know what.

p, Gene Corman; d, Roger Corman; w, John Corrington, Joyce Corrington; ph, Michael Reed, Peter Allwork, Peter Pechowski, Seamus Corcoran (DeLuxe Color); m, Hugo Friedhofer; ed, George Van Noy, Alan Collins; art d, Jim Murakami; set d, Maureen Roche; cos, Charles Guerin, Dymphna McKenna; spec eff, Peter Dawson; makeup, Toni Delaney.

War/Action   **(PR:C MPAA:GP)**

VON RYAN'S EXPRESS***½   (1965) 117m P-R Productions/FOX c

Frank Sinatra (Col. Joseph L. Ryan), Trevor Howard (Maj. Eric Fincham), Raffaela Carra (Gabriella), Brad Dexter (Sgt. Bostick), Sergio Fantoni (Capt. Oriani), John Leyton (Orde), Edward Mulhare (Constanzo), Wolfgang Preiss (Maj. von Klemment), James Brolin (Pvt. Ames), John Van Dreelen (Col. Gortz), Adolfo Celi (Battaglia), Vito Scotti (Italian Train Engineer), Richard Bakalyan (Cpl. Giannini), Michael Goodliffe (Capt. Stein), Michael St. Clair (Sgt. Dunbar), Ivan Triesault (Von Kleist), Jacques Stanislavski (Gortz's Aide), Al Wyatt, Buzz Henry, John Day, James Sikking (American Soldiers), Eric Micklewood (Ransom), John Mitory (Oriani's Aide), Benito Prezia (Italian Corporal), Dominick Delgarde (Italian Soldier), Barry Ford (Ransom's Batman), Gino Gottarelli (Gortz's 2nd Aide), Peter Hellman (Pilot), Michael Romanoff (Italian Nobleman), Walter Linden (German Captain), Bard Stevens (German Sergeant), Ernesto Melinari (Italian Tailor), Bob Rosen (POW Who Opens Sweatbox), Don Grant 'Don Glut'.

At a mostly British prisoner-of-war camp in Italy, Howard is the ranking officer, but his attempts to improve conditions and lead escapes have failed at every turn. He is jealous when he is forced to turn over leadership of the camp to Sinatra, an American flier just shot down and placed in the camp. Sinatra quickly earns the contempt of the other prisoners, who accuse him of cooperating with the enemy and dub him "Von Ryan." Their scorn turns to respect, though, when Sinatra is placed in the camp sweatbox for demanding better conditions. Later, the Italian war effort collapses and–with the help of their Italian captors–the men simply walk out of camp. Soon, though, the Germans arrive on the scene to take up where their allies failed. The prisoners commandeer a train headed for Switzerland. For a time, with the help of sympathetic Italians, their ruses are successful, but eventually the Germans catch on and set out after the train, strafing it with airplanes and sending an armored train after it. In a rather startling scene, Sinatra machine-pistols the only woman in the cast, collaborator Carra, as she races to unrealized safety after betraying the plan. After a final furious skirmish the train makes the last few hundred yards to safety. Sinatra runs to catch the train, but a burst from a German submachine gun cuts him down and the other men can only look back as they cross the Swiss border. A good performance by Sinatra and a better one by Howard highlight this action-filled war movie. The story, once it gets aboard the train, moves quickly but the film keeps itself light, realizing the basic absurdity of its premise. Technically the film is impressive, particularly the duel between the train and the airplanes attacking it in the mountains of northern Italy. No moralizing here, just a straight-ahead war story that should please action fans.

p, Saul David; d, Mark Robson; w, Wendell Mayes, Joseph Landon (based on the novel by Joseph Westheimer); ph, William H. Daniels (CinemaScope, DeLuxe Color); m, Jerry Goldsmith; ed, Dorothy Spencer; art d, Jack Martin Smith, Hilyard Brown; set d, Walter M. Scott, Raphael Bretton; spec eff, L.B. Abbott, Emil Kosa, Jr.; makeup, Ben Nye, Roy Stork.

War   **Cas.**   **(PR:C   MPAA:NR)**

VOODOO BLOOD BATH   (SEE: I EAT YOUR SKIN, 1971)

VOODOO GIRL   (SEE: SUGAR HILL, 1974)

VOODOO HEARTBEAT zero   (1972) 88m TWI National c

Ray Molina, Philip Ahn, Ern Dugo, Mary Martinez, Ebby Rhodes, Forrest Duke, Mike Zapata, Stan Mason, Ray Molina, Jr, Mike Meyers.

A truly awful vampire picture about spies who are searching for a serum with which to achieve eternal youth. Instead of making them young, however, it transforms them into bloodsucking deviates. Shot in Las Vegas with an inordinate amount of bikini clad girls performing voodoo rituals. You won't find a more ridiculous vampire than the middle-aged, sideburned Molina who dresses conservatively in his bloodstained suit and tie. Too weird for words.

p, Ray Molina; d&w, Charles Nizet.

Horror   **(PR:O   MPAA:R)**

VOODOO ISLAND*   (1957) 76m Bel-Air/UA bw (AKA: SILENT DEATH)

Boris Karloff (Dr. Phillip Knight), Beverly Tyler (Sara Adams, Knight's Secretary), Murvyn Vye (Barney Finch), Elisha Cook (Martin Schuyler), Rhodes Reason (Matthew Gunn), Jean Engstrom (Claire Winter), Frederick Ledebur (The Ruler), Glenn Dixon (Mitchell), Owen Cunningham (Howard Carlton), Herbert Patterson (Dr. Wilding), Jerome Frank (Vickers).

A terrible film in which Karloff plays a scholarly type who likes to go about disproving supernatural occurrences with scientific fact. He is called upon to investigate the possible island site for a large resort hotel; the island is rumored to be infested with zombies. Sure enough, after Karloff and company witness plants eating people and members of the expedition becoming zombies (for no apparent reason), the scientist's thoughts about supernatural phenomena are given a vast reworking. Had more effort been put into developing plot motivation and explaining some of the strange events, the picture could have fared a bit better. As is, it is better left unseen. A certain amount of fuss was made over the film's special effects flora, said by its creators to be over-sized carbon copies of the real carnivorous things. Filmed on the Hawaiian island of Kauai, the picture was made in two versions to allow for the inclusion of some sexier scenes for European consumption.

p, Howard W. Koch; d, Reginald Le Borg; w, Richard Landau; ph, William Margulies; m, Les Baxter; ed, John F. Schreyer; spec eff, Jack Rabin, Louis De Witt; makeup, Ted Coodley.

Horror   **(PR:A   MPAA:NR)**

VOODOO MAN*½   (1944) 62m MON bw

Bela Lugosi (Dr. Richard Marlowe), John Carradine (Job), George Zucco (Nicolas), Michael Ames [Tod Andrews] (Ralph Dawson), Wanda McKay (Betty Benton), Ellen Hall (Mrs. Evelyn Marlowe), Louise Currie (Sally Saunders), Henry Hall (Sheriff), Dan White (Deputy), Pat McKee (Grego), Terry Walker (Alice), Mici Gota (Housekeeper), Mary Currier (Mrs. Benton), Ethelreda Leopold, Claire James, Dorothy Bailer (Zombies), Ralph Little-field.

Only the skill of Lugosi could make anything of this ridiculous picture in which he plays a scientist whose desire to keep his dead wife alive has him going about kidnaping pretty young things and turning them into zombies. Atrociously cast as the doctor's assistant, Carradine is a thoroughly unconvincing blockhead. More effort should have been made in putting life into this production instead of the dead woman.

p, Sam Katzman, Jack Dietz; d, William Beaudine; w, Robert Charles; ph, Marcel Le Picard; ed, Carl Pierson; md, Edward J. Kay; art d, Dave Milton.

Horror   **Cas.**   **(PR:A   MPAA:NR)**

VOODOO TIGER*½   (1952) 67m COL bw

Johnny Weissmuller (Jungle Jim), Jean Byron (Phyllis Bruce), James Seay (Abel Peterson), Jeanne Dean (Shalimar), Charles Horvath (Wombulu), Robert Bray (Maj. Bill Green), Michael Fox (Carl Werner), John Cason

(Jerry Masters), Paul Hoffman (Michael Kovacs), Richard Kipling (Commissioner Kingston), Frederic Berest (Native Chief), William R. Klein (CoPilot), Alex Montoya (Native Leader), Rick Vallin (Sgt. Bono), Tamba.

Donning a khaki outfit to perform his Dark Continent heroics as Jungle Jim, Weissmuller thwarts the attempts of Nazis and American hoods (with a few headhunters thrown in for good measure) to uncover an art treasure stolen from France during WW II and hidden deep in the jungle. This routine fare comes complete with the usual leaf-and-lion footage. The highlight occurs when Dean attempts a rather risque native dance. (See JUNGLE JIM series, Index.)

p, Sam Katzman; d, Spencer Gordon Bennet; w, Samuel Newman (based on the comic strip "Jungle Jim"); ph, William Whitley; ed, Gene Havlick; md, Mischa Bakaleinikoff; art d, Paul Palmentola; set d, Sidney Clifford.

Adventure   **(PR:A   MPAA:NR)**

VOODOO WOMAN*   (1957) 77m Carmel/AIP c

Marla English (Marilyn Blanchard), Tom Conway (Dr. Roland Gerard), Touch [Mike] Connors (Ted Bronson), Lance Fuller (Rick/Harry), Mary Ellen Kaye (Susan), Paul Durov (Marcel, Innkeeper), Martin Wilkins (Chaka), Norman Willis (Harry West), Otis Greene (Bobo), Emmett E. Smith (Gandor), Paul Blaisdell (Monster), Giselle D'Arc (Singer), Jean Davis (Native Girl).

One of Cahn's more shabby productions has Conway a mad scientist trying to create the perfect woman, though his interest is not so much carnal as murderous. To his mind the perfect distaff creation will be the one that obeys his telepathic commands to kill. To arrive at this end, he does the odious deed of turning the beautiful gold-hunter English into a grotesquely ugly monster. Very bad!

p, Alex Gordon; d, Edward L. Cahn; w, Russell Bender, V.I. Voss; ph, Frederick E. West; m, Darrell Calker; ed, Ronald Sinclair; m/l, "Black Voodoo," Calker, John Blackburn (sung by Giselle D'arc).

Horror/Fantasy   **(PR:A   MPAA:NR)**

VOR SONNENUNTERGANG**   (1961, Ger) 102m CCC-Filmkunst/Casino bw

Hans Albers (Mathias Clausen), Annemarie Duringer (Inken Peters), Martin Held (Erich Klamroth), Hannelore Schroth (Ottilie Klamroth), Claus Biederstaedt (Egert Clausen), Maria Becker (Bettina Clausen), Erich Schellow (Wolfgang Clausen), Inge Langen (Paula Clausen), Wolfgang Preiss (Dr. Hahnefield), Hans Nielsen (Dr. Steynity), Johanna Hofer (Frau Peters).

Albers plays a wealthy industrialist unable to find the needed affection or love once his wife dies. Though an affair with a younger woman puts some life back into the man, the disapproval of his family causes this relationship to dissolve. A biting look at the hypocrisy of the wealthy. Released in West Germany in 1956, this film was based on the play by Gerhart Hauptmann which also provided the inspiration for DER HERRSCHER (1937).

p, Artur Brauner; d, Gottfried Reinhardt; w, Jochen Huth (based on the play "Vor Sonnenuntergang" by Gerhart Hauptmann); ph, Kurt Hasse; m, Werner Eisbrenner.

Drama   **(PR:A   MPAA:NR)**

VORTEX   (SEE: DAY TIME ENDED, THE, 1980, Span.)

VORTEX*½   (1982) 90m B Movies c

James Russo (Anthony Demmer), Lydia Lunch (Angel Powers), Bill Rice (Frederick Fields), Ann Magnasen (Pamela Fleming), Brent Collins (Peter), Bill Corsair (John Allen), Tom Webber (Ron Gavers), Haoui Montaug (Harry), Scott B (Carlo/Cop), Richard France (Therapist), Chris Strang (Tarman), Richard Prince (Vito), David Kennedy (Congressman White), Kal Eric (Bodyguard), Gideon Horowitz, Christof Kohlhofer (Doctors), Dani Johnson (Patient/Teletypist), Bill Landis, Andy Whyland (Patients), Dick Miller.

Scott B and Beth B had long been making successful short films that correspond to the artistic attitudes of the New Wave movement of the 1970s and 1980s when they undertook this 16mm project. Their earlier films were harsh, flashy in technique, and insightfully pessimistic, and this attempt to make a commercially viable picture using the same techniques was a hard task to take on. Only by taking a camp approach could they hope to be successful, but "camp" can date quickly and only time will tell if this film will appeal to future audiences. A film noirish atmosphere is created to show detective Lunch (a popular underground musician and poet) plow her way through the plans of a corporate businessman who seeks government defense contracts through real "corporate wars" and the manipulation of politicians. Though not without its merits, especially in the form of Lunch, a really stunning performer, this picture is more tedious than entertaining.

d&w, Scott B., Beth B.; ph, Steven Fierberg; m, Adele Bertei, Richard Edson, Lydia Lunch, Scott B., Beth B.; ed, Scott B., Beth B.; art d, Tom Surgal; set d, John Loggia; makeup, J. Aspinal, A. Gargiulo.

Experimental/Crime   **Cas.**   **(PR:O   MPAA:NR)**

VOSKRESENIYE   (SEE: RESURRECTION, 1963, USSR)

VOTE FOR HUGGETT   (1948, Brit.) 84m Gainsborough/GFD bw

Jack Warner (*Joe Huggett*), Kathleen Harrison (*Ethel Huggett*), Susan Shaw (*Susan Huggett*), Petula Clark (*Pet Huggett*), David Tomlinson (*Harold Hinchley*), Diana Dors (*Diana*), Peter Hammond (*Peter Hawtrey*), Amy Veness (*Grandma*), Hubert Gregg (*Maurice Lever*), John Blythe (*Gowan*), Anthony Newley (*Dudley*), Charles Victor (*Mr. Hall*), Adrianne Allen (*Mrs. Hall*), Frederick Piper (*Mr. Bentley*), Empsie Bowman, Isa Bowman, Nellie Bowman (*Old Ladies*), Eliot Makeham, Clive Morton, Norman Shelley, Lyn Evans, Hal Osmond, Elizabeth Hunt, Ferdy Mayne.

Warner, the head of the Huggett household, decides to get into politics, promising to construct a war memorial. Her runs into difficulties when his wife, Harrison, refuses to let him use her part of the land for the memorial. Dors, Harrison's niece, forges her aunt's signature on the deal and gets Warner into a fix. Trouble is averted when Shaw, Warner's daughter, discovers Dors' wrongdoing and keeps Warner from losing the election. (See: HUGGETT FAMILY series, Index.)

p, Betty Box; d, Ken Annakin; w, Mabel Constanduros, Denis Constanduros, Allan Mackinnon; ph, Reginald Wyer; cos, Yvonne Gaffin.

Comedy   (PR:A   MPAA:NR)

VOULEZ-VOUS DANSER AVEC MOI
                (SEE: COME DANCE WITH ME, 1960, Fr.)

VOW, THE   (1947, USSR.) 103 Tbilissi/Artkino bw

Mikhail Gelovani (*Joseph Stalin*), S. Chiatsintova (*The Mother*), N. Bogoliubov (*Alexander*), D. Pavlov (*Sergei*), S. Bogoliubova (*Olg*), T. Makharova (*Xenia*), N. Plotnikov (*Yermilov*), V. Soloviev (*Ruzayev*), S. Blinnikov (*Baklan*), G. Sagardze (*Georgi*), P. Ismatov (*Tugunbayev*), M. Shtraugh (*U.S. Correspondent*), N. Chapligin (*British Correspondent*), I. Nabatov (*French Minister Georges Bonnet*), A. Mansvetov, N. Konovalov, A Gribov, N. Rizhov, G. Musheghian, Y. Yurlev, V. Mironov, A. Khbilya, F. Biazhevich, M. Sidorkin, A. Sovolev, T. Beinikevich (*Soviet Leaders*).

Well-produced and nicely executed picture that was victim of the propaganda of Soviet Realism. It depicts Stalin as a righteous follower of Lenin with a firm belief in the Russian people's ability to contend with the Nazi onslaught. For a change, the U.S. is given good representation, though in the rather dubious form of a newspaperman who is a good ol' boy deep down, able to get along in a brotherly fashion with the Soviets. (In Russian; English Subtitles)

d, Makail Chiaureli; w, Chiaureli, N. Pavlenko; ph, A. Kesmatov; m, A. Balanchiavadze; English subtitles, C. Clement.

War/History   (PR:A   MPAA:NR)

VOYAGE, THE   (1974, Ital.) 101m Champion SPA c (IL VIAGGIO; AKA: THE JOURNEY; THE TRIP)

Sophia Loren (*Adriana De Mauro*), Richard Burton (*Cesar Braggi*), Ian Bannen (*Antonio Braggi*), Renato Pinciroli (*Dr. Mascione*), Daniele Pitani (*Notary*), Barbara Pilavin (*Signora De Mauro*), Sergio Bruni (*Armando Gill*), Ettore Geri (*Rinaldo*), Olga Romanelli (*Clementina*), Annabella Incontrera (*Simona*), Paolo Lena (*Nandino*), Danile Vergas (*Notary Salierno*), Richard Mangana (*Dr. Carlini*), Barrie Simmons (*Dr. De Paolo*), Franco Lauriano (*Notary's Clerk*), Antonio Anelli (*Puccini*).

This barely tolerable Loren-Burton soap opera takes place among the wealthy classes in turn-of-the-century Sicily. Loren is in love with Burton, but marries his brother Bannen instead. It turns out that Burton had promised his father on his deathbed to let Bannen marry the girl. Bannen is a weak-willed individual who handily ends up dead in an auto wreck. Loren is left free to mourn until Burton shows up to help her out. Since his beloved suffers from dizzy spells, Burton takes her to specialists. In the best of bad movie traditions, the doctors declare Loren has an incurable disease that should do her in by the final reel. Burton spends the rest of the time pitching woo, and proposed to Loren in the romantic confines of a gondola. Loren's mother is furious about this, and Burton angrily agrues with her on the telephone. As they bicker, Loren conveniently has a heart attack and dies in Burton's grief-stricken arms. Loren and Burton are boring in the leads, adding nothing to the already wretched material. De Sica, in yet another greatly disappointing effort, manages to evoke the period with some degree of success but the lifeless treatment of the story is something one would expect from a hack director, not a pioneering master in Italian cinema. This may have been the result of De Sica's ill health, which closed the production for a time. His long-time smoking habit had finally cought up with him and he had to be operated on for emphysema. He died after the film was completed, making this the great director's final work, though the far superior A BRIEF VACATION, made previous to this, would be his last film released in America. Burton took off a weekend during production, flying across the North Pole to be at the bedside of his wife, Elizabeth Taylor. Though their well-publicized marriage was coming to an end, she has requested him to come when she underwent emergency surgery. Burton made a 12-hour flight to Los Angeles, spent a night at the hospital, then made another 12-hour flight over the Pole back to the Rome location. "I felt like death, and looked it," he later recalled, but he made good on his promise not to miss a day of shooting.

p, Carlo Ponti; d, Vittorio De Sica; w, Diego Fabbri, Massimo Franciosa, Luisa Montagnana (based on the novel by Luigi Pirandello); ph, Ennio Guarnieri (Eastmancolor); m, Manuel De Sica, ed, Kim Arcalli; prod d, Luigi Scaccianoce; art d, Paolo Biagetti; set d, Bruno Cesari; cos, Marcel Escoffier.

Drama   (PR:O   MPAA:NR)

VOYAGE BEYOND THE SUN   (SEE: SPACE MONSTER, 1965)

VOYAGE IN A BALLOON   (SEE: STOWAWAY IN THE SKY, 1962, Fr.)

VOYAGE OF SILENCE½   (1968, Fr.) 89m Fildebroc-Les Productions Artistes Assoc ies/Lopert bw (O SALTO; LE SAUT)

Marco Pico (*Antonio Ferreira*), Henrique de Sousa (*Alberto*), Americo Trindade (*Americo*), Antonio Passalia (*Carlos*), Ludmila Mikael (*Dominique the Nurse*), Heitor Fernandes, Joao Neto, Antonio Gonzalves, Jose Belchior, Jose Borges, Antonio Lopez, Luis Oliveira, Alfredo Neto.

A young man's dream of leaving his poor Portuguese village for the gold-paved streets of Paris results in a hard dose of reality when the man actually undertakes the journey. Pico plays the Portuguese carpenter who makes a rough journey across Spain hoping to obtain work in Paris, something promised him by his friend Passalia. However, he discovers his friend to be anything but sincere, as Pico goes through one hardship after another, only to end up poorer than he started out.

p, Philippe de Broca; d, Christian de Chalonges; w, Chalonges, Roberto Bodegas; ph, Alain Derobe; m, Luis Cilia; ed, Helene Arnal; art d, Claude Pignot; makeup, Simone Knapp.

Drama   (PR:A   MPAA:NR)

VOYAGE OF THE DAMNED½   (1976, Brit.) 155m Associated General/AE c

Faye Dunaway (*Denise Kreisler*), Max Von Sydow (*Capt. Schroeder*), Oskar Werner (*Dr. Kreisler*), Malcolm McDowell (*Max Gunter*), Orson Welles (*Estedes*), James Mason (*Remos*), Lee Grant (*Lillian Rosen*), Ben Gazzara (*Morris Troper*), Katharine Ross (*Mira Hauser*), Luther Adler (*Prof. Weiler*), Paul Koslo (*Aaron Pozner*), Michael Constantine (*Clasing*), Nehemiah Persoff (*Mr. Hauser*), Jose Ferrer (*Benitez*), Fernando Rey (*Cuban President*), Lynne Frederick (*Anna Rosen*), Maria Schell (*Mrs. Hauser*), Helmut Griem (*Otto Schiendick*), Victor Spinetti (*Dr. Strauss*), Julie Harris (*Alice Feinchild*), Janet Suzman (*Leni Strauss*), Wendy Hiller (*Rebecca Weiler*), Sam Wanamaker (*Carl Rosen*), Denholm Elliott (*Adm. Wilhelm Canaris*).

A ponderous, overlong, star-studded film based on a shocking true story. It resembles SHIP OF FOOLS in a few ways as it seeks to establish too many characters involved in interrelated vignettes. The impact of the potentially powerful screenplay is diminished by Rosenberg's heavy-handed direction that tries to tell too much and doesn't succeed in giving us enough. It's 1939 and the Nazis have loaded a liner with a group of Jewish refugees and sent them off to Havana, Cuba, knowing that they would be refused entry by the Cuban president, Rey. The whole thing is a publicity stunt for the Nazis, who want to prove that no country will accept the wretched refuse of Jews that they seek to eliminate with their infamous "Final Solution." The ship is refused in Cuba and must journey back to Germany and certain death for the passengers. Aboard are a sophisticated couple, Dunaway and Werner; the ship's non-Nazi captain, Von Sydow; Adler and Hiller, a senior citizen professor and his spouse; Persoff and Schell, a couple who are hopefully looking forward to reuniting with their daughter, Ross, who has since become a hooker in Havana; a disbarred attorney, Wanamaker; and his wife and daughter, Grant and Frederick. Besides Rey in Cuba are Welles, an industrialist; Mason, a minister sympathetic to the Jews; a local bureaucrat, Ferrer; and Gazzara, the man who heads the local Jewish agency. McDowell is a cabin boy on the ship and the action cuts quickly between all of the above until you can't tell the refugees without a scorecard. It was to be a TV mini-series and looks it. Oscar nominations went to Grant, Schifrin's score (which includes a snippet of Glenn Miller's "Moonlight Serenade" to establish the period), and the screenplay by Butler and Shagan. The huge cast seem to be confused about which scene they are in and the attempt at making this an "important" story falls dead. Shagan likes to tackle tough subjects and when he succeeds, as in SAVE THE TIGER, he's terrific. When he flops, as in this and his screenplay for his excellent book THE FORMULA, it could make you get a headache. One-note and often monotonous, VOYAGE OF THE DAMNED failed to dock at many theaters and eventually sailed out to sea.

p, Robert Fryer; d, Stuart Rosenberg; w, Steve Shagan, David Butler (based on the book by Max Morgan-Witts, Gordon Thomas); ph, Billy Williams

(Eastmancolor); m, Lalo Schifrin; ed, Tom Priestley; prod d, Wilfred Shingleton; art d, Jack Stephens; cos, Betty Adamson, John Billing, Phyllis Dalton.

War Drama   **Cas.**   **(PR:A-C MPAA:PG)**

VOYAGE TO AMERICA½** (1952, Fr.) 82m Martin J. Lewis bw (LE VOYAGE EN AMERIQUE)

Yvonne Printemps (*Clotilde Fournier*), Pierre Fresnay (*Gaston Fournier*), Oliver Hussenot (*Soalhat*), Jane Morlet (*Marie*), Lisette Lebon (*Marguerite*), Claude Laydu (*Francois*).

None of America is shown in this enjoyable tale about a middle-aged, provincial French couple who get it into their heads to take a plane trip across the Atlantic. Since the couple, Printemps and Fresnay, have led a fairly sheltered life in their small village, the new experiences they encounter as they go about preparing for and actually setting off on their vacation make for some pretty ironic situations and a good time for all. One trip worth taking. (In French; English subtitles.)

p, Fred Orain; d, Henri Lavorel; w, Lavorel, Roland Laudenbach; ph, Henri Alekan; m, Francis Poulenc.

Comedy   **(PR:A MPAA:NR)**

VOYAGE TO PREHISTORY
      (SEE: JOURNEY TO THE BEGINNING OF TIME, 1966, Czech.)

VOYAGE TO THE BOTTOM OF THE SEA
                (1961) 105m Windsor/FOX c

Walter Pidgeon (*Adm. Harriman Nelson*), Joan Fontaine (*Dr. Susan Hiller*), Barbara Eden (*Cathy Connors*), Peter Lorre (*Commodore Lucius Emery*), Robert Sterling (*Capt. Lee Crane*), Michael Ansara (*Miguel Alvarez*), Frankie Avalon (*Chip Romano*), Regis Toomey (*Dr. Jamieson*), John Litel (*Adm. Crawford*), Howard McNear (*Congressman Parker*), Henry Daniell (*Dr. Zucco*), Mark Slade (*Smith*), Charles Tannen (*Gleason*), Delbert Monroe (*Kowski*), Anthony Monaco (*Cookie*), Robert Easton (*Sparks*), Jonathan Gilmore (*Young*), David McLean (*Ned Thompson*), Larry Gray (*Dr. Newmar*), George Diestel (*Lt. Hodges*), Skip Ward, Michael Ford (*Crew Members*), Art Baker (*UN Commentator*), Kendrick Huxham (*U.N. Chairman*), Dr. John Giovanni (*Italian Delegate*).

The inspiration for the long-running television series of the same name, which for once shows that a TV version can be better than the costly movie that spawned it. An excellent cast, featuring the likes of Pidgeon, Fontaine, and Lorre, is given the most inane caricatures with which to fill, along with predictable situations and trite dialog to waste dtheir talent on. As a whole the script itself is only redeemed through the captivating special effects and expensively designed sets. Pidgeon is the inventor of a nuclear submarine designed to reach depths greater than man has previously ever been able to reach. (This capacity is only required once, while evading submarines which are trying to blow it up.) Going against the wishes of the United Nations, Pidgeon decides to save the world by launching missiles against the Van Allen radiation belt, which has gone out of control and is threatening to melt the world. He sees this mission through despite the efforts of the other ships and Fontaine's efforts to sabotage the mission. One of the more exciting scenes, though it too is predictable, is the attack of a giant squid.

p&d, Irwin Allen; w, Allen, Charles Bennett (based on the story by Allen); ph, Winton C. Hoch (CinemaScope, DeLuxe Color); m, Paul Sawtell, Bert Shefter; ed, George Boemler; art d, Jack Martin Smith, Herman A. Blumenthal; set d, Walter M. Scott, John Sturtevant; cos, Paul Zastupnevich; spec eff, L.B. Abbott; m/l, Russell Faith; makeup, Ben Nye.

Fantasy   **Cas.**   **(PR:A MPAA:NR)**

VOYAGE TO THE END OF THE UNIVERSE½** (1963, Czech.) 81m Barrandov-Ceskosloven sky Film/AIP bw (IKARIE XB-1; IKARIA XB-1 AKA: ICARUS XB-1)

Dennis Stephans [Zdenek Stephanek] (*Expedition Commander Vladimir Abajev*), Francis Smolen [Erantisek Smdik] (*Astronomer Anthony Hopkins*), Dana Meredith [Dana Medricka] (*Nina Kirova*), IreneKova [Irena Kasikova] (*Brigit*), Rodney Lucas [Radovan Lukavsky] (*MacDonald*), Otto Lack [Otto Lackovic] (*Michael*), Myron March [Miroslav Machacek] (*Marcel Bernard*), Joseph Adams [Josef Adamovic] (*Zdenek Lorenic*), Rudolph Dial [Rudolf Deyl] (*Ervin Herold*), John Rose [Jaroslav Rozsival] (*Doctor*), Martin Tapin [Martin Tapak] (*Peter Kubes*), Jerry Tullis [Jiri Vrstala] (*Erik Svensson*), John Mares [Jaroslav Mares] (*Milek Wertbowsky*), Marcella Martin [Marcela Martinkova] (*Stefa*), Svatava Hubenakova [MacDonald's Wife], Renza Nova (*Ruzena Urbanova*), Jan Morris [Jan Cmiral], Joe Irwin [Vjaceslav Irmanov], Ludek Munzar, Emilie Vasayova.

Traveling in an enormous spaceship, its crew of 50 seeks a safe haven. They find a ghost spaceship–peopled with skeletons still garbed in fancy uniforms–which has drifted aimlessly for a hundred years. Armed with nuclear devices, the drifting ship proves dangerous to its discoverers; two are killed in an accidental blast. Other dangers threaten; the explorers must put the ship on automatic pilot to navigate past a dark star whose radiation induces sleep. They are helped by a magnetic beam radiating from a mysterious

green planet. Believing the latter to be the home they have sought, they approach the planet and see...the Statue of Liberty. A well-made, intelligent film which is enjoyable despite the dubbed voices, the recutting, and the ending which was added for U.S. consumption.

p, Rudolph Wohl; d, Jindrich Polak; w, Polak, Pavel Juracek; ph, Jan Kalis (CinemaScope); m, Danny List; ed, Josef Dobrichovsky, Helena Lehovcova, Ruzena Hejskova; md, Frantisek Belfin; art d, Jan Zazvorka, Bohumil Dudar; spec eff, Kalis, Milan Nejedly, Jiri Hlupy, Pavel Necesal, Karel Cisarovsky, Frantisek Zemlicka; cos, Esther Smith, John Scales, Don Demore; makeup, Rudolph Hammer.

Fantasy   **(PR:A MPAA:NR)**

VOYAGE TO THE PLANET OF PREHISTORIC WOMEN*
      (1966) 78m Filmgroup c (AKA: GILL WOMAN; GILL WOMEN OF VENUS)

Mamie Van Doren (*Moana*), Mary Mark, Paige Lee.

A rehash job, made–along with VOYAGE TO A PREHISTORIC PLANET (1965)–from a film, PLANETA BURG (AKA: STORM PLANET), coproducer Corman bought from the Russians. Astronauts land on Venus where they encounter the likes of dreamy looking women such as Van Doren–in a good role for her because she's not required to act–as well as nasty monsters. Van Doren and company turn out to be all right when they help the astronauts get back to Earth. More interesting to see for the result of splicing together parts of another film than for its own intrinsic worth. This was Peter Bogdanovich's first helming effort, though he preferred using a pseudonym.

p, Norman D. Wells, Roger Corman; d, Derek Thomas (Peter Bogdanovich); w, Henry Ney.

Fantasy   **(PR:A MPAA:NR)**

VOYAGE TO THE PREHISTORIC PLANET*
      (1965) 80m Filmgroup-AIP c (AKA: VOYAGE TO A PREHISTORIC PLANET)

Basil Rathbone (*Prof. Hartman*), Faith Domergue (*Marcia*), Marc Shannon, Christopher Brand, John Bix, Lewis Keane, Robert Chanta.

More interesting than the actual movie is the manner in which wheeler-dealer Roger Corman managed to create this picture. Taking footage from his recent Russian possession PLANETA BURG (AKA: STORM PLANET) combined with extra footage shot during the filming of QUEEN OF BLOOD, VOYAGE TO A PREHISTORIC PLANET was born. VOYAGE TO THE PLANET OF PREHISTORIC WOMEN was created out of the same material as this feature. The resulting picture was a very unoriginal tale about astronauts going to Venus where they encounter incredible perils, and are in danger of losing their lives until finally rescued. The special effects, originally from the Russian footage, look decent.

p, George Edwards; d&w, John Sebastian (Curtis Harrington); ph, Vilis Lapenieks.

Fantasy   **(PR:A MPAA:NR)**

VOYNA I MIR   (SEE: WAR AND PEACE, 1968, USSR)

VRAZDA PO CESKU   (SEE: MURDER CZECH STYLE, 1968, Czech.)

VRAZDA PO NASEM   (SEE: MURDER CZECH STYLE, 1968, Czech.)

VREDENS DAG   (SEE: DAY OF WRATH, 1948, Den.)

VROODER'S HOOCH   (SEE: CRAZY WORLD OF JULIUS VROODER, THE, 1974)

VU DU PONT   (SEE: VIEW FROM THE BRIDGE, A, 1962, Fr./Ital.)

VULCAN AFFAIR, THE   (SEE: TO TRAP A SPY, 1966)

VULCANO   (SEE: VOLCANO, 1950, Ital.)

VULTURE, THE**   (1937, Brit.) 67m WB-FN bw

Claude Hulbert (*Cedric Gull*), Lesley Brook (*Sylvia*), Hal Walters (*Stiffy Mason*), Frederick Burtwell (*Jenkinson*), George Merritt (*Spicer*), Arthur Hardy (*Li Fu*), Archibald Batty (*McBride*), George Carr (*Charlie Yen*).

Hulbert plays a correspondence course private detective who is hot on the trail of a gang of jewel thieves led by the notorious "Vulture." He follows his clues to Chinatown where he goes under cover as a Chinaman, and smashes their crime ring. A likable comedy with some genuinely funny moments.

p, Irving Asher; d, Ralph Ince; w, Stafford Dickens; ph, Basil Emmott.

Crime/Comedy (PR:A MPAA:NR)

VULTURE, THE*½ (1967, U.S./Brit./Can.) 91m Homeric-Iliad-Film Financial/PAR bw

Robert Hutton (*Eric Lutyens*), Akim Tamiroff (*Prof. Koniglich*), Broderick Crawford (*Brian Stroud*), Diane Clare (*Trudy Lutyens*), Philip Friend (*The Vicar*), Patrick Holt (*Jarvis*), Annette Carell (*Ellen West*), Edward Caddick (*The Sexton*), Gordon Sterne (*Edward Stroud*), Keith McConnell (*Police Supt. Wendell*), Margaret Robinson (*Nurse*), Monty Landis (*Bus Driver*), Gordon Tanner, Arnold Diamond, Murray Hayne, Roy Hanlon, Peter Elliott, George Tovey.

An 18th-century Spanish seaman had cursed the descendants of his killer, the Cornish squire who had him buried alive along with his pet, a giant bird. Crawford, the current squire, scoffs at the legend even when the mutilated carcass of a sheep is discovered in what appears to be the nest of a giant vulture. Crawford's brother-in-law Hutton, a scientist, discovers that Tamiroff-a descendant of the seaman-is responsible. In attempting to fuse himself with his ancestor through atomic transmutation-but forgetting about the buried bird-Tamiroff has accidentally managed to meld himself with the carrion-eating creature, creating a big bird with the face of a man. Crawford and his brother Sterne both fall victim to the vulture. When Hutton's wife Clare is carried off by the bird, she manages to fell it with a pistol shot. Ridiculous casting makes this one a laugh riot. Originally filmed in color, this was released in the U.S. only in black-and-white.

p,d&w, Lawrence Huntington; ph, Stephen Dade; m, Eric Spear; ed, John S. Smith; art d, Duncan Sutherland; makeup, Geoffrey Rodway.

Horror (PR:C MPAA:NR)

VULTURES OF THE LAW (SEE: SON OF THE PLAINS, 1931)

VYNALEZ ZKAZY (SEE: FABULOUS WORLD OF JULES VERNE, 1961, Czech.)

VZROSLYYE DETI (SEE: GROWN-UP CHILDREN, 1963, USSR)